The Norton Anthology
of English Literature
REVISED

VOLUME 1

The Norton Anthology
of English Literature
REVISED

M. H. Abrams, *General Editor*
Professor of English, Cornell University

E. Talbot Donaldson
Professor of English, Yale University

Hallett Smith
*Professor of English and Chairman, Division of the Humanities,
California Institute of Technology*

Robert M. Adams
Professor of English, University of California at Los Angeles

Samuel Holt Monk
Professor Emeritus, University of Minnesota

George H. Ford
*Professor of English and Chairman, Department of English,
University of Rochester*

David Daiches
*Professor of English and Dean of the School of English and American Studies,
University of Sussex*

VOLUME 1

W · W · NORTON & COMPANY · INC · New York

Beowulf, a new prose translation by E. Talbot Donaldson. Copyright © 1966 by
W. W. Norton & Company, Inc. Reprinted by permission of the publisher.
The Book of Beasts, by T. H. White. Copyright © 1954 by T. H. White. Selection
reprinted by permission of G. P. Putnam's Sons.
Boswell on the Grand Tour: Germany and Switzerland, 1764, edited by Frederick
A. Pottle. Copyright © 1928, 1953, by Yale University. Selection reprinted by
permission of McGraw-Hill Book Company, Inc.
Chaucer's Poetry: An Anthology for the Modern Reader, edited by E. T. Donald-
son. Copyright © 1958 by The Ronald Press Company. Selections reprinted by
permission of the publishers.
The Poems of Sir Philip Sidney, edited by William A. Ringler, Jr. Copyright ©
1962 by Oxford University Press. Selections reprinted by permission of the
Clarendon Press, Oxford
Sir Gawain and the Green Knight, a new verse translation by Marie Borroff.
Copyright © 1967 by W. W. Norton & Company, Inc. Reprinted by permission
of the publisher.
Utopia, by Thomas More. Translated and edited by H. V. S. Ogden. Copyright ©
1949 by Appleton-Century-Crofts, Inc. Selections reprinted by permission of the
publishers.

Book design by John Woodlock

PRINTED IN THE UNITED STATES OF AMERICA

8   9   0

Contents

The Seventeenth Century (1603–1660) · 861

Preface
to the Revised Edition

The first edition of the *Norton Anthology* was the result of two decades of experimentation with the indispensable course that introduces students to the greatness and variety of English literature. The response to that edition has amply justified the principles that guided its design. These are: that an introductory anthology ought to make possible a study in depth of all the major writers (other than novelists) in the historical context of the chief literary modes and traditions of their times; that the student deserves the most accurate texts of these writers, edited to make them immediately accessible and printed in a format manageable to the hand and inviting to the eye; and that the editorial materials should make the anthology self-sufficient, assist precise and sensitive reading, and enhance an intelligent delight in literature as literature.

Out of their experience with this book, many teachers and scholars volunteered comments, suggestions, and corrections; many others answered requests for information about their procedures and preferences generously and in detail. As the result of this accumulating information, based on actual use of the anthology in teaching, the editors are now able to provide in this revised edition a substantial improvement on the first.

A few selections (assigned very little or not at all) have been eliminated; a far greater number have been added. A number of works originally represented only in part are now complete, among them *Beowulf*, Book I of *The Faerie Queene*, *Absalom and Achitophel*, and *The Marriage of Heaven and Hell*. New titles have been added for all the major writers and for most of the lesser writers. Many of these are long works, reprinted *in toto*: Chaucer's *Wife of Bath's Tale*, Milton's *Samson Agonistes* (in addition to a larger representation of *Paradise Lost*), Swift's *Argument against Abolishing Christianity* and Part IV (in addition to Part II) of *Gulliver's Travels*, Blake's *Book of Thel*, Wordsworth's *Ruined Cottage*, Coleridge's *Eolian Harp*, Byron's *Vision of Judgment*, Shelley's *Mont Blanc* and *Triumph of Life*, and Keat's *Fall of Hyperion*. Other important additions have been made to the work of many poets—especially to Skelton, Wyatt, Sidney, Spenser, Ralegh, and Shakespeare in the Elizabethan age; to Tennyson's *In Memoriam* and the poems of Browning and Arnold; and to Hardy, Hopkins, Yeats, Housman, Edward Thomas, Owen, and Dylan Thomas among other more recent poets. New prose selections are included for Caxton, Browne, Johnson, Lamb, Carlyle, Newman, Mill, Conrad, and Eliot. D. H. Lawrence (as befits a major writer) is now represented by substantial examples of his writing in a variety of genres. The list of contemporary poets has been augmented by Edwin Muir and Robert Graves.

The "Topics" in literary, critical, or intellectual history appended to the selections for each period have proved widely useful in various ways—as additional reading, as convenient illustrations for points made in lectures, as materials for discussion, or as starting places for written reports. In the second edition we add three new Topics: one on "Medieval Views of Life on Earth"; another, in the Restoration and Eighteenth Century, on "The General and the Particular," which is documented by writings from Aristotle and Horace to William Blake; and a third, on "Literature Since Mid-Century: Anti-Culture and the New Traditionalism," which illustrates, through the writings of Samuel Beckett and some contemporary British poets, a central opposition in the literature of the present day.

By an improvement in the quality of the paper, these and many other additions have been made without increasing appreciably the bulk of the volumes and without impairing the visibility and open layout of the texts. Poetry in this anthology can still be read as it was written to be read: in a single column and with comfortable margins.

We also continue faithful to the principle that texts for undergraduates should be no less scrupulously chosen and edited than texts for the scholar. Accordingly we offer new, more sensitive, and more accurate translations of *Beowulf* and of *Sir Gawain and the Green Knight*. We use William Ringler's edition of Sir Philip Sidney's poetry and the David Erdman and Harold Bloom edition of William Blake. Shelley's *Triumph of Life* is the revised version recently published by Donald H. Reiman, and Wordsworth's great but neglected narrative poem, *The Ruined Cottage*, is a new and improved version edited from an unpublished manuscript by Jonathan Wordsworth.

Each editor has reconsidered all his introductory essays and footnotes and has rewritten many of them in the light of recent scholarship and criticism. The comprehensive introductions and the full glossing of archaisms and allusions have freed the student from reliance on a reference library and enabled him to carry and read the book anywhere—in class, at home in his own room, or under a tree. Actual use of the anthology in teaching has confirmed our original opinion that, in selected instances, the notes should also provide a modicum of guidance in interpretation; for some of the works here are among the most complex and difficult in the language, and of those assigned to the student, only a fraction can be discussed adequately in class. Experience has shown that these editorial aids do not displace the teacher but open possibilities to the student's own judgment and suggest points of departure for commentary and dialogue in the classroom. All the bibliographical guides at the end of the volumes, designed to encourage students to read further on their own, have been brought up to date. As a convenience to the student wishing to develop his own library of literary history and criticism, a dagger symbol indicates the books currently available in paperback.

We have continued the editorial procedures which have proved their utility in the earlier edition. In each of the historical and biographical introductions we list and identify the dates of crucial importance at the beginning and limit further chronological references to those the student needs to orient himself. In order, however, to specify the interrelations of individual works, we place after each selection, where the facts are known, the date of composition on the left and the date of first publication in book form on the right; the latter is sometimes preceded by the date of first appearance in a periodical publication. The writings of authors such as Chaucer, Skelton, Spenser, or Burns, which contain a large proportion of unfamiliar words, have been glossed in the margin, where the translation can be assimilated with least impediment to the flow of the reading. Whenever a portion of text has been omitted, the omission is indicated by three asterisks. Titles supplied by the editors are enclosed in square brackets.

All texts are printed in the form which makes them most immediately available to their particular audience. We have thus normalized spellings and capitalization according to modern American usage, but only in those instances in which the change does not alter semantic, phonological, or metric qualities. The verse of Spenser and of Hopkins and the prose of Joyce, Shaw, Carlyle, and Keats (in his letters) have been reproduced in their original form; only the minimal changes necessary for ready intelligibility have been made in the writings etched by William Blake; and in all writers, significant deviations from the norm (Keats's "faery," for example) have been left unaltered. The works of Chaucer and other writers in Middle English not too difficult for the novice have also been left in the original language, but each word is consistently spelled in that variant of its scribal form that is closest to modern English When we have altered punctuation it has been on the conservative principle that a change should be made only when the old punctuation would mislead a modern reader.

In the process of compiling both editions of this anthology, the editors incurred obligations to scores of teachers throughout the country who volunteered useful suggestions or gave essential information when asked. To each of these—too numerous to list here— we owe our thanks. We wish especially to acknowledge the wise counsel, in preparing the first edition, of W. R. Keast, now president of Wayne State University, and the detailed and helpful critiques toward revising that edition provided by a number of teacher-scholars: William Alfred (Harvard University); Harold Bloom (Yale University); Jack M. Davis (University of Connecticut); Peter Elbow (University of California, Berkeley); James Gindin (University of Michigan); David D. Harvey (State University of New York at Albany); Robert W. Hill, Jr. (Middlebury College); Arthur Hoffman (Syracuse University); David Kalstone (Rutgers, The State University); Robert Kimbrough (University of Wisconsin); R. M. Lumiansky (University of Pennsylvania); Hugh Maclean (State University of New York at Albany); Thomas Moser (Stanford University); Stephen M. Parrish (Cornell University); S. P. Rosenbaum (University of Toronto); and Clarence Tracy (University of British Columbia). Howard L. Anderson (Michigan State University) was of special assistance on the bibliography for the Eighteenth Century, and Richard L. Greene (Wesleyan University, Connecticut) provided the editors with a comprehensive and most helpful list of corrections and suggestions. George P. Brockway and John Benedict, of W. W. Norton & Company, Inc. —assisted ably by Eleanor Brooks, Kathleen Calkins, and S. H. Dammacco—have contributed immensely, by encouragement, caveats, and hard editorial work, to mitigate the chronic dilemmas in the endeavor to represent, justly and accurately, the work of all the major English writers in a single volume.

M. H. ABRAMS

The Norton Anthology
of English Literature
REVISED

VOLUME 1

The Middle Ages

(To 1485)

The medieval period in English literature extends for more than 800 years, from Cædmon's *Hymn* at the end of the 7th century to *Everyman* at the end of the 15th. So long a period, comprehending vast changes in culture, inevitably lacks a single, dominant literary motif. Historians used to divide the medieval period into two parts, calling the earlier centuries the Dark Ages in order to distinguish their quality from that of the later centuries, when European civilization attained one of the summits of its history. Misleading as such a distinction is—for the Dark Ages were only relatively dark—it is nevertheless true that in England the Middle Ages embraced two quite different periods of literary history, the Old English (or Anglo-Saxon) and the Middle English, sharply divided from each other by the Norman duke William's conquest of the island in 1066. Both English culture and the English language changed radically in the years following this event—though not entirely as a result of it—and English literature inevitably changed with them.

Adequate study of Old English and Middle English literature requires, of course, some familiarity with the early stages and development of our language, but it cannot be expected that the reader will stop and devote a year to this sort of preparation. For this reason, the Old English texts printed in this book are given in translation, as are the Middle English

1

texts in the more difficult regional dialects. Other Middle English texts, such as Geoffrey Chaucer's, appear in the original, but have been re-spelled in a way that it is hoped will aid the reader. Analyses of the sounds and grammar of Middle English, and of Old and Middle English prosody, appear at the end of this introduction.

THE GERMANIC PEOPLES

The Anglo-Saxon invasion of the island of Britain which began in the first half of the 5th century was a phase of a great folk migration that had been going on for some centuries and was to continue for several more—the movement of the Germanic tribes from the northeast of Europe into areas of the Roman Empire in the west, south, and south-east. The invaders of Britain, although they are now called collectively the Anglo-Saxons, consisted in fact of three tribes, the Angles, the Saxons, and the Jutes. Although independent, these tribes were closely allied to one another by their common Germanic heritage, which they shared also with the many other tribes that had already invaded or were to invade the whole of western Europe, tribes such as the Goths, Vandals, Danes, Franks, Norwegians, and Burgundians. In prehistoric times the ancestors of all these tribes had spoken a common language, and in historical times their individual tongues amounted to little other than variant dialects of a common language. They shared, moreover, the same primitive culture, the customs of one tribe differing little from those of another.

In its earliest period Germanic society had probably been organized by families: the head of the family was chieftain over his close kinsmen, and together they formed an independent political entity. With the pass-ing of time, the unit of society tended to grow larger as a number of families gathered around a single superior chief—or "king," to use the word derived from the Old Germanic name for chief. The unit never grew to be very large except on those relatively rare occasions when some par-ticularly successful king attracted others to him in order to perform a great military exploit; and such larger unions rarely endured long after the completion of the venture for which they had been formed. The normal order of society consisted of a number of small bands, the males of which were very closely associated with their king. If these bands did not always live at peace with one another, they still shared a sense of community and Germanic kinship, especially in the face of a common enemy, such as the Romans or Celts whose lands they were invading. Since the Germanic folk was migratory, many kings had, properly speaking, no kingdoms; and if kingdoms did come into being, they were apt to disappear after the death of the particular king who had founded them. This divisiveness, along with the related impermanence of kingdoms, seems to have been especially characteristic of the Anglo-Saxons: long after they had settled in England that small island was still broken up into a bewildering num-ber of kingdoms, some of them very short-lived, and a coherent union of all Englishmen was not achieved until after the Norman Conquest. It is true that from earliest times the kingdoms in England south of the Hum-ber River tended to confederate loosely under a single overlord, as did the kingdoms north of the Humber, but there was constant flux in these con-federations. It is perhaps characteristic of Germanic society that the division between north and south bore little correlation to the original settling places of the Angles, Saxons, and Jutes: apparently common Germanic relationship, combining with geographical convenience, was more cohesive than narrower tribal relationships.

THE PRIMITIVE HEROIC IDEAL

The same general organization of many kings coexisting within a common culture had been characteristic of that other migratory people, the Greeks—or Achaeans, to give them their more ancient and accurate name —who had moved down from the north of Europe and overrun the region of the eastern Mediterranean, where they founded many small kingdoms. The idea of kingship was equally important to both the Achaean and the Germanic peoples—so important that the ideal of kingly behavior was perhaps the chief spiritual force behind the civilizations they developed, the creative power that, in their earliest periods, shaped their history and their literature. It is generally called the heroic ideal; put most simply, the heroic ideal was excellence. The hero-king strove to do better than anyone else the things that an essentially migratory life demanded: to sail a ship through a storm, to swim a river or a bay, to tame a horse, to choose a camp site and set firm defenses, in times of peace even to plow a field or build a hall, but always and above all, to fight. Skill and courage were the primary qualities that a king had to have in order to realize the practical ideal of success in a community enterprise involving warfare.

In its original form the ideal was appropriate only to kings, but because society was so closely knit, all members of the tribe tended to imitate it. In general, of course, this ideal of conduct remained aristocratic, though without that quality of unreality and remoteness from the rigors of daily life that we associate with the idea of aristocracy in late medieval times. The king was not the distant apex of a vast, formally gradated society, but the active leader of a small number of fellow warriors who, as members of his household, beheld all that he did. A successful king won from his retainers complete loyalty. It was their duty to defend him in battle, and history records a number of occasions on which warriors gave up their own lives while defending or avenging their king's life. In return for their service, the king gave his retainers gifts from the spoil that had been accumulated in warfare. Royal generosity—one of the aspects of heroic behavior—was a most important quality, for it symbolized the excellence of the king's rule, implying on the one hand that his retainers deserved what they were given because of their loyalty to him, and, on the other, that he himself was worthy of such loyalty. In this way also the heroic ideal had a very practical bearing on the life of the people whom the king ruled.

While the heroic life might well win practical success for a king, it had also another, perhaps more important, end—enduring fame. In cultures whose religion, unlike Christianity, offers no firm promise of rewards in an afterlife, a name that will live on after one's death serves as the closest substitute for immortality. Thus arises the heroic paradox, still latent in our own civilization, that by dying gloriously one may achieve immortality. The poet who could sing the story of his heroic life was, of course, the agent upon whom the hero depended for his fame, and a good poet—or bard, to use the customary term for the poet of heroic life— was a valued member of a primitive court. Alexander, visiting the tomb of Achilles, is said to have expressed envy of the ancient hero-king because he had had a Homer to celebrate his deeds. The poetic form which primitive bards evolved for their heroic narratives is called "epic"; it is characterized by a solemn dignity of tone and elevation of style. Their poems were not written down, but transmitted through oral recitation; and when a bard recited a poem, he probably relied partly on his memory and partly on his ability to improvise and to make use of standard poetic formulas. It follows that the great majority of poems have failed to come down to us. In Greek there have survived Homer's two great epics, the *Iliad* and the *Odyssey*, while from Germanic culture the chief survivor is the Old English *Beowulf*. Yet enough has been preserved to show the enduring popularity of heroic stories throughout the migratory phase of the two peoples, and a single hero, such as Theodoric the Ostrogoth, might be made the subject of heroic poems composed many years after his death and among tribes widely separated from his own, sharing with him only a common racial heritage. The immortality that primitive heroes had sought was achieved through poetry, and poetry in turn enriched the cultural tradition of the heroes' race, so that later men might find in the old heroic tales an inspiration for their own lives.

CHRISTIANITY AND THE SPREAD OF WRITTEN CULTURE

When the Anglo-Saxons came to Britain in the 5th century, they brought with them from the mainland both their pagan religion and their ancient folk traditions. Since they had not yet learned to make written records, we have no Anglo-Saxon documents dating from the early period: traditions were passed from generation to generation by word of mouth, and were preserved only in men's memories. Not until they had been converted to Christianity in the 7th century did the Anglo-Saxons begin to write things down; and as Christian converts they naturally wrote little of the religion they had abandoned, so that we do not know how they worshiped Woden, Thunor, and Tig. After their conversion, their poets tended to rework the ancient Germanic traditions in Christian terms, thereby burying the pagan past beneath the Christian present. Yet such a poem as *Beowulf*, composed by a Christian poet during the first half of the 8th century, still reflects an attitude toward life that the poet and his hearers had inherited from earliest English and pre-English times, long before the conversion to Christianity.

The people of the island that the pagan Anglo-Saxons seized were Christians, for the original British (Celtic) inhabitants had already been converted, as had the Romans, whose forces had occupied the island since the 1st century and whose final withdrawal at the beginning of the 5th had opened the doors to the Anglo-Saxons. For 150 years after the coming of the Anglo-Saxons Christianity was maintained only in the remoter parts of Britain where the invaders had failed to penetrate. In the year 597, however, St. Augustine was sent by Pope Gregory as a missionary to King Ethelbert of Kent, one of the various kingdoms into which England was divided, and within 75 years of Augustine's arrival the island was once more predominantly Christian. Ethelbert himself was one of the first Englishmen to become converted—and it is indicative of the relationship between Christianity and writing that our first specimen of the Old English (Anglo-Saxon) language is a code of laws promulgated by this first English Christian king. Missionaries from the ecclesiastical center that Augustine established at Canterbury gradually brought the southern kingdoms to Christianity, while in the north the conversion was largely accomplished by missions from Ireland, which had escaped the Anglo-Saxon invasions and remained Christian, and from the island of Iona in the Hebrides, a center of Celtic Christianity.

Although the cultural records of Anglo-Saxon England after the conversion are mainly anonymous, the names of several Englishmen who made important contributions to their civilization have survived. The earliest of these is Bede, the great churchman whose *Ecclesiastical History of the English People*, composed in Latin, was completed in 731, perhaps at the very time the poet of *Beowulf* was working on his epic. Bede's *History*, despite its author's lack of interest in matters not directly connected with the church, is our most important source for knowledge of the earlier Anglo-Saxon period. Bede also wrote a large number of Latin works on such subjects as science, grammar, and theology, which enjoyed a wide audience throughout the Middle Ages. In the year of Bede's death, 735, was born one who was also to become a great churchman: Alcuin, not so distinguished or prolific a writer as Bede, but a man of wide culture who became the friend and advisor of the Frankish Emperor Charlemagne, whom he assisted in making the Frankish court a great center of learning. Thus one might say that by the year 800 English culture had developed so richly that it began to flow back over its insular boundaries to the continent of Europe.

Anglo-Saxon culture received its greatest impetus from a man who was not of the clergy: Alfred, king of the West Saxons from 871 to 899 and the greatest single name in Anglo-Saxon history. This most active king, who for a time united all the kingdoms of southern England and beat off those new Germanic invaders, the Vikings, was a great patron of literature. Insofar as he had leisure, he was himself a translator of various books from Latin, including two tracts of Pope Gregory, Orosius' *History of the World*, and, most important, Boethius' *De Consolatione* (*Consolation of Philosophy*), the early 6th-century Roman work whose heroic stoicism has proved especially congenial to the English temperament. Under Alfred's direction, Bede's *History* was also translated into Old English, and the *Anglo-Saxon Chronicle*, a year-by-year record of important events in England, was begun. Furthermore we owe the preservation of most of the surviving earlier English works, including *Beowulf*, to copies that were made of them in the West Saxon dialect as a result of the impetus that Alfred gave to literary pursuits. Though the political stability that Alfred achieved was not long-lived (within 167 years of his death England fell first into the control of the Scandinavians and then into the control of the Normans), the culture he nurtured so lovingly was maintained at a high level until the very end of the Old English period.

OLD ENGLISH POETRY

Written literature in English, as we think of it, began, then, with the re-establishment of Christianity on English soil in the 7th century, although writing was no doubt at first only an adjunct to memory and the oral tradition, not a substitute for them. Unfortunately, because most works in Old English survive in copies made many years after their original composition—which was itself often unwritten—it is not possible to assign them accurate dates or even to arrange them in any convenient chronology. All the poems in Old English of whatever date employ the same alliterative verse form. A more detailed analysis of this appears in the section on "Old and Middle English Prosody," but it should be indicated here that alliterative verse differs from the rhyming verse which is more familiar today in that the verse unit is the single line in which two or more words begin with the same sound, as in the following lines (from a verse translation of *Beowulf*):

> From a friendless foundling, feeble and wretched,
> He grew to a terror as time brought change.

Surely Cædmon's *Hymn* is among the earliest of Old English literary works to have been preserved, and it is probable that the purely secular poem *Widsith* should be assigned to the same period, the second half of the 7th century. Although *Widsith* is not reprinted in this anthology, it bears discussion here because of the interesting light it sheds on the importance, to the Anglo-Saxons of the earlier period, of oral literature based on their Germanic traditions. The poem consists mainly of a monologue by a professional bard—or *scop*, to use the Old English term—in which he catalogues various eminent Germanic kings and mentions his services to some of them, while boasting of the rich rewards he has received. Although a number of these kings belonged to the remotest periods of the Germanic past, the speaker refers to them as having lived within his own lifetime: this means that they must have had enduring life in the folk memory of the poem's 7th-century audience. The poem shows that the heroic actions of their legendary forebears served as examples of noble behavior to the Anglo-Saxons—furnished them with something like an ethical code which not even the more specific and widely different code provided by Christianity could entirely replace. A bard such as the one in *Widsith* would expect to be well rewarded for his work, for he held the mirror of the past up to his audience and also expressed that fame of the dead and that praise of the living which were the chief ends of the heroic life.

The *scop* of *Widsith* took his Anglo-Saxon listeners back to that Germanic past to which they looked for the values by which they lived. But Christianity brought another past with it—the alien past of the far-off worlds of the Old and New Testaments. It was necessary for the Christian poets to supplement familiar Anglo-Saxon history and its values—since they could hardly hope to replace them—with the unfamiliar history of the new belief, and in order to make this alien world intelligible they treated it in the same epic terms with which earlier poets had been accustomed to treat Germanic history. The alliterative verse form of Old English was primarily associated with heroic narrative; in adopting this verse for Christian subjects, the new poets naturally adopted its heroic formulas and its heroic attitudes. In Old English religious poetry—especially in what we suppose to be the earlier works—Moses and St. Andrew, Christ and God the Father, share the attributes of a Beowulf, appear as heroes who performed famous deeds. The Anglo-Saxon historian Bede tells us that after Cædmon had received the gift of song he sang of many of the great events of the Old and New Testaments, in order "to draw men away from the love of sin, and to excite in them devotion to welldoing and perseverance therein": so far as purpose and topics are concerned, all the surviving Old English religious poetry might well have been composed by Cædmon, even though nothing can be ascribed to him with assurance except his *Hymn*. There have been preserved a large number of works dealing, most of them in heroic terms, with the crucial incidents of Christian and pre-Christian history and serving, just as pagan poetry did, to guide men's present actions by the example of the glorious past. From the Old Testament there are stories of Genesis, Exodus, Daniel, and Judith. Based on the New Testament and its Apocrypha are poems on the deaths of the apostles, on the Harrowing of Hell, on Doomsday, and on the Crucifixion, which is the subject of the most splendid of all Old English religious poems, the *Dream of the Rood*. From early Christian legend there are stories of saints such as Juliana and Helena and of mystical wonders such as the Phoenix. We can assign authorship to only four of these poems (Cynewulf, who signed these four, is otherwise unknown), and we cannot place them accurately within the period between 700 and 1000.

Although there is much of interest and of value in these religious poems, the true Anglo-Saxon genius was for the epic narrative dealing either with ancient legendary heroes of the Teutonic past or with more recent historical events. The first is represented by *Beowulf*, the greatest of English and Germanic epics and the only surviving Old English one; it was probably composed in its present form during the first half of the 8th century. Historical events are memorialized by the *Battle of Brunanburg*, which celebrates King Athelstan's victory over invading Scots and Vikings in the year 937, and, more impressively, by the *Battle of Maldon*, which describes the defeat of the heroic English defenders by a band of Vikings in 991. These defenders were, of course, Christians, but their losing fight is described in the high tradition of Germanic heroism. Doubtless other epics were composed and recited, if not written down, and we possess one or two narrative fragments dealing with ancient Germanic legends that may have been parts of epics or at least of heroic lays.

It is unnecessary here to list all the items of Old English verse which have survived to us, but mention should be made of three impressive shorter pieces: the *Wanderer*, the *Seafarer*, and *Deor*. These laments— a genre in which the Anglo-Saxons seem to have excelled—are informed by that sad consciousness of the transience of all earthly good so characteristic of *Beowulf*: in the first two, the older pagan sense of fatal doom is effectively fused with the Christian moral doctrine of transience; in *Deor* a *scop*, deprived of the position he has held at his lord's court, finds what bleak consolation he can in the fact that the joys and woes of famous people before him have also passed away.

THE SPIRIT OF OLD ENGLISH POETRY

To the modern reader, Old English poetry may seem alien because it lacks so many of the qualities that we expect to find in poetry. Its world is a dark one, and it may seem also a narrow one with narrow laws that exclude all but sardonic laughter—a world circumscribed by fatal doom. Men in the mead-hall are said by the poets to be cheerful, but even there they think of struggle in war: of possible triumph and more possible failure. Nor does romantic love, one of the principal themes of later literature, appear even in the incidental way that we find it in the ancient poetry of Greece and Rome, although the few scraps of Old English poetry that deal with the relations between men and women show that the subject was not unknown to Anglo-Saxon poets. In general men seem seldom to relax: clothed always in their armor, they are ready to go forth and test their courage against fate. (They are, indeed, so habitually seen as warriors that in the earlier poetry some of the words for "man" and "warrior" are interchangeable.) Their world lacks the softer qualities of life Depressing as this world may seem, it is re-created in Old English poetry with extraordinary intensity, with high spiritual excitement. This excitement is achieved in part by the frequent use of ironic understatement—a feature of English literature that time did not obliterate; it remains as congenial to Chaucer and Malory as to the author of *Beowulf*. Actions and things are often spoken of as less than they really are because, apparently, the speaker wishes to suggest that they are more—or perhaps other—than they are: "They cared not for battle," says the author of the *Battle of Maldon* about those cowardly Englishmen who fled the fight. The poet is apt to hint at the potentialities of things, either for good or bad, rather than to describe the things themselves. Even the "kenning," that formalized compound metaphor common to Old Germanic poetry, often achieves this effect of suggesting potentials ironically—"whale's-road" or "swan's-path" for the sea that was so perilous for men lacking the physical equipment of whales and swans. The dignity the Anglo-Saxons assigned to poetry, which was, after all, the repository of the ancient traditions by which they were accustomed to live, apparently prevented the humor latent in ironic understatement from reaching any expression more overt than a grim smile. Yet if the hilarity that understatement achieves in the works of Chaucer is more attractive to us today than Anglo-Saxon somberness, the grandeur with which Old English poetry garbed its subtle and intense depiction of the nature of reality remains enormously impressive.

THE NORMAN CONQUEST AND ITS EFFECTS

In the year 1066 England was once more invaded and conquered by a Germanic people, though one whose culture had become widely different from that of their remote kinsmen, the Anglo-Saxons. The Normans—the name is actually a form of "Norsemen"—were the descendants of Scandinavian adventurers who at the beginning of the 10th century had seized a wide part of northern France. A highly adaptable nation, they had adopted the language of the land they had settled in and had set up a powerful state which, while its ruler was technically a duke subject to the king of France, was actually an independent political entity. The invasion of England was led by the energetic Duke William who saw in England's lack of unity and of strong leadership an opportunity to extend his own dominion. At the decisive Battle of Hastings, fought near the spot on the English channel where the Normans landed, the English were defeated and their leader Harold was killed. Thereafter William's forces overran much of England, and the Norman duke became its king and insured the succession to his descendants. But, kings of England though they were, he and his followers were not as much interested in the country he had won (though they were constantly fighting the Welsh, the Scots, and their own barons for control of parts or the whole of it) as they were in their continental possessions: the Conqueror (1066–87), his son William Rufus (1087–1100), Henry I (1100–35), Steven (1135–54), Henry II (1154–89), Richard I (1189–99), and John (1199–1216) were mostly absentee rulers—and their presence within the kingdom was seldom less troublesome for it than their absence from it. It was not, indeed, until the 13th century, with the reign of Henry III (1216–72, the fifth generation from the Conqueror) that England became the principal concern of its kings. And until the very end of the Middle Ages any given English monarch was capable of asserting and trying to make good his continental claims, as Edward III did in France in the 14th century and Henry V and Edward IV did in the 15th. But, despite temporary successes, none was able to maintain his overseas authority for very long, and the kings of England eventually became perforce English.

The immediate effect of the Norman Conquest upon English literature was to remove it from the care of the aristocracy and to deprive it of that cohesive spirit that it had possessed in Old English times. The great aristocratic households, which were the centers of pre-Conquest cultural activity, were broken up or parceled out to the Conqueror's Norman barons, and the English aristocracy itself was either wholly displaced or forced into service with the invaders. For a time, even the English language seems to have fallen into disuse as a vehicle for written literature, for very little survives of Middle English from before the year 1200. Initially, men of education who continued to produce literary works wrote either in Latin or in Anglo-Norman, the dialect of French that was spoken by the new rulers of England. But since the practical Normans were less preoccupied with culture than the English, the literature in the latter language is not especially distinguished and was not very long-lived: not much was written in Anglo-Norman after the reign of Edward I (1272–1307), who might properly be called only the second of England's truly resident kings. Latin, which had always been and continued to be the language of the international church, produced a fairly rich literature in England, especially during the 12th century; but throughout the Middle Ages, Latin literature remained essentially conservative and remote, not much dealing with the subjects that are of importance in the development of vernacular literature. Perhaps the chief exception to this generalization is the work of Geoffrey of Monmouth who, probably during the reign of Steven, produced his *History of the Kings of Britain:* this collection of largely legendary material contains the first full literary treatment of the story of King Arthur and is a most important source of the legend eventually to occupy so prominent a place in English literature.

A POPULAR LITERATURE

Although literature in English was necessarily neglected by the aristocracy in the century after the Conquest, it must have been carried on at least orally among the people, by men who were unable to write: such men had, of course, always practiced literature in their fashion, but had left few traces, since the learned did not think their productions worth transcribing. But when English literature begins to reappear after the hiatus between the Conquest and the end of the 12th century, the larger part of it carries the stamp of popular or at least semi-popular origin, and indeed, considered in the bulk, Middle English literature is a popular literature. Its origin in the orders of society below the very top provides its most striking contrast with Old English: most Old English literature seems to be uttered by a single aristocratic voice, grave, decorous, responsible, speaking in terms of high communal aspirations; Middle English literature, on the other hand, is uttered by a medley of very different voices, dealing with a wide range of topics in a great diversity of styles and tones and genres. Originality of thought, to be sure, is not a very common feature of this literature, for no matter how diverse the voices may be, they often seem to be saying precisely the same things as each other. Yet, while it lacks the authority, the cohesiveness, and the grandeur of Old English, Middle English has its compensations for the reader. Because its writers addressed themselves to a popular audience they achieved a greater immediacy, a greater recognizability than one finds in Old English: a modern reader experiences little trouble in understanding the world of most Middle English literature. The change is perhaps most obvious in the narrative of adventure, where the idealized hero of Old English yields place to the more sympathetic if less admirable man who not only fights and fights again, but also laughs and cries, plays games, and, above all, falls in and sometimes out of love—the nonaristocratic man who was the readier to supplant the epic hero because a mature Christianity places as much value on a plain man's soul as it does on an epic hero's. In dealing with this new kind of hero the writer's imaginative perspective was broadened as much, perhaps, as his ability to see deeply was decreased. The portrayal of life in Middle English literature is often shallow, yet it is a life in which we see much that is familiar: sometimes, when it is portrayed as lively and gay, colorful, full of surprise, its attractiveness will earn our active appreciation; and even when some austere moralist reduces human experience to mere wretchedness we may experience amid the overlying gloom the sudden charm of poignancy. Lack of profound vision does not prevent an accurate presentation of the details of life from being pleasing and sometimes moving. And humor—the chief virtue of Middle English literature—is apt to flash everywhere, even in the most solemn and foreboding of moralizations.

Thus the new perspective reveals a broader horizon—too broad, indeed, and too clouded with distractions to enable the average writer to bring everything into clear focus. It takes a powerfully disciplined mind to comprehend infinite variety in a single artistic vision: happily, English popular literature was ultimately to produce such a mind in Geoffrey Chaucer, the greatest poet in Middle English and one of the greatest in English. Chaucer was by birth nonaristocratic, a bourgeois, and one of the chief excellences of his work was its fusion of essentially popular English elements with aristocratic elements borrowed from other literatures. And popular literature had, of course, preserved and even enhanced the old oral tradition, in which the poet, by speaking directly to the audience, tends to "perform" his poem and so to become a dramatic character within it—a tendency that was to find its fullest artistic development in Chaucer's *Canterbury Tales,* whose many speakers unite in a drama larger and more enthralling than English literature had previously seen.

WRITINGS RELIGIOUS AND SECULAR

It is a truism that the greater portion of Middle English that has survived is religious, but, like all truisms, this one is in many ways misleading. The church did indeed have a virtual monopoly on literacy during much of the later Middle Ages, for the average person who had learned to read and write probably had done so because he had signified his intention (not always fulfilled) of becoming a cleric—that is, an ecclesiast, performing one of the many functions of the church: otherwise, he would probably not have received any but the most elementary kind of education. Furthermore, the church not only had this direct claim upon the services of the majority of literate men but also was itself a large producer of books in the physical sense (books were actually hand-written manuscripts) as well as a maintainer (especially in its monasteries) of libraries. Therefore it is only natural that religious literature should bulk so large. Yet much secular literature has also survived, and it is probable that much more has not. Some that has survived was produced, in accordance with an ancient paradox, by writers who could not write or did not trouble to—professional storytellers such as minstrels who committed to memory tales that they had heard others recite or had composed themselves: such literature had to depend for survival on the special interest of some literate hearer who wished to possess the story himself. And even secular literature which was committed to writing might sometimes be lost because of the low esteem in which it was held by the more austere clerics who would enforce St. Paul's precept that everything that is written ought to express specific Christian doctrine: secular works that failed to embody this principle might well be removed from library shelves to make way for works containing doctrine.

The Pauline precept, while it was certainly not heeded by all medieval writers, did exert a good deal of influence on literature. History, which presumably tells the truth about man's past, was considered naturally doctrinal, so that the historian needed to make no apology for his writing. But insistence upon historical truth left no place for what we should call fiction, the narrative of imagined happenings—and the medieval literary imagination was thus theoretically limited to rhetorical enhancement of statements of truth. In order to circumvent so large an inhibition on the use of the imagination medieval writers adopted various stratagems. In the first place, fiction could simply be made to assume the guise of history, and that it was frequently made to do so is reflected in the fact that our word "story," meaning any narrative whether true or false, is merely a by-form of the word "history." Medieval romances, for instance, generally purport to be true, and the fact that they often concern genuine historical characters such as Alexander the Great or Charlemagne lends credibility to the most unlikely events that occur in them. Furthermore, as in Old English times, there was no clear distinction between history and folk-tradition—any legend of long persistence became "historical," as King Arthur did when he was clothed in the respectability of Geoffrey of Monmouth's Latin narrative.

But for a writer who wished to make up a new story or to retell an old one that was a palpable fiction, some other sanction had to be found. The most ancient of these sanctions was allegorization: the Fathers of the Church had justified the reading and enjoyment of the great pagan poems such as the *Aeneid* on the grounds that the obviously fictional narrative concealed moral truth that was not unconformable to Christian doctrine —thus the trials of the Trojan Aeneas could be read as a metaphor for the trials of the Christian soul. A writer who wished to satisfy both his creative imagination and the need for doctrine might work backward from this method of interpretation and produce his own allegorizable fiction: hence the popularity, especially among learned ecclesiastical writers, of personification allegory, in which the allegory is self-explanatory since the actors bear the names of the psychological and moral qualities that they represent. Other writers, less ambitious, preferred to justify their retelling of old stories by appending allegorical interpretations to bring out covert doctrine—interpretations that are often more ingenious than persuasive. Probably the easiest and most popular of all methods of justification was the simple one of adding a moral at the end of a tale in the manner of an Aesopian fable: there have survived several large collections of stories thus moralized by pious clerks for the edification of the populace; in these, however, the moral often seems like a desperate afterthought whose import is no match for the sheer narrative interest of what has gone before. But this genre of storytelling, technically called the *exemplum*, became one of the richest forms of medieval narrative, attaining its culmination in Chaucer's Pardoner's Tale (printed below)—in which, however, the narrative interest still tends to outweigh the moral intent.

THE QUALITY OF MIDDLE ENGLISH LITERATURE

Middle English literature, as a whole, lacks originality. This lack—which, stated another way, amounts to repetitiveness—is partly due to the attempt by so many writers, both religious and secular, to make their works reflect the unchanging principles of medieval Christian doctrine (an attempt which, of course, also tends to blur any clear distinction between the religious and the secular). Until the end of the 14th century Christian teaching was primarily concerned with the issue of personal salvation—that is, it put more emphasis on the moral and spiritual responsibilities of the individual than it did on his ethical or social responsibilities. Medieval idealism characteristically looked to the world to come for the only answer to men's troubles and considered the reformation of this world neither possible nor especially desirable. Sin was seen not so much as a disease poisoning society on earth as something which jeopardized each man's future. Even William Langland, who in his more passionate moments expresses powerful indignation at the existence of remediable social evils, in the long run seems to recommend that the individual Christian not try to reform the world, but. patiently endure it. So constant is the attitude that life in this world is only a waiting period before we enter something better (or worse) that the modern reader is apt to get the impression of the Middle Ages as a period of intellectual and social stasis, a period in which time was standing still. And the fact is that not only in specifically moral and doctrinal literature, whose premises are timeless, but also in ephemeral literature designed primarily to entertain, one senses this unchangingness: a romance at the beginning of the 13th century is only a little more primitive than one written in the 15th (with which it shares its plot), and at the very end of the period Malory is still peopling with his knights a never-never land of chivalry that had its origin in 12th-century France.

Now it is perfectly clear that between 1066 and 1485 England underwent large political and social changes—in such matters as the development of feudalism, the gradual evolution of Parliament, the growth of cities and of the middle class along with the increase in foreign trade, and in many other similar phenomena. But apparently the changes occurred too slowly to produce much intellectual awareness of them on the part of writers. The great exception is, of course, Chaucer, whose pages are informed, especially in his handling of the bourgeois, by an excited sense of the novelty of social life in his own times; Langland's poem also possesses something of this—though without Chaucer's tone of approval; and Langland himself, when he describes the social structure of the kingdom, fails to recognize the existence of the bourgeoisie, characteristically subsuming them under the title of commons, which he thought consisted or should consist mostly of farmers. But in an age where most people, perhaps, were born in the same village where their grandfathers had been born and lived virtually the same lives, doing the same work with the same tools, enjoying the same sports and the same festivals, large slow-moving change is probably bound to be virtually imperceptible, and if perceived disapproved. And it is necessary to remember that no century since the Middle Ages has failed to produce far more changes than all the four centuries of the later Middle Ages put together and that compared to the changes that have taken place in society in the last fifty years the Middle Ages does indeed represent a vast stasis.

But if in a broad historical sense change was imperceptible, in the daily life of medieval man it was all too visible. Indeed, the inevitability of change—for the worse, even in the lives of men already apparently wholly wretched—is one of the most insistently repetitive themes of Middle English literature. Nor is this theme to be thought of merely as an expression of the world-hating doctrine discussed above: rather, the theme and the world-hating doctrine itself are both largely the result of the violence of life in the Middle Ages, a violence not matched again in history until our own times. Famine, war, pestilence, and death—these are the riders who passed through the streets of medieval cities and villages by night and day. Probably not all Englishmen led lives as precarious as their rulers, but the fact that eight of the eighteen kings who reigned in England between 1066 and 1485 died deaths of violence or deaths resulting from violent activity is not uncharacteristic of the time: the Conqueror, dead in 1087 while fighting in France, of an injury caused by the pommel of his horse's saddle —a type of injury that was still mortally wounding knights four centuries later; his son, William II, struck by an arrow while hunting in the New Forest in 1100; Richard I, the Lion-Hearted, struck by an arrow in battle in 1199; Edward II, murdered in 1327; Richard II, murdered in 1400 in the year following his deposition by Henry IV; Henry VI, murdered in 1471; Edward V, one of the Princes in the Tower, murdered in 1483; and Richard III, killed fighting at Bosworth Field in 1485. Meanwhile men hardly less august were also constantly meeting death in battle, or by murder, or by accident, or, not infrequently, on the scaffold before a fascinated populace. The chroniclers who record these events say little of the lower orders of society, but constant warfare against enemies at home and abroad, the depredations of the powerful in supplying themselves from the fruits of the poor man's toil, the fearful severity of the laws combined with the failure to enforce them against the strong; and, especially after the middle of the 14th century, recurrent pestilence compounded by famine —all these explain why change for the worst seems to have been the unchanging expectation of medieval men. And, even in the temporary absence of these, the coldness and darkness of an English winter for people living in badly insulated dwellings with only minimal heat and light might well seem to make life a bleak perpetual twilight.

In view of the violence prevalent during most of the period, it is perhaps extraordinary that so much literature was produced. But even in the worst of times things are not always and everywhere at their worst; Spring does come, and some people come through life almost untouched by disasters that seem historically to be omnipresent, while others live through them to experience periods of peace or experience periods of peace before disaster overtakes them. And the fact is that a curious normality permeates the best Middle English literature—which is, indeed, in general less preoccupied with its age's violence than we are with ours, probably because it never conceived of a time when violence was not a fact of life. Despite the constant warning that they were under to expect change for the worse, men in the Middle Ages seem, in their daily lives, to have pursued the same pleasures that we pursue today—pursued them with rather more relish because they were rarer: this is clear both from the accounts of those who approved of the pursuit as well as of those who did not. As the general violence suggests, medieval society was in many ways more primitive than our own—or more frankly primitive—and may thus seem to us more childlike. People took tremendous pleasure in color, in dress, in ritual, in parades, in spectacles, in elaborate food and drink (when they could get them), in all those aspects of life that children especially love, and most adults do not scorn. Like children, medieval men were subject to emotional extremes —wept more quickly than we do, went more quickly from weeping to laughter and back again; were headstrong and hasty, quick to sin zestfully and repent heartily and then to sin and repent again. Yet it is a mistake to overemphasize the childishness of medieval men: their life was physically more limited than ours, without our comforts, our mobility, our communications; it was even more precarious, more uncertain; but as it is reflected in the best writers, such as Chaucer, their life was lived very richly and perhaps with greater awareness and greater savor than ours.

THE EARLIER LITERATURE

There has survived very little literature that was written in English between the Conquest and the beginning of the 13th century. But that the

Norman invasion did not cause a complete discontinuity in English is evident from a number of facts. During the 12th century, for instance, "modernized" copies were made of late Old English homilies and of King Alfred's translation of Boethius. Furthermore, what is probably the earliest original Middle English prose work reveals a level of artistry impossible to any writer who was not working in a highly developed tradition of prose writing. This is the *Ancrene Riwle*, or "Rule for Anchoresses" (i.e., female religious recluses), written probably during the second half of the 12th century. This is the product of a mind at once highly sophisticated and deeply devout—warm, humorous, earthy—and a stylist so brilliant that English prose is able to offer nothing comparable until Malory's *Morte Darthur* some three centuries later. Probably the *Ancrene Riwle* originated in the west of England in an area that somehow managed to retain throughout the period of the Conquest the high level of English culture achieved by the West Saxon kingdom under Alfred.

One of the earliest major Middle English poems that has survived also points to a continuity between Old and Middle English. This is Layamon's *Brut*, composed between 1175 and 1205 in an alliterative prosody that is recognizably descended from the Old English poetic measure—and alliterative poetry was to flourish throughout the Middle English period, especially during the so-called 14th-century "alliterative revival" which culminates in *Gawain and the Green Knight* and in Langland's *Piers Plowman*. But the *Brut* is also interesting because it contains the first treatment in English of the Arthurian legend. Layamon's immediate source was a Norman poem by Wace, which in turn was based on Geoffrey of Monmouth's *History of the Kings of Britain*, the Latin work mentioned earlier. When Layamon began his poem, he had intended to make use also of Bede's genuine history of England, but he soon found the past described by legend more interesting to him. According to post-Conquest tradition, England had been founded by a descendant of the Trojan Aeneas, the founder of Rome, and the old name of the island, Britain, was supposedly derived from the name of its founder, Brutus (hence the title *Brut*). Of the mythical kings of England who succeeded Brutus the most famous was Arthur. The *Brut* develops the Arthurian legend somewhat beyond its sources, but Layamon was not only the first English writer to treat Arthurian material extensively, but also the only Englishman other than Geoffrey to add anything of significance to the legend. In France Chrétien de Troyes had in several romances already invested the legend with that curious charm it was still to possess in Malory, and after Chrétien, Arthur continued to be a favorite hero in French literature, from which all later English treatments, with the possible exception of *Sir Gawain and the Green Knight*, are drawn. In origin the legend was probably mainly Celtic—i.e., Welsh and Irish—and was carried to France by those Celts who migrated from England to Brittany at the time of the Anglo-Saxon invasions. In Layamon's village on the Severn River near Wales, Welsh stories of Arthur may still have been current, and it was perhaps this that impelled him to concentrate on the legendary king. It is interesting that not only was this most English of heroes given immortality by French writers, but also that the historical Arthur who lies behind him was a defender of the island against those

Anglo-Saxons who were the ancestors of the Englishmen who adopted him as their traditional hero.

Both Layamon and the poet of *Beowulf* dealt with legendary materials which they thought of as history. Layamon's treatment is, however, different from the epic mode of *Beowulf*: it moves toward the genre, originated by the Middle Ages, known as "romance." The romance has certain typical features: it generally concerns knights (though not always) and involves a large amount of fighting as well as miscellaneous adventures; it makes liberal use of the improbable, often of the supernatural; it does not avoid the subject of romantic love, though it does not always include it; characterization is standardized, so that heroes, heroines, and wicked lords could easily move from one romance to another without causing any disturbance in the narrative; the plots consist of a vast number of events, and the same event is apt to occur several times within the same romance. In general, artistic unity is rarely striven for, and even more rarely attained.

Popular as it was in medieval England, Middle English romance is very likely to disappoint the modern reader. In the first place, very few accomplished poets—the author of *Sir Gawain and the Green Knight* is the principal exception—turned their hand to romance; it was apparently left largely to minstrels and other uncultivated versifiers addressing a semi-literate audience, most often in dog-trot verse full of windy clichés. The great age of medieval romance had been the 12th and early 13th centuries, and its chief breeding ground had been aristocratic society in France, where such poets as Chrétien de Troyes spun their marvelously sophisticated tales, and the genre was also not neglected by the somewhat less aristocratic Anglo-Norman writers. The Middle English purveyors of romance, functioning before nonaristocratic audiences in the second half of the 13th and in the 14th centuries, introduced the French romances into English, so that the majority of the hundred or more English romances that have survived are either proved or suspected adaptations from the French. The result of the lag in time and change in audience is artistically unfortunate, though often unintentionally amusing. Aristocratic ideals of behavior of a different era and an alien society were replaced by patterns of behavior that would be easily comprehended by bourgeois and lower-class Englishmen. Heroes who have all the accouterments of the most chivalrous of knights are apt to behave in the crudest fashion, whether they are fighting, eating, or making love: they act as a petty bourgeois might if suddenly given the chance to enjoy the high scale of living of chivalric aristocracy with no education in how such a life should be conducted. Nevertheless, it is often agreeable to watch the blunt Englishman who replaced the aristocratic hero react with practical common sense to the extravagant situations in which the poem has placed him.

All the various subject matters of medieval romance are represented in Middle English, most of them in very undistinguished form. It is particularly surprising that the later Arthurian romances are so poor; besides *Sir Gawain and the Green Knight*, which stands by itself, only two are of value: the stanzaic *Morte Arthur* (after 1400), a lively, readable, if unsubstantial account of the love of Lancelot and Guinevere, drawn, with some originality, from the French; and the alliterative *Morte Arthure* (ca. 1360) a tale of Arthur's wars stemming from Geoffrey of Monmouth, which in its vigor, at least, harks back to Old English heroic poetry: Malory used both of these to supplement his French sources in his own prose *Morte Darthur.*

Of the rather few secular poems not in the romance genre the earliest and best is the *Owl and the Nightingale*, probably written during the last years of the 12th century. This poem, written in rhyming couplets with alternate syllabic stress, a form that Middle English writers early borrowed from the French, consists of a debate between the two birds of the title, a dispute arising not from an intellectual disagreement but from natural hostility. The poem comes to no conclusion, though it suggests many, since the birds associate themselves with some large and enduring human issues. Between the rich humorousness and earthiness of this poem and some of Chaucer's there is a close kinship, but, unhappily, from the two centuries that separate its poet from Chaucer there has survived no other secular poem of such excellence. *Dame Sirith,* the only non-Chaucerian fabliau (a realistic verse short story) in English, is lively enough, but crude in comparison with such a work as Chaucer's *Miller's Tale.* Some of the secular lyrics are excellent, to be sure, but they are in short supply. Indeed, when one considers the English tradition of secular literature before Chaucer, his achievement seems even more extraordinary.

THE FLOWERING OF MIDDLE ENGLISH

The great age of Middle English literature was the last quarter of the 14th century. Here we have, writing probably at the same moment, the author of *Gawain,* the author of *Piers Plowman,* and the author of the *Canterbury Tales.* Not only did the poet of *Gawain* produce the best romance in Middle English, but he was also an accomplished religious poet; his Biblical narrative in alliterative verse, *Patience,* the story of Jonah, is perhaps the best of its kind since Anglo-Saxon times. In the *Pearl* he combined elegy with theology to produce the most moving religious poem— and the most finely wrought poem—of the English later Middle Ages. And if, as some suppose, he also wrote *St. Erkenwald,* a charming story of a miraculous event in the life of a saint, then he is also responsible for giving ultimate distinction to that most undistinguished and most voluminous genre, the saints' legends. William Langland's achievement in *Piers Plowman* is important both in literature and in history, since he faced squarely in great poetry the great issues of his day—and these became the great issues of the following century and a half: imitations of *Piers Plowman* which borrow both Piers himself and Langland's anti-ecclesiastical satire played an important part in bringing on the reformation of the church which Langland prophesied but would have deplored. Geoffrey Chaucer's achievement was greatest of all: while he is entirely rooted in the soil of the English Middle Ages, his art carries him well out of the Middle Ages to make him one of the two or three greatest poets in English.

This sudden florescence may have been partly due to an increase in patronage of literature by the well-to-do. Chaucer was a "court poet" who seems to have been encouraged not only by John of Gaunt but perhaps also by Gaunt's father, Edward III (died 1377), as well as by his nephew Richard II (deposed 1399) and, in the last year of the poet's life, by Gaunt's son, Henry IV. The *Gawain* poet probably wrote for a provincial aristocratic court, remote from London but no less interested in literary art. Even William Langland seems to have enjoyed patronage, but from what source it is hard to be sure: it is probable that at one time or another he was sheltered by monasteries, and it is not unlikely that he ended his life in one. In any case, English literature is fortunate that these three great contemporary poets all found encouragement from one source or another.

History is often unnecessarily harsh with lesser writers who had the misfortune to be roughly contemporary with the great, and so, perhaps, it has been with Chaucer's friend, the poet John Gower. Gower, a far more typically medieval writer than Chaucer, wrote three considerable works which, linguistically at least, summarized the English Middle Ages: one was in Latin, one in Norman French, and one in English. The last of these, the *Confessio Amantis* ("Lover's Confession"), is, like the *Canterbury Tales*, a series of stories which might now seem better than they do if Chaucer's tales did not offer so high a standard of comparison. But, despite his occasional tediousness, Gower is greatly superior to the English poets of the next generation such as John Lydgate and Thomas Hoccleve, who, in the dying years of the Middle Ages, seemed determined to perpetuate the worst medieval vices of endless expatiation, flat moralization, and bad verse. They claimed Chaucer as their master, but he had far more to teach than they were able to learn.

THE FIFTEENTH CENTURY

England in the 15th century produced no major writer except Sir Thomas Malory (d.1471), who, if the old identification is correct, epitomizes in his career the troublous times of the Wars of the Roses: in his long sojourn in prison toward the end of his life, he whiled away the time by compiling his great *Morte Darthur*. Earlier in the century, another prisoner had similarly entertained himself: King James I of Scotland, incarcerated in London from 1406 to 1424, wrote the *King's Quair* or *King's Book*, an agreeable love poem which is a far better Chaucerian imitation than James's English contemporaries were able to achieve. And indeed, all the better poets of the century are Scots, the so-called Scottish Chaucerians, especially Robert Henryson and William Dunbar, whose poetry often reflects Chaucer's satirical spirit and his characteristic liveliness.

Despite the paucity of major literary names in the English kingdom, the 15th century was a period in which popular literature flourished. Some of the best lyrics, both religious and secular, date from this time; and this was also the century during which many of the ballads were composed. It was also a period of much activity in the drama. The mystery plays, which had probably been well established in the preceding century, continued to be performed widely, and the cycles that have been preserved from York, Chester, and Wakefield date from the 15th century. The same years saw the development of the morality play, culminating at the very end of the century in *Everyman*. The authors of the plays, ballads, and lyrics of the century are nameless; aside from the plays, manuscripts of which were kept only by the towns in which the performances were given, these anonymous works were probably transmitted orally and only haphazardly written down. Fortunately for the future history of English literature, Malory's *Morte Darthur* did not have to depend on the chance survival of a manuscript; it was printed in 1485 by William Caxton, who had introduced printing by movable type to England less than ten years earlier. But for Caxton, Malory would have been unknown until 1934, when a manuscript of his work finally came to light.

To assign a specific date, as historians must, for the end of an era that extends for more than eight centuries is an arbitrary act. Nevertheless, some events that took place close to the year 1485 give some justification for naming this date as the end of the English Middle Ages. In literature, the printing houses of Caxton and his followers were to effect an important change, replacing the old relationship of speaker to hearer with the new relationship of writer to reader. Henry VII's accession to the throne in 1485 restored political stability which gave men leisure for intellectual activities, and his court attracted humanist scholars who brought with them the "New Learning"—in particular, the knowledge of Greek and Greek thought which was to revitalize English culture. And under the next monarch, Henry VIII, England was to separate itself from the Church of Rome, and, for better or for worse, from a vital part of its medieval heritage. Yet beneath the surface of the Renaissance the reader will still detect much that remains from the Middle Ages.

MEDIEVAL ENGLISH

The medieval works in this book were composed in two different states of our language: Old English, the language which took shape among the Germanic settlers of England and preserved its integrity until the Norman Conquest radically altered English civilization; and Middle English, the earliest records of which date from the early 12th century and which gave way to Modern English shortly after the introduction of printing at the end of the 15th century. Old English is a very heavily inflected language (that is, the words change form, to indicate changes in usage, such as person, number, tense, case, mood, etc. Most languages have some inflection—for example, the personal pronouns in Modern English have different forms when used as objects—but a "heavily inflected" language is one in which almost all classes of words undergo elaborate patterns of change). Its vocabulary is almost entirely Germanic. In Middle English, the inflectional system is weakened; and a large number of words were introduced into it from France, so that many of the older native words disappeared. Because of the difficulty of Old English, all selections from it in this book have been given in translation. In order that the reader may see an example of the language, *Cædmon's Hymn* has been printed in the original, together with an interlinear translation. The present discussion, then, is concerned only with Middle English.

The chief difficulty with Middle English for the modern reader is caused not by its inflections so much as by its spelling, which may be described as a rough-and-ready phonetic system, and by the fact that it is not a single standardized language, but consists of a number of regional dialects each with its own peculiarities of sound and its own systems for representing sounds in writing. The Midland dialect—the dialect of London and of Chaucer, and the ancestor of our own standard speech—

differs greatly from the dialect spoken in the west of England (the original dialect of *Piers Plowman*), and from that of the northwest (*Sir Gawain and the Green Knight*), and from that of the north (*The Second Shepherd's Play*); and these dialects differ from one another. In this book, the long texts composed in the more difficult dialects have been translated or modernized; and those which, like Chaucer, *Everyman*, the lyrics, and the ballads, appear in the original, have been respelled in a way that it is hoped will aid the reader. The remarks which follow apply chiefly to Chaucer's Midland English, though certain non-Midland dialectal variations are noted if they occur in some of the other selections.

I. THE SOUNDS OF MIDDLE ENGLISH: GENERAL RULES

The following general analysis of the sounds of Middle English will enable the reader who has not time for detailed study to read Middle English aloud so as to preserve some of its most essential characteristics, without, however, giving heed to many important details. Section II, Detailed Analysis, is designed for the reader who wishes to go more deeply into the pronunciation of Middle English.

Middle English differs from Modern English in three principal respects: 1. the pronunciation of the long vowels *a, e, i* (or *y*), *o*, and *u* (spelled *ou, ow*); 2. the fact that Middle English final *e* is often sounded; 3. the fact that all Middle English consonants are sounded.

1. Long Vowels

Middle English vowels are long when they are doubled (*aa, ee, oo*) or when they are terminal (*he, to, holy*); *a, e,* and *o* are long when followed by a single consonant plus a vowel (*name, mete, note*). Middle English vowels are short when they are followed by two consonants.

Long *a* is sounded like the *a* in Modern English "father": *maken, maad*.

Long *e* may be sounded like the *a* in Modern English "name" (ignoring the distinction between the close and open vowel): *be, sweete*.

Long *i* (or *y*) is sounded like the *i* in Modern English "machine": *lif, whit; myn, holy*.

Long *o* may be sounded like the *o* in Modern English "note" (again ignoring the distinction between the close and open vowel): *do, soone*.

Long *u* (spelled *ou, ow*) is sounded like the *oo* in Modern English "goose": *hous, flowr*.

Note that in general Middle English long vowels are pronounced like long vowels in modern languages other than English. Short vowels and diphthongs, however, may be pronounced as in Modern English.

2. Final e

In Middle English syllabic verse, final *e* is sounded like the *a* in "sofa" to provide a needed unstressed syllable: *Another Nonnë with hire haddë she*. But (cf. *hire* in the example) final *e* is suppressed when not needed for the meter. It is commonly silent before words beginning with a vowel or *h*.

3. Consonants

Middle English consonants are pronounced separately in all combinations—*gnat: g-nat; knave: k-nave; write: w-rite; folk: fol-k*. In a simplified system of pronunciation the combination *gh* as in *night* or *thought* may be treated as if it were silent.

II. THE SOUNDS OF MIDDLE ENGLISH: DETAILED ANALYSIS

1. *Simple Vowels*

Sound	Pronunciation	Example
long *a* (spelled *a, aa*)	*a* in "father"	*maken, maad*
short *a*	*o* in "hot"	*cappe*
long *e* close (spelled *e, ee*)	*a* in "name"	*be, sweete*
long *e* open (spelled *e, ee*)	*e* in "there"	*mete, heeth*
short *e*	*e* in "set"	*setten*
final *e*	*a* in "sofa"	*large*
long *i* (spelled *i, y*)	*i* in "machine"	*lif, myn*
short *i*	*i* in "wit"	*wit*
long *o* close (spelled *o, oo*)	*o* in "note"	*do, soone*
long *o* open (spelled *o, oo*)	*oa* in "broad"	*go, goon*
short *o*	*o* in "oft"	*pot*
long *u* when spelled *ou, ow*	*oo* in "goose"	*hous, flowr*
long *u* when spelled *u*	*u* in "pure"	*vertu*
short *u* (spelled *u, o*)	*u* in "full"	*ful, love*

Doubled vowels and terminal vowels are always long, while single vowels before two consonants other than *th, ch* are always short. The vowels *a, e,* and *o* are long before a single consonant followed by a vowel: *nāmë, sēkë* (sick), *hōly*. In general, words that have descended into Modern English reflect their original Middle English quantity: *līven* (to live), but *līf* (life).

The close and open sounds of long *e* and long *o* may often be identified by the Modern English spellings of the words in which they appear. Original long close *e* is generally represented in Modern English by *ee*: "sweet," "knee," "teeth," "see" have close *e* in Middle English, but so does "be"; original long open *e* is generally represented in Modern English by *ea*: "meat," "heath," "sea," "great," "breath" have open *e* in Middle English. Similarly, original long close *o* is now generally represented by *oo*: "soon," "food," "good," but also "do," "to"; original long open *o* is represented either by *oa* or by *o*: "coat," "boat," "moan," but also "go," "bone," "foe," "home." Notice that original close *o* is now almost always pronounced like the *oo* in "goose," but that original open *o* is almost never so pronounced; thus it is often possible to identify the Middle English vowels through Modern English sounds.

The nonphonetic Middle English spelling of *o* for short *u* has been preserved in a number of Modern English words ("love," "son," "come"), but in others *u* has been restored: "sun" (*sonne*), "run" (*ronne*).

For the treatment of final *e*, see above, General Rules, section 2.

2. *Diphthongs*

Sound	Pronunciation	Example
ai, ay, ei, ay	between *ai* in "aisle" and *ay* in "day"	*saide, day, veine, preye*
au, aw	*ou* in "out"	*chaunge, bawdy*
eu, ew	*ew* in "few"	*newe*

| *oi, oy* | *oy* in "joy" | *joye, point* |
| *ou, ow* | *ou* in "thought" | *thought, lowe* |

Note that in words with *ou, ow* which in Modern English are sounded with the *ou* of "about," the combination indicates not the diphthong but the simple vowel long *u* (see above, Simple Vowels).

3. *Consonants*

In general, all consonants except *h* were always sounded in Middle English, including consonants that have become silent in Modern English, such as the *g* in *gnaw*, the *k* in *knight*, the *l* in *folk*, and the *w* in *write*. In noninitial *gn*, however, the *g* was silent as in Modern English "sign." Initial *h* was silent in short common English words and in words borrowed from French, and may have been almost silent in all words. The combination *gh* as in *night* or *thought* was sounded like the *ch* of German *ich* or *nach*. Note that Middle English *gg* represents both the hard sound of "dagger" and the soft sound of "bridge."

III. PARTS OF SPEECH AND GRAMMAR

1. *Nouns*

The plural and possessive of nouns end in *es*, formed by adding *s* or *es* to the singular: *knight, knightes; roote, rootes*; a final consonant is frequently doubled before *es: bed, beddes*. A common irregular plural is *yën*, from *yë*, eye.

2. *Pronouns*

The chief differences from Modern English are as follows:

Modern English	Middle English
I	*I, ich* (*ik* is a northern form)
you (singular)	*thou* (subjective); *thee* (objective)
her	*hir(e), her(e)*
its	*his*
you (plural)	*ye* (subjective); *you* (objective)
their	*hir*
them	*hem*

In formal speech, the second person plural is often used for the singular. The possessive adjectives *my, thy* take *n* before a word beginning with a vowel or *h: thyn yë, myn host*.

3. *Adjectives*

Adjectives ending in a consonant add final *e* when they stand before the noun they modify and after another modifying word such as *the, this, that*, or nouns or pronouns in the possessive: *a good hors*, but *the* (*this, my, the kinges*) *goode hors*. They also generally add *e* when standing before and modifying a plural noun, a noun in the vocative, or any proper noun: *goode men, oh goode man, faire Venus*.

Adjectives are compared by adding *er(e)* for the comparative, *est(e)* for the superlative. Sometimes the stem vowel is shortened or altered in the process: *sweete, swettere, swettest; long, lenger, lengest*.

4. *Adverbs*

Adverbs are formed from adjectives by adding *e, ly*, or *liche*; the adjective *fair* thus yields *faire, fairly, fairliche*.

5. *Verbs*

Middle English verbs, like Modern English verbs, are either "weak" or "strong." Weak verbs form their preterites and past participles with a *t* or *d* suffix and preserve the same stem vowel throughout their systems, though it is sometimes shortened in the preterite and past participle: *love, loved; bend, bent; hear, heard; meet, met.* Strong verbs do not use the *t* or *d* suffix, but vary their stem vowel in the preterite and past participle: *take, took, taken; begin, began, begun; find, found, found.*

The inflectional endings are the same for Middle English strong verbs and weak verbs except in the preterite singular and the imperative singular. In the following paradigms, the weak verbs *loven* (to love) and *heeren* (to hear), and the strong verbs *taken* (to take) and *ginnen* (to begin) serve as models.

	Present Indicative	Preterite Indicative
I	*love, heere*	*loved(e), herde*
	take, ginne	*took, gan*
thou	*lovest, heerest*	*lovedest, herdest*
	takest, ginnest	*tooke, gonne*
he, she, it	*loveth, heereth*	*loved(e), herde*
	taketh, ginneth	*took, gan*
we, ye, they	*love(n) (th), heere(n) (th)*	*loved(e) (en), herde(n)*
	take(n) (th), ginne(n) (th)	*tooke(n), gonne(n)*

The present plural ending *eth* is southern, while the *e(n)* ending is Midland and characteristic of Chaucer. In the north, *s* may appear as the ending of all persons of the present. In the weak preterite, when the ending *e* gave a verb three or more syllables, it was frequently dropped. Note that in certain strong verbs like *ginnen* there are two distinct stem vowels in the preterite: even in Chaucer's time, however, one of these had begun to replace the other, and Chaucer occasionally writes *gan* for all persons of the preterite.

	Present Subjunctive	Preterite Subjunctive
Singular	*love, heere*	*lovede, herde*
	take, ginne	*tooke, gonne*
Plural	*love(n), heere(n)*	*lovede(n), herde(n)*
	take(n), ginne(n)	*tooke(n), gonne(n)*

In verbs like *ginnen*, which have two stem vowels in the indicative preterite, it is the vowel of the plural and of the second person singular that is used for the preterite subjunctive.

The imperative singular of most weak verbs is *e*: *(thou) love*, but of some weak verbs and all strong verbs, the imperative singular is without termination: *(thou) heer, taak, gin.* The imperative plural of all verbs is either *e* or *eth*: *(ye) love(th), heere(th), take(th), ginne(th).*

The infinitive of verbs is *e* or *en*: *love(n), heere(n), take(n), ginne(n).*

The past participle of weak verbs is the same as the preterite without inflectional ending: *loved, herd.* In strong verbs the ending is either *e* or *en*: *take(n), gonne(n).* The prefix *y* often appears on past participles: *yloved, yherd, ytake(n).*

OLD AND MIDDLE ENGLISH PROSODY

All the poetry of Old English is in the same verse form. The verse unit is the single line, since rhyme was not used to link one line to another, except very occasionally in late Old English. The organizing device of the line is alliteration, the beginning of several words with the same sound ("Foemen fled"). The Old English alliterative line contains four principal stresses, and is divided into two half-lines of two stresses each by a strong medial caesura, or pause. These two half-lines are linked to each other by the alliteration: at least one of the two stressed words in the first half-line, and usually both of them, begin with the same sound as the first stressed word of the second half-line (the second stressed word is generally non-alliterative). The fourth line of *Beowulf* is an example:

> Oft Scyld Scefing   sceaþena þreatum.

For further examples, see *Cædmon's Hymn*, printed below. It will be noticed that any vowel alliterates with any other vowel. In addition to the alliteration, the length of the unstressed syllables and their number and pattern is governed by a highly complex set of rules. When sung or intoned—as it was—to the rhythmic strumming of a harp, Old English poetry must have been wonderfully impressive in the dignified, highly formalized way which aptly fits both its subject matter and tone.

The majority of Middle English verse is either in alternately stressed rhyming verse, adapted from French after the Conquest, or in alliterative verse that is descended from Old English. The latter preserves the caesura of Old English and in its purest form the same alliterative system, the two stressed words of the first half-line (or at least one of them) alliterating with the first stressed word in the second half-line. But most of the alliterative poets allowed themselves a number of deviations from the norm. All four stressed words may alliterate, as in the first line of *Piers Plowman:*

> In a summer season   when soft was the sun.

Or the line may contain five, six, or even more stressed words, of which all or only the basic minimum may alliterate:

> A fair field full of folk   found I therebetween.

There is no rule determining the number of unstressed syllables, and at times some poets are apt to ignore alliteration entirely. As in Old English, any vowel may alliterate with any other vowel; furthermore, since initial *h* was silent or lightly pronounced in Middle English, words beginning with *h* are treated as though they began with the following vowel.

There are two general types of stressed verse with rhyme. In the more common, stressed and unstressed syllables alternate regularly: x X x X x X; or, with two unstressed syllables intervening: x x X x x X x x X; or a combination of the two: x x X x X x x X (of the reverse patterns, only X x X x X x is common in English). There is also a line which can only be defined as containing a predetermined number of stressed syllables but an irregular number and pattern of unstressed syllables. Much Middle English verse has to be read without expectation of regularity: some of this was evidently composed in the irregular meter, but some was probably originally composed according to a strict metrical system which has been obliterated by scribes careless of fine points. One receives the impression that many of the lyrics—as well as the *Second Shepherd's Play*—were at least composed with regular syllabic alternation. In the ballads, on the other hand, and in the play *Everyman*, only the number of stresses is predetermined (and perhaps not even this in *Everyman*), but not the number or placement of unstressed syllables.

In pre-Chaucerian verse the number of stresses, whether regularly or irregularly alternated, was most often four, though sometimes the number was three, and rose in some poems to seven. Rhyme in Middle English as in Modern English may be either between adjacent or alternate lines, or may occur in more complex patterns. The *Canterbury Tales* are in rhymed couplets, the line containing five stresses with regular alternation —technically known as iambic pentameter, the standard English poetic line, perhaps introduced into English by Chaucer. In reading Chaucer and much pre-Chaucerian verse one must remember that the final *e*, which is silent in Modern English, was pronounced at any time in order to provide a needed unstressed syllable. Evidence seems to indicate that it was also pronounced at the end of the line, even though it thus produced a line with eleven syllables. Although he was a very regular metricist, Chaucer used various conventional devices which are apt to make the reader stumble until he understands them. Final *e* is often not pronounced before a word beginning with a vowel or *h*, and may be suppressed whenever metrically convenient. The same medial and terminal syllables that are slurred in Modern English are apt to be suppressed in Chaucer's English: *Canterb'ry* for *Canterbury*; *ev'r* (perhaps *e'er*) for *evere*. The plural in *es* may either be syllabic or reduced to *s* as in Modern English. Despite these seeming irregularities, Chaucer's verse is not difficult to read if one constantly bears in mind the basic pattern of the iambic pentameter line.

Old English Poetry

CÆDMON'S HYMN

Cædmon's *Hymn* is one of the oldest of preserved English poems, having been written between 658 and 680. Bede, the great cleric of Old English times, tells the story of its composition in his *Ecclesiastical History of the English People* (completed in 731). Cædmon, a Northumbrian lay-man, had all his life felt himself incompetent in the art of verse, and when, according to the custom that was used at feasts, the harp was passed around the table so that each guest might entertain the others with a song, Cædmon always found a pretext to take himself from the table before the harp reached him. One night when he had thus avoided sing-ing, he fell asleep in the stable where he had gone to tend the animals. He dreamed that someone came to him and said, "Cædmon, sing me something," and when Cædmon excused himself, the other insisted that he sing, directing him to celebrate the beginning of created things. Cædmon at once sang the *Hymn*. On waking, he remembered his verses; and there-after, Bede tells us, he was able to express any given sacred topic in ex-cellent poetry after only a few hours of work. He became a monk and devoted his life to the composition of Christian verse, but none of the religious poetry in Old English that has been preserved may surely be ascribed to him except his first short work.

The poem is given here in a West Saxon form with a literal interlinear translation. In Old English spelling, æ (as in Cædmon's name and line 3) is a vowel symbol that has not survived; it represented both a short *a* sound and a long open *e* sound. þ (line 2) and ð both represented the sound *th*. The large space in the middle of the line indicates the caesura.

Cædmon's Hymn

Nu sculon herigean   heofonrices   Weard
Now we must praise   heaven-kingdom's Guardian,

Meotodes meahte   and his modgeþanc
the Creator's might   and his mind-plans,

weorc Wuldor-Fæder   swa he wundra gehwæs
the work of the Glory-Father,   when he of wonders of every one,

ece　Drihten eternal Lord,	or　　　　onstealde the beginning established.[1]
He ærest sceop He first　created	ielda[2]　bearnum for men's sons
heofon to hrofe heaven as a roof,	halig Scyppend holy Creator;
ða　middangeard then middle-earth	moncynnes Weard mankind's　Guardian,
ece　Drihten eternal Lord,	æfter　teode afterwards made—
firum　foldan for men earth,	Frea　aelmihtig Master almighty.

THE DREAM OF THE ROOD

The *Dream of the Rood* (i.e., of the Cross) is the finest of a rather large number of religious poems in Old English. Neither its author nor its date of composition is known. It appears in a late 10th-century manuscript located in Vercelli in northern Italy, a manuscript made up of Old English religious poems and sermons. The poet Cynewulf, about whom nothing is surely known except that he wrote four Old English homiletic poems (two of them found in the Vercelli manuscript), has sometimes been credited with the *Dream*, but on no very convincing evidence. The poem may antedate its manuscript by almost three centuries, for some passages from the Rood's speech were carved, with some variations, in runes on a stone cross early in the 8th century: this is the famous Ruthwell Cross, which is preserved near Dumfries in southern Scotland. The precise relation of the poem to this cross is, however, uncertain.

The homiletic tone of the Dreamer's meditation may seem anticlimactic after the intensity, so terse and exciting, of the Rood's address to him, but the former is nevertheless an admirable frame for the latter. The experience of the Cross—its humiliation at the hands of those who changed it from tree to instrument of punishment for criminals, its humility when the young hero Christ mounts upon it, and its pride as the restored "tree of glory"—has a suggestive relevance to the condition of the sad, lonely, sin-stained Dreamer. In the Cross's experience, hope has replaced torment; when, at the end of the poem, the Dreamer describes Christ's triumphant

1. I.e., "established the beginning of every one of wonders."
2. The later manuscript copies read *eorþan*, "earth," for *ælda* (West Saxon *ielda*), "men's."

progress from hell to heaven, the verse recaptures some of the excitement of the Cross's address, reflecting the Dreamer's response to the hope that has been brought him.

The Dream of the Rood[1]

Behold, I shall tell of a most marvelous dream—what I dreamed at midnight, when men and their voices were at rest. It seemed to me that I saw a tree, more wonderful than any other, reach high aloft, bathed in light, brightest of wood. All that beacon[2] was covered with gold. Four gems were set where it met the earth, and five more stood on it high about the crosspiece. There looked upon it many hosts of angels, fair in the form God gave them of old. This was surely no felon's gallows, for holy spirits beheld it, men upon earth, and all this glorious creation. Wonderful was the triumphant tree, and I stained with sin, wounded with wrongdoing. I saw the tree of wonder, adorned with clothes, shine brilliantly, decked with gold; splendidly had jewels covered the Lord's tree. But through that gold I might see wretches' ancient agony, for now it began to bleed upon the right side. I was sadly troubled, afraid of that fair sight. I saw that beacon, changeable, alter in clothes and in color: now was it wet with moisture, drenched with blood's flowing, now adorned with treasure. But I lay there a long while looking upon the Saviour's tree, troubled in mind, until I heard it give voice; the noblest of trees began to speak.

"It was long ago—still I remember it—that I was hewn down at the wood's edge, taken from my stump. Fierce foes seized me, shaped me into the spectacle that they wished, bade me lift their felons. Men carried me on their shoulders to a hill where they set me down; foes enough fastened me there. Then I saw the Master of Mankind hasten with all his heart because he wished to climb upon me. I did not dare against God's word bow or break, though I saw earth's surface tremble. All foemen I might have felled, but I stood fast. The young hero stripped himself—he who was God almighty—strong and stouthearted. He climbed upon the high gallows, valiant, in the sight of many, for he would redeem mankind. I shook when the warrior embraced me, yet I dared not bow to earth, fall to the ground's surface: I must stand fast. A cross was I raised; I lifted up the Mighty King, Lord of the Heavens; I dared not bend. They pierced me with dark nails—on me are the wounds seen, open hateful gashes. Nor did I dare do harm to any of them. They mocked

1. This prose translation, by the present editor, has been based in general on the edition of the poem by J. C. Pope, *Seven Old English Poems* (1966).

2. The Old English word *beacen* means also "token" or "sign" and "battle standard."

us both together. I was all wet with blood shed from the sides of that man by the time that he had sent forth his spirit. Many bitter things I had endured on the hill. I saw the God of Hosts cruelly racked. Darkness had covered with its mists the Ruler's body, the bright splendor. Shadow came forth, dark under the clouds. All creation wept, bewailed the King's fall: Christ was on Cross.

"Yet from afar, ready and willing, there came some to the Lord.[3] I saw all this. Sore was I troubled, yet I bent to the hands of the men, with all my heart humble. They took Almighty God, lifted him from his great torment. The warriors let me stand, stained with blood. I was all wounded with arrows. They laid him down, limb-weary, stood at his body's head, gazed upon Heaven's Lord; and he rested him there a while, exhausted after the great struggle. In the sight of his slayer[4] warriors began to build him an earth-home, carved it out of bright stone, set therein the Wielder of Triumphs. Then they began to sing for him a song of lament, sad in the evening. Then would they depart, tired, from the great Lord. He rested with small host; yet we[5] stood in our places a good while, weeping. The song of the men rose up. The body grew cold, the spirit's fair dwelling. Then they began to fell us to the earth—that was a fearful fate. They buried us in a deep pit. Yet thanes[6] of the Lord, friends, heard of me there[7] . . . decked me with gold and silver.

"Thou might now understand, man beloved of me, that I had endured suffering of evils, of grievous sorrows. Now is the happy time come that far and wide men upon earth adore me, and all this glorious creation prays to this beacon. On me the Son of God suffered for a while; therefore now I tower glorious under the heavens, and I may heal every one of those that hold me in awe. Once I was made the hardest of torments, most loathsome to men, before I made open the true road to life for all who have voices. Lo, the Lord of Glory honored me above all the trees of the wood, the Ruler of Heaven, just as his mother also, Mary herself, Almighty God for the sake of all men honored above all woman's kind.

"Now I bid thee, man beloved of me, that thou tell this vision to men. Reveal with thy words that it is the tree of glory on which Almighty God suffered for mankind's many sins and for the deeds done by Adam long ago. Death he tasted there; yet the Lord rose again in his great might to help mankind. Then he ascended into Heaven; but he will come again hither to seek mankind on doomsday, the Lord himself, Almighty God, and his angels with him, that at

---

3. According to John xix.38–39, it was Joseph of Arimathaea and Nicodemus who received Christ's body from the Cross.
4. I.e., the Cross.
5. I.e., Christ's Cross and those on which the two thieves were crucified.
6. Members of the King's body of warriors.
7. A number of lines describing the finding of the Cross have apparently been lost here.

that time he who has the power to judge may judge each one as in this transitory life he deserves. Nor may any be unafraid of the word that the Ruler will speak. Before his multitude he will ask where the man is who in the name of the Lord would taste bitter death as he did on the Cross. But then they will be afraid and will little know what they may begin to answer to Christ. Yet there need not any be afraid who bears on his breast the best of beacons. For through the Cross shall every soul who thinks to dwell with the Lord seek his kingdom[8] in his earthly journey."

Then blithe-hearted, confident, I prayed to the Cross, there where I was alone, without company. My heart was drawn away from earth's paths. Often I endured weariness of spirit. Now is there hope of life, that I may seek the tree of triumph, honor it more often than other men, since I am alone. Great is the desire of my heart for the Cross, and my hope of protection rests in it. I have not many powerful friends on earth, for they have gone from the joys of the world, sought for themselves the King of Glory; now they live in Heaven with the High Father, dwell in glory. And every day I expect the time when the Lord's Cross that I beheld here on earth shall fetch me in this transitory life and bring me where bliss is great, joy in Heaven, where the Lord's folk are set at the feast, where bliss is eternal. And may it place me where I may thereafter dwell in glory, enjoy with the saints their delight. May the Lord be my friend, who here on earth suffered for man's sins on the gallows tree. He redeemed us and granted us life, a heavenly home. Hope was restored, with glory and bliss, to those who suffered in fire.[9] The Son was victorious in that foray, mighty and successful. Then he came with many, a host of spirits, into God's kingdom, the All-Powerful Ruler, and the angels and all the saints who then dwelt in Heaven rejoiced when their Ruler, Almighty God, came where his home was.

8. I.e., the Lord's.
9. This and the following sentences refer to the Harrowing (i.e., pillaging) of Hell: after His death upon the Cross, Christ descended into hell, from which He released the souls of certain of the patriarchs and prophets, conducting them triumphantly to heaven.

BEOWULF

Beowulf, the oldest of the great long poems written in English, was probably composed more than twelve hundred years ago, in the first half of the eighth century. Its author may have been a native of what was then West Mercia, the West Midlands of England today, though the late tenth-century manuscript, which alone preserves the poem, originated in the south in the kingdom of the West Saxons. In 1731, before any modern transcription of the text had been made, the manuscript was seriously damaged in the fire that destroyed the building in London which housed the extraordinary collection of medieval English manuscripts made by Sir Robert Bruce Cotton (1571–1631). As a result of the fire and of subsequent deterioration of the manu-

script, a number of lines and words have been lost from the poem, but even
if the manuscript had not been damaged, the poem would still have been
difficult, because the poetic Old English (or Anglo-Saxon) in which it was
written is itself hard, the style is allusive, the ideas often seem remote and
strange to modern perceptions, and because the text was inevitably corrupted during the many transcriptions which must have intervened in the
two and a half centuries between the poem's composition and the copying
of the extant manuscript. Yet despite its difficulty, the somber grandeur of
Beowulf is still capable of stirring the hearts of readers, and because of its excellence as well as its antiquity, the poem merits the high position that it is
generally assigned in the study of English poetry.

While the poem itself is English in language and origin, it deals not with
native Englishmen, but with their Germanic forebears, especially with two
south Scandinavian tribes, the Danes and the Geats, who lived on the
Danish island of Zealand and in southern Sweden, respectively. Thus, the
historical period it concerns—insofar as it may be said to refer to history at all
—is some two centuries before the poem was written; that is, it concerns a
time following the initial invasion of England by Germanic tribes in 449,
but before the Anglo-Saxon migration was completed, and perhaps before
the arrival of the ancestors of the audience to whom the poem was sung:
this audience may have considered itself to be of the same Geatish stock as
the hero, Beowulf. The one datable fact of history mentioned in the poem
is a raid on the Franks made by Hygelac, the king of the Geats at the time
Beowulf was a young man, and this raid occurred in the year 520. Yet
despite their antiquity, the poet's materials must have been very much alive
to his audience, for the elliptical way in which he alludes to events not directly concerned with his plot demands of the listener a wide knowledge of
traditional Germanic history. This knowledge was probably kept alive by
other heroic poetry, of which little has been preserved in English, though
much must once have existed. As it stands, *Beowulf* is not only unique as
an example of the Old English epic, but is also the greatest of the surviving
epics composed by the Germanic peoples.

It is generally agreed that the poet who put the old materials into their
present form was a Christian, and that his poem reflects a Christian tradition: the conversion of the Germanic settlers in England had largely been
completed during the century preceding the one in which the poet wrote.
But there is little general agreement as to how clearly *Beowulf* reflects a
Christian tradition or, conversely, the actual nature of the Christian tradition that it is held to reflect. Many specifically Christian references occur,
especially to the Old Testament: God is said to be the Creator of all things
and His will seems recognized (sporadically if not systematically) as being
identical with Fate (*wyrd*); Grendel is described as a descendant of Cain,
and the sword that Beowulf finds in Grendel's mother's lair has engraved
on it the story of the race of giants and their destruction by flood; the dead
await God's judgment, and Hell and the Devil are ready to receive the souls
of Grendel and his mother, while believers will find the Father's embrace;
Hrothgar's speech of advice to Beowulf (section XXV) seems to reflect
patristic doctrine in its emphasis on conscience and the Devil's lying in wait
for the unwary. Yet there is no reference to the New Testament—to Christ
and His Sacrifice which are the real bases of Christianity in any intelligible
sense of the term. Furthermore, readers may well feel that the poem achieves

rather little of its emotional power through invocation of Christian values or of values that are consonant with Christian doctrine as we know it. Perhaps the sense of tragic waste which pervades the Finnsburg episode (section XVI) springs from a Christian perception of the insane futility of the primitive Germanic thirst for vengeance; and the facts that Beowulf's chief adversaries are not men but monsters and that before his death he is able to boast that as king of the Geats he did not seek wars with neighboring tribes may reflect a Christian's appreciation for peace among men. But while admitting such values, the poet also invokes many others of a very different order, values that seem to belong to an ancient, pagan, warrior society of the kind described by the Roman historian Tacitus at the end of the first century. It should be noted that even Hrothgar's speech about conscience is directed more toward making Beowulf a good Germanic leader of men than a good Christian. One must, indeed, draw the conclusion from the poem itself that while Christian is a correct term for the religion of the poet and of his audience, it was a Christianity that had not yet by any means succeeded in obliterating an older pagan tradition, which still called forth powerful responses from men's hearts, despite the fact that many aspects of this tradition must be abhorrent to a sophisticated Christian. In this connection it is well to recall that the missionaries from Rome who initiated the conversion of the English proceeded in a conciliatory manner, not so much uprooting paganism in order to plant Christianity as planting Christianity in the faith that it would ultimately choke out the weeds of paganism. And the English clung long to some of their ancient traditions: for instance, the legal principle of the payment of *wergild* (defined below) remained in force until the Norman Conquest, four centuries after the conversion of the English.

In the warrior society whose values the poem constantly invokes, the most important of human relationships was that which existed between the warrior—the thane—and his lord, a relationship based less on subordination of one man's will to another's than on mutual trust and respect. When a warrior vowed loyalty to his lord, he became not so much his servant as his voluntary companion, one who would take pride in defending him and fighting in his wars. In return, the lord was expected to take affectionate care of his thanes and to reward them richly for their valor: a good king, one like Hrothgar or Beowulf, is referred to by such poetic epithets as "protector of warriors" and "dispenser of treasure" or "ring-giver," and the failure of bad kings is ascribed to their ill-temper and avarice, both of which alienate them from their retainers. The material benefit of this arrangement between lord and thane is obvious, yet under a good king the relationship seems to have had a significance more spiritual than material. Thus the treasure that an ideal Germanic king seizes from his enemies and rewards his retainers with is regarded as something more than mere wealth that will serve the well-being of its possessor; rather, it is a kind of visible proof that all parties are realizing themselves to the full in a spiritual sense—that the men of this band are congenially and successfully united with one another. The symbolic importance of treasure is illustrated by the poet's remark that the gift Beowulf gave the Danish coast-guard brought the latter honor among his companions, and even more by the fact that although Beowulf dies while obtaining a great treasure for his people, such objects as are removed from the dragon's hoard are actually buried with him as a fitting sign of his ultimate achievement.

The relationship between kinsmen was also of deep significance to this society and provides another emotional value for Old English heroic poetry. If one of his kinsmen had been slain, a man had the special duty of either killing the slayer or exacting from him the payment of *wergild* ("manprice"): each rank of society was evaluated at a definite price, which had to be paid to the dead man's kinsmen by the killer who wished to avoid their vengeance—even if the killing had been accidental. Again, the money itself had less significance as wealth than as a proof that the kinsmen had done what was right. Relatives who failed either to exact *wergild* or to take vengeance could never be happy, having found no practical way of satisfying their grief for their kinsmen's death. "It is better for a man to avenge his friend than much mourn," Beowulf says to the old Hrothgar, who is bewailing Aeschere's killing by Grendel's mother. And one of the most poignant passages in the poem describes the sorrow of King Hrethel after one of his sons had accidentally killed another: by the code of kinship Hrethel was forbidden to kill or to exact compensation from a kinsman, yet by the same code he was required to do one or the other in order to avenge the dead. Caught in this curious dilemma, Hrethel became so disconsolate that he could no longer face life.

It is evident that the need to take vengeance would create never-ending feuds, which the practice of marrying royal princesses to the kings or princes of hostile tribes did little to mitigate, though the purpose of such marriages was to replace hostility by alliance. Hrothgar wishes to make peace with the Heatho-Bards by marrying his daughter to their king, Ingeld, whose father was killed by the Danes; but as Beowulf predicts, sooner or later the Heatho-Bards' desire for vengeance on the Danes will erupt, and there will be more bloodshed. And the Danish princess Hildeburh, married to Finn of the Jutes, will see her son and her brother both killed while fighting on opposite sides in a battle at her own home, and ultimately will see her husband killed by the Danes in revenge for her brother's death. Beowulf himself is, for a Germanic hero, curiously free of involvement in feuds of this sort, though he does boast that he avenged the death of his king, Heardred, on his slayer Onela. Yet the potentiality—or inevitability—of sudden attack, sudden change, swift death is omnipresent in *Beowulf*; men seem to be caught in a vast web of reprisals and counterreprisals from which there is little hope of escape. This is the aspect of the poem which is apt to make the most powerful impression on the reader—its strong sense of doom.

Beowulf himself is chiefly concerned not with tribal feuds but with fatal evil both less and more complex. Grendel and the dragon are threats to the security of the lands they infest just as human enemies would be, but they are not part of the social order and presumably have no one to avenge their deaths (that Grendel's mother appeared as an avenger seems to have been a surprise both to Beowulf and to the Danes). On the other hand, because they are outside the normal order of things, they require of their conqueror something greater than normal warfare requires. In each case, it is the clear duty of the king and his companions to put down the evil But the Danish

Hrothgar is old and his companions unenterprising, and excellent though Hrothgar has been in the kingship, he nevertheless lacks the quality that later impels the old Beowulf to fight the dragon that threatens his people. The poem makes no criticism of Hrothgar for this lack; he merely seems not to be the kind of man—one might almost say he was not fated—to develop his human potential to the fullest extent that Fate would permit: that is Beowulf's role. In undertaking to slay Grendel, and later Grendel's mother, Beowulf is testing his relationship with unknowable destiny. At any time, as he is fully aware, his luck may abandon him and he may be killed, as, indeed, he is in the otherwise successful encounter with the dragon. But whether he lives or dies, he will have done all that any man could do to develop his character heroically. It is this consciousness of testing Fate that probably explains the boasting that modern readers of heroic poetry often find offensive. When he boasts, Beowulf is not only demonstrating that he has chosen the heroic way of life, but is also choosing it, for when he invokes his former courage as pledge of his future courage, his boast becomes a vow; the hero has put himself in a position from which he cannot withdraw.

Courage is the instrument by which the hero realizes himself. "Fate often saves an undoomed man when his courage is good," says Beowulf in his account of his swimming match: that is, if Fate has not entirely doomed a man in advance, courage is the quality that can perhaps influence Fate against its natural tendency to doom him now. It is this complex statement (in which it is hard to read the will of God for Fate) that Beowulf's life explores: he will use his great strength in the most courageous way by going alone, even unarmed, against monsters. Doom, of course, ultimately claims him, but not until he has fulfilled to its limits the pagan ideal of a heroic life. And despite the desire he often shows to Christianize pagan virtues, the Christian poet remains true to the older tradition when, at the end of his poem, he leaves us with the impression that Beowulf's chief reward is pagan immortality: the memory in the minds of later men of a hero's heroic actions. The poem itself is, indeed, a noble expression of that immortality.

TRIBES AND GENEALOGIES

I. The Danes (Bright-, Half-, Ring-, Spear-, North-, East-, South-, West-Danes; Scyldings, Honor-, Victor-, War-Scyldings; Ing's friends).

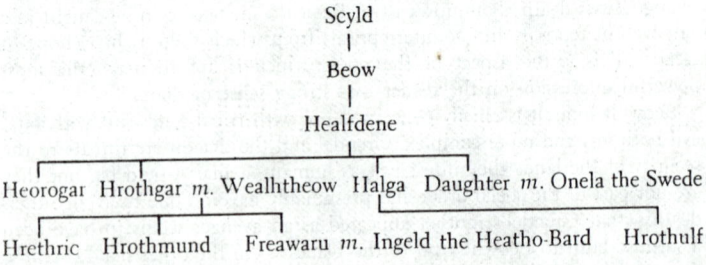

Scyld
|
Beow
|
Healfdene

Heorogar Hrothgar *m.* Wealhtheow Halga Daughter *m.* Onela the Swede

Hrethric Hrothmund Freawaru *m.* Ingeld the Heatho-Bard Hrothulf

II. The Geats (Sea-, War-, Weather-Geats)

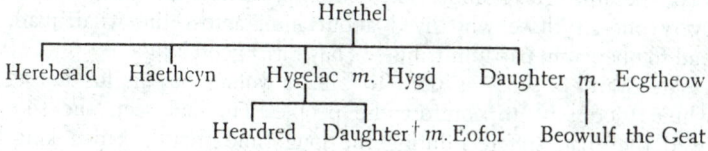

III. The Swedes.

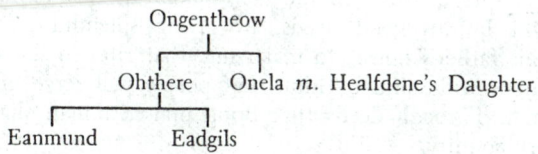

IV. Miscellaneous.

A. The Half-Danes (also called Scyldings) involved in the fight at Finnsburg may represent a different tribe from the Danes of paragraph I, above. Their king Hoc had a son, Hnaef, who succeeded him, and a daughter Hildeburh, who married Finn, king of the Jutes.

B. The Jutes or Frisians are represented as enemies of the Danes in the fight at Finnsburg and as allies of the Franks or Hugas at the time Hygelac the Geat made the attack in which he lost his life and from which Beowulf swam home. Also allied with the Franks at this time were the Hetware.

C. The Heatho-Bards (i.e., "Battle-Bards") are represented as inveterate enemies of the Danes. Their king Froda had been killed in an attack on the Danes, and Hrothgar's attempt to make peace with them by marrying his daughter Freawaru to Froda's son Ingeld failed when the latter attacked Heorot. The attack was repulsed, though Heorot was burned.

Beowulf[1]

[Prologue: The Earlier History of the Danes]

Yes, we have heard of the glory of the Spear-Danes' kings in the old days—how the princes of that people did brave deeds.

Often Scyld Scefing[2] took mead-benches away from enemy bands, from many tribes, terrified their nobles—after the time

---

† The daughter of Hygelac who was given to Eofor may have been born to him by a former wife, older than Hygd.

1. The translation into modern English, by the editor (1966), is based on F. Klaeber's third edition of the poem (1950); in general, the emendations suggested by J. C. Pope, *The Rhythm of Beowulf*, second edition (1966), have been adopted. The division into sections headed by roman numerals is that of the manuscript, which makes, however, no provision for Section XXX.

2. The meaning is probably "son of Sceaf," although Scyld's origins are mysterious.

that he was first found helpless.[3] He lived to find comfort for that, became great under the skies, prospered in honors until every one of those who lived about him, across the whale-road, had to obey him, pay him tribute. That was a good king.

Afterwards a son was born to him, a young boy in his house, whom God sent to comfort the people: He had seen the sore need they had suffered during the long time they lacked a king. Therefore the Lord of Life, the Ruler of Heaven, gave him honor in the world: Beow[4] was famous, the glory of the son of Scyld spread widely in the Northlands. In this way a young man ought by his good deeds, by giving splendid gifts while still in his father's house, to make sure that later in life beloved companions will stand by him, that people will serve him when war comes. Through deeds that bring praise, a man shall prosper in every country.

Then at the fated time Scyld the courageous went away into the protection of the Lord. His dear companions carried him down to the sea-currents, just as he himself had bidden them do when, as protector of the Scyldings,[5] he had ruled them with his words —long had the beloved prince governed the land. There in the harbor stood the ring-prowed ship, ice-covered and ready to sail, a prince's vessel. Then they laid down the ruler they had loved, the ring-giver, in the hollow of the ship, the glorious man beside the mast. There was brought great store of treasure, wealth from lands far away. I have not heard of a ship more splendidly furnished with war-weapons and battle-dress, swords and mail-shirts. On his breast lay a great many treasures that should voyage with him far out into the sea's possession. They provided him with no lesser gifts, treasure of the people, than those had done who at his beginning first sent him forth on the waves, a child alone. Then also they set a golden standard high over his head, let the water take him, gave him to the sea. Sad was their spirit, mournful their mind. Men cannot truthfully say who received that cargo, neither counsellors in the hall nor warriors under the skies.

(I) Then in the cities was Beo of the Scyldings beloved king of the people, long famous among nations (his father had gone elsewhere, the king from his land), until later great Healfdene was born to him. As long as he lived, old and fierce in battle, he upheld the glorious Scyldings. To him all told were four children born into the world, to the leader of the armies:

---

3. As is made clear shortly below, Scyld arrived in Denmark as a child alone in a ship loaded with treasures.
4. Although the manuscript reads "Beowulf," most scholars now agree that it

should read "Beow." Beo was the grandfather of the Danish king Hrothgar.
5. I.e., the Danes ("descendants of Scyld").

Heorogar and Hrothgar and the good Halga. I have heard tell that [. . . was On]ela's queen,[6] beloved bed-companion of the Battle-Scylfing.

[*Beowulf and Grendel*]

[THE HALL HEOROT IS ATTACKED BY GRENDEL]

Then Hrothgar was given success in warfare, glory in battle, so that his retainers gladly obeyed him and their company grew into a great band of warriors. It came to his mind that he would command men to construct a hall, a mead-building large[r] than the children of men had ever heard of, and therein he would give to young and old all that God had given him, except for common land and men's bodies.[7] Then I have heard that the work was laid upon many nations, wide through this middle-earth, that they should adorn the folk-hall. In time it came to pass—quickly, as men count it—that it was finished, the largest of hall-dwellings. He gave it the name of Heorot,[8] he who ruled wide with his words. He did not forget his promise: at the feast he gave out rings, treasure. The hall stood tall, high and wide-gabled: it would wait for the fierce flames of vengeful fire;[9] the time was not yet at hand for sword-hate between son-in-law and father-in-law to awaken after murderous rage.

Then the fierce spirit[1] painfully endured hardship for a time, he who dwelt in the darkness, for every day he heard loud mirth in the hall; there was the sound of the harp, the clear song of the scop.[2] There he spoke who could relate the beginning of men far back in time, said that the Almighty made earth, a bright field fair in the water that surrounds it, set up in triumph the lights of the sun and the moon to lighten land-dwellers, and adorned the surfaces of the earth with branches and leaves, created also life for each of the kinds that move and breathe.—Thus these warriors lived in joy, blessed, until one began to do evil deeds, a hellish enemy. The grim spirit was called Grendel, known as a rover of the borders, one who held the moors, fen and fastness. Unhappy creature, he lived for a time in the home of the monsters' race, after God had condemned them as kin of Cain. The Eternal Lord avenged the murder in

---

6. The text is faulty, so that the name of Healfdene's daughter has been lost; her husband Onela was a Swedish (Scylfing) king.
7. Or "men's lives." Apparently slaves, along with public land, were not in the king's power to give away.
8. I.e., "Hart."
9. The destruction by fire of Heorot occurred at a later time than that of

the poem's action, probably during the otherwise unsuccessful attack of the Heatho-Bard Ingeld on his father-in-law Hrothgar, mentioned in the next clause.
1. I.e., Grendel.
2. The "scop" was the Anglo-Saxon minstrel, who recited poetic stories to the accompaniment of a harp.

which he slew Abel. Cain had no pleasure in that feud, but He banished him far from mankind, the Ruler, for that misdeed. From him sprang all bad breeds, trolls and elves and monsters—likewise the giants who for a long time strove with God: He paid them their reward for that.

(II.) Then, after night came, Grendel went to survey the tall house—how, after their beer-drinking, the Ring-Danes had disposed themselves in it. Then he found therein a band of nobles asleep after the feast: they felt no sorrow, no misery of men. The creature of evil, grim and fierce, was quickly ready, savage and cruel, and seized from their rest thirty thanes. From there he turned to go back to his home, proud of his plunder, sought his dwelling with that store of slaughter.

Then in the first light of dawning day Grendel's war-strength was revealed to men: then after the feast weeping arose, great cry in the morning. The famous king, hero of old days, sat joyless; the mighty one suffered, felt sorrow for his thanes, when they saw the track of the foe, of the cursed spirit: that hardship was too strong, too loathsome and long-lasting. Nor was there a longer interval, but after one night Grendel again did greater slaughter—and had no remorse for it—vengeful acts and wicked: he was too intent on them. Thereafter it was easy to find the man who sought rest for himself elsewhere, farther away, a bed among the outlying buildings—after it was made clear to him, told by clear proof, the hatred of him who now controlled the hall.[3] *litote* (Whoever escaped the foe held himself afterwards farther off and more safely. Thus Grendel held sway and fought against right, one against all, until the best of houses stood empty. It was a long time, the length of twelve winters, that the lord of the Scyldings suffered grief, all woes, great sorrows. Therefore, sadly in songs, it became well-known to the children of men that Grendel had fought a long time with Hrothgar, for many half-years maintained mortal spite, feud, and enmity—constant war. He wanted no peace with any of the men of the Danish host, would not withdraw his deadly rancor, or pay compensation: no counselor there had any reason to expect splendid repayment at the hands of the slayer.[4] For the monster was relentless, the dark death-shadow, against warriors old and young, lay in wait and ambushed them. In the perpetual darkness he held to the misty moors: men do not know where hell-demons direct their footsteps.

Thus many crimes the enemy of mankind committed, the ter-

---

3. I.e., Grendel.
4. According to old Germanic law, a slayer could achieve peace with his victim's kinsmen only by paying them *wergild,* i.e., compensation for the life of the slain man.

rible walker-alone, cruel injuries one after another. In the dark nights he dwelt in Heorot, the richly adorned hall. He might not approach the throne, [receive] treasure, because of the Lord; He had no love for him.[5]

This was great misery to the lord of the Scyldings, a breaking of spirit. Many a noble sat often in council, sought a plan, what would be best for strong-hearted men to do against the awful attacks. At times they vowed sacrifices at heathen temples, with their words prayed that the soul-slayer[6] would give help for the distress of the people. Such was their custom, the hope of heathens; in their spirits they thought of Hell, they knew not the Ruler, the Judge of Deeds, they recognized not the Lord God, nor indeed did they know how to praise the Protector of Heaven, the glorious King. Woe is him who in terrible trouble must thrust his soul into the fire's embrace, hope for no comfort, not expect change. Well is the man who after his death-day may seek the Lord and find peace in the embrace of the Father.

[THE COMING OF BEOWULF TO HEOROT]

(III.) So in the cares of his times the son of Healfdene constantly brooded, nor might the wise warrior set aside his woe. Too harsh, hateful and long-lasting was the hardship that had come upon the people, distress dire and inexorable, worst of night-horrors.

A thane of Hygelac,[7] a good man among the Geats, heard in his homeland of Grendel's deeds: of mankind he was the strongest of might in the time of this life, noble and great. He bade that a good ship be made ready for him, said he would seek the war-king over the swan's road, the famous prince, since he had need of men. Very little did wise men blame him for that adventure, though he was dear to them; they urged the brave one on, examined the omens. From the folk of the Geats the good man had chosen warriors of the bravest that he could find; one of fifteen he led the way, the warrior sought the wooden ship, the sea-skilled one the land's edge. The time had come: the ship was on the waves, the boat under the cliff. The warriors eagerly climbed on the prow—the sea-currents eddied, sea against sand; men bore bright weapons into the ship's bosom, splendid armor. Men pushed the well-braced ship from shore, warriors on a well-wished voyage. Then over the sea-waves,

---

5. Behind this obscure passage seems to lie the idea that Grendel, unlike Hrothgar's thanes, could not approach the throne to receive gifts from the king, having been condemned by God as an outlaw.

6. I.e., the Devil. Despite this assertion that the Danes were heathen, their king, Hrothgar, speaks consistently as a Christian.

7. I.e., Beowulf the Geat, whose king was Hygelac.

blown by the wind, the foam-necked boat traveled, most like a bird, until at good time on the second day the curved prow had come to where the seafarers could see land, the sea-cliffs shine, towering hills, great headlands. Then was the sea crossed, the journey at end. Then quickly the men of the Geats climbed upon the shore, moored the wooden ship; mail-shirts rattled, dress for battle. They thanked God that the wave-way had been easy for them.

Then from the wall the Scyldings' guard who should watch over the sea-cliffs saw bright shields borne over the gangway, armor ready for battle; strong desire stirred him in mind to learn what the men were. He went riding on his horse to the shore, thane of Hrothgar, forcefully brandished a great spear in his hands, with formal words questioned them: "What are you, bearers of armor, dressed in mail-coats, who thus have come bringing a tall ship over the sea-road, over the water to this place? Lo, for a long time I have been guard of the coast, held watch by the sea so that no foe with a force of ships might work harm on the Danes' land: never have shield-bearers more openly undertaken to come ashore here; nor did you know for sure of a word of leave from our warriors, consent from my kinsmen. I have never seen a mightier warrior on earth than is one of you, a man in battle-dress. That is no retainer made to seem good by his weapons—unless his appearance belies him, his unequalled form. Now I must learn your lineage before you go any farther from here, spies on the Danes' land. Now you far-dwellers, sea-voyagers, hear what I think: you must straightway say where you have come from."

(IV.) To him replied the leader, the chief of the band unlocked his word-hoard: "We are men of the Geatish nation and Hygelac's hearth-companions. My father was well-known among the tribes, a noble leader named Ecgtheow. He lived many winters before he went on his way, an old man, from men's dwellings. Every wise man wide over the earth readily remembers him. Through friendly heart we have come to seek your lord, the son of Healfdene, protector of the people. Be good to us and tell us what to do: we have a great errand to the famous one, the king of the Danes. And I too do not think that anything ought to be kept secret: you know whether it is so, as we have indeed heard, that among the Scyldings I know not what foe, what dark doer of hateful deeds in the black nights, shows in terrible manner strange malice, injury and slaughter. In openness of heart I may teach Hrothgar remedy for that, how he, wise and good, shall overpower the foe—if change is ever to come to him, relief from evil's distress—and how his surging cares may be made to cool. Or else ever after he will suffer tribulations, constraint, while the best of houses remains there on its high place."

The guard spoke from where he sat on his horse, brave officer: "A sharp-witted shield-warrior who thinks well must be able to judge each of the two things, words and works. I understand this: that here is a troop friendly to the Scyldings' king. Go forward, bearing weapons and war-gear. I will show you the way; I shall also bid my fellow-thanes honorably to hold your boat against all enemies, your new-tarred ship on the sand, until again over the sea-streams it bears its beloved men to the Geatish shore, the wooden vessel with curved prow. May it be granted by fate that one who behaves so bravely pass whole through the battle-storm."

Then they set off. The boat lay fixed, rested on the rope, the deep-bosomed ship, fast at anchor. Boar-images [8] shone over cheek-guards gold-adorned, gleaming and fire-hardened—the war-minded boar held guard over fierce men. The warriors hastened, marched together until they might see the timbered hall, stately and shining with gold; for earth-dwellers under the skies that was the most famous of buildings in which the mighty one waited—its light gleamed over many lands. The battle-brave guide pointed out to them the shining house of the brave ones so that they might go straight to it. Warrior-like he turned his horse, then spoke words: "It is time for me to go back. The All-Wielding Father in His grace keep you safe in your undertakings. I shall go back to the sea to keep watch against hostile hosts."

(V.) The road was stone-paved, the path showed the way to the men in ranks. War-corselet shone, hard and hand-wrought, bright iron rings sang on their armor when they first came walking to the hall in their grim gear. Sea-weary they set down their broad shields, marvelously strong protections, against the wall of the building. Then they sat down on the bench—mail-shirts, warrior's clothing, rang out. Spears stood together, seamen's weapons, ash steel-gray at the top. The armed band was worthy of its weapons.

Then a proud-spirited man [9] asked the warriors there about their lineage: "Where do you bring those gold-covered shields from, gray mail-shirts and visored helmets, this multitude of battle-shafts? I am Hrothgar's herald and officer. I have not seen strangers—so many men—more bold. I think that it is for daring—not for refuge, but for greatness of heart—that you have sought Hrothgar." The man known for his courage replied to him; the proud man of the Geats, hardy under helmet, spoke

8. Carved images of boars (sometimes represented as clothed like human warriors) were placed on helmets in the belief that they would protect the wearer in battle.

9. Identified below as Wulfgar.

words in return: "We are Hygelac's table-companions. Beowulf is my name. I will tell my errand to Healfdene's son, the great prince your lord, if, good as he is, he will grant that we might address him." Wulfgar spoke—he was a man of the Wendels, his bold spirit known to many, his valor and wisdom: "I will ask the lord of the Danes about this, the Scyldings' king, the ring-giver, just as you request—will ask the glorious ruler about your voyage, and will quickly make known to you the answer the good man thinks best to give me."

He returned at once to where Hrothgar sat, old and hoary, with his company of earls. The man known for his valor went forward till he stood squarely before the Danes' king: he knew the custom of tried retainers. Wulfgar spoke to his lord and friend: "Here have journeyed men of the Geats, come far over the sea's expanse. The warriors call their chief Beowulf. They ask that they, my prince, might exchange words with you. Do not refuse them your answer, gracious Hrothgar. From their war-gear they seem worthy of earls' esteem. Strong indeed is the chief who has led the warriors here."

(VI.) Hrothgar spoke, protector of the Scyldings: "I knew him when he was a boy. His father was called Ecgtheow: Hrethel of the Geats [1] gave him his only daughter for his home. Now has his hardy offspring come here, sought a fast friend. Then, too, seafarers who took gifts there to please the Geats used to say that he has in his handgrip the strength of thirty men, a man famous in battle. Holy God of His grace has sent him to us West-Danes, as I hope, against the terror of Grendel. I shall offer the good man treasures for his daring. Now make haste, bid them come in together to see my company of kinsmen. In your speech say to them also that they are welcome to the Danish people."

Then Wulfgar went to the hall's door, gave the message from within: "The lord of the East-Danes, my victorious prince, has bidden me say to you that he knows your noble ancestry, and that you brave-hearted men are welcome to him over the sea-swells. Now you may come in your war-dress, under your battle helmets, to see Hrothgar. Let your war-shields, your wooden spears, await here the outcome of the talk."

Then the mighty one rose, many a warrior about him, a company of strong thanes. Some waited there, kept watch over the weapons as the brave one bade them. Together they hastened, as the warrior directed them, under Heorot's roof. The war-leader, hardy under helmet, advanced till he stood on the hearth. Beowulf spoke, his mail-shirt glistened, armor-net woven by the blacksmith's

---

1. Hrethel was the father of Hygelac and Beowulf's grandfather and guardian.

skill: "Hail, Hrothgar! I am kinsman and thane of Hygelac. In my youth I have set about many brave deeds. The affair of Grendel was made known to me on my native soil: sea-travelers say that this hall, best of buildings, stands empty and useless to all warriors after the evening-light becomes hidden beneath the cover of the sky. Therefore my people, the best wise earls, advised me thus, lord Hrothgar, that I should seek you because they know what my strength can accomplish. They themselves looked on when, bloody from my foes, I came from the fight where I had bound five, destroyed a family of giants, and at night in the waves slain water-monsters, suffered great pain, avenged an affliction of the Weather-Geats on those who had asked for trouble—ground enemies to bits. And now alone I shall settle affairs with Grendel, the monster, the demon. Therefore, lord of the Bright-Danes, protector of the Scyldings, I will make a request of you, refuge of warriors, fair friend of nations, that you refuse me not, now that I have come so far, that alone with my company of earls, this band of hardy men, I may cleanse Heorot. I have also heard say that the monster in his recklessness cares not for weapons. Therefore, so that my liege lord Hygelac may be glad of me in his heart, I scorn to bear sword or broad shield, yellow wood, to the battle, but with my grasp I shall grapple with the enemy and fight for life, foe against foe. The one whom death takes can trust the Lord's judgment. I think that if he may accomplish it, unafraid he will feed on the folk of the Geats in the war-hall as he has often done on the flower of men. You will not need to hide my head [2] if death takes me, for he will have me blood-smeared; he will bear away my bloody flesh meaning to savor it, he will eat ruthlessly, the walker alone, will stain his retreat in the moor; no longer will you need trouble yourself to take care of my body. If battle takes me, send to Hygelac the best of war-clothes that protects my breast, finest of mail-shirts. It is a legacy of Hrethel, the work of Weland.[3] Fate always goes as it must." (Danes)

(VII.) Hrothgar spoke, protector of the Scyldings: "For deeds done, my friend Beowulf, and for past favors you have sought us. A fight of your father's brought on the greatest of feuds. With his own hands he became the slayer of Heatholaf among the Wylfings. After that the country of the Weather-Geats might not keep him, for fear of war. From there he sought the folk of the South-Danes, the Honor-Scyldings, over the sea-swell. At that time I was first ruling the Danish people and, still in my youth, held the wide kingdom, hoard-city of heroes. Heorogar had died then, gone from life, my older brother, son of Healfdene—he was better than I. Afterwards I paid blood-money to end the feud;

2. I.e., "bury my body."   3. The blacksmith of the Norse gods.

over the sea's back I sent to the Wylfings old treasures; he [4] swore oaths to me.

"It is a sorrow to me in spirit to say to any man what Grendel has brought me with his hatred—humiliation in Heorot, terrible violence. My hall-troop, warrior-band, has shrunk; fate has swept them away into Grendel's horror. (God may easily put an end to the wild ravager's deeds!) Full often over the ale-cups warriors made bold with beer have boasted that they would await with grim swords Grendel's attack in the beer-hall. Then in the morning this mead-hall was a hall shining with blood, when the day lightened, all the bench-floor blood-wet, a gore-hall. I had fewer faithful men, beloved retainers, for death had destroyed them. Now sit down to the feast and unbind your thoughts, your famous victories, as heart inclines."

[THE FEAST AT HEOROT]

Then was a bench cleared in the beer-hall for the men of the Geats all together. Then the stout-hearted ones went to sit down, proud in their might. A thane did his work who bore in his hands an embellished ale-cup, poured the bright drink. At times a scop sang, clear-voiced in Heorot. There was joy of brave men, no little company of Danes and Weather-Geats.

(VIII.) Unferth spoke, son of Ecglaf, who sat at the feet of the king of the Scyldings, unbound words of contention—to him was Beowulf's undertaking, the brave seafarer, a great vexation, for he would not allow that any other man of middle-earth should ever achieve more glory under the heavens than himself: "Are you that Beowulf who contended with Breca, competed in swimming on the broad sea, where for pride you explored the water, and for foolish boast ventured your lives in the deep? Nor might any man, friend nor enemy, keep you from the perilous venture of swimming in the sea. There you embraced the sea-streams with your arms, measured the sea-ways, flung forward your hands, glided over the ocean; the sea boiled with waves, with winter's swell. Seven nights you toiled in the water's power. He overcame you at swimming, had more strength. Then in the morning the sea bore him up among the Heathoraemas; from there he sought his own home, dear to his people, the land of the Brondings, the fair stronghold, where he had folk, castle, and treasures. All his boast against you the son of Beanstan carried out in deed. Therefore I expect the worse results for you—though you have prevailed everywhere in battles, in grim war—if you dare wait near Grendel a night-long space."

Beowulf spoke, the son of Ecgtheow: "Well, my friend Unferth, drunk with beer you have spoken a great many things

4. Ecgtheow, whose feud with the Wylfings Hrothgar had settled.

about Breca—told about his adventures. I maintain the truth that I had more strength in the sea, hardship on the waves, than any other man. Like boys we agreed together and boasted—we were both in our first youth—that we would risk our lives in the salt sea, and that we did even so. We had naked swords, strong in our hands, when we went swimming; we thought to guard ourselves against whale-fishes. He could not swim at all far from me in the flood-waves, be quicker in the water, nor would I move away from him. Thus we were together on the sea for the time of five nights until the flood drove us apart, the swelling sea, coldest of weathers, darkening night, and the north wind battle-grim turned against us: rough were the waves. The anger of the sea-fishes was roused. Then my body-mail, hard and hand-linked, gave me help against my foes; the woven war-garment, gold-adorned, covered my breast. A fierce cruel attacker dragged me to the bottom, held me grim in his grasp, but it was granted me to reach the monster with my sword-point, my battle-blade. The war-stroke destroyed the mighty sea-beast—through my hand.

(IX.) "Thus often loathsome assailants pressed me hard. I served them with my good sword, as the right was. They had no joy at all of the feast, the malice-workers, that they should eat me, sit around a banquet near the sea-bottom. But in the morning, sword-wounded they lay on the shore, left behind by the waves, put to sleep by the blade, so that thereafter they would never hinder the passage of sea-voyagers over the deep water. Light came from the east, bright signal of God, the sea became still so that I might see the headlands, the windy walls of the sea. Fate often saves an undoomed man when his courage is good. In any case it befell me that I slew with my sword nine sea-monsters. I have not heard tell of a harder fight by night under heaven's arch, nor of a man more hard-pressed in the sea-streams. Yet I came out of the enemies' grasp alive, weary of my adventure. Then the sea bore me onto the lands of the Finns, the flood with its current, the surging waters.

"I have not heard say of you any such hard matching of might, such sword-terror. Breca never yet in the games of war—neither he nor you—achieved so bold a deed with bright swords (I do not much boast of it), though you became your brothers' slayer, your close kin; for that you will suffer punishment in hell, even though your wit is keen. I tell you truly, son of Ecglaf, that Grendel, awful monster, would never have performed so many terrible deeds against your chief, humiliation in Heorot, if your spirit, your heart, were so fierce in fight as you claim. But he has noticed that he need not much fear the hostility, not much dread the terrible sword-storm of your people, the Victory-Scyldings.

He exacts forced levy, shows mercy to none of the Danish people; but he is glad, kills, carves for feasting, expects no fight from the Spear-Danes. But I shall show him soon now the strength and courage of the Geats, their warfare. Afterwards he will walk who may, glad to the mead, when the morning light of another day, the bright-clothed sun, shines from the south on the children of men."

Then was the giver of treasure in gladness, gray-haired and battle-brave. The lord of the Bright-Danes could count on help. The folk's guardian had heard from Beowulf a fast-resolved thought.

There was laughter of warriors, voices rang pleasant, words were cheerful. Wealhtheow came forth, Hrothgar's queen, mindful of customs, gold-adorned, greeted the men in the hall; and the noble woman offered the cup first to the keeper of the land of the East-Danes, bade him be glad at the beer-drinking, beloved of the people. In joy he partook of feast and hall-cup, king famous for victories. Then the woman of the Helmings went about to each one of the retainers, young and old, offered them the costly cup, until the time came that she brought the mead-bowl to Beowulf, the ring-adorned queen, mature of mind. Sure of speech she greeted the man of the Geats, thanked God that her wish was fulfilled, that she might trust in some man for help against deadly deeds. He took the cup, the warrior fierce in battle, from Wealhtheow, and then spoke, one ready for fight— Beowulf spoke, the son of Ecgtheow: "I resolved, when I set out on the sea, sat down in the sea-boat with my band of men, that I should altogether fulfill the will of your people or else fall in slaughter, fast in the foe's grasp. I shall achieve a deed of manly courage or else have lived to see in this mead-hall my ending day." These words were well-pleasing to the woman, the boast of the Geat. Gold-adorned, the noble folk-queen went to sit by her lord.

Then there were again as at first strong words spoken in the hall, the people in gladness, the sound of a victorious folk, until, in a little while, the son of Healfdene wished to seek his evening rest. He knew of the battle in the high hall that had been plotted by the monster, plotted from the time that they might see the light of the sun until the night, growing dark over all things, the shadowy shapes of darkness, should come gliding, black under the clouds. The company all arose. Then they saluted each other, Hrothgar and Beowulf, and Hrothgar wished him good luck, control of the wine-hall, and spoke these words: "Never before, since I could raise hand and shield, have I entrusted to any man the great hall of the Danes, except now to you. Hold now and guard the best of houses: remember your fame, show your great courage, keep watch against the fierce foe. You will not lack what you wish if you survive that deed of valor."

[THE FIGHT WITH GRENDEL]

(X.) Then Hrothgar went out of the hall with his company of warriors, the protector of the Scyldings. The war-chief would seek the bed of Wealhtheow the queen. The King of Glory—as men had learned—had appointed a hall-guard against Grendel; he had a special mission to the prince of the Danes: he kept watch against monsters.

And the man of the Geats had sure trust in his great might, the favor of the Ruler. Then he took off his shirt of armor, the helmet from his head, handed his embellished sword, best of irons, to an attendant, bade him keep guard over his war-gear. Then the good warrior spoke some boast-words before he went to his bed, Beowulf of the Geats: "I claim myself no poorer in war-strength, war works, than Grendel claims himself. Therefore I will not put him to sleep with a sword, so take away his life, though surely I might. He knows no good tools with which he might strike against me, cut my shield in pieces, though he is strong in fight. But we shall forgo the sword in the night—if he dare seek war without weapon—and then may wise God, Holy Lord, assign glory on whichever hand seems good to Him."

The battle-brave one laid himself down, the pillow received the earl's head, and about him many a brave seaman lay down to hall-rest. None of them thought that he would ever again seek from there his dear home, people or town where he had been brought up; for they knew that bloody death had carried off far too many men in the wine-hall, folk of the Danes. But the Lord granted to weave for them good fortune in war, for the folk of the Weather-Geats, comfort and help that they should quite overcome their foe through the might of one man, through his sole strength: the truth has been made known that mighty God has always ruled mankind.

There came gliding in the black night the walker in darkness. The warriors slept who should hold the horned house—all but one. It was known to men that when the Ruler did not wish it the hostile creature might not drag them away beneath the shadows. But he, lying awake for the fierce foe, with heart swollen in anger awaited the outcome of the fight.

(XI.) Then from the moor under the mist-hills Grendel came walking, wearing God's anger. The foul ravager thought to catch some one of mankind there in the high hall. Under the clouds he moved until he could see most clearly the wine-hall, treasure-house of men, shining with gold. That was not the first time that he had sought Hrothgar's home. Never before or since in his life-days did he find harder luck, hardier hall-thanes. The creature deprived of joy came walking to the hall. Quickly the door gave way, fastened with fire-forged bands, when he touched it with his hands. Driven by evil desire, swollen with rage, he tore it open, the hall's mouth. After that the foe at once stepped onto the shining floor, advanced angrily. From his eyes came a light not fair, most like a flame. He saw many men in the hall, a band of kinsmen all asleep together, a company of war-men. Then his heart laughed: dreadful monster, he thought that before the day came he would divide the life from the body of every one of them, for there had come to him a hope of full-feasting. It was not his fate that when that night was over he should feast on more of mankind.

The kinsman of Hygelac, mighty man, watched how the evil-doer would make his quick onslaught. Nor did the monster mean to delay it, but, starting his work, he suddenly seized a sleeping man, tore at him ravenously, bit into his bone-locks, drank the blood from his veins, swallowed huge morsels; quickly he had eaten all of the lifeless one, feet and hands. He stepped closer, then felt with his arm for the brave-hearted man on the bed, reached out towards him, the foe with his hand; at once in fierce response Beowulf seized it and sat up, leaning on his own arm. Straightway the fosterer of crimes knew that he had not en-countered on middle-earth, anywhere in this world, a harder hand-grip from another man. In mind he became frightened, in his spirit: not for that might he escape the sooner. His heart was eager to get away, he would flee to his hiding-place, seek his rabble of devils. What he met there was not such as he had ever before met in the days of his life. Then the kinsman of Hygelac, the good man, thought of his evening's speech, stood upright and laid firm hold on him: his fingers cracked. The giant was pulling away, the earl stepped forward. The notorious one thought to move farther away, wherever he could, and flee his way from there to his fen-retreat; he knew his fingers' power to be in a hateful grip. That was a painful journey that the loathsome de-spoiler had made to Heorot. The retainers' hall rang with the noise—terrible drink [5] for all the Danes, the house-dwellers, every brave man, the earls. Both were enraged, fury-filled, the two who meant to control the hall. The building resounded. Then was it much wonder that the wine-hall withstood them joined in fierce

5. The metaphor reflects the idea that the chief purpose of a hall such as Heorot was as a place for men to feast in.

fight, that it did not fall to the ground, the fair earth-dwelling; but it was so firmly made fast with iron bands, both inside and outside, joined by skillful smith-craft. There started from the floor—as I have heard say—many a mead-bench, gold-adorned, when the furious ones fought. No wise men of the Scyldings ever before thought that any men in any manner might break it down, splendid with bright horns, have skill to destroy it, unless flame should embrace it, swallow it in fire. Noise rose up, sound strange enough. Horrible fear came upon the North-Danes, upon every one of those who heard the weeping from the wall, God's enemy sing his terrible song, song without triumph—the hell-slave bewail his pain. There held him fast he who of men was strongest of might in the days of this life.

[XII.] Not for anything would the protector of warriors let the murderous guest go off alive: he did not consider his life-days of use to any of the nations. There more than enough of Beowulf's earls drew swords, old heirlooms, wished to protect the life of their dear lord, famous prince, however they might. They did not know when they entered the fight, hardy-spirited warriors, and when they thought to hew him on every side, to seek his soul, that not any of the best of irons on earth, no war-sword, would touch the evil-doer: for with a charm he had made victory-weapons useless, every sword-edge. His departure to death from the time of this life was to be wretched, and the alien spirit was to travel far off into the power of fiends. Then he who before had brought trouble of heart to mankind, committed many crimes—he was at war with God—found that his body would do him no good, for the great-hearted kinsman of Hygelac had him by the hand. Each was hateful to the other alive. The awful monster had lived to feel pain in his body, a huge wound in his shoulder was exposed, his sinews sprang apart, his bone-locks broke. Glory in battle was given to Beowulf. Grendel must flee from there, mortally sick, seek his joyless home in the fen-slopes. He knew the more surely that his life's end had come, the full number of his days. For all the Danes was their wish fulfilled after the bloody fight. Thus he who had lately come from far off, wise and stout-hearted, had purged Heorot, saved Hrothgar's house from affliction. He rejoiced in his night's work, a deed to make famous his courage. The man of the Geats had fulfilled his boast to the East-Danes; so too he had remedied all the grief, the malice-caused sorrow that they had endured before, and had had to suffer from harsh necessity, no small distress. That was clearly proved when the battle-brave man set the hand up under the curved roof—the arm and the shoulder: there all together was Grendel's grasp.

[CELEBRATION AT HEOROT]

(XIII.) Then in the morning, as I have heard, there was many a warrior about the gift-hall. Folk-chiefs came from far and near over the wide-stretching ways to look on the wonder, the footprints of the foe. Nor did his going from life seem sad to any of the men who saw the tracks of the one without glory—how, weary-hearted, overcome with injuries, he moved on his way from there to the mere [6] of the water-monsters with life-failing footsteps, death-doomed and in flight. There the water was boiling with blood, the horrid surge of waves swirling, all mixed with hot gore, sword-blood. Doomed to die he had hidden, then, bereft of joys, had laid down his life in his fen-refuge, his heathen soul: there hell took him.

From there old retainers—and many a young man, too— turned back in their glad journey to ride from the mere, high-spirited on horseback, warriors on steeds. There was Beowulf's fame spoken of; many a man said—and not only once—that, south nor north, between the seas, over the wide earth, no other man under the sky's expanse was better of those who bear shields, more worthy of ruling. Yet they found no fault with their own dear lord, gracious Hrothgar, for he was a good king. At times battle-famed men let their brown horses gallop, let them race where the paths seemed fair, known for their excellence. At times a thane of the king, a man skilled at telling adventures, songs stored in his memory, who could recall many of the stories of the old days, wrought a new tale in well-joined words; this man undertook with his art to recite in turn Beowulf's exploit, and skillfully to tell an apt tale, to lend words to it.

He spoke everything that he had heard tell of Sigemund's valorous deeds, many a strange thing, the strife of Waels's son,[7] his far journeys, feuds and crimes, of which the children of men knew nothing—except for Fitela with him, to whom he would tell everything, the uncle to his nephew, for they were always friends in need in every fight. Many were the tribes of giants that they had laid low with their swords. For Sigemund there sprang up after his death-day no little glory—after he, hardy in war, had killed the dragon, keeper of the treasure-hoard: under the hoary stone the prince's son had ventured alone, a daring deed, nor was Fitela with him. Yet it turned out well for him, so that his sword went through the gleaming worm and stood fixed in the wall, splendid weapon: the dragon lay dead of the murdering stroke. Through his courage the great warrior had brought it about that he might at his own wish enjoy the ring-hoard. He

6. Lake. 7. Waels was Sigemund's father.

loaded the sea-boat, bore into the ship's bosom the bright treasure, offspring of Waels. The hot dragon melted.

He was adventurer most famous, far and wide through the nations, for deeds of courage—he had prospered from that before, the protector of warriors—after the war-making of Heremod had come to an end, his strength and his courage.[8] Among the Jutes Heremod came into the power of his enemies, was betrayed, quickly dispatched. Surging sorrows had oppressed him too long: he had become a great care to his people, to all his princes; for many a wise man in former times had bewailed the journey of the fierce-hearted one—people who had counted on him as a relief from affliction—that that king's son should prosper, take the rank of his father, keep guard over the folk, the treasure and stronghold, the kingdom of heroes, the home of the Scyldings. The kinsman of Hygelac became dearer to his friends, to all mankind: crime took possession of Heremod.

Sometimes racing their horses they passed over the sand-covered ways. By then the morning light was far advanced, hastening on. Many a stout-hearted warrior went to the high hall to see the strange wonder. The king himself walked forth from the women's apartment, the guardian of the ring-hoards, secure in his fame, known for his excellence, with much company; and his queen with him passed over the path to the mead-hall with a troop of attendant women.

(XIV.) Hrothgar spoke—he had gone to the hall, taken his stand on the steps, looked at the high roof shining with gold, and at Grendel's hand: "For this sight may thanks be made quickly to the Almighty: I endured much from the foe, many griefs from Grendel: God may always work wonder upon wonder, the Guardian of Heaven. It was not long ago that I did not expect ever to live to see relief from any of my woes—when the best of houses stood shining with blood, stained with slaughter, a far-reaching woe for each of my counselors, for every one, since none thought he could ever defend the people's stronghold from its enemies, from demons and evil spirits. Now through the Lord's might a warrior has accomplished the deed that all of us with our skill could not perform. Yes, she may say, whatever woman brought forth this son among mankind—if she still lives —that the God of Old was kind to her in her child-bearing. Now, Beowulf, best of men, in my heart I will love you as a son: keep well this new kinship. To you will there be no lack

---

8. Heremod was an unsuccessful king of the Danes, one who began brilliantly but became cruel and avaricious, ultimately having to take refuge among the Jutes, who put him to death. His reputation was thus overshadowed by that of Sigemund.

of the good things of the world that I have in my possession. Full often I have made reward for less, done honor with gifts to a lesser warrior, weaker in fighting. With your deeds you yourself have made sure that your glory will be ever alive. May the Almighty reward you with good—as just now he has done."

Beowulf spoke, the son of Ecgtheow: "With much good will we have achieved this work of courage, that fight, have ventured boldly against the strength of the unknown one. I should have wished rather that you might have seen him, your enemy brought low among your furnishings. I thought quickly to bind him on his deathbed with hard grasp, so that because of my hand-grip he should lie struggling for life—unless his body should escape. I could not stop his going, since the Lord did not wish it, nor did I hold him firmly enough for that, my life-enemy: he was too strong, the foe in his going. Yet to save his life he has left his hand behind to show that he was here—his arm and shoulder; nor by that has the wretched creature bought any comfort, none the longer will the loathsome ravager live, hard-pressed by his crimes, for a wound has clutched him hard in its strong grip, in deadly bonds. There, like a man outlawed for guilt, he shall await the great judgment, how the bright Lord will decree for him."

Then was the warrior more silent in boasting speech of war-like deeds, the son of Ecglaf,[9] after the nobles had looked at the hand, now high on the roof through the strength of a man, the foe's fingers. The end of each one, each of the nail-places, was most like steel; the hand-spurs of the heathen warrior were monstrous spikes. Everyone said that no hard thing would hurt him, no iron good from old times would harm the bloody battle-hand of the monster.

(XV.) Then was it ordered that Heorot be within quickly adorned by hands. Many there were, both men and women, who made ready the wine-hall, the guest-building. The hangings on the walls shone with gold, many a wondrous sight for each man who looks on such things. That bright building was much damaged, though made fast within by iron bonds, and its door-hinges sprung; the roof alone came through unharmed when the monster, out-lawed for his crimes, turned in flight, in despair of his life. That is not easy to flee from—let him try it who will—but driven by need one must seek the place prepared for earth-dwellers, soul-bearers, the sons of men, the place where, after its feasting, one's body will sleep fast in its death-bed.

Then had the proper time come that Healfdene's son should go to the hall; the king himself would share in the feast. I have

---

9. I.e., Unferth, who had taunted Beowulf the night before.

never heard that a people in a larger company bore themselves better about their treasure-giver. Men who were known for courage sat at the benches, rejoiced in the feast. Their kinsmen, stout-hearted Hrothgar and Hrothulf, partook fairly of many a mead-cup in the high hall. Heorot within was filled with friends: the Scylding-people had not then known treason's web.[1]

Then the son of Healfdene gave Beowulf a golden standard to reward his victory—a decorated battle-banner—a helmet and mail-shirt: many saw the glorious, costly sword borne before the war-rior. Beowulf drank of the cup in the mead-hall. He had no need to be ashamed before fighting men of those rich gifts. I have not heard of many men who gave four precious, gold-adorned things to another on the ale-bench in a more friendly way. The rim around the helmet's crown had a head-protection, wound of wire, so that no battle-hard sharp sword might badly hurt him when the shield-warrior should go against his foe. Then the people's protector commanded eight horses with golden bridles to be led into the hall, within the walls. The saddle of one of them stood shining with hand-ornaments, adorned with jewels: that had been the war-seat of the high king when the son of Healfdene would join sword-play: never did the warfare of the wide-known one fail when men died in battle. And then the prince of Ing's friends [2] yielded possession of both, horses and weapons, to Beowulf: he bade him use them well. So generously the famous prince, guardian of the hoard, repaid the warrior's battle-deeds with horses and treasure that no man will ever find fault with them—not he that will speak truth according to what is right.

(XVI.) Then further the lord gave treasure to each of the men on the mead-bench who had made the sea-voyage with Beowulf, gave heirlooms; and he commanded that gold be paid for the one whom in his malice Grendel had killed—as he would have killed more if wise God and the man's courage had not forestalled that fate. The Lord guided all the race of men then, as he does now. Yet is discernment everywhere best, fore-thought of mind. Many a thing dear and loath he shall live to see who here in the days of trouble long makes use of the world.

There was song and music together before Healfdene's battle-leader, the wooden harp touched, tale oft told, when Hrothgar's scop should speak hall-pastime among the mead-benches . . . [of] Finn's retainers when the sudden disaster fell upon them. . . .[3]

1. A reference to the later history of the Danes, when, after Hrothgar's death, his nephew Hrothulf apparently drove his son and successor Hrethric from the throne.
2. Ing was a legendary Danish king, and his "friends" are the Danes.
3. The lines introducing the scop's song seem faulty. The story itself is re-counted in a highly allusive way, and many of its details are obscure, though some help is offered by an independent version of the story given in a frag-mentary Old English lay called *The Fight at Finnsburg*.

The hero of the Half-Danes, Hnaef of the Scyldings, was fated to fall on Frisian battlefield. And no need had Hildeburh [4] to praise the good faith of the Jutes: blameless she was deprived of her dear ones at the shield-play, of son and brother; wounded by spears they fell to their fate. That was a mournful woman. Not without cause did Hoc's daughter lament the decree of destiny when morning came and she might see, under the sky, the slaughter of kinsmen—where before she had the greatest of world's joy. The fight took away all Finn's thanes except for only a few, so that he could in no way continue the battle on the field against Hengest, nor protect the survivors by fighting against the prince's thane. But they offered them peace-terms,[5] that they should clear another building for them, hall and high seat, that they might have control of half of it with the sons of the Jutes; and at givings of treasure the son of Folcwalda [6] should honor the Danes each day, should give Hengest's company rings, such gold-plated treasure as that with which he would cheer the Frisians' kin in the high hall. Then on both sides they confirmed the fast peace-compact. Finn declared to Hengest, with oaths deep-sworn, unfeigned, that he would hold those who were left from the battle in honor in accordance with the judgment of his counselors, so that by words or by works no man should break the treaty nor because of malice should ever mention that, princeless, the Danes followed the slayer of their own ring-giver, since necessity forced them. If with rash speech any of the Frisians should insist upon calling to mind the cause of murderous hate, then the sword's edge should settle it.

The funeral pyre was made ready and gold brought up from the hoard. The best of the warriors of the War-Scyldings [7] was ready on the pyre. At the fire it was easy to see many a blood-stained battle-shirt, boar-image all golden—iron-hard swine—many a noble destroyed by wounds: more than one had died in battle. Then Hildeburh bade give her own son to the flames on Hnaef's pyre, burn his blood vessels, put him in the fire at the shoulder of

---

4. Hildeburh, daughter of the former Danish king Hoc and sister of the ruling Danish king Hnaef, was married to Finn, king of the Jutes (Frisians). Hnaef with a party of Danes made what was presumably a friendly visit to Hildeburh and Finn at their home Finnsburg, but during a feast a quarrel broke out between the Jutes and the Danes (since the scop's sympathies are with the Danes, he ascribes the cause to the bad faith of the Jutes), and in the ensuing fight Hnaef and his nephew, the son of Finn and Hildeburh, were killed, along with many other Danes and Jutes.

5. It is not clear who proposed the peace terms, but in view of the teller's Danish sympathies, it was probably the Jutes that sought the uneasy truce from Hengest, who became the Danes' leader after Hnaef's death. The truce imposed upon Hengest and the Danes the intolerable condition of having to dwell in peace with the Jutish king who was responsible for the death of their own king.

6. I.e., Finn.

7. I.e., Hnaef.

his uncle. The woman mourned, sang her lament. The warrior took his place.[8] The greatest of death-fires wound to the skies, roared before the barrow. Heads melted as blood sprang out—wounds opened wide, hate-bites of the body. Fire swallowed them—greediest of spirits—all of those whom war had taken away from both peoples: their strength had departed.

(XVII.) Then warriors went to seek their dwellings, bereft of friends, to behold Friesland, their homes and high city.[9] Yet Hengest stayed on with Finn for a winter darkened with the thought of slaughter, all desolate. He thought of his land, though he might not drive his ring-prowed ship over the water—the sea boiled with storms, strove with the wind, winter locked the waves in ice-bonds—until another year came to men's dwellings, just as it does still, glorious bright weather always watching for its time. Then winter was gone, earth's lap fair, the exile was eager to go, the guest from the dwelling: [yet] more he thought of revenge for his wrongs than of the sea-journey—if he might bring about a fight where he could take account of the sons of the Jutes with his iron. So he made no refusal of the world's custom when the son of Hunlaf[1] placed on his lap Battle-Bright, best of swords: its edges were known to the Jutes. Thus also to war-minded Finn in his turn cruel sword-evil came in his own home, after Guthlaf and Oslaf complained of the grim attack, the injury after the sea-journey, assigned blame for their lot of woes: breast might not contain the restless heart. Then was the hall reddened from foes' bodies, and thus Finn slain, the king in his company, and the queen taken. The warriors of the Scyldings bore to ship all the hall-furnishings of the land's king, whatever of necklaces, skillfully wrought treasures, they might find at Finn's home. They brought the noble woman on the sea-journey to the Danes, led her to her people.

The lay was sung to the end, the song of the scop. Joy mounted again, bench-noise brightened, cup-bearers poured wine from wonderful vessels. Then Wealhtheow came forth to walk under gold crown to where the good men sat, nephew and uncle: their friendship was then still unbroken, each true to the other.[2] There too Unferth the spokesman sat at the feet of the prince

---

8. The line is obscure, but it perhaps means that the body of Hildeburh's son was placed on the pyre.
9. This seems to refer to the few survivors on the Jutish side.
1. The text is open to various interpretations. The one adopted here assumes that the Dane Hunlaf, brother of Guthlaf and Oslaf, had been killed in the fight, and that ultimately Hunlaf's son demanded vengeance by the sym-

bolical act of placing his father's sword in Hengest's lap, while at the same time Guthlaf and Oslaf reminded Hengest of the Jutes' treachery. It is not clear whether the subsequent fight in which Finn was killed was waged by the Danish survivors alone, or whether the party first went back to Denmark and then returned to Finnsburg with reinforcements.
2. See section XV, note 1, above.

of the Scyldings: each of them trusted his spirit, that he had much courage, though he was not honorable to his kinsmen at sword-play. Then the woman of the Scyldings spoke:

"Take this cup my noble lord, giver of treasure. Be glad, gold-friend of warriors, and speak to the Geats with mild words, as a man ought to do. Be gracious to the Geats, mindful of gifts [which] [3] you now have from near and far. They have told me that you would have the warrior for your son. Heorot is purged, the bright ring-hall. Enjoy while you may many rewards, and leave to your kinsmen folk and kingdom when you must go forth to look on the Ruler's decree. I know my gracious Hrothulf, that he will hold the young warriors in honor if you, friend of the Scyldings, leave the world before him. I think he will repay our sons with good if he remembers all the favors we did to his pleasure and honor when he was a child."

Then she turned to the bench where her sons were, Hrethric and Hrothmund, and the sons of the warriors, young men together. There sat the good man Beowulf of the Geats beside the two brothers.

(XVIII.) The cup was borne to him and welcome offered in friendly words to him, and twisted gold courteously bestowed on him, two arm-ornaments, a mail-shirt and rings, the largest of necklaces of those that I have heard spoken of on earth. I have heard of no better hoard-treasure under the heavens since Hama carried away to his bright city the necklace of the Brosings,[4] chain and rich setting: he fled the treacherous hatred of Eormenric, got eternal favor. This ring Hygelac of the Geats,[5] grandson of Swerting, had on his last venture, when beneath his battle-banner he defended his treasure, protected the spoils of war: fate took him when for pride he sought trouble, feud with the Frisians. Over the cup of the waves the mighty prince wore that treasure, precious stone. He fell beneath his shield; the body of the king came into the grasp of the Franks, his breast-armor and the neck-ring together. Lesser warriors plundered the fallen after the war-harvest: people of the Geats held the place of corpses.

The hall was filled with noise. Wealhtheow spoke, before the company she said to him: "Wear this ring, beloved Beowulf, young man, with good luck, and make use of this mail-shirt from

3. The text seems corrupt.
4. The Brisings' (Brosings') necklace had been worn by the goddess Freya. Nothing more is known of this story of Hama, who seems to have stolen the necklace from the famous Gothic king Eormenric.

5. Beowulf is later said to have presented the necklace to Hygelac's queen, Hygd, though here Hygelac is said to have been wearing it on his ill-fated expedition against the Franks and Frisians, into whose hands it fell at his death.

the people's treasure, and prosper well; make yourself known with your might, and be kind of counsel to these boys: I shall remember to reward you for that. You have brought it about that, far and near, for a long time all men shall praise you, as wide as the sea surrounds the shores, home of the winds. While you live, prince, be prosperous. I wish you well of your treasure. Much favored one, be kind of deeds to my son. Here is each earl true to other, mild of heart, loyal to his lord; the thanes are at one, the people obedient, the retainers cheered with drink do as I bid."

Then she walked to her seat. There was the best of feasts, men drank wine. They did not know the fate, the grim decree made long before, as it came to pass to many of the earls after evening had come and Hrothgar had gone to his chambers, the noble one to his rest. A great number of men remained in the hall, just as they had often done before. They cleared the benches from the floor. It was spread over with beds and pillows. One of the beer-drinkers, ripe and fated to die, lay down to his hall-rest. They set at their heads their battle-shields, bright wood; there on the bench it was easy to see above each man his helmet that towered in battle, his ringed mail-shirt, his great spear-wood. It was their custom to be always ready for war whether at home or in the field, in any case at any time that need should befall their liege lord: that was a good nation.

[GRENDEL'S MOTHER'S ATTACK]

(XIX.) Then they sank to sleep. One paid sorely for his evening rest, just as had often befallen them when Grendel guarded the gold-hall, wrought wrong until the end came, death after misdeeds. It came to be seen, wide-known to men, that after the bitter battle an avenger still lived for an evil space: Grendel's mother, woman, monster-wife, was mindful of her misery, she who had to dwell in the terrible water, the cold currents, after Cain became sword-slayer of his only brother, his own father's son. Then Cain went as an outlaw to flee the cheerful life of men, marked for his murder, held to the wasteland. From him sprang many a devil sent by fate. Grendel was one of them, hateful outcast who at Heorot found a waking man waiting his warfare. There the monster had laid hold upon him, but he was mindful of the great strength, the large gift God had given him, and relied on the Almighty for favor, comfort and help. By that he overcame the foe, subdued the hell-spirit. Then he went off wretched, bereft of joy, to seek his dying-place, enemy of mankind. And his mother, still greedy and gallows-grim, would go on a sorrowful venture, avenge her son's death.

Then she came to Heorot where the Ring-Danes slept throughout the hall. Then change came quickly to the earls there, when
Grendel's mother made her way in. The attack was the less terrible
by just so much as is the strength of women, the war-terror of a
wife, less than an armed man's when a hard blade, forge-ham-
mered, a sword shining with blood, good of its edges, cuts the
stout boar on a helmet opposite. Then in the hall was hard-edged
sword raised from the seat, many a broad shield lifted firmly in
hand: none thought of helmet, of wide mail-shirt, when the terror
seized him. She was in haste, would be gone out from there,
protect her life after she was d scovered. Swiftly she had taken
fast hold on one of the nobles, then she went to the fen. He
was one of the men between the seas most beloved of Hrothgar
in the rank of retainer, a noble shield-warrior whom she destroyed
at his rest, a man of great repute. Beowulf was not there, for
earlier, after the treasure-giving, another lodging had been appointed for the renowned Geat. Outcry arose in Heorot: she
had taken, in its gore, the famed hand. Care was renewed, come
again on the dwelling. That was not a good bargain, that on both
sides they had to pay with the lives of friends.

Then was the old king, the hoary warrior, of bitter mind when
he learned that his chief thane was lifeless, his dearest man dead.
Quickly Beowulf was fetched to the bed-chamber, man happy
in victory. At daybreak together with his earls he went, the
noble champion himself with his retainers, to where the wise one
was, waiting to know whether after tidings of woe the All-Wielder
would ever bring about change for him. The worthy warrior
walked over the floor with his retainers—hall-wood resounded
—that he might address words to the wise prince of Ing's friends,
asked if the night had been pleasant according to his desires.

(XX.) Hrothgar spoke, protector of the Scyldings: "Ask not
about pleasure. Sorrow is renewed to the people of the Danes:
Aeschere is dead, Yrmenlaf's elder brother, my speaker of wisdom and my bearer of counsel, my shoulder-companion when we
used to defend our heads in battle, when troops clashed, beat on
boar-images. Whatever an earl should be, a man good from old
times, such was Aeschere. Now a wandering murderous spirit has
slain him with its hands in Heorot. I do not know by what
way the awful creature, glorying in its prey, has made its retreat,
gladdened by its feast. She has avenged the feud—that last night
you killed Grendel with hard hand-grips, savagely, because too
long he had diminished and destroyed my people. He fell in
the fight, his life forfeited, and now the other has come, a mighty
worker of wrong, would avenge her kinsman, and has carried far
her revenge—as many a thane may think who weeps in his

spirit for his treasure-giver, bitter sorrow in heart. Now the hand lies lifeless that was strong in support of all your desires.

"I have heard landsmen, my people, hall-counselors, say this, that they have seen two such huge walkers in the wasteland holding to the moors, alien spirits. One of them, so far as they could clearly discern, was the likeness of a woman. The other wretched shape trod the tracks of exile in the form of a man, except that he was bigger than any other man. Land-dwellers in the old days named him Grendel. They know of no father, whether in earlier times any was begotten for them among the dark spirits. They hold to the secret land, the wolf-slopes, the windy headlands, the dangerous fen-paths where the mountain stream goes down under the darkness of the hills, the flood under the earth. It is not far from here, measured in miles, that the mere stands; over it hang frost-covered woods, trees fast of root close over the water. There each night may be seen fire on the flood, a fearful wonder. Of the sons of men there lives none, old of wisdom, who knows the bottom. Though the heath-stalker, the strong-horned hart, harassed by hounds makes for the forest after long flight, rather will he give his life, his being, on the bank than save his head by entering. That is no pleasant place. From it the surging waves rise up black to the heavens when the wind stirs up awful storms, until the air becomes gloomy, the skies weep. Now once again is the cure in you alone. You do not yet know the land, the perilous place, where you might find the seldom-seen creature: seek if you dare. I will give you wealth for the feud, old treasure, as I did before, twisted gold—if you come away."

(XXI.) Beowulf spoke, the son of Ecgtheow: "Sorrow not, wise warrior. It is better for a man to avenge his friend than much mourn. Each of us must await his end of the world's life. Let him who may get glory before death: that is best for the warrior after he has gone from life. Arise, guardian of the kingdom, let us go at once to look on the track of Grendel's kin. I promise you this: she will not be lost under cover, not in the earth's bosom nor in the mountain woods nor at the bottom of the sea, go where she will. This day have patience in every woe—as I expect you to."

Then the old man leapt up, thanked God, the mighty Lord, that the man had so spoken. Then was a horse bridled for Hrothgar, a curly-maned mount. The wise king moved in state; the band of shield-bearers marched on foot. The tracks were seen wide over the wood-paths where she had gone on the ground, made her way forward over the dark moor, borne lifeless the best of retainers of those who watched over their home with Hrothgar. The son of noble forebears [6] moved over the steep

6. I.e., Hrothgar.

rocky slopes, narrow paths where only one could go at a time, an unfamiliar trail, steep hills, many a lair of water-monsters. He went before with a few wise men to spy out the country, until suddenly he found mountain trees leaning out over hoary stone, a joyless wood: water lay beneath, bloody and troubled. It was pain of heart for all the Danes to suffer, for the friends of the Scyldings, for many a thane, grief to each earl when on the cliff over the water they came upon Aeschere's head. The flood boiled with blood—the men looked upon it—with hot gore. Again and again the horn sang its urgent war-song. The whole troop sat down to rest. Then they saw on the water many a snake-shape, strong sea-serpents exploring the mere, and water-monsters lying on the slopes of the shore such as those that in the morning often attend a perilous journey on the paths of the sea, serpents and wild beasts.

These fell away from the shore, fierce and rage-swollen: they had heard the bright sound, the war-horn sing. One of them a man of the Geats with his bow cut off from his life, his water-warring, after the hard war-arrow stuck in his heart: he was weaker in swimming the lake when death took him. Straightway he was hard beset on the waves with barbed boar-spears, strongly surrounded, pulled up on the shore, strange spawn of the waves. The men looked on the terrible alien thing.

Beowulf put on his warrior's dress, had no fear for his life. His war-shirt, hand-fashioned, broad and well-worked, was to explore the mere: it knew how to cover his body-cave so that foe's grip might not harm his heart, or grasp of angry enemy his life. But the bright helmet guarded his head, one which was to stir up the lake-bottom, seek out the troubled water—made rich with gold, surrounded with splendid bands, as the weapon-smith had made it in far-off days, fashioned it wonderfully, set it about with boar-images so that thereafter no sword or battle-blade might bite into it. And of his strong supports that was not the least which Hrothgar's spokesman [7] lent to his need: Hrunting was the name of the hilted sword; it was one of the oldest of ancient treasures; its edge was iron, decorated with poison-stripes, hardened with battle-sweat. Never had it failed in war any man of those who grasped it in their hands, who dared enter on danger-ous enterprises, onto the common meeting place of foes: this was not the first time that it should do work of courage. Surely the son of Ecglaf, great of strength, did not have in mind what, drunk with wine, he had spoken, when he lent that weapon to a better sword-fighter. He did not himself dare to risk his life under the warring waves, to engage his courage: there he lost his glory,

7. I.e., Unferth.

his name for valor. It was not so with the other when he had armed himself for battle.

[BEOWULF ATTACKS GRENDEL'S MOTHER]

(XXII.) Beowulf spoke, the son of Ecgtheow: "Think now, renowned son of Healfdene, wise king, now that I am ready for the venture, gold-friend of warriors, of what we said before, that, if at your need I should go from life, you would always be in a father's place for me when I am gone: be guardian of my young retainers, my companions, if battle should take me. The treasure you gave me, beloved Hrothgar, send to Hygelac. The lord of the Geats may know from the gold, the son of Hrethel may see when he looks on that wealth, that I found a ring-giver good in his gifts, enjoyed him while I might. And let Unferth have the old heirloom, the wide-known man my splendid-waved sword, hard-edged: with Hrunting I shall get glory, or death will take me."

After these words the man of the Weather-Geats turned away boldly, would wait for no answer: the surging water took the warrior. Then was it a part of a day before he might see the bottom's floor. Straightway that which had held the flood's tract a hundred half-years, ravenous for prey, grim and greedy, saw that some man from above was exploring the dwelling of monsters. Then she groped toward him, took the warrior in her awful grip. Yet not the more for that did she hurt his hale body within: his ring-armor shielded him about on the outside so that she could not pierce the war-dress, the linked body-mail, with hateful fingers. Then as she came to the bottom the sea-wolf bore the ring-prince to her house so that—no matter how brave he was —he might not wield weapons; but many monsters attacked him in the water, many a sea-beast tore at his mail-shirt with war-tusks, strange creatures afflicted him. Then the earl saw that he was in some hostile hall where no water harmed him at all, and the flood's onrush might not touch him because of the hall-roof. He saw firelight, a clear blaze shine bright.

Then the good man saw the accursed dweller in the deep, the mighty mere-woman. He gave a great thrust to his sword—his hand did not withhold the stroke—so that the etched blade sang at her head a fierce war-song. Then the stranger found that the battle-lightning would not bite, harm her life, but the edge failed the prince in his need: many a hand-battle had it endured before, often sheared helmet, war-coat of man fated to die: this was the first time for the rare treasure that its glory had failed.

But still he was resolute, not slow of his courage, mindful of fame, the kinsman of Hygelac. Then, angry warrior, he threw away the sword, wavy-patterned, bound with ornaments, so that it lay on the ground, hard and steel-edged: he trusted in his strength, his mighty hand-grip. So ought a man to do when he thinks to get long-lasting praise in battle: he cares not for his life. Then he seized by the hair Grendel's mother—the man of the War-Geats did not shrink from the fight. Battle-hardened, now swollen with rage, he pulled his deadly foe so that she fell to the floor. Quickly in her turn she repaid him his gift with her grim claws and clutched at him: then weary-hearted, the strongest of warriors, of foot-soldiers, stumbled so that he fell. Then she sat upon the hall-guest and drew her knife, broad and bright-edged. She would avenge her child, her only son. The woven breast-armor lay on his shoulder: that protected his life, withstood entry of point or of edge. Then the son of Ecgtheow would have fared amiss under the wide ground, the champion of the Geats, if the battle-shirt had not brought help, the hard war-net—and holy God brought about victory in war; the wise Lord, Ruler of the Heavens, decided it with right, easily, when Beowulf had stood up again.

XXIII. Then he saw among the armor a victory-blessed blade, an old sword made by the giants, strong of its edges, glory of warriors: it was the best of weapons, except that it was larger than any other man might bear to war-sport, good and adorned, the work of giants. He seized the linked hilt, he who fought for the Scyldings, savage and slaughter-bent, drew the patterned-blade; desperate of life, he struck angrily so that it bit her hard on the neck, broke the bone-rings. The blade went through all the doomed body. She fell to the floor, the sword was sweating, the man rejoiced in his work.

The blaze brightened, light shone within, just as from the sky heaven's candle shines clear. He looked about the building; then he moved along the wall, raised his weapon hard by the hilt, Hygelac's thane, angry and resolute: the edge was not useless to the warrior, for he would quickly repay Grendel for the many attacks he had made on the West-Danes—many more than the one time when he slew in their sleep fifteen hearth-companions of Hrothgar, devoured men of the Danish people while they slept, and another such number bore away, a hateful prey. He had paid him his reward for that, the fierce champion, for there he saw Grendel, weary of war, lying at rest, lifeless with the wounds he had got in the fight at Heorot. The body bounded wide when it suffered the blow after death, the hard sword-swing; and thus he cut off his head.

At once the wise men who were watching the water with Hrothgar saw that the surging waves were troubled, the lake stained with blood. Gray-haired, old, they spoke together of the good warrior, that they did not again expect of the chief that he would come victorious to seek their great king; for many agreed on it, that the sea-wolf had destroyed him.

Then came the ninth hour of the day. The brave Scyldings left the hill. The gold-friend of warriors went back to his home. The strangers sat sick at heart and stared at the mere. They wished—and did not expect—that they would see their beloved lord himself.

Then the blade began to waste away from the battle-sweat, the war-sword into battle-icicles. That was a wondrous thing, that it should all melt, most like the ice when the Father loosens the frost's fetters, undoes the water-bonds—He Who has power over seasons and times: He is the true Ruler. Beowulf did not take from the dwelling, the man of the Weather-Geats, more treasures —though he saw many there—but only the head and the hilt, bright with jewels. The sword itself had already melted, its patterned blade burned away: the blood was too hot for it, the spirit that had died there too poisonous. Quickly he was swimming, he who had lived to see the fall of his foes; he plunged up through the water. The currents were all cleansed, the great tracts of the water, when the dire spirit left her life-days and this loaned world.

Then the protector of seafarers came toward the land, swimming stout-hearted; he had joy of his sea-booty, the great burden he had with him. They went to meet him, thanked God, the strong band of thanes, rejoiced in their chief that they might see him again sound. Then the helmet and war-shirt of the mighty one were quickly loosened. The lake drowsed, the water beneath the skies, stained with blood. They went forth on the foot-tracks, glad in their hearts, measured the path back, the known ways, men bold as kings. They bore the head from the mere's cliff, toilsomely for each of the great-hearted ones: four of them had trouble in carrying Grendel's head on spear-shafts to the gold-hall —until at last they came striding to the hall, fourteen bold warriors of the Geats; their lord, high-spirited, walked in their company over the fields to the mead-hall.

Then the chief of the thanes, man daring in deeds, enriched by new glory, warrior dear to battle, came in to greet Hrothgar. Then Grendel's head was dragged by the hair over the floor to where men drank, a terrible thing to the earls and the woman with them, an awful sight: the men looked upon it.

[FURTHER CELEBRATION AT HEOROT]

(XXIV.) Beowulf spoke, the son of Ecgtheow: "Yes, we have brought you this sea-booty, son of Healfdene, man of the Scyldings, gladly, as evidence of glory—what you look on here. Not easily did I come through it with my life, the war under water, not without trouble carried out the task. The fight would have been ended straightway if God had not guarded me. With Hrunting I might not do anything in the fight, though that is a good weapon. But the Wielder of Men granted me that I should see hanging on the wall a fair, ancient great-sword—most often He has guided the man without friends—that I should wield the weapon. Then in the fight when the time became right for me I hewed the house-guardians. Then that war-sword, wavy-patterned, burnt away as their blood sprang forth, hottest of battle-sweats. I have brought the hilt away from the foes. I have avenged the evil deeds, the slaughter of Danes, as it was right to do. I promise you that you may sleep in Heorot without care with your band of retainers, and that for none of the thanes of your people, old or young, need you have fear, prince of the Scyldings—for no life-injury to your men on that account, as you did before."

Then the golden hilt was given into the hand of the old man, the hoary war-chief—the ancient work of giants. There came into the possession of the prince of the Danes, after the fall of devils, the work of wonder-smiths. And when the hostile-hearted creature, God's enemy, guilty of murder, gave up this world, and his mother too, it passed into the control of the best of worldly kings between the seas, of those who gave treasure in the Northlands.

Hrothgar spoke—he looked on the hilt, the old heirloom, on which was written the origin of ancient strife, when the flood, rushing water, slew the race of giants—they suffered terribly: that was a people alien to the Everlasting Lord. The Ruler made them a last payment through water's welling. On the sword-guard of bright gold there was also rightly marked through rune-staves, set down and told, for whom that sword, best of irons, had first been made, its hilt twisted and ornamented with snakes. Then the wise man spoke, the son of Healfdene—all were silent: "Lo, this may one say who works truth and right for the folk, recalls all things far distant, an old guardian of the land: that this earl was born the better man. Glory is raised up over the far ways—your glory over every people, Beowulf my friend. All of it, all your strength, you govern steadily in the wisdom of your heart. I shall fulfill my friendship to you, just as we spoke before. You shall become a comfort, whole and long-lasting, to your people, a help to warriors.

"So was not Heremod to the sons of Ecgwela, the Honor-Scyldings. He grew great not for their joy, but for their slaughter, for the destruction of Danish people. With swollen heart he killed his table-companions, shoulder-comrades, until he turned away from the joys of men, alone, notorious king, although mighty God had raised him in power, in the joys of strength, had set him up over all men. Yet in his breast his heart's thought grew blood-thirsty: no rings did he give to the Danes for glory. He lived joyless to suffer the pain of that strife, the long-lasting harm of the people. Teach yourself by him, be mindful of munificence. Old of winters, I tell this tale for you.

"It is a wonder to say how in His great spirit mighty God gives wisdom to mankind, land and earlship—He possesses power over all things. At times He lets the thought of a man of high lineage move in delight, gives him joy of earth in his homeland, a stronghold of men to rule over, makes regions of the world so subject to him, wide kingdoms, that in his unwisdom he may not himself have mind of his end. He lives in plenty; illness and age in no way grieve him, neither does dread care darken his heart, nor does enmity bare sword-hate, for the whole world turns to his will—he knows nothing worse—(XXV.) until his portion of pride increases and flourishes within him; then the watcher sleeps, the soul's guardian; that sleep is too sound, bound in its own cares, and the slayer most near whose bow shoots treacherously. Then is he hit in the heart, beneath his armor, with the bitter arrow—he cannot protect himself—with the crooked dark commands of the accursed spirit. What he has long held seems to him too little, angry-hearted he covets, no plated rings does he give in men's honor, and then he forgets and regards not his destiny because of what God, Wielder of Heaven, has given him before, his portion of glories. In the end it happens in turn that the loaned body weakens, falls doomed; another takes the earl's ancient treasure, one who recklessly gives precious gifts, does not fearfully guard them.

"Keep yourself against that wickedness, beloved Beowulf, best of men, and choose better—eternal gains. Have no care for pride, great warrior. Now for a time there is glory in your might: yet soon it shall be that sickness or sword will diminish your strength, or fire's fangs, or flood's surge, or sword's swing, or spear's flight, or appalling age; brightness of eyes will fail and grow dark; then it shall be that death will overcome you, warrior.

"Thus I ruled the Ring-Danes for a hundred half-years under the skies, and protected them in war with spear and sword against many nations over middle-earth, so that I counted no one as my adversary underneath the sky's expanse. Well, disproof of that came to me in my own land, grief after my joys, when Grendel, ancient adversary, came to invade my home. Great sorrow of heart I have always suffered for his persecution. Thanks be to the Ruler, the Eternal Lord, that after old strife I have come to see in my lifetime, with my own eyes, his blood-stained head. Go now to your seat, have joy of the glad feast, made famous in battle. Many of our treasures will be shared when morning comes."

The Geat was glad at heart, went at once to seek his seat as the wise one bade. Then was a feast fairly served again, for a second time, just as before, for those famed for courage, sitting about the hall.

Night's cover lowered, dark over the warriors. The retainers all arose. The gray-haired one would seek his bed, the old Scylding. It pleased the Geat, the brave shield-warrior, immensely that he should have rest. Straightway a hall-thane led the way on for the weary one, come from far country, and showed every courtesy to the thane's need, such as in those days seafarers might expect as their due.

Then the great-hearted one rested; the hall stood high, vaulted and gold-adorned; the guest slept within until the black raven, blithe-hearted, announced heaven's joy. Then the bright light came passing over the shadows. The warriors hastened, the nobles were eager to set out again for their people. Bold of spirit, the visitor would seek his ship far thence.

Then the hardy one bade that Hrunting be brought to the son of Ecglaf,[8] that he take back his sword, precious iron. He spoke thanks for that loan, said that he accounted it a good war-friend, strong in battle; in his words he found no fault at all with the sword's edge: he was a thoughtful man. And then they were eager to depart, the warriors ready in their armor. The prince who had earned honor of the Danes went to the high seat where the other was: the man dear to war greeted Hrothgar.

[Beowulf Returns Home]

(XXVI.) Beowulf spoke, the son of Ecgtheow: "Now we sea-travelers come from afar wish to say that we desire to seek Hygelac. Here we have been entertained splendidly according to our desire: you have dealt well with us. If on earth I might in any way earn more of your heart's love, prince of warriors, than I have done before with warlike deeds, I should be ready at once. If beyond the sea's expanse I hear that men dwelling near threaten you with terrors, as those who hated you did before, I shall bring you a thousand thanes, warriors to your aid. I know of Hygelac, lord of the Geats, though he is young as a guardian of the people, that he will further me with words and works so that I may do you honor and bring spears to help you, strong support where you have need of men. If Hrethric, king's son, decides to come to the court of the Geats, he can find many friends there;

8. I.e., Unferth.

far countries are well sought by him who is himself strong."

Hrothgar spoke to him in answer: "The All-Knowing Lord sent those words into your mind: I have not heard a man of so young age speak more wisely. You are great of strength, mature of mind, wise of words. I think it likely if the spear, sword-grim war, takes the son of Hrethel, sickness or weapon your prince, the people's ruler, and you have your life, that the Sea-Geats will not have a better to choose as their king, as guardian of their treasure, if you wish to hold the kingdom of your kinsmen. So well your heart's temper has long pleased me, beloved Beowulf. You have brought it about that peace shall be shared by the peoples, the folk of the Geats and the Spear-Danes, and enmity shall sleep, acts of malice which they practiced before; and there shall be, as long as I rule the wide kingdom, sharing of treasures, many a man shall greet his fellow with good gifts over the sea-bird's baths; the ring-prowed ship will bring gifts and tokens of friendship over the sea. I know your people, blameless in every respect, set firm after the old way both as to foe and to friend."

Then the protector of earls, the kinsman of Healfdene, gave him there in the hall twelve precious things; he bade him with these gifts seek his own dear people in safety, quickly come back. Then the king noble of race, the prince of the Scyldings, kissed the best of thanes and took him by his ncek: tears fell from the gray-haired one. He had two thoughts of the future, the old and wise man, one more strongly than the other—that they would not see each other again, bold men at council. The man was so dear to him that he might not restrain his breast's welling, for fixed in his heartstrings a deep-felt longing for the beloved man burned in his blood. Away from him Beowulf, warrior glorious with gold, walked over the grassy ground, proud of his treasure. The sea-goer awaited its owner, riding at anchor. Then on the journey the gift of Hrothgar was oft-praised: that was a king blameless in all things until age took from him the joys of his strength—old age that has often harmed many.

(XXVII.) There came to the flood the band of brave-hearted ones, of young men. They wore mail-coats, locked limb-shirts. The guard of the coast saw the coming of the earls, just as he had done before. He did not greet the guests with taunts from the cliff's top, but rode to meet them, said that the return of the warriors in bright armor in their ship would be welcome to the people of the Weather-Geats. There on the sand the broad sea-boat was loaded with armor, the ring-prowed ship with horses and rich things. The mast stood high over Hrothgar's hoard-gifts. He gave the boat-guard a sword wound with gold, so that thereafter on the mead-bench he was held the worthier for the treasure, the heirloom. The boat moved out to furrow the deep water, left the land of the Danes. Then on the mast a sea-cloth, a sail, was made fast by a rope. The boat's beams creaked: wind did not keep the sea-floater from its way over the waves. The sea-goer moved, foamy-necked floated forth over the swell, the ship with bound prow over the sea-currents until they might see the cliffs of the Geats, the well-known headlands. The ship pressed ahead, borne by the wind, stood still at the land. Quickly the harbor-guard was at the sea-side, he who had gazed for a long time far out over the currents, eager to see the beloved men. He [9] moored the deep ship in the sand, fast by its anchor ropes, lest the force of the waves should drive away the fair wooden vessel. Then he bade that the prince's wealth be borne ashore, armor and plated gold. It was not far for them to seek the giver of treasure, Hygelac son of Hrethel, where he dwelt at home near the sea-wall, himself with his retainers.

The building was splendid, its king most valiant, set high in the hall, Hygd [1] most youthful, wise and well-taught, though she had lived within the castle walls few winters, daughter of Hae-reth. For she was not niggardly, nor too sparing of gifts to the men of the Geats, of treasures. Modthryth,[2] good folk-queen, did dreadful deeds [in her youth]: no bold one among her retainers dared venture—except her great lord—to set his eyes on her in daylight, but [if he did] he should reckon deadly bonds pre-pared for him, arresting hands: that straightway after his seizure the sword awaited him, that the patterned blade must settle it, make known its death-evil. Such is no queenly custom for a woman to practice, though she is peerless—that one who weaves peace [3] should take away the life of a beloved man after pretended injury. However the kinsman of Hemming stopped that: [4] ale-drinkers gave another account, said that she did less harm to the people, fewer injuries, after she was given, gold-adorned, to the young warrior, the beloved noble, when by her father's teach-ing she sought Offa's hall in a voyage over the pale sea. There on the throne she was afterwards famous for generosity, while living made use of her life, held high love toward the lord of

9. Beowulf.
1. Hygd is Hygelac's young queen. The suddenness of her introduction here is perhaps due to a faulty text.
2. A transitional passage introducing the contrast between Hygd's good be-havior and Modthryth's bad behavior as young women of royal blood seems to have been lost. Modthryth's practice of having those who looked into her face put to death may reflect the folk-motif of the princess whose unsuccessful suitors are executed, though the text does not say that Modthryth's victims were suitors. Modthryth's "great lord" was probably her father.
3. Daughters of kings were frequently given in marriage to the king of a hostile nation in order to bring about peace; hence Modthryth may be called "one who weaves peace."
4. Offa, an Angle king who, according to legend ruled Mercia in England; who Hemming was—besides being Offa's forebear—is not known.

warriors, [who was] of all mankind the best, as I have heard, between the seas of the races of men. Since Offa was a man brave of wars and gifts, wide-honored, he held his native land in wisdom. From him sprang Eomer to the help of warriors, kinsman of Hemming, grandson of Garmund, strong in battle.[5]

(XXVIII.) Then the hardy one came walking with his troop over the sand on the sea-plain, the wide shores. The world-candle shone, the sun moved quickly from the south. They made their way, strode swiftly to where they heard that the protector of earls, the slayer of Ongentheow,[6] the good young war-king, was dispensing rings in the stronghold. The coming of Beowulf was straightway made known to Hygelac, that there in his home the defender of warriors, his comrade in battle, came walking alive to the court, sound from the battle-play. Quickly the way within was made clear for the foot-guests, as the mighty one bade.

Then he sat down with him, he who had come safe through the fight, kinsman with kinsman, after he had greeted his liege lord with formal speech, loyal, with vigorous words. Haereth's daughter moved through the hall-building with mead-cups, cared lovingly for the people, bore the cup of strong drink to the hands of the warriors. Hygelac began fairly to question his companion in the high hall, curiosity pressed him, what the adventures of the Sea-Geats had been. "How did you fare on your journey, beloved Beowulf, when you suddenly resolved to seek distant combat over the salt water, battle in Heorot? Did you at all help the wide-known woes of Hrothgar, the famous prince? Because of you I burned with seething sorrows, care of heart—had no trust in the venture of my beloved man. I entreated you long that you should in no way approach the murderous spirit, should let the South-Danes themselves settle the war with Grendel. I say thanks to God that I may see you sound."

Beowulf spoke, the son of Ecgtheow: "To many among men it is not hidden, lord Hygelac, the great encounter—what a fight we had, Grendel and I, in the place where he made many sorrows for the Victory-Scyldings, constant misery. All that I avenged, so that none of Grendel's kin over the earth need boast of that clash at night—whoever lives longest of the loathsome kind, wrapped in malice. There I went forth to the ring-hall to greet Hrothgar. At once the famous son of Healfdene, when he knew my purpose, gave me a seat with his own sons. The company was in joy:

5. Offa, the only person that may be identified as English in this English poem, receives high praise; apparently the names of his father Garmund and son Eomer would strike a responsive chord in the poet's audience.

6. Ongentheow was a Scylfing (Swedish) king, whose story is fully told below, sections XL and XLI. In fact Hygelac was not his slayer, but is called so because he led the attack on the Scylfings in which Ongentheow was killed.

I have not seen in the time of my life under heaven's arch more mead-mirth of hall-sitters. At times the famous queen, peace-pledge of the people, went through all the hall, cheered the young men; often she would give a man a ring-band before she went to her seat. At times Hrothgar's daughter bore the ale-cup to the retainers, to the earls throughout the hall. I heard hall-sitters name her Freawaru when she offered the studded cup to warriors. Young and gold-adorned, she is promised to the fair son of Froda.[7] That has seemed good to the lord of the Scyldings, the guardian of the kingdom, and he believes of this plan that he may, with this woman, settle their portion of deadly feuds, of quarrels.[8] Yet most often after the fall of a prince in any nation the deadly spear rests but a little while, even though the bride is good.

"It may displease the lord of the Heatho-Bards and each thane of that people when he goes in the hall with the woman, [that while] the noble sons of the Danes, her retainers, [are] feasted,[9] the heirlooms of their ancestors will be shining on them [1]—the hard and wave-adorned treasure of the Heatho-Bards, [which was theirs] so long as they might wield those weapons, (XXIX.) until they led to the shield-play, to destruction, their dear companions and their own lives. Then at the beer he [2] who sees the treasure, an old ash-warrior who remembers it all, the spear-death of warriors—grim is his heart—begins, sad of mind, to tempt a young fighter in the thoughts of his spirit, to awaken war-evil, and speaks this word:

" 'Can you, my friend, recognize that sword, the rare iron-blade, that your father, beloved man, bore to battle his last time in armor, where the Danes slew him, the fierce Scyldings, got possession of the battle-field, when Withergeld [3] lay dead, after the fall of warriors? Now here some son of his murderers walks in the hall, proud of the weapon, boasts of the murder, and wears the treasure that you should rightly possess.' So he will provoke and remind at every chance with wounding words until that moment comes that the woman's thane,[4] forfeiting life, shall lie dead, blood-smeared from the sword-bite, for his father's deeds. The other escapes with his life, knows the land well. Then on both sides the oath of the earls will be broken;

7. I.e., Ingeld, who succeeded his father a king of the Heatho-Bards.
8. I.e., the feud between the Danes and Heatho-Bards.
9. The text is faulty here.
1. I.e., the weapons and armor which had once belonged to the Heatho-Bards and were captured by the Danes will be worn by the Danish attendants of Hrothgar's daughter Freawaru when she goes to the Heatho-Bards to marry king Ingeld.
2. I.e., some old Heatho-Bard warrior.
3. Apparently a leader of the Heatho-Bards in their unsuccessful war with the Danes.
4. I.e., the Danish attendant of Freawaru who is wearing the sword of his Heatho-Bard attacker's father.

then deadly hate will well up in Ingeld, and his wife-love after the surging of sorrows will become cooler. Therefore I do not think the loyalty of the Heatho-Bards, their part in the alliance with the Danes, to be without deceit—do not think their friendship fast.

"I shall speak still more of Grendel, that you may readily know, giver of treasure, what the hand-fight of warriors came to in the end. After heaven's jewel had glided over the earth, the angry spirit came, awful in the evening, to visit us where, unharmed, we watched over the hall. There the fight was fatal to Hondscioh, deadly to one who was doomed. He was dead first of all, armed warrior. Grendel came to devour him, good young retainer, swallowed all the body of the beloved men. Yet not for this would the bloody-toothed slayer, bent on destruction, go from the gold-hall empty-handed; but, strong of might, he made trial of me, grasped me with eager hand. His glove [5] hung huge and wonderful, made fast with cunning clasps: it had been made all with craft, with devil's devices and dragon's skins. The fell doer of evils would put me therein, guiltless, one of many. He might not do so after I had stood up in anger. It is too long to tell how I repaid the people's foe his due for every crime. My prince, there with my deeds I did honor to your people. He slipped away, for a little while had use of life's joy. Yet his right hand remained as his spoor in Heorot, and he went from there abject, mournful of heart sank to the mere's bottom.

"The lord of the Scyldings repaid me for that bloody combat with much plated gold, many treasures, after morning came and we sat down to the feast. There was song and mirth. The old Scylding, who has learned many things, spoke of times far-off. At times a brave one in battle touched the glad wood, the harp's joy; at times he told tales, true and sad; at times he related strange stories according to right custom; at times, again, the great-hearted king, bound with age, the old warrior, would begin to speak of his youth, his battle-strength. His heart welled within when, old and wise, he thought of his many winters. Thus we took pleasure there the livelong day until another night came to men.

"Then in her turn Grendel's mother swiftly made ready to take revenge for his injuries, made a sorrowful journey. Death had taken her son, war-hate of the Weather-Geats. The direful woman avenged her son, fiercely killed a warrior: there the life of Aeschere departed, a wise old counselor. And when morning came the folk of the Danes might not burn him, death-weary, in the fire, nor place him on the pyre, beloved man: she had borne

5. Apparently a large glove that could be used as a pouch.

his body away in fiend's embrace beneath the mountain stream. That was the bitterest of Hrothgar's sorrows, of those that had long come upon the people's prince. Then the king, sore-hearted, implored me by your life [6] that I should do a man's work in the tumult of the waters, venture my life, finish a glorious deed. He promised me reward. Then I found the guardian of the deep pool, the grim horror, as is now known wide. For a time there we were locked hand in hand. Then the flood boiled with blood, and in the war-hall I cut off the head of Grendel's mother with a mighty sword. Not without trouble I came from there with my life. I was not fated to die then, but the protector of earls again gave me many treasures, the son of Healfdene.

(XXXI.) "Thus the king of that people lived with good customs. I had lost none of the rewards, the meed of my might, but he gave me treasures, the son of Healfdene, at my own choice. I will bring these to you, great king, show my good will. On your kindnesses all still depends: I have few close kinsmen besides you, Hygelac."

Then he bade bring in the boar-banner—the head-sign—the helmet towering in battle, the gray battle-shirt, the splendid sword —afterwards spoke words: "Hrothgar, wise king, gave me this armor; in his words he bade that I should first tell you about his gift: he said that king Heorogar,[7] lord of the Scyldings, had had it for a long time; not for that would he give it, the breast-armor, to his son, bold Heoroweard, though he was loyal to him. Use it all well!"

I have heard that four horses, swift and alike, followed that treasure, fallow as apples. He gave him the gift of both horses and treasure. So ought kinsmen do, not weave malice-nets for each other with secret craft, prepare death for comrades. To Hygelac his nephew was most true in hard fights, and each one mindful of helping the other. I have heard that he gave Hygd the neck-ring, the wonderfully wrought treasure, that Wealhtheow had given him—gave to the king's daughter as well three horses, supple and saddle-bright. After the gift of the necklace, her breast was adorned with it.

Thus Beowulf showed himself brave, a man known in battles, of good deeds, bore himself according to discretion. Drunk, he slew no hearth-companions. His heart was not savage, but he held the great gift that God had given him, the most strength of all mankind, like one brave in battle. He had long been despised,[8] so that the sons of the Geats did not reckon him brave, nor

6. I.e., "in your name."
7. Hrothgar's elder brother, whom Hrothgar succeeded as king.

8. Beowulf's poor reputation as a young man is mentioned only here.

would the lord of the Weather-Geats do him much gift-honor on the mead-bench. They strongly suspected that he was slack, a young man unbold. Change came to the famous man for each of his troubles.

Then the protector of earls bade fetch in the heirloom of Hrethel,[9] king famed in battle, adorned with gold. There was not then among the Geats a better treasure in sword's kind. He laid that in Beowulf's lap, and gave him seven thousand [hides of land], a hall and a throne. To both of them alike land had been left in the nation, home and native soil: to the other more especially wide was the realm, to him who was higher in rank.

[Beowulf and the Dragon]

Afterwards it happened, in later days, in the crashes of battle, when Hygelac lay dead and war-swords came to slay Heardred[1] behind the shield-cover, when the Battle-Scylfings, hard fighters, sought him among his victorious nation, attacked bitterly the nephew of Hereric—then the broad kingdom came into Beowulf's hand. He held it well fifty winters—he was a wise king, an old guardian of the land—until in the dark nights a certain one, a dragon, began to hold sway, which on the high heath kept watch over a hoard, a steep stone-barrow. Beneath lay a path unknown to men. By this there went inside a certain man [who made his way near to the heathen hoard; his hand took a cup, large, a shining treasure. The dragon did not afterwards conceal it though in his sleep he was tricked by the craft of the thief. That the people discovered, the neighboring folk—that he was swollen with rage].[2]

(XXXII.) Not of his own accord did he who had sorely harmed him[3] break into the worm's hoard, not by his own desire, but for hard constraint; the slave of some son of men fled hostile blows, lacking a shelter, and came there, a man guilty of wrong-doing. As soon as he saw him,[4] great horror arose in the stranger; [yet the wretched fugitive escaped the terrible worm . . . When the sudden shock came upon him, he carried off a precious cup.][5] There were many such ancient treasures in the earth-house, as in the old days some one of mankind had prudently hidden there the huge legacy of a noble race, rare treasures. Death had taken them all in earlier times, and the only one of the nation of people who still survived, who walked

---

9. Hygelac's father.
1. Hygelac's son Heardred, who succeeded Hygelac as king, was killed by the Swedes (Heatho-Scylfings) in his own land, as is explained more fully below, section XXXIII. His uncle Hereric was perhaps Hygd's brother.

2. This part of the manuscript is badly damaged, and the text within brackets is highly conjectural.
3. The dragon.
4. The dragon.
5. Several lines of the text have been lost.

there longest, a guardian mourning his friends, supposed the same of himself as of them—that he might little while enjoy the long-got treasure. A barrow stood all ready on the shore near the sea-waves, newly placed on the headland, made fast by having its entrances skillfully hidden. The keeper of the rings carried in the part of his riches worthy of hoarding, plated gold; he spoke few words:

"Hold now, you earth, now that men may not, the possession of earls. What, from you good men got it first! War-death has taken each man of my people, evil dreadful and deadly, each of those who has given up this life, the hall-joys of men. I have none who wears sword or cleans the plated cup, rich drinking vessel. The company of retainers has gone elsewhere. The hard helmet must be stripped of its fair-wrought gold, of its plating. The polishers are asleep who should make the war-mask shine. And even so the coat of mail, which withstood the bite of swords after the crashing of the shields, decays like its warrior. Nor may the ring-mail travel wide on the war-chief beside his warriors. There is no harp-delight, no mirth of the singing wood, no good hawk flies through the hall, no swift horse stamps in the castle court. Baleful death has sent away many races of men."

So, sad of mind, he spoke his sorrow, alone of them all, moved joyless through day and night until death's flood reached his heart. The ancient night-ravager found the hoard-joy standing open, he who burning seeks barrows, the smooth hateful dragon who flies at night wrapped in flame. Earth-dwellers much dread him. He it is who must seek a hoard in the earth where he will guard heathen gold, wise for his winters: he is none the better for it.

So for three hundred winters the harmer of folk held in the earth one of its treasure-houses, huge and mighty, until one man angered his heart. He bore to his master a plated cup, asked his lord for a compact of peace: thus was the hoard searched, the store of treasures diminished. His requests were granted the wretched man: the lord for the first time looked on the ancient work of men. Then the worm woke; cause of strife was renewed: for then he moved over the stones, hard-hearted beheld his foe's footprints—with secret stealth he had stepped forth too near the dragon's head. (So may an undoomed man who holds favor from the Ruler easily come through his woes and misery.) The hoard-guard sought him eagerly over the ground, would find the man who had done him injury while he slept. Hot and fierce-hearted, often he moved all about the outside of the barrow. No man at all was in the emptiness. Yet he took joy in the thought of war, in the work of fighting. At times he turned back into the barrow, sought his rich cup. Straightway he found that some man had tampered with his gold, his splendid treasure. The hoard-guard waited restless until evening came; then the barrow-keeper was in rage: he would requite that precious drinking cup with vengeful fire. Then the day was gone—to the joy of the worm. He would not wait long on the sea-wall, but set out with fire, ready with flame. The beginning was terrible to the folk on the land, as the ending was soon to be sore to their giver of treasure.

(XXXIII.) Then the evil spirit began to vomit flames, burn bright dwellings; blaze of fire rose, to the horror of men; there the deadly flying thing would leave nothing alive. The worm's warfare was wide-seen, his cruel malice, near and far—how the destroyer hated and hurt the people of the Geats. He winged back to the hoard, his hidden hall, before the time of day. He had circled the land-dwellers with flame, with fire and burning. He had trust in his barrow, in his war and his wall: his expectation deceived him.

Then the terror was made known to Beowulf, quickly in its truth, that his own home, best of buildings, had melted in surging flames, the throne-seat of the Geats. That was anguish of spirit to the good man, the greatest of heart-sorrows. The wise one supposed that he had bitterly offended the Ruler, the Eternal Lord, against old law. His breast within boiled with dark thoughts— as was not for him customary. The fiery dragon with his flames had destroyed the people's stronghold, the land along the sea, the heart of the country. Because of that the war-king, the lord of the Weather-Geats, devised punishment for him. The protector of fighting men, lord of earls, commanded that a wonderful battle-shield be made all of iron. Well he knew that the wood of the forest might not help him—linden against flame. The prince good from old times was to come to the end of the days that had been lent him, life in the world, and the worm with him, though he had long held the hoarded wealth. Then the ring-prince scorned to seek the far-flier with a troop, a large army. He had no fear for himself of the combat, nor did he think the worm's war-power anything great, his strength and his courage, because he himself had come through many battles before, dared perilous straits, clashes of war, after he had purged Hrothgar's hall, victorious warrior, and in combat crushed to death Grendel's kin, loathsome race.

Nor was that the least of his hand-combats where Hygelac was slain, when the king of the Geats, the noble lord of the people, the son of Hrethel, died of sword-strokes in the war-storm among the Frisians, laid low by the blade. From there Beowulf came away by means of his own strength, performed a feat of swimming; he had on his arm the armor of thirty earls when he turned back to the sea. There was no need for the Hetware [6] to exult in the foot-battle when they bore their shields against him: few came again from that warrior to seek their homes. Then the son of Ecgtheow swam over the water's expanse, forlorn and alone, back to his people. There Hygd offered him hoard and kingdom, rings and a prince's throne. She had no trust in her son, that he could hold his native throne against foreigners now that Hygelac was dead. By no means the sooner might the lordless ones get consent from the noble that he would become lord of Heardred or that he would accept royal power.[7] Yet he held him up among the people by friendly counsel, kindly with honor, until he became older,[8] ruled the Weather-Geats.

Outcasts from over the sea sought him, sons of Ohthere.[9] They had rebelled against the protector of the Scylfings, the best of the sea-kings of those who gave treasure in Sweden, a famous lord. For Heardred that became his life's limit: because of his hospitality there the son of Hygelac got his life's wound from the strokes of a sword. And the son of Ongentheow went back to seek his home after Heardred lay dead, let Beowulf hold the royal throne, rule the Geats: that was a good king.

(XXXIV.) In later days he was mindful of repaying the prince's fall, became the friend of the destitute Eadgils; [1] with folk he supported the son of Ohthere over the wide sea, with warriors and weapons. Afterwards he got vengeance by forays that brought with them cold care: he took the king's life.

Thus he had survived every combat, every dangerous battle, every deed of courage, the son of Ecgtheow, until that one day when he should fight with the worm. Then, one of twelve, the lord of the Geats, swollen with anger, went to look on the dragon. He had learned then from what the feud arose, the fierce malice to men: the glorious cup had come to his possession from the hand of the finder: he was the thirteenth of that company, the man who had brought on the beginning of the war, the sad-hearted slave—wretched, he must direct them to the place. Against his will he went to where he knew of an earth-hall, a barrow beneath the ground close to the sea-surge, to the strug-

---

6. I.e., a tribe, with whom the Frisians were allied.
7. I.e., Beowulf refused to take the throne from the rightful heir Heardred.
8. I.e., Beowulf supported the young Heardred.
9. Ohthere succeeded his father Ongentheow as king of the Scylfings (Swedes), but after his death his brother Onela seized the throne, driving out Ohthere's sons Eanmund and Eadgils. They were given refuge at the Geatish court by Heardred, whom Onela attacked for this act of hospitality. In the fight Eanmund and Heardred were killed, and Onela left the kingdom in Beowulf's charge.
1. The surviving son of Ohthere was befriended by Beowulf, who supported him in his successful attempt to gain the Swedish throne and who killed the usurper Onela.

gling waves: within, it was full of ornaments and gold chains. The terrible guardian, ready for combat, held the gold treasure, old under the earth. It was no easy bargain for any man to obtain. Then the king, hardy in fight, sat down on the headland; there he saluted his hearth-companions, gold-friend of the Geats. His mind was mournful, restless and ripe for death: very close was the fate which should come to the old man, seek his soul's hoard, divide life from his body; not for long then was the life of the noble one wound in his flesh.

Beowulf spoke, the son of Ecgtheow: "In youth I lived through many battle-storms, times of war. I remember all that. I was seven winters old when the lord of treasure, the beloved king of the folk, received me from my father: King Hrethel had me and kept me, gave me treasure and feast, mindful of kinship. During his life I was no more hated by him as a man in his castle than any of his own sons, Herebeald and Haethcyn, or my own Hygelac. For the eldest a murder-bed was wrongfully spread through the deed of a kinsman, when Haethcyn struck him down with an arrow from his horned bow—his friend and his lord—missed the mark and shot his kinsman dead, one brother the other, with the bloody arrowhead. That was a fatal fight, without hope of recompense, a deed wrongly done, baffling to the heart; yet it had happened that a prince had to lose life unavenged.

"So it is sad for an old man to endure that his son should ride young on the gallows. Then he may speak a story, a sorrowful song, when his son hangs for the joy of the raven, and, old in years and knowing, he can find no help for him. Always with every morning he is reminded of his son's journey elsewhere. He cares not to wait for another heir in his hall, when the first through death's force has come to the end of his deeds. Sorrowful he sees in his son's dwelling the empty wine-hall, the windy resting place without joy—the riders sleep, the warriors in the grave. There is no sound of the harp, no joy in the dwelling, as there was of old. (XXXV.) Then he goes to his couch, sings a song of sorrow, one alone for one gone. To him all too wide has seemed the land and the dwelling.

"So the protector of the Weather-Geats bore in his heart swelling sorrow for Herebeald. In no way could he settle his feud with the life-slayer; not the sooner could he wound the warrior with deeds of hatred, though he was not dear to him. Then for the sorrow that had too bitterly befallen him he gave up the joys of men, chose God's light. To his sons he left—as a happy man does—his land and his town when he went from life.

"Then there was battle and strife of Swedes and Geats, over

the wide water a quarrel shared, hatred between hardy ones, after Hrethel died. And the sons of Ongentheow [2] were bold and active in war, wanted to have no peace over the seas, but about Hreosnabeorh often devised awful slaughter. That my friends and kinsmen avenged, both the feud and the crime, as is well-known, though one of them bought it with his life, a hard bargain: the war was mortal to Haethcyn, lord of the Geats.[3] Then in the morning, I have heard, one kinsman avenged the other on his slayer with the sword's edge, when Ongentheow attacked Eofor: the war-helm split, the old Scylfing fell mortally wounded: his hand remembered feuds enough, did not withstand the life-blow.

"I repaid in war the treasures that he [4] gave me—with my bright sword, as was granted me by fate: he had given me land, a pleasant dwelling. There was not any need for him, any reason, that he should have to seek among the Gifthas or the Spear-Danes or in Sweden in order to buy with treasure a worse warrior. I would always go before him in the troop, alone in the front. And so all my life I shall wage battle while this sword endures that has served me early and late ever since I became Daeghrefn's slayer in the press—the warrior of the Hugas.[5] He could not bring armor to the king of the Frisians, breast ornament, but fell in the fight, keeper of the standard, a noble man. Nor was my sword's edge his slayer, but my warlike grip broke open his heart-streams, his bone-house. Now shall the sword's edge, the hand and hard blade, fight for the hoard."

[BEOWULF ATTACKS THE DRAGON]

Beowulf spoke, for the last time spoke words in boast: "In my youth I engaged in many wars. Old guardian of the people, I shall still seek battle, perform a deed of fame, if the evil-doer will come to me out of the earth-hall."

Then he saluted each of the warriors, the bold helmet-bearers, for the last time—his own dear companions. "I would not bear sword, weapon, to the worm, if I knew how else according to my boast I might grapple with the monster, as I did of old with Grendel. But I expect here hot battle-fire, steam and poison. Therefore I have on me shield and mail-shirt. I will not flee a foot-step from the barrow-ward, but it shall be with us at the wall as fate allots, the ruler of every man. I am confident in

2. I.e., the Swedes Onela and Ohthere: the reference is, of course, to a time earlier than that referred to in section XXXIII, note 9.
3. Haethcyn had succeeded his father Hrethel as king of the Geats after his accidental killing of his brother Herebeald. When Haethcyn was killed while

attacking the Swedes, he was succeeded by Hygelac, who, as the next sentence relates, avenged Haethcyn's death on Ongentheow. The death of Ongentheow is described below; sections XL and XLI.
4. Hygelac.
5. I.e., the Franks.

heart, so I forgo help against the war-flier. Wait on the barrow, safe in your mail-shirts, men in armor—which of us two may better bear wounds after our bloody meeting. This is not your venture, nor is it right for any man except me alone that he should spend his strength against the monster, do this man's deed. By my courage I shall get gold, or war will take your king, dire life-evil."

Then the brave warrior arose by his shield; hardy under helmet he went in his mail-shirt beneath the stone-cliffs, had trust in his strength—that of one man: such is not the way of the cowardly. Then he saw by the wall—he who had come through many wars, good in his great-heartedness, many clashes in battle when troops meet together—a stone arch standing, through it a stream bursting out of the barrow: there was welling of a current hot with killing fires, and he might not endure any while unburnt by the dragon's flame the hollow near the hoard. Then the man of the Weather-Geats, enraged as he was, let a word break from his breast. Stout-hearted he shouted; his voice went roaring, clear in battle, in under the gray stone. Hate was stirred up, the hoard's guard knew the voice of a man. No more time was there to ask for peace. First the monster's breath came out of the stone, the hot war-steam. The earth resounded. The man below the barrow, the lord of the Geats, swung his shield against the dreadful visitor. Then the heart of the coiled thing was aroused to seek combat. The good war-king had drawn his sword, the old heirloom, not blunt of edge. To each of them as they threatened destruction there was terror of the other. Firm-hearted he stood with his shield high, the lord of friends, while quickly the worm coiled itself; he waited in his armor. Then, coiling in flames, he came gliding on, hastening to his fate. The good shield protected the life and body of the famous prince, but for a shorter while than his wish was. There for the first time, the first day in his life, he might not prevail, since fate did not assign him such glory in battle. The lord of the Geats raised his hand, struck the shining horror so with his forged blade that the edge failed, bright on the bone, but less surely than its folk-king had need, hard-pressed in perils. Then because of the battle-stroke the barrow-ward's heart was savage, he exhaled death-fire—the war-flames sprang wide. The gold-friend of the Geats boasted of no great victories: the war blade had failed, naked at need, as it ought not to have done, iron good from old times. That was no pleasant journey, not one on which the famous son of Ecgtheow would wish to leave his land; against his will he must take up a dwelling-place elsewhere—as every man must give up the days that are lent him.

It was not long until they came together again, dreadful foes. The hoard-guard took heart, once more his breast swelled with his breathing. Encircled with flames, he who before had ruled a folk felt harsh pain. Nor did his companions, sons of nobles, take up their stand in a troop about him with the courage of fighting men, but they crept to the wood, protected their lives. In only one of them the heart surged with sorrows: nothing can ever set aside kinship in him who means well.

(XXXVI.) He was called Wiglaf, son of Weohstan, a rare shield-warrior, a man of the Scylfings,[6] kinsman of Aelfhere. He saw his liege lord under his war-mask suffer the heat. Then he was mindful of the honors he had given him before, the rich dwelling-place of the Waegmundings, every folk-right such as his father possessed. He might not then hold back, his hand seized his shield, the yellow linden-wood; he drew his ancient sword. Among men it was the heirloom of Eanmund, the son of Ohthere:[7] Weohstan had become his slayer in battle with sword's edge—an exile without friends; and he bore off to his kin the bright-shining helmet, the ringed mail-armor, the old sword made by giants that Onela had given him,[8] his kinsman's war-armor, ready battle-gear: he did not speak of the feud, though he had killed his brother's son.[9] He[1] held the armor many half-years, the blade and the battle-dress, until his son might do manly deeds like his old father. Then he gave him among the Geats war-armor of every kind, numberless, when, old, he went forth on the way from life. For the young warrior this was the first time that he should enter the war-storm with his dear lord. His heart's courage did not slacken, nor did the heirloom of his kinsman fail in the battle. That the worm found when they had come together.

Wiglaf spoke, said many fit words to his companions—his mind was mournful: "I remember that time we drank mead, when we

6. Though in the next sentence Wiglaf is said to belong to the family of the Waegmundings, the Geatish family to which Beowulf belonged, he is here called a Scylfing (Swede), and immediately below his father Weohstan is represented as having fought for the Swede Onela in his attack on the Geats. But for a man to change his nation was not unusual, and Weohstan, who may have had both Swedish and Geatish blood, had evidently become a Geat long enough before to have brought up his son Wiglaf as one. The identity of Aelfhere is not known.

7. See above, section XXXIII, note 9. Not only did Weohstan support Onela's attack on the Geat king Heardred, but

actually killed Eanmund whom Heardred was supporting, and it is Eanmund's sword that Wiglaf is now wielding.

8. The spoils of war belonged to the victorious king, who apportioned them among his fighters: thus Onela gave Weohstan the armor of Eanmund, whom Weohstan had killed.

9. This ironic remark points out that Onela did not claim *wergild* or seek vengeance from Weohstan, as in other circumstances he ought to have done inasmuch as Weohstan had killed Onela's close kinsman, his nephew Eanmund: but Onela was himself trying to kill Eanmund.

1. Weohstan.

promised our lord in the beer-hall—him who gave us these rings— that we would repay him for the war-arms if a need like this befell him—the helmets and the hard swords. Of his own will he chose us among the host for this venture, thought us worthy of fame—and gave me these treasures—because he counted us good war-makers, brave helm-bearers, though our lord intended to do this work of courage alone, as keeper of the folk, because among men he had performed the greatest deeds of glory, daring actions. Now the day has come that our liege lord has need of the strength of good fighters. Let us go to him, help our war-chief while the grim terrible fire persists. God knows of me that I should rather that the flame enfold my body with my gold-giver. It does not seem right to me for us to bear our shields home again unless we can first fell the foe, defend the life of the prince of the Weather-Geats. I know well that it would be no recompense for past deeds that he alone of the company of the Geats should suffer pain, fall in the fight. For us both shall there be a part in the work of sword and helmet, of battle-shirt and war-clothing."

Then he waded through the deadly smoke, bore his war-helmet to the aid of his king, spoke in few words: "Beloved Beowulf, do all well, for, long since in your youth, you said that you would not let your glory fail while you lived. Now, great-spirited noble, brave of deeds, you must protect your life with all your might. I shall help you."

After these words, the worm came on, angry, the terrible malice-filled foe, shining with surging flames, to seek for the second time his enemies, hated men. Fire advanced in waves; shield burned to the boss; mail-shirt might give no help to the young spear-warrior; but the young man went quickly under his kinsman's shield when his own was consumed with flames. Then the war-king was again mindful of fame, struck with his war-sword with great strength so that it stuck in the head-bone, driven with force. Naegling broke, the sword of Beowulf failed in the fight, old and steel-gray. It was not ordained for him that iron edges might help in the combat. Too strong was the hand that I have heard strained every sword with its stroke, when he bore wound-hardened weapon to battle: he was none the better for it.

Then for the third time the folk-harmer, the fearful fire-dragon, was mindful of feuds, set upon the brave one when the chance came, hot and battle-grim seized all his neck with his sharp fangs: he was smeared with life-blood, gore welled out in waves.

(XXXVII.) Then, I have heard, at the need of the folk-king the earl at his side made his courage known, his might and his keenness—as was natural to him. He took no heed for that head,[2] but the hand of the brave man was burned as he helped his kinsman, as the man in armor struck the hateful foe a little lower down, so that the sword sank in, shining and engraved; and then the fire began to subside. The king himself then still controlled his senses, drew the battle-knife, biting and war-sharp, that he wore on his mail-shirt: the protector of the Weather-Geats cut the worm through the middle. They felled the foe, courage drove his life out, and they had destroyed him together, the two noble kinsmen. So ought a man be, a thane at need. To the prince that was the last moment of victory for his own deeds, of work in the world.

Then the wound that the earth-dragon had caused began to burn and to swell; at once he felt dire evil boil in his breast, poison within him. Then the prince, wise of thought, went to where he might sit on a seat near the wall. He looked on the work of giants, how the timeless earth-hall held within it stone-arches fast on pillars. Then with his hands the thane, good without limit, washed him with water, blood-besmeared, the famous prince, his beloved lord, sated with battle; and he unfastened his helmet.

Beowulf spoke—despite his wounds spoke, his mortal hurts. He knew well he had lived out his days' time, joy on earth; all passed was the number of his days, death very near. "Now I would wish to give my son my war-clothing, if any heir after me, part of my flesh, were granted. I held this people fifty winters. There was no folk-king of those dwelling about who dared approach me with swords, threaten me with fears. In my land I awaited what fate brought me, held my own well, sought no treacherous quarrels, nor did I swear many oaths unrightfully. Sick with life-wounds, I may have joy on all this, for the Ruler of Men need not blame me for the slaughter of kinsmen when life goes from my body. Now quickly go to look at the hoard under the gray stone, beloved Wiglaf, now that the worm lies sleeping from sore wounds, bereft of his treasure. Be quick now, so that I may see the ancient wealth, the golden things, may clearly look on the bright curious gems; so that for that, because of the treasure's richness, I may the more easily leave life and nation I have long held."

(XXXVIII.) Then I have heard that the son of Weohstan straightway obeyed his lord, sick with battle-wounds, according to the words he had spoken, went wearing his ring-armor, woven battle-shirt, under the barrow's roof. Then he saw, as he went

---

2. I.e., the dragon's flame-breathing head.

by the seat, the brave young retainer, triumphant in heart, many precious jewels, glittering gold lying on the ground, wonders on the wall, and the worm's lair, the old night-flier's—cups standing there, vessels of men of old, with none to polish them, stripped of their ornaments. There was many a helmet old and rusty, many an arm-ring skillfully twisted. (Easily may treasure, gold in the ground, betray each one of the race of men, hide it who will.) Also he saw a standard all gold hang high over the hoard, the greatest of hand-wonders, linked with fingers' skill. From it came a light so that he might see the ground, look on the works of craft. There was no trace of the worm, for the blade had taken him. Then I have heard that one man in the mound pillaged the hoard, the old work of giants, loaded in his bosom cups and plates at his own desire. He took also the standard, brightest of banners. The sword of the old lord—its edge was iron—had already wounded the one who for a long time had been guardian of the treasure, waged his fire-terror, hot for the hoard, rising up fiercely at midnight, till he died in the slaughter.

The messenger was in haste, eager to return, urged on by the treasures. Curiosity tormented him, whether eagerly seeking he should find the lord of the Weather-Geats, strength gone, alive in the place where he had left him before. Then with the treasures he found the great prince, his lord, bleeding, at the end of his life. Again he began to sprinkle him with water until this word's point broke through his breast-hoard—he spoke, the king, old man in sorrow, looked on the gold: "I speak with my words thank to the Lord of All for these treasures, to the King of Glor Eternal Prince, for what I gaze on here, that I might get su for my people before my death-day. Now that I have bought hoard of treasures with my old life, you attend to the peo needs hereafter: I can be here no longer. Bid the battle-renov make a mound, bright after the funeral fire, on the sea's It shall stand high on Hronesness as a reminder to my so that sea-travelers later will call it Beowulf's barrow they drive their ships far over the darkness of the seas."

He took off his neck the golden necklace, bold-hearte gave it to the thane, to the young spear-warrior—gold helmet, ring, and mail-shirt, bade him use them well. "Y last left of our race, of the Waegmundings. Fate has all my kinsmen, earls in their strength, to destin have to go after." That was the last word of the the thoughts of his heart, before he should tast pyre, hot hostile flames. The soul went from his the doom of those fast in truth.

[*Beowulf's Funeral*]

(XXXIX.) Then sorrow came to the young man that he saw him whom he most loved on the earth, at the end of his life, suffering piteously. His slayer likewise lay dead, the awful earth-dragon bereft of life, overtaken by evil. No longer should the coiled worm rule the ring-hoard, for iron edges had taken him, hard and battle-sharp work of the hammers, so that the wide-flier, stilled by wounds, had fallen on the earth near the treasure-house. He did not go flying through the air at midnight, proud of his property, showing his aspect, but he fell to earth through the work of the chief's hands. Yet I have heard of no man of might on land, though he was bold of every deed, whom it should prosper to rush against the breath of the venomous foe or disturb with hands the ring-hall, if he found the guard awake who lived in the barrow. The share of the rich treasures became Beowulf's, paid for by death: each of the two had journeyed to the end of life's loan.

Then it was not long before the battle-slack ones left the woods, ten weak troth-breakers together, who had not dared fight with their spears in their liege lord's great need. But they bore their shields, ashamed, their war-clothes, to where the old man lay, looked on Wiglaf. He sat wearied, the foot-soldier near the shoulders of his lord, would waken him with water: it gained him nothing. He might not, though he much wished it, hold life in his chieftain on earth nor change anything of the Ruler's: the judgment of God would control the deeds of every man, just as it still does now. Then it was easy to get from the young man a grim answer to him who before had lost courage. Wiglaf spoke, the son of Weohstan, a man sad at heart, looked on the unloved ones:

"Yes, he who will speak truth may say that the liege lord who gave you treasure, the war-gear that you stand in there, when he used often to hand out to hall-sitters on the ale-benches, a prince to his thanes, helmets and war-shirts such as he could find mightiest anywhere, both far and near—that he quite threw away the war-gear, to his distress when war came upon him. The folk-king had no need to boast of his war-comrades. Yet God, Ruler of Victories, granted him that he might avenge himself, alone with his sword, when there was need for his courage. I was able to give him little life-protection in the fight, and yet beyond my power I did begin to help my kinsman. The deadly foe was ever the weaker after I struck him with my sword, fire poured less strongly from his head. Too few defenders thronged about the prince when the hard time came upon him. Now

there shall cease for your race the receiving of treasure and the giving of swords, all enjoyment of pleasant homes, comfort. Each man of your kindred must go deprived of his land-right when nobles from afar learn of your flight, your inglorious deed. Death is better for any earl than a life of blame."

(XL.) Then he bade that the battle-deed be announced in the city, up over the cliff-edge, where the band of warriors sat the whole morning of the day, sad-hearted, shield-bearers in doubt whether it was the beloved man's last day or whether he would come again. Little did he fail to speak of new tidings, he who rode up the hill, but spoke to them all truthfully: "Now the joy-giver of the people of the Weathers, the lord of the Geats, is fast on his death-bed, lies on his slaughter-couch through deeds of the worm. Beside him lies his life-enemy, struck down with dagger-wounds—with his sword he might not work wounds of any kind on the monster. Wiglaf son of Weohstan sits over Beowulf, one earl by the lifeless other, in weariness of heart holds death-watch over the loved and the hated.

"Now may the people expect a time of war, when the king's fall becomes wide-known to the Franks and the Frisians. A harsh quarrel was begun with the Hugas when Hygelac came traveling with his sea-army to the land of the Frisians, where the Hetware assailed him in battle, quickly, with stronger forces, made the mailed warrior bow; he fell in the ranks: that chief gave no treasure to his retainers. Ever since then the good will of the Merewioing king has been denied us.

"Nor do I expect any peace or trust from the Swedish people, for it is wide-known that Ongentheow took the life of Haethcyn, Hrethel's son, near Ravenswood when in their over-pride the people of the Geats first went against the War-Scylfings. Straightway the wary father of Ohthere,[3] old and terrible, gave a blow in return, cut down the sea-king,[4] rescued his wife, old woman of times past, bereft of her gold, mother of Onela and Ohthere, and then he followed his life-foes until they escaped, lordless, painfully, to Ravenswood. Then with a great army he besieged those whom the sword had left, weary with wounds, often vowed woes to the wretched band the livelong night, said that in the morning he would cut them apart with sword-blades, [hang] some on gallows-trees as sport for birds. Relief came in turn to the sorry-hearted together with dawn when they heard Hygelac's horn and trumpet, his sound as the good man came on their track with a body of retainers. (XLI.) Wide-seen was the bloody track of Swedes and

---

3. I.e., Ongentheow.
4. I.e., Haethcyn, king of the Geats. Haethcyn's brother Hygelac, who succeeded him, was not present at this battle, but arrived after the death of Haethcyn with reinforcements to relieve the survivors and to pursue Ongentheow in his retreat to his city.

Geats, the slaughter-strife of men, how the peoples stirred up the feud between them. Then the good man went with his kinsmen, old and much-mourning, to seek his stronghold: the earl Ongentheow moved further away. He had heard of the warring of Hygelac, of the war-power of the proud one. He did not trust in resistance, that he might fight off the sea-men, defend his hoard against the war-sailors, his children and wife. Instead he drew back, the old man behind his earth-wall.

"Then pursuit was offered to the people of the Swedes, the standards of Hygelac overran the stronghold as Hrethel's people pressed forward to the citadel. There Ongentheow the gray-haired was brought to bay by sword-blades, and the people's king had to submit to the judgment of Eofor alone. Wulf [5] son of Wonred had struck him angrily with his weapon so that for the blow the blood sprang forth in streams beneath his hair. Yet not for that was he afraid, the old Scylfing, but he quickly repaid the assault with worse exchange, the folk-king, when he turned toward him. The strong son of Wonred could not give the old man a return blow, for Ongentheow had first cut through the helmet of his head so that he had to sink down, smeared with blood—fell on the earth: he was not yet doomed, for he recovered, though the wound hurt him. The hardy thane of Hygelac,[6] when his brother lay low, let his broad sword, old blade made by giants, break the great helmet across the shield-wall; then the king bowed, the keeper of the folk was hit to the quick.

"Then there were many who bound up the brother, quickly raised him up after it was granted them to control the battle-field. Then one warrior stripped the other, took from Ongentheow his iron-mail, hard-hilted sword, and his helmet, too; he bore the arms of the hoary one to Hygelac. He accepted that treasure and fairly promised him rewards among the people, and he stood by it thus: the lord of the Geats, the son of Hrethel, when he came home, repaid Wulf and Eofor for their battle-assault with much treasure, gave each of them a hundred thousand [units] of land and linked rings: there was no need for any man on middle-earth to blame him for the rewards, since they had performed great deeds. And then he gave Eofor his only daughter as a pledge of friendship—a fair thing for his home.

"That is the feud and the enmity, the death-hatred of men, for which I expect that the people of the Swedes, bold shield-warriors after the fall of princes, will set upon us after they learn that our prince has gone from life, he who before held hoard and

---

5. The two sons of Wonred, Wulf and Eofor, attacked Ongentheow in turn. Wulf was struck down but not killed by the old Swedish king, who was then slain by Eofor.

6. I.e., Eofor.

kingdom against our enemies, did good to the people, and further still, did what a man should. Now haste is best, that we look on the people's king there and bring him who gave us rings on his way to the funeral pyre. Nor shall only a small share melt with the great-hearted one, but there is a hoard of treasure, gold uncounted, grimly purchased, and rings bought at the last now with his own life. These shall the fire devour, flames enfold—no earl to wear ornament in remembrance, nor any bright maiden add to her beauty with neck-ring; but mournful-hearted, stripped of gold, they shall walk, often, not once, in strange countries—now that the army-leader has laid aside laughter, his game and his mirth. Therefore many a spear, cold in the morning, shall be grasped with fingers, raised by hands; no sound of harp shall waken the warriors, but the dark raven, low over the doomed, shall tell many tales, say to the eagle how he fared at the feast when with the wolf he spoiled the slain bodies."

Thus the bold man was a speaker of hateful news, nor did he much lie in his words or his prophecies. The company all arose. Without joy they went below Earnaness [7] to look on the wonder with welling tears. Then they found on the sand, soulless, keeping his bed of rest, him who in former times had given them rings. Then the last day of the good man had come, when the war-king, prince of the Weather-Geats, died a wonderful death. First they saw the stranger creature, the worm lying loathsome, opposite him in the place. The fire-dragon was grimly terrible with his many colors, burned by the flames; he was fifty feet long in the place where he lay. Once he had joy of the air at night, came back down to seek his den. Then he was made fast by death, had made use of the last of his earth-caves. Beside him stood cups and pitchers, plates and rich swords lay eaten through by rust, just as they had been there in the bosom of the earth for a thousand winters. Then that huge heritage, gold of men of old, was wound in a spell, so that no one of men must touch the ring-hall unless God himself, the True King of Victories—He is men's protection—should grant to whom He wished to open the hoard—whatever man seemed fit to Him.

(XLII.) Then it was seen that the act did not profit him who wrongly kept hidden the handiworks under the wall. The keeper had first slain a man like few others, then the feud had been fiercely avenged. It is a wonder where an earl famed for courage may reach the end of his allotted life—then may dwell no longer in the mead-hall, man with his kin. So it was with Beowulf when he sought quarrels, the barrow's ward: he himself did not then know in what way his parting with the world should come. The

7. The headland near where Beowulf had fought the dragon.

great princes who had put it [8] there had laid on it so deep a curse until doomsday that the man who should plunder the place should be guilty of sins, imprisoned in idol-shrines, fixed with hell-bonds, punished with evils—unless the Possessor's favor were first shown the more clearly to him who desired the gold.

Wiglaf spoke, the son of Weohstan: "Often many a man must suffer distress for the will of one man, as has happened to us. We might by no counsel persuade our dear prince, keeper of the kingdom, not to approach the gold-guardian, let him lie where he long was, live in his dwelling to the world's end. He held to his high destiny. The hoard has been made visible, grimly got. What drove the folk-king thither was too powerfully fated. I have been therein and looked at it all, the rare things of the chamber, when it was granted me—not at all friendly was the journey that I was permitted beneath the earth-wall. In haste I seized with my hands a huge burden of hoard-treasures, of great size, bore it out here to my king. He was then still alive, sound-minded and aware. He spoke many things, old man in sorrow, and bade greet you, commanded that for your lord's deeds you make a high barrow in the place of his pyre, large and conspicuous, since he was of men the worthiest warrior through the wide earth, while he might enjoy wealth in his castle.

"Let us now hasten to see and visit for the second time the heap of precious jewels, the wonder under the walls. I shall direct you so that you may look on enough of them from near at hand—rings and broad gold. Let the bier be made ready, speedily prepared, when we come out, and then let us carry our prince, beloved man, where he shall long dwell in the Ruler's protection."

Then the son of Weohstan, man brave in battle, bade command many warriors, men who owned houses, leaders of the people, that they carry wood from afar for the pyre for the good man. "Now shall flame eat the chief of warriors—the fire shall grow dark—who often survived the iron-shower when the storm of arrows driven from bow-strings passed over the shield-wall—the shaft did its task, made eager by feather-gear served the arrowhead."

And then the wise son of Weohstan summoned from the host thanes of the king, seven together, the best; one of eight warriors, he went beneath the evil roof. One who walked before bore a torch in his hands. Then there was no lot to decide who should plunder that hoard, since the men could see that every part of it rested in the hall without guardian, lay wasting. Little did any man mourn that hastily they should bear out the rare treasure.

8. The treasure.

Also they pushed the dragon, the worm, over the cliff-wall, let the wave take him, the flood enfold the keeper of the treasure. Then twisted gold was loaded on a wagon, an uncounted number of things, and the prince, hoary warrior, borne to Hronesness.

(XLIII.) Then the people of the Geats made ready for him a funeral pyre on the earth, no small one, hung with helmets, battle-shields, bright mail-shirts, just as he had asked. Then in the midst they laid the great prince, lamenting their hero, their beloved lord. Then warriors began to awaken on the barrow the greatest of funeral-fires; the wood-smoke climbed, black over the fire; the roaring flame mixed with weeping—the wind-surge died down—until it had broken the bone-house, hot at its heart. Sad in spirit they lamented their heart-care, the death of their liege lord. [And the Geatish woman, wavy-haired, sang a sorrowful song about Beowulf, said] [9] again and again that she sorely feared for herself invasions of armies, many slaughters, terror of troops, humiliation, and captivity. Heaven swallowed the smoke.

Then the people of the Weather-Geats built a mound on the promontory, one that was high and broad, wide-seen by seafarers, and in ten days completed a monument for the bold in battle, surrounded the remains of the fire with a wall, the most splendid that men most skilled might devise. In the barrow they placed rings and jewels, all such ornaments as troubled men had earlier taken from the hoard. They let the earth hold the wealth of earls, gold in the ground, where now it still dwells, as useless to men as it was before. Then the brave in battle rode round the mound, children of nobles, twelve in all, would bewail their sorrow and mourn their king, recite dirges and speak of the man. They praised his great deeds and his acts of courage, judged well of his prowess. So it is fitting that man honor his liege lord with words, love him in heart when he must be led forth from the body. Thus the people of the Geats, his hearth-companions, lamented the death of their lord. They said that he was of world-kings the mildest of men and the gentlest, kindest to his people, and most eager for fame.

9. The manuscript is badly damaged and the interpretation conjectural.

THE WANDERER

The lament of *The Wanderer* is an excellent example of the elegiac mood so common in Old English poetry. The loss of a lord, of companions in arms, of a mead-hall (in which Anglo-Saxon life realized itself to the full) are themes that enhance the melancholy tone of *Beowulf* as they are the emotional basis for such a poem as the present one. But nowhere more poignantly expressed than in *The Wanderer* is the loneliness of the exile in search of a new lord and hall: this is what Beowulf's father, Ecgtheow, would have suffered, had it not been for Hrothgar's hospitality. To the wretched seeker all weather is wintry, for nature seems to conspire to match a man's mood as he moves over the water from one land to another, yearning for a home and kin to replace those vanished ones that still fill his thoughts.

As is true of most Old English elegiac laments, both the language and the structure of *The Wanderer* are difficult. The poem begins with a speaker who voices hope of finding comfort after many tribulations, one who is identified as an "earth-walker." After the interruption, this wanderer continues to speak—to himself—of his long search for a new home, describing how he must keep his thoughts locked within him while he makes his search. But these thoughts form the most vivid and moving part of his soliloquy—how, floating upon the sea, dazed with sorrow and fatigue, he imagines that he sees his old companions, and how, as he wakens to reality, they vanish over the water like sea-birds.

The second part of the poem, beginning with the seventh paragraph ("Therefore I cannot think why * * * "), expands the theme from one man to all men in a world wasted by war and time. It is possible that the speaker of this part of the poem is the same as that of the earlier part, but it is also possible, as John C. Pope has recently argued, that the poet meant the second part to be assigned to a different speaker, one of a more thoughtful turn of mind who draws philosophical implications from the experience of the first. The second speaker derives such cold comfort as he can from asking the old question, *Ubi sunt?*—where are they who were once so glad to live? And he concludes with the thought that this "resting place of earth" shall be emptied of mankind. This man, "wise in heart," sits apart at the council, apparently as an indication of his detachment from life. The poem concludes with a characteristic Old English injunction to practice restraint on earth, place hope only in heaven.

The Wanderer is preserved only in the Exeter Book, a manuscript copied about 975, which contains the largest surviving collection of Old English poetry.

The Wanderer[1]

"Often the lone-dweller lives to find favor, mildness of the Lord, though long over the water-way, troubled in heart, he has had to stir with his arms the frost-cold sea, tread the tracks of exile. Fully fixed is his fate."

So spoke the earth-walker, mindful of hardships, of cruel war-slaughters—and the fall of dear kinsmen.

1. The translation by the editor is based on the text edited by J. C. Pope in *Seven Old English Poems* (1966); the indication of a new speaker at the beginning of the seventh paragraph is also adopted from Pope.

"Often before the dawn of each day, alone, I have had to speak my cares: there is now none of the living to whom I dare clearly say my heart's thought. I know for truth that it is an excellent custom in a man that he lock fast his heart's coffer, keep his mind's hoard-case closed, purpose what he will. The weary-hearted may not withstand fate, nor the torn spirit bring help. Therefore those eager for fame often bind sorrowful thought fast in their breast-coffer.

"So I, often wretched with care, deprived of my homeland, far from dear kinsmen, had to fasten my heart's thought with fetters—after the time, in years long past, that I covered my gold-friend in the darkness of earth; and thence downcast I crossed over the woven waves, winter-sad, yearning for a hall, sought a giver of treasure—where, far or near, I might find one who should know of my people or would comfort me friendless, receive me with gladness. He who has felt it knows how cruel a companion is sorrow to him who has no beloved protectors. The path of exile attends him, not twisted gold—frozen are the thoughts in his heart-case, no joy of earth. He remembers the hall-warriors and the taking of treasure—how in his youth his gold-friend made him accustomed to feasting. All delight ends.

"Indeed, he who must long forgo the counsel-words of a beloved lord knows how it will seem to him in his mind, when together sorrow and sleep often bind the poor lone-dweller, that he is embracing and kissing his liege lord and laying his hands and head on his knee, as in the old days when sometimes he shared in the gift-giving. Then the lordless man wakens again, sees before him the yellow waves, the sea-birds bathe, spread their feathers, frost and snow fall, mingled with hail.

"Then the wounds of his heart are deeper, sore for want of his dear one. Sorrow is made new as memory of kinsmen moves through his mind: he greets them with glad words, eagerly looks on them, a company of warriors. They fade again, moving away over the water: such fleeting ones' spirit brings there no well-known voices. Care is renewed in him who many and often times must send his weary heart over the woven waves."

"Therefore I cannot think why my heart's thought should not grow dark when through this world I consider all the life of men—with what terrible swiftness they forgo the hall-floor, bold young retainers. So each day this middle-earth fails and falls. Indeed, no man may become wise before he has had a share of winters in the kingdom of this world. The wise must be patient, must never be too hot-hearted, nor too hasty of speech, nor too weak of wars, nor too wanting of thought, nor too fearful, nor too glad, nor too greedy for wealth, nor ever too eager of boast before he has clear knowing.

A man must wait, when he speaks boast, until, sure-minded, he knows clearly whither the thought of hearts will turn.

"The wise warrior must observe how ghostly it will be when all the wealth of this world stands waste, as now here and there through this middle-earth walls stand blown by the wind, covered with frost-fall, the dwellings storm-beaten. The wine-halls totter, the lord lies bereft of joy, all the company has fallen, bold men beside the wall. Some war took away, bore them on their way forth; one a bird carried off over the deep sea, one the gray wolf shared with death, another a man with sad face hid in an earth-pit.

"So the Creator of men's generations laid waste this dwelling-ground until the old works of giants stood idle, empty of the sound of the stronghold's keepers. Therefore the wise in heart thinks deeply on this wall-place and this dark life, remembers the great number of deadly combats long ago, and speaks these words: 'Where has the horse gone? Where the young warrior? Where is the giver of treasure? What has become of the seats for the feasts? Where are the joys of the hall? Alas, the bright cup! Alas, the mailed warrior! Alas, the prince's glory! How has that time gone, vanished beneath night's cover, just as if it had never been! The wall, wonderfully high, adorned with snake-images, stands now over the old traces of the beloved company. Might of the ash-spears has carried away the earls, weapons greedy for slaughter—Fate the mighty, and storms beat on the stone walls, thick-falling snow binds the earth; winter's roar, when darkness comes, the night-shadow falls, sends from the north harsh hailstones in hatred of men. All the kingdom of earth is wretched, work of the fates changes the world under the skies. Here wealth is fleeting, here friend is fleeting, here man is fleeting, here woman is fleeting—all this resting place of earth shall be emptied.' "

So spoke the wise in heart, sat apart at the council. Good is he who keeps his pledge, must never man utter too quickly the passion of his breast, unless he knows first how to achieve remedy, an earl with his valor. Well will it be with him who seeks favor, support from the Father in heaven, where for us the only stronghold stands.

THE BATTLE OF MALDON

The *Battle of Maldon* celebrates an event of the year 991, when a large party of Scandinavian raiders met the English defense forces on the estuary of the Blackwater River (the Pant of the poem), near Maldon in Essex. The Vikings had made a number of successful raids on seaports in the vicinity, after which they had encamped on an island near the mouth of the river. The island, since it was accessible from the mainland by a causeway that might be used only at low tide, provided a natural base from which the Vikings could continue their hit-and-run depredations on the countryside. Birhtnoth, the Earl of Essex, who was leader of the English militia, took up his position at the end of the causeway and from there was able to prevent the enemy from crossing to the mainland. As the poem relates, however, in his "overconfidence" he allowed them free passage so that a battle might take place. As a result, he was himself killed, and many of the defenders took to their heels; but the earl's retinue —his close associates and retainers—continued to fight bravely until they were overwhelmed. In the incomplete form in which the poem has come down to us we do not hear of the ultimate defeat of the English, though the grim tone and in particular the famous speech of Birhtwold prepare us for the disaster.

The unknown poet of late Anglo-Saxon times was apparently well versed in heroic English poetry of the type of *Beowulf*, and he does a brilliant job of adapting traditional epic mannerisms to his description of a local battle of no particular historical importance, which involved people with whom he was acquainted. The defense forces were actually no more than a home guard: inexperienced farmers and laborers conscripted for the local defense, together with a small group of aristocrats who were acquainted with heroic martial tradition but had not before had the opportunity to behave heroically. Since the defeat of the Scandinavians at Brunanburg in 937, the kingdom had enjoyed a long, peaceful respite from attack; the present Viking raid was, indeed, the beginning of a new and bloody era during which the realm that Alfred had consolidated weakened badly under Ethelred "the Unready." Godric and his brothers, who, according to the poem, fled from the battle, are representative of those Englishmen who preferred to pay tribute rather than to fight. But Birhtnoth and his retinue are of the traditional tough fiber, and it is especially in their speeches and single combats that the poet uses the epic style, contenting himself elsewhere with a forceful but generally realistic narrative of what occurred. Birhtnoth's decision to let the Vikings cross the river is treated in the epic manner as an instance of heroic overconfidence, like Beowulf's refusal to use his sword against the unarmed Grendel —but in this case it is a gesture that leads to tragic doom. Probably Birhtnoth had a practical motive for his rashness: if the Vikings were prevented from raiding here, they would simply sail along the coast to a less well-defended spot in order to continue their depredations. Only their destruction would insure general peace; but from the local point of view, Birhtnoth's permitting the enemy to come where he could fight with them might well appear as the rashly noble act of a traditional hero.

The poem was written down in a manuscript that was reduced to charred fragments in the same fire that damaged the *Beowulf* manuscript. Fortunately, a transcript had been made of it before the fire, and on this modern editions depend. Even before the manuscript was burned the poem must have lacked a number of lines at its beginning and end, though most scholars feel that nothing very substantial has been lost.

The Battle of Maldon[1]

Then he[2] commanded each of his warriors to leave his horse, drive it far away, and walk forward, trusting in his hands and in his good courage. When Offa's kinsman[3] understood that the earl would not put up with cowardice, he let his beloved hawk fly from his hand toward the woods and advanced to the battle: by this men might know that the youth would not weaken in the fight once he had taken up his weapons. Eadric wished also to serve his lord the earl in the battle; he carried his spear forward to the conflict. He was of good heart as long as he might hold shield and broad-sword in his hands; he carried out the vow that he had made, now that he was to fight before his lord.

Then Birhtnoth began to place his men at their stations; he rode about and advised them, taught the troops how they should stand and hold the place and bade them grasp their shields aright, firm in their hands, and have no fear. When he had arranged his folk properly, he alighted among them where it seemed best to him, where he knew his retainers to be most loyal.

Then the Vikings' herald stood on the river bank, cried out loudly, spoke words, boastfully proclaimed the seafarers' message to the earl where he stood on the shore: "Bold seamen have sent me to thee, have commanded me to say to thee that thou must quickly send treasure in order to protect thyself; and it is better for you to buy off this spear-assault with tribute than to have us give you harsh war. There is no need for us to destroy one another, if you are rich enough to pay. With the gold we will confirm truce. If thou that art highest here decide upon this, that thou wilt ransom thy people, and in return for peace give the seamen money in the amount they request, and receive peace from us, we will go to ship with the tribute, set sail on the sea, and keep peace with you."

Birhtnoth spoke, raised his shield, his slender ash-spear, uttered words, angry and resolute gave him answer: "Dost thou hear, sea-farer, what this folk says? They will give you spears for tribute, poisoned point and old sword, heriot[4] that avails you not in battle. Sea-wanderers' herald, take back our answer, speak to thy people a message far more hateful, that here stands with his host an undis-

---

1. In this prose translation by the present editor, a few liberties have been taken with the text in order to make clear the references of some of the loosely used Old English terms for "warrior." The translation is in general based on the text in J. C. Pope's *Seven Old English Poems* (1966).
2. Earl Birhtnoth, commander of the

English defense forces.
3. Offa is mentioned later in the poem as one of Birhtnoth's principal retainers; his young kinsman is not otherwise identified.
4. The weapons a tenant received from his lord; they were returned to the lord upon the tenant's death.

graced earl who will defend this country, my lord Æthelred's[5] homeland, folk and land. Heathen shall fall in the battle. It seems to me too shameful that you should go to ship with our tribute unfought, now that you have come thus far into our land. Not so easily shall you get treasure: point and edge shall first reconcile us, grim battle-play, before we give tribute."

Then he ordered the men to bear their shields, go forward so that they all stood on the river bank. Because of the water neither band could come to the other: after the ebb, the floodtide came flowing in; currents met and crossed. It seemed to them too long a time before they might bear their spears together. On the river Pant they stood in proud array, the battle-line of the East Saxons and the men from the ash-ships. Nor might any of them injure another, unless one should receive death from the flight of an arrow.

The tide went out. The seamen stood ready, many Vikings eager for war. The earl, protector of men, bade a war-hard warrior—he was named Wulfstan, of bold lineage—to hold the bridge:[6] he was Ceola's son, who with his spear pierced the first man bold enough to step upon the bridge. There stood with Wulfstan fearless fighters, Ælfhere and Maccus, bold men both who would not take flight from the ford, but defended themselves stoutly against the enemy as long as they might wield weapons.

When the loathed strangers saw that, and understood clearly that they would face bitter bridge-defenders there, they began to prefer words to deeds,[7] prayed that they might have access to the bank, pass over the ford and lead their forces across. Then in his overconfidence the earl began to yield ground—too much ground— to the hateful people: Birhthelm's son began to call over the cold water while warriors listened: "Now the way is laid open for you. Come straightway to us, as men to battle. God alone knows which of us may be master of the field."

The slaughter-wolves advanced, minded not the water, a host of Vikings westward over the Pant, over the bright water bore their shields: sailors to land brought shields of linden. Opposite stood Birhtnoth with his warriors, ready for the fierce invaders. He ordered his men to form a war-hedge[8] with their shields and to hold the formation fast against the enemy. Now was combat near, glory in battle. The time had come when doomed men should fall. Shouts were raised; ravens circled, the eagle eager for food. On earth there was uproar.

They let the file-hard spears fly from their hands, grim-ground

5. King Ethelred "the Unready," who reigned from 978 to 1016.
6. Not a bridge in the modern sense, but probably a stone causeway, under water even at low tide; immediately below, it is called a ford.

7. Literally, "to practice deception"— an overstatement due to the poet's scorn for fighters who refused to do things the hard heroic way.
8. A wall of shields (a common defensive formation).

javelins. Bows were busy, shield felt point. Bitter was the battle-rush. On either side warriors fell, young men lay dead. Wulfmær was wounded, chose the slaughter-bed: kinsman of Birhtnoth—his sister's son—he was cruelly hewn down with swords. Then requital was made to the Vikings: I have heard that Eadweard struck one fiercely with his sword, withheld not the stroke, so that the warrior fell doomed at his feet; for this his lord gave the chamberlain[9] thanks when he had opportunity. Thus men stood firm in the battle, stern of purpose. Eagerly all these armed fighters contended with one another to see who could be the first with his weapon's point to take life from doomed man. The slain fell, carrion, to the earth. The defenders stood fast; Birhtnoth urged them on, bade each man who would win glory from the Danes to give his whole heart to the battle.

A war-hard Viking advanced, raised up his weapon, his shield to defend himself, moved against Birhtnoth. As resolute as the churl,[1] the earl advanced toward him. Each of them meant harm to the other. Then the seaman threw his southern-made[2] spear so that the fighters' chief was wounded. But he thrust the spear with his shield so that the shaft split and the spearhead broke off and sprang away.[3] The war-chief was maddened; with his spear he stabbed the proud Viking that had given him the wound. Wise in war was the host's leader: he let his spear go through the man's neck, guided his hand so that he mortally wounded the raider. Then he quickly stabbed another, breaking through the mail-shirt: in the breast, quite through the corselet, was this one wounded; at his heart stood the poisoned point. The earl was the blither; the bold man laughed, gave thanks to God that the Lord had given him this day's work.

One of the Vikings loosed a javelin from his hand, let it fly from his fist, and it sped its way through Æthelred's noble thane. By the earl's side stood a lad not yet grown, a boy in the battle, son of Wulfstan, Wulfmær the young, who plucked full boldly the bloody spear from the warrior. He sent the hard spear flying back again: its point went in, and on the earth lay the man who had sorely wounded his lord. Then an armed Viking stepped toward the earl. He wished to seize the earl's war-gear, make booty of rings and ornamented sword. Then Birhtnoth took his sword from its sheath, broad and bright-edged, and struck at his assailant's coat of mail. Too soon one of the seafarers hindered him, wounded the earl in his arm. Then the gold-hilted sword fell to the earth: he might not hold the hard blade, wield his weapon. Yet he spoke

---

9. I.e., Eadweard.
1. Here "churl" means something like "villain."
2. Apparently the Vikings preferred weapons made in England or France—the "south."
3. The maneuver described frees the spear from the wounded man's body and enables him to take retaliatory action.

words, the hoar battle-leader, encouraged his men, bade them go forward stoutly together. He might no longer stand firm on his feet. He looked toward Heaven and spoke: "I thank thee, Ruler of Nations, for all the joys that I have had in the world. Now, gentle Lord, I have most need that thou grant my spirit grace, that my soul may travel to thee—under thy protection, Prince of Angels, depart in peace. I beseech thee that fiends of hell harm it not." Then the heathen warriors slew him and both the men who stood by him; Ælfnoth and Wulfmær both were laid low; close by their lord they gave up their lives.

Then there retired from the battle those who did not wish to be there. The son of Odda was the first to flee. Godric went from the fight and left the good man that had given him many a steed. He leaped upon the horse that his lord had owned, upon trappings that he had no right to, and both his brothers galloped with him, Godwine and Godwig cared not for battle, but went from the war and sought the wood, fled to its fastness and saved their lives—and more men than was in any way right, if they remembered all the favors he had done for their benefit. So Offa had said to him that day at the meeting he had held in the place, that many there spoke boldly who would not remain firm at need.

The folk's leader had fallen, Æthelred's earl: all his hearth-companions saw that their lord lay dead. Then the proud thanes advanced; men without fear pressed eagerly on. They all desired either of two things, to leave life or avenge the man they loved. Thus Ælfric's son urged them on; the warrior young of winters spoke words; Ælfwine it was who spoke, and spoke boldly: "Remember the speeches we have spoken so often over our mead,[4] when we raised boast on the bench, heroes in the hall, about hard fighting. Now may the man who is bold prove that he is. I will make my noble birth known to all, that I was of great kin in Mercia. My grandfather was named Ealhelm, a wise earl, worldly-prosperous. Thanes among that people shall not have reason to reproach me that I would go from this band of defenders, seek my home, now that my lord lies hewn down in battle. To me that is greatest of griefs: he was both my kinsman and my lord." Then he went forward, bent on revenge, and with the point of his spear pierced one of the pirate band, so that he lay on the earth, destroyed by the weapon. Then Ælfwine began to encourage his comrades, friends and companions, to go forward.

Offa spoke, shook his ash-spear: "Lo, thou, Ælfwine, hast encouraged us all, thanes in need. Now that our lord the earl lies on the earth, there is need for us all that each one of us encourage

4. Boasting of prowess while drinking is a common element in Old English poetry.

the other, warriors to battle, as long as he may have and hold weapon, hard sword, spear and good blade. The coward son of Odda, Godric, has betrayed us all; when he rode off on that horse, on that proud steed, many a man thought that he was our lord. Therefore here on the field folk were dispersed, the shield-wall broken. Curses on his action, by which he caused so many men here to flee."

Leofsunu spoke, raised the linden buckler, his shield to defend himself; he answered the warrior: "I promise that I will not flee a footstep hence, but I will go forward, avenge my dear lord in the fight. Steadfast warriors about Sturmer[5] need not reproach me with their words that now that my patron is dead I would go lordless home, abandon the battle. But weapon, point and iron, shall take me." Full wrathful he went forward, fought fiercely; flight he despised.

Then Dunnere spoke, shook his spear; humble churl,[6] he cried over all, bade each warrior avenge Birhtnoth: "He who intends to avenge his lord on the folk may not hesitate nor care for life." Then they advanced: they cared not for life. The retainers began to fight hardily, fierce spear-bearers, and prayed God that they might avenge their patron and bring destruction to their enemies.

The hostage[7] began to help them eagerly. He was of bold kin among the Northumbrians, the son of Ecglaf; his name was Æscferth. He did not flinch at the war-play, but threw spears without pause. Now he hit shield, now he pierced man: each moment he caused some wound, as long as he might wield weapons.

Eadweard the Long still stood in the line, ready and eager, spoke boasting words, how he would not flee a footstep nor turn back, now that his chief lay dead. He broke the shield-wall and fought against the foe until he had worthily avenged his treasure-giver on the seamen—before he himself lay on the slaughter-bed.

So also did Æthelric, noble companion, eager and impetuous; he fought most resolutely, this brother of Sibirht, as did many another: they split the hollow shield and defended themselves boldly [8]. . . The shield's rim broke and the mail-shirt sang one of horror's songs. Then in the battle Offa struck the seafarer so that he fell on the earth, and there Gadd's kinsman himself sought the ground: Offa was quickly hewn down in the fight. He had, however, performed what he had promised his lord, what he had vowed before to his ring-giver, that they should either both ride to the town, hale to their home, or fall among the host, die of wounds in the slaughter-

5. The Essex village where the speaker lived.
6. I.e., freeman of the lowest rank.
7. Among Germanic peoples, hostages of high rank generally fought on the side of the warriors who held them in hostage.
8. Apparently a description of a Viking's attack on Offa has been lost.

place. He lay as a thane should, near his lord.

Then there was a crash of shields. The seamen advanced, enraged by the fight. Spear oft pierced life-house of doomed man. Then Wistan advanced: Thurstan's son fought against the men. He was the slayer of three of them in the throng before the son of Wigelm [9] lay dead in the carnage. There was stubborn conflict. Warriors stood fast in the fight. Fighting men fell, worn out with wounds: slain fell among slain.

All the while Oswold and Eadwold, brothers both, encouraged the men, with their words bade their dear kinsmen that they should stand firm at need, wield their weapons without weakness.

Birhtwold spoke, raised his shield—he was an old retainer—shook his ash-spear; full boldly he exhorted the men: "Purpose shall be the firmer, heart the keener, courage shall be the more, as our might lessens.[1] Here lies our lord all hewn down, good man on ground. Ever may he lament who now thinks to turn from war-play. I am old of life; from here I will not turn, but by my lord's side, by the man I loved, I intend to lie."

So also the son of Æthelgar encouraged them all to the battle: this Godric oft let spear go, slaughter-shaft fly on the Vikings; thus he advanced foremost among the folk, hewed and laid low until he died in the fighting: he was not that Godric who fled the battle.

---

9. Identification uncertain: perhaps Offa was the son of Wigelm.
1. These famous lines appear thus in the original: "Hige sceal þe heardra, heorte þe cenre, / mod sceal þe mare, þe ure mægen lytlaþ."

GEOFFREY CHAUCER
(ca. 1343–1400)

1370: The *Book of the Duchess* (first important extant poem).
1372: First Italian journey: contact with Italian literature.
1385: *Troilus and Criseide*.
1386: *Canterbury Tales* begun.

Social thought in the Middle Ages lagged far behind social realities. Medieval England did not recognize the existence of any class between the aristocracy, a relatively small group that attained its position by birth alone, and the commons, which included everyone not of high birth. There was, theoretically, no way by which one might advance from the commons to the aristocracy. But in actual fact there existed a large and increasingly important middle class that was constantly infiltrating the aristocracy, and it was into this middle class that Chaucer was born. He was the son of a well-to-do wine merchant, and probably spent his boyhood in the down-to-earth atmosphere of London's Vintry, the wine-merchandising area; here, despite the privileges, especially in the way of education, that his father's wealth secured for him, he must have mixed daily with other commoners of all sorts. He might well have passed his whole life there, counting casks and money; but in his early teens he was sent to serve as a page in one of the great aristocratic households of England, that of Lionel of Antwerp, a son of the reigning monarch, Edward III. The rest of his life Chaucer spent in close association with the ruling nobility of the kingdom, not only with Lionel, but with his more powerful brother John of Gaunt; with their father King Edward; with their nephew Richard II, who succeeded to the throne in 1377; and finally with John's son Henry IV, who deposed his cousin and became king in 1399. Chaucer's wife Philippa was a member of the households of Edward's queen and of John of Gaunt's second wife, Constance of Castile, and she was doubtless of higher birth than the poet. A Thomas Chaucer, who was probably their son, was an eminent man in the next generation, and an Alice Chaucer, quite possibly Chaucer's granddaughter, was sufficiently important in her day to have been married successively to the Earl of Salisbury and the Duke of Norfolk. The theoretically unbridgeable gap between the commons and the aristocracy was thus ably bridged by the poet.

In order to accomplish this, Chaucer must have been able in other ways than as a poet, though doubtless his extraordinary poetic ability was of great service to his advancement. Yet if one were to rely merely on the preserved historical records, one would have little reason to suspect that the Geoffrey Chaucer they keep mentioning ever wrote a line of verse. We catch glimpses of him serving as a page in Lionel's household (1357); as a soldier getting himself captured by the French in one of Edward III's many sallies to the continent (1359); of his being the well-beloved *vallectus* of Edward III (1367)—despite the term, which means "valet," Chaucer's duties were hardly menial—and the well-beloved servant of John of Gaunt (1374), and of receiving substantial rewards for his services; of his being sent to Italy to assist in arranging a trade agreement with the Genoese (1372), and to France, perhaps to assist in getting a royal bride for young Prince Richard (1377); of his receiving a rent-free house on the city wall of London (1374); of his keeping, "in his own hand," the accounts for which he was responsible as Controller of the Customs and Subsidies on Wool for the port of London (1374–86)—and the wool trade was England's largest trade; of other trips abroad on official business; of his becoming Justice of the Peace and Knight of the Shire (Member of Parliament) for the county of Kent (1385–86); of his erect-ing grandstands, inventorying pots and pans, and getting himself robbed as Clerk of the King's Works (1389–91); of his being appointed deputy forester of one of the royal preserves in Somerset (1391); and—throughout his life—of his receiving grants and annuities, or having them confirmed by royal act when a new king took the throne, or asking that butts of wine given him by the crown be transformed into cash, or merely asking for money or more money. We last glimpse him, in the final months of his life, renting a house in the garden of Westminster Abbey, within a stone's throw of Westminster Hall, the ancient seat of English government.

CHAUCER'S LITERARY CAREER

It might seem that a man so busy would have had little time to write poetry, but Chaucer seems to have been an assiduous versifier all his adult life. Unfortunately, few of his poems can be precisely dated, and some have not been preserved. Probably among his earliest works was a trans-lation of the *Roman de la Rose*, a 13th-century French poem that exercised a profound influence on Chaucer's work. The first part of the *Roman* is an allegory, written by Guillaume de Lorris, which tells, in the form of a dream, the progress of a youthful love affair. Guillaume left the poem unfinished, but an enormous sequel was added to it after Guillaume's death by Jean de Meun: in this sequel the young courtier finally wins his lady (the rose), but not until Jean has discussed at great length many of the issues considered important by medieval intellectuals. The poem is a mixture of highly diverse elements, and it is characteristic of Chaucer's love of variety that he was able to assimilate into his own work both the courtly emotionalism of Guillaume and the philosophical, often satiric, detachment of Jean. Of a 14th-century English translation of the French poem only a fragment has come down to us, and that without any men-tion of the translator's name; scholars are generally agreed that the first 1700 lines of this fragment are Chaucer's.

Chaucer's work on the *Roman* is thought to have been done during the 60's. During this decade he probably made other translations from the French, and kept on sharpening his rhetorical tools. At the end of the decade he produced his first major work (and the only one of his poems that can be accurately dated): the *Book of the Duchess*, probably com-pleted in early 1370, an elegy for John of Gaunt's first wife, the lovely Blanche of Lancaster, who died in 1369. This is at once one of Chaucer's most derivative and most original poems: many of its octosyllabic lines are translated directly from various works by Jean Froissart, a French poet contemporary with Chaucer, and from his countryman Guillaume de Machaut as well as from other Frenchmen; yet the plan of the work is imaginative and daring, and as a whole the elegy is on a level of excellence never attained by the poets from whom Chaucer is borrowing. It is also interesting to observe how that tact which was later to earn Chaucer his status as a minor diplomat controls the direction of the poem and gives it artistic form.

In the first period of his literary activity Chaucer's specific poetic models were French, but a knowledge of writings in Latin lies behind virtually everything he wrote—although the Latin writers Chaucer read were not the same as those which we should study today. He probably had a more than adequate knowledge of the *Aeneid* and of Ovid in the original, but it is likely that he knew the other classical authors mostly through French translations and paraphrases. He was directly familiar with a number of (to us) cumbersome medieval Latin poems. Certainly his favorite Latin writer was Boethius, the 6th-century Roman whose *Consolation of Philosophy*, written while its author was in prison awaiting his execution, became one of the most valued of books for the whole Middle Ages, which never failed to find inspiration and comfort in its nobly stoic doctrine. Chaucer's own philosophical attitude, that of living wholeheartedly in the world while remaining spiritually detached from it, is at least partially a legacy from Boethius. His wooden but painstaking prose translation of the *Consolation*, probably made during the 70's, is only one of innumerable indications of Chaucer's reverence for the Roman writer.

The journey that Chaucer made to Italy in 1372 was in all likelihood a milestone in his literary development. Hitherto the influences upon him had been largely French and Latin, and while he may have read Italian before, it is likely that it was his Italian journey that immersed him in the works of Dante, Petrarch, and Boccaccio—the last two still alive at the time of Chaucer's visit, though he probably did not meet them. Between Chaucer and the greatest of the Italian writers, Dante, there was a large dissimilarity of temperament; yet if Chaucer could not assimilate *The Divine Comedy*, he nevertheless appreciated its austere moral grandeur, and his work shows its influences in subtle, oblique ways. Moreover, one of his funniest poems, the *House of Fame*, written sometime while he was in the customs (1374–86), may be read as a lighthearted imitation of the *Comedy*, though not a wholly successful one. From the works of Petrarch, also a writer of alien temperament, Chaucer obtained less, though he accords him respect on the several occasions when he mentions him. It was Boccaccio, whose cast of mind was far more congenial to Chaucer than the more sober Dante and Petrarch, who was to provide the source for some of Chaucer's finest poems— though his name is never mentioned in Chaucer's works. Many of the *Canterbury Tales* are indebted to one or another of Boccaccio's works, as is his lovely, cryptic love vision, the *Parliament of Fowls* (between 1375 and 1385). And his longest poem, *Troilus and Criseide*, probably completed about 1385, is an adaptation of Boccaccio's *Il Filostrato* ("The

Love-Stricken"). The Italian work is one of considerable stature, which Chaucer reworked into one of the greatest love poems in any language. Even if he had never written the *Canterbury Tales, Troilus* would have secured Chaucer a place among the great English poets.

Chaucer probably began work on the *Canterbury Tales* in 1386, and this was his chief literary interest until his death. The old tripartite division of Chaucer's literary career which assigns him a French period (to 1372), and an Italian period (1372–85), calls this last period of his life "English." But it was not English in the same sense as the earlier periods were French and Italian (i.e., dominated by French and Italian models), for the fact is that Chaucer from the beginning to the end stands apart from the mainstream of English literature. In the Rhyme of Sir Thopas, which he assigns himself in the *Canterbury Tales*, the wonderful fun he makes of popular Middle English romances shows his intimate knowledge of them; and undoubtedly he had read much English writing of all kinds. Yet his notion of literary art seems to have excluded many of the common characteristics—and the characteristic vices—of what had been and was being written in English, so that it is difficult to relate his work to that of his fellow English writers. His friend John Gower is a case in point: like Chaucer, he wrote a collection of English narrative poems in his *Confessio Amantis* ("The Lover's Confession"), and Chaucer tells some of the same stories in the *Canterbury Tales* and in the *Legend of Good Women*. The last, which may have interrupted Chaucer's work on the *Canterbury Tales* in the late 80's, was apparently assigned him by some eminent person; in order to make amends for his portrait of the unfaithful Criseide, he had to write a series of short poems celebrating famous faithful women. To make each story prove exactly the same point and nothing more is something that the conventional Gower had no trouble in doing. Yet Chaucer was able to complete the tales of only nine solemnly steadfast ladies before giving up in something like despair, and the most amusing thing about his narratives is his evident exasperation with having to make everything accord to a single formula. He could not bring himself to use the simple moralistic technique of conventional English poetry, and what Gower treats seriously appears in Chaucer often to be bordering on burlesque. Every comparison between Chaucer and run-of-the-mill English poetry either so exalts him as to make the act of comparison ludicrous or else, when Chaucer is trying to behave conventionally, shows him writing with his left hand. Chaucer had no really "English" period; English poetry had little to teach the first great English poet.

CHAUCER'S ART

The extraordinary variety of the *Canterbury Tales* as well as their number might well have demanded their author's full energy and attention during the last fourteen years of his life, but while he was at work on them he continued, almost to the end, to perform what seem to have been full-time jobs having nothing to do with literaure. Doubtless this practical business prevented him from achieving more than the 22 tales he finished; and it probably made him search his old papers for tales that he could work in without substantial revision. Yet if it reduced his literary output—which, even so, is enormous—this lifelong involvement with the practical is one of the chief reasons for his greatness as a poet. From his birth to his death he dealt continually with all sorts of people, the highest and the lowest, and his wonderfully observant mind made the most of this ever-present opportunity. His wide reading gave him plots and ideas, but his experience gave him people. As a commoner himself he had a sympathy with and understanding of the lower classes that few men who attained his ultimate station might boast of—and the lower classes must have accepted him. Similarly, he seems to have won full acceptance from the proud and important personages with whom he associated at court, and this he could not have won if he had not understood them perfectly. He understands both the high and the low, but he remains curiously detached from both, and it is detachment, perfectly balanced in his poetry by sympathy, which distinguishes Chaucer's art. Although he was born a commoner, he did not live as a commoner; and although he was accepted by the aristocracy, he must always have been conscious of the fact that he did not really belong to that society of which birth alone could make one a true member. Medieval aristocratic society arrogated to itself all idealism, and Chaucer characteristically regards life in terms of aristocratic ideals; but he never lost the ability, which for the poorer class was also a positive necessity, of regarding life as a purely practical matter. The art of being at once involved in and detached from a given situation is peculiarly Chaucer's.

In the physical realm, double vision results in a blurred image, but not so in Chaucer's poetic world, where images have often an extraordinary clarity, as if reality itself were made more real. His Prioress in the *Canterbury Tales* is an example of the basic human paradox which places what people are in opposition to what they think they are or pretend to be: Chaucer shows us clearly her inability to be what she professes to be, a nun; shows also the inadequacy of what she thinks a nun ought to be, a lady; and shows the great human charm of what she is, a woman. The elements of the portrait are divided between the critical and the admiring: a heavily satiric poet might well enhance the critical comment, so that our ultimate impression would be of the Prioress' weakness, while a sentimental one might enhance her amiable side so as to make that the aspect which we should remember. But in Chaucer's handling the reality comprehends both sides of the Prioress, expresses the paradox without attempting to resolve it. He appears to have been a man who had no illusions about the world or its inhabitants, but was nevertheless deeply fond of them both, and thought it worth while to keep the world spinning as well as possible, either by telling stories of high artistic truth or by counting pots and pans.

The text given here is from the present editor's *Chaucer's Poetry: An Anthology for the Modern Reader* (1958). For the *Canterbury Tales* the Hengwrt Manuscript has provided the textual basis. The spelling has been altered to improve consistency, and has been modernized in so far as is possible without distorting the phonological values of the Middle English. Discussions of Middle English pronunciation, grammar, and prosody will be found in the introduction to the period.

The Canterbury Tales   Chaucer's original plan for the *Canterbury Tales* projected about 120 stories, two for each pilgrim to tell on the way to Canterbury and two more on the way back. Chaucer actually completed only 22, though two more exist in fragments; a modification of the original plan is seen in the assignment of one of the completed tales to a pilgrim who was not a member of the group that assembled at Southwark. The work was probably first conceived in 1386, when Chaucer was living in Greenwich, some miles east of London. From his house he might have been able to see the pilgrim road that led toward the shrine of the famous English saint, Thomas à Becket, the Archbishop of Canterbury who was murdered in his cathedral in 1170. Medieval pilgrims were notorious tale-tellers (liars, according to the austere Langland), and the sight and sound of the bands riding toward Canterbury may well have suggested to Chaucer the idea of using a fictitious pilgrimage as a "framing" device for a number of stories. Collections of stories linked by such a device were common in the later Middle Ages. Chaucer's contemporary John Gower had used one in his *Confessio Amantis*; earlier in the century Boccaccio had placed the hundred tales of his *Decameron* in the mouths of ten characters, each of whom told a tale a day for ten days; and another Italian, Giovanni Sercambi, had placed a series of stories in the mouth of the leader of a group of persons journeying on horseback. Even if, as seems likely, Chaucer was unaware of the Italian precedents, the device of the framing fiction was in the air.

Chaucer's artistic exploitation of the device is, however, altogether his own. In Gower and Sercambi, one speaker relates all the stories; and in Boccaccio, the relationship between any one of the ten speakers and the story he tells is haphazard, so that reassignment of all the stories to different speakers would not materially change the effect. But in the best of the *Canterbury Tales* there is a fascinating accord between the narrator and his story, so that the story takes on rich overtones from what we have learned of its teller in the General Prologue and elsewhere, and the character himself grows and is revealed by his story. Chaucer conducts two fictions simultaneously—that of the individual tale and that of the pilgrim to whom he has assigned it. He develops the second fiction not only through the General Prologue but also through the "links," the interchanges among the pilgrims between stories. These interchanges sometimes lead to animosities. Thus the Miller's Tale offends the Reeve, who, formerly a carpenter, sees himself slandered in the figure of the Miller's silly, cuckolded carpenter; and the Reeve replies with a story that scores a miller who seems very like the pilgrim Miller. Similarly the Friar and the Summoner quarrel at the end of the Wife of Bath's Prologue, so that when the Friar is called upon he tells a tale most offensive to the Summoner, who in turn retaliates with an even more offensive story about a friar. The effect of each of these tales is enhanced by the animus of its teller, while the description of the animus in the links is exciting in itself: we are given at once a story and a drama. Furthermore, the Wife of Bath's monstrous feminism sets up resonances that are felt through all the succeeding tales. Indeed, so powerful are these resonances that some see in them a thematic unifying device: the question of marriage that the Wife introduces is further treated from two opposing points of view by the Clerk and the Merchant, and is finally settled by the common sense of the Franklin. In addition to such artistic stratagems as these, the personality and mind of the reporter—a half-burlesque version of Chaucer himself—permeates the poem and enriches its meaning.

The composition of none of the tales can be accurately dated; most of them were written during the last fourteen years of Chaucer's life, though some which fail to fit their tellers may be much earlier. The popularity of the poem in late medieval England is attested by the number of surviving manuscripts: more than 80, mostly from the 15th century. It was also twice printed by Caxton, and often reprinted by Caxton's early successors. The manuscripts reflect the unfinished state of the poem—the fact that when he died Chaucer had not made up his mind about a number of details, and hence left many inconsistencies. The poem appears in the manuscripts as nine or ten "fragments" or blocks of tales; the order of the poems within each fragment is generally the same, but the order of the fragments themselves varies widely. The fragment containing the General Prologue, the Knight's, Miller's and Reeve's Tales, and the Cook's unfinished tale, always comes first, and the fragment consisting of the Parson's Tale and the Retraction always comes last; but the others, such as that containing the Wife of Bath, the Friar, and the Summoner, or that consisting of the Physician and Pardoner, or the longest fragment consisting of six tales concluding with the Nun's Priest's, are by no means stable in relation to one another. Either of two orders seems as satisfactory a solution as the unfinished state of the poem will allow. According to these, the selections in this book would run: General Prologue, Miller, Wife of Bath, Pardoner, Nun's Priest (or Nun's Priest, Wife of Bath, Pardoner), Parson. For pedagogical reasons—since it represents a certain extreme of Chaucer's art—the Miller's Tale has here been placed out of order.

THE GENERAL PROLOGUE

Chaucer did not need to make a pilgrimage himself in order to meet the types of people that his fictitious pilgrimage includes, for most of them had long inhabited literature as well as life: the ideal Knight, who had fought against the pagans in all the great battles of the last half-century; his son the Squire, a lover out of any love poem; the Prioress without a vocation but with the dogs and jewelry that satirical literature was always condemning nuns for; the hunting Monk and flattering Friar, chief butts of medieval satirists; the too-busy and too-rich lawyer; the prosperous Franklin; the fraudulent Doctor; the Wife—or Archwife—of Bath; the austere Parson; and so on down through the lower orders to that flamboyant hypocrite, the Pardoner, a living vice. One meets all these types in medieval literature, and, since literature imitates life, one might have met them also in medieval society, as Chaucer, with his wide experience, undoubtedly did. Indeed, it has been argued that in some of his portraits he is drawing real people; but the appearance of doing so is actually a function of his art, which is able to endow types with a reality we generally associate only with people we know. Chaucer achieves this effect largely by persuading us that his own interest lies only in the visible, in what actually met his eye on the pilgrimage. He pretends to let the salient features of each pilgrim leap out directly at the reader, and does not seem to mind if some of his descriptions are from top to toe, others all toe and no top. This imitation of the way our minds actually perceive reality may make us fail to notice the care with which Chaucer has selected his details in order to give an integrated sketch of the person being described. While they are generally not full-blown literary symbols, most of these details give something more than   verisimilitude to the description; actually, they mediate between the world of types and the world of real people. Independent bourgeois women of the time were often makers of cloth, so that the Wife of Bath's proficiency at the trade is, in one way, merely part of her historical reality; yet the first weaver of cloth was the unparadised Eve, and her descendant is an unregenerate member of the distaff side. The Franklin's red face and white beard are in the same way merely individualizing factors in the portrait; yet the red face and white beard seem always to associate themselves with a man of good will who likes good living, and since Chaucer's time they have become the distinguishing marks of a kind of mythic Franklin, Santa Claus.

The rich suggestiveness of the details is what makes the portraits worth reading again and again. One may begin by enjoying the bright if flat photographic image of reality that the reporter creates, but one will find that the initial appearance of flatness is deceptive, and that the more one rereads the more complex and significant the portraits become. Here, as elsewhere in his work, Chaucer shows himself to be a rival to Shakespeare in the art of providing entertainment on the most primitive level, and at the same time, of significantly increasing the reader's ability to comprehend reality.

From THE CANTERBURY TALES
The General Prologue

Whan that April with his° showres soote°   *its / sweet*
The droughte of March hath perced to the roote,
And bathed every veine[1] in swich° licour,°   *such / liquid*
Of which vertu[2] engendred is the flowr;
5 Whan Zephyrus[3] eek° with his sweete breeth   *also*
Inspired hath in every holt° and heeth°   *grove / field*
The tendre croppes,° and the yonge sonne[4]   *shoots*
Hath in the Ram his halve cours yronne,
And smale fowles maken melodye
10 That sleepen al the night with open yë°—   *eye*
So priketh hem° Nature in hir corages[5]—   *them*

1. I.e., in plants.
2. By the power of which.
3. The west wind.
4. The sun is young because it has run

only halfway through its course in Aries, the Ram—the first sign of the zodiac in the solar year.
5. Their hearts.

Thanne longen folk to goon° on pilgrimages,　　　　　*go*
And palmeres[6] for to seeken straunge strondes
To ferne halwes, couthe° in sondry londes;　　　　　*known*
15 And specially from every shires ende
Of Engelond to Canterbury they wende,
The holy blisful martyr[7] for to seeke
That hem hath holpen° whan that they were seke.°　*helped / sick*
Bifel that in that seson on a day,
20 In Southwerk[8] at the Tabard as I lay,
Redy to wenden on my pilgrimage
To Canterbury with ful° devout corage,　　　　　　*very*
At night was come into that hostelrye
Wel nine and twenty in a compaignye
25 Of sondry folk, by aventure° yfalle　　　　　　　*chance*
In felaweshipe, and pilgrimes were they alle
That toward Canterbury wolden° ride.　　　　　　*would*
The chambres and the stables weren wide,
And wel we weren esed° at the beste.[9]　　*accommodated*
30 And shortly, whan the sonne was to reste,[1]
So hadde I spoken with hem everichoon°　　　　*every one*
That I was of hir felaweshipe anoon,°　　　　　*at once*
And made forward[2] erly for to rise,
To take oure way ther as[3] I you devise.°　　　　*describe*
35　But nathelees,° whil I have time and space,[4]　*nevertheless*
Er° that I ferther in this tale pace,°　　　　*before / pass*
Me thinketh it accordant to resoun[5]
To telle you al the condicioun
Of eech of hem, so as it seemed me,
40 And whiche they were, and of what degree,
And eek in what array that they were inne:
And at a knight thanne° wol I first biginne.　　　*then*
　A Knight ther was, and that a worthy man,
That fro the time that he first bigan
45 To riden out, he loved chivalrye,
Trouthe[6] and honour, freedom and curteisye.
Ful worthy was he in his lordes werre,°　　　　　*war*
And therto hadde he riden, no man ferre,°　　　*further*
As wel in Cristendom as hethenesse,°　　　*heathen lands*
50 And[7] evere honoured for his worthinesse.
　At Alisandre[8] he was whan it was wonne;

6. Palmers, wide-ranging pilgrims—especially those who sought out the "straunge strondes" (foreign shores) of the Holy Land. "Ferne halwes": far-off shrines.
7. St. Thomas à Becket, murdered in Canterbury Cathedral in 1170.
8. Southwark, site of the Tabard Inn, was then a suburb of London, south of the Thames River.
9. In the best possible way.
1. Had set.

2. I.e., (we) made an agreement.
3. "Ther as": where.
4. I.e., opportunity.
5. It seems to me according to reason.
6. Integrity. "Freedom" is here generosity of spirit, while "curteisye" is courtesy.
7. I.e., and he was.
8. The Knight has taken part in campaigns fought against all three groups of pagans who threatened Europe during the 14th century: the Moslems in

Ful ofte time he hadde the boord bigonne[9]
Aboven alle nacions in Pruce;
In Lettou had he reised,° and in Ruce,   *campaigned*
55 No Cristen man so ofte of his degree;
In Gernade at the sege eek hadde he be
Of Algezir, and riden in Belmarye;
At Lyeis was he, and at Satalye,
Whan they were wonne; and in the Grete See[1]
60 At many a noble armee° hadde he be. *assembly of forces*
  At mortal batailes[2] hadde he been fifteene,
And foughten for oure faith at Tramissene
In listes[3] thries,° and ay° slain his fo. *thrice / always*
  This ilke° worthy Knight hadde been also *same*
65 Somtime with the lord of Palatye[4]
Again° another hethen in Turkye;   *against*
And everemore he hadde a soverein pris.° *reputation*
And though that he were worthy,[5] he was wis,
And of his port° as meeke as is a maide. *demeanor*
70 He nevere yit no vilainye° ne saide   *rudeness*
In al his lif unto no manere wight:[6]
He was a verray,° parfit,° gentil knight. *true / perfect*
But for to tellen you of his array,
His hors° were goode, but he was nat gay. *horses*
75 Of fustian° he wered° a gipoun[7] *thick cloth / wore*
Al bismotered with his haubergeoun,[8]
For he was late come from his viage,° *expedition*
And wente for to doon his pilgrimage.
  With him ther was his sone, a yong Squier,[9]
80 A lovere and a lusty bacheler,
With lokkes crulle° as they were laid in presse. *curly*
Of twenty yeer of age he was, I gesse.
Of his stature he was of evene° lengthe, *moderate*
And wonderly delivere,° and of greet° strengthe. *agile / great*
85 And he hadde been som time in chivachye[1]
In Flandres, in Artois, and Picardye,
And born him wel as of so litel space,[2]

the Near East, from whom Alexandria was seized after a famous siege; the northern barbarians in Prussia, Lithuania, and Russia; and the Moors in North Africa. The place names in the following lines refer to battlegrounds in these continuing wars.
9. Sat in the seat of honor at military feasts.
1. The Mediterranean.
2. Tournaments fought to the death.
3. Lists, tournament grounds.
4. "The lord of Palatye" was a pagan: alliances of convenience were often made during the Crusades between Christians and pagans.
5. I.e., a valiant knight.
6. "No manere wight": any sort of per-

son. In Middle English, negatives are multiplied for emphasis, as in these two lines: "nevere," "no," "ne," "no."
7. Tunic worn underneath the coat of mail.
8. All rust-stained from his hauberk (coat of mail).
9. The vague term "Squier" (Squire) here seems to be the equivalent of "bacheler," a young knight still in the service of an older one.
1. On cavalry expeditions. The places in the next line are sites of skirmishes in the constant warfare between the English and the French.
2. I.e., considering the little time he had been in service.

In hope to stonden in his lady° grace. — *lady's*
Embrouded° was he as it were a mede,[3] — *embroidered*
90 Al ful of fresshe flowres, white and rede;° — *red*
Singing he was, or floiting,° al the day: — *whistling*
He was as fressh as is the month of May.
Short was his gowne, with sleeves longe and wide.
Wel coude he sitte on hors, and faire ride;
95 He coude songes make, and wel endite,° — *compose verse*
Juste[4] and eek daunce, and wel portraye° and write. — *sketch*
So hote° he loved that by nightertale[5] — *hotly*
He slepte namore than dooth a nightingale.
Curteis he was, lowely,° and servisable, — *humble*
100 And carf biforn his fader at the table.[6]

　A Yeman[7] hadde he and servants namo° — *no more*
At that time, for him liste[8] ride so;
And he[9] was clad in cote and hood of greene.
A sheef of pecok arwes,° bright and keene, — *arrows*
105 Under his belt he bar° ful thriftily;° — *bore / properly*
Wel coude he dresse° his takel° yemanly:[1] — *tend to / gear*
His arwes drouped nought with fetheres lowe.
And in his hand he bar a mighty bowe.
A not-heed° hadde he with a brown visage. — *close-cut head*
110 Of wodecraft wel coude° he al the usage. — *knew*
Upon his arm he bar a gay bracer,[2]
And by his side a swerd° and a bokeler,[3] — *sword*
And on that other side a gay daggere,
Harneised° wel and sharp as point of spere; — *mounted*
115 A Cristophre[4] on his brest of silver sheene;° — *bright*
An horn he bar, the baudrik[5] was of greene.
A forster° was he soothly,° as I gesse. — *forester / truly*

　Ther was also a Nonne, a Prioresse,[6]
That of hir smiling was ful simple and coy.
120 Hir gretteste ooth was but by sainte Loy!° — *Eloi*
And she was cleped° Madame Eglantine. — *named*
Ful wel she soong° the service divine, — *sang*
Entuned° in hir nose ful semely;[7] — *chanted*
And Frenssh she spak ful faire and fetisly,° — *elegantly*
125 After the scole° of Stratford at the Bowe[8]— — *school*
For Frenssh of Paris was to hire unknowe.
At mete° wel ytaught was she withalle:° — *meals / besides*

---

3. Mead, meadow.
4. Joust, fight in a tournament.
5. At night.
6. It was a squire's duty to carve his lord's meat.
7. The "Yeman" (Yeoman) is an independent commoner who acts as the Knight's military servant; "he" is the Knight.
8. "Him liste": it pleased him to.
9. I.e., the Yeoman.
1. In a workmanlike way.

2. Wristguard for archers.
3. Buckler (a small shield).
4. St. Christopher medal.
5. Baldric (a supporting strap).
6. The Prioress is the mother superior of her nunnery. "Simple and coy": sincere and mild.
7. In a seemly manner.
8. The French learned in a convent school in Stratford-at-the-Bow, a suburb of London, was evidently not up to the Parisian standard.

She leet° no morsel from hir lippes falle,	let
Ne wette hir fingres in hir sauce deepe;	
130 Wel coude she carve a morsel, and wel keepe°	take care
That no drope ne fille° upon hir brest.	should fall
In curteisye was set ful muchel hir lest.[9]	
Hir over-lippe wiped she so clene	
That in hir coppe° ther was no ferthing° seene	cup / bit
135 Of grece,° whan she dronken hadde hir draughte;	grease
Ful semely after hir mete she raughte.°	reached
And sikerly° she was of greet disport,[1]	certainly
And ful plesant, and amiable of port,°	mien
And pained hire to countrefete cheere[2]	
140 Of court, and to been statlich° of manere,	dignified
And to been holden digne[3] of reverence.	
But, for to speken of hir conscience,	
She was so charitable and so pitous°	merciful
She wolde weepe if that she saw a mous	
145 Caught in a trappe, if it were deed° or bledde.	dead
Of[4] smale houndes hadde she that she fedde	
With rosted flessh, or milk and wastelbreed;°	fine white bread
But sore wepte she if oon of hem were deed,	
Or if men smoot it with a yerde smerte;[5]	
150 And al was conscience and tendre herte.	
Ful semely hir wimpel° pinched° was,	headdress / pleated
Hir nose tretis,° hir yën° greye as glas,	well-formed / eyes
Hir mouth ful smal, and therto° softe and reed,°	moreover / red
But sikerly° she hadde a fair forheed:	certainly
155 It was almost a spanne brood,[6] I trowe,°	believe
For hardily,° she was nat undergrowe.	assuredly
Ful fetis° was hir cloke, as I was war;°	becoming / aware
Of smal° coral aboute hir arm she bar	dainty
A paire[7] of bedes, gauded al with greene,	
160 And theron heeng° a brooch of gold ful sheene,°	hung / bright
On which ther was first writen a crowned A,[8]	
And after, *Amor vincit omnia.*[9]	
Another Nonne with hire hadde she	
That was hir chapelaine,° and preestes three.[1]	secretary
165 A Monk ther was, a fair for the maistrye,[2]	
An outridere[3] that loved venerye,°	hunting
A manly man, to been an abbot able.°	worthy

9. I.e., her chief delight lay in good manners.
1. Of great good cheer.
2. And took pains to imitate the behavior.
3. And to be considered worthy.
4. I.e., some.
5. If someone struck it with a rod sharply.
6. A handsbreadth wide.
7. String (i.e., a rosary); "gauded al with greene": provided with green beads to mark certain prayers.
8. An *A* with an ornamental crown on it.
9. A Latin motto meaning "Love conquers all."
1. Although he here awards this charming lady three priests, Chaucer later reduces the number to one.
2. I.e., a superlatively fine one.
3. A monk charged with supervising property distant from the monastery.

Ful many a daintee° hors hadde he in stable, *fine*
And whan he rood,° men mighte his bridel heere *rode*
170 Ginglen° in a whistling wind as clere *jingle*
And eek as loude as dooth the chapel belle
Ther as this lord was kepere of the celle.[4]
The rule of Saint Maure or of Saint Beneit,[5]
By cause that it was old and somdeel strait—
175 This ilke Monk leet olde thinges pace,° *pass away*
And heeld° after the newe world the space.[6] *held*
He yaf nought of that text a pulled hen[7]
That saith that hunteres been° nought holy men, *are*
Ne that a monk, whan he is recchelees,[8]
180 Is likned til° a fissh that is waterlees— *to*
This is to sayn, a monk out of his cloistre;
But thilke° text heeld he nat worth an oystre. *that same*
And I saide his opinion was good:
What° sholde he studye and make himselven wood° *why / crazy*
185 Upon a book in cloistre alway to poure,
Or swinke° with his handes and laboure, *work*
As Austin bit?[9] How shal the world be served?
Lat Austin have his swink to him reserved!
Therfore he was a prikasour° aright. *hard rider*
190 Grehoundes he hadde as swift as fowl in flight.
Of priking° and of hunting for the hare *riding*
Was al his lust,° for no cost wolde he spare. *pleasure*
I sawgh his sleeves purfiled° at the hand *fur-lined*
With gris,° and that the fineste of a land; *gray fur*
195 And for to festne his hood under his chin
He hadde of gold wrought a ful curious[1] pin:
A love-knotte in the grettere° ende ther was. *greater*
His heed was balled,° that shoon as any glas, *bald*
And eek his face, as he hadde been anoint:
200 He was a lord ful fat and in good point;[2]
His yën steepe,° and rolling in his heed, *protruding*
That stemed as a furnais of a leed,[3]
His bootes souple,° his hors in greet estat°— *supple / condition*
Now certainly he was a fair prelat.[4]
205 He was nat pale as a forpined° gost: *wasted away*
A fat swan loved he best of any rost.
His palfrey° was as brown as is a berye. *saddle horse*
A Frere[5] ther was, a wantoune and a merye,

---

4. Keeper of an outlying cell (branch) of the monastery.
5. St. Maurus and St. Benedict, authors of monastic rules. "Somdeel strait": somewhat strict.
6. I.e., in his own lifetime (?).
7. He didn't give a plucked hen for that text.
8. Reckless, careless of rule.
9. I.e., as St. Augustine bids. St. Augus-

tine had written that monks should perform manual labor.
1. Of careful workmanship.
2. In good shape, plump.
3. That glowed like a furnace with a pot in it.
4. Prelate (an important churchman).
5. The "Frere" (Friar) is a member of one of the four religious orders whose members live by begging; as a "limi-

A limitour, a ful solempne° man.	*pompous*
210 In alle the ordres foure is noon that can°	*knows*
So muche of daliaunce° and fair langage:	*flirtation*
He hadde maad ful many a mariage	
Of yonge wommen at his owene cost;	
Unto his ordre he was a noble post.[6]	
215 Ful wel biloved and familier was he	
With frankelains over al[7] in his contree,	
And with worthy wommen of the town—	
For he hadde power of confessioun,	
As saide himself, more than a curat,°	*parish priest*
220 For of° his ordre he was licenciat.[8]	*by*
Ful swetely herde he confessioun,	
And plesant was his absolucioun.	
He was an esy man to yive penaunce	
Ther as he wiste to have[9] a good pitaunce;°	*donation*
225 For unto a poore ordre for to yive	
Is signe that a man is wel yshrive;[1]	
For if he yaf, he dorste make avaunt°	*boast*
He wiste that a man was repentaunt;	
For many a man so hard is of his herte	
230 He may nat weepe though him sore smerte:[2]	
Therfore, in stede of weeping and prayeres,	
Men mote° yive silver to the poore freres.[3]	*may*
His tipet° was ay farsed° ful of knives	*scarf / packed*
And pinnes, for to yiven faire wives;	
235 And certainly he hadde a merye note;	
Wel coude he singe and playen on a rote;°	*fiddle*
Of yeddinges he bar outrely the pris.[4]	
His nekke whit was as the flowr-de-lis;°	*lily*
Therto he strong was as a champioun.	
240 He knew the tavernes wel in every town,	
And every hostiler° and tappestere,°	*innkeeper / barmaid*
Bet° than a lazar[5] or a beggestere.	*better*
For unto swich a worthy man as he	
Accorded nat, as by his facultee,[6]	
245 To have with sike° lazars aquaintaunce:	*sick*
It is nat honeste,° it may nought avaunce,°	*dignified / profit*
For to delen with no swich poraile,[7]	

tour" (line 209) he has been granted exclusive begging rights within a certain limited area.

6. I.e., pillar.

7. I.e., with franklins everywhere. Franklins were well-to-do country men.

8. I.e., licensed to hear confessions.

9. Where he knew he would have.

1. Shriven, absolved.

2. Though he is sorely grieved.

3. Before granting absolution, the confessor must be sure the sinner is contrite; moreover, the absolution is contingent upon the sinner's performance

of an act of satisfaction. In the case of Chaucer's Friar, a liberal contribution served both as proof of contrition and as satisfaction.

4. He absolutely took the prize for ballads.

5. Leper; "beggestere": female beggar.

6. It was not suitable because of his position.

7. I.e., poor people. The oldest order of friars had been founded by St. Francis to administer to the spiritual needs of precisely those classes the Friar avoids.

But al with riche, and selleres of vitaile;°   *foodstuffs*
And over al ther as profit sholde arise,
250 Curteis he was, and lowely of servise.
Ther was no man nowher so vertuous:°   *efficient*
He was the beste beggere in his hous.°   *friary*
And yaf a certain ferme for the graunt:[8]
Noon of his bretheren cam ther in his haunt.[9]
255 For though a widwe° hadde nought a sho,°   *widow / shoe*
So plesant was his *In principio*[1]
Yit wolde he have a ferthing° er he wente;   *small coin*
His purchas was wel bettre than his rente.[2]
And rage he coude as it were right a whelpe;[3]
260 In love-dayes[4] ther coude he muchel° helpe,   *much*
For ther he was nat lik a cloisterer,
With a thredbare cope, as is a poore scoler,
But he was lik a maister[5] or a pope.
Of double worstede was his semicope,°   *short robe*
265 And rounded as a belle out of the presse.°   *bell-mold*
Somwhat he lipsed° for his wantounesse°   *lisped / affectation*
To make his Englissh sweete upon his tonge;
And in his harping, whan he hadde songe,°   *sung*
His yën twinkled in his heed aright
270 As doon the sterres° in the frosty night.   *stars*
This worthy limitour was cleped Huberd.

    A Marchant was ther with a forked beerd,
In motelee,[6] and hye on hors he sat,
Upon his heed a Flandrissh° bevere hat,   *Flemish*
275 His bootes clasped faire and fetisly.°   *elegantly*
His resons° he spak ful solempnely,   *opinions*
Souning° alway th'encrees of his winning.   *sounding*
He wolde the see were kept for any thing[7]
Bitwixen Middelburgh and Orewelle.
280 Wel coude he in eschaunge sheeldes[8] selle.
This worthy man ful wel his wit bisette:°   *employed*
Ther wiste° no wight that he was in dette,   *knew*
So statly° was he of his governaunce,[9]   *dignified*
With his bargaines,[1] and with his chevissaunce.
285 Forsoothe he was a worthy man withalle;
But, sooth to sayn, I noot° how men him calle.   *don't know*

---

8. And he paid a certain rent for the privilege of begging.
9. Assigned territory.
1. A friar's usual salutation (John i.1): "In the beginning (was the Word)."
2. I.e., the money he got through such activity was more than his regular income.
3. And he could flirt wantonly, as if he were a puppy.
4. Days appointed for the settlement of lawsuits out of court.
5. A man of recognized learning.

6. Motley, a cloth of mixed color.
7. I.e., he wished the sea to be guarded at all costs. The sea route between Middelburgh (in the Netherlands) and Orwell (in Suffolk) was vital to the Merchant's export and import of wool—the basis of England's chief trade at the time.
8. Shields, *ecus* (French coins): he could speculate profitably (if illegally) in foreign exchange.
9. The management of his affairs.
1. Bargainings; "chevissaunce": borrowing.

A Clerk[2] ther was of Oxenforde also
That unto logik hadde longe ygo.[3]
As lene was his hors as is a rake,
290 And he was nought right fat, I undertake,
But looked holwe,° and therto sobrely.   *hollow*
Ful thredbare was his overeste courtepy,[4]
For he hadde geten him yit no benefice,
Ne was so worldly for to have office.°   *secular employment*
295 For him was levere[5] have at his beddes heed
Twenty bookes, clad in blak or reed,
Of Aristotle and his philosophye,
Than robes riche, or fithele,° or gay sautrye.[6]   *fiddle*
But al be that he was a philosophre[7]
300 Yit hadde he but litel gold in cofre;°   *coffer*
But al that he mighte of his freendes hente,°   *take*
On bookes and on lerning he it spente,
And bisily gan for the soules praye
Of hem that yaf him wherwith to scoleye.°   *study*
305 Of studye took he most cure° and most heede.   *care*
Nought oo° word spak he more than was neede,   *one*
And that was said in forme[8] and reverence,
And short and quik,° and ful of heigh sentence:[9]   *lively*
Souning° in moral vertu was his speeche,   *resounding*
310 And gladly wolde he lerne, and gladly teche.
    A Sergeant of the Lawe,[1] war and wis,
That often hadde been at the Parvis[2]
Ther was also, ful riche of excellence.
Discreet he was, and of greet reverence—
315 He seemed swich, his wordes weren so wise.
Justice he was ful often in assise°   *circuit courts*
By patente[3] and by plein° commissioun.   *full*
For his science° and for his heigh renown   *knowledge*
Of fees and robes hadde he many oon.
320 So greet a purchasour° was nowher noon;   *speculator in land*
Al was fee simple[4] to him in effect—
His purchasing mighte nat been infect.[5]
Nowher so bisy a man as he ther nas;°   *was not*
And yit he seemed bisier than he was.
325 In termes[6] hadde he caas and doomes alle

2. The Clerk is a student at Oxford; in order to become a student, he would have had to signify his intention of becoming a cleric, but he was not bound to proceed to a position of responsibility in the church.
3. Who had long since matriculated in philosophy.
4. Outer cloak. "Benefice": ecclesiastical living.
5. He would rather.
6. Psaltery (a kind of harp).
7. The word may also mean "alchemist."

8. With decorum.
9. Elevated thought.
1. The Sergeant is not only a practicing lawyer, but one of the high justices of the nation. "War and wis": wary and wise.
2. The "Paradise," a meeting place for lawyers and their clients.
3. Royal warrant.
4. "Fee simple": owned outright without legal impediments.
5. Invalidated on a legal technicality.
6. I.e., by heart. "Caas and doomes": lawcases and decisions.

That from the time of King William[7] were falle.
Therto he coude endite and make a thing,[8]
Ther coude no wight pinchen° at his writing;   *cavil*
And every statut coude° he plein° by rote.[9]   *knew / entire*
₃₃₀ He rood but hoomly ° in a medlee cote,[1]   *unpretentiously*
Girt with a ceint of silk, with barres smale.
Of his array telle I no lenger tale.
   A Frankelain[2] was in his compaignye:
Whit was his beerd as is the dayesye;°   *daisy*
₃₃₅ Of his complexion he was sanguin.[3]
Wel loved he by the morwe a sop in win.[4]
To liven in delit° was evere his wone,°   *sensual delight / wont*
For he was Epicurus[5] owene sone,
That heeld opinion that plein° delit   *full*
₃₄₀ Was verray felicitee parfit.
An housholdere and that a greet was he:
Saint Julian[6] he was in his contree.
His breed, his ale, was always after oon;[7]
A bettre envined° man was nevere noon.   *wine-stocked*
₃₄₅ Withouten bake mete was nevere his hous,
Of fissh and flessh, and that so plentevous°   *plenteous*
It snewed° in his hous of mete and drinke,   *snowed*
Of alle daintees that men coude thinke.
After° the sondry sesons of the yeer   *according to*
₃₅₀ So chaunged he his mete[8] and his soper.
Ful many a fat partrich hadde he in mewe,°   *cage*
And many a breem,° and many a luce° in stewe.[9]   *carp / pike*
Wo was his cook but if his sauce were
Poinant° and sharp, and redy all his gere.   *pungent*
₃₅₅ His table dormant in his halle alway
Stood redy covered all the longe day.[1]
At sessions[2] ther was he lord and sire.
Ful ofte time he was Knight of the Shire.
An anlaas° and a gipser° al of silk   *dagger / purse*
₃₆₀ Heeng at his girdel,[3] whit as morne° milk.   *morning*
A shirreve° hadde he been, and countour.[4]   *sheriff*
Was nowher swich a worthy vavasour.[5]

7. I.e., the Conqueror (reigned 1066–
87).
8. Compose and draw up a deed.
9. By heart.
1. A coat of mixed color. "Ceint": belt;
"barres": transverse stripes.
2. The "Frankelain" (Franklin) is a
prosperous country man, whose lower-
class ancestry is no impediment to the
importance he has attained in his
county.
3. A reference to the fact that the
Franklin's temperament is dominated
by blood as well as to his red face.
4. I.e., in the morning he was very fond
of a piece of bread soaked in wine.
5. The Greek philosopher whose teach-

ing is popularly believed to make pleasure the chief goal of life.
6. The patron saint of hospitality.
7. Always of the same high quality.
8. Dinner; "soper": supper.
9. Fishpond.
1. Tables were usually dismounted
when not in use, but the Franklin kept
his mounted and set ("covered"), hence
"dormant."
2. I.e., sessions of the justices of the
peace. "Knight of the Shire": county
representative in Parliament.
3. Hung at his belt.
4. Auditor of county finances.
5. Member of an upper, but not an
aristocratic, feudal class.

An Haberdasshere and a Carpenter,
A Webbe,° a Dyere, and a Tapicer°—   *weaver / tapestry-maker*
365 And they were clothed alle in oo liveree⁶
Of a solempne and greet fraternitee.
Ful fresshe and newe hir gere apiked° was;   *polished*
Hir knives were chaped° nought with bras,   *mounted*
But al with silver; wrought ful clene and weel
370 Hir girdles and hir pouches everydeel.°   *altogether*
Wel seemed eech of hem a fair burgeis°   *burgher*
To sitten in a yeldehalle° on a dais.   *guildhall*
Everich, for the wisdom that he can,⁷
Was shaply° for to been an alderman.   *suitable*
375 For catel° hadde they ynough and rente,°   *property / income*
And eek hir wives wolde it wel assente—
And elles certain were they to blame:
It is ful fair to ⊙en ycleped "Madame,"
And goon to vigilies⁸ all bifore,
380 And have a mantel royalliche ybore.⁹
    A Cook they hadde with hem for the nones,¹
To boile the chiknes with the marybones,°   *marrowbones*
And powdre-marchant tart and galingale.²
Wel coude he knowe° a draughte of London ale.   *recognize*
385 He coude roste, and seethe,° and broile, and frye,   *boil*
Maken mortreux,° and wel bake a pie.   *stews*
But greet harm was it, as it thoughte° me,   *seemed to*
That on his shine a mormal° hadde he.   *ulcer*
For blankmanger,³ that made he with the beste.
390   A Shipman was ther, woning° fer by weste—   *dwelling*
For ought I woot,° he was of Dertemouthe.⁴   *know*
He rood upon a rouncy° as he couthe,⁵   *large nag*
In a gowne of falding° to the knee.   *heavy wool*
A daggere hanging on a laas° hadde he   *strap*
395 Aboute his nekke, under his arm adown.
The hote somer hadde maad his hewe° al brown;   *color*
And certainly he was a good felawe.
Ful many a draughte of win hadde he drawe⁶
Fro Burdeuxward,⁷ whil that the chapman sleep:
400 Of nice° conscience took he no keep;°   *fastidious / heed*
If that he faught and hadde the hyer hand,
By water he sente hem hoom to every land.
But of his craft, to rekene wel his tides,

---

6. In one livery, i.e., the uniform of their "fraternitee" or guild, a partly religious, partly social organization.
7. Was capable of.
8. Feasts held on the eve of saints' days. "Al bifore": i.e., at the head of the procession.
9. Royally carried.
1. For the occasion.
2. "Powdre-marchant" and "galingale" are flavoring materials.
3. An elaborate stew.
4. Dartmouth, a port in the southwest of England.
5. As best he could.
6. Drawn, i.e., stolen.
7. From Bordeaux; i.e., while carrying wine from Bordeaux (the wine center of France). "Chapman sleep": merchant slept.

His stremes° and his daungers° him bisides,[8]   *currents / hazards*
405 His herberwe° and his moone, his lodemenage,[9]   *anchorage*
There was noon swich from Hulle to Cartage.[1]
Hardy he was and wis to undertake;
With many a tempest hadde his beerd been shake;
He knew alle the havenes° as they were   *harbors*
410 Fro Gotlond to the Cape of Finistere,[2]
And every crike° in Britaine° and in Spaine.   *inlet / Brittany*
His barge ycleped was the Maudelaine.°   *Magdalene*
    With us ther was a Doctour of Physik:°   *medicine*
In al this world ne was ther noon him lik
415 To speken of physik and of surgerye,
For° he was grounded in astronomye,°   *because / astrology*
He kepte° his pacient a ful greet deel[3]   *tended to*
In houres[4] by his magik naturel.
Wel coude he fortunen the ascendent
420 Of his images[5] for his pacient.
He knew the cause of every maladye,
Were it of hoot or cold or moiste or drye,
And where engendred and of what humour:[6]
He was a verray parfit praktisour.[7]
425 The cause yknowe,° and of his harm the roote,   *known*
Anoon he yaf the sike man his boote.°   *remedy*
    Ful redy hadde he his apothecaries
To senden him drogges° and his letuaries,°   *drugs / medicines*
For eech of hem made other for to winne:
430 Hir frendshipe was nought newe to biginne.
Wel knew he the olde Esculapius,[8]
And Deiscorides and eek Rufus,
Olde Ipocras, Hali, and Galien,
Serapion, Razis, and Avicen,

8. Around him.
9. Pilotage.
1. From Hull (in northern England) to
Cartagena (in Spain).
2. From Gotland (an island in the Baltic) to Finisterre (the westernmost
point in Spain).
3. Closely.
4. I.e., the astrologically important
hours (when conjunctions of the planets
might help his recovery). "Magik naturel": natural—as opposed to black—
magic.
5. Assign the propitious time, according to the position of stars, for using
talismanic images. Such images, representing either the patient himself or
points in the zodiac, were thought to
be influential on the course of the disease.
6. Diseases were thought to be caused
by a disturbance of one or another of
the four bodily "humors," each of
which, like the four elements, was a
compound of two of the elementary

qualities mentioned in line 422: the
melancholy humor, seated in the black
bile was cold and dry (like earth); the
sanguine, seated in the blood, hot and
moist (like air); the choleric, seated
in the yellow bile, hot and dry (like
fire); the phlegmatic, seated in the
phlegm, cold and moist (like water).
7. True perfect practitioner.
8. The Doctor is familiar with the
treatises that the Middle Ages attributed to the "great names" of medical
history, whom Chaucer names in lines
431–36: the purely legendary Greek
demigod Aesculapius; the Greeks Dioscorides, Rufus, Hippocrates, Galen,
and Serapion; the Persians Hali and
Rhazes; the Arabians Avicenna and
Averroës; the early Christians John (?)
of Damascus and Constantine Afer; the
Scotsman Bernard Gordon; the Englishmen John of Gatesden and Gilbert, the
former an early contemporary of Chaucer.

435 Averrois, Damascien, and Constantin,
Bernard, and Gatesden, and Gilbertin.
Of his diete mesurable° was he,   *moderate*
For it was of no superfluitee,
But of greet norissing° and digestible.   *nourishment*
440 His studye was but litel on the Bible.
In sanguin° and in pers° he clad was al,   *blood-red / blue*
Lined with taffata and with sendal;°   *silk*
And yit he was but esy of dispence;°   *expenditure*
He kepte that he wan in pestilence.[9]
445 For° gold in physik is a cordial,[1]   *because*
Therfore he loved gold in special.

    A good Wif was ther of biside Bathe,
But she was somdeel deef, and that was scathe.°   *a pity*
Of cloth-making she hadde swich an haunt,°   *practice*
450 She passed° hem of Ypres and of Gaunt.[2]   *surpassed*
In al the parissh wif ne was ther noon
That to the offring[3] bifore hire sholde goon,
And if ther dide, certain so wroth° was she   *angry*
That she was out of alle charitee.
455 Hir coverchiefs ful fine were of ground°—   *texture*
I dorste° swere they weyeden° ten pound   *dare / weighed*
That on a Sonday weren° upon hir heed.   *were*
Hir hosen weren of fin scarlet reed,°   *red*
Ful straite yteyd,[4] and shoes ful moiste° and newe.   *unworn*
460 Bold was hir face and fair and reed of hewe.
She was a worthy womman al hir live:
Housbondes at chirche dore[5] she hadde five,
Withouten other compaignye in youthe—
But therof needeth nought to speke as nouthe.°   *now*
465 And thries hadde she been at Jerusalem;
She hadde passed many a straunge° streem;   *foreign*
At Rome she hadde been, and at Boloigne,
In Galice at Saint Jame, and at Coloigne:[6]
She coude° muchel of wandring by the waye.   *knew*
470 Gat-toothed° was she, soothly for to saye.   *gap-toothed*
Upon an amblere[7] esily she sat,
Ywimpled° wel, and on hir heed an hat   *veiled*
As brood as is a bokeler or a targe,[8]
A foot-mantel° aboute hir hipes large,   *riding skirt*
475 And on hir feet a paire of spores° sharpe.   *spurs*
In felaweshipe wel coude she laughe and carpe:°   *talk*

9. He saved the money he made during the plague time.
1. A stimulant. Gold was thought to have some medicinal properties.
2. Ypres and Ghent ("Gaunt") were Flemish cloth-making centers.
3. The offering in church, when the congregation brought its gifts forward.
4. Tightly laced.
5. In medieval times, weddings were performed at the church door.
6. Rome; Boulogne (in France); St. James (of Compostella) in Galicia (Spain); Cologne (in Germany): all sites of shrines much visited by pilgrims.
7. Horse with an easy gait.
8. "Bokeler" and "targe": small shields.

Of remedies of love she knew parchaunce,°   *as it happened*
For she coude of that art the olde daunce.[9]
   A good man was ther of religioun,
480 And was a poore Person° of a town,   *parson*
But riche he was of holy thought and werk.
He was also a lerned man, a clerk,
   That Cristes gospel trewely° wolde preche;   *faithfully*
   His parisshens° devoutly wolde he teche.   *parishioners*
485 Benigne he was, and wonder° diligent,   *wonderfully*
And in adversitee ful pacient,
And swich he was preved° ofte sithes.°   *proved / times*
Ful loth were him to cursen for his tithes,[1]
But rather wolde he yiven, out of doute,[2]
490 Unto his poore parisshens aboute
Of his offring[3] and eek of his substaunce:°   *property*
He coude in litel thing have suffisaunce.°   *sufficiency*
Wid was his parissh, and houses fer asonder,
But he ne lafte° nought for rain ne thonder,   *neglected*
495 In siknesse nor in meschief,° to visite   *misfortune*
The ferreste° in his parissh, muche and lite,[4]   *farthest*
Upon his feet, and in his hand a staf.
This noble ensample° to his sheep he yaf   *example*
That first he wroughte,[5] and afterward he taughte.
500 Out of the Gospel he tho° wordes caughte,°   *those / took*
And this figure he added eek therto:
That if gold ruste, what shal iren do?
For if a preest be foul, on whom we truste,
No wonder is a lewed° man to ruste.   *uneducated*
505 And shame it is, if a preest take keep,°   *heed*
A shiten° shepherde and a clene sheep.   *befouled*
Wel oughte a preest ensample for to yive
By his clennesse how that his sheep sholde live.
He sette nought his benefice[6] to hire
510 And leet his sheep encombred in the mire
And ran to London, unto Sainte Poules,[7]
To seeken him a chaunterye[8] for soules,
Or with a bretherhede to been withholde,[9]
But dwelte at hoom and kepte wel his folde,
515 So that the wolf ne made it nought miscarye:
He was a shepherde and nought a mercenarye.

---

9. I.e., she knew all the tricks of that trade.
1. He would be most reluctant to invoke excommunication in order to collect his tithes.
2. Without doubt.
3. The offering made by the congregation of his church was at the Parson's disposal.
4. Great and small.
5. I.e., he practiced what he preached.
6. I.e., his parish. A priest might rent his parish to another and take a more profitable position. "Leet": i.e., he did not leave.
7. St. Paul's Cathedral.
8. Chantry, i.e., a foundation that employed priests for the sole duty of saying masses for the souls of certain persons. St. Paul's had many of them.
9. Or to be employed by a brotherhood; i.e., to take a lucrative and fairly easy position as chaplain with a parish guild.

And though he holy were and vertuous,
He was to sinful men nought despitous,°   *scornful*
Ne of his speeche daungerous° ne digne,°   *disdainful / haughty*
520 But in his teching discreet and benigne,
To drawen folk to hevene by fairnesse
By good ensample—this was his bisinesse.
But it° were any persone obstinat,   *if there*
What so he were, of heigh or lowe estat,
525 Him wolde he snibben° sharply for the nones:[1]   *scold*
A bettre preest I trowe° ther nowher noon is.   *believe*
He waited after[2] no pompe and reverence,
Ne maked him a spiced conscience,[3]
But Cristes lore° and his Apostles twelve   *teaching*
530 He taughte, but first he folwed it himselve.
    With him ther was a Plowman, was his brother,
That hadde ylad° of dong° ful many a fother.[4]   *carried / dung*
A trewe swinkere° and a good was he,   *worker*
Living in pees° and parfit charitee.   *peace*
535 God loved he best with al his hoole° herte   *whole*
At alle times, though him gamed or smerte,[5]
And thanne his neighebor right as himselve.
He wolde thresshe, and therto dike° and delve,   *dig ditches*
For Cristes sake, for every poore wight,
540 Withouten hire, if it laye in his might.
His tithes payed he ful faire and wel,
Bothe of his propre swink[6] and his catel.°   *property*
In a tabard° he rood upon a mere.°   *short coat / mare*
    Ther was also a Reeve° and a Millere,   *estate manager*
545 A Somnour, and a Pardoner[7] also,
A Manciple,° and myself—ther were namo.   *steward*
    The Millere was a stout carl° for the nones.   *fellow*
Ful big he was of brawn° and eek of bones—   *muscle*
That preved[8] wel, for overal ther he cam
550 At wrastling he wolde have alway the ram.[9]
He was short-shuldred, brood,° a thikke knarre.° *broad / bully*
Ther was no dore that he nolde heve of harre,[1]
Or breke it at a renning° with his heed.°   *running / head*
His beerd as any sowe or fox was reed,°   *red*
555 And therto brood, as though it were a spade;
Upon the cop° right of his nose he hade   *ridge*
A werte,° and theron stood a tuft of heres,   *wart*
Rede as the bristles of a sowes eres;
His nosethirles° blake were and wide.   *nostrils*

1. On any occasion.
2. I.e., expected.
3. Nor did he assume an overfastidious conscience.
4. Load.
5. Whether he was pleased or grieved.
6. His own work.
7. "Somnour" (Summoner): server of summonses to the ecclesiastical court; Pardoner: dispenser of papal pardons. See lines 625 and 671, and notes, below.
8. Proved, i.e., was evident.
9. A ram was frequently offered as the prize in wrestling.
1. He would not heave off (its) hinge.

560 A swerd and a bokeler° bar° he by his side.   *shield / bore*
His mouth as greet was as a greet furnais.°   *furnace*
He was a janglere° and a Goliardais,[2]   *chatterer*
And that was most of sinne and harlotries.°   *obscenities*
Wel coude he stelen corn and tollen thries[3]—
565 And yit he hadde a thombe[4] of gold, pardee.°   *by heaven*
A whit cote and a blew hood wered° he.   *wore*
A baggepipe wel coude he blowe and soune,°   *sound*
And therwithal° he broughte us out of towne.   *therewith*
   A gentil Manciple[5] was ther of a temple,
570 Of which achatours° mighte take exemple   *buyers of food*
For to been wise in bying of vitaile;°   *victuals*
For wheither that he paide or took by taile,[6]
Algate he waited so in his achat[7]
That he was ay biforn[8] and in good stat.
575   Now is nat that of God a ful fair grace
That swich a lewed° mannes wit shal pace°   *ignorant / surpass*
The wisdom of an heep of lerned men?
Of maistres° hadde he mo than thries ten   *masters*
That weren of lawe expert and curious,°   *cunning*
580 Of whiche ther were a dozeine in that hous
Worthy to been stiwardes of rente° and lond   *income*
Of any lord that is in Engelond,
To make him live by his propre good[9]
In honour dettelees but if[1] he were wood,°   *insane*
585 Or live as scarsly° as him list° desire,   *sparely / it pleases*
And able for to helpen al a shire
In any caas° that mighte falle° or happe,   *event / befall*
And yit this Manciple sette hir aller cappe![2]
   The Reeve[3] was a sclendre° colerik man;   *slender*
590 His beerd was shave as neigh° as evere he can;   *close*
His heer was by his eres ful round yshorn;
His top was dokked[4] lik a preest biforn;
Ful longe were his legges and ful lene,
Ylik a staf, ther was no calf yseene.°   *visible*
595 Wel coude he keepe° a gerner° and a binne—   *guard / granary*
Ther was noon auditour coude on him winne.[5]
Wel wiste° he by the droughte and by the rain   *knew*
The yeelding of his seed and of his grain.

2. Goliard, teller of ribald stories.
3. Take toll thrice—i.e., deduct from the grain far more than the lawful percentage.
4. Thumb. The narrator seems to be questioning the validity of the adage that (only) an honest miller has a golden thumb.
5. The Manciple is the steward of a community of lawyers in London (a "temple").
6. By talley, i.e., on credit.
7. Always he was on the watch in his purchasing.
8. I.e., ahead of the game. "Stat": financial condition.
9. His own money.
1. Out of debt unless.
2. This Manciple made fools of them all.
3. The Reeve is the superintendent of a large farming estate; "colerik" (choleric) describes a man whose dominant humor is yellow bile (choler)—i.e., a hot-tempered man.
4. Cut short: the clergy wore the head partially shaved.
5. I.e., find him in default.

	His lordes sheep, his neet,° his dayerye,	*cattle*
600	His swin, his hors, his stoor,° and his pultrye	*stock*
	Was hoolly° in this Reeves governinge,	*wholly*
	And by his covenant yaf⁶ the rekeninge,	
	Sin° that his lord was twenty yeer of age.	*since*
	There coude no man bringe him in arrerage.⁷	
605	Ther nas baillif, hierde, nor other hine,	
	That he ne knew his sleighte and his covine⁸—	
	They were adrad° of him as of the deeth.°	*afraid / plague*
	His woning° was ful faire upon an heeth;°	*dwelling / meadow*
	With greene trees shadwed was his place.	
610	He coude bettre than his lord purchace.°	*acquire goods*
	Ful riche he was astored° prively.°	*stocked / secretly*
	His lord wel coude he plesen subtilly,	
	To yive and lene° him of his owene good,°	*lend / property*
	And have a thank, and yit a cote and hood.	
615	In youthe he hadde lerned a good mister:°	*occupation*
	He was a wel good wrighte, a carpenter.	
	This Reeve sat upon a ful good stot°	*stallion*
	That was a pomely° grey and highte° Scot.	*dapple / was named*
	A long surcote° of pers° upon he hade,⁹	*overcoat / blue*
620	And by his side he bar° a rusty blade.	*bore*
	Of Northfolk was this Reeve of which I telle,	
	Biside a town men clepen Baldeswelle.°	*Bawdswell*
	Tukked¹ he was as is a frere aboute,	
	And evere he rood the hindreste of oure route.²	
625	A Somnour³ was ther with us in that place	
	That hadde a fir-reed° cherubinnes⁴ face,	*fire-red*
	For saucefleem° he was, with yën narwe,	*pimply*
	And hoot° he was, and lecherous as a sparwe,°	*hot / sparrow*
	With scaled° browes blake and piled⁵ beerd:	*scabby*
630	Of his visage children were aferd.°	*afraid*
	Ther nas quiksilver, litarge, ne brimstoon,	
	Boras, ceruce, ne oile of tartre noon,⁶	
	Ne oinement that wolde clense and bite,	
	That him mighte helpen of his whelkes° white,	*blotches*
635	Nor of the knobbes° sitting on his cheekes.	*lumps*
	Wel loved he garlek, oinons, and eek leekes,	
	And for to drinke strong win reed as blood.	
	Thanne wolde he speke and crye as he were wood;°	*mad*

6. And according to his contract he gave.
7. Convict him of being in arrears financially.
8. There was no bailiff (i.e., foreman), shepherd, nor other farm laborer whose craftiness and plots he didn't know.
9. "Upon he hade": he had on.
1. With clothing tucked up.
2. Hindmost of our group.
3. The "Somnour" (Summoner) is an employee of the ecclesiastical court, whose defined duty is to bring to court persons whom the archdeacon—the justice of the court—suspects of offenses against canon law. By this time, however, summoners had generally transformed themselves into corrupt detectives who spied out offenders and blackmailed them by threats of summonses.
4. Cherub's, often depicted in art with a red face.
5. Uneven, partly hairless.
6. These are all ointments for diseases affecting the skin, probably diseases of venereal origin.

And whan that he wel dronken hadde the win,
640 Thanne wolde he speke no word but Latin:
A fewe termes hadde he, two or three,
That he hadde lerned out of som decree;
No wonder is—he herde it al the day,
And eek ye knowe wel how that a jay°   *parrot*
645 Can clepen "Watte"[7] as wel as can the Pope—
But whoso coude in other thing grope,°   *examine*
Thanne hadde he spent all his philosophye;[8]
Ay *Questio quid juris*[9] wolde he crye.
    He was a gentil harlot° and a kinde;   *rascal*
650 A bettre felawe sholde men nought finde:
He wolde suffre,° for a quart of win,   *permit*
A good felawe to have his concubin
A twelfmonth, and excusen him at the fulle;[1]
Ful prively a finch eek coude he pulle.[2]
655 And if he foond° owher° a good felawe   *found / anywhere*
He wolde techen him to have noon awe
In swich caas of the Ercedekenes curs,[3]
But if[4] a mannes soule were in his purs,
For in his purs he sholde ypunisshed be.
660 "Purs is the Ercedekenes helle," saide he.
    But wel I woot he lied right in deede:
Of cursing° oughte eech gilty man drede,   *excommunication*
For curs wol slee° right as assoiling° savith—   *slay / absolution*
And also war him of a *significavit*.[5]
665 In daunger[6] hadde he at his owene gise°   *disposal*
The yonge girles of the diocise,
And knew hir conseil,° and was al hir reed.[7]   *secrets*
A gerland hadde he set upon his heed
As greet as it were for an ale-stake;[8]
670 A bokeler hadde he maad him of a cake.
    With him ther rood a gentil Pardoner[9]
Of Rouncival, his freend and his compeer,°   *comrade*
That straight was comen fro the Court of Rome.
Ful loude he soong,° "Com hider, love, to me."   *sang*
675 This Somnour bar to him a stif burdoun:[1]

7. Call out: "Walter"—like modern parrots' "Polly."
8. I.e., learning.
9. "What point of law does this investigation involve?": a phrase frequently used in ecclesiastical courts.
1. "At the fulle": fully. Ecclesiastical courts had jurisdiction over many offenses which today would come under civil law, including sexual offenses.
2. "To pull a finch" is to have carnal dealings with a woman.
3. Archdeacon's sentence of excommunication.
4. "But if": unless.
5. And also one should be careful of a *significavit* (the writ which transferred the guilty offender from the ecclesiastical to the civil arm for punishment).
6. Under his domination.
7. Was their chief source of advice.
8. A tavern was signalized by a pole ("ale-stake"), rather like a modern flagpole, projecting from its front wall; on this hung a garland, or "bush."
9. A Pardoner dispensed papal pardon for sins to those who contributed to the charitable institution that he was licensed to represent; this Pardoner purported to be collecting for the hospital of Roncesvalles ("Rouncival") in Spain, which had a London branch.
1. I.e., provided him with a strong vocal accompaniment.

Was nevere trompe° of half so greet a soun.   *trumpet*
  This Pardoner hadde heer as yelow as wex,
But smoothe it heeng° as dooth a strike° of
    flex;°   *hung / hank / flax*
By ounces² heenge his lokkes that he hadde,
680 And therwith he his shuldres overspradde,°   *overspread*
But thinne it lay, by colpons,° oon by oon;   *strands*
But hood for jolitee° wered° he noon,   *nonchalance / wore*
For it was trussed up in his walet:°   *pack*
Him thoughte he rood al of the newe jet.°   *fashion*
685 Dischevelee° save his cappe he rood al bare.   *with hair down*
Swiche glaring yën hadde he as an hare.
A vernicle³ hadde he sowed upon his cappe,
His walet biforn him in his lappe,
Bretful° of pardon, comen from Rome al hoot.°   *brimful / hot*
690 A vois he hadde as smal° as hath a goot;°   *fine / goat*
No beerd hadde he, ne nevere sholde have;
As smoothe it was as it were late yshave:
I trowe° he were a gelding or a mare.   *believe*
But of his craft, fro Berwik into Ware,⁴
695 Ne was ther swich another pardoner;
For in his male° he hadde a pilwe-beer°   *bag / pillowcase*
Which that he saide was Oure Lady veil;
He saide he hadde a gobet° of the sail   *piece*
That Sainte Peter hadde whan that he wente
700 Upon the see, til Jesu Crist him hente.°   *seized*
He hadde a crois° of laton,° ful of stones,   *cross / brassy metal*
And in a glas he hadde pigges bones,
But with thise relikes⁵ whan that he foond°   *found*
A poore person° dwelling upon lond,⁶   *parson*
705 Upon° a day he gat° him more moneye   *in / got*
Than that the person gat in monthes twaye;
And thus with feined° flaterye and japes°   *false / tricks*
He made the person and the peple his apes.°   *dupes*
But trewely to tellen at the laste,
710 He was in chirche a noble ecclesiaste;
Wel coude he rede a lesson and a storye,°   *liturgical narrative*
But alderbest° he soong an offertorye,   *best of all*
For wel he wiste° whan that song was songe,   *knew*
He moste° preche and wel affile° his tonge   *must / sharpen*
715 To winne silver, as he ful wel coude—
Therfore he soong the merierly° and loude.   *more merrily*
    Now have I told you soothly in a clause⁷
Th'estaat, th'array, the nombre, and eek the cause

---

2. I.e., thin strands.
3. Portrait of Christ's face as it was said to have been impressed on St. Veronica's handkerchief.
4. Probably towns south and north of London.

5. Relics—i.e., the pigs' bones which the Pardoner represented as saints' bones.
6. "Upon lond": upcountry.
7. I.e., in a short space.

Why that assembled was this compaignye
720 In Southwerk at this gentil hostelrye
That highte the Tabard, faste° by the Belle;[8]   *close*
But now is time to you for to telle
How that we baren us[9] that ilke° night   *same*
Whan we were in that hostelrye alight;
725 And after wol I telle of oure viage,°   *trip*
And al the remenant of oure pilgrimage.
But first I praye you of youre curteisye
That ye n'arette it nought my vilainye[1]
Though that I plainly speke in this matere
730 To telle you hir wordes and hir cheere,°   *behavior*
Ne though I speke hir wordes proprely;°   *accurately*
For this ye knowen also wel as I:
Who so shal telle a tale after a man
He moot° reherce,° as neigh as evere he can,   *must / repeat*
735 Everich a word, if it be in his charge,°   *responsibility*
Al speke he[2] nevere so rudeliche and large,°   *broadly*
Or elles he moot telle his tale untrewe,
Or feine° thing, or finde° wordes newe;   *falsify / devise*
He may nought spare[3] although he were his brother:
740 He moot as wel saye oo word as another.
Crist spak himself ful brode° in Holy Writ,   *broadly*
And wel ye woot no vilainye is it;
Eek Plato saith, who so can him rede,
The wordes mote be cosin to the deede.
745   Also I praye you to foryive it me
Al° have I nat set folk in hir degree   *although*
Here in this tale as that they sholde stonde:
My wit is short, ye may wel understonde.
   Greet cheere made oure Host[4] us everichoon,
750 And to the soper sette he us anoon.°   *at once*
He served us with vitaile° at the beste.   *food*
Strong was the win, and wel to drinke us leste.°   *it pleased*
A semely man oure Hoste was withalle
For to been a marchal[5] in an halle;
755 A large man he was, with yën steepe,°   *prominent*
A fairer burgeis° was ther noon in Chepe[6]—   *burgher*
Bold of his speeche, and wis, and wel ytaught,
And of manhood him lakkede right naught.
Eek therto he was right a merye man,
760 And after soper playen he bigan,
And spak of mirthe amonges othere thinges—
Whan that we hadde maad oure rekeninges[7]—

---

8. Another tavern in Southwark.
9. Bore ourselves.
1. That you do not charge it to my lack of decorum.
2. Although he speak.
3. I.e., spare anyone.
4. The Host is the landlord of the

Tabard Inn.
5. Marshal, one who was in charge of feasts.
6. Cheapside, bourgeois center of London.
7. Had paid our bills.

And saide thus, "Now, lordinges, trewely,
Ye been to me right welcome, hertely.°   *heartily*
765 For by my trouthe, if that I shal nat lie,
I sawgh nat this yeer so merye a compaignye
At ones in this herberwe° as is now.   *inn*
Fain° wolde I doon you mirthe, wiste I[8] how.   *gladly*
And of a mirthe I am right now bithought,
770 To doon you ese, and it shal coste nought.
    "Ye goon to Canterbury—God you speede;
The blisful martyr quite you youre meede.[9]
And wel I woot as ye goon by the waye
Ye shapen you[1] to talen° and to playe,   *converse*
775 For trewely, confort ne mirthe is noon
To ride by the waye domb as stoon;°   *stone*
And therfore wol I maken you disport
As I saide erst,° and doon you som confort;   *before*
And if you liketh alle, by oon assent,
780 For to stonden at[2] my juggement,
And for to werken as I shal you saye,
Tomorwe whan ye riden by the waye—
Now by my fader° soule that is deed,   *father's*
But° ye be merye I wol yive you myn heed!°   *unless / head*
785 Holde up youre handes withouten more speeche."
    Oure counseil was nat longe for to seeche;°   *seek*
Us thoughte it was nat worth to make it wis,[3]
And graunted him withouten more avis,°   *deliberation*
And bade him saye his voirdit° as him leste.[4]   *verdict*
790 "Lordinges," quod he, "now herkneth for the beste;
But taketh it nought, I praye you, in desdain.
This is the point, to spoken short and plain,
That eech of you, to shorte with oure waye
In this viage, shal tellen tales twaye°—   *two*
795 To Canterburyward, I mene it so,
And hoomward he shal tellen othere two,
Of aventures that whilom° have bifalle;   *once upon a time*
And which of you that bereth him best of alle—
That is to sayn, that telleth in this cas
800 Tales of best sentence° and most solas°—   *purport / delight*
Shal have a soper at oure aller cost,[5]
Here in this place, sitting by this post,
Whan that we come again fro Canterbury.
And for to make you the more mury°   *merry*
805 I wol myself goodly° with you ride—   *kindly*
Right at myn owene cost—and be youre gide.
And who so wol my juggement withsaye°   *contradict*
Shal paye al that we spende by the waye.

8. If I knew.
9. Pay you your reward.
1. "Shapen you": intend.
2. Abide by.
3. We didn't think it worthwhile to make an issue of it.
4. It pleased.
5. At the cost of us all.

And if ye vouche sauf that it be so,
810 Telle me anoon, withouten wordes mo,°   *more*
And I wol erly shape me[6] therfore."
   This thing was graunted and oure othes swore
With ful glad herte, and prayden[7] him also
That he wolde vouche sauf for to do so,
815 And that he wolde been oure governour,
And of oure tales juge and reportour,°   *accountant*
And sette a soper at a certain pris,°   *price*
And we wol ruled been at his devis,°   *disposal*
In heigh and lowe; and thus by oon assent
820 We been accorded to his juggement.
And therupon the win was fet° anoon;   *fetched*
We dronken and to reste wente eechoon
Withouten any lenger° taryinge.   *longer*
   Amorwe° whan that day bigan to springe   *in the morning*
825 Up roos oure Host and was oure aller cok,[8]
And gadred us togidres in a flok,
And forth we riden, a litel more than pas,°   *a step*
Unto the watering of Saint Thomas;[9]
And ther oure Host bigan his hors arreste,°   *halt*
830 And saide, "Lordes, herkneth if you leste:°   *it please*
   Ye woot youre forward° and it you recorde:[1]   *agreement*
If evensong and morwesong° accorde,°   *morningsong / agree*
Lat see now who shal telle the firste tale.
As evere mote I drinken win or ale,
835 Who so be rebel to my juggement
Shal paye for al that by the way is spent.
Now draweth cut[2] er that we ferrer twinne:
He which that hath the shorteste shal biginne.
   "Sire Knight," quod he, "my maister and my lord,
840 Now draweth cut, for that is myn accord.°   *will*
Cometh neer," quod he, "my lady Prioresse,
And ye, sire Clerk, lat be youre shamefastnesse°—   *modesty*
Ne studieth nought. Lay hand to, every man!"
   Anoon to drawen every wight bigan,
845 And shortly for to tellen as it was,
Were it by aventure, or sort, or cas,[3]
The soothe° is this, the cut fil° to the Knight;   *truth / fell*
Of which ful blithe and glad was every wight,
And telle he moste° his tale, as was resoun,   *must*
850 By forward and by composicioun,[4]
As ye han herd. What needeth wordes mo?
And whan this goode man sawgh that it was so,
As he that wis was and obedient

---

6. Prepare myself.
7. I.e., we prayed.
8. Was rooster for us all.
9. A watering place near Southwark.
1. You recall it.

2. I.e., draw lots; "ferrer twinne": go farther.
3. Whether it was luck, fate, or chance.
4. By agreement and compact.

To keepe his forward by his free assent,
855 He saide, "Sin I shal biginne the game,
What, welcome be the cut, in Goddes name!
Now lat us ride, and herkneth what I saye."
And with that word we riden forth oure waye,
And he bigan with right a merye cheere°   *countenance*
860 His tale anoon, and saide as ye may heere.

The Wife of Bath's Prologue and Tale

The Prologue [1]

Experience, though noon auctoritee
Were in this world, is right ynough for me
To speke of wo that is in mariage:
For lordinges,° sith I twelf yeer was of age—   *gentlemen*
5 Thanked be God that is eterne on live—
Housbondes at chirche dore² I have had five
(If I so ofte mighte han wedded be),
And alle were worthy men in hir degree.
But me was told, certain, nat longe agoon is,
10 That sith that Crist ne wente nevere but ones

1. The Wife of Bath is the remarkable culmination of many centuries of an antifeminism that was particularly nurtured by the medieval church. In their eagerness to exalt the spiritual ideal of chastity, certain theologians developed an idea of womankind that was nothing less than monstrous. According to these, insatiable lecherousness and indomitable shrewishness (plus a host of attendant vices) were characteristic of women. This notion was given most eloquent expression by St. Jerome in his attack (written about A.D. 400) on the monk Jovinian, who had uttered some good words for matrimony, and it is Jerome that the Wife of Bath comes forward not, curiously enough, to refute, but to confirm. The first part of her Prologue is a mass of quotations from that part of Jerome's tract where he is appealing to St. Paul's Epistle (I Corinthians vii) for antimatrimonial authority. On the narrow issue of her right to remarry, to be sure, the Wife finds fault—rather mildly—with Jerome, but on the more central issue of why she wishes to marry and remarry she expresses no disagreement with him. Yet in the failure to defend herself and refute the saint, she somehow manages to make the latter's point of view look a good deal sillier than she looks herself; and instead of embodying the satire on womanhood that one would ex-

pect because of her origins in antifeminist literature, she becomes instead a satirist of the grotesquely woman-hating men who had first defined her personality.

More important, because of the extraordinary vitality that Chaucer has imparted to her, the Wife of Bath by the end of her Prologue comes to bear a less significant relation to satire than she does to reality itself. Making the best of the world in which they have arbitrarily been placed is the occupation of both the Wife of Bath and the reader, and it is in doing this that the Wife ceases to be a monstrosity of fiction and becomes alive—wonderfully alive, both to the potentialities of which she and her world are capable and to the limitations that even in her world time and age place upon her. It is especially in the attitude with which she regards these limitations that her fiction becomes most true to life, since they are also the limitations imposed by the real world. Despite the loss of youth and beauty, her best weapons, she faces her future not only with a woman's ability to endure and enjoy what she cannot reshape, but also with a zest for life on its own terms that is almost more than human.
2. The actual wedding ceremony was celebrated at the church door, not in the chancel.

To wedding in the Cane[3] of Galilee,
That by the same ensample° taughte he me   *example*
That I ne sholde wedded be but ones.
Herke eek,° lo, which° a sharp word for the nones,[4]   *also / what*
15 Biside a welle, Jesus, God and man,
Spak in repreve° of the Samaritan: *reproof*
"Thou hast yhad five housbondes," quod he,
"And that ilke° man that now hath thee   *same*
Is nat thyn housbonde." Thus saide he certain.
20 What that he mente therby I can nat sayn,
But that I axe° why the fifthe man   *ask*
Was noon housbonde to the Samaritan?[5]
How manye mighte she han in mariage?
Yit herde I nevere tellen in myn age
25 Upon this nombre diffinicioun.°   *definition*
Men may divine° and glosen° up and down,   *guess / interpret*
But wel I woot,° expres,° withouten lie,   *know / expressly*
God bad us for to wexe[6] and multiplye:
That gentil text can I wel understonde.
30 Eek wel I woot° he saide that myn housbonde   *know*
Sholde lete° fader and moder and take to me,[7]   *leave*
But of no nombre mencion made he—
Of bigamye or of octogamye:[8]
Why sholde men thanne speke of it vilainye?
35 Lo, here the wise king daun° Salomon: *master*
I trowe° he hadde wives many oon,[9]   *believe*
As wolde God it leveful° were to me   *permissible*
To be refresshed half so ofte as he.
Which yifte[1] of God hadde he for alle his wives!
40 No man hath swich that in this world alive is.
God woot this noble king, as to my wit,°   *knowledge*
The firste night hadde many a merye fit°   *bout*
With eech of hem, so wel was him on live.[2]
Blessed be God that I have wedded five,
45 Of whiche I have piked out the beste,[3]
Bothe of hir nether° purs and of hir cheste.°   *lower / moneybox*
Diverse scoles maken parfit° clerkes,   *perfect*
And diverse practikes[4] in sondry werkes
Maken the werkman parfit sikerly:°   *certainly*
50 Of five housbondes scoleying° am I.   *schooling*
Welcome the sixte whan that evere he shal![5]

3. Cana (see John ii.1).
4. To the purpose.
5. Christ was actually referring to a sixth man who was not married to the Samaritan woman (cf. John iv.6 ff.).
6. I.e., increase. See Genesis i.28.
7. See Matthew xix.5.
8. I.e., of two or even eight marriages. The Wife is referring to successive, rather than simultaneous marriages.
9. Solomon had 700 wives and 300 concubines (I Kings xi.3).
1. What a gift.
2. I.e., so pleasant a life he had.
3. Whom I have cleaned out of everything worthwhile.
4. Practical experiences.
5. I.e., shall come along.

For sith I wol nat kepe me chast in al,
Whan my housbonde is fro the world agoon,
Som Cristen man shal wedde me anoon.°   *right away*
55 For thanne th'Apostle⁶ saith that I am free
To wedde, a Goddes half,⁷ where it liketh me.
He said that to be wedded is no sinne:
Bet° is to be wedded than to brinne.°   *better / burn*
What rekketh me⁸ though folk saye vilainye
60 Of shrewed° Lamech⁹ and his bigamye?   *cursed*
I woot wel Abraham was an holy man,
And Jacob eek, as fer as evere I can,°   *know*
And eech of hem hadde wives mo than two,
And many another holy man also.
65   Where can ye saye in any manere age
That hye God defended° mariage   *prohibited*
By expres word? I praye you, telleth me.
Or where comanded he virginitee?
I woot as wel as ye, it is no drede,°   *doubt*
70 Th'Apostle, whan he speketh of maidenhede,°   *maidenhood*
He saide that precept therof hadde he noon:
Men may conseile a womman to be oon,°   *single*
But conseiling nis no comandement.
He putte it in oure owene juggement.
75 For hadde God comanded maidenhede,
Thanne hadde he dampned° wedding with the
      deede;¹   *condemned*
And certes, if ther were no seed ysowe,
Virginitee, thanne wherof sholde it growe?
Paul dorste nat comanden at the leeste
80 A thing of which his maister yaf° no heeste.°   *gave / command*
The dart² is set up for virginitee:
Cacche whoso may, who renneth° best lat see.   *runs*
But this word is nought take of³ every wight,
But ther as⁴ God list° yive it of his might.   *it pleases*
85 I woot wel that th'Apostle was a maide,°   *virgin*
But nathelees, though that he wroot and saide
He wolde that every wight were swich° as he,   *such*
Al nis but conseil to virginitee;
And for to been a wif he yaf me leve
90 Of indulgence; so nis it no repreve°   *disgrace*
To wedde me⁵ if that my make° die,   *mate*
Withouten excepcion of bigamye⁶——

6. St. Paul.
7. On God's behalf; "it liketh me": I
please.
8. What do I care.
9. The first man whom the Bible mentions as having two wives (Genesis
iv.19–24).

1. I.e., at the same time.
2. I.e., prize in a race.
3. Understood for, i.e., applicable to.
4. Where.
5. For me to marry.
6. I.e., without there being any legal objection on the score of remarriage.

Al° were it good no womman for to touche   *although*
(He mente as in his bed or in his couche,
95 For peril is bothe fir° and tow° t'assemble—   *fire / flax*
Ye knowe what this ensample may resemble).[7]
This al and som,[8] he heeld virginitee
More parfit than wedding in freletee.°   *frailty*
(Freletee clepe I but if[9] that he and she
100 Wolde leden al hir lif in chastitee.)
I graunte it wel, I have noon envye
Though maidenhede preferre° bigamye:°   *excel / remarriage*
It liketh hem to be cleue in body and gost.°   *spirit*
Of myn estaat ne wol I make no boost;
105 For wel ye knowe, a lord in his houshold
Ne hath nat every vessel al of gold:
Some been of tree,° and doon hir lord servise.   *wood*
God clepeth folk to him in sondry wise,
And everich hath of God a propre[1] yifte,
110 Som this, som that, as him liketh shifte.°   *ordain*
Virginitee is greet perfeccioun,
And continence eek with devocioun,
But Crist, that of perfeccion is welle,°   *source*
Bad nat every wight he sholde go selle
115 Al that he hadde and yive it to the poore,
And in swich wise folwe him and his fore:[2]
He spak to hem that wolde live parfitly°—   *perfectly*
And lordinges, by youre leve, that am nat I.
I wol bistowe the flour of al myn age
120 In th'actes and in fruit of mariage.
Telle me also, to what conclusioun°   *end*
Were membres maad of generacioun
And of so parfit wis a wrighte ywrought?[3]
Trusteth right wel, they were nat maad for nought.
125 Glose° whoso wol, and saye bothe up and down   *interpret*
That they were maked for purgacioun
Of urine, and oure bothe thinges smale
Was eek to knowe a femele from a male,
And for noon other cause—saye ye no?
130 Th'experience woot it is nought so.
So that the clerkes be nat with me wrothe,
I saye this, that they been maad for bothe—
That is to sayn, for office° and for ese   *excretion*
Of engendrure, ther we nat God displese.
135 Why sholde men elles in hir bookes sette
That man shal yeelde[4] to his wif hir dette?

---

7. I.e., what this metaphor may apply
to.
8. This is all there is to it.
9. Frailty I call it unless.
1. I.e., his own.

2. Matthew xix.21. "Fore": footsteps.
3. And wrought by so perfectly wise a
maker.
4. I.e., pay.

Now wherwith sholde he make his payement
If he ne used his sely° instrument?   *innocent*
Thanne were they maad upon a creature
140 To purge urine, and eek for engendrure.
    But I saye nought that every wight is holde,°   *bound*
That hath swich harneis° as I to you tolde,   *equipment*
To goon and usen hem in engendrure:
Thanne sholde men take of chastitee no cure.°   *heed*
145 Crist was a maide° and shapen as a man,   *virgin*
And many a saint sith that the world bigan,
Yit lived they evere in parfit chastitee.
I nil envye no virginitee:
Lat hem be breed° of pured° whete seed,   *bread / refined*
150 And lat us wives hote° barly breed—   *be called*
And yit with barly breed, Mark telle can,
Oure Lord Jesu refresshed many a man.[5]
In swich estaat as God hath cleped us
I wol persevere: I nam nat precious.°   *fastidious*
155 In wifhood wol I use myn instrument
As freely° as my Makere hath it sent.   *generously*
If I be daungerous,° God yive me sorwe: *stand-offish*
Myn housbonde shal it han both eve and morwe,°   *morning*
Whan that him list[6] come forth and paye his dette.
160 An housbonde wol I have, I wol nat lette,[7]
Which shal be bothe my dettour° and my thral,°   *debtor / slave*
And have his tribulacion withal
Upon his flessh whil that I am his wif.
I have the power during al my lif
165 Upon his propre° body, and nat he: *own*
Right thus th'Apostle tolde it unto me,
And bad oure housbondes for to love us weel.
Al this sentence° me liketh everydeel.°   *purport / entirely*

[AN INTERLUDE]

    Up sterte° the Pardoner and that anoon: *started*
170 "Now dame," quod he, "by God and by Saint John,
Ye been a noble prechour in this cas.
I was aboute to wedde a wif: allas,
What° sholde I bye° it on my flessh so dere?   *why / purchase*
Yit hadde I levere wedde no wif toyere."°   *this year*
175 "Abid," quod she, "my tale is nat bigonne.
Nay, thou shalt drinken of another tonne,°   *tun*
Er that I go, shal savoure wors than ale.
And whan that I have told thee forth my tale
Of tribulacion in mariage,
180 Of which I am expert in al myn age—

5. In the descriptions of the miracle
of the loaves and fishes, it is actually
John, not Mark, who mentions barley
bread (vi.9).
6. When he wishes to.
7. I will make no difficulty.

This is to saye, myself hath been the whippe—
Thanne maistou chese° wheither thou wolt sippe   *choose*
Of thilke° tonne that I shal abroche:°   *this same / broach*
Be war of it, er thou too neigh approche,
185 For I shal telle ensamples mo than ten.
'Whoso that nile° be war by othere men,   *would not*
By him shal othere men corrected be.'
Thise same wordes writeth Ptolomee:
Rede in his *Almageste* and take it there."[8]
190 "Dame, I wolde praye you if youre wil it were,"
Saide this Pardoner, "as ye bigan,
Telle forth youre tale; spareth for no man,
And teche us yonge men of youre practike."°   *mode of operation*
"Gladly," quod she, "sith it may you like;°   *please*
195 But that I praye to al this compaignye,
If that I speke after my fantasye,[9]
As taketh nat agrief° of that I saye,   *amiss*
For myn entente nis but for to playe."

[THE WIFE CONTINUES]

Now sire, thanne wol I telle you forth my tale.
200 As evere mote I drinke win or ale,
I shal saye sooth: tho° housbondes that I hadde,   *those*
As three of hem were goode, and two were badde.
The three men were goode, and riche, and olde;
Unnethe° mighte they the statut holde   *with difficulty*
205 In which they were bounden unto me—
Ye woot wel what I mene of this, pardee.
As help me God, I laughe whan I thinke
How pitously anight I made hem swinke;°   *work*
And by my fay,° I tolde of it no stoor:[1]   *faith*
210 They hadde me yiven hir land and hir tresor;
Me needed nat do lenger diligence
To winne hir love or doon hem reverence.
They loved me so wel, by God above,
That I ne tolde no daintee of[2] hir love.
215 A wis womman wol bisye hire evere in oon[3]
To gete hire love, ye, ther as she hath noon.
But sith I hadde hem hoolly in myn hand,
And sith that they hadde yiven me al hir land,
What° sholde I take keep° hem for to plese,   *why / care*
220 But it were for my profit and myn ese?
I sette hem so awerke,° by my fay,°   *awork / faith*
That many a night they songen° wailaway.   *sang*

8. The *Almagest,* an astronomical work by the Greek astronomer and mathematician Ptolemy (second century A.D.), contains no such aphorism. The aphorism does, however, appear in a collection ascribed to him.
9. If I speak according to my whim.
1. I set no store by it.
2. Set no value on.
3. Busy herself constantly.

The bacon was nat fet° for hem, I trowe,   *brought back*
That some men han in Essexe at Dunmowe.[4]
225 I governed hem so wel after° my lawe   *according to*
That eech of hem ful blisful was and fawe°   *glad*
To bringe me gaye thinges fro the faire;
They were ful glade whan I spak hem faire,
For God it woot, I chidde° hem spitously.°   *chided / cruelly*
230   Now herkneth how I bar me[5] proprely:
Ye wise wives, that conne understonde,
Thus sholde ye speke and bere him wrong on honde[6]—
For half so boldely can ther no man
Swere and lie as a womman can.
235 I saye nat this by wives that been wise,
But if it be whan they hem misavise.[7]
A wis wif, if that she can hir good,[8]
Shal bere him on hande the cow is wood,[9]
And take witnesse of hir owene maide
240 Of hir assent.[1] But herkneth how I saide:
    "Sire olde cainard,° is this thyn array?[2]   *sluggard*
Why is my neighebores wif so gay?
She is honoured overal ther she gooth:
I sitte at hoom; I have no thrifty° cloth.   *decent*
245 What doostou at my neighebores hous?
Is she so fair? Artou so amorous?
What roune° ye with oure maide, benedicite?[3]   *whisper*
Sire olde lechour, lat thy japes° be.   *tricks, intrigues*
And if I have a gossib° or a freend,   *confidant*
250 Withouten gilt ye chiden as a feend,
If that I walke or playe unto his hous.
Thou comest hoom as dronken as a mous,
And prechest on thy bench, with yvel preef.[4]
Thou saist to me, it is a greet meschief°   *misfortune*
255 To wedde a poore womman for costage.[5]
And if that she be riche, of heigh parage,°   *descent*
Thanne saistou that it is a tormentrye
To suffre hir pride and hir malencolye.
And if that she be fair, thou verray knave,
260 Thou saist that every holour° wol hire have: *whoremonger*
She may no while in chastitee abide
That is assailed upon eech a side.
    "Thou saist som folk desiren us for richesse,

4. The Dunmow flitch was awarded to the couple who after a year of marriage could claim no quarrels, no regrets, and the desire, if freed, to remarry one another.
5. Bore myself, behaved.
6. Accuse him falsely.
7. When they make a mistake.
8. If she knows what's good for her.
9. Shall persuade him the chough has gone crazy. The chough, or jackdaw, was popularly supposed to tell husbands of their wives' infidelity.
1. And call as a witness her maid, who is on her side.
2. I.e., is this how you behave?
3. Bless me.
4. I.e., (may you have) bad luck.
5. Because of the expense.

Som[6] for oure shap, and som for oure fairnesse,
265 And som for she can outher° singe or daunce,   *either*
And som for gentilesse and daliaunce,°   *flirtatiousness*
Som for hir handes and hir armes smale°—   *slender*
Thus gooth al to the devel by thy tale![7]
Thou saist men may nat keepe[8] a castel wal,
270 It may so longe assailed been overal.°   *everywhere*
And if that she be foul, thou saist that she
Coveiteth° every man that she may see;   *desires*
For as a spaniel she wol on him lepe,
Til that she finde som man hire to chepe.°   *buy*
275 Ne noon so grey goos gooth ther in the lake,
As, saistou, wol be withoute make;°   *mate*
And saist it is an hard thing for to weelde°   *possess*
A thing that no man wol, his thankes, heelde.[9]
Thus saistou, lorel,° whan thou goost to bedde,   *loafer*
280 And that no wis man needeth for to wedde,
Ne no man that entendeth° unto hevene—   *aims*
With wilde thonder-dint[1] and firy levene
Mote thy welked nekke be tobroke![2]
Thou saist that dropping° houses and eek smoke   *leaking*
285 And chiding wives maken men to flee
Out of hir owene hous: a, benedicite,
What aileth swich an old man for to chide?
Thou saist we wives wil oure vices hide
Til we be fast,[3] and thanne we wol hem shewe—
290 Wel may that be a proverbe of a shrewe!°   *villain*
Thou saist that oxen, asses, hors,° and houndes,   *horses*
They been assayed at diverse stoundes;°   *times*
Bacins, lavours,° er that men hem bye,   *washbowls*
Spoones, stooles, and al swich housbondrye,°   *household goods*
295 And so be° pottes, clothes, and array°—   *are / clothing*
But folk of wives maken noon assay
Til they be wedded—olde dotard shrewe!
And thanne, saistou, we wil oure vices shewe.
Thou saist also that it displeseth me
300 But if that thou wolt praise my beautee,
And but thou poure alway upon my face,
And clepe me 'Faire Dame' in every place,
And but thou make a feeste on thilke day
That I was born, and make me fressh and gay,
305 And but thou do to my norice° honour,   *nurse*
And to my chamberere within my bowr,[4]
And to my fadres folk, and his allies[5]—

6. "Som," in this and the following lines, means "one."
7. I.e., according to your story.
8. I.e., keep safe.
9. No man would willingly hold.
1. Thunderbolt; "levene": lightning.

2. May thy withered neck be broken!
3. I.e., married.
4. And to my chambermaid within my bedroom.
5. Relatives by marriage.

Thus saistou, olde barel-ful of lies.
And yit of our apprentice Janekin,
310 For his crispe° heer, shining as gold so fin,   *curly*
And for he squiereth me bothe up and down,
Yit hastou caught a fals suspecioun;
I wil° him nat though thou were deed° tomorwe. *want / dead*
    "But tel me this, why hidestou with sorwe[6]
315 The keyes of thy cheste away fro me?
It is my good° as wel as thyn, pardee.   *property*
What, weenestou° make an idiot of oure dame? *do you think to*
Now by that lord that called is Saint Jame,
Thou shalt nought bothe, though thou were wood,° *furious*
320 Be maister of my body and of my good:
That oon thou shalt forgo, maugree thine yën.[7]
    "What helpeth it of me enquere° and spyen?   *inquire*
I trowe thou woldest loke° me in thy cheste.   *lock*
Thou sholdest saye, 'Wif, go wher thee leste.° *it may please*
325 Taak youre disport. I nil leve° no tales: *believe*
I knowe you for a trewe wif, dame Alis.'
We love no man that taketh keep or charge[8]
Wher that we goon: we wol been at oure large.[9]
Of alle men yblessed mote he be
330 The wise astrologen° daun Ptolomee,   *astronomer*
That saith this proverbe in his *Almageste*:
'Of alle men his wisdom is the hyeste
That rekketh° nat who hath the world in honde.' *cares*
By this proverbe thou shalt understonde,
335 Have thou[1] ynough, what thar° thee rekke or care *need*
How merily that othere folkes fare?
For certes, olde dotard, by youre leve,
Ye shal han queinte° right ynough at eve: *pudendum*
He is too greet a nigard that wil werne°   *refuse*
340 A man to lighte a candle at his lanterne;
He shal han nevere the lasse° lighte, pardee.   *less*
Have thou ynough, thee thar nat plaine thee.[2]
    "Thou saist also that if we make us gay
With clothing and with precious array,
345 That it is peril of oure chastitee,
And yit with sorwe thou moste enforce thee,[3]
And saye thise wordes in th'Apostles name:
'In habit° maad with chastitee and shame   *clothing*
Ye wommen shal apparaile you,' quod he,
350 'And nat in tressed heer[4] and gay perree,°   *jewelry*
As perles ne with gold ne clothes riche.'[5]
After thy text, ne after thy rubriche,[6]

---

6. I.e., with sorrow to you.
7. Despite your eyes—i.e., despite anything you can do about it.
8. Notice or interest.
9. I.e., liberty.
1. If you have.

2. I.e., you need not complain.
3. Strengthen your position.
4. I.e., elaborate hairdo.
5. See I Timothy ii.9.
6. Rubric, i.e., direction.

I wol nat werke as muchel as a gnat.
Thou saidest this, that I was lik a cat:
355 For whoso wolde senge° a cattes skin, — singe
Thanne wolde the cat wel dwellen in his in;° — lodging
And if the cattes skin be slik° and gay, — sleek
She wol nat dwelle in house half a day,
But forth she wol, er any day be dawed,[7]
360 To shewe her skin and goon a-caterwawed.° — caterwauling
This is to saye, if I be gay, sire shrewe,
I wol renne° out, my borel° for to shewe. — run / clothing
Sire olde fool, what helpeth[8] thee t'espyen?
Though thou praye Argus with his hundred yën
365 To be my wardecors,° as he can best, — bodyguard
In faith, he shal nat keepe° me but me lest:[9] — guard
Yit coude I make his beerd,[1] so mote I thee.° — thrive
  "Thou saidest eek that ther been thinges three,
The whiche thinges troublen al this erthe,
370 And that no wight may endure the ferthe.° — fourth
O leve° sire shrewe, Jesu shorte° thy lif! — dear / shorten
Yit prechestou and saist an hateful wif
Yrekened is for oon of thise meschaunces.
Been ther nat none othere resemblaunces
375 That ye may likne youre parables to,[2]
But if[3] a sely° wif be oon of tho? — innocent
  "Thou liknest eek wommanes love to helle,
To bareine° land ther water may nat dwelle; — barren
Thou liknest it also to wilde fir—
380 The more it brenneth,° the more it hath desir — burns
To consumen every thing that brent° wol be; — burned
Thou saist right° as wormes shende° a tree, — just / destroy
Right so a wif destroyeth hir housbonde—
This knowen they that been to wives bonde."° — bound
385 Lordinges, right thus, as ye han understonde,
Bar I stifly mine olde housbondes on honde[4]
That thus they saiden in hir dronkenesse—
And al was fals, but that I took witnesse
On Janekin and on my nece also.
390 O Lord, the paine I dide hem and the wo,
Ful giltelees, by Goddes sweete pine!° — suffering
For as an hors I coude bite and whine;° — whinny
I coude plaine° and° I was in the gilt, — complain / if
Or elles often time I hadde been spilt.° — ruined
395 Whoso that first to mille comth first grint.° — grinds

---

7. Has dawned.
8. What does it help.
9. Unless I please.
1. I.e., deceive him.
2. Isn't there something else appropriate that you can apply your metaphors to?
3. Unless.
4. I rigorously accused my old husbands.

I plained first: so was oure werre stint.[5]
They were ful glade to excusen hem ful blive°   *quickly*
Of thing of which they nevere agilte hir live.[6]
Of wenches wolde I beren hem on honde,
400 Whan that for sik[7] they mighte unnethe° stonde,   *scarcely*
Yit tikled I his herte for that he
Wende° I hadde had of him so greet cheertee.[8]   *thought*
I swoor that al my walking out by nighte
Was for to espye wenches that he dighte.[9]
405 Under that colour[1] hadde I many a mirthe.
For al swich wit is yiven us in oure birthe:
Deceite, weeping, spinning God hath yive
To wommen kindely° whil they may live.   *naturally*
And thus of oo thing I avaunte me:[2]
410 At ende I hadde the bet° in eech degree,   *better*
By sleighte or force, or by som manere thing,
As by continuel murmur° or grucching;°   *complaint / grumbling*
Namely° abedde hadden they meschaunce: *especially*
Ther wolde I chide and do hem no plesaunce;[3]
415 I wolde no lenger in the bed abide
If that I felte his arm over my side,
Til he hadde maad his raunson° unto me;   *ransom*
Thanne wolde I suffre him do his nicetee.°   *lust*
And therfore every man this tale I telle:
420 Winne whoso may, for al is for to selle;
With empty hand men may no hawkes lure.
For winning° wolde I al his lust endure,   *profit*
And make me a feined appetit—
And yit in bacon[4] hadde I nevere delit.
425 That made me that evere I wolde hem chide;
For though the Pope hadde seten° hem biside,   *sat*
I wolde nought spare hem at hir owene boord.
For by my trouthe, I quitte° hem word for word.   *repaid*
As help me verray God omnipotent,
430 Though I right now sholde make my testament,
I ne owe hem nat a word that it nis quit.
I broughte it so aboute by my wit
That they moste yive it up as for the beste,
Or elles hadde we nevere been in reste;
435 For though he looked as a wood° leoun,   *furious*
Yit sholde he faile of his conclusioun.°   *object*
   Thanne wolde I saye, "Goodelief, taak keep,[5]
How mekely looketh Wilekin, oure sheep!

5. Our war brought to an end.
6. Of a thing in which they never offended in their lives.
7. I.e., sickness.
8. Affection.
9. Had intercourse with.

1. I.e., excuse.
2. Boast.
3. Show them no affection.
4. I.e., old meat.
5. Good friend, take notice.

Com neer my spouse, lat me ba° thy cheeke— — *kiss*
440 Ye sholden be al pacient and meeke,
And han a sweete-spiced[6] conscience,
Sith ye so preche of Jobes pacience;
Suffreth alway, sin ye so wel can preche;
And but ye do, certain, we shal you teche
445 That it is fair to han a wif in pees.
Oon of us two moste bowen, doutelees,
And sith a man is more resonable
Than womman is, ye mosten been suffrable.° — *patient*
What aileth you to grucche° thus and grone? — *grumble*
450 Is it for ye wolde have my queinte° allone? — *pudendum*
Why, taak it al—lo, have it everydeel.° — *altogether*
Peter, I shrewe° you but ye love it weel. — *curse*
For if I wolde selle my bele chose,[7]
I coude walke as fressh as is a rose;
455 But I wol keepe it for youre owene tooth.° — *taste*
Ye be to blame. By God, I saye you sooth!"
Swiche manere° wordes hadde we on honde. — *kind of*
Now wol I speke of my ferthe° housbonde. — *fourth*
     My ferthe housbonde was a revelour—
460 This is to sayn, he hadde a paramour°— — *mistress*
And I was yong and ful of ragerye,° — *wantonness*
Stibourne° and strong and joly as a pie:° — *untamable / magpie*
How coude I daunce to an harpe smale,° — *gracefully*
And singe, ywis,° as any nightingale, — *indeed*
465 Whan I hadde dronke a draughte of sweete win.
Metellius, the foule cherl, the swin,
That with a staf birafte° his wif hir lif — *deprived*
For° she drank win, though I hadde been his wif, — *because*
Ne sholde nat han daunted me fro drinke;
470 And after win on Venus moste° I thinke, — *must*
For also siker° as cold engendreth hail, — *sure*
A likerous° mouth moste han a likerous° tail: — *greedy / lecherous*
In womman vinolent° is no defence— — *bibulous*
This knowen lechours by experience.
475   But Lord Crist, whan that it remembreth me[8]
Upon my youthe and on my jolitee,
It tikleth me aboute myn herte roote—
Unto this day it dooth myn herte boote° — *good*
That I have had my world as in my time.
480 But age, allas, that al wol envenime,° — *poison*
Hath me biraft[9] my beautee and my pith—
Lat go, farewel, the devel go therwith!
The flour is goon, ther is namore to telle:
The bren° as I best can now moste I selle; — *husks*
485 But yit to be right merye wol I fonde.° — *strive*

---

6. I.e., delicate.   8. When I look back.
7. Fair thing.   9. Has taken away from me.

Now wol I tellen of my ferthe housbonde.
    I saye I hadde in herte greet despit
That he of any other hadde delit,
But he was quit,° by God and by Saint Joce: *paid back*
490 I made him of the same wode a croce[1]—
Nat of my body in no foul manere—
But, certainly, I made folk swich cheere
That in his owene grece I made him frye,
For angre and for verray jalousye.
495 By God, in erthe I was his purgatorye,
For which I hope his soule be in glorye.
    For God it woot, he sat ful ofte and soong°   *sang*
Whan that his sho ful bitterly him wroong.°   *pinched*
Ther was no wight save God and he that wiste°   *knew*
500 In many wise how sore I him twiste.
He deide whan I cam fro Jerusalem,
And lith ygrave under the roode-beem,[2]
Al° is his tombe nought so curious[3]   *although*
As was the sepulcre of him Darius,
505 Which that Apelles wroughte subtilly:[4]
It nis but wast to burye him preciously.°   *expensively*
Lat him fare wel, God yive his soule reste;
He is now in his grave and in his cheste.
    Now of my fifthe housbonde wol I telle—
510 God lete his soule nevere come in helle—
And yit he was to me the moste shrewe:[5]
That feele I on my ribbes al by rewe,[6]
And evere shal unto myn ending day.
But in oure bed he was so fressh and gay,
515 And therwithal so wel coulde he me glose°   *wheedle*
Whan that he wolde han my bele chose,
That though he hadde me bet° on every boon,°   *beaten / bone*
He coude winne again my love anoon.°   *immediately*
I trowe I loved him best for that he
520 Was of his love daungerous[7] to me.
We wommen han, if that I shal nat lie,
In this matere a quainte fantasye:
Waite what[8] thing we may nat lightly° have,   *easily*
Therafter wol we crye al day and crave;
525 Forbede us thing, and that desiren we;
Preesse on us faste, and thanne wol we flee.
With daunger oute we al oure chaffare:[9]
Greet prees° at market maketh dere° ware,   *crowd / expensive*

---

1. I made him a cross of the same wood. The proverb has much the same sense as the one quoted in line 493.
2. And lies buried under the rood beam (the crucifix beam running between nave and chancel).
3. Carefully wrought.
4. According to medieval legend, the artist Apelles decorated the tomb of Darius, king of the Persians.
5. Worst rascal.
6. In a row.
7. I.e., he played hard to get.
8. "Waite what": whatever.
9. With coyness, we spread out our merchandise.

And too greet chepe is holden at litel pris.[1]
530 This knoweth every womman that is wis.
　　My fifthe housbonde—God his soule blesse!—
Which that I took for love and no richesse,
He somtime was a clerk at Oxenforde,
And hadde laft° scole and wente at hoom to boorde　　　*left*
535 With my gossib,° dwelling in oure town—　　　*confidante*
God have hir soule!—hir name was Alisoun;
She knew myn herte and eek my privetee°　　　*secrets*
Bet° than oure parissh preest, as mote I thee.°　　　*better / thrive*
To hire biwrayed° I my conseil° al,　　　*disclosed / secrets*
540 For hadde myn housbonde pissed on a wal,
Or doon a thing that sholde han cost his lif,
To hire,° and to another worthy wif,　　　*her*
And to my nece which I loved weel,
I wolde han told his conseil everydeel;°　　　*entirely*
545 And so I dide ful often, God it woot,
That made his face often reed° and hoot°　　　*red / hot*
For verray shame, and blamed himself for he
Hadde told to me so greet a privetee.
　　And so bifel that ones in a Lente—
550 So often times I to my gossib wente,
For evere yit I loved to be gay,
And for to walke in March, Averil, and May,
From hous to hous, to heere sondry tales—
That Janekin clerk and my gossib dame Alis
555 And I myself into the feeldes wente.
Myn housbonde was at London al that Lente:
I hadde the better leiser for to playe,
And for to see, and eek for to be seye°　　　*seen*
Of lusty folk—what wiste I wher my grace°　　　*luck*
560 Was shapen° for to be, or in what place?　　　*destined*
Therfore I made my visitaciouns
To vigilies[2] and to processiouns,
To preching eek, and to thise pilgrimages,
To playes of miracles and to mariages,
565 And wered upon[3] my gaye scarlet gites°—　　　*dress*
Thise wormes ne thise motthes ne thise mites,
Upon my peril, frete° hem neveradeel:　　　*ate*
And woostou why? For they were used weel.
　　Now wol I tellen forth what happed me.
570 I saye that in the feeldes walked we,
Til trewely we hadde swich daliaunce,°　　　*flirtation*
This clerk and I, that of my purveyaunce°　　　*foresight*
I spak to him and saide him how that he,
If I were widwe, sholde wedde me.

---

1. Too good a bargain is held at little　　2. Feasts preceding a saint's day.
value.　　3. Wore.

575 For certainly, I saye for no bobaunce,°   *boast*
     Yit was I nevere withouten purveyaunce
     Of mariage n'of othere thinges eek:
     I holde a mouses herte nought worth a leek
     That hath but oon hole for to sterte° to,   *run*
580 And if that faile thanne is al ydo.[4]
     I bar him on hand[5] he hadde enchaunted me
     (My dame taughte me that subtiltee);
     And eek I saide I mette° of him al night: *dreamed*
     He wolde han slain me as I lay upright,°   *supine*
585 And al my bed was ful of verray blood—
     "But yit I hope that ye shul do me good;
     For blood bitokeneth gold, as me was taught."
     And al was fals, I dremed of it right naught,
     But as I folwed ay my dames° lore°   *mother's / teaching*
590 As wel of that as othere thinges more.
     But now sire—lat me see, what shal I sayn?
     Aha, by God, I have my tale again.
       Whan that my ferthe housbonde was on beere,°   *bier*
     I weep° algate,° and made sory cheere,   *wept / anyhow*
595 As wives moten,° for it is usage,°   *must / custom*
     And with my coverchief covered my visage;
     But for I was purveyed° of a make.°   *provided / mate*
     I wepte but smale, and that I undertake.°   *guarantee*
       To chirche was myn housbonde born amorwe[6]
600 With neighebores that for him maden sorwe,
     And Janekin oure clerk was oon of tho.
     As help me God, whan that I saw him go
     After the beere, me thoughte he hadde a paire
     Of legges and of feet so clene[7] and faire,
605 That al myn herte I yaf unto his hold.°   *possession*
     He was, I trowe,° twenty winter old,   *believe*
     And I was fourty, if I shal saye sooth—
     But yit I hadde alway a coltes tooth:[8]
     Gat-toothed° was I, and that bicam me weel;   *gap-toothed*
610 I hadde the prente[9] of Sainte Venus seel.
     As help me God, I was a lusty oon,
     And fair and riche and yong and wel-bigoon,°   *well-situated*
     And trewely, as mine housbondes tolde me,
     I hadde the beste quoniam° mighte be.   *pudendum*
615 For certes I am al Venerien[1]
     In feeling, and myn herte is Marcien:
     Venus me yaf my lust, my likerousnesse,°   *lecherousness*
     And Mars yaf me my sturdy hardinesse.

---

4. I.e., the game is up.
5. I pretended to him.
6. In the morning.
7. I.e., neat.

8. I.e., youthful appetites.
9. Print, i.e., a birthmark; "seel": seal.
1. Astrologically influenced by Venus; "Marcien": influenced by Mars.

Myn ascendent was Taur[2] and Mars therinne—
620 Allas, allas, that evere love was sinne!
I folwed ay° my inclinacioun   ever
By vertu of my constellacioun;[3]
That made me I coude nought withdrawe
My chambre of Venus from a good felawe.
625 Yit have I Martes° merk upon my face,   Mars'
And also in another privee place.
For God so wis° be my savacioun,°   surely / salvation
I loved nevere by no discrecioun,
But evere folwede myn appetit,
630 Al were he short or long or blak or whit;
I took no keep,° so that he liked° me,   heed / pleased
How poore he was, ne eek of what degree.
    What sholde I saye but at the monthes ende
This joly clerk Janekin that was so hende°   nice
635 Hath wedded me with greet solempnitee,°   splendor
And to him yaf I al the land and fee°   property
That evere was me yiven therbifore—
But afterward repented me ful sore:
He nolde suffre no thing of my list.°   pleasure
640 By God, he smoot° me ones on the list°   struck / ear
For that I rente° out of his book a leef,   tore
That of the strook° myn ere weex° al deef.   blow / grew
Stibourne° I was as is a leonesse,   stubborn
And of my tonge a verray jangleresse,°   blabbermouth
645 And walke I wolde, as I hadde doon biforn,
From hous to hous, although he hadde it[4] sworn;
For which he often times wolde preche,
And me of olde Romain geestes° teche,   stories
How he Simplicius Gallus lafte° his wif,   left
650 And hire forsook for terme of al his lif,
Nought but for open-heveded he hire sey[5]
Looking out at his dore upon a day.
    Another Romain tolde he me by name
That, for his wif was at a someres° game   summer's
655 Withouten his witing,° he forsook hire eke;   knowledge
And thanne wolde he upon his Bible seeke
That ilke proverbe of Ecclesiaste[6]
Where he comandeth and forbedeth faste°   strictly
Man shal nat suffre his wif go roule° aboute;   roam
660 Thanne wolde he saye right thus withouten doute:
"Whoso that buildeth his hous al of salwes,°   willow sticks
And priketh° his blinde hors over the falwes,[7]   rides

---

2. My birth sign was the constellation
Taurus.
3. I.e., horoscope.
4. I.e., the contrary.

5. Just because he saw her bareheaded.
6. Ecclesiasticus (xxv.25).
7. Plowed land.

And suffreth his wif to go seeken halwes,°   *shrines*
Is worthy to be hanged on the galwes."°   *gallows*
665 But al for nought—I sette nought an hawe[8]
Of his proverbes n'of his olde sawe;
N'I wolde nat of him corrected be:
I hate him that my vices telleth me,
And so doon mo, God woot, of us than I.
670 This made him with me wood al outrely:[9]
I nolde nought forbere° him in no cas.   *submit to*
   Now wol I saye you sooth, by Saint Thomas,
Why that I rente° out of his book a leef,   *tore*
For which he smoot me so that I was deef.
675 He hadde a book that gladly night and day
For his disport he wolde rede alway.
He cleped it *Valerie*[1] *and Theofraste*,
At which book he lough° alway ful faste,   *laughed*
And eek ther was somtime a clerk at Rome,
680 A cardinal, that highte Saint Jerome,
That made a book[2] again Jovinian;
In which book eek ther was Tertulan,[3]
Crysippus, Trotula, and Helouis,
That was abbesse nat fer fro Paris;
685 And eek the Parables of Salomon,[4]
Ovides *Art*, and bookes many oon—
And alle thise were bounden in oo volume.
And every night and day was his custume,
Whan he hadde leiser and vacacioun
690 From other worldly occupacioun
To reden in this book of wikked wives.
He knew of hem mo legendes and lives
Than been of goode wives in the Bible.
For trusteth wel, it is an impossible°   *impossibility*
695 That any clerk wol speke good of wives,
But if it be of holy saintes lives,
N'of noon other womman nevere the mo—
Who painted the leon, tel me who?[5]
By God, if wommen hadden writen stories,
700 As clerkes han within hir oratories,

8. I did not rate at the value of a haw-thorn berry.
9. Entirely.
1. I.e., the *Letter of Valerius Concern-ing Not Marrying*, by Walter Map; "*Theofraste*": Theophrastus' *Book Concerning Marriage*. Medieval manu-scripts often contained a number of different works, sometimes, as here, dealing with the same subject.
2. St. Jerome's antifeminist *Reply to Jovinian*; "again": against.
3. Tertullian, author of treatises on sexual modesty. Crysippus (or Chrysip-pus), in the next line, is mentioned by Jerome as an antifeminist; Trotula was a female doctor whose presence here is unexplained; "Helouis" is Eloise, whose love affair with the great scholar Abe-lard was a medieval scandal.
4. The Biblical Book of Proverbs; "Ovides *Art*": Ovid's *Art of Love*.
5. In one of Aesop's fables, the lion, shown a picture of a man killing a lion, asked who painted the picture. Had a lion been the artist, of course, the roles would have been reversed.

They wolde han writen of men more wikkednesse
Than al the merk⁶ of Adam may redresse.
The children of Mercurye and Venus⁷
Been in hir werking° ful contrarious:°   *operation / opposed*
705 Mercurye loveth wisdom and science,
And Venus loveth riot° and dispence;°   *parties / expenditures*
And for hir diverse disposicioun
Each falleth in otheres exaltacioun,⁸
And thus, God woot, Mercurye is desolat
710 In Pisces wher Venus is exaltat,⁹
And Venus falleth ther Mercurye is raised:
Therfore no womman of no clerk is praised.
The clerk, whan he is old and may nought do
Of Venus werkes worth his olde sho,°   *shoe*
715 Thanne sit° he down and writ° in his dotage   *sits / writes*
That wommen can nat keepe hir mariage.
    But now to purpose why I tolde thee
That I was beten for a book, pardee:
Upon a night Janekin, that was oure sire,¹
720 Redde on his book as he sat by the fire
Of Eva first, that for hir wikkednesse
Was al mankinde brought to wrecchednesse,
For which that Jesu Crist himself was slain
That boughte° us with his herte blood again—   *redeemed*
725 Lo, heer expres of wommen may ye finde
That womman was the los° of al mankinde.²   *ruin*
    Tho° redde he me how Sampson loste his heres: *then*
Sleeping his lemman° kitte° it with hir sheres,   *mistress / cut*
Thurgh which treson loste he bothe his yën.
730 Tho redde he me, if that I shal nat lien,
Of Ercules and of his Dianire,³
That caused him to sette himself afire.
    No thing forgat he the sorwe and wo
That Socrates hadde with his wives two—
735 How Xantippa caste pisse upon his heed:
This sely° man sat stille as he were deed;   *silly*
He wiped his heed, namore dorste he sayn
But "Er that thonder stinte,° comth a rain."   *stops*
    Of Pasipha⁴ that was the queene of Crete—
740 For shrewednesse° him thoughte the tale sweete—   *malice*

6. Mark, sex.
7. I.e., clerks and women, astrologically ruled by Mercury and Venus respectively.
8. Because of their contrary positions (as planets), each one descends (in the belt of the zodiac) as the other rises; hence one loses its power as the other becomes dominant.
9. I.e., Mercury is deprived of power in Pisces (the sign of the Fish), where Venus is most powerful.
1. My husband.
2. The stories of wicked women Chaucer drew mainly from St. Jerome and Walter Map.
3. Dejanira unwittingly gave Hercules a poisoned shirt, which hurt him so much that he committed suicide by fire.
4. Pasiphaë, who fell in love with a bull.

Fy, speek namore, it is a grisly thing
Of hir horrible lust and hir liking.°   *pleasure*
    Of Clytermistra[5] for hir lecherye
That falsly made hir housbonde for to die,
745 He redde it with ful good devocioun.
    He tolde me eek for what occasioun
Amphiorax[6] at Thebes loste his lif:
Myn housbonde hadde a legende of his wif
Eriphylem, that for an ouche° of gold   *trinket*
750 Hath prively unto the Greckes told
Wher that hir housbonde hidde him in a place,
For which he hadde at Thebes sory grace.
Of Livia[7] tolde he me and of Lucie:
They bothe made hir housbondes for to die,
755 That oon for love, that other was for hate;
Livia hir housbonde on an even late
Empoisoned hath for that she was his fo;
Lucia likerous° loved hir housbonde so   *lecherous*
That for° he sholde alway upon hire thinke,   *in order that*
760 She yaf him swich a manere love-drinke
That he was deed er it were by the morwe.[8]
And thus algates° housbondes han sorwe.   *constantly*
    Thanne tolde he me how oon Latumius
Complained unto his felawe Arrius
765 That in his gardin growed swich a tree,
On which he saide how that his wives three
Hanged hemself for herte despitous.[9]
    "O leve° brother," quod this Arrius,   *dear*
"Yif me a plante of thilke blessed tree,
770 And in my gardin planted shal it be."
    Of latter date of wives hath he red
That some han slain hir housbondes in hir bed
And lete hir lechour dighte[1] hire al the night,
Whan that the cors° lay in the floor upright;°   *corpse / supine*
775 And some han driven nailes in hir brain
Whil that they sleepe, and thus they han hem slain;
Some han hem yiven poison in hir drinke.
He spak more harm than herte may bithinke,°   *imagine*
And therwithal he knew of mo proverbes
780 Than in this world ther growen gras or herbes:
"Bet is," quod he, "thyn habitacioun
Be with a leon or a foul dragoun

---

5. Clytemnestra, who, with her lover
Aegisthus, slew her husband Agamemnon.
6. Amphiaraus, betrayed by his wife
Eriphyle and forced to go to the war
against Thebes.
7. Livia murdered her husband in behalf of her lover Sejanus. "Lucie": Lucilla, who was said to have poisoned
her husband, the poet Lucretius, with a
potion designed to keep him faithful.
8. He was dead before it was near
morning.
9. For malice of heart.
1. Have intercourse with.

Than with a womman using° for to chide." *accustomed*
"Bet is," quod he, "hye in the roof abide
785 Than with an angry wif down in the hous:
They been so wikked° and contrarious, *perverse*
They haten that hir housbondes loveth ay."
He saide, "A womman cast° hir shame away *casts*
Whan she cast of° hir smok,"[2] and ferthermo, *off*
790 "A fair womman, but she be chast also,
Is like a gold ring in a sowes nose."
Who wolde weene,° or who wolde suppose *think*
The wo that in myn herte was and pine?° *suffering*
And whan I sawgh he wolde nevere fine° *end*
795 To reden on this cursed book al night,
Al sodeinly three leves have I plight° *snatched*
Out of his book right as he redde, and eke
I with my fist so took[3] him on the cheeke
That in oure fir he fil° bakward adown. *fell*
800 And up he sterte as dooth a wood° leoun, *raging*
And with his fist he smoot me on the heed° *head*
That in the floor I lay as I were deed.
And whan he sawgh how stille that I lay,
He was agast, and wolde have fled his way,
805 Til atte laste out of my swough° I braide:° *swoon / started*
"O hastou slain me, false thief?" I saide,
"And for my land thus hastou mordred° me? *murdered*
Er I be deed° yit wol I kisse thee." *dead*
And neer he cam and kneeled faire adown,
810 And saide, "Dere suster Alisoun,
As help me God, I shal thee nevere smite.
That I have doon, it is thyself to wite.° *blame*
Foryif it me, and that I thee biseeke."
And yit eftsoones° I hitte him on the cheeke, *again*
815 And saide, "Thief, thus muchel am I wreke.° *avenged*
Now wol I die: I may no lenger speke."
But at the laste with muchel care and wo
We fille[4] accorded by us selven two.
He yaf me al the bridel° in myn hand, *bridle*
820 To han the governance of hous and land,
And of his tonge and his hand also;
And made[5] him brenne° his book anoonright tho. *burn*
And whan that I hadde geten unto me
By maistrye° al the sovereinetee,° *skill / dominion*
825 And that he saide, "Myn owene trewe wif,
Do as thee lust° the terme of al thy lif; *it pleases*
Keep thyn honour, and keep eek myn estat,"
After that day we hadde nevere debat.

---

2. Undergarment.   4. I.e., became.
3. I.e., hit.   5. I.e., I made.

God help me so, I was to him as kinde
830 As any wif from Denmark unto Inde,
And also trewe, and so was he to me.
I praye to God that sit° in majestee,   *sits*
So blesse his soule for his mercy dere.
Now wol I saye my tale if ye wol heere.

[ANOTHER INTERRUPTION]

835   The Frere lough° whan he hadde herd al this: *laughed*
"Now dame," quod he, "so have I joye or blis,
This is a long preamble of a tale."
And whan the Somnour herde the Frere gale,°   *exclaim*
"Lo," quod the Somnour, "Goddes armes two,
840 A frere wol entremette him[6] everemo!
Lo, goode men, a flye and eek a frere
Wol falle in every dissh and eek matere.
What spekestou of preambulacioun?
What, amble or trotte or pisse or go sitte down!
845 Thou lettest° oure disport in this manere."   *hinder*
    "Ye, woltou so, sire Somnour?" quod the Frere.
"Now by my faith, I shal er that I go
Telle of a somnour swich a tale or two
That al the folk shal laughen in this place."
850   "Now elles, Frere, I wol bishrewe° thy face,"   *curse*
Quod this Somnour, "and I bishrewe me,
But if I telle tales two or three
Of freres, er I come to Sidingborne,[7]
That I shal make thyn herte for to moorne—
855 For wel I woot thy pacience is goon."
    Oure Hoste cride, "Pees, and that anoon!"
And saide, "Lat the womman telle hir tale:
Ye fare as folk that dronken been of ale.
Do, dame, tel forth youre tale, and that is best."
860   "Al redy, sire," quod she, "right as you lest°—   *it pleases*
If I have licence of this worthy Frere."
"Yis, dame," quod he, "tel forth and I wol heere."

6. Intrude himself.
7. Sittingbourne (a town forty miles from London).

The Tale[1]

In th'olde dayes of the King Arthour,
Of which that Britouns° speken greet honour,   *Bretons*
865 Al was this land fulfild of faïrye:[2]
The elf-queene with hir joly compaignye
Daunced ful ofte in many a greene mede°—   *meadow*
This was the olde opinion as I rede;
I speke of many hundred yeres ago.
870 But now can no man see none elves mo,
For now the grete charitee and prayeres
Of limitours,[3] and othere holy freres,
That serchen every land and every streem,
As thikke as motes in the sonne-beem,
875 Blessing halles, chambres, kichenes, bowres,
Citees, burghes,° castels, hye towres,   *townships*
Thropes, bernes, shipnes,[4] dayeries—
This maketh that ther been no faïries.
For ther as wont to walken was an elf
880 Ther walketh now the limitour himself,
In undermeles° and in morweninges,°   *afternoons / mornings*
And saith his Matins and his holy thinges,
As he gooth in his limitacioun.[5]
Wommen may go saufly° up and down: *safely*
885 In every bussh or under every tree
Ther is noon other incubus[6] but he,
And he ne wol doon hem but dishonour.

And so bifel it that this King Arthour
Hadde in his hous a lusty bacheler,
890 That on a day cam riding fro river,[7]
And happed° that, allone as he was born,   *it happened*

1. The story of the knight who fully realizes what women most desire only after having been told it in a number of ways was popular in Chaucer's time and a natural one for him to assign to the Wife of Bath, whose well-loved fifth husband had also been slow to learn. But Chaucer reshaped the tale in such a way as to make it fit the Wife and her thesis even more closely. In the other medieval versions of the story the knight is guiltless of any offense to womanhood, and in several of them he is Sir Gawain, traditional model of chivalric courtesy, who weds the hideous hag to save not his own life but that of his lord, King Arthur. Chaucer has made the knight a most ill-behaved and ill-mannered man who needs to learn what women most desire as much in order to redeem his disagreeably virile character as to save his neck. Because within her story he is the sole male in a world of women, Dame Alice is able not only to prove conclusively the value of woman's sovereignty, but also to pay her respects to a world of men that had preached antifeminism, a world here represented by a single rapist.

The story is suited to the Wife's own character psychologically as well as dramatically, for she, like the old hag, had wedded a young man—though unlike the hag she could not restore her former beauty. But if there is a touch of melancholy in the incompleteness of this similarity, it is sharply dispelled by the Wife's final comments, which reassert the sturdy fighting spirit that permeates her Prologue.
2. I.e., filled full of supernatural creatures.
3. Friars licenced to beg in a certain territory.
4. Thorps (villages), barns, stables.
5. I.e., the friar's assigned area. His "holy thinges" are prayers.
6. A spirit that lies with mortal women. "Ne * * * but" in the next line means "only."
7. Hawking, usually carried out on the banks of a stream.

He sawgh a maide walking him biforn;
Of which maide anoon, maugree hir heed,[8]
By verray force he rafte° hir maidenheed;   *deprived her of*
895 For which oppression° was swich clamour,   *rape*
And swich pursuite° unto the King Arthour,   *petitioning*
That dampned was this knight for to be deed[9]
By cours of lawe, and sholde han lost his heed—
Paraventure° swich was the statut tho—   *perhaps*
900 But that the queene and othere ladies mo
So longe prayeden the king of grace,
Til he his lif him graunted in the place,
And yaf him to the queene, al at hir wille,
To chese° wheither she wolde him save or spille.[1]   *choose*
905 The queene thanked the king with al hir might,
And after this thus spak she to the knight,
Whan that she saw hir time upon a day:
"Thou standest yit," quod she, "in swich array°   *condition*
That of thy lif yit hastou no suretee.°   *guarantee*
910 I graunte thee lif if thou canst tellen me
What thing it is that wommen most desiren:
Be war and keep thy nekke boon° from iren.   *bone*
And if thou canst nat tellen me anoon,
Yit wol I yive thee leve for to goon
915 A twelfmonth and a day to seeche° and lere°   *search / learn*
An answere suffisant° in this matere,   *satisfactory*
And suretee wol I han er that thou pace,°   *pass*
Thy body for to yeelden in this place."
    Wo was this knight, and sorwefully he siketh.°   *sighs*
920 But what, he may nat doon al as him liketh,
And atte laste he chees° him for to wende,   *chose*
And come again right at the yeres ende,
With swich answere as God wolde him purveye,°   *provide*
And taketh his leve and wendeth forth his waye.
925 He seeketh every hous and every place
Wher as he hopeth for to finde grace,
To lerne what thing wommen love most.
But he ne coude arriven in no coost[2]
Wher as he mighte finde in this matere
930 Two creatures according in fere.[3]
    Some saiden wommen loven best richesse;
Some saide honour, some saide jolinesse;°   *wantonness*
Some riche array, some saiden lust° abedde,   *pleasure*
And ofte time to be widwe and wedde.
935 Some saide that oure herte is most esed
Whan that we been yflatered and yplesed—
He gooth ful neigh the soothe, I wol nat lie:
A man shal winne us best with flaterye,

8. Despite her head, i.e., despite any-   1. Put to death.
thing she could do.   2. I.e., country.
9. This knight was condemned to death.   3. Agreeing together.

And with attendance and with bisinesse°   *assiduousness*
940 Been we ylimed,° bothe more and lesse.   *ensnared*
    And some sayen that we loven best
For to be free, and do right as us lest,°   *it pleases*
And that no man repreve° us of oure vice,   *reprove*
But saye that we be wise and no thing nice.°   *foolish*
945 For trewely, ther is noon of us alle,
If any wight wol clawe us on the galle,°   *sore spot*
That we nil kike° for° he saith us sooth: *kick / because*
Assaye and he shal finde it that so dooth.
For be we nevere so vicious withinne,
950 We wol be holden° wise and clene of sinne.   *considered*
    And some sayn that greet delit han we
For to be holden stable and eek secree,[4]
And in oo purpos stedefastly to dwelle,
And nat biwraye° thing that men us telle—   *disclose*
955 But that tale is nat worth a rake-stele.°   *rake handle*
Pardee, we wommen conne no thing hele:°   *conceal*
Witnesse on Mida.° Wol ye heere the tale?   *Midas*
    Ovide, amonges othere thinges smale,
Saide Mida hadde under his longe heres,
960 Growing upon his heed, two asses eres,
The whiche vice° he hidde as he best mighte   *defect*
Ful subtily from every mannes sighte,
That save his wif ther wiste° of it namo.   *knew*
He loved hire most and trusted hire also.
965 He prayed hire that to no creature
She sholde tellen of his disfigure.°   *deformity*
    She swoor him nay, for al this world to winne,
She nolde do that vilainye or sinne
To make hir housbonde han so foul a name:
970 She nolde nat telle it for hir owene shame.
But nathelees, hir thoughte that she dyde°   *would die*
That she so longe sholde a conseil° hide;   *secret*
Hire thoughte it swal° so sore aboute hir herte   *swelled*
That nedely som word hire moste asterte,[5]
975 And sith she dorste nat telle it to no man,
Down to a mareis° faste° by she ran—   *marsh / close*
Til she cam there hir herte was afire—
And as a bitore[6] bombleth in the mire,
She laide hir mouth unto the water down:
980 "Biwray° me nat, thou water, with thy soun,"°   *betray / sound*
Quod she. "To thee I telle it and namo:°   *to no one else*
Myn housbonde hath longe asses eres two.
Now is myn herte al hool,[7] now is it oute.
I mighte no lenger keepe it, out of doute."
985 Here may ye see, though we a time abide,

---

4. Reliable and also close-mouthed.
5. Of necessity some word must escape her.
6. Bittern, a heron. "Bombleth": makes a booming noise.
7. I.e., sound.

Yit oute it moot:° we can no conseil hide.   *must*
The remenant of the tale if ye wol heere,
Redeth Ovide, and ther ye may it lere.[8]
    This knight of which my tale is specially,
990 Whan that he sawgh he mighte nat come therby—
This is to saye what wommen loven most—
Within his brest ful sorweful was his gost,°   *spirit*
But hoom he gooth, he mighte nat sojurne:°   *delay*
The day was come that hoomward moste° he turne.   *must*
995 And in his way it happed him to ride
In al this care under a forest side,
Wher as he sawgh upon a daunce go
Of ladies foure and twenty and yit mo;
Toward the whiche daunce he drow ful yerne,[9]
1000 In hope that som wisdom sholde he lerne.
But certainly, er he cam fully there,
Vanisshed was this daunce, he niste° where.   *knew not*
No creature sawgh he that bar° lif,   *bore*
Save on the greene he sawgh sitting a wif—
1005 A fouler wight ther may no man devise.°   *imagine*
Again[1] the knight this olde wif gan rise,
And saide, "Sire knight, heer forth lith° no way.°   *lies / road*
Telle me what ye seeken, by youre fay.°   *faith*
Paraventure it may the better be:
1010 Thise olde folk conne° muchel thing," quod she.   *know*
    "My leve moder,"° quod this knight, "certain,   *mother*
I nam but deed but if that I can sayn
What thing it is that wommen most desire.
Coude ye me wisse,° I wolde wel quite youre hire."[2]   *teach*
1015 "Plight me thy trouthe here in myn hand," quod she.
"The nexte thing that I requere° thee,   *require of*
Thou shalt it do, if it lie in thy might,
And I wol telle it you er it be night."
    "Have heer my trouthe," quod the knight. "I graunte."
1020 "Thanne," quod she, "I dar me wel avaunte°   *boast*
Thy lif is sauf,° for I wol stande therby.   *safe*
Upon my lif the queene wol saye as I.
Lat see which is the pruddeste° of hem alle   *proudest*
That wereth on[3] a coverchief or a calle°   *headdress*
1025 That dar saye nay of that I shal thee teche.
Lat us go forth withouten lenger speeche."
Tho rouned° she a pistel° in his ere,   *whispered / sentence*
And bad him to be glad and have no fere.
    Whan they be comen to the court, this knight
1030 Saide he hadde holde his day as he hadde hight,°   *promised*
And redy was his answere, as he saide.
Ful many a noble wif, and many a maide,

---

8. Learn. The reeds disclosed the secret
by whispering *"aures asinelli"* (asses'
ears).
9. Drew very quickly.

1. I.e., to meet.
2. Repay your trouble.
3. That wears.

And many a widwe—for that they been wise—
The queene hirself sitting as justise,
1035 Assembled been this answere for to heere,
And afterward this knight was bode° appere.   *bidden to*
To every wight comanded was silence,
And that the knight sholde telle in audience°   *pen hearing*
What thing that worldly wommen loven best.
1040 This knight ne stood nat stille as dooth a best,°   *beast*
But to his question anoon answerde
With manly vois that al the court it herde.
    "My lige° lady, generally," quod he,   *liege*
"Wommen desire to have sovereinetee°   *dominion*
1045 As wel over hir housbonde as hir love,
And for to been in maistrye him above.
This is youre moste desir though ye me kille.
Dooth as you list:° I am here at youre wille."   *please*
In al the court ne was ther wif ne maide
1050 Ne widwe that contraried° that he saide,   *contradicted*
But saiden he was worthy han° his lif.   *to have*
    And with that word up sterte° that olde wif,   *started*
Which that the knight sawgh sitting on the greene;
"Mercy," quod she, "my soverein lady queene,
1055 Er that youre court departe, do me right.
I taughte this answere unto the knight,
For which he plighte me his trouthe there
The firste thing I wolde him requere°   *require*
He wolde it do, if it laye in his might.
1060 Bifore the court thanne praye I thee, sire knight,"
Quod she, "that thou me take unto thy wif,
For wel thou woost that I have kept° thy lif.   *saved*
If I saye fals, say nay, upon thy fay."
    This knight answerde, "Allas and wailaway,
1065 I woot right wel that swich was my biheeste.°   *promise*
For Goddes love, as chees° a newe requeste: *choose*
Taak al my good and lat my body go."
    "Nay thanne," quod she, "I shrewe° us bothe two.   *curse*
For though that I be foul and old and poore,
1070 I nolde for al the metal ne for ore
That under erthe is grave° or lith° above,   *buried / lies*
But if thy wif I were and eek thy love."
    "My love," quod he. "Nay, my dampnacioun!°   *damnation*
Allas, that any of my nacioun⁴
1075 Sholde evere so foule disparaged° be."   *disgraced*
But al for nought, th'ende is this, that he
Constrained was: he needes moste hire wedde,
And taketh his olde wif and gooth to bedde.
    Now wolden some men saye, paraventure,
1080 That for my necligence I do no cure⁵
To tellen you the joy and al th'array

4. I.e., family.   5. I do not take the trouble.

That at the feeste was that ilke day.
To which thing shortly answere I shal:
I saye ther nas no joye ne feeste at al;
1085 Ther nas but hevinesse and muche sorwe.
For prively he wedded hire on morwe,[6]
And al day after hidde him as an owle,
So wo was him, his wif looked so foule.
    Greet was the wo the knight hadde in his thought:
1090 Whan he was with his wif abedde brought,
He walweth° and he turneth to and fro.   *tosses*
His olde wif lay smiling everemo,
And saide, "O dere housbonde, benedicite,°   *bless me*
Fareth° every knight thus with his wif as ye?   *behaves*
1095 Is this the lawe of King Arthures hous?
Is every knight of his thus daungerous?°   *stand-offish*
I am youre owene love and youre wif;
I am she which that saved hath youre lif;
And certes yit ne dide I you nevere unright.
1100 Why fare ye thus with me this firste night?
Ye faren like a man hadde lost his wit.
What is my gilt? For Goddes love, telle it,
And it shal been amended if I may."
    "Amended!" quod this knight. "Allas, nay, nay,
1105 It wol nat been amended neveremo.
Thou art so lothly° and so old also,   *loathsome*
And therto comen of so lowe a kinde,°   *race*
That litel wonder is though I walwe and winde.° *turn*
So wolde God myn herte wolde breste!"°   *break*
1110   "Is this," quod she, "the cause of youre unreste?"
"Ye, certainly," quod he. "No wonder is."
    "Now sire," quod she, "I coude amende al this,
If that me liste, er it were dayes three,
So° wel ye mighte bere you[7] unto me.   *provided that*
1115   "But for ye speken of swich gentilesse
As is descended out of old richesse—
That therfore sholden ye be gentilmen—
Swich arrogance is nat worth an hen.
Looke who that is most vertuous alway,
1120 Privee and apert,[8] and most entendeth ay
To do the gentil deedes that he can,
Taak him for the gretteste° gentilman.   *greatest*
Crist wol° we claime of him oure gentilesse,   *desires that*
Nat of oure eldres for hir 'old richesse.'[9]
1125 For though they yive us al hir heritage,
For which we claime to been of heigh parage,°   *descent*
Yit may they nat biquethe for no thing
To noon of us hir vertuous living,
That made hem gentilmen ycalled be,

6. In the morning.   8. Privately and publicly.
7. Behave.   9. See Chaucer's *Gentilesse,* line 16.

1130 And bad[1] us folwen hem in swich degree.
    "Wel can the wise poete of Florence,
That highte Dant,[2] speken in this sentence;°   *topic*
Lo, in swich manere rym is Dantes tale:
'Ful selde° up riseth by his braunches[3] smale   *seldom*
1135 Prowesse° of man, for God of his prowesse   *excellence*
Wol that of him we claime oure gentilesse.'
For of oure eldres may we no thing claime
But temporel thing that man may hurte and maime.
Eek every wight woot this as wel as I,
1140 If gentilesse were planted natureelly
Unto a certain linage down the line,
Privee and apert, thanne wolde they nevere fine°   *cease*
To doon of gentilesse the faire office°—   *function*
They mighte do no vilainye or vice.
1145   "Taak fir and beer° it in the derkeste hous   *bear*
Bitwixe this and the Mount of Caucasus,
And lat men shette° the dores and go thenne,°   *shut / thence*
Yit wol the fir as faire lie[4] and brenne°   *burn*
As twenty thousand men mighte it biholde:
1150 His° office natureel ay wol it holde,   *its*
Up° peril of my lif, til that it die.   *upon*
Heer may ye see wel how that genterye°   *gentility*
Is nat annexed° to possessioun,[5]   *related*
Sith folk ne doon hir operacioun
1155 Alway, as dooth the fir, lo, in his kinde.°   *nature*
For God it woot, men may wel often finde
A lordes sone do shame and vilainye;
And he that wol han pris of his gentrye,[6]
For he was boren° of a gentil hous,   *born*
1160 And hadde his eldres noble and vertuous,
And nil himselven do no gentil deedes,
Ne folwen his gentil auncestre that deed° is,   *dead*
He nis nat gentil, be he duc or erl—
For vilaines sinful deedes maken a cherl.
1165 Thy gentilesse[7] nis but renomee°   *renown*
Of thine auncestres for hir heigh bountee,°   *magnanimity*
Which is a straunge° thing for thy persone.   *alien*
For gentilesse[8] cometh fro God allone.
Thanne comth oure verray gentilesse of grace:
1170 It was no thing biquethe us with oure place.
Thenketh how noble, as saith Valerius,[9]
Was thilke Tullius Hostilius
That out of poverte° roos to heigh noblesse.   *poverty*
Redeth Senek,° and redeth eek Boece:°   *Seneca / Boethius*
1175 Ther shul ye seen expres that no drede° is   *doubt*

---

1. I.e., they bade.
2. Dante; see his *Convivio*.
3. I.e., by its own efforts.
4. I.e., remain.
5. I.e., inheritable property.
6. Have credit for his noble birth.
7. I.e., the gentility you claim.
8. I.e., true gentility.
9. A Roman historian.

That he is gentil that dooth gentil deedes.
And therfore, leve housbonde, I thus conclude:
Al were it that mine auncestres weren rude,[1]
Yit may the hye God—and so hope I—
1180 Graunte me grace to liven vertuously.
Thanne am I gentil whan that I biginne
To liven vertuously and waive° sinne.   *avoid*
    "And ther as ye of poverte me repreve,°   *reprove*
The hye God, on whom that we bileve,
1185 In wilful° poverte chees° to live his lif;   *voluntary / chose*
And certes every man, maiden, or wif
May understonde that Jesus, hevene king,
Ne wolde nat chese° a vicious living.   *choose*
Glad poverte is an honeste° thing, certain;   *honorable*
1190 This wol Senek and othere clerkes sayn.
Whoso that halt him paid of[2] his poverte,
I holde him riche al hadde he nat a sherte.°   *shirt*
He that coveiteth[3] is a poore wight,
For he wolde han that is nat in his might;
1195 But he that nought hath, ne coveiteth° have,   *desires to*
Is riche, although we holde him but a knave.
Verray poverte it singeth proprely.°   *appropriately*
Juvenal saith of poverte, 'Merily
The poore man, whan he gooth by the waye,
1200 Biforn the theves he may singe and playe.'
Poverte is hateful good, and as I gesse,
A ful greet bringere out of bisinesse;[4]
A greet amendere eek of sapience
To him that taketh it in pacience;
1205 Poverte is thing, although it seeme elenge,°   *wretched*
Possession that no wight wol chalenge;[5]
Poverte ful often, whan a man is lowe,
Maketh[6] his God and eek himself to knowe;
Poverte a spectacle° is, as thinketh me,   *pair of spectacles*
1210 Thurgh which he may his verray freendes see.
And therfore, sire, sin that I nought you greve,
Of my poverte namore ye me repreve.°   *reproach*
    "Now sire, of elde° ye repreve me: *old age*
And certes sire, though noon auctoritee
1215 Were in no book, ye gentils of honour
Sayn that men sholde an old wight doon favour,
And clepe him fader for youre gentilesse—
And auctours[7] shal I finden, as I gesse.
    "Now ther ye saye that I am foul and old:
1220 Thanne drede you nought to been a cokewold,°   *cuckold*
For filthe and elde, also mote I thee,[8]
Been grete wardeins° upon chastitee.   *guardians*

1. I.e., low born.
2. Considers himself satisfied with.
3. I.e., suffers desires.
4. I.e., cares.
5. Claim as his property.
6. I.e., makes him.
7. I.e., authorities.
8. So may I thrive.

But nathelees, sin I knowe your delit,
I shal fulfille youre worldly appetit.
1225 "Chees now," quod she, "oon of thise thinges twaye:
To han me foul and old til that I deye
And be to you a trewe humble wif,
And nevere you displese in al my lif,
Or elles ye wol han me yong and fair,
1230 And take youre aventure° of the repair⁹   chance
That shal be to youre hous by cause of me—
Or in som other place, wel may be.
Now chees youreselven wheither° that you liketh."   whichever
This knight aviseth him¹ and sore siketh;°   sighs
1235 But atte laste he saide in this manere:
"My lady and my love, and wif so dere,
I putte me in youre wise governaunce:
Cheseth° yourself which may be most plesaunce²   choose
And most honour to you and me also.
1240 I do no fors the wheither³ of the two,
For as you liketh it suffiseth° me."   satisfies
"Thanne have I gete° of you maistrye," quod she,   got
"Sin I may chese and governe as me lest?"°   it pleases
"Ye, certes, wif," quod he. "I holde it best."
1245 "Kisse me," quod she. "We be no lenger wrothe.
For by my trouthe, I wol be to you bothe—
This is to sayn, ye, bothe fair and good.
I praye to God that I mote sterven wood,⁴
But° I to you be al so good and trewe   unless
1250 As evere was wif sin that the world was newe.
And but I be tomorn° as fair to seene   tomorrow morning
As any lady, emperisse, or queene,
That is bitwixe the eest and eek the west,
Do with my lif and deeth right as you lest:
1255 Caste up the curtin, looke how that it is."
    And whan the knight sawgh verraily al this,
That she so fair was and so yong therto,
For joye he hente° hire in his armes two;   took
His herte bathed in a bath of blisse;
1260 A thousand time arewe° he gan hire kisse,   in a row
And she obeyed him in every thing
That mighte do him plesance or liking.°   pleasure
And thus they live unto hir lives ende
In parfit° joye. And Jesu Crist us sende   perfect
1265 Housbondes meeke, yonge, and fresshe abedde—
And grace t'overbide° hem that we wedde.   outlive
And eek I praye Jesu shorte° hir lives   shorten
That nought wol be governed by hir wives,
And olde and angry nigardes of dispence°—   expenditure
1270 God sende hem soone a verray° pestilence!   veritable

9. I.e., visits.   3. I do not care whichever.
1. Considers.   4. Die mad.
2. Pleasure.

The Pardoner's Prologue and Tale[1]
The Introduction

Oure Hoste gan to swere as he were wood;°   *insane*
"Harrow,"° quod he, "by nailes[2] and by blood,   *help*

1. The Pardoner is the chief actor in a grim comedy which shows how a clever hypocrite exploits Christian principles in order to enrich himself—and which, in the Epilogue, suggests that the exploiter of Christian principles is not immune to their operation. The medieval pardoner's function was to collect money for charitable enterprises supported by branches of the church and to act as the Pope's agent in rewarding donors with some temporal remission of their sins. According to theological doctrine, St. Peter—and through him his papal successors—received from Christ the papal power to make a gift of mercy from God's infinite treasury to those of the faithful that had earned special favor, such as contributors to charity. The charitable enterprises themselves—generally hospitals—hired pardoners to raise money, but the pardoners had also to be licensed by the Pope to pass on to contributors the papal indulgence. By canon law pardoners were permitted to work only in a prescribed area; within that area they might visit churches during Sunday service, briefly explain their mission, receive contributions, and, in the Pope's name, issue indulgence, which was considered not a sale, but a free gift made in return for a free gift. In actual fact pardoners seem seldom to have behaved as the law required them. Since a parish priest was forbidden to exclude properly licensed pardoners, they made their way into churches at will, and once there did not confine themselves to a mere statement of their business, but rather, in order to make the congregation free of its gifts, preached highly emotive sermons and boasted of the extraordinary efficacy of their own particular pardon, claiming for it powers that not even the Pope could have invested it with. An honest pardoner, if such existed, was entitled to a percentage of his collections; dishonest pardoners took more than their share, and some took everything; indeed, some were complete frauds, bearing forged credentials which, in an age when even clerical illiteracy was common, were no less impressive than if they had been real.

While Chaucer's Pardoner belongs, as he boastfully tells us, to the most dishonest class of fund-gatherers, he is an extremely able one. His text is always the same: *Radix malorum est cupiditas*, "The love of money is the root of all evil," and he uses it most effectively in order to frighten his hearers into a generosity that will fulfill his own cupidity. The Pardoner's audacious description of his behavior in a parish church is followed by a sample sermon on his invariable text. Aware that his audience is more interested in narrative than in the moralization one expects of a sermon he first introduces the three dissolute young men of his *exemplum*, that is, of the story which is to illustrate concretely the sermon's point. Having titillated his hearers with the promise of a lurid story, he proceeds to the moralization; curiously enough, this does not concern the sin of avarice, but drunkenness, gluttony, lechery, gambling, and cursing. Yet the apparent lack of logic serves the Pardoner's deeper purpose, for these are the sins people find it exciting to hear about. When his audience has thus been emotionally prepared by a discussion of the debauchees' more flamboyant sins, the Pardoner tells his *exemplum* of the destructiveness of avarice, shutting it off at the moment of highest interest, and concluding with a demand to the congregation for money in return for his pardon.

The story of the young men who seek Death only to find him in a treasure that had made them forget him is a masterpiece of irony, and indeed the Pardoner is in all ways a master ironist. So highly developed is his own sense of irony that it enables him to feel superior not only to other men but to God, for he dares to exempt himself from the effect of his Christian text. Yet the brief Epilogue seems to show that God's irony, like His other attributes, is supreme. The one fact that the Pardoner's candid confession has concealed—that it was perhaps spoken in order to conceal—is that he is a eunuch. When in the Epilogue his proud avarice leads him to see if he can get money from the pilgrims to whom he has revealed his hypocrisy, the Pardoner's secret is revealed by the Host's coarse response, and the verbal facility by which he maintains his superiority fails him.

2. I.e., God's nails.

This was a fals cherl and a fals justise.[3]
As shameful deeth as herte may devise
5 Come to thise juges and hir advocats.
Algate° this sely° maide is slain, allas! *at an rate / innocent*
Allas, too dere boughte she beautee!
Wherfore I saye alday° that men may see *always*
The yiftes of Fortune and of Nature
10 Been cause of deeth to many a creature.
As bothe yiftes that I speke of now,
Men han ful ofte more for harm than prow.° *benefit*
 "But trewely, myn owene maister dere,
This is a pitous tale for to heere.
15 But nathelees, passe over, is no fors:[4]
I praye to God so save thy gentil cors,° *body*
And eek thine urinals and thy jurdones,[5]
Thyn ipocras[6] and eek thy galiones,
And every boiste° ful of thy letuarye°— *box / medicine*
20 God blesse hem, and oure lady Sainte Marye.
So mote I theen,[7] thou art a propre man,
And lik a prelat, by Saint Ronian![8]
Saide I nat wel? I can nat speke in terme.[9]
But wel I woot, thou doost° myn herte to erme° *make / grieve*
25 That I almost have caught a cardinacle.[1]
By corpus bones,[2] but if I have triacle,° *medicine*
Or elles a draughte of moiste° and corny° ale, *fresh / malty*
Or but I heere anoon° a merye tale, *at once*
Myn herte is lost for pitee of this maide.
30 "Thou bel ami,[3] thou Pardoner," he saide,
"Tel us som mirthe or japes° right anoon." *joke*
 "It shal be doon," quod he, "by Saint Ronion.
But first," quod he, "here at this ale-stake[4]
I wol bothe drinke and eten of a cake."
35 And right anoon thise gentils gan to crye,
"Nay, lat him telle us of no ribaudye.° *ribaldry*
Tel us som moral thing that we may lere,° *learn*
Som wit,[5] and thanne wol we gladly heere."
 "I graunte, ywis," quod he, "but I moot thinke
40 Upon som honeste° thing whil that I drinke." *decent*

---

3. The Host has been affected by the Physician's sad tale of the Roman maiden Virginia, whose great beauty caused a judge to attempt to obtain her person by means of a trumped-up lawsuit in which he connived with a "churl" who claimed her as his slave; in order to preserve her chastity, her father killed her.
4. I.e., never mind.
5. Jordans (chamber pots): the Host is somewhat confused in his endeavor to use technical medical terms.
6. A medicinal drink named after Hippocrates; "galiones": a medicine, prob-

ably invented on the spot by the Host, named after Galen.
7. So might I thrive.
8. St. Ronan or St. Ninian, with a possible play on "runnion" (sexual organ).
9. Speak in technical idiom.
1. Apparently a cardiac condition, confused in the Host's mind with a cardinal.
2. An illiterate oath, mixing "God's bones" with *corpus dei*. "But if": unless.
3. Fair friend.
4. Sign of a tavern.
5. I.e., something with significance.

The Prologue

Lordinges—quod he—in chirches whan I preche,
I paine me[6] to han an hautein° speeche,   *loud*
And ringe it out as round as gooth a belle,
For I can al by rote[7] that I telle.
45 My theme is alway oon,[8] and evere was:
Radix malorum est cupiditas.[9]
First I pronounce whennes° that I come,   *whence*
And thanne my bulles[1] shewe I alle and some:
Oure lige lordes seel on my patente,[2]
50 That shewe I first, my body to warente,°   *keep safe*
That no man be so bold, ne preest ne clerk,
Me to destourbe of Cristes holy werk.
And after that thanne telle I forth my tales[3]—
Bulles of popes and of cardinales,
55 Of patriarkes and bisshopes I shewe,
And in Latin I speke a wordes fewe,
To saffron with[4] my predicacioun,°   *preaching*
And for to stire hem to devocioun.
Thanne shewe I forth my longe crystal stones,° *jars*
60 Ycrammed ful of cloutes° and of bones—   *rags*
Relikes been they, as weenen° they eechoon. *suppose*
Thanne have I in laton° a shulder-boon   *zinc*
Which that was of an holy Jewes sheep.
"Goode men," I saye, "take of my wordes keep:° *notice*
65 If that this boon be wasshe in any welle,
If cow, or calf, or sheep, or oxe swelle,
That any worm hath ete or worm ystonge,[5]
Take water of that welle and wassh his tonge,
And it is hool[6] anoon. And ferthermoor,
70 Of pokkes° and of scabbe and every soor°   *pox / sore*
Shal every sheep be hool that of this welle
Drinketh a draughte. Take keep eek° that I telle: *also*
If that the goode man that the beestes oweth° *owns*
Wol every wike,° er that the cok him croweth, *week*
75 Fasting drinken of this welle a draughte—
As thilke° holy Jew oure eldres taughte—   *that same*
His beestes and his stoor° shal multiplye.   *stock*
"And sire, also it heleth jalousye:
For though a man be falle in jalous rage,
80 Lat maken with this water his potage,°   *soup*
And nevere shal he more his wif mistriste,° *mistrust*

6. Take pains.
7. I know all by heart.
8. I.e., the same.
9. Avarice is the root of evil (I Timothy vi.10).
1. Episcopal mandates; "alle and some": each and every one.

2. I.e., the Pope's seal on my papal license.
3. I go on with my yarn.
4. To add spice to.
5. That has eaten or been bitten by any worm.
6. I.e., sound.

Though he the soothe of hir defaute wiste,[7]
Al hadde she[8] taken preestes two or three.
  "Here is a mitein° eek that ye may see: *mitten*
85 He that his hand wol putte in this mitein
He shal have multiplying of his grain,
Whan he hath sowen, be it whete or otes—
So that he offre pens or elles grotes.[9]
  "Goode men and wommen, oo thing warne I you:
90 If any wight be in this chirche now
That hath doon sinne horrible, that he
Dar nat for shame of it yshriven° be,   *absolved*
Or any womman, be she yong or old,
That hath ymaked hir housbonde cokewold,°   *cuckold*
95 Swich folk shal have no power ne no grace
To offren to[1] my relikes in this place;
And whoso findeth him out of swich blame,
He wol come up and offre in Goddes name,
And I assoile° him by the auctoritee   *absolve*
100 Which that by bulle ygraunted was to me."
  By this gaude° have I wonne, yeer by yeer,   *trick*
An hundred mark[2] sith° I was pardoner.   *since*
I stonde lik a clerk in my pulpet,
And whan the lewed° peple is down yset,   *ignorant*
105 I preche so as ye han herd bifore,
And telle an hundred false japes° more.   *tricks*
Thanne paine I me[3] to strecche forth the nekke,
And eest and west upon the peple I bekke[4]
As dooth a douve,° sitting on a berne;°   *dove / barn*
110 Mine handes and my tonge goon so yerne°   *fast*
That it is joye to see my bisinesse.
Of avarice and of swich cursednesse°   *sin*
Is al my preching, for to make hem free°   *generous*
To yiven hir pens, and namely° unto me,   *especially*
115 For myn entente is nat but for to winne,[5]
And no thing for correccion of sinne:
I rekke° nevere whan that they been beried°   *care / buried*
Though that hir soules goon a-blakeberied.[6]
For certes, many a predicacioun°   *sermon*
120 Comth ofte time of yvel entencioun:
Som for plesance of folk and flaterye,
To been avaunced° by ypocrisye,   *promoted*
And som for vaine glorye, and som for hate;
For whan I dar noon otherways debate,°   *fight*
125 Thanne wol I stinge him with my tonge smerte
In preching, so that he shal nat asterte°   *escape*

7. Knew the truth of her infidelity.   3. I take pains.
8. Even if she had.   4. I.e., I shake my head.
9. Pennies, groats, coins.   5. Only to gain.
1. To make gifts in reverence of.   6. Go blackberrying, i.e., go to hell.
2. Marks (pecuniary units).

To been defamed falsly, if that he
Hath trespassed to[7] my bretheren or to me.
For though I telle nought his propre name,
130 Men shal wel knowe that it is the same
By signes and by othere circumstaunces.
Thus quite° I folk that doon us displesaunces;[8]   *pay back*
Thus spete° I out my venim under hewe°   *spit / color*
Of holinesse, to seeme holy and trewe.
135 But shortly myn entente I wol devise:°   *describe*
I preche of no thing but for coveitise;
Therfore my theme is yit and evere was
Radix malorum est cupiditas.
      Thus can I preche again that same vice
140 Which that I use, and that is avarice.
But though myself be gilty in that sinne,
Yit can I make other folk to twinne°   *separate*
From avarice, and sore to repente—
But that is nat my principal entente:
145 I preche no thing but for coveitise.
Of this matere it oughte ynough suffise.
      Thanne telle I hem ensamples[9] many oon
Of olde stories longe time agoon,
For lewed° peple loven tales olde—   *ignorant*
150 Swiche thinges can they wel reporte and holde.[1]
What, trowe° ye that whiles I may preche,   *believe*
And winne gold and silver for° I teche,   *because*
That I wol live in poverte wilfully?
Nay, nay, I thoughte° it nevere, trewely,   *intended*
155 For I wol preche and begge in sondry landes;
I wol nat do no labour with mine handes,
Ne make baskettes and live therby,
By cause I wol nat beggen idelly.[2]
I wol none of the Apostles countrefete:°   *imitate*
160 I wol have moneye, wolle,° cheese, and whete,   *wool*
Al were it[3] yiven of the pooreste page,
Or of the pooreste widwe in a village—
Al sholde hir children sterve[4] for famine.
Nay, I wol drinke licour of the vine
165 And have a joly wenche in every town.
But herkneth, lordinges, in conclusioun,
Youre liking° is that I shal telle a tale: *pleasure*
Now have I dronke a draughte of corny ale,
By God, I hope I shal you telle a thing
170 That shal by reson been at youre liking;
For though myself be a ful vicious man,
A moral tale yit I you telle can,

7. Injured.
8. Do us discourtesies.
9. *Exempla* (stories illustrating moral principles).

1. Repeat and remember.
2. I.e., without profit.
3. Even though it were.
4. Even though her children should die.

Which I am wont to preche for to winne.
Now holde youre pees, my tale I wol biginne.

The Tale

175 In Flandres whilom° was a compaignye   *once*
Of yonge folk that haunteden° folye—   *practiced*
As riot, hasard, stewes,[5] and tavernes,
Wher as with harpes, lutes, and giternes°   *guitars*
They daunce and playen at dees° bothe day and night, *dice*
180 And ete also and drinke over hir might,[6]
Thurgh which they doon the devel sacrifise
Within that develes temple in cursed wise
By superfluitee° abhominable.   *overindulgence*
Hir othes been so grete and so dampnable
185 That it is grisly for to heere hem swere:
Oure blessed Lordes body they totere[7]—
Hem thoughte that Jewes rente° him nought ynough. *tore*
And eech of hem at otheres sinne lough.°   *laughed*
And right anoon thanne comen tombesteres,° *dancing girls*
190 Fetis° and smale,° and yonge frutesteres,[8] *shapely / neat*
Singeres with harpes, bawdes,° wafereres[9]—   *pimps*
Whiche been the verray develes officeres,
To kindle and blowe the fir of lecherye
That is annexed unto glotonye:[1]
195 The Holy Writ take I to my witnesse
That luxure° is in win and dronkenesse.   *lechery*
Lo, how that dronken Lot[2] unkindely°   *unnaturally*
Lay by his doughtres two unwitingly:
So dronke he was he niste° what he wroughte. *didn't know*
200 Herodes, who so wel the stories soughte,[3]
Whan he of win was repleet at his feeste,
Right at his owene table he yaf his heeste°   *command*
To sleen° the Baptist John, ful giltelees.   *slay*
Senek[4] saith a good word doutelees:
205 He saith he can no difference finde
Bitwixe a man that is out of his minde
And a man which that is dronkelewe,°   *drunken*
But that woodnesse, yfallen in a shrewe,[5]
Persevereth lenger than dooth dronkenesse.
210 O glotonye, ful of cursednesse!°   *wickedness*
O cause first of oure confusioun!°   *downfall*
O original of oure dampnacioun,°   *damnation*
Til Crist hadde bought° us with his blood again! *redeemed*

5. Wild parties, gambling, brothels.
6. Beyond their capacity.
7. Tear apart (a reference to oaths sworn by parts of His body, such as "God's bones!" or "God's teeth!").
8. Fruit-selling girls.
9. Girl cake-vendors.
1. I.e., closely related to gluttony.

2. For Lot, see Genesis xix.30–36.
3. For the story of Herod and St. John the Baptist, see Mark vi.17–29. "Who so * * * soughte": i.e., whoever looked it up in the Gospel would find.
4. Seneca, the Roman Stoic philosopher.
5. But that madness, occurring in a wicked man.

Lo, how dere, shortly for to sayn,
215 Abought° was thilke° cursed vilainye; °paid for / that same
Corrupt was al this world for glotonye:
Adam oure fader and his wif also
Fro Paradis to labour and to wo
Were driven for that vice, it is no drede.° °doubt
220 For whil that Adam fasted, as I rede,
He was in Paradis; and whan that he
Eet° of the fruit defended° on a tree, °ate / forbidden
Anoon he was out cast to wo and paine.
O glotonye, on thee wel oughte us plaine!° °complain
225   O, wiste a man[6] how manye maladies
Folwen of excesse and of glotonies,
He wolde been the more mesurable° °moderate
Of his diete, sitting at his table.
Allas, the shorte throte, the tendre mouth,
230 Maketh that eest and west and north and south,
In erthe, in air, in water, men to swinke,° °work
To gete a gloton daintee mete and drinke.
Of this matere, O Paul, wel canstou trete:
"Mete unto wombe,° and wombe eek unto mete, °belly
235 Shal God destroyen bothe," as Paulus saith.[7]
Allas, a foul thing is it, by my faith,
To saye this word, and fouler is the deede
Whan man so drinketh of the white and rede[8]
That of his throte he maketh his privee° °privy
240 Thurgh thilke cursed superfluitee.° °overindulgence
   The Apostle[9] weeping saith ful pitously,
"Ther walken manye of which you told have I—
I saye it now weeping with pitous vois—
They been enemies of Cristes crois,° °cross
245 Of whiche the ende is deeth—wombe is hir god!"[1]
O wombe, O bely, O stinking cod,° °bag
Fulfilled° of dong° and of corrupcioun! °filled full / dung
At either ende of thee foul is the soun.° °sound
How greet labour and cost is thee to finde!° °provide for
250 Thise cookes, how they stampe[2] and straine and grinde,
And turnen substance into accident[3]
To fulfillen al thy likerous° talent!° °dainty / appetite
Out of the harde bones knokke they
The mary,° for they caste nought away °marrow
255 That may go thurgh the golet[4] softe and soote.° °sweetly
Of spicerye° of leef and bark and roote °spices
Shal been his sauce ymaked by delit,

---

6. If a man knew.
7. See I Corinthians vi.13.
8. I.e., white and red wines.
9. I.e., St. Paul.
1. See Philippians iii.18.
2. Pound.

3. A philosophic joke, depending on the distinction between inner reality (substance) and outward appearance (accident).
4. Through the gullet.

To make him yit a newer appetit.
But certes, he that haunteth swiche delices°   *pleasures*
260 Is deed° whil that he liveth in tho° vices.   *dead / those*
   A lecherous thing is win, and dronkenesse
Is ful of striving° and of wrecchednesse.   *quarreling*
O dronke man, disfigured is thy face!
Sour is thy breeth, foul artou to embrace!
265 And thurgh thy dronke nose seemeth the soun
As though thou saidest ay,° "Sampsoun, Sampsoun."   *always*
And yit, God woot,° Sampson drank nevere win.[5]   *knows*
Thou fallest as it were a stiked swin;[6]
Thy tonge is lost, and al thyn honeste cure,
270 For dronkenesse is verray sepulture°   *burial*
Of mannes wit° and his discrecioun.   *intelligence*
In whom that drinke hath dominacioun
He can no conseil° keepe, it is no drede.°   *secrets / doubt*
Now keepe you fro the white and fro the rede—
275 And namely° fro the white win of Lepe[7]   *particularly*
That is to selle in Fisshstreete or in Chepe:[8]
The win of Spaine creepeth subtilly
In othere wines growing faste° by,   *close*
Of which ther riseth swich fumositee°   *heady fumes*
280 That whan a man hath dronken draughtes three
And weeneth° that he be at hoom in Chepe,   *supposes*
He is in Spaine, right at the town of Lepe,
Nat at The Rochele ne at Burdeux town;[9]
And thanne wol he sayn, "Sampsoun, Sampsoun."
285   But herkneth, lordinges, oo° word I you praye,   *one*
That alle the soverein actes,[1] dar I saye,
Of victories in the Olde Testament,
Thurgh verray God that is omnipotent,
Were doon in abstinence and in prayere:
290 Looketh° the Bible and ther ye may it lere.°   *behold / learn*
   Looke Attila, the grete conquerour,[2]
Deide° in his sleep with shame and dishonour,   *died*
Bleeding at his nose in dronkenesse:
A capitain sholde live in sobrenesse.
295   And overal this, aviseth you[3] right wel
What was comanded unto Lamuel[4]—
Nat Samuel, but Lamuel, saye I—
Redeth the Bible and finde it expresly,
Of win-yiving° to hem that han[5] justise: *wine-serving*

5. Before Samson's birth an angel told his mother that he would be a Nazarite throughout his life; members of this sect took no strong drink.
6. Stuck pig. "Honeste cure": care for self-respect.
7. A town in Spain.
8. Fishstreet and Cheapside in the London market district.
9 The Pardoner is joking about the illegal custom of adulterating fine wines of Bordeaux and La Rochelle with strong Spanish wine.
1. Distinguished deeds.
2. Attila was the leader of the Huns who captured Rome in the 5th century.
3. Consider.
4. Lemuel's mother told him that kings should not drink (Proverbs xxxi.4–5).
5. I.e., administer.

300 Namore of this, for it may wel suffise.
    And now that I have spoken of glotonye,
Now wol I you defende° hasardrye:°   *prohibit / gambling*
Hasard is verray moder° of lesinges,°   *mother / lies*
And of deceite and cursed forsweringes,
305 Blaspheme of Crist, manslaughtre, and wast° also   *waste*
Of catel° and of time; and ferthermo,   *property*
It is repreve° and contrarye of honour   *disgrace*
For to been holden a commune hasardour,°   *gambler*
And evere the hyer he is of estat
310 The more is he holden desolat.[6]
If that a prince useth hasardrye,
In alle governance and policye
He is, as by commune opinioun,
Yholde the lasse° in reputacioun.   *less*
315   Stilbon, that was a wis embassadour,
Was sent to Corinthe in ful greet honour
Fro Lacedomye° to make hir alliaunce,   *Sparta*
And whan he cam him happede° parchaunce   *it happened*
That alle the gretteste° that were of that lond   *greatest*
320 Playing at the hasard he hem foond,   *found*
For which as soone as it mighte be
He stal him[7] hoom again to his contree,
And saide, "Ther wol I nat lese° my name,   *lose*
N'I wol nat take on me so greet defame°   *dishonor*
325 You to allye unto none hasardours:
Sendeth othere wise embassadours,
For by my trouthe, me were levere[8] die
Than I you sholde to hasardours allye.
For ye that been so glorious in honours
330 Shal nat allye you with hasardours
As by my wil, ne as by my tretee."°   *treaty*
This wise philosophre, thus saide he.
    Looke eek that to the king Demetrius
The King of Parthes,° as the book[9] saith us,   *Parthians*
335 Sente him a paire of dees° of gold in scorn,   *dice*
For he hadde used hasard therbiforn,
For which he heeld his glorye or his renown
At no value or reputacioun.
    Lordes may finden other manere play
340 Honeste° ynough to drive the day away.   *honorable*
    Now wol I speke of othes false and grete
A word or two, as olde bookes trete:
    Greet swering is a thing abhominable,
And fals swering is yit more reprevable.°   *reprehensible*
345 The hye God forbad swering at al—

6. I.e., dissolute.
7. He stole away.
8. I had rather.
9. The book that relates this and the previous incident is the *Policraticus* of the 12th-century Latin writer, John of Salisbury.

Witnesse on Mathew.[1] But in special
Of swering saith the holy Jeremie,[2]
"Thou shalt swere sooth thine othes and nat lie,
And swere in doom[3] and eek in rightwisnesse,
350 But idel swering is a cursednesse."°   *wickedness*
    Biholde and see that in the firste Table[4]
Of hye Goddes heestes° honorable   *commandments*
How that the seconde heeste of him is this:
"Take nat my name in idel or amis."
355 Lo, rather° he forbedeth swich swering   *sooner*
Than homicide, or many a cursed thing.
I saye that as by ordre thus it stondeth—
This knoweth that[5] his heestes understondeth
How that the seconde heeste of God is that.
360 And fertherover,° I wol thee telle al plat°   *moreover / flat*
That vengeance shal nat parten° from his hous   *depart*
That of his othes is too outrageous.
"By Goddes precious herte!" and "By his nailes!"°   *fingernails*
And "By the blood of Crist that is in Hailes,[6]
365 Sevene is my chaunce, and thyn is cink and traye!"[7]
"By Goddes armes, if thou falsly playe
This daggere shal thurghout thyn herte go!"
This fruit cometh of the bicche bones[8] two—
Forswering, ire, falsnesse, homicide.
370 Now for the love of Crist that for us dyde,
Lete° youre othes bothe grete and smale.   *leave*
But sires, now wol I telle forth my tale.
    Thise riotoures° three of whiche I telle,   *revelers*
Longe erst er prime[9] ronge of any belle,
375 Were set hem in a taverne to drinke,
And as they sat they herde a belle clinke
Biforn a cors° was caried to his grave.   *corpse*
That oon of hem gan callen to his knave:°   *servant*
"Go bet,"[1] quod he, "and axe° redily°   *ask / promptly*
380 What cors is this that passeth heer forby,
And looke° that thou reporte his name weel."°   *be sure / well*
    "Sire," quod this boy, "it needeth neveradeel:[2]
It was me told er ye cam heer two houres.
He was, pardee, an old felawe of youres,
385 And sodeinly he was yslain tonight,°   *last night*
Fordronke° as he sat on his bench upright;   *very drunk*
Ther cam a privee° thief men clepeth° Deeth,   *stealthy / call*
That in this contree al the peple sleeth,°   *slays*

1. "But I say unto you, Swear not at all" (Matthew v.34).
2. Jeremiah (iv.2).
3. Equity; "rightwisnesse": righteousness.
4. I.e., the first four of the Ten Commandments.
5. I.e., he that.

6. An abbey in Gloucestershire supposed to possess some of Christ's blood.
7. Five and three.
8. I.e., damned dice.
9. Long before 9 A.M.
1. Better, i.e., quick.
2. It isn't a bit necessary.

And with his spere he smoot his herte atwo,
390 And wente his way withouten wordes mo.
He hath a thousand slain this° pestilence.   *during this*
And maister, er ye come in his presence,
Me thinketh that it were necessarye
For to be war of swich an adversarye;
395 Beeth redy for to meete him everemore:
Thus taughte me my dame.° I saye namore."   *mother*
    "By Sainte Marye," saide this taverner,
"The child saith sooth, for he hath slain this yeer,
Henne° over a mile, within a greet village,   *hence*
400 Bothe man and womman, child and hine³ and page.
I trowe° his habitacion be there.   *believe*
To been avised° greet wisdom it were   *wary*
Er that he dide a man a dishonour."
    "Ye, Goddes armes," quod this riotour,
405 "Is it swich peril with him for to meete?
I shal him seeke by way and eek by streete,⁴
I make avow to Goddes digne° bones.   *worthy*
Herkneth, felawes, we three been alle ones:°   *of one mind*
Lat eech of us holde up his hand to other
410 And eech of us bicome otheres brother,
And we wol sleen this false traitour Deeth.
He shal be slain, he that so manye sleeth,
By Goddes dignitee, er it be night."
    Togidres han thise three hir trouthes plight⁵
415 To live and dien eech of hem with other,
As though he were his owene ybore° brother.   *born*
And up they sterte,° al dronken in this rage,   *started*
And forth they goon towardes that village
Of which the taverner hadde spoke biforn.
420 And many a grisly ooth thanne han they sworn,
And Cristes blessed body they torente:°   *tore apart*
Deeth shal be deed° if that they may him hente.°   *dead / catch*
    Whan they han goon nat fully half a mile,
Right as they wolde han treden° over a stile,   *stepped*
425 An old man and a poore with hem mette;
This olde man ful mekely hem grette,°   *greeted*
And saide thus, "Now lordes, God you see."⁶
    The pruddeste° of thise riotoures three   *proudest*
Answerde again, "What, carl° with sory grace,   *churl*
430 Why artou al forwrapped save thy face?
Why livestou so longe in so greet age?"
    This olde man gan looke in his visage,
And saide thus, "For° I ne can nat finde   *because*
A man, though that I walked into Inde,
435 Neither in citee ne in no village,

---

3. Farm laborer.
4. By highway and byway.
5. Pledged their words of honor.
6. May God protect you.

That wolde chaunge his youthe for myn age;
And therfore moot I han myn age stille,
As longe time as it is Goddes wille.
"Ne Deeth, allas, ne wol nat have my lif.
₄₄₀ Thus walke I lik a restelees caitif,°   *captive*
And on the ground which is my modres° gate   *mother's*
I knokke with my staf bothe erly and late,
And saye, 'Leve° moder, leet me in: *dear*
Lo, how I vanisshe, flessh and blood and skin.
₄₄₅ Allas, whan shal my bones been at reste?
Moder, with you wolde I chaunge° my cheste[7]   *exchange*
That in my chambre longe time hath be,
Ye, for an haire-clout[8] to wrappe me.'
But yit to me she wol nat do that grace,
₄₅₀ For which ful pale and welked° is my face.   *withered*
But sires, to you it is no curteisye
To speken to an old man vilainye,°   *rudeness*
But° he trespasse° in word or elles in deede.   *unless / offend*
In Holy Writ ye may yourself wel rede,
₄₅₅ 'Agains[9] an old man, hoor° upon his heed,   *hoar*
Ye shal arise.'[1] Wherfore I yive you reed,°   *advice*
Ne dooth unto an old man noon harm now,
Namore than that ye wolde men dide to you
In age, if that ye so longe abide.
₄₆₀ And God be with you wher ye go° or ride: *walk*
I moot go thider as I have to go."
    "Nay, olde cherl, by God thou shalt nat so,"
Saide this other hasardour anoon.
"Thou partest nat so lightly,° by Saint John!   *easily*
₄₆₅ Thou speke° right now of thilke traitour Deeth,   *spoke*
That in this contree alle oure freendes sleeth:
Have here my trouthe, as thou art his espye,
Tel wher he is, or thou shalt it abye,°   *pay for*
By God and by the holy sacrament!
₄₇₀ For soothly thou art oon of his assent[2]
To sleen us yonge folk, thou false thief."
    "Now sires," quod he, "if that ye be so lief°   *anxious*
To finde Deeth, turne up this crooked way,
For in that grove I lafte° him, by my fay,°   *left / faith*
₄₇₅ Under a tree, and ther he wol abide:
Nat for youre boost° he wol him no thing hide.   *boast*
See ye that ook?° Right ther ye shal him finde.   *oak*
God save you, that boughte again[3] mankinde,
And you amende." Thus saide this olde man.
₄₈₀   And everich of thise riotoures ran
Til he cam to that tree, and ther they founde

---

7. Chest for one's belongings, used here as the symbol for life—or perhaps a coffin.
8. Haircloth, for a winding sheet.
9. In the presence of.
1. Cf. Leviticus xix.32.
2. I.e., one of his party.
3. Redeemed.

Of florins° fine of gold ycoined rounde   *coins*
Wel neigh an eighte busshels as hem thoughte—
Ne lenger thanne after Deeth they soughte,
485 But eech of hem so glad was of the sighte,
For that the florins been so faire and brighte,
That down they sette hem by this precious hoord.
The worste of hem he spak the firste word:
    "Bretheren," quod he, "take keep° what that I saye: *heed*
490 My wit is greet though that I bourde° and playe.   *joke*
This tresor hath Fortune unto us yiven
In mirthe and jolitee oure lif to liven,
And lightly° as it cometh so wol we spende.   *easily*
Ey, Goddes precious dignitee, who wende⁴
495 Today that we sholde han so fair a grace?
But mighte this gold be caried fro this place
Hoom to myn hous—or elles unto youres—
For wel ye woot that al this gold is oures—
Thanne were we in heigh felicitee.
500 But trewely, by daye it mighte nat be:
Men wolde sayn that we were theves stronge,°   *flagrant*
And for oure owene tresor doon us honge.⁵
This tresor moste ycaried be by nighte,
As wisely and as slyly as it mighte.
505 Therfore I rede° that cut° amonges us alle   *advise / lots*
Be drawe, and lat see wher the cut wol falle;
And he that hath the cut with herte blithe
Shal renne° to the town, and that ful swithe,°   *run / quickly*
And bringe us breed and win ful prively;
510 And two of us shal keepen° subtilly   *guard*
This tresor wel, and if he wol nat tarye,
Whan it is night we wol this tresor carye
By oon assent wher as us thinketh best."
That oon of hem the cut broughte in his fest°   *fist*
515 And bad hem drawe and looke wher it wol falle;
And it fil° on the yongeste of hem alle,   *fell*
And forth toward the town he wente anoon.
And also° soone as that he was agoon,°   *as / gone away*
That oon of hem spak thus unto that other:
520 "Thou knowest wel thou art my sworen brother;
Thy profit wol I telle thee anoon:
Thou woost wel that oure felawe is agoon,
And here is gold, and that ful greet plentee,
That shal departed° been among us three.   *divided*
525 But nathelees, if I can shape° it so   *arrange*
That it departed were among us two,
Hadde I nat doon a freendes turn to thee?"
    That other answerde, "I noot⁶ how that may be:

---

4. Who would have supposed.   6. Don't know.
5. Have us hanged.

He woot that the gold is with us twaye.
530 What shal we doon? What shal we to him saye?"
"Shal it be conseil?"[7] saide the firste shrewe.°   *villain*
"And I shal telle in a wordes fewe
What we shul doon, and bringe it wel aboute."
"I graunte," quod that other, "out of doute,
535 That by my trouthe I wol thee nat biwraye."°   *expose*
"Now," quod the firste, "thou woost wel we be twaye,
And two of us shal strenger° be than oon: *stronger*
Looke whan that he is set that right anoon
Aris as though thou woldest with him playe,
540 And I shal rive° him thurgh the sides twaye,   *pierce*
Whil that thou struglest with him as in game,
And with thy daggere looke thou do the same;
And thanne shal al this gold departed be,
My dere freend, bitwixe thee and me.
545 Thanne we may bothe oure lustes° al fulfille,   *desires*
And playe at dees° right at oure owene wille."   *dice*
And thus accorded been thise shrewes twaye
To sleen the thridde, as ye han herd me saye.
This yongeste, which that wente to the town,
550 Ful ofte in herte he rolleth up and down
The beautee of thise florins newe and brighte.
"O Lord," quod he, "if so were that I mighte
Have al this tresor to myself allone,
Ther is no man that liveth under the trone°   *throne*
555 Of God that sholde live so merye as I."
And at the laste the feend oure enemy
Putte in his thought that he sholde poison beye,°   *buy*
With which he mighte sleen his felawes twaye—
Forwhy° the feend foond him in swich livinge   *because*
560 That he hadde leve° him to sorwe bringe:[8]   *permission*
For this was outrely° his fulle entente,   *plainly*
To sleen hem bothe, and nevere to repente.
And forth he gooth—no lenger wolde he tarye—
Into the town unto a pothecarye,°   *apothecary*
565 And prayed him that he him wolde selle
Som poison that he mighte his rattes quelle,°   *kill*
And eek ther was a polcat[9] in his hawe°   *yard*
That, as he saide, his capons hadde yslawe,°   *slain*
And fain he wolde wreke him[1] if he mighte
570 On vermin that destroyed him[2] by nighte.
The pothecarye answerde, "And thou shalt have
A thing that, also° God my soule save,   *as*
In al this world there is no creature
That ete or dronke hath of this confiture°—   *mixture*

---

7. A secret.
8. Christian doctrine teaches that the devil may not tempt men except with God's permission.
9. A weasel-like animal.
1. He would gladly avenge himself.
2. I.e., were ruining his farming.

575 Nat but the mountance° of a corn° of whete—   *amount / grain*
     That he ne shal his lif anoon forlete.°   *lose*
     Ye, sterve° he shal, and that in lasse° while   *die / less*
     Than thou wolt goon a paas[3] nat but a mile,
     The poison is so strong and violent."
580 This cursed man hath in his hand yhent°   *taken*
     This poison in a box and sith° he ran   *then*
     Into the nexte streete unto a man
     And borwed of him large botels three,
     And in the two his poison poured he—
585 The thridde he kepte clene for his drinke,
     For al the night he shoop him[4] for to swinke°   *work*
     In carying of the gold out of that place.
     And whan this riotour with sory grace
     Hadde filled with win his grete botels three,
590 To his felawes again repaireth he.
       What needeth it to sermone of it more?
     For right as they had cast° his deeth bifore,   *plotted*
     Right so they han him slain, and that anoon.
     And whan that this was doon, thus spak that oon:
595 "Now lat us sitte and drinke and make us merye,
     And afterward we wol his body berye."°   *bury*
     And with that word it happed him par cas[5]
     To take the botel ther the poison was,
     And drank, and yaf his felawe drinke also,
600 For which anoon they storven° bothe two.   *died*
       But certes I suppose that Avicen
     Wroot nevere in no canon ne in no *fen*[6]
     Mo wonder signes[7] of empoisoning
     Than hadde thise wrecches two er hir ending:
605 Thus ended been thise homicides two,
     And eek the false empoisonere also.
       O cursed sinne of alle cursednesse!
     O traitours homicide, O wikkednesse!
     O glotonye, luxure,° and hasardrye!   *lechery*
610 Thou blasphemour of Crist with vilainye
     And othes grete of usage° and of pride!   *habit*
     Allas, mankinde, how may it bitide
     That to thy Creatour which that thee wroughte,
     And with his precious herte blood thee boughte,°   *redeemed*
615 Thou art so fals and so unkinde,° allas?   *unnatural*
       Now goode men, God foryive you youre trespas,
     And ware° you fro the sinne of avarice: *guard*
     Myn holy pardon may you alle warice°—   *save*
     So that ye offre nobles or sterlinges,[8]

3. Take a walk.
4. He was preparing.
5. By chance.
6. The *Canon of Medicine*, by Avicenna, an 11th-century Arabic philosopher, was divided into sections called "*fens.*"
7. More wonderful symptoms.
8. "Nobles" and "sterlinges" were valuable coins.

620 Or elles silver brooches, spoones, ringes.
Boweth your heed under this holy bulle!
Cometh up, ye wives, offreth of youre wolle!°   *wool*
Youre name I entre here in my rolle: anoon
Into the blisse of hevene shul ye goon.
625 I you assoile° by myn heigh power—   *absolve*
Ye that wol offre—as clene and eek as cleer
As ye were born.—And lo, sires, thus I preche.
And Jesu Crist that is oure soules leeche°   *physician*
So graunte you his pardon to receive,
630 For that is best—I wol you nat deceive.

The Epilogue

"But sires, oo word forgat I in my tale:
I have relikes and pardon in my male°   *bag*
As faire as any man in Engelond,
Whiche were me yiven by the Popes hond.
635 If any of you wol of devocioun
Offren and han myn absolucioun,
Come forth anoon, and kneeleth here adown,
And mekely receiveth my pardoun;
Or elles taketh pardon as ye wende,
640 Al newe and fressh at every miles ende—
So that ye offre alway newe and newe[9]
Nobles or pens whiche that be goode and trewe.
It is an honour to everich that is heer
That ye have a suffisant° pardoner   *competent*
645 T'assoile you in contrees as ye ride,
For aventures whiche that may bitide:
Paraventure ther may falle oon or two
Down of his hors and breke his nekke atwo;
Looke which a suretee° is it to you alle   *safeguard*
650 That I am in youre felaweshipe yfalle
That may assoile you, bothe more and lasse,[1]
Whan that the soule shal fro the body passe.
I rede° that oure Hoste shal biginne,   *advise*
For he is most enveluped° in sinne.   *involved*
655 Com forth, sire Host, and offre first anoon,
And thou shalt kisse the relikes everichoon,°   *each one*
Ye, for a grote: unbokele° anoon thy purs."   *unbuckle*
"Nay, nay," quod he, "thanne have I Cristes curs!
Lat be," quod he, "it shal nat be, so theech!°   *may I thrive*
660 Thou woldest make me kisse thyn olde breech°   *breeches*
And swere it were a relik of a saint,
Though it were with thy fundament depeint.°   *stained*
But, by the crois which that Sainte Elaine foond,[2]

9. Over and over.
1. Both high and low (i.e., everybody).
2. I.e., by the cross that St. Helena

found. Helena, mother of Constantine
the Great, was reputed to have found
the True Cross.

I wolde I hadde thy coilons° in myn hond,   *testicles*
665 In stede of relikes or of saintuarye.°   *relic-box*
Lat cutte hem of: I wol thee helpe hem carve.
They shal be shrined in an hogges tord."°   *turd*
This Pardoner answerde nat a word:
So wroth he was no word ne wolde he saye.
670 "Now," quod oure Host, "I wol lenger playe
With thee, ne with noon other angry man."
But right anoon the worthy Knight bigan,
Whan that he sawgh that al the peple lough,°   *laughed*
"Namore of this, for it is right ynough.
675 Sire Pardoner, be glad and merye of cheere,
And ye, sire Host that been to me so dere,
I praye you that ye kisse the Pardoner,
And Pardoner, I praye thee, draw thee neer,
And as we diden lat us laughe and playe."
680 Anoon they kiste and riden forth hir waye.

The Nun's Priest's Tale[1]

A poore widwe somdeel stape° in age   *advanced*
Was whilom° dwelling in a narwe[2] cotage,   *once upon a time*
Biside a grove, stonding in a dale:
This widwe of which I telle you my tale,
5 Sin thilke° day that she was last a wif,   *that same*
In pacience ladde° a ful simple lif.   *led*

1. The Nun's Priest's Tale is an example of the literary genre known as the "beast fable," in which animals behave like human beings. The beast fable is inevitably injurious to man's dignity, since to pretend that animals behave like men is to suggest that men behave like animals, for a pig cannot look like a man unless a man in some way looks like a pig. In the Nun's Priest's Tale, as in its French source, the history of Reynard the Fox, the beast fable is combined with the mock heroic, and the result is doubly injurious to man's dignity. The elevated language of true heroic poetry means to enhance the splendid deeds of men of great stature, while the elevated language of mock heroic, by treating the trivial as if it were sublime, reveals man's lack of dignity in the awful gulf that separates the idealized language from the petty action it describes; and when the petty action is carried on not even by men, but by animals masquerading as men (that is, by men reduced to the status of animals), the loss of human dignity is even greater.
  The nominal hero of the Tale is Chauntecleer, a fowl of courtly bearing, profound learning, and superior crowing. This rooster is, like Achilles or Aeneas, made the center of a "great" action—which, however, takes up a relatively small portion of the total number of lines in the poem. The hero of the larger portion, and the real hero of the poem, is rhetoric, which is responsible for all Chauntecleer's importance, though it almost drowns his story in its vast tumid flow. Rhetoric as employed by the Nun's Priest includes not only elevated speech, but proverbs, saws, conventional similes—all the clichés of formal language and thought. Epic mannerisms abound; proverbs fly thick and fast and contradict one another with impunity; sententious generalizations about the tragic inevitability of certain events, the bad counsel given by women, and the folly of heeding flattery are successively used to account for Chauntecleer's near-fall; and throughout the tale learned pedantry invokes rhetorical tradition to footnote the least original of ideas. All rhetoric's ordering devices achieve a fine disorder.
2. I.e., small.

For litel was hir catel° and hir rente,°   *property / income*
By housbondrye° of swich as God hire sente   *economy*
She foond° hirself and eek hir doughtren two.   *provided for*
10 Three large sowes hadde she and namo,
Three kin,° and eek a sheep that highte Malle.   *cows*
Ful sooty was hir bowr° and eek hir halle,   *bedroom*
In which she eet ful many a slendre° meel;   *scanty*
Of poinant° sauce hire needed neveradeel: *pungent*
15 No daintee morsel passed thurgh hir throte—
Hir diete was accordant to hir cote.°   *cottage*
Repleccioun° ne made hire nevere sik: *overeating*
Attempre° diete was al hir physik,°   *moderate / medicine*
And exercise and hertes suffisaunce.°   *contentment*
20 The goute lette hire nothing for to daunce,[3]
N'apoplexye shente° nat hir heed.°   *hurt / head*
No win ne drank she, neither whit ne reed:°   *red*
Hir boord° was served most with whit and blak,[4]   *table*
Milk and brown breed, in which she foond no lak;[5]
25 Seind bacon, and somtime an ey° or twaye,   *egg*
For she was as it were a manere daye.[6]
A yeerd° she hadde, enclosed al withoute   *yard*
With stikkes, and a drye dich aboute,
In which she hadde a cok heet° Chauntecleer: *named*
30 In al the land of crowing nas° his peer.   *was not*
His vois was merier than the merye orgon
On massedayes that in the chirche goon;[7]
Wel sikerer[8] was his crowing in his logge°   *dwelling*
Than is a clok or an abbeye orlogge;°   *timepiece*
35 By nature he knew eech ascensioun
Of th'equinoxial[9] in thilke town:
For whan degrees fifteene were ascended,
Thanne crew[1] he that it mighte nat been amended
His comb was redder than the fin coral,
40 And batailed° as it were a castel wal;   *battlemented*
His bile° was blak, and as the jeet° it shoon;   *bill / jet*
Like asure[2] were his legges and his toon;°   *toes*
His nailes whitter° than the lilye flowr,   *whiter*
And lik the burned° gold was his colour.   *burnished*
45 This gentil cok hadde in his governaunce
Sevene hennes for to doon al his plesaunce,°   *pleasure*
Whiche were his sustres and his paramours,[3]
And wonder like to him as of colours;

3. The gout didn't hinder her at all from dancing.
4. I.e., milk and bread.
5. Found no fault. "Seind": scorched (i.e., broiled).
6. I.e., a kind of dairymaid.
7. I.e., is played.
8. More reliable.
9. I.e., he knew by instinct each step in the progression of the celestial equator. The celestial equator was thought to make a 360-degree rotation around the earth every 24 hours; therefore a progression of 15 degrees would be equal to the passage of an hour (line 37).
1. Crowed; "amended": improved.
2. Lapis lazuli.
3. His sisters and his mistresses.

Of whiche the faireste hewed° on hir throte   *colored*
50 Was cleped faire damoisele Pertelote:
Curteis she was, discreet, and debonaire,°   *meek*
And compaignable,[4] and bar° hirself so faire,   *bore*
Sin thilke day that she was seven night old,
That trewely she hath the herte in hold
55 Of Chauntecleer, loken° in every lith.°   *locked / limb*
He loved hire so that wel was him therwith.[5]
But swich a joye was it to heere hem singe,
Whan that the brighte sonne gan to springe,
In sweete accord *My Lief is Faren in Londe*[6]—
60 For thilke time, as I have understonde,
Beestes and briddes couden speke and singe.
    And so bifel that in a daweninge,
As Chauntecleer among his wives alle
Sat on his perche that was in the halle,
65 And next him sat this faire Pertelote,
This Chauntecleer gan gronen in his throte,
As man that in his dreem is drecched° sore.   *troubled*
    And whan that Pertelote thus herde him rore,
She was agast, and saide, "Herte dere,
70 What aileth you to grone in this manere?
Ye been a verray slepere,[7] fy, for shame!"
    And he answerde and saide thus, "Madame,
I praye you that ye take it nat agrief.°   *amiss*
By God, me mette I was in swich meschief[8]
75 Right now, that yit myn herte is sore afright.
Now God," quod he, "my swevene recche aright,[9]
And keepe my body out of foul prisoun!
Me mette how that I romed up and down
Within oure yeerd, wher as I sawgh a beest,
80 Was lik an hound and wolde han maad arrest[1]
Upon my body, and han had me deed.[2]
His colour was bitwixe yelow and reed,
And tipped was his tail and bothe his eres
With blak, unlik the remenant° of his heres;°   *rest / hairs*
85 His snoute smal, with glowing yën twaye.
Yit of his look for fere almost I deye:°   *die*
This caused me my groning, doutelees."
    "Avoi,"° quod she, "fy on you, hertelees!°   *fie / coward*
Allas," quod she, "for by that God above,
90 Now han ye lost myn herte and al my love!
I can nat love a coward, by my faith.
For certes, what so any womman saith,
We alle desiren, if it mighte be,

---

4. Companionable.
5. That he was well contented.
6. A popular song of the time.
7. Sound sleeper.
8. I dreamed that I was in such misfortune.
9. Interpret my dream correctly (i.e.,
in an auspicious manner).
1. Would have laid hold.
2. I.e., killed me.

To han housbondes hardy, wise, and free,°   *generous*
95 And secree,° and no nigard, ne no fool,   *discreet*
Ne him that is agast of every tool,°   *weapon*
Ne noon avauntour.° By that God above,   *boaster*
How dorste ye sayn for shame unto youre love
That any thing mighte make you aferd?
100 Have ye no mannes herte and han a beerd?
Allas, and conne° ye been agast of swevenes?°   *can / dreams*
No thing, God woot, but vanitee[3] in swevene is!
Swevenes engendren of replexiouns,[4]
And ofte of fume° and of complexiouns,°   *gas / bodily humors*
105 Whan humours been too habundant in a wight.[5]
Certes, this dreem which ye han met° tonight   *dreamed*
Comth of the grete superfluitee
Of youre rede colera,[6] pardee,
Which causeth folk to dreden° in hir dremes   *fear*
110 Of arwes,° and of fir with rede lemes,°   *arrows / flames*
Of rede beestes, that they wol hem bite,
Of contek,° and of whelpes grete and lite[7]—   *strife*
Right° as the humour of malencolye[8]   *just*
Causeth ful many a man in sleep to crye
115 For fere of blake beres° or boles° blake,   *bears / bulls*
Or elles blake develes wol hem take.
Of othere humours coude I tell also
That werken many a man in sleep ful wo,
But I wol passe as lightly° as I can.   *quickly*
120 Lo, Caton,[9] which that was so wis a man,
Saide he nat thus? 'Ne do no fors of[1] dremes.'
Now, sire," quod she, "whan we flee fro the bemes,[2]
For Goddes love, as take som laxatif.
Up° peril of my soule and of my lif,   *upon*
125 I conseile you the beste, I wol nat lie,
That bothe of colere and of malencolye
Ye purge you; and for° ye shal nat tarye,   *in order that*
Though in this town is noon apothecarye,
I'shal myself to herbes techen you,
130 That shal been for youre hele[3] and for youre prow,
And in oure yeerd tho herbes shal I finde,
The whiche han of hir propretee by kinde°   *nature*
To purge you binethe and eek above.
Foryet° nat this, for Goddes owene love.   *forget*
135 Ye been ful colerik° of complexioun;   *bilious*

3. I.e., empty illusion.
4. Dreams have their origin in over-eating.
5. I.e., when humors are too abundant in a person. Pertelote's diagnosis is based on the familiar concept that an overabundance of one of the bodily humors in a person affected his temperament.
6. Red bile.
7. And of big and little dogs.
8. I.e., black bile.
9. Dionysius Cato, supposed author of a book of maxims used in elementary education.
1. Pay no attention to.
2. Fly down from the rafters.
3. Health; "prow": benefit.

Ware° the sonne in his ascencioun   *beware that*
Ne finde you nat repleet° of humours hote;°   *filled / hot*
And if it do, I dar wel laye° a grote   *bet*
That ye shul have a fevere terciane,[4]
140 Or an agu that may be youre bane.°   *death*
A day or two ye shul han digestives
Of wormes, er ye take youre laxatives
Of lauriol, centaure, and fumetere,[5]
Or elles of ellebor° that groweth there,   *hellebore*
145 Of catapuce, or of gaitres beries,[6]
Of herbe-ive° growing in oure yeerd ther merye is.[7] *herb ivy*
Pekke hem right up as they growe and ete hem in.
Be merye, housbonde, for youre fader kin!
Dredeth no dreem: I can saye you namore."
150   "Madame," quod he, "graunt mercy of youre lore.[8]
But nathelees, as touching daun° Catoun,   *master*
That hath of wisdom swich a greet renown,
Though that he bad no dremes for to drede,
By God, men may in olde bookes rede
155 Of many a man more of auctoritee°   *authority*
Than evere Caton was, so mote I thee,°   *thrive*
That al the revers sayn of his sentence,°   *opinion*
And han wel founden by experience
That dremes been significaciouns
160 As wel of joye as tribulaciouns
That folk enduren in this lif present.
Ther needeth make of this noon argument:
The verray preve[9] sheweth it in deede.
   "Oon of the gretteste auctour[1] that men rede
165 Saith thus, that whilom two felawes wente
On pilgrimage in a ful good entente,
And happed so they comen in a town,
Wher as ther was swich congregacioun
Of peple, and eek so strait of herbergage,[2]
170 That they ne founde as muche as oo cotage
In which they bothe mighte ylogged° be;   *lodged*
Wherfore they mosten° of necessitee   *must*
As for that night departe° compaignye.   *part*
And eech of hem gooth to his hostelrye,
175 And took his logging as it wolde falle.°   *befall*
That oon of hem was logged in a stalle,
Fer° in a yeerd, with oxen of the plough;   *far away*
That other man was logged wel ynough,
As was his aventure° or his fortune,   *lot*

4. Tertian (recurring every other day).
5. Of laureole, centaury, and fumitory. These, and the herbs mentioned in the next lines, were all common medieval medicines used as cathartics.
6. Of caper berry or of gaiter berry.
7. Where it is pleasant.
8. Many thanks for your instruction.
9. Actual experience.
1. I.e., one of the greatest authors (perhaps Cicero).
2. And also such a shortage of lodging.

180 That us governeth alle as in commune.
And so bifel that longe er it were day,
This man mette° in his bed, ther as he lay,   *dreamed*
How that his felawe gan upon him calle,
And saide, 'Allas, for in an oxes stalle
185 This night I shal be mordred° ther I lie!   *murdered*
Now help me, dere brother, or I die!
In alle haste com to me,' he saide.
    "This man out of his sleep for fere abraide,°   *started up*
But whan that he was wakened of his sleep,
190 He turned him and took of this no keep:°   *heed*
Him thoughte his dreem nas but a vanitee.
Thus twies in his sleeping dremed he,
And atte thridde time yit his felawe
Cam, as him thoughte, and saide, 'I am now slawe:°   *slain*
195 Bihold my bloody woundes deepe and wide.
Aris up erly in the morwe tide[3]
And atte west gate of the town,' quod he,
'A carte ful of dong° ther shaltou see,   *dung*
In which my body is hid ful prively:
200 Do thilke carte arresten boldely.[4]
My gold caused my mordre, sooth to sayn'—
And tolde him every point how he was slain,
With a ful pitous face, pale of hewe.
And truste wel, his dreem he foond° ful trewe,   *found*
205 For on the morwe° as soone as it was day,   *morning*
To his felawes in° he took the way,   *lodging*
And whan that he cam to this oxes stalle,
After his felawe he bigan to calle.
    "The hostiler° answerde him anoon,   *innkeeper*
210 And saide, 'Sire, youre felawe is agoon:°   *gone away*
As soone as day he wente out of the town.'
    "This man gan fallen in suspecioun,
Remembring on his dremes that he mette;°   *dreamed*
And forth he gooth, no lenger wolde he lette,°   *tarry*
215 Unto the west gate of the town, and foond
A dong carte, wente as it were to donge° lond,   *put manure on*
That was arrayed in that same wise
As ye han herd the dede° man devise;   *dead*
And with an hardy herte he gan to crye,
220 'Vengeance and justice of this felonye!
My felawe mordred is this same night,
And in this carte he lith° gaping upright!°   *lies / supine*
I crye out on the ministres,' quod he,
'That sholde keepe and rulen this citee.
225 Harrow,° allas, here lith my felawe slain!'   *help*
What sholde I more unto this tale sayn?
The peple up sterte° and caste the carte to grounde,   *started*

---

3. In the morning.   4. Boldly have this same cart stopped.

And in the middel of the dong they founde
The dede man that mordred was al newe.[5]
230 "O blisful God that art so just and trewe,
Lo, how that thou biwrayest° mordre alway!   *disclose*
Mordre wol out, that see we day by day:
Mordre is so wlatsom° and abhominable   *loathsome*
To God that is so just and resonable,
235 That he ne wol nat suffre it heled° be,   *concealed*
Though it abide a yeer or two or three.
Mordre wol out: this my conclusioun.
And right anoon ministres of that town
Han hent° the cartere and so sore him pined,[6]   *seized*
240 And eek the hostiler so sore engined,°   *racked*
That they biknewe° hir wikkednesse anoon,   *confessed*
And were anhanged° by the nekke boon.   *hanged*
Here may men seen that dremes been to drede.[7]
  "And certes, in the same book I rede—
245 Right in the nexte chapitre after this—
I gabbe° nat, so have I joye or blis—   *lie*
Two men that wolde han passed over see
For certain cause into a fer contree,
If that the wind ne hadde been contrarye
250 That made hem in a citee for to tarye,
That stood ful merye upon an haven° side—   *harbor's*
But on a day again° the even tide   *toward*
The wind gan chaunge, and blewe right as hem leste:[8]
Jolif° and glad they wenten unto reste,   *merry*
255 And casten hem[9] ful erly for to saile.
  "But to that oo man fil° a greet mervaile: *befell*
That oon of hem, in sleeping as he lay,
Him mette[1] a wonder dreem again the day:
Him thoughte a man stood by his beddes side,
260 And him comanded that he sholde abide,
And saide him thus, 'If thou tomorwe wende,
Thou shalt be dreint:° my tale is at an ende.'   *drowned*
  "He wook and tolde his felawe what he mette,
And prayed him his viage° to lette;°   *voyage / delay*
265 As for that day he prayed him to bide.
  "His felawe that lay by his beddes side
Gan for to laughe, and scorned him ful faste.°   *hard*
'No dreem,' quod he, 'may so myn herte agaste°   *terrify*
That I wol lette° for to do my thinges.°   *delay / business*
270 I sette nat a straw by thy dreminges,[2]
For swevenes been but vanitees and japes:[3]
Men dreme alday° of owles or of apes,[4]   *constantly*

---

5. Recently.
6. Tortured.
7. Worthy of being feared.
8. Just as they wished.
9. Determined.

1. He dreamed.
2. I don't care a straw for your dreamings.
3. Dreams are but illusions and frauds.
4. I.e., of absurdities.

And of many a maze° therwithal—   *delusion*
Men dreme of thing that nevere was ne shal.[5]
275 But sith I see that thou wolt here abide,
And thus forsleuthen° wilfully thy tide,°   *waste / time*
Good woot, it reweth me;[6] and have good day.'
And thus he took his leve and wente his way.
But er that he hadde half his cours ysailed—
280 Noot I nat why ne what meschaunce it ailed—
But casuelly the shippes botme rente,[7]
And ship and man under the water wente,
In sighte of othere shippes it biside,
That with hem sailed at the same tide.
285 And therfore, faire Pertelote so dere,
By swiche ensamples olde maistou lere°   *learn*
That no man sholde been too recchelees°   *careless*
Of dremes, for I saye thee doutelees
That many a dreem ful sore is for to drede.
290 "Lo, in the lif of Saint Kenelm[8] I rede—
That was Kenulphus sone, the noble king
Of Mercenrike°—how Kenelm mette a thing   *Mercia*
A lite° er he was mordred on a day.   *little*
His mordre in his avision° he sey.°   *dream / saw*
295 His norice° him expounded everydeel°   *nurse / entirely*
His swevene, and bad him for to keepe him[9] weel
For traison, but he nas but seven yeer old,
And therfore litel tale hath he told
Of any dreem,[1] so holy was his herte.
300 By God, I hadde levere than my sherte[2]
That ye hadde rad° his legende as have I.   *read*
"Dame Pertelote, I saye you trewely,
Macrobeus,[3] that writ the *Avisioun*
In Affrike of the worthy Scipioun,
305 Affermeth° dremes, and saith that they been   *confirms*
Warning of thinges that men after seen.
"And ferthermore, I praye you looketh wel
In the Olde Testament of Daniel,
If he heeld° dremes any vanitee.[4]   *considered*
310 "Rede eek of Joseph[5] and ther shul ye see
Wher° dremes be somtime—I saye nat alle—   *whether*
Warning of thinges that shul after falle.
"Looke of Egypte the king daun Pharao,
His bakere and his botelere° also,   *butler*

5. I.e., shall be.
6. I'm sorry.
7. I don't know why nor what was the trouble with it—but accidentally the ship's bottom split.
8. Kenelm succeeded his father as king of Mercia at the age of 7, but was slain by his aunt (in 821).
9. Guard himself.
1. Therefore he has set little store by any dream.
2. I.e., I'd give my shirt.
3. Macrobius wrote a famous commentary on Cicero's account in *De Republica* of the dream of Scipio Africanus Minor; the commentary came to be regarded as a standard authority on dream lore.
4. See Daniel vii.
5. See Genesis xxxvii.

315 Wher they ne felte noon effect in dremes.[6]
Whoso wol seeke actes of sondry remes°　　　*realms*
May rede of dremes many a wonder thing.
　"Lo Cresus, which that was of Lyde° king,　　*Lydia*
Mette° he nat that he sat upon a tree,　　　*dreamed*
320 Which signified he sholde anhanged° be?　　*hanged*
　"Lo here Andromacha, Ectores° wif,　　　*Hector's*
That day that Ector sholde lese° his lif,　　　*lose*
She dremed on the same night biforn
How that the lif of Ector sholde be lorn,°　　　*lost*
325 If thilke° day he wente into bataile;　　　*that same*
She warned him, but it mighte nat availe:°　　*do any good*
He wente for to fighte nathelees,
But he was slain anoon° of Achilles.　　　*right away*
But thilke tale is al too long to telle,
330 And eek it is neigh day, I may nat dwelle.
Shortly I saye, as for conclusioun,
That I shal han of this avisioun[7]
Adversitee, and I saye ferthermoor
That I ne telle of[8] laxatives no stoor,
335 For they been venimes,° I woot it weel:　　　*poisons*
I hem defye, I love hem neveradeel.°　　　*not a bit*
　"Now lat us speke of mirthe and stinte° al this.　　*stop*
Madame Pertelote, so have I blis,
Of oo thing God hath sente me large grace:
340 For whan I see the beautee of youre face—
Ye been so scarlet reed° aboute youre yën—　　*red*
It maketh al my drede for to dien.
For also siker° as *In principio*,[9]　　　*certain*
Mulier est hominis confusio.[1]
345 Madame, the sentence° of this Latin is,　　*meaning*
'Womman is mannes joye and al his blis.'
For whan I feele anight youre softe side—
Al be it that I may nat on you ride,
For that oure perche is maad so narwe, allas—
350 I am so ful of joye and of solas°　　　*delight*
That I defye bothe swevene and dreem."
And with that word he fleigh° down fro the beem,　*flew*
For it was day, and eek his hennes alle,
And with a "chuk" he gan hem for to calle,
355 For he hadde founde a corn lay in the yeerd.
Real° he was, he was namore aferd:°　　*regal / afraid*
He fethered[2] Pertelote twenty time,
And trad[3] hire as ofte er it was prime.

6. See Genesis xxxix–xli.
7. Divinely inspired dream (as opposed to the more ordinary "swevene" or "dreem").
8. Set by.
9. A tag from the Gospel of St. John which gives the essential premises of Christianity: "In the beginning was the Word."
1. Woman is man's ruination.
2. I.e., embraced.
3. Trod, copulated with; "prime": 9 A.M.

He looketh as it were a grim leoun,
360 And on his toes he rometh up and down:
Him deined[4] nat to sette his foot to grounde.
He chukketh whan he hath a corn yfounde,
And to him rennen° thanne his wives alle.   *run*
Thus royal, as a prince is in his halle,
365 Leve I this Chauntecleer in his pasture,
And after wol I telle his aventure.
    Whan that the month in which the world bigan,
That highte March, whan God first maked man,
Was compleet, and passed were also,
370 Sin March bigan, thritty dayes and two,[5]
Bifel that Chauntecleer in al his pride,
His sevene wives walking him biside,
Caste up his yën to the brighte sonne,
That in the signe of Taurus hadde yronne
375 Twenty degrees and oon and somwhat more,
And knew by kinde,° and by noon other lore,   *nature*
That it was prime, and crew with blisful stevene.°   *voice*
"The sonne," he saide, "is clomben[6] up on hevene
Fourty degrees and oon and more, ywis.
380 Madame Pertelote, my worldes blis,
Herkneth thise blisful briddes° how they singe,   *birds*
And see the fresshe flowres how they springe:
Ful is myn herte of revel and solas."
But sodeinly him fil° a sorweful cas,°   *befell / chance*
385 For evere the latter ende of joye is wo—
God woot that worldly joye is soone ago,
And if a rethor° coude faire endite,   *rhetorician*
He in a cronicle saufly° mighte it write,   *safely*
As for a soverein notabilitee.[7]
390 Now every wis man lat him herkne me:
This storye is also° trewe, I undertake,   *as*
As is the book of *Launcelot de Lake*,[8]
That wommen holde in ful greet reverence.
Now wol I turne again to my sentence.°   *main point*
395   A colfox[9] ful of sly iniquitee,
That in the grove hadde woned° yeres three,   *dwelled*
By heigh imaginacion forncast,[1]
The same night thurghout the hegges° brast°   *hedges / burst*
Into the yeerd ther Chauntecleer the faire
400 Was wont, and eek his wives, to repaire;

4. He deigned.
5. The rhetorical time-telling is perhaps burlesque; it can be read as yielding the date April 3, though May 3 seems intended from lines 374–75: on May 3 the sun would have passed some twenty degrees through Taurus (the Bull), the second sign of the zodiac; the sun would be forty degrees from the horizon at 9 o'clock in the morning.
6. Has climbed.
7. Indisputable fact.
8. Romances of the courteous knight Lancelot of the Lake were very popular.
9. Fox with black markings.
1. Predestined by divine planning.

And in a bed of wortes° stille he lay   *cabbages*
Til it was passed undren° of the day,   *midmorning*
Waiting his time on Chauntecleer to falle,
As gladly doon thise homicides alle,
405 That in await liggen to mordre² men.
O false mordrour, lurking in thy den!
O newe Scariot!³ Newe Geniloun!
False dissimilour!° O Greek Sinoun,⁴   *dissembler*
That broughtest Troye al outrely° to sorwe!   *utterly*
410 O Chauntecleer, accursed be that morwe°   *morning*
That thou into the yeerd flaugh° fro the bemes!   *flew*
Thou were ful wel ywarned by thy dremes
That thilke day was perilous to thee;
But what that God forwoot° moot° needes be, *foreknows / must*
415 After° the opinion of certain clerkes: *according to*
Witnesse on him that any parfit° clerk is   *perfect*
That in scole is greet altercacioun
In this matere, and greet disputisoun,°   *disputation*
And hath been of an hundred thousand men.
420 But I ne can nat bulte° it to the bren,°   *sift / husks*
As can the holy doctour Augustin,
Or Boece, or the bisshop Bradwardin⁵—
Wheither that Goddes worthy forwiting°   *foreknowledge*
Straineth me nedely⁶ for to doon a thing
425 ("Nedely" clepe I simple necessitee),
Or elles if free chois be graunted me
To do that same thing or do it nought,
Though God forwoot° it er that I was wrought;   *foreknew*
Or if his witing° straineth neveradeel,   *knowledge*
430 But by necessitee condicionel⁷—
I wol nat han to do of swich matere:
My tale is of a cok, as ye may heere,
That took his conseil of his wif with sorwe,
To walken in the yeerd upon that morwe
435 That he hadde met° the dreem that I you tolde.   *dreamed*
Wommenes conseils been ful ofte colde,⁸
Wommanes conseil broughte us first to wo,
And made Adam fro Paradis to go,
Ther as he was ful merye and wel at ese.
440 But for I noot° to whom it mighte displese   *don't know*
If I conseil of wommen wolde blame,

2. That lie in ambush to murder.
3. Judas Iscariot. "Geniloun" is Ganelon, who betrayed Roland to the Saracens (in the medieval French epic *The Song of Roland*).
4. Sinon, who persuaded the Trojans to take the Greeks' wooden horse into their city—with, of course, the result that the city was destroyed.
5. St. Augustine, Boethius (6th-century Roman philosopher, whose *Consolation of Philosophy* was translated by Chaucer), and Thomas Bradwardine (Archbishop of Canterbury, d. 1349) were all concerned with the interrelationship between man's free will and God's foreknowledge.
6. Constrains me necessarily.
7. Boethius' "conditional necessity" permitted a large measure of free will.
8. I.e., baneful.

Passe over, for I saide it in my game°—   *sport*
Rede auctours where they trete of swich matere,
And what they sayn of wommen ye may heere—
₄₄₅ Thise been the cokkes wordes and nat mine:
I can noon harm of no womman divine.°   *guess*
  Faire in the sond° to bathe hire merily   *sand*
Lith° Pertelote, and alle hir sustres by,   *lies*
Again° the sonne, and Chauntecleer so free°   *in / noble*
₄₅₀ Soong° merier than the mermaide in the see—   *sang*
For Physiologus[9] saith sikerly
How that they singen wel and merily.
  And so bifel that as he caste his yë
Among the wortes on a boterflye,°   *butterfly*
₄₅₅ He was war of this fox that lay ful lowe.
No thing ne liste him[1] thanne for to crowe,
But cride anoon "Cok cok!" and up he sterte,°   *started*
As man that[2] was affrayed in his herte—
For naturelly a beest desireth flee
₄₆₀ Fro his contrarye[3] if he may it see,
Though he nevere erst° hadde seen it with his yë.   *before*
This Chauntecleer, whan he gan him espye,
He wolde han fled, but that the fox anoon
Saide, "Gentil sire, allas, wher wol ye goon?
₄₆₅ Be ye afraid of me that am youre freend?
Now certes, I were worse than a feend
If I to you wolde° harm or vilainye.   *meant*
I am nat come youre conseil° for t'espye,   *secrets*
But trewely the cause of my cominge
₄₇₀ Was only for to herkne how that ye singe:
For trewely, ye han as merye a stevene°   *voice*
As any angel hath that is in hevene.
Therwith ye han in musik more feelinge
Than hadde Boece,[4] or any that can singe.
₄₇₅ My lord your fader—God his soule blesse!—
And eek youre moder, of hir gentilesse,°   *gentility*
Han in myn hous ybeen, to my grete ese.
And certes sire, ful fain° wolde I you plese.   *gladly*
  "But for men speke of singing, I wol saye,
₄₈₀ So mote I brouke[5] wel mine yën twaye,
Save ye, I herde nevere man so singe
As dide youre fader in the morweninge.
Certes, it was of herte[6] al that he soong.°   *sang*
And for to make his vois the more strong,
₄₈₅ He wolde so paine him[7] that with bothe his yën

---

9. Supposed author of a bestiary, a book of moralized zoology describing both natural and supernatural animals (including mermaids).
1. He wished.
2. Like one who.

3. I.e., his natural enemy.
4. Boethius also wrote a treatise on music.
5. So might I enjoy the use of.
6. Heartfelt.
7. Take pains.

He moste winke,[8] so loude wolde he cryen;
And stonden on his tiptoon therwithal,
And strecche forth his nekke long and smal;
And eek he was of swich discrecioun
490 That ther nas no man in no regioun
That him in song or wisdom mighte passe.
I have wel rad° in *Daun Burnel the Asse*[9]   read
Among his vers how that ther was a cok,
For a preestes sone yaf him a knok[1]
495 Upon his leg whil he was yong and nice,°   foolish
He made him for to lese° his benefice.[2]   lose
But certain, ther nis no comparisoun
Bitwixe the wisdom and discrecioun
Of youre fader and of his subtiltee.
500 Now singeth, sire, for sainte° charitee!   holy
Lat see, conne° ye youre fader countrefete?"°   can / imitate
    This Chauntecleer his winges gan to bete,
As man that coude his traison nat espye,
So was he ravisshed with his flaterye.
505 Allas, ye lordes, many a fals flatour°   flatterer
Is in youre court, and many a losengeour,°   deceiver
That plesen you wel more, by my faith,
Than he that soothfastnesse° unto you saith!   truth
Redeth Ecclesiaste[3] of flaterye.
510 Beeth war, ye lordes, of hir trecherye.
    This Chauntecleer stood hye upon his toos,
Strecching his nekke, and heeld his yën cloos,
And gan to crowe loude for the nones;°   occasion
And daun Russel the fox sterte° up atones,   jumped
515 And by the gargat° hente° Chauntecleer,   throat / seized
And on his bak toward the wode him beer,°   bore
For yit ne was ther no man that him sued.°   followed
    O destinee that maist nat been eschued!°   eschewed
Allas that Chauntecleer fleigh° fro the bemes!   flew
520 Allas his wif ne roughte nat of[4] dremes!
And on a Friday fil° al this meschaunce!   befell
    O Venus that art goddesse of plesaunce,
Sin that thy servant was this Chauntecleer,
And in thy service dide al his power—
525 More for delit than world[5] to multiplye—
Why woldestou suffre him on thy day[6] to die?
    O Gaufred,[7] dere maister soverein,

8. He had to shut his eyes.
9. Master Brunellus, a discontented donkey, was the hero of a 12th-century satirical poem by Nigel Wireker.
1. Because a priest's son gave him a knock.
2. The offended cock neglected to crow so that his master, now grown to manhood, overslept, missing his ordination

and losing his benefice.
3. The Book of Ecclesiasticus, in the Apocrypha.
4. Didn't care for.
5. I.e., population.
6. Friday is Venus' day.
7. Geoffrey of Vinsauf, a famous medieval rhetorician, who wrote a lament on the death of Richard I in which he

That, whan thy worthy king Richard was slain
With shot,[8] complainedest his deeth so sore,
530 Why ne hadde I now thy sentence and thy lore,[9]
The Friday for to chide as diden ye?
For on a Friday soothly slain was he.
Thanne wolde I shewe you how that I coude plaine[1]
For Chauntecleres drede and for his paine.
535   Certes, swich cry ne lamentacioun
Was nevere of ladies maad whan Ilioun°   *Ilium, Troy*
Was wonne, and Pyrrus[2] with his straite swerd,
Whan he hadde hent° King Priam by the beerd   *seized*
And slain him, as saith us *Eneidos*,[3]
540 As maden alle the hennes in the cloos,°   *yard*
Whan they hadde seen of Chauntecleer the sighte.
But sovereinly[4] Dame Pertelote shrighte°   *shrieked*
Ful louder than dide Hasdrubales[5] wif
Whan that hir housbonde hadde lost his lif,
545 And that the Romains hadden brend° Cartage: *burned*
She was so ful of torment and of rage°   *madness*
That wilfully unto the fir she sterte,°   *jumped*
And brende hirselven with a stedefast herte.
    O woful hennes, right so criden ye
550 As, whan that Nero brende the citee
Of Rome, criden senatoures wives
For that hir housbondes losten alle hir lives:[6]
Withouten gilt this Nero hath hem slain.
Now wol I turne to my tale again.
555   The sely° widwe and eek hir doughtres two   *innocent*
Herden thise hennes crye and maken wo,
And out at dores sterten° they anoon,   *leaped*
And sien° the fox toward the grove goon,   *saw*
And bar upon his bak the cok away,
560 And criden, "Out, harrow,° and wailaway,   *help*
Ha, ha, the fox," and after him they ran,
And eek with staves many another man;
Ran Colle oure dogge, and Talbot and Gerland,[7]
And Malkin with a distaf in hir hand,
565 Ran cow and calf, and eek the verray hogges,
Sore aferd° for berking of the dogges   *frightened*
And shouting of the men and wommen eke.
They ronne° so hem thoughte hir herte breke;[8]   *ran*
They yelleden as feendes doon in helle;

scolded Friday, the day on which the king died.
8. I.e., a missile.
9. Thy wisdom and thy learning.
1. Lament.
2. Pyrrhus was the Greek who slew Priam, king of Troy. "Straite": rigorous, unsparing.
3. As the *Aeneid* tells us.

4. Splendidly.
5. Hasdrubal was king of Carthage when it was destroyed by the Romans.
6. According to the legend, Nero not only set fire to Rome (in A.D. 64) but also put many senators to death.
7. Two other dogs.
8. Would break.

570 The dokes° criden as men wolde hem quelle;°   *ducks / kill*
The gees for fere flowen° over the trees;   *flew*
Out of the hive cam the swarm of bees;
So hidous was the noise, a, benedicite,°   *bless me*
Certes, he Jakke Straw⁹ and his meinee°   *company*
575 Ne made nevere shoutes half so shrille
Whan that they wolden any Fleming kille,
As thilke day was maad upon the fox:
Of bras they broughten bemes° and of box,°   *trumpets / boxwood*
Of horn, of boon,° in whiche they blewe and pouped,¹   *bone*
580 And therwithal they skriked² and they houped—
It seemed as that hevene sholde falle.
      Now goode men, I praye you herkneth alle:
Lo, how Fortune turneth° sodeinly   *reverses, overturns*
The hope and pride eek of hir enemy.
585 This cok that lay upon the foxes bak,
In al his drede unto the fox he spak,
And saide, "Sire, if that I were as ye,
Yit sholde I sayn, as wis° God helpe me,   *surely*
'Turneth ayain, ye proude cherles alle!
590 A verray pestilence upon you falle!
Now am I come unto this wodes side,
Maugree your heed,³ the cok shal here abide.
I wol him ete, in faith, and that anoon.' "
      The fox answerde, "In faith, it shal be doon."
595 And as he spak that word, al sodeinly
The cok brak from his mouth deliverly,°   *nimbly*
And hye upon a tree he fleigh° anoon.   *flew*
      And whan the fox sawgh that he was agoon,
"Allas," quod he, "O Chauntecleer, allas!
600 I have to you," quod he, "ydoon trespas,
In as muche as I maked you aferd
Whan I you hente° and broughte out of the yeerd.   *seized*
But sire, I dide it in no wikke° entente: *wicked*
Come down, and I shal telle you what I mente.
605 I shal saye sooth to you, God help me so."
      "Nay thanne," quod he, "I shrewe° us bothe two: *curse*
But first I shrewe myself, bothe blood and bones,
If thou bigile me ofter than ones;
Thou shalt namore thurgh thy flaterye
610 Do° me to singe and winken with myn yë.   *cause*
For he that winketh whan he sholde see,
Al wilfully, God lat him nevere thee."°   *thrive*
      "Nay," quod the fox, "but God yive him meschaunce
That is so undiscreet of governaunce°   *self-control*
615 That jangleth° whan he sholde holde his pees."   *chatters*

9. One of the leaders of the Peasant's   1. Tooted.
Revolt in 1381, which was partially di-   2. Shrieked; "houped": whooped.
rected against the Flemings living in   3. Despite your head—i.e., despite any-
London.   thing you can do.

Lo, swich it is for to be recchelees°   *careless*
And necligent and truste on flaterye.
But ye that holden this tale a folye
As of a fox, or of a cok and hen,
620 Taketh the moralitee, goode men.
For Saint Paul saith that al that writen is
To oure doctrine it is ywrit, ywis:[4]
Taketh the fruit, and lat the chaf be stille.
Now goode God, if that it be thy wille,
625 As saith my lord, so make us alle goode men,
And bringe us to his hye blisse. Amen.

The Miller's Tale[1]

The Introduction

Whan that the Knight hadde thus his tale ytold,[2]
In al the route° nas ther yong ne old   *group*
That he ne saide it was a noble storye,
And worthy for to drawen° to memorye,   *recall*
5 And namely° the gentils everichoon.   *especially*
Oure Hoste lough° and swoor, "So mote I goon,[3]   *laughed*
This gooth aright: unbokeled is the male.°   *pouch*
Lat see now who shal telle another tale.
For trewely the game is wel bigonne.
10 Now telleth ye, sire Monk, if that ye conne,°   *can*
Somwhat to quite° with the Knightes tale."   *repay*
The Millere, that for dronken[4] was al pale,
So that unnethe° upon his hors he sat,   *with difficulty*
He nolde avalen° neither hood ne hat,   *doff*
15 Ne abiden no man for his curteisye,
But in Pilates vois[5] he gan to crye,

4. See Romans xv.4.
1. The Miller's Tale belongs to the literary genre known as the "fabliau," a short story in verse that generally involves bourgeois or lower-class characters in an outrageous, often obscene plot, which is, however, realistically handled by the narrator. The fabliau is peculiarly French, and aside from the three or four examples in Chaucer there are few representatives of it in English. Yet Chaucer was supreme in this kind of tale as in many others, and the Miller's Tale is generally considered the best-told fabliau in any language.

Two originally separate plots are the basis of the Miller's Tale, both of them probably already old in Chaucer's time. In the first, a student—students are often the heroes of fabliaux and were probably often their authors—creates an opportunity to sleep with a woman by persuading her husband that Noah's flood is about to be repeated; and in the second, a lover who has been tricked into a humiliatingly misdirected kiss takes a dreadful vengeance on his tormentor. Whether or not Chaucer first united these traditional plots is not clear, but in any case their union, culminating in the scorched student's cry of "Water!" is a brilliant stroke, and brilliantly handled by Chaucer.
2. The Knight's Tale is actually the first one told on the Canterbury pilgrimage, immediately following the General Prologue.
3. So might I walk.
4. I.e., drunkenness.
5. The harsh voice usually associated with the character of Pontius Pilate in the mystery plays.

And swoor, "By armes[6] and by blood and bones,
I can° a noble tale for the nones,   *know*
With which I wol now quite the Knightes tale."
20 Oure Hoste sawgh that he was dronke of ale,
And saide, "Abide, Robin, leve° brother,   *dear*
Som bettre man shal telle us first another.
Abide, and lat us werken thriftily."°   *with propriety*
"By Goddes soule," quod he, "that wol nat I,
25 For I wol speke or elles go my way."
Oure Host answerde, "Tel on, a devele way![7]
Thou art a fool; thy wit is overcome."
"Now herkneth," quod the Millere, "alle and some.[8]
But first I make a protestacioun°   *public affirmation*
30 That I am dronke: I knowe it by my soun.°   *tone of voice*
And therfore if that I mis° speke or saye,   *amiss*
Wite it[9] the ale of Southwerk; I you praye;
For I wol telle a legende and a lif
Bothe of a carpenter and of his wif,
35 How that a clerk hath set the wrightes cappe."[1]
The Reeve answerde and saide, "Stint thy clappe![2]
Lat be thy lewed° dronken harlotrye.°   *ignorant / obscenity*
It is a sinne and eek° a greet folye   *also*
To apairen° any man or him defame,   *injure*
40 And eek to bringen wives in swich fame.°   *report*
Thou maist ynough of othere thinges sayn."
This dronken Millere spak ful soone again,
And saide, "Leve° brother Osewold,   *dear*
Who hath no wif, he is no cokewold.°   *cuckold*
45 But I saye nat therfore that thou art oon.
Ther ben ful goode wives many oon,°   *a one*
And evere a thousand goode ayains oon badde.
That knowestou wel thyself but if thou madde.°   *rave*
Why artou angry with my tale now?
50 I have a wif, pardee, as wel as thou,
Yit nolde° I, for the oxen in my plough,   *would not*
Take upon me more than ynough
As deemen of myself that I were oon:
I wol bileve wel that I am noon.
55 An housbonde shal nought been inquisitif
Of Goddes privetee,° nor of his wif.   *secrets*
So[3] he may finde Goddes foison° there,   *plenty*
Of the remenant° needeth nought enquere."°   *rest / inquire*
What sholde I more sayn but this Millere
60 He nolde his wordes for no man forbere,
But tolde his cherles tale in his manere.
M'athinketh° that I shal reherce° it here,   *I regret / repeat*

6. I.e., by God's arms.
7. I.e., in the devil's name.
8. Each and every one.
9. Blame it on.

1. I.e., how a clerk made a fool of a
carpenter.
2. Stop your chatter.
3. Provided that.

And therfore every gentil wight I praye,
Deemeth nought, for Goddes love, that I saye
65 Of yvel entente, but for° I moot reherse   *because*
Hir tales alle, be they bet° or werse,   *better*
Or elles falsen° som of my matere.   *falsify*
And therfore, whoso list it nought yheere
Turne over the leef, and chese° another tale,   *choose*
70 For he shal finde ynowe,° grete and smale,   *enough*
Of storial[4] thing that toucheth gentilesse,°   *gentility*
And eek moralitee and holinesse:
Blameth nought me if that ye chese amis.
The Millere is a cherl, ye knowe wel this,
75 So was the Reeve eek, and othere mo,
And harlotrye° they tolden bothe two.   *ribaldry*
Aviseth you,[5] and putte me out of blame:
And eek men shal nought maken ernest of game.

The Tale

Whilom° ther was dwelling at Oxenforde   *once upon a time*
80 A riche gnof° that gestes heeld to boorde,[6]   *boor*
And of his craft he was a carpenter.
With him ther was dwelling a poore scoler,
Hadde lerned art,[7] but al his fantasye°   *interest*
Was turned for to lere° astrologye,   *learn*
85 And coude a certain of conclusiouns,
To deemen by interrogaciouns,[8]
If that men axed° him in certain houres   *asked*
Whan that men sholde have droughte or elles showres,
Or if men axed him what shal bifalle
90 Of every thing—I may nat rekene hem alle.
This clerk was cleped° hende[9] Nicholas.   *called*
Of derne love he coude, and of solas,[1]
And therto he was sly and ful privee,°   *secretive*
And lik a maide meeke for to see.
95 A chambre hadde he in that hostelrye
Allone, withouten any compaignye,
Ful fetisly ydight[2] with herbes swoote,°   *sweet*
And he himself as sweete as is the roote
Of licoris or any setewale.[3]
100 His *Almageste*[4] and bookes grete and smale,
His astrelabye,[5] longing for his art,
His augrim stones,[6] layen faire apart

4. Historical, i.e., true.
5. Take heed.
6. I.e., took in boarders.
7. Who had completed the first stage of university education (the trivium).
8. I.e., and he knew a number of propositions on which to base astrological analyses (which would reveal the matters in ll. 87–90).
9. Handy, sly, attractive.

1. I.e., he knew about secret love and pleasurable practices.
2. Elegantly furnished.
3. Setwall, a spice.
4. 2nd-century treatise by Ptolemy, still the standard astronomy textbook.
5. Astrolabe, an astronomical instrument. "Longing for": belonging to.
6. Counters used in arithmetic.

On shelves couched° at his beddes heed;   *set*
His presse° ycovered with a falding reed;[7]   *storage chest*
105 And al above ther lay a gay sautrye,°   *psaltery*
On which he made a-nightes melodye
So swetely that al the chambre roong,°   *rang*
And *Angelus ad Virginem*[8] he soong,
And after that he soong the *Kinges Note:*
110 Ful often blessed was his merye throte.
And thus this sweete clerk his time spente
After his freendes finding and his rente.[9]

    This carpenter hadde wedded newe° a wif   *lately*
Which that he loved more than his lif.
115 Of eighteteene yeer she was of age;
Jalous he was, and heeld hire narwe in cage,
For she was wilde and yong, and he was old,
And deemed himself been lik a cokewold.[1]
He knew nat Caton,[2] for his wit was rude,
120 That bad men sholde wedde his similitude:[3]
Men sholde wedden after hir estat,[4]
For youthe and elde° is often at debat.   *age*
But sith that he was fallen in the snare,
He moste endure, as other folk, his care.

125   Fair was this yonge wif, and therwithal
As any wesele° hir body gent and smal.[5]   *weasel*
A ceint she wered, barred[6] al of silk;
A barmcloth° as whit as morne milk   *apron*
Upon hir lendes,° ful of many a gore;°   *loins / strip of cloth*
130 Whit was hir smok,° and broiden[7] al bifore   *undergarment*
And eek bihinde, on hir coler° aboute,   *collar*
Of° col-blak silk, withinne and eek withoute;   *with*
The tapes° of hir white voluper°   *ribbons / cap*
Were of the same suite of[8] hir coler;
135 Hir filet° brood° of silk and set ful hye;   *headband / broad*
And sikerly° she hadde a likerous° yë;   *certainly / wanton*
Ful smale ypulled[9] were hir browes two,
And tho were bent,° and blake as any slo.°   *arching / sloeberry*
She was ful more blisful on to see
140 Than is the newe perejonette° tree,   *pear*
And softer than the wolle° is of a wether;°   *wool / ram*
And by hir girdel° heeng° a purs of lether,   *belt / hung*
Tasseled with silk and perled with latoun.[1]

7. Red coarse wool.
8. "The Angel's Address to the Virgin," a hymn; *"Kinges Note"*: probably a popular song of the time.
9. In accordance with his friends' provision and his own income.
1. I.e., suspected of himself that he was like a cuckold.
2. Dionysius Cato, the supposed author of a book of maxims used in elementary education.
3. Commanded that one should wed his equal.
4. Men should marry according to their condition.
5. Slender and delicate.
6. A belt she wore, with transverse stripes.
7. Embroidered.
8. I.e., the same pattern as.
9. Delicately plucked.
1. I.e., with brassy spangles on it.

In al this world, to seeken up and down,
145 Ther nis no man so wis that coude thenche°   *imagine*
So gay a popelote° or swich° a wenche.   *doll / such*
Ful brighter was the shining of hir hewe
Than in the Towr[2] the noble° yforged newe.   *gold coin*
But of hir song, it was as loud and yerne°   *lively*
150 As any swalwe sitting on a berne.°   *barn*
Therto she coude skippe and make game[3]
As any kide or calf folwing his dame.°   *mother*
Hir mouth was sweete as bragot or the meeth,[4]
Or hoord of apples laid in hay or heeth.°   *heather*
155 Winsing° she was as is a joly° colt,   *skittish / high-spirited*
Long as a mast, and upright° as a bolt.°   *straight / arrow*
A brooch she bar upon hir lowe coler
As brood as is the boos° of a bokeler;°   *boss / shield*
Hir shoes were laced on hir legges hye.
160 She was a primerole,° a piggesnye,°   *cowslip / pig's eye*
For any lord to leggen° in his bedde,   *lay*
Or yit for any good yeman to wedde.

Now sire, and eft° sire, so bifel the cas   *again*
That on a day this hende Nicholas
165 Fil° with this yonge wif to rage° and playe,   *happened / flirt*
Whil that hir housbonde was at Oseneye[5]
(As clerkes been ful subtil and ful quainte),°   *clever*
And prively he caughte hire by the queinte,°   *pudendum*
And saide, "Ywis, but if ich° have my wille,   *I*
170 For derne° love of thee, lemman, I spille,"°   *secret / die*
And heeld hire harde by the haunche-bones,
And saide, "Lemman,° love me al atones,[6]   *mistress*
Or I wol dien, also° God me save."   *so*
And she sproong° as a colt dooth in a trave,[7]   *sprang*
175 And with hir heed she wried° faste away;   *twisted*
She saide, "I wol nat kisse thee, by my fay.°   *faith*
Why, lat be," quod she, "lat be, Nicholas!
Or I wol crye 'Out, harrow,° and allas!'   *help*
Do way youre handes, for your curteisye!"
180 This Nicholas gan mercy for to crye,
And spak so faire, and profred him so faste,[8]
That she hir love him graunted atte laste,
And swoor hir ooth by Saint Thomas of Kent[9]
That she wolde been at his comandement,
185 Whan that she may hir leiser[1] wel espye.
"Myn housbonde is so ful of jalousye
That but ye waite° wel and been privee,   *be on guard*
I woot right wel I nam but deed," quod she.

2. The Tower of London.   6. Right now.
3. Play.   7. Frame for a restive horse.
4. "Bragot" and "meeth" are honey   8. I.e., pushed himself so vigorously.
drinks.   9. Thomas à Becket.
5. A town near Oxford.   1. I.e., opportunity.

"Ye moste been ful derne as in this cas."

190 "Nay, therof care thee nought," quod Nicholas.

"A clerk hadde litherly biset his while,[2]

But if he coude a carpenter bigile."

And thus they been accorded and ysworn

To waite° a time, as I have told biforn.　　　　　*watch for*

195 Whan Nicholas hadde doon this everydeel,

And thakked° hire upon the lendes° weel,　　　*patted / loins*

He kiste hire sweete, and taketh his sautrye,

And playeth faste, and maketh melodye.

Thanne fil° it thus, that to the parissh chirche,　　*befell*

200 Cristes owene werkes for to wirche,°　　　　　*perform*

This goode wif wente on an haliday:°　　　　　*holy day*

Hir forheed shoon as bright as any day,

So was it wasshen whan she leet° hir werk.　　　　*left*

Now was ther of that chirche a parissh clerk,

205 The which that was ycleped° Absolon:　　　　　*called*

Crul° was his heer, and as the gold it shoon,　　　*curly*

And strouted° as a fanne[3] large and brode;　　*spread out*

Ful straight and evene lay his joly shode.[4]

His rode° was reed, his yën greye as goos.°　　*complexion / goose*

210 With Poules window corven[5] on his shoos,

In hoses° rede he wente fetisly.°　　　*stockings / elegantly*

Yclad he was ful smale° and proprely,　　　　　*finely*

Al in a kirtel° of a light waget°—　　　　　*tunic / blue*

Ful faire and thikke been the pointes[6] set—

215 And therupon he hadde a gay surplis,°　　　　　*surplice*

As whit as is the blosme upon the ris.°　　　　　*bough*

A merye child° he was, so God me save.　　　　　*lad*

Wel coude he laten° blood, and clippe, and shave,　*let*

And maken a chartre of land, or acquitaunce;[7]

220 In twenty manere° coude he trippe and daunce　　　*ways*

After the scole of Oxenforde tho,

And with his legges casten° to and fro,　　　　　*prance*

And playen songes on a smal rubible;°　　　　　*fiddle*

Therto he soong somtime a loud quinible,[8]

225 And as wel coude he playe on a giterne:°　　　　　*guitar*

In al the town nas brewhous ne taverne

That he ne visited with his solas,°　　　　　*entertainment*

Ther any gailard tappestere[9] was.

But sooth to sayn, he was somdeel squaimous°　　*squeamish*

230 Of farting, and of speeche daungerous,°　　　　*fastidious*

This Absolon, that joly° was and gay,　　　*pretty, amorous*

Gooth with a cencer° on the haliday,　　　*incense-burner*

2. Poorly employed his time.
3. Wide-mouthed basket for separating grain from chaff.
4. Parting of the hair.
5. Carved with intricate designs, like the tracery in the windows of St. Paul's.
6. Laces for fastening the tunic and holding up the hose.
7. Legal release.
8. Part requiring a very high voice.
9. Gay barmaid.

Cencing the wives of the parissh faste,
And many a lovely look on hem he caste,
235 And namely° on this carpenteres wif: *especially*
To looke on hire him thoughte a merye lif.
She was so propre° and sweete and likerous,[1]   *neat*
I dar wel sayn, if she hadde been a mous,
And he a cat, he wolde hire hente° anoon.   *pounce on*
240 This parissh clerk, this joly Absolon,
Hath in his herte swich a love-longinge°   *lovesickness*
That of no wif ne took he noon offringe—
For curteisye he saide he wolde noon.
The moone, whan it was night, ful brighte shoon,°   *shone*
245 And Absolon his giterne° hath ytake—   *guitar*
For paramours° he thoughte for to wake—   *love*
And forth he gooth, jolif° and amorous,   *pretty*
Til he cam to the carpenteres hous,
A litel after cokkes hadde ycrowe,
250 And dressed him up by a shot-windowe[2]
That was upon the carpenteres wal.
He singeth in his vois gentil and smal,°   *dainty*
"Now dere lady, if thy wille be,
I praye you that ye wol rewe° on me,"   *have pity*
255 Ful wel accordant to his giterninge.[3]
This carpenter awook and herde him singe,
And spak unto his wif, and saide anoon,
"What, Alison, heerestou nought Absolon
That chaunteth thus under oure bowres° wal?"   *bedroom's*
260 And she answerde hir housbonde therwithal,
"Yis, God woot, John, I heere it everydeel."
    This passeth forth. What wol ye bet than weel?[4]
Fro day to day this joly Absolon
So woweth° hire that him is wo-bigoon: *woos*
265 He waketh° al the night and al the day;   *stays awake*
He kembed° his lokkes brode[5] and made him gay;   *combed*
He woweth hire by menes and brocage,[6]
And swoor he wolde been hir owene page;°   *personal servant*
He singeth, brokking° as a nightingale;   *trilling*
270 He sente hire piment,[7] meeth, and spiced ale,
And wafres° piping hoot out of the gleede;°   *pastries / coals*
And for she was of towne,[8] he profred meede°—   *bribe*
For som folk wol be wonnen for richesse,
And som for strokes,° and som for gentilesse.   *blows*
275 Somtime to shewe his lightnesse and maistrye,[9]
He playeth Herodes[1] upon a scaffold° hye.   *platform, stage*

---

1. Wanton, appetizing.
2. Took his position by a hinged window.
3. In harmony with his guitar-playing.
4. Better than well.
5. I.e., wide-spreading.

6. By intermediaries and mediation.
7. Spiced wine; "meeth": mead.
8. Since she was a town woman.
9. Facility and virtuosity.
1. Herod, a role traditionally played as a bully in the mystery plays.

But what availeth him as in this cas?
She loveth so this hende Nicholas
That Absolon may blowe the bukkes horn;[2]
280 He ne hadde for his labour but a scorn.
And thus she maketh Absolon hir ape,[3]
And al his ernest turneth til a jape.°   *joke*
Ful sooth is this proverbe, it is no lie;
Men saith right thus: "Alway the nye slye
285 Maketh the ferre leve to be loth."[4]
For though that Absolon be wood° or wroth,   *furious*
By cause that he fer was from hir sighte,
This nye° Nicholas stood in his lighte.   *nearby*
       Now beer° thee wel, thou hende Nicholas,   *bear*
290 For Absolon may waile and singe allas.
       And so bifel it on a Saterday
This carpenter was goon til Oseney,
And hende Nicholas and Alisoun
Accorded been to this conclusioun,
295 That Nicholas shal shapen° hem a wile°   *arrange / trick*
This sely[5] jalous housbonde to bigile,
And if so be this game wente aright,
She sholden sleepen in his arm al night—
For this was his desir and hire° also.   *hers*
300 And right anoon, withouten wordes mo,
This Nicholas no lenger wolde tarye,
But dooth ful softe unto his chambre carye
Bothe mete and drinke for a day or twaye,
And to hir housbonde bad hire for to saye,
305 If that he axed after Nicholas,
She sholde saye she niste° wher he was—   *didn't know*
Of al that day she sawgh him nought with yë:
She trowed° that he was in maladye,   *believed*
For for no cry hir maide coude him calle,
310 He nolde answere for no thing that mighte falle.°   *happen*
       This passeth forth al thilke° Saterday   *this*
That Nicholas stille in his chambre lay,
And eet,° and sleep,° or dide what him leste,[6]   *ate / slept*
Til Sonday that the sonne gooth to reste.
315   This sely carpenter hath greet mervaile
Of Nicholas, or what thing mighte him aile,
And saide, "I am adrad,° by Saint Thomas,   *afraid*
It stondeth nat aright with Nicholas.
God shilde° that he deide sodeinly!   *forbid*
320 This world is now ful tikel,° sikerly: *changeable*
I sawgh today a corps yborn to chirche
That now a° Monday last I sawgh him wirche.°   *on / work*

2. Blow the buck's horn, i.e., go without reward.
3. I.e., thus she makes a fool of Absolon.
4. Always the sly man at hand makes
the distant dear one hated.
5. "Poor innocent."
6. He wanted.

Go up," quod he unto his knave° anoon, *manservant*
"Clepe° at his dore or knokke with a stoon.° *call / stone*
325 Looke how it is and tel me boldely."
 This knave gooth him up ful sturdily,
And at the chambre dore whil that he stood
He cride and knokked as that he were wood,° *mad*
"What? How? What do ye, maister Nicholay?
330 How may ye sleepen al the longe day?"
But al for nought: he herde nat a word.
An hole he foond ful lowe upon a boord,
Ther as the cat was wont in for to creepe,
And at that hole he looked in ful deepe,
335 And atte laste he hadde of him a sighte.
 This Nicholas sat evere caping° uprighte *gaping*
As he hadde kiked° on the newe moone. *gazed*
Adown he gooth and tolde his maister soone
In what array° he saw this ilke° man. *condition / same*
340 This carpenter to blessen him⁷ bigan,
And saide, "Help us, Sainte Frideswide!
A man woot litel what him shal bitide.
This man is falle, with his astromye,⁸
In som woodnesse° or in som agonye. *madness*
345 I thoughte ay° wel how that it sholde be: *always*
Men sholde nought knowe of Goddes privetee.
Ye, blessed be alway a lewed° man *ignorant*
That nought but only his bileve° can.° *creed / knows*
So ferde° another clerk with astromye: *fared*
350 He walked in the feeldes for to prye
Upon the sterres,° what ther sholde bifalle, *stars*
Til he was in a marle-pit⁹ yfalle—
He saw nat that. But yit, by Saint Thomas,
Me reweth sore¹ for hende Nicholas.
355 He shal be rated of² his studying,
If that I may, by Jesus, hevene king!
Get me a staf that I may underspore,° *pry up*
Whil that thou, Robin, hevest° up the dore. *heave*
He shal³ out of his studying, as I gesse."
360 And to the chambre dore he gan him dresse.⁴
His knave was a strong carl° for the nones,° *fellow / purpose*
And by the haspe he haaf° it up atones: *heaved*
Into° the floor the dore fil° anoon. *on / fell*
This Nicholas sat ay as stille as stoon,
365 And evere caped up into the air.
This carpenter wende° he were in despair, *thought*
And hente° him by the shuldres mightily, *seized*
And shook him harde, and cride spitously,° *roughly*

7. Cross himself.
8. Illiterate form of "astronomye."
9. Pit from which a fertilizing clay is dug.

1. I sorely pity.
2. Scolded for.
3. I.e., shall come.
4. Took his stand.

"What, Nicholay, what, how! What! Looke adown!
370 Awaak and thenk on Cristes passioun![5]
I crouche[6] thee from elves and fro wightes."
Therwith the nightspel saide he anoonrightes[7]
On foure halves° of the hous aboute, *sides*
And on the thresshfold° on the dore withoute: *threshold*
375 "Jesu Crist and Sainte Benedight,° *Benedict*
Blesse this hous from every wikked wight!
For nightes nerye the White Pater Noster.[8]
Where wentestou, Sainte Petres soster?"° *sister*
And at the laste this hende Nicholas
380 Gan for to sike° sore, and saide, "Allas, *sigh*
Shal al the world be lost eftsoones° now?" *again*
 This carpenter answerde, "What saistou?
What, thenk on God as we doon, men that swinke."[9]
 This Nicholas answerde, "Fecche me drinke,
385 And after wol I speke in privetee
Of certain thing that toucheth me and thee.
I wol telle it noon other man, certain."
 This carpenter gooth down and comth again,
And broughte of mighty ale a large quart,
390 And when that eech of hem hadde dronke his part,
This Nicholas his dore faste shette,° *shut*
And down the carpenter by him he sette,
And saide, "John, myn hoste lief° and dere, *beloved*
Thou shalt upon thy trouthe° swere me here *word of honor*
395 That to no wight thou shalt this conseil° wraye;° *secret / disclose*
For it is Cristes conseil that I saye,
And if thou telle it man,[1] thou art forlore,° *lost*
For this vengeance thou shalt have therfore,
That if thou wraye me, thou shalt be wood." [2]
400 "Nay, Crist forbede it, for his holy blood,"
Quod tho this sely° man. "I nam no labbe,[3] *innocent*
And though I saye, I nam nat lief to gabbe.[4]
Say what thou wilt, I shal it nevere telle
To child ne wif, by him that harwed helle."[5]
405 "Now John," quod Nicholas, "I wol nought lie.
I have yfounde in myn astrologye,
As I have looked in the moone bright,
That now a Monday next, at quarter night,[6]
Shal falle a rain, and that so wilde and wood,° *furious*
410 That half so greet was nevere Noees° flood. *Noah's*
This world," he saide, "in lasse° than an hour *less*

---

5. I.e., the Crucifixion.
6. Make the sign of the cross on;
"wightes": wicked creatures.
7. The night-charm he said right away.
8. I.e., the White Lord's Prayer defend
(us). This personification was considered a powerful beneficent spirit.
9. Work.

1. To anyone.
2. Go mad.
3. Blabbermouth.
4. And though I say it myself, I don't
like to gossip.
5. By Him that despoiled hell—i.e.,
Christ.
6. I.e., shortly before dawn.

Shal al be dreint,° so hidous is the showr.   *drowned*
Thus shal mankinde drenche° and lese° hir lif." *drown / lose*
  This carpenter answerde, "Allas, my wif!
415 And shal she drenche? Allas, myn Alisoun!"
For sorwe of this he fil almost[7] adown,
And saide, "Is there no remedye in this cas?"
  "Why yis, for[8] Gode," quod hende Nicholas,
"If thou wolt werken after lore and reed[9]—
420 Thou maist nought werken after thyn owene heed;° *head*
For thus saith Salomon that was ful trewe,
'Werk al by conseil and thou shalt nought rewe.'° *be sorry*
And if thou werken wolt by good conseil,
I undertake, withouten mast or sail,
425 Yit shal I save hire and thee and me.
Hastou nat herd how saved was Noee
Whan that oure Lord hadde warned him biforn
That al the world with water sholde be lorn?"° *lost*
  "Yis," quod this carpenter, "ful yore ago."
430   "Hastou nat herd," quod Nicholas, "also
The sorwe of Noee with his felaweshipe?
Er that he mighte gete his wif to shipe,
Him hadde levere,[1] I dar wel undertake,
At thilke time than alle his wetheres blake
435 That she hadde had a ship hirself allone.[2]
And therfore woostou° what is best to doone? *do you know*
This axeth° haste, and of an hastif° thing *requires / urgent*
Men may nought preche or maken tarying.
Anoon go gete us faste into this in° *lodging*
440 A kneeding trough or elles a kimelin° *brewing tub*
For eech of us, but looke that they be large,° *wide*
In whiche we mowen swimme as in a barge,[3]
And han therinne vitaile suffisaunt[4]
But for a day—fy° on the remenaunt! *fie*
445 The water shal aslake° and goon away *diminish*
Aboute prime[5] upon the nexte day.
But Robin may nat wite° of this, thy knave, *know*
Ne eek thy maide Gille I may nat save.
Axe nought why, for though thou axe me,
450 I wol nought tellen Goddes privetee.° *secrets*
Suffiseth thee, but if thy wittes madde,° *go mad*
To han° as greet a grace as Noee hadde. *have*
Thy wif shal I wel saven, out of doute.
Go now thy way, and speed thee heraboute.
455 But whan thou hast for hire° and thee and me *her*

7. Almost fell.
8. I.e., by.
9. Act according to learning and advice.
1. He had rather. "Wetheres": rams. I.e., he'd have given all the rams he had.

2. The reluctance of Noah's wife to board the ark is a traditional comic theme in the mystery plays.
3. In which we can float as in a vessel.
4. Sufficient food.
5. 9 A.M.

Ygeten us thise kneeding-tubbes three,
Thanne shaltou hangen hem in the roof ful hye,
That no man of oure purveyance° espye.   *foresight*
And whan thou thus hast doon as I have said,
460 And hast oure vitaile faire in hem ylaid,
And eek an ax to smite the corde atwo,
Whan that the water comth that we may go,
And broke an hole an heigh[6] upon the gable
Unto the gardinward,[7] over the stable,
465 That we may freely passen forth oure way,
Whan that the grete showr is goon away,
Thanne shaltou swimme as merye, I undertake,
As dooth the white doke° after hir drake.   *duck*
Thanne wol I clepe,° 'How, Alison? How, John?   *call*
470 Be merye, for the flood wol passe anoon.'
And thou wolt sayn, 'Hail, maister Nicholay!
Good morwe, I see thee wel, for it is day!'
And thanne shal we be lordes al oure lif
Of al the world, as Noee and his wif.
475 But of oo thing I warne thee ful right:
Be wel avised on that ilke night
That we been entred into shippes boord
That noon of us ne speke nought a word,
Ne clepe, ne crye, but been in his prayere,
480 For it is Goddes owene heeste dere.[8]
Thy wif and thou mote hange fer atwinne,[9]
For that bitwixe you shal be no sinne—
Namore in looking than ther shal in deede.
This ordinance is said: go, God thee speede.
485 Tomorwe at night whan men been alle asleepe,
Into oure kneeding-tubbes wol we creepe,
And sitten there, abiding Goddes grace.
Go now thy way, I have no lenger space°   *time*
To make of this no lenger sermoning.
490 Men sayn thus: 'Send the wise and say no thing.'
Thou art so wis it needeth thee nat teche:
Go save oure lif, and that I thee biseeche."
    This sely carpenter gooth forth his way:
Ful ofte he saide allas and wailaway,
495 And to his wif he tolde his privetee,
And she was war,° and knew it bet° than he,   *aware / better*
What al this quainte cast° was for to saye.°   *trick / mean*
But nathelees she ferde° as she wolde deye,   *acted*
And saide, "Allas, go forth thy way anoon.
500 Help us to scape,° or we been dede eechoon.   *escape*
I am thy trewe verray wedded wif:
Go, dere spouse, and help to save oure lif."

6. On high.   8. Precious commandment.
7. Toward the garden.   9. Far apart.

Lo, which a greet thing is affeccioun!°   *emotion*
Men may dien of imaginacioun,
505 So deepe° may impression be take.   *deeply*
This sely carpenter biginneth quake;
Him thinketh verrailiche° that he may see   *truly*
Noees flood come walwing° as the see   *rolling*
To drenchen° Alison, his hony dere.   *drown*
510 He weepeth, waileth, maketh sory cheere;
He siketh° with ful many a sory swough,°   *sighs / breath*
And gooth and geteth him a kneeding-trough,
And after a tubbe and a kimelin,
And prively he sente hem to his in,°   *dwelling*
515 And heeng° hem in the roof in privetee;   *hung*
His owene hand he made laddres three,
To climben by the ronges° and the stalkes°   *rungs / uprights*
Unto the tubbes hanging in the balkes,°   *rafters*
And hem vitailed,° bothe trough and tubbe,   *victualed*
520 With breed and cheese and good ale in a jubbe,°   *jug*
Suffising right ynough as for a day.
But er that he hadde maad al this array,
He sente his knave, and eek his wenche also,
Upon his neede[1] to London for to go.
525 And on the Monday whan it drow to[2] nighte,
He shette° his dore withouten candel-lighte,   *shut*
And dressed° alle thing as it sholde be,   *arranged*
And shortly up they clomben° alle three.   *climbed*
They seten° stille wel a furlong way.[3]   *sat*
530   "Now, Pater Noster, clum,"[4] saide Nicholay,
And "Clum" quod John, and "Clum" saide Alisoun.
This carpenter saide his devocioun,
And stille he sit° and biddeth his prayere,   *sits*
Awaiting on the rain, if he it heere.°   *might hear*
535   The dede sleep, for wery bisinesse,
Fil° on this carpenter right as I gesse   *fell*
Aboute corfew time,[5] or litel more.
For travailing of his gost[6] he groneth sore,
And eft° he routeth,° for his heed mislay.[7]   *then / snores*
540   Down of the laddre stalketh Nicholay,
And Alison ful softe adown she spedde:
Withouten wordes mo they goon to bedde
Ther as the carpenter is wont to lie.
Ther was the revel and the melodye,
545 And thus lith° Alison and Nicholas   *lies*
In bisinesse of mirthe and of solas,°   *pleasure*
Til that the belle of Laudes[8] gan to ringe,

1. On an errand for him.
2. Drew toward.
3. The time it takes to go a furlong (i.e., a few minutes).
4. Hush (?).
5. Probably about 8 P.M.
6. Affliction of his spirit.
7. Lay in the wrong position.
8. The first church service of the day.

And freres in the chauncel° gonne singe.   *chancel*
  This parissh clerk, this amorous Absolon,
550 That is for love alway so wo-bigoon,
Upon the Monday was at Oseneye,
With compaignye him to disporte and playe,
And axed upon caas⁹ a cloisterer
Ful prively after John the carpenter;
555 And he drow him apart out of the chirche,
And saide, "I noot:¹ I sawgh him here nought wirche
Sith Saterday. I trowe that he be went
For timber ther oure abbot hath him sent.
For he is wont for timber for to go,
560 And dwellen atte grange² a day or two.
Or elles he is at his hous, certain.
Where that he be I can nought soothly sayn."
  This Absolon ful jolif was and light,³
And thoughte, "Now is time to wake al night,
565 For sikerly,° I sawgh him nought stiringe   *certainly*
Aboute his dore sin day bigan to springe.
So mote° I thrive, I shal at cokkes crowe   *may*
Ful prively knokken at his windowe
That stant° ful lowe upon his bowres⁴ wal.   *stands*
570 To Alison now wol I tellen al
My love-longing,° for yet I shal nat misse   *lovesickness*
That at the leeste way⁵ I shal hire kisse.
Som manere confort shal I have, parfay.°   *in faith*
My mouth hath icched al this longe day:
575 That is a signe of kissing at the leeste.
Al night me mette⁶ eek I was at a feeste.
Therfore I wol go sleepe an hour or twaye,
And al the night thanne wol I wake and playe."
  Whan that the firste cok hath crowe, anoon
580 Up rist° this joly lovere Absolon,   *rises*
And him arrayeth gay at point devis.⁷
But first he cheweth grain⁸ and licoris,
To smellen sweete, er he hadde kembd° his heer.   *combed*
Under his tonge a trewe-love⁹ he beer,°   *bore*
585 For therby wende° he to be gracious.°   *supposed / pleasing*
He rometh° to the carpenteres hous,   *strolls*
And stille he stant° under the shot-windowe—   *stands*
Unto his brest it raughte,° it was so lowe—   *reached*
And ofte he cougheth with a semisoun.°   *small sound*
590 "What do ye, hony-comb, sweete Alisoun,
My faire brid,¹ my sweete cinamome?
Awaketh, lemman° myn, and speketh to me.   *mistress*

9. By chance; "cloisterer": here, a member of the religious order of Osney Abbey.
1. Don't know; "wirche": work.
2. The outlying farm belonging to the abbey.
3. Was very amorous and gay.
4. Bower's, bedroom's.
5. I.e., at least.
6. I dreamed.
7. To perfection.
8. Grain of paradise (a spice).
9. Sprig of a clover-like plant.
1. Bird or bride.

Wel litel thinken ye upon my wo
That for your love I swete° ther I go.   *sweat*
595 No wonder is though that I swelte° and swete: *melt*
I moorne as doth a lamb after the tete.°   *tit*
Ywis, lemman, I have swich love-longinge,
That lik a turtle° trewe is my moorninge: *dove*
I may nat ete namore than a maide."
600 "Go fro the windowe, Jakke fool," she saide.
"As help me God, it wol nat be com-pa-me.°   *come-kiss-me*
I love another, and elles I were to blame,
Wel bet° than thee, by Jesu, Absolon.   *better*
Go forth thy way or I wol caste a stoon,
605 And lat me sleepe, a twenty devele way."[2]
"Allas," quod Absolon, "and wailaway,
That trewe love was evere so yvele biset.[3]
Thanne kis me, sin that it may be no bet,
For Jesus love and for the love of me."
610 "Woltou thanne go thy way therwith?" quod she.
"Ye, certes, lemman," quod this Absolon.
"Thanne maak thee redy," quod she. "I come anoon."
And unto Nicholas she saide stille,°   *quietly*
"Now hust,° and thou shalt laughen al thy fille."   *hush*
615 This Absolon down sette him on his knees,
And said, "I am a lord at alle degrees,[4]
For after this I hope ther cometh more.
Lemman, thy grace, and sweete brid, thyn ore!"°   *mercy*
The windowe she undooth, and that in haste.
620 "Have do," quod she, "come of and speed thee faste,
Lest that oure neighebores thee espye."
This Absolon gan wipe his mouth ful drye:
Derk was the night as pich or as the cole,
And at the windowe out she putte hir hole,
625 And Absolon, him fil no bet ne wers,[5]
But with his mouth he kiste hir naked ers,
Ful savourly,° er he were war of this.   *with relish*
Abak he sterte,° and thoughte it was amis,   *started*
For wel he wiste a womman hath no beerd.
630 He felte a thing al rough and longe yherd,°   *haired*
And saide, "Fy, allas, what have I do?"
"Teehee," quod she, and clapte the windowe to.
And Absolon gooth forth a sory pas.[6]
"A beerd, a beerd!" quod hende Nicholas,
635 "By Goddes corpus,° this gooth faire and weel."   *body*
This sely Absolon herde everydeel,
And on his lippe he gan for anger bite,
And to himself he saide, "I shal thee quite."°   *repay*
Who rubbeth now, who froteth° now his lippes   *wipes*
640 With dust, with sond,[7] with straw, with cloth, with chippes,

2. In the name of twenty devils.   5. It befell him neither better nor worse.
3. Ill-used.   6. I.e., walking sadly.
4. In every way.   7. Sand.

But Absolon, that saith ful ofte allas?
"My soule bitake° I unto Satanas,°   *commit / Satan*
But me were levere[8] than all this town," quod he,
"Of this despit° awroken° for to be.   *insult / avenged*
645 Allas," quod he, "allas I ne hadde ybleint!"°   *turned aside*
His hote love was cold and al yqueint,°   *quenched*
For fro that time that he hadde kist hir ers
Of paramours he sette nought a kers,[9]
For he was heled° of his maladye.   *cured*
650 Ful ofte paramours he gan defye,°   *renounce*
And weep° as dooth a child that is ybete.   *wept*
A softe paas[1] he wente over the streete
Until° a smith men clepen daun Gervais,[2]   *to*
That in his forge smithed plough harneis:°   *equipment*
655 He sharpeth shaar and cultour[3] bisily.
This Absolon knokketh al esily,°   *quietly*
And saide, "Undo, Gervais, and that anoon."°   *at once*
     "What, who artou?" "It am I, Absolon."
"What, Absolon? What, Cristes sweete tree!
660 Why rise ye so rathe?° Ey, benedicite,°   *early / bless me*
What aileth you? Som gay girl, God it woot,
Hath brought you thus upon the viritoot.[4]
By Sainte Note, ye woot wel what I mene."
     This Absolon ne roughte nat a bene[5]
665 Of al his play. No word again he yaf:
He hadde more tow on his distaf[6]
Than Gervais knew, and saide, "Freend so dere,
This hote cultour in the chimenee° here,   *fireplace*
As lene[7] it me: I have therwith to doone.
670 I wol bringe it thee again ful soone."
     Gervais answerde, "Certes, were it gold,
Or in a poke nobles alle untold,[8]
Thou sholdest have, as I am trewe smith.
Ey, Cristes fo,[9] what wol ye do therwith?"
675   "Therof," quod Absolon, "be as be may.
I shal wel telle it thee another day,"
And caughte the cultour by the colde stele.°   *handle*
Ful softe out at the dore he gan to stele,
And wente unto the carpenteres wal:
680 He cougheth first and knokketh therwithal
Upon the windowe, right as he dide er.°   *before*
     This Alison answerde, "Who is ther
That knokketh so? I warante[1] it a thief."
     "Why, nay," quod he, "God woot, my sweete lief,°   *dear*

---

8. I had rather.
9. He didn't care a piece of cress for woman's love.
1. I.e., quiet walk.
2. Master Gervais.
3. He sharpens plowshare and coulter (the turf-cutter on a plow).
4. I.e., on the prowl.
5. Didn't care a bean.
6. I.e., more on his mind.
7. I.e., please lend.
8. Or gold coins all uncounted in a bag.
9. Foe, i.e., Satan.
1. I.e., wager.

685 I am thyn Absolon, my dereling.
Of gold," quod he, "I have thee brought a ring—
My moder yaf it me, so God me save;
Ful fin it is and therto wel ygrave:°   *engraved*
This wol I yiven thee if thou me kisse."

690   This Nicholas was risen for to pisse,
And thoughte he wolde amenden[2] al the jape:°   *joke*
He sholde kisse his ers er that he scape.
And up the windowe dide he hastily,
And out his ers he putteth prively,

695 Over the buttok to the haunche-boon.
   And therwith spak this clerk, this Absolon,
"Speek, sweete brid, I noot nought wher thou art."
This Nicholas anoon leet flee[3] a fart
As greet as it hadde been a thonder-dent°   *thunderbolt*

700 That with the strook he was almost yblent,°   *blinded*
And he was redy with his iren hoot,°   *hot*
And Nicholas amidde the ers he smoot:°   *smote*
Of gooth the skin an hande-brede° aboute;   *handsbreadth*
The hote cultour brende so his toute°   *buttocks*

705 That for the smert he wende for to[4] die;
As he were wood° for wo he gan to crye,   *crazy*
"Help! Water! Water! Help, for Goddes herte!"
   This carpenter out of his slomber sterte,
And herde oon cryen "Water!" as he were wood,

710 And thoughte, "Allas, now cometh Noweles[5] flood!"
He sette him up withoute wordes mo,
And with his ax he smoot the corde atwo,
And down gooth al: he foond neither to selle
Ne breed ne ale til he cam to the celle,[6]

715 Upon the floor, and ther aswoune° he lay.   *in a faint*
   Up sterte hire[7] Alison and Nicholay,
And criden "Out" and "Harrow" in the streete.
The neighebores, bothe smale and grete,
In ronnen for to gauren° on this man   *gape*

720 That aswoune lay bothe pale and wan,
For with the fal he brosten° hadde his arm;   *broken*
But stonde he moste° unto his owene harm,   *must*
For whan he spak he was anoon bore down[8]
With° hende Nicholas and Alisoun: *by*

725 They tolden every man that he was wood—
He was agast so of Noweles flood,
Thurgh fantasye, that of his vanitee°   *folly*
He hadde ybought him kneeding-tubbes three,
And hadde hem hanged in the roof above,

730 And that he prayed hem, for Goddes love,

---

2. Improve on.
3. Let fly.
4. Thought he would.
5. The carpenter is confusing Noah and Noel (Christmas).
6. He found time to sell neither bread nor ale until he arrived at the foundation.
7. Started.
8. Refuted.

To sitten in the roof, *par compaignye*.[9]
   The folk gan laughen at his fantasye.
Into the roof they kiken° and they cape,°   *peer / gape*
And turned al his harm unto a jape,°   *joke*
735 For what so that this carpenter answerde,
   It was for nought: no man his reson° herde;   *argument*
With othes grete he was so sworn adown,
That he was holden° wood in al the town,   *considered*
For every clerk anoonright heeld with other:
740 They saide, "The man was wood, my leve brother,"
   And every wight gan laughen at this strif.°   *fuss*
Thus swived° was the carpenteres wif   *slept with*
For al his keeping° and his jalousye,   *guarding*
And Absolon hath kist hir nether° yë,   *lower*
745 And Nicholas is scalded in the toute:
   This tale is doon, and God save al the route!°   *company*

From The Parson's Tale[1]

The Introduction

By that[2] the Manciple hadde his tale al ended,
The sonne fro the south line[3] was decended

9. For company's sake.
1. Among the moral writers of the later Middle Ages the pilgrimage was so commonly treated as an allegory of man's life that Chaucer's audience must have been surprised to find the *Canterbury Tales* so little allegorical. At the end of his life, however, and at the end of his work, Chaucer seems to have been caught up in the venerable allegory. Some ten months before his death he rented a house in the garden of Westminster Abbey, and it is possible that during these months—perhaps when he felt his death approaching—he fell under the influence of the monks of Westminster. In any case, in the Parson's Tale, and in its short Introduction and in the Retraction that follows it, Chaucer seems to be making an end for two pilgrimages that had become one, that of his fiction and that of his life.

   In the Introduction to the tale we find the 29 pilgrims moving through a nameless little village as the sun sinks to within 29 degrees of the horizon. The atmosphere contains something of both the chill and the urgency of a late autumn afternoon, and we are surprised to find that the pilgrimage is almost over, that there is need for haste in order to make that "good end" that every medieval Christian hoped for. This delicately suggestive passage, rich with allegorical overtones, introduces an extremely long sermon on penitence and the seven deadly sins, probably

translated by Chaucer from French or Latin some years earlier, before he had begun the *Canterbury Tales*. The other stories have many echoes of it: for instance, in the selection printed here one sees the germ of ideas that reappear—in highly altered form—in the Wife of Bath. The sermon is at times not without animation, but in general Chaucer provides no exception to the statement that Middle English prose is inferior to Middle English verse. But then the intent of the sermon is didactic, not artistic, and according to the more rigorous theologians of the time, didactic intent is infinitely more important than artistic expression.

   It is to this doctrine that Chaucer yielded at the end of his life. The Retraction which follows and concludes the Parson's Tale offers Chaucer's apology for having written all the works on which his reputation as a great poet depends, not only such stories as the Miller's Tale, but also his loveliest and seemingly most harmless poems. Yet a readiness to deny his own reality before the reality of his God is implicit in many of Chaucer's works, and the placement of the Retraction within the artistic structure of the *Canterbury Tales* suggests that while Chaucer denied his art, he seems to have recognized that he and it were inseparable.

2. By the time that.
3. I.e., the line that runs some 28 de-

So lowe, that he nas nat to my sighte
Degrees nine and twenty as in highte.
5 Four of the clokke it was, so as I gesse,
For elevene foot, or litel more or lesse,
My shadwe was at thilke time as there,
Of swich feet as° my lengthe parted° were   *as if / divided*
In sixe feet equal of proporcioun.[4]
10 Therwith the moones exaltacioun[5]—
I mene Libra—alway gan ascende,
As we were entring at a thropes° ende.   *village's*
For which oure Host, as he was wont to gie°   *lead*
As in this caas oure joly compaignye,
15 Saide in this wise, "Lordinges everichoon,
Now lakketh us no tales mo than oon:
Fulfild is my sentence° and my decree;   *purpose*
I trowe° that we han herd of eech degree;   *believe*
Almost fulfild is al myn ordinaunce.
20 I praye to God, so yive him right good chaunce
That telleth this tale to us lustily.
Sire preest," quod he, "artou a vicary,°   *vicar*
Or arte a Person? Say sooth, by thy fay.°   *faith*
Be what thou be, ne breek° thou nat oure play,   *break*
25 For every man save thou hath told his tale.
Unbokele and shew us what is in thy male!°   *bag*
For trewely, me thinketh by thy cheere°   *expression*
Thou sholdest knitte up wel a greet matere.
Tel us a fable anoon, for cokkes bones!"
30   This Person answerde al atones,[6]
"Thou getest fable noon ytold for me,
For Paul, that writeth unto Timothee,
Repreveth° hem that waiven soothfastnesse,[7]   *reproves*
And tellen fables and swich wrecchednesse.
35 Why sholde I sowen draf° out of my fest,°   *chaff / fist*
Whan I may sowen whete if that me lest?[8]
For which I saye that if you list to heere
Moralitee and vertuous matere,
And thanne that ye wol yive me audience,
40 I wol ful fain,° at Cristes reverence,   *gladly*
Do you plesance leveful° as I can.   *lawful*
But trusteth wel, I am a southren man:
I can nat geeste Rum-Ram-Ruf by lettre[9]—
Ne, God woot, rym holde° I but litel bettre.   *consider*
45 And therfore, if you list, I wol nat glose;[1]

grees to the south of the celestial equator and parallel to it.
4. This detailed analysis merely says
that the shadows are lengthening.
5. I.e., the astrological sign in which
the moon's influence was dominant.
"Libra": the constellation of the
Scales.
6. Immediately.

7. Depart from truth. See I Timothy
i.4.
8. It pleases me.
9. I.e., I cannot tell stories in the
alliterative measure (without rhyme):
this form of poetry was not common
in southeastern England.
1. I.e., speak in order to please.

I wol you telle a merye tale in prose,
To knitte up al this feeste and make an ende.
And Jesu for his grace wit me sende
To shewe you the way in this viage°   *journey*
50 Of thilke parfit glorious pilgrimage
That highte Jerusalem celestial.
And if ye vouche sauf, anoon I shal
Biginne upon my tale, for which I praye
Telle youre avis:° I can no bettre saye.   *opinion*
55 But nathelees, this meditacioun
I putte it ay under correccioun
Of clerkes, for I am nat textuel:[2]
I take but the sentence,° trusteth wel.   *meaning*
Therfore I make protestacioun°   *public acknowledgment*
60 That I wol stonde to correccioun."
    Upon this word we han assented soone,
For, as it seemed, it was for to doone
To enden in som vertuous sentence,°   *doctrine*
And for to yive him space and audience;
65 And bede[3] oure Host he sholde to him saye
That alle we to telle his tale him praye.
    Oure Hoste hadde the wordes for us alle:
"Sire preest," quod he, "now faire you bifalle:
Telleth," quod he, "youre meditacioun.
70 But hasteth you; the sonne wol adown.
Beeth fructuous,° and that in litel space,°   *fruitful / time*
And to do wel God sende you his grace.
Saye what you list, and we wol gladly heere."
And with that word he saide in this manere.

[The Remedy Against Lechery]

Now cometh the remedye agains leccherye, and that is generally chastitee and continence that restraineth alle the desordeinee mevinges[4] that comen of flesshly talentes. And evere the grettere merite shal he han that most restraineth the wikkede eschaufinges of the ardor[5] of this sinne. And this is in two maneres, that is to sayn, chastitee in mariage and chastitee of widwehood. Now shaltou understonde that matrimoine is leveful[6] assembling of man and of woman that receiven by vertu of the sacrement the bond thurgh which they may nat be departed[7] in al hir lif—that is to sayn, whil that they liven bothe. This, as saith the book, is a ful greet sacrement. God maked it, as I have said, in Paradis, and wolde himself be born in mariage. And for to halwen[8] mariage he was at a wedding wheras he turned water into win, which was the firste miracle that

---

2. Literal, faithful to the letter.
3. I.e., we bade.
4. Inordinate urges. "Talentes": desires.
5. The wicked blazings up of the fire.
6. Permissible.
7. Separated.
8. Sanctify.

he wroughte in erthe biforn his disciples. Trewe effect of mariage clenseth fornicacion and replenissheth holy chirche of[9] good linage, for that is the ende of mariage. And it chaungeth deedly[1] sinne into venial sinne bitwixe hem that been ywedded, and maketh the hertes al oon[2] of hem that been ywedded, as wel as the bodies. This is verray[3] mariage that was establisshed by God er that sinne bigan, whan naturel lawe was in his righte point[4] in Paradis. And it was ordained that oo[5] man sholde have but oo womman, and oo womman but oo man, as saith Saint Augustin, by manye reasons.

First, for mariage is figured[6] bitwixe Crist and holy chirche. And that other[7] is for a man is heed of a womman—algate, by ordinance[8] it sholde be so. For if a womman hadde mo[9] men than oon, thanne sholde she have mo hedes than oon, and that were an horrible thing bifore God. And eek a womman ne mighte nat plese too many folk atones. And also ther ne sholde nevere be pees ne reste amonges hem, for everich[1] wolde asken his owene thing. And fertherover,[2] no man ne sholde knowe his owne engendrure,[3] ne who sholde have his heritage. And the womman sholde been the lesse biloved fro the time that she were conjoint[4] to manye men.

Now cometh how that a man sholde bere him[5] with his wif, and namely in two thinges, that is to sayn, in suffrance[6] and in reverence, as shewed Crist whan he made first womman. For he ne made hire nat of the heed of Adam for[7] she sholde nat claime too greet lordshipe. For theras the womman hath the maistrye[8] she maketh too muche desray. Ther needen none ensamples of this: the experience of day by day oughte suffise. Also certes God ne made nat womman of the foot of Adam for she ne sholde nat been holden too lowe: for she can nat paciently suffre. But God made womman of the rib of Adam for womman sholde be felawe unto man. Man sholde bere him to his wif in faith, in trouthe, and in love, as saith Saint Paul[9] that a man sholde loven his wif as Crist loved holy chirche, that loved it so wel that he deide for it: so sholde a man for his wif, if it were neede.

Now how that a womman sholde be subjet to hir housbonde, that telleth Saint Peter.[1] First, in obedience; and eek, as saith the decree, a woman that is wif, as longe as she is a wif, she hath noon auctoritee to swere ne to bere witnesse withoute leve[2] of hir hous-

---

9. With.
1. Deadly.
2. I.e., in union.
3. True.
4. I.e., in its natural working order.
5. One.
6. I.e., symbolizes the relationship.
7. Second; "heed": head.
8. At any rate, by proper management.
9. More.
1. Each.

2. Moreover.
3. Children.
4. Joined.
5. Behave. "Namely": especially.
6. Patience.
7. In order that.
8. Domination; "desray": disturbance.
9. In Ephesians v.25.
1. See I Peter iii.1.
2. Permission.

bonde that is hir lord—algate, he sholde be so by reson. She sholde eek serven him in alle honestee, and been attempree[3] of hir array. I woot wel that they sholde setten hir entente[4] to plesen hir housbondes, but nat by hir quaintise[5] of array. Saint Jerome saith that wives that been appareiled in silk and in precious purpre[6] ne mowe nat clothen hem in Jesu Crist. Loke what saith Saint John eek in this matere. Saint Gregorye eek saith that no wight seeketh precious array but only for vaineglorye, to been honoured the more bifore the peple. It is a greet folye a womman to have a fair array outward and in hireself be foul inward. A wif sholde eek be mesurable[7] in looking and in bering and in laughing, and discreet in alle hir wordes and hir deedes. And aboven alle worldly thing she sholde loven hir housbonde with al hir herte and to him be trewe of hir body. So sholde an housbonde eek be to his wif. For sith[8] that al the body is the housbondes, so sholde hir herte been, or elles ther is bitwixe hem two as in that no parfit[9] mariage. Thanne shal men understonde that for three thinges a man and his wif flesshly mowen[1] assemble. The firste is in entente of engendrure of[2] children to the service of God: for certes that is the cause final of matrimoine. Another cause is to yeelden everich[3] of hem to other the dette of hir bodies, for neither of hem hath power of his owene body. The thridde[4] is for to eschewe leccherye and vilainye. The ferthe[5] is forsoothe deedly sinne. As to the firste, it is meritorye;[6] the seconde also for, as saith the decree, that she hath merite of chastitee that yeeldeth to hir housbonde the dette of hir body, ye, though it be again hir liking and the lust[7] of hir herte. The thridde manere is venial sinne: and trewely, scarsly may ther any of thise be withoute venial sinne, for the corrupcion and the delit.[8] The ferthe manere is for to understonde, as if they assemble only for amorous love and for noon of the foresaide causes, but for to accomplisshe thilke brenning[9] delit, they rekke nevere how ofte. Soothly it is deedly sinne. And yit, with sorwe, some folk wol painen hem[1] more to doon than to hir appetit suffiseth. * * *

Another remedye agayns leccherye is specially to withdrawen swiche[2] thinges as yive occasion to thilke vilainye, as ese, eting, and drinking. For certes whan the pot boileth strongly, the beste remedye is to withdrawe the fir. Sleeping longe in greet quiete is eek a greet norice[3] to leccherye.

3. Modest.
4. Do their best.
5. Extravagance.
6. Royal scarlet; "mowe": may.
7. Modest; "bering": behavior.
8. Since.
9. Perfect.
1. May.
2. With desire to beget.
3. Pay each.

4. Third.
5. Fourth.
6. Meritorious.
7. Desire.
8. On account of the impurity and bodily delight.
9. That burning.
1. Exert themselves.
2. Such.
3. Nurse.

Another remedye agains leccherye is that a man or a womman eschewe the compaignye of hem by whiche he douteth[4] to be tempted. For albeit so that the deede be withstonden, yit is ther greet temptacion. Soothly, a whit wal, although it brenne[5] nought fully by stiking of a candele, yit is the wal blak of the leit.[6] Ful ofte time I rede that no man truste in his owene perfeccion but[7] he be stronger than Sampson and holier than David and wiser than Salomon. * * *

Chaucer's Retraction

Now praye I to hem alle that herkne this litel tretis[8] or rede, that if ther be any thing in it that liketh[9] hem, that therof they thanken oure Lord Jesu Crist, of whom proccedeth al wit[1] and al goodnesse. And if ther be any thing that displese him, I praye hem also that they arrette it to the defaute of myn unconning,[2] and nat to my wil, that wolde ful fain have said bettre if I hadde had conning. For oure book saith, "Al that is writen is writen for oure doctrine,"[3] and that is myn entente. Wherfore I biseeke[4] you mekely, for the mercy of God, that ye praye for me that Crist have mercy on me and foryive me my giltes, and namely[5] of my translacions and enditinges of worldly vanitees, the whiche I revoke in my retraccions: as is the *Book of Troilus;* the *Book* also *of Fame;* the *Book of the Five and Twenty Ladies;*[6] the *Book of the Duchesse;* the *Book of Saint Valentines Day of the Parlement of Briddes;* the *Tales of Canterbury,* thilke that sounen into[7] sinne; the *Book of the Leon;*[8] and many another book, if they were in my remembrance, and many a song and many a leccherous lay: that Crist for his grete mercy foryive me the sinne. But of the translacion of Boece[9] *De Consolatione,* and othere bookes of legendes of saintes, and omelies,[1] and moralitee, and devocion, that thanke I oure Lord Jesu Crist and his blisful Moder and alle the saintes of hevene, biseeking hem that they from hennes[2] forth unto my lives ende sende me grace to biwaile my giltes and to studye to the salvacion of my soule, and graunte me grace of verray penitence, confession, and satisfaccion to doon in this present lif, thurgh the benigne grace of him that is king of kinges and preest over alle preestes, that boughte[3] us with the precious blood of his herte, so that I may

4. Fears.
5. Burn; "stiking": application.
6. Flame.
7. Unless.
8. Hear this little treatise.
9. Pleases.
1. Understanding.
2. Ascribe it to the defaute of my lack of skill.
3. Romans xv.4.
4. Beseech.

5. Especially. "Enditinges": compositions.
6. I.e., the *Legend of Good Women.*
7. Those that tend toward.
8. The *Book of the Lion* has not been preserved.
9. Boethius.
1. Homilies.
2. Hence.
3. Redeemed.

been oon of hem at the day of doom that shulle be saved. *Qui cum patre et Spiritu Sancto vivis et regnas Deus per omnia saecula.*[4] *Amen.*

1386–1400

Lyrics and Occasional Verse[1]
To Rosamond[2]

Madame, ye been of alle beautee shrine
As fer as cercled is the mapemounde:[3]
For as the crystal glorious ye shine,
And like ruby been youre cheekes rounde.
5 Therwith ye been so merye and so jocounde
That at a revel whan that I see you daunce
It is an oinement unto my wounde,
Though ye to me ne do no daliaunce.[4]

For though I weepe of teres ful a tine,°   *tub*
10 Yit may that wo myn herte nat confounde;
Youre semy° vois, that ye so smale outtwine,[5]   *small*
Maketh my thought in joye and blis habounde:°   *abound*
So curteisly I go with love bounde
That to myself I saye in my penaunce,[6]
15 "Suffiseth me to love you, Rosemounde,
Though ye to me ne do no daliaunce."

Was nevere pik walwed in galauntine[7]
As I in love am walwed and vwounde,
For which ful ofte I of myself divine
20 That I am trewe Tristam[8] the secounde;

4. Who with the Father and the Holy Spirit livest and reignest God forever.
1. As a man of accomplishments who was often at court, Chaucer must, like other courtiers, have been called upon to write both occasional verses and lyrics. Of the handful of these shorter poems that have survived, several of the best are included here: they reveal the ways in which Chaucer handled some of the poetic modes and attitudes of his time. These modes—particularly the lyric strain, which seeks expression in a brief form—seem to have been uncongenial to his temperament. Some, in fact, might well be termed "anti-lyrics"; these are the poems where the extreme conventions of the courtly-love lyric become a framework in which Chaucer's irony and indirection may be brought into immediate play. Chaucer's best work, however, is in his longer poems, for irony and indirection are qualities which can be given proper development only if the poet has ample room to work in.
2. This lyric extends the extravagant images of the stylized courtly-love lyric to outrageous lengths: a lover might well weep a flood of tears but would hardly measure them by the tubful (line 9), and he might be overwhelmed with love—but not like a fish buried in sauce (line 17). The general imperturbability of tone contrasts ironically with the grotesque metaphors.
3. I.e., to the farthest circumference of the map of the world.
4. I.e., show me no encouragement.
5. That you so delicately spin out.
6. I.e., pangs of unrequited love.
7. Pike rolled in galantine sauce.
8. The famous lover of Isolt (Iseult, Isolde) in medieval legend, renowned for his constancy.

My love may not refreide nor affounde;[9]
I brenne° ay in amorous plesaunce: *burn*
Do what you list, I wol youre thral° be founde,   *slave*
Though ye to me ne do no daliaunce.

To His Scribe Adam[1]

Adam scrivain,° if evere it thee bifalle   *scribe*
Boece[2] or *Troilus* for to writen newe,
Under thy longe lokkes thou moste[3] have the scalle,°   *scurf*
But after my making thou write more trewe,[4]
5 So ofte a day I moot° thy werk renewe,   *must*
It to correcte, and eek to rubbe and scrape:
And al is thurgh thy necligence and rape.°   *haste*

Complaint to His Purse[5]

To you. my purs, and to noon other wight,
Complaine I, for ye be my lady dere.
I am so sory, now that ye be light,
For certes, but if[6] ye make me hevy cheere,
5 Me were as lief[7] be laid upon my beere;°   *bier*
For which unto youre mercy thus I crye:
Beeth hevy again, or elles moot° I die.   *must*

Now voucheth sauf this day er it be night
That I of you the blisful soun may heere,
10 Or see youre colour, lik the sonne bright,
That of yelownesse hadde nevere peere.
Ye be my life, ye be myn hertes steere,°   *rudder, guide*
Queene of confort and of good compaignye:
Beeth hevy again, or elles moot I die.

15 Ye purs, that been to me my lives light
And saviour, as in this world down here,

9. Cool nor chill.
1. This *jeu d'esprit*, called forth by the inefficiency of his amanuensis, is written in the verse form of Chaucer's great poem *Troilus and Criseide*.
2. I.e., Chaucer's translation of Boethius' *De Consolatione*. "*Troilus*": *Troilus and Criseide*.
3. I.e., may you.
4. Unless you write more accurately what I've composed.
5. In this variation on the courtly-love lyric the conventional language of love is both used and misused to express love of cash. Ladies, like coins, should be golden, and like purses they should not be "light" (i.e., fickle). On the other hand, they should not be heavy, as purses should be. The poem is in the characteristic three-stanza *ballade* form, with the usual "envoy" addressed to a noble patron. In this case the patron apparently heard the complaint, for, three days after his accession (in 1399), King Henry IV renewed and increased the pension Chaucer had received from Richard II.
6. Unless.
7. I'd just as soon.

Out of this tonne[8] helpe me thurgh your might,
Sith that ye wol nat be my tresorere;°   *disburser*
For I am shave as neigh° as any frere.°   *close / friar*
20 But yit I praye unto youre curteisye:
Beeth hevy again, or elles moot I die.

Envoy to Henry IV

O conquerour of Brutus Albioun,[9]
Which that by line and free eleccioun
Been verray king, this song to you I sende:
25 And ye, that mowen° alle oure harmes amende,   *may*
Have minde upon my supplicacioun.

Merciless Beauty[1]

1

Youre yën two wol slee° me sodeinly: *slay*
I may the beautee of hem nat sustene,°   *withstand*
So woundeth it thurghout myn herte keene.°   *keenly*

And but° youre word wol helen hastily   *unless*
5 Myn hertes wounde, whil that it is greene,[2]
Youre yën two wol slee me sodeinly:
I may the beautee of hem nat sustene.

Upon my trouthe, I saye you faithfully
That ye been of my lif and deeth the queene,
10 For with my deeth the trouthe shal be seene.
Youre yën two wol slee me sodeinly:
I may the beautee of hem nat sustene,
So woundeth it thurghout myn herte keene.

2

So hath youre beautee fro youre herte chaced
15 Pitee, that me ne availeth nought to plaine:°   *complain*
For Daunger halt[3] youre mercy in his chaine.

Giltelees my deeth thus han ye me purchased;°   *procured*
I saye you sooth, me needeth nought to feine:°   *dissemble*
So hath youre beautee fro youre herte chaced
20 Pitee, that me ne availeth nought to plaine.

8. Tun, meaning "predicament."
9. Britain (Albion) was supposed to have been founded by Brutus, the grandson of Aeneas, the founder of Rome.
1. The first two sections of this poem employ the typical imagery and extravagant emotion of courtly-love lyrics—the power of the lady's eyes to slay the lover, for instance, and the struggle between her native pity and her "daunger" (haughtiness). But it ends where a real lyric could never end: the poet's self-congratulation, at the failure of his affair, on his unimpaired health.
2. I.e., fresh.
3. Haughtiness holds.

Allas, that nature hath in you compaced°   *enclosed*
So greet beautee that no man may attaine
To mercy, though he sterve° for the paine.   *die*
   So hath youre beautee fro youre herte chaced
25 Pitee, that me ne availeth nought to plaine:
For Daunger halt youre mercy in his chaine.

3

Sin I fro Love escaped am so fat,
I nevere thenke° to been in his prison lene: *intend*
Sin I am free, I counte him nat a bene.[4]

30 He may answere and saye right this and that;
I do no fors,[5] I speke right as I mene:
   Sin I fro Love escaped am so fat,
I nevere thenke to been in his prison lene.

Love hath my name ystrike° out of his sclat,°   *struck / slate*
35 And he is strike out of my bookes clene
For everemo; ther is noon other mene.°   *solution*
   Sin I fro Love escaped am so fat,
I nevere thenke to been in his prison lene:
Sin I am free, I counte him nat a bene.

Gentilesse[6]

The firste fader and findere° of gentilesse,   *founder*
What° man desireth gentil for to be   *whatever*
Moste folwe his traas,° and alle his wittes dresse[7]   *path*
Vertu to sue,° and vices for to flee: *follow*
5 For unto vertu longeth° dignitee,   *belongs*
And nought the revers, saufly° dar I deeme,   *safely*
Al were he[8] mitre, crowne, or diademe.

This firste stok was ground of rightwisnesse,°   *righteousness*
Trewe of his word, sobre, pietous,[9] and free,
10 Clene of his gost,° and loved bisinesse   *spirit*
Against the vice of slouthe,° in honestee;   *sloth*
And but his heir love vertu as dide he,
He is nat gentil, though he riche° seeme,   *noble*
Al were he mitre, crowne, or diademe.

---

4. I don't consider him worth a bean.
5. I don't care.
6. The virtue of "gentilesse" combined a courtesy of manner with a courtesy of mind. That it is not the inevitable adjunct of aristocratic birth (though most appropriate to it) was a medieval commonplace, to which Chaucer here gives succinct—if conventional—expression. It is important to observe, however, that the moral democracy implied by this doctrine was never transferred by the Middle Ages to the political or even the social realm.
7. I.e., must follow his (the first father's) path and dispose all his (own) wits.
8. Even if he wear.
9. Merciful; "free": generous.

15 Vice may wel be heir to old richesse,
But ther may no man, as ye may wel see,
Biquethe his heir his vertuous noblesse:
That is appropred° unto no degree   *exclusively assigned*
But to the firste fader in majestee,
20 That maketh his heir him that wol him queme,°   *please*
Al were he mitre, crowne, or diademe.

Truth[1]

Flee fro the prees° and dwelle with soothfastnesse;   *crowd*
Suffise unto° thy thing, though it be smal;   *to be content with*
For hoord hath[2] hate, and climbing tikelnesse;°   *insecurity*
Prees hath envye, and wele° blent° overal.   *prosperity / blinds*
5 Savoure° no more than thee bihoove shal;   *relish*
Rule wel thyself that other folk canst rede:°   *advise*
And Trouthe shal delivere,[3] it is no drede.°   *doubt*

Tempest thee nought al crooked to redresse[4]
In trust of hire[5] that turneth as a bal;
10 Muche wele stant in litel bisinesse;[6]
Be war therfore to spurne ayains an al.[7]
Strive nat as dooth the crokke° with the wal.   *pot*
Daunte° thyself that dauntest otheres deede: *master*
And Trouthe shal delivere, it is no drede.

15 That thee is sent, receive in buxomnesse;°   *obedience*
The wrastling for the world axeth° a fal;   *asks for*
Here is noon hoom, here nis but wildernesse:
Forth, pilgrim, forth! Forth, beest, out of thy stal!
Know thy countree, looke up, thank God of al.
20 Hold the heigh way and lat thy gost° thee lede: *spirit*
And Trouthe shal delivere, it is no drede.

Therfore, thou Vache,[8] leve thyn olde wrecchednesse
Unto the world; leve[9] now to be thral.
Crye him mercy that of his heigh goodnesse
25 Made thee of nought, and in especial

1. Taking as his theme Christ's words to his disciples (in John viii.32), "And ye shall know the truth, and the truth shall make you free," Chaucer plays upon the triple meaning that the Middle English word "trouthe" seems to have had for him: the religious truth of Christianity, the moral virtue of integrity, and the philosophical idea of reality. By maintaining one's faith and one's integrity, one rises superior to the vicissitudes of this world and comes eventually to know reality—which is not, however, of this world.

2. Hoarding causes.
3. I.e., truth shall make you free.
4. Do not disturb yourself to straighten all that's crooked.
5. Fortune, who turns like a ball in that she is always presenting a different aspect to men.
6. Peace of mind stands in little anxiety.
7. I.e. to kick against the pricks.
8. Probably Sir Philip de la Vache, with a pun on the French for "cow."
9. I.e. cease.

Draw unto him, and pray in general,
For thee and eek for othere, hevenelich meede:°   *reward*
And Trouthe shal delivere, it is no drede.

SIR GAWAIN AND THE GREEN KNIGHT

N.W. dialect

(ca. 1375–1400)

Nothing is known about the author of *Sir Gawain and the Green Knight* except that he probably wrote the three religious poems (*Patience*, *Purity*, and *Pearl*) preserved in the same manuscript as *Sir Gawain* (no other copies of any of the poems have come to light); and he may also have written a fifth poem, which, like the others, is alliterative, but is preserved in a different manuscript—a charming legend of St. Erkenwald. The dialect of *Sir Gawain* points to an origin in provincial England, about 150 miles northwest of the capital: thus of the three great poets of late medieval England, two, the authors of *Sir Gawain* and *Piers Plowman*, were representatives of cultural centers remote from the royal court at London where Chaucer spent his life. We know almost nothing about these provincial centers, but the works that emanated from them demonstrate a high level of culture. The poet of *Sir Gawain*, indeed, was a most sophisticated and urbane writer, and even though his language (a dialect most difficult for us today and probably difficult for London men in his own time) and his alliterative measure would have been considered barbaric by Chaucer's London audience, the subtlety of his perceptions and the delicacy with which he handles his narrative is not unworthy of Chaucer himself. And although it is impossible to date the poem with any accuracy, its author must have been an almost exact contemporary of Chaucer.

It is possible that the plot of *Sir Gawain* came ready-made to the poet, who may have found it in some lost French poem or have heard it recited in English—perhaps even in Welsh—in his own country. The motif of the green man's decapitation originates in very ancient folklore, probably in a vegetation myth in which the beheading would have been a ritual death that insured the return of spring to the earth and the regrowth of the crops. But this primitive theme has been entirely rationalized by the late medieval poet, who sees in his inherited plot an opportunity to study how successfully Gawain, as a man wholly dedicated to Christian ideals, maintains those ideals when he is subjected to unusual pressures. The poem is a rare combination: at once a comedy—even a satire—of manners and a profoundly Christian view of man's character and his destiny. The court of King Arthur is presented, in the most grandiose and laudatory of language, as the place where the ideal of chivalry has reached its zenith, where all is courtesy and martial prowess in defense of the right. The praise bestowed by the poet upon this court may seem excessive, and indeed the sequel suggests that the author made it so intentionally. For when the court is invaded by the Green Knight, arrogant, monstrous, and yet exasperatingly reasonable, it suddenly seems to become slightly unreal, as if, the Green Knight insultingly implies, its reputation were founded more on fiction than on fact—as if the poets that celebrated it had been working harder to enhance its glory than the knights themselves. In any case, the court is to receive a testing, which is naturally entrusted to the most courteous and valiant knight of the Round Table (in this most English of Arthurian romances Gawain has not been replaced as the best of knights by the continental-born Lancelot).

Once Gawain has set out to keep his promise to the Green Knight, his humiliation—and by inference that of the court—begins: in describing Gawain's adventures the poet, for all his epic enhancement and overt praise for the hero, actually tells a tale of his increasing helplessness. First of all Gawain's courtesy fails him—not, to be sure, in the sense that he relinquishes it, but in the sense that it involves him in a profoundly embarrassing and dangerous situation with the lady: it results in trouble instead of the serenity that courtesy, as the diplomat's virtue, is supposed to procure. Then the second of his great virtues, his martial prowess, is denied to him by the promise he has made not to defend himself against the Green Knight's return stroke. Thus betrayed by or cut off from the two qualities that he supposes to have made him the splendid knight people think him to be, he also, with very human lack of logic, momentarily cuts himself off from the power that has actually permitted those qualities to flourish in him. For when the pressures increase, St. Mary's knight, no longer able to rely on himself, relies not on St. Mary but on a belt of supposed magical powers, which he must accept from the lady with ignominy and hide from her lord with dishonesty. When the Green Knight spares his life there is revealed to Gawain his own real impoverishment, the complete incapacity of the greatest of Arthur's knights to help himself. He has found that without God's grace the virtues which he has made particularly his own are of no use to him—that, indeed, he no longer possesses them. The poem ends happily; but the baldric that the courtiers wear in honor of Gawain's adventure is a reminder that what God asks of men is not primarily courtly or martial prowess, but a humble and a contrite heart.

This didactic point is made with a most Chaucer-like indirection, a fine irony that strips Gawain of his pretensions but leaves him his charm and shows him sympathy for the really quite unfair nature of his predicament—and which also enjoys, and makes the reader enjoy, the embarrassment the hero is made to suffer. *Sir Gawain* is one of the latest and certainly the best of the Middle English romances; yet its greatness lies in the fact that, without ever ceasing to be a romance, a fiction full of the most exquisite comic touches, it is something much larger, one of the really significant literary achievements of the Middle Ages.

Sir Gawain and the Green Knight [1]

Part I

Since the siege and the assault was ceased at Troy,
The walls breached and burnt down to brands and ashes,
The knight that had knotted the nets of deceit
Was impeached for his perfidy, proven most true,[2]
It was high-born Aeneas and his haughty race   5
That since prevailed over provinces, and proudly reigned
Over well-nigh all the wealth of the West Isles.[3]
Great Romulus [4] to Rome repairs in haste;
With boast and with bravery builds he that city
And names it with his own name, that it now bears.   10
Ticius [5] to Tuscany, and towers raises,
Langobard in Lombardy lays out homes,
And far over the French Sea, Felix Brutus [6]
On many broad hills and high Britain he sets,
                    most fair.   15
    Where war and wrack and wonder
    By shifts have sojourned there,
    And bliss by turns with blunder
    In that land's lot had share.

And since this Britain was built by this baron great,   20
Bold boys bred there, in broils delighting,
That did in their day many a deed most dire.
More marvels have happened in this merry land
Than in any other I know, since that olden time,
But of those that here built, of British kings,   25
King Arthur was counted most courteous of all,
Wherefore an adventure I aim to unfold,
That a marvel of might some men think it,
And one unmatched among Arthur's wonders.
If you will listen to my lay but a little while,   30
As I heard it in hall, I shall hasten to tell
                    anew.
    As it was fashioned featly
    In tale of derring-do,
    And linked in measures meetly   35
    By letters tried and true.

1. The Modern English translation is by Marie Borroff (1967), who has reproduced the alliterative meter of the original as well as the "bob and wheel," the five-line rhyming group that concludes each of the long irregular stanzas.
2. The treacherous knight is either Aeneas himself or Antenor, both of whom were, according to medieval tradition, traitors to their city Troy; but Aeneas was actually tried ("impeached") by the Greeks for his refusal to hand over to them his sister Polyxena.
3. Perhaps western Europe.
4. The legendary founder of Rome is here given Trojan ancestry, like Aeneas.
5. Not otherwise known. "Langobard" was the reputed founder of Lombardy.
6. Great-grandson of Aeneas and legendary founder of Britain; not elsewhere given the name Felix (Latin "happy").

This king lay at Camelot [7] at Christmastide;
Many good knights and gay his guests were there,
Arrayed of the Round Table [8] rightful brothers,
With feasting and fellowship and carefree mirth.   40
There true men contended in tournaments many,
Joined there in jousting these gentle knights,
Then came to the court for carol-dancing,
For the feast was in force full fifteen days,
With all the meat and the mirth that men could devise,   45
Such gaiety and glee, glorious to hear,
Brave din by day, dancing by night.
High were their hearts in halls and chambers,
These lords and these ladies, for life was sweet.
In peerless pleasures passed they their days,   50
The most noble knights known under Christ,
And the loveliest ladies that lived on earth ever,
And he the comeliest king, that that court holds,
For all this fair folk in their first age
                              were still.   55
          Happiest of mortal kind,
          King noblest famed of will;
          You would now go far to find
          So hardy a host on hill.

While the New Year was new, but yesternight come,   60
This fair folk at feast two-fold was served,
When the king and his company were come in together,
The chanting in chapel achieved and ended.
Clerics and all the court acclaimed the glad season,
Cried Noel anew, good news to men;   65
Then gallants gather gaily, hand-gifts to make,
Called them out clearly, claimed them by hand,
Bickered long and busily about those gifts.
Ladies laughed aloud, though losers they were,
And he that won was not angered, as well you will know.[9]   70
All this mirth they made until meat was served;
When they had washed them worthily, they went to their seats,
The best seated above, as best it beseemed,
Guenevere the goodly queen gay in the midst
On a dais well-decked and duly arrayed   75
With costly silk curtains, a canopy over,
Of Toulouse and Turkestan tapestries rich,
All broidered and bordered with the best gems
Ever brought into Britain, with bright pennies
                              to pay.   80

7. Capital of Arthur's kingdom, presumably located in southwest England or southern Wales.
8. According to legend, Merlin made the Round Table after a dispute broke out among Arthur's knights about precedence: it seated 100 knights. The table described in the poem is not round.
9. The dispensing of New Year's gifts seems to have involved kissing.

> Fair queen, without a flaw,
> She glanced with eyes of grey.
> A seemlier that once he saw,
> In truth, no man could say.

But Arthur would not eat till all were served;   85
So light was his lordly heart, and a little boyish;
His life he liked lively—the less he cared
To be lying for long, or long to sit,
So busy his young blood, his brain so wild.
And also a point of pride pricked him in heart,   90
For he nobly had willed, he would never eat
On so high a holiday, till he had heard first
Of some fair feat or fray some far-borne tale,
Of some marvel of might, that he might trust,
By champions of chivalry achieved in arms,   95
Or some suppliant came seeking some single knight
To join with him in jousting, in jeopardy each
To lay life for life, and leave it to fortune
To afford him on field fair hap or other.
Such is the king's custom, when his court he holds   100
At each far-famed feast amid his fair host
> so dear.
> > The stout king stands in state
> > Till a wonder shall appear;
> > He leads, with heart elate,   105
> > High mirth in the New Year.

So he stands there in state, the stout young king,
Talking before the high table [1] of trifles fair.
There Gawain the good knight by Guenevere sits,
With Agravain à la dure main on her other side,   110
Both knights of renown, and nephews of the king.
Bishop Baldwin above begins the table,
And Yvain, son of Urien, ate with him there.
These few with the fair queen were fittingly served;
At the side-tables sat many stalwart knights.   115
Then the first course comes, with clamor of trumpets
That were bravely bedecked with bannerets bright,
With noise of new drums and the noble pipes.
Wild were the warbles that wakened that day
In strains that stirred many strong men's hearts.   120
There dainties were dealt out, dishes rare,
Choice fare to choose, on chargers so many
That scarce was there space to set before the people
The service of silver, with sundry meats,
> on cloth.   125
> > Each fair guest freely there
> > Partakes, and nothing loth;

---

1. The high table is on a dais; the side tables (line 115) are on the main floor and run along the walls at a **right** angle with the high table.

Twelve dishes before each pair;
Good beer and bright wine both.

Of the service itself I need say no more,   130
For well you will know no tittle was wanting.
Another noise and a new was well-nigh at hand,
That the lord might have leave his life to nourish;
For scarce were the sweet strains still in the hall,
And the first course come to that company fair,   135
There hurtles in at the hall-door an unknown rider,
One the greatest on ground in growth of his frame:
From broad neck to buttocks so bulky and thick,
And his loins and his legs so long and so great,
Half a giant on earth I hold him to be,   140
But believe him no less than the largest of men,
And that the seemliest in his stature to see, as he rides,
For in back and in breast though his body was grim,
His waist in its width was worthily small,
And formed with every feature in fair accord   145
                  was he.
            Great wonder grew in hall
              At his hue most strange to see,
            For man and gear and all
              Were green as green could be.   150

And in guise all of green, the gear and the man:
A coat cut close, that clung to his sides,
And a mantle to match, made with a lining
Of furs cut and fitted—the fabric was noble,
Embellished all with ermine, and his hood beside,   155
That was loosed from his locks, and laid on his shoulders.
With trim hose and tight, the same tint of green,
His great calves were girt, and gold spurs under
He bore on silk bands that embellished his heels,
And footgear well-fashioned, for riding most fit.   160
And all his vesture verily was verdant green;
Both the bosses on his belt and other bright gems
That were richly ranged on his raiment noble
About himself and his saddle, set upon silk,
That to tell half the trifles would tax my wits,   165
The butterflies and birds embroidered thereon
In green of the gayest, with many a gold thread.
The pendants of the breast-band, the princely crupper,
And the bars of the bit were brightly enameled;
The stout stirrups were green, that steadied his feet,   170
And the bows of the saddle and the side-panels both,
That gleamed all and glinted with green gems about.
The steed he bestrides of that same green
                so bright.
            A green horse great and thick;   175
            A headstrong steed of might;

> In broidered bridle quick,
> Mount matched man aright.

Gay was this goodly man in guise all of green,
And the hair of his head to his horse suited;   180
Fair flowing tresses enfold his shoulders;
A beard big as a bush on his breast hangs,
That with his heavy hair, that from his head falls,
Was evened all about above both his elbows,
That half his arms thereunder were hid in the fashion   185
Of a king's cap-à-dos,[2] that covers his throat.
The mane of that mighty horse much to it like,
Well curled and becombed, and cunningly knotted
With filaments of fine gold amid the fair green,
Here a strand of the hair, here one of gold;   190
His tail and his foretop twin in their hue,
And bound both with a band of a bright green
That was decked adown the dock with dazzling stones
And tied tight at the top with a triple knot
Where many bells well burnished rang bright and clear.   195
Such a mount in his might, nor man on him riding,
None had seen, I dare swear, with sight in that hall
> so grand.
> As lightning quick and light
> He looked to all at hand;   200
> It seemed that no man might
> His deadly dints withstand.

Yet had he no helm, nor hauberk neither,
Nor plate, nor appurtenance appending to arms,
Nor shaft pointed sharp, nor shield for defense,   205
But in his one hand he had a holly bob
That is goodliest in green when groves are bare,
And an ax in his other, a huge and immense,
A wicked piece of work in words to expound:
The head on its haft was an ell long;   210
The spike of green steel, resplendent with gold;
The blade burnished bright, with a broad edge,
As well shaped to shear as a sharp razor;
Stout was the stave in the strong man's gripe,
That was wound all with iron to the weapon's end,   215
With engravings in green of goodliest work.
A lace lightly about, that led to a knot,
Was looped in by lengths along the fair haft,
And tassels thereto attached in a row,
With buttons of bright green, brave to behold.   220
This horseman hurtles in, and the hall enters;

---

2. The word *capados* occurs in this form in Middle English only in *Gawain*, here and in line 572. The translator has interpreted it, as the poet apparently did also, as *cap-à-dos*—i.e., a garment covering its wearer "from head to back," on the model of *cap-à-pie*, "from head to foot," referring to armor.

Riding to the high dais, recked he no danger;
Not a greeting he gave as the guests he o'erlooked,
Nor wasted his words, but "Where is," he said,
"The captain of this crowd? Keenly I wish   225
To see that sire with sight, and to himself say
          my say."
      He swaggered all about
      To scan the host so gay;
      He halted, as if in doubt   230
      Who in that hall held sway.

There were stares on all sides as the stranger spoke,
For much did they marvel what it might mean
That a horseman and a horse should have such a hue,
Grow green as the grass, and greener, it seemed,   235
Than green fused on gold more glorious by far.
All the onlookers eyed him, and edged nearer,
And awaited in wonder what he would do,
For many sights had they seen, but such a one never,
So that phantom and faerie the folk there deemed it,   240
Therefore chary of answer was many a champion bold,
And stunned at his strong words stone-still they sat
In a swooning silence in the stately hall.
As all were slipped into sleep, so slackened their speech
          apace.   245
      Not all, I think, for dread,
      But some of courteous grace
      Let him who was their head
      Be spokesman in that place.

Then Arthur before the high dais that entrance beholds,   250
And hailed him, as behooved, for he had no fear,
And said "Fellow, in faith you have found fair welcome;
The head of this hostelry Arthur am I;
Leap lightly down, and linger, I pray,
And the tale of your intent you shall tell us after."   255
"Nay, so help me," said the other, "He that on high sits,
To tarry here any time, 'twas not mine errand;
But as the praise of you, prince, is puffed up so high,
And your court and your company are counted the best,
Stoutest under steel-gear on steeds to ride,   260
Worthiest of their works the wide world over,
And peerless to prove in passages of arms,
And courtesy here is carried to its height,
And so at this season I have sought you out.
You may be certain by the branch that I bear in hand   265
That I pass here in peace, and would part friends,
For had I come to this court on combat bent,
I have a hauberk at home, and a helm beside,
A shield and a sharp spear, shining bright,

And other weapons to wield, I ween well, to boot,   270
But as I willed no war, I wore no metal.
But if you be so bold as all men believe,
You will graciously grant the game that I ask
                          by right."
                    Arthur answer gave   275
                    And said, "Sir courteous knight,
                    If contest here you crave,
                    You shall not fail to fight."

"Nay, to fight, in good faith, is far from my thought;
There are about on these benches but beardless children,   280
Were I here in full arms on a haughty steed,
For measured against mine, their might is puny.
And so I call in this court for a Christmas game,
For 'tis Yule and New Year, and many young bloods about;
If any in this house such hardihood claims,   285
Be so bold in his blood, his brain so wild,
As stoutly to strike one stroke for another,
I shall give him as my gift this gisarme noble,
This ax, that is heavy enough, to handle as he likes,
And I shall bide the first blow, as bare as I sit.   290
If there be one so wilful my words to assay,
Let him leap hither lightly, lay hold of this weapon;
I quitclaim it forever, keep it as his own,
And I shall stand him a stroke, steady on this floor,
So you grant me the guerdon to give him another,   295
                          sans blame.
                    In a twelvemonth and a day
                    He shall have of me the same;
                    Now be it seen straightway
                    Who dares take up the game."   300

If he astonished them at first, stiller were then
All that household in hall, the high and the low;
The stranger on his green steed stirred in the saddle,
And roisterously his red eyes he rolled all about,
Bent his bristling brows, that were bright green,   305
Wagged his beard as he watched who would arise.
When the court kept its counsel he coughed aloud,
And cleared his throat coolly, the clearer to speak:
"What, is this Arthur's house," said that horseman then,
"Whose fame is so fair in far realms and wide?   310
Where is now your arrogance and your awesome deeds,
Your valor and your victories and your vaunting words?
Now are the revel and renown of the Round Table
Overwhelmed with a word of one man's speech,
For all cower and quake, and no cut felt!"   315
With this he laughs so loud that the lord grieved;
The blood for sheer shame shot to his face,
                          and pride.

With rage his face flushed red,
And so did all beside.   320
Then the king as bold man bred
Toward the stranger took a stride.

And said "Sir, now we see you will say but folly,
Which whoso has sought, it suits that he find.
No guest here is aghast of your great words.   325
Give to me your gisarme, in God's own name,
And the boon you have begged shall straight be granted."
He leaps to him lightly, lays hold of his weapon;
The green fellow on foot fiercely alights.
Now has Arthur his ax, and the haft grips,   330
And sternly stirs it about, on striking bent.
The stranger before him stood there erect,
Higher than any in the house by a head and more;
With stern look as he stood, he stroked his beard,
And with undaunted countenance drew down his coat,   335
No more moved nor dismayed for his mighty dints
Than any bold man on bench had brought him a drink
                    of wine.
                Gawain by Guenevere
                Toward the king doth now incline:
                "I beseech, before all here,   340
                That this melee may be mine."

"Would you grant me the grace," said Gawain to the king,
"To be gone from this bench and stand by you there,
If I without discourtesy might quit this board,   345
And if my liege lady misliked it not,
I would come to your counsel before your court noble.
For I find it not fit, as in faith it is known,
When such a boon is begged before all these knights,
Though you be tempted thereto, to take it on yourself   350
While so bold men about upon benches sit,
That no host under heaven is hardier of will,
Nor better brothers-in-arms where battle is joined;
I am the weakest, well I know, and of wit feeblest;
And the loss of my life would be least of any;   355
That I have you for uncle is my only praise;
My body, but for your blood, is barren of worth;
And for that this folly befits not a king,
And 'tis I that have asked it, it ought to be mine,
And if my claim be not comely let all this court judge, 360
                    in sight."
                The court assays the claim,
                And in counsel all unite
                To give Gawain the game
                And release the king outright.   365

Then the king called the knight to come to his side,

And he rose up readily, and reached him with speed,
Bows low to his lord, lays hold of the weapon,
And he releases it lightly, and lifts up his hand,
And gives him God's blessing, and graciously prays   370
That his heart and his hand may be hardy both.
"Keep, cousin," said the king, "what you cut with this day,
And if you rule it aright, then readily, I know,
You shall stand the stroke it will strike after."
Gawain goes to the guest with gisarme in hand,   375
And boldly he bides there, abashed not a whit.
Then hails he Sir Gawain, the horseman in green:
"Recount we our contract, ere you come further.
First I ask and adjure you, how you are called
That you tell me true, so that trust it I may."   380
"In good faith," said the good knight, "Gawain am I
Whose buffet befalls you, whate'er betide after,
And at this time twelvemonth take from you another
With what weapon you will, and with no man else
          alive."   385
            The other nods assent:
            "Sir Gawain, as I may thrive,
            I am wondrous well content
            That you this dint shall drive."

"Sir Gawain," said the Green Knight, "By God, I rejoice   390
That your fist shall fetch this favor I seek,
And you have readily rehearsed, and in right terms,
Each clause of my covenant with the king your lord,
Save that you shall assure me, sir, upon oath,
That you shall seek me yourself, wheresoever you deem   395
My lodgings may lie, and look for such wages
As you have offered me here before all this host."
"What is the way there?" said Gawain, "Where do you dwell?
I heard never of your house, by Him that made me,
Nor I know you not, knight, your name nor your court.   400
But tell me truly thereof, and teach me your name,
And I shall fare forth to find you, so far as I may,
And this I say in good certain, and swear upon oath."
"That is enough in New Year, you need say no more,"
Said the knight in the green to Gawain the noble,   405
"If I tell you true, when I have taken your knock,
And if you handily have hit, you shall hear straightway
Of my house and my home and my own name;
Then follow in my footsteps by faithful accord.
And if I spend no speech, you shall speed the better: 410
You can feast with your friends, nor further trace
          my tracks.
            Now hold your grim tool steady
            And show us how it hacks."
            "Gladly, sir; all ready,"   415
            Says Gawain; he strokes the ax.

The Green Knight upon ground girds him with care:
Bows a bit with his head, and bares his flesh:
His long lovely locks he laid over his crown,
Let the naked nape for the need be shown.   420
Gawain grips to his ax and gathers it aloft—
The left foot on the floor before him he set—
Brought it down deftly upon the bare neck,
That the shock of the sharp blow shivered the bones
And cut the flesh cleanly and clove it in twain,   425
That the blade of bright steel bit into the ground.
The head was hewn off and fell to the floor;
Many found it at their feet, as forth it rolled;
The blood gushed from the body, bright on the green,
Yet fell not the fellow, nor faltered a whit,   430
But stoutly he starts forth upon stiff shanks,
And as all stood staring he stretched forth his hand,
Laid hold of his head and heaved it aloft,
Then goes to the green steed, grasps the bridle,
Steps into the stirrup, bestrides his mount,   435
And his head by the hair in his hand holds,
And as steady he sits in the stately saddle
As he had met with no mishap, nor missing were
                his head.
       His bulk about he haled,   440
       That fearsome body that bled;
       There were many in the court that quailed
       Before all his say was said.

For the head in his hand he holds right up;
Toward the first on the dais directs he the face,   445
And it lifted up its lids, and looked with wide eyes,
And said as much with its mouth as now you may hear:
"Sir Gawain, forget not to go as agreed,
And cease not to seek till me, sir, you find,
As you promised in the presence of these proud knights.   450
To the Green Chapel come, I charge you, to take
Such a dint as you have dealt—you have well deserved
That your neck should have a knock on New Year's morn.
The Knight of the Green Chapel I am well-known to many,
Wherefore you cannot fail to find me at last;   455
Therefore come, or be counted a recreant knight."
With a roisterous rush he flings round the reins,
Hurtles out at the hall-door, his head in his hand,
That the flint-fire flew from the flashing hooves.
Which way he went, not one of them knew   460
Nor whence he was come in the wide world
                so fair.
       The king and Gawain gay
       Make game of the Green Knight there,
       Yet all who saw it say   465
       'Twas a wonder past compare.

Though high-born Arthur at heart had wonder,
He let no sign be seen, but said aloud
To the comely queen, with courteous speech,
"Dear dame, on this day dismay you no whit;   470
Such crafts are becoming at Christmastide,
Laughing at interludes, light songs and mirth,
Amid dancing of damsels with doughty knights.
Nevertheless of my meat now let me partake,
For I have met with a marvel, I may not deny."   475
He glanced at Sir Gawain, and gaily he said,
"Now, sir, hang up your ax, that has hewn enough,"
And over the high dais it was hung on the wall
That men in amazement might on it look,
And tell in true terms the tale of the wonder.   480
Then they turned toward the table, these two together,
The good king and Gawain, and made great feast,
With all dainties double, dishes rare,
With all manner of meat and minstrelsy both,
Such happiness wholly had they that day   485
              in hold.
        Now take care, Sir Gawain,
        That your courage wax not cold
        When you must turn again
        To your enterprise foretold.   490

Part II

This adventure had Arthur of handsels first
When young was the year, for he yearned to hear tales;
Though they wanted for words when they went to sup,
Now are fierce deeds to follow, their fists stuffed full.
Gawain was glad to begin those games in hall,   495
But if the end be harsher, hold it no wonder,
For though men are merry in mind after much drink,
A year passes apace, and proves ever new:
First things and final conform but seldom.
And so this Yule to the young year yielded place,   500
And each season ensued at its set time;
After Christmas there came the cold cheer of Lent,
When with fish and plainer fare our flesh we reprove;
But then the world's weather with winter contends:
The keen cold lessens, the low clouds lift;   505
Fresh falls the rain in fostering showers
On the face of the fields; flowers appear.
The ground and the groves wear gowns of green;
Birds build their nests, and blithely sing
That solace of all sorrow with summer comes   510
            ere long.
        And blossoms day by day

Bloom rich and rife in throng;
Then every grove so gay
Of the greenwood rings with song.   515

And then the season of summer with the soft winds,
When Zephyr sighs low over seeds and shoots;
Glad is the green plant growing abroad,
When the dew at dawn drops from the leaves,
To get a gracious glance from the golden sun.   520
But harvest with harsher winds follows hard after,
Warns him to ripen well ere winter comes;
Drives forth the dust in the droughty season,
From the face of the fields to fly high in air.
Wroth winds in the welkin wrestle with the sun,   525
The leaves launch from the linden and light on the ground,
And the grass turns to gray, that once grew green.
Then all ripens and rots that rose up at first,
And so the year moves on in yesterdays many,
And winter once more, by the world's law,   530
          draws nigh.
        At Michaelmas [3] the moon
        Hangs wintry pale in sky;
        Sir Gawain girds him soon
        For travails yet to try.   535

Till All-Hallows' Day [4] with Arthur he dwells,
And he held a high feast to honor that knight
With great revels and rich, of the Round Table.
Then ladies lovely and lords debonair
With sorrow for Sir Gawain were sore at heart;   540
Yet they covered their care with countenance glad:
Many a mournful man made mirth for his sake.
So after supper soberly he speaks to his uncle
Of the hard hour at hand, and openly says,
"Now, liege lord of my life, my leave I take;   545
The terms of this task too well you know—
To count the cost over concerns me nothing.
But I am bound forth betimes to bear a stroke
From the grim man in green, as God may direct."
Then the first and foremost came forth in throng: 550
Yvain and Eric and others of note,
Sir Dodinal le Sauvage, the Duke of Clarence,
Lionel and Lancelot and Lucan the good,
Sir Bors and Sir Bedivere, big men both,
And many manly knights more, with Mador de la Porte.   555
All this courtly company comes to the king
To counsel their comrade, with care in their hearts;
There was much secret sorrow suffered that day
That one so good as Gawain must go in such wise

---

3. September 29.   4. All Saints' Day, November 1.

To bear a bitter blow, and his bright sword 560
    lay by.
   He said, "Why should I tarry?"
   And smiled with tranquil eye;
   "In destinies sad or merry,
   True men can but try." 565

He dwelt there all that day, and dressed in the morning;
Asked early for his arms, and all were brought.
First a carpet of rare cost was cast on the floor
Where much goodly gear gleamed golden bright;
He takes his place promptly and picks up the steel, 570
Attired in a tight coat of Turkestan silk
And a kingly cap-à-dos, closed at the throat,
That was lavishly lined with a lustrous fur.
Then they set the steel shoes on his sturdy feet
And clad his calves about with comely greaves, 575
And plate well-polished protected his knees,
Affixed with fastenings of the finest gold.
Fair cuisses enclosed, that were cunningly wrought,
His thick-thewed thighs, with thongs bound fast,
And massy chain-mail of many a steel ring 580
He bore on his body, above the best cloth,
With brace burnished bright upon both his arms,
Good couters and gay, and gloves of plate,
And all the goodly gear to grace him well
    that tide. 585
   His surcoat blazoned bold;
   Sharp spurs to prick with pride;
   And a brave silk band to hold
   The broadsword at his side.

When he had on his arms, his harness was rich, 590
The least latchet or loop laden with gold;
So armored as he was, he heard a mass,
Honored God humbly at the high altar.
Then he comes to the king and his comrades-in-arms,
Takes his leave at last of lords and ladies, 595
And they clasped and kissed him, commending him to Christ.
By then Gringolet was girt with a great saddle
That was gaily agleam with fine gilt fringe,
New-furbished for the need with nail-heads bright;
The bridle and the bars bedecked all with gold; 600
The breast-plate, the saddlebow, the side-panels both,
The caparison and the crupper accorded in hue,
And all ranged on the red the resplendent studs
That glittered and glowed like the glorious sun.
His helm now he holds up and hastily kisses, 605
Well-closed with iron clinches, and cushioned within;

It was high on his head, with a hasp behind,
And a covering of cloth to encase the visor,
All bound and embroidered with the best gems
On broad bands of silk, and bordered with birds,   610
Parrots and popinjays preening their wings,
Lovebirds and love-knots as lavishly wrought
As many women had worked seven winters thereon,
                    entire.
            The diadem costlier yet   615
            That crowned that comely sire,
            With diamonds richly set,
            That flashed as if on fire.

Then they showed forth the shield, that shone all red,
With the pentangle [5] portrayed in purest gold.   620
About his broad neck by the baldric he casts it,
That was meet for the man, and matched him well.
And why the pentangle is proper to that peerless prince
I intend now to tell, though detain me it must.
It is a sign by Solomon sagely devised   625
To be a token of truth, by its title of old,
For it is a figure formed of five points,
And each line is linked and locked with the next
For ever and ever, and hence it is called
In all England, as I hear, the endless knot.   630
And well may he wear it on his worthy arms,
For ever faithful five-fold in five-fold fashion
Was Gawain in good works, as gold unalloyed,
Devoid of all villainy, with virtues adorned
                    in sight.   635
            On shield and coat in view
            He bore that emblem bright,
            As to his word most true
            And in speech most courteous knight.

And first, he was faultless in his five senses,   640
Nor found ever to fail in his five fingers,
And all his fealty was fixed upon the five wounds
That Christ got on the cross, as the creed tells;
And wherever this man in melee took part,
His one thought was of this, past all things else,   645
That all his force was founded on the five joys [6]
That the high Queen of heaven had in her child.
And therefore, as I find, he fittingly had
On the inner part of his shield her image portrayed,
That when his look on it lighted, he never lost heart.   650
The fifth of the five fives followed by this knight

---

5. A five-pointed star, formed by five lines which are drawn without lifting the pencil from the paper, supposed to have mystical significance; as Solomon's sign (line 625) it was enclosed in a circle.
6. The Annunciation, Nativity, Resurrection, Ascension, and Assumption.

Were beneficence boundless and brotherly love
And pure mind and manners, that none might impeach,
And compassion most precious—these peerless five
Were forged and made fast in him, foremost of men.   655
Now all these five fives were confirmed in this knight,
And each linked in other, that end there was none,
And fixed to five points, whose force never failed,
Nor assembled all on a side, nor asunder either,
Nor anywhere at an end, but whole and entire   660
However the pattern proceeded or played out its course.
And so on his shining shield shaped was the knot
Royally in red gold against red gules,
That is the peerless pentangle, prized of old
                           in lore.   665
          Now armed is Gawain gay,
          And bears his lance before,
          And soberly said good day,
          He thought forevermore.

He struck his steed with the spurs and sped on his way   670
So fast that the flint-fire flashed from the stones.
When they saw him set forth they were sore aggrieved,
And all sighed softly, and said to each other,
Fearing for their fellow, "Ill fortune it is
That you, man, must be marred, that most are worthy!   675
His equal on this earth can hardly be found;
To have dealt more discreetly had done less harm,
And have dubbed him a duke, with all due honor.
A great leader of lords he was like to become,
And better so to have been than battered to bits,   680
Beheaded by an elf-man,[7] for empty pride!
Who would credit that a king could be counseled so,
And caught in a cavil in a Christmas game?"
Many were the warm tears they wept from their eyes
When goodly Sir Gawain was gone from the court   685
                     that day.
          No longer he abode,
          But speedily went his way
          Over many a wandering road,
          As I heard my author say.   690

Now he rides in his array through the realm of Logres,[8]
Sir Gawain, God knows, though it gave him small joy!
All alone must he lodge through many a long night
Where the food that he fancied was far from his plate;
He had no mate but his mount, over mountain and plain,   695
Nor man to say his mind to but almighty God,
Till he had wandered well-nigh into North Wales.
All the islands of Anglesey he holds on his left,

7. Supernatural being.
8. One of the names for Arthur's kingdom.

And follows, as he fares, the fords by the coast,
Comes over at Holy Head, and enters next   700
The Wilderness of Wirral ⁹—few were within
That had great good will toward God or man.
And earnestly he asked of each mortal he met
If he had ever heard aught of a knight all green,
Or of a Green Chapel, on ground thereabouts,   705
And all said the same, and solemnly swore
They saw no such knight all solely green
                        in hue.
                 Over country wild and strange
                 The knight sets off anew;
                 Often his course must change   710
                 Ere the Chapel comes in view.

Many a cliff must he climb in country wild;
Far off from all his friends, forlorn must he ride;
At each strand or stream where the stalwart passed   715
'Twere a marvel if he met not some monstrous foe,
And that so fierce and forbidding that fight he must.
So many were the wonders he wandered among
That to tell but the tenth part would tax my wits.
Now with serpents he wars, now with savage wolves,   720
Now with wild men of the woods, that watched from the rocks,
Both with bulls and with bears, and with boars besides,
And giants that came gibbering from the jagged steeps.
Had he not borne himself bravely, and been on God's side,
He had met with many mishaps and mortal harms.   725
And if the wars were unwelcome, the winter was worse,
When the cold clear rains rushed from the clouds
And froze before they could fall to the frosty earth.
Near slain by the sleet he sleeps in his irons
More nights than enough, among naked rocks,   730
Where clattering from the crest the cold stream ran
And hung in hard icicles high overhead.
Thus in peril and pain and predicaments dire
He rides across country till Christmas Eve,
                        our knight.   735
                 And at that holy tide
                 He prays with all his might
                 That Mary may be his guide
                 Till a dwelling comes in sight.

By a mountain next morning he makes his way   740
Into a forest fastness, fearsome and wild;
High hills on either hand, with hoar woods below,
Oaks old and huge by the hundred together.
The hazel and the hawthorn were all intertwined

9. Gawain went from Camelot north to   east across the Dee to the forest of
the northern coast of Wales, opposite   Wirral in Chesire.
the islands of Anglesey; there he turned

With rough raveled moss, that raggedly hung,   745
With many birds unblithe upon bare twigs
That peeped most piteously for pain of the cold.
The good knight on Gringolet glides thereunder
Through many a marsh and mire, a man all alone;
He feared for his default, should he fail to see   750
The service of that Sire that on that same night
Was born of a bright maid, to bring us His peace.
And therefore sighing he said, "I beseech of Thee, Lord,
And Mary, thou mildest mother so dear,
Some harborage where haply I might hear mass   755
And Thy matins tomorrow—meekly I ask it,
And thereto proffer and pray my pater and ave
                    and creed."
            He said his prayer with sighs,
            Lamenting his misdeed;   760
            He crosses himself, and cries
            On Christ in his great need.

No sooner had Sir Gawain signed himself thrice
Than he was ware, in the wood, of a wondrous dwelling,
Within a moat, on a mound, bright amid boughs   765
Of many a tree great of girth that grew by the water—
A castle as comely as a knight could own,
On grounds fair and green, in a goodly park
With a palisade of palings planted about
For two miles and more, round many a fair tree.   770
The stout knight stared at that stronghold great
As it shimmered and shone amid shining leaves,
Then with helmet in hand he offers his thanks
To Jesus and Saint Julian,[1] that are gentle both,
That in courteous accord had inclined to his prayer;   775
"Now fair harbor," said he, "I humbly beseech!"
Then he pricks his proud steed with the plated spurs,
And by chance he has chosen the chief path
That brought the bold knight to the bridge's end
                    in haste.   780
            The bridge hung high in air;
            The gates were bolted fast;
            The walls well-framed to bear
            The fury of the blast.

The man on his mount remained on the bank   785
Of the deep double moat that defended the place.
The wall went in the water wondrous deep,
And a long way aloft it loomed overhead.
It was built of stone blocks to the battlements' height,
With corbels under cornices in comeliest style;   790
Watch-towers trusty protected the gate,

1. Patron saint of hospitality.

With many a lean loophole, to look from within:
A better-made barbican the knight beheld never.
And behind it there hoved a great hall and fair:
Turrets rising in tiers, with tines [2] at their tops,   795
Spires set beside them, splendidly long,
With finials [3] well-fashioned, as filigree fine.
Chalk-white chimneys over chambers high
Gleamed in gay array upon gables and roofs;
The pinnacles in panoply, pointing in air,   800
So vied there for his view that verily it seemed
A castle cut of paper for a king's feast.
The good knight on Gringolet thought it great luck
If he could but contrive to come there within
To keep the Christmas feast in that castle fair   805
          and bright.
              There answered to his call
              A porter most polite;
              From his station on the wall
              He greets the errant knight.   810

"Good sir," said Gawain, "Wouldst go to inquire
If your lord would allow me to lodge here a space?"
"Peter!" said the porter, "For my part, I think
So noble a knight will not want for a welcome!"
Then he bustles off briskly, and comes back straight,   815
And many servants beside, to receive him the better.
They let down the drawbridge and duly went forth
And kneeled down on their knees on the naked earth
To welcome this warrior as best they were able.
They proffered him passage—the portals stood wide—   820
And he beckoned them to rise, and rode over the bridge.
Men steadied his saddle as he stepped to the ground,
And there stabled his steed many stalwart folk.
Now come the knights and the noble squires
To bring him with bliss into the bright hall.   825
When his high helm was off, there hied forth a throng
Of attendants to take it, and see to its care;
They bore away his brand and his blazoned shield;
Then graciously he greeted those gallants each one,
And many a noble drew near, to do the knight honor.   830
All in his armor into hall he was led,
Where fire on a fair hearth fiercely blazed.
And soon the lord himself descends from his chamber
To meet with good manners the man on his floor.
He said, "To this house you are heartily welcome: 835
What is here is wholly yours, to have in your power
          and sway."
           "Many thanks," said Sir Gawain;
           "May Christ your pains repay!"

2. Spikes.   3. Gable ornaments.

The two embrace amain   840
As men well met that day.

Gawain gazed on the host that greeted him there,
And a lusty fellow he looked, the lord of that place:
A man of massive mold, and of middle age;
Broad, bright was his beard, of a beaver's hue,   845
Strong, steady his stance, upon stalwart shanks,
His face fierce as fire, fair-spoken withal,
And well-suited he seemed in Sir Gawain's sight
To be a master of men in a mighty keep.
They pass into a parlor, where promptly the host   850
Has a servant assigned him to see to his needs,
And there came upon his call many courteous folk
That brought him to a bower where bedding was noble,
With heavy silk hangings hemmed all in gold,
Coverlets and counterpanes curiously wrought,   855
A canopy over the couch, clad all with fur,
Curtains running on cords, caught to gold rings,
Woven rugs on the walls of eastern work,
And the floor, under foot, well-furnished with the same.
With light talk and laughter they loosed from him then 860
His war-dress of weight and his worthy clothes.
Robes richly wrought they brought him right soon,
To change there in chamber and choose what he would.
When he had found one he fancied, and flung it about,
Well-fashioned for his frame, with flowing skirts,   865
His face fair and fresh as the flowers of spring,
All the good folk agreed, that gazed on him then,
His limbs arrayed royally in radiant hues,
That so comely a mortal never Christ made
                    as he.   870
            Whatever his place of birth,
            It seemed he well might be
            Without a peer on earth
            In martial rivalry.

A couch before the fire, where fresh coals burned,   875
They spread for Sir Gawain splendidly now
With quilts quaintly stitched, and cushions beside,
And then a costly cloak they cast on his shoulders
Of bright silk, embroidered on borders and hems,
With furs of the finest well-furnished within,   880
And bound about with ermine, both mantle and hood;
And he sat at that fireside in sumptuous estate
And warmed himself well, and soon he waxed merry.
Then attendants set a table upon trestles broad,
And lustrous white linen they laid thereupon,   885
A saltcellar of silver, spoons of the same.
He washed himself well and went to his place,
Men set his fare before him in fashion most fit.

There were soups of all sorts, seasoned with skill,
Double-sized servings, and sundry fish,   890
Some baked, some breaded, some broiled on the coals,
Some simmered, some in stews, steaming with spice,
And with sauces to sup that suited his taste.
He confesses it a feast with free words and fair;
They requite him as kindly with courteous jests,   895
         well-sped.
      "Tonight you fast [4] and pray;
      Tomorrow we'll see you fed."
      The knight grows wondrous gay
      As the wine goes to his head.   900

Then at times and by turns, as at table he sat,
They questioned him quietly, with queries discreet,
And he courteously confessed that he comes from the court,
And owns him of the brotherhood of high-famed Arthur,
The right royal ruler of the Round Table,   905
And the guest by their fireside is Gawain himself,
Who has happened on their house at that holy feast.
When the name of the knight was made known to the lord,
Then loudly he laughed, so elated he was,
And the men in that household made haste with joy   910
To appear in his presence promptly that day,
That of courage ever-constant, and customs pure,
Is pattern and paragon, and praised without end:
Of all knights on earth most honored is he.
Each said solemnly aside to his brother,   915
"Now displays of deportment shall dazzle our eyes
And the polished pearls of impeccable speech;
The high art of eloquence is ours to pursue
Since the father of fine manners is found in our midst.
Great is God's grace, and goodly indeed,   920
That a guest such as Gawain he guides to us here
When men sit and sing of their Savior's birth
         in view.
      With command of manners pure
      He shall each heart imbue;   925
      Who shares his converse, sure,
      Shall learn love's language true."

When the knight had done dining and duly arose,
The dark was drawing on; the day nigh ended.
Chaplains in chapels and churches about   930
Rang the bells aright, reminding all men
Of the holy evensong of the high feast.
The lord attends alone; his fair lady sits
In a comely closet, secluded from sight.
Gawain in gay attire goes thither soon;   935

4. Gawain is said to be "fasting" because the meal, though elaborate, consisted only of fish dishes, appropriate to a fasting day.

The lord catches his coat, and calls him by name,
And has him sit beside him, and says in good faith
No guest on God's earth would he gladlier greet.
For that Gawain thanked him; the two then embraced
And sat together soberly the service through. 940
Then the lady, that longed to look on the knight,
Came forth from her closet with her comely maids.
The fair hues of her flesh, her face and her hair
And her body and her bearing were beyond praise,
And excelled the queen herself, as Sir Gawain thought. 945
He goes forth to greet her with gracious intent;
Another lady led her by the left hand
That was older than she—an ancient, it seemed,
And held in high honor by all men about.
But unlike to look upon, those ladies were, 950
For if the one was fresh, the other was faded:
Bedecked in bright red was the body of one;
Flesh hung in folds on the face of the other;
On one a high headdress, hung all with pearls;
Her bright throat and bosom fair to behold, 955
Fresh as the first snow fallen upon hills;
A wimple the other one wore round her throat;
Her swart chin well swaddled, swathed all in white;
Her forehead enfolded in flounces of silk
That framed a fair fillet, of fashion ornate, 960
And nothing bare beneath save the black brows,
The two eyes and the nose, the naked lips,
And they unsightly to see, and sorrily bleared.
A beldame, by God, she may well be deemed,
                              of pride! 965
    She was short and thick of waist,
    Her buttocks round and wide;
    More toothsome, to his taste,
    Was the beauty by her side.

When Gawain had gazed on that gay lady, 970
With leave of her lord, he politely approached;
To the elder in homage he humbly bows;
The lovelier he salutes with a light embrace.
He claims a comely kiss, and courteously he speaks;
They welcome him warmly, and straightway he asks 975
To be received as their servant, if they so desire.
They take him between them; with talking they bring him
Beside a bright fire; bade then that spices
Be freely fetched forth, to refresh them the better,
And the good wine therewith, to warm their hearts. 980
The lord leaps about in light-hearted mood;
Contrives entertainments and timely sports;
Takes his hood from his head and hangs it on a spear,
And offers him openly the honor thereof
Who should promote the most mirth at that Christmas feast; 985

"And I shall try for it, trust me—contend with the best,
Ere I go without my headgear by grace of my friends!"
Thus with light talk and laughter the lord makes merry
To gladden the guest he had greeted in hall
                that day.   990
      At the last he called for light
      The company to convey;
      Gawain says goodnight
      And retires to bed straightway.

On the morn when each man is mindful in heart   995
That God's son was sent down to suffer our death,
No household but is blithe for His blessed sake;
So was it there on that day, with many delights.
Both at larger meals and less they were lavishly served
By doughty lads on dais, with delicate fare;   1000
The old ancient lady, highest she sits;
The lord at her left hand leaned, as I hear;
Sir Gawain in the center, beside the gay lady,
Where the food was brought first to that festive board,
And thence throughout the hall, as they held most fit,   1005
To each man was offered in order of rank.
There was meat, there was mirth, there was much joy,
That to tell all the tale would tax my wits,
Though I pained me, perchance, to paint it with care;
But yet I know that our knight and the noble lady   1010
Were accorded so closely in company there,
With the seemly solace of their secret words,
With speeches well-sped, spotless and pure,
That each prince's pastime their pleasures far
               outshone.   1015
      Sweet pipes beguile their cares,
      And the trumpet of martial tone;
      Each tends his affairs
      And those two tend their own.

That day and all the next, their disport was noble,   1020
And the third day, I think, pleased them no less;
The joys of St. John's Day [5] were justly praised,
And were the last of their like for those lords and ladies;
Then guests were to go in the gray morning,
Wherefore they whiled the night away with wine and
    with mirth,   1025
Moved to the measures of many a blithe carol;
At last, when it was late, took leave of each other,
Each one of those worthies, to wend his way.
Gawain bids goodbye to his goodly host
Who brings him to his chamber, the chimney beside,   1030
And detains him in talk, and tenders his thanks
And holds it an honor to him and his people

5. December 27.

That he has harbored in his house at that holy time
And embellished his abode with his inborn grace.
"As long as I may live, my luck is the better   1035
That Gawain was my guest at God's own feast!"
"Noble sir," said the knight, "I cannot but think
All the honor is your own—may heaven requite it!
And your man to command I account myself here
As I am bound and beholden, and shall be, come   1040
            what may."
        The lord with all his might
        Entreats his guest to stay;
        Brief answer makes the knight:
        Next morning he must away.   1045

Then the lord of that land politely inquired
What dire affair had forced him, at that festive time,
So far from the king's court to fare forth alone
Ere the holidays wholly had ended in hall.
"In good faith," said Gawain, "you have guessed the truth: 1050
On a high errand and urgent I hastened away,
For I am summoned by myself to seek for a place—
I would I knew whither, or where it might be!
Far rather would I find it before the New Year
Than own the land of Logres, so help me our Lord!   1055
Wherefore, sir, in friendship this favor I ask,
That you say in sober earnest, if something you know
Of the Green Chapel, on ground far or near,
Or the lone knight that lives there, of like hue of green.
A certain day was set by assent of us both   1060
To meet at that landmark, if I might last,
And from now to the New Year is nothing too long,
And I would greet the Green Knight there, would God but allow,
More gladly, by God's Son, than gain the world's wealth!
And I must set forth to search, as soon as I may;   1065
To be about the business I have but three days
And would as soon sink down dead as desist from my errand."
Then smiling said the lord, "Your search, sir, is done,
For we shall see you to that site by the set time.
Let Gawain grieve no more over the Green Chapel;   1070
You shall be in your own bed, in blissful ease,
All the forenoon, and fare forth the first of the year,
And make the goal by midmorn, to mind your affairs,
            no fear!
        Tarry till the fourth day   1075
        And ride on the first of the year.
        We shall set you on your way;
        It is not two miles from here."

Then Gawain was glad, and gleefully he laughed:

"Now I thank you for this, past all things else!   1080
Now my goal is here at hand! With a glad heart I shall
Both tarry, and undertake any task you devise."
Then the host seized his arm and seated him there;
Let the ladies be brought, to delight them the better,
And in fellowship fair by the fireside they sit;   1085
So gay waxed the good host, so giddy his words,
All waited in wonder what next he would say.
Then he stares on the stout knight, and sternly he speaks:
"You have bound yourself boldly my bidding to do—
Will you stand by that boast, and obey me this once?" 1090
"I shall do so indeed," said the doughty knight;
"While I lie in your lodging, your laws will I follow."
"As you have had," said the host, "many hardships abroad
And little sleep of late, you are lacking, I judge,
Both in nourishment needful and nightly rest;   1095
You shall lie abed late in your lofty chamber
Tomorrow until mass, and meet then to dine
When you will, with my wife, who will sit by your side
And talk with you at table, the better to cheer
      our guest.   1100
   A-hunting I will go
   While you lie late and rest."
   The knight, inclining low,
   Assents to each behest.

"And Gawain," said the good host, "agree now to this: 1105
Whatever I win in the woods I will give you at eve,
And all you have earned you must offer to me;
Swear now, sweet friend, to swap as I say,
Whether hands, in the end, be empty or better."
"By God," said Sir Gawain, "I grant it forthwith!   1110
If you find the game good, I shall gladly take part."
"Let the bright wine be brought, and our bargain is done,"
Said the lord of that land—the two laughed together.
Then they drank and they dallied and doffed all constraint,
These lords and these ladies, as late as they chose,   1115
And then with gaiety and gallantries and graceful adieux
They talked in low tones, and tarried at parting.
With compliments comely they kiss at the last;
There were brisk lads about with blazing torches
To see them safe to bed, for soft repose   1120
      long due.
   Their covenants, yet awhile,
   They repeat, and pledge anew;
   That lord could well beguile
   Men's hearts, with mirth in view.   1125

Part III

Long before daylight they left their beds;
Guests that wished to go gave word to their grooms,
And they set about briskly to bind on saddles,
Tend to their tackle, tie up trunks.
The proud lords appear, appareled to ride,⁣ 1130
Leap lightly astride, lay hold of their bridles,
Each one on his way to his worthy house.
The liege lord of the land was not the last
Arrayed there to ride, with retainers many;
He had a bite to eat when he had heard mass; 1135
With horn to the hills he hastens amain.
By the dawn of that day over the dim earth,
Master and men were mounted and ready.
Then they harnessed in couples the keen-scented hounds,
Cast wide the kennel-door and called them forth, 1140
Blew upon their bugles bold blasts three;
The dogs began to bay with a deafening din,
And they quieted them quickly and called them to heel,
A hundred brave huntsmen, as I have heard tell,
        together. 1145
    Men at stations meet;
    From the hounds they slip the tether;
    The echoing horns repeat,
    Clear in the merry weather.

At the clamor of the quest, the quarry trembled; 1150
Deer dashed through the dale, dazed with dread;
Hastened to the high ground, only to be
Turned back by the beaters, who boldly shouted.
They harmed not the harts, with their high heads,
Let the bucks go by, with their broad antlers, 1155
For it was counted a crime, in the close season,
If a man of that demesne should molest the male deer.
The hinds were headed up, with "Hey!" and "Ware!"
The does with great din were driven to the valleys.
Then you were ware, as they went, of the whistling of arrows; 1160
At each bend under boughs the bright shafts flew
That tore the tawny hide with their tapered heads.
Ah! they bray and they bleed, on banks they die,
And ever the pack pell-mell comes panting behind;
Hunters with shrill horns hot on their heels— 1165
Like the cracking of cliffs their cries resounded.
What game got away from the gallant archers
Was promptly picked off at the posts below
When they were harried on the heights and herded to the streams:
The watchers were so wary at the waiting-stations, 1170
And the greyhounds so huge, that eagerly snatched,
And finished them off as fast as folk could see
        with sight.
    The lord, now here, now there,

Spurs forth in sheer delight.   1175
And drives, with pleasures rare,
The day to the dark night.

So the lord in the linden-wood leads the hunt
And Gawain the good knight in gay bed lies,
Lingered late alone, till daylight gleamed,   1180
Under coverlet costly, curtained about.
And as he slips into slumber, slyly there comes
A little din at his door, and the latch lifted,
And he holds up his heavy head out of the clothes;
A corner of the curtain he caught back a little   1185
And waited there warily, to see what befell.
Lo! it was the lady, loveliest to behold,
That drew the door behind her deftly and still
And was bound for his bed—abashed was the knight,
And laid his head low again in likeness of sleep;   1190
And she stepped stealthily, and stole to his bed,
Cast aside the curtain and came within,
And set herself softly on the bedside there,
And lingered at her leisure, to look on his waking.
The fair knight lay feigning for a long while,   1195
Conning in his conscience what his case might
Mean or amount to—a marvel he thought it.
But yet he said within himself, "More seemly it were
To try her intent by talking a little."
So he started and stretched, as startled from sleep,   1200
Lifts wide his lids in likeness of wonder,
And signs himself swiftly, as safer to be,
                with art.
        Sweetly does she speak
        And kindling glances dart,   1205
        Blent white and red on cheek
        And laughing lips apart.

"Good morning, Sir Gawain," said that gay lady,
"A slack sleeper you are, to let one slip in!
Now you are taken in a trice—a truce we must make,   1210
Or I shall bind you in your bed, of that be assured."
Thus laughing lightly that lady jested.
"Good morning, good lady," said Gawain the blithe,
"Be it with me as you will; I am well content!
For I surrender myself, and sue for your grace,   1215
And that is best, I believe, and behooves me now."
Thus jested in answer that gentle knight.
"But if, lovely lady, you misliked it not,
And were pleased to permit your prisoner to rise,
I should quit this couch and accoutre me better,   1220
And be clad in more comfort for converse here."
"Nay, not so, sweet sir," said the smiling lady;
"You shall not rise from your bed; I direct you better:
I shall hem and hold you on either hand,

And keep company awhile with my captive knight. 1225
For as certain as I sit here, Sir Gawain you are,
Whom all the world worships, whereso you ride;
Your honor, your courtesy are highest acclaimed
By lords and by ladies, by all living men;
And lo! we are alone here, and left to ourselves: 1230
My lord and his liegemen are long departed,
The household asleep, my handmaids too,
The door drawn, and held by a well-driven bolt,
And since I have in this house him whom all love,
I shall while the time away with mirthful speech 1235
                  at will.
        My body is here at hand,
        Your each wish to fulfill;
        Your servant to command
        I am, and shall be still." 1240

"In good faith," said Gawain, "my gain is the greater,
Though I am not he of whom you have heard;
To arrive at such reverence as you recount here
I am one all unworthy, and well do I know it.
By heaven, I would hold me the happiest of men 1245
If by word or by work I once might aspire
To the prize of your praise—'twere a pure joy!"
"In good faith, Sir Gawain," said that gay lady,
"The well-proven prowess that pleases all others,
Did I scant or scout it, 'twere scarce becoming. 1250
But there are ladies, believe me, that had liefer far
Have thee here in their hold, as I have today,
To pass an hour in pastime with pleasant words,
Assuage all their sorrows and solace their hearts,
Than much of the goodly gems and gold they possess. 1255
But laud be to the Lord of the lofty skies,
For here in my hands all hearts' desire
                  doth lie."
        Great welcome got he there
        From the lady who sat him by; 1260
        With fitting speech and fair
        The good knight makes reply.

"Madame," said the merry man, "Mary reward you!
For in good faith, I find your beneficence noble.
And the fame of fair deeds runs far and wide, 1265
But the praise you report pertains not to me,
But comes of your courtesy and kindness of heart."
"By the high Queen of heaven" (said she) "I count it not so,
For were I worth all the women in this world alive,
And all wealth and all worship were in my hands, 1270
And I should hunt high and low, a husband to take,
For the nurture I have noted in thee, knight, here,
The comeliness and courtesies and courtly mirth—
And so I had ever heard, and now hold it true—

No other on this earth should have me for wife." 1275
"You are bound to a better man," the bold knight said,
"Yet I prize the praise you have proffered me here,
And soberly your servant, my sovereign I hold you,
And acknowledge me your knight, in the name of Christ."
So they talked of this and that until 'twas nigh noon, 1280
And ever the lady languishing in likeness of love.
With feat words and fair he framed his defence,
For were she never so winsome, the warrior had
The less will to woo, for the wound that his bane
                         must be. 1285
                    He must bear the blinding blow,
                    For such is fate's decree;
                    The lady asks leave to go;
                    He grants it full and free.

Then she gaily said goodbye, and glanced at him, laughing, 1290
And as she stood, she astonished him with a stern speech:
"Now may the Giver of all good words these glad hours repay!
But our guest is not Gawain—forgot is that thought."
"How so?" said the other, and asks in some haste,
For he feared he had been at fault in the forms of his speech. 1295
But she held up her hand, and made answer thus:
"So good a knight as Gawain is given out to be,
And the model of fair demeanor and manners pure,
Had he lain so long at a lady's side,
Would have claimed a kiss, by his courtesy, 1300
Through some touch or trick of phrase at some tale's end."
Said Gawain, "Good lady, I grant it at once!
I shall kiss at your command, as becomes a knight,
And more, lest you mislike, so let be, I pray."
With that she turns toward him, takes him in her arms, 1305
Leans down her lovely head, and lo! he is kissed.
They commend each other to Christ with comely words,
He sees her forth safely, in silence they part,
And then he lies no later in his lofty bed,
But calls to his chamberlain, chooses his clothes, 1310
Goes in those garments gladly to mass,
Then takes his way to table, where attendants wait,
And made merry all day, till the moon rose
                         in view
                    Was never knight beset 1315
                    'Twixt worthier ladies two:
                    The crone and the coquette;
                    Fair pastimes they pursue.

And the lord of the land rides late and long,
Hunting the barren hind over the broad heath. 1320
He had slain such a sum, when the sun sank low,
Of does and other deer, as would dizzy one's wits.
Then they trooped in together in triumph at last,
And the count of the quarry quickly they take.

The lords lent a hand with their liegemen many,   1325
Picked out the plumpest and put them together
And duly dressed the deer, as the deed requires.
Some were assigned the assay of the fat:
Two fingers'-width fully they found on the leanest.
Then they slit the slot open and searched out the paunch,   1330
Trimmed it with trencher-knives and tied it up tight.
They flayed the fair hide from the legs and trunk,
Then broke open the belly and laid bare the bowels,
Deftly detaching and drawing them forth.
And next at the neck they neatly parted   1335
The weasand [6] from the windpipe, and cast away the guts.
At the shoulders with sharp blades they showed their skill,
Boning them from beneath, lest the sides be marred;
They breached the broad breast and broke it in twain,
And again at the gullet they begin with their knives,   1340
Cleave down the carcass clear to the breach;
Two tender morsels they take from the throat,
Then round the inner ribs they rid off a layer
And carve out the kidney-fat, close to the spine,
Hewing down to the haunch, that all hung together,   1345
And held it up whole, and hacked it free,
And this they named the numbles,[7] that knew such terms
                         of art.
              They divide the crotch in two,
              And straightway then they start   1350
              To cut the backbone through
              And cleave the trunk apart.

With hard strokes they hewed off the head and the neck,
Then swiftly from the sides they severed the chine,
And the corbie's bone [8] they cast on a branch.   1355
Then they pierced the plump sides, impaled either one
With the hock of the hind foot, and hung it aloft,
To each person his portion most proper and fit.
On a hide of a hind the hounds they fed
With the liver and the lights,[9] the leathery paunches,   1360
And bread soaked in blood well blended therewith.
High horns and shrill set hounds a-baying,
Then merrily with their meat they make their way home,
Blowing on their bugles many a brave blast.
Ere dark had descended, that doughty band   1365
Was come within the walls where Gawain waits
                    at leisure.
              Bliss and hearth-fire bright
              Await the master's pleasure;
              When the two men met that night,   1370
              Joy surpassed all measure.

6. Esophagus.   ("corbies").
7. The other internal organs.   9. Lungs.
8. A bit of gristle assigned to the ravens

Then the host in the hall his household assembles,
With the dames of high degree and their damsels fair.
In the presence of the people, a party he sends
To convey him his venison in view of the knight.   1375
And in high good-humor he hails him then,
Counts over the kill, the cuts on the tallies,
Holds high the hewn ribs, heavy with fat.
"What think you, sir, of this? Have I thriven well?
Have I won with my woodcraft a worthy prize?"   1380
"In good earnest," said Gawain, "this game is the finest
I have seen in seven years in the season of winter."
"And I give it to you, Gawain," said the goodly host,
"For according to our covenant, you claim it as your own."
"That is so," said Sir Gawain, "the same say I: 1385
What I worthily have won within these fair walls,
Herewith I as willingly award it to you."
He embraces his broad neck with both his arms,
And confers on him a kiss in the comeliest style.
"Have here my profit, it proved no better;   1390
Ungrudging do I grant it, were it greater far."
"Such a gift," said the good host, "I gladly accept—
Yet it might be all the better, would you but say
Where you won this same award, by your wits alone."
"That was no part of the pact; press me no further,   1395
For you have had what behooves; all other claims
                  forbear."
        With jest and compliment
        They conversed, and cast off care;
        To the table soon they went;   1400
        Fresh dainties wait them there.

And then by the chimney-side they chat at their ease;
The best wine was brought them, and bounteously served;
And after in their jesting they jointly accord
To do on the second day the deeds of the first: 1405
That the two men should trade, betide as it may,
What each had taken in, at eve when they met.
They seal the pact solemnly in sight of the court;
Their cups were filled afresh to confirm the jest;
Then at last they took their leave, for late was the hour,   1410
Each to his own bed hastening away.
Before the barnyard cock had crowed but thrice
The lord had leapt from his rest, his liegemen as well.
Both of mass and their meal they made short work:
By the dim light of dawn they were deep in the woods   1415
                  away.
        With huntsmen and with horns
        Over plains they pass that day;
        They release, amid the thorns,
        Swift hounds that run and bay.   1420

Soon some were on a scent by the side of a marsh;
When the hounds opened cry, the head of the hunt
Rallied them with rough words, raised a great noise.
The hounds that had heard it came hurrying straight
And followed along with their fellows, forty together.   1425
Then such a clamor and cry of coursing hounds
Arose, that the rocks resounded again.
Hunters exhorted them with horn and with voice;
Then all in a body bore off together
Between a mere in the marsh and a menacing crag,   1430
To a rise where the rock stood rugged and steep,
And boulders lay about, that blocked their approach.
Then the company in consort closed on their prey:
They surrounded the rise and the rocks both,
For well they were aware that it waited within,   1435
The beast that the bloodhounds boldly proclaimed.
Then they beat on the bushes and bade him appear,
And he made a murderous rush in the midst of them all;
The best of all boars broke from his cover,
That had ranged long unrivaled, a renegade old,   1440
For of tough-brawned boars he was biggest far,
Most grim when he grunted—then grieved were many,
For three at the first thrust he threw to the earth,
And dashed away at once without more damage.
With "Hi!" "Hi!" and "Hey!" "Hey!" the others followed,   1445
Had horns at their lips, blew high and clear.
Merry was the music of men and of hounds
That were bound after this boar, his bloodthirsty heart
                    to quell.
          Often he stands at bay,   1450
          Then scatters the pack pell-mell;
          He hurts the hounds, and they
          Most dolefully yowl and yell.

Men then with mighty bows moved in to shoot,
Aimed at him with their arrows and often hit,   1455
But the points had no power to pierce through his hide,
And the barbs were brushed aside by his bristly brow;
Though the shank of the shaft shivered in pieces,
The head hopped away, wheresoever it struck.
But when their stubborn strokes had stung him at last,   1460
Then, foaming in his frenzy, fiercely he charges,
Hies at them headlong that hindered his flight,
And many feared for their lives, and fell back a little.
But the lord on a lively horse leads the chase;
As a high-mettled huntsman his horn he blows;   1465
He sounds the assembly and sweeps through the brush,
Pursuing this wild swine till the sunlight slanted.
All day with this deed they drive forth the time
While our lone knight so lovesome lies in his bed,

Sir Gawain safe at home, in silken bower   1470
                                       so gay.
                         The lady, with guile in heart,
                         Came early where he lay;
                         She was at him with all her art
                         To turn his mind her way.   1475

She comes to the curtain and coyly peeps in;
Gawain thought it good to greet her at once,
And she richly repays him with her ready words,
Settles softly at his side, and suddenly she laughs,
And with a gracious glance, she begins on him thus: 1480
"Sir, if you be Gawain, it seems a great wonder—
A man so well-meaning, and mannerly disposed,
And cannot act in company as courtesy bids,
And if one takes the trouble to teach him, 'tis all in vain.
That lesson learned lately is lightly forgot,   1485
Though I painted it as plain as my poor wit allowed."
"What lesson, dear lady?" he asked all alarmed;
"I have been much to blame, if your story be true."
"Yet my counsel was of kissing," came her answer then,
"Where favor has been found, freely to claim   1490
As accords with the conduct of courteous knights."
"My dear," said the doughty man, "dismiss that thought;
Such freedom, I fear, might offend you much;
It were rude to request if the right were denied."
"But none can deny you," said the noble dame,   1495
"You are stout enough to constrain with strength, if you choose,
Were any so ungracious as to grudge you aught."
"By heaven," said he, "you have answered well,
But threats never throve among those of my land,
Nor any gift not freely given, good though it be.   1500
I am yours to command, to kiss when you please;
You may lay on as you like, and leave off at will."
                         With this,
                         The lady lightly bends
                         And graciously gives him a kiss;   1505
                         The two converse as friends
                         Of true love's trials and bliss.

"I should like, by your leave," said the lovely lady,
"If it did not annoy you, to know for what cause
So brisk and so bold a young blood as you,   1510
And acclaimed for all courtesies becoming a knight—
And name what knight you will, they are noblest esteemed
For loyal faith in love, in life as in story;
For to tell the tribulations of these true hearts,
Why, 'tis the very title and text of their deeds,   1515
How bold knights for beauty have braved many a foe,
Suffered heavy sorrows out of secret love,
And then valorously avenged them on villainous churls

And made happy ever after the hearts of their ladies.
And you are the noblest knight known in your time; 1520
No household under heaven but has heard of your fame,
And here by your side I have sat for two days
Yet never has a fair phrase fallen from your lips
Of the language of love, not one little word!
And you, that with sweet vows sway women's hearts, 1525
Should show your winsome ways, and woo a young thing,
And teach by some tokens the craft of true love.
How! are you artless, whom all men praise?
Or do you deem me so dull, or deaf to such words?
                    Fie! Fie! 1530
        In hope of pastimes new
        I have come where none can spy;
        Instruct me a little, do,
        While my husband is not nearby."

"God love you, gracious lady!" said Gawain then; 1535
"It is a pleasure surpassing, and a peerless joy,
That one so worthy as you would willingly come
And take the time and trouble to talk with your knight
And content you with his company—it comforts my heart.
But to take to myself the task of telling of love, 1540
And touch upon its texts, and treat of its themes
To one that, I know well, wields more power
In that art, by a half, than a hundred such
As I am where I live, or am like to become,
It were folly, fair dame, in the first degree! 1545
In all that I am able, my aim is to please,
As in honor behooves me, and am evermore
Your servant heart and soul, so save me our Lord!"
Thus she tested his temper and tried many a time,
Whatever her true intent, to entice him to sin, 1550
But so fair was his defense that no fault appeared,
Nor evil on either hand, but only bliss
                    they knew.
        They linger and laugh awhile;
        She kisses the knight so true, 1555
        Takes leave in comeliest style
        And departs without more ado.

Then he rose from his rest and made ready for mass,
And then a meal was set and served, in sumptuous style;
He dallied at home all day with the dear ladies, 1560
But the lord lingered late at his lusty sport;
Pursued his sorry swine, that swerved as he fled,
And bit asunder the backs of the best of his hounds
When they brought him to bay, till the bowmen appeared
And soon forced him forth, though he fought for dear life, 1565
So sharp were the shafts they shot at him there.
But yet the boldest drew back from his battering head,

Till at last he was so tired he could travel no more,
But in as much haste as he might, he makes his retreat
To a rise on rocky ground, by a rushing stream.   1570
With the bank at his back he scrapes the bare earth,
The froth foams at his jaws, frightful to see.
He whets his white tusks—then weary were all
Those hunters so hardy that hoved round about
Of aiming from afar, but ever they mistrust   1575
        his mood.
      He had hurt so many by then
        That none had hardihood
        To be torn by his tusks again,
        That was brainsick, and out for blood.   1580

Till the lord came at last on his lofty steed,
Beheld him there at bay before all his folk;
Lightly he leaps down, leaves his courser,
Bares his bright sword, and boldly advances;
Straight into the stream he strides towards his foe.   1585
The wild thing was wary of weapon and man;
His hackles rose high; so hotly he snorts
That many watched with alarm, lest the worst befall.
The boar makes for the man with a mighty bound
So that he and his hunter came headlong together   1590
Where the water ran wildest—the worse for the beast,
For the man, when they first met, marked him with care,
Sights well the slot, slips in the blade,
Shoves it home to the hilt, and the heart shattered,
And he falls in his fury and floats down the water,   1595
        ill-sped.
        Hounds hasten by the score
        To maul him, hide and head;
        Men drag him in to shore
        And dogs pronounce him dead.   1600

With many a brave blast they boast of their prize,
All hallooed in high glee, that had their wind;
The hounds bayed their best, as the bold men bade
That were charged with chief rank in that chase of renown.
Then one wise in woodcraft, and worthily skilled,   1605
Began to dress the boar in becoming style:
He severs the savage head and sets it aloft,
Then rends the body roughly right down the spine;
Takes the bowels from the belly, broils them on coals,
Blends them well with bread to bestow on the hounds.   1610
Then he breaks out the brawn in fair broad flitches,
And the innards to be eaten in order he takes.
The two sides, attached to each other all whole,
He suspended from a spar that was springy and tough;
And so with this swine they set out for home;   1615
The boar's head was borne before the same man

That had stabbed him in the stream with his strong arm,
right through.
He thought it long indeed
Till he had the knight in view;
At his call, he comes with speed
To claim his payment due.

1620

The lord laughed aloud, with many a light word,
When he greeted Sir Gawain—with good cheer he speaks.
They fetch the fair dames and the folk of the house;
He brings forth the brawn, and begins the tale
Of the great length and girth, the grim rage as well,
Of the battle of the boar they beset in the wood.
The other man meetly commended his deeds
And praised well the prize of his princely sport,
For the brawn of that boar, the bold knight said,
And the sides of that swine surpassed all others.
Then they handled the huge head; he owns it a wonder,
And eyes it with abhorrence, to heighten his praise.
"Now, Gawain," said the good man, "this game becomes yours
By those fair terms we fixed, as you know full well."
"That is true," returned the knight, "and trust me, fair friend,
All my gains, as agreed, I shall give you forthwith."
He clasps him and kisses him in courteous style,
Then serves him with the same fare a second time.
"Now we are even," said he, "at this evening feast,
And clear is every claim incurred here to date,
and debt."
"By Saint Giles!" the host replies,
"You're the best I ever met!
If your profits are all this size,
We'll see you wealthy yet!"

1625

1630

1635

1640

1645

Then attendants set tables on trestles about,
And laid them with linen; light shone forth,
Wakened along the walls in waxen torches.
The service was set and the supper brought;
Royal were the revels that rose then in hall
At that feast by the fire, with many fair sports:
Amid the meal and after, melody sweet,
Carol-dances comely and Christmas songs,
With all the mannerly mirth my tongue may describe.
And ever our gallant knight beside the gay lady;
So uncommonly kind and complaisant was she,
With sweet stolen glances, that stirred his stout heart,
That he was at his wits' end, and wondrous vexed;
But he could not in conscience her courtship repay,
Yet took pains to please her, though the plan might
go wrong.
When they to heart's delight
Had reveled there in throng,

1650

1655

1660

1665

> To his chamber he calls the knight,
> And thither they go along.

And there they dallied and drank, and deemed it good sport
To enact their play anew on New Year's Eve,
But Gawain asked again to go on the morrow,　　　　　　　1670
For the time until his tryst was not two days.
The host hindered that, and urged him to stay,
And said, "On my honor, my oath here I take
That you shall get to the Green Chapel to begin your chores
By dawn on New Year's Day, if you so desire.　　　　　　1675
Wherefore lie at your leisure in your lofty bed,
And I shall hunt hereabouts, and hold to our terms,
And we shall trade winnings when once more we meet,
For I have tested you twice, and true have I found you;
Now think this tomorrow: the third pays for all;　　　　　1680
Be we merry while we may, and mindful of joy,
For heaviness of heart can be had for the asking."
This is gravely agreed on and Gawain will stay.
They drink a last draught and with torches depart
> 　　　　　　to rest.　　　　　　　　　　　　　　1685
> 　　　To bed Sir Gawain went;
> 　　　His sleep was of the best;
> 　　　The lord, on his craft intent,
> 　　　Was early up and dressed.

After mass, with his men, a morsel he takes;　　　　　　1690
Clear and crisp the morning; he calls for his mount;
The folk that were to follow him afield that day
Were high astride their horses before the hall gates.
Wondrous fair were the fields, for the frost was light;
The sun rises red amid radiant clouds,　　　　　　　　1695
Sails into the sky, and sends forth his beams.
They let loose the hounds by a leafy wood;
The rocks all around re-echo to their horns;
Soon some have set off in pursuit of the fox,
Cast about with craft for a clearer scent;　　　　　　　1700
A young dog yaps, and is yelled at in turn;
His fellows fall to sniffing, and follow his lead,
Running in a rabble on the right track,
And he scampers all before; they discover him soon,
And when they see him with sight they pursue him the faster,　1705
Railing at him rudely with a wrathful din.
Often he reverses over rough terrain,
Or loops back to listen in the lee of a hedge;
At last, by a little ditch, he leaps over the brush,
Comes into a clearing at a cautious pace,　　　　　　　1710
Then he thought through his wiles to have thrown off the hounds
Till he was ware, as he went, of a waiting-station
Where three athwart his path threatened him at once,
> 　　　　　　all gray.

Quick as a flash he wheels   1715
And darts off in dismay;
With hard luck at his heels
He is off to the wood away.

Then it was heaven on earth to hark to the hounds
When they had come on their quarry, coursing together!   1720
Such harsh cries and howls they hurled at his head
As all the cliffs with a crash had come down at once.
Here he was hailed, when huntsmen met him;
Yonder they yelled at him, yapping and snarling;
There they cried "Thief!" and threatened his life,   1725
And ever the harriers at his heels, that he had no rest.
Often he was menaced when he made for the open,
And often rushed in again, for Reynard was wily;
And so he leads them a merry chase, the lord and his men,
In this manner on the mountains, till midday or near,   1740
While our hero lies at home in wholesome sleep
Within the comely curtains on the cold morning.
But the lady, as love would allow her no rest,
And pursuing ever the purpose that pricked her heart,
Was awake with the dawn, and went to his chamber   1735
In a fair flowing mantle that fell to the earth,
All edged and embellished with ermines fine;
No hood on her head, but heavy with gems
Were her fillet and the fret [1] that confined her tresses;
Her face and her fair throat freely displayed;   1730
Her bosom all but bare, and her back as well.
She comes in at the chamber-door, and closes it with care,
Throws wide a window—then waits no longer,
But hails him thus airily with her artful words,
                         with cheer: 1745
          "Ah, man, how can you sleep?
          The morning is so clear!"
          Though dreams have drowned him deep,
          He cannot choose but hear.

Deep in his dreams he darkly mutters   1750
As a man may that mourns, with many grim thoughts
Of that day when destiny shall deal him his doom
When he greets his grim host at the Green Chapel
And must bow to his buffet, bating all strife.
But when he sees her at his side he summons his wits,   1755
Breaks from the black dreams, and blithely answers.
That lovely lady comes laughing sweet,
Sinks down at his side, and salutes him with a kiss.
He accords her fair welcome in courtliest style;
He sees her so glorious, so gaily attired,   1760
So faultless her features, so fair and so bright,

1. Ornamental net.   •

His heart swelled swiftly with surging joys.
They melt into mirth with many a fond smile,
And there was bliss beyond telling between those two,
               at height.   1765
          Good were their words of greeting;
          Each joyed in other's sight;
          Great peril attends that meeting
          Should Mary forget her knight.

For that high-born beauty so hemmed him about,   1770
Made so plain her meaning, the man must needs
Either take her tendered love or distastefully refuse.
His courtesy concerned him, lest crass he appear,
But more his soul's mischief, should he commit sin
And belie his loyal oath to the lord of that house.   1775
"God forbid!" said the bold knight, "That shall not befall!"
With a little fond laughter he lightly let pass
All the words of special weight that were sped his way;
"I find you much at fault," the fair one said,
"Who can be cold toward a creature so close by your side,   1780
Of all women in this world most wounded in heart,
Unless you have a sweetheart, one you hold dearer,
And allegiance to that lady so loyally knit
That you will never love another, as now I believe.
And, sir, if it be so, then say it, I beg you;   1785
By all your heart holds dear, hide it no longer
               with guile."
          "Lady, by Saint John,"
          He answers with a smile,
          "Lover have I none,   1790
          Nor will have, yet awhile."

"Those words," said the woman, "are the worst of all,
But I have had my answer, and hard do I find it!
Kiss me now kindly; I can but go hence
To lament my life long like a maid lovelorn."   1795
She inclines her head quickly and kisses the knight,
Then straightens with a sigh, and says as she stands,
"Now, dear, ere I depart, do me this pleasure:
Give me some little gift, your glove or the like,
That I may think on you, man, and mourn the less."   1800
"Now by heaven," said he, "I wish I had here
My most precious possession, to put it in your hands,
For your deeds, beyond doubt, have often deserved
A repayment far passing my power to bestow.
But a love-token, lady, were of little avail;   1805
It is not to your honor to have at this time
A glove as a guerdon from Gawain's hand;
And I am here on an errand in unknown realms
And have no bearers with baggage with becoming gifts,
Which distresses me, madame, for your dear sake.   1810

A man must keep within his compass: account it neither grief
                      nor slight."
            "Nay, noblest knight alive,"
            Said that beauty of body white,
            "Though you be loath to give,   1815
            Yet you shall take, by right."

She reached out a rich ring, wrought all of gold,
With a splendid stone displayed on the band
That flashed before his eyes like a fiery sun;
It was worth a king's wealth, you may well believe.   1820
But he waved it away with these ready words:
"Before God, good lady, I forego all gifts;
None have I to offer, nor any will I take."
And she urged it on him eagerly, and ever he refused,
And vowed in very earnest, prevail she would not.   1825
And she sad to find it so, and said to him then,
"If my ring is refused for its rich cost—
You would not be my debtor for so dear a thing—
I shall give you my girdle; you gain less thereby."
She released a knot lightly, and loosened a belt   1830
That was caught about her kirtle, the bright cloak beneath,
Of a gay green silk, with gold overwrought,
And the borders all bound with embroidery fine,
And this she presses upon him, and pleads with a smile,
Unworthy though it were, that it would not be scorned.   1835
But the man still maintains that he means to accept
Neither gold nor any gift, till by God's grace
The fate that lay before him was fully achieved.
"And be not offended, fair lady, I beg,
And give over your offer, for ever I must   1840
                decline.
            I am grateful for favor shown
            Past all deserts of mine,
            And ever shall be your own
            True servant, rain or shine."   1845

"Now does my present displease you," she promptly inquired,
"Because it seems in your sight so simple a thing?
And belike, as it is little, it is less to praise,
But if the virtue that invests it were verily known,
It would be held, I hope, in higher esteem.   1850
For the man that possesses this piece of silk,
If he bore it on his body, belted about,
There is no hand under heaven that could hew him down,
For he could not be killed by any craft on earth."
Then the man began to muse, and mainly he thought   1855
It was a pearl for his plight, the peril to come
When he gains the Green Chapel to get his reward:
Could he escape unscathed, the scheme were noble!
Then he bore with her words and withstood them no more,

And she repeated her petition and pleaded anew,   1860
And he granted it, and gladly she gave him the belt,
And besought him for her sake to conceal it well,
Lest the noble lord should know—and the knight agrees
That not a soul save themselves shall see it thenceforth
               with sight.   1865
      He thanked her with fervent heart,
      As often as ever he might;
      Three times, before they part,
      She has kissed the stalwart knight.

Then the lady took her leave, and left him there,   1870
For more mirth with that man she might not have.
When she was gone, Sir Gawain got from his bed,
Arose and arrayed him in his rich attire;
Tucked away the token the temptress had left,
Laid it reliably where he looked for it after.   1875
And then with good cheer to the chapel he goes,
Approached a priest in private, and prayed to be taught
To lead a better life and lift up his mind,
Lest he be among the lost when he must leave this world.
And shamefaced at shrift he showed his misdeeds   1880
From the largest to the least, and asked the Lord's mercy,
And called on his confessor to cleanse his soul,
And he absolved him of his sins as safe and as clean
As if the dread Day of Judgment should dawn on the morrow.
And then he made merry amid the fine ladies   1885
With deft-footed dances and dalliance light,
As never until now, while the afternoon wore
               away.
      He delighted all around him,
      And all agreed, that day,   1890
      They never before had found him
      So gracious and so gay.

Now peaceful be his pasture, and love play him fair!
The host is on horseback, hunting afield;
He has finished off this fox that he followed so long: 1895
As he leapt a low hedge to look for the villain
Where he heard all the hounds in hot pursuit,
Reynard comes racing out of a rough thicket,
And all the rabble in a rush, right at his heels.
The man beholds the beast, and bides his time,   1900
And bares his bright sword, and brings it down hard,
And he blenches from the blade, and backward he starts;
A hound hurries up and hinders that move,
And before the horse's feet they fell on him at once
And ripped the rascal's throat with a wrathful din.   1905
The lord soon alighted and lifted him free,
Swiftly snatched him up from the snapping jaws,
Holds him over his head, halloos with a will,

And the dogs bayed the dirge, that had done him to death.
Hunters hastened thither with horns at their lips,   1910
Sounding the assembly till they saw him at last.
When that comely company was come in together,
All that bore bugles blew them at once,
And the others all hallooed, that had no horns.
It was the merriest medley that ever a man heard,   1915
The racket that they raised for Sir Reynard's soul
                         that died.
             Their hounds they praised and fed,
             Fondling their heads with pride,
             And they took Reynard the Red   1920
             And stripped away his hide.

And then they headed homeward, for evening had come,
Blowing many a blast on their bugles bright.
The lord at long last alights at his house,
Finds fire on the hearth where the fair knight waits,   1925
Sir Gawain the good, that was glad in heart.
With the ladies, that loved him, he lingered at ease;
He wore a rich robe of blue, that reached to the earth
And a surcoat lined softly with sumptuous furs;
A hood of the same hue hung on his shoulders;   1930
With bands of bright ermine embellished were both.
He comes to meet the man amid all the folk,
And greets him good-humoredly, and gaily he says,
"I shall follow forthwith the form of our pledge
That we framed to good effect amid fresh-filled cups."   1935
He clasps him accordingly and kisses him thrice,
As amiably and as earnestly as ever he could.
"By heaven," said the host, "you have had some luck
Since you took up this trade, if the terms were good."
"Never trouble about the terms," he returned at once,   1940
"Since all that I owe here is openly paid."
"Marry!" said the other man, "mine is much less,
For I have hunted all day, and nought have I got
But this foul fox pelt, the fiend take the goods!
Which but poorly repays those precious things   1945
That you have cordially conferred, those kisses three
                         so good."
                  "Enough!" said Sir Gawain;
                  "I thank you, by the rood!"
                  And how the fox was slain   1950
                  He told him, as they stood.

With minstrelsy and mirth, with all manner of meats,
They made as much merriment as any men might
(Amid laughing of ladies and light-hearted girls,
So gay grew Sir Gawain and the goodly host)   1955
Unless they had been besotted, or brainless fools.
The knight joined in jesting with that joyous folk,

Until at last it was late; ere long they must part,
And be off to their beds, as behooved them each one.
Then politely his leave of the lord of the house   1960
Our noble knight takes, and renews his thanks:
"The courtesies countless accorded me here,
Your kindness at this Christmas, may heaven's King repay!
Henceforth, if you will have me, I hold you my liege,
And so, as I have said, I must set forth tomorrow,   1965
If I may take some trusty man to teach, as you promised,
The way to the Green Chapel, that as God allows
I shall see my fate fulfilled on the first of the year."
"In good faith," said the good man, "with a good will
Every promise on my part shall be fully performed."   1970
He assigns him a servant to set him on the path,
To see him safe and sound over the snowy hills,
To follow the fastest way through forest green
                 and grove.
         Gawain thanks him again,   1975
         So kind his favors prove,
         And of the ladies then
         He takes his leave, with love.

Courteously he kissed them, with care in his heart,
And often wished them well, with warmest thanks,   1980
Which they for their part were prompt to repay.
They commend him to Christ with disconsolate sighs;
And then in that hall with the household he parts—
Each man that he met, he remembered to thank
For his deeds of devotion and diligent pains,   1985
And the trouble he had taken to tend to his needs;
And each one as woeful, that watched him depart,
As he had lived with him loyally all his life long.
By lads bearing lights he was led to his chamber
And blithely brought to his bed, to be at his rest.   1990
How soundly he slept, I presume not to say,
For there were matters of moment his thoughts might well
                 pursue.
         Let him lie and wait;
         He has little more to do,   1995
         Then listen, while I relate
         How they kept their rendezvous.

Part IV

Now the New Year draws near, and the night passes,
The day dispels the dark, by the Lord's decree;
But wild weather awoke in the world without: 2000
The clouds in the cold sky cast down their snow
With great gusts from the north, grievous to bear.
Sleet showered aslant upon shivering beasts;

The wind warbled wild as it whipped from aloft,
And drove the drifts deep in the dales below. 2005
Long and well he listens, that lies in his bed;
Though he lifts not his eyelids, little he sleeps;
Each crow of the cock he counts without fail.
Readily from his rest he rose before dawn,
For a lamp had been left him, that lighted his chamber. 2010
He called to his chamberlain, who quickly appeared,
And bade him get him his gear, and gird his good steed,
And he sets about briskly to bring in his arms,
And makes ready his master in manner most fit.
First he clad him in his clothes, to keep out the cold, 2015
And then his other harness, made handsome anew,
His plate-armor of proof, polished with pains,
The rings of his rich mail rid of their rust,
And all was fresh as at first, and for this he gave thanks
              indeed. 2020
        With pride he wears each piece,
        New-furbished for his need:
        No gayer from here to Greece;
        He bids them bring his steed.

In his richest raiment he robed himself then: 2025
His crested coat-armor, close-stitched with craft,
With stones of strange virtue on silk velvet set;
All bound with embroidery on borders and seams
And lined warmly and well with furs of the best.
Yet he left not his love-gift, the lady's girdle; 2030
Gawain, for his own good, forgot not that:
When the bright sword was belted and bound on his haunches,
Then twice with that token he twined him about.
Sweetly did he swathe him in that swatch of silk,
That girdle of green so goodly to see, 2035
That against the gay red showed gorgeous bright.
Yet he wore not for its wealth that wondrous girdle,
Nor pride in its pendants, though polished they were,
Though glittering gold gleamed at the tips,
But to keep himself safe when consent he must 2040
To endure a deadly dint, and all defense
              denied.
        And now the bold knight came
        Into the courtyard wide;
        That folk of worthy fame 2045
        He thanks on every side.

Then was Gringolet girt, that was great and huge,
And had sojourned safe and sound, and savored his fare;
He pawed the earth in his pride, that princely steed.
The good knight draws near him and notes well his look, 2050
And says sagely to himself, and soberly swears,
"Here is a household in hall that upholds the right!"

The man that maintains it, may happiness be his!
Likewise the dear lady, may love betide her!
If thus they in charity cherish a guest   2055
That are honored here on earth, may they have His reward
That reigns high in heaven—and also you all;
And were I to live in this land but a little while,
I should willingly reward you, and well, if I might."
Then he steps into the stirrup and bestrides his mount;   2060
His shield is shown forth; on his shoulder he casts it;
Strikes the side of his steed with his steel spurs,
And he starts across the stones, nor stands any longer
                    to prance.
            On horseback was the swain   2065
            That bore his spear and lance;
            "May Christ this house maintain
            And guard it from mischance!"

The bridge was brought down, and the broad gates
Unbarred and carried back upon both sides;   2070
He commended him to Christ, and crossed over the planks;
Praised the noble porter, who prayed on his knees
That God save Sir Gawain, and bade him good day,
And went on his way alone with the man
That was to lead him ere long to that luckless place   2075
Where the dolorous dint must be dealt him at last.
Under bare boughs they ride, where steep banks rise,
Over high cliffs they climb, where cold snow clings;
The heavens held aloof, but heavy thereunder
Mist mantled the moors, moved on the slopes.   2080
Each hill had a hat, a huge cape of cloud;
Brooks bubbled and broke over broken rocks,
Flashing in freshets that waterfalls fed.
Roundabout was the road that ran through the wood
Till the sun at that season was soon to rise,   2085
                    that day.
            They were on a hilltop high;
            The white snow round them lay;
            The man that rode nearby
            Now bade his master stay.   2090

"For I have seen you here safe at the set time,
And now you are not far from that notable place
That you have sought for so long with such special pains.
But this I say for certain, since I know you, sir knight,
And have your good at heart, and hold you dear—   2095
Would you heed well my words, it were worth your while—
You are rushing into risks that you reck not of:
There is a villain in yon valley, the veriest on earth,
For he is rugged and rude, and ready with his fists,
And most immense in his mold of mortals alive,   2100
And his body bigger than the best four

That are in Arthur's house, Hector [2] or any.
He gets his grim way at the Green Chapel;
None passes by that place so proud in his arms
That he does not dash him down with his deadly blows,   2105
For he is heartless wholly, and heedless of right,
For be it chaplain or churl that by the Chapel rides,
Monk or mass-priest or any man else,
He would as soon strike him dead as stand on two feet.
Wherefore I say, just as certain as you sit there astride,   2110
You cannot but be killed, if his counsel holds,
For he would trounce you in a trice, had you twenty lives
for sale.
He has lived long in this land
And dealt out deadly bale;   2115
Against his heavy hand
Your power cannot prevail.

"And so, good Sir Gawain, let the grim man be;
Go off by some other road, in God's own name!
Leave by some other land, for the love of Christ,
And I shall get me home again, and give you my word   2120
That I shall swear by God's self and the saints above,
By heaven and by my halidom [3] and other oaths more,
To conceal this day's deed, nor say to a soul
That ever you fled for fear from any that I knew."
"Many thanks!" said the other man—and demurring he speaks—   2125
"Fair fortune befall you for your friendly words!
And conceal this day's deed I doubt not you would,
But though you never told the tale, if I turned back now,
Forsook this place for fear, and fled, as you say,   2130
I were a caitiff coward; I could not be excused.
But I must to the Chapel to chance my luck
And say to that same man such words as I please,
Befall what may befall through Fortune's will
or whim.   2135
Though he be a quarrelsome knave
With a cudgel great and grim,
The Lord is strong to save:
His servants trust in Him."

"Marry," said the man, "since you tell me so much,   2140
And I see you are set to seek your own harm,
If you crave a quick death, let me keep you no longer!
Put your helm on your head, your hand on your lance,
And ride the narrow road down yon rocky slope
Till it brings you to the bottom of the broad valley.   2145
Then look a little ahead, on your left hand,
And you will soon see before you that self-same Chapel,
And the man of great might that is master there.

2. Either the Trojan hero or one of   3. Holiness or, more likely, patron
Arthur's knights.   saints.

Now goodbye in God's name, Gawain the noble!
For all the world's wealth I would not stay here,   2150
Or go with you in this wood one footstep further!"
He tarried no more to talk, but turned his bridle,
Hit his horse with his heels as hard as he might,
Leaves the knight alone, and off like the wind
                 goes leaping.   2155
        "By God," said Gawain then,
        "I shall not give way to weeping;
        God's will be done, amen!
        I commend me to His keeping."

He puts his heels to his horse, and picks up the path;   2160
Goes in beside a grove where the ground is steep,
Rides down the rough slope right to the valley;
And then he looked a little about him—the landscape was wild,
And not a soul to be seen, nor sign of a dwelling,
But high banks on either hand hemmed it about,   2165
With many a ragged rock and rough-hewn crag;
The skies seemed scored by the scowling peaks.
Then he halted his horse, and hoved there a space,
And sought on every side for a sight of the Chapel,
But no such place appeared, which puzzled him sore,   2170
Yet he saw some way off what seemed like a mound,
A hillock high and broad, hard by the water,
Where the stream fell in foam down the face of the steep
And bubbled as if it boiled on its bed below.
The knight urges his horse, and heads for the knoll;   2175
Leaps lightly to earth; loops well the rein
Of his steed to a stout branch, and stations him there.
He strides straight to the mound, and strolls all about,
Much wondering what it was, but no whit the wiser;
It had a hole at one end, and on either side,   2180
And was covered with coarse grass in clumps all without,
And hollow all within, like some old cave,
Or a crevice of an old crag—he could not discern
                 aright.
        "Can this be the Chapel Green?   2185
        Alack!" said the man, "Here might
        The devil himself be seen
        Saying matins at black midnight!"

"Now by heaven," said he, "it is bleak hereabouts;
This prayer-house is hideous, half-covered with grass!   2190
Well may the grim man mantled in green
Hold here his orisons, in hell's own style!
Now I feel it is the Fiend, in my five wits,
That has tempted me to this tryst, to take my life;
This is a Chapel of mischance, may the mischief take it!   2195
As accursed a country church as I came upon ever!"

With his helm on his head, his lance in his hand,
He stalks toward the steep wall of that strange house.
Then he heard, on the hill, behind a hard rock,
Beyond the brook, from the bank, a most barbarous din: 2200
Lord! it clattered in the cliff fit to cleave it in two,
As one upon a grindstone ground a great scythe!
Lord! it whirred like a mill-wheel whirling about!
Lord! it echoed loud and long, lamentable to hear!
Then "By heaven," said the bold knight, "That business
up there 2205
Is arranged for my arrival, or else I am much
misled.
Let God work! Ah me!
All hope of help has fled!
Forfeit my life may be 2210
But noise I do not dread."

Then he listened no longer, but loudly he called,
"Who has power in this place, high parley to hold?
For none greets Sir Gawain, or gives him good day;
If any would a word with him, let him walk forth 2215
And speak now or never, to speed his affairs."
"Abide," said one on the bank above over his head,
"And what I promised you once shall straightway be given."
Yet he stayed not his grindstone, nor stinted its noise,
But worked awhile at his whetting before he would rest, 2220
And then he comes around a crag, from a cave in the rocks,
Hurtling out of hiding with a hateful weapon,
A Danish [4] ax devised for that day's deed,
With a broad blade and bright, bent in a curve,
Filed to a fine edge—four feet it measured 2225
By the length of the lace that was looped round the haft.
And in form as at first, the fellow all green,
His lordly face and his legs, his locks and his beard,
Save that firm upon two feet forward he strides,
Sets a hand on the ax-head, the haft to the earth; 2230
When he came to the cold stream, and cared not to wade,
He vaults over on his ax, and advances amain
On a broad bank of snow, overbearing and brisk
of mood.
Little did the knight incline
When face to face they stood; 2235
Said the other man, "Friend mine,
It seems your word holds good!"

"God love you, Sir Gawain!" said the Green Knight then,
"And well met this morning, man, at my place! 2240
And you have followed me faithfully and found me betimes,
And on the business between us we both are agreed:

4. I.e., long-bladed.

Twelve months ago today you took what was yours,
And you at this New Year must yield me the same.
And we have met in these mountains, remote from all eyes: 2245
There is none here to halt us or hinder our sport;
Unhasp your high helm, and have here your wages;
Make no more demur than I did myself
When you hacked off my head with one hard blow."
"No, by God," said Sir Gawain, "that granted me life,   2250
I shall grudge not the guerdon, grim though it prove;
Bestow but one stroke, and I shall stand still,
And you may lay on as you like till the last of my part
                              be paid."
              He proffered, with good grace,   2255
              His bare neck to the blade,
              And feigned a cheerful face:
              He scorned to seem afraid.

Then the grim man in green gathers his strength,
Heaves high the heavy ax to hit him the blow.   2260
With all the force in his frame he fetches it aloft,
With a grimace as grim as he would grind him to bits;
Had the blow he bestowed been as big as he threatened,
A good knight and gallant had gone to his grave.
But Gawain at the great ax glanced up aside   2265
As down it descended with death-dealing force,
And his shoulders shrank a little from the sharp iron.
Abruptly the brawny man breaks off the stroke,
And then reproved with proud words that prince among knights.
"You are not Gawain the glorious," the green man said,   2270
"That never fell back on field in the face of the foe,
And now you flee for fear, and have felt no harm:
Such news of that knight I never heard yet!
I moved not a muscle when you made to strike,
Nor caviled at the cut in King Arthur's house;   2275
My head fell to my feet, yet steadfast I stood,
And you, all unharmed, are wholly dismayed—
Wherefore the better man I, by all odds,
                              must be."
              Said Gawain, "Strike once more;   2280
              I shall neither flinch nor flee;
              But if my head falls to the floor
              There is no mending me!"

"But go on, man, in God's name, and get to the point!
Deliver me my destiny, and do it out of hand,   2285
For I shall stand to the stroke and stir not an inch
Till your ax has hit home—on my honor I swear it!"
"Have at thee then!" said the other, and heaves it aloft,
And glares down as grimly as he had gone mad.
He made a mighty feint, but marred not his hide;   2290

Withdrew the ax adroitly before it did damage.
Gawain gave no ground, nor glanced up aside,
But stood still as a stone, or else a stout stump
That is held in hard earth by a hundred roots.
Then merrily does he mock him, the man all in green: 2295
"So now you have your nerve again, I needs must strike;
Uphold the high knighthood that Arthur bestowed,
And keep your neck-bone clear, if this cut allows!"
Then was Gawain gripped with rage, and grimly he said,
"Why, thrash away, tyrant, I tire of your threats; 2300
You make such a scene, you must frighten yourself.
Said the green fellow, "In faith, so fiercely you speak
That I shall finish this affair, nor further grace
    allow."
    He stands prepared to strike 2305
    And scowls with both lip and brow;
    No marvel if the man mislike
    Who can hope no rescue now.

He gathered up the grim ax and guided it well:
Let the barb at the blade's end brush the bare throat;
He hammered down hard, yet harmed him no whit 2310
Save a scratch on one side, that severed the skin;
The end of the hooked edge entered the flesh,
And a little blood lightly leapt to the earth.
And when the man beheld his own blood bright on the snow, 2315
He sprang a spear's length with feet spread wide,
Seized his high helm, and set it on his head,
Shoved before his shoulders the shield at his back,
Bares his trusty blade, and boldly he speaks—
Not since he was a babe born of his mother 2320
Was he once in this world one-half so blithe—
"Have done with your hacking—harry me no more!
I have borne, as behooved, one blow in this place;
If you make another move I shall meet it midway
And promptly, I promise you, pay back each blow 2325
    with brand.
    One stroke acquits me here;
    So did our covenant stand
    In Arthur's court last year—
    Wherefore, sir, hold your hand!" 2330

He lowers the long ax and leans on it there,
Sets his arms on the head, the haft on the earth,
And beholds the bold knight that bides there afoot,
How he faces him fearless, fierce in full arms,
And plies him with proud words—it pleases him well. 2335
Then once again gaily to Gawain he calls,
And in a loud voice and lusty, delivers these words:
"Bold fellow, on this field your anger forbear!

No man has made demands here in manner uncouth,
Nor done, save as duly determined at court.   2340
I owed you a hit and you have it; be happy therewith!
The rest of my rights here I freely resign.
Had I been a bit busier, a buffet, perhaps,
I could have dealt more directly, and done you some harm.
First I flourished with a feint, in frolicsome mood,   2345
And left your hide unhurt—and here I did well
By the fair terms we fixed on the first night;
And fully and faithfully you followed accord:
Gave over all your gains as a good man should.
A second feint, sir, I assigned for the morning   2350
You kissed my comely wife—each kiss you restored.
For both of these there behooved but two feigned blows
                              by right.
              True men pay what they owe;
                No danger then in sight.   2355
              You failed at the third throw,
                So take my tap, sir knight.

"For that is my belt about you, that same braided girdle,
My wife it was that wore it; I know well the tale,
And the count of your kisses and your conduct too,   2360
And the wooing of my wife—it was all my scheme!
She made trial of a man most faultless by far
Of all that ever walked over the wide earth;
As pearls to white peas, more precious and prized,
So is Gawain, in good faith, to other gay knights.   2365
Yet you lacked, sir, a little in loyalty there,
But the cause was not cunning, nor courtship either,
But that you loved your own life; the less, then, to blame."
The other stout knight in a study stood a long while,
So gripped with grim rage that his great heart shook.   2370
All the blood of his body burned in his face
As he shrank back in shame from the man's sharp speech.
The first words that fell from the fair knight's lips:
"Accursed be a cowardly and covetous heart!
In you is villainy and vice, and virtue laid low!"   2375
Then he grasps the green girdle and lets go the knot,
Hands it over in haste, and hotly he says:
"Behold there my falsehood, ill hap betide it!
Your cut taught me cowardice, care for my life,
And coveting came after, contrary both   2380
To largesse and loyalty belonging to knights.
Now am I faulty and false, that fearful was ever
Of disloyalty and lies, bad luck to them both!
                              and greed.
              I confess, knight, in this place,   2385
              Most dire is my misdeed;
              Let me gain back your good grace,
              And thereafter I shall take heed."

Then the other laughed aloud, and lightly he said,
"Such harm as I have had, I hold it quite healed.   2390
You are so fully confessed, your failings made known,
And bear the plain penance of the point of my blade,
I hold you polished as a pearl, as pure and as bright
As you had lived free of fault since first you were born.
And I give you, sir, this girdle that is gold-hemmed   2395
And green as my garments, that, Gawain, you may
Be mindful of this meeting when you mingle in throng
With nobles of renown—and known by this token
How it chanced at the Green Chapel, to chivalrous knights.
And you shall in this New Year come yet again   2400
And we shall finish out our feast in my fair hall,
> > > > with cheer."
> > > > He urged the knight to stay,
> > > > And said, "With my wife so dear
> > > > We shall see you friends this day,   2405
> > > > Whose enmity touched you near."

"Indeed," said the doughty knight, and doffed his high helm,
And held it in his hands as he offered his thanks,
"I have lingered long enough—may good luck be yours,
And He reward you well that all worship bestows!   2410
And commend me to that comely one, your courteous wife,
Both herself and that other, my honoured ladies,
That have trapped their true knight in their trammels so quaint.
But if a dullard should dote, deem it no wonder,
And through the wiles of a woman be wooed into sorrow,   2415
For so was Adam by one, when the world began,
And Solomon by many more, and Samson the mighty—
Delilah was his doom, and David thereafter
Was beguiled by Bathsheba, and bore much distress;
Now these were vexed by their devices—'twere a very joy   2420
Could one but learn to love, and believe them not.
For these were proud princes, most prosperous of old,
Past all lovers lucky, that languished under heaven,
> > > > bemused.
> > > > And one and all fell prey   2425
> > > > To women that they had used;
> > > > If I be led astray,
> > > > Methinks I may be excused.

"But your girdle, God love you! I gladly shall take
And be pleased to possess, not for the pure gold,   2430
Nor the bright belt itself, nor the beauteous pendants,
Nor for wealth, nor worldly state, nor workmanship fine,
But a sign of excess it shall seem oftentimes
When I ride in renown, and remember with shame
The faults and the frailty of the flesh perverse,   2435
How its tenderness entices the foul taint of sin;
And so when praise and high prowess have pleased my heart,
A look at this love-lace will lower my pride.

But one thing would I learn, if you were not loath,
Since you are lord of yonder land where I have long sojourned   2440
With honor in your house—may you have His reward
That upholds all the heavens, highest on throne!
How runs your right name?—and let the rest go."
"That shall I give you gladly," said the Green Knight then;
"Bercilak de Hautdesert this barony I hold,   2445
Through the might of Morgan le Faye,[5] that lodges at my house,
By subtleties of science and sorcerers' arts,
The mistress of Merlin,[6] she has caught many a man,
For sweet love in secret she shared sometime
With that wizard, that knows well each one of your knights   2450
                    and you.
                Morgan the Goddess, she,
                So styled by title true;
                None holds so high degree
                That her arts cannot subdue.   2455

"She guided me in this guise to your glorious hall,
To assay, if such it were, the surfeit of pride
That is rumored of the retinue of the Round Table.
She put this shape upon me to puzzle your wits,
To afflict the fair queen, and frighten her to death   2460
With awe of that elvish man that eerily spoke
With his head in his hand before the high table.
She was with my wife at home, that old withered lady,
Your own aunt [7] is she, Arthur's half-sister,
The Duchess' daughter of Tintagel, that dear King Uther   2465
Got Arthur on after, that honored is now.
And therefore, good friend, come feast with your aunt;
Make merry in my house; my men hold you dear,
And I wish you as well, sir, with all my heart,
As any mortal man, for your matchless faith."   2470
But the knight said him nay, that he might by no means.
They clasped then and kissed, and commended each other
To the Prince of Paradise, and parted with one
                    assent.
                Gawain sets out anew;   2475
                Toward the court his course is bent;
                And the knight all green in hue,
                Wheresoever he wished, he went.

Wild ways in the world our worthy knight rides
On Gringolet, that by grace had been granted his life.   2480
He harbored often in houses, and often abroad,
And with many valiant adventures verily he met
That I shall not take time to tell in this story.

5. Arthur's half-sister, an enchantress
who sometimes abetted him, sometimes
made trouble for him.
6. The wise magician who had helped
Arthur become king.

7. Morgan was the daughter of Igraine,
Duchess of Tintagel, and her husband
the Duke; Igraine conceived Arthur
when his father Uther lay with her
through one of Merlin's trickeries.

The hurt was whole that he had had in his neck,
And the bright green belt on his body he bore,   2485
Oblique, like a baldric, bound at his side,
Below his left shoulder, laced in a knot,
In betokening of the blame he had borne for his fault;
And so to court in due course he comes safe and sound.
Bliss abounded in hall when the high-born heard   2490
That good Gawain was come; glad tidings they thought it.
The king kisses the knight, and the queen as well,
And many a comrade came to clasp him in arms,
And eagerly they asked, and awesomely he told,
Confessed all his cares and discomfitures many,   2495
How it chanced at the Chapel, what cheer made the knight,
The love of the lady, the green lace at last.
The nick on his neck he naked displayed
That he got in his disgrace at the Green Knight's hands,
                  alone.   2500
        With rage in heart he speaks,
        And grieves with many a groan;
        The blood burns in his cheeks
        For shame at what must be shown.

"Behold, sir," said he, and handles the belt,   2505
"This is the blazon of the blemish that I bear on my neck;
This is the sign of sore loss that I have suffered there
For the cowardice and coveting that I came to there;
This is the badge of false faith that I was found in there,
And I must bear it on my body till I breathe my last.   2510
For one may keep a deed dark, but undo it no whit,
For where a fault is made fast, it is fixed evermore."
The king comforts the knight, and the court all together
Agree with gay laughter and gracious intent
That the lords and the ladies belonging to the Table,   2515
Each brother of that band, a baldric should have,
A belt borne oblique, of a bright green,
To be worn with one accord for that worthy's sake.
So that was taken as a token by the Table Round,
And he honored that had it, evermore after,   2520
As the best book of knighthood bids it be known.
In the old days of Arthur this happening befell;
The books of Brutus' deeds bear witness thereto
Since Brutus, the bold knight, embarked for this land
After the siege ceased at Troy and the city fared   2525
                amiss.
        Many such, ere we were born,
        Have befallen here, ere this.
        May He that was crowned with thorn
        Bring all men to His bliss! Amen.   2530

Hony Soyt Qui Mal Pense [8]

8. "Shame be to the man who has evil in his mind." This is the motto of the Order of the Garter, founded ca. 1350: apparently a copyist of the poem associated this order with the one founded to honor Gawain.

PIERS PLOWMAN
(B Text, ca. 1377)

St. dialect

The large number of manuscripts in which the *Vision of Piers Plowman* has been preserved indicates its wide popularity from the end of the 14th century up to the reign of Elizabeth I. Yet celebrated as the poem was, we know little about its origin. It exists in three versions, which scholars refer to as the A, B, and C Texts. The first, about 2,400 lines long, stops at a rather inconclusive point in the action; the second is a revision of the first plus an extension of more than 4,000 lines; and the third is a revision of the second. The name frequently associated with the poem is William Langland, but who he was and whether he wrote all three versions is not known. The little that can be inferred about him suggests that he came from the west of England and was probably a native of the Malvern Hills area in which the poem is set and where many of the surviving manuscripts were copied. If he wrote all three versions, then his interests and opinions must have changed while he was at work, for the versions differ from one another in many respects; but if more than one poet was involved, then it is extraordinary that all three versions share the same highly individual style and reflect the same curious and interesting poetic personality. Whatever its origin, the poem was avidly read and studied by a great many people. Within four years of the writing of the second version—which scholars have good evidence to date 1377, the year of Edward III's death and Richard II's accession to the throne—it had become so well known that the leaders of the Peasants' Revolt of 1381 used phrases borrowed from it as part of the rhetoric of the rebellion. The poem must therefore have managed to catch the imagination of a number of readers.

Piers Plowman has the form of a dream vision, a common medieval type in which the author presents his story under the guise of having dreamed it. Most dream visions concern romantic love; *Piers Plowman* also concerns love, but in this instance the love is theological. The dream vision generally involves allegory, not only because one expects from a dream the unrealistic, the fanciful, but also because men have always suspected that dreams relate the truth in a disguised form—that they are natural allegories. *Piers Plowman* is perhaps the greatest of English allegories, though the reader who expects to find in it the kind of definite and clear statement that allegory makes in the morality *Everyman* will be disappointed; allegory here is used not so much in order to define the known, as the character "Good Deeds" does in that play, as to explore the unknown, in particular the great spiritual mysteries of Christianity. When handling these the poet's imagination (for convenience let us assume a single poet, Langland) is apt to soar into a mode of expression that stimulates and excites the reader's imagination while, perhaps, bewildering his intellect (as in Passus I, lines 151 ff. on the Incarnation). Langland's theme is nothing less than the history of Christianity as it unfolds both in the world of the Old and New Testaments and in the heart of the individual Christian—two seemingly distinct realms between which the poet's allegory moves with dizzying rapidity. The ideas of the work are entirely orthodox; but the poet is so passionate that he handles the orthodox as if it were something fresh and exciting.

It is this passion to which he owes his popularity, particularly in the centuries following his own. One of his major themes is the corruption of the clergy, which was for Langland too evident a feature of the recent history of Christianity on earth; when he considers clerical corruption, the reservoir of his passion is opened, and he pours out savagely indignant satire. Since this issue was to become one of the many tangled issues that led ultimately to the separation of the English church from Rome, Langland's castigation of it made his poem almost a textbook of propaganda for the use of the English reformers. Probably nothing would have brought more horror to the poet's orthodox soul; even the papal schism that so disgusted him in his own time would have seemed preferable to this fragmentation of the church. It was probably his passion, too, as it is aroused when he contemplates the sufferings of the poor, that made his poem popular with the rebels of 1381, who, though confused in their motives, were eager to correct certain social abuses that Langland had touched upon. If he was alive to witness it, this use of his poem must also have horrified him, for he is, in his intellectual statements, the least revolutionary of poets. These historical developments are direct results of Langland's peculiar art: his own emotional power is constantly leading him into apparent contradictions and opening him to general misunderstanding. One might observe that Chaucer's portraits of the Monk, Friar, Summoner, and Pardoner are, in their total statement, as devastating as any satire Langland wrote; but because of the extreme control with which they are written, no one has ever ranked Chaucer among the anticlerical reformers— indeed, he has scarcely been given credit for a very real criticism of corruption.

The selections from *Piers Plowman* presented here include a part of the Prologue which contains the well-known vision of the "field full of folk," a passage largely satirical; and the first Passus (or "step," as Langland calls the sections of his poem), wherein the Dreamer, in his habitual pose of the man who has to have everything explained to him, is instructed by Lady Holy Church in the basic essentials of Christianity. These excerpts show the author in several of his characteristic moods, though perhaps exercising better control over his material and expression than he sometimes displays. The hero, Piers Plowman, does not appear until more than a thousand lines later: a simple, honest farmer, in the course of the poem he comes to assume aspects of Adam, Moses, Christ, St. Peter, and the best of the popes. In general he represents both the humanity that Christ redeemed and the humanity that Christ took in order to make the redemption. It is in Piers that the divine meets the human, and that the history of Christianity in the world and its history in the human heart become one and the same. This theme of the accessibility of the divine to the human is presented in its simplest form by the first Passus.

From The Vision of Piers Plowman[1]
From *The Prologue*

In a summer season when soft was the sun,
I shaped me into shrouds[2] as if I a shepherd were,
In habit like a hermit, unholy of works,
Went wide in this world, wonders to hear.
5 But on a May morning, on Malvern Hills,
There befell me a ferly,[3] of fairy it seemed.
I was weary of wandering, and went me to rest
Under a broad bank by a brook's side;
And as I lay and leaned° and looked in the
    waters,   *stretched out*
10 I slumbered into a sleeping, it sounded so merry.
Then did I meet° a marvelous dream,   *dream*
That I was in a wilderness, wist° I never where;   *knew*
As I beheld into the east, on high to the sun,
I saw a tower on a toft,° trily° made;   *hill / splendidly*
15 A deep dale beneath, a dungeon° therein,   *prison-tower*
With deep ditches and dark and dreadful of sight.
A fair field full of folk found I therebetween,
Of all manner of men, the mean° and the rich,   *poor*
Working and wandering as the world asks.
20 Some put them[4] to the plow, played full seldom,
In setting° and in sowing sweated full hard,   *planting*
And won° what wasters with gluttony destroy.   *earned*
And some put them to pride, appareled them thereafter,
In countenance of clothing came disguised.[5]
25 In prayers and penance put them many,
All for love of our Lord lived full strait,°   *austerely*
In hope for to have heaven-rich[6] bliss;
Such as anchorites and hermits that hold them in their cells
And covet not in country to kair° about,   *wander*
30 For no lickerish° livelihood their likam° to please.   *dainty / body*
And some chose chaffer;° they achieved the
    better—   *merchandise*
At least it seems to our sight that such men thrive.
And some mirths to make, as minstrels can,

1. The present editor has chosen the B Text for the basis of his modernization, but in the Prologue he has followed the structure of the A Text in omitting a long, interesting, but rather technical passage added by B. The preference for B depends on a few passages where that version appears superior in expression. The modernization has retained a number of archaic words either in order to preserve the alliteration or because no modern word conveys the same idea so economically. Note that the modernizer has used words beginning with the now silent consonants *w* and *k* as though those consonants were still pronounced: *w-rought, k-now*, etc. The text is based on a new edition of the B Text now in preparation.
2. I dressed in long clothes.
3. Marvel. "Of fairy": i.e., supernatural.
4. Applied themselves.
5. Came decked out in showy clothing.
6. Of the kingdom of heaven.

And get gold with their glee°—guiltless, I believe. *singing*
35 But japers° and janglers,° Judas' children, *jokers / loudmouths*
Feign them fantasies[7] and make fools of themselves—
And have their wit at will to work if they would:
What Paul preaches of them, I will not prove it here:
Qui loquitur turpiloquium[8] is Lucifer's hind.° *servant*
40 Bidders° and beggars fast about went *tramps*
With their belly and their bag brimful crammed;
Faited° for their food, fought at the alehouse: *feigned illness*
In gluttony, God knows, go they to bed,
And rise with ribaldry, those Robert's knaves;[9]
45 Sleep and sloth pursue them ever.
Pilgrims and palmers[1] plighted them together
To seek Saint James[2] and saints at Rome:
They went forth on their way with many wise tales,
And had leave to tell lies all their life after.
50 Hermits in a heap with hooked staves
Went to Walsingham,[3] and their wenches after;
Great lubbers and long that loath were to sweat
Clothed them in copes[4] to be known from others,
And held forth as hermits, their ease to have.
55 I found there friars, all the four orders,
Preached to the people for profit of their bellies,
Glozed° the Gospel as them good seemed, *interpreted*
For covetousness of copes construed it as they would;
Many of these Masters[5] may clothe them at pleasure,
60 For their money and their merchandise march together.[6]
For since Charity[7] has been a chapman and chief to shrive lords,
Many ferlies° have befallen in a few years: *wonders*
Unless Holy Church and hi° hold better together, *they*
The most mischief on mold° is mounting well fast. *earth*
65 There preached a pardoner[8] as if he a priest were,
Brought forth a bull° with bishop's seals, *papal license*
And said that himself might absolve them all
Of falseness in fasting, of vows they had broken.
Unlearned men believed him well and liked his words,
70 Came up kneeling to kiss his bulls.
He banged them with his brevet[9] and bleared their eyes,
And raked in with his ragman[1] rings and brooches.

---

7. Pretend to suffer (religious) halluci-
nations.
8. "Who speaks slander" (the text is
not St. Paul's).
9. I.e., robbers.
1. Experienced, often professional, pilgrims.
2. I.e., the famous shrine to him at
Compostella, Spain.
3. English town, site of a famous shrine
of the Virgin Mary.
4. Hermits' or friars' garments.
5. I.e., Masters of Divinity.

6. I.e., their income consists of what
they make by their sales (of shrift).
7. The ideal of the friars—as stated by
St. Francis, founder of the Franciscans
—was simply charity.
8. An official empowered to pass on
from the Pope temporal indulgence for
their sins to persons who contributed to
charitable enterprises; pardoners often
abused their office: see Chaucer's Pardoner, General Prologue, lines 671 ff.
9. Pardoner's license.
1. Documents rolled up.

Thus they give their gold gluttons to maintain,
And lend° it to losels° that lechery practice.   *give / rascals*
75 Were the bishop blessed and worth both his ears,
His seal should not be sent to deceive the people.
But it is not by[2] the bishop that the boy° preaches,   *knave*
For the parish priest and the pardoner part° the silver,   *divide*
That to the poor of the parish should be paid otherwise.
80 Parsons and parish priests complained to the bishop
That their parishes were poor since the pestilence time,[3]
To have a license and leave at London to dwell,
And sing[4] there for simony, for silver is sweet.[5]

* * *

Yet hoved° there a hundred in hoves[6] of silk,   *lingered*
85 Sergeants[7] they seemed that served at the bar,
Pleaded for pennies[8] and impounded the law,
And not for love of our Lord unloosed their lips once:
You might better measure mist on Malvern Hills
Than get a "mum" from their mouth till money is showed.
90 Barons and burgesses and bondmen also
I saw in this assembly, as you shall hear after;
Bakers and brewers and butchers many,
Woolen-websters° and weavers of linen,   *weavers of wool*
Tailors and tinkers and tollers[9] in markets,
95 Masons and miners and many other trades;
Of all kinds of living laborers leapt forth some,
Such as dikers[1] and delvers that do their deed° ill,   *work*
And drive forth the day with *"Dieu save Dame Emme."*[2]
Cooks and their knaves° cried, "Hot pies, hot!"   *servants*
100 Taverners to them told the same story:
"White wine of Alsace and wine of Gascony,
Of the Rhine and of Rochelle, the roast to wash down."
All this saw I sleeping, and seven times more.

From *Passus I*

What this mountain means, and the murky dale,
And the field full of folk, I shall you fair show.
A lovely lady of lere° in linen clothed   *face*
Came down from a castle and called me fair,
5 And said, "Son, sleepest thou? Seest thou these people,

2. I.e., by permission of.
3. Since 1349, England had suffered a number of epidemics of the plague, which had produced famines and depopulated the countryside.
4. I.e., sing masses: wealthy persons, especially in London, set up foundations to pay priests to sing masses for their own souls and those of their relatives. "Simony": abuse of ecclesiastical office; a priest who had charge of a parish was canonically prohibited from exercising any other salaried function
in the church.
5. At this point the B Text adds 125 lines, here omitted, to the A Text.
6. Scarves worn by lawyers.
7. Sergeants-of-law, important lawyers.
8. Pennies were fairly valuable coins in medieval England. "Impounded": i.e., took possession of.
9. Tax collectors who collected fees from merchants using public markets.
1. Ditchdiggers.
2. "God save Dame Emma"; apparently a popular song.

How busy they be about the maze?
The most part of these people that pass on this earth,
Have they worship[3] in this world, they want no better:
Of other heaven than here have they no care."
10 I was afraid of her face, though she fair was,
And said, "Mercy, madam, what may this be to mean?"
"The tower on the toft," quoth she, "Truth is therein,
And wants you to work as his word teaches.
For he is father of faith, formed you all
15 Both with fell° and with face, and gave you five wits   *skin*
For to worship him with while that you are here.
And therefore he ordered the earth to help you each one,
Of woolen, of linen, of livelihood at need,
In measurable° manner to make you at ease;   *moderate*
20 And commanded of his courtesy in common three things:
Are none needful but they, and name them I will,
And reckon them by reason[4]—repeat thou them after:
The first is vesture from chill thee to save,
And meat at meals for misease[5] of thyself,
25 And drink when thou driest—but do not out of reason,
Lest thou worth° the worse when thou work shouldest.   *should be*
For Lot in his lifedays through liking of drink
Did with his daughters what the Devil liked,
Delighted him in drink as the Devil would,
30 And lechery him laught° and he lay by them
both;[6]   *took possession of*
And all he witted° wine that wicked deed.[7]   *blamed on*

* * *

Through wine and through women there was Lot disgraced,
And there begat in gluttony girls° that were churls.   *brats*
Therefore dread delectable drink and thou shalt do the better:
35 Measure° is medicine though thou much yearn;   *moderation*
It is not all good to the ghost° that the gut asks,   *spirit*
Nor livelihood to thy likam° that lief° is to thy
soul.   *body / dear*
Believe not thy likam, for a liar him teaches:
That is the wretched world that would thee betray.
40 For the Fiend and thy flesh follow thee together,
And that sullies thy soul: set this in thy heart.
And for thou shouldest beware, I wiss° thee the best."   *teach*
"Madam, mercy," quoth I, "I love well your words.
But the money of this mold° that men hold so fast,   *earth*
45 Tell me to whom, madam, that treasure belongs?"
"Go to the Gospel and see what God said himself,
When the people apposed[8] him with a penny in the temple—

3. I.e., prosperity.
4. In order.
5. I.e., to prevent discomfort.
6. For the events in Lot's story alluded to here, see Genesis xix.30–38.

7. The poet's quotation in Latin of Genesis xix.32 is here omitted.
8. Questioned. The incident she retells here is in Matthew xxii.17–21.

Whether they should therewith worship the king Caesar.
And God asked of hem° of whom spoke the writing *them*
50 And the image alike that thereon stood.
'Caesar's,' they said, 'we see well each one.'
'*Reddite Caesari*,'[9] said God, 'what to Caesar belongs,
Et quae sunt dei deo,'[1] or else you do ill.
For rightfully Reason should rule you all,
55 And Kind Wit[2] be warden your wealth to guard,
And tutor° of your treasure, and take° it you at
  need, *overseer / give*
For husbandry° and he hold together." *economy*
Then I frained° her fair, for Him that her made, *asked*
"That dungeon in the dale that dreadful is of sight,
60 What may it be to mean, madam, I you beseech?"
"That is the Castle of Care: whoso comes therein
May ban° that he born was with body or with soul. *curse*
Therein wons° a wight° that Wrong is called, *dwells / creature*
Father of falsehood, and founded it himself.
65 Adam and Eve he egged to ill,
Counseled Cain to kill his brother,
Judas he japed° with Jewish silver, *tricked*
And after on an eldertree he hanged himself.
He is letter[3] of love and lies to them all:
70 Those who trust on his treasure betrays he soonest."
Then had I wonder in my wit what woman it was
That such wise words of Holy Writ showed,
And halsed° her on the High Name, ere she thence
  went, *conjured*
What she were witterly° that wissed° me so fair. *truly / taught*
75 "Holy Church I am," quoth she, "thou oughtest me to know:
I underfong[4] thee first and thee faith taught,
And thou broughtest me borrows° my bidding to fulfill, *pledges*
And to love me loyally the while thy life endures."
Then I kneeled on my knees and cried to her for grace,
80 And prayed her piteously to pray for my sins,
And also ken° me kindly° on Christ to believe, *teach / sincerely*
That I might work his will who wrought me as a man.
"Teach me to no treasure, but tell me this same:
How I may save my soul, thou that sacred art held."
85 "When all treasures are tried, Truth is the best:
I do it on *Deus caritas* to deem the sooth.[5]
It is as dear a drury° as dear God himself. *love token*
Who is true of his tongue and tells nothing else,
And does the works that accord therewith, and wills no man ill,

---

9. This, like the other Biblical quotations in the poem, is from the Latin Vulgate version of the Bible. In the King James version this phrase is "Render unto Caesar."
1. "And unto God the things that are God's."
2. Natural, God-given intelligence.
3. Obstructer, i.e., enemy.
4. Undertook responsibility for.
5. I rely on the text "God is love" (I John iv.8) to arrive at the truth.

90 He is a god by the Gospel, on ground and aloft,
And like to our Lord by Saint Luke's words.[6]
The clerks that know this should ken it about,
For Christian and unchristian claim it[7] both.
Kings and knights should keep to it by reason,
95 Ride and rap° down in realms about   *strike*
And take transgressors and tie them fast,
Till Truth has determined their trespass° to the end.   *wrongdoing*
And that is the profession apertly[8] that appends to knights,
And not to fast one Friday in fivescore° winter,   *one hundred*
100 But hold with him and with her that ask all truth,
And never leave them for love nor for latching° of silver.   *getting*
For David in his days dubbed knights,
And made them swear on their sword to serve Truth ever,
And whoso passes that point[9] is apostate° to the order.   *traitor*
105 But Christ, King of Kings, knighted ten,[1]
Cherubim and seraphim, seven more such and another,
And gave them might in his majesty—the merrier he thought
    it—
And over his mean meiny[2] made them archangels,
Taught them by the Trinity Truth to know,
110 To be buxom° at his bidding—he bade them nought
    else.   *obedient*
Lucifer with legions learned it in heaven—
He was loveliest to look at after our Lord himself;
But because he broke buxomness his bliss did he lose,
And fell from that fellowship in a fiend's likeness,
115 Into a deep dark hell, to dwell there forever;
And more thousands mid° him than man could number   *with*
Leaped out with Lucifer in loathly form,
For they believed in their lord that lied in this manner:
Ponam pedem in aquilone et similis ero altissimo.[3]
120 And all that hoped it might be so no heaven might them hold,
But they fell out in fiend's likeness full nine days together,
Till God of his goodness gan° pause and stop,   *did*
And made heaven stable, and it stood quiet.
When these wicked went out, wonderwise they fell,
125 Some in air, some in earth, and some in hell deep;
But Lucifer lowest lies of them all:
For pride that he put out[4] his pain has no end.
And all that work with Wrong, wend they shall
After their death day to dwell with that fiend.

6. What text the poet had in mind is unclear.
7. I.e., the truth.
8. Obviously; "appends": belongs.
9. I.e., does otherwise.
1. I.e., ten orders of heavenly beings: seraphim, cherubim, thrones, dominions, virtues, powers, principalities, archangels, angels, and the nameless order that fell with Lucifer.
2. Lower orders.
3. The Latin may be translated: "I shall set my foot in the north and I shall be like the most high"; cf. Isaiah xiv.13–14. This passage and Revelation xii.7–9 are the chief sources for the story of Lucifer's fall.
4. Exhibited.

130 But those that work well as Holy Writ tells,
And end, as I said ere, in Truth that is the best,
May be sure that their souls shall wend to heaven,
Where Truth is in Trinity and gives thrones to them all.
Therefore I say as I said before by sight of these texts,
135 When all treasures are tried, Truth is the best:
Learn° it to these lewd° men, for lettered men know   *teach / ignorant*
    it,
That Truth is treasure the triest° on earth."   *best*
"Yet have I no kind knowing,"[5] quoth I, "you must ken me
    better
By what craft[6] in my corse° it commences, and where?"   *body*
140 "Thou doting daff,"° quoth she, "dull are thy wits: *dunce*
Too little Latin learnedest thou, lad, in thy youth.
Heu mihi, quia sterilem duxi vitam iuvenilem.[7]
It is a kind knowing," quoth she, "that kens in thy heart
For to love thy Lord liefer° than thyself;   *dearer*
145 No deadly sin to do, die though thou shouldest;
This I trow° be truth: who can teach thee better,   *think*
Look thou suffer him to say, and sithen° learn it after.   *then*
For thus witnesses his word, work thou thereafter.
For Truth tells that love is treacle[8] of heaven:
150 May no sin be on him seen who that spice° uses.   *medicament*
And all his works he wrought with love as he pleased,
And learned it[9] Moses as the liefest thing and most like heaven,
And also the plant of peace, most precious of virtues.[1]
For heaven might not hold it, it was so heavy of itself
155 Till it had of the earth eaten its fill.
And when it had first of this fold° flesh and blood taken, *earth*
Was never leaf upon linden lighter thereafter,
And portative° and piercing as the point of a
    needle,   *quick-moving*
That might no armor it obstruct, nor no high walls.
160 Therefore is love leader of the Lord's folk of heaven,
And a mean° as the mayor is between the many and the
    king.   *mediator*
Just so is love a leader and the law shapes:
Upon man for his misdeeds the merciment° he imposes.   *fine*
And for to know it kindly,° it[2] commences by force, *naturally*
165 And in the heart there is its head and its high source.
For of kind knowing in heart there commences a power,
And that falls° from the Father that formed us all,   *originates*
Looked on us with love and let his Son die
Meekly for our misdeeds to amend us all;
170 And yet willed he them no woe that wrought him that pain,

---

5. Natural understanding. "Ken":
teach.
6. I.e., process.
7. "Alas for me, that I have passed my
youth without profit."

8. Powerful medicine.
9. Love, which as the passage goes on
becomes embodied in Christ.
1. I.e., most efficacious of powers.
2. I.e., love.

But meekly with mouth Mercy he besought
To have pity on that people that pained° him to death.   *tortured*
Here mightest thou see example in himself alone
That he was mighty, and meek, and mercy did grant
175 To them that hanged him high and his heart pierced.
Therefore I rede° you rich, have ruth° on the poor: *advise / pity*
Though you are mighty to moot,³ be meek in your works,
For the same measure that you mete,° amiss or else,   *weigh out*
You shall be weighed therewith when you wend hence:
180 *Eadem mensura qua mensi fueritis remetietur vobis.*⁴
For though you are true of your tongue, and truly win,
And as chaste as a child that in church weeps,
Unless you love loyally and lend° the poor—   *give to*
Such goods as God you sends goodly share—
185 You have no more merit in Mass nor in hours⁵
Than Malkin of her maidenhead that no man desires.⁶
For James the gentle enjoined in his books
That faith without the fait° is feebler than nothing,   *deed*
And as dead as a doornail unless the deed accords:
190 *Fides sine operibus mortua est.*⁷
Therefore chastity without charity shall be chained in hell:
It is as lewd° as a lamp that has no light in it.   *useless*
Many chaplains are chaste, but charity they lack:
Are none harder than hi° when hi are promoted—   *they*
195 Unkind to their kin and to all Christian people,
Chew up their charity⁸ and chide after more:
Such chastity without charity shall be chained in hell!
Many curators° keep them clean of their bodies: *parish priests*
They are enclosed in covetousness—they cannot creep out,
200 So hard has avarice hasped° them together.   *clamped*
And that is no truth of the Trinity, but treachery of hell,
And a lesson to unlearned men the later to give.
For these words were written in the Gospel:
'*Date et dabitur vobis,*⁹ for I deal° you all: *give to*
205 And that is the lock of love that lets out my grace
To comfort the careworn encumbered with sin.'
Love is leech° of life and next our Lord's self,   *doctor*
And also the graith gate¹ that goes into heaven.
Therefore I say as I said before by sight of these texts:
210 When all treasures are tried, Truth is the best.
Now I have told thee what Truth is, that no treasure is better,
I may no longer linger with thee; now look thee our Lord."

---

3. Powerful in lawsuits.
4. Cf. Luke vi.38: "For with the same measure that ye mete withal it shall be measured to you again."
5. Other church services.
6. Malkin, proverbially a loose wench, here appears as chaste because undesirable.
7. Cf. James ii.26: "Faith without works is dead."
8. I.e., what they have been given.
9. Cf. Luke vi.38: "Give, and it shall be given unto you."
1. Narrow path.

MIDDLE ENGLISH LYRICS

The best of the Middle English lyrics, both religious and secular, seem re-markably fresh despite the fact that in both theme and form they are ex-tremely conventional—at times almost stylized. The song of spring (the French *reverdie*), the love lyric and love complaint, the celebration of the Virgin Mary, the witty satire of women, the meditation upon Calvary—even the rollicking verse in praise of good food, good drink, and good liv-ing—are members of ancient genres, most of which had developed in France (some of the poems here printed closely parallel French lyrics). The poet's love in *Alison* is conventional even in her name, which is that of the Wife of Bath and of the heroine of the Miller's Tale, and the poet could have written her praise without ever having loved anything more feminine than books, which contained hundreds of ladies with Alison's charms. The fact that most of them would have been blue-eyed blondes might make love for a black-eyed brunette seem daringly realistic, but conventions set up anti-conventions which become as rigid as their older antitheses. Yet those who feel that such a lyric as *Alison* is the genuine complaint of a 13th-century English lad are right in their reactions as readers if wrong in fact, for the poem re-creates excellently the excitement of young love—and the time must have been full of young men yearning for black-eyed Alisons.

It is the same with the spring songs. Spring returns in much the same literary terms in poem after poem, year after year, century after century, but the best medieval spring songs also vigorously reproduce the actual excite-ment of its natural return every March and April. For while every good poet brings something of his own observing to the tradition he is following, the writers of medieval lyrics are especially distinguished for their unself-consciousness and immediacy. Just as there was no consciousness on the part of the medieval man of anachronism—historical differences in time or place—there seems to have been no self-consciousness about his attempts to express himself in poetic terms: convention apparently liberated him, instead of oppressing him in the way it is often supposed to do. It is with perfect naturalness that the poet of *Sunset on Calvary* relives the scene, standing with the mother Mary beside the cross on which her Son hangs; or the poet of *I Sing of a Maiden* visualizes the mystery of the Virgin Birth in terms of the most natural of mysteries, the falling dew; or the poet of *Adam Lay Bound* cheerfully regards Adam's sin and its dire consequences as a kind of childish naughtiness and punishment that had the tremendous effect of bringing Christ to earth. The very simplicity of the poet's attitude achieves the most striking artistic results.

Several of the poems printed here depend on traditions that are no longer alive. The *Corpus Christi Carol* relies upon the ancient fertility myth of the Fisher King which had been caught up and Christianized in Ar-thurian legend. *I Have a Young Sister* is a riddling poem that is reminiscent of the Old English riddles, though its clues, highly suggestive sexual sym-bols, are of a fully developed sophistication.

It is impossible to date the individual lyrics with any certainty. Perhaps the oldest is the *Cuckoo Song*, which is probably of the 12th century, and one may guess that the other spring songs are of the late 13th or early 14th; but some of the best of the lyrics (*I Sing of a Maiden, Adam Lay Bound*) may be of the 15th century. In general, we know only that the poems must be earlier than the manuscripts in which they appear, but because of the fact that an early lyric might have been reworded by a late scribe in such a way as to make it appear late, we can rarely tell by how many years any given lyric preceded the manuscript that records it. The sources of the texts printed here are too diverse to be listed. Spelling has been normalized as in the selections from Chaucer.

Fowls in the Frith

Fowles° in the frith,°	*birds / woods*
The fisshes in the flood,	
And I mon waxe wood:[1]	
Much sorwe° I walke with	*sorrow*
5 For beste[2] of boon° and blood.	*bone*

Alison

Bitweene° Merch and Averil,	*in the seasons of*
When spray biginneth to springe,	
The litel fowl hath hire wil°	*pleasure*
On hire leod[3] to singe.	
5 Ich° libbe° in love-longinge	*I / live*
For semlokest° of alle thinge.	*seemliest, fairest*
Heo° may me blisse bringe:	*she*
Ich am in hire baundoun.°	*power*
An hendy hap ich habbe yhent,[4]	
10 Ichoot° from hevene it is me sent:	*I know*
From alle[5] wommen my love is lent,°	*removed*
And light° on Alisoun.	*alights*
On hew° hire heer° is fair ynough,	*hue / hair*
Hire browe browne, hire yë° blake;	*eye*
15 With lossum cheere heo on me lough;[6]	
With middel smal and wel ymake.	
But° heo me wolle to hire take	*Unless*
For to been hire owen make,°	*mate*
Longe to liven ichulle° forsake,	*I will*
20 And feye° fallen adown.	*dead*
An hendy hap, etc.	

1. Must go mad.
2. Probably "the best," i.e., his lady. The meaning "beast" is, however, not impossible.
3. In her language.
4. A gracious chance I have received.
5. I.e., all other.
6. With lovely face she on me smiled.

Nightes when I wende° and wake,   *turn*
Forthy° mine wonges° waxeth wan: *therefore / cheeks*
Levedy,° al for thine sake   *lady*
25 Longinge is ylent me on.[7]
In world nis noon so witer° man   *clever*
That al hire bountee° telle can;   *excellence*
Hire swire° is whittere° than the swan,   *neck / whiter*
    And fairest may° in town.   *maid*
30   An hendy, etc.

Ich am for wowing° al forwake,°   *wooing / worn out from waking*
Wery so water in wore.[8]
Lest any reve me[9] my make
Ich habbe y-yerned yore.[1]
35 Bettere is tholien° while° sore   *endure / for a time*
Than mournen evermore.
Geinest under gore,[2]
    Herkne to my roun:°   *song*
    An hendy, etc.

My Lief Is Faren in Londe

My lief is faren in londe[3]—
Allas, why is she so?
And I am so sore bonde°   *bound*
I may nat come her to.
5 She hath myn herte in holde
Wherever she ride or go°—   *walk*
With trewe love a thousand folde.

Western Wind

Westron wind, when will thou blow?
The small rain down can rain.
Christ, that my love were in my arms,
And I in my bed again.

I Have a Young Sister

I have a yong suster
    Fer° biyonde the see;   *far*
Manye be the druries°   *gifts*
    That she sente me.

7. Longing has come upon me.
8. Perhaps "millpond."
9. Deprive me.

1. I have been worrying long since.
2. Fairest beneath clothing.
3. My beloved has gone away.

5 She sente me the cherye
  Withouten any stoon,°   *stone*
And so she dide the dove
  Withouten any boon.°   *bone*

  She sente me the brere°   *briar*
10 Withouten any rinde;°   *bark*
She bad me love my lemman°   *mistress*
  Withoute longinge.

How sholde any cherye
  Be withoute stoon?
15 And how sholde any dove
  Be withoute boon?

How sholde any brere
  Be withoute rinde?
How sholde I love my lemman
20 Withoute longinge?

Whan the cherye was a flowr,
  Thanne hadde it no stoon;
Whan the dove was an ey,°   *egg*
  Thanne hadde it no boon.

25 Whan the brere was unbred,°   *ungrown*
  Thanne hadde it no rinde;
Whan the maiden hath that° she loveth,   *what*
  She is withoute longinge.

Spring Has Come with Love

Lenten is come with love to towne,
  With blosmen° and with briddes roune,[4]   *blossoms*
  That al this blisse bringeth;
Dayes-yës[5] in thise dales,
5 Notes sweete of nightegales—
  Eech fowl song singeth.
The threstelcok him threteth oo.[6]
Away is here° winter wo   *their*
  When woderove[7] springeth.
10 Thise fowles singeth ferly fele[8]
And wliteth on here winne wele,[9]
  That al the wode° ringeth.   *wood*

  The rose raileth hire rode,[1]
  The leves on the lighte wode
15 Waxen° al with wille.°   *grow / joy*

4. Birds' song.
5. Daisies ("day's-eyes").
6. The thrush chatters constantly.
7. A sweet-smelling plant.
8. Wondrous many.
9. And warble of their joyous state.
1. Arrays her face.

The moone mandeth hire blee,[2]
The lilye is lossum° to see,   *lovely*
  The fenil[3] and the fille;
Woweth° thise wilde drakes,   *woo*
20 Males mirgeth° here makes°   *gladden / mates*
  As streem that striketh stille;°   *flows continually*
Moody meneth—so dooth mo:[4]
Ichoot° ich am oon of tho   *I know*
  For love that liketh ille.[5]

25 The moone mandeth hire light,
So dooth the seemly sunne bright,
  When briddes singeth breme.°   *loudly*
Dewes donketh° the downes,°   *dampen / hills*
Deeres with here derne rounes,
30   Doomes forto deeme.[6]
Wormes° woweth under cloude,°   *snakes / stones*
Wommen waxeth wonder proude,
  So wel it wol hem seeme.[7]
If me shal wante wille of oon,[8]
35 This winne wele[9] I wol forgoon,
  And wight° in wode be fleme.°   *creature / exiled*

The Cuckoo Song

Sumer is ycomen in,
Loude sing cuckou!
Groweth seed and bloweth meed,[1]
And springth the wode° now.   *wood*
5 Sing cuckou!

Ewe bleteth after lamb,
Loweth after calve cow,
Bulloc sterteth,° bucke verteth,°   *leaps / breaks wind*
Merye sing cuckou!
10 Cuckou, cuckou,
Wel singest thou cuckou:
Ne swik° thou never now!   *cease*

2. Sends forth her complexion (i.e., her light).
3. Fennel, an herb; "fille" is probably also an herb.
4. Mournful things complain—so do others.
5. That is ill pleased because of love.
6. These lines probably mean: "Animals make their secret sounds / in order to settle their (love) affairs."
7. This seems to them good.
8. If I must do without my pleasure in one.
9. Joyous state.
1. The meadow blossoms.

Tell Me, Wight in the Broom

"Say me, wight in the broom,° shrub
What is me for to doon?
Ich° have the werste bonde° I / husband
That is in any londe."

5 "If thy bonde is ille,° bad
Hold thy tonge stille."

The Henpecked Husband

How! hay! it is noon lees:° lie
I dar not° saye when she saith "Pees!"° nothing / hush

Yonge men, I warne you everichoon:° every one
Olde wives take ye noon.° none
For I myself have oon at hoom—
    I dar not sayn when she saith "Pees!"

5 Whan I come fro the plow at noon,
In a riven° dissh my mete is doon.² broken
I dar not asken oure dame a spoon—
    I dar not sayn when she saith "Pees!"

If I aske oure dame breed,
10 She taketh a staf and breketh myn heed,
And dooth° me runnen under the bed— makes
    I dar not sayn when she saith "Pees!"

If I aske oure dame fleissh,° meat
She breketh myn heed with a dissh:
15 "Boy, thou art not worth a rissh!"° rush
    I dar not sayn when she saith "Pees!"
If I aske our dame cheese,
"Boy," she saith al at ese,
"Thou art not worth half a pese."° pea
20   I dar not sayn when she saith "Pees!"

I Am of Ireland

Ich am of Irlonde,
And of the holy londe
    Of Irlonde.

2. I.e., my food is served.

Goode sire, praye ich thee,
5 For of° sainte charitee,   *sake of*
Com and dance with me
    In Irlonde.

Sunset on Calvary

Now gooth sunne under wode:[4]
Me reweth,[5] Marye, thy faire rode.°   *face*
Now gooth sunne under tree:
Me reweth, Marye, thy sone and thee.

I Sing of a Maiden

I sing of a maiden
    That is makelees:°   *matchless*
King of alle kinges
    To° her sone she chees.°   *as / chose*

5 He cam also° stille   *as*
    Ther° his moder° was   *where / mother*
As dewe in Aprille
    That falleth on the gras.

He cam also stille
10 To his modres bowr
As dewe in Aprille
    That falleth on the flowr.

He cam also stille
    Ther his moder lay
15 As dewe in Aprille
    That falleth on the spray.

Moder and maiden
    Was nevere noon but she:
Wel may swich° a lady   *such*
20 Godes moder be.

4. Wood, i.e., the Cross.   5. I pity.

Adam Lay Bound

Adam lay ybounden, bounden in a bond,
Four thousand winter thoughte he not too long;
And al was for an apple, an apple that he took,
As clerkes finden writen in hire book.
5 Ne hadde[6] the apple taken been, the apple taken been,
Ne hadde nevere Oure Lady have been hevene Queen.
Blessed be the time that apple taken was:
Therfore we mown° singen *Deo Gratias*.[7]   *may*

The Corpus Christi Carol

Lully, lullay, lully, lullay,
The faucon° hath borne my make° away.   *falcon / mate*

He bare him up, he bare him down,
He bare him into an orchard brown.

5 In that orchard ther was an hall
That was hanged with purple and pall.°   *black velvet*

And in that hall ther was a bed:
It was hanged with gold so red.

And in that bed ther lith° a knight,   *lies*
10 His woundes bleeding by day and night.

By that beddes side ther kneeleth a may,°   *maid*
And she weepeth both night and day.

And by that beddes side ther standeth a stoon:°   *stone*
Corpus Christi[8] writen theron.

6. Had not.   8. Body of Christ.
7. Thanks be to God.

THE SECOND SHEPHERDS' PLAY

η. dialect   (ca. 1385)

The *Second Shepherds' Play* is the finest example in English of a medieval mystery play. The word "mystery" in this context refers to the spiritual mystery of Christ's redemption of mankind, and mystery plays are dramatizations of incidents of the Old Testament, which foretells that redemption, and of the New, which recounts it. In England the mysteries were generally composed in cycles containing as many as 48 individual plays; a typical cycle would begin with the Creation, continue with the Fall of Man, and proceed through the most significant events of the Old Testament, such as the Flood, to the New Testament, which provided plays on the Nativity, the chief events of Christ's life, the Crucifixion, the Harrowing of Hell (based on sources now deemed apocryphal), and the Last Judgment. This kind of drama had its origin within the very walls of the medieval church, in the liturgical dialogue that had long been a characteristic feature of formal Christian worship. The exchanges between priest and congregation in the celebration of the Mass are essentially dramatic, as are also the exchanges between several sections of the choir in the singing of an anthem. By a natural elaboration of these dialogues, the texts of which are based on Biblical or Apocryphal sources, a church drama came into being—indeed, it ultimately developed so fully that there was no longer room for it within the liturgy; it then had to be presented separately. In England it was given a home in the churchyard, but as it became increasingly secularized and increasingly pervaded by the rough popular humor of medieval minstrelsy, it lost its place even in the churchyard. By the time of their fullest development, the mysteries were acted in the streets of the town.

Despite secularization and separation from the church proper, mystery plays never lost their religious impulse. They were generally performed at the time of one of two great church festivals—Whitsuntide, the week following the seventh Sunday after Easter, or Corpus Christi, a week later—and their performance was one of the important ways in which the unlearned layman of the Middle Ages participated directly in the celebration of his religion. Every trade in urban society had its guild, an organization combining the functions of a modern club, trade union, and religious society, and each of these guilds had its traditional play to perform on the days when the cycles were presented. In certain of the towns each company had a wagon which served as a stage. The wagon would proceed from one strategic point in the town to another, and the play would be performed a number of times on the same day: the spectators gathered at any one strategic point would never be without a play before them, and might see the whole cycle without moving. In other towns, however, the plays were probably acted out in sequence at a single place—an innyard or some other such natural theater.

The *Second Shepherds' Play*, which was probably played at Wakefield in Yorkshire, is a member of one of the four great cycles of English mysteries that have been preserved in their entirety; from what must have originally been a great number of other cycles we possess only a few individual pieces. The Wakefield cycle has two plays for shepherds; it is the second which is reprinted below. The artistic level of most of the Middle English mysteries is not high: a kind of rough piety, at times mixed with a crude humor, is characteristic of most of them, though there are happy exceptions. The happiest of these are c ain of the Wakefield plays, which display a sophisticated artistic intelligence at work beneath the apparent naïveté. This intelligence belonged undoubtedly to one individual, who probably revised traditional plays. His identity is not known, but because of his achievement scholars refer to him as the Wakefield Master. He was probably a highly educated cleric stationed in the vicinity of Wakefield, perhaps a friar of a nearby priory. He appreciated the rough humor and rough piety of the traditional plays, but he also knew how to refine both qualities without appearing to do so, and, more important, he knew how to combine the humorous and the religious so that the former serves the latter rather than detracting from it. In the *Second Shepherds' Play*, by linking the comic subplot of Mak and Gill with the solemn story of Christ's nativity, the Wakefield Master has produced a dramatic parable of what the Nativity means in Christian history and in Christian hearts. No one will fail to observe the parallelism between the stolen sheep, ludicrously disguised as Mak's latest heir, lying in the cradle, and the real Lamb of God, born in the stable among beasts. A complex of relationships based upon this relationship suggests itself. But perhaps the most important point is that the charity twice shown by the shepherds—in the first instance to the supposed son of Mak and in the second instance to Mak and Gill when they decide to let them off with only the mildest of punishments—is rewarded when they are invited to visit the Christ Child, the embodiment of charity. The bleak beginning of the play, with its series of individual complaints, is ultimately balanced by the optimistic ending, which sees the shepherds once again singing together in harmony.

Characterization in the mystery plays is usually rather slight, except in the case of stereotypes like Noah's stubborn wife or the ranting Herod (both mentioned in Chaucer's Miller's Tale). Mak therefore stands high above the generality and is perhaps the best humorous character outside of Chaucer's works in this period. A braggart of the worst kind, he has something of Falstaff's charm; and he resembles Falstaff also in his grotesque attempts to maintain the last shreds of his dignity when he is caught in a lie. Most readers will be glad that the shepherds do not carry out their threat to have the death penalty invoked for his crime.

The Second Shepherds' Play[1]

Dramatis Personae

COLL	GILL
GIB	ANGEL
DAW	MARY
MAK	

[*A moor.*]

[*Enter* COLL.]

COLL. Lord, what[2] these weathers are cold, and I am ill happed;
    I am nearhand dold,° so long have I napped;   *numb*
    My legs they fold,° my fingers are chapped.   *give way*
    It is not as I would, for I am all lapped°   *wrapped*
5   In sorrow:
      In storms and tempest,
      Now in the east, now in the west,
      Woe is him has never rest
      Midday nor morrow.

10 But we silly° husbands° that walks on the
        moor,   *poor / farmers*
    In faith we are nearhands out of the door.[3]
    No wonder, as it stands, if we be poor,
    For the tilth° of our lands lies fallow as the
        floor,   *arable part*
      As ye ken.°   *know*
15   We are so hammed,
      Fortaxed, and rammed,
      We are made hand-tamed
      With these gentlery-men.[4]

    Thus they reave us[5] our rest—Our Lady them wary!°   *curse*
20   These men that are lord-fest,[6] they cause the plow tarry.
    That men say is for the best, we find it contrary.
    Thus are husbands oppressed in point to miscarry.[7]
      On live

---

1. The text is based on that given by A. W. Pollard in *The Towneley Plays* (1897), but has been freely edited. Spelling has been normalized except where rhyme makes changes impossible. Since the original text has no indications of scenes and only four stage directions, written in Latin, appropriate scenes of action and additional stage directions have been added; the four original stage directions are identified in the footnotes.

2. How; "ill happed": badly covered.
3. I.e., homeless.
4. We are so hamstrung, overtaxed, and beaten down (that) we are made slaves by these highborn men. Coll is complaining of the peasant's hard lot, at the mercy of the agents of the Crown and of the wealthy landholders.
5. Deprive us of.
6. Attached to lords.
7. To the point of ruin. "On live": in life.

Thus hold they us under,
25 Thus they bring us in blunder,°   *trouble*
It were a great wonder
And° ever should we thrive.   *if*

There shall come a swain as proud as a po:°   *peacock*
He must borrow my wain,° my plow also;   *wagon*
30 Then I am full fain° to grant ere he go.   *glad*
Thus live we in pain, anger, and woe,
By night and by day.
He must have if he lang° it,   *wants*
If I should forgang it:[8]
35 I were better be hanged
Than once say him nay.[9]

For may he get a paint-sleeve[1] or a brooch nowadays,
Woe is him that him grieve or once again-says.°   *gainsays*
Dare no man him reprieve, what mastery he maes.[2]
40 And yet may no man lieve° one word that he says,   *believe*
No letter.
He can make purveyance[3]
With boast and bragance,°   *bragging*
And all is through maintenance°   *protection*
45 Of men that are greater.

It does me good, as I walk thus by mine one,°   *self*
Of this world for to talk in manner of moan.
To my sheep will I stalk, and hearken anon,
There abide on a balk,° or sit on a stone,   *grassy mound*
50 Full soon;
For I trow,° pardie,°   *think / by God*
True men if they be,
We get more company
Ere it be noon.

[*Enter* GIB, *who at first does not see* COLL.]
55 GIB. Benste and Dominus,[4] what may this bemean?°   *mean*
Why fares this world thus? Such have we not seen.
Lord, these winds are spiteous° and the weathers full
keen   *cruel*
And the frosts so hideous they water mine een,°   *eyes*
No lie.
60 Now in dry, now in wet,
Now in snow, now in sleet,
When my shoon° freeze to my feet   *shoes*
It is not all easy.

8. Even if I have to do without it.
9. In the manuscript, this stanza follows the next.
1. Embroidered sleeve (i.e., sign of authority).

2. No one dares to reprove him, no
matter what force he uses.
3. Requisition (of private property).
4. Bless us and Lord.

But as far as I ken,° or yet as I go,°   *see / walk*
65   We silly wedmen dree mickle woe;⁵
      We have sorrow then and then⁶—it falls oft so.
      Silly Capple,⁷ our hen, both to and fro
            She cackles;
            But begin she to croak,
70   To groan or to cluck,
            Woe is him our cock,
                  For he is in the shackles.

      These men that are wed have not all their will:
      When they are full hard stead⁸ they sigh full still;
75   God wot° they are led full hard and full ill;   *knows*
      In bower nor in bed they say nought theretill.°   *thereagainst*
            This tide°   *time*
            My part have I fun;°   *found, learned*
            I know my lesson:
80   Woe is him that is bun,°   *bound*
                  For he must abide.

      But now late in our lives—a marvel to me,
      That I think my heart rives° such wonders to see;   *splits*
      What that destiny drives it should so be⁹—
85   Some men will have two wives, and some men three
            In store.
            Some are woe¹ that has any,
            But so far can° I,   *know*
            Woe is him that has many,
90   For he feels sore.

      But young men a-wooing, for God that you
                  bought,°   *redeemed*
      Be well ware of wedding and think in your thought:
      "Had I wist"° is a thing, it serves of nought.   *known*
      Mickle° still° mourning has wedding home
                  brought,   *much / continual*
95   And griefs
            With many a sharp shower,°   *fight*
            For thou may catch in an hour
            That° shall savor° full sour   *what / taste*
                  As long as thou lives.

100   For as ever read I 'pistle,° I have one to my fere²   *Epistle*
      As sharp as a thistle, as rough as a brere;°   *briar*
      She is browed like a bristle, with a sour-loten cheer;³
      Had she once wet her whistle she could sing full clear
                  Her Pater Noster.

5. We poor married men suffer much
woe.
6. Constantly.
7. I.e., one's wife.
8. Beset; "still": constantly.

9. What destiny causes must occur.
1. I.e., wretched.
2. As my mate.
3. She has brows like pig's bristles and
a sour-looking face.

105　　　She is great as a whale;
　　　　　She has a gallon of gall:
　　　　　By Him that died for us all,
　　　　　　　I would I had run to° I had lost her.　　　　*until*

COLL.　Gib, look over the raw!° Full deafly ye stand!　*hedge*
110 GIB.　Yea, the devil in thy maw, so tariand!⁴
　　　　　Saw thou awhere° of Daw?　　　　　　　*anywhere*
COLL.　　　　　　　　　　　Yea, on a
　　　　　lea-land°　　　　　　　　　　*pasture land*
　　　　　Heard I him blaw.⁵ He comes here at hand,
　　　　　　Not far.
　　　　　Stand still.
GIB.　　　　　　　Why?
115 COLL.　For he comes, hope° I.　　　　　　*think*
GIB.　　　He will make us both a lie
　　　　　　But if⁶ we be ware.

[Enter DAW, *who does not see the others.]*
DAW.　Christ's cross me speed, and Saint Nicholas!
　　　　　Thereof had I need: it is worse than it was.
120　　　Whoso could take heed and let the world pass,
　　　　　It is ever in dread° and brickle° as glass,　*doubt / brittle*
　　　　　　And slithes.°　　　　　　　　*slips away*
　　　　　This world foor° never so,　　　　　　*behaved*
　　　　　With marvels mo° and mo,　　　　　　*more*
125　　　Now in weal, now in woe,
　　　　　　And all thing writhes.°　　　　　*changes*

　　　　　Was never sin° Noah's flood such floods seen,　*since*
　　　　　Winds and rains so rude and storms so keen:
　　　　　Some stammered, some stood in doubt,⁷ as I
　　　　　　ween.°　　　　　　　　　　*suppose*
130　　　Now God turn all to good! I say as I mean.
　　　　　　For ponder:
　　　　　These floods so they drown
　　　　　Both in fields and in town,
　　　　　And bears all down,
135　　　　And that is a wonder.

　　　　　We that walk on the nights, our cattle to keep,
　　　　　We see sudden° sights when other men sleep. *unexpected*
　　　　　Yet methink my heart lights: I see shrews peep.⁸
　　　　　[He sees the others, but does not hail them.]
　　　　　Ye are two tall wights.° I will give my sheep　*creatures*
140　　　　A turn.
　　　　　But full ill have I meant:⁹

---

4. Yes, the devil take thy guts for being so late.
5. Blow (his horn).
6. Unless.

7. The line apparently refers to men's
behavior at the time of Noah's flood.
8. I see rascals are watching.
9. But that is a poor idea.

As I walk on this bent°   *field*
I may lightly° repent,   *quickly*
   My toes if I spurn.°   *stub*

145 Ah, sir, God you save, and master mine!
A drink fain would I have, and somewhat to dine.

COLL. Christ's curse, my knave, thou art a lither hine![1]

GIB. What, the boy list° rave! Abide unto sine.[2]   *wants to*
   We have made it.[3]

150   Ill thrift on thy pate!
I Though the shrew° came late   *rascal*
   Yet is he in state
   To dine, if he had it.

DAW. Such servants as I, that sweats and swinks,°   *toil*
155 Eats our bread full dry, and that me forthinks.°   *angers*
We are oft wet and weary when master-men winks,° *sleep*
Yet comes full lately° both dinners and drinks.   *tardily*
   But nately°   *profitably*
   Both our dame and our sire,
160   When we have run in the mire,
   They can nip at our hire,[4]
   And pay us full lately.

But here my troth, master, for the fare° that ye
   make°   *food / provide*
I shall do thereafter: work as I take.[5]
165 I shall do a little, sir, and among° ever
   lake,°   *meanwhile / play*
For yet lay my supper never on my stomach
   In fields.
   Whereto should I threap?°   *haggle*
   With my staff can I leap,[6]
170   And men say, "Light cheap
   Litherly foryields."[7]

COLL. Thou were an ill lad to ride a-wooing
With a man that had but little of spending.[8]

GIB. Peace, boy, I bade—no more jangling,
175 Or I shall make thee full rad,° by the heaven's
   King,   *quickly*
   With thy gauds.°   *tricks*
   Where are our sheep, boy? We scorn.[9]

DAW. Sir, this same day at morn
   I them left in the corn
180   When they rang Lauds.[1]

---

1. Thou art a worthless servant.
2. Wait till later.
3. I.e., had dinner.
4. They can deduct from our wages.
5. I.e., work in the same way as I am paid.
6. I.e., run away.
7. A cheap bargain repays badly (a proverb).
8. You would be a bad servant for a poor man to take wooing with him.
9. I.e., waste time.
1. Rang the bells for the church service held at dawn.

They have pasture good, they cannot go wrong.

COLL. That is right. By the rood,° these nights are long!   *cross*
Yet I would, ere we yode,° one gave us a song.   *went*

GIB. So I thought as I stood, to mirth° us   *cheer / meanwhile*
among.°

185 DAW.   I grant.

COLL. Let me sing the tenory.°   *tenor*

GIB. And I the treble so hee.°   *high*

DAW. Then the mean° falls to me.   *middle part*
Let see how you chant.

[They sing.—Enter MAK *with a cloak over his clothes.*[2]]

190 MAK. Now, Lord, for thy names seven, that made both moon
and starns[3]
Well mo than I can neven,° thy will, Lord, of me tharns.[4]
I am all uneven°—that moves oft my harns.[5]   *at odds*
Now would God I were in heaven, for there weep no
barns°   *children*
So still.°   *continually*

195 COLL. Who is that pipes so poor?

MAK. [*aside*] Would God ye wist° how I foor!° *knew / fared*
[*aloud*] Lo, a man that walks on the moor
And has not all his will.

GIB. Mak, where has thou gane?° Tell us tiding.   *gone*

200 DAW. Is he come? Then ilkane[6] take heed to his thing.
[*Snatches a cloak from him.*]

MAK. What! Ich[7] be a yeoman, I tell you, of the king,
The self and the same, sond° from a great
lording   *messenger*
And sich.°   *suchlike*
Fie on you! Goth hence
205 Out of my presence:
I must have reverence.
Why, who be ich?

COLL. Why make ye it so quaint? Mak, ye do wrang.[8]

GIB. But, Mak, list ye saint? I trow that ye lang.[9]

210 DAW. I trow the shrew can paint[1]—the devil might him hang!

MAK. Ich shall make complaint and make you all to
thwang°   *be flogged*
At a word,
And tell even° how ye doth.   *exactly*

2. Mak's entrance is a stage direction in the original MS.
3. Stars.
4. Well more than I can name, thy will, Lord, falls short in regard to me.
5. That often disturbs my brains.
6. Each one; "thing": possessions. The stage direction here is in the MS.

7. I (the southern form): Mak is pretending to be an important person from the south.
8. Why do you behave in such an unfriendly manner? Mak, you do wrong.
9. But, Mak, do you want to act as if you were a saint? I guess you do.
1. I think the shrew can play tricks.

COLL.   But Mak, is that sooth?
215   Now take out that southern tooth,[2]
        And set in a turd!

GIB.   Mak, the devil in your ee![3] A stroke would I lean you!

DAW.   Mak, know ye not me? By God, I could teen° you.   *vex*

MAK.   God look° you all three: Methought I had seen you. *guard*
220   Ye are a fair company.

COLL.   Can ye now mean you?[4]

GIB.   Shrew, peep![5]
        Thus late as thou goes,
        What will men suppose?
        Thou has an ill nose[6]
225   Of stealing of sheep.

MAK.   And I am true as steel, all men wate.°   *know*
        But a sickness I feel that holds me full hate:° *hot, feverish*
        My belly fares not weel, it is out of estate.

DAW.   Seldom lies the devil dead by the gate.[7]
230 MAK.   Therefore
        Full sore am I and ill
        If I stand stone-still:
        I eat not a needill[8]
        This month and more.

235 COLL. How fares thy wife? By my hood, how fares sho?°   *she*

MAK.   Lies waltering,° by the rood, by the fire, lo!   *lounging*
        And a house full of brood.° She drinks well, too: *children*
        Ill speed other good that she will do![9]
          But sho
240   Eats as fast as she can;
        And ilk° year that comes to man   *every*
        She brings forth a lakan,°   *baby*
        And some years two.

        But were I now more gracious° and richer by
           far,   *prosperous*
245   I were eaten out of house and of harbar.°   *home*
        Yet is she a foul douce,° if ye come nar:[1] *sweetheart*
        There is none that trows° nor knows a
           war°   *imagines / worse*
          Than ken° I.   *know*
        Now will ye see what I proffer:
250   To give all in my coffer
        Tomorn at next[2] to offer
        Her head-masspenny.[3]

---

2. Now stop speaking like a southerner.
3. Eye; "lean": lend.
4. Remember.
5. Rascal, watch out.
6. Noise, i.e., reputation.
7. Road (i.e., the devil is always on the move).

8. Needle, i.e., a little bit.
9. I.e., that's the only good thing she does.
1. I.e., near the truth.
2. "Tomorn at next": tomorrow.
3. The penny paid for a mass for her departed spirit.

GIB. I wot° so forwaked° is none in this shire. *know / sleepless*
      I would sleep if° I taked less to my hire. *even if*
255 DAW. I am cold and naked and would have a fire.
      I am weary forraked° and run in the mire. *from walking*
          Wake thou.[4]
GIB.   Nay, I will lie down by,
          For I must sleep, truly.
260 DAW. As good a man's son was I
          As any of you.

      But Mak, come hither, between shall thou lie down.
MAK. Then might I let you bedeen of that ye would rown,[5]
          No dread.° *doubt*
265   From my top to my toe,
      [*Saying his prayers.*]
          Manus tuas commendo
          Pontio Pilato.[6]
          Christ's cross me speed!

      [*He gets up as the others sleep and speaks.*][7]
      Now were time for a man that lacks what he would
270   To stalk privily than° unto a fold, *then*
      And nimbly to work than, and be not too bold,
      For he might abuy° the bargain if it were told *pay for*
          At the ending.
          Now were time for to reel:° *move spryly*
275   But he needs good counseel
          That fain would fare weel° *well*
          And has but little spending.

      [*He casts a spell.*]
      But about you a circill,° as round as a moon, *circle*
      To° I have done that° I will, till that it be *until / what*
          noon, *until / what*
280   That ye lie stone-still to that I have done;
      And I shall say theretill° of good words a *moreover / few*
          foon:° *moreover / few*
          "On height,
          Over your heads my hand I lift.
          Out go your eyes! Fordo your sight!"[8]
285   But yet I must make better shift
          And it be right.[9]

      Lord, what° they sleep hard—that may ye all hear. *how*
      Was I never a shephard, but now will I lear.° *learn*
      If the flock be scar'd, yet shall I nip near.
290   How! Draws hitherward! Now mends our cheer

4. You stay awake.
5. Then I might hinder you if you
wanted to whisper together.
6. Mak's prayer means, "Thy hands I
commend to Pontius Pilate."

7. One of the original stage directions.
8. May your sight be rendered power-
less.
9. If it is to be all right.

From sorrow.
A fat sheep, I dare say!
A good fleece, dare I lay!°   *bet*
Eft-quit° when I may,   *repay*
295   But this will I borrow.
[*Exit with sheep.*]

[MAK's *house*. MAK *speaks outside the door.*]

MAK. How, Gill, art thou in? Get us some light.
GILL. [*within*] Who makes such a din this time of the night?
I am set for to spin; I hope not I might[1]
Rise a penny to win—I shrew° them on height!   *curse*
300   So fares
A housewife that has been
To be raised thus between:[2]
Here may no note° be seen   *completed work*
For such small chares.°   *chores*

305 MAK. Good wife, open the heck!° Sees thou not what I
    bring?   *door*
GILL. I may thole thee draw the sneck.[3] Ah, come in, my
    sweeting.
MAK. Yea, thou thar not reck of[4] my long standing.
[*She opens the door.*]
GILL. By the naked neck art thou like for to hing.°   *hang*
MAK.   Do way!
310   I am worthy° my meat,   *worthy of*
For in a strait° can I get   *pinch*
More than they that swink° and sweat   *work*
All the long day.

Thus it fell to my lot, Gill, I had such grace.
315 GILL. It were a foul blot to be hanged for the case.
MAK. I have 'scaped,° Jelot,[5] oft as hard a glase.°   *escaped / blow*
GILL. But "So long goes the pot to the water," men says,
    "At last
Comes it home broken."
320 MAK.   Well know I the token,
But let it never be spoken!
But come and help fast.

I would he were flain,° I list° well eat: *skinned / wish*
This twelvemonth was I not so fain of one sheep-meat.
325 GILL. Come they ere he be slain, and hear the sheep bleat—
MAK. Then might I be taen°—that were a cold sweat!   *taken*
    Go spar°   *fasten*
    The gate° door.   *street*

1. I don't think I could.
2. This is what happens to anyone who's been a housewife—to be got up all the time.
3. I may let you draw the latch.
4. You need not care about.
5. I.e., Gill.

GILL.   Yes, Mak,
   For and° they come at thy back—   *if*
330 MAK. Then might I buy,° for all the pack,   *have to pay*
   The devil of the war.°   *worse*

GILL. A good bourd have I spied, sin thou can none:[6]
   Here shall we him hide, to° they be gone,   *until*
   In my cradle. Abide, let me alone,
335 And I shall lie beside in childbed and groan.
MAK. Thou red,°   *get ready*
   And I shall say thou was light°   *delivered*
   Of a knave-child° this night.   *boy child*
GILL. Now well is me day bright
340   That ever was I bred.[7]

   This is a good guise° and a fair cast:° *method / trick*
   Yet a woman's advise helps at the last.
   I wot° never who spies: again go thou fast.   *know*
MAK. But° I come ere they rise, else blows a cold blast. *unless*
345 I will go sleep.
   Yet sleeps all this meny,°   *company*
   And I shall go stalk privily,
   As it had never been I
    That carried their sheep.

   [The moor. The shepherds are waking.]

350 COLL. *Resurrex a mortruus!*[8] Have hold my hand!
   Judas carnas dominus![9] I may not well stand.
   My foot sleeps, by Jesus, and I walter°
     fastand.°   *lie / fasting*
   I thought that we laid us full near England.
GIB. Ah, yea?
355   Lord, what° I have slept weel!°   *how / well*
   As fresh as an eel,
   As light I me feel
    As leaf on a tree.

DAW. Benste° be herein! So my body quakes, *blessing*
360   My heart is out of skin, what-so° it
     makes.°   *whatever / causes*
   Who makes all this din? So my brows blakes,[1]
   To the door will I win. Hark, fellows, wakes!
    We were four:
    See ye awhere of Mak now?
365 COLL. We were up ere thou.

6. A good trick have I found, since
you know none.
7. Now it was a good day that I was
born.
8. An illiterate oath referring, apparently, to Christ's Resurrection from the
dead.
9. Judas, (in?)carnate lord.
1. The meaning is probably "my eyes
are dim." Daw's head may be under a
blanket.

GIB. Man, I give God avow
Yet yede he naw're.[2]

DAW. Methought he was lapped° in a wolfskin.   *covered*
COLL. So are many happed° now, namely°
within.   *clad / especially*
370 DAW. When we had long napped, methought with a gin°   *snare*
A fat sheep he trapped, but he made no din.
GIB. Be still:
Thy dream makes thee wood.°   *mad*
It is but phantom, by the rood.°   *cross*
375 COLL. Now God turn all to good,
If it be his will.

GIB. Rise, Mak, for shame! Thou lies right lang.°   *long*
MAK. Now Christ's holy name be us amang!°   *among*
What is this? For Saint Jame, I may not well gang.°   *walk*
380 I trow° I be the same. Ah, my neck has lain
wrang.°   *think / wrong*
    [*One of them twists his neck.*]
Enough!
Mickle thank! Sin yestereven
Now, by Saint Strephen,[3]
I was flayed with a sweven[4]—
385 My heart out of slough.°   *skin*

I thought Gill began to croak and travail full sad,°   *hard*
Well-near at the first cock, of a young lad,
For to mend° our flock—then be I never glad: *increase*
I have tow on my rock[5] more than ever I had.
390 Ah, my head!
A house full of young tharms!°   *guts*
The devil knock out their harns!°   *brains*
Woe is him has many barns,°   *children*
And thereto little bread.

395 I must go home, by your leave, to Gill, as I thought.
I pray you look° my sleeve, that I steal nought.   *examine*
I am loath you to grieve or from you take aught.
DAW. Go forth! Ill might thou chieve!° Now would I we
sought[6]   *prosper*
This morn
400 That we had all our store.
COLL. But I will go before.
Let us meet.
GIB.   Whore?°   *where*
DAW. At the crooked thorn.

2. He's gone nowhere yet.
3. Probably St. Stephen.
4. I was terrified by a dream.
5. Flax on my distaff (i.e., trouble).
6. I want us to seek.

[MAK's *house.* MAK *at the door.*]

MAK.	Undo this door! Who is here? How long shall I stand?	
405 GILL.	Who makes such a bere?° Now walk in the	
	weniand![7]	*clamor*
MAK.	Ah, Gill, what cheer? It is I, Mak, your husband.	
GILL.	Then may we see here the devil in a band,[8]	
	Sir Guile!	
	Lo, he comes with a lote°	*noise*
410	As he were holden in the throat:	
	I may not sit at my note°	*work*
	A hand-long° while.	*short*
MAK.	Will ye here what fare[9] she makes to get her a glose?	
	And does nought but lakes° and claws her toes?	*plays*
415 GILL.	Why, who wanders? Who wakes? Who comes? Who	
	goes?	
	Who brews? Who bakes? What makes me thus	
	hose?°	*hoarse*
	And than°	*then*
	It is ruth° to behold,	*pity*
	Now in hot, now in cold,	
420	Full woeful is the household	
	That wants° a woman.	*lacks*
	But what end has thou made with the herds,°	
	Mak?	*shepherds*
MAK.	The last word that they said when I turned my back,	
	They would look that they had their sheep all the pack.	
425	I hope[1] they will not be well paid when they their sheep	
	lack.	
	Pardie!°	*by God*
	But how-so the game goes,	
	To me they will suppose,°	*suspect*
	And make a foul nose,°	*noise*
430	And cry out upon me.	
	But thou must do as thou hight.°	*promised*
GILL.	I accord me theretill.[2]	
	I shall swaddle him right in my cradill.	
	If it were a greater sleight, yet could I help till.[3]	
	I will lie down straight.° Come, hap°	
	me.	*straightway / cover*
MAK.	I will.	
435 GILL.	Behind	
	Come Coll and his marrow;°	*mate*
	They will nip us full narrow.	

MAK.   But I may cry "Out, harrow,"°   *help*
         The sheep if they find.

440 GILL. Hearken ay when they call—they will come anon.
         Come and make ready all, and sing by thine one.°   *self*
         Sing "lullay"° thou shall, for I must groan,   *lullaby*
         And cry out by the wall on Mary and John
              For sore.°   *pain*
445   Sing "lullay" on fast
              When thou hears at the last,
              And but I play a false cast,[4]
              Trust me no more.

[The moor.]

DAW.   Ah, Coll, good morn. Why sleeps thou not?
450 COLL. Alas that ever I was born! We have a foul blot:
         A fat wether° have we lorn.°   *ram / lost*
DAW.   Marry, God's forbot![5]
GIB.   Who should do us that scorn? That were a foul spot!
COLL.   Some shrew.°   *rascal*
           I have sought with my dogs
455   All Horbury shrogs,°   *thickets*
           And of fifteen hogs
           Found I but one ewe.[6]

DAW.   Now trow me,° if ye will, by Saint Thomas of
              Kent,   *believe*
         Either Mak or Gill was at that assent.°   *conspiracy*
460 COLL. Peace, man, be still! I saw when he went.
         Thou slanders him ill, thou ought to repent
              Good speed.
GIB.   Now as ever might I thee,°   *thrive*
              If I should even here dee,°   *die*
465   I would say it were he
              That did that same deed.

DAW.   Go we thither, I read,° and run on our feet.   *advise*
         Shall I never eat bread the sooth to I weet.[7]
COLL.   Nor drink in my head, with him till I meet.
470 GIB. I will rest in no stead° till that I him greet,   *place*
              My brother.
              One I will hight:[8]
              Till I see him in sight
              Shall I never sleep one night
475   There° I do another.   *where*

---

4. Unless I play a false trick.
5. God forbid.
6. And with fifteen young sheep I found only a ewe (i.e., the wether was missing).
7. Until I know the truth.
8. One thing will I promise.

[MAK'S *house.* MAK *and* GILL *within, she in bed groaning,*
he singing a lullaby; the shepherds enter outside the door.]

DAW. Will ye hear how they hack?[9] Our sire list croon.
COLL. Heard I never none crack° so clear out of tune.   song
     Call on him.
GIB.   Mak, undo your door soon!°   at once
MAK. Who is that spake, as° it were noon,   as if
480   On loft?[1]
     Who is that, I say?
DAW.   Good fellows, were it day.[2]
MAK.   As far as ye may,
     [*opening*] Good,° speaks soft   good men

485   Over a sick woman's head, that is at malease.[3]
     I had liefer° be dead ere she had any
        disease.°   rather / distress
GILL. Go to another stead, I may not well wheeze:°   breathe
     Each foot that ye tread goes through my nese.°   nose
     So, hee!°   scat
490 COLL. Tell us, Mak, if you may,
     How fare ye, I say?
MAK.   But are ye in this town today?
     Now how fare ye?

     Ye have run in the mire and are wet yit.
495   I shall make you a fire if you will sit.
     A nurse would I hire—Think ye one[4] yit?
     Well quit is my hire—my dream, this is it
     A season.[5]
     I have barns,° if ye knew,   children
500   Well mo° than enew:°   more / enough
     But we must drink as we brew,
     And that is but reason.

     I would ye dined ere ye yode.° Methink that ye
        sweat.   went
GIB. Nay, neither mends our mood[6] drink nor meat.
505 MAK. Why, sir, ails you aught but good?[7]
DAW.   Yea, our sheep that we get
     Are stolen as they yode:° our loss is great.   walked
MAK.   Sirs, drinks!
     Had I been thore°   there
     Some should have bought° it full sore.   paid for
510 COLL. Marry, some men trows° that ye wore,°   think / were
     And that us forthinks.°   disturbs

---

9. Bellow. "List": wants to.
1. Loudly..
2. Good companions, if it were daytime.
3. That feels badly.
4. Can you think of one?

5. Right on time.
6. Appeases our anger.
7. Is there anything wrong with you?
"Get": tend.

GIB. Mak, some men trows that it should be ye.

DAW. Either ye or your spouse, so say we.

MAK. Now if you have suspouse° to Gill or to me,   *suspicion*

515   Come and ripe° the house, and then may ye see   *search*

    Who had her[8]—

    If I any sheep fot,°   *fetched*

    Either cow or stot[9]—

    And Gill my wife rose not

520   Here sin she laid her.

    As I am true and leal,° to God here I pray   *just*

    That this be the first meal that I shall eat this day.

COLL. Mak, as I have sele,[1] advise thee, I say:

    [*They begin the search.*]

    He learned timely to steal that could not say nay.

525 GILL.   I swelt!°   *die*

    Out, thieves, from my wones!°   *dwelling*

    Ye come to rob us for the nones.[2]

MAK.   Hear ye not how she groans?

    Your hearts should melt.

530 GILL. Out, thieves, from my barn!° Nigh him not thore![3]   *child*

MAK. Wist ye how she had farn,[4] your hearts would be sore.

    You do wrong, I you warn, that thus comes before

    To a womman that has farn°—but I say no

        more.   *been in labor*

GILL.   Ah, my middill!

535   I pray to God so mild,

    If ever I you beguiled,

    That I eat this child

    That lies in this cradill.

MAK. Peace, woman, for God's pain, and cry not so!

540   Thou spills° thy brain and makes me full woe.   *spoil*

GIB. I trow our sheep be slain. What find ye two?

DAW. All work we in vain; as well may we go.

    But hatters,[5]

    I can find no flesh,

545   Hard nor nesh,°   *soft*

    Salt nor fresh,

    But two tome° platters.   *empty*

    Quick cattle[6] but this, tame nor wild,

    None, as have I bliss, as loud as he smiled.[7]

    [*Approaches the cradle.*]

550 GILL. No, so God me bliss,° and give me joy of my child!   *bless*

8. I.e., the sheep.
9. Either female or male.
1. Happiness; "advise thee": take thought.
2. You come for the purpose of robbing us.

3. Approach him not there.
4. If you knew how she had fared.
5. Except for clothing.
6. Livestock.
7. Smelled as badly as he (the baby).

COLL. We have marked° amiss—I hold us beguiled.　　　*aimed*

GIB.　　Sir, don!°　　　　　　　　　　　　　　　*thoroughly*
　　　Sir—Our Lady him save—
　　　Is your child a knave?[8]

555　MAK.　　Any lord might him have,
　　　　This child, to his son.

　　　When he wakens he kips,° that joy is to see.　*kicks*
DAW.　In good time to his hips, and in sely.[9]
　　　But who were his gossips,° so soon ready?　*godparents*
560　MAK. So fair fall their lips—

COLL.　　　　　　Hark, now, a lee.°　　　　*lie*

MAK.　　So God them thank,
　　　Perkin, and Gibbon Waller, I say,
　　　And gentle John Horne, in good fay°—　　　*faith*
　　　He made all the garray
565　　　With the great shank.[1]

GIB. Mak, friends will we be, for we are all one.°　*in accord*

MAK. We? Now I hold for me, for mends get I none.[2]
　　　Farewell all three, all glad[3] were ye gone.

DAW. Fair words may there be, but love is there none
570　　　This year.
　　　[They go out the door.]

COLL. Gave ye the child anything?

GIB. I trow not one farthing.

DAW. Fast again will I fling.°　　　　　　　　*dash*
　　　Abide ye me there.

575　Mak, take it to no grief if I come to thy barn.°　*child*

MAK. Nay, thou does me great reprief,[4] and foul has thou farn.

DAW. Thy child it will not grief, that little day-starn°　*day star*
　　　Mak, with your leaf,° let me give your barn　*leave*
　　　But sixpence.

580　MAK.　Nay, do way, he sleeps.

DAW.　Methinks he peeps.°　　　　　　　　*opens his eyes*

MAK.　When he wakens he weeps.
　　　I pray you go hence.

DAW. Give me leave him to kiss, and lift up the clout.[5]
　　　[Lifts the cover.]
585　　　What the devil is this? He has a long snout.
　　　[The others re-enter.]

COLL. He is marked[6] amiss. We wot ill about.

GIB. Ill-spun weft, ywis, ay comes foul out.[7]

8. Boy (although Mak takes the word in its alternate meaning of "rascal").
9. Perhaps "that's the best thing for him."
1. He made all the trouble with his long legs (the reference is obscure).
2. Now I'll remain apart, for I get no apology.
3. I.e., I would be glad.
4. Shame; "farn": behaved.
5. Cover.
6. Fashioned. "We wot ill about": we know mischief has been at work.
7. An ill-spun web, indeed, always comes out badly.

Aye, so!
He is like to our sheep.

590 DAW. How, Gib, may I peep?
COLL. I trow kind will creep
Where it may not go.[8]

GIB. This was quaint gaud and a fair cast.[9]
It was a high fraud.
DAW.   Yea, sirs, was't.
595 Let burn this bawd and bind her fast.
A false scaud° hang at the last: scold
So shall thou.
Will you see how they swaddle
His four feet in the middle?
600 Saw I never in cradle
A hornèd lad ere now.

MAK. Peace bid I! What, let be your fare!°   fuss
I am he that him gat,° and yond woman him bare.   begot
COLL. What devil shall he hat?° Mak? Lo, Gib, Mak's
heir!   be named
605 GIB. Let be all that: now God give him care°—   sorrow
I sawgh.[1]
GILL. A pretty child is he
As sits on a woman's knee,
A dillydown, pardie,
610 To gar° a man laugh.   make

DAW. I know him by the earmark—that is a good token.
MAK. I tell you, sirs, hark, his nose was broken.
Sithen° told me a clark that he was
forspoken.°   later / bewitched
COLL. This is a false wark.° I would fain be
wroken.°   work / avenged
615 Get wapen.°   weapon
GILL. He was taken with° an elf—   by
I saw it myself—
When the clock struck twelf
He was forshapen.°   transformed

620 GIB. Ye two are well feft sam in a stead.[2]
DAW. Sin[3] they maintain their theft, let do them to dead.
MAK. If I trespass eft,° gird° off my head.   again / cut
With you will I be left.[4]
COLL.   Sirs, do my read:°   advice
For this trespass
625 We will neither ban° ne flite,°   curse / wrangle

8. I think kinship will creep where it
can't walk (i.e., only a parent could
love this child).
9. This was a strange trick and a fine
dodge.

1. Probably "I saw it."
2. I.e., you two birds of a feather properly flock together.
3. Since; "dead": death.
4. I put myself in your mercy.

Fight nor chite,° chide
But have done as tite,° quickly
And cast him in canvas.
[*They toss* MAK *in a blanket.*]

[*The moor.*]

COLL. Lord, what° I am sore, in point for to brist!° how / burst
630   In faith, I may no more—therefore will I rist.° rest
GIB. As a sheep of seven score⁵ he weighed in my fist:
For to sleep aywhore° methink that I list.° anywhere / want
DAW.   Now I pray you
Lie down on this green.
635 COLL. On these thieves yit I mean.° think
DAW. Whereto should ye teen?° worry
Do as I say you.

[*An* ANGEL *sings* Gloria in Excelsis *and then speaks.*]⁶
ANGEL. Rise, herdmen hend,° for now is he born gentle
That shall take fro the fiend that Adam had lorn;⁷
640 That warlock° to shend,° this night is he
born. devil / confound
God is made your friend now at this morn
He beheests.° promises
At Bedlem° go see: Bethlehem
There lies that free,° noble one
645 In a crib full poorly,
Betwixt two beasts.
[*Exit.*]

COLL. This was a quaint steven⁸ that ever yet I hard.° heard
It is a marvel to neven° thus to be scar'd.° tell of / scared
GIB. Of God's Son of heaven he spake upward.° on high
650 All the wood on a leven methought that he gard
Appear.⁹
DAW. He spake of a barn° child
In Bedlem, I you warn.
COLL. That betokens yond starn.¹
655   Let us seek him there.

GIB. Say, what was his song? Heard ye not how he cracked it,²
Three breves³ to a long?
DAW.   Yea, marry, he hacked it.
Was no crochet° wrong, nor nothing that lacked it.⁴ note
COLL. For to sing us among, right as he knacked° it, trilled
660   I can.° know how
GIB.   Let see how ye croon!

5. 140 pounds.
6. One of the original stage directions.
7. What Adam had brought to ruin.
8. Fine voice.
9. I thought he made the whole wood seem full of light.
1. That's what yonder star means.
2. Sang it out.
3. Short notes; "hacked": sang loud.
4. It lacked.

Can ye bark at the moon?

DAW.   Hold your tongues! Have done!

COLL.   Hark after, than!

665 GIB.   To Bedlem he bade that we should gang:°   *go*
      I am full rad° that we tarry too lang.°   *afraid / long*

DAW. Be merry and not sad; of mirth is our sang:
      Everlasting glad to meed may we fang.[5]

COLL.   Without nose°   *noise*
670   Hie we thither forthy°   *therefore*
      To that child and that lady;
        If° we be wet and weary,   *though*
          We have it not to lose.[6]

GIB.   We find by the prophecy—let be your din!—
675   Of David and Isay, and mo than I min,[7]
      That prophesied by clergy° that in a virgin   *learning*
      Should he light° and lie, to sloken° our sin *alight / quench*
        And slake° it,   *relieve*
        Our kind,[8] from woe,
680   For Isay said so:
       Ecce virgo
        Concipiet[9] a child that is naked.

DAW. Full glad may we be and° we abide that day   *if*
      That lovely to see, that all mights may.[1]
685   Lord, well were me for once and for ay
      Might I kneel on my knee, some word for to say
        To that child.
        But the angel said
        In a crib was he laid,
690   He was poorly arrayed,
        Both mean° and mild.   *lowly*

COLL. Patriarchs that has been, and prophets beforn,
      That desired to have seen this child that is born,
      They are gone full clean—that have they lorn.[2]
695   We shall see him, I ween,° ere it be morn,   *think*
        To token.[3]
        When I see him and feel,
        Then wot I full weel[4]
        It is true as steel
700   That prophets have spoken:

      To so poor as we are that he would appear,
      First find, and declare by his messenger.

5. Eternal joy as our reward may we receive.
6. We must not neglect it.
7. Of David and Isaiah and more than I remember.
8. I.e., mankind.
9. Behold, a virgin shall conceive (Isaiah vii.14).

1. I.e., when we see that lovely one who is all-powerful.
2. That (sight) have they lost.
3. As a sign.
4. Then know I full well.

GIB. Go we now, let us fare, the place is us near.

DAW. I am ready and yare,° go we in fere[5]   *prepared*
705   To that bright.°   *glorious one*
         Lord, if thy wills be—
         We are lewd° all three—   *ignorant*
         Thou grant us some kins glee[6]
         To comfort thy wight.°   *creature*

[*A stable in Bethlehem.*]

710 COLL. Hail, comely and clean! Hail, young child!
         Hail Maker, as I mean, of° a maiden so mild!   *born of*
         Thou has waried,° I ween, the warlock° so
              wild.   *put a curse on / devil*
         The false guiler of teen,[7] now goes he beguiled.
              Lo, he merries!
715   Lo, he laughs, my sweeting!
              A well fair meeting!
         I have holden my heting:°   *promise*
         Have a bob° of cherries.   *bunch*

GIB.   Hail, sovereign Saviour, for thou has us sought!
720   Hail freely food[8] and flower, that all thing has wrought!
       Hail, full of favor, that made all of nought!
       Hail! I kneel and I cower.° A bird have I brought   *crouch*
              To my barn.°   *child*
       Hail, little tiny mop!°   *baby*
725   Of our creed thou art crop.°   *head*
       I would drink on thy cup,
              Little day-starn.

DAW.   Hail, darling dear, full of Godhead!
       I pray thee be near when that I have need.
730   Hail, sweet is thy cheer°—my heart would bleed   *face*
       To see thee sit here in so poor weed,°   *clothing*
              With no pennies.
       Hail! Put forth thy dall!°   *hand*
       I bring thee but a ball:
735   Have and play thee withal,
              And go to the tennis.

MARY. The Father of heaven, God omnipotent,
       That set all on seven,[9] his Son has he sent.
       My name could he neven, and light ere he went.[1]
740   I conceived him full even through might as he meant.[2]
              And now is he born.
              He[3] keep you from woe!

---

5. Together.
6. Some kind of cheer.
7. The false grievous deceiver.
8. Noble child.
9. Who created everything perfectly.

1. My name did he name, and alighted ere he went.
2. I conceived him through his power, just as he intended.
3. May he.

                I shall pray him so.
                Tell forth as ye go,
745   And min on⁴ this morn.

    COLL.   Farewell, lady, so fair to behold,
            With thy child on thy knee.
    GIB.   But he lies full cold.
            Lord, well is me. Now we go, thou behold.
    DAW.   Forsooth, already it seems to be told
750   Full oft.
    COLL.   What grace we have fun!°   *received*
    GIB.   Come forth, now are we won!°   *redeemed*
    DAW.   To sing are we bun:°   *bound*
            Let take on loft.⁵
            [*They sing.*]

4. Remember.   5. Let's raise our voices.

EVERYMAN
(ca. 1485)

Everyman is the best surviving example of that kind of medieval drama
which is known as the morality play. Moralities apparently evolved side by
side with the mysteries and in England were, like them, acted by trade
guilds, though they were composed individually and not in cycles. They
too have a primarily religious purpose, though their method of attaining
it is different. The mysteries endeavored to make the Christian religion
more real to the unlearned by dramatizing significant events in Biblical
history and by showing what these events meant in terms of human experience. The moralities, on the other hand, employed allegory to dramatize the moral struggle that Christianity envisions as present in every man:
the actors are every man and the qualities within him, good or bad, and
the plot consists of his various reactions to these qualities as they push
and pull him one way or another—that is, in Christian terms, toward
heaven or toward hell. The intent of the morality is more overtly didactic
than the mystery, but most of the moralities share with the mysteries a
good deal of rough humor. This is perhaps more evident in other plays
of the genre than in *Everyman*, where the chief humor lies in the undue
haste with which the hero's friends abandon him when he calls on them
for help.

  Everyman inculcates its austere lesson by the simplicity and directness
of its language and of its approach. A fine sense of inevitability is built
up as Everyman is stripped, one by one, of those apparent goods on
which he had relied. First he is deserted by his patently false friends: his
casual companions, his kinsmen, and his wealth. Receiving some comfort
from his enfeebled good deeds, he falls back on them and on his other
resources—his strength, his beauty, his intelligence, and his knowledge—

qualities which, when properly used, help to make an integrated man. These assist him through the crisis in which he must make up his book of accounts, but at the end, when he must go to the grave, all desert him save his good deeds alone. While the play contains rather too much direct sermonizing, it makes most effectively its grim point that man can take with him from this world nothing that he has received, only what he has given.

In *Everyman* allegory appears in its most meticulously worked-out form. Each actor has his allegorical significance defined by his name and behaves entirely within the limits of that definition. The onlooker takes a good deal of intellectual satisfaction in watching the nice operation of the allegorical equations. On the other hand, one might object that allegory, when so neatly handled, sacrifices for a kind of mathematical regularity the suggestiveness that inheres in the far looser allegory of such a work as *Piers Plowman*, which stimulates the imagination more than it satisfies the intellect. Nevertheless, when it is well staged and well acted, *Everyman*, despite its uncompromising didacticism, is a powerful drama.

The play was written near the end of the 15th century. It is probably a translation of a Flemish play, though it is not impossible that the Flemish play is the translation and the English *Everyman* the original.

Everyman[1]

Dramatis Personae

MESSENGER	KNOWLEDGE
GOD	CONFESSION
DEATH	BEAUTY
EVERYMAN	STRENGTH
FELLOWSHIP	DISCRETION
KINDRED	FIVE-WITS
COUSIN	ANGEL
GOODS	DOCTOR
GOOD DEEDS	

HERE BEGINNETH A TREATISE HOW THE HIGH FATHER OF
HEAVEN SENDETH DEATH TO SUMMON EVERY CREATURE
TO COME AND GIVE ACCOUNT OF THEIR LIVES IN THIS
WORLD, AND IS IN MANNER OF A MORAL PLAY

[*Enter* MESSENGER.]

MESSENGER. I pray you all give your audience,
    And hear this matter with reverence,
    By figure[2] a moral play,

1. The text is based upon the earliest printing of the play (no manuscript is known) by John Skot about 1530, as reproduced by W. W. Greg (Louvain, 1904). The spelling has been modernized except where modernization would spoil the rhyme, and modern punctuation has been added. The stage directions have been amplified.
2. In form.

The Summoning of Everyman called it is,
5   That of our lives and ending shows
How transitory we be all day.[3]
The matter is wonder precious,
But the intent of it is more gracious
And sweet to bear away.
10   The story saith: Man, in the beginning
Look well, and take good heed to the ending,
Be you never so gay.
You think sin in the beginning full sweet,
Which in the end causeth the soul to weep,
15   When the body lieth in clay.
Here shall you see how fellowship and jollity,
Both strength, pleasure, and beauty,
Will fade from thee as flower in May.
For ye shall hear how our Heaven-King
20   Calleth Everyman to a general reckoning.
Give audience and hear what he doth say.
      [*Exit* MESSENGER.—*Enter* GOD.]
GOD. I perceive, here in my majesty,
How that all creatures be to me unkind,°   *thoughtless*
Living without dread in worldly prosperity.
25   Of ghostly° sight the people be so blind,   *spiritual*
Drowned in sin, they know me not for their God.
In worldly riches is all their mind:
They fear not of my righteousness the sharp rod;
My law that I showed when I for them died
30   They forget clean, and shedding of my blood red.
I hanged between two,[4] it cannot be denied:
To get them life I suffered to be dead.
I healed their feet, with thorns hurt was my head.
I could do no more than I did, truly—
35   And now I see the people do clean forsake me.
They use the seven deadly sins damnable,
As pride, coveitise,° wrath, and lechery[5]   *avarice*
Now in the world be made commendable.
And thus they leave of angels the heavenly company.
40   Every man liveth so after his own pleasure,
And yet of their life they be nothing sure.
I see the more that I them forbear,
The worse they be from year to year:
All that liveth appaireth° fast.   *degenerates*
45   Therefore I will, in all the haste,
Have a reckoning of every man's person.
For, and° I leave the people thus alone   *if*
In their life and wicked tempests,

---

3. Always.
4. I.e., the two thieves between whom Christ was crucified.
5. The other three deadly sins are envy, gluttony, and sloth.

Verily they will become much worse than beasts;
50 For now one would by envy another up eat.
Charity do they all clean forgeet.
I hoped well that every man
In my glory should make his mansion,
And thereto I had them all elect.° chosen
55 But now I see, like traitors deject,° abased
They thank me not for the pleasure that I to° them
  meant, for
Nor yet for their being that I them have lent.
I proffered the people great multitude of mercy,
And few there be that asketh it heartily.° sincerely
60 They be so cumbered° with worldly riches encumbered
That needs on them I must do justice—
On every man living without fear.
Where art thou, Death, thou mighty messenger?
  [*Enter* DEATH.]
DEATH. Almighty God, I am here at your will,
65 Your commandment to fulfill.
GOD. Go thou to Everyman,
And show him, in my name,
A pilgrimage he must on him take,
Which he in no wise may escape;
70 And that he bring with him a sure reckoning
Without delay or any tarrying.
DEATH. Lord, I will in the world go run over all,[6]
And cruelly out-search both great and small.
  [*Exit* GOD.]
Everyman will I beset that liveth beastly
75 Out of God's laws, and dreadeth not folly.
He that loveth riches I will strike with my dart,
His sight to blind, and from heaven to depart°— separate
Except that Almsdeeds be his good friend—
In hell for to dwell, world without end
80 Lo, yonder I see Everyman walking:
Full little he thinketh on my coming;
His mind is on fleshly lusts and his treasure,
And great pain it shall cause him to endure
Before the Lord, Heaven-King.
  [*Enter* EVERYMAN.]
85 Everyman, stand still! Whither art thou going
Thus gaily? Hast thou thy Maker forgeet?° forgotten
EVERYMAN. Why askest thou?
Why wouldest thou weet?° know
DEATH. Yea, sir, I will show you:
90 In great haste I am sent to thee
From God out of his majesty.
EVERYMAN. What! sent to me?

6. Everywhere.

DEATH. Yea, certainly.
    Though thou have forgot him here,
95   He thinketh on thee in the heavenly sphere,
    As, ere we depart, thou shalt know.
EVERYMAN. What desireth God of me?
DEATH. That shall I show thee:
    A reckoning he will needs have
100   Without any longer respite.
EVERYMAN. To give a reckoning longer leisure I crave.
    This blind° matter troubleth my wit.   *unexpected*
DEATH. On thee thou must take a long journay:
    Therefore thy book of count° with thee thou bring, *accounts*
105   For turn again thou cannot by no way.
    And look thou be sure of thy reckoning,
    For before God thou shalt answer and shew
    Thy many bad deeds and good but a few—
    How thou hast spent thy life and in what wise,
110   Before the Chief Lord of Paradise.
    Have ado that we were in that way,[7]
    For weet thou well thou shalt make none attornay.[8]
EVERYMAN. Full unready I am such reckoning to give.
    I know thee not. What messenger art thou?
115 DEATH. I am Death that no man dreadeth,[9]
    For every man I 'rest,° and no man spareth;   *arrest*
    For it is God's commandment
    That all to me should be obedient.
EVERYMAN. O Death, thou comest when I had thee least in
        mind.
120   In thy power it lieth me to save:
    Yet of my good° will I give thee, if thou will be kind, *goods*
    Yea, a thousand pound shalt thou have—
    And defer this matter till another day.
DEATH. Everyman, it may not be, by no way.
125   I set nought by[1] gold, silver, nor riches,
    Nor by pope, emperor, king, duke, nor princes,
    For, and° I would receive gifts great,   *if*
    All the world I might get.
    But my custom is clean contrary:
130   I give thee no respite. Come hence and not tarry!
EVERYMAN. Alas, shall I have no longer respite?
    I may say Death giveth no warning.
    To think on thee it maketh my heart sick,
    For all unready is my book of reckoning.
135   But twelve year and I might have a biding,[2]
    My counting-book I would make so clear
    That my reckoning I should not need to fear.

---

7. I.e., let's get started at once.
8. I.e., none to appear in your stead.
9. That fears nobody.

1. I care nothing for.
2. If I might have a delay for just twelve years.

Wherefore, Death, I pray thee, for God's mercy,
Spare me till I be provided of remedy.
140 DEATH. Thee availeth not to cry, weep, and pray;
But haste thee lightly° that thou were gone that   quickly
   journay,
And prove° thy friends, if thou can.   test
For weet° thou well the tide° abideth no man,   know / time
And in the world each living creature
145 For Adam's sin must die of nature.[3]
EVERYMAN. Death, if I should this pilgrimage take
And my reckoning surely make,
Show me, for saint° charity,   holy
Should I not come again shortly?
150 DEATH. No, Everyman. And thou be once there,
Thou mayst never more come here,
Trust me verily.
EVERYMAN. O gracious God in the high seat celestial,
Have mercy on me in this most need!
155 Shall I have no company from this vale terrestrial
Of mine acquaintance that way me to lead?
DEATH. Yea, if any be so hardy
That would go with thee and bear thee company.
Hie° thee that thou were gone to God's magnificence,   hasten
160 Thy reckoning to give before his presence.
What, weenest° thou thy life is given thee,   suppose
And thy worldly goods also?
EVERYMAN. I had weened so, verily.
DEATH. Nay, nay, it was but lent thee.
165 For as soon as thou art go,
Another a while shall have it and then go therefro,
Even as thou hast done.
Everyman, thou art mad! Thou hast thy wits° five,   senses
And here on earth will not amend thy live![4]
170 For suddenly I do come.
EVERYMAN. O wretched caitiff! Whither shall I flee
That I might 'scape this endless sorrow?
Now, gentle Death, spare me till tomorrow,
That I may amend me
175 With good advisement.°   preparation
DEATH. Nay, thereto I will not consent,
Nor no man will I respite,
But to the heart suddenly I shall smite,
Without any advisement.
180 And now out of thy sight I will me hie:
See thou make thee ready shortly,
For thou mayst say this is the day
That no man living may 'scape away.
   [*Exit* DEATH.]

3. Naturally.   4. In thy life.

EVERYMAN. Alas, I may well weep with sighs deep:
185   Now have I no manner of company
    To help me in my journey and me to keep.°   *guard*
    And also my writing[5] is full unready—
    How shall I do now for to excuse me?
    I would to God I had never be geet![6]
190   To my soul a full great profit it had be.
    For now I fear pains huge and great.
    The time passeth: Lord, help, that all wrought!
    For though I mourn, it availeth nought.
    The day passeth and is almost ago:°   *gone by*
195   I wot° not well what for to do.   *know*
    To whom were I best my complaint to make?
    What and I to Fellowship thereof spake,
    And showed him of this sudden chance?
    For in him is all mine affiance,°   *trust*
200   We have in the world so many a day
    Be good friends in sport and play.
    I see him yonder, certainly.
    I trust that he will bear me company.
    Therefore to him will I speak to ease my sorrow.
        [*Enter* FELLOWSHIP.]
205   Well met, good Fellowship, and good morrow!
FELLOWSHIP. Everyman, good morrow, by this day!
    Sir, why lookest thou so piteously?
    If anything be amiss, I pray thee me say,
    That I may help to remedy.
210 EVERYMAN. Yea, good Fellowship, yea:
    I am in great jeopardy.
FELLOWSHIP. My true friend, show to me your mind.
    I will not forsake thee to my life's end
    In the way of good company.
215 EVERYMAN. That was well spoken, and lovingly!
FELLOWSHIP. Sir, I must needs know your heaviness.°   *sorrow*
    I have pity to see you in any distress.
    If any have you wronged, ye shall revenged be,
    Though I on the ground be slain for thee,
220   Though that I know before that I should die.
EVERYMAN. Verily, Fellowship, gramercy.°   *many thanks*
FELLOWSHIP. Tush! by thy thanks I set not a stree.°   *straw*
    Show me your grief and say no more.
EVERYMAN. If I my heart should to you break,°   *disclose*
225   And then you to turn your mind fro me,
    And would not me comfort when ye hear me speak,
    Then should I ten times sorrier be.
FELLOWSHIP. Sir, I say as I will do, indeed.
EVERYMAN. Then be you a good friend at need.
230   I have found you true herebefore.

5. I.e., ledger.   6. Been begotten.

FELLOWSHIP. And so ye shall evermore.
    For, in faith, and thou go to hell,
    I will not forsake thee by the way.
EVERYMAN. Ye speak like a good friend. I believe you well.
235 I shall deserve° it, and° I may.   *repay / if*
FELLOWSHIP. I speak of no deserving, by this day!
    For he that will say and nothing do
    Is not worthy with good company to go.
    Therefore show me the grief of your mind,
240 As to your friend most loving and kind.
EVERYMAN. I shall show you how it is:
    Commanded I am to go a journay,
    A long way, hard and dangerous,
    And give a strait° count,° without delay,   *strict / accounting*
245 Before the high judge Adonai.[7]
    Wherefore I pray you bear me company,
    As ye have promised, in this journay.
FELLOWSHIP. This is matter indeed! Promise is duty—
    But, and I should take such a voyage on me,
250 I know it well, it should be to my pain.
    Also it maketh me afeard, certain.
    But let us take counsel here, as well as we can—
    For your words would fear° a strong man.   *frighten*
EVERYMAN. Why, ye said if I had need,
255 Ye would me never forsake, quick ne dead,
    Though it were to hell, truly.
FELLOWSHIP. So I said, certainly.
    But such pleasures° be set aside, the sooth to say.   *jokes*
    And also, if we took such a journay,
260 When should we again come?
EVERYMAN. Nay, never again, till the day of doom.
FELLOWSHIP. In faith, then will not I come there!
    Who hath you these tidings brought?
EVERYMAN. Indeed, Death was with me here.
265 FELLOWSHIP. Now by God that all hath bought,°   *redeemed*
    If Death were the messenger,
    For no man that is living today
    I will not go that loath° journay—   *loathsome*
    Not for the father that begat me!
270 EVERYMAN. Ye promised otherwise, pardie.°   *by God*
FELLOWSHIP. I wot well I said so, truly.
    And yet, if thou wilt eat and drink and make good cheer,
    Or haunt to women the lusty company,[8]
    I would not forsake you while the day is clear,
275 Trust me verily!
EVERYMAN. Yea, thereto ye would be ready—
    To go to mirth, solace,° and play: *pleasure*

---

7. I.e., God.
8. Or frequent the lusty company of women.

Your mind to folly will sooner apply°   *attend*
Than to bear me company in my long journey.
280 FELLOWSHIP. Now in good faith, I will not that way.
But, and thou will murder or any man kill,
In that I will help thee with a good will.
EVERYMAN. O that is simple° advice, indeed!   *foolish*
Gentle fellow, help me in my necessity:
285 We have loved long, and now I need—
And now, gentle Fellowship, remember me!
FELLOWSHIP. Whether ye have loved me or no,
By Saint John, I will not with thee go!
EVERYMAN. Yet I pray thee take the labor and do so much for
me,
290 To bring me forward,[9] for saint charity,
And comfort me till I come without the town.
FELLOWSHIP. Nay, and thou would give me a new gown,
I will not a foot with thee go.
But, and thou had tarried, I would not have left thee so.
295 And as now, God speed thee in thy journey!
For from thee I will depart as fast as I may.
EVERYMAN. Whither away, Fellowship? Will thou forsake me?
FELLOWSHIP. Yea, by my fay!° To God I betake°
thee.   *faith / commend*
EVERYMAN. Farewell, good Fellowship! For thee my heart is
sore.
300 Adieu forever—I shall see thee no more.
FELLOWSHIP. In faith, Everyman, farewell now at the ending:
For you I will remember that parting is mourning.
[*Exit* FELLOWSHIP.]
EVERYMAN. Alack, shall we thus depart° indeed—   *part*
Ah, Lady, help!—without any more comfort?
305 Lo, Fellowship forsaketh me in my most need!
For help in this world whither shall I resort?
Fellowship herebefore with me would merry make,
And now little sorrow for me doth he take.
It is said, "In prosperity men friends may find
310 Which in adversity be full unkind."
Now whither for succor shall I flee,
Sith° that Fellowship hath forsaken me?   *since*
To my kinsmen I will, truly,
Praying them to help me in my necessity.
315 I believe that they will do so,
For kind will creep where it may not go.[1]
I will go 'say°—for yonder I see them—   *assay*
Where° be ye now my friends and kinsmen.   *whether*
[*Enter* KINDRED *and* COUSIN.]
KINDRED. Here be we now at your commandment:

9. Escort me.   not walk (i.e., kinsmen will suffer hard-
1. For kinship will creep where it can-   ship for one another).

320   Cousin, I pray you show us your intent
In any wise, and not spare.
COUSIN. Yea, Everyman, and to us declare
If ye be disposed to go anywhither.
For, weet° you well, we will live and die togither.   *know*
325 KINDRED. In wealth and woe we will with you hold,
For over his kin a man may be bold.[2]
EVERYMAN. Gramercy,° my friends and kinsmen
    kind.   *much thanks*
Now shall I show you the grief of my mind.
I was commanded by a messenger
330 That is a high king's chief officer:
He bade me go a pilgrimage, to my pain—
And I know well I shall never come again.
Also I must give a reckoning strait,°   *strict*
For I have a great enemy that hath me in wait,[3]
335 Which intendeth me to hinder.
KINDRED. What account is that which ye must render?
That would I know.
EVERYMAN. Of all my works I must show
How I have lived and my days spent;
340 Also of ill deeds that I have used
In my time sith life was me lent,
And of all virtues that I have refused.
Therefore I pray you go thither with me
To help me make mine account, for saint charity.
345 COUSIN. What, to go thither? Is that the matter?
Nay, Everyman, I had liefer fast[4] bread and water
All this five year and more!
EVERYMAN. Alas, that ever I was bore!°   *born*
For now shall I never be merry
350 If that you forsake me.
KINDRED. Ah, sir, what? Ye be a merry man:
Take good heart to you and make no moan.
But one thing I warn you, by Saint Anne,
As for me, ye shall go alone.
355 EVERYMAN. My Cousin, will you not with me go?
COUSIN. No, by Our Lady! I have the cramp in my toe:
Trust not to me. For, so God me speed,
I will deceive you in your most need.
KINDRED. It availeth you not us to 'tice.°   *entice*
360 Ye shall have my maid with all my heart:
She loveth to go to feasts, there to be nice,°   *wanton*
And to dance, and abroad to start.[5]
I will give her leave to help you in that journey,
If that you and she may agree.

---

2. I.e., for a man may make demands
of his kinsmen.
3. I.e., Satan lies in ambush for me.

4. I.e., rather fast on.
5. To go gadding about.

365 EVERYMAN. Now show me the very effect° of your mind: *bent*
    Will you go with me or abide behind?
  KINDRED. Abide behind? Yea, that will I and I may!
    Therefore farewell till another day.
        [*Exit* KINDRED.]
  EVERYMAN. How should I be merry or glad?
370   For fair promises men to me make,
    But when I have most need they me forsake.
    I am deceived. That maketh me sad.
  COUSIN. Cousin Everyman, farewell now,
    For verily I will not go with you;
375   Also of mine own an unready reckoning
    I have to account—therefore I make tarrying.
    Now God keep thee, for now I go.
        [*Exit* COUSIN.]
  EVERYMAN. Ah, Jesus, is all come hereto?°   *to this*
    Lo, fair words maketh fools fain:°   *glad*
380   They promise and nothing will do, certain.
    My kinsmen promised me faithfully
    For to abide with me steadfastly,
    And now fast away do they flee.
    Even so Fellowship promised me.
385   What friend were best me of to provide?
    I lose my time here longer to abide.
    Yet in my mind a thing there is:
    All my life I have loved riches;
    If that my Good° now help me might,   *Goods*
390   He would make my heart full light.
    I will speak to him in this distress.
    Where art thou, my Goods and riches?
  GOODS. [*within*] Who calleth me? Everyman? What, hast thou
    haste?
    I lie here in corners, trussed and piled so high,
395   And in chests I am locked so fast—
    Also sacked in bags—thou mayst see with thine eye
    I cannot stir, in packs low where I lie.
    What would ye have? Lightly° me say.   *quickly*
  EVERYMAN. Come hither, Good, in all the haste thou may,
400   For of counsel I must desire thee.
        [*Enter* GOODS.]
  GOODS. Sir, and° ye in the world have sorrow or adversity,   *if*
    That can I help you to remedy shortly.
  EVERYMAN. It is another disease° that grieveth me: *distress*
    In this world it is not, I tell thee so.
405   I am sent for another way to go,
    To give a strait count general
    Before the highest Jupiter[6] of all.
    And all my life I have had joy and pleasure in thee:

6. I.e., God.

Therefore I pray thee go with me,
410 For, peradventure, thou mayst before God Almighty
My reckoning help to clean and purify.
For it is said ever among[7]
That money maketh all right that is wrong.
GOODS. Nay, Everyman, I sing another song:
415 I follow no man in such voyages.
For, and I went with thee,
Thou shouldest fare much the worse for me;
For because on me thou did set thy mind,
Thy reckoning I have made blotted and blind,°   *illegible*
420 That thine account thou cannot make truly—
And that hast thou for the love of me.
EVERYMAN. That would grieve me full sore,
When I should come to that fearful answer.
Up, let us go thither together.
425 GOODS. Nay, not so, I am too brittle, I may not endure.
I will follow no man one foot, be ye sure.
EVERYMAN. Alas, I have thee loved and had great pleasure
All my life-days on good and treasure.
GOODS. That is to thy damnation, without leasing,°   *lie*
430 For my love is contrary to the love everlasting.
But if thou had me loved moderately
    during,°   *in the meanwhile*
As to the poor to give part of me,
Then shouldest thou not in this dolor be,
Nor in this great sorrow and care.
435 EVERYMAN. Lo, now was I deceived ere I was ware,
And all I may wite° misspending of time.   *blame on*
GOODS. What, weenest° thou that I am thine?   *suppose*
EVERYMAN. I had weened so.
GOODS. Nay, Everyman, I say no.
440 As for a while I was lent thee;
A season thou hast had me in prosperity.
My condition° is man's soul to kill;   *disposition*
If I save one, a thousand I do spill.°   *ruin*
Weenest thou that I will follow thee?
445 Nay, from this world, not verily.
EVERYMAN. I had weened otherwise.
GOODS. Therefore to thy soul Good is a thief;
For when thou art dead, this is my guise°—   *custom*
Another to deceive in the same wise
450 As I have done thee, and all to his soul's repreef.°   *shame*
EVERYMAN. O false Good, cursed thou be,
Thou traitor to God, that hast deceived me
And caught me in thy snare!
GOODS. Marry, thou brought thyself in care,°   *sorrow*
455 Whereof I am glad;

7. Now and then.

I must needs laugh, I cannot be sad.

EVERYMAN. Ah, Good, thou hast had long my heartly° love;   *sincere*

I gave thee that which should be the Lord's above.

But wilt thou not go with me, indeed?

460   I pray thee truth to say.

GOODS. No, so God me speed!

Therefore farewell and have good day.

[*Exit* GOODS.]

EVERYMAN. Oh, to whom shall I make my moan

For to go with me in that heavy° journay?   *sorrowful*

465   First Fellowship said he would with me gone:°   *go*

His words were very pleasant and gay,

But afterward he left me alone.

Then spake I to my kinsmen, all in despair,

And also they gave me words fair—

470   They lacked no fair speaking,

But all forsake me in the ending.

Then went I to my Goods that I loved best,

In hope to have comfort; but there had I least,

For my Goods sharply did me tell

475   That he bringeth many into hell.

Then of myself I was ashamed,

And so I am worthy to be blamed:

Thus may I well myself hate.

Of whom shall I now counsel take?

480   I think that I shall never speed

Till that I go to my Good Deed.

But alas, she is so weak

That she can neither go° nor speak.   *walk*

Yet will I venture° on her now.   *gamble*

485   My Good Deeds, where be you?

GOOD DEEDS. [*speaking from the ground*] Here I lie, cold in the ground:

Thy sins hath me sore bound

That I cannot stear.°   *stir*

EVERYMAN. O Good Deeds, I stand in fear:

490   I must you pray of counsel,

For help now should come right well.

GOOD DEEDS. Everyman, I have understanding

That ye be summoned, account to make,

Before Messiah of Jer'salem King.

495   And you do by me,[8] that journey with you will I take.

EVERYMAN. Therefore I come to you my moan to make.

I pray you that ye will go with me.

GOOD DEEDS. I would full fain, but I cannot stand, verily.

EVERYMAN. Why, is there anything on you fall?°   *fallen*

500 GOOD DEEDS. Yea, sir, I may thank you of all:

8. I.e., if you do what I say.

    If ye had perfectly cheered me,
    Your book of count full ready had be.
        [GOOD DEEDS *shows him the account book.*]
    Look, the books of your works and deeds eke,°   *also*
    As how they lie under the feet,
505   To your soul's heaviness.°   *distress*
EVERYMAN. Our Lord Jesus help me!
    For one letter here I cannot see.
GOOD DEEDS. There is a blind° reckoning in time of
        distress!   *illegible*
EVERYMAN. Good Deeds, I pray you help me in this need,
510   Or else I am forever damned indeed.
    Therefore help me to make reckoning
    Before the Redeemer of all thing
    That King is and was and ever shall.
GOOD DEEDS. Everyman, I am sorry of° your fall   *for*
515   And fain would help you and I were able.
EVERYMAN. Good Deeds, your counsel I pray you give me.
GOOD DEEDS. That shall I do verily,
    Though that on my feet I may not go;
    I have a sister that shall with you also,
520   Called Knowledge, which shall with you abide
    To help you to make that dreadful reckoning.
        [*Enter* KNOWLEDGE.]
KNOWLEDGE. Everyman, I will go with thee and be thy guide,
    In thy most need to go by thy side.
EVERYMAN. In good condition I am now in everything,
525   And am whole content with this good thing,
    Thanked be God my Creator.
GOOD DEEDS. And when she hath brought you there
    Where thou shalt heal thee of thy smart,°   *pain*
    Then go you with your reckoning and your Good Deeds to-
        gether
530   For to make you joyful at heart
    Before the blessed Trinity.
EVERYMAN. My Good Deeds, gramercy!
    I am well content, certainly,
    With your words sweet.
535 KNOWLEDGE. Now go we together lovingly
    To Confession, that cleansing river.
EVERYMAN. For joy I weep—I would we were there!
    But I pray you give me cognition,°   *knowledge*
    Where dwelleth that holy man Confession?
540 KNOWLEDGE. In the House of Salvation:
    We shall find him in that place
    That shall us comfort, by God's grace.
        [KNOWLEDGE *leads* EVERYMAN *to* CONFESSION.]
    Lo, this is Confession: kneel down and ask mercy,
    For he is in good conceit° with God Almighty.   *esteem*

545 EVERYMAN. [*kneeling*] O glorious fountain that all uncleanness
        doth clarify,[9]
        Wash from me the spots of vice unclean,
        That on me no sin may be seen.
        I come with Knowledge for my redemption,
        Redempt° with heart and full contrition,   *redeemed*
550   For I am commanded a pilgrimage to take
        And great accounts before God to make.
        Now I pray you, Shrift, mother of Salvation,
        Help my Good Deeds for my piteous exclamation.
   CONFESSION. I know your sorrow well, Everyman:
555   Because with Knowledge ye come to me,
        I will you comfort as well as I can,
        And a precious jewel I will give thee,
        Called Penance, voider° of adversity.   *expeller*
        Therewith shall your body chastised be—
560   With abstinence and perseverance in God's service.
        Here shall you receive that scourge of me,
        Which is penance strong° that ye must endure,   *harsh*
        To remember thy Saviour was scourged for thee
        With sharp scourges, and suffered it patiently.
565   So must thou ere thou 'scape that painful pilgrimage.
        Knowledge, keep° him in this voyage,   *guard*
        And by that time Good Deeds will be with thee.
        But in any wise be secure° of mercy—   *certain*
        For your time draweth fast—and ye will saved be.
570   Ask God mercy and he will grant, truly.
        When with the scourge of penance man doth him°   *himself*
          bind,
        The oil of forgiveness then shall he find.
   EVERYMAN. Thanked be God for his gracious work,
        For now I will my penance begin.
575   This hath rejoiced and lighted my heart,
        Though the knots[1] be painful and hard within.
   KNOWLEDGE. Everyman, look your penance that ye fulfill,
        What pain that ever it to you be;
        And Knowledge shall give you counsel at will
580   How your account ye shall make clearly.
   EVERYMAN. O eternal God, O heavenly figure,
        O way of righteousness, O goodly vision,
        Which descended down in a virgin pure
        Because he would every man redeem,
585   Which Adam forfeited by his disobedience;
        O blessed Godhead, elect and high Divine,°   *divinity*
        Forgive my grievous offense!
        Here I cry thee mercy in this presence:
        O ghostly Treasure, O Ransomer and Redeemer,

9. Purify.
1. I.e., the knots on the scourge (whip) of penance. "Within": i.e., to my senses.

590 Of all the world Hope and Conduiter,°   *guide*
Mirror of joy, Foundator° of mercy,   *Founder*
Which enlumineth° heaven and earth thereby,   *lights up*
Hear my clamorous complaint, though it late be;
Receive my prayers, of thy benignity.

595 Though I be a sinner most abominable,
Yet let my name be written in Moses' table.[2]
O Mary, pray to the Maker of all thing
Me for to help at my ending,
And save me from the power of my enemy,

600 For Death assaileth me strongly.
And Lady, that I may by mean of thy prayer
Of your Son's glory to be partner—
By the means of his passion I it crave.
I beseech you help my soul to save.

605 Knowledge, give me the scourge of penance:
My flesh therewith shall give acquittance.° *satisfaction for sins*
I will now begin, if God give me grace.

KNOWLEDGE. Everyman, God give you time and
     space!°   *opportunity*
Thus I bequeath you in the hands of our Saviour:

610 Now may you make your reckoning sure.

EVERYMAN. In the name of the Holy Trinity
My body sore punished shall be:
Take this, body, for the sin of the flesh!
Also° thou delightest to go gay and fresh,   *as*

615 And in the way of damnation thou did me bring,
Therefore suffer now strokes of punishing!
Now of penance I will wade the water clear,
To save me from purgatory, that sharp fire.

GOOD DEEDS. I thank God, now can I walk and go,

620 And am delivered of my sickness and woe.
Therefore with Everyman I will go, and not spare:
His good works I will help him to declare.

KNOWLEDGE. Now, Everyman, be merry and glad:
Your Good Deeds cometh now, ye may not be sad.

625 Now is your Good Deeds whole and sound,
Going° upright upon the ground.   *walking*

EVERYMAN. My heart is light, and shall be evermore.
Now will I smite faster than I did before.

GOOD DEEDS. Everyman, pilgrim, my special friend,

630 Blessed be thou without end!
For thee is preparate° the eternal glory.   *prepared*
Ye have me made whole and sound:
Therefore I will bide by thee in every stound.°   *trial*

EVERYMAN. Welcome, my Good Deeds! Now I hear thy voice,

635 I weep for very sweetness of love.

---

2. "Moses' table" is here the tablet on which are recorded those who have been baptized and have done penance.

KNOWLEDGE. Be no more sad, but ever rejoice:
    God seeth thy living in his throne above.
    Put on this garment to thy behove,°   *advantage*
    Which is wet with your tears—
610   Or else before God you may it miss
    When ye to your journey's end come shall.
EVERYMAN. Gentle Knowledge, what do ye it call?
KNOWLEDGE. It is a garment of sorrow;
    From pain it will you borrow:°   *redeem*
645   Contrition it is
    That getteth forgiveness;
    It pleaseth God passing° well.   *surpassingly*
GOOD DEEDS. Everyman, will you wear it for your heal?° *welfare*
EVERYMAN. Now blessed be Jesu, Mary's son,
650   For now have I on true contrition.
    And let us go now without tarrying.
    Good Deeds, have we clear our reckoning?
GOOD DEEDS. Yea, indeed, I have it here.
EVERYMAN. Then I trust we need not fear.
655   Now friends, let us not part in twain.
KNOWLEDGE. Nay, Everyman, that will we not, certain.
GOOD DEEDS. Yet must thou lead with thee
    Three persons of great might.
EVERYMAN. Who should they be?
660 GOOD DEEDS. Discretion and Strength they hight,°   *are called*
    And thy Beauty may not abide behind.
KNOWLEDGE. Also ye must call to mind
    Your Five-Wits° as for your counselors.   *senses*
GOOD DEEDS. You must have have them ready at all hours.
665 EVERYMAN. How shall I get them hither?
KNOWLEDGE. You must call them all togither,
    And they will be here incontinent.°   *at once*
EVERYMAN. My friends, come hither and be present,
    Discretion, Strength, my Five-Wits, and Beauty!
      [*They enter.*]
670 BEAUTY. Here at your will we be all ready.
    What will ye that we should do?
GOOD DEEDS. That ye would with Everyman go
    And help him in his pilgrimage.
    Advise you:[3] will ye with him or not in that voyage?
675 STRENGTH. We will bring him all thither,
    To his help and comfort, ye may believe me.
DISCRETION. So will we go with him all togither.
EVERYMAN. Almighty God, loved° might thou be!   *praised*
    I give thee laud that I have hither brought
680   Strength, Discretion, Beauty, and Five-Wits—lack I
        nought—
    And my Good Deeds, with Knowledge clear,

3. Take thought.

All be in my company at my will here:
I desire no more to my business.

STRENGTH. And I, Strength, will by you stand in distress,
685 Though thou would in battle fight on the ground.

FIVE-WITS. And though it were through the world round,
We will not depart for sweet ne sour.

BEAUTY. No more will I, until death's hour,
Whatsoever thereof befall.

690 DISCRETION. Everyman, advise you first of all:
Go with a good advisement° and deliberation.   *preparation*
We all give you virtuous° monition°   *confident / prediction*
That all shall be well.

EVERYMAN. My friends, hearken what I will tell;
695 I pray God reward you in his heaven-sphere;
Now hearken all that be here,
For I will make my testament,
Here before you all present:
In alms half my good° I will give with my hands twain, *goods*
700 In the way of charity with good intent;
And the other half, still⁴ shall remain,
I 'queath° to be returned there it ought to be.   *bequeath*
This I do in despite of the fiend of hell,
To go quit out of his perel,⁵
705 Ever after and this day.

KNOWLEDGE. Everyman, hearken what I say:
Go to Priesthood, I you advise,
And receive of him, in any wise,⁶
The holy sacrament and ointment° togither; *extreme unction*
710 Then shortly see ye turn again hither:
We will all abide you here.

FIVE-WITS. Yea, Everyman, hie you that ye ready were.
There is no emperor, king, duke, ne baron,
That of God hath commission
715 As hath the least priest in the world being:
For of the blessed sacraments pure and bening°   *benign*
He beareth the keys, and thereof hath the cure°   *care*
For man's redemption—it is ever sure—
Which God for our souls' medicine
720 Gave us out of his heart with great pine,°   *torment*
Here in this transitory life for thee and me.
The blessed sacraments seven there be:
Baptism, confirmation, with priesthood° good,   *ordination*
And the sacrament of God's precious flesh and blood,
725 Marriage, the holy extreme unction, and penance:
These seven be good to have in remembrance,
Gracious sacraments of high divinity.

EVERYMAN. Fain° would I receive that holy body,   *gladly*

4. I.e., which still.
5. In order to go free of danger from
him.
6. At all costs.

And meekly to my ghostly° father I will go.   *spiritual*

730 FIVE-WITS. Everyman, that is the best that ye can do:
        God will you to salvation bring.
        For priesthood exceedeth all other thing:
        To us Holy Scripture they do teach,
        And converteth man from sin, heaven to reach;
735   God hath to them more power given
        Than to any angel that is in heaven.
        With five words[7] he may consecrate
        God's body in flesh and blood to make,
        And handleth his Maker between his hands.
740   The priest bindeth and unbindeth all bands,[8]
        Both in earth and in heaven.
        Thou ministers° all the sacraments seven;   *administer*
        Though we kiss thy feet, thou were worthy;
        Thou art surgeon that cureth sin deadly;
745   No remedy we find under God
        But all only priesthood.[9]
        Everyman, God gave priests that dignity
        And setteth them in his stead among us to be.
        Thus be they above angels in degree.

          [*Exit* EVERYMAN.]

750 KNOWLEDGE. If priests be good, it is so, surely.
        But when Jesu hanged on the cross with great smart,°   *pain*
        There he gave out of his blessed heart
        The same sacrament in great torment,
        He sold them not to us, that Lord omnipotent:
755   Therefore Saint Peter the Apostle doth say
        That Jesu's curse hath all they
        Which God their Saviour do buy or sell,[1]
        Or they for any money do take or tell.[2]
        Sinful priests giveth the sinners example bad:
760   Their children sitteth by other men's fires, I have heard;
        And some haunteth women's company
        With unclean life, as lusts of lechery.
        These be with sin made blind.

    FIVE-WITS. I trust to God no such may we find.
765   Therefore let us priesthood honor,
        And follow their doctrine for our souls' succor.
        We be their sheep and they shepherds be
        By whom we all be kept in surety.
        Peace, for yonder I see Everyman come,
770   Which hath made true satisfaction.

7. The five words ("For this is my body") spoken by the priest when he offers the wafer at communion.
8. A reference to the power of the keys, inherited by the priesthood from St. Peter, who received it from Christ (Matthew xvi.19) with the promise that whatever St. Peter bound or loosed on earth would be bound or loosed in heaven.
9. Except from priesthood alone.
1. To give or receive money for the sacraments is simony, named after Simon, who wished to buy the gift of the Holy Ghost and was cursed by St. Peter.
2. Or who, for any sacrament, take or count out money.

GOOD DEEDS. Methink it is he indeed.
   [*Re-enter* EVERYMAN.]
EVERYMAN. Now Jesu be your alder speed![3]
   I have received the sacrament for my redemption,
   And then mine extreme unction.
775   Blessed be all they that counseled me to take it!
   And now, friends, let us go without longer respite.
   I thank God that ye have tarried so long.
   Now set each of you on this rood° your hond   *cross*
   And shortly follow me:
780   I go before there° I would be. God be our guide!   *where*
STRENGTH. Everyman, we will not from you go
   Till ye have done this voyage long.
DISCRETION. I, Discretion, will bide by you also.
KNOWLEDGE. And though this pilgrimage be never so
     strong,°   *harsh*
785   I will never part you fro.
STRENGTH. Everyman, I will be as sure by thee
   As ever I did by Judas Maccabee.[4]
EVERYMAN. Alas, I am so faint I may not stand—
   My limbs under me doth fold!
790   Friends, let us not turn again to this land,
   Not for all the world's gold.
   For into this cave must I creep
   And turn to earth, and there to sleep.
BEAUTY. What, into this grave, alas?
795 EVERYMAN. Yea, there shall ye consume,° more and lass.[5] *decay*
BEAUTY. And what, should I smother here?
EVERYMAN. Yea, by my faith, and nevermore appear.
   In this world live no more we shall,
   But in heaven before the highest Lord of all.
800 BEAUTY. I cross out all this! Adieu, by Saint John—
   I take my tape in my lap and am gone.[6]
EVERYMAN. What, Beauty, whither will ye?
BEAUTY. Peace, I am deaf—I look not behind me,
   Not and thou wouldest give me all the gold in thy chest.
   [*Exit* BEAUTY.]
805 EVERYMAN. Alas, whereto may I trust?
   Beauty goeth fast away fro me—
   She promised with me to live and die!
STRENGTH. Everyman, I will thee also forsake and deny.
   Thy game liketh° me not at all.   *pleases*
810 EVERYMAN. Why then, ye will forsake me all?
   Sweet Strength, tarry a little space.
STRENGTH. Nay, sir, by the rood of grace,
   I will hie me from thee fast,

---

3. The prosperer of you all.
4. Judas Maccabaeus was an enormously powerful warrior in the defense of Israel against the Syrians in late Old Testament times.
5. More and less (i.e., all of you).
6. I tuck my skirts in my belt and am off.

Though thou weep till thy heart tobrast.°   *break*

815 EVERYMAN. Ye would ever bide by me, ye said.

STRENGTH. Yea, I have you far enough conveyed!°   *escorted*

Ye be old enough, I understand,

Your pilgrimage to take on hand:

I repent me that I hither came.

820 EVERYMAN. Strength, you to displease I am to blame,[7]

Yet promise is debt, this ye well wot.°   *know*

STRENGTH. In faith, I care not:

Thou art but a fool to complain;

You spend your speech and waste your brain.

825 Go, thrust thee into the ground.

[*Exit* STRENGTH.]

EVERYMAN. I had weened° surer I should you have

found.   *supposed*

He that trusteth in his Strength

She him deceiveth at the length.

Both Strength and Beauty forsaketh me—

830 Yet they promised me fair and lovingly.

DISCRETION. Everyman, I will after Strength be gone:

As for me, I will leave you alone.

EVERYMAN. Why Discretion, will ye forsake me?

DISCRETION. Yea, in faith, I will go from thee.

835 For when Strength goeth before,

I follow after evermore.

EVERYMAN. Yet I pray thee, for the love of the Trinity,

Look in my grave once piteously.

DISCRETION. Nay, so nigh will I not come.

840 Farewell everyone!

[*Exit* DISCRETION.]

EVERYMAN. O all thing faileth save God alone—

Beauty, Strength, and Discretion.

For when Death bloweth his blast

They all run fro me full fast.

845 FIVE-WITS. Everyman, my leave now of thee I take.

I will follow the other, for here I thee forsake.

EVERYMAN. Alas, then may I wail and weep,

For I took you for my best friend.

FIVE-WITS. I will no longer thee keep.°   *watch over*

850 Now farewell, and there an end!

[*Exit* FIVE-WITS.]

EVERYMAN. O Jesu, help, all hath forsaken me!

GOOD DEEDS. Nay, Everyman, I will bide with thee:

I will not forsake thee indeed;

Thou shalt find me a good friend at need.

855 EVERYMAN. Gramercy, Good Deeds! Now may I true friends

see.

They have forsaken me every one—

7. I'm to blame for displeasing you.

I loved them better than my Good Deeds alone.
Knowledge, will ye forsake me also?

KNOWLEDGE. Yea, Everyman, when ye to Death shall go,
860   But not yet, for no manner of danger.

EVERYMAN. Gramercy, Knowledge, with all my heart!

KNOWLEDGE. Nay, yet will I not from hence depart
Till I see where ye shall become.[8]

EVERYMAN. Methink, alas, that I must be gone
865   To make my reckoning and my debts pay,
For I see my time is nigh spent away.
Take example, all ye that this do hear or see,
How they that I best loved do forsake me,
Except my Good Deeds that bideth truly.

870 GOOD DEEDS. All earthly things is but vanity.
Beauty, Strength, and Discretion do man forsake,
Foolish friends and kinsmen that fair spake—
All fleeth save Good Deeds, and that am I.

EVERYMAN. Have mercy on me, God most mighty,
875   And stand by me, thou mother and maid, holy Mary!

GOOD DEEDS. Fear not: I will speak for thee.

EVERYMAN. Here I cry God mercy!

GOOD DEEDS. Short our end, and 'minish our pain.[9]
Let us go, and never come again.

880 EVERYMAN. Into thy hands, Lord, my soul I commend:
Receive it, Lord, that it be not lost.
As thou me boughtest,° so me defend,   *redeemed*
And save me from the fiend's boast,
That I may appear with that blessed host
885   That shall be saved at the day of doom.
In manus tuas, of mights most,
Forever *commendo spiritum meum.*[1]

      [EVERYMAN *and* GOOD DEEDS *descend into the grave.*]

KNOWLEDGE. Now hath he suffered that we all shall endure,
The Good Deeds shall make all sure.
890   Now hath he made ending,
Methinketh that I hear angels sing
And make great joy and melody
Where Everyman's soul received shall be.

ANGEL. [*within*] Come, excellent elect° spouse to Jesu![2] *chosen*
895   Here above thou shalt go
Because of thy singular virtue.
Now the soul is taken the body fro,
Thy reckoning is crystal clear:
Now shalt thou into the heavenly sphere—
900   Unto the which all ye shall come
That liveth well before the day of doom.

---

8. Till I see what shall become of you.
9. I.e., make our dying quick and diminish our pain.
1. "Into thy hands, O greatest of powers, I commend my spirit forever."
2. Man's soul is often referred to as the bride of Jesus.

[*Enter* DOCTOR.³]

DOCTOR. This memorial° men may have in mind: *reminder*
　　　Ye hearers, take it of worth,⁴ old and young,
　　　And forsake Pride, for he deceiveth you in the end.
905　And remember Beauty, Five-Wits, Strength, and Discretion,
　　　They all at the last do Everyman forsake,
　　　Save his Good Deeds there doth he take—
　　　But beware, for and they be small,
　　　Before God he hath no help at all—
910　None excuse may be there for Everyman.
　　　Alas, how shall he do than?° *then*
　　　For after death amends may no man make,
　　　For then mercy and pity doth him forsake.
　　　If his reckoning be not clear when he doth come,
915　God will say, "*Ite, maledicti, in ignem eternum!*"⁵
　　　And he that hath his account whole and sound,
　　　High in heaven he shall be crowned,
　　　Unto which place God bring us all thither,
　　　That we may live body and soul togither.
920　Thereto help, the Trinity!
　　　Amen say ye, for saint charity.

3. The Doctor is the learned theologian who explains the meaning of the play.
4. Prize it.
5. "Depart, ye cursed, into everlasting fire."

POPULAR BALLADS

Ballads are anonymous narrative songs that have been preserved by oral transmission. Although any stage of a given culture may produce ballads, they are most characteristic of primitive societies such as that of the American frontier in the 18th and 19th centuries or that of the English-Scottish border region in the later Middle Ages. These northern English songs, even divorced from the tunes to which they were once sung, are narrative poems of great literary interest.

The origins of the popular (or folk) ballad are much disputed. The theory that they were first composed by communal effort, taking shape as the songs with which primitive people accompanied ritual dances, no longer seems plausible. On the other hand, the forms in which the ballads have come down to us show that they have been subjected to a continuing process of revision, both conscious and unconscious, by those through whose lips and memories they passed. Though the English ballads were probably composed during the 500-year period from 1200 to 1700, few of them were printed before the 18th century and some not until the 19th. Bishop Thomas Percy (1729–1811) was among the first to take a literary interest in ballads, stimulated by his chance discovery of a 17th-century manuscript in which a number of them had been copied down among a great welter of Middle English verse. Percy's publication of this material in his *Reliques of Ancient English Poetry* inspired others, notably

Sir Walter Scott, to go to the living source of the ballads and to set them down on paper at the dictation of the border people among whom the old songs were still being sung. These collectors often found that one ballad was remembered differently by different people: for instance, when one speaks of *Sir Patrick Spens* one is actually speaking of a number of poems that tell the same story in slightly or widely different words. If a single original form by a single author lies behind this diversity, it is too far back in the mists of time to be recovered.

A work that is the product of a consciously artistic mind will not ordinarily be improved by the revision that most ballads have been subjected to, but some of the ballads are probably better in their revised form than they were in their original form. The distinctive quality that popular ballads share is spareness: they are apt to deal only with the culminating incident or climax of a plot, to describe that event with intense compression, to put the burden of narration on allusive monologue or dialogue, and to avoid editorial comment. This concentration upon the bare essential is precisely that quality that the fallible human memory is likely not only to preserve but also to enhance, for the effort of remembering causes a sloughing-off of what is not strictly relevant. Some of the best of the ballads may have thus been refined in their transmission through men's minds, gaining rather than losing artistic stature.

The fact that ballads were originally songs is important to their development. The simplicity of the tunes to which they were sung not only influenced the distinctive verse form—normally a quatrain with four stresses per line—but also encouraged a corresponding simplicity in the narrative itself, and made individualizing flourishes impossible. Furthermore, the choral practice of using refrains and other kinds of repetitions probably lent the ballad one of its most impressive qualities, for while the actual narratives are tightly compressed, ballads rarely develop in an unbroken line. The reader—originally, the hearer—is constantly made to pause by a repeated phrase, or even by nonsense syllables, which provide suspense in a very primitive and effective form. The progress to a foreknown, foredoomed conclusion is paradoxically made to seem more inevitable, more urgent, by such relaxations of narrative tension. The use of repetition and refrain also imparts to the ballads something of the quality of incantation, of ritual, of liturgy—all of which are, of course, themselves closely allied with music.

Most of the best ballads have as their subject a tragic incident, often a murder or accidental death, generally involving supernatural elements. These motifs are a part of the common legacy of European folklore, and many of the English ballads have counterparts in other languages. To this class belong, among the selections chosen for inclusion here, *Lord Randall, Edward, Barbara Allan,* the *Wife of Usher's Well,* the *Three Ravens,* and—though not in its present form—*Sir Patrick Spens.* Not all the ballads with folklore motifs are tragic, however, for *Thomas Rhymer* has a happy ending. This ballad has gone through an added stage of evolution, for it is a shortening—a reduction to ballad form—of a romance which is preserved in a longer and more sophistication form; but the romance itself had its origin in some ancient folk tale, and there may have been an earlier ballad on the same theme, with, perhaps, a less happy conclusion.

Some ballads have as their subject actual historical incidents. Two late songs, the *Bonny Earl of Murray* and *Bonny George Campbell*, lament the political murders of two popular 16th-century Scots nobles. The presumably much older ballad *Sir Patrick Spens* may be based on a historical incident of the end of the 13th century. Yet all three of these achieve that mood of sadness that is characteristic of the best of the tragic stories derived from ancient folklore. The quasi-historical Robin Hood ballads, which form a large class by themselves, are less impressive. Most of them seem to have been composed relatively late and hence not to have gone through many stages of oral transmission; they lack the better ballads' intensity, often exhibiting an expansive development that is not free from chattiness. They are probably the work of minstrels who exploited the old folklore figure of Robin Hood by making him a symbol of that rebellion against authority that their own hearers perhaps longed for but did not dare to undertake. In the ballads Robin Hood is placed in a kind of never-never land of English history, where he can strike down tyrants with impunity, but often with far too much gloating: the attractive folklore figure of a natural, freedom-loving man has been burdened with too many political and social implications.

St. *Steven and King Herod* is hardly a ballad in the same sense as the other poems discussed here. It was probably not transmitted orally, for it contains Latin, and it shows none of the characteristic signs of having passed through more than a single stage of composition. Its author was probably a learned cleric who was exploiting the ballad form for religious purposes—an exploitation so successful as to earn the poem classification as a true ballad despite its evident artificiality.

The great collection of English ballads is that of F. J. Child, *The English and Scottish Popular Ballads*, first published in 1882. The numbers under which Child lists the various versions of each of the ballads printed here are given in footnotes to the individual titles. The versions chosen for this anthology are those which the editor considers the most effective as poetry. Spelling has been modernized; the majority of the northernisms in the originals have been retained.

Lord Randall[1]

"Oh where ha'e ye been, Lord Randall my son?
O where ha'e ye been, my handsome young man?"
   "I ha'e been to the wild wood: mother, make my bed soon,
   For I'm weary wi' hunting, and fain° wald° lie
     down."   *gladly / would*

5 "Where gat ye your dinner, Lord Randall my son?
Where gat ye your dinner, my handsome young man?"
   "I dined wi' my true love; mother, make my bed soon,
   For I'm weary wi' hunting, and fain wald lie down."

"What gat ye to your dinner, Lord Randall my son?
10 What gat ye to your dinner, my handsome young man?"
   "I gat eels boiled in broo:° mother, make my bed
     soon,   *broth*
   For I'm weary wi' hunting and fain wald lie down."

"What became of your bloodhounds, Lord Randall my son?
What became of your bloodhounds, my handsome young man?"
15   "O they swelled and they died: mother, make my bed soon,
   For I'm weary wi' hunting and fain wald lie down."

"O I fear ye are poisoned, Lord Randall my son!
O I fear ye are poisoned, my handsome young man!"
   "O yes, I am poisoned: mother, make my bed soon,
20   For I'm sick at the heart, and I fain wald lie down."

Edward[2]

"Why does your brand sae drap wi' bluid,[3]
     Edward, Edward?
Why does your brand sae drap wi' bluid,
   And why sae sad gang° ye, O?"   *go*
5 "O I ha'e killed my hawk sae guid,
     Mither, mither,
O I ha'e killed my hawk sae guid,
   And I had nae mair° but he, O."   *more*

"Your hawkes bluid was never sae reid,°   *red*
10   Edward, Edward.
Your hawkes bluid was never sae reid,
   My dear son I tell thee, O."

---

1. Child, No. 12.   3. I.e., why does your sword so drip
2. Child, No. 13.   with blood?

"O I ha'e killed my reid-roan° steed,   chestnut
        Mither, mither,
15 O I ha'e killed my reid-roan steed,
        That erst° was sae fair and free, O."   before

"Your steed was auld° and ye ha'e gat mair,   old
        Edward, Edward.
    Your steed was auld and ye ha'e gat mair:
20   Som other dule° ye dree,° O."   grief / suffer
"O I ha'e killed my fader dear,
        Mither, mither,
    O I ha'e killed my fader dear,
        Alas and wae° is me, O!"   woe

25 "And whatten° penance wul ye dree for that,   what sort of
        Edward, Edward?
    And whatten penance wul ye dree for that,
        My dear son, now tell me, O?"
    "I'll set my feet in yonder boat,
30   Mither, mither,
    I'll set my feet in yonder boat,
        And I'll fare over the sea, O."

"And what wul ye do wi' your towers and your ha',
        Edward, Edward?
35 And what wul ye do wi' your towers and your ha',
        That were sae fair to see, O?"
    "I'll let thame stand til they down fa',
        Mither, mither,
    I'll let thame stand til they down fa',
40   For here never mair maun° I be, O."   must

"And what wul ye leave to your bairns° and your wife,   children
        Edward, Edward,
    And what wul ye leave to your bairns and your wife,
        Whan ye gang over the sea, O?"
45 "The warldes room⁴ late° them beg thrae° life,   let / through
        Mither, mither,
    The warldes room late them beg thrae life,
        For thame never mair wul I see, O."

"And what wul ye leave to your ain° mither dear,   own
50   Edward, Edward?
    And what wul ye leave to your ain mither dear,
        My dear son, now tell me, O?"
    "The curse of hell frae° me sal° ye bear,   from / shall
        Mither, mither,
55 The curse of hell frae me sal ye bear,
        Sic° counseils ye gave to me, O."   such

4. The world's space.

Barbara Allan[1]

It was in and about the Martinmas[2] time,
 When the green leaves were a-fallin',
That Sir John Graeme in the West Country
 Fell in love with Barbara Allan.

5 He sent his man down through the town
 To the place where she was dwellin':
"O haste and come to my master dear,
 Gin° ye be Barbara Allan."   *if*

O slowly, slowly rase° she up,   *rose*
10 To the place where he was lyin',
And when she drew the curtain by:
 "Young man, I think you're dyin'."

"O it's I'm sick, and very, very sick,
 And 'tis a' for Barbara Allan."
15 "O the better for me ye sal° never be,   *shall*
 Though your heart's blood were a-spillin'.

"O dinna ye mind,[3] young man," said she,
 "When ye the cups were fillin',
That ye made the healths gae° round and round, *go*
20 And slighted Barbara Allan?"

He turned his face unto the wall,
 And death with him was dealin':
"Adieu, adieu, my dear friends all,
 And be kind to Barbara Allan."

25 And slowly, slowly, rase she up,
 And slowly, slowly left him;
And sighing said she could not stay,
 Since death of life had reft° him.   *deprived*

She had not gane° a mile but twa,°   *gone / two*
30 When she heard the dead-bell knellin',
And every jow° that the dead-bell ga'ed[4]   *stroke*
 It cried, "Woe to Barbara Allan!"

"O mother, mother, make my bed,
 O make it soft and narrow:
35 Since my love died for me today,
 I'll die for him tomorrow."

---

1. Child, No. 84.
2. November 11.
3. Don't you remember.
4. I.e., made.

The Wife of Usher's Well[1]

There lived a wife at Usher's Well,
    And a wealthy wife was she;
She had three stout and stalwart sons,
    And sent them o'er the sea.

5 They hadna' been a week from her,
    A week but barely ane,°   *one*
When word came to the carlin° wife   *old*
    That her three sons were gane.°   *gone*

They hadna' been a week from her,
10   A week but barely three,
When word came to the carlin wife
    That her sons she'd never see.

"I wish the wind may never cease,
    Nor fashes° in the flood,   *disturbances*
15 Till my three sons come hame° to me, *home*
    In earthly flesh and blood."

It fell about the Martinmas,[2]
    When nights are lang and mirk,°   *dark*
The carlin wife's three sons came hame,
20   And their hats were o' the birk.[3]

It neither grew in sike° nor ditch,   *field*
    Nor yet in ony sheugh,°   *furrow*
But at the gates o' Paradise
    That birk grew fair eneugh.

25 "Blow up the fire, my maidens,
    Bring water from the well:
For a' my house shall feast this night,
    Since my three sons are well."

And she has made to them a bed,
30   She's made it large and wide,
And she's ta'en her mantle her about,
    Sat down at the bedside.

Up then crew the red, red cock,
    And up and crew the gray.
35 The eldest to the youngest said,
    " 'Tis time we were away."[4]

1. Child, No. 79.
2. November 11.
3. Birch: those returning from the dead were thought to wear vegetation on their heads.
4. Dead men must return to their graves at cockcrow.

The cock he hadna' crawed but once,
    And clapped his wings at a',
When the youngest to the eldest said,
₄₀   "Brother, we must awa'.°"   *away*

"The cock doth craw, the day doth daw,°   *dawn*
    The channerin'° worm doth chide: *fretting*
Gin° we be missed out o' our place,   *if*
    A sair pain we maun bide.⁵

₄₅ "Fare ye weel,° my mother dear,   *well*
    Fareweel to barn and byre.°   *cow house*
And fare ye weel, the bonny lass
    That kindles my mother's fire."

The Three Ravens[1]

There were three ravens sat on a tree,
    Down a down, hay down, hay down,
There were three ravens sat on a tree,
    With a down,
₅ There were three ravens sat on a tree,
They were as black as they might be,
    With a down, derry, derry, derry, down, down.

The one of them said to his mate,
"Where shall we our breakfast take?

₁₀ "Down in yonder green field
There lies a knight slain under his shield.

"His hounds they lie down at his feet,
So well they can their master keep.

"His hawks they fly so eagerly,°   *fiercely*
₁₅ There's no fowl° dare him come nigh."   *bird*

Down there comes a fallow° doe,   *red-brown*
As great with young as she might go.°   *walk*

She lift up his bloody head,
And kissed his wounds that were so red.

₂₀ She got him up upon her back,
And carried him to earthen lake.°   *pit*

She buried him before the prime;[2]
She was dead herself ere evensong time.

5. A sore pain we must abide.   2. The first hour of the morning.
1. Child, No. 26.

God send every gentleman
25 Such hawks, such hounds, and such a lemman.°   *mistress*

Bonny George Campbell[3]

High upon Highlands
   And low upon Tay,
Bonny George Campbell
   Rade° out on a day.   *rode*

5 Saddled and bridled
   And gallant rade he:
Hame° cam his guid horse,   *home*
   But never cam he.

Out cam his auld mither,
10   Greeting fu' sair,[4]
And out cam his bonny bride,
   Riving° her hair.   *tearing*

Saddled and bridled
   And booted rade he:
15 Toom° hame cam the saddle,   *empty*
   But never cam he.

"My meadow lies green,
   And my corn is unshorn,
My barn is to build,
20   And my babe is unborn."

Saddled and bridled
   And booted rade he;
Toom hame cam the saddle,
   But never cam he.

Sir Patrick Spens[1]

The king sits in Dumferline town,
   Drinking the blude-reid° wine: *blood-red*
"O whar will I get a guid sailor
   To sail this ship of mine?"

3. Child, No. 210. The form printed here is a composite, made up from several variant versions by the ballad- collector Motherwell. 4. Weeping full sore. 1. Child, No. 58.

5 Up and spak an eldern° knicht,   *ancient*
    Sat at the king's richt knee:
"Sir Patrick Spens is the best sailor
    That sails upon the sea."

The king has written a braid° letter   *broad*
10   And signed it wi' his hand,
And sent it to Sir Patrick Spens,
    Was walking on the sand.

The first line that Sir Patrick read,
    A loud lauch° lauched he;   *laugh*
15 The next line that Sir Patrick read,
    The tear blinded his ee.°   *eye*

"O wha° is this has done this deed,   *who*
    This ill deed done to me,
To send me out this time o' the year,
20   To sail upon the sea?

"Make haste, make haste, my mirry men all,
    Our guid ship sails the morn."
"O say na° sae,° my master dear,   *not / so*
    For I fear a deadly storm.

25 "Late late yestre'en I saw the new moon
    Wi' the auld° moon in her arm,   *old*
And I fear, I fear, my dear master,
    That we will come to harm."

O our Scots nobles were richt laith°   *loath*
30   To weet° their cork-heeled shoon,°   *wet / shoes*
But lang owre° a' the play were played   *ere*
    Their hats they swam aboon.°   *above*

O lang, lang may their ladies sit,
    Wi' their fans into their hand,
35 Or e'er they see Sir Patrick Spens
    Come sailing to the land.

O lang, lang may the ladies stand,
    Wi' their gold kembs° in their hair,   *combs*
Waiting for their ain° dear lords,   *own*
40   For they'll see thame na mair.°   *more*

Half o'er,[2] half o'er to Aberdour
    It's fifty fadom° deep,   *fathoms*
And there lies guid Sir Patrick Spens,
    Wi' the Scots lords at his feet.

2. Halfway over.

The Bonny Earl of Murray[1]

Ye Highlands and ye Lawlands,°   *Lowlands*
    O where have you been?
They have slain the Earl of Murray,
    And they laid him on the green.

5 "Now wae° be to thee, Huntly,[2]   *woe*
    And wherefore did you sae?°   *so*
I bade you bring him wi' you,
    But forbade you him to slay."

He was a braw° gallant,   *brave*
10   And he rid[3] at the ring;
And the bonny Earl of Murray,
    O he might have been a king.

He was a braw gallant,
    And he played at the ba';°   *ball*
15 And the bonny Earl of Murray
    Was the flower amang them a'.

He was a braw gallant,
    And he played at the glove;[4]
And the bonny Earl of Murray,
20   O he was the queen's love.

O lang will his lady
    Look o'er the Castle Down,
Ere she see the Earl of Murray
    Come sounding[5] through the town.

Thomas Rhymer[1]

True Thomas lay on Huntly bank;
    A ferly° he spied wi' his ee;°   *wonder / eye*
And there he saw a lady bright
    Come riding down by the Eildon Tree.[2]

5 Her shirt was o' the grass-green silk,
    Her mantle o' the velvet fine;
At ilka° tett° of her horse's mane   *every / braid*
    Hung fifty sil'er bells and nine.

---

1. Child, No. 181.
2. Huntly, who slew Murray in 1592, had been ordered by King James VI of Scotland (the speaker of this stanza) to arrest the earl.
3. Rode. "The ring" was a hanging ring which mounted knights tried to impale on their spears.

4. Either the goal in a race or else a lady's favor.
5. Blowing horns.
1. I e., Thomas the Minstrel. Child, No. 37.
2. Trees in folklore are often frequented by supernatural beings.

True Thomas he pulled off his cap
    And louted° low down to his knee: *bowed*
"All hail, thou mighty Queen of Heaven!
    For thy peer on earth I never did see."

"O no, O no, Thomas," she said,
    "That name does not belang to me;
I am but the Queen of fair Elfland,
    That am hither come to visit thee.

"Harp° and carp,° Thomas," she said,   *play / speak*
    "Harp and carp along wi' me;
And if ye dare to kiss my lips,
    Sure of your body I will be."

"Betide me weal, betide me woe,
    That weird° shall never daunten me."   *fate*
Sine° he has kissed her rosy lips,   *then*
    All underneath the Eildon Tree.

"Now ye maun° go wi' me," she said,   *must*
    "True Thomas, ye maun go wi' me;
And ye maun serve me seven years
    Through weal or woe, as may chance to be."

She mounted on her milk-white steed;
    She's ta'en True Thomas up behind;
And ay whene'er her bridle rung,
    The steed flew swifter than the wind.

O they rade° on and farther on;   *rode*
    The steed gaed° swifter than the wind,   *went*
Until they reached a desert wide,
    And living land was left behind.

"Light down, light down now, True Thomas,
    And lean your head upon my knee.
Abide and rest a little space,
    And I will show you ferlies three.

"O see ye not yon narrow road,
    So thick beset with thorns and briars?
That is the path of righteousness,
    Though after it but few inquires.

"And see ye not that braid,° braid road   *broad*
    That lies across that lily leven?[3]
That is the path of wickedness,
    Though some call it the road to heaven.

"And see not ye that bonny road
    That winds about the ferny brae?°   *hillside*

---

3. Probably "lawn."

That is the road to fair Elfland,
    Where thou and I this night maun gae.°   *go*

"But Thomas, ye maun hold your tongue,
    Whatever ye may hear or see;
55 For if you speak word in Elfenland,
    Ye'll ne'er get back to your ain° country."   *own*

O they rade on and farther on,
    And they waded through rivers aboon° the knee,   *above*
And they saw neither sun nor moon,
60   But they heard the roaring of the sea.

It was mirk,° mirk night, and there was nae stern-light,[4] *dark*
    And they waded through red blude to the knee,
For a' the blude that's shed on earth
    Rins° through the springs o' that country.   *runs*

65 Sine they came onto a garden green,
    And she pulled an apple frae° a tree.   *from*
"Take this for thy wages, True Thomas,
    It will give thee the tongue that never can lee."°   *lie*

"My tongue is mine ain," True Thomas said;
70   "A gudely° gift ye wad° gi'e to me!   *goodly / would*
I neither dought° to buy nor sell   *feared*
    At fair or tryst° where I may be.   *meeting place*

"I dought neither speak to prince or peer,
    Nor ask of grace frae fair lady."
75 "Now hold thy peace," the lady said,
    "For as I say, so must it be."

He has gotten a coat of the even° cloth,   *smooth*
    And a pair of shoes of velvet green;
And till seven years were gane and past,
80   True Thomas on earth was never seen.

Robin Hood and the Three Squires[1]

There are twelve months in all the year,
    As I hear many men say,
But the merriest month in all the year
    Is the merry month of May.

5 Now Robin Hood is to Nottingham gone,
    With a link-a-down and a-day,
And there he met a silly° old woman,   *poor, innocent*
    Was weeping on the way.

4. No starlight.   1. Child, No. 140.

"What news? what news, thou silly old woman?
    What news hast thou for me?"
Said she, "There's three squires in Nottingham town,
    Today is condemned to dee."°   *die*

"O have they parishes burnt?" he said,
    "Or have they ministers slain?
15 Or have they robbed any virgin,
    Or with other men's wives have lain?"

"They have no parishes burnt, good sir,
    Nor yet have ministers slain,
Nor have they robbed any virgin,
    Nor with other men's wives have lain."

"O what have they done?" said bold Robin Hood,
    "I pray thee tell to me."
"It's for slaying of the king's fallow° deer,   *brown-red*
    Bearing their longbows with thee."

25 "Dost thou not mind,° old woman," he said,   *remember*
    "Since thou made me sup and dine?
By the truth of my body," quoth bold Robin Hood,
    "You could not tell it in better time."
Now Robin Hood is to Nottingham gone,
30   *With a link-a-down and a-day,*
And there he met with a silly old palmer,[2]
    Was walking along the highway.

"What news? what news, thou silly old man?
    What news, I do thee pray?"
35 Said he, "Three squires in Nottingham town
    Are condemned to die this day."

"Come change thine apparel with me, old man,
    Come change thine apparel for mine.
Here is forty shillings in good silver,
40   Go drink it in beer or wine."

"O thine apparel is good," he said,
    "And mine is ragged and torn.
Wherever you go, wherever you ride,
    Laugh ne'er an old man to scorn."

45 "Come change thine apparel with me, old churl,
    Come change thine apparel with mine:
Here are twenty pieces of good broad gold,
    Go feast thy brethren with wine."

Then he put on the old man's hat,
50   It stood full high on the crown:
"The first bold bargain that I come at,
    It shall make thee come down."

---

2. A poor old palmer: a palmer was one who had made the pilgrimage to the Holy Land.

Then he put on the old man's cloak,
 Was patched black, blue, and red:
55 He thought it no shame all the day long
 To wear the bags of bread.

Then he put on the old man's breeks,°   *underbreeches*
 Was patched from ballup³ to side:
"By the truth of my body," bold Robin can° say,   *did*
60 "This man loved little pride."

Then he put on the old man's hose,°   *tights*
 Were patched from knee to wrist:
"By the truth of my body," said bold Robin Hood,
 "I'd laugh if I had any list."°   *desire*

65 Then he put on the old man's shoes,
 Were patched both beneath and aboon:°   *above*
Then Robin Hood swore a solemn oath,
 "It's good habit° that makes a man."   *clothing*

Now Robin Hood is to Nottingham gone,
70 *With a link-a-down and a-down,*
And there he met with the proud sheriff,
 Was walking along the town.

"O Christ you save, O sheriff," he said,
 "O Christ you save and see:
75 And what will you give to a silly old man
 Today will your hangman be?"

"Some suits, some suits," the sheriff he said,
 "Some suits I'll give to thee;
Some suits, some suits, and pence thirteen,
80 Today's a hangman's fee."

Then Robin he turns him round about,
 And jumps from stock° to stone: *stump*
"By the truth of my body," the sheriff he said,
 "That's well jumped, thou nimble old man."

85 "I was ne'er a hangman in all my life,
 Nor yet intends to trade.
But cursed be he," said bold Robin,
 "That first a hangman was made.

"I've a bag for meal, and a bag for malt,
90 And a bag for barley and corn,
A bag for bread, and a bag for beef,
 And a bag for my little small horn.

"I have a horn in my pocket:
 I got it from Robin Hood;
95 And still when I set it to my mouth,
 For thee it blows little good."

3. I.e., center.

"O wind° thy horn, thou proud fellow: *blow*
 Of thee I have no doubt;°   *fear*
I wish that thou give such a blast
100 Till both thy eyes fall out."

The first loud blast that he did blow,
 He blew both loud and shrill,
A hundred and fifty of Robin Hood's men
 Came riding over the hill.

105 The next loud blast that he did give,
 He blew both loud and amain,
And quickly sixty of Robin Hood's men
 Came shining[4] over the plain.

"O who are those," the sheriff he said,
110 "Come tripping over the lea?"°   *meadow*
"They're my attendants," brave Robin did say,
 "They'll pay a visit to thee."

They took the gallows from the slack,°   *hollow*
 They set it in the glen;
115 They hanged the proud sheriff on that,
 Released their own three men.

St. Steven and King Herod[1]

Saint Steven was a clerk
 In King Herodes hall,
And served him of bread and cloth
 As every king befall.[2]

5 Steven out of kitchen came
 With boar's head on hand;
He saw a star was fair and bright
 Over Bedlem° stand.   *Bethlehem*

He cast adown the boar's head
10 And went into the hall:
"I forsake thee, King Herodes,
 And thy works all.

"I forsake thee, King Herodes,
 And thy works all:
15 There is a child in Bedlem born
 Is better than we all."

"What aileth thee, Steven?
 What is thee befall?
Lacketh thee either meat or drink
20 In King Herodes hall?"

---

4. I.e., making a brave show.   2. As is appropriate to every king.
1. Child, No. 22.

"Lacketh me neither meat ne drink
    In King Herodes hall:
There is a child in Bedlem born
    Is better than we all."

25 "What aileth thee, Steven?
    Art thou wood, or ginnest weede?[3]
Lacketh thee either gold or fee°   *property*
    Or any rich weed?"°   *clothing*

"Lacketh me neither gold ne fee
30   Ne none rich weed:
There is a child in Bedlem born
    Shall help us at our need."

"That is also° sooth,° Steven,   *as / true*
    Also sooth, ywis,°   *indeed*
35 As this capon crow shal
    That lith° here in my dish."   *lies*

That word was not so soon said,
    That word in that hall,
The capon crew *Christus natus est*[4]
40   Among the lords all.

"Riseth up, my tormentors,
    By two and all by one,
And leadeth Steven out of this town,
    And stoneth him with stone."

45 Tooken they Steven,
    And stoned him in the way;
And therefore is his even[5]
    Christ's own day.

3. Art thou insane or beginning to go   4. Christ is born.
mad?   5. Eve: the day before his feast day.

SIR THOMAS MALORY

(ca. 1405–1471)

1451:   First of a long series of arrests and imprison-
               ments.
ca. 1469–70:   *Morte Darthur* completed in prison.
1485:   *Morte Darthur* printed by William Caxton.

The little that we know of Malory (and that the Malory discussed here was
indeed the Malory who wrote the *Morte Darthur* is an assumption that has
recently been challenged severely though by no means fatally) suggests a
man of violent temperament much given to lawless action. He seems to

have been a respectable enough person in his youth, but in 1451 he got into difficulties with the law that lasted the rest of his life. In that year he was arrested in order to prevent his doing injury—presumably further injury—to a priory in Lincolnshire, and shortly thereafter he was accused of a number of criminal acts. These included escaping from prison after his first arrest, twice breaking into and plundering the Abbey of Coombe, extorting money from various persons, and committing rape. Malory pleaded innocent of all charges, and it is indeed possible that he was less guilty of (or had more provocation for) the crimes than the records make it appear. The years of the Wars of the Roses were violent ones, when a supporter of the party out of power was apt to be subjected to much persecution by the ruling group; such a man might at times feel himself justified in taking the law into his own hands in order to recover what had wrongfully been taken from him. But one suspects that Malory took the law into his own hands with unnecessary enthusiasm.

How much time Malory passed in prison is not known, but he was surely a prisoner in 1468 after he had supported an unsuccessful Lancastrian revolt against the Yorkist king, Edward IV, who specifically excluded Malory from two amnesties granted to the Lancastrians. It was probably in prison that he became engaged on the *Morte Darthur;* he was still in prison when he completed it, and may have died there. The book was printed (and edited) in 1485 by William Caxton, the first English printer. A manuscript of it that has recently come to light helps us to a better text than Caxton's.

Arthurian romance, of which Malory's book is a compilation, is a body of highly diverse narrative materials which originated at various times among various peoples and which only gradually became associated with the name of Arthur. Arthur himself was probably a British or Roman-British king who resisted the Anglo-Saxon invasions of England in the 6th century, but his historical reality is less important than the legendary role he played as the great figure around whom the medieval ideal of chivalry flourished. At its simplest, chivalry is the code that governs the actions of the knight-adventurer who rides out in search of wrongs that he may right—typically in search of ladies whom he may rescue from monsters, churls, and wicked (non-Arthurian) knights. The ideal was invented and given a local habitation in the brilliantly imaginative and idealistic 12th century. History had, of course, never witnessed such knights, such ladies, nor such a landscape as that on which their adventures took place, and when chivalry was first invented it was already placed in the past. Man's urge to devise an idealized past seems to be recurrent, for the Camelot of Arthur has its counterpart in the Sherwood Forest of Robin Hood and in the American West. All three of these fictions have the same ideal: that of maintaining order in an essentially lawless land by the efforts of the individual, who fights for the right against seemingly overwhelming odds. Naïve as the practice of this ideal may seem in the Arthurian fiction, the ideal itself has made an important contribution to civilization—though if one imitates literally the Arthurian practice of enforcing the right by violence, as Malory's life suggests that he did, one will find oneself not maintaining order, but disrupting it.

The Arthurian milieu attracted to itself all sorts of diverse motifs, such as the remnants of primitive pagan religious rites, heavily moralized Christianity, an elaborate and in general flagrantly immoral code of romantic love, and others equally miscellaneous. In 13th-century France the amorphous Arthurian material was given a kind of order in a series of prose narratives. Long and often rather vaguely told, these formed the chief material which Malory further edited and ordered while translating it into English.

His book is attractive, however, not only because it is the best and most complete treatment of the story of Arthur and his knights, but also because it is one of the greatest pieces of prose in English. Malory was the first English writer to make prose as sensitive an instrument of narrative as English poetry had always been. One has only to turn from a page of Chaucer's prose to a page of Malory's to be struck by the naturalness and lack of self-consciousness of the later writer. Indeed, Malory achieves in his prose that wonderful impression of simplicity that Chaucer achieves only in his poetry. No matter how extravagant the adventure Malory is recounting, he always manages to give it a hard base of realism. He is in particular a master of naturalistic dialogue, with which he keeps his narrative close to earth. And both he and the majority of his characters are masters of understatement who express themselves, in moments of great emotional tension, with a bare minimum of words. The result is highly provocative to the reader's imagination, which is made, in a sense, to do the writer's work for him. This appeal to the reader's creative imagination probably explains why the *Morte Darthur* brings forth such widely differing responses from its readers, who agree, perhaps, only in their affection for the work.

"The Death of Arthur"—the incident that gives the book its title, though the book itself concerns the whole life of Arthur—is one of Malory's finest passages, and the one on which Tennyson based a famous *Idyll*. Largely at the insistence of his nephew Gawain, Arthur has been in France, futilely besieging his friend Lancelot in a halfhearted attempt to punish him for having been Queen Guinevere's lover. Word comes to the King that his bastard son Mordred has seized the kingdom, and Arthur leads his forces back to England. Mordred attacks them upon their landing, and Gawain is mortally wounded and dies, though not before he has repented for having insisted that Arthur fight Lancelot and has written Lancelot to come to the aid of his former lord.

From Morte Darthur[1]
[*The Death of Arthur*]

So upon Trinity Sunday at night King Arthur dreamed a wonderful dream, and in his dream him seemed[2] that he saw upon a chafflet a chair, and the chair was fast to a wheel, and thereupon sat King Arthur in the richest cloth of gold that might be made.

1. The selection here given is from the section of the book that Caxton called Book XXI, Chaps. 3–7, with omissions. The text has been based on the Winchester MS., with some readings introduced from the Caxton edition; spelling has been modernized and modern punctuation added.
2. It seemed to him. "Chafflet": scaffold.

And the King thought there was under him, far from him, an hideous deep black water, and therein was all manner of serpents, and worms, and wild beasts, foul and horrible. And suddenly the King thought that the wheel turned upside down, and he fell among the serpents, and every beast took him by a limb. And then the King cried as he lay in his bed, "Help, help!"

And then knights, squires, and yeomen awaked the king, and then he was so amazed that he wist[3] not where he was. And then so he awaked[4] until it was nigh day, and then he fell on slumbering again, not sleeping nor thoroughly waking. So the King seemed[5] verily that there came Sir Gawain unto him with a number of fair ladies with him. So when King Arthur saw him, he said, "Welcome, my sister's son. I weened ye had been dead. And now I see thee on-live, much am I beholden unto Almighty Jesu. Ah, fair nephew and my sister's son, what been these ladies that hither be come with you?"

"Sir," said Sir Gawain, "all these be ladies for whom I have foughten for when I was man living. And all these are tho[6] that I did battle for in righteous quarrels, and God hath given them that grace, at their great prayer, because I did battle for them for their right, that they should bring me hither unto you. Thus much hath given me leave God, for to warn you of your death. For and ye fight as tomorn[7] with Sir Mordred, as ye both have assigned,[8] doubt ye not ye must be slain, and the most party of your people on both parties. And for the great grace and goodness that Almighty Jesu hath unto you, and for pity of you and many mo[9] other good men there shall be slain, God hath sent me to you of his special grace to give you warning that in no wise ye do battle as tomorn, but that ye take a treatise[1] for a month-day. And proffer you largely,[2] so that tomorn ye put in a delay. For within a month shall come Sir Lancelot with all his noble knights and rescue you worshipfully and slay Sir Mordred and all that ever will hold with him."

Then Sir Gawain and all the ladies vanished. And anon the King called upon his knights, squires, and yeomen, and charged them wightly[3] to fetch his noble lords and wise bishops unto him. And when they were come the King told them of his avision,[4] that Sir Gawain had told him and warned him that, and he fought on the morn, he should be slain. Then the King commanded Sir Lucan the Butler[5] and his brother Sir Bedivere the Bold, with two bish-

3. Knew.
4. Lay awake.
5. It seemed to the King.
6. Those.
7. If you fight tomorrow.
8. Decided.
9. More. "There": i.e., who there.
1. Treaty, truce. "For a month-day":
for a month from today.
2. Make generous offers.
3. Quickly.
4. Dream.
5. "Butler" here is probably only a title of high rank, although it was originally used to designate the officer who had charge of wine for the king's table.

ops with them, and charged them in any wise to take a treatise for a month-day with Sir Mordred. "And spare not: proffer him lands and goods as much as ye think reasonable."

So then they departed and came to Sir Mordred where he had a grim host of an hundred thousand, and there they entreated[6] Sir Mordred long time. And at the last Sir Mordred was agreed for to have Cornwall and Kent by King Arthur's days,[7] and after that, all England, after the days of King Arthur.

Then were they condescended[8] that King Arthur and Sir Mordred should meet betwixt both their hosts, and everich[9] of them should bring fourteen persons. And so they came with this word unto Arthur. Then said he, "I am glad that this is done," and so he went into the field.

And when King Arthur should depart, he warned all his host that, and they see any sword drawn, "Look ye come on fiercely and slay that traitor Sir Mordred, for I in no wise trust him." In like wise Sir Mordred warned his host that "And ye see any manner of sword drawn, look that ye come on fiercely, and so slay all that ever before you standeth, for in no wise I will not trust for this treatise." And in the same wise said Sir Mordred unto his host, "For I know well my father will be avenged upon me."

And so they met as their pointment[1] was and were agreed and accorded thoroughly. And wine was fetched and they drank together. Right so came an adder out of a little heath-bush, and it stung a knight in the foot. And so when the knight felt him so stung, he looked down and saw the adder. And anon he drew his sword to slay the adder, and thought[2] none other harm. And when the host on both parties saw that sword drawn, then they blew beams,[3] trumpets, and horns, and shouted grimly. And so both hosts dressed them[4] together. And King Arthur took his horse and said, "Alas, this unhappy day!" and so rode to his party, and Sir Mordred in like wise.

And never since was there never seen a more dolefuller battle in no Christian land, for there was but rushing and riding, foining[5] and striking; and many a grim word was there spoken of either to other, and many a deadly stroke. But ever King Arthur rode throughout the battle[6] of Sir Mordred many times and did full nobly, as a noble king should do, and at all times he fainted never. And Sir Mordred did his devoir[7] that day and put himself in great peril.

And thus they fought all the long day, and never stinted[8] till the noble knights were laid to the cold earth. And ever they fought still

---

6. Dealt with.
7. During King Arthur's lifetime.
8. Agreed.
9. Each.
1. Arrangement.
2. Meant.

3. Trumpets.
4. Prepared to come.
5. Lunging.
6. Battalion.
7. Knightly duty.
8. Stopped.

till it was near night, and by then was there an hundred thousand laid dead upon the down. Then was King Arthur wood-wroth[9] out of measure when he saw his people so slain from him. And so he looked about him and could see no mo[1] of all his host, and good knights left no mo on-live, but two knights: the t'one[2] was Sir Lucan the Butler and [the other] his brother Sir Bedivere. And yet they were full sore wounded.

"Jesu, mercy," said the King, "where are all my noble knights become?[3] Alas that ever I should see this doleful day! For now," said King Arthur, "I am come to mine end. But would to God," said he, "that I wist[4] now where were that traitor Sir Mordred that has caused all this mischief."

Then King Arthur looked about and was ware where stood Sir Mordred leaning upon his sword among a great heap of dead men.

"Now give me my spear," said King Arthur unto Sir Lucan, "for yonder I have espied the traitor that all this woe hath wrought."

"Sir, let him be," said Sir Lucan, "for he is unhappy.[5] And if ye pass this unhappy day ye shall be right well revenged upon him. And, good lord, remember ye of your night's dream, and what the spirit of Sir Gawain told you tonight, and yet God of his great goodness hath preserved you hitherto. And for God's sake, my lord, leave off by this,[6] for, blessed be God, ye have won the field: for yet we been here three on-live, and with Sir Mordred is not one on-live. And therefore if ye leave off now, this wicked day of destiny is past."

"Now, tide[7] me death, tide me life," said the King, "now I see him yonder alone, he shall never escape mine hands. For at a better avail[8] shall I never have him."

"God speed you well!" said Sir Bedivere.

Then the King got his spear in both his hands and ran toward Sir Mordred, crying and saying, "Traitor, now is thy deathday come!"

And when Sir Mordred saw King Arthur he ran until him with his sword drawn in his hand, and there King Arthur smote Sir Mordred under the shield, with a foin[9] of his spear, throughout the body more than a fathom.[1] And when Sir Mordred felt that he had his death's wound, he thrust himself with the might that he had up to the burr[2] of King Arthur's spear, and right so he smote his father King Arthur with his sword holden in both his hands, upon the side of the head, that the sword pierced the helmet and

---

9. Mad with rage.
1. Others.
2. That one, i.e., the first.
3. What has become of all my noble knights?
4. Knew.
5. I.e., unlucky for you.

6. I.e., with this much accomplished.
7. Betide.
8. Advantage.
9. Thrust.
1. Six feet.
2. Hand guard.

the tay[3] of the brain. And therewith Sir Mordred dashed down stark dead to the earth.

And noble King Arthur fell in a swough[4] to the earth, and there he swooned oftentimes, and Sir Lucan and Sir Bedivere ofttimes heaved him up. And so, weakly betwixt them, they led him to a little chapel not far from the seaside, and when the King was there, him thought him reasonably eased. Then heard they people cry in the field. "Now go thou, Sir Lucan," said the King, "and do me to wit[5] what betokens that noise in the field."

So Sir Lucan departed, for he was grievously wounded in many places. And so as he yede[6] he saw and harkened by the moonlight how that pillers[7] and robbers were come into the field to pill and to rob many a full noble knight of brooches and bees[8] and of many a good ring and many a rich jewel. And who that were not dead all out[9] there they slew them for their harness and their riches. When Sir Lucan understood this work, he came to the King as soon as he might and told him all what he had heard and seen. "Therefore by my read,"[1] said Sir Lucan, "it is best that we bring you to some town."

"I would it were so," said the King, "but I may not stand, my head works[2] so. Ah, Sir Lancelot," said King Arthur, "this day have I sore missed thee. And alas that ever I was against thee, for now have I my death, whereof Sir Gawain me warned in my dream."

Then Sir Lucan took up the King the t'one party[3] and Sir Bedivere the other party; and in the lifting up the King swooned and in the lifting Sir Lucan fell in a swoon that part of his guts fell out of his body, and therewith the noble knight's heart burst. And when the King awoke he beheld Sir Lucan how he lay foaming at the mouth and part of his guts lay at his feet.

"Alas," said the King, "this is to me a full heavy[4] sight to see this noble duke so die for my sake, for he would have holpen[5] me that had more need of help than I. Alas that he would not complain him for[6] his heart was so set to help me. Now Jesu have mercy upon his soul."

Then Sir Bedivere wept for the death of his brother.

"Now leave this mourning and weeping, gentle knight," said the King, "for all this will not avail me. For wit thou well, and[7] I might live myself, the death of Sir Lucan would grieve me evermore. But my time passeth on fast," said the King. "Therefore," said King

---

3. Edge.
4. Swoon.
5. Let me know.
6. Walked.
7. Plunderers.
8. Bracelets.
9. Entirely. "Harness": armor.

1. Advice.
2. Aches.
3. On one side.
4. Sorrowful.
5. Helped.
6. Because.
7. If.

Arthur unto Sir Bedivere, "take thou here Excalibur[8] my good sword and go with it to yonder water's side; and when thou comest there I charge thee throw my sword in that water and come again and tell me what thou sawest there."

"My lord," said Sir Bedivere, "your commandment shall be done, and [I shall] lightly[9] bring you word again."

So Sir Bedivere departed. And by the way he beheld that noble sword, that the pommel[1] and the haft was all precious stones. And then he said to himself, "If I throw this rich sword in the water, thereof shall never come good, but harm and loss." And then Sir Bedivere hid Excalibur under a tree. And so, as soon as he might, he came again unto the King and said he had been at the water and had thrown the sword into the water.

"What saw thou there?" said the King.

"Sir," he said, "I saw nothing but waves and winds."

"That is untruly said of thee," said the King. "And therefore go thou lightly again and do my commandment; as thou art to me lief[2] and dear, spare not, but throw it in."

Then Sir Bedivere returned again and took the sword in his hand. And yet him thought[3] sin and shame to throw away that noble sword. And so eft[4] he hid the sword and returned again and told the King that he had been at the water and done his commandment.

"What sawest thou there?" said the King.

"Sir," he said, "I saw nothing but waters wap and waves wan."[5]

"Ah, traitor unto me and untrue," said King Arthur, "now hast thou betrayed me twice. Who would have weened that thou that hast been to me so lief and dear, and thou art named a noble knight, and would betray me for the riches of this sword. But now go again lightly, for thy long tarrying putteth me in great jeopardy of my life, for I have taken cold. And but if thou do now as I bid thee, if ever I may see thee I shall slay thee mine[6] own hands, for thou wouldest for my rich sword see me dead."

Then Sir Bedivere departed and went to the sword and lightly took it up, and so he went to the water's side; and there he bound the girdle[7] about the hilts, and threw the sword as far into the water as he might. And there came an arm and an hand above the water and took it and clutched it, and shook it thrice and brandished; and then vanished away the hand with the sword into the

---

8. The sword which Arthur had received as a young man from the Lady of the Lake; it is presumably she who catches it when Bedivere finally throws it into the water.
9. Quickly.
1. Rounded knob on the hilt; "haft": handle.

2. Beloved.
3. It seemed to him.
4. Again.
5. The phrase seems to mean "waters wash the shore and waves grow dark."
6. I.e., with mine.
7. Sword belt.

water. So Sir Bedivere came again to the King and told him what he saw.

"Alas," said the King, "help me hence, for I dread me I have tarried overlong."

Then Sir Bedivere took the King upon his back and so went with him to that water's side. And when they were at the water's side, even fast[8] by the bank hoved[9] a little barge with many fair ladies in it; and among them all was a queen; and all they had black hoods, and all they wept and shrieked when they saw King Arthur.

"Now put me into that barge," said the King; and so he did softly. And there received him three ladies with great mourning, and so they set them[1] down. And in one of their laps King Arthur laid his head, and then the queen said, "Ah, my dear brother, why have ye tarried so long from me? Alas, this wound on your head hath caught overmuch cold." And anon they rowed fromward the land, and Sir Bedivere beheld all tho ladies go froward him.

Then Sir Bedivere cried and said, "Ah, my lord Arthur, what shall become of me, now ye go from me and leave me here alone among mine enemies?"

"Comfort thyself," said the King, "and do as well as thou mayest, for in me is no trust for to trust in. For I must into the vale of Avilion[2] to heal me of my grievous wound. And if thou hear nevermore of me, pray for my soul."

But ever the queen and ladies wept and shrieked that it was pity to hear. And as soon as Sir Bedivere had lost the sight of the barge he wept and wailed and so took[3] the forest, and went all that night. And in the morning he was ware betwixt two holts hoar[4] of a chapel and an hermitage.[5] * * *

Thus of Arthur I find no more written in books that been authorized,[6] neither more of the very certainty of his death heard I never read,[7] but thus was he led away in a ship wherein were three queens: that one was King Arthur's sister, Queen Morgan la Fée, the t'other[8] was the Queen of North Wales, and the third was the Queen of the Waste Lands. * * *

Now more of the death of King Arthur could I never find but that these ladies brought him to his burials,[9] and such one was buried there that the hermit bore witness that sometime was Bishop

---

8. Close.
9. Waited.
1. I.e., they sat.
2. A legendary island, sometimes identified with the earthly paradise.
3. Took to. "Went": walked.
4. Ancient copses.
5. In the passage here omitted, Sir Bedivere meets the former Bishop of Canterbury, now a hermit, who describes how on the previous night a company of ladies had brought to the chapel a dead body, asking that it be buried. Sir Bedivere exclaims that the dead man must have been King Arthur, and vows to spend the rest of his life there in the chapel as a hermit.
6. That have authority.
7. Tell.
8. The second.
9. Grave.

360 · *William Caxton* [*Introduction*

of Canterbury.[1] But yet the hermit knew not in certain that he was verily the body of King Arthur, for this tale Sir Bedivere, a Knight of the Table Round, made it to be written. Yet some men say in many parts of England that King Arthur is not dead, but had by the will of our Lord Jesu into another place. And men say that he shall come again and he shall win the Holy Cross. Yet I will not say that it shall be so, but rather I will say, Here in this world he changed his life. And many men say that there is written upon his tomb this verse: *Hic iacet Arthurus, rex quondam, rexque futurus.*[2]

1469–70   1485

1. Of whom the hermit, who was formerly Bishop of Canterbury, bore witness.

2. "Here lies Arthur, who was once king and king will be again."

WILLIAM CAXTON

(ca. 1422–1491)

In his early years Caxton was a prosperous merchant who traded mostly in the low countries. In 1470, at the command of his patroness, Margaret of Burgundy, he completed a translation into English of the French *Recueil des Histoires de Troie* (i.e., collection of the stories of Troy), which he had begun earlier in his leisure time. This work, circulated in manuscript, became so popular that the demand for it exceeded the number of copies that could be readily produced by scribes. Caxton thereupon went to Cologne, where he studied the newly developed art of printing, and subsequently set up a press at Bruges in Belgium. In 1475 he printed his translation of the Troy book (the first book printed in English), and in the next year returned to England, where he established England's first printing press, in London. Among his first publications were Chaucer's *Canterbury Tales* (1478; second edition about 1484). In 1485 he printed Malory's work, with the Preface reproduced here.

A shrewd publisher and practiced writer, as well as a pioneer printer, Caxton gives a most astute and inviting account of Malory's work and the personage after whom it was named. Caxton himself evidently put small credence in the historicity of Arthur, but by appearing—in all modesty—to have been overwhelmed by the faith that eminent people had in Arthur's existence, as well as by the survival of certain relics that seemed to support such faith, he encourages the reader to lay aside his own skepticism (although the warning remains: "ye are at your liberty" to accept or reject the truth of Malory's narrative). In describing the work itself, Caxton is careful to emphasize its exemplary qualities, "the noble acts of chivalry" that knights performed in the old days, from which one may learn virtuous conduct; but he is also careful not to suppress the fact—though he presents it in tantalizing subordination—that the book contains much that is exemplary only in the negative sense: "cowardice, murder, hate, * * * and sin," which for some might, perhaps, enhance the book's appeal.

Preface to *Morte Darthur*

After that I had accomplished and finished divers histories as well of contemplation as of other historial and worldly acts of great conquerors and princes, and also certain books of ensamples [1] and doctrine, many noble and divers gentlemen of this royalme of England camen and demanded me many and ofttimes wherefore that I have not do [2] made and imprint the noble history of the Saint Grail and of the most renommed [3] Christian king, first and chief of the three best Christian, and worthy,[4] king Arthur, which ought most to be remembered among us Englishmen tofore all other Christian kings.

For it is notoirly [5] known through the universal world that there been nine worthy and the best that ever were, that is to wit, three Paynims,[6] three Jews, and three Christian men. As for the Paynims, they were tofore the Incarnation of Christ, which were named, the first Hector of Troy, of whom th'istory is common both in ballad and in prose, the second Alexander the Great, and the third Julius Caesar, Emperor of Rome, of whom th'istories been well known and had.[7] And as for the three which also were tofore th'Incarnation of our Lord, of whom the first was Duke Joshua which brought the children of Israel into the land of behest,[8] the second David, king of Jerusalem, and the third Judas Maccabeus, of these three the Bible rehearseth all their noble histories and acts. And sith [9] the said Incarnation have been three noble Christian men stalled [1] and admitted through the universal world into the number of the nine best and worthy of whom was first the noble Arthur, whose noble acts I purpose to write in this present book here following. The second was Charlemagne, or Charles the Great, of whom th'istory is had in many places, both in French and English; and the third and last was Godefroy of Bouillon, of whose acts and life I made a book unto th'excellent prince and king of noble memory, King Edward the Fourth.

The said noble gentlemen instantly required [2] me t'imprint th'istory of the said noble king and conqueror king Arthur and of his knights, with th'istory of the Saint Grail and of the death and end-

1. Exemplary stories.
2. Caused to be.
3. Renowned.
4. I.e., one of the Nine Worthies
5. Notoriously.
6. Pagans.

7. Available.
8. Promised Land.
9. Since.
1. Assigned.
2. Urgently requested.

ing of the said Arthur, affirming that I ought rather t'imprint his acts and noble feats than of Godefroy of Bouillon or any of the other eight, considering that he was a man born within this royalme and king and emperor of the same, and that there been in French divers and many noble volumes of his acts, and also of his knights.

To whom I answered that divers men hold opinion that there was no such Arthur and that all such books as been made of him been but feigned and fables, because that some chronicles make of him no mention ne remember him nothing, ne of his knights.

Whereto they answered, and one in special said, that in him that should say or think that there was never such a king called Arthur might well be aretted [3] great folly and blindness, for he said that there were many evidences of the contrary. First, ye may see his sepulture [4] in the monastery of Glastonbury; and also in *Polychronicon*,[5] in the fifth book, the sixth chapter, and in the seventh book, the twenty-third chapter, where his body was buried, and after founden and translated [6] into the said monastery. Ye shall see also in th'istory of Bochas,[7] in his book *De Casu Principum*, part of his noble acts, and also of his fall. Also Galfridus, in his British book,[8] recounteth his life. And in divers places of England many remembrances been yet of him and shall remain perpetually, and also of his knights: first, in the abbey of Westminster, at Saint Edward's shrine, remaineth the print of his seal in red wax, closed in beryl, in which is written PATRICIUS ARTHURUS BRITANNIE GALLIE GERMANIE DACIE IMPERATOR; [9] item, in the castle of Dover ye may see Gawain's skull and Cradok's mantle; at Winchester, the Round Table; in other places Lancelot's sword and many other things.

Then, all these things considered, there can no man reasonably gainsay but there was a king of this land named Arthur. For in all places, Christian and heathen, he is reputed and taken for one of the nine worthy, and the first of the three Christian men. And also he is more spoken of beyond the sea, mo [1] books made of his noble acts, than there be in England; as well in Dutch, Italian, Spanish, and Greekish, as in French. And yet of record remain in witness of him in Wales, in the town of Camelot, the great stones and marvelous works of iron lying under the ground, and royal vaults, which divers now living hath seen. Wherefore it is a marvel why he is no

---

3. Imputed.
4. Burial place.
5. A Latin history by Ranulph Higden (d. 1364), an English translation of which was printed by Caxton in 1482.
6. Carried
7. The Italian Giovanni Boccaccio (d. 1375), whose book *Concerning the Falls of Illustrious Men* ("Concerning the Fall of Princes," according to Caxton) was a favorite of the later Middle Ages.

8. Geoffrey of Monmouth, whose *History of the Kings of Britain* (ca. 1136), begins with the story of the founding of Britain by Brutus, Aeneas' great-grandson, who was believed to have given his name to Britain: hence Caxton's "Brutish."
9. The Noble Arthur, Emperor of Britain, Gaul, Germany, and Dacia.
1. More.

more renommed in his own country, save only it accordeth to the word of God, which saith that no man is accept for a prophet in his own country.

Then, all these things foresaid alleged,[2] I could not well deny but that there was such a noble king named Arthur, and reputed one of the nine worthy, and first and chief of the Christian men. And many noble volumes be made of him and of his noble knights in French, which I have seen and read beyond the sea, which been not had in our maternal tongue. But in Welsh been many, and also in French, and some in English, but nowhere nigh all. Wherefore, such as have late been drawn out briefly into English, I have, after the simple cunning that God hath sent to me, under the favor and correction of all noble lords and gentlemen, emprised[3] to imprint a book of the noble histories of the said king Arthur and of certain of his knights, after a copy unto me delivered, which copy sir Thomas Malory did take out of certain books of French and reduced it into English.

And I, according to my copy, have done set it[4] in imprint to the intent that noble men may see and learn the noble acts of chivalry, the gentle and virtuous deeds that some knights used in tho[5] days, by which they came to honor, and how they that were vicious were punished and oft put to shame and rebuke; humbly beseeching all noble lords and ladies with all other estates, of what estate or degree they been of, that shall see and read in this said book and work, that they take the good and honest acts in their remembrance, and to follow the same; wherein they shall find many joyous and pleasant histories and noble and renommed acts of humanity, gentleness, and chivalries. For herein may be seen noble chivalry, courtesy, humanity, friendliness, hardiness, love, friendship, cowardice, murder, hate, virtue, and sin. Do after the good and leave the evil, and it shall bring you to good fame and renommee.[6]

And for to pass the time this book shall be pleasant to read in, but for to give faith and belief that all is true that is contained herein, ye be at your liberty. But all is written for our doctrine, and for to beware that we fall not to vice ne sin, but t'exercise and follow virtue, by which we may come and attain to good fame and renommee in this life, and after this short and transitory life to come unto everlasting bliss in heaven; the which He grant us that reigneth in heaven, the Blessed Trinity. AMEN.

Then, to proceed forth in this said book, which I direct unto all noble princes, lords and ladies, gentlemen or gentlewomen, that desire to read or hear read of the noble and joyous history of the great conqueror and excellent king, king Arthur, sometime king of this

2. Having been cited.   5. Those.
3. Undertaken.   6. Renown.
4. Have caused it to be set.

noble royalme then called Britain, I, William Caxton, simple person, present this book following which I have emprised t'imprint: and treateth of the noble acts, feats of arms of chivalry, prowess, hardiness, humanity, love, courtesy, and very [7] gentleness, with many wonderful histories and adventures.

1485

7. True.

Topic in Medieval Literature

MEDIEVAL ATTITUDES TOWARD
LIFE ON EARTH

Unto the woman he said, I will greatly multiply thy sorrow and thy conception; in sorrow thou shalt bring forth children; and thy desire shall be to thy husband, and he shall rule over thee.

And unto Adam he said, Because thou hast hearkened unto the voice of thy wife, and hast eaten of the tree, of which I commanded thee, saying, Thou shalt not eat of it: cursed is the ground for thy sake; in sorrow shalt thou eat of it all the days of thy life;

Thorns also and thistles shall it bring forth to thee; and thou shalt eat the herb of the field:

In the sweat of thy face shalt thou eat bread, till thou return unto the ground; for out of it wast thou taken: for dust thou art, and unto dust shalt thou return.

Genesis iii.16–19

The words with which the Lord God cursed Adam and Eve after their transgression formed, for many articulate men in the Middle Ages, an accurate image of human life: something which was wretched because the Creator had made it so. Such thinkers believed that man had to acknowledge the wretchedness of his life and feel contempt for the world in which he lived in order to attain spiritual salvation. Christianity, by teaching that eternal life in heaven is the reward for right behavior on earth, exalts the values of the future life over those of the present. Many medieval men, characteristically extremist, tended to make of the relative an absolute: if the life to come is perfectly good, then it seemed logical to suppose that the present life must be perfectly bad, so that even what seems good about it must, in fact, be evil. Had not Christ promised the Kingdom of Heaven to those who were most wretched on earth, and warned that a rich man would have great difficulty getting into heaven? Therefore it seemed to many a fair inference that those who were not miserable forfeited the Kingdom of Heaven. Thus by the Old Testament and the New, wretchedness seemed confirmed as the inevitable and proper condition for mankind.

But even in an era when life was—from the modern point of view—wretched for most men in fact as well as in theory, the average man was reluctant to stop pursuing whatever apparent goods life had to offer. It thus became the responsibility of his spiritual and moral mentors to try to persuade him to scorn the present while making sure of the future. The title of a late 12th-century tract by Pope Innocent III—*Contempt for the World; or, The Wretchedness of the Human Condition*—would serve to describe a very large amount of medieval writing designed to give the reader a correct set of values. Characteristic literary expressions of this doctrine, as well as modifications and contradictions of it, are given in the selections below.

Contempt for the World

The noblest statement of the proposition that life's goods are unreal fails to invoke the Christian doctrine of a life to come in order to validate its argument, although its author seems to have been a Christian: this is Boethius' *Consolation of Philosophy*, composed about 523 while the writer, an eminent Roman citizen, was in prison awaiting execution for "crimes against the state"—actually for having upheld older Roman political ideals against the reigning emperor, Theodoric the Ostrogoth. According to Boethius' stoic teaching, the man who refuses to commit himself to life's seeming goods makes himself spiritually invulnerable to its ills. Although this triumph over the world is a spiritual one, it takes place while man is alive and in the world. Boethius envisages neither future reward nor future punishment. More orthodox Christian writers could, of course, stress the surpassing importance of the world to come in their disparagement of this world. Yet a surprising number of them chose not to do so, but instead took a gloomy satisfaction in reminding the reader that he is dust, that all his pleasures are dusty, and that he will return to dust. If there is any mention of a life to come, it is apt to take the form of a threat of eternal damnation. The very frequent expression of such obstinate defeatism probably helped to popularize Boethius, who does offer positive aid to the suffering spirit. Thus in literature Boethius' ideas are often restated as a kind of general consolation for the ills of life: by reminding us that all men must suffer woe and must die, the writer hopes to comfort us for our specific griefs and losses. Even in this watered-down Boethianism there is a wholesome perspective that is lacking to those monitory poems which can see only man's earthiness.

BOETHIUS: *From* The Consolation of Philosophy[1]

[*Triumph over the World*]

Whoever is unstained of virtue, constant and well-ordered of life, who has put proud chance under foot and looks upright upon either kind of Fortune, may keep his countenance undisturbed. Neither the rage of the sea nor its threats, as it stirs upward the swell from its depths, shall move that man. Neither the unstable mountain that is called Vesuvius, which writhes out smoking fires through its broken

1. Based on Chaucer's Middle English rendering (Book I, Meter 4).

chimneys, nor the track of the thunderbolt that is wont to smite high towers shall move that man. Wherefore then, O wretches, do you dread tyrants who, villainous and mad, are without any strength? Hope for no thing, and dread nought; and so shall you disarm the wrath of the impotent tyrant. But whoever quaking dreads or desires a thing that is not constant in its own right, that man has cast away his shield and is moved from his place, and entangles himself in the chain with which he may be dragged.

Earth Took of Earth [2]

Erthe took of erthe erthe with wogh;°	*harm*
Erthe other erthe to the erthe drogh;°	*drew*
Erthe laide erthe in erthen throgh:°	*coffin*
Thanne hadde erthe of erthe erthe ynogh.°	*enough*

Earth upon Earth [3]

Memento homo quod cinis es et in cinerem reverteris.

Erthe out of erthe is wonderly wrought;
Erthe hath of erthe a dignitee of nought;
Erthe upon erthe hath set al his thought
How that erthe upon erthe may be heigh° brought.   *high*

5   Erthe upon erthe wolde be a king;
How erthe shal [4] to erthe thinketh he no thing;
When erthe biddeth erthe his rents home bring,[5]
Then shal erthe from erthe have a pitous parting.

Erthe upon erthe winneth castels and towrs;
10 Then saith erthe unto erthe, "This is al ours."
When erthe upon erthe hath bigged° up his bowrs,   *built*
Then shal erthe for erthe suffre sharp showrs.°   *onslaughts*

Erthe gooth° upon erthe as molde° upon molde;   *walks / dirt*
So gooth erthe upon erthe al glittering in golde,
15 Lik as erthe unto erthe never go sholde;
Yet shal erthe unto erthe rather° than he wolde.   *sooner*

Why that erthe loveth erthe wonder me think,
Or why that erthe for erthe swete° wil or swink:°   *sweat / labor*
When erthe upon erthe is brought within brink,[6]
20 Then shal erthe have of erthe a wonder foul stink.

2. The earliest of a great number of English "earth" poems (early 13th century).
3. A late 14th-century specimen of an "earth" poem. The epigraph is translated, "Remember, man, that thou art dust, and unto dust thou shalt return" (cf. Genesis iii.19).
4. I.e., shall go.
5. I.e., show what he has gained.
6. I.e., grave.

GEOFFREY CHAUCER: [A Thoroughfare Full of Woe][7]

No man myghte gladen Theseus
Savyng his olde fader Egeus
That knew this worldes transmutacioun,
As he hadde seyn° it chaungen up and down,   seen
5 Joye after wo, and wo after gladnesse,
And shewed hem ensample and lyknesse:
"Right as ther deyed° nevere man," quod he,   died
"That he ne lyved in erthe in som degree,
Right so ther lyved nevere man," he seyde,
10 "In al this world that som tyme he ne deyde.
This world nys but a thurghfare ful of wo,
And we been pilgrymes passynge to and fro:
Deeth is an ende of every worldly soore."

The Goddess Fortune   The image of the goddess Fortune is one
of the Middle Age's chief literary devices for persuading the reader that
this world is a sorry one. Fortune is a legacy from pagan Rome who was
used to good effect by Boethius in his *Consolation* and to less good effect
by hundreds of writers following Boethius. She is generally imagined as
constantly turning a vertical wheel that has chairs fastened on its rim; in
one of these chairs man rides, sometimes on the ascendant or at the apex
of the wheel's orbit, but always in the end dashed down to its lowest point,
where he ends his life in misery. (For one vivid description of Fortune, see
King Arthur's dream, as told by Malory). In the *Consolation* Fortune
is made the means by which Boethius persuades the reader to put no trust
in the seeming goods of life and to accept its ills without complaint. Ultimately, Boethius tells us, Fortune is merely the agent of the benevolent
Prime Mover who governs the universe. Translated into specifically Christian terms, Fortune should become the agent of God, exercising his inscru-
table will on earth, as she appears in Dante. But once again the full and
mature vision proved beyond the capability of the majority of medieval
writers, in whom Fortune becomes a purely malevolent power whose function is to make life miserable. Writers, the piety of whose motives it is
impossible to doubt, interpreted all history as proving nothing more than
that Fortune holds all men in her malicious sway. Works such as Boccaccio's *Falls of Illustrious Men*, Chaucer's Monk's Tale, and Lydgate's *Falls
of Princes* consist of a series of biographies of eminent men betrayed by
Fortune—"tragedies," according to the medieval definition. Though these
writers thought that they were serving Christianity and mankind, in their
enthusiasm for railing at Fortune they often seal themselves up within a

7. From the Knight's Tale, A2837-49 (in complete editions). Theseus, lord of
Athens, is grieving at the death of his knight Arcite.

moral vacuum: a man becomes a "tragic" figure merely by falling from high to low, and it does not matter that he might richly deserve his fall, so that Nero's life is as tragic as that of the worthiest of heroes. In the general disparagement of life's values, even those values which lie at the heart of Christianity tended to disappear.

BOETHIUS: *From* The Consolation of Philosophy[1]

[*Fortune Defends Herself*]

O man, wherefore do you recriminate me with your daily complaints? What wrong have I done you? What goods have I bereft you of that were yours? Strive or argue with me concerning the possession of riches or of dignities before whatever judge you will, and if you may show me that any mortal man has ever received any of those things as his and his alone, then will I grant freely that those same things were yours which you now seek.

When nature brought you forth out of your mother's womb I received you naked and wanting all things, and I nourished you with my riches, and was ready and eager to sustain you through my favor: and now that makes you impatient with me. And I surrounded you with all the abundance of all the goods that are in my control. Now it pleases me to withdraw my hand. You have had grace such as one has who has made use of someone else's goods: you have no right to complain as if you had really lost all your possessions. Why do you complain then? I have done you no wrong. Riches, honors, and other such things are of my right. They are my servants and recognize me as their mistress. They come with me, and depart when I turn away. I can confidently say that if those things whose loss you complain of had been yours, you would not have lost them.

Shall I alone, then, be forbidden to exercise my right? Surely it is permissible for the sky to bring bright day and after that to cover the day with dark night. The year too has leave to apparel the face of the earth now with fruit, now with flowers, and sometimes to destroy them with rain and cold. And the sea has a right sometimes to be calm and blandishing with smooth water, and sometimes to be horrible with waves and winds. But the desire of man, which cannot be quenched—shall it force me to be steadfast, although steadfastness is strange to my ways? Such is my nature, and this game I play continually: I turn the whirling wheel and the circle spins. I am glad to change the lowest to the highest, and the highest to the lowest. Mount up if you will, provided you do so under this condition, that you will not maintain that I do you wrong though you descend down when the rules of my game require it.

1. Based on Chaucer's Middle English rendition (Book II, Prose 2).

DANTE: [Fortune an Agent of God's Will] [2]

"Master," said I to him, "now tell me further, this Fortune, on which thou touchest to me, what is it, which has the goods of the world so in its clutches?"

And he to me: "O foolish creatures, how great is that ignorance which harms you! I would have thee now receive my opinion concerning her. He whose wisdom transcends all, made the heavens, and gave them their guides, so that every part shines on every part, distributing equally the light. In like wise for the splendors of the world, He ordained a general ministress and guide, who should from time to time transfer the vain goods from race to race, and from one blood to another, beyond the resistance of human wit. Wherefore one race rules, and another languishes, pursuant to her judgment, which is hidden like the snake in the grass. Your wisdom has no withstanding of her: she foresees, judges, and pursues her reign, as theirs the other gods. Her permutations have no truce; necessity compels her to be swift, so often comes he who obtains a turn. This is she who is so set upon the cross, even by those who ought to give her praise, giving her blame amiss and ill report. But she is blessed and hears this not: with the other Primal Creatures she turns her sphere, and blessed she rejoices."

GEOFFREY CHAUCER: [The Monk's Definition of Tragedy] [3]

I wol biwaille in manere of tragedie	
The harm of hem that stoode in heigh degree	
And fillen° so that ther nas no remedie	*fell*
To brynge hem out of hire adversitee.	
5 For certeyn, whan that Fortune list° to flee,	*desires*
Ther may no man the cours of hire withholde:	
Lat no man triste° on blynde prosperitee;	*trust*
Beth war by this ensamples trewe and olde.	

2. From *Inferno* VII.48 ff., in Charles Eliot Norton's translation. Dante is discussing Fortune with Virgil, his guide through Hell.

3. From the Monk's Tale, B² 3181-88.

GEOFFREY CHAUCER: [The Tragedy of Pierre de Lusignan] [4]

O worthy Petro, kyng of Cipre°, also   *Cyprus*
That Alisaundre wan by heigh maistrie,[5]
Ful many an hethen wroghtestow ful wo,
Of which thyne owene liges° hadde envie,   *lieges*
5 And for no thyng but for thy chivalrie
They in thy bed han slayn thee by the morwe: [6]
Thus kan Fortune hire wheel governe and gye°,   *guide*
And out of joye bryngen men to sorwe.

4. King of Cyprus, whose recapture of Alexandria from the Saracens in 1365 was considered one of the great feats of Christendom; he was ultimately murdered by one of his followers. His life thus provides an apt demonstration of the turn of Fortune's wheel. The Monk's Tale, B[2] 3581-8.
5. That won Alexandria by great force.
6. In the morning.

"Life is Sweet"   Disgust for the world, no matter how pious the motives of those who express it, must to some extent deny the Bible's statement that the work of the Creator is good, a fact that will be at least occasionally evident to all men's senses. That earth's beauty continued to inspire joy in medieval hearts is attested by such lyrics as *Spring Has Come* (p. 286), which occur in profusion in all the vernaculars. On a more exalted plane, William Langland in *Piers Plowman* pays reverence to the divine Creator's ordering of nature, and in so doing brings the reader a comforting sense of the closeness of God to His handiwork on earth. But while earth's beauty is one proof of life's potential goodness, a far more powerful one is young love. Such lyrics as *Alison* (p. 284), of which there are a number, suggest that to try to teach hatred of the world to a lover is a lost cause; and the hero of the French romance *Aucassin and Nicolete* says that he will gladly pay for his earthly love with an eternity of hell. Other poets rebut the moralists with rollicking poems in praise of good eating and good drinking, and one—probably a monk—takes refuge from the austerities of life in splendid fantasy, in which he pictures an earthly paradise, the *Land of Cockaigne*, where all life's forbidden pleasures are freely and joyously practiced.

[A Vision of Nature in *Piers Plowman*] [1]

And sleeping I saw all this, and soon came Kind [2]
And named me by name, and bade me note well,
And through the wonders of this world wise to become.

1. From the B Text: XI.312-21, 336-46, 354-59. The translation is the present editor's.
2. Nature.

And on a mountain called Middle-earth, as it seemed to me then,
I was fetched forth through natural forms to learn   5
Of every creature, Kind, my Creator to love.
I saw the sun and the sea and the sand after,
And where birds and beasts by their mates were moving:
Wild worms in woods, and wonderful fowls,
With flecked feathers and of varied colors.   10

* * *

Birds I beheld that in bushes made nests—
Had never man the mastery to make the smallest.
I wondered from whom or where the magpie
Learned to lay the sticks in which she lays and broods:
Has no carpenter the craft to construct her nest so well;   15
If any mason could make a mold for it, it would be much wonder.
And yet I marveled more how many other birds
Covered and concealed full craftily their eggs
In marshes and in moors, in mires and waters,
For fear of other fowls and for wild beasts,   20
And for men should not find them when they from them went.

* * *

And soon I looked upon the sea, and so forth on the stars:
I saw many marvels which may not be told now.
I saw flowers in the field and their fair colors,
And how among the green grass grew so many hues,   25
And some sour and some sweet—wonder strange I thought it;
On their kind and their color to comment would take long.

From Aucassin and Nicolete [3]

[Aucassin Renounces Paradise]

In Paradise what have I to win? Therein I seek not to enter, but only to have Nicolete, my sweet lady that I love so well. For into Paradise go none but such folk as I shall tell thee now: Thither go these same old priests, and halt old men and maimed, who all day and night cower continually before the altars, and in the crypts; and such folk as wear old amices [4] and old clouted frocks, and naked folk and shoeless, and covered with sores, perishing of hunger and thirst, and of cold, and of little ease. These be they that go into Paradise, with them have I naught to make. But into Hell would I fain go; for into Hell fare the goodly clerks, and goodly knights that fall in tourneys and great wars, and stout men at arms, and all men noble. With these would I liefly go. And thither pass the sweet ladies and courteous that have two lovers or three, and their lords also thereto. Thither goes the gold, and the silver, and cloth of vair, and cloth

3. From Andrew Lang's translation. Aucassin makes this reply to someone who
has warned him that if he finds his lost
lady he will run the risk of sinning with
her and thus of losing Paradise.
4. Cloaks worn by the clergy.

of gris,[5] and harpers, and makers, and the prince of this world. With these I would gladly go, let me but have with me Nicolete, my sweetest lady.

From The Land of Cockaigne [6]

Far out in the ocean west of Spain
There is a land that's called Cockaigne.
There is no land beneath the air
With Cockaigne's excellence can compare.
Though Paradise is merry and bright,   5
Cockaigne is the fairer site.
What has Paradise got to show,
Where only fruit and green trees grow?
Though it has joy and pleasure sweet,
There's only apples for you to eat;   10
It has no hall, no bower, no bench,
And only water your thirst to quench;
There's little company there for you:
Elijah and Enoch are the only two; [7]
And well you know that men no more   15
Than a pair can be a dreadful bore.

In Cockaigne is food and drink
Got without trouble or sweat or swink.[8]
The food is choice, the drink is fine,
At lunch, at tea time, or when you dine.   20
There is no doubt, I make it clear,
There is no land on earth its peer;
Beneath the sky such joy and bliss
No land can show to compare with this.

There is many a lovely sight: 25
It's always day, there is no night;
There is no ill will, grudge, or strife;
There is no death, but only life;
There is no lack of food or cloth;
No man is there with woman wroth.   30

There is no serpent, wolf, nor fox,
Horse nor sheep, cow nor ox;
No pigs or goats does it enclose:
There's no need there to hold your nose.

5. Gray and gray-and-white fur, probably of squirrels.
6. The translation is the present editor's, based on the text given in R. H. Robbins' *Historical Poems of the XIVth and XVth Centuries* (1959).
7. On Biblical evidence, they were the only mortals to have been "translated" alive to Paradise (Genesis v.24, II Kings xi.11-12, Hebrews xi.5).
8. Labor.

Of stable or stud there is no trace: 35
This is a wholly pleasant place.
There is no fly, no flea, no louse,
In clothes, in town, in bed, in house.
There is no thunder, sleet, nor hail,
No ugly worm or slimy snail.   40
There is no storm, no rain, no wind;
There is no man or woman blind;
But all is pleasure, joy, and glee:
Well is the man that there may be.

There are rivers great and fine,   45
Of oil, of milk, of honey and wine.
Water is used there for no thing
Except to look at, and washing.
There're fruits for every appetite,
For all is comfort and delight.   50

Also there is an abbey fair:
White and gray monks both live there.
It has many bowers and halls—
All of pastry are the walls,
Of flesh, of fish, of choicest meat,   55
The tastiest that man could eat.
Of sugar cakes are the shingles all,
Of church, of cloister, bower and hall;
The pinnacles are fat puddings,
Fit to be served to princes or kings.   60
You may eat whatever you will:
It is your right to take your fill,
For all is common to young or old,
To strong, to fierce, to meek, to bold.

* * *

So many and various are the birds,   65
To name them all I lack the words—
Throstle, thrush, and nightingale,
Woodpecker, partridge, lark, and quail,
That are always singing with all their might—
They keep it up both day and night.   70
And another thing I mustn't omit:
The geese, fresh roasted from the spit,
Fly to the abbey—God it wot—
And cry out, "Geese all hot, all hot!"
They bring of stuffing a great supply,   75
The best prepared that you could buy.

The tender larks, as is well known,
Fly to a watering mouth on their own,
All fixed up in an elegant stew,
With a sauce designed to titillate you.   80

There is no need to order drink:
Just take enough without more swink.

When the monks have gone to Mass,
All the windows that are of glass
Turn themselves into crystal bright   85
To give the monks a better light.
And when the Mass has all been said
And the prayers have all been read,
The crystal turns back into glass,
Of the same sort that it earlier was.   90

The younger monks, day upon day,
After dinner go out to play:
There is no hawk or bird so fast,
Nor that better flies in the airy vast,
Than the young monks, high of mood,   95
Sailing on wings of sleeves and hood.

When the Abbot sees them soar,
It always makes his pleasure more.
But when the monks their flight prolong,
He summons them to evensong.   100
Yet still the monks come not to ground,
But keep on flying round and round.

When the Abbot thus does learn
That flying monks his summons spurn,
He takes what maiden he can find   105
And upward turns her white behind,
And beats the tabors with his hand,
To make his monks alight on land.

When his monks that sight espy,
Down to the maiden quick they fly,   110
And to the wench they too attend,
And spank her on her white rear end.
And after all their thirsty swink,
Meekly the monks go home to drink,
And in an orderly formation   115
Parade toward their night's collation.

                    *   *   *

A monk who will be stallion good
And knows how best to set his hood,
Shall have—and no man interfere—
Twelve wives for each and every year.   120
And not through grace, but all through right,
With which to make himself delight.

And of these monks who can sleep best,
And give his body greatest rest,

Has cause to hope, with God's good aid,   125
Soon Father Abbot to be made.

Whoso will come that land unto,
Full great penance must he do.
Seven whole years in hogs' manure
He must wade—of that I'm sure—   130
And all that time up to the chin:
And thus he shall to that land win.

Lordings good and kind and true,
May you to earth not say adieu
Before you've had a proper chance   135
To undergo all that penance,
So that you may that land attain,
And nevermore come here again.
Let's pray to God it may so be;
Amen, for holy charity.   140

"Beauty That Must Die"   Some of the most poignant poetry of
the Middle Ages results from a combination of two extreme attitudes toward life, expressing at once appreciation for the beauty of the world and
acknowledgment that this beauty is so transitory that, viewed against the
background of eternity, it is scarcely more than an illusion. In poetry of
this sort, an important part is often played by the *ubi sunt* device, which
takes its name from the first two words of the Latin sentence, *Ubi sunt qui
ante nos fuerunt?* ("Where are they who before us were?"). In asking the
question the poet evokes for a moment the splendor of life, symbolized by
famous persons of the past, and then, by his inevitably grim answer, condemns it to death. The tone of such poems will vary from the austerely
monitory to the hauntingly sad, depending upon how the poet describes the
"they" of the question, and how he phrases his answer: whether he sides
with death or with life or tries to balance delicately between them.

[Ubi Sunt Qui ante Nos Fuerunt?]

Where beeth they biforen us weren,
Houndes ledden and hawkes beren,°   bore
   And hadden feeld and wode?
The riche ladies in hir bowr,
That wereden ° gold in hir tressour,°   wore / hair
   With hir brighte rode,°   faces

Eten and drunken and maden hem glad;
Hir lif was al with gamen ylad; [1]

1. With pleasure led.

Men kneeleden hem biforen:
10   They beren hem wel swithe hye.[2]
And in a twinkling of an ye
Hir soules weren forloren.

FRANÇOIS VILLON: The Ballad of Dead Ladies[3]

Tell me now in what hidden way is
    Lady Flora the lovely Roman?[4]
Where's Hipparchia, and where is Thaïs,[5]
    Neither of them the fairer woman?
    Where is Echo, beheld of no man,   5
Only heard on river and mere—
    She whose beauty was more than human?[6] . . .
But where are the snows of yesteryear?

Where's Héloise, the learned nun,
    For whose sake Abeillard, I ween,   10
Lost manhood and put priesthood on?[7]
    (From Love he won such dule and teen[1])
    And where, I pray you, is the queen[8]
Who willed that Buridan should steer
    Sewed in a sack's mouth down the Seine? . . .   15
But where are the snows of yesteryear?

White Queen Blanche, like a queen of lilies,
    With a voice like any mermaidén[9]—
Bertha Broadfoot, Beatrice, Alice,
    And Ermengarde, the lady of Maine[1]—   20
    And that good Joan whom Englishmen

2. Very proudly.
3. Villon (b. 1431), a French poet and vagabond, regarded as the first and one of the greatest of French lyrists. This translation of his *Ballade du Temps Jadis* is by Dante Gabriel Rossetti.
4. Probably the Roman goddess of flowers and spring, later thought of as a wealthy and beautiful woman.
5. Hipparchia was the wife of Crates, Greek Cynic philosopher (3rd century B.C.). Thaïs is either the courtesan who accompanied Alexander the Great on his Asian expedition or the Egyptian courtesan who became a saint.
6. Echo was the nymph who pined away for Narcissus until nothing was left of her except her voice.
7. Héloise fell in love with her teacher, Pierre Abelard (1079-1142), scholastic philosopher and theologian; they were secretly married in order not to hinder Abelard's advancement in the church. Héloise's uncle, in revenge, had Abelard emasculated in order to make him canonically incapable of ecclesiastical preferment. Abelard became a monk and Héloise a nun. "Dule and teen": grief and pain.
8. Marguerite de Bourgogne, heroine of the legend of the Tour de Nesle, according to which she had her numerous lovers killed and thrown into the Seine; Jean Buridan, rector of the University of Paris, escaped.
9. Perhaps Blanche of Castille, mother of Louis IX of France (1226-70).
1. Names of famous medieval ladies; Bertha Broadfoot was mother of Charlemagne, king of the Franks and emperor of the West (742-814).

At Rouen doomed and burned her there [2]—
 Mother of God, where are they then? . . .
But where are the snows of yesteryear?

Nay, never ask this week, fair lord,   25
 Where they are gone, nor yet this year,
Except with this for an overword—
 "But where are the snows of yesteryear?"

GEOFFREY CHAUCER: [This Worlde That Passeth
   Soone as Floures Faire][3]

O yonge fresshe folkes, he or she,
In which that love up groweth with youre age,
Repeyreth home fro worldly vanitee,
And of youre herte up casteth the visage
5 To thilke God that after his ymage
Yow made, and thynketh al nys but a faire,
This worlde that passeth soone as floures faire;

And loveth hym the which that right for love
Upon a crois oure soules for to beye
10 First starf and roos and sit in hevene above:
For he nyl° falsen no wight, dar I leye,° *will not/wager*
That wol his herte al holly on hym leye—
And syn° he best to love is and most meke, *since*
What nedeth feynede loves for to seke?

2. Joan of Arc; she saved France from
conquest but was later imprisoned and
burned at the stake for heresy and

witchcraft in 1431.
3. From *Troilus and Criseide*, V.1835-48.

The Sixteenth Century

(1485-1603)

1485: Accession of Henry VII inaugurates age of the Tudor sovereigns.

1509: Accession of Henry VIII.

1517: Martin Luther's Wittenberg Theses; beginning of the Reformation.

1535: Henry VIII acknowledged "Supreme Head on Earth" of the English church.

1557: Publication of *Tottel's Miscellany*, containing poems by Sir Thomas Wyatt, Henry Howard Earl of Surrey, and others.

1558: Accession of Queen Elizabeth I.

1576: The Theatre, the first permanent structure in England for the presentation of plays, is built.

1588: Defeat of the Spanish Armada.

1603: Death of Elizabeth I; accession of James I, first of the Stuart line.

ENGLAND UNDER HENRY VII

The 16th century in England is the age of the Tudor sovereigns. There were three generations of them; they ruled England from 1485 to 1603. Before the first Tudor, the Earl of Richmond who became Henry VII, won his crown by defeating Richard III at Bosworth field, the country had for more than thirty years been torn by a dynastic strife between the houses of York and Lancaster. Henry VII was Lancastrian, but he married Elizabeth of the house of York, sister of Edward V and niece of the Yorkist king he defeated, Richard III. The barons, impoverished and divided by the dynastic wars, could not effectively oppose the power of the crown, and the church, the other great force in society, was closer to alliance with royal power than to opposition. So Tudor government meant, in comparison with what had gone before and with other conceivable alternatives, a government of strong central authority, of order, and of practical solutions to problems.

About a decade before Henry VII won his throne, the art of printing from movable type, a German invention, had been introduced into England by William Caxton (ca. 1422–91), who had learned and practiced it in the Low Countries. Literacy had been increasing during the 15th century, so that many more people could read than in Chaucer's time. It is estimated that some 30 per cent of the people could read English in the early 15th century and some 60 per cent by 1530. Printing of course made books cheaper and more plentiful, and accordingly there were more opportunities to read and more incentive to learn to read.

Seven years after Henry VII became king, Columbus discovered America, and a few years later Vasco da Gama reached the Orient by sailing around the Cape of Good Hope. The English were not pioneers in the discovery and exploration of the western hemisphere, but the consequences of new discoveries were to affect their place in the world profoundly, for in the next century they became great colonizers and merchants.

Significant changes in trade and in the arts of war also marked the early years of the Tudor regime. Henry VII made commercial treaties with European countries; England, which had always been a sheep-raising country, began to manufacture and export significant amounts of cloth. As lands were enclosed to permit grazing on a larger scale, people were driven off the land to the cities, London grew into a metropolitan market, and business in the modern sense began to develop. At the same time the old feudal structure began to break down, partly because the introduction of firearms had made obsolete the old armored knight on horseback, as well as the English bowman who had won such famous victories in France under King Henry V. The "new men" who supported the Tudors and profited from their favor could adapt themselves more easily to a changed society than could the survivors of the great families of the feudal 15th century.

Yet it would be a mistake to visualize these changes as sudden and dramatic. Although Caxton introduced printed books, and was an author and translator as well as a printer, his publications consisted of long prose romances translated from the French, collections of moral sayings, and other works—such as Malory's *Morte Darthur*—that were medieval rather than modern. And even though the armored knight was obsolete, for a century jousts and tournaments took place at court and the approved code of behavior was the traditional code of chivalry. As often in an age of spectacular novelty, full of significance for the future, men's minds looked back instead of forward. Confronted with innovation, they dreamed of an idealized past instead of looking forward to an uncertain future. The best writers of the time of Henry VII were imitators of Chaucer, who had died about a century before. They were Scottish rather than English: William Dunbar (ca. 1460–ca. 1520), Gavin Douglas (1475–1522), and Sir David Lindsay (1485–1555) Even the English writers looked back; a typical one is Stephen Hawes (1474–1523), who imitated not Chaucer but John Lydgate, monk of Bury.

HUMANISM

During the 15th century a few English clerics and government officials had journeyed to Italy and had seen something of the extraordinary cultural and intellectual movement flourishing in the city-states there. But it was only near the end of the century that Italian influence came to be important, and it was not until the accession of Henry VIII to the throne in 1509 that a notable renaissance took place in England.

Humanism was a revolt against the other-worldly orientation of medieval philosophy and religion. The humanists turned to newly recovered Greek manuscripts for inspiration and enlightenment; they saw in the ancient classics a more "modern" and more desirable world than the one they lived in. They proposed to reform education in the direction of Ciceronian *humanitas*, to make men realize their human capabilities as individuals, to free them from the shackles of Scholasticism and the view that, as Chaucer had expressed it, "this world nis but a thurghfare ful of wo."

The thesis of humanism was that man's proper role in the world was action, not contemplation. Wealth and power were not necessarily evil, since they might provide the means of achieving good. The mind and the will had to be properly disciplined, but they were to be used positively, not renounced for the sake of the salvation of the soul. Passion, striving for glory, the aspiring mind were to be encouraged when the motives were noble, and becoming the master of the earth and thereby achieving benefits for mankind was a noble motive. The Italian humanists studied the Greek text of the new Testament (St. Jerome's Latin text, the Vulgate, was the official text of the church). In Florence, under the patronage of Lorenzo de Medici, such scholars of Plato as Marsilio Ficino (1433–99) and Pico della Mirandola (1463–94) created the liveliest intellectual atmosphere in Europe.

The humanist influence began to reach England slightly before the beginning of the 16th century. The Dutch scholar Desiderius Erasmus (ca. 1466–1536) wrote in 1499 about his first visit to England,

I have met with so much kindness and so much learning, not backward and trivial, but deep, accurate, ancient, Latin and Greek, that but for the curiosity of seeing it, I do not so much care for Italy. When I hear my Colet [John Colet, 1467–1519, Lecturer on the New Testament at Oxford and founder of St. Paul's School], I seem to be listening to Plato himself. In Grocyn [William Grocyn, 1446–1519, Lecturer in Greek at Oxford], who does not marvel at such a perfect round of learning? What can be more acute, profound, and delicate than the judgment of Linacre? [Thomas Linacre, physician and scholar, tutor to princes] What has nature ever created more gentle, more sweet, more happy than the genius of Thomas More?

The masterpiece of English humanism was More's *Utopia*, written in Latin, though More's English prose, his *Richard III* and his controversial pamphlets, is more important for the period. (It was easier, one must remember, for a scholar of this time to write in Latin than in English.) The *History of Richard III*, which drew upon what he had learned from Cardinal Morton as a young page in Morton's household, was a justification of the Tudor dynasty by blackening its immediate predecessor. Another important humanist historian was the naturalized Italian, Polydore Vergil (ca. 1470–1555), who, like More, defended Henry VII's right to the throne but also attacked the medieval legends of Brutus, the mythical founder of Britain, and the stories of King Arthur and his Round Table. Humanism was to have a profound effect upon English intellectual life, education, and writing all through the 16th century. Queen Elizabeth herself, with her command of languages and her practical sense of the problems of government, was a typical product of a humanistic education.

Elizabethan education was based upon the medieval *trivium* (grammar, logic, and rhetoric) and *quadrivium* (arithmetic, geometry, astronomy, and music). Grammar was of course Latin grammar, and the rhetoric that went with it was a rigorous discipline in all the stylistic devices used by classical authors. The purpose was a utilitarian one—to train the student to speak and write good Latin, the language of diplomacy, of the professions, and of all higher learning. But the books read and studied rhetorically were not considered mere exhibitions of literary style; from the *Sententiae Pueriles* for beginners, on up through Terence, Virgil, Horace, and Cicero's *De Officiis*, the works were studied for the moral, political, and philosophical content they offered. Elizabethan schoolmasters might use the system of double translation, from English into Latin and then from Latin back into English, to develop facility and rhetorical elegance, but they well knew that the rapid development from child into man (so much more rapid than we consider either feasible or desirable) required moral instruction, and this was to be found in the Latin classics. It was a mission of the English humanists like Colet, Elyot, and Ascham to persuade the English gentry that their sons should be bred to this kind of learning as the most suitable preparation for public service.

Although Sir Thomas More had turned naturally to Latin in writing his *Utopia*, the choice was not as easy for succeeding generations. In fact, the question of whether to write in English or in Latin became a question of great seriousness. The vernaculars seemed relatively new and unstable to learned men, and with their great desire for eternal fame it was natural that they should concern themselves about the durability of their medium. Furthermore, the age of the humanists had emphasized the value of the classical languages; Cicero and the other masters of rhetoric were imitated in their own tongues. But in Italy, France, and England alike, there came to be a revolt against this sterile and slavish imitation of the classics. It is the contention of Joachim Du Bellay's *Défense et Illustration de la Langue Française* (1549) that the value of a language is not inherent in the language itself, but depends upon what great and fine works are written in that language; furthermore, and this is even more important, the feeling of nationality itself dictates that the vernacular should be used. If the tongue of the people is not so refined and polished as the Greek or Latin, all the more reason why men of learning should improve it by studying it and writing their most ambitious works in it. Roger Ascham (1515–68), tutor to Princess Elizabeth, included in his book on archery called *Toxophilus* (1545) a defense of writing in English, though he said it would be easier for him to write in Latin or Greek. He dedicated the book to King Henry, and his patriotic motives are expressed in verses addressed to England:

> Stick to the truth, and evermore thou shall
> Through Christ, King Henry, the book and the bow,
> All manner of enemies quite overthrow.

Richard Mulcaster (ca. 1530–1611), principal of the Merchant Taylors' School and teacher of Edmund Spenser, said:

I do write in my natural English tongue, because though I make the learned my judges, which understand Latin, yet I mean good to the unlearned, which understand but English. * * * For is it not indeed a marvelous bondage, to become servants to one tongue for learning's sake the most of our time, with loss of most time, whereas we may have the very same treasure in our own tongue, with the gain of most time? our own bearing the joyful title of our liberty and freedom, the Latin tongue remembering us of our thralldom and bondage? I love Rome, but London better; I favor Italy, but England more; I honor the Latin, but I worship the English.

THE REFORMATION—HENRY VIII, EDWARD VI, AND MARY

Humanists like Erasmus advocated and practiced a scholarly and critical study of the Scriptures; humanists like More were opposed to corrupt and ignorant clergy and such abuses as the sale of papal indulgences and pardons. But when, after Martin Luther nailed his famous Theses to the church door in Wittenberg in 1517, the Reformation itself gathered force, Erasmus and More drew back. Humanism and Reformation for a while seemed to be hostile forces.

What was the Reformation? From the point of view of those who supported it, it was a return to pure Christianity—cleansing the church of all the filth and idolatry that had accumulated over the centuries. From a less partisan point of view it was the break-up of western Christendom, the secularization of society, the establishment of princely ascendancy over the church, and consequently the identification of religious feelings with patriotic, nationalistic ones. From the point of view of the Catholic Church it was, of course, damnable heresy.

In England, one cannot say that the Reformation had an ideological basis. There had been John Wycliffe and the Lollard movement, a popular protest in the time of Chaucer, but little of this survived in the second decade of the 16th century. The split with the Church of Rome was caused by a man who considered himself a Catholic champion against Luther and his opinions: Henry VIII, who for writing a book against Luther had been given the title "Defender of the Faith" by Pope Leo X. Henry's motives were dynastic, not religious; he needed a legitimate son and he could not get one without the divorce which Rome refused him. He insisted upon being Supreme Head of the English church and requiring oaths of allegiance to him in that role; Sir Thomas More, his Lord Chancellor, resigned and finally gave up his life rather than sign such an oath. More's successor, Thomas Cromwell, dissolved the monasteries and distributed the property to a group of people who thereafter would not side with Rome. And though under Henry the great English translator of the Bible, William Tyndale, was persecuted, driven out of England, and finally martyred in 1536, it was also in Henry's reign that the Scriptures in English were made available in The Great Bible of 1539 to anyone who could read.

Under Henry's son, the child king Edward VI (b. 1537; reigned 1547–53), the English Reformation, which had taken place for political reasons, acquired a strong religious and spiritual force. Protestant theologians from the Continent swarmed to England, the Book of Common Prayer was published in 1549 and 1552, and by 1553, the year of the boy king's death, the 42 Articles which officially defined the beliefs of the English church were thoroughly Protestant.

The successor to the young Protestant king was his older sister Mary, half-Spanish and devoutly Catholic, who married her cousin, Philip II of Spain. The leading Protestants either fled to the Continent or were burned at the stake as heretics; ideologically the Reformation could be reversed, but some of its practical consequences, like the distribution of monastery lands, could not. A Spaniard on the throne of England was not popular, and Mary, whose accession had been opposed by the Council which had proclaimed Lady Jane Grey queen, and whose throne was challenged by a rebellion led by Sir Thomas Wyatt the Younger, son of the poet, dared not press her people too far. She could herself return to Roman allegiance but she could not undo the work of her father and brother. The most necessary thing to do was something she could not do—produce an heir. (Had she done so, England and the United States would probably be Catholic countries today.) Her reign was short, and the Protestant exiles swarmed back at her death to be a potent force in English society during the long reign of Mary's half sister, Elizabeth.

NATIONALISM—ELIZABETH I

Elizabeth Tudor, who ascended the throne in 1558 and ruled until 1603, was one of the most remarkable political geniuses ever produced by a people which has not been barren of political geniuses. Vain, difficult, and headstrong, she nevertheless had a very shrewd instinct about her country's strengths and weaknesses, and she identified herself with her country as no previous ruler had done. Although she was susceptible to the flattery of her courtiers and favorites, she nevertheless entrusted power to such solid men as William Cecil and Francis Walsingham. Cecil (1520–98) was her chief and most trusted Secretary. He devoted his great talents with unswerving loyalty to preserving a balance of forces in England, maintaining the queen's supremacy over ambitious nobles, and extracting money from the Commons to run the government. Walsingham (ca. 1530–90), a gifted diplomat and administrator, was her principal architect of foreign policy.

England's weakness was its politico-religious division. The Catholics, who had never been reformed and who adhered to the pro-Spanish faction of the previous reign, and the Protestant exiles, whose sojourn on the Continent had only sharpened their zeal for the eradication of papistry everywhere in Europe, were the extremes. Between them were the majority of Englishmen whose main desire was for order (remembering the civil conflicts of the previous century), and for these Englishmen Elizabeth, in her person and her policy, became the symbol and the cause.

England's strength lay in its middle position in the balance of power in Europe—it could throw its weight either way in the power contest between Spain and France; it could support or fail to support the Protestant uprising in the Low Countries. Moreover the queen was unmarried, and the general assumption was that of course she would marry, since as her father had undoubtedly taught her, one of a monarch's major duties is to provide an unquestioned, strong, legitimate heir to the throne. As long as she was capable of bearing children, Elizabeth's possible marriage was an important factor in European diplomacy. By the time it was too late to marry, England was strong and united, capable of shaking off (in 1588) the attempt of the Spanish king, Philip II, to invade the country. What unified England more than anything else was the papal bull of 1570, excommunicating Elizabeth and relieving her subjects of their loyalty to her. This bull, had it taken effect, would have brought to the throne Mary Queen of Scots, Catholic by faith and French by culture—an insupportable thought; Englishmen rallied to their queen and she became a symbol of Englishness and nationalism. The adulation of her, in the face of trouble on the Scottish border, near-chaos in Ireland, and varying threats from the Continent, grew to almost religious heights; her beauty (which was exaggerated), her wisdom (which generally did not need exaggeration), and her divine mission to guide England became articles of faith. In 1588 the defeat of the great Spanish Armada, the mightiest invasion fleet ever mounted against England, seemed to justify that faith.

In matters of religion Elizabeth chose a middle way which satisfied neither the Catholics nor the Puritans. She imposed a form of service, compelled her subjects to attend it, and left their consciences to themselves. The effect was again nationalistic; in the settled and established Elizabethan church, Christians looked toward neither Rome nor Geneva as the prime source of authority, but to the throne of their own sovereign.

The desire for commercial profit also strengthened nationalistic feelings. In 1493 the Pope had divided the new world between the Spanish and the Portuguese by drawing a line from pole to pole (hence Brazil speaks Portuguese today and the rest of Latin America speaks Spanish): the English were not in the picture. But by the end of Edward VI's reign the Company of Merchant Adventurers was founded and Englishmen had become interested in Asia and North America. As Protestantism progressed, many fishing fleets lacked work, for the sale of fish depended in great part upon the Catholic practice of eating no meat on Fridays and other fast days. So they turned to piracy, preying on Spanish ships which were returning laden with wealth from the New World. This business soon became a private undeclared war, with the queen and her courtiers investing in these raids privately but accepting no responsibility for them. The greatest of many dazzling exploits was the voyage of Francis Drake in 1577-80: he sailed through the Straits of Magellan, pillaged Spanish towns on the Pacific, reached as far north as San Francisco, crossed to the Philippines and returned around the Cape of Good Hope; he came back with £1,000,000 in treasure, and his investors earned a dividend of 5,000 per cent. Queen Elizabeth knighted him on the deck of his ship, *The Golden Hind.*

More than anything else, the mere survival of Elizabeth for so long provided the opportunity for nationalistic consciousness and feeling to become established. When she came to the throne in 1558 she was 25 years old; her sister had reigned only five years and her brother only six, but she would remain queen for almost 45 years. The second half of the 16th century is very appropriately called the Elizabethan age.

DRAMATIC LITERATURE

The dramatic literature of the age of Elizabeth is the greatest cultural achievement of the period. It grew out of the drama of the medieval church, but it was more directly influenced by the popular morality plays which continued to be performed on down to 1600. The emphasis in the moralities—as in the earlier mystery and miracle plays—was, of course, religious, and the plays were usually presented on church festival days. But by the end of the 15th century, plays with secular plots and characters began to be written, usually for presentation after a courtly dinner—or, if they were short enough, between the courses. Plays of this nature are now called "interludes"; the earliest known is *Fulgens and Lucrece*, by Henry

Medwall, produced in 1497 at Lambeth Palace. Several members of Sir Thomas More's circle wrote interludes, especially his brother-in-law John Rastell (1475–1536) and his nephew John Heywood (ca. 1497–ca. 1580). Heywood in particular made his interludes "merry" by introducing broad comic scenes on the model of contemporary French farce. The interlude was essentially courtly entertainment; it reached its height under Henry VIII, and remained popular down into the reign of Elizabeth. As it decayed, the Devils and other vicious characters of the old morality plays were fused into a single "Vice," who became essentially a comic character. Some late interludes, like John Bale's *King John* (ca. 1561), had political themes, a development that was to be important later in Elizabethan tragedies and chronicle history plays.

Classical Latin drama, particularly the tragedies of Seneca and the comedies of Plautus and Terence, began to influence English drama in the 60's. Students at schools and universities read and sometimes acted Latin plays, and it was an easy step from that to writing and producing imitations in English. Seneca's tragedies were constructed in five acts and were characterized by violent and bloody plots, resounding rhetorical speeches, and the presence of ghosts among the cast of characters; the first English tragedy based on these models was *Gorboduc, or Ferrex and Porrex*, by two lawyers, Thomas Sackville and Thomas Norton, produced at the Inner Temple in 1561 and later before the queen. Like Bale's *King John*, it has a political theme—the ruinous consequences of leaving a country without an heir to the throne.

Even earlier (ca. 1550), a schoolmaster, Nicholas Udall, had written a classical comedy in English, called *Ralph Roister Doister*, for his students to act. About the same time a play called *Gammer Gurton's Needle*, classical in form but thoroughly English in content, with much knockabout horseplay and native English provincial humor, was being acted before the scholars of Christ's College, Cambridge. In the first of these comedies the classical *miles gloriosus* (cowardly braggart soldier) makes his appearance in English; the type was to have its supreme fulfillment in Sir John Falstaff of Shakespeare's 1 and 2 *Henry IV*.

The fusion of classical form with English content brought about the possibility of a mature and artistic drama. But such drama must have an audience, a theater, and professional actors, or it will remain only a possibility. The earliest English drama had been acted by members of the clergy in the church; the mystery and miracle plays had been acted by amateurs —members of the local trade guilds—ordinarily on wagons in the streets of the towns. Moralities and interludes were produced by semi-amateur groups who traveled about, or by the servants of a lord in the hall of his castle. (See *The Second Shepherds' Play* and *Everyman* in this volume.) By 1450 one professional group was on tour. But there was no guild of actors, and they tended to be classed with jugglers, acrobats, mountebanks, and other traveling entertainers of dubious character; in 1545 actors were classified by statute as idle rogues and vagabonds and, as such, subject to arrest. Some noblemen maintained a company of actors as their personal servants, wearing livery and the badge of their masters. They could travel and practice their craft when not needed by their lords, and they were of course exempt from the statute. So it came about that the professional acting companies of Shakespeare's time, including Shakespeare's own, attached themselves to a nobleman and were technically his servants, even though virtually all of their time was devoted to, and their income came from, the public.

To reach a public audience they set up a platform in the courtyard of an enclosed inn, so the spectators could watch them from the ground of the courtyard or from the windows of the inn. The most profitable audiences could of course be collected in London innyards, particularly on Sundays. Their behavior was perhaps not very orderly; at any rate the City authorities, Puritans as they were, argued that such crowds contributed to riot, fire, accidents, ungodliness (especially on Sunday), absence from work (on weekdays), and the spread of the plague. The Puritans generally thought the drama vain and wicked: plays sometimes contained oaths and blasphemy, and it was morally shocking that men and boys put on female clothes to enact the roles of women.

To escape from the London authorities and to avoid sharing their profits with innkeepers, the Earl of Leicester's Men built in 1576 their own building outside the City limits in Shoreditch, and called it The Theatre. In general structure it resembled the innyards in which the plays had earlier been performed: it was open to the sky (except for sheltered galleries on three sides), and the stage very probably consisted of a large raised platform jutting out into the middle of the arena. A structure of this kind would place different requirements on actors than would our more intimate indoor theaters of today, and the style of acting was probably more declamatory and rhetorical. Other theaters followed, in Shoreditch and also in Southwark across the Thames, close to the pits where bull-baiting and bear-baiting satisfied the public taste for a more primitive kind of entertainment.

The companies were what would now be called "repertory companies" —that is, they filled the roles of each play from members of their own group, not employing outsiders, and they performed a number of different plays on consecutive days, not continuing a single play for a "run." Actors were shareholders in the profits of the company. Boys were apprenticed to actors just as they would be apprenticed to master craftsmen in a guild, and they took the women's parts in the plays until their voices changed. The plays might be bought for the company from a hack-writer or groups of hack-writers; or, as in Shakespeare's company, the Lord Chamberlain's Men, the company might have one of its members who could supply it with some (but by no means all) of its plays. The text remained the property of the company, but a popular play was eagerly sought by the printers, and the company sometimes had trouble achieving effective control over its rights in the play.

Public performance, though profitable, was not the only goal of the acting companies. The queen and the court must be entertained, especially at the holiday season or when foreign dignitaries paid a visit, and the rewards, both in money and prestige, of being selected to perform at court were great. There is a legend that Shakespeare wrote *The Merry Wives of Windsor* at the specific command of the queen, who found Falstaff amusing and wanted to see him in love, and it is quite clear that he wrote *Macbeth* with the Scottish interests of King James I in mind. The court audience was important in other ways. The best plays of the 1580's, a series of prose comedies by John Lyly, were written for the court circle and performed by a boys' company from one of the schools for choristers. Such performances, and others, could be put on in "private" theaters, indoors under a roof, with artificial lighting, like the "private" theater in Blackfriars which Shakespeare's company used. Lyly's comedies, such as *Endymion* and *Sapho and Phao*, were sophisticated, witty, and topical, masking under mythological or historical names actual persons of the queen's court.

It was for the courtly audience, also, that the first strain of real poetry was introduced into English drama. What Marlowe scornfully called the "jigging veins of rhyming mother wits / And such conceits as clownage keeps in pay" prevailed until George Peele's *Arraignment of Paris* (before 1584), an extravagantly flattering tribute to the queen in lovely verse, was acted by the Children of the Chapel. The 80's and 90's were to see such mighty poets as Marlowe and Shakespeare devote their genius to the stage.

Thomas Kyd, a friend of Marlowe, wrote a Senecan revenge play called *The Spanish Tragedy* which was popular for years, and probably also an early version of *Hamlet*, now lost. At the turn of the century Ben Jonson was beginning his great series of satirical comedies, such as *Every Man in His Humor* (1598), *Volpone* (1609), and *The Alchemist* (1610), and his less popular classical tragedies. Thomas Dekker (*The Shoemaker's Holiday*, 1599) and Thomas Heywood (*A Woman Killed With Kindness*, 1603) were successful playwrights who appealed to a middle-class audience. After James I came to the throne in 1603 the split between the tastes of the aristocratic audiences and the common people became more marked. Francis Beaumont and John Fletcher collaborated in comedies (*The Knight of the Burning Pestle*, ca. 1607) and tragedies (*The Maid's Tragedy*, ca. 1609) appealing to the taste of the court. Sensational plots set in the decadent courts of Italy provided material for John Webster (*The Duchess of Malfi*, ca. 1613) and Thomas Middleton (*Women Beware Women*, ca. 1621), and the same violence of action and morbidity of sentiment may be found in John Ford (*The Broken Heart*, ca. 1633) and James Shirley (*The Cardinal*, 1641) not long before the closing of the theaters and the beginning of the Civil Wars in 1642.

POET, PATRON, AND PUBLISHER

In the court the greatest opportunities existed, but there also were the greatest disappointments to be found. "It was overrun with place-seekers," writes M. St. Clare Byrne in *Elizabethan Life in Town and Country*, "but it was also undeniably the focus of the national life. It drew to it the clever mountebanks, but also the real vigor and talent. It captured and stimulated men's imaginations, even if eventually it disheartened and disgusted them." Men like Sir Christopher Hatton and Sir Walter Ralegh leaped from obscurity to great power and prominence as a result of their success as courtiers, but it must not be forgotten that they had other abilities than the gallantry and dancing which have made them famous in anecdote. The security of the courtier was always precarious, and there was scarcely one of Queen Elizabeth's courtiers who did not know, at some time or other, the harshness of the sovereign's disapproval. The great guide and conduct book for the courtier was Castiglione's *Il Cortegiano* (1528, translated into English by Sir Thomas Hoby in 1561), and according to its theses the function of the courtier was to give good and honest advice to the prince. But, as Sir Philip Sidney found out when he tried to advise the queen against a French marriage, advice is not always relished by a monarch whose powers over any individual subject are almost absolute. As a result there was a long tradition of literature against court life, comparing it unfavorably to the country life of the retired and obscure man. Sir Thomas Wyatt's verse epistles to Sir Francis Bryan and John Poins are early examples of this attitude, and it runs all through the period. Of course the fact that there was a "tradition" means that everything unfavorable said about the court should not be taken at its face value. But enough evidence exists to show that there was a definite feeling that court life was too precarious, too superficial, too corrupt, too hypocritical. From the time of Wyatt to the time of Ralegh the bitter tone is consistent.

For literary men like Edmund Spenser and Lyly, men who by birth were not in a position to be real courtiers, the court offered a faint hope of livelihood, notice, and encouragement. But for these two, at any rate, it was a source of bitter disappointment. Lyly's long wait for the office of the Revels and Spenser's disillusionment after hoping for court favor (reflected in *Mother Hubberds Tale* and *Colin Clouts Come Home Againe*) tell the story. Much of the satire of the period is directed against the superficiality and treachery of the court atmosphere. "A thousand hopes, but all nothing," wailed Lyly, "a hundred promises, but yet nothing."

Although most of the literature which is still considered worth reading shows the predominant influences of the court, it would be a mistake to underestimate the influence of the City of London on the literary taste and production of the period. London had grown tremendously since the time of Chaucer. Instead of a population of about 50,000 it had 93,276 in 1563 and 224,275 in 1605. It was by far the most important city in the realm, and the political history of the 17th century is understandable only if one recognizes the great power the City had, even as against the Crown. The printing presses were located in London, the publishers were located in London, and the mass of the middle-class population which set the style for literature written for the ordinary man lived in London. The middle class found among the university men some writers who catered to them: Thomas Heywood is a good example. And although Thomas Nashe scornfully rejects the claim of the bourgeois to have any literary taste at all or to have any ability at producing literature, still the class had its own writers, like Thomas Deloney, and it knew what it liked—books of instruction, romances, religious tracts, and sensational ballads. Whether the aristocrats admitted it or not, the standards and tastes of the middle class affected all writing, all publishing, and all literary success. For finally the writer saw his work exhibited on the stalls of St. Paul's churchyard, and the customers who frequented that center of the book trade were more often members of the middle class than of the court circle. Louis B. Wright has shown (in his *Middle-Class Culture in Elizabethan England*) how extensive and profound was the influence of the citizenry upon the writing and publication of books, and how bourgeois standards of edification and utility dictated to most of the authors of the time.

Next to the court and the City, the most important sources of literature were of course the two universities. In Elizabeth's reign they were old-fashioned in their curriculum, poor in discipline, and undistinguished in learning, in comparison with what they had been a generation before. There was a great shortage of ministers in the country, partly because of the poor living standard provided for members of the clergy and partly because of the loss of ministers through the religious changes of the middle of the century. Hence the universities were attempting to train ministers exclusively. The university man had either to get a fellowship and remain in academic life (which almost always meant taking holy orders), to enter the church and get a poor living, or to go into law or medicine. The career of a professional man of letters as such did not exist: literature was regarded as an adjunct, not a primary occupation.

The university graduate who came to London to make a literary career for himself faced a very difficult situation. It is best pictured, perhaps, in the Cambridge trilogy of *Parnassus* plays, performed at the end of the century but fairly faithfully reflecting conditions which held good during the whole period. It was the university wits, to be sure, who gave to the drama some of the classical form it needed, and who inaugurated the great literary vogue of the 90's. But the lives of Nashe and Marlowe, of Robert Greene and George Peele, do not suggest that the path was easy. The diary of Philip Henslowe, a leading theatrical manager, has entry after entry showing university graduates in prison or in debt or even at best miserably eking out an existence patching plays.

Financial rewards for writing and publishing prose or poetry came mostly in the form of gifts from patrons—in reality the old system of master and servant which had come down from the Middle Ages and had not changed much with the invention of printing. The writer by a dedication hoped for a suitable reward, and in an age when honor and vanity were motives much more sharply defined or observed than they are today, this procedure sometimes worked. Yet the patron whose vanity was amply satisfied by his own conceit and would not reward an author for a dedication remained a constant irritation to the writers of the time, and we hear many complaints that the age is degenerate because patrons are not more munificent. There were some generous and literary-minded patrons, notably Sir Philip Sidney and his sister Mary, the Countess of Pembroke. Shakespeare's relations with his patron, the Earl of Southampton, little as we know about them, were apparently satisfactory, as the dedication to *The Rape of Lucrece* (1594) is much warmer and more personal than the earlier one, to *Venus and Adonis* (1593). But the experience of Robert Greene is perhaps more typical than that of Shakespeare in this respect. He had sixteen different patrons for seventeen books; this suggests that he was not fortunate in finding favor or support from any one. A fraudulent practice grew up of printing the book and then printing off separate dedications, so that an impecunious author could deceive several patrons each into thinking that he was the one to be honored by the volume. Two or three pounds seems to have been the usual reward for the dedication of a pamphlet or small volume of verse. Ben Jonson, who fared much better than most of his contemporaries, sums up the matter, for poets at least, when he says: "Poetry in this latter age hath proved but a mean mistress to such as have wholly addicted themselves to her, or given their names up to her family. Those who have but saluted her on the way, and now and then tendered their visits, she hath done much for, and advanced in the way of their own professions (both the law and the gospel) beyond all they could have hoped or done for themselves without her favor."

The other possible source of reward, besides the patron, was the publisher. And rewards from the publisher in the 16th century were nothing at all like the rewards from that source now. In the first place there was no such thing as copyright, and no such thing, in the ordinary way, as royalties paid according to the sale of the book. An author sold his manuscript to the publisher outright, for what seems now like a ridiculously low price—for a pamphlet or small book of poetry, usually forty shillings.

The writer's troubles were not over when he had written his book, gone through the difficulty of finding a publisher, and finally come to terms with him for the sale of it. He still had to face the many and stringent regulations of the press by political and ecclesiastical authorities, and the fact that he had sold the manuscript did not exempt him from responsibility for what was in it. The authorities were, first, the Privy Council and the Court of Star Chamber, the highest political authority in the realm below the queen; then the Court of High Commission, the supreme ecclesiastical authority, which sometimes supervised matters which had only the slightest connection with religion; then the Stationers' Company, with whom a book had to be registered but who supervised and protected the publisher and printer rather than the author.

The principal rules governing the publication of books were that the number of printers (not publishers) was strictly limited; that nothing could be printed except in the City of London and the Universities of Oxford and Cambridge; that everything printed must receive the imprimatur of the Archbishop of Canterbury and the Bishop of London or their representatives; and that everything published in London must be entered in the registers of the Stationers' Company, if any kind of property protection were desired for it. An example of the regulation which reached back of the publisher to the author himself can be seen in the history of John Stubbs, who protested against Elizabeth's projected French marriage in a pamphlet called *The Discovery of a Gaping Gulf* (1579). For writing this pamphlet, Stubbs was condemned to have his right hand cut off with one stroke of a butcher's cleaver. When the execution had taken place, Stubbs took off his hat with his left hand and cried "God save the queen!"

Almost every writer of the period got into some sort of trouble for publishing a book. It might be prison, it might be merely a reprimand, it might be an investigation by the Star Chamber. It was dangerous to put pen to paper, and it was so unprofitable that it is a wonder that any original writing was published at all. Yet the Elizabethan age is an extremely prolific one in writing and publishing. The *Short Title Catalogue* of the Bibliographical Society, which lists works and editions published between 1475 and 1640, includes over 26,000 items, and it does not include all that were published.

To suppose that poetry, or even prose, circulated only in printed form would be a mistake. The 16th century was the first century of the printed book, and the older way, of circulating in manuscript, lingered on into the 17th century. This was particularly true of poets of gentle or noble rank.

Sidney is the most prominent example. Sir John Harington, in his translation of Ariosto's *Orlando Furioso* in 1591, mentions a sonnet of Sidney's "which many I am sure have read"; that particular sonnet was not published until seven years later. Many people kept commonplace books in which they would copy down poems from borrowed manuscript copies. Professional scribes made a living by copying manuscripts, for authors or for readers. There are even complaints by printers of the hoarding of literary manuscripts by "their grand possessors." There is a difference, which has not always been appreciated, between the poetry of the professional poets who wrote for print and the gentle or noble poets who wrote for circulation in manuscript among their cultivated friends.

ART, NATURE, AND POETRY

Elizabethan taste had some very definite and particular characteristics of its own, and the student who wishes to read Elizabethan literature in the spirit of its own time must adjust his mind to the differences between the aesthetic principles of the 16th century and those of our own day. In the 16th century there still remained much of the medieval awareness of the arts as *crafts*, and every writer of the period shows an amazing knowledge of the techniques of many crafts or "mysteries" now unfamiliar. Shakespeare is not an isolated example, and it has been often noticed that his works show an intimate knowledge of such matters as gardening, hawking, dressmaking, archery, building, and so on. Managing the great horse in the tournament was an art. Sailing was an art. Planting a kitchen garden was an art. What they had in common was that they all used the materials of nature but exploited the ingenuity of man's mind. The same fundamental characteristic was thought to apply to the art or craft of writing.

We have been taught by the Romantic movement to glorify nature and to regard the works of art as attempts, usually unsuccessful, to emulate nature. This conception would have seemed strange indeed to the Elizabethans. They recognized, of course, that nature was the cause and basis of all; but that seemed to them no reason why the ingenuity of man should not be used in enabling nature to outdo herself. In *The Winter's Tale* Polixenes is amused at the naïveté of Perdita, who protests that she will have no streaked carnations or gillyflowers in her garden because

> I have heard it said
> There is an art which in their piedness shares
> With great creating nature.

"Say there be," replies Polixenes,

> Yet nature is made better by no mean
> But nature makes that mean. So, over that art
> Which you say adds to nature, is an art
> That nature makes. You see, sweet maid, we marry
> A gentler scion to the wildest stock
> And make conceive a bark of baser kind
> By bud of nobler race. This is an art
> Which does mend nature—change it rather; but
> The art itself is nature.

There was no uneasiness in the Elizabethan mind about a possible conflict between art and nature, for the reason that Polixenes gives. And the improvement by device, by arrangement, by art, of something naturally beautiful extended to all aspects of life, so that there was felt to be no great gulf between literature and the sports of the field or the arts of the kitchen. George Puttenham, in discussing ornament in his *Art of English Poesy* (1589), compares poetry to dress and to jewelry:

And as we see in these great Madames of honor, be they for personage or otherwise never so comely and beautiful, yet if they want their courtly habiliments or at leastwise such other apparel as custom and civility have ordained to cover their naked bodies, would be half ashamed or greatly out of countenance to be seen in that sort, and perchance do then think themselves more amiable in every man's eye when they be in their richest attire, suppose of silks or tissues and costly embroideries, than when they go in cloth or in any other plain and simple apparel. Even so cannot our vulgar Poesy show itself either gallant or gorgeous, if any limb be left naked and bare and not clad in his kindly clothes and colors, such as may convey them somewhat out of sight, that is, from the common course of ordinary speech and capacity of the vulgar judgment, and yet being artificially handled must needs yield it much more beauty and commendation. This ornament we speak of is given to it by figures and figurative speeches, which be the flowers, as it were, and colors that a poet setteth upon his language by art, as the embroiderer doth his stone and pearl or passements of gold upon the stuff of a princely garment, or as th' excellent painter bestoweth the rich Orient colors upon his table of portrait.

"Artificially" is used by Puttenham, and by the other Elizabethans, as a word of praise. It means "done with artifice, with skill, with art." And the word "curious" meant to the Elizabethans "skillfully, elaborately, or beautifully wrought" or, in a more general sense, "excellent or fine."

The Elizabethan garden was designed as a square, filled with elaborate and intricate, but perfectly regular, design. Francis Bacon protests at gardens which include plots of different colored earths, so arranged as to form a design even without the flowers planted in them; he says he sees enough of this kind of thing in confections and tarts. Yet the very protest shows that his taste was perhaps not typical, and a contemporary might well have asked him why a garden should not look like a confection from the baker's—they were both samples of the art of design. Some Elizabethans had their houses built in the shape of an E, out of honor to the queen, and one man, John Thorpe, designed his house in the form of his own initials. These instances were extreme, of course, but they show the tendency.

Contrapuntal music (composed of several independent melodies joined together), which was sung by the Elizabethans in an accomplished amateur manner, was an intricate kind of music, with elaborate patterns and complex harmonies. The composer Thomas Morley (ca. 1557–1603) says of the madrigal:

As for the music, it is, next unto the motet, the most artificial and to men of understanding most delightful. If therefore you will compose in this kind you must possess yourself with an amorous humor * * * so that you must in your music be wavering like the wind, sometime wanton, sometime grave and staid, otherwhile effeminate; you may maintain points and revert them, use triplaes and show the very uttermost of your variety, and the more variety you show the better shall you please.

But a rigid form was to control all of this extravagance, just as the square border of a garden and the regularity of the pattern controlled the exuberance of the curves in the "knot" or design.

All of this has its counterpart in poetry. The geometrical design is present in such poems as the one by Arthur Gorges which begins

Your face	Your tongue	Your wit
So fair	So sweet	So sharp
First bent	Then drew	So hit
Mine eye	Mine ear	My heart * * *

(It can be read both ways, across and down.) The balance and antithesis in Lyly's prose style is an example of the same kind of literary interest. The sestina, a poem in which the last words of each line in the first stanza are repeated in a different order in each of the following stanzas, was a form used by Sidney and other craftsmen in poetry.

The verse forms used by the Elizabethans range from the extremely simple four-line ballad stanza through the rather complicated form of the sonnet to the elaborate and beautiful 18-line stanza of Spenser's *Epithalamion*. A stanza such as

> The man of life upright
> Whose guileless heart is free
> From all dishonest deeds
> Or thought of vanity

might have been written by any one of many poets at almost any time in the 16th century; it happened to have been written by a fine craftsman, Thomas Campion, near the end of it. Henry Howard, Earl of Surrey, who introduced blank verse into English and helped introduce the sonnet in the reign of Henry VIII, was also a practitioner of a form of iambic couplet in which the first line had twelve syllables and the second fourteen:

> The young man eke that feels his bones with pains oppressed,
> How he would be a rich old man, to live and lie at rest.

This verse form, called "poulter's measure" (because a poulter's dozen was supposed to be sometimes twelve and sometimes fourteen), was the most common verse form in the 60's and 70's. Its dreary monotony in long stretches is matched only by the "fourteener" couplet of fourteen syllables in a line. We still have examples of these forms in our hymnbooks; when each line of poulter's measure is printed as two lines, the hymnbooks call it "short meter"; when they so divide fourteeners they call it "common meter."

Sonnets, which the Elizabethans often called "quatorzains," using the term "sonnet" loosely for any short poem, are fourteen-line poems in iambic pentameter with elaborate rhyme schemes. The most common Italian form, which Wyatt, Sidney, and others imitated, was divided structurally into the octave (first eight lines) and the sestet (last six). A typical rhyme scheme was *abba abba cdecde*. The so-called English sonnet, introduced by Surrey and practiced by Shakespeare, is structurally three quatrains and a couplet: *abab cdcd efef gg*. Spenser, the most experimental and the most gifted prosodist of the century, preferred a form that is harder to write and richer in rhymes: *abab bcbc cdcd ee*.

The six-line stanza and the seven-line rhyme royal or Troilus stanza, both practiced by Chaucer, survived into the 16th century. Shakespeare used the former in *Venus and Adonis* and the latter in *The Rape of Lucrece*; that popular collection of historical poems, *The Mirror for Magistrates*, features rhyme royal.

An innovation was Spenser's nine-line stanza, called after him the "Spenserian stanza," which added to the Italian ottava rima (*abab bc bc*) an additional line of twelve syllables, an Alexandrine, rhyming with the preceding line. This is the stanza form which serves so well the large descriptive and narrative requirements of *The Faerie Queene*. The elaborate scheme of the stanza Spenser devised for his *Epithalamion* perhaps illustrates the height of Elizabethan craftsmanship in verse. Its eighteen lines rhyme *ababcc*, then various combinations in the second six, and finally three couplets. Lines 6, 11, and 16 are short, having only six syllables contrasted to the pentameter's ten, and the last line is an Alexandrine, as in the Spenserian stanza.

GENRES AND CONVENTIONS IN POETRY

A literary convention is a pattern that has become habitual and arouses certain expectations in the reader. For the Elizabethan poet available conventions enabled him to assume particular responses from his audience and to show his learning by his exploitation of these well-known patterns and his virtuosity by his ingenious elaborations of them. It must not be supposed that these conventions were lifeless forms, so stale with use that they no longer carried meaning or conviction. They were charged with values, with associations. They related writer and reader to other times, other languages, other cultures.

The pastoral convention presented a simple and idealized world, inhabited by shepherds and shepherdesses, concerned not at all with war or politics or commerce. Its business consisted of tending the flocks, friendly poetic contests among shepherds, love, and the pursuit of contentment rather than fame or fortune.

Pastoral lyrics expressed the joys of pastoral life or disappointment in love. Pastoral eclogues were dialogues between shepherds in which a poetic contest was staged, or there was serious, satirical comment on abuses in the great world concealed in the disguise of the homely local concerns of country folk. There were also, of course, pastoral dramas and pastoral romances (prose fiction) which embodied the same values of *otium* (leisure), freedom from pride and ambition, and the pursuit of humble contentment.

Another popular convention was that of the mythological-erotic poem, derived from Ovid mainly but influenced by Italian imitations of him. In the middle ages Ovid's poetry had been allegorized and interpreted morally —the same process that has overtaken the love songs in the Song of Solomon in the Old Testament. This process continued on into the 17th century, but a newer treatment of the convention returned to the frank sensuality of the Latin amatory poets and allowed for elaborate mythological decoration of the narrative without worrying about moral propriety or allegorical interpretation. Such poems appealed to a courtly taste; they validated the senses and they asserted the primacy of physical beauty and the imagination. Shakespeare in *Venus and Adonis* and Marlowe in *Hero and Leander* were among the poets who practiced in this convention.

Sometimes related to the Ovidian tradition but separate from it in origin was the convention of the complaint poem. This goes back to a medieval genre represented by works of the Italian Boccaccio and his English imitators, Lydgate and the authors of *The Mirror for Magistrates*. The complaint poem is essentially tragic and moral. In it the ghost of someone who fell from high place bemoans his fate and warns others. If the ghost is a woman, like Daniel's Rosamund, her fall was caused by the frailty of her sex and the poem may be related to the Ovidian tradition. Another kind of poem, which came both from Ovid and the *Mirror for Magistrates* tradition, was the heroical epistle, practised notably by Drayton.

The Elizabethan sonnet, which reached the height of its vogue in the last decade of the 16th century, depended upon a convention established by Petrarch and followed by his many imitators in Italy and France. In this tradition the poet complains of his lady's coldness; he describes the contrary states of feeling the lover experiences; and he writes sonnets on the conventional themes of sleep, absence, originality, renunciation, and others. The purposes of the love sonneteers differed, of course, but what they had in common might be described as an ambition to give dignity and power to the theme of love by the elaborate rhetorical and stylistic devices available in the Petrarchan tradition. Lesser poets often produced nothing but standard conceits served up in fourteen-line helpings, but major poets such as Sidney, Spenser, and Shakespeare wrote sonnets of power and originality that stand out as major poetic products of the Elizabethan Age.

The conventional forms for satire were less well fixed in the 16th century than in some later periods, though there is a good deal of Elizabethan satirical verse. Some examples belong to a medieval tradition coming down from *Piers Plowman*, which was believed to be the only English masterpiece in satire until satires by the "university wits" in the tradition of the Latin satirists Persius and Juvenal began to appear, and some were written by young John Donne and circulated only in manuscript until after the poet's death in 1631. The epigram was a form that flourished, both in the classical tradition of Martial and in the lyric form of words for a madrigal; the famous *The Silver Swan* (p. 847) is an example.

Poetry for music also followed some conventions: the dance song of course had its definite rhythms and refrains, and many well-known tunes provided the formula by which poet after poet composed new words. In the polyphonic madrigal, the same phrases tend to be repeated again and again, while the words often get lost in the music because various voices sing different words at the same time. As a result, the poem written as a madrigal is usually short and simple both in language and ideas. The "ayre," however, is a song written for a single voice to a lute accompaniment and is usually sung straight through. Since the words are much more intelligible, the thought can be more complex. While the poem is often a good deal longer than the madrigal (since the same melody is repeated over and over), the poem is divided into repetitive stanzas.

There were conventions as well for the heroic poem, of which Spenser's *Faerie Queene* is the prime example. The classical epics of Homer and Virgil had their influence, but so did the romantic Italian epics of Ariosto and Tasso. Chapman's Homer and Harington's Ariosto were regarded by contemporaries as something more than translation, having much of the interest and significance of original poems.

The major conventions in poetry did not stifle originality; they served as both an ordering device and a challenge that stimulated the poet to something fresh and new. When these conventions were alive for writers and readers, they had significance in themselves, which was an essential part of the total significance of the poem. Knowledge of the more important Elizabethan conventions is not simply of scholarly interest; it is essential to the experience of the poem as a poem.

ELIZABETHAN MOODS AND ATTITUDES

The English Renaissance was no sharp break with the past. Attitudes and feelings which had been characteristic of the 15th or 14th centuries persisted well down into the era of humanism and Reformation. George Gascoigne, the leading writer of the 1570's, has in many ways a medieval point of view, and the popular collection of verse tales of the fall of princes called *The Mirror for Magistrates* (first published in 1559, and reprinted with additions in 1563, 1587, and 1610) derives from Lydgate and Boccaccio. Even a lyric by that flamboyant and "modern" Elizabethan, Sir Walter Ralegh, may embody a sentiment of the vanity and transitoriness of all earthly ambitions and achievements. The Dance of Death and related images were still living symbols to the Elizabethan imagination; witness Shakespeare's *Richard II* (III.ii.152–70):

> And nothing can we call our own but death
> And that small model of the barren earth
> Which serves as paste and cover to our bones.
> For God's sake let us sit upon the ground
> And tell sad stories of the death of kings!
> How some have been deposed; some slain in war;
> Some haunted by the ghosts they have deposed;
> Some poisoned by their wives; some sleeping killed—
> All murthered; for within the hollow crown
> That rounds the mortal temples of a king
> Keeps Death his court, and there the antic sits,
> Scoffing his state and grinning at his pomp;
> Allowing him a breath, a little scene,
> To monarchize, be feared, and kill with looks;
> Infusing him with self and vain conceit,
> As if this flesh which walls about our life
> Were brass impregnable: and humored thus,
> Comes at the last, and with a little pin
> Bores through the castle wall, and farewell king!

Yet there was at the same time a spirit of joy and gaiety, of innocence and lightheartedness, that future ages were to look back on as "merry England." This spirit is popular, it comes from the folk and from the persistent love of Englishmen for their countryside; it is spontaneous, yet it seems somehow stable and permanent. Perhaps its best expression is in the songs of Shakespeare's plays:

> When daffodils begin to peer,
> With heigh! the doxy over the dale,
> Why, then comes in the sweet o' the year;
> For the red blood reigns in the winter's pale.

or

> When daisies pied and violets blue
> And ladysmocks all silver-white
> And cuckoobuds of yellow hue
> Do paint the meadows with delight.

The mood of pastoral, as we have already seen in our notice of that convention, is generally one of quiet contentment, of reflective leisure, of the enjoyment of a simple, idealized world. Marlowe's *Passionate Shepherd to His Love* beautifully invokes this world.

There was of course also among the Elizabethans the opposite mood: the burning desire for conquest, for achievement, for surmounting all obstacles. The Elizabethans called it "the aspiring mind." The great projector of this mood is Christopher Marlowe, who has his heroes fling themselves into the pursuit of power—

> Is it not passing brave to be a king
> And ride in triumph through Persepolis?—

or into the lust for gold—

> Infinite riches in a little room—

or into the search for knowledge—

> All things that move between the quiet poles
> Shall be at my command; emperors and kings
> Are but obeyed in their several provinces,
> Nor can they raise the wind or rend the clouds;
> But his dominion that excels in this
> Stretcheth as far as doth the mind of man.

Marlowe's heroes are defeated finally, all of them, but their fiery spirit in assaulting the limits of the possible echoes after they are gone.

The Elizabethan spirit has been described as "sensuous, comprehensive, extravagant, disorderly, thirsty for beauty, abounding in the zest for life." This is part of the truth, but not all of it. Fundamentally, the thought and feeling of Shakespeare's contemporaries was far more deeply affected by Christian humanism than by the extravagances of Marlowe. We need to remember Ben Jonson, with his classical principles of structure and decorum and his ideal of the balanced man. Jonson was in every respect more typical of his age than Shakespeare. His emphasis upon learning, his reconciliation of ancient models and English content, and his critical responsibility truly represent the ideal English poet of his time, as Sidney would have visualized him. Because his major work was done after 1603, he is represented in the 17th-century section of this anthology.

The second generation of English humanists—men like Roger Ascham (1515–68, tutor to Queen Elizabeth), Sir John Cheke (1514–57, professor of Greek at Cambridge), and Thomas Wilson (1525–81, rhetorician and translator)—combined an earnest Protestant Christianity with their classical learning, and Ascham vigorously opposed the more secular, pagan humanism that was coming out of Italy. These men shaped the University of Cambridge, which in turn shaped many men. It was an Oxford man, however—Richard Hooker—who provided in his great work, *The Laws of Ecclesiastical Polity* (1593 and later), the supreme masterpiece of English Christian humanism. In so far as his doctrine is concerned, Spenser is a Christian humanist, and the label can justly be applied to John Milton, both in content and in form.

If the beginning of the Tudor era showed more links with the past than with the future, it is equally true that the end of Elizabeth's reign prefigured some of the conflict and uncertainty of the time to come. "The disenchantment of the Elizabethans" is a phrase that has been used to describe it. In 1599, the year of Spenser's death, occurred the abortive revolt of the Earl of Essex. Elizabeth was old, a peaceful succession was by no means assured, and the rifts in society which were to mean civil war in the midcentury were already present. An outbreak of satire and epigrams had to be stopped by the authorities. Some of the cynical undercurrent in Shakespeare's *Hamlet* and *Troilus and Cressida* reflects the spirit of the time. John Donne was already writing his poems, and a very different age, the 17th century, was in the offing. In 1603 Elizabeth, the last of the Tudors, died, and to the immense relief of anxious Englishmen, the succession took place peacefully. The new monarch was the Protestant James VI of Scotland, who became James I of England.

Man and Society

The 16th century carried along in its stream so many currents of thought, some ancient and some new, some Christian and some Stoic or skeptic, some systematic and some whimsically personal, that any concise description of them is bound to be oversimplified. Curious minds speculated about everything known or believed in the universe, yet there was a pervading sense that some kinds of knowledge were forbidden. There was a feeling that new discoveries had been made and more were possible, yet men felt an underlying conviction that somehow all wisdom could be encompassed in the writings of classical antiquity and the scriptures. But for all its diversity of views, the 16th century generally held doctrines about man, nature, and order in society in sharp contrast to those held in the 20th.

The view of man held by 16th-century thinkers was essentially a conservative one. It derived from ancient sources and was not fundamentally different from that which had been held in the Middle Ages. The basic concept was that of order, an order which was all-pervasive and reflected a major attribute of God. Presiding over this order was nature, a kind of deputy of God, or, in another sense, one of his manifestations. God gave two books to man; one was the Bible and the other was nature; they revealed the same truth.

This natural order was not devised by man, nor imposed by him; it was always there and remained to be discovered. Man's only function was to conform to it. This was his purpose in life, as everything had a purpose: "God and nature create nothing that has not its use," said Aristotle, and use implies purpose. As one Elizabethan poet wrote,

> I'll ne'er believe that the arch-architect
> With all these fires the heavenly arches decked
> Only for show, and with these glistering shields
> T' amaze poor shepherds watching in the fields.

There were three areas in which this order prevailed, but they were all related and they resembled each other: the great cosmos, the world of created things, and human society. A truth discovered about one realm was applicable to the others.

The Elizabethans were of course aware of mutability and change; their world, for all its basic order, was not static. But change was confined to the center of the universe, our earth, with its four elements arranged in order of weight—earth, water, air, and fire. Out beyond the element of fire began the celestial part of the universe, made of purer stuff and therefore unchanging. This outer area, divided into eight (or sometimes nine) concentric spheres, shed a considerable influence on the sublunary world below.

Each sphere, made of some transparent material, carried a heavenly body—the moon, Mercury, Venus, the sun, Mars, Jupiter, Saturn, and finally the fixed stars. These spheres rotated at different speeds and by rubbing against each other produced celestial sounds, the music of the spheres. The harmony of this music was an instance of fundamental law.

Within the cosmic order, the arrangement of all things was hierarchical. It could be thought of as a ladder or a great chain of being. At the top was God, just below him the angels, then man, then woman, then the animals, then plant life, then inorganic nature, then chaos. This ranking was part of the divine plan and was inherent in fundamental law. Human society had a similar organization and for the same reason. It was governed by three kinds of temporal law: natural law, the law of nations (which derives from natural law), and finally civil law, which dealt with the particular customs of individual countries. They all rested, in greater or less degree, upon divine sanction. Accordingly, the system of government in England, with its king and lords and commons, might differ from the system in another country, but it still represented the will of God for England. Just as there were stars of various magnitudes in the heavens and categories of animals on the earth, so there were four classes of Englishmen: gentlemen, citizens, yeoman artificers, and laborers.

Any disruption of this order and degree produced confusion which was like a return to chaos and an undoing of God's creation; it could not last because it was unnatural. Accordingly the Elizabethans dreaded social upheaval and revolution for religious and scientific as well as political reasons. Any attempt to change established order, whether of kings and magistrates or of bishops and priests, was viewed with horror as a violation of God's plan and a defiance of the laws of nature.

Man himself occupied a unique position in creation. God had made three kinds of creatures: the angelical, who were pure intelligence; the brutal, who were pure "sense" or instinct, without "discourse of reason"; and the human, who had some attributes of both. Man could, because of his unique position, move gradually upward to the angelic level, but this had become much more difficult since the Fall in the Garden of Eden. Since then it was much more likely that he would move downward toward the condition of beasts. There was available to him, however, Divine Grace, by means of which he could, if he would, reverse the effects of the Fall—a reversal which remains within man's capacity, even though the human will itself had been weakened and corrupted by the Fall.

Standing halfway between angels and beasts, man was in a precarious position. His physiology also suggested his critical instability. In the center of him lay his soul, immortal and undamageable, though capable of punishment and reward. But that soul was, during life, the prisoner of a body which was controlled by the four humors. Unless these were in perfect balance, sense would triumph over intellect in one way or another. Choler, which was related to the element fire, made a man wrathful; blood, related to the element air, made him sanguine and over-optimistic; phlegm, related to water, made him silent and morose; and melancholy, related to earth, made him despondent.

It is easy to see that such a creature would have to be rigorously disciplined by his education and rigorously controlled by his governmental system. Yet education was feasible, and, in the 16th century, most important. The individual could be trained and developed because there was, running through the universe, a fundamental harmony. To unite one's self with this harmony was worth any discipline and a lifetime's endeavor. The most popular of all ancient moral treatises, Cicero's *De Officiis*, had explained man's great opportunity: "It is no mean manifestation of Nature and Reason that man is the only animal that has a feeling for order, for propriety, for moderation in word and deed. And so no other animal has a sense of beauty, loveliness, harmony in the visible world."

SIR THOMAS MORE
(1478–1535)

1514–16: Writing *Utopia*.
1532: Resigns as Lord Chancellor after refusing to take oath to support Act of Succession and Supremacy.

More's famous philosophical romance *Utopia* (the name means "nowhere") is the father of a whole class of writings, from Bacon's *New Atlantis* (1626), through Swift's *Gulliver's Travels* (1726), Butler's *Erewhon* (1872), and Bellamy's *Looking Backward* (1888), to the "science fiction" stories of the present. But More's book has its own ancestry. It derives in part from Plato's *Republic* (and hence is philosophical) and in part from the accounts of travelers like Amerigo Vespucci (1507) and hence is romantic. It is a major monument of the great Christian humanist awakening of which Pico della Mirandola (1463–94), Desiderius Erasmus (ca. 1466–1536), and More himself were the most brilliant figures. Since the first of these was Italian, the second Dutch, and the third English, the movement was obviously international; *Utopia* was written in Latin, the international language.

Utopia represents itself as a traveler's tale, told by a veteran mariner (who is also a philosopher) to a group of somewhat skeptical companions as they sit in a garden one afternoon in Antwerp, in Holland. It is divided into two books. In the first, written in dialogue form, the corruption of European civil life is criticized. In the second, the traveler Raphael Hythloday describes the institutions of Utopia, with many ironic references to the real world with which the listeners are familiar.

Utopia is thus not presented as a mere dream or impractical fancy, as the modern use of the word "utopian" sometimes suggests. It is the fruit of More's serious thought—though he was never wholly serious—on the great social problems of his time. More felt, very strongly, the value of the ideals embodied in the rules of the monastic orders. Yet he was himself a man of the world, a lawyer and negotiator; he saw how far from realization in practice were the social ideals he admired. Central to his thought is the idea of community of property, for which he had a precedent in Plato as well as in the rules of the monastic orders; no fundamental reform in society is possible until private property is abolished. Yet it is typical of More's carefully balanced method that a standard defense of private property is put into the mouth of More as a character in the dialogue, against the position of the main speaker, Hythloday.

More's life was even more remarkable than his writings. He was born in London, the son of a prominent lawyer; as a boy he served in Archbishop Morton's household, then proceeded to Oxford and the Inns of Court. He became a friend of Erasmus, the great humanist, scholar, and editor of the New Testament; it was to More that Erasmus dedicated his satire *The Praise of Folly*. Soon after he wrote *Utopia* More rose to positions of great responsibility under King Henry VIII: Master of Requests, Privy Councillor, Speaker of the House of Commons, and finally Lord Chancellor. In 1532, after the king's marriage to Anne Boleyn, More refused to take the oath for the Act of Succession and Supremacy. Although he had compromised before, as any successful administrator must, his conscience would not permit him to assert that any temporal lord, even Henry, could or ought to be head of that spiritual body, the church. From the point of view of the government, his refusal was treason, and he was condemned to death; efforts, including those of his wife, to reconcile him with Henry failed, and in 1535 he was executed. No death in English history is more famous: as he mounted the shaky steps to the scaffold, he said to the sheriff's officer, "I pray you, Master Lieutenant, see me safe up, and for my coming down let me shift for myself"; as he put his head on the block he moved his beard aside, remarking that his beard had done the king no offense. He was of course certain that he was not dying for treason, but in and for the faith of the Catholic Church. Four hundred years later he was canonized by the church as St. Thomas More.

From Utopia[1]

From *Book I*

The most victorious and triumphant King of England, Henry the Eighth of that name, in all royal virtues a prince most peerless, had recently some differences with Charles,[2] the most serene Prince of Castile, and sent me into Flanders to negotiate and compose matters between them. I was colleague and companion to that incomparable man, Cuthbert Tunstall,[3] whom the king lately made Master of the Rolls to the great satisfaction of all. I will say nothing of this man, not because I fear the testimony of a friend will be questioned, but because his learning and virtues are greater than I can describe. And also they are so well-known that they do not need my commenda-

---

1. The translation from which these selections are taken is by H. S. V. Ogden (1949).
2. The future Emperor Charles V; the differences had to do with the wool trade. The negotiations took place in 1515 and 1516.
3. Cuthbert Tunstall, later Bishop of London and of Durham, was one of More's closest friends.

tion, unless I would, according to the proverb, "Show the sun with a lantern."

The men appointed by the prince to treat with us, all excellent men, met us at Bruges according to agreement. The chief man among them and their leader was the Margrave of Bruges, a distinguished man. But the wisest and best spoken was George Temse, the Provost of Cassel, a man eloquent both by nature and training, very learned in the law, and most skillful in affairs through his capacity and long practice. After we had met several times and could not come to an agreement, they went to Brussels for some days to learn their prince's pleasure.

Meanwhile I went to Antwerp, since our business permitted it. Of those who visited me while I was there, Peter Giles[4] was more congenial to me than any of the others. He was a native of Antwerp, a man much respected there and worthy of the highest regard. I do not know of a more cultivated or a better bred young man anywhere. He is, indeed, the best and most learned of men, and besides, very courteous to all. To his intimates he is so loving, so trustworthy, and so deeply affectionate that it would be very hard to find another friend like him anywhere. No man is more modest or more candid. No man unites more simplicity with prudence. His conversation is so pleasant, and so witty without vulgarity, that the fervent desire I felt to see my native country and my wife and children (from whom I had been away more than four months) was much eased by his company.

One day after I had heard mass at Notre Dame, the most beautiful and most frequented church in Antwerp, I was about to return to my lodgings when I happened to see him talking with a stranger, a man well advanced in years. The stranger had a sunburned face, a long beard, and a cloak hanging carelessly from his shoulders. From his appearance and clothing I took him to be a seaman. When Peter saw me, he approached and greeted me. As I was returning his salutation, he took me aside, and pointing to the stranger, said, "Do you see that man? I was just thinking of bringing him to you."

"He would have been very welcome on your account," I answered.

"And on his own, too," he said, "if you knew him, for there is no man alive who can tell you so much about unknown peoples and countries. And I know that you are most eager for such information."

"Then," said I, "I did not guess badly, for at first sight I took him for a seaman."

---

4. Peter Giles, or Petrus Aegidius, was town clerk of Antwerp, a humanist and friend of Erasmus. He arranged for the first printing of *Utopia*.

"No," he replied, "you are mistaken, for he has sailed not as the sailor Palinurus, but as Ulysses, or rather as Plato.[5] This Raphael, surnamed Hythloday (for so he is called), though not ignorant of the Latin tongue, is eminently learned in the Greek. He has applied himself more particularly to Greek because he has given himself wholly to philosophy, in which he knew that the Romans have left us nothing that is valuable except what is to be found in Seneca and Cicero. He was so desirous of seeing the world that he divided his patrimony among his brothers (he is Portuguese by birth), and threw in his lot with Americus Vespucius. He took part in the last three of Vespucius's four voyages, accounts of which are now published. But he did not return home with him on the last voyage. After much effort, he won permission from Americus to be one of the twenty-four who were left in a fort at the farthest place at which they touched in their last voyage. Being left thus was highly gratifying to a man who gave more thought to his travels than to his burial place, and who often used to say that one who has no grave is covered by the sky and that the road to heaven is equally short from all places.

"Yet this disposition of mind would have cost him dear if God had not been very gracious to him. After the departure of Vespucius he traveled over many countries with five companions from the fort. At last by singular good fortune he got to Ceylon and from thence to Calcutta, where he very happily found some Portuguese ships. And so, beyond anyone's expectation, he came back to his own country."

When Peter had told me this, I thanked him for his kindness in wishing to make me acquainted with a man whose conversation he knew would be so acceptable to me, and I turned toward Raphael. Upon that Raphael and I greeted one another. And after the ordinary civilities of strangers upon their first meeting, we all went to my house. There in the garden we sat down on a grassy bank and conversed.

He told us that when Vespucius had sailed away, he and his companions that had stayed behind in the fort often met the people of the country, and by fair and gentle speech gradually won their favor. Before long they came to dwell with them quite safely and even familiarly. He also told us that they were esteemed by the prince (I have forgotten his name and his country), who furnished them plentifully with all things necessary, and who also gave them the means of traveling, both boats when they went by

5. Palinurus, Aeneas' pilot, fell overboard when asleep and drowned. He is here contrasted with Ulysses, who was regarded as the type of the thoughtful, observant traveler. Plato is cited as the profound philosopher; his *Republic* strongly influenced *Utopia*. Raphael Hythloday is an invented character; his last name is coined from Greek words meaning "a skilled conveyer of trifles or nonsense."

water and wagons when they traveled overland. He sent with them a faithful guide who was to introduce and recommend them to such other princes as they had a mind to see. After many days' journey, they came to towns and cities, and to commonwealths that were both well peopled and happily governed.

Under the equator and as far on both sides of it as the sun moves, there lie vast deserts parched with the perpetual heat of the sun. The whole region is desolate and gloomy, savage and uncultivated, inhabited by wild beasts and serpents, and by a few men as wild and dangerous as the beasts themselves. As they went on, conditions gradually grew milder. The heat was less burning, the earth greener, and even the beasts less fierce. At last they found nations, cities, and towns that had mutual commerce among themselves and with their neighbors, and that traded by sea and land with remote countries. From then on, he said, they were able to visit many lands on all sides, for they were welcome on board any ship about to make a voyage.

The first vessels that they saw were flat-bottomed, with sails made of close-woven reeds and wicker, or in some places of leather. Farther on they found ships made with round keels and canvas sails, in all ways like our ships. The seamen were skillful both in sailing and in navigation. They were most grateful to him, Raphael said, for showing them the use of the compass, of which they had been ignorant. For that reason they had sailed with great caution and only in summer. Now they have such confidence in the compass that they no longer fear winter, and are carefree rather than safe. This discovery, which they thought so much to their advantage, may become the cause of much mischief to them through their imprudence.

It would take too long to set forth all that Raphael told us he had observed, and it would be a digression from our present purpose. Perhaps in another place we shall tell more about the things that are worth knowing, especially about the wise and prudent institutions that he observed among the civilized nations. We asked him many questions about such things and he answered us very willingly. We made no inquiries, however, about monsters, which are common enough. Scyllas, ravenous harpies,[6] and cannibals are easy to find anywhere, but it is not so easy to find states that are well and wisely governed.

While he told us of many things which are amiss among those new-found nations, he also reckoned up not a few things from which patterns might be taken for correcting the errors of our

---

6. "Scyllas" were horrible monsters, like that which dwelt in a cave in the rock Scylla in the *Odyssey;* she had twelve feet and six heads, with three rows of teeth in each head. "Harpies" were large birds with faces of women pale with hunger and long, sharp claws.

own cities and kingdoms. These I shall treat in another place,[7] as I have said. Now I intend to relate only what he told us about the manners and laws of the Utopians, first setting forth the occasion that led us to speak of that commonwealth. Raphael had been talking very wisely about the numerous errors and also the wise institutions found both among those nations and us, speaking as intimately about the customs and government of each place he had visited as though he had lived there all his life. Peter was struck with admiration.

"I wonder, Master Raphael," he said, "why you do not enter some king's service, for I know of no prince who would not be eager to have you. Your learning and your knowledge of places and men would entertain him pleasantly, while your advice and your examples would be invaluable. Thus you would serve your own interest and be useful to all your friends."

"I am not greatly concerned about my friends," he said, "for I have already done my duty toward them. While I was still young and healthy, I distributed among my relations and friends the possessions which other men do not part with till they are old and sick (and then only grudgingly and because they can no longer keep them). I think my friends should rest content with this and not expect that for their sake I should enslave myself to any king whatsoever."

"Well said," Peter replied, "but I do not mean that you should be a slave to any king, only that you should be of service to him."

"The difference is a mere matter of words," Raphael replied.

"As you will," said Peter, "but I do not see any other way in which you can be so useful either to your friends or to the public, to say nothing of making yourself happier."

"Happier?" exclaimed Raphael. "Would a way of life so abhorrent to my nature make my life happier? Now I live as I will, and I believe very few courtiers can say that. As a matter of fact, there are so many men courting the favor of the great that it will be no great loss if they have to do without me or others like me."

Then I said, "It is clear, Master Raphael, that you desire neither wealth nor power, and indeed I value and admire such a man much more than I do any of the great men in the world. Yet I think, if you would give your time and effort to public affairs, you would do a thing worthy of a generous and philosophical nature like yours, even though you might not enjoy it. You could best perform such a service by belonging to the council of some great prince, whom you would urge on to whatever is noble and just. I know you would do this, if you were in such a post. And your efforts would be effective, because a people's welfare or misery

7. See Book II below.

flows wholly from their prince, as from a never-failing spring. Your learning is so full, even when not combined with experience, and your experience so great, even without learning, that you would be an exceptional councilor to any king whatsoever."

"You are doubly mistaken, my dear More," said he, "both in your opinion of me and in your estimate of the situation itself. I do not have that capacity which you fancy to be in me, and if I had it, the public would not be any better off through the sacrifice of my leisure; for most princes apply themselves to warlike pursuits (in which I have no skill or interest) rather than to the useful arts of peace. They are generally more set on acquiring new kingdoms rightly or wrongly, than on governing well those that they already have. Moreover the councilors of kings are so wise that they need no advice from others (or at least so it seems to themselves). At the same time they accept and even applaud the most absurd statements of men whose favor they seek for the sake of standing well with the prince. It is natural that each man should flatter himself by thinking his own opinions best. The old crow loves his young and the ape his cubs. Now in a court made up of those who envy all others and admire only themselves, if a man should propose something that he had read in history or observed in his travels, the other councilors would fear that their whole reputation for wisdom was in danger, and that they would be regarded as plain fools unless they could show his suggestion was weak and defective. If all else failed, they would take refuge in the retort that such and such things pleased our ancestors and would that we could match their wisdom! With this they would settle down as though they had said the last word on the subject and as though there were a terrible danger in finding a man wiser than our ancestors in anything. We readily follow whatever they did, as though it were necessarily best. But if something better is proposed, we seize the excuse of reverence for past times and cling to it doggedly. I have met with these proud, absurd, and morose judgments in many places, and once even in England. * * * "

From *Book II*

1. THEIR COUNTRY AND AGRICULTURE

The island of Utopia is two hundred miles in breadth in the middle part where it is widest, and it is nowhere much narrower than this except toward the two ends. These ends, drawn around in a five-hundred-mile curve, make the island crescent-shaped. Between the horns of the crescent, which are some eleven miles apart, the sea comes in and spreads into a great bay. Being well secured from the wind, the bay does not rage with great waves, but is quite like a lake. This makes nearly the whole inner coast a harbor, greatly facilitating mutual trade. But the entrance into the bay, what with shallows on one side and rocks on the other, is very dangerous. Near the middle there is one rock that rises above the water, and so is not dangerous. On the top of it a tower has been built, in which a garrison is kept. The other rocks lie under water and are very treacherous. The channels are known only to the Utopians, so if any stranger should chance to enter the bay without one of their pilots, he would run a great danger of shipwreck. Even they themselves could not enter safely if some marks on the coast did not direct their way. If these were shifted even a little, any fleet coming against them, no matter how great it was, would certainly be lost.

On the other side of the island there are likewise many harbors, and the coast is so fortified by nature and art that a small number of men could hold off the attack of a great force. They say (and the appearance of the place bears this out) that their land was once not an island. But Utopus, who conquered the country and gave it his name (it was previously called Abraxa),[1] brought its rude and uncivilized inhabitants to such a high level of culture and humanity that now they excel all other people in that part of the world. When he had subdued them, he cut a channel fifteen miles long where their land joined the continent and thus brought the sea entirely around their land. He not only forced the natives to work at it, but his soldiers too, so that the natives would not think they were treated like slaves. By putting so many men to work, he finished the project quickly, and the neighbors, who at first had laughed at his folly, were struck with admiration and terror at his success.

There are fifty-four cities on the island, all large and well built, and with the same language, customs, institutions, and laws. All of them are built on the same plan, as far as the location permits. The nearest are at least twenty-four miles apart, and those that are farthest are not so far but that a man can go on foot from one city to the next in a day.

Once a year each city sends three of its wisest elders to Amaurot[2] to consult about their common concerns. Amaurot is the chief city of the island and lies near its center, so that it is the most convenient place for the elders to meet. Every city has enough ground assigned to it so that it has at least ten miles of farm land in every direction. Where the cities are farther apart, they have more ground. No city desires to enlarge its bounds, for the inhabitants consider themselves husbandmen rather than landlords. They have built houses all over the countryside, well designed and fur-

1. From Greek, "not small."
2. The name is coined from a Greek adjective meaning "dim, obscure"—a suitable name for the capital of "Nowhere."

nished with farm equipment. These houses are inhabited by citizens who come to the country by turns to dwell in them. No country household has fewer than forty men and women in it, besides two bondmen.[3] A master and mistress, serious and mature persons, are in charge of each household. A magistrate is placed over every thirty households. Every year twenty from each household move back to the city, after completing a two-year turn in the country. In their place twenty others are sent out from town, to learn farm work from those that have already been in the country for a year and are somewhat skilled in it. In turn they must teach those who come the following year. If they were all equally ignorant of farm work and new to it, they might damage the crops through ignorance. This custom of shifting the farm workers is established in order that no one will have to do this hard work against his will for more than two years, but many of them ask to stay longer because they take a natural delight in farm life.

The farm workers till the soil, care for the cattle, hew wood, and take it to the city by land or water, as is most convenient. They breed an enormous number of chickens by a marvelous method. Men hatch the eggs, not hens, by keeping them in a warm place at an even temperature. The chicks, as soon as they come out of the shell, recognize and follow men instead of their mothers.

They raise very few horses, but these are full of mettle and are kept only for exercising the youth in the art of horsemanship. For the work of plowing and hauling they employ only oxen. They think horses are stronger than oxen, but they find that oxen can hold out longer and are less subject to disease, and so can be kept with less cost and effort. Moreover, when they are too old for work, they can be used for meat.

They raise grain only for bread. They drink wine, apple or pear cider, or water, sometimes clear, but often mixed with honey or licorice, of which they have an abundance. Although they know just how much grain each city and its district will consume, they sow more grain and breed more cattle than they need for their own use, and share the surplus with their neighbors. When they need goods on the farms which they do not make there, they get them from the town magistrates without giving anything in exchange. This is not inconvenient, since most of them go to town once a month, especially on holidays. When harvest time comes, the country magistrates notify the towns how many hands will be needed. The harvesters come at the right time, and commonly get in the whole harvest in one fair day.

---

3. More provides for a few bondmen or slaves in Utopia, to perform tasks unfit for citizens, such as slaughtering. Bondage is usually a punishment for serious crimes.

7. THEIR GOLD AND SILVER, AND HOW THEY KEEP IT

Therefore[4] they have accumulated an inestimable amount of gold and silver, but they do not keep it in the form of treasure. I am reluctant to tell you how they keep it, for fear you will not believe me. I would not have believed it myself if anyone had told me about it—not unless I had seen it with my own eyes. It is almost always true that the more different anything is from what people are used to, the harder it is to believe. In view of the fact that the Utopians' customs are so different from ours, a shrewd judge will not be surprised to find that they do not use gold and silver at all as we do. Since they keep gold and silver only for grave contingencies, they take care that in the meantime no one shall value these metals more than they deserve. Iron is obviously greatly superior to either. Men can no more do without iron than without fire and water. But gold and silver have no indispensable qualities. Human folly has made them precious only because of their scarcity. Nature, like a wise and generous parent, has placed the best things everywhere and in the open, such as air and water and the earth itself, but she has hidden vain and useless things in remote and faraway places.

If they kept their gold and silver guarded in a tower, foolish people might suspect the prince and senate[5] of deceiving the citizens and aiming at some advantage for themselves. If they made plate and wrought-metal work out of them, they would not want to give up such articles and melt them down to pay mercenaries. To solve the problem, they have thought out a plan as much in accord with their institutions as it is contrary to ours. The plan seems incredible to us (except to those of us who are very wise), because we regard gold as of great value and hoard it carefully. While their eating and drinking utensils are made of china and glass, beautiful but inexpensive, their chamber pots and stools both in their public halls and their homes are made of gold and silver. They also use these metals for the chains and fetters of their bondmen. They hang gold rings from the ears of criminals, place gold rings on their fingers, gold collars around their necks, and gold crowns on their heads. Thus they hold gold and silver up to scorn in every way.

The result is that when there is need to part with these metals, which others give up as painfully as if their vitals were being torn out, none of the Utopians regard it as any more than the loss of a penny, so to speak. They find pearls on their shores and

4. More has explained (in a section here omitted) that the Utopians hire mercenary soldiers in time of war and pay them very highly; enemy soldiers often desert to them.

5. The prince, as More has earlier explained, is chosen for life by the senate, whose members are selected by an assembly, whose members in turn are elected from households.

diamonds and carbuncles[6] on certain rocks, but they do not search for them. If they find them by chance, they polish them and adorn their younger children with them. As children they take pride and pleasure in such ornaments, and consequently put them aside when they are older and observe that only children use such baubles. This results from their own sense of propriety and not from their parents' commands, just as our children throw away their nuts,[7] amulets, and dolls, when they grow up.

Different customs and institutions produce quite different ideas and attitudes, a truth I never saw better illustrated than in the behavior of the Anemolian[8] ambassadors, who came to Amaurot while I was there. Because they came to discuss important business, three citizens from each city had come to Amaurot ahead of time. The ambassadors from neighboring states, at least those who had been there before, knew that fine clothing was not esteemed among the Utopians, that silk was scorned, and that gold was considered a shameful thing. They came as plainly clothed as possible. But when the Anemolians, who lived far away and had little intercourse with the Utopians, saw that all the people wore the same coarse clothing, they took it for granted that they did not have anything else. They themselves, being a proud rather than a wise people, decided to dress themselves gloriously like gods and dazzle the eyes of the poor Utopians by the splendor of their garb. The three ambassadors made their entry accompanied by a hundred attendants, all dressed in varicolored clothing, many in silk. Since they were nobles at home, the ambassadors wore cloaks of cloth of gold, necklaces and earrings of gold, gold rings on their fingers, caps hung with gold chains studded with pearls and other jewels, in short decked out with all those things which among the Utopians were considered badges of slavery, signs of punishment, or toys for children. It was a sight to see how high they held their heads when they compared their clothing with that of the Utopians, for the people had swarmed out into the streets. It was no less amusing to think how far they were from creating the impression which they had expected to make, for in the eyes of all the Utopians, except for those few who had visited other states, all this pomp and splendor seemed shameful. The Utopians saluted all the lowest people as lords and paid no respect at all to the ambassadors themselves, because they seemed to be dressed as slaves with their gold chains. And you might have seen children, who had already thrown away their pearls and gems, nudge their mothers upon seeing the jewels in the ambassadors' caps, and say, "Look, mother! See that big fool who wears pearls and gems, as if he were a little boy!"

6. Rubies.   8. Coined from the Greek for "windy."
7. Marbles.

Then she would say seriously, "Hush, my boy. I think he is one of the ambassadors' fools." Others found fault with the golden chains for being useless and so light that any slave might break them, and so loose that a person when he wished could shake them off, and run away. But after the ambassadors had spent one day and then another there, and had seen the great quantity of cheap gold and silver which was scorned as much by the Utopians as it was held in respect by the Anemolians, and when they had learned also that there was more gold and silver in the chains and fetters of a single slave than in the apparel of all three ambassadors, then their feathers fell. Somewhat shamefacedly they laid aside all the finery in which they had strutted, but they did so willingly, as they had conversed with the Utopians and learned their customs and ideas.

12. THEIR MARRIAGE CUSTOMS

A woman is not married before eighteen, nor a man before twenty-two. If a man (or woman) is convicted of an illict affair before marriage, he is severely punished and marriage is denied him for his whole life, unless a prince's pardon remits the punishment. The master and mistress of the household in which the offense has occured are in disgrace for having been remiss in their duty. The reason for punishing this offense so severely is the fear that few would unite in married love, to spend their whole lives with one person and put up with all the annoyances of marriage, unless they were rigorously restrained from promiscuity.

In the choice of wives they carefully follow a custom which seemed to us foolish and absurd. Before marriage some responsible and honorable woman, either a virgin or a widow, presents the woman naked to her suitor and after that some upright man presents the suitor naked to the woman. We laughed at this and condemned it as foolish. On the contrary they wonder at the stupidity of other people, who are exceedingly cautious in matters involving only a little money. For example, men will refuse to buy a colt, unless they take off its saddle and harness, which might conceal a sore. But in the choice of a mate, on which one's happiness depends for the rest of one's life, they act carelessly. They leave all but a hand's-breadth of the woman's face covered with clothing and judge her by it, so that in marrying a couple runs a great risk of mutual dislike if later anything in either's body should offend the other. Not all men are so wise that they consider only a woman's behavior. And even wise men think that physical beauty in wives adds not a little to the virtues of the mind. Certainly some deformity may lurk underneath clothing which will alienate a man from his wife when it is too late to be separated from her. If such a deformity is discovered after marriage, a man must bear his lot, so the Utopians think care ought to be taken by law that no one be deceived.

There is all the more reason for their taking this precaution, because in that part of the world they alone are monogamists. Their marriages are broken only by death. They do not allow divorce except for adultery or insufferable waywardness on the part of either spouse. The injured person is given permission to change spouses by the senate, but the guilty party is considered disreputable and for the rest of his life is forbidden to remarry. They do not allow a husband to put away his wife against her will because of some bodily misfortune. They consider it a matter of cruelty and disloyalty to desert one's spouse when most in need of comfort, especially in old age (which is itself really a sickness, since it brings sickness in its train). It happens occasionally that when a married couple cannot agree well together and when they have found other persons with whom they hope to live more happily, they separate by mutual consent and contract new marriages, but only with the consent of the senate. Such divorces are not allowed unless the senators and their wives have made careful inquiry into the grounds for it. They allow them unwillingly, for they know that it weakens the love of married couples to leave the door open to easy new marriages.

They punish adulterers with the severest bondage. If both parties are married, they are divorced, and the injured persons may be married to one another or to someone else. But if either of the injured parties continues to love the undeserving spouse, then the couple may live together in marriage, provided the innocent person is willing to share in the labor to which bondmen are condemned. Sometimes it happens that the repentance of the guilty person so moves the prince to pity that he grants both of them freedom once more. If anyone commits adultery a second time, his punishment is death.

16. THE RELIGION OF THE UTOPIANS

There are different kinds of religion throughout the island, as well as in each city. Some worship the sun as a god, others the moon, and still others some one of the planets. Others worship some man pre-eminent in virtue or glory, not only as a god, but as the supreme god. But by far the greatest number of the Utopians, and among these the wisest, worship none of these. They think there is one unknown, eternal, infinite, and unknowable deity, transcending human comprehension and pervading the whole universe not physically but in virtue and power. Him they call Father of all. They acknowledge that from Him alone comes the beginning,

increase, progress, change, and end of all things. They do not offer
divine honors to any other god.

Though they hold different beliefs on other matters of religion,
all the Utopians agree with their wiser sort in this, that there is
only one supreme power, the Maker and Ruler of the universe,
whom they all call in their native language Mithra. But they differ
as to who he is; some think he is one god, others another. But
whatever god each person regards as the chief god, they all agree
in thinking that God is the very Being to whose power and majesty
the supremacy over all things is attributed by universal consent.

By degrees all the Utopians are coming to forsake their various
superstitions and to agree upon this one religion that seems to
excel the others in reason. No doubt the other religions would have
vanished long ago, had it not happened that whenever one of the
Utopians who was planning to change his religion met with misfortune, the rest regarded it not as an accident but as something
sent by a divinity as a punishment for the desertion of his worship.

We told them of the name, doctrine, manner of life, and miracles
of Christ, and of the wonderful constancy of the many martyrs,
who willingly sacrificed their blood to bring so many nations far
and wide to Christianity. You will hardly believe with what favorably disposed minds they received this account, either because God
secretly incited them or because this religion is most like the belief
already very strong among them. I thought that they were also
somewhat influenced by learning that Christ instituted community
of goods and that this custom was still in practice among the most
sincere of the Christians. Whatever the reason, many came over
to our religion and were baptized. Two of our number had died
and none of us four survivors, I regret to say, were priests, so though
they received instruction in other matters they did not receive
those sacraments which in our religion only priests can administer.
But they understand them and long for them ardently. In fact, they
argue vigorously with one another as to whether a man chosen from
among them without the Pope's authorization would have the true
character of a priest. Though they seemed determined to choose
such a one, they had not chosen him at the time of my leaving.

Those among them that have not yet accepted the Christian
religion do not restrain others from it nor abuse the converts to it.
While I was there, only one man among the Christians was punished. This newly baptized convert, in spite of all our advice, was
preaching in public on the Christian worship more zealously than
wisely. He grew so heated that he not only put our worship before
all others, but also condemned all other rites as profane and loudly
denounced their celebrants as wicked and impious men fit for hell-
fire. After he had been preaching these things for a long time, they

seized him. They convicted him not on a charge of disparaging their religion, but of arousing public disorder among the people, and sentenced him to exile. For they count it among their oldest institutions that no man shall be made to suffer for his religion.

In the early days King Utopus learned that before his coming the inhabitants had quarreled violently over religion. He found that it was easy to conquer them all, because the different sects in fighting for their country fought by themselves instead of together. Therefore after his victory he decreed that each man might follow whatever religion he wished and might try to persuade others to join it amicably and temperately and without bitterness toward others. If persuasion failed, a person was forbidden to use force or to indulge in wrangling. If anyone argued for his religion contentiously, he was to be punished by exile or bondage.

Utopus made this law partly for the sake of peace, which he saw was in danger of being completely destroyed by constant strife and implacable hatred, and partly for the sake of religion. He did not venture to make dogmatic decisions in regard to religion, perhaps from some idea that God likes and inspires a variety and multiplicity of worship. He deemed it foolish and insolent for anyone to try to make all men accept his own beliefs by force and by threats. If one religion is true and the others false, and if men use reason and moderation, he clearly foresaw that the truth would prevail by its own strength. But if men fight and riot, as evil and headstrong men will do, then the best and holiest religion in the world will be crowded out by the emptiest superstitions, like wheat choked by thorns and briars. So he imposed no one religion on his people, and left each man free to believe what he would, with one exception. He made a solemn and severe law against any who sink so far below the dignity of human nature as to think that the soul dies with the body, or that the universe is carried along by chance without an over-ruling providence.

The Utopians believe that after this life there are punishments for wickedness and rewards for virtue. They consider one who thinks otherwise as hardly a man, since he has degraded the human soul to the low level of a beast's body. Such a man they do not count fit for human society, for if he dares, he will scorn all its laws and customs. Who can doubt that a man who fears nothing but the law and apprehends nothing after death would secretly flout his country's laws or break them by force to satisfy his greed? Therefore no preferment is awarded to one with such views, and no magistracy or any public responsibility is entrusted to him. Instead, he is generally looked down upon as a man of worthless and sordid nature. Yet they do not punish such a man further, for they are persuaded that no one can make himself believe anything at will. Nor do they force him by threats to conceal his thoughts, and so open the door to deceit and lying, which they detest as the next thing to fraud. But they take care that he does not argue for his opinions, especially before the common people. They permit and even encourage him to discuss these matters with their priests and other serious men, in full confidence that finally his mad opinions will yield to reason.

There are others, in fact a considerable number, who go to the opposite extreme, and believe that the souls of animals are immortal, though not comparable with the human soul in excellence nor capable of as great happiness. These men are not thought to be bad or altogether lacking in reason, and their opinion is not discouraged.

Almost all the Utopians believe so firmly that man's happiness after death is endless, that they lament sickness but not death. They only mourn a man's death if they see that he parts with life reluctantly. This they take as a very bad sign, as if his soul dreaded death because of hopelessness or from some secret and guilty foreboding of impending punishment. The coming of a man who does not run gladly at the call, but is dragged off like a shirker, cannot be pleasing to God. They feel horror at such a death, and after carrying out the body in sorrow and with silent prayers to God mercifully to pardon the man's weakness, they bury the body in the earth. When a man dies cheerfully and full of good hope, they do not grieve, but follow the body singing, earnestly commending the man's soul to God. Then they cremate him reverently rather than sadly, and in the place where the funeral pyre was made, they set up a tombstone with the dead man's honors engraved upon it. When they return from the funeral, they relate his life and good deeds, and no part of his life is more frequently nor more gladly rehearsed than his cheerful death.

They think that remembering his good qualities is a powerful incitement to virtue among the living and the most pleasing honor to the dead. For they believe that the dead are present among us and hear the talk about themselves, though they are invisible through the dullness of human sight. They think that the dead, in keeping with their happy condition, can go where they want, and in affectionate loyalty visit those they loved and esteemed during their lives. They also believe that in good men these affections, like other good things, are increased rather than decreased after death, and that the dead come among the living observing their words and deeds. Consequently they enter into their undertakings all the more confidently because of their trust in such protectors. And they are deterred from secret wrongdoing by the belief that their forefathers are present.

They laugh at auguries and other superstitious forms of divination that are common among other nations. But they revere miracles which cannot flow from the powers of nature, looking on them as the works and witnesses of God. They say that such miracles have frequently occurred among them. Sometimes they have won safety and success amid great dangers and uncertainties through public prayers offered with assured confidence.

They hold that the careful observation of nature and the reflection on it and the reverence that arises from this is a kind of worship very pleasing to God. * * *

Now I have described to you as truthfully as I could the structure of this commonwealth, which I think the best, and indeed the only one which can rightfully be called by that name. In other places where they speak of the common good, every man is looking out for his own good. But in Utopia where there is no private property and where they zealously pursue the public business, there the name commonwealth is doubly deserved. Elsewhere, even though the state is prosperous, most men know that they may die of hunger if they do not look out for themselves, and so they are forced to take care of themselves rather than other people. In Utopia where everything belongs to everybody, they know that if the public warehouses and granaries are full, no one will lack anything for his personal use. Among them there is no maldistribution of goods, nor is anyone poor and indigent. When no one owns anything, all are rich. What greater riches can there be than to live cheerfully and serenely, free from all anxieties, without worries about making a living and unvexed by the complaints of one's wife about money? No one has to worry about his son's being poor, or about his daughter's dowry. Each man's livelihood and happiness are secure, and the same is true of all his relations, his wife, sons, grandsons, great-grandsons, and the whole line of descendants that highborn men assume will follow them. Why should he look forward to less, since those who can no longer work are cared for as well as those who do?

How could anyone dare to compare the justice of the Utopians with that of other nations? If there is any trace of justice or equity among other nations, may I perish among them! What justice is there in this, that a nobleman, a goldsmith,[9] a moneylender, or some other man who does nothing at all for a living or does something that is of no use to the public, lives a sumptuous and elegant life? In the meantime a servant, a driver, a blacksmith, or a farmer works as hard as a beast at labor so necessary that the commonwealth could not last a year without it. Yet they earn so poor a living and lead such miserable lives that their condition seems worse than that of draft animals. Beasts do not work so incessantly and do not live

9. I.e., a banker.

much worse—in fact they live better—and they have no worries about the future. But workingmen are burdened with barren and fruitless toil, and live in fear of want in their old age. Their daily wage is insufficient to support them for the present, so they can have no surplus to lay up for the future.

Is not a government unjust and ungrateful that squanders rich rewards on noblemen (as they are called), goldsmiths, and others that do not work but live only by flattery or by catering to useless pleasures? And is it just for a government to ignore the welfare of farmers, charcoal burners, servants, drivers, and blacksmiths, without whom the commonwealth could not exist at all? After their best years have been consumed by labor and they are worn out by age and sickness, they are still penniless, and the thankless state, unmindful of their many great services, rewards them with nothing but a miserable death. Furthermore the rich constantly try to whittle away something from the pitiful wages of the poor by private fraud and even by public laws. To pay so little to men who deserve the best from the state is in itself unjust, yet it is made "just" legally by passing a law.

So when I weigh in my mind all the other states which flourish today, so help me God, I can discover nothing but a conspiracy of the rich, who pursue their own aggrandizement under the name and title of the Commonwealth. They devise ways and means to keep safely what they have unjustly acquired, and to buy up the toil and labor of the poor as cheaply as possible and oppress them. When these schemes of the rich become established by the government, which is meant to protect the poor as well as the rich, then they are law. With insatiable greed these wicked men divide among themselves the goods which would have been enough for all.

And yet they are far short of the happiness of the Utopians, who have abolished the use of money, and with it greed. What evils they avoid! What a multitude of crimes they prevent! Everyone knows that frauds, thefts, quarrels, contentions, uprisings, murders, betrayals, and poisonings (evils which are commonly punished rather than checked by the severities of the law) would wither away if money were eradicated! Fear, anxiety, worry, care, toil, and sleepless nights would disappear at the same time as money! Even poverty, which seems to need money more than anything else for its relief, would vanish if money were gone.

To see this more clearly, consider this one example. Take some poor and unfruitful year in which hunger has carried off many thousands of men. If the barns of the rich were searched at the end of the year, I maintain that enough grain would be found to feed everyone, and to save those who died from the famine and from the plague caused by the famine. How easily the bare needs of life might be provided, if money, which is meant to procure us the necessities of life, did not itself deter us! Certainly rich men know this. They also know that it would be more practicable to provide the necessities of life for everyone than to supply superfluities for a few, and much better to eradicate our innumerable evils than to be burdened with great concentrations of wealth.

If that one monster pride, the first and foremost of all evils, did not forbid it, the whole world would doubtless have adopted the laws of the Utopians long before this, drawn on by a rational perception of what each man's true interest is or else by the authority of Christ our Saviour, who in His great wisdom knows what is best and in His loving-kindness bids us do it. Pride measures her prosperity not by her own goods but by others' wants. Pride would not deign to be a goddess, if there were no inferiors she could rule and triumph over. Her happiness shines brightly only in comparison to others' misery, and their poverty binds them and hurts them the more as her wealth is displayed. Pride is the infernal serpent that steals into the hearts of men, thwarting and holding them back from choosing the better way of life.

Pride is far too deeply rooted in men's hearts to be easily torn out. I am glad, therefore, that the Utopians have achieved their social organization, which I wish all mankind would imitate. Their institutions give their commonwealth a moral and social foundation for living happy lives, and as far as man can predict, these institutions will last forever. Because they have rooted out ambition and strife along with other vices, they are in no danger of civil wars, which have ruined many states that seemed secure. And as long as they maintain sound institutions and domestic harmony, they can never be overcome by the envious rulers near by, who have often attempted their ruin in vain.

Thus Raphael finished speaking. I admit that not a few things in the manners and laws of the Utopians seemed very absurd to me: their way of waging war, their religious customs, as well as other matters, but especially the keystone of their entire system, namely, their communal living without the use of money. This one thing takes away all the nobility, magnificence, splendor, and majesty which public opinion commonly regards as the true ornaments of a nation. But I saw that Raphael was tired with talking, and I was not sure that he could bear contradiction in these matters. I remembered that he had spoken ill of certain men who feared they would not be thought wise unless they could find something to criticize in other men's opinions.

So with praise for the Utopian institutions and for his account of them, I took him by the hand and led him in to supper, adding that we would find some other time for considering these things more thoroughly and for talking with him in greater detail about them. I hope that such an opportunity may come sometime. Meanwhile I cannot agree with everything that he said, though he was singularly well informed and also highly experienced in worldly affairs. Yet I must confess that there are many things in the Utopian Commonwealth that I wish rather than expect to see followed among our citizens. *understatement*

1514–16   1516

THE BOOK OF HOMILIES

King Edward VI ascended the throne in 1547 at the age of 9. His Council of Regency, which ruled in his name, was concerned primarily with two matters: to ensure obedience to the royal authority and to further the Protestant cause (the boy king was Supreme Head of the English Church). The Council prohibited preaching except under special license, and sent to every parish in the kingdom a copy of *Certain Sermons or Homilies appointed by the King's Majesty to be declared and read by all Parsons, Vicars, and Curates every Sunday in their Churches where they have cure.* The tenth homily in this volume is on order and obedience; it is basic to an understanding of Elizabethan attitudes on politics, religion, and the nature of the universe. Shakespeare heard such homilies in church from childhood on.

From An Exhortation Concerning Good Order and Obedience to Rulers and Magistrates

Almighty God hath created and appointed all things, in heaven, earth, and waters, in a most excellent and perfect order. In heaven he hath appointed distinct orders and states of archangels and angels. In earth he hath assigned kings, princes, and other governors under them, all in good and necessary order. The water above is kept and raineth down in due time and season. The sun, moon, stars, rainbow, thunder, lightning, clouds, and all birds of the air do keep their order. The earth, trees, seeds, plants, herbs, corn, grass, and all manner of beasts keep them in their order. All parts of the whole year, as winter, summer, months, nights, and days, continue in their order. All kinds of fishes in the sea, rivers, and waters, with all fountains, springs, yea, the seas themselves, keep their comely course and order. And man himself also, hath all his parts, both within and without, as soul, heart, mind, memory, understanding, reason, speech withal, and singular corporal members of his body in a profitable, necessary, and pleasant order. Every de-

gree of people in their vocation, calling, and office hath appointed
to them their duty and order. Some are in high degree, some in
low, some kings and princes, some inferiors and subjects, priests
and laymen, masters and servants, fathers and children, husbands
and wives, rich and poor, and everyone have need of other; so that
in all things is to be lauded and praised the goodly order of God,
without the which no house, no city, no commonwealth can continue and endure. For where there is no right order, there reigneth
all abuse, carnal liberty, enormity, sin, and Babylonical confusion.
Take away kings, princes, rulers, magistrates, judges, and such states
of God's order, no man shall ride or go by the highway unrobbed,
no man shall sleep in his own house or bed unkilled, no man shall
keep his wife, children, and possessions in quietness; all things shall
be common, and there must needs follow all mischief and utter destruction, both of souls, bodies, goods, and commonwealths. But
blessed be God, that we in this realm of England feel not the horrible calamities, miseries, and wretchedness which all they undoubtedly feel and suffer that lack this goodly order. And praised be God
that we know the great excellent benefit of God showed towards
us in this behalf. God hath sent us his high gift, our most dear
sovereign lord King Edward the Sixth, with godly, wise and, honorable council, with other superiors and inferiors in a beautiful
order. Wherefore, let us subjects do our bounden duties, giving
hearty thanks to God and praying for the preservation of this godly
order. Let us all obey even from the bottom of our hearts all their
godly proceedings, laws, statutes, proclamations, and injunctions,
with all other godly orders. Let us consider the scriptures of the
Holy Ghost which persuade and command us all obediently to
be subject, first and chiefly, to the King's majesty, supreme head
over all, and next, to his honorable council, and to all other noblemen, magistrates, and officers which by God's goodness be placed
and ordered; for Almighty God is the only author and provider
of this forenamed state and order, as it is written of God in the
book of Proverbs: "Through me, kings do reign; through me councilors make just laws; through me do princes bear rule and all judges
of the earth execute judgment. I am loving to them that love
me."[1] * * *

The wicked judge Pilate said to Christ, "Knowest thou not that
I have power to crucify thee and have power also to loose thee?"
Jesus answered, "Thou couldst have no power at all against me,
except it were given thee from above."[2] Whereby Christ taught us
plainly that even the wicked rulers have their power and authority
from God. And therefore it is not lawful for their subjects by force
to resist them, although they abuse their power; much less then
is it lawful for subjects to resist their godly and Christian princes

1. Proverbs viii.15–17.   2. John xix.10–11.

which do not abuse their authority but use the same to God's glory and to the profit and commodity of God's people. The holy apostle St. Peter commandeth servants to be obedient to their masters, not only if they be good and gentle but also if they be evil and froward, affirming that the vocation and calling of God's people is to be patient, and of the suffering side. And there he bringeth in the patience of our saviour Christ to persuade obedience to governors, yea, although they be wicked and wrongdoers. * * *

Let us all therefore fear the most detestable vice of rebellion, ever knowing and remembering that he that resisteth common authority, resisteth God and his ordinance, as it may be proved by many other mo [3] places of holy scripture. And here let us take heed that we understand not these or such other like places, which so straitly command obedience to superiors and so straitly punish rebellion, and disobedience to the same, to be meant in any condition of the pretended power of the Bishop of Rome. For truly the scripture of God alloweth no such usurped power, full of enormities, abusions, and blasphemies. But the true meaning of these and such places be to extol and set forth God's true ordinance and the authority of God's anointed kings and of their officers appointed under them. * * *

3. More. 　　　　　　　　　　　　　　　　　　　　　　1547

SIR THOMAS HOBY
(1530–1566)

One of the great and influential books of the Renaissance was *Il Cortegiano* ("The Courtier") published in Italian by Count Baldasarre Castiglione (1478–1529) in 1528 and soon translated into all the other European languages. The English translation, by the humanist and diplomat Sir Thomas Hoby, was first published in 1561, but it was written earlier, probably during the reign of Queen Mary (1553–58) when Hoby lived abroad as a Protestant exile. The style of the translation makes it an important landmark in English prose; Hoby, like his master Sir John Cheke, prefers words from the native Anglo-Saxon element of the language, rather than borrowings from French or Italian.

The book attempts to present, in the form of dialogues between actual persons living at the court of the Duke of Urbino in the years 1504–8, a full description of the qualities and characteristics of the ideal courtier. Spenser's friend Gabriel Harvey, in his copy of Hoby's translation, summarized the contents of this great "courtesy book" as follows: "Above all things it importeth a courtier to be graceful and lovely in countenance and behavior; fine and discreet in discourse and entertainment; skillful and expert in letters and arms; active and gallant in every courtly exercise;

nimble and speedy of body and mind; resolute, industrious and valorous in action; as profound and invincible in action as is possible; and withal ever generously bold, wittily pleasant, and full of life in his sayings and doings." Shakespeare's Hamlet was such an ideal courtier, as Ophelia testifies when she attributes to him

> The courtier's, soldier's, scholar's, eye, tongue, sword;
> The expectancy and rose of the fair state,
> The glass of fashion and the mold of form.

The Elizabethans thought of Sir Philip Sidney as the example of an ideal courtier in real life.

Probably the most famous passage in *The Courtier* is Peter Bembo's discourse on love in Book IV. Its theme is essentially Platonic—that is, that love is not the mere gratification of the senses, but is the yearning of the soul after beauty. Furthermore, the beautiful is always ultimately identical with the good. Love properly understood is therefore a kind of ladder by which the soul progresses from lower to higher things. As he pursues his theme Bembo becomes more enraptured and ends with a prayer to Love as a god; although the dialogue form permits criticism of Bembo's doctrine, the eloquence of his speech carries the day.

From The Courtier

From *Book I*

[GRACE]

Bound am I not (quoth the Count) to teach you to have a good grace,[1] nor anything else, saving only to show you what a perfect Courtier ought to be. Neither will I take upon me to teach you this perfection, since a while ago I said that the Courtier ought to have the feat of wrestling and vaulting, and such other things, the which how I should be able to teach them, not having learned them myself. I am sure ye know it all. It sufficeth that as a good soldier can speak his mind to an armorer, of what fashion, of what temper and goodness he will have his harness, and for all that cannot teach him to make it, nor to hammer or temper it, so perhaps I am able to tell you what a perfect Courtier ought to be, but not to teach you how ye should do to be one. Notwithstanding, to fulfill your request in what I am able, although it be (in manner) in a proverb that *Grace is not to be learned*, I say unto you, whoso mindeth to be gracious or to have a good grace in the exercises of the body (presupposing first that he be not of nature unapt) ought to begin betimes, and to learn his principles of cunning men. The which thing

---

1. "Grace" had a wide range of meanings for Elizabethans, and many puns were made on the word. Most simply, it refers to a natural, easy manner, especially in doing something that is difficult. The Italian word is *sprezza-* *tura*. But grace had also a religious meaning—that favor from God which is neither earned nor deserved. The "Count" is Count Lodovico Canossa ("Count Lewis"), later Bishop of Bayeux.

how necessary a matter Philip, king of Macedonia, thought it, a man may gather in that his will was that Aristotle, so famous a philosopher, and perhaps the greatest that ever hath been in the world, should be the man that should instruct Alexander, his son, in the first principles of letters. And of men whom we know nowadays, mark how well and with what a good grace Sir Galeazzo Sanseverino, master of the horse to the French king, doth all exercises of the body; and that because, beside the natural disposition of person that is in him, he hath applied all his study to learn of cunning men, and to have continually excellent men about him, and, of every one, to choose the best of that they have skill in. For as in wrestling, in vaulting, and in learning to handle sundry kind of weapons he hath taken for his guide our Master Peter Mount, who (as you know) is the true and only master of all artificial force and sleight, so in riding, in jousting, and in every other feat, he hath always had before his eyes the most perfectest that hath been known to be in those professions.

He therefore that will be a good scholar, beside the practicing of good things, must evermore set all his diligence to be like his master, and, if it were possible, change himself into him. And when he hath had some entry, it profiteth him much to behold sundry men of that profession; and, governing himself with that good judgment that must always be his guide, go about to pick out, sometime of one and sometime of another, sundry matters. And even as the bee in the green meadows flieth always about the grass choosing out flowers, so shall our Courtier steal this grace from them that to his seeming[2] have it, and from each one that parcel that shall be most worthy praise. And not do as a friend of ours whom you all know, that thought he resembled much King Ferdinand the younger, of Aragon, and regarded not to resemble him in any other point but in the often lifting up his head, wrying[3] therewithal a part of his mouth, the which custom the king had gotten by infirmity. And many such there are that think they do much, so they resemble a great man in somewhat and take many times the thing in him that worst becometh him.

But I, imagining with myself often times how this grace cometh, leaving apart such as have it from above, find one rule that is most general which in this part (methink) taketh place in all things belonging to a man in word or deed above all other. And that is to eschew as much as a man may, and as a sharp and dangerous rock, *Affectation* or curiosity,[4] and, to speak a new word, to use in everything a certain *Recklessness*,[5] to cover art withal, and seem what-

2. Opinion.
3. Twisting awry.
4. Over-fastidiousness.
5. Hoby translates badly here. The Italian word is *sprezzatura*, which means ℗ natural, easy grace. "Art": artifice.

soever he doth and sayeth to do it without pain, and, as it were, not minding it. And of this do I believe grace is much derived, for in rare matters and well brought to pass every man knoweth the hardness of them, so that a readiness therein maketh great wonder. And contrariwise to use force, and, as they say, to hale by the hair, giveth a great disgrace and maketh everything, how great soever it be, to be little esteemed. Therefore that may be said to be a very art that appeareth not to be art; neither ought a man to put more diligence in anything than in covering it, for in case it be open, it loseth credit clean, and maketh a man little set by. And I remember that I have read in my days that there were some most excellent orators which among other their cares enforced themselves to make every man believe that they had no sight in letters, and dissembling their cunning, made semblant their orations to be made very simply, and rather as nature and truth made them, than study and art, the which if it had been openly known would have put a doubt in the people's mind, for fear lest he beguiled them. You may see then how to show art and such bent study taketh away the grace of everything.

From *Book IV*

[LOVE]

Then the Lord Gaspar:[6] "I remember," quoth he, "that these lords yesternight, reasoning of the Courtier's qualities, did allow him to be a lover; and in making rehearsal[7] of as much as hitherto hath been spoken, a man may pick out a conclusion that the Courtier which with his worthiness and credit must incline his prince to virtue must in manner of necessity be aged, for knowledge cometh very seldom time before years, and specially in matters that be learned with experience. I cannot see, when he is well drawn in years, how it will stand well with him to be a lover, considering, as it hath been said the other night, love frameth not with old men, and the tricks that in young men be gallantness, courtesy, and preciseness so acceptable to women, in them are mere follies and fondness[8] to be laughed at, and purchase him that useth them hatred of women and mocks of others. Therefore, in case this your Aristotle, an old Courtier, were a lover and practiced the feats that young lovers do, as some that we have seen in our days, I fear me he would forget to teach his prince; and peradventure boys would mock him behind his back, and women would have none other delight in him but to make him a jesting-stock."

6. Gasparo Pallavicino, whose attitude in the dialogue is usually that of the woman-hater.

7. Reviewing.

8. Foolishness.

Then said the Lord Octavian:[9] "Since all the other qualities appointed to the Courtier are meet for him, although he be old, methink we should not then bar him from this happiness to love."

"Nay rather," quoth the Lord Gaspar, "to take this love from him is a perfection over and above, and a making him to live happily out of misery and wretchedness."

M. Peter Bembo[1] said: "Remember you not, my Lord Gaspar, that the Lord Octavian declared the other night in his device of pastimes, although he be not skillful in love, to know yet that there be some lovers which reckon the disdains, the angers, the debates and torments which they receive of their ladies, sweet? Whereupon he required to be taught the cause of this sweetness. Therefore, in case our Courtier, though he be old, were kindled with those loves that be sweet without any bitter smack, he should feel no misery nor wretchedness at all. And being wise, as we set case[2] he is, he should not be deceived in thinking to be meet for him whatsoever were meet for young men, but in loving should perhaps love after a sort that might not only not bring him in slander, but to much praise and great happiness, without any loathsomeness at all, the which very seldom or in manner never happeneth to young men; and so should he neither lay aside the teaching of his prince, nor yet commit anything that should deserve the mocking of boys."

Then spake the Duchess:[3] "I am glad, M. Peter, that you have not been much troubled in our reasonings this night, for now we may be the bolder to give you in charge to speak, and to teach the Courtier this so happy a love, which bringeth with it neither slander nor any inconvenience; for perhaps it shall be one of the necessariest and profitablest qualities that hitherto hath been given him; therefore speak, of good fellowship, as much as you know therein."

M. Peter laughed and said: "I would be loath, madam, where I say it is lawful for old men to love, it should be an occasion for these ladies to think me old; therefore hardily[4] give ye this enterprise to another."

The Duchess answered: "You ought not to refuse to be counted old in knowledge, though ye be young in years. Therefore say on, and excuse yourself no more."

M. Peter said: "Surely, madam, if I must entreat upon this matter, I must first go ask counsel of my hermit[5] Lavinello."

The Lady Emilia[6] said then half in anger: "There is never a one

---

9. Ottaviano Fregoso, a soldier, later Doge of Genoa.
1. Poet, Platonist, grammarian, and historian; later a cardinal. He is here the philosopher of love. "M.": Master.
2. Assume.
3. Elizabetta Gonzaga, wife of the Duke of Urbino.
4. By all means.
5. I.e., spiritual advisor; cf. Friar Laurence in *Romeo and Juliet*.
6. Lady Emilia Pio, friend and confidante of the Duchess.

in all the company so disobedient as you be, M. Peter, therefore should the Duchess do well to chastise you somewhat for it."

M. Peter said smiling: "For love of God, madam, be not angry with me, for I will say whatever you will have me."

"Go to, say on then," answered the Lady Emilia.

Then M. Peter after a while's silence, somewhat settling himself as though he should entreat upon a weighty matter, said thus: "My Lords, to show that old men may love not only without slander, but otherwhile[7] more happily than young men, I must be enforced to make a little discourse to declare what love is, and wherein consisteth the happiness that lovers may have. Therefore I beseech you give the hearing with heedfulness, for I hope to make you understand that it were not unfitting for any man here to be a lover, in case he were fifteen or twenty years elder than M. Morello."[8]

And here, after they had laughed awhile, M. Peter proceeded: "I say, therefore, that according as it is defined of the wise men of old time, love is nothing else but a certain coveting to enjoy beauty; and forsomuch as coveting longeth for nothing but for things known, it is requisite that knowledge go evermore before coveting, which of his own nature willeth the good, but of himself is blind and knoweth it not. Therefore hath nature so ordained that to every virtue of knowledge there is annexed a virtue of longing. And because in our soul there be three manner[9] ways to know, namely, by sense, reason, and understanding: of sense ariseth appetite or longing, which is common to us with brute beasts; of reason ariseth election or choice, which is proper to man; of understanding, by the which man may be partner with angels, ariseth will. Even as therefore the sense knoweth not but sensible matters and that which may be felt, so the appetite or coveting only desireth the same; and even as the understanding is bent but to behold things that may be understood, so is that will only fed with spiritual goods. Man of nature endowed with reason, placed, as it were, in the middle between these two extremities, may, through his choice inclining to sense or reaching to understanding, come nigh to the coveting, sometime of the one, sometime of the other part. In these sorts therefore may beauty be coveted, the general name whereof may be applied to all things, either natural or artificial, that are framed in good proportion and due temper,[1] as their nature beareth. But speaking of the beauty that we mean, which is only it that appeareth in bodies, and especially in the face of man, and moveth this fervent coveting which we call love, we will term it an influence of the heavenly

---

7. Occasionally.
8. Morello da Ortona, a courtier and musician; later a speaker in the dialogue.

9. Kinds of.
1. The right mixture or combination of elements.

bountifulness, the which for all it stretcheth over all things that be created (like the light of the sun), yet when it findeth out a face well proportioned, and framed with a certain lively agreement of several colors, and set forth with lights and shadows, and with an orderly distance and limits of lines, thereinto it distilleth itself and appeareth most well favored, and decketh out and lighteneth the subject where it shineth with a marvelous grace and glistering, like the sunbeams that strike against beautiful plate of fine gold wrought and set with precious jewels, so that it draweth unto it men's eyes with pleasure, and piercing through them imprinteth himself in the soul, and with an unwonted sweetness all to-stirreth[2] her and de-lighteth, and setting her on fire maketh her to covet him. When the soul then is taken with coveting to enjoy this beauty as a good thing, in case she suffer herself to be guided with the judgment of sense, she falleth into most deep errors, and judgeth the body in which beauty is discerned to be the principal cause thereof; where-upon to enjoy it she reckoneth it necessary to join as inwardly as she can with that body, which is false; and therefore whoso think-eth in possessing the body to enjoy beauty, he is far deceived, and is moved to it, not with true knowledge by the choice of reason, but with false opinion by the longing of sense. Whereupon the pleasure that followeth it is also false and of necessity full of errors. And therefore into one of the two vices run all those lovers that satisfy their unhonest lusts with the women whom they love; for either as soon as they come to the coveted end, they not only feel a fullness and loathsomeness, but also conceive a hatred against the right beloved, as though longing repented him of his offense and acknowledged the deceit wrought him by the false judgment of sense, that made him believe the ill to be good, or else they continue in the very same coveting and greediness, as though they were not indeed come to the end which they sought for. And albeit through the blind opinion that hath made them drunken (to their seeming) in that instant they feel a contentation,[3] as the diseased otherwhile, that dream they drink of some clear spring, yet they are not satisfied, nor leave off so. And because of possessing coveted goodness there arises always quietness and satisfaction in the possessor's mind, in case this were the true and right end of their coveting, when they possess it they would be at quietness and throughly satisfied, which they be not: but rather deceived through that likeness, they forth-with return again to unbridled coveting, and with the very same trouble which they felt at the first, they fall again into the raging and most burning thirst of the thing, that they hope in vain to possess perfectly. These kind of lovers therefore love most unluckily

2. Moves violently.   3. Satisfied condition.

for either they never come by their covetings, which is a great unluckiness, or else if they do come by them, they find they come by
their hurt and end their misery with other greater miseries, for both
in the beginning and middle of this love, there is never other thing
felt but afflictions, torments, griefs, pining travail, so that to be wan,
vexed with continual tears and sighs, to live with a discontented
mind, to be always dumb, or to lament, to covet death, in conclusion to be most unlucky are the properties which, they say, belong to lovers. The cause therefore of this wretchedness in men's
minds is principally sense, which in youthful age beareth most sway,
because the lustiness of the flesh and of the blood in that season
adds unto him even so much force as it withdraweth from reason.
Therefore doth it easily train the soul to follow appetite or longing,
for when she seeth herself drowned in the earthly prison, because
she is set in the office to govern the body, she cannot of herself
understand plainly at the first the truth of spiritual beholding.
Wherefore to compass the understanding of things, she must go
beg the beginning at the senses, and therefore she believeth them
and giveth ear to them, and is contented to be led by them, especially
when they have so much courage, that (in a manner) they enforce
her, and because they are deceitful they fill her with errors and false
opinions. Whereupon most commonly it happeneth that young men
be wrapped in this sensual love, which is a very rebel against reason,
and therefore they make themselves unworthy to enjoy the favors
and benefits which love bestows upon his true subjects, neither in
love feel they any other pleasures than what beasts without reason
do, but much more grievous afflictions. Setting case therefore this
to be so, which is most true, I say that the contrary chanceth to
them of a more ripe age. For in case they, when the soul is not now
so much weighted down with the bodily burden, and when the
natural burning assuageth and draweth to a warmth, if they be inflamed with beauty, and to it bend their coveting guided by reasonable choice, they be not deceived, and possess beauty perfectly, and
therefore through the possessing of it, always goodness ensueth to
them. Because beauty is good and consequently the true love of
it is most good and holy, and evermore bringeth forth good fruits
in the souls of them that with the bridle of reason restrain the ill
disposition of sense, the which old men can much sooner do than
young. It is not therefore out of reason to say that old men may also
love without slander and more happily than young men, taking notwithstanding this name old, not for the age at the pit's brink, nor
when the canals of the body be so feeble, that the soul cannot
through them work her feats, but when knowledge in us is in his
right strength. And I will not also hide this from you: namely, that
I suppose where sensual love in every age is naught, yet in young

men it deserveth excuse, and perhaps in some case lawful; for although it puts them in afflictions, dangers, travails, and the unfortunateness that is said, yet are there many that to win them the goodwill of their ladies practice virtuous things, which for all they be not bent to a good end, yet are they good of themselves; and so of that much bitterness they pick out a little sweetness, and through the adversities which they sustain, in the end they acknowledge their error. As I judge therefore those young men that bridle their appetites, and love with reason, to be godly; so do I hold excused such as yield to sensual love, whereunto they be so inclined through the weakness and frailties of man—so they show therein meekness, courtesy, and prowess, and the other worthy conditions that these Lords have spoken of; and when those youthful years be gone and past, leave it off clean, keeping aloof from this sensual coveting as from the lowermost step of the stairs, by which a man may ascend to true love. But in case after they draw in years once, they reserve in their cold heart the fire of appetites, and bring stout reason in subjection to feeble sense, it cannot be said how much they are to be blamed: for like men without sense they deserve with an everlasting shame to be put in the number of unreasonable living creatures, because the thoughts and ways of sensual love be far unfitting for ripe age."

Here Bembo paused awhile, and when all things were whist[4] M. Morello of Ortona said: "And in case there were some old man more fresh and lusty and of a better complexion than many young men, why would you not have it lawful for him to love with the love that young men love?"

The Duchess laughed, and said: "If the love of young men be so unlucky, why would you, M. Morello, that old men should also love with this unluckiness? But in case you were old, as these men say you be, you would not thus procure the hurt of old men."

M. Morello answered: "The hurt of old men, meseemeth, M. Peter Bembo procureth, who will have them to love after a sort that I for my part understand not; and, methink, the possessing of this beauty which he praiseth so much, without the body, is a dream."

"Do you believe, M. Morello," quoth then Count Lewis, "that beauty is always so good a thing as M. Peter Bembo speaketh of?"

"Not I, in good sooth," answered M. Morello. "But I remember rather that I have seen many beautiful women of a most ill inclination, cruel and spiteful, and it seemeth that, in a manner, it happeneth always so, for beauty maketh them proud, and pride, cruel."

Count Lewis said, smiling: "To you perhaps they seem cruel,

4. Quiet.

because they content you not with it that you would have. But cause
M. Peter Bembo to teach you in what sort old men ought to covet
beauty, and what to seek at their ladies' hands, and what to content
themselves withal; and in not passing out of these bounds you shall
see that they shall be neither proud nor cruel, and will satisfy you
with what you shall require."

M. Morello seemed then somewhat out of patience, and said:
"I will not know the thing that toucheth[5] me not. But cause you
to be taught how the young men ought to covet this beauty that are
not so fresh and lusty as old men be."

Here Sir Frederick,[6] to pacify M. Morello and to break their talk,
would not suffer Count Lewis to make answer, but interrupting him
said: "Perhaps M. Morello is not altogether out of the way in saying
that beauty is not always good, for the beauty of women is many
times cause of infinite evils in the world—hatred, war, mortality,
and destruction, whereof the razing of Troy can be a good witness;
and beautiful women for the most part be either proud and cruel,
as is said, or unchaste; but M. Morello would find no fault with that.
There be also many wicked men that have the comeliness of a beautiful countenance, and it seemeth that nature hath so shaped them
because they may be the readier to deceive, and that this amiable
look were like a bait that covereth the hook."

Then M. Peter Bembo: "Believe not," quoth he, "but beauty is
always good."

Here Count Lewis, because he would return again to his former
purpose, interrupted him and said: "Since M. Morello passeth not
to understand that which is so necessary for him, teach it me, and
show me how old men may come by this happiness of love, for I
will not care to be counted old, so it may profit me."

M. Peter Bembo laughed, and said: "First will I take the error
out of these gentlemen's mind, and afterward will I satisfy you
also." So beginning afresh: "My Lords," quoth he, "I would not
that with speaking ill of beauty, which is a holy thing, any of us
as profane and wicked should purchase him the wrath of God.
Therefore, to give M. Morello and Sir Frederick warning, that they
lose not their sight, as Stesichorus[7] did—a pain most meet for whoso
dispraiseth beauty—I say that beauty cometh of God and is like
a circle, the goodness whereof is the center. And therefore, as there
can be no circle without a center, no more can beauty be without
goodness. Whereupon doth very seldom an ill soul dwell in a

---

5. Concerns.
6. Federico Fregoso, later Archbishop
of Salerno.
7. "A notable poet which lost his sight

for writing against Helena [Helen of
Troy] and recanting had his sight restored him again" [Hoby's note].

beautiful body. And therefore is the outward beauty a true sign of the inward goodness, and in bodies this comeliness is imprinted, more and less, as it were, for a mark of the soul, whereby she is outwardly known; as in trees, in which the beauty of the buds giveth a testimony of the goodness of the fruit. And the very same happeneth in bodies, as it is seen that palmisters by the visage know many times the conditions and otherwhile the thoughts of men. And, which is more, in beasts also a man may discern by the face the quality of the courage, which in the body declareth itself as much as it can. Judge you how plainly in the face of a lion, a horse, and an eagle, a man shall discern anger, fierceness, and stoutness; in lambs and doves, simpleness and very innocency; the crafty subtlety in foxes and wolves; and the like, in a manner, in all other living creatures. The foul,[8] therefore, for the most part be also evil, and the beautiful good. Therefore it may be said that beauty is a face pleasant, merry, comely, and to be desired for goodness; and foulness a face dark, uglesome, unpleasant, and to be shunned for ill. And in case you will consider all things, you shall find that whatsoever is good and profitable hath also evermore the comeliness of beauty. Behold the state of this great engine of the world,[9] which God created for the health and preservation of everything that was made: the heaven round beset with so many heavenly lights; and in the middle the earth environed with the elements and upheld with the very weight of itself; the sun, that compassing about giveth light to the whole, and in winter season draweth to the lowermost sign, afterward by little and little climbeth again to the other part; the moon, that of him taketh her light, according as she draweth nigh or goeth farther from him; and the other five stars that diversely keep the very same course. These things among themselves have such force by the knitting together of an order so necessarily framed that, with altering them any one jot, they should all be loosed and the world would decay. They have also such beauty and comeliness that all the wits men have cannot imagine a more beautiful matter.

"Think now of the shape of man, which may be called a little world, in whom every parcel of his body is seen to be necessarily framed by art and not by hap, and then the form altogether most beautiful, so that it were a hard matter to judge whether the members (as the eyes, the nose, the mouth, the ears, the arms, the breast, and in like manner the other parts) give either more profit to the countenance and the rest of the body, or comeliness. The

8. Ugly.
9. The following description is a summary of the Ptolemaic universe with the earth at the center; the elements of earth, water, air, fire surrounding the earth; the various crystalline spheres each containing sun, moon, or a planet; and the hard outer shell, the *Primum Mobile* (first mover).

like may be said of all other living creatures. Behold the feathers of fowls, the leaves and boughs of trees, which be given them of nature to keep them in their being, and yet have they withal a very great sightliness. Leave nature, and come to art. What thing is so necessary in sailing vessels as the forepart, the sides, the main yards, the mast, the sails, the stern, oars, anchors, and tacklings? All these things notwithstanding are so wellfavored in the eye that unto whoso beholdeth them they seem to have been found out as well for pleasure as for profit. Pillars and great beams uphold high buildings and palaces, and yet are they no less pleasureful unto the eyes of the beholders than profitable to the buildings. When men began to build, in the middle of temples and houses they reared the ridge of the roof, not to make the works to have a better show, but because the water might the more commodiously avoid[1] on both sides; yet unto profit there was forthwith adjoined a fair sightliness, so that if, under the sky where there falleth neither hail nor rain, a man should build a temple without a reared ridge, it is to be thought that it could have neither a sightly show nor any beauty. Beside other things, therefore, it giveth a great praise to the world in saying that it is beautiful. It is praised in saying the beautiful heaven, beautiful earth, beautiful sea, beautiful rivers, beautiful woods, trees, gardens, beautiful cities, beautiful churches, houses, armies. In conclusion, this comely and holy beauty is a wondrous setting out of everything. And it may be said that good and beautiful be after a sort one self thing, especially in the bodies of men; of the beauty whereof the nighest cause, I suppose, is the beauty of the soul; the which, as a partner of the right and heavenly beauty, maketh sightly and beautiful whatever she toucheth, and most of all, if the body, where she dwelleth, be not of so vile a matter that she cannot imprint in it her property. Therefore beauty is the true monument and spoil of the victory of the soul, when she with heavenly influence beareth rule over material and gross nature, and with her light overcometh the darkness of the body. It is not, then, to be spoken that beauty maketh women proud or cruel, although it seem so to M. Morello. Neither yet ought beautiful women to bear the blame of that hatred, mortality, and destruction which the unbridled appetites of men are the cause of. I will not now deny but it is possible also to find in the world beautiful women unchaste; yet not because beauty inclineth them to unchaste living, for it rather plucketh them from it, and leadeth them into the way of virtuous conditions, through the affinity that beauty hath with goodness; but otherwhile ill bringing up, the continual provocations of lovers' tokens, poverty, hope, deceits, fear, and a thousand other matters, overcome the steadfast-

1. Escape.

ness, yea, of beautiful and good women; and for these and like causes may also beautiful men become wicked."

Then said the Lord Cesar:[2] "In case the Lord Gaspar's saying be true of yesternight, there is no doubt but the fair women be more chaste than the foul."

"And what was my saying?" quoth the Lord Gaspar.

The Lord Cesar answered: "If I do well bear in mind, your saying was that the women that are sued to always refuse to satisfy him that sueth to them, but those that are not sued to, sue to others. There is no doubt but the beautiful women have always more suitors, and be more instantly laid at in love, than the foul. Therefore the beautiful always deny, and consequently be more chaste than the foul, which, not being sued to, sue unto others."

M. Peter Bembo laughed, and said: "This argument cannot be answered to."

Afterward he proceeded: "It chanceth also, oftentimes, that as the other senses, so the sight is deceived and judgeth a face beautiful which indeed is not beautiful. And because in the eyes and in the whole countenance of some woman a man beholdeth otherwhile a certain lavish wantonness painted, with dishonest flickerings, many, whom that manner delighteth because it promiseth them an easiness to come by the thing that they covet, call it beauty; but indeed it is a cloaked unshamefastness,[3] unworthy of so honorable and holy a name."

M. Peter Bembo held his peace, but those lords still were earnest upon him to speak somewhat more of this love and of the way to enjoy beauty aright, and at the last: "Methink," quoth he, "I have showed plainly enough that old men may love more happily than young, which was my drift; therefore it belongeth not to me to enter any farther."

Count Lewis answered: "You have better declared the unluckiness of young men than the happiness of old men, whom you have not as yet taught what way they must follow in this love of theirs; only you have said that they must suffer themselves to be guided by reason, and the opinion of many is that it is unpossible for love to stand with reason."

Bembo notwithstanding sought to make an end of reasoning, but the Duchess desired him to say on, and he began thus afresh: "Too unlucky were the nature of man, if our soul, in which this so fervent coveting may lightly arise, should be driven to nourish it with that only which is common to her with beasts, and could not turn it to the other noble part, which is proper to her. Therefore, since it is so your pleasure, I will not refuse to reason upon this noble matter.

2. Lord Cesar Gonzaga, cousin of Cas-   3. Immodesty.
tiglione.

And because I know myself unworthy to talk of the most holy mysteries of Love, I beseech him to lead my thought and my tongue so that I may show this excellent Courtier how to love contrary to the wonted manner of the common ignorant sort. And even as from my childhood I have dedicated all my whole life unto him, so also now that my words may be answerable to the same intent, and to the praise of him: I say, therefore, that since the nature of man in youthful age is so much inclined to sense, it may be granted the Courtier, while he is young, to love sensually; but in case afterward also, in his riper years, he chance to be set on fire with this coveting of love, he ought to be good and circumspect, and heedful that he beguile not himself to be led willfully into the wretchedness that in young men deserveth more to be pitied than blamed and contrariwise in old men, more to be blamed than pitied. Therefore when an amiable countenance of a beautiful woman cometh in his sight, that is accompanied with noble conditions and honest behaviors, so that, as one practiced in love, he wotteth well that his hue hath an agreement with hers, as soon as he is aware that his eyes snatch that image and carry it to the heart, and that the soul beginneth to behold it with pleasure, and feeleth within herself the influence that stirreth her and by little and little setteth her in heat, and that those lively spirits that twinkle out through the eyes put continually fresh nourishment to the fire, he ought in this beginning to seek a speedy remedy and to raise up reason, and with her to fence the fortress of his heart, and to shut in such wise the passages against sense and appetites that they may enter neither with force nor subtle practice. Thus, if the flame be quenched, the jeopardy is also quenched. But in case it continue or increase, then must the Courtier determine, when he perceiveth he is taken, to shun throughly[4] all filthiness of common love, and so enter into the holy way of love with the guide of reason, and first consider that the body where that beauty shineth is not the fountain from whence beauty springeth, but rather because beauty is bodiless and, as we have said, an heavenly shining beam, she loseth much of her honor when she is coupled with that vile subject and full of corruption, because the less she is partner thereof, the more perfect she is, and, clean sundered from it, is most perfect. And as a man heareth not with his mouth, nor smelleth with his ears, no more can he also in any manner wise enjoy beauty, nor satisfy the desire that she stirreth up in our minds, with feeling, but with the sense unto whom beauty is the very butt to level at, namely, the virtue of seeing. Let him lay aside, therefore, the blind judgment of the sense, and enjoy with his eyes the brightness, the comeliness, the loving sparkles, laughters, gestures, and all the other pleasant furnitures of beauty, especially with hearing the sweetness

4. Completely.

of her voice, the tunableness of her words, the melody of her singing and playing on instruments (in case the woman beloved be a musician), and so shall he with most dainty food feed the soul through the means of these two senses which have little bodily substance in them and be the ministers of reason, without entering farther toward the body with coveting unto any longing otherwise than honest. Afterward let him obey, please, and honor with all reverence his woman, and reckon her more dear to him than his own life, and prefer all her commodities[5] and pleasures before his own, and love no less in her the beauty of the mind than of the body. Therefore let him have a care not to suffer her to run into any error, but with lessons and good exhortations seek always to frame her to modesty, to temperance, to true honesty, and so to work that there may never take place in her other than pure thoughts and far wide from all filthiness of vices. And thus in sowing of virtue in the garden of that mind, he shall also gather the fruits of most beautiful conditions, and savor them with a marvelous good relish. And this shall be the right engendering and imprinting of beauty in beauty, the which some hold opinion to be the end of love. In this manner shall our Courtier be most acceptable to his lady, and she will always show herself toward him tractable, lowly,[6] and sweet in language, and as willing to please him as to be beloved of him; and the wills of them both shall be most honest and agreeable, and they consequently shall be most happy."

Here M. Morello: "The engendering," quoth he, "of beauty in beauty aright were the engendering of a beautiful child in a beautiful woman; and I would think it a more manifest token a great deal that she loved her lover, if she pleased him with this than with the sweetness of language that you speak of."

M. Peter Bembo laughed, and said: "You must not, M. Morello, pass your bounds. I may tell you it is not a small token that a woman loveth when she giveth unto her lover her beauty, which is so precious a matter; and by the ways that be a passage to the soul (that is to say, the sight and the hearing) sendeth the looks of her eyes, the image of her countenance, and the voice of her words, that pierce into the lover's heart and give a witness of her love."

M. Morello said: "Looks and words may be, and oftentimes are, false witnesses. Therefore whoso hath not a better pledge of love, in my judgment he is in an ill assurance. And surely I looked still that you would have made this woman of yours somewhat more courteous and free toward the Courtier than my Lord Julian[7] hath made his; but meseemeth ye be both of the property of those judges

5. Conveniences.
6. Modest.
7. Giuliano de Medici, youngest son of Lorenzo the Magnificent, commander-in-chief of the papal armies, and a speaker in the dialogue.

that, to appear wise, give sentence against their own."

Bembo said: "I am well pleased to have this woman much more courteous toward my Courtier not young than the Lord Julian's is to the young; and that with good reason, because mine coveteth but honest matters, and therefore may the woman grant him them all without blame. But my Lord Julian's woman, that is not so assured of the modesty of the young man, ought to grant him the honest matters only, and deny him the dishonest. Therefore more happy is mine, that hath granted him whatsoever he requireth, than the other, that hath part granted and part denied. And because you may moreover the better understand that reasonable love is more happy than sensual, I say unto you that selfsame things in sensual ought to be denied otherwhile, and in reasonable granted; because in the one they be honest, and in the other dishonest. Therefore the woman, to please her good lover, besides the granting him merry countenances, familiar and secret talk, jesting, dallying, hand-in-hand, may also lawfully and without blame come to kissing, which in sensual love, according to the Lord Julian's rules, is not lawful. For since a kiss is a knitting together both of body and soul, it is to be feared lest the sensual lover will be more inclined to the part of the body than of the soul; but the reasonable lover wotteth well that although the mouth be a parcel[8] of the body, yet is it an issue for the words that be the interpreters of the soul, and for the inward breath, which is also called the soul; and therefore hath a delight to join his mouth with the woman's beloved with a kiss—not to stir him to any unhonest desire, but because he feeleth that that bond is the opening of an entry to the souls, which, drawn with a coveting the one of the other, pour themselves by turn the one into the other's body, and be so mingled together that each of them hath two souls, and one alone so framed of them both ruleth, in a manner, two bodies. Whereupon a kiss may be said to be rather a coupling together of the soul than of the body, because it hath such force in her that it draweth her unto it, and, as it were, separateth her from the body. For this do all chaste lovers covet a kiss as a coupling of souls together. And therefore Plato, the divine lover, saith that in kissing his soul came as far as his lips to depart out of the body. And because the separating of the soul from the matters of the sense; and the thorough coupling of her with matters of understanding, may be betokened by a kiss, Solomon saith[9] in his heavenly book of ballads, 'Oh that he would kiss me with a kiss of his mouth,' to express the desire he had that his soul might be ravished through heavenly love to the beholding of heavenly beauty in such manner that, coupling herself inwardly with it, she might forsake the body."

8. Part.   9. In Song of Solomon i.2.

When Bembo had hitherto spoken with such vehemency that a man would have thought him, as it were, ravished and beside himself, he stood still without once moving, holding his eyes toward heaven as astonied,[1] when the Lady Emilia, which together with the rest gave most diligent ear to this talk, took him by the plait of his garment and, plucking him a little, said, "Take heed, M. Peter, that these thoughts make not your soul also to forsake the body." "Madam," answered M. Peter, it should not be the first miracle that love hath wrought in me."

1561

1. Enraptured.

RICHARD HOOKER
(1554–1600)

Out of the long and bitter controversy over the government of the church in 16th-century England emerged one literary masterpiece. It is a long work in eight books called *Of the Laws of Ecclesiastical Polity* (that is, the governmental system of the church). The author was Richard Hooker, a scholar and minister who accomplished the extraordinary feat of engaging in the bitterest dispute of his time and maintaining a calm, reasonable manner. In 1585 Hooker was Master of the Temple (in modern terms, a dean of a law school); one of his subordinates was a Puritan lecturer named Walter Travers. Between them a running debate developed on the burning question of how the church should be governed. The Puritan view was that no organization or authority in the church was valid unless it was based clearly and specifically upon the Bible; the whole hierarchical system of the English church, with its deacons, priests, bishops, and archbishops, was accordingly wrong. The position Hooker undertook to defend was that the Scriptures, or divine revelation, are not the only guide given to men for organizing and administering the Christian church. A more important guide is the law of nature, which is also divinely given; this law can be discovered by the use of human reason.

In his great book, which grew out of his controversy with Travers, Hooker therefore had to explain how the law of nature justified the existing organization of the English church. Book I of *Ecclesiastical Polity* deals with laws in general and their various kinds, picturing a universe operating under natural and divine law and founded upon reason. Book II deals with the nature, authority, and adequacy of Scripture. Book III concerns the scriptural bases for worship and government. Book IV defends the rites and ceremonies of the English church, and Book V, longer than the first four together, is a commentary on *The Book of Common Prayer*. Books VI, VII, and VIII deal with various embodiments of authority—elders, bishops, kings, and popes.

Hooker was a close and effective reasoner; he relied not upon the fiery invective or impassioned rhetoric which characterized most disputants of his time, but rather upon a calm, reasonable, tolerant approach. His defense of existing ecclesiastical practices went back to fundamental principles, to a philosophy of nature and of man's place in it, of his relation to God and to his fellow men. It is this world view which makes Hooker's book of interest when the controversy over church organization has long since died down. And the prose in which Hooker sets forth his world view is the finest prose of the Elizabethan age. King James I is quoted by Izaak Walton, Hooker's 17th-century biographer, as saying, "I observe there is in Mr. Hooker no affected language; but a grave, comprehensive, clear manifestation of reason, and that backed with the authority of the Scriptures, the fathers and schoolmen, and with all law both sacred and civil. And, though others may write well, yet in the next age they will be forgotten; but doubtless there is in every page of Mr. Hooker's book the picture of a divine soul, such pictures of truth and reason, and drawn in so sacred colors, that they shall never fade but give an immortal memory to the author."

From Of the Laws of Ecclesiastical Polity
From *The Preface*

[ON MODERATION IN CONTROVERSY]

* * * Amongst ourselves, there was in King Edward's days some question moved by reason of a few men's scrupulosity touching certain things.[1] And beyond seas, of them which fled in the days of Queen Mary, some contenting themselves abroad with the use of their own service book at home authorized before their departure out of the realm, others liking better the common prayer book of the Church of Geneva translated, those smaller contentions before begun were by this mean somewhat increased. Under the happy reign of Her Majesty which now is, the greatest matter a while contended for was the wearing of the cap and surplice,[2] till there came *Admonitions Directed unto the High Court of Parliament*, by men who, concealing their names, thought it glory enough to discover their minds and affections, which were now universally bent even against all the orders and laws wherein this Church is found unconformable to the platform of Geneva. Concerning the defender of which admonitions, all that I mean to say is this: "There will come a time when three words uttered with charity and meekness shall

1. During the short reign of the boy king, Edward VI (1547–53), the reformation begun under Henry VIII was carried further. Services were held in English, images were banished from the church, and the use of holy water was forbidden. During the following reign of Mary, a Catholic, many Protestant reformers fled abroad and there were influenced by the Calvinist doctrines and practices of the "Church of Geneva."

2. The extreme Protestants or "Puritans" were opposed to the daily wearing of cap and gown by the clergy and the wearing of the surplice in church. This "Vestiarian controversy" was at its height in the 1560's. The *"Admonitions Directed unto the High Court of Parliament,"* by John Field and Thomas Wilcox (1572), attacked not only conventional clerical dress but the Prayer Book, episcopacy, and the whole structure of the Church of England.

receive a far more blessed reward than three thousand volumes written with disdainful sharpness of wit." But the manner of men's writing must not alienate our hearts from the truth if it appear they have the truth, as the followers of the same defender do think he hath, and in that persuasion they follow him no otherwise than himself doth Calvin, Beza[3] and others, with the like persuasion that they in this cause had the truth. We being as fully persuaded otherwise, it resteth that some kind of trial be used to find out which part is in error.

The first mean whereby Nature teacheth men to judge good from evil, as well in laws as in other things, is the force of their own discretion. Hereunto therefore Saint Paul referreth oftentimes his own speech to be considered by them that heard him, "I speak as to them which have understanding; judge ye what I say."[4] Again, afterward, "Judge in yourselves, is it comely that a woman pray uncovered?" The exercise of this kind of judgment our Saviour requireth in the Jews.[5] In them of Berea the Scripture commendeth it. Finally, whatsoever we do, if our own secret judgment consent not unto it as fit and good to be done, the doing of it, to us, is sin, although the thing itself be allowable. Saint Paul's rule therefore generally is, "Let every man in his own mind be fully persuaded of that thing which he either alloweth or doth."[6] Some things are so familiar and plain that truth from falsehood and good from evil is most easily discerned in them, even by men of no deep capacity. And of that nature, for the most part are things absolutely unto all men's salvation necessary, either to be held or denied, either to be done or avoided. For which cause Saint Augustine acknowledgeth that they are not only set down, but also plainly set down in scripture, so that he which heareth or readeth may, without any great difficulty, understand. Other things also there are belonging, though in a lower degree of importance, unto the offices of Christian men, which, because they are more obscure, more intricate and hard to be judged of, therefore God hath appointed some to spend their whole time principally in the study of things divine, to the end that in these more doubtful cases their understanding might be a light to direct others. "If the understanding power or faculty of the soul be," saith the Grand Physician,[7] "like unto the bodily sight, not of equal sharpness in all, what can be more convenient than that, even as the dark-sighted man is directed by the clear about things visible, so likewise in matters of deeper discourse the wise

3. John Calvin (1509–64) and Theodore Beza (1519–1605), two leading Protestant reformers on the Continent.
4. I Corinthians x.15. The next quotation is from I Corinthians xi.13.
5. See Luke xii.57. "Them of Berea": the inhabitants of the Macedonian city of Berea who "received the word with all readiness of mind" when Paul preached to them, according to Acts xiv.10–11.
6. See Romans xiv.5.
7. I.e., Galen, Greek physician of the 2d century A.D., whose works were long accepted as the highest medical authority.

in heart do show the simple where his way lieth?" In the doubtful cases of law, what man is there who seeth not how requisite it is that professors of skill in that faculty be our directors? So is it in all other kinds of knowledge. And even in this kind likewise the Lord hath himself appointed that "the Priest's lips should preserve knowledge, and that other men should seek the truth at his mouth, because he is the messenger of the Lord of Hosts."[8] Gregory Nazianzen, offended at the people's too great presumption in controlling the judgment of them to whom in such cases they should rather have submitted their own, seeketh by earnest entreaty to stay them within their bounds: "Presume not, ye that are sheep, to make yourselves guides of them that should guide you; neither seek ye to overskip the fold which they about you have pitched. It sufficeth for your part, if ye can well frame yourselves to be ordered. Take not upon you to judge your judges, nor to make them subject to your laws who should be a law to you. For God is not a God of sedition and confusion but of order and of peace." But ye will say that if the guides of the people be blind, the common sort of men must not close up their own eyes and be led by the conduct of such; if the priest be partial in the law, the flock must not therefore depart from the ways of sincere truth, and in simplicity yield to be followers of him for his place' sake and office over them. Which thing, though in itself most true, is in your defense notwithstanding weak; because the matter wherein ye think that ye see and imagine that your ways are sincere is of far deeper consideration than any one amongst five hundred of you conceiveth. Let the vulgar sort amongst you know that there is not the least branch of the cause wherein they are so resolute but to the trial of it a great deal more appertaineth than their concept doth reach unto. I write not this in disgrace of the simplest that way given,[9] but I would gladly they knew the nature of that cause wherein they think themselves thoroughly instructed and are not; by means whereof they daily run themselves, without feeling their own hazard, upon the dint of the Apostle's sentence against evil speakers as touching things wherein they are ignorant.[1] If it be granted a thing unlawful for private men, not called into public consultation, to dispute which is the best state of civil polity, with a desire of bringing in some other kind than that under which they already live, for of such disputes I take it his meaning was—if it be a thing confessed that of such questions they cannot determine without rashness, inasmuch as a great part of them consisteth in special circumstances, and for one kind as many reasons may be brought as for another—is there any reason in the

8. See Malachi ii.7. "Gregory Nazianzen" is St. Gregory of Nazianzus, a 4th-century bishop.
9. I.e., I am not disparaging ordinary, uneducated people.
1. Ignorant people run the risk of the condemnation of the apostle Peter: "But these, as natural brute beasts, made to be taken and destroyed, speak evil of the things that they understand not; and shall utterly perish in their own corruption" (II Peter ii.12).

world why they should better judge what kind of regiment[2] ecclesiastical is the fittest? For in the civil state more insight and, in those affairs, more experience a great deal needs be granted them, than in this they can possibly have. When they which write in defense of your discipline and commend it unto the highest[3] not in the least cunning manner, are forced notwithstanding to acknowledge that with whom the truth is they know not, they are not certain—what certainty or knowledge can the multitude have thereof? Weigh what doth move the common sort so much to favor this innovation and it shall soon appear unto you that the force of particular reasons which for your several opinions are alleged is a thing whereof the multitude never did nor could consider as to be therewith wholly carried; but certain general inducements are used to make salable your cause in gross; and when once men have cast a fancy towards it, any slight declaration of specialties will serve to lead forward men's inclinable and prepared minds. The method of winning the people's affection unto a general liking of "the Cause," for so ye term it, hath been this: First, in the hearing of the multitude, the faults, especially of higher callings, are ripped up with marvelous exceeding severity and sharpness of reproof, which being oftentimes done, begetteth a great good opinion of integrity, zeal, and holiness to such constant reprovers of sin as by likelihood would never be so much offended at that which is evil, unless themselves were singularly good. The next thing hereunto is to impute all faults and corruptions wherewith the world aboundeth unto the kind of ecclesiastical government established. Wherein, as by reproving faults, they purchased unto themselves with the multitude a name to be virtuous; so by finding out this kind of cause they obtain to be judged wise above others, whereas in truth unto the form even of Jewish government, which the Lord himself, they all confess, did establish, with like show of reason they might impute those faults which the prophets condemn in the governors of that commonwealth as to the English kind of regiment ecclesiastical (whereof also God himself though in other sort is author), the stains and blemishes found in our state, which springing from the root of human frailty and corruption, not only are, but have always been more or less—yea, and for anything we know to the contrary will be till the world's end— complained of, what form of government soever take place. Having gotten thus much sway in the hearts of men, a third step is to propose their own form of church government as the only sovereign remedy of all evils, and to adorn it with all the glorious titles that may be. And the nature, as of men that have sick bodies, so likewise

---

2. Government.
3. I.e., Queen Elizabeth. The *Humble Petition of the Commonalty* (1588) said, "we are very babes and children, not knowing our right hand from our left in matters that concern the Kingdom of Heaven." "Cunning": learned.

of the people in the crazedness of their minds possessed with dislike and discontentment at things present, is to imagine that anything the virtue whereof they hear commended would help them, but that most which they least have tried. The fourth degree of inducement is by fashioning the very notions and conceits[4] of men's minds in such sort that when they read the Scriptures they may think that everything soundeth towards the advancement of that discipline and to the utter disgrace of the contrary. Pythagoras, by bringing up his scholars in the speculative knowledge of numbers, made their conceits therein so strong that when they came to the contemplation of things natural they imagined that in every particular thing they even beheld, as it were with their eyes, how the elements of number gave essence and being to the works of nature. A thing in reason impossible, which notwithstanding through their misfashioned preconceit appeared unto them no less certain than if nature had written it in the very foreheads of all the creatures of God. * * *

From *Book I, Chapter 3*
[THE LAW OF NATURE]

* * * Now if Nature should intermit her course and leave altogether, though it were but for a while, the observation of her own laws; if those principal and mother elements of the world, whereof all things in this lower world are made, should lose the qualities which they now have; if the frame of that heavenly arch erected over our heads should loosen and dissolve itself; if celestial spheres should forget their wonted motions and by irregular volubility turn themselves any way as it might happen; if the prince of the lights of heaven which now as a giant doth run his unwearied course, should as it were through a languishing faintness begin to stand and to rest himself; if the moon should wander from her beaten way, the times and seasons of the year blend themselves by disordered and confused mixture, the winds breathe out their last gasp, the clouds yield no rain, the earth be defeated of heavenly influence, the fruits of the earth pine away as children at the withered breasts of their mother no longer able to yield them relief, what would become of man himself, whom these things now do all serve? See we not plainly that obedience of creatures unto the law of Nature is the stay of the whole world? Notwithstanding with Nature it cometh sometimes to pass as with art. Let Phidias[5] have rude and obstinate stuff to carve, though his art do that it should, his work will lack that beauty which otherwise in fitter matter it might have had. He that striketh an instrument with skill may cause notwith-

---

4. Concepts.

5. The greatest of ancient Greek sculptors (5th century B.C.).

standing a very unpleasant sound if the string whereon he striketh chance to be uncapable of harmony. In the matter whereof natural things consist, that of Theophrastus[6] taketh place, "much of it is oftentimes such as will by no means yield to receive that impression which were best and most perfect." Which defect in the matter of things natural, they who gave themselves unto the contemplation of Nature among the heathen observed often; but the true original cause thereof divine malediction,[7] laid for the sin of man upon those creatures which God had made for the use of man. This, being an article of that saving truth which God hath revealed unto his church, was above the reach of their merely natural capacity and understanding. But howsoever these swervings are now and then incident into the course of Nature, nevertheless so constantly the laws of Nature are by natural agents observed, that no man denieth but those things which Nature worketh are wrought either always or for the most part after one and the same manner. * * *

From *Book I, Chapter 8*

[ON COMMON SENSE]

* * * The general and perpetual voice of men is as the sentence[8] of God himself. For that which all men have at all times learned, Nature herself must needs have taught, and God being the author of Nature, her voice is but his instrument. By her from Him we receive whatsoever in such sort we learn. Infinite duties there are, the goodness whereof is by this rule sufficiently manifested, although we had no warrant besides to approve them. The apostle St. Paul having speech concerning the heathen saith of them "They are a law unto themselves."[9] His meaning is, that by force of the light of reason wherewith God illuminateth everyone which cometh into the world, men being enabled to know truth from falsehood, and good from evil, do thereby learn in many things what the will of God is; which will himself not revealing by any extraordinary means unto them, but they by natural discourse attaining the knowledge thereof, seem the makers of those laws which indeed are his, and they but only the finders of them out. A law therefore generally taken is a directive rule unto goodness of operation. The rule of divine operations outward is the definite appointment of God's own wisdom set down within himself. The rule of natural agents that work by simple necessity is the determination of the wisdom of God, known to God himself, the principal director of them, but not unto them that are directed to execute the same. The rule of natural agents which work after a sort of their own accord, as the

6. Greek writer of the 3rd century B.C., a follower of Aristotle and inventor of the type of essay called the "character," which in concise form delineated a type of person.

7. God's curse in Eden, which fell not only upon sinful man but upon the earth as well.
8. Wisdom.
9. Romans ii.14.

beasts do, is the judgment of common sense or fancy concerning the sensible[1] goodness of those objects wherewith they are moved. The rule of ghostly or immaterial natures, as spirits and angels, is their intuitive intellectual judgment concerning the amiable beauty and high goodness of that object, which with unspeakable joy and delight doth set them on work. The rule of voluntary agents on earth is the sentence that reason giveth concerning the goodness of those things which they are to do. And the sentences which reason giveth are some more, some less general, before it come to define in particular actions what is good. The main principles of reason are in themselves apparent. For to make nothing evident of itself unto man's understanding were to take away all possibility of knowing anything. And herein that of Theophrastus is true, "They that seek a reason of all things do utterly overthrow reason." * * *

From *Book I, Chapter* 9

[NATURE, RIGHTEOUSNESS, AND SIN]

Now the due observation of this law which reason teacheth us cannot but be effectual unto their great good that observe the same. For we see the whole world and each part thereof so compacted[2] that as long as each thing performeth only that work which is natural unto it, it thereby preserveth both other things and also itself. Contrariwise, let any principal thing, as the sun or moon, or any one of the heavens or elements, but once cease or fail, or swerve, and who does not easily conceive that the sequel thereof would be ruin both to itself and whatsoever dependeth upon it? And is it possible that man, being not only the noblest creature in the world, but even a very world in himself, his transgressing the law of his nature should draw no manner of harm after it? Yes, tribulation and anguish unto every soul that doth evil. Good doth follow unto all things by observing the course of their nature, and on the contrary side, evil by not observing it, but not unto natural agents that good which we call reward, not that evil which we properly term punishment. The reason whereof is because amongst creatures in this world, only man's observation of the law of his nature is Righteousness, only man's transgression Sin. And the reason of this is his manner of observing or transgressing the law of his nature. He doth not otherwise than voluntarily the one or the other. What we do against our wills, or constrainedly, we are not properly said to do it, because the motive cause of doing it is not in ourselves, but carrieth us, as if the wind should drive a feather in the air, we no whit furthering that whereby we are driven. In such cases therefore the evil which is done moveth compassion; men are pitied for it, as being rather miserable in such respect than culpable. * * *

---

1. Perceptible by the senses.   2. Agreed.

From *Book I, Chapter 10*

[THE FOUNDATIONS OF SOCIETY]

That which hitherto we have set down is, I hope, sufficient to show their brutishness which imagine that religion and virtue are only as men will accompt of[3] them, that we might make as much accompt, if we would, of the contrary, without any harm unto ourselves, and that in Nature they are as indifferent one as the other. We see then how Nature itself teacheth laws and statutes to live by. The laws which have been hitherto mentioned do bind men absolutely, even as they are men, although they have never any settled fellowship, never any solemn agreement amongst themselves what to do or not to do. But forasmuch as we are not by ourselves sufficient to furnish ourselves with competent store of things needful for such a life as our nature doth desire, a life fit for the dignity of man, therefore to supply those defects and imperfections which are in us living single and solely, by ourselves, we are naturally induced to seek communion and fellowship with others. This was the cause of men's uniting themselves at the first in politic societies, which societies could not be without government, nor government without a distinct kind of law from that which hath been already declared. Two foundations there are which bear up public societies, the one a natural inclination whereby all men desire a sociable life and fellowship, the other an order expressly or secretly agreed upon, touching the manner of their union in living together. The latter is that which we call the law of a commonweal,[4] the very soul of a politic body, the parts whereof are by law animated, held together and set on work in such actions as the common good requireth. Laws politic, ordained for external order and regiment amongst men, are never framed as they should be, unless presuming the will of man to be inwardly obstinate, rebellious, and averse from all obedience unto the sacred laws of his nature—in a word, unless presuming man to be in regard of his depraved mind little better than a wild beast—they do accordingly provide notwithstanding so to frame his outward actions that they be no hindrance unto the common good for which societies are instituted; unless they do this, they are not perfect. It resteth therefore that we consider how Nature findeth out such laws of government as serve to direct even nature depraved to a right end. All men desired to lead in this world an happy life. That life is led most happily, wherein all virtue is exercised without impediment or let. The Apostle[5] in exhorting men to contentment, although they have in this world no more than very bare food and raiment, giveth us thereby to understand that those are even the lowest of things necessary; that if we should be stripped of all those

3. Value.
4. Commonwealth. Originally the "common good."
5. Paul, in I Timothy vi.8.

things without which we might possibly be, yet these must be left, that destitution in these is such an impediment, as till it be removed, suffereth not the mind of man to admit any other care. For this cause first God assigned Adam maintenance of life and then appointed him a law to observe. For this cause after men began to grow to a number, the first thing we read they gave themselves unto was the tilling of the earth and the feeding of cattle. Having by this mean whereon to live, the principal actions of their life afterward are noted by the exercise of their religion. True it is that the Kingdom of God must be the first thing in our purposes and desires. But inasmuch as righteous life presupposeth life, inasmuch as to live virtuously it is impossible except we live, therefore the first impediment which naturally we endeavor to remove is penury and want of things without which we cannot live. Unto life many implements are necessary; moe,[6] if we seek, as all men naturally do, such a life as hath in it joy, comfort, delight and pleasure. To this end we see how quickly sundry arts mechanical were found out in the very prime of the world. As things of greatest necessity are always first provided for, so things of greatest dignity are most accompted of by all such as judge rightly. Although therefore riches be a thing which every man wisheth, yet no man of judgment can esteem it better to be rich than wise, virtuous, and religious. If we be both or either of these, it is not because we are so born. For into the world we come as empty of the one as of the other, as naked in mind as we are in body. Both which necessities of man had at the first no other helps and supplies than only domestical, such as that which the prophet[7] implieth, saying, "Can a mother forget her child?", such as that which the Apostle[8] mentioneth, saying, "He that careth not for his own is worse than an infidel"; such as that concerning Abraham, "Abraham will command his sons and his household after him that they keep the way of the Lord."[9] But neither that which we learn of ourselves, nor that which others teach us, can prevail where wickedness and malice have taken deep root. If therefore when there was but as yet one only family in the world, no means of instruction human or divine could prevent effusion of blood, how could it be chosen but that when families were multiplied and increased upon earth, after separation each providing for itself, envy, strife, contention, and violence must grow amongst them? For hath not Nature furnished man with wit and valor, as it were with armor, which may be used as well unto extreme evil as good? Yea, were they not used by the rest of the world unto evil, unto the contrary only by Seth, Enoch, and those few the rest in that line?[1] We all

6. More.
7. Isaiah (xlix.17).
8. Paul, in I Timothy v.8.
9. Genesis xviii.19.
1. The virtuous line of Seth is described in Genesis iv.25–26. It was in the time of Seth and his son Enos that "men began to call upon the name of the Lord."

make complaint of the iniquity of our times; not unjustly, for the days are evil. But compare them with those times wherein there were no civil societies, with those times wherein there was as yet no manner of public regiment established, with those times wherein there were not above eight persons righteous living upon the face of the earth, and we have surely good cause to think that God hath blessed us exceedingly and hath made us behold most happy days. To take away all such mutual grievances, injuries, and wrongs, there was no way but only by growing into composition and agreement amongst themselves by ordaining some kind of government public and by yielding themselves subject thereunto, that unto whom they granted authority to rule and govern, by them the peace, tranquility, and happy estate of the rest might be procured. * * *

From *Book I, Chapter* 12

[THE NEED FOR LAW]

* * * The first principles of the law of nature are easy: hard it were to find men ignorant of them; but concerning the duty which Nature's law doth require at the hands of men in a number of things particular, so far hath the natural understanding even of sundry whole nations been darkened, that they have not discerned—no, not gross iniquity—to be sin. Again, being so prone as we are to fawn upon ourselves, and to be ignorant as much as may be of our own deformities, without the feeling sense whereof we are most wretched, even so much the more because not knowing them we cannot as much as desire to have them taken away, how should our festered sores be cured but that God hath delivered a law as sharp as the two-edged sword, piercing the very closest and most unsearchable corners of the heart which the law of nature can hardly, human laws by no means possible, reach unto? Hereby we know even secret concupiscence to be sin, and are made fearful to offend, though it be but in a wandering cogitation. * * *

1593

WILLIAM SHAKESPEARE

[Ulysses' Speech on Degree[5]]

Troy, yet upon his basis, had been down,
    And the great Hector's sword had lacked a master,

5. From *Troilus and Cressida* (I.iii. 75–137). In a council of the Greeks, Ulysses, their wisest member, explains why they are failing to capture Troy: the authority of Agamemnon, the Greek leader, has broken down. Order and degree, Ulysses insists, are fundamental principles of nature. In line 50 he addresses Agamemnon directly, as chairman of the meeting.

But for these instances.[6]
The specialty of rule hath been neglected.
And look how many Grecian tents do stand   5
Hollow upon this plain, so many hollow factions.
When that the general is not like the hive
To whom the foragers shall all repair,
What honey is expected? Degree being vizarded,[7]
The unworthiest shows as fairly in the mask.   10
The heavens themselves, the planets, and this center,[8]
Observe degree, priority, and place,
Insisture, course, proportion, season, form,
Office, and custom, in all line of order.[9]
And therefore is the glorious planet Sol   15
In noble eminence enthroned and sphered
Amidst the other,[1] whose medicinable eye
Corrects the ill aspécts of planets evil,[2]
And posts like the commandment of a king,
Sans check to good and bad. But when the planets   20
In evil mixture to disorder wander,
What plagues and what portents, what mutiny,
What raging of the sea, shaking of earth,
Commotion in the winds, frights, changes, horrors,
Divert and crack, rend and deracinate,[3]   25
The unity and married calm of states
Quite from their fixture![4] Oh, when degree is shaked,
Which is the ladder to all high designs,
The enterprise is sick! How could communities,
Degrees in schools and brotherhoods in cities,   30
Peaceful commerce from dividable shores,
The primogenitive[5] and due of birth,
Prerogative of age, crowns, scepters, laurels,
But by degree, stand in authentic place?
Take but degree away, untune that string,   35
And hark, what discord follows! Each thing meets
In mere oppugnancy.[6] The bounded waters
Should lift their bosoms higher than the shores,
And make a sop[7] of all this solid globe.
Strength should be lord of imbecility,[8]   40
And the rude son should strike his father dead.
Force should be right, or rather, right and wrong,
Between whose endless jar justice resides,
Should lose their names, and so should justice too.
Then everything includes itself in power,   45
Power into will, will into appetite,

6. Reasons. "Specialty of rule": discipline.
7. I.e., rank being obscured.
8. The earth.
9. I.e., all in order. "Insisture": regularity; "office": function.
1. Others; "medicinable": healing.
2. I.e., their positions relative to other planets; a planet's aspect determined whether its astrological influence would be good or bad.
3. Uproot.
4. Stability.
5. The right of the eldest son to inherit.
6. Complete opposition.
7. A piece of bread soaked with liquor.
8. Weakness.

And appetite, a universal wolf,
So doubly seconded with will and power,
Must make perforce a universal prey,
And last eat up himself. Great Agamemnon,   50
This chaos, when degree is suffocate,
Follows the choking.
And this neglection of degree it is
That by a pace goes backward, with a purpose
It hath to climb. The general's disdained   55
By him one step below, he by the next,
That next by him beneath. So every step,
Exampled by the first pace that is sick[9]
Of his superior, grows to an envious fever
Of pale and bloodless emulation.   60
And 'tis that fever that keeps Troy on foot,
Not her own sinews. To end a tale of length,
Troy in our weakness stands, not in her strength.

                                                            1603

9. Envious.

SIR THOMAS WYATT THE ELDER
(1503–1542)

Wyatt was born at Allington Castle in Kent, and educated at St. John's College, Cambridge. He spent most of his life as a courtier and diplomat, serving King Henry VIII as Clerk of the King's Jewels and as ambassador to Spain and to the Emperor Charles V. He was also a member of various missions to France and Italy. He spent much of his adult life abroad; his interest in foreign literature, especially Italian, is evident from his translations and imitations of poems by the Italian sonneteers Petrarch, Sannazaro, Alamanni, and others. The life of a courtier under Henry VIII was not a calm life: Wyatt was twice arrested and imprisoned, once in 1536, after a quarrel with the Duke of Suffolk, and again in 1541, when he was charged with treason, lodged in the Tower of London, and stripped of all his property. On both occasions he was fortunate enough to regain the king's favor and receive a pardon. His praise of quiet retired life in the country and the cynical comments about foreign courts in his verse epistle to John Poins derive from his own experience.

For all his travel abroad, Wyatt remained essentially an Englishman. His poetry includes not only the sonnets, based upon Italian models, but also many delightful lyrics with short stanzas and refrains in the manner of the native English "ballet" (pronounced to rhyme with *mallet*) or dance-song. Wyatt's own temperament and disposition show more clearly in these English poems than in the sonnets. The lover in the Petrarchan sonnet is usually in a mood of doleful despair; the typical poem is essentially a complaint, though the interest lies in following the elaborately worked out "conceits" or comparisons. The lover is abject, he is the lady's slave; her coldness is a perpetual torture to him. In the ballets, however, a rather gay, manly independence is the characteristic note.

The sonnet, a 14-line poem with a complicated rhyme scheme, was introduced into English by Wyatt. He took his subject matter from Petrarch's sonnets, for the most part, but his rhyme schemes came from other Italian models. The most common rhyme scheme in Wyatt's sonnets is *abba abba cddc ee*; the usual Italian structure of an octave (first eight lines) followed after a turn in the sense by a sestet (last six lines) was already beginning to break down into the "English" structure for the sonnet, three quatrains and a couplet.

Although Wyatt intended to publish a collection of his poems, he never did so. In fact, very little of his verse was published until after his death. In aristocratic circles poems circulated in manuscript and were copied by hand; the general public usually saw courtiers' poems only when some enterprising publisher acquired manuscripts, perhaps already formed into a collection, and printed them as a miscellany. An early volume of this sort, called *The Court of Venus*, published a few Wyatt poems before 1540. A dozen such collections were published during the second half of the 16th century, with titles like *A Paradise of Dainty Devices*, *A Handful of*

Pleasant Delights, and *A Gorgeous Gallery of Gallant Inventions*. By far the most important of these miscellanies was issued by the printer Richard Tottel in 1557 (15 years after Wyatt's death) with the title *Songs and Sonnets written by the Right Honorable Lord Henry Howard late Earl of Surrey and other*. Until modern times it was always called simply *Songs and Sonnets* (Shakespeare has his Master Slender in *The Merry Wives of Windsor* say "I had rather than forty shillings I had my book of Songs and Sonnets here"); but now it is always referred to as *Tottel's Miscellany*. The printer, Richard Tottel, addressed the reader in an interesting epistle:

That to have well written in verse, yea and in small parcels, deserveth great praise, the works of divers Latins, Italians and other do prove sufficiently. That our tongue is able in that kind to do as praiseworthily as the rest, the honorable style of the noble Earl of Surrey and the weightiness of the deep-witted Sir Thomas Wyatt the Elder's verse, with several graces in sundry good English writers, do show abundantly. It resteth now, gentle reader, that thou think it not ill done to publish, to the honor of the English tongue, and for profit of the studious of English eloquence, those works which the ungentle hoarders up of such treasure have heretofore envied thee. And for this point, good reader, thine own profit and pleasure in these presently, and moe hereafter, shall answer for my defence. If perhaps some mislike the stateliness of style, removed from the rude skill of common ears, I ask help of the learned to defend their learned friends, the authors of this work. And I exhort the unlearned, by reading to be more skilfull, and to purge that swinelike grossness that maketh the sweet marjoram not to smell to their delight.

The anthology includes 271 poems—97 attributed to Wyatt, 40 to Surrey, 40 to Nicholas Grimald, and 94 to "Uncertain Authors." It is surely one of the most important books in the history of English literature, for it was the channel through which the main currents of European Renaissance poetry flowed into the British Isles. In it the sonnet, blank verse, *terza rima*, ottava rima, rondeau, and other forms were naturalized into English, and suddenly the ragged, undisciplined, pedestrian verse of the first part of the century became antiquated. When Wyatt was a boy it was possible for Alexander Barclay, an ambitious and by no means uneducated poet, to write verse like this:

> The famous poets with the muses nine
> With wit inspired, fresh, pregnant and divine,
> Say boldly endite in style substantial;
> Some in poems high and historical,
> Some them delight in heavy tragedies
> And some in wanton or merry comedies.

Wyatt was not primarily concerned with regularity of accent and smoothness of rhythm. By the time *Tottel's Miscellany* was published, Wyatt's rather rough and vigorous metrical practice was felt to be crude, and Tottel's editor smoothed out the versification. We reprint *They Flee from Me* in the versions of the Egerton manuscript and of Tottel. The Egerton manuscript (E. MS.) contains poems in Wyatt's own hand and corrections in his hand of scribal texts. The Devonshire manuscript (D. MS.) was not apparently in the poet's possession, but some of its texts seem earlier than Egerton's and it furnishes additional poems.

The Long Love That in My Thought Doth Harbor[1]

The long love that in my thought doth harbor,
And in my heart doth keep his residence,
Into my face presseth with bold pretense
And therein campeth, spreading his banner.[2]
She that me learns to love and suffer   5
And wills that my trust and lust's negligence[3]
Be reined by reason, shame, and reverence
With his hardiness taketh displeasure.
Wherewithal unto the heart's forest he fleeth,
Leaving his enterprise with pain and cry,   10
And there him hideth, and not appeareth.
What may I do, when my master feareth,
But in the field with him to live and die?
For good is the life ending faithfully.

E. MS.

Farewell, Love

Farewell, Love, and all thy laws forever,
Thy baited hooks shall tangle me no more;
Senec and Plato call me from thy lore,
To perfect wealth my wit for to endeavor.[4]
In blind error when I did persever,   5
Thy sharp repulse, that pricketh ay so sore,
Hath taught me to set in trifles no store
And 'scape forth since liberty is lever.[5]
Therefore farewell, go trouble younger hearts,
And in me claim no more authority;   10
With idle youth go use thy property,
And thereon spend thy many brittle darts.
For hitherto though I have lost all my time,
Me lusteth[6] no longer rotten boughs to climb.

E. MS.

---

1. Wyatt's version of Petrarch's *Sonnetto in Vita* 91; his younger friend, the Earl of Surrey, also translated it (see *Love, That Doth Reign and Live Within My Thought*).
2. I.e., the poet's blush. The first four lines of this sonnet contain the "conceit" (or elaborately sustained metaphor) of love as a kind of warrior who "harbors" in the speaker's thought, lives in his heart, and occasionally invades his face "with bold pretense" (i.e., making bold claim). He flaunts his warlike presence by means of the "banner." Elaborate metaphors of this kind are found often in Elizabethan love poetry; sometimes an entire sonnet will turn on one conceit. "Learns": teaches.
3. I.e., my open and careless revelation of my love. "Shame": modesty, shamefastness.
4. I.e.. "Senec" (Seneca, the Roman moral philosopher and tragedian) and Plato call him to educate his mind to perfect well-being ("wealth").
5. More pleasing, dearer.
6. I care.

I Find No Peace[7]

I find no peace and all my war is done,
I fear and hope, I burn and freeze like ice,
I fly above the wind, yet can I not arise,
And naught I have and all the world I seize on;
That looseth nor locketh holdeth me in prison,[8]   5
And holdeth me not; yet can I 'scape nowise;
Nor letteth me live nor die at my devise,[9]
And yet of death it giveth none occasion.
Without eyen[1] I see; and without tongue I plain;
I desire to perish, and yet I ask health;   10
I love another, and thus I hate myself;
I feed me in sorrow, and laugh in all my pain.
Likewise displeaseth me both death and life,
And my delight is causer of this strife.

                              E. MS.

Madam, Withouten Many Words

Madam, withouten many words,
Once[2] I am sure ye will or no,
And if ye will, then leave your bordes,[3]
And use your wit and show it so.

And with a beck ye shall me call,   5
And if of one that burneth alway
Ye have any pity at all,
Answer him fair with yea or nay.

If it be yea I shall be fain,
If it be nay, friends as before;   10
Ye shall another man obtain
And I mine own and yours no more.

                              E. MS.

7. In the opening lines of this sonnet, translated from Petrarch, *Sonnetto in Vita* 90, Wyatt reveals the early 16th-century preference for one-syllable words in poetry, which George Gascoigne justified by remarking that "the more monosyllables that you use, the truer Englishman you shall seem."
8. I.e., love that keeps no jail but yet imprisons me. The whole sonnet is a series of paradoxes; it represents a popular Petrarchan convention.
9. Wish.
1. Eyes; "plain": complain.
2. Sometime.
3. Jests.

Whoso List to Hunt[1]

Whoso list [2] to hunt, I know where is an hind.
But as for me, alas, I may no more.
The vain travail hath wearied me so sore
I am of them that farthest cometh behind.
Yet may I, by no means, my wearied mind   5
Draw from the deer, but as she fleeth afore,
Fainting I follow. I leave off therefore,
Since in a net I seek to hold the wind.
Whoso list her hunt, I put him out of doubt,
As well as I, may spend his time in vain.   10
And graven with diamonds in letters plain
There is written, her fair neck round about,
"*Noli me tangere*, for Caesar's I am,
And wild for to hold, though I seem tame."

E. MS.

My Lute, Awake!

My lute, awake! Perform the last
Labor that thou and I shall waste,
And end that I have now begun;
For when this song is sung and past,
My lute, be still, for I have done.   5

As to be heard where ear is none,
As lead to grave in marble stone [3]
My song may pierce her heart as soon.
Should we then sigh or sing or moan?
No, no, my lute, for I have done.   10

The rocks do not so cruelly
Repulse the waves continually
As she my suit and affection.
So that I am past remedy,
Whereby my lute and I have done.   15

Proud of the spoil that thou hast got
Of simple hearts, thorough love's shot;
By whom, unkind, thou hast them won,
Think not he hath his bow forgot,
Although my lute and I have done.   20

1. An adaptation of Petrarch, *Rime* 190, perhaps influenced by commentators on Petrarch, who said that *Noli me tangere quia Caesaris sum* ("Touch me not, for I am Caesar's") was inscribed on the collars of Caesar's hinds which were then set free and were presumably safe from hunters. Wyatt's sonnet is usually supposed to refer to Anne Boleyn, in whom Henry VIII became interested in 1526.
2. Cares.
3. I.e., when sound may be heard with no ear to hear it, or when soft lead is able to carve ("grave") hard marble.

Vengeance shall fall on thy disdain
That makest but game on earnest pain.
Think not alone under the sun
Unquit [4] to cause thy lovers plain,
Although my lute and I have done.   25

Perchance thee lie withered and old
The winter nights that are so cold,
Plaining in vain unto the moon.
Thy wishes then dare not be told.
Care then who list,[5] for I have done.   30

And then may chance thee to repent
The time that thou hast lost and spent
To cause thy lovers sigh and swoon.
Then shalt thou know beauty but lent,
And wish and want as I have done.   35

Now cease, my lute. This is the last
Labor that thou and I shall waste,
And ended is that we begun.
Now is this song both sung and past;
My lute, be still, for I have done.   40

E. MS.

They Flee from Me

They flee from me, that sometime did me seek,
With naked foot stalking in my chamber.
I have seen them, gentle, tame, and meek,
That now are wild, and do not remember
That sometime they put themselves in danger   5
To take bread at my hand; and now they range,
Busily seeking with a continual change.

Thankéd be fortune it hath been otherwise,
Twenty times better; but once in special,
In thin array, after a pleasant guise,   10
When her loose gown from her shoulders did fall,
And she me caught in her arms long and small,[1]
And therewithall sweetly did me kiss
And softly said, "Dear heart, how like you this?"

It was no dream, I lay broad waking.   15
But all is turned, thorough my gentleness,
Into a strange fashion of forsaking;
And I have leave to go, of her goodness,

4. Unrevenged. "Plain": to complain.   1. Slender.
5. Likes.

And she also to use newfangleness.[2]
But since that I so kindely[3] am servéd,   20
I fain would know what she hath deservéd.

E. MS.

The Lover Showeth How He Is Forsaken of Such as He Sometime Enjoyed

They flee from me, that sometime did me seek
With naked foot stalking within my chamber.
Once have I seen them gentle, tame, and meek
That now are wild, and do not once remember
That sometime they have put themselves in danger   5
To take bread at my hand, and now they range,
Busily seeking in continual change.

Thankéd be fortune, it hath been otherwise,
Twenty times better; but once especial,
In thin array, after a pleasant guise,   10
When her loose gown did from her shoulders fall,
And she me caught in her arms long and small,
And therewithal, so sweetly did me kiss
And softly said, "Dear heart, how like you this?"

It was no dream, for I lay broad awaking.   15
But all is turned now, through my gentleness,
Into a bitter fashion of forsaking.
And I have leave to go, of her goodness,
An she also to use newfangleness.
But since that I unkindly so am servéd,   20
How like you this, what hath she now deservéd?

Tottel, 1557

Divers Doth Use

Divers doth use, as I have heard and know,
When that to change their ladies do begin,
To mourne and wail, and never for to lin,[4]
Hoping thereby to pease[5] their painful woe.
And some there be, that when it chanceth so   5
That women change and hate where love hath been,
They call them false and think with words to win

2. Fickleness.
3. Naturally, but with an ironic suggestion of the modern meaning of
"kindly."
4. Cease.
5. Appease, relieve.

The hearts of them which otherwhere doth grow.
But as for me, though that by chance indeed
Change hath outworn the favor that I had,   10
I will not wail, lament, nor yet be sad,
Nor call her false that falsely did me feed,
But let it pass, and think it is of kind [6]
That often change doth please a woman's mind.

                                        D. MS.

Tangled I Was in Love's Snare

Tangled I was in love's snare,
Oppressed with pain, torment with care,
Of grief right sure, of joy full bare,
Clean in despair by cruelty—
But ha! ha! ha! full well is me,   5
For I am now at liberty.

The woeful day so full of pain,
The weary night all spent in vain,
The labor lost for so small gain,
To write them all it will not be.   10
But ha! ha! ha! full well is me,
For I am now at liberty.

Everything that fair doth show,
When proof is made it proveth not so,
But turneth mirth to bitter woe;   15
Which in this case full well I see.
But ha! ha! ha! full well is me,
For I am now at liberty.

Too great desire was my guide
And wanton will went by my side;   20
Hope ruléd still, and made me bide
Of love's craft th' extremity.
But ha! ha! ha! full well is me,
For I am now at liberty.

With feignéd words which were but wind   25
To long delays I was assigned;
Her wily looks my wits did blind;
Thus as she would I did agree.
But ha! ha! ha! full well is me,
For I am now at liberty.   30

Was never bird tangled in lime [7]
That brake away in better time

6. Nature.   bark, used to catch small birds.
7. A sticky substance made from holly

Than I, that rotten boughs did climb,
And had no hurt, but 'scapéd free.
Now ha! ha! ha! full well is me,   35
For I am now at liberty.

1557

Mine Own John Poins[1]

Mine own John Poins, since ye delight to know
The cause why that homeward I me draw,
And flee the press of courts, whereso they go,
Rather than to live thrall, under the awe
Of lordly looks, wrapped within my cloak,   5
To will and lust[2] learning to set a law;
It is not for because I scorn and mock
The power of them to whom Fortune hath lent
Charge over us, of right to strike the stroke.[3]
But true it is that I have always meant   10
Less to esteem them than the common sort,
Of outward things that judge in their intent
Without regard what doth inward resort.
I grant sometime that of glory the fire
Doth touch my heart; me list not to report   15
Blame by honor, and honor to desire.[4]
But how may I this honor now attain
That cannot dye the color black a liar?
My Poins, I cannot frame me tune to feign,
To cloak the truth, for praise without desert,   20
Of them that list all vice for to retain.
I cannot honor them that sets their part
With Venus and Bacchus all their life long;[5]
Nor hold my peace of them, although I smart.
I cannot crouch nor kneel to do so great a wrong,   25
To worship them like God on earth alone,
That are as wolves these sely[6] lambs among.
I cannot with my words complain and moan
Nor suffer naught, nor smart without complaint,
Nor turn the word that from my mouth is gone;   30
I cannot speak and look like a saint,

1. A friend of Wyatt's. This verse epistle of informal satire is based upon the
tenth satire of the Italian Luigi Alamanni, but personalized and Angli-
cized in detail by Wyatt. It was apparently written during Wyatt's banishment from court in 1536.
2. Pleasure.
3. I.e., my retirement from court is not
because I scorn great and powerful
princes. But (lines 10–13) I esteem

them less than do the "common sort"
of people, who judge by externals only.
4. I.e., I do not wish to attack honor,
nor to call dishonorable desire honorable.
5. I.e., I cannot honor those who devote themselves to Venus (goddess of
love-making) and Bacchus (god of
drinking).
6. Innocent.

Use wiles for wit, or make deceit a pleasure;
And call craft counsel, for profit still to paint;
I cannot wrest the law to fill the coffer,
With innocent blood to feed myself fat,　　　　　　35
And do most hurt where most help I offer.
I am not he that can allow the state
Of high Caesar, and damn Cato[7] to die,
That with his death did 'scape out of the gate
From Caesar's hands, if Livy[8] do not lie,　　　　　40
And would not live where liberty was lost,
So did his heart the common weal[9] apply.
I am not he, such eloquence to boast
To make the crow in singing as the swan,
Nor call the lion of coward beasts the most,　　　　45
That cannot take a mouse as the cat can;
And he that dieth of hunger of the gold,
Call him Alexander,[1] and say that Pan
Passeth Apollo in music manifold;[2]
Praise Sir Thopas for a noble tale,　　　　　　　50
And scorn the story that the Knight told;[3]
Praise him for counsel that is drunk of ale;
Grin when he laugheth that beareth all the sway,
Frown when he frowneth, and groan when he is pale;
On others' lust to hang both night and day—　　　55
None of these points would ever frame in me;
My wit is naught: I cannot learn the way;
And much the less of things that greater be
That asken help of colors of device[4]
To join the mean with each extremity.　　　　　　60
With nearest virtue to cloak alway the vice,
And as to purpose, likewise it shall fall
To press the virtue that it may not rise;
As drunkenness, good fellowship to call;
The friendly foe, with his double face,　　　　　　65
Say he is gentle and courteous therewithal;
And say that favel[5] hath a goodly grace
In eloquence; and cruelty to name
Zeal of justice, and change in time and place;
And he that suff'reth offense without blame,　　　70
Call him pitiful, and him true and plain
That raileth reckless to every man's shame,
Say he is rude that cannot lie and feign,
The lecher a lover, and tyranny

7. Cato the Younger, the famous Roman patriot who committed suicide rather than submit to Caesar.
8. Titus Livius (59 B.C.–A.D. 17), the great Roman historian.
9. The common good, or the state.
1. Alexander yearned for more worlds to conquer.
2. Pan's music was simple and rustic, played on "Pan's pipes."
3. The silly tale of Sir Thopas, in Chaucer's *Canterbury Tales*, is told by Chaucer himself, until the Host forces him to stop. The Knight's Tale is the most courtly and dignified of the tales.
4. Tricks of rhetoric.
5. Flattery.

To be the right of a prince's reign.   75
I cannot, I: no, no, it will not be.
This is the cause that I could never yet
Hang on their sleeves, that weigh, as thou mayst see,
A chip of chance more than a pound of wit.
This maketh me at home to hunt and hawk,   80
And in foul weather at my book to sit,
In frost and snow then with my bow to stalk.
No man doth mark whereso I ride or go.
In lusty leas[6] at liberty I walk,
And of these news I feel nor weal nor woe,   85
Save that a clog doth hang yet at my heel.[7]
No force for that, for it is ordered so
That I may leap both hedge and dike full well;
I am not now in France, to judge the wine,
With sav'ry sauce those delicates[8] to feel;   90
Nor yet in Spain, where one must him incline,
Rather than to be, outwardly to seem.
I meddle not with wits that be so fine;
Nor Flanders' cheer[9] letteth not my sight to deem
Of black and white, nor taketh my wit away   95
With beastliness, they beasts do so esteem.
Nor am I not where Christ is given in prey
For money, poison, and treason—at Rome[1]
A common practice, uséd night and day.
But here I am in Kent and Christendom,   100
Among the Muses, where I read and rhyme;
Where, if thou list, my Poins, for to come,
Thou shalt be judge how I do spend my time.

                                                        E. MS.

6. Pleasant fields.
7. "I feel neither happiness nor unhappiness about current political affairs, except that a 'clog' (i.e., his
confinement on parole to his estate)
keeps me from traveling far." Note
that "news" is a plural in Elizabethan
English. "No force": no matter.
8. Delicacies.

9. I.e., the drinking for which Flemings
were notorious in the 16th century;
"letteth": hinders, prevents.
1. In *Tottel's Miscellany*, published in
the reign of the Catholic Queen Mary,
these lines were altered as follows:
"where *truth* is given in prey / For
money, poison and treason; *of some*."

HENRY HOWARD, EARL OF SURREY

(1517–1547)

Surrey was the eldest son of the Duke of Norfolk, who was the premier
English nobleman and the chief bulwark of the old aristocracy against the
rising tide of "new men" and the Reformed religion. Surrey was descended
from kings on both sides of his family; he was brought up with Henry
VIII's illegitimate son, the Duke of Richmond, who married Surrey's sister.
Some stories indicate that Surrey was a proud, high-spirited youth, not

above wandering about the streets at night, in the company of Sir Thomas Wyatt's son, using stone-bows to break the windows of sober sleeping citizens. Surrey, like his father and grandfather, was an able soldier, and the Howards were called upon whenever military brilliance was needed. But their fortunes at court depended upon Henry's queens; the Howards were in high favor when Surrey's cousin, Catherine Howard, was queen, but they were low on Fortune's wheel when the queen was Jane Seymour, the mother of the future king.

Surrey's importance as a poet rests upon his continuing the practice of the sonnet in English as instituted by Wyatt and establishing a form for it which was used by Shakespeare and has become known as the "English" sonnet form: three quatrains and a couplet, rhyming *abab cdcd efef gg*. Even more significantly, he was the first English poet to publish in blank verse—unrhymed iambic pentameter—a verse form that has so flourished in the succeeding four centuries that it seems almost indigenous and inevitable to the language. The work in which he used this "strange meter," as the publisher called it, was a translation of part of Virgil's *Aeneid*. Book IV was published in 1554 and Book II in 1557. Surrey was of course a courtier poet, interested in circulating his poems in manuscript rather than in printing them, but he did publish a poetic tribute to Wyatt. The bulk of his poetry first appeared in *Tottel's Miscellany*.

Surrey shows a more regular maintenance of normal accent than Wyatt, and he is often more fluent and musical. His poetic diction is clear and consistent, and in many ways Surrey indicates the direction in which the main stream of English verse will flow. Yet he often seems less vivid and vigorous than Wyatt, and he perhaps takes the figurative language he uses less seriously.

Love, That Doth Reign and Live Within My Thought[1]

Love, that doth reign and live within my thought,
And built his seat within my captive breast,
Clad in the arms wherein with me he fought,
Oft in my face he doth his banner rest.
But she that taught me love and suffer pain,   5
My doubtful hope and eke[2] my hot desire
With shamefast look to shadow and refrain,
Her smiling grace converteth straight to ire.
And coward Love, then, to the heart apace
Taketh his flight, where he doth lurk and plain,[3]   10
His purpose lost, and dare not show his face.
For my lord's guilt thus faultless bide I pain,
Yet from my lord shall not my foot remove:
Sweet is the death that taketh end by love.

                                                                 1557

1. Compare this version of Petrarch's *Sonnetto in Vita* 91 with Wyatt's translation of the same original (*The Long Love That in My Thought Doth Harbor*, printed earlier in this anthology).
2. Also; "shamefast": modest.
3. Complain.

The Soote Season[4]

The soote season, that bud and bloom forth brings,   *a*
With green hath clad the hill and eke the vale;   *b*
The nightingale with feathers new she sings;   *a*
The turtle to her make[5] hath told her tale.   *b*
Summer is come, for every spray now springs;   *a*   5
The hart hath hung his old head on the pale;   *b*
The buck in brake his winter coat he flings,   *a*
The fishes float with new repairéd scale;   *b*
The adder all her slough away she slings,   *a*
The swift swallow pursueth the fliés small;   *b*   10
The busy bee her honey now she mings.[6]   *a*
Winter is worn, that was the flowers' bale.[7]   *b*
And thus I see among these pleasant things,   *a*
Each care decays, and yet my sorrow springs.   *a*

1557

Alas! So All Things Now Do Hold Their Peace[7a]

Alas! so all things now do hold their peace,
Heaven and earth disturbéd in no thing;
The beasts, the air, the birds their song do cease,
The nightés chare[8] the stars about doth bring.
Calm is the sea, the waves work less and less;   5
So am not I, whom love, alas, doth wring,
Bringing before my face the great increase
Of my desires, whereat I weep and sing,
In joy and woe, as in a doubtful ease.
For my sweet thoughts sometime do pleasure bring,   10
But by and by the cause of my disease[9]
Gives me a pang that inwardly doth sting,
When that I think what grief it is again
To live and lack the thing should rid my pain.

1557

Give Place, Ye Lovers, Here Before

Give place, ye lovers, here before
That spent your boasts and brags in vain;
My lady's beauty passeth more

---

4. In this adaptation from Petrarch's *Sonnetto in Morte* 42, Surrey has changed the details of nature from Italian to English. Note that the sonnet has only two rhymes. "Soote": sweet. fragrant.
5. Turtledove to her mate.

6. Remembers.
7. Harm.
7a. Translated from Petrarch's *Sonnetto in Vita* 113.
8. From Italian *carro* (the Great Bear).
9. Dis-ease, i.e., discomfort.

The best of yours, I dare well sayn [1]
Than doth the sun the candlelight,   5
Or brightest day the darkest night,

And thereto hath a troth as just [2]
As had Penelope the fair,
For what she saith, ye may it trust
As it by writing sealéd were,   10
And virtues hath she many moe
Than I with pen have skill to show.

I could rehearse, if that I wold, [3]
The whole effect of Nature's plaint,
When she had lost the perfect mold   15
The like to whom she could not paint;
With wringing hands how she did cry
And what she said, I know it, I.

I know she swore, with raging mind,
Her kingdom only set apart,   20
There was no loss, by law of kind, [4]
That could have gone so near her heart;
And this was chiefly all her pain:
She could not make the like again.

Sith [5] nature thus gave her the praise   25
To be the chiefest work she wrought,
In faith, methinks some better ways
On your behalf might well be sought
Than to compare, as ye have done,
To match the candle with the sun.   30

1557

My Friend, the Things That Do Attain [6]

My friend, the things that do attain
The happy life be these, I find:
The riches left, not got with pain;
The fruitful ground; the quiet mind;

The equal friend; no grudge, no strife;   5
No charge of rule, nor governance;
Without disease, the healthy life;
The household of continuance;

1. Say.
2. Constancy as firm.
3. Would.
4. Nature.
5. Since.

6. A translation of an epigram by the Latin poet Martial (X.47). The theme, a glorification of "the mean estate," is very common in Elizabethan literature.

The mean diet, no dainty fare;
Wisdom joined with simpleness;   10
The night dischargéd of all care,
Where wine the wit may not oppress:

The faithful wife, without debate;
Such sleeps as may beguile the night;
Content thyself with thine estate,   15
Neither wish death, nor fear his might.

1547

From The Fourth Book of Virgil[1]

ENTREATING OF THE LOVE BETWEEN AENEAS AND DIDO, TRANSLATED
INTO ENGLISH AND DRAWN INTO A STRANGE METER BY HENRY LATE
EARL OF SURREY, WORTHY TO BE EMBRACED

[*The Hunt*]

Then from the seas the dawning gan arise.
The sun once up, the chosen youth gan throng
Unto the gates; the hayes[2] so rarely knit,
The hunting staves with their broad heads of steel,
And of Massile[3] the horsemen, forth they brake;   5
Of scenting hounds a kennel huge likewise.
And at the threshold of her chamber door
The Carthage lords did there the queen await;
The trampling steed, with gold and purple decked,
Chawing the foamy bit, there fiercely stood.   10
Then issued she, backed with a great rout,[4]
Clad in a cloak of Tyre embroidered rich.
Her quiver hung behind her back, her tresses
Wound up with gold, her purple vestures eke
Buttoned with gold. The Troyans of her train   15
Before her go, with gladsome Iulus.[5]
Aeneas eke, the goodliest of the rout,
Makes one of them and joineth close the throngs;
Like when Apollo leaveth Lycia,
His wintering place, and Xanthus' floods likewise,[6] 20
To visit Delos, his mother's mansion,
For to repair and furnish new her choir,
The Candians and folk of Driopis,
And painted Agathyrsies shout and cry,[7]

---

1. These are lines 129–68 in Virgil.
2. Nets.
3. Massilia (Marseilles).
4. Band, troop.
5. Son of Aeneas.
6. Lycia is a country on the south coast of Asia Minor; Xanthus, the chief river of Lycia. Delos, an island, was Apollo's birthplace.
7. "Candians": Cretans. "Driopis" is Doris, in Greece; the "Agathyrsies" were tattooed people from Transylvania.

Environing the altars round about,   25
When he walks upon Mount Cynthus' top,[8]
His sparkled tresses he pressed with garlands soft
Of tender leaves, and trusséd up in gold,
His quivering darts clattering behind his back—
So fresh and lusty did Aeneas seem,   30
Such lordly port in countenance present.
   But to the hills and wild holts[9] when they came,
From the rock's top then driven, savage roes
Avail[1] the hill, above to the other side,
Through the wide lands, whereas their course,   35
The harts likewise, in troops taking their flight,
Raising the dust, the mountains fast forsake.
The child Iulus, blithe of his swift steed,
Amidst the plain now pricks by them, now these,
And to encounter wisheth oft in mind   40
The foaming boar, instead of timorous beasts,
Or lion brown might from the hill descend.
   In the meanwhile the heavens gan rumble sore;
In tail thereof, a mingled shower with hail.
The Tyrian folk and eke the Troyan youth   45
And Venus' nephew the cottages for fear
Sought round about; the floods fell from the hills.
Dido, a den, the Troyan prince likewise
Chanced upon. Our mother then, the Earth,
And Juno that hath charge of marriage,   50
First tokens gave with burning gledes[2] of flame,
And, privy to the wedlock, lightning skies,
And the nymphs wailed from the mountain's top.

                                                        1554

8. A mountain in Delos, where both   1. Gain.
Apollo and Artemis were born.   2. Coals, embers.
9. Woods.

SIR PHILIP SIDNEY
(1554–1586)

Sir Philip Sidney—courtier, soldier, scholar, poet, friend, and patron—seemed to the Elizabethans to embody all the traits of character and personality they admired: he was Castiglione's *Il Cortegiano* come to life. When he was killed in battle in the Low Countries at the age of 32, all England mourned.

   He was the son of Sir Henry Sidney, thrice Lord Deputy of Ireland, and of a sister of Robert Dudley, Earl of Leicester, the most spectacular and powerful of all the queen's subjects. He entered Shrewsbury School in 1564, at the age of 10, on the same day as Fulke Greville, who became his lifelong friend and biographer. Greville said of Sidney, "though I lived with him and knew him from a child, yet I never knew him other than a man—with such staidness of mind, lovely and familiar gravity, as carried grace and reverence above greater years." Although he attended Oxford, he left without taking a degree. His education was completed by extended travels on the Continent, where he had opportunities to meet the most important men of the time and to be witness to such crucial events as the Massacre of St. Bartholomew's Day, August 23, 1572. Sidney's family background and education were Protestant, but this slaughter of the French Huguenots undoubtedly strengthened his Protestant sympathies. Another important influence was his friendship with the scholar-diplomat Hubert Languet.

On his return to England he lived the life of a prominent courtier, serving occasionally on diplomatic missions and actively encouraging literary men such as Edward Dyer, Fulke Greville, and, most importantly, the young Edmund Spenser, who dedicated *The Shepheardes Calender* to him as "the president of noblesse and of chevalree." So strong were Sidney's Protestant convictions that he incurred the queen's displeasure by opposing her projected marriage to the Duke of Anjou; this led to his dismissal from court for a time. He retired to Wilton, the estate of his beloved sister Mary, Countess of Pembroke, and there he wrote, at her request and for her entertainment, a pastoral romance called *Arcadia*.

Sidney's romance exists in two forms, called the "Old Arcadia" and the "New Arcadia." The "New Arcadia" was published in fragmentary form, almost three books, in 1590. In 1593 the Countess of Pembroke republished it with slight changes and added the last three books of the "Old Arcadia," but the first three books of the earlier version remained in manuscript until the 20th century. As William Ringler says, "The *Arcadia*, in both its old and new forms, is the most important original work of English prose fiction produced before the 18th century." The romance's complicated plot is full of oracles, disguisings, mistaken identity, melodramatic incidents and tangled love situations. Some episodes are of political interest, and Sidney clearly put more of his serious thought on statecraft into it than he pretends when he describes the book as mere entertainment. The *Arcadia* also contains many poems—eclogues and songs which are interspersed throughout the narrative; they represent Sidney's experimental and exploratory ventures into verse. A good example is the double sestina, "Ye Goatherd Gods."

In 1579, the same year in which he dedicated *The Shepheardes Calender* to Sidney, Spenser wrote to his friend Gabriel Harvey, "New books I hear of none but only of one that writing a certain book called *The School of Abuse*, and dedicating it to Master Sidney, was for his labor scorned, if at least it be in the goodness of that nature to scorn." The book referred to was by Stephen Gosson; it was an attack upon poets and players from a narrowly Puritan point of view. Sidney did not specifically answer Gosson's attack, but he must have had it in mind when he composed, at some uncertain date, a major piece of critical prose which was published after his death under the titles *The Defense of Poesy* and *An Apology for Poetry*. In this long essay Sidney systematically defends poetry (indeed all imaginative literature) against its attackers. He points out the antiquity of poetry, and its prestige in the ancient world. He establishes its universality. He cites the names given to poets by the Romans (*vates* or prophet) and the

Greeks (*poietes* or maker) to indicate their ancient dignity. But, he says, the real defense of the poet depends not upon what he has been but upon what he does. All arts depend upon works of nature, but the poet, supreme among artists, can make another nature, new and more beautiful. "Nature never set forth the earth in so rich tapestry as divers poets have done, neither with pleasant rivers, fruitful trees, sweet-smelling flowers, nor whatsoever else may make the too much loved earth more lovely." Moreover, the poet presents virtues and vices in a more lively and telling way than nature does; his function is to teach and delight at the same time. He is superior to the philosopher and the historian, because he is more concrete than the one and more universal than the other. Sidney shows himself to be a thorough student of Aristotle when he explains poetry as an art of imitation in which the artist imitates not merely what is, but also what might be. He refutes the charge that poets are liars by stating that "the poet nothing affirmeth," and he maintains that poetry does not abuse man's wits by arousing base desires but that man's wits abuse poetry. Then Sidney surveys the English literary scene as it looked to him. He found little to praise: Surrey's lyrics, the *Mirror for Magistrates*, Spenser's *Shepheardes Calender* (though he disliked Spenser's use of antique language). The drama was generally bad (he was writing before the great achievements of the Elizabethans), and its failure to observe the classical unities of time and place was, for Sidney, a particular weakness. He concludes by a general defense of English as a language suitable for poetry and a humorous defiance of those who will not be converted by his defense. Despite the seriousness and logical rigor of Sidney's essay, it has many delightful personal touches. His manner is graceful and easy; it exhibits that *sprezzatura*, or casualness in doing something difficult perfectly, which Castiglione had held up as an ideal in *The Courtier.*

Sidney's *Astrophel and Stella* ("Starlover and Star") is the first of the great Elizabethan sonnet cycles. These collections, imitative of Petrarch or of his French imitators, were based upon a well-understood convention. The poet undertook to display all the contrary feelings of a lover—hope and despair, tenderness and bitterness, exultation and modesty, by the use of "conceits" or ingenious comparisons. Many of these became traditional, and eventually, stale: the poet who complained that in love he both burned and froze, or that his sighs were the winds driving his ship on a tossing sea, was echoing many an earlier poet. So Sidney protests, in the role of Astrophel, that he uses no standard conventional phrases; his verse is original and comes from the heart. (This pretense is also conventional.) But what gives Sidney's sonnets their extraordinary vigor and freshness is Sidney's ability to dramatize. He uses dialogue, is often colloquial, and he heightens the situation as much as he can within the fourteen lines.

The sonnet cycle has a framework of plot, but it does not tell a story. Yet there is a rather mysterious story hinted at in Sidney's cycle, and some of these hints point to what may be an actual episode in the poet's life. Penelope Devereux, Lady Rich, is supposed to be the original of Stella, and some of the sonnets contain puns on the name "Rich." On the other hand, Stella is virtuous in the sonnets, and refuses Astrophel anything more than a kiss, whereas the historical Penelope Devereux was apparently a different kind of woman. But there is little profit in speculating on the events behind an Elizabethan sonnet cycle; as Sidney said in his *Apology*, "the poet nothing affirmeth."

Sidney called poetry his "unelected vocation," and he did not publish it himself. His view of himself was probably more that of patron than of artist. Yet his achievement as the author of the most important work of prose fiction in his age, the most important piece of literary criticism, and the most important sonnet cycle surely qualify him as a major author. The texts here printed have been reviewed against those in William Ringler's newly authoritative edition, *The Poems of Sir Philip Sidney* (1962).

Ye Goatherd Gods[1]

STREPHON. Ye goatherd gods, that love the grassy mountains,
Ye nymphs which haunt the springs in pleasant valleys,
Ye satyrs joyed with free and quiet forests,
Vouchsafe your silent ears to plaining music,
Which to my woes gives still an early morning,   5
And draws the dolor on till weary evening.

KLAIUS. O Mercury,[2] foregoer to the evening,
O heavenly huntress of the savage mountains,
O lovely star, entitled of the morning,
While that my voice doth fill these woeful valleys,   10
Vouchsafe your silent ears to plaining music,
Which oft hath Echo tired in secret forests.

STREPHON. I, that was once free burgess[3] of the forests,
Where shade from sun, and sport I sought in evening,
I, that was once esteemed for pleasant music,   15
Am banished now among the monstrous mountains
Of huge despair, and foul affliction's valleys,
Am grown a screech owl to myself each morning.

KLAIUS. I, that was once delighted every morning,
Hunting the wild inhabiters of forests,   20
I, that was once the music of these valleys,
So darkened am that all my day is evening,

1. From Sidney's pastoral-heroic romance, the *Arcadia*. The poem is a dialogue between two shepherds, Strephon and Klaius, both of whom are in love with the absent Urania. Sidney, of course, knew no shepherds like this: the figures and the landscape in the poem belong to the pastoral tradition of an elegant idealized country life— usually Greek.

The form of the poem is basically that of the sestina, which has six-line stanzas and a final triplet of three lines; the terminal words of each stanza are the same, but rearranged according to a definite pattern, and all six terminal words must appear in the final triplet. Sestinas usually have six stanzas, but Sidney has here created a double sestina, of twelve stanzas. The *Arcadia* has about eighty interpolated poems, some of them ingenious metrical experiments like this one.

2. The evening star. The "huntress" is Diana, the moon; the "lovely star" is Lucifer, the morning star.

3. Citizen.

Heartbroken so that molehills seem high mountains
And fill the vales with cries instead of music.

STREPHON. Long since, alas, my deadly swannish[4] music   25
Hath made itself a crier of the morning,
And hath with wailing strength climbed highest mountains;
Long since my thoughts more desert be than forests,
Long since I see my joys come to their evening,
And state[5] thrown down to overtrodden valleys.   30

KLAIUS. Long since the happy dwellers of these valleys
Have prayed me leave my strange exclaiming music
Which troubles their day's work and joys of evening;
Long since I hate the night, more hate the morning;
Long since my thoughts chase me like beasts in forests   35
And make me wish myself laid under mountains.

STREPHON. Meseems I see the high and stately mountains
Transform themselves to low dejected valleys;
Meseems I hear in these ill-changéd forests
The nightingales do learn of owls their music;   40
Meseems I feel the comfort of the morning
Turned to the mortal serene[6] of an evening.

KLAIUS. Meseems I see a filthy cloudy evening
As soon as sun begins to climb the mountains;
Meseems I feel a noisome[7] scent, the morning   45
When I do smell the flowers of these valleys;
Meseems I hear, when I do hear sweet music,
The dreadful cries of murdered men in forests.

STREPHON. I wish to fire the trees of all those forests;
I give the sun a last farewell each evening;   50
I curse the fiddling finders-out of music;
With envy I do hate the lofty mountains
And with despite despise the humble valleys;
I do detest night, evening, day, and morning.

KLAIUS. Curse to myself my prayer is, the morning;   55
My fire is more than can be made with forests,
My state more base than are the basest valleys.
I wish no evenings more to see, each evening;
Shaméd, I hate myself in sight of mountains
And stop mine ears, lest I grow mad with music.   60

STREPHON. For she whose parts maintained a perfect music,
Whose beauties shined more than the blushing morning,
Who much did pass[8] in state the stately mountains,

---

4. Doleful, like the song supposedly
sung by the swan just before its death.
5. High position.
6. Deadly dew.

7. Stinking. "The morning": i.e., in
the morning.
8. Surpass.

In straightness passed the cedars of the forests,
Hath cast me, wretch, into eternal evening   65
By taking her two suns from these dark valleys.

KLAIUS. For she, to whom compared, the Alps are valleys,
She, whose least word brings from the spheres their music,
At whose approach the sun rose in the evening,
Who where she went bare[9] in her forehead morning,   70
Is gone, is gone, from these our spoiled forests,
Turning to deserts our best pastured mountains.

STREPHON. These mountains witness shall, so shall these valleys,
These forests eke, made wretched by our music,

KLAIUS.   Our morning hymn is this, and song at evening.   75
1577-1580   1593

Thou Blind Man's Mark

Thou blind man's mark,[1] thou fool's self-chosen snare,
Fond fancy's scum, and dregs of scattered thought;
Band[2] of all evils, cradle of causeless care;
Thou web of will, whose end is never wrought;
Desire, desire! I have too dearly bought,   5
With price of mangled mind, thy worthless ware;
Too long, too long, asleep thou hast me brought,
Who should my mind to higher things prepare.
But yet in vain thou hast my ruin sought;
In vain thou madest me to vain things aspire;   10
In vain thou kindlest all thy smoky fire;
For virtue hath this better lesson taught—
Within myself to seek my only hire,
Desiring naught but how to kill desire.

1581   1598

Leave Me, O Love

Leave me, O love which reachest but to dust;
And thou, my mind, aspire to higher things;
Grow rich in that which never taketh rust,
Whatever fades but fading pleasure brings.
Draw in thy beams, and humble all thy might   5
To that sweet yoke where lasting freedoms be;
Which breaks the clouds and opens forth the light,

9. Bore.   2. Swaddling band.
1. Target.

That doth both shine and give us sight to see.
O take fast hold; let that light be thy guide
In this small course which birth draws out to death,   10
And think how evil becometh him to slide,
Who seeketh heav'n, and comes of heav'nly breath.[3]
Then farewell, world; thy uttermost I see;
Eternal Love, maintain thy life in me.

1581   1598

From Astrophel and Stella[1]

1

Loving in truth, and fain[2] in verse my love to show,
That the dear she might take some pleasure of my pain,
Pleasure might cause her read, reading might make her know,
Knowledge might pity win, and pity grace obtain,
I sought fit words to paint the blackest face of woe: 5
Studying inventions fine, her wits to entertain,
Oft turning others' leaves, to see if thence would flow
Some fresh and fruitful showers upon my sunburnt brain.
But words came halting[3] forth, wanting Invention's stay;
Invention, Nature's child, fled stepdame Study's blows;   10
And others' feet still seemed but strangers in my way.
Thus, great with child to speak, and helpless in my throes,
Biting my truant pen, beating myself for spite:
"Fool," said my Muse to me, "look in thy heart, and write!"

5

It is most true that eyes are formed to serve
The inward light,[4] and that the heavenly part
Ought to be king, from whose rules who do swerve,
Rebels to nature, strive for their own smart.
It is most true, what we call Cupid's dart   5
An image is, which for ourelves we carve,
And, fools, adore in temple of our heart,
Till that good god make church and churchman starve.
True, that true beauty virtue is indeed,
Whereof this beauty can be but a shade,   10
Which elements with mortal mixture breed.[5]
True, that on earth we are but pilgrims made,
And should in soul up to our country move.
True, and yet true that I must Stella love.

3. I.e., and think how evil it is for one who is seeking heaven and has a divine spirit or soul in him to descend to earthly things.
1. The first sonnet is one of six in the cycle that are written in hexameters.
2. Desirous.
3. Limping. "Stay": crutch, support.
4. I.e., the soul. The concessions made in the argument of this sonnet are to Platonic and Christian doctrines as opposed to romantic love.
5. This beauty is a mixture of the four elements (earth, air, water, fire) and as such is mortal. According to Platonic doctrine the only true beauty (identical with virtue) is a divine idea or essence and is immortal.

6

Some lovers speak, when they their Muses entertain,
Of hopes begot by fear, of wot[6] not what desires,
Of force of heavenly beams infusing hellish pain,
Of living deaths, dear wounds, fair storms, and freezing fires;
Someone his song in Jove and Jove's strange tales attires,   5
Bordered with bulls and swans, powdered with golden rain;[7]
Another humbler wit to shepherd's pipe[8] retires,
Yet hiding royal blood full oft in rural vein.
To some a sweetest plaint a sweetest style affords,
While tears pour out his ink, and sighs breathe out his words,   10
His paper pale despair, and pain his pen doth move.
I can speak what I feel, and feel as much as they,[9]
But think that all the map of my state I display
When trembling voice brings forth, that I do Stella love.

10

Reason, in faith thou art well served, that still
Wouldst brabbling [1] be with sense and love in me;
I rather wished thee climb the Muses' hill,
Or reach the fruit of nature's choicest tree,
Or seek heaven's course, or heaven's inside to see.   5
Why shouldst thou toil our thorny soil to till?
Leave sense, and those which sense's objects be;
Deal thou with powers of thoughts; leave love to will.
But thou wouldst needs fight both with love and sense,
With sword of wit, giving wounds of dispraise,   10
Till downright blows did foil thy cunning fence; [2]
For soon as they strake thee with Stella's rays,
Reason, thou kneel'dst, and offeredst straight to prove
By reason good, good reason her to love.

18

With what sharp checks I in myself am shent,[3]
When into Reason's audit I do go,
And by just counts myself a banckrout [4] know
Of all those goods, which heaven to me hath lent;
Unable quite to pay even Nature's rent,   5
Which unto it by birthright I do owe;
And which is worse, no good excuse can show,
But that my wealth I have most idly spent.
My youth doth waste, my knowledge brings forth toys,[5]
My wit doth strive those passions to defend,   10

6. Know.
7. In classical mythology Jove courted Europa in the shape of a bull, Leda as a swan, and Danaë as a golden shower.
8. In the pastoral convention the poet pretends to be a shepherd and his poems are the songs he plays on his oaten or reed pipe.
9. I.e., the Petrarchan sonneteers in Italy and France, whose literary conventions he had been describing. As a matter of fact, he utilizes some of these conventions himself and is not so direct and simple as he would have us believe here and in sonnets 1 and 74.

1. Quarreling.
2. Skill at fencing.
3. Disgraced; "checks": reproofs.
4. Bankrupt.
5. Trifles, i.e. these poems.

Which for reward spoil it with vain annoys.
I see my course to lose myself doth bend:
I see and yet no greater sorrow take,
Then that I lose no more for Stella's sake.

21

Your words, my friend, right healthful caustics, blame
My young mind marred, whom Love doth windlass [6] so,
That mine own writings like bad servants show
My wits, quick in vain thoughts, in virtue lame;
That Plato I read for nought, but if he tame   5
Such coltish gyres,[7] that to my birth I owe
Nobler desires, lest else that friendly foe,
Great expectation, wear a train of shame.
For since mad March great promise made of me,
If now the May of my years much decline,   10
What can be hoped my harvest time will be?
Sure you say well; your wisdom's golden mine
Dig deep with learning's spade; now tell me this,
Hath this world ought so fair as Stella is?

31

With how sad steps, Oh Moon, thou climb'st the skies!
How silently, and with how wan a face!
What, may it be that even in heavenly place
That busy archer [8] his sharp arrows tries?
Sure, if that long-with-love-acquainted eyes   5
Can judge of love, thou feel'st a lover's case,
I read it in thy looks; thy languished grace,
To me, that feel the like, thy state descries.
Then, even of fellowship, Oh Moon, tell me,
Is constant love deemed there but want of wit?   10
Are beauties there as proud as here they be?
Do they above love to be loved, and yet
Those lovers scorn whom that love doth possess?
Do they call virtue there ungratefulness? [9]

39

Come sleep! Oh sleep, the certain knot of peace,
The baiting place [1] of wit, the balm of woe,
The poor man's wealth, the prisoner's release,
The indifferent judge between the high and low;
With shield of proof [2] shield me from out the prease   5
Of those fierce darts Despair at me doth throw;
Oh make in me those civil wars to cease;
I will good tribute pay, if thou do so.
Take thou of me smooth pillows, sweetest bed,
A chamber deaf to noise and blind to light,   10
A rosy garland and a weary head;

---

6. Ambush, ensnare.
7. Youthful gyrations.
8. Cupid.
9. I.e., do they   gratefulness

virtue there (as they do here)?
1. A place for refreshment on a journey.
2. Proven strength. "Prease": press, crowd.

And if these things, as being thine by right,
Move not thy heavy grace, thou shalt in me,
Livelier than elsewhere, Stella's image see.

41

Having this day my horse, my hand, my lance
Guided so well that I obtained the prize,[3]
Both by the judgment of the English eyes
And of some sent from that sweet enemy, France,
Horsemen my skill in horsemanship advance,   5
Town-folks my strength; a daintier judge applies
His praise to sleight which from good use [4] doth rise;
Some lucky wits impute it but to chance;
Others, because of both sides I do take
My blood from them who did excel in this,[5]   10
Think nature me a man-at-arms did make.
How far they shoot awry! The true cause is,
Stella looked on, and from her heavenly face
Sent forth the beams which made so fair my race.

64

No more, my dear, no more these counsels try;
Oh, give my passions leave to run their race;
Let Fortune lay on me her worst disgrace;
Let folk o'ercharged with brain against me cry;
Let clouds bedim my face, break in mine eye;   5
Let me no steps but of lost labor trace;
Let all the earth with scorn recount my case;
But do not will me from my Love to flie.
I do not envy Aristotle's wit,[6]
Nor do aspire to Caesar's bleeding fame,   10
Nor ought do care, though some above me sit,
Nor hope nor wish another course to frame,
But that which once may win thy cruel heart:
Thou art my wit, and thou my virtue art.

71

Who will in fairest book of Nature know,
How Virtue may best lodged in beauty be,
Let him but learn of Love to read in thee,
Stella, those fair lines, which true goodness show.
There shall he find all vices' overthrow,   5
Not by rude force, but sweetest sovereignty
Of reason, from whose light those night birds [7] fly;
That inward sun in thine eyes shineth so.
And not content to be Perfection's heir

---

3. At an actual tournament in the summer of 1581.
4. Cleverness which from experience.
5. I.e., because my ancestors on both sides were distinguished in the tournament.
6. Wisdom.
7. Night birds, like owls, conventionally symbolized vices.

Thyself, dost strive all minds that way to move,   10
Who mark in thee what is in thee most fair.
So while thy beauty draws the heart to love,
As fast thy Virtue bends that love to good:
"But ah," desire still cries, "give me some food."

74

I never drank of Aganippe well,
Nor ever did in shade of Tempe sit,[8]
And Muses scorn with vulgar brains to dwell;
Poor layman I, for sacred rites unfit.
Some do I hear of poets' fury tell,   5
But, God wot, wot not what they mean by it;
And this I swear by blackest brook of hell,[9]
I am no pick-purse of another's wit.
How falls it then that with so smooth an ease
My thoughts I speak; and what I speak doth flow   10
In verse, and that my verse best wits doth please?
Guess we the cause. What, is it thus? Fie, no.
Or so? Much less. How then? Sure thus it is:
My lips are sweet, inspired with Stella's kiss.

1582   1591

From An Apology for Poetry

* * * There is no art delivered to mankind that hath not the
works of nature for his principal object, without which they could
not consist, and on which they so depend, as they become actors
and players, as it were, of what nature will have set forth. So doth
the astronomer look upon the stars, and, by that he seeth, setteth
down what order nature hath taken therein.[1] So do the geometrician
and arithmetician in their diverse sorts of quantities. So doth the
musician in times tell you which by nature agree,[2] which not. The
natural philosopher thereon[3] hath his name, and the moral philosopher standeth upon the natural virtues, vices, and passions of man;
and "follow nature," saith he, "therein, and thou shalt not err." The
lawyer saith what men have determined; the historian what men
have done. The grammarian speaketh only of the rules of speech;
and the rhetorician and logician, considering what in nature will
soonest prove and persuade, thereon give artificial rules, which still
are compassed within the circle of a question according to the
proposed matter.[4] The physician weigheth the nature of a man's

8. Aganippe: a well at the foot of Mt.
Helicon in Greece, sacred to the Muses;
Tempe: a valley beside Mt. Olympus,
sacred to Apollo, the god of song.
9. The river Styx.
1. I.e., according to that which he
sees, he sets down what arrangements
nature has made.
2. Which musical measures fit together

naturally.
3. I.e., from studying nature; the "natural philosopher" is what we would call
a scientist. "Standeth upon": takes as
his subject matter.
4. I.e., which apply only to the particular situation for which the rule was
devised. "Weigheth": studies, considers.

body, and the nature of things helpful or hurtful unto it. And the metaphysic, though it be in the second and abstract notions, and therefore be counted supernatural, yet doth he indeed build upon the depth of nature. Only the poet, disdaining to be tied to any such subjection, lifted up with the vigor of his own invention, doth grow in effect another nature, in making things either better than nature bringeth forth, or, quite anew, forms such as never were in nature, as the Heroes,[5] Demigods, Cyclops, Chimeras, Furies, and such like: so as he goeth hand in hand with nature, not enclosed within the narrow warrant of her gifts, but freely ranging only within the zodiac of his own wit.

Nature never set forth the earth in so rich tapestry as divers poets have done—neither with pleasant rivers, fruitful trees, sweet-smelling flowers, nor whatsoever else may make the too much loved earth more lovely. Her[6] world is brazen, the poets only deliver a golden. But let those things alone, and go to man—for whom as the other things are, so it seemeth in him her uttermost cunning is employed—and know whether she have brought forth so true a lover as Theagenes, so constant a friend as Pylades, so valiant a man as Orlando, so right a prince as Xenophon's Cyrus,[7] so excellent a man every way as Virgil's Aeneas. Neither let this be jestingly conceived, because the works of the one be essential, the other in imitation or fiction; for any understanding knoweth the skill of the artificer standeth in that idea or foreconceit of the work, and not in the work itself. And that the poet hath that idea is manifest, by delivering them forth in such excellency as he hath imagined them. Which delivering forth also is not wholly imaginative, as we are wont to say by them that build castles in the air: but so far substantially it worketh, not only to make a Cyrus, which had been but a particular excellency, as nature might have done, but to bestow a Cyrus upon the world, to make many Cyruses, if they will learn aright why and how that maker made him.

Neither let it be deemed too saucy a comparison to balance the highest point of man's wit with the efficacy of nature; but rather give right honor to the heavenly Maker of that maker,[8] who, having made man to his own likeness, set him beyond and over all the works of that second nature: which in nothing he showeth so much as in poetry, when with the force of a divine breath he bringeth

5. Sidney uses the word in its Greek sense, meaning a deified man; "Cyclops": one-eyed giants in Homer's *Odyssey;* "Chimeras": fire-breathing monsters, with lion's head, goat's body, and serpent's tail.

6. I.e., nature's. "Brazen": a reference to the traditional idea that the first age of man was the Golden Age, and that deterioration then followed through the Silver Age and the Brazen Age down to the present Iron Age.

7. Theagenes: hero of Heliodorus' Greek romance *Aethiopica;* Pylades was the constant friend of the Greek hero Orestes; Orlando: hero of Ariosto's *Orlando Furioso;* Cyrus: hero of Xenophon's *Cyropaedia.*

8. Sidney had earlier explained that the word "poet" comes from the Greek word for "maker." The "maker" is then in a role like that of God, but on a lower level—an anticipation of the idea of the poet as creator.

things forth far surpassing her doings, with no small argument to the incredulous of that first accursed fall of Adam, since our erected wit[9] maketh us know what perfection is, and yet our infected will keepeth us from reaching unto it.[1] But these arguments will by few be understood, and by fewer granted. Thus much (I hope) will be given me, that the Greeks with some probability of reason gave him the name above all names of learning. Now let us go to a more ordinary opening[2] of him, that the truth may be more palpable: and so I hope, though we get not so unmatched a praise as the etymology of his names will grant, yet his very description, which no man will deny, shall not justly be barred from a principal commendation.

Poesy therefore is an art of imitation, for so Aristotle termeth it[3] in his word *mimesis*, that is to say, a representing, counterfeiting, or figuring forth—to speak metaphorically, a speaking picture; with this end, to teach and delight. Of this have been three several kinds.

The chief, both in antiquity and excellency, were they that did imitate the inconceivable excellencies of God. Such were David in his Psalms; Solomon in his Song of Songs, in his Ecclesiastes, and Proverbs; Moses and Deborah in their Hymns; and the writer of Job, which, beside other, the learned Emanuel Tremellius and Franciscus Junius[4] do entitle the poetical part of the Scripture. Against these none will speak that hath the Holy Ghost in due holy reverence. In this kind, though in a full wrong divinity, were Orpheus, Amphion, Homer in his Hymns, and many other, both Greeks and Romans, and this poesy must be used by whosoever will follow St. James's counsel in singing psalms when they are merry, and I know is used with the fruit of comfort by some, when, in sorrowful pangs of their death-bringing sins, they find the consolation of the never-leaving goodness.

The second kind is of them that deal with matters philosophical: either moral, as Tyrtaeus, Phocylides, and Cato;[5] or natural, as Lucretius and Virgil's *Georgics*; or astronomical, as Manilius and Pontanus; or historical, as Lucan; which who mislike, the fault is in their judgments quite out of taste, and not in the sweet food of sweetly uttered knowledge.

9. I.e., our elevated, undebased intelligence.
1. The "will" is "infected" because corrupted and weakened by original sin in the Fall.
2. Analysis or explanation. Sidney goes on to explain poetry as an art of imitation, following Aristotle. There are three kinds: divine poetry, which imitates the excellencies of God; philosophical poetry, which imitates learning; and a third kind, which we generally call simple "poetry," and which imitates life as it might be and should be, for the purpose of conveying instruction and delight.
3. In the *Poetics* 1.2, but Sidney is probably drawing here on Scaliger's *Poetice* I.i.
4. Two 16th-century Protestant scholars who published a Latin translation of the Bible in 1575–80.
5. Dionysius Cato was the reputed author of *Disticha de moribus*, four books of epigrammatic moral precepts in Latin hexameters used as a textbook in Elizabethan schools.

But because this second sort is wrapped within the fold of the proposed subject, and takes not the course of his own invention, whether they properly be poets or no let grammarians dispute; and go to the third, indeed right [6] poets, of whom chiefly this question ariseth, betwixt whom and these second is such a kind of difference as betwixt the meaner sort of painters, who counterfeit only such faces as are set before them, and the more excellent, who, having no law but wit, bestow that in colors upon you which is fittest for the eye to see, as the constant though lamenting look of Lucretia, when she punished in herself another's fault [7] (wherein he painteth not Lucretia whom he never saw, but painteth the outward beauty of such a virtue). For these third be they which most properly do imitate to teach and delight, and to imitate borrow nothing of what is, hath been, or shall be; but range, only reined with learned discretion, into the divine consideration of what may be, and should be. These be they that, as the first and most noble sort may justly be termed *vates*,[8] so these are waited on in the excellentest languages and best understandings, with the foredescribed name of poets; for these indeed do merely make to imitate, and imitate both to delight and teach, and delight to move men to take that goodness in hand, which without delight they would fly as from a stranger, and teach, to make them know that goodness whereunto they are moved: which being the noblest scope to which ever any learning was directed, yet want there not idle tongues to bark at them.

These be subdivided into sundry more special denominations. The most notable be the heroic, lyric, tragic, comic, satiric, iambic, elegiac, pastoral, and certain others, some of these being termed according to the matter they deal with, some by the sorts of verses they liked best to write in; for indeed the greatest part of poets have appareled their poetical inventions in that numbrous [9] kind of writing which is called verse—indeed but appareled, verse being but an ornament and no cause to poetry, since there have been many most excellent poets that never versified, and now swarm many versifiers that need never answer to the name of poets. For Xenophon,[1] who did imitate so excellently as to give us *effigiem iusti imperii*, "the portraiture of a just Empire," under name of Cyrus (as Cicero saith of him), made therein an absolute heroical poem. So did Heliodorus in his sugared invention of that picture of love in Theagenes and Chariclea;[2] and yet both these writ in

6. Real.
7. Lucretia was the wife of L. Tarquinius Colatinus, outraged by Sextus, son of Tarquinius Superbus. See Shakespeare *The Rape of Lucrece*.
8. A *vates* was originally a prophet or oracle; later the term was used for a poet.
9. Not "numerous," but in "numbers" or metrical lines.
1. Xenophon's *Cyropaedia* is an idealized and romanticized biography, in prose, of Cyrus the Great.
2. See note 7, page 478.

prose: which I speak to show that it is not rhyming and versing that maketh a poet—no more than a long gown maketh an advocate, who though he pleaded in armor should be an advocate and no soldier. But it is that feigning notable images of virtues, vices, or what else, with that delightful teaching, which must be the right describing note to know a poet by, although indeed the Senate of Poets hath chosen verse as their fittest raiment, meaning, as in matter they passed all in all, so in manner to go beyond them—not speaking (table-talk fashion or like men in a dream) words as they chanceably fall from the mouth, but peizing [3] each syllable of each word by just proportion according to the dignity of the subject.

Now therefore it shall not be amiss first to weigh this latter sort of poetry by his works, and then by his parts, and, if in neither of these anatomies [4] he be condemnable, I hope we shall obtain a more favorable sentence. This purifying of wit, this enriching of memory, enabling of judgment, and enlarging of conceit, which commonly we call learning, under what name soever it come forth, or to what immediate end soever it be directed, the final end is to lead and draw us to as high a perfection as our degenerate souls, made worse by their clayey lodgings, can be capable of. This, according to the inclination of the man, bred many formed impressions. For some that thought this felicity principally to be gotten by knowledge and no knowledge to be so high and heavenly as acquaintance with the stars, gave themselves to astronomy; others, persuading themselves to be demigods if they knew the causes of things, became natural and supernatural philosophers; some an admirable delight drew to music; and some the certainty of demonstration to the mathematics. But all, one and other, having this scope—to know, and by knowledge to lift up the mind from the dungeon of the body to the enjoying his own divine essence. But when by the balance of experience it was found that the astronomer looking to the stars might fall into a ditch, that the inquiring philosopher might be blind in himself, and the mathematician might draw forth a straight line with a crooked heart, then, lo, did proof, the overruler of opinions, make manifest that all these are but serving sciences, which, as they have each a private end in themselves, so yet are they all directed to the highest end of the mistress-knowledge, by the Greeks called *architectonike*, which stands (as I think) in the knowledge of a man's self, in the ethic and politic consideration, with the end of well doing and not of well knowing only:— even as the saddler's next end is to make a good saddle, but his farther end to serve a nobler faculty, which is horsemanship; so the horseman's to soldiery, and the soldier not only to have the skill, but to perform the practice of a soldier. So that, the ending

3. Weighing.   4. Analyses.

end of all earthly learning being virtuous action, those skills, that most serve to bring forth that, have a most just title to be princes over all the rest.[5] * * *

But since I have run so long a career in this matter, methinks, before I give my pen a full stop, it shall be but a little more lost time to inquire why England (the mother of excellent minds) should be grown so hard a stepmother to poets, who certainly in wit ought to pass all other, since all only proceedeth from their wit, being indeed makers of themselves, not takers of others. How can I but exclaim,

Musa, mihi causas memora, quo numine laeso![8]

Sweet poesy, that hath anciently had kings, emperors, senators, great captains, such as, besides a thousand others, David, Adrian, Sophocles, Germanicus,[9] not only to favor poets, but to be poets; and of our nearer times can present for her patrons a Robert, King of Sicily, the great King Francis of France, King James of Scotland;[1] such cardinals as Bembus and Bibiena; such famous preachers and teachers as Beza and Melancthon; so learned philosophers as Fracastorius and Scaliger; so great orators as Pontanus and Muretus; so piercing wits as George Buchanan;[2] so grave counselors as, besides many, but before all, that Hospital of France,[3] than whom (I think) that realm never brought forth a more accomplished judgment, more firmly builded upon virtue—I say these, with numbers of others, not only to read others' poesies, but to poetize for others' reading—that poesy, thus embraced in all other places, should only find in our time a hard welcome in England, I think the very earth lamenteth it, and therefore decketh our soil with fewer laurels than it was accustomed. For heretofore poets have in England also

5. In the omitted portion Sidney compares the poet with the moral philosopher, who gives precepts, and the historian, who gives examples; the poet is their superior because he gives both. The poet can invent, but the historian is "captived to the truth of a foolish world." The moral philosopher may teach more systematically, but the poet affects the feelings and therefore influences action. The poet is the monarch of the human sciences. Sidney defends the various kinds of literature and refutes the traditional complaints that poets tell lies, that poetry is effeminate, that poetry abuses man's wit, and that Plato banished poets from his commonwealth. He calls for laurels for poets instead of abuse of their art.
8. "O Muse, call to mind the causes: what divinity was injured?" (*Aeneid* I.8).
9. Adrian is the Emperor Hadrian; Sophocles, the great Greek dramatist, was also a general; Germanicus, 1st-

century Roman emperor, translated poetry.
1. Robert d'Anjou, King of Naples, friend of Petrarch and Boccaccio; Francis I of France was a great patron of arts and letters; King James I of Scotland was author of the *King's Quair*.
2. Pietro Cardinal Bembo, a stylist and man of letters (he also appears in Castiglione's *Courtier*); Bernardo da Bibbiena, a writer of comedy and private secretary to Lorenzo de Medici. Theodore Beza and Philip Melancthon were prominent European Protestant theologians. Fracastorius and Julius Caesar Scaliger were famous Italian scholars. John Jovius Pontanus was an Italian medieval poet; Muretus was the Latinized name of Marc Antoine Muret, French scholar and writer. George Buchanan was the foremost Scottish writer of the 16th century.
3. Michel de l'Hospital, Chancellor of France and defender of the Huguenots.

flourished, and, which is to be noted, even in those times when the trumpet of Mars did sound loudest. And now that an overfaint quietness should seem to strew the house for poets,[4] they are almost in as good reputation as the mountebanks at Venice. Truly even that, as of the one side it giveth great praise to poesy, which like Venus (but to better purpose) hath rather be troubled in the net with Mars than enjoy the homely quiet of Vulcan;[5] so serves it for a piece of a reason why they are less grateful to idle England, which now can scarce endure the pain of a pen. Upon this necessarily followeth, that base men with servile wits undertake it, who think it enough if they can be rewarded of the printer. And so as Epaminondas is said, with the honor of his virtue, to have made an office, by his exercising it, which before was contemptible, to become highly respected,[6] so these, no more but setting their names to it, by their own disgracefulness disgrace the most graceful poesy. For now, as if all the Muses were got with child, to bring forth bastard poets, without any commission they do post over the banks of Helicon, till they make the readers more weary than posthorses, while, in the meantime, they,

Queis meliore luto finxit praecordia Titan,[7]

are better content to suppress the outflowing of their wit than, by publishing them, to be accounted knights of the same order. But I that, before ever I durst aspire unto the dignity, am admitted into the company of the paper-blurrers, do find the very true cause of our wanting estimation is want of desert, taking upon us to be poets in despite of Pallas. Now, wherein we want desert were a thank-worthy labor to express: but if I knew, I should have mended my-self. But I, as I never desired the title, so have I neglected the means to come by it. Only, overmastered by some thoughts, I yielded an inky tribute unto them. Marry, they that delight in poesy itself should seek to know what they do, and how they do, and, especially, look themselves in an unflattering glass of reason, if they be inclina-ble unto it. For poesy must not be drawn by the ears; it must be gen-tly led, or rather it must lead; which was partly the cause that made the ancient-learned affirm it was a divine gift, and no human skill: since all other knowledges lie ready for any that hath strength of wit; a poet no industry can make, if his own genius be not carried unto it; and therefore is it an old proverb, *Orator fit, Poeta nascitur.*[8]

---

4. I.e., now that peace has strewn rushes on the floor to make poets com-fortable. "Mountebanks": vendors of quack medicines.
5. Vulcan discovered his wife Venus in bed with Mars; he entrapped them in a net and called the other gods to see them, expecting the lovers to suffer ridicule and shame, but he was the victim of their laughter himself.
6. He was sewer commissioner in Thebes.
7. "Whose hearts Titan [Prometheus] had formed of better clay" (Juvenal, *Satires* XIV.34–35).
8. "An orator is made, but a poet must be born one."

Yet confess I always that as the fertilest ground must be manured, so must the highest-flying wit have a Daedalus[9] to guide him. That Daedalus, they say, both in this and in other, hath three wings to bear itself up into the air of due commendation: that is, Art, Imitation, and Exercise. But these, neither artificial rules nor imitative patterns, we much cumber ourselves withal. Exercise indeed we do, but that very fore-backwardly: for where we should exercise to know, we exercise as having known: and so is our brain delivered of much matter which never was begotten by knowledge. For, there being two principal parts—matter to be expressed by words and words to express the matter—in neither we use Art or Imitation rightly. Our matter is *Quodlibet*[1] indeed, though wrongly performing Ovid's verse,

> *Quicquid conabar dicere, versus erit:*

never marshaling it into an assured rank, that almost the readers cannot tell where to find themselves.

Chaucer, undoubtedly, did excellently in his *Troilus and Cressida*; of whom, truly, I know not whether to marvel more, either that he in that misty time could see so clearly, or that we in this clear age walk so stumblingly after him. Yet had he great wants, fit to be forgiven in so reverent antiquity. I account the *Mirror of Magistrates*[2] meetly furnished of beautiful parts, and in the Earl of Surrey's *Lyrics* many things tasting of a noble birth, and worthy of a noble mind. The *Shepherd's Calendar* hath much poetry in his Eclogues, indeed worthy the reading, if I be not deceived. That same framing of his style to an old rustic language I dare not allow, since neither Theocritus in Greek, Virgil in Latin, nor Sannazaro in Italian[3] did affect it. Besides these, do I not remember to have seen but few (to speak boldly) printed, that have poetical sinews in them: for proof whereof, let but most of the verses be put in prose, and then ask the meaning; and it will be found that one verse did but beget another, without ordering at the first what should be at the last; which becomes a confused mass of words, with a tingling sound of rhyme, barely accompanied with reason.

Our tragedies and comedies (not without cause cried out against), observing rules neither of honest civility nor of skillful poetry, excepting *Gorboduc*[4] (again, I say, of those that I have seen), which

---

9. The legendary craftsman who invented wings for himself and his son Icarus. Icarus did not follow his father's instructions and fell into the sea.
1. "Anything you please." The phrase following may be translated, "Whatever I try to write will become verse."
2. A large collection of Elizabethan poems on the downfall of princes and men of power. The "beautiful parts" were probably in Sackville's Induction to it.
3. Three models for pastoral poetry.
4. A Senecan play by Thomas Sackville and Thomas Norton, published in 1565 and called the first regular English tragedy. The tragedies of the Roman dramatist Seneca (5 B.C.–A.D. 65) are written in a highly rhetorical, declamatory style.

notwithstanding, as it is full of stately speeches and well-sounding phrases, climbing to the height of Seneca's style, and as full of notable morality, which it doth most delightfully teach, and so obtain the very end of poesy, yet in truth it is very defectious in the circumstances, which grieveth me, because it might not remain as an exact model of all tragedies. For it is faulty both in place and time, the two necessary companions of all corporal actions. For where the stage should always represent but one place, and the uttermost time presupposed in it should be, both by Aristotle's precept and common reason, but one day, there is both many days, and many places, inartificially imagined. But if it be so in *Gorboduc*, how much more in all the rest, where you shall have Asia of the one side, and Afric of the other, and so many other under-kingdoms, that the player, when he cometh in, must ever begin with telling where he is, or else the tale will not be conceived? Now ye shall have three ladies walk to gather flowers, and then we must believe the stage to be a garden. By and by we hear news of shipwreck in the same place, and then we are to blame if we accept it not for a rock. Upon the back of that comes out a hideous monster, with fire and smoke, and then the miserable beholders are bound to take it for a cave. While in the meantime two armies fly in, represented with four swords and bucklers,[5] and then what hard heart will not receive it for a pitched field? Now, of time they are much more liberal, for ordinary it is that two young princes fall in love. After many traverses,[6] she is got with child, delivered of a fair boy; he is lost, groweth a man, falls in love, and is ready to get another child; and all this in two hours' space: which, how absurd it is in sense, even sense may imagine, and art hath taught, and all ancient examples justified, and, at this day, the ordinary players in Italy will not err in. Yet will some bring in an example of *Eunuchus* in Terence,[7] that containeth matter of two days, yet far short of twenty years. True it is, and so was it to be played in two days, and so fitted to the time it set forth. And though Plautus hath in one place done amiss, let us hit with him, and not miss with him. But they will say, How then shall we set forth a story, which containeth both many places and many times? And do they not know that a tragedy is tied to the laws of poesy, and not of history; not bound to follow the story, but, having liberty, either to feign a quite new matter, or to frame the history to the most tragical conveniency? Again, many things may be told which cannot be showed, if they know the difference betwixt reporting and representing. As, for example, I may speak (though I am here) of Peru, and in speech digress from that to the description of Calicut; but in action I

---

5. Shields.
6. Difficulties, mishaps.
7. Terence (195–159 B.C.) and Plautus

(251–184 B.C.) were the chief Latin writers of comedy.

cannot represent it without Pacolet's horse.[8] And so was the manner
the ancients took, by some Nuncius[9] to recount things done in
former time or other place. Lastly, if they will represent an history,
they must not (as Horace saith) begin *ab ovo*,[1] but they must come
to the principal point of that one action which they will represent.
By example this will be best expressed. I have a story of young
Polydorus,[2] delivered for safety's sake, with great riches, by his
father Priam to Polymnestor, king of Thrace, in the Trojan war
time. He, after some years, hearing the overthrow of Priam, for
to make the treasure his own, murdereth the child. The body of the
child is taken up by Hecuba. She, the same day, findeth a sleight
to be revenged most cruelly of the tyrant. Where now would one of
our tragedy writers begin, but with the delivery of the child? Then
should he sail over into Thrace, and so spend I know not how
many years, and travel numbers of places. But where doth Euripides?
Even with the finding of the body, leaving the rest to be told by
the spirit of Polydorus. This need no further to be enlarged; the
dullest wit may conceive it.

But besides these gross absurdities, how all their plays be neither
right tragedies, nor right comedies, mingling kings and clowns, not
because the matter so carrieth it, but thrust in clowns by head and
shoulders, to play a part in majestical matters, with neither decency
nor discretion,[3] so as neither the admiration and commiseration,
nor the right sportfulness, is by their mongrel tragicomedy obtained.
I know Apuleius[4] did somewhat so, but that is a thing recounted
with space of time, not represented in one moment: and I know
the ancients have one or two examples of tragicomedies, as Plautus
hath *Amphitruo*.[5] But, if we mark them well, we shall find, that
they never, or very daintily, match hornpipes[6] and funerals. So
falleth it out that, having indeed no right comedy, in that comical
part of our tragedy we have nothing but scurrility, unworthy of
any chaste ears, or some extreme show of doltishness, indeed fit to
lift up a loud laughter, and nothing else: where the whole tract
of a comedy should be full of delight, as the tragedy should be
still maintained in a well-raised admiration. But our comedians
think there is no delight without laughter; which is very wrong,
for though laughter may come with delight, yet cometh it not of
delight, as though delight should be the cause of laughter; but
well may one thing breed both together. Nay, rather in themselves

8. A magic horse in the French romance *Valentine and Orson*. "Calicut":
Calcutta.
9. Messenger.
1. From the beginning (literally, "from
the egg").
2. In Euripides' *Hecuba*.
3. Mingling of social levels (kings and
clowns) was thought to be a violation
of the principle of decorum.
4. Not a dramatist, but the 2nd-century
Roman author of the popular satirical
novel, *The Golden Ass*.
5. *Amphitruo* is tragicomic only in that
it contains gods and heroes; otherwise
it is pure comedy.
6. Merry tunes for country dances.

they have, as it were, a kind of contrariety: for delight we scarcely do but in things that have a conveniency to ourselves or to the general nature: laughter almost ever cometh of things most disproportioned to ourselves and nature. Delight hath a joy in it, either permanent or present. Laughter hath only a scornful tickling. For example, we are ravished with delight to see a fair woman, and yet are far from being moved to laughter. We laugh at deformed creatures, wherein certainly we cannot delight. We delight in good chances, we laugh at mischances; we delight to hear the happiness of our friends, or country, at which he were worthy to be laughed at that would laugh. We shall, contrarily, laugh sometimes to find a matter quite mistaken and go down the hill against the bias, in the mouth of some such men, as for the respect of them one shall be heartily sorry, yet he cannot choose but laugh; and so is rather pained than delighted with laughter. Yet deny I not but that they may go well together. For as in Alexander's picture well set out we delight without laughter, and in twenty mad antics we laugh without delight, so in Hercules, painted with his great beard and furious countenance, in woman's attire, spinning at Omphale's commandment,[7] it breedeth both delight and laughter. For the representing of so strange a power in love procureth delight: and the scornfulness of the action stirreth laughter. But I speak to this purpose, that all the end of the comical part be not upon such scornful matters as stirreth laughter only, but, mixed with it, that delightful teaching which is the end of poesy. And the great fault even in that point of laughter, and forbidden plainly by Aristotle, is that they stir laughter in sinful things, which are rather execrable than ridiculous; or in miserable, which are rather to be pitied than scorned. For what is it to make folks gape at a wretched beggar, or a beggarly clown; or, against law of hospitality, to jest at strangers, because they speak not English so well as we do? What do we learn? Since it is certain

> *Nil habet infelix paupertas durius in se,*
> *Quam quod ridiculos homines facit.*[8]

But rather a busy loving courtier, a heartless threatening Thraso, a self-wise-seeming schoolmaster, an awry-transformed traveler—these if we saw walk in stage names, which we play naturally, therein were delightful laughter, and teaching delightfulness: as in the other, the tragedies of Buchanan do justly bring forth a divine admiration. But I have lavished out too many words of this play matter. I do it because, as they are excelling parts of poesy, so is

---

7. Hercules was so infatuated with Omphale, queen of Lydia, that he submitted to being dressed as a female slave and forced to spin wool.

8. "Unfortunate poverty has in itself nothing harder to bear than that it makes men ridiculous" (Juvenal, *Satires* III.152–53).

there none so much used in England, and none can be more pitifully abused; which, like an unmannerly daughter showing a bad education, causeth her mother Poesy's honesty to be called in question.

Other sorts of poetry almost have we none, but that lyrical kind of songs and sonnets: which, Lord, if He gave us so good minds, how well it might be employed, and with how heavenly fruit, both private and public, in singing the praises of the immortal beauty, the immortal goodness of that God who giveth us hands to write and wits to conceive; of which we might well want words, but never matter; of which we could turn our eyes to nothing, but we should ever have new budding occasions. But truly many of such writings as come under the banner of unresistible love, if I were a mistress, would never persuade me they were in love; so coldly they apply fiery speeches, as men that had rather read lovers' writings, and so caught up certain swelling phrases (which hang together like a man which once told me the wind was at northwest, and by south, because he would be sure to name winds enough), than that in truth they feel those passions, which easily (as I think) may be betrayed by that same forcibleness, or *energia* (as the Greeks call it) of the writer. But let this be a sufficient though short note, that we miss the right use of the material point of poesy.

Now, for the outside of it, which is words, or (as I may term it) diction, it is even well worse. So is that honey-flowing matron Eloquence appareled, or rather disguised, in a courtesan-like painted affectation: one time with so farfetched words, they may seem monsters, but must seem strangers, to any poor Englishman; another time, with coursing of a letter,[9] as if they were bound to follow the method of a dictionary; another time, with figures and flowers,[1] extremely winter-starved. But I would this fault were only peculiar to versifiers, and had not as large possession among prose-printers, and (which is to be marveled) among many scholars, and (which is to be pitied) among some preachers. Truly I could wish, if at least I might be so bold to wish in a thing beyond the reach of my capacity, the diligent imitators of Tully[2] and Demosthenes (most worthy to be imitated) did not so much keep Nizolian paperbooks[3] of their figures and phrases, as by attentive translation (as it were) devour them whole, and make them wholly theirs. For now they cast sugar and spice upon every dish that is served to the table, like those Indians, not content to wear earrings at the fit and nat-

---

9. Alliteration.
1. Of rhetoric.
2. Cicero.
3. Marius Nizolius or Nizzoli (1498?–1576), Italian rhetorician and lexicographer, published a collection of Ciceronian phrases in 1535. Ascham mentions the keeping of similar books in *The Scholemaster*.

ural place of the ears, but they will thrust jewels through their nose and lips, because they will be sure to be fine. Tully, when he was to drive out Catiline, as it were with a thunderbolt of eloquence, often used that figure of repetition, *Vivit. Vivit? Immo in Senatum venit,*[4] etc. Indeed, inflamed with a well-grounded rage, he would have his words (as it were) double out of his mouth, and so do that artificially which we see men do in choler naturally. And we, having noted the grace of those words, hale them in sometime to a familiar epistle, when it were too much choler to be choleric.

Now for similitudes in certain printed discourses, I think all Herbarists,[5] all stories of beasts, fowls, and fishes are rifled up, that they come in multitudes to wait upon any of our conceits; which certainly is as absurd a surfeit to the ears as is possible: for the force of a similitude not being to prove anything to a contrary disputer, but only to explain to a willing hearer; when that is done, the rest is a most tedious prattling, rather over-swaying the memory from the purpose whereto they were applied, than any whit informing the judgment, already either satisfied, or by similitudes not to be satisfied. For my part, I do not doubt, when Antonius and Crassus, the great forefathers of Cicero in eloquence, the one (as Cicero testifieth of them) pretended not to know art, the other not to set by it, because with a plain sensibleness they might win credit of popular ears; which credit is the nearest step to persuasion; which persuasion is the chief mark of oratory—I do not doubt (I say) but that they used these knacks very sparingly; which, who doth generally use, any man may see doth dance to his own music; and so be noted by the audience more careful to speak curiously than to speak truly.

Undoubtedly (at least to my opinion undoubtedly) I have found in divers small-learned courtiers a more sound style than in some professors of learning: of which I can guess no other cause, but that the courtier, following that which by practice he findeth fittest to nature, therein (though he know it not) doth according to art, though not by art: where the other, using art to show art, and not to hide art (as in these cases he should do), flieth from nature, and indeed abuseth art.

But what? Methinks I deserve to be pounded for straying from poetry to oratory: but both have such an affinity in this wordish consideration, that I think this digression will make my meaning receive the fuller understanding—which is not to take upon me to teach poets how they should do, but only, finding myself sick among the rest, to show some one or two spots of the common in-

---

4. Sidney quotes rather freely from memory a line from Cicero (*Catiline*, 1, 2): "He lives, nay more, he comes into the Senate."

5. Writers who, like Lyly, introduce botanical and zoological analogies into their writing.

fection grown among the most part of writers: that, acknowledging ourselves somewhat awry, we may bend to the right use both of matter and manner; whereto our language giveth us great occasion, being indeed capable of any excellent exercising of it. I know some will say it is a mingled language. And why not so much the better, taking the best of both the other? Another will say it wanteth grammar. Nay truly, it hath that praise, that it wanteth not grammar: for grammar it might have, but it needs it not; being so easy of itself, and so void of those cumbersome differences of cases, genders, moods, and tenses, which I think was a piece of the Tower of Babylon's curse, that a man should be put to school to learn his mother tongue. But for the uttering sweetly and properly the conceits of the mind, which is the end of speech, that hath it equally with any other tongue in the world: and is particularly happy in compositions of two or three words together, near the Greek, far beyond the Latin: which is one of the greatest beauties can be in a language.

Now, of versifying there are two sorts, the one ancient, the other modern: the ancient marked the quantity of each syllable, and according to that framed his verse; the modern observing only number [6] (with some regard of the accent), the chief life of it standeth in that like sounding of the words, which we call rhyme. Whether of these be the most excellent, would bear many speeches. The ancient, no doubt, more fit for music, both words and tune observing quantity, and more fit lively to express divers passions, by the low and lofty sound of the well-weighed syllable. The latter likewise, with his rhyme, striketh a certain music to the ear: and, in fine, since it doth delight, though by another way, it obtains the same purpose: there being in either sweetness, and wanting in neither majesty. Truly the English, before any other vulgar language I know, is fit for both sorts: for, for the ancient, the Italian is so full of vowels that it must ever be cumbered with elisions; the Dutch so, of the other side, with consonants, that they cannot yield the sweet sliding fit for a verse; the French, in his whole language, hath not one word that hath his accent in the last syllable saving two, called *antepenultima*; and little more hath the Spanish: and, therefore, very gracelessly may they use dactyls. The English is subject to none of these defects.

Now, for the rhyme, though we do not observe quantity, yet we observe the accent very precisely: which other languages either cannot do, or will not do so absolutely. That *caesura*, or breathing place in the midst of the verse, neither Italian nor Spanish have, the French, and we, never almost fail of. Lastly, even the very

6. "Quantity" meant length or duration of a syllable; by "number" Sidney   means merely counting the syllables.

rhyme itself the Italian cannot put in the last syllable, by the French named the "masculine rhyme," but still in the next to the last, which the French call the "female," or the next before that, which the Italians term *sdrucciola*. The example of the former is *buono: suono*, of the *sdrucciola, femina: semina*. The French, of the other side, hath both the male, as *bon: son*, and the female, as *plaise: taise*, but the *sdrucciola* he hath not: where the English hath all three, as *due: true; father: rather; motion: potion*;[1] with much more which might be said, but that I find already the triflingness of this discourse is much too much enlarged.

So that since the ever-praiseworthy poesy is full of virtue-breeding delightfulness, and void of no gift that ought to be in the noble name of learning; since the blames laid against it are either false or feeble; since the cause why it is not esteemed in England is the fault of poet-apes, not poets; since, lastly, our tongue is most fit to honor poesy, and to be honored by poesy; I conjure you all that have had the evil luck to read this ink-wasting toy of mine, even in the name of the Nine Muses, no more to scorn the sacred mysteries of poesy, no more to laugh at the name of "poets," as though they were next inheritors to fools, no more to jest at the reverent title of a "rhymer"; but to believe, with Aristotle, that they were the ancient treasurers of the Grecians' divinity; to believe, with Bembus, that they were first bringers-in of all civility; to believe, with Scaliger, that no philosopher's precepts can sooner make you an honest man than the reading of Virgil; to believe, with Clauserus,[2] the translator of Cornutus, that it pleased the heavenly Deity, by Hesiod and Homer, under the veil of fables, to give us all knowledge, logic, rhetoric, philosophy, natural and moral, and *Quid non?*;[3] to believe, with me, that there are many mysteries contained in poetry, which of purpose were written darkly, lest by profane wits it should be abused; to believe, with Landin,[4] that they are so beloved of the gods that whatsoever they write proceeds of a divine fury; lastly, to believe themselves, when they tell you they will make you immortal by their verses.

Thus doing, your name shall flourish in the printers' shops; thus doing, you shall be of kin to many a poetical preface; thus doing, you shall be most fair, most rich, most wise, most all; you shall dwell upon superlatives. Thus doing, though you be *libertino patre natus*,[5] you shall suddenly grow *Herculea proles*,[6]

1. These were three-syllable words in Elizabethan pronunciation.
2. Conrad Clauser (ca. 1520–1611), a German scholar; he translated a Greek treatise by Cornutus, who was a contemporary of Nero's.
3. What not.

4. Cristofero Landino, 15th-century Italian scholar and onetime tutor to Lorenzo de Medici.
5. "Born of a freed slave father."
6. I.e., a descendent of Hercules. The next phrase means "if my songs are of any avail" (*Aeneid* IX.446).

Si quid mea carmina possunt.

Thus doing, your soul shall be placed with Dante's Beatrix, or Virgil's Anchises. But if (fie of such a but) you be born so near the dull-making cataract of Nilus[7] that you cannot hear the planet-like music of poetry, if you have so earth-creeping a mind that it cannot lift itself up to look to the sky of poetry, or rather, by a certain rustical disdain, will become such a mome[8] as to be a Momus of poetry; then, though I will not wish unto you the ass's ears of Midas,[9] nor to be driven by a poet's verses (as Bubonax[1] was) to hang himself, nor to be rhymed to death, as is said to be done in Ireland;[2] yet thus much curse I must send you, in the behalf of all poets, that while you live, you live in love, and never get favor for lacking skill of a sonnet, and, when you die, your memory die from the earth for want of an epitaph.

1595

7. According to Cicero, people living near the cataracts of the Nile became deaf from the noise. "Planet-like music": the music of the spheres was supposed to be the most beautiful of all music.
8. A stupid person; "Momus": a critic.
9. He was given ass's ears because he preferred Pan's playing to Apollo's.
1. Bupalus, a sculptor, was so ashamed when his works were satirized by the poet Hipponax that he hanged himself. Sidney fuses the two names.
2. There was a popular tradition that Irish bards could cause death by their incantations.

EDMUND SPENSER
(1552–1599)

1579: Publication of *The Shepheardes Calender*.
1580: In Ireland, where he remains for the rest of his life.
1590: First three books of *The Faerie Queene* published.

The greatest nondramatic poet of the English Renaissance, Edmund Spenser, was born in London, probably in 1552, and attended the Merchant Taylors' School under its famous headmaster Richard Mulcaster. In 1569 he went to Cambridge as a "sizar" or poor scholar. His Cambridge experience strongly colored the rest of his life; it was at the university that Spenser began as a poet by translating some poems for a volume of anti-Catholic propaganda. His work, then and later, reflects the strong Puritanical environment of Cambridge where the popular preacher Thomas Cartwright was beginning to make the authorities uneasy. Spenser's friendship with Gabriel Harvey, a Cambridge don, humanist, pamphleteer, and eccentric, also began at the university. Some correspondence between Harvey and Spenser, published in 1580, shows that they were interested in theories of poetry and in experiments in quantitative versification in English; it also shows that Spenser had ambitious plans as a poet.

He proceeded through the university, receiving the degree of B.A. in 1573 and M.A. in 1576. He then entered upon a series of positions in the retinues of prominent men, including Dr. John Young, Bishop of Rochester; the Earl of Leicester, the queen's favorite; and finally, Lord Grey of Wilton, Lord Deputy of Ireland. During his employment in Leicester's household he came to know Sir Philip Sidney and his friend Sir Edward Dyer, courtiers who were interested in promoting a new English poetry. Spenser's own contribution to the movement is *The Shepheardes Calender*, published in 1579 and dedicated to Sidney in the verses:

To His Booke

Goe little booke: thy selfe present,
As child whose parent is unkent,
To him that is the president
Of noblesse and of chevalree.
And if that Envie barke at thee,
As sure it will, for succoure flee
Under the shadow of his wing
And, asked who thee forth did bring,
A shepheardes swaine saye did thee sing,
All as his straying flocke he fedde;
And when his honor has thee redde,
Crave pardon for my hardy hedde.
But if that any aske thy name,
Say thou wert base begot with blame,
For thy thereof thou takest shame.
And when thou art past jeopardee,
Come tell me what was said of mee
And I will send more after thee.

Immerito [Unworthy].

The *Calender* consists of twelve pastoral eclogues, one for each month of the year. Each is prefaced by an illustrative woodcut representing the characters or theme of the poem and picturing the appropriate sign of the zodiac for that month in the clouds above. The eclogue was a classical form, practiced by Virgil and others; it presents, usually in dialogue between shepherds, the moods and feelings and attitudes of the simple life. But often the pastoral eclogue criticizes the world as it is by reflection from the world as it might be, and in Spenser, as in other Renaissance poets, the eclogue at times becomes didactic or satirical. Though it pretends to represent simple shepherds, it is really commenting on contemporary affairs. The eclogues of the *Calender* are divided by its commentator, "E. K.," into three groups— plaintive, recreative, and moral. Of the moral eclogues, the final and climactic one is *October*, which deals with the problem of poetry in modern life and the responsibility of the poet in time—in an important way, the theme of the whole *Calender*. It looks forward to related themes in Milton's *Lycidas*.

Spenser used a deliberately archaic language, partly out of homage to Chaucer, whom he refers to as Tityrus, the god of shepherds, "who taught me, homely as I can, to make." But Spenser also used this language to get a rustic effect. The patron to whom the *Calender* is dedicated did not approve; Sidney wrote in his *Apology for Poetry*, "The Shepheardes Calendar hath much poetry in his Eclogues, indeed worthy the reading, if I be not deceived. That same framing of his style to an old rustic language I dare not allow, since neither Theocritus in Greek, Virgil in Latin, nor Sannazaro in Italian did affect it." Another classical purist, Ben Jonson, growled that Spenser "writ no language," but that he would have him read for his matter. It would be a pity to follow Jonson's advice too literally, for Spenser's skillful use of many verse forms and his extraordinary musical effects indicate that here indeed is a poet to inaugurate the "new poetry" of the Elizabethan age.

There are thirteen different meters in *The Shepheardes Calender:* three kinds of couplet; three kinds of four-line stanza; three kinds of six-line stanza; stanzas of eight, nine, and ten lines; and a sestina. Some of these Spenser invented, some he adapted, but most of them were novel: only three or four were at all common in 1579. Spenser was a prolific experimenter: of the thirteen different meters in the *Calender* he used only three in his later poems. He went on to make further innovations—the special rhyme scheme of the Spenserian sonnet, richer than any other; the remarkably beautiful adaptation of Italian *canzone* forms for the *Epithalamion* and *Prothalamion*, and the nine-line stanza of *The Faerie Queene*, with its extraordinary six-foot line at the end, are only the most famous. Spenser is sometimes called the "poet's poet" because so many later English poets have learned the art of versification from him. In the 19th century alone his influence may be seen in Shelley's *Revolt of Islam*, Byron's *Childe Harold's Pilgrimage*, Keats's *Eve of St. Agnes*, and Tennyson's *The Lotos Eaters*.

The year after the publication of *The Shepheardes Calender* Spenser went to Ireland to serve Lord Grey; he spent the rest of his life there, except for two visits to England. He was at work on his great romantic epic, *The Faerie Queene*, when Sir Walter Ralegh visited him at Kilcolman Castle; the result was a trip to England and the publication, in 1590, of the first three books of *The Faerie Queene*. After that there was no question that Edmund Spenser was "the prince of poets in his time." He published a volume of poems called *Complaints*; a pastoral sequel to some of the eclogues in *The Shepheardes Calender* called *Colin Clouts Come Home Againe* (1595), which gave his views of the English court on his visit there in 1590; a sonnet cycle, *Amoretti*, and two marriage poems, *Epithalamion* and *Prothalamion*, but he completed only six of his projected twelve books of *The Faerie Queene*: in 1596 the first three books appeared again, with alterations, together with Books IV, V, and VI; the so-called "Mutability Cantos" first appeared in the edition of 1609.

In the second half of the decade, Ireland was torn by revolt and civil war; Spenser's castle was destroyed, and the poet was sent to England with messages from the besieged garrison in Ireland. He died in Westminster on January 13, 1599, and was buried near his beloved Chaucer in what is now called the Poets' Corner of Westminster Abbey.

Spenser is a complex genius who cannot be put into neatly labeled categories. He is, for instance, strongly influenced by Renaissance Neoplatonism, but remains always firmly grounded in earthiness and practicality. In *The Faerie Queene* he reaches toward the highest ideals of the Renaissance but knows, at the same time, what it is to want to remain an animal. He is a lover and celebrator of physical beauty, and he is sternly moral. His "morality" is, however, not of the repressive sort; it arises from his understanding of right action and of the temptations that entrap men as they try to achieve such action. Spenser was strongly influenced by Puritanism in his early days; he always remained a thoroughgoing Protestant; the Roman Catholic Church is made a villain in *The Faerie Queene*—and yet his understanding of faith and of sin has its roots in the great Catholic thinkers. He is profoundly English and patriotic; in him nationality and religion were inextricably joined. In the Proem to Book V of *The Faerie Queene* he characteristically looks back to the antique world and compares his own time with it most unfavorably. Yet his strongest links are not with the past, despite his love of Chaucer and his deliberately antique language: his closest affinity is with Milton, who was born nine years after Spenser's death. Milton called Spenser a better teacher than Scotus or Aquinas. He recognized Spenser, his great predecessor, as, like himself, a Christian humanist and British poet-prophet.

Spenser's poetry is always printed in the original spelling and punctuation (although a few of the most confusing punctuation marks have been altered in the present text), since it was a deliberate choice on Spenser's part that his language should seem antique. (A modern reader who read Shakespeare or the King James version of the Bible in the original spelling would not find as much difference in Spenser, but he would find some.) Furthermore, Spenser uses his spelling to suggest rhymes to the eye, sometimes to suggest etymologies, often incorrectly. The fact that Spenser's spelling is inconsistent is simply typical of his time; in the 16th century a man varied the spelling of even his name to suit convenience or a whim.

From THE SHEPHEARDES CALENDER[1]

October

Argument

In Cuddie[2] is set out the perfecte paterne of a Poete, whiche finding no maintenaunce of his state and studies, complayneth of

1. When *The Shepheardes Calender* was published in 1579, each of the twelve eclogues was followed by a "Glosse," which contained explications of difficult or archaic words, together with learned discussions of—and disagreements with —Spenser's ideas, imagery, and poetics. The Glosses are by one "E. K.," whose identity has never been satisfactorily ascertained. Although certain scholars have suggested that E. K. was Spenser himself, it is equally possible that he was a friend.

E. K.'s editorial apparatus is usually printed along with the poems from the *Calender*. In the text that follows, the present editor has incorporated the glosses into the footnotes, abridging only some of E. K.'s longer exegeses, anecdotes, and tags from classical and

contemporary authors; the original spelling has also been retained. E. K. first discusses the poem's sources: "This Aeglogue is made in imitation of Theocritus his xvi. Idilion, wherein hee reproved the Tyranne Hiero of Syracuse for his nigardise towarde Poetes, in whome is the power to make men immortal for theyr good dedes, or shameful for their naughty lyfe. And the lyke also is in Mantuane. The style hereof as also that in Theocritus, is more loftye then the rest, and applyed to the heighte of Poeticall witte." Actually Spenser's eclogue owes very little to Theocritus, but it does draw heavily upon the fifth eclogue of Baptista Spagnuoli, called Mantuan.

2. "I doubte whether by Cuddie be specified the authour selfe, or some

the contempte of Poetrie, and the causes thereof: Specially having
bene in all ages, and even amongst the most barbarous alwayes of
singular accounpt[3] and honor, and being indede so worthy and
commendable an arte: or rather no arte, but a divine gift and heavenly instinct not to bee gotten by laboure and learning, but adorned
with both: and poured into the witte by a certaine ἐνθουσιασμὸς[4]
and celestiall inspiration, as the Author hereof els where at large
discourseth, in his booke called the *English Poete*, which booke
being lately come to my hands, I mynde also by Gods grace upon
further advisement to publish.

PIERS

Cuddie, for shame hold up thy heavye head,
And let us cast with what delight to chace,
And weary thys long lingring Phoebus race.[5]
Whilome° thou wont the shepheards laddes to leade,   *formerly*
5 In rymes, in ridles, and in bydding base:[6]
Now they in thee, and thou in sleepe art dead.

CUDDIE

Piers, I have pyped erst° so long with payne,   *up to now*
That all mine Oten reedes[7] bene rent and wore:
And my poore Muse hath spent her sparéd store,
10 Yet little good hath got, and much lesse gayne.
Such pleasaunce makes the Grashopper so poore,
And ligge so layd,[8] when Winter doth her straine:

The dapper[9] ditties, that I wont devise,
To feede youthes fancie, and the flocking fry,[1]
15 Delighten much: what I the bett forthy?
They han the pleasure, I a sclender prise.
I beate the bush, the byrds to them doe flye:
What good thereof to Cuddie can arise?

PIERS

Cuddie, the prayse is better, then the price,
20 The glory eke much greater then the gayne:
O what an honor is it, to restraine
The lust of lawlesse youth with good advice:[2]

other. For in the eyght Aeglogue the
same person was brought in, singing a
Cantion of Colins making, as he sayth.
So that some doubt, that the persons be
different" [E. K.'s Glosse].
3. Account, reputation.
4. The Greek word from which "enthusiasm" derives; it means inspiration. The *"English Poete"* is a lost work
by Spenser, apparently never published.
5. I.e., let us see how we may pass the
day pleasantly.
6. A popular game, here probably a
poetry contest.
7. "Avena" [E. K.'s Glosse]. Avena
means "stalks" and was used by Virgil
(*Eclogues* I.2) to signify the shepherd's
pipe. E. K. thinks Spenser's "oten

reeds" translates Avena.
8. "Lye so faynt and unlustie" [E. K.'s
Glosse]. The reference is to the fable
of the industrious ant and the carefree
grasshopper.
9. "Pretye" [E. K.'s Glosse].
1. "Frye is a bold Metaphore, forced
from the spawning fishes. For the multitude of young fish be called the frye"
[E. K.'s Glosse]. In the next line,
"what * * * for thy?" means, "what
better am I for this reason?"
2. "This place seemeth to conspyre with
Plato, who in his first booke *de Legibus*
sayth, that the first invention of Poetry
was of very vertuous intent * * *"
[E. K.'s Glosse].

Or pricke° them forth with pleasaunce of thy vaine,   *stimulate*
Whereto thou list their traynéd° willes entice.   *ensnared*

25 Soone as thou gynst to sette thy notes in frame,
   O how the rurall routes° to thee doe cleave: *crowds*
   Seemeth thou dost their soule of sence bereave,[3]
   All as the shepheard, that did fetch his dame
   From Plutoes balefull bowre withouten leave:
30 His musicks might the hellish hound did tame.

CUDDIE

So praysen babes the Peacoks spotted traine,
And wondren at bright Argus blazing eye:[4]
But who rewards him ere the more forthy?
Or feedes him once the fuller by a graine?
35 Sike° prayse is smoke, that sheddeth in the skye,   *such*
   Sike words bene wynd, and wasten soone in vayne.

PIERS

Abandon then the base and viler clowne,°   *rustic*
Lyft up thy selfe out of the lowly dust:
And sing of bloody Mars, of wars, of giusts,°   *jousts*
40 Turne thee to those, that weld° the awful crowne.   *wield*
   To doubted[5] Knights, whose woundlesse armour rusts,
   And helmes unbruzéd wexen dayly browne.

There may thy Muse display her fluttryng wing,[6]
And stretch herselfe at large from East to West:
45 Whither thou list in fayre Elisa rest,
   Or if thee please in bigger notes to sing,
   Advaunce the worthy whome shee loveth best,
   That first the white beare to the stake did bring.[7]

3. "What the secrete working of Musick is in the myndes of men, as well appeareth, hereby, that some of the auncient Philosophers, and those the moste wise, as Plato. and Pythagoras held for opinion, that the mynd was made of a certaine harmonie and musicall nombers, for the great compassion and likenes of affection in thone and in the other * * * So that it is not incredible which the Poete here sayth, that Musick can bereave the soule of sence" [E. K.'s Glosse]. The "shepheard" in the next line is "Orpheus: of whom is sayd, that by his excellent skil in Musick and Poetry, he recovered his wife Eurydice from hell" [E. K.'s Glosse].

4. "Of Argus is before said, that Juno to him committed hir husband Jupiter his Paragon Iô, bicause he had an hundred eyes: but afterwarde Mercury wyth hys Musick lulling Argus asleepe, slew him and brought Iô away, whose eyes it is sayd that Juno for his eternall memory placed in her byrd the Peacocks tayle. For those coloured spots indeede resemble eyes" [E. K.'s Glosse].

5. Redoubted, dreaded. The knights' "armour" is "woundlesse" because "unwounded in warre, [they] doe rust through long peace" [E. K.'s Glosse].

6. "A poeticall metaphore: whereof the meaning is, that if the Poet list showe his skill in matter of more dignitie, then is the homely Aeglogue, good occasion is him offered of higher veyne and more Heroicall argument, in the person of our most gratious soveraign, whom (as before) he calleth Elisa. Or if mater of knighthoode and chevalrie please him better, that there be many Noble and valiaunt men, that are both worthy of his payne in theyr deserved prayses, and also favourers of hys skil and faculty" [E. K.'s Glosse].

7. "He meaneth (as I guesse) the most honorable and renowmed the Erle of Leycester * * * " [E. K.'s Glosse]. Leicester's device was the bear and ragged staff.

And when the stubborne stroke of stronger stounds,°   *efforts*
50 Has somewhat slackt the tenor of thy string:[8]
Of love and lustihead tho mayst thou sing,
And carrol lowde, and leade the Myllers rownde,[9]
All° were Elisa one of thilke same ring.   *although*
So mought our Cuddies name to Heaven sownde.

CUDDIE

55 Indeede the Romish Tityrus,[1] I heare,
Through his Mecaenas left his Oaten reede,
Whereon he earst° had taught his flocks to feede,   *before*
And laboured lands to yield the timely eare,
And eft did sing of warres and deadly drede,[2]
60 So as the Heavens did quake his verse to here.

But ah Mecaenas is yclad in claye,
And great Augustus long ygoe is dead:
And all the worthies liggen wrapt in leade,
That matter made for Poets on to play:
65 For ever, who in derring doe[3] were dreade,
The loftie verse of hem was lovéd aye.[4]

But after vertue gan for age to stoupe,
And mighty manhode brought a bedde of ease:[5]
The vaunting Poets found nought worth a pease,
70 To put in preace[6] among the learned troupe.
Tho gan the streames of flowing wittes to cease,
And sonnebright honour pend in shamefull coupe.[7]

And if that any buddes of Poesie,
Yet of the old stocke gan to shoote agayne:

8. "That is when thou chaungest thy verse from stately discourse, to matter of more pleasaunce and delight" [E. K.'s Glosse].
9. "A kind of daunce" [E. K.'s Glosse]. "Ring," in the next line, E. K. explains as a "company of dauncers."
1. "Well knowen to be Virgile, who by Mecaenas means was brought into the favour of the Emperor Augustus, and by him moved to write in loftier kinde, then he erst had doen" [E. K.'s Glosse].
2. "In these three verses are the three severall workes of Virgile intended. For in teaching his flocks to feede, is meant his Aeglogues. In labouring of lands, is hys Bucoliques. In singing of wars and deadly dreade, is his divine Aeneis figured" [E. K.'s Glosse].
3. "In manhoode and chevalrie" [E. K.'s Glosse].
4. "He sheweth the cause, why Poetes were wont be had in such honor of noble men; that is, that by them their worthines and valor shold through

theyr famous Posies be commended to al posterities. Wherefore it is sayd, that Achilles had never bene so famous, as he is, but for Homeres immortal verses. Which is the only advantage, which he had of Hector. * * * As also that Alexander destroying Thebes, when he was enformed that the famous Lyrick Poet Pindarus was borne in that citie, not onely commaunded streightly, that no man should upon payne of death do any violence to that house by fire or otherwise: but also specially spared most, and some highly rewarded, that were of hys kinne. * * * Such honor have Poetes alwayes found in the sight of princes and noble men. Which this author here very well sheweth, as els where more notably" [E. K.'s Glosse].
5. "He sheweth the cause of contempt of Poetry to be idlenesse and basenesse of mynd" [E. K.'s Glosse].
6. Put in press, crowd in among.
7. Coop. E. K. explains the phrase as "shut up in slouth, as in a coope or cage."

75 Or it mens follies mote be forst to fayne,
    And rolle with rest in rymes of rybaudrye:
    Or as it sprong, it wither must agayne:
    Tom Piper makes us better melodie.[8]

PIERS

    O pierlesse Poesye, where is then thy place?
80 If nor in Princes pallace thou doe sitt:
    (And yet is Princes pallace the most fitt)
    Ne brest of baser birth[9] doth thee embrace.
    Then make thee winges of thine aspyring wit,
    And, whence thou camst, flye backe to heaven apace.

CUDDIE

85 Ah Percy it is all to weake and wanne,
    So high to sore, and make so large a flight:
    Her peecéd pyneons[1] bene not so in plight,
    For Colin fittes such famous flight to scanne:
    He, were he not with love so ill bedight,
90 Would mount as high, and sing as soote as Swanne.[2]

PIERS

    Ah fon,° for love does teach him climbe so hie,   *fool*
    And lyftes him up out of the loathsome myre:
    Such immortall mirrhor,[3] as he doth admire,
    Would rayse ones mynd above the starry skie.
95 And cause a caytive corage[4] to aspire,
    For lofty love doth loath a lowly eye.

CUDDIE

    All otherwise the state of Poet stands,
    For lordly love is such a Tyranne fell:
    That where he rules, all power he doth expell.
100 The vaunted verse a vacant head demaundes,
    Ne wont with crabbéd care the Muses dwell.
    Unwisely weaves, that takes two webbes in hand.

    Who ever casts to compasse weightye prise,
    And thinks to throwe out thondring words of threate:
105 Let powre in lavish cups and thriftie bitts of meate,[5]
    For Bacchus fruite is frend to Phoebus wise.

---

8. "An Ironicall Sarcasmus, spoken in derision of these rude wits, whych make more account of a ryming rybaud, then of skill grounded upon learning and judgment" [E. K.'s Glosse].
9. "The meaner sort of men" [E. K.'s Glosse].
1. Patched-up wings. "Unperfect skil. Spoken wyth humble modestie" [E. K.'s Glosse]. "Colin fittes": it is appropriate for Colin (Spenser).
2. "The comparison seemeth to be strange: for the swanne hath ever wonne small commendation for her swete singing: but it is sayd of the learned that the swan a little before hir death, singeth most pleasantly, as prophecying by a secrete instinct her neere destinie * * * " [E. K.'s Glosse].
3. "Beauty, which is an excellent object of Poeticall spirites * * * " [E. K.'s Glosse].
4. "A base and abject minde" [E. K.'s Glosse].
5. I.e., let him pour lavish drink and nourishing ("thrifty") food.

And when with Wine the braine begins to sweate,
The nombers flowe as fast as spring doth ryse.

Thou kenst not Percie howe the ryme should rage.
110 O if my temples were distaind° with wine,[6]   *distended*
And girt in girlonds of wild Yvie twine,
How I could reare the Muse on stately stage,
And teache her tread aloft in bus-kin[7] fine,
With queint Bellona[8] in her equipage.

115 But ah my corage cooles ere it be warme,
For thy, content us in thys humble shade:
Where no such troublous tydes° han us assayde,   *seasons*
Here we our slender pipes may safely charme.[9]

PIERS

And when my Gates shall han their bellies layd:[1]
120 Cuddie shall have a Kidde to store his farme.

Cuddies Embleme.[2]
Agitante calescimus illo &c.

1579

6. "He seemeth here to be ravished with a Poetical furie. For (if one rightly mark) the numbers rise so ful, and the verse groweth so big, that it seemeth he hath forgot the meanenesse of shepheards state and stile" [E. K.'s Glosse]. E. K. adds an explanation of "wild Yvie" in the next line: "For it is dedicated to Bacchus and therefore it is sayd that the Maenades (that is Bacchus franticke priestes) used in theyr sacrifice to carry *Thyrsos*, which were pointed staves or Javelins, wrapped about with yvie."
7. "It was the maner of Poetes and plaiers in tragedies to were buskins, as also in Comedies to use stockes and light shoes. So that the buskin in Poetry is used for tragical matter * * * " [E. K.'s Glosse].
8. "Strange Bellona; the goddesse of battaile, that is Pallas, which may therefore wel be called queint for that (as Lucian saith) when Jupiter hir father was in traveile of her, he caused his sonne Vulcane with his axe to hew his head. Out of which leaped forth lustely a valiant damsell armed at all poyntes, whom seeing Vulcane so faire and comely, lightly leaping to her, proferred her some cortesie, which the Lady disdeigning, shaked her speare at him, and threatned his saucinesse. Therefore such straungenesse is well applyed to her" [E. K.'s Glosse]. E. K. also glosses "equipage": order.
9. "Temper and order. For Charmes were wont to be made by verses as Ovid sayth, *Aut si carminibus*" [E. K.'s Glosse]. E. K. had a slip of memory: the fragment is not in Ovid.
1. I.e., when my goats bear their young.
2. An "embleme" is a motto or relevant quotation. The Latin line, of which Spenser gives the first three words here, is from Ovid, *Fasti* vi.5: "There is a god within us; it is from his stirring that we feel warm." E. K. comments on the quotation: "Hereby is meant, as also in the whole course of this Aeglogue, that Poetry is a divine instinct and unnatural rage passing the reache of comen reason. Whom Piers answereth *Epiphonematicos* [by way of summary] as admiring the excellencye of the skyll whereof in Cuddie hee hadde alreadye hadde a taste."

The Faerie Queene

Spenser's masterpiece is a poem peculiarly characteristic of its age. It is a "courtesy book," like Castiglione's *Courtier*, intended to "fashion a gentleman or noble person" by exhibiting the traits such a person should have. Only six of the twelve projected books were finished. These exhibit the virtues of Holiness, Temperance, Chastity, Friendship, Justice, and Courtesy. A fragment of another book, the cantos on Mutability, also survives. But whereas the ordinary courtesy book was a piece of explanation and exhortation, *The Faerie Queene* is also a poem, and, as Elizabethans all believed, a poem teaches by delighting. Spenser's great work is full of adventures and marvels, dragons, witches, enchanted trees, giants, jousting knights, and castles; a romantic epic, like Ariosto's *Orlando Furioso* (1516). But it is also an allegory, like Tasso's *Gerusalemme Liberata* (1575); the heroes of the several books represent the virtues portrayed in those books. The Redcrosse Knight in Book I is of course St. George, the patron saint of England, but he also represents Holiness, as Sir Guyon in Book II represents Temperance (not simply abstinence in drinking but self-control under all the temptations of the senses). The heroes do not have the virtues they represent at the beginning of their adventures—they acquire them in the course of the book. Spenser explains his allegorical method in a preliminary letter to Sir Walter Ralegh; however he does not explain what would be obvious to every contemporary reader, the many conventional symbols and attributes which would identify his characters. For example, when a woman appears who has a miter, wears scarlet clothes, and comes from the river Tiber, the reader is supposed to know immediately that she represents the Roman Catholic Church, which had been so often identified by Protestant preachers with the Whore of Babylon in the Book of Revelation.

Book I of *The Faerie Queene* is in a way an epitome of the whole poem, or the part of it Spenser completed. It is almost entirely self-contained; it has been called a miniature epic in itself. It consists of twelve cantos, as Virgil's *Aeneid* consists of twelve books. The introductory lines are intended to remind the reader of Virgil, who began with pastoral poetry and moved on to the epic, as Spenser is now doing.

The theme is not arms and the man, however, but something more romantic—"Fierce warres and faithfull loves." The scenery, too, is not classical but romantic. There are plains and forests and caves and castles and magical trees and springs; one meets dwarfs and giants and lions and pilgrims and magicians and Saracens or "paynims" (with French names). An accurate map of Faerie Land is impossible but unnecessary; if you are going somewhere you just start out and, after many adventures, get there. A clear, pleasant stream may be dangerous to drink because it produces loss of strength. Any stranger you meet is more than likely to be a villain and to be in disguise.

The good people are subject to the Faerie Queene and are called Faeries or Elves. They are human beings, though not much individualized. They undergo the trials and tribulations men undergo in the ordinary world, but these events are told in a romantic, fantastic way in order to arouse wonder. The bad creatures, people and monsters, are various vices, evils, and temptations, often revealed to the reader by their names or by the short verse summaries at the beginning of each canto but not revealed to the hero until he has conquered them. Houses, castles, and animals also stand for abstract virtues or vices. The world of Faerie Land is a visual world in which the meaning of something is made fully evident by its appearance when stripped of all disguise.

Read as romantic narrative, the plot of Book I is a series of chivalric adventures undertaken by the Redcrosse Knight culminating in his killing the dragon, rescuing Una's parents, and winning her as his bride. Read as spiritual allegory, the book tells the story of the Christian's struggle for salvation—his wandering between the evil extremes of pride and despair, his encounter with the seven deadly sins, his separation from and reunion with the one true faith, the purgation of his sinfulness, and his final salvation by divine grace added to heroic effort.

The poem can be enjoyed on many levels, and it may, in fact, work on several of these levels at a time. In addition to being—most especially— a heroic poem and a spiritual allegory, it also embodies many religious and political aspects of Spenser's own England; a "political allegory" runs all through Book I. This is a romantic, "medieval," heroic, religious, political, magical world, and the reader entering it must be prepared to move as the story moves, taking the meanings on whatever level seems most viable at the moment. Spenser is not a great explainer; more usually, he gives the reader a scene or a surface, and lets the full allegorical import work its way out.

Moreover, that scene or surface may draw on the riches of literary and pictorial traditions. Entire episodes may be adopted from the Italian romantic epics of Ariosto and Tasso and, either through them or independently, from Homer, Virgil, or Ovid (this was an age when borrowing and reworking earlier materials was praiseworthy in a poet). Places, such as Lucifera's castle; individual attributes, such as Una's lamb or Speranza's anchor; even names or colors came to Spenser from the classics, from theologians, from liturgical tradition, from the village pulpit, from folk tales and pageants, from tapestries, paintings, and emblem books. In our notes we have attempted to show what some of the sources were—but more important is the understanding that these traditions had a life for Spenser and his readers; they could flow together, separate, recombine.

The strangeness of *The Faerie Queene* becomes, on closer acquaintance, a source of delight. No work of the English Renaissance is more exuberant, more fertile, more full.

From THE FAERIE QUEENE
A Letter of the Authors

EXPOUNDING HIS WHOLE INTENTION IN THE COURSE OF THIS WORKE:
WHICH FOR THAT IT GIVETH GREAT LIGHT TO THE READER; FOR THE
BETTER UNDERSTANDING IS HEREUNTO ANNEXED

*To the Right noble, and Valorous, Sir Walter Raleigh knight,
Lo. Wardein of the Stanneryes, and her Majesties liefetenaunt
of the County of Cornewayll*

Sir knowing how doubtfully all Allegories may be construed, and
this booke of mine, which I have entituled the *Faery Queene*, being a continued Allegory, or darke conceit, I have thought good as
well for avoyding of gealous opinions and misconstructions, as also
for your better light in reading thereof, (being so by you commanded,) to discover unto you the general intention and meaning,
which in the whole course thereof I have fashioned, without expressing of any particular purposes or by-accidents[1] therein occasioned. The generall end therefore of all the booke is to fashion[2] a
gentleman or noble person in vertuous and gentle discipline:
Which for that I conceived shoulde be most plausible and pleasing,
being coloured with an historicall fiction, the which the most part
of men delight to read, rather for variety of matter, then for profite
of the ensample: I chose the historye of King Arthure, as most fitte
for the excellency of his person, being made famous by many mens
former workes, and also furthest from the daunger of envy, and
suspition of present time.[3] In which I have followed all the antique
Poets historicall, first Homere, who in the Persons of Agamemnon
and Ulysses hath ensampled a good governour and a vertuous man,
the one in his *Ilias*, the other in his *Odysseis*: then Virgil, whose
like intention was to doe in the person of Aeneas: after him Ariosto
comprised them both in his Orlando: and lately Tasso dissevered
them againe, and formed both parts in two persons, namely that
part which they in Philosophy call Ethice, or vertues of a private
man, coloured in his Rinaldo: The other named Politice in his
Godfredo.[4] By ensample of which excellente Poets, I labour to
pourtraict in Arthure, before he was king, the image of a brave
knight, perfected in the twelve private morall vertues, as Aristotle

1. Secondary matters.
2. I.e., to represent (secondarily, to educate).
3. I.e., free from current political controversy.
4. Lodovico Ariosto (1474–1533) was
author of the epic-romance *Orlando Fu-*
rioso, first published in complete form
in 1532; Torquato Tasso (1544–95)
published his chivalric romance *Rinaldo*
in 1562 and the epic *Gerusalemme Lib-*
erata (centered on the heroic figure of
Count Godfredo) in 1581.

hath devised,[5] the which is the purpose of these first twelve bookes: which if I finde to be well accepted, I may be perhaps encouraged, to frame the other part of polliticke vertues in his person, after that hee came to be king. To some I know this Methode will seeme displeasaunt, which had rather have good discipline delivered plainly in way of precepts, or sermoned at large, as they use, then thus clowdily enwrapped in Allegoricall devises. But such, me seeme, should be satisfide with the use of these dayes, seeing all things accounted by their showes, and nothing esteemed of, that is not delightfull and pleasing to commune sence. For this cause is Xenophon preferred before Plato, for that the one in the exquisite depth of his judgment, formed a Commune welth [6] such as it should be, but the other in the person of Cyrus and the Persians fashioned a governement such as might best be: So much more profitable and gratious is doctrine by ensample, then by rule. So have I laboured to doe in the person of Arthure: whome I conceive after his long education by Timon, to whom he was by Merlin delivered to be brought up, so soone as he was borne of the Lady Igrayne, to have seene in a dream or vision the Faery Queen, with whose excellent beauty ravished, he awaking resolved to seeke her out, and so being by Merlin armed, and by Timon throughly instructed, he went to seeke her forth in Faerye land. In that Faery Queene I meane glory in my generall intention, but in my particular I conceive the most excellent and glorious person of our soveraine the Queene, and her kingdome in Faery land. And yet in some places els, I doe otherwise shadow [7] her. For considering she beareth two persons, the one of a most royall Queene or Empresse, the other of a most vertuous and beautifull Lady, this latter part in some places I doe express in Belphoebe, fashioning her name according to your owne excellent conceipt of Cynthia,[8] (Phoebe and Cynthia being both names of Diana.) So in the person of Prince Arthure I sette forth magnificence in particular, which vertue for that (according to Aristotle and the rest) it is the perfection of all the rest, and conteineth in it them all, therefore in the whole course I mention the deedes of Arthure applyable to that vertue, which I write of in that booke. But of the xii. other vertues, I make xii. other knights the patrones, for the more variety of the history. Of which these three bookes contayn three, The first of the knight of the Redcrosse, in whome I expresse Holynes: The seconde of Sir Guyon, in whome I sette forth Temperaunce: The third of Brito-

---

5. Aristotle did not devise twelve private moral virtues: Spenser was in fact relying upon more modern philosophers—his friend Lodowick Bryskett and the Italian Piccolomini. That Spenser actually planned a poem four times as long as the six books we now have rather staggers the imagination, but his language is plain.
6. The allusion is to Plato's *Republic* and Xenophon's *Cyropaedia*.
7. Picture, portray.
8. Ralegh's poem *Cynthia* praised Queen Elizabeth.

martis a Lady knight, in whome I picture Chastity. But because the
beginning of the whole worke seemeth abrupte and as depending
upon other antecedents, it needs that ye know the occasion of these
three knights severall adventures. For the Methode of a Poet historical is not such, as of an Historiographer. For an Historiographer
discourseth of affayres orderly as they were donne, accounting as
well the times as the actions, but a Poet thrusteth into the middest, even where it most concerneth him, and there recoursing to
the thinges forepaste, and divining of thinges to come, maketh a
pleasing Analysis of all. The beginning therefore of my history, if
it were to be told by an Historiographer, should be the twelfth
booke, which is the last, where I devise that the Faery Queene
kept her Annuall feaste xii. dayes, uppon which xii. severall dayes,
the occasions of the xii. severall adventures hapned, which being
undertaken by xii. severall knights, are in these xii books severally
handled and discoursed. The first was this. In the beginning of the
feaste, there presented him selfe a tall clownishe [9] younge man,
who falling before the Queen of Faeries desired a boone (as the
manner then was) which during that feast she might not refuse:
which was that hee might have the atchievement of any adventure,
which during that feaste should happen, that being graunted, he
rested him on the floore, unfitte through his rusticity for a better
place. Soone after entred a faire Ladye in mourning weedes, riding
on a white Asse, with a dwarfe behind her leading a warlike steed,
that bore the Armes of a knight, and his speare in the dwarfes
hand. Shee falling before the Queene of Faeries, complayned that
her father and mother an ancient King and Queene, had bene by
an huge dragon many years shut up in a brasen Castle, who thence
suffred them not to yssew: and therefore besought the Faery
Queene to assygne her some one of her knights to take on him that
exployt. Presently that clownish person upstarting, desired that adventure: whereat the Queene much wondering, and the Lady much
gainesaying, yet he earnestly importuned his desire. In the end the
Lady told him that unlesse that armour which she brought, would
serve him (that is the armour of a Christian man specified by Saint
Paul v. Ephes.) that he could not succeed in that enterprise, which
being forthwith put upon him with dewe furnitures [1] thereunto,
he seemed the goodliest man in al that company, and was well
liked of the Lady. And eftesoones taking on him knighthood, and
mounting on that straunge Courser, he went forth with her on that
adventure: where beginneth the first booke, vz.

A gentle knight was pricking on the playne. &c.

The second day ther came in a Palmer bearing an Infant with

---

9. Rustic-looking.   1. Suitable equipment.

bloody hands, whose Parents he complained to have bene slayn by an Enchaunteresse called Acrasia: and therfore craved of the Faery Queene, to appoint him some knight, to performe that adventure, which being assigned to Sir Guyon, he presently went forth with that same Palmer: which is the beginning of the second booke and the whole subject thereof. The third day there came in, a Groome who complained before the Faery Queene, that a vile Enchaunter called Busirane had in hand a most faire Lady called Amoretta, whom he kept in most grievous torment, because she would not yield him the pleasure of her body. Whereupon Sir Scudamour the lover of that Lady presently tooke on him that adventure. But being unable to performe it by reason of the hard Enchauntments, after long sorrow, in the end met with Britomartis, who succoured him, and reskewed his love.

But by occasion hereof, many other adventures are intermedled, but rather as Accidents, then intendments.[2] As the love of Britomart, the overthrow of Marinell, the misery of Florimell, the vertuousnes of Belphoebe, the lasciviousnes of Hellenora, and many the like.

Thus much Sir, I have briefly overronne to direct your understanding to the wel-head of the History, that from thence gathering the whole intention of the conceit, ye may as in a handfull gripe al the discourse, which otherwise may happily[3] seeme tedious and confused. So humbly craving the continuaunce of your honorable favour towards me, and th'eternall establishment of your happines, I humbly take leave.

23. January, 1589
Yours most humbly affectionate.
ED. SPENSER.

The First Booke of the Faerie Queene

CONTAYNING
The Legende of the
Knight of the Red Crosse,
OR
OF HOLINESSE

1

Lo I the man, whose Muse whilome did maske,
     As time her taught, in lowly Shepheards weeds,[4]

---

2. That is, there are episodes that are merely romantic and not specifically allegorical. Characters are often types, not symbols.
3. By chance.
4. I.e., behold me, the poet who appropriately appeared before ("whilome") as a writer of humble pastoral (i.e., *The Shepheardes Calender*). These lines are imitated from the verses prefixed to Virgil's *Aeneid*.

Am now enforst a far unfitter taske,
For trumpets sterne to chaunge mine Oaten reeds,[5]
5   And sing of Knights and Ladies gentle deeds;
Whose prayses having slept in silence long,[6]
Me, all too meane, the sacred Muse areeds °   appoints
To blazon broad emongst her learned throng:
Fierce warres and faithfull loves shall moralize my song.

2

10 Helpe then, O holy Virgin chiefe of nine,[7]
Thy weaker Novice to performe thy will,
Lay forth out of thine everlasting scryne [8]
The antique rolles, which there lye hidden still,
Of Faerie knights and fairest Tanaquill,[9]
15 Whom that most noble Briton Prince [1] so long
Sought through the world, and suffered so much ill,
That I must rue his undeservéd wrong:
O helpe thou my weake wit, and sharpen my dull tong.

3

And thou most dreaded impe [2] of highest Jove,
20 Faire Venus sonne, that with thy cruell dart
At that good knight so cunningly didst rove,°   shoot
That glorious fire it kindled in his hart,
Lay now thy deadly Heben ° bow apart,   ebony
And with thy mother milde come to mine ayde:
25 Come both, and with you bring triumphant Mart,[3]
In loves and gentle jollities arrayd,
After his murdrous spoiles and bloudy rage allayd.

4

And with them eke,° O Goddesse heavenly bright,   also
Mirrour of grace and Majestie divine,
30 Great Lady of the greatest Isle, whose light
Like Phoebus lampe throughout the world doth shine,
Shed thy faire beames into my feeble eyne,
And raise my thoughts too humble and too vile,°   lowly
To thinke of that true glorious type ° of thine,   pattern
35 The argument of mine afflicted stile:
The which to heare, vouchsafe, O dearest dred [4] a-while.

Canto I

The Patron of true Holinesse,
Foule Errour doth defeate:
Hypocrisie him to entrappe,
Doth to his home entreate.

---

5. To write heroic poetry, of which the trumpet is a symbol, instead of pastoral poetry like *The Shepheardes Calender*, symbolized by the humble shepherd's pipe ("Oaten reeds").
6. Lines 5 and 6 are imitated from the opening lines of Ariosto's *Orlando Furioso*.

7. Clio, the Muse of history; "weaker": too weak.
8. A chest for papers.
9. I.e., Gloriana.
1. I.e., Arthur.
2. Child, i.e., Cupid.
3. Mars, god of war and lover of Venus.
4. Object of awe.

1

A Gentle Knight was pricking ° on the plaine,　　　　　*cantering*
　　Ycladd in mightie armes and silver shielde,
　　Wherein old dints of deepe wounds did remaine,
　　The cruell markes of many a bloudy fielde;
5　　Yet armes till that time did he never wield: [5]
　　His angry steede did chide his foming bitt,
　　As much disdayning to the curbe to yield:
　　Full jolly ° knight he seemd, and faire did sitt,　　　　*courageous*
As one for knightly giusts ° and fierce encounters　　*tourneys, jousts*
　　fitt.

2

10　But on his brest a bloudie Crosse he bore,
　　The deare remembrance of his dying Lord,
　　For whose sweete sake that glorious badge he wore,
　　And dead as living ever him adored:
　　Upon his shield the like was also scored,
15　For soveraine hope, which in his helpe he had:
　　Right faithfull true he was in deede and word,
　　But of his cheere [6] did seeme too solemne sad; °　　*serious*
Yet nothing did he dread, but ever was ydrad.°　　*dreaded, feared*

3

Upon a great adventure he was bond,
20　That greatest Gloriana to him gave,
　　That greatest Glorious Queene of Faerie Lond,
　　To winne him worship, and her grace to have,
　　Which of all earthly things he most did crave;
　　And ever as he rode, his hart did earne °　　　　　*yearn*
25　To prove his puissance in battell brave
　　Upon his foe, and his new force to learne;
Upon his foe, a Dragon horrible and stearne.

4

A lovely Ladie rode him faire beside,
　　Upon a lowly Asse more white then snow,
30　Yet she much whiter, but the same did hide
　　Under a vele, that wimpled ° was full low,　　　　　*folded*
　　And over all a blacke stole she did throw,
　　As one that inly mournd: so was she sad,
　　And heavie sat upon her palfrey slow:
35　Seeméd in heart some hidden care she had,
And by her in a line a milke white lambe she lad.[7]

---

5. Redcrosse wears the armor of the Christian man, as Spenser explained in the letter to Ralegh: "put on the whole armor of God, that ye may be able to stand against the wiles of the devil" (Ephesians vi.10–22). The armor bears the dents of every Christian's fight against evil; Redcrosse himself is as yet untried.
6. Facial expression.

7. The lady will be called by name in line 405; she is Una, short for *Una Vera Fides,* "The One True Faith" (if it is true it can only be *one*). But, like other figures, she may bear other roles and attributes. Therefore she may also be the Church of England, with whom Redcrosse, in his role as Britain (St. George) will be united. Her parents typify all mankind—originally lords of

5

So pure an innocent, as that same lambe,
  She was in life and every vertuous lore,
  And by descent from Royall lynage came
40 Of ancient Kings and Queenes, that had of yore
  Their scepters stretcht from East to Westerne shore,
  And all the world in their subjection held;
  Till that infernall feend with foule uprore
  Forwasted all their land, and them expeld:
45 Whom to avenge, she had this Knight from far compeld.°   *summoned*

6

Behind her farre away a Dwarfe did lag,
  That lasie seemd in being ever last,
  Or wearied with bearing of her bag
  Of needments at his backe.[8] Thus as they past,
50 The day with cloudes was suddeine overcast,
  And angry Jove an hideous storme of raine
  Did poure into his Lemans[9] lap so fast,
  That every wight° to shrowd° it did constrain,   *creature/cover*
And this faire couple eke ° to shroud themselves were fain.   *also*

7

55 Enforst to seeke some covert nigh at hand,
  A shadie grove not far away they spide,
  That promist ayde the tempest to withstand:
  Whose loftie trees yclad with sommers pride,
  Did spred so broad, that heavens light did hide,
60 Not perceable with power of any starre:
  And all within were pathes and alleies wide,
  With footing worne, and leading inward farre:
Faire harbour that them seemes; so in they entred arre.

8

And foorth they passe, with pleasure forward led,
65 Joying to heare the birdes sweete harmony,
  Which therein shrouded from the tempest dred,
  Seemd in their song to scorne the cruell sky.
  Much can° they prayse the trees, so straight and hy,   *did*
  The sayling Pine, the Cedar proud and tall,

Eden, now fallen. She is veiled because fallen man cannot see the one truth but only fragments thereof, and she is sad because man is fallen. It is a characteristic Spenserian subtlety that Una enters the poem under a veil and only appears to the Redcrosse Knight, unveiled and radiant, in Canto vii. The "lowly Asse" she rides (line 29) is a figure of humility (cf. Christ's entry into Jerusalem), and the "lambe" is that of innocence. Having filled its symbolic function, the lamb does not appear in the poem again. C. S. Lewis, in *The Allegory of Love* (pp. 310–11) discusses another aspect of Spenser's alle-gorical imagination that this passage reveals: "the lady was commonly represented leading her lamb in the pageants [local religious dramas] of St. George and the dragon." That is, many of the associations evoked in *The Faerie Queene* are not merely literary but "popular, homely, patriotic."
8. The Dwarfe is sometimes taken as Redcrosse's conscience—useful in emergencies, otherwise forgotten or lost. In addition, or alternatively, the Dwarfe may represent common sense or common prudence.
9. His lover, i.e., the earth.

70   The vine-prop Elme, the Poplar never dry,
          The builder Oake, sole king of forrests all,
        The Aspine good for staves, the Cypresse funerall.

                              9
        The Laurell, meed° of mightie Conquerours   *reward*
          And Poets sage, the Firre that weepeth still,
75   The Willow worne of forlorne Paramours,
          The Eugh obedient to the benders will,
          The Birch for shaftes, the Sallow for the mill,
          The Mirrhe sweete bleeding in the bitter wound,
          The warlike Beech, the Ash for nothing ill,
80   The fruitfull Olive, and the Platane round,
        The carver Holme, the Maple seeldom inward sound.[1]

                             10
        Led with delight, they thus beguile the way,
          Untill the blustring storme is overblowne;
          When weening° to returne, whence they did stray,   *supposing*
85   They cannot finde that path, which first was showne,
          But wander too and fro in wayes unknowne,
          Furthest from end then, when they neerest weene,
          That makes them doubt, their wits be not their owne:
          So many pathes, so many turnings seene,
90   That which of them to take, in diverse doubt they been.

                             11
        At last resolving forward still to fare,
          Till that some end they finde or° in or out,   *either*
          That path they take, that beaten seemd most bare,
          Which when by tract[2] they hunted had throughout,
95   And like to lead the labyrinth about;°   *out of*
          At length it brought them to a hollow cave,
          Amid the thickest woods. The Champion stout
          Eftsoones° dismounted from his courser brave,   *forthwith*
        And to the Dwarfe a while his needlesse spere he gave.

                             12
100   "Be well aware," quoth then that Ladie milde,
          "Least suddaine mischiefe ye too rash provoke:
          The danger hid, the place unknowne and wilde,
          Breedes dreadfull doubts: Oft fire is without smoke,
          And perill without show: therefore your stroke
105   Sir knight with-hold, till further triall made."
          "Ah Ladie," said he, "shame were to revoke
          The forward footing for° an hidden shade: *because of*
        Vertue gives her selfe light, through darkenesse for to wade."

                             13
        "Yea but," quoth she, "the perill of this place
110   I better wot then you, though now too late

---

1. In these lines, Spenser has been imitating Chaucer's catalogue of trees in
the *Parliament of Fowls;* the convention goes back to Ovid.
2. By following the track.

To wish you backe returne with foule disgrace,
Yet wisedome warnes, whilest foot is in the gate,
To stay the steepe, ere forcéd to retrate.
This is the wandring wood, this Errours den,
A monster vile, whom God and man does hate:
Therefore I read° beware.". "Fly fly," quoth then   *advise*
The fearefull Dwarfe: "this is no place for living men."

14

But full of fire and greedy hardiment,°   *boldness*
The youthfull knight could not for ought be staide,
But forth unto the darksome hole he went,
And lookéd in: his glistring armor made
A litle glooming light, much like a shade,
By which he saw the ugly monster plaine,
Halfe like a serpent horribly displaide,[3]
But th' other halfe did womans shape retaine,
Most lothsom, filthie, foule, and full of vile disdaine.

15

And as she lay upon the durtie ground,
Her huge long taile her den all overspred,
Yet was in knots and many boughtes° upwound,   *coils*
Pointed with mortall sting. Of her there bred
A thousand yong ones, which she dayly fed,
Sucking upon her poisonous dugs, eachone
Of sundry shapes, yet all ill favoréd:
Soone as that uncouth° light upon them shone,   *unfamiliar*
Into her mouth they crept, and suddain all were gone.

16

Their dam upstart, out of her den effraide,
And rushéd forth, hurling her hideous taile
About her curséd head, whose folds displaid
Were stretcht now forth at length without
   entraile.°   *winding, coiling*
She lookt about, and seeing one in mayle
Arméd to point, sought backe to turne againe;
For light she hated as the deadly bale,°   *evil*
Ay wont in desert darknesse to remaine,
Where plaine none might her see, nor she see any plaine.

17

Which when the valiant Elfe[4] perceived, he lept
As Lyon fierce upon the flying pray,
And with his trenchand° blade her boldly kept   *cutting*
From turning backe, and forcéd her to stay:
Therewith enragéd she loudly gan to bray,

3. That Errour (or theological, doctrinal heresy) is half serpent reminds us of the primal error in Eden, which the serpent instigated. "Errour," at first glance, may not seem an important demon; here Lewis is helpful in reminding us that "Spenser is writing in an age of religious doubt and controversy when the avoidance of error is a problem as pressing as, and in a sense prior to, the conquest of sin" (*Allegory of Love*, p. 334). The description echoes both classical and Biblical monsters (cf. Revelation ix.7–10).

4. Knight of Faerie Land.

150 And turning fierce, her speckled taile advaunst,
Threatning her angry sting, him to dismay:
Who nough aghast, his mightie hand enhaunst:° *lifted up*
The stroke down from her head unto her shoulder glaunst.

18

Much daunted with that dint, her sence was dazd,
155 Yet kindling rage, her selfe she gathered round,
And all attonce her beastly body raizd
With doubled forces high above the ground:
Tho° wrapping up her wrethéd sterne arownd, *then*
Lept fierce upon his shield, and her huge traine° *tail*
160 All suddenly about his body wound,
That hand or foot to stirre he strove in vaine:
God helpe the man so wrapt in Errours endlesse traine.

19

His Lady sad to see his sore constraint,
Cride out, "Now now Sir knight, shew what ye bee,
165 Add faith unto your force, and be not faint:
Strangle her, else she sure will strangle thee."
That when he heard, in great perplexitie,
His gall did grate for griefe° and high disdaine, *wrath*
And knitting all his force got one hand free,
170 Wherewith he grypt her gorge° with so great paine, *neck*
That soone to loose her wicked bands did her constraine.

20

Therewith she spewd out of her filthy maw
A floud of poyson horrible and blacke,
Full of great lumpes of flesh and gobbets raw,
175 Which stunck so vildly, that it forst him slacke
His grasping hold, and from her turne him backe:
Her vomit full of bookes and papers[5] was,
With loathly frogs and toades, which eyes did lacke,
And creeping sought way in the weedy gras:
180 Her filthy parbreake° all the place defiléd has.[6] *vomit*

21

As when old father Nilus gins to swell
With timely pride above the Aegyptian vale,
His fattie° waves do fertile slime outwell, *rich*
And overflow each plaine and lowly dale:
185 But when his later spring gins to avale,° *subside*
Huge heapes of mudd he leaves, wherein there breed
Ten thousand kindes of creatures, partly male
And partly female of his fruitfull seed;
Such ugly monstrous shapes elswhere may no man reed.° *see*

---

5. The reference is to books and pamphlets of Catholic propaganda, particularly attacks on Queen Elizabeth in 1588—and, indeed, to violent religious controversy of any kind.

6. Revelation xvi.13: "And I saw three unclean spirits like frogs come out of the mouth of the dragon, and out of the mouth of the beast, and out of the mouth of the false prophet."

22

190 The same so sore annoyéd has the knight,
    That welnigh chokéd with the deadly stinke,
    His forces faile, ne can no longer fight.
    Whose corage when the feend perceived to shrinke,
195   She pouréd forth out of her hellish sinke
    Her fruitfull curséd spawne of serpents small,
    Deforméd monsters, fowle, and blacke as inke,
    Which swarming all about his legs did crall,
And him encombred sore, but could not hurt at all.

23

As gentle Shepheard in sweete even-tide,
200   When ruddy Phoebus gins to welke° in west,   *sink*
    High on an hill, his flocke to vewen wide,
    Markes which do byte their hasty supper best;
    A cloud of combrous gnattes do him molest,
    All striving to infixe their feeble stings,
205   That from their noyance he no where can rest,
    But with his clownish° hands their tender wings   *rustic*
He brusheth oft, and oft doth mar their murmurings.

24

Thus ill bestedd,° and fearfull more of shame,   *situated*
    Then of the certaine perill he stood in,
210   Halfe furious unto his foe he came,
    Resolved in minde all suddenly to win,
    Or soone to lose, before he once would lin;°   *cease, stop*
    And strooke at her with more then manly force,
    That from her body full of filthie sin
215   He raft° her hatefull head without remorse;   *cut away*
A streame of cole black bloud forth gushéd from her corse.

25

Her scattred brood, soone as their Parent deare
    They saw so rudely falling to the ground,
    Groning full deadly, all with troublous feare,
220   Gathred themselves about her body round,
    Weening their wonted entrance to have found
    At her wide mouth: but being there withstood
    They flockéd all about her bleeding wound,
    And suckéd up their dying mothers blood,
225 Making her death their life, and eke° her hurt their good.   *also*

26

That detestable sight him much amazde,
    To see th' unkindly Impes of heaven accurst,
    Devoure their dam; on whom while so he gazd,
    Having all satisfide their bloudy thurst,
230   Their bellies swolne he saw with fulnesse burst,
    And bowels gushing forth: well worthy end
    Of such as drunke her life, the which them nurst;
    Now needeth him no lenger labour spend,
His foes have slaine themselves, with whom he should contend.

27

235 His Ladie seeing all, that chaunst, from farre
    Approcht in hast to greet his victorie,
    And said, "Faire knight, borne under happy starre,
    Who see your vanquisht foes before you lye;
    Well worthy be you of that Armorie,[7]
240   Wherein ye have great glory wonne this day,
    And prooved your strength on a strong enimie,
    Your first adventure: many such I pray,
And henceforth ever wish, that like succeed it may."

28

    Then mounted he upon his Steede againe,
245   And with the Lady backward sought to wend;
    That path he kept, which beaten was most plaine,
    Ne ever would to any by-way bend,
    But still did follow one unto the end,
    The which at last out of the wood them brought.
250 So forward on his way (with God to frend[8])
    He passéd forth, and new adventure sought;
Long way he travelléd, before he heard of ought.

29

    At length they chaunst to meet upon the way
    An aged Sire, in long blacke weedes yclad,[9]
255   His feete all bare, his beard all hoarie gray,
    And by his belt his booke he hanging had;
    Sober he seemde, and very sagely sad,°   *pensive*
    And to the ground his eyes were lowly bent,
    Simple in shew, and voyde of malice bad,
260   And all the way he prayéd, as he went,
And often knockt his brest, as one that did repent.[1]

30

    He faire the knight saluted, louting° low,   *bowing*
    Who faire him quited,° as that courteous was: *answered*
    And after askéd him, if he did know
265   Of straunge adventures, which abroad did pas.
    "Ah my deare Sonne," quoth he, "how should, alas,
    Silly° old man, that lives in hidden cell,   *innocent*
    Bidding° his beades all day for his trespas,   *telling*
    Tydings of warre and worldly trouble tell?
270 With holy father sits not with such things to mell.°   *meddle*

---

7. I.e., Christian armor.
8. With God as friend.
9. Dressed in long black garments.
1. The Sire is in reality Archimago (arch, or head, magician)—i.e., hypocrisy, the archdeceiver, Satan, idolatry of the Roman Catholic Church. He is disguised as a holy man, as evil is so often under the guise of good in Christian thought and legend. Note (especially in lines 312–15) that his "holiness" is in talking, not in doing, and that he is far too reminiscent of the Catholic monasteries to be trustworthy. The black magician in hermit's disguise often appears in medieval romance and in Italian romance epics.

31

"But if of daunger which hereby doth dwell,
    And homebred evill ye desire to heare,
    Of a straunge man I can you tidings tell,
    That wasteth all this countrey farre and neare."
275 "Of such," said he, "I chiefly do inquere,
    And shall you well reward to shew the place,
    In which that wicked wight his dayes doth weare:
    For to all knighthood it is foule disgrace,
That such a cursed creature lives so long a space."

32

280 "Far hence," quoth he, "in wastfull° wildernesse   desolate
    His dwelling is, by which no living wight
    May ever passe, but thorough great distresse."
    "Now," sayd the Lady, "draweth toward night,
    And well I wote, that of your later° fight   recent
285 Ye all forwearied be: for what so strong,
    But wanting rest will also want of might?
    The Sunne that measures heaven all day long,
At night doth baite° his steedes the Ocean waves emong. feed, refresh

33

"Then with the Sunne take Sir, your timely rest,
290 And with new day new worke at once begin:
    Untroubled night they say gives counsell best."
    "Right well Sir knight ye have adviséd bin,"
    Quoth then that aged man; "the way to win
    Is wisely to advise: now day is spent;
295 Therefore with me ye may take up your In°   lodging
    For this same night." The knight was well content:
So with that godly father to his home they went.

34

A little lowly Hermitage it was,
    Downe in a dale, hard by a forests side,
300 Far from resort of people, that did pas
    In travell to and froe: a little wyde°   apart
    There was an holy Chappell edifyde,°   built
    Wherein the Hermite dewly wont° to say   was wont
    His holy things each morne and eventyde:
305 Thereby a Christall streame did gently play,
Which from a sacred fountaine welléd forth alway.

35

Arrivéd there, the little house they fill,
    Ne looke for entertainement, where none was:
    Rest is their feast, and all things at their will;
310 The noblest mind the best contentment has.
    With faire discourse the evening so they pas:
    For that old man of pleasing wordes had store,
    And well could file his tongue as smooth as glas;
    He told of Saintes and Popes, and evermore
315 He strowd an *Ave-Mary* after and before.

36

The drouping Night thus creepeth on them fast,
   And the sad humour[2] loading their eye liddes,
   As messenger of Morpheus[3] on them cast
   Sweet slombring deaw, the which to sleepe them biddes.
320   Unto their lodgings then his guestes he riddes:°   *leads*
   Where when all drownd in deadly sleepe he findes,
   He to his study goes, and there amiddes
   His Magick bookes and artes of sundry kindes,
He seekes out mighty charmes, to trouble sleepy mindes.

37

325 Then choosing out few wordes most horrible
   (Let none them read), thereof did verses frame,
   With which and other spelles like terrible,
   He bade awake blacke Plutoes griesly Dame,[4]
   And curséd heaven, and spake reprochfull shame
330   Of highest God, the Lord of life and light;
   A bold bad man, that dared to call by name
   Great Gorgon, Prince of darknesse and dead night,
At which Cocytus quakes, and Styx[5] is put to flight.

38

And forth he cald out of deepe darknesse dred
335   Legions of Sprights, the which like little flyes
   Fluttring about his ever damnéd hed,
   A-waite whereto their service he applyes,
   To aide his friends, or fray° his enimies: *frighten*
   Of those he chose out two, the falsest twoo,
340   And fittest for to forge true-seeming lyes;
   The one of them he gave a message too,
The other by him selfe staide other worke to doo.

39

He making speedy way through spedséd° ayre,   *dispersed*
   And through the world of waters wide and deepe,
345   To Morpheus house doth hastily repaire.
   Amid the bowels of the earth full steepe,
   And low, where dawning day doth never peepe,
   His dwelling is; there Tethys[6] his wet bed
   Doth ever wash, and Cynthia[7] still doth steepe
350   In silver deaw his ever-drouping hed,
Whiles sad Night over him her mantle black doth spred.

40

Whose double gates he findeth lockéd fast,
   The one faire framed of burnisht Yvory,
   The other all with silver overcast;
355   And wakefull dogges before them farre do lye,

2. Heavy moisture.
3. The god of sleep.
4. I.e., Proserpine.
5. Rivers of hell.
6. The wife of Ocean.
7. I.e., Diana, the goddess of the moon.

Watching to banish Care their enimy,
Who oft is wont to trouble gentle Sleepe.
By them the Sprite doth passe in quietly,
And unto Morpheus comes, whom drownéd deepe
360 In drowsie fit he findes: of nothing he takes keepe.°   *notice*

41

And more, to lulle him in his slumber soft,
A trickling streame from high rocke tumbling downe
And ever-drizling raine upon the loft,
Mixt with a murmuring winde, much like the sowne
365 Of swarming Bees, did cast him in a swowne:°   *faint*
No other noyse, nor peoples troublous cryes,
As still° are wont t'annoy the walléd towne,   *always*
Might there be heard: but carelesse Quiet lyes,
Wrapt in eternall silence farre from enemyes.[8]

42

370 The messenger approching to him spake,
But his wast° wordes returnd to him in vaine: *wasted*
So sound he slept, that nought mought him awake.
Then rudely he him thrust, and pusht with paine,
Whereat he gan to stretch: but he againe
375 Shooke him so hard, that forced him to speake.
As one then in a dreame, whose dryer braine[9]
Is tost with troubled sights and fancies weake,
He mumbled soft, but would not all his silence breake.

43

The Sprite then gan more boldly him to wake,
380 And threatned unto him the dreaded name
Of Hecate:[1] whereat he gan to quake,
And lifting up his lumpish head, with blame
Halfe angry askéd him, for what he came.
"Hither," quoth he, "me Archimago sent,
385 He that the stubborne Sprites can wisely tame,
He bids thee to him send for his intent
A fit false dreame, that can delude the sleepers sent."°   *senses*

44

The God obayde, and calling forth straight way
A diverse° dreame out of his prison darke,   *misleading*
390 Delivered it to him, and downe did lay
His heavie head, devoide of carefull carke,[2]
Whose sences all were straight benumbd and starke.
He backe returning by the Yvorie dore,[3]

8. Spenser is imitating descriptions of the house of Morpheus in Chaucer, Ovid, and other ancient writers, but he achieves originality, particularly by means of the sound effects in stanza 41.
9. According to the old physiology, old people and other light sleepers had too little moisture in the brain.
1. Queen of Hades.
2. Anxious concerns.
3. False dreams came through the ivory door, true dreams through the gate of horn (Homer, *Odyssey* XIX.562–67; Virgil, *Aeneid* VI.893–96).

Remounted up as light as chearefull Larke,
395 And on his litle winges the dreame he bore
In hast unto his Lord, where he him left afore.

45

Who all this while with charmes and hidden artes,
Had made a Lady of that other Spright,
And framed of liquid ayre her tender partes
400 So lively,° and so like in all mens sight,   *lifelike*
That weaker° sence it could have ravisht quight   *too weak*
The maker selfe for all his wondrous witt,
Was nigh beguiléd with so goodly sight:
Her all in white he clad, and over it
405 Cast a blacke stole, most like to seeme for Una[4] fit.

46

Now when that ydle dreame was to him brought
Unto that Elfin knight he bad him fly,
Where he slept soundly void of evill thought
And with false shewes abuse his fantasy,°   *imagination*
410 In sort as[5] he him schooléd privily:
And that new creature borne without her dew[6]
Full of the makers guile, with usage sly
He taught to imitate that Lady trew,
Whose semblance she did carrie under feignéd hew.°   *form*

47

415 Thus well instructed, to their worke they hast
And comming where the knight in slomber lay
The one upon his hardy head him plast,
And made him dreame of loves and lustfull play
That nigh his manly hart did melt away,
420 Bathéd in wanton blis and wicked joy:
Then seeméd him his Lady by him lay,
And to him playnd,° how that false wingéd boy   *complained*
Her chast hart had subdewd, to learne Dame pleasures toy.

48

And she her selfe of beautie soveraigne Queene
425 Faire Venus seemde unto his bed to bring
Her, whom he waking evermore did weene
To be the chastest flowre, that ay° did spring   *ever*
On earthly braunch, the daughter of a king,
Now a loose Leman° to vile service bound: *paramour*
430 And eke the Graces seeméd all to sing,
Hymen iô Hymen, dauncing all around,
Whilst freshest Flora her with Yvie girlond crownd.[7]

4. The lady is now given her name.
5. In the way.
6. Unnaturally.
7. The three graces of classical mythology were personifications of grace and beauty, yet here they sing a call to the pleasures of the marriage bed (Hymen was god of marriage). On Flora, cf. E.K.'s Glosse to the March eclogue: "the Goddesse of flowres, but indede (as saith Tacitus) a famous harlot."

49

In this great passion of unwonted lust,
  Or wonted feare of doing ought amis,
435   He started up, as seeming to mistrust
  Some secret ill, or hidden foe of his:
  Lo there before his face his Lady is,
  Under blake stole hyding her bayted hooke,
  And as halfe blushing offred him to kis,
440   With gentle blandishment and lovely looke,
Most like that virgin true, which for her knight him took.

50

All cleane dismayd to see so uncouth sight,
  And halfe enragéd at her shamelesse guise,
  He thought have slaine her in his fierce despight:°   *indignation*
445   But hasty heat tempring with sufferance wise,
  He stayde his hand, and gan himselfe advise
  To prove his sense, and tempt her faignéd truth.
  Wringing her hands in wemens pitteous wise,
  Tho can she[8] weepe, to stirre up gentle ruth,°   *pity*
450 Both for her noble bloud, and for her tender youth.

51

And said, "Ah Sir, my liege Lord and my love,
  Shall I accuse the hidden cruell fate,
  And mightie causes wrought in heaven above,
  Or the blind God, that doth me thus amate,°   *dismay*
455   For° hopéd love to winne me certaine hate?   *instead of*
  Yet thus perforce he bids me do, or die.
  Die is my dew: yet rew my wretched state
  You, whom my hard avenging destinie
Hath made judge of my life or death indifferently.

52

460 "Your owne deare sake forst me at first to leave
  My Fathers kingdome," There she stopt with teares;
  Her swollen hart her speach seemd to bereave,
  And then againe begun, "My weaker yeares
  Captived to fortune and frayle worldly feares,
465   Fly to your faith for succour and sure ayde:
  Let me not dye in languor and long teares.
  "Why Dame," quoth he, "what hath ye thus dismayd?
What frayes ye, that were wont to comfort me affrayd?"

53

 "Love of your selfe," she said, "and deare° constraint   *dire*
470   Lets me not sleepe, but wast the wearie night
  In secret anguish and unpittied plaint,
  Whiles you in carelesse sleepe are drownéd quight."
  Her doubtfull words made that redoubted knight
  Suspect her truth: yet since no untruth he knew,

8. Then she began to.

475   Her fawning love with foule disdainefull spight
      He would not shend,° but said, "Deare dame I rew,   *reject*
  That for my sake unknowne such griefe unto you grew.

54

  "Assure your selfe, it fell not all to ground;
    For all so deare as life is to my hart,
480   I deeme your love, and hold me to you bound;
    Ne let vaine feares procure your needlesse smart,
    Where cause is none, but to your rest depart."
    Not all content, yet seemd she to appease°   *cease*
    Her mournefull plaintes, beguiléd of her art,
485   And fed with words, that could not chuse but please,
  So slyding softly forth, she turnd as to her ease.

55

  Long after lay he musing at her mood,
    Much grieved to thinke that gentle Dame so light,
    For whose defence he was to shed his blood.
490   At last dull wearinesse of former fight
    Having yrockt a sleepe his irkesome spright,°   *spirit*
    That troublous dreame gan freshly tosse his braine,
    With bowres, and beds, and Ladies deare delight:[9]
    But when he saw his labour all was vaine,
495 With that misforméd spright he backe returnd againe.

Canto II

The guilefull great Enchaunter parts
The Redcrosse Knight from Truth:
Into whose stead faire falshood steps,
And workes him wofull ruth.

1

By this the Northerne wagoner had set
    His seven fold teame behind the stedfast starre,[1]
    That was in Ocean waves yet never wet,
    But firme is fixt, and sendeth light from farre
5   To all, that in the wide deepe wandring arre.
    And chearefull Chaunticlere with his note shrill
    Had warnéd once, that Phoebus fiery carre[2]
    In hast was climbing up the Easterne hill,
Full envious that night so long his roome did fill.

2

10 When those accurséd messengers of hell,
    That feigning dreame, and that faire-forgéd Spright
    Came to their wicked maister, and gan tell
    Their bootelesse° paines, and ill succeeding night: *useless*
    Who all in rage to see his skilfull might

---

9. Redcrosse has been unable to distinguish the false Una from the true because his reason has been clouded by desire (see I.ii.6).

1. I.e., by this time the Big Dipper had set behind the North Star.
2. The chariot of the sun.

15   Deluded so, gan threaten hellish paine
      And sad Prosérpines wrath, them to affright.
      But when he saw his threatning was but vaine,
    He cast about, and searcht his balefull° bookes againe.   *deadly*

3

    Eftsoones he tooke that miscreated faire,
20   And that false other Spright, on whom he spred
      A seeming body of the subtile aire,
      Like a young Squire, in loves and lusty-hed
      His wanton dayes that ever loosely led,
      Without regard of armes and dreaded fight:
25   Those two he tooke, and in a secret bed,
      Covered with darknesse and misdeeming° night,   *misleading*
    Them both together laid, to joy in vaine delight.

4

    Forthwith he runnes with feignéd faithfull hast
      Unto his guest, who after troublous sights
30   And dreames, gan now to take more sound repast,°   *rest*
      Whom suddenly he wakes with fearefull frights,
      As one aghast with feends or damnéd sprights,
      And to him cals, "Rise rise unhappy Swaine,
      That here wex old in sleepe, whiles wicked wights
35   Have knit themselves in Venus shamefull chaine;
    Come see, where your false Lady doth her honour staine."

5

    All in amaze he suddenly up start
      With sword in hand, and with the old man went;
      Who soone him brought into a secret part,
40   Where that false couple were full closely ment°   *mingled*
      In wanton lust and lewd embracément:
      Which when he saw, he burnt with gealous fire,
      The eye of reason was with rage yblent,°   *blinded*
      And would have slaine them in his furious ire,
45   But hardly was restreinéd of that aged sire.

6

    Returning to his bed in torment great,
      And bitter anguish of his guiltie sight,
      He could not rest, but did his stout heart eat,
      And wast his inward gall with deepe despight,
50   Yrkesome of life, and too long lingring night.
      At last faire Hesperus[3] in highest skie
      Had spent his lampe, and brought forth dawning light
      Then up he rose, and clad him hastily;
    The Dwarfe him brought his steed: so both away do fly.[4]

7

55   Now when the rosy-fingred Morning faire,
      Weary of aged Tithones[5] saffron bed,

---

3. The evening star.
4. Reason and discrimination are defeated, and so "Holiness" is separated

from the one true faith.
5. The husband of Aurora, goddess of the dawn.

Had spred her purple robe through deawy aire,
And the high hils Titan° discoveréd,   *the sun*
The royall virgin shooke off drowsy-hed,
60 And rising forth out of her baser° bowre,   *humbler*
Lookt for her knight, who far away was fled,
And for her Dwarfe, that wont to wait each houre;
Then gan she waile and weepe, to see that woefull stowre.°   *affliction*

8

And after him she rode with so much speede
65 As her slow beast could make; but all in vaine:
For him so far had borne his light-foot steede,
Prickéd with wrath and fiery fierce disdaine,
That him to follow was but fruitlesse paine;
Yet she her weary limbes would never rest,
70 But every hill and dale, each wood and plaine
Did search, sore grievéd in her gentle brest,
He so ungently left her, whom she lovéd best.

9

But subtill Archimago, when his guests
He saw divided into double parts,
75 And Una wandring in woods and forrests,
Th' end of his drift, he praisd his divelish arts
That had such might over true meaning harts;
Yet rests not so, but other meanes doth make,
How he may worke unto her further smarts:
80 For her he hated as the hissing snake,
And in her many troubles did most pleasure take.

10

He then devisde himselfe how to disguise;
For by his mightie science° he could take   *knowledge*
As many formes and shapes in seeming wise,
85 As ever Proteus to himselfe could make:
Sometime a fowle, sometime a fish in lake,
Now like a foxe, now like a dragon fell,°   *fierce*
That of himselfe he oft for feare would quake,
And oft would flie away. O who can tell
90 The hidden power of herbes, and might of Magicke spell?

11

But now seemde best, the person to put on
Of that good knight, his late beguiléd guest:
In mighty armes he was yclad anon,
And silver shield: upon his coward brest
95 A bloudy crosse, and on his craven crest
A bounch of haires discolourd diversly:
Full jolly knight he seemde, and well addrest,
And when he sate upon his courser free,
Saint George himself ye would have deeméd him to be.[6]

---

6. Archimago, in disguising himself as Holiness, takes on the role of the Anti-Christ.

12

But he the knight, whose semblaunt° he did beare,   *likeness*
  The true Saint George was wandred far away,
  Still flying from his thoughts and gealous feare;
  Will was his guide,[7] and griefe led him astray.
  At last him chaunst to meete upon the way
  A faithlesse Sarazin° all armed to point,   *Saracen*
  In whose great shield was writ with letters gay
  Sans foy:[8] full large of limbe and every joint
He was, and caréd not for God or man a point.

13

He had a faire companion of his way,
  A goodly Lady clad in scarlot red,
  Purfled° with gold and pearle of rich assay,   *decorated*
  And like a Persian mitre on her hed
  She wore, with crownes and owches° garnishéd,   *brooches*
  The which her lavish lovers to her gave;
  Her wanton palfrey all was overspred
  With tinsell trappings, woven like a wave,
Whose bridle rung with golden bels and bosses brave.

14

With faire disport° and courting dalliaunce   *diversion*
  She intertainde her lover all the way:
  But when she saw the knight his speare advaunce,
  She soone left off her mirth and wanton play,
  And bad her knight addresse him to the fray:
  His foe was nigh at hand. He prickt° with pride   *pranced*
  And hope to winne his Ladies heart that day,
  Forth spurréd fast: adowne his coursers side
The red bloud trickling staind the way, as he did ride.

15

The knight of the Redcrosse when him he spide,
  Spurring so hote with rage dispiteous,
  Gan fairely couch° his speare, and towards ride: *lower*
  Soone meete they both, both fell and furious,
  That daunted with their forces hideous,
  Their steeds do stagger, and amazéd stand,
  And eke themselves too rudely rigorous,
  Astonied° with the stroke of their owne hand,   *stunned*
Do backe rebut,° and each to other yeeldeth land.   *recoil*

16

As when two rams stird with ambitious pride,
  Fight for the rule of the rich fleecéd flocke,
  Their hornéd fronts so fierce on either side
  Do meete, that with the terrour of the shocke

7. Will was his guide; but will, of all the human faculties, is least fitted to be one's guide; it should itself be under the guidance of intelligence or truth.
8. Redcrosse's victory over the monster Errour did not give him the discrimination to pierce the deceptions of either Archimago or the false Una. His second trial will be against Sans foy—"without faith," atheism.

140　Astonied both, stand sencelesse as a blocke,
　　Forgetfull of the hanging victory:
　　So stood these twaine, unmovéd as a rocke,
　　Both staring fierce, and holding idely
The broken reliques of their former cruelty.

17

145　The Sarazin sore daunted with the buffe
　　Snatcheth his sword, and fiercely to him flies;
　　Who well it wards, and quyteth° cuff with cuff:　　　*requites*
　　Each others equall puissaunce envies,
　　And through their iron sides with cruell spies°　　　*looks*
150　Does seeke to perce: repining courage yields
　　No foote to foe. The flashing fier flies
　　As from a forge out of their burning shields,
And streames of purple bloud new dies the verdant fields.

18

　　"Curse on that Crosse," quoth then the Sarazin,
155　"That keepes thy body from the bitter fit;°　　　*stroke*
　　Dead long ygoe I wote thou haddest bin,
　　Had not that charme from thee forwarnéd it:
　　But yet I warne thee now assuréd sitt,
　　And hide thy head." Therewith upon his crest
160　With rigour so outrageous he smitt,
　　That a large share it hewd out of the rest,
And glauncing downe his shield, from blame him fairely blest.[9]

19

　　Who thereat wondrous wroth, the sleeping spark
　　Of native vertue gan eftsoones revive,
165　And at his haughtie helmet making mark,
　　So hugely stroke, that it the steele did rive,
　　And cleft his head. He tumbling downe alive,
　　With bloudy mouth his mother earth did kis,
　　Greeting his grave: his grudging ghost did strive
170　With the fraile flesh; at last it flitted is,
Whither the soules do fly of men, that live amis.

20

　　The Lady when she saw her champion fall,
　　Like the old ruines of a broken towre,
　　Staid not to waile his woefull funerall,
175　But from him fled away with all her powre;
　　Who after her as hastily gan scowre,°　　　*scurry*
　　Bidding the Dwarfe with him to bring away
　　The Sarazins shield, signe of the conqueroure.
　　Her soone he overtooke, and bad to stay,
180　For present cause was none of dread her to dismay.

21

　　She turning backe with ruefull countenaunce,
　　Cride, "Mercy mercy Sir vouchsafe to show
　　On silly° Dame, subject to hard mischaunce,　　　*innocent*

9. Preserved him from harm.

And to your mighty will." Her humblesse low
In so ritch weedes and seeming glorious show,
Did much emmove his stout heroicke heart,
And said, "Deare dame, your suddein overthrow
Much rueth° me; but now put feare apart,   *grieves*
And tell, both who ye be, and who that tooke your part."

22

Melting in teares, then gan she thus lament;
"The wretched woman, whom unhappy howre
Hath now made thrall to your commandément,
Before that angry heavens list to lowre,
And fortune false betraide me to your powre
Was (O what now availeth that I was!)
Borne the sole daughter of an Emperour,
He that the wide West under his rule has,
And high hath set his throne, where Tiberis doth pas.[1]

23

"He in the first flowre of my freshest age,
Betrothéd me unto the onely haire°   *heir*
Of a most mighty king, most rich and sage;
Was never Prince so faithfull and so faire,
Was never Prince so meeke and debonaire;°   *gracious*
But ere my hopéd day of spousall shone,
My dearest Lord fell from high honours staire,
Into the hands of his accursed fone,°   *foes*
And cruelly was slaine, that shall I ever mone.

24

"His blessed body spoild of lively breath,
Was afterward, I know not how, convaid
And fro me hid: of whose most innocent death
When tidings came to me unhappy maid,
O how great sorrow my sad soule assaid.°   *afflicted*
Then forth I went his woefull corse to find,
And many yeares throughout the world I straid,

1. The Tiber River runs through Rome. The lady's admission that she is the daughter of Rome (and hence the Roman Catholic Church) is an immediate clue to the fact that she is evil. Her appearance, as described in stanza 13, was, however, also full of clues. She resembles the Whore of Babylon (Revelation xvii.3–4): "and I saw a woman sit upon a scarlet coloured beast, full of names of blasphemy, having seven heads and ten horns. And the woman was arrayed in purple and scarlet colour, and decked with gold and precious stones and pearls, having a golden cup in her hand full of abominations and filthiness of her fornication." Her father, she says, is ruler of the West—but Una's father had the rule of both East *and* West (I.i.5): on the historical plane, the true church once embraced east and west whereas the false rules only the west; truth is universal and comprehends falsehood, which is partial. As the false church, she wears the pope's miter. The Roman church is an embodiment of villainy and evil in *The Faerie Queene* because this was a time of violent Protestant-Catholic controversy in both Europe and England, which had led to exchanges of Protestant and Catholic monarchs, bloodshed, and burnings; England had only recently emerged from its own religious strife. Popular fear of Catholicism was very real, and Spenser draws partly on the "bogey" images of this fear in erecting his figures of evil.

215   A virgin widow, whose deepe wounded mind
    With love, long time did languish as the striken hind.[2]

25

"At last it chauncéd this proud Sarazin
    To meete me wandring, who perforce me led
    With him away, but yet could never win
220   The fort, that Ladies hold in soveraigne dread.
    There lies he now with foule dishonour dead,
    Who whiles he livde, was calléd proud Sans foy,
    The eldest of three brethren, all three bred
    Of one bad sire, whose youngest is Sans joy,
225 And twixt them both was borne the bloudy bold Sans loy.[3]

26

"In this sad plight, friendlesse, unfortunate,
    Now miserable I Fidessa dwell,
    Craving of you in pitty of my state,
    To do none° ill, if please ye not do well."   *no*
230   He in great passion all this while did dwell,
    More busying his quicke eyes, her face to view,
    Then his dull eares, to heare what she did tell;
    And said, "Faire Lady hart of flint would rew
The undeservéd woes and sorrowes, which ye shew.

27

235 "Henceforth in safe assuraunce may ye rest,
    Having both found a new friend you to aid,
    And lost an old foe, that did you molest:
    Better new friend than an old foe is[4] said."
    With chaunge of cheare the seeming simple maid
240   Let fall her eyen, as shamefast to the earth,
    And yeelding soft, in that she nought gain-said,
    So forth they rode, he feining seemely merth,
And she coy lookes: so dainty they say maketh derth.[5]

28

Long time they thus together traveiléd,
245   Till weary of their way, they came at last,
    Where grew two goodly trees, that faire did spred
    Their armes abroad, with gray mosse overcast,
    And their greene leaves trembling with every blast,°   *breeze*
    Made a calme shadow far in compasse round:

2. Her story is full of lies, inasmuch as she is not a "virgin widow," while Christ, the "Prince," is not "hid"; she is unaware that he has risen from the dead.

3. Literally, "without law." Sans foy means "without faith"; Sans joy, "without joy." *The Faerie Queene* is full of characters who come in sets—opposing principles or double and triple incarnations of the same principle. Una and this lady (falsely named Fidessa, or "faith"), for example, are in opposition;

the three Saracens form a triad of degenerative qualities that Holiness must defeat. For Holiness, even untried, to defeat atheism ("without faith") was comparatively easy.

4. I.e., it is.

5. Proverbial: "what's dear is rare." Here, "coyness creates unsatisfied desire." Redcrosse is unaware of the falsehoods in the lady's story—as England was seduced again to the false church during the reign of Mary.

250 The fearefull Shepheard often there aghast
       Under them never sat, ne wont there sound
His mery oaten pipe, but shund th' unlucky ground.

29

But this good knight soone as he them can spie,
       For the coole shade him thither hastly got:
255   For golden Phoebus now ymounted hie,
       From fiery wheeles of his faire chariot
       Hurléd his beame so scorching cruell hot,
       That living creature mote it not abide;
       And his new Lady it enduréd not.
260   There they alight, in hope themselves to hide
From the fierce heat, and rest their weary limbs a tide.°   time

30

Faire seemely pleasaunce each to other makes,
       With goodly purposes there as they sit:
       And in his falséd fancy he her takes
265   To be the fairest wight that livéd yit;
       Which to expresse, he bends his gentle wit,
       And thinking of those braunches greene to frame
       A girlond for her dainty forehead fit,
       He pluckt a bough; out of whose rift there came
270 Small drops of gory bloud, that trickled downe the same.

31

Therewith a piteous yelling voyce was heard,
       Crying, "O spare with guilty hands to teare
       My tender sides in this rough rynd embard,°   imprisoned
       But fly, ah fly far hence away, for feare
275   Least to you hap, that happened to me heare,
       And to this wretched Lady, my deare love,
       O too deare love, love bought with death too deare."
       Astond he stood, and up his haire did hove°   heave, raise
And with that suddein horror could no member move.

32

280 At last whenas the dreadfull passion
       Was overpast, and manhood well awake,
       Yet musing at the straunge occasion,
       And doubting much his sence, he thus bespake;
       "What voyce of damnéd Ghost from Limbo[6] lake,
285   Or guilefull spright wandring in empty aire,
       Both which fraile men do oftentimes mistake,°   mislead
       Sends to my doubtfull eares these speaches rare,
And ruefull plaints, me bidding guiltlesse bloud to spare?"

33

Then groning deepe, "Nor damned Ghost," quoth he,
290   "Nor guilefull sprite to thee these wordes doth speake,
       But once a man Fradubio,° now a tree,   Doubt
       Wretched man, wretched tree; whose nature weake,

6. The abode of lost spirits.

A cruell witch her curséd will to wreake,
Hath thus transformed, and plast in open plaines,
295 Where Boreas° doth blow full bitter bleake,   *the North Wind*
And scorching Sunne does dry my secret vaines:
For though a tree I seeme, yet cold and heat me paines."

34

"Say on Fradubio then, or° man, or tree,"   *whether*
Quoth then the knight, "by whose mischievous arts
300 Art thou misshapéd thus, as now I see?
He oft finds med'cine, who his griefe imparts;
But double griefs afflict concealing harts,
As raging flames who striveth to suppresse."
"The author then," said he, "of all my smarts,
305 Is one Duessa[7] a false sorceresse,
That many errant° knights hath brought to wretchednesse. *wandering*

35

"In prime of youthly yeares, when corage hot
The fire of love and joy of chevalree
First kindled in my brest, it was my lot
310 To love this gentle Lady, whom ye see,
Now not a Lady, but a seeming tree;
With whom as once I rode accompanyde,
Me chauncéd of a knight encountred bee,
That had a like faire Lady by his syde,
315 Like a faire Lady, but did fowle Duessa hyde.

36

"Whose forgéd beauty he did take in hand,[8]
All other Dames to have exceeded farre;
I in defence of mine did likewise stand,
Mine, that did then shine as the Morning starre:
320 So both to battell fierce arraungéd arre,
In which his harder fortune was to fall
Under my speare: such is the dye° of warre: *hazard*
His Lady left as a prise martiall,[9]
Did yield her comely person, to be at my call.

37

325 "So doubly loved of Ladies unlike faire,
Th' one seeming such, the other such indeede,
One day in doubt I cast for to compare,
Whether° in beauties glorie did exceede;   *which one (of two)*
A Rosy girlond was the victors meede:°   *reward*
330 Both seemde to win, and both seemde won to bee,
So hard the discord was to be agreede.
Fraelissa° was as faire, as faire mote bee,   *Frailty*
And ever false Duessa seemde as faire as shee.

38

"The wicked witch now seeing all this while
335 The doubtfull ballaunce equally to sway,

7. Duessa means "two," of double nature.
8. He maintained.
9. Spoil of battle.

What not by right, she cast to win by guile,
And by her hellish science raisd streight way
A foggy mist, that overcast the day,
And a dull blast, that breathing on her face,
340 Dimmed her former beauties shining ray,
And with foule ugly forme did her disgrace:
Then was she faire alone, when none was faire in place.[1]

39

"Then cride she out, 'Fye, fye, deforméd wight,
Whose borrowed beautie now appeareth plaine
345 To have before bewitchéd all mens sight;
O leave her soone, or let her soone be slaine.'
Her lothly visage viewing with disdaine,
Eftsoones I thought her such, as she me told,
And would have kild her; but with faignéd paine,
350 The false witch did my wrathfull hand withhold;
So left her, where she now is turnd to tréen mould.[2]

40

"Thens forth I tooke Duessa for my Dame,
And in the witch unweeting° joyd long time,   *unknowingly*
Ne ever wist, but that she was the same,
355 Till on a day (that day is every Prime,[3]
When Witches wont do penance for their crime)
I chaunst to see her in her proper hew,
Bathing her selfe in origane and thyme:[4]
A filthy foule old woman I did vew,
360 That ever to have toucht her, I did deadly rew.

41

"Her neather partes misshapen, monstruous,
Were hidd in water, that I could not see,
But they did seeme more foule and hideous,
Then womans shape man would beleeve to bee.
365 Thens forth from her most beastly companie
I gan refraine, in minde to slip away,
Soone as appeard safe opportunitie:
For danger great, if not assured decay°   *destruction*
I saw before mine eyes, if I were knowne to stray.

42

370 "The divelish hag by chaunges of my cheare°   *countenance*
Perceived my thought, and drownd in sleepie night,
With wicked herbes and ointments did besmeare
My bodie all, through charmes and magicke might,
That all my senses were bereavéd quight:
375 Then brought she me into this desert waste,
And by my wretched lovers side me pight,°   *pitched*
Where now enclosd in wooden wals full faste,
Banisht from living wights, our wearie dayes we waste."

1. Perhaps, "when nobody else was fair."
2. The form of a tree.
3. The first appearance of the new moon.
4. Two kinds of herbs; they were associated, in classical tradition, with witches like Scylla, Circe, and Medea.

43

"But how long time," said then the Elfin knight,
380   "Are you in this misforméd house to dwell?"
   "We may not chaunge," quoth he, "this evil plight,
   Till we be bathéd in a living well;
   That is the terme prescribéd by the spell."
   "O how," said he, "mote I that well out find,
385   That may restore you to your wonted well?"°   *well-being*
   "Time and suffiséd fates to former kynd
Shall us restore, none else from hence may us unbynd."[5]

44

The false Duessa, now Fidessa hight,°   *called*
   Heard how in vaine Fradubio did lament,
390   And knew well all was true. But the good knight
   Full of sad feare and ghastly dreriment,°   *gloom*
   When all this speech the living tree had spent,
   The bleeding bough did thrust into the ground,
   That from the bloud he might be innocent,
395   And with fresh clay did close the wooden wound:
Then turning to his Lady, dead with feare her found.

45

Her seeming dead he found with feignéd feare,
   As all unweeting of that well she knew,[6]
   And paynd himselfe with busie care to reare
400   Her out of carelesse° swowne. Her eylids blew   *unconscious*
   And dimméd sight with pale and deadly hew.
   At last she up gan lift: with trembling cheare
   Her up he tooke, too simple and too trew,
   And oft her kist. At length all passéd feare,[7]
405 He set her on her steede, and forward forth did beare.

Canto III

   Forsaken Truth long seekes her love,
     And makes the Lyon mylde,
   Marres° blind Devotions mart,° and fals   *spoils / business*
     In hand of leachour vylde.

1

Nought is there under heav'ns wide hollownesse,
   That moves more deare compassion of mind,

---

5. The tale of a man imprisoned in a tree is paralleled by Virgil's *Aeneid* III. 27–42 and Ariosto's *Orlando Furioso* VI.26–53. His hesitation between Frae-lissa and Duessa parallels Redcrosse's own spiritual state between Una and Duessa (the real name of "Fidessa," as line 388 casually informs us). The very name "Duessa" (two) reveals her falsity next to Una ("one"). Note that Fra-dubio ("father doubt") cannot warn Redcrosse against Duessa, who is present at the whole recital: doubt is not; per-haps, a trustworthy help to Holiness. Doubt and frailty can only be helped by baptism (lines 381–82).
6. I.e., pretending ignorance of what she knew well.
7. I.e., having passed all fear.

Then beautie brought t'unworthy° wretchednesse   *undeserved*
Through envies snares or fortunes freakes unkind:
5   I, whether lately through her brightnesse blind,
Or through alleageance and fast fealtie,
Which I do owe unto all woman kind,
Feele my heart perst° with so great agonie,   *pierced*
When such I see, that all for pittie I could die.

2

10 And now it is empassionéd so deepe,
For fairest Unas sake, of whom I sing,
That my fraile eyes these lines with teares do steepe,
To thinke how she through guilefull handeling,
Though true as touch,° though daughter of a king,   *touchstone*
15 Though faire as ever living wight was faire,
Though nor in word nor deede ill meriting,
Is from her knight divorcéd in despaire
And her due loves derived° to that vile witches share.   *diverted*

3

Yet she most faithfull Ladie all this while
20 Forsaken, wofull, solitarie mayd
Farre from all peoples prease,° as in exile,   *press, crowd*
In wildernesse and wastfull deserts strayd,
To seeke her knight; who subtilly betrayd
Through that late vision, which th' Enchaunter wrought,
25 Had her abandond. She of nought affrayd,
Through woods and wastnesse wide him daily sought;
Yet wishéd tydings none of him unto her brought.

4

One day nigh wearie of the yrkesome way,
From her unhastie beast she did alight,
30 And on the grasse her daintie limbes did lay
In secret shadow,° farre from all mens sight: *shade*
From her faire head her fillet she undight,[8]
And laid her stole aside. Her angels face
As the great eye of heaven shynéd bright,
35 And made a sunshine in the shadie place;
Did never mortall eye behold such heavenly grace.

5

It fortunéd out of the thickest wood
A ramping Lyon rushéd suddainly,
Hunting full greedie after salvage blood;[9]
40 Soone as the royall virgin he did spy,
With gaping mouth at her ran greedily,
To have attonce devoured her tender corse:
But to the pray when as he drew more ny,
His bloudie rage asswagéd with remorse,
45 And with the sight amazd, forgat his furious forse.

8. She took off her headband.   9. Wild game.

6

In stead thereof he kist her wearie feet,
    And lickt her lilly hands with fawning tong,
    As[1] he her wrongéd innocence did weet.°   *understand*
    O how can beautie maister the most strong,
50   And simple truth subdue avenging wrong?
    Whose yeelded pride and proud submission,
    Still dreading death, when she had markéd long,
    Her hart gan melt in great compassion,
And drizling teares did shed for pure affection.

7

55 "The Lyon Lord of everie beast in field,"
    Quoth she, "his princely puissance° doth abate   *power*
    And mightie proud to humble weake does yield,
    Forgetfull of the hungry rage, which late
    Him prickt, in pittie of my sad estate:°   *condition*
60   But he my Lyon, and my noble Lord,
    How does he find in cruell hart to hate
    Her that him loved, and ever most adord,
As the God of my life? why hath he me abhord?"

8

Redounding teares did choke th'end of her plaint,
65   Which softly ecchoed from the neighbour wood;
    And sad to see her sorrowfull constraint°   *affliction*
    The kingly beast upon her gazing stood;
    With pittie calmd, downe fell his angry mood.
    At last in close hart shutting up her paine,
70   Arose the virgin borne of heavenly brood,°   *parentage*
    And to her snowy Palfrey got againe,
To seeke her strayéd Champion, if she might attaine.°   *overtake*

9

The Lyon would not leave her desolate,
    But with her went along, as a strong gard
75   Of her chast person, and a faithfull mate
    Of her sad troubles and misfortunes hard:
    Still when she slept, he kept both watch and ward,
    And when she wakt, he waited diligent,
    With humble service to her will prepard:
80   From her faire eyes he tooke commaundement,
And ever by her lookes conceivéd her intent.[2]

10

Long she thus traveiléd through deserts wyde,
    By which she thought her wandring knight shold pas,
    Yet never shew of living wight espyde;
85   Till that at length she found the troden gras,

---

1. As though.
2. Whereas Redcrosse, the man, has confusedly abandoned truth, the lion, king of beasts, an animal under nature's law, follows truth instinctively. Lions revere the heroine in the romance *Sir Bevis of Hamptoun* and accompany the heroes of other medieval romances; they have long been associated with the British crown.

In which the tract° of peoples footing was,　　　　*track*
　　Under the steepe foot of a mountaine hore;°　　*gray*
　　The same she followes, till at last she has
　　A damzell spyde slow footing her before,
90 That on her shoulders sad° a pot of water bore.　*heavy*

11

To whom approching she to her gan call,
　　To weet, if dwelling place were nigh at hand;
　　But the rude° wench her answered nought at all,　*ignorant*
　　She could not heare, nor speake, nor understand;
95 Till seeing by her side the Lyon stand,
　　With suddaine feare her pitcher downe she threw,
　　And fled away: for never in that land
　　Face of faire Ladie she before did vew,
And that dread Lyons looke her cast in deadly° hew.　*deathlike*

12

00 Full fast she fled, ne ever lookt behynd,
　　As if her life upon the wager lay,
　　And home she came, whereas her mother blynd
　　Sate in eternall night: nought could she say,
　　But suddaine catching hold, did her dismay
05 With quaking hands, and other signes of feare:
　　Who full of ghastly fright and cold affray,
　　Gan shut the dore. By this arrivéd there
Dame Una, wearie Dame, and entrance did requere.°　*request*

13

　　Which when none yeelded, her unruly Page
10 With his rude clawes the wicket° open rent,　　*door*
　　And let her in; where of his cruell rage
　　Nigh dead with feare, and faint astonishment,
　　She found them both in darkesome corner pent;°　*huddled*
　　Where that old woman day and night did pray
15 Upon her beades devoutly penitent;
　　Nine hundred *Pater nosters* every day,
And thrise nine hundred *Aves* she was wont to say.[3]

14

And to augment her painefull pennance more,
　　Thrise every weeke in ashes she did sit,
20 And next her wrinkled skin rough sackcloth wore,
　　And thrise three times did fast from any bit:°　*food*
　　But now for feare her beads she did forget.
　　Whose needlesse dread for to remove away,
　　Faire Una framéd words and count'nance fit:
25 Which hardly doen, at length she gan them pray,
That in their cotage small, that night she rest her may.

3. "Them both" will be named in line 157. The old lady's name, Corceca, means "blind devotion." The (obviously Catholic) prayers that the two mouth are motivated by fear, not faith. Her daughter's name, "Abessa," suggests the monastic orders (i.e., "abbess") and (from *ab esse*, "non-being," "withdrawal") that she is superstition. Her timorous reaction to the Lyon was typically excessive, and her pitcher of water was perhaps emblematic of her fickle state.

15

    The day is spent, and commeth drowsie night,
      When every creature shrowded is in sleepe;
      Sad Una downe her laies in wearie plight,
130   And at her feet the Lyon watch doth keepe:
      In stead of rest, she does lament, and weepe
      For the late losse of her deare lovéd knight,
      And sighes, and grones, and evermore does steepe
      Her tender brest in bitter teares all night,
135 All night she thinks too long, and often lookes for light.

16

    Now when Aldeboran was mounted hie
    Above the shynie Cassiopeias chaire,[4]
      And all in deadly sleepe did drownéd lie,
      One knockéd at the dore, and in would fare;
140   He knockéd fast,° and often curst, and sware,   *insistently*
      That readie entrance was not at his call:
      For on his backe a heavy load he bare
      Of nightly stelths and pillage severall,
    Which he had got abroad by purchase° criminall.   *acquisition*

17

145 He was to weete[5] a stout and sturdie thiefe,
      Wont to robbe Churches of their ornaments,
      And poore mens boxes[6] of their due reliefe,
      Which given was to them for good intents;
      The holy Saints of their rich vestiments
150   He did disrobe, when all men carelesse slept,
      And spoild the Priests of their habiliments,°   *vestments*
      Whiles none the holy things in safety kept;
    Then he by cunning sleights in at the window crept.

18

    And all that he by right or wrong could find,
155   Unto this house he brought, and did bestow
      Upon the daughter of this woman blind,
      Abessa daughter of Corceca slow,
      With whom he whoredome usd, that few did know,
      And fed her fat with feast of offerings,
160   And plentie, which in all the land did grow;
      Ne sparéd he to give her gold and rings:
    And now he to her brought part of his stolen things.

19

    Thus long the dore with rage and threats he bet,°   *beat*
      Yet of those fearefull women none durst rize,
165   The Lyon frayéd° them, him in to let: *terrify*
      He would no longer stay him to advize,
      But open breakes the dore in furious wize,

4. Aldebaran, in the constellation Taurus, mounts over the constellation Cassiopeia.
5. In fact.
6. A box for alms for the poor, especially one placed near the door of a church.

And entring is; when that disdainfull beast
    Encountring fierce, him suddaine doth surprize,
70   And seizing° cruell clawes on trembling brest,   *fastening*
Under his Lordly foot him proudly hath supprest.[7]

20

Him booteth not resist,[8] nor succour call,
    His bleeding hart is in the vengers hand,
    Who streight him rent in thousand peeces small,
75   And quite dismembred hath: the thirstie land
    Drunke up his life; his corse left on the strand.°   *ground*
    His fearefull friends weare out the wofull night,
    Ne dare to weepe, nor seeme to understand
    The heavie hap,° which on them is alight,   *lot*
80 Affraid, least to themselves the like mishappen might.

21

Now when broad day the world discovered° has,   *revealed*
    Up Una rose, up rose the Lyon eke,
    And on their former journey forward pas,
    In wayes unknowne, her wandring knight to seeke,
85   With paines farre passing that long wandring Greeke,
    That for his love refuséd deitie;[9]
    Such were the labours of this Lady meeke,
    Still seeking him, that from her still did flie,
Then furthest from her hope, when most she weenéd nie.[1]

22

90 Soone as she parted thence, the fearefull twaine,
    That blind old woman and her daughter deare
    Came forth, and finding Kirkrapine there slaine,
    For anguish great they gan to rend their heare,
    And beat their brests, and naked flesh to teare.
95   And when they both had wept and wayld their fill,
    Then forth they ranne like two amazéd deare,
    Halfe mad through malice, and revenging will,[2]
To follow her, that was the causer of their ill.

23

Whom overtaking, they gan loudly bray,
100 With hollow howling, and lamenting cry,
    Shamefully at her rayling all the way,
    And her accusing of dishonesty,°   *unchastity*
    That was the flowre of faith and chastity;
    And still amidst her rayling, she[3] did pray,
105 That plagues, and mischiefs, and long misery

---

7. The thief is named Kirkrapine (in line 192), which means "church robbery." That he brings illgotten gains to the house of superstition may represent the accumulation of the monastic estates and their sheltering under the privileges of the Roman church. By this interpretation, the lion becomes Henry VIII, who expropriated the monasteries.
8. It does no good to resist.
9. Odysseus, who renounced immortality and the love of the nymph Calypso for his wife Penelope.
1. Believed near.
2. Desire of revenge.
3. I.e., Corceca.

Might fall on her, and follow all the way,
And that in endlesse error° she might ever stray.   *wandering*

24

But when she saw her prayers nought prevaile,
  She backe returnéd with some labour lost;
210 And in the way as she did weepe and waile,
    A knight her met in mighty armes embost,°   *encased*
    Yet knight was not for all his bragging bost,
    But subtill Archimag, that Una sought
    By traynes° into new troubles to have tost: *tricks*
215 Of that old woman tydings he besought,
If that of such a Ladie she could tellen ought.

25

Therewith she gan her passion to renew,
  And cry, and curse, and raile, and rend her heare,
  Saying, that harlot she too lately knew,
220 That causd her shed so many a bitter teare,
    And so forth told the story of her feare:
    Much seeméd he to mone her haplesse chaunce,
    And after for that Ladie did inquere;
    Which being taught, he forward gan advaunce
225 His fair enchaunted steed, and eke his charméd launce.

26

Ere long he came, where Una traveild slow,
  And that wilde Champion wayting° her besyde: *attending*
  Whom seeing such, for dread he durst not show
  Himselfe too nigh at hand, but turnéd wyde
230 Unto an hill; from whence when she him spyde,
    By his like seeming shield, her knight by name
    She weend it was, and towards him gan ryde:
    Approching nigh, she wist° it was the same,   *believed*
And with faire fearefull humblesse towards him shee came.

27

235 And weeping said, "Ah my long lackéd Lord,
  Where have ye bene thus long out of my sight?
  Much fearéd I to have bene quite abhord,
  Or ought° have done, that ye displeasen might,   *aught*
  That should as death unto my deare hart light:[4]
240 For since mine eye your joyous sight did mis,
    My chearefull day is turnd to chearelesse night,
    And eke my night of death the shadow is;
But welcome now my light, and shining lampe of blis."

28

He thereto meeting[5] said, "My dearest Dame,
245 Farre be it from your thought, and fro my will,
  To thinke that knighthood I so much should shame,
  As you to leave, that have me lovéd still,
  And chose in Faery court of meere° goodwill,   *pure*
  Where noblest knights were to be found on earth:

---

4. I.e., be as a death-blow to my sad   5. Answering in like manner.
heart.

The earth shall sooner leave her kindly° skill   *natural*
  To bring forth fruit, and make eternall derth,°   *desert*
Then I leave you, my liefe, yborne of heavenly berth.

29

"And sooth to say, why I left you so long,
  Was for to seeke adventure in strange place,
  Where Archimago said a felon strong
  To many knights did daily worke disgrace;
  But knight he now shall never more deface:
Good cause of mine excuse; that mote° ye please   *may*
Well to accept, and evermore embrace
My faithfull service, that by land and seas
Have vowd you to defend, now then your plaint appease."

30

His lovely° words her seemd due recompence   *loving*
  Of all her passéd paines: one loving howre
  For many yeares of sorrow can dispence:°   *make amends*
  A dram of sweet is worth a pound of sowre:
  She has forgot, how many a wofull stowre°   *trouble*
For him she late endured; she speakes no more
Of past: true is, that true love hath no powre
To looken backe; his eyes be fixt before.
Before her stands her knight, for whom she toyld so sore.

31

Much like, as when the beaten marinere,
  That long hath wandred in the Ocean wide,
  Oft soust° in swelling Tethys[6] saltish teare,   *soaked*
  And long time having tand his tawney hide
  With blustring breath of heaven, that none can bide,
  And scorching flames of fierce Orions hound,[7]
Soone as the port from farre he has espide,
His chearefull whistle merrily doth sound,
And Nereus crownes with cups;[8] his mates him pledg° around.   *toast*

32

Such joy made Una, when her knight she found;
  And eke th'enchaunter joyous seemd no lesse,
  Then the glad marchant, that does vew from ground.
  His ship farre come from watrie wildernesse,
  He hurles out vowes, and Neptune oft doth blesse:
  So forth they past, and all the way they spent
Discoursing of her dreadfull late distresse,
In which he askt her, what the Lyon ment:
Who told her all that fell° in journey as she went.   *befell*

33

They had not ridden farre, when they might see
  One pricking towards them with hastie heat,

---

6. The wife of Ocean; here, Ocean.
7. Sirius, the dog star, symbolizing hot weather (the "dog days").

8. Nereus is god of the Mediterranean, to whom the mariner in gratitude makes libations.

Full strongly armd, and on a courser free,
That through his fiercenesse fomed all with sweat,
And the sharpe yron° did for anger eat,   bit
When his hot ryder spurd his chaufféd° side;   heated
295   His looke was sterne, and seeméd still to threat
Cruell revenge, which he in hart did hyde,
And on his shield Sans loy⁹ in bloudie lines was dyde.

34

When nigh he drew unto this gentle payre
And saw the Red-crosse, which the knight did beare,
300   He burnt in fire, and gan eftsoones prepare
Himselfe to battell with his couchéd speare.
Loth was that other, and did faint through feare,
To taste th'untryed dint of deadly steele;
But yet his Lady did so well him cheare,
305   That hope of new good hap he gan to feele;
So bent° his speare, and spurnd his horse with yron heele.   lowered

35

But that proud Paynim° forward came so fierce,   pagan
And full of wrath, that with his sharp-head speare
Through vainely crosséd shield¹ he quite did pierce,
310   And had his staggering steede not shrunke for feare,
Through shield and bodie eke he should him beare:°   thrust
Yet so great was the puissance of his push,
That from his saddle quite he did him beare:
He tombling rudely downe to ground did rush,
315   And from his goréd wound a well of bloud did gush.²

36

Dismounting lightly from his loftie steed,
He to him lept, in mind to reave° his life,   take
And proudly said, "Lo there the worthie meed
Of him, that slew Sans foy with bloudie knife;
320   Henceforth his ghost freed from repining strife,
In peace may passen over Lethe³ lake,
When mourning altars purgd° with enemies life,   cleansed
The blacke infernall Furies⁴ doen aslake:°   appease
Life from Sans foy thou tookst, Sans loy shall from thee take."

37

325   Therewith in haste his helmet gan unlace,
Till Una cride, "O hold that heavie hand,
Deare Sir, what ever that thou be in place:⁵
Enough is, that thy foe doth vanquisht stand
Now at thy mercy: Mercie not withstand:

---

9. The name means "without law." Law here is not, of course, merely state law, but the law of the cosmos, of nature, of civil government, and of man—the law that holds all life, both above the earth and on it, together. Hence "Sans loy" stands for the loss of all order, or chaos.
1. The cross on Archimago's shield was false and did not give him the protection the Redcrosse knight received in his fight with Sans foy; see I.ii.18.
2. This is true poetic justice: lawlessness defeats the devil.
3. A river in Hades whose water when drunk caused forgetfulness.
4. Spirits of discord and revenge.
5. Whoever you are.

30 For he is one the truest knight alive,
    Though conquered now he lie on lowly land,
    And whilest him fortune favourd, faire did thrive
In bloudie field: therefore of life him not deprive."

38

Her piteous words might not abate his rage,
35   But rudely rending up his helmet, would
    Have slaine him straight: but when he sees his age,
    And hoarie head of Archimago old,
    His hastie hand he doth amazéd hold,
    And halfe ashaméd, wondred at the sight:
40   For the old man well knew he, though untold,
    In charmes and magicke to have wondrous might,
Ne ever wont in field, ne in round lists[6] to fight.

39

And said, "Why Archimago, lucklesse syre,
    What doe I see? what hard mishap is this,
45   That hath thee hither brought to taste mine yre?
    Or thine the fault, or mine the error is,
    In stead of foe to wound my friend amis?"
    He answered nought, but in a traunce still lay,
    And on those guilefull dazéd eyes of his
50 The cloud of death did sit. Which doen away,[7]
He left him lying so, ne would no lenger stay.

40

But to the virgin comes, who all this while
    Amaséd stands, her selfe so mockt° to see   *deceived*
    By him, who has the guerdon° of his guile,   *reward*
55   For so misfeigning her true knight to bee:
    Yet is she now in more perplexitie,
    Left in the hand of that same Paynim bold,
    From whom her booteth not at all to flie;
    Who by her cleanly garment catching hold,
60 Her from her Palfrey pluckt, her visage to behold.

41

But her fierce servant full of kingly awe
    And high disdaine, whenas his soveraine Dame
    So rudely handled by her foe he sawe,
    With gaping jawes full greedy at him came,
65   And ramping on his shield, did weene° the same   *intend*
    Have reft away with his sharpe rending clawes
    But he was stout, and lust did now inflame
    His corage more, that from his griping pawes
He hath his shield redeemed, and foorth his swerd he drawes.

42

70 O then too weake and feeble was the forse
    Of salvage beast, his puissance to withstand:
    For he was strong, and of so mightie corse,

6. Enclosures for fighting tournaments.   7. When he recovered from the swoon.

As ever wielded speare in warlike hand,
And feates of armes did wisely understand.
375   Eftsoones he perced through his chaufed chest
With thrilling° point of deadly yron brand,°   *penetrating / sword*
And launcht° his Lordly hart: with death opprest   *pierced*
He roared aloud, whiles life forsooke his stubborne brest.[8]

43

Who now is left to keepe the forlorne maid
380   From raging spoile of lawlesse victors will?
Her faithfull gard removed, her hope dismaid,
Her selfe a yeelded pray to save or spill.°   *destroy*
He now Lord of the field, his pride to fill,
With foule reproches, and disdainfull spight
385   Her vildly entertaines, and will or nill,
Beares her away upon his courser light:
Her prayers nought prevaile; his rage is more of might.

44

And all the way, with great lamenting paine,
And piteous plaints she filleth his dull° eares,   *deaf*
390   That stony hart could riven have in twaine,
And all the way she wets with flowing teares:
But he enraged with rancor, nothing heares.
Her servile beast yet would not leave her so,
But followes her farre off, ne ought he feares,
395   To be partaker of her wandring woe,
More mild in beastly kind,° then that her beastly foe.   *nature*

Canto IV

*To sinfull house of Pride, Duessa
guides the faithfull knight,
Where brothers death to wreak° Sansjoy   avenge
doth chalenge him to fight.*

1

Young knight, what ever that dost armes professe,
And through long labours huntest after fame,
Beware of fraud, beware of ficklenesse,
In choice, and change of thy deare lovéd Dame,
5   Least thou of her beleeve too lightly blame,
And rash misweening doe thy hart remove:
For unto knight there is no greater shame,
Then lightnesse and inconstancie in love;
That doth this Redcrosse knights ensample° plainly prove.   *example*

2

10 Who after that he had faire Una lorne,°   *lost*
Through light misdeeming of her loialtie,   *misjudging*
And false Duessa in her sted had borne,

8. Nature's law is, perhaps, defenseless against human lawlessness. Sans loy's killing of the lion might also be taken as the momentary triumph of Catholicism under Mary Tudor.

Called Fidess', and so supposd to bee;
Long with her traveild, till at last they see
15 A goodly building, bravely garnishéd,°   *adorned*
The house of mightie Prince it seemd to bee:
And towards it a broad high way[9] that led,
All bare through peoples feet, which thither traveiléd.

3

Great troupes of people traveild thitherward
20 Both day and night, of each degree and place,°   *rank*
But few returnéd, having scapéd hard,
With balefull beggerie, or foule disgrace,
Which ever after in most wretched case,
Like loathsome lazars,° by the hedges lay.   *lepers*
25 Thither Duessa bad him bend his pace:
For she is wearie of the toilesome way,
And also nigh consuméd is the lingring day.

4

A stately Pallace built of squaréd bricke,
Which cunningly was without morter laid,
30 Whose wals were high, but nothing strong, nor thick,
And golden foile° all over them displaid,   *thin layer*
That purest skye with brightnesse they dismaid°:   *outdid*
High lifted up were many loftie towres,
And goodly galleries farre over laid,[1]
35 Full of faire windowes, and delightfull bowres;
And on the top a Diall told the timely howres.[2]

5

It was a goodly heape° for to behould,   *building*
And spake the praises of the workmans wit;
But full great pittie, that so faire a mould°   *structure*
40 Did on so weake foundation ever sit:
For on a sandie hill, that still did flit,°   *give way*
And fall away, it mounted was full hie,
That every breath of heaven shakéd it:
And all the hinder parts, that few could spie,
45 Were ruinous and old, but painted cunningly.

6

Arrivéd there they passéd in forth right;
For still to all the gates stood open wide,
Yet charge of them was to a Porter hight°   *committed*
Cald Malvenù,[3] who entrance none denide:
50 Thence to the hall, which was on every side
With rich array and costly arras dight:[4]
Infinite sorts of people did abide

9. "Broad is the way that leadeth to destruction" (Matthew vii.13).
1. Placed above.
2. The clock ("Diall") is illustrative of the power of time over the life of this world, as it is lived in the House of Pride. This proud elegant castle is reminiscent of Alcina's palace in *Orlando Furioso* VI.
3. The name means "unwelcome." In courtly-love allegories, the porter is often called "Bienvenu" or "Bel-accueil" ("welcome").
4. Decorated with costly wall hangings.

There waiting long, to win the wishéd sight
Of her, that was the Lady of that Pallace bright.

7

55 By them they passe, all gazing on them round,
  And to the Presence° mount; whose glorious vew   *reception hall*
  Their frayle amazéd senses did confound:
  In living Princes court none ever knew
  Such endlesse richesse, and so sumptuous shew;
60   Ne Persia selfe, the nourse of pompous pride
  Like ever saw. And there a noble crew
  Of Lordes and Ladies stood on every side,
Which with their presence faire, the place much beautifide.

8

High above all a cloth of State[5] was spred,
65   And a rich throne, as bright as sunny day,
  On which there sate most brave embellishéd[6]
  With royall robes and gorgeous array,
  A mayden Queene, that shone as Titans° ray,   *the sun's*
  In glistring gold, and peerelesse pretious stone:
70   Yet her bright blazing beautie did assay°   *attempt*
  To dim the brightnesse of her glorious throne,
As envying her selfe, that too exceeding shone.

9

Exceeding shone, like Phoebus fairest childe,
  That did presume his fathers firie wayne,°   *chariot*
75 And flaming mouthes of steedes unwonted wilde
  Through highest heaven with weaker° hand to rayne;   *too weak*
  Proud of such glory and advancement vaine,
  While flashing beames do daze his feeble eyen,
  He leaves the welkin° way most beaten plaine,   *skyey*
80 And rapt° with whirling wheeles, inflames the skyen,   *carried away*
With fire not made to burne, but fairely for to shyne.[7]

10

So proud she shynéd in her Princely state,°   *throne*
  Looking to heaven; for earth she did disdayne,
  And sitting high; for lowly° she did hate: *lowliness*
85 Lo underneath her scornefull feete, was layne
  A dreadfull Dragon with an hideous trayne,°   *tail*
  And in her hand she held a mirrhour bright,[8]
  Wherein her face she often vewéd fayne,
  And in her selfe-loved semblance tooke delight;
90 For she was wondrous faire, as any living wight.

---

5. Canopy.
6. Handsomely clad.
7. Phaëthon tried to drive the chariot of Phoebus, his father, but set the skies on fire and fell, as Lucifer (Satan) fell from heaven. Lucifera (Pride) shines like Phaëthon (line 82), which suggests a similar fate. Although her House does not fall, it is seen first as glorious, then for what it really is.
8. Pride, and figures associated with her in Renaissance literature and art, often hold a mirror, emblematic of self-love.

11

Of griesly Pluto she the daughter was,
    And sad Proserpina the Queene of hell;
    Yet did she thinke her pearelesse worth to pas
    That parentage, with pride so did she swell,
95 And thundring Jove, that high in heaven doth dwell,
    And wield° the world, she clayméd for her syre,   *govern*
    Or if that any else did Jove excell:
    For to the highest she did still aspyre,
Or if ought higher were then that, did it desyre.

12

And proud Lucifera men did her call,
    That made her selfe a Queene, and crownd to be,
    Yet rightfull kingdome she had none at all,
    Ne heritage of native soveraintie,
    But did usurpe with wrong and tyrannie
05 Upon the scepter, which she now did hold:
    Ne ruld her Realmes with lawes, but pollicie,°   *conspiracy*
    And strong advizement of six wisards old,
That with their counsels bad her kingdome did uphold.

13

Soone as the Elfin knight in presence came,
    And false Duessa seeming Lady faire,
    A gentle Husher,° Vanitie by name   *usher*
    Made rowme, and passage for them did prepaire:
    So goodly brought them to the lowest staire
15 Of her high throne, where they on humble knee
    Making obeyssance, did the cause declare,
    Why they were come, her royall state to see,
To prove° the wide report of her great Majestee.   *verify*

14

With loftie eyes, halfe loth to looke so low,
    She thankéd them in her disdainefull wise,
20 Ne other grace vouchsaféd them to show
    Of Princesse worthy, scarse them bad arise
    Her Lordes and Ladies all this while devise
    Themselves to setten forth to straungers sight:
    Some frounce° their curléd haire in courtly guise,   *frizzle*
25 Some prancke° their ruffes, and others trimly dight°   *display/adjust*
Their gay attire: each others greater pride does spight.

15

Goodly they all that knight do entertaine,
    Right glad with him to have increast their crew:
    But to Duess' each one himselfe did paine
    All kindnesse and faire courtesie to shew;
30 For in that court whylome° her well they knew: *formerly*
    Yet the stout Faerie mongst the middest° crowd   *thickest*
    Thought all their glorie vaine in knightly vew,
    And that great Princesse too exceeding prowd,
35 That to strange knight no better countenance allowd.

16

Suddein upriseth from her stately place
    The royall Dame, and for her coche doth call:

All hurtlen° forth, and she with Princely pace,   *rush*
As faire Aurora in her purple pall,°   *robe*
140 Out of the East the dawning day doth call:
So forth she comes: her brightnesse brode° doth blaze;   *abroad*
The heapes of people thronging in the hall,
Do ride° each other, upon her to gaze: *crowd*
Her glorious glitterand° light doth all mens eyes amaze.   *glittering*

17

145 So forth she comes, and to her coche does clyme,
Adornéd all with gold, and girlonds gay,
That seemd as fresh as Flora in her prime,
And strove to match, in royall rich array,
Great Junos golden chaire,° the which they say   *chariot*
150 The Gods stand gazing on, when she does ride
To Joves high house through heavens bras-pavéd way
Drawne of faire Pecocks, that excell in pride,
And full of Argus eyes their tailes dispredden wide.[9]

18

But this was drawne of six unequall beasts,
155 On which her six sage Counsellours did ryde,
Taught to obay their bestiall beheasts,
With like conditions to their kinds applyde:[1]
Of which the first, that all the rest did guyde,
Was sluggish Idlenesse the nourse of sin;
160 Upon a slouthfull Asse he chose to ryde,
Arayd in habit blacke, and amis° thin,   *hood, cape*
Like to an holy Monck, the service to begin.

19

And in his hand his Portesse° still he bare,   *breviary*
That much was worne, but therein little red,
165 For of devotion he had little care,
Still drownd in sleepe, and most of his dayes ded;
Scarse could he once uphold his heavie hed,
To looken, whether it were night or day:
May seeme the wayne° was very evill led,   *chariot*
170 When such an one had guiding of the way,
That knew not, whether right he went, or else astray.

20

From worldly cares himselfe he did esloyne,°   *withdraw*
And greatly shunnéd manly exercise,
From every worke he chalengéd essoyne,°   *excuse*
175 For contemplation sake: yet otherwise,
His life he led in lawlesse riotise;
By which he grew to grievous malady;
For in his lustlesse° limbs through evill guise°   *feeble/living*

9. The many-eyed monster Argus was set by Juno to watch Jupiter's love Io. When Mercury killed Argus, his eyes were put in the peacock's tail feathers.
1. The "sage Counsellours" do not guide their beasts, but are guided by them (i.e., by their bestial "kinds," or natures). This procession of the seven deadly sins—of which Pride is the queen, the chief sin—had a long tradition in medieval art and literature. And see Marlowe's *Dr. Faustus* (II.ii.111–64).

A shaking fever raignd continually:
Such one was Idlenesse, first of this company.

21

And by his side rode loathsome Gluttony,
  Deforméd creature, on a filthie swyne,
  His belly was up-blowne with luxury,
  And eke with fatnesse swollen were his eyne,
  And like a Crane his necke was long and fyne,°   thin
  With which he swallowd up excessive feast,
    For want whereof poore people oft did pyne;°   starve
  And all the way, most like a brutish beast,
He spuéd up his gorge, that all did him deteast.

22

In greene vine leaves he was right fitly clad;
  For other clothes he could not weare for heat,
  And on his head an yvie girland had,
  From under which fast trickled downe the sweat:
  Still as he rode, he somewhat° still did eat,   something
  And in his hand did beare a bouzing can,
  Of which he supt so oft, that on his seat
  His dronken corse he scarse upholden can,
In shape and life more like a monster, then a man.[2]

23

Unfit he was for any worldly thing,
  And eke unhable once° to stirre or go,°   at all/walk
  Not meet to be of counsell to a king,
  Whose mind in meat and drinke was drownéd so,
  That from his friend he seldome knew his fo:
  Full of diseases was his carcas blew,°   livid
  And a dry dropsie through his flesh did flow:
  Which by misdiet daily greater grew:
Such one was Gluttony, the second of that crew.

24

And next to him rode lustfull Lechery,
  Upon a bearded Goat, whose rugged haire,
  And whally° eyes (the signe of gelosy,)   greenish
  Was like the person selfe, whom he did beare:
  Who rough, and blacke, and filthy did appeare,
  Unseemely man to please faire Ladies eye;
  Yet he of Ladies oft was lovéd deare,
  When fairer faces were bid standenby:°   away
O who does know the bent of womens fantasy?

25

In a greene gowne he clothéd was full faire,
  Which underneath did hide his filthinesse,
  And in his hand a burning hart he bare,
  Full of vaine follies, and new fanglenesse:°   fickleness
  For he was false, and fraught with ficklenesse,

2. The drunken old Silenus of Greek mythology (see Ovid's *Metamorphoses*) is
echoed here.

And learnéd had to love with secret lookes,
And well could daunce, and sing with ruefulnesse,
And fortunes tell, and read in loving° bookes,   *erotic*
225 And thousand other wayes, to bait his fleshly hookes.

26

Inconstant man, that lovéd all he saw,
And lusted after all, that he did love,
Ne would his looser life be tide to law,
But joyd weake wemens hearts to tempt and prove°   *try*
230 If from their loyall loves he might then move;
Which lewdnesse fild him with reprochfull paine
Of that fowle evill,[3] which all men reprove,
That rots the marrow, and consumes the braine:
Such one was Lecherie, the third of all this traine.

27

235 And greedy Avarice by him did ride,
Upon a Camell loaden all with gold;
Two iron coffers hong on either side,
With precious mettall full, as they might hold,
And in his lap an heape of coine he told;°   *counted*
240 For of his wicked pelfe his God he made,
And unto hell him selfe for money sold;
Accursed usurie was all his trade,
And right and wrong ylike in equall ballaunce waide.[4]

28

His life was nigh unto deaths doore yplast,
245 And thread-bare cote, and cobled shoes he ware,
Ne scarse good morsell all his life did tast,
But both from backe and belly still did spare,
To fill his bags, and richesse to compare;°   *acquire*
Yet chylde ne kinsman living had he none
250 To leave them to; but thorough daily care
To get, and nightly feare to lose his owne,
He led a wretched life unto him selfe unknowne.

29

Most wretched wight, whom nothing might suffise,
Whose greedy lust did lacke in greatest store,°   *plenty*
255 Whose need had end, but no end covetise,
Whose wealth was want, whose plenty made him pore,
Who had enough, yet wishéd ever more;
A vile disease, and eke in foote and hand
A grievous gout tormented him full sore,
260 That well he could not touch, nor go, nor stand:
Such one was Avarice, the fourth of this faire band.

30

And next to him malicious Envie rode,
Upon a ravenous wolfe, and still did chaw

---

3. I.e., syphilis.   4. I.e., made no distinction between right
                                   and wrong.

Betweene his cankred teeth a venemous tode,
That all the poison ran about his chaw;°   *jaw*
But inwardly he chawéd his owne maw°   *entrails*
At neighbours wealth, that made him ever sad;
For death it was, when any good he saw,
And wept, that cause of weeping none he had,
But when he heard of harme, he wexéd wondrous glad.

31

All in a kirtle of discolourd say⁵
   He clothéd was, ypainted full of eyes;
   And in his bosome secretly there lay
   An hatefull Snake, the which his taile uptyes
   In many folds, and mortall sting implyes.°   *enfolds*
   Still as he rode, he gnasht his teeth, to see
   Those heapes of gold with griple° Covetyse,   *grasping*
   And grudgéd at the great felicitie
Of proud Lucifera, and his owne companie.

32

He hated all good workes and vertuous deeds,
   And him no lesse, that any like did use,
   And who with gracious bread the hungry feeds,
   His almes for want of faith he doth accuse;
   So every good to bad he doth abuse:°   *twist*
   And eke the verse of famous Poets witt
   He does backebite, and spightfull poison spues
   From leprous mouth on all, that ever writt:
Such one vile Envie was, that fifte in row did sitt.

33

And him beside rides fierce revenging Wrath,
   Upon a Lion, loth for to be led;
   And in his hand a burning brond° he hath,   *sword*
   The which he brandisheth about his hed;
   His eyes did hurle forth sparkles fiery red,
   And staréd sterne on all, that him beheld,
   As ashes pale of hew and seeming ded;
   And on his dagger still his hand he held,
Trembling through hasty rage, when choler° in him sweld.   *anger*

34

His ruffin° raiment all was staind with blood,   *disarranged*
   Which he had spilt, and all to rags yrent,°   *torn*
   Through unadviséd rashnesse woxen wood,⁶
   For of his hands he had no governement,°   *control*
   Ne cared for bloud in his avengement:
   But when the furious fit was overpast,
   His cruell facts° he often would repent;   *actions*
   Yet wilfull man he never would forecast,
How many mischieves should ensue his heedlesse hast.

---

5. Jacket of many-colored wool.   6. Grown insane.

35

Full many mischiefes follow cruell Wrath;
   Abhorréd bloudshed, and tumultuous strife,
   Unmanly° murder, and unthrifty scath,°   *inhuman/damage*
310   Bitter despight, with rancours rusty knife,
   And fretting griefe the enemy of life;
   All these, and many evils moe° haunt ire,   *more*
   The swelling Splene,° and Frenzy raging rife,   *malice*
   The shaking Palsey, and Saint Fraunces fire:[7]
315 Such one was Wrath, the last of this ungodly tire.°   *train*

36

And after all, upon the wagon beame
   Rode Sathan, with a smarting whip in hand,
   With which he forward lasht the laesie teme,
   So oft as Slowth still in the mire did stand.
320   Huge routs of people did about them band,
   Showting for joy, and still before their way
   A foggy mist had covered all the land;
   And underneath their feet, all scattered lay
Dead sculs and bones of men, whose life had gone astray.

37

325 So forth they marchen in this goodly sort,
   To take the solace° of the open aire,   *recreation*
   And in fresh flowring fields themselves to sport;
   Emongst the rest rode that false Lady faire,
   The fowle Duessa, next unto the chaire
330   Of proud Lucifera, as one of the traine:
   But that good knight would not so nigh repaire,°   *approach*
   Him selfe estraunging from their joyaunce vaine,
Whose fellowship seemd far unfit for warlike swaine.

38

So having solacéd themselves a space
335   With pleasaunce of the breathing° fields yfed,   *fragrant*
   They backe returnéd to the Princely Place;
   Whereas an errant knight in armes ycled,°   *clad*
   And heathnish shield, wherein with letters red
   Was writ Sans joy, they new arrivéd find:
340   Enflamed with fury and fiers hardy-hed,°   *audacity*
   He seemd in hart to harbour thoughts unkind,
And nourish bloudy vengeaunce in his bitter mind.[8]

39

Who when the shaméd shield[9] of slaine Sans foy
   He spied with that same Faery champions page,
345 Bewraying° him, that did of late destroy   *revealing*

7. St. Anthony's fire, erysipelas, or the
flaming itch; appropriate to Wrath.
8. Sans joy ("without joy") stands, not
simply for gloom or "no fun," but for
accidie, loss of heart. Redcrosse's high-
minded rejection of the seven deadly sins
(lines 331–33) does not protect him
from this darkness of the spirit.
9. With the arms reversed. See below,
line 369.

His eldest brother, burning all with rage
He to him leapt, and that same envious gage[1]
Of victors glory from him snatcht away:
But th'Elfin knight, which ought° that warlike   owned/trophy
 wage,°
Disdaind to loose the meed he wonne in fray,
And him rencountring fierce, reskewd the noble pray.

40

Therewith they gan to hurtlen° greedily,   skirmish
 Redoubted battaile ready to darrayne,°   contest
 And clash their shields, and shake their swords on hy,
 That with their sturre they troubled all the traine;
 Till that great Queene upon eternall paine
 Of high displeasure, that ensewen might,
 Commaunded them their fury to refraine,
 And if that either to that shield had right,
In equall lists they should the morrow next it fight.

41

"Ah dearest Dame," quoth then the Paynim bold,
 "Pardon the errour of enragéd wight,
 Whom great griefe made forget the raines to hold
 Of reasons rule, to see this recreant knight,
 No knight, but treachour full of false despight
 And shamefull treason, who through guile hath slayn
 The prowest° knight, that ever field did fight,   bravest
 Even stout Sans foy (O who can then refrayn?)
Whose shield he beares renverst, the more to heape disdayn.

42

"And to augment the glorie of his guile,
 His dearest love[2] the faire Fidessa loe
 Is there possessed of° the traytour vile,   by
 Who reapes the harvest sowen by his foe,
 Sowen in bloudy field, and bought with woe:
 That brothers hand shall dearely well requight
 So be, O Queene, you equall favour showe."
 Him litle answerd th'angry Elfin knight:
He never meant with words, but swords to plead his right.

43

But threw his gauntlet as a sacred pledge,
 His cause in combat the next day to try:
 So been they parted both, with harts on edge,
 To be avenged each on his enimy.
 That night they pas in joy and jollity,
 Feasting and courting both in bowre and hall;
 For Steward was excessive Gluttonie,
 That of his plenty pouréd forth to all;
Which doen,° the Chamberlain Slowth did to rest them call.   done

1. Envied prize.   2. I.e. Sans foy's.

44

Now whenas darkesome night had all displayd
  Her coleblacke curtein over brightest skye,
390   The warlike youthes on dayntie couches layd,
  Did chace away sweet sleepe from sluggish eye,
  To muse on meanes of hopéd victory.
  But whenas Morpheus[3] had with leaden mace
  Arrested all that courtly company,
395   Up-rose Duessa from her resting place,
And to the Paynims lodging comes with silent pace.

45

Whom broad awake she finds, in troublous fit,°   *mood*
  Forecasting, how his foe he might annoy,
  And him amoves with speaches seeming fit:
400   "Ah deare Sans joy, next dearest to Sans foy,
  Cause of my new griefe, cause of my new joy,
  Joyous, to see his ymage in mine eye,
  And greeved, to thinke how foe did him destroy,
  That was the flowre of grace and chevalrye;
405 Lo his Fidessa to thy secret faith I flye."

46

With gentle wordes he can° her fairely greet,   *did*
  And bad say on the secret of her hart.
  Then sighing soft, "I learne that litle sweet
  Oft tempred is," quoth she, "with muchell smart:
410   For since my brest was launcht° with lovely dart   *pierced*
  Of deare Sans foy, I never joyéd howre,
  But in eternall woes my weaker hart
  Have wasted, loving him with all my powre,
And for his sake have felt full many an heavie stowre.°   *grief*

47

415 "At last when perils all I weenéd past,
  And hoped to reape the crop of all my care,
  Into new woes unweeting° I was cast,   *unknowing*
  By this false faytor,° who unworthy ware   *deceiver*
  His worthy shield, whom he with guilefull snare
420   Entrappéd slew, and brought to shamefull grave.
  Me silly° maid away with him he bare,   *innocent*
  And ever since hath kept in darksome cave,
For that I would not yeeld, that° to Sans foy I gave.   *what*

48

"But since faire Sunne hath sperst° that lowring clowd,   *dispersed*
425   And to my loathéd life now shewes some light,
  Under your beames I will me safely shroud,
  From dreaded storme of his disdainfull spight:
  To you th'inheritance belongs by right
  Of brothers prayse, to you eke longs° his love.   *belongs*
430   Let not his love, let not his restlesse spright°   *ghost*
  Be unrevenged, that calles to you above
From wandring Stygian[4] shores, where it doth endlesse move."

---

3. The god of sleep.   4. Of the river Styx, in the underworld.

49

Thereto said he, "Faire Dame be nought dismaid
  For sorrowes past; their griefe is with them gone:
35 Ne yet of present perill be affraid;
  For needlesse feare did never vantage° none, *aid*
  And helplesse hap it booteth not to mone.
  Dead is Sans-foy, his vitall paines are past,
  Though greevéd ghost for vengeance deepe do grone:
40 He lives, that shall him pay his dewties° last, *rites*
And guiltie Elfin bloud shall sacrifice in hast."

50

"O but I feare the fickle freakes,"⁵ quoth shee,
  "Of fortune false, and oddes of armes in field."
  "Why dame," quoth he, "what oddes can ever bee,
45 Where both do fight alike, to win or yield?"
  "Yea but," quoth she, "he beares a charméd shield,
  And eke enchaunted armes, that none can perce,
  Ne none can wound the man, that does them wield."
  "Charmd or enchaunted," answerd he then ferce,° *fiercely*
50 "I no whit reck, ne you the like need to reherce.° *recount*

51

"But faire Fidessa, sithens° fortunes guile, *since*
  Or enimies powre hath now captivéd you,
  Returne from whence ye came, and rest a while
  Till morrow next, that I the Elfe subdew,
5 And with Sans foyes dead dowry you endew."⁶
  "Ay me, that is a double death," she said,
  "With proud foes sight my sorrow to renew:
  Where ever yet I be, my secrete aid
Shall follow you." So passing forth she him obaid.

Canto V

*The faithfull knight in equall field
subdewes his faithlesse foe,
Whom false Duessa saves, and for
his cure to hell does goe.*

1

The noble hart, that harbours vertuous thought,
  And is with child of glorious great intent,
  Can never rest, untill it forth have brought
  Th'eternall brood of glorie excellent:⁷
5 Such restlesse passion did all night torment
  The flaming corage of that Faery knight,
  Devizing, how that doughtie turnament
  With greatest honour he atchieven might;
Still did he wake, and still did watch for dawning light.

5. Unpredictable tricks.
6. I.e., endow you with the dowry of the dead Sans foy.
7. That good is manifested only in action, not in mere intent, is an important commonplace of Renaissance thinking.

2

10 At last the golden Oriental gate
    Of greatest heaven gan to open faire,
    And Phoebus fresh, as bridegrome to his mate,
    Came dauncing forth, shaking his deawie haire:
    And hurld his glistring beames through gloomy aire.
15   Which when the wakeful Elfe perceived, streight way
    He started up, and did him selfe prepaire,
    In sun-bright armes, and battailous array:
For with that Pagan proud he combat will that day.

3

And forth he comes into the commune hall,
20   Where earely waite him many a gazing eye,
    To weet what end to straunger knights may fall.
    There many Minstrales maken melody,
    To drive away the dull melancholy,
    And many Bardes, that to the trembling chord
25   Can tune their timely° voyces cunningly,   *measured*
    And many Chroniclers, that can record
Old loves, and warres for ladies doen by many a Lord.

4

Soone after comes the cruell Sarazin,
    In woven maile all arméd warily,
30   And sternly lookes at him, who not a pin
    Does care for looke of living creatures eye.
    They bring them wines of Greece and Araby,
    And daintie spices fetcht from furthest Ynd,°   *India*
    To kindle heat of courage privily:°   *within*
35   And in the wine a solemne oth they bynd
T'observe the sacred lawes of armes, that are assynd.

5

At last forth comes that far renowméd Queene,
    With royall pomp and Princely majestie;
    She is ybrought unto a paléd° greene,   *fenced*
40   And placéd under stately canapee,°   *canopy*
    The warlike feates of both those knights to see.
    On th'other side in all mens open vew
    Duessa placéd is, and on a tree
    Sans-foy his shield is hangd with bloudy hew:
45 Both those the lawrell girlonds to the victor dew.

6

A shrilling trompet sownded from on hye,
    And unto battaill bad them selves addresse:
    Their shining shieldes about their wrestes° they tye,   *wrists*
    And burning blades about their heads do blesse,°   *brandish*
50   The instruments of wrath and heavinesse:
    With greedy force each other doth assayle,
    And strike so fiercely, that they do impresse

Deepe dinted furrowes in the battred mayle;
The yron walles to ward their blowes are weake and fraile.

7

The Sarazin was stout, and wondrous strong,
    And heapéd blowes like yron hammers great:
    For after bloud and vengeance he did long.
    The knight was fiers, and full of youthly heat:
    And doubled strokes, like dreaded thunders threat:
    For all for prayse and honour he did fight.
    Both stricken strike, and beaten both do beat,
    That from their shields forth flyeth firie light,
And helmets hewen deepe, shew marks of eithers might.

8

So th'one for wrong, the other strives for right:
    As when a Gryfon[8] seizéd of his pray,
    A Dragon fiers encountreth in his flight,
    Through widest ayre making his ydle way,
    That would his rightfull ravine° rend away: *prey*
    With hideous horrour both together smight,
    And souce° so sore, that they the heavens affray: *strike*
    The wise Southsayer° seeing so sad sight,   *soothsayer*
Th'amazéd vulgar tels of warres and mortall fight.

9

So th'one for wrong, the other strives for right,
    And each to deadly shame would drive his foe:
    The cruell steele so greedily doth bight
    In tender flesh, that streames of bloud down flow,
    With which the armes, that earst so bright did show,
    Into a pure vermillion now are dyde:
    Great ruth in all the gazers harts did grow,
    Seeing the goréd woundes to gape so wyde,
That victory they dare not wish to either side.

10

At last the Paynim chaunst to cast his eye,
    His suddein° eye, flaming with wrathfull fyre,   *darting*
    Upon his brothers shield, which hong thereby:
    Therewith redoubled was his raging yre,
    And said, "Ah wretched sonne of wofull syre,
    Doest thou sit wayling by black Stygian lake,
    Whilest here thy shield is hangd for victors hyre,°   *reward*
    And sluggish german[9] doest thy forces slake,
To after-send his foe, that him may overtake?

11

"Goe caytive° Elfe, him quickly overtake,   *wretched*
    And soone redeeme from his long wandring woe;
    Goe guiltie ghost, to him my message make,
    That I his shield have quit° from dying foe."   *rescued*

8. A legendary monster, half eagle, half   9. I.e., his brother (Sans foy).
lion.

95　Therewith upon his crest he stroke him so,
　　That twise he reeléd, readie twise to fall;
　　End of the doubtfull battell deeméd tho°　　　　　　　　*then*
　　The lookers on, and lowd to him gan call
　　The false Duessa, "Thine the shield, and I, and all."[1]

12

100　Soone as the Faerie heard his Ladie speake,
　　Out of his swowning dreame he gan awake,
　　And quickning° faith, that earst was woxen weake,　　*vitalizing*
　　The creeping deadly cold away did shake:
　　Tho moved with wrath, and shame, and Ladies sake,
105　Of all attonce he cast° avengd to bee,　　　　　　　*determined*
　　And with so'exceeding furie at him strake,
　　That forcéd him to stoupe upon his knee;
　　Had he not stoupéd so, he should have cloven bee,

13

　　And to him said, "Goe now proud Miscreant,
110　Thy selfe thy message doe° to german deare,　　　　*give*
　　Alone he wandring thee too long doth want:
　　Goe say, his foe thy shield with his doth beare."
　　Therewith his heavie hand he high gan reare,
　　Him to have slaine; when loe a darkesome clowd
115　Upon him fell: he no where doth appeare,
　　But vanisht is. The Elfe him cals alowd,
　　But answer none receives: the darknes him does shrowd.[2]

14

　　In haste Duessa from her place arose,
　　And to him running said, "O prowest° knight,　　　　*bravest*
120　That ever Ladie to her love did chose,
　　Let now abate the terror of your might,
　　And quench the flame of furious despight,
　　And bloudie vengeance; lo th'infernall powres
　　Covering your foe with cloud of deadly night,
125　Have borne him hence to Plutoes balefull bowres.
　　The conquest yours, I yours, the shield, and glory yours."

15

　　Not all so satisfide, with greedie eye
　　He sought all round about, his thirstie blade
　　To bath in bloud of faithlesse enemy;
130　Who all that while lay hid in secret shade:
　　He standes amazéd, how he thence should fade.
　　At last the trumpets Triumph sound on hie,
　　And running Heralds humble homage made,
　　Greeting him goodly with new victorie,
135　And to him brought the shield, the cause of enmitie.

1. Duessa is, of course, calling to Sans joy, but Redcrosse (lines 100 ff.) hears her as "Fidessa."
2. This inconclusive ending to the fight is a traditional epic device. Cf., in *Iliad* III, the battle between Menelaus and Paris and *Paradise Lost* IV. In Tasso's *Gerusalemme Liberata* (VII.44–45) the enchantress Armida protects Rambaldo in like manner.

16

Wherewith he goeth to that soveraine Queene,
  And falling her before on lowly knee,
  To her makes present of his service seene:[3]
  Which she accepts, with thankes, and goodly gree,°   *favor*
40 Greatly advauncing° his gay chevalree.   *extolling*
  So marcheth home, and by her takes the knight,
  Whom all the people follow with great glee,
  Shouting, and clapping all their hands on hight,
That all the aire it fils, and flyes to heaven bright.

17

45 Home is he brought, and laid in sumptuous bed:
  Where many skilfull leaches° him abide,°   *doctors/attend*
  To salve his hurts, that yet still freshly bled.
  In wine and oyle they wash his woundes wide,
  And softly can embalme° on every side.   *anoint*
50 And all the while, most heavenly melody
  About the bed sweet musicke did divide,[4]
  Him to beguile of griefe and agony:
And all the while Duessa wept full bitterly.

18

As when a wearie traveller that strayes
55 By muddy shore of broad seven-mouthéd Nile,
  Unweeting of the perillous wandring wayes,
  Doth meet a cruell craftie Crocodile,
  Which in false griefe hyding his harmefull guile,
  Doth weepe full sore, and sheddeth tender teares:
60 The foolish man, that pitties all this while
  His mournefull plight, is swallowed up unwares,
Forgetfull of his owne, that mindes anothers cares.

19

So wept Duessa untill eventide,
  That° shyning lampes in Joves high house were light: *when*
65 Then forth she rose, ne lenger would abide,
  But comes unto the place, where th'Hethen knight
  In slombring swownd nigh voyd of vitall spright,
  Lay covered with inchaunted cloud all day:
  Whom when she found, as she him left in plight,
70 To wayle his woefull case she would not stay,
But to the easterne coast of heaven makes speedy way.

20

Where griesly Night, with visage deadly sad,
  That Phoebus chearefull face durst never vew,
  And in a foule blacke pitchie mantle clad,
75 She findes forth comming from her darkesome mew,°   *den*
  Where she all day did hide her hated hew.
  Before the dore her yron charet stood,

3. Proved. Redcrosse's act of idolatrous
worship to Lucifera bodes ill for his spiritual health.
4. Played variations.

Alreadie harnesséd for journey new;
And cole blacke steedes yborne of hellish brood,
180 That on their rustie bits did champ, as they were wood.[5]

21

Who when she saw Duessa sunny bright,
Adornd with gold and jewels shining cleare,
She greatly grew amazéd at the sight,
And th'unacquainted light began to feare:
185 For never did such brightnesse there appeare,
And would have backe retyred to her cave,
Untill the witches speech she gan to heare,
Saying, "Yet O thou dreaded Dame, I crave
Abide, till I have told the message, which I have."

22

190 She stayd, and foorth Duessa gan proceede,
"O thou most auncient Grandmother of all,
More old then Jove, whom thou at first didst breede,
Or that great house of Gods caelestiall,
Which wast begot in Daemogorgons hall,[6]
195 And sawst the secrets of the world unmade,[7]
Why suffredst thou thy Nephewes° deare to fall   grandsons
With Elfin sword, most shamefully betrade?
Lo where the stout Sans joy doth sleepe in deadly shade.

23

"And him before, I saw with bitter eyes
200 The bold Sans foy shrinke underneath his speare;
And now the pray of fowles in field he lyes,
Nor wayld of friends, nor laid on groning beare,°   bier
That whylome was to me too dearely deare.
O what of Gods then boots it to be borne,
205 If old Aveugles sonnes so evill heare?[8]
Or who shall not great Nightes children scorne,
When two of three her Nephews are so fowle forlorne.

24

"Up then, up dreary Dame, of darknesse Queene,
Go gather up the reliques of thy race,
210 Or else goe them avenge, and let be seene,
That dreaded Night in brightest day hath place,
And can the children of faire light deface."°   destroy
Her feeling speeches some compassion moved
In hart, and chaunge in that great mothers face:
215 Yet pittie in her hart was never proved
Till then: for evermore she hated, never loved.

25

And said, "Deare daughter rightly may I rew
The fall of famous children borne of mee,

---

5. Mad. The description of night echoes not only descriptions in classical poetry but also the world of popular superstition in the English countryside.
6. I.e., in Chaos.
7. Before it was made.
8. I.e., are so badly thought of. "Aveugle" means "blind"; he is son of Night and father of Sans foy, Sans joy, and Sans loy.

And good successes, which their foes ensew:°   *attend*
220 But who can turne the streame of destinee,
    Or breake the chayne of strong necessitee,
    Which fast is tyde to Joves eternall seat?[9]
    The sonnes of Day he favoureth, I see,
    And by my ruines thinkes to make them great:
225 To make one great by others losse, is bad excheat.°   *profit*

26

"Yet shall they not escape so freely all;
    For some shall pay the price of others guilt:
    And he the man that made Sans foy to fall,
    Shall with his owne bloud price that[1] he hath spilt.
230 But what art thou, that telst of Nephews kilt?"
    "I that do seeme not I, Duessa am,"
    Quoth she, "how ever now in garments gilt,
    And gorgeous gold arayd I to thee came;
Duessa I, the daughter of Deceipt and Shame."

27

235 Then bowing downe her agéd backe, she kist
    The wicked witch, saying; "In that faire face
    The false resemblance of Deceipt, I wist°   *knew*
    Did closely lurke; yet so true-seeming grace
    It carried, that I scarse in darkesome place
240 Could it discerne, though I the mother bee
    Of falshood, and root of Duessaes race.
    O welcome child, whom I have longd to see,
And now have seene unwares. Lo now I go with thee."

28

Then to her yron wagon she betakes,
245 And with her beares the fowle welfavour'd witch:
    Through mirkesome aire her readie way she makes.
    Her twyfold° Teme, of which two blacke as pitch,   *twofold*
    And two were browne, yet each to each unlich,°   *unlike*
    Did softly swim away, ne ever stampe,
250 Unlesse she chaunst their stubborne mouths to twitch;
    Then foming tarre, their bridles they would champe,
And trampling the fine element,[2] would fiercely rampe.°   *rear*

29

So well they sped, that they be come at length
    Unto the place, whereas the Paynim lay,
255 Devoid of outward sense, and native strength,
    Coverd with charméd cloud from vew of day,
    And sight of men, since his late luckelesse fray.
    His cruell wounds with cruddy° bloud congealed,   *clotted*
    They binden up so wisely, as they may,

---

9. The golden chain of concord or design that binds the entire universe; the image goes back as far as Homer (*Iliad* VIII.18–27) and was given classic statement by Boethius (*Consolation of Philosophy* II.8). Cf. ix.1.
1. I.e., pay for what.
2. The air.

260 And handle softly, till they can be healed:
So lay him in her charet, close in night concealed.

30

And all the while she stood upon the ground,
    The wakefull dogs did never cease to bay,
    As giving warning of th'unwonted sound,
265 With which her yron wheeles did them affray,
    And her darke griesly looke them much dismay;
    The messenger of death, the ghastly Owle
    With drearie shriekes did also her bewray;°   *reveal*
    And hungry Wolves continually did howle,
270 At her abhorréd face, so filthy and so fowle.

31

Thence turning backe in silence soft they stole,
    And brought the heavie corse with easie pace
    To yawning gulfe of deepe Avernus hole.[3]
    By that same hole an entrance darke and bace
275 With smoake and sulphure hiding all the place,
    Descends to hell: there creature never past,
    That backe returnéd without heavenly grace;
    But dreadfull Furies, which their chaines have brast,°   *burst*
And damnéd sprights sent forth to make ill° men aghast.   *evil*

32

280 By that same way the direfull dames doe drive
    Their mournefull charet, fild with rusty blood,
    And downe to Plutoes house are come bilive:°   *quickly*
    Which passing through, on every side them stood
    The trembling ghosts with sad amazéd mood,
285 Chattring their yron teeth, and staring wide
    With stonie eyes; and all the hellish brood
    Of feends infernall flockt on every side,
To gaze on earthly wight, that with the Night durst ride.

33

They pas the bitter waves of Acheron,
290 Where many soules sit wailing woefully,
    And come to fiery flood of Phlegeton,
    Whereas the damnéd ghosts in torments fry,
    And with sharpe shrilling shriekes doe bootlesse cry,
    Cursing high Jove, the which them thither sent.
295 The house of endlesse paine is built thereby,
    In which ten thousand sorts of punishment
The curséd creatures doe eternally torment.

34

Before the threshold dreadfull Cerberus
    His three deforméd heads did lay along,°   *down*

---

3. In classical mythology, Avernus is
Hell, where Pluto reigns (line 282).
Acheron (line 289) and Phlegeton (line
291) are rivers in Hell. Cerberus (line
298), the three-headed dog, is guardian
there. Stanzas 31–35 recall much of
Aeneas's descent into Hell (Virgil, *Aeneid* VI.200, 239–40).

43

"Not so," quoth she; "but sith that heavens king
30 From hope of heaven hath thee excluded quight,
  Why fearest thou, that canst not hope for thing,
  And fearest not, that more thee hurten might,
  Now in the powre of everlasting Night?
  Goe to then, O thou farre renowméd sonne
35 Of great Apollo, shew thy famous might
  In medicine, that else° hath to thee wonne   *already*
 Great paines, and greater praise, both never to be donne."° *ended*

44

Her words prevaild: And then the learnéd leach°   *doctor*
  His cunning hand gan to his wounds to lay,
40 And all things else, the which his art did teach:
  Which having seene, from thence arose away
  The mother of dread darknesse, and let stay
  Aveugles sonne there in the leaches cure,
  And backe returning tooke her wonted way,
45 To runne her timely race,[2] whilst Phoebus pure
 In westerne waves his wearie wagon did recure.° *refresh*

45

The false Duessa leaving noyous° Night,   *harmful*
  Returnd to stately pallace of dame Pride;
  Where when she came, she found the Faery knight
50 Departed thence, albe° his woundes wide   *although*
  Not throughly heald, unreadie were to ride.
  Good cause he had to hasten thence away;
  For on a day his wary Dwarfe had spide,
  Where in a dongeon deepe huge numbers lay
5 Of caytive° wretched thrals,° that wayléd night *captive/slaves*
  and day.[3]

46

A ruefull sight, as could be seene with eie;
  Of whom he learnéd had in secret wise
  The hidden cause of their captivitie,
  How mortgaging their lives to Covetise,
60 Through wastfull Pride, and wanton Riotise,
  They were by law of that proud Tyrannesse[4]
  Provokt with Wrath, and Envies false surmise,
  Condemnéd to that Dongeon mercilesse,
 Where they should live in woe, and die in wretchednesse.

47

65 There was that great proud king of Babylon,[5]
  That would compell all nations to adore,
  And him as onely God to call upon,
  Till through celestiall doome° throwne out of dore, *judgment*
  Into an Oxe he was transformed of yore:
70 There also was king Croesus,[6] that enhaunst° *exalted*

2. Her measured (nightly) journey.
3. The Dwarfe here acts as a "wary" conscience.
4. I.e., Lucifera, whose "law" is that of destruction by sin. The noble sinners named in stanzas 47–50 exemplify a theme common to Renaissance morality, the fall of princes.
5. Nebuchadnezzar (Daniel iii–iv).
6. King of Lydia, famous for his riches.

His heart too high through his great riches store;
And proud Antiochus,[7] the which advaunst
His curséd hand gainst God, and on his altars daunst.

48

And them long time before, great Nimrod[8] was,
425   That first the world with sword and fire warrayd;°   *ravaged*
  And after him old Ninus farre did pas°   *surpass*
  In princely pompe, of all the world obayd;
  There also was that mightie Monarch layd
  Low under all, yet above all in pride,
430   That name of native° syre did fowle upbrayd,   *natural*
  And would as Ammons sonne[8a] be magnifide,
Till scornd of God and man a shamefull death he dide.

49

All these together in one heape were throwne,
  Like carkases of beasts in butchers stall.
435   And in another corner wide were strowne
  The antique ruines of the Romaines fall:[9]
  Great Romulus the Grandsyre of them all,
  Proud Tarquin, and too lordly Lentulus,
  Stout Scipio, and stubborne Hanniball,
440   Ambitious Sylla, and sterne Marius,
High Caesar, great Pompey, and fierce Antonius.

50

Amongst these mighty men were wemen mixt,
  Proud wemen, vaine, forgetfull of their yoke:
  The bold Semiramis,[1] whose sides transfixt
445   With sonnes owne blade, her fowle reproches spoke;
  Faire Sthenoboea,[2] that her selfe did choke
  With wilfull cord, for wanting° of her will;   *lacking*
  High minded Cleopatra, that with stroke
  Of Aspes sting her selfe did stoutly kill:
450 And thousands moe the like, that did that dongeon fill.

51

Besides the endlesse routs of wretched thralles,
  Which thither were assembled day by day,
  From all the world after their wofull falles,
  Through wicked pride, and wasted wealthes decay.
455   But most of all, which in that Dongeon lay
  Fell from high Princes courts, or Ladies bowres,
  Where they in idle pompe, or wanton play,
  Consuméd had their goods, and thriftlesse howres,
And lastly throwne themselves into these heavy stowres.°   *disasters*

7. King of Syria, who tried to stamp out the Jewish religion (I Maccabees i.20–24).
8. A mighty hunter, associated with the Tower of Babel (Genesis x.9). Founder of Nineveh.
8a. Alexander the Great, occasionally worshiped as the son of Jupiter Ammon.
9. Romulus, founder of Rome; Tarquin, Roman tyrant; Lentulus, a conspirator with Catiline; Scipio, Roman general, conqueror of Carthage; Hannibal, Carthaginian general; Sulla, Roman civil war general; Marius, Sulla's rival; Julius Caesar; Pompey the Great; and Mark Anthony. All are memorialized in Plutarch's *Lives*.
1. Wife of Ninus.
2. Queen of King Proetus of Argos, who fell vainly in love with Bellerophon.

52

Whose case whenas the carefull Dwarfe had tould,
   And made ensample of their mournefull sight
   Unto his maister, he no lenger would
   There dwell in perill of like painefull plight,
   But early rose, and ere that dawning light
   Discovered had the world to heaven wyde,
   He by a privie Posterne° tooke his flight,   *gate*
   That of no envious eyes he mote be spyde:[3]
For doubtlesse death ensewd, if any him descryde.

53

Scarse could he footing find in that fowle way,
   For many corses, like a great Lay-stall°   *rubbish heap*
   Of murdred men which therein strowéd lay,
   Without remorse, or decent funerall:
   Which all through that great Princesse pride did fall
   And came to shamefull end. And them beside
   Forth ryding underneath the castell wall,
   A donghill of dead carkases he spide,
The dreadfull spectacle° of that sad house of Pride.   *example*

Canto VI

From lawlesse lust by wondrous grace
fayre Una is releast:
Whom salvage nation does adore,
   and learnes her wise beheast.°   *bidding*

1

As when a ship, that flyes faire under saile,
   An hidden rocke escapéd hath unwares,
   That lay in waite her wrack for to bewaile,
   The Marriner yet halfe amazéd stares
   At perill past, and yet in doubt ne dares
   To joy at his foole-happie oversight:
   So doubly is distrest twixt joy and cares
   The dreadlesse courage° of this Elfin knight,   *heart*
Having escapt so sad ensamples in his sight.

2

Yet sad he was that his too hastie speed
   The faire Duess' had forst him leave behind;
   And yet more sad, that Una his deare dreed° *object of reverence*
   Her truth had staind with treason so unkind;°   *unnatural*
   Yet crime in her could never creature find,
   But for his love, and for her owne selfe sake,
   She wandred had° from one to other Ynd,   *would have*
   Him for to seeke, ne ever would forsake,
Till her unwares the fierce Sansloy did overtake.

3. Redcrosse entered the House of Pride from above; he leaves it from below.

3

Who after Archimagoes fowle defeat,
20 Led her away into a forrest wilde,
    And turning wrathfull fire to lustfull heat,
    With beastly sin thought her to have defilde,
    And made the vassall of his pleasures vilde.°   *vile*
    Yet first he cast by treatie,° and by traynes,°   *persuasion/tricks*
25 Her to perswade, that stubborne fort to yilde:
    For greater conquest of hard love he gaynes,
That workes it to his will, then he that it constraines.°   *forces*

4

With fawning wordes he courted her a while,
    And looking lovely,° and oft sighing sore,   *lovingly*
30 Her constant hart did tempt with diverse guile:
    But wordes, and lookes, and sighes she did abhore,
    As rocke of Diamond stedfast evermore.[4]
    Yet for to feed his fyrie lustfull eye,
    He snatcht the vele, that hong her face before;
35 Then gan her beautie shine, as brightest skye,
And burnt his beastly hart t'efforce° her chastitye.   *violate*

5

So when he saw his flatt'ring arts to fayle,
    And subtile engines bet° from batteree,   *beaten*
    With greedy force he gan the fort assayle,
40 Whereof he weend possesséd soone to bee,
    And win rich spoile of ransackt chastetee.
    Ah heavens, that do this hideous act behold,
    And heavenly virgin thus outragéd see,
    How can ye vengeance just so long withhold,
45 And hurle not flashing flames upon that Paynim bold?

6

The pitteous maden carefull° comfortlesse,   *full of cares*
    Does throw out thrilling shriekes, and shrieking cryes,
    The last vaine helpe of womens great distresse,
    And with loud plaints importuneth the skyes,
50 That molten starres do drop like weeping eyes;
    And Phoebus flying so most shamefull sight,
    His blushing face in foggy cloud implyes,°   *buries*
    And hides for shame. What wit of mortall wight
Can now devise to quit a thrall[5] from such a plight?

7

55 Eternall providence exceeding thought,
    Where none appeares can make her selfe a way:
    A wondrous way it for this Lady wrought,
    From Lyons clawes to pluck the gripéd pray.
    Her shrill outcryes and shriekes so loud did bray,
60 That all the woodes and forestes did resownd;

4. The diamond was traditionally per-
fect; Arthur's shield (I.vii.33) is also   made of diamond.
5. Release a victim.

A troupe of Faunes and Satyres far away
    Within the wood were dauncing in a rownd,
Whiles old Sylvanus slept in shady arber sownd.[6]

8

Who when they heard that pitteous strainéd voice,
    In hast forsooke their rurall meriment,
    And ran towards the far rebownded noyce,
    To weet, what wight so loudly did lament.
    Unto the place they come incontinent:°   *immediately*
    Whom when the raging Sarazin espide,
    A rude, misshapen, monstrous rablement,
    Whose like he never saw, he durst not bide,
But got his ready steed, and fast away gan ride.[7]

9

The wyld woodgods arrivéd in the place,
    There find the virgin dolefull desolate,
    With ruffled rayments, and faire blubbred face,
    As her outrageous foe had left her late,
    And trembling yet through feare of former hate;
    All stand amazéd at so uncouth° sight,   *strange*
    And gin to pittie her unhappie state,
    All stand astonied at her beautie bright,
In their rude eyes unworthie° of so wofull plight.   *undeserving*

10

She more amazed, in double dread doth dwell,
    And every tender part for feare does shake:
    As when a greedie Wolfe through hunger fell
    A seely° Lambe farre from the flocke does take,   *innocent*
    Of whom he meanes his bloudie feast to make,
    A Lyon spyes fast running towards him,
    The innocent pray in hast he does forsake,
    Which quit from death yet quakes in every lim
With chaunge of feare, to see the Lyon looke so grim.

11

Such fearefull fit assaid° her trembling hart,   *afflicted*
    Ne word to speake, ne joynt to move she had:
    The salvage nation feele her secret smart,
    And read her sorrow in her count'nance sad;
    Their frowning forheads with rough hornes yclad,
    And rusticke horror[8] all a side doe lay,
    And gently grenning, shew a semblance glad
    To comfort her, and feare to put away,
Their backward bent knees teach[9] her humbly to obay.

---

6. Fauns and satyrs, creatures with men's bodies above the waist and goats' bodies below, noted in classical mythology for their sensuality, engage here in "rurall meriment"; Sylvanus, Roman god of the woods, is traditionally associated with fauns.

7. The "woodgods," like the Lyon of Canto iii, bear some natural goodness—unlike Sans loy, who is alien to nature. They perhaps represent religious belief and practice before Christianity.
8. Rough manner.
9. I.e., teach them.

12

100 The doubtfull Damzell dare not yet commit
    Her single° person to their barbarous truth,°   *solitary/honesty*
    But still twixt feare and hope amazd does sit,
    Late learnd what harme to hastie trust ensu'th,
    They in compassion of her tender youth,
105   And wonder of her beautie soveraine,
    Are wonne with pitty and unwonted ruth,
    And all prostrate upon the lowly plaine,
Do kisse her feete, and fawne on her with count'nance faine.° *pleasant*

13

Their harts she ghesseth by their humble guise,
110   And yieldes her to extremitie of time;[1]
    So from the ground she fearelesse doth arise,
    And walketh forth without suspect of crime:
    They all as glad, as birdes of joyous Prime,°   *springtime*
    Thence lead her forth, about her dauncing round,
115   Shouting, and singing all a shepheards ryme,
    And with greene braunches strowing all the ground,
Do worship her, as Queene, with olive girlond cround.

14

And all the way their merry pipes they sound,
    That all the woods with doubled Eccho ring,
120   And with their hornéd feet do weare the ground,
    Leaping like wanton kids in pleasant Spring.
    So towards old Sylvanus they her bring;
    Who with the noyse awakéd, commeth out,
    To weet the cause, his weake steps governing
125   An agéd limbs on Cypresse stadle° stout,   *staff*
And with an yvie twyne his wast is girt about.

15

Far off he wonders, what them makes so glad,
    Or° Bacchus merry fruit[2] they did invent,°   *whether/find*
    Or Cybeles franticke rites[3] have made them mad;
130   They drawing nigh, unto their God present
    That flowre of faith and beautie excellent.
    The God himselfe vewing that mirrhour rare,
    Stood long amazd, and burnt in his intent;[4]
    His owne faire Dryope now he thinkes not faire,
135 And Pholoe fowle, when her to this he doth compaire.[5]

16

The woodborne people fall before her flat,
    And worship her as Goddesse of the wood;
    And old Sylvanus selfe bethinkes not, what
    To thinke of wight so faire, but gazing stood,

1. I.e., necessity of the time.
2. Wine grapes.
3. Orgiastic dances in worship of Cybele, goddess of the powers of Nature.
4. Glowed with intense concentration. Una is a "mirrhour rare" in that she reflects heavenly beauty.
5. Dryope and Pholoe were nymphs loved by Faunus and Pan; for Spenser, the names "Faunus," "Pan," and "Sylvanus" were apparently interchangeable.

In doubt to deeme her borne of earthly brood;
Sometimes Dame Venus selfe he seemes to see,
But Venus never had so sober mood;
Sometimes Diana he her takes to bee,
But misseth bow, and shaftes, and buskins° to her knee.   *soft boots*

17

By vew of her he ginneth to revive
His ancient love, and dearest Cyparisse,[6]
And calles to mind his pourtraiture alive,[7]
How faire he was, and yet not faire to this,
And how he slew with glauncing dart amisse
A gentle Hynd, the which the lovely boy
Did love as life, above all worldly blisse;
For griefe whereof the lad n'ould° after joy,   *would not*
But pynd away in anguish and selfe-wild annoy.°   *suffering*

18

The wooddy Nymphes, faire Hamadryades[8]
Her to behold do thither runne apace,
And all the troupe of light-foot Naiades,[9]
Flocke all about to see her lovely face:
But when they vewéd have her heavenly grace,
They envie her in their malitious mind,
And fly away for feare of fowle disgrace:
But all the Satyres scorne their woody kind,
And henceforth nothing faire, but her on earth they find.

19

Glad of such lucke, the luckelesse lucky maid,
Did her content to please their feeble eyes,
And long time with that salvage people staid,
To gather breath in many miseries.
During which time her gentle wit she plyes,
To teach them truth, which worshipt her in vaine,
And made her th'Image of Idolatryes;
But when their bootlesse zeale she did restraine
From her own worship, they her Asse would worship fayn.[1]

20

It fortunéd a noble warlike knight
By just occasion to that forrest came,
To seeke his kindred, and the lignage right,°   *true*
From whence he tooke his well deservéd name:
He had in armes abroad wonne muchell fame,
And fild far landes with glorie of his might,
Plaine, faithfull, true, and enimy of shame,
And ever loved to fight for Ladies right,
But in vaine glorious frayes he litle did delight.

---

6. A fair youth, beloved of Sylvanus, turned into a cypress tree.
7. I.e., his appearance when alive.
8. Nymphs whose lives depended upon the trees with which they were associated.
9. Water nymphs.
1. I.e., willingly. Natural goodness can give some recognition, albeit only externally, to Una. Though Una does her best to teach the satyrs true religion, they are idolaters even in the truth.

21

A Satyres sonne yborne in forrest wyld,
 By straunge adventure as it did betyde,
 And there begotten of a Lady myld,
 Faire Thyamis the daughter of Labryde,
185 That was in sacred bands of wedlocke tyde
 To Therion, a loose unruly swayne;[2]
 Who had more joy to raunge the forrest wyde,
 And chase the salvage beast with busie payne,[3]
Then serve his Ladies love, and wast in pleasures vayne.

22

190 The forlorne mayd did with loves longing burne,
 And could not lacke° her lovers company,   **be without**
 But to the wood she goes, to serve her turne,
 And seeke her spouse, that from her still does fly,
 And followes other game and venery:[4]
195 A Satyre chaunst her wandring for to find,
 And kindling coles of lust in brutish eye,
 The loyall links of wedlocke did unbind,
And made her person thrall unto his beastly kind.

23

So long in secret cabin there he held
200 Her captive to his sensuall desire,
 Till that with timely fruit her belly sweld,
 And bore a boy unto that salvage sire:
 Then home he suffred her for to retire,
 For ransome leaving him the late borne childe;
205 Whom till to ryper yeares he gan aspire,°   **grow up**
 He noursled up in life and manners wilde,
Emongst wild beasts and woods, from lawes of men exilde.

24

For all he taught the tender ymp,° was but   **child**
 To banish cowardize and bastard° feare;   **base**
210 His trembling hand he would him force to put
 Upon the Lyon and the rugged Beare,
 And from the she Beares teats her whelps to teare;
 And eke wyld roring Buls he would him make
 To tame, and ryde their backes not made to beare;
215 And the Robuckes in flight to overtake,
That every beast for feare of him did fly and quake.

25

Thereby so fearelesse, and so fell° he grew,   **fierce**
 That his owne sire and maister of his guise[5]

2. "Thyamis" means "passion," "Therion," "wild beast." Their child Satyrane
(he is named in line 249) ought to be
a savage creature, but instead his natural
goodness welcomes and reveres truth and
grace in Una with a higher understand-

ing than the lion or the woodgods can
give.
3. Painstaking care.
4. The word means both "hunting" and
"sexual play."
5. Teacher of his manners.

Did often tremble at his horrid° vew,   rough
20   And oft for dread of hurt would him advise,
The angry beasts not rashly to despise,
Nor too much to provoke; for he would learne°   teach
The Lyon stoup to him in lowly wise,
(A lesson hard) and make the Libbard° sterne   leopard
25 Leave roaring, when in rage he for revenge did earne.°   yearn

                              26
And for to make his powre approvéd° more,   extended
    Wyld beasts in yron yokes he would compell;
The spotted Panther, and the tuskéd Bore,
The Pardale° swift, and the Tigre cruell;   panther
30   The Antelope, and Wolfe both fierce and fell;
And them constraine in equall teme to draw.
Such joy he had, their stubborne harts to quell,
And sturdie courage tame with dreadfull aw,
That his beheast they feauréd, as a tyrans law.

                              27
35 His loving mother came upon a day
    Unto the woods, to see her little sonne;
And chaunst unwares to meet him in the way,
After his sportes, and cruell pastime donne,
When after him a Lyonesse did runne,
40   That roaring all with rage, did lowd requere°   demand
Her children deare, whom he away had wonne:
The Lyon whelpes she saw how he did beare,
And lull in rugged armes, withouten childish feare.

                              28
The fearefull Dame all quakéd at the sight,
45   And turning backe, gan fast to fly away,
Untill with love revokt° from vaine affright,   restrained
She hardly yet perswaded was to stay,
And then to him these womanish words gan say;
"Ah Satyrane, my dearling, and my joy,
50   For love of me leave off this dreadfull play;
To dally thus with death, is no fit toy,
Go find some other play-fellowes, mine own sweet boy."

                              29
In these and like delights of bloudy game
    He traynéd was, till ryper yeares he raught,°   reached
55   And there abode, whilst any beast of name
Walkt in that forest, whom he had not taught
To feare his force: and then his courage haught°   high
Desird of forreine foemen to be knowne,
And far abroad for straunge adventures sought:
60   In which his might was never overthrowne,
But through all Faery lond his famous worth was blown.

30

Yet evermore it was his manner faire,
    After long labours and adventures spent,
    Unto those native woods for to repaire,
265   To see his sire and ofspring° auncient.   *origin*
    And now he thither came for like intent;
    Where he unwares the fairest Una found,
    Straunge Lady, in so straunge habiliment,
    Teaching the Satyres, which her sat around,
270 Trew sacred lore, which from her sweet lips did redound.

31

He wondred at her wisedome heavenly rare,
    Whose like in womens wit he never knew;
    And when her curteous deeds he did compare,
    Gan her admire, and her sad sorrowes rew,
275   Blaming of Fortune, which such troubles threw,
    And joyd to make proofe of her crueltie
    On gentle Dame, so hurtlesse,° and so trew: *harmless*
    Thenceforth he kept her goodly company,
And learnd her discipline of faith and veritie.

32

280 But she all vowd unto the Redcrosse knight,
    His wandring perill closely° did lament,   *secretly*
    Ne in this new acquaintaunce could delight,
    But her deare heart with anguish did torment,
    And all her wit in secret counsels spent,
285   How to escape. At last in privie wise
    To Satyrane she shewéd her intent;
    Who glad to gain such favour, gan devise,
How with that pensive Maid he best might thence arise.°   *depart*

33

So on a day when Satyres all were gone,
290   To do their service to Sylvanus old,
    The gentle virgin left behind alone
    He led away with courage stout and bold.
    Too late it was, to Satyres to be told,
    Or ever hope recover her againe:
295   In vaine he seekes that having cannot hold.
    So fast he carried her with carefull paine,[6]
That they the woods are past, and come now to the plaine.

34

The better part now of the lingring day,
    They traveild had, when as they farre espide
300   A wearie wight forwandring° by the way,   *wandering along*
    And towards him they gan in hast to ride,
    To weet of newes, that did abroad betide,
    Or tydings of her knight of the Redcrosse.
    But he them spying, gan to turne aside,

6. Painstaking care.

305 For feare as seemd, or for some feignéd losse;
    More greedy they of newes, fast towards him do crosse.

35

    A silly° man, in simple weedes forworne,°   simple/worn out
        And solid with dust of the long dried way;
        His sandales were with toilesome travell torne,
310   And face all tand with scorching sunny ray,
        As he had traveild many a sommers day,
        Through boyling sands of Arabie and Ynde;
        And in his hand a Jacobs staffe,⁷ to stay
        His wearie limbes upon: and eke behind,
315   His scrip° did hang, in which his needments he did bind.   bag

36

    The knight approching nigh, of him inquerd
        Tydings of warre, and of adventures new;
        But warres, nor new adventures none he herd.
        Then Una gan to aske, if ought he knew,
320   Or heard abroad of that her champion trew,
        That in his armour bare a croslet° red.   small cross
        "Aye me, Deare dame," quoth he, "well may I rew
        To tell the sad sight, which mine eies have red:°   beheld
        These eyes did see that knight both living and eke ded."

37

325 That cruell word her tender hart so thrild,°   pierced
        That suddein cold did runne through every vaine,
        And stony horrour all her sences fild
        With dying fit, that downe she fell for paine.
        The knight her lightly rearéd up againe,
330   And comforted with curteous kind reliefe:
        Then wonne from death, she bad him tellen plaine
        The further processe° of her hidden griefe;   account
        The lesser pangs can beare, who hath endured the chiefe.

38

    Then gan the Pilgrim thus, "I chaunst this day,
335   This fatall day, that shall I ever rew,
        To see two knights in travell on my way
        (A sory sight) arraunged in battell new,
        Both breathing vengeaunce, both of wrathfull hew:
        My fearefull flesh did tremble at their strife,
340   To see their blades so greedily imbrew,°   thrust
        That drunke with bloud, yet thristed after life:
    What more? the Redcrosse knight was slaine with Paynim knife."

39

    "Ah dearest Lord," quoth she, "how might that bee,
        And he the stoutest knight, that ever wonne?"°   fought
345   "Ah dearest dame," quoth he, "how might I see
        The thing, that might not be, and yet was donne?"
        "Where is," said Satyrane, "that Paynims sonne,
        That him of life, and us of joy hath reft?"

---

7. I.e., pilgrim's staff.

"Not far away," quoth he, "he hence doth wonne°   *stay*
350   Foreby a fountaine, where I late him left
Washing his bloudy wounds, that through° the steele were cleft." *by*

40

Therewith the knight thence marchéd forth in hast,
    Whiles Una with huge heavinesse opprest,
    Could not for sorrow follow him so fast;
355   And soone he came, as he the place had ghest,
    Whereas that Pagan proud him selfe did rest,
    In secret shadow by a fountaine side:
    Even he it was, that earst would have supprest°   *violated*
    Faire Una: whom when Satyrane espide,
360 With fowle reprochfull words he boldly him defide.

41

And said, "Arise thou cursed Miscreaunt,
    That hast with knightlesse guile and trecherous train°   *deceit*
    Faire knighthood fowly shamed, and doest vaunt
    That good knight of the Redcrosse to have slain:
365   Arise, and with like treason now maintain
    Thy guilty wrong, or else thee guilty yield."
    The Sarazin this hearing, rose amain,°   *at once*
    And catching up in hast his three square[8] shield,
    And shining helmet, soone him buckled to the field.

42

370 And drawing nigh him said, "Ah misborne° Elfe,   *base-born*
    In evill houre thy foes thee hither sent,
    Anothers wrongs to wreake upon thy selfe:
    Yet ill thou blamest me, for having blent°   *stained*
    My name with guile and traiterous intent;
375   That Redcrosse knight, perdie, I never slew,
    But had he beene, where earst his armes were lent,
    Th' enchaunter vaine his errour should not rew:
    But thou his errour shalt, I hope now proven trew."[9]

43

Therewith they gan, both furious and fell,
380   To thunder blowes, and fiersly to assaile
    Each other bent his enimy to quell,°   *kill*
    That with their force they perst both plate and maile,
    And made wide furrowes in their fleshes fraile,
    That it would pitty° any living eie.   *bring pity to*
385   Large floods of bloud adowne their sides did raile:°   *flow*
    But floods of bloud could not them satisfie:
    Both hungred after death: both chose to win, or die.

---

8. Triangular.
9. I.e., had Redcrosse been where his arms were, the enchanter Archimago would not have to regret his error in fighting me. But you will now repeat his error in fighting me and demonstrate what an error it is.

44

So long they fight, and fell revenge pursue,
That fainting each, themselves to breathen let,
₃₉₀   And oft refreshéd, battell oft renue:
As when two Bores with rancling malice met,
Their gory sides fresh bleeding fiercely fret,°   *tear*
Til breathlesse both them selves aside retire,
Where foming wrath, their cruell tuskes they whet,
₃₉₅   And trample th'earth, the whiles they may respire
Then backe to fight againe, new breathéd and entire.°   *refreshed*

45

So fiersly, when these knights had breathéd once,
They gan to fight returne, increasing more
Their puissant force, and cruell rage attonce,
₄₀₀   With heapéd strokes more hugely, then before,
That with their drerie° wounds and bloudy gore   *dreadful*
They both deforméd, scarsely could be known.
By this sad Una fraught with anguish sore,
Led with their noise, which through the aire was thrown,
₄₀₅ Arrived, where they in erth their fruitles bloud had sown.

46

Whom all so soone as that proud Sarazin
Espide, he gan revive the memory
Of his lewd lusts, and late attempted sin,
And left the doubtfull battell hastily,
₄₁₀   To catch her, newly offred to his eie:
But Satyrane with strokes him turning, staid,
And sternely bad him other businesse plie,
Then hunt the steps of pure unspotted Maid:
Wherewith he all enraged, these bitter speaches said.

47

₄₁₅ "O foolish faeries sonne, what furie mad
Hath thee incenst, to hast thy dolefull fate?
Were it not better, I that Lady had,
Then that thou hadst repented it too late?
Most sencelesse man he, that himselfe doth hate,
₄₂₀   To love another. Lo then for thine ayd
Here take thy lovers token on thy pate."
So they to fight; the whiles the royall Mayd
Fled farre away, of that proud Paynim sore afrayd.

48

But that false Pilgrim, which that leasing° told,   *lying*
₄₂₅ Being in deed old Archimage, did stay
In secret shadow, all this to behold,
And much rejoycéd in their bloudy fray:
But when he saw the Damsell passe away
He left his stond,° and her pursewd apace,   *place*

430 In hope to bring her to her last decay.° *destruction*
 But for to tell her lamentable cace,
 And eke this battels end, will need another place.

Canto VII

The Redcrosse knight is captive made
By Gyaunt proud opprest,
Prince Arthur meets with Una great-
ly with those newes distrest.

1

What man so wise, what earthly wit so ware,° *wary*
  As to descry° the crafty cunning traine, *perceive*
  By which deceipt doth maske in visour faire,
  And cast her colours dyéd deepe in graine,
5 To seeme like Truth, whose shape she well can faine,
  And fitting gestures to her purpose frame,
  The guiltlesse man with guile to entertaine?° *receive*
  Great maistresse of her art was that false Dame,
The false Duessa, clokéd with Fidessaes name.

2

10 Who when returning from the drery Night,
  She fownd not in that perilous house of Pryde,
  Where she had left, the noble Redcrosse knight,
  Her hopéd pray, she would no lenger bide,
  But forth she went, to seeke him far and wide.
15 Ere long she fownd, whereas° he wearie sate, *where*
  To rest him selfe, foreby° a fountaine side, *beside*
  Disarméd all of yron-coted Plate,
And by his side his steed the grassy forage ate.

3

He feedes upon the cooling shade, and bayes° *bathes*
20 His sweatie forehead in the breathing wind,
  Which through the trembling leaves full gently playes
  Wherein the cherefull birds of sundry kind
  Do chaunt sweet musick, to delight his mind:
  The Witch approaching gan him fairely greet,
25 And with reproch of carelesnesse unkind
  Upbrayd, for leaving her in place unmeet,° *unfitting*
With fowle words tempring faire, soure gall with hony sweet.

4

Unkindnesse past, they gan of solace treat,
  And bathe in pleasaunce of the joyous shade,
30 Which shielded them against the boyling heat,
  And with greene boughes decking a gloomy glade,
  About the fountaine like a girlond made;
  Whose bubbling wave did ever freshly well,
  Ne ever would through fervent° sommer fade: *hot*
35 The sacred Nymph, which therein wont to dwell,
Was out of Dianes favour, as it then befell.

5

The cause was this: one day when Phoebe[1] fayre
    With all her band was following the chace,
    This Nymph, quite tyred with heat of scorching ayre
40   Sat downe to rest in middest of the race:
    The goddesse wroth gan fowly her disgrace,°   *scold*
    And bad the waters, which from her did flow,
    Be such as she her selfe was then in place.[2]
    Thenceforth her waters waxéd dull and slow,
45 And all that drunke thereof, did faint and feeble grow.

6

Hereof this gentle knight unweeting was,
    And lying downe upon the sandie graile,°   *gravel*
    Drunke of the streame, as cleare as cristall glas;
    Eftsoones his manly forces gan to faile,
50   And mightie strong was turnd to feeble fraile.
    His chaungéd powres at first themselves not felt,
    Till crudled° cold his corage° gan assaile,   *curdled/vigor*
    And chearefull bloud in faintnesse chill did melt,
    Which like a fever fit through all his body swelt.°   *raged*

7

55 Yet goodly court he made still to his Dame,
    Pourd out in loosnesse on the grassy grownd,
    Both carelesse of his health, and of his fame:
    Till at the last he heard a dreadfull sownd,
    Which through the wood loud bellowing, did rebownd,
60   That all the earth for terrour seemed to shake,
    And trees did tremble. Th'Elfe therewith astownd,°   *amazed*
    Upstarted lightly from his looser make,°   *companion*
    And his unready weapons gan in hand to take.[3]

8

But ere he could his armour on him dight,
65   Or get his shield, his monstrous enimy
    With sturdie steps came stalking in his sight,
    An hideous Geant horrible and hye,
    That with his talnesse seemd to threat the skye,
    The ground eke groned under him for dreed;
70   His living like saw never living eye,
    Ne durst behold: his stature did exceed
    The hight of three the tallest sonnes of mortall seed.

9

The greatest Earth his uncouth mother was,
    And blustring Aeolus his boasted sire,[4]
75   Who with his breath, which through the world doth pas,
    Her hollow womb did secretly inspire,°   *breathe into*

1. I.e., Diana, goddess of the moon.
2. At that time.
3. Redcrosse is weakened by his encounter with the despair of Sans joy; he has been seduced by falsehood, Duessa; he has drunk of the waters of spiritual sloth: he is thus, now, an easy victim.

4. Aeolus was keeper of the winds. His son, the giant, is Orgoglio (named in line 122), which means "pride." That this sin, pride of the flesh, unchristian and unreasonable, should be the son of the gross earth and the "blustring" wind seems appropriate.

And fild her hidden caves with stormie yre,
That she conceived; and trebling the dew time,
In which the wombes of women do expire,°   *bring forth*
80   Brought forth this monstrous masse of earthly slime,
Puft up with emptie wind, and fild with sinfull crime.

10

So growen great through arrogant delight
Of th'high descent, whereof he was yborne,
And through presumption of his matchlesse might,
85   All other powres and knighthood he did scorne.
Such now he marcheth to this man forlorne,
And left to losse:° his stalking steps are stayde   *destruction*
Upon a snaggy Oke, which he had torne
Out of his mothers bowelles, and it made
90 His mortall mace, wherewith his foemen he dismayde.

11

That when the knight he spide, he gan advance
With huge force and insupportable mayne,[5]
And towardes him with dreadfull fury praunce;
Who haplesse, and eke hopelesse, all in vaine
95   Did to him pace, sad battaile to darrayne,°   *contest*
Disarmd, disgrast, and inwardly dismayde,[6]
And eke so faint in every joynt and vaine,
Through that fraile° fountaine, which him feeble made,   *enfeebling*
That scarsely could he weeld his bootlesse° single blade.   *futile*

12

100 The Geaunt strooke so maynly° mercilesse,   *mightily*
That could have overthrowne a stony towre,
And were not heavenly grace, that him did blesse,
He had beene pouldred° all, as thin as flowre: *powdered*
But he was wary of that deadly stowre,
105   And lightly lept from underneath the blow:
Yet so exceeding was the villeins powre,
That with the wind it did him overthrow,
And all his sences stound,° that still he lay full low.   *stunned*

13

As when that divelish yron Engin[7] wrought
110   In deepest Hell, and framd by Furies skill,   *explosive*
With windy Nitre and quick° Sulphur fraught,
And ramd with bullet round, ordaind to kill,
Conceiveth fire, the heavens it doth fill
With thundring noyse, and all the ayre doth choke,
115   That none can breath, nor see, nor heare at will,
Through smouldry cloud of duskish stincking smoke,
That th'onely breath[8] him daunts, who hath escapt the stroke.

---

5. Irresistable power.   7. I.e., cannon.
6. Dis-made, dissolved.   8. I.e., the blast alone.

14

So daunted when the Geaunt saw the knight,
    His heavie hand he heavéd up on hye,
120   And him to dust thought to have battred quight,
    Untill Duessa loud to him gan crye;
    "O great Orgoglio, greatest under skye,
    O hold thy mortall hand for Ladies sake,
    Hold for my sake, and do him not to dye,
125   But vanquisht thine eternall bondslave make,
And me thy worthy meed unto thy Leman take."[9]

15

He hearkned, and did stay from further harmes,
    To gayne so goodly guerdon,° as she spake: *reward*
    So willingly she came into his armes,
130   Who her as willingly to grace° did take,   *favor*
    And was possesséd of his new found make.°   *mate*
    Then up he tooke the slombred sencelesse corse,
    And ere he could out of his swowne awake,
    Him to his castle brought with hastie forse,
135 And in a Dongeon deepe him threw without remorse.

16

From that day forth Duessa was his deare,
    And highly honourd in his haughtie eye,
    He gave her gold and purple pall° to weare,   *robe*
    And triple crowne set on her head full hye,[1]
140   And her endowd with royall majestye:
    Then for to make her dreaded more of men,
    And peoples harts with awfull terrour tye,
    A monstrous beast ybred in filthy fen
He chose, which he had kept long time in darksome den.

17

145 Such one it was, as that renowméd Snake
    Which great Alcides in Stremona slew,
    Long fostred in the filth of Lerna lake,
    Whose many heads out budding ever new,
    Did breed him endlesse labour to subdew:[2]
150   But this same Monster much more ugly was;
    For seven great heads out of his body grew,
    An yron brest, and backe of scaly bras,
And all embrewd° in bloud, his eyes did shine as glas.   *stained*

9. I.e., take me, your worthy reward, as your mistress.
1. Duessa is attired like the Whore of Babylon in Revelation xvii.3–4; the triple crown is that of the papacy. See i.13, also i.22 and note.
2. The nine-headed Lernean hydra slain by Hercules (Alcides). The seven-headed monster is the red dragon of Revelation: "behold a great red dragon, having seven heads and ten horns, and seven crowns upon his heads * * * [whose] tail drew the third part of the stars of heaven, and did cast them to the earth * * * [he is] that old serpent, called the Devil, and Satan, which deceiveith the whole world" (xii.3–4,9). Pictures of the Beast of the Apocalypse illustrate medieval literature on the vices. On the historical plane, Spenser associates it with the Roman church.

18

His tayle was strechéd out in wondrous length,
That to the house of heavenly gods it raught,°   reached
And with extorted powre, and borrowed strength,
The ever-burning lamps from thence it brought,
And prowdly threw to ground, as things of nought;
And underneath his filthy feet did tread
The sacred things, and holy heasts° foretaught.   commandments
Upon this dreadfull Beast with sevenfold head
He set the false Duessa, for more aw and dread.

19

The wofull Dwarfe, which saw his maisters fall,
Whiles he had keeping of his grasing steed,
And valiant knight become a caytive thrall,
When all was past, tooke up his forlorne weed,[3]
His mightie armour, missing most at need;
His silver shield, now idle maisterlesse;
His poynant° speare, that many made to bleed,   piercing
The ruefull moniments of heavinesse,
And with them all departes, to tell his great distresse.

20

He had not travaild long, when on the way
He wofull Ladie, wofull Una met,[4]
Fast flying from the Paynims greedy pray,°   clutch
Whilest Satyrane him from pursuit did let:°   prevent
Who when her eyes she on the Dwarfe had set,
And saw the signes, that deadly tydings spake,
She fell to ground for sorrowfull regret,
And lively breath her sad brest did forsake,
Yet might her pitteous hart be seene to pant and quake.

21

The messenger of so unhappie newes
Would faine have dyde: dead was his hart within,
Yet outwardly some little comfort shewes:
At last recovering hart, he does begin
To rub her temples, and to chaufe her chin,
And every tender part does tosse and turne:
So hardly he the flitted life does win,
Unto her native prison[5] to retourne:
Then gins her grievéd ghost° thus to lament and mourne.   spirit

22

"Ye dreary instruments of dolefull sight,
That doe this deadly spectacle behold,
Why do ye lenger feed on loathéd light,
Or liking find to gaze on earthly mould,°   form
Sith cruell fates the carefull° threeds unfould,   anguished
The which my life and love together tyde?

---

3. Abandoned garment.
4. Only in Faerie Land could the Dwarfe
find Una so soon after Redcrosse's fortunes are at their lowest.
5. I.e., the body.

Now let the stony dart of senselesse cold
Perce to my hart, and pas through every side,
And let eternall night so sad sight fro me hide.

23

"O lightsome day, the lampe of highest Jove,
    First made by him, mens wandring wayes to guyde,
    When darknesse he in deepest dongeon drove,
    Henceforth thy hated face for ever hyde,
    And shut up heavens windowes shyning wyde:
    For earthly sight can nought but sorrow breed,
    And late repentance, which shall long abyde:
    Mine eyes no more on vanitie shall feed,
But seeléd up with death, shall have their deadly meed."[6]

24

Then downe againe she fell unto the ground;
    But he her quickly rearéd up againe:
    Thrise did she sinke adowne in deadly swownd,
    And thrise he her revived with busie paine:
    At last when life recovered had the raine,°   *rein*
    And over-wrestled his strong enemie,
    With foltring tong, and trembling every vaine,
    "Tell on," quoth she, "the wofull Tragedie,
The which these reliques sad present unto mine eie.

25

"Tempestuous fortune hath spent all her spight,
    And thrilling sorrow throwne his utmost dart;
    Thy sad tongue cannot tell more heavy plight,
    Then that I feele, and habour in mine hart:
    Who hath endured the whole, can beare each part.
    If death it be, it is not the first wound,
    That launchéd° hath my brest with bleeding smart.   *pierced*
    Begin, and end the bitter balefull stound;°   *disaster*
If lesse, then that I feare, more favour I have found."

26

Then gan the Dwarfe the whole discourse declare,
    The subtill traines of Archimago old;
    The wanton loves of false Fidessa faire,
    Bought with the bloud of vanquisht Paynim bold:
    The wretched payre transformed to treen mould;[7]
    The house of Pride, and perils round about;
    The combat, which he with Sans joy did hould;
    The lucklesse conflict with the Gyant stout,
Wherein captived, of life or death he stood in doubt.

27

She heard with patience all unto the end,
    And strove to maister sorrowfull assay,[8]
    Which greater grew, the more she did contend,
    And almost rent her tender hart in tway;

6. Reward of death.
7. Shape of a tree.
8. I.e., attack of sorrow.

And love fresh coles unto her fire did lay:
240 For greater love, the greater is the losse.
Was never Ladie lovéd dearer° day,   *more dearly*
Then she did love the knight of the Redcrosse;
For whose deare sake so many troubles her did tosse.

28

At last when fervent sorrow slakéd was,
245 She up arose, resolving him to find
Alive or dead: and forward forth doth pas,
All as the Dwarfe the way to her assynd:°   *showed*
And evermore in constant carefull mind
She fed her wound with fresh renewéd bale;°   *anguish*
250 Long tost with stormes, and bet° with bitter wind,   *beat*
High over hils, and low adowne the dale,
She wandred many a wood, and measurd many a vale.

29

At last she chauncéd by good hap to meet
A goodly knight,[9] faire marching by the way
255 Together with his Squire, arayéd meet:
His glitterand° armour shinéd farre away,   *glittering*
Like glauncing light of Phoebus brightest ray;
From top to toe no place appearéd bare,
That deadly dint of steele endanger may:
260 Athwart his brest a bauldrick° brave he ware,   *sash*
That shynd, like twinkling stars, with stons most pretious rare.

30

And in the midst thereof one pretious stone
Of wondrous worth, and eke of wondrous mights,
Shapt like a Ladies head,[1] exceeding shone,
265 Like Hesperus° emongst the lesser lights,   *evening star*
And strove for to amaze the weaker sights;
Thereby his mortall blade full comely hong
In yvory sheath, ycarved with curious slights;°   *patterns*
Whose hilts were burnisht gold, and handle strong
270 Of mother pearle, and buckled with a golden tong.°   *pin*

31

His haughtie helmet, horrid° all with gold,   *bristling*
Both glorious brightnesse, and great terrour bred;
For all the crest a Dragon did enfold
With greedie pawes, and over all did spred

9. Prince Arthur, the supreme hero of the entire *Faerie Queene*. As Spenser explained to Ralegh, "So in the person of Prince Arthure I sette forth magnificence in particular, which vertue for that (according to Aristotle and the rest) it is the perfection of all the rest, and conteineth in it them all." Since, he says, "I mention [in each book] the deeds of Arthur appliable to that vertue which I write of in that book," and since the "virtue" in Book I is Holiness, Arthur will be not unlike Christ, or the power of Christian grace, in the ensuing episodes.
1. I.e., that of the Faerie Queene, Gloriana.

275   His golden wings: his dreadfull hideous hed
          Close couchéd on the bever,° seemed to throw   *visor*
          From flaming mouth bright sparkles fierie red,
          That suddeine horror to faint harts did show;
      And scaly tayle was stretcht adowne his backe full low.

                              32
280 Upon the top of all his loftie crest,
          A bunch of haires discolourd° diversly,   *dyed*
          With sprincled pearle, and gold full richly drest,
          Did shake, and seemed to daunce for jollity,
          Like to an Almond tree ymounted hye
285   On top of greene Selinis all alone,
          With blossomes brave bedeckéd daintily;
          Whose tender locks do tremble every one
      At every little breath, that under heaven is blowne.

                              33
      His warlike shield all closely covered was,
290   Ne might of mortall eye be ever seene;
          Not made of steele, nor of enduring bras,
          Such earthly mettals soone consuméd bene:
          But all of Diamond perfect pure and cleene°   *clear*
          It framéd was, one massie entire mould,
295   Hewen out of Adamant rocke with engines keene,
          That point of speare it never percen could,
      Ne dint of direfull sword divide the substance would.[2]

                              34
      The same to wight he never wont disclose,
          But° when as monsters huge he would dismay,   *except*
300   Or daunt unequall armies of his foes,
          Or when the flying heavens he would affray;
          For so exceeding shone his glistring ray,
          That Phoebus golden face it did attaint,°   *dim*
          As when a cloud his beames doth over-lay;
305   And silver Cynthia° wexéd pale and faint,   *the moon*
      As when her face is staynd with magicke arts constraint.°   *force*

                              35
      No magicke arts hereof had any might,
          Nor bloudie wordes of bold Enchaunters call,
          But all that was not such, as seemd in sight,
310   Before that shield did fade, and suddeine fall:
          And when him list the raskall routes[3] appall,
          Men into stones therewith he could transmew,°   *change*
          And stones to dust, and dust to nought at all;
          And when him list the prouder lookes subdew,
315   He would them gazing blind, or turne to other hew.°   *form*

---

2. The diamond—unflawed, unpierce-
able, translucent—is emblematic of the
perfect faith which is Arthur's shield. Cf.
Ephesians vi.16: "Above all, taking the

shield of faith, wherewith ye shall be
able to quench all the fiery darts of the
wicked."
3. Unruly mobs.

36

Ne let it seeme, that credence this exceedes,
For he that made the same, was knowne right well
To have done much more admirable deedes.
It Merlin was, which whylome° did excell   *formerly*
320 All living wightes in might of magicke spell:
Both shield, and sword, and armour all he wrought
For this young Prince, when first to armes he fell;
But when he dyde, the Faerie Queene it brought
To Faerie lond, where yet it may be seene, if sought.[4]

37

325 A gentle youth, his dearely lovéd Squire
His speare of heben° wood behind him bare,   *ebony*
Whose harmefull head, thrice heated in the fire,
Had riven many a brest with pikehead square;
A goodly person, and could menage° faire   *control*
330 His stubborne steed with curbéd canon bit,[5]
Who under him did trample as the aire,
And chauft,° that any on his backe should sit;   *fretted*
The yron rowels into frothy fome he bit.

38

When as this knight nigh to the Ladie drew,
335 With lovely court he gan her entertaine;
But when he heard her answers loth, he knew
Some secret sorrow did her heart distraine:°   *oppress*
Which to allay, and calme her storming paine,
Faire feeling words he wisely gan display,
340 And for her humour fitting purpose faine,[6]
To tempt the cause it selfe for to bewray;
Wherewith emmoved, these bleeding words she gan to say.

39

"What worlds delight, or joy of living speach
Can heart, so plunged in sea of sorrowes deepe,
345 And heapéd with so huge misfortunes, reach?
The carefull° cold beginneth for to creepe,   *afflicting*
And in my heart his yron arrow steepe,
Soone as I thinke upon my bitter bale:
Such helplesse harmes yts better hidden keepe,
350 Then rip up griefe, where it may not availe,
My last left comfort is, my woes to weepe and waile."

40

"Ah Ladie deare," quoth then the gentle knight,
"Well may I weene, your griefe is wondrous great;
For wondrous great griefe groneth in my spright,°   *spirit*
355 Whiles thus I heare you of your sorrowes treat.
But wofull Ladie let me you intrete,
For to unfold the anguish of your hart:
Mishaps are maistred by advice discrete,

---

4. I.e., Arthur's virtues may be seen still in Queen Elizabeth's England.

5. Cannon-bit; a smooth, round bit.

6. I.e., suited his manner to her mood.

And counsell mittigates the greatest smart;
360 Found never helpe, who never would his hurts impart."

41

"O but," quoth she, "great griefe will not be tould,
   And can more easily be thought, then said."
   "Right so"; quoth he, "but he, that never would,
   Could never: will to might gives greatest aid."
365   "But grief," quoth she, "does greater grow displaid,
   If then it find not helpe, and breedes despaire."
   "Despaire breedes not," quoth he, "where faith is staid."°   *firm*
   "No faith so fast," quoth she, "but flesh does paire."°   *impair*
"Flesh may empaire," quoth he, "but reason can repaire."

42

370 His goodly reason, and well guided speach
   So deepe did settle in her gratious thought,
   That her perswaded to disclose the breach,
   Which love and fortune in her heart had wrought,
   And said; "Faire Sir, I hope good hap hath brought
375   You to inquire the secrets of my griefe,
   Or that your wisedome will direct my thought,
   Or that your prowesse can me yield reliefe:
Then heare the storie sad, which I shall tell you briefe.

43

"The forlorne Maiden, whom your eyes have seene
380   The laughing stocke of fortunes mockeries,
   Am th'only daughter of a King and Queene,
   Whose parents deare, whilest equall destinies
   Did runne about,[7] and their felicities
   The favourable heavens did not envy,
385   Did spread their rule through all the territories,
   Which Phison and Euphrates floweth by,
And Gehons golden waves doe wash continually.[8]

44

"Till that their cruell curséd enemy,
   An huge great Dragon horrible in sight,
390   Bred in the loathly lakes of Tartary,°   *Tartarus (Hell)*
   With murdrous ravine,° and devouring might   *destruction*
   Their kingdome spoild, and countrey wasted quight:
   Themselves, for feare into his jawes to fall,
   He forst to castle strong to take their flight,
395   Where fast embard in mightie brasen wall,
He has them now foure yeres besiegd to make them thrall.

45

"Full many knights adventurous and stout
   Have enterprizd that Monster to subdew;
   From every coast that heaven walks about,
400   Have thither come the noble Martiall crew,
   That famous hard atchievements still pursew,

7. I.e., while impartial destinies surrounded them.

8. These three rivers flow in the Garden
of Eden (Genesis ii.11–14).

Yet never any could that girlond win,
But all still shronke,° and still he greater grew: quailed
All they for want of faith, or guilt of sin,
405 The pitteous pray of his fierce crueltie have bin.

46

"At last yledd° with farre reported praise,   led
Which flying fame throughout the world had spread,
Of doughtie knights, whom Faery land did raise,
That noble order hight° of Maidenhed,[9]   called
410 Forthwith to court of Gloriane I sped,
Of Gloriane great Queene of glory bright,
Whose kingdomes seat Cleopolis is red,[1]
There to obtaine some such redoubted knight,
That Parents deare from tyrants powre deliver might.

47

415 "It was my chance (my chance was faire and good)
There for to find a fresh unprovéd knight,
Whose manly hands imbrewed in guiltie blood
Had never bene, ne ever by his might
Had throwne to ground the unregarded right:
420 Yet of his prowesse proofe he since hath made
(I witnesse am) in many a cruell fight;
The groning ghosts of many one dismaide
Have felt the bitter dint of his avenging blade.

48

"And ye the forlorne reliques of his powre,
425 His byting sword, and his devouring speare,
Which have enduréd many a dreadfull stowre,°   conflict
Can speake his prowesse, that did earst you beare,
And well could rule: now he hath left you heare,
To be the record of his ruefull losse,
430 And of my dolefull disaventurous deare:[2]
O heavie record of the good Redcrosse,
Where have you left your Lord, that could so well you tosse?

49

"Well hopéd I, and faire beginnings had,
That he my captive langour should redeeme,[3]
435 Till all unweeting, an Enchaunter bad
His sence abusd, and made him to misdeeme
My loyalty, not such as it did seeme;
That° rather death desire, then such despight.   I, who
Be judge ye heavens, that all things right esteeme,
440 How I him loved, and love with all my might,
So thought I eke of him, and thinke I thought aright.

9. Historically, the Order of the Garter. Its emblem shows St. George killing the dragon.
1. Named. "Cleopolis" means "famous city." In the historical allegory, it is London, as Gloriana is Elizabeth. In other contexts, however, it may be Camelot or the earthly counterpart of the New Jerusalem.
2. Unfortunate lover.
3. I.e., relieve my state, captive to sadness.

50

"Thenceforth me desolate he quite forsooke,
  To wander, where wilde fortune would me lead,
  And other bywaies he himselfe betooke,
445 Where never foot of living wight did tread,
  That brought not backe the balefull body dead;[4]
  In which him chauncéd false Duessa meete,
  Mine onely foe, mine onely deadly dread,
  Who with her witchcraft and misseeming° sweete, *deception*
450 Inveigled him to follow her desires unmeete.° *improper*

51

"At last by subtill sleights she him betraid
  Unto his foe, a Gyant huge and tall,
  Who him disarméd, dissolute,° dismaid, *enfeebled*
  Unwares surprised, and with mightie mall° *club*
455 The monster mercilesse him made to fall,
  Whose fall did never foe before behold;
  And now in darkesome dungeon, wretched thrall,
  Remedilesse, for aie° he doth him hold; *ever*
This is my cause of griefe, more great, then may be told."

52

460 Ere she had ended all, she gan to faint:
  But he her comforted and faire bespake,
  "Certes, Madame, ye have great cause of plaint,
  That stoutest heart, I weene, could cause to quake.
  But be of cheare, and comfort to you take:
465 For till I have acquit° your captive knight, *freed*
  Assure your selfe, I will you not forsake."
  His chearefull words revived her chearelesse spright,
So forth they went, the Dwarfe them guiding ever right.

Canto VIII

Faire virgin to redeeme her deare
brings Arthur to the fight:
Who slayes the Gyant, wounds the beast,
and strips Duessa quight.

1

Ay me, how many perils doe enfold
  The righteous man, to make him daily fall?
  Were not, that heavenly grace doth him uphold,
  And stedfast truth acquite him out of all.
5 Her love is firme, her care continuall,
  So oft as he through his owne foolish pride,
  Or weaknesse is to sinfull bands° made thrall: *bonds*
  Else should this Redcrosse knight in bands have dyde,
For whose deliverance she this Prince doth thither guide.

4. I.e., who returned alive.

2

10 They sadly traveild thus, untill they came
     Nigh to a castle builded strong and hie:
     Then cryde the Dwarfe, "lo yonder is the same,
     In which my Lord my liege doth lucklesse lie,
     Thrall to that Gyants hatefull tyrannie:
15   Therefore, deare Sir, your mightie powres assay."
     The noble knight alighted by and by[5]
     From loftie steede, and bad the Ladie stay,
To see what end of fight should him befall that day.

3

     So with the Squire, th'admirer of his might,
20   He marchéd forth towards that castle wall;
     Whose gates he found fast shut, ne living wight
     To ward° the same, nor answere commers call.   guard
     Then tooke that Squire an horne of bugle small,[6]
     Which hong adowne his side in twisted gold,
25   And tassels gay. Wyde wonders over all
     Of that same hornes great vertues weren told,
Which had approvéd° bene in uses manifold.   demonstrated

4

     Was never wight, that heard that shrilling sound,
     But trembling feare did feele in every vaine;
30   Three miles it might be easie heard around,
     And Ecchoes three answered it selfe againe:
     No false enchauntment, nor deceiptfull traine
     Might once abide the terror of that blast,
     But presently was voide and wholly vaine:
35   No gate so strong, no locke so firme and fast,
But with that percing noise flew open quite, or brast.°   burst

5

     The same before the Geants gate he blew,
     That all the castle quakéd from the ground,
     And every dore of freewill open flew.
40   The Gyant selfe dismaiéd with that sownd,
     Where he with his Duessa dalliance° fownd,   amorous play
     In hast came rushing forth from inner bowre,
     With staring countenance sterne, as one astownd,
     And staggering steps, to weet, what suddein stowre°   disturbance
45 Had wrought that horror strange, and dared his dreaded powre.

6

     And after him the proud Duessa came,
     High mounted on her manyheaded beast,
     And every head with fyrie tongue did flame,
     And every head was crownéd on his creast,
50   And bloudie mouthéd with late cruell feast.[7]
     That when the knight beheld, his mightie shild

5. Immediately.
6. A "bugle" is a wild ox; the "wide wonders" (marvelous tales) told of the horn connect it with the horn of Roland and the ram's horn of Joshua, with which he razed the walls of Jericho (Joshua vi.5).
7. Evidently the St. Bartholomew's Day Massacre of 1572, in which the French Huguenots (Protestants) were slaughtered.

Upon his manly arme he soone addrest,°   *adjusted*
And at him fiercely flew, with courage fild,°   *filled*
And eger greedinesse° through every member thrild.   *desire*

7

55 Therewith the Gyant buckled him to fight,
   Inflamed with scornefull wrath and high disdaine,
   And lifting up his dreadfull club on hight,
   All armed with ragged snubbes° and knottie graine,   *snags*
   Him thought at first encounter to have slaine.
60   But wise and warie was that noble Pere,°   *peer*
   And lightly leaping from so monstrous maine,°   *force*
   Did faire avoide the violence him nere;
It booted nought, to thinke, such thunderbolts to beare.[8]

8

Ne shame he thought to shunne so hideous might:
65   The idle° stroke, enforcing furious way,   *inaccurate*
   Missing the marke of his misaymèd sight
   Did fall to ground, and with his° heavie sway°   *its/force*
   So deepely dinted in the driven clay,
   That three yardes deepe a furrow up did throw:
70   The sad earth wounded with so sore assay,°   *assault*
   Did grone full grievous underneath the blow,
And trembling with strange feare, did like an earthquake show.

9

As when almightie Jove in wrathfull mood,
   To wreake° the guilt of mortall sins is bent,   *punish*
75   Hurles forth his thundring dart with deadly food,[9]
   Enrold in flames, and smouldring dreriment,
   Through riven cloudes and molten firmament;
   The fierce threeforkèd engin° making way,   *weapon*
   Both loftie towres and highest trees hath rent,
80   And all that might his angrie passage stay,
And shooting in the earth, casts up a mount of clay.

10

His boystrous° club, so buried in the ground,   *huge*
   He could not rearen up againe so light,
   But that the knight him at avantage found,
85   And whiles he strove his combred clubbe to quight°   *release*
   Out of the earth, with blade all burning bright
   He smote off his left arme, which like a blocke
   Did fall to ground, deprived of native might;
   Large streames of bloud out of the trunckèd stocke
90 Forth gushèd, like fresh water streame from riven rocke.[1]

11

Dismaièd with so desperate deadly wound,
   And eke impatient of[2] unwonted paine,
   He loudly brayd with beastly yelling sound,
   That all the fields rebellowèd againe;

8. The ensuing battle may be taken as the struggle of the Protestant against the Roman church—or that of Christian grace against evil, the Antichrist.

9. Hatred (feud).
1. Cf. Exodus xvii.6, where Moses smites the rock and water flows forth.
2. Agonized by.

95 As great a noyse, as when in Cymbrian plaine
     An heard of Bulles, whom kindly° rage doth sting,   *natural*
     Do for the milkie mothers want complaine,[3]
     And fill the fields with troublous bellowing,
     The neighbour woods around with hollow murmur ring.

12

100 That when his deare Duessa heard, and saw
     The evill stownd,° that daungerd her estate,   *blow*
     Unto his aide she hastily did draw
     Her dreadfull beast, who swolne with bloud of late
     Came ramping forth with proud presumpteous gate,
105 And threatned all his heads like flaming brands.°   *torches*
     But him the Squire made quickly to retrate,
     Encountring fierce with single° sword in hand,   *only*
     And twixt him and his Lord did like a bulwarke stand,

13

     The proud Duessa full of wrathfull spight,
110 And fierce disdaine, to be affronted so,
     Enforst her purple beast with all her might
     That stop° out of the way to overthroe,   *obstacle*
     Scorning the let° of so unequall foe: *obstruction*
     But nathemore° would that courageous swayne   *never the more*
115 To her yeeld passage, gainst his Lord to goe,
     But with outrageous strokes did him restraine,
     And with his bodie bard the way atwixt them twaine.

14

     Then tooke the angrie witch her golden cup,
     Which still she bore, replete with magick artes;[4]
120 Death and despeyre did many thereof sup,
     And secret poyson through their inner parts,
     Th' eternall bale of heavie wounded harts;
     Which after charmes and some enchauntments said,
     She lightly sprinkled on his weaker° parts;   *too weak*
125 Therewith his sturdie courage soone was quayd,°   *quelled*
     And all his senses were with suddeine dread dismayd.

15

     So downe he fell before the cruell beast,
     Who on his necke his bloudie clawes did seize,
     That life nigh crusht out of his panting brest:
130 No powre he had to stirre, nor will to rize.
     That when the carefull° knight gan well avise,   *watchful*
     He lightly left the foe, with whom he fought,
     And to the beast gan turne his enterprise;
     For wondrous anguish in his hart it wrought,
135 To see his lovéd Squire into such thraldome brought.

16

     And high advauncing his bloud-thirstie blade,

---

3. I.e., mourn the cows' absence.
4. Cf. the golden cup of the woman in Revelation, which is "full of abominations" (xvii.4), the chalice of the Roman church, and the cup of Circe (in *Odys-sey* X).

Stroke one of those deforméd heads so sore,[5]
   That of his puissance proud ensample made;
   His monstrous scalpe° downe to his teeth it tore   *skull*
140   And that misforméd shape mis-shapéd more:
   A sea of bloud gusht from the gaping wound,
   That her gay garments staynd with filthy gore,
   And overflowéd all the field around;
That over shoes in bloud he waded on the ground.

17

145 Thereat he roaréd for exceeding paine,
   That to have heard, great horror would have bred,
   And scourging th' emptie ayre with his long traine,
   Through great impatience° of his grievéd hed   *agony*
   His gorgeous ryder from her loftie sted
150   Would have cast downe, and trod in durtie myre,
   Had not the Gyant soone her succouréd;
   Who all enraged with smart and franticke yre,
Came hurtling in full fierce, and forst the knight retyre.

18

The force, which wont in two to be disperst,
155   In one alone left hand he now unites,
   Which is through rage more strong then both were erst;
   With which his hideous club aloft he dites,°   *raises*
   And at his foe with furious rigour smites,
   That strongest Oake might seeme to overthrow:
160   The stroke upon his shield so heavie lites,
   That to the ground it doubleth him full low:
What mortall wight could ever beare so monstrous blow?

19

And in his fall his shield, that covered was,
   Did loose his vele° by chaunce, and open flew: *veil*
165   The light whereof, that heavens light did pas,°   *surpass*
   Such blazing brightnesse through the aier threw,
   That eye mote not the same endure to vew.
   Which when the Gyaunt spyde with staring° eye,   *awed*
   He downe let fall his arme, and soft withdrew
170   His weapon huge, that heavéd was on hye
For to have slaine the man, that on the ground did lye.

20

And eke the fruitfull-headed° beast, amazed   *many-headed*
   At flashing beames of that sunshiny shield,
   Became starke blind, and all his senses dazed,
175   That downe he tumbled on the durtie field,
   And seemed himselfe as conqueréd to yield.
   Whom when his maistresse proud perceived to fall,
   Whiles yet his feeble feet for faintnesse reeld,
   Unto the Gyant loudly she gan call,
180 "O helpe Orgoglio, helpe, or else we perish all."

5. "I saw one of [the beast's] heads as it were wounded to death" (Revelation xiii.3).

21

At her so pitteous cry was much amooved
    Her champion stout, and for to ayde his frend,
    Againe his wonted angry weapon prooved:°   *tried*
    But all in vaine: for he has read his end
185   In that bright shield, and all their forces spend
    Themselves in vaine: for since that glauncing° sight,   *flashing*
    He hath no powre to hurt, nor to defend;
    As where th' Almighties lightning brond does light,
It dimmes the dazéd eyen, and daunts the senses quight.

22

190 Whom when the Prince, to battell new addrest,
    And threatning high his dreadfull stroke did see,
    His sparkling blade about his head he blest,°   *waved*
    And smote off quite his right leg by the knee,
    That downe he tombled; [6] as an aged tree,
195   High growing on the top of rocky clift,
    Whose hartstrings with keene steele nigh hewen be,
    The mightie trunck halfe rent, with ragged rift
Doth roll adowne the rocks, and fall with fearefull drift.°   *impact*

23

Or as a Castle rearéd high and round,
200   By subtile engins and malitious slight°   *magic*
    Is underminéd from the lowest ground,
    And her foundation forst,° and feebled quight,   *shattered*
    At last downe falles, and with her heapéd hight
    Her hastie ruine does more heavie make,
205   And yields it selfe unto the victours might;
    Such was this Gyaunts fall, that seemed to shake
The stedfast globe of earth, as it for feare did quake.

24

The knight then lightly leaping to the pray,
    With mortall steele him smot againe so sore,
210   That headlesse his unweldy bodie lay,
    All wallowd in his owne fowle bloudy gore,
    Which flowéd from his wounds in wondrous store.
    But soone as breath out of his breast did pas,
    That huge great body, which the Gyaunt bore,
215   Was vanisht quite, and of that monstrous mas
Was nothing left, but like an emptie bladder was.

25

Whose grievous fall, when false Duessa spide,
    Her golden cup she cast unto the ground,
    And crownéd mitre rudely threw aside;
220   Such percing griefe her stubborne hart did wound,
    That she could not endure that dolefull stound,°   *sorrow*
    But leaving all behind her, fled away:
    The light-foot Squire her quickly turned around,
    And by hard meanes enforcing her to stay,
225 So brought unto his Lord, as his deservéd pray.

---

6. Pride is not defeated all at once, but step by step; for the image of the tree,
cf. *Aeneid* II.626–31, among other sources.

26

The royall Virgin, which beheld from farre,
  In pensive plight, and sad perplexitie,
  The whole atchievement° of this doubtfull warre,   *course*
  Came running fast to greet his victorie,
230 With sober gladnesse, and myld modestie,
  And with sweet joyous cheare him thus bespake;
  "Faire braunch of noblesse, flowre of chevalrie,
  That with your worth the world amazéd make,
How shall I quite° the paines, ye suffer for my sake?   *requite*

27

235 "And you [7] fresh bud of vertue springing fast,
  Whom these sad eyes saw nigh unto deaths dore,
  What hath poore Virgin for such perill past,
  Wherewith you to reward? Accept therefore
  My simple selfe, and service evermore;
240 And he that high does sit, and all things see
  With equall° eyes, their merites to restore,°   *impartial/reward*
  Behold what ye this day have done for mee,
And what I cannot quite, requite with usuree.

28

"But sith the heavens, and your faire handeling°   *conduct*
245 Have made you maister of the field this day,
  Your fortune maister eke with governing,[8]
  And well begun end all so well, I pray,
  Ne let that wicked woman scape away;
  For she it is, that did my Lord bethrall,
250 My dearest Lord, and deepe in dongeon lay,
  Where he his better dayes hath wasted all.
O heare, how piteous he to you for ayd does call."

29

Forthwith he gave in charge unto his Squire,
  That scarlot whore to keepen carefully;
255 Whiles he himselfe with greedie ° great desire   *eager*
  Into the Castle entred forcibly,
  Where living creature none he did espye;
  Then gan he lowdly through the house to call:
  But no man cared to answere to his crye.
260 There raignd a solemne silence over all,
Nor voice was heard, nor wight was seene in bowre or hall.

30

At last with creeping crooked pace forth came
  An old old man, with beard as white as snow,
  That on a staffe his feeble steps did frame,
265 And guide his wearie gate both too and fro:
  For his eye sight him failéd long ygo,
  And on his arme a bounch of keyes he bore,
  The which unuséd rust did overgrow:
  Those were the keyes of every inner dore,
270 But he could not them use, but kept them still in store.

---

7. I.e., the Squire. Una's reward to the Squire who has done such faithful service in the war against Pride is itself an exemplary act of humility.
8. Secure your good fortune also by prudent management.

31

But very uncouth sight was to behold,
How he did fashion his untoward° pace,   *awkward*
For as he forward mooved his footing old,
So backward still was turned his wrincled face,
275 Unlike to men, who ever as they trace,
Both feet and face one way are wont to lead.
This was the auncient keeper of that place,
And foster father of the Gyant dead;
His name Ignaro did his nature right aread.[9]

32

280 His reverend haires and holy gravitie
The knight much honord, as beseeméd well,[1]
And gently askt, where all the people bee,
Which in that stately building wont to dwell.
Who answerd him full soft, he could not tell.
285 Againe he askt, where that same knight was layd,
Whom great Orgoglio with his puissaunce fell
Had made his caytive thrall; againe he sayde,
He could not tell: ne ever other answere made.

33

Then askéd he, which way he in might pas:
290 He could not tell, againe he answeréd.
Thereat the curteous knight displeaséd was,
And said, "Old sire, it seemes thou hast not red °   *recognized*
How ill it sits with [2] that same silver hed
In vaine to mocke, or mockt in vaine to bee:
295 But if thou be, as thou art pourtrahéd
With natures pen, in ages grave degree,[3]
Aread in graver wise, what I demaund of thee."

34

His answere likewise was, he could not tell.
Whose sencelesse speach, and doted ignorance
300 When as the noble Prince had markéd well,
He ghest his nature by his countenance,
And calmd his wrath with goodly temperance.
Then to him stepping, from his arme did reach
Those keyes, and made himselfe free enterance.
305 Each dore he opené without any breach;°   *forcing*
There was no barre to stop, nor foe him to empeach.°   *hinder*

35

There all within full rich arayd he found,
With royall arras and resplendent gold.
And did with store of every thing abound,
310 That greatest Princes presence might behold.
But all the floore (too filthy to be told)
With bloud of guiltlesse babes, and innocents trew,

---

9. Make known. Doting ignorance ("Ig-naro") is a fit servant for pride and the false church; he has his counterparts in Abessa and Corceca.
1. Seemed proper.
2. I.e., suits.
3. I.e., dignity.

Which there were slaine, as sheepe out of the fold,
Defiléd was, that dreadfull was to vew,
315 And sacred° ashes over it was strowéd new.   *accursed*

36

And there beside of marble stone was built
An Altare, carved with cunning imagery,
On which true Christians bloud was often spilt,
And holy Martyrs often doen to dye,[4]
320 With cruell malice and strong tyranny:
Whose blessed sprites from underneath the stone
To God for vengeance cryde continually,[5]
And with great griefe were often heard to grone,
That hardest heart would bleede, to heare their piteous mone.

37

325 Through every rowme he sought, and every bowr,
But no where could he find that wofull thrall:
At last he came unto an yron doore,
That fast was lockt, but key found not at all
Emongst that bounch, to open it withall;
330 But in the same a little grate was pight,°   *placed*
Through which he sent his voyce, and lowd did call
With all his powre, to weet, if living wight
Were houséd therewithin, whom he enlargen° might.   *release*

38

Therewith an hollow, dreary, murmuring voyce
335 These piteous plaints and dolours did resound;
"O who is that, which brings me happy choyce°   *chance*
Of death, that here lye dying every stound,°   *moment*
Yet live perforce in balefull darkenesse bound?
For now three Moones have changéd thrice their hew,°   *shape*
340 And have beene thrice hid underneath the ground,
Since I the heavens chearefull face did vew,
O welcome thou, that doest of death bring tydings trew."

39

Which when that Champion heard, with percing point
Of pitty deare° his hart was thrilléd sore,   *extreme*
345 And trembling horrour ran through every joynt,
For ruth of gentle knight so fowle forlore:
Which shaking off, he rent that yron dore,
With furious force, and indignation fell;°   *fierce*
Where entred in, his foot could find no flore,
350 But all a deepe descent, as darke as hell,
That breathéd ever forth a filthie banefull smell.

40

But neither darkenesse fowle, nor filthy bands,
Nor noyous smell his purpose could withhold,
(Entire affection hateth nicer° hands)   *too fastidious*

---

4. Put to death.
5. "And when he had opened the fifth seal, I saw under the altar the souls of them that were slain for the word of God, and for the testimony which they held: And they cried with a loud voice, saying, How long, O Lord, holy and true, dost thou not judge and avenge our blood on them that dwell on the earth?" (Revelation vi.9–10).

355 But that with constant zeale, and courage bold,
After long paines and labours manifold,
He found the meanes that Prisoner up to reare;
Whose feeble thighes, unhable to uphold
His pinéd° corse, him scarse to light could beare,   *wasted*
360 A ruefull spectacle of deathe and ghastly drere.°   *wretchedness*

41

His sad dull eyes deepe sunck in hollow pits,
Could not endure th' unwonted sunne to view;
His bare thin cheekes for want of better bits,°   *food*
And empty sides deceivéd° of their dew,   *cheated*
365 Could make a stony hart his hap to rew;
His rawbone armes, whose mighty brawnéd bowrs°   *muscles*
Were wont to rive steele plates, and helmets hew,
Were cleane consumed, and all his vitall powres
Decayd, and all his flesh shronk up like withered flowres.

42

370 Whom when his Lady saw, to him she ran
With hasty joy: to see him made her glad,
And sad to view his visage pale and wan,
Who earst in flowres of freshest youth was clad.
Tho° when her well of teares she wasted had,   *then*
375 She said, "Ah dearest Lord, what evill starre
On you hath fround, and pourd his influence bad,
That of your selfe ye thus berobbéd arre,
And this misseeming hew⁶ your manly looks doth marre?

43

"But welcome now my Lord, in wele or woe,
380 Whose presence I have lackt to long a day;
And fie on Fortune mine avowéd foe,
Whose wrathfull wreakes° them selves do now alay.   *punishments*
And for these wrongs shall treble penaunce pay
Of treble good: good growes of evils priefe."⁷
385 The chearelesse man, whom sorrow did dismay,°   *unnerve*
Had no delight to treaten° of his griefe;   *speak*
His long enduréd famine needed more reliefe.

44

"Faire Lady," then said that victorious knight,⁸
"The things, that grievous were to do, or beare,
390 Them to renew, I wote, breeds no delight;
Best musicke breeds delight in loathing eare:
But th'onely good, that growes of passéd feare,
Is to be wise, and ware° of like agein.   *wary*
This dayes ensample hath this lesson deare
395 Deepe written in my heart with yron pen,
That blisse may not abide in state of mortall men.

45

"Henceforth sir knight, take to you wonted strength,
And maister these mishaps with patient might;

---

6. Unseemly shape.   8. I.e., Arthur.
7. Endurance of evil.

Loe where your foe lyes stretcht in monstrous length,
400 And loe that wicked woman in your sight,[9]
The roote of all your care, and wretched plight,
Now in your powre, to let her live, or dye."
"To do her dye," quoth Una, "were despight,°   spiteful
And shame t'avenge so weake an enimy;
405 But spoile her of her scarlot robe, and let her fly."

46

So as she bad, that witch they disaraid,
And robd of royall robes, and purple pall,
And ornaments that richly were displaid;
Ne sparéd they to strip her naked all.
410 Then when they had despoild her tire° and call,°   robe/headdress
Such as she was, their eyes might her behold,
That her misshapéd parts did them appall,
A loathly, wrinckled hag, ill favoured, old,
Whose secret filth good manners biddeth not be told.

47

415 Her craftie head was altogether bald,
And as in hate of honorable eld,°   age
Was overgrowne with scurfe and filthy scald;°   scabs
Her teeth out of her rotten gummes were feld,°   fallen
And her sowre breath abhominably smeld;
420 Her dried dugs, like bladders lacking wind,
Hong downe, and filthy matter from them weld;
Her wrizled skin as rough, as maple rind,
So scabby was, that would have loathd all womankind.

48

Her neather parts, the shame of all her kind,[1]
425 My chaster Muse for shame doth blush to write;
But at her rompe she growing had behind
A foxes taile, with dong all fowly dight;°   covered
And eke her feete most monstrous were in sight;
For one of them was like an Eagles claw,
430 With griping talaunts armd to greedy fight,
The other like a Beares uneven° paw: rough
More ugly shape yet never living creature saw.[2]

49

Which when the knights beheld, amazd they were,
And wondred at so fowle deforméd wight.
435 "Such then," said Una, "as she seemeth here,
Such is the face of falshood, such the sight
Of fowle Duessa, when her borrowed light
Is laid away, and counterfesaunce° knowne."   disguise
Thus when they had the witch disrobéd quight,
440 And all her filthy feature° open showne,   form
They let her goe at will, and wander wayes unknowne.

9. Over there.
1. I.e., womankind.
2. Cf. Duessa with the House of Pride:
fair above, foul below. Her filthiness is
like that of Alcina in Ariosto's *Orlando
Furioso*, VII.71–73. Cf. also Revelation

xvii.16: "these shall hate the whore, and
shall make her desolate and naked."
Foxes (cf. line 427) were noted for
cunning; eagles and bears (lines 429,
431) for rapacity, cruelty, and brutality.

50

She flying fast from heavens hated face,
  And from the world that her discovered wide,
  Fled to the wastfull wildernesse apace,
445 From living eyes her open shame to hide,
  And lurkt in rocks and caves long unespide.
  But that faire crew of knights, and Una faire
  Did in that castle afterwards abide,
  To rest them selves, and weary powres repaire,
450 Where store they found of all, that dainty was and rare.

Canto IX

His loves and lignage Arthur tells:
The knights knit friendly bands:
Sir Trevisan flies from Despayre,
Whom Redcrosse knight withstands.

1

O goodly golden chaine,[3] wherewith yfere°   together
  The vertues linkéd are in lovely wize:
  And noble minds of yore allyéd were,
  In brave poursuit of chevalrous emprize,°   adventure
5 That none did others safety despize,
  Nor aid envy° to him, in need that stands,   begrudge
  But friendly each did others prayse devize
  How to advaunce with favourable hands,
As this good Prince redeemd the Redcrosse knight from bands.°bonds

2

10 Who when their powres, empaird through labour long,
  With dew repast they had recuréd° well,   restored
  And that weake captive wight now wexéd strong,
  Them list no lenger there at leasure dwell,
  But forward fare, as their adventures fell,
15 But ere they parted, Una faire besought
  That straunger knight his name and nation tell;
  Least so great good, as he for her had wrought,
Should die unknown, and buried be in thanklesse thought.

3

"Faire virgin," said the Prince, "ye me require
20 A thing without the compas[4] of my wit:
  For both the lignage and the certain Sire,
  From which I sprong, from me are hidden yit.
  For all so soone as life did me admit
  Into this world, and shewéd heavens light,
25 From mothers pap I taken was unfit:°   unsuitably
  And streight delivered to a Faery knight,
To be upbrought in gentle thewes° and martiall might.   manners

3. Stanza 1 opens with an invocation of
the golden chain of love or concord
which binds the world and the human
race together (cf. v.25 and note). It

will be reaffirmed in stanza 19 when the
two knights exchange symbolic gifts and
shake hands in token of fellowship.
4. I.e., beyond the reach of.

4

"Unto old Timon⁵ he me brought bylive,°   *immediately*
  Old Timon, who in youthly yeares hath beene
30 In warlike feates th'expertest man alive,
  And is the wisest now on earth I weene;
  His dwelling is low in a valley greene,
  Under the foot of Rauran mossy hore,°   *gray*
  From whence the river Dee as silver cleene°   *pure*
35 His tombling billowes rolls with gentle rore:⁶
There all my dayes he traind me up in vertuous lore.

5

"Thither the great Magicien Merlin came,
  As was his use, ofttimes to visit me:
  For he had charge my discipline to frame,
40 And Tutours nouriture° to oversee.   *training*
  Him oft and oft I askt in privitie,
  Of what loines and what lignage I did spring:
  Whose aunswere bad me still assuréd bee,
  That I was sonne and heire unto a king,
45 As time in her just terme⁷ the truth to light should bring."

6

"Well worthy impe,"° said then the Lady gent,°   *offspring/gentle*
  "And Pupill fit for such a Tutours hand.
  But what adventure, or what high intent
  Hath brought you hither into Faery land,
50 Aread° Prince Arthur, crowne of Martiall band?"   *declare*
  "Full hard it is," quoth he, "to read aright
  The course of heavenly cause, or understand
  The secret meaning of th'eternall might,
That rules mens wayes, and rules the thoughts of living wight.

7

55 "For whither he through fatall° deepe foresight   *prophetic*
  Me hither sent, for cause to me unghest,
  Or that fresh bleeding wound, which day and night
  Whilome° doth rancle in my riven brest,   *incessantly*
  With forcéd fury following his° behest,   *its*
60 Me hither brought by wayes yet never found,
  You to have helpt I hold my selfe yet blest."
  "Ah curteous knight," quoth she, "what secret wound
Could ever find,° to grieve the gentlest hart on ground?"   *succeed*

8

"Deare Dame," quoth he, "you sleeping sparkes awake,
65 Which trubled once, into huge flames will grow,
  Ne ever will their fervent fury slake
  Till living moysture into smoke do flow,
  And wasted° life do lye in ashes low.   *consumed*
  Yet sithens° silence lesseneth not my fire,   *since*

5. The name means "Honor."
6. The hill Rauran is in Wales; the river Dee also flows in, and forms part of the boundary of Wales. The Tudors (Queen Elizabeth's family) were originally Welsh, and the legends of Arthur had their beginnings in the Celtic mythology of early Wales.
7. Due course.

70   But told it flames, and hidden it does glow,
      I will revele, what ye so much desire:
Ah Love, lay downe thy bow, the whiles I may respire.°   *breathe*

9

"It was in freshest flowre of youthly yeares,
    When courage first does creepe in manly chest,
75   Then first the coale of kindly° heat appeares   *of nature*
    To kindle love in every living brest;
    But me had warnd old Timons wise behest,
    Those creeping flames by reason to subdew,
    Before their rage grew to so great unrest,
80   As miserable lovers use to rew,
Which still wex old in woe, whiles woe still wexeth new.

10

"That idle name of love, and lovers life,
    As losse of time, and vertues enimy
    I ever scornd, and joyd to stirre up strife,
85   In middest of their mournfull Tragedy,
    Ay wont to laugh, when them I heard to cry,
    And blow the fire, which them to ashes brent:°   *burned*
    Their God himselfe, grieved at my libertie,
    Shot many a dart at me with fiers intent,
90   But I them warded all with wary government.[8]

11

"But all in vaine: no fort can be so strong,
    Ne fleshly brest can arméd be so sound,
    But will at last be wonne with battrie° long,   *siege*
    Or unawares at disavantage found;
95   Nothing is sure, that growes on earthly ground:
    And who most trustes in arme of fleshly might,
    And boasts, in beauties chaine not to be bound,
    Doth soonest fall in disaventrous° fight.   *disastrous*
And yeeldes his caytive neck to victours most° despight.   *greatest*

12

100 "Ensample make of him your haplesse joy,
    And of my selfe now mated,° as ye see;   *overcome*
    Whose prouder° vaunt that proud avenging boy   *too proud*
    Did soone pluck downe, and curbd my libertie.
    For on a day prickt° forth with jollitie   *rode*
105   Of looser life, and heat of hardiment,°   *boldness*
    Raunging the forest wide on courser free,
    The fields, the floods, the heavens with one consent
Did seeme to laugh° on me, and favour mine intent.   *smile*

13

"For-wearied with my sports, I did alight
110   From loftie steed, and downe to sleepe me layd;
    The verdant gras my couch did goodly dight,°   *make*
    And pillow was my helmet faire displayd:

8. I.e., self-control. The descriptions here of Cupid's archery and of the siege of the castle of chastity (in the next stanza) have many echoes from the courtly-love traditions.

Whiles every sence the humour sweet embayd,°   *pervaded*
And slombring soft my hart did steale away,
115   Me seeméd, by my side a royall Mayd
Her daintie limbes full softly down did lay:
So faire a creature yet saw never sunny day.

14

"Most goodly glee° and lovely blandishment°   *pleasure/compliment*
She to me made, and bad me love here deare,
120   For dearely sure her love was to me bent,
As when just time expiréd[9] should appeare.
But whether dreames delude, or true it were,
Was never hart so ravisht with delight,
Ne living man like words did ever heare,
125   As she to me delivered all that night;
And at her parting said, She Queene of Faeries hight.[1]

15

"When I awoke, and found her place devoyd,°   *empty*
And nought but presséd gras, where she had lyen,
I sorrowed all so much, as earst I joyd,
130   And washéd all her place with watry eyen.
From that day forth I loved that face divine;
From that day forth I cast in carefull mind,
To seeke her out with labour, and long tyne,°   *hardship*
And never vow to rest, till her I find,
135   Nine monethes I seeke in vaine yet ni'll° that vow unbind."   *will not*

16

Thus as he spake, his visage wexéd pale,
And chaunge of hew great passion did bewray;
Yet still he strove to cloke his inward bale,°   *grief*
And hide the smoke, that did his fire display,
140   Till gentle Una thus to him gan say;
"Oh happy Queene of Faeries, that hast found
Mongst many, one that with his prowesse may
Defend thine honour, and thy foes confound:
True Loves are often sown, but seldom grow on ground."

17

145   "Thine, O then," said the gentle Redcrosse knight,
"Next to that Ladies love, shalbe the place,
O fairest virgin, full of heavenly light,
Whose wondrous faith, exceeding earthly race,
Was firmest fixt in mine extremest case.
150   And you, my Lord, the Patrone° of my life,   *protector*
Of that great Queene may well gaine worthy grace:
For onely worthy you through prowes priefe[2]
Yf living man mote worthy be, to be her liefe."°   *love*

9. The right occasion having arisen.
1. Was called. Gloriana is also, in the two principal allegories, Queen Elizabeth and Heavenly Grace. This is one of the passages where the "faery" nature of *The Faerie Queene* makes itself strongly felt. In the background are many folk-tales and ballads of a hero bewitched by the Queen of Faery. Note further the complex layering, by which Arthur, who is a character in Faery, has entered this world through a vision in a dream.
2. Demonstration of prowess.

18

So diversly discoursing of their loves,
155 The golden Sunne his glistring head gan shew,
And sad remembraunce now the Prince amoves,
With fresh desire his voyage to pursew:
Als° Una earnd° her traveill to renew.   *so/yearned*
Then those two knights, fast friendship for to bynd,
160 And love establish each to other trew,
Gave goodly gifts, the signes of gratefull mynd,
And eke as pledges firme, right hands together joynd.

19

Prince Arthur gave a boxe of Diamond sure,°   *flawless*
Embowd° with gold and gorgeous ornament,   *bound*
165 Wherein were closd few drops of liquor pure,
Of wondrous worth, and vertue excellent,
That any wound could heale incontinent:°   *immediately*
Which to requite, the Redcrosse knight him gave
A booke, wherein his Saveours testament
170 Was writ with golden letters rich and brave;
A worke of wondrous grace, and able soules to save.

20

Thus beene they parted, Arthur on his way
To seeke his love, and th'other for to fight
With Unas foe, that all her realme did pray.°   *prey upon*
175 But she now weighing the decayéd plight,
And shrunken synewes of her chosen knight,
Would not a while her forward course pursew,
Ne bring him forth in face of dreadfull fight,
Till he recovered had his former hew:
180 For him to be yet weake and wearie well she knew.

21

So as they traveild, lo they gan espy
An arméd knight towards them gallop fast,
That seeméd from some fearéd foe to fly,
Or other griesly thing, that him agast.°   *scared*
185 Still as he fled, his eye was backward cast,
As if his feare still followed him behind;
Als flew his steed, as he his bands had brast,
And with his wingéd heeles did tread the wind,
As he had beene a fole of Pegasus his kind.[3]

22

190 Nigh as he drew, they might perceive his head
To be unarmd, and curld uncombéd heares
Upstaring stiffe, dismayd with uncouth dread;
Nor drop of bloud in all his face appeares
Nor life in limbe: and to increase his feares,
195 In fowle reproch° of knighthoods faire degree,°   *disgrace/position*
About his neck an hempen rope he weares,
That with his glistring armes does ill agree;[4]
But he of rope or armes has now no memoree.

---

3. I.e., like Pegasus (a flying horse).
4. The rope around his neck suggests attempts (past and future) at suicide—the reason for which becomes clear a few stanzas later.

23

The Redcrosse knight toward him crosséd fast,
    To weet, what mister° wight was so dismayd: *kind of*
    There him he finds all sencelesse and aghast,
    That of him selfe he seemd to be afrayd;
    Whom hardly he from flying forward stayd,
    Till he these wordes to him deliver might;
    "Sir knight, aread who hath ye thus arayd,
    And eke from whom make ye this hasty flight:
For never knight I saw in such misseeming° plight."   *unseemly*

24

He answerd nought at all, but adding new
    Feare to his first amazment, staring wide
    With stony eyes, and hartlesse hollow hew,
    Astonisht stood, as one that had aspide
    Infernall furies, with their chaines untide.
    Him yet againe, and yet againe bespake
    The gentle knight; who nought to him replide,
    But trembling every joynt did inly quake,
And foltring tongue at last these words seemd forth to shake.

25

"For Gods deare love, Sir knight, do me not stay;
    For loe he comes, he comes fast after mee."
    Eft° looking backe would faine have runne away;   *again*
    But he him forst to stay, and tellen free
    The secret cause of his perplexitie:
    Yet nathemore° by his bold hartie speach,   *not at all*
    Could his bloud-frosen hart emboldned bee,
    But through his boldnesse rather feare did reach,
Yet forst, at last he made through silence suddein breach.

26

"And am I now in safetie sure," quoth he,
    "From him, that would have forcéd me to dye?
    And is the point of death now turnd fro mee,
    That I may tell this haplesse history?"
    "Feare nought:" quoth he, "no daunger now is nye."
    "Then shall I you recount a ruefull cace,"
    Said he, "the which with this unlucky eye
    I late beheld, and had not greater grace
Me reft from it, had bene partaker of the place.[5]

27

"I lately chaunst (Would I had never chaunst)
    With a faire knight to keepen companee,
    Sir Terwin hight, that well himselfe advaunst
    In all affaires, and was both bold and free,
    But not so happie as mote happie bee:
    He loved, as was his lot, a Ladie gent,°   *noble*
    That him againe° loved in the least degree: *in return*
    For she was proud, and of too high intent,°   *ambition*
And joyd to see her lover languish and lament.

5. I.e., shared the same fate.

28

"From whom returning sad and comfortlesse,
245   As on the way together we did fare,
    We met that villen (God from him me blesse°) *defend*
    That curséd wight, from whom I scapt why leare,° *recently*
    A man of hell, that cals himselfe Despaire;[6]
    Who first us greets, and after faire areedes° *tells*
250   Of tydings strange, and of adventures rare:
    So creeping close, as Snake in hidden weedes,
Inquireth of our states, and of our knightly deedes.

29

"Which when he knew, and felt our feeble harts
    Embost° with bale,° and bitter byting griefe, *exhausted/sorrow*
255   Which love had launchéd with his deadly darts,
    With wounding words and termes of foule repriefe° *insult*
    He pluckt from us all hope of due reliefe,
    That earst us held in love of lingring life;
    Then hopelesse hartlesse, gan the cunning thiefe
260   Perswade us die, to stint° all further strife: *end*
To me he lent this rope, to him a rustie knife.

30

"With which sad instrument of hastie death,
    That wofull lover, loathing lenger° light, *longer*
    A wide way made to let forth living breath.
265   But I more fearefull, or more luckie wight,
    Dismayd with that deforméd dismall sight,
    Fled fast away, halfe dead with dying feare:[7]
    Ne yet assured of life by you, Sir knight,
    Whose like infirmitie like chaunce may beare:
270   But God you never let his charméd speeches heare."

31

"How may a man," said he, "with idle speach
    Be wonne, to spoyle the Castle of his health?"
    "I wote," quoth he, "whom triall° late did teach, *experience*
    That like would not[8] for all this worldes wealth:
275   His subtill tongue, like dropping honny, mealt'th° *melts*
    Into the hart, and searcheth every vaine,
    That ere one be aware, by secret stealth
    His powre is reft, and weaknesse doth remaine.
O never Sir desire to try° his guilefull traine." *test*

32

280   "Certes," said he, "hence shall I never rest,
    Till I that treachours art have heard and tride;
    And you Sir knight, whose name mote° I request, *might*
    Of grace do me unto his cabin guide."

---

6. Redcrosse has hitherto been the victim of pride and rashness; here, another spiritual vice, directly contrary, is met—the temptation to the ultimate Christian sin, the despair of God's grace. Such despair was a concern to Renaissance writers of religious and medical works. Robert Burton, in his *Anatomy* *of Melancholy* (1621), wrote that the despair "which concerns God * * * [is] opposite to hope, and a most pernicious sin * * * The part affected is the whole soul" ("Religious Melancholy," II.i.2).
7. Fear of death.
8. I.e., would not do the like again.

"I that hight Trevisan," quoth he, "will ride
285 Against my liking backe, to doe you grace:
 But nor for gold nor glee° will I abide   *glitter*
 By you, when ye arrive in that same place;
For lever° had I die, then see his deadly face."   *rather*

33

Ere long they come, where that same wicked wight
290 His dwelling has, low in an hollow cave,
 Farre underneath a craggie clift ypight,°   *placed*
 Darke, dolefull, drearie, like a greedie grave,
 That still for carrion carcases doth crave:
 On top whereof aye dwelt the ghastly Owle,
295 Shrieking his balefull note, which ever drave
 Farre from that haunt all other chearefull fowle;
And all about it wandring ghostes did waile and howle.

34

And all about old stockes and stubs of trees,
 Whereon nor fruit, nor leafe was ever seene,
300 Did hang upon the ragged rocky knees;°   *crags*
 On which had many wretches hangéd beene,
 Whose carcases were scattered on the greene,
 And throwne about the cliffs. Arrivéd there,
 That bare-head knight for dread and dolefull teene,° *grief*
305 Would faine have fled, ne durst approachen neare,
But th'other forst him stay, and comforted in feare.

35

That darkesome cave they enter, where they find
 That ccurséd man, low sitting on the ground,
 Musing full sadly in his sullein mind;
310 His griesie° lockes, long growen, and unbound, *gray*
 Disordred hong about his shoulders round,
 And hid his face; through which his hollow eyne
 Lookt deadly dull, and staréd as astound;
 His raw-bone cheekes through penurie and pine,° *starvation*
315 Were shronke into his jawes, as° he did never dine. *as if*

36

His garment nought but many ragged clouts,°   *cloths*
 With thornes together pind and patchéd was,
 The which his naked sides he wrapt abouts;
 And him beside there lay upon the gras
320 A drearie corse, whose life away did pas,
 All wallowd in his owne yet luke-warme blood,
 That from his wound yet welléd fresh alas;
 In which a rustie knife fast fixéd stood,
And made an open passage for the gushing flood.

37

325 Which piteous spectacle, approving trew
 The wofull tale that Trevisan had told,
 When as the gentle Redcrosse knight did vew,
 With firie zeale he burnt in courage bold,

Him to avenge, before his bloud were cold,
330 And to the villein said, "Thou damnéd wight,
The author of this fact,° we here behold,   deed
What justice can but judge against thee right,
With thine owne bloud to price° his bloud, here   pay for
    shed in sight?"

38

"What franticke fit," quoth he,[9] "hath thus distraught
335 Thee, foolish man, so rash a doome° to give?   judgment
What justice ever other judgement taught,
But he should die, who merites not to live?
None else to death this man despayring drive,°   drove
But his owne guiltie mind deserving death.
340 Is then unjust to each his due to give?
Or let him die, that loatheth living breath?
Or let him die at ease, that liveth here uneath°?   uneasily

39

"Who travels by the wearie wandring way,
To come unto his wishéd home in haste,
345 And meetes a flood, that doth his passage stay,
Is not great grace to helpe him over past,
Or free his feet, that in the myre sticke fast?
Most envious man, that grieves at neighbours good,
And fond,° that joyest in the woe thou hast,   foolish
350 Why wilt not let him passe, that long hath stood
Upon the banke, yet wilt thy selfe not passe the flood?

40

"He there does now enjoy eternall rest
And happie ease, which thou doest want and crave,
And further from it daily wanderest:
355 What if some litle paine the passage have,
That makes fraile flesh to feare the bitter wave?
Is not short paine well borne, that brings long ease,
And layes the soule to sleepe in quiet grave?
Sleepe after toyle, port after stormie seas,
360 Ease after warre, death after life does greatly please."[1]

41

The knight much wondred at his suddeine° wit,   quick
And said, "The terme of life is limited,
Ne may a man prolong, nor shorten it;
The souldier may not move from watchfull sted,°   position
365 Nor leave his stand, untill his Captaine bed."°   commands
"Who life did limit by almightie doome,"
Quoth he,[2] "knowes best the termes establishéd;
And he, that points the Centonell his roome,°   station
Doth license him depart at sound of morning droome.

---

9. I.e., Despaire.
1. Despaire's arguments on behalf of suicide as against a painful life are derived, like those of Hamlet in his third soliloquy (*Hamlet* III.i.56–88), princi-

pally from Seneca, Marcus Aurelius, and the ancient stoics, and from Old Testament utterings on divine justice.
2. I.e., Despaire.

42

370 "Is not his deed, what ever thing is donne,
    In heaven and earth? did not he all create
    To die againe? all ends that was begonne.
    Their times in his eternall booke of fate
    Are written sure, and have their certaine date.
375 Who then can strive with strong necessitie,
    That holds the world in his° still chaunging state,   *its*
    Or shunne the death ordaynd by destinie?
When houre of death is come, let none aske whence, nor why.

43

"The lenger life, I wote° the greater sin,   *know*
380 The greater sin, the greater punishment:
    All those great battels, which thou boasts to win,
    Through strife, and bloud-shed, and avengement,
    Now praysd, hereafter deare thou shalt repent:
    For life must life, and bloud must bloud repay.
385 Is not enough thy evill life forespent?
    For he, that once hath misséd the right way,
The further he doth goe, the further he doth stray.

44

"Then do no further goe, no further stray,
    But here lie downe, and to thy rest betake,
390 Th'ill to prevent, that life ensewen may.[3]
    For what hath life, that may it lovéd make,
    And gives not rather cause it to forsake?
    Feare, sicknesse, age, losse, labour, sorrow, strife,
    Paine, hunger, cold, that makes the hart to quake;
395 And ever fickle fortune rageth rife,
All which, and thousands mo° do make a loathsome life.   *more*

45

"Thou wretched man, of death hast greatest need,
    If in true ballance thou wilt weigh thy state:
    For never knight, that daréd warlike deede,
400 More lucklesse disaventures did amate:°   *appall*
    Witnesse the dongeon deepe, wherein of late
    Thy life shut up, for death so oft did call;
    And though good lucke prolongéd hath thy date,°   *span of life*
    Yet death then, would the like mishaps forestall,
405 Into the which hereafter thou maiest happen fall.

46

"Why then doest thou, O man of sin, desire
    To draw thy dayes forth to their last degree?
    Is not the measure of thy sinfull hire[4]
    High heapéd up with huge iniquitie,
410 Against the day of wrath,[5] to burden thee?
    Is not enough that to this Ladie milde
    Thou falséd hast thy faith with perjurie,
    And sold thy selfe to serve Duessa vilde,°   *vile*
With whom in all abuse thou hast thy selfe defilde?

3. I.e., to prevent the evil that will en-   4. Service to sin.
sue in the rest of your life.   5. Judgment Day.

47

415 "Is not he just, that all this doth behold
From highest heaven, and beares an equall° eye?   *impartial*
Shall he thy sins up in his knowledge fold,
And guiltie be of thine impietie?
Is not his law, Let every sinner die:
420 Die shall all flesh? what then must needs be donne,
Is it not better to doe willinglie,
Then linger, till the glasse be all out ronne?
Death is the end of woes: die soone, O faeries sonne."

48

The knight was much enmovéd with his speach,
425 That as a swords point through his hart did perse,
And in his conscience made a secret breach,
Well knowing true all, that he did reherse°   *recount*
And to his fresh remembrance did reverse°   *bring back*
The ugly vew of his deforméd crimes,
430 That all his manly powres it did disperse,
As he were charméd with inchaunted rimes,
That oftentimes he quakt, and fainted oftentimes.

49

In which amazement, when the Miscreant
Perceivéd him to waver weake and fraile,
435 Whiles trembling horror did his conscience dant,°   *daunt*
And hellish anguish did his soule assaile,
To drive him to despaire, and quite to quaile,°   *be dismayed*
He shewed him painted in a table° plaine,   *picture*
The damnéd ghosts, that doe in torments waile,
440 And thousand feends that doe them endlesse paine
With fire and brimstone, which for ever shall remaine.

50

The sight whereof so throughly him dismaid,
That nought but death before his eyes he saw,
And ever burning wrath before him laid,
445 By righteous sentence of th'Almighties law:
Then gan the villein him to overcraw,°   *exult over*
And brought unto him swords, ropes, poison, fire,
And all that might him to perdition draw;
And bad him choose, what death he would desire:
450 For death was due to him, that had provokt Gods ire.[6]

51

But when as none of them he saw him take,
He to him raught° a dagger sharpe and keene,   *reached*
And gave it him in hand: his hand did quake,
And tremble like a leafe of Aspin greene,
455 And troubled bloud through his pale face was seene
To come, and goe with tydings from the hart,
As it a running messenger had beene.
At last resolved to worke his finall smart,
He lifted up his hand, that backe againe did start.

6. Hamlet turned aside from suicide because of fear of the unknown; here, however, Redcrosse is tempted by the powerfully exciting allurement of death.

52

Which when as Una saw, through every vaine
 The crudled cold ran to her well of life,
 As in a swowne: but soone relived° againe,   *revived*
 Out of his hand she snatcht the curséd knife,
 And threw it to the ground, enragéd rife,°   *deeply*
 And to him said, "Fie, fie, faint harted knight,
 What meanest thou by this reprochfull strife?
 Is this the battell, which thou vauntst to fight
With the fire-mouthéd Dragon, horrible and bright?

53

"Come, come away, fraile, feeble, fleshly wight,
 Ne let vaine words bewitch thy manly hart,
 Ne divelish thoughts dismay thy constant spright.
 In heavenly mercies hast thou not a part?
 Why shouldst thou then despeire, that chosen art?
 Where justice growes, there grows eke greater grace,
 The which doth quench the brond of hellish smart,
 And that accurst hand-writing doth deface.°   *blot out*
Arise, Sir knight arise, and leave this curséd place."[7]

54

So up he rose, and thence amounted streight.
 Which when the carle° beheld, and saw his guest   *churl*
 Would safe depart, for all his subtill sleight,
 He chose an halter from among the rest,
 And with it hung himselfe, unbid unblest.
 But death he could not worke himselfe thereby;
 For thousand times he so himselfe had drest,°   *made ready*
 Yet nathelesse it could not doe him die,
Till he should die his last, that is eternally.[8]

Canto X

*Her faithfull knight faire Una brings
to house of Holinesse,
Where he is taught repentance, and
the way to heavenly blesse.°*   *bliss*

1

What man is he, that boasts of fleshly might,
 And vaine assurance of mortality,°   *immortality*
 Which all so soone, as it doth come to fight,
 Against spirituall foes, yeelds by and by,[1]
 Or from the field most cowardly doth fly?
 Ne let the man ascribe it to his skill,
 That thorough grace hath gainéd victory.
 If any strength we have, it is to ill,

---

7. Una reminds Redcrosse of God's mercy, the "greater grace" conspicuously missing from Despaire's eloquent speeches.
8. Despaire cannot kill himself. Compare his fruitless suicide attempts with Aesculapius's equally fruitless attempts "himself with salves to health for to restore" (I.v.40).
1. Immediately.

But all the good is Gods, both power and eke will.[2]

2

By that, which lately hapned, Una saw,
  That this her knight was feeble, and too faint;
  And all his sinews woxen weake and raw,°   *unready*
  Through long enprisonment, and hard constraint,
  Which he enduréd in his late restraint,
  That yet he was unfit for bloudie fight:
  Therefore to cherish him with diets daint,°   *dainty*
  She cast to bring him, where he chearen° might,   *be cheered*
Till he recovered had his[3] late decayéd plight.

3

There was an auntient house not farre away,
  Renowmd throughout the world for sacred lore,
  And pure unspotted life: so well they say
  It governd was, and guided evermore,
  Through wisedome of a matrone grave and hore;°   *gray-haired*
  Whose onely joy was to relieve the needes
  Of wretched soules, and helpe the helpelesse pore:
  All night she spent in bidding of her bedes,[4]
And all the day in doing good and godly deedes.

4

Dame Caelia[5] men did her call, as thought
  From heaven to come, or thither to arise,
  The mother of three daughters, well upbrought
  In goodly thewes,° and godly exercise: *habits*
  The eldest two most sober, chast, and wise,
  Fidelia and Speranza virgins were,
  Though spousd,° yet wanting wedlocks solemnize;   *bethrothed*
  But faire Charissa to a lovely fere°   *mate*
Was linckéd, and by him had many pledges dere.[6]

5

Arrivéd there, the dore they find fast lockt;
  For it was warely watchéd night and day,
  For feare of many foes: but when they knockt,
  The Porter opened unto them streight way:
  He was an agéd syre, all hory gray,
  With lookes full lowly cast, and gate full slow,
  Wont on a staffe his feeble steps to stay,
  Hight Humilta.° They passe in stouping low;   *humility*
For streight and narrow was the way, which he did show.[7]

---

2. "For by grace are ye saved through faith; and that not of yourselves: it is the gift of God: Not of works, lest any men should boast" (Ephesians ii.8–9).
3. I.e., from his.
4. Saying prayers.
5. The name means "heavenly."
6. I.e., many children. The daughters' names mean "faith," "hope," and "charity." Cf. with them the three Saracens, Sans foy, Sans joy, and Sans loy: "faith" is the answer to atheism; "hope," the answer to empty despair; and "charity" (the highest law that embraces all other laws) the answer to chaos. "And now abideth faith, hope, charity, these three; but the greatest of these is charity" (I Corinthians xiii.13). Canto x, in which Spenser's didactic purpose is expressed with particular directness, is especially rich in scriptural references and echoes. Many aspects of the House of Holiness oppose their counterparts in the House of Pride (Canto iv).
7. "Strait is the gate, and narrow is the way, which leadeth unto life, and few there be that find it" (Matthew vii.14).

6

Each goodly thing is hardest to begin,
 But entred in a spacious court they see,
 Both plaine, and pleasant to be walkéd in,
 Where them does meete a francklin° faire and free,   *freeholder*
50 And entertaines with comely courteous glee,
 His name was Zele, that him right well became,
 For in his speeches and behaviour hee
 Did labour lively to expresse the same,
And gladly did them guide, till to the Hall they came.

7

55 There fairely them receives a gentle Squire,
 Of milde demeanure, and rare courtesie,
 Right cleanly clad in comely sad° attire;   *sober*
 In word and deede that shewed great modestie,
 And knew his good° to all of each degree,   *proper respect*
60 Hight Reverence. He them with speeches meet
 Does faire entreat; no courting nicetie,°   *affectation*
 But simple true, and eke unfainéd sweet,
As might become a Squire so great persons to greet.

8

And afterwards them to his Dame he leades,
65 That agéd Dame, the Ladie of the place:
 Who all this while was busie at her beades:
 Which doen, she up arose with seemely grace,
 And toward them full matronely did pace.
 Where when that fairest Una she beheld,
70 Whom well she knew to spring from heavenly race,
 Her hart with joy unwonted inly sweld,
As feeling wondrous comfort in her weaker eld.°   *older age*

9

And her embracing said, "O happie earth,
 Whereon thy innocent feet doe ever tread,
75 Most vertuous virgin borne of heavenly berth,
 That to redeeme thy woefull parents head,
 From tyrans rage, and ever-dying dread,[8]
 Hast wandred through the world now long a day;
 Yet ceasest not thy wearie soles to lead,
80 What grace hath thee now hither brought this way?
Or doen thy feeble feet unweeting hither stray?

10

"Strange thing it is an errant° knight to see   *wandering*
 Here in this place, or any other wight,
 That hither turnes his steps. So few there bee,
85 That chose the narrow path, or seeke the right:
 All keepe the broad high way, and take delight
 With many rather for to go astray,
 And be partakers of their evill plight,
 Then with a few to walke the rightest way;
90 O foolish men, why haste ye to your owne decay?"

8. Continuing fear of death.

11

"Thy selfe to see, and tyred limbs to rest,
    O matrone sage," quoth she, "I hither came,
    And this good knight his way with me addrest,
    Led with thy prayses and broad-blazéd fame,
95 That up to heaven is blowne." The auncient Dame
    Him goodly greeted in her modest guise,
    And entertaynd them both, as best became,
    With all the court'sies, that she could devise,
Ne wanted ought, to shew her bounteous or wise.

12

100 Thus as they gan of sundry things devise,°   *talk*
    Loe two most goodly virgins came in place,
    Ylinkéd arme in arme in lovely° wise,   *loving*
    With countenance demure, and modest grace,
    They numbred even steps and equall pace:
105 Of which the eldest, that Fidelia hight,
    Like sunny beames threw from her Christall face,
    That could have dazd the rash beholders sight,
And round about her head did shine like heavens light.[9]

13

She was araiéd all in lilly white,
110 And in her right hand bore a cup of gold,
    With wine and water fild up to the hight,
    In which a Serpent did himselfe enfold,
    That horrour made to all, that did behold;
    But she no whit did chaunge her constant mood:[1]
115 And in her other hand she fast did hold
    A booke, that was both signd and seald with blood,
Wherein darke things were writ, hard to be understood.[2]

14

Her younger sister, that Speranza hight,
    Was clad in blew, that her beseeméd well;
120 Not all so chearefull seeméd she of sight,[3]
    As was her sister; whether dread did dwell,
    Or anguish in her hart, is hard to tell:
    Upon her arme a silver anchor[4] lay,
    Whereon she leanéd ever, as befell:
125 And ever up to heaven, as she did pray,
Her stedfast eyes were bent, ne swarvéd other way.

15

They seeing Una, towards her gan wend,

9. Cf. the brightness of Arthur's shield, unveiled (viii.19).
1. Expression. The serpent in the cup is a symbol of St. John the Evangelist, whose faith was so great he could drink venom without harm. Contrast Duessa's cup (viii.14). The symbolic details in these portraits appear also in the allegorical figures in other works of Renaissance literature and art—particular'y the emblem books.
2. The New Testament. See II Peter iii.16: "in which are some things hard to be understood, which they that are unlearned and unstable wrest, as they do also the other scriptures, unto their own destruction." Peter says this of St. Paul's writings, but it could also be said of many other parts of the New Testament—which is "signed and sealed with [the] blood" of Christ and the martyrs.
3. In appearance.
4. The iconographic symbol of hope.

Who them encounters with like courtesie;
Many kind speeches they betwene them spend,
And greatly joy each other well to see:
Then to the knight with shamefast° modestie   *humble*
They turne themselves, at Unas meeke request,
And him salute with well beseeming glee;
Who faire them quites,° as him beseeméd best,   *returns the salute*
And goodly gan discourse of many a noble gest.°   *achievement*

16

Then Una thus; "But she your sister deare;
The deare Charissa where is she become?
Or wants she health, or busie is elsewhere?"
"Ah no," said they, "but forth she may not come:
For she of late is lightned of her wombe,
And hath encreast the world with one sonne more,[5]
That her to see should be but troublesome."
"Indeede," quoth she, "that should her trouble sore,
But thankt be God, that her encrease so° evermore."   *truly*

17

Then said the aged Caelia, "Deare dame,
And you good Sir, I wote that of your toyle,
And labours long, through which ye hither came,
Ye both forwearied be: therefore a whyle
I read° you rest, and to your bowres recoyle."[6]   *suggest*
Then calléd she a Groome, that forth him led
Into a goodly lodge, and gan despoile°   *disrobe*
Of puissant armes, and laid in easie bed;
His name was meeke Obedience rightfully aréd.°   *understood*

18

Now when their wearie limbes with kindly° rest,   *natural*
And bodies were refresht with due repast,
Faire Una gan Fidelia faire request,
To have her knight into her schoolehouse plaste,
That of her heavenly learning he might taste,
And heare the wisedome of her words divine.
She graunted, and that knight so much agraste,°   *favored*
That she him taught celestiall discipline,
And opened his dull eyes, that light mote in them shine.

19

And that her sacred Booke, with bloud[7] ywrit,
That none could read, except she did them teach,
She unto him discloséd every whit,
And heavenly documents° thereout did preach,   *doctrines*
That weaker whit of man could never reach,
Of God, of grace, of justice, of free will,
That wonder was to heare her goodly speach:
For she was able, with her words to kill,
And raise againe to life the hart, that she did thrill.°   *pierce*

5. Charity, the fruitful virtue, is often depicted pictorially as a mother with children.

6. Retire to your rooms.

7. I.e., the blood of Christ.

20

And when she list poure out her larger spright,[8]
    She would commaund the hastie Sunne to stay,
    Or backward turne his course from heavens hight;
175   Sometimes great hostes of men she could dismay,
    Dry-shod to passe, she parts the flouds in tway;
    And eke huge mountaines from their native seat
    She would commaund, themselves to beare away,
    And throw in raging sea with roaring threat.
180 Almightie God her gave such powre, and puissance great.[9]

21

The faithfull knight now grew in litle space,
    By hearing her, and by her sisters lore,
    To such perfection of all heavenly grace,
    That wretched world he gan for to abhore,
185   And mortall life gan loath, as thing forelore,
    Greeved with remembrance of his wicked wayes,
    And prickt with anguish of his sinnes so sore,
    That he desirde to end his wretched dayes:
So much the dart of sinfull guilt the soule dismayes.

22

190 But wise Speranza gave him comfort sweet,
    And taught him how to take assuréd hold
    Upon her silver anchor, as was meet;
    Else had his sinnes so great, and manifold
    Made him forget all that Fidelia told.
195   In this distresséd doubtfull agonie,
    When him his dearest Una did behold,
    Disdeining life, desiring leave to die,
She found her selfe assayld with great perplexitie.

23

And came to Caelia to declare her smart,
200   Who well acquainted with that commune plight,
    Which sinfull horror[1] workes in wounded hart,
    Her wisely comforted all that she might,
    With goodly counsell and advisement right;
    And streightway sent with carefull diligence,
205   To fetch a Leach,° the which had great insight   *doctor*
    In that disease of grievéd conscience,
And well could cure the same; His name was Patience.

24

Who comming to that soule-diseaséd knight,
    Could hardly him intreat, to tell his griefe:
210   Which knowne, and all that noyd° his heavie spright   *troubled*
    Well searcht, eftsoones he gan apply reliefe
    Of salves and med'cines, which had passing priefe,[2]

---

8. Full spiritual power.
9. Joshua made the sun stand still (Joshua x.12); Hezekiah made it turn backwards (II Kings xx.10); Gideon was victorious over the Midianites (Judges vii.7); Moses led the Israelites through the parted waters of the Red Sea (Exodus xiv.21–31); faith, said Christ, can move mountains (Matthew xxi.21). All these are miracles of faith.
1. Horror of sin.
2. Which had extraordinary power.

And thereto added words of wondrous might:[3]
　By which to ease he him recuréd briefe,°　　　　　　　*speedily*
5　And much asswaged the passion° of his plight,　　　　*suffering*
That he his paine endured, as seeming now more light.

25

But yet the cause and root of all his ill,
　Inward corruption, and infected sin,
　Not purged nor heald, behind remainéd still,
0　And festring sore did rankle yet within,
　Close° creeping twixt the marrow and the skin.　　　　*secretly*
　Which to extirpe,° he laid him privily　　　　　　　*extirpate*
　Downe in a darkesome lowly place farre in,
　Whereas he meant his corrosives to apply,
5　And with streight° diet tame his stubborne malady.　　*strict*

26

In ashes and sackcloth he did array
　His daintie corse, proud humors[4] to abate,
　And dieted with fasting every day,
　The swelling of his wounds to mitigate,
0　And made him pray both earely and eke late:
　And ever as superfluous flesh did rot
　Amendment readie still at hand did wayt,
　To pluck it out wth pincers firie whot,°　　　　　　*hot*
That soone in him was left no one corrupted jot.

27

5　And bitter Penance with an yron whip,
　Was wont him once to disple° every day:　　　　　　*discipline*
　And sharpe Remorse his hart did pricke and nip,
　That drops of bloud thence like a well did play;
　And sad Repentance uséd to embay°　　　　　　　　*bathe*
0　His bodie in salt water smarting sore,
　The filthy blots of sinne to wash away.[5]
　So in short space they did to health restore
The man that would not live, but earst° lay at deathes dore.　*before*

28

In which his torment often was so great,
5　That like a Lyon he would cry and rore,
　And rend his flesh, and his owne synewes eat.
　His own deare Una hearing evermore
　His ruefull shriekes and gronings, often tore
　Her guiltlesse garments, and her golden heare,
0　For pitty of his paine and anguish sore;
　Yet all with patience wisely she did beare;
For well she wist, his crime could else be never cleare.

29

Whom thus recovered by wise Patience,
　And trew Repentance they to Una brought:
5　Who joyous of his curéd conscience,
　Him dearely kist, and fairely eke besought

---

3. I.e., absolution, or spiritual counsel-
ing generally.
4. Passions—i.e., pride.

5. "Wash me throughly from mine iniquity, and cleanse me from my sin"
(Psalms li.2).

Himselfe to chearish,° and consuming thought   *cheer*
To put away out of his carefull brest.
By this Charissa, late in child-bed brought,
260   Was woxen strong, and left her fruitfull nest;
To her faire Una brought this unacquainted guest.

30

She was a woman in her freshest age,
Of wondrous beauty, and of bountie° rare,   *virtue*
With goodly grace and comely personage,
265   That was on earth not easie to compare;
Full of great love, but Cupids wanton snare
As hell she hated, chast in worke and will;
Her necke and breasts were ever open bare,
That ay thereof her babes might sucke their fill;
270 The rest was all in yellow robes arayéd still.[6]

31

A multitude of babes about her hong,
Playing their sports, that joyd her to behold,
Whom still she fed, whiles they were weake and young,
But thrust them forth still, as they wexéd old:
275   And on her head she wore a tyre° of gold,   *headdress*
Adornd with gemmes and owches° wondrous faire,   *jewels*
Whose passing° price uneath° was to be told;   *surpassing/scarcely*
And by her side there sate a gentle paire
Of turtle doves, she sitting in an yvorie chaire.

32

280 The knight and Una entring, faire her greet,
And bid her joy of that her happie brood;
Who them requites with court'sies seeming meet,°   *appropriate*
And entertaines with friendly chearefull mood.
Then Una her besought, to be so good,
285   As in her vertuous rules to schoole her knight,
Now after all his torment well withstood,
In that sad° house of Penaunce, where his spright   *solemn*
Had past the paines of hell, and long enduring night.

33

She was right joyous of her just request,
290   And taking by the hand that Faeries sonne,
Gan him instruct in every good behest,
Of love, and righteousnesse, and well to donne,[7]
And wrath, and hatred warely to shonne,
That drew on men Gods hatred, and his wrath,
295   And many soules in dolours° had fordonne:°   *misery/destroyed*
In which when him she well instructed hath,
From thence to heaven she teacheth him the ready path.

34

Wherein his weaker° wandring steps to guide,   *too weak*
An auncient matrone she to her does call,

6. Her yellow (saffron) robe is the emblem of fruitfulness. That she is "chast in work and will" and hates "Cupids wanton snare" does not contradict her "multitude of babes"; Spenser is distinguishing between *eros* and *agape*, sexual love and Christian love.
7. I.e., right action.

Whose sober lookes her wisedome well describe:°   *made known*
  Her name was Mercie, well knowne over all,
  To be both gratious, and eke liberall:
  To whom the carefull charge of him she gave,
  To lead aright, that he should never fall
In all his wayes through this wide worldés wave,°   *expanse*
That Mercy in the end his righteous soule might save.

35

The godly Matrone by the hand him beares
  Forth from her presence, by a narrow way,
  Scattred with bushy thornes, and ragged breares,°   *briers*
  Which still before him she removed away,
  That nothing might his ready passage stay:
  And ever when his feet encombred were,
  Or gan to shrinke, or from the right to stray,
  She held him fast, and firmely did upbeare,
As carefull Nourse her child from falling oft does reare.

36

Eftsoones unto an holy Hospitall,°   *retreat*
  That was fore°by the way, she did him bring,   *close*
  In which seven Bead-men[8] that had vowéd all
  Their life to service of high heavens king
  Did spend their dayes in doing godly thing:
  Their gates to all were open evermore,
  That by the wearie way were traveiling,
  And one sate wayting ever them before,
To call in commers-by, that needy were and pore.

37

The first of them that eldest was, and best,°   *chief*
  Of all the house had charge and governement,
  As Guardian and Steward of the rest:
  His office was to give entertainement
  And lodging, unto all that came, and went:
  Not unto such, as could him feast againe,
  And double quite,° for that he on them spent,   *repay*
  But such, as want of harbour° did constraine: *shelter*
Those for Gods sake his dewty was to entertaine.

38

The second was as Almner° of the place,   *almoner*
  His office was, the hungry for to feed,
  And thristy give to drinke, a worke of grace:
  He feard not once him selfe to be in need,
  Ne cared to hoord for those, whom he did breede:[9]
  The grace of God he layd up still in store,
  Which as a stocke he left unto his seede;
  He had enough, what need him care for more?
And had he lesse, yet some he would give to the pore.

39

The third had of their wardrobe custodie,
  In which were not rich tyres,° nor garments gay,   *robes*

---

8. Men of prayer.   9. I.e., his children.

345 The plumes of pride, and wings of vanitie,
  But clothes meet to keepe keene could° away,   *cold*
  And naked nature seemely to aray;
  With which bare wretched wights he dayly clad,
  The images of God in earthly clay;
350 And if that no spare clothes to give he had,
His owne coate he would cut, and it distribute glad.

40

The fourth appointed by his office was,
  Poore prisoners to relieve with gratious ayd,
  And captives to redeeme with price of bras,°   *money*
355 From Turkes and Sarazins, which them had stayd;° *held captive*
  And though they faultie were, yet well he wayd,
  That God to us forgiveth every howre
  Much more then that, why° they in bands were layd, *for which*
  And he that harrowd hell[1] with heavie stowre,
360 The faultie soules from thence brought to his heavenly bowre.

41

The fift had charge sicke persons to attend,
  And comfort those, in point of death which lay;
  For them most needeth comfort in the end,
  When sin, and hell, and death do most dismay
365 The feeble soule departing hence away.
  All is but lost, that living we bestow,°   *store up*
  If not well ended at our dying day.
  O man have mind of that last bitter throw;°   *throe*
For as the tree does fall, so lyes it ever low.

42

370 The sixt had charge of them now being dead,
  In seemely sort their courses to engrave,°   *bury*
  And deck with dainty flowres their bridall bed,
  That to their heavenly spouse both sweet and brave
  They might appeare, when he their soules shall save.
375 The wondrous workemanship of Gods owne mould,° *image*
  Whose face he made, all beasts to feare, and gave
  All in his hand, even dead we honour should.
Ah dearest God me graunt, I dead be not defould.° *abused*

43

The seventh now after death and buriall done,
380 Had charge the tender Orphans of the dead
  And widowes ayd, least they should be undone:
  In face of judgement[2] he their right would plead,
  Ne ought the powre of mighty men did dread
  In their defence, nor would for gold or fee
385 Be wonne their rightfull causes downe to tread:

---

1. I.e., Christ, who journeyed to hell to deliver those good people who lived before his time, according to a popular story in the Middle Ages. It originated in the apocryphal gospel of Nicodemus.
2. I.e., in court.
3. Always freely. The seven Bead-men here correspond to, and perform, the seven works of charity, or corporal mercy: lodging the homeless, feeding the hungry, clothing the naked, redeeming the captive, comforting the sick, honoring the dead, and succoring the orphan. Cf. the seven deadly sins in the House of Pride.

And when they stood in most necessitee,
He did supply their want, and gave them ever free.[3]

44

There when the Elfin knight arrivéd was,
    The first and chiefest of the seven, whose care
    Was guests to welcome, towardes him did pas:
    Where seeing Mercie, that his steps up bare,°   *supported*
    And always led, to her with reverence rare
    He humbly louted° in meeke lowlinesse,   *bowed*
    And seemely welcome for her did prepare:
For of their order she was Patronesse,
Albe° Charissa were their chiefest founderesse.   *although*

45

There she awhile him stayes, him selfe to rest,
    That to the rest more able he might bee:
    During which time, in every good behest
    And godly worke of Almes and charitee
    She him instructed with great industree;
    Shortly therein so perfect he became,
    That from the first unto the last degree,
His mortall life he learnéd had to frame
In holy righteousnesse, without rebuke or blame.

46

Thence forward by that painfull way they pas,
    Forth to an hill, that was both steepe and hy;
    On top whereof a sacred chappell was,
    And eke a litle Hermitage thereby,
    Wherein an agéd holy man did lye,
    That day and night said his devotion,
    Ne other worldly busines did apply;
His name was heavenly Contemplation;
Of God and goodnesse was his meditation.

47

Great grace that old man to him given had;
    For God he often saw from heavens hight,
    All° were his earthly eyen both blunt° and bad,   *although/dim*
    And through great age had lost their kindly° sight,   *natural*
    Yet wondrous quick and persant° was his spright,   *piercing*
    As Eagles eye, that can behold the Sunne:
    That hill they scale with all their powre and might,
    That his frayle thighes nigh wearie and fordonne°   *exhausted*
Gan faile, but by her helpe the top at last he wonne.

48

There they do finde that godly agéd Sire,
    With snowy lockes adowne his shoulders shed,
    As hoarie frost with spangles doth attire
    The mossy braunches of an Oke halfe ded.
    Each bone might through his body well be red,°   *observed*
    And every sinew seene through his long fast:
    For nought he cared his carcas long unfed;
His mind was full of spirituall repast,
And pyned° his flesh, to keepe his body low and chast.   *starved*

49

Who when these two approching he aspide,
   At their first presence grew agrievéd sore,
435   That forst him lay his heavenly thoughts aside;
   And had he not that Dame respected more,°   *greatly*
   Whom highly he did reverence and adore,
   He would not once have movéd for the knight.
   They him saluted standing far afore;°   *away*
440   Who well them greeting, humbly did requight,
And asked, to what end they clomb° that tedious height. *had climbed*

50

"What end," quoth she, "should cause us take such paine,
   But that same end, which every living wight
   Should make his marke, high heaven to attaine?
445   Is not from hence the way, that leadeth right
   To that most glorious house, that glistreth bright
   With burning starres, and everliving fire,
   Whereof the keyes are to thy hand behight°   *entrusted*
   By wise Fidelia? she doth thee require,
450 To shew it to this knight, according his desire."

51

"Thrise happy man," said then the father grave,
   "Whose staggering steps thy steady hand doth lead,
   And shewes the way, his sinfull soule to save.
   Who better can the way to heaven aread.
455   Then thou thy selfe, that was both borne and bred
   In heavenly throne, where thousand Angels shine?
   Thou doest the prayers of the righteous sead°   *offspring*
   Present before the majestie divine,
And his avenging wrath to clemencie incline.

52

460 "Yet since thou bidst, thy pleasure shalbe donne.
   Then come thou man of earth, and see the way,
   That never yet was seene of Faeries sonne,
   That never leads the traveiler astray,
   But after labours long, and sad delay,
465   Brings them to joyous rest and endlesse blis.
   But first thou must a season fast and pray,
   Till from her bands the spright assoiléd° is,   *released*
And have her strength recured° from fraile infirmitis." *recovered*

53

That done, he leads him to the highest Mount;
470   Such one, as that same mighty man of God,
   The bloud-red billowes like a walléd front
   On either side disparted with his rod,
   Till that his army dry-foot through them yod,°   *went*
   Dwelt fortie dayes upon; where writ in stone
475   With bloudy letters by the hand of God,
   The bitter doome° of death and balefull mone   *judgment*
He did receive, whiles flashing fire about him shone.

54

Or like that sacred hill, whose head full hie,

Adornd with fruitfull Olives all arownd,
80 Is, as it were for endlesse memory
Of that deare Lord, who oft thereon was fownd,
For ever with a flowring girlond crownd:
Or like that pleasaunt Mount, that is for ay
Through famous Poets verse each where° renownd,   *everywhere*
85 On which the thrise three learned Ladies play
Their heavenly notes, and make full many a lovely lay.[4]

55

From thence, far off he unto him did shew
A litle path, that was both steepe and long,
Which to a goodly Citie led his vew;
90 Whose wals and towres were builded high and strong
Of perle and precious stone, that earthly tong
Cannot describe, nor wit of man can tell;
Too high a ditty° for my simple song;   *subject*
The Citie of the great king hight it well,
95 Wherein eternall peace and happinesse doth dwell.

56

As he thereon stood gazing, he might see
The blessed Angels to and fro descend
From highest heaven, in gladsome companee,
And with great joy into that Citie wend,
100 As commonly° as friend does with his frend.[5]   *generally*
Whereat he wondred much, and gan enquere,
What stately building durst so high extend
Her loftie towres unto the starry sphere,
And what unknowen nation there empeopled were.

57

105 "Faire knight," quoth he, "Hierusalem that is,
The new Hierusalem, that God has built
For those to dwell in, that are chosen his,
His chosen people purged from sinfull guilt,
With pretious bloud, which cruelly was spilt
110 On cursèd tree, of that unspotted lam,
That for the sinnes of all the world was kilt:
Now are they Saints all in that Citie sam,°   *together*
More deare unto their God, then younglings to their dam."[6]

58

"Till now," said then the knight, "I weenèd well,
115 That great Cleopolis,[7] where I have beene,

4. The mountain is successively compared to Mount Sinai (lines 469–77), where Moses, after parting the "bloud-red billowes" of the Red Sea, received the tablets of the laws of Judaism; to the Mount of Olives (lines 478–82), associated with Christ; and to Mount Parnassus (lines 483–86), where dwelled the nine muses of art and poetry. This last has the effect of equating poetry with the profoundest religious experience—a tradition that Sidney's *Apology* also incorporates.

5. Cf. Jacob's ladder: "And he dreamed, and behold a ladder set up on the earth, and the top of it reached to heaven; and behold the angels of God ascending and descending on it" (Genesis xxviii.12).
6. The New Jerusalem is described in Revelation xxi–xxii; "the nations of them which are saved shall walk in the light of it" (xxi.24).
7. London, Camelot—and here, the earthly counterpart of the Heavenly Kingdom.

In which that fairest Faerie Queene doth dwell,
The fairest Citie was, that might be seene;
And that bright towre all built of christall cleene,°   *clear*
Panthea,[8] seemd the brightest thing, that was:
520   But now by proofe all otherwise I weene;
For this great Citie that does far surpas,
And this bright Angels towre quite dims that towre of glas."

59

"Most trew," then said the holy aged man;
"Yet is Cleopolis for earthly frame,°   *structure*
525   The fairest peece, that eye beholden can:
And well beseemes all knights of noble name,
That covet in th'immortall booke of fame
To be eternizéd, that same to haunt,°   *frequent*
And doen their service to that soveraigne Dame,
530   That glorie does to them for guerdon° graunt: *reward*
For she is heavenly borne, and heaven may justly vaunt.°   *claim*

60

"And thou faire ymp, sprong out from English race,
How ever now accompted° Elfins sonne,   *accounted*
Well worthy doest thy service for her grace,°   *favor*
535   To aide a virgin desolate foredonne.
But when thou famous victorie hast wonne,
And high emongst all knights has hong thy shield,
Thenceforth the suit° of earthly conquest shonne,   *pursuit*
And wash thy hands from guilt of bloudy field:
540 For bloud can nought but sin, and wars but sorrowes yield.

61

"Then seeke this path, that I to thee presage,°   *point out*
Which after all to heaven shall thee send;
Then peaceably thy painefull pilgrimage
To yonder same Hierusalem do bend,
545   Where is for thee ordaind a blessed end:
For thou emongst those Saints, whom thou doest see,
Shalt be a Saint, and thine owne nations frend
And Patrone: thou Saint George shalt calléd bee,
Saint George of mery England, the signe of victoree."[9]

62

550 "Unworthy wretch," quoth he, "of so great grace,
How dare I thinke such glory to attaine?"
"These that have it attaind, were in like cace,"
Quoth he, "as wretched, and lived in like paine."
"But deeds of armes must I at last be faine,
555   And Ladies love to leave so dearely bought?"
"What need of armes, where peace doth ay remaine,"
Said he, "and battailes none are to be fought?
As for loose loves are vaine, and vanish into nought."

8. Reminiscent of the temple of glass in Chaucer's *Hous of Fame;* perhaps intended to represent Richmond Palace or Westminster Abbey.
9. Spenser's conception of St. George,
patron saint of England, draws on the *Legenda Aurea* (translated by Caxton in 1487); on pictures, tapestries, and pageants; and on folklore.

63

"O let me not," quoth he, "then turne againe
50   Backe to the world, whose joyes so fruitlesse are;
  But let me here for aye in peace remaine,
  Or streight way on that last long voyage fare,
  That nothing may my present hope empare."°   *impair*
  "That may not be," said he, "ne maist thou yit
55   Forgo that royall maides bequeathéd care,°   *charge*
  Who did her cause into thy hand commit,
Till from her curséd foe thou have her freely quit."°   *released*

64

"Then shall I soone," quoth he, "so God me grace,
  Abet° that virgins cause disconsolate,   *support*
70   And shortly backe returne unto this place
  To walke this way in Pilgrims poore estate.
  But now aread, old father, why of late
  Didst thou behight me borne of English blood,
  Whom all a Faeries sonne doen nominate?"°   *name*
75   "That word shall I," said he, "avouchen° good,   *prove*
Sith to thee is unknowne the cradle of thy brood.

65

"For well I wote, thou springst from ancient race
  Of Saxon kings, that have with mightie hand
  And many bloudie battailes fought in place°   *there*
80   High reard their royall throne in Britane land,
  And vanquisht them, unable to withstand:
  From thence a Faerie thee unweeting reft,[1]
  There as thou slepst in tender swadling band,
  And her base Elfin brood there for thee left.
85 Such men do Chaungelings call, so chaungd by Faeries theft.

66

"Thence she thee brought into this Faerie lond,
  And in an heapéd furrow did thee hyde,
  Where thee a Ploughman all unweeting fond,
  As he his toylesome teme that way did guyde,
90   And brought thee up in ploughmans state to byde,
  Whereof Georgos he thee gave to name;[2]
  Till prickt with courage, and thy forces pryde,
  To Faery court thou cam'st to seeke for fame,
And prove thy puissaunt armes, as seemes thee best became."°   *suited*

67

95 "O holy Sire," quoth he, "how shall I quight
  The many favours I with thee have found,
  That has my name and nation red aright,
  And taught the way that does to heaven bound?"°   *go*
  This said, adowne he lookéd to the ground,
100   To have returnd, but dazéd were his eyne,
  Through passing° brightnesse, which did quite confound   *surpassing*
  His feeble sence, and too exceeding shyne.
So darke are earthly things compard to things divine.

1. Secretly stole.
2. *Georgos* is Greek for "farmer" (cf. Virgil's *Georgics,* on farming).

68

At last whenas himselfe he gan to find,
605   To Una back he cast him to retire;
  Who him awaited still with pensive mind.
  Great thankes and goodly meed° to that good syre,   *gift*
  He thence departing gave for his paines hyre.°   *reward*
  So came to Una, who him joyd to see,
610   And after litle rest, gan him desire,
  Of her adventure mindfull for to bee.
So leave they take of Caelia, and her daughters three.

Canto XI

The knight with that old Dragon fights
two dayes incessantly:
The third him overthrowes, and gayns
most glorious victory.

1

High time now gan it wex° for Una faire,   *develop*
  To thinke of those her captive Parents deare,
  And their forwasted kingdome to repaire:³
  Whereto whenas they now approachéd neare,
5   With hartie words her knight she gan to cheare,
  And in her modest manner thus bespake;
  "Deare knight, as deare, as ever knight was deare,
  That all these sorrowes suffer for my sake,
High heaven behold the tedious toyle, ye for me take.

2

10 "Now are we come unto my native soyle,
  And to the place, where all our perils dwell;
  Here haunts that feend, and does his dayly spoyle,
  Therefore henceforth be at your keeping well,⁴
  And ever ready for your foeman fell.
15   The sparke of noble courage now awake,
  And strive your excellent selfe to excell;
  That shall ye evermore renowméd make,
Above all knights on earth, that batteill undertake."

3

And pointing forth, "lo yonder is," said she,
20   "The brasen towre in which my parents deare
  For dread of that huge feend emprisond be,
  Whom I from far see on the walles appeare,
  Whose sight my feeble° soule doth greatly cheare: *melancholy*
  And on the top of all I do espye
25   The watchman wayting tydings glad to heare,
  That O my parents might I happily
Unto you bring, to ease you of your misery."

4

With that they heard a roaring hideous sound,

---

3. I.e., to restore their kingdom, laid   4. I.e., be alert to your responsibilities.
waste (by the dragon) to health.

That all the ayre with terrour filléd wide,
And seemd uneath° to shake the stedfast ground. *almost*
Eftsoones that dreadfull Dragon they espide,
Where stretcht he lay upon the sunny side
Of a great hill, himselfe like a great hill.
But all so soone, as he from far descride
Those glistring armes, that heaven with light did fill,
He rousd himselfe full blith,° and hastned them *eagerly/*
 untill.° *toward*

5

Then bad the knight his Lady yede° aloofe, *step*
And to an hill her selfe withdraw aside,
From whence she might behold that battailes proof° *outcome*
And eke be safe from daunger far descryde:
She him obayd, and turnd a little wyde.° *aside*
Now I thou sacred Muse,[5] most learned Dame,
Faire ympe° of Phoebus, and his aged bride,[6] *child*
The Nourse of time, and everlasting fame,
That warlike hands ennoblest with immortall name;

6

O gently come into my feeble brest,
Come gently, but not with that mighty rage,
Wherewith the martiall troupes thou doest infest,° *arouse*
And harts of great Heroës doest enrage,
That nought their kindled courage may aswage,
Soone as thy dreadfull trompe begins to sownd;
The God of warre with his fiers equipage
Thou doest awake, sleepe never he so sownd,
And scaréd nations doest with horrour sterne astown.° *appall*

7

Faire Goddesse lay that furious fit° aside, *mood*
Till I of warres and bloudy Mars do sing[7]
And Briton fields with Sarazin bloud bedyde,
Twixt that great faery Queene and Paynim king,
That with their horrour heaven and earth did ring,
A worke of labour long, and endlesse prayse:
But now a while let downe that haughtie string,
And to my tunes thy second tenor rayse,[8]
That I this man of God his godly armes may blaze.° *describe*

8

By this the dreadfull Beast drew nigh to hand,
Halfe flying, and halfe footing in his hast,
That with his largenesse measuréd much land,
And made wide shadow under his huge wast;° *girth*
As mountaine doth the valley overcast.
Approching nigh, he rearéd high afore
His body monstrous, horrible, and vast,
Which to increase his wondrous greatnesse more,
Was swolne with wrath, and poyson, and with bloudy gore.

5. Calliope, muse of epic poetry, or Clio, muse of history.
6. I.e., Mnemosyne (memory).
7. Spenser refers to a projected book of *The Faerie Queene* which he never wrote.

8. The "haughtie" (high-pitched) mode would be appropriate to a large-scale epic war; the "second tenor" (lower in pitch) to this present battle.

9

And over, all with brasen scales was armd,
    Like plated coate of steele, so couchéd neare,[9]
75   That nought mote perce, ne might his corse be harmd
    With dint of sword, nor push of pointed speare;
    Which as an Eagle, seeing pray appeare,
    His aery Plumes doth rouze,° full rudely dight,   *shake*
    So shakéd he, that horrour was to heare,
80   For as the clashing of an Armour bright,
Such noyse his rouzéd scales did send unto the knight.

10

His flaggy° wings when forth he did display,   *drooping*
    Were like two sayles, in which the hollow wynd
    Is gathered full, and worketh speedy way:
85   And eke the pennes,° that did his pineons bynd,   *quills*
    Were like mayne-yards, with flying canvas lynd,
    With which whenas him list the ayre to beat,
    And there by force unwonted passage find,
    The cloudes before him fled for terrour great,
90   And all the heavens stood still amazéd with his threat.

11

His huge long taylc wound up in hundred foldes,
    Does overspred his long bras-scaly backe,
    Whose wreathéd boughts° when ever he unfoldes,   *coils*
    And thicke entangled knots adown does slacke,
95   Bespotted as with shields of red and blacke,
    It sweepeth all the land behind him farre,
    And of three furlongs does but litle lacke;
    And at the point two stings in-fixéd arre,
Both deadly sharpe, that sharpest steele exceeden farre.

12

100 But stings and sharpest steele did far exceed[1]
    The sharpnesse of his cruell rending clawes;
    Dead was it sure, as sure as death in deed,
    What ever thing does touch his ravenous pawes,
    Or what within his reach he ever drawes.
105   But his most hideous head my toung to tell
    Does tremble: for his deepe devouring jawes
    Wide gapéd, like the griesly mouth of hell,
Through which into his darke abisse all ravin° fell.[2]   *prey, booty*

13

And that more wondrous was, in either jaw
110   Three ranckes of yron teeth enraungéd were,
    In which yet trickling bloud and gobbets raw
    Of late devouréd bodies did appeare,
    That sight thereof bred cold congealéd feare:
    Which to increase, and all at once to kill,
115   A cloud of smoothering smoke and sulphur seare°   *burning*

9. Closely overlaid.
1. I.e., were far exceeded by.
2. In emphasizing the deathly, hellish aspects of the dragon, this stanza reveals the stakes of the battle: holiness v. sin, the Protestant v. the Catholic churches, life v. death.

Out of his stinking gorge° forth steeméd still,   maw
That all the ayre about with smoke and stench did fill.

14

His blazing eyes, like two bright shining shields,
 Did burne with wrath, and sparkled living fyre;
As two broad Beacons, set in open fields,
 Send forth their flames farre off to every shyre,
 And warning give, that enemies conspyre,
 With fire and sword the region to invade;
 So flamed his eyne with rage and rancorous yre:
But farre within, as in a hollow glade,
Those glaring lampes were set, that made a dreadfull shade.[3]

15

So dreadfully he towards him did pas,
 Forelifting up aloft his speckled brest,
 And often bounding on the bruséd gras,
As for great joyance of his newcome guest.
 Eftsoones he gan advance his haughtie crest,
 As chawfféd° Bore his bristles doth upreare,   vexed
 And shoke his scales to battell readie drest;
That made the Redcrosse knight nigh quake for feare,
As bidding bold defiance to his foeman neare.

16

The knight gan fairely couch° his steadie speare,   rest, aim
 And fiercely ran at him with rigorous might:
 The pointed steele arriving rudely theare,
 His harder hide would neither perce, nor bight,
But glauncing by forth passéd forward right;
 Yet sore amovéd with so puissant push,
 The wrathfull beast about him turnéd light,°   quickly
 And him so rudely passing by, did brush
With his long tayle, that horse and man to ground did rush.

17

Both horse and man up lightly rose againe,
 And fresh encounter towards him addrest:
 But th' idle stroke yet backe recoyld in vaine,
 And found no place his° deadly point to rest.   its
Exceeding rage enflamed the furious beast,
 To be avengéd of so great despight;°   outrage
 For never felt his imperceable brest
 So wondrous force, from hand of living wight;
Yet had he proved° the powre of many a puissant knight.   tested

18

Then with his waving wings displayéd wyde,
 Himselfe up high he lifted from the ground,
 And with strong flight did forcibly divide
The yielding aire, which nigh too feeble found
Her flitting partes, and element unsound,

---

3. Cf. among other echoes, the great beast of Revelation (xiii.2): "And the beast which I saw was like unto a leopard, and his feet were as the feet of a bear, and his mouth as the mouth of a lion: and the dragon gave him his power, and his seat, and great authority."

To beare so great a weight: he cutting way
160   With his broad sayles, about him soaréd round:
   At last low stouping with unweldie sway,[4]
Snatcht up both horse and man, to beare them quite away.

19

Long he them bore above the subject plaine,[5]
   So farre as Ewghen[6] bow a shaft may send,
165   Till struggling strong did him at last constraine,
   To let them downe before his flightés end:
   As hagard° hauke presuming to contend   *untrained*
   With hardie fowle, above his hable might,[7]
   His wearie pounces° all in vaine doth spend,   *claws*
170   To trusse° the pray too heavie for his flight;   *seize*
Which comming downe to ground, does free it selfe by fight.

20

He so disseizéd of his gryping grosse,[8]
   The knight his thrillant° speare againe assayd   *piercing*
   In his bras-plated body to embosse,°   *plunge*
175   And three mens strength unto the stroke he layd;
   Wherewith the stiffe beame quakéd, as affrayd,
   And glauncing from his scaly necke, did glyde
   Close under his left wing, then broad displayd.
   The percing steele there wrought a wound full wyde,
180 That with the uncouth smart the Monster lowdly cryde.

21

He cryde, as raging seas are wont to rore,
   When wintry storme his wrathfull wreck does threat,
   The rolling billowes beat the ragged shore,
   As they the earth would shoulder from her seat,
185   And greedie gulfe does gape, as he would eat
   His neighbour element[9] in his revenge:
   Then gin the blustring brethren[1] boldly threat,
   To move the world from off his stedfast henge,°   *hinge*
And boystrous battell make, each other to avenge.

22

190 The steely head stucke fast still in his flesh,
   Till with his cruell clawes he snatcht the wood,
   And quite a sunder broke. Forth flowéd fresh
   A gushing river of blacke goarie blood,
   That drownéd all the land, whereon he stood;
195   The stream thereof would drive a water-mill.
   Trebly augmented was his furious mood
   With bitter sense of his deepe rooted ill,
That flames of fire he threw forth from his large noséthrill.

23

His hideous tayle then hurléd he about,
200   And therewith all enwrapt the nimble thyes

---

4. Ponderous force.
5. I.e., the ground below.
6. Yewen, of yew.
7. Able power.

8. Freed from his formidable grip.
9. I.e., earth.
1. I.e., the winds.

Of his froth-fomy steed, whose courage stout
  Striving to loose the knot, that fast him tyes,
  Himselfe in streighter bandes too rash implyes,
  That to the ground he is perforce constraynd
  To throw his rider: who can° quickly ryse   *began to*
  From off the earth, with durty bloud distaynd,
For that reprochfull fall right fowly he disdaynd.

24

And fiercely tooke his trenchand° blade in hand,   *sharp*
  With which he stroke so furious and so fell,
  That nothing seemd the puissance could withstand:
  Upon his crest the hardned yron fell,
  But his more hardned crest was armd so well,
  That deeper dint therein it would not make;
  Yet so extremely did the buffe him quell,°   *dismay*
  That from thenceforth he shund the like to take,
But when he saw them come, he did them still forsake.° *avoid*

25

The knight was wrath to see his stroke beguyld,
  And smote againe with more outrageous might;
  But backe againe the sparckling steele recoyld,
  And left not any marke, where it did light;
  As if in Adamant rocke it had bene pight.°   *struck against*
  The beast impatient of his smarting wound,
  And of so fierce and forcible despight,
  Thought with his wings to stye° above the ground; *mount*
But his late wounded wing unserviceable found.

26

Then full of griefe and anguish vehement,
  He lowdly brayd, that like was never heard,
  And from his wide devouring oven sent
  A flake° of fire, that flashing in his beard,   *flash*
  Him all amazd, and almost made affeard;
  The scorching flame sore swingéd° all his face, *singed*
  And through his armour all his bodie seard,
  That he could not endure so cruell cace,
But thought his armes to leave, and helmet to unlace.

27

Not that great Champion of the antique world,
  Whom famous Poetes verse so much doth vaunt,
  And hath for twelve huge labours high extold,
  So many furies and sharpe fits did haunt,
  When him the poysoned garment did enchaunt
  With Centaures bloud, and bloudie verses charmed,
  As did this knight twelve thousand dolours daunt,
  Whom fyrie steele now burnt, that earst him armed,
That erst him goodly armed, now most of all him harmed.[2]

2. Redcrosse's fire-baptism is compared to the burning shirt of Nessus, which killed Hercules, "that great Champion of the antique world" (line 235); the meta-phor of warfare and battle is here supplemented, as often in Spenser, by a metaphor of healing and purgation.

28

Faint, wearie, sore, emboylèd, grievèd, brent°   *burned*
245   With heat, toyle, wounds, armes, smart, and inward fire
     That never man such mischiefes did torment;
     Death better were, death did he oft desire,
     But death will never come, when needes require.
     Whom so dismayd when that his foe beheld,
250   He cast to suffer him no more respire,°   *rest*
     But gan his sturdie sterne° about to weld,°   *tail/lash*
And him so strongly stroke, that to the ground him feld.

29

It fortunéd (as faire it then befell)
     Behind his backe unweeting, where he stood,
255   Of auncient time there was a springing well,
     From which fast trickled forth a silver flood,
     Full of great vertues, and for med'cine good.
     Whylome,° before that cursèd Dragon got   *formerly*
     That happie land, and all with innocent blood
260   Defyld those sacred waves, it rightly hot°   *was called*
The Well of Life, ne yet his° vertues had forgot.   *its*

30

For unto life the dead it could restore,
     And guilt of sinfull crimes cleane wash away,
     Those that with sicknesse were infected sore,
265   It could recure, and aged long decay
     Renew, as one were borne that very day.
     Both Silo this, and Jordan did excell,
     And th' English Bath, and eke the german Spau,
     Ne can Cephise, nor Hebrus match this well:
270   Into the same the knight backe overthrowen, fell.[3]

31

Now gan the golden Phoebus for to steepe
     His fierie face in billowes of the west,
     And his faint steedes watred in Ocean deepe,
     Whiles from their journall° labours they did rest,   *daily*
275   When that infernall Monster, having kest°   *cast*
     His wearie foe into that living well,
     Can° high advaunce his broad discoloured brest,   *did*
     Above his wonted pitch,° with countenance fell,   *height*
And clapt his yron wings, as victor he did dwell.°   *remain*

32

280   Which when his pensive Ladie saw from farre,
     Great woe and sorrow did her soule assay,°   *attack*
     As weening that the sad end of the warre,
     And gan to highest God entirely° pray,   *earnestly*
     That fearéd chaunce° from her to turne away;   *fate*

3. In the old English metrical romance *Sir Bevis of Hampton*, the hero is saved in his fight with a dragon by a healing well; "a pure river of water of life" is also described in Revelation xxii.1–2. The Well of Life, with its baptismal powers of renewal, is successively compared to waters of the Bible, of England and Europe, and of classical antiquity. In Siloam (Silo) a blind man was cured by Christ (John ix.7); the crossing of the river Jordan saved the Jews (Deuteronomy xxvii.2–9), and Christ was baptized therein (Matthew iii.16); "Bath" and "Spau" (Spa) were famed for their medicinal waters; "Cephise" and "Hebrus" in Greece were noted for their clear streams.

85   With folded hands and knees full lowly bent
      All night she watcht, ne once adowne would lay
      Her daintie limbs in her sad dreriment,
But praying still did wake, and waking did lament.

33

    The morrow next gan early to appeare,
290   That Titan[4] rose to runne his daily race;
      But early ere the morrow next gan reare
      Out of the sea faire Titans deawy face,
      Up rose the gentle virgin from her place,
      And lookéd all about, if she might spy
295   Her loved knight to move his manly pace:
      For she had great doubt of his safety,
Since late she saw him fall before his enemy.

34

    At last she saw, where he upstarted brave
      Out of the well, wherein he drenchéd lay;
300   As Eagle fresh out of the Ocean wave,
      Where he hath left his plumes all hoary gray,
      And deckt himselfe with feathers youthly gay,
      Like Eyas° hauke up mounts unto the skies,   *young*
      His newly budded pineons to assay,
305   And marveiles at himselfe, still as he flies:
So new this new-borne knight to battell new did rise.

35

    Whom when the damnéd feend so fresh did spy,
      No wonder if he wondred at the sight,
      And doubted, whether his late enemy
310   It were, or other new suppliéd knight.
      He, now to prove his late renewéd might,
      High brandishing his bright deaw-burning blade,
      Upon his crested scalpe so sore did smite,
      That to the scull a yawning wound it made:
315 The deadly dint his dulléd senses all dismaid.

36

    I wote not, whether the revenging steele
      Were hardnéd with that holy water dew,
      Wherein he fell, or sharper edge did feele,
      Or his baptizéd hands now greater° grew;   *stronger*
320   Or other secret vertue did ensew;
      Else never could the force of fleshly arme,
      Ne molten mettall in his bloud embrew:°   *plunge*
      For till that stownd° could never wight him harme, *stunning blow*
By subtilty, nor slight,° nor might, nor mighty charme.   *trickery*

37

325   The cruell wound enragéd him so sore,
      That loud he yelléd for exceeding paine;
      As hundred ramping Lyons seemed to rore,
      Whom ravenous hunger did there to constraine:
      Then gan he tosse aloft his stretchéd traine,
330   And therewith scourge the buxome° aire so sore,   *yielding*

---

4. When the sun.

That to his force to yeelden it was faine;
Ne ought° his sturdie strokes might stand afore,   *anything*
That high trees overthrew, and rocks in peeces tore.

38

The same advauncing high above his head,
335 With sharpe intended° sting so rude him smot,   *shot out*
That to the earth him drove, as stricken dead,
Ne living wight would have him life behot:°   *granted*
The mortall sting his angry needle shot
Quite through his shield, and in his shoulder seasd,
340 Where fast it stucke, ne would there out be got:
The griefe thereof him wondrous sore diseasd,°   *afflicted*
Ne might his ranckling paine with patience be appeasd.[5]

39

But yet more mindfull of his honour deare,
Then of the grievous smart, which him did wring,°   *torment*
345 From loathéd soile he can° him lightly reare,   *began to*
And strove to loose the farre infixéd sting:
Which when in vaine he tryde with struggeling,
Inflamed with wrath, his raging blade he heft,
And strooke so strongly, that the knotty string
350 Of his huge taile he quite a sunder cleft,
Five joynts thereof he hewd, and but the stump him left.

40

Hart cannot thinke, what outrage, and what cryes,
With foule enfouldred[6] smoake and flashing fire,
The hell-bred beast threw forth unto the skyes,
355 That all was coveréd with darknesse dire:
Then fraught with rancour, and engorgéd° ire,   *choking*
He cast at once him to avenge for all,
And gathering up himselfe out of the mire,
With his uneven wings did fiercely fall
360 Upon his sunne-bright shield, and gript it fast withall.

41

Much was the man encombred with his hold,
In feare to lose his weapon in his paw,
Ne wist yet, how his talents° to unfold;   *talons*
Nor harder was from Cerberus greedie jaw
365 To plucke a bone, then from his cruell claw
To reave° by strength the gripéd gage° away: *seize/prize*
Thrise he assayd it from his foot to draw,
And thrise in vaine to draw it did assay,
It booted nought to thinke, to robbe him of his pray.

42

370 Tho when he saw no power might prevaile,
His trustie sword he cald to his last aid,
Wherewith he fiercely did his foe assaile,
And double blowes about him stoutly laid,
That glauncing fire out of the yron plaid;
375 As sparckles from the Andvile use to fly,

5. Redcrosse's wound suggests Christ's   6. Hurled out like thunder.
wounded side.

When heavie hammers on the wedge are swaid;°   *struck*
Therewith at last he forst him to unty°   *loosen*
One of his grasping feete, him to defend thereby.

43

The other foot, fast fixéd on his shield,
380   Whenas no strength, nor stroks mote him constraine
To loose, ne yet the warlike pledge to yield,
He smot thereat with all his might and maine,
That nought so wondrous puissance might sustaine;
Upon the joynt the lucky steele did light,
385   And made such way, that hewd it quite in twaine;
The paw yet misséd not his minisht° might,   *lessened*
But hong still on the shield, as it at first was pight.

44

For griefe thereof, and divelish despight,
From his infernall fournace forth he threw
390   Huge flames, that dimméd all the heavens light,
Enrold in duskish smoke and brimstone blew;
As burning Aetna from his boyling stew°   *cauldron*
Doth belch out flames, and rockes in peeces broke,
And ragged ribs of mountaines molten new
395   Enwrapt in coleblacke clouds and filthy smoke,
That all the land with stench, and heaven with horror choke.

45

The heate whereof, and harmefull pestilence
So sore him noyd,° that forst him to retire   *troubled*
A little backward for his best defence,
400   To save his bodie from the scorching fire,
Which he from hellish entrailes did expire.°   *breathe out*
It chaunst (eternall God that chaunce did guide)
As he recoyléd backward, in the mire
His nigh forwearied feeble feet did slide,
405   And downe he fell, with dread of shame sore terrifide.

46

There grew a goodly tree him faire beside,
Loaden with fruit and apples rosie red,
As they in pure vermilion had beene dide,
Whereof great vertues over all were red:°   *declared*
410   For happie life to all, which thereon fed,
And life eke everlasting did befall:
Great God it planted in that blessed sted°   *place*
With his almightie hand, and did it call
The Tree of Life, the crime of our first fathers fall.[7]

47

415 In all the world like was not to be found,
Save in that soile, where all good things did grow,
And freely sprong out of the fruitfull ground,
As incorrupted Nature did them sow,

7. In Genesis ii.9 appears the Tree of Life which God planted in the Garden of Eden. The "crime of our first fathers fall" is that Adam, in being banished from Eden, separated himself—and us—from the tree. The tree appears again in the New Jerusalem (Revelation xxii.2).

Till that dread Dragon all did overthrow.
Another like faire tree eke grew thereby,
Whereof who so did eat, eftsoones did know
Both good and ill: O mornefull memory:
That tree through one mans fault hath doen us all to dy.[8]

48

From that first tree forth flowd, as from a well,
A trickling streame of Balme, most soveraine
And daintie deare,[9] which on the ground still fell,
And overflowéd all the fertill plaine,
As it had deawéd bene with timely° raine: seasonable
Life and long health that gratious° ointment gave,   full of grace
And deadly woundes could heale, and reare againe
The senselesse corse appointed° for the grave.   made ready
Into that same he fell: which did from death him save.[1]

49

For nigh thereto the ever damnéd beast
Durst not approch, for he was deadly made,[2]
And all that life preservéd, did detest:
Yet he it oft adventured to invade.
By this the drouping day-light gan to fade,
And yeeld his roome to sad succeeding night,
Who with her sable mantle gan to shade
The face of earth, and wayes of living wight,
And high her burning torch set up in heaven bright.

50

When gentle Una saw the second fall
Of her deare knight, who wearie of long fight,
And faint through losse of bloud, moved not at all,
But lay as in a dreame of deepe delight,
Besmeard with pretious Balme, whose vertuous might
Did heale his wounds, and scorching heat alay,
Againe she stricken was with sore affright,
And for his safetie gan devoutly pray;
And watch the noyous° night, and wait for joyous day.   afflicting

51

The joyous day gan early to appeare,
And faire Aurora from the deawy bed
Of aged Tithone gan her selfe to reare,[3]
With rosie cheekes, for shame as blushing red;
Her golden lockes for haste were loosely shed
About her eares, when Una her did marke
Clymbe to her charet, all with flowers spred,
From heaven high to chase the chearelesse darke;
With merry note her loud salutes the mounting larke.

---

8. I.e., killed us. The tree described here is the Tree of Knowledge of Good and Evil in the Garden of Eden.
9. Precious.
1. A healing balm flowing from the tree of mercy is used by Seth to anoint Adam in the apocryphal Gospel of Nicodemus. This same balm is used later by Christ

and is understood to be His blood. Christ's blood was shed to redeem mankind from eternal damnation.
2. I.e., a child of death.
3. Aurora is goddess of the dawn, Tithonus her husband ("aged" because he was granted everlasting life without everlasting youth).

52

460 Then freshly up arose the doughtie knight,
    All healéd of his hurts and woundés wide,
    And did himselfe to battell readie dight;
    Whose early foe awaiting him beside
    To have devourd, so soone as day he spyde,
465 When now he saw himselfe so freshly reare,
    As if late fight had nought him damnifyde,°   *injured*
    He woxe dismayd, and gan his fate to feare;
Nathlesse° with wonted rage he him advauncéd neare.   *nevertheless*

53

    And in his first encounter, gaping wide,
470 He thought attonce him to have swallowed quight,
    And rusht upon him with outragious pride;
    Who him r'encountring fierce, as hauke in flight,
    Perforce rebutted° backe. The weapon bright   *drove*
    Taking advantage of his open jaw,
475 Ran through his mouth with so importune° might,   *violent*
    That deepe emperst his darksome hollow maw,
And back retyrd, his life bloud forth with all did draw.

54

    So downe he fell, and forth his life did breath,
    That vanisht into smoke and cloudés swift;
480 So downe he fell, that th' earth him underneath
    Did grone, as feeble so great load to lift;
    So downe he fell, as an huge rockie clift,
    Whose false° foundation waves have washt away,   *insecure*
    With dreadfull poyse° is from the mayneland rift, *falling weight*
485 And rolling downe, great Neptune doth dismay;
So downe he fell, and like an heapéd mountaine lay.

55

    The knight himselfe even trembled at his fall,
    So huge and horrible a masse it seemed;
    And his deare Ladie, that beheld it all,
490 Durst not approch for dread, which she misdeemed,°   *misjudged*
    But yet at last, when as the direfull feend
    She saw not stirre, off-shaking vaine affright,
    She nigher drew, and saw that joyous end:
    Then God she praysd, and thankt her faithfull knight,
495 That had atchieved so great a conquest by his might.

Canto XII

Faire Una to the Redcrosse knight
betrouthéd is with joy:
Though false Duessa it to barre
her false sleights doe imploy.

1

Behold I see the haven nigh at hand,
    To which I meane my wearie course to bend;

Vere the maine shete, and beare up with the land,[4]
The which afore is fairely to be kend,°   *recognized*
5   And seemeth safe from stormes, that may offend;
There this faire virgin wearie of her way
Must landed be, now at her journeyes end:
There eke my feeble barke° a while may stay,   *ship*
Till merry wind and weather call her thence away.

2

10 Scarsely had Phoebus in the glooming East
Yet harnesséd his firie-footed teeme,
Ne reard above the earth his flaming creast,
When the last deadly smoke aloft did steeme,
That signe of last outbreathéd life did seeme
15 Unto the watchman on the castle wall;
Who thereby dead that balefull Beast did deeme,
And to his Lord and Ladie lowd gan call,
To tell, how he had seene the Dragons fatall fall.

3

Uprose with hastie joy, and feeble speed
20 That aged Sire, the Lord of all that land,
And lookéd forth, to weet, if true indeede
Those tydings were, as he did understand,
Which whenas true by tryall he out fond,
He bad to open wyde his brazen gate,
25 Which long time had bene shut, and out of hond[5]
Proclayméd joy and peace through all his state;
For dead now was their foe, which them forrayéd late.[6]

4

Then gan triumphant Trompets sound on hie,
That sent to heaven the ecchoéd report
30 Of their new joy, and happie victorie
Gainst him, that had them long opprest with tort,°   *wrong*
And fast imprisonéd in siegéd fort.
Then all the people, as in solemne feast,
To him assembled with one full consort,[7]
35 Rejoycing at the fall of that great beast,
From whose eternall bondage now they were releast.

5

Forth came that auncient Lord and aged Queene,
Arayd in antique robes downe to the ground,
And sad° habiliments right well beseene;°   *dignified/proper*
40 A noble crew about them waited round
Of sage and sober Peres, all gravely gownd;
Whom farre before did march a goodly band
Of tall young men, all hable armes to sownd,[8]
But now they laurell braunches bore in hand;
45 Glad signe of victorie and peace in all their land.

---

4. Release the mainsail line and sail toward the land. The metaphor in this
stanza echoes many classical authors and
Chaucer's *Troilus and Criseyde* (II.1–7).

5. Straightway.
6. Had recently ravaged.
7. All together.
8. Able to fight with weapons.

6

Unto that doughtie Conquerour they came,
   And him before themselves prostrating low,
   Their Lord and Patrone loud did him proclaime,
   And at his feet their laurell boughes did throw.
50 Soone after them all dauncing on a row
   The comely virgins came, with girlands dight,
   As fresh as flowres in medow greene do grow,
   When morning deaw upon their leaves doth light:
And in their hands sweet Timbrels° all upheld   *tambourines*
    on hight.

7

55 And them before, the fry° of children young   *crowd*
   Their wanton° sports and childish mirth did play,   *playful*
   And to the Maydens sounding tymbrels sung
   In well attunéd notes, a joyous lay,
   And made delightfull musicke all the way,
60 Untill they came, where that faire virgin stood;
   As faire Diana in fresh sommers day
   Beholds her Nymphes, enraunged in shadie wood,
Some wrestle, some do run, some bathe in christall flood.

8

So she beheld those maydens meriment
65 With chearefull vew; who when to her they came,
   Themselves to ground with gratious humblesse bent,
   And her adored by honorable name,
   Lifting to heaven her everlasting fame:
   Then on her head they set a girland greene,
70 And crownéd her twixt earnest and twixt game; [9]
   Who in her selfe-resemblance well beseene,[1]
Did seeme such, as she was, a goodly maiden Queene.

9

And after all, the raskall many° ran,   *mob*
   Heapéd together in rude rablement,
75 To see the face of that victorious man:
   Whom all admired, as from heaven sent,
   And gazd upon with gaping wonderment.
   But when they came, where that dead Dragon lay,
   Stretcht on the ground in monstrous large extent,
80 The sight with idle° feare did them dismay,   *baseless*
Ne durst approch him nigh, to touch, or once assay.

10

Some feard, and fled; some feard and well it faynd;
   One that would wiser seeme, then all the rest,
   Warnd him not touch, for yet perhaps remaynd
85 Some lingring life within his hollow brest,
   Or in his wombe might lurke some hidden nest
   Of many Dragonets, his fruitfull seed;
   Another said, that in his eyes did rest
   Yet sparckling fire, and bad thereof take heed;
90 Another said, he saw him move his eyes indeed.

9. I.e., half in fun.   1. I.e., looking appropriately like herself.

11

One mother, when as her foolehardie chyld
   Did come too neare, and with his talants play,
   Halfe dead through feare, her litle babe revyld,°   *scolded*
   And to her gossips° gan in counsell say;   *women friends*
95   "How can I tell, but that his talants may
   Yet scratch my sonne, or rend his tender hand?"
   So diversly themselves in vaine they fray;°   *scare*
   Whiles some more bold, to measure him nigh stand,
To prove° how many acres he did spread of land.   *determine*

12

100 Thus flockéd all the folke him round about,
   The whiles that hoarie king, with all his traine,
   Being arrivéd, where that champion stout
   After his foes defeasance° did remaine,   *defeat*
   Him goodly greetes, and faire does entertaine,
105   With princely gifts of yvorie and gold,
   And thousand thankes him yeelds for all his paine.
   Then when his daughter deare he does behold,
Her dearely doth imbrace, and kisseth manifold.°   *many times*

13

And after to his Pallace he them brings,
110   With shaumes,[2] and trompets, and with Clarions sweet;
   And all the way the joyous people sings,
   And with their garments strowes the pavéd street:
   Whence mounting up, they find purveyance° meet   *provisions*
   Of all, that royall Princes court became,°   *suited*
115   And all the floore was underneath their feet
   Bespred with costly scarlot of great name,[3]
On which they lowly sit, and fitting purpose frame.

14

What needs me tell their feast and goodly guize,°   *mode of life*
   In which was nothing riotous nor vaine?
120   What needs of daintie dishes to devize,°   *talk*
   Of comely services, or courtly trayne?
   My narrow leaves cannot in them containe
   The large discourse[4] of royall Princes state.
   Yet was their manner then but bare and plaine:
125   For th' antique world excesse and pride did hate;[5]
Such proud luxurious pompe is swollen up but late.

15

Then when with meates and drinkes of every kinde
   Their fervent appetites they quenchéd had,
   That auncient Lord gan fit occasion finde,
130   Of straunge adventures, and of perils sad,
   Which in his travell him befallen had,
   For to demaund of his renowméd guest:
   Who then with utt'rance grave, and count'nance sad,
   From point to point, as is before exprest,
135 Discourst his voyage long, according his request.

2. Ancient wind instrument like an oboe.
3. I.e., famous scarlet cloth.
4. I.e., full description.
5. The question of "excesse" will be paramount in Book II, "The Legend of Sir Guyon, or of Temperance."

16

Great pleasure mixt with pittifull° regard,   *sympathetic*
  That godly King and Queene did passionate,[6]
  Whiles they his pittifull adventures heard,
  That oft they did lament his lucklesse state,
140 And often blame the too importune fate,
  That heapd on him so many wrathfull wreakes:°   *injuries*
  For never gentle knight, as he of late,
    So tosséd was in fortunes cruell freakes;
And all the while salt teares bedeawd the hearers cheaks.

17

145 Then said that royall Pere in sober wise:
  "Deare Sonne, great beene the evils, which ye bore
  From first to last in your late enterprise,
  That I note,° whether prayse, or pitty more: *know not*
  For never living man, I weene, so sore
150 In sea of deadly daungers was distrest;
  But since now safe ye seiséd° have the shore,   *reached*
    And well arrivéd are (high God be blest),
Let us devize of ease and everlasting rest."

18

"Ah dearest Lord," said then that doughty knight,
155 "Of ease or rest I may not yet devize;
  For by the faith, which I to armes have plight,
  I bounden am streight after this emprize,°   *enterprise*
  As that your daughter can ye well advize,
  Backe to returne to that great Faerie Queene,
160 And her to serve six yeares in warlike wize,
  Gainst that proud Paynim king, that workes her teene:°   *sorrow*
Therefore I ought crave pardon, till I there have beene."[7]

19

"Unhappie falles that hard necessitie,"
  Quoth he, "the troubler of my happie peace,
165 And vowéd foe of my felicitie;
  Ne I against the same can justly preace:°   *press*
  But since that band° ye cannot now release,   *obligation*
  Nor doen undo (for vowes may not be vaine),
  Soone as the terme of those six yeares shall cease,
170 Ye then shall hither backe returne againe,
The marriage to accomplish vowd betwixt you twain.

20

"Which for my part I covet to performe,
  In sort as through the world I did proclame,
  That who so kild that monster most deforme,
175 And him in hardy battaile overcame,
  Should have mine onely daughter to his Dame,°   *wife*

---

6. I.e., did feel and express.
7. That the marriage of Redcrosse and Una cannot be made final here and now signifies primarily that the final Christian triumph, the marriage of Christ and the true church will be achieved only at the end of time, the Day of Judgment. Meanwhile, the struggle against evil (and the Roman Church) continues.

And of my kingdome heire apparaunt bee:
Therefore since now to thee perteines the same,
By dew desert of noble chevalree,
180 Both daughter and eke kingdome, lo I yield to thee."

21

Then forth he calléd that his daughter faire,
The fairest Un' his onely daughter deare,
His onely daughter, and his onely heyre;
Who forth proceeding with sad° sober cheare,° *grave/countenance*
185 As bright as doth the morning starre appeare
Out of the East, with flaming lockes bedight,° *bedecked*
To tell that dawning day is drawing neare,
And to the world does bring long wishéd light;
So faire and fresh that Lady shewd her selfe in sight.

22

190 So faire and fresh, as freshest flowre in May;
For she had layd her mournefull stole aside,
And widow-like sad wimple° throwne away, *veil*
Wherewith her heavenly beautie she did hide,
Whiles on her wearie journey she did ride;
195 And on her now a garment she did weare,
All lilly white, withoutten spot, or pride,° *ornament*
That seemed like silke and silver woven neare,° *tightly*
But neither silke nor silver therein did appeare.[8]

23

The blazing brightnesse of her beauties beame,
200 And glorious light of her sunshyny face[9]
To tell, were as to strive against the streame.
My ragged rimes are all too rude and bace,
Her heavenly lineaments for to enchace.° *adorn*
Ne wonder; for her owne deare lovéd knight,
205 All° were she dayly with himselfe in place, *although*
Did wonder much at her celestiall sight:
Oft had he seene her faire, but never so faire dight.

24

So fairely dight, when she in presence came,
She to her Sire made humble reverence,
210 And bowéd low, that her right well became,
And added grace unto her excellence:
Who with great wisdome, and grave eloquence
Thus gan to say. But eare° he thus had said, *ere*
With flying speede, and seeming great pretence,° *importance*
215 Came running in, much like a man dismaid,
A Messenger with letters, which his message said.

---

8. "The marriage of the Lamb is come, and his wife hath made herself ready. And to her was granted that she should be arrayed in fine linen, clean and white: for the fine linen is the righteousness of saints" (Revelation xix.7–8).
9. Revelation xxi.9, 11 describes the New Jerusalem as "the bride, the Lamb's wife * * * her light was like unto a store most precious." Contemplation showed Redcrosse the "real New Jerusalem" (xi.505–13); by these allusions, Spenser associates it with Una and her father's kingdom, Eden (now restored).

25

All in the open hall amazéd stood,
 At suddeinnesse of that unwarie° sight,   *unexpected*
 And wondred at his breathlesse hastie mood.
220 But he for nought would stay his passage right°   *direct*
 Till fast° before the king he did alight;   *close*
 Where falling flat, great humblesse he did make,
 And kist the ground, whereon his foot was pight;° *placed*
 Then to his hands that writ° he did betake,   *document*
225 Which he disclosing, red thus, as the paper spake.

26

"To thee, most mighty king of Eden faire,
 Her greeting sends in these sad lines addrest,
 The wofull daughter, and forsaken heire
 Of that great Emperour of all the West;
230 And bids thee be advizéd for the best,
 Ere thou thy daughter linck in holy band
 Of wedlocke to that new unknowen guest:
 For he already plighted his right hand
Unto another love, and to another land.

27

235 "To me sad mayd, or rather widow sad,
 He was affiauncéd long time before,
 And sacred pledges he both gave, and had,
 False erraunt knight, infamous, and forswore:
 Witnesse the burning Altars, which° he swore, *by which*
240 And guiltie heavens of[1] his bold perjury,
 Which though he hath polluted oft of yore,
 Yet I to them for judgement just do fly,
And them conjure t' avenge this shamefull injury.

28

"Therefore since mine he is, or° free or bond,   *whether*
245 Or false or trew, or living or else dead,
 Withhold, O soveraine Prince, your hasty hond
 From knitting league with him, I you aread;° *advise*
 Ne wene° my right with strength adowne to tread, *think*
 Through weakenesse of my widowhed, or woe:
250 For truth is strong, her rightfull cause to plead,
 And shall find friends, if need requireth soe,
So bids thee well to fare, Thy neither friend, nor foe, Fidessa."

29

When he these bitter byting words had red,
 The tydings straunge did him abashéd make,
255 That still he sate long time astonishéd
 As in great muse, ne word to creature spake.
 At last his solemne silence thus he brake,
 With doubtfull eyes fast fixéd on his guest:
 "Redoubted knight, that for mine onely sake
260 Thy life and honour late adventurest,
Let nought be hid from me, that ought to be exprest.

---

1. I.e., and heavens polluted by.

30

"What meane these bloudy vowes, and idle threats,
 Throwne out from womanish impatient mind?
 What heavens? what altars? what enragéd heates
265 Here heapéd up with termes of love unkind,°   *unnatural*
 My conscience cleare with guilty bands[2] would bind?
 High God be witnesse, that I guiltlesse ame.
 But if your selfe, Sir knight, ye faultie find,
 Or wrappéd be in loves of former Dame,
270 With crime do not it cover, but disclose the same."

31

To whom the Redcrosse knight this answere sent,
 "My Lord, my King, be nought hereat dismayd,
 Till well ye wote by grave intendiment,[3]
 What woman, and wherefore doth me upbrayd
275 With breach of love, and loyalty betrayd.
 It was in my mishaps, as hitherward
 I lately traveild, that unwares I strayd
 Out of my way, through perils straunge and hard;
 That day should faile me, ere I had them all declard.

32

280 "There did I find, or rather I was found
 Of this false woman, that Fidessa hight,
 Fidessa hight the falsest Dame on ground,
 Most false Duessa, royall richly dight,
 That easie was t' invegle° weaker sight: *deceive*
285 Who by her wicked arts, and wylie skill,
 Too fasle and strong for earthly skill or might,
 Unwares me wrought unto her wicked will,
And to my foe betrayd, when least I fearéd ill."

33

Then steppéd forth the goodly royall Mayd,
290 And on the ground her selfe prostrating low,
 With sober countenaunce thus to him sayd:
 "O pardon me, my soveraigne Lord, to show
 The secret treasons, which of late I know
 To have bene wroght by that false sorceresse.
295 She onely she it is, that earst did throw
 This gentle knight into so great distresse,
That death him did awaite in dayly wretchednesse.

34

"And now it seemes, that she subornéd hath
 This craftie messenger with letters vaine,
300 To worke new woe and improvided scath,[4]
 By breaking of the band betwixt us twaine;
 Wherein she uséd hath the practicke paine[5]
 Of this false footman, clokt with simplenesse,
 Whom if ye please for to discover plaine,
305 Ye shall him Archimago find, I ghesse,
The falsest man alive; who tries shall find no lesse."

2. I.e., bonds of guilt.   4. Unexpected harm.
3. I.e., serious investigation.   5. Treacherous skill.

35

The king was greatly movéd at her speach,
    And all with suddein indignation fraight,°   *laden*
    Bad° on that Messenger rude hands to reach.   *bade*
    Eftsoones the Gard, which on his state did wait,
    Attacht that faitor° false, and bound him strait: *impostor*
    Who seeming sorely chaufféd° at his band,   *angered*
    As chainéd Beare, whom cruell dogs do bait,
    With idle force did faine them to withstand,
And often semblaunce made to scape out of their hand.

36

But they him layd full low in dungeon deepe,
    And bound him hand and foote with yron chaines.
    And with continuall watch did warely keepe;
    Who then would thinke, that by his subtile trains
    He could escape fowle death or deadly paines?[6]
    Thus when that Princes wrath was pacifide,
    He gan renew the late forbidden banes,[7]
    And to the knight his daughter deare he tyde,
With sacred rites and vowes for ever to abyde.

37

His owne two hands the holy knots did knit,
    That none but death for ever can devide;
    His owne two hands, for such a turne most fit,
    The housling° fire did kindle and provide,   *sacramental*
    And holy water thereon sprinckled wide;[8]
    At which the bushy Teade° a groome did light,   *marriage torch*
    And sacred lampe in secret chamber hide,
    Where it should not be quenchéd day nor night,
For feare of evill fates, but burnen ever bright.

38

Then gan they sprinckle all the posts with wine,
    And made great feast to solemnize that day;
    They all perfumde with frankensense divine,
    And precious odours fetcht from far away,
    That all the house did sweat with great aray:
    And all the while sweete Musicke did apply
    Her curious° skill, the warbling notes to play,   *intricate*
    To drive away the dull Melancholy;
The whiles one sung a song of love and jollity.

39

During the which there was an heavenly noise
    Heard sound through all the Pallace pleasantly,

6. "And he laid hold on the dragon, that old serpent, which is the Devil, and Satan, and bound him a thousand years, And cast him into the bottomless pit, and shut him up, and set a seal upon him, that he should deceive the nations no more, till the thousand years should be fulfilled: and after that he must be loosed a little season" (Revelation xx.2–3).
7. Banns, i.e., announcements of marriage.

8. So marriages in ancient times were solemnized with sacramental fire and water. Plutarch (*Roman Questions* 1) explains the practice on four counts, of which two may especially have interested Spenser: (a) fire is masculine and active, water feminine and relatively passive; (b) as fire and water are most usefully productive in combination, so the joining of male and female in marriage appropriately completes society.

345   Like as it had bene many an Angels voice,
    Singing before th' eternall majesty,
    In their trinall triplicities[9] on hye;
    Yet wist no creature, whence that heavenly sweet°   *delight*
    Proceeded, yet each one felt secretly°   *inwardly*
350   Himselfe thereby reft of his sences meet,°   *proper*
And ravishéd with rare impression in his sprite.[10]

40

Great joy was made that day of young and old,
    And solemne feast proclaimd throughout the land,
    That their exceeding merth may not be told:
355   Suffice it heare by signes to understand
    The usuall joyes at knitting of loves band.
    Thrise happy man the knight himselfe did hold,
    Possesséd of his Ladies hart and hand,
    And ever, when his eye did her behold,
360   His heart did seeme to melt in pleasures manifold.

41

Her joyous presence and sweet company
    In full content he there did long enjoy,
    Ne wicked envie, ne vile gealosy
    His deare delights were able to annoy:
365   Yet swimming in that sea of blisfull joy,
    He nought forgot, how he whilome had sworne,
    In case he could that monstrous beast destroy,
    Unto his Faerie Queene backe to returne:
The which he shortly did, and Una left to mourne.

42

370   Now strike your sailes ye jolly Mariners,
    For we be come unto a quiet rode,°   *harbor*
    Where we must land some of our passengers,
    And light this wearie vessell of her lode.
    Here she a while may make her safe abode,
375   Till she repairéd have her tackles spent,°   *worn out*
    And wants supplide. And then againe abroad
    On the long voyage whereto she is bent:
Well may she speede and fairely finish her intent.

From Book II, Canto XII[1]

[*The Bower of Bliss*]

42

370   Thence passing forth, they shortly do arrive,
    Whereas the Bowre of Blisse was situate;

---

9. The "trinall triplicities" are the nine angelic orders, divided, according to the pseudo-Areopagite, into three groups of three, the whole hierarchy corresponding to the nine spheres of the universe; what is heard in this stanza is, therefore, the music of the spheres.
10. Spirit. "Let us be glad and rejoice, and give honor to him: for the marriage of the Lamb is come" (Revelation xix.6).

In Revelation, the marriage of Christ and the New Jerusalem signalizes the general redemption.
1. Book II is the story of Sir Guyon, who represents and becomes the virtue of Temperance (or moderation, self-control) as Redcrosse represented, and became, Holiness; his companion is a "palmer," a "sage and sober" pilgrim. In the present selection from the last

A place pickt out by choice of best alive,[2]
That natures worke by art can imitate:
In which what ever in this worldly state
Is sweet, and pleasing unto living sense,
Or that may dayntiest fantasie aggrate,°   *please, satisfy*
Was pouréd forth with plentifull dispence,°   *liberality*
And made there to abound with lavish affluence.

43

Goodly it was encloséd round about,
  Aswell their entred guestes to keepe within,
  As those unruly beasts to hold without;
  Yet was the fence thereof but weake and thin;
  Nought feard their force, that fortilage° to win,   *fortalice, fort*
  But wisedomes powre, and temperaunces might,[3]
  By which the mightiest things efforcéd bin:°   *were*
  And eke the gate was wrought of substaunce light,
Rather for pleasure, then for battery or fight.

44

Yt framéd was of precious yvory,
  That seemd a worke of admirable wit;
  And therein all the famous history
  Of Jason and Medaea was ywrit;
  Her mighty charmes, her furious loving fit,
  His goodly conquest of the golden fleece,
  His falséd faith, and love too lightly flit,
  The wondred° Argo, which in venturous peece   *admired*
First through the Euxine seas bore all the flowr of Greece.

45

Ye might have seene the frothy billowes fry°   *foam*
  Under the ship, as thorough them she went,

Canto, they visit and destroy the Bower of Bliss. The Bower functions, much as Lucifera's palace or Orgoglio's·dungeon did in Book I, as an allegorical locale where a symbolic action takes place. Spenser had first shown his readers the Bower in Canto v; there Cymochles is found reclining "amidst a flock of Damzelles"; they are half-naked, wantonly flirtatious, while he,"like an Adder lurking in the weedes, / His wandring thought in deep desire does steepe." That was, however, only a preliminary glimpse.

The "Bower of Bliss," perhaps the most famous of Spenser's "set pieces," has been variously interpreted. In *The Allegory of Love*, C. S. Lewis argues convincingly that the Bower "is not a picture of lawless, that is, unwedded love as opposed to lawful love. It is a picture, one of the most powerful ever painted, of the whole sexual nature in disease. There is not a kiss or an embrace in the island: only male prurience and female provocation" (p. 332). This is especially true of Acrasia, the mistress of the Bower, whose name means both "excess" and "impotence"; she is seen (stanzas 77–79) statically posed, doing nothing, only *appearing* as the archetypal seductress. The Bower is certainly a place where sexuality is sterile, as the Garden of Adonis (in the following selection) is a place where it is fertile. Some readers may find, however, that imagery partly overflows moral intention. For example, the two girls bathing in a pool (stanzas 63–68) are assuredly pin-ups out of a man's magazine of the mid-20th century—and yet Spenser compares them to the morning star and to the Venus of Cyprus (lines 577–80).

2. I.e., the best living artists. The imitating of nature by art had been foreshadowed in Canto v, where "art, striving to compare / with nature, did an Arber greene dispred" (II.v.272–73). Nature is important to Sir Guyon, as it was not to Redcrosse, because temperance is attainable by unaided nature, whereas holiness requires the help of grace.

3. The fear is not of the physical force of Guyon and the Palmer but of the virtuous power of their temperance and wisdom.

That seemd the waves were into yvory,
Or yvory into the waves were sent;
And other where the snowy substaunce sprent
With vermell,° like the boyes bloud therein shed,   *vermilion*
A piteous spectacle did represent,
And otherwhiles° with gold besprinkeléd;   *elsewhere*
Yt seemd th' enchaunted flame, which did Creüsa wed.[4]

46

All this, and more might in that goodly gate
Be red; that ever open stood to all,[5]
Which thither came: but in the Porch there sate
A comely personage of stature tall,
And semblaunce° pleasing, more than naturall,   *appearance*
That travellers to him seemd to entize;
His looser° garment to the ground did fall,   *too loose*
And flew about his heeles in wanton wize,
Not fit for speedy pace, or manly exercize.

47

They in that place him Genius° did call: *guiding spirit*
Not that celestiall powre, to whom the care
Of life, and generation of all
That lives, pertaines in charge particulare,
Who wondrous things concerning our welfare,
And straunge phantomes doth let us oft forsee,
And oft of secret ill bids us beware:
That is our Selfe, whom though we do not see,
Yet each doth in him selfe it well perceive to bee.

48

Therefore a God him sage Antiquity
Did wisely make, and good Agdistes call:
But this same was to that quite contrary,
The foe of life, that good envyes° to all,   *grudges*
That secretly doth us procure to fall,
Through guilefull semblaunts,° which he makes us see.   *illusions*
He of this Gardin had the governall,
And Pleasures porter was devizd° to bee,   *considered*
Holding a staffe in hand for more formalitee.

49

With diverse flowres he daintily was deckt,
And strowéd round about, and by his side
A mighty mazer° bowle of wine was set,   *drinking*
As if it had to him bene sacrifide;
Wherewith all new-come guests he gratifide:

---

4. Jason, in his ship the *Argo*, sought the Golden Fleece of the king of Colchis; the witch Medea, the king's daughter, fell in love with him and used "her mighty charmes" to help him obtain it (lines 392–93). The "boyes bloud" (line 402) refers to Absyrtus, Medea's younger brother, whose body she cut into pieces and scattered, to delay her father's pursuit by making him stop to collect the fragments. Later, Jason deserted Medea for Creüsa; in revenge, Medea gave the girl a dress which burst into fire when she put it on; the flame consumed and thus "wed" her (line 405). This tale of unnatural "furious loving," with all its attendant violence, is appropriate to the Bower.

5. "Wide is the gate, and broad is the way, that leadeth to destruction, and many there be which go in thereat" (Matthew vii.13).

So did he eke Sir Guyon passing by:
But he his idle curtesie defide,
    And overthrew his bowle disdainfully;
And broke his staffe, with which he charméd semblants sly.[6]

50

Thus being entred, they behold around
    A large and spacious plaine, on every side
    Strowed with pleasauns,° whose faire grassy ground   *gardens*
Mantled with greene, and goodly beautifide
    With all the ornaments of Floraes pride,
    Wherewith her mother Art, as halfe in scorne
Of niggard Nature, like a pompous bride
    Did decke her, and too lavishly adorne,
When forth from virgin bowre she comes in th' early morne.[7]

51

Thereto the Heavens alwayes Joviall,°   *propitious*
    Lookt on them lovely,° still in stedfast state,   *lovingly*
    Ne suffred storme nor frost on them to fall,
Their tender buds or leaves to violate,
    Nor scorching heat, nor cold intemperate
    T' afflict the creatures, which therein did dwell,
But the milde aire with season moderate
    Gently attempred, and disposd so well,
That still it breathéd forth sweet spirit and holesome smell.

52

More sweet and holesome, then the pleasaunt hill
    Of Rhodope, on which the Nimphe, that bore
    A gyaunt babe, her selfe for griefe did kill;
Or the Thessalian Tempe, where of yore
    Faire Daphne Phoebus hart with love did gore;
    Or Ida, where the Gods loved to repaire,
When ever they their heavenly bowres forlore;[8]
    Or sweet Parnasse, the haunt of Muses faire;
Or Eden selfe, if ought with Eden mote compaire.

53

Much wondred Guyon at the faire aspect
    Of that sweet place, yet suffred no delight
    To sincke into his sence, nor mind affect,
But passéd forth, and lookt still forward right,°   *straight ahead*
    Bridling his will, and maistering his might:
    Till that he came unto another gate;
No gate, but like one, being goodly dight
    With boughes and braunches, which did broad dilate°   *spread out*
Their clasping armes, in wanton wreathings intricate.

6. I.e., raised deceitful apparitions. The rod and bowl are traditional emblems of enchantment (cf. for example, Duessa's cup, in I.viii.14).

7. Art no longer merely imitates nature but undertakes to supplant it, by excess.

8. Deserted. The nymph Rhodope, who had a "gyaunt babe," Athos, by Neptune (lines 460–62), was turned into a mountain; Daphne, another nymph, charmed Apollo so that he pursued her until she prayed for aid and was turned into a laurel tree; Mount Ida was the scene of the rape of Ganymede and the judgment of Paris, and the gods watched the Trojan War from its heights. These are all allusions to violent and unhappy passion—and yet the Bower is also compared to Mt. Parnassus, home of the Muses, and to the Garden of Eden.

54

So fashionéd a Porch with rare device,
   Archt over head with an embracing vine,
480   Whose bounches hanging downe, seemed to entice
   All passers by, to tast their lushious wine
   And did themselves into their hands incline,
   As freely offering to be gatheréd:
   Some deepe empurpled as the Hyacint,
485   Some as the Rubine, laughing sweetly red,
Some like faire Emeraudes, not yet well ripenéd.

55

And them amongst, some were of burnisht gold,
   So made by art, to beautifie the rest,
   Which did themselves emongst the leaves enfold,
490   As lurking from the vew of covetous guest,
   That the weake bowes, with so rich load opprest,
   Did bowe adowne, as over-burdenéd.
   Under that Porch a comely dame did rest,
   Clad in faire weedes,° but fowle disorderéd,   *garments*
495 And garments loose, that seemd unmeet for womanhed.° *womanhood*

56

In her left hand a Cup of gold she held,
   And with her right the riper° fruit did reach,   *overripe*
   Whose sappy liquor, that with fulnesse sweld,
   Into her cup she scruzd,° with daintie breach   *crushed*
500   Of her fine fingers, without fowle empeach,°   *hindrance*
   That so faire wine-presse made the wine more sweet:
   Thereof she usd to give to drinke to each,
   Whom passing by she happenéd to meet:
It was her guise,° all Straungers goodly so to greet.   *custom*

57

505 So she to Guyon offred it to tast;
   Who taking it out of her tender hond,
   The cup to ground did violently cast,
   That all in peeces it was broken fond,°   *found*
   And with the liquor stainéd all the lond.°   *land*
510   Whereat Excesse exceedingly was wroth,
   Yet no'te° the same amend, ne yet withstond, *knew not how to*
   But suffered him to passe, all° were she loth;   *although*
Who nought regarding her displeasure forward goth.

58

There the most daintie Paradise on ground,
515   It selfe doth offer to his sober eye,
   In which all pleasures plenteously abound,
   And none does others happinesse envye:
   The painted flowres, the trees upshooting hye,
   The dales for shade, the hilles for breathing space,
520   The trembling groves, the Christall running by;
   And that, which all faire workes doth most aggrace,° *add grace to*
The art, which all that wrought, appearéd in no place.

59

One would have thought (so cunningly, the rude,
    And scornéd parts were mingled with the fine)
    That nature had for wantonesse ensude°   *imitated*
    Art, and that Art at nature did repine;°   *complain*
    So striving each th' other to undermine,
    Each did the others worke more beautifie;
    So diff'ring both in willes, agreed in fine:[9]
    So all agreed through sweete diversitie,
This Gardin to adorne with all varietie.

60

And in the midst of all, a fountaine stood,
    Of richest substaunce, that on earth might bee,
    So pure and shiny, that the silver flood
    Through every channell running one might see;
    Most goodly it with curious imageree
    Was over-wrought, and shapes of naked boyes,
    Of which some seemd with lively jollitee,
    To fly about, playing their wanton toyes,°   *sports*
Whilest others did them selves embay° in liquid joyes.   *drench*

61

And over all, of purest gold was spred,
    A trayle of yvie in his native hew:
    For the rich metall was so colouréd,
    That wight, who did not well avised vew,
    Would surely deeme it to be yvie trew:[1]
    Low his lascivious armes adown did creepe,
    That themselves dipping in the silver dew,
    Their fleecy flowres they tenderly did steepe,
Which° drops of Christall seemd for wantones° *on which/wantonness*
        to weepe.

62

Infinit streames continually did well
    Out of this fountaine, sweet and faire to see,
    The which into an ample laver° fell,   *basin*
    And shortly grew to so great quantitie,
    That like a little lake it seemd to bee;
    Whose depth exceeded not three cubits hight,
    That through the waves one might the bottom see,
    All pavéd beneath with Jasper shining bright,
That seemd the fountaine in that sea did sayle upright.

63

And all the margent round about was set,
    With shady Laurell trees, thence to defend°   *ward off*
    The sunny beames, which on the billowes bet,
    And those which therein bathéd, mote offend.
    As Guyon hapned by the same to wend,
    Two naked Damzelles he therein espyde,

9. I.e., at the end. Art and nature harmonize with each other in effect, although antagonistic in intention.

1. The golden ivy has attracted much critical comment as an image of artifice with a touch of the repellent about it.

565   Which therein bathing, seeméd to contend,
    And wrestle wantonly, ne cared to hyde,
  Their dainty parts from vew of any, which them eyde.

64

  Sometimes the one would lift the other quight
    Above the waters, and then downe againe
570   Her plong, as over maisteréd by might,
    Where both awhile would coveréd remaine,
    And each the other from to rise restraine;
    The whiles their snowy limbes, as through a vele,
    So through the Christall waves appearéd plaine:
575   Then suddeinly both would themselves unhele,°   *uncover*
  And th' amarous sweet spoiles to greedy eyes revele.

65

  As that faire Starre, the messenger of morne,
    His deawy face out of the sea doth reare:
    Or as the Cyprian goddesse,[2] newly borne
580   Of th' Oceans fruitfull froth, did first appeare:
    Such seeméd they, and so their yellow heare
    Christalline humour[3] droppéd downe apace.
    Whom such when Guyon saw, he drew him neare,
    And somewhat gan relent his earnest pace,
585 His stubborne brest gan secret pleasaunce to embrace.

66

  The wanton Maidens him espying, stood
    Gazing a while at his unwonted guise;°   *manner*
    Then th' one her selfe low duckéd in the flood,
    Abasht, that her a straunger did avise:°   *see*
590   But th' other rather higher did arise,
    And her two lilly paps aloft displayd,
    And all, that might his melting hart entise
    To her delights, she unto him bewrayed:°   *revealed*
  The rest hid underneath, him more desirous made.

67

595 With that, the other likewise up arose,
    And her faire lockes, which formerly were bownd
    Up in one knot, she low adowne did lose: °   *loosen*
    Which flowing long and thick, her clothed arownd,
    And th' yvorie in golden mantle gownd:
600   So that faire spectacle from him was reft,
    Yet that, which reft it, no lesse faire was fownd:
    So hid in lockes and waves from lookers theft,
  Nought but her lovely face she for his looking left.

68

  Withall she laughéd, and she blusht withall,
605   That blushing to her laughter gave more grace,
    And laughter to her blushing, as did fall:
    Now when they spide the knight to slacke his pace,
    Them to behold, and in his sparkling face

2. Venus (one of whose principal   3. Clear liquid.
shrines was on the island of Cyprus).

The secret signes of kindled lust appeare,
Their wanton meriments they did encreace,
And to him beckned, to approach more neare,
And shewd him many sights, that courage cold could reare.[4]

69

On which when gazing him the Palmer saw,
He much rebukt those wandring eyes of his,
And counseld well, him forward thence did draw.
Now are they come nigh to the Bowre of blis
Of her fond favorites so named amis:
When thus the Palmer: "Now Sir, well avise;°   *take care*
For here the end of all our travell is:
Here wonnes° Acrasia, whom we must surprise,   *dwells*
Else she will slip away, and all our drift° despise."   *plan, effort*

70

Eftsoones they heard a most melodious sound,
Of all that mote delight a daintie eare,
Such as attonce might not on living ground,
Save in this Paradise, be heard elswhere:
Right hard it was, for wight, which did it heare,
To read, what manner musicke that mote bee:
For all that pleasing is to living eare,
Was there consorted in one harmonee,
Birdes, voyces, instruments, windes, waters, all agree.

71

The joyous birdes shrouded in chearefull shade,
Their notes unto the voyce attempred° sweet;   *attuned*
Th' Angelicall soft trembling voyces made
To th' instruments divine respondence meet:°   *fitting*
The silver sounding instruments did meet°   *join*
With the base murmure of the waters fall:
The waters fall with difference discreet,°   *suitable*
Now soft, now loud, unto the wind did call:
The gentle warbling wind low answered to all.[5]

72

There, whence that Musick seeméd heard to bee,
Was the faire Witch her selfe now solacing,
With a new Lover, whom through sorceree
And witchcraft, she from farre did thither bring:
There she had him now layd a slombering,
In secret shade, after long wanton joyes:
Whilst round about them pleasauntly did sing
Many faire Ladies, and lascivious boyes,
That ever mixt their song with light licentious toyes.

---

4. That could arouse a cold spirit.
5. Taste, sight, smell, and sound are all titillated here; little is said, however, of touching. Acrasia, whom we are about to see, bears many resemblances to Circe (not only the cool figure of *Odyssey* X, but the much more witchlike and seductive creature painted by Ovid) and to the enchantresses of Italian romance who derive from Circe, such as Acratia in Trissino's *L'Italia Liberata* and Armida in Tasso's *Gerusalemme Liberata*. In fact, much of the description in Canto xii is imitated from Armida's garden in that poem, and the rose song of stanzas 74 and 75 (a classic statement of the *carpe-diem* theme) is a direct translation.

73

And all that while, right over him she hong,
With her false eyes fast fixéd in his sight,
As seeking medicine, whence she was stong,
Or greedily depasturing° delight: *feeding on*
And oft inclining downe with kisses light,
For feare of waking him, his lips bedewd,
And through his humid eyes did sucke his spright,
Quite molten into lust and pleasure lewd;
Wherewith she sighéd soft, as if his case she rewd.° *pitied*

74

The whiles some one did chaunt this lovely lay:
"Ah see, who so faire thing doest faine° to see   *delight*
In springing flowre the image of thy day;
Ah see the Virgin Rose, how sweetly shee
Doth first peepe forth with bashfull modestee
That fairer seemes, the lesse ye see her may
Lo see soone after, how more bold and free
Her baréd bosome she doth broad display;
Loe see soone after, how she fades, and falles away.

75

"So passeth, in the passing of a day,
Of mortall life the leafe, the bud, the flowre,
Ne more doth flourish after first decay,
That earst was sought to decke both bed and bowre,
Of many a Ladie, and many a Paramowre: °   *lover*
Gather therefore the Rose, whilest yet is prime
For soone comes age, that will her pride deflowre:
Gather the Rose of love, whilest yet is time,
Whilest loving thou mayst lovéd be with equal crime."

76

He ceast, and then gan all the quire of birdes
Their diverse notes t' attune unto his lay,
As in approvance of his pleasing words.
The constant paire heard all, that he did say,
Yet swarved not, but kept their forward way,
Through many covert groves, and thickets close,
In which they creeping did at last display°   *discover*
That wanton Ladie, with her lover lose,°   *loose*
Whose sleepie head she in her lap did soft dispose.

77

Upon a bed of Roses she was layd,[6]
As faint through heat, or dight to pleasant sin,
And was arayd, or rather disarayd,
All in a vele of silke and silver thin,
That hid no whit her alablaster skin,
But rather shewd more white, if more might bee:
More subtile web Arachne° cannot spin,   *the spider*
Nor the fine nets, which oft we woven see
Of scorched deaw, do not in th' aire more lightly flee.° *float*

6. Prepared for.

78

Her snowy brest was bare to readie spoyle
  Of hungry eies, which n'ote° therewith be fild,   *could not*
  And yet through languor of her late sweet toyle,
  Few drops, more cleare than Nectar, forth distild,
  That like pure Orient perles adowne it trild,°   *trickled*
  And her faire eyes sweet smyling in delight,
  Moystened their fierie beames, with which she thrild
  Fraile harts, yet quenchéd not; like starry light
Which sparckling on the silent waves, does seeme more bright.

79

The young man sleeping by her, seemd to bee
  Some goodly swayne of honorable place,°   *rank*
  That certés it great pittie was to see
  Him his nobilitie so foule deface;°   *disgrace*
  A sweet regard, and amiable grace,
  Mixed with manly sternnesse did appeare
  Yet sleeping, in his well proportioned face,
  And on his tender lips the downy heare
Did now but freshly spring, and silken blossomes beare.

80

His warlike armes, the idle instruments
  Of sleeping praise, were hong upon a tree,
  And his brave shield, full of old moniments,
  Was fowly ra'st,[7] that none the signes might see;
  Ne for them, ne for honour caréd hee,
  Ne ought, that did to his advauncement tend,
  But in lewd loves, and wastfull luxuree,
  His dayes, his goods, his bodie he did spend:
O horrible enchantment, that him so did blend.°   *blind*

81

The noble Elfe,[8] and carefull Palmer drew
  So nigh them, minding nought, but lustfull game,
  That suddein forth they on them rusht, and threw
  A subtile net, which onely for the same
  The skilfull Palmer formally° did frame.   *scientifically*
  So held them under fast, the whiles the rest
  Fled all away for feare of fowler shame.
  The faire Enchauntresse, so unwares opprest,
Tryde all her arts, and all her sleights, thence out to wrest.

82

And eke her lover strove: but all in vaine;
  For that same net so cunningly was wound,
  That neither guile, nor force might it distraine.°   *tear*
  They tooke them both, and both them strongly bound
  In captive bandes, which there they readie found:
  But her in chaines of adamant he tyde;
  For nothing else might keepe her safe and sound;

---

7. Erased. The removal of the emblems
from his shield was the last disgrace of
a knight.
8. Knight of fairyland.

But Verdant[9] (so he hight) he soone untyde,
And counsell sage in steed thereof to him applyde.

83

But all those pleasant bowres and Pallace brave,
740   Guyon broke downe, with rigour pittilesse;
Ne ought their goodly workmanship might save
Them from the tempest of his wrathfulnesse,
But that their blisse he turned to balefulnesse:
Their groves he feld, their gardins did deface,
745   Their arbers spoyle, their Cabinets° suppresse,   *summerhouses*
Their banket houses burne, their buildings race,°   *raze*
And of the fairest late, now made the fowlest place.

84

Then led they her away, and eke that knight
They with them led, both sorrowfull and sad:
750   The way they came, the same retourned they right,
Till they arrivéd, where they lately had
Charmed those wild-beasts, that raged with furie mad.
Which now awaking, fierce at them gan fly,
As in their mistresse reskew, whom they lad;°   *lead*
755   But them the Palmer soone did pacify.
Then Guyon askt, what meant those beastes, which there did ly.

85

Said he, "These seeming beasts are men indeed,
Whom this Enchauntresse hath transforméd thus,
Whylome her lovers, which her lusts did feed,
760   Now turned into figures hideous,
According to their mindes like monstruous."[1]
"Sad end," quoth he, "of life intemperate,
And mournefull meed of joyes delicious:
But Palmer, if it mote thee so aggrate,°   *please*
765 Let them returnéd be unto their former state."

86

Streight way he with his vertuous staffe them strooke,
And streight of beasts they comely men became;
Yet being men they did unmanly looke,
And staréd ghastly, some for inward shame,
770   And some for wrath, to see their captive Dame:
But one above the rest in speciall,
That had an hog beene late, hight Grille by name,
Repinéd greatly, and did him miscall,°   *abuse*
That had from hoggish forme him brought to naturall.

87

775 Said Guyon, "See the mind of beastly man,
That hath so soone forgot the excellence
Of his creation, when he life began,
That now he chooseth, with vile difference,°   *change*
To be a beast, and lacke intelligence."

9. The name means "green" and may refer, therefore, to a young man in the springtime of his sensuality.
1. Circe had changed Odysseus' companions into swine, but Odysseus was empowered to release them. Cf. also the animals upon which the sins rode in I.v.

780   To whom the Palmer thus, "The donghill kind
         Delights in filth and foule incontinence:
         Let Grill be Grill, and have his hoggish mind,
  But let us hence depart, whilest wether serves and wind."

From Book III, Canto VI[1]

[*The Garden of Adonis*]

30

   In that same Gardin all the goodly flowres,
       Wherewith dame Nature doth her beautifie,
       And decks the girlonds of her paramoures,
265   Are fetcht: there is the first seminarie°   *genetic source*
       Of all things, that are borne to live and die,
       According to their kindes. Long worke it were,
       Here to account the endlesse progenie
       Of all the weedes,° that bud and blossome there;   *plants*
270 But so much as doth need, must needs be counted here.

31

   It sited was in fruitfull soyle of old,
       And girt in with two walles on either side;
       The one of yron, the other of bright gold,
       That none might thorough breake, nor overstride:
275   And double gates it had, which opened wide,
       By which both in and out men moten° pas;   *could*
       Th' one faire and fresh, the other old and dride:
       Old Genius the porter of them was,
  Old Genius, the which a double nature has.

32

280 He letteth in, he letteth out to wend,°   *go*
       All that to come into the world desire;
       A thousand thousand naked babes attend
       About him day and night, which doe require,
       That he with fleshly weedes would them attire:[2]
285   Such as him list, such as eternall fate
       Ordainéd hath, he clothes with sinfull mire,[3]
       And sendeth forth to live in mortall state,
  Till they againe returne backe by the hinder gate.

1. The "hero" of Book III is the lady Britomart, the representative of Chastity. By "chastity" is meant, however, not abstinence but a love that is devoted and active. The "Garden of Adonis" passage here reprinted is the "allegorical core" of the book, but unlike Orgoglio's castle or the Bower of Bliss, the knight does not enter upon any symbolic action therein; in fact, Britomart does not even appear.

     The Garden of Adonis is part of a long literary tradition of earthly paradises, among them Homer's Garden of Alcinous (*Odyssey* VII) and Chaucer's Garden of Nature in the *Parliament of Fowls* (lines 120–308), and of gardens in courtly-love allegories. The broadly Neoplatonic ideas in stanzas 30–50 parallel classical and later sources such as the Myth of Er in Plato's *Republic,* the *Enneads* of Plotinus, and Arthur Golding's translation of Ovid's *Metamorphoses*. In Spenser's Garden all living things are formed and re-formed; as the center of generation and regeneration, it is the axis upon which the idea of love, as the life-producing power, turns. The Garden exhibits a picture of what love would be if man were not what he is.

2. The "naked babes" may be taken as the "seeds" from which all life springs, or as souls in the pre-existent state. "Weedes" are clothes, so "fleshly weedes" are, here, the body.

3. I.e., the flesh.

33

After that they againe returnéd beene,
290   They in that Gardin planted be againe;
    And grow afresh, as they had never seene
    Fleshly corruption, nor mortall paine.
    Some thousand yeares so doen they there remaine;
    And then of him are clad with other hew,°   *form*
295   Or sent into the chaungefull world againe,
    Till thither they returne, where first they grew:
So like a wheele around they runne from old to new.

34

Ne needs there Gardiner to set, or sow,
    To plant or prune: for of their owne accord
300   All things, as they created were, doe grow,
    And yet remember well the mightie word,
    Which first was spoken by th' Almightie lord,
    That bad them to increase and multiply:
    Ne doe they need with water of the ford,°   *stream*
305   Or of the clouds to moysten their roots dry;
For in themselves eternall moisture they imply.°   *contain*

35

Infinite shapes of creatures there are bred,
    And uncouth° formes, which none yet ever knew,   *strange*
    And every sort is in a sundry° bed   *separate*
310   Set by it selfe, and ranckt in comely rew:°   *row, rank*
    Some fit for reasonable soules t' indew,°   *put on*
    Some made for beasts, some made for birds to weare,
    And all the fruitfull spawne of fishes hew
    In endlesse rancks along enraungéd were,
315   That seemed the Ocean could not containe them there.

36

Daily they grow, and daily forth are sent
    Into the world, it to replenish more;
    Yet is the stocke not lessenéd, nor spent,
    But still remaines in everlasting store,
320   As it at first created was of yore.
    For in the wide wombe of the world there lyes,
    In hatefull darkenesse and in deepe horrore,
    An huge eternall Chaos, which supplyes
The substances of natures fruitfull progenyes.

37

325   All things from thence doe their first being fetch,
    And borrow matter, whereof they are made,
    Which when as forme and feature it does ketch,[4]
    Becomes a bodie, and doth then invade°   *enter*
    The state of life, out of the griesly shade.
330   That substance is eterne, and bideth so,
    Ne when the life decayes, and forme does fade,
    Doth it consume, and into nothing go,
But chaungéd is, and often altred to and fro.

---

4. I.e., when it takes shape and outline.

38

The substance is not chaungéd, nor alteréd,
335   But th' only forme and outward fashion;°   *appearance*
    For every substance is conditionéd
    To change her hew, and sundry formes to don,
    Meet for her temper and complexion:
    For formes are variable and decay,
340   By course of kind,° and by occasion;   *nature*
    And that faire flowre of beautie fades away,
As doth the lilly fresh before the sunny ray.[5]

39

Great enimy to it, and to all the rest,
    That in the Gardin of Adonis springs,
345   Is wicked Time, who with his scyth addrest,°   *armed*
    Does mow the flowring herbes and goodly things,
    And all their glory to the ground downe flings,
    Where they doe wither, and are fowly mard:
    He flyes about, and with his flaggy° wings   *drooping*
350   Beates downe both leaves and buds without regard,
Ne ever pittie may relent his malice hard.

40

Yet pittie often did the gods relent,
    To see so faire things mard, and spoyléd quight:
    And their great mother Venus did lament
355   The losse of her deare brood, her deare delight:
    Her hart was pierst with pittie at the sight,
    When walking through the Gardin, them she spyde,
    Yet no'te[6] she find redresse for such despight.
    For all that lives, is subject to that law:
360 All things decay in time, and to their end do draw.

41

But were it not, that Time their troubler is,
    All that in this delightfull Gardin growes,
    Should happie be, and have immortall blis,
    For here all plentie, and all pleasure flowes,
365   For sweet love gentle fits° emongst them throwes,   *impulses*
    Without fell rancor, or fond gealosie;
    Franckly each paramour° his leman° knowes,   *lover / sweetheart*
    Each bird his mate, ne any does envie
Their goodly meriment, and gay felicite.

42

370 There is continuall spring, and harvest there
    Continuall, both meeting at one time:[7]
    For both the boughes doe laughing blossomes beare,
    And with fresh colours decke the wanton Prime,°   *Spring*
    And eke attonce the heavy trees they clime,
375   Which seeme to labour under their fruits lode:

5. While stanzas 30–35 emphasized the cyclical process of all life, stanzas 36–38 describe the indestructible substance that persists through the cycles.
6. Did not know how to.
7. The sexuality of the Garden is life-giving—unlike the sexuality of the Bower of Bliss, which was life-destroying. The Garden is untroubled by seasonal change, like other perfect gardens in Renaissance and medieval literature, which are types of an ideal world.

The whiles the joyous birdes make their pastime
Emongst the shadie leaves, their sweet abode,
And their true loves without suspition tell abrode.

43

Right in the middest of that Paradise,
380   There stood a stately Mount, on whose round top
A gloomy grove of mirtle trees did rise,
Whose shadie boughes sharpe steele did never lop,
Nor wicked beasts their tender buds did crop,
But like a girlond compasséd the hight,
385   And from their fruitfull sides sweet gum did drop,
That all the ground with precious deaw bedight,
Threw forth most dainty odours, and most sweet delight.

44

And in the thickest covert of that shade,
There was a pleasant arbour, not by art,
390   But of the trees owne inclination made,[8]
Which knitting their rancke° braunches part to part,   *dense*
With wanton yvie twyne entrayld athwart,
And Eglantine, and Caprifole[9] emong,
Fashiond above within their inmost part,
395   That nether Phœbus beams could through them throng,
Nor Aeolus sharp blast could worke them any wrong.

45

And all about grew every sort of flowre,
To which sad lovers were transformed of yore;
Fresh Hyacinthus, Phoebus paramoure,
400   And dearest love,
Foolish Narcisse, that likes the watry shore,
Sad Amaranthus, made a flowre but late,
Sad Amaranthus, in whose purple gore
Me seemes I see Amintas wretched fate,
405   To whom sweet Poets verse hath given endlesse date.[1]

46

There wont faire Venus often to enjoy
Her deare Adonis joyous company,
And reape sweet pleasure of the wanton boy;
There yet, some say, in secret he does ly,
410   Lappéd in flowres and pretious spycery,
By her hid from the world, and from the skill°   *knowledge*
Of Stygian Gods, which doe her love envy;

8. Unlike the Bower of Bliss, where art rivaled or supplanted nature, Venus's bower is entirely natural.
9. Honeysuckle or woodbine.
1. Hyacinthus was a youth loved by Apollo and Zephyrus; returning the love of the former, he was killed out of jealousy by the latter, and the flower known by his name sprang from his blood. Narcissus, enamored of his own reflection in a pool, died and was also transformed into a flower. "Amintas" is Spenser's name for Sir Philip Sidney, on whose death Spenser, like all the other poets of his day, produced a poem. All these young men, turned into flowers after being cut off in the flower of their lives, suggest the quality of Adonis's Garden; it is the place where unfulfilled potentialities are renewed, and spiritual vitality is restored to wounded ideals. "Amaranthus" completes this idea, for its name means, in Greek, the "undying, unfading flower"; it symbolizes spiritual immortality for Adonis and his group of handsome, unfulfilled young men.

But she her selfe, when ever that she will,
Possesseth him, and of his sweetnesse takes her fill.

47

415 And sooth it seemes they say: for he may not
For ever die, and ever buried bee
In balefull night, where all things are forgot;
All° be he subject to mortalitie,   *although*
Yet is eterne in mutabilitie,
420 And by succession made perpetuall,
Transforméd oft, and chaungéd diverslie:
For him the Father of all formes they call;
Therefore needs mote he live, that living gives to all.[2]

48

There now he liveth in eternall blis,
425 Joying his goddesse, and of her enjoyd:
Ne feareth he hence forth that foe of his,
Which with his cruell tuske him deadly cloyd:°   *pierced*
For that wilde Bore, the which him once annoyd,°   *injured*
She firmely hath emprisonéd for ay,
430 That her sweet love his malice mote avoyd,
In a strong rocky Cave; which is they say,
Hewen underneath that Mount, that none him losen may.[3]

49

There now he lives in everlasting joy,
With many of the Gods in company,
435 Which thither haunt, and with the wingéd boy[4]
Sporting himselfe in safe felicity:
Who when he hath with spoiles and cruelty
Ransackt the world, and in the wofull harts
Of many wretches set his triumphes hye,
440 Thither resorts, and laying his sad darts
Aside, with faire Adonis playes his wanton parts.

50

And his true love faire Psyche with him playes,
Faire Psyche to him lately reconcyld,
After long troubles and unmeet upbrayes,°   *reproaches*
445 With which his mother Venus her revyld,°   *scolded*
And eke himselfe her cruelly exyld:[5]
But now in stedfast love and happy state
She with him lives, and hath him borne a chyld,
Pleasure, that doth both gods and men aggrate,°   *gratify*
450 Pleasure, the daughter of Cupid and Psyche late.

2. Adonis might be taken to symbolize the changing forms of matter, which cannot be destroyed but remain "eterne in mutabilitie," line 419.
3. "Losen": set free. This stanza retells the myth of Venus and Adonis. The boar may stand for animal passion, violence, and disorder.
4. I.e., Cupid—who, it should be noted, never appeared in the Bower of Bliss.
5. Psyche, a beautiful princess, was visited by her lover Cupid only at night. Curious to see him, she lighted a lamp while he was asleep accidentally dropped some hot oil on him, and awakened him. He was angry at her lack of trust and left her; she wandered in search of him and endured many hardships imposed by Venus, who was jealous of her beauty. She was finally reunited with Cupid and made immortal. Her story has been taken to represent the arduous purification, by trial and misfortune, of the human soul.

From Book VII, Mutabilitie[1]

The VIII Canto, Unperfite

When I bethinke me on that speech whyleare,
  Of Mutability,[2] and well it way:
  Me seemes, that though she all unworthy were
  Of the Heav'ns Rule; yet very sooth to say,
5   In all things else she beares the greatest sway.
  Which makes me loath this state of life so tickle,°   *precarious*
  And love of things so vaine to cast away;
  Whose flowring pride, so fading and so fickle,
Short Time shall soone cut down with his consuming sickle.

2

10 Then gin I thinke on that which Nature sayd,
  Of that same time when no more Change shall be,
  But stedfast rest of all things firmely stayd
  Upon the pillours of Eternity,
  That is contrayr to Mutabilitie:
15 For, all that moveth, doth in Change delight:
  But thence-forth all shall rest eternally
  With Him that is the God of Sabbaoth hight:
O that great Sabbaoth God, graunt me that Sabaoths sight.[3]

                            1590, 1596, 1609

From Amoretti[4]

Sonnet 1

Happy ye leaves when as those lilly hands,
  Which hold my life in their dead doing[5] might,
  Shall handle you and hold in loves soft bands,
  Lyke captives trembling at the victors sight.
5 And happy lines, on which with starry light,
  Those lamping eyes will deigne sometimes to look
  And reade the sorrowes of my dying spright,°   *spirit*
  Written with teares in harts close° bleeding book.   *secret*
  And happy rymes bathed in the sacred brooke,

1. Cantos VI and VII and two stanzas of Canto VIII, called the "Mutability Cantos," were first published in 1609, ten years after Spenser's death. According to the title page, they "appear to be parcel of some following Book of *The Faerie Queene*, under the legend of Constancie." These cantos give Spenser's reflections, influenced perhaps by Lucretius, on change and permanence in the world—a subject enthralling to the Elizabethan imagination.
2. Before an assembly of the gods the Titaness Mutability had pleaded that since all things are subject to change, she should be goddess over all.
3. A play on *sabaoth* (Hebrew: "hosts," "armies") and "Sabbath," day of rest.

4. I.e., "little loves" or "little love poems." They are sonnets to a woman named Elizabeth—probably Elizabeth Boyle, who became Spenser's second wife. The sequence, or cycle, tells of a courtship (*Epithalamion*, with which they were published, is a song for a wedding). The *Amoretti* draws, like other sonnet cycles, upon characteristic and conventional themes and conceits; what is characteristically Spenserian about them is his understanding, and yoking, of the spirit and the flesh; see, for example, lines 9–12 of Sonnet 1. The rhyme scheme is *abab bcbc cdcd ee*, a difficult pattern requiring four words for two of the rhymes.
5. I.e., killing.

10   Of Helicon[6] whence she derivéd is,
     When ye behold that Angels blessed looke,
     My soules long lackéd foode, my heavens blis.
     Leaves, lines, and rymes, seeke her to please alone,
     Whom if ye please, I care for other none.

Sonnet 34

     Lyke as a ship that through the ocean wyde,
     By conduct of some star doth make her way,
     Whenas a storme hath dimd her trusty guyde,
     Out of her course doth wander far astray.
5   So I whose star, that wont with her bright ray,
     Me to direct, with cloudes is overcast,
     Doe wander now in darknesse and dismay,
     Through hidden perils round about me plast.°   placed
     Yet hope I well, that when this storme is past
10   My Helice[7] the lodestar of my lyfe
     Will shine again, and looke on me at last,
     With lovely light to cleare my cloudy grief.
     Till then I wander carefull° comfortlesse,   full of cares
     In secret sorow and sad pensivenesse.

Sonnet 35

     My hungry eyes through greedy covetize,
     Still to behold the object of their paine,
     With no contentment can themselves suffize:
     But having pine° and having not complaine.   starve
5   For lacking it they cannot lyfe sustayne,
     And having it they gaze on it the more:
     In their amazement lyke Narcissus[8] vaine
     Whose eyes him starved: so plenty makes me poore.
     Yet are mine eyes so filled with the store°   abundance
10   Of that faire sight, that nothing else they brooke,
     But lothe the things which they did like before,
     And can no more endure on them to looke.
     All this worlds glory seemeth vayne to me,
     And all their showes but shadowes, saving she.

Sonnet 37

     What guyle is this, that those her golden tresses,
     She doth attyre under a net of gold:
     And with sly° skill so cunningly them dresses,   clever
     That which is gold or heare, may scarse be told?
5   Is it that mens frayle eyes, which gaze too bold,
     She may entangle in that golden snare:
     And being caught may craftily enfold,
     Theyr weaker harts, which are not wel aware?
     Take heed therefore, myne eyes, how ye doe stare
10   Henceforth too rashly on that guilefull net,

6. The "sacred brooke" is the Hippocrene, which flows from Mount Helicon, the mountain sacred to the Muses. It not only inspires the poet but here represents heaven, where his beloved originated.
7. The Big Dipper or North Star.
8. The beautiful youth in mythology who fell in love with his own reflection.

In which if ever ye entrappéd are,
Out of her bands ye by no means shall get.
Fondnesse° it were for any being free,   *foolishness*
To covet fetters, though they golden bee.

Sonnet 54

Of this worlds theatre in which we stay,
My love like the spectator ydly sits
Beholding me that all the pageants play,
Disguysing diversly my troubled wits.
5 Sometimes I joy when glad occasion fits,
And mask in myrth lyke to a comedy:
Soone after when my joy to sorrow flits,
I waile and make my woes a tragedy.
Yet she, beholding me with constant eye,
10 Delights not in my merth nor rues my smart:
But when I laugh she mocks, and when I cry
She laughs and hardens evermore her heart.
What then can move her? if nor merth nor mone,°   *moan*
She is no woman, but a sencelesse stone.

Sonnet 59

Thrise happie she, that is so well assured
Unto her selfe and setled so in hart:
That nether will for better be allured,
Ne feard with worse to any chaunce to start:
5 But like a steddy ship doth strongly part
The raging waves and keepes her course aright:
Ne ought ° for tempest doth from it depart,   *at all*
Ne ought for fayrer weathers false delight.
Such selfe assurance need not feare the spight
10 Of grudging foes, ne favour seek of friends:
But in the stay of her owne stedfast might,
Nether to one her self nor other bends.
Most happy she that most assured doth rest,
But he most happy who such one loves best.

Sonnet 68

Most glorious Lord of lyfe, that on this day,[9]
Didst make thy triumph over death and sin:
And having harrowed hell,[1] didst bring away
Captivity thence captive us to win:
5 This joyous day, deare Lord, with joy begin,
And grant that we for whom thou diddest dye
Being with thy deare blood clene washt from sin,
May live for ever in felicity.
And that thy love we weighing worthily,
10 May likewise love thee for the same againe:

9. Easter Day.
1. In the apocryphal gospels, Christ descended into hell and led out those who had lived before his time that de- served to be saved. "Captivity thence captive" is a Biblical phrase, as in Judges v.12 and Ephesians iv.8.

And for thy sake that all lyke deare didst buy,
With love may one another entertayne.
So let us love, deare love, lyke as we ought,
Love is the lesson which the Lord us taught.[2]

Sonnet 70

Fresh spring the herald of loves mighty king,
In whose cote armour[3] richly are displayd
All sorts of flowers the which on earth do spring
In goodly colours gloriously arrayd.
5 Goe to my love, where she is carelesse layd,
Yet in her winters bowre not well awake:
Tell her the joyous time wil not be staid
Unlesse she doe him by the forelock take.
Bid her therefore her selfe soone ready make,
10 To wayt on love amongst his lovely crew:
Where every one that misseth then her make,°   *mate, lover*
Shall be by him amearest with penance dew.[4]
Make hast therefore sweet love, whilest it is prime,°*early morning*
For none can call againe the passéd time.

Sonnet 75[5]

One day I wrote her name upon the strand,
But came the waves and washéd it away:
Agayne I wrote it with a second hand,
But came the tyde, and made my paynes his pray.
5 "Vayne man," sayd she, "that doest in vaine assay,
A mortall thing so to immortalize,
For I my selve shall lyke to this decay,
And eek my name bee wypéd out lykewize."
"Not so," quod° I, "let baser things devize   *quoth*
10 To dy in dust, but you shall live by fame:
My verse your vertues rare shall eternize,
And in the heavens wryte your glorious name.
Where whenas death shall all the world subdew,
Our love shall live, and later life renew."

Sonnet 79

Men call you fayre, and you doe credit° it,   *believe*
For that your selfe ye dayly such doe see:
But the trew fayre, that is the gentle wit,
And vertuous mind, is much more praysd of me.
5 For all the rest, how ever fayre it be,
Shall turne to nought and loose that glorious hew:
But onely that is permanent and free
From frayle corruption, that doth flesh ensew.°   *outlast*
That is true beautie: that doth argue you

2. Cf. John xv.12: "This is my commandment, That ye love one another, as I have loved you."
3. Coat of arms.
4. I.e., have suitable penance imposed upon him.
5. The theme here expressed is an ancient and traditional one. Cf. Shakespeare's Sonnet 55, "Not marble, nor the gilded monuments."

10 To be divine and borne of heavenly seed:
   Derived from that fayre Spirit, from whom al true
   And perfect beauty did at first proceed.
   He onely fayre, and what he fayre hath made:
   All other fayre, lyke flowres, untymely fade.

1595

Epithalamion[1]

Ye learned sisters which have oftentimes
Beene to me ayding, others to adorne:[2]
Whom ye thought worthy of your gracefull rymes,
That even the greatest did not greatly scorne
5 To heare theyr names sung in your simple layes,
But joyéd in theyr prayse.
And when ye list your owne mishaps to mourne,
Which death, or love, or fortunes wreck did rayse,
Your string could soone to sadder tenor° turne,   mood
10 And teach the woods and waters to lament
   Your dolefull dreriment.°   sorrow
Now lay those sorrowfull complaints aside,
And having all your heads with girland crownd,
Helpe me mine owne loves prayses to resound,
15 Ne let the same of° any be envide: by
So Orpheus did for his owne bride,[3]
So I unto my selfe alone will sing,
The woods shall to me answer and my Eccho ring.

Early before the worlds light giving lampe,
20 His golden beame upon the hils doth spred,

1. An epithalamion is a wedding song or poem; its Greek name conveys that it was sung on the threshold of the bridal chamber. The genre was widely practiced by the Latin poets, particularly Catullus. Catullus wrote two kinds of epithalamion: one in an elevated ceremonial style, the other in a more private, lyric style; it is the latter style that Spenser follows. Common elements are the invocation to the Muses, the bringing home of the bride, the singing and dancing at the wedding party, and the preparations for the wedding night. The reader should be aware that the poem's merit is not in its "originality" but in its evocative, many-layered commingling of the conventions. Spenser blends with these conventional elements his own Irish setting and native folklore.
   In addition, the *Epithalamion* is highly structured. First there is an introductory stanza, then two 10-stanza sections on each side of the two central stanzas about the church ceremony itself. Each of the 10-stanza sections is divided into units of 3-4-3. As A. Kent Hieatt has pointed out in his book, *Short Time's Endless Monument* (1960), the poem also has a surprising and complex numerical structure that reinforces the motif of the passage of time. For example, the poem has exactly 365 long lines (composed of five or more metrical feet) matching the number of days in the year. There are 24 stanzas, counting the envoy, matching the hours of one day and night. Of these stanzas, the first 16 describe the course of the day, in which the woods echo the various sounds; the last 8 describe the night, a time of silence in which the woods no longer echo. At the summer solstice (cf. line 266 and note) in the latitude of Ireland, night in fact falls after 16 hours of daylight.
   To point to these elements of high artistry is not, of course, to explain why the *Epithalamion* is one of the great poems of the language. The subtle time structure serves to reinforce the idea implicit throughout the poem that this marriage has reference to all marriages; it emphasizes the endless cycle of time, measured by the passing of the hours and the years—as against which marriage, as a Christian sacrament, stands firm, "eterne in mutabilitie."
2. I.e., to write poems in praise of others (e.g., Queen Elizabeth in *The Faerie Queene*). The "learned sisters" are the Muses.
3. Orpheus, the most famous musician of classical antiquity, was equally famous for his love for his wife Eurydice.

Having disperst the nights unchearefull dampe,
Doe ye awake, and with fresh lustyhed°   *vigor*
Go to the bowre° of my belovéd love,   *bedchamber*
My truest turtle dove,
25   Bid her awake; for Hymen[4] is awake,
And long since ready forth his maske to move,
With his bright Tead[5] that flames with many a flake,°   *spark*
And many a bachelor to waite on him,
In theyr fresh garments trim.
30   Bid her awake therefore and soone her dight,°   *dress*
For lo the wishéd day is come at last,
That shall for al the paynes and sorrowes past,
Pay to her usury of long delight:
And whylest she doth her dight,
35   Doe ye to her of joy and solace sing,
That all the woods may answer and your eccho ring.

Bring with you all the Nymphes that you can heare[6]
Both of the rivers and the forrests greene:
And of the sea that neighbours to her neare,
40   Al with gay girlands goodly wel beseene.[7]
And let them also with them bring in hand,
Another gay girland
For my fayre love of lillyes and of roses,
Bound truelove wize[8] with a blew silke riband.
45   And let them make great store of bridale poses,°   *posies*
And let them eeke bring store of other flowers
To deck the bridale bowers.
And let the ground whereas her foot shall tread,
For feare the stones her tender foot should wrong
50   Be strewed with fragrant flowers all along,
And diapred lyke the discolored mead. [9]
Which done, doe at her chamber dore awayt,
For she will waken strayt, °   *straightway*
The whiles doe ye this song unto her sing,
55   The woods shall to you answer and your Eccho ring.

Ye Nymphes of Mulla[1] which with careful heed,
The silver scaly trouts doe tend full well,
And greedy pikes which use therein to feed,
(Those trouts and pikes all others doo excell)
60   And ye likewise, which keepe the rushy lake,
Where none doo fishes take,
Bynd up the locks the which hang scatterd light,
And in his waters which your mirror make,
Behold your faces as the christall bright,
65   That when you come whereas my love doth lie,
No blemish she may spie.

4. The god of marriage, who leads a "maske" or procession at weddings.
5. A ceremonial torch, associated with marriages since classical times.
6. I.e., that can hear you.
7. I.e., beautified.
8. I.e., in a love knot.
9. I.e., ornamented like the many-colored meadow.
1. The vale of Mulla, near Spenser's home in Ireland.

And eke ye lightfoot mayds which keepe the deere.[2]
That on the hoary mountayne use to towre,
And the wylde wolves which seeke them to devoure,
70   With your steele darts doo chace from comming neer
Be also present heere,
To helpe to decke her and to help to sing,
That all the woods may answer and your eccho ring.

Wake, now my love, awake; for it is time,
75   The Rosy Morne long since left Tithones bed,
All ready to her silver coche to clyme,
And Phoebus gins to shew his glorious hed.
Hark how the cheerefull birds do chaunt theyr laies
And carroll of loves praise.
80   The merry Larke hir mattins° sing aloft,   *morning prayers*
The thrust replyes, the Mavis descant[3] playes,
The Ouzell shrills, the Ruddock warbles soft,
So goodly all agree with sweet consent,
To this dayes merriment.
85   Ah my deere love why doe ye sleepe thus long,
When meeter were that ye should now awake,
T' awayt the comming of your joyous make,°   *mate*
And hearken to the birds lovelearnéd song,
The deawy leaves among.
90   For they of joy and pleasance to you sing,
That all the woods them answer and theyr eccho ring.

My love is now awake out of her dreame,
And her fayre eyes like stars that dimméd were
With darksome cloud, now shew theyr goodly beams
95   More bright then Hesperus° his head doth rere.   *evening star*
Come now ye damzels, daughters of delight,
Helpe quickly her to dight,
But first come ye fayre houres which were begot
In Joves sweet paradice, of Day and Night,
100 Which doe the seasons of the yeare allot,
And al that ever in this world is fayre
Doe make and still repayre.[4]
And ye three handmayds of the Cyprian Queene,[5]
The which doe still adorne her beauties pride,
105 Helpe to addorne my beautifullest bride:
And as ye her array, still throw betweene°   *now and then*
Some graces to be seene,
And as ye use to Venus, to her sing,
The whiles the woods shal answer and your eccho ring.

110 Now is my love all ready forth to come,
Let all the virgins therefore well awayt,

2. I.e., all wild animals, kept by the forest nymphs. To "towre" (a falconry term) is to occupy heights.
3. A melody or counterpoint written above a musical theme—a soprano obbligato. The "Mavis" is the thrush. The "Ouzell" is the blackbird (which sings in England); the "Ruddock," the European robin. The birds' concert is a convention of medieval love poetry.
4. In the passage of the hours, all things on earth change. "Still": continuously.
5. The Graces attending on Venus ("Cyprian Queene"), representing brightness, joy, and bloom.

And ye fresh boyes that tend upon her groome
Prepare your selves; for he is comming strayt.
Set all your things in seemely good aray°   order
115 Fit for so joyfull day,
The joyfulst day that ever sunne did see.
Faire Sun, shew forth thy favourable ray,
And let thy lifull° heat not fervent be   lifegiving
For feare of burning her sunshyny face,
120 Her beauty to disgrace.
O fayrest Phoebus, father of the Muse,
If ever I did honour thee aright,
Or sing the thing, that mote° they mind delight,   might
Doe not thy servants simple boone refuse,
125 But let this day let this one day be myne,
Let all the rest be thine.
Then I thy soverayne prayses loud wil sing,
That all the woods shal answer and theyr eccho ring.

Harke how the Minstrels gin to shrill aloud
130 Their merry Musick that resounds from far,
The pipe, the tabor, and the trembling Croud,[6]
That well agree withouten breach or jar.°   discord
But most of all the Damzels doe delite,
When they their tymbrels° smyte,   tambourines
135 And thereunto doe daunce and carrol sweet,
That all the sences they doe ravish quite,
The whyles the boyes run up and downe the street,
Crying aloud with strong confuséd noyce,
As if it were one voyce.
140 *Hymen iô Hymen, Hymen*[7] they do shout,
That even to the heavens theyr shouting shrill
Doth reach, and all the firmament doth fill,
To which the people standing all about,
As in approvance doe thereto applaud
145 And loud advaunce her laud,°   praise
And evermore they *Hymen Hymen* sing,
That al the woods them answer and theyr eccho ring.

Loe where she comes along with portly° pace   stately
Lyke Phoebe from her chamber of the East,
150 Arysing forth to run her mighty race,[8]
Clad all in white, that seemes° a virgin best.   suits
So well it her beseems that ye would weene
Some angell she had beene.
Her long loose yellow locks lyke golden wyre,
155 Sprinckled with perle, and perling° flowres a tweene,   winding
Doe lyke a golden mantle her attyre,

---

6. Primitive fiddle; the "tabor" is a small drum. Spenser here designates Irish, not classical, instruments and music for the classical masque or ballet.
7. The name of the god of marriage, used as a conventional exclamation at weddings.
8. Phoebe is the moon, a virgin like the bride; the reference to her antici-pates the night.

And being crownéd with girland greene,
Seeme lyke some mayden Queene.
Her modest eyes abashéd to behold
160 So many gazers, as on her do stare,
Upon the lowly ground affixéd are.
Ne dare lift up her countenance too bold,
But blush to heare her prayses sung so loud,
So farre from being proud.
165 Nathlesse doe ye still loud her prayses sing.
That all the woods may answer and your eccho ring.

Tell me ye merchants daughters did ye see
So fayre a creature in your towne before,
So sweet, so lovely, and so mild as she,
170 Adornd with beautyes grace and vertues store,
Her goodly eyes lyke Saphyres shining bright,
Her forehead yvory white,
Her cheekes lyke apples which the sun hath rudded,°   *made red*
Her lips lyke cherryes charming men to byte,
175 Her brest like to a bowle of creame uncrudded,°   *uncurdled*
Her paps lyke lyllies budded,
Her snowie necke lyke to a marble towre,
And all her body like a pallace fayre,
Ascending uppe with many a stately stayre,
180 To honors seat and chastities sweet bowre.[9]
Why stand ye still ye virgins in amaze,
Upon her so to gaze,
Whiles ye forget your former lay to sing,
To which the woods did answer and your eccho ring.

185 But if ye saw that which no eyes can see,
The inward beauty of her lively spright,°   *soul*
Garnisht with heavenly guifts of high degree,
Much more then would ye wonder at that sight,
And stand astonisht lyke to those which red°   *discern*
190 Medusaes mazeful hed.[1]
There dwels sweet love and constant chastity,
Unspotted fayth and comely womanhood,
Regard of honour and mild modesty,
There vertue raynes as Queene in royal throne,
195 And giveth lawes alone.
The which the base° affections doe obay,   *lower*
And yeeld theyr services unto her will,
Ne thought of thing uncomely ever may
Thereto approch to tempt her mind to ill.
200 Had ye once seene these her celestiall threasures,
And unrevealéd pleasures,
Then would ye wonder and her prayses sing,
That al the woods should answer and your echo ring.

9. The head, where the higher faculties are. The catalogue of qualities is a convention in love poetry. Cf. also The Song of Solomon iv–viii.

1. Medusa, one of the Gorgons, had serpents instead of hair (hence a "mazeful hed"): the effect on a beholder was to turn him to stone.

Open the temple gates unto my love,
205 Open them wide that she may enter in,
And all the postes adorne as doth behove,[2]
And all the pillours deck with girlands trim,
For to recyve this Saynt with honour dew,
That commeth in to you.
210 With trembling steps and humble reverence,
She commeth in, before th' almighties vew,
Of her ye virgins learne obedience,
When so ye come into those holy places,
To humble your proud faces:
215 Bring her up to th' high altar, that she may
The sacred ceremonies there partake,
The which do endless matrimony make,
And let the roring Organs loudly play
The praises of the Lord in lively notes,
220 The whiles with hollow throates
The Choristers the joyous Antheme sing,
That al the woods may answere and their eccho ring.

Behold whiles she before the altar stands
Hearing the holy priest that to her speakes
225 And blesseth her with his two happy hands,
How the red roses flush up in her cheekes,
And the pure snow with goodly vermill stayne,
Like crimsin dyde in grayne,°   *fast color*
That even th' Angels which continually,
230 About the sacred Altare doe remaine,
Forget their service and about her fly,
Ofte peeping in her face that seemes more fayre,
The more they on it stare.
But her sad° eyes still fastened on the ground,   *modest*
235 Are governéd with goodly modesty,
That suffers not one looke to glaunce awry,
Which may let in a little thought unsownd.
Why blush ye love to give to me your hand,
The pledge of all our band?°   *bond, tie*
240 Sing ye sweet Angels, Alleluya sing,
That all the woods may answere and your eccho ring.

Now al is done; bring home the bride againe,
Bring home the triumph of our victory,
Bring home with you the glory of her gaine,[3]
245 With joyance bring her and with jollity.
Never had man more joyfull day then this,
Whom heaven would heape with blis.
Make feast therefore now all this live long day,
This day for ever to me holy is,
250 Poure out the wine without restraint or stay,
Poure not by cups, but by the belly full,

2. As is proper. The doorposts were trimmed for weddings in classical times, and the custom was often referred to in classical and medieval love poetry.
3. I.e., the glory of gaining her.

Poure out to all that wull,°   *want it*
And sprinkle all the postes and wals with wine,
That they may sweat, and drunken be withall.
255 Crowne ye God Bacchus with a coronall,°   *flower garland*
And Hymen also crowne with wreathes of vine,
And let the Graces daunce unto the rest;
For they can doo it best:
The whiles the maydens doe theyr carroll sing,
260 To which the woods shal answer and theyr eccho ring.

Ring ye the bels, ye young men of the towne,
And leave your wonted labors for this day:
This day is holy; doe ye write it downe,
That ye for ever it remember may.
265 This day the sunne is in his chiefest hight,
With Barnaby the bright,[4]
From whence declining daily by degrees,
He somewhat loseth of his heat and light,
When once the Crab[5] behind his back he sees.
270 But for this time it ill ordainéd was,
To chose the longest day in all the yeare,
And shortest night, when longest fitter weare:
Yet never day so long, but late° would passe.   *at last*
Ring ye the bels, to make it weare away,
275 And bonefiers make all day,
And daunce about them, and about them sing:
That all the woods may answer, and your eccho ring.

Ah when will this long weary day have end,
And lende me leave to come unto my love?
280 How slowly do the houres theyr numbers spend?
How slowly does sad Time his feathers move?
Hast thee O fayrest Planet to thy home
Within the Westerne fome:
Thy tyred steedes long since have need of rest.
285 Long though it be, at last I see it gloome,
And the bright evening star with golden creast
Appeare out of the East.
Fayre childe of beauty, glorious lampe of love
That all the host of heaven in rankes doost lead,
290 And guydest lovers through the nightés dread,
How chearefully thou lookest from above,
And seemst to laugh atweene thy twinkling light
As joying in the sight
Of these glad many which for joy doe sing,
295 That all the woods them answer and their echo ring.

Now ceasse ye damsels your delights forepast;
Enough is it, that all the day was youres:
Now day is doen, and night is nighing fast:
Now bring the Bryde into the brydall boures.

4. St. Barnabas' Day, at the time of the summer solstice.
5. The constellation Cancer between Gemini and Leo. The sun, passing through the zodiac, leaves the Crab behind toward the end of July.

300 Now night is come, now soone her disaray,
And in her bed her lay;
Lay her in lillies and in violets,
And silken courteins over her display,°   *spread*
And odourd sheetes, and Arras° coverlets.   *tapestry*
305 Behold how goodly my faire love does ly
In proud humility;
Like unto Maia,[6] when as Jove her tooke,
In Tempe, lying on the flowry gras,
Twixt sleepe and wake, after she weary was,
310 With bathing in the Acidalian brooke.
Now it is night, ye damsels may be gon,
And leave my love alone,
And leave likewise your former lay to sing:
The woods no more shal answere, nor your echo ring.

315 Now welcome night, thou night so long expected,
That long daies labour doest at last defray,°   *pay*
And all my cares, which cruell love collected,
Hast sumd in one, and cancelléd for aye:
Spread thy broad wing over my love and me,
320 That no man may us see,
And in thy sable mantle us enwrap,
From feare of perrill and foule horror free.
Let no false treason seeke us to entrap,
Nor any dread disquiet once annoy
325 The safety of our joy:
But let the night be calme and quietsome,
Without tempestuous storms or sad afray:
Lyke as when Jove with fayre Alcmena[7] lay,
When he begot the great Tirynthian groome:
330 Or lyke as when he with thy selfe[8] did lie,
And begot Majesty.
And let the mayds and yongmen cease to sing:
Ne let the woods them answer, nor theyr eccho ring.

Let no lamenting cryes, nor dolefull teares,
335 Be heard all night within nor yet without.
Ne let false whispers, breeding hidden feares,
Breake gentle sleepe with misconceivéd dout.
Let no deluding dreames, nor dreadful sights
Make sudden sad affrights;
340 Ne let housefyres, nor lightnings helpelesse harmes,
Ne let the Pouke,[9] nor other evill sprights,
Ne let mischivous witches with theyr charmes,
Ne let hob Goblins, names whose sence we see not,
Fray us with things that be not.
345 Let not the shriech Oule, nor the Storke be heard:

6. The eldest and most beautiful of the Pleiades.
7. The mother of Hercules ("the great Tirynthian groome").
8. I.e., night.
9. Puck, Robin Goodfellow—here more powerful and evil than Shakespeare made him.

Nor the night Raven that still deadly yels,[1]
Nor damnéd ghosts cald up with mighty spels,
Nor griesly vultures make us once affeard:
Ne let th'unpleasant Quyre of Frogs still croking
350 Make us to wish theyr choking.
   Let none of these theyr drery accents sing;
   Ne let the woods them answer, nor theyr eccho ring.

   But let stil Silence trew night watches keepe,
   That sacred peace may in assurance rayne,
355 And tymely sleep, when it is tyme to sleepe,
   May poure his limbs forth on your[2] pleasant playne,
   The whiles an hundred little wingéd loves,[3]
   Like divers fethered doves,
   Shall fly and flutter round about your bed,
360 And in the secret darke, that none reproves,
   Their prety stealthes shal worke, and snares shal spread
   To filch away sweet snatches of delight,
   Conceald through covert night.
   Ye sonnes of Venus, play your sports at will,
365 For greedy pleasure, carelesse of your toyes,°   *frivolities*
   Thinks more upon her paradise of joyes,
   Then what ye do, albe it good or ill.
   All night therefore attend your merry play,
   For it will soone be day:
370 Now none doth hinder you, that say or sing,
   Ne will the woods now answer, nor your Eccho ring.

   Who is the same, which at my window peepes?
   Or whose is that faire face, that shines so bright,
   Is it not Cinthia,[4] she that never sleepes,
375 But walkes about high heaven al the night?
   O fayrest goddesse, do thou not envy
   My love with me to spy:
   For thou likewise didst love, though now unthought,° *unsuspected*
   And for a fleece of woll,° which privily,   *wool*
380 The Latmian shephard[5] once unto thee brought,
   His pleasures with thee wrought,
   Therefore to us be favorable now;
   And sith of wemens labours thou hast charge,[6]
   And generation goodly dost enlarge,
385 Encline thy will t' effect our wishfull vow,
   And the chast wombe informe with timely seed,
   That may our comfort breed:
   Till which we cease our hopefull hap to sing,
   Ne let the woods us answere, nor our Eccho ring.

1. The owl and the night raven were
birds of ill omen; the stork, in Chaucer's
Parliament of Fowls, is called an avenger
of adultery. "Still": always.
2. I.e., Night's.
3. Cupids (or amoretti).
4. I.e., the moon.
5. Endymion, beloved by the moon.

The "fleece of woll," however, comes
from another story—that of Pan's en-
ticement of the moon.
6. Diana (the moon, "Cinthia") is,
as Lucina, patroness of births; the "labours" are, of course, those of childbirth.

₃₉₀ And thou great Juno, which with awful might
The lawes of wedlock still dost patronize,
And the religion of the faith first plight
With sacred rites hast taught to solemnize:
And eeke for comfort often callèd art
₃₉₅ Of women in their smart,°   *labor*
Eternally bind thou this lovely band,
And all thy blessings unto us impart.
And thou glad Genius,[7] in whose gentle hand,
The bridale bowre and geniall bed remaine,
₄₀₀ Without blemish or staine,
And the sweet pleasures of theyr loves delight
With secret ayde doest succour and supply,
Till they bring forth the fruitfull progeny,
Send us the timely fruit of this same night.
₄₀₅ And thou fayre Hebe,[8] and thou Hymen free,
Grant that it may be so.
Til which we cease your further prayse to sing,
Ne any woods shal answer, nor your Eccho ring.

And ye high heavens, the temple of the gods,
₄₁₀ In which a thousand torches flaming bright
Doe burne, that to us wretched earthly clods,
In dreadful darknesse lend desired light;
And all ye powers which in the same remayne,
More than we men can fayne,
₄₁₅ Poure out your blessing on us plentiously,
And happy influence upon us raine,
That we may raise a large posterity,
Which from the earth, which they may long possesse,
With lasting happinesse,
₄₂₀ Up to your haughty pallaces may mount,
And for the guerdon of theyr glorious merit
May heavenly tabernacles there inherit,
Of blessed Saints for to increase the count.
So let us rest, sweet love, in hope of this,
₄₂₅ And cease till then our tymely joyes to sing,
The woods no more us answer, nor our eccho ring.

Song made in lieu of many ornaments,
With which my love should duly have bene dect,
Which cutting off through hasty accidents,
₄₃₀ Ye would not stay your dew time to expect,
But promist both to recompens,
Be unto her a goodly ornament,
And for short time an endlesse moniment.[9]

₁₅₉₅

7. Patron of sex, pregnancy, reproduction. Cf. Genius in the Garden of Adonis (*The Faerie Queene* III.vi.31).
8. Patron of youth and freedom.
9. The envoy is traditionally apologetic in tone: the poem is offered as a substitute for wedding presents ("ornaments") that did not arrive in time for the wedding. But this elaborate poem is itself a "goodly ornament," for (in a final reference to the theme of time and eternity) it stands as a timeless monument of art to the passing day which it celebrates.

CHRISTOPHER MARLOWE
(1564–1593)

ca. 1587: *Tamburlaine* produced, introducing blank verse, "Marlowe's mighty line," to the stage.
ca. 1592–93: *Dr. Faustus*

Christopher Marlowe was born two months before William Shakespeare. He was the son of a Canterbury shoemaker; in 1580 he went to Corpus Christi College, Cambridge, on a scholarship which was ordinarily awarded to students preparing for the ministry. He held the scholarship for the maximum time, six years, but did not take holy orders. Instead, he began to write plays. When he came to supplicate for his Master of Arts degree in 1587, the university was about to deny it to him on the grounds that he intended to go abroad to Reims, the center of Catholic intrigue and propaganda against Elizabeth, and remain there. But the Privy Council intervened and requested that, since Marlowe had done the queen good service, he be granted his degree at the next commencement "because it is not Her Majesty's pleasure that anyone employed as he had been in matters touching the benefit of his country should be defamed by those that are ignorant in the affairs he went about." Although much sensational information about Marlowe has been discovered in modern times, we are still "ignorant in the affairs he went about."

Before he left Cambridge, he had certainly written his tremendously successful play *Tamburlaine* and perhaps also, in collaboration with his younger Cambridge contemporary, Thomas Nashe, the tragedy of *Dido, Queen of Carthage*. *Tamburlaine*, which soon was followed by a sequel (*Tamburlaine*, Part II), dramatizes the exploits of a 14th-century Scythian shepherd who conquered much of the known world, as Alexander had before him. In some 16th-century narratives Tamburlaine is represented as the type of modern (i.e., Renaissance) man, and in others he is portrayed as God's Scourge. In Marlowe's play he is the vehicle for the expression of boundless energy and ambition, the impulse to strive constantly upward to absolute power. When one of his victims accuses him of bloody cruelty, Tamburlaine answers that ambition to rule is embedded in the laws of nature and in basic human psychology:

> Nature, that framed us of four elements
> Warring within our breasts for regiment,
> Doth teach us all to have aspiring minds;
> Our souls, whose faculties can comprehend
> The wondrous architecture of the world
> And measure every planet's wandering course,
> Still climbing after knowledge infinite,
> And always moving as the restless spheres,

> Wills us to wear ourselves and never rest
> Until we reach the ripest fruit of all,
> That perfect bliss and sole felicity,
> The sweet fruition of an earthly crown.

The English theater had heard nothing like this before. Here is a resonant, rhetorical blank verse, eminently suited to projection from the stage, and appropriate also, as it turned out, for the robust talents of the actor Edward Alleyn who happily appeared in time to portray Marlowe's heroes.

From the time of his first great success, when he was 23, Marlowe had only six years to live. They were not calm years. In 1589 he was involved in a brawl with one William Bradley, in which the poet Thomas Watson intervened and killed Bradley. Both poets were jailed, but Watson got off on a plea of self-defense and Marlowe was released. In 1591 Marlowe was living in London with the playwright Thomas Kyd, who later gave information to the Privy Council accusing Marlowe of atheism and treason. On May 30, 1593, at the inn of the Widow Bull in Deptford, Marlowe was killed by a dagger thrust in an argument over the bill. In these six violent years, Marlowe composed five more plays: his sequel to *Tamburlaine; The Massacre at Paris;* two major tragedies, *The Jew of Malta* and *Dr. Faustus;* and a chronicle history play, *Edward II.* We do not know when he did his verse translations, of the *Amores* of Ovid and the first book of Lucan's *Pharsalia,* or the more original *Hero and Leander.* When he died, in 1593, he had created an immortal place for himself in English drama and poetry; if his contemporary, William Shakespeare, had died at the same age he would scarcely be known today.

Marlowe's major tragedies, *Tamburlaine, The Jew of Malta,* and *Dr. Faustus,* all portray a hero who passionately seeks power—the power of rule, the power of money, and the power of knowledge, respectively. Each of the heroes is an "overreacher," striving beyond the bounds of human capacity, or at least the limits imposed upon human achievement. The plots show these heroes finally defeated, but, as in all high tragedy, the values for which the hero stood emerge larger than the forces which defeat him.

From Hero and Leander[1]

From *The First Sestiad*

> On Hellespont, guilty of true love's blood,
> In view and opposite, two cities stood,

1. *Hero and Leander* is a poem of the mythological-erotic type which was highly popular in the 1590's, especially among readers of the aristocratic or courtier class. Shakespeare's *Venus and Adonis* is another example of the genre, for which the great classical model was Ovid. Marlowe, however, based his poem somewhat remotely upon a Greek original by Musaeus, an Alexandrian poet and grammarian of the 5th century A.D. Although the subject matter was drawn from classical authors, the qualities sought in these poems by Elizabethan poets and readers were their own: a richness of detail in the descriptions, exuberance of fancy and vividness in mythological invention, sensuous appeal in the erotic passages, and the conveying of a kind of remoteness which makes the action seem to take place in a recognizable but idealized world.

The poem is divided into "Sestiads"

Sea-borderers, disjoined by Neptune's might;
The one Abydos, the other Sestos hight.[2]
At Sestos Hero dwelt; Hero the fair, 5
Whom young Apollo courted for her hair,
And offered as a dower his burning throne,
Where she should sit for men to gaze upon.
The outside of her garments were of lawn,[3]
The lining purple silk, with gilt stars drawn; 10
Her wide sleeves green, and bordered with a grove
Where Venus in her naked glory strove
To please the careless and disdainful eyes
Of proud Adonis, that before her lies;[4]
Her kirtle blue, whereon was many a stain, 15
Made with the blood of wretched lovers slain.[5]
Upon her head she ware a myrtle wreath,
From whence her veil reached to the ground beneath.
Her veil was artificial flowers and leaves,
Whose workmanship both man and beast deceives; 20
Many would praise the sweet smell as she passed,
When 'twas the odor which her breath forth cast;
And there for honey, bees have sought in vain,
And, beat from thence, have lighted there again.
About her neck hung chains of pebble-stone, 25
Which, lightened by her neck, like diamonds shone.
She ware no gloves, for neither sun nor wind
Would burn or parch her hands, but to her mind[6]
Or warm or cool them, for they took delight
To play upon those hands, they were so white. 30
Buskins[7] of shells all silvered, uséd she,
And branched with blushing coral to the knee,
Where sparrows perched, of hollow pearl and gold,
Such as the world would wonder to behold;
Those with sweet water oft her handmaid fills, 35
Which, as she went, would chirrup through the bills.
Some say, for her the fairest Cupid pined,
And looking in her face, was strooken blind.
But this is true: so like was one the other,
As he imagined Hero was his mother;[8] 40
And oftentimes into her bosom flew,
About her naked neck his bare arms threw,
And laid his childish head upon her breast,
And with still panting rocked, there took his rest.

(i.e., cantos), a word coined from Hero's city, Sestos, which was opposite Abydos on the Hellespont (see lines 1–4). Marlowe completed only the First Sestiad (of which the initial 176 lines are here reprinted), and the Second. George Chapman later finished the poem.
2. Called.
3. A kind of fine linen or thin cambric.
4. Venus's love for the reluctant young hunter, Adonis, and his death in the boar hunt are told by Ovid and by Shakespeare in *Venus and Adonis*. "Kirtle": skirt.
5. The extravagant claim is made that many "wretched lovers" had committed suicide at her feet beca se Hero would not have them.
6. As she wished.
7. High shoes or boots.
8. I.e., Venus.

So lovely fair was Hero, Venus' nun,[9] 45
As Nature wept, thinking she was undone,
Because she took more from her than she left
And of such wondrous beauty her bereft;
Therefore, in sign her treasure suffered wrack,
Since Hero's time hath half the world been black. 50
Amorous Leander, beautiful and young,
(Whose tragedy divine Musaeus[1] sung)
Dwelt at Abydos; since him dwelt there none
For whom succeeding times make greater moan.
His dangling tresses that were never shorn, 55
Had they been cut and unto Colchos[2] borne,
Would have allured the vent'rous youth of Greece
To hazard more than for the Golden Fleece.
Fair Cynthia[3] wished his arms might be her sphere;
Grief makes her pale, because she moves not there. 60
His body was as straight as Circe's wand;[4]
Jove might have sipped out nectar from his hand.
Even as delicious meat is to the taste,
So was his neck in touching, and surpassed
The white of Pelops' shoulder.[5] I could tell ye 65
How smooth his breast was, and how white his belly,
And whose immortal fingers did imprint
That heavenly path, with many a curious[6] dint,
That runs along his back; but my rude pen
Can hardly blazon forth the loves of men, 70
Much less of powerful gods; let it suffice
That my slack[7] muse sings of Leander's eyes,
Those orient cheeks and lips, exceeding his
That leapt into the water for a kiss
Of his own shadow, and despising many, 75
Died ere he could enjoy the love of any.[8]
Had wild Hippolytus[9] Leander seen,
Enamored of his beauty had he been;
His presence made the rudest peasant melt,
That in the vast uplandish country dwelt; 80
The barbarous Thracian soldier, moved with naught,
Was moved with him, and for his favor sought.
Some swore he was a maid in man's attire,
For in his looks were all that men desire:
A pleasant smiling cheek, a speaking[1] eye, 85

9. The connotations of these two words are contradictory; Marlowe gets a similar effect elsewhere in the poem. Hero is a maiden in attendance at the temple of Venus, who is, of course, the goddess of love.
1. I.e., the author of the Greek poem upon which *Hero and Leander* is remotely based. He was sometimes confused with a legendary early Musaeus, supposed son of Orpheus—hence Marlowe calls him "divine."
2. A country in Asia where the Argo-nauts ("the ven'trous youth of Greece") found the Golden Fleece.
3. The moon; "sphere": orbit.
4. The wand with which Circe, in the *Odyssey*, turned men into beasts.
5. Pelops, according to Ovid, had a shoulder of ivory.
6. Exquisite.
7. Dull. "Orient": shining.
8. An allusion to Narcissus.
9. Like Adonis, he preferred hunting to love.
1. Expressive.

A brow for love to banquet royally;
And such as knew he was a man, would say,
"Leander, thou art made for amorous play;
Why art thou not in love, and loved of all?
Though thou be fair, yet be not thine own thrall." 90
　　The men of wealthy Sestos every year,
For his sake whom their goddess held so dear,
Rose-cheeked Adonis, kept a solemn feast.
Thither resorted many a wandering guest
To meet their loves; such as had none at all 95
Came lovers home from this great festival;
For every street, like to a firmament,
Glistered with breathing stars, who, where they went,
Frighted the melancholy earth, which deemed
Eternal heaven to burn, for so it seemed 100
As if another Phaëton[2] had got
The guidance of the sun's rich chariot.
But, far above the loveliest, Hero shined,
And stole away the enchanted gazer's mind;
For like sea nymphs' inveigling harmony, 105
So was her beauty to the standers by.
Nor that night-wandering pale and watery star[3]
(When yawning dragons draw her thirling[4] car
From Latmus' mount up to the gloomy sky,
Where, crowned with blazing light and majesty, 110
She proudly sits) more over-rules[5] the flood
Than she the hearts of those that near her stood.
Even as when gaudy nymphs pursue the chase,
Wretched Ixion's shaggy-footed race,[6]
Incensed with savage heat, gallop amain 115
From steep pine-bearing mountains to the plain,
So ran the people forth to gaze upon her,
And all that viewed her were enamored on her.
And as in fury of a dreadful fight,
Their fellows being slain or put to flight, 120
Poor soldiers stand with fear of death dead-strooken,
So at her presence all, surprised and tooken,
Await the sentence of her scornful eyes;
He whom she favors lives, the other dies.
There might you see one sigh, another rage, 125
And some, their violent passions to assuage,
Compile sharp satires; but alas, too late,
For faithful love will never turn to hate.
And many, seeing great princes were denied,
Pined as they went, and thinking on her, died. 130

2. A son of the sun god, he drove his father's chariot across the sky and almost burned up the world.
3. The moon.
4. Flying like a spear. Latmus was the mountain where the moon visited her lover, Endymion.
5. Rules over.
6. I.e., the centaurs, fathered by Ixion upon a cloud. For his presumption in loving Juno, Ixion was chained to a wheel—hence "wretched."

On this feast day, oh, curséd day and hour!
Went Hero thorough[7] Sestos, from her tower
To Venus' temple, where unhappily,
As after chanced, they did each other spy.
So fair a church as this had Venus none;   135
The walls were of discolored[8] jasper stone,
Wherein was Proteus carved, and o'erhead
A lively[9] vine of green sea-agate spread,
Where, by one hand, light-headed Bacchus hung,
And with the other, wine from grapes out-wrung.   140
Of crystal shining fair the pavement was;
The town of Sestos called it Venus' glass;
There might you see the gods in sundry shapes,
Committing heady[1] riots, incest, rapes;
For know that underneath this radiant floor   145
Was Danae's statue in a brazen tower;[2]
Jove slyly stealing from his sister's bed
To dally with Idalian Ganymed,[3]
And for his love Europa bellowing loud,
And tumbling with the rainbow in a cloud;   150
Blood-quaffing Mars heaving the iron net
Which limping Vulcan and his Cyclops set;[4]
Love kindling fire to burn such towns as Troy
Silvanus weeping for the lovely boy[5]
That now is turned into a cypress tree,   155
Under whose shade the wood-gods love to be.
And in the midst a silver altar stood;
There Hero sacrificing turtles'[6] blood,
Veiled to the ground, veiling her eyelids close,
And modestly they opened as she rose;   160
Thence flew love's arrow with the golden head,[7]
And thus Leander was enamoréd.
Stone still he stood, and evermore he gazed,
Till with the fire that from his countenance blazed,
Relenting Hero's gentle heart was strook;   165
Such force and virtue hath an amorous look.

   It lies not in our power to love or hate,
For will in us is overruled by fate.
When two are stripped, long ere the course begin
We wish that one should lose, the other win;   170
And one especially do we affect[8]

---

7. Through.
8. Of various colors.
9. Lifelike.
1. Passionate, violent. In the next lines, specific examples of the "riots, incest, rapes" are given.
2. Danae, imprisoned in a tower, was visited by Jove in the form of a shower of gold. "His sister's": i.e., Juno's; she was also Jove's wife.
3. A beautiful youth whom Jove kidnaped from Mt. Ida (hence "Idalian"). In order to seduce Europa, Jove took the form of a "bellowing" bull.
4. Vulcan used a net to trap Venus, his wife, and Mars, "blood-quaffing" god of war, in the act of love.
5. I.e., Cyparissus, beloved of the wood god Sylvanus.
6. Turtledoves, symbolic of constancy in love.
7. The "golden head" of some of Cupid's arrows produced love; he had others, of lead, that produced dislike.
8. Have affection for.

Of two gold ingots, like in each respect.
The reason no man knows, let it suffice,
What we behold is censured by our eyes.
Where both deliberate, the love is slight;   175
Who ever loved, that loved not at first sight?[9]

* * *

1598

The Passionate Shepherd to His Love[1]

Come live with me and be my love,
And we will all the pleasures prove[2]
That valleys, groves, hills, and fields,
Woods, or steepy mountain yields.

And we will sit upon the rocks,   5
Seeing the shepherds feed their flocks,
By shallow rivers to whose falls
Melodious birds sing madrigals.

And I will make thee beds of roses
And a thousand fragrant posies,   10
A cap of flowers, and a kirtle
Embroidered all with leaves of myrtle;

A gown made of the finest wool
Which from our pretty lambs we pull;
Fair lined slippers for the cold,   15
With buckles of the purest gold;

A belt of straw and ivy buds,
With coral clasps and amber studs:
And if these pleasures may thee move,
Come live with me, and be my love.   20

The shepherds' swains shall dance and sing
For thy delight each May morning:
If these delights thy mind may move,
Then live with me and be my love.

1599, 1600

9. Shakespeare quotes this line in *As You Like It* (III.v.82).
1. This pastoral lyric of invitation is one of the most famous of Elizabethan songs, and a few lines from it are sung in Shakespeare's *Merry Wives of Windsor*. Many poets have written replies to it, the finest of which is by that other great Elizabethan romantic, Sir Walter Ralegh.
2. Test, experience.

Dr. Faustus   The date of Marlowe's *Dr. Faustus* is in dispute. Some authorities date it during the last year of the playwright's life, between the spring of 1592 and that of 1593, but others think it belongs in 1588–89, not long after the second part of *Tamburlaine*. The story was a striking one, often retold in ballad and pamphlet, and the play, which includes some of Marlowe's most magnificent poetry, was a theatrical success. In popular legend John Faustus, a Doctor of Divinity, sold his soul to the devil for further knowledge, of magic particularly, and was damned for it; Marlowe used as his source material a rather simple-minded German narrative called, in its English translation, *The History of the Damnable Life and Deserved Death of Doctor John Faustus*. He turned it into a powerful projection of the Renaissance lust for knowledge, set against the medieval insistence upon salvation as the individual's main and guiding concern upon earth. In the *Faustbook* which was his source, many farcical episodes showed the hero playing pranks with his newly-won power; whether Marlowe wrote the comic scenes in *Faustus* or turned them over to a collaborator like Samuel Rowley we cannot be sure. Recent critics have replied to the standard objection that the poetic and prose parts of the play conflict with each other by arguing that the discrepancy is intentionally ironic.

Some of the intellectual background of the play requires explanation for a 20th-century reader. He must understand that devils are real and are sometimes called "spirits"; that when Faustus asks for power to be a spirit and go invisible he is taking on some attributes of a devil, though of course he keeps his human soul; and that when he acquires Helen, who is a spirit, as his paramour, he has committed the sin of demoniality (intercourse with devils) and is beyond repentance. But although Marlowe's play should be read in the context of the thought and belief of the Middle Ages and Renaissance, it has also a timeless interest. The Faust legend has a relevant meaning in many periods; Goethe made it the subject of his masterpiece in the 19th century and Thomas Mann has treated it again in the 20th.

The text of *Dr. Faustus* has come down to us in two forms, both corrupt. It is one of the major triumphs of modern literary scholarship that Sir W. W. Greg, in his parallel-text edition of the two quartos and his conjectural reconstruction of what Marlowe and his collaborator originally wrote, has made *Dr. Faustus* a comprehensible play. The text here printed is based upon Greg's work.

The Tragical History
of the Life and Death of Doctor Faustus

Dramatis Personae

CHORUS
DR. JOHN FAUSTUS, *of the University of Wittenberg*
WAGNER, *his servant*
GOOD ANGEL *and* BAD ANGEL
VALDES *and* CORNELIUS, *magicians and friends of* FAUSTUS
THREE SCHOLARS, *students at the university*
LUCIFER, MEPHISTOPHILIS, *and* BELZEBUB, *devils*
ROBIN *and* DICK, *rustic clowns*
THE SEVEN DEADLY SINS

POPE ADRIAN

RAYMOND, *King of Hungary*

BRUNO, *a rival Pope, appointed by the* EMPEROR

CARDINALS OF FRANCE *and* PADUA

ARCHBISHOP OF RHEIMS

MARTINO, FREDERICK, *and* BENVOLIO, *gentlemen at the* EMPEROR'S
court

CAROLUS (CHARLES) THE FIFTH, EMPEROR

DUKE OF SAXONY

DUKE *and* DUCHESS OF VANHOLT

HORSE-COURSER

CARTER

HOSTESS *of a tavern*

OLD MAN

SPIRITS *of* DARIUS, ALEXANDER *and his* PARAMOUR, *and* HELEN OF
TROY

ATTENDANTS, MONKS *and* FRIARS, SOLDIERS, PIPER, *two* CUPIDS

Act I

[Enter CHORUS.[1]]

CHO. Not marching in the fields of Trasimene[2]
    Where Mars did mate the warlike Carthagens,
    Nor sporting in the dalliance of love
    In courts of kings where state[3] is overturned,
    Nor in the pomp of proud audacious deeds   5
    Intends our Muse to vaunt his heavenly verse:
    Only this, gentles, we must now perform,
    The form of Faustus' fortunes good or bad.
    And so to patient judgments we appeal
    And speak for Faustus in his infancy.   10
    Now is he born, his parents base of stock,
    In Germany within a town called Rhode:[4]
    At riper years to Wittenberg he went
    Whereas his kinsmen chiefly brought him up;
    So much he profits in divinity,   15
    The fruitful plot of scholarism graced,[5]
    That shortly he was graced with Doctor's name,
    Excelling all whose sweet delight disputes[6]
    In th' heavenly matters of theology,
    Till, swollen with cunning,[7] of a self-conceit,   20
    His waxen wings did mount above his reach
    And melting, heavens conspired his overthrow.[8]

1. A single actor who recited a prologue to an act or a whole play, and
occasionally delivered an epilogue.
2. The battle of Lake Trasimene (217
B.C.) was one of the Carthaginian leader
Hannibal's great victories. "Mate":
join with.
3. Political power.
4. Roda. Wittenberg, in the next line,
was the famous university where Martin Luther studied, as did Shakespeare's

Hamlet and Horatio; "whereas":
where.
5. Grazed. In line 17 "graced" refers
to the Cambridge word for permission
to proceed to a degree.
6. The usual academic exercises were
disputations, which took the place of
examinations.
7. Learning.
8. The reference is to the Greek myth
of Icarus, who flew too near the sun

For, falling to a devilish exercise
And glutted more with learning's golden gifts,
He surfeits upon cursèd necromancy;[9]   25
Nothing so sweet as magic is to him,
Which he prefers before his chiefest bliss[1]—
And this the man that in his study sits.
　　[*Draws the curtain[2] and exit.*]

SCENE 1

　　[FAUSTUS *in his study.*]
FAUST. Settle thy studies, Faustus, and begin
　　To sound the depth of that thou wilt profess.
　　Having commenced, be a divine in show,
　　Yet level[3] at the end of every art
　　And live and die in Aristotle's works: 5
　　Sweet Analytics,[4] 'tis thou hast ravished me!   [*Reads.*]
　　Bene disserere est finis logicis—
　　Is to dispute well logic's chiefest end?
　　Affords this art no greater miracle?
　　Then read no more; thou hast attained the end.   10
　　A greater subject fitteth Faustus' wit:
　　Bid *ὸν χαὶ μὴ ὸν*[5] farewell, Galen come,
　　Seeing *ubi desinit philosophus, ibi incipit medicus;*[6]
　　Be a physician, Faustus, heap up gold
　　And be eternized for some wondrous cure.   [*Reads.*] 15
　　Summum bonum medicinae sanitas[7]—
　　The end of physic is our bodies' health:
　　Why, Faustus, hast thou not attained that end?
　　Is not thy common talk sound aphorisms?[8]
　　Are not thy bills hung up as monuments   20
　　Whereby whole cities have escaped the plague
　　And thousand desperate maladies been cured?
　　Yet art thou still but Faustus, and a man.
　　Couldst thou make men to live eternally
　　Or, being dead, raise them to life again,   25
　　Then this profession were to be esteemed.
　　Physic, farewell. Where is Justinian?[9]   [*Reads.*]
　　Si una eademque res legatur duobus,
　　Alter rem, alter valorem rei, etc.[1]—

on wings of feathers and wax made by his father Daedalus. The wax melted and he fell into the sea and was drowned.
9. Black magic.
1. The salvation of his soul.
2. The curtain to the inner stage, behind the main stage, which serves here as Faustus' study. "Draws" here means "draws apart."
3. "Commenced": graduated, i.e., received the doctor's degree; "in show": in external appearance; "level": aim.
4. The title of a treatise on logic by Aristotle. The Latin means, "To carry on a disputation well is the end or purpose of logic."
5. "Being and not being," i.e., philosophy. Galen: the ancient authority on medicine (2nd century A.D.).
6. "Where the philosopher leaves off the physician begins."
7. "Good health is the object of medicine" (or "physic").
8. I.e., reliable medical pronouncements. "Bills": prescriptions.
9. Roman emperor and authority on law (483–565), author of the *Institutes.*
1. "If something is bequeathed to two persons, one shall have the thing itself, the other something of equal value." The next Latin phrase means:

A pretty case of paltry legacies!   30
Exhaereditare filium non potest pater nisi—
Such is the subject of the Institute
And universal body of the law.
This study fits a mercenary drudge
Who aims at nothing but external trash,   35
Too servile and illiberal for me.
When all is done, divinity is best.
Jerome's Bible,[2] Faustus, view it well: [*Reads.*]
Stipendium peccati mors est—Ha! *Stipendium, etc.*
The reward of sin is death? That's hard.   40
Si pecasse negamus, fallimur, et nulla est in nobis veritas[3]—
If we say that we have no sin
We deceive ourselves, and there's no truth in us.
Why then belike
We must sin and so consequently die,   45
Aye, we must die an everlasting death.
What doctrine call you this, *Che sera, sera:*[4]
What will be, shall be? Divinity, adieu!
These metaphysics[5] of magicians
And necromantic books are heavenly: 50
Lines, circles, signs, letters, and characters—
Aye, these are those that Faustus most desires.
O what a world of profit and delight,
Of power, of honor, of omnipotence,
Is promised to the studious artisan![6]   55
All things that move between the quiet[7] poles
Shall be at my command. Emperors and kings
Are but obeyed in their several provinces,
Nor can they raise the wind or rend the clouds;
But his dominion that exceeds in this   60
Stretcheth as far as doth the mind of man.
A sound magician is a demigod:
Here tire my brains to gain a deity!
Wagner!
            [*Enter* WAGNER.]
Commend me to my dearest friends,   65
The German Valdes and Cornelius;
Request them earnestly to visit me.
WAG. I will, sir.   [*Exit.*]
FAUST. Their conference will be a greater help to me
Than all my labors, plod I ne'er so fast.   70
        [*Enter the* GOOD ANGEL *and the* BAD ANGEL.]
G. ANG. O Faustus, lay that damnéd book aside
And gaze not on it, lest it tempt thy soul

"A father cannot disinherit his son un-   lines.
less."   4. Translated in the first half of the
2. The Latin translation, or "Vulgate,"   next line.
of St. Jerome (ca. 340–420). The Latin   5. Basic principles.
(Romans vi.23) is translated in line   6. I.e., a master of the occult arts,
40.   such as necromancy.
3. I John i.8, translated in the next two   7. Unmoving.

And heap God's heavy wrath upon thy head.
Read, read the Scriptures! That is blasphemy.
B. ANG. Go forward, Faustus, in that famous art   75
   Wherein all nature's treasury is contained:
   Be thou on earth, as Jove[8] is in the sky,
   Lord and commander of these elements.
      [*Exeunt* ANGELS.]
FAUST. How am I glutted with conceit[9] of this!
   Shall I make spirits fetch me what I please,   80
   Resolve me of all ambiguities,
   Perform what desperate enterprise I will?
   I'll have them fly to India[1] for gold,
   Ransack the ocean for orient pearl,
   And search all corners of the new-found world[2]   85
   For pleasant fruits and princely delicates;
   I'll have them read me strange philosophy
   And tell the secrets of all foreign kings;
   I'll have them wall all Germany with brass
   And make swift Rhine circle fair Wittenberg;   90
   I'll have them fill the public schools[3] with silk
   Wherewith the students shall be bravely clad;
   I'll levy soldiers with the coin they bring,
   And chase the Prince of Parma[4] from our land
   And reign sole king of all our provinces;   95
   Yea, stranger engines for the brunt of war
   Than was the fiery keel[5] at Antwerp's bridge
   I'll make my servile spirits to invent!
      [*Enter* VALDES *and* CORNELIUS.]
   Come, German Valdes and Cornelius,
   And make me blest with your sage conference.   100
   Valdes, sweet Valdes and Cornelius,
   Know that your words have won me at the last
   To practice magic and concealéd arts;
   Yet not your words only, but mine own fantasy
   That will receive no object,[6] for my head   105
   But ruminates on necromantic skill.
   Philosophy is odious and obscure,
   Both law and physic are for petty wits,
   Divinity is basest of the three,
   Unpleasant, harsh, contemptible, and vile;   110
   'Tis magic, magic, that hath ravished me!
   Then, gentle friends, aid me in this attempt,
   And I, that have with concise syllogisms

8. God (a common substitution in Elizabethan drama).
9. Filled with the idea.
1. "India" could mean the West Indies, America, or Ophir (in the east).
2. The western hemisphere.
3. The university lecture rooms.
4. The Duke of Parma was the Spanish governor general of the Low Countries from 1579 to 1592.
5. A reference to the burning ship sent by the Netherlanders in 1585 against the barrier on the river Scheldt which Parma had built as a part of the blockade of Antwerp.
6. That will pay no attention to physical reality.

Graveled[7] the pastors of the German church,
And made the flowering pride of Wittenberg   115
Swarm to my problems[8] as the infernal spirits
On sweet Musaeus when he came to hell,
Will be as cunning as Agrippa[9] was
Whose shadows made all Europe honor him.

VALD. Faustus, these books, thy wit, and our experience   120
Shall make all nations to canonize us.
As Indian Moors[1] obey their Spanish lords
So shall the spirits of every element
Be always serviceable to us three:
Like lions shall they guard us when we please.   125
Like Almain rutters[2] with their horsemen's staves,
Or Lapland giants trotting by our sides;
Sometimes like women, or unwedded maids,
Shadowing more beauty in their airy brows
Than in the white breasts of the queen of love;   130
From Venice shall they drag huge argosies
And from America the golden fleece
That yearly stuffs old Philip's[3] treasury,
If learned Faustus will be resolute.

FAUST. Valdes, as resolute am I in this   135
As thou to live; therefore object it not.[4]

CORN. The miracles that magic will perform
Will make thee vow to study nothing else.
He that is grounded in astrology,
Enriched with tongues, well seen[5] in minerals,   140
Hath all the principles magic doth require.
Then doubt not, Faustus, but to be renowned
And more frequented for this mystery[6]
Than heretofore the Delphian oracle.
The spirits tell me they can dry the sea   145
And fetch the treasure of all foreign wrecks—
Aye, all the wealth that our forefathers hid
Within the massy[7] entrails of the earth.
Then tell me, Faustus, what shall we three want?

FAUST. Nothing, Cornelius. O this cheers my soul!   150
Come, show me some demonstrations magical
That I may conjure in some lusty[8] grove
And have these joys in full possession.

VALD. Then haste thee to some solitary grove
And bear wise Bacon's[9] and Albanus' works,   155

---

7. Confounded.
8. Lectures in logic and mathematics. Musaeus was a mythical singer, son of Orpheus; it was, however, the latter who charmed the denizens of hell with his music.
9. Cornelius Agrippa, German author of *The Vanity and Uncertainty of Arts and Sciences*, popularly supposed to have the power of calling up shades ("shadows") of the dead.

1. I.e., dark-skinned American Indians.
2. German horsemen.
3. Philip II, king of Spain.
4. I.e., don't make it a condition.
5. Expert.
6. Craft. The "Delphian oracle" was the oracle of Apollo at Delphi, much frequented in antiquity.
7. Massive.
8. Flourishing, beautiful.
9. Roger Bacon, the medieval friar and

The Hebrew Psalter and New Testament;
And whatsoever else is requisite
We will inform thee ere our conference cease.

CORN. Valdes, first let him know the words of art,
    And then, all other ceremonies learned,   160
    Faustus may try his cunning by himself.

VALD. First I'll instruct thee in the rudiments,
    And then wilt thou be perfecter than I.

FAUST. Then come and dine with me, and after meat
    We'll canvass every quiddity[1] thereof;   165
    For ere I sleep I'll try what I can do:
    This night I'll conjure[2] though I die therefore.   [*Exeunt.*]

SCENE 2

    [*Enter two* SCHOLARS.]

1 SCH. I wonder what's become of Faustus, that was wont to make our schools ring with *sic probo*.[3]

2 SCH. That shall we presently know; here comes his boy.[4]
    [*Enter* WAGNER *carrying wine*.]

1 SCH. How now, sirrah; where's thy master?

WAG. God in heaven knows.   5

2 SCH. Why, dost not thou know then?

WAG. Yes, I know; but that follows not.

1 SCH. Go to, sirrah; leave your jesting and tell us where he is.

WAG. That follows not by force of argument, which you, being licentiate,[5] should stand upon; therefore acknowledge your   10 error and be attentive.

2 SCH. Then you will not tell us?

WAG. You are deceived, for I will tell you. Yet if you were not dunces you would never ask me such a question, for is he not *corpus naturale*, and is not that *mobile*?[6] Then wherefore   15 should you ask me such a question? But that I am by nature phlegmatic,[7] slow to wrath and prone to lechery (to love, I would say), it were not for you to come within forty foot of the place of execution,[8] although I do not doubt to see you both hanged the next sessions. Thus having triumphed over   20 you, I will set my countenance like a precisian,[9] and begin to speak thus: Truly, my dear brethren, my master is within at dinner with Valdes and Cornelius, as this wine, if it could speak, would inform your worships; and so the Lord bless you, preserve you, and keep you, my dear brethren.   25
    [*Exit.*]

scientist, popularly thought a magician. "Albanus" is Pietro d'Albano, 13th-century alchemist.
1. Essential feature.
2. Call up spirits.
3. "Thus I prove," a phrase in scholastic disputation.
4. Poor student earning his keep.
5. I.e., graduate students.
6. *Corpus naturale et mobile* (natural, movable matter) was a scholastic defi-

nition of the subject matter of physics. Wagner is here parodying the language of learning he hears around the university.
7. Dominated by the phlegm, one of the four humors of medieval medicine and psychology.
8. I.e., the dining room.
9. A Puritan. The rest of his speech is in the style of the Puritans.

1 SCH. O Faustus, then I fear that which I have long suspected,
    That thou art fallen into that damnéd art
    For which they two are infamous throughout the world.
2 SCH. Were he a stranger, not allied to me,
    The danger of his soul would make me mourn.   30
    But come, let us go and inform the Rector,[1]
    It may be his grave counsel may reclaim him.
1 SCH. I fear me nothing will reclaim him now.
2 SCH. Yet let us see what we can do.

                                            [Exeunt.]

SCENE 3

    [Enter FAUSTUS *to conjure.]*
FAUST. Now that the gloomy shadow of the night,
    Longing to view Orion's drizzling look,[2]
    Leaps from the antarctic world unto the sky
    And dims the welkin[3] with her pitchy breath,
    Faustus, begin thine incantations   5
    And try if devils will obey thy hest,
    Seeing thou has prayed and sacrificed to them.
    Within this circle is Jehovah's name
    [He draws the circle[4] on the ground.]
    Forward and backward anagrammatized,
    The breviated names of holy saints,   10
    Figures of every adjunct[5] to the heavens
    And characters of signs and erring stars,
    By which the spirits are enforced to rise.
    Then fear not, Faustus, but be resolute
    And try the uttermost magic can perform.   *[Thunder.]* 15
    Sint mihi dei Acherontis propitii! Valeat numen triplex
    Iehovae! Ignei aerii aquatici terreni spiritus, salvete! Orientis
    princeps Lucifer Belzebub, inferni ardentis monarcha, et De-
    mogorgon, propitiamus vos, ut appareat et surgat Mephistophi-
    lis![6]   20
    *[*FAUSTUS *pauses. Thunder still.]*
    Quid tu moraris?[7] *Per Iehovam, Gehennam et consecratam*
    aquam quam nunc spargo, signumque crucis quod nunc facio,
    et per vota nostra, ipse nunc surgat nobis dicatus Mephistophi-
    lis!

---

1. The head of a German university.
2. Orion appears at the beginning of winter. The phrase is a reminiscence of Virgil.
3. Sky.
4. I.e., the magic circle on the ground within which the spirits rise.
5. Heavenly body, thought to be joined to the solid firmament. "Characters of signs" are signs of the zodiac and the planets; "erring": wandering.
6. This first part of the incantation means: "May the gods of the lower regions favor me! Goodbye to the Trin-ity! Hail, spirits of fire, air, water, and earth! Prince of the East, Belzebub, monarch of burning hell, and Demogorgon, we pray to you that Mephistophilis may appear and rise."
7. Nothing has happened, so Faustus asks, "What are you waiting for?" and continues to conjure: "By Jehovah, Gehenna, and the holy water which I now sprinkle, and the sign of the cross which I now make, and by our vows, may Mephistophilis himself now rise to serve us."

[MEPHISTOPHILIS *in the shape of a dragon rises from the
earth outside the circle.*]

I charge thee to return and change thy shape;   25
Thou art too ugly to attend on me.
Go, and return an old Franciscan friar;
That holy shape becomes a devil best.   [*Exit* MEPH.]
I see there's virtue in my heavenly words:
Who would not be proficient in this art?   30
How pliant is this Mephistophilis,
Full of obedience and humility!
Such is the force of magic and my spells.
Now, Faustus, thou art conjurer laureate
That canst command great Mephistophilis: 35
Quin redis, Mephistophilis, fratris imagine![8]
[*Re-enter* MEPHISTOPHILIS *like a Friar.*]
MEPH. Now, Faustus, what wouldst thou have me do?
FAUST. I charge thee wait upon me whilst I live
To do whatever Faustus shall command,
Be it be make the moon drop from her sphere   40
Or the ocean to overwhelm the world.
MEPH. I am a servant to great Lucifer
And may not follow thee without his leave:
No more than he commands must we perform.
FAUST. Did not he charge thee to appear to me?   45
MEPH. No, I came now hither of my own accord.
FAUST. Did not my conjuring speeches raise thee?
Speak!
MEPH. That was the cause, but yet *per accidens,*[9]
For when we hear one rack[1] the name of God,   50
Abjure the Scriptures and his Saviour Christ,
We fly in hope to get his glorious soul;
Nor will we come unless he use such means
Whereby he is in danger to be damned;
Therefore the shortest cut for conjuring.   55
Is stoutly to abjure the Trinity
And pray devoutly to the prince of hell.
FAUST. So I have done, and hold this principle,
There is no chief but only Belzebub
To whom Faustus doth dedicate himself.   60
This word "damnation" terrifies not me
For I confound hell in Elysium;
My ghost be with the old philosophers![2]
But leaving these vain trifles of men's souls—
Tell me, what is that Lucifer thy lord?   65
MEPH. Arch-regent and commander of all spirits.
FAUST. Was not that Lucifer an angel once?
MEPH. Yes, Faustus, and most dearly loved of God.

8. "Return, Mephistophilis, in the shape of a friar."
9. By the immediate, not ultimate, cause.
1. Torture (by anagrammatizing).

2. I.e., I regard heaven and hell indifferently; if the old (pre-Christian) philosophers are damned, let me be damned with them.

FAUST. How comes it, then, that he is prince of devils? 70
MEPH. O, by aspiring pride and insolence,
 For which God threw him from the face of heaven.
FAUST. And what are you that live with Lucifer?
MEPH. Unhappy spirits that fell with Lucifer,
 Conspired against our God with Lucifer, 75
 And are forever damned with Lucifer.
FAUST. Where are you damned?
MEPH. In hell.
FAUST. How comes it, then, that thou art out of hell?
MEPH. Why, this is hell, nor am I out of it: 80
 Thinkst thou that I who saw the face of God
 And tasted the eternal joys of heaven
 Am not tormented with ten thousand hells
 In being deprived of everlasting bliss?
 O Faustus, leave these frivolous demands 85
 Which strike a terror to my fainting soul!
FAUST. What, is great Mephistophilis so passionate[3]
 For being deprivéd of the joys of heaven?
 Learn thou of Faustus manly fortitude
 And scorn those joys thou never shalt possess. 90
 Go, bear these tidings to great Lucifer:
 Seeing Faustus hath incurred eternal death
 By desperate thoughts against Jove's deity,
 Say he surrenders up to him his soul
 So he will spare him four and twenty years, 95
 Letting him live in all voluptuousness,
 Having thee ever to attend on me:
 To give me whatsoever I shall ask,
 To tell me whatsoever I demand,
 To slay mine enemies and aid my friends, 100
 And always be obedient to my will.
 Go, and return to mighty Lucifer,
 And meet me in my study at midnight
 And then resolve me of thy master's mind.[4]
MEPH. I will, Faustus. [*Exit.*] 105
FAUST. Had I as many souls as there be stars
 I'd give them all for Mephistophilis!
 By him I'll be great emperor of the world,
 And make a bridge thorough the moving air
 To pass the ocean with a band of men; 110
 I'll join the hills that bind the Afric shore
 And make that country continent to Spain,
 And both contributory to my crown;
 The Emperor[5] shall not live but by my leave,
 Nor any potentate of Germany. 115
 Now that I have obtained what I desire
 I'll live in speculation[6] of this art
 Till Mephistophilis return again. [*Exit.*]

3. Overcome by emotion. 5. The Holy Roman Emperor.
4. Give me his decision. 6. Contemplation.

SCENE 4

[*Enter* WAGNER *and the* CLOWN ⟨ROBIN.⟩[7]]

WAG. Come hither, sirrah boy.

CLOWN. Boy! O disgrace to my person! Zounds, boy in your face!
You have seen many boys with such pickadevaunts, I am sure.[8]

WAG. Sirrah, hast thou no comings in?[9]

CLOWN. Yes, and goings out too; you may see, sir.   5

WAG. Alas, poor slave. See how poverty jests in his nakedness: the
villain's out of service, and so hungry that I know he would
give his soul to the devil for a shoulder of mutton, though it
were blood-raw.

CLOWN. Not so, neither; I had need to have it well-roasted, and 10
good sauce to it, if I pay so dear, I can tell you.

WAG. Sirrah, wilt thou be my man and wait on me? And I will
make thee go like *Qui mihi discipulus*.[1]

CLOWN. What, in verse?

WAG. No, slave, in beaten silk and staves-acre.[2]   15

CLOWN. Staves-acre! that's good to kill vermin. Then, belike, if
I serve you I shall be lousy.

WAG. Why, so thou shalt be, whether thou dost it or no; for,
sirrah, if thou dost not presently bind thyself to me for seven
years, I'll turn all the lice about thee into familiars[3] and make 20
them tear thee in pieces.

CLOWN. Nay, sir, you may save yourself a labor, for they are as
familiar with me as if they paid for their meat and drink, I can
tell you.

WAG. Well, sirrah, leave your jesting and take these guilders.[4]   25

CLOWN. Yes, marry, sir, and I thank you, too.

WAG. So, now thou art to be at an hour's warning whenever and
wheresoever the devil shall fetch thee.

CLOWN. Here, take your guilders again, I'll none of 'em.

WAG. Not I, thou art pressed;[5] prepare thyself, for I will presently 30
raise up two devils to carry thee away. Banio! Belcher!

CLOWN. Belcher? And Belcher come here I'll belch him. I am not
afraid of a devil.

[*Enter two* DEVILS, *and the* CLOWN *runs up and down crying*.]

WAG. How now, sir! Will you serve me now?

CLOWN. Aye, good Wagner, take away the devil then.   35

WAG. Spirits, away!   [DEVILS *exeunt*.]

7. Not a court jester (as in some of Shakespeare's plays), but the older-fashioned stock character, a rustic buffoon. The name "Robin" has been interpolated by later editors of the text; all such interpolations, introduced for clarity of understanding, are indicated by the special brackets used here.
8. The point of the Clown's retort is that he is a man and wears a beard ("pickadevaunt"). "Zounds": an oath ("God's wounds").
9. Income, but the Clown then puns on the literal meaning.
1. "You who are my pupil" (the opening phrase of a poem on how students should behave, from Lily's *Latin Grammar*). Wagner means, "like a proper servant of a learned man."
2. A kind of delphinium used for killing vermin.
3. Familiar spirits, demons.
4. Money.
5. Impressed, i.e., hired.

Now, sirrah, follow me.

CLOWN. I will, sir. But hark you, master, will you teach me this conjuring occupation?

WAG. Aye, sirrah, I'll teach thee to turn thyself to a dog, or a cat, or a mouse, or a rat, or anything.   40

CLOWN. A dog, or a cat, or a mouse, or a rat! O brave[6] Wagner!

WAG. Villain, call me Master Wagner; and see that you walk attentively, and let your right eye be always diametrally[7] fixed upon my left heel, that thou mayst *quasi vestigiis nostris insistere.*[8]   45

CLOWN. Well, sir, I warrant you.   [*Exeunt.*]

Act II

SCENE 1

[*Enter* FAUSTUS *in his study.*]

FAUST. Now, Faustus, must thou needs be damned,
Canst not be saved.
What boots[9] it, then, to think of God or heaven?
Away with such vain fancies, and despair—
Despair in God and trust in Belzebu[h].   5
Now go not backward, no, be resolute!
Why waverest? Something soundeth in mine ears:
"Abjure this magic, turn to God again!"
Aye, and Faustus will turn to God again.
To God? He loves thee not;   10
The God thou servest is thine own appetite,
Wherein is fixed the love of Belzebub.
To him I'll build an altar and a church
And offer lukewarm blood of newborn babes.
[*Enter* GOOD ANGEL *and* BAD ANGEL.]

G. ANG. Sweet Faustus, leave that execrable art.   15

B. ANG. Go forward, Faustus, in that famous art.

FAUST. Contrition, prayer, repentance—what of them?

G. ANG. O they are means to bring thee unto heaven!

B. ANG. Rather illusions, fruits of lunacy,
That makes men foolish that do use them most.   20

G. ANG. Sweet Faustus, think of heaven and heavenly things.

B. ANG. No, Faustus, think of honor and of wealth.
[⟨*Exeunt* ANGELS.⟩]

FAUST. Of wealth!
Why, the signiory of Emden[1] shall be mine.
When Mephistophilis shall stand by me   25
What power can hurt me? Faustus, thou art safe;
Cast no more doubts. Come, Mephistophilis,
And bring glad tidings from great Lucifer.
Is't not midnight? Come, Mephistophilis!

6. Marvelous, wonderful.
7. Diametrically.
8. A pedantic way of saying "follow

my footsteps."
9. Avails.
1. A wealthy German trade center.

Veni, veni, Mephistophile![2]   30
    [*Enter* MEPHISTOPHILIS.]
Now tell me what saith Lucifer, thy lord?
MEPH. That I shall wait on Faustus whilst I live,
  So he will buy my service with his soul.
FAUST. Already Faustus hath hazarded that for thee.
MEPH. But, Faustus, thou must bequeath it solemnly   35
  And write a deed of gift with thine own blood,
  For that security craves Lucifer.
  If thou deny it, I must back to hell.
FAUST. Stay, Mephistophilis, and tell me what good
  Will my soul do thy lord?
MEPH.   Enlarge his kingdom.   40
FAUST. Is that the reason why he tempts us thus?
MEPH. *Solamen miseris socios habuisse doloris.*[3]
FAUST. Why, have you any pain that tortures others?
MEPH. As great as have the human souls of men.
  But tell me, Faustus, shall I have thy soul?   45
  And I will be thy slave, and wait on thee,
  And give thee more than thou hast wit to ask.
FAUST. Aye, Mephistophilis, I'll give it him.
MEPH. Then, Faustus, stab thine arm courageously,
  And bind thy soul that at some certain day   50
  Great Lucifer may claim it as his own,
  And then be thou as great as Lucifer.
FAUST. Lo, Mephistophilis, for love of thee
    [*Stabbing his arm.*]
  I cut mine arm, and with my proper[4] blood
  Assure my soul to be great Lucifer's.   55
  Chief lord and regent of perpetual night,
  View here the blood that trickles from mine arm
  And let it be propitious for my wish!
MEPH. But, Faustus,
  Write it in manner of a deed of gift.   60
FAUST. Aye, so I do. [*Writes.*] But, Mephistophilis,
  My blood congeals and I can write no more.
MEPH. I'll fetch thee fire to dissolve it straight.   [*Exit.*]
FAUST. What might the staying of my blood portend?
  Is it unwilling I should write this bill?[5]   65
  Why streams it not, that I may write afresh?
  "Faustus gives to thee his soul"—ah, there it stayed.
  Why shouldst thou not? Is not thy soul thine own?
  Then write again: "Faustus gives to thee his soul."
    [*Enter* MEPHISTOPHILIS *with a chafer*[6] *of fire.*]
MEPH. See, Faustus, here is fire; set it on.   70
FAUST. So: now the blood begins to clear again;
  Now will I make an end immediately.   [⟨*Writes.*⟩]

---

2. "Come, come, Mephistophilis!"   5. Contract.
3. "Misery loves company."   6. A portable grate.
4. Own.

MEPH. [*aside*] What will not I do to obtain his soul!

FAUST. *Consummatum est*[7]—this bill is ended;
And Faustus hath bequeathed his soul to Lucifer. 75
But what is this inscription on mine arm?
"*Homo, fuge!*"[8] Whither should I fly?
If unto God, he'll throw me down to hell.
My senses are deceived; here's nothing writ.
O yes, I see it plain: even here is writ 80
"*Homo, fuge!*" Yet shall not Faustus fly.

MEPH. I'll fetch him somewhat to delight his mind. [*Exit.*]
[*Re-enter* MEPHISTOPHILIS *with* DEVILS, *giving crowns and
rich apparel to* FAUSTUS, *and dance, and then depart.*]

FAUST. What means this show?
Speak, Mephistophilis.

MEPH. Nothing, Faustus, but to delight thy mind 85
And let thee see what magic can perform.

FAUST. But may I raise such spirits when I please?

MEPH. Aye, Faustus, and do greater things than these.

FAUST. Then, Mephistophilis, receive this scroll,
A deed of gift of body and of soul; 90
But yet conditionally that thou perform
All covenant-articles between us both.

MEPH. Faustus, I swear by hell and Lucifer
To effect all promises between us made.

FAUST. Then hear me read it, Mephistophilis. [⟨*Reads.*⟩] 95
"On these conditions following:
First, that Faustus may be a spirit in form and substance.
Secondly, that Mephistophilis shall be his servant and at his
command.
Thirdly, that Mephistophilis shall do for him, and bring him 100
whatsoever.
Fourthly, that he shall be in his chamber or house invisible.
Lastly, that he shall appear to the said John Faustus at all
times, in what form or shape soever he please.
I, John Faustus of Wittenberg, Doctor, by these presents do 105
give both body and soul to Lucifer, Prince of the East, and his
minister Mephistophilis, and furthermore grant unto them,
that four and twenty years being expired, the articles above
written inviolate, full power to fetch or carry the said John
Faustus, body and soul, flesh, blood, or goods, into their habi- 110
tation wheresoever.

By me John Faustus."

MEPH. Speak, Faustus, do you deliver this as your deed?

FAUST. Aye, take it, and the devil give thee good of it.

MEPH. Now, Faustus, ask what thou wilt. 115

FAUST. First will I question with thee about hell.
Tell me, where is the place that men call hell?

MEPH. Under the heavens.

7. "It is finished." A blasphemy, as these are the words of Christ on the Cross (see John xix.30).
8. "O man, flee!"

FAUST.   Aye, but whereabout?

MEPH. Within the bowels of these elements,
  Where we are tortured and remain forever.   120
  Hell hath no limits, nor is circumscribed
  In one self place, for where we are is hell,
  And where hell is there must we ever be;
  And, to be short, when all the world dissolves
  And every creature shall be purified,   125
  All places shall be hell that is not heaven.

FAUST. I think hell's a fable.

MEPH. Aye, think so, till experience change thy mind.

FAUST. Why, thinkst thou that Faustus shall be damned?

MEPH. Aye, of necessity, for here's the scroll   130
  In which thou hast given thy soul to Lucifer.

FAUST. Aye, and body too; but what of that?
  Thinkst thou that Faustus is so fond[9] to imagine
  That after this life there is any pain?
  No, these are trifles and mere old wives' tales.   135

MEPH. But I am an instance to prove the contrary,
  For I tell thee I am damned and now in hell.

FAUST. Nay, and this be hell I'll willingly be damned.
  What, sleeping, eating, walking, and disputing?
  But leaving off this, let me have a wife,   140
  The fairest maid in Germany,
  For I am wanton and lascivious
  And cannot live without a wife.

MEPH. I prithee, Faustus, talk not of a wife.[1]

FAUST. Nay, sweet Mephistophilis, fetch me one, for I will have 145
one.

MEPH. Well, thou shalt have a wife. Sit there till I come. [⟨*Exit.*⟩]
    [*Re-enter* MEPHISTOPHILIS *with a* DEVIL *dressed like a
    woman, with fireworks.*]

FAUST. What sight is this?

MEPH. Now Faustus, how dost thou like thy wife?

FAUST. Here's a hot whore indeed! No, I'll no wife.   150

MEPH. Marriage is but a ceremonial toy,
  And if thou lovest me, think no more of it.
  I'll cull thee out the fairest courtesans
  And bring them every morning to thy bed;
  She whom thine eye shall like thy heart shall have,   155
  Were she as chaste as was Penelope,[2]
  As wise as Saba, or as beautiful
  As was bright Lucifer before his fall.
  Hold, take this book: peruse it thoroughly.
  The iterating[3] of these lines brings gold,   160
  The framing[4] of this circle on the ground

9. Foolish.
1. Mephistophilis cannot produce a wife for Faustus because marriage is a sacrament.
2. The wife of Ulysses, famed for chastity and fidelity. "Saba": the Queen of Sheba.
3. Repeating.
4. Drawing.

Brings whirlwinds, tempests, thunder, and lightning;
Pronounce this thrice devoutly to thyself
And men in harness shall appear to thee,
Ready to execute what thou desirest.   165

FAUST. Thanks, Mephistophilis, yet fain would I have a book
wherein I might behold all spells and incantations, that I
might raise up spirits when I please.

MEPH. Here they are in this book.   [*There turn to them.*]

FAUST. Now would I have a book where I might see all characters 170
and planets of the heavens, that I might know their motions
and dispositions.

MEPH. Here they are too.   [*Turn to them.*]

FAUST. Nay, let me have one book more, and then I have done,
wherein I might see all plants, herbs, and trees that grow upon 175
the earth.

MEPH. Here they be.

FAUST. O thou art deceived!

MEPH. Tut, I warrant thee.   [*Turn to them.*]
          [⟨*Exeunt.*⟩]⁵

SCENE 2

[*Enter* FAUSTUS *in his study and* MEPHISTOPHILIS.]

FAUST. When I behold the heavens then I repent
And curse thee, wicked Mephistophilis,
Because thou hast deprived me of those joys.

MEPH. 'Twas thine own seeking, Faustus, thank thyself.
But thinkest thou heaven is such a glorious thing?   5
I tell thee, Faustus, it is not half so fair
As thou or any man that breathes on earth.

FAUST. How provest thou that?

MEPH. 'Twas made for man; then he's more excellent.

FAUST. If heaven was made for man 'twas made for me.   10
I will renounce this magic and repent.

[*Enter* GOOD ANGEL *and* BAD ANGEL.]

G. ANG. Faustus, repent; yet God will pity thee.

B. ANG. Thou art a spirit; God cannot pity thee.

FAUST. Who buzzeth in mine ears I am a spirit?⁶
Be I a devil, yet God may pity me.
Yea, God will pity me, if I repent.   15

B. ANG. Aye, but Faustus never shall repent.
          [*Exeunt* ANGELS.]

FAUST. My heart is hardened; I cannot repent.
Scarce can I name salvation, faith, or heaven,
But fearful echoes thunder in mine ears: 20
"Faustus, thou are damned!" Then guns and knives,
Swords, poison, halters, and envenomed steel

---

5. After this a comic scene has been
lost from the text. In it, apparently the
Clown, Robin, stole one of Faustus'
conjuring books and left Wagner's serv-

ice. He then became an hostler at an
inn.
6. Evil spirit, devil.

Are laid before me to dispatch myself,
And long ere this I should have done the deed
Had not sweet pleasure conquered deep despair.   25
Have I not made blind Homer sing to me
Of Alexander's love and Oenon's death,[7]
And hath not he that built the walls of Thebes
With ravishing sound of his melodious harp[8]
Made music with my Mephistophilis?   30
Why should I die, then, or basely despair?
I am resolved Faustus shall not repent.
Come, Mephistophilis, let us dispute again
And reason of divine astrology.
Speak, are there many spheres above the moon?   35
Are all celestial bodies but one globe
As is the substance of this centric earth?[9]

MEPH. As are the elements, such are the heavens,
Even from the moon unto the empyreal orb,
Mutually folded in each other's spheres,   40
And jointly move upon one axletree
Whose termine[1] is termed the world's wide pole;
Nor are the names of Saturn, Mars, or Jupiter
Feigned, but are erring stars.

FAUST. But tell me, have they all one motion, both *situ et tem-*   45
pore?[2]

MEPH. All move from east to west in four and twenty hours upon
   the poles of the world, but differ in their motions upon the
   poles of the zodiac.[3]

FAUST. These slender questions Wagner can decide.   50
   Hath Mephistophilis no greater skill?
   Who knows not the double motion of the planets?
   That the first is finished in a natural day;
   The second thus, Saturn in thirty years, Jupiter in twelve, Mars
   in four, the Sun, Venus, and Mercury in a year, the Moon in   55
   twenty-eight days. These are freshmen's suppositions. But tell
   me, hath every sphere a dominion or *intelligentia?*[4]

MEPH. Aye.

FAUST. How many heavens or spheres are there?

MEPH. Nine: the seven planets, the firmament, and the empyreal   60
   heaven.

7. Alexander is another name for Paris, the lover of Oenone; later he deserted her and abducted Helen, causing the Trojan War. Oenone refused to heal the wounds Paris received in battle, and when he died of them she killed herself in remorse.
8. I.e., the legendary musician Amphion.
9. "Faustus asks whether all the apparently different heavenly bodies form really one globe, like the earth. Mephistophilis answers that like the elements, which are separate but combined, the heavenly bodies are separate, though their spheres are infolded, and they move on one axletree. Hence we are not in error in giving individual names to Saturn, Mars, or Jupiter; they are separate planets" (F. S. Boas). The "empyreal orb," or outermost sphere, was also called the empyrean.
1. End.
2. In position and time.
3. I.e., the common axletree on which all the spheres revolve.
4. I.e., an angel or intelligence (thought to be the source of motion in each sphere).

FAUST. But is there not *coelum igneum, et crystallinum?*[5]

MEPH. No, Faustus, they be but fables.

FAUST. Resolve me then in this one question: why are not con- 65
junctions, oppositions, aspects, eclipses, all at one time, but in
some years we have more, in some less?

MEPH. *Per inequalem motum respectu totius.*[6]

FAUST. Well, I am answered. Tell me, who made the world?

MEPH. I will not.

FAUST. Sweet Mephistophilis, tell me. 70

MEPH. Move me not, Faustus.

FAUST. Villain, have I not bound thee to tell me anything?

MEPH. Aye, that is not against our kingdom; this is.
Thou art damned; think thou of hell.

FAUST. Think, Faustus, upon God that made the world! 75

MEPH. Remember this! [*Exit.*]

FAUST. Aye, go, accursèd spirit, to ugly hell;
'Tis thou has damned distressèd Faustus' soul.
Is 't too late?
[*Enter* GOOD ANGEL *and* BAD ANGEL.]

B. ANG. Too late. 80

G. ANG. Never too late, if Faustus will repent.

B. ANG. If thou repent, devils will tear thee in pieces.

G. ANG. Repent, and they shall never raze[7] thy skin.
[*Exeunt* ANGELS.]

FAUST. O Christ, my Saviour! my Saviour!
Help to save distressèd Faustus' soul. 85
[*Enter* LUCIFER, BELZEBUB, *and* MEPHISTOPHILIS.]

LUC. Christ cannot save thy soul, for he is just;
There's none but I have interest in the same.

FAUST. O what art thou that lookst so terrible?

LUC. I am Lucifer,
And this is my companion prince in hell. 90

FAUST. O Faustus, they are come to fetch thy soul!

BEL. We are come to tell thee thou dost injure us.

LUC. Thou call'st on Christ, contrary to thy promise.

BEL. Thou shouldst not think on God.

LUC. Think on the devil. 95

BEL. And his dam too.[8]

FAUST. Nor will I henceforth. Pardon me in this,
And Faustus vows never to look to heaven,
Never to name God or pray to him,
To burn his Scriptures, slay his ministers, 100
And make my spirits pull his churches down.

LUC. So shalt thou show thyself an obedient servant, and we will
highly gratify thee for it.

BEL. Faustus, we are come from hell in person to show thee some

---

5. The "heaven of fire" and the "crystalline sphere," introduced by some of
the old authorities to explain the pre-
cession of the equinoxes.
6. "Because of their unequal velocities

within the system."
7. Scratch.
8. "The devil and his dam" was a common colloquial expression.

pastime. Sit down, and thou shalt behold the Seven Deadly 105
Sins appear to thee in their own proper shapes and likeness.

FAUST. That sight will be as pleasant to me as Paradise was to
Adam, the first day of his creation.

LUC. Talk not of Paradise or Creation, but mark the show. Go,
Mephistophilis, fetch them in. 110

[*Enter the* SEVEN DEADLY SINS,[9] *led by a piper.*]

Now, Faustus, question them of their names and dispositions.

FAUST. That shall I soon. What art thou, the first?

PRIDE. I am Pride. I disdain to have any parents. I am like to
Ovid's flea:[1] I can creep into every corner of a wench; sometimes like a periwig I sit upon her brow; next like a necklace 115
I hang about her neck; then like a fan of feathers I kiss her
lips; and then turning myself to a wrought smock[2] do what I
list. But fie, what a smell is here! I'll not speak another word
except the ground be perfumed and covered with cloth of
arras.[3] 120

FAUST. Thou art a proud knave indeed. What art thou, the
second?

COVET. I am Covetousness, begotten of an old churl in a leather
bag; and, might I now obtain my wish, this house, you and
all, should turn to gold, that I might lock you safe into my 125
chest. O my sweet gold!

FAUST. And what art thou, the third?

ENVY. I am Envy, begotten of a chimney-sweeper and an oyster-
wife. I cannot read, and therefore wish all books were burned.
I am lean with seeing others eat. O that there would come a 130
famine over all the world, that all might die, and I live alone;
then thou shouldst see how fat I'd be! But must thou sit and
I stand? Come down, with a vengeance!

FAUST. Out, envious wretch! But what art thou, the fourth?

WRATH. I am Wrath. I had neither father nor mother; I leapt 135
out of a lion's mouth when I was scarce an hour old, and ever
since have run up and down the world with these case of
rapiers, wounding myself when I could get none to fight withal.
I was born in hell; and look to it, for some of you shall be my
father. 140

FAUST. And what art thou, the fifth?

GLUT. I am Gluttony. My parents are all dead, and the devil a
penny they have left me but a small pension, and that buys
me thirty meals a day and ten bevers[4]—a small trifle to suffice
nature. I come of a royal pedigree: my father was a gammon[5] 145
of bacon, and my mother was a hogshead of claret wine. My

---

9. The Seven Deadly Sins are pride,
avarice, gluttony, lust, sloth, envy, and
anger. (They are deadly because other
sins grow out of them.) They were
frequently represented in medieval
plays, sometimes in the rather grimly
comic tone used here; in the old morality plays all the characters, not
merely the sins, were abstractions.

1. A salacious medieval poem *Carmen
de Pulice* ("The Flea") was attributed
to Ovid.
2. A decorated or ornamented petticoat.
3. Arras in Flanders exported fine cloth
used for tapestry hangings.
4. Snacks.
5. The lower side of pork, including
the leg.

godfathers were these: Peter Pickle-herring and Martin Martle-
mas-beef. But my godmother, O, she was a jolly gentlewoman,
and well beloved in every good town and city: her name was
mistress Margery March-beer. Now, Faustus, thou hast heard 150
all my progeny;[6] wilt thou bid me to supper?

FAUST. Not I. Thou wilt eat up all my victuals.

GLUT. Then the devil choke thee!

FAUST. Choke thyself, glutton. What art thou, the sixth?

SLOTH. Heigh ho! I am Sloth. I was begotten on a sunny bank, 155
where I have lain ever since, and you have done me great injury
to bring me from thence; let me be carried thither again by
Gluttony and Lechery. Heigh ho! I'll not speak word more for
a king's ransom.

FAUST. And what are you, mistress minx, the seventh and last? 160

LECHERY. Who, I, sir? I am one that loves an inch of raw mutton[7] better than an ell of fried stockfish, and the first letter
of my name begins with Lechery.

LUC. Away, to hell, away! On, piper![8]

   [*Exeunt the* SINS.]

FAUST. O how this sight doth delight my soul! 165

LUC. Tut, Faustus, in hell is all manner of delight.

FAUST. O might I see hell and return again safe, how happy were
I then!

LUC. Faustus, thou shalt. At midnight I will send for thee. In
meantime peruse this book, and view it throughly, and thou 170
shalt turn thyself into what shape thou wilt.

FAUST. Thanks, mighty Lucifer; this will I keep as chary[9] as my
life.

LUC. Now Faustus, farewell.

FAUST. Farewell, great Lucifer. Come, Mephistophilis. 175

   [*Exeunt* OMNES.]

          SCENE 3

   [*Enter the* CLOWN ⟨ROBIN⟩.]

ROBIN. What, Dick, look to the horses there till I come again.
I have gotten one of Dr. Faustus' conjuring books, and now
we'll have such knavery as 't passes.

   [*Enter* DICK.]

DICK. What, Robin, you must come away and walk the horses.

ROBIN. I walk the horses! I scorn 't, faith: I have other matters 5
in hand; let the horses walk themselves and they will. "A *per
se*[1] a; t, h, e, the; o *per se* o; deny orgon, gorgon." Keep further
from me, O thou illiterate and unlearned hostler.

---

6. Ancestry, lineage.
7. Frequently a word of indecent meaning in Elizabethan English; here it
means the penis. "Ell": 45 inches;
"stockfish": dried cod.
8. The command to the piper who led
the procession of the Deadly Sins onto
the stage to strike up a tune for their

exit.
9. Carefully.
1. "A by itself," a method of reading
the letters of the alphabet taught to
children. Robin's semi-literacy is being
satirized. "Deny orgon, gorgon" is a
parody of Faustus' invocation of Demogorgon in I.iii.

DICK. 'Snails,[2] what has thou got there? a book? Why, thou canst not tell ne'er a word on 't.   10

ROBIN. That thou shalt see presently. Keep out of the circle, I say, lest I send you into the ostry[3] with a vengeance.

DICK. That's like, faith! You had best leave your foolery, for an my master come, he'll conjure you, faith.

ROBIN. My master conjure me! I'll tell thee what; an my master 15
come here, I'll clap as fair a pair of horns on 's head as e'er thou sawest in thy life.[4]

DICK. Thou needst not do that, for my mistress hath done it.

ROBIN. Aye, there be of us here have waded as deep into matters as other men, if they were disposed to talk.   20

DICK. A plague take you! I thought you did not sneak up and down after her for nothing. But I prithee tell me in good sadness, Robin, is that a conjuring book?

ROBIN. Do but speak what thou 't have me do, and I'll do 't. If thou 't dance naked, put off thy clothes, and I'll conjure about 25
thee presently. Or if thou 't but to the tavern with me, I'll give thee white wine, red wine, claret wine, sack, muscadine, malmesey, and whippincrust,[5] hold-belly-hold, and we'll not pay one penny for it.

DICK. O brave! Prithee let's to it presently, for I am as dry as a dog. 30

ROBIN. Come then, let's away.   [*Exeunt.*]

Act III

[*Enter* CHORUS.]
CHO. Learned Faustus,
    To find the secrets of astronomy
    Graven in the book of Jove's high firmament,
    Did mount himself to scale Olympus' top.
    Where sitting in a chariot burning bright   5
    Drawn by the strength of yokéd dragons' necks,
    He views the clouds, the planets, and the stars,
    The tropics, zones, and quarters of the sky
    From the bright circle of the hornéd moon
    Even to the height of *Primum Mobile;*[6]   10
    And whirling round with this circumference
    Within the concave compass of the pole,
    From east to west his dragons swiftly glide
    And in eight days did bring him home again.
    Not long he stayed within his quiet house   15
    To rest his bones after his weary toil
    But new exploits do hale him out again;
    And mounted then upon a dragon's back
    That with his wings did part the subtle air,
    He now is gone to prove cosmography[7]   20

2. I.e., God's nails (on the Cross).
3. Stable.
4. A wife's infidelity was supposed in legend, and in the standard Elizabethan joke, to cause her husband to grow horns.
5. Robin's pronunciation of "hippocras," a spiced wine.
6. The outermost sphere, the empyrean.
7. I.e., to test the accuracy of maps.

That measures coasts and kingdoms of the earth:
And, as I guess, will first arrive at Rome
To see the Pope and manner of his court
And take some part of holy Peter's feast,
The which this day is highly solemnized.   25
　　[*Exit.*]

SCENE 1

[*Enter* FAUSTUS *and* MEPHISTOPHILIS.]
FAUST. Having now, my good Mephistophilis,
　Passed with delight the stately town of Trier[8]
　Environed round with airy mountain tops,
　With walls of flint and deep-entrenchéd lakes,[9]
　Not to be won by any conquering prince;   5
　From Paris next coasting the realm of France,
　We saw the river Maine fall into Rhine,
　Whose banks are set with groves of fruitful vines;
　Then up to Naples, rich Campania,
　With buildings fair and gorgeous to the eye,   10
　Whose streets straight forth and paved with finest brick
　Quarter the town in four equivalents.
　There saw we learned Maro's[1] golden tomb,
　The way he cut, an English mile in length,
　Thorough a rock of stone in one night's space.   15
　From thence to Venice, Padua, and the rest,
　In midst of which a sumptuous temple[2] stands
　That threats the stars with her aspiring top,
　Whose frame is paved with sundry colored stones
　And roofed aloft with curious work in gold.   20
　Thus hitherto hath Faustus spent his time.
　But tell me now, what resting place is this?
　Hast thou, as erst I did command,
　Conducted me within the walls of Rome?
MEPH. I have, my Faustus, and for proof thereof   25
　This is the goodly palace of the Pope,
　And 'cause we are no common guests
　I choose his privy chamber for our use.
FAUST. I hope his Holiness will bid us welcome.
MEPH. All's one, for we'll be bold with his venison.   30
　But now, my Faustus, that thou mayst perceive
　What Rome contains for to delight thine eyes,
　Know that this city stands upon seven hills
　That underprop the groundwork of the same;
　Just through the midst runs flowing Tiber's stream,   35
　With winding banks that cut it in two parts
　Over the which four stately bridges lean

---

8. Treves (in Prussia).
9. Moats.
1. Virgil's. In medieval legend the Roman poet Virgil was considered a magician, and a tunnel ("way") on the
promontory of Posilippo at Naples, near
his tomb, was accredited to his magical
powers.
2. I.e., St. Mark's in Venice.

That make safe passage to each part of Rome.
Upon the bridge called Ponte Angelo
Erected is a castle passing strong,   40
Where thou shalt see such store of ordnance
As that the double cannons forged of brass
Do match the number of the days contained
Within the compass of one complete year;
Besides the gates and high pyramides[3]   45
That Julius Caesar brought from Africa.

FAUST. Now by the kingdoms of infernal rule,
  Of Styx, Acheron, and the fiery lake
  Of ever-burning Phlegethon,[4] I swear
  That I do long to see the monuments   50
  And situation of bright-splendent Rome.
  Come, therefore, let's away.

MEPH. Nay, stay, my Faustus; I know you'd see the Pope
  And take some part of holy Peter's feast,
  The which in state and high solemnity   55
  This day is held through Rome and Italy
  In honor of the Pope's triumphant victory.

FAUST. Sweet Mephistophilis, thou pleasest me;
  Whilst I am here on earth let me be cloyed
  With all things that delight the heart of man.   60
  My four and twenty years of liberty
  I'll spend in pleasure and in dalliance,
  That Faustus' name, whilst this bright frame doth stand,
  May be admiréd through the furthest land.

MEPH. 'Tis well said, Faustus; come then, stand by me   65
  And thou shalt see them come immediately.

FAUST. Nay, stay, my gentle Mephistophilis,
  And grant me my request, and then I go.
  Thou knowst, within the compass of eight days
  We viewed the face of heaven, of earth, of hell;   70
  So high our dragons soared into the air
  That, looking down, the earth appeared to me
  No bigger than my hand in quantity.
  There did we view the kingdoms of the world,
  And what might please mine eye I there beheld.   75
  Then in this show let me an actor be,
  That this proud Pope may Faustus' cunning see.

MEPH. Let it be so, my Faustus, but first stay
  And view their triumphs[5] as they pass this way,
  And then devise what best contents thy mind,   80
  By cunning of thine art to cross the Pope
  Or dash the pride of this solemnity,
  To make his monks and abbots stand like apes
  And point like antics[6] at his triple crown,

3. *Py-rám-i-des,* a singular noun, meaning an obelisk.
4. Classical names for rivers of the underworld; symbolic of hell, they are appropriate as oaths for Faustus.
5. Parades.
6. Grotesque figures.

To beat the beads about the friars' pates   85
Or clap huge horns upon the cardinals' heads,
Or any villainy thou canst devise,
And I'll perform it, Faustus. Hark, they come!
This day shall make thee be admired in Rome.

> [*Enter the* CARDINALS *and* BISHOPS, *some bearing crosiers,
> some the pillars;* MONKS *and* FRIARS *singing their proces-
> sion; then the* POPE *and* RAYMOND, *King of Hungary,
> with* BRUNO *led in chains.*][7]

POPE. Cast down our footstool.

RAY.   Saxon Bruno, stoop,   90
Whilst on thy back his Holiness ascends
St. Peter's chair and state pontifical.

BRUNO. Proud Lucifer, that state belongs to me;
But thus I fall, to Peter, not to thee.

POPE. To me and Peter shalt thou groveling lie   95
And crouch before the papal dignity.
Sound trumpets, then, for thus St. Peter's heir
From Bruno's back ascends St. Peter's chair.

> [*A flourish while he ascends.*]

Thus as the gods creep on with feet of wool
Long ere with iron hands they punish men,   100
So shall our sleeping vengeance now arise
And smite with death thy hated enterprise.
Lord Cardinals of France and Padua,
Go forthwith to our holy consistory
And read among the statutes decretal   105
What, by the holy council held at Trent,[8]
The sacred synod hath decreed for him
That doth assume the papal government
Without election and a true consent.
Away and bring us word with speed.   110

1 CARD. We go, my lord.   [*Exeunt* CARDINALS.]

POPE. Lord Raymond—

FAUST. Go, haste thee, gentle Mephistophilis,
Follow the cardinals to the consistory,
And as they turn their superstitious books,   115
Strike them with sloth and drowsy idleness
And make them sleep so sound that in their shapes
Thyself and I may parley with this Pope,
This proud confronter of the Emperor,[9]
And in despite of all his holiness   120
Restore this Bruno to his liberty

---

7. "Crosiers": crosses borne before prelates; "the pillars" (of silver), however, are known to have been used by only two English cardinals, Wolsey and De la Pole. "Raymond, King of Hungary" is unknown to history. "Bruno" is likewise fictitious; he is the German pretender to the papal throne over whom the Pope has just triumphed (line 57).

8. The famous council of the Catholic Church which lasted from 1545 to 1563.

9. Holy Roman Emperor. Faustus refers to the conflict between the Pope and the Emperor; the former was victorious and captured the Emperor's choice for Pope, "Saxon Bruno."

And bear him to the states of Germany.
MEPH. Faustus, I go.
FAUST.   Dispatch it soon.
  The Pope shall curse that Faustus came to Rome.
    [*Exeunt* FAUSTUS *and* MEPHISTOPHILIS.]
BRUNO. Pope Adrian, let me have some right of law;   125
  I was elected by the Emperor.
POPE. We will depose the Emperor for that deed
  And curse the people that submit to him;
  Both he and thou shalt stand excommunicate
  And interdict from church's privilege   130
  And all society of holy men.
  He grows too proud in his authority,
  Lifting his lofty head above the clouds,
  And like a steeple overpeers the church,
  But we'll pull down his haughty insolence.   135
  And as Pope Alexander,[1] our progenitor,
  Trod on the neck of German Frederick,
  Adding this golden sentence to our praise,
  That Peter's heirs should tread on emperors
  And walk upon the dreadful adder's back,   140
  Treading the lion and the dragon down,
  And fearless spurn the killing basilisk;[2]
  So will we quell that haughty schismatic,
  And by authority apostolical
  Depose him from his regal government.   145
BRUNO. Pope Julius swore to princely Sigismond,
  For him and the succeeding popes of Rome,
  To hold the emperors their lawful lords.
POPE. Pope Julius did abuse the church's rights,
  And therefore none of his decrees can stand.   150
  Is not all power on earth bestowed on us?
  And therefore though we would we cannot err.
  Behold this silver belt, whereto is fixed
  Seven golden keys fast sealed with seven seals
  In token of our sevenfold power from heaven,   155
  To bind or loose, lock fast, condemn, or judge,
  Resign or seal, or whatso pleaseth us.
  Then he and thou and all the world shall stoop,
  Or be assuréd of our dreadful curse
  To light as heavy as the pains of hell.   160
    [*Enter* FAUSTUS *and* MEPHISTOPHILIS *like cardinals.*]
MEPH. Now tell me, Faustus, are we not fitted well?
FAUST. Yes, Mephistophilis, and two such cardinals
  Ne'er served a holy pope as we shall do.
  But whilst they sleep within the consistory
  Let us salute his reverend Fatherhood.   165
RAY. Behold, my lord, the cardinals are returned.

1. Pope Alexander III (1159–81) com-   2. A mythical monster capable of kill-
pelled the **Emperor Frederick Barba-**   ing by a look.
rossa to submit to him.

POPE. Welcome, grave fathers, answer presently;[3]
    What have our holy council there decreed
    Concerning Bruno and the Emperor
    In quittance of their late conspiracy   170
    Against our state and papal dignity?
FAUST. Most sacred patron of the church of Rome,
    By full consent of all the synod
    Of priests and prelates it is thus decreed:
    That Bruno and the German Emperor   175
    Be held as lollards[4] and bold schismatics
    And proud disturbers of the church's peace.
    And if that Bruno by his own assent,
    Without enforcement of the German peers,
    Did seek to wear the triple diadem   180
    And by your death to climb St. Peter's chair,
    The statutes decretal have thus decreed:
    He shall be straight condemned of heresy
    And on a pile of fagots burned to death.
POPE. It is enough. Here, take him to your charge   185
    And bear him straight to Ponte Angelo,
    And in the strongest tower enclose him fast.
    Tomorrow, sitting in our consistory
    With all our college of grave cardinals,
    We will determine of his life or death.   190
    Here, take his triple crown along with you
    And leave it in the church's treasury.
    Make haste again, my good lord cardinals,
    And take our blessing apostolical.
MEPH. So, so. Was never devil thus blessed before!   195
FAUST. Away, sweet Mephistophilis, be gone;
    The cardinals will be plagued for this anon.
        [*Exeunt* FAUSTUS *and* MEPHISTOPHILIS *with* BRUNO.]
POPE. Go presently and bring a banquet forth,
    That we may solemnize St. Peter's feast
    And with Lord Raymond, King of Hungary,   200
    Drink to our late and happy victory.   [*Exeunt.*]

SCENE 2

    [*The banquet is brought in, and then enter* FAUSTUS *and*
    MEPHISTOPHILIS *in their own shapes.*]
MEPH. Now Faustus, come prepare thyself for mirth;
    The sleepy cardinals are hard at hand
    To censure Bruno, that is posted hence
    And on a proud-paced steed as swift as thought
    Flies o'er the Alps to fruitful Germany,   5
    There to salute the woeful Emperor.
FAUST. The Pope will curse them for their sloth today
    That slept both Bruno and his crown away.

---

3. Immediately.
4. Protestants, usually English follow-   ers of Wycliffe, the 14th-century religious reformer.

But now, that Faustus may delight his mind
And by their folly make some merriment,   10
Sweet Mephistophilis, so charm me here
That I may walk invisible to all
And do whate'er I please unseen of any.
MEPH. Faustus, thou shalt; then kneel down presently,
    Whilst on thy head I lay my hand   15
    And charm thee with this magic wand.
    First wear this girdle, then appear
    Invisible to all are here.
    The planets seven, the gloomy air,
    Hell, and the Furies' forkéd hair,   20
    Pluto's blue fire and Hecate's[5] tree
    With magic spells so compass thee
    That no eye may thy body see.
    So, Faustus, now, for all their holiness,
    Do what thou wilt thou shalt not be discerned.   25
FAUST. Thanks, Mephistophilis. Now friars, take heed
    Lest Faustus make your shaven crowns to bleed.
MEPH. Faustus, no more; see where the cardinals come.
    [*Enter* POPE *and all the lords, with* KING RAYMOND *and
    the* ARCHBISHOP OF RHEIMS. *Enter the two* CARDINALS
    with a book.]
POPE. Welcome, lord cardinals; come, sit down.
    Lord Raymond, take your seat. Friars, attend,   30
    And see that all things be in readiness
    As best beseems this solemn festival.
1 CARD. First may it please your sacred holiness
    To view the sentence of the reverend synod
    Concerning Bruno and the Emperor.   35
POPE. What needs this question? Did I not tell you
    Tomorrow we would sit i' th' consistory
    And there determine of his punishment?
    You brought us word, even now, it was decreed
    That Bruno and the curséd Emperor   40
    Were by the holy council both condemned
    For loathéd lollards and base schismatics;
    Then wherefore would you have me view that book?
1 CARD. Your Grace mistakes; you gave us no such charge.
RAY. Deny it not; we all are witnesses   45
    That Bruno here was late delivered you,
    With his rich triple crown to be reserved
    And put into the church's treasury
BOTH CARD. By holy Paul we saw them not.
POPE. By Peter, you shall die   50
    Unless you bring them forth immediately.

---

5. The goddess of magic and witch-craft, whose name the Elizabethans pronounced *Héc-at*. She is not known to have any special "tree"; the word may be a mistake for "three," since she was often represented as a triple god-dess—of heaven, earth, and hell.

Hale them to prison! Lade their limbs with gyves![6]
False prelates, for this hateful treachery,
Cursed be your souls to hellish misery. [*Exeunt* CARDINALS.]
FAUST. So they are safe. Now, Faustus, to the feast;   55
The Pope had never such a frolic guest.
POPE. Lord Archbishop of Rheims, sit down with us.
ARCH. I thank your Holiness.
FAUST. Fall to! The devil choke you an you spare!
POPE. Who's that spoke? Friars, look about.   60
Lord Raymond, pray fall to. I am beholden
To the Bishop of Milan for this so rare a present.
FAUST. I thank you, sir.
        [FAUSTUS *snatches the meat from the* POPE.]
POPE. How now! Who snatched the meat from me? Villains,
why speak you not?   65
FRIAR. Here's nobody, if it like your Holiness.
POPE. My good Lord Archbishop, here's a most dainty dish
Was sent me from a cardinal in France.
FAUST. I'll have that, too.
        [FAUSTUS *snatches the dish from the* POPE.]
POPE. What lollards do attend our Holiness   70
That we receive such great indignity?
Fetch me some wine.
FAUST. Aye, pray do, for Faustus is adry.
POPE. Lord Raymond, I drink unto your Grace.
FAUST. I pledge your Grace.   75
        [FAUSTUS *snatches the cup from the* POPE.]
POPE. My wine gone, too? Ye lubbers, look about
And find the man that doth this villainy,
Or by my sanctitude you all shall die.
I pray, my lords, have patience at this troublesome banquet.
ARCH. Please your Holiness, I think it be some ghost crept out of   80
purgatory and now is come unto your Holiness for his pardon.
POPE. It may be so;
Go then, command our priests to sing a dirge
To lay the fury of this same troublesome ghost.
Once again, my lord, fall to.   85
        [*The* POPE *crosses himself.*]
FAUST. How now!
Must every bit be spicéd with a cross?
Well, use that trick no more, I would advise you.
        [*The* POPE *crosses himself.*]
Well, there's the second time; aware the third;
I give you fair warning.   90
        [*The* POPE *crosses himself again.*]
Nay then, take that!
        [FAUSTUS *hits the* POPE *a box on the ear.*]
POPE. O, I am slain! Help me, my lords!
O come and help to bear my body hence!

6. I.e., load their limbs with prisoners' shackles.

Damned be his soul forever for this deed.
   [*Exeunt the* POPE *and his train.*]
MEPH. Now Faustus, what will you do now? For I can tell you 95
  you'll be cursed with bell, book, and candle.[7]
FAUST. Bell, book, and candle; candle, book, and bell
  Forward and backward, to curse Faustus to hell!
   [*Enter all the* FRIARS *with bell, book, and candle to sing
   the dirge.*]
FRIAR. Come, brethren, let's about our business with good devo-
tion.   100
   [ALL *sing this:*]
  Cursèd be he that stole away his Holiness' meat from the
  table—*maledicat dominus!*[8]
  Cursèd be he that struck his Holiness a blow on the face—
  maledicat dominus!
  Cursèd be he that took Friar Sandelo a blow on the face— 105
  maledicat dominus!
  Cursèd be he that disturbeth our holy dirge—*maledicat dominus!*
  Cursèd be he that took away his Holiness' wine—*maledicat
  dominus! Et omnes sancti!*[9] Amen.   110
   [FAUSTUS *and* MEPHISTOPHILIS *beat the* FRIARS, *and fling
  fireworks among them, and so exeunt.*]

SCENE 3

   [*Enter* CLOWN ⟨ROBIN⟩ *and* DICK *with a cup.*]
DICK. Sirrah Robin, we were best look that your devil can answer
  the stealing of this same cup, for the vintner's boy follows us
  at the hard heels.
ROBIN. 'Tis no matter, let him come! An he follow us I'll so con-
  jure him as he was never conjured in his life, I warrant him. 5
  Let me see the cup.
   [*Enter* VINTNER.]
DICK. Here 'tis. Yonder he comes. Now, Robin, now or never
  show thy cunning.
VINT. O, are you here? I am glad I have found you. You are a
  couple of fine companions! Pray, where's the cup you stole 10
  from the tavern?
ROBIN. How, how? We steal a cup? Take heed what you say! We
  look not like cup-stealers, I can tell you.
VINT. Never deny it, for I know you have it, and I'll search you.
ROBIN. Search me? Aye, and spare not. Hold the cup, Dick! 15
  Come, come; search me, search me.
VINT. Come on, sirrah, let me search you now.
DICK. Aye, aye, do; do. Hold the cup, Robin. I fear not your
  searching. We scorn to steal your cups, I can tell you.
VINT. Never outface me for the matter, for sure the cup is be- 20
  tween you two.

---

7. The traditional paraphernalia for
cursing and excommunication.

8. "May the Lord curse him!"
9. And all saints (also curse him).

ROBIN. Nay, there you lie. 'Tis beyond us both.

VINT. A plague take you! I thought 'twas your knavery to take it
away. Come, give it me again.

ROBIN. Aye, much! When, can you tell?[1] Dick, make me a circle, 25
and stand close at my back and stir not for thy life. Vintner,
you shall have your cup anon. Say nothing, Dick. O *per se* O;
Demogorgon, Belcher and Mephistophilis!

    [*Enter* MEPHISTOPHILIS.]

MEPH. Monarch of hell, under whose black survey
  Great potentates do kneel with awful fear, 30
  Upon whose altars thousand souls do lie,
  How am I vexéd with these villains' charms!
  From Constantinople am I hither brought
  Only for pleasure of these damnéd slaves.   [*Exit* VINTNER.]

ROBIN. By Lady, sir, you have had a shrewd journey of it; will it 35
please you to take a shoulder of mutton to supper and a tester[2]
in your purse, and go back again?

DICK. Aye, I pray you heartily, sir; for we called you but in jest,
I promise you.

MEPH. To purge the rashness of this curséd deed, 40
  First be thou turnéd to this ugly shape:
  For apish deeds transforméd to an ape.

ROBIN. O brave! an ape! I pray, sir, let me have the carrying of
him about to show some tricks.

MEPH. And so thou shalt. Be thou transformed to a dog and 45
carry him upon thy back. Away! Be gone!

ROBIN. A dog! That's excellent! Let the maids look well to their
porridge pots, for I'll into the kitchen presently. Come, Dick,
come.

    [*Exit* ROBIN *and* DICK.]

MEPH. Now with the flames of ever-burning fire 50
  I'll wing myself and forthwith fly amain
  Unto my Faustus, to the Great Turk's court.   [*Exit.*]

Act IV

    [*Enter* CHORUS.]

CHO. When Faustus had with pleasure ta'en the view
  Of rarest things and royal courts of kings,
  He stayed his course and so returnéd home,
  Where such as bear his absence but with grief,
  I mean his friends and nearest companións, 5
  Did gratulate his safety with kind words,
  And in their conference of what befell
  Touching his journey through the world and air,
  They put forth questions of astrology
  Which Faustus answered with such learned skill 10
  As they admired and wondered at his wit.
  Now is his fame spread forth in every land:

---

1. A common Elizabethan scornful re-   2. Sixpence.
tort.

Amongst the rest the Emperor is one,
Carolus the Fifth,[3] at whose palace now
Faustus is feasted 'mongst his noblemen.   15
What there he did in trial of his art
I leave untold, your eyes shall see performed.   [*Exit.*]

SCENE 1

[*Enter* MARTINO *and* FREDERICK *at several doors.*[4]]

MART. What ho! Officers, gentlemen!
  Hie to the presence to attend the Emperor.
  Good Frederick, see the rooms be voided straight;
  His Majesty is coming to the hall.
  Go back, and see the state in readiness.   5
FRED. But where is Bruno, our elected Pope,
  That on a fury's back came post from Rome?
  Will not his Grace consort[5] the Emperor?
MART. O yes, and with him comes the German conjurer,
  The learned Faustus, fame of Wittenberg,   10
  The wonder of the world for magic art;
  And he intends to show great Carolus
  The race of all his stout progenitors
  And bring in presence of his majesty
  The royal shapes and warlike semblances   15
  Of Alexander and his beauteous paramour.[6]
FRED. Where is Benvolio?
MART. Fast asleep, I warrant you;
  He took his rouse with stoups[7] of Rhenish wine
  So kindly yesternight to Bruno's health   20
  That all this day the sluggard keeps his bed.
FRED. See, see; his window's ope; we'll call to him.
MART. What ho, Benvolio!

  [*Enter* BENVOLIO *above at a window, in his nightcap,
  buttoning.*]

BENV. What a devil ail you two?
MART. Speak softly, sir, lest the devil hear you;   25
  For Faustus at the court is late arrived
  And at his heels a thousand furies wait
  To accomplish whatsoever the Doctor please.
BENV. What of this?
MART. Come, leave thy chamber first and thou shalt see   30
  This conjurer perform such rare exploits
  Before the Pope[8] and royal Emperor
  As never yet was seen in Germany.
BENV. Has not the Pope enough of conjuring yet?
  He was upon the devil's back late enough,   35
  And if he be so far in love with him
  I would he would post home to Rome with him again.

3. I.e., Emperor Charles V (1519–56). Thaïs.
4. I.e., at different entrances.   7. Drank many full glasses.
5. Accompany.   8. Bruno.
6. Alexander the Great and his mistress

FRED. Speak, wilt thou come and see this sport?

BENV. Not I.

MART. Wilt thou stand in thy window and see it, then? 40

BENV. Aye, and I fall not asleep i' th' meantime.

MART. The Emperor is at hand, who comes to see
What wonders by black spells may compassed be.

BENV. Well, go you to the Emperor. I am content for this once
to thrust my head out a window, for they say if a man be drunk 45
overnight the devil cannot hurt him in the morning. If that be
true, I have a charm in my head shall control him as well as the
conjurer, I warrant you.

> [*Exit* MARTINO *and* FREDERICK.]

SCENE 2

> [*A sennet.*[9] *Enter* CHARLES THE GERMAN EMPEROR, BRUNO,
> *the* DUKE OF SAXONY, FAUSTUS, MEPHISTOPHILIS, FRED-
> ERICK, MARTINO *and* ATTENDANTS. BENVOLIO *remains at
> his window.*]

EMP. Wonder of men, renowned magician,
Thrice-learned Faustus, welcome to our court.
This deed of thine, in setting Bruno free
From his and our professéd enemy,
Shall add more excellence unto thine art 5
Than if by powerful necromantic spells
Thou couldst command the world's obedience.
Forever be beloved of Carolus;
And if this Bruno thou hast late redeemed
In peace possess the triple diadem 10
And sit in Peter's chair despite of chance,
Thou shalt be famous through all Italy
And honored of the German Emperor.

FAUST. These gracious words, most royal Carolus,
Shall make poor Faustus to his utmost power 15
Both love and serve the German Emperor
And lay his life at holy Bruno's feet.
For proof whereof, if so your Grace be pleased,
The Doctor stands prepared by power of art
To cast his magic charms that shall pierce through 20
The ebon gates of ever-burning hell
And hale the stubborn furies from their caves
To compass whatsoe'er your Grace commands.

BENV. [*aside*] Blood! He speaks terribly, but for all that I do not
greatly believe him. He looks as like a conjurer as the Pope to 25
a costermonger.[1]

EMP. Then Faustus, as thou late didst promise us,
We would behold that famous conqueror,
Great Alexander and his paramour,
In their true shapes and state majestical, 30
That we may wonder at their excellence.

9. A trumpet signal.　　　　　1. Fruitseller.

FAUST. Your Majesty shall see them presently.
Mephistophilis, away!
And with a solemn noise of trumpets' sound
Present before this royal Emperor   35
Great Alexander and his beauteous paramour.
MEPH. Faustus, I will.   [*Exit.*]
BENV. [*aside*] Well, master Doctor, an your devils come not away
quickly, you shall have me asleep presently. Zounds, I could eat
myself for anger to think I have been such an ass all this while   40
to stand gaping after the devil's governor, and can see nothing.
FAUST. [*aside*] I'll make you feel something anon if my art fail me
not.—
My lord, I must forewarn your Majesty
That when my spirits present the royal shapes   45
Of Alexander and his paramour,
Your Grace demand no questions of the King,
But in dumb silence let them come and go.
EMP. Be it as Faustus please; we are content.
BENV. [*aside*] Aye, Aye, and I am content, too. And thou bring   50
Alexander and his paramour before the Emperor, I'll be Ac-
taeon[2] and turn myself into a stag.
FAUST. [*aside*] And I'll play Diana and send you the horns pres-
ently.
    [*Sennet. Enter at one door the emperor* ALEXANDER, *at the
    other* DARIUS. *They meet;* DARIUS *is thrown down;* ALEX-
    ANDER *kills him, takes off his crown and, offering to go
    out, his* PARAMOUR *meets him; he embraceth her and sets*
    DARIUS' *crown upon her head and, coming back, both
    salute the* EMPEROR, *who, leaving his state,[3] offers to em-
    brace them, which* FAUSTUS *seeing, suddenly stays him.
    Then trumpets cease and music sounds.*]
FAUST. My gracious lord, you do forget yourself;   55
These are but shadows, not substantial.
EMP. O pardon me; my thoughts are ravished so
With sight of this renownéd Emperor
That in mine arms I would have compassed him.
But Faustus, since I may not speak to them   60
To satisfy my longing thoughts at full,
Let me this tell thee: I have heard it said
That this fair lady, whilst she lived on earth,
Had on her neck a little wart or mole.
How may I prove that saying to be true?   65
FAUST. Your Majesty may boldly go and see.
EMP. Faustus, I see it plain;
And in this sight thou better pleasest me
Than if I gained another monarchy.
FAUST. Away, be gone!   [*Exit* SHOW.] 70
See, see, my gracious lord, what strange beast is yon, that

2. The hunter of classical legend who   into a stag and pursued by his own
happened to see the goddess Diana   hounds.
bathing. In punishment he was changed   3. Throne.

thrusts its head out at the window!

EMP. O wondrous sight! See, Duke of Saxony, two spreading horns most strangely fastened upon the head of young Benvolio.

SAX. What, is he asleep, or dead? 75

FAUST. He sleeps, my lord, but dreams not of his horns.

EMP. This sport is excellent. We'll call and wake him. What ho! Benvolio!

BENV. A plague upon you! Let me sleep a while. 80

EMP. I blame thee not to sleep, much, having such a head of thine own.

SAX. Look up, Benvolio. 'Tis the Emperor calls.

BENV. The Emperor! Where? O zounds, my head!

EMP. Nay, and thy horns hold 'tis no matter for thy head, for 85 that's armed sufficiently.

FAUST. Why, how now, sir knight! What, hanged by the horns? This is most horrible. Fie, fie! Pull in your head, for shame! Let not all the world wonder at you.

BENV. Zounds, Doctor, is this your villainy? 90

FAUST. O, say not so, sir. The Doctor has no skill,
No art, no cunning to present these lords
Or bring before this royal Emperor
The mighty monarch, warlike Alexander?
If Faustus do it, you are straight resolved 95
In bold Actaeon's shape to turn a stag?
And therefore, my lord, so please your Majesty,
I'll raise a kennel of hounds shall hunt him so
As all his footmanship shall scarce prevail
To keep his carcass from their bloody fangs. 100
Ho, Belimote, Argiron, Asterote!

BENV. Hold, hold! Zounds, he'll raise up a kennel of devils, I think, anon. Good my lord, entreat for me. 'Sblood, I am never able to endure these torments.

EMP. Then good master Doctor, 105
Let me entreat you to remove his horns;
He has done penance now sufficiently.

FAUST. My gracious lord, not so much for injury done to me, as to delight your Majesty with some mirth, hath Faustus justly requited this injurious knight; which, being all I desire, I am 110 content to remove his horns.—Mephistophilis, transform him. —And hereafter, sir, look you speak well of scholars.

BENV. [*aside*] Speak well of ye! 'Sblood, and scholars be such cuckoldmakers to clap horns of honest men's heads o' this order, I'll ne'er trust smooth faces and small ruffs[4] more. But an 115 I be not revenged for this, would I might be turned to a gaping oyster and drink nothing but salt water!

EMP. Come, Faustus. While the Emperor lives,
In recompense of this thy high desert,

4. I.e., scholars, who were often smooth-shaven and did not wear the large "ruffs" (collars) of courtiers. But Faustus has a beard; see the next scene.

Thou shalt command the state of Germany 120
And live beloved of mighty Carolus. [*Exeunt* OMNES.]

SCENE 3

[*Enter* BENVOLIO, MARTINO, FREDERICK, *and* SOLDIERS.]

MART. Nay, sweet Benvolio, let us sway thy thoughts
From this attempt against the conjurer.
BENV. Away! You love me not to urge me thus.
Shall I let slip so great an injury
When every servile groom jests at my wrongs 5
And in their rustic gambols proudly say,
"Benvolio's head was graced with horns today"?
O, may these eyelids never close again
Till with my sword I have that conjurer slain.
If you will aid me in this enterprise, 10
Then draw your weapons and be resolute;
If not, depart. Here will Benvolio die,
But Faustus' death shall quit[5] my infamy.
FRED. Nay, we will stay with thee, betide what may,
And kill that Doctor if he come this way. 15
BENV. Then gentle Frederick, hie thee to the grove
And place our servants and our followers
Close in an ambush there behind the trees.
By this I know the conjurer is near;
I saw him kneel and kiss the Emperor's hand 20
And take his leave laden with rich rewards.
Then, soldiers, boldly fight. If Faustus die,
Take you the wealth, leave us the victory.
FRED. Come, soldiers, follow me unto the grove;
Who kills him shall have gold and endless love. 25
[*Exit* FREDERICK *with the* SOLDIERS.]
BENV. My head is lighter than it was by th' horns,
But yet my heart's more ponderous than my head
And pants until I see that conjurer dead.
MART. Where shall we place ourselves, Benvolio?
BENV. Here will we stay to bide the first assault. 30
O, were that damnéd hell-hound but in place
Thou soon shouldst see me quit my foul disgrace.
[*Enter* FREDERICK.]
FRED. Close, close! The hated conjurer is at hand
And all alone comes walking in his gown;
Be ready then and strike the peasant down. 35
BENV. Mine be that honor then. Now, sword, strike home!
For horns he gave I'll have his head anon.
[*Enter* FAUSTUS *wearing a false head.*]
MART. See, see, he comes.
BENV.   No words; this blow ends all;
Hell take his soul, his body thus must fall.
FAUST. O! 40

5. Avenge.

FRED. Groan you, master Doctor?

BENV. Break may his heart with groans. Dear Frederick, see
    Thus will I end his griefs immediately.
        [*Cuts off the false head.*]

MART. Strike with a willing hand! His head is off.

BENV. The devil's dead; the furies now may laugh.   45

FRED. Was this that stern aspect, that awful frown,
    Made the grim monarch of infernal spirits
    Tremble and quake at his commanding charms?

MART. Was this that damnéd head whose art conspired
    Benvolio's shame before the Emperor?   50

BENV. Aye, that's the head, and here the body lies
    Justly rewarded for his villainies.

FRED. Come, let's devise how we may add more shame
    To the black scandal of his hated name.

BENV. First, on his head, in quittance of my wrongs,   55
    I'll nail huge forkéd horns and let them hang
    Within the window where he yoked me first,
    That all the world may see my just revenge.

MART. What use shall we put his beard to?

BENV. We'll sell it to a chimney-sweeper; it will wear out ten   60
    birchen brooms, I warrant you.

FRED. What shall his eyes do?

BENV. We'll pull out his eyes, and they shall serve for buttons to
    his lips to keep his tongue from catching cold.

MART. An excellent policy. And now, sirs, having divided him,   65
    what shall the body do?
        [FAUSTUS *rises.*]

BENV. Zounds, the devil's alive again!

FRED. Give him his head, for God's sake!

FAUST. Nay, keep it. Faustus will have heads and hands,
    Aye, all your hearts, to recompense this deed.   70
    Knew you not, traitors, I was limited
    For four and twenty years to breathe on earth?
    And had you cut my body with your swords
    Or hewed this flesh and bones as small as sand,
    Yet in a minute had my spirit returned   75
    And I had breathed a man made free from harm.
    But wherefore do I dally my revenge?
    Asteroth, Belimoth, Mephistophilis!
        [*Enter* MEPHISTOPHILIS *and other* DEVILS.]
    Go, horse these traitors on your fiery backs
    And mount aloft with them as high as heaven,   80
    Then pitch them headlong to the lowest hell.
    Yet stay, the world shall see their misery,
    And hell shall after plague their treachery.
    Go, Belimoth, and take this caitiff[6] hence
    And hurl him in some lake of mud and dirt;   85
    Take thou this other, drag him through the woods

6. Wretch.

Amongst the pricking thorns and sharpest briars,
Whilst with my gentle Mephistophilis
This traitor flies unto some steepy rock
That rolling down may break the villain's bones   90
As he intended to dismember me.
Fly hence, dispatch my charge immediately.
FRED. Pity us, gentle Faustus; save our lives!
FAUST. Away!
FRED. He must needs go that the devil drives.   95
                    [*Exeunt* SPIRITS *with the* KNIGHTS.]
        [*Enter the ambushed* SOLDIERS.]
1 SOLD. Come, sirs, prepare yourselves in readiness;
Make haste to help these noble gentlemen;
I heard them parley with the conjurer.
2 SOLD. See where he comes; dispatch, and kill the slave!
FAUST. What's here? An ambush to betray my life?   100
Then, Faustus, try thy skill. Base peasants, stand!
For lo, these trees remove at my command
And stand as bulwarks 'twixt yourselves and me
To shield me from your hated treachery;
Yet to encounter this, your weak attempt,   105
Behold an army comes incontinent.[7]
        [FAUSTUS *strikes the door, and enter a* DEVIL *playing on a
        drum; after him another bearing an ensign, and divers
        with weapons;* MEPHISTOPHILIS *with fireworks. They set
        upon the* SOLDIERS *and drive them out. Exeunt.*]

SCENE 4

        [*Enter at several doors* BENVOLIO, FREDERICK, *and* MAR-
        TINO, *their heads and faces bloody and besmeared with
        mud and dirt, all having horns on their heads.*]
MART. What ho, Benvolio!
BENV. Here! What, Frederick, ho!
FRED. O help me, gentle friend. Where is Martino?
MART. Dear Frederick, here—
Half smothered in a lake of mud and dirt   5
Through which the furies dragged me by the heels.
FRED. Martino, see! Benvolio's horns again.
MART. O misery! How now, Benvolio!
BENV. Defend me, heaven! Shall I be haunted still?
MART. Nay, fear not, man; we have no power to kill.   10
BENV. My friends transforméd thus! O hellish spite!
Your heads are all set with horns.
FRED. You hit it right;
It is your own you mean; feel on your head.
BENV. Zounds, horns again!   15
MART. Nay, chafe not, man; we are all sped.[8]
BENV. What devil attends this damned magician
That spite of spite our wrongs are doubléd?

7. Immediately.   8. Don't fret, man, we are all done for.

FRED. What may we do that we may hide our shames?

BENV. If we should follow him to work revenge, 20
 He'd join long asses' ears to those huge horns
 And make us laughingstocks to all the world.

MART. What shall we then do, dear Benvolio?

BENV. I have a castle joining near these woods,
 And thither we'll repair and live obscure 25
 Till time shall alter this our brutish shapes.
 Sith black disgrace hath thus eclipsed our fame,
 We'll rather die with grief than live with shame.

[Exeunt OMNES.]

SCENE 5

[Enter FAUSTUS and the HORSE-COURSER.⁹]

HOR. I beseech your Worship, accept of these forty dollars.¹

FAUST. Friend, thou canst not buy so good a horse for so small a
 price. I have no great need to sell him, but if thou likest him
 for ten dollars more, take him, because I see thou hast a good
 mind to him. 5

HOR. I beseech you, sir, accept of this; I am a very poor man and
 have lost very much of late by horseflesh, and this bargain will
 set me up again.

FAUST. Well, I will not stand with thee; give me the money. Now,
 sirrah, I must tell you that you may ride him o'er hedge and 10
 ditch and spare him not; but—do you hear?—in any case ride
 him not into the water.

HOR. How, sir, not into the water? Why, will he not drink of all
 waters?

FAUST. Yes, he will drink of all waters, but ride him not into the 15
 water; o'er hedge and ditch or where thou wilt, but not into the
 water. Go bid the hostler deliver him unto you, and remember
 what I say.

HOR. I warrant you, sir. O joyful day! Now am I a made man forever.
 [Exit.] 20

FAUST. What art thou, Faustus, but a man condemned to die?
 Thy fatal time draws to a final end;
 Despair doth drive distrust into my thoughts.
 Confound these passions with a quiet sleep.
 Tush, Christ did call the thief upon the cross;² 25
 Then rest thee, Faustus, quiet in conceit.

[He sits to sleep in his chair.]
 [Enter the HORSE-COURSER wet.]

HOR. O, what a cozening Doctor was this! I riding my horse into
 the water, thinking some hidden mystery had been in the horse,
 I had nothing under me but a little straw, and had much ado
 to escape drowning. Well, I'll go rouse him and make him give 30

9. Horse-trader, traditionally a sharp bargainer or cheat.
1. Common German coins; the word originally comes from the German *Joachimsthaler.*
2. In Luke xxiii.39–43 one of the two thieves crucified with Jesus is promised Paradise. "In conceit": in mind.

me my forty dollars again. Ho! sirrah Doctor, you cozening
scab! Master Doctor, awake and arise, and give me my money
again, for your horse is turned to a bottle[3] of hay. Master Doctor—

    [*He pulls off his leg.*]

    Alas, I am undone! What shall I do? I have pulled off his leg. 35

FAUST. O help! Help! The villain hath murdered me!

HOR. Murder or not murder, now he has but one leg I'll outrun
him and cast this leg into some ditch or other.

    [*Exit.*]

FAUST. Stop him, stop him, stop him! Ha ha ha! Faustus hath his
leg again, and the horse-courser a bundle of hay for his forty 40
dollars.

    [*Enter* WAGNER.]

FAUST. How now, Wagner! What news with thee?

WAG. If it please you, the Duke of Vanholt doth earnestly entreat
your company and hath sent some of his men to attend you
with provision fit for your journey. 45

FAUST. The Duke of Vanholt's an honorable gentleman, and one
to whom I must be no niggard of my cunning. Come, away!

SCENE 6

    [*Enter* ROBIN, DICK, HORSE-COURSER, *and a* CARTER.]

CART. Come, my masters, I'll bring you to the best beer in Europe— What ho, Hostess!—Where be these whores?[4]

    [*Enter* HOSTESS.]

HOST. How now! What lack you? What, my old guests, welcome.

ROBIN. Sirrah Dick, dost thou know why I stand so mute?

DICK. No, Robin, why is 't? 5

ROBIN. I am eighteen pence on the score,[5] but say nothing; see if
she have forgotten me.

HOST. Who's this that stands so solemnly by himself? What, my
old guest!

ROBIN. O, hostess, how do you do? I hope my score stands still. 10

HOST. Aye, there's no doubt of that, for methinks you make no
haste to wipe it out.

DICK. Why, hostess, I say, fetch us some beer.

HOST. You shall presently; look up into th' hall. There, ho!

    [*Exit.*]

DICK. Come, sirs; what shall we do now till mine hostess comes? 15

CART. Marry, sir, I'll tell you the bravest tale how a conjurer
served me. You know Dr. Faustus?

HOR. Aye, a plague take him! Here's some on 's have cause to
know him. Did he conjure thee too?

CART. I'll tell you how he served me. As I was going to Witten- 20
berg t' other day, he met me and asked me what he should give
me for as much hay as he could eat. Now, sir, I, thinking that
a little would serve his turn, bade him take as much as he

---

3. Bundle.
4. I.e., the hostess and maids of the
inn.
5. Charged, not paid for.

would for three farthings. So he presently gave me my money and fell to eating; and, as I am a cursen man, he never left eat- 25 ing till he had eat up all my load of hay.

ALL. O monstrous; eat a whole load of hay!

ROBIN. Yes, yes; that may be, for I have heard of one that has eat a load of logs.[6]

HOR. Now, sirs, you shall hear now villainously he served me. I 30 went to him yesterday to buy a horse of him, and he would by no means sell him under forty dollars. So, sir, because I knew him to be such a horse as would run over hedge and ditch and never tire, I gave him his money. So, when I had my horse, Dr. Faustus bade me ride him night and day and spare him no 35 time; "But," quoth he, "in any case ride him not into the water." Now sir, I thinking the horse had had some quality that he would not have me know of, what did I but ride him into a great river, and when I came just in the midst my horse vanished away and I sat straddling upon a bottle of hay. 40

ALL. O brave Doctor!

HOR. But you shall hear how bravely I served him for it. I went me home to his house, and there I found him asleep; I kept a hallowing and whooping in his ears, but all could not wake him. I seeing that, took him by the leg and never rested pull- 45 ing till I had pulled me his leg quite off, and now 'tis at home in mine hostry.[7]

DICK. And has the Doctor but one leg then? That's excellent, for one of his devils turned me into the likeness of an ape's face.

CART. Some more drink, hostess! 50

ROBIN. Hark you, we'll into another room and drink awhile, and then we'll go seek out the Doctor.

[*Exeunt* OMNES.]

SCENE 7

[*Enter the* DUKE OF VANHOLT, *his* DUCHESS, FAUSTUS, *and* MEPHISTOPHILIS.]

DUKE. Thanks, master Doctor, for these pleasant sights; nor know I how sufficiently to recompense your great deserts in erecting that enchanted castle in the air, the sight whereof so delighted me as nothing in the world could please me more.

FAUST. I do think myself, my good lord, highly recompensed that 5 it pleaseth your Grace to think but well of that which Faustus hath performed. But gracious lady, it may be that you have taken no pleasure in those sights; therefore I pray you tell me what is the thing you most desire to have; be it in the world it shall be yours. I have heard that great-bellied women do long 10 for things that are rare and dainty.

DUCH. True, master Doctor, and since I find you so kind, I will make known unto you what my heart desires to have; and were it now summer, as it is January, a dead time of winter, I would

6. Comic expression for being drunk   7. Inn.
—to carry a jag (or load) of logs.

request no better meat than a dish of ripe grapes. 15

FAUST. This is but a small matter.—Go, Mephistophilis, away!—
  [*Exit* MEPHISTOPHILIS.]
  Madam, I will do more than this for your content.
  [*Enter* MEPHISTOPHILIS *again with the grapes.*]
  Here, now taste ye these; they should be good, for they come
  from a far country, I can tell you.

DUKE. This makes me wonder more than all the rest, that at this 20
  time of year, when every tree is barren of his fruit, from whence
  you had these ripe grapes.

FAUST. Please it your Grace, the year is divided into two circles
  over the whole world, so that when it is winter with us, in the
  contrary circle it is likewise summer with them, as in India, 25
  Saba,[8] and such countries that lie far east, where they have
  fruit twice a year. From whence, by means of a swift spirit that
  I have, I had these grapes brought as you see.

DUCH. And trust me they are the sweetest grapes that e'er I tasted.
  [*The* CLOWNS *bounce*[9] *at the gate within.*]

DUKE. What rude disturbers have we at the gate? 30
  Go pacify their fury, set it ope,
  And then demand of them what they would have.
  [*They knock again and call out to talk with* FAUSTUS.]

A SERVANT. Why, how now, masters, what a coil[1] is there!
  What is the reason you disturb the Duke?

DICK. We have no reason for it, therefore a fig[2] for him! 35

SERV. Why, saucy varlets! Dare you be so bold?

HOR. I hope, sir, we have wit enough to be more bold than welcome.

SERV. It appears so; Pray be bold elsewhere
  And trouble not the Duke. 40

DUKE. What would they have?

SERV. They all cry out to speak with Dr. Faustus.

CART. Aye, and we will speak with him.

DUKE. Will you, sir? Commit[3] the rascals!

DICK. Commit with us? He were as good commit with his father 45
  as commit with us.

FAUST. I do beseech your Grace, let them come in;
  They are good subject for a merriment.

DUKE. Do as thou wilt, Faustus; I give thee leave.

FAUST. I thank your Grace.
  [*Enter* ROBIN, DICK, CARTER, *and* HORSE-COURSER.]
                Why, how now, my good friends? 50
  'Faith you are too outrageous; but come near,
  I have procured your pardons. Welcome all!

ROBIN. Nay, sir, we will be welcome for our money, and we will
  pay for what we take. What ho! Give 's half a dozen of beer
  here, and be hanged. 55

---

8. Sheba.
9. Bang.
1. Disturbance.
2. An obscene gesture, implying con-

tempt.
3. Put in jail. Dick puns on its other
meaning ("commit adultery"), from
the Ten Commandments.

FAUST. Nay, hark you, can you tell me where you are?

CART. Aye, marry, can I; we are under heaven.

SERV. Aye, but, sir saucebox, know you in what place?

HOR. Aye, aye, the house is good enough to drink in. Zounds, fill us some beer, or we'll break all the barrels in the house and dash out all your brains with your bottles.

FAUST. Be not so furious; come, you shall have beer.

My lord, beseech you give me leave awhile;

I'll gage my credit 'twill content your Grace.

DUKE. With all my heart, kind Doctor, please thyself;

Our servants and our court's at thy command.

FAUST. I humbly thank your Grace. Then fetch some beer.

HOR. Aye, marry, there spake a doctor indeed; and, faith, I'll drink a health to thy wooden leg for that word.

FAUST. My wooden leg! What dost thou mean by that?

CART. Ha ha ha, dost hear him, Dick? He has forgot his leg.

HOR. Aye, he does not stand much upon that.

FAUST. No, faith, not much upon a wooden leg.

CART. Good lord, that flesh and blood should be so frail with your worship! Do you not remember a horse-courser you sold a horse to?

FAUST. Yes, I remember I sold one a horse.

CART. And do you remember you bid he should not ride him into the water?

FAUST. Yes, I do very well remember that.

CART. And do you remember nothing of your leg?

FAUST. No, in good sooth.

CART. Then I pray remember your courtesy.

FAUST. I thank you, sir.

CART. 'Tis not so much worth. I pray you tell me one thing.

FAUST. What's that?

CART. Be both of your legs bedfellows every night together?

FAUST. Wouldst thou make a colossus[4] of me, that thou askest me such questions?

CART. No, truly, sir, I would make nothing of you, but I would fain know that.

[*Enter* HOSTESS *with drink.*]

FAUST. Then I assure thee certainly they are.

CART. I thank you; I am fully satisfied.

FAUST. But wherefore dost thou ask?

CART. For nothing, sir; but methinks you should have a wooden bedfellow to one of 'em.

HOR. Why, do you hear, sir, did not I pull off one of your legs when you were asleep?

FAUST. But I have it again now I am awake; look you here, sir.

ALL. O horrible! Had the doctor three legs?

CART. Do you remember, sir, how you cozened me and eat up my load of——

---

4. The huge statue which stood at the entrance to the harbor at Rhodes; boats sailed between its legs, and Dr. Faustus is suggesting that the clowns are making his legs as important.

[FAUSTUS *charms him dumb.*]

DICK. Do you remember how you made me wear an ape's——

HOR. You whoreson conjuring scab, do you remember how you
cozened me of a ho——   105

ROBIN. Ha' you forgotten me? You think to carry it away with
your hey-pass and your re-pass;[5] do you remember the dog's
fa——

[*Exeunt* CLOWNS.]

HOST. Who pays for the ale? Hear you, master Doctor, now you
have sent away my guests, I pray who shall pay me for my   110
a——

[*Exit* HOSTESS.]

DUCH. My lord,
We are much beholding to this learned man.

DUKE. So are we, madam, which we will recompense
With all the love and kindness that we may;   115
His artful sport drives all sad thoughts away.   [*Exeunt.*]

Act V

SCENE 1

[*Thunder and lightning. Enter* DEVILS *with covered dishes;*
MEPHISTOPHILIS *leads them into* FAUSTUS' *study. Then
enter* WAGNER.]

WAG. I think my master means to die shortly;
He has made his will and given me his wealth,
His house, his goods, and store of golden plate,
Besides two thousand ducats ready coined.
And yet I wonder, for if death were nigh   5
He would not banquet and carouse and swill
Amongst the students as even now he doth,
Who are at supper with such belly-cheer
As Wagner ne'er beheld in all his life.
See where they come; belike the feast is ended.   [*Exit.*] 10

[*Enter* FAUSTUS *and* MEPHISTOPHILIS *with two or three*
SCHOLARS.]

1 SCH. Master Doctor Faustus, since our conference about fair
ladies, which was the beautifullest in all the world, we have determined with ourselves that Helen of Greece was the ad-
mirablest lady that ever lived. Therefore, master Doctor, if
you will do us that favor as to let us see that peerless dame of 15
Greece whom all the world admires for majesty, we should
think ourselves much beholding unto you.

FAUST. Gentlemen,
For that I know your friendship is unfeigned,
And Faustus' custom is not to deny   20
The just requests of those that wish him well,
You shall behold that peerless dame of Greece,
No otherways for pomp and majesty

5. Traditional exclamations of a conjurer.

Than when Sir Paris crossed the seas with her
And brought the spoils to rich Dardania.[6]   25
Be silent, then, for danger is in words.

    [*Music sounds, and* HELEN *passeth over the stage.*]

2 SCH. Too simple is my wit to tell her praise
Whom all the world admires for majesty.

3 SCH. No marvel though the angry Greeks pursued
With ten years' war the rape of such a queen   30
Whose heavenly beauty passeth all compare.

1 SCH. Since we have seen the pride of Nature's works
And only paragon of excellence,
Let us depart, and for this glorious deed
Happy and blest be Faustus evermore.   35

FAUST. Gentlemen, farewell; the same I wish to you.

                       [*Exeunt* SCHOLARS.]

    [*Enter an* OLD MAN.]

OLD MAN. O gentle Faustus, leave this damnéd art,
This magic, that will charm thy soul to hell
And quite bereave[7] thee of salvation.
Though thou hast now offended like a man,   40
Do not persevere in it like a devil.
Yet, yet, thou hast an amiable soul
If sin by custom grow not into nature;
Then, Faustus, will repentance come too late;
Then thou art banished from the sight of heaven.   45
No mortal can express the pains of hell.
It may be this my exhortation
Seems harsh and all unpleasant; let it not;
For, gentle son, I speak it not in wrath
Or envy of thee, but in tender love   50
And pity of thy future misery,
And so have hope that this my kind rebuke,
Checking thy body, may amend thy soul.

FAUST. Where art thou, Faustus? Wretch, what hast thou done?
Damned art thou, Faustus, damned! Despair and die.   55

    [MEPHISTOPHILIS *gives him a dagger.*]

Hell claims his right, and with a roaring voice
Says, "Faustus, come; thine hour is almost come!"
And Faustus now will come to do thee right.

OLD MAN. O stay, good Faustus, stay thy desperate steps!
I see an angel hovers o'er thy head   60
And with a vial full of precious grace
Offers to pour the same into thy soul:
Then call for mercy and avoid despair.

FAUST. Ah my sweet friend, I feel thy words
To comfort my distresséd soul.   65
Leave me awhile to ponder on my sins.

OLD MAN. Faustus, I leave thee, but with grief of heart,
Fearing the ruin of thy hopeless soul.   [*Exit.*]

6. Troy.   7. Deprive.

FAUST. Accurséd Faustus, where is mercy now?
    I do repent and yet I do despair: 70
    Hell strives with grace for conquest in my breast.
    What shall I do to shun the snares of death?
MEPH. Thou traitor, Faustus, I arrest thy soul
    For disobedience to my sovereign lord.
    Revolt, or I'll in piecemeal tear thy flesh.   75
FAUST. I do repent I e'er offended him.
    Sweet Mephistophilis, entreat thy lord
    To pardon my unjust presumption,
    And with my blood again I will confirm
    The former vow I made to Lucifer.   80
MEPH. Do it then, Faustus, with unfeignéd heart
    Lest greater danger do attend thy drift.
FAUST. Torment, sweet friend, that base and aged man
    That durst dissuade me from thy Lucifer,
    With greatest torments that our hell affords.   85
MEPH. His faith is great; I cannot touch his soul;
    But what I may afflict his body with
    I will attempt, which is but little worth.
FAUST. One thing, good servant, let me crave of thee
    To glut the longing of my heart's desire: 90
    That I might have unto my paramour
    That heavenly Helen which I saw of late,
    Whose sweet embracings may extinguish clear
    These thoughts that do dissuade me from my vow,
    And keep mine oath I made to Lucifer.   95
MEPH. This, or what else my Faustus shall desire
    Shall be performed in twinkling of an eye.
          [*Enter* HELEN *again, passing over between two* CUPIDS.]
FAUST. Was this the face that launched a thousand ships
    And burnt the topless[8] towers of Ilium?
    Sweet Helen, make me immortal with a kiss.   100
    Her lips sucks forth my soul—see where it flies!
    Come, Helen, come, give me my soul again.
    Here will I dwell, for heaven is in these lips
    And all is dross that is not Helena.
          [*Enter* OLD MAN *and stands watching* FAUSTUS.]
    I will be Paris, and for love of thee   105
    Instead of Troy shall Wittenberg be sacked,
    And I will combat with weak Menelaus
    And wear thy colors on my pluméd crest;
    Yea, I will wound Achilles in the heel
    And then return to Helen for a kiss.   110
    O thou art fairer than the evening air
    Clad in the beauty of a thousand stars!
    Brighter art thou than flaming Jupiter
    When he appeared to hapless Semele,[9]

8. So high they seemed to have no tops.
9. A Theban girl, loved by Jupiter and destroyed by the fire of his lightning when he appeared to her in his full splendor.

More lovely than the monarch of the sky 115
In wanton Arethusa's azured arms,[1]
And none but thou shalt be my paramour!
    [*Exeunt* ALL *except the* OLD MAN.]
OLD MAN. Accurséd Faustus, miserable man,
  That from thy soul exclud'st the grace of heaven
  And fliest the throne of his tribunal seat. 120
    [*Enter the* DEVILS *to torment him.*]
Satan begins to sift me with his pride.[2]
As in this furnace God shall try my faith,
My faith, vile hell, shall triumph over thee!
Ambitious fiends, see how the heavens smiles
At your repulse, and laughs your state to scorn. 125
Hence, hell! for hence I fly unto my God.   [*Exeunt.*]

SCENE 2

    [*Thunder. Enter* LUCIFER, BELZEBUB, *and* MEPHISTOPHI-
    LIS.]
LUC. Thus from infernal Dis[3] do we ascend
  To view the subjects of our monarchy,
  Those souls which sin seals the black sons of hell.
  'Mong which as chief, Faustus, we come to thee,
  Bringing with us lasting damnation 5
  To wait upon thy soul; the time is come
  Which makes it forfeit.
MEPH.   And this gloomy night
  Here in this room will wretched Faustus be.
BEL. And here we'll stay
  To mark him how he doth demean himself. 10
MEPH. How should he but with desperate lunacy?
  Fond worldling, now his heart-blood dries with grief,
  His conscience kills it, and his laboring brain
  Begets a world of idle fantasies
  To overreach the devil, but all in vain. 15
  His store of pleasure must be sauced with pain.
  He and his servant Wagner are at hand;
  Both come from drawing Faustus' latest will.
  See where they come!
    [*Enter* FAUSTUS *and* WAGNER.]
FAUST. Say, Wagner, thou hast perused my will; 20
  How dost thou like it?
WAG.   Sir, so wondrous well
  As in all humble duty I do yield
  My life and lasting service for your love.
    [*Enter the* SCHOLARS.]
FAUST. Gramercies, Wagner.—Welcome, gentlemen.
1 SCH. Now, worthy Faustus, methinks your looks are changed. 25

1. Arethusa was the nymph of a foun-   of the sky."
tain, as well as the fountain itself; no   2. I.e., to test me with his strength.
classical myth, however, records her   3. The underworld.
love affair with Jupiter, the "monarch

FAUST. Ah, gentlemen!

2 SCH. What ails Faustus?

FAUST. Ah, my sweet chamber-fellow, had I lived with thee, then had I lived still, but now must die eternally. Look, sirs! Comes he not? Comes he not? 30

1 SCH. O my dear Faustus, what imports this fear?

2 SCH. Is all our pleasure turned to melancholy?

3 SCH. He is not well with being over-solitary.

2 SCH. If it be so, we'll have physicians, and Faustus shall be cured. 35

3 SCH. 'Tis but a surfeit,[4] sir; fear nothing.

FAUST. A surfeit of deadly sin that hath damned both body and soul.

2 SCH. Yet, Faustus, look up to heaven: remember God's mercies are infinite. 40

FAUST. But Faustus' offense can ne'er be pardoned; the Serpent that tempted Eve may be saved, but not Faustus. Ah, gentlemen, hear me with patience, and tremble not at my speeches. Though my heart pants and quivers to remember that I have been a student here these thirty years, O would I had never seen 45 Wittenberg, never read book! And what wonders I have done all Germany can witness, yea all the world, for which Faustus hath lost both Germany and the world, yea heaven itself— heaven the seat of God, the throne of the blessed, the kingdom of joy, and must remain in hell forever, hell, ah hell, forever! 50 Sweet friends, what shall become of Faustus, being in hell forever?

3 SCH. Yet, Faustus, call on God.

FAUST. On God, whom Faustus hath abjured? on God, whom Faustus hath blasphemed? Ah, my God, I would weep, but the 55 devil draws in my tears! Gush forth, blood, instead of tears, yea life and soul! O he stays my tongue; I would lift up my hands but, see, they hold 'em, they hold 'em!

ALL. Who, Faustus?

FAUST. Why, Lucifer and Mephistophilis. 60

Ah, gentlemen, I gave them my soul for my cunning.

ALL. God forbid!

FAUST. God forbade it indeed, but Faustus hath done it: for vain pleasure of four and twenty years hath Faustus lost eternal joy and felicity. I writ them a bill with mine own blood; the date 65 is expired, this is the time, and he will fetch me.

1 SCH. Why did not Faustus tell us of this before, that divines might have prayed for thee?

FAUST. Oft have I thought to have done so, but the devil threatened to tear me in pieces if I named God, to fetch both body 70 and soul if I once gave ear to divinity; and now 'tis too late. Gentlemen, away, lest you perish with me!

2 SCH. O what may we do to save Faustus?

FAUST. Talk not of me, but save yourselves and depart.

4. Indigestion; the effects of overindulgence.

3 SCH. God will strengthen me: I will stay with Faustus.   75
1 SCH. Tempt not God, sweet friend, but let us into the next
     room, and there pray for him.
FAUST. Aye, pray for me, pray for me! And what noise soever ye
     hear, come not unto me, for nothing can rescue me.
2 SCH. Pray thou, and we will pray that God may have mercy   80
     upon thee.
FAUST. Gentlemen, farewell. If I live till morning I'll visit you;
     if not, Faustus is gone to hell.
ALL. Faustus, farewell.   [*Exeunt* SCHOLARS.]
MEPH. Aye, Faustus, now hast thou no hope of heaven;   85
     Therefore despair, think only upon hell,
     For that must be thy mansion, there to dwell.
FAUST. O thou bewitching fiend, 'twas thy temptation
     Hath robbed me of eternal happiness.
MEPH. I do confess it, Faustus, and rejoice.   90
     'Twas I, that when thou wert i' the way to heaven
     Damned up thy passage; when thou tookest the book
     To view the scriptures, then I turned the leaves
     And led thine eye.
     What, weepst thou? 'tis too late. Despair, farewell!   95
     Fools that will laugh on earth must weep in hell.   [*Exit.*]
          [*Enter the* GOOD ANGEL *and the* BAD ANGEL *at several
          doors.*]
G. ANG. Ah Faustus, if thou hadst given ear to me,
     Innumerable joys had followed thee,
     But thou didst love the world.
B. ANG.   Gave ear to me
     And now must taste hell's pains perpetually.   100
G. ANG. O what will all thy riches, pleasures, pomps
     Avail thee now?
B. ANG.   Nothing but vex thee more,
     To want in hell, that had on earth such store.
          [*Music while the throne descends.*[5]]
G. ANG. O, thou hast lost celestial happiness,
     Pleasures unspeakable, bliss without end.   105
     Hadst thou affected sweet divinity
     Hell or the devil had had no power on thee.
     Hadst thou kept on that way, Faustus, behold
     In what resplendent glory thou hadst sit
     In yonder throne, like those bright shining saints,   110
     And triumphed over hell; that hast thou lost.
     And now, poor soul, must thy good angel leave thee;
     The jaws of hell are open to receive thee.
          [*Exit. Hell is discovered.*]
B. ANG. Now Faustus, let thine eyes with horror stare
     Into that vast perpetual torture-house.   115
     There are the furies, tossing damnéd souls

5. A throne suspended by ropes descended to the stage near the end of
many Elizabethan plays and was an
expected theatrical display. Here the
throne clearly symbolizes heaven, as
the next speech shows.

On burning forks; their bodies boil in lead.
There are live quarters[6] broiling on the coals
That ne'er can die; this ever-burning chair
Is for o'ertortured souls to rest them in;   120
These that are fed with sops of flaming fire
Were gluttons and loved only delicates
And laughed to see the poor starve at their gates.
But yet all these are nothing; thou shalt see
Ten thousand tortures that more horrid be.   125

FAUST. O, I have seen enough to torture me.

B. ANG. Nay, thou must feel them, taste the smart of all;
He that loves pleasure must for pleasure fall.
And so I leave thee, Faustus, till anon;
Then wilt thou tumble in confusión.[7]   130
      [*Exit. The clock strikes eleven.*]

FAUST. Ah, Faustus,
Now hast thou but one bare hour to live
And then thou must be damned perpetually!
Stand still, you ever-moving spheres of heaven,
That time may cease and midnight never come;   135
Fair Nature's eye, rise, rise again, and make
Perpetual day; or let this hour be but
A year, a month, a week, a natural day,
That Faustus may repent and save his soul!
O lente lente currite noctis equi.[8]   140
The stars move still, time runs, the clock will strike,
The devil will come, and Faustus must be damned.
O, I'll leap up to my God! Who pulls me down?
See, see, where Christ's blood streams in the firmament!—
One drop would save my soul—half a drop! ah, my Christ!   145
Rend not my heart for naming of my Christ;
Yet will I call on him—O, spare me, Lucifer!
Where is it now? 'Tis gone; and see where God
Stretcheth out his arm and bends his ireful brows.
Mountains and hills, come, come and fall on me   150
And hide me from the heavy wrath of God,
No, no—
Then will I headlong run into the earth:
Earth, gape! O no, it will not harbor me.
You stars that reigned at my nativity,   155
Whose influence hath allotted death and hell,
Now draw up Faustus like a foggy mist
Into the entrails of yon laboring clouds
That when they vomit forth into the air,
My limbs may issue from their smoky mouths,   160
So that my soul may but ascend to heaven.
      [*The watch strikes.*]
Ah, half the hour is past; 'twill all be past anon.

6. Bodies.
7. Destruction, perdition.
8. "Slowly, slowly run, O horses of the night," adapted from a line in Ovid's *Amores.*

O God,
If thou wilt not have mercy on my soul,
Yet for Christ's sake whose blood hath ransomed me   165
Impose some end to my incessant pain:
Let Faustus live in hell a thousand years,
A hundred thousand, and at last be saved!
O, no end is limited to damnéd souls!
Why wert thou not a creature wanting soul?   170
Or why is this immortal that thou hast?
Ah, Pythagoras' *metempsychosis*[9]—were that true,
This soul should fly from me, and I be changed
Unto some brutish beast. All beasts are happy,
For when they die   175
Their souls are soon dissolved in elements,
But mine must live still[1] to be plagued in hell.
Cursed be the parents that engendered me!
No, Faustus, curse thyself, curse Lucifer
That hath deprived thee of the joys of heaven.   180
          [*The clock strikes twelve.*]
It strikes, it strikes! Now, body, turn to air
Or Lucifer will bear thee quick[2] to hell!
          [*Thunder and lightning.*]
O soul, be changed to little water drops
And fall into the ocean, ne'er be found.
My God, my God, look not so fierce on me!   185
          [*Enter* DEVILS.]
Adders and serpents, let me breathe awhile!
Ugly hell, gape not—come not, Lucifer—
I'll burn my books—ah, Mephistophilis!
          [*Exeunt* DEVILS *with* FAUSTUS.]

                         SCENE 3

          [*Enter the* SCHOLARS.]
1 SCH. Come, gentlemen, let us go visit Faustus,
      For such a dreadful night was never seen
      Since first the world's creation did begin,
      Such fearful shrieks and cries were never heard.
      Pray heaven the Doctor have escaped the danger.   5
2 SCH. O, help us heaven! See, here are Faustus' limbs
      All torn asunder by the hand of death.
3 SCH. The devils whom Faustus served have torn him thus;
      For 'twixt the hours of twelve and one, methought
      I heard him shriek and call aloud for help.   10
      At which self[3] time the house seemed all on fire
      With dreadful horror of these damnéd fiends.
2 SCH. Well, gentlemen, though Faustus' end be such
      As every Christian heart laments to think on,
      Yet for he was a scholar once admired   15

9. Pythagoras' doctrine of the trans-   2. Alive.
migration of souls.   3. Same, exact.
1. Always.

For wondrous knowledge in our German schools,
We'll give his mangled limbs due burial;
And all the students, clothed in mourning black,
Shall wait upon his heavy[4] funeral [*Exeunt.*]
    [*Enter* CHORUS.]
CHO. Cut is the branch that might have grown full straight, 20
And burnéd is Apollo's laurel bough[5]
That sometime grew within this learnéd man.
Faustus is gone: regard his hellish fall,
Whose fiendful fortune may exhort the wise
Only to wonder at[6] unlawful things 25
Whose deepness doth entice such forward wits
To practice more than heavenly power permits. [*Exit.*]
                                              1604, 1616

4. Tragic, sorrowful.
5. Laurel is a symbol of wisdom and learning; Apollo was the god of divination, one of whose shrines was the oracle at Delphi. The image, though it
sounds classical, is really Marlowe's.
6. I.e., to be content with observing with awe. "Fiendful fortune": devilish fate.

WILLIAM SHAKESPEARE
(1564–1616)

ca. 1588–92: In London as actor and playwright.
ca. 1592–98: Devotes himself mainly to chronicle histories and comedies.
ca. 1601–9: Period of the great tragedies and romantic comedies.
ca. 1610: Retires to Stratford.

William Shakespeare was born in Stratford-on-Avon in April (probably April 23), 1564. His father was a citizen of some prominence who became an alderman and bailiff, but who later suffered financial reverses. Shakespeare presumably attended the Stratford grammar school, where he could have acquired a respectable knowledge of Latin, but he did not proceed to Oxford or Cambridge. There are legends about Shakespeare's youth but no documented facts. The first record we have of his life after his christening is that of his marriage in 1582 to Anne Hathaway. A daughter was born to the young Shakespeares in 1583 and twins, a boy and a girl, in 1585. We possess no information about his activities for the next seven years, but by 1592 he was in London as an actor and apparently well-known as a playwright, for Robert Greene refers to him resentfully in *A Groatsworth of Wit* as "an upstart crow, beautified with our feathers," who, "being an absolute *Johannes Factotum*, is in his own conceit the only Shake-scene in a country."

At this time, there were several companies of actors in London and in the provinces. What connection Shakespeare had with one or more of them before 1592 is conjectural, but we do know of his long and fruitful connection with the most successful troupe, the Lord Chamberlain's Men, who later, when James I came to the throne, became the King's Men. Shakespeare not only acted with this company, but eventually became a leading shareholder and the principal playwright. The company included some of the most famous actors of the day, such as Richard Burbage, who no doubt created the roles of Hamlet, Lear, and Othello, and Will Kempe and Robert Armin, who acted Shakespeare's clowns and fools. In 1599 the Chamberlain's Men built and occupied that best known of Elizabethan theaters, the Globe.

Shakespeare did not, in his early years, confine himself to the theater. In 1593 he published a mythological-erotic poem, *Venus and Adonis*, dedicated to the Earl of Southampton; in the next year he dedicated a "graver labor," *The Rape of Lucrece*, to the same noble patron. By 1597 Shakespeare had so prospered that he was able to purchase New Place, a handsome house in Stratford; he could now call himself a gentleman, as his father had been granted a coat of arms in the previous year.

Our first record of the playwright's actual work occurs in Francis Meres' *Palladis Tamia: Wit's Treasury* (1598), in which Meres compared English poets with the ancients; of Shakespeare he says, "As Plautus and Seneca are accounted the best for Comedy and Tragedy among the Latins, so Shakespeare among the English is the most excellent in both kinds for the stage." He goes on to list *Richard II, Richard III, Henry IV, King John, Titus Andronicus*, and *Romeo and Juliet* for tragedy and *Two Gentlemen of Verona, The Comedy of Errors, A Midsummer Night's Dream, The Merchant of Venice, Love's Labor's Lost*, and the unknown (or perhaps retitled) *Love's Labor's Won* as comedy. All of the plays Meres lists as tragedy (except for *Romeo and Juliet* and the very early *Titus Andronicus*) we would call chronicle history plays, a popular kind of drama based upon history books like Raphael Holinshed's *Chronicle* and presenting dramatically the events in the reigns of various English kings. About the turn of the century Shakespeare wrote his great romantic comedies, *As You Like It, Twelfth Night*, and *Much Ado About Nothing*, and his concluding history play in the Prince Hal series, *Henry V*. The next decade was the period of the great tragedies: *Hamlet, Macbeth, Othello, King Lear*, and *Antony and Cleopatra*.

About 1610 Shakespeare apparently retired to Stratford, though he continued to write, both by himself (*The Tempest*) and in collaboration (*Henry VIII*). This is the period of the "romances" or "tragicomedies," which include, besides *The Tempest, Cymbeline* and *The Winter's Tale*. Aside from his two early nondramatic poems, Shakespeare devoted his genius primarily to the stage. Meres mentioned in 1598, however, that he was known for "his sugared sonnets among his private friends"; the sonnets were published in 1609, apparently without his authorization. He contributed the strange and beautiful poem, *The Phoenix and the Turtle*, to an anthology in 1601.

The plays contain some of the finest songs ever written. They are of various types: the aubade, or morning song, the gay pastoral invitation, love songs of various kinds, the ballad sung by wandering minstrels, and the funeral dirge. They illustrate many sides of Shakespeare's genius—his incomparable lyric gift, his ready humor, and his marvelous sensitivity to the sights and sounds of English life, especially the life of the country.

The sonnets are Shakespeare's contribution to a popular vogue, but his cycle is quite unlike the other sonnet sequences of his day. Shakespeare's cycle suggests a story, though the details are vague, and there is doubt even whether the sonnets as published in 1609 are in the correct order. Certain motifs are clear: a series celebrating the beauty of a young man and urging him to marry; some sonnets to a lady; some sonnets (like 144) about a strange triangle of love involving two men and a woman; sonnets on the destructive power of time and the permanence of poetry; sonnets about a rival poet; and incidental sonnets of moral insight, like 129 and 146. The biographical background of the sonnets has aroused much speculation, but very little of it is convincing. The poems themselves are what is important. Though the vocabulary is often simple, the metaphorical style of the sonnets is rich. "Shall I compare thee to a summer's day" is a question which might lead to a very ordinary conceit; instead it introduces a profound meditation on time, change, and beauty.

The structure of the sonnet frequently reinforces the power of the metaphors; each quatrain in 73 develops an image of lateness, of approaching extinction—of a season, of a day, and of a fire, but they also apply to a life. The three quatrains may be equally and successively at work preparing for the conclusion in the couplet, or the first eight lines may contain a catalogue and the last six turn in quite a different direction, as in sonnet 29. The rhetorical strategy of the sonnets is also worth careful attention. Some begin with a purported reminiscence; some are imperative; others make an almost proverbial statement, then elaborate it. The imagery comes from a wide variety of sources: gardening, navigation, law, farming, business, pictorial art, astrology, domestic affairs. The moods are also not confined to what the Renaissance thought were those of the despairing Petrarchan lover; they include delight, pride, melancholy, shame, disgust, fear. It is evident that the poet of the sonnets is also the author of the great plays.

When Shakespeare died, in Stratford in 1616, no collected edition of his plays had been published. Some of them had been printed in separate editions ("quartos") without his editorial supervision, sometimes from his manuscripts, sometimes from playhouse prompt books, sometimes from pirated texts secured by shorthand reports of a performance or from reconstruction from memory by an actor or spectator.

In 1623, two members of Shakespeare's company, John Heminges and Henry Condell, published the great collection of all the plays they considered authentic; it is called the First Folio. They printed the best texts they had, according to their lights. The Folio contains an epistle "to the great variety of readers" which urges us to read Shakespeare again and again; if we do not like him, say Heminges and Condell, it is evident that we do not understand him. Another preliminary document in the First Folio is a poem by Shakespeare's great rival, critic, and opposite, Ben Jonson. In it he asserts the superiority of Shakespeare not only to other English playwrights but to the Greek and Latin masters. Jonson first states what has come to be a universal opinion:

> Triumph, my Britain, thou hast one to show
> To whom all scenes of Europe homage owe.
> He was not of an age, but for all time!

SONGS FROM THE PLAYS
When Daisies Pied[1]

SPRING

When daisies pied and violets blue
   And ladysmocks all silver-white
And cuckoobuds of yellow hue
   Do paint the meadows with delight,
The cuckoo then, on every tree,   5
Mocks married men;[2] for thus sings he,
               Cuckoo;
Cuckoo, cuckoo: Oh word of fear,
Unpleasing to a married ear!

When shepherds pipe on oaten straws,[3]   10
   And merry larks are plowmen's clocks,
When turtles tread,[4] and rooks, and daws,
   And maidens bleach their summer smocks,
The cuckoo then, on every tree,
Mocks married men; for thus sings he,   15
               Cuckoo;
Cuckoo, cuckoo: Oh word of fear,
Unpleasing to a married ear!

WINTER

When icicles hang by the wall
   And Dick the shepherd blows his nail[5]   20
And Tom bears logs into the hall,
   And milk comes frozen home in pail,
When blood is nipped and ways be foul,
Then nightly sings the staring owl,
             Tu-who;   25
Tu-whit, tu-who: a merry note,
While greasy Joan doth keel[6] the pot.

When all aloud the wind doth blow,
   And coughing drowns the parson's saw,[7]
And birds sit brooding in the snow,   30
   And Marian's nose looks red and raw,
When roasted crabs[8] hiss in the bowl,
Then nightly sings the staring owl,
             Tu-who;
Tu-whit, tu-who: a merry note   35
While greasy Joan doth keel the pot.

1. This song concludes *Love's Labour's Lost* (1594–95), one of Shakespeare's earliest comedies. Announced as a "Dialogue * * * in praise of the Owl and the Cuckoo," it provides a lyric commentary on the bittersweet mood that dominates the play's last scene. "Pied": variegated.
2. The cuckoo's song—"Cuckoo!"—is taken to mean "Cuckold!"

3. The reed pipes played by shepherds.
4. Turtledoves mate. The "larks" are "plowmen's clocks" because they sing at sunrise.
5. Warms his fingers by blowing on them.
6. Stir, to prevent boiling over.
7. Wise saying.
8. Crabapples.

Tell Me Where Is Fancy Bred[9]

Tell me where is fancy bred,
Or in the heart or in the head?
How begeot, how nourishéd?
    Reply, reply.
It is engendered in the eyes,   5
With gazing fed; and fancy dies
In the cradle where it lies.
    Let us all ring fancy's knell:
I'll begin it—Ding, dong, bell.
Ding, dong, bell.   10

Sigh No More, Ladies[1]

Sigh no more, ladies, sigh no more,
    Men were deceivers ever;
One foot in sea, and one on shore,
    To one thing constant never.
      Then sigh not so,   5
      But let them go,
And be you blithe and bonny,
Converting all your sounds of woe
Into Hey nonny, nonny.

Sing no more ditties, sing no mo   10
    Of dumps [2] so dull and heavy;
The fraud of men was ever so,
    Since summer first was leavy.
      Then sigh not so,
      But let them go,   15
And be you blithe and bonny,
Converting all your sounds of woe
Into Hey nonny, nonny.

Under the Greenwood Tree[3]

Under the greenwood tree
Who loves to lie with me,

---

9. *The Merchant of Venice* (1596–97) III.ii.63 ff.; sung while Bassanio is trying to choose between the caskets of gold, silver, and lead—one of which contains the token that will enable him to gain Portia as his wife. The song is perhaps intended to help Bassanio's choice: notice the number of words that rhyme with "lead." "Fancy" is a superficial love or liking for something attractive.
1. *Much Ado About Nothing* (1598–99) II.iii.64 ff.
2. Sad songs.
3. *As You Like It* (1599–1600) II.v.1 ff.; this song provides a comment on the happy existence of the banished Duke and his followers in the Forest of Arden, where life is "more sweet / Than that of painted pomp."

And turn his merry note
Unto the sweet bird's throat,[4]
Come hither. come hither, come hither: 5
   Here shall he see
   No enemy
But winter and rough weather.

Who doth ambition shun
And loves to live i' the sun,   10
Seeking the food he eats,
And pleased with what he gets,
Come hither. come hither, come hither:
   Here shall he see
   No enemy   15
But winter and rough weather.

Blow, Blow, Thou Winter Wind[5]

Blow, blow, thou winter wind,
Thou art not so unkind
   As man's ingratitude;
Thy tooth is not so keen,
Because thou art not seen,   5
   Although thy breath be rude.
Heigh-ho! sing, heigh-ho! unto the green holly:
Most friendship is feigning, most loving mere folly:
   Then, heigh-ho, the holly!
   This life is most jolly.   10

Freeze, freeze, thou bitter sky,
That dost not bite so nigh
   As benefits forgot:
Though thou the waters warp,[6]
Thy sting is not so sharp   15
   As friend remembered not.
Heigh-ho! sing, etc.

Oh Mistress Mine[7]

Oh mistress mine! where are you roaming?
Oh! stay and hear; your true love's coming,
   That can sing both high and low.
Trip no further, pretty sweeting;
Journeys end in lovers meeting,   5
   Every wise man's son doth know.

What is love? 'tis not hereafter;
Present mirth hath present laughter;
   What's to come is still unsure:

---

4. I.e., improvise his song in harmony with the bird's.
5. Also from *As You Like It* II.vii. 174 ff. The contrast here between na-ture and man's willful behavior is one of the continuing themes of the play.
6. I.e., roughen by freezing.
7. *Twelfth Night* (1601–2) II.iii.40 ff.

In delay there lies no plenty;   10
    Then come kiss me, sweet and twenty,
        Youth's a stuff will not endure.

Take, Oh, Take Those Lips Away[8]

Take, Oh, take those lips away,
    That so sweetly were forsworn;
And those eyes, the break of day,
    Lights that do mislead the morn:
But my kisses bring again, bring again;   5
Seals of love, but sealed in vain, sealed in vain.

Fear No More the Heat o' the Sun[9]

Fear no more the heat o' the sun,
    Nor the furious winter's rages;
Thou thy worldly task hast done,
    Home art gone, and ta'en thy wages:
Golden lads and girls all must,   5
As [1] chimney-sweepers, come to dust.

Fear no more the frown o' the great;
    Thou art past the tyrant's stroke;
Care no more to clothe and eat;
    To thee the reed is as the oak: 10
The scepter, learning, physic, must
All follow this, and come to dust.

Fear no more the lightning flash,
    Nor the all-dreaded thunder stone;[2]
Fear not slander, censure rash;   15
    Thou hast finished joy and moan:
All lovers young, all lovers must
Consign to thee, and come to dust.

No exorciser harm thee!
Nor no witchcraft charm thee!   20
Ghost unlaid forbear thee!
Nothing ill come near thee!
Quiet consummation have;
And renownéd be thy grave!

When Daffodils Begin to Peer[3]

When daffodils begin to peer,
    With heigh! the doxy[4] over the dale,

8. *Measure for Measure* (1604) IV.i.
1 ff.; Mariana's desolation at being
jilted by her lover Angelo is poignantly
conveyed in this song, which is sung
at her first entrance.
9. A lament for the supposedly dead
Imogen, sung in *Cymbeline* IV.ii.258 ff.
1. Like.
2. The sound of thunder was commonly
thought to be caused by the falling of
stones or meteorites.
3. *The Winter's Tale* (1610–11) IV.
iii.1 ff. Autolycus, ballad-singer, ped-
dler, and rogue, makes his entrance
singing this song, which not only effectively establishes his character but
also helps to move the play from the
wintry mood of the earlier scenes to
the spring mood of the later scenes.
4. Girl or mistress (thieves' slang).

Why, then comes in the sweet o' the year;
    For the red blood reigns in the winter's pale.[5]

The white sheet bleaching on the hedge,[6]   5
    With heigh! the sweet birds, Oh, how they sing!
Doth set my pugging[7] tooth on edge;
    For a quart of ale is a dish for a king.

The lark, that tirra-lirra chants,
    With heigh! with heigh! the thrush and the jay,   10
Are summer songs for me and my aunts,[8]
    While we lie tumbling in the hay.

Full Fathom Five[9]

Full fathom five thy father lies;
    Of his bones are coral made;
Those are pearls that were his eyes:
    Nothing of him that doth fade,
But doth suffer a sea change   5
Into something rich and strange.
Sea nymphs hourly ring his knell:
    Ding-dong.
Hark! now I hear them—Ding-dong, bell.

Where the Bee Sucks, There Suck I[1]

Where the bee sucks, there suck I:
In a cowslip's bell I lie;
There I couch when owls do cry.
On the bat's back I do fly
After summer merrily.   5
Merrily, merrily shall I live now
Under the blossom that hangs on the bough.

Sonnets

3

Look in thy glass, and tell the face thou viewest
Now is the time that face should form another,
Whose fresh repair if now thou not renewest,

---

5. A pun on (1) a territory over which one has jurisdiction (2) lacking in color.
6. Laundry, dried or bleached on hedges, was sometimes stolen by passing vagabonds like Autolycus.
7. Thieving.
8. Girls or mistresses.
9. *The Tempest* (1611–12) I.ii.396 ff. Ariel, the airy spirit of the enchanted isle, sings this song to Ferdinand, prince of Naples. Ferdinand wonders at it: "The ditty does remember my drowned father. / This is no mortal business, nor no sound/ That the earth owes [owns]."
1. Also from *The Tempest* V.i.88 ff.: Ariel is happily anticipating the freedom of his future life.

Thou dost beguile the world, unbless some mother.
For where is she so fair whose uneared[2] womb   5
Disdains the tillage of thy husbandry?
Or who is he so fond[3] will be the tomb
Of his self-love, to stop posterity?
Thou art thy mother's glass,[4] and she in thee
Calls back the lovely April of her prime;   10
So thou through windows of thine age shalt see,
Despite of wrinkles, this thy golden time.
But if thou live rememb'red not to be,
Die single, and thine image dies with thee.

12

When I do count the clock that tells the time
And see the brave[5] day sunk in hideous night,
When I behold the violet past prime
And sable curls all silver'd o'er with white,
When lofty trees I see barren of leaves,   5
Which erst[6] from heat did canopy the herd,
And summer's green all girded up in sheaves
Borne on the bier with white and bristly beard—
Then of thy beauty do I question make
That thou among the wastes of time must go,   10
Since sweets and beauties do themselves forsake
And die as fast as they see others grow,
And nothing 'gainst Time's scythe can make defense
Save breed,[7] to brave him when he takes thee hence.

18

Shall I compare thee to a summer's day?
Thou art more lovely and more temperate:
Rough winds do shake the darling buds of May,
And summer's lease hath all too short a date:
Sometime too hot the eye of heaven shines   5
And often is his gold complexion dimmed;
And every fair from fair sometimes declines,
By chance or nature's changing course untrimmed;[8]
But thy eternal summer shall not fade,
Nor lose possession of that fair thou ow'st;[9]   10
Nor shall death brag thou wander'st in his shade,
When in eternal lines to time thou grow'st:
So long as men can breathe, or eyes can see,
So long lives this, and this gives life to thee.[1]

2. Unplowed.
3. Foolish.
4. Mirror.
5. Splendid.
6. Formerly.
7. Offspring; "to brave": to defy.
8. Stripped of gay apparel.

9. Ownest.
1. The boast of immortality for one's verse was a Renaissance convention and goes back to the classics. It implies, not egotism on the part of the poet, but a faith in the permanence of poetry.

29

When, in disgrace with fortune and men's eyes,
I all alone beweep my outcast state,
And trouble deaf heaven with my bootless[2] cries,
And look upon myself, and curse my fate,
Wishing me like to one more rich in hope,   5
Featured like him, like him with friends possessed,
Desiring this man's art and that man's scope,
With what I most enjoy contented least;
Yet in these thoughts myself almost despising,
Haply I think on thee—and then my state,[3]   10
Like to the lark at break of day arising
From sullen earth, sings hymns at heaven's gate;
For thy sweet love remembered such wealth brings
That then I scorn to change my state with kings.[4]

30

When to the sessions[5] of sweet silent thought
I summon up remembrance of things past,
I sigh the lack of many a thing I sought,
And with old woes new wail[6] my dear time's waste:
Then can I drown an eye, unused to flow,   5
For precious friends hid in death's dateless[7] night,
And weep afresh love's long since canceled woe,
And moan the expense [8] of many a vanished sight:
Then can I grieve at grievances foregone,[9]
And heavily from woe to woe tell o'er   10
The sad account of fore-bemoanèd moan,
Which I new pay as if not paid before.
But if the while I think on thee, dear friend,
All losses are restored and sorrows end.

55

Not marble, nor the gilded monuments
Of princes, shall outlive this powerful rhyme;
But you shall shine more bright in these contents
Than unswept stone, besmeared with sluttish time.[1]
When wasteful war shall statues overturn,   5
And broils root out the work of masonry,
Nor Mars his[2] sword nor war's quick fire shall burn
The living record of your memory.
'Gainst death and all-oblivious enmity[3]

---

2. Futile.
3. Condition, state of mind; but in line 14 there is a pun on "state" meaning chair of state, throne.
4. This sonnet and the next are companion pieces, one dealing with present troubles, the other with those past.
5. Sittings of court; "summon up" (line 2) continues the metaphor.
6. Bewail anew.

7. Endless.
8. Loss.
9. Old subjects for grief. "Tell": count.
1. I.e., than in a stone tomb or effigy which time wears away and covers with dust.
2. Mars's.
3. The enmity of oblivion, of being forgotten.

Shall you pace forth; your praise shall still find room   10
Even in the eyes of all posterity
That wear this world out to the ending doom.[4]
So, till the judgment that yourself arise,
You live in this, and dwell in lovers' eyes.

56

Sweet love, renew thy force; be it not said
Thy edge should blunter be than appetite,
Which but today by feeding is allayed,
Tomorrow sharpened in his former might.
So, love, be thou: although today thou fill   5
Thy hungry eyes even till they wink[5] with fullness,
Tomorrow see again, and do not kill
The spirit of love with a perpetual dullness.
Let this sad int'rim like the ocean be
Which parts the shore where two contracted new[6]   10
Come daily to the banks, that, when they see
Return of love, more blest may be the view;
Or call it winter, which, being full of care,
Makes summer's welcome thrice more wished, more rare.

60

Like as the waves make towards the pebbled shore,
So do our minutes hasten to their end;
Each changing place with that which goes before,
In sequent toil all forwards do contend.[7]
Nativity, once in the main[8] of light,   5
Crawls to maturity, wherewith being crowned,
Crooked eclipses 'gainst his glory fight,
And time that gave doth now his gift confound.
Time doth transfix the flourish[9] set on youth
And delves the parallels in beauty's brow,   10
Feeds on the rarities of nature's truth,
And nothing stands but for his scythe to mow.
And yet to times in hope[1] my verse shall stand,
Praising thy worth, despite his cruel hand.

71

No longer mourn for me when I am dead
Than you shall hear the surly sullen bell[2]
Give warning to the world that I am fled
From this vile world, with vilest worms to dwell:

4. Judgment Day. The next line is paraphrased, "Until you rise from the dead
on Judgment Day."
5. Close (not momentarily).
6. A newly engaged couple.
7. Toiling and following each other,
the waves struggle to press forward.
8. Broad expanse.

9. Remove the embellishment. "Delves
the parallels": digs the parallel furrows
(wrinkles). To "flourish" is also to
blossom.
1. Future times.
2. The bell was tolled to announce the
death of a member of the parish—
one stroke for each year of his life.

Nay, if you read this line, remember not 5
The hand that writ it; for I love you so,
That I in your sweet thoughts would be forgot,
If thinking on me then should make you woe.
Oh, if, I say, you look upon this verse
When I perhaps compounded am with clay, 10
Do not so much as my poor name rehearse,
But let your love even with my life decay;
Lest the wise world should look into your moan,
And mock you with me after I am gone. ·

73

That time of year thou mayst in me behold
When yellow leaves, or none, or few, do hang
Upon those boughs which shake against the cold,
Bare ruined choirs, where late the sweet birds sang.
In me thou see'st the twilight of such day 5
As after sunset fadeth in the west;
Which by and by black night doth take away,
Death's second self that seals up all in rest.
In me thou see'st the glowing of such fire,
That on the ashes of his youth doth lie, 10
As the deathbed whereon it must expire,
Consumed with that which it was nourished by.[3]
This thou perceiv'st, which makes thy love more strong,
To love that well which thou must leave ere long.

87

Farewell: thou art too dear[4] for my possessing,
And like enough thou know'st thy estimate.[5]
The charter[6] of thy worth gives thee releasing;
My bonds in thee are all determinate.[7]
For how do I hold thee but by thy granting, 5
And for that riches where is my deserving?
The cause of this fair gift in me is wanting,
And so my patent [8] back again is swerving.
Thyself thou gav'st, thy own worth then not knowing,
Or me, to whom thou gav'st it, else mistaking; 10
So thy great gift, upon misprision[9] growing,
Comes home again, on better judgment making.
Thus have I had thee as a dream doth flatter,
In sleep a king, but waking no such matter.

94

They that have power to hurt and will do none,
That do not do the thing they most do show,[1]

3. Choked by the ashes of that which once nourished its flame.
4. Expensive, beloved.
5. Value.
6. Deed, contract for property.
7. Expired.
8. Title.
9. Mistake, oversight.
1. Seem to do.

Who, moving others, are themselves as stone,
Unmovéd, cold, and to temptation slow;
They rightly do inherit heaven's graces
And husband nature's riches from expense; [2]
They are the lords and owners of their faces,
Others but stewards of their excellence.
The summer's flower is to the summer sweet,
Though to itself it only live and die,
But if that flower with base infection meet,
The basest weed outbraves his dignity:
For sweetest things turn sourest by their deeds;
Lilies that fester smell far worse than weeds. [3]

97

How like a winter hath my absence been
From thee, the pleasure of the fleeting year!
What freezings have I felt, what dark days seen!
What old December's bareness everywhere!
And yet this time removed was summer's time,
The teeming autumn big with rich increase,
Bearing the wanton burthen of the prime, [4]
Like widowed wombs after their lords' decease;
Yet this abundant issue seemed to me
But hope of orphans and unfathered fruit;
For summer and his pleasures wait on thee,
And, thou away, the very birds are mute;
Or, if they sing, 'tis with so dull a cheer
That leaves look pale, dreading the winter's near.

98

From you have I been absent in the spring,
When proud-pied[5] April, dressed in all his trim,
Hath put a spirit of youth in everything,
That heavy Saturn[6] laughed and leaped with him.
Yet nor the lays of birds, nor the sweet smell
Of different flowers in odor and in hue,
Could make me any summer's story tell,
Or from their proud lap pluck them where they grew;
Nor did I wonder at[7] the lily's white,
Nor praise the deep vermilion in the rose;
They were but sweet, but figures of delight,
Drawn after you, you pattern of all those.
Yet seemed it winter still, and, you away,
As with your shadow I with these did play.

---

2. I.e., they do not squander nature's gifts.
3. This line appears in *Edward III* (II. i.451), an apocryphal Shakespearean play licensed December 1, 1595.
4. Spring, which has engendered the lavish crop ("wanton burthen") that autumn is now left to bear.
5. Magnificent in many colors.
6. God of melancholy.
7. Admire.

104

To me, fair friend, you never can be old,
For as you were when first your eye I eyed
Such seems your beauty still. Three winters cold
Have from the forests shook three summers' pride,
Three beauteous springs to yellow autumn turned   5
In process [8] of the seasons have I seen,
Three April perfumes in three hot Junes burned,
Since first I saw you fresh, which yet are green.
Ah, yet doth beauty, like a dial-hand,[9]
Steal from his figure, and no pace perceived;   10
So your sweet hue, which methinks still doth stand,
Hath motion, and mine eye may be deceived:
For fear of which, hear this, thou age unbred:[1]
Ere you were born was beauty's summer dead.

106

When in the chronicle of wasted [2] time
I see descriptions of the fairest wights,
And beauty making beautiful old rhyme
In praise of ladies dead and lovely knights,
Then, in the blazon[3] of sweet beauty's best,   5
Of hand, of foot, of lip, of eye, of brow,
I see their antique pen would have expressed
Even such a beauty as you master now.
So all their praises are but prophecies
Of this our time, all you prefiguring;   10
And, for they looked but with divining eyes,
They had not skill enough your worth to sing:[4]
For we, which now behold these present days,
Have eyes to wonder, but lack tongues to praise.

107

Not mine own fears, nor the prophetic soul
Of the wide world dreaming on things to come,[5]
Can yet the lease of my true love control,
Supposed as forfeit to a confinéd doom.[6]
The mortal moon hath her eclipse endured,   5
And the sad augurs mock their own presage;[7]
Incertainties now crown themselves assured,
And peace[8] proclaims olives of endless age.

8. Procession.
9. Hand of a watch.
1. Unborn generation.
2. Past.
3. Display.
4. Because ("for") they were able *only* ("but") to foresee prophetically.
5. This sonnet refers to contemporary events and the prophecies, common in Elizabethan almanacs, of disaster.
6. I.e., can yet put an end to my love, which I thought doomed to early forfeiture.

7. The "mortal moon" is Queen Elizabeth; her "eclipse" is probably her climacteric year, her 63rd (thought significant because the product of two "significant" numbers, 7 and 9), which ended in September, 1596. The sober astrologers ("sad augurs") now ridicule their own predictions ("presage") of catastrophe, since they turned out to be false.
8. Probably an agreement between Henry IV of France and Elizabeth.

Now with the drops of this most balmy time
My love looks fresh, and death to me subscribes,[9]   10
Since, spite of him, I'll live in this poor rhyme,
While he insults o'er dull and speechless tribes:
And thou in this shalt find thy monument,
When tyrants' crests and tombs of brass are spent.

110[1]

Alas, 'tis true I have gone here and there
And made myself a motley[2] to the view,
Gored[3] mine own thoughts, sold cheap what is most dear,
Made old offenses of affections new;[4]
Most true it is that I have looked on truth   5
Askance and strangely; but, by all above,
These blenches[5] gave my heart another youth,
And worse essays[6] proved thee my best of love.
Now all is done, have what shall have no end:
Mine appetite I never more will grind[7]   10
On newer proof, to try an older friend,
A god in love, to whom I am confined.
Then give me welcome, next my heaven the best,
Even to thy pure and most most loving breast.

116

Let me not to the marriage of true minds
Admit impediments.[8] Love is not love
Which alters when it alteration finds,
Or bends with the remover to remove:
Oh, no! it is an ever-fixèd mark,   5
That looks on tempests and is never shaken;
It is the star to every wandering bark,
Whose worth's unknown, although his height[9] be taken.
Love's not Time's fool, though rosy lips and cheeks
Within his[1] bending sickle's compass come;   10
Love alters not with his brief hours and weeks,
But bears it out even to the edge of doom.[2]
If this be error and upon me proved,
   I never writ, nor no man ever loved.

118

   Like as, to make our appetites more keen,
   With eager[3] compounds we our palate urge;

9. Submits.
1. This is the second in a group of sonnets that deal with the poet's absence from the friend and an unfaithfulness to him. The first three lines may refer to Shakespeare's career as an actor.
2. A clown (with a varicolored costume).
3. Wounded.
4. Offended by changing old friends for new.
5. Offenses.
6. Trials of what is worse.

7. Whet.
8. From the Marriage Service: "If any of you know cause or just impediment why these persons should not be joined together * * * "
9. The star's value is not known, though the star's "height" (altitude) may be known and used for practical navigation.
1. I.e., Time's (as also in line 11).
2. Brink of the Last Judgment.
3. Bitter.

As, to prevent our maladies unseen,
We sicken to shun sickness when we purge:[4]
Even so, being full of your ne'er-cloying sweetness,   5
To bitter sauces did I frame my feeding;
And, sick of welfare,[5] found a kind of meetness
To be diseased ere that there was true needing.
Thus policy in love, t' anticipate
The ills that were not, grew to faults assuréd,   10
And brought to medicine a healthful state,
Which, rank of goodness, would by ill be curéd.
But thence I learn, and find the lesson true,
Drugs poison him that so fell sick of you.

121

'Tis better to be vile than vile esteemed
When not to be receives reproach of being,[6]
And the just pleasure lost, which is so deemed
Not by our feeling but by others' seeing.
For why should others' false adulterate eyes
Give salutation to my sportive blood?[7]
Or on my frailties why are frailer spies,[8]
Which in their wills count bad what I think good?
No, I am that I am; and they that level[9]
At my abuses reckon up their own: 10
I may be straight though they themselves be bevel;[1]
By their rank thoughts my deeds must not be shown,
Unless this general evil they maintain:
All men are bad and in their badness reign.

129

Th' expense of spirit in a waste of shame
Is lust in action;[2] and till action, lust
Is perjured, murderous, bloody, full of blame,
Savage, extreme, rude, cruel, not to trust;
Enjoyed no sooner but despiséd straight: 5
Past reason hunted; and no sooner had,
Past reason hated, as a swallowed bait,
On purpose laid to make the taker mad:
Mad in pursuit, and in possession so;
Had, having, and in quest to have, extreme;   10
A bliss in proof[3] and proved, a very woe;

4. Take cathartics.
5. Replete with well-being; as in "rank of goodness" (line 12). "Sick of" does not have the modern meaning "tired of"; it rather means "sick with," here and in line 14.
6. I.e., it is better to be vicious than to be thought vicious when the innocent are thought vicious.
7. Others' falsified, lewdly corrupt eyes tempt me.

8. Men with more frailties.
9. Aim.
1. Crooked, slanting.
2. The word order here is inverted and slightly obscures the meaning. Lust, when put into action, expends "spirit" (life, vitality) in a "waste" (desert, with a possible pun on "waist," also) of shame.
3. A bliss during the experience.

Before, a joy proposed; behind, a dream.
All this the world well knows; yet none knows well
To shun the heaven that leads men to this hell.

130

My mistress' eyes are nothing like the sun;[4]
Coral is far more red than her lips' red;
If snow be white, why then her breasts are dun;
If hairs be wires, black wires grow on her head.
I have seen roses damasked,[5] red and white,   5
But no such roses see I in her cheeks;
And in some perfumes is there more delight
Than in the breath that from my mistress reeks.
I love to hear her speak, yet well I know
That music hath a far more pleasing sound;   10
I grant I never saw a goddess go;[6]
My mistress, when she walks, treads on the ground.
And yet, by heaven, I think my love as rare
As any she belied with false compare.

138

When my love swears that she is made of truth,
I do believe her, though I know she lies,
That she might think me some untutored youth,
Unlearnèd in the world's false subtleties.
Thus vainly thinking that she thinks me young,   5
Although she knows my days are past the best,[7]
Simply I credit her false-speaking tongue:
On both sides thus is simple truth suppressed.
But wherefore says she not she is unjust?[8]
And wherefore say not I that I am old?   10
Oh, love's best habit[9] is in seeming trust,
And age in love loves not to have years told.
Therefore I lie with her and she with me,
And in our faults by lies we flattered be.

144

Two loves I have of comfort and despair,
Which like two spirits do suggest me still:[1]
The better angel is a man right fair,
The worser spirit a woman, colored ill.[2]
To win me soon to hell, my female evil   5
Tempteth my better angel from my side,
And would corrupt my saint to be a devil,

---

4. An anti-Petrarchan sonnet. All of the details commonly attributed by other Elizabethan sonneteers to their ladies are here denied to the poet's mistress.
5. Variegated. The damask rose (supposedly from Damascus, originally) is pink.
6. Walk.

7. Shakespeare was 35 or younger when he wrote this sonnet (it first appeared in *The Passionate Pilgrim*, 1599). "Simply": like a simpleton.
8. Unfaithful.
9. Appearance, deportment.
1. Tempt me constantly.
2. Dark.

Wooing his purity with her foul pride.
And whether that my angel be turned fiend
Suspect I may, yet not directly tell;   10
But being both from[3] me, both to each friend,
I guess one angel in another's hell.
Yet this shall I ne'er know, but live in doubt,
Till my bad angel fire[4] my good one out.

146

Poor soul, the center of my sinful earth,
Lord of[5] these rebel powers that thee array,[6]
Why dost thou pine within and suffer dearth,
Painting thy outward walls so costly gay?
Why so large cost, having so short a lease,   5
Dost thou upon thy fading mansion spend?
Shall worms, inheritors of this excess,
Eat up thy charge? Is this thy body's end?
Then, soul, live thou upon thy servant's loss,
And let that pine to aggravate thy store;[7]   10
Buy terms[8] divine in selling hours of dross;
Within be fed, without be rich no more.
So shalt thou feed on death, that feeds on men,
And death once dead, there's no more dying then.

The Phoenix and the Turtle[1]

Let the bird of loudest lay,[2]
On the sole Arabian tree,
Herald sad and trumpet be,
To whose sound chaste wings obey.

3. Away from; "each": each other.
4. Drive out by fire.
5. An emendation. The Quarto repeats the last three words of line 1. Other suggestions are "Thrall to," "Starv'd by," "Press'd by," and leaving the repetition but dropping "that 'thee" in line 2
6. Dress out, often used in a military sense.
7. Let "that" (i.e., the body) deteriorate to increase ("aggravate") the soul's riches ("thy store").
8. Long periods; "dross": refuse, rubbish.
1. First published in Robert Chester's *Love's Martyr, or Rosalin's Complaint* (1601). It is part of an appendix containing "divers poetical essays" by other poets, all supposedly dealing with the same subject. This subject has something to do with a Welsh knight, Sir John Salusbury, and his lady. But Shakespeare's poem is not consistent with the other poems in the volume, for some of them celebrate the birth of offspring to the phoenix and the turtle, whereas Shakespeare says the birds died leaving no posterity. The phoenix is a legendary bird of Arabia: it perishes in flames and a new one arises from the ashes; only one is alive at a time. Queen Elizabeth, the Virgin Queen, was sometimes symbolized by the unique and virginal phoenix. The "turtle" (turtledove) is common in Elizabethan imagery as the most loving of birds. Bird poems were traditionally allegorical, from Chaucer's time on down, but the key to this allegory (if it is one) has been lost.
2. Cry or song. This stanza might be paraphrased, "Let the bird with the loudest voice proclaim from the perch of the phoenix ('Arabian tree'); all gentle birds ('chaste wings') will respond to the summons."

But thou shrieking harbinger,   5
Foul precurrer of the fiend,[3]
Augur of the fever's end,
To this troop come thou not near!

From this session interdict
Every fowl of tyrant wing,   10
Save the eagle, feathered king:
Keep the obsequy so strict.

Let the priest in surplice white,
That defunctive music can,[4]
Be the death-divining swan,   15
Lest the requiem lack his right.

And thou treble-dated[5] crow,
That thy sable gender mak'st
With the breath thou giv'st and tak'st,[6]
'Mongst our mourners shalt thou go.   20

Here the anthem doth commence:
Love and constancy is dead,
Phoenix and the turtle fled
In a mutual flame from hence.

So they loved as love in twain   25
Had the essence but in one;[7]
Two distincts, division none:
Number there in love was slain.

Hearts remote, yet not asunder;
Distance, and no space was seen   30
'Twixt this turtle and his queen;
But in them[8] it were a wonder.

So between them love did shine
That the turtle saw his right[9]
Flaming in the phoenix' sight: 35
Either was the other's mine.[1]

Property[2] was thus appalled,
That the self was not the same;
Single nature's double name
Neither two nor one was called.   40

---

3. Forerunner of the devil. "Harbinger": precursor. The screech owl is probably meant.
4. I.e., skilled in funeral ("defunctive") music. The swan was supposed to sing only once, just before its death.
5. Living three lifetimes.
6. "Sable gender": black offspring. The crow was supposed to conceive and lay its eggs through the bill.
7. They were originally two, but by love were united into one. Since one is singular, and not a number, "Number there in love was slain."
8. In any other case than theirs.
9. What was due him, love returned.
1. Rich source of wealth or treasure.
2. Peculiar or essential quality. "Property" is "appalled" to find that personality ("self") is obliterated in the union of the two. Accordingly it is impossible to say whether they were two or one.

Reason, in itself confounded,
Saw division grow together,[3]
To themselves yet either neither,
Simple were so well compounded;

That it cried, "How true a twain   45
Seemeth this concordant one!
Love hath reason, reason none,
If what parts can so remain."[4]

Whereupon it made this threne[5]
To the phoenix and the dove,   50
Co-supremes and stars of love,
As chorus to their tragic scene.

Threnos

Beauty, truth, and rarity,
Grace in all simplicity,
Here enclosed in cinders lie.   55

Death is now the phoenix' nest;
And the turtle's loyal breast
To eternity doth rest,

Leaving no posterity:
'Twas not their infirmity,   60
It was married chastity.

Truth may seem, but cannot be;
Beauty brag, but 'tis not she:[6]
Truth and Beauty buried be.

To this urn let those repair   65
That are either true or fair;
For these dead birds sigh a prayer.

1601

---

1 Henry IV   The title page of the first quarto edition of Shakespeare's *1 Henry IV*, published in 1598, reads:"THE HISTORY OF HENRIE THE FOURTH; With the the battell at Shrewsburie, *betweene the King and Lord* Henry Percy, surnamed Henrie Hotspur of the North. *With the humorous conceits of Sir John Falstalffe.*" It had been performed on the stage and at court before publication, and from that time to this it has remained one of Shakespeare's most popular plays.

Shakespeare had already inaugurated a new dramatic type by writing

3. Reason, which discriminates parts of a thing, is here confounded because the two parts are merged. Each element lost its identity in being fused with the other.
4. Love is more reasonable than reason, because it has proved that the separateness of entities (one of reason's laws) does not always hold true.
5. Threnody, funeral song.
6. Whatever may appear hereafter as truth or beauty will be only illusion. Real truth and beauty lie buried here.

four plays dealing with fairly recent English history, and had then gone back to a period two centuries earlier to portray, in *Richard II*, the downfall of the weak, effeminate and poetic young King Richard ("that sweet lovely rose," as he is called in this play) at the hands of the hard, efficient Bolingbroke, who came to the throne as Henry IV. Before this seizure of the crown there had been a prophecy, put by Shakespeare into the mouth of the Bishop of Carlisle in *Richard II* (IV.i.136–44), of the dire consequences to follow:

> And if you crown him, let me prophesy,
> The blood of English shall manure the ground
> And future ages groan for this foul act;
> Peace shall go sleep with Turks and infidels,
> And in this seat of peace tumultuous wars
> Shall kin with kin and kind with kind confound;
> Disorder, horror, fear, and mutiny
> Shall here inhabit, and this land be called
> The field of Golgotha and dead men's skulls.

Shakespeare drew his historical material from the prose chronicle histories, specifically Raphael Holinshed's *Chronicles of England, Scotland, and Ireland*, Samuel Daniel's historical poem *Civil Wars*, and an earlier play, either the popular farcical piece called *The Famous Victories of Henry V* or a lost play which was its source. His sources gave him the portrait of a gay and reckless Prince of Wales and his roistering companions. Chief of these was a fat knight, Sir John Oldcastle; Shakespeare at first used this name, but later, because of protests from the descendants of that Protestant martyr, changed the name to Sir John Falstaff. This character, whose "humorous conceits" are advertised on the title page, is one of the greatest comic creations in all literature. Shakespeare continued to exploit his inexhaustible exuberance through a sequel, *The Second Part of Henry IV*, and a comedy of middle-class life, supposed to have been written at Queen Elizabeth's command, *The Merry Wives of Windsor*.

The ominous wars of Carlisle's prophecy could thus be mixed with hilarious fooling, but *1 Henry IV* succeeds, not only as a comedy, but as a serious play about character and history. The real hero is not King Henry IV, nor the fat Falstaff, but Prince Hal, the handsome playboy who in time of crisis reforms and saves his father's throne. He is the prince who later became Henry V, the English national hero who reconquered France.

Shakespeare's theme in all his history plays is the importance of order and degree, of the disruptive effects of civil strife and rebellion. But as he matured as a dramatist (and *1 Henry IV* stands at the beginning of his great period of maturity), he found character to be more interesting than the philosophy or events of history. How to demonstrate the kind of character that would make the English national hero was his problem, and he solved it by a method of comparison and contrast, utilizing four men of different types. At one extreme is Falstaff, who loves to eat, drink, joke, and dramatize himself, and to whom anything as intangible as honor is a mere word, a breath of air. Opposite in every way is Hotspur, fiery and impatient, completely ambitious for honor and fame, scornful of the soft, civilized arts of poetry and music, a hardheaded fanatic. A third type is the wild Welshman Glendower, a believer in magic and a practitioner of it, an accomplished poet yet a valiant, if superstitious, warrior, and an egotist like his ally Hotspur. Finally there is Prince Hal, whose sense of humor rivals Falstaff's, but who turns out to be the match for Hotspur in valor and his superior in knightly courtesy. It is worth noting that Shakespeare changed history in order to make this dramatic contrast: in Holinshed's *Chronicle* Hotspur is older than Prince Hal's father, but Shakespeare makes them contemporaries. It is in the excesses of the other three that we see the merits of the Prince's character illuminated. The four characters represent not only men but ways of life. And these ways of life are all relevant to fundamental questions about social and political responsibility, honor, and loyalty to a cause.

Some background in 15th-century English history, as Shakespeare understood it, is needed if we are to respond readily to the play. Henry Hereford, called Bolingbroke, was in exile in France when his father, John of Gaunt, died. He returned to England to claim his inheritance, and profited from the aid of the Percy family, powerful nobles in the north. The two brothers, Henry Percy, Earl of Northumberland, and Thomas Percy, Earl of Worcester, together with Northumberland's son Henry (called Hotspur) received Bolingbroke's oath at Doncaster (see V.i.32–58) to seize only his inheritance. But King Richard II was in Ireland fighting, having named Edmund Mortimer, Earl of March, his successor if he did not return. In the confused situation in England, Bolingbroke was able to collect enough power so that on Richard's return he could force him to abdicate and then have him killed in prison. Various troubles on the borders made the throne of the new king (Henry IV) insecure. Hotspur managed to defeat the Scots under Douglas at Holmédon (see I.i.62–75) and took many important prisoners. But Mortimer, in fighting against Glendower in Wales, was taken captive and married Glendower's daughter. Henry IV refused to ransom Mortimer, and the indignation of Mortimer's brother-in-law, Hotspur, led him to refuse to turn over his prisoners to the king. So came the conspiracy into being—and such a formidable opposition as that of the Percies, Douglas, Glendower, and certain disaffected churchmen like the Archbishop of York meant a critical danger to Henry's throne. The Battle of Shrewsbury, the climax of this play, decides the conflict.

Much critical comment has been devoted to the character of Falstaff. He has certain resemblances to the traditional *miles gloriosus* (braggart soldier) of Latin comedy, but he far transcends the type; he sometimes resembles the Vice, a comic character in the old morality plays, who is usually an allegorical personification of extreme self-indulgence or of a particular sin; and he often uses, or parodies, the language of the Puritans. Critics differ on whether Falstaff is really a coward or not, and on the question of how much he expects his lies to be believed. But everyone agrees about his inexhaustible vitality and resiliency. It is not surprising that he, like other immortal characters in literature, remains something of a mystery.

The First Part of
King Henry the Fourth

Dramatis Personae

KING HENRY THE FOURTH

HENRY, *Prince of Wales*
PRINCE JOHN OF LANCASTER   } *Sons to the* KING
EARL OF WESTMORELAND

SIR WALTER BLUNT

THOMAS PERCY, *Earl of Worcester*

HENRY PERCY, *Earl of Northumberland*

HENRY PERCY, *surnamed* HOTSPUR, *his son*

EDMUND MORTIMER, *Earl of March*

RICHARD SCROOP, *Archbishop of York*

ARCHIBALD, *Earl of Douglas*

OWEN GLENDOWER

SIR RICHARD VERNON

SIR MICHAEL, *a friend to the* ARCHBISHOP OF YORK

SIR JOHN FALSTAFF

POINS

GADSHILL

PETO

BARDOLPH

LADY PERCY, *wife to* HOTSPUR, *and sister to* MORTIMER

LADY MORTIMER, *daughter to* GLENDOWER, *and wife to* MORTIMER

MISTRESS QUICKLY, *hostess of a tavern in Eastcheap*

LORDS, OFFICERS, SHERIFF, VINTNER, CHAMBERLAIN, DRAWERS, *two*
CARRIERS, TRAVELERS, *and* ATTENDANTS

Act I

SCENE 1

[*Enter the* KING, PRINCE JOHN OF LANCASTER, THE EARL OF
WESTMORELAND, SIR WALTER BLUNT, *with others.*]

KING. So shaken as we are, so wan with care,
   Find we a time for frighted peace to pant,[1]
   And breathe short-winded accents of new broils[2]
   To be commenced in stronds afar remote.
   No more the thirsty entrance[3] of this soil   5
   Shall daub her lips with her own children's blood;
   No more shall trenching war channel her fields,
   Nor bruise her flowerets with the arméd hoofs
   Of hostile paces:[4] those opposéd eyes,
   Which, like the meteors of a troubled heaven,   10
   All of one nature, of one substance bred,
   Did lately meet in the intestine shock[5]
   And furious close of civil butchery,
   Shall now, in mutual well-beseeming ranks,

1. I.e., let us allow peace to catch her
breath.
2. I.e., news of new wars; "stronds":
strands, regions.
3. Surface.
4. The tread of war horses.
5. Internal violence; "close": encounter.

March all one way and be no more opposed   15
Against acquaintance, kindred, and allies.
The edge of war, like an ill-sheathéd knife,
No more shall cut his master: therefore, friends,
As far as to the sepulcher of Christ,
Whose soldier now, under whose blessed cross   20
We are impresséd and engaged to fight,
Forthwith a power[6] of English shall we levy,
Whose arms were molded in their mother's womb
To chase these pagans in those holy fields
Over whose acres walked those blessed feet   25
Which fourteen hundred years ago were nailed
For our advantage on the bitter cross.
But this our purpose now is twelve month old,
And bootless[7] 'tis to tell you we will go.
Therefore we meet not now:[8] then let me hear   30
Of you, my gentle cousin Westmoreland,
What yesternight our council did decree
In forwarding this dear expedience.[9]

WEST. My liege, this haste was hot in question,[1]
And many limits of the charge set down   35
But yesternight, when all athwart[2] there came
A post from Wales loaden with heavy news,
Whose worst was that the noble Mortimer,
Leading the men of Herefordshire to fight
Against the irregular[3] and wild Glendower,   40
Was by the rude hands of that Welshman taken,
A thousand of his people butcheréd,
Upon whose dead corpse[4] there was such misuse,
Such beastly shameless transformatión,
By those Welshwomen done as may not be   45
Without much shame retold or spoken of.

KING. It seems then that the tidings of this broil
Brake off our business for the Holy Land.

WEST. This matched with other did, my gracious lord,
For more uneven and unwelcome news   50
Came from the north, and thus it did import:
On Holyrood Day[5] the gallant Hotspur there,
Young Harry Percy, and brave Archibald,
That ever-valiant and approvéd Scot,
At Holmedon met,   55
Where they did spend a sad and bloody hour;
As by discharge of their artillery,
And shape of likelihood,[6] the news was told;
For he that brought them[7] in the very heat

6. Army. He is planning a crusade, in expiation of his guilt for the death of Richard II.
7. Useless.
8. I.e., that is not the reason for our present meeting. "Cousin": kinsman.
9. Important, urgent matter.
1. Actively discussed. "Limits of the charge": assignment of commands.
2. Interrupting, crossing our purpose. "Post": messenger.
3. Guerilla.
4. Bodies.
5. Holy Cross Day (Sept. 14).
6. Probable inference. "As": since.
7. I.e., the news (usually a plural in Shakespeare). "Pride": height; literally, the top of a falcon's flight.

And pride of their contention did take horse,   60
  Uncertain of the issue any way.
KING. Here is a dear, a true industrious friend,
  Sir Walter Blunt, new lighted from his horse,
  Stained with the variation of each soil
  Betwixt that Holmedon and this seat of ours;   65
  And he hath brought us smooth and welcome news.
  The Earl of Douglas is discomfited;
  Ten thousand bold Scots, two and twenty knights
  Balked[8] in their own blood did Sir Walter see
  On Holmedon's plains. Of prisoners Hotspur took   70
  Mordake Earl of Fife, and eldest son
  To beaten Douglas, and the Earl of Athol,
  Of Murray, Angus, and Menteith;
  And is not this an honorable spoil,
  A gallant prize? ha, cousin, is it not?   75
WEST. In faith,
  It is a conquest for a prince to boast of.
KING. Yea, there thou mak'st me sad and mak'st me sin
  In envy that my Lord Northumberland
  Should be the father to so blest a son,   80
  A son who is the theme of honor's tongue,
  Amongst a grove the very straightest plant,
  Who is sweet Fortune's minion[9] and her pride;
  Whilst I, by looking on the praise of him,
  See riot and dishonor stain the brow   85
  Of my young Harry. O that it could be proved
  That some night-tripping fairy had exchanged
  In cradle-clothes our children where they lay,
  And called mine Percy, his Plantagenet!
  Then would I have his Harry, and he mine.   90
  But let him from my thoughts. What think you, coz,
  Of this young Percy's pride? The prisoners
  Which he in this adventure hath surprised
  To his own use he keeps, and sends me word
  I shall have none but Mordake Earl of Fife.   95
WEST. This is his uncle's teaching, this is Worcester,
  Malevolent to you in all aspects,[1]
  Which makes him prune himself,[2] and bristle up
  The crest of youth against your dignity.
KING. But I have sent for him to answer this;   100
  And for this cause awhile we must neglect
  Our holy purpose to Jerusalem.
  Cousin, on Wednesday next our council we
  Will hold at Windsor, so inform the lords;
  But come yourself with speed to us again,   105
  For more is to be said and to be done
  Than out of anger can be utterèd.
WEST. I will, my liege.   [*Exeunt.*]

8. Heaped.
9. Favorite.
1. Hostile in every way. The figure is from astrology.

2. Plume himself. "Bristle up" and "crest" continue the image, which is that of a fighting cock.

SCENE 2

[*Enter* HENRY, PRINCE OF WALES, *and* SIR JOHN FALSTAFF.]

FAL. Now Hal, what time of day is it, lad?

PRINCE. Thou art so fat-witted with drinking of old sack,[3] and un-
buttoning thee after supper, and sleeping upon benches after
noon, that thou hast forgotten to demand that truly which
thou wouldst truly know. What a devil hast thou to do with   5
the time of the day? Unless hours were cups of sack, and minutes capons, and clocks the tongues of bawds, and dials the
signs of leaping-houses,[4] and the blessed sun himself a fair hot
wench in flame-colored taffeta, I see no reason why thou
shouldst be so superfluous to demand the time of the day.   10

FAL. Indeed you come near me now, Hal, for we that take purses
go by the moon and the seven stars, and not by Phoebus,[5] he,
"that wandering knight so fair." And I prithee, sweet wag,
when thou art king, as, God save thy grace—majesty I should
say, for grace[6] thou wilt have none—   15

PRINCE. What, none?

FAL. No, by my troth, not so much as will serve to be prologue
to an egg and butter.

PRINCE. Well, how then? come, roundly, roundly.[7]

FAL. Marry then, sweet wag, when thou art king, let not us that   20
are squires of the night's body[8] be called thieves of the day's
beauty; let us be Diana's foresters, gentlemen of the shade,
minions of the moon; and let men say we be men of good
government, being governed as the sea is, by our noble and
chaste mistress the moon, under whose countenance we steal.   25

PRINCE. Thou sayest well, and it holds well too, for the fortune
of us that are the moon's men doth ebb and flow like the sea,
being governed as the sea is by the moon. As for proof now:
a purse of gold most resolutely snatched on Monday night and
most dissolutely spent on Tuesday morning, got with swearing   30
"Lay by" and spent with crying "Bring in," now in as low an
ebb as the foot of the ladder and by and by in as high a flow
as the ridge of the gallows.[9]

FAL. By the Lord thou sayest true, lad. And is not my hostess of
the tavern a most sweet wench?   35

PRINCE. As the honey of Hybla,[1] my old lad of the castle. And is
not a buff jerkin a most sweet robe of durance?[2]

3. Sherry.
4. Whorehouses.
5. The sun. Falstaff then quotes from
a popular ballad.
6. A triple pun: (1) "your Grace,"
the correct manner of addressing a
prince or duke; (2) the divine influence
which produces sanctity; and (3) a
short prayer before a meal—hence
Falstaff's allusion to "egg and butter,"
a common hasty breakfast.
7. Plainly.
8. Two puns are involved: a "squire
of the body" was an attendant on a
knight, and "body" would be pronounced *bawdy*. "Beauty" also puns
with "booty" (which thieves take);

Diana is, of course, the moon goddess.
9. "Lay by": i.e., hand over (a robber's command to his victim); "bring
in": a customer's command for more
drink at a tavern. The "foot of the
ladder" is at the bottom of the gallows
(robbery was a hanging offense);
the "ridge" is the crosspiece at the
top.
1. A town in Sicily, famous for honey;
"old lad of the castle" is a reference
to Falstaff's original name, Oldcastle.
2. A "buff jerkin" was the leather
jacket worn by a sheriff's sergeant;
"durance" is a pun: (1) lasting quality
and (2) imprisonment.

FAL. How now, how now, mad wag! what, in thy quips and thy quiddities?[3] what a plague have I to do with a buff jerkin?

PRINCE. Why, what a pox have I to do with my hostess of the tavern? 40

FAL. Well, thou hast called her to a reckoning many a time and oft.

PRINCE. Did I ever call for thee to pay thy part?

FAL. No, I'll give thee thy due, thou hast paid all there. 45

PRINCE. Yea, and elsewhere, so far as my coin would stretch, and where it would not I have used my credit.

FAL. Yea, and so used it that were it not here apparent that thou art heir apparent[4]—but I prithee, sweet wag, shall there be gallows standing in England when thou art king? and resolu- 50 tion thus fobbed as it is with the rusty curb of old father antic the law?[5] Do not thou, when thou art king, hang a thief.

PRINCE. No, thou shalt.

FAL. Shall I? O rare! By the Lord, I'll be a brave judge.

PRINCE. Thou judgest false already; I mean thou shalt have the 55 hanging of the thieves and so become a rare hangman.

FAL. Well, Hal, well; and in some sort it jumps with my humor[6] as well as waiting in the court, I can tell you.

PRINCE. For obtaining of suits?[7]

FAL. Yea, for obtaining of suits, whereof the hangman hath no 60 lean wardrobe. 'Sblood,[8] I am as melancholy as a gib cat or a lugged bear.

PRINCE. Or an old lion, or a lover's lute.

FAL. Yea, or the drone of a Lincolnshire bagpipe.

PRINCE. What sayest thou to a hare, or the melancholy of Moor- 65 ditch?[9]

FAL. Thou hast the most unsavory similes and art indeed the most comparative,[1] rascalliest, sweet young prince. But Hal, I prithee, trouble me no more with vanity. I would to God thou and I knew where a commodity of good names were to be 70 bought. An old lord of the council rated[2] me the other day in the street about you, sir, but I marked him not; and yet he talked very wisely, but I regarded him not; and yet he talked wisely, and in the street too.

PRINCE. Thou didst well, for wisdom cries out in the streets and 75 no man regards it.[3]

FAL. O, thou hast damnable iteration[4] and art indeed able to corrupt a saint. Thou hast done much harm upon me, Hal, God forgive thee for it! Before I knew thee, Hal, I knew noth-

3. Quibbles.
4. "Here" and "heir" would pun in Elizabethan pronunciation.
5. "Resolution": bravery; "fobbed": cheated; "antic": a clown.
6. I.e., agrees with my disposition.
7. Special favors, but "clothing" in the next line. The hangman was given the clothes of his victims.
8. God's blood, a common oath. "Gib cat": tomcat; "lugged": baited (in the bear-baiting pits a bear was attacked by

dogs as a public amusement).
9. The "hare" was traditionally associated with melancholy; Moorditch was a foul-smelling ditch on the outskirts of London.
1. Affecting wit, dealing in comparisons.
2. Scolded, berated.
3. Prince Hal is quoting Proverbs i. 20 and 24.
4. Repetition, especially of sacred texts.

ing, and now am I, if a man should speak truly, little better 80
than one of the wicked. I must give over this life, and I will
give it over; by the Lord, an[5] I do not, I am a villain; I'll be
damned for never a king's son in Christendom.

PRINCE. Where shall we take a purse tomorrow, Jack?

FAL. Zounds, where thou wilt, lad; I'll make one; an I do not, 85
call me villain and baffle[6] me.

PRINCE. I see a good amendment of life in thee—from praying
to purse-taking.

FAL. Why, Hal, 'tis my vocation,[7] Hal; 'tis no sin for a man to
labor in his vocation. 90

[*Enter* POINS.]

Poins! Now shall we know if Gadshill[8] have set a match. O, if
men were to be saved by merit, what hole in hell were hot
enough for him? This is the most omnipotent villain that ever
cried "stand" to a true man.

PRINCE. Good morrow, Ned. 95

POINS. Good morrow, sweet Hal. What says Monsieur Remorse?
what says Sir John Sack and Sugar? Jack! how agrees the devil
and thee about thy soul, that thou soldest him on Good Friday last for a cup of Madeira and a cold capon's leg?

PRINCE. Sir John stands to his word; the devil shall have his bar- 100
gain, for he was never yet a breaker of proverbs; he will give
the devil his due.

POINS. Then art thou damned for keeping thy word with the
devil.

PRINCE. Else he had been damned for cozening[9] the devil. 105

POINS. But my lads, my lads, tomorrow morning by four o'clock,
early at Gadshill, there are pilgrims going to Canterbury with
rich offerings, and traders riding to London with fat purses.
I have vizards[1] for you all, you have horses for yourselves; Gadshill lies tonight in Rochester; I have bespoke supper tomorrow 110
night in Eastcheap; we may do it as secure as sleep. If you will
go, I will stuff your purses full of crowns; if you will not, tarry
at home and be hanged.

FAL. Hear ye, Yedward, if I tarry at home and go not, I'll hang
you for going. 115

POINS. You will, chops?[2]

FAL. Hal, wilt thou make one?

PRINCE. Who, I rob? I a thief? not I, by my faith.

FAL. There's neither honesty, manhood, nor good fellowship in
thee, nor thou camest not of the blood royal,[3] if thou darest 120

---

5. If.

6. A knight in the days of chivalry was "baffled" or disgraced by having his shield hung upside down. Falstaff may mean "hang me up by the heels." "Zounds": a common oath, a contraction of "by God's wounds" (i.e., Jesus' wounds on the Cross).

7. Falstaff is here making fun of the Puritan doctrine of "calling" or vocation, based on the parable of the talents (see Matthew xxv.25 ff.).

8. Gadshill is both a man and a place: the place is a hill 27 miles from London on the road to Rochester; it was notorious for robberies. The man, so called from the place, is the thieves' "setter," who arranges when and where the robbery will occur.

9. Cheating.

1. Masks.

2. Fat face.

3. A pun: the coin called a "royal" was worth ten shillings. "Stand for" also puns: it means both "represent" and "fight for."

not stand for ten shillings.

PRINCE. Well then, once in my days I'll be a madcap.

FAL. Why, that's well said.

PRINCE. Well, come what will, I'll tarry at home.

FAL. By the Lord, I'll be a traitor then, when thou art king.   125

PRINCE. I care not.

POINS. Sir John, I prithee leave the prince and me alone; I will
lay him down such reasons for this adventure that he shall go.

FAL. Well, God give thee the spirit of persuasion and him the
ears of profiting, that what thou speakest may move and what   130
he hears may be believed, that the true prince may, for recreation sake, prove a false thief; for the poor abuses of the time
want countenance.[4] Farewell; you shall find me in Eastcheap.

PRINCE. Farewell, thou latter spring, farewell, Allhallown summer![5]

　　[⟨*Exit* FALSTAFF.⟩][6]

POINS. Now, my good sweet honey lord, ride with us tomorrow;   135
I have a jest to execute that I cannot manage alone. Falstaff,
Bardolph, Peto, and Gadshill shall rob those men that we have
already waylaid; yourself and I will not be there, and when
they have the booty, if you and I do not rob them, cut this
head off from my shoulders.   140

PRINCE. How shall we part with them in setting forth?

POINS. Why, we will set forth before or after them, and appoint
them a place of meeting, wherein it is at our pleasure to fail,
and then will they adventure upon the exploit themselves,
which they shall have no sooner achieved but we'll set upon   145
them.

PRINCE. Yea, but 'tis like that they will know us by our horses, by
our habits,[7] and by every other appointment to be ourselves.

POINS. Tut, our horses they shall not see—I'll tie them in the
wood; our vizards we will change after we leave them: and,   150
sirrah, I have cases of buckram for the nonce,[8] to immask our
noted outward garments.

PRINCE. Yea, but I doubt they will be too hard for us.

POINS. Well, for two of them, I know them to be as true-bred
cowards as ever turned back; and for the third, if he fight   155
longer than he sees reason, I'll forswear arms. The virtue of this
jest will be the incomprehensible lies that this same fat rogue
will tell us when we meet at supper: how thirty at least he
fought with; what wards,[9] what blows, what extremities he endured; and in the reproof of this lies the jest.   160

PRINCE. Well, I'll go with thee. Provide us all things necessary

---

4. A satirical reference to the common
complaint that the nobility did not
properly give "countenance" to (i.e.,
encourage) good causes, and to the
Puritan habit of attacking the "abuses
of the time." This entire speech parodies the language of the Puritans.
5. I.e., Indian summer. The two epithets are intended to suggest how unseasonable it is for Falstaff, an old
man, to be engaged in youthful, hood-

lum exploits.
6. This stage direction, like some others
in the play, does not appear in the
earliest editions; it was added by a
later editor. All such interpolated directions are indicated in our text by
the special brackets used here.
7. Clothes.
8. I.e., outer clothes (of a coarse, stiff
cloth) for the occasion.
9. Guards in fencing.

and meet me tomorrow night[1] in Eastcheap; there I'll sup.
Farewell.

POINS. Farewell, my lord.   [*Exit* POINS.]

PRINCE. I know you all, and will awhile uphold   165
The unyoked humor[2] of your idleness;
Yet herein will I imitate the sun,
Who doth permit the base contagious clouds
To smother up his beauty from the world,
That, when he please again to be himself,   170
Being wanted, he may be more wondered at
By breaking through the foul and ugly mists
Of vapors that did seem to strangle him.
If all the year were playing holidays,
To sport would be as tedious as to work;   175
But when they seldom come, they wished for come,
And nothing pleaseth but rare accidents.
So, when this loose behavior I throw off
And pay the debt I never promiséd,
By how much better than my word I am,   180
By so much shall I falsify men's hopes,
And like bright metal on a sullen ground,[3]
My reformation, glittering o'er my fault,
Shall show more goodly and attract more eyes
Than that which hath no foil[4] to set it off.   185
I'll so offend to make offense a skill,[5]
Redeeming time when men think least I will.   [*Exit.*]

SCENE 3

[*Enter the* KING, NORTHUMBERLAND, WORCESTER, HOT-
SPUR, SIR WALTER BLUNT, *with others.*]

KING. My blood hath been too cold and temperate,
Unapt to stir at these indignities,
And you have found me,[6] for accordingly
You tread upon my patience; but be sure
I will from henceforth rather be myself,   5
Mighty and to be feared, than my condition,[7]
Which hath been smooth as oil, soft as young down,
And therefore lost that title of respect
Which the proud soul ne'er pays but to the proud.

WOR. Our house, my sovereign liege, little deserves   10
The scourge of greatness to be used on it,

---

1. Either the text should read "tonight" (before the robbery) or else
Shakespeare intends to show Prince
Hal's mind intent, not on the robbery,
but on its aftermath. The soliloquy of
the Prince that follows has provoked
much critical discussion. Read psychologically, it makes Hal seem like a
prig and a self-conscious schemer, but
this surely was not Shakespeare's intention. Rather, the speech belongs to
the old dramatic convention in which
the speaker steps out of character for
a moment to deliver a message from
the playwright to the audience.
2. Undisciplined whim.
3. Dull background.
4. I.e., contrast.
5. Piece of good policy. "Redeeming
time": making good use of time, following the advice given to Christians
in a non-Christian world. See Ephesians
v.16.
6. Discovered this to be true.
7. Disposition.

And that same greatness too which our own hands
Have holp[8] to make so portly.
NORTH. My lord—
KING. Worcester, get thee gone, for I do see   15
  Danger and disobedience in thine eye;
  O, sir, your presence is too bold and peremptory,
  And majesty might never yet endure
  The moody frontier of a servant brow.[9]
  You have good leave to leave us; when we need   20
  Your use and counsel we shall send for you.   [*Exit* WOR.]
  You were about to speak.   [⟨*to* NORTH.⟩]
NORTH.   Yea, my good lord.
  Those prisoners in your highness' name demanded,
  Which Harry Percy here at Holmedon took,
  Were, as he says, not with such strength denied   25
  As is delivered to your majesty.
  Either envy therefore or misprisión[1]
  Is guilty of this fault, and not my son.
HOT. My liege, I did deny no prisoners.
  But I remember, when the fight was done,   30
  When I was dry with rage and extreme toil,
  Breathless and faint, leaning upon my sword,
  Came there a certain lord, neat and trimly dressed,
  Fresh as a bridegroom, and his chin new reaped
  Showed like a stubble-land at harvest-home;   35
  He was perfuméd like a milliner,[2]
  And 'twixt his finger and his thumb he held
  A pouncet box,[3] which ever and anon
  He gave his nose and took 't away again;
  Who therewith angry, when it next came there,   40
  Took it in snuff;[4] and still he smiled and talked,
  And as the soldiers bore dead bodies by,
  He called them untaught knaves, unmannerly,
  To bring a slovenly[5] unhandsome corse
  Betwixt the wind and his nobility.   45
  With many holiday and lady terms[6]
  He questioned me; amongst the rest, demanded
  My prisoners in your majesty's behalf.
  I then, all smarting with my wounds being cold,
  To be so pestered with a popinjay,[7]   50
  Out of my grief and my impatience
  Answered neglectingly I know not what,
  He should, or he should not; for he made me mad
  To see him shine so brisk and smell so sweet

8. Helped; "portly": stately.
9. I.e., a servant's brow showing defiance, like a fortification ("frontier").
1. "Envy": malice; "misprision": mistake.
2. Not a maker of hats, but a dealer in perfumes, women's gloves, etc.
3. Perfume box.
4. I.e., was annoyed at it, with a pun on "snuffing it up."
5. Nasty, disgusting; "corse": corpse, body.
6. Affected and effeminate language (not "everyday" English).
7. Parrot.

And talk so like a waiting-gentlewoman 55
Of guns and drums and wounds—God save the mark!—
And telling me the sovereign'st thing on earth
Was parmaceti[8] for an inward bruise,
And that it was great pity, so it was,
This villanous saltpeter[9] should be digged 60
Out of the bowels of the harmless earth,
Which many a good tall[1] fellow had destroyed
So cowardly, and but for these vile guns
He would himself have been a soldier.
This bald[2] unjointed chat of his, my lord, 65
I answered indirectly as I said,
And I beseech you, let not his report
Come current[3] for an accusation
Betwixt my love and your high majesty.

BLUNT. The circumstance considered, good my lord, 70
Whate'er Lord Harry Percy then had said
To such a person and in such a place,
At such a time, with all the rest retold,
May reasonably die and never rise
To do him wrong or any way impeach 75
What then he said, so he unsay it now.

KING. Why, yet[4] he doth deny his prisoners,
But with pioviso and exceptión,
That we at our own charge shall ransom straight
His brother-in-law, the foolish Mortimer, 80
Who, on my soul, hath willfully betrayed
The lives of those that he did lead to fight
Against that great magician, damned Glendower,
Whose daughter, as we hear, the Earl of March
Hath lately married. Shall our coffers then 85
Be emptied to redeem a traitor home?
Shall we buy treason? and indent with fears,[5]
When they have lost and forfeited themselves?
No, on the barren mountains let him starve;
For I shall never hold that man my friend 90
Whose tongue shall ask me for one penny cost
To ransom home revolted Mortimer.

HOT. Revolted Mortimer!
He never did fall off, my sovereign liege,
But by the chance of war. To prove that true 95
Needs no more but one tongue for all those wounds,
Those mouthéd wounds[6] which valiantly he took
When on the gentle Severn's sedgy bank
In single opposition, hand to hand,

8. Spermaceti, whale oil used as an ointment.
9. Used in gunpowder.
1. Brave.
2. Trivial. "Indirectly": negligently.
3. Be considered valid.
4. I.e., even after all this (the strong use of "yet"). "But": except.

5. Enter into a contract with cowards.
6. Wounds are often likened to mouths in Shakespeare. The image may derive from their appearance and from the idea that they could speak as witnesses to what caused them. Cf. *Julius Caesar* III.ii.229–31 and *Richard III* I.ii. 55–56.

He did confound the best part of an hour 100
In changing hardiment[7] with great Glendower;
Three times they breathed[8] and three times did they drink
Upon agreement of swift Severn's flood,
Who then, affrighted with their bloody looks,
Ran fearfully among the trembling reeds, 105
And hid his crisp[9] head in the hollow bank
Bloodstainéd with these valiant combatants.
Never did bare and rotten policy[1]
Color her working with such deadly wounds,
Nor never could the noble Mortimer 110
Receive so many, and all willingly;
Then let not him be slandered with revolt.

KING. Thou dost belie him, Percy, thou dost belie him;
He never did encounter with Glendower.
I tell thee, 115
He durst as well have met the devil alone
As Owen Glendower for an enemy.
Art thou not ashamed? But, sirrah,[2] henceforth
Let me not hear you speak of Mortimer;
Send me your prisoners with the speediest means, 120
Or you shall hear in such a kind from me
As will displease you. My Lord Northumberland,
We license your departure with your son.
Send us your prisoners, or you will hear of it.
[*Exeunt* KING, ⟨BLUNT, *and train.*⟩]

HOT. An if the devil come and roar for them 125
I will not send them; I will after straight
And tell him so, for I will ease my heart
Albeit I make a hazard of my head.

NORTH. What, drunk with choler?[3] stay and pause awhile.
Here comes your uncle.
[*Enter* WORCESTER.]

HOT. Speak of Mortimer! 130
Zounds, I will speak of him, and let my soul
Want mercy if I do not join with him;
Yea, on his part[4] I'll empty all these veins,
And shed my dear blood drop by drop in the dust,
But I will lift the downtrod Mortimer 135
As high in the air as this unthankful king,
As this ingrate and cankered[5] Bolingbroke.

NORTH. Brother, the king hath made your nephew mad.

WOR. Who struck this heat up after I was gone?

HOT. He will, forsooth, have all my prisoners; 140
And when I urged the ransom once again
Of my wife's brother, then his cheek looked pale,
And on my face he turned an eye of death,

7. Testing prowess and exchanging blows. "Confound": spend.
8. Paused for breath.
9. I.e., curly (because of the waves).
1. Craftiness or conspiracy; "color": disguise.
2. A form of "Sir," but used familiarly, and sometimes, as here, with a tone of contempt. "Speak of": i.e., even mention (an emphatic sense of "speak").
3. Anger.
4. Behalf.
5. Ungrateful and malignant.

Trembling even at the name of Mortimer.

WOR. I cannot blame him; was not he proclaimed 145
By Richard, that dead is, the next of blood?

NORTH. He was—I heard the proclamatión;
And then it was when the unhappy king
(Whose wrongs in us God pardon!⁶) did set forth
Upon his Irish expeditión; 150
From whence he intercepted did return
To be deposed and shortly murderéd.

WOR. And for whose death we in the world's wide mouth
Live scandalized and foully spoken of.

HOT. But soft, I pray you; did King Richard then 155
Proclaim my brother⁷ Edmund Mortimer
Heir to the crown?

NORTH. He did; myself did hear it.

HOT. Nay, then I cannot blame his cousin king
That wished him on the barren mountains starve.
But shall it be that you, that set the crown 160
Upon the head of this forgetful man
And for his sake wear the detested blot
Of murderous subornation⁸—shall it be
That you a world of curses undergo,
Being the agents, or base second means,⁹ 165
The cords, the ladder, or the hangman rather?
O pardon me that I descend so low
To show the line and the predicament
Wherein you range¹ under this subtle king!
Shall it for shame be spoken in these days, 170
Or fill up chronicles in time to come,
That men of your nobility and power
Did gage² them both in an unjust behalf,
As both of you—God pardon it!—have done,
To put down Richard, that sweet lovely rose, 175
And plant this thorn, this canker,³ Bolingbroke?
And shall it in more shame be further spoken,
That you are fooled, discarded, and shook off
By him for whom these shames ye underwent?
No; yet time serves wherein you may redeem 180
Your banished honors and restore yourselves
Into the good thoughts of the world again,
Revenge the jeering and disdained⁴ contempt
Of this proud king, who studies day and night
To answer all the debt he owes to you 185
Even with the bloody payment of your deaths:
Therefore, I say—

WOR. Peace, cousin, say no more;
And now I will unclasp a secret book,

6. I.e., God pardon in us the wrongs we did to him.
7. Brother-in-law.
8. I.e., the stain of aiding and abetting murder.
9. Tools, helpers.
1. I.e., to show the position and the category (or class) in which you are placed.
2. Pledge; "behalf": cause.
3. "Canker" meant not only a wild rose but also a diseased spot (a cancer).
4. Disdainful.

And to your quick-conceiving discontents
I'll read you matter deep and dangerous, 190
As full of peril and adventurous spirit
As to o'er-walk a current roaring loud
On the unsteadfast footing of a spear.[5]

HOT. If he fall in, good night, or sink or swim;
Send danger from the east unto the west, 195
So honor cross it from the north to south,
And let them grapple; O, the blood more stirs
To rouse a lion than to start[6] a hare!

NORTH. Imagination of some great exploit
Drives him beyond the bounds of patience. 200

HOT. By heaven, methinks it were an easy leap
To pluck bright honor from the pale-faced moon,
Or dive into the bottom of the deep,
Where fathom line could never touch the ground,
And pluck up drownèd honor by the locks, 205
So he that doth redeem her thence might wear
Without corrival[7] all her dignities;
But out upon this half-faced fellowship![8]

WOR. He apprehends a world of figures[9] here,
But not the form of what he should attend. 210
Good cousin, give me audience for a while.

HOT. I cry you mercy.

WOR.   Those same noble Scots
That I have prisoners—

HOT.   I'll keep them all;
By God, he shall not have a Scot of them;
No, if a Scot would save his soul he shall not. 215
I'll keep them, by this hand.

WOR.   You start away
And lend no ear unto my purposes.
Those prisoners you shall keep.

HOT.   Nay, I will; that's flat.
He said he would not ransom Mortimer,
Forbade my tongue to speak of Mortimer, 220
But I will find him when he lies asleep,
And in his ear I'll holla "Mortimer!"
Nay,
I'll have a starling shall be taught to speak[1]
Nothing but "Mortimer," and give it him 225
To keep his anger still in motion.

WOR. Hear you, cousin, a word.

HOT. All studies here I solemnly defy,
Save how to gall[2] and pinch this Bolingbroke;
And that same sword-and-buckler[3] Prince of Wales, 230
But that I think his father loves him not

5. A spear laid down as a foot-bridge.
6. Arouse, in hunting.
7. Rival.
8. Miserable sharing (of honor) with someone else.
9. Rhetorical figures of speech.

1. Starlings used to be taught to speak, as parrots are now.
2. Irritate.
3. Weapons used not by gentlemen but by servants or rustic clowns.

And would be glad he met with some mischance,
I would have him poisoned with a pot of ale.[4]
WOR. Farewell, kinsman; I'll talk to you
 When you are better tempered to attend.   235
NORTH. Why, what a wasp-stung and impatient fool
 Art thou to break into this woman's mood,
 Tying thine ear to no tongue but thine own!
HOT. Why, look you, I am whipped and scourged with rods,
 Nettled and stung with pismires,[5] when I hear 240
 Of this vile politician Bolingbroke.
 In Richard's time—what do you call the place?—
 A plague upon it, it is in Gloucestershire—
 'Twas where the madcap duke his uncle kept,[6]
 His uncle York, where I first bowed my knee 245
 Unto this king of smiles, this Bolingbroke—
 'Sblood!—
 When you and he came back from Ravenspurgh.
NORTH. At Berkeley castle.
HOT. You say true. 250
 Why, what a candy deal of courtesy
 This fawning greyhound[7] then did proffer me!
 "Look when his infant fortune came to age,"
 And "gentle Harry Percy," and "kind cousin";
 O, the devil take such cozeners![8] God forgive me! 255
 Good uncle, tell your tale; I have done.
WOR. Nay, if you have not, to it again;
 We will stay your leisure.
HOT.   I have done, i' faith.
WOR. Then once more to your Scottish prisoners.
 Deliver them up without their ransom straight, 260
 And make the Douglas' son your only mean
 For powers in Scotland, which, for divers reasons
 Which I shall send you written, be assured
 Will easily be granted. You, my lord, [⟨*to* NORTHUMBERLAND⟩]
 Your son in Scotland being thus employed, 265
 Shall secretly into the bosom creep
 Of that same noble prelate well beloved,
 The archbishop.
HOT. Of York, is it not?
WOR. True; who bears hard 270
 His brother's death at Bristol, the Lord Scroop.
 I speak not this in estimation,[9]
 As what I think might be, but what I know
 Is ruminated, plotted, and set down,
 And only stays but to behold the face 275
 Of that occasion that shall bring it on.

4. The drink of the lower classes.
5. Ants.
6. Lived.
7. A complex image which occurs in Shakespeare several times (cf. *Hamlet* III.ii.65–67 and *Antony and Cleopatra* IV.xii.20–23). The idea of fawning or flattery called up to Shakespeare's mind the image of a dog begging for sweetmeats ("candy").
8. Cheaters, with of course a pun on the word "cousin."
9. I.e., guessing.

HOT. I smell it; upon my life, it will do well.

NORTH. Before the game is afoot, thou still let'st slip.[1]

HOT. Why, it cannot choose but be a noble plot;
  And then the power of Scotland and of York   280
  To join with Mortimer, ha?

WOR.   And so they shall.

HOT. In faith, it is exceedingly well aimed.

WOR. And 'tis no little reason bids us speed,
  To save our heads by raising of a head;[2]
  For, bear ourselves as even as we can,   285
  The king will always think him in our debt,
  And think we think ourselves unsatisfied,
  Till he hath found a time to pay us home;
  And see already how he doth begin
  To make us strangers to his looks of love.   290

HOT. He does, he does; we'll be revenged on him.

WOR. Cousin, farewell. No further go in this
  Than I by letters shall direct your course.
  When time is ripe, which will be suddenly,
  I'll steal to Glendower and Lord Mortimer,   295
  Where you and Douglas and our powers at once,
  As I will fashion it, shall happily meet,
  To bear our fortunes in our own strong arms,
  Which now we hold at much uncertainty.

NORTH. Farewell, good brother; we shall thrive, I trust.   300

HOT. Uncle, adieu; O, let the hours be short
  Till fields and blows and groans applaud our sport!   [*Exeunt.*]

Act II

SCENE 1

[*Enter a* CARRIER *with a lantern in his hand.*]

FIRST CAR. Heigh-ho! an it be not four by the day, I'll be hanged;
  Charles' wain[3] is over the new chimney, and yet our horse not
  packed. What, ostler!

OST. [*within*] Anon, anon.

FIRST CAR. I prithee, Tom, beat Cut's saddle,[4] put a few flocks   5
  in the point; poor jade, is wrung in the withers out of all cess.[5]
      [*Enter another* CARRIER.]

SEC. CAR. Peas and beans are as dank here as a dog, and that is the
  next way to give poor jades the bots;[6] this house is turned upside down since Robin Ostler died.

FIRST CAR. Poor fellow, never joyed since the price of oats rose;   10
  it was the death of him.

SEC. CAR. I think this be the most villainous house in all London

---

1. An image from hunting. The meaning is: "You always ('still') release the dogs before we are ready to pursue the game."
2. Raising an army.
3. The constellation of the Great Bear or Big Dipper.
4. The saddle was beaten to make it soft; "Cut" is a name for a horse with a docked tail. "Flocks in the point": pieces of wool under the point of the saddle.
5. I.e., is sore in the shoulders excessively.
6. I.e., that is the easiest way to give poor nags worms in the stomach.

road for fleas; I am stung like a tench.[7]

FIRST CAR. Like a tench! by the mass, there is ne'er a king christen[8] could be better bit than I have been since the first cock.   15

SEC. CAR. Why, they will allow us ne'er a jordan, and then we leak in your chimney, and your chamber-lye breeds fleas like a loach.[9]

FIRST CAR. What, ostler! come away and be hanged, come away!   20

SEC. CAR. I have a gammon[1] of bacon and two razes of ginger, to be delivered as far as Charing Cross.

FIRST CAR. God's body! the turkeys in my pannier[2] are quite starved. What, ostler! A plague on thee, hast thou never an eye in thy head? canst not hear? An 'twere not as good deed as   25
drink to break the pate on thee, I am a very villain. Come and be hanged! hast no faith in thee?

[*Enter* GADSHILL.]

GADS. Good morrow, carriers. What's o'clock?

FIRST CAR. I think it be two o'clock.

GADS. I prithee lend me thy lantern to see my gelding in the   30
stable.

FIRST CAR. Nay, by God, soft; I know a trick worth two of that, i' faith.

GADS. I pray thee lend me thine.

SEC. CAR. Aye, when? canst tell?[3] Lend me thy lantern, quoth   35
he? marry, I'll see thee hanged first.

GADS. Sirrah carrier, what time do you mean to come to London?

SEC. CAR. Time enough to go to bed with a candle, I warrant thee. Come, neighbor Mugs, we'll call up the gentlemen; they will along with company, for they have great charge.[4]   40

[*Exeunt* ⟨CARRIERS.⟩]

GADS. What ho! chamberlain!

CHAM. [*within*] At hand, quoth pickpurse.

GADS. That's even as fair as At hand, quoth the chamberlain, for thou variest no more from picking of purses than giving direction[5] doth from laboring; thou layest the plot how.   45

[*Enter* CHAMBERLAIN.]

CHAM. Good morrow, Master Gadshill. It holds current[6] that I told you yesternight; there's a franklin[7] in the weald of Kent hath brought three hundred marks with him in gold—I heard him tell it to one of his company last night at supper—a kind of auditor,[8] one that hath abundance of charge too, God   50
knows what. They are up already and call for eggs and butter;

---

7. A fish covered with red spots, like fleabites.
8. Christian king.
9. "Jordan": chamber pot; "chamber-lye": urine. The "loach" is a fish which breeds prolifically.
1. Haunch; "razes": roots.
2. Basket.
3. A colloquial expression of contemptuous refusal.
4. Valuable cargo.
5. A pun: "giving direction" means

supervising, as contrasted with "laboring," but it was also the name for informing thieves about the journeys of prospective victims (laying "the plot how").
6. Remains true.
7. A freeholder, just below a gentleman in rank. "Weald of Kent": a section of that county, formerly wooded.
8. Revenue officer; "abundance of charge": considerable property.

they will away presently.[9]

GADS. Sirrah, if they meet not with Saint Nicholas' clerks,[1] I'll give thee this neck.

CHAM. No, I'll none of it; I pray thee, keep that for the hang- 55
man, for I know thou worshipest Saint Nicholas as truly as a man of falsehood may.

GADS. What talkest thou to me of the hangman? if I hang, I'll make a fat pair of gallows; for if I hang, old Sir John hangs with me, and thou knowest he is no starveling. Tut! there are 60
other Trojans[2] that thou dreamest not of, the which for sport sake are content to do the profession some grace, that would, if matters should be looked into, for their own credit sake make all whole. I am joined with no foot land-rakers,[3] no long-staff sixpenny strikers, none of these mad mustachio purple- 65
hued maltworms,[4] but with nobility and tranquility, burgo-masters and great oneyers, such as can hold in, such as will strike sooner than speak, and speak sooner than drink, and drink sooner than pray; and yet, zounds, I lie, for they pray continually to their saint, the commonwealth, or rather, not 70
pray to her but prey on her, for they ride up and down on her and make her their boots.[5]

CHAM. What, the commonwealth their boots? will she hold out water in foul way?

GADS. She will, she will; justice hath liquored her. We steal as in 75
a castle, cocksure; we have the receipt of fern seed,[6] we walk invisible.

CHAM. Nay, by my faith, I think you are more beholding to the night than to fern seed for your walking invisible.

GADS. Give me thy hand; thou shalt have a share in our purchase,[7] 80
as I am a true man.

CHAM. Nay, rather let me have it, as you are a false thief.

GADS. Go to; *homo* is a common name to all men. Bid the ostler bring my gelding out of the stable. Farewell, you muddy[8] knave.

[Exeunt.]

SCENE 2

[Enter PRINCE *and* POINS.]

POINS. Come shelter, shelter; I have removed Falstaff's horse, and he frets like a gummed velvet.[9]

PRINCE. Stand close.

[Enter FALSTAFF.]

FAL. Poins! Poins, and be hanged! Poins!

PRINCE. Peace, ye fat-kidneyed rascal! what a brawling dost thou 5
keep!

FAL. Where's Poins, Hal?

9. At once.
1. Highwaymen.
2. Roisterers, good fellows.
3. Footpads; "sixpenny strikers": small-time thieves.
4. Flushed, swaggering barflies. "Oneyers": dignitaries; "hold in": keep secret.
5. Booty.

6. I.e., we have the recipe for fern seed (supposed to make one invisible). "Liquored": greased.
7. Takings.
8. Muddle-headed.
9. Cheap velvet was treated with gum to make the pile stiff; as a result it soon fretted or wore away. "Stand close": hide.

PRINCE. He is walked up to the top of the hill; I'll go seek him.
　　　[⟨*He pretends to go, but hides onstage with* POINS.⟩]
FAL. I am accursed to rob in that thief's company; the rascal
　　hath removed my horse, and tied him I know not where. If
　　I travel but four foot by the squier[1] further afoot, I shall break
　　my wind. Well, I doubt not but to die a fair death for all this,
　　if I 'scape hanging for killing that rogue. I have forsworn his
　　company hourly any time this two and twenty years, and yet
　　I am bewitched with the rogue's company. If the rascal have
　　not given me medicines to make me love him, I'll be hanged;
　　it could not be else; I have drunk medicines. Poins! Hal! a
　　plague upon you both! Bardolph! Peto! I'll starve ere I'll rob
　　a foot further. An 'twere not as good a deed as drink to turn
　　true man and to leave these rogues, I am the veriest varlet
　　that ever chewed with a tooth. Eight yards of uneven ground
　　is threescore and ten miles afoot with me, and the stony-hearted
　　villains know it well enough; a plague upon it when thieves
　　cannot be true one to another! [*They whistle.*] Whew! A
　　plague upon you all! Give me my horse, you rogues; give me
　　my horse, and be hanged!
PRINCE. Peace, ye fat-guts! lie down; lay thine ear close to the
　　ground and list if thou canst hear the tread of travelers.
FAL. Have you any levers to lift me up again, being down?
　　'Sblood, I'll not bear my own flesh so far afoot again for all
　　the coin in thy father's exchequer. What a plague mean ye to
　　colt[2] me thus?
PRINCE. Thou liest; thou art not colted, thou art uncolted.
FAL. I prithee, good Prince, Hal, help me to my horse, good king's
　　son.
PRINCE. Out, ye rogue! shall I be your ostler?
FAL. Go hang thyself in thine own heir-apparent garters! If I be
　　ta'en, I'll peach for this. An I have not ballads made on you
　　all and sung to filthy tunes, let a cup of sack be my poison;
　　when a jest is so forward, and afoot too! I hate it.
　　　[*Enter* GADSHILL, ⟨BARDOLPH *and* PETO *with him.*⟩]
GADS. Stand.
FAL. So I do, against my will.
POINS. O, 'tis our setter; I know his voice. Bardolph, what news?
BARD. Case[3] ye, case ye, on with your vizards; there's money of
　　the king's coming down the hill; 'tis going to the king's ex-
　　chequer.
FAL. You lie, you rogue; 'tis going to the king's tavern.
GADS. There's enough to make us all.
FAL. To be hanged.
PRINCE. Sirs, you four shall front them in the narrow lane; Ned
　　Poins and I will walk lower; if they 'scape from your encounter,
　　then they light on us.
PETO. How many be there of them?
GADS. Some eight or ten.
FAL. Zounds, will they not rob us?

1. Ruler, yardstick.　　　　　　3. Mask.
2. Trick.

PRINCE. What, a coward, Sir John Paunch?

FAL. Indeed, I am not John of Gaunt your grandfather, but yet no coward, Hal.

PRINCE. Well, we leave that to the proof.

POINS. Sirrah Jack, thy horse stands behind the hedge; when thou 60 needest him, there thou shalt find him. Farewell, and stand fast.

FAL. Now cannot I strike him, if I should be hanged.

PRINCE. [⟨*aside to* POINS⟩] Ned, where are our disguises?

POINS. [⟨*aside*⟩] Here, hard by; stand close. 65

　　　　　[⟨*Exeunt* PRINCE *and* POINS.⟩]

FAL. Now, my masters, happy man be his dole,[4] say I; every man to his business.

　　　　　[*Enter the* TRAVELERS.]

FIRST TRAV. Come, neighbor, the boy shall lead our horses down the hill; we'll walk afoot awhile, and ease our legs.

THIEVES. Stand! 70

TRAVELERS. Jesus bless us!

FAL. Strike; down with them; cut the villains' throats. Ah, whoreson caterpillars,[5] bacon-fed knaves, they hate us youth! Down with them, fleece them.

TRAVELERS. O, we are undone, both we and ours forever! 75

FAL. Hang ye, gorbellied[6] knaves, are ye undone? No, ye fat chuffs, I would your store were here! On, bacons, on! What, ye knaves, young men must live! You are grand jurors, are ye? we'll jure ye, faith.

　　　　　[*Here they rob them and bind them. Exeunt.*]

　　　　[*Enter the* PRINCE *and* POINS.]

PRINCE. The thieves have bound the true men. Now could thou 80 and I rob the thieves and go merrily to London; it would be argument[7] for a week, laughter for a month, and a good jest forever.

POINS. Stand close; I hear them coming.

　　　　　[*Enter the* THIEVES *again.*]

FAL. Come, my masters, let us share, and then to horse before 85 day. An the Prince and Poins be not two arrant cowards, there's no equity stirring;[8] there's no more valor in that Poins than in a wild duck.

PRINCE. Your money!

POINS. Villains! 90

　　　　　[*As they are sharing, the* PRINCE *and* POINS *set upon them; they all run away; and* FALSTAFF, *after a blow or two, runs away too, leaving the booty behind them.*]

PRINCE. Got with much ease. Now merrily to horse;

The thieves are all scattered and possessed with fear

So strongly that they dare not meet each other;

Each takes his fellow for an officer.

Away, good Ned. Falstaff sweats to death, 95

---

4. I.e., good luck!
5. "Caterpillars of the commonwealth" was a common phrase, referring to rogues. Falstaff here applies ridiculously inappropriate terms to the travelers

and to himself (e.g., "youth").
6. Fat; "chuffs": misers.
7. Subject of stories.
8. There's no justice.

And lards the lean earth as he walks along;
Were 't not for laughing, I should pity him.

POINS. How the rogue roared!   [*Exeunt.*]

SCENE 3

[*Enter* HOTSPUR, *alone, reading a letter.*]

HOT. "But for mine own part, my lord, I could be well contented
to be there, in respect of the love I bear your house." "He
could be contented"; why is he not, then? "In respect of the
love he bears our house," he shows in this, he loves his own
barn better than he loves our house. Let me see some more. 5
"The purpose you undertake is dangerous." Why, that's certain. 'Tis dangerous to take a cold, to sleep, to drink; but I tell
you, my lord fool, out of this nettle, danger, we pluck this
flower, safety. "The purpose you undertake is dangerous, the
friends you have named uncertain, the time itself unsorted,[9] 10
and your whole plot too light for the counterpoise of so great
an opposition." Say you so, say you so? I say unto you again,
you are a shallow cowardly hind,[1] and you lie. What a lack-
brain is this! By the Lord, our plot is a good plot as ever was
laid, our friends true and constant; a good plot, good friends, 15
and full of expectation; an excellent plot, very good friends.
What a frosty-spirited rogue is this! Why, my lord of York[2]
commends the plot and the general course of the action.
Zounds, an I were now by this rascal I could brain him with
his lady's fan. Is there not my father, my uncle, and myself? 20
Lord Edmund Mortimer, my lord of York, and Owen Glendower? is there not besides the Douglas? have I not all their
letters to meet me in arms by the ninth of the next month, and
are they not some of them set forward already? What a pagan
rascal is this, an infidel! Ha! you shall see now in very sincerity 25
of fear and cold heart, will he to the king and lay open all our
proceedings. O, I could divide myself and go to buffets,[3] for
moving such a dish of skim milk with so honorable an action!
Hang him! let him tell the king. We are prepared; I will set
forward tonight. 30

[*Enter his* LADY.]

How now, Kate! I must leave you within these two hours.

LADY. O, my good lord, why are you thus alone?
For what offense have I this fortnight been
A banished woman from my Harry's bed?
Tell me, sweet lord, what is 't that takes from thee 35
Thy stomach,[4] pleasure, and thy golden sleep?
Why dost thou bend thine eyes upon the earth,
And start so often when thou sit'st alone?
Why hast thou lost the fresh blood in thy cheeks,
And given my treasures and my rights of thee 40
To thick-eyed musing and cursed melancholy?
In thy faint slumbers I by thee have watched
And heard thee murmur tales of iron wars,

9. Unsuitable.
1. Peasant.
2. The Archbishop of York.

3. Split myself in two and let the parts fight each other; "moving": urging.
4. Appetite.

Speak terms of manage[5] to thy bounding steed,
Cry "Courage! to the field!" And thou hast talked   45
Of sallies and retires, of trenches, tents,
Of palisadoes, frontiers, parapets,
Of basilisks, of cannon, culverin,[6]
Of prisoners' ransom and of soldiers slain,
And all the currents of a heady fight.   50
Thy spirit within thee hath been so at war
And thus hath so bestirred thee in thy sleep
That beads of sweat have stood upon thy brow
Like bubbles in a late-disturbèd stream,
And in thy face strange motions have appeared   55
Such as we see when men restrain their breath
On some great sudden hest.[7] O, what portents are these?
Some heavy business hath my lord in hand
And I must know it, else he loves me not.

HOT. What, ho!
    [⟨*Enter* SERVANT.⟩]
               Is Gilliams with the packet gone?   60
SERV. He is, my lord, an hour ago.
HOT. Hath Butler brought those horses from the sheriff?
SERV. One horse, my lord, he brought even now.
HOT. What horse? a roan, a crop-ear, is it not?
SERV. It is, my lord.
HOT.   That roan shall be my throne.   65
  Well, I will back[7a] him straight; O Esperance![8]
  Bid Butler lead him forth into the park.   [⟨*Exit* SERVANT.⟩]
LADY. But hear you, my lord.
HOT. What say'st thou, my lady?
LADY. What is it carries you away?   70
HOT. Why, my horse, my love, my horse.
LADY. Out, you mad-headed ape!
  A weasel hath not such a deal of spleen[9]
  As you are tossed with. In faith
  I'll know your business, Harry, that I will.   75
  I fear my brother Mortimer doth stir
  About his title, and hath sent for you
  To line[1] his enterprise; but if you go—
HOT. So far afoot, I shall be weary, love.
LADY. Come, come, you paraquito, answer me   80
  Directly unto this question that I ask;
  In faith, I'll break thy little finger, Harry,
  An if thou wilt not tell me all things true.
HOT. Away,
  Away, you trifler! Love! I love thee not,   85

---

5. Horsemanship.
6. Three kinds of artillery (named here in decreasing order of weight).
7. Command.
7a. Mount.
8. The battle cry of the Percies:
"Hope!"
9. The spleen was supposed to be the source of sudden and violent emotions; the weasel was considered a very impetuous animal.
1. Support.

I care not for thee, Kate; this is no world
To play with mammets and to tilt with lips;
We must have bloody noses and cracked crowns,[2]
And pass them current too. God's me, my horse!
What say'st thou, Kate? what wouldst thou have with me? 90
LADY. Do you not love me? do you not, indeed?
Well, do not then, for since you love me not
I will not love myself. Do you not love me?
Nay, tell me if you speak in jest or no.
HOT. Come, wilt thou see me ride? 95
And when I am o' horseback, I will swear
I love thee infinitely. But hark you, Kate,
I must not have you henceforth question me
Whither I go, nor reason whereabout;
Whither I must, I must; and, to conclude, 100
This evening must I leave you, gentle Kate.
I know you wise, but yet no farther wise
Than Harry Percy's wife; constant you are,
But yet a woman, and for secrecy
No lady closer; for I well believe 105
Thou wilt not utter what thou dost not know,
And so far will I trust thee, gentle Kate.
LADY. How! so far?
HOT. Not an inch further. But hark you, Kate,
Whither I go, thither shall you go too; 110
Today will I set forth, tomorrow you.
Will this content you, Kate?
LADY.   It must of force.   [*Exeunt.*]

SCENE 4

[*Enter the* PRINCE *and* POINS.]

PRINCE. Ned, prithee come out of that fat[3] room, and lend me
thy hand to laugh a little.
POINS. Where hast been, Hal?
PRINCE. With three or four loggerheads[4] amongst three or fourscore hogsheads. I have sounded the very bass string of humil- 5
ity. Sirrah, I am sworn brother to a leash of drawers,[5] and can
call them all by their christen names, as Tom, Dick, and Francis. They take it already upon their salvation, that though I be
but Prince of Wales, yet I am the king of courtesy, and tell me
flatly I am no proud Jack, like Falstaff, but a Corinthian,[6] a lad 10
of mettle, a good boy—by the Lord, so they call me—and when
I am king of England I shall command all the good lads in
Eastcheap. They call drinking deep, dyeing scarlet, and when
you breathe in your watering[7] they cry "hem!" and bid you
play it off. To conclude, I am so good a proficient in one quar- 15
ter of an hour that I can drink with any tinker in his own lan-

---

2. Broken heads, with a pun on
"crowns" as coins. "Mammets": breasts.
3. Vat. This establishes that the scene is
a tavern.

4. Blockheads.
5. Group of tapsters, waiters.
6. Good fellow.
7. Drinking.

guage during my life. I tell thee, Ned, thou hast lost much honor, that thou wert not with me in this action. But, sweet Ned—to sweeten which name of Ned, I give thee this penny- 20 worth of sugar, clapped even now into my hand by an under- skinker,[8] one that never spake other English in his life than "Eight shillings and sixpence," and "You are welcome," with this shrill addition, "Anon, anon, sir! Score a pint of bastard in the Half-Moon,"[9] or so. But, Ned, to drive away the time till Falstaff come, I prithee do thou stand in some by-room, 25 while I question my puny drawer to what end he gave me the sugar, and do thou never leave calling "Francis," that his tale to me may be nothing but "Anon." Step aside, and I'll show thee a precedent.

POINS. Francis! 30

PRINCE. Thou art perfect.

POINS. Francis! [⟨*Exit* POINS.⟩]

    [*Enter* DRAWER.]

FRAN. Anon, anon, sir. Look down into the Pomgarnet,[1] Ralph.

PRINCE. Come hither, Francis.

FRAN. My lord? 35

PRINCE. How long hast thou to serve,[2] Francis?

FRAN. Forsooth, five years, and as much as to—

POINS. [*within*] Francis!

FRAN. Anon, anon, sir.

PRINCE. Five year! by'r Lady, a long lease for the clinking of 40 pewter. But, Francis, darest thou be so valiant as to play the coward with thy indenture and show it a fair pair of heels and run from it?

FRAN. O Lord, sir, I'll be sworn upon all the books in England, I could find in my heart— 45

POINS. [*within*] Francis!

FRAN. Anon, sir.

PRINCE. How old art thou, Francis?

FRAN. Let me see—about Michaelmas next I shall be—

POINS. [*within*] Francis! 50

FRAN. Anon, sir. Pray stay a little, my lord.

PRINCE. Nay, but hark you, Francis: for the sugar thou gavest me, 'twas a pennyworth, was't not?

FRAN. O Lord, I would it had been two!

PRINCE. I will give thee for it a thousand pound; ask me when 55 thou wilt, and thou shalt have it.

POINS. [*within*] Francis!

FRAN. Anon, anon.

PRINCE. Anon, Francis? No, Francis, but tomorrow, Francis; or Francis, o' Thursday, or indeed, Francis, when thou wilt. But, 60

8. Assistant waiter.
9. I.e., charge a pint of "bastard" (a sweet Spanish wine) to a customer in the room called "Half-Moon." "Anon": immediately (the reply of a servant when called, equivalent to "Coming!").

1. Pomegranate (another room in the tavern).
2. I.e., to finish out his apprenticeship, usually a seven-year period under an "indenture" or agreement.

Francis!

FRAN. My lord?

PRINCE. Wilt thou rob this leathern-jerkin,[3] crystal-button, not-
pated, agate-ring, puke-stocking, caddis-garter, smooth-tongue,
Spanish-pouch—   65

FRAN. O Lord, sir, who do you mean?

PRINCE. Why, then, your brown bastard is your only drink, for
look you, Francis, your white canvas doublet will sully. In Bar-
bary, sir, it cannot come to so much.[4]

FRAN. What, sir?   70

POINS. [*within*] Francis!

PRINCE. Away, you rogue, dost thou not hear them call?
[*Here they both call him; the drawer stands amazed,
not knowing which way to go.*]
[*Enter* VINTNER.]

VINT. What, stand'st thou still, and hear'st such a calling? Look
to the guests within. [*Exit* FRANCIS.] My lord, old Sir John with
half-a-dozen more are at the door; shall I let them in?   75

PRINCE. Let them alone awhile, and then open the door. [*Exit*
VINTNER.] Poins!
[*Enter* POINS.]

POINS. Anon, anon, sir.

PRINCE. Sirrah, Falstaff and the rest of the thieves are at the door;
shall we be merry?   80

POINS. As merry as crickets, my lad. But hark ye, what cunning
match have you made with this jest of the drawer? come, what's
the issue?

PRINCE. I am now of all humors[5] that have showed themselves
humors since the old days of goodman Adam to the pupil[6] age   85
of this present twelve o'clock at midnight.
[⟨*Enter* FRANCIS.⟩]
What's o'clock, Francis?

FRAN. Anon, anon, sir.   [⟨*Exit.*⟩]

PRINCE. That ever this fellow should have fewer words than a
parrot, and yet the son of a woman! His industry is upstairs   90
and downstairs, his eloquence the parcel[7] of a reckoning. I am
not yet of Percy's mind, the Hotspur of the north, he that kills
me some six or seven dozen of Scots at a breakfast, washes his
hands, and says to his wife "Fie upon this quiet life! I want
work." "O my sweet Harry," says she, "how many hast thou   95
killed today?" "Give my roan horse a drench," says he, and
answers "Some fourteen," an hour after, "a trifle, a trifle."
I prithee, call in Falstaff; I'll play Percy, and that damned
brawn shall play Dame Mortimer his wife. "Rivo!"[8] says the
drunkard. Call in ribs, call in tallow.   100
[*Enter* FALSTAFF, ⟨GADSHILL, BARDOLPH, *and* PETO, FRAN-

---

3. Leather-jacketed; "not-pated": with
short hair; "puke": dark gray; "cad-
dis": worsted tape.
4. Deliberate nonsense to confuse
Francis, and one of the first instances
of doubletalk in English literature.

5. Temperaments, dispositions.
6. Youthful.
7. Item.
8. Drink up!

CIS *following with wine.*)]

POINS. Welcome, Jack; where hast thou been?

FAL. A plague of all cowards, I say, and a vengeance too, marry and amen! Give me a cup of sack, boy. Ere I lead this life long, I'll sew nether stocks[9] and mend them and foot them too. A plague of all cowards! Give me a cup of sack, rogue. Is there no virtue extant? [*He drinks.*] 105

PRINCE. Didst thou ever see Titan[1] kiss a dish of butter, pitiful-hearted butter that melted at the sweet tale of the sun's? If thou didst, then behold that compound.

FAL. You rogue, here's lime in this sack too;[2] there is nothing but 110 roguery to be found in villainous man, yet a coward is worse than a cup of sack with lime in it. A villainous coward! Go thy ways, old Jack, die when thou wilt; if manhood, good manhood, be not forgot upon the face of the earth, then am I a shotten herring.[3] There lives not three good men unhanged in Eng- 115 land, and one of them is fat and grows old. God help the while; a bad world, I say. I would I were a weaver; I could sing psalms[4] or anything. A plague of all cowards, I say still.

PRINCE. How now, woolsack, what mutter you?

FAL. A king's son! If I do not beat thee out of thy kingdom with 120 a dagger of lath, and drive all thy subjects afore thee like a flock of wild geese, I'll never wear hair on my face more. You Prince of Wales!

PRINCE. Why, you whoreson round man, what's the matter?

FAL. Are not you a coward? answer me to that; and Poins there? 125

POINS. Zounds, ye fat paunch, an ye call me coward, by the Lord I'll stab thee.

FAL. I call thee coward! I'll see thee damned ere I call thee coward; but I would give a thousand pound I could run as fast as thou canst. You are straight enough in the shoulders, you 130 care not who sees your back; call you that backing of your friends? A plague upon such backing! give me them that will face me. Give me a cup of sack; I am a rogue if I drunk today.

PRINCE. O villain! thy lips are scarce wiped since thou drunkest last. 135

FAL. All's one for that. [*He drinks.*] A plague of all cowards, still say I.

PRINCE. What's the matter?

FAL. What's the matter! there be four of us here have ta'en a thousand pound this day morning. 140

PRINCE. Where is it, Jack? where is it?

FAL. Where is it? taken from us it is—a hundred upon poor four of us.

PRINCE. What, a hundred, man?

FAL. I am a rogue if I were not at half-sword[5] with a dozen of 145 them two hours together. I have 'scaped by miracle. I am

9. Stockings.
1. The sun.
2. Lime was used to make wine sparkle.
3. A herring that has cast its spawn and is lean.
4. Protestant weavers from Flanders were notorious for singing psalms.
5. At half a sword's length.

eight times thrust through the doublet, four through the hose, my buckler cut through and through, my sword hacked like a handsaw—*ecce signum!*[6] I never dealt better since I was a man; all would not do. A plague of all cowards! Let them speak; if they speak more or less than truth, they are villains and the sons of darkness.

PRINCE. Speak, sirs; how was it?

GADS. We four set upon some dozen—

FAL. Sixteen at least, my lord.

GADS. And bound them.

PETO. No, no, they were not bound.

FAL. You rogue, they were bound, every man of them, or I am a Jew else, an Ebrew Jew.

GADS. As we were sharing, some six or seven fresh men set upon us—

FAL. And unbound the rest, and then come in the other.

PRINCE. What, fought you with them all?

FAL. All! I know not what you call all, but if I fought not with fifty of them, I am a bunch of radish; if there were not two or three and fifty upon poor old Jack, then am I no two-legged creature.

PRINCE. Pray God you have not murdered some of them.

FAL. Nay, that's past praying for; I have peppered two of them. Two I am sure I have paid, two rogues in buckram suits. I tell thee what, Hal, if I tell thee a lie, spit in my face, call me horse. Thou knowest my old ward;[7] here I lay, and thus I bore my point. Four rogues in buckram let drive at me—

PRINCE. What, four? thou saidst but two even now.

FAL. Four, Hal; I told thee four.

POINS. Aye, aye, he said four.

FAL. These four came all a-front, and mainly[8] thrust at me. I made me no more ado but took all their seven points in my target,[9] thus.

PRINCE. Seven? why, there were but four even now.

FAL. In buckram.

POINS. Aye, four, in buckram suits.

FAL. Seven, by these hilts, or I am a villain else.

PRINCE. Prithee, let him alone; we shall have more anon.

FAL. Dost thou hear me, Hal?

PRINCE. Aye, and mark thee too, Jack.

FAL. Do so, for it is worth the listening to. These nine in buckram that I told thee of—

PRINCE. So, two more already.

FAL. Their points being broken—

POINS. Down fell their hose.[1]

FAL. Began to give me ground; but I followed me close, came in foot and hand, and with a thought seven of the eleven I paid.

6. Here's the proof!
7. Defense; "here I lay": this was my stance.
8. Strongly.

9. Shield.
1. Poins puns on the other meaning of "points": the laces used to tie up trousers ("hose").

PRINCE. O monstrous! eleven buckram men grown out of two!

FAL. But, as the devil would have it, three misbegotten knaves 195
in Kendal green came at my back and let drive at me, for it
was so dark, Hal, that thou couldst not see thy hand.

PRINCE. These lies are like their father that begets them—gross
as a mountain, open, palpable. Why, thou clay-brained guts,
thou knotty-pated fool, thou whoreson, obscene, greasy tallow- 200
catch²—

FAL. What, art thou mad? art thou mad? is not the truth the
truth?

PRINCE. Why, how couldst thou know these men in Kendal green,
when it was so dark thou couldst not see thy hand? come, tell 205
us your reason. What sayest thou to this?

POINS. Come, your reason, Jack, your reason.

FAL. What, upon compulsion? Zounds, an I were at the strap-
pado,³ or all the racks in the world, I would not tell you on
compulsion. Give you a reason on compulsion! if reasons⁴ 210
were as plentiful as blackberries, I would give no man a reason
upon compulsion, I.

PRINCE. I'll be no longer guilty of this sin; this sanguine coward,
this bed-presser, this horseback-breaker, this huge hill of
flesh— 215

FAL. 'Sblood, you starveling, you eelskin, you dried neat's tongue,
you bull's pizzle, you stockfish!⁵ O for breath to utter what is
like thee! you tailor's yard, you sheath, you bow case, you vile
standing-tuck⁶—

PRINCE. Well, breathe awhile, and then to it again; and when 220
thou hast tired thyself in base comparisons, hear me speak
but this.

POINS. Mark, Jack.

PRINCE. We two saw you four set on four and bound them, and
were masters of their wealth. Mark now, how a plain tale shall 225
put you down. Then did we two set on you four; and, with a
word, outfaced you from your prize, and have it, yea, and can
show it you here in the house; and, Falstaff, you carried your
guts away as nimbly, with as quick dexterity, and roared for
mercy and still run and roared, as ever I heard bullcalf. What a 230
slave art thou, to hack thy sword as thou hast done, and then
say it was in fight! What trick, what device, what starting-
hole,⁷ canst thou now find out to hide thee from this open
and apparent shame?

POINS. Come, let's hear, Jack; what trick hast thou now? 235

FAL. By the Lord, I knew ye as well as he that made ye. Why,
hear you, my masters: was it for me to kill the heir apparent?
should I turn upon the true prince? why, thou knowest I am

---

2. Piece of tallow from which chandlers made candles.
3. A method of torture; "racks":
another method.
4. A pun on the word "raisin," which
was spelled and pronounced like "reason" in Elizabethan England.
5. I.e., you ox tongue, you bull's penis,
you dried cod!
6. Stiff rapier.
7. Evasion.

as valiant as Hercules; but beware instinct; the lion will not
touch the true prince.[8] Instinct is a great matter; I was now
a coward on instinct. I shall think the better of myself and
thee during my life; I for a valiant lion, and thou for a true
prince. But, by the Lord, lads, I am glad you have the money.
Hostess, clap to the doors; watch tonight, pray tomorrow.
Gallants, lads, boys, hearts of gold, all the titles of good fellowship come to you! What, shall we be merry? shall we have a
play extempore?

PRINCE. Content; and the argument[9] shall be thy running away.

FAL. Ah, no more of that, Hal, an thou lovest me!

     [*Enter* HOSTESS.]

HOST. O Jesu, my lord the prince!

PRINCE. How now, my lady the hostess! what sayest thou to me?

HOST. Marry, my lord, there is a nobleman of the court at door
would speak with you; he says he comes from your father.

PRINCE. Give him as much as will make him a royal[1] man, and
send him back again to my mother.

FAL. What manner of man is he?

HOST. An old man.

FAL. What doth gravity out of his bed at midnight? Shall I give
him his answer?

PRINCE. Prithee, do, Jack.

FAL. Faith, and I'll send him packing.   [*Exit.*]

PRINCE. Now, sirs. By 'r Lady, you fought fair; so did you, Peto;
so did you, Bardolph; you are lions too, you ran away upon
instinct, you will not touch the true prince; no, fie!

BARD. Faith, I ran when I saw others run.

PRINCE. Faith, tell me now in earnest, how came Falstaff's sword
so hacked?

PETO. Why, he hacked it with his dagger, and said he would
swear truth out of England but he would make you believe it
was done in fight, and persuaded us to do the like.

BARD. Yea, and to tickle our noses with speargrass to make them
bleed, and then to beslubber our garments with it and swear
it was the blood of true men. I did that I did not this seven
year before, I blushed to hear his monstrous devices.

PRINCE. O villain, thou stolest a cup of sack eighteen years ago,
and wert taken with the manner,[2] and ever since thou hast
blushed extempore. Thou hadst fire[3] and sword on thy side,
and yet thou rannest away; what instinct hadst thou for it?

BARD. My lord, do you see these meteors? do you behold these
exhalations?

PRINCE. I do.

BARD. What think you they portend?

PRINCE. Hot livers and cold purses.[4]

---

8. In many medieval romances the lion,
as king of beasts, shows respect for
royalty.
9. Plot or story.
1. A "royal" was half of a pound
sterling, a "noble" was a third.

2. In the act.
3. "Fire" and the allusions to "meteors" and "exhalations" (shooting stars)
refer to Bardolph's red nose.
4. I.e., drunkenness and poverty.

BARD. Choler, my lord, if rightly taken.

PRINCE. No, if rightly taken, halter.   285

[*Enter* FALSTAFF.]

Here comes lean Jack, here comes bare-bone. How now, my
sweet creature of bombast,[5] how long is 't ago, Jack, since thou
sawest thine own knee?

FAL. My own knee! when I was about thy years, Hal, I was not
an eagle's talon in the waist; I could have crept into any alder-   290
man's thumb ring. A plague of sighing and grief—it blows a
man up like a bladder. There's villainous news abroad; here
was Sir John Bracy from your father; you must to the court
in the morning. That same mad fellow of the north, Percy, and
he of Wales, that gave Amamon[6] the bastinado and made   295
Lucifer cuckold and swore the devil his true liegeman upon the
cross of a Welsh hook[7]—what a plague call you him?

POINS. O, Glendower.

FAL. Owen, Owen, the same; and his son-in-law Mortimer, and
old Northumberland, and that sprightly Scot of Scots, Doug-   300
las, that runs o' horseback up a hill perpendicular—

PRINCE. He that rides at high speed and with his pistol kills a
sparrow flying.

FAL. You have hit it.

PRINCE. So did he never the sparrow.   305

FAL. Well, that rascal hath good mettle in him; he will not run.

PRINCE. Why, what a rascal art thou then, to praise him so for
running!

FAL. O' horseback, ye cuckoo; but afoot he will not budge a foot.

PRINCE. Yes, Jack, upon instinct.   310

FAL. I grant ye, upon instinct. Well, he is there too, and one
Mordake, and a thousand blue-caps[8] more. Worcester is stolen
away tonight; thy father's beard is turned white with the news;
you may buy land now as cheap as stinking mackerel.

PRINCE. Why then, it is like, if there come a hot June, and this   315
civil buffeting hold, we shall buy maidenheads as they buy
hobnails, by the hundreds.

FAL. By the mass, lad, thou sayest true; it is like we shall have
good trading that way. But tell me, Hal, art not thou horrible
afeard? thou being heir apparent, could the world pick thee   320
out three such enemies again as that fiend Douglas, that spirit
Percy, and that devil Glendower? Art thou not horribly afraid?
doth not thy blood thrill at it?

PRINCE. Not a whit, i' faith; I lack some of thy instinct.

FAL. Well, thou wilt be horribly chid tomorrow when thou com-   325
est to thy father; if thou love me, practice an answer.

PRINCE. Do thou stand for[9] my father and examine me upon the
particulars of my life.

FAL. Shall I? Content. This chair shall be my state,[1] this dagger

5. Padding, stuffing.
6. A devil. "Bastinado": a beating,
cudgelling.
7. A long spear with a hook on it.

8. Scots.
9. Represent.
1. Throne.

my scepter, and this cushion my crown.   330

PRINCE. Thy state is taken for a joint-stool,[2] thy golden scepter for a leaden dagger, and thy precious rich crown for a pitiful bald crown!

FAL. Well, an the fire of grace be not quite out of thee, now shalt thou be moved. Give me a cup of sack to make my eyes   335 look red, that it may be thought I have wept, for I must speak in passion, and I will do it in King Cambyses'[3] vein.

PRINCE. Well, here is my leg.[4]

FAL. And here is my speech. Stand aside, nobility.

HOST. O Jesu, this is excellent sport, i' faith!   340

FAL. Weep not, sweet queen, for trickling tears are vain.

HOST. O, the father, how he holds his countenance!

FAL. For God's sake, lords, convey my tristful queen,
For tears do stop the floodgates of her eyes.

HOST. O Jesu, he doth it as like one of these harlotry players as   345 ever I see!

FAL. Peace, good pint pot, peace, good ticklebrain. Harry, I do not only marvel where thou spendest thy time, but also how thou art accompanied, for though the camomile,[5] the more it is trodden on the faster it grows, so youth, the more it is   350 wasted the sooner it wears. That thou art my son, I have partly thy mother's word, partly my own opinion, but chiefly a villainous trick of thine eye and a foolish hanging of thy nether lip that doth warrant[6] me. If then thou be son to me, here lies the point; why, being son to me, art thou so pointed at? Shall   355 the blessed sun of heaven prove a micher[7] and eat blackberries? a question not to be asked. Shall the son of England prove a thief and take purses? a question to be asked. There is a thing, Harry, which thou hast often heard of and it is known to many in our land by the name of pitch. This pitch, as an-   360 cient writers do report, doth defile; so doth the company thou keepest: for, Harry, now I do not speak to thee in drink but in tears, not in pleasure but in passion, not in words only, but in woes also: and yet there is a virtuous man whom I have often noted in thy company, but I know not his name.   365

PRINCE. What manner of man, an it like your majesty?

FAL. A goodly portly man, i' faith, and a corpulent; of a cheerful look, a pleasing eye and a most noble carriage, and, as I think, his age some fifty, or, by 'r Lady, inclining to threescore; and now I remember me, his name is Falstaff. If that man should   370 be lewdly given, he deceiveth me, for, Harry, I see virtue in his looks. If then the tree may be known by the fruit, as the fruit by the tree, then, peremptorily I speak it, there is virtue in that Falstaff; him keep with, the rest banish. And tell me

---

2. An ordinary stool, made by a joiner (carpenter).
3. Like the bombastic hero of the old play *Cambyses*.
4. I.e., he bows, makes an obeisance.
5. An aromatic herb. The style in this speech is a parody of Euphuism, the ornate, elaborate, balanced style made popular by Lyly's *Euphues*.
6. Assure.
7. Truant.

now, thou naughty varlet, tell me, where hast thou been this 375
month?

PRINCE. Dost thou speak like a king? Do thou stand for me, and
I'll play my father.

FAL. Depose me? if thou dost it half so gravely, so majestically,
both in word and matter, hang me up by the heels for a 380
rabbit-sucker[8] or a poulter's hare.

PRINCE. Well, here I am set.[9]

FAL. And here I stand; judge, my masters.

PRINCE. Now, Harry, whence come you?

FAL. My noble lord, from Eastcheap. 385

PRINCE. The complaints I hear of thee are grievous.

FAL. 'Sblood, my lord, they are false: nay, I'll tickle ye for a
young prince, i' faith.

PRINCE. Swearest thou, ungracious boy? thenceforth ne'er look
on me. Thou art violently carried away from grace; there is a 390
devil haunts thee in the likeness of an old fat man; a tun[1] of
man is thy companion. Why dost thou converse with that
trunk of humors, that bolting-hutch[2] of beastliness, that swollen parcel of dropsies, that huge bombard of sack, that stuffed
cloak-bag of guts, that roasted Manningtree[3] ox with the pud- 395
ding in his belly, that reverend vice, that gray iniquity, that
father ruffian, that vanity in years? Wherein is he good, but to
taste sack and drink it? wherein neat and cleanly, but to carve
a capon and eat it? wherein cunning, but in craft? wherein
crafty, but in villainy? wherein villainous, but in all things? 400
wherein worthy, but in nothing?

FAL. I would your grace would take me with you; whom means
your grace?

PRINCE. That villainous abominable misleader of youth, Falstaff,
that old white-bearded Satan. 405

FAL. My lord, the man I know.

PRINCE. I know thou dost.

FAL. But to say I know more harm in him than in myself were
to say more than I know. That he is old the more the pity, his
white hairs do witness it; but that he is, saving your reverence, 410
a whoremaster, that I utterly deny. If sack and sugar be a
fault, God help the wicked! if to be old and merry be a sin,
then many an old host that I know is damned; if to be fat be
to be hated, then Pharaoh's lean kine[4] are to be loved. No,
my good lord, banish Peto, banish Bardolph, banish Poins, 4 5
but for sweet Jack Falstaff, kind Jack Falstaff, true Jack Falstaff,
valiant Jack Falstaff, and therefore more valiant, being as he is
old Jack Falstaff, banish not him thy Harry's company, banish not him thy Harry's company; banish plump Jack, and ban-

---

8. Suckling rabbit.
9. Seated.
1. Large barrel.
2. Trough; "bombard": leather wine
vessel.
3. Town in Essex, noted for barbecues;

"pudding": sausage. The "vice" was
a comic character in the old morality
plays. Falstaff is in some respects a
descendant of this type-character.
4. In the dream Joseph interpreted.
See Genesis xli.19–21.

ish all the world.

PRINCE. I do, I will. [⟨*A knocking heard.*⟩]

[⟨*Exeunt* HOSTESS *and* BARDOLPH.⟩]

[*Enter* BARDOLPH, *running.*]

BARD. O, my lord, my lord, the sheriff with a most monstrous watch is at the door.

FAL. Out, ye rogue! Play out the play; I have much to say in the behalf of that Falstaff.

[*Enter the* HOSTESS.]

HOST. O Jesu, my lord, my lord!

FAL. Heigh, heigh! the devil rides upon a fiddlestick;[5] what's the matter?

HOST. The sheriff and all the watch are at the door; they are come to search the house. Shall I let them in?

FAL. Dost thou hear, Hal? never call a true piece of gold a counterfeit; thou art essentially mad, without seeming so.[6]

PRINCE. And thou a natural coward, without instinct.

FAL. I deny your major;[7] if you will deny the sheriff, so; if not, let him enter. If I become not a cart as well as another man, a plague on my bringing up! I hope I shall as soon be strangled with a halter as another.[8]

PRINCE. Go hide thee behind the arras;[9] the rest walk up above. Now, my masters, for a true face and good conscience.

FAL. Both which I have had; but their date is out,[1] and therefore I'll hide me.

PRINCE. Call in the sheriff.

[*Exeunt* ⟨*all except the* PRINCE *and* POINS.⟩]

[*Enter* SHERIFF *and the* CARRIER.]

Now, master sheriff, what is your will with me?

SHER. First pardon me, my lord. A hue and cry

Hath followed certain men unto this house.

PRINCE. What men?

SHER. One of them is well known, my gracious lord,

A gross fat man.

CAR.   As fat as butter.

PRINCE. The man, I do assure you, is not here,

For I myself at this time have employed him,

And, sheriff, I will engage my word to thee

That I will by tomorrow dinnertime

Send him to answer thee or any man

For anything he shall be charged withal;

And so let me entreat you leave the house.

SHER. I will, my lord. There are two gentlemen

---

5. I.e., there's a commotion.
6. I.e., don't give a true man (me, Falstaff) away as a thief. He goes on to accuse the prince, in his reversal of values in the play scene, of being out of his mind, though he appears rational.
7. Your major premise (that I, Falstaff, am a coward).
8. I.e., I hope my fat neck will not

make the process of strangling on the gallows longer for me than for the rest of you. The "cart" is the wagon on which criminals were taken to be hanged.
9. The hangings or draperies. On the Elizabethan stage these would conceal the inner stage. "Up above": on the balcony.
1. Lease has expired.

Have in this robbery lost three hundred marks.

PRINCE. It may be so; if he have robbed these men
　　He shall be answerable; and so farewell.

SHER. Good night, my noble lord.　　　　　　　　　　　　　460

PRINCE. I think it is good morrow, is it not?

SHER. Indeed, my lord, I think it be two o'clock.
　　　　[*Exeunt* ⟨SHERIFF *and* CARRIER.⟩]

PRINCE. This oily rascal is known as well as Paul's.² Go call him
　　forth.

POINS. Falstaff!—Fast asleep behind the arras, and snorting like　465
　　a horse.

PRINCE. Hark, how hard he fetches breath. Search his pockets.
　　[*He searcheth his pockets, and findeth certain papers.*] What
　　hast thou found?

POINS. Nothing but papers, my lord.　　　　　　　　　　　470

PRINCE. Let's see what they be: read them.

POINS. [*reads*] "Item, a capon.　.　.　.　.　2*s.* 2*d.*
　　　　　　　Item, sauce.　.　.　.　.　.　　　4*d.*
　　　　　　　Item, sack, two gallons.　.　5*s.* 8*d.*
　　　　　　　Item, anchovies and sack　　　　　　475
　　　　　　　　after supper.　.　.　.　.　2*s.* 6*d.*
　　　　　　　Item, bread.　.　.　.　.　.　　ob."³

PRINCE. O monstrous! but one halfpennyworth of bread to this
　　intolerable deal of sack! What there is else, keep close; we'll
　　read it at more advantage; there let him sleep till day. I'll to　480
　　the court in the morning. We must all to the wars, and thy
　　place shall be honorable. I'll procure this fat rogue a charge
　　of foot,⁴ and I know his death will be a march of twelvescore.
　　The money shall be paid back again with advantage. Be with
　　me betimes⁵ in the morning, and so good morrow, Poins.　485

POINS. Good morrow, good my lord.　　　　　　[*Exeunt.*]

Act III

SCENE 1

[*Enter* HOTSPUR, WORCESTER, LORD MORTIMER, *and* OWEN
GLENDOWER.]

MORT. These promises are fair, the parties sure,
　　And our induction⁶ full of prosperous hope.

HOT. Lord Mortimer, and cousin Glendower,
　　Will you sit down?
　　And uncle Worcester; a plague upon it,
　　I have forgot the map.

GLEND.　　　　　　　No, here it is.
　　Sit, cousin Percy, sit, good cousin Hotspur,
　　For by that name as oft as Lancaster
　　Doth speak of you, his cheek looks pale and with

2. St. Paul's Cathedral.　　　　　　score": i.e., 240 yards.
3. Oble, a halfpenny.　　　　　　　5. Early.
4. Company　of　infantry.　"Twelve-　6. Initial step.

A rising sigh he wisheth you in heaven.   10
HOT. And you in hell as often as he hears Owen Glendower spoke
    of.
GLEND. I cannot blame him; at my nativity
    The front[7] of heaven was full of fiery shapes,
    Of burning cressets, and at my birth   15
    The frame and huge foundation of the earth
    Shaked like a coward.
HOT. Why, so it would have done at the same season if your
    mother's cat had but kittened, though yourself had never been
    born.   20
GLEND. I say the earth did shake when I was born.
HOT. And I say the earth was not of my mind,
    If you suppose as fearing you it shook.
GLEND. The heavens were all on fire, the earth did tremble.
HOT. O then the earth shook to see the heavens on fire,   25
    And not in fear of your nativity.
    Diseaséd nature oftentimes breaks forth
    In strange eruptions; oft the teeming earth
    Is with a kind of colic pinched and vexed
    By the imprisoning of unruly wind   30
    Within her womb, which for enlargement striving
    Shakes the old beldam[8] earth and topples down
    Steeples and moss-grown towers. At your birth
    Our grandam earth, having this distemperature,[9]
    In passion shook.
GLEND.   Cousin, of many men   35
    I do not bear these crossings. Give me leave
    To tell you once again that at my birth
    The front of heaven was full of fiery shapes,
    The goats ran from the mountains, and the herds
    Were strangely clamorous to the frighted fields.   40
    These signs have marked me extraordinary,
    And all the courses of my life do show
    I am not in the roll of common men.
    Where is he living, clipped in with[1] the sea
    That chides the banks of England, Scotland, Wales,   45
    Which calls me pupil or hath read to me?
    And bring him out that is but woman's son
    Can trace me in the tedious ways of art[2]
    And hold me pace in deep experiments.
HOT. I think there's no man speaks better Welsh. I'll to dinner.   50
MORT. Peace, cousin Percy; you will make him mad.
GLEND. I can call spirits from the vasty deep.
HOT. Why, so can I, or so can any man;
    But will they come when you do call for them?
GLEND. Why, I can teach you, cousin, to command   55
    The devil.

---

7. The forehead. "Cressets": lamps.
8. Old woman.
9. Ailment.

1. Within the limits of.
2. Follow me in practicing difficult
magic.

HOT. And I can teach thee, coz, to shame the devil
  By telling truth; tell truth and shame the devil.[3]
  If thou have power to raise him, bring him hither,
  And I'll be sworn I have power to shame him hence.   60
  O, while you live, tell truth and shame the devil!
MORT. Come, come, no more of this unprofitable chat.
GLEND. Three times hath Henry Bolingbroke made head
  Against my power, thrice from the banks of Wye
  And sandy-bottomed Severn have I sent him   65
  Bootless[4] home and weather-beaten back.
HOT. Home without boots, and in foul weather too!
  How 'scapes he agues,[5] in the devil's name?
GLEND. Come, here is the map; shall we divide our right
  According to our threefold order ta'en?[6]   70
MORT. The archdeacon hath divided it
  Into three limits very equally:
  England, from Trent and Severn hitherto,
  By south and east is to my part assigned;
  All westward, Wales beyond the Severn shore,   75
  And all the fertile land within that bound,
  To Owen Glendower; and, dear coz, to you
  The remnant northward lying off from Trent;
  And our indentures tripartite are drawn,
  Which being sealéd interchangeably,   80
  A business that this night may execute,
  Tomorrow, cousin Percy, you and I
  And my good Lord of Worcester will set forth
  To meet your father[7] and the Scottish power,
  As is appointed us, at Shrewsbury.   85
  My father Glendower is not ready yet,
  Nor shall we need his help these fourteen days.
  Within that space you may have drawn together
  Your tenants, friends, and neighboring gentlemen.
GLEND. A shorter time shall send me to you, lords,   90
  And in my conduct shall your ladies come,
  From whom you now must steal and take no leave,
  For there will be a world of water shed
  Upon the parting of your wives and you.
HOT. Methinks my moiety,[8] north from Burton here,   95
  In quantity equals not one of yours;
  See how this river comes me cranking[9] in,
  And cuts me from the best of all my land
  A huge half-moon, a monstrous cantle[1] out.
  I'll have the current in this place dammed up;   100
  And here the smug[1a] and silver Trent shall run

---

3. A proverb.
4. Unsuccessful; but Hotspur takes it in the other sense.
5. Fevers and chills.
6. Divide our property according to the arrangement for division into three parts.
7. Father-in-law.
8. Part, share.
9. Curving.
1. Corner.
1a. Smooth.

In a new channel, fair and evenly;
It shall not wind with such a deep indent
To rob me of so rich a bottom[2] here.
GLEND. Not wind? it shall, it must; you see it doth.   105
MORT. Yea, but
Mark how he bears his course, and runs me up
With like advantage on the other side;
Gelding the opposéd continent[3] as much
As on the other side it takes from you.   110
WOR. Yea, but a little charge will trench him here
And on this north side win this cape of land,
And then he runs straight and even.
HOT. I'll have it so; a little charge will do it.
GLEND. I'll not have it altered.
HOT.   Will not you?   115
GLEND. No, nor you shall not.
HOT.   Who shall say me nay?
GLEND. Why, that will I.
HOT. Let me not understand you then; speak it in Welsh.
GLEND. I can speak English, lord, as well as you,
For I was trained up in the English court,   120
Where, being but young, I framéd to the harp
Many an English ditty lovely well
And gave the tongue a helpful ornament,
A virtue that was never seen in you.
HOT. Marry,   125
And I am glad of it with all my heart;
I had rather be a kitten and cry mew
Than one of these same meter ballad-mongers;
I had rather hear a brazen canstick turned,[4]
Or a dry wheel grate on the axletree,   130
And that would set my teeth nothing on edge,
Nothing so much as mincing[5] poetry;
'Tis like the forced gait of a shuffling nag.
GLEND. Come, you shall have Trent turned.
HOT. I do not care; I'll give thrice so much land   135
To any well-deserving friend;
But in the way of bargain, mark ye me,
I'll cavil[6] on the ninth part of a hair.
Are the indentures drawn? shall we be gone?
GLEND. The moon shines fair; you may be away by night.   140
I'll haste the writer, and withal
Break with[7] your wives of your departure hence.
I am afraid my daughter will run mad,
So much she doteth on her Mortimer.   [*Exit.*]
MORT. Fie, cousin Percy, how you cross my father!
HOT. I cannot choose; sometime he angers me   145

2. Valley.
3. I.e., cutting off from the opposite side.
4. A brass candlestick turned on a lathe.
5. Affected.
6. Quibble.
7. Inform.

With telling me of the moldwarp[8] and the ant,
Of the dreamer Merlin and his prophecies,
And of a dragon and a finless fish,
A clip-winged griffin and a molten raven,   150
A couching lion and a ramping[9] cat,
And such a deal of skimble-skamble stuff
As puts me from my faith. I tell you what;
He held me last night at least nine hours
In reckoning up the several devils' names   155
That were his lackeys. I cried "hum" and "well, go to,"
But marked him not a word. O, he is as tedious
As a tired horse, a railing[1] wife,
Worse than a smoky house. I had rather live
With cheese and garlic in a windmill,[2] far,   160
Than feed on cates and have him talk to me
In any summer house in Christendom.

MORT. In faith, he is a worthy gentleman,
Exceedingly well read, and profited
In strange concealments,[3] valiant as a lion   165
And wondrous affable and as bountiful
As mines of India. Shall I tell you, cousin?
He holds your temper[4] in a high respect
And curbs himself even of his natural scope
When you come 'cross his humor; faith, he does.   170
I warrant you that man is not alive
Might so have tempted him as you have done
Without the taste of danger and reproof;
But do not use it oft, let me entreat you.

WOR. In faith, my lord, you are too willful-blame,   175
And since your coming hither have done enough
To put him quite beside his patience.
You must needs learn, lord, to amend this fault.
Though sometimes it show greatness, courage, blood[5]—
And that's the dearest grace it renders you—   180
Yet oftentimes it doth present harsh rage,
Defect of manners, want of government,[6]
Pride, haughtiness, opinion, and disdain;
The least of which haunting a nobleman
Loseth men's hearts and leaves behind a stain   185
Upon the beauty of all parts besides,
Beguiling them of commendation.

HOT. Well, I am schooled; good manners be your speed!
Here come our wives, and let us take our leave.

8. Mole. According to the chronicler Holinshed there were prophecies in which Henry IV was referred to as "a moldwarp, cursed of God." Merlin was the famous prophet of King Arthur's court; many later prophecies were attributed to him.
9. "Couching" and "ramping" are Hotspur's versions of the heraldic terms "couchant" (lying down) and "ramp-

ant" (erect, on hind feet).
1. Nagging.
2. Cheese and garlic would be smelly, and the living quarters in a mill would be noisy. "Cates": delicacies.
3. Experienced in secret mysteries.
4. Character.
5. Breeding, blood-lines.
6. Self-control. "Opinion": arrogance.

[*Enter* GLENDOWER *with the ladies.*]

MORT. This is the deadly spite that angers me; 190
My wife can speak no English, I no Welsh.

GLEND. My daughter weeps; she will not part with you,
She'll be a soldier too, she'll to the wars.

MORT. Good father, tell her that she and my aunt Percy
Shall follow in your conduct speedily. 195

[GLENDOWER SPEAKS *to her in Welsh, and she answers
him in the same.*]

GLEND. She is desperate here; a peevish self-willed harlotry,[7] one
that no persuasion can do good upon.

[*The lady speaks in Welsh.*]

MORT. I understand thy looks; that pretty Welsh
Which thou pour'st down from these swelling heavens[8]
I am too perfect in; and, but for shame, 200
In such a parley should I answer thee.

[*The lady speaks again in Welsh.*]

I understand thy kisses and thou mine,
And that's a feeling disputation,
But I will never be a truant, love,
Till I have learned thy language, for thy tongue 205
Makes Welsh as sweet as ditties highly penned,
Sung by a fair queen in a summer's bower,
With ravishing division,[9] to her lute.

GLEND. Nay, if you melt, then will she run mad.

[*The lady speaks again in Welsh.*]

MORT. O, I am ignorance itself in this! 210

GLEND. She bids you on the wanton rushes[1] lay you down
And rest your gentle head upon her lap,
And she will sing the song that pleaseth you
And on your eyelids crown the god of sleep,
Charming your blood with pleasing heaviness, 215
Making such difference 'twixt wake and sleep
As is the difference betwixt day and night
The hour before the heavenly-harnessed team[2]
Begins his golden progress in the east.

MORT. With all my heart I'll sit and hear her sing; 220
By that time will our book,[3] I think, be drawn.

GLEND. Do so;
And those musicians that shall play to you
Hang in the air a thousand leagues from hence,
And straight they shall be here; sit, and attend. 225

HOT. Come, Kate, thou art perfect in lying down; come, quick,
quick, that I may lay my head in thy lap.

LADY P. Go, ye giddy goose.

---

7. Wench; used affectionately, not
seriously (Juliet's father applies the
same phrase to her in *Romeo and
Juliet*).
8. I.e., tears from her eyes. "Answer
thee": cry likewise.
9. Musical variation.
1. The dry reeds used as a floor covering
in Elizabethan England.
2. The horses of the sun.
3. The indenture.

[The music plays.]

HOT. Now I perceive the devil understands Welsh,
And 'tis no marvel, he is so humorous.[4]   230
By 'r Lady, he is a good musician.

LADY P. Then should you be nothing but musical, for you are altogether governed by humors. Lie still, ye thief, and hear the
lady sing in Welsh.

HOT. I had rather hear Lady, my brach,[5] howl in Irish.   235

LADY P. Wouldst thou have thy head broken?

HOT. No.

LADY P. Then be still.

HOT. Neither; 'tis a woman's fault.[6]

LADY P. Now God help thee.   240

HOT. To the Welsh lady's bed.

LADY P. What's that?

HOT. Peace! she sings.

[Here the lady sings a Welsh song.]

HOT. Come, Kate, I'll have your song too.

LADY P. Not mine, in good sooth.   245

HOT. Not yours, in good sooth! Heart! you swear like a comfit-
maker's[7] wife. "Not you, in good sooth," and "as true as I
live," and "as God shall mend me," and "as sure as day,"
And givest such sarcenet[8] surety for thy oaths
As if thou never walk'st further than Finsbury.   250
Swear me, Kate, like a lady as thou art,
A good mouth-filling oath, and leave "in sooth,"
And such protest of pepper-gingerbread,[9]
To velvet-guards and Sunday citizens.
Come, sing.   255

LADY P. I will not sing.

HOT. 'Tis the next way to turn tailor, or be redbreast teacher.[1]
An the indentures be drawn, I'll away within these two hours;
and so, come in when ye will.   *[Exit.]*

GLEND. Come, come, Lord Mortimer, you are as slow   260
As hot Lord Percy is on fire to go.
By this our book is drawn; we will but seal,
And then to horse immediately.

MORT.   With all my heart. *[Exeunt.]*

SCENE 2

[Enter the KING, PRINCE OF WALES, *and others.]*

KING. Lords, give us leave; the Prince of Wales and I

---

4. Capricious, governed by humors.
5. My bitch hound, Lady.
6. Hotspur sarcastically reverses the usual saying about women and talkativeness.
7. Confectioner's.
8. Thin silk. Finsbury: a recreation ground outside London, frequented by citizens and their wives on Sundays, but not by ladies of Lady Percy's class.
9. I.e., such tame oaths, as crumbly and unsubstantial as gingerbread. "Velvet-guards": respectable people of the middle class, who wore velvet stripes on their clothes; "Sunday citizens": city folk out for a stroll on Sunday.
1. I.e., it is the easiest way to become a tailor (supposedly tailors sang at their work) or a person who teaches birds to sing. Hotspur is equally scornful of music and of people who work for a living.

Must have some private conference; but be near at hand,
For we shall presently have need of you.　　[*Exeunt* LORDS.]
I know not whether God will have it so
For some displeasing service I have done, 5
That, in his secret doom, out of my blood[2]
He'll breed revengement and a scourge for me;
But thou dost in thy passages[3] of life
Make me believe that thou art only marked
For the hot vengeance and the rod of heaven 10
To punish my mistreadings.[4] Tell me else,
Could such inordinate and low desires,
Such poor, such bare, such lewd,[5] such mean attempts,
Such barren pleasures, rude society
As thou art matched withal and grafted to 15
Accompany the greatness of thy blood
And hold their level with thy princely heart?

PRINCE. So please your majesty, I would I could
Quit[6] all offenses with as clear excuse
As well as I am doubtless I can purge 20
Myself of many I am charged withal;
Yet such extenuation let me beg,
As, in reproof of many tales devised
(Which oft the ear of greatness needs must hear)
By smiling pickthanks[7] and base newsmongers, 25
I may, for some things true, wherein my youth
Hath faulty wandered and irregular,
Find pardon on my true submissión.

KING. God pardon thee; yet let me wonder, Harry,
At thy affections, which doth hold a wing 30
Quite from the flight of all thy ancestors.
Thy place in council thou hast rudely lost,
Which by thy younger brother is supplied,
And art almost an alien to the hearts
Of all the court and princes of my blood. 35
The hope and expectation of thy time[8]
Is ruined, and the soul of every man
Prophetically do forethink thy fall.
Had I so lavish of my presence been,
So common-hackneyed in the eyes of men, 40
So stale and cheap to vulgar company,
Opinion,[9] that did help me to the crown,
Had still kept loyal to possessión
And left me in reputeless banishment,
A fellow of no mark nor likelihood. 45
By being seldom seen, I could not stir

2. Through my son.
3. Actions.
4. False steps, misdeeds.
5. Low.
6. Acquit myself of. "Doubtless": sure.
7. Flatterers; "newsmongers": tattle-
tales.
8. Lifetime.
9. Popularity, public opinion. "Possession": i.e., the possessor, Richard II.

But like a comet I was wondered at,
That men would tell their children "This is he";
Others would say "Where, which is Bolingbroke?"
And then I stole all courtesy from heaven,   50
And dressed myself in such humility
That I did pluck allegiance from men's hearts,
Loud shouts and salutations from their mouths,
Even in the presence of the crownéd king.
Thus did I keep my person fresh and new,   55
My presence like a robe pontifical,
Ne'er seen but wondered at; and so my state,[1]
Seldom but sumptuous, showed like a feast
And wan[2] by rareness such solemnity.
The skipping king, he ambled up and down   60
With shallow jesters and rash bavin wits,[3]
Soon kindled and soon burnt, carded his state,
Mingled his royalty with capering fools,
Had his great name profanéd with their scorns
And gave his countenance[4] against his name   65
To laugh at gibing boys and stand the push
Of every beardless vain comparative,[5]
Grew a companion to the common streets,
Enfeoffed himself to popularity,[6]
That, being daily swallowed by men's eyes,   70
They surfeited with honey and began
To loathe the taste of sweetness, whereof a little
More than a little is by much too much.
So when he had occasion to be seen
He was but as the cuckoo is in June,[7]   75
Heard, not regarded, seen, but with such eyes
As, sick and blunted with community,[8]
Afford no extraordinary gaze
Such as is bent on sunlike majesty
When it shines seldom in admiring eyes,   80
But rather drowsed and hung their eyelids down,
Slept in his face[9] and rendered such aspéct
As cloudy men use to their adversaries,
Being with his presence glutted, gorged, and full.
And in that very line, Harry, standest thou,   85
For thou hast lost thy princely privilege
With vile participation.[1] Not an eye
But is a-weary of thy common sight,

1. Public ceremonial appearances.
2. Won. "Such solemnity": i.e., the greatest possible majestic effect (an intensive use of "such"). King Henry's theory of public relations is of course not based upon the assumption of a democratic society.
3. "Rash": quick; "bavin": brushwood; the image is explained in the next line. "Carded his state": degraded his royal dignity; "card" also means "to adulterate wine."
4. Authority; "name": reputation.
5. Shallow satirical pretender to wit.
6. Made himself the common property of the public.
7. The cuckoo is noticed in April, when its song is first heard; by June it is commonplace.
8. Commonness.
9. I.e., yawned in his face. "Aspect": looks; "cloudy": sullen.
1. Association with vile companions.

Save mine, which hath desired to see thee more,
Which now doth that I would not have it do, 90
Make blind itself with foolish tenderness.
PRINCE. I shall hereafter, my thrice gracious lord,
Be more myself.
KING.   For all the world
As thou art to this hour was Richard then
When I from France set foot at Ravenspurgh, 95
And even as I was then is Percy now.
Now, by my scepter and my soul to boot,
He hath more worthy interest to the state
Than thou the shadow of succession;[2]
For of no right, nor color like to right, 100
He doth fill fields with harness in the realm,
Turns head against the lion's arméd jaws,[3]
And, being no more in debt to years than thou,
Leads ancient lords and reverend bishops on
To bloody battles and to bruising arms. 105
What never-dying honor hath he got
Against renownéd Douglas! whose high deeds,
Whose hot incursions and great name in arms
Holds from all soldiers chief majority
And military title capital[4] 110
Through all the kingdoms that acknowledge Christ.
Thrice hath this Hotspur, Mars in swaddling clothes,
This infant warrior, in his enterprises
Discomfited great Douglas, ta'en him once,
Enlargéd[5] him and made a friend of him, 115
To fill the mouth of deep defiance up[6]
And shake the peace and safety of our throne.
And what say you to this? Percy, Northumberland,
The Archbishop's grace of York, Douglas, Mortimer,
Capitulate[7] against us and are up. 120
But wherefore do I tell these news to thee?
Why, Harry, do I tell thee of my foes,
Which art my nearest and dearest enemy?
Thou that art like enough through vassal fear,
Base inclination and the start of spleen,[8] 125
To fight against me under Percy's pay,
To dog his heels and curtsy at his frowns,
To show how much thou art degenerate.
PRINCE. Do not think so; you shall not find it so;
And God forgive them that so much have swayed 130
Your majesty's good thoughts away from me.

2. I.e., Hotspur's claim to the throne is more solid, because of his achievements, than is Hal's, which rests only on shadowy rights of succession by birth. "Color": false pretense.
3. I.e., takes military action against the king's army. "Harness": armor.
4. Has the greatest reputation among soldiers. "Incursions": raids; "majority": superiority.
5. Freed.
6. I.e., to make the voice of defiance full in volume.
7. Make agreements; "up": in arms.
8. Unreasoning impulse.

I will redeem all this on Percy's head
And in the closing of some glorious day
Be bold to tell you that I am your son,
When I will wear a garment all of blood   135
And stain my favors[9] in a bloody mask,
Which, washed away, shall scour my shame with it;
And that shall be the day, whene'er it lights,
That this same child of honor and renown,
This gallant Hotspur, this all-praiséd knight,   140
And your unthought-of Harry chance to meet.
For every honor sitting on his helm—
Would they were multitudes, and on my head
My shames redoubled!—for the time will come
That I shall make this northern youth exchange   145
His glorious deeds for my indignities.
Percy is but my factor,[1] good my lord,
To engross up glorious deeds on my behalf,
And I will call him to so strict account,
That he shall render every glory up,   150
Yea, even the slightest worship[2] of his time,
Or I will tear the reckoning from his heart.
This in the name of God I promise here,
The which if He be pleased I shall perform,
I do beseech your majesty, may salve   155
The long-grown wounds of my intemperance;
If not, the end of life cancels all bands,[3]
And I will die a hundred thousand deaths
Ere break the smallest parcel of this vow.
KING. A hundred thousand rebels die in this;   160
    Thou shalt have charge and sovereign trust herein.
        [*Enter* BLUNT.]
    How now, good Blunt? thy looks are full of speed.
BLUNT. So hath the business that I come to speak of.
    Lord Mortimer of Scotland hath sent word
    That Douglas and the English rebels met   165
    The eleventh of this month at Shrewsbury;
    A mighty and a fearful head[4] they are,
    If promises be kept on every hand,
    As ever offered foul play in a state.
KING. The Earl of Westmoreland set forth today,   170
    With him my son, Lord John of Lancaster,
    For this advertisement[5] is five days old.
    On Wednesday next, Harry, you shall set forward;
    On Thursday we ourselves will march. Our meeting
    Is Bridgenorth and, Harry, you shall march   175
    Through Gloucestershire, by which account,[6]

9. Features.
1. Agent; "engross up": collect, acquire.
2. Honor.
3. Bonds, debts.
4. Power.
5. News.
6. Method. "Our business valued": according to estimates.

Our business valued, some twelve days hence
Our general forces at Bridgenorth shall meet.
Our hands are full of business: let's away;
Advantage feeds him fat while men delay.[7] [*Exeunt.*] 180

SCENE 3

[*Enter* FALSTAFF *and* BARDOLPH.]

FAL. Bardolph, am I not fallen away vilely since this last action?[8]
do I not bate? do I not dwindle? Why, my skin hangs about
me like an old lady's loose gown; I am withered like an old
applejohn.[9] Well, I'll repent, and that suddenly, while I am
in some liking; I shall be out of heart shortly, and then I shall 5
have no strength to repent. An I have not forgotten what the
inside of a church is made of, I am a peppercorn, a brewer's
horse. The inside of a church! Company, villainous company,
hath been the spoil of me.

BARD. Sir John, you are so fretful you cannot live long. 10

FAL. Why, there is it; come sing me a bawdy song, make me
merry. I was as virtuously given as a gentleman need to be:
virtuous enough; swore little; diced not above seven times a
week; went to a bawdyhouse not above once in a quarter—of an
hour; paid money that I borrowed three or four times; lived 15
well and in good compass; and now I live out of all order, out
of all compass.

BARD. Why, you are so fat, Sir John, that you must needs be out
of all compass, out of all reasonable compass, Sir John.

FAL. Do thou amend thy face, and I'll amend my life; thou art 20
our admiral,[1] thou bearest the lantern in the poop, but 'tis in
the nose of thee; thou art the Knight of the Burning Lamp.

BARD. Why, Sir John, my face does you no harm.

FAL. No, I'll be sworn; I make as good use of it as many a man
doth of a death's-head or a *memento mori*.[2] I never see thy 25
face but I think upon hell-fire and Dives[3] that lived in purple,
for there he is in his robes, burning, burning. If thou wert any
way given to virtue, I would swear by thy face; my oath should
be "By this fire, that's God's angel"; but thou art altogether
given over, and wert indeed, but for the light in thy face, the 30
son of utter darkness. When thou rannest up Gadshill in the
night to catch my horse, if I did not think thou hadst been an
ignis fatuus[4] or a ball of wildfire, there's no purchase in money.
O, thou art a perpetual triumph,[5] an everlasting bonfire light!
Thou hast saved me a thousand marks in links[6] and torches, 35
walking with thee in the night betwixt tavern and tavern, but

---

7. I.e., the rebels' "advantage" (opportunity) grows as the king's men delay.
8. I.e., the Gadshill robbery; "bate":
lose weight.
9. A keeping apple with a wrinkled
skin. "In some liking": in good condition.
1. Flagship.

2. I.e., a skull or some other reminder
of death.
3. The rich man who would not give
food to Lazarus and was punished in
hell for it. See Luke xvi.19–31.
4. Will-o'-the-wisp; "wildfire": a firework used for military purposes.
5. Illumination at a public festival.
6. Small torches carried at night.

the sack that thou hast drunk me would have bought me lights as good cheap at the dearest chandler's[7] in Europe. I have maintained that salamander of yours with fire any time this two and thirty years, God reward me for it.   40

BARD. 'Sblood, I would my face were in your belly!

FAL. God-a-mercy! so should I be sure to be heartburned.

[*Enter* HOSTESS.]

How now, Dame Partlet[8] the hen! have you inquired yet who picked my pocket?

HOST. Why, Sir John, what do you think, Sir John? do you think   45
I keep thieves in my house? I have searched, I have inquired, so has my husband, man by man, boy by boy, servant by servant; the tithe[9] of a hair was never lost in my house before.

FAL. Ye lie, hostess; Bardolph was shaved and lost many a hair, and I'll be sworn my pocket was picked. Go to, you are a   50
woman, go.

HOST. Who, I? no, I defy thee; God's light, I was never called so in mine own house before.

FAL. Go to, I know you well enough.

HOST. No, Sir John; you do not know me, Sir John. I know   55
you, Sir John; you owe me money, Sir John, and now you pick a quarrel to beguile me of it; I bought you a dozen of shirts to your back.

FAL. Dowlas,[1] filthy dowlas; I have given them away to bakers' wives, and they have made bolters of them.   60

HOST. Now, as I am a true woman, holland[2] of eight shillings an ell. You owe money here besides, Sir John, for your diet and by-drinkings,[3] and money lent you, four and twenty pound.

FAL. He had his part of it; let him pay.

HOST. He? alas, he is poor; he hath nothing.   65

FAL. How! poor? look upon his face; what call you rich? let them coin his nose, let them coin his cheeks; I'll not pay a denier.[4] What, will you make a younker of me? shall I not take mine ease in mine-inn but I shall have my pocket picked? I have lost a seal ring of my grandfather's worth forty mark.[5]   70

HOST. O Jesu, I have heard the prince tell him I know not how oft that that ring was copper.

FAL. How! the prince is a Jack,[6] a sneak-up; 'sblood, an he were here, I would cudgel him like a dog if he would say so.

[*Enter the* PRINCE ⟨*and* POINS⟩, *marching, and* FALSTAFF *meets them playing upon his truncheon like a fife.*]

How now, lad, is the wind in that door, i' faith? must we all   75
march?

---

7. Candlemaker's. "Salamanders" were lizards that supposedly lived in fire and ate it.
8. A nickname from the hen in Chaucer's Nun's Priest's Tale; in Shakespeare's time a conventional name for a scolding woman.
9. Tenth part.
1. A coarse cloth. "Bolters": sieves for

flour.
2. Fine linen; "ell": 45 inches.
3. Drinks between meals.
4. French penny, worth a tenth of an English penny. "Younker": youngster, novice.
5. A mark was worth two-thirds of a pound.
6. Rascal; "sneak-up": a sneak.

BARD. Yea, two and two, Newgate fashion.[7]

HOST. My lord, I pray you hear me.

PRINCE. What sayest thou, Mistress Quickly? How doth thy husband? I love him well; he is an honest man.　　　　　　80

HOST. Good my lord, hear me.

FAL. Prithee let her alone, and list to me.

PRINCE. What sayest thou, Jack?

FAL. The other night I fell asleep here behind the arras and had my pocket picked; this house is turned bawdyhouse, they pick　85 pockets.

PRINCE. What didst thou lose, Jack?

FAL. Wilt thou believe me, Hal? three or four bonds of forty pound apiece, and a seal ring of my grandfather's.

PRINCE. A trifle, some eightpenny matter.　　　　　　90

HOST. So I told him, my lord, and I said I heard your grace say so; and, my lord, he speaks most vilely of you, like a foul-mouthed man as he is, and said he would cudgel you.

PRINCE. What, he did not?

HOST. There's neither faith, truth, nor womanhood in me else.　95

FAL. There's no more faith in thee than in a stewed prune,[8] nor no more truth in thee than in a drawn fox, and for womanhood Maid Marian may be the deputy's wife of the ward to thee.[9] Go, you thing, go.

HOST. Say, what thing, what thing?　　　　　　100

FAL. What thing! why, a thing to thank God on.

HOST. I am no thing to thank God on, I would thou shouldst know it; I am an honest man's wife, and, setting thy knighthood aside,[1] thou art a knave to call me so.

FAL. Setting thy womanhood aside, thou art a beast to say other-　105 wise.

HOST. Say, what beast, thou knave, thou?

FAL. What beast? why, an otter.

PRINCE. An otter, Sir John, why an otter?

FAL. Why, she's neither fish nor flesh, a man knows not where　110 to have her.[2]

HOST. Thou art an unjust man in saying so; thou or any man knows where to have me, thou knave, thou!

PRINCE. Thou sayest true, hostess, and he slanders thee most grossly.　　　　　　115

HOST. So he doth you, my lord, and said this other day you ought[3] him a thousand pound.

PRINCE. Sirrah, do I owe you a thousand pound?

FAL. A thousand pound, Hal! A million. Thy love is worth a mil-

7. Chained together, like prisoners at Newgate.

8. Stewed prunes were commonly served in bawdyhouses, as a supposed protection against venereal disease. "Drawn": hunted.

9. "Maid Marian" was a female character of low morals in the popular Robin Hood plays; a "deputy's wife of the ward" would be a respectable woman.

1. I.e., ignoring, or intending no disrespect to, the rank of knighthood. Falstaff intentionally misunderstands the phrase.

2. I.e., how to understand her. But the Hostess' retort is, unconsciously, equivalent to saying that she is completely promiscuous.

3. Owed.

lion; thou owest me thy love.   120

HOST. Nay, my lord, he called you Jack, and said he would cudgel
     you.

FAL. Did I, Bardolph?

BARD. Indeed, Sir John, you said so.

FAL. Yea, if he said my ring was copper.   125

PRINCE. I say 'tis copper; darest thou be as good as thy word now?

FAL. Why, Hal, thou knowest, as thou art but man, I dare; but
     as thou art prince, I fear thee as I fear the roaring of the lion's
     whelp.

PRINCE. And why not as the lion?   130

FAL. The king himself is to be feared as the lion; dost thou think
     I'll fear thee as I fear thy father? Nay, an I do, I pray God my
     girdle[4] break.

PRINCE. O, if it should, how would thy guts fall about thy knees!
     But, sirrah, there's no room for faith, truth, nor honesty in this 135
     bosom of thine; it is all filled up with guts and midriff. Charge
     an honest woman with picking thy pocket! Why, thou whore-
     son, impudent, embossed rascal,[5] if there were anything in thy
     pocket but tavern-reckonings, memorandums of bawdyhouses,
     and one poor pennyworth of sugar candy to make thee long-   140
     winded, if thy pocket were enriched with any other injuries but
     these, I am a villain. And yet you will stand to it, you will not
     pocket up wrong; art thou not ashamed?

FAL. Dost thou hear, Hal? thou knowest in the state of innocency
     Adam fell, and what should poor Jack Falstaff do in the days 145
     of villainy? Thou seest I have more flesh than another man,
     and therefore more frailty. You confess then, you picked my
     pocket?

PRINCE. It appears so by the story.

FAL. Hostess, I forgive thee; go make ready breakfast, love thy 150
     husband, look to thy servants, cherish thy guests; thou shalt
     find me tractable to any honest reason; thou seest I am pacified
     still. Nay, prithee begone. [*Exit* HOSTESS.] Now, Hal, to the
     news at court; for the robbery, lad, how is that answered?

PRINCE. O, my sweet beef, I must still be good angel to thee; the 155
     money is paid back again.

FAL. O, I do not like that paying back; 'tis a double labor.

PRINCE. I am good friends with my father and may do anything.

FAL. Rob me the exchequer the first thing thou doest, and do it
     with unwashed hands too.   160

BARD. Do, my lord.

PRINCE. I have procured thee, Jack, a charge of foot.[6]

FAL. I would it had been of horse. Where shall I find one that
     can steal well? O for a fine thief, of the age of two and twenty
     or thereabouts! I am heinously unprovided. Well, God be 165
     thanked for these rebels, they offend none but the virtuous; I

---

4. Belt.
5. Swollen rascal; "embossed" was also
a technical term in hunting, applied to
a deer which was exhausted and foaming at the mouth.
6. Command of a company of foot-
soldiers. "Horse": cavalry.

laud them, I praise them.

PRINCE. Bardolph!

BARD. My lord?

PRINCE. Go bear this letter to Lord John of Lancaster, to my 170
brother John; this to my Lord of Westmoreland. [*Exit* BAR-
DOLPH.] Go, Poins, to horse, to horse; for thou and I have
thirty miles to ride yet ere dinnertime. [*Exit* POINS.] Jack, meet
me tomorrow in the Temple Hall at two o'clock in the after-
noon. 175
There shalt thou know thy charge, and there receive
Money and order for their furniture.[7]
The land is burning, Percy stands on high,
And either we or they must lower lie. [⟨*Exit.*⟩]

FAL. Rare words, brave world! Hostess, my breakfast, come. 180
O, I could wish this tavern were my drum![7a] [*Exit.*]

Act IV

SCENE 1

[*Enter* HOTSPUR, WORCESTER, *and* DOUGLAS.]

HOT. Well said, my noble Scot. If speaking truth
In this fine age were not thought flattery,
Such attribution should the Douglas have
As not a soldier of this season's stamp
Should go so general current[8] through the world. 5
By God, I cannot flatter; I do defy
The tongues of soothers,[9] but a braver place
In my heart's love hath no man than yourself;
Nay, task me to my word,[1] approve me, lord.

DOUG. Thou art the king of honor; 10
No man so potent breathes upon the ground
But I will beard him.[2]

HOT.   Do so, and 'tis well.
[*Enter a* MESSENGER *with letters.*]
What letters hast thou there?—I can but thank you.

MESS. These letters come from your father.

HOT. Letters from him! why comes he not himself? 15

MESS. He cannot come, my lord; he is grievous sick.

HOT. Zounds! how has he the leisure to be sick
In such a justling[3] time? Who leads his power?
Under whose government come they along?

MESS. His letters bears his mind, not I, my lord. 20

WOR. I prithee tell me, doth he keep his bed?

MESS. He did, my lord, four days ere I set forth,
And at the time of my departure thence

7. Furnishings, equipment.
7a. Headquarters.
8. I.e., that not a soldier of this year's
coinage should achieve such currency.
"Attribution": praise.
9. Flatterers; "braver": more distin-

guished.
1. Compare my actions with my speech.
"Approve": prove, test.
2. I.e., I will take on anybody, however powerful.
3. Turbulent.

He was much feared by[4] his physiciáns.

WOR. I would the state of time had first been whole   25
    Ere he by sickness had been visited;
    His health was never better worth than now.

HOT. Sick now! droop now! this sickness doth infect
    The very lifeblood of our enterprise;
    'Tis catching hither, even to our camp.   30
    He writes me here that inward sickness—
    And that his friends by deputation could not
    So soon be drawn,[5] nor did he think it meet
    To lay so dangerous and dear a trust
    On any soul removed but on his own.   35
    Yet doth he give us bold advertisement
    That with our small conjunction[6] we should on
    To see how fortune is disposed to us;
    For, as he writes, there is no quailing now,
    Because the king is certainly possessed[7]   40
    Of all our purposes. What say you to it?

WOR. Your father's sickness is a maim to us.

HOT. A perilous gash, a very limb lopped off;
    And yet in faith it is not; his present want[8]
    Seems more than we shall find it. Were it good   45
    To set the exact wealth of all our states
    All at one cast, to set so rich a main[9]
    On the nice hazard of one doubtful hour?
    It were not good, for therein should we read
    The very bottom and the soul of hope,[1]   50
    The very list, the very utmost bound
    Of all our fortunes.

DOUG.   Faith, and so we should,
    Where now remains a sweet reversión.[2]
    We may boldly spend upon the hope of what
    Is to come in;   55
    A comfort of retirement[3] lives in this.

HOT. A rendezvous, a home to fly unto,
    If that the devil and mischance look big
    Upon the maidenhead of our affairs.[4]

WOR. But yet I would your father had been here.   60
    The quality and hair[5] of our attempt
    Brooks no division; it will be thought
    By some that know not why he is away
    That wisdom, loyalty, and mere dislike
    Of our proceedings kept the earl from hence.   65

---

4. Feared for by. "State of time": public affairs.
5. Could not quickly be organized under a deputy. "Soul removed": other person.
6. Unified forces.
7. Informed.
8. Our present awareness of his absence.
9. Stake, in betting; "nice hazard": risky chance.
1. Foundation and essence of our expectations. "List": limit.
2. A fund to be inherited in the future.
3. Sustaining place to fall back on.
4. I.e., threaten the beginning of our affairs.
5. Character; "brooks": allows.

And think how such an apprehensión
May turn the tide of fearful factión[6]
And breed a kind of question in our cause,
For well you know we of the offering[7] side
Must keep aloof from strict arbitrement,   70
And stop all sight-holes, every loop[8] from whence
The eye of reason may pry in upon us.
This absence of your father's draws a curtain,
That shows the ignorant a kind of fear
Before not dreamt of.

HOT.   You strain too far.   75
I rather of his absence make this use:
It lends a luster and more great opinion,
A larger dare to our great enterprise,
Than if the earl were here, for men must think,
If we without his help can make a head   80
To push against a kingdom, with his help
We shall o'erturn it topsy-turvy down.
Yet all goes well, yet all our joints are whole.

DOUG. As heart can think; there is not such a word
Spoke of in Scotland as this term of fear.   85

[*Enter* SIR RICHARD VERNON.]

HOT. My cousin Vernon, welcome, by my soul!

VER. Pray God my news be worth a welcome, lord.
The Earl of Westmoreland, seven thousand strong,
Is marching hitherwards; with him Prince John.

HOT. No harm; what more?

VER.   And further I have learned   90
The king himself in person is set forth,
Or hitherwards intended speedily,
With strong and mighty preparatión.

HOT. He shall be welcome too. Where is his son,
The nimble-footed madcap Prince of Wales,   95
And his comrades that daft[9] the world aside
And bid it pass?

VER.   All furnished, all in arms,
All plumed like estridges[1] that with the wind
Bated, like eagles having lately bathed,
Glittering in golden coats like images,   100
As full of spirit as the month of May,
And gorgeous as the sun at midsummer,
Wanton as youthful goats, wild as young bulls.
I saw young Harry, with his beaver[2] on,
His cushes on his thighs, gallantly armed,   105
Rise from the ground like feathered Mercury,
And vaulted with such ease into his seat,

---

6. Conspiracy.
7. Challenging. "Arbitrement": investigation.
8. Loophole.
9. Push.

1. Ostriches; "bated": fluttering their wings.
2. Helmet. "Cushes": cuisses, armor for the thighs.

As if an angel dropped down from the clouds,
To turn and wind[3] a fiery Pegasus
And witch the world with noble horsemanship.   110
HOT. No more, no more. Worse than the sun in March
  This praise doth nourish agues.[4] Let them come;
  They come like sacrifices in their trim,
  And to the fire-eyed maid of smoky war[4a]
  All hot and bleeding will we offer them;   115
  The mailéd Mars shall on his altar sit
  Up to the ears in blood. I am on fire
  To hear this rich reprisal[5] is so nigh
  And yet not ours. Come, let me taste my horse,
  Who is to bear me like a thunderbolt   120
  Against the bosom of the Prince of Wales;
  Harry to Harry shall, hot horse to horse,
  Meet and ne'er part till one drop down a corse.
  O that Glendower were come!
VER.   There is more news;
  I learned in Worcester, as I rode along,   125
  He cannot draw his power this fourteen days.
DOUG. That's the worst tidings that I hear of yet.
WOR. Aye, by my faith, that bears a frosty sound.
HOT. What may the king's whole battle[6] reach unto?
VER. To thirty thousand.
HOT.   Forty let it be;   130
  My father and Glendower being both away,
  The powers of us may serve so great a day.
  Come, let us take a muster speedily;
  Doomsday is near; die all, die merrily.
DOUG. Talk not of dying; I am out out of fear   135
  Of death or death's hand for this one-half year.   [*Exeunt.*]

SCENE 2

[*Enter* FALSTAFF *and* BARDOLPH.]
FAL. Bardolph, get thee before to Coventry; fill me a bottle of
  sack, our soldiers shall march through. We'll to Sutton Co'fil'[6a]
  tonight.
BARD. Will you give me money, captain?
FAL. Lay out, lay out.   5
BARD. This bottle makes an angel.[7]
FAL. An if it do, take it for thy labor; and if it make twenty, take
  them all; I'll answer the coinage. Bid my lieutenant Peto
  meet me at town's end.
BARD. I will, captain; farewell.   [*Exit.*]   10
FAL. If I be not ashamed of my soldiers, I am a soused gurnet.[8]
  I have misused the king's press damnably. I have got in ex-

---

3. Direct. "Pegasus": winged horse.
4. Fevers. Malaria was thought to be caused by vapors from the marshes, drawn up by the sun in spring.
4a. Bellona, goddess of war.
5. Prize.

6. Army.
6a. Sutton Coldfield, about 25 miles from Coventry.
7. Ten shillings' worth.
8. Pickled anchovy. "Press": the draft or impressment of soldiers into service.

change of a hundred and fifty soldiers three hundred and odd pounds. I press me none but good householders, yeomen's sons, inquire me out contracted bachelors, such as had been asked twice on the banns,[9] such a commodity[1] of warm slaves as had as lieve hear the devil as a drum, such as fear the report of a caliver worse than a struck fowl or a hurt wild duck. I pressed me none but such toasts-and-butter[2] with hearts in their bellies no bigger than pins' heads, and they have bought out their services, and now my whole charge consists of ancients,[3] corporals, lieutenants, gentlemen of companies, slaves as ragged as Lazarus in the painted cloth where the glutton's dogs licked his sores, and such as indeed were never soldiers, but discarded unjust serving-men, younger sons to younger brothers, revolted tapsters and ostlers trade-fallen,[4] the cankers of a calm world and a long peace, ten times more dishonorable ragged than an old-fac'd ancient,[5] and such have I to fill up the rooms of them that have bought out their services, that you would think that I had a hundred and fifty tattered prodigals lately come from swine-keeping, from eating draff[6] and husks. A mad fellow met me on the way and told me I had unloaded all the gibbets and pressed the dead bodies. No eye hath seen such scarecrows. I'll not march through Coventry with them, that's flat; nay, and the villains march wide betwixt the legs, as if they had gyves[7] on, for indeed I had the most of them out of prison. There's but a shirt and a half in all my company, and the half shirt is two napkins tacked together and thrown over the shoulders like a herald's coat without sleeves, and the shirt, to say the truth, stolen from my host at Saint Alban's, or the red-nose innkeeper of Daventry. But that's all one; they'll find linen enough on every hedge.[8]

[*Enter the* PRINCE *and the Lord of* WESTMORELAND.]

PRINCE. How now, blown Jack! how now, quilt!

FAL. What, Hal, how now, mad wag! what a devil dost thou in Warwickshire? My good Lord of Westmoreland, I cry you mercy; I thought your honor had already been at Shrewsbury.

WEST. Faith, Sir John, 'tis more than time that I were there, and you too; but my powers are there already. The king, I can tell you, looks for us all; we must away all night.

FAL. Tut, never fear me; I am as vigilant as a cat to steal cream.

PRINCE. I think, to steal cream indeed, for thy theft hath already made thee butter. But tell me, Jack, whose fellows are these that come after?

FAL. Mine, Hal, mine.

PRINCE. I did never see such pitiful rascals.

---

9. Notice of approaching marriage, announced three times publicly in church before the marriage could take place.
1. "Commodity": collection; "warm": well-to-do; "caliver": musket.
2. Sissies.
3. Ensigns.
4. Hostlers out of work; "cankers":

canker worms.
5. Frayed flag.
6. Garbage. The prodigal son, in the Bible, fed on husks before returning to the paternal board.
7. Leg-irons.
8. Laundry was customarily hung on hedges to dry.

FAL. Tut, tut, good enough to toss,[9] food for powder, food for
    powder; they'll fill a pit as well as better; tush, man, mortal
    men, mortal men.

WEST. Aye, but, Sir John, methinks they are exceeding poor and
    bare, too beggarly.   60

FAL. Faith, for their poverty I know not where they had that,
    and for their bareness I am sure they never learned that of me.

PRINCE. No, I'll be sworn, unless you call three fingers on the
    ribs bare. But, sirrah, make haste; Percy is already in the field.

FAL. What, is the king encamped?   65

WEST. He is, Sir John; I fear we shall stay too long.

FAL. Well,
    To the latter end of a fray and the beginning of a feast
    Fits a dull fighter and a keen guest.   *[Exeunt.]*

SCENE 3

[*Enter* HOTSPUR, WORCESTER, DOUGLAS, *and* VERNON.]

HOT. We'll fight with him tonight.

WOR.   It may not be.

DOUG. You give him then advantage.

VER.   Not a whit.

HOT. Why say you so? looks he not for supply?

VER. So do we.

HOT.   His is certain, ours is doubtful.

WOR. Good cousin, be advised; stir not tonight.   5

VER. Do not, my lord.

DOUG.   You do not counsel well;
    You speak it out of fear and cold heart.

VER. Do me no slander, Douglas; by my life,
    And I dare well maintain it with my life,
    If well-respected honor bid me on,   10
    I hold as little counsel with weak fear
    As you, my lord, or any Scot that this day lives.
    Let it be seen tomorrow in the battle
    Which of us fears.

DOUG.   Yea, or tonight.

VER.   Content.

HOT. Tonight, say I.   15

VER. Come, come, it may not be. I wonder much,
    Being men of such great leading as you are,
    That you foresee not what impediments
    Drag back our expedition;[1] certain horse
    Of my cousin Vernon's are not yet come up,   20
    Your uncle Worcester's horse came but today,
    And now their pride and mettle is asleep,
    Their courage with hard labor tame and dull,
    That not a horse is half the half of himself.

HOT. So are the horses of the enemy   25

---

9. I.e., on a pike, or long spear.   1. Retard our speed.

In general, journey-bated[2] and brought low;
The better part of ours are full of rest.

WOR. The number of the king exceedeth ours;
For God's sake, cousin, stay till all come in.

[*The trumpet sounds a parley. Enter* SIR WALTER BLUNT.]

BLUNT. I come with gracious offers from the king,   30
If you vouchsafe me hearing and respect.

HOT. Welcome, Sir Walter Blunt; and would to God
You were of our determinatión!
Some of us love you well, and even those some
Envy your great deservings and good name   35
Because you are not of our quality,[3]
But stand against us like an enemy.

BLUNT. And God defend[4] but still I should stand so,
So long as out of limit and true rule
You stand against anointed majesty.   40
But to my charge. The king hath sent to know
The nature of your griefs, and whereupon
You conjure from the breast of civil peace
Such bold hostility, teaching his duteous land
Audacious cruelty. If that the king   45
Have any way your good deserts forgot,
Which he confesseth to be manifold,
He bids you name your griefs, and with all speed
You shall have your desires with interest
And pardon absolute for yourself and these   50
Herein misled by your suggestión.

HOT. The king is kind, and well we know the king
Knows at what time to promise, when to pay.
My father and my uncle and myself
Did give him that same royalty he wears;   55
And when he was not six and twenty strong,
Sick in the world's regard, wretched and low,
A poor unminded outlaw sneaking home,
My father gave him welcome to the shore;
And when he heard him swear and vow to God   60
He came but to be Duke of Lancaster,
To sue his livery[5] and beg his peace,
With tears of innocency and terms of zeal,
My father, in kind heart and pity moved,
Swore him assistance and performed it too.   65
Now when the lords and barons of the realm
Perceived Northumberland did lean to him,
The more and less came in with cap and knee,
Met him in boroughs, cities, villages,
Attended him on bridges, stood in lanes,   70
Laid gifts before him, proffered him their oaths,

2. Tired from travel.
3. Fellowship, party.
4. Forbid; "still": always.

5. I.e., claim title to his late father's
lands (held by King Richard II).

Gave him their heirs as pages, followed him
Even at the heels in golden multitudes.
He presently, as greatness knows itself,
Steps me a little higher than his vow,   75
Made to my father while his blood was poor
Upon the naked shore at Ravenspurgh,
And now, forsooth, takes on him to reform
Some certain edicts and some strait[6] decrees
That lie too heavy on the commonwealth,   80
Cries out upon abuses, seems to weep
Over his country's wrongs, and by this face,
This seeming brow of justice, did he win
The hearts of all that he did angle for;
Proceeded further, cut me off the heads   85
Of all the favorites that the absent king
In deputation left behind him here,
When he was personal[7] in the Irish war.

BLUNT. Tut, I came not to hear this.

HOT.   Then to the point.
In short time after he deposed the king,   90
Soon after that deprived him of his life,
And in the neck of that tasked[8] the whole state;
To make that worse, suffered his kinsman March
(Who is, if every owner were well placed,
Indeed his king) to be engaged[9] in Wales,   95
There without ransom to lie forfeited;
Disgraced[1] me in my happy victories,
Sought to entrap me by intelligence,[2]
Rated mine uncle from the council board,
In rage dismissed my father from the court,   100
Broke oath on oath, committed wrong on wrong,
And in conclusion drove us to seek out
This head of safety,[3] and withal to pry
Into his title, the which we find
Too indirect for long continuance.   105

BLUNT. Shall I return this answer to the king?

HOT. Not so, Sir Walter; we'll withdraw awhile.
Go to the king, and let there be impawned[4]
Some surety for a safe return again,
And in the morning early shall mine uncle   110
Bring him our purposes; and so farewell.

BLUNT. I would you would accept of grace and love.

HOT. And may be so we shall.

BLUNT.   Pray God you do.   [*Exeunt.*]

6. Strict.
7. Actively participating in person.
8. I.e., immediately after that, (he) taxed.
9. Pawned as a hostage.

1. I.e., did not favor.
2. Spying; "rated": angrily dismissed.
3. Army for our safety.
4. Pledged; "surety": guarantee.

SCENE 4

[*Enter the* ARCHBISHOP OF YORK *and* SIR MICHAEL.]

ARCH. Hie, good Sir Michael; bear this sealéd brief[5]
    With wingéd haste to the lord marshal,
    This to my cousin Scroop, and all the rest
    To whom they are directed. If you knew
    How much they do import you would make haste.   5
SIR M. My good lord,
    I guess their tenor.
ARCH.   Like enough you do.
    Tomorrow, good Sir Michael, is a day
    Wherein the fortune of ten thousand men
    Must bide the touch;[6] for, sir, at Shrewsbury,   10
    As I am truly given to understand,
    The king with mighty and quick-raiséd power
    Meets with Lord Harry; and I fear, Sir Michael,
    What with the sickness of Northumberland,
    Whose power was in the first proportión,[7]   15
    And what with Owen Glendower's absence thence,
    Who with them was a rated[8] sinew too
    And comes not in, o'er-ruled by prophecies—
    I fear the power of Percy is too weak
    To wage an instant trial with the king.   20
SIR M. Why, my good lord, you need not fear;
    There is Douglas and Lord Mortimer.
ARCH. No, Mortimer is not there.
SIR M. But there is Mordake, Vernon, Lord Harry Percy,
    And there is my Lord of Worcester and a head   25
    Of gallant warriors, noble gentlemen.
ARCH. And so there is; but yet the king hath drawn
    The special head[9] of all the land together:
    The Prince of Wales, Lord John of Lancaster,
    The noble Westmoreland, and warlike Blunt,   30
    And many more corrivals[1] and dear men
    Of estimation and command in arms.
SIR M. Doubt not, my lord, they shall be well opposed.
ARCH. I hope no less, yet needful 'tis to fear,
    And to prevent the worst, Sir Michael, speed;   35
    For if Lord Percy thrive not, ere the king
    Dismiss his power, he means to visit[2] us,
    For he hath heard of our confederacy,
    And 'tis but wisdom to make strong against him;
    Therefore make haste. I must go write again   40
    To other friends; and so farewell, Sir Michael.   [*Exeunt.*]

---

5. Letter.
6. Stand the test.
7. The largest part.
8. Highly regarded.

9. Principal army.
1. Associates; "dear": noble.
2. Attack.

Act V

SCENE 1

[*Enter the* KING, PRINCE OF WALES, PRINCE JOHN OF
LANCASTER, SIR WALTER BLUNT, *and* FALSTAFF.]

KING. How bloodily the sun begins to peer
  Above yon busky[3] hill! The day looks pale
  At his distemperature.[4]
PRINCE.   The southern wind
  Doth play the trumpet to his purposes,[5]
  And by his hollow whistling in the leaves   5
  Foretells a tempest and a blustering day.
KING. Then with the losers let it sympathize,
  For nothing can seem foul to those that win.
    [*The trumpet sounds. Enter* WORCESTER ⟨*and* VERNON.⟩]
  How now, my lord of Worcester! 'Tis not well
  That you and I should meet upon such terms   10
  As now we meet. You have deceived our trust
  And made us doff our easy robes of peace,
  To crush[6] our old limbs in ungentle steel;
  This is not well, my lord, this is not well.
  What say you to it? will you again unknit   15
  This churlish knot of all-abhorréd war
  And move in that obedient orb[7] again
  Where you did give a fair and natural light,
  And be no more an exhaled meteor,[8]
  A prodigy of fear and a portent   20
  Of broachéd mischief to the unborn times?[9]
WOR. Hear me, my liege:
  For mine own part I could be well content
  To entertain the lag end of my life
  With quiet hours, for I do protest   25
  I have not sought the day of this dislike.
KING. You have not sought it! how comes it then?
FAL. Rebellion lay in his way, and he found it.
PRINCE. Peace, chewet,[1] peace!
WOR. It pleased your majesty to turn your looks   30
  Of favor from myself and all our house,
  And yet I must remember[2] you, my lord,
  We were the first and dearest of your friends.
  For you my staff of office did I break
  In Richard's time, and posted day and night   35
  To meet you on the way and kiss your hand

---

3. Wooded.
4. I.e., the sun's illness or malevolence.
5. I.e., the sun's intentions; the southern wind supports them.
6. Enfold, cramp.
7. Regular orbit, as of a planet.
8. Meteors were thought to be made of gas exhaled by a planet and were com-

monly associated with civil commotion.
9. I.e., of harm or disaster opened up ("broached") to plague the future. Note that "mischief" conveyed a stronger meaning to Shakespeare than it does to us.
1. Chattering bird.
2. Remind.

When yet you were in place and in account
Nothing so strong and fortunate as I.
It was myself, my brother, and his son
That brought you home and boldly did outdare   40
The dangers of the time. You swore to us,
And you did swear that oath at Doncaster,
That you did nothing purpose 'gainst the state
Nor claim no further than your new-fall'n right,
The seat of Gaunt, dukedom of Lancaster.   45
To this we swore our aid. But in short space
It rained down fortune showering on your head
And such a flood of greatness fell on you,
What with our help, what with the absent king,
What with the injuries of a wanton time,   50
The seeming sufferances[3] that you had borne,
And the contrarious winds that held the king
So long in his unlucky Irish wars
That all in England did repute him dead;
And from this swarm of fair advantages   55
You took occasion to be quickly wooed
To gripe the general sway[4] into your hand,
Forgot your oath to us at Doncaster,
And being fed by us you used us so
As that ungentle gull[5] the cuckoo's bird   60
Useth the sparrow, did oppress our nest,
Grew by our feeding to so great a bulk
That even our love durst not come near your sight
For fear of swallowing;[6] but with nimble wing
We were enforced for safety sake to fly   65
Out of your sight and raise this present head,
Whereby we stand opposéd by such means
As you yourself have forged against yourself
By unkind usage, dangerous countenance,[7]
And violation of all faith and troth   70
Sworn to us in your younger enterprise.
KING. These things indeed you have articulate,[8]
Proclaimed at market crosses, read in churches,
To face the garment of rebellión
With some fine color that may please the eye   75
Of fickle changelings and poor discontents,
Which gape and rub the elbow at the news
Of hurlyburly innovatión;
And never yet did insurrection want
Such water colors to impaint his cause,   80
Nor moody beggars starving for a time
Of pellmell havoc and confusión.
PRINCE. In both our armies there is many a soul

---

3. Sufferings.
4. Seize power over the whole state.
5. Rude nestling; the cuckoo hatches its young in other birds' nests.
6. Being swallowed.
7. Threatening looks.
8. Drawn up in detail.

Shall pay full dearly for this encounter,
If once they join in trial. Tell your nephew   85
The Prince of Wales doth join with all the world
In praise of Henry Percy; by my hopes,
This present enterprise set off his head,[9]
I do not think a braver gentleman,
More active-valiant or more valiant-young,   90
More daring or more bold, is now alive
To grace this latter age with noble deeds.
For my part, I may speak it to my shame,
I have a truant been to chivalry—
And so I hear he doth account me too—   95
Yet this before my father's majesty:
I am content that he shall take the odds
Of his great name and estimátion,
And will, to save the blood on either side,
Try fortune with him in a single fight.   100
KING. And, Prince of Wales, so dare we venture thee,
Albeit considerations infinite
Do make[1] against it. No, good Worcester, no,
We love our people well; even those we love
That are misled upon your cousin's part;   105
And, will they take the offer of our grace,
Both he and they and you, yea, every man
Shall be my friend again and I'll be his.
So tell your cousin, and bring me word
What he will do; but if he will not yield,   110
Rebuke and dread correction wait on[2] us
And they shall do their office. So, be gone;
We will not now be troubled with reply.
We offer fair; take it advisedly.
    [*Exit* WORCESTER ⟨*and* VERNON.⟩]
PRINCE. It will not be accepted, on my life;   115
The Douglas and the Hotspur both together
Are confident against the world in arms.
KING. Hence, therefore, every leader to his charge,
For on their answer will we set on them,
And God befriend us, as our cause is just!   120
    [*Exeunt all but the* PRINCE *and* FALSTAFF.]
FAL. Hal, if thou see me down in the battle and bestride me, so;
    'tis a point of friendship.
PRINCE. Nothing but a colossus can do thee that friendship. Say
    thy prayers, and farewell.
FAL. I would 'twere bedtime, Hal, and all well.   125
PRINCE. Why, thou owest God a death.   [⟨*Exit.*⟩]
FAL. 'Tis not due yet; I would be loath to pay him before his day.
    What need I be so forward with him that calls not on me?
    Well, 'tis no matter; honor pricks me on. Yea, but how if honor

---

9. Deducted from his account.   2. Accompany.
1. Weigh.

prick me off when I come on? How then? can honor set to a 130
leg? No. Or an arm? No. Or take away the grief of a wound?
No. Honor hath no skill in surgery, then? No. What is honor?
A word. What is in that word honor? what is that honor? Air.
A trim reckoning!³ Who hath it? He that died o' Wednesday.
Doth he feel it? No. Doth he hear it? No. 'Tis insensible,⁴ 135
then? Yea, to the dead. But will it not live with the living? No.
Why? Detraction will not suffer it. Therefore I'll none of it;
Honor is a mere scutcheon.⁵ And so ends my catechism. [*Exit.*]

SCENE 2

[*Enter* WORCESTER *and* SIR RICHARD VERNON.]

WOR. O no, my nephew must not know, Sir Richard,
    The liberal and kind offer of the king.
VER. 'Twere best he did.
WOR.   Then are we all undone
    It is not possible, it cannot be,
    The king should keep his word in loving us;   5
    He will suspect us still and find a time
    To punish this offense in other faults.
    Suspicion all our lives shall be stuck full of eyes,
    For treason is but trusted like the fox
    Who, ne'er so tame, so cherished and locked up,   10
    Will have a wild trick of his ancestors;
    Look how we can, or sad or merrily,
    Interpretation will misquote our looks,
    And we shall feed like oxen at a stall,
    The better cherished, still the nearer death.   15
    My nephew's trespass may be well forgot;
    It hath the excuse of youth and heat of blood
    And an adopted name of privilege,⁶
    A harebrained Hotspur, governed by a spleen.
    All his offenses live upon my head   20
    And on his father's; we did train him on,
    And, his corruption being ta'en from us,⁷
    We, as the spring of all, shall pay for all.
    Therefore, good cousin, let not Harry know
    In any case the offer of the king.   25
VER. Deliver what you will; I'll say 'tis so.
    Here comes your cousin.

[*Enter* HOTSPUR ⟨*and* DOUGLAS.⟩]

HOT. My uncle is returned;
    Deliver up my Lord of Westmoreland.
    Uncle, what news?   30
WOR. The king will bid you battle presently.⁸
DOUG. Defy him by the Lord of Westmoreland.

3. A fine totaling of the bill.
4. Not capable of being felt.
5. A coat of arms, as often put on a tombstone.
6. A nickname which gives him privileges. "Spleen": impetuous temperament.
7. Being attributed to. "Train": entice.
8. Immediately.

HOT. Lord Douglas, go you and tell him so.
DOUG. Marry, and shall, and very willingly.   [*Exit.*]
WOR. There is no seeming mercy in the king.   35
HOT. Did you beg any? God forbid!
WOR. I told him gently of our grievances,
    Of his oath-breaking, which he mended thus,
    By now forswearing° that he is forsworn;
    He calls us rebels, traitors, and will scourge   40
    With haughty arms this hateful name in us.
        [*Enter* DOUGLAS.]
DOUG. Arm, gentlemen, to arms! for I have thrown
    A brave defiance in King Henry's teeth,
    And Westmoreland, that was engaged,[1] did hear it,
    Which cannot choose but bring him quickly on.   45
WOR. The Prince of Wales stepped forth before the king,
    And, nephew, challenged you to single fight.
HOT. O, would the quarrel lay upon our heads,
    And that no man might draw short breath today
    But I and Harry Monmouth! Tell me, tell me,   50
    How showed his tasking?[2] seemed it in contempt?
VER. No, by my soul; I never in my life
    Did hear a challenge urged more modestly,
    Unless a brother should a brother dare
    To gentle exercise and proof of arms.   55
    He gave you all the duties of a man,
    Trimmed up your praises with a princely tongue,
    Spoke your deservings like a chronicle,
    Making you ever better than his praise
    By still dispraising praise valued with you;   60
    And, which became him like a prince indeed,
    He made a blushing cital[3] of himself,
    And chid his truant youth with such a grace
    As if he mastered there a double spirit
    Of teaching and of learning instantly.   65
    There did he pause; but let me tell the world,
    If he outlive the envy of this day,
    England did never owe[4] so sweet a hope,
    So much misconstrued in his wantonness.
HOT. Cousin, I think thou art enamoured   70
    On his follies; never did I hear
    Of any prince so wild a libertine.
    But be he as he will, yet once ere night
    I will embrace him with a soldier's arm,
    That he shall shrink under my courtesy.   75
    Arm, arm with speed; and, fellows, soldiers, **friends,**
    Better consider what you have to do
    Than I, that have not well the gift of tongue,

9. Swearing falsely.   3. Mention, recital.
1. Held as a hostage.   4. Own. "Wantonness": **frivolity.**
2. Challenge.

Can lift your blood up with persuasión.
    [*Enter a* MESSENGER.]
MESS. My lord, here are letters for you.   80
HOT. I cannot read them now.
  O gentlemen, the time of life is short!
  To spend that shortness basely were too long,
  If life did ride upon a dial's point,[5]
  Still ending at the arrival of an hour;   85
  And if we live, we live to tread on kings,
  If die, brave death when princes die with us!
  Now, for our consciences, the arms are fair,
  When the intent of bearing them is just.
      [*Enter another* MESSENGER.]
MESS. My lord, prepare; the king comes on apace.   90
HOT. I thank him that he cuts me from my tale,
  For I profess not talking; only this—
  Let each man do his best; and here draw I
  A sword whose temper I intend to stain
  With the best blood that I can meet withal   95
  In the adventure of this perilous day.
  Now, Esperance! Percy![6] and set on.
  Sound all the lofty instruments of war,
  And by that music let us all embrace;
  For, heaven to earth,[7] some of us never shall   100
  A second time do such a courtesy.
    [*The trumpets sound. They embrace and exeunt.*]

SCENE 3

[*The* KING *enters with his power. Alarum*[8] *to the battle.
Then enter* DOUGLAS *and* SIR WALTER BLUNT.]
BLUNT. What is thy name, that in the battle thus
  Thou crossest me? what honor dost thou seek
  Upon my head?
DOUG.   Know then, my name is Douglas,
  And I do haunt thee in the battle thus
  Because some tell me that thou art a king.[9]   5
BLUNT. They tell thee true.
DOUG. The Lord of Stafford dear[1] today hath bought
  Thy likeness, for instead of thee, King Harry,
  This sword hath ended him; so shall it thee,
  Unless thou yield thee as my prisoner.   10
BLUNT. I was not born a yielder, thou proud Scot,
  And thou shalt find a king that will revenge
  Lord Stafford's death.   [*They fight.* DOUGLAS *kills* BLUNT.]
    [*Enter* HOTSPUR.]

---

5. Hand of a clock; "still": always.
Hotspur's meaning (in lines 83–85)
is that a base life would be too long
even if it lasted only an hour.
6. Hope, Percy! (the family motto).
7. I.e., the odds are heaven to earth

that.
8. Trumpet signal.
9. Blunt and others are dressed to look
like the king.
1. Expensively.

HOT. O Douglas, hadst thou fought at Holmedon thus,
   I never had triumphed upon a Scot.   15
DOUG. All's done, all's won; here breathless lies the king.
HOT. Where?
DOUG. Here.
HOT. This, Douglas? No, I know this face full well;
   A gallant knight he was, his name was Blunt;   20
   Semblably furnished like the king himself.
DOUG. Ah fool, go with thy soul whither it goes!
   A borrowed title hast thou bought too dear;
   Why didst thou tell me that thou wert a king?
HOT. The king hath many marching in his coats.   25
DOUG. Now, by my sword, I will kill all his coats;
   I'll murder all his wardrobe, piece by piece,
   Until I meet the king.
HOT.   Up and away!
   Our soldiers stand full fairly for the day.   [*Exeunt.*]
      [*Alarum. Enter* FALSTAFF *alone.*]
FAL. Though I could 'scape shot-free[2] at London, I fear the shot   30
   here; here's no scoring but upon the pate. Soft, who are you?
   Sir Walter Blunt; there's honor for you, here's no vanity! I
   am as hot as molten lead, and as heavy too; God keep lead out
   of me! I need no more weight than mine own bowels. I have
   led my ragamuffins where they are peppered; there's not three   35
   of my hundred and fifty left alive, and they are for the town's
   end, to beg during life. But who comes here?
      [*Enter the* PRINCE.]
PRINCE. What, stand'st thou idle here? lend me thy sword;
   Many a nobleman lies stark and stiff
   Under the hoofs of vaunting enemies,   40
   Whose deaths are yet unrevenged; I prithee, lend me thy sword.
FAL. O Hal, I prithee give me leave to breathe awhile. Turk Greg-
   ory[3] never did such deeds in arms as I have done this day. I
   have paid Percy, I have made him sure.
PRINCE. He is indeed, and living to kill thee. I prithee, lend me   45
   thy sword.
FAL. Nay, before God, Hal, if Percy be alive, thou get'st not
   my sword; but take my pistol if thou wilt.
PRINCE. Give it me; what, is it in the case?
FAL. Aye, Hal; 'tis hot, 'tis hot; there's that will sack a city.   50
      [*The* PRINCE *draws it out, and finds it to be a bottle of
      sack.*]
PRINCE. What, is it a time to jest and dally now?
      [*He throws the bottle at him. Exit.*]
FAL. Well, if Percy be alive, I'll pierce him. If he do come in my
   way, so; if he do not, if I come in his willingly, let him make a

---

2. Scot-free, without paying the bill at
a tavern; "scoring" continues the pun;
it means (1) marking up a charge;
(2) cutting with a sword.

3. Falstaff combines Pope Gregory
VII, of whom fantastic stories were
told, with "Turk" (the Turks were
noted for ferocity).

carbonado[4] of me. I like not such grinning honor as Sir Walter
hath; give me life, which if I can save, so; if not, honor comes   55
unlooked for, and there's an end.   [*Exit.*]

SCENE 4

[*Alarum. Excursions.*[5] *Enter the* KING, *the* PRINCE, PRINCE
JOHN OF LANCASTER, *and* EARL OF WESTMORELAND.]

KING. I prithee,
  Harry, withdraw thyself; thou bleed'st too much.
  Lord John of Lancaster, go you with him.
LAN. Not I, my lord, unless I did bleed too.
PRINCE. I beseech your majesty, make up,[6]   5
  Lest your retirement do amaze your friends.
KING. I will do so.
  My Lord of Westmoreland, lead him to his tent.
WEST. Come, my lord, I'll lead you to your tent.
PRINCE. Lead me, my lord? I do not need your help,   10
  And God forbid a shallow scratch should drive
  The Prince of Wales from such a field as this,
  Where stained nobility lies trodden on,
  And rebels' arms triumph in massacres!
LAN. We breathe too long; come, cousin Westmoreland,   15
  Our duty this way lies; for God's sake, come.
          [⟨*Exeunt* PRINCE JOHN *and* WESTMORELAND.⟩]
PRINCE. By God, thou hast deceived me, Lancaster;
  I did not think thee lord of such a spirit.
  Before, I loved thee as a brother, John,
  But now I do respect thee as my soul.   20
KING. I saw him hold Lord Percy at the point
  With lustier maintenance than I did look for
  Of such an ungrown warrior.
PRINCE.   O, this boy
  Lends mettle to us all!   [*Exit.*]
          [*Enter* DOUGLAS.]
DOUG. Another king! they grow like Hydra's heads.[7]   25
  I am the Douglas, fatal to all those
  That wear those colors on them; what art thou,
  That counterfeit'st the person of a king?
KING. The king himself, who, Douglas, grieves at heart
  So many of his shadows thou hast met   30
  And not the very king. I have two boys
  Seek Percy and thyself about the field,
  But seeing thou fall'st on me so luckily
  I will assay thee; so defend thyself.
DOUG. I fear thou art another counterfeit,   35
  And yet, in faith, thou bearest thee like a king;
  But mine I am sure thou art, whoe'er thou be,

4. A cubed steak.
5. Brief appearances and exits of soldiers fighting.
6. Advance; "amaze": dismay.

7. The heads of this fabulous monster
grew back faster than they could be
cut off.

And thus I win thee.
> [*They fight; the* KING *being in danger, enter* PRINCE OF
> WALES.]

PRINCE. Hold up thy head, vile Scot, or thou art like
Never to hold it up again! the spirits   40
Of valiant Shirley, Stafford, Blunt, are in my arms;
It is the Prince of Wales that threatens thee,
Who never promiseth but he means to pay.
> [*They fight;* DOUGLAS *flieth.*]

Cheerly, my lord; how fares your grace?
Sir Nicholas Gawsey hath for succor sent,   45
And so hath Clifton; I'll to Clifton straight.

KING. Stay, and breathe awhile.
Thou hast redeemed thy lost opinión,
And showed thou makest some tender of[8] my life
In this fair rescue thou hast brought to me.   50

PRINCE. O God, they did me too much injury
That ever said I hearkened for your death.
If it were so, I might have let alone
The insulting hand of Douglas over you,
Which would have been as speedy in your end   55
As all the poisonous potions in the world
And saved the treacherous labor of your son.

KING. Make up to Clifton; I'll to Sir Nicholas Gawsey.   [*Exit.*]
> [*Enter* HOTSPUR.]

HOT. If I mistake not, thou art Harry Monmouth.

PRINCE. Thou speak'st as if I would deny my name.   60

HOT. My name is Harry Percy.

PRINCE.   Why then I see
A very valiant rebel of the name.
I am the Prince of Wales, and think not, Percy,
To share with me in glory any more:
Two stars keep not their motion in one sphere,[9]   65
Nor can one England brook a double reign
Of Harry Percy and the Prince of Wales.

HOT. Nor shall it, Harry, for the hour is come
To end the one of us; and would to God
Thy name in arms were now as great as mine!   70

PRINCE. I'll make it greater ere I part from thee,
And all the budding honors on thy crest
I'll crop to make a garland for my head.

HOT. I can no longer brook thy vanities.   [*They fight.*]
> [*Enter* FALSTAFF.]

FAL. Well said, Hal, to it, Hal! Nay, you shall find no boy's play 75
here, I can tell you.
> [*Enter* DOUGLAS; *he fighteth with* FALSTAFF, *who falls
> down as if he were dead.* ⟨*Exit* DOUGLAS.⟩ *The* PRINCE
> *killeth* PERCY.]

8. I.e., you have some concern for.   9. Orbit. "Brook": endure.
"Opinion": reputation.

HOT. O Harry, thou hast robbed me of my youth!
    I better brook the loss of brittle life
    Than those proud titles thou hast won of me;
    They wound my thoughts worse than thy sword my flesh; 80
    But thought's the slave of life, and life time's fool,
    And time, that takes survey of all the world,
    Must have a stop. O, I could prophesy,
    But that the earthy and cold hand of death
    Lies on my tongue; no, Percy, thou art dust, 85
    And food for—   [⟨*Dies.*⟩]
PRINCE. For worms, brave Percy; fare thee well, great heart!
    Ill-weaved ambition, how much art thou shrunk!
    When that this body did contain a spirit
    A kingdom for it was too small a bound, 90
    But now two paces of the vilest earth
    Is room enough; this earth that bears thee dead
    Bears not alive so stout[1] a gentleman.
    If thou wert sensible of courtesy,
    I should not make so dear[2] a show of zeal; 95
    But let my favors hide thy mangled face[3]
    And, even in thy behalf, I'll thank myself
    For doing these fair rites of tenderness.
    Adieu, and take thy praise with thee to heaven;
    Thy ignominy sleep with thee in the grave, 100
    But not remembered in thy epitaph!
        [*He spieth* FALSTAFF *on the ground.*]
    What, old acquaintance, could not all this flesh
    Keep in a little life? Poor Jack, farewell;
    I could have better spared a better man.
    O, I should have a heavy miss of thee, 105
    If I were much in love with vanity!
    Death hath not struck so fat a deer today,
    Though many dearer,[4] in this bloody fray.
    Emboweled will I see thee by and by;
    Till then in blood by noble Percy lie.   [*Exit.*] 110
FAL. [*rising up*] Emboweled! if thou embowel me today, I'll give
    you leave to powder[5] me and eat me tomorrow. 'Sblood, 'twas
    time to counterfeit, or that hot termagant[6] Scot had paid me
    scot and lot too. Counterfeit? I lie, I am no counterfeit; to die
    is to be a counterfeit, for he is but the counterfeit of a man 115
    who hath not the life of a man; but to counterfeit dying when
    a man thereby liveth is to be no counterfeit, but the true and
    perfect image of life indeed. The better part[7] of valor is discre-
    tion, in the which better part I have saved my life. Zounds, I
    am afraid of this gunpowder Percy, though he be dead; how if 120
    he should counterfeit too and rise? By my faith, I am afraid he
    would prove the better counterfeit. Therefore I'll make him

1. Valiant.
2. Open.
3. Prince Hal here covers Hotspur's face with a scarf.
4. Nobler. "Emboweled": embalmed.
5. Pickle.
6. Violent; "scot and lot": completely.
7. Quality, not "portion."

sure; yea, and I'll swear I killed him. Why may not he rise as
well as I? Nothing confutes me but eyes, and nobody sees me.
Therefore, sirrah [*stabbing him*], with a new wound in your 125
thigh, come you along with me.

       [*He takes up* HOTSPUR *on his back.*]
  [*Enter the* PRINCE *and* JOHN OF LANCASTER.]

PRINCE. Come, brother John, full bravely hast thou fleshed[8]
 Thy maiden sword.

LAN.   But soft, whom have we here?
 Did you not tell me this fat man was dead?

PRINCE. I did; I saw him dead,   130
 Breathless and bleeding on the ground. Art thou alive?
 Or is it fantasy[9] that plays upon our eyesight?
 I prithee speak; we will not trust our eyes
 Without our ears; thou art not what thou seem'st.

FAL. No, that's certain, I am not a double man; but if I be not 135
Jack Falstaff, then am I a Jack.[1] There is Percy [*throwing the
body down*]; if your father will do me any honor, so; if not, let
him kill the next Percy himself. I look to be either earl or duke,
I can assure you.

PRINCE. Why, Percy I killed myself and saw thee dead.   140

FAL. Didst thou? Lord, Lord, how this world is given to lying! I
grant you I was down and out of breath, and so was he; but we
rose both at an instant and fought a long hour by Shrewsbury
clock. If I may be believed, so; if not, let them that should reward valor bear the sin upon their own heads. I'll take it upon 145
my death, I gave him this wound in the thigh; if the man were
alive and would deny it, zounds, I would make him eat a piece
of my sword.

LAN. This is the strangest tale that ever I heard.

PRINCE. This is the strangest fellow, brother John.   150
 Come, bring your luggage nobly on your back;
 For my part, if a lie may do thee grace,
 I'll gild it with the happiest terms I have.

    [*A retreat is sounded.*]
 The trumpet sounds retreat;[2] the day is ours.
 Come, brother, let us to the highest[3] of the field,   155
 To see what friends are living, who are dead.

   [*Exeunt* ⟨PRINCE OF WALES *and* LANCASTER.⟩]

FAL. I'll follow, as they say, for reward. He that rewards me, God
reward him! If I do grow great,[4] I'll grow less, for I'll purge and
leave sack, and live cleanly as a nobleman should do. [*Exit.*]

SCENE 5

[*The trumpets sound. Enter the* KING, PRINCE OF WALES,
PRINCE JOHN OF LANCASTER, EARL OF WESTMORELAND,
with WORCESTER *and* VERNON *prisoners.*]

8. Initiated.
9. Illusion.
1. I.e., a worthless fellow.
2. The signal to stop pursuit of the

defeated enemy.
3. Highest part.
4. I.e., become "either earl or duke."
"Purge": take cleansing medicines.

KING. Thus ever did rebellion find rebuke.
　Ill-spirited Worcester, did not we send grace,
　Pardon, and terms of love to all of you?
　And wouldst thou turn our offers contrary,
　Misuse the tenor of thy kinsman's trust?　　　　　　　5
　Three knights upon our party slain today,
　A noble earl and many a creature else
　Had been alive this hour,
　If like a Christian thou hadst truly borne
　Betwixt our armies true intelligence.　　　　　　　10
WOR. What I have done my safety urged me to,
　And I embrace this fortune patiently,
　Since not to be avoided it falls on me.
KING. Bear Worcester to the death and Vernon too;
　Other offenders we will pause upon.　　　　　　　15
　　　　[*Exeunt* WORCESTER *and* VERNON (*guarded.*)]
　How goes the field?
PRINCE. The noble Scot, Lord Douglas, when he saw
　The fortune of the day quite turned from him,
　The noble Percy slain, and all his men
　Upon the foot of fear,[5] fled with the rest,　　　　　20
　And falling from a hill he was so bruised
　That the pursuers took him. At my tent
　The Douglas is, and I beseech your grace
　I may dispose of him.
KING.　　　　　　　With all my heart.
PRINCE. Then, brother John of Lancaster, to you　　　25
　This honorable bounty shall belong;
　Go to the Douglas and deliver him
　Up to his pleasure, ransomless and free;
　His valor shown upon our crests today
　Hath taught us how to cherish such high deeds　　　30
　Even in the bosom of our adversaries.
LAN. I thank your grace for this high courtesy,
　Which I shall give away immediately.
KING. Then this remains, that we divide our power.
　You, son John and my cousin Westmoreland,　　　35
　Towards York shall bend you with your dearest[6] speed
　To meet Northumberland and the prelate Scroop,
　Who, as we hear, are busily in arms;
　Myself and you, son Harry, will towards Wales
　To fight with Glendower and the Earl of March.　　40
　Rebellion in this land shall lose his sway,
　Meeting the check of such another day;
　And since this business so fair is done,
　Let us not leave till all our own be won.　　　[*Exeunt.*]
　　　　　　　　　　　　　　　　　　　　　1598

5. Fleeing in panic.　　　　　　　6. Greatest.

Sixteenth-Century Lyrics

The 16th century was one of the great ages for lyric poetry in English. As J. J. Jusserand puts it, in his *Literary History of the English People*, "Indefatigable, the poets now sing verses worthy of remembrance, on every subject, amorous, religious, epic, satirical, pastoral, didactic, moving from the world of insects to the world of heroes. Songs rise naturally to their lips, no one knows why, they do not know why."

The lyrics written by courtiers, in the first half of the century as well as later, were poems intended to be set to music and sung. In the courts of all the Tudor sovereigns music flourished; skill in composition was an excellent qualification for a servant, and noblemen, even crowned heads themselves, pursued the art. Sometimes a courtly poet would compose new words to a popular tune. The songs of Wyatt and other courtiers collected in *Tottel's Miscellany* are only a remnant of the large amount of lyrical verse written in the courts of Henry VIII and Edward VI. The courtly "makers," as they have been called, were of course able to imitate and borrow foreign stanza forms and popular themes from the poetry of Italy and France. But at their best they wrote lyrics in the native English tradition also, and the fusing of native and foreign strains may well be the best reason for the flourishing of lyric poetry in the last decades of the century.

In Shakespeare's *Twelfth Night*, the Duke calls upon a court jester to repeat a song he has heard him sing:

> O fellow, come, the song we had last night.
> Mark it, Cesario; it is old and plain.
> The spinsters and the knitters in the sun,
> And the free maids that weave their thread with bones,
> Do use to chant it. It is silly sooth,
> And dallies with the innocence of love
> Like the old age.

Singing at court is pictured here; moreover, it is part of a play, thereby illustrating another source of lyric poetry in Elizabethan England: the drama. Acting companies used boys to play their female parts, and often these boys had been trained as singers; the playwright would provide them opportunities to display their talents. In Thomas Dekker's play of craftsmen's life, *The Shoemakers' Holiday*, the workers sing while they cobble shoes, and Shakespeare's gravedigger, in *Hamlet*, sings while he works.

The popular ballad, with its simple four-line stanza form, of anonymous or perhaps composite authorship, can be traced back to the 15th century, and, with the invention of printing, a more commercial form, the broadside ballad, became popular. Copies of broadside ballads were sold by traveling peddlers like Autolycus in Shakespeare's *Winter's Tale;* they were often crude affairs, and exploited the latest murder or scandal like the sensational newspaper of modern times.

At the other extreme were the two kinds of art song, the madrigal and the air. A madrigal is a song for two or more voices in counterpoint, usually a setting of a poem expressing the woes of the Petrarchan lover, although any subject is possible. The music is highly imitative of the meaning of the words, but since the separate voices are usually not on the same word at the same time, it is often difficult to understand a madrigal being sung. There is evidence that many Elizabethans could sing a part in a madrigal at sight—a feat which now requires a high degree of musical training. The words must be contained within one rather short stanza, since the music is so closely adapted to the meaning and since phrases are repeated many times in the different voices.

The air, a much less complicated musical form, used words arranged in stanzas; it was a single, recurring melody for the voice with a three-part accompaniment on the lute. Words written for the lute-song or air were much more frequently excellent lyric poems than the words written for madrigals, which tended to be not much more than epigrams. The finest poet of airs was Thomas Campion, who was also a composer. He had a remarkably sensitive ear and a thorough understanding of the problems of versification and musical setting. The genius of Campion and of Ben Jonson solved the vexed problem of whether English quantitative verse (verse which relies upon length and duration of syllables, rather than accent) could be successful.

The 16th century produced more anonymous lyrics than it did lyrics the authors of which can be identified. There are several reasons for this. The Elizabethan period shared the medieval idea that pride of individual authorship was unimportant. Moreover many poems circulated in manuscript and were copied into manuscript books one after the other, without particular care for identifying authorship. Sometimes publishers obtained such collections and printed them, either not knowing or not caring about the authorship of individual poems. The first great 16th-century anthology, *Tottel's Miscellany* (1557), has a large number of poems attributed to "Uncertain Authors," only a few of whom have been identified up to the present time; a very popular anthology at the end of the century, *The Phoenix Nest*, gives no name at all for some poems and attributes others to "Ignoto."

Another reason for the survival of anonymous poems was that they were often the lyrics for songs. The composer published his musical settings with the words, so that they could be sung, but few publishers gave credit to the author of the words. An exception was Thomas Campion. There was a casualness about authorship that seems strange to us. Aristocrats and courtiers, though they wrote poetry, often did not wish to be known as writers—it would seem beneath them. On the other hand, the art was less specialized in those days: lawyers, statesmen, explorers, parsons, soldiers, merchants—it was a rare Elizabethan who would not try his hand at a verse.

JOHN SKELTON
(ca. 1460–1529)

According to one of the jest-book tales, John Skelton suddenly interrupted one of his sermons to ask the members of his congregation why they had complained that he kept a fair wench in the rectory. To be sure, he said, he did keep a fair wench; she was fairer than his parishioners' wives and had given him a son. Holding the child up naked before the congregation, he exclaimed, "How say you, neighbors all? Is not this child as fair as is the best of all yours? It hath nose, eyes, hands, and feet, as well as any of yours. It is not like a pig, nor a calf, nor like no foul nor no monstrous beast. If I had brought forth this child without arms or legs, or that it were deformed being a monstrous thing, I would never have blamed you to have complained to the Bishop of me, but to complain without a cause! I say as I said before, in my antetheme, *vos estis*, you be, and have been, and will and shall be knaves to complain of me without a cause reasonable."

Many and colorful were the stories circulated about the mad wag Skelton —who was also the major poet of the first quarter of the century, with the title of Poet Laureate from both Oxford and Cambridge. He was famous as a rhetorician and a translator, and he was also, for a time, tutor to the young Henry VIII. He took orders and, after writing *The Bowge of Court*, a satire on courtiers and court life, retired about 1504, became rector of the parish church at Diss, in Norfolk. By 1512 he had returned to the court, appointed King's Orator. He moved to a house in the sanctuary of Westminster in 1518, and shortly thereafter began his vituperous attacks upon Cardinal Wolsey, the great prelate-statesman, beginning with *Colin Clout* (1519) and continuing with *Speak, Parrot* (1521) and *Why Come Ye Not to Court?* (1522–23). Wolsey had him imprisoned for a time but later released him.

While in retirement at Diss, he began to write poetry in a "plain style" that rejected ornate rhetorical devices and aureate language. His satires gain some of their most startling effects by mixing high and low styles. These "open satires," as they are called, are written in short rhymed lines that to the modern ear resemble doggerel, although something like this form was probably familiar enough to readers of medieval satire. A Skeltonic line may have from two to five beats, and the lines can keep on rhyming until the resources of the language give out. To many of his poems, particularly the satires, this strange meter is singularly appropriate. *The Tunning of Elinour Rumming* is, for example, a wonderfully disordered, clattering portrait of an alewife that reminds one of Brueghel's paintings in its realism, and the Skeltonics do much to contribute to the effect of disorder. The lines give the voice of the narrator of the satires a breathless urgency much admired by Robert Graves and W. H. Auden, among other modern poets. Skelton's satires draw upon a long tradition of medieval anti-clerical satire, but he brings a fresh voice to the genre.

Skelton's lyrics also partake of traditional medieval modes which the poet makes his own. To the three-part song *Mannerly Margery*, a traditional ballad of the clerk and the serving-maid, he gives an ironic ending. His rather salacious *Lullay, Lullay* is a parody on traditional lullabies in which the Virgin Mary rocks the Christ child in her lap. In such poems we hear a genuine music and find, as always, the impress of the distinctive character of their author.

From Colin Clout[1]

And if ye stand in doubt
Who brought this rhyme about,
My name is Colin Clout.
I purpose to shake out
5   All my conning° bag,   *learning*
Like a clerkly hag.[2]
For though my rhyme be ragged,
Tattered and jagged,
Rudely rain-beaten,
10   Rusty and moth-eaten,
If ye take well therewith,
It hath in it some pith.
For, as far as I can see,
It is wrong with each degree.
15   For the temporality°   *laymen*
Accuseth the spirituality;
The spiritual again
Doth grudge and complain
Upon the temporal men;
20   Thus, each of other blother°   *babble*
The one against the other.
Alas, they make me shudder!
For in hugger-mugger°   *haste*
The Church is put in fault;
25   The prelates been so haut,°   *haughty*
They say, and look so high
As though they wouldé fly
Above the starry sky.

1519

Upon a Dead Man's Head

That was sent to him from an honorable gentlewoman for a token, Skelton, Laureate, devised this ghostly[3] *meditation in English covenable,*[4] *in sentence, commendable, lamentable, lacrimable, profitable for the soul.*

1. These are lines 47–74, comprising part of the introductory matter. Colin Clout, the narrator, here introduces the theme of the whole long poem, in the characteristically jagged Skeltonic line.
2. Old scholar.
3. Spiritual.
4. Suitable; "in sentence": in meaning.

Your ugly token
My mind hath broken
From worldly lust;
For I have discussed,
5   We are but dust
And die we must.

It is general
To be mortal;
I have well espied
10   No man may him hide
From Death hollow-eyed
With sinews wyderéd°   *withered*
With bones shyderéd,°   *shattered*
With his worm-eaten maw
15   And his ghastly jaw
Gaping aside,
Naked of hide,
Neither flesh nor fell.°   *skin*

Then, by my counsel
20   Look that ye spell°   *study*
Well this gospel,
For whereso we dwell
Death will us quell
And with us mell.°   *mix*

25   For all our pampered paunches
There may no fraunchis°   *franchise*
Nor worldly bliss
Redeem us from this:
Our days be dated
30   To be checkmated
With draughtes of death
Stopping our breath;
Our eyen sinking,
Our bodies stinking,
35   Our gummes grinning,
Our soules brinning.°   *burning*

To whom, then, shall we sue
For to have rescue
But to sweet Jesu
40   On us then for to rue?
O goodly child
Of Mary mild
Then be our shield,
That we be not exiled
45   To the dyne° dale   *dark*

Of bootless bale[5]
Nor to the lake
Of fiendes° black.   devils

But grant us grace
50   To see thy face
And to purchase
Thine heavenly place
And thy palace
Full of solace
55   Above the sky
That is so high,
Eternally
To behold and see
The Trinity.

                                                    Amen.
Myrres vous y.[6]

ca.1498

Mannerly Margery Milk and Ale[7]

Aye, beshrew you, by my fay,[8]
These wanton clerks be nice° alway,   foolish
Avaunt, avaunt, my popinjay!
"What, will you do nothing but play?"
5   Tilly vally straw, let be I say!
Gup,[9] Christian Clout, gup, Jack of the Vale!
With Mannerly Margery milk and ale.

"By God, ye be a pretty pode,°   toad
And I love you an whole cartload."
10   Straw, James Foder, ye play the fode,°   deceiver, seducer
I am no hackney for your rod:°   riding
Go watch a bull, your back is broad!
Gup, Christian Clout, gup, Jack of the Vale!
With Mannerly Margery milk and ale.

15   Ywis° ye deal uncourteously;   certainly
What, would ye frumple° me? now fie!   rumple, tumble
"What, and ye shall not be my pigsny?"°   darling
By Christ, ye shall not, no hardily:
I will not be japped° bodily!   tricked, deceived
20   Gup, Christian Clout, gup, Jack of the Vale!
With Mannerly Margery milk and ale.

"Walk forth your way, ye cost me naught;
Now have I found that I have sought:

5. Irremediable sorrow.
6. See yourself in it.
7. The clerk's lines are in quotation marks; Margery sings the rest, except the chorus lines, which are sung by a bass.
8. "Beshrew": curse (not used seriously); "fay": faith.
9. Contracted from "go up."

The best cheap flesh that ever I bought."
25 Yet, for his love that hath all wrought,
Wed me, or else I die for thought.
Gup, Christian Clout, your breath is stale!
Go, Mannerly Margery milk and ale!
Gup, Christian Clout, gup, Jack of the Vale!
30 With Mannerly Margery milk and ale.

ca. 1510   1523

Lullay, Lullay, Like a Child

With lullay, lullay, like a child,
Thou sleepest too long, thou art beguiled.°   *deceived*

"My darling dear, my daisy flower,
Let me," quod° he, "lie in your lap."   *quoth*
5 "Lie still," quod she, "my paramour,
Lie still, hardily,° and take a nap."   *confidently*
His head was heavy, such was his hap,
All drowsy dreaming, drowned in sleep,
That of his love he took no keep.
10 With hey, lullay, lullay, like a child,
Thou sleepest too long, thou art beguiled.

With ba, ba, ba![1] and bas, bas, bas!
She cherished him, both cheek and chin,
That he wist never where he was,
15 He had forgotten all deadly sin.
He wanted wit her love to win,
He trusted her payment and lost all his pay;
She left him sleeping and stale° away,   *stole*
With hey, lullay, lullay, like a child,
20 Thou sleepest too long, thou art beguiled.

The rivers rough, the waters wan,
She sparéd not to wet her feet;
She waded over, she found a man
That halséd° her heartily and kissed her sweet—   *embraced*
25 Thus after her cold she caught a heat.
"My lief," she said, "routeth[2] in his bed;
Ywis° he hath an heavy head."   *certainly*
With hey, lullay, lullay, like a child,

Thou sleepest too long, thou are beguiled.
30 What dreamest thou, drunkard, drowsy pate?
Thy lust and liking is from thee gone.
Thou blinkard blowboll,[3] thou wakest too late.

---

1. The "by" of *lullaby;* "bas, bas, bas":   2. My lover snores.
kiss, kiss, kiss.   3. Blink-eyed drunkard.

Behold thou liest, luggard,° alone!   *sluggard*
Well may thou sigh, well may thou groan,
35   To deal with her so cowardly.
Ywis, pole-hatchet,° she bleared thine eye.   *barfly*

1490–1503

SIR EDWARD DYER
(1543–1607)

Dyer was a courtier, a friend of Sir Philip Sidney, and a patron of poets.
Since he published nothing himself, not much poetry has survived that
can be confidently assigned to him. But his contemporaries, such as Nashe,
thought that he was the first "that repurified poetry from arts pedantism
[presumably the learned language of the university] and that instructed
it to speak courtly." His best-known lyric, *My Mind to Me a Kingdom Is*,
is one of the great expressions in English of the ideal of *otium* or the contented mind. It is of course related to the idyllic simplicity of pastoral,
and to the glorification of the mean estate (moderate living) in Surrey's
poem *My Friend, the Things That Do Attain*.

My Mind to Me a Kingdom Is

My mind to me a kingdom is;
    Such present joys therein I find
That it excels all other bliss
    That earth affords or grows by kind.[1]
Though much I want[2] which most would have,   5
Yet still my mind forbids to crave.

No princely pomp, no wealthy store,
    No force to win the victory,
No wily wit to salve a sore,
    No shape to feed a loving eye;   10
To none of these I yield as thrall.
For why[3] my mind doth serve for all.

I see how plenty suffers oft,
    And hasty climbers soon do fall;
I see that those which are aloft   15
    Mishap doth threaten most of all;
They get with toil, they keep with fear.
Such cares my mind could never bear.

Content I live, this is my stay;
    I seek no more than may suffice;   20
I press to bear no haughty sway;
    Look, what I lack my mind supplies;

1. Nature.   3. Because.
2. Lack.

Lo, thus I triumph like a king,
Content with that my mind doth bring.
Some have too much, yet still do crave;
   I little have, and seek no more.   25
They are but poor, though much they have,
   And I am rich with little store.
They poor, I rich; they beg, I give;
They lack, I leave; they pine, I live.   30

I laugh not at another's loss;
   I grudge not at another's gain;
No worldly waves my mind can toss;
   My state at one doth still remain.
I fear no foe, I fawn no friend;   35
I loathe not life, nor dread my end.

Some weigh their pleasure by their lust,
   Their wisdom by their rage of will;
Their treasure is their only trust;
   A cloakéd craft their store of skill.
But all the pleasure that I find   40
Is to maintain a quiet mind.

My wealth is health and perfect ease;
   My conscience clear my choice defense;
I neither seek by bribes to please,
   Nor by deceit to breed offense.   45
Thus do I live; thus will I die.
Would all did so as well as I!

1588

SIR WALTER RALEGH
(1552–1618)

The brilliant and versatile Ralegh was a soldier, courtier, poet, philosopher, explorer and colonizer, student of science, and historian. He is
popularly known now as the founder of Virginia and the introducer of
tobacco into Europe, but in his own time he was known for his skeptical
mind, his great favor with the queen, his hatred of Spain, and, to Edmund
Spenser and others, his poetry. The major part of his verse has not survived; it was a long poem to the queen called *Cynthia*; it was never printed
and we have only a few stanzas in manuscript. Some of his shorter poems
were very popular and were printed in anthologies or songbooks. His reply
to Marlowe's *Passionate Shepherd* is only one of several such answers; both
Donne and Herrick wrote them, but Ralegh's is the best. His poem *The
Lie*, with its attacks upon social classes and institutions, in its turn provoked many answers. *Farewell, False Love* is an early poem of Ralegh's
which was set to music by the composer William Byrd in 1588.
    From 1603 to his execution in 1618 Ralegh was kept imprisoned in the
Tower of London by King James, except for a period in 1617, when he

made his ill-fated last voyage to Guiana. He studied science and wrote his *History of the World.* As a passionate man, like Hotspur and Hamlet, he of course had enemies, but by 1618 popular sympathy was so much in his favor that, as the modern historian G. M. Trevelyan has said, "the ghost of Ralegh pursued the house of Stuart to the scaffold."

The Nymph's Reply to the Shepherd

If all the world and love were young,
And truth in every shepherd's tongue,
These pretty pleasures might me move
To live with thee and be thy love.

Time drives the flocks from field to fold   5
When rivers rage and rocks grow cold,
And Philomel[1] becometh dumb;
The rest complains of cares to come.

The flowers do fade, and wanton fields
To wayward winter reckoning yields;   10
A honey tongue, a heart of gall,
Is fancy's spring, but sorrow's fall.

Thy gowns, thy shoes, thy beds of roses,
Thy cap, thy kirtle,[2] and thy posies
Soon break, soon wither, soon forgotten—   15
In folly ripe, in reason rotten.

Thy belt of straw and ivy buds,
Thy coral clasps and amber studs,
All these in me no means can move
To come to thee and be thy love.   20

But could youth last and love still breed,
Had joys no date[3] nor age no need,
Then these delights my mind might move
To live with thee and be thy love.

[On the Life of Man]

What is our life? a play of passion;
Our mirth the music of division;[4]
Our mothers' wombs the tiring-houses[5] be
Where we are dressed for this short comedy.
Heaven the judicious sharp spectator is,   5

1. The nightingale.
2. Skirt, outer petticoat.
3. Ending.
4. The more rapid accompaniment to,
or variation on, a musical theme.
5. Dressing rooms in an Elizabethan theater.

That sits and marks still who doth act amiss;
Our graves that hide us from the searching sun
Are like drawn curtains when the play is done.
Thus march we, playing, to our latest rest,
Only we die in earnest—that's no jest.   10

1612

[Sir Walter Ralegh to His Son]

Three things there be that prosper up apace
And flourish, whilst they grow asunder far,
But on a day, they meet all in one place,
And when they meet, they one another mar;
And they be these: the wood, the weed, the wag.   5
The wood is that which makes the gallow tree;
The weed is that which strings the hangman's bag;
The wag, my pretty knave, betokeneth thee.
Mark well, dear boy, whilst these assemble not,
Green springs the tree, hemp grows, the wag is wild,   10
But when they meet, it makes the timber rot;
It frets the halter, and it chokes the child.
Then bless thee, and beware, and let us pray
We part not with thee at this meeting day.

ca. 1600

Walsinghame[6]

"As you came from the holy land
    of Walsinghame,
Met you not with my true love
    by the way as you came?"

"How shall I know your true love,   5
    that have met many one
As I went to the holy land,
    that have come, that have gone?"

"She is neither white nor brown,
    but as the heavens fair: 10
There is none hath a form so divine
    in the earth or the air."

"Such an one did I meet, good sir,
    such an angelic face,
Who like a queen, like a nymph, did appear   15
    by her gait, by her grace."

6. A priory popular for pilgrimages before its destruction in 1538. There were several traditional ballads on the subject; Ralegh's imitation is a dialogue between an old man and a pilgrim. They speak alternately, until the last four stanzas, when the pilgrim speaks.

"She hath left me here all alone,
 all alone as unknown,
Who sometimes did lead me with herself,
 and me loved as her own." 20

"What's the cause that she leaves you alone
 and a new way doth take,
Who loved you once as her own
 and her joy did you make?"

"I have loved her all my youth, 25
 but now, old, as you see;
Love likes not the falling fruit
 from the withered tree."

"Know that love is a careless child
 and forgets promise past; 30
He is blind, he is deaf when he list
 and in faith never fast.

"His desire is a dureless[7] content
 and a trustless joy;
He is won with a world of despair 35
 and is lost with a toy.

"Of womenkind such indeed is the love,
 (or the word 'love' abused)
Under which many childish desires
 and conceits are excused. 40

"But Love is a durable fire
 in the mind ever burning—
Never sick, never old, never dead,
 from itself never turning."

The Lie

Go, soul, the body's guest,
Upon a thankless errand;
Fear not to touch the best;
The truth shall be thy warrant.
Go, since I needs must die, 5
And give the world the lie.

Say to the court, it glows
And shines like rotten wood;
Say to the church, it shows
What's good, and doth no good. 10
If church and court reply,
Then give them both the lie.

7. Transient.

Tell potentates, they live
Acting by others' action;
Not loved unless they give,
Not strong but by a faction.
If potentates reply,
Give potentates the lie.

Tell men of high condition,
That manage the estate,
Their purpose is ambition,
Their practice only hate.
And if they once reply,
Then give them all the lie.

Tell them that brave it[8] most,
They beg for more by spending,
Who, in their greatest cost,
Seek nothing but commending.
And if they make reply,
Then give them all the lie.

Tell zeal it wants devotion;
Tell love it is but lust;
Tell time it is but motion;
Tell flesh it is but dust.
And wish them not reply,
For thou must give the lie.

Tell age it daily wasteth;
Tell honor how it alters;
Tell beauty how she blasteth;
Tell favor how it falters.
And as they shall reply,
Give every one the lie.

Tell wit how much it wrangles
In tickle[9] points of niceness;
Tell wisdom she entangles
Herself in overwiseness.
And when they do reply,
Straight give them both the lie.

Tell physic of her boldness;
Tell skill it is pretension;
Tell charity of coldness;
Tell law it is contention.
And as they do reply,
So give them still the lie.

Tell fortune of her blindness;
Tell nature of decay;
Tell friendship of unkindness;
Tell justice of delay.

15

20

25

30

35

40

45

50

55

---

8. I.e., those who spend much on clothes.   9. Delicate.

And if they will reply,
Then give them all the lie.   60

Tell arts they have no soundness,
But vary by esteeming;
Tell schools they want profoundness,
And stand too much on seeming.
If arts and schools reply,   65
Give arts and schools the lie.

Tell faith it's fled the city;
Tell how the country erreth;
Tell manhood shakes off pity;
Tell virtue least preferreth.   70
And if they do reply,
Spare not to give the lie.

So when thou hast, as I
Commanded thee, done blabbing—
Although to give the lie   75
Deserves no less than stabbing—
Stab at thee he that will,
No stab the soul can kill.

ca. 1592

Farewell, False Love

Farewell, false love, the oracle of lies,
A mortal foe and enemy to rest;
An envious boy, from whom all cares arise,
A bastard vile, a beast with rage possessed;
A way of error, a temple full of treason,   5
In all effects contrary unto reason.

A poisoned serpent covered all with flowers,
Mother of sighs and murtherer of repose,
A sea of sorrows from whence are drawn such showers
As moisture lends to every grief that grows;   10
A school of guile, a net of deep deceit,
A gilded hook that holds a poisoned bait.

A fortress foiled[1] which reason did defend,
A siren song, a fever of the mind,
A maze wherein affection finds no end,   15
A raging cloud that runs before the wind,
A substance like the shadow of the sun,
A goal of grief for which the wisest run.

A quenchless fire, a nurse of trembling fear,
A path that leads to peril and mishap;   20
A true retreat of sorrow and despair,
An idle boy that sleeps in pleasure's lap,

1. Overthrown.

A deep distrust of that which certain seems,
A hope of that which reason doubtful deems.

Sith[2] then thy trains my younger years betrayed,   25
And for my faith ingratitude I find,
And sith repentance hath my wrongs bewrayed[3]
Whose course was ever contrary to kind—
False love, desire, and beauty frail, adieu!
Dead is the root whence all these fancies grew.   30

                                                                          1588

The Author's Epitaph, Made By Himself[4]

Even such is time, which takes in trust
Our youth, our joys, and all we have,
And pays us but with age and dust,
Who in the dark and silent grave
When we have wandered all our ways   5
Shuts up the story of our days,
And from which earth, and grave, and dust
The Lord shall raise me up, I trust.

                                                                          1628

2. Since; "trains": tricks, stratagems.
3. Revealed.
4. In the 17th century it was thought that Ralegh composed this poem the night before his execution and wrote it in his Bible. It is actually a version of the last stanza of a love poem, "Nature, That Washed Her Hands in Milk" (about 1592). Only the first three words and the final couplet are changed.

ROBERT SOUTHWELL
(1561–1595)

Father Robert Southwell, S.J., was the younger son of a prominent English family who went to the English seminary for Catholics at Douai as a youth, then to Rome, where he entered the Society of Jesus. In 1586 he returned to England. His mission was a dangerous one, and he probably foresaw the martyrdom he was to suffer in 1595. He wrote a good deal of religious prose and verse; the most famous of his lyrics is *The Burning Babe*. Ben Jonson remarked to William Drummond of Hawthornden that if he had written *The Burning Babe* he would have been willing to destroy many of his own poems.

The Burning Babe

As I in hoary winter's night stood shivering in the snow,
Surprised I was with sudden heat which made my heart to glow;

And lifting up a fearful eye to view what fire was near,
A pretty babe all burning bright did in the air appear;
Who, scorchéd with excessive heat, such floods of tears did shed   5
As though his floods should quench his flames which with his tears
    were fed.
"Alas," quoth he, "but newly born in fiery heats I fry,[1]
Yet none approach to warm their hearts or feel my fire but I!
My faultless breast the furnace is, the fuel wounding thorns,
Love is the fire, and sighs the smoke, the ashes shame and scorns;   10
The fuel justice layeth on, and mercy blows the coals,
The metal in this furnace wrought are men's defiléd souls,
For which, as now on fire I am to work them to their good,
So will I melt into a bath to wash them in my blood."
With this he vanished out of sight and swiftly shrunk away,   15
And straight I calléd unto mind that it was Christmas day.

                              1602

1. Burn.

SAMUEL DANIEL
(1562–1619)

Samuel Daniel, translator, historian, and poet, was a follower of the Countess of Pembroke, Sidney's sister. He wrote classical tragedies, a verse history
of the *Civil Wars Between the Two Houses of Lancaster and York* (1594–
1609), a late defense of learning in *Musophilus*, and one of the better
Elizabethan sonnet cycles, *Delia* (1592). His *Defense of Rhyme* (1603),
written in answer to Thomas Campion's criticisms of the use of rhyme, is
an important contribution to the critical debates of the time. As a lyric
poet, Daniel is restrained, quiet, and eloquent.

From Delia

33

When men shall find thy flower, thy glory pass,
And thou, with careful brow sitting alone,
Receivéd hast this message from thy glass,
That tells thee truth, and says that all is gone,
Fresh shalt thou see in me the wounds thou madest,   5
Though spent thy flame, in me the heat remaining,
I that have loved thee thus before thou fadest,
My faith shall wax, when thou art in thy waning.
The world shall find this miracle in me,
That fire can burn when all the matter's spent;   10
Then what my faith hath been thyself shall see,
And that thou wast unkind thou mayst repent.
Thou mayst repent that thou hast scorned my tears,
When winter snows upon thy golden hairs.

45

Care-charmer Sleep, son of the sable Night,
Brother to Death, in silent darkness born,
Relieve my languish and restore the light;
With dark forgetting of my cares, return.
And let the day be time enough to mourn   5
The shipwreck of my ill-adventured youth;
Let waking eyes suffice to wail their scorn
Without the torment of the night's untruth.
Cease, dreams, th' imagery of our day desires,
To model forth the passions of the morrow;   10
Never let rising sun approve you liars,
To add more grief to aggravate my sorrow.
Still let me sleep, embracing clouds in vain,
And never wake to feel the day's disdain.

46

Let others sing of knights and paladins
In aged accents and untimely[1] words,
Paint shadows in imaginary lines
Which well the reach of their high wits records;
But I must sing of thee and those fair eyes.   5
Authentic shall my verse in time to come,
When yet th' unborn shall say, "Lo where she lies,
Whose beauty made him speak that else was dumb."
These are the arks, the trophies I erect,
That fortify thy name against old age;   10
And these thy sacred virtues must protect
Against the dark and time's consuming rage.
Though th' error of my youth they shall discover,
Suffice, they show I lived and was thy lover.

                                                      1592

1. Obsolete.

MICHAEL DRAYTON
(1563–1631)

Drayton's long career as a poet extended from the early 1590's until well on in the 17th century. He was born about a year earlier than Shakespeare and in the same county, Warwickshire. He collaborated in plays, wrote sonnets, pastorals, odes, poetic epistles, and a versified history called *The Barons' Wars*, but he intended as his masterpiece a 30,000-line historical-geographical poem about the English countryside called *Poly-Olbion*. His lifelong devotion to Anne Goodere, Lady Rainsford, is memorialized in his sonnets to a lady called Idea. He revised his sonnets and added to them as they were republished, so one can trace his development from an Elizabethan to a 17th-century poet. He wrote of himself:

> "My muse is rightly of the English strain
> That cannot long one fashion entertain."

From Idea

6

How many paltry, foolish, painted things,
That now in coaches trouble every street,
Shall be forgotten, whom no poet sings,
Ere they be well wrapped in their winding sheet?
Where[1] I to thee eternity shall give
When nothing else remaineth of these days,
And queens hereafter shall be glad to live
Upon the alms of thy superfluous praise.
Virgins and matrons, reading these my rhymes,
Shall be so much delighted with thy story
That they shall grieve they lived not in these times
To have seen thee, their sex's only glory;
So shalt thou fly above the vulgar throng,
Still to survive in my immortal song.

1619

37

Dear, why should you command me to my rest
When now the night doth summon all to sleep?
Methinks this time becometh lovers best;
Night was ordained together friends to keep.
How happy are all other living things
Which, though the day disjoin by several flight,
The quiet evening yet together brings,
And each returns unto his love at night.
O thou, that art so courteous else to all,
Why shouldst thou, Night, abuse me only thus,
That every creature to his kind doth call
And yet 'tis thou dost only sever us.
Well could I wish it would be ever day
If when night comes you bid me go away.

1602

50

As in some countries far removed from hence
The wretched creature destinéd to die,
Having the judgment due to his offense,
By surgeons begged, their art on him to try;
Which on the living work without remorse,
First make incision on each mastering[2] vein,
Then staunch the bleeding, then trans-pierce the corse,
And with their balms recure the wounds again;
Then poison, and with physic him restore;
Not that they fear the hopeless man to kill,
But their experience to increase the more;

---

1. Whereas.   2. Master, principal.

Even so my mistress works upon my ill
By curing me and killing me each hour
Only to show her beauty's sovereign power.

1605

61

Since there's no help, come let us kiss and part;
Nay, I have done, you get no more of me,
And I am glad, yea glad with all my heart
That thus so cleanly I myself can free;
Shake hands forever, cancel all our vows,   5
And when we meet at any time again,
Be it not seen in either of our brows
That we one jot of former love retain.
Now at the last gasp of love's latest breath,
When, his pulse failing, passion speechless lies,   10
When faith is kneeling by his bed of death,
And innocence is closing up his eyes;
Now if thou wouldst, when all have given him over,
From death to life thou mightst him yet recover.

1619

THOMAS NASHE
(1567–1601)

Nashe was a graduate of Cambridge. He wrote one of the best Elizabethan novels, *The Unfortunate Traveler*, and a number of plays, usually in collaboration. He was chiefly known in his time, however, for his breezy, vigorous pamphlets in a running battle with Gabriel Harvey. This quarrel became so violent that in 1599 the authorities ordered that "all Nashe's books and Doctor Harvey's books be taken wheresoever they may be found and that none of their books ever be printed hereafter." The two lyrics of very different moods, *Spring, the Sweet Spring* and *A Litany*, are songs from *A Pleasant Comedy Called Summer's Last Will and Testament*, acted before the Archbishop of Canterbury in his palace at Croydon in 1592 and published in 1600.

Spring, the Sweet Spring

Spring, the sweet spring, is the year's pleasant king,
Then blooms each thing, then maids dance in a ring,
Cold doth not sting, the pretty birds do sing:
    Cuckoo, jug-jug, pu-we, to-witta-woo![1]

---

1. The calls of the cuckoo, the nightin-   tively.
gale, the lapwing, and the owl respec-

The palm and may make country houses gay,   5
Lambs frisk and play, the shepherds pipe all day,
And we hear aye birds tune this merry lay:
  Cuckoo, jug-jug, pu-we, to-witta-woo!

The fields breathe sweet, the daisies kiss our feet,
Young lovers meet, old wives a-sunning sit,   10
In every street these tunes our ears do greet:
  Cuckoo, jug-jug, pu-we, to-witta-woo!
    Spring, the sweet spring!

1592   1600

A Litany in Time of Plague

Adieu, farewell, earth's bliss;
This world uncertain is;
Fond[2] are life's lustful joys;
Death proves them all but toys;[3]
None from his darts can fly;   5
I am sick, I must die.
  Lord, have mercy on us!

Rich men, trust not in wealth,
Gold cannot buy you health;
Physic himself must fade.   10
All things to end are made,
The plague full swift goes by;
I am sick, I must die.
  Lord, have mercy on us!

Beauty is but a flower   15
Which wrinkles will devour;
Brightness falls from the air;
Queens have died young and fair;
Dust hath closed Helen's eye.
I am sick, I must die.   20
  Lord, have mercy on us!

Strength stoops unto the grave,
Worms feed on Hector brave;
Swords may not fight with fate,
Earth still holds ope her gate.   25
"Come, come!" the bells do cry.
I am sick, I must die.
  Lord, have mercy on us.

Wit with his wantonness
Tasteth death's bitterness;   30
Hell's executioner
Hath no ears for to hear
What vain art can reply.

---

2. Foolish.   3. Trifles.

I am sick, I must die.
    Lord, have mercy on us.   35

Haste, therefore, each degree,
To welcome destiny;
Heaven is our heritage,
Earth but a player's stage;
Mount we unto the sky.   40
I am sick, I must die.
    Lord, have mercy on us.

THOMAS CAMPION
(1567–1620)

Thomas Campion was a law student, a physician, a composer, and a poet. His first poetic attempts were in Latin. His love of classical, quantitative versification carried over into his English poems and songs, as well as into his critical theory, which he expounded in his *Observations in the Art of English Poesy*. (In quantitative verse the syllables are arranged in pattern according to their length and duration, rather than according to accent or stress; cf. Campion's *Rose-Cheeked Laura*.) But his greatest achievement as a lyric poet—and he is one of the very best in the language—comes from the fact that he was both poet and composer. He says in the preface to one of his books, "I have chiefly aimed to couple my words and notes lovingly together, which will be much for him to do that hath not power over both."

My Sweetest Lesbia[1]

My sweetest Lesbia, let us live and love,
And though the sager sort our deeds reprove,
Let us not weigh them. Heaven's great lamps do dive
Into their west, and straight again revive,
But soon as once set is our little light,   5
Then must we sleep one ever-during night.

If all would lead their lives in love like me,
Then bloody swords and armor should not be;
No drum nor trumpet peaceful sleeps should move,
Unless alarm came from the camp of love.   10
But fools do live, and waste their little light,
And seek with pain their ever-during night.

1. Imitated and partly translated from a poem by Catullus (87–ca. 54 B.C.), the Latin lyric poet who often celebrated the charms of Lesbia in his verses. This and the two lyrics which follow appeared in *A Book of Airs*, which contains Campion's first work as a composer.

When timely death my life and fortune ends,
Let not my hearse be vexed with mourning friends,
But let all lovers, rich in triumph, come   15
And with sweet pastimes grace my happy tomb;
And Lesbia, close up thou my little light,
And crown with love my ever-during night.

                                                        1601

When to Her Lute Corinna Sings

When to her lute Corinna sings,
Her voice revives the leaden strings,
And doth in highest notes appear
As any challenged echo clear;
But when she doth of mourning speak,   5
Ev'n with her sighs the strings do break.

And as her lute doth live or die,
Led by her passion, so must I:
For when of pleasure she doth sing,
My thoughts enjoy a sudden spring,   10
But if she doth of sorrow speak,
Ev'n from my heart the strings do break.

                                                        1601

When Thou Must Home to Shades of Underground

When thou must home to shades of underground,
And there arrived, a new admiréd guest,
The beauteous spirits do engirt thee round,
White Iope,[2] blithe Helen, and the rest,
To hear the stories of thy finished love   5
From that smooth tongue whose music hell can move,

Then wilt thou speak of banqueting delights,
Of masques and revels which sweet youth did make,
Of tourneys and great challenges of knights,
And all these triumphs for thy beauty's sake;   10
When thou hast told these honors done to thee,
Then tell, Oh tell, how thou didst murther me.

                                                        1601

Rose-cheeked Laura[3]

Rose-cheeked Laura, come,
Sing thou smoothly with thy beauty's

2. Daughter of Aeolus, also known as
Cassiopeia.
3. Written by Campion to illustrate
his theories of versification in *Observa-*
tions in the Art of English Poesy, this
song is a brilliant example of the way
in which quantitative verse can be made
musically effective in English.

Silent music, either other
  Sweetly gracing.

Lovely forms do flow   5
From concent[4] divinely framed;
Heav'n is music, and thy beauty's
  Birth is heavenly.

These dull notes we sing
Discords need for helps to grace them;   10
Only beauty purely loving
  Knows no discord,

But still moves delight,
Like clear springs renewed by flowing,
Ever perfect, ever in themselves   15
  Eternal.

           1602

What If a Day

What if a day, or a month, or a year
Crown thy delights with a thousand sweet contentings?
Cannot a chance of a night or an hour
Cross thy desires with as many sad tormentings?
   Fortune, honor, beauty, youth   5
   Are but blossoms dying;
   Wanton pleasure, doting love
   Are but shadows flying.
   All our joys are but toys,
   Idle thoughts deceiving;   10
   None have power of an hour
   In their lives' bereaving.

Earth's but a point to the world, and a man
Is but a point to the world's compared centure;[5]
Shall then the point of a point be so vain   15
As to triumph in a sely[6] point's adventure?
   As is hazard that we have,
   There is nothing biding;
   Days of pleasure are like streams
   Through fair meadows gliding.   20
   Weal and woe, time doth go,
   Time is never turning;
   Secret fates guide our states,
   Both in mirth and mourning.

           1606

4. Playing or singing together in harmony.
5. Circumference (literally, a belt or
girdle).
6. Innocent, insignificant.

Never Love Unless You Can

Never love unless you can
Bear with all the faults of man;
Men sometimes will jealous be,
Though but little cause they see,
And hang the head, as discontent,   5
And speak what straight they will repent.

Men that but one saint adore
Make a show of love to more;
Beauty must be scorned in none,
Though but truly served in one;   10
For what is courtship but disguise?
True hearts may have dissembling eyes.

Men when their affairs require
Must a while themselves retire,
Sometimes hunt, and sometimes hawk,   15
And not ever sit and talk.
If these and such like you can bear,
Then like, and love, and never fear.

1617

There Is a Garden in Her Face

There is a garden in her face,
Where roses and white lilies grow,
A heavenly paradise is that place,
Wherein all pleasant fruits do flow.
There cherries grow, which none may buy   5
Till "Cherry ripe!"[7] themselves do cry.

Those cherries fairly do enclose
Of orient pearl a double row;
Which when her lovely laughter shows,
They look like rosebuds filled with snow.   10
Yet them nor peer nor prince can buy,
Till "Cherry ripe!" themselves do cry.

Her eyes like angels watch them still;
Her brows like bended bows do stand,
Threatening with piercing frowns to kill   15
All that attempt with eye or hand
Those sacred cherries to come nigh,
Till "Cherry ripe!" themselves do cry.

1617

7. A familiar cry of London street vendors.

ANONYMOUS LYRICS[1]

Back and Side Go Bare, Go Bare[2]

Back and side go bare, go bare,
   Both foot and hand go cold;
But, belly, God send thee good ale enough,
   Whether it be new or old.

I cannot eat but little meat,   5
   My stomach is not good;
But sure I think that I can drink
   With him that wears a hood.[3]
Though I go bare, take ye no care,
   I am nothing a-cold;   10
I stuff my skin so full within
   Of jolly good ale and old.
Back and side go bare, go bare, etc.

I love no roast but a nut-brown toast,[4]
   And a crab laid in the fire;   15
A little bread shall do me stead,
   Much bread I not desire.
No frost nor snow, no wind, I trow,[5]
   Can hurt me if I would,
I am so wrapped, and throughly lapped   20
   Of jolly good ale and old.
Back and side go bare, etc.

And Tib my wife, that as her life
   Loveth well good ale to seek,
Full oft drinks she, till ye may see   25
   The tears run down her cheeks.
Then doth she troll[6] to me the bowl,
   Even as a maltworm should,
And saith, "Sweetheart, I took my part
   Of this jolly good ale and old."   30
Back and side go bare, etc.

Now let them drink, till they nod and wink,
   Even as good fellows should do;
They shall not miss to have the bliss
   Good ale doth bring men to;   35
And all poor souls that have scoured bowls
   Or have them lustily trolled,

---

1. For discussion, see the introduction to the Lyrics section.
2. One of the best of English drinking songs, this is sung in *Gammer Gurton's Needle*, a pioneer play in the development of native English comedy. The play is often ascribed to a "Mr. S., Master of Art," who probably wrote it for performance at Cambridge University.
3. Specifically, with a monk; generally, with anybody.
4. Toast was often dipped in beverages; "crab": crab apple.
5. Think, suppose.
6. Pass.

God save the lives of them and their wives,
  Whether they be young or old.

Back and side go bare, go bare,   40
  Both foot and hand go cold;
But, belly, God send thee good ale enough,
  Whether it be new or old.

                                        1575

Though Amaryllis Dance in Green[7]

Though Amaryllis dance in green
    Like fairy queen;
    And sing full clear
Corinna can, with smiling, cheer.
Yet since their eyes make heart so sore,   5
Heigh ho, heigh ho, 'chill[8] love no more.

My sheep are lost for want of food,
    And I so wood,[9]
    That all the day
I sit and watch a herdmaid gay,
Who laughs to see me sigh so sore,   10
Heigh ho, heigh ho, 'chill love no more.

Her loving looks, her beauty bright
    Is such delight,
    That all in vain
I love to like and lose my gain,   15
For her that thanks me not therefor,
Heigh ho, heigh ho, 'chill love no more.

Ah wanton eyes, my friendly foes,
    And cause of woes,   20
    Your sweet desire
Breeds flames of ice and freeze in fire.
Ye scorn to see me weep so sore,
Heigh ho, heigh ho, 'chill love no more.

Love ye who list, I force him not,   25
    Sith, God it wot,
    The more I wail,
The less my sighs and tears prevail.
What shall I do but say therefore,
Heigh ho, heigh ho, 'chill love no more.   30

                                        1588

---

7. William Byrd set this anonymous lyric to music in his song book entitled *Psalms, Sonnets, and Songs of Sadness and Piety*. It is a "ballet"— a dance-song of short stanzas with refrain—an appropriate form for this quaint rustic song of the renunciation of love.
8. The rustic dialect form for "I will": (i)ch (w)ill.
9. Frantic.

Come Away, Come, Sweet Love![1]

Come away, come, sweet love! The golden morning breaks;
All the earth, all the air of love and pleasure speaks.
    Teach thine arms then to embrace,
    And sweet rosy lips to kiss,
    And mix our souls in mutual bliss;   5
    Eyes were made for beauty's grace,
    Viewing, rueing love-long pain,
    Procured by beauty's rude disdain.

Come away, come, sweet love! The golden morning wastes,
While the sun from his sphere his fiery arrows casts   10
    Making all the shadows fly,
    Playing, staying in the grove
    To entertain the stealth of love.
    Thither, sweet love, let us hie,
    Flying, dying in desire,   15
    Winged with sweet hopes and heavenly fire.

Come away, come, sweet love! Do not in vain adorn
Beauty's grace, that should rise like to the naked morn.
    Lilies on the riverside
    And fair Cyprian[2] flowers new-blown   20
    Desire no beauties but their own,
    Ornament is nurse of pride;
    Pleasure measure love's delight.
    Haste then, sweet love, our wishéd flight!

                    1597

Thule, the Period of Cosmography[3]

Thule, the period of cosmography,
    Doth vaunt of Hecla,[4] whose sulphurious fire
Doth melt the frozen clime and thaw the sky;
    Trinacrian Aetna's[5] flames ascend not higher.
These things seem wondrous, yet more wondrous I,   5
Whose heart with fear doth freeze, with love doth fry.

The Andalusian[6] merchant, that returns
    Laden with cochineal and China dishes,
Reports in Spain how strangely Fogo[7] burns

---

1. An aubade (or morning song to one's lady), set to music by John Dowland in his *First Book of Songs or Airs*. Dowland (1563–1626) was a famous composer and lutenist.
2. Pertaining to Venus, the Cyprian goddess; hence, spring flowers.
3. "Thule" or "Ultima Thule" was a general name for the Arctic; "period of cosmography" suggests the end point of navigation, a full stop. This remark-able poem, which draws upon Elizabethan interest in exploration and discovery to illustrate the conventional pangs of a ·lover, first appeared in a book of madrigals by Thomas Weelkes.
4. A volcano in Iceland.
5. Mt. Etna, a volcano in Sicily ("Trinacria").
6. From southern Spain. "Cochineal": a red dye.
7. Fuego, a volcano in Guatemala

Amidst an ocean full of flying fishes.   10
These things seem wondrous, yet more wondrous I,
Whose heart with fear doth freeze, with love doth fry.

1600

Madrigal[8]

My love in her attire doth show her wit,
    It doth so well become her;
For every season she hath dressings fit,
    For winter, spring, and summer.
    No beauty she doth miss   5
    When all her robes are on;
    But beauty's self she is
    When all her robes are gone.

1602

Weep You No More, Sad Fountains[9]

Weep you no more, sad fountains;
    What need you flow so fast?
Look how the snowy mountains
    Heaven's sun doth gently waste.
    But my sun's heavenly eyes   5
        View not your weeping,
        That now lie sleeping
    Softly, now softly lies
        Sleeping.

Sleep is a reconciling,   10
    A rest that peace begets.
Doth not the sun rise smiling
    When fair at even he sets?
    Rest you then, rest, sad eyes,
        Melt not in weeping   15
    While she lies sleeping
    Softly, now softly lies
        Sleeping.

1603

8. This sophisticated courtly lyric was printed in an anthology entitled *A Poetical Rhapsody* (1602).
9. This anonymous lyric comes from another song book of John Dowland's (his *Third and Last Book of Songs or Airs*). Like a number of other song-book lyrics which were apparently written only with the object of being set to music, its versification is quantitative.

The Silver Swan[1]

The silver swan, who living had no note,
When death approached, unlocked her silent throat;
Leaning her breast against the reedy shore,
Thus sung her first and last, and sung no more:
"Farewell, all joys; Oh death, come close mine eyes;   5
More geese than swans now live, more fools than wise."

1612

1. From Orlando Gibbons' *First Set of Madrigals and Motets*. In this short lyric, Gibbons, who was one of the last of the madrigalists, may be mourning the demise of his art.

Topic in Sixteenth-Century Literature

THE DEVELOPMENT OF PROSE STYLE

English writers of the 16th century were self-consciously puzzled about the state of their language. They knew that it had changed markedly in the past two centuries, but they were not sure whether too rapid a change was good. They were aware also that its vocabulary was being influenced by other modern languages, especially French and Italian. They wondered whether it should be more like Latin, the international language of learning, or whether it should be true to its own native genius. The spread of printing meant that people who were not learned (who did not know Latin) could afford English books and would therefore read, as they had not done before. Notable defenses of the vernacular tongues of Italian and French had been published; some Englishmen felt that an equally valid defense of English could be made.

As early as 1543 a translator, Peter Betham, proclaimed that he thought translators ought to use the usual terms of our English tongue, not borrowing terms from other languages, because, as he said, continual borrowing without repayment would make the language, as it would make a man, bankrupt. Furthermore, he deplored what he called "inkhorn" terms, learned words derived from Latin or invented by authors—words so obscure that he thought the ordinary Englishman would not be able to understand them. To be sure, he admitted, a few words of foreign origin must be allowed, since languages are clearly interlaced with each other, but the good writer of English is the one who follows Chaucer and other old writers, keeping English in its native tradition. The most notable theorist of language reform in the middle of the century was the famous classical scholar, Sir John Cheke, Regius Professor of Greek at Cambridge. His theory of phonetic spelling is demonstrated in his letter to the translator Sir Thomas Hoby.

The most important translations of the 16th century were the renderings of the Bible into the vernaculars. In England William Tyndale began his translation in 1523; he had to do it surreptitiously and outside the country; he finally suffered martyrdom for his efforts. In 1530 a royal proclamation condemned Tyndale's translation and all other versions in the vulgar tongue. Then in 1535 Miles Coverdale published, in Zürich, the first complete Bible in English. By this time the official attitude was changing, and in 1540 the so-called Great Bible was published, the first English Bible issued with official sanction—evidence of the extent of the breach between the English church and the Church of Rome.

The Geneva Bible (1560) was the work of Protestant refugees who fled to the Continent in the reign of the Catholic Queen Mary. It was the first Bible to divide the chapters into verses in the modern manner, and the first English Bible to be printed in Roman type rather than the old black letter or Gothic type. It was handy in size, and in many instances more accurate than its predecessors, but the marginal commentary was strongly biased in the Protestant direction. The Bishops' Bible (1568) was an attempt on the part of the Elizabethan church to counter the extreme Protestantism of the Geneva Bible. The bishops who sponsored it could indeed insist that their Bible be the official one used in churches, but the people continued to read the Geneva Bible at home, and its influence remained very great throughout the century. A Catholic translation into English, based upon the Latin Vulgate, was a belated concession to the demand for the Scriptures in the vernacular. It was published by English refugees abroad, the New Testament at Rheims in 1582 and the Old Testament at Douai in 1609–10. Though it was outside the main English tradition, it was not without its influence upon the King James Version which was to follow.

King James did not like the popular Geneva Bible (some of its commentary was not highly favorable to kings). As a part of the religious settlement which took place early in his reign, he authorized a group of translators to make a new version of the Bible in English. The resulting work has been called "the noblest monument of English prose"; it owes more to Tyndale than to any other predecessor, but it has extraordinary beauties of its own. Where the Bishops' Bible reads, "He is such a man as hath good experience of sorrows and infirmities," and the Geneva Bible reads, "a man full of sorrows and hath experience of infirmities," the King James version reaches the final perfection of "a man of sorrows, and acquainted with grief" (Isaiah liii.3).

Most educated writers learned their prose style, however, not from English models but from Latin, since the study of grammar in school was the study of Latin grammar, and the models and examples were from Cicero and other Romans like him. James Sutherland in *On English Prose* has suggested that this training was not wholly bad: "If you wish to raise the general level of prose composition, you cannot do better than base your style on the artificial, periodic prose of the Ciceronians, for that sort of writing is easiest to learn and to teach." He goes on to quote an "eagerly attempted but only half-learnt" exercise in Ciceronian English, the first sentence of Edward Halle's chronicle, *The Union of the Two Noble and Illustre Families of Lancaster and York* (1542):

What mischief hath insurged in realms by intestine division, what depopulation hath insued in countries by civil dissension, what detestable murder hath been committed in cities by separate factions, and what calamity hath insued in famous regions by domestical discord and unnatural controversy, Rome hath felt, Italy can testify, France can bear witness. Beame [Bohemia] can tell, Scotland may write, Denmark can show, and especially this noble realm of England can apparently declare and make demonstration.

By 1570 Halle's English was denounced as "indenture English" by Ascham, and all through the period certain writers carried on a sporadic campaign for more direct, plain prose that could be understood by the ordinary man. Among the learned, moreover, an anti-Ciceronian element preferred the Latin style of Seneca and Tacitus or the French style of Montaigne. These writers wished to put more emphasis on matter and less on manner; they believed the cast of mind of the writer, the individual turns of his thought closely revealed in his phrases, to be infinitely preferable to the rhetorical flourishes of a Roman orator.

Classical eloquence survived, of course, down to the prose of Browne and Milton in the next century. It had long outgrown the crudity of the time of Edward Halle. The periodic sentence which begins our selection from Richard Hooker's essay on the law of nature (p. 444) is almost 200 words in length; it contains half a dozen dependent clauses before the main clause is reached, several of which have lengthy subordinate elements within them; yet Hooker's sentence is not too long for the matter it contains, and he has the artistic tact to follow it with short sentences and to vary sentence structure as well as length. The change in the course of 50 years is notable, aside from the fact that Hooker was a genius and Halle was not.

Problems of style are of course related to the kind of audience a writer is attempting to reach. In the 1580's John Lyly delighted ladies at court with an elaborately ornate style called "Euphuism" (after the title of Lyly's book *Euphues*). The style existed before and after Lyly, but he brought it to its extreme and his success made a fad of it. The style is based upon classical and medieval rhetorical devices such as *isocolon* (successive phrases or clauses equal in length), *parison* (successive phrases or clauses identical in structure), and *paromoion* (successive phrases or clauses, or corresponding syllables, alike in sound). These schemes are used in combination, and the additional effects of repetition, antithesis, rhetorical questions, and exclamations are also combined with them. The content as well as the style is ornamented, particularly in three ways: *exempla*, or incidents from history or poetry, are used to illustrate a point; *sententiae* or proverbs are frequent; and *similia*, or similes, are drawn from science or pseudo-science, either traditional or invented by the author himself. Less artificial than Euphuism, but still formal and suited to a courtly taste, is the style of Sir Philip Sidney's *Arcadia*. One can see how much Sidney felt that a romance intended for courtly ladies like his sister, the Countess of Pembroke, required a special style, by comparing the artificial style of the *Arcadia* with the directness of his *Apology* (see p. 477).

Of course pamphleteers and journalists, appealing to a popular rather than a courtly audience, much more nearly approximated the style of everyday English speech. The Puritan Philip Stubbes, in attacking the popular sport of football, may string many epithets together as though he were orating or preaching, but he keeps his sentences short and uncomplicated and he uses vigorous active verbs. And a popularizer like William Bullein, appealing to quite unlearned readers, casts his matter into the form of a dialogue in common speech.

SIR JOHN CHEKE: [Our Own Tongue Clean and Pure]¹

A LETTER OF SYR I. CHEEKES TO HIS LOUING FRIND MAYSTER THOMAS HOBY

For your opinion of my gud will vnto you as you wriit,² you can not be deceiued: for submitting your doinges to mi iudgement, I thanke you: for taking this pain of your translation, you worthilie deseru great thankes of all sortes. I haue taken sum pain at your request cheflie in your preface, not in the reading of it for that was pleasaunt vnto me boath for the roundnes of your saienges and welspeakinges³ of the saam, but in changing certein wordes which might verie well be let aloan, but that I am verie curious in mi freendes matters, not to determijn, but to debaat what is best. Whearin, I seek not the bestnes haplie bi truth, but bi mijn own phansie, and shew of goodnes.

I am of this opinion that our own tung shold be written cleane and pure, vnmixt and vnmangeled with borowing of other tunges, wherein if we take not heed by tijm, euer borowing and neuer paying, she shall be fain to keep her house as bankrupt. For then doth our tung naturallie and praisablie vtter her meaning, whan she bouroweth no counterfeitnes of other tunges to attire her self withall, but vseth plainlie her own, with such shift as nature, craft, experiens and folowing of other excellent⁴ doth lead her vnto, and if she want at ani tijm (as being vnperfight⁵ she must) yet let her borrow with suche bashfulnes that it mai appeer that if either the mould of our own tung could serue vs to fascion a woord of our own, or if the old denisoned⁶ wordes could content and ease this neede, we wold not boldly venture of vnknowen wordes. This I say not for reproof of you, who haue scarslie and necessarily vsed whear occasion serueth a strange word so, as it seemeth to grow out of the matter and not to be sought for: but for mijn own defens, who might be counted ouerstraight a deemer of thinges, if I gaue not thys accompt to you, mi freend and wijs, of mi marring this your handiwork. But I am called awai, I prai you pardon mi shortnes,

---

1. Sir John Cheke (1514–57) was tutor to King Edward VI, Regius Professor of Greek at Cambridge, and an ardent reformer of Greek pronunciation and English spelling. His letter to Hoby, prefixed to Hoby's translation of Castiglione's *Courtier* (not published until 1561), is here printed in its original spelling, to show Cheke's attempted reforms. His purist doctrine about diction (using only native words) was fortunately not followed by Elizabethan writers; although

a pedantry, it reveals the concern of early humanists over English prose style.
2. Write. A double vowel (including *ij*) indicates a long sound in Cheke's attempt at phonetic spelling.
3. Cheke's native equivalent for the word "eloquence," borrowed from the Latin *eloquentia*. See the doctrine in the next paragraph.
4. Supply the word "models."
5. Unperfect.
6. Admitted to citizenship.

the rest of mi saienges should be but praise and exhortacion in this your doinges, which at moar leisor I shold do better.

From my house in Woodstreete

the 16. of Iuly, 1557.

Yours assured

IOAN CHEEK

THE BIBLE: Translations of the Twenty-third Psalm[7]

From *The Great Bible*

The Lord is my shepherd; therefore can I lack nothing. He shall feed me in a green pasture, and lead me forth beside the waters of comfort. He shall convert my soul, and bring me forth in the paths of righteousness for his name's sake. Yea, though I walk through the valley of the shadow of death, I will fear no evil, for thou art with me. Thy rod and thy staff comfort me. Thou shalt prepare a table before me against them that trouble me; thou hast anointed my head with oil, and my cup shall be full. But thy loving-kindness and mercy shall follow me all the days of my life and I will dwell in the house of the Lord forever.

1539–40

From A *Latin-English Psalter*

The Lord governeth me, and I shall lack nothing; in a place of pasture even there hath he set me.

Upon the water of refection hath he nourished me; my soul hath he converted.

He hath led me forth upon the paths of righteousness, even for his own name's sake.

For though I walk in the midst of the shadow of death, I will fear no evil, for thou art with me.

Thy rod and thy staff, those have comforted me.

Thou hast prepared a table before me, against them that trouble me.

Thou hast soupled[8] my head in oil; my cup is also full and exceeding fair.

And thy mercy shall go with me all the days of my life.

That I also may dwell in the house of the Lord long and many days.

1540

7. To demonstrate the stylistic problems involved in Bible translation, we print the familiar Twenty-third Psalm as it appeared in the Great Bible, in a contemporary Latin-English psalter, in the popular or vulgar versified psalm-book of Sternhold and Hopkins, in the extremely Puritan Geneva Bible of 1560, in the Anglican Bishops' Bible of 1568, the Catholic Bible in English, the Douai version of 1609, and the King James version of 1611.

8. Anointed.

From *Thomas Sternhold and John Hopkins' Psalm-Book*

My shepherd is the living Lord; nothing, therefore, I need.
In pastures fair, with waters calm, he set me for to feed.
He did convert and glad my soul, and brought my mind in frame
To walk in paths of righteousness for his most holy name.

Yea, though I walk in vale of death, yet will I fear none ill;   5
Thy rod, thy staff doth comfort me, and thou art with me still.
And in the presence of my foes, my table thou hast spread;
Thou shalt, O Lord, fill full my cup and eke anoint my head.

Through all my life thy favor is so frankly showed to me
That in thy house forevermore my dwelling place shall be.   10

1567

From *The Geneva Bible*

The Lord is my shepherd; I shall not want.
He maketh me to rest in green pasture, and leadeth me by the still
    waters.
He restoreth my soul and leadeth me in the paths of righteousness
    for his Name's sake.
Yea, though I should walk through the valley of the shadow of death,
    I will fear no evil, for thou art with me; thy rod and thy staff, they
    comfort me.
Thou dost prepare a table before me in the sight of mine adversaries;
    thou dost anoint mine head with oil, and my cup runneth over.
Doubtless kindness and mercy shall follow me all the days of my life,
    and I shall remain a long season in the house of the Lord.

1560

From *The Bishops' Bible*

God is my shepherd, therefore I can lack nothing; he will cause me
to repose myself in pasture full of grass, and he will lead me unto
calm waters.
He will convert my soul; he will bring me forth into the paths of
righteousness for his name's sake.
Yea, though I walk through the valley of the shadow of death, I
will fear no evil, for thou art with me; thy rod and thy staff be the
things that do comfort me.
Thou wilt prepare a table before me in the presence of mine adversaries; thou hast anointed my head with oil, and my cup shall be
brimful.
Truly felicity and mercy shall follow me all the days of my life, and
I will dwell in the house of God for a long time.

1568

From *The Douai Bible*

Our Lord ruleth me, and nothing shall be wanting to me; in place of pasture there he hath placed me.

Upon the water of refection he hath brought me up; he hath converted my soul.

He hath conducted me upon the paths of justice, for his name.

For, although I shall walk in the midst of the shadow of death, I will not fear evils because thou art with me.

Thy rod and thy staff, they have comforted me.

Thou hast prepared in my sight a table against them that trouble me.

Thou hast fatted my head with oil, and my chalice inebriating how goodly is it!

And thy mercy shall follow me all the days of my life

And that I may dwell in the house of the Lord in longitude of days.

1609

From *The Authorized or King James Bible*

The Lord is my shepherd; I shall not want.

He maketh me to lie down in green pastures: he leadeth me beside the still waters.

He restoreth my soul: he leadeth me in the paths of righteousness for his name's sake.

Yea, though I walk through the valley of the shadow of death, I will fear no evil: for thou art with me; thy rod and thy staff they comfort me.

Thou preparest a table before me in the presence of mine enemies: thou anointest my head with oil; my cup runneth over.

Surely goodness and mercy shall follow me all the days of my life: and I will dwell in the house of the Lord forever.

1611

JOHN LYLY: *From* Euphues: The Anatomy of Wit[9]

* * * Gentlewoman, my acquaintance being so little, I am afraid my credit will be less, for that they commonly are soonest believed, that are best beloved, and they liked best, whom we have known longest, nevertheless the noble mind suspecteth no guile without cause, neither condemneth any wight without proof, having there-

9. This passage is a speech by Euphues to Lucilla. Lucilla is the lady-love of Euphues' friend Philautus, but Philautus has been called away and Euphues seizes the opportunity to woo Lucilla himself. (He succeeds, but not for long; Lucilla is no more true to him than she had been to Philautus.)

fore notice of your heroical heart, I am the better persuaded of my good hap. So it is, Lucilla, that coming to Naples but to fetch fire, as the byword is, not to make my place of abode, I have found such flames that I can neither quench them with the water of free will, neither cool them with wisdom. For as the hop the pole being never so high groweth to the end, or as the dry beech kindled at the root, never leaveth until it come to the top, or as one drop of poison disperseth itself into every vein, so affection having caught hold of my heart, and the sparkles of love kindled my liver, will suddenly though secretly flame up into my head, and spread itself into every sinew. It is your beauty (pardon my abrupt boldness), lady, that hath taken every part of me prisoner, and brought me unto this deep distress, but seeing women when one praiseth them for their deserts, deem that he flattereth them to obtain his desire, I am here present to yield myself to such trial, as your courtesy in this behalf shall require: Yet will you commonly object this to such as serve you and starve to win your good will, that hot love is soon cold, that the bavin[1] though it burn bright, is but a blaze, that scalding water if it stand a while turneth almost to ice, that pepper though it be hot in the mouth is cold in the maw, that the faith of men though it try in their words, it freezeth in their works: Which things, Lucilla, albeit they be sufficient to reprove the lightness of someone, yet can they not convince everyone of lewdness, neither ought the constancy of all to be brought in question through the subtilty of a few. For although the worm entereth almost into every wood, yet he eateth not the cedar tree: Though the stone cylindrus[2] at every thunderclap roll from the hill, yet the pure sleek stone[3] mounteth at the noise, though the rust fret the hardest steel, yet doth it not eat into the emerald, though polypus[4] change his hue, yet the salamander keepeth his color, though Proteus transform himself into every shape, yet Pygmalion retaineth his old form,[5] though Aeneas were too fickle to Dido, yet Troilus was too faithful to Cressida, though others seem counterfeit in their deeds, yet, Lucilla, persuade yourself that Euphues will be always current in his dealings. But as the true gold is tried by the touch, the pure flint by the stroke of the iron, so the loyal heart of the faithful lover is known by the trial of his lady: of the which trial, Lucilla, if you shall account Euphues worthy, assure yourself, he will be as ready to offer himself a sacrifice for your sweet sake, as yourself shall be

---

1. Brushwood.
2. Lyly is inventing his own pseudo-science, though the name is given to a precious stone in Pliny.
3. A polishing stone. Lyly's meaning is obscure.
4. A transparent jellyfish, seeming to take on the color of whatever rock it adheres to. Lyly is appropriating from

Erasmus' *Similia*.
5. Proteus was a sea god in Greek mythology who continually changed his form; Pygmalion was the legendary sculptor who fell in love with one of his own statues. Here Lyly seems to attribute to him the durability of his marble.

willing to employ him in your service. Neither doth he desire to be trusted any way, until he shall be tried every way, neither doth he crave credit at the first, but a good countenance till time his desire shall be made manifest by his deserts. Thus not blinded by light affection, but dazzled with your rare perfection, and boldened by your exceeding courtesy, I have unfolded mine entire love, desiring you, having so good leisure, to give so friendly an answer, as I may receive comfort, and you commendation. * * *

1579

SIR PHILIP SIDNEY: *From* Arcadia[6]

* * * The joy which wrought into Pygmalion's mind, while he found his beloved image was softer and warmer in his folded arms, till at length it accomplished his gladness with a perfect woman's shape (still beautified with the former perfections), was even such, as by each degree of Zelmane's words creepingly entered into Philoclea: till her pleasure was fully made up with the manifesting of his being: which was such as in hope did overcome Hope. Yet Doubt would fain have played his part in her mind, and called in question how she should be assured that Zelmane was Pyrocles. But Love straight stood up and deposed that a lie could not come from the mouth of Zelmane. Besides, a certain spark of honor, which rose in her well-disposed mind, made her fear to be alone with him, with whom alone she desired to be (with all the other contradictions growing in those minds, which neither absolutely climb the rock of virtue, nor freely sink into the sea of vanity), but that spark soon gave place, or at least gave no more light in her mind, than a candle doth in the sun's presence. But even sick with a surfeit of joy, and fearful of she knew not what (as he that newly finds huge treasures doubts whether he sleep or no; or like a fearful deer, which then looks most about, when he comes to the best feed) with a shrugging kind of tremor through all her principal parts, she gave these affectionate words for answer. * * *

1590

PHILIP STUBBES: *From* The Anatomy of Abuses[7]

* * * For as concerning football playing, I protest unto you it may rather be called a friendly kind of fight, than a play or recrea-

6. In this passage Sidney relates the feelings of one of his heroines, Philoclea, when she realizes that Zelmane, the Amazon, is really her lover Pyrocles in disguise.

7. Philip Stubbes (ca. 1555–ca. 1611) was a writer of edifying books of small literary merit but of considerable pop-

tion; a bloody and murdering practice, than a fellowly sport or pastime. For doth not everyone lie in wait for his adversary, seeking to overthrow him and to pick[8] him on his nose, though it be upon hard stones, in ditch or dale, in valley or hill, or what place soever it be he careth not, so he have him down. And he that can serve the most of this fashion, he is counted the only fellow, and who but he? So that by this means, sometimes their necks are broken, sometimes their backs, sometimes their legs, sometime their arms, sometime one part thrust out of joint, sometime another, sometime their noses gush out with blood, sometime their eyes start out, and sometimes hurt in one place, sometimes in another. But whosoever 'scapeth away the best goeth not scot-free, but is either sore wounded, crazed,[9] and bruised, so as he dieth of it, or else 'scapeth very hardly. And no marvel, for they have the sleights to meet one betwixt two, to dash him against the heart with their elbows, to hit him under the short ribs with their gripped fists, and with their knees to catch him upon the hip, and to pick him on his neck, with an hundred such murdering devices. And hereof groweth envy, malice, rancor, choler, hatred, displeasure, enmity, and what not else: and sometimes fighting, brawling, contention, quarrel-picking, murder, homicide, and great effusion of blood, as experience daily teacheth. * * *

1583

WILLIAM BULLEIN: *From* A Dialogue Against
the Pestilence[1]
[*Travelers' Tales*]

CIVIS. I pray you, gentle master, I cannot tell what to call you, nor of what country you are.

MENDAX. Sir, I was born near unto Tunbridge, where fine knives are made; my name is Mendax, a younger brother lineally descended

ularity. His famous *Anatomy of Abuses* is a Puritanical attack upon all of the popular amusements of the time. Stubbes is a good example of the Puritan preachers and propagandists, who often developed a vigorous, plain prose for purposes of controversy.
8. Throw.
9. Crushed.
1. William Bullein was a physician and writer on medical subjects for ordinary middle-class readers. He died in 1576. The title of one of his books will give a good idea of his purpose and method: *A new book entitled The Government of Health, wherein is uttered many notable rules for man's preservation, with sundry simples and other matters, no less fruitful than profitable, collect out of many approved authors. Reduced into the form of a dialogue for the better understanding of the unlearned.* In his attempt to simulate actual speech in his dialogue and to appeal to unlearned readers, Bullein used short sentences, proverbs and familiar expressions, and a simple vocabulary. He was not without literary skill, however, as his satire on the lying traveler shows. Here, "Civis" (Latin, a citizen) learns about the wonders of travel from "Mendax" (Latin, a liar).

of an ancient house before the conquest. We give three whetstones in gules, with no difference,[2] and upon our crest a left hand, with a horn upon the thumb, and a knife in the hand. The supporters are a fox on the one side, and a friar on the other side. And of late I traveled into Terra Florida, whereas[3] I felt both wealth and woe; the black ox never trod upon my foot before; a dog hath but a day. We are born all to travail, and as for me I have but little to lose. Yet I am a gentleman, and cannot find it in my heart to play the slave, or go to cart; I never could abide it, by the mass.

CIVIS. You speak like a wise man. I perceive by your behavior that you have been well brought up. I pray you, where is that land?

MENDAX. Many hundred miles beyond Torrida Zona, or the equinoctial line, in the longitude near unto the pole antarctic; it is seventeen thousand miles long, and is in the part named America; and by the way are the islands called Fortunata or Canaria, whose west parts be situated in the third climate.

CIVIS. It was a dangerous travel into that country. Where landed you? At what place?

MENDAX. We sailed to the islands of Portum Sanctum, and then to Madeira, in which were sundry countries and islands, as Eractelenty, Magnefortis, Grancanary, Teneriffe, Palme Ferro, etc. And our captain went with his soldiers to land. And at our first coming near unto a river in one of these islands, as we refreshed ourselves among the date trees, in the land of the palms, by the sweet wells, we did, to the great fear of us all, see a great battle between the dragon and the unicorn; and, as God would, the unicorn thrust the dragon to the heart; and, again, the dragon with his tail stung the unicorn to death. Here is a piece of his horn; the blood of dragons is rich; that battle was worth two hundred marks to our captain. Then we traveled further into Teneriffe, into an exceeding high mountain, above the middle region, whereas we had great plenty of alum, and might well hear an heavenly harmony among the stars. The moon was near hand[4] us with marvelous heat; and when we came down, at the hill-foot grew many gross herbs, as lovage, laserpitium, acanthus, and solanum: and whether it was by the eating of solanum or no, there was a very mighty man naked and hairy, in a great sleep, whom we gently suffered to lie still. He had a great beard in which a bird did breed and brought her young ones meat. Our captain declared unto us that the spials[5] had viewed the land, and how that our enemies were at hand. The next day most fearful people painted with sundry colors approached in strange

---

2. We bear on our coat of arms three whetstones (symbolic of lying; an old custom was to hang a whetstone around the neck of a liar); "gules": red; "difference": an addition or alteration in a coat of arms. The "horn upon the thumb" and "knife" are the tools of a pickpocket (the horn was to protect the pickpocket's thumb while cutting a purse). The "fox" and the "friar" represent cunning and deceit.
3. Where.
4. Close by.
5. Spies.

beasts' skins, with flint so were their shafts and darts, with whom we fought and slew and took some, and yet the people so assaulted us that with much difficulty we recovered our barks. And then we sailed forth, and chanced to let fall our sounding-lead new-tallowed, whereupon did stick gold. With all speed we sent down our divers, and so within three days we gathered thirty hogsheads of fine gold, besides two butts of orient pearls; all the shore was full of coral. From thence we sailed to the great isle called Madagastat, in Scorea, where were kings, Mahometans by religion, black as devils. Some had no heads, but eyes in their breasts.[6] Some, when it rained, covered all the whole body with one foot. The land did abound in elephants' teeth; the men did eat camels' and lions' flesh. Musk and civet in every place did abound, and the mother of pearl, whereof the people made their platters to put in their meat; they dwell among spice; the ground is moist with oil of precious trees. Plenty of wine out of grapes as big as this loaf; much pepper; they cannot tell what to do with sugar; but that their merchants of Maabar, twenty days' journey off, do come and take of their goods frankly for nothing; but some of them do bring iron to make edge tools, for which they have for one pound twelve pound of fine gold. Their pots, pans, and all vessel is clean gold garnished with diamonds. I did see swine feed in them.

CIVIS. Did you see no strange fowls there and fishes?

MENDAX. In the isle called Ruc, in the great Can's land, I did see mermaids and satyrs with other fishes by night come four miles from the sea, and climbed into trees, and did eat dates and nutmegs, with whom the apes and baboons had much fighting, yelling, and crying. The people of that land do live by eating the flesh of women. In this land did I see an ape play at tick-tack[7] and after at Irish on the tables with one of that land; and also a parrot give one of their gentlewomen a checkmate at chess.

CIVIS. God keep me from those cruel people.

MENDAX. But, sir, as for birds, they are not only infinite in numbers, but also in kinds; some voices most sweet and some most fearful; nightingales as big as geese, owls greater than some horse; and there are birds that do lie in a rock where dragons are, whose feathers on their wings are thirty foot long, the quill as big as a cannon royal. Also I heard parrots dispute in philosophy, fresh in Greek.

CIVIS. I pray you is there any plenty of precious stones?

MENDAX. Very many, but hard to come by; but in the island Zanzibar is much plenty of ambergris, that they make clay for their houses withal; there, if we had holden together like friends, we might have gotten a great kingdom. O my heart, it maketh it bleed when I do remember it; every man is but for himself; you may con-

6. Shakespeare's *Othello* told Desdemona about seeing such fabulous men
on his travels. See *Othello* I.iii.144–45.

7. An old form of backgammon.
"Irish": a similar game.

sider what division is; emeralds, rubies, turkies,[8] diamonds, and sapphires were sold when we came thither first for the weight of iron; a thousand rich turkesses were sold for fourpence, to be short, one with another, after three shillings[9] fourpence a peck. Our men gathered up carbuncles and diamonds with rakes under the spice trees.

CIVIS. How chance you brought none home into this realm?

MENDAX. Oh, sir, we filled two ships with fine gold, three ships with ambergris, musk, and unicorns' horns, and two tall barks with precious stones, and sailed by the adamant stones, which will draw iron unto them, and so cast away the greatest riches in Heathenness or Christendom. After that cruel chance, we came upon the mainland of Cuba, in the great and mighty land of America, whereas the people called the Cannibals do dwell in caves, rocks, and woods; thereas women will eat their own children, and one man another, and they are giants most high and fearful. All go naked; they neither know good humanity, human policy, religion, law, nor chastity. One is equal with another; the strongest of body are chief, for there all is ruled by force, and not through reason, after the manner of swine. Children love their fathers no more than pigs do the boars, for they say lust causeth generation. And when their parents are very old, they bring them to an exceeding high mountain whereas is a great tower builded upon a rock, under which tower is the golden mine, in which mine there be two great monstrous dragons keeping the same, which will never suffer the children to come to receive the benefits of that place until such time as they have slain their parents and cast their flesh into the cave and wash the dragons' images, which are within that tower, made of precious wood, with the blood of their said parents. From thence we traveled into an island whereas it never raineth but once a year, and that is in the month of July, whereas Nilus runneth by giving benefit unto the plain country, whereas spice of all kinds doth grow. In that island doth grow hops most plentifully, which they do call Lupilum. A little before our coming was a great wind which had shaken down much fruit and precious spice and many hundred cartloads of good hops, after which fell down plenty of rain, raising a mighty flood; incontinent succeeded a burning heat, for it is under the equinoctial line, or Torrida Zona. In fine, through this concoction[1] of the sun moving this boiling of the water, through the help of much spice, I never drank such hippocras,[2] wine, nor beer. The Flemings have found out the commodity, and care to transport no more hops hither unto us. And if good luck had been our good lord, we had made ourselves and all the Christian kingdoms forever. * * *

1564

8. "Turkies" and "turkesses" both mean "turquoises."
9. In fact, wholesale, about three shill-

ings.
1. Alternation of matter by moist heat.
2. Wine flavored with spices.

The Seventeenth Century

(1603-1660)

1603: Death of Elizabeth Tudor, accession of James Stuart.
1605: Gunpowder Plot: Guy Fawkes and the last desperate effort of Catholic extremists.
1620: First emigration of Pilgrims to the New World.
1625: Death of James I, accession of Charles I.
1642: Outbreak of the English Civil War; closing of the theaters.
1649: Execution of Charles I, beginning of Cromwellian Protectorate.
1660: End of the Protectorate, Restoration of Charles II.

"THIS OTHER EDEN"

An unnaturally farsighted Englishman who surveyed his circumstances in 1605 (looking backward and projecting forward in time, casting his eye outward through space) might well have congratulated himself and his nation on their peculiarly favored position. England had escaped early and relatively undamaged from the medieval turbulence of dynastic and regional feuds. The Wars of the Roses had been for the most part noblemen's squabbles, fought by little bands of knights and retainers in the semi-privacy of back fields; they were not wars of populations, with large-scale burning, looting, and cattle-killing, such as were commonplace on the Continent. And in 1485 the Tudor settlement had imposed the "king's peace" upon England so successfully that civil strife on any large scale did not occur in the 16th century. Under Henry VIII, the church too had undergone a relatively peaceful reformation, imposed from above and carried out below, with docility, if not always with enthusiasm, by populace and clergy. Thus the English church had entered on its historic "middle way," between Catholicism as practiced in Rome and Presbyterianism as practiced in Scotland; and this way it took, not violently or divisively, but through the typical English arts of compromise and consensus. Pacification had been, over the past hundred years, a notable tendency throughout England, in both church and state. In 1588 the social order was put to the test of the Spanish Armada, a test which it passed triumphantly, almost (it appeared to contemporaries) miraculously. Finally, in 1603, the peaceful and even popular accession of James Stuart, Elizabeth Tudor's

Scottish cousin, had seemed to assure the continuance of the same practical compromises and domestic discipline which had been so successful in the past.

Looking over at the Continent, our Englishman might shudder at visible evidence of the disasters which his country had happily escaped. Climaxing generations of religious strife, which was invariably bloody, fanatical, and destructive, the Thirty Years' War (1618–48) was about to break out in Germany, and it would shortly involve most other Continental countries. The French Protestants, known as Huguenots, were struggling desperately and dangerously for their existence. By fire and flood, the Dutch had just won a precarious independence from Spain; and the fragile prosperity of the Spanish golden age itself was just collapsing under the impact of an exploding inflation. Italy was prostrate and fragmented, Portugal in political and social decadence. Everywhere abroad political strife, religious dissension, and economic distress clouded the horizon. In England alone peace, harmony, and prosperity seemed to prevail, and their prevailing bore visible fruit. The English yeoman ate good beef, drank stout ale, and wore leather shoes, while his Continental counterpart ate black bread, drank sour wine, and wore wooden sabots. Such prosperity could not be undeserved. How could one doubt that God was preparing His Englishmen for some great and special destiny?

The island nation from which our speculative Englishman surveyed Europe with so much complacency was tightly organized into two coextensive and almost completely comprehensive bodies, the church and the state. Neither was threatened by visible enemies of any magnitude. A few dissenting voices might, indeed, be heard within the church; a certain number of English subjects even dared to exist outside the English church, maintaining their ancient allegiance to Rome. But the old Catholic families, though socially powerful, were politically torpid; and rash, radical Catholics, like Guy Fawkes (who formed the Gunpowder Plot, to blow up Parliament, in 1605), were without any popular support at all. There were also, within the church, a certain number of hyper-Protestant critics who wished to make the Reformation more thorough; they were first called "Presbyterians" and were just now coming to be called "Puritans" because of their desire to "purify" Anglican church discipline. But their numbers were small, their influence uncertain, and their energies largely devoted to reforming, not to replacing or rivaling the English church. Those who felt bitterly enough about the inadequacies of the Anglican discipline were free to go to Holland or America; and in 1620, the search for religious freedom actually began to lead men to the New World, though in negligible numbers. But by and large the English church, during the first part of the 17th century, was in reputable if not flourishing estate. It included some of the most learned scholars in the world; its faults of discipline and fabric were relatively venial; and its stability, under the Crown, must have seemed beyond challenge.

As for the political strength of the regime, it too must have seemed unshakable. For if there were a few Puritans in the church and an uncertain number of Catholics outside of it, there was no Englishman of the early 17th century who challenged the root idea of monarchy. Democracy was an idea as terrible as communism, from which it seemed to be only a stage removed. Nobody believed in liberalism, progress, or social change; in fact, the reformers of the age were vociferous in demanding a return to the original foundation of things. All the progress of this revolutionary age was to take place under the paradoxical battle cry of "back, back to the good old days." But this paradox was only latent in 1605, and the staunch, provincial conservatism of the English country gentleman must have seemed like a bulwark against radical social change of any sort.

To be sure, a few signs of truculent independence had appeared in the House of Commons during the last years of Elizabeth's reign. The Commons had shown an increasing tendency to take the order of business into their own hands, and to put off the government demands for "supply," i.e., fresh taxes, until certain grievances had been investigated. But these grievances did not seem, in 1605, like momentous matters. Various petty domestic monopolies, granted by the government to the detriment of local interests; a foreign policy rather too lenient toward Catholic Spain and not sufficiently vigorous in behalf of the Continental Protestants; an occasional greedy minister, a conniving churchman—who could suppose a revolt would some day spring from causes like these? Who could suppose that by midcentury the fabric of both church and state would be furiously rent? What possible reason ·could be found for anticipating that a kingdom, peaceable and settled for a century and a half, would suddenly depose a lawful monarch, cut off his head and his succession, set up a new tyranny and tear it down again in order to call back the murdered monarch's wandering son, and then finally eject the whole line for a second time less than thirty years after calling it back? Toward the end of the century Dryden remarked half-humorously that Englishmen were naturally crazy; once every twenty years, by natural instinct, they were bound to have a revolution. But this was true only in the 17th century; the 18th and 19th centuries were to be even more placid, dynastically, than the 16th.

CHURCH AND CONSTITUTION

The turmoil into which 17th-century England was so unexpectedly plunged involved basic issues of religious and political authority. The English church and the English state as they existed at the turn of the century were essentially authoritarian institutions, modified by the discretion of the Tudor monarchs. In an effort to disturb her subjects' religious consciences as little as possible, Queen Elizabeth and her bishops had tolerated a wide variety of opinions and even practices within the English church. In the state, too, authoritarianism concealed itself. The royal prerogative (that is, essentially, the royal privilege of taking independent action) had never been clearly defined, and it continued to be exercised, but Queen Elizabeth was careful not to alarm her subjects by acting in any serious matter without the advice and opinion of her council and of her predominantly loyal and obedient parliaments. The system in both church and state could be described as absolutism tempered by political discretion and deliberate vagueness.

But James and Charles Stuart possessed none of Elizabeth Tudor's tact and flexibility; James especially had a pedantic need for clarity, which was in the highest degree inexpedient politically. Both the Stuart kings tried to stamp out Presbyterianism, Puritanism, and all forms of dissent and organized protest within the church. They tried to impose new restrictions on a parliament already restive under the restraints which had become traditional under Elizabeth. Being consistent men, and devoid of political sense, they tended to see every minor grievance as an incipient case of treachery or heresy, to be vigorously repressed. But they did not have the machinery to carry out a policy of wholesale repression. The Puritans, forbidden to organize directly for the reform of the church, undertook a long-term program of indirect propaganda. They used the pulpit to preach, not the overthrow of the English church, but a new way of life, a life of godly, disciplined endeavor, of sober yet dedicated activity. Under strict Presbyterian discipline as Calvin had conceived it, this way of life would have been imposed on the entire population, by a potent mixture of lay and clerical authority, acting through individual church synods and local councils. Such a rigid system had in fact been installed in Geneva and in parts of Scotland. But in England, where the discipline could not be imposed from above (although the preachers were free to talk about it in a general way), it became the subject of popular agitation from below; and so each man formed his own idea of what the godly discipline would be like. While every man could see that the existing institution was faulty as compared with his private ideal, not very many reformers could appreciate that their own ultimate ideals were wildly incompatible with one another.

Thus the Puritan movement developed into a powerful destructive force, so far as its original enemy, the Anglican Church, was concerned; but as soon as that enemy was defeated (ca. 1642), the inner disagreements of Puritanism came to the surface. A national convention was called, known as the Westminster Assembly from its place of sitting in Westminster Hall. Convoked in 1643 to reform the national church of England, it sat for nearly six years; and the longer its members sat, the less they could agree upon. Meanwhile, in the country at large, sects, segments, and schisms multiplied. Arians, Baptists, Anabaptists, Shakers, Quakers, Diggers, Levelers, Fifth Monarchy Men, and many other groups of true believers proliferated. About 1643, a conservative Presbyterian named Thomas Edwards started to list them all in a book which he called, picturesquely, *Gangraena*. But history outran the historian. Even while the first volume of *Gangraena* was passing through the press, enough new sects sprang up to call for a second volume; and after a third volume, Edwards gave up in despair. Men who believed in a single unified national church were naturally distressed by the sects. But it would be a mistake to ignore the existence of a sizable body of Englishmen who rejoiced in the sectarian squabbles and even helped provoke them, because they frankly preferred either no church government at all or a very weak and docile one. These "Erastians" (so called from Thomas Erastus, a 16th-century Swiss theologian who advocated the supremacy of the state in ecclesiastical matters) were not a very vocal, or highly organized, or even a very active group. But of all parties, they were that for which the Puritan revolutionary movement held fewest heartaches. John Selden typified their cool unconcern. He often stopped by the Westminster Assembly to watch the assembled parsons quoting texts at one another; like the Persian princes, he said, he liked to see the wild asses fight.

From the beginning of the century, political opposition to the Stuart regime was concentrated among the lawyers and the gentry, that class of rural landlords which contributed so largely to the membership of Elizabeth's augmented House of Commons. Sporadic moves were made in the parliaments of James I to investigate particular abuses, and a determined fight was waged by lawyers and judges to maintain the supremacy of the common law against the aggressions of the ecclesiastical lawyers. But these were piecemeal and essentially defensive maneuvers; and gradually a concerted strategy was evolved for putting pressure on the king. The House of Commons simply refused to vote any taxes unless the king took steps toward a general reform of abuses in church and state. It is never hard or even unpleasant to refuse taxes. The last parliaments of James voted him less and less money. And almost from the day his son Charles I ascended the throne, the parliaments cut the king's income (not merely his personal income, but the whole budget of executive government) to a trickle. About 1630, Charles resolved to do without parliaments altogether, and for the next eleven years, he managed to govern through his own personal agencies. The two arms of his policy were the church, under Archbishop William Laud (1573–1645), and the army, under Thomas Wentworth, Earl of Strafford (1593–1641). Between themselves these two agents of the king's power referred laconically to the royal program as "Thorough." "Thorough" was royal absolutism, government without Parliament.

Lacking a regular income, which only Parliament could vote, Charles I and his aides were bound to improvise ways of levying money. Various medieval taxes, long since obsolete, were revived during the 1630's and put into effect because they did not require parliamentary approval. "Ship money" and "tonnage and poundage," two levies imposed by prerogative power, did something to fill the king's empty coffers; they also roused widespread fears that men's estates might be taken from them arbitrarily. Adding to these fears was the act of the administration in fostering the swift growth of ecclesiastical and prerogative courts. These courts, notably Archbishop Laud's revived and expanded Star Chamber, dispensed a speedier justice than the old courts of common law, a more arbitrary justice, and one more concerned with equity than with precedent. Any property owner looks with dismay upon a legal system which elevates equity above precedent. Thus disaffection grew throughout the land like a festering sore, though on the surface all remained placid.

The structure of "Thorough" was shaky at best, depending as it did on the almost unaided vigilance and energy of two highly placed men; in 1639 it was rocked by a rash effort to impose episcopal discipline on the strongly Presbyterian Scots. They reacted angrily by raising an army and invading England. Their aim was not to conquer; but they were well aware that they would have good friends in Parliament, if that were ever called into session. Charles had to call it; it was convened, refused to vote supplies, and was dissolved three weeks later, having earned the name of the Short Parliament. Its successor was convened within a year and sat for twenty years—earning the name of the Long Parliament. Strongly Puritan in feeling, it first acted to call Laud and Strafford to account. Both men were imprisoned and ultimately executed; the prerogative courts were abolished forever, "Thorough" was wiped from the face of the earth, and

Parliament began reforming the abuses in church and state about which many of its members had long been clamoring. As the reformers set enthusiastically to work, the king, despairing of his future with men so radical, left London and raised his banner at Nottingham. In August, 1642, open civil war broke out.

From a military point of view, the wars between the king and his Parliament were no equal contest. After a few preliminary successes, the king's forces were steadily ground down by the Parliament's superior money, manpower, and supplies. Actually, the greatest obstacle to Parliamentary victory was the divided loyalty of its military commanders. To most Englishmen there was something profoundly shocking in the idea of fighting against an anointed king to whom one had sworn eternal allegiance. What would one do if one met him on the battlefield—fire or kneel down and beg his pardon? But as always in civil wars, the more resolved and desperate men moved quickly to the fore. On the Parliamentary side, these shortly came to consist of soldiers the like of whom had never before been seen in English warfare. The Puritan regiments were no band of starveling cutthroats, out for plunder, pay, and drink; they carried Bibles in their pockets, and sang psalms before entering battle. But they were terrible agents of the Lord's will, who feared neither king nor bishop nor cavalry; and they defeated the royal armies with brutal ease. Before long the king himself was prisoner. But it was one thing to beat the king on the field and another thing to make peace with him. A treaty between the king and his Parliament was legally unthinkable, and in practice very difficult. Neither side really trusted the other, and after protracted negotiations, the Parliamentary leaders resolved to rid themselves of Charles Stuart, once and for all. Expelling its moderate members, the House of Commons reduced itself to a small minority of hard-core radicals (about 50 out of an original 325 members). This remainder, known derisively to its enemies as the Rump, constituted itself a court of justice, tried its sovereign as an enemy of the English people, and on January 30, 1649, had him beheaded. In a very direct way, this solved the problem of making peace with the king; but it left no clear or effective source of political power in England. For a short time, the Rump tried to govern on its own; but it proved incapable, and Cromwell took the power in his own hands, establishing what was, in effect, a military dictatorship—the Protectorate.

Thus the Puritan Revolution failed in its two major aims, of establishing responsible civil government and achieving a purified, uniform religious discipline. So long as Cromwell stayed in power, gaining military and diplomatic triumphs abroad, there was no changing the government. But as soon as Cromwell died in 1658, his regime started to weaken. Powerful forces in the community began secret negotiations with the government of Charles II, who had been in exile at Paris. Finally, in 1660, the new monarch and his court returned to take up the government of England. Out of retirement came the bishops, archbishops, deacons, and other Anglican officials. Parliamentary elections were called for and a new parliament convened. Charles II was crowned king of England in the ancient ritual. Evidently the *form* of Restoration government would be pretty much the same as before the wars. Time would show, however, that the Revolution and Civil Wars had altered the course of history very considerably. Neither church nor state could be returned to the pre-revolutionary condition. There remained a sizable body of Dissenters, who refused to return to the Anglican church. And the new Parliament, though loyal to the point of fanaticism, had no intention of allowing Charles II to think himself independent, as Charles I had done.

SOCIAL AND INTELLECTUAL TRENDS

The political and religious conflicts of the 17th century began as a search for certainty, and though often distracted from it, reverted at their finest moments to a conflict of intellectual principles. Terrifying as this conflict must have been, especially for men accustomed to the leisurely security of the Elizabethan state, it was responsible for the enormous intellectual vitality of the early 17th century. One can trace its impact in many fields of study. This was the great age of English polemical divinity. The art is lost today, but in its time it called forth vast learning, acuteness, and complexity of mind. In Hooker, Andrewes, Laud, Ussher, and Chillingworth, the English church boasted a group of controversialists before whom the greatest Catholic apologists of the age, Baronius and Bellarmine, might have paused in respect. And 17th-century learning was not confined to the clergy. A lawyer like Sir Edward Coke was more than a great lawyer, a great judge, even a great legal scholar; as a result of his studies he was able to recast the common law of England into a shape which it holds to this day. His friend John Selden was very likely the most learned man of his day; he was an Orientalist, a lawyer and legal historian, a rabbinical student, an editor, a scholar of heraldry, and an able parliamentarian. Other students of the past, famous in their day throughout Europe, were Sir Robert Cotton and William Camden. But the mind of the 17th century reached forward as well as backward, it was capacious as well as subtle. The most noted exponent of scientific method in the century was Francis Bacon. Edward Herbert, Thomas Hobbes, and James Harrington were philosophers of originality, whose thought exercised powerful influence on ages to come. Robert Boyle and William Harvey represent names well known in physical and medical research. William Gilbert laid open the principles of magnetism in a scientific classic published during the first year of the century; and in the last years of the Protectorate, John Wallis laid the foundations of the differential calculus. In most fields of intellectual activity, the first half of the 17th century was an age of reaching and grasping, of intellectual strain and fresh discovery.

For all its complexity of detail, the general development of English society during the period 1603–60 is simple enough to be described in a few phrases. A strict, inclusive, hierarchical, and authoritarian pattern of life was shattered. After a period of uncertainty and experiment, the old system was restored in a looser version, more spacious than any of the individual parties considered ideal, yet still rigid enough to preserve the fundamentals of private property, social order, and Christian control.

Politically and socially, the change accomplished by the Puritan Revolution was one of *degree*; government after the Restoration was like Elizabethan government, only more tolerant of differences. But culturally and intellectually, the change was one of *kind*, as far-reaching as any in the history of thought. The English community changed from one founded on the concepts of uniformity, hierarchy, and relation to one founded on the concepts of multiplicity, disparity, and toleration. Intellectually and imaginatively, the Commonwealth and Protectorate are a vast dividing line. Dryden spoke of the Elizabethans as "the giant race before the flood"; and he was right. In the quality of his imagination, in the structure of the world he took for granted, Dryden was farther removed from Shakespeare than Shakespeare was from Chaucer.

For the Elizabethan, when he looked at the world about him, viewed it (as had many a medieval philosopher before him) through the veil of a great nostalgia for order. In the Elizabethan view, every creature, from the highest archangel to the lowest worm, had his place in the great order of divine appointments; and by being a worm or an archangel to the height of his powers, he echoed forth the supreme goodness of the Almighty. Man was not only united to every other creature in the cosmos by a "great Chain of Being," which assigned to him a middle position, subordinate to some creatures and superior to others; within his own nature, some elements were superior to others. Reason, which ruled in man, made him natural lord over passion, which ruled—for example—in woman. The king was "head" of the body politic; in him reason ruled, as it ought, over the passionate and tumultuous multitude. Whether one looked high or low on the great Chain of Being, one found that the universal principle of analogy rendered all modes and levels of existence systematically correspondent to one another. The king was to his subjects as Michael was to the other archangels, as the bishop was to his pastors, as the Archbishop of Canterbury was to his bishops, as the lion was to other beasts, as the eagle was to other birds, as the diamond was to other stones, as gold was to other metals. Within every category and species, there was an order of excellence; and though the noblest lion was less than the lowest man, yet he was a monarch of his species. That the king was "father of his country" was a metaphor, to be sure; but that a father was "king of his family" was also a metaphor, and both were metaphors derived from the central fact that God the Father was King of Kings.

Now a world view like this, insubstantial as it appears to modern reason, offered many securities and assurances. In Elizabethan minds, it seems to have existed halfway between a fact and a hope. Shakespeare caused Ulysses to expound it dramatically but inconclusively in that puzzling, bitter tragicomedy, *Troilus and Cressida*. Raphael explained it to Adam in Milton's *Paradise Lost* (V.469–505), but of course he was speaking of the universe before the Fall. It was less a description of fact than an ideal.

During the 17th century, this world view came under attack from two main directions and was substantially demolished. The Puritans seized on the ancient doctrine of the Christian calling, and with their usual emphasis on a direct relation between God and the individual soul, declared that every man must decide for himself what God intended him to have as his "calling" on earth. If he thought the squire, or the constable, or King Charles I was a sinner, the Puritan's calling required him to oppose that sinner with might and main. Across the fine strands of analogy and hierarchy which bound together an earlier cosmos, the Puritan brushed a rougher, simpler division, a division between saints and sinners, between those who are of God's party and those who are of Satan's. The older social creed was shattered by that of an individual seeker, a fighter.

The other enemy of the Elizabethan world view, less hostile by intent, but more deadly in its ultimate effects, was scientific method. Most 17th-century scientists were pious men, who shrank from the idea that their work might harm religion. And yet Galileo's validation of Copernicus' theory—that the sun, the other stars, and the planets did not all revolve around the earth—wrought havoc in the analogical universe. It rendered conceivable a plurality, perhaps even an infinity of worlds; and so destroyed the symmetry of this one. Conversely, men came to think it most improbable that the God who created the universe of intergalactic space was so fanciful as to make this world along the intricate ingenious lines envisaged by the Elizabethans.

The analogical universe, informed with moral meaning, largely disappeared, then, in the course of the 17th century; and though God did not forthwith disappear from the universe, He withdrew behind it. He had been constantly at man's elbow, issuing (through His signatures in the natural world) veiled warnings, encouragements, demands; He was to become personally remote, yet powerful in His established laws, like the architect of an ancient house.

The tendency of 17th-century thought was to dissociate God increasingly from the intimate texture of the world, its day-to-day functioning. The growing scientism of the age tended also to dissociate the world of man's thought from that of his feeling. Astrology gave way to astronomy, alchemy to chemistry, and the immense corpus of "curious learning," accumulated from generation to generation, and cherished less because it was presumed true than because it was thought instructive, was subjected to the cruel test of fact. The new science enabled the scientist to understand the world better, and to manipulate it more accurately, than ever before; but it deprived the ordinary man of a structure, a framework, a set of ordered directives for his life. The test of truth gradually changed, under the double impulsion of scientific method and prolonged, inconclusive sectarian conflict, from conformity with a large-scale view, philosophical or religious, to conformity with experimental data, manipulative fact. "The truth" became something objective, public, general, impersonal; a man's private insights, the feelings of a poet, an "enthusiast," an individual, were something secondary. T. S. Eliot has described the sort of divorce between thought and feeling which he feels the 17th century inaugurated as the work of Dryden and Milton; but in fact the names of these poets are mere symbols for vast processes, anonymous and ill-defined, which affected the intellectual weather of the age. The pursuit of the heavenly kingdom gave way to the pursuit of earthly prosperity; the ideal of strenuous intellectual and spiritual effort gave way to the ideal of gentlemanly good taste; the rule of the saints gave way to the rule of the well-to-do and respectable. Truth, instead of standing on a rough, high hill up which each man must find his own difficult way (cf. Donne, *Satire III*, lines 79–82), became plain, natural, easy, and common to all. Wit, instead of being serious intellectual work, became the pointed enunciation of commonplaces.

For, tied in with all these intellectual and spiritual changes, and very likely underlying them, is a single social shift of immense import. England in the course of the 17th century became increasingly bourgeois. The City tradesman, who was a figure of ridicule and contempt for Ben Jonson and Shakespeare (in different manifestations he is Bottom the Weaver in *A Midsummer Night's Dream* and Corvino the Raven in *Volpone*," became by the century's end a respectable member of the cultured community. During the last half of the 17th century, chivalry faded as an ideal, and pragmatic common sense flourished. The courtier, like Sir Philip Sidney (1554–86) gave way, as the characteristic leader of his society, to an 18th-century Whig landlord with good commercial connections in the City. The word "Whig," which first came into prominence in the last years of the 17th century, connotes all sorts of particulars, both as to creed and social position. Broadly, it implies a landed oligarchy, closely allied with the money power; jealous of the royal prerogative and hostile to popular democracy; strong for property rights and gradual social evolution; Low-Church or latitudinarian in religion, and protectionist in its economic policies. But to be ruled by Whigs is to be ruled frankly by an interest, not a principle.

As it advanced toward the 18th century, England changed markedly its social tone. The ancient and indigenous art of madrigal-singing died out. Henry Purcell, England's last composer of note before Sir Edward Elgar, died in 1695; and the English musical tradition was replaced by professionals imported from Germany and Italy, and by the hymns of Isaac Watts and John Wesley. The Maypoles were torn down throughout England, the fairy legends were dismissed as idle or sinful, the folk culture fell under blighting disapproval. Middle-class antipathy for the stage, though deeply rooted and of long standing, was less immediate in its destructive effects; yet by 1700, as a regular way for a writer to make a reputable living, the stage had all but ceased to exist. During the great age of English drama, the stage and the court (closely allied as they were) had represented the main sources from which a writer could anticipate reward for his work. (Jonson and Dryden, the two professional authors of the 17th century, wrote primarily for the stage and the court; a man like Milton, who could appeal to neither, went substantially unrewarded.) But after the exile of the house of Stuart, in 1688, England was governed for better than a century by monarchs who spoke English only as a second language. Thus royal patronage for literature dried up. Lacking court patronage and a dependable source of theatrical income, authors betook themselves to hack work or hired out to political parties. The immediate result of either choice was a definite lowering of literary tone.

The suppression of "pagan superstitions" like Maypoles and folk songs, the cold hand of morality laid on the stage, the instituting of the glum English Nonconformist Sunday, all suggest a new if rather grim power in religion as a repressive force. No doubt it was so. But in matters of money, in their power to censure or direct economic matters, the clergy had lost ground. The advent of large-scale banking and joint-stock enterprise removed much economic conduct from the realm of personal behavior; in addition, the idea of clerical interference in the nation's economic life called forth hateful memories of Laud and "Thorough." Thus the power of clergymen to adjudicate economic matters shrank, as their power over personal life, of the lower orders in particular, grew. On balance, this was no gain for the men of the cloth. There was much more talk at the end of the century regarding "contempt of the clergy" than there had been in 1600.

The alliance of physical science and the money interest was a supreme social fact at the end of the century. Material improvements, like street-lighting, canals, water supplies, coal mines, banking facilities, and good roads, were matters of general concern in 1700, as dynastic diplomacy, the rise and fall of royal favorites, and ecclesiastical intrigues had been the characteristic concerns of 1600. Behind the dramatic clash of Anglican and Puritan, behind the comings and goings of the house of Stuart, behind the slogans and heroisms associated with the rise and fall of Cromwell, one notes the steady growth in influence of the power of money as against the power of land. (This process is never clearcut, because money is always transforming itself into land by the simple process of purchase; but the struggle can usefully be thought of as new money and new land asserting themselves against old land and the authority that goes with it.) What the 17th century was busy consolidating was that Whig oligarchy which was to rule England almost uninterruptedly from the Glorious Revolution of 1688 till the Reform Bill of 1832.

THE ELIZABETHAN LITERARY HERITAGE

The 17th century naturally inherited a full quota of literary genres and traditions from the previous age. No clearcut line separates the drama produced under James and Charles Stuart from that produced under Elizabeth Tudor, though during the first thirty years of the century, tragicomedy, pastoral romance, and the masque grew steadily in popularity. The trage-dies of John Ford, John Webster, and Cyril Tourneur are dark and horrify-ing productions, shot through with moments of powerful poetic statement. The great comic artist of the age was of course Ben Jonson, though many of his later plays were described unkindly as his "dotages." After the the-aters were closed (by the Puritans in 1642) and reopened (by Charles II in 1660), taste turned to broad sexual comedy (William Wycherley, *The Country Wife*) or to the comedy of manners (George Etherege, *The Man of Mode, or Sir Fopling Flutter*); while tragedy assumed the pompous, in-flated manner known as "heroic tragedy."

The Elizabethans had rung most of the available changes on the sonnet of courtly or romantic love, and 17th-century sonneteers tuned their in-struments to new pitches—devotion for Donne, politics for Milton. After undergoing a number of interesting vocational variations (fishermen's eclogues, shoemakers' eclogues, and the like), the pastoral reached high-water mark in *Lycidas* (1637); and throughout the middle years of the century, religious and meditative lyrics expanded sharply in importance. The Elizabethan lyric, generally gay and musical, grew graver though no less melodious under the Stuarts; the ode, the elegy, and the epigram, forms deliberately modeled on classical originals, enjoyed the periodic re-vivals one would anticipate in an age of great classical scholarship, and underwent interesting adaptations by Ben Jonson, John Donne, and Abraham Cowley. As the lyric impulse gradually faded, discursive and social modes of poetry came to the fore. A major development in verse genres was the advent of formal satire, which began about 1590 and de-veloped steadily until it became the literary mode most characteristic of the Restoration and early 18th century. Though exploited with complete success only by Milton, the epic retained its traditional position as the supreme literary form. But Milton's use of blank verse for nondramatic poems was a major technical innovation, which would be emulated, not only in future epics, but in discursive and narrative poems of many different sorts. Another major technical development was the gradual emergence, after many hesitant and uncoordinated steps, of the heroic couplet, that razorsharp, double-edged weapon which Dryden handled with such cool assurance.

In prose, though the 17th century inherited a number of traditional forms, it had to invent several more; for prose, in the early stages of a culture, generally develops more slowly and with greater difficulty than verse. Long before 1600 the design and pattern of a sermon had been pretty thoroughly worked out; so had some techniques of religious controversy and various modes of devotional and meditative prose. Elsewhere relatively little had been accomplished in English prose. Setting aside chronicles and other such compilations, there were few distinguished histories in English before Edward Hyde, first Earl of Clarendon, began his *History of the Rebellion* in 1650; even fewer full-length English biographies before Izaak Walton began his biography of John Donne in 1640; no informal English essays before Francis Bacon began his in 1597; no character sketches before Joseph Hall produced his in 1608. In all these genres, the 17th century had by 1660 produced, not simply examples, but masterpieces. Yet the 17th century was not, in prose any more than in verse, an age of startling novelties. Most of the genres which it introduced into English had a history in other languages. Even in the matter of prose style, the 17th century built on foundations solidly laid by the craftsmen of two centuries. The great work of the 17th-century prose writers was to enrich, diversify, perhaps even to individualize English style. They applied their native tongue to science and philosophy, and made of it an instrument as precise as Latin; they applied it to meditative and speculative themes, and found it richly expressive. They applied it to the work of political and social persuasion, and created a practical common-sense prose idiom. In only two major areas is the period substantially barren. Perhaps feeling that "mere fables" failed to meet the urgent needs of the age, the early 17th century created next to no prose fiction. And, apparently not needing to do so, the writers of the age created no literary criticism of significance. Jonson is the only notable critic in the early century; and he writes no essays, only notebook entries. Milton's criticism, often suggestive, is more often a simple rationalization of his own practice; and Thomas Hobbes belongs, by influence and affinity, to the Restoration. In both fiction and criticism, then, the writers of the 17th century inherited more from the age of Elizabeth than they transmitted to that of Charles II.

But if they did not expound very much original criticism, the writers of the early 17th century clung all the more earnestly to critical standards which they had inherited; and in reading their poetry, it is important to bear in mind some of the ideals which helped to shape it. However contradictory they seem, the age took them seriously and knew how to reconcile them artfully. One major ideal was that of *copia* or fullness; a poet was expected to have a full supply of imagery, based on traditional knowledge, with which to render his subject graphic and vivid. The epic poet, particularly, was expected to be a man of universal learning; he must know all the arts and sciences of war and peace, in order to display the ideal man in action. In addition to this discursive knowledge, the poet was expected also to show individual ingenuity and acuteness of mind. The word "originality" did not yet exist in criticism; but all men agreed that the poet's imagery must be fresh and unhackneyed—some even thought that it might be his proper function to surprise. Yet an ideal of stylistic chastity also prevailed; not only were many 17th-century poems notably restrained in the matter of decoration, those which fell into the trap of over-ingenuity were often subjected to cruel mockery. Even with regard to a matter as simple as harmony, contradictory standards stood side by side. Poets like Spenser and Shakespeare were praised enthusiastically for writing smooth and mellifluous verse; other poets, like Donne and George Chapman, were praised with equal enthusiasm for writing deliberately rough and difficult lines.

The key to these apparent contradictions lies in the important 17th-century concept of decorum. Socially, "decorum" is propriety or sedateness. But in its critical context the word was used in the 17th century to describe what was fitting, seemly, or in keeping with the particular poetic kind, or genre. Thus rough lines were decorous in a satire, because the satire was supposed to be spoken by a rough, discontented person, intent on telling rough truths. But these same lines would be thoroughly indecorous in a traditional love poem. Some of Donne's roughest and bawdiest poems may thus be described as perfect examples of decorum—style, subject, imagery, occasion, and imagined speaker are all of a piece. One need not think the concept of decorum an ultimate answer to all questions of literary tone, style, and structure to see that because of the great variety of recognized poetic kinds, it granted the poets of the 17th century a remarkable range of literary freedoms only vaguely tempered by responsibility. More elaborate critical doctrines have sometimes accomplished less.

METAPHYSICAL, CAVALIER, AND SPENSERIAN POETRY

The early 17th century was an age of intellectual conflict. Men sought for certainty, not just because it was pleasant to have, but because on it they could build structures of compulsion; they exploded other men's certainties to prevent them from erecting other structures. It was an age of intellectual mine and countermine.

The poetry of the age represents several distinct responses to this universal search for certainty. "Metaphysical" poetry, that written by John Donne and his followers, is so called for a curious complex of irrelevant reasons; the adjective was not even invented until Samuel Johnson published his *Life of Cowley* in 1779, many years after all the metaphysical poets were dead. But it has caught on, because it implies what no reader of John Donne can fail to recognize in an instant—that his is a sinewy, searching style, rooted in the conception of a "difficult" image often derived from Scholastic concepts. Its larger structure is that of an argument; its tone is frequently paradoxical. It tries to reach through conventional ideas, beyond the mere surface of things, by sheer force of intellectual energy. This is characteristic of the whole metaphysical school. The basic idiom of metaphysical poetry is daring, colloquial, and passionate; its meter is often deliberately rough, with many short syllables irregularly spaced, as in the rhythms of everyday speech. This poetry delights in ingenious, knotty, many-sided metaphors, which the age itself referred to as "conceits."

The word "conceit" derives, not from the notion of egotism in the author, but from the Italian *concetto*; it is most closely allied to the English "concept." In this sense, it is an almost separable unit of intellectual or verbal ingenuity, which occurs in a poem but can be detached from it and appreciated separately. A frequent early form was the conventional physical comparison of the Petrarchan sonnet (one's mistress has eyes like diamonds, lips like cherries, hair like golden wire, and so forth) The most famous conceit in English verse is doubtless the comparison of two separated lovers to the legs of a compass, which occurs at the end of Donne's *Valediction: Forbidding Mourning*. Even bolder is the conceit by Richard Crashaw which describes Christ as clad in the garment of his own blood, which has been taken from the purple wardrobe on his side (*On Our Crucified Lord, Naked and Bloody*). These are extreme examples of the conceit—the latter example is grotesque. Metaphysical poetry, with its restless intellectual manner, found the witty, exaggerated conceit particularly useful as a means of making complex, compressed assertions about a world which appeared divided if not fragmented, and of displaying at the same time the individuality of the poet. The metaphysical conceit is often consciously odd and far-fetched; hence it takes some getting used to. But its ultimate effect is one of highly compressed, sharply angled perspectives on an object of contemplation, glittering and intellectually provocative.

The second major poetic school was conservative rather than extravagant. Poets who had no taste for exploding the Elizabethan decorative image into a metaphysical conceit tended to chasten it, under classical influence, into a correct and restrained mode of verse quite new to English literary experience. Pruning off the redundant modifiers and subordinate grammatical clauses, eliminating the Spenserian surplus of expletives ("doth run," "do eat," and the like), and cutting down on a profusion of unaccented syllables and run-on lines, Ben Jonson and his followers produced verse which had the special Latin quality of being "lapidary." At its best their poetry gave the impression of being written to be carved in marble. Restrained in feeling, deliberately limited in its subject matter, intellectually thin but meticulously clear and incisive in expression, the poems of Jonson are models of this style. A song like *Queen and Huntress*, or *Still To Be Neat*, or *Drink to Me Only* is unadorned to the point of plainness, chaste in its diction, and silvery-pure in its feeling. It is strong syntactically—i.e., closely knit in its grammar—as a poem by Donne is strong metaphorically. One of the few critical terms in which the age had any confidence was "strong lines." On the whole, the early 17th century liked strong lines; and though it did not distinguish them clearly, liked them strong in two very different ways. Jonson's poems were strong in their compressed and muscular syntax; Donne's through the energy of their startling and far-reaching conceits.

Influential as it has proved in the 20th century, the metaphysical school of Donne by no means overpowered the 17th century. George Herbert, Richard Crashaw, and Henry Vaughan, all metaphysicals, are generally ranked among the finest of English devotional poets. But they were all retiring men personally, with very individual styles which could not be imitated or widely adapted. Herbert died young, while Crashaw was in exile and Vaughan a recluse during the greater part of their active poetical lives. Like Herbert's, Andrew Marvell's poems were published only after his death (1681), and too late to exercise any influence on the poetry of the age. Abraham Cowley was the single metaphysical poet who won great popular fame during his lifetime. He did so by coarsening and degrading the style; and immediately after his death in 1667, his poetry suffered a calamitous revaluation, from which it has never recovered. In a word, metaphysical poetry had something of a vogue in what we would call the "intellectual circles" of the early century; but being at its best subtle and allusive, it was almost always a private and, one might almost say, unsocial poetry. Between 1600 and 1900, it is only a rare and unusually catholic critic like Coleridge, who will be found suggesting that its virtues outweighed its defects.

The severe, restrained style of Ben Jonson, on the other hand, proved one of the root inspirations for poets of the later 17th and 18th centuries. To be sure, the sort of beautifully phrased but social and conventional poem which Jonson wrote had a tendency in the hands of lesser practitioners to reduce itself to the elegant verbal trifle. Many of the "Sons of Ben," disciples who gathered round Jonson during the 1620's and early 1630's, spent their energies on these gallant, fluffy compliments; and a certain group of them (Lovelace, Herrick, Carew, Waller, Suckling) have been memorialized by literary historians under the name of "the Cavalier poets." Some jocose critic has remarked that Cavalier poetry is poetry that sounds as if it had been written while falling off a horse. The slander is not wholly unfair; for the Cavalier poets did try to give the impression that their flawless little trifles were dashed off quite without effort. Out of the inherited code of the gentleman, they laid primary emphasis on just one secondary feature, his *sprezzatura*, or fine, careless elegance; and as a result they contributed one more chapter to the decline of a heroic ideal. One has only to contrast Sir Philip Sidney with Sir John Suckling to sense that the latter brings us very close to a Restoration gentleman-doll, a Sir Fopling Flutter. Still, if gentlemen had less and less to express as the century advanced, the polished Jonsonian style offered them more and more elegant ways to express it. At their best, the Cavalier poets wrote poems of unexampled neatness. And the "reforming of our numbers" (that is, the polishing of English metrics) accomplished by Cavalier poets like Edmund Waller and Sir John Denham paved the way for many of the achievements of Dryden and his followers during the Restoration and 18th century.

The metaphysical style of Donne and the neoclassical style of Jonson are two characteristically 17th-century developments of poetic art; and most poets of the early century wrote in one (or occasionally both) of these styles. But a third strain persists well into the century, of Spenserian or post-Spenserian style. Most of the post-Spenserians are not distinguished poets at all. William Browne of Tavistock produces something very close to doggerel, and the brothers Fletcher (Giles and Phineas) are scarcely more important than he as literary artists. But this relatively old-fashioned Spenserian manner, surviving past its time into the 17th century, bore fruit when Milton grafted onto it his own highly individual style. Allegorical romance, imbued with moral feeling and narrated in ornate verse, was the essence of the Spenserian manner. Milton may have adopted it as a flexible vehicle, capable of absorbing the immense burden of his classical learning; or he may have thought it the best model for a narrative poet, who must work to a large scale, in a steady and uniform style. In any event, he enriched the manner with formal diction and rhetorical patterns, stiffened it with strict Latin syntax, and, liberating it from rhyme and stanza, taught it to branch out boldly into verse paragraphs. All these developments were to have an enormous and permanent influence on English poetry.

PROSE: GORGEOUS, DIGNIFIED, AND PLAIN

As it became steadily less ornate in the course of the century, prose became steadily more practical, popular, and common-sense. A spectacular development of the age of Elizabeth was the use of gorgeous and gallant devices in prose. Writers were fascinated by old saws and wise adages, by puns, parallels, alliterations; they rejoiced in new and fancy coinages. This highly adorned and artificial prose style, called "Euphuism," was not much more than a courtier's freak. But it had more enduring analogues in the witty and conceited style of pulpit oratory which prevailed for a while at the beginning of the century. Men like Lancelot Andrewes and John Donne preached to sophisticated and learned auditories, who were quick to catch a Greek, Latin, or Hebrew allusion, avid after ingenious puns, and delighted by a display of metaphorical fireworks or intellectual gymnastics. The preachers responded with fantastic shows of verbal virtuosity. Among the most spectacular of their performances were the seventeen sermons on the Nativity which Lancelot Andrewes preached before King James and his court on successive Christmases, and the sermon popularly titled *Death's Duel* which John Donne preached in 1631 before a crowded auditory at St. Paul's. Preaching of this sort represented one particularly valid use of gorgeous prose, and the tradition continued till late in the century. Long, rolling periods, complex metaphors, Latinate construction, formal balance, and florid, deliberate flights of rhetorical fancy are found in the prose of Jeremy Taylor, even after the Restoration, when a chaster diction and more conversational tone had come into general use.

But the greatest exponents of gorgeous prose were not clergymen at all. Sir Thomas Browne, a country doctor and rural magistrate of reflective disposition, about midcentury set down in some of the most polyphonic prose ever penned his ruminations on time, death, order, decay, eternity, and the grounds of religious belief. Discursive, witty, and fantastically learned, Browne is a prose poet, and his best effects come from the sense of a soaring, sensuous-intellectual imagination, quizzical and passionate, skeptical and credulous, which revels in the fabulous darkness of antiquity and holds passionately to the promises of eternity, till the shoddy continuum of the present comes to seem fragile and fantastic indeed.

The other master of gorgeous, learned prose in English was John Milton. Much of his prose work is devoted to controversy, and this material cannot be read today without profound discomfort. Heavily armored with Latin and learning, Milton did not have a mind or a style flexible enough for controversy. In the field of polemical journalism lesser men, with a shrewder sense of how to appeal to the popular mind, could write rings around him. But when he fancied himself mounted upon such a rostrum as the ancient Athenian Areopagus, a free citizen of a free nation, delivering his mind freely to the citizens at large on a matter of public moment, his style and his thought took on a nobility for which his own age, and ours, do not furnish many parallels. When he is worthy of himself, Milton the prose-writer pours forth an impetuous, complicated rhetoric, in which the complexity and learning of the mind do not seem like irrelevant distractions, far less like hampering armor; they are marks of genuine authority.

But gorgeous prose, with its emphasis on rhetorical figures and external decoration, stood clearly apart from the main intellectual concern of the 17th century—the search for grounds of certainty. The real work of forging intellectual tools for use in the everyday work of exposition and persuasion demanded a less elaborate, a less distracting diction. A model of such diction in the "middle style" had been bequeathed to the age in the work of Richard Hooker. Undertaking to disentangle the Puritan-Anglican quarrel of personalities and irrelevancies, Hooker had laid down the grounds of intellectual certainty in broad philosophical terms. *Of the Laws of Ecclesiastical Polity* (1593) is a forbidding title for a splendid book, learned and strongly argued. Its sonorous and dignified yet flexible prose struck exactly that note of persuasive reasonableness which for many years was to be the prevailing mode of public discourse in English. Writers of many faiths, and on many topics, made use of a prose style deriving more or less directly from Hooker. Above all, they learned from Hooker the art of various tone, which enabled them now to rise to dignified rhetorical periods, now to descend to homely illustrations, without abandoning their broad persuasive purpose.

The need for clear, accurate, and forceful communication produced all sorts of experiments in simple prose throughout the century. Bacon was particularly conscious of the need for a natural, informal style, and made the *Essays* into examples of it. The root inspiration here is the condensed, aphoristic manner characteristic of Seneca, the Roman philosopher. Bacon does not really succeed in molding a smooth or consecutive prose style out of his successive aphorisms. Each individual sentence has the air of starting afresh and ending abruptly before it is really under way. But it is forceful, and above all it is clear writing. Other men attempted Senecan prose; opposing its short, jog-trot gait to the long, loping swing of Ciceronian periods, they sometimes called it "the Senecan amble." But the lack of emphasis in this prose (most fully evident in the somewhat eccentric version of it produced by Robert Burton in his *Anatomy of Melancholy*), is ultimately as fatiguing as the pounding periods of the gorgeous style; and it is more confusing. Of all the Senecans, Bacon is most successful in keeping the line of his thought uncluttered by particulars (he is most truly a Senecan and least an ambler); but even he now and then succumbs to the lack of variety inherent in the style.

The outstanding 17th-century influence on English prose style was, naturally, the Civil War. In the course of the conflict, men were driven to look for more and more effective means of persuasion. Techniques of controversy which had served very well when theologian glittered darkly against theologian proved cumbersome when applied to the mass media. One of Milton's early tracts appeared under the forbidding title of *Animadversions upon the Remonstrant's Defense Against Smectymnuus*. But plainer, bolder, more provocative titles soon drove out the heavily armored controversialists. *A Hue and Cry After the Fundamental Liberties of England*—the purchaser of such a pamphlet had some idea of what to expect for his tuppence. For a nation of Bible-reading controversialists engaged in a civil war subjected the English language to an extraordinary double strain. The powerful poetic metaphors of Biblical style stirred the hearts and souls of men to great imaginings. Their plain English common sense, on the other hand, tested these dreams against considerations of homely, down-to-earth realism. When any Englishman might appoint himself a judge of public affairs and religious truth, matters of public concern and religious faith had to be stated in ordinary English. One outcome of the popular discussion of public issues was the rise of periodical journalism—communication reduced to the lowest common denominator. A happier result was a certain lustiness and amplitude about the post-Restoration English prose styles. Never pruned, clipped, or formalized by an official academy, English prose grew by taking over metaphors from farm and forge, from shop and barn. It grew too by adapting itself to the casual rhythms and unpretentious periods of colloquial speech. This extraordinary fusion of elements—the colloquial with the elegant, the learned with the vulgar, the taut with the casual—distinguishes the prose style of Jonathan Swift, and marks the end toward which 17th-century prose is moving.

JOHN DONNE
(1572–1631)

1601: Secret marriage to Ann More.
1615: Sacred orders.
1633: First publication of *Songs and Sonnets*.

There are two distinct but related authors known as John Donne. First is the scandalous young spark, who wrote bawdy and cynical verses—Jack Donne, the rake. Then there is the gravely witty, passionately religious divine, who wrote verses to his God as ardent as those he had once addressed to his mistresses. This is Dr. John Donne, the Dean of St. Paul's. Yet the key to both men is the same; it is a kind of restless, searching energy, which scorns the easy platitude and the smooth, empty phrase; which is vivid, immediate, troubling; and which makes the reading of Donne's poetry an imaginative and intellectual struggle and an all-absorbing experience.

Donne was born into an old Roman Catholic family, at a time when anti-Catholic feeling in England was near its height. His faith barred him from many of the usual avenues of success, and his point of view was always that of an insecure outsider. Though he attended both Oxford and Cambridge Universities, as well as Lincoln's Inn (where barristers got their training), he never took any academic degrees and never practiced law. After quietly abandoning Catholicism some time during the 1590's, he had scruples about becoming an Anglican. He had no gift for commerce, and though he inherited money from his father (who died when Donne was only 4), it was far from enough to render him independent. Hence he had to make his way in the world indirectly—by wit, charm, learning, valor, and above all, favor. Partly from sheer intellectual curiosity, he read enormously in divinity, medicine, law, and the classics; he wrote to display his learning and wit. He traveled on the Continent, especially, it would seem, to Spain; even in later years, he was an inveterate voyager. With Ralegh and Essex he took part in two hit-and-run expeditions against Cadiz and the Azores. He put himself in the way of court employment, danced attendance on great court ladies, and generally lived the life of a brilliant young man hopeful of preferment.

When in 1598 Donne was appointed private secretary to Sir Thomas Egerton, the Lord Keeper, his prospects for worldly advancement seemed good. He sat in Elizabeth's last parliament and moved in court circles. But in 1601 he secretly married Lady Egerton's niece, 16-year-old Ann More, and thereby ruined his own worldly hopes. The marriage turned out happily, but Donne's imprudence was never forgiven. Sir George More had Donne imprisoned and dismissed from his post; and for the next dozen years, the poet had to struggle at a series of makeshift employments to support his growing family. As a man of 35, Donne was no longer the brilliant young gallant of the 1590's; sick, poor, and unhappy, he was composing, but not publishing, a treatise on the lawfulness of suicide (*Biathanatos*). As he approached 40, he was engaged with Thomas Morton, Dean of Gloucester, in composing anti-Catholic polemics (*Pseudo-Martyr*, 1610; *Ignatius his Conclave*, 1611). In return for patronage from Sir Robert Drury, he wrote in 1611 and 1612 a pair of long poems, *The Anniversaries*, on the death of Sir Robert's daughter Elizabeth. None of these activities represent a full employment of Donne's volcanic intellectual energy. To be sure, Donne's social position need not be painted too blackly. He had friends among the courtiers, politicians, poets, and clergy—Mrs. Magdalen Herbert and her sons George and Edward, Ben Jonson, Sir Henry Goodyere, and Sir Henry Wotton among them. He was never quite without resources. Yet, broadly speaking, the middle years of Donne's life were a period of searching, uncertainty, and unhappiness.

Though Donne had flatly refused in 1607 to take Anglican orders, King James was certain that he would some day make a great Anglican preacher. Hence he declared that Donne could have no preferment or employment from him, except in the church. Finally, in 1615, Donne overcame his scruples, not the least of which was the fear of seeming ambitious, and entered the ministry. He was promptly appointed Reader in Divinity at Lincoln's Inn. In the 17th century, among court circles and at the Inns of Court where lawyers congregated, preaching was at once a form of spiritual devotion, an intellectual exercise, and a dramatic entertainment. Donne's metaphorical style, bold erudition, and dramatic wit at once established him as a great preacher in an age of great preachers. Fully 160 of his sermons survive. In 1621 he was made Dean of St. Paul's, where he preached to great congregations of "City" lawyers, courtiers, merchants, and tradesmen. In addition, his private devotions were published in 1624, and he continued to write sacred poetry till the very end of his life. Obsessed with the idea of death, Donne preached what was called his own funeral sermon just a few weeks before he died, and is supposed to have written the last, and one of the greatest, of his poems on his deathbed. He even had his portrait painted in his shroud.

The poetry of Donne represents a sharp break with that written by his predecessors and most of his contemporaries. Much Elizabethan verse is decorative and flowery in its quality. Its images adorn, its meter is mellifluous. Image harmonizes with image, and line swells almost predictably into line. Donne's poetry, on the other hand, is written very largely in *conceits*—concentrated images which involve an element of dramatic contrast, of strain, or of intellectual difficulty. Most of the traditional "flowers of rhetoric" disappear completely. For instance, in his love poetry one never encounters bleeding hearts, cheeks like roses, lips like cherries, teeth like pearls, or Cupid shooting the arrows of love. The tears which flow in *A Valediction: of Weeping* are different from, and more complex than, the ordinary saline fluid of unhappy lovers; they are ciphers, naughts, symbols of the world's emptiness without the beloved; or else, suddenly reflecting her image, they are globes, worlds, they contain the sum of things. The poet who plays with conceits not only displays his own ingenuity; he may see into the nature of the world as deeply as the philosopher. Donne's conceits in particular leap continually in a restless orbit from the personal to the cosmic and back again.

Donne's rhythms are colloquial and various. He likes to twist and distort not only ideas, but metrical patterns and grammar itself. In the satires, which Renaissance writers understood to be "harsh" and "crabbed" as a genre, Donne's distortions often threaten to choke off the stream of expression entirely. But in the lyrics (both those which are worldly and those which are religious in theme), as in the elegies and sonnets, the verse never fails of a complex and memorable melody. Donne had an unusual gift, rather like that of a modern poet, T. S. Eliot, for striking off phrases which ring in the mind like a silver coin. They are two masters of the colloquial style, removed alike from the dignified, weighty manner of Milton and the sugared sweetness of the Elizabethans.

Donne and his followers are known to literary history as the "metaphysical school" of poets. Strictly speaking, this is a misnomer; there was no organized group of poets who imitated Donne, and if there had been, they would not have called themselves "metaphysical" poets. That term was invented by Dryden and Dr. Johnson. But the influence of Donne's poetic style was widely felt, especially by men whose taste was formed before 1660. George Herbert, Richard Crashaw, Henry Vaughan, Andrew Marvell, and Abraham Cowley are only the best known of those on whom Donne's influence is recognizable. The great change of taste which took place in 1660 threw Donne and the "conceited" style out of fashion; during the 18th and 19th centuries both he and his followers were rarely read and still more rarely appreciated. Finally, in the late 19th and early 20th centuries, three new editions of Donne appeared, of which Sir H. J. C. Grierson's, published in 1912, was quickly accepted as standard. By clarifying and purifying the often-garbled text, Grierson did a great deal to make Donne's poetry more available to the modern reader. Almost at once it started to exert an influence on modern poetic practice, the modern poets being hungry for a "tough" style which would free them from the worn-out rhetoric of late 19th-century romanticism. And Donne's status among the English poets quickly climbed from that of a curiosity to that of an acknowledged master.

Modern criticism, particularly, has rejoiced in the revival of Donne and the metaphysicals. Endlessly patient of subtle paradoxes and ambiguities, the new critics have succeeded in bringing out the rich sensibility and subtly intellectual music which underlie Donne's abrupt and muscular manner. Whether he writes of love or devotion, Donne's peculiar blend of wit and seriousness—of intense feeling, darting thought, and vast erudition—creates a fascination quite beyond the reach of easier styles and less strenuous minds. His poems, like his mind, are overwhelmingly mobile. Some of his poems are burlesques of traditional poetic modes. Platonic love places woman on a pedestal where she is to be worshiped spiritually; *Love's Alchemy* tears her down. Petrarch and his followers assured their readers that love was immutable, immortal, infinite; *The Indifferent* proclaims that it is a trifling game. Yet Donne can take the old forms seriously still. *The Undertaking* is in the spirit of serious Platonic love, and *The Good-Morrow* is an extravagant Petrarchan compliment. Indeed, Donne's mind is so mobile that a single poem may change points of view, and, beginning in passion, end in defiance (*The Funeral*).

The poems of Donne occasionally appear willful or shocking because they mention unconventional topics under unconventional circumstances. Corpses rotting in graves turn up in love poems, alongside geometrical compasses and astronomical data. The soul's union with God is described under the image of rape. The shock value of these images is sometimes exploited for its own sake. But just as often, Donne has a perfectly serious point to make. In *The Relic* that "bracelet of bright hair about the bone" is more than a macabre touch; the image of a spiritual marriage, it is shown triumphing by a miracle over death. In *The Sun Rising* the poet addresses the sun itself as a "busy old fool"; and this is audacious cleverness, but it also defines a psychological situation. The speaker, as he lies in bed with his mistress, feels himself exalted far above the sun—he looks down from an immense psychological height. Thus the wit is dramatically revealing as well as just shocking.

The first editors of Donne's poetry divided his work into about a dozen groupings, sometimes including only a single longer poem in a group. The *Songs and Sonnets*, which open the volume, are generally amorous in theme; the *Divine Poems*, which close it, are described in their title. In between, and harder to categorize, fall such sizable groups as the five satires, eighteen epigrams, twenty elegies, and 34 verse letters. There are also four epithalamia, or marriage songs, seven epicedes (i.e., mortuary poems) and obsequies on the death of sundry personages, and about a dozen epigrams. In short, Donne, whom Grierson shrewdly characterized as one of the great talkers in English verse, wrote in almost all the customary forms and on all the customary occasions of his day.

With three or four exceptions (the two *Anniversaries*, an *Elegy on Prince Henry*, and a trifle on Coryat's *Crudities*), none of the poetry on which Donne's reputation stands today appeared in print during his lifetime. Yet his poems were widely read and well known. The explanation of this paradox lies in the custom of circulating little clusters of manuscript poems among the witty and cultured circles of Elizabethan and Jacobean society. Hard poems imply small audiences. When one could hope for no more than a thousand or so readers, at best, and when most of them were concentrated in London and the two universities, publication became an unnecessary luxury. Copied out by hand, and gathered together in little bundles, the poems of Donne enjoyed a subterranean popularity, in the boudoir and in the law library, where they were doubtless hidden behind heavier and more respectable volumes. Donne himself had little reason to quarrel with this arrangement. Many of the poems for which he was admired would have constituted black marks on his reputation as an earnest and godly divine. Hence they were deliberately kept out of print during his later years.

Of the poems which follow, the *Hymn to God, My God, in my Sickness* and *Holy Sonnet 5* first appeared in 1635; while *Holy Sonnet 18* saw the light of day only in 1899, when Sir Edmund Gosse published his *Life of John Donne*. All the other poems bear a publication date of 1633; and as for date of composition, almost all of them might be assigned a question mark. We must guess at their dates from the scanty marks of internal evidence. Early scholars took for granted that all the bawdy, cynical, and lecherous poems were written by young Jack Donne, while all the somber, penitent, devotional poems were written by the godly divine. The more we learn about the matter (and progress is astonishingly slow), the less this easy division seems to stand up. But then, the less we believe John Donne underwent a tremendous conversion experience, the less important problems of exact dating become. It is one mind throughout, whatever different facet happens to be showing.

The basic text which follows is that of Sir Herbert Grierson (1912), but it has been modified, wherever sensible improvement seemed possible, and sometimes supplemented, by that of Miss Helen Gardner (*Divine Poems*, 1952, and *The Elegies and the Songs and Sonnets*, 1964).

The Good-Morrow

I wonder, by my troth, what thou and I
Did, till we loved? Were we not weaned till then,
But sucked on country pleasures, childishly?
Or snorted we in the seven sleepers' den?[1]
'Twas so; But this, all pleasures fancies be.   5
If ever any beauty I did see,
Which I desired, and got, 'twas but a dream of thee.

And now good morrow to our waking souls,
Which watch not one another out of fear;
For love all love of other sights controls,   10
And makes one little room an everywhere.
Let sea-discoverers to new worlds have gone,
Let maps to other,[2] worlds on worlds have shown,
Let us possess one world; each hath one, and is one.

My face in thine eye, thine in mine appears,[3]   15
And true plain hearts do in the faces rest;
Where can we find two better hemispheres
Without sharp North, without declining West?
Whatever dies was not mixed equally;[4]
If our two loves be one, or thou and I   20
Love so alike that none do slacken, none can die.

1633

Song

Go and catch a falling star,
Get with child a mandrake root,[5]

1. Both Christian and Mohammedan authors recite the legend of seven youths of Ephesus, who hid in a cave from the persecutions of Decius, and slept there for 187 years. "Sucked" and "snorted" are words carefully chosen for their impact on the love poem.
2. I.e., let us concede that maps to other investigators have shown, etc. ("other" is an archaic plural form). In line 14 an alternative reading is "Let us possess *our* world" (from Miss Gardner).
3. Reflected in the pupils of one another's eyes, the lovers are, and possess, worlds of their own.
4. Scholastic philosophy taught that when the elements were imperfectly ("not equally") mixed, matter was mortal and mutable; but when they were perfectly mixed, it was undying and unchanging. The dividing line between these two natures was the sphere of the moon.
5. The mandrake root, or mandragora, forked like the lower part of the human body, was highly reputed as an aphrodisiac; to get one with child is a supreme impossibility.

Tell me where all past years are,
  Or who cleft the Devil's foot,
Teach me to hear mermaids[6] singing,   5
Or to keep off envy's stinging,
    And find
    What wind
Serves to advance an honest mind.

If thou beest born to strange sights,   10
  Things invisible to see,
Ride ten thousand days and nights,
  Till age snow white hairs on thee,
Thou, when thou return'st, wilt tell me
All strange wonders that befell thee,   15
    And swear
    No where
Lives a woman true, and fair.

If thou find'st one, let me know,
  Such a pilgrimage were sweet;   20
Yet do not, I would not go,
  Though at next door we might meet;
Though she were true when you met her,
And last till you write your letter,
    Yet she   25
    Will be
False, ere I come, to two, or three.

1633

The Undertaking

I have done one braver thing
  Than all the Worthies[1] did,
And yet a braver thence doth spring,
  Which is, to keep that hid.

It were but madness now t' impart   5
  The skill of specular stone,[2]
When he which can have learned the art
  To cut it, can find none.

So, if I now should utter this,
  Others (because no more   10

6. Identified with the sirens, whose song only the wily Odysseus survived.

1. According to medieval legend, the Nine Worthies, or supreme heroes of history, included three Jews (Joshua, David, Judas Maccabeus), three pagans (Hector, Alexander, Julius Caesar), and three Christians (Arthur, Charlemagne, Godfrey of Bouillon).

2. A transparent or translucent material, reputed to have been used in antiquity for mirrors (in Latin, *speculae*), but no longer known. •

Such stuff to work upon, there is)
    Would love but as before.

But he who loveliness within
    Hath found, all outward loathes,
For he who color loves, and skin,   15
    Loves but their oldest clothes.

If, as I have, you also do
    Virtue attired in woman see,
And dare love that, and say so too,
    And forget the He and She;   20

And if this love, though placéd so,
    From profane men you hide,
Which will no faith on this bestow,
    Or, if they do, deride;

Then you have done a braver thing   25
    Than all the Worthies did;
And a braver thence will spring,
    Which is, to keep that hid.

                      1633

The Indifferent

I can love both fair and brown,[1]
Her whom abundance melts, and her whom want betrays,
Her who loves loneness best, and her who masks and plays,
Her whom the country formed, and whom the town,
Her who believes, and her who tries,[2]   5
Her who still weeps with spongy eyes,
And her who is dry cork, and never cries;
I can love her, and her, and you, and you,
I can love any, so she be not true.

Will no other vice content you?   10
Will it not serve your turn to do as did your mothers?
Or have you all old vices spent, and now would find out others?
Or doth a fear that men are true torment you?
O we are not, be not you so;
Let me, and do you, twenty know.   15
Rob me, but bind me not, and let me go.
Must I, who came to travail[3] thorough you
Grow your fixed subject, because you are true?

Venus heard me sigh this song,
And by love's sweetest part, variety, she swore,   20
She heard not this till now; and that it should be so no more.

1. Both blonde and brunette.
2. "Attempts to believe" and "tries things out."
3. "Grief, sorrow," but also "journey, travel."

She went, examined, and returned ere long,
And said, Alas, some two or three
Poor heretics in love there be,
Which think to 'stablish dangerous constancy.   25
But I have told them, Since you will be true,
You shall be true to them who are false to you.

                                                        1633

The Canonization

For God's sake hold your tongue, and let me love,
 Or chide my palsy, or my gout,
My five gray hairs, or ruined fortune, flout,
  With wealth your state, your mind with arts improve,
   Take you a course, get you a place,[1]   5
   Observe His Honor, or His Grace,
Or the King's real, or his stamped face[2]
  Contemplate; what you will, approve,[3]
  So you will let me love.

Alas, alas, who's injured by my love?   10
 What merchant's ships have my sighs drowned?
Who says my tears have overflowed his ground?
  When did my colds a forward spring remove?[4]
   When did the heats which my veins fill
   Add one man to the plaguy bill?[5]   15
Soldiers find wars, and lawyers find out still
 Litigious men, which quarrels move,
 Though she and I do love.

Call us what you will, we are made such by love;
 Call her one, me another fly,
We're tapers too, and at our own cost die,[6]   20
  And we in us find the eagle and the dove.[7]
   The phoenix riddle hath more wit

1. "Take you a course": not necessarily of physic or instruction, but in the general sense of "settling yourself in life." A "place" is an appointment, at court or elsewhere.
2. On coins.
3. Put to proof, find by experience.
4. By freezing it up.
5. Deaths from the hot-weather plague were recorded, by parish, in weekly lists.
6. Like the "fly," a symbol of transitory life, we are burned up in "tapers," which consume themselves. There is a hint here of the old superstition that every act of intercourse subtracts a day from one's life. (To "die," in the punning terminology of the 17th century, was to consummate the act of sex.)
7. The eagle and the dove are symbols of earthly wisdom (strength) and heavenly meekness (purity), the latter paradoxically more powerful than the former. The phoenix, in general mythology, was a fabulous Arabian bird, only one of which existed at any one time. After living a thousand years, it lit its own funeral pyre, jumped in, and sang its funeral song as it was consumed— then rose triumphantly from its ashes, a new bird. Thus it was a symbol of immortality, as .well as of desire rising from its own exhaustion. "Eagle" and "dove" are also alchemical terms for processes leading to the rise of "phoenix," a stage in the transmutation of metals.

By us: we two being one, are it.
So, to one neutral thing both sexes fit.   25
   We die and rise the same, and prove
   Mysterious by this love.

We can die by it, if not live by love,
   And if unfit for tombs and hearse
Our legend be, it will be fit for verse;   30
   And if no piece of chronicle we prove,
     We'll build in sonnets pretty rooms;
     As well a well-wrought urn becomes
The greatest ashes, as half-acre tombs,
   And by these hymns,[8] all shall approve   35
   Us canonized for love:

And thus invoke us: You whom reverend love
   Made one another's hermitage;
You, to whom love was peace, that now is rage;
   Who did the whole world's soul contract,[8a] and drove   40
     Into the glasses of your eyes
     (So made such mirrors, and such spies,
That they did all to you epitomize)
   Countries, towns, courts: Beg from above
   A pattern of your love![9]   45

1633

Twicknam Garden[1]

Blasted with sighs, and surrounded with tears,
   Hither I come to seek the spring,
   And at mine eyes, and at mine ears,
Receive such balms as else cure everything;
   But oh, self traitor, I do bring   5
The spider love, which transubstantiates all,
   And can convert manna to gall;[2]
And that this place may thoroughly be thought
   True paradise, I have the serpent brought.

'Twere wholesomer for me that winter did   10
   Benight the glory of this place,
   And that a grave frost did forbid

8. Donne's own poems, transformed into hymns in a new love-religion; "all": posterity.
8a. In line 40 Miss Gardner reads "extract" for "contract."
9. The poet and his mistress, turned to saints, are implored by the rest of the population to get from heaven ("above") a pattern of their love for general distribution. "Countries, towns, courts" are objects of the verb "drove"; the notion that eyes both see and reflect the outside world, and so "contain" it doubly, was very delightful to Donne.
1. The poem takes its title from the country house at Twickenham Park, of Lucy, Countess of Bedford; she was one of Donne's patrons.
2. Love is a spider because it infuses its poison into every experience, turning one substance into another ("transubstantiates all"), and converting "manna," the essence of sweetness, to "gall," the essence of bitterness.

These trees to laugh and mock me to my face;
    But that I may not this disgrace
Endure, nor leave this garden, Love, let me   15
    Some senseless piece of this place be;
Make me a mandrake, so I may groan here,[3]
    Or a stone fountain weeping out my year.

Hither with crystal vials, lovers, come
    And take my tears, which are love's wine,   20
    And try your mistress' tears at home,
For all are false that taste not just like mine;
    Alas, hearts do not in eyes shine,
Nor can you more judge woman's thoughts by tears,
    Than by her shadow what she wears.   25
O perverse sex, where none is true but she,
    Who's therefore true, because her truth kills me.

                                        1633

The Apparition

When by thy scorn, O murderess, I am dead,
And that thou thinkst thee free
From all solicitation from me,
Then shall my ghost come to thy bed,
And thee, feigned vestal,[4] in worse arms shall see;   5
Then thy sick taper will begin to wink,
And he whose thou art then, being tired before,
Will, if thou stir, or pinch to wake him, think
    Thou call'st for more,
And in false sleep will from thee shrink,   10
And then, poor aspen wretch,[5] neglected thou
Bathed in a cold quicksilver sweat[6] wilt lie
    A verier ghost than I;
What I will say, I will not tell thee now,
Lest that preserve thee; and since my love is spent,   15
I had rather thou shouldst painfully repent,
Than by my threatenings rest still innocent.

                                        1633

Love's Alchemy

Some that have deeper digged love's mine than I,
Say where his centric happiness doth lie;

---

3. The mandrake, also called mandragora, was popularly thought to shriek when uprooted.
4. In Roman history the "vestals" were sacred virgins.
5. Aspen leaves flutter in the slightest breeze.
6. Sweating in terror; with an added innuendo from the circumstance that quicksilver (mercury) was a stock prescription for venereal disease.

I have loved, and got, and told,
But should I love, get, tell, till I we old,
I should not find that hidden mystery;   5
    O, 'tis imposture all:
And as no chemic yet the elixir got,[1]
    But glorifies his pregnant pot,[2]
    If by the way to him befall
Some odoriferous thing, or medicinal;   10
    So lovers dream a rich and long delight,
    But get a winter-seeming summer's night.

Our ease, our thrift, our honor, and our day,
Shall we for this vain bubble's shadow pay?
    Ends love in this, that my man   15
Can be as happy as I can if he can
Endure the short scorn of a bridegroom's play?
    That loving wretch that swears,
'Tis not the bodies marry, but the minds,
    Which he in her angelic finds,   20
    Would swear as justly that he hears,
In that day's rude hoarse minstrelsy, the spheres.[3]
    Hope not for mind in women; at their best
    Sweetness and wit they are, but mummy, possessed.[4]

                                  1633

The Flea

Mark but this flea, and mark in this,
How little that which thou deniest me is;
Me it sucked first, and now sucks thee,
And in this flea our two bloods mingled be;
Thou know'st that this cannot be said   5
A sin, or shame, or loss of maidenhead,
    Yet this enjoys before it woo,
    And pampered swells with one blood made of two,
    And this, alas, is more than we would do.[1]

Oh stay, three lives in one flea spare,   10
Where we almost, nay more than married, are.
This flea is you and I, and this

1. "Chemic": alchemist; "the elixir":
a magic medicine sought by alchemists
and reputed to heal all ills.
2. Praises his fertile (and womb-
shaped) retort.
3. The perfect harmony of the planets,
moving in concentric crystalline spheres,
is contrasted with the charivari, a boisterous serenade for pots, pans, and
trumpets, performed on the wedding
night.
4. Almost all punctuation for the last

two lines represents conjectures by modern editors. There might equally well be
commas after "best" and "wit." The
last word, "possessed," may modify
"mummy," meaning "mummy with a
demon in it," or else "they," meaning
"women who, when you have possessed
them, are nothing but dried mummy."
1. I.e., we, alas, don't dare hope for
this consummation of our love, which
the flea freely accepts. The idea of
swelling suggests that of pregnancy.

Our marriage bed and marriage temple is;
Though parents grudge, and you, we are met,
And cloistered in these living walls of jet,   15
  Though use[2] make you apt to kill me
  Let not to that, self-murder added be,
  And sacrilege, three sins in killing three.

Cruel and sudden, hast thou since
Purpled thy nail, in blood of innocence?[3]   20
Wherein could this flea guilty be,
Except in that drop which it sucked from thee?
Yet thou triumph'st, and say'st that thou
Find'st not thy self nor me the weaker now;
  'Tis true, then learn how false fears be;   25
  Just so much honor, when thou yield'st to me,
  Will waste, as this flea's death took life from thee.

                                                        1633

The Bait[4]

Come live with me and be my love,
And we will some new pleasures prove,
Of golden sands and crystal brooks,
With silken lines and silver hooks.

There will the river whispering run,   5
Warmed by thine eyes more than the sun.
And there th' enamored fish will stay,
Begging themselves they may betray.

When thou wilt swim in that live bath,
Each fish, which every channel hath,   10
Will amorously to thee swim,
Gladder to catch thee, than thou him.

If thou, to be so seen, beest loath,
By sun or moon, thou darkenest both;
And if myself have leave to see,   15
I need not their light, having thee.

Let others freeze with angling reeds,
And cut their legs with shells and weeds,
Or treacherously poor fish beset
With strangling snare, or windowy net.   20

Let coarse bold hands from slimy nest
The bedded fish in banks out-wrest,

2. Custom.
3. Like Herod, Donne's mistress has
slaughtered the innocents, and is now
clothed in imperial purple.
4. This poem is Donne's response to

Marlowe's *Passionate Shepherd to His
Love*. Another of the many replies was
Ralegh's *Nymph's Reply to the Shep-
herd*.

Or curious traitors, sleave-silk flies,[5]
Bewitch poor fishes' wandering eyes.

For thee, thou needest no such deceit,   25
For thou thyself art thine own bait;
That fish that is not catched thereby,
Alas, is wiser far than I.

1633

A Valediction: Forbidding Mourning[1]

As virtuous men pass mildly away,
    And whisper to their souls to go,
Whilst some of their sad friends do say
    The breath goes now, and some say, No;

So let us melt, and make no noise,   5
    No tear-floods, nor sigh-tempests move,
'Twere profanation of our joys
    To tell the laity our love.

Moving of th' earth brings harms and fears,
    Men reckon what it did and meant;   10
But trepidation of the spheres,
    Though greater far, is innocent.[2]

Dull sublunary[3] lovers' love
    (Whose soul[4] is sense) cannot admit
Absence, because it doth remove
    Those things which elemented[5] it.   15

But we by a love so much refined
    That our selves know not what it is,
Inter-assuréd of the mind,
    Care less, eyes, lips, and hands to miss.   20

Our two souls therefore, which are one,
    Though I must go, endure not yet
A breach, but an expansion,
    Like gold to airy thinness beat.

5. Flies of unraveled silk, floss-silk.

1. The particularly serious and steady tone of this poem may be due to the circumstances of its composition. Izaak Walton tells us it was addressed to Donne's wife on the occasion of his trip to the Continent in 1612. Donne had many forebodings of misfortune, which were verified when his wife gave birth to a stillborn child during his absence.

2. I.e., earthquakes are thought to threaten evil consequences, but the variations of the spheres from true circularity, though they involve greater motions, are not considered sinister. "Trepidation of the spheres" (literally, "shuddering") was an additional arbitrary motion of the eighth sphere, introduced into the Ptolemaic system about the year 950 to account for certain celestial phenomena which were really due to the wobbling of the earth on its axis.

3. Beneath the moon, therefore mundane and subject to change.

4. Essence.

5. Composed.

If they be two, they are two so   25
    As stiff twin compasses are two;
Thy soul, the fixed foot, makes no show
    To move, but doth, if th' other do.

And though it in the center sit,
    Yet when the other far doth roam,   30
It leans and hearkens after it,
    And grows erect, as it comes home.

Such wilt thou be to me, who must
    Like th' other foot, obliquely run;
Thy firmness makes my circle just,   35
    And makes me end where I begun.[6]

1633

The Ecstasy

Where, like a pillow on a bed,
    A pregnant bank swelled up to rest
The violet's reclining head,
    Sat we two, one another's best.
Our hands were firmly cemented   5
    With a fast balm, which thence did spring.
Our eye-beams twisted, and did thread
    Our eyes upon one double string;[1]
So to intergraft our hands, as yet
    Was all our means to make us one;   10
And pictures in our eyes to get
    Was all our propagation.
As 'twixt two equal armies, Fate
    Suspends uncertain victory,
Our souls (which to advance their state,   15
    Were gone out) hung 'twixt her and me.
And whilst our souls negotiate there,
    We like sepulchral statues lay;
All day the same our postures were,
    And we said nothing all the day.   20
If any, so by love refined
    That he soul's language understood,
And by good love were grown all mind,
    Within convenient distance stood,
He (though he know not which soul spake,   25
    Because both meant, both spake the same)
Might thence a new concoction[2] take,

6. The circle is an emblem of perfection; cf. also the motto of Mary, Queen of Scots, "In my end is my beginning." An excitingly complex, if perhaps overly medieval, reading of the poem is offered by John Freccero in *ELH*, XXX (December, 1963), 335–376.

1. Joining hands and eyes is the only intercourse of the two lovers: "eye-beams" are invisible shafts of light, thought of as going out of the eyes and so enabling one to see things.
2. Purified mixture.

And part far purer than he came.
This ecstasy doth unperplex,[3]
   We said, and tell us what we love;   30
We see by this it was not sex;
   We see we saw not what did move;[4]
But as all several souls contain
   Mixture of things, they know not what,
Love these mixed souls doth mix again,   35
   And makes both one, each this and that.
A single violet transplant,
   The strength, the colour, and the size
(All which before was poor, and scant)
   Redoubles still, and multiplies.   40
When love, with one another so
   Interinanimates two souls,
That abler soul, which thence doth flow,
   Defects of loneliness controls.[5]
We then, who are this new soul, know,   45
   Of what we are composed, and made,
For, th' atomies[6] of which we grow,
   Are souls, whom no change can invade.
But O alas, so long, so far
   Our bodies why do we forbear?   50
They are ours, though they are not we; we are
   The intelligences, they the sphere.[7]
We owe them thanks because they thus,
   Did us to us at first convey,
Yielded their forces, sense, to us,   55
   Nor are dross to us, but allay.[8]
On man heaven's influence works not so
   But that it first imprints the air,[9]
So soul into the soul may flow,
   Though it to body first repair.   60
As our blood labors to beget
   Spirits as like souls as it can,[1]
Because such fingers need to knit
   That subtle knot which makes us man:
So must pure lovers' souls descend   65
   T' affections, and to faculties
Which sense may reach and apprehend;

3. I.e., separate and clarify.
4. I.e., we see that we did not understand before what motivated ("did move") us.
5. The "abler soul" which derives from the union of two lesser ones can eliminate the loneliness with which each in itself is afflicted.
6. Atoms.
7. Medieval astronomers believed that the planets, set in crystalline spheres, were inhabited by "intelligences" which guided and controlled them. Similarly, Donne says, our bodies are guided and controlled by our selves.
8. "Dross" is an impurity which weakens metal, "allay" (alloy) an impurity which strengthens it. Our bodies contribute sensation ("sense") to the soul, and so reinforce it.
9. Astrological influences were thought to work on man through the surrounding air.
1. "Animal spirits" were thought to be begotten by the blood, to serve as intermediaries between body and soul.

Else a great Prince in prison lies.
To our bodies turn we then, that so
　　Weak men on love revealed may look;　　　　　70
Love's mysteries in souls do grow,
　　But yet the body is his book.[2]
And if some lover, such as we,
　　Have heard this dialogue of one,[3]
Let him still mark us; he shall see　　　　　75
　　Small change when we are to bodies gone.

　　　　　　　　　　　　　　　　1633

Lovers' Infiniteness

If yet I have not all[4] thy love,
Dear, I shall never have it all;
I cannot breathe one other sigh to move,
Nor can entreat one other tear to fall;
All my treasure, which should purchase thee,　　　5
Sighs, tears, and oaths, and letters, I have spent.
Yet no more can be due to me
Than at the bargain made was meant;
If then thy gift of love were partial,
That some to me, some should to others fall,　　　10
　　Dear, I shall never have thee all.

Or if then thou gavest me all,
All was but all which thou hadst then;
But if in thy heart since there be or shall
New love created be by other men,　　　15
Which have their stocks entire, and can in tears,
In sighs, in oaths, and letters outbid me,
This new love may beget new fears,
For this love was not vowed by thee.
And yet it was, thy gift being general;　　　20
The ground, thy heart, is mine; whatever shall
　　Grow there, dear, I should have it all.

Yet I would not have all yet.
He that hath all can have no more;
And since my love doth every day admit　　　25
New growth, thou shouldst have new rewards in store.
Thou canst not every day give me thy heart;
If thou canst give it, then thou never gavest it.
Love's riddles are, that though thy heart depart,

2. I.e., love, a god within man, puts forth in the body a book where his mysteries may be read (as God the Creator put forth the book of Nature and the book of Scripture).
3. The characteristic Donne poem might be described as a "dialogue of one."
4. The influence of Donne's legal training is very clear here; the poem is a series of technical verbal quibbles on the word "all."

It stays at home, and thou with losing savest it.   30
But we will have a way more liberal
Than changing hearts, to join them;[5] so we shall
    Be one, and one another's all.

1633

The Sun Rising

    Busy old fool, unruly sun,
      Why dost thou thus,
Through windows and through curtains call on us?
Must to thy motions lovers' seasons run?
    Saucy pedantic wretch, go chide   5
      Late school boys and sour prentices,
  Go tell court huntsmen that the King will ride,
  Call country ants to harvest offices;[1]
Love, all alike, no season knows nor clime,
Nor hours, days, months, which are the rags of time.   10

    Thy beams, so reverend and strong
      Why shouldst thou think?
I could eclipse and cloud them with a wink,
But that I would not lose her sight so long;
    If her eyes have not blinded thine,   15
      Look, and tomorrow late, tell me,
  Whether both th' Indias of spice and mine[2]
  Be where thou leftst them, or lie here with me.
Ask for those kings whom thou saw'st yesterday,
And thou shalt hear, All here in one bed lay.   20

    She is all states, and all princes, I,
      Nothing else is.
Princes do but play us; compared to this,
All honor's mimic, all wealth alchemy.[3]
    Thou, sun, art half as happy as we,   25
      In that the world's contracted thus;
  Thine age asks ease, and since thy duties be
  To warm the world, that's done in warming us.
Shine here to us, and thou art everywhere;
This bed thy center is,[4] these walls, thy sphere.   30

1633

5. To join hearts is more liberal than to "change" (exchange) them; "liberal" implies amorous generosity, also relief from legal hairsplitting.
1. Harvest chores, duties.

2. The India of "spice" is East India, that of "mine" (gold), the West Indies.
3. I.e., metaphorically, fraudulent.
4. The "center" of the sun's orbit.

Air and Angels

Twice or thrice had I loved thee,
Before I knew thy face or name;
So in a voice, so in a shapeless flame,
Angels affect us oft, and worshiped be;
     Still when, to where thou wert, I came,   5
Some lovely glorious nothing I did see.
     But since my soul, whose child love is,
Takes limbs of flesh, and else could nothing do,
     More subtle than the parent is
Love must not be, but take a body too;   10
     And therefore what thou wert, and who,
       I bid love ask, and now
That it assume thy body I allow,
And fix itself in thy lip, eye, and brow.

Whilst thus to ballast love I thought,   15
And so more steadily to have gone,
With wares which would sink admiration,
I saw I had love's pinnace overfraught;[1]
     Every thy hair[2] for love to work upon
Is much too much, some fitter must be sought;   20
     For, nor in nothing, nor in things
Extreme and scatt'ring[3] bright, can love inhere.
     Then as an angel, face and wings
Of air, not pure as it, yet pure doth wear,
     So thy love may be my love's sphere.[4]   25
       Just such disparity
As is 'twixt air and angels' purity,
'Twixt women's love and men's will ever be.

                    1633

Break of Day[5]

'Tis true, 'tis day; what though it be?
O wilt thou therefore rise from me?

1. Her physical beauty (his "wares") would sink admiration—i.e., overwhelm wonder itself. This is too much ballast for love's "pinnace" (a small boat).
2. I.e., each hair of thine.
3. Diffused, dazzling.
4. Some Scholastic philosophers held that angels, when they appeared to men, assumed a body of air. Such a body, though pure, was less so than the angel's spiritual being. Similarly, women's love, which Donne thinks *less* pure than that of men, may still serve as the receptacle ("sphere") for the love of men.
5. Modeled on the Provençal aubade, or song of the lovers' parting at dawn, this poem is a departure for Donne in that it assumes a feminine point of view. As a rule, he is among the most consistently masculine of poets.

Why should we rise, because 'tis light?
Did we lie down, because 'twas night?
Love, which in spite of darkness brought us hither,   5
Should in despite of light keep us together.

Light hath no tongue, but is all eye;
If it could speak as well as spy,
This were the worst that it could say,
That being well, I fain would stay,   10
And that I loved my heart and honor so,
That I would not from him, that had them, go.

Must business thee from hence remove?
O, that's the worst disease of love.
The poor, the foul, the false, love can   15
Admit, but not the busied man.
He which hath business, and makes love, doth do
Such wrong, as when a married man doth woo.

                                     1633

A Valediction: Of Weeping

          Let me pour forth
My tears before thy face whilst I stay here,
For thy face coins them, and thy stamp they bear,
And by this mintage they are something worth,
           For thus they be   5
           Pregnant of thee;
Fruits of much grief they are, emblems of more—
When a tear falls, that Thou falls which it bore,
So thou and I are nothing then, when on a diverse shore.[1]

          On a round ball   10
A workman that hath copies by, can lay
An Europe, Afric, and an Asia,
And quickly make that, which was nothing, all;[2]
           So doth each tear
           Which thee doth wear,   15
A globe, yea world, by that impression grow,
Till thy tears mixed with mine do overflow
This world; by waters sent from thee, my heaven dissolvéd so.[3]

          O more than moon,
Draw not up seas to drown me in thy sphere;   20

1. The loss of the lovers in their separation is figured in the fall of a tear which contains the image of the mistress.
2. I.e., on a blank globe an artist can draw the world, and so convert a cipher, the image of nothingness, to the whole world.
3. In describing Creation, Genesis i.6–7 makes mention of certain heavenly waters, some above and some below the firmament. Their existence and function has been much debated by Bible scholars.

Weep me not dead, in thine arms, but forbear
To teach the sea what it may do too soon.
    Let not the wind
    Example find
To do me more harm than it purposeth;   25
Since thou and I sigh one another's breath,
Whoe'er sighs most is cruelest, and hastes the other's death.[4]

              1633

The Funeral

Whoever comes to shroud me, do not harm
    Nor question much
That subtle wreath of hair which crowns my arm;
The mystery, the sign you must not touch,
    For 'tis my outward soul,   5
Viceroy to that, which then to heaven being gone,
    Will leave this to control,
And keep these limbs, her provinces, from dissolution.

For if the sinewy thread[1] my brain lets fall
    Through every part   10
Can tie those parts and make me one of all;
These hairs, which upward grew, and strength and art
    Have from a better brain,
Can better do it; except she meant that I
    By this should know my pain,   15
As prisoners then are manacled, when they're condemned to die.

Whate'er she meant by it, bury it with me,
    For since I am
Love's martyr, it might breed idolatry,
If into others' hands these relics came;   20
    As 'twas humility[2]
To afford to it all that a soul can do,
    So 'tis some bravery,
That since you would save none of me, I bury some of you.

              1633

The Relic

    When my grave is broke up again
    Some second guest to entertain
    (For graves have learned that woman-head[1]
    To be to more than one a bed),

4. The breath of life has been interchanged between the lovers.
1. The spinal cord and nervous system.
2. It was humility to grant, in the first thirteen and a half lines of the poem, that her hair could act as a soul; it is also "bravery" (defiance) to bury a part of the mistress in revenge for her cruelty.
1. I.e., characteristic of women. On the re-use of graves, see Sir Thomas Browne's *Urn-Burial* and *Hamlet* V.i.

And he that digs it, spies 5
A bracelet of bright hair about the bone,
Will he not let us alone,
And think that there a loving couple lies,
Who thought that this device might be some way
To make their souls, at the last busy day, 10
Meet at this grave, and make a little stay?

If this fall in a time, or land,
Where mis-devotion[2] doth command,
Then he that digs us up, will bring
Us to the Bishop and the King, 15
To make us relics; then
Thou shalt be a Mary Magdalen, and I
A something else thereby;[3]
All women shall adore us, and some men;
And since at such time, miracles are sought, 20
I would have that age by this paper taught
What miracles we harmless lovers wrought.

First, we loved well and faithfully,
Yet knew not what we loved, nor why,
Difference of sex no more we knew, 25
Than our guardian angels do;
Coming and going, we
Perchance might kiss, but not between those meals;[4]
Our hands ne'er touched the seals,
Which nature, injured by late law, sets free:
These miracles we did; but now, alas, 30
All measure and all language I should pass,
Should I tell what a miracle she was.

1633

To the Countess of Bedford[1]

MADAM,
Reason is our soul's left hand, faith her right,
By these we reach divinity, that's you;

2. False devotion, superstition. Donne
seems to have in mind Roman Catholicism.
3. The rhythm of "something else"
suggests the complete but blasphemous
parallel, "Jesus Christ."
4. The kiss of salutation and parting
was, in the 17th century, a peculiarly
English custom; the passage that follows seems to suggest some greater intimacy, permitted by nature, but unjustly abridged by "late law." It is hard

to imagine what Donne had in mind
here; he was not opposed to the sacrament of matrimony, and the laws of
marriage could not be called "late,"
i.e., recent.
1. The social relations implied in this
verse letter offer an interesting puzzle.
Lucy, Countess of Bedford, was a gay,
rich, clever, and decorative lady in a
very worldly court; Donne was an eager, clever climber; not yet in holy or-

Their loves, who have the blessings of your light,
Grew from their reason, mine from fair faith grew.

But as, although a squint left-handedness   5
Be ungracious, yet we cannot want[2] that hand,
So would I, not to increase, but to express
My faith, as I believe, so understand.[3]

Therefore I study you first in your saints,
Those friends whom your election glorifies,   10
Then in your deeds, accesses, and restraints,
And what you read, and what yourself devise.

But soon the reasons why you are loved by all
Grow infinite, and so pass reason's reach,
Then back again to implicit faith I fall,   15
And rest on what the catholic[4] voice doth teach;

That you are good: and not one heretic
Denies it: if he did, yet you are so.
For, rocks which high-topped and deep-rooted stick,
Waves wash, not undermine, nor overthrow.   20

In every thing there naturally grows
A balsamum,[5] to keep it fresh and new,
If 'twere not injured by extrinsic blows;
Your birth and beauty are this balm in you.

But you of learning and religion,   25
And virtue, and such ingredients, have made
A mithridate,[6] whose operation
Keeps off, or cures, what can be done or said.

Yet, this is not your physic[7] but your food,
A diet fit for you; for you are here   30
The first good angel, since the world's frame stood,
That ever did in woman's shape appear.

Since you are then God's masterpiece, and so
His factor[8] for our loves; do as you do,

ders, disgraced by his rash marriage,
and, as he clearly says in the poem,
altogether unknown to the lady. His
poem is in the audacious, semi-blas-
phemous tone of courtly adulation;
would her response have taken the
form of an invitation to dinner, an
assignation, a religious homily, or a
bank note? Donne wrote numerous verse
letters, including several later ones to
the Countess of Bedford.
2. Do without, lack.
3. He requests the pleasure of her acquaintance.
4. Universal.
5. Paracelsus and other early physicians have much to say of a natural

balsam, or balm, which preserves life
and cures all human ailments.
6. From Mithridates, the Persian king,
who (it is related) ate poisons in small
doses to render himself immune from
large ones; hence, an immunizing dose.
7. Medicine.
8. A factor is one who does business for
another, an agent. The sense of the last
stanza is dark. "Home" (line 35) and
"there" (line 37) certainly refer to
heaven; he is, then, asking her to become a saint and intervene with God
in his behalf, rather than help him in a
worldly sense, the shape of which remains rather ill-defined.

Make your return home gracious; and bestow   35
This life on that; so make one life of two.
    For so God help me, I would not miss you there
For all the good which you can do me here.

1633

Elegy IV. The Perfume[1]

Once, and but once found in thy company,
All thy supposed escapes are laid on me;
And as a thief at bar is questioned there
By all the men that have been robbed that year,
So am I (by this traitorous means surprised),   5
By thy hydroptic[2] father catechized.
Though he had wont to search with glazéd eyes,
As though he came to kill a cockatrice,[3]
Though he hath often sworn that he would remove
Thy beauty's beauty, and food of our love,   10
Hope of his goods, if I with thee were seen,
Yet close and secret as our souls we have been.
Though thy immortal mother, which doth lie
Still buried in her bed, yet will not die,
Takes this advantage to sleep out day light,   15
And watch thy entries and returns all night,
And when she takes thy hand, and would seem kind,
Doth search what rings and armlets she can find,
And, kissing, notes the color of thy face,
And, fearing lest thou art swollen, doth thee embrace;   20

1. In Latin poetry, an elegy is not necessarily a funeral lament, but may be simply a discursive or reflective poem written in elegiac meter (alternating dactylic pentameters and hexameters). In English, the genre has been even vaguer, partly because this metrical pattern is unusual; and many early poems in pentameter couplets have been classified as elegies simply because they discussed some matter more or less consecutively and seriously. Twenty poems by Donne are customarily grouped together as elegies; they are not so rough as the satires nor so clearly musical as many of the *Songs and Sonnets*, but to find any other common denominator will not be easy. They include dramatic sketches and monologues, short stories in verse, satires, jokes, epigrams, and simple love lyrics. Apparently they were written over a considerable period of time, and with no single purpose or unifying theme in mind.

    Elegy IV is rowdy and cynical, with a "low" point of view and a sour, suspicious eye for everyone's worst motives—including the poet's own. The poem is addressed to the speaker's mistress, a girl living with her parents. (Others of the elegies are to married women, court ladies, or to nobody in particular.) The circumstances of the poem suggest a middle-class family, probably of merchant status; the poet assumes the part of an adventurer, ruthless and greedy. Clearly Donne is playing here with a situation. Hence the word "escapes," meaning "sexual lapses," is not really an insult, for the whole situation is that of a comic story of sexual misadventure.

2. Thirsty for information, curious; with the additional overtone of "dropsical," i.e., swollen with disease and money, flabby.

3. The cockatrice, or basilisk, was a fabulous beast, reputed to kill its enemies by its very glance; the girl's father is so suspicious of the speaker that he scarcely looks at him. In this situation of unmasked social warfare, the speaker can admit that for him the beauty of the girl's beauty (i.e., its essence) is hope of her father's goods.

And to try if thou long, doth name strange meats,
And notes thy paleness, blushing, sighs, and sweats;[4]
And politicly[5] will to thee confess
The sins of her own youth's rank lustiness;
Yet Love these sorceries did remove, and move   25
Thee to gull[6] thine own mother for my love.
Thy little brethren, which like fairy sprites
Oft skipped into our chamber, those sweet nights,
And kissed and ingled[7] on thy father's knee,
Were bribed next day to tell what they did see: 30
The grim, eight-foot-high, iron-bound serving-man,
That oft names God in oaths, and only then,
He that to bar the first gate doth as wide
As the great Rhodian Colossus[8] stride,
Which, if in hell no other pains there were,   35
Makes me fear hell, because he must be there:
Though by thy father he were hired to this,
Could never witness any touch or kiss.
But O, too common ill, I brought with me
That which betrayed me to my enemy,   40
A loud perfume, which at my entrance cried
Even at thy father's nose, so we were spied.
When, like a tyrant king that in his bed
Smelt gunpowder, the pale wretch shiveréd.[9]
Had it been some bad smell, he would have thought   45
That his own feet, or breath, that smell had wrought.
But as we, in our isle imprisonéd,
Where cattle only, and divers dogs are bred,
The precious unicorns strange monsters call,
So thought he good, strange, that had none at all.[1]   50
I taught my silks their whistling to forbear,
Even my oppressed shoes dumb and speechless were,
Only thou bitter-sweet, whom I had laid
Next me, me traitorously hast betrayed,
And unsuspected hast invisibly   55
At once fled unto him, and stayed with me.
Base excrement of earth, which dost confound
Sense from distinguishing the sick from sound;
By thee the silly amorous sucks his death
By drawing in a leprous harlot's breath;   60
By thee the greatest stain to man's estate
Falls on us, to be called effeminate;

---

4. All the stock tests for pregnancy are being applied.
5. With policy (in order to provoke a counter-confession from her daughter).
6. Fool, deceive.
7. Fondled, caressed.
8. The giant statue of Apollo at Rhodes was one of the seven wonders of the ancient world.
9. The reference may be to James I and the Gunpowder Plot, which would date the poem sometime after 1605.
1. I.e., knowing only local cattle, we think unicorns strange, even though they are precious; so he, who had no proper sense of smell, thought even a good odor strange. Only in Donne's poetry do we find rarefied reflections like this rising from the smell of a man's feet.

Though you be much loved in the prince's hall,
There, things that seem exceed substantial;[2]
Gods, when ye fumed on altars,[3] were pleased well   65
Because you were burnt, not that they liked your smell;
You are loathsome all, being taken simply alone,
Shall we love ill things joined, and hate each one?[4]
If you were good, your good doth soon decay;
And you are rare, that takes the good away.[5]   70
All my perfumes I give most willingly
To embalm thy father's corpse; What? will he die?[6]

1633

2. I.e., at court more attention is paid to empty appearances than to matters of substance.
3. Incense.
4. The ingredients in perfume are often unpleasant individually; why should we like the end product?
5. I.e., that (your rarity) spoils any good you may possess.
6. The word "corpse" gives the speaker sudden hope.

Satire III, Religion

For the first time in English literary history, the mode of satire flourished in the last decade of Elizabeth's reign and under the first two Stuarts. Many social circumstances contributed to its popularity: a surplus of clever young men without jobs, bitter antipathies between social classes and groups, and a general spirit of disillusion and doubt which has been characterized as "Jacobean melancholy."

Out of this mood of prolonged doubt, search, and obstinate questioning came the five satires of John Donne. *Satire III, Religion* is not a satire in the customary sense of a mocking attack on some person or custom. It is a strenuous, inconclusive discussion of an acute theological problem: How may a man recognize the true church, to which all Christians claim to belong? The person to whom it is addressed is evidently a man without specific religious commitment, but with a great and anxious interest in religion, and a specially nervous feeling that the claims of Roman Catholicism may be justified. He has been a sailor, a soldier, a bit of a rake, a bit of a theologian; he has more than a smattering of law. In many small ways, he reminds us of young Jack Donne himself. But the most characteristic thing about this poem on the search for certainty is the toughness of mind which it evinces throughout. Donne's images have a raw, contemptuous force, his phrasing is clipped, his grammar and his meter are twisted by the energy of his argument. He has no easy answer for the question raised, and makes no effort to charm or lull the reader. His poem is sheer display of intellectual force, a pointed, inconclusive game of mind.

Satire III, Religion

Kind pity chokes my spleen; brave scorn forbids
Those tears to issue which swell my eyelids;
I must not laugh, nor weep sins, and be wise,

Can railing then cure these worn maladies?
Is not our mistress, fair Religion,   5
As worthy of all our souls' devotion,
As virtue was to the first blinded age?[1]
Are not heaven's joys as valiant to assuage
Lusts, as earth's honor was to them?[2] Alas,
As we do them in means, shall they surpass   10
Us in the end, and shall thy father's spirit
Meet blind philosophers in heaven, whose merit
Of strict life may be imputed faith,[3] and hear
Thee, whom he taught so easy ways and near
To follow, damned? O, if thou dar'st, fear this;   15
This fear great courage and high valor is.
Dar'st thou aid mutinous Dutch,[4] and dar'st thou lay
Thee in ships, wooden sepulchers, a prey
To leaders' rage, to storms, to shot, to dearth?
Dar'st thou dive seas and dungeons of the earth?   20
Hast thou courageous fire to thaw the ice
Of frozen North discoveries? and thrice
Colder than salamanders,[5] like divine
Children in the oven,[6] fires of Spain, and the line,
Whose countries limbecks to our bodies be,   25
Canst thou for gain bear?[7] And must every he
Which cries not, "Goddess!" to thy mistress, draw,[8]
Or eat thy poisonous words? Courage of straw!
O desperate coward, wilt thou seem bold, and
To thy foes and his[9] (who made thee to stand   30
Sentinel in his world's garrison) thus yield,
And for forbidden wars, leave th' appointed field?
Know thy foes: The foul Devil (whom thou
Strivest to please) for hate, not love, would allow
Thee fain his whole realm to be quit;[1] and as   35
The world's all parts[2] wither away and pass,
So the world's self, thy other loved foe, is
In her decrepit wane, and thou, loving this,
Dost love a withered and worn strumpet; last,

1. The age of paganism, blind to the light of Christianity, but capable of following natural morality ("virtue").
2. I.e., hope of heaven should be as powerful ("valiant") an antidote to sin in us as earthly honor was to "them"—the pagans.
3. Even without Christian faith, pagan philosophers may achieve heaven (see *The Divine Comedy, Paradiso* XX) by an extraordinary display of virtue which causes faith to be imputed to them.
4. The Dutch continually enlisted English volunteers in their rebellious wars against the Spaniards. Donne had never fought in Flanders, though he had sailed twice against the Spaniards, to Cadiz and the Azores.
5. The salamander was traditionally so cold-blooded that it could live even in a fire.
6. The "divine children in the oven" are Shadrach, Meshach, and Abednego, rescued from the fiery furnace in Daniel iii.
7. The object of "bear" is "fires of Spain, and the line"—Inquisitorial and equatorial heats, which roast men as chemists heat materials in "limbecks" (alembics, or retorts for distilling).
8. I.e., fight a duel.
9. God's.
1. I.e., the Devil would gladly give you a free hand with his whole kingdom.
2. All parts of the world. It was a common belief in the 17th century that the world was getting old and decrepit.

Flesh (itself's death) and joys which flesh can taste,   40
Thou lovest; and thy fair goodly soul, which doth
Give this flesh power to taste joy, thou dost loathe.
Seek true religion. O, where? Mirreus,[3]
Thinking her unhoused here, and fled from us,
Seeks her at Rome; there, because he doth know   45
That she was there a thousand years ago.
He loves her rags so, as we here obey
The statecloth[4] where the Prince sat yesterday.
Crantz to such brave loves will not be enthralled,
But loves her only, who at Geneva is called   50
Religion—plain, simple, sullen, young,
Contemptuous, yet unhandsome; as among
Lecherous humors,[5] there is one that judges
No wenches wholesome but coarse country drudges.
Graius stays still at home here, and because   55
Some preachers, vile ambitious bawds, and laws
Still new, like fashions, bid him think that she
Which dwells with us, is only perfect, he
Embraceth her whom his Godfathers will
Tender to him, being tender, as wards still   60
Take such wives as their guardians offer, or
Pay values.[6] Careless Phrygius doth abhor
All, because all cannot be good, as one
Knowing some women whores, dares marry none.
Graccus loves all as one, and thinks that so   65
As women do in divers countries go
In divers habits, yet are still one kind,
So doth, so is religion; and this blind-
ness too much light breeds; but unmoved thou
Of force must one, and forced but one allow;   70
And the right;[7] ask thy father which is she,
Let him ask his; though truth and falsehood be
Near twins, yet truth a little elder is;
Be busy to seek her, believe me this,
He's not of none, nor worst, that seeks the best.[8]   75
To adore, or scorn an image, or protest,
May all be bad; doubt wisely; in strange way
To stand inquiring right, is not to stray;
To sleep, or run wrong, is. On a huge hill,
Cragged and steep, Truth stands, and he that will   80

3. The imaginary characters in this passage represent different creeds. "Mirreus" is a Roman Catholic, "Crantz" a Geneva Presbyterian, "Graius" an Erastian (i.e., believing in any religion sponsored by the state), "Phrygius" a skeptic, and "Graccus" a Universalist.
4. The royal canopy, a symbol of kingly power.
5. Tempers, temperaments.
6. Young men (of "tender" years) might reject the wives offered ("tendered") them by their guardians; but, if they did so, had to pay "values," i.e. fines.
7. I.e., being blind to the differences between religions, Graccus has too much light to see anything (lines 68–69). But the poet insists that without being swayed by human pressures, we must find just one true religion, "the right" true religion.
8. The man who seeks the best church is neither an unbeliever nor the worst sort of believer.

Reach her, about must, and about must go,
And what the hill's suddenness resists, win so;
Yet strive so, that before age, death's twilight,
Thy soul rest, for none can work in that night.
To will[9] implies delay, therefore now do.   85
Hard deeds, the body's pains; hard knowledge too
The mind's endeavors reach,[1] and mysteries
Are like the sun, dazzling, yet plain to all eyes.
Keep the truth which thou hast found; men do not stand
In so ill case here, that God hath with his hand   90
Signed kings' blank charters to kill whom they hate,
Nor are they vicars, but hangmen to fate.[2]
Fool and wretch, wilt thou let thy soul be tied
To man's laws, by which she shall not be tried
At the last day? O, will it then boot thee   95
To say a Philip, or a Gregory,
A Harry, or a Martin taught thee this?[3]
Is not this excuse for mere contraries
Equally strong? Cannot both sides say so?
That thou mayest rightly obey power, her bounds know;   100
Those passed, her nature and name is changed; to be
Then humble to her is idolatry.[4]
As streams are, power is; those blest flowers that dwell
At the rough stream's calm head, thrive and do well,
But having left their roots, and themselves given   105
To the stream's tyrannous rage, alas, are driven
Through mills, and rocks, and woods, and at last, almost
Consumed in going, in the sea are lost.
So perish souls, which more choose men's unjust
Power from God claimed, than God himself to trust.   110

                                                          1633

Good Friday, 1613. Riding Westward

Let man's soul be a sphere, and then, in this,
The intelligence that moves, devotion is,[1]
And as the other spheres, by being grown
Subject to foreign motions, lose their own,
And being by others hurried every day,   5

9. To intend a future action.
1. I.e., the body's pains achieve ("reach") hard deeds; the mind's endeavors will reach hard knowledge.
2. Human authority does not represent divine justice on earth; men are not God's vicars on earth (the hit here is at both the Pope and the secular monarch), but his hangmen at best—agents through whom his justice is fulfilled without carte blanche ("blank charters") to use their own judgments.
3. "Philip" is Philip II of Spain, and "Gregory" any one of several Pope Gregories (VII, XIII, XIV); "Harry" is England's Henry VIII, and "Martin" is Martin Luther. Laymen and clergy, Protestants and Catholics, all are covered. "Boot": profit.
4. I.e., when the true limits of ecclesiastical power have been passed, obedience becomes idolatry.
1. As intelligences guide the visible planets, devotion is or should be the guiding principle of man's life.

Scarce in a year their natural form obey;
Pleasure or business, so, our souls admit
For their first mover, and are whirled by it.[2]
Hence is 't, that I am carried towards the West
This day, when my soul's form bends towards the East.   10
There I should see a Sun,[3] by rising, set,
And by that setting endless day beget:
But that Christ on this cross did rise and fall,
Sin had eternally benighted all.
Yet dare I almost be glad I do not see   15
That spectacle, of too much weight for me.
Who sees God's face, that is self-life, must die;
What a death were it then to see God die?
It made his own lieutenant, Nature, shrink;
It made his footstool crack, and the sun wink.[4]   20
Could I behold those hands which span the poles,
And tune all spheres at once, pierced with those holes?
Could I behold that endless height which is
Zenith to us, and our antipodes,[5]
Humbled below us? Or that blood which is   25
The seat of all our souls, if not of His,
Make dirt of dust, or that flesh which was worn
By God, for his apparel, ragg'd and torn?
If on these things I durst not look, durst I
Upon his miserable mother cast mine eye,   30
Who was God's partner here, and furnished thus
Half of that sacrifice which ransomed us?
Though these things, as I ride, be from mine eye,
They are present yet unto my memory,
For that looks towards them; and Thou look'st towards me,   35
O Saviour, as Thou hang'st upon the tree.
I turn my back to Thee but to receive
Corrections, till Thy mercies bid Thee leave.
O think me worth Thine anger; punish me;
Burn off my rusts and my deformity;   40
Restore Thine image so much, by Thy grace,
That Thou may'st know me, and I'll turn my face.

           1633

From Holy Sonnets[1]

1

Thou hast made me, and shall Thy work decay?
Repair me now, for now mine end doth haste;

2. I.e., spheres are deflected from their true orbits by outside influences; so our souls are deflected by business or pleasure.
3. The sun-Son pun was an ancient one. Christ, the Son of God, set when he rose on the Cross, and his setting (death) gave rise to the Christian era.
4. An earthquake and eclipse supposedly accompanied the Crucifixion.
5. "Zenith" and "antipodes" are the highest and farthest reach of heaven.
1. Several of the *Holy Sonnets* contain specific indications of date; number 17

I run to death, and death meets me as fast,
And all my pleasures are like yesterday.
I dare not move my dim eyes any way,   5
Despair behind, and death before doth cast
Such terror, and my feeble flesh doth waste
By sin in it, which it towards hell doth weigh.
Only Thou art above, and when towards Thee
By Thy leave I can look, I rise again;   10
But our old subtle foe so tempteth me
That not one hour myself I can sustain.
Thy grace may wing me to prevent his art,
And Thou like adamant draw mine iron heart.[2]

                                                    1633

5

I am a little world made cunningly
Of elements, and an angelic sprite;[3]
But black sin hath betrayed to endless night
My world's both parts, and O, both parts must die.
You which beyond that heaven which was most high   5
Have found new spheres, and of new lands can write,[4]
Pour new seas in mine eyes, that so I might
Drown my world with my weeping earnestly,
Or wash it if it must be drowned no more.[5]
But O, it must be burnt! Alas, the fire   10
Of lust and envy have burnt it heretofore,
And made it fouler; let their flames retire,
And burn me, O Lord, with a fiery zeal
Of Thee and Thy house, which doth in eating heal.[6]

                                                    1635

7

At the round earth's imagined corners,[7] blow
Your trumpets, angels; and arise, arise

makes reference to the recent death of Donne's wife (August 15, 1617) and number 18 may have been inspired by the Elector Palatine's defeat (October 29, 1620). But most are considerably earlier (1609–10). They are nineteen in number, conventional in their rhyme scheme and broad metrical pattern, but rhythmically bold, powerful in their imagery, and marked by deep emotional coloring. Donne's religion was never a secure or comfortable experience; his *Holy Sonnets* are documents which mingle anguished despair with no less anguished hope. And in a sonnet like *Holy Sonnet 14,* his faith rises to a series of knotted paradoxes involving coercion and submission, which would be revolting were it not for the full and evident sincerity of the mind to which they were inevitable.

2. "Wing": strengthen; "prevent":

counteract; "adamant": loadstone. Note throughout the sonnets a combination of strong imperatives and protestations of abject helplessness which determines the tone of Donne's religious feeling.
3. Both body and soul—the former made of "elements," the latter "angelic sprite" (spirit).
4. Donne asks the astronomers and explorers to find new oceans for tears to weep or waters to wash away his sins.
5. God promised (Genesis ix.11) after Noah's experience that the earth would never again be flooded.
6. See Psalm lxix.9: "For the zeal of thine house hath eaten me up." The passage involves three sorts of flame—those of the Last Judgment; those of lust and envy; and those of zeal, which alone heal.
7. Donne may have been thinking of

From death, you numberless infinities
Of souls, and to your scattered bodies go;
All whom the flood did, and fire shall, o'erthrow,   5
All whom war, dearth, age, agues, tyrannies,
Despair, law, chance hath slain, and you whose eyes
Shall behold God, and never taste death's woe.[8]
But let them sleep, Lord, and me mourn a space;
For, if above all these, my sins abound,   10
'Tis late to ask abundance of Thy grace
When we are there. Here on this lowly ground,
Teach me how to repent; for that's as good
As if Thou hadst sealed my pardon with Thy blood.

1633

10

Death, be not proud, though some have calléd thee
Mighty and dreadful, for thou art not so;
For those whom thou think'st thou dost overthrow
Die not, poor Death, nor yet canst thou kill me.
From rest and sleep, which but thy pictures be,   5
Much pleasure; then from thee much more must flow,
And soonest our best men with thee do go,
Rest of their bones, and soul's delivery.[9]
Thou art slave to fate, chance, kings, and desperate men,
And dost with poison, war, and sickness dwell,   10
And poppy or charms can make us sleep as well
And better than thy stroke; why swell'st[1] thou then?
One short sleep past, we wake eternally
And death shall be no more; Death, thou shalt die.

1633

14

Batter my heart, three-personed God; for You
As yet but knock, breathe, shine, and seek to mend;
That I may rise and stand, o'erthrow me, and bend
Your force to break, blow, burn, and make me new.
I, like an usurped town, to another due,   5
Labor to admit You, but O, to no end;
Reason, Your viceroy in me, me should defend,
But is captived, and proves weak or untrue.
Yet dearly I love You, and would be loved fain,
But am bethrothed unto Your enemy.   10
Divorce me, untie or break that knot again;
Take me to You, imprison me, for I,

the angels on old maps, who blow their trumpets to the four points of the compass. See also Revelation vii.1.
8. See Matthew xvi.28, Mark ix.1, and Luke ix.27, where the worthies are described who ascended directly to heaven from this life.
9. I.e., our best men go with you to find rest for their bones and freedom ("delivery") for their souls.
1. Puff up with pride.

Except You enthrall me, never shall be free,
Nor ever chaste, except You ravish me.

1633

18

Show me, dear Christ, Thy spouse so bright and clear.[2]
What! is it she which on the other shore
Goes richly painted? or which, robbed and tore,
Laments and mourns in Germany and here?[3]
Sleeps she a thousand, then peeps up one year?   5
Is she self-truth, and errs? now new, now outwore?
Doth she, and did she, and shall she evermore
On one, on seven, or on no hill appear?[4]
Dwells she with us, or like adventuring knights
First travel[5] we to seek, and then make love?   10
Betray, kind husband, Thy spouse to our sights,
And let mine amorous soul court Thy mild dove,
Who is most true and pleasing to Thee then
When she is embraced and open to most men.

1899

A Hymn to Christ, at the Author's Last Going into Germany[6]

In what torn ship soever I embark,
That ship shall be my emblem of Thy ark;
What sea soever swallow me, that flood
Shall be to me an emblem of Thy blood;
Though Thou with clouds of anger do disguise   5
Thy face, yet through that mask I know those eyes,
    Which, though they turn away sometimes,
        They never will despise.

I sacrifice this island unto Thee,
And all whom I loved there, and who loved me;   10
When I have put our seas twixt them and me,
Put Thou Thy seas betwixt my sins and Thee.
As the tree's sap doth seek the root below
In winter, in my winter now I go

2. "What are the marks of a true church?" was a deeply fought field of interdenominational debate in the 17th century. Few Anglican clergymen would have expressed an indecision as universal as Donne's in this sonnet. Its skepticism, and a sense that versifying did not beseem a clergyman, kept the sonnet out of all 17th-century editions.
3. The Church of Rome is "she which goes richly painted on the other shore";

she is contrasted with the reformed churches "in Germany and here."
4. The Mount of Olives, the seven hills of Rome, and (perhaps) by Lake Geneva or in the town of Canterbury.
5. The 17th-century spelling, *travaile*, includes the idea of labor.
6. Donne went to Germany as chaplain to the Earl of Doncaster in 1619; the mission was a diplomatic one, to the King and Queen of Bohemia.

Where none but Thee, th' eternal root   15
    Of true love, I may know.

Nor Thou nor Thy religion dost control
The amorousness of an harmonious soul,
But Thou would'st have that love Thyself; as Thou
Art jealous, Lord, so I am jealous now;   20
Thou lov'st not, till from loving more,[7] Thou free
My soul; whoever gives, takes liberty;
    Oh, if Thou car'st not whom I love,
      Alas, Thou lov'st not me.

Seal then this bill of my divorce to all   25
On whom those fainter beams of love did fall;
Marry those loves, which in youth scattered be
On fame, wit, hopes (false mistresses), to Thee.
Churches are best for prayer that have least light:
To see God only, I go out of sight;   30
    And to 'scape stormy days, I choose
      An everlasting night.

                  1633

Hymn to God My God, in My Sickness[1]

Since I am coming to that holy room
    Where, with Thy choir of saints for evermore,
I shall be made Thy music; as I come
    I tune the instrument here at the door,
    And what I must do then, think here before.   5

Whilst my physicians by their love are grown
    Cosmographers, and I their map, who lie
Flat on this bed, that by them may be shown
    That this is my southwest discovery[2]
    Per fretum febris,[3] by these straits to die,   10

I joy, that in these straits, I see my West;[4]
    For, though their currents yield return to none,
What shall my West hurt me? As West and East
    In all flat maps (and I am one) are one,
    So death doth touch the resurrection.   15

Is the Pacific Sea my home? Or are
    The Eastern riches? Is Jerusalem?

---

7. From loving elsewhere. Donne is playing with the idea, "To give me true love you must take away my freedom to love elsewhere."

1. Izaak Walton, Donne's first biographer, says this poem was written March 23, 1631, eight days before Donne's death.

2. The Straits of Magellan, or something spiritual which is analogous to them.

3. I.e., through the straits of fever.

4. Where the sun sets, hence where life ends.

Anyan,[5] and Magellan, and Gibraltar,
  All straits, and none but straits, are ways to them,
  Whether where Japhet dwelt, or Cham, or Shem.[6]   20

We think that Paradise and Calvary,
  Christ's cross, and Adam's tree, stood in one place;
Look, Lord, and find both Adams met in me;
  As the first Adam's sweat surrounds my face,
  May the last Adam's blood my soul embrace.   25

So, in his purple wrapped,[7] receive me, Lord;
  By these his thorns give me his other crown;
And, as to others' souls I preached Thy word,
  Be this my text, my sermon to mine own;
  Therefore that he may raise the Lord throws down.   30

1635

⤹A Hymn to God the Father[1]

Wilt Thou forgive that sin where I begun,
  Which is my sin, though it were done before?
Wilt Thou forgive that sin through which I run,
  And do run still, though still I do deplore?
    Refrain When Thou hast done, Thou hast not done,   5
      For I have more.

Wilt Thou forgive that sin which I have won
  Others to sin? and made my sin their door?
Wilt Thou forgive that sin which I did shun
  A year or two, but wallowed in a score?   10
    When Thou hast done, Thou hast not done,
      For I have more.

I have a sin of fear, that when I have spun
  My last thread, I shall perish on the shore;
Swear by Thy self, that at my death Thy Son   15
  Shall shine as he shines now and heretofore;
    And, having done that, Thou hast done,
      I fear no more.

1633

5. The Bering Straits.
6. Japhet, Cham (Ham), and Shem were the three sons of Noah by whom the world was repopulated after the Flood (Genesis x). The descendants of Japhet were thought to inhabit Europe, those of Ham Africa, and those of Shem Asia.

7. The purple of Christ is his blood; also a royal garment.
1. Even in poetry of unquestioned seriousness, Donne's mind expressed itself naturally in puns; there are several in this short hymn, which Walton tells us was written during Donne's illness of 1623.

Prose One volume of average size contains handily the complete poetical works of John Donne; his prose works would fill out at least fifteen such. Of this prose material, much will seem to the modern reader intolerably heavy going. Donne's formal preaching was tailored to the tastes of his age. He divides and subdivides his text, and regularly cites ancient ecclesiastical authorities in their original Latin. Sermons in the 17th century were expected to be vigorous intellectual exercises, and Donne's auditors obviously relished the rigor of the game. This was a game at which Donne had been practicing since youth—like most of his contemporaries, he read the Bible as a lawyer reads a contract—but its exhilarations are largely reserved for specialists.

Donne's most viable prose performances remain those which reveal his character as a poet. Thoughts of disease, death, and damnation rarely failed to stir in him a penitential fervor in which he became, as it were, representative of his audience and of humanity at large. His genius was irresistibly dramatic, even self-dramatizing; his prose contains a frequent confessional strain. At his most characteristic, he is the spokesman before God of a virile, vulnerable, unconquerable humanity.

From Paradoxes and Problems[1]

Paradox VI. *That It Is Possible to Find Some Virtue in Women*

I am not of that seared[2] impudence that I dare defend women, or pronounce them good; yet we see physicians allow some virtue in every poison. Alas! why should we except women? since certainly they are good for physic[3] at least, so as some wine is good for a fever. And though they be the occasioners of many sins, they are also the punishers and revengers of the same sins: for I have seldom seen one which consumes his substance and body upon them, escapes diseases or beggary; and this is their justice. And if *suum cuique dare*[4] be the fulfilling of all civil justice, they are most just; for they deny that which is theirs to no man.

Tanquam non liceat nulla puella negat.[5]

And who may doubt of great wisdom in them, that doth but observe with how much labor and cunning our justicers and other dispensers of the laws study to embrace them: and how zealously our preachers dehort[6] men from them, only by urging their subtleties and policies and wisdom, which are in them? Or who can deny them a good measure of fortitude, if he consider how valiant men they have overthrown, and being themselves overthrown, how much and how patiently they bear? And though they be most

1. In 1633, two years after Donne's death, a volume of his *Juvenilia*, or youthful productions, appeared. The "Paradoxes and Problems," as they are subtitled, are bits of logical horse-play, loaded with legal aphorisms perversely misapplied, and perfectly impudent in their cheerful, brassy assurance. This is the mood, and sometimes the mode, of many of the *Songs and Sonnets; Go and Catch a Falling Star* involves a playful misuse of logic akin to that of Paradox VI.
2. Insensitive, unfeeling.
3. As a medicine, to cure a morbid condition.
4. "To give each his own."
5. "So long as it's forbidden, no girl will deny it."
6. Discourage, draw away.

intemperate, I care not, for I undertook to furnish them with some virtue, not with all. Necessity, which makes even bad things good, prevails also for them, for we must say of them, as of some sharp pinching laws: If men were free from infirmities, they were needless. These or none must serve for reasons, and it is my great happiness that examples prove not rules, for to confirm this opinion, the world yields not one example.

Problem II. Why Puritans Make Long Sermons?

It needs not for perspicuousness, for God knows they are plain enough: nor do all of them use sem-brief accents, for some of them have crotchets enough.[7] It may be they intend not to rise like glorious tapers and torches, but like thin-wretched-sick-watching-candles, which languish and are in a divine consumption from the first minute, yea in their snuff, and stink when others are in their more profitable glory. I have thought sometimes that out of conscience they allow "Long measure to coarse ware."[8] And sometimes that, usurping in that place a liberty to speak freely of kings, they would reign as long as they could. But now I think they do it out of a zealous imagination that it is their duty to preach on till their auditory wake.

Problem VI. Why Hath the Common Opinion Afforded Women Souls?

It is agreed that we have not so much from them as any part of either our mortal souls of sense or growth;[9] and we deny souls to others equal to them in all but in speech, for which they are beholding to their bodily instruments: for perchance an ox's heart, or a goat's, or a fox's, or a serpent's would speak just so, if it were in the breast, and could move that tongue and jaws. Have they so many advantages and means to hurt us (for, ever their loving destroyed us) that we dare not displease them, but give them what they will? And so when some call them Angels, some Goddesses, and the Palpulian heretics make them bishops,[1] we descend so much with the stream to allow them souls? Or do we somewhat (in this dignifying of them) flatter princes and great personages, that are so much governed by them? Or do we in that easiness and

7. The sem-brief (now spelled *semibreve*) is, in modern music, the longest note in ordinary use, a whole note; the crotchet is a note with half the value of a minim, a very short note indeed. But Donne is also playing with another meaning of "crotchet": a cranky idea on an unimportant point.
8. I.e., extra quantity to atone for poor quality.
9. 17th-century anatomy imputed to man several vital principles in addi-tion to his immortal soul. The "animal spirits" and "vital spirits" which governed man's senses and his growth might be referred to freely as "souls."
1. "Palpulians," a nonsense word, is probably a misprint for "Peputians." The Montanist sect, which centered at Pepuza in Phrygia, admitted women to the offices of deacon and sometimes of priest; Donne exaggerates when he mentions bishops.

prodigality, wherein we daily lose our own souls to we care not whom, so labor to persuade ourselves, that sith a woman hath a soul, a soul is no great matter? Or do we lend them souls but for use,[2] since they for our sakes give their souls again, and their bodies to boot? Or perchance because the devil (who is all soul) doth most mischief, and for convenience and proportion, because they would come nearer him, we allow them some souls, and so as the Romans naturalized some provinces in revenge, and made them Romans only for the burden of the commonwealth; so we have given women souls only to make them capable of damnation?

1633

From Devotions upon Emergent Occasions[1]

Meditation XIV

Idque notant criticis medici evenisse diebus.[2]

The physicians observe these accidents to have fallen upon the critical days.

I would not make man worse than he is, nor his condition more miserable than it is. But could I though I would? As a man cannot flatter God nor overpraise him, so a man cannot injure man nor undervalue him. Thus much must necessarily be presented to his remembrance, that those false happinesses which he hath in this world have their times and their seasons and their critical days; and they are judged and denominated according to the times when they befall us. What poor elements are our happinesses made of if time, time which we can scarce consider to be anything, be an essential part of our happiness! All things are done in some place; but if we consider place to be no more but the next hollow superficies[3] of the air, alas! how thin and fluid a thing is air, and how thin a film is a superficies, and a superficies of air! All things are done in time too; but if we consider time to be but the measure of motion, and howsoever it may seem to have three stations, past, present, and future, yet the first and last of these are not (one is not now, and the other is not yet) and that which you call *present* is not now the same that it was when you began to call it so in this line (before you sound that word *present* or that monosyllable

2. I.e., usury. Donne is suggesting that women's souls are only rented, to yield a profit to men.
1. The *Private Devotions* were written during an attack of illness in the winter of 1623. They describe in detail the stages of Donne's disease and recovery; each stage comprises a meditation on the human condition, an expostulation and debate with God, and a prayer to Him. The book was published almost immediately it was written, and to

great effect—the blend of private feeling and public moralizing rendering it particularly accessible to 17th-century readers. And its eloquent periods have provided a title for at least one major modern novel (see Meditation XVII). "Emergent" occasions are those which arise casually or unexpectedly.
2. Donne's Latin epigraphs are followed by his English translations, some of them very free ones indeed.
3. Surface.

now, the present and the now is past). If this imaginary half-nothing, time, be of the essence of our happinesses, how can they be thought durable? Time is not so; how can they be thought to be? Time is not so; not so considered in any of the parts thereof. If we consider eternity, into that time never entered; eternity is not an everlasting flux of time, but time is a short parenthesis in a long period; and eternity had been the same as it is, though time had never been. If we consider, not eternity, but perpetuity; not that which had no time to begin in, but which shall outlive time and be, when time shall be no more, what a minute is the life of the durablest creature compared to that! and what a minute is man's life in respect of the sun's or of a tree! and yet how little of our life is occasion, opportunity to receive good in; and how little of that occasion do we apprehend and lay hold of! How busy and perplexed a cobweb is the happiness of man here, that must be made up with a watchfulness to lay hold upon occasion, which is but a little piece of that which is nothing, time! And yet the best things are nothing without that. Honors, pleasures, possessions presented to us out of time, in our decrepit and distasted[4] and unapprehensive age, lose their office and lose their name; they are not honors to us that shall never appear nor come abroad into the eyes of the people to receive honor from them who give it; nor pleasures to us who have lost our sense to taste them; nor possessions to us who are departing from the possession of them. Youth is their critical day; that judges them, that denominates them, that inanimates and informs them, and makes them honors and pleasures and possessions; and when they come in an unapprehensive age, they come as a cordial when the bell rings out,[5] as a pardon when the head is off. We rejoice in the comfort of fire, but does any man cleave to it at midsummer? We are glad of the freshness and coolness of a vault, but does any man keep his Christmas there? or are the pleasures of the spring acceptable in autumn? If happiness be in the season or in the climate, how much happier then are birds than men, who can change the climate and accompany and enjoy the same season ever.

Meditation XVII

Nunc lento sonitu dicunt, morieris.

Now this bell tolling softly for another, says to me, Thou must die.

Perchance he for whom this bell tolls may be so ill as that he knows not it tolls for him; and perchance I may think myself so much better than I am, as that they who are about me and see my state may have caused it to toll for me, and I know not that. The church is catholic, universal, so are all her actions; all that she does

---

4. Having lost the sense of taste.
5. A "cordial" (medicine) which arrives

when the parish bell is already tolling is a bit too late.

belongs to all. When she baptizes a child, that action concerns me; for that child is thereby connected to that body which is my head too,[6] and ingrafted into that body whereof I am a member. And when she buries a man, that action concerns me: all mankind is of one author and is one volume; when one man dies, one chapter is not torn out of the book, but translated[7] into a better language; and every chapter must be so translated. God employs several translators; some pieces are translated by age, some by sickness, some by war, some by justice; but God's hand is in every translation, and his hand shall bind up all our scattered leaves again for that library where every book shall lie open to one another. As therefore the bell that rings to a sermon calls not upon the preacher only, but upon the congregation to come, so this bell calls us all; but how much more me, who am brought so near the door by this sickness. There was a contention as far as a suit[8] (in which piety and dignity, religion and estimation,[9] were mingled) which of the religious orders should ring to prayers first in the morning; and it was determined that they should ring first that rose earliest. If we understand aright the dignity of this bell that tolls for our evening prayer, we would be glad to make it ours by rising early, in that application, that it might be ours as well as his whose indeed it is. The bell doth toll for him that thinks it doth; and though it intermit again, yet from that minute that that occasion wrought upon him, he is united to God. Who casts not up his eye to the sun when it rises? but who takes off his eye from a comet when that breaks out? Who bends not his ear to any bell which upon any occasion rings? but who can remove it from that bell which is passing a piece of himself out of this world? No man is an island, entire of itself; every man is a piece of the continent, a part of the main.[1] If a clod be washed away by the sea, Europe is the less, as well as if a promontory were, as well as if a manor of thy friend's or of thine own were. Any man's death diminishes me because I am involved in mankind, and therefore never send to know for whom the bell tolls; it tolls for thee. Neither can we call this a begging of misery or a borrowing of misery, as though we were not miserable enough of ourselves but must fetch in more from the next house, in taking upon us the misery of our neighbors. Truly it were an excusable covetousness if we did; for affliction is a treasure, and scarce any man hath enough of it. No man hath affliction enough that is not matured and ripened by it and made fit for God by that affliction. If a man carry treasure in bullion, or in a wedge of gold, and have none coined

6. I.e., the Christian church is the head of all men, as well as a body composed of its members.
7. Literally, "carried across"; hence, on the spiritual level, exalted from one sphere to another.
8. Controversy which went as far as a lawsuit.
9. Self-esteem.
1. Mainland.

into current money, his treasure will not defray[2] him as he travels. Tribulation is treasure in the nature of it, but it is not current money in the use of it, except we get nearer and nearer our home, heaven, by it. Another man may be sick too, and sick to death, and this affliction may lie in his bowels as gold in a mine and be of no use to him; but this bell that tells me of his affliction digs out and applies that gold to me, if by this consideration of another's danger I take mine own into contemplation and so secure myself by making my recourse to my God, who is our only security.

1623   1624

From Sermon LXXVI[3]

[*On Falling out of God's Hand*]

* * * When God's hand is bent to strike, "it is a fearful thing to fall into the hands of the living God";[4] but to fall out of the hands of the living God is a horror beyond our expression, beyond our imagination. That God should let my soul fall out of his hand into a bottomless pit and roll an unremovable stone upon it and leave it to that which it finds there (and it shall find that there which it never imagined till it came thither) and never think more of that soul, never have more to do with it; that of that providence of God that studies the life of every weed and worm and ant and spider and toad and viper there should never, never any beam flow out upon me; that that God who looked upon me when I was nothing and called me when I was not, as though I had been, out of the womb and depth of darkness, will not look upon me now, when though a miserable and a banished and a damned creature, yet I am his creature still and contribute something to his glory even in my damnation; that that God who hath often looked upon me in my foulest uncleanness and when I had shut out the eye of the day, the sun, and the eye of the night, the taper, and the eyes of all the world with curtains and windows and doors, did yet see me and see me in mercy by making me see that he saw me and sometimes brought me to a present remorse and (for that time) to a

2. Pay his expenses.

3. Of Donne's estimated 180 sermons, the extraordinary total of 160 survive —monumental evidence that he was both a prolific and a popular preacher. The reasons for his popularity are clear: the sermons are not only rich in learning and curious lore; they are characteristically personal and powerful in their phrasing. Concepts which Donne used in his poems continually recur in the sermons, and the fuller context of the prose often sheds useful light on the meaning of the poetry. Our present selection comes from the concluding part of a sermon preached "to the Earl of Carlisle and his company, at Sion" on the text, Mark xvi.16: "He that believeth not, shall be damned." The date is some time after 1623, when Sion College was founded in London by Dr. Thomas White.

4. Hebrews x.31.

forbearing of that sin, should so turn himself from me to his glorious
saints and angels as that no saint nor angel nor Christ Jesus himself
should ever pray him to look towards me, never remember[5] him that
such a soul there is; that that God who hath so often said to my soul,
Quare morieris? why wilt thou die? and so often sworn to my
soul, *Vivit Dominus,* as the Lord liveth, I would not have thee die
but live, will neither let me die nor let me live, but die an everlasting life and live an everlasting death; that that God who, when
he could not get into me by standing and knocking, by his ordinary
means of entering, by his word, his mercies, hath applied his judgments and hath shaked the house, this body, with agues and palsies,
and set this house on fire with fevers and calentures,[6] and frighted
the master of the house, my soul, with horrors and heavy apprehensions and so made an entrance into me; that that God should
frustrate all his own purposes and practices upon me and leave me
and cast me away as though I had cost him nothing; that this God
at last should let this soul go away as a smoke, as a vapor, as a
bubble; and that then this soul cannot be a smoke, a vapor, nor a
bubble, but must lie in darkness as long as the Lord of light is light
itself, and never spark of that light reach to my soul; what Tophet is
not paradise, what brimstone is not amber, what gnashing is not a
comfort, what gnawing of the worm is not a tickling, what torment
is not a marriage bed to this damnation, to be secluded eternally,
eternally, eternally from the sight of God? * * *

1640

5. Remind.   6. Fever with delirium.

BEN JONSON
(1572–1637)

1598:   *Every Man in His Humor,* Jonson's first play.
1616:   Jonson appointed poet laureate; publishes his
          Works.
1618–19: Journey to Scotland; conversations with Drummond
          of Hawthornden.

Ben Jonson played a vast part in the literary life of the 17th century. His
special blend of satiric realism, romantic sentiment, and classical correctness
was a root inspiration for nearly 200 years; his impact was felt on the stage,
as well as in poetry, criticism, and standards of literary taste generally. He
was in effect the precursor of English neoclassicism.

Jonson's father, a clergyman, died shortly after his son was born. Adopted
in infancy by a bricklayer, Ben was educated for several years by William

Camden, the great Elizabethan antiquary, at Westminster School. He learned a great deal from Camden, and picked up much more of his splendid erudition on his own; for though he later received honorary degrees from both Oxford and Cambridge, he never attended either university. Instead, after leaving Westminster School, he seems to have worked for a while at the trade of bricklaying, and then to have entered the army. In Flanders, where the Dutch, allies of England, were warring for their liberty against the Spaniards, he fought singlehanded with one of the enemy before the massed armies, and killed his man. Returning to England about 1595, he began to work as an actor and playwright, and conquered the stage as vigorously as he had done the foreign foe. Hot of head and quick of hand, he was jailed for killing a fellow actor in a duel, jailed for insulting the Scotch at a time when King James was newly arrived on the throne from Scotland, and furiously embroiled in a series of literary wars with his fellow playwrights. But as he grew older, he grew mellower; and he succeeded in becoming literary dictator of London, not by the length of his sword or the sharpness of his pen, but by gaining the friendship of men like Donne, Shakespeare, Francis Beaumont, John Selden, John Fletcher, and Bacon. In addition, he engaged the affection of younger men (poets like Robert Herrick, Thomas Carew, and Sir John Suckling, speculative thinkers like Lord Falkland and Sir Kenelm Digby), who delighted to christen themselves "Sons of Ben." Sons of Ben provided the nucleus of the entire "Cavalier school" of English lyric poets.

The first of Jonson's great plays was *Every Man in His Humor*, in which Shakespeare acted a leading role. It was also the first of the so-called "comedies of humors," in which the prevailing eccentricities and ruling passions (i.e., "humors") of characters were exposed to satiric deflation. Though Jonson's classical tragedy *Sejanus* (1603) has been generally discounted as overloaded with antiquarian lore, *Volpone* (1606) and *The Alchemist* (1610) are two supreme satiric comedies of the English stage. Meanwhile, starting in 1605, Jonson began to write for the court a series of masques—elaborate and very expensive spectacles involving music, song, and dance, built around a moral allegory, and culminating in a compliment to the king or queen. Thus he became closely involved with the life of the court, a connection which was formalized in 1616, when he was appointed poet laureate with a substantial pension from the king. In 1618 he made a walking tour to Scotland, where he was entertained by William Drummond of Hawthornden, who recorded a good deal of his rather opinionated conversation. Perhaps because his later plays were generally unsuccessful on the stage, Jonson developed a tendency to vilify the taste of the age while applauding his own integrity, in a way that laid him open to satire. Yet even those who mocked him, admired; and he vindicated himself by leaving among his posthumous papers poetry as fine and delicate as any he had ever written—for example, the lovely *Sad Shepherd*, a pastoral drama. His death was universally mourned as the end of an era, for he was the last of the great Elizabethans as well as the first precursor of neoclassicism. His body lies in Westminster Abbey under the laconic, ambiguous inscription, "O Rare Ben Jonson."

In lyric poetry, as elsewhere, Jonson's primary debt was to the classics. His epigrams and satires have the tart and crackling energy of Martial's;

his songs and lyrical productions move with an elegant softness reminiscent of Catullus; he can turn a compliment or grace a playful little occasion with all the suavity of Horace. In all these qualities, as in the terse, masculine rhythms of his verse and the strong energy of his syntax, Jonson drew upon the Latin tongue for the advantage of his native English. He is one of the great discipliners of our speech; he reformed a diction overrun with sprawling, florid, intertangled metaphors into one capable of the chiseled phrase. His best work is always chaste and clear of outline, specific and strong in its language, bold in its effects. *Queen and Huntress* has a trochaic severity of meter which contrasts finely with the silver purity of its images. The tribute *To Penshurst* manages to describe, not just a building, but a way of life, an image of the great society which combines simplicity and elegance as Jonson himself combined them. This is done with complex, though unobtrusive, art. Note, for instance, how the description rises through the scale of creatures, from vegetables to animals to pretty girls— who carry emblems of themselves in the form of ripe fruit—to the lord of the manor, and finally to the king himself. Each person is in his place, each is in harmony with general nature, all things are ordered according to an architecture of full proportion; so that a kind of heroic image of the just society rises out of a simple description of a country house.

There is, indeed, a kind of Roman splendor about Jonson's writing, to which the typographers themselves have generally responded. When he published his *Works* in 1616 (the word is a translation of Latin *Opera*, a title previously applied only to the complete works of classical poets), the folio was one of the most elegant ever printed; and he has continued to appear in volumes of ripe, imperial dignity ever since.

To Penshurst[1]

Thou art not, Penshurst, built to envious show,
Of touch[2] or marble; nor canst boast a row
Of polished pillars, or a roof of gold;
Thou hast no lantern, whereof tales are told,
Or stair, or courts; but stand'st an ancient pile,   5
And, these[3] grudged at, art reverenced the while.
Thou joy'st in better marks, of soil, of air,
Of wood, of water; therein thou art fair.
Thou hast thy walks for health, as well as sport;
Thy mount, to which the dryads[4] do resort,   10
Where Pan and Bacchus their high feasts have made,
Beneath the broad beech and the chestnut shade;
That taller tree, which of a nut was set
At his great birth where all the Muses met.[5]

1. The country seat of the Sidney family (famous for Sir Philip) in Kent; Jonson's is one of the first English poems celebrating a specific place (later examples are *Cooper's Hill* by John Denham and *Windsor Forest* by Alexander Pope).

2. Touchstone, i.e., basanite, a pure black, finely grained, and therefore expensive variety of basalt.
3. More pretentious houses.
4. Wood nymphs.
5. Sir Philip Sidney was born at Penshurst; an oak tree, planted the day of

There in the writhéd bark are cut the names   15
Of many a sylvan,[6] taken with his flames;
And thence the ruddy satyrs oft provoke
The lighter fauns to reach thy Lady's Oak.[7]
Thy copse too, named of Gamage,[8] thou hast there,
That never fails to serve thee seasoned deer   20
When thou wouldst feast or exercise thy friends.
The lower land, that to the river bends,
Thy sheep, thy bullocks, kine, and calves do feed;
The middle grounds thy mares and horses breed.
Each bank doth yield thee conies;[9] and the tops,   25
Fertile of wood, Ashore and Sidney's copse,[1]
To crown thy open table, doth provide
The purpled pheasant with the speckled side;
The painted partridge lies in every field,
And for thy mess is willing to be killed.   30
And if the high-swollen Medway[2] fail thy dish,
Thou hast thy ponds, that pay thee tribute fish,
Fat aged carps that run into thy net,
And pikes, now weary their own kind to eat,
As loath the second draught or cast to stay,   35
Officiously at first themselves betray;
Bright eels that emulate them, and leap on land
Before the fisher, or into his hand.
Then hath thy orchard fruit, thy garden flowers,
Fresh as the air, and new as are the hours.   40
The early cherry, with the later plum,
Fig, grape, and quince, each in his time doth come;
The blushing apricot and woolly peach
Hang on thy walls, that every child may reach.
And though thy walls be of the country stone,   45
They are reared with no man's ruin, no man's groan;
There's none that dwell about them wish them down;
But all come in, the farmer and the clown,[3]
And no one empty-handed, to salute
Thy lord and lady, though they have no suit.   50
Some bring a capon, some a rural cake,
Some nuts, some apples; some that think they make
The better cheeses bring them, or else send
By their ripe daughters, whom they would commend
This way to husbands, and whose baskets bear   55
An emblem of themselves in plum or pear.
But what can this (more than express their love)

his birth, is still shown as "Sidney's oak."
6. Woodsman.
7. Lady Leicester's oak, named after a lady of the house who once entered into labor under its branches. "Provoke": challenge to a race.
8. Lady Barbara Gamage gave her name to a grove near the entrance of the park.
9. Rabbits.
1. "Ashore and Sidney's copse" are little woods and spinneys, lovingly enumerated by Jonson. They still survive, under their ancient names.
2. The local river.
3. Yokel.

Add to thy free provisions, far above
The need of such? whose liberal board doth flow
With all that hospitality doth know;   60
Where comes no guest but is allowed to eat,
Without his fear, and of thy lord's own meat;
Where the same beer and bread, and selfsame wine,
That is his lordship's shall be also mine,
And I not fain to sit (as some this day   65
At great men's tables), and yet dine away.[4]
Here no man tells[5] my cups; nor, standing by,
A waiter doth my gluttony envy,
But gives me what I call, and lets me eat;
He knows below he shall find plenty of meat.   70
Thy tables hoard not up for the next day;
Nor, when I take my lodging, need I pray
For fire, or lights, or livery;[6] all is there,
As if thou then wert mine, or I reigned here:
There's nothing I can wish, for which I stay.[7]   75
That found King James when, hunting late this way
With his brave son, the prince, they saw thy fires
Shine bright on every hearth, as the desires
Of thy Penates[8] had been set on flame
To entertain them; or the country came   80
With all their zeal to warm their welcome here.
What (great I will not say, but) sudden cheer
Didst thou then make 'em! and what praise was heaped
On thy good lady then, who therein reaped
The just reward of her high housewifery;   85
To have her linen, plate, and all things nigh,
When she was far; and not a room but dressed
As if it had expected such a guest!
These, Penshurst, are thy praise, and yet not all.
Thy lady's noble, fruitful, chaste withal.   90
His children thy great lord may call his own,
A fortune in this age but rarely known.
They are, and have been, taught religion; thence
Their gentler spirits have sucked innocence.
Each morn and even they are taught to pray,   95
With the whole household, and may, every day,
Read in their virtuous parents' noble parts
The mysteries of manners, arms, and arts.
Now, Penshurst, they that will proportion[9] thee
With other edifices, when they see   100
Those proud, ambitious heaps, and nothing else,
May say their lords have built, but thy lord dwells.

1616

---

4. Because the tables were so large, different courses might be served at different ends—hence the possibility of sitting at a man's table, yet dining away.
5. Counts.
6. Rations, food.
7. Wait.
8. Roman household gods. A room in the house is still known as "King James's room."
9. Compare.

To the Memory of My Beloved Master
William Shakespeare
AND WHAT HE HATH LEFT US[1]

To draw no envy, Shakespeare, on thy name,
Am I thus ample to thy book and fame,
While I confess thy writings to be such
As neither man nor Muse can praise too much.
'Tis true, and all men's suffrage.[2] But these ways   5
Were not the paths I meant unto thy praise:
For silliest ignorance on these may light,
Which, when it sounds at best, but echoes right;
Or blind affection,[3] which doth ne'er advance
The truth, but gropes, and urgeth all by chance;   10
Or crafty malice might pretend this praise,
And think to ruin where it seemed to raise.
These are as some infamous bawd or whore
Should praise a matron. What could hurt her more?
But thou art proof against them, and, indeed,   15
Above th' ill fortune of them, or the need.
I therefore will begin. Soul of the age!
The applause! delight! the wonder of our stage!
My Shakespeare, rise; I will not lodge thee by
Chaucer or Spenser, or bid Beaumont lie   20
A little further to make thee a room:[4]
Thou art a monument without a tomb,
And art alive still while thy book doth live,
And we have wits to read and praise to give.
That I not mix thee so, my brain excuses,   25
I mean with great, but disproportioned[5] Muses;
For, if I thought my judgment were of years,
I should commit thee surely with thy peers,
And tell how far thou didst our Lyly outshine,
Or sporting Kyd, or Marlowe's mighty line.[6]   30
And though thou hadst small Latin and less Greek,[7]
From thence to honor thee I would not seek
For names, but call forth thund'ring Aeschylus,
Euripides, and Sophocles to us,

1. This poem was prefixed to the first folio of Shakespeare's plays, published in 1623.
2. Agreement, consent.
3. Prejudice.
4. Chaucer, Spenser, and Francis Beaumont were buried in Westminster Abbey; Shakespeare, of course, in Stratford. Jonson endorses the separation; Shakespeare should not be crowded.
5. Not comparable.
6. John Lyly, Thomas Kyd, and Christopher Marlowe, Elizabethan dramatists put in the shade by Shakespeare.
7. Shakespeare had, by modern standards, a very adequate command of Latin; Jonson is speaking from the lofty height of his own remarkable scholarship. Shakespeare's French and Italian (he was competent in both tongues) Jonson does not think worthy of mention.

Pacuvius, Accius, him of Cordova dead,[8]   35
To life again, to hear thy buskin[9] tread
And shake a stage; or, when thy socks were on,
Leave thee alone for the comparison
Of all that insolent Greece or haughty Rome
Sent forth, or since did from their ashes come.   40
Triumph, my Britain; thou hast one to show
To whom all scenes[1] of Europe homage owe.
He was not of an age, but for all time!
And all the Muses still were in their prime
When like Apollo he came forth to warm   45
Our ears, or like a Mercury to charm.
Nature herself was proud of his designs,
And joyed to wear the dressing of his lines,
Which were so richly spun, and woven so fit,
As, since, she will vouchsafe no other wit: 50
The merry Greek, tart Aristophanes,
Neat Terence, witty Plautus[2] now not please,
But antiquated and deserted lie,
As they were not of Nature's family.
Yet must I not give Nature all; thy Art,   55
My gentle Shakespeare, must enjoy a part.
For though the poet's matter Nature be,
His Art doth give the fashion; and that he
Who casts to write a living line must sweat
(Such as thine are) and strike the second heat   60
Upon the muses' anvil; turn the same,
And himself with it, that he thinks to frame,
Or for the laurel he may gain a scorn;
For a good poet's made as well as born.
And such wert thou! Look how the father's face   65
Lives in his issue; even so the race
Of Shakespeare's mind and manners brightly shines
In his well-turned and true-filed lines,
In each of which he seems to shake a lance,[3]
As brandished at the eyes of ignorance.   70
Sweet swan of Avon, what a sight it were
To see thee in our waters yet appear,
And make those flights upon the banks of Thames
That so did take Eliza and our James![4]
But stay; I see thee in the hemisphere   75
Advanced and made a constellation there![5]
Shine forth, thou star of poets, and with rage

8. Marcus Pacuvius and Lucius Accius (2nd century B.C.) and "him of Cordova," Seneca the Younger (1st century A.D.), the greatest of the Latin tragedians. Only fragments survive of the plays of Pacuvius and Accius; Jonson's comparisons are more pedantic, in these instances, than relevant.
9. The symbol of tragedy, as contrasted with "socks" (in the next line), symbols of comedy.

1. Stages.
2. Aristophanes, the great Greek satirist and comic writer; Terence and Plautus (3rd and 2nd centuries B.C.), Roman writers of comedy.
3. Pun on Shake-speare.
4. Queen Elizabeth and King James.
5. Heroes and demigods were typically exalted after death to a place among the stars.

Or influence[6] chide or cheer the drooping stage,
Which, since thy flight from hence, hath mourned like night,
And despairs day, but for thy volume's light.   80
                                                                1623

To William Camden[1]

Camden, most reverend head, to whom I owe
All that I am in arts, all that I know
(How nothing's that!), to whom my country owes
The great renown and name wherewith she goes;[2]
Than thee the age sees not that thing more grave,   5
More high, more holy, that she more would crave.
What name, what skill, what faith hast thou in things!
What sight in searching the most antique springs!
What weight and what authority in thy speech!
Man scarce can make that doubt, but thou canst teach.[3]   10
Pardon free truth and let thy modesty,
Which conquers all, be once overcome by thee.
Many of thine, this better could than I;
But for[4] their powers, accept my piety.

                                                                1616

On My First Daughter

Here lies, to each her parents' ruth,[5]
Mary, the daughter of their youth;
Yet all heaven's gifts being heaven's due,
It makes the father less to rue.
At six months' end she parted hence   5
With safety of her innocence;
Whose soul heaven's queen, whose name she bears,
In comfort of her mother's tears,
Hath placed amongst her virgin-train:
Where, while that severed doth remain,   10
This grave partakes the fleshly birth;
Which cover lightly, gentle earth!

                                                                1616

---

6. "Rage" and "influence" describe the supposed effects of the planets on earthly affairs. "Rage" also implies poetic inspiration.
1. Camden (1551–1623), a famous antiquary and historical scholar, had been Jonson's schoolmaster.
2. Camden's antiquarian studies in *Britannia* (1586) and *Remains of a Greater Work Concerning Britain* (1605) ran into several editions and were translated abroad.
3. I.e., man can scarcely ask a question to which you don't know the answer.
4. But in lieu of.
5. Grief. There is no sure identification of Jonson's daughter, nor a positive date of composition for the poem.

On My First Son

Farewell, thou child of my right hand,[6] and joy;
My sin was too much hope of thee, loved boy:
Seven years thou wert lent to me, and I thee pay,
Exacted by thy fate, on the just day.
O could I lose all father[7] now! for why   5
Will man lament the state he should envy,
To have so soon 'scaped world's and flesh's rage,
And, if no other misery, yet age?
Rest in soft peace, and asked, say, "Here doth lie
Ben Jonson his best piece of poetry."   10
For whose sake henceforth all his vows be such
As what he loves may never like too much.[8]

                                        1616

To John Donne

Donne, the delight of Phoebus and each Muse,
Who, to thy one, all other brains refuse;[9]
Whose every work, of thy most early wit,
Came forth example and remains so yet;
Longer a-knowing than most wits do live,   5
And which no affection praise enough can give.
To it[1] thy language, letters, arts, best life,
Which might with half mankind maintain a strife.
All which I meant to praise, and yet I would,
But leave, because I cannot as I should.   10

                                        1616

It Was a Beauty That I Saw[2]

It was a beauty that I saw,
So pure, so perfect, as the frame

6. "Child of the right hand" is a literal translation of the Hebrew name "Benjamin," which implies the meanings "dexterous" or "fortunate." The boy was born in 1596, and died on his birthday in 1603.
7. Relinquish all thoughts of being a father.
8. The obscure grammar of the last lines seems to refer back to the feeling in line 2, that too much affection is fatal to the loved one.
9. The word "refuse" could imply a reproach against Donne's obscurity, a notion of egotism ("refusal" involving preference of one over others), or the idea of welding (re-fusing) lesser minds to a greater.
1. The verb "add" is understood.
2. In *The New Inn* IV.4, this song is sung by Lovel.

Of all the universe was lame
To that one figure, could I draw
Or give least line of it a law.   5
A skein of silk without a knot,
A fair march made without a halt,
A curious[3] form without a fault,
A printed book without a blot:
All beauty, and without a spot.   10

1629

Epitaph on Elizabeth, L. H.[4]

Wouldst thou hear what man can say
In a little? Reader, stay.
Underneath this stone doth lie
As much beauty as could die;
Which in life did harbor give   5
To more virtue than doth live.
If at all she had a fault,
Leave it buried in this vault.
One name was Elizabeth;
Th' other, let it sleep with death: 10
Fitter, where it died, to tell,
Than that it lived at all. Farewell!

1616

An Elegy

Though beauty be the mark of praise,
    And yours of whom I sing be such
    As not the world can praise too much,
Yet is 't your virtue now I raise.

A virtue, like allay,[5] so gone   5
    Throughout your form as, though that move
    And draw and conquer all men's love,
This subjects you to love of one.

Wherein you triumph yet; because
    'Tis of yourself, and that you use   10
    The noblest freedom, not to choose
Against or faith or honor's laws.

3. Elaborate.
4. The subject of this epitaph may have been Elizabeth, Lady Hatton; but, in fact, her name has slept with death.
5. Alloy. The thought is that her beauty makes her loved by all, while her virtue confines her to a single lover (her husband?). Jonson here is in an unusually metaphysical mood.

But who should less expect from you,
   In whom alone Love lives again?
   By whom he is restored to men,   15
And kept, and bred, and brought up true.

His falling temples you have reared,
   The withered garlands ta'en away;
   His altars kept from the decay
That envy wished, and nature feared;   20

And on them burn so chaste a flame,
   With so much loyalties' expense,
   As Love, t' acquit such excellence,
Is gone himself into your name.[6]

And you are he; the deity   25
   To whom all lovers are designed
   That would their better objects find;
Among which faithful troop am I.

Who, as an offspring[7] at your shrine,
   Have sung this hymn, and here entreat   30
   One spark of your diviner heat
To light upon a love of mine.

Which, if it kindle not, but scant
   Appear, and that to shortest view,
   Yet give me leave t' adore in you   35
What I in her am grieved to want.[8]

                               1640

Slow, Slow, Fresh Fount[9]

Slow, slow, fresh fount, keep time with my salt tears;
Yet slower, yet, O faintly, gentle springs!
List to the heavy part the music bears,
Woe weeps out her division,[1] when she sings.
    Droop herbs and flowers;
    Fall grief in showers;   5
Our beauties are not ours. O, I could still,
Like melting snow upon some craggy hill,

6. To repay the lady's devotion, Love himself has entered her name; from these lines it has been conjectured that the poem was addressed to Lady Covell.
7. Perhaps "descendant," more likely a wandering offshoot of the "faithful troop."
8. Can Jonson possibly be saying here that his own mistress is a poor copy of the lady to whom this poem is addressed? This hardly seems complimentary to either lady, though it is in the Donne tradition of bold, witty truthtelling.
9. From the satiric comedy *Cynthia's Revels* (1600). It deals with the sin of self-love, and this famous lyric is a lament sung by Echo for Narcissus, who was entranced by his own image and ultimately transformed into a flower.
1. Grief, but also a rapid, melodic passage of music.

Drop, drop, drop, drop,[2]   10
Since nature's pride is now a withered daffodil.

                                                              1600

Queen and Huntress[3]

Queen and huntress, chaste and fair,
Now the sun is laid to sleep,
Seated in thy silver chair,
State in wonted manner keep;
Hesperus entreats thy light,   5
Goddess excellently bright.

Earth, let not thy envious shade
Dare itself to interpose;
Cynthia's shining orb was made
Heaven to clear, when day did close.   10
Bless us then with wishèd sight,
Goddess excellently bright.

Lay thy bow of pearl apart,
And thy crystal-shining quiver;
Give unto the flying hart   15
Space to breathe, how short soever.
Thou that mak'st a day of night,
Goddess excellently bright.

                                                              1600

Gypsy Songs[4]

1

The faery beam upon you,
The stars to glister on you;
    A moon of light
    In the noon of night,
Till the fire-drake[5] hath o'ergone you!   5
The wheel of fortune guide you,
The boy with the bow[6] beside you;
    Run ay in the way
    Till the bird of day,
And the luckier lot betide you!   10

2. This line shows how far Jonson could go in adapting his verse to the needs of a composer.
3. Also from *Cynthia's Revels*, this song is sung by Hesperus, the evening star, to Cynthia, or Diana, goddess of chastity and the moon—with whom Queen Elizabeth was, almost automatically, equated.
4. From one of Jonson's masques, *The Gypsies Metamorphosed*.
5. I.e., till the will-o'-the-wisp has passed you by.
6. Cupid.

2

To the old, long life and treasure!
To the young, all health and pleasure!
  To the fair, their face
  With eternal grace
And the soul to be loved at leisure!   5
To the witty, all clear mirrors;
To the foolish, their dark errors;
  To the loving sprite,
  A secure delight;
To the jealous, his own false terrors!   10

1621

Though I Am Young and Cannot Tell[7]

Though I am young, and cannot tell
  Either what Death or Love is well,
Yet I have heard they both bear darts,
  And both do aim at human hearts.
And then again, I have been told   5
  Love wounds with heat, as Death with cold;
So that I fear they do but bring
  Extremes to touch, and mean one thing.

As in a ruin[8] we it call
  One thing to be blown up, or fall;   10
Or to our end like way may have
  By a flash of lightning, or a wave;
So Love's inflaméd shaft or brand
  May kill as soon as Death's cold hand;
Except Love's fires the virtue have   15
  To fright the frost out of the grave.

1641

Song: To Celia[9]

Drink to me only with thine eyes,
  And I will pledge with mine;
Or leave a kiss but in the cup,
  And I'll not look for wine.

7. This song is sung in *The Sad Shepherd* by Caroline; the pastoral simplicity of her character is caught in the naïve monosyllables of the poem.
8. Demolition, explosion.
9. These famous lines are a patchwork of five separate passages in the *Epistles* of Philostratus, a Greek sophist of the 3rd century A.D. Jonson very carefully reworded the phrases (there are several early MS. versions of the poem) into this classic lyric.

The thirst that from the soul doth rise, 5
Doth ask a drink divine:
But might I of Jove's nectar sup,
I would not change for thine.

I sent thee late a rosy wreath,
Not so much honoring thee, 10
As giving it a hope, that there
It could not withered be.
But thou thereon did'st only breathe,
And sent'st it back to me;
Since when it grows and smells, I swear, 15
Not of itself, but thee.

1616

Come, My Celia[1]

Come, my Celia, let us prove,[2]
While we can, the sports of love;
Time will not be ours forever;
He at length our good will sever.
Spend not then his gifts in vain. 5
Suns that set may rise again;
But if once we lose this light,
'Tis with us perpetual night.
Why should we defer our joys?
Fame and rumor are but toys. 10
Cannot we delude the eyes
Of a few poor household spies,
Or his easier ears beguile,
So removéd by our wile?
'Tis no sin love's fruit to steal; 15
But the sweet thefts to reveal,
To be taken, to be seen,
These have crimes accounted been.

1606

The Triumph of Charis[3]

See the chariot at hand here of Love,
Wherein my lady rideth!
Each that draws is a swan or a dove,

1. This song is sung by Volpone, in the comedy of the same name. It paraphrases a poem by Catullus.
2. Experience.
3. *A Celebration of Charis* consists of ten loosely connected lyrics, which were printed as a unit, amid a posthumous collection of Jonson's lyric poetry. The *Triumph* is the fourth of the ten poems.

And well the car Love guideth.
As she goes, all hearts do duty   5
    Unto her beauty;
And, enamored, do wish, so they might
    But enjoy such a sight,
That they still were to run by her side,
Through swords, through seas, whither she would ride.   10

Do but look on her eyes; they do light
    All that Love's world compriseth!
Do but look on her hair; it is bright
    As Love's star when it riseth!
Do but mark, her forehead's smoother   15
    Than words that soothe her!
And from her arched brows, such a grace
    Sheds itself through the face,
As alone there triumphs to the life
All the gain, all the good, of the elements' strife.   20

Have you seen but a bright lily grow,
    Before rude hands have touched it?
Ha' you marked but the fall o' the snow
    Before the soil hath smutched it?
Ha' you felt the wool o' the beaver?   25
    Or swan's down ever?
Or have smelt o' the bud o' the brier?
    Or the nard[4] in the fire?
Or have tasted the bag o' the bee?
O so white, O so soft, O so sweet is she![5]
                                      30

1640

Still to Be Neat[6]

Still to be neat, still to be dressed,
As you were going to a feast;
Still to be powdered, still perfumed;
Lady, it is to be presumed,
Though art's hid causes are not found,   5
All is not sweet, all is not sound.

Give me a look, give me a face
That makes simplicity a grace;
Robes loosely flowing, hair as free;
Such sweet neglect more taketh me   10
Then all th' adulteries of art.
They strike mine eyes, but not my heart.

1609

4. I.e., spikenard, an aromatic Oriental
bush.
5. This last stanza, expanded from the
Latin epigrammatist Martial, was so
pleasing to Jonson that he used it in
several different poems.
6. In *Epicoene, or The Silent Woman*,
this song is sung by Clerimont.

Ode to Himself[7]

Come leave the loathéd stage,
   And the more loathsome age,
Where pride and impudence, in faction knit,
    Usurp the chair of wit!
Indicting and arraigning every day   5
    Something they call a play.
   Let their fastidious, vain
   Commission of the brain
Run on and rage, sweat, censure, and condemn;
They were not made for thee, less thou for them.   10

Say that thou pour'st them wheat,
   And they will acorns eat;
'Twere simple fury still thyself to waste
    On such as have no taste!
To offer them a surfeit of pure bread,   15
    Whose appetites are dead!
   No, give them grains their fill,
   Husks, draff to drink and swill:[8]
If they love lees, and leave the lusty wine,
Envy them not; their palate's with the swine.   20

No doubt some moldy tale,
   Like *Pericles*,[9] and stale
As the shrieve's crusts, and nasty as his fish—
    Scraps, out every dish
Thrown forth and raked into the common tub,   25
    May keep up the Play-club:
   There, sweepings do as well
   As the best-ordered meal;
For who the relish of these guests will fit
Needs set them but the alms basket of wit.   30

And much good do 't you then:
   Brave plush and velvet men
Can feed on orts;[1] and, safe in your stage clothes,
    Dare quit, upon your oaths,
The stagers and the stage-wrights too, your peers,[2]   35
    Of larding your large ears
   With their foul comic socks,

---

7. The failure of Jonson's *The New Inn* (1629) inspired this heroic assault on criticism and the public taste.
8. Jonson gets into one line three words which suggest pig-food.
9. Shakespeare's play, at least in part (printed 1609), which Jonson compares to poorhouse fare.

1. Scraps.
2. This fourth stanza turns toward an attack on the players and playwrights themselves, whom Jonson holds responsible for the low state of public taste. His anger here comes close to incoherence, and the plain sense of the stanza is most unclear.

Wrought upon twenty blocks;
Which, if they are torn, and turned, and patched enough,
The gamesters share your guilt, and you their stuff.   40

   Leave things so prostitute
   And take th' Alcaic lute;[3]
Or thine own Horace, or Anacreon's lyre;
   Warm thee by Pindar's fire:
And though thy nerves be shrunk, and blood be cold,   45
   Ere years have made thee old,
   Strike that disdainful heat
   Throughout, to their defeat,
As curious fools, and envious of thy strain,
May, blushing, swear no palsy's in thy brain.   50

   But when they hear thee sing
   The glories of thy king,
His zeal to God and his just awe o'er men,
   They may, blood-shaken then,
Feel such a flesh-quake to possess their powers   55
   As they shall cry, "Like ours,
   In sound of peace or wars,
   No harp e'er hit the stars
In tuning forth the acts of his sweet reign,
And raising Charles his chariot 'bove his Wain."[4]   60

1629   1640

The Vision of Delight[1]

Presented at Court in Christmas, 1617

THE SCENE—*A Street in Perspective of Fair Building Discovered.*

DELIGHT *is seen to come as afar off, accompanied with* GRACE, LOVE,
HARMONY, REVEL, SPORT, LAUGHTER. WONDER *following.*

       DELIGHT *spake in song* (*stylo recitativo*):
Let us play, and dance, and sing,
   Let us now turn every sort

3. That of Alcaeus. who lived ca. 600
B.C., and became famous, along with
Horace, Anacreon, and Pindar, among
the greatest lyric poets.
4. Jonson's poetry will elevate the
chariot of Charles I (symbol of his
royal power) above Charles's Wain
(the seven bright stars of Ursa Major)
among the constellations.
1. The sort of extravagant allegorical
entertainment represented by *The Vision
of Delight* was enormously popular at
the court of James I. The parts were
taken by courtiers, there was usually
only a single representation of each
masque, and enormous sums of money
were expended on the *décor*. The three

traditional elements of the masque are
spectacle, allegory, and compliment; it
is of the essence that the mythological-
allegorical world of the masque should
finally be converted into the "actual"
world of the court, just as Delight
promises to do in the first four lines of
her first speech.
   Jonson's stage directions, being partly
descriptive (for the reader), partly instructive (for the performer), are rather
casual about observing consistency of
tense. The chief actor in *The Vision of
Delight* was George Villiers. newly
created Marquis of Buckingham;
among the audience was an American
visitor, Pocahontas.

Of the pleasures of the spring
  To the graces of a court.

From air, from cloud, from dreams, from toys,[2]   5
  To sounds, to sense, to love, to joys;
Let your shows[3] be new, as strange,
  Let them oft and sweetly vary;
Let them haste so to their change,
  As the seers may not tarry;   10
Too long to expect the pleasingest sight
  Doth take away from the delight.

Here the first ANTIMASQUE[4] *entered.*
A *she-monster delivered of six* BURRATINES, *that dance with six*
PANTALOONS; *which done,*
                        DELIGHT *spoke again:*
Yet hear what your Delight doth pray:
  All sour and sullen looks away,
  That are the servants of the day;   15
Our sports are of the humorous[5] Night,
  Who feeds the stars that give her light,
  And useth (than her wont) more bright,[6]
To help the vision of DELIGHT.

Here the NIGHT *rises, and took her chariot bespangled with stars.*
                        DELIGHT *proceeds:*
See, see her scepter and her crown   20
  Are all of flame, and from her gown
  A train of light comes waving down.
This night in dew she will not steep
  The brain, nor lock the sense in sleep;
  But all awake with Phantoms keep,   25
And those to make DELIGHT more deep.

By this time the NIGHT *and* MOON *being both risen,* NIGHT, *hovering
over the place, sang:*

Break, Fancy, from thy cave of cloud,
  And spread thy purple wings;
Now all thy figures are allowed,
  And various shapes of things;   30
Create of airy forms a stream;
  It must have blood, and naught of fleam,[7]
And though it be a waking dream;
THE CHOIR: Yet let it like an odor rise
          To all the senses here,   35

2. Trifles.
3. Displays.
4. The "good" characters—Delight and her following—are the "masque"; the "antimasque" comprises grotesques who threaten and oppose them. "Burratines" are puppet-figures; "pantaloons" are clowns. Both names come from the Italian, and there is a possibility that

Jonson modeled this masque in its entirety on an Italian original.
5. Whimsical.
6. I.e., and remains (is accustomed to be, "useth") brighter than usual.
7. Phlegm, the dull, muddy humor. Fancy (fantasy) must be of a hot, sanguine humor ("must have blood") to present lively pictures.

And fall like sleep upon their eyes,
Or music in their ear.

The scene here changed to cloud, and FANCY, *breaking forth, spake:*[8]

Bright Night, I obey thee, and am come at thy call,
But it is no one dream that can please these all;
Wherefore I would know what dreams would delight 'em;   40
For never was Fancy more loath to affright 'em.
And Fancy, I tell you, has dreams that have wings,
And dreams that have honey, and dreams that have stings;
Dreams of the maker, and dreams of the teller,
Dreams of the kitchen, and dreams of the cellar: 45
Some that are tall, and some that are dwarfs,
Some that are haltered, and some that wear scarfs;
Some that are proper, and signify o' thing,
And some another, and some that are nothing:
For say the French verdingale and the French hood   50
Were here to dispute; must it be understood,
A feather, for a wisp, were a fit moderator?[9]
Your ostrich, believe it, is no faithful translator
Of perfect Utopian; and then, 'twere an odd piece
To see the conclusion peep forth at a codpiece.[1]   55
      The political pudding hath still his two ends,
Though the bellows and the bagpipe were ne'er so good friends;
And who can report what offense it would be
For the squirrel to see a dog climb a tree?
If a dream should come in now, to make you afeard,   60
With a windmill on 's head, and bells at his beard,
Would you straight wear your spectacles here at your toes,
And your boots on your brows, and your spurs on your nose?[2]
Your whale he will swallow a hogshead for a pill;
But the maker o' the mouse-trap is he that hath skill.   65
And the nature of the onion is to draw tears,
As well as the mustard; peace, pitchers have ears,
And shuttlecocks wings; these things, do not mind 'em.
If the bell have any sides, the clapper will find 'em;
There's twice so much music in beating the tabor   70
As in the stockfish,[3] and somewhat less labor.
Yet all this while, no proportion is boasted
'Twixt an egg and an ox, though both have been roasted,
For grant the most barbers can play o' the cittern,[4]
Is it requisite a lawyer should plead to a gittern?   75

8. Fancy's speech is almost a parody of metaphysical poetry, a series of glaring, brilliant metaphors, jumbled together without making much sense.
9. I.e., the vast hooped petticoat and the full French hood would overwhelm a wispy feather which tried to mediate their quarrel.
1. A flap, often ornamented, concealing an opening in the front of men's breeches; fashionable in the 15th and 16th centuries.

2. Fancy's mind runs on dreams with fantastic consequences, dreams which might scare an audience "out of its wits."
3. Dried codfish, which had to be pounded into a pulp before it was edible. "Tabor": drum. The logic of Fancy is purposely erratic and obscure.
4. Zither. "Gittern" (in the next line) is a guitar.

You will say now, the morris-bells[5] were but bribes
To make the heel forget that ever it had kibes;[6]
I say, let the wine make never so good jelly,
The conscience of the bottle is much in the belly.
For why? do but take common council in your way,   80
And tell me who'll then set a bottle of hay
Before the old usurer, and to his horse
A slice of salt-butter, perverting the course
Of civil society?[7] Open that gap,
And out skip your fleas, four and twenty at a clap,   85
With a chain and a trundle-bed following at the heels,
And will they not cry then, the world runs a wheels:
As for example, a belly and no face,
With the bill of a shoveler,[8] may here come in place;
The haunches of a drum, with the feet of a pot,   90
And the tail of a Kentishman to it; why not?
Yet would I take the stars to be cruel,
If the crab and the ropemaker ever fight duel,[9]
On any dependence, be it right, be it wrong.
But mum; a thread may be drawn out too long.   95

Here the second ANTIMASQUE *of* FANTASMS *came forth, which danced.*

FANCY *proceeded:*
Why, this, you will say, was fantastical now,
As the cock and the bull, the whale and the cow;
    But vanish away, I have change to present you,
And such as (I hope) will more truly content you:
    Behold the gold-haired Hour[1] descending here,   100
That keeps the gate of heaven, and turns the year,
    Already with her sight, how she doth cheer,
And makes another face of things appear.

Here one of the HOURS *descending, the whole scene changed to the Bower of* ZEPHYRUS, *whilst* PEACE *sang, as followeth:*

Why look you so, and all turn dumb
    To see the opener of the New Year come?   105
My presence rather should invite
    And aid and urge and call to your delight.
The many pleasures that I bring
    Are all of youth, of heat, of life, of spring,
And were prepared to warm your blood,   110
    Not fix it thus, as if you statues stood.

5. Bells worn by morris-dancers.
6. Sores.
7. Fancy's argument has vaguely to do with the proper uses of things; if it weren't for the arrangements of civil society, everything would be topsy-turvy, and we would get all sorts of monstrous combinations.
8. A bird with a wide, flat beak.
9. A crab is a tool used by ropemakers to twist yarn; the point is that no man should fall out with the tools of his trade.
1. Fancy has shown, as in dreams, the decay and disintegration of things which takes places under the aegis of Night and the old year; the Hour now brings forth spring, dawn, and a new era for everyone.

THE CHOIR: We see, we hear, we feel, we taste,
We smell the change in every flower,
We only wish that all could last,
And be as new still as the hour.   115

The song ended, WONDER *spake:*

WONDER must speak or break. What is this? Grows
The wealth of Nature here, or Art? It shows
As if Favonius,[2] father of the spring,
Who, in the verdant meads, doth reign sole king,
Had roused him here, and shook his feathers, wet   120
With purple-swelling nectar; and had let
The sweet and fruitful dew fall on the ground
To force out all the flowers that might be found.
    Or a Minerva with her needle had
Th' enamoured earth with all her riches clad,   125
And made the downy Zephyr as he flew
Still to be followed with the spring's best hue.[3]
    The gaudy peacock boasts not in his train
So many lights and shadows, nor the rain-
Resolving Iris,[4] when the sun doth court her,   130
Nor purple pheasant while his aunt[5] doth sport her
To hear him crow; and with a perchéd[6] pride
Wave his discolored neck and purple side.
    I have not seen the place could more surprise;
It looks (methinks) like one of nature's eyes,   135
Or her whole body set in art. Behold!
How the blue bind-weed doth itself enfold
With honeysuckle, and both these entwine
Themselves with bryony[7] and jessamine
To cast a kind and odoriferous shade!   140

FANCY:

How better than they are are all things made
By WONDER![8] But a while refresh thine eye,
I'll put thee to thy oftener What and Why?

Here (*to a loud music*) *the Bower opens, and the* MASQUERS *discovered,*[9] *as the glories of the spring.*

WONDER *again spake:*

Thou wilt indeed; what better change appears?
Whence is it that the air so sudden clears   145
And all things in a moment turn so mild?

2. Sometimes called Zephyrus, a god of the west wind and hence of spring.
3. Athena or Minerva, though often represented with spear and shield, was a famous needlewoman (witness the story of Arachne), and is here imagined as embroidering the spring.
4. I.e., the rainbow.
5. Doxy, mistress; a term from thieve's slang.
6. Lofty.
7. A wild vine, often credited with magic powers.
8. The allegorical meaning of Jonson's characters comes out in a speech like this, which at the same time paves the way for the masque's climactic compliment.
9. Unmasked.

Whose breath or beams have got proud earth with child
Of all the treasures that great Nature's worth,
And makes her every minute to bring forth?
How comes it winter is so quite forced hence,   150
And locked up under ground? that every sense
Hath several objects? trees have got their heads,
The fields their coats? that now the shining meads
Do boast the paunce,[1] the lily, and the rose;
And every flower doth laugh as Zephyr blows?   155
That seas are now more even than the land?
The rivers run as smoothéd by his hand;
Only their heads are crispéd[2] by his stroke.
How plays the yearling with his brow scarce broke[3]
Now in the open grass? and frisking lambs   160
Make wanton salts[4] about their dry-sucked dams,
Who to repair their bags do rob the fields?
    How is 't each bough a several[5] music yields?
The lusty throstle, early nightingale
Accord in tune, though vary in their tale?   165
The chirping swallow, called forth by the sun,
And crested lark doth his division run?
The yellow bees the air with murmur fill?
The finches carol, and the turtles bill?
Whose power is this? What God?

FANCY:
                    Behold a king   170
Whose presence maketh this perpetual spring,
The glories of which spring grow in that bower,
And are the marks and beauties of his power.

To which the CHOIR *answered:*

'Tis he, 'tis he, and no power else,
That makes all this what Fancy tells;   175
    The founts, the flowers, the birds, the bees,
The herds, the flocks, the grass, the trees,
Do all confess him; but most these
Who call him lord of the four seas,
King of the less and greater isles,[6]   180
And all those happy when he smiles.
    Advance, his favor calls you to advance,
And do your (this night's) homage in a dance.

Here they danced their ENTRY, *after which they sung again:*

Again, again; you cannot be
Of such a true delight too free,   185

1. Pansy.
2. Curled.
3. By budding horns.
4. Leaps.
5. Separate.

6. James was king of Ireland ("the less") and England ("the greater isle"), and laid claim to sovereignty over the "four seas" surrounding England.

Which who once saw would ever sea;
And if they could the object prize,
Would while it lasts not think to rise,
    But wish their bodies were all eyes.

They danced their MAIN DANCE, *after which they sung:*

In curious knots and mazes so
The spring at first was taught to go;   190
And Zephyr when he came to woo
His Flora had their motions too,
    And thence did Venus learn to lead
    Th' Idalian brawls,[7] and so to tread,   195
As if the wind, not she, did walk;
Nor pressed a flower, nor bowed a stalk.

They danced with LADIES, *and the whole* REVELS[8] *followed; after
which* AURORA *appeared (the* NIGHT *and* MOON *descended) and this*
EPILOGUE *followed:*

AURORA:

I was not wearier where I lay
By frozen Tithon's side tonight[9]
Than I am willing now to stay
And be a part of your delight.   200
    But I am urgéd by the day,
Against my will, to bid you come away.

THE CHOIR:

    They yield to Time, and so must all.
As Night to sport, Day doth to action call,   205
    Which they the rather do obey,
Because the Morn with roses strews the way.

Here they danced their going off, and ended.

1631

7. The dances of Venus on Mt. Ida were legendary in antiquity. "Brawls" had a less rowdy connotation in the 17th century than the word bears today.
8. Procession of masquers.
9. Aurora was the unwilling bride of chilly old Tithonus (who was granted eternal life without the privilege of eternal youth); hence she was eager to come to the morning's entertainment, and now is reluctant to leave it.

ROBERT HERRICK
(1591–1674)

Robert Herrick was the son of a Cheapside goldsmith, who died shortly
after the poet's birth; in 1607, Herrick was apprenticed to his uncle, Sir
William Herrick, who was also a goldsmith and jeweler to the king. Thus
the poet was a Londoner, from the very heart of the London middle class.
In 1617, at the advanced age (for those days) of 26, he received his B.A.
degree at Cambridge; he was granted an M.A. in 1620, and was ordained

in 1623. But his real education came from his association with Ben Jonson, to whom he was deeply devoted. He was one of the "Sons of Ben," who foregathered in London taverns for rich hours of literary talk, suitably spiced with Canary wine; and in these happy, unprofitable pastimes he idled away some half-dozen years after he left the university. But circumstances pressed; one could not be a Son of Ben forever; and in 1629, with his fortieth birthday looming on the horizon, Herrick accepted the church living of Dean Prior in Devonshire, and moved there.

It was a great wrench for Herrick to leave London. He found the Devonshire folk rough, warty, and uncivil; and they, for their part, did not know what to make of a parson who wrote verses to "Saint Ben," and who reared, figuratively if not literally, an altar to Pan in the garden of the vicarage. How Herrick resolved in his own mind the conflict between a Pauline calling and a Horatian temperament is not easy to say; but he seems to have balanced happily, if precariously, between the two aspects of the situation. Surrounded by a crowd of imaginary mistresses with exotic names like Julia, Corinna, Perilla, Anthea, Electra, and Myrrha, but comfortably attended by an actual maidservant named Prudence Baldwin, Herrick lived out the existence of a bachelor clergyman, and wrote his verses. (Incidentally, the fact that all his imaginary ladies had namesakes beloved of ancient Greek or Roman poets illustrates the saturation of his mind in classical antiquity.) After a while he even came to delight in Devonshire, its pink milkmaids, quaint superstitions, and rural delicacies, such as clotted cream and fresh strawberries.

In 1647, dispossessed by the Puritans, Herrick came down to London with the products of his muse, and had them published early in 1648 in a fat little octavo volume with two titles, *Hesperides* for the secular poems, and *Noble Numbers* for those with sacred subjects. *Hesperides*, referring to the fabulous golden islands of the western ocean, embodies a melancholy reflection on the fact that his living was in the West Country. Altogether, there were 1,200 poems in Herrick's volume, a lyric cornucopia. But England at the time was in a fever of excitement over the trial and execution of Charles I. Herrick's rich harvest of verses disappeared in silence and oblivion, not to be revived till the 19th century; and Herrick himself, though he returned to Dean Prior in 1662, and survived to the ripe old age of 83, never ventured again on publication.

Though he published only one volume, Herrick covered in that single tome all the topics that interested him, from the agreeable glisten of Julia's satins to his relations with the Almighty. Politics, the place of man in the universe, and the darker aspects of passion interested him not at all. His poetry was never scaled to the heroic dimension; even in the *Noble Numbers*, where his seriousness is unquestioned, he contents himself with an urgent, docile piety. The surface polish of his poems, their relatively modest themes, and their classical balance have caused Herrick to be commonly classified with the "Cavaliers"—poets like Sir John Suckling and Edmund Waller, who turned off airy, graceful trifles with gentlemanly unconcern. There is something painful about describing the plump and sedentary Herrick as a galloping Cavalier; but in terms of poetic style, he belongs nowhere else.

The unique quality of Herrick's poetry may be described as the consciously naïve delight of a highly sophisticated man in natural things. He is a playful poet, but never a careless one; a master of the polished trifle, which, after one sees how many facets have been polished, turns out not to be a trifle at all. From Ben Jonson he learned the art of epigram—the brief, pointed, inevitable statement that seems to have been not so much written on paper as carved in marble. But his own private, wayward wit is more intimate and less didactic than Ben's; one can see its playful delicacy in a poem like the invitation to Corinna to go a-Maying, where the ideas of "church" and "sin" are joyously perverted, and then happily rearranged. And, generally, Herrick brings a richness of ornament to the handling of the most modest and hackneyed themes, which marks him as one of the great lyric artists—a goldsmith and jeweler of language, beyond all comparison in English.

The Argument[1] of His Book

I sing of brooks, of blossoms, birds, and bowers,
Of April, May, of June, and July flowers.
I sing of Maypoles, hock carts, wassails, wakes,[2]
Of bridegrooms, brides, and of their bridal cakes.
I write of youth, of love, and have access   5
By these to sing of cleanly wantonness.[3]
I sing of dews, of rains, and, piece by piece,
Of balm, of oil, of spice, and ambergris.[4]
I sing of times trans-shifting, and I write
How roses first came red and lilies white.   10
I write of groves, of twilights, and I sing
The court of Mab and of the fairy king.[5]
I write of hell; I sing (and ever shall)
Of heaven, and hope to have it after all.

                                                                  1648

Discontents in Devon[6]

More discontents I never had
    Since I was born, than here,
Where I have been, and still am sad,
    In this dull Devonshire;

1. Subject matter.
2. "Hock carts" carried home the last load of the harvest; therefore adorned and celebrated. "Wakes": festive, not funerary occasions, to commemorate the dedication of a parish church.
3. Good fun, but already tinged with the lascivious overtone the word carries today.
4. Ambergris is used in making per-
fumes; hence it carries the overtone of something rare and delectable.
5. Mab was by long-standing tradition queen of the fairies and wife of King Oberon. See Shakespeare, *A Midsummer Night's Dream*.
6. As a Londoner, Herrick was for a long time miserable in his parsonage at Dean Prior, Devonshire.

Yet justly too I must confess,   5
    I ne'er invented such
Ennobled numbers for the press,
    Than where I loathed so much.

                                    1648

Delight in Disorder

A sweet disorder in the dress
Kindles in clothes a wantonness.[7]
A lawn[8] about the shoulders thrown
Into a fine distractión;
An erring[9] lace, which here and there   5
Enthralls the crimson stomacher;[1]
A cuff neglectful, and thereby
Ribbons to flow confusedly;
A winning wave, deserving note,
In the tempestuous petticoat;   10
A careless shoestring, in whose tie
I see a wild civility;
Do more bewitch me than when art
Is too precise[2] in every part.

                                    1648

Upon Julia's Clothes

Whenas in silks my Julia goes,
Then, then, methinks, how sweetly flows
That liquefaction of her clothes.

Next, when I cast mine eyes, and see
That brave[3] vibration, each way free,   5
O, how that glittering taketh me!

                                    1648

To the Virgins, to Make Much of Time

Gather ye rosebuds while ye may,
    Old time is still a-flying;

---

7. Most of the terms used to describe the ladies' clothing have an ethical or social overtone.
8. A scarf of fine linen.
9. Wandering, floating.
1. The lower part of the bodice.

2. "Precise" and "precision" were terms used freely of Puritans; Herrick, in praising feminine disarray, is defining the "sprezzatura," or careless grace, of his own cavalier art.
3. Glorious, splendid.

And this same flower that smiles today
   Tomorrow will be dying.

The glorious lamp of heaven, the sun,   5
   The higher he's a-getting,
The sooner will his race be run,
   And nearer he's to setting.

That age is best which is the first,
   When youth and blood are warmer;   10
But being spent, the worse, and worst
   Times still succeed the former.

Then be not coy, but use your time,
   And, while ye may, go marry;
For, having lost but once your prime,   15
   You may forever tarry.

1648

Upon a Child That Died

Here she lies, a pretty bud,
Lately made of flesh and blood,
Who as soon fell fast asleep
As her little eyes did peep.
Give her strewings, but not stir   5
The earth that lightly covers her.

1648

Another Grace for a Child

Here a little child I stand,
Heaving up my either hand;
Cold as paddocks[4] though they be,
Here I lift them up to Thee,
For a benison[5] to fall   5
On our meat and on us all. Amen.

1648

↘ Corinna's Going A-Maying

Get up! get up for shame! the blooming morn
Upon her wings presents the god unshorn.[1]
See how Aurora throws her fair

---

4. Frogs.
5. Blessing.
1. Apollo, the sun god, whose hair (the rays of the sun) is never cut. For a discussion of the poem, and Apollo's rôle in it, see Cleanth Brooks, *The Well-Wrought Urn* (New York, 1947), Ch. 4.

Fresh-quilted colors through the air:[2]
Get up, sweet slug-a-bed, and see   5
The dew bespangling herb and tree.
Each flower has wept and bowed toward the east
Above an hour since, yet you not dressed;
    Nay, not so much as out of bed?
    When all the birds have matins said,   10
    And sung their thankful hymns, 'tis sin,
    Nay, profanation to keep in,
Whenas a thousand virgins on this day
Spring, sooner than the lark, to fetch in May.[3]

Rise, and put on your foliage, and be seen   15
To come forth, like the springtime, fresh and green,
    And sweet as Flora.[4] Take no care
    For jewels for your gown or hair;
    Fear not; the leaves will strew
    Gems in abundance upon you;   20
Besides, the childhood of the day has kept,
Against you come, some orient[5] pearls unwept;
    Come and receive them while the light
    Hangs on the dew-locks of the night,
    And Titan[6] on the eastern hill   25
    Retires himself, or else stands still
Till you come forth. Wash, dress, be brief in praying:
Few beads[7] are best when once we go a-Maying.

Come, my Corinna, come; and, coming, mark
How each field turns a street,[8] each street a park   30
    Made green and trimmed with trees; see how
    Devotion gives each house a bough
    Or branch: each porch, each door ere this,
    An ark, a tabernacle is,[9]
Made up of whitethorn neatly interwove,   35
As if here were those cooler shades of love.
    Can such delights be in the street
    And open fields, and we not see 't?
    Come, we'll abroad; and let's obey
    The proclamation made for May,   40

2. Aurora, goddess of the dawn, is both tossing her blankets aside, like one anxious to be up, and spreading over the earth a freshly composed coverlet of light.
3. On May-Day morning, it was the custom to gather whitethorn blossoms and trim the house with them (see below, lines 30–35).
4. Flora, the Roman goddess of flowers and vegetation, had her festival in the spring.
5. Eastern, as pearls come from the Orient, but also rosy and glowing like the rising sun. "Against": until.
6. The sun.
7. A casual term for prayers, but with overtones of the old (Catholic) religion, which in the next stanza is playfully converted into, and identified with, the worship of nature.
8. Turns into a street.
9. The doorways, ornamented with whitethorn, are like the Hebrew Ark of the Covenant; May sprigs are the central mystery of the religion of nature.

And sin no more, as we have done, by staying;
But, my Corinna, come, let's go a-Maying.

There's not a budding boy or girl this day
But is got up and gone to bring in May;
    A deal of youth, ere this, is come 45
    Back, and with whitethorn laden home.
    Some have dispatched their cakes and cream
    Before that we have left to dream;
And some have wept, and wooed, and plighted troth,
And chose their priest, ere we can cast off sloth. 50
    Many a green-gown[1] has been given,
    Many a kiss, both odd and even;[2]
    Many a glance, too, has been sent
    From out the eye, love's firmament;
Many a jest told of the keys betraying 55
This night, and locks picked; yet we're not a-Maying.

Come, let us go while we are in our prime,
And take the harmless folly of the time.
    We shall grow old apace, and die
    Before we know our liberty. 60
    Our life is short, and our days run
    As fast away as does the sun;
And, as a vapor or a drop of rain
Once lost, can ne'er be found again;
    So when or you or I are made 65
    A fable, song, or fleeting shade,
    All love, all liking, all delight
    Lies drowned with us in endless night.
Then while time serves, and we are but decaying,
Come, my Corinna, come, let's go a-Maying. 70

1648

Oberon's Feast[1]

    Shapcot![2] to thee the fairy state
    I, with discretion, dedicate,
    Because thou prizest things that are
    Curious and unfamiliar.
    Take first the feast; these dishes gone, 5
    We'll see the fairy court anon.

    A little mushroom table spread,
    After short prayers, they set on bread;

---

1. Got by rolling in the grass.
2. Kisses are odd and even in kissing games.
1. Oberon, the king of the fairies, was a popular figure in rural mythology as well as in literature (see *A Midsummer Night's Dream*).
2. Probably Herrick's friend Thomas Shapcot(t), a Devonshire lawyer.

A moon-parched grain of purest wheat,
With some small glittering grit[3] to eat   10
His choice bits with; then in a trice
They make a feast less great than nice.[4]
But all this while his eye is served,
We must not think his ear was sterved;[5]
But that there was in place to stir   15
His spleen,[6] the chirring grasshopper,
The merry cricket, puling fly,
The piping gnat for minstrelsy.
And now we must imagine first,
The elves present to quench his thirst   20
A pure seed-pearl of infant dew,
Brought and besweetened in a blue
And pregnant violet; which done,
His kitling[7] eyes begin to run
Quite through the table, where he spies   25
The horns of papery butterflies,
Of which he eats, and tastes a little
Of that we call the cuckoo's spittle.[8]
A little fuzz-ball pudding stands
By, yet not blessed by his hands,   30
That was too coarse; but then forthwith
He ventures boldly on the pith
Of sugared rush, and eats the sag
And well-bestrutted[9] bee's sweet bag,
Gladding his palate with some store   35
Of emmets' eggs;[1] what would he more?
But beards of mice, a newt's stewed thigh,
A bloated earwig, and a fly;
With the red-capped worm that's shut
Within the concave of a nut,   40
Brown as his tooth. A little moth,
Late fattened in a piece of cloth;
With withered cherries, mandrake's ears,[2]
Mole's eyes; to these[3] the slain stag's tears;
The unctuous dewlaps of a snail;   45
The broke-heart of a nightingale
O'ercome in music;[4] with a wine
Ne'er ravished from the flattering vine,
But gently pressed from the soft side

---

3. Chaff, flour dust.
4. Delicate.
5. Neglected.
6. The seat of all emotions, more usually anger, but also, as here, laughter.
7. Little, tiny.
8. A frothy secretion, given off by various insects on grass and branches.
9. "Sag / And well-bestrutted": filled to the point of bulging.
1. Ant eggs.
2. Mandrakes (mandragoras), being half-animal, half-vegetable, have very small ears indeed; moles (in the next line) have tiny, weak eyes. The point is that Oberon's food must be not only curious but very dainty.
3. The word "add" is understood.
4. Herrick is thinking of an ancient story about a nightingale which tried to outsing a musician with a lyre, and died in the attempt. Such a broken heart would be the epitome of sweetness.

Of the most sweet and dainty bride,[5]   50
Brought in a dainty daisy, which
He fully quaffs up to bewitch
His blood to height; this done, commended
Grace by his priest; the feast is ended.

                                                    1648

His Return to London

From the dull confines of the drooping West,
To see the day spring from the pregnant East,
Ravished in spirit, I come, nay more, I fly
To thee, blest place of my nativity!
Thus, thus with hallowed foot I touch the ground   5
With thousand blessings by thy fortune crowned.
O fruitful genius! that bestowest here
An everlasting plenty, year by year;
O place! O people! Manners framed to please
All nations, customs, kindreds, languages!   10
I am a free-born Roman;[1] suffer then
That I amongst you live a citizen.
London my home is: though by hard fate sent
Into a long and irksome banishment;
Yet since called back; henceforward let me be,   15
O native country, repossessed by thee!
For, rather than I'll to the West return,
I'll beg of thee first here to have mine urn.
Weak I am grown, and must in short time fall;
Give thou my sacred relics burial.[2]   20

                                                    1648

To the Water Nymphs Drinking at the Fountain

Reach with your whiter hands to me
    Some crystal of the spring;
And I about the cup shall see
    Fresh lilies flourishing.

Or else, sweet nymphs, do you but this—   5
    To the glass your lips incline;
And I shall see by that one kiss
    The water turned to wine.

                                                    1648

5. Bridewort (sometimes called mead-ow-sweet) is the source of the fairy vintage.
1. A Roman born in the city was said to be "free of it," i.e., entitled to its liberties.
2. As a priest and a poet, Herrick might without immodesty claim that his "rel-ics" were sacred.

Upon Prue, His Maid

In this little urn is laid
Prudence Baldwin, once my maid,
From whose happy spark here let
Spring the purple violet.

1648

Upon His Spaniel Tracy

Now thou art dead, no eye shall ever see,
For shape and service, spaniel like to thee.
This shall my love do, give thy sad death one
Tear, that deserves of me a million.

1648

The Pillar of Fame

Fame's pillar here at last we set,
Out-during marble, brass, or jet;
   Charmed and enchanted so
   As to withstand the blow
     Of o v e r t h r o w;   5
     Nor shall the seas,
     O r   o u t r a g e s
     Of storms, o'erbear
     What we uprear;
     Tho' kingdoms fall,   10
   This pillar never shall
   Decline or waste at all;
But stand for ever by his own
Firm and well-fixed foundation.

To his book's end this last line he'd have placed: 15
Jocund his Muse was, but his life was chaste.[3]

1648

3. The poem is a shaped verse, like those of George Herbert; it makes a typographical picture of its subject. The claim of the last line was probably cor- rect: in any case, it was his last word on the subject, for this is the final poem in *Hesperides*.

GEORGE HERBERT
(1593–1633)

George Herbert was the fifth son of an ancient and distinguished Welsh family. His father died when he was young, and he was brought up by his mother, Magdalen Herbert, a friend of Donne's, and a lady eminent both for her piety and her love of letters. After taking his degrees with distinction at the University of Cambridge, George Herbert was elected Public Orator of the university. It was a post carrying dignity and even some authority: its incumbent was called on to express, in the florid Latin of the day, the sentiments of the university on public occasions. Other men had used the post as a steppingstone to high political office; and Herbert seems to have had this idea, at least briefly, in mind. But the death of his patrons, and the bent of his own temper, soon drew him in another direction. In 1626 he took a minor office in the church; in 1629 he married Jane Danvers; and in 1630 he accepted the living of Bemerton, in Salisbury, and took orders.

Many younger sons of highly connected houses entered the church in those days—picking up a sinecure here and a nonresident ministry there; accepting the pay, and letting the work be done by underpaid curates; filling the offices of the church, perhaps without scandal, but also without the least breath of spiritual fervor. At Bemerton, on the contrary, George Herbert became at once what the age delighted to recognize as "a learned, godly, and painful divine." He preached and prayed; he rebuilt the church out of his own pocket; he visited the poor, consoled the sick, and sat by the bed of the dying—administering true pastoral care to the plowman and the peer alike. "Holy Mr. Herbert" became the talk of the countryside in the three short years of his ministry, before he died of consumption. And during these years, he completed the volume of poems known as *The Temple*, which was published shortly after his death, in 1633, by the friend to whom it had been left. His fame rests on this volume, and all our selections are taken from it.

As a poet, Herbert is quiet, inward, subtle, graceful, and neat. Working within the great tradition of Christian types and imagery, he delights in using quaint devices and homely images. But his spiritual feeling is to an extraordinary degree pure and fresh and free. Donne may be described as the poet of religious doubt, of strain, of anxiety; Herbert is the poet of religious faith, of submission, of acceptance. Both are classified as "metaphysical" poets; both use "conceited" and ingenious images; but Herbert, in a poem like *Love*, for example, allows his meaning to unfold from the situation gently like a flower, where Donne would be tugging at it or arguing with a mock opponent. Herbert is never flashy, nor even strongly dramatic; like the church he served, he is devoted to the quiet middle way. Yet his quiet is never the quiet of emotional poverty or torpor. Herbert's moods are as changeable as the English weather; but underneath them one hears the uninterrupted murmur of prayer, the serene wisdom of a thousand years of faith. The ancient forms were ever George Herbert's chief delight; his poetry, from which the concept of "freshness" is rarely absent, is like the parish church—an intricate, ancient structure, rich in traditional designs, which is open for the humblest and simplest person to enter.

Easter Wings[1]

Lord, who createdst man in wealth and store,[2]
  Though foolishly he lost the same,
    Decaying more and more
      Till he became
        Most poor: 5
        With thee
      O let me rise
    As larks, harmoniously,
  And sing this day thy victories:
Then shall the fall further the flight in me.   10

My tender age in sorrow did begin:
  And still with sicknesses and shame
    Thou didst so punish sin,
      That I became
        Most thin.   15
        With thee
      Let me combine,
    And feel this day thy victory;
  For, if I imp[3] my wing on thine,
Affliction shall advance the flight in me.   20

1633

Virtue

Sweet day, so cool, so calm, so bright,
  The bridal of the earth and sky:
The dew shall weep thy fall tonight;
  For thou must die.

Sweet rose, whose hue, angry and brave,[4]   5

---

1. This poem and *The Altar* (p. 955) are "shaped verses," which represent, by the typographical shape of the poem on the page, some part of the subject. Though sometimes condemned as "false wit," this sort of poem has appealed to an occasional author from Hellenistic times to the present. Among recent examples are *Vision and Prayer* by Dylan Thomas and *Un Coup de Dés* by Stéphane Mallarmé. The most amazing poet in this mode was a Byzantine pedant, Publius Optatian Porphyry,

who printed his poems in two colors of ink, and got them to represent triremes and other complicated objects. Early editions of Herbert print *Easter Wings* with the lines running vertically.
2. Abundance.
3. Graft (a technical term from falconry).
4. "Angry": having the hue of anger, red. "Brave": splendid. Both adjectives indicate the arrogant yet pathetic defiance of beauty in the face of time.

Bids the rash gazer wipe his eye:
Thy root is ever in its grave,
    And thou must die.

Sweet spring, full of sweet days and roses,
  A box where sweets[5] compacted lie;   10
My music shows ye have your closes,[6]
    And all must die.

Only a sweet and virtuous soul,
  Like seasoned timber, never gives;
But though the whole world turn to coal,[7]   15
    Then chiefly lives.

                    1633

Jordan (I) [1]

Who says that fictions only and false hair
Become a verse? Is there in truth no beauty?
Is all good structure in a winding stair?
May no lines pass, except they do their duty
    Not to a true, but painted chair?[2]   5

Is it no verse, except enchanted groves
And sudden arbors shadow coarse-spun lines?[3]
Must purling streams refresh a lover's loves?
Must all be veiled while he that reads, divines,
    Catching the sense at two removes?   10

Shepherds are honest people; let them sing:
Riddle who list, for me, and pull for prime:[4]
I envy no man's nightingale or spring;

5. Perfumes.
6. Concluding cadences. The expression shows that Herbert intended his poem to be sung—as it has, in fact, often been.
7. Be reduced to a cinder at the Last Judgment. See II Peter iii.10.
1. Both poems titled *Jordan* are about complexity and simplicity; "crossing Jordan" is of course a symbol for entering into the Promised Land, and it seems likely that Herbert means to indicate by his title that for one who has crossed the river (i.e., come into God's country), many worldly complexities cease to be necessary or desirable.
2. May no poems ("lines") pass as good unless they make a reverence ("do their duty") to a false throne? It has often been the custom for men to bow before a throne, whether it was oc-

cupied or not (see Donne, *Satire III*, lines 47–48); but to require bowing to a throne in a painting (i.e., an artificial throne), would be excessive. Herbert implies that earthly love is a mere painted imitation of divine love.
3. "Sudden": i.e., that appear unexpectedly (an artificial effect much sought after in landscape gardening). "Shadow": overshadow, cause to be overlooked. Herbert is suggesting that flashy dramatic effects obscure poor craftsmanship. So far as it applies to anyone in particular, "coarse-spun lines" may be taken as referring to Donne.
4. To draw a lucky card in the card game of "primero." Herbert implies that anyone who understands one of the complex poems he is describing (and parodying) has made a wild and lucky guess.

Nor let them punish me with loss of rhyme,
 Who plainly say, *My God, My King.*   15
                1633

Jordan (II)

When first my lines of heavenly joys made mention,
 Such was their luster, they did so excel,
That I sought out quaint words, and trim invention;
 My thoughts began to burnish,[1] sprout, and swell,
Curling with metaphors a plain intention,   5
 Decking the sense, as if it were to sell.[2]

Thousands of notions in my brain did run,
 Offering their service, if I were not sped:[3]
I often blotted what I had begun;
 This was not quick[4] enough, and that was dead. 10
Nothing could seem too rich to clothe the sun,
 Much less those joys which trample on his head.[5]

As flames do work and wind when they ascend,
 So did I weave myself into the sense;
But while I bustled, I might hear a friend   15
 Whisper, "How wide[6] is all this long pretense!
There is in love a sweetness ready penned:
 Copy out only that, and save expense."

                1633

Denial

  When my devotions could not pierce
    Thy silent ears;
  Then was my heart broken, as was my verse:
    My breast was full of fears
    And disorder: 5

  My bent thoughts, like a brittle bow,
    Did fly asunder:
  Each took his way; some would to pleasure go,
    Some to the wars and thunder
    Of alarms.   10

  As good go anywhere, they say,
    As to benumb

---

1. Expand, burgeon.
2. For sale.
3. Suited, supplied.
4. Lively, alive.

5. The "joys which trample on" the sun's head are those of the Son.
6. Irrelevant, "wide of the mark."

Both knees and heart in crying night and day,
 Come, come, my God, O come!
  But no hearing.   15

O that thou shouldst give dust a tongue
 To cry to thee,
And then not hear it crying! All day long
 My heart was in my knee,[1]
  But no hearing.   20

Therefore my soul lay out of sight,
 Untuned, unstrung:
My feeble spirit, unable to look right,
 Like a nipped blossom, hung
  Discontented.   25

O cheer and tune my heartless breast;
 Defer no time,
That so thy favors granting my request,
 They and my mind may chime,[2]
  And mend my rhyme.   30

        1633

The Altar

A broken ALTAR, Lord, thy servant rears,
Made of a heart, and cemented with tears:
 Whose parts are as thy hand did frame;
 No workman's tool hath touched the same.[3]
    A HEART alone   5
    Is such a stone,
    As nothing but
    Thy power doth cut.
    Wherefore each part
    Of my hard heart   10
    Meets in this frame,
    To praise thy Name:
 That, if I chance to hold my peace,
 These stones to praise thee may not cease.[4]
Oh let thy blessed SACRIFICE be mine, 15
And sanctify this ALTAR to be thine.

        1633

1. I.e., my heart was bowed and bent, like my knee, in reverence.
2. Agree. The rhyming of the last two lines, coming to restore the harmony of this stanza, illustrates Herbert's hope of harmony with God.
3. A reference to Exodus xx.25, in which the Lord enjoins Moses to build an altar without using cut stone or any tools. Herbert's book was titled *The Temple*, and many individual poems are about particular parts of a church— the porch, the windows, the floor, the lock and key, or the altar.
4. Herbert wants his poem to praise God whether or not it is being read or spoken. There is also a reference to Luke xix.40: "I tell you that, if these should hold their peace, the stones would immediately cry out." Herbert's poetry, like Milton's, is rich to overflowing in Scriptural echoes.

The Flower

How fresh, oh Lord, how sweet and clean
Are thy returns! even as the flowers in spring;
 To which, besides their own demesne,[1]
The late-past frosts tributes of pleasure bring.
   Grief melts away   5
   Like snow in May,
 As if there were no such cold thing.

 Who would have thought my shriveled heart
Could have recovered greenness? It was gone
 Quite underground; as flowers depart   10
To see their mother-root, when they have blown,[2]
   Where they together
   All the hard weather,
 Dead to the world, keep house unknown.

 These are thy wonders, Lord of power,   15
Killing and quickening, bringing down to hell
 And up to heaven in an hour;
Making a chiming of a passing-bell.[3]
   We say amiss
   This or that is:[4]   20
 Thy word is all, if we could spell.

 Oh that I once past changing were,
Fast in thy Paradise, where no flower can wither!
 Many a spring I shoot up fair,
Offering[5] at heaven, growing and groaning thither; 25
   Nor doth my flower
   Want a spring shower,[6]
 My sins and I joining together.

 But while I grow in a straight line,
Still upwards bent, as if heaven were mine own, 30
 Thy anger comes, and I decline:
What frost to that? what pole is not the zone
   Where all things burn,
   When thou dost turn,
 And the least frown of thine is shown?[7]   35

1. Estate of one's own (here, beauty or pleasure). The word, spelled *demean* in the original text, may also be a short form of "demeanor," i.e., bearing.
2. Bloomed.
3. The passing-bell, intended to mark the death of a parishioner, is tolled in a monotone; a chiming offers pleasant variety.
4. I.e., that a thing exists in its own nature.
5. Aiming.
6. The tears of contrition produced by the "joining together" of the poet's conscience and his sins.
7. Lines 32–35 may be paraphrased: "What cold compares to God's anger? Compared to God's wrath, what polar chill would not seem like the heat of the equator?"

And now in age I bud again,
After so many deaths I live and write;
  I once more smell the dew and rain,
And relish versing. Oh, my only light,
      It cannot be   40
      That I am he
On whom thy tempests fell all night.

These are thy wonders, Lord of love,
To make us see we are but flowers that glide;[8]
  Which when we once can find and prove,[9]   45
Thou hast a garden for us where to bide;
      Who would be more,
      Swelling through store,
Forfeit their Paradise by their pride.

                    1633

The Collar

I struck the board[1] and cried, "No more;
    I will abroad!
What? shall I ever sigh and pine?
My lines and life are free, free as the road,
  Loose as the wind, as large as store.   5
      Shall I be still in suit?[2]
Have I no harvest but a thorn
To let me blood, and not restore
What I have lost with cordial[3] fruit?
      Sure there was wine   10
Before my sighs did dry it; there was corn
  Before my tears did drown it.
Is the year only lost to me?
  Have I no bays[4] to crown it,
No flowers, no garlands gay? all blasted?   15
    All wasted?
Not so, my heart; but there is fruit,
    And thou hast hands.
Recover all thy sigh-blown age
On double pleasures: leave thy cold dispute   20
Of what is fit and not. Forsake thy cage,
    Thy rope of sands,[5]
Which petty thoughts have made, and made to thee
Good cable, to enforce and draw,

---

8. Pass silently away.
9. Experience.
1. Table.
2. In attendance, waiting on someone for a favor.
3. Giving heart's ease, restorative.

4. The poet's wreath, here used as a general symbol of festivity.
5. Christian restrictions on behavior, which the "petty thoughts" of the docile believer have made "good cable," i.e., strong.

And be thy law,   25
While thou didst wink[6] and wouldst not see.
Away! take heed;
I will abroad.
Call in thy death's-head[7] there; tie up thy fears.
He that forbears   30
To suit and serve his need,
Deserves his load."
But as I raved and grew more fierce and wild
At every word,
Methought I heard one calling, *Child!*   35
And I replied, *My Lord.*

1633

The Pulley

When God at first made man,
Having a glass of blessings standing by,
"Let us," said he, "pour on him all we can.
Let the world's riches, which dispersèd lie,
Contract into a span."   5

So strength first made a way;
Then beauty flowed, then wisdom, honor, pleasure.
When almost all was out, God made a stay,
Perceiving that, alone of all his treasure,
Rest in the bottom lay.[1]   10

"For if I should," said he,
"Bestow this jewel also on my creature,
He would adore my gifts instead of me,
And rest in Nature, not the God of Nature;
So both should losers be.   15

"Yet let him keep the rest,
But keep them with repining restlessness.
Let him be rich and weary, that at least,
If goodness lead him not, yet weariness
May toss him to my breast."   20

Discipline

Throw away thy rod,
Throw away thy wrath:

6. Shut your eyes (to the real weakness of the church's injunctions).
7. The skull which reminds the penitent of approaching death.
1. "Rest" in the poem has two senses ("remainder" and "repose"); Herbert works them against one another. This seesaw suggests the pulley, which can draw us to God one way or the other.

O my God,
Take the gentle path.

For my heart's desire   5
Unto thine is bent:
            I aspire
To a full consent.

Not a word or look
I affect to own,   10
            But by book,
And thy book alone.[2]

Though I fail, I weep:
Though I halt in pace,
            Yet I creep   15
To the throne of grace.

Then let wrath remove;
Love will do the deed:
            For with love
Stony hearts will bleed.   20

Love is swift of foot;
Love's a man of war,[3]
            And can shoot,
And can hit from far.

Who can 'scape his bow?   25
That which wrought on thee,
            Brought thee low,
Needs must work on me.

Throw away thy rod;
Though man frailties hath,   30
            Thou art God:
Throw away thy wrath.

                                                                    1633

Prayer (I)

Prayer, the church's banquet, angels' age,[1]
    God's breath in man returning to his birth,
    The soul in paraphrase, heart in pilgrimage,
    The Christian plummet sounding heaven and earth;

2. Disclaiming all independence, Herbert describes himself as an actor, who will speak only "by the book."
3. The jubilant song sung by Moses in Exodus xv calls the Lord "a man of war"; but Herbert is thinking also, and without any apparent sense of contradiction, about Cupid, another divine bowman.
1. The age of angels is infinite; hence prayer puts us in touch with infinity.

Engine against th' Almighty, sinner's tower,   5
  Reverséd thunder, Christ-side-piercing spear,[2]
  The six-days' world transposing in an hour,[3]
A kind of tune, which all things hear and fear;

Softness, and peace, and joy, and love, and bliss,
  Exalted manna, gladness of the best,   10
  Heaven in ordinary,[4] man well dressed,
The Milky Way, the bird of Paradise,

  Church bells beyond the stars heard, the soul's blood,
  The land of spices; something understood.

                                                  1633

Ana ${Mary \atop Army}$ gram

How well her name an *Army* doth present,
  In whom the Lord of Hosts did pitch his tent!

                                                  1633

Sin's Round

Sorry I am, my God, sorry I am
That my offenses course it in a ring.
My thoughts are working like a busy flame,
Until their cockatrice [5] they hatch and bring:
And when they once have perfected their draughts,[6]   5
My words take fire from my inflaméd thoughts.

My words take fire from my inflaméd thoughts,
Which spit it forth like the Sicilian hill.[7]
They vent [8] the wares, and pass them with their faults,
And by their breathing ventilate [9] the ill.   10
But words suffice not, where are lewd intentions:
My hands do join to finish the inventions.

2. Prayer is a spear which pierces Christ's side and touches his heart.
3. An hour of prayer can transform a universe which took six days to create.
4. I.e., Heaven in the regular course of worldly life.
5. A fabulous creature, sometimes identified with the basilisk, hatched by a viper out of a cock's egg and partaking of both natures, but infinitely more deadly than either. Here it is an image for sin.

6. This word, always pronounced and sometimes spelled *drafts* nowadays, was pronounced in the 17th century to rhyme with "naughts."
7. Mt. Etna, a volcano.
8. Vend; also "let forth" or "give vent to."
9. Increase, augment; also "give breath to." The word is a reminder that the cockatrice could kill creatures simply by breathing on them.

My hands do join to finish the inventions:
And so my sins ascend three stories high,[1]
As Babel grew, before there were dissensions. 15
Yet ill deeds loiter not: for they supply
New thoughts of sinning: wherefore, to my shame,
Sorry I am, my God, sorry I am.

1633

Aaron

Holiness on the head,
Light and perfections on the breast,
Harmonious bells below, raising the dead
To lead them unto life and rest:
  Thus are true Aarons dressed.[2] 5

Profaneness in my head,
Defects and darkness in my breast,
A noise of passions ringing me for dead
Unto a place where is no rest:
  Poor priest, thus am I dressed. 10

Only another head
I have, another heart and breast,
Another music, making live, not dead,
Without whom I could have no rest:
  In him I am well dressed. 15

Christ is my only head,
My alone only heart and breast,
My only music, striking me even dead,
That to the old man I may rest,
  And be in him new dressed.[3] 20

So, holy in my head,
Perfect and light in my dear breast,
My doctrine tuned by Christ, who is not dead,
But lives in me while I do rest,
  Come, people; Aaron's dressed. 25

1633

Love (III)

Love bade me welcome: yet my soul drew back,
  Guilty of dust and sin.

1. I.e., thoughts, words, hands—like the Tower of Babel.
2. Exodus xxviii describes in great detail the garments to be worn by Aaron as high priest. Note that there are five letters in the name "Aaron," five stanzas in the poem, and five lines in each stanza.
3. As the clapper strikes the bell and makes music of it, Christ strikes the priest, killing the Old Adam (the "old man," i.e., human frailty) in him, and raising the regenerate soul.

But quick-eyed Love, observing me grow slack [4]
    From my first entrance in,
Drew nearer to me, sweetly questioning   5
    If I lacked anything.[5]

"A guest," I answered, "worthy to be here":
    Love said, "You shall be he."
"I, the unkind, ungrateful? Ah, my dear,
    I cannot look on thee."   10
Love took my hand, and smiling did reply,
    "Who made the eyes but I?"

"Truth, Lord; but I have marred them; let my shame
    Go where it doth deserve."
"And know you not," says Love, "who bore the blame?"   15
    "My dear, then I will serve."
"You must sit down," says Love, "and taste my meat."
    So I did sit and eat.

             1633

---

4. Backward.
5. The first question of shopkeepers and tavern waiters to an entering customer would be, "What d'ye lack?" (i.e., want).

RICHARD CRASHAW
(ca. 1613–1649)

A figure almost unique in English literary history, Richard Crashaw belongs to a tradition which is Roman Catholic, Continental (specifically Italian), and Counter-Reformation. Because there is so little like it in English, his verse has undergone wildly fluctuating judgments, alternately ridiculed and admired—and usually in extremes—ever since it appeared.

Crashaw, the son of a Puritan clergyman, revolted against everything in his father's background except the Christian religion itself. After a successful career at Peterhouse College, Cambridge, he took orders in the English church in 1638; but his sympathies had long since drawn him toward the ritual party, the party of Laud, episcopacy, and anti-Calvinism. During the Civil Wars he was ejected from his fellowship, went abroad, was converted to Roman Catholicism (in our own day, an equivalent action would be for the son of a Republican senator to become a Communist agent), and was appointed a canon in the famous shrine of the Virgin at Loreto. Here he died suddenly (there were some melodramatic stories of poisoning) before attaining his 40th year. He had published a book of *Sacred Epigrams* (in Latin and Greek) in 1634; a volume titled *Steps to the Temple (with other delights of the Muses)* in 1646; and in 1652 his final writings were collected under the title *Carmen Deo Nostro* ("A Song to Our Lord"). A conscientious craftsman, Crashaw took great pains to revise his poems, and most of them exist in several versions.

The peculiar quality of Crashaw's verse is determined by his taste, which was formed on contemporary Italian models, notably the great *concettisto* ("writer of conceits") Giambattista Marini, whose long poem, *The Massacre of the Innocents*, Crashaw partially translated. One result of this influence is that Crashaw's own poems are deliberately artificial and deliberately lacking in formal structure. There are certain recurrent themes in Crashaw's poetry; he loves to describe divine love in human terms, and his poetry is rich in wounds and kisses, blood and milk, nests and breasts, ecstasy and surrender. But he feels free to repeat these elements at will, to string his extravagant metaphors loosely together, and to combine them with almost grotesque effects. His best poems culminate, like the great cantata *In the Holy Nativity* or the concluding section of *The Flaming Heart*, in a swirling, grandiose phantasmagoria of sensual and spiritual ecstasy. In effect, this verse is like nothing so much as one of the great baroque churches of Rome, where ornate theatricalities work on every hand to dissolve everyday solidities into a vision of florid, artificial grandeur.

In the Holy Nativity of Our Lord God[1]

A HYMN SUNG AS BY THE SHEPHERDS

CHORUS

Come, we shepherds, whose blest sight
    Hath met love's noon in nature's night;
Come, lift we up our loftier song
And wake the sun[2] that lies too long.

To all our world of well-stolen joy   5
He[3] slept, and dreamt of no such thing;
    While we found out heaven's fairer eye,
And kissed the cradle of our King.
    Tell him he rises now too late
To show us aught worth looking at.   10

    Tell him we now can show him more
Than he e'er showed to mortal sight,
    Than he himself e'er saw before,
Which to be seen needs not his light:[4]
    Tell him, Tityrus, where th' hast been;   15
Tell him, Thyrsis, what th' hast seen.

TITYRUS

Gloomy night embraced the place
    Where the noble Infant lay.
    The Babe looked up and showed His face:
In spite of darkness, it was day.   20
    It was Thy day, Sweet! and did rise,
Not from the east, but from Thine eyes.

1. This poem originally appeared, in a very different version, in *Steps to the Temple;* the much improved version reprinted here is from *Carmen Deo Nostro,* six years later.
2. Christ the sun-Son is the noontime (i.e., the high point) of love, encountered, paradoxically, in "nature's night" (of wintertime and paganism).
3. The sun (i.e., nature's sun).
4. I.e., sunlight. Christ himself is more than nature and is visible without the light of nature—sense, reason, and the inferior faculties.

CHORUS: It was Thy day, Sweet, etc.

THYRSIS

Winter chid aloud, and sent
The angry North to wage his wars.   25
The North forgot his fierce intent,
And left perfumes instead of scars.
By those sweet eyes' persuasive powers,
Where he meant frost, he scattered flowers.

CHORUS: By those sweet eyes', etc.   30

BOTH

We saw Thee in Thy balmy nest,
Young Dawn of our eternal day!
We saw Thine eyes break from their east,
And chase the trembling shades away.
We saw Thee, and we blest the sight;   35
We saw Thee by Thine own sweet light.

CHORUS: We saw Thee, etc.

TITYRUS

"Poor world," said I, "what wilt thou do
To entertain this starry Stranger?
Is this the best thou canst bestow—   40
A cold and not too cleanly manger?
Contend, ye powers of heaven and earth,
To fit a bed for this huge birth!"

CHORUS: Contend, ye powers, etc.

THYRSIS

"Proud world," said I, "cease your contest,   45
And let the mighty Babe alone.
The phoenix builds the phoenix' nest;
Love's architecture is his own.
The Babe whose birth embraves[5] this morn
Made His own bed ere He was born."   50

CHORUS: The Babe whose, etc.

TITYRUS

I saw the curled drops, soft and slow,
Come hovering o'er the place's head,
Offering their whitest sheets of snow
To furnish the fair Infant's bed;   55
"Forbear," said I; "be not too bold;
Your fleece is white, but 'tis too cold."

CHORUS: "Forbear," said I, etc.

THYRSIS

I saw the obsequious[6] seraphims

5. Makes splendid, glorifies.   and purifying ministers of Jehovah.
6. Obedient, devoted. Seraphim are fiery

Their rosy fleece of fire bestow,   60
  For well they now can spare their wings,
Since Heaven itself lies here below.
  "Well done," said I; "but are you sure
Your down, so warm, will pass for pure?"

    CHORUS: "Well done," said I, etc.   65

TITYRUS

No, no, your King's not yet to seek
Where to repose His royal head;
  See, see how soon His new-bloomed cheek
'Twixt's mother's breasts is gone to bed.
  "Sweet choice," said we! "no way but so,   70
Not to lie cold, yet sleep in snow."

    CHORUS: "Sweet choice," said we, etc.

BOTH

We saw Thee in Thy balmy nest,
Bright Dawn of our eternal day!
  We saw Thine eyes break from their east,   75
And chase the trembling shades away.
  We saw Thee, and we blest the sight;
We saw Thee by Thine own sweet light.

    CHORUS: We saw Thee, etc.

FULL CHORUS

Welcome, all wonders in one sight!   80
Eternity shut in a span.
  Summer in winter. Day in night.
Heaven in earth, and God in man!
  Great little one! whose all-embracing birth
Lifts earth to heaven, stoops heaven to earth.   85

Welcome; though nor to gold nor silk,
To more than Caesar's birthright is:
  Two sister-seas of virgin milk,
With many a rarely tempered kiss,
  That breathes at once both maid and mother,   90
Warms in the one, cools in the other.

Welcome, though not to those gay flies,[7]
Gilded i' th' beams of earthly kings,
  Slippery souls in smiling eyes;
But to poor shepherds, homespun things,   95
  Whose wealth's their flock, whose wit, to be
Well read in their simplicity.

Yet when young April's husband-showers
Shall bless the fruitful Maia's bed,[8]
  We'll bring the first-born of her flowers   100

7. Courtiers, who flutter around the light of royalty—fragile, glittering, short-lived creatures ("slippery souls"), who exist only so long as someone smiles on them.

8. April is the husband, generating flowers in May, the wife.

To kiss Thy feet, and crown Thy head.
To Thee, dread Lamb! whose love must keep
The shepherds more than they the sheep;

To Thee, meek Majesty! soft King
Of simple graces and sweet loves,   105

Each of us his lamb will bring,
Each his pair of silver doves;
Till burnt at last in fire of Thy fair eyes,
Ourselves become our own best sacrifice.[9]

1646, 1652

From The Flaming Heart

UPON THE BOOK AND PICTURE OF THE SERAPHICAL SAINT
TERESA,[1] AS SHE IS USUALLY EXPRESSED WITH
A SERAPHIM BESIDE HER

* * *

O heart! the equal poise of love's both parts,[2]   75
Big alike with wounds and darts,
Live in these conquering leaves;[3] live all the same;
And walk through all tongues one triumphant flame.
Live here, great heart; and love and die and kill,
And bleed and wound; and yield and conquer still.   80
Let this immortal life, where'er it comes,
Walk in a crowd of loves and martyrdoms.
Let mystic deaths wait on 't, and wise souls be
The love-slain witnesses of this life of thee:
O sweet incendiary! show here thy art,   85
Upon this carcass of a hard, cold heart;[4]
Let all thy scattered shafts of light, that play
Among the leaves of thy large books of day,[5]
Combined against this breast, at once break in
And take away from me myself and sin!   90
This gracious robbery shall thy bounty be,
And my best fortunes such fair spoils of me.[6]
O thou undaunted daughter of desires!
By all thy dower of lights and fires;
By all the eagle in thee, all the dove;[7]   95
By all thy lives and deaths of love;
By thy large draughts of intellectual day,
And by thy thirsts of love more large than they;

9. Since divine love is a fire, our best
sacrifice is the burnt offering of ourselves.
1. St. Teresa (1515–82) was a Spanish
mystic, famous for her passionate visions and holy labors. Crashaw's poem
doubtless owes something to the great
statue of the saint by Bernini in Santa
Maria della Vittoria, at Rome.
2. In the heart are combined both parts
of love, the passive ("wounds") and
the active ("darts").

3. I.e., the leaves of St. Teresa's book.
4. After being Saint Teresa's, the heart
is now Crashaw's.
5. Books filled with intellectual and
spiritual light.
6. I.e., my best fortune will be to be
despoiled in this way.
7. The eagle symbolizes wisdom, for
its lofty flight and ability to look into
the sun's eye; the dove symbolizes
mercy. Cf. Donne's *Canonization*, line
22.

By all thy brim-filled bowls of fierce desire,
By thy last morning's draught of liquid fire;   100
By the full kingdom of that final kiss
That seized thy parting soul, and sealed thee His;
By all the heavens thou hast in Him,
Fair sister of the seraphim,
By all of Him we have in thee,   105
Leave nothing of myself in me!
Let me so read thy life that I
Unto all life of mine may die!

       1652

On Our Crucified Lord, Naked and Bloody

Th' have left Thee naked, Lord, O that they had;
This garment too I would they had denied.
Thee with Thyself they have too richly clad,
Opening the purple wardrobe of Thy side.
    O never could be found garments too good   5
    For Thee to wear, but these, of Thine own blood.

       1646

To the Infant Martyrs[1]

Go, smiling souls, your new-built cages[2] break,
In heaven you'll learn to sing, ere here to speak,
Nor let the milky fonts that bathe your thirst
       Be your delay;
The place that calls you hence is, at the worst,   5
       Milk all the way.[3]

       1646

I Am the Door

And now Th' art set wide ope, the spear's sad art,
Lo! hath unlocked Thee at the very heart;
    He to himself (I fear the worst)
      And his own hope
Hath shut these doors of heaven, that durst   5
      Thus set them ope.

       1646

1. This poem, and the five which follow, were originally published in Latin, as sacred epigrams; but also appeared in *Steps to the Temple*, translated into English.
2. I.e., the bodies which confine them to an earthly existence.
3. The Milky Way will replace their mothers' milk, at the worst; at best, they may rise even higher in the heavens.

Luke 11

Blessed be the paps which Thou hast sucked.

Suppose He had been tabled at thy teats,
    Thy hunger feels not what He eats;
He'll have his teat ere long (a bloody one),
    The Mother then must suck the Son.

1646

Upon the Infant Martyrs

To see both blended in one flood,
    The mothers' milk, the children's blood,
Make me doubt if heaven will gather
Roses hence, or lilies rather.

1646

Luke 7

She began to wash His feet with tears and wipe them with the hairs of her head.

Her eyes' flood licks His feet's fair stain,
Her hairs' flame licks that up again.
This flame thus quenched hath brighter beams;
This flood thus stained fairer streams.

1646

On the Wounds of Our Crucified Lord

O these wakeful wounds of Thine!
    Are they mouths? or are they eyes?
Be they mouths, or be they eyne,[1]
    Each bleeding part some one supplies.[2]

Lo! a mouth, whose full-bloomed lips   5
    At too dear a rate are roses.
Lo! a bloodshot eye! that weeps
    And many a cruel tear discloses.

O thou that on this foot hast laid
    Many a kiss and many a tear,   10

1. An old plural form of "eyes."   2. I.e., each wound of Christ's supplies either an eye or a mouth.

Now thou shalt have all repaid,
  Whatsoe'er thy charges were.

This foot hath got a mouth and lips
  To pay the sweet sum of thy kisses;
To pay thy tears, an eye that weeps   15
  Instead of tears such gems as this is.

The difference only this appears
  (Nor can the change offend),
The debt is paid in ruby-tears
  Which thou in pearls didst lend.   20

                                              1646

HENRY VAUGHAN
(1621–1695)

The doctrines of mystic correspondence (i.e., of analogical relations between the world of creatures and the world of spirits), which had been
publicly accepted philosophy in the Middle Ages, and which the genius of
Donne had daringly revitalized in the late 16th century, faded during the
17th century before the rising rationalism and materialism which culminated in John Locke and Isaac Newton. One of the last figures to give
expression to the old philosophy was a Welsh country doctor with an interest in the occult—Henry Vaughan.

The record of Vaughan's public career is not very clear or very spectacular. He went up to Oxford in 1638, but left without a degree; read
law in London, and wrote some conventionally dissipated poems in the
amatory vein of the Cavaliers; and soldiered briefly during the Civil Wars
on the king's side. Having taken up the study of medicine, he retired to
Wales about 1647 and set up practice; and there he published the two
volumes on which his reputation rests—*Olor Iscanus* in 1651, and *Silex
Scintillans*, published in 1650 and reissued in much augmented form in
1655. The first title means "The Swan of Usk," and expresses Vaughan's
resolve to be a singer of his native Wales (Usk is a small Welsh river near
his home). *Silex Scintillans*, or "The Fiery Flint," is a volume of devotional verse, written under the general influence of George Herbert, and
making in its title a reference to the poet's own heart; it is a flint from
which God's steel has struck sparkles of glory and of verse. From this
volume all the present selections are drawn.

This last title is a specially apt one, for Vaughan's best poems start with
a brilliant phrase or series of phrases and trail off into relatively prosaic
statements. Sparkles of brightness attend almost all his writing, glowing
and fading under the wavering breath of his inspiration. He is a most uneven poet; but there is a kind of silver purity about Vaughan's best
poetry, an exalted intellectual agitation, which is like nothing else in English. Perhaps for the modern reader it does not much matter that the cock

was once considered in esoteric circles an emblem of the Resurrection. But the excitement which this concept engenders in Vaughan's poem *Cock Crowing* can be sensed by anyone. The doctrine of pre-existence which he hints at in *The Retreat* and the complex symbolic structure which animates *Regeneration* are informed with the same feeling. It is not exactly mysticism, but it is equally removed from rationalism.

Vaughan's poetry is animated by a spiritual philosophy at once traditional and private, the outlines of which can be traced in technical volumes published by his twin brother Thomas. The details of this philosophy need not be sketched here, but its effect is to enrich the material, palpable world with all sorts of spiritual signs and meanings. Heaven, for Vaughan, lies very close behind the veil interposed by material things, and its radiance shines for a few brief moments through Vaughan's verses before it fades into the common light of day. For Vaughan himself the gleam was only momentary; and though he published a last volume of verse in 1678 (*Thalia Rediviva*), the last forty years of his life were as barren of the magic feeling which touched him during the 1650's as the first 25 had been. He died in obscurity and isolation among the hills of his beloved Wales, just in time to escape seeing his brother Thomas caricatured as a type of the learned idiot by a brash young satirist named Jonathan Swift (*A Tale of a Tub*, Sections V and X).

The Retreat

Happy those early days! when I
Shined in my angel infancy.
Before I understood this place
Appointed for my second race,[1]
Or taught my soul to fancy aught   5
But a white, celestial thought;
When yet I had not walked above
A mile or two from my first love,
And looking back, at that short space,
Could see a glimpse of His bright face;   10
When on some gilded cloud or flower
My gazing soul would dwell an hour,
And in those weaker glories spy
Some shadows of eternity;
Before I taught my tongue to wound   15
My conscience with a sinful sound,
Or had the black art to dispense
A several[2] sin to every sense,
But felt through all this fleshly dress
Bright shoots of everlastingness.   20
   O, how I long to travel back,
And tread again that ancient track!

1. The "second race" suggests, dimly,   2. Different.
a doctrine of pre-existence.

That I might once more reach that plain
Where first I left my glorious train,
From whence th' enlightened spirit sees   25
That shady city of palm trees.[3]
But, ah! my soul with too much stay[4]
Is drunk, and staggers in the way.
Some men a forward motion love;
But I by backward steps would move,   30
And when this dust falls to the urn,
In that state I came, return.

1650

Cock-Crowing

Father of lights! what sunny seed,
What glance of day hast Thou confined
Into this bird? To all the breed
This busy ray Thou hast assigned;
  Their magnetism [5] works all night,   5
  And dreams of paradise and light.

Their eyes watch for the morning hue;
Their little grain,[6] expelling night,
So shines and sings as if it knew
The path unto the house of light.   10
  It seems their candle, howe'er done,
  Was tinned [7] and lighted at the sun.

If such a tincture, such a touch,
So firm a longing can empower,
Shall Thy own image think it much   15
To watch for Thy appearing hour?
  If a mere blast so fill the sail,
  Shall not the breath of God prevail?

O Thou immortal light and heat!
Whose hand so shines through all this frame [8]   20
That, by the beauty of the seat,
We plainly see who made the same,
  Seeing Thy seed abides in me,
  Dwell Thou in it, and I in Thee!

To sleep without Thee is to die;   25
Yea, 'tis a death partakes of hell:

3. The New Jerusalem, the Heavenly City (see Deuteronomy xxxiv.3).
4. Delay.
5. Vaughan, as a Hermetic philosopher, believed in mysterious "sympathetic" attractions between earthly and spiritual things, symbolized here by the special affinity of cocks for the dawn.
6. Dye, tincture; also "seed." The spiritual vitality of the bird repels darkness.
7. Given its brilliance.
8. Of the universe. "The seat": the earth.

For where Thou dost not close the eye,
It never opens, I can tell.[9]
    In such a dark Egyptian border,
      The shades of death dwell, and disorder.   30

If joys, and hopes, and earnest throes,
And hearts whose pulse beats still for light
Are given to birds; who, but Thee, knows
A love-sick soul's exalted flight?
      Can souls be tracked by any eye   35
      But His who gave them wings to fly?

Only this veil [1] which Thou hast broke,
And must be broken yet in me,
This veil, I say, is all the cloak
And cloud which shadows Thee from me.   40
      This veil Thy full-eyed love denies,
      And only gleams and fractions spies.

O take it off! make no delay;
But brush me with Thy light that I
May shine unto a perfect day,   45
And warm me at Thy glorious eye!
      O take it off, or till it flee,
      Though with no lily,[2] stay with me!

1655

Regeneration

A ward, and still in bonds, one day
    I stole abroad;
It was high spring, and all the way
    Primrosed and hung with shade;
      Yet was it frost within,   5
        And surly winds
Blasted my infant buds, and sin
    Like clouds eclipsed my mind.

Stormed thus, I straight perceived my spring
    Mere stage and show,   10
My walk a monstrous, mountained thing,
    Roughcast with rocks and snow;
      And as a pilgrim's eye,
        Far from relief,
Measures the melancholy sky,   15
    Then drops and rains for grief,

9. If God does not give sleep, with His blessing, man dies (his "eye never opens") and he goes to hell.
1. The veil of physical existence which shadows the unseen world from us.
2. A reference to the Song of Solomon ii.16: "My beloved is mine, and I am his: he feedeth among the lilies."

So sighed I upwards still; at last
    'Twixt steps and falls
I reached the pinnacle, where placed
    I found a pair of scales;   20
    I took them up and laid
        In th' one, late pains;
The other smoke and pleasures weighed,
    But proved the heavier grains.[3]

With that some cried, "Away!" Straight I   25
    Obeyed, and led
Full east, a fair, fresh field could spy;
    Some called it Jacob's bed,[4]
    A virgin soil which no
        Rude feet ere trod,   30
Where, since he stepped there, only go
    Prophets and friends of God.

Here I reposed; but scarce well set,
    A grove descried
Of stately height, whose branches met   35
    And mixed on every side;
    I entered, and once in,
        Amazed to see 't,
Found all was changed, and a new spring
    Did all my senses greet.   40

The unthrift sun shot vital gold,
    A thousand pieces,
And heaven its azure did unfold,
    Checkered with snowy fleeces;
    The air was all in spice,   45
        And every bush
A garland wore; thus fed my eyes,
    But all the ear lay hush.[5]

Only a little fountain lent
    Some use for ears,   50
And on the dumb shades language spent,
    The music of her tears;
    I drew her near, and found
        The cistern full
Of divers stones, some bright and round,   55
    Others ill-shaped and dull.[6]

The first, pray mark, as quick as light
    Danced through the flood,

3. Vaughan's spiritual adventure can only be described darkly. After his purgatorial ascent, smoke and pleasures prove heavier than "late pains"; i.e., the vanity of his mind outweighs its recent turning to repentance.
4. Jacob, who wrestled with an angel and ascended directly to heaven on a ladder, is here a type of the mystical visionary.
5. Quiet.
6. The stones may be thoughts, images, and concepts in the "little fountain" of inspiration; the imagery is no doubt tinged with alchemical symbolism, as well.

But the last, more heavy than the night,
　　Nailed to the center stood;　　　　60
I wondered much, but tired
　　At last with thought,
My restless eye that still desired
　　As strange an object brought.

It was a bank of flowers, where I descried,　　65
　　Though 'twas midday,
Some fast asleep, others broad-eyed
　　And taking in the ray;
Here, musing long, I heard
　　A rushing wind　　　　70
Which still increased, but whence it stirred
　　No where I could not find.

I turned me round, and to each shade
　　Dispatched an eye
To see if any leaf had made　　　　75
　　Least motion or reply,
But while I listening sought
　　My mind to ease
By knowing where 'twas, or where not,
　　It whispered, "Where I please."[5]　　80

"Lord," then said I, "on me one breath,
And let me die before my death!"

　　　　　　1650

Peace

My soul, there is a country
　　Far beyond the stars,
Where stands a wingéd sentry
　　All skillful in the wars.
There, above noise and danger,　　　　5
　　Sweet Peace sits crowned with smiles,
And One born in a manger
　　Commands the beauteous files.[6]
He is thy gracious friend,
　　And (O my soul, awake!)　　　　10
Did in pure love descend
　　To die here for thy sake.
If thou canst get but thither,
　　There grows the flower of peace,

5. John iii.8: "The wind bloweth where it listeth, and thou hearest the sound thereof, but canst not tell whence it cometh, and whither it goeth: so is every one that is born of the Spirit." Cf. also the inspiring breath by which God breathed life into man (Genesis ii.7).
6. Ranks.

The rose that cannot wither, 15
   Thy fortress and thy ease.
Leave, then, thy foolish ranges; [7]
   For none can thee secure
But One who never changes,
   Thy God, thy life, thy cure. 20

1650

Corruption

Sure it was so. Man in those early days
   Was not all stone and earth;
He shined a little, and by those weak rays
   Had some glimpse of his birth.
He saw heaven o'er his head, and knew from whence 5
   He came, condemnéd, hither;
And, as first love draws strongest, so from hence
   His mind sure progressed thither.
Things here were strange unto him: sweat and till,
   All was a thorn or weed: 10
Nor did those last, but (like himself) died still
   As soon as they did seed.
They seemed to quarrel with him, for that act
   That felled him foiled them all:
He drew the curse upon the world, and cracked 15
   The whole frame with his fall.[1]
This made him long for home, as loath to stay
   With murmurers and foes;
He sighed for Eden, and would often say,
   "Ah! what bright days were those!" 20
Nor was heaven cold unto him; for each day
   The valley or the mountain
Afforded visits, and still paradise lay
   In some green shade or fountain.
Angels lay leiger[2] here; each bush and cell, 25
   Each oak and highway knew them;
Walk but the fields, or sit down at some well,
   And he was sure to view them.
Almighty Love! where art Thou now? Mad man
   Sits down and freezeth on;
He raves, and swears to stir nor fire, nor fan, 30
   But bids the thread be spun.[3]
I see, Thy curtains are close-drawn; Thy bow
   Looks dim, too, in the cloud;
Sin triumphs still, and man is sunk below 35
   The center, and his shroud.
All's in deep sleep and night: thick darkness lies
   And hatcheth o'er Thy people—

7. Rovings.
1. Compare *Paradise Lost* X.650 ff.
2. As resident ambassadors (from heaven).

3. Man is willing to do none of the work of salvation, but expects all the rewards.

But hark! what trumpet's that? what angel cries,
   "Arise! thrust in Thy sickle"?[4]

                       40

                   1650

The World

I saw eternity the other night
Like a great ring of pure and endless light,
     All calm as it was bright;
And round beneath it, Time, in hours, days, years,
     Driven by the spheres,[1]
Like a vast shadow moved, in which the world
     And all her train were hurled.
The doting lover in his quaintest[2] strain
     Did there complain;
Near him, his lute, his fancy, and his flights,[3]
     Wit's sour delights,
With gloves and knots,[4] the silly snares of pleasure,
     Yet his dear treasure,
All scattered lay, while he his eyes did pour
     Upon a flower.

The darksome statesman, hung with weights and woe,
Like a thick midnight fog, moved there so slow
     He did nor stay nor go;
Condemning thoughts, like sad eclipses, scowl
     Upon his soul,
And clouds of crying witnesses without
     Pursued him with one shout.
Yet digged the mole, and, lest his ways be found,
     Worked underground,
Where he did clutch his prey. But One did see
     That policy:[5]
Churches and altars fed him; perjuries
     Were gnats and flies;
It rained about him blood and tears; but he
     Drank them as free.[6]

The fearful miser on a heap of rust
Sat pining all his life there, did scarce trust
     His own hands with the dust;
Yet would not place[7] one piece above, but lives
     In fear of thieves.
Thousands there were as frantic as himself,
     And hugged each one his pelf:

4. Revelation xiv.15: "And another angel came out of the temple, crying with a loud voice to him that sat on the cloud, 'Thrust in thy sickle and reap * * * '" The time to harvest is now.
1. The concentric spheres of Ptolemaic astronomy.
2. Most elaborate.
3. Light arrows, as used by Cupid.
4. Love knots.
5. Strategy. The "mole" (i.e., the "darksome statesman," line 16) worked underground to avoid detection; but He who marks the fall of a sparrow was not deceived.
6. I.e., as freely as they rained.
7. Invest.

The downright epicure placed heaven in sense,[8]
    And scorned pretense;
While others, slipped into a wide excess,   40
    Said little less;
The weaker sort, slight, trivial wares enslave,
    Who think them brave;[9]
And poor, despiséd Truth sat counting by[1]
    Their victory.   45
Yet some, who all this while did weep and sing,
And sing and weep, soared up into the ring;
    But most would use no wing.
"O fools!" said I, "thus to prefer dark night
    Before true light!   50
To live in grots and caves, and hate the day
    Because it shows the way,
The way which from this dead and dark abode
    Leads up to God,
A way where you might tread the sun and be   55
    More bright than he!"
But, as I did their madness so discuss,
    One whispered thus:
"This ring the bridegroom did for none provide,
    But for His bride."[2]   60

      1650

They Are All Gone into the World of Light!

They are all gone into the world of light!
    And I alone sit lingering here;
Their very memory is fair and bright,
    And my sad thoughts doth clear.[3]

It glows and glitters in my cloudy breast   5
    Like stars upon some gloomy grove,
Or those faint beams in which this hill is dressed
    After the sun's remove.

I see them walking in an air of glory,
    Whose light doth trample on my days;   10
My days, which are at best but dull and hoary,
    Mere glimmering and decays.

O holy hope, and high humility,
    High as the heavens above!
These are your walks, and you have showed them me   15
    To kindle my cold love.

Dear, beauteous death! the jewel of the just,
    Shining nowhere but in the dark;

---

8. Found his heaven in the senses.
9. Fine, flashy.
1. Watching.
2. See Revelation xix.7–9 and xxi for the marriage of the Lamb and the bride (Christ and His church).
3. Brighten.

What mysteries do lie beyond thy dust,
 Could man outlook that mark! [4]   20

He that hath found some fledged bird's nest may know
 At first sight if the bird be flown;
But what fair well [5] or grove he sings in now,
 That is to him unknown.
And yet, as angels in some brighter dreams   25
 Call to the soul when man doth sleep,
So some strange thoughts transcend our wonted themes,
 And into glory peep.

If a star were confined into a tomb,
 Her captive flames must needs burn there;   30
But when the hand that locked her up gives room,
 She'll shine through all the sphere.

O Father of eternal life, and all
 Created glories under Thee!
Resume Thy spirit from this world of thrall [6]   35
 Into true liberty!

Either disperse these mists, which blot and fill
 My perspective [7] still as they pass;
Or else remove me hence unto that hill [8]
 Where I shall need no glass.
                                        40
                                   1655

Man

Weighing the steadfastness and state
Of some mean things which here below reside,
Where birds, like watchful clocks, the noiseless date
 And intercourse of times divide,
Where bees at night get home and hive, and flowers,   5
 Early as well as late,
Rise with the sun and set in the same bowers;

I would (said I) my God would give
The staidness of these things to man! for these
To His divine appointments ever cleave,   10
 And no new business breaks their peace;
The birds nor sow nor reap, yet sup and dine;
 The flowers without clothes live,
Yet Solomon was never dressed so fine.[1]

Man hath still either toys or care;[2]   15
He hath no root, nor to one place is tied,
But ever restless and irregular
 About this earth doth run and ride.

4. Limit.
5. Spring.
6. I.e., take back the spirit which you have made from this world of slavery.
7. Literally, "telescope," but more freely, "distant vision."
8. Sion hill (figuratively, Abraham's bosom).
1. Cf. Matthew vi.26–29.
2. Diversions or grief.

He knows he hath a home, but scarce knows where;
   He says it is so far   20
That he hath quite forgot how to go there.
  He knocks at all doors, strays and roams,
Nay, hath not so much wit as some stones[3] have,
Which in the darkest nights point to their homes,
   By some hid sense their Maker gave;   25
Man is the shuttle, to whose winding quest
    And passage through these looms
God ordered motion, but ordained no rest.

1650

3. Loadstones.

ANDREW MARVELL
(1621–1678)

Andrew Marvell was one of those quiet men of wit and spirit whose voice generally goes unheard during the storm and turmoil of revolution. He attended Cambridge; but after graduating B.A. in 1638 and traveling abroad for some years, he disappears from the biographer's view, turning up around 1650 as tutor to the daughter of Sir Thomas Fairfax, Lord-General of the Parliamentary forces. Here, at the family seat in Yorkshire, Nun Appleton House, Marvell seems to have written many if not most of his English poems. They are playful miniatures, for the most part, which display a genius for catching in a phrase some glancing overtone of serious, almost profound, reflection. Yet their learning, like their serious intent, is hidden beneath a graceful, humorous surface, and they suggest that Marvell must have been a delightful tutor to the little girl who was growing up to be the daughter of a great house.

In 1657 Marvell was appointed assistant to the blind Latin Secretary for the Commonwealth, John Milton; and in his quiet way, he seems to have been responsible after the Restoration for saving Milton from imprisonment and possible execution. Starting in 1659, Marvell was returned M.P. for his home town of Hull, and he continued to represent it in a businesslike way until his death. He was a good committee man, though not a public speaker, and devoted to the interests of Hull. His letters to his constituents are valuable historical documents; but one would never guess from reading them that their author was an accomplished poet.

And in fact, when Marvell died, he was known to the world simply as the author of a few rough-and-ready satires in prose and verse which had been printed during the Restoration. His "serious" verse was only published three years after his death, by a woman who gave herself out as his widow but had really been his housekeeper. The reputation of these poems has made its way slowly, but steadily; and it has never stood higher than in our own time. For it is now clear that Marvell's is the most major minor verse in English. Playful, casual, and witty in tone, always light on its metrical feet and exact in its diction, it displays depth and intellectual hardness in unexpected places; its texture is extraordinarily rich. One need only glance at the famous *To His Coy Mistress* to see these qualities exemplified. At first it looks like a dozen other poems on the *carpe diem* theme: slight, singsong, and semi-serious, it urges on the lady enjoyment of the present hour. But soon the four-beat couplet is made to sound deep and hollow, is made to reverberate like a bell as well as pattering like a nursery rhyme; and a vision of the grinning grave and the deserts of eternity rises out of Marvell's gallant compliments to a pretty girl. It is a slight thing—yet its three paragraphs are nailed to the stiff logic of the syllogism, and its delicately balanced feelings reach out to embrace more than, for so slight a structure, seems possible.

The Garden

How vainly men themselves amaze
To win the palm, the oak, or bays,[1]
And their incessant labors see
Crowned from some single herb, or tree,
Whose short and narrow-vergéd shade   5
Does prudently their toils upbraid;
While all flowers and all trees do close[2]
To weave the garlands of repose!

Fair Quiet, have I found thee here,
And Innocence, thy sister dear?   10
Mistaken long, I sought you then
In busy companies of men.
Your sacred plants, if here below,
Only among the plants will grow;
Society is all but rude   15
To this delicious solitude.

No white nor red was ever seen
So amorous as this lovely green.
Fond lovers, cruel as their flame,
Cut in these trees their mistress' name: 20
Little, alas, they know or heed
How far these beauties hers exceed!
Fair trees, wheresoe'er your barks I wound,
No name shall but your own be found.[3]

When we have run our passion's heat,   25
Love hither makes his best retreat.
The gods, that mortal beauty chase,
Still in a tree did end their race:
Apollo hunted Daphne so,
Only that she might laurel grow;[4]   30

1. Crowns, respectively, for athletics, civic merit, and poetry. "Amaze": bewilder.
2. Unite.
3. Marvell proposes to carve on the bark of trees, not "Sylvia" or "Laura," but "Beech" and "Oak."
4. Ovid tells (in *Metamorphoses*) how Apollo hunted Daphne until she turned into a laurel, and how Pan pursued Syrinx until she became a reed, out of which he made Panpipes.

And Pan did after Syrinx speed,
Not as a nymph, but for a reed.

What wondrous life is this I lead!
Ripe apples drop about my head;
The luscious clusters of the vine   35
Upon my mouth do crush their wine;
The nectarine and curious[5] peach
Into my hands themselves do reach;
Stumbling on melons, as I pass,
Insnared with flowers, I fall on grass.   40

Meanwhile the mind, from pleasure less,[6]
Withdraws into its happiness;
The mind, that ocean where each kind
Does straight its own resemblance find;[7]
Yet it creates, transcending these,   45
Far other worlds and other seas,
Annihilating all that's made
To a green thought in a green shade.[8]

Here at the fountain's sliding foot,
Or at some fruit tree's mossy root,   50
Casting the body's vest[9] aside,
My soul into the boughs does glide:
There, like a bird, it sits and sings,
Then whets[1] and combs its silver wings,
And, till prepared for longer flight,   55
Waves in its plumes the various light.[2]

Such was that happy garden-state,
While man there walked without a mate:
After a place so pure and sweet,
What other help could yet be meet!   60
But 'twas beyond a mortal's share
To wander solitary there:
Two paradises 'twere in one
To live in paradise alone.

How well the skillful gardener drew   65
Of flowers and herbs this dial[3] new,
Where, from above, the milder sun

---

5. Exquisite.
6. Diminished and drawn in on itself to savor the pleasure.
7. Every creature on earth was popularly supposed to have its counterpart in the ocean; thus the mind is an ocean because it contains a counterpart to everything on earth.
8. The garden is a symbol of the contemplative life as contrasted with the active life; and green, distinguished from the white of innocence and the red of passion (line 17), connotes a way of life which is cool and detached from human concerns.
9. Vestment, garment.
1. Preens.
2. The many-colored light of this world, contrasted with the white radiance of eternity.
3. Clock. While the growth and decline of the garden measure the passage of time, the sun, a milder clock, runs through the zodiac, or constellation of the seasons.

Does through a fragrant zodiac run;
  And as it works, th' industrious bee
Computes its time as well as we!   70
How could such sweet and wholesome hours
  Be reckoned but with herbs and flowers?

                                                                1681

The Mower, Against Gardens

Luxurious man,[1] to bring his vice in use,
  Did after him the world seduce,
And from the fields the flowers and plants allure,
  Where Nature was most plain and pure.
He first enclosed within the gardens square   5
  A dead and standing pool of air,
And a more luscious earth for them did knead,
  Which stupefied them while it fed.
The pink grew then as double as his mind;[2]
  The nutriment did change the kind.   10
With strange perfumes he did the roses taint;
  And flowers themselves were taught to paint.
The tulip white did for complexion seek,
  And learned to interline its cheek;
Its onion root they then so high did hold,   15
  That one was for a meadow sold:[3]
Another world was searched through oceans new,
  To find the marvel of Peru;[4]
And yet these rarities might be allowed
  To man, that sovereign thing and proud,   20
Had he not dealt between the bark and tree,[5]
  Forbidden mixtures there to see.
No plant now knew the stock from which it came;
  He grafts upon the wild the tame,
That the uncertain and adulterate fruit   25
  Might put the palate in dispute.
His green seraglio has its eunuchs too,
  Lest any tyrant him outdo;
And in the cherry he does Nature vex,
  To procreate without a sex.   30
'Tis all enforced, the fountain and the grot,
  While the sweet fields do lie forgot,
Where willing Nature does to all dispense

1. Luxury-loving, voluptuous man, who wants to popularize ("bring in use") his own vices.
2. The double pink or carnation is a product of sophisticated, therefore hypocritical ("double"), minds.
3. A great boom in tulip bulbs took place in Holland during the 17th century; Marvell's line was therefore, on occasion, strictly accurate.
4. *Mirabilis Jalapa,* the four o'clock, a flower found originally in South America.
5. By grafting.

A wild and fragrant innocence;
And fauns and fairies do the meadows till   35
    More by their presence than their skill.
Their statues polished by some ancient hand,
    May to adorn the gardens stand;
But, howsoe'er the figures do excel,
    The gods themselves with us do dwell.   40

1681

The Mower's Song

My mind was once the true survey[1]
Of all these meadows fresh and gay,
And in the greenness of the grass
Did see its hopes as in a glass;
    When Juliana came, and she,   5
What I do to the grass, does to my thoughts and me.

But these, while I with sorrow pine,
Grew more luxuriant still and fine,
That not one blade of grass you spied,
But had a flower on either side;   10
    When Juliana came, and she,
What I do to the grass, does to my thoughts and me.

Unthankful meadows, could you so
A fellowship so true forego,
And in your gaudy May-games[2] meet,   15
While I lay trodden under feet?
    When Juliana came, and she,
What I do to the grass, does to my thoughts and me.

But what you in compassion ought,
Shall now by my revenge be wrought;   20
And flowers, and grass, and I, and all
Will in one common ruin fall;
    For Juliana comes, and she,
What I do to the grass, does to my thoughts and me.

And thus, ye meadows, which have been   25
Companions of my thoughts more green,
Shall now the heraldry become
With which I shall adorn my tomb;
    For Juliana comes, and she,
What I do to the grass, does to my thoughts and me.   30

1681

1. Map, image.
2. May Day was the season of indulgence; "gaudy" implies feasting and jollity on the part of the gaily colored meadows, while the hapless mower is crushed underfoot, spurned by Juliana.

Bermudas

Where the remote Bermudas ride,
In th' ocean's bosom unespied,
From a small boat that rowed along,
The listening winds received this song:

"What should we do but sing His praise,   5
That led us through the watery maze
Unto an isle so long unknown,
And yet far kinder than our own?
Where He the huge sea monsters wracks,
That lift the deep upon their backs;[1]   10
He lands us on a grassy stage,
Safe from the storms, and prelate's rage.[2]
He gave us this eternal spring
Which here enamels everything,
And sends the fowls to us in care,   15
On daily visits through the air;
He hangs in shades the orange bright,
Like golden lamps in a green night,
And does in the pomegranates close
Jewels more rich than Ormus[3] shows;   20
He makes the figs our mouths to meet,
And throws the melons at our feet;
But apples[4] plants of such a price,
No tree could ever bear them twice;
With cedars, chosen by His hand,   25
From Lebanon, He stores the land;
And makes the hollow seas, that roar,
Proclaim the ambergris[5] on shore;
He cast (of which we rather boast)
The Gospel's pearl upon our coast,   30
And in these rocks for us did frame
A temple, where to sound His name.
O! let our voice His praise exalt,
Till it arrive at heaven's vault,
Which, thence (perhaps) rebounding, may   35
Echo beyond the Mexique Bay."[6]

Thus sung they in the English boat,
An holy and a cheerful note;

1. See Milton's use of the same sea fable in *Paradise Lost* I.203 ff. "Wracks": shipwrecks, destroys.
2. Storms at sea are quietly equated with bishops as sources of peril.
3. Pearl- and jewel-trading center in the Persian Gulf.
4. Pineapples.
5. "Proclaim," a kind of learned joke, suggests the seas roaring to announce their bounty. Ambergris is an expensive, mysterious, soapy substance found in sperm whales and used in the manufacture of perfumes (see *Moby Dick*, Chapter XCII).
6. The Gulf of Mexico.

And all the way, to guide their chime,
With falling oars they kept the time.   40

1681

A Dialogue Between the Soul and Body

SOUL. O, who shall from this dungeon raise
        A soul enslaved so many ways?
        With bolts of bones, that fettered stands
        In feet; and manacled in hands.
        Here blinded with an eye; and there   5
        Deaf with the drumming of an ear;
        A soul hung up, as 'twere, in chains
        Of nerves,[1] and arteries, and veins;
        Tortured, besides each other part,
        In a vain head and double heart?   10

BODY.   O, who shall me deliver whole
        From bonds of this tyrannic soul?
        Which, stretched upright, impales me so
        That mine own precipice[2] I go;
        And warms and moves this needless frame[3]   15
        (A fever could but do the same),
        And, wanting where[4] its spite to try,
        Has made me live to let me die.
        A body that could never rest
        Since this ill spirit it possessed.   20

SOUL.   What magic could me thus confine
        Within another's grief to pine?
        Where, whatsoever it complain,
        I feel, that cannot feel,[5] the pain;
        And all my care itself employs,   25
        That to preserve which me destroys;
        Constrained not only to endure
        Diseases, but, what's worse, the cure;
        And, ready oft the port to gain,
        Am shipwrecked into health again.   30

BODY.   But Physic[6] yet could never reach
        The maladies thou me dost teach;
        Whom first the cramp of hope does tear,
        And then the palsy shakes of fear;
        The pestilence of love does heat,   35
        Or hatred's hidden ulcer eat;
        Joy's cheerful madness does perplex,

---

1. Sinews.
2. Possession of a soul is the reason why man walks erect, facing the heavens, instead of prowling the earth like a brute; but it is also the reason why he can fall and be damned, as brutes cannot; so the soul is an interior precipice.
3. This frame, which does not need it.
4. Lacking an object.
5. The soul can "feel" (sympathize) even though it "cannot feel" (has no power of physical sensation).
6. Medicine.

Or sorrow's other madness vex;
Which knowledge forces me to know,
And memory will not forego; 40
What but a soul could have the wit
To build me up for sin so fit?
So architects do square and hew
Green trees that in the forest grew.[7]

1681

Mourning

You, that decipher out the fate
    Of human offsprings from the skies,
What mean these infants which, of late,
    Spring from the stars of Chlora's eyes?

Her eyes confused, and doubled o'er 5
    With tears suspended ere they flow,
Seem bending upwards to restore
    To Heaven, whence it came, their woe.

When, molding of the watery spheres,[1]
    Slow drops untie themselves away, 10
As if she with those precious tears
    Would strew the ground where Strephon lay.

Yet some affirm, pretending art,
    Her eyes have so her bosom drowned,
Only to soften, near her heart, 15
    A place to fix another wound.

And while vain pomp does her restrain
    Within her solitary bower,
She courts herself in amorous rain,
    Herself both Danaë and the shower.[2] 20

Nay others, bolder, hence esteem
    Joy now so much her master grown,
That whatsoever does but seem
    Like grief is from her windows thrown.

Nor that she pays, while she survives, 25
    To her dead love this tribute due,
But casts abroad these donatives[3]
    At the installing of a new.

How wide they dream! the Indian slaves,
    That sink for pearl through seas profound, 30

7. The body asserts that it has been trimmed and squared to an alien purpose, instead of being allowed to grow freely and naturally, as in the forest.

1. Taking the shape of watery spheres.
2. Zeus wooed Danaë in a shower of gold.
3. Largesse, gifts of public charity.

Would find her tears yet deeper waves
And not of one the bottom sound.

I yet my silent judgment keep,
  Disputing not what they believe;
But sure as oft as women weep   35
  It is to be supposed they grieve.

1681

To His Coy Mistress

    Had we but world enough, and time,
This coyness, lady, were no crime.
We would sit down, and think which way
To walk, and pass our long love's day.
Thou by the Indian Ganges' side   5
Shouldst rubies find; I by the tide
Of Humber would complain.[1] I would
Love you ten years before the flood,
And you should, if you please, refuse
Till the conversion of the Jews.[2]   10
My vegetable love should grow
Vaster than empires and more slow;
An hundred years should go to praise
Thine eyes, and on thy forehead gaze;
Two hundred to adore each breast,   15
But thirty thousand to the rest;
An age at least to every part,
And the last age should show your heart.
For, lady, you deserve this state,[3]
Nor would I love at lower rate.   20
    But at my back I always hear
Time's wingèd chariot hurrying near;
And yonder all before us lie
Deserts of vast eternity.
Thy beauty shall no more be found,   25
Nor, in thy marble vault, shall sound
My echoing song; then worms shall try
That long-preserved virginity,
And your quaint honor turn to dust,
And into ashes all my lust: 30
The grave's a fine and private place,
But none, I think, do there embrace.
    Now therefore, while the youthful hue

1. Compared to the gorgeous Oriental
Ganges, the Humber (which flows
through Marvell's home town of Hull)
is a dull and unassuming little stream.
"Complain" implies songs of plaintive
love.
2. According to popular chronology, the
Jews were to be converted just before
the Last Judgment.
3. Dignity.

Sits on thy skin like morning dew,[4]
And while thy willing soul transpires[5]   35
At every pore with instant fires,
Now let us sport us while we may,
And now, like amorous birds of prey,
Rather at once our time devour
Than languish in his slow-chapped[6] power.   40
Let us roll all our strength and all
Our sweetness up into one ball,
And tear our pleasures with rough strife
Thorough the iron gates of life:
Thus, though we cannot make our sun   45
Stand still, yet we will make him run.

1681

The Definition of Love

My Love is of a birth as rare
As 'tis, for object, strange and high;
It was begotten by Despair
Upon Impossibility.

Magnanimous Despair alone   5
Could show me so divine a thing,
Where feeble Hope could ne'er have flown
But vainly flapped its tinsel wing.

And yet I quickly might arrive
Where my extended soul is fixed;[1]   10
But Fate does iron wedges drive,
And always crowds itself betwixt.

For Fate with jealous eye does see
Two perfect loves, nor lets them close;[2]
Their union would her ruin be,   15
And her tyrannic power depose.[3]

And therefore her decrees of steel
Us as the distant poles have placed
(Though Love's whole world on us doth wheel),
Not by themselves to be embraced,   20

Unless the giddy heaven fall,
And earth some new convulsion tear,
And, us to join, the world should all
Be cramped into a planisphere.[4]

4. The text reads "glew"—an odious reading. "Lew" (meaning "warmth") has also been suggested, but it was obsolete long before Marvell wrote.
5. Breathes forth. "Instant fires": immediate, present enthusiasm.
6. Slow-jawed. Time is envisaged as slowly chewing up the world and the people in it.
1. Marvell thinks of his soul as having gone out of his body ("extended") and attached ("fixed") itself to his mistress.
2. Unite.
3. Fate, and its agents Time and Change, would none of them have any power against a perfect mixture of the elements.
4. A flat sphere, literally absurd, but describing a kind of astrological projection in which the world was represented in two dimensions and the poles were united.

As lines, so loves oblique may well   25
Themselves in every angle greet;[5]
    But ours, so truly parallel,
    Though infinite, can never meet.

Therefore the love which us doth bind,
But Fate so enviously debars,   30
    Is the conjunction of the mind,
    And opposition of the stars.[6]

1681

An Horatian Ode

UPON CROMWELL'S RETURN FROM IRELAND [1]

The forward youth that would appear,
Must now forsake his Muses dear,
    Nor in the shadows sing
    His numbers languishing:

'Tis time to leave the books in dust,   5
And oil the unuséd armor's rust;
    Removing from the wall
    The corselet of the hall.[2]

So restless Cromwell could not cease
In the inglorious arts of peace,   10
    But through adventurous war
    Urgéd his active star;

And, like the three-forked lightning, first
Breaking the clouds where it was nursed,
    Did thorough his own side   15
    His fiery way divide:[3]

5. "Oblique" includes the meaning of "deviating from right conduct or thought"; oblique loves, like oblique lines, touch in angles (corners), but Marvell's love and the lady's, being parallel and perfect, can never touch.
6. "Conjunction" and "opposition" are technical terms from astronomy, here yoked to Marvell's "definition."
1. Cromwell returned from conquering Ireland in May, 1650, about 18 months after the execution of Charles I. The two events were vaguely but persistently connected: Cromwell's victory over the Irish was somehow a "vindication" of his career to this point, a sign that God did not disapprove of his laying violent hands on the sacred person of the monarch. The title phrase, "An Horatian Ode," promises a poem of cool and balanced judgment, not "enthusiastic" or heroic like the odes of Pindar. For the

political background of Marvell's poem, see John M. Wallace, "Marvell's Horatian Ode," *PMLA* 77 (1962), 33–45.
2. The "forward youth" who removes armor from the wall owes something to a similar figure in the first book of Lucan's *Pharsalia*, which is also a poem about force, justice, and civil war. Andrew Marvell was not by any means dropping books and picking up armor in 1650.
3. Cromwell had begun as a relatively inconspicuous Presbyterian, but soon became the leader of the more radical group variously known as the "Rump" or the "Independents." The "three-forked lightning" he wields identifies him with Zeus; and his giving birth (to himself, presumably) through his own side (party, of course, but a part of the body, too) might remind a reader of Athena's birth through Zeus's ear.

For 'tis all one to courage high,
The emulous, or enemy;
    And with such, to enclose,
    Is more than to oppose;   20

Then burning through the air he went,
And palaces and temples rent;
    And Caesar's head at last
    Did through his laurels blast.[4]

'Tis madness to resist or blame   25
The face of angry Heaven's flame;
    And if we would speak true,
    Much to the man is due,

Who from his private gardens, where
He lived reservéd and austere,   30
    As if his highest plot
    To plant the bergamot;[5]

Could by industrious valor climb
To ruin the great work of Time,
    And cast the kingdom old,   35
    Into another mold;

Though Justice against Fate complain,
And plead the ancient rights in vain;
    But those do hold or break,
    As men are strong or weak.   40

Nature that hateth emptiness,
Allows of penetration less,
    And therefore must make room
    Where greater spirits come.

What field of all the civil wars   45
Where his were not the deepest scars?
    And Hampton shows what part
    He had of wiser art;[6]

Where, twining subtle fears with hope,
He wove a net of such a scope   50
    That Charles himself might chase
    To Caresbrooke's narrow case,

4. Laurels were used for royal crowns precisely because they were supposed to protect from lightning. "Caesar," of course, is Charles I. Cromwell's acts with his thunderbolt (smashing palaces, temples, and at last Caesar's head through its laurels) suggest a tyrannical God. Yet Caesar was a tyrant too.
5. Bergamot is a variety of pear; but its etymology (from the Turkish, "prince's pear") may conceal the insinuation that Cromwell had been plotting for power even in his early days of "private" life. The whole poem is full of puns (cf. "enclose," line 19, "mold," line 36) for the reader to seek out.
6. Hampton Court, where Charles I was confined shortly before his execution. It was popularly said that Cromwell connived at his momentary escape to Carisbrooke Castle on the Isle of Wight in order to convince the doubtful Parliament that the king could not be trusted and must be executed.

That thence the royal actor borne,
The tragic scaffold might adorn;
    While round the arméd bands
    Did clap their bloody hands.   55

He nothing common did or mean
Upon that memorable scene,
    But with his keener eye
    The ax's edge did try;[7]   60

Nor called the gods with vulgar spite
To vindicate his helpless right;
    But bowed his comely head
    Down, as upon a bed.

This was that memorable hour,   65
Which first assured the forcéd power;
    So when they did design
    The capitol's first line,

A bleeding head where they begun,
Did fright the architects to run;   70
    And yet in that the state
    Foresaw its happy fate.[8]

And now the Irish are ashamed
To see themselves in one year tamed;
    So much one man can do,   75
    That does both act and know.

They can affirm his praises best,
And have, though overcome, confessed
    How good he is, how just,
    And fit for highest trust.   80

Nor yet grown stiffer with command,
But still in the republic's hand—
    How fit he is to sway,
    That can so well obey.

He to the Commons' feet presents   85
A kingdom for his first year's rents;
    And, what he may, forbears
    His fame to make it theirs;

And has his sword and spoils ungirt,
To lay them at the public's skirt: 90
    So, when the falcon high
    Falls heavy from the sky,

7. Latin uses one word, *acies*, for the front of a battle line, the edge of a sword- or ax-blade, and the beam of an eye.
8. When foundations were being dug for the temple of Jupiter at Rome, Pliny tells us, the workmen uncovered a bloody head. They at first thought it an ill omen but then were persuaded to consider it a token that Rome would be the head (*caput*) of an empire; hence the name of the temple, Jupiter Capitolinus, and of the hill on which it stood, the Capitoline. The tale may well imply a generic relation between civilization and violence.

She, having killed, no more does search,
But on the next green bough to perch;
    Where, when he first does lure,   95
    The falconer has her sure.

What may not then our isle presume,
While victory his crest does plume!
    What may not others fear,
    If thus he crown each year!   100

A Caesar he ere long to Gaul,
To Italy an Hannibal,
    And to all states not free,
    Shall climactéric be.[9]

The Pict no shelter now shall find   105
Within his party-colored mind,
    But from this valor sad,
    Shrink underneath the plaid;[1]

Happy if in the tufted brake
The English hunter him mistake,   110
    Nor lay his hounds in near
    The Caledonian[2] deer.

But thou, the war's and fortune's son,
March indefatigably on;
    And for the last effect,   115
    Still keep thy sword erect;[3]

Besides the force it has to fright
The spirits of the shady night,
    The same arts that did gain
    A power must it maintain.[4]   120

1681

9. Neither Caesar nor Hannibal brought, or pretended to bring, freedom to the lands they attacked. "Climactéric": a period of crucial change in human life (for better or worse), popularly supposed to occur when 9 joined with 7 in man's age, i.e., in his 63rd year.
1. Early inhabitants of Scotland were called Picts because their warriors painted themselves many colors (Latin, *pictus*: painted); Marvell is playing with an image of the Scotch as divided by factions (parties) into as many colors as Scotch plaids.
2. Scotch.
3. The sword is being carried "erect," i.e., with the bare blade up, not the cross of the handle. Naked power, not religion, is to be the ensign of Cromwell's rule.
4. The last lines of the poem seem to paraphrase a saying of Christ's to the effect that they who take the sword shall perish with the sword (Matthew xxvi.52); from Cromwell's point of view, it is not a very reassuring ending to the poem. Yet when the poem was printed, in 1681, the censor of Charles II thought it politically subversive, and had it physically cut out of all the copies of Marvell's poems except (fortunately) one.

JOHN MILTON
(1608–1674)

> 1637:   *Lycidas.*
> 1640–60: The pamphlet wars.
> 1651:   Blindness.
> 1667:   *Paradise Lost.*

The life of John Milton falls conveniently into three divisions. There is a period of youthful education and apprenticeship, which culminates in the writing of *Lycidas* (1637) and Milton's foreign travels (1638–39). There is a period of prose and controversy (1640–60), when almost all his verse was occasional, and when his major preoccupations were political and social; and finally, there are the last fourteen years of his life, when he returned to literature, a mature and somewhat embittered figure, to publish his three great poems, *Paradise Lost* (1667), *Paradise Regained* (1671), and *Samson Agonistes* (1671).

Milton was born at Bread Street in Cheapside, the elder son of what we would nowadays probably call a real-estate man. From the beginning, Milton showed prodigious gifts as a student of languages. At St. Paul's School he mastered Latin and Greek, and before long he was adept in most modern European tongues, as well as Hebrew. Sent to Christ's College, Cambridge, he proceeded B.A. in 1629 and M.A. in 1632, meanwhile continuing to read voraciously and writing (too infrequently for his own satisfaction) an occasional poem. In the normal course of events, a career like this would have culminated in ordination to the ministry and a position in the church. Both Milton and his parents seem to have anticipated this. But after taking his M.A., Milton, who disliked the trend of civil and religious affairs in England, did not take orders; instead, he retired to his father's country house at Horton in Buckinghamshire, and for five more years, under his own direction, read day and night. It seems likely that Milton, in his time, read just about everything that was ever written in English, Latin, Greek, and Italian. (Of course, he had the Bible by heart.) In 1634 he wrote, at the invitation of a nearby noble family, the masque known as *Comus*; and in 1637 he contributed to a volume memorializing a college classmate the elegy of *Lycidas*. Finally, in 1638, his most indulgent father sent this most voracious of students abroad, to put the finishing touches on an already splendid education. For two years, Milton traveled on the Continent, visiting famous literary figures and scenes; then, hearing rumors of impending troubles in England, he returned home in 1639.

Of Milton's complex and troubled career in controversy we need not say much. It too is divided in three phases. He began by publishing anti-prelatical tracts, against the government of the church by bishops. These are rough, knockabout, name-calling tracts in the style of the times, which take a popular position on a relatively popular issue. But Milton's next venture procured him a reputation as a radical. In June, 1642, he married Mary Powell. Within six weeks, she left him, to return to her parents' house; and from 1643 to 1645, Milton published a series of pamphlets advocating that divorce be granted on the grounds of incompatibility. Clearly his personal situation had influenced his social judgment; just as clearly, respectable Englishmen, who were disturbed by the troubles of the time, were bound to feel that "divorce at pleasure" represented the end of all social order, the coming of complete anarchy. Milton not only effected no change in the divorce laws, he largely discredited himself by his divorce pamphlets. His last undertaking was more worthy of his gifts. After the execution of Charles I, in 1649, he published a series of Latin disputations against Continental critics of the regime, defending the actions of Parliament in executing Charles. In the middle of this work, he went blind, as the result of eyestrain continued over many years. By the use of secretaries and amanuenses, however, he was able to fulfill his duties as Latin Secretary to Cromwell's Council of State, and to contribute very substantially to the diplomatic dignity of the new government.

Meanwhile, his first wife returned to him, and having born him three daughters, died in 1652. In 1656 Milton married Katharine Woodcock, who died in childbirth, in 1658. Finally, in 1660, the whole political movement for which Milton had sacrificed so much, went to smash. Though Milton boldly published pamphlets in its support to the very last minute, the Good Old Cause was defeated, and Charles II recalled from his travels. For a time under the Restoration, Milton was imprisoned and in danger of his life; but friends intervened, and he escaped with a fine and the loss of most of his property.

In 1663 Milton married his third wife, Elizabeth Minshull; and in blindness, poverty, defeat, and relative isolation, he set about completing a poem "justifying the ways of God to men," which he had first envisaged many years before. It was published in 1667, as *Paradise Lost*; and despite the many difficulties which it presented, despite its unfamiliar meter (blank verse was rare outside drama), despite the unpopularity of its attitudes and Milton's reputation as a dangerous man, it was recognized at once as a supreme epic achievement. In 1671 Milton published *Paradise Regained*, an epic poem in four books describing Christ's temptation in the wilderness, and *Samson Agonistes*, a "closet" tragedy (i.e., not intended for the stage). He died, of complications arising from gout, in 1674.

In the writings of Milton, the work of two tremendous intellectual and social movements comes to a head. The Renaissance is responsible for the rich and complex texture of Milton's style, the multiplicity of its classical references, its wealth of ornament and decoration. *Paradise Lost*, being an epic, not only challenges comparison with Homer and Virgil, it undertakes to encompass the whole life of mankind—war, love, religion, Hell, Heaven, the cosmos. It is a poem vastly capacious of worldly experience. On the other hand, the Reformation speaks with equal, if not greater, authority in Milton's earnest and individually-minded Christianity. The great epic, which resounds with the grandeur and multiplicity of the world, is also a poem the central actions of which take place inwardly, at the core of man's conscience. Adam's fate culminates in an act of passive suffering, not of active heroism. He does not kill Hector or Turnus, much less Satan, he picks up the burden of worldly existence, and triumphs over his guilt by admitting it and repenting of it.

These two contrasting aspects of Milton's life and thought place him among the Christian humanists. His literary art places him in the small circle of great epic writers.

L'Allegro[1]

Hence loathéd Melancholy
   Of Cerberus[2] and blackest midnight born,
In Stygian[3] cave forlorn
   'Mongst horrid shapes, and shrieks, and sights unholy,
Find out some uncouth cell,   5
   Where brooding Darkness spreads his jealous wings,
And the night-raven sings;
   There under ebon shades, and low-browed rocks,
As ragged as thy locks,
   In dark Cimmerian[4] desert ever dwell.   10
But come thou goddess fair and free,
In Heaven yclept Euphrosyne,[5]
And by men, heart-easing Mirth,
Whom lovely Venus at a birth
With two sister Graces more   15
To ivy-crownéd Bacchus bore;[6]
Or whether (as some sager sing)[7]
The frolic wind that breathes the spring,
Zephyr with Aurora playing,
As he met her once a-Maying,   20
There on beds of violets blue,
And fresh-blown[8] roses washed in dew,

1. *L'Allegro* and *Il Penseroso* are a pair of companion-poems, probably written around 1630 or 1631, in those dancing tetrameter couplets which are so hard to keep from degenerating into singsong, and so delightful when controlled. Milton's handling of this difficult meter may be compared with virtuoso performances like those of Marvell (*To·His Coy Mistress*), Keats (*Lines on the Mermaid Tavern*) and A. E. Housman (*Terence, This Is Stupid Stuff*).

The titles are almost untranslatable, which is why Milton did not translate them. But within the framework of two contrasted days, we see the cheerful, sociable man, and the melancholy, contemplative man in their typical spiritual attitudes. Milton's interest in the typical accounts for the striking generality of the pictures: "And every shepherd tells his tale / Under the hawthorn in the dale"—there is no effort to create an individual shepherd in a particular setting. All the shepherds in all the dales for miles around are telling one story or another, each under his own hawthorn bush. But Milton's focus is on the mind that sees, and on the tone which it casts over a landscape. The cheerful man infuses his world with contagious cheerfulness; the melancholy man casts over the events of his day (which, as events, are not very different) a pervasive veil of melancholy. The backgrounds of this complex contemplative mood may be explored in Burton's famous *Anatomy of Melancholy;* in a more recent book, Erwin Panofsky's study, *Albrecht Dürer,* where it occurs in connection with Dürer's magnificent engraving of Melancholia; or in Saxl, Panofsky, and Klibansky's immense study, *Saturn and Melancholy* (1964). There is a history of literary cheerfulness, too—*The Happy Man,* by Maren Sofie Røstvig (1954).

Milton's poems stand in contrast to one another, but the contrasts are shaded, not glaring; there is no effort to "decide" the conflict, or to make melancholy black and cheerfulness convivial. Both poems exist in a reflective half-light, as little idyls of description which for sheer elegance and charm have rarely been equaled.

2. The three-headed hell-hound of classical mythology.

3. I.e., near the river Styx, the river of the underworld.

4. The Cimmerians, who gave their name to Crimea, were supposed to live on the outer edge of the world, in perpetual twilight.

5. Euphrosyne, Aglaia, and Thalia were the Graces, daughters (according to one story) of Zeus himself, and goddesses of beauty and delight. "Yclept": called.

6. Bacchus is god of wine.

7. The "sager" (poets) who describe the Graces as born of Zephyr and Aurora are in fact John Milton himself; he invented this version of the myth.

8. Newly opened.

Filled her with thee a daughter fair,
So buxom,[9] blithe, and debonair.
Haste thee nymph, and bring with thee   25
Jest and youthful Jollity,
Quips and Cranks,[1] and wanton Wiles,
Nods, and Becks, and wreathéd Smiles,
Such as hang on Hebe's[2] cheek,
And love to live in dimple sleek;   30
Sport that wrinkled Care derides,
And Laughter, holding both his sides.
Come, and trip it as ye go
On the light fantastic toe,
And in thy right hand lead with thee,   35
The mountain nymph, sweet Liberty;
And if I give thee honor due,
Mirth, admit me of thy crew
To live with her and live with thee,
In unreprovéd pleasures free;   40
To hear the lark begin his flight,
And, singing, startle the dull night,
From his watch-tower in the skies,
Till the dappled dawn doth rise;
Then to come[3] in spite of sorrow,   45
And at my window bid good morrow,
Through the sweetbriar, or the vine,
Or the twisted eglantine.
While the cock with lively din,
Scatters the rear of darkness thin,   50
And to the stack, or the barn door,
Stoutly struts his dames before;
Oft listening how the hounds and horn
Cheerly rouse the slumbering morn,
From the side of some hoar hill,   55
Through the high wood echoing shrill.
Sometime walking not unseen
By hedgerow elms, on hillocks green,
Right against the eastern gate,
Where the great sun begins his state,[4]   60
Robed in flames, and amber light,
The clouds in thousand liveries dight;[5]
While the plowman near at hand,
Whistles o'er the furrowed land,
And the milkmaid singeth blithe,   65
And the mower whets his scythe,
And every shepherd tells his tale,
Under the hawthorn in the dale.
Straight mine eye hath caught new pleasures
Whilst the landscape round it measures,   70

9. Lively.
1. Jokes. "Becks": curtseys.
2. Goddess of youth and cupbearer to
the other gods.

3. I.e., then admit me to come.
4. Procession.
5. Dressed.

Russet lawns and fallows gray,
Where the nibbling flocks do stray,
Mountains on whose barren breast
The laboring clouds do often rest;
Meadows trim with daisies pied,[6]   75
Shallow brooks, and rivers wide.
Towers and battlements it sees
Bosomed high in tufted trees,
Where perhaps some beauty lies,
The cynosure[7] of neighboring eyes.   80
Hard by, a cottage chimney smokes,
From betwixt two aged oaks,
Where Corydon and Thyrsis[8] met,
Are at their savory dinner set
Of herbs, and other country messes,   85
Which the neat-handed Phyllis dresses;
And then in haste her bower she leaves,
With Thestylis to bind the sheaves;
Or if the earlier season lead
To the tanned haycock in the mead.   90
Sometimes with secure delight
The upland hamlets will invite,
When the merry bells ring round
And the jocund rebecks[9] sound
To many a youth and many a maid,   95
Dancing in the checkered shade;
And young and old come forth to play
On a sunshine holiday,
Till the livelong daylight fail;
Then to the spicy nut-brown ale,   100
With stories told of many a feat,
How fairy Mab[1] the junkets eat;
She was pinched and pulled, she said,
And he, by Friar's lantern led,
Tells how the drudging goblin[2] sweat   105
To earn his cream-bowl, duly set,
When in one night, ere glimpse of morn,
His shadowy flail hath threshed the corn
That ten day-laborers could not end;
Then lies him down the lubber fiend,[3]   110
And, stretched out all the chimney's length,
Basks at the fire his hairy strength;
And crop-full out of doors he flings
Ere the first cock his matin rings.

6. Dappled.
7. Literally, the bright polestar, by which mariners steer; here, a splendid, eminent object, much gazed at.
8. Since the days of Theocritus, the names "Corydon," "Thyrsis," "Phyllis," and "Thestylis" have been traditional shepherds' names.
9. A rebeck is a small three-stringed fiddle; "jocund" implies a festive occasion.
1. Queen Mab, wife of Oberon, the fairy king. "She" and "he" in the next two lines are country folk, telling of their experiences with the fairies.
2. Robin Goodfellow, alias Puck, Pook, or Hobgoblin. "Friar's lantern": will-o'-the-wisp.
3. Oafish spirit.

Thus done the tales, to bed they creep,   115
By whispering winds soon lulled asleep.
Towered cities please us then,
And the busy hum of men,
Where throngs of knights and barons bold,
In weeds[4] of peace high triumphs hold,   120
With store of ladies, whose bright eyes
Rain influence,[5] and judge the prize
Of wit, or arms, while both contend
To win her grace, whom all commend.
There let Hymen[6] oft appear   125
In saffron robe, with taper clear,
And pomp, and feast, and revelry,
With masque, and antique pageantry;
Such sights as youthful poets dream
On summer eves by haunted stream.   130
Then to the well-trod stage anon,
If Jonson's learned sock[7] be on,
Or sweetest Shakespeare, fancy's child,
Warble his native wood-notes wild.
And ever against eating cares[8]   135
Lap me in soft Lydian airs,[9]
Married to immortal verse
Such as the meeting soul may pierce
In notes, with many a winding bout[1]
Of linkéd sweetness long drawn out,   140
With wanton heed, and giddy cunning,
The melting voice through mazes running;
Untwisting all the chains that tie
The hidden soul of harmony;
That Orpheus' self[2] may heave his head   145
From golden slumber on a bed
Of heaped Elysian flowers, and hear
Such strains as would have won the ear
Of Pluto, to have quite set free
His half-regained Eurydice.   150
These delights if thou canst give,
Mirth, with thee I mean to live.

ca. 1631   1645

4. Garments. "Triumphs": festive ceremonies.
5. The ladies' eyes are stars, and so
have astrological influence over the
men.
6. Roman god of marriage, wearing a
yellow ("saffron") robe.
7. A low-heeled slipper, worn by actors
in classical comedy, and often contrasted
with the buskin (high-heeled boot) appropriate to tragedy. The contrast of
Jonson as a "learned" poet with Shakespeare as a "natural" one was conventional.
8. "Eating cares" is but one of many
classical phrases in the poem; it is

from Horace, *Odes* II.xi.18 (*curas
edaces*).
9. "Lydian" airs in music would be
soft, languishing, sensual—unlike the
chaste Dorian and brisk Ionian.
1. A musical "run" passage.
2. Orpheus went to the underworld to
regain his wife Eurydice, and by his
music dissolved the guardians of Hades
in tears. But as they left, he violated
the condition of her release by looking
back at her, and so lost her again.
Milton uses the Orpheus story again
in *Il Penseroso*, *Lycidas*, and *Paradise
Lost* VII.32 ff.

Il Penseroso

Hence vain deluding Joys,
  The brood of Folly without father bred.
How little you bestead,[3]
  Or fill the fixéd mind with all your toys;[4]
Dwell in some idle brain,   5
  And fancies fond[5] with gaudy shapes possess,
As thick and numberless
  As the gay motes that people the sunbeams,
Or likest hovering dreams,
  The fickle pensioners[6] of Morpheus' train.   10
But hail thou Goddess, sage and holy,
Hail, divinest Melancholy,
Whose saintly visage is too bright
To hit[7] the sense of human sight;
And therefore to our weaker view,   15
O'erlaid with black, staid Wisdom's hue.
Black, but such as in esteem,
Prince Memnon's sister[8] might beseem,
Or that starred Ethiope queen[9] that strove
To set her beauty's praise above   20
The sea nymphs, and their powers offended.
Yet thou art higher far descended;
Thee bright-haired Vesta long of yore
To solitary Saturn bore;[1]
His daughter she (in Saturn's reign   25
Such mixture was not held a stain).
Oft in glimmering bowers and glades
He met her, and in secret shades
Of woody Ida's inmost grove,
While yet there was no fear of Jove.   30
Come pensive nun, devout and pure,
Sober, steadfast, and demure,
All in a robe of darkest grain,[2]
Flowing with majestic train,
And sable stole of cypress lawn[3]   35
Over thy decent shoulders drawn.
Come, but keep thy wonted state,

3. Avail, help.
4. Trifles.
5. Foolish.
6. Followers. Morpheus is the god of sleep; the melancholy man feels the cheerful man lives in a dream.
7. Suit, agree with.
8. Memnon in *Odyssey* XI was a handsome Ethiopian prince who fought for Troy; his sister, mentioned not by Homer but by later commentators, was Hemera.
9. Cassiopeia, who was "starred" (i.e., turned into a constellation) for bragging that her daughter Andromeda or she herself (Milton follows this second version) was more beautiful than the sea nymphs.
1. Vesta was a goddess of purity; Milton invented the story of her connection with Saturn on Mt. Ida in Crete, and of her giving birth to Melancholy. But Saturn helps out the poem because he was a primitive deity (hence melancholy is "natural") and because a saturnine complexion is said to show a dark and melancholy disposition.
2. Color.
3. "Cypress": a dark, delicate cloth (originally Cyprus, from the island; but the cypress is also the tree of death). "Lawn": a transparent, gauzy material, much like crape. "Decent": comely, proper.

With even step and musing gait,
And looks commercing with the skies,
Thy rapt soul sitting in thine eyes: 40
There held in holy passion still,
Forget thyself to marble, till
With a sad leaden downward cast,
Thou fix them on the earth as fast.
And join with thee calm Peace and Quiet,   45
Spare Fast, that oft with gods doth diet,
And hears the Muses in a ring
Aye round about Jove's altar sing.
And add to these retired Leisure,
That in trim gardens takes his pleasure;   50
But first, and chiefest, with thee bring,
Him that yon soars on golden wing,
Guiding the fiery-wheeléd throne,
The cherub Contemplation;[4]
And the mute Silence hist along   55
'Less Philomel[5] will deign a song,
In her sweetest, saddest plight,
Smoothing the rugged brow of night,
While Cynthia[6] checks her dragon yoke
Gently o'er th' accustomed oak;   60
Sweet bird that shunn'st the noise of folly,
Most musical, most melancholy!
Thee chantress oft the woods among,
I woo to hear thy evensong;
And missing thee, I walk unseen   65
On the dry smooth-shaven green,
To behold the wandering moon,
Riding near her highest noon,
Like one that had been led astray
Through the Heaven's wide pathless way;   70
And oft as if her head she bowed,
Stooping through a fleecy cloud.
Oft on a plat[7] of rising ground,
I hear the far-off curfew sound,
Over some wide-watered shore,   75
Swinging slow with sullen roar;
Or if the air will not permit,
Some still removéd place will fit,
Where glowing embers through the room
Teach light to counterfeit a gloom   80
Far from all resort of mirth,
Save the cricket on the hearth,
Or the bellman's[8] drowsy charm,

---

4. The cherub Contemplation is suggested by the Biblical vision of Ezekiel.
5. The nightingale, whose song is traditionally one of grief. "Hist": summon.
6. Goddess of the moon, and of the underworld as well, she drives a pair of sleepless dragons.
7. Plot, flat open space.
8. The night watchman in little villages rang a bell to call the hours.

To bless the doors from nightly harm;
Or let my lamp at midnight hour   85
Be seen in some high lonely tower,
Where I may oft outwatch the Bear,[9]
With thrice great Hermes,[1] or unsphere
The spirit of Plato to unfold
What worlds, or what vast regions hold   90
The immortal mind that hath forsook
Her mansion in this fleshly nook;
And of those demons[2] that are found
In fire, air, flood, or underground,
Whose power hath a true consent[3]   95
With planet, or with element.
Some time let gorgeous Tragedy
In sceptered pall[4] come sweeping by,
Presenting Thebes', or Pelops' line,
Or the tale of Troy divine.[5]   100
Or what (though rare) of later age
Ennobled hath the buskined[6] stage.
But, O sad virgin, that thy power
Might raise Musaeus[7] from his bower,
Or bid the soul of Orpheus[8] sing   105
Such notes as, warbled to the string,
Drew iron tears down Pluto's cheek,
And made Hell grant what Love did seek.
Or call up him[9] that left half told
The story of Cambuscan bold,   110
Of Camball, and of Algarsife,
And who had Canacee to wife,
That owned the virtuous[1] ring and glass,
And of the wondrous horse of brass,
On which the Tartar king did ride;   115
And if aught else great bards beside
In sage and solemn tunes have sung,
Of tourneys and of trophies hung,
Of forests and enchantments drear,
Where more is meant than meets the ear.[2]   120

9. Since the Great Bear never sets, outwatching it is a major enterprise.
1. The Egyptian god Thoth or Hermes, to whom were attributed various esoteric books of the 3rd and 4th centuries A.D.; under the name of Hermes Trismegistus he later became a patron of magicians and alchemists. To "unsphere" Plato is to call Plato by magical means back to earth from the sphere he now inhabits.
2. Not devils, but classical beings akin to heroes, halfway between gods and men. There were four sorts of demons, corresponding to the four elements, each with a corresponding planet.
3. Mysterious agreement.
4. Royal robe (from Latin *palla*, the robe of tragic actors).
5. Tragedies about the royal line of Thebes would include Sophocles' Oedipus cycle; those about the line of Pelops, Aeschylus' *Oresteia;* and those about Troy, Euripides' *Trojan Women.*
6. The buskin of tragedy, contrasted with the sock of comedy.
7. A mythical poet-priest of the pre-Homeric age, supposedly son or pupil of the equally mythical Orpheus.
8. For the story of Orpheus, see *L'Allegro,* line 145, and note.
9. I.e., Chaucer, who in the Squire's Tale left the tale of Cambuscan half told.
1. Having special power.
2. A capsule description of allegory.

Thus, Night, oft see me in thy pale career,
Till civil-suited morn appear,[3]
Not tricked and frounced as she was wont,
With the Attic boy to hunt,
But kerchiefed in a comely cloud,   125
While rocking winds are piping loud,
Or ushered with a shower still,
When the gust hath blown his fill,
Ending on the rustling leaves,
With minute-drops from off the eaves.   130
And when the sun begins to fling
His flaring beams, me, Goddess, bring
To archéd walks of twilight groves,
And shadows brown that Sylvan[4] loves
Of pine or monumental oak,   135
Where the rude ax with heavéd stroke,
Was never heard the nymphs to daunt,
Or fright them from their hallowed haunt.
There in close covert by some brook,
Where no profaner eye may look,   140
Hide me from day's garish eye,
While the bee with honeyed thigh,
That at her flowery work doth sing,
And the waters murmuring
With such consort[5] as they keep,   145
Entice the dewy-feathered sleep;
And let some strange mysterious dream,
Wave at his wings in airy stream,
Of lively portraiture displayed,
Softly on my eyelids laid.[6]   150
And as I wake, sweet music breathe
Above, about, or underneath,
Sent by some spirit to mortals good,
Or th' unseen genius[7] of the wood.
But let my due feet never fail   155
To walk the studious cloister's pale,[8]
And love the high embowéd roof,
With antic[9] pillars massy proof,
And storied windows[1] richly dight,
Casting a dim religious light.   160
There let the pealing organ blow,
To the full-voiced choir below,

3. The goddess Aurora, who once fell in love with Cephalus ("the Attic boy," line 124), and used to go hunting with him. "Tricked and frounced": adorned and frizzled.
4. Roman god of the woodlands.
5. Accompaniment.
6. Milton's syntax gets loose and dreamy too, here. He means, "Let some strange dream wave at the wings of sleep, while a stream of vivid pictures passes softly over my eyelids."
7. Guardian angel.
8. Enclosure.
9. I.e., covered with quaint, grotesque, or antic carvings; but "antique," which derives from the same Latin root, was not excluded from the sense. "Massy proof": massive and strong.
1. I.e., with stories told by stained-glass images. "Dight": dressed.

In service high, and anthems clear,
As may with sweetness, through mine ear,
Dissolve me into ecstasies,   165
And bring all heaven before mine eyes.
And may at last my weary age
Find out the peaceful hermitage,
The hairy gown and mossy cell,
Where I may sit and rightly spell[2]   170
Of every star that Heaven doth show,
And every herb that sips the dew
Till old experience do attain
To something like prophetic strain.
These pleasures, Melancholy, give,   175
And I with thee will choose to live.

ca. 1631   1645

At a Solemn Music

Blest pair of Sirens,[3] pledges of Heaven's joy,
Sphere-born harmonious sisters, Voice and Verse,
Wed your divine sounds, and mixed power employ
Dead things with inbreathed sense able to pierce,
And to our high-raised fantasy [4] present   5
That undisturbed song of pure consent,[5]
Aye sung before the sapphire-colored throne
To him that sits thereon
With saintly shout and solemn jubilee,
Where the bright seraphim in burning row   10
Their loud uplifted angel-trumpets blow,
And the cherubic host in thousand choirs
Touch their immortal harps of golden wires,
With those just spirits that wear victorious palms,[6]
Hymns devout and holy psalms   15
Singing everlastingly; [7]
That we on earth with undiscording voice
May rightly answer that melodious noise;
As once we did, till disproportioned sin
Jarred against nature's chime, and with harsh din   20
Broke the fair music that all creatures made
To their great Lord, whose love their motion swayed
In perfect diapason, whilst they stood
In first obedience, and their state of good.[8]

2. Study. The melancholy man wants to think his way into the cosmos until he becomes a prophet.
3. The Sirens, enticing mermaids who lured men to destruction (*Odyssey* XII), were traditionally sweet but evilly intentioned singers; Milton's Sirens are "blest," i.e., not only "happy" but "of good omen."
4. Imagination.
5. Harmony, agreement.
6. The saints wear palms in token of their victory over sin.
7. "Singing" modifies "spirits" (line 14), and takes as an object "hymns devout and holy psalms" (line 15). Milton is practicing at balancing the masses of his long sentences on a Latin grammar and word order.
8. Before man fell, the whole cosmos was in moral and intellectual concord ("diapason"), hence the music of the spheres could be heard on earth.

O may we soon again renew that song,   25
And keep in tune with Heaven, till God ere long
To his celestial consort us unite,
To live with him, and sing in endless morn of light.

1632   1645

Songs from Comus

Sweet Echo[1]

Sweet Echo, sweetest nymph that liv'st unseen
    Within thy airy shell
    By slow Meander's[2] margent green,
And in the violet-embroidered vale
    Where the lovelorn nightingale   5
Nightly to thee her sad song mourneth well.
Canst thou not tell me of a gentle pair
    That likest thy Narcissus[3] are?
      O if thou have
      Hid them in some flowery cave,   10
        Tell me but where
Sweet queen of parley, daughter of the sphere,[4]
So mayest thou be translated to the skies,
And give resounding grace to all Heaven's harmonies.

Sabrina Fair[5]

Sabrina fair
    Listen where thou art sitting
Under the glassy, cool, translucent wave,
    In twisted braids of lilies knitting
The loose train of thy amber-dropping hair;   5
    Listen for dear honor's sake,
    Goddess of the silver lake,
      Listen and save.

By the Rushy-fringed Bank

[*Sabrina rises, attended by water nymphs, and sings*]

    By the rushy-fringéd bank,
Where grows the willow and the osier[6] dank,
    My sliding chariot stays,
Thick set with agate, and the azurn sheen
Of turquoise blue, and emerald green   5
    That in the channel strays;
    Whilst from off the waters fleet

1. To keep up her courage, the Lady in Milton's masque, *Comus*, sings this song to Echo when she is alone and benighted in a dark forest.

2. A Near-Eastern river, famous for its many twistings and turnings.

3. The lady is looking for her two brothers ("a gentle pair"); they are like Narcissus (with whom Echo fell in love and because of whom she pined away to an empty voice) in being handsome, not in admiring themselves.

4. Echo is "queen of parley," i.e., of speech, because she talked so much. The flaw for which she was punished becomes a ground for compliment. She is "daughter of the sphere" because her "airy shell" is the arch of the sky.

5. The song is sung by the Attendant Spirit, to invoke the aid of Sabrina (goddess of the river Severn and patroness of chastity) in freeing the Lady from Comus' magic charms.

6. Osier is actually a variety of willow; but the name sounds much danker and moister than willow alone.

Thus I set my printless feet
O'er the cowslip's velvet head,
That bends not as I tread;   10
Gentle swain, at thy request
    I am here.

1634   1637

Lycidas   This poem is a pastoral elegy; that is, it uses the sometimes artificial imagery supplied by an idyllic shepherd's existence to bewail the loss of a friend. Among its many predecessors in the Renaissance and in classical antiquity are poems by Spenser, Ronsard, Castiglione, Mantuan, Petrarch, Virgil, Theocritus, Moschus, and Bion; its successors include poems like *Adonais* by Shelley and *Thyrsis* by Matthew Arnold. T. P. Harrison and H. J. Leon have collected in *The Pastoral Elegy* (1939) a selection of poems from the tradition.

All pastoral poems enjoy the privilege of saying something about the world as a whole while seeming to talk simply of an artificial play-society; they are irresistibly allegorical. They have certain conventions—the swain (i.e., the shepherd) is ignorant but unspoiled, naturally virtuous, inherently poetic; life is pleasant and easy, yet just for this reason the basic human preoccupations stand out. The pastoral elegy has a further list of conventions—a history of past friendship, a questioning of destiny, a procession of mourners, a laying-on of flowers, a consolation, and usually a refrain. Milton adapted all but the last of these to *Lycidas*.

Edward King, who was the occasion of the poem if not its subject, was a fellow student of Milton's at Cambridge. Milton says he was a poet, and he was in the church. While proceeding to his new parish in Ireland, he was drowned, in 1637; and Milton joined with his schoolfellows, the following year, to produce a little memorial volume. *Justa Edouardo King* includes 35 poems, mostly in Latin; only *Lycidas* is of literary consequence.

It is written in a flowing, extended manner, with many run-on lines and great impetus, predominantly in pentameter, but with many variations of line length, and an irregular rhyme scheme including ten unrhymed lines and two perfectly formed stanzas of ottava rima. Many of these technical qualities are reminiscent of the Italian *canzone* or song, but most of them had been exemplified previously in Spenser's *Epithalamion*.

There are usually taken to be three explicit climaxes in *Lycidas*, each having to do with an aspect of the shepherd's life and with a problem which Milton wished to pose regarding the meaning of existence. Apollo answers his first question about the reward of poetry; St. Peter answers a second question, about the spiritual shepherd who betrays his flock; and finally Lycidas is translated into the Christian Paradise, to be at one with the Lamb of God, the Good Shepherd, the supreme giver of poetic fame, and the proper subject of all song. Subordinate patterns of imagery include vegetation and nature deities, water and water gods, who serve an immense variety of purposes.

Lycidas

IN THIS MONODY[1] THE AUTHOR BEWAILS A LEARNED FRIEND,
UNFORTUNATELY DROWNED IN HIS PASSAGE FROM CHESTER
ON THE IRISH SEAS, 1637. AND BY OCCASION FORETELLS
THE RUIN OF OUR CORRUPTED CLERGY,
THEN IN THEIR HEIGHT.

Yet once more, O ye laurels, and once more
Ye myrtles brown, with ivy never sere,[2]
I come to pluck your berries harsh and crude,[3]
And with forced fingers rude,
Shatter your leaves before the mellowing year.   5
Bitter constraint, and sad occasion dear,[4]
Compels me to disturb your season due;
For Lycidas is dead, dead ere his prime,
Young Lycidas, and hath not left his peer.
Who would not sing for Lycidas? He knew   10
Himself to sing, and build the lofty rhyme.
He must not float upon his watery bier
Unwept, and welter to the parching wind,
Without the meed[5] of some melodious tear.
  Begin then, sisters of the sacred well[6]   15
That from beneath the seat of Jove doth spring,
Begin, and somewhat loudly sweep the string.
Hence with denial vain, and coy excuse;
So may some gentle Muse
With lucky words favor my destined urn,[7]   20
And as he passes turn,
And bid fair peace be to my sable shroud.
For we were nursed upon the selfsame hill,
Fed the same flock, by fountain, shade, and rill.
  Together both, ere the high lawns[8] appeared   25
Under the opening eyelids of the morn,
We drove afield, and both together heard
What time the grayfly winds her sultry horn,[9]
Battening our flocks with the fresh dews of night,
Oft till the star that rose at evening bright   30
Toward Heaven's descent had sloped his westering wheel.

1. A song sung in Greek drama by a single voice.
2. "Laurels" for the crown of poetry given by Apollo; "myrtles" for the undying love granted by Venus; "ivy," the plant of Bacchus. All three plants are evergreens associated with poetic inspiration.
3. Unripe.
4. Heartfelt, profoundly moving; but also, in the 17th century, with overtones of "dire."
5. Reward.
6. The nine sister Muses were reported to dwell by various springs or "wells"; most likely Milton had in mind that of Aganippe near Mt. Helicon.
7. The speaker suggests that if he sings for Lycidas, "some gentle Muse" (i.e., poet) may some day sing for him.
8. Upland pastures.
9. I.e., heard the grayfly when she buzzes ("winds her sultry horn"). "Battening": feeding.

Meanwhile the rural ditties were not mute,
Tempered to th' oaten flute,[1]
Rough satyrs danced, and fauns with cloven heel
From the glad sound would not be absent long,   35
And old Damoetas[2] loved to hear our song.
　　But O the heavy change, now thou art gone,
Now thou art gone, and never must return!
Thee, shepherd, thee the woods and desert caves,
With wild thyme and the gadding[3] vine o'ergrown,   40
And all their echoes mourn.
The willows and the hazel copses green
Shall now no more be seen,
Fanning their joyous leaves to thy soft lays.
As killing as the canker[4] to the rose,   45
Or taint-worm to the weanling herds that graze,
Or frost to flowers that their gay wardrobe wear,
When first the white thorn blows;[5]
Such, Lycidas, thy loss to shepherd's ear.
　　Where were ye, nymphs,[6] when the remorseless deep   50
Closed o'er the head of your loved Lycidas?
For neither were ye playing on the steep,
Where your old Bards, the famous Druids[7] lie,
Nor on the shaggy top of Mona high,[8]
Nor yet where Deva spreads her wizard stream: 55
Ay me! I fondly dream—
Had ye been there—for what could that have done?
What could the Muse[9] herself that Orpheus bore,
The Muse herself, for her inchanting[1] son
Whom universal Nature did lament,   60
When by the rout[2] that made the hideous roar,
His gory visage down the stream was sent,
Down the swift Hebrus to the Lesbian shore?
　　Alas! What boots[3] it with incessant care
To tend the homely slighted shepherd's trade,   65
And strictly meditate the thankless Muse?[4]

1. Traditional Panpipes, played by shepherds.
2. A type name from pastoral poetry, possibly referring to some specific tutor at Cambridge.
3. Straggling.
4. Cankerworm.
5. Blossoms (as in the surviving expression, "full-blown").
6. Nature deities.
7. The Druids, priestly poet-kings of Celtic Britain, worshiped the forces of nature. They lie dead in their burying ground on the mountain ("steep") Kerig-y-Druidion in Wales.
8. "Mona" is the island of Anglesey. "Deva" is the river Dee in Cheshire. The Dee was magic ("wizard") because the size and position of its shifting stream foretold prosperity or dearth for the land. All the places mentioned in lines 52–55 are in the West Country, near where King drowned.
9. Calliope, Muse of epic poetry, was the mother of Orpheus.
1. "Inchanting" implies both song and magic; the root word survives as "incantation."
2. Orpheus was torn to pieces by a mob ("rout") of screaming Thracian women, who threw his gory head into the river Hebrus, down which it floated, still singing, and out to Lesbos in the Aegean. The fate of Orpheus and the Druids suggests that nature everywhere is indifferent to the destruction of the poet.
3. Profits.
4. Study to write poetry (the phrase is Virgil's).

Were it not better done as others use,
To sport with Amaryllis in the shade,
Or with the tangles of Neaera's hair?[5]
Fame is the spur that the clear spirit doth raise   70
(That last infirmity of noble mind)
To scorn delights, and live laborious days;
But the fair guerdon[6] when we hope to find,
And think to burst out into sudden blaze,
Comes the blind Fury[7] with th' abhorréd shears,   75
And slits the thin spun life. "But not the praise,"
Phoebus[8] replied, and touched my trembling ears;
"Fame is no plant that grows on mortal soil,
Not in the glistering foil[9]
Set off to th' world, nor in broad rumor lies,   80
But lives and spreads aloft by those pure eyes,
And perfect witness of all-judging Jove;
As he pronounces lastly on each deed,
Of so much fame in Heaven expect thy meed."

O fountain Arethuse,[1] and thou honored flood,   85
Smooth-sliding Mincius, crowned with vocal reeds,
That strain I heard was of a higher mood.
But now my oat[2] proceeds,
And listens to the herald of the sea[3]
That came in Neptune's plea.   90
He asked the waves, and asked the felon winds,
"What hard mishap hath doomed this gentle swain?"
And questioned every gust of rugged wings
That blows from off each beakéd promontory;
They knew not of his story,   95
And sage Hippotades[4] their answer brings,
That not a blast was from his dungeon strayed,
The air was calm, and on the level brine,
Sleek Panope[5] with all her sisters played.
It was that fatal and perfidious bark   100
Built in th' eclipse,[6] and rigged with curses dark,

5. "Amaryllis" and "Neaera," conventional names for pretty nymphs, a passing hour's diversion for idle shepherds.
6. Reward.
7. Atropos, one of the three Fates, bearing scissors with which she cuts the thread of human life. Milton, to suggest the bitterness of death, makes her an avenging Fury.
8. Phoebus Apollo, god of poetic inspiration. Touching the ears of one's hearers was a traditional Roman way of asking them to remember something that had been said (Virgil, *Eclogues* VI; Horace, *Satires* I.ix.77).
9. Cheap, flashy metal, used to add glitter to glass gems.
1. Arethusa was a fountain in Sicily, Mincius a river in Lombardy, the former associated with the pastorals of Theocritus, the latter with those of Virgil. Arethusa was originally a nymph who went bathing in the river Alpheus, in Arcadian Greece. The river god grew enamored, and gave chase; she dove into the ocean and fled undersea to Sicily, where she came up as a fountain. Milton plays here with the idea of his pastoral going underground while the "strain of a higher mood" (line 87) is heard.
2. Pipe, hence song.
3. Neptune's "herald" is Triton, pleading his master's innocence in the death of Lycidas.
4. Aeolus, god of winds, and son of Hippotas.
5. The chief Nereid or sea nymph.
6. I.e., time of the worst possible luck.

That sunk so low that sacred head of thine.
    Next Camus,[7] reverend sire, went footing slow,
His mantle hairy, and his bonnet sedge,
Inwrought with figures dim, and on the edge   105
Like to that sanguine flower inscribed with woe.[8]
"Ah! who hath reft," quoth he, "my dearest pledge?"
Last came and last did go
The pilot of the Galilean lake,[9]
Two massy keys he bore of metals twain   110
(The golden opes, the iron shuts amain[1]).
He shook his mitered locks,[2] and stern bespake:
"How well could I have spared for thee, young swain,
Enow[3] of such as for their bellies' sake,
Creep and intrude, and climb into the fold!   115
Of other care they little reckoning make,
Than how to scramble at the shearers' feast,
And shove away the worthy bidden guest.
Blind mouths![4] That scarce themselves know how to hold
A sheep-hook,[5] or have learned aught else the least   120
That to the faithful herdsman's art belongs!
What recks it them?[6] What need they? They are sped;
And when they list,[7] their lean and flashy songs
Grate on their scrannel[8] pipes of wretched straw.
The hungry sheep look up, and are not fed,   125
But swoln with wind, and the rank mist they draw,
Rot inwardly, and foul contagion spread,
Besides what the grim wolf with privy paw[9]
Daily devours apace, and nothing said.
But that two-handed engine at the door[1]   130
Stands ready to smite once, and smite no more."
    Return, Alpheus,[2] the dread voice is past,

---

7. God of the river Cam (properly, Granta), representing the ancient University of Cambridge, but slow and shaggy like the stream.
8. The bonnet and mantle of Camus have marks of woe on the edge like the *AI AI* supposedly found on the hyacinth, a "sanguine flower" sprung from the blood of a youth killed accidentally by Apollo.
9. St. Peter, originally a fisherman on Lake Tiberias in Galilee, was first founder and bishop of the Christian church; his keys open and shut the gates to heaven.
1. Literally "in full force," "exceedingly"; in this context, "for good," "once and for all."
2. He wears the bishop's miter.
3. An old plural form of "enough," used here with contemptuous intensification, as if to say, "enough and more than enough."
4. This audacious metaphor, as of tapeworms, takes on new depth when one notes that the word *episcopus* (bishop)

originally meant "over-seer" and a "pastor" is properly one who feeds his flock.
5. The bishop's staff, or crozier, is made in the form of a shepherd's crook.
6. What do they care? "They are sped": i.e., they have prospered in a worldly sense; but also, "their doom is sealed."
7. Choose (that is, choose to play on their pipes, as shepherds should); but with the secondary meaning of "listen."
8. Harsh, meager. Milton's is the first recorded literary use of the word in English; it existed previously only in a North-Country dialect.
9. I.e., Roman Catholicism, whose agents operated in secret.
1. Many guesses as to the specific meaning of the "two-handed engine" are on record; it may be St. Peter's keys, the two houses of Parliament, or a big sword, but there is no harm in letting it remain an indistinct, apocalyptic instrument of revenge.
2. With the return of Alpheus, the pastoral mode of the poem revives (see

That shrunk thy streams; return, Sicilian muse,
And call the vales, and bid them hither cast
Their bells and flowerets of a thousand hues.   135
Ye valleys low where the mild whispers use,[3]
Of shades and wanton winds, and gushing brooks,
On whose fresh lap the swart star[4] sparely looks,
Throw hither all your quaint enameled eyes,
That on the green turf suck the honeyed showers,   140
And purple all the ground with vernal flowers.
Bring the rathe[5] primrose that forsaken dies.
The tufted crow-toe, and pale jessamine,
The white pink, and the pansy freaked[6] with jet,
The glowing violet,   145
The musk-rose, and the well attired woodbine.
With cowslips wan that hang the pensive head,
And every flower that sad embroidery wears:
Bid amaranthus[7] all his beauty shed,
And daffadillies fill their cups with tears,   150
To strew the laureate hearse[8] where Lycid lies.
For so to interpose a little ease,
Let our frail thoughts dally with false surmise.[9]
Ay me! Whilst thee the shores and sounding seas
Wash far away, where'er thy bones are hurled,   155
Whether beyond the stormy Hebrides,[1]
Where thou perhaps under the whelming tide
Visit'st the bottom of the monstrous world;
Or whether thou, to our moist vows denied,
Sleep'st by the fable of Bellerus old,[2]   160
Where the great vision of the guarded mount
Looks toward Namancos and Bayona's hold:[3]
Look homeward angel now, and melt with ruth:[4]
And, O ye dolphins,[5] waft the hapless youth.
Weep no more, woeful shepherds, weep no more,   165
For Lycidas your sorrow is not dead,

above, lines 85–87), and a catalogue of flowers serves, as in Castiglione's *Alcon*, to "interpose a little ease."
3. I.e., are used or accustomed to be heard.
4. The Dog Star, Sirius, which during the heats of late summer "looks sparely" (witheringly) on the vegetation.
5. Early.
6. Flecked (the early verb survives in our word "freckle").
7. The amaranth is an imaginary flower that never fades; but for Lycidas it will.
8. Bier decked with laurels (see line 1).
9. The "false surmise" is that the body of Lycidas has been recovered and can receive Christian burial.
1. Islands off the coast of Scotland, representing the northern terminus of the Irish Sea.
2. The fabulous giant Bellerus is supposed to lie buried on Land's End in Cornwall.
3. St. Michael's Mount, in Cornwall, from which the archangel is envisioned as looking south, over miles of open Atlantic, across the Bay of Biscay, to Bayona and the stronghold of Namancos in northern Spain, where the historical Catholic enemy of Protestant England lay entrenched.
4. Michael is implored to look homeward, relaxing his stern guard for a moment of grief and pity ("ruth").
5. Dolphins, admirable sea beasts, brought the Greek poet Arion safely ashore for love of his verses, and also wafted the dead body of Melicertes to land, where he was promptly transformed to a sea god, Palaemon.

Sunk though he be beneath the watery floor,
So sinks the day-star[6] in the ocean bed,
And yet anon repairs his drooping head,
And tricks[7] his beams, and with new-spangled ore,   170
Flames in the forehead of the morning sky:
So Lycidas sunk low, but mounted high,
Through the dear might of him that walked the waves,
Where other groves, and other streams along,
With nectar pure his oozy locks he laves,   175
And hears the unexpressive nuptial song,[8]
In the blest kingdoms meek of joy and love.
There entertain him all the saints above,
In solemn troops and sweet societies
That sing, and singing in their glory move,   180
And wipe the tears forever from his eyes.
Now, Lycidas, the shepherds weep no more;
Henceforth thou art the genius[9] of the shore,
In thy large recompense, and shalt be good
To all that wander in that perilous flood.   185
    Thus sang the uncouth swain[1] to th' oaks and rills,
While the still morn went out with sandals gray;
He touched the tender stops of various quills,[2]
With eager thought warbling his Doric[3] lay:
And now the sun had stretched out all the hills,   190
And now was dropped into the western bay;
At last he rose, and twitched his mantle blue:
Tomorrow to fresh woods, and pastures new.

                      1637

How Soon Hath Time

How soon hath Time, the subtle thief of youth,
    Stoln on his wing my three and twentieth year!
    My hasting days fly on with full career,
    But my late spring no bud or blossom show'th.
Perhaps my semblance might deceive the truth,   5
    That I to manhood am arrived so near,
    And inward ripeness doth much less appear,
    That some more timely-happy spirits endu'th.[1]
Yet be it less or more, or soon or slow,
    It shall be still in strictest measure even[2]   10

6. The sun.
7. Dresses.
8. Inexpressible hymn of joy, sung at "the marriage supper of the Lamb" (Revelation xix).
9. One who by divine appointment haunts a locality (in this case, "the shore") where he suffered and died, protecting others who might undergo a fate like his own.

1. Unlettered shepherd (a stock convention of this supremely literary form).
2. The oaten stalks of Panpipes.
3. Rustic, simple.
1. Endoweth.
2. Equal, adequate. Whenever it appears and however much it amounts

To that same lot, however mean or high,
Toward which Time leads me, and the will of Heaven;
All is, if I have grace to use it so,
As ever in my great Taskmaster's eye.[3]

1631   1645

When the Assault Was Intended to the City[4]

Captain or Colonel,[5] or Knight in Arms,
Whose chance on these defenseless doors may seize,
If deed of honor did thee ever please,
Guard them, and him within protect from harms.
He can requite thee; for he knows the charms   5
That call fame on such gentle acts as these,
And he can spread thy name o'er lands and seas,
Whatever clime the sun's bright circle warms.
Lift not thy spear against the Muses' bower:
The great Emathian conqueror bid spare   10
The house of Pindarus, when temple and tower
Went to the ground;[6] and the repeated air
Of sad Electra's poet had the power
To save th' Athenian walls from ruin bare.[7]

1642   1645

A Book Was Writ of Late Called *Tetrachordon*

A book was writ of late called *Tetrachordon*,[8]
And woven close, both matter, form, and style;
The subject new: it walked the town a while,
Numb'ring good intellects; now seldom pored on.
Cries the stall-reader, "Bless us! what a word on   5
A title-page is this!"; and some in file
Stand spelling false,[9] while one might walk to Mile-
End Green. Why is it harder, sirs, than Gordon,

to, Milton's inner growth will be adequate to the destiny which time and
heaven are preparing.
3. The last two lines are enigmatic;
their sense depends on whether one
reads the "all" of line 13 as referring
to time or talent.
4. During the campaign of 1642, the
king's forces seemed at one point in a
position to assault London. This sonnet
is a half-humorous plea that the poet's
house be spared, though the idea that
the Muse might and should protect her
spokesman was thoroughly congenial to
Milton (cf. *Lycidas*). Fortunately the
king's armies turned back without a battle, and the poem's persuasive powers
were never tested.
5. Colonel: pronounced with three syllables.

6. Alexander the Great gave orders that
Pindar's house be spared when Thebes
was captured. Emathian: Macedonian.
7. Plutarch is authority for the story
that when the Spartans had defeated
Athens and were about to raze the walls
of the city, they were stopped by an
Athenian officer, who recited the opening chorus of Euripides' *Electra*.
8. The title of Milton's third tract
on divorce (published with the fourth,
Colasterion, in 1645). It was called
"Tetrachordon," a Greek term for the
four-tone scale in music, because the
tract expounded and sought to harmonize the four chief biblical passages on
marriage and divorce.
9. Misinterpreting. Mile-End Green was
at the East End of London.

Colkitto, or Macdonnel, or Galasp?[1]
    Those rugged names to our like mouths grow sleek   10
    That would have made Quintilian[2] stare and gasp.
Thy age, like ours, O soul of Sir John Cheke,
    Hated not learning worse than toad or asp,
    When thou taught'st Cambridge and King Edward Greek.[3]

1645–46   1673

On the New Forcers of Conscience Under the Long Parliament[1]

Because you have thrown off your prelate lord,[2]
    And with stiff vows renounced his liturgy,
    To seize the widowed whore Plurality[3]
    From them whose sin ye envied, not abhorred,
Dare ye for this adjure the civil sword   5
    To force our consciences that Christ set free,
    And ride us with a classic hierarchy[4]
    Taught ye by mere A. S. and Rutherford?[5]
Men whose life, learning, faith, and pure intent
    Would have been held in high esteem with Paul   10
    Must now be named and printed heretics
By shallow Edwards and Scotch what d'ye call:[6]
    But we do hope to find out all your tricks,
    Your plots and packing worse than those of Trent,[7]
                That so the Parliament   15
May with their wholesome and preventive shears
Clip your phylacteries,[8] though balk your ears,
And succor our just fears

1. Scottish names made familiar through Scotland's involvement in the Civil War.
2. The great 1st-century Roman authority on rhetoric, who disapproved of barbarous words.
3. Sir John Cheke (1514–57) was the first to teach Greek at Cambridge; he was also tutor to Edward VI. In *Tetrachordon* Milton praises Edward's reign (1547–53) as the "best and purest" age of the English Reformation, and he commends Cheke's learning and piety. But even then, Milton is saying, a man of learning had to contend with much ignorant hostility and suspicion.
1. "The new forcers of conscience" are Presbyterians, whom Milton at first supported against the Episcopalians (Church-of-England men). Now, under the Puritan-dominated Long Parliament, he finds them as bad as their predecessors ("whose sin ye envied, not abhorred"). The sonnet proper has 14 lines followed by two "tails" of three lines each; in Italy, where it was common, this was called a *sonnetto caudato*, or "tailed sonnet."
2. Bishop.
3. I.e., the comfortable, and sometimes necessary, practice of one priest's holding several livings at once.
4. A church discipline made up on the Presbyterian model of synods or classes, ecclesiastical governing boards with strong powers over the laity.
5. Adam Stuart and Samuel Rutherford, Presbyterian pamphleteers, whose full names Milton does not deign to give.
6. Thomas Edwards, alarmed by the spread of heresies, began to describe them in a book picturesquely titled *Gangraena* (1645–46). Before giving up in despair, he wrote three fat volumes, including a denunciation of Milton, whom he described unjustly as an advocate of "divorce at pleasure." "Scotch what d'ye call" is Milton's humanistic sneer at the unpronounceability of Scottish names.
7. I.e., of the Council of Trent, held by the Papacy in consequence of the Reformation; it was widely reported to have been the scene of political jockeying.
8. Little scrolls, containing texts from the Pentateuch, worn by orthodox Jews to remind them of the Law. Milton uses them here as symbols of superstition.

When they shall read this clearly in your charge:
New presbyter is but *old priest* writ large.   20
ca. 1646   1673

On the Late Massacre in Piedmont[1]

Avenge, O Lord, thy slaughtered saints, whose bones
   Lie scattered on the Alpine mountains cold,
   Even them who kept thy truth so pure of old
   When all our fathers worshiped stocks and stones,
Forget not: in thy book record their groans   5
   Who were thy sheep and in their ancient fold
   Slain by the bloody Piemontese that rolled
   Mother with infant down the rocks. Their moans
The vales redoubled to the hills, and they
   To Heaven. Their martyred blood and ashes sow   10
   O'er all th' Italian fields where still doth sway
The triple tyrant:[2] that from these may grow
   A hundredfold, who having learnt thy way
   Early may fly the Babylonian woe.[3]
1655   1673

Lawrence, of Virtuous Father Virtuous Son[1]

Lawrence, of virtuous father virtuous son,
   Now that the fields are dank and ways are mire,
   Where shall we sometimes meet, and by the fire
   Help waste a sullen day, what may be won
From the hard season gaining? Time will run   5
   On smoother, till Favonius[2] reinspire
   The frozen earth, and clothe in fresh attire
   The lily and rose, that neither sowed nor spun.
What neat repast shall feast us, light and choice,
   Of Attic taste,[3] with wine, whence we may rise   10

Mutilation by having one's ears cut off was a common punishment for sedition, and several Presbyterian leaders had suffered it. Milton's MS. read, "Clip ye as close as marginal P——'s ears," but the jeer was too brutal. William Prynne, whose books had many footnotes in the margins, and whose ears had twice been cropped, had suffered for a cause in which Milton at the time believed; and his final version of the line is gentler.
1. The Waldenses were a heretical sect, probably of Eastern origin by way of Venice; they lived in the valleys of northern Italy ("the Piedmont") and southern France, professing a creed which was particularly akin to Protestantism in its avoidance of graven images ("stocks and stones"). The understanding which had allowed them freedom of worship was terminated in 1655, and the massacre which ensued was widely protested by the Protestant powers of Europe. Milton, as Latin secretary to Cromwell, wrote several indignant letters.
2. I.e., the Pope, wearing his tiara with three crowns.
3. Protestants in Milton's day frequently identified the Roman Church with the "whore of Babylon" (Revelation xvii, xviii).
1. The "virtuous father" was Henry Lawrence, author of theological tracts and Lord President of Cromwell's Council for a time; his son, Edward Lawrence, became a member of parliament but died at the age of 24.
2. The west wind of spring.
3. I.e., "light and choice" (line 9), also flavored with wit.

To hear the lute well touched, or artful voice
Warble immortal notes and Tuscan[4] air?
He who of those delights can judge, and spare[5]
To interpose them oft, is not unwise.

1655   1673

When I Consider How My Light Is Spent[1]

When I consider how my light is spent
  Ere half my days, in this dark world and wide,
  And that one talent which is death to hide,
  Lodged with me useless, though my soul more bent
To serve therewith my Maker, and present   5
  My true account, lest he returning chide;
  "Doth God exact day-labor, light denied?"
  I fondly[2] ask; but Patience to prevent
That murmur, soon replies, "God doth not need
  Either man's work or his own gifts; who best   10
  Bear his mild yoke, they serve him best. His state
Is kingly. Thousands at his bidding speed
  And post o'er land and ocean without rest:
  They also serve who only stand and wait."

1655   1673

Methought I Saw My Late Espoused Saint

Methought I saw my late espousèd saint
  Brought to me like Alcestis[1] from the grave,
  Whom Jove's great son to her glad husband gave,
  Rescued from death by force though pale and faint.
Mine, as whom washed from spot of childbed taint,   5
  Purification in the old law did save,[2]
  And such, as yet once more I trust to have
  Full sight of her in Heaven without restraint,
Came vested all in white, pure as her mind.
  Her face was veiled, yet to my fancied sight,   10

---

4. Italian, and specifically Florentine, calling to mind the carnival songs composed by such men as Lorenzo the Magnificent.
5. "Spare": in one possible sense, afford, spare time; in another, refrain, limit oneself (from too frequent interposing). The poem contains quite as many reinings-in of appetite as invitations to indulgence; it balances out to a very sober festivity or festive sobriety.
1. Milton's sonnet on his blindness is very close, in theme, to that on his 23rd birthday. But the absolute repose of the latter sonnet's final line is beyond anything in the earlier one.
2. Foolishly. "Prevent": forestall.
1. Alcestis, wife of Admetus, was rescued from the underworld by Hercules ("Jove's great son").
2. The old law, prescribing periods for the purification of women after childbirth, is found in Leviticus xii. The compression of line 5 is perhaps extreme; expanded, it would read, "My wife, like the woman whom when washed from spot of childbed taint," etc.

Love, sweetness, goodness, in her person shined
So clear, as in no face with more delight.
But O, as to embrace me she inclined,
I waked, she fled, and day brought back my night.

1658   1673

From Of Education[1]

* * * I shall detain you no longer in the demonstration of what
we should not do, but straight conduct ye to a hillside, where I will
point ye out the right path of a virtuous and noble education;
laborious indeed at the first ascent, but else so smooth, so green,
so full of goodly prospect and melodious sounds on every side, that
the harp of Orpheus was not more charming. I doubt not but ye
shall have more ado to drive our dullest and laziest youth, our stocks
and stubs,[2] from the infinite desire of such a happy nurture, than we
have now to haul and drag our choicest and hopefulest wits to that
asinine[3] feast of sow-thistles and brambles which is commonly
set before them, as all the food and entertainment of their tenderest and most docible[4] age. I call, therefore, a complete and generous education, that which fits a man to perform justly, skillfully,
and magnanimously all the offices, both private and public, of peace
and war. And how all this may be done between twelve and one-and-
twenty, less time than is now bestowed in pure trifling at grammar
and sophistry, is to be thus ordered.

First, to find out a spacious house and ground about it fit for
an academy, and big enough to lodge a hundred and fifty persons,
whereof twenty or thereabout may be attendants, all under the
government of one who shall be thought of desert sufficient, and
ability either to do all or wisely to direct and oversee it done. This
place should be at once both school and university, not needing a
remove to any other house of scholarship, except it be some peculiar[5]

1. Written in the form of an open
letter to Samuel Hartlib (a noted educational reformer of the 17th century), *Of Education* was the product
of Milton's leisure hours, and of an
occasion. Hartlib had published in
1642 a book called *A Reformation of
Schools*, putting forward some ideas
derived from the Bohemian pedagogue
John Comenius. On the whole, Hartlib,
like Comenius, was interested in simple,
easy schemes of education for everyone. Milton's proposal, which appeared
as a tract on June 5, 1644, was courteous enough but definitely modeled on
different lines. Characteristically, Milton called for a limited and intensive

educational operation aimed at training
a few distinguished leaders. But for
them it was necessary to know nothing
less than everything. Milton's aim was
the humanistic one of producing a complete man who could design a building, storm a city, write an epic, or cure
a lame knee. To the noble confidence
of this program one can still respond,
even though the details of the program
itself appear antiquated.
2. Backward students.
3. Stupid; and, of course (reinforcing
the metaphor), fit for donkeys.
4. Docile, teachable.
5. Set apart for particular studies.

college of law or physic, where they mean to be practitioners; but as for those general studies which take up all our time from Lily[6] to the commencing, as they term it, Master of Art, it should be absolute. After this pattern, as many edifices may be converted to this use as shall be needful in every city throughout this land, which would tend much to the increase of learning and civility everywhere. This number, less or more, thus collected, to the convenience of a foot-company or interchangeably two troops of cavalry, should divide their day's work into three parts, as it lies orderly: their studies, their exercise, and their diet.

For their studies: first, they should begin with the chief and necessary rules of some good grammar, either that now used, or any better; and while this is doing, their speech is to be fashioned to a distinct and clear pronunciation, as near as may be to the Italian, especially in the vowels. For we Englishmen, being far northerly, do not open our mouths in the cold air wide enough to grace a southern tongue; but are observed by all other nations to speak exceeding close and inward, so that to smatter Latin with an English mouth is as ill a hearing as law French.[7] Next, to make them expert in the usefulest points of grammar, and withal to season them and win them early to the love of virtue and true labor, ere any flattering seducement or vain principle seize them wandering, some easy and delightful book of education would be read to them, whereof the Greeks have store, as Cebes, Plutarch, and other Socratic discourses;[8] but in Latin we have none of classic authority extant, except the two or three first books of Quintilian[9] and some select pieces elsewhere. But here the main skill and groundwork will be to temper[1] them such lectures and explanations upon every opportunity, as may lead and draw them in willing obedience, inflamed with the study of learning and the admiration of virtue, stirred up with high hopes of living to be brave men and worthy patriots, dear to God and famous to all ages: that they may despise and scorn all their childish and ill-taught qualities, to delight in manly and liberal exercises; which he who hath the art and proper eloquence to catch them with, what with mild and effectual persua-

6. William Lily, first headmaster of St. Paul's School, was responsible for the elementary Latin grammar one encountered as a schoolboy beginning Latin. Milton is describing education from the level we should call the beginning of junior high school through college.
7. Norman French terms in English law-courts grated harshly on Milton's humanistic ear.
8. *The Picture* by Cebes describes and recommends the path to virtue and learning (its author's dates are highly uncertain). The book of Plutarch which Milton has in mind might be his essay on *The Education of Children* or perhaps the biographies; his moral essays are reserved for a later stage in the student's education. By "other Socratic discourses" Milton may mean either discourses using the Socratic method of question and answer or discourses teaching Socratic (i.e., Platonic) doctrine.
9. Quintilian wrote a famous book of instructions in oratory (1st century A.D.) which greatly influenced Milton's ideas on education.
1. Afford.

sions, and what with the intimation of some fear, if need be, but chiefly by his own example, might in a short space gain them to an incredible diligence and courage, infusing into their young breasts such an ingenuous and noble ardor as would not fail to make many of them renowned and matchless men. At the same time, some other hour of the day might be taught them the rules of arithmetic; and, soon after, the elements of geometry, even playing, as the old manner was. After evening repast till bedtime their thoughts would be best taken up in the easy grounds of religion and the story of Scripture. The next step would be to the authors of agriculture, Cato, Varro, and Columella,[2] for the matter is most easy; and if the language be difficult, so much the better; it is not a difficulty above their years. And here will be an occasion of inciting and enabling them hereafter to improve the tillage of their country, to recover the bad soil, and to remedy the waste that is made of good; for this was one of Hercules' praises. Ere half these authors be read, which will soon be with plying hard and daily, they cannot choose but be masters of any ordinary prose: so that it will be then seasonable for them to learn in any modern author the use of the globes and all the maps, first with the old names and then with the new; or they might be then capable to read any compendious method of natural philosophy: and, at the same time, might be entering into the Greek tongue, after the same manner as was before prescribed in the Latin; whereby the difficulties of grammar being soon overcome, all the historical physiology of Aristotle and Theophrastus[3] are open before them and, as I may say, under contribution. The like access will be to Vitruvius, to Seneca's *Natural Questions*, to Mela, Celsus, Pliny, or Solinus.[4] And having thus passed the principles of arithmetic, geometry, astronomy, and geography, with a general compact[5] of physics, they may descend in mathematics to the instrumental science of trigonometry, and from thence to fortification, architecture, enginery,[6] or navigation. And in natural philosophy they may proceed leisurely from the history of meteors, minerals, plants, and living creatures, as far as anatomy. Then also in course might be read to them out of some not tedious writer the institution of physic;[7] that they may

2. In the 2nd and 1st centuries B.C. and the 1st century A.D., all three wrote books about farming; during the Renaissance these treatises were customarily bound together.

3. Aristotle's *Natural History of Animals* would naturally be supplemented by his pupil Theophrastus' *Inquiry into Plants.*

4. Vitruvius wrote not only of architecture, but of engineering problems; Celsus was famous for a book on medicine; Seneca and Pliny were natural historians; Mela and Solinus wrote general descriptions of the world. All these authors were of the 1st century A.D. except Solinus, who was of the 3rd.

5. Digest.

6. I.e., mechanics.

7. Instruction in medicine. Milton's pupils must learn the four "humors" (blood, phlegm, choler, and melancholy or black choler) and their "tempers" and "seasons" (i.e., mixtures and timings), in order to avoid a "crudity" (an upset stomach resulting from an ill mixture of humors).

know the tempers, the humors, the seasons, and how to manage a crudity; which he who can wisely and timely do is not only a great physician to himself and to his friends, but also may at some time or other save an army by this frugal and expenseless means only, and not let the healthy and stout bodies of young men rot away under him for want of this discipline; which is a great pity, and no less a shame to the commander. To set forward all these proceedings in nature and mathematics, what hinders but that they may procure, as oft as shall be needful, the helpful experiences of hunters, fowlers, fishermen, shepherds, gardeners, apothecaries; and in the other sciences, architects, engineers, mariners, anatomists; who, doubtless, would be ready, some for reward and some to favor such a hopeful seminary. And this will give them such a real tincture of natural knowledge as they shall never forget, but daily augment with delight. Then also those poets which are now counted most hard will be both facile and pleasant: Orpheus, Hesiod, Theocritus, Aratus, Nicander, Oppian, Dionysius; and, in Latin, Lucretius, Manilius, and the rural part of Virgil.[8]

By this time, years and good general precepts will have furnished them more distinctly with that act of reason which in ethics is called *proairesis*,[9] that they may with some judgment contemplate upon moral good and evil. Then will be required a special reinforcement of constant and sound indoctrinating to set them right and firm, instructing them more amply in the knowledge of virtue and the hatred of vice; while their young and pliant affections are led through all the moral works of Plato, Xenophon, Cicero, Plutarch, Laertius, and those Locrian remnants;[1] but still to be reduced in their nightward studies, wherewith they close the day's work, under the determinate sentence of David or Solomon, or the evangels and apostolic Scriptures.[2] Being perfect in the knowledge of personal duty, they may then begin the study of economics.[3] And either now or before this they may have easily learned at any odd hour the Italian tongue. And soon after, but with wariness and good antidote, it would be wholesome enough to let them taste some choice comedies, Greek, Latin, or Italian; those tragedies also that treat of household matters, as *Trachiniae*, *Alcestis*, and the

---

8. All these poets were didactic in character; for instance, the Hellenistic cultists who wrote under the mythical name of Orpheus created a poem called *Lithica* on the magic properties of precious stones; Oppian and Dionysius of Alexandria (2nd century A.D.) wrote on fishes and geography, Manilius (1st century A.D.) on astrology.
9. An Aristotelian term transliterated by Milton from the *Nicomachean Ethics* (II.iv.3) to suggest the idea of reason as choice.
1. Plato's dialogues, Plutarch's *Moralia*, and Cicero's moral essays all prescribe the principles of ethical behavior. Diogenes Laertius (ca. 150 A.D.) and Xenophon, the disciple of Socrates, are authorities on the lives of the philosophers. The "Locrian remnants" are a forgery, supposed to be by Plato's teacher, Timaeus of Locri, and titled *On the Soul of the World*.
2. In the evening all this pagan learning is shown to be subsumed in the Bible, the last word ("determinate sentence") of the Proverbs, Psalms, and apostolic Epistles.
3. Not the dismal science, but household management.

like. The next remove must be to the study of politics; to know the beginning, end, and reasons of political societies, that they may not, in a dangerous fit of the commonwealth, be such poor, shaken, uncertain reeds, of such a tottering conscience as many of our great counselors have lately shown themselves, but steadfast pillars of the state. After this they are to dive into the grounds of law and legal justice, delivered first and with best warrant by Moses; and, as far as human prudence can be trusted, in those extolled remains of Grecian law-givers, Lycurgus, Solon, Zaleucus, Charondas; and thence to all the Roman edicts and tables, with their Justinian; and so down to the Saxon and common laws of England and the statutes. Sundays also and every evening may be now understandingly spent in the highest matters of theology and church history, ancient and modern; and ere this time the Hebrew tongue at a set hour might have been gained, that the Scriptures may be read in their own original; whereto it would be no impossibility to add the Chaldee and the Syrian dialect.[4] When all these employments are well conquered, then will the choice histories, heroic poems, and Attic tragedies of stateliest and most regal argument, with all the famous political orations, offer themselves; which, if they were not only read, but some of them got by memory, and solemnly pronounced with right accent and grace, as might be taught, would endue them even with the spirit and vigor of Demosthenes or Cicero, Euripides or Sophocles. And now, lastly, will be the time to read with them those organic arts which enable men to discourse and write perspicuously, elegantly, and according to the fitted style of lofty, mean, or lowly. Logic, therefore, so much as is useful, is to be referred to this due place, with all her well-couched heads and topics, until it be time to open her contracted palm into a graceful and ornate rhetoric taught out of the rule of Plato, Aristotle, Phalereus, Cicero, Hermogenes, Longinus.[5] To which poetry would be made subsequent, or, indeed, rather precedent, as being less subtle and fine, but more simple, sensuous, and passionate; I mean not here the prosody of a verse, which they could not but have hit on before among the rudiments of grammar, but that sublime art which in Aristotle's *Poetics*, in Horace, and the Italian commentaries of Castelvetro, Tasso, Mazzoni,[6] and others, teaches what the laws are of a true epic poem, what of a dramatic, what of a lyric, what decorum is, which is the grand masterpiece to observe. This would make them soon perceive

---

4. Many passages of the Bible are more thoroughly understood by the man who can compare the Hebrew text with its Aramaic and Syriac versions.
5. Logic is a closed fist, say Aristotle and Cicero; rhetoric is an open palm. Phalereus and Hermogenes (2nd centuries B.C. and A.D. respectively) wrote

treatises on rhetoric.
6. Only Castelvetro wrote what is properly speaking a commentary on Aristotle; but Tasso's *Discourse on Epic Poetry* and Mazzoni's *Defense of the "Divine Comedy" of Dante* were important critical documents for Milton the poet.

what despicable creatures our common rhymers and play-writers be; and show them what religious, what glorious and magnificent use might be made of poetry, both in divine and human things. From hence, and not till now, will be the right season of forming them to be able writers and composers in every excellent matter, when they shall be thus fraught with an universal insight into things.[7] Or whether they be to speak in Parliament or Council, honor and attention would be waiting on their lips. There would then also appear in pulpits other visages, other gestures, and stuff otherwise wrought than what we now sit under, ofttimes to as great a trial of our patience as any other that they preach to us. These are the studies wherein our noble and our gentle youth ought to bestow their time in a disciplinary way from twelve to one-and-twenty, unless they rely more upon their ancestors dead than upon themselves living. In which methodical course it is so supposed they must proceed by the steady pace of learning onward, as at convenient times for memory's sake to retire back into the middle ward,[8] and sometimes into the rear of what they have been taught, until they have confirmed and solidly united the whole body of their perfected knowledge, like the last embattling of a Roman legion. Now will be worth the seeing what exercises and what recreations may best agree and become these studies.

Their Exercise

The course of study hitherto briefly described is, what I can guess by reading, likest to those ancient and famous schools of Pythagoras, Plato, Isocrates, Aristotle, and such others, out of which were bred such a number of renowned philosophers, orators, historians, poets, and princes all over Greece, Italy, and Asia, besides the flourishing studies of Cyrene and Alexandria. But herein it shall exceed them, and supply a defect as great as that which Plato noted in the commonwealth of Sparta; whereas that city trained up their youth most for war, and these in their academies and Lyceum all for the gown,[9] this institution of breeding which I here delineate shall be equally good both for peace and war. Therefore, about an hour and a half ere they eat at noon should be allowed them for exercise, and due rest afterwards; but the time for this may be enlarged at pleasure, according as their rising in the morning shall be early. The exercise which I commend first is the exact use of their weapon, to guard, and to strike safely with edge or point; this will keep them healthy, nimble, strong, and well in breath, is also the likeliest means to make them grow large and

7. Note how late the art of composition occurs in Milton's curriculum. He felt that students should not be asked, or even allowed, to write about anything till they had mastered the subject.

8. Milton's metaphor comes from the sport of fencing; the various "wards" represent so many postures of attack or defense.

9. The academic gown, i.e., study.

tall, and to inspire them with a gallant and fearless courage, which, being tempered with seasonable lectures and precepts to them of true fortitude and patience, will turn into a native and heroic valor, and make them hate the cowardice of doing wrong. They must be also practiced in all the locks and grips of wrestling, wherein Englishmen were wont to excel, as need may often be in fight to tug, to grapple, and to close. And this, perhaps, will be enough wherein to prove and heat their single strength. The interim of unsweating themselves regularly, and convenient rest before meat, may both with profit and delight be taken up in recreating and composing their travailed spirits with the solemn and divine harmonies of music heard or learned; either while the skillful organist plies his grave and fancied descant in lofty fugues,[1] or the whole symphony with artful and unimaginable touches adorn and grace the well-studied chords of some choice composer; sometimes the lute or soft organ-stop, waiting on[2] elegant voices, either to religious, martial, or civil ditties; which, if wise men and prophets be not extremely out,[3] have a great power over dispositions and manners, to smooth and make them gentle from rustic harshness and distempered passions. The like also would not be inexpedient after meat, to assist and cherish nature in her first concoction, and send their minds back to study in good tune and satisfaction. Where having followed it close under vigilant eyes until about two hours before supper, they are, by a sudden alarum or watchword, to be called out to their military motions, under sky or covert, according to the season, as was the Roman wont; first on foot, then, as their age permits, on horseback, to all the art of cavalry; that having in sport, but with much exactness and daily muster, served out the rudiments of their soldiership in all the skill of embattling, marching, encamping, fortifying, besieging, and battering, with all the helps of ancient and modern stratagems, tactics, and warlike maxims, they may, as it were out of a long war, come forth renowned and perfect commanders in the service of their country. They would not then, if they were trusted with fair and hopeful armies, suffer them for want of just and wise discipline to shed away from about them like sick feathers, though they be never so oft supplied; they would not suffer their empty and unrecruitable colonels of twenty men in a company to quaff out or convey into secret hoards, the wages of a delusive list and a miserable remnant;[4] yet in the meanwhile to be overmastered with a score or two of drunkards, the only soldiery left about them, or else to comply with all rapines and violences. No, certainly, if they knew aught of that

1. I.e., while the organist plays variations on a theme in the form of a fugue. "Symphony": orchestra.
2. Accompanying.
3. Mistaken.
4. Milton is indignant with colonels who cannot recruit more than twenty men to a company, or who deliberately hold down the rosters so they can collect (and drink up) the pay of the absentees.

knowledge that belongs to good men or good governors, they would not suffer these things. But to return to our own institute: besides these constant exercises at home, there is another opportunity of gaining experience to be won from pleasure itself abroad; in those vernal seasons of the year, when the air is calm and pleasant, it were an injury and sullenness against nature not to go out and see her riches and partake in her rejoicing with heaven and earth. I should not, therefore, be a persuader to them of studying much then, after two or three years that they have well laid their grounds, but to ride out in companies with prudent and staid guides to all quarters of the land, learning and observing all places of strength, all commodities of building and of soil, for towns and tillage, harbors, and ports for trade. Sometimes taking sea as far as to our navy, to learn there also what they can in the practical knowledge of sailing and of sea fight. These ways would try all their peculiar gifts of nature; and if there were any secret excellence among them, would fetch it out and give it fair opportunities to advance itself by, which could not but mightily redound to the good of this nation, and bring into fashion again those old admired virtues and excellencies, with far more advantage now in this purity of Christian knowledge. Nor shall we then need the monsieurs of Paris to take our hopeful youth into their slight and prodigal custodies, and send them over back again transformed into mimics, apes, and kickshaws.[5] But if they desire to see other countries at three or four and twenty years of age, not to learn principles, but to enlarge experience and make wise observation, they will by that time be such as shall deserve the regard and honor of all men where they pass, and the society and friendship of those in all places who are best and most eminent. And perhaps then other nations will be glad to visit us for their breeding, or else to imitate us in their own country.

Now, lastly, for their diet there cannot be much to say, save only that it would be best in the same house; for much time else would be lost abroad, and many ill habits got; and that it should be plain, healthful, and moderate, I suppose is out of controversy. Thus, Mr. Hartlib, you have a general view in writing, as your desire was, of that which at several times I had discoursed with you concerning the best and noblest way of education; not beginning, as some have done, from the cradle, which yet might be worth many considerations, if brevity had not been my scope. Many other circumstances also I could have mentioned; but this, to such as have the worth in them to make trial, for light and direction may be enough. Only I believe that this is not a bow for every man to shoot in that counts himself a teacher, but will require sinews almost equal to

5. A corruption of *quelque chose*, a thing of no real value, hence a trifling person.

those which Homer gave Ulysses; yet I am withal persuaded that it may prove much more easy in the assay[6] than it now seems at distance, and much more illustrious: howbeit not more difficult than I imagine, and that imagination presents me with nothing but very happy and very possible according to best wishes; if God have so decreed, and this age have spirit and capacity enough to apprehend.

1644

From Areopagitica[1]

* * * In Athens, where books and wits were ever busier than in any other part of Greece, I find but only two sorts of writings which the magistrate cared to take notice of: those either blasphemous and atheistical, or libelous. Thus the books of Protagoras were by the judges of Areopagus commanded to be burnt, and himself banished the territory for a discourse begun with his confessing not to know *whether there were gods, or whether not.*[2] And against defaming, it was decreed that none should be traduced by name, as was the manner of Vetus Comoedia,[3] whereby we may guess how they censured libeling: and this course was quick enough, as Cicero writes, to quell both the desperate wits of other atheists, and the open way of defaming, as the event showed. Of other sects and

6. In experience.

1. *Areopagitica* appeared on November 24, 1644. The title means "things to be said before the Areopagus." The Areopagus was an ancient, powerful, and much-respected tribunal in Athens, before which Isocrates, in 355 B.C., delivered a famous speech. Milton's title implies a comparison between the Areopagus and the English Parliament, and this comparison may be thought to validate, in some degree, the florid, oratorical tone of the tract.

Areopagitica is a plea for the liberty of unlicensed printing; its occasion was a severe ordinance for the control of printing which had been passed by Parliament on June 14, 1643. This ordinance, however disagreeable at the moment, was no striking novelty in English history. On the contrary, control of the press had been actively exercised by all the Tudors and both the early Stuarts. The aim of this government regulation was traditionally defined as the preservation of order and uniformity in church and state; but it also had an economic motive. Unlicensed printers threatened a monopoly enjoyed by the twenty licensed printers of London. Thus the censorship laws familiar to Englishmen had generally been strictly defined and had bristled with penalties. But to enforce them

was another matter entirely. Tudor and Stuart police forces being what they were, few printers or authors had to worry about the consequences of going to print without a license. As a matter of fact, *Areopagitica* was itself unlicensed, Milton's third unlicensed pamphlet since the passage of the Ordinance for Printing only seventeen months before.

Thus the practical effects of the Ordinance for Printing were less important (particularly, we may be sure, in Milton's eyes) than the principle involved. Having taken the lead in destroying the licensing system of the Stuarts, Parliament was now setting up a censorship of its own. After a long prologue, Milton's first approach to his subject was to undertake a condensed history of censorship, intended to discredit the institution by showing that only degenerate cultures ever made use of it.

2. It was in the 5th century B.C. that the sophist Protagoras of Abdera was censured in the manner described; Cicero wrote approvingly of this action in his treatise *On the Nature of the Gods* I.xxiii.

3. The "Old Comedy" of Aristophanes dealt with individuals, unlike the "New Comedy" of Menander, which dealt with types.

opinions, though tending to voluptuousness and the denying of Divine Providence, they took no heed. Therefore we do not read that either Epicurus, or that libertine school of Cyrene, or what the Cynic impudence uttered, was ever questioned by the laws.[4] Neither is it recorded that the writings of those old comedians were suppressed, though the acting of them were forbid; and that Plato commended the reading of Aristophanes, the loosest of them all, to his royal scholar Dionysius,[5] is commonly known, and may be excused, if holy Chrysostom, as is reported, nightly studied so much the same author and had the art to cleanse a scurrilous vehemence into the style of a rousing sermon.[6] * * *

And that the primitive councils and bishops were wont only to declare what books were not commendable, passing no further, but leaving it to each one's conscience to read or to lay by, till after the year 800, is observed already by Padre Paolo, the great unmasker of the Trentine Council.[7] After which time the Popes of Rome, engrossing what they pleased of political rule into their own hands, extended their dominion over men's eyes, as they had before over their judgments, burning and prohibiting to be read what they fancied not; yet sparing in their censures, and the books not many which they so dealt with: till Martin the Fifth, by his bull, not only prohibited, but was the first that excommunicated the reading of heretical books; for about that time Wycliffe and Huss[8] growing terrible, were they who first drove the papal court to a stricter policy of prohibiting. Which course Leo the Tenth and his successors followed, until the Council of Trent and the Spanish Inquisition engendering together brought forth, or perfected, those catalogues and expurging indexes,[9] that rake through the entrails of many an old good author with a violation worse than any could

---

4. Epicurus (4th and 3rd centuries B.C.) thought the gods had no influence on human affairs, but he did not deny their existence; therefore he was free of censorship. Aristippus of Cyrene, the pupil of Socrates, was like Epicurus in making pleasure the end of life. His school was known, from the Greek word for "pleasure," as the school of Hedonism; but, like Epicurus, he is misunderstood as a sensualist. Diogenes was the most famous of the Cynics, who often affected a rude and truculent disposition ("Cynic impudence"). All these philosophers flourished in and about the 4th century B.C.
5. That Plato told Dionysius, tyrant of Syracuse, to read Aristophanes is an ancient tradition. St. John Chrysostom, archbishop of Constantinople in the 4th century, is said to have hated the stage plays of his own day but profited from a constant perusal of Aristophanes.
6. After working his way through the various cities of Greece and the meager records of Roman censorship, Milton takes his readers to the ages of primitive Christianity, where he finds no positive censorship, merely an occasional recommendation of certain books to be read or not to be read.
7. Father Paolo Sarpi (d. 1623) was a Venetian historian who opposed papal claims to secular authority. His *History of the Council of Trent* was favorite reading matter for Protestants, since it described in graphic detail the "plots and packing" which went on behind the scenes of the Counter-Reformation. See Milton's sonnet *On the New Forcers of Conscience*, line 14.
8. John Wycliffe (d. 1384) was an English church reformer and translator of the Bible; John Huss (burned at the stake in 1415) was a Bohemian reformer of similar tendencies.
9. Literally from the Latin, *indices expurgatorii*, lists of books forbidden to Catholics.

be offered to his tomb.

Nor did they stay in matters heretical, but any subject that was not to their palate, they either condemned in a Prohibition, or had it straight into the new purgatory of an Index. To fill up the measure of encroachment, their last invention was to ordain that no book, pamphlet, or paper should be printed (as if St. Peter had bequeathed them the keys of the press also out of paradise) unless it were approved and licensed under the hands of two or three glutton friars. For example:[1]

Let the Chancellor Cini be pleased to see if in this present work be contained aught that may withstand the printing.
      Vincent Rabatta, Vicar of Florence.

I have seen this present work, and find nothing athwart the Catholic faith and good manners: in witness whereof I have given, etc.
      Nicolò Cini, Chancellor of Florence.

Attending the precedent relation, it is allowed that this present work of Davanzati may be printed.
      Vincent Rabatta, etc.

It may be printed, July 15.
      Friar Simon Mompei d'Amelia, Chancellor
       of the holy office in Florence.

Sure they have a conceit,[2] if he of the bottomless pit had not long since broke prison, that this quadruple exorcism would bar him down. I fear their next design will be to get into their custody the licensing of that which they say Claudius intended,[3] but went not through with. Vouchsafe to see another of their forms, the Roman stamp:

Imprimatur, If it seem good to the reverend master of the holy palace.
      Belcastro, Vicegerent.

Imprimatur, Friar Nicolò Rodolphi, Master of the holy palace.

Sometimes five Imprimaturs are seen together dialogue-wise in the piazza of one title page, complimenting and ducking each to other with their shaven reverences, whether the author, who stands by in perplexity at the foot of his epistle, shall to the press or to the sponge.[4] These are the pretty responsories, these are the dear antiphonies, that so bewitched of late our prelates and their chaplains

---

1. Milton's examples come from a book on *The English Schism*, translated by Bernardo Davanzati from the original of an English Jesuit.
2. Notion.
3. The Roman historian Suetonius says that Claudius once planned to tax the act of breaking wind. Milton's note refers to this impractical scheme in the decent obscurity of a learned language.
4. I.e., the eraser. In the next sentence, "responsories" and "antiphonies" are ecclesiastical services after the pattern of a dialogue.

with the goodly echo they made; and besotted us to the gay imitation of a lordly Imprimatur, one from Lambeth House, another from the west end of Paul's;[5] so apishly Romanizing, that the word of command still was set down in Latin; as if the learned grammatical pen that wrote it would cast no ink without Latin; or perhaps, as they thought, because no vulgar tongue was worthy to express the pure conceit of an Imprimatur; but rather, as I hope, for that our English, the language of men ever famous and foremost in the achievements of liberty, will not easily find servile letters enow to spell such a dictatory presumption English.[6] * * *

Good and evil we know in the field of this world grow up together almost inseparably; and the knowledge of good is so involved and interwoven with the knowledge of evil, and in so many cunning resemblances hardly to be discerned, that those confused seeds which were imposed on Psyche as an incessant labor to cull out and sort asunder,[7] were not more intermixed. It was from out the rind of one apple tasted, that the knowledge of good and evil, as two twins cleaving together, leaped forth into the world. And perhaps this is that doom which Adam fell into of knowing good and evil, that is to say of knowing good by evil.

As therefore the state of man now is, what wisdom can there be to choose, what continence to forbear without the knowledge of evil? He that can apprehend and consider vice with all her baits and seeming pleasures, and yet abstain, and yet distinguish, and yet prefer that which is truly better, he is the true wayfaring[8] Christian. I cannot praise a fugitive and cloistered virtue, unexercised and unbreathed, that never sallies out and sees her adversary, but slinks out of the race where that immortal garland[9] is to be run for, not without dust and heat. Assuredly we bring not innocence into the world, we bring impurity much rather; that which purifies us is trial, and trial is by what is contrary. That virtue therefore which is but a youngling in the contemplation of evil, and knows not the utmost that vice promises to her followers, and rejects it, is but a blank virtue, not a pure; her whiteness is but an excremental[1] whiteness; which was the reason why our sage and serious poet Spenser (whom I dare be known to think a better teacher than Scotus or Aquinas),[2]

5. Lambeth House is the Archbishop of Canterbury's London home. "Paul's" is St. Paul's Cathedral, headquarters of the Bishop of London. Under the prerogative government of Charles, these were the two chief censors.
6. Having finished with the history of censorship, Milton proceeds to argue more generally that the institution itself is evil and unchristian. As God left man free to choose among the many physical foods of this world, urging only temperance, so he left him free to pick and choose among ideas.
7. Angry at her son Cupid's love for

Psyche, Venus set Psyche to sorting out a vast mound of mixed seeds; but the ants took pity on her, and did the work. See Apuleius, *The Golden Ass*.
8. There has been debate whether this word should be read "wayfaring" or "warfaring," but in the image of Christian life as a pilgrimage, a crusade, the two ideas are united.
9. The crown of righteousness, the garland of virtue.
1. Exterior (like a whited sepulcher, covering corruption within).
2. Duns Scotus and Thomas Aquinas, taken as types of the Scholastic theo-

describing true temperance under the person of Guyon, brings him in with his palmer through the cave of Mammon and the bower of earthly bliss, that he might see and know, and yet abstain.

Since therefore the knowledge and survey of vice is in this world so necessary to the constituting of human virtue, and the scanning of error to the confirmation of truth, how can we more safely, and with less danger, scout into the regions of sin and falsity than by reading all manner of tractates and hearing all manner of reason? And this is the benefit which may be had of books promiscuously read.

But of the harm that may result hence, three kinds are usually reckoned. First, is feared the infection that may spread; but then all human learning and controversy in religious points must remove out of the world, yea, the Bible itself; for that ofttimes relates blasphemy not nicely,[3] it describes the carnal sense of wicked men not unelegantly, it brings in holiest men passionately murmuring against Providence through all the arguments of Epicurus:[4] in other great disputes it answers dubiously and darkly to the common reader: and ask a Talmudist what ails the modesty of his marginal Keri, that Moses and all the prophets cannot persuade him to pronounce the textual Chetiv.[5] For these causes we all know the Bible itself put by the papist into the first rank of prohibited books. The ancientest Fathers must be next removed, as Clement of Alexandria, and that Eusebian book of evangelic preparation, transmitting our ears through a hoard of heathenish obscenities to receive the Gospel.[6] Who finds not that Irenaeus, Epiphanius, Jerome, and others discover[7] more heresies than they well confute, and that oft for heresy which is the truer opinion?[8] * * *

Impunity and remissness, for certain, are the bane of a commonwealth; but here the great art lies, to discern in what the law is to bid restraint and punishment, and in what things persuasion only is to work. If every action which is good or evil in man at ripe years were to be under pittance[9] and prescription and compulsion, what were virtue but a name, what praise could be then due to

logian. The passage of Spenser referred to is *Faerie Queene* II.vii.

3. Daintily.

4. See the Book of Ecclesiastes.

5. "Keri" are the marginal comments of rabbinical scholars on the "Chetiv" of the Bible, the text itself. When the text was too free-spoken for later commentators, Keri was sometimes read in place of Chetiv.

6. Eusebius' *Preparatio Evangelica*, like many early Christian books of polemic, describes heathen wickedness in fascinating detail, as an encouragement to Christan faith. St. Irenaeus, St. Epiphanius, St. Jerome, and even that ancient and edifying convert, Clement of Alexandria, are all subject to this charge.

7. Describe (and so preserve, report).

8. Milton now argues that books cannot pervert men unless they are given force and vitality by a teacher, who, if he is a good teacher, needs no books. A fool, he urges, can find material for his folly in the best books, and a wise man material for his wisdom in the worst. Plato, indeed, recommended censorship in his *Republic;* but in real life one cannot censor books without censoring ballads, fiddlers, clothing, conversation, and social life as a whole.

9. Rationing.

well-doing, what gramercy[1] to be sober, just, or continent?

Many there be that complain of Divine Providence for suffering Adam to transgress; foolish tongues! when God gave him reason, he gave him freedom to choose, for reason is but choosing; he had been else a mere artificial Adam, such an Adam as he is in the motions.[2] We ourselves esteem not of that obedience, or love, or gift, which is of force: God therefore left him free, set before him a provoking object, ever almost in his eyes; herein consisted his merit, herein the right of his reward, the praise of his abstinence. Wherefore did he create passions within us, pleasures round about us, but that these rightly tempered are the very ingredients of virtue? They are not skillful considerers of human things, who imagine to remove sin by removing the matter of sin; for, besides that it is a huge heap increasing under the very act of diminishing, though some part of it may for a time be withdrawn from some persons, it cannot from all, in such a universal thing as books are; and when this is done, yet the sin remains entire. Though ye take from a covetous man all his treasure, he has yet one jewel left, ye cannot bereave him of his covetousness. Banish all objects of lust, shut up all youth into the severest discipline that can be exercised in any hermitage, ye cannot make them chaste that came not thither so: such great care and wisdom is required to the right managing of this point.

Suppose we could expel sin by this means; look how much we thus expel of sin, so much we expel of virtue: for the matter of them both is the same; remove that, and ye remove them both alike. This justifies the high providence of God, who, though he commands us temperance, justice, continence, yet pours out before us, even to a profuseness, all desirable things, and gives us minds that can wander beyond all limit and satiety. Why should we then affect a rigor contrary to the manner of God and of nature, by abridging or scanting those means, which books freely permitted are, both to the trial of virtue and the exercise of truth?[3] * * *

Well knows he who uses to consider, that our faith and knowledge thrives by exercise, as well as our limbs and complexion.[4] Truth is compared in Scripture to a streaming fountain; if her waters flow not in a perpetual progression, they sicken into a muddy pool of conformity and tradition. A man may be a heretic in the truth; and if he believe things only because his pastor says so, or the Assembly so determines, without knowing other reason, though his

1. Reward, thanks.
2. Puppet shows.
3. Censorship, Milton urges, is a vulgar, mechanical job; no man of intelligence will undertake it, and a dunderhead will make serious blunders. Finally, to put stupid men in authority over intelligent ones will discourage the pursuit of learning on every hand, except so far as censorship, by giving authority to banned books, will encourage men to seek out and cling to perverse opinions.
4. Constitution, regarded as the proper mingling of certain qualities in one's body.

belief be true, yet the very truth he holds becomes his heresy. There is not any burden that some would gladlier post off to another than the charge and care of their religion. There be, who knows not that there be, of Protestants and professors[5] who live and die in as arrant an implicit faith as any lay papist of Loretto.[6] A wealthy man, addicted to his pleasure and to his profits, finds religion to be a traffic so entangled, and of so many piddling accounts, that of all mysteries he cannot skill[7] to keep a stock going upon that trade. What should he do? Fain he would have the name to be religious, fain he would bear up with his neighbors in that. What does he therefore, but resolves to give over toiling, and to find himself out some factor,[8] to whose care and credit he may commit the whole managing of his religious affairs; some divine of note and estimation that must be. To him he adheres, resigns the whole warehouse of his religion, with all the locks and keys, into his custody; and indeed makes the very person of that man his religion; esteems his associating with him a sufficient evidence and commendatory of his own piety. So that a man may say his religion is now no more within himself, but is become a dividual[9] movable, and goes and comes near him, according as that good man frequents the house. He entertains him, gives him gifts, feasts him, lodges him; his religion comes home at night, prays, is liberally supped, and sumptuously laid to sleep, rises, is saluted, and after the malmsey, or some well-spiced brewage, and better breakfasted than He whose morning appetite would have gladly fed on green figs between Bethany and Jerusalem,[1] his religion walks abroad at eight, and leaves his kind entertainer in the shop trading all day without his religion.

Another sort there be who, when they hear that all things shall be ordered, all things regulated and settled, nothing written but what passes through the custom-house of certain publicans that have the tonnaging and poundaging[2] of all free-spoken truth, will straight give themselves up into your hands, make 'em and cut 'em out what religion ye please: there be delights, there be recreations and jolly pastimes that will fetch the day about from sun to sun, and rock the tedious year as in a delightful dream. What need they torture their heads with that which others have taken so strictly and so unalterably into their own purveying? These are the fruits which a dull ease and cessation of our knowledge will bring forth among the people. How goodly and how to be wished were

---

5. "Professors" in this context are people professing the Protestant faith.
6. A famous Catholic shrine.
7. Trades he cannot manage.
8. Agent.
9. I.e., separate or separable. Milton is describing the common institution of the household chaplain.

1. Mark xi.12–13. Jesus, hungry, found nothing but leaves on the fig tree, for the time of the figs was not yet.
2. "Publicans": tax collectors. Tonnage and poundage were excise taxes levied illegally by the king before 1641, and therefore specially odious to Milton's readers.

such an obedient unanimity as this, what a fine conformity would it starch us all into! Doubtless a staunch and solid piece of framework, as any January could freeze together.[3] * * *

Truth indeed came once into the world with her Divine Master, and was a perfect shape most glorious to look on: but when he ascended, and his apostles after him were laid asleep, then straight arose a wicked race of deceivers, who, as that story goes of the Egyptian Typhon with his conspirators, how they dealt with the good Osiris,[4] took the virgin Truth, hewed her lovely form into a thousand pieces, and scattered them to the four winds. From that time ever since, the sad friends of Truth, such as durst appear, imitating the careful search that Isis made for the mangled body of Osiris, went up and down gathering up limb by limb, still as they could find them. We have not yet found them all, Lords and Commons, nor ever shall do, till her Master's second coming; he shall bring together every joint and member, and shall mold them into an immortal feature of loveliness and perfection. Suffer not these licensing prohibitions to stand at every place of opportunity, forbidding and disturbing them that continue seeking, that continue to do our obsequies to the torn body of our martyred saint. We boast our light; but if we look not wisely on the sun itself, it smites us into darkness. Who can discern those planets that are oft combust,[5] and those stars of brightest magnitude that rise and set with the sun, until the opposite motion of their orbs bring them to such a place in the firmament where they may be seen evening or morning? The light which we have gained was given us, not to be ever staring on, but by it to discover onward things more remote from our knowledge. It is not the unfrocking of a priest, the unmitering of a bishop, and the removing him from off the Presbyterian shoulders, that will make us a happy nation. No, if other things as great in the church, and in the rule of life both economical[6] and political, be not looked into and reformed, we have looked so long upon the blaze that Zwinglius[7] and Calvin hath beaconed up to us, that we are stark blind.

There be who perpetually complain of schisms and sects, and make it such a calamity that any man dissents from their maxims. 'Tis their own pride and ignorance which causes the disturbing, who neither will hear with meekness, nor can convince; yet all must be suppressed which is not found in their syntagma.[8] They are the

---

3. To set barriers in the way of fresh truths implies that a nation has all the truth it needs; but this, Milton argues, is far from the case. England has no grounds for smugness; the nation needs every bit of truth it can discover.
4. Plutarch tells, in his *Isis and Osiris*, of Typhon's scattering the fragments of his brother Osiris, and of Isis' efforts

to recover them.
5. Literally, burned up; in astrology, so close to the sun as not to be visible.
6. Domestic.
7. Zwingli and Calvin, both radical Swiss reformers, were mainstays of the Presbyterian cause, which Milton was already feeling to be a little narrow.
8. Compilation of beliefs, creed.

troublers, they are the dividers of unity, who neglect and permit not others to unite those dissevered pieces which are yet wanting to the body of Truth. To be still searching what we know not by what we know, still closing up truth to truth as we find it (for all her body is homogeneal and proportional), this is the golden rule in theology as well as in arithmetic, and makes up the best harmony in a church; not the forced and outward union of cold and neutral and inwardly divided minds.

Lords and Commons of England, consider what nation it is whereof ye are, and whereof ye are the governors: a nation not slow and dull, but of a quick, ingenious and piercing spirit, acute to invent, subtle and sinewy to discourse, not beneath the reach of any point, the highest that human capacity can soar to. Therefore the studies of learning in her deepest sciences have been so ancient and so eminent among us, that writers of good antiquity and ablest judgment have been persuaded that even the school of Pythagoras and the Persian wisdom took beginning from the old philosophy of this island.[9] And that wise and civil Roman, Julius Agricola, who governed once here for Caesar, preferred the natural wits of Britain before the labored studies of the French. Nor is it for nothing that the grave and frugal Transylvanian sends out yearly from as far as the mountainous borders of Russia, and beyond the Hercynian wilderness, not their youth, but their staid men, to learn our language and our theologic arts.

Yet that which is above all this, the favor and the love of heaven, we have great argument[1] to think in a peculiar manner propitious and propending towards us. Why else was this nation chosen before any other, that out of her, as out of Zion,[2] should be proclaimed and sounded forth the first tidings and trumpet of Reformation to all Europe? And had it not been the obstinate perverseness of our prelates against the divine and admirable spirit of Wycliffe, to suppress him as a schismatic and innovator, perhaps neither the Bohemian Huss and Jerome,[3] no, nor the name of Luther or of Calvin, had been ever known: the glory of reforming all our neighbors had been completely ours. But now, as our obdurate clergy have with violence demeaned[4] the matter, we are become hitherto the latest and backwardest scholars of whom God offered to have made us the teachers. Now once again by all concurrence of signs, and by the general instinct of holy and devout men, as they daily

---

9. So far as it concerns Pythagoras and the Persians, this sentence is better patriotism than it is intellectual history. Agricola's opinion of the British intellect (referred to next), is found in Tacitus' *Life of Agricola;* "civil" means "cultured, civilized." The Transylvanians, being Protestants, did sometimes come to England from "beyond the Hercynian wilderness" (the Harz mountains) to study.
1. Reason. "Propending": inclining, favorable.
2. Mt. Zion, in Jerusalem, the site of the temple, the holy of holies.
3. Jerome of Prague (martyred in 1416) was a follower of Huss and so of Wycliffe.
4. Conducted.

and solemnly express their thoughts, God is decreeing to begin some new and great period in his church, even to the reforming of Reformation itself; what does he then but reveal himself to his servants, and as his manner is, first to his Englishmen? I say, as his manner is, first to us, though we mark not the method of his counsels, and are unworthy. Behold now this vast city: a city of refuge, the mansion house of liberty, encompassed and surrounded with his protection; the shop of war hath not there more anvils and hammers waking, to fashion out the plates[5] and instruments of armed justice in defense of beleaguered truth, than there be pens and heads there, sitting by their studious lamps, musing, searching, revolving new notions and ideas wherewith to present, as with their homage and their fealty, the approaching Reformation: others as fast reading, trying all things, assenting to the force of reason and convincement.

What could a man require more from a nation so pliant and so prone to seek after knowledge? What wants there to such a towardly[6] and pregnant soil, but wise and faithful laborers, to make a knowing people, a nation of prophets, of sages, and of worthies? We reckon more than five months yet to harvest; there need not be five weeks; had we but eyes to lift up, the fields are white already.[7] Where there is much desire to learn, there of necessity will be much arguing, much writing, many opinions; for opinion in good men is but knowledge in the making. Under these fantastic terrors of sect and schism we wrong the earnest and zealous thirst after knowledge and understanding which God hath stirred up in this city.

What some lament of, we rather should rejoice at, should rather praise this pious forwardness among men, to reassume the ill-deputed care of their religion into their own hands again. A little generous prudence, a little forbearance of one another, and some grain of charity might win all these diligences to join, and unite into one general and brotherly search after truth; could we but forgo this prelatical tradition of crowding free consciences and Christian liberties into canons and precepts of men. I doubt not, if some great and worthy stranger should come among us, wise to discern the mold and temper of a people, and how to govern it, observing the high hopes and aims, the diligent alacrity of our extended thoughts and reasonings in the pursuance of truth and freedom, but that he would cry out as Pyrrhus did, admiring the Roman docility and courage: "If such were my Epirots, I would not despair the greatest design that could be attempted, to make a church or kingdom happy."[8] Yet these are the men cried out against for schismat-

---

5. Plate mail, armor plate.
6. Favorable.
7. Milton is paraphrasing Christ's words to the disciples (John iv.35).

8. Though King Pyrrhus of Epirus beat the Roman armies at Heraclea in 280 B.C., he was much impressed by their discipline.

ics and sectaries;[9] as if, while the temple of the Lord was building, some cutting, some squaring the marble, others hewing the cedars, there should be a sort of irrational men, who could not consider there must be many schisms and many dissections[1] made in the quarry and in the timber, ere the house of God can be built. And when every stone is laid artfully together, it cannot be united into a continuity, it can but be contiguous in this world; neither can every piece of the building be of one form; nay rather the perfection consists in this, that out of many moderate varieties and brotherly dissimilitudes that are not vastly disproportional, arises the goodly and the graceful symmetry that commends the whole pile and structure. Let us therefore be more considerate builders, more wise in spiritual architecture, when great reformation is expected. For now the time seems come, wherein Moses the great prophet may sit in heaven rejoicing to see that memorable and glorious wish of his fulfilled, when not only our seventy elders, but all the Lord's people, are become prophets.[2] * * *

Methinks I see in my mind a noble and puissant nation rousing herself like a strong man after sleep, and shaking her invincible locks: methinks I see her as an eagle mewing[3] her mighty youth, and kindling her undazzled eyes at the full midday beam; purging and unscaling her long-abused sight at the fountain itself of heavenly radiance; while the whole noise of timorous and flocking birds, with those also that love the twilight, flutter about, amazed at what she means, and in their envious gabble would prognosticate a year of sects and schisms.[4] * * *

1644

9. Sectarians, dividers of the church.
1. Milton puns on the literal meanings of "schisms" and "dissections" ("split" and "cut up") to press the image of the church as a temple built of believers.
2. In Numbers xi.29, Moses expressed the wish that all the Lord's people (not just the council of "seventy," or Sanhedrin) were prophets.
3. Molting, shaking off. Or the word may be "newing," i.e., renewing.
4. With this vigorous expression of idealistic optimism, Milton's argument subsides into a few last repetitions and afterthoughts. In practical terms, it was not a successful argument; the ordinance against which it protested was not repealed, though it was never effectively enforced, being, in effect, unenforceable. In time, Milton himself became, temporarily, a licenser of news sheets under Cromwell. But this biographical fact need not and must not be taken as a retraction or limitation of the position assumed in *Areopagitica*, which moves throughout on a plane of policy far removed from mundane considerations of practical politics.

Paradise Lost   The entry into *Paradise Lost* is easy—deceptively so. Carried along by the impetus of Satan's tremendous adventures, readers are apt to forget there is any other part to the poem. Indeed, while we are getting acclimated to the Miltonic world, there is no reason to hold back our sympathy with Satan, our admiration for his heroic energy. It is energy in a bad cause, clearly; but it is energy, it is heroically exercised, and there is as yet no source of virtuous power to oppose or offset it. With the

appearance of Christ the Son, at the opening of Book III, we begin to see
in heavenly Love the counterpoise of Satan's hellish Hate; and in Book
IV, as we are introduced not only to Adam and Eve but to Paradise, our
sympathies gradually shift. Satan is no longer a glamorous underdog, fighting his adventurous way through the universe against enormous odds; he
is a menacing vulture, a cormorant, a toad, a snake. He is not only dangerous, he is dull; whatever richness and variety he discovers in the universe serve only to produce in him envious hatred and destructiveness. His
sin is incestuous, as the allegory of Sin and Death points out; it breeds
out of itself ever fresh occasions of sin. Adam and Eve, who are weaker,
less active, and less spectacular in every way, finally outweigh Satan in
our interest and sympathy simply because they can respond to life, and
to the terrifying experience of guilt, more vigorously than Satan can.

Seen overall—from above, as it were—*Paradise Lost* is a vast but delicately balanced structure. The adventure of Satan in Books I–III balances
the history of mankind in Books X–XII. Book IV, the entry of Satan (and
the reader) into Paradise, balances Book IX, describing the loss of Paradise. Books V and VI, describing the destructive war in Heaven, balance
as on a fulcrum against Books VII and VIII, which describe the Creation
and deal with the problems of understanding it.

Within the poem's larger structure, there are all sorts of secondary balances which the knowing reader will recognize for himself. The consult
in Hell (Book II) is paralleled by a consult in Heaven (Book III); the
Heavenly Trinity of Father, Son, and Holy Ghost is paralleled by a diabolic
trinity of Satan, Sin, and Death. Satan's fall parallels Adam's fall, and the
parallel is prolonged into that extended series of falls and recoveries which
is the history of mankind. Moloch contrasts with Mammon; the Son's
mercy with the Father's justice; Raphael's affability with Michael's severity;
and so on, almost without limit.

The structure of the poem is at once massive and delicate; its language
is also both rich and strong. Milton's range of classical reference and gift
for epithet are undoubtedly staggering at first view, and his long, complexly subordinated sentences are sometimes hard to follow. Footnotes,
alas, provide the only proper solution to this problem. But one need not
equal, or even follow, all Milton's learning in order to appreciate his poem,
especially at a first reading. The poem progresses as through a garden of
metaphor and reference which stretches away on either side of one, as
far as the eye can see; on a first tour, it is enough to get the general prospect clear, without learning the name of each particular blossom. Ultimately, the reader who is experienced in the poem comes to appreciate
its details—epic similes like Leviathan the seabeast (I.201), no less than
the one-eyed Arimaspians and the gryphon (II.944)—its epithets and
circumlocutions like Mulciber (I.740), who is Vulcan, and Amram's son
(I.339) who is Moses—without sense of strain or strangeness. Milton himself moved securely through the literatures of half a dozen languages and
as many cultures; it is one of the supreme rewards of literary study to be
able to follow him with an equivalent security.

Paradise Lost is at once a deeply traditional and a boldly original poem.
Milton takes pains to fulfill the traditional prescriptions of the epic form;
he gives us love, war, supernatural characters, a descent into Hell, a cata-

logue of warriors, all the conventional items of epic machinery. Yet no poem in which the climax of the central action is a woman eating a piece of fruit can be a conventional epic. Similarly, Milton himself defined his own moral purpose as being to "justify the ways of God to men." This seems no more than conventionally meek. Yet we cannot even think of equating the message of Milton's poem with Pope's injunction to "submit" because "whatever is is right." The way of life which Adam and Eve take up as the poem ends is that of the Christian pilgrimage through this world. Paradise was no place or condition in which to exercise Christian heroism as Milton conceives it. Expelled from Eden, our first "grand parents" pick up the burdens of humanity as we know them, sustained by a faith which we also know, and go forth to seek a blessing which we do not know yet. They are to become wayfaring, warfaring Christians, like John Milton; and in this condition, with its weaknesses and strivings and inevitable defeats, there is a glory that no devil can ever understand. Thus Milton strikes, humanly as well as artistically, a grand resolving chord. It is the careful, triumphant balancing and tempering of this conclusion which makes Milton's poem the noble architecture it is; and which makes of the end a richer, if not a more exciting, experience than the beginning.

From PARADISE LOST

Book I

The Argument[1]

   This first book proposes, first in brief, the whole subject, man's disobedience, and the loss thereupon of Paradise, wherein he was placed: then touches the prime cause of his fall, the serpent, or rather Satan in the serpent; who, revolting from God, and drawing to his side many legions of angels, was, by the command of God, driven out of Heaven, with all his crew, into the great deep. Which action passed over, the poem hastens into the midst of things;[2] presenting Satan, with his angels, now fallen into Hell—described here not in the center (for heaven and earth may be supposed as yet not made, certainly not yet accursed), but in a place of utter darkness, fitliest called Chaos. Here Satan with his angels lying on the burning lake, thunderstruck and astonished, after a certain space recovers, as from confusion; calls up him who, next in order and dignity, lay by him: they confer of their miserable fall. Satan awakens all his legions, who lay till then in the same manner confounded. They rise: their numbers; array of battle; their

1. *Paradise Lost* appeared originally without any sort of prose aid to the reader; but, since many readers found the poem hard going, the printer asked Milton for some prose "Arguments" or summary explanations of the action in the various books, and prefixed them to later issues of the poem. We reprint those for the first two books and the ninth.
2. Adapted from Horace's prescription that the epic poet should start *"in medias res."*

chief leaders named, according to the idols known afterwards in Canaan and the countries adjoining. To these Satan directs his speech; comforts them with hope yet of regaining Heaven; but tells them, lastly, of a new world and new kind of creature to be created, according to an ancient prophecy, or report, in Heaven; for that angels were long before this visible creation was the opinion of many ancient fathers.[3] To find out the truth of this prophecy, and what to determine[4] thereon, he refers to a full council. What his associates thence attempt. Pandemonium, the palace of Satan, rises, suddenly built out of the deep: the infernal peers there sit in council.

Of man's first disobedience, and the fruit[5]
Of that forbidden tree whose mortal[6] taste
Brought death into the world, and all our woe,
With loss of Eden, till one greater Man[7]
Restore us, and regain the blissful seat,   5
Sing, Heavenly Muse,[8] that, on the secret top
Of Oreb, or of Sinai, didst inspire
That shepherd who first taught the chosen seed
In the beginning how the Heavens and Earth
Rose out of Chaos: or, if Sion hill[9]   10
Delight thee more, and Siloa's brook that flowed
Fast[1] by the oracle of God, I thence
Invoke thy aid to my adventurous song,
That with no middle flight intends to soar
Above th' Aonian mount,[2] while it pursues   15
Things unattempted yet in prose or rhyme.
And chiefly thou, O Spirit,[3] that dost prefer
Before all temples th' upright heart and pure,
Instruct me, for thou know'st; thou from the first
Wast present, and, with mighty wings outspread,   20
Dovelike sat'st brooding[4] on the vast abyss,

3. I.e., Church Fathers, the Christian writers of the first three centuries of the church.
4. I.e., what action to take upon their information.
5. Eve's apple, of course; but also all the consequences of eating it.
6. Deadly; but also "to mortals" (i.e., human beings).
7. Christ, the second Adam.
8. In Greek mythology, Urania, Muse of astronomy and epic poetry; but here identified, by references to Oreb and Sinai, with the Holy Spirit of the Bible, which inspired Moses ("that shepherd") to write Genesis and the other four books of the Pentateuch for the instruction of the Jews ("the chosen seed").
9. The hill of Sion and the brook of Siloa are two features of the landscape around Jerusalem likely to appeal to a Muse, whose natural haunts are springs and mountains (see *Lycidas*,

line 15). Milton's aim is to show that poetry is everywhere recognized as an inspiration close to that of religion.
1. Close.
2. Helicon, home of the classical Muses; Milton is deliberately courting comparison with Homer and Virgil.
3. The Spirit is an impulse or voice of God, by which the Hebrew prophets were directly inspired.
4. A composite of phrases and ideas from Genesis i.2 ("And the earth was without form, and void; and darkness was upon the face of the deep. And the Spirit of God moved upon the face of the waters"); Matthew iii.16 ("and he saw the Spirit of God descending like a dove, and lighting upon him"); and Luke iii.22 ("and the Holy Ghost descended in a bodily shape like a dove upon him"). Milton's mind as he wrote was impregnated with expressions from the King James Bible, only a few of which can be indicated in the notes.

And mad'st it pregnant: what in me is dark
Illumine; what is low, raise and support;
That, to the height of this great argument,[5]
I may assert Eternal Providence,   25
And justify the ways of God to men.
   Say first (for Heaven hides nothing from thy view,
Nor the deep tract of Hell), say first what cause
Moved our grand[6] parents, in that happy state,
Favored of Heaven so highly, to fall off   30
From their Creator, and transgress his will
For[7] one restraint, lords of the world besides?[8]
Who first seduced them to that foul revolt?
   Th' infernal serpent; he it was, whose guile,
Stirred up with envy and revenge, deceived   35
The mother of mankind, what time[9] his pride
Had cast him out from Heaven, with all his host
Of rebel angels, by whose aid, aspiring
To set himself in glory above his peers,[1]
He trusted to have equaled the Most High,   40
If he opposed; and with ambitious aim
Against the throne and monarchy of God,
Raised impious war in Heaven and battle proud,
With vain attempt. Him the Almighty Power
Hurled headlong flaming from th' ethereal sky,   45
With hideous ruin and combustion, down
To bottomless perdition, there to dwell
In adamantine chains and penal fire,
Who durst defy th' Omnipotent to arms.
   Nine times the space that measures day and night   50
To mortal men, he with his horrid crew,
Lay vanquished, rolling in the fiery gulf,
Confounded though immortal. But his doom
Reserved him to more wrath; for now the thought
Both of lost happiness and lasting pain   55
Torments him; round he throws his baleful[2] eyes,
That witnessed huge affliction and dismay,
Mixed with obdúrate pride and steadfast hate.
At once, as far as angels ken,[3] he views
The dismal situation waste and wild: 60
A dungeon horrible, on all sides round,
As one great furnace flamed; yet from those flames
No light,[4] but rather darkness visible

5. Theme.
6. First in importance; by implication, in time also.
7. Because of.
8. In every other respect.
9. I.e., at the time when.
1. His equals. The sentence mimics Satan's action, piling clause loosely upon clause, and building ever higher, till "with vain attempt" (line 44) brings the whole structure crashing down. It is a dramatic entry into "the midst of things," where epics begin. Book VI will recount more largely the war in Heaven, in the full narrative form which Aeneas used to tell Dido of the last days of Troy.
2. Malignant, as well as suffering.
3. As far as angels can see.
4. Omitting the verb conveys abruptly the paradox: fire-without-light.

Served only to discover sights of woe,
Regions of sorrow, doleful shades, where peace 65
And rest can never dwell, hope never comes
That comes to all,[5] but torture without end
Still urges,[6] and a fiery deluge, fed
With ever-burning sulphur unconsumed.
Such place Eternal Justice had prepared 70
For those rebellious; here their prison ordained
In utter[7] darkness, and their portion set,
As far removed from God and light of Heaven
As from the center[8] thrice to th' utmost pole.
O how unlike the place from whence they fell! 75
There the companions of his fall, o'erwhelmed
With floods and whirlwinds of tempestuous fire,
He soon discerns; and, weltering by his side,
One next himself in power, and next in crime,
Long after known in Palestine, and named 80
Beëlzebub.[9] To whom th' arch-enemy,
And thence in Heaven called Satan,[1] with bold words
Breaking the horrid silence, thus began:
    "If thou beëst he—but O how fallen! how changed
From him who, in the happy realms of light 85
Clothed with transcendent brightness, didst outshine
Myriads, though bright! if he whom mutual league,
United thoughts and counsels, equal hope
And hazard in the glorious enterprise,
Joined with me once, now misery hath joined 90
In equal ruin; into what pit thou seest[2]
From what height fallen, so much the stronger proved
He with his thunder:[3] and till then who knew
The force of those dire arms? Yet not for those,
Nor what the potent Victor in his rage 95
Can else inflict, do I repent, or change,
Though changed in outward luster, that fixed mind,
And high disdain from sense of injured merit,

5. The phrase echoes an expression in Dante ("All hope abandon, ye who enter here"), but Milton expresses it as a logical absurdity. Hope comes to "all" but not to Helldwellers; they are not included in "all."
6. Afflicts.
7. "Complete" but also "outer."
8. The earth. Milton makes use in *Paradise Lost* of two images of the cosmos: (1) the earth is the center of the *created* (Ptolemaic) cosmos of nine concentric spheres; but (2) the earth and the whole created cosmos are a mere appendage, hanging from Heaven by a golden chain, in the larger, aboriginal, and less shapely cosmos. In the present passage, the fall from Heaven to Hell (through the aboriginal universe) is described as thrice as far as the distance (in the created universe)
from the center (earth) to the outer-most sphere.
9. A Phoenician deity, or Baal (the name means "Lord of flies"); tradi-tionally, a prince of devils and enemy of Jehovah. The Phoenician Baal, a sun god, had many aspects and so many names; most Baals were nature deities. But in the poem's time scheme all this lies in the future; Beelzebub's angelic name, whatever it was, has been erased from the Book of Life, and as he has not yet got another one, he must be called by the name he will have later on.
1. In Hebrew, the name means "Ad-versary."
2. Satan's syntax, like that of a man recovering from a stunning blow, is not of the clearest.
3. God with his thunderbolts.

That with the Mightiest raised me to contend,
And to the fierce contentions brought along   100
Innumerable force of spirits armed,
That durst dislike his reign, and, me preferring,
His utmost power with adverse power opposed
In dubious battle on the plains of Heaven,
And shook his throne. What though the field be lost?   105
All is not lost: the unconquerable will,
And study[4] of revenge, immortal hate,
And courage never to submit or yield:
And what is else not to be overcome?[5]
That glory never shall his wrath or might   110
Extort from me. To bow and sue for grace
With suppliant knee, and deify his power[6]
Who, from the terror of this arm, so late
Doubted his empire[7]—that were low indeed;
That were an ignominy and shame beneath   115
This downfall; since, by fate, the strength of gods,[8]
And this empyreal substance, cannot fail;
Since, through experience of this great event,
In arms not worse, in foresight much advanced,
We may with more successful hope resolve   120
To wage by force or guile eternal war,
Irreconcilable to our grand Foe,
Who now triúmphs, and in th' excess of joy
Sole reigning holds the tyranny[9] of Heaven."
    So spake th' apostate angel, though in pain,   125
Vaunting aloud, but racked with deep despair;
And him thus answered soon his bold compeer:[1]
    "O prince, O chief of many thronéd powers,
That led th' embattled seraphim[2] to war
Under thy conduct, and, in dreadful deeds   130
Fearless, endangered Heaven's perpetual King,
And put to proof his high supremacy,
Whether upheld by strength, or chance, or fate![3]
Too well I see and rue the dire event[4]

4. Pursuit.
5. I.e., what else does it mean not to be beaten? "That glory" is the glory of hearing Satan confess himself overcome.
6. I.e., deify the power of him who. Milton sometimes writes English as if it were an inflected language.
7. I.e., doubted whether he could maintain his empire.
8. The essence of Satan's fault is his claim to the position of a god, subject to fate but to nothing else. His substance is "empyreal" (heavenly, from the empyrean), and cannot be destroyed; but, as he learns in the poem, it can be confounded by God's greater power and weakened by its own corruption and self-contradictions. "Fail":

cease to exist.
9. The accusation is bold, but one of the aims of the poem is to show that Satan is a tyrant and God is not. The next two lines start this dramatic process by suggesting that Satan's brave exterior is merely a front.
1. Comrade and equal.
2. According to tradition, there were nine orders of angels—seraphim, cherubim, thrones, dominions, virtues, powers, principalities, archangels, and angels; but Milton does not use these systematic categories systematically.
3. The devils can conceive of any reason for God's continuing rule, except goodness and justice.
4. Outcome.

That with sad overthrow and foul defeat   135
Hath lost us Heaven, and all this mighty host
In horrible destruction laid thus low,
As far as gods and heavenly essences
Can perish: for the mind and spirit remains
Invincible, and vigor soon returns,   140
Though all our glory extinct, and happy state
Here swallowed up in endless misery.
But what if he our Conqueror (whom I now
Of force[5] believe almighty, since no less
Than such could have o'erpowered such force as ours)   145
Have left us this our spirit and strength entire,
Strongly to suffer and support our pains,
That we may so suffice[6] his vengeful ire,
Or do him mightier service as his thralls
By right of war, whate'er his business be,   150
Here in the heart of Hell to work in fire,
Or do his errands in the gloomy deep?
What can it then avail though yet we feel
Strength undiminished, or eternal being
To undergo eternal punishment?"   155
    Whereto with speedy words th' arch-fiend[7] replied:
"Fallen cherub, to be weak is miserable,
Doing or suffering:[8] but of this be sure,
To do aught good never will be our task,
But ever to do ill our sole delight,   160
As being the contrary to his high will
Whom we resist. If then his providence
Out of our evil seek to bring forth good,
Our labor must be to pervert that end,
And out of good still to find means of evil;   165
Which oft times may succeed, so as perhaps
Shall grieve him, if I fail not,[9] and disturb
His inmost counsels from their destined aim.
But see! the angry Victor hath recalled
His ministers of vengeance and pursuit   170
Back to the gates of Heaven; the sulphurous hail,
Shot after us in storm, o'erblown hath laid
The fiery surge that from the precipice
Of Heaven received us falling; and the thunder,
Winged with red lightning and impetuous rage,   175
Perhaps hath spent his shafts, and ceases now
To bellow through the vast and boundless deep.
Let us not slip[1] th' occasion, whether scorn
Or satiate fury yield it from our Foe.
Seest thou yon dreary plain, forlorn and wild,   180
The seat of desolation, void of light,

5. Perforce, necessarily.
6. Satisfy.
7. A fiend is an enemy, one who hates; the word is an antonym of "friend."
8. Whether one is active or passive.
9. "Unless I'm mistaken" (direct from the Latin, *ne fallor*).
1. I.e., let slip.

Save what the glimmering of these livid flames
Casts pale and dreadful? Thither let us tend
From off the tossing of these fiery waves;
There rest, if any rest can harbor there;   185
And, reassembling our afflicted powers,[2]
Consult how we may henceforth most offend
Our enemy, our own loss how repair,
How overcome this dire calamity,
What reinforcement we may gain from hope,   190
If not, what resolution from despair."[3]

    Thus Satan, talking to his nearest mate,
With head uplift above the wave, and eyes
That sparkling blazed; his other parts besides,
Prone on the flood, extended long and large,   195
Lay floating many a rood,[4] in bulk as huge
As whom[5] the fables name of monstrous size,
Titanian or Earth-born, that warred on Jove,
Briareos or Typhon,[6] whom the den
By ancient Tarsus held, or that sea beast   200
Leviathan,[7] which God of all his works
Created hugest that swim th' ocean-stream.
Him, haply, slumbering on the Norway foam,
The pilot of some small night-foundered[8] skiff,
Deeming some island, oft, as seamen tell,   205
With fixéd anchor in his scaly rind,
Moors by his side under the lee, while night
Invests[9] the sea, and wishéd morn delays.
So stretched out huge in length the arch-fiend lay,
Chained on the burning lake; nor ever thence   210
Had risen or heaved his head, but that the will
And high permission of all-ruling Heaven
Left him at large to his own dark designs,
That with reiterated crimes he might
Heap on himself damnation, while he sought   215
Evil to others, and enraged might see
How all his malice served but to bring forth
Infinite goodness, grace, and mercy shown
On man by him seduced, but on himself

---

2. Stricken armies.
3. Of the last nine lines of Satan's speech, no less than five rhyme. Milton may have felt the need for something like the couplet with which blank-verse dramatists cut off their scenes.
4. An old unit of measure, between six and eight yards.
5. I.e., as those whom.
6. Both the Titans, led by Briareos, and the earth-born Giants, represented by Typhon (who lived in Cilicia near Tarsus), fought with Jove. Briareos was said to have a hundred hands, and Typhon a hundred heads; and both were said, by different authors, to have

been punished for their rebellion (like Satan for his) by being thrown into the underworld. Briareos and Typhon are still heard grumbling from time to time under Mt. Etna.
7. The great sea monster of Isaiah xxvii.1 or Job xli; for Milton and us, simply a whale, but scaly (line 206).
8. Overtaken by darkness.
9. Wraps, covers. The story of sailors mooring to whales was an old one, but the reference to Norway suggests that Milton was thinking of a recently translated version by Olaus Magnus, the Swedish historian.

Treble confusion, wrath, and vengeance poured.   220
   Forthwith upright he rears from off the pool
His mighty stature; on each hand the flames
Driven backward slope their pointing spires,[1] and, rolled
In billows, leave i' th' midst a horrid[2] vale.
Then with expanded wings he steers his flight   225
Aloft, incumbent on[3] the dusky air,
That felt unusual weight; till on dry land
He lights, if it were land that ever burned
With solid, as the lake with liquid fire,
And such appeared in hue; as when the force   230
Of subterranean wind transports a hill
Torn from Pelorus,[4] or the shattered side
Of thundering Etna, whose combustible
And fueled entrails, thence conceiving fire,
Sublimed[5] with mineral fury, aid the winds,   235
And leave a singéd bottom all involved[6]
With stench and smoke. Such resting found the sole
Of unblest feet. Him followed his next mate,
Both glorying to have 'scaped the Stygian[7] flood
As gods, and by their own recovered strength,   240
Not by the sufferance[8] of supernal power.
   "Is this the region, this the soil, the clime,"
Said then the lost archangel, "this the seat
That we must change[9] for Heaven? this mournful gloom
For that celestial light? Be it so, since he   245
Who now is sovereign can dispose and bid
What shall be right: farthest from him is best,
Whom reason hath equaled, force hath made supreme
Above his equals.[1] Farewell, happy fields,
Where joy forever dwells! Hail, horrors! hail,   250
Infernal world! and thou, profoundest Hell,
Receive thy new possessor, one who brings
A mind not to be changed by place or time.
The mind is its own place, and in itself
Can make a Heaven of Hell, a Hell of Heaven.   255
What matter where, if I be still the same,
And what I should be, all but less[2] than he
Whom thunder hath made greater? Here at least
We shall be free; th' Almighty hath not built
Here for his envy, will not drive us hence: 260
Here we may reign secure; and, in my choice,
To reign is worth ambition, though in Hell:

1. Points of flame.
2. Not simply "ghastly," but in the Latin sense, "bristling."
3. Resting upon.
4. Pelorus and Etna are volcanic mountains in Sicily, which Milton pictures as exploding under pressure of underground winds.
5. Kindled.
6. Wrapped.
7. Of the river Styx, i.e., demonic, hellish.
8. Permission.
9. Exchange.
1. Satan likes to think that by "reason" he is God's equal; this only shows how far he is from "right reason."
2. Second only to. The expression "all but less than" telescopes "all but equal to" and "only less than."

Better to reign in Hell than serve in Heaven.
But wherefore let we then our faithful friends,
Th' associates and copartners of our loss,   265
Lie thus astonished[3] on th' oblivious pool,
And call them not to share with us their part
In this unhappy mansion, or once more
With rallied arms to try what may be yet
Regained in Heaven, or what more lost in Hell?"   270
    So Satan spake; and him Beëlzebub
Thus answered: "Leader of those armies bright
Which, but th' Omnipotent, none could have foiled!
If once they hear that voice, their liveliest pledge
Of hope in fears and dangers, heard so oft   275
In worst extremes, and on the perilous edge[4]
Of battle, when it raged, in all assaults
Their surest signal, they will soon resume
New courage and revive, though now they lie
Groveling and prostrate on yon lake of fire,   280
As we erewhile, astounded and amazed;
No wonder, fallen such a pernicious height!"
    He scarce had ceased when the superior fiend
Was moving toward the shore; his ponderous shield,
Ethereal temper,[5] massy, large, and round,   285
Behind him cast. The broad circumference
Hung on his shoulders like the moon, whose orb
Through optic glass the Tuscan artist[6] views
At evening, from the top of Fesolè,
Or in Valdarno, to descry new lands,   290
Rivers, or mountains, in her spotty globe.
His spear, to equal which the tallest pine
Hewn on Norwegian hills, to be the mast
Of some great admiral,[7] were but a wand,
He walked with, to support uneasy steps   295
Over the burning marl,[8] not like those steps
On Heaven's azure; and the torrid clime
Smote on him sore besides, vaulted with fire.
Nathless[9] he so endured, till on the beach
Of that inflaméd[1] sea he stood, and called   300
His legions, angel forms, who lay entranced,
Thick as autumnal leaves that strow the brooks
In Vallombrosa,[2] where th' Etrurian shades

3. Stunned. The epithet "oblivious" is transferred from the fallen angels to the pool in which they have fallen.
4. Not the fringe of battle but the front line (Latin *acies*).
5. With the qualities of ether, which, being the fifth element, is not subject to change, corruption, or decay.
6. Galileo, who looked through a telescope ("optic glass") from the hill town of Fiesole outside Florence in the Val

d'Arno, is the only contemporary mentioned by Milton in *Paradise Lost*.
7. Not the naval commander, but his flagship, usually the biggest of the fleet.
8. Soil.
9. A compressed, archaic form of "not the less."
1. Flaming, of course, but also fevered.
2. Literally, "Shady Valley," a few miles from Florence.

High over-arched embower;[3] or scattered sedge
Afloat, when with fierce winds Orion armed   305
Hath vexed the Red-Sea coast, whose waves o'erthrew
Busiris and his Memphian chivalry,
While with perfidious hatred they pursued
The sojourners of Goshen, who beheld
From the safe shore their floating carcasses   310
And broken chariot wheels.[4] So thick bestrown,
Abject and lost, lay these, covering the flood,
Under amazement of their hideous change.
He called so loud that all the hollow deep
Of Hell resounded: "Princes, potentates,   315
Warriors, the flower of Heaven, once yours, now lost,
If such astonishment as this can seize
Eternal spirits! or have ye chosen this place
After the toil of battle to repose
Your wearied virtue,[5] for the ease you find   320
To slumber here, as in the vales of Heaven?
Or in this abject posture have ye sworn
To adore the Conqueror, who now beholds
Cherub and seraph rolling in the flood
With scattered arms and ensigns,[6] till anon   325
His swift pursuers from Heaven-gates discern
Th' advantage, and descending tread us down
Thus drooping, or with linkéd thunderbolts
Transfix us to the bottom of this gulf?
Awake, arise, or be forever fallen!"   330
    They heard, and were abashed, and up they sprung
Upon the wing, as when men wont to watch
On duty, sleeping found by whom they dread,
Rouse and bestir themselves ere well awake.
Nor did they not perceive[7] the evil plight   335
In which they were, or the fierce pains not feel;
Yet to their general's voice they soon obeyed
Innumerable. As when the potent rod
Of Amram's son,[8] in Egypt's evil day,
Waved round the coast, up called a pitchy cloud   340
Of locusts, warping[9] on the eastern wind,
That o'er the realm of impious Pharaoh hung
Like night, and darkened all the land of Nile;

3. I.e., form bowers by enclosing space.
4. Orion is a constellation, visible chiefly in late summer and autumn, hence associated with storms; in the Red Sea, where sedge grows thick, these storms result in much floating seaweed. This reminds Milton of how the sea must have looked after the Israelites ("sojourners of Goshen") passed through it while escaping from Egypt, when it was covered with the littered corpses of Pharaoh ("Busiris") and his pursuing horsemen ("Memphian chivalry").
5. Strength, but Satan's sarcasm makes use of the other connotation too.
6. Standards, battle flags.
7. The double negatives make a positive: they did indeed perceive both plight and pains. (Latin, *neque non*, "nor . . . not," "and.")
8. Moses, who drew down a plague of locusts on Egypt (Exodus x.12–15). Milton's learned locution is designed to keep Moses out of Hell, as well as from appearing too often in the poem (cf. above, 307–11).
9. Floating.

So numberless were those bad angels seen
Hovering on wing under the cope[1] of Hell,   345
'Twixt upper, nether, and surrounding fires;
Till, as a signal given, th' uplifted spear
Of their great sultan[2] waving to direct
Their course, in even balance down they light
On the firm brimstone, and fill all the plain: 350
A multitude like which the populous North[3]
Poured never from her frozen loins to pass
Rhene or the Danaw, when her barbarous sons
Came like a deluge on the South, and spread
Beneath Gibraltar to the Libyan sands.   355
Forthwith, from every squadron and each band,
The heads and leaders thither haste where stood
Their great commander; godlike shapes, and forms
Excelling human; princely dignities,
And powers that erst in Heaven sat on thrones,   360
Though of their names in Heavenly records now
Be no memorial, blotted out and rased[4]
By their rebellion from the Books of Life.
Nor had they yet among the sons of Eve
Got them new names, till, wandering o'er the Earth,   365
Through God's high sufferance for the trial of man,
By falsities and lies the greatest part
Of mankind they corrupted to forsake
God their Creator, and th' invisible
Glory of him that made them to transform   370
Oft to the image of a brute, adorned
With gay religions[5] full of pomp and gold,
And devils to adore for deities.
Then were they known to men by various names,
And various idols through the heathen world.   375
    Say, Muse, their names then known, who first, who last,[6]
Roused from the slumber on that fiery couch,
At their great emperor's call, as next in worth
Came singly[7] where he stood on the bare strand,
While the promiscuous crowd stood yet aloof.   380
    The chief were those who, from the pit of Hell
Roaming to seek their prey on Earth, durst fix
Their seats, long after, next the seat of God,[8]

1. Roof.
2. A first use of the image, which will be reinforced later, of Satan as an Oriental despot.
3. The barbarian invasions of falling Rome began with crossings of the Rhine ("Rhene") and Danube ("Danaw") Rivers, and spread across Spain, via Gibraltar, to North Africa.
4. Erased. See above, line 81. Though reluctant to state the view strongly, Milton believed all the pagan deities had been devils in disguise.

5. Ceremonies.
6. The catalogue of gods here is an epic convention; Homer catalogues ships, Virgil warriors.
7. One at a time. The diabolical aristocrats rally round Satan, while the "promiscuous crowd," the vulgar gods, stand apart.
8. The first group of devils come from the Near East, close neighbors and intimate enemies of Jehovah at Jerusalem.

Their altars by his altar, gods adored
Among the nations round, and durst abide   385
Jehovah thundering out of Sion, throned
Between the cherubim; yea, often placed
Within his sanctuary itself their shrines,
Abominations; and with curséd things
His holy rites and solemn feasts profaned,   390
And with their darkness durst affront his light.
First, Moloch,[9] horrid king, besmeared with blood
Of human sacrifice, and parents' tears;
Though, for the noise of drums and timbrels loud,
Their children's cries unheard, that passed through fire   395
To his grim idol. Him the Ammonite[1]
Worshiped in Rabba and her watery plain,
In Argob and in Basan, to the stream
Of utmost Arnon. Nor content with such
Audacious neighborhood, the wisest heart   400
Of Solomon he led by fraud to build
His temple right against the temple of God
On that opprobrious hill,[2] and made his grove
The pleasant valley of Hinnom, Tophet thence
And black Gehenna called, the type of Hell.   405
Next Chemos,[3] th' obscene dread of Moab's sons,
From Aroar to Nebo and the wild
Of southmost Abarim; in Hesebon
And Horonaim, Seon's realm, beyond
The flowery dale of Sibma clad with vines,   410
And Elealè to th' Asphaltic pool:
Peor[4] his other name, when he enticed
Israel in Sittim, on their march from Nile,
To do him wanton rites, which cost them woe.
Yet thence his lustful orgies he enlarged   415
Even to that hill of scandal, by the grove
Of Moloch homicide,[5] lust hard by hate,
Till good Josiah drove them thence to Hell.
With these came they who, from the bordering flood
Of old Euphrates to the brook that parts   420

---

9. A sun god, sometimes represented as a roaring bull or with a calf's head, within whose brazen image living children were often burned as sacrifices (for a lurid fictional account, see Flaubert's *Salammbô*). "Timbrels": tambourines.

1. The Ammonites lived east of the Jordan, and Milton uses uncouth place names ("Rabba," "Argob," "Basan," "utmost Arnon") to suggest wildness.

2. The rites of Moloch on "that opprobrious hill" (the Mount of Olives) right opposite the Jewish temple, and in the valley of Hinnom, so polluted these places that they were turned into the refuse dump of Jerusalem. Thus they became "types" (analogies) of Hell, under the names "Tophet" and "Gehenna."

3. Chemos or Chemosh was another name for Moloch, used in Moab, a nation lying south and east of the Dead Sea ("th' Asphaltic pool"). Many of the geographical names clustered here come from Isaiah xv–xvi.

4. For the story of how Peor seduced "Israel in Sittim," see Numbers xxv.

5. An epithet was often joined to a god's name as a surname (e.g., *Jupiter Tonans*, Jove the Thunderer); Milton's epithet involves almost a parody, Moloch the Mankiller. The story of "good Josiah" and his campaign against pagan gods is told in II Kings xxiii.

Egypt from Syrian ground,[6] had general names
Of Baalim and Ashtaroth, those male,
These feminine.[7] For spirits, when they please,
Can either sex assume, or both; so soft
And uncompounded is their essence pure,   425
Not tied or manacled with joint or limb,
Nor founded on the brittle strength of bones,
Like cumbrous flesh; but, in what shape they choose,
Dilated or condensed, bright or obscure,
Can execute their airy purposes,   430
And works of love or enmity fulfill.
For those the race of Israel oft forsook
Their Living Strength,[8] and unfrequented left
His righteous altar, bowing lowly down
To bestial gods; for which their heads as low   435
Bowed down in battle, sunk before the spear
Of despicable foes. With these in troop
Came Astoreth, whom the Phoenicians called
Astartè, queen of heaven, with crescent horns;
To whose bright image nightly by the moon   440
Sidonian virgins[9] paid their vows and songs;
In Sion also not unsung, where stood
Her temple on th' offensive mountain,[1] built
By that uxorious king[2] whose heart, though large,
Beguiled by fair idolatresses, fell   445
To idols foul. Thammuz[3] came next behind,
Whose annual wound in Lebanon allured
The Syrian damsels to lament his fate
In amorous ditties all a summer's day,
While smooth Adonis[4] from his native rock   450
Ran purple to the sea, supposed with blood
Of Thammuz yearly wounded: the love tale
Infected Sion's daughters with like heat,
Whose wanton passions in the sacred porch
Ezekiel[5] saw, when, by the vision led,   455
His eye surveyed the dark idolatries
Of alienated Judah. Next came one
Who mourned in earnest, when the captive ark

6. Palestine lies between the Euphrates and "the brook Besor" (I Samuel xxx.10).

7. I.e., plural forms, masculine and feminine respectively, for Baal and Astarte. As Baals were aspects of the sun god, Astartes (Ishtars) were manifestations of the moon goddess.

8. The Jews lost battles, Milton says, when they neglected Jehovah.

9. Sidon and Tyre were the chief cities of Phoenicia.

1. The Mount of Olives again (see above, lines 403 and 416).

2. Solomon, who "loved many strange women" (I Kings xi.1–8).

3. A Syrian god, who was supposed to have been killed by a boar in Lebanon; annual festivals mourned his death and celebrated his revival, imitating the cycle of vegetable life. In his Greek form he was Adonis, god of the solar year.

4. A Lebanese river, named after the deity because every spring it turned blood-red with sedimentary mud.

5. Ezekiel complained that the Jewish women of his day were worshiping Thammuz (Ezekiel viii.14).

Maimed his brute image, head and hands lopped off,
In his own temple, on the grunsel-edge,[6]   460
Where he fell flat, and shamed his worshipers:
Dagon his name, sea monster, upward man
And downward fish; yet had his temple high
Reared in Azotus, dreaded through the coast
Of Palestine, in Gath and Ascalon,   465
And Accaron and Gaza's frontier bounds.[7]
Him followed Rimmon, whose delightful seat
Was fair Damascus, on the fertile banks
Of Abbana and Pharphar, lucid streams.
He also 'gainst the house of God was bold: 470
A leper once he lost, and gained a king,
Ahaz,[8] his sottish conqueror, whom he drew
God's altar to disparage and displace
For one of Syrian mode, whereon to burn
His odious offerings, and adore the gods   475
Whom he had vanquished. After these appeared
A crew who, under names of old renown,
Osiris, Isis, Orus,[9] and their train,
With monstrous shapes[1] and sorceries abused
Fanatic Egypt and her priests to seek   480
Their wandering gods disguised in brutish forms
Rather than human. Nor did Israel 'scape
Th' infection, when their borrowed gold composed
The calf in Oreb;[2] and the rebel king
Doubled that sin in Bethel and in Dan,   485
Likening his Maker to the grazéd ox[3]—
Jehovah, who, in one night, when he passed
From Egypt marching, equaled[4] with one stroke
Both her first-born and all her bleating gods.
Belial[5] came last; than whom a spirit more lewd   490
Fell not from Heaven, or more gross to love
Vice for itself. To him no temple stood
Or altar smoked; yet who more oft than he
In temples and at altars, when the priest

6. When the Philistines stole the ark of God, they tried to store it in the temple of their sea god, Dagon; but in the morning the mutilated statue of Dagon was found on the threshold ("grunsel-edge"). See I Samuel v.1–5.
7. Milton names the five chief cities of the Philistines as places where Dagon was worshiped.
8. A Syrian general, Naaman, was cured of leprosy and converted from worship of Rimmon by the waters of the Jordan (II Kings v). King Ahaz "turned from the house of the Lord for the king of Assyria" (II Kings xvi).
9. The second group of devils includes those from Egypt.
1. Monstrous, because often represented with animals' heads.

2. Aaron made a golden calf in the wilderness (Exodus xxxii); Milton thought it an idol of the Egyptian god Apis because the gold of which it was made had been borrowed from the Egyptians.
3. Jeroboam, "the rebel king," doubled Aaron's sin by making *two* golden calves (I Kings xii.28–30).
4. Leveled. See Exodus xii.12 for Jehovah's vengeance on the first-born of Egypt and their gods.
5. Belial was never worshiped as a god; his name was originally an abstract noun meaning "wickedness"; hence used mainly in set phrases like "sons of Belial." He comes last, because weak and slothful.

Turns atheist, as did Eli's sons,[6] who filled 495
With lust and violence the house of God?
In courts and palaces he also reigns,
And in luxurious cities, where the noise
Of riot ascends above their loftiest towers,
And injury and outrage; and, when night 500
Darkens the streets, then wander forth the sons
Of Belial, flown[7] with insolence and wine.
Witness the streets of Sodom,[8] and that night
In Gibeah, when the hospitable door
Exposed a matron, to avoid worse rape. 505

These were the prime in order and in might;
The rest were long to tell, though far renowned,
Th' Ionian gods, of Javan's issue held
Gods, yet confessed later than Heaven and Earth,
Their boasted parents;[9] Titan, Heaven's first-born, 510
With his enormous brood, and birthright seized
By younger Saturn; he from mightier Jove,
His own and Rhea's son, like measure found;
So Jove usurping reigned.[1] These, first in Crete
And Ida known, thence on the snowy top 515
Of cold Olympus ruled the middle air,
Their highest heaven; or on the Delphian cliff,
Or in Dodona, and through all the bounds
Of Doric land; or who with Saturn old
Fled over Adria to th' Hesperian fields, 520
And o'er the Celtic roamed the utmost isles.

All these and more came flocking; but with looks
Downcast and damp,[2] yet such wherein appeared
Obscure some glimpse of joy, to have found their chief
Not in despair, to have found themselves not lost 525
In loss itself; which on his countenance cast
Like doubtful hue.[3] But he, his wonted pride
Soon recollecting, with high words, that bore
Semblance of worth, not substance, gently raised
Their fainting courage, and dispelled their fears: 530
Then straight commands that, at the warlike sound

---

6. The misdeeds of Eli's sons, and the epithet "sons of Belial" applied to them, will be found in I Samuel ii. 12–17.
7. Flushed.
8. In Sodom and Gibeah ancient outrages befell, described in Genesis xix and Judges xix.
9. Though considered ancient by the Greeks ("Javan's issue," i.e., offspring of Javan, son of Japhet, son of Noah) and worshiped as the first children of "Heaven" (Uranus) and "Earth" (Ge), the Titans, Milton says, were actually confessed to be of a later age.
1. Cronos or Saturn, one of the Titans, deposed his elder brother, married his

sister Rhea, and ruled until Zeus, who had been reared in secret on Mt. Ida in Crete, overthrew his own father and came to rule on Mt. Olympus. Zeus was also worshiped in Delphos, Dodona, and throughout the "Doric (Grecian) land." Meanwhile Saturn (lines 519–21), after his downfall, fled across the Adriatic Sea ("Adria") to Italy ("th' Hesperian fields"), crossed "the Celtic" (fields) of France, and finally reached Britain ("the utmost isles").
2. Depressed.
3. Their comfort is the chilly one of finding themselves not completely annihilated; and at first it is reflected in Satan's face.

Of trumpets loud and clarions,[4] be upreared
His mighty standard. That proud honor claimed
Azazel[5] as his right, a cherub tall:
Who forthwith from the glittering staff unfurled   535
Th' imperial ensign; which, full high advanced,
Shone like a meteor streaming to the wind,
With gems and golden luster rich emblazed,
Seraphic arms and trophies; all the while
Sonorous metal[6] blowing martial sounds·   540
At which the universal host up sent
A shout that tore Hell's concave,[7] and beyond
Frighted the reign of Chaos and old Night.[8]
All in a moment through the gloom were seen
Ten thousand banners rise into the air,   545
With orient[9] colors waving: with them rose
A forest huge of spears; and thronging helms
Appeared, and serried[1] shields in thick array
Of depth immeasurable. Anon they move
In perfect phalanx to the Dorian[2] mood   550
Of flutes and soft recorders; such as raised
To height of noblest temper heroes old
Arming to battle, and instead of rage
Deliberate valor breathed, firm, and unmoved
With dread of death to flight or foul retreat;   555
Nor wanting power to mitigate and swage[3]
With solemn touches troubled thoughts, and chase
Anguish and doubt and fear and sorrow and pain
From mortal or immortal minds. Thus they,
Breathing united force with fixéd thought,   560
Moved on in silence to soft pipes that charmed
Their painful steps o'er the burnt soil. And now
Advanced in view they stand, a horrid[4] front
Of dreadful length and dazzling arms, in guise
Of warriors old, with ordered spear and shield,   565
Awaiting what command their mighty chief
Had to impose. He through the arméd files
Darts his experienced eye, and soon traverse[5]
The whole battalion views, their order due,
Their visages and stature as of gods;   570
Their number last he sums. And now his heart
Distends with pride, and hardening in his strength
Glories; for never, since created man,[6]
Met such embodied force as, named with these,

4. Small, shrill, treble trumpets.
5. Among the historians of angels and devils, a traditional diabolic leader.
6. Reverberant trumpets.
7. Vault.
8. Disorder and darkness, the first materials of the cosmos, still maintain a kingdom between Heaven and Hell.
9. Lustrous, like the colors of a pearl.
1. Locked together.

2. Severe, simple. The shrill trumpet, which first roused the courage of the devils, now gives way to firm, martial tones, played on instruments of softer timbre, in the Spartan manner.
3. Assuage.
4. Bristling.
5. Across. Satan glances, like a reviewing officer, down the files and columns.
6. I.e., since the creation of man.

Could merit more than that small infantry 575
Warred on by cranes:[7] though all the giant brood
Of Phlegra with th' heroic race were joined
That fought at Thebes and Ilium, on each side
Mixed with auxiliar[8] gods; and what resounds
In fable or romance of Uther's son, 580
Begirt with British and Armoric knights;
And all who since, baptized or infidel,
Jousted in Aspramont, or Montalban,
Damasco, or Marocco, or Trebisond;
Or whom Biserta sent from Afric shore 585
When Charlemagne with all his peerage fell
By Fontarabbia.[9] Thus far these beyond
Compare of mortal prowess, yet observed[1]
Their dread commander. He, above the rest
In shape and gesture proudly eminent, 590
Stood like a tower. His form had yet not lost
All her[2] original brightness, nor appeared
Less than archangel ruined, and th' excess
Of glory obscured: as when the sun new-risen
Looks through the horizontal[3] misty air 595
Shorn of his beams, or from behind the moon,
In dim eclipse,[4] disastrous twilight sheds
On half the nations, and with fear of change
Perplexes monarchs. Darkened so, yet shone
Above them all th' archangel; but his face 600
Deep scars of thunder had entrenched, and care
Sat on his faded cheek, but under brows
Of dauntless courage, and considerate[5] pride
Waiting revenge. Cruel his eye, but cast
Signs of remorse and passion,[6] to behold 605
The fellows of his crime, the followers rather
(Far other once beheld in bliss), condemned
Forever now to have their lot in pain;
Millions of spirits for his fault amerced[7]
Of Heaven, and from eternal splendors flung 610

[margin: description of Satan]

7. The pygmies had periodic fights with the cranes, which (according to Pliny) they won by riding to battle on pigs and goats. This would make them cavalry; but Milton wanted the pun on "infants." His idea is that, compared with the devils, all other armies that ever were would look puny.
8. Allied.
9. The Giants of Greek mythology were born at Phlegra (line 577); Milton imagines them joined with the Seven who fought against Thebes, and the whole Greek host that besieged Troy ("Ilium"), plus the various gods who helped on both sides. He even adds the knights "British or Armoric" (from Brittany) who fought with King Arthur ("Uther's son"), and includes a list of proper names taken from the cycles of romance and suggesting vast, remote armies. Fontarabbia, the best known, was reputed to be the scene of Roland's last stand in the *Chanson de Roland;* Milton thus mingles the fall of Charlemagne with that of his best-known knight.
1. Obeyed.
2. *Forma,* in Latin, is feminine; hence "her."
3. The rays of the sun, as it first rises over the horizon, are almost horizontal.
4. Time of ill omen. "Disastrous": threatening disaster.
5. Thoughtful, conscious.
6. Compassion.
7. Deprived.

For his revolt; yet faithful how they stood,
Their glory withered; as, when Heaven's fire
Hath scathed the forest oaks or mountain pines,
With singéd top their stately growth, though bare,
Stands on the blasted heath. He now prepared   615
To speak; whereat their doubled ranks they bend
From wing to wing, and half enclose him round
With all his peers: attention held them mute.
Thrice he essayed, and thrice, in spite of scorn,
Tears, such as angels weep, burst forth: at last   620
Words interwove with sighs found out their way:
    "O myriads of immortal spirits! O powers
Matchless, but with th' Almighty!—and that strife
Was not inglorious, though th' event[8] was dire,
As this place testifies, and this dire change,   625
Hateful to utter. But what power of mind,
Foreseeing or presaging, from the depth
Of knowledge past or present, could have feared
How such united force of gods, how such
As stood like these, could ever know repulse?   630
For who can yet believe, though after loss,
That all these puissant[9] legions, whose exile
Hath emptied Heaven, shall fail to reascend,
Self-raised, and repossess their native seat?
For me, be witness all the host of Heaven,   635
If counsels different,[1] or danger shunned
By me, have lost our hopes. But he who reigns
Monarch in Heaven, till then as one secure
Sat on his throne, upheld by old repute,
Consent or custom, and his regal state   640
Put forth at full, but still his strength concealed,
Which tempted our attempt,[2] and wrought our fall.
Henceforth his might we know, and know our own,
So as not either to provoke, or dread
New war provoked: our better part remains   645
To work in close design,[3] by fraud or guile,
What force effected not; that he no less
At length from us may find, who overcomes
By force hath overcome but half his foe.
Space may produce new worlds; whereof so rife   650
There went a fame[4] in Heaven that he ere long
Intended to create, and therein plant
A generation whom his choice regard
Should favor equal to the sons of Heaven.
Thither, if but to pry, shall be perhaps   655
Our first eruption—thither, or elsewhere;

8. Outcome, result.
9. Potent, powerful.
1. Contradictory or even selfish, but also, in an obsolete sense, delaying.
2. Satan is an inveterate punster and player on words.
3. I.e., our best choice is to achieve by secret schemes.
4. Rumor. "Rife": common.

For this infernal pit shall never hold
Celestial spirits in bondage, nor th' abyss
Long under darkness cover. But these thoughts
Full counsel must mature. Peace is despaired,   660
For who can think submission? War, then, war
Open or understood,[5] must be resolved."

He spake; and, to confirm his words, outflew
Millions of flaming swords, drawn from the thighs
Of mighty cherubim; the sudden blaze   665
Far round illumined Hell. Highly they raged
Against the Highest, and fierce with graspéd arms
Clashed on their sounding shields the din of war,[6]
Hurling defiance toward the vault of Heaven.

There stood a hill not far, whose grisly[7] top   670
Belched fire and rolling smoke; the rest entire
Shone with a glossy scurf,[8] undoubted sign
That in his womb was hid metallic ore,
The work of sulphur.[9] Thither, winged with speed,
A numerous brigade hastened: as when bands   675
Of pioneers,[1] with spade and pickax armed,
Forerun the royal camp, to trench a field,
Or cast a rampart. Mammon led them on,
Mammon, the least erected[2] spirit that fell
From Heaven; for even in Heaven his looks and thoughts   680
Were always downward bent, admiring more
The riches of Heaven's pavement, trodden gold,
Than aught divine or holy else enjoyed
In vision beatific. By him first
Men also, and by his suggestion taught,   685
Ransacked the center, and with impious hands
Rifled the bowels of their mother Earth
For treasures better hid. Soon had his crew
Opened into the hill a spacious wound,
And digged out ribs[3] of gold. Let none admire   690
That riches grow in Hell; that soil may best
Deserve the precious bane. And here let those
Who boast in mortal things, and wondering tell
Of Babel, and the works of Memphian kings,
Learn how their greatest monuments of fame   695
And strength, and art, are easily outdone
By spirits reprobate,[4] and in an hour
What in an age they, with incessant toil
And hands innumerable, scarce perform.

5. Agreed-upon, tacit, hence secret.
6. Like Roman legionaries, the fallen angels applaud by beating swords on shields.
7. Horrible.
8. Crust.
9. Sulphur and mercury were considered the basic substances of all metals.
1. Sappers, engineers.
2. Elevated. Mammon is not a god but an abstract word meaning "wealth"; cf. Belial.
3. Bars, of course, but also with a hit at Eve, who was a "precious bane" (sweet poison) dug out of Adam's side. "Admire": wonder.
4. The tower of Babel and the Pyramids of Egypt ("works of Memphian kings") are easily outdone by the devils ("spirits reprobate").

Nigh on the plain, in many cells prepared, 700
That underneath had veins of liquid fire
Sluiced from the lake, a second multitude
With wondrous art founded the massy ore,
Severing each kind, and scummed the bullion-dross.
A third as soon had formed within the ground 705
A various mold, and from the boiling cells
By strange conveyance filled each hollow nook;[5]
As in an organ, from one blast of wind,
To many a row of pipes the soundboard breathes.
Anon out of the earth a fabric huge 710
Rose like an exhalation, with the sound
Of dulcet symphonies and voices sweet,
Built like a temple, where pilasters[6] round
Were set, and Doric pillars[7] overlaid
With golden architrave; nor did there want 715
Cornice or frieze, with bossy[8] sculptures graven;
The roof was fretted[9] gold. Not Babylon
Nor great Alcairo such magnificence
Equaled in all their glories,[1] to enshrine
Belus or Serapis their gods, or seat 720
Their kings, when Egypt with Assyria strove
In wealth and luxury. Th' ascending pile
Stood fixed[2] her stately height; and straight the doors,
Opening their brazen folds, discover, wide
Within, her ample spaces o'er the smooth 725
And level pavement: from the archéd roof,
Pendent by subtle magic, many a row
Of starry lamps and blazing cressets,[3] fed
With naphtha and asphaltus, yielded light
As from a sky. The hasty multitude 730
Admiring entered; and the work some praise,
And some the architect. His hand was known
In Heaven by many a towered structure high,
Where sceptered angels held their residence,
And sat as princes, whom the súpreme King 735
Exalted to such power, and gave to rule,
Each in his hierarchy, the orders bright.
Nor was his name unheard or unadored
In ancient Greece; and in Ausonian land
Men called him Mulciber;[4] and how he fell 740

5. After melting the gold with fire from the lake and pouring it into molds, the devils cause their building to rise by a sort of spiritual-musical magic.
6. Columns set in a wall.
7. Doric pillars are severe and plain.
8. Embossed.
9. Patterned.
1. At Babylon in Assyria there were temples to "Belus" or Baal; at Alcairo (modern Cairo, ancient Memphis) in Egypt, they were to Osiris, one of whose names was Serapis (here, but not ordi-

narily, accented on the first syllable).
2. Complete; "straight": straightway.
3. Basketlike lamps, hung from the ceiling.
4. Hephaestus, or Vulcan, was sometimes known in "Ausonian land" (Italy) by the secondary epithet of "Mulciber." The story of Jove's tossing him out of Heaven is told, to the accompaniment of much Homeric laughter, in *Iliad* I. Milton calls him by a secondary name because he is a little uneasy at having to put a "good" Greek deity in Hell.

From Heaven they fabled, thrown by angry Jove
Sheer o'er the crystal battlements: from morn
To noon he fell, from noon to dewy eve,
A summer's day, and with the setting sun
Dropped from the zenith, like a falling star, 745
On Lemnos, th' Aegean isle. Thus they relate,
Erring;[5] for he with this rebellious rout
Fell long before; nor aught availed him now
To have built in Heaven high towers; nor did he 'scape
By all his engines, but was headlong sent, 750
With his industrious crew, to build in Hell.
    Meanwhile the wingéd heralds, by command
Of sovereign power, with awful ceremony
And trumpet's sound, throughout the host proclaim
A solemn council forthwith to be held 755
At Pandemonium,[6] the high capital
Of Satan and his peers.[7] Their summons called
From every band and squaréd regiment
By place or choice the worthiest; they anon
With hundreds and with thousands trooping came 760
Attended. All access was thronged, the gates
And porches wide, but chief the spacious hall
(Though like a covered field, where champions bold
Wont ride in armed, and at the soldan's[8] chair
Defied the best of paynim chivalry 765
To mortal combat, or career with lance),
Thick swarmed, both on the ground and in the air,
Brushed with the hiss of rustling wings. As bees
In springtime, when the sun with Taurus[9] rides,
Pour forth their populous youth about the hive 770
In clusters; they among fresh dews and flowers
Fly to and fro, or on the smoothéd plank,
The suburb of their straw-built citadel,
New rubbed with balm, expatiate, and confer[1]
Their state-affairs: so thick the airy crowd 775
Swarmed and were straitened; till, the signal given,
Behold a wonder! They but now who seemed
In bigness to surpass Earth's giant sons,
Now less than smallest dwarfs, in narrow room
Throng numberless—like that pygmean race 780
Beyond the Indian mount;[2] or faery elves,
Whose midnight revels, by a forest side
Or fountain, some belated peasant sees,

5. Milton tells the story, and gives it
six lines of splendid poetry (740–46),
but in the end condemns it as a corrupt
version of the Biblical truth.
6. "Pandemonium" means literally
"All-Demons"; an inversion of Pantheon, "All-Gods."
7. Nobility.
8. Sultan's. "Paynim": pagan.

9. The sun is in the Zodiacal sign of
Taurus from April 19 to May 20.
1. Spread out and discuss, bring together. The simile of bees prepares for
the sudden contraction of the devils'
size; they can shrink or dilate at will.
2. The pygmies were supposed to live
beyond the Himalayas, "the Indian
mount."

Or dreams he sees, while overhead the Moon
Sits arbitress,[3] and nearer to the Earth 785
Wheels her pale course; they, on their mirth and dance
Intent, with jocund[4] music charm his ear;
At once with joy and fear his heart rebounds.
Thus incorporeal spirits to smallest forms
Reduced their shapes immense, and were at large, 790
Though without number still, amidst the hall
Of that infernal court. But far within,
And in their own dimensions like themselves,
The great seraphic lords and cherubim
In close recess and secret conclave sat, 795
A thousand demigods on golden seats,
Frequent and full.[5] After short silence then,
And summons read, the great consult began.

Book II

The Argument

The consultation begun, Satan debates whether another battle be to be hazarded for the recovery of Heaven: some advise it, others dissuade. A third proposal is preferred, mentioned before by Satan —to search the truth of that prophecy or tradition in Heaven concerning another world, and another kind of creature, equal or not much inferior to themselves, about this time to be created. Their doubt who shall be sent on this difficult search: Satan, their chief, undertakes alone the voyage; is honored and applauded. The council thus ended, the rest betake them several ways and to several employments, as their inclinations lead them, to entertain[1] the time till Satan return. He passes on his journey to Hell-gates; finds them shut, and who sat there to guard them; by whom at length they are opened, and discover[2] to him the great gulf between Hell and Heaven. With what difficulty he passes through, directed by Chaos, the power of that place, to the sight of this new world which he sought.

High on a throne of royal state, which far
Outshone the wealth of Ormus[3] and of Ind,
Or where the gorgeous East with richest hand
Showers on her kings barbaric pearl and gold,
Satan exalted sat, by merit raised 5
To that bad eminence; and, from despair

3. Witness.
4. Merry.
5. Crowded ("frequent") and in full complement ("full"); all present and accounted for.

1. Pass.
2. Disclose.
3. An island in the Persian Gulf, modern Hormuz, famous for pearls. "Ind": India

Thus high uplifted beyond hope, aspires
Beyond thus high, insatiate to pursue
Vain war with Heaven; and, by success[4] untaught,
His proud imaginations thus displayed: 10
    "Powers and dominions, deities of Heaven!
For since no deep within her gulf can hold
Immortal vigor, though oppressed and fallen,
I give not Heaven for lost: from this descent
Celestial virtues rising will appear   15
More glorious and more dread than from no fall,
And trust themselves to fear no second fate.
Me though just right, and the fixed laws of Heaven
Did first create your leader, next, free choice,
With what besides, in council or in fight,   20
Hath been achieved of merit, yet this loss
Thus far at least recovered, hath much more
Established in a safe unenvied throne
Yielded with full consent.[5] The happier state
In Heaven, which follows dignity, might draw   25
Envy from each inferior; but who here
Will envy whom the highest place exposes
Foremost to stand against the Thunderer's aim,
Your bulwark, and condemns to greatest share
Of endless pain? Where there is then no good   30
For which to strive, no strife can grow up there
From faction; for none sure will claim in Hell
Precédence, none, whose portion is so small
Of present pain, that with ambitious mind
Will covet more. With this advantage then   35
To union, and firm faith, and firm accord,
More than can be in Heaven, we now return
To claim our just inheritance of old,
Surer to prosper than prosperity
Could have assured us;[6] and by what best way,   40
Whether of open war or covert guile,
We now debate; who can advise, may speak."
    He ceased, and next him Moloch, sceptered king,
Stood up, the strongest and the fiercest spirit
That fought in Heaven, now fiercer by despair.   45
His trust was with th' Eternal to be deemed
Equal in strength, and rather than be less
Cared not to be at all; with that care lost
Went all his fear: of God, or Hell, or worse
He recked[7] not, and these words thereafter spake: 50

---

4. Outcome, result; experience of either sort, good or bad.
5. He lays claim to the throne by just right, fixed laws, free choice—and the fact that no one else will want such a dangerous job.
6. Note the play on "sure—prosper—prosperity—assured." An Elizabethan critic famous for his picturesque terminology, George Puttenham, calls this figure *"epanalepsis,* or the echo sound, otherwise the slow return." It is a favorite device of Milton's.
7. Cared.

"My sentence[8] is for open war: of wiles,
More unexpert,[9] I boast not: them let those
Contrive who need, or when they need, not now.
For while they sit contriving, shall the rest,
Millions that stand in arms, and longing wait   55
The signal to ascend, sit lingering here
Heaven's fugitives, and for their dwelling place
Accept this dark opprobrious den of shame,
The prison of his tyranny who reigns
By our delay? No! let us rather choose,   60
Armed with Hell-flames and fury, all at once
O'er Heaven's high towers to force resistless way,
Turning our tortures into horrid arms
Against the Torturer; when to meet the noise
Of his almighty engine[1] he shall hear   65
Infernal thunder, and for lightning see
Black fire and horror shot with equal rage
Among his angels, and his throne itself
Mixed with Tartarean[2] sulphur, and strange fire,
His own invented torments. But perhaps   70
The way seems difficult and steep to scale
With upright wing against a higher foe.
Let such bethink them, if the sleepy drench[3]
Of that forgetful lake benumb not still,
That in our proper motion[4] we ascend   75
Up to our native seat; descent and fall
To us is adverse. Who but felt of late,
When the fierce foe hung on our broken rear
Insulting,[5] and pursued us through the deep,
With what compulsion and laborious flight   80
We sunk thus low? Th' ascent is easy then;
Th' event[6] is feared: should we again provoke
Our stronger,[7] some worse way his wrath may find
To our destruction; if there be in Hell
Fear to be worse destroyed! What can be worse   85
Than to dwell here, driven out from bliss, condemned
In this abhorréd deep to utter woe;
Where pain of unextinguishable fire
Must exercise us without hope of end,
The vassals[8] of his anger, when the scourge   90
Inexorably, and the torturing hour,
Calls us to penance? More destroyed than thus,
We should be quite abolished, and expire.
What fear we then? what[9] doubt we to incense

8. Judgment.
9. Inexperienced. Moloch never had to be clever, and is proud of it.
1. The thunderbolt.
2. Tartarus is a classical name for Hell.
3. A draught of physic, as for animals; hence, used contemptuously here.
4. Natural impulse.

5. With the Latin sense of stamping or dancing on.
6. Outcome.
7. The word "enemy" is understood.
8. Servants, underlings; but perhaps also—or alternatively—"vessels."
9. Why.

His utmost ire? Which, to the height enraged,   95
Will either quite consume us, and reduce
To nothing this essential,[1] happier far
Than miserable to have eternal being!
Or if our substance be indeed divine,
And cannot cease to be, we are at worst   100
On this side nothing;[2] and by proof we feel
Our power sufficient to disturb his Heaven,
And with perpetual inroads to alarm,
Though inaccessible, his fatal throne:
Which, if not victory, is yet revenge."   105
　　He ended frowning, and his look denounced
Desperate revenge, and battle dangerous
To less than gods.[3] On th' other side up rose
Belial, in act more graceful and humane;
A fairer person lost not Heaven; he seemed   110
For dignity composed, and high exploit.
But all was false and hollow; though his tongue
Dropped manna,[4] and could make the worse appear
The better reason, to perplex and dash
Maturest counsels: for his thoughts were low,   115
To vice industrious, but to nobler deeds
Timorous and slothful: yet he pleased the ear,
And with persuasive accent thus began:
　　"I should be much for open war, O peers,
As not behind in hate, if what was urged   120
Main reason to persuade immediate war,
Did not dissuade me most, and seem to cast
Ominous conjecture on the whole success;[5]
When he who most excels in fact of arms,
In what he counsels, and in what excels   125
Mistrustful, grounds his courage on despair
And utter dissolution, as the scope
Of all his aim, after some dire revenge.
First, what revenge? The towers of Heaven are filled
With arméd watch, that render all access   130
Impregnable; oft on the bordering deep
Encamp their legions, or with óbscure wing
Scout far and wide into the realm of Night,
Scorning surprise. Or could we break our way
By force, and at our heels all Hell should rise   135
With blackest insurrection, to confound
Heaven's purest light, yet our great enemy
All incorruptible would on his throne

---

1. Essence.
2. I.e., we are now as badly off as we can be without being nothing, and so need have no fear.
3. Only gods could have withstood Moloch.
4. His tongue was honeyed. To "make the worse appear / The better reason" was characteristic of Sophists—hollow, mercenary logic-choppers of ancient Greece. "Dash": confuse.
5. As above, line 9, outcome. "Fact": feat.

Sit unpolluted, and th' ethereal mold[6]
Incapable of stain would soon expel   140
Her mischief, and purge off the baser fire,
Victorious. Thus repulsed, our final hope
Is flat despair: we must exasperate
Th' almighty Victor to spend all his rage,
And that must end us, that must be our cure,   145
To be no more. Sad cure! for who would lose,
Though full of pain, this intellectual being,
Those thoughts that wander through eternity,
To perish rather, swallowed up and lost
In the wide womb of uncreated Night,   150
Devoid of sense and motion? And who knows,
Let this be good,[7] whether our angry Foe
Can give it, or will ever? How he can
Is doubtful; that he never will is sure.
Will he, so wise, let loose at once his ire,   155
Belike[8] through impotence, or unaware,
To give his enemies their wish, and end
Them in his anger, whom his anger saves
To punish endless? 'Wherefore cease we then?'
Say they who counsel war, 'we are decreed,   160
Reserved and destined to eternal woe;
Whatever doing, what can we suffer more,
What can we suffer worse?' Is this then worst,
Thus sitting, thus consulting, thus in arms?
What when we fled amain,[9] pursued and strook   165
With Heaven's afflicting thunder, and besought
The deep to shelter us? this Hell then seemed
A refuge from those wounds. Or when we lay
Chained on the burning lake? that sure was worse.
What if the breath that kindled those grim fires,   170
Awaked, should blow them into sevenfold rage,
And plunge us in the flames? or from above
Should intermitted[1] vengeance arm again
His red right hand to plague us? What if all
Her[2] stores were opened, and this firmament   175
Of Hell should spout her cataracts of fire,
Impendent[3] horrors, threatening hideous fall
One day upon our heads; while we perhaps
Designing or exhorting glorious war,
Caught in a fiery tempest shall be hurled,   180
Each on his rock transfixed, the sport and prey
Of racking whirlwinds, or forever sunk
Under yon boiling ocean, wrapped in chains;

6. Substance. "Ethereal" substance, derived from "ether," is thought to be incorruptible.
7. I.e., suppose it is good to be destroyed.
8. Ironically, in the sense of "I dare say."
9. Headlong. "Strook": struck.
1. Momentarily suspended.
2. Those of Hell.
3. In the Latin sense, hanging down, threatening.

There to converse with everlasting groans,
Unrespited, unpitied, unreprieved,   185
Ages of hopeless end! This would be worse.
War therefore, open or concealed, alike
My voice dissuades; for what can force or guile[4]
With him, or who deceive his mind, whose eye
Views all things at one view? He from Heaven's height   190
All these our motions[5] vain, sees and derides,
Not more almighty to resist our might
Than wise to frustrate all our plots and wiles.
Shall we then live thus vile, the race of Heaven
Thus trampled, thus expelled to suffer here   195
Chains and these torments? Better these than worse,
By my advice; since fate inevitable
Subdues us, and omnipotent decree,
The Victor's will. To suffer, as to do,
Our strength is equal,[6] nor the law unjust   200
That so ordains: this was at first resolved,
If we were wise, against so great a foe
Contending, and so doubtful what might fall.
I laugh, when those who at the spear are bold
And venturous, if that fail them, shrink and fear   205
What yet they know must follow, to endure
Exile, or ignominy, or bonds, or pain,
The sentence of their Conqueror. This is now
Our doom; which if we can sustain and bear,
Our súpreme Foe in time may much remit   210
His anger, and perhaps, thus far removed,
Not mind us not offending, satisfied
With what is punished;[7] whence these raging fires
Will slacken, if his breath stir not their flames.
Our purer essence then will overcome   215
Their noxious vapor, or inured[8] not feel,
Or changed at length, and to the place conformed
In temper and in nature, will receive
Familiar the fierce heat, and void of pain;
This horror will grow mild, this darkness light;   220
Besides what hope the never-ending flight
Of future days may bring, what chance, what change
Worth waiting, since our present lot appears
For happy though but ill, for ill not worst,[9]
If we procure not to ourselves more woe."   225
     Thus Belial, with words clothed in reason's garb,

4. The verb "accomplish" or "achieve" is omitted.
5. Proposals, plots.
6. I.e., passive endurance and active energy are both in the devils' power. Belial points out, with dangerous good sense, that they must have known from the beginning that they might have to exercise both (lines 201–3).

7. A Latinism, *quod punitum est;* God will be satisfied with the punishment that has been inflicted.
8. Accustomed.
9. I.e., from the point of view of happiness, the devils are but ill off; from the point of view of evil, they could be worse. This is diabolic relativism.

Counseled ignoble ease and peaceful sloth,
Not peace; and after him thus Mammon spake:
  "Either to disenthrone the King of Heaven
We war, if war be best, or to regain   230
Our own right lost: him to unthrone we then
May hope, when everlasting Fate shall yield
To fickle Chance, and Chaos judge the strife.
The former, vain to hope, argues[1] as vain
The latter; for what place can be for us   235
Within Heaven's bound, unless Heaven's Lord supreme
We overpower? Suppose he should relent
And publish grace to all, on promise made
Of new subjection; with what eyes could we
Stand in his presence humble, and receive   240
Strict laws imposed, to celebrate his throne
With warbled hymns, and to his Godhead sing
Forced Halleluiahs; while he lordly sits
Our envied Sovereign, and his altar breathes
Ambrosial odors and ambrosial flowers,   245
Our servile offerings? This must be our task
In Heaven, this our delight; how wearisome
Eternity so spent in worship paid
To whom we hate! Let us not then pursue,
By force impossible, by leave obtained   250
Unácceptable, though in Heaven, our state
Of spendid vassalage;[2] but rather seek
Our own good from ourselves, and from our own
Live to ourselves, though in this vast recess,
Free, and to none accountable, preferring   255
Hard liberty before the easy yoke
Of servile pomp. Our greatness will appear
Then most conspicuous, when great things of small,
Useful of hurtful, prosperous of adverse,
We can create, and in what place soe'er   260
Thrive under evil, and work ease out of pain
Through labor and endurance. This deep world
Of darkness do we dread? How oft amidst
Thick clouds and dark doth Heaven's all-ruling Sire
Choose to reside, his glory unobscured,   265
And with the majesty of darkness round
Covers his throne; from whence deep thunders roar,
Mustering their rage, and Heaven resembles Hell!
As he our darkness, cannot we his light
Imitate when we please? This desert soil   270
Wants[3] not her hidden luster, gems, and gold;
Nor want we skill or art, from whence to raise
Magnificence; and what can Heaven show more?

---

1. Proves.
2. Servitude.
3. Lacks. Mammon proposes a tawdry
imitation-Heaven in Hell; this is the
ultimate in diabolic degradation.

Our torments also may in length of time
Become our elements, these piercing fires   275
As soft as now severe, our temper changed
Into their temper; which must needs remove
The sensible[4] of pain. All things invite
To peaceful counsels, and the settled state
Of order, how in safety best we may   280
Compose our present evils, with regard
Of what we are and where, dismissing quite
All thoughts of war. Ye have what I advise."
    He scarce had finished, when such murmur filled
Th' assembly, as when hollow rocks retain   285
The sound of blustering winds, which all night long
Had roused the sea, now with hoarse cadence lull
Seafaring men o'erwatched,[5] whose bark by chance,
Or pinnace, anchors in a craggy bay
After the tempest: such applause was heard   290
As Mammon ended, and his sentence pleased,
Advising peace; for such another field
They dreaded worse than Hell; so much the fear
Of thunder and the sword of Michaël[6]
Wrought still within them; and no less desire   295
To found this nether empire, which might rise
By policy, and long process of time,
In emulation opposite to Heaven.
Which when Beëlzebub perceived, than whom,
Satan except, none higher sat, with grave   300
Aspect he rose, and in his rising seemed
A pillar of state; deep on his front[7] engraven
Deliberation sat and public care;
And princely counsel in his face yet shone,
Majestic though in ruin. Sage he stood   305
With Atlantean[8] shoulders fit to bear
The weight of mightiest monarchies; his look
Drew audience and attention still as night
Or summer's noontide air, while thus he spake:
    "Thrones and imperial powers, offspring of Heaven,   310
Ethereal virtues; or these titles now
Must we renounce, and, changing style, be called
Princes of Hell? For so the popular vote
Inclines, here to continue, and build up here
A growing empire—Doubtless! while we dream,   315
And know not that the King of Heaven hath doomed
This place our dungeon, not our safe retreat
Beyond his potent arm, to live exempt
From Heaven's high jurisdiction, in new league

---

4. Sense, sensation.
5. Tired out with watching.
6. The warrior angel, chief stay of the
angelic armies.
7. Forehead, brow.

8. Worthy of Atlas, one of the Titans,
who as a punishment for rebellion was
condemned to stand in North Africa
and hold up the heavens.

Banded against his throne, but to remain   320
In strictest bondage, though thus far removed,
Under th' inevitable curb, reserved
His captive multitude. For he, be sure,
In height or depth, still first and last will reign
Sole King, and of his kingdom lose no part   325
By our revolt, but over Hell extend
His empire, and with iron scepter rule
Us here, as with his golden those in Heaven.
What⁹ sit we then projecting peace and war?
War hath determined us,¹ and foiled with loss   330
Irreparable; terms of peace yet none
Vouchsafed or sought; for what peace will be given
To us enslaved, but custody severe,
And stripes, and arbitrary punishment
Inflicted? and what peace can we return,   335
But, to our power,² hostility and hate,
Untamed reluctance,³ and revenge, though slow,
Yet ever plotting how the Conqueror least
May reap his conquest, and may least rejoice
In doing what we most in suffering feel?⁴   340
Nor will occasion want, nor shall we need
With dangerous expedition to invade
Heaven, whose high walls fear no assault or siege,
Or ambush from the deep. What if we find
Some easier enterprise? There is a place   345
(If ancient and prophetic fame⁵ in Heaven
Err not), another world, the happy seat
Of some new race called *Man*, about this time
To be created like to us,⁶ though less
In power and excellence, but favored more   350
Of him who rules above; so was his will
Pronounced among the gods, and by an oath,
That shook Heaven's whole circumference, confirmed.
Thither let us bend all our thoughts, to learn
What creatures there inhabit, of what mold,   355
Or substance, how endured,⁷ and what their power,
And where their weakness, how attempted⁸ best,
By force or subtlety. Though Heaven be shut,
And Heaven's high Arbitrator sit secure
In his own strength, this place may lie exposed,   360
The utmost border of his kingdom, left
To their defense who hold it;⁹ here, perhaps,

---

9. Why.
1. I.e., war has decided the question for (but also, limited) us.
2. I.e., to the best of our power.
3. Resistance (in the Latin sense, struggling back).
4. How God may get least pleasure from our pain—a devil's view of the deity.

5. Report, rumor.
6. The created (Ptolemaic) cosmos only came into existence after the fall of Satan, and the fallen angels, being otherwise occupied, could not know of it.
7. Endowed.
8. Attacked, but also "tempted."
9. To be defended by the occupants.

Some advantageous act may be achieved
By sudden onset: either with Hell-fire
To waste[1] his whole creation, or possess   365
All as our own, and drive, as we were driven,
The puny habitants; or if not drive,
Seduce them to our party, that their God
May prove their foe, and with repenting hand
Abolish his own works. This would surpass   370
Common revenge, and interrupt his joy
In our confusion, and our joy upraise
In his disturbance; when his darling sons,
Hurled headlong to partake with us, shall curse
Their frail original,[2] and faded bliss,   375
Faded so soon! Advise if this be worth
Attempting, or to sit in darkness here
Hatching vain empires." Thus Beëlzebub
Pleaded his devilish counsel, first devised
By Satan, and in part proposed; for whence,   380
But from the author of all ill could spring
So deep a malice, to confound[3] the race
Of mankind in one root, and Earth with Hell
To mingle and involve, done all to spite
The great Creator? But their spite still serves   385
His glory to augment. The bold design
Pleased highly those infernal states, and joy
Sparkled in all their eyes; with full assent
They vote: whereat his speech he thus renews:
    "Well have ye judged, well ended long debate,   390
Synod of gods, and, like to what ye are,
Great things resolved; which from the lowest deep
Will once more lift us up, in spite of Fate,
Nearer our ancient seat; perhaps in view
Of those bright confines, whence with neighboring arms   395
And opportune excursion we may chance
Re-enter Heaven; or else in some mild zone
Dwell not unvisited of Heaven's fair light,
Secure, and at the brightening orient beam
Purge off this gloom; the soft delicious air,   400
To heal the scar of these corrosive fires,
Shall breathe her balm. But first, whom shall we send
In search of this new world? whom shall we find
Sufficient? who shall tempt[4] with wandering feet
The dark, unbottomed, infinite abyss,   405
And through the palpable obscure[5] find out
His uncouth way, or spread his airy flight
Upborn with indefatigable wings

1. Lay waste.
2. Originator, parent; or, perhaps,
"their original condition."
3. Destroy, ruin. Adam, the first man,
is the "root" of mankind.
4. Try, attempt (from Latin *temptare*).
5. Darkness so thick it can be felt.
"Uncouth": strange, new.

Over the vast abrupt,[6] ere he arrive
The happy isle?[7] What strength, what art, can then   410
Suffice, or what evasion bear him safe
Through the strict senteries[8] and stations thick
Of angels watching round? Here he had need
All circumspection, and we now no less
Choice in our suffrage;[9] for on whom we send   415
The weight of all, and our last hope, relies."
    This said, he sat; and expectation held
His look suspense,[1] awaiting who appeared
To second, or oppose, or undertake
The perilous attempt; but all sat mute,   420
Pondering the danger with deep thoughts; and each
In others' countenance read his own dismay,
Astonished. None among the choice and prime
Of those Heaven-warring champions could be found
So hardy as to proffer or accept   425
Alone the dreadful voyage; till at last
Satan, whom now transcendent glory raised
Above his fellows, with monarchal pride
Conscious of highest worth, unmoved thus spake:
    "O progeny of Heaven, empyreal thrones!   430
With reason hath deep silence and demur[2]
Seized us, though undismayed. Long is the way
And hard, that out of Hell leads up to light;
Our prison strong, this huge convex[3] of fire,
Outrageous to devour, immures us round   435
Ninefold,[4] and gates of burning adamant,
Barred over us, prohibit all egress.
These passed, if any pass, the void profound
Of unessential[5] Night receives him next,
Wide gaping, and with utter loss of being   440
Threatens him, plunged in that abortive gulf.
If thence he 'scape into whatever world,
Or unknown region, what remains him less[6]
Than unknown dangers and as hard escape?
But I should ill become this throne, O peers,   445
And this imperial sovereignty, adorned
With splendor, armed with power, if aught proposed
And judged of public moment,[7] in the shape
Of difficulty or danger, could deter
Me from attempting. Wherefore do I assume   450

6. Chaos; a striking example of sound imitating sense.
7. Wherever man is (for the fallen angels do not yet know of Earth).
8. Old spelling of *sentries*, necessary here for the meter.
9. Care in our voting.
1. I.e., everyone sat waiting in suspense.
2. Delay.
3. Vault.

4. Walls us in with nine thicknesses. See below, lines 645 ff.
5. Without real being, darkness being merely the absence of light. The "abortive gulf" expresses again this completely negative quality of Chaos and Night.
6. I.e., what awaits him except.
7. Importance.

These royalties,[8] and not refuse to reign,
Refusing to accept as great a share
Of hazard as of honor, due alike
To him who reigns, and so much to him due
Of hazard more, as he above the rest   455
High honored sits?[9] Go therefore, mighty powers,
Terror of Heaven, though fallen; intend[1] at home,
While here shall be our home, what best may ease
The present misery, and render Hell
More tolerable; if there be cure or charm   460
To respite, or deceive, or slack the pain
Of this ill mansion; intermit no watch
Against a wakeful foe, while I abroad
Through all the coasts of dark destruction seek
Deliverance for us all: this enterprise   465
None shall partake with me." Thus saying, rose
The monarch, and prevented[2] all reply;
Prudent, lest, from his resolution raised,[3]
Others among the chief might offer now
(Certain to be refused) what erst they feared,   470
And, so refused, might in opinion stand
His rivals, winning cheap the high repute
Which he through hazard huge must earn. But they
Dreaded not more th' adventure than his voice
Forbidding; and at once with him they rose;   475
Their rising all at once was as the sound
Of thunder heard remote. Towards him they bend
With awful[4] reverence prone; and as a god
Extol him equal to the Highest in Heaven.
Nor failed they to express how much they praised,   480
That for the general safety he despised
His own; for neither do the spirits damned
Lose all their virtue; lest bad men should boast
Their specious deeds on Earth, which glory excites,
Or close ambition varnished o'er with zeal.[5]   485
    Thus they their doubtful consultations dark
Ended, rejoicing in their matchless chief:
As when from mountain tops the dusky clouds
Ascending, while the north wind sleeps, o'erspread
Heaven's cheerful face, the lowering element   490
Scowls o'er the darkened landscape snow or shower;
If chance the radiant sun with farewell sweet
Extend his evening beam, the fields revive,

8. Insignia of royalty. "Refusing": i.e., if I refuse.
9. Satan's argument, simple though entangled in rhetoric, is that rulers must share in the dangers as well as the rewards of an enterprise.
1. Undertake, endeavor.
2. Forestalled, anticipated.
3. After their courage had been raised by his resolution.
4. Full of respect and awe.
5. The sense is that damned spirits still retain some virtues; lest bad men boast of good deeds they have done out of glory and ambition, Milton has shown us that devils do just as much. "Specious": pretending virtue. "Close": secret.

The birds their notes renew, and bleating herds
Attest their joy, that hill and valley rings.   495
O shame to men! Devil with devil damned
Firm concord holds, men only disagree
Of creatures rational, though under hope
Of heavenly grace; and, God proclaiming peace,[6]
Yet live in hatred, enmity, and strife   500
Among themselves, and levy cruel wars,
Wasting the earth, each other to destroy:
As if (which might induce us to accord)
Man had not hellish foes enow[7] besides,
That day and night for his destruction wait!   505
    The Stygian council thus dissolved; and forth
In order came the grand infernal peers.
Midst came their mighty paramount,[8] and seemed
Alone th' antagonist of Heaven, nor less
Than Hell's dread emperor, with pomp supreme,   510
And godlike imitated state; him round
A globe[9] of fiery seraphim enclosed
With bright emblazonry,[1] and horrent arms.
Then of their session ended they bid cry
With trumpets' regal sound the great result: 515
Toward the four winds four speedy cherubim
Put to their mouths the sounding alchemy[2]
By herald's voice explained; the hollow abyss
Heard far and wide, and all the host of Hell
With deafening shout, returned them loud acclaim.   520
Thence more at ease their minds and somewhat raised
By false presumptuous hope, the rangèd[3] powers
Disband; and, wandering, each his several way
Pursues, as inclination or sad choice
Leads him perplexed where he may likeliest find   525
Truce to his restless thoughts, and entertain
The irksome hours, till his great chief return.
Part on the plain, or in the air sublime,[4]
Upon the wing, or in swift race contend,
As at th' Olympian games or Pythian fields;[5]   530
Part curb their fiery steeds, or shun the goal
With rapid wheels, or fronted brígades form.
As when, to warn proud cities, war appears
Waged in the troubled sky, and armies rush
To battle in the clouds;[6] before each van   535
Prick forth the airy knights, and couch their spears

6. I.e., though God proclaims peace.
7. I.e., enough; the old plural emphatic form.
8. Champion, chief.
9. Band or crowd.
1. Decorated shields. "Horrent": bristling.
2. I.e., resonant trumpets (made of the alloy brass by a marriage of metals which Milton associates with alchemy).

3. Arrayed in ranks.
4. Aloft, uplifted (the adjective modifies the flyer, not the air).
5. The Olympic games were held at Olympia, the Pythian games at Delphi. To "shun the goal" is to drive a chariot as close as possible around a column without hitting it.
6. Warfare in the skies at night, portending trouble on earth. "Prick": spur.

Till thickest legions close; with feats of arms
From either end of Heaven the welkin[7] burns.
Others with vast Typhoean[8] rage more fell
Rend up both rocks and hills, and ride the air   540
In whirlwind; Hell scarce holds the wild uproar.
As when Alcides, from Oechalia crowned
With conquest, felt th' envenomed robe, and tore
Through pain up by the roots Thessalian pines,
And Lichas from the top of Oeta threw   545
Into th' Euboic sea.[9] Others more mild,
Retreated in a silent valley, sing
With notes angelical to many a harp
Their own heroic deeds and hapless fall
By doom of battle; and complain that Fate   550
Free Virtue should enthrall to Force or Chance.
Their song was partial,[1] but the harmony
(What could it less when spirits immortal sing?)
Suspended[2] Hell, and took with ravishment
The thronging audience. In discourse more sweet   555
(For eloquence the soul, song charms the sense)
Others apart sat on a hill retired,
In thoughts more elevate, and reasoned high
Of providence, foreknowledge, will, and fate,
Fixed fate, free will, foreknowledge absolute,   560
And found no end, in wandering mazes lost.
Of good and evil much they argued then,
Of happiness and final misery,
Passion and apathy,[3] and glory and shame,
Vain wisdom all, and false philosophy![4]   565
Yet with a pleasing sorcery could charm
Pain for a while or anguish, and excite
Fallacious hope, or arm th' obduréd[5] breast
With stubborn patience as with triple steel.
Another part, in squadrons and gross[6] bands,   570
On bold adventure to discover wide
That dismal world, if any clime perhaps
Might yield them easier habitation, bend
Four ways their flying march, along the banks
Of four infernal rivers that disgorge   575

7. Sky.
8. Like that of Typhon, the hundred-headed Titan. See above, I.199.
9. Hercules, returning in triumph from Oechalia, prepared to sacrifice to the gods on top of Mt. Oeta, and sent to his wife Dejanira for a new robe. She had been told by the dying Nessus, a centaur whom Hercules had killed, that centaur's blood would preserve her husband's love. So she sent Hercules a robe anointed with the blood of Nessus. The "envenomed robe" tortured him into a frenzy, and before he died, he threw Lichas, who had brought it, together with a good part of Mt. Oeta itself, into the sea of Euboea.
1. Prejudiced.
2. Held in suspense.
3. Feeling and lack of feeling; the angels are dabbling in Stoicism.
4. Milton means, not that the subjects themselves are vain (he himself, in the present poem, has a good deal to say on these topics), but that the very premises with which devils start are bound to land them in error.
5. Hardened.
6. Solid, dense.

Into the burning lake their baleful streams:[7]
Abhorréd Styx, the flood of deadly hate;
Sad Acheron of sorrow, black and deep;
Cocytus, named of lamentation loud
Heard on the rueful stream; fierce Phlegethon   580
Whose waves of torrent fire inflame with rage.
Far off from these a slow and silent stream,
Lethe, the river of oblivion, rolls
Her watery labyrinth, whereof who drinks
Forthwith his former state and being forgets,   585
Forgets both joy and grief, pleasure and pain.
Beyond this flood a frozen continent
Lies dark and wild, beat with perpetual storms
Of whirlwind and dire hail, which on firm land
Thaws not, but gathers heap,[8] and ruin seems   590
Of ancient pile; all else deep snow and ice,
A gulf profound as that Serbonian bog[9]
Betwixt Damiata and Mount Casius old,
Where armies whole have sunk: the parching air
Burns frore,[1] and cold performs th' effect of fire.   595
Thither by harpy-footed[2] Furies haled,
At certain revolutions[3] all the damned
Are brought; and feel by turns the bitter change
Of fierce extremes, extremes by change more fierce,
From beds of raging fire to starve[4] in ice   600
Their soft ethereal warmth, and there to pine
Immovable, infixed, and frozen round
Periods of time; thence hurried back to fire.
They ferry over this Lethean sound
Both to and fro, their sorrow to augment,   605
And wish and struggle, as they pass, to reach
The tempting stream, with one small drop to lose
In sweet forgetfulness all pain and woe,
All in one moment, and so near the brink;
But Fate withstands, and to oppose th' attempt   610
Medusa[5] with Gorgonian terror guards
The ford, and of itself the water flies
All taste of living wight, as once it fled
The lips of Tantalus.[6] Thus roving on
In cónfused march forlorn, th' adventurous bands   615

7. The four rivers are traditional in hellish geography; Milton takes pains to distinguish them by the original meanings of their Greek names (Styx means "hateful," Acheron "woeful," etc.).
8. In a heap, so that it looks like the ruin of an old building ("ancient pile").
9. Lake Serbonis, once famous for its quicksands but today dried up, used to lie on the coast of Egypt, just east of the Nile, between Damiata and Mt. Cassius.

1. Frosty.
2. With hooked claws.
3. I.e., of time.
4. Benumb.
5. One of the three Gorgons, women with snaky hair, scaly bodies, and boar's tusks, the very sight of whose faces changed men to stone.
6. Tantalus, afflicted with a raging thirst, stood in the middle of a lake, the water of which always eluded his grasp (hence, "tantalize").

With shuddering horror pale, and eyes aghast
Viewed first their lamentable lot, and found
No rest. Through many a dark and dreary vale
They passed, and many a region dolorous,
O'er many a frozen, many a fiery alp,[7]   620
Rocks, caves, lakes, fens, bogs, dens, and shades of death,
A universe of death, which God by curse
Created evil, for evil only good,
Where all life dies, death lives, and Nature breeds,
Perverse, all monstrous, all prodigious things,   625
Abominable, unutterable, and worse
Than fables yet have feigned, or fear conceived,
Gorgons, and Hydras, and Chimeras[8] dire.
    Meanwhile the adversary of God and man,
Satan with thoughts inflamed of highest design,   630
Puts on swift wings,[9] and toward the gates of Hell
Explores his solitary flight; sometimes
He scours the right hand coast, sometimes the left;
Now shaves with level wing the deep, then soars
Up to the fiery concave[1] towering high.   635
As when far off at sea a fleet descried
Hangs in the clouds, by equinoctial winds
Close sailing from Bengala,[2] or the isles
Of Ternate and Tidore,[3] whence merchants bring
Their spicy drugs; they on the trading flood   640
Through the wide Ethiopian[4] to the Cape
Ply stemming nightly toward the pole: so seemed
Far off the flying fiend. At last appear
Hell bounds, high reaching to the horrid roof,
And thrice threefold the gates; three folds were brass,   645
Three iron, three of adamantine rock,
Impenetrable, impaled with circling fire,
Yet unconsumed. Before the gates there sat
On either side a formidable shape;[5]
The one seemed woman to the waist, and fair,   650
But ended foul in many a scaly fold
Voluminous and vast, a serpent armed
With mortal sting. About her middle round
A cry[6] of Hellhounds never-ceasing barked

---

7. A "fiery alp" is a volcano.
8. The Hydra was a serpent with nine heads, which was slain by Hercules; the Chimera was a fire-breathing creature, part lion, part dragon, part goat. They exemplify abominations of nature.
9. Satan does not fasten on his wings; he takes swiftly to wing.
1. Vault.
2. An old form of "Bengal."
3. Two of the Molucca or "Spice" Islands, modern Indonesia.
4. The Indian Ocean, east of Africa. "The Cape" is of course the Cape of Good Hope; "the pole," the South Pole.
5. The allegorical figures of Sin and Death are founded on James i.15: "Then when lust hath conceived, it bringeth forth sin: and sin, when it is finished, bringeth forth death." But the incestuous relations of Sin and Death are Milton's own invention. Physically, Sin is modeled on Virgil's or Ovid's, with some touches adopted from Spenser's Error; Death is a traditional figure, vague and vast.
6. Pack.

With wide Cerberean[7] mouths full loud, and rung   655
A hideous peal; yet, when they list, would creep,
If aught disturbed their noise, into her womb,
And kennel there, yet there still barked and howled
Within unseen. Far less abhorred than these
Vexed Scylla,[8] bathing in the sea that parts   660
Calabria from the hoarse Trinacrian shore;
Nor uglier follow the night-hag,[9] when, called
In secret, riding through the air she comes,
Lured with the smell of infant blood, to dance
With Lapland witches, while the laboring moon   665
Eclipses at their charms. The other shape,
If shape it might be called that shape had none
Distinguishable in member, joint, or limb,
Or substance might be called that shadow seemed,
For each seemed either; black it stood as night,   670
Fierce as ten Furies, terrible as Hell,
And shook a dreadful dart; what seemed his head
The likeness of a kingly crown had on.
Satan was now at hand, and from his seat
The monster moving onward came as fast,   675
With horrid strides; Hell trembled as he strode.
Th' undaunted fiend what this might be admired,[1]
Admired, not feared; God and his Son except,
Created thing nought valued he nor shunned;
And with disdainful look thus first began: 680
    "Whence and what art thou, execrable shape,
That dar'st, though grim and terrible, advance
Thy miscreated front[2] athwart my way
To yonder gates? Through them I mean to pass,
That be assured, without leave asked of thee.   685
Retire, or taste thy folly, and learn by proof,
Hell-born, not to contend with spirits of Heaven."
    To whom the goblin, full of wrath, replied:
"Art thou that traitor angel, art thou he,
Who first broke peace in Heaven, and faith, till then   690
Unbroken, and in proud rebellious arms
Drew after him the third part of Heaven's sons
Conjured[3] against the Highest, for which both thou
And they, outcast from God, are here condemned
To waste eternal days in woe and pain?   695
And reckon'st thou thyself with spirits of Heaven,
Hell-doomed, and breath'st defiance here and scorn,
Where I reign king, and, to enrage thee more,

7. Like Cerberus, the traditional hound
of Hell.
8. Circe out of jealousy threw poison
into the water where Scylla bathed, in
the straits between Calabria and Sicily
("Trinacria"); as a result of the poisons, Scylla developed a ring of barking, snapping dogs around her waist.

9. Hecate, goddess of sorcery. She attends the orgies of witches in the home
of all witchcraft, Lapland, whither she
is drawn by the blood of babies sacrificed for the occasion.
1. Wondered.
2. Misshapen forehead, or face.
3. Sworn together by an oath.

Thy king and lord? Back to thy punishment,
False fugitive, and to thy speed add wings,   700
Lest with a whip of scorpions I pursue
Thy ling'ring, or with one stroke of this dart
Strange horror seize thee, and pangs unfelt before."
   So spake the grisly terror, and in shape,
So speaking and so threatening, grew tenfold   705
More dreadful and deform. On th' other side,
Incensed with indignation, Satan stood
Unterrified, and like a comet burned
That fires the length of Ophiucus[4] huge
In th' Arctic sky, and from his horrid hair   710
Shakes pestilence and war. Each at the head
Leveled his deadly aim; their fatal hands
No second stroke intend,[5] and such a frown
Each cast at th' other, as when two black clouds,
With Heaven's artillery fraught,[6] come rattling on   715
Over the Caspian,[7] then stand front to front
Hovering a space, till winds the signal blow
To join their dark encounter in mid-air:
So frowned the mighty combatants, that Hell
Grew darker at their frown; so matched they stood;   720
For never but once more was either like
To meet so great a foe.[8] And now great deeds
Had been achieved, whereof all Hell had rung,
Had not the snaky sorceress that sat
Fast by Hell-gate, and kept the fatal key,   725
Ris'n, and with hideous outcry rushed between.
   "O father, what intends thy hand," she cried,
"Against thy only son?[9] What fury, O son,
Possesses thee to bend that mortal dart
Against thy father's head? and know'st for whom?   730
For Him who sits above and laughs the while
At thee ordained his drudge, to execute
Whate'er his wrath, which he calls Justice, bids;
His wrath which one day will destroy ye both!"
   She spake, and at her words the hellish pest   735
Forbore, then these to her Satan returned:
   "So strange thy outcry, and thy words so strange
Thou interposest, that my sudden hand,
Prevented,[1] spares to tell thee yet by deeds
What it intends, till first I know of thee,   740
What thing thou art, thus double-formed, and why,
In this infernal vale first met, thou call'st

---

4. A vast Northern constellation, "The Serpent-Holder" (also called "Serpentarius"). Satan will soon appear as a snake; and, like a comet, he portends "pestilence and war."
5. I.e., the first stroke will do the business.
6. Loaded with thunderbolts.

7. The Caspian is a particularly stormy area.
8. I.e., the Son of God.
9. Sin, Death, and Satan, in their various interrelations, parody obscenely the relations between God and the Son, Adam and Eve.
1. Forestalled.

Me father, and that phantasm call'st my son?
I know thee not, nor ever saw till now
Sight more detestable than him and thee."   745
    T' whom thus the portress of Hell-gate replied:
"Hast thou forgot me then, and do I seem
Now in thine eye so foul? once deemed so fair
In Heaven, when at th' assembly, and in sight
Of all the seraphim with thee combined   750
In bold conspiracy against Heaven's King,
All on a sudden miserable pain
Surprised thee; dim thine eyes, and dizzy swum
In darkness, while thy head flames thick and fast
Threw forth, till on the left side opening wide,   755
Likest to thee in shape and countenance bright,
Then shining heavenly-fair, a goddess armed
Out of thy head I sprung.[2] Amazement seized
All th' host of Heaven; back they recoiled afraid
At first, and called me *Sin*, and for a sign   760
Portentous held me; but, familiar grown,
I pleased, and with attractive graces won
The most averse, thee chiefly, who full oft
Thyself in me thy perfect image viewing
Becam'st enamored;[3] and such joy thou took'st   765
With me in secret, that my womb conceived
A growing burden. Meanwhile war arose,
And fields were fought in Heaven; wherein remained
(For what could else?) to our almighty Foe
Clear victory, to our part loss and rout   770
Through all the empyrean. Down they fell,
Driven headlong from the pitch[4] of Heaven, down
Into this deep, and in the general fall
I also; at which time this powerful key
Into my hand was given, with charge to keep   775
These gates forever shut, which none can pass
Without my opening. Pensive here I sat
Alone, but long I sat not, till my womb
Pregnant by thee, and now excessive grown,
Prodigious motion felt and rueful throes.   780
At last this odious offspring whom thou seest,
Thine own begotten, breaking violent way,
Tore through my entrails, that, with fear and pain
Distorted, all my nether shape thus grew
Transformed; but he, my inbred enemy,   785
Forth issued, brandishing his fatal dart,
Made to destroy. I fled, and cried out *Death!*
Hell trembled at the hideous name, and sighed
From all her caves, and back resounded *Death!*

2. As Athena sprang full-grown from
the head of Zeus.
3. Sin looks attractive at first, being
a lovely woman at the top of her body;
but she is a serpent below, and ends in
a "mortal sting," i.e., death.
4. Peak.

I fled; but he pursued (though more, it seems, 790
Inflamed with lust than rage) and, swifter far,
Me overtook, his mother, all dismayed,
And in embraces forcible and foul
Engendering with me, of that rape begot
These yelling monsters, that with ceaseless cry 795
Surround me, as thou sawest, hourly conceived
And hourly born, with sorrow infinite
To me; for when they list, into the womb
That bred them they return, and howl, and gnaw
My bowels, their repast; then, bursting forth 800
Afresh, with conscious terrors vex me round,
That rest or intermission none I find.
Before mine eyes in opposition sits
Grim Death, my son and foe, who sets them on,
And me his parent would full soon devour 805
For want of other prey, but that he knows
His end with mine involved; and knows that I
Should prove a bitter morsel, and his bane,
Whenever that shall be; so Fate pronounced.
But thou, O father, I forewarn thee, shun 810
His deadly arrow; neither vainly hope
To be invulnerable in those bright arms,
Though tempered heavenly; for that mortal dint,
Save he who reigns above, none can resist."[5]
     She finished, and the subtle fiend his lore 815
Soon learned, now milder, and thus answered smooth:
"Dear daughter, since thou claimest me for thy sire,
And my fair son here show'st me, the dear pledge
Of dalliance had with thee in Heaven, and joys
Then sweet, now sad to mention, through dire change 820
Befallen us unforeseen, unthought of; know
I come no enemy, but to set free
From out this dark and dismal house of pain,
Both him and thee, and all the Heavenly host
Of spirits that, in our just pretenses[6] armed, 825
Fell with us from on high. From them I go
This uncouth errand sole,[7] and one for all
Myself expose, with lonely steps to tread
Th' unfounded deep, and through the void immense
To search with wandering quest a place foretold 830
Should be, and, by concurring signs, ere now
Created vast and round, a place of bliss
In the purlieus[8] of Heaven, and therein placed
A race of upstart creatures, to supply
Perhaps our vacant room, though more removed, 835
Lest Heaven, surcharged[9] with potent multitude,

5. I.e., only God is immune to death.   8. Outskirts, suburbs.
6. Grievances.   9. Too full. "Broils": controversies.
7. Alone on a desolate journey.

Might hap to move new broils. Be this, or aught
Than this more secret, now designed, I haste
To know; and, this once known, shall soon return,
And bring ye to the place where thou and Death   840
Shall dwell at ease, and up and down unseen
Wing silently the buxom¹ air, embalmed
With odors: there ye shall be fed and filled
Immeasurably; all things shall be your prey."
He ceased, for both seemed highly pleased, and Death   845
Grinned horrible a ghastly smile, to hear
His famine² should be filled, and blessed his maw
Destined to that good hour. No less rejoiced
His mother bad, and thus bespake her sire:
    "The key of this infernal pit, by due   850
And by command of Heaven's all-powerful King
I keep, by him forbidden to unlock
These adamantine gates; against all force
Death ready stands to interpose his dart,
Fearless to be o'ermatched by living might.   855
But what owe I to his commands above
Who hates me, and hath hither thrust me down
Into this gloom of Tartarus profound,
To sit in hateful office here confined,
Inhabitant of Heaven and heavenly-born,   860
Here in perpetual agony and pain,
With terrors and with clamors compassed round
Of mine own brood that on my bowels feed?
Thou art my father, thou my author, thou
My being gav'st me; whom should I obey   865
But thee? whom follow? Thou wilt bring me soon
To that new world of light and bliss, among
The gods who live at ease, where I shall reign
At thy right hand voluptuous,³ as beseems
Thy daughter and thy darling, without end."   870
    Thus saying, from her side the fatal key,
Sad instrument of all our woe, she took;
And, towards the gate rolling her bestial train,⁴
Forthwith the huge portcullis high up-drew,
Which but herself not all the Stygian powers⁵   875
Could once have moved; then in the keyhole turns
Th' intricate wards, and every bolt and bar
Of massy iron or solid rock with ease
Unfastens: on a sudden open fly
With impetuous recoil and jarring sound   880
Th' infernal doors, and on their hinges grate

---

1. Yielding. "Embalmed": made fragrant, but also with a thought of the
process associated with death.
2. Hunger, belly.
3. As the Son sits at God's right hand,
Sin will sit at Satan's; a blasphemous

parody, showed up by the word "voluptuous."
4. I.e., accompanied by her yelping offspring.
5. The powers of Hell.

Harsh thunder, that the lowest bottom shook
Of Erebus.[6] She opened, but to shut
Excelled[7] her power; the gates wide open stood,
That with extended wings a bannered host,   885
Under spread ensigns[8] marching, might pass through
With horse and chariots ranked in loose array;
So wide they stood, and like a furnace-mouth
Cast forth redounding[9] smoke and ruddy flame.
Before their eyes in sudden view appear   890
The secrets of the hoary deep, a dark
Illimitable ocean, without bound,
Without dimension; where length, breadth, and height,
And time and place are lost; where eldest Night
And Chaos, ancestors of Nature, hold   895
Eternal anarchy, amidst the noise
Of endless wars, and by confusion stand.
For Hot, Cold, Moist, and Dry, four champions fierce
Strive here for mastery, and to battle bring
Their embryon atoms;[1] they around the flag   900
Of each his faction, in their several clans,
Light-armed or heavy, sharp, smooth, swift, or slow,
Swarm populous, unnumbered as the sands
Of Barca or Cyrene's torrid soil,[2]
Levied to side with warring winds, and poise[3]   905
Their lighter wings. To whom these most adhere,
He rules a moment; Chaos[4] umpire sits,
And by decision more embroils the fray
By which he reigns: next him, high arbiter,
Chance governs all. Into this wild abyss,   910
The womb of Nature and perhaps her grave,
Of neither sea, nor shore, nor air, nor fire,
But all these in their pregnant causes[5] mixed
Confusedly, and which thus must ever fight,
Unless th' Almighty Maker them ordain   915
His dark materials to create more worlds,[6]
Into this wild abyss the wary fiend
Stood on the brink of Hell and looked awhile,
Pondering his voyage; for no narrow frith[7]
He had to cross. Nor was his ear less pealed[8]   920
With noises loud and ruinous (to compare
Great things with small) than when Bellona[9] storms,

6. Another classical name for Hell.
7. Exceeded. That Sin cannot shut Hell
gate, though she can open it, is sym-
bolical.
8. Standards, flags.
9. Billowing.
1. The four elements, fire, earth, water,
and air, struggle endlessly in Chaos.
"Embryon": embryo, unformed.
2. Barca and Cyrene were cities built
on the shifting sands of North Africa.
3. Give weight to.

4. Chaos is both the place where confusion reigns and personified confusion
itself.
5. Chaos is not organized to the point
of being matter; it is the seeds of all
forms of matter.
6. God must impose order on Chaos to
create worlds from it.
7. Channel, firth.
8. Rung.
9. Goddess of war.

With all her battering engines bent to raze
Some capital city; or less than if this frame
Of Heaven were falling, and these elements   925
In mutiny had from her axle torn
The steadfast Earth. At last his sail-broad vans[1]
He spreads for flight, and in the surging smoke
Uplifted spurns the ground; thence many a league,
As in a cloudy chair ascending, rides   930
Audacious; but that seat soon failing, meets
A vast vacuity: all unawares,
Fluttering his pennons[2] vain, plumb down he drops
Ten thousand fathom deep, and to this hour
Down had been falling, had not by ill chance   935
The strong rebuff[3] of some tumultuous cloud,
Instinct[4] with fire and niter, hurried him
As many miles aloft; that fury stayed,
Quenched in a boggy Syrtis,[5] neither sea,
Nor good dry land, nigh foundered on he fares,   940
Treading the crude consistence, half on foot,
Half flying; behoves[6] him now both oar and sail.
As when a gryphon through the wilderness
With wingéd course o'er hill or moory dale,
Pursues the Arimaspian, who by stealth   945
Had from his wakeful custody purloined
The guarded gold:[7] so eagerly the fiend
O'er bog or steep, through strait, rough, dense, or rare,
With head, hands, wings, or feet pursues his way,
And swims, or sinks, or wades, or creeps, or flies. 950
At length a universal hubbub wild
Of stunning sounds and voices all confused
Borne through the hollow dark, assaults his ear
With loudest vehemence. Thither he plies
Undaunted, to meet there whatever power   955
Or spirit of the nethermost abyss
Might in that noise reside, of whom to ask
Which way the nearest coast of darkness lies
Bordering on light; when straight behold the throne
Of Chaos, and his dark pavilion spread   960
Wide on the wasteful deep! With him enthroned
Sat sable-vested Night, eldest of things,
The consort of his reign; and by them stood
Orcus and Ades,[8] and the dreaded name

1. Wings.
2. Pinions, from Latin *pennae,* "wings."
3. Puff or blast.
4. Filled. "Niter": saltpeter.
5. Quicksand, from the North African gulfs, famous for their shifting sandbars.
6. Befits.
7. Gryphons, fabulous creatures, half-eagle, half-dragon, lived in northern Europe, and were said to hoard gold. When it was stolen from them by the one-eyed Arimaspians, they pursued these curious malefactors, hopping, flapping, and squawking. The story is a piece of moralized medieval natural history, directed against the love of money.
8. Latin and Greek names of Pluto, god of Hell.

Of Demogorgon;[9] Rumor next and Chance, 965
And Tumult and Confusion all embroiled,
And Discord with a thousand various mouths.
  T' whom Satan, turning boldly, thus: "Ye powers
And spirits of this nethermost abyss,
Chaos and ancient Night, I come no spy, 970
With purpose to explore or to disturb
The secrets of your realm; but by constraint
Wandering this darksome desert, as my way
Lies through your spacious empire up to light,
Alone and without guide, half lost, I seek 975
What readiest path leads where your gloomy bounds
Confine with[1] Heaven; or if some other place
From your dominion won, th' Ethereal King
Possesses lately, thither to arrive
I travel this profound.[2] Direct my course: 980
Directed, no mean recompense it brings
To your behoof,[3] if I that region lost,
All usurpation thence expelled, reduce
To their original darkness and your sway
(Which is my present journey[4]), and once more 985
Erect the standard there of ancient Night.
Yours be th' advantage all, mine the revenge!"
  Thus Satan; and him thus the anarch[5] old,
With faltering speech and visage incomposed,[6]
Answered: "I know thee, stranger, who thou art, 990
That mighty leading angel, who of late
Made head against Heaven's King, though overthrown.
I saw and heard; for such a numerous host
Fled not in silence through the frighted deep
With ruin upon ruin, rout on rout, 995
Confusion worse confounded; and Heaven-gates
Poured out by millions her victorious bands,
Pursuing. I upon my frontiers here
Keep residence; if all I can will serve,
That little which is left so to defend 1000
Encroached on still through our intestine broils[7]
Weakening the scepter of old Night: first Hell,
Your dungeon, stretching far and wide beneath;
Now lately Heaven and Earth,[8] another world
Hung o'er my realm, linked in a golden chain 1005
To that side Heaven from whence your legions fell.
If that way be your walk, you have not far;

9. A mysterious subdeity, stronger than Fate itself, first invented by Boccaccio. Cf. Shelley's *Prometheus Unbound.*
1. Border on.
2. Deep pit.
3. On your behalf.
4. I.e., the purpose of my present journey.
5. Chaos is not "monarch" of his realm, but "anarch," i.e., nonruler.

6. Disturbed.
7. I.e., our territory is continually shrinking because of our civil wars ("intestine broils").
8. Our human world and its sky have been carved out of Chaos. The sky is distinguished from "Heaven" as used in line 1006, meaning the abode of the blessed, the Empyrean.

So much the nearer danger. Go, and speed!
Havoc and spoil and ruin are my gain."
    He ceased; and Satan stayed not to reply,   1010
But, glad that now his sea should find a shore,
With fresh alacrity and force renewed
Springs upward, like a pyramid of fire,
Into the wild expanse, and through the shock
Of fighting elements, on all sides round   1015
Environed, wins his way; harder beset
And more endangered, than when Argo[9] passed
Through Bosporus betwixt the jostling rocks;
Or when Ulysses on the larboard shunned
Charybdis, and by th' other whirlpool steered: 1020
So he with difficulty and labor hard
Moved on: with difficulty and labor he;
But, he once past, soon after when man fell,
Strange alteration! Sin and Death amain,[1]
Following his track (such was the will of Heaven),   1025
Paved after him a broad and beaten way
Over the dark abyss, whose boiling gulf
Tamely endured a bridge of wondrous length
From Hell continued reaching th' utmost orb[2]
Of this frail world; by which the spirits perverse   1030
With easy intercourse pass to and fro
To tempt or punish mortals, except whom
God and good angels guard by special grace.
But now at last the sacred influence
Of light appears, and from the walls of Heaven   1035
Shoots far into the bosom of dim Night
A glimmering dawn. Here Nature first begins
Her farthest verge,[3] and Chaos to retire,
As from her outmost works a broken foe
With tumult less and with less hostile din;   1040
That[4] Satan with less toil, and now with ease
Wafts on the calmer wave by dubious light,
And, like a weather-beaten vessel, holds[5]
Gladly the port, though shrouds and tackle torn;
Or in the emptier waste, resembling air,   1045
Weighs his spread wings, at leisure to behold
Far off th' empyreal Heaven, extended wide
In circuit, undetermined[6] square or round,

9. Jason and his fifty Argonauts, sailing through the Bosporus to the Black Sea in pursuit of the Golden Fleece, had to pass through the Symplegades, or clashing rocks. Ulysses also had a tight squeeze to pass between Scylla and Charybdis, where Italy almost touches Sicily. Charybdis was a whirlpool, but Scylla, the dog-monster who ate alive six of Ulysses' best men, is called by Milton "th' other whirlpool."
1. At full speed, vigorously.
2. The world is surrounded by nine spheres, the whole construction comprising the created universe. The bridge built by Sin and Death ends on the outermost of these spheres.
3. Threshold. The end of Chaos is the beginning of (created) Nature.
4. So that.
5. Makes for.
6. Heaven is so vast that simply by looking at it one cannot tell its shape. Of course it is really round, the circle being an emblem of perfection.

With opal towers and battlements adorned
Of living sapphire, once his native seat;   1050
And fast by, hanging in a golden chain,
This pendant world,[7] in bigness as a star
Of smallest magnitude close by the moon.
Thither, full fraught with mischievous revenge,
Accursed, and in a cursèd hour, he hies.   1055

From Book III
[The Consult in Heaven]

Hail, holy Light, offspring of Heaven first-born!
Or of th' Eternal coeternal beam,
May I express thee unblamed?[1] since God is light,
And never but in unapproachèd light
Dwelt from eternity, dwelt then in thee,   5
Bright effluence of bright essence increate![2]
Or hear'st thou rather[3] pure ethereal stream,
Whose fountain who shall tell? Before the sun,
Before the heavens, thou wert, and at the voice
Of God, as with a mantle, didst invest[4]   10
The rising world of waters dark and deep,
Won from the void and formless infinite!
Thee I revisit now with bolder wing,
Escaped the Stygian pool, though long detained
In that obscure sojourn, while in my flight,   15
Through utter and through middle darkness[5] borne,
With other notes than to th' Orphean lyre[6]
I sung of Chaos and eternal Night;
Taught by the Heavenly Muse[7] to venture down
The dark descent, and up to reascend,   20
Though hard and rare. Thee I revisit safe,
And feel thy sovereign vital lamp; but thou
Revisit'st not these eyes, that roll in vain
To find thy piercing ray, and find no dawn;
So thick a drop serene[8] hath quenched their orbs,   25
Or dim suffusion veiled. Yet not the more
Cease I to wander where the Muses haunt
Clear spring, or shady grove, or sunny hill,

7. Homer first showed the world as hanging from Heaven by a golden chain (*Iliad* VIII). As Milton uses the image, it has a symbolic meaning as well; earth is dependent on Heaven. The world which hangs from Heaven is not just our earth, but earth and all its nine spheres, the created cosmos, as described by Ptolemy.
1. Milton feels some hesitation at calling Light coeternal with God himself; his reasons follow.

2. Uncreated, i.e., eternal.
3. I.e., would you rather be called. The construction is a Latinism.
4. Occupy.
5. Hell and Chaos.
6. One of the so-called Orphean Hymns is *To Night*. But Milton's darkness, being Christian, is deeper and wider.
7. Urania.
8. One medical theory about blindness attributed it to a *gutta serena*, another to a *suffusio nigra*.

Smit with the love of sacred song;[9] but chief
Thee, Sion,[1] and the flowery brooks beneath,   30
That wash thy hallowed feet, and warbling flow,
Nightly I visit: nor sometimes forget[2]
Those other two equaled with me in fate,[3]
So were I equaled with them in renown,
Blind Thamyris and blind Maeonides,   35
And Tiresias and Phineus, prophets old:[4]
Then feed on thoughts that voluntary move
Harmonious numbers; as the wakeful bird[5]
Sings darkling, and, in shadiest covert hid,
Tunes her nocturnal note. Thus with the year   40
Seasons return; but not to me returns
Day, or the sweet approach of even or morn,
Or sight of vernal bloom, or summer's rose,
Or flocks, or herds, or human face divine;
But cloud instead and ever-during dark   45
Surrounds me, from the cheerful ways of men
Cut off, and, for the book of knowledge fair,
Presented with a universal blank
Of Nature's works, to me expunged and rased,[6]
And wisdom at one entrance quite shut out.   50
So much the rather thou, Celestial Light,
Shine inward, and the mind through all her powers
Irradiate; there plant eyes; all mist from thence
Purge and disperse, that I may see and tell
Of things invisible to mortal sight.   55
        Now had th' Almighty Father from above,
From the pure empyrean where he sits
High throned above all height, bent down his eye,
His own works and their works at once to view:
About him all the sanctities of Heaven   60
Stood thick as stars, and from his sight[7] received
Beatitude past utterance; on his right
The radiant image of his glory sat,
His only Son. On Earth he first beheld
Our two first parents, yet the only two   65
Of mankind, in the happy garden placed,
Reaping immortal fruits of joy and love,
Uninterrupted joy, unrivaled love,

9. The phrase is Virgilian, *"ingenti per-cussus amore"* (*Georgics* II.476), but the adjective "sacred" is Milton's own reservation.
1. The mountain of Scriptural inspiration, with its brooks Siloa and Kidron.
2. I.e., and never forget: therefore always remember.
3. Blind like me.
4. Thamyris was a blind Thracian poet, who lived before Homer. "Maeonides" is an epithet of Homer, either as a son of Maeon or as a native of Maeonia. Tiresias was the blind prophet of

Thebes (cf. *Oedipus Rex*); Phineus was another blind prophet and soothsayer (*Aeneid* III). For Milton poetry and prophesy were intimately joined; blindness of the outer eye rendered more acute the sight of the inner eye; and the very thought of these matters moved him, as he says, spontaneously to verse.
5. The nightingale. "Darkling": at night.
6. Shaved off (like a Roman tablet), erased.
7. From sight of him.

In blissful solitude. He then surveyed
Hell and the gulf between, and Satan there   70
Coasting the wall of Heaven on this side Night,
In the dun air sublime,[8] and ready now
To stoop, with wearied wings and willing feet,
On the bare outside of this world, that seemed
Firm land embosomed without firmament,   75
Uncertain which, in ocean or in air.
Him God beholding from his prospect high,
Wherein past, present, future, he beholds,
Thus to his only Son foreseeing spake:
    "Only-begotten Son, seest thou what rage   80
Transports our adversary? whom no bounds
Prescribed, no bars of Hell, nor all the chains
Heaped on him there, nor yet the main abyss
Wide interrupt,[9] can hold; so bent he seems
On desperate revenge, that shall redound   85
Upon his own rebellious head. And now,
Through all restraint broke loose, he wings his way
Not far off Heaven, in the precincts of light,
Directly towards the new-created world,
And man there placed, with purpose to essay   90
If him by force he can destroy, or, worse,
By some false guile pervert: and shall pervert;
For man will hearken to his glozing lies,
And easily transgress the sole command,
Sole pledge of his obedience; so will fall   95
He and his faithless progeny. Whose fault?
Whose but his own? Ingrate, he had of me
All he could have; I made him just and right,
Sufficient to have stood, though free to fall.
Such I created all th' ethereal powers   100
And spirits, both them who stood and them who failed:
Freely they stood who stood, and fell who fell.
Not free, what proof could they have given sincere[1]
Of true allegiance, constant faith, or love,
Where only what they needs must do appeared,   105
Not what they would? What praise could they receive,
What pleasure I, from such obedience paid,
When Will and Reason (Reason also is Choice),
Useless and vain, of freedom both despoiled,
Made passive both, had served Necessity,   110
Not me? They, therefore, as to right belonged,
So were created, nor can justly accuse
Their Maker, or their making, or their fate,

8. From the aspect of God's radiance
the air is "dun," i.e., dusky; Satan is
literally "sublime" in it, i.e., lifted up,
aloft. But from where Satan hangs,
outside the world's outer shell, he cannot be sure the world and its nine concentric spheres are not a single solid
(line 75). The points of view are precisely distinguished.
9. Dividing, in between.
1. The delayed modifier is a favorite
stylistic device of Milton's. "Sincere"
goes with "proof."

As if predestination overruled
Their will, disposed by absolute decree   115
Or high foreknowledge. They themselves decreed
Their own revolt, not I. If I foreknew,
Foreknowledge had no influence on their fault,
Which had no less proved certain unforeknown.[2]
So without least impulse or shadow of fate,   120
Or aught by me immutably foreseen,
They trespass, authors to themselves in all,
Both what they judge and what they choose; for so
I formed them free, and free they must remain
Till they enthrall themselves: I else must change   125
Their nature, and revoke the high decree
Unchangeable, eternal, which ordained
Their freedom; they themselves ordained their fall.
The first sort[3] by their own suggestion fell,
Self-tempted, self-depraved; man falls, deceived   130
By the other first: man, therefore, shall find grace;
The other, none. In mercy and justice both,[4]
Through Heaven and Earth, so shall my glory excel;
But mercy, first and last, shall brightest shine."

    Thus while God spake ambrosial fragrance filled   135
All Heaven, and in the blessed spirits elect
Sense of new joy ineffable diffused.
Beyond compare the Son of God was seen
Most glorious; in him all his Father shone
Substantially expressed;[5] and in his face   140
Divine compassion visibly appeared,
Love without end, and without measure grace;
Which uttering, thus he to his Father spake:
    "O Father, gracious was that word which closed
Thy sovereign sentence, that man should find grace; 145
For which both Heaven and Earth shall high extol
Thy praises, with th' innumerable sound
Of hymns and sacred songs, wherewith thy throne
Encompassed shall resound thee ever blest.
For, should man finally be lost, should man,   150
Thy creature late so loved, thy youngest son,
Fall circumvented thus by fraud, though joined
With his own folly? That be from thee far,
That far be from thee, Father, who art judge
Of all things made, and judgest only right!   155
Or shall the adversary[6] thus obtain
His end, and frustrate thine? shall he fulfill
His malice, and thy goodness bring to naught

2. I.e., if I had not foreknown it.
3. The bad angels, Satan and his crew.
4. Mercy and justice are two key terms
in the poem. Their personifications
here are separate: God is justice (he
claims to be merciful, but his speech
does not have this tone at all), the

Son is mercy; but by Book XII Milton
intends to show their identity.
5. God himself cannot be directly apprehended, except through the Son.
6. "Satan" in Hebrew means "Adversary."

Or proud return, though to his heavier doom,
Yet with revenge accomplished, and to Hell   160
Draw after him the whole race of mankind,
By him corrupted? Or wilt thou thyself
Abolish thy creation, and unmake,
For him, what for thy glory thou hast made?
So should thy goodness and thy greatness both   165
Be questioned and blasphemed without defense."
    To whom the great Creator thus replied:
"O Son, in whom my soul hath chief delight,
Son of my bosom, Son who art alone
My word, my wisdom, and effectual might,   170
All hast thou spoken as my thoughts are, all
As my eternal purpose hath decreed.[7]
Man shall not quite be lost, but saved who will;
Yet not of will in him, but grace in me
Freely vouchsafed. Once more I will renew   175
His lapséd powers, though forfeit, and enthralled
By sin to foul exorbitant desires:
Upheld by me, yet once more he shall stand
On even ground against his mortal foe,
By me upheld,[8] that he may know how frail   180
His fallen condition is, and to me owe
All his deliverance, and to none but me.
Some I have chosen of peculiar grace,
Elect above the rest; so is my will:
The rest shall hear me call, and oft be warned   185
Their sinful state,[9] and to appease betimes
Th' incenséd Deity, while offered grace
Invites; for I will clear their senses dark
What may suffice,[1] and soften stony hearts
To pray, repent, and bring obedience due.   190
To prayer, repentance, and obedience due,
Though but endeavored with sincere intent,
Mine ear shall not be slow, mine eye not shut.
And I will place within them as a guide
My umpire Conscience; whom if they will hear,   195
Light after light well used they shall attain,[2]
And to the end persisting, safe arrive.
This my long sufferance, and my day of grace,
They who neglect and scorn shall never taste;
But hard be hardened, blind be blinded more,   200
That they may stumble on, and deeper fall;
And none but such from mercy I exclude.
But yet all is not done. Man, disobeying,

---

7. The Lord's speech is notably rhythmic and even rhymed.
8. Note the ambiguity: the second "by
me upheld" (line 180) may modify
either "he" (line 178) or "his mortal
foe" (line 179). Both divine and hellish energy are ultimately divine.
9. I.e., warned about their sinful state.
1. I.e., as much as need be.
2. By using light well, they will reach
even more light, and, in the end, salvation.

Disloyal, breaks his fealty, and sins
Against the high supremacy of Heaven, 205
Affecting[3] godhead, and so, losing all,
To expiate his treason hath naught left,
But, to destruction sacred and devote,[4]
He with his whole posterity must die;
Die he or Justice must; unless for him 210
Some other, able and as willing,[5] pay
The rigid satisfaction, death for death.
Say, heavenly powers, where shall we find such love?
Which of ye will be mortal, to redeem
Man's mortal crime,[6] and just, th' unjust to save? 215
Dwells in all Heaven charity so dear?"
　　He asked, but all the heavenly choir stood mute,[7]
And silence was in Heaven: on man's behalf
Patron or intercessor none appeared,
Much less that durst upon his own head draw 220
The deadly forfeiture, and ransom set.
And now without redemption all mankind
Must have been lost, adjudged to Death and Hell
By doom severe, had not the Son of God,
In whom the fullness dwells of love divine, 225
His dearest mediation[8] thus renewed:
　　"Father, thy word is passed, man shall find grace;
And shall Grace not find means, that finds her way,
The speediest of thy wingéd messengers,
To visit all thy creatures, and to all 230
Comes unprevented,[9] unimplored, unsought?
Happy for man, so coming! He her aid
Can never seek, once dead in sins and lost;
Atonement for himself, or offering meet,
Indebted and undone, hath none to bring. 235
Behold me, then: me for him, life for life,
I offer; on me let thine anger fall;
Account me man: I for his sake will leave
Thy bosom, and this glory next to thee
Freely put off, and for him lastly die 240
Well pleased; on me let Death wreak all his rage.
Under his gloomy power I shall not long
Lie vanquished. Thou hast given me to possess
Life in myself forever; by thee I live;
Though now to Death I yield, and am his due, 245
All that of me can die, yet, that debt paid,
Thou wilt not leave me in the loathsome grave
His prey, nor suffer my unspotted soul

3. Pretending to.
4. Dedicated, given up to.
5. I.e., able to pay, and as willing as he is able.
6. Note that "mortal" means "human" (line 214) but "deadly" (line 215).
7. The silence of the good angels in face of a difficult task parallels that of the devils in the "great consult" (II. 420–26).
8. Intercession.
9. Unforestalled.

Forever with corruption there to dwell;
But I shall rise victorious, and subdue   250
My vanquisher, spoiled of his vaunted spoil.
Death his death's wound shall then receive, and stoop[1]
Inglorious, of his mortal sting disarmed;
I through the ample air in triumph high
Shall lead Hell captive maugre[2] Hell, and show   255
The powers of darkness bound. Thou, at the sight
Pleased, out of Heaven shalt look down and smile,
While, by thee raised, I ruin[3] all my foes,
Death last, and with his carcass glut the grave;
Then, with the multitude of my redeemed,   260
Shall enter Heaven, long absent, and return,
Father, to see thy face, wherein no cloud
Of anger shall remain, but peace assured
And reconcilement: wrath shall be no more
Thenceforth, but in thy presence joy entire."   265
    His words here ended; but his meek aspéct
Silent yet spake, and breathed immortal love
To mortal men, above which only shone
Filial obedience: as a sacrifice
Glad to be offered, he attends the will   270
Of his great Father. Admiration[4] seized
All Heaven, what this might mean, and whither tend,
Wondering; but soon th' Almighty thus replied:
    "O thou in Heaven and Earth the only peace
Found out for mankind under wrath,[5] O thou   275
My sole complacence![6] well thou know'st how dear
To me are all my works; nor man the least,
Though last created, that for him I spare
Thee from my bosom and right hand, to save,
By losing thee a while, the whole race lost!   280
Thou, therefore, whom thou only canst redeem,
Their nature also to thy nature join;[7]
And be thyself man among men on Earth,
Made flesh, when time shall be, of virgin seed,
By wondrous birth; be thou in Adam's room   285
The head of all mankind, though Adam's son.[8]
As in him perish all men, so in thee,
As from a second root, shall be restored

1. Be humbled, fall.
2. In spite of (French, *malgré*). The Son's triumph is represented in a series of fantastic paradoxes—a vanquisher vanquished, a spoiler spoiled, death dead, Hell captured in all Hell's despite.
3. In the Latin sense, throw down.
4. Wonder, curiosity.
5. The Lord is looking to the future, when mankind will be under his wrath.
6. Contentment.
7. I.e., join the nature of those people (mankind) whom you alone can save to your own nature; in other words,

"Become a man and suffer the pains of mortality." The antecedent of "whom" is, loosely construed, the "their" which follows it.
8. Adam is, properly, the "Old Adam"; Christ is the Second Adam (there was an old tradition that the Forbidden Tree and the Cross of Christ stood on the same spot). The Son of God, who long antedates the creation of Adam, and who is actually the first created being (III.383), is historical Jesus Christ in one sense, an eternal spiritual principle in another.

As many as are restored; without thee, none.
His crime makes guilty all his sons;[9] thy merit,   290
Imputed, shall absolve them who renounce
Their own both righteous and unrighteous deeds,[1]
And live in thee transplanted, and from thee
Receive new life. So man, as is most just,
Shall satisfy for man, be judged and die,   295
And dying rise, and, rising, with him raise
His brethren, ransomed with his own dear life.
So heavenly love shall outdo hellish hate,
Giving to death, and dying to redeem,
So dearly to redeem, what hellish hate   300
So easily destroyed, and still destroys
In those who, when they may, accept not grace.
Nor shalt thou, by descending to assume
Man's nature, lessen or degrade thine own.
Because thou hast, though throned in highest bliss   305
Equal to God, and equally enjoying
Godlike fruition,[2] quitted all to save
A world from utter loss, and hast been found
By merit more than birthright Son of God,[3]
Found worthiest to be so by being good,   310
Far more than great or high; because in thee
Love hath abounded more than glory abounds;
Therefore thy humiliation shall exalt
With thee thy manhood also to this throne:
Here shalt thou sit incarnate, here shalt reign   315
Both God and man, Son both of God and man,
Anointed[4] universal King. All power
I give thee; reign forever, and assume
Thy merits; under thee, as Head Supreme,
Thrones, princedoms, powers, dominions, I reduce: 320
All knees to thee shall bow of them that bide
In Heaven, or Earth, or under Earth in Hell.
When thou, attended gloriously from Heaven,
Shalt in the sky appear, and from thee send
The summoning archangels to proclaim   325
Thy dread tribunal, forthwith from all winds[5]
The living, and forthwith the cited dead
Of all past ages, to the general doom
Shall hasten; such a peal shall rouse their sleep.
Then, all thy saints assembled, thou shalt judge   330
Bad men and angels; they arraigned shall sink
Beneath thy sentence; Hell, her numbers full,

9. The intense legalism of the Deity is apparent.
1. I.e., the merit of Christ, imputed to men, frees from original sin those who renounce their own deeds both good and bad and hope to be saved by faith.
2. Godlike pleasures, rewards.
3. An audacious doctrine, that Christ was Son of God by merit. Satan, one notes, was sultan of Hell on the same principle.
4. "The Anointed," in Hebrew, is the Messiah.
5. From all directions. "Cited": summoned.

Thenceforth shall be forever shut. Meanwhile
The world shall burn, and from her ashes spring
New Heaven and Earth, wherein the just shall dwell,[6]   335
And, after all their tribulations long,
See golden days, fruitful of golden deeds,
With Joy and Love triúmphing, and fair Truth.
Then thou thy regal scepter shalt lay by;
For regal scepter then no more shall need;[7]   340
God shall be all in all. But all ye gods,[8]
Adore him who, to compass all this, dies;
Adore the Son, and honor him as me."
   No sooner had th' Almighty ceased, but all
The multitude of angels, with a shout   345
Loud as from numbers without number, sweet
As from blest voices, uttering joy, Heaven rung[9]
With jubilee, and loud hosannas filled
Th' eternal regions. Lowly reverent
Towards either throne[1] they bow, and to the ground   350
With solemn adoration down they cast
Their crowns, inwove with amarant[2] and gold;
Immortal amarant, a flower which once
In Paradise, fast by the Tree of Life,
Began to bloom, but soon for man's offense   355
To Heaven removed, where first it grew, there grows
And flowers aloft, shading the Fount of Life,
And where the River of Bliss through midst of Heaven
Rolls o'er Elysian[3] flowers her amber stream.
With these, that never fade, the spirits elect   360
Bind their resplendent locks, enwreathed with beams.
Now in loose garlands thick thrown off, the bright
Pavement, that like a sea of jasper shone,
Empurpled with celestial roses smiled.
Then, crowned again, their golden harps they took,   365
Harps ever tuned, that glittering by their side
Like quivers hung; and with preamble sweet
Of charming symphony they introduce
Their sacred song, and waken raptures high:
No voice exempt,[4] no voice but well could join   370
Melodious part; such concord is in Heaven.
   Thee, Father, first they sung, Omnipotent,
Immutable, Immortal, Infinite,[5]

---

6. The burning of the earth is based on II Peter iii.12, 13.
7. Be needed.
8. In addressing the angels as gods, the Lord is merely indicating their share in his divinity; the word is not literal.
9. "Multitude" (line 345) is subject of the sentence, "rung" the verb, and "Heaven" the object.
1. Those of God and the Son.
2. Or "amaranth"; in Greek, "unwithering"—an unfading flower and hence a

type of immortality, which could not continue on earth after man became subject to death.
3. Milton draws freely, and with no sense of incongruity, on pagan properties for his Christian Heaven. "Amber": not "yellow," but "clear." Milton's epithets are not always visually strong.
4. Abstaining.
5. Joshua Sylvester, in translating the long, pedestrian poem of Du Bartas on the creation, makes use of this line. It

Eternal King; thee, Author of all being,
Fountain of light, thyself invisible   375
Amidst the glorious brightness where thou sitt'st
Throned inaccessible, but when thou shad'st
The full blaze of thy beams, and through a cloud
Drawn round about thee like a radiant shrine
Dark with excessive bright thy skirts appear,[6]   380
Yet dazzle Heaven, that brightest seraphim
Approach not, but with both wings veil their eyes.
Thee next they sang, of all creation first,
Begotten Son, divine similitude,
In whose conspicuous countenance, without cloud   385
Made visible, th' Almighty Father shines,
Whom else[7] no creature can behold: on thee
Impressed th' effulgence of his glory abides;
Transfused on thee his ample spirit rests.
He Heaven of Heavens, and all the powers therein,   390
By thee created; and by thee threw down
Th' aspiring dominations.[8] Thou that day
Thy Father's dreadful thunder didst not spare,
Nor stop thy flaming chariot wheels, that shook
Heaven's everlasting frame, while o'er the necks   395
Thou drov'st of warring angels disarrayed.
Back from pursuit, thy powers with loud acclaim
Thee only extolled, Son of thy Father's might,
To execute fierce vengeance on his foes.
Not so on man: him, through their malice fallen,   400
Father of mercy and grace, thou didst not doom
So strictly, but much more to pity incline.
No sooner did thy dear and only Son
Perceive thee purposed not to doom frail man
So strictly, but much more to pity inclined,[9]   405
He, to appease thy wrath, and end the strife
Of mercy and justice in thy face discerned,
Regardless of the bliss wherein he sat
Second to thee, offered himself to die
For man's offense. O unexampled love!   410
Love nowhere to be found less than divine!
Hail, Son of God, Savior of men! Thy name
Shall be the copious matter of my[1] song
Henceforth, and never shall my harp thy praise
Forget, nor from thy Father's praise disjoin!   415

is the only example, and not a very
striking one, of Milton's paralleling an
English predecessor for ten consecutive
syllables.
6. In this hymn, for the first time, we
get a sense of the majesty and mystery
of the Godhead; hitherto, he has been
rather querulous and legalistic.
7. Except for whom (if it were not for
the Son, no creature could see God).
8. I.e., the rebel angels.

9. A "than" or "but" is understood at
the end of line 405. The repetition
(lines 402, 405) suggests the choral
nature of the psalm. Note in 407 the
re-emphasis on a conflict of mercy and
justice.
1. Either the angels are singing as a
single chorus, or Milton wishes to associate himself with them; possibly both.
The change of pronoun is deliberate and
striking.

Summary   The consult in Heaven, which occupies the first half of Book III, has momentarily interrupted Milton's account of Satan's journey. During the latter half of Book III, he continues to describe this journey. Satan, passing through the dim air outside the firmament, lights on the outer shell of the created cosmos, in a barren, windy place later to be known as the Paradise of Fools. He finds a passageway leading down through the concentric crystal spheres in which the planets are set, and spirals down toward Earth, at the center of this smaller cosmos, hung on a chain in the midst of the larger cosmos. But to find Eden he needs directions, and so, disguising himself as an inquisitive but virtuous angel, he imposes on Uriel, the archangel of the sun. Uriel gives him instructions, and Satan stops near Mt. Niphates, in Armenia.

From Book IV

Summary   On the point of entering Paradise, Satan is momentarily overcome by remorse, fear, envy, and despair; but in a dramatic soliloquy, he reasons himself back into resolution, and pushes forward.

[*Satan's Entry into Paradise*]

So on he fares, and to the border comes
Of Eden, where delicious Paradise,
Now nearer, crowns with her enclosure green,
As with a rural mound, the champaign[1] head
Of a steep wilderness, whose hairy sides   135
With thicket overgrown, grotesque[2] and wild,
Access denied; and overhead up grew
Insuperable height of loftiest shade,
Cedar, and pine, and fir, and branching palm,
A sylvan scene, and, as the ranks ascend   140
Shade above shade, a woody theater[3]
Of stateliest view. Yet higher than their tops
The verdurous wall of Paradise up sprung;
Which to our general sire[4] gave prospect large
Into his nether empire neighboring round.   145
And higher than that wall a circling row
Of goodliest trees, laden with fairest fruit,
Blossoms and fruits at once of golden hue,
Appeared, with gay enameled colors mixed;
On which the sun more glad impressed his beams   150
Than in fair evening cloud, or humid bow,[5]

1. From French *champs*, open countryside. Paradise is an open garden on top of a hill straddling a river in the east of Eden.
2. One of the earliest uses of the word in English to mean "romantic" or "picturesque."
3. As if in a Greek amphitheater, the trees are set row on row.
4. Adam.
5. The rainbow. There is a thick wall of trees around Paradise, which "access denied"; then above them, the shaggy sides of Paradise itself ("the verdurous wall"), and above it the garden of fruit trees.

When God hath showered the earth: so lovely seemed
That landscape. And of pure now purer air[6]
Meets his approach, and to the heart inspires
Vernal delight and joy, able to drive[7]   155
All sadness but despair. Now gentle gales,
Fanning their odoriferous wings, dispense
Native perfumes, and whisper whence they stole
Those balmy spoils. As when to them who sail
Beyond the Cape of Hope, and now are past   160
Mozambic, off at sea northeast winds blow
Sabean odors from the spicy shore
Of Araby the Blest,[8] with such delay
Well pleased they slack their course, and many a league
Cheered with the grateful smell old Ocean smiles;   165
So entertained those odorous sweets the fiend
Who came their bane, though with them better pleased
Than Asmodeus with the fishy fume
That drove him, though enamored, from the spouse
Of Tobit's son,[9] and with a vengeance sent   170
From Media post to Egypt, there fast bound.
    Now to th' ascent of that steep savage[1] hill
Satan had journeyed on, pensive and slow;
But further way found none; so thick entwined,
As one continued brake, the undergrowth   175
Of shrubs and tangling bushes had perplexed
All path of man or beast that passed that way.
One gate there only was, and that looked east
On th' other side. Which when th' arch-felon saw,
Due entrance he disdained, and, in contempt,   180
At one slight bound high overleaped all bound[2]
Of hill or highest wall, and sheer within
Lights on his feet. As when a prowling wolf,
Whom hunger drives to seek new haunt for prey,
Watching where shepherds pen their flocks at eve,   185
In hurdled cotes[3] amid the field secure,
Leaps o'er the fence with ease into the fold;
Or as a thief, bent to unhoard the cash
Of some rich burgher, whose substantial doors,
Cross-barred and bolted fast, fear no assault,   190
In at the window climbs, or o'er the tiles;

6. After breathing pure air, Satan now breathes even purer.
7. Scatter.
8. Coasting up East Africa after doubling the Cape of Good Hope, Milton supposes off "Mozambic" (Mozambique) one might meet "Sabean" (i.e., as from Sheba) odors coming from "Araby the Blest" (Arabia Felix). This is the fantasy of a man who learned his geography from medieval atlases and Diodorus Siculus, for the distance between Mozambique and Arabia is close to 2,000 miles.

9. Milton retells briefly here the story of Tobias, Tobit's son, who married Sara and was saved from the fate of her seven previous husbands by the advice of Raphael, who showed him how to make a fishy smell that would drive away the devil Asmodeus. See the Book of Tobit among the Apocrypha.
1. Wooded, entangled (from Latin, *silvaticus*, through Italian *selvaggio*, and French *sauvage*).
2. Satan enters Paradise, not only illegally, but with a contemptuous pun.
3. Pens made of woven reeds.

So clomb[4] this first grand thief into God's fold:
So since into his church lewd[5] hirelings climb.
Thence up he flew, and on the Tree of Life,
The middle tree and highest there that grew,   205
Sat like a cormorant; yet not true life
Thereby regained, but sat devising death
To them who lived; nor on the virtue thought
Of that life-giving plant, but only used
For prospect,[6] what, well used, had been the pledge   200
Of immortality. So little knows
Any, but God alone, to value right
The good before him, but perverts best things
To worst abuse, or to their meanest use.

        Beneath him, with new wonder, now he views,   205
To all delight of human sense exposed,
In narrow room Nature's whole wealth; yea, more,
A Heaven on Earth; for blissful Paradise
Of God the garden was, by him in the east
Of Eden planted. Eden stretched her line   210
From Auran eastward to the royal towers
Of great Seleucia, built by Grecian kings,
Or where the sons of Eden long before
Dwelt in Telassar.[7] In this pleasant soil
His far more pleasant garden God ordained.   215
Out of the fertile ground he caused to grow
All trees of noblest kind for sight, smell, taste;
And all amid them stood the Tree of Life,
High eminent, blooming ambrosial fruit
Of vegetable gold; and next to life,   220
Our death, the Tree of Knowledge, grew fast by—
Knowledge of good, bought dear by knowing ill.
Southward through Eden went a river large,
Nor changed his course, but through the shaggy hill
Passed underneath engulfed; for God had thrown   225
That mountain, as his garden-mold,[8] high raised
Upon the rapid current, which, through veins
Of porous earth with kindly[9] thirst up drawn,
Rose a fresh fountain, and with many a rill
Watered the garden; thence united fell   230
Down the steep glade, and met the nether flood,
Which from his darksome passage now appears,

4. Old past tense of "climb," but used with a special feeling of ungainly energy. The whole metaphor, of God as a rich citizen hoarding Adam and Eve from Satan the second-story-man, is instinct with comic feeling. On the devil as a thief, see John x.1.
5. Base.
6. Perspective, lookout.
7. By suggesting alternate boundaries of Eden, Milton invokes a hazy sense of the richness, vastness, and antiquity of the Middle East. "Auran" is an area in Syria, to the south of Damascus; "Seleucia" lies near modern Bagdad, a powerful city founded by one of Alexander's generals (hence, "built by Grecian kings"); and "Telassar" is another Near Eastern kingdom, this one probably on the east bank of the Euphrates.
8. The mountain is God's topsoil, out of which grows Paradise. The river (traditionally Tigris) flowed under the hill.
9. Natural.

And now, divided into four main streams,
Runs diverse, wandering many a famous realm
And country, whereof here needs no account;[1]   235
But rather to tell how, if art could tell,
How, from that sapphire fount the crispéd[2] brooks,
Rolling on orient pearl and sands of gold,
With mazy error[3] under pendant shades
Ran nectar, visiting each plant, and fed   240
Flowers worthy of Paradise; which not nice[4] art
In beds and curious knots, but Nature boon[5]
Poured forth profuse on hill, and dale, and plain,
Both where the morning sun first warmly smote
The open field, and where the unpierced shade   245
Embrowned[6] the noontide bowers. Thus was this place,
A happy rural seat of various view:[7]
Groves whose rich trees wept odorous gums and balm;
Others whose fruit, burnished with golden rind,
Hung amiable[8]—Hesperian fables true,   250
If true, here only—and of delicious taste.
Betwixt them lawns, or level downs, and flocks
Grazing the tender herb, were interposed,
Or palmy hillock; or the flowery lap
Of some irriguous[9] valley spread her store,   255
Flowers of all hue, and without thorn the rose.[1]
Another side, umbrageous[2] grots and caves
Of cool recess, o'er which the mantling vine
Lays forth her purple grape, and gently creeps
Luxuriant; meanwhile murmuring waters fall   260
Down the slope hills dispersed, or in a lake,
That to the fringéd bank with myrtle crowned
Her crystal mirror holds, unite their streams.
The birds their choir apply;[3] airs, vernal airs,
Breathing the smell of field and grove, attune   265
The trembling leaves, while universal Pan,[4]
Knit with the Graces and the Hours in dance,
Led on th' eternal spring.[5] Not that fair field
Of Enna, where Proserpin gathering flowers,
Herself a fairer flower, by gloomy Dis   270
Was gathered, which cost Ceres all that pain

1. Milton has in mind Genesis ii.10; but the expression "whereof here needs no account" dodges many questions about the correct translation of this passage.
2. Wavy, ruffled.
3. From Latin *errare*, "wandering."
4. Particular, careful.
5. Liberal, bounteous.
6. Darkened.
7. Aspect.
8. Lovely. These were real golden apples like those said to have existed in the Hesperides, fabulous islands of the Western Ocean; Paradise was the only place where the fable of the Hesperides was literally true.
9. Well-watered.
1. Figuratively and literally, there was no need for thorns in Paradise.
2. Shady.
3. Practice their song. "Airs" may be either "breezes" or "melodies," and probably are both.
4. The god of all nature. "Pan" in Greek means "all" but it is also the name of the goat-legged nature god.
5. The god of nature dances with the Graces and Hours, an image of perfect harmony.

To seek her through the world; nor that sweet grove
Of Daphne,[6] by Orontes and th' inspired
Castalian spring, might with this Paradise
Of Eden strive; nor that Nyseian isle,   275
Girt with the river Triton, where old Cham,
Whom Gentiles Ammon call and Libyan Jove,
Hid Amalthea, and her florid son,
Young Bacchus, from his stepdame Rhea's eye;[7]
Nor, where Abassin kings their issue guard,   280
Mount Amara[8] (though this by some supposed
True Paradise) under the Ethiop line
By Nilus' head, enclosed with shining rock,
A whole day's journey high, but wide remote
From this Assyrian garden, where the fiend   285
Saw undelighted all delight, all kind
Of living creatures, new to sight and strange.
Two of far nobler shape, erect and tall,
Godlike erect,[9] with native honor clad
In naked majesty, seemed lords of all,   290
And worthy seemed; for in their looks divine,
The image of their glorious Maker, shone
Truth, wisdom, sanctitude severe and pure—
Severe, but in true filial freedom[1] placed,
Whence true authority in men; though both   295
Not equal, as their sex not equal seemed.
For contemplation he and valor formed,
For softness she and sweet attractive grace;
He for God only, she for God in him.[2]
His fair large front[3] and eye sublime declared   300
Absolute rule; and hyacinthine[4] locks
Round from his parted forelock manly hung

6. Milton is comparing Paradise with the famous beauty spots of antiquity. Enna in Sicily was a lovely meadow from which "Proserpin" was kidnapped by "gloomy Dis" (i.e., Pluto); her mother Ceres sought her throughout the world. The grove of Daphne, near Antioch and the Orontes river in the Near East, had a spring called "Castalia" in imitation of the Muses' fountain near Delphi.

7. The isle of Nysa in the river Triton in Tunisia was where Ammon hid Bacchus, his bastard child by Amalthea, from the eye of his wife Rhea. "Florid" (wine-flushed) Bacchus, when he grew up, received the name of Dionysus in honor of his birthplace. The identification of the Egyptian god Ammon or Hammon with Cham or Ham, the son of Noah, is a piece of comparative anthropology on Milton's part.

8. Finally, Paradise ("this Assyrian garden," line 285) is finer than the palaces atop Mt. Amara, where the "Abassin" (Abyssinian) kings had a splendid palace. Milton's authority for this exotic scene was Peter Heylyn (*Cosmographie* IV.lxiv), from whom he took several phrases direct. His passage then had a continuing influence on the names and phrasings of Coleridge's *Kubla Khan*.

9. By emphasizing the word "erect," Milton means to distinguish man from the beasts of the field, who went "prone."

1. Though almost a paradox, the phrase suggests Milton's idea that true freedom always involves respect for authority and hierarchy. Cf. Eve's foolish question, "For, inferior, who is free?" (IX.825).

2. Milton's ideas on the relations between the sexes were strict for his day, though not as strict as they now appear.

3. Forehead.

4. A classical metaphor, often applied to hair, and implying "brown" or perhaps "flowing," but actually not very definite in its import.

Clustering, but not beneath his shoulders broad:
She, as a veil down to the slender waist,
Her unadornéd golden tresses wore   305
Disheveled, but in wanton ringlets waved
As the vine curls her tendrils,[5] which implied
Subjection, but required with gentle sway,
And by her yielded, by him best received,
Yielded with coy[6] submission, modest pride,   310
And sweet, reluctant, amorous delay.
Nor those mysterious parts were then concealed;
Then was not guilty shame. Dishonest shame
Of Nature's works, honor dishonorable,
Sin-bred, how have ye troubled all mankind   315
With shows instead, mere shows of seeming pure,
And banished from man's life his happiest life,
Simplicity and spotless innocence!
So passed they naked on, nor shunned the sight
Of God or angel; for they thought no ill;   320
So hand in hand they passed, the loveliest pair
That ever since in love's embraces met:
Adam the goodliest man of men since born
His sons; the fairest of her daughters Eve.[7]
Under a tuft of shade that on a green   325
Stood whispering soft, by a fresh fountain-side,
They sat them down; and, after no more toil
Of their sweet gardening labor than sufficed
To recommend cool Zephyr,[8] and make ease
More easy, wholesome thirst and appetite   330
More grateful, to their supper fruits they fell,
Nectarine fruits, which the compliant boughs
Yielded them, sidelong as they sat recline
On the soft downy bank damasked with flowers.
The savory pulp they chew, and in the rind,   335
Still as they thirsted scoop the brimming stream;
Nor gentle purpose,[9] nor endearing smiles
Wanted, nor youthful dalliance, as beseems
Fair couple linked in happy nuptial league,
Alone as they. About them frisking played   340
All beasts of th' earth, since wild, and of all chase[1]
In wood or wilderness, forest or den.
Sporting the lion ramped,[2] and in his paw
Dandled the kid; bears, tigers, ounces, pards,[3]
Gamboled before them; th' unwieldly elephant,   345
To make them mirth, used all his might, and wreathed

5. Eve's hair is curly, abundant, un-controlled; like the vegetation in Para-dise, it clings seductively about a severe and masculine virtue.
6. Shy.
7. Logically these constructions are ab-surd; Adam was not born since his day, Eve was not one of her own daughters.

Milton combines comparative with su-perlative forms for emphatic effect.
8. I.e., to make a cool breeze welcome.
9. Conversation. "Wanted": lacked.
1. Who lurk in every sort of cover.
2. Reared up.
3. Lynxes and leopards.

His lithe proboscis; close the serpent sly,
Insinuating,[4] wove with Gordian twine
His braided train,[5] and of his fatal guile
Gave proof unheeded. Others on the grass   350
Couched and now filled with pasture, gazing sat,
Or bedward ruminating;[6] for the sun,
Declined, was hasting now with prone career
To th' ocean isles,[7] and in th' ascending scale
Of Heaven the stars that usher evening rose: 355
When Satan, still in gaze as first he stood,
Scarce thus at length failed speech recovered sad:[8]
    "O Hell! what do mine eyes with grief behold?
Into our room of bliss thus high advanced
Creatures of other mold, Earth-born perhaps,   360
Not spirits, yet to heavenly spirits bright
Little inferior; whom my thoughts pursue
With wonder, and could love; so lively shines
In them divine resemblance, and such grace
The hand that formed them on their shape hath poured.[9]   365
Ah! gentle pair, ye little think how nigh
Your change approaches, when all these delights
Will vanish, and deliver ye to woe,
More woe, the more your taste is now of joy:
Happy, but for so happy[1] ill secured   370
Long to continue, and this high seat, your Heaven,
Ill fenced for Heaven to keep out such a foe
As now is entered; yet no purposed foe
To you, whom I could pity thus forlorn,
Though I unpitied. League with you I seek,   375
And mutual amity, so strait, so close,
That I with you must dwell, or you with me,
Henceforth.[2] My dwelling, haply, may not please,
Like this fair Paradise, your sense; yet such
Accept your Maker's work; he gave it me,   380
Which I as freely give. Hell shall unfold,
To entertain you two, her widest gates,
And send forth all her kings; there will be room,
Not like these narrow limits, to receive
Your numerous offspring; if no better place,   385
Thank him who puts me, loath, to this revenge
On you, who wrong me not, for him who wronged.[3]

4. Writhing and twisting, but with a glance at the Tempter's rhetorical techniques.
5. Checkered body. "Gordian twine": knots, like the Gordian knot, cut by Alexander the Great.
6. The animals are chewing their cuds before bedtime; in Paradise, where the animal kingdom is not yet subject to death, they are perforce vegetarians.
7. The Azores.
8. The choked, laborious line mirrors Satan's heavy, congested mind.
9. Though Satan's moral values are topsy-turvy ("Evil, be thou my Good," he has said in the first part of Book IV), his aesthetic values are strictly orthodox.
1. Such happiness.
2. Though it starts in simple admiration, Satan's friendship for mankind is, at the end, rather grisly and sardonic. The turning point seems to be "though I unpitied" (line 375)—the reaction of a spoiled child.
3. I.e., it is not my fault; Satan's favorite phrase.

And, should I at your harmless innocence
Melt, as I do, yet public reason just—
Honor and empire with revenge enlarged   390
By conquering this new world—compels me now
To do what else, though damned, I should abhor."[4]
    So spake the fiend, and with necessity,
The tyrant's plea, excused his devilish deeds.
Then from his lofty stand on that high tree   395
Down he alights among the sportful herd
Of those four-footed kinds, himself now one,
Now other, as their shape served best his end
Nearer to view his prey, and unespied,
To mark what of their state he more might learn   400
By word or action marked. About them round
A lion now he stalks with fiery glare;
Then as a tiger, who by chance hath spied
In some purlieu[5] two gentle fawns at play,
Straight couches close; then, rising, changes oft   405
His couchant watch, as one who chose his ground,
Whence rushing he might surest seize them both
Griped in each paw * * *

4. Satan's final reason for destroying Adam and Eve is thoroughly Satanic; it is *ragione di stato*, reason of state, the public interest.
5. The outskirt of a forest. Note that Satan can and does enter any animal he wants; it is only for the special purposes of the temptation that he finds the serpent specially convenient.

Summary   By eavesdropping on Adam and Eve, Satan learns of the prohibited Tree of Knowledge; this weakness he resolves to exploit. Meanwhile Uriel, rendered suspicious by Satan's fierce demeanor outside Paradise, reports to Gabriel, the angel specially assigned to guard mankind, that a diabolic intruder may be near. Gabriel promises to search him out. After Adam and Eve say their evening prayers and retire, Gabriel divides his night watch into groups, assigning Ithuriel and Zephon to guard closely the bower of Adam and Eve. They find Satan whispering in the ear of the sleeping Eve, and bring him before Gabriel. A battle impends, but is averted by a heavenly signal, and Satan flees out of Paradise.

Book V. *Summary*   In the morning Eve is distressed by her dreams of the previous night, which she relates to Adam; he comforts her. Meanwhile God dispatches Raphael to warn man of the approaching danger. Raphael arrives about noon, and dines with Adam and Eve. He then warns his hosts of the need to remain obedient, and, to explain the risks they run, recounts the story of Satan's revolt and fall. He describes how Satan, pretending that God's creation of the Son was an offense to angelic dignity, persuaded a host of his fellow angels to withdraw their allegiance to God and set up a camp in the north. When open war on God was announced, however, one of these angels was able to repent. The seraph Abdiel, though scorned by his fellows, denounced the rebellion and returned, heroically alone, to the camp of God's followers.

Book VI. Summary   Continuing the story of the war in Heaven, Raphael describes the assembling of the armies and a first skirmish in which Satan is both insulted and wounded by Abdiel. After the first day's battle, the evil angels retire discomfited; but overnight Satan invents cannon with which, on the second day, the good angels are put to some disorder. In the fury of the fight, however, they pull up mountains by the roots and bury the cannon beneath them; thus the issue remains inconclusive. On the third day, God withdraws all his armies and sends the Son alone into battle; the Son drives his enemies irresistibly over the wall of Heaven, and after falling nine days through Chaos they are swallowed up in Hell.

From Book VII

[*The Invocation*][1]

Descend from Heaven, Urania, by that name
If rightly thou art called,[2] whose voice divine
Following, above th' Olympian hill I soar,
Above the flight of Pegasean wing![3]
The meaning, not the name I call: for thou   5
Nor of the Muses nine, nor on the top
Of old Olympus dwell'st, but heavenly born,
Before the hills appeared, or fountain flowed,
Thou with eternal Wisdom didst converse,
Wisdom thy sister, and with her didst play   10
In presence of th' Almighty Father,[4] pleased
With thy celestial song. Up led by thee
Into the Heaven of Heavens I have presumed,
An earthly guest, and drawn empyreal air,
Thy tempering;[5] with like safety guided down,   15
Return me to my native element:
Lest from this flying steed unreined (as once
Bellerophon,[6] though from a lower clime),
Dismounted, on th' Aleian field I fall,
Erroneous[7] there to wander and forlorn.   20

1. To start the second half of his poem, Milton must counterbalance the destruction of the war in Heaven with the creation by God of a new universe, centering on the Earth. Book VII is devoted to this topic; and to approach so vast a subject, Milton once more invokes his Muse.
2. Milton has only the names of classical Muses with which to invoke the spiritual principles of Christian theology. Properly the Muse of astronomy, Urania is also the symbol of heavenly love and of divine wisdom; Milton here renews the invocation he made in Book I.
3. Pegasus, the flying horse of poetry, suggests (in connection with Bellero-

phon, line 18) Milton's sense of his own perilous audacity in writing so vast a poem.
4. In Proverbs viii.30, Wisdom is made to speak of "playing always before God" previous even to the Creation. Milton makes his Muse coeval with divine wisdom.
5. Tempered by thee.
6. Bellerophon tried to explore the stars astride Pegasus the flying horse; but Zeus sent a gadfly to sting Pegasus, and his rider, after falling onto the Aleian plain in Lycia, wandered about there till he died.
7. From Latin *errare*, "to wander," as well as "to be mistaken."

Half yet remains unsung, but narrower bound
Within the visible diurnal sphere;
Standing on Earth, not rapt above the pole,
More safe I sing with mortal voice, unchanged
To hoarse or mute, though fall'n on evil days,   25
On evil days though fall'n, and evil tongues;
In darkness, and with dangers compassed round,
And solitude; yet not alone, while thou
Visit'st my slumbers nightly, or when morn
Purples the east:[8] still govern thou my song,   30
Urania, and fit audience find, though few.
But drive far off the barbarous dissonance
Of Bacchus and his revelers, the race
Of that wild rout that tore the Thracian bard[9]
In Rhodope, where woods and rocks had ears   35
To rapture, till the savage clamor drowned
Both harp and voice; nor could the Muse defend
Her son. So fail not thou, who thee implores:
For thou art heavenly, she an empty dream.

8. Milton composed mostly at night or very early in the morning.
9. The Thracian Bacchantes, female worshipers of Bacchus, tore Orpheus to pieces in Rhodope, though even the rocks and trees were so impressed with his music that they refused to be used against the poet. See *Lycidas*, lines 58–63. Orpheus was son of Calliope, the epic Muse.

Summary   At Adam's request, Raphael continues his narration and describes how God, to replace the fallen angels, created the world, its creatures, and finally man, in the course of six days; the story of the creation concludes, on the seventh day, with a chorus of thanksgiving by the angels.

Book VIII. Summary   Adam asks Raphael why so many and such splendid stars seem to be at the service of the earth, which appears smaller and less noble than they; at this point Eve leaves her husband and his guest to continue the discussion alone. Raphael proposes various astronomical possibilities but gives no conclusive answer to Adam's question, urging him instead to confine his curiosity to more practical matters. Adam now, at Raphael's request, describes his own recollections of his creation, as well as his first meeting and marriage with Eve. In the course of the story, he shows a somewhat exaggerated deference for Eve, which the angel rebukes; Adam is to be the head of the family, and follow his own judgment, not his wife's. Repeating his admonitions to beware of temptation, Raphael departs.

Book IX

The Argument

Satan, having compassed the Earth, with meditated guile returns as a mist by night into Paradise; enters into the serpent sleeping. Adam and Eve in the morning go forth to their labors, which Eve proposes to divide in several places, each laboring apart: Adam consents not, alleging the danger lest that enemy of whom they were forewarned should attempt her found alone. Eve, loath to be thought not circumspect or firm enough, urges her going apart, the rather desirous to make trial of her strength; Adam at last yields. The serpent finds her alone: his subtle approach, first gazing, then speaking, with much flattery extolling Eve above all other creatures. Eve, wondering to hear the serpent speak, asks how he attained to human speech and such understanding not till now; the serpent answers that by tasting of a certain tree in the garden he attained both to speech and reason, till then void of both. Eve requires him to bring her to that tree, and finds it to be the Tree of Knowledge forbidden: the serpent, now grown bolder, with many wiles and arguments induces her at length to eat. She, pleased with the taste, deliberates a while whether to impart thereof to Adam or not; at last brings him of the fruit; relates what persuaded her to eat thereof. Adam, at first amazed, but perceiving her lost, resolves, through vehemence of love, to perish with her, and, extenuating[1] the trespass, eats also of the fruit. The effects thereof in them both; they seek to cover their nakedness; then fall to variance and accusation of one another.

> No more of talk where God[2] or angel guest
> With man, as with his friend, familiar used
> To sit indulgent, and with him partake
> Rural repast, permitting him the while
> Venial[3] discourse unblamed. I now must change   5
> Those notes to tragic; foul distrust, and breach
> Disloyal, on the part of man, revolt
> And disobedience; on the part of Heaven,
> Now alienated, distance and distaste,
> Anger and just rebuke, and judgment given,   10
> That brought into this world a world of woe,
> Sin and her shadow Death, and Misery,
> Death's harbinger. Sad task! yet argument
> Not less but more heroic than the wrath
> Of stern Achilles on his foe pursued   15
> Thrice fugitive about Troy wall; or rage
> Of Turnus for Lavinia disespoused;
> Or Neptune's ire, or Juno's, that so long
> Perplexed the Greek, and Cytherea's son:[4]

1. Not "diminishing" or "excusing" as in customary English usage, but carrying further, drawing out.
2. God, of course, has not been lunching with Adam; but since man is about to fall, the age is now over when such an occasion could be contemplated.
3. Permissible.
4. In the *Iliad* (**XXII**), Achilles pursues Hector three times around Troy wall before catching him. In the *Aeneid*, Aeneas must fight with Turnus for the hand of Lavinia. Neptune (or Poseidon) was unfriendly to Odysseus (the Greek); Juno (or Hera) to Aeneas, who was Cytherea's, i.e., Aphrodite's, son by Anchises.

If answerable style I can obtain 20
Of my celestial Patroness,[5] who deigns
Her nightly visitation unimplored,
And dictates to me slumbering, or inspires
Easy my unpremeditated verse,[6]
Since first this subject for heroic song 25
Pleased me, long choosing and beginning late,[7]
Not sedulous by nature to indite
Wars, hitherto the only argument
Heroic deemed, chief mastery to dissect[8]
With long and tedious havoc fabled knights 30
In battles feigned (the better fortitude
Of patience and heroic martyrdom
Unsung), or to describe races and games,
Or tilting furniture,[9] emblazoned shields,
Impresses quaint, caparisons and steeds, 35
Bases and tinsel trappings, gorgeous knights
At joust and tournament; then marshaled feast
Served up in hall with sewers and seneschals:[1]
The skill of artifice or office mean;
Not that which justly gives heroic name 40
To person or to poem. Me, of these
Nor skilled nor studious, higher argument
Remains,[2] sufficient of itself to raise
That name,[3] unless an age too late, or cold
Climate, or years, damp my intended wing 45
Depressed; and much they may if all be mine,
Not hers who brings it nightly to my ear.
     The sun was sunk, and after him the star
Of Hesperus, whose office is to bring
Twilight upon the Earth, short arbiter 50
'Twixt day and night, and now from end to end
Night's hemisphere had veiled the horizon round,
When Satan, who late fled before the threats
Of Gabriel out of Eden,[4] now improved
In meditated fraud and malice, bent 55
On man's destruction, mauger what might hap
Of heavier on himself,[5] fearless returned.

---

5. The muse, Urania.
6. Milton, we are told by his nephew Edward Philips, used to wake up in the morning with lines of poetry full-formed in his head; he would then dictate them to an amanuensis.
7. Milton's early plans for epics, preserved in manuscript, did center on national heroes; his choice of a sacred subject is a novelty within the epic tradition. "Sedulous": eager.
8. I.e., in describing wars one's chief task is to dissect; dissect, in its strict Latin sense of "cut apart," but perhaps also with a comic overtone from the anatomy table.

9. The equipment of tournaments; "impresses quaint": elaborate devices on shields; "bases": trappings for horses.
1. Waiters and stewards.
2. I.e., for me, when these things are set aside which I neither can nor want to do, there remains a higher argument.
3. I.e., the name heroic poet. "Age too late": not Milton's age, but the age of the world. Milton felt a "cold climate," by forcing people to keep their mouths shut and mumble, was inimical to epic poetry. "Damp": stupefy, benumb.
4. At the end of Book IV.
5. Despite the peril of heavier (punishments).

By night he fled, and at midnight returned
From compassing the Earth—cautious of day
Since Uriel, regent of the sun, descried   60
His entrance, and forewarned the Cherubim
That kept their watch.[6] Thence, full of anguish, driven,
The space of seven continued nights he rode
With darkness; thrice the equinoctial line[7]
He circled, four times crossed the car of Night   65
From pole to pole, traversing each colure;
On the eighth returned, and on the coast averse
From entrance or cherubic watch by stealth
Found unsuspected way. There was a place   70
(Now not, though sin, not time, first wrought the change)
Where Tigris, at the foot of Paradise,
Into a gulf shot under ground, till part
Rose up a fountain by the Tree of Life.
In with the river sunk, and with it rose,   75
Satan, involved in rising mist; then sought
Where to lie hid. Sea he had searched and land
From Eden over Pontus, and the pool
Maeotis, up beyond the river Ob;[8]
Downward as far antarctic; and, in length,   80
West from Orontes to the ocean barred
At Darien, thence to the land where flows
Ganges and Indus.[9] Thus the orb he roamed
With narrow search, and with inspection deep
Considered every creature, which of all   85
Most opportune might serve his wiles, and found
The serpent subtlest beast of all the field.[1]
Him, after long debate, irresolute
Of thoughts revolved,[2] his final sentence chose
Fit vessel, fittest imp[3] of fraud, in whom   90
To enter, and his dark suggestions hide
From sharpest sight; for in the wily snake
Whatever sleights none would suspicious mark,
As from his wit and native subtlety
Proceeding, which, in other beasts observed,   95
Doubt[4] might beget of diabolic power
Active within beyond the sense of brute.

6. At the beginning of Book IV. These connections with Book IV not only bridge the intervening narration, but emphasize a balancing of the whole epic; see the headnote.
7. The equator. The colures are the two great circles of the celestial sphere which intersect at the poles. By circling the globe, either from east to west or over the north and south poles, Satan can remain continually hidden in darkness.
8. Pontus is the Black Sea, the pool Maeotis the swamps of the Sea of Azov;

the river Ob flows north through Siberia into the Arctic Ocean.
9. Flying west from Orontes in Syria, Satan now crosses the Atlantic to the Isthmus of Panama (Darien), then crosses the Pacific and southeast Asia to India.
1. Genesis iii.1 describes the serpent as the subtlest beast of the field.
2. I.e., unable to decide among his revolving thoughts. "Sentence": decision.
3. Graft, offshoot.
4. Suspicion.

Thus he resolved, but first from inward grief
His bursting passion into plaints thus poured:
　　"O Earth, how like to Heaven, if not preferred
More justly, seat worthier of Gods, as built　　　　100
With second thought, reforming what was old!
For what God, after better, worse would build?
Terrestrial Heaven, danced round by other Heavens,
That shine, yet bear their bright officious lamps,
Light above light, for thee alone, as seems,　　　　105
In thee concent'ring all their precious beams
Of sacred influence![5] As God in Heaven
Is center, yet extends to all, so thou
Cent'ring receiv'st from all those orbs; in thee,
Not in themselves, all their known virtue appears,　　110
Productive in herb, plant, and nobler birth
Of creatures animate with gradual life
Of growth, sense, reason,[6] all summed up in man.
With what delight could I have walked thee round,
If I could joy in aught; sweet interchange　　　　115
Of hill and valley, rivers, woods, and plains,
Now land, now sea, and shores with forest crowned,
Rocks, dens, and caves! But I in none of these
Find place or refuge; and the more I see
Pleasures about me, so much more I feel　　　　120
Torment within me, as from the hateful siege[7]
Of contraries; all good to me becomes
Bane,[8] and in Heaven much worse would be my state.
But neither here seek I, no, nor in Heaven,
To dwell, unless by mastering Heaven's Supreme;　　125
Nor hope to be myself less miserable
By what I seek, but others to make such
As I, though thereby worse to me redound.
For only in destroying I find ease
To my relentless thoughts, and him [9] destroyed,　　130
Or won to what may work his utter loss,
For whom all this was made, all this [1] will soon
Follow, as to him linked in weal or woe:
In woe then, that destruction wide may range!
To me shall be the glory sole among　　　　135
The infernal Powers, in one day to have marred
What he, Almighty styled, six nights and days
Continued making, and who knows how long
Before had been contriving? though perhaps
Not longer than since I in one night freed　　　　140

---

5. Satan, like Adam in Book VIII, is impressed that so many heavenly bodies center on (and "serve") the earth—as the old Ptolemaic astronomy taught that they did. "Officious": dutiful.
6. The sacred influence of the stars was thought to generate and foster life within the earth.
7. Conflict.
8. Poison.
9. I.e., man.
1. I.e., the created cosmos.

From servitude inglorious well-nigh half
Th' angelic name, and thinner left the throng
Of his adorers. He, to be avenged,
And to repair his numbers thus impaired,
Whether such virtue,[2] spent of old, now failed   145
More angels to create (if they at least
Are his created),[3] or to spite us more,
Determined to advance into our room
A creature formed of earth, and him endow,
Exalted from so base original,   150
With heavenly spoils, our spoils. What he decreed
He effected; man he made, and for him built
Magnificent this World, and Earth his seat,
Him lord pronounced, and, O indignity!
Subjected to his service angel-wings   155
And flaming ministers, to watch and tend
Their earthy charge. Of these the vigilance
I dread, and to elude, thus wrapt in mist
Of midnight vapor, glide obscure, and pry
In every bush and brake, where hap may find   160
The serpent sleeping, in whose mazy folds
To hide me, and the dark intent I bring.
O foul descent! that I, who erst contended
With Gods to sit the highest, am now constrained
Into a beast, and, mixed with bestial slime,   165
This essence to incarnate and imbrute,[4]
That to the height of deity aspired!
But what will not ambition and revenge
Descend to? Who aspires must down as low
As high he soared, obnoxious,[5] first or last,   170
To basest things. Revenge, at first though sweet,
Bitter ere long back on itself recoils.
Let it; I reck not, so it light well aimed,
Since higher I fall short, on him who next
Provokes my envy, this new favorite   175
Of Heaven, this man of clay, son of despite,
Whom, us the more to spite,[6] his Maker raised
From dust: spite then with spite is best repaid."
    So saying, through each thicket, dank or dry,
Like a black mist low-creeping, he held on   180
His midnight search, where soonest he might find
The serpent. Him fast sleeping soon he found,
In labyrinth of many a round self-rolled,
His head the midst, well stored with subtle wiles:
Not yet in horrid shade or dismal den,   185

2. Strength, energy.
3. Satan never raises this question, whether angels are created or independent beings, without hesitating over it.
4. Satan's incarnation in a snake is a grotesque parody of the Son of God's incarnation in Christ.
5. Subject to.
6. Satan sees God in his own image, as a spiteful creature.

Nor nocent [7] yet, but on the grassy herb,
Fearless, unfeared, he slept. In at his mouth
The devil entered, and his brutal sense,
In heart or head, possessing soon inspired
With act intelligential; but his sleep   190
Disturbed not, waiting close[8] th' approach of morn.
    Now, whenas sacred light began to dawn
In Eden on the humid flowers, that breathed
Their morning incense, when all things that breathe
From th' Earth's great altar send up silent praise   195
To the Creator, and his nostrils fill
With grateful smell, forth came the human pair,
And joined their vocal worship to the choir
Of creatures wanting voice; that done, partake
The season,[9] prime for sweetest scents and airs;   200
Then cómmune how that day they best may ply
Their growing work; for much their work outgrew
The hands' dispatch of two gardening so wide:
And Eve first to her husband thus began:
    "Adam, well may we labor still [1] to dress   205
This garden, still to tend plant, herb, and flower,
Our pleasant task enjoined; but, till more hands
Aid us, the work under our labor grows,
Luxurious by restraint: what we by day
Lop overgrown, or prune, or prop, or bind,   210
One night or two with wanton growth derides,
Tending to wild. Thou, therefore, now advise,
Or hear what to my mind first thoughts present.
Let us divide our labors; thou where choice
Leads thee, or where most needs, whether to wind   215
The woodbine round this arbor, or direct
The clasping ivy where to climb; while I
In yonder spring [2] of roses intermixed
With myrtle find what to redress till noon.
For, while so near each other thus all day   220
Our task we choose, what wonder if so near
Looks intervene and smiles, or objects new
Casual discourse draw on, which intermits
Our day's work, brought to little, though begun
Early, and th' hour of supper comes unearned!"   225
    To whom mild answer Adam thus returned:
"Sole Eve, associate sole, to me beyond
Compare above all living creatures dear!
Well hast thou motioned,[3] well thy thoughts employed
How we might best fulfil the work which here   230
God hath assigned us, nor of me shalt pass

7. Harmful.
8. In secret.
9. I.e., go forth into the morning air.
"Prime": the best.

1. Continually.
2. Growth.
3. Suggested.

Unpraised; for nothing lovelier can be found
In woman than to study household good,
And good works in her husband to promote.[4]
Yet not so strictly hath our Lord imposed   235
Labor as to debar us when we need
Refreshment, whether food or talk between,
Food of the mind, or this sweet intercourse
Of looks and smiles; for smiles from reason flow,
To brute denied, and are of love the food,   240
Love, not the lowest end of human life.
For not to irksome toil, but to delight,
He made us, and delight to reason joined.
These paths and bowers doubt not but our joint hands
Will keep from wilderness with ease, as wide   245
As we need walk, till younger hands ere long
Assist us. But, if much converse perhaps
Thee satiate, to short absence I could yield;
For solitude sometimes is best society,
And short retirement urges sweet return.   250
But other doubt possesses me, lest harm
Befall thee, severed from me; for thou know'st
What hath been warned us, what malicious foe,
Envying our happiness, and of his own
Despairing, seeks to work us woe and shame   255
By sly assault, and somewhere nigh at hand
Watches, no doubt, with greedy hope to find
His wish and best advantage, us asunder,[5]
Hopeless to circumvent us joined, where each
To other speedy aid might lend at need.   260
Whether his first design be to withdraw
Our fealty from God, or to disturb
Conjugal love, than which perhaps no bliss
Enjoyed by us excites his envy more;
Or this, or worse,[6] leave not the faithful side   265
That gave thee being, still shades thee and protects.
The wife, where danger or dishonor lurks,
Safest and seemliest by her husband stays,
Who guards her, or with her the worst endures."
    To whom the virgin [7] majesty of Eve,   270
As one who loves, and some unkindness meets,
With sweet austere composure thus replied:
    "Offspring of Heaven and Earth, and all Earth's lord!
That such an enemy we have, who seeks
Our ruin, both by thee informed I learn,   275
And from the parting angel overheard,

4. Proverbs xxxi is devoted to the praise of a good wife, and Milton doubtless had it in mind here.
5. I.e., to find us apart, which will an-swer his wishes and serve his advantage.
6. I.e., whether this or something worse be his intent.
7. Unspotted.

As in a shady nook I stood behind,
Just then returned at shut of evening flowers.
But that thou shouldst my firmness therefore doubt
To God or thee, because we have a foe   280
May tempt it, I expected not to hear.
His violence thou fear'st not, being such
As we, not capable of death or pain,
Can either not receive, or can repel.
His fraud is, then, thy fear; which plain infers   285
Thy equal fear that my firm faith and love
Can by his fraud be shaken or seduced:
Thoughts, which how found they harbor in thy breast,
Adam, misthought of her to thee so dear?" [8]

      To whom, with healing words, Adam replied: 290
"Daughter of God and man, immortal Eve,
For such thou art, from sin and blame entire; [9]
Not diffident of thee do I dissuade
Thy absence from my sight, but to avoid
Th' attempt itself, intended by our foe.   295
For he who tempts, though in vain, at least asperses [1]
The tempted with dishonor foul, supposed
Not incorruptible of faith, not proof
Against temptation. Thou thyself with scorn
And anger wouldst resent the offered wrong,   300
Though ineffectual found; misdeem not, then,
If such affront I labor to avert
From thee alone, which on us both at once
The enemy, though bold, will hardly dare;
Or, daring, first on me th' assault shall light.   305
Nor thou his malice and false guile contemn——
Subtle he needs must be who could seduce
Angels—nor think superfluous others' aid.
I from the influence of thy looks receive
Access in every virtue; [2] in thy sight   310
More wise, more watchful, stronger, if need were
Of outward strength; while shame, thou looking on,
Shame to be overcome or overreached, [3]
Would utmost vigor raise, and raised unite.
Why shouldst not thou like sense within thee feel   315
When I am present, and thy trial choose
With me, best witness of thy virtue tried?"
      So spake domestic Adam in his care
And matrimonial love; but Eve, who thought
Less[4] attributed to her faith sincere,   320

---

8. I.e., these thoughts were misthought
of (misapplied to) her to thee so dear
(me).
9. "Entire" is from Latin *integer*, untouched. "Diffident": the usual English
meaning is "shy," "timid"; Milton emphasizes the Latin roots, *dis* + *fides* =

mistrustful.
1. The word is from Latin *spargere*, to
sprinkle, with overtones from English
"aspersion," an ugly insinuation.
2. Extra strength.
3. Overpowered or outwitted.
4. Too little.

Thus her reply with accent sweet renewed:
"If this be our condition, thus to dwell
In narrow circuit straitened by a foe,
Subtle or violent, we not endued
Single with like defence wherever met,   325
How are we happy, still in fear of harm?
But harm precedes not sin: only our foe
Tempting affronts us with his foul esteem
Of our integrity: his foul esteem
Sticks no dishonor on our front,[5] but turns   330
Foul on himself; then wherefore shunned or feared
By us, who rather double honor gain
From his surmise proved false, find peace within,
Favor from Heaven, our witness, from th' event?
And what is faith, love, virtue, unassayed   335
Alone, without exterior help sustained?
Let us not then suspect our happy state
Left so imperfect by the Maker wise
As not secure to single or combined.
Frail is our happiness, if this be so;   340
And Eden were no Eden, thus exposed."
    To whom thus Adam fervently replied:
"O woman, best are all things as the will
Of God ordained them; his creating hand
Nothing imperfect or deficient left   345
Of all that he created, much less man,
Or aught that might his happy state secure,
Secure from outward force. Within himself
The danger lies, yet lies within his power;
Against his will he can receive no harm.   350
But God left free the will; for what obeys
Reason is free; and reason he made right,
But bid her well beware, and still erect,[6]
Lest, by some fair appearing good surprised,
She dictate false, and misinform the will   355
To do what God expressly hath forbid.
Not then mistrust, but tender love, enjoins
That I should mind [7] thee oft; and mind thou me.
Firm we subsist, yet possible to swerve,
Since reason not impossibly may meet   360
Some specious object by the foe suborned,
And fall into deception unaware,
Not keeping strictest watch, as she was warned.
Seek not temptation, then, which to avoid
Were better, and most likely if from me   365

5. Forehead.
6. Remain alert.

7. Remind; in the next phrase, "mind" means "obey."

Thou sever not: trial will come unsought.
Wouldst thou approve thy constancy, approve [8]
First thy obedience; th' other who can know,
Not seeing thee attempted, who attest?
But if thou think trial unsought may find   370
Us both securer than thus warned thou seem'st,
Go; for thy stay, not free, absents thee more.
Go in thy native innocence; rely
On what thou hast of virtue; summon all;
For God towards thee hath done his part: do thine.'   375
    So spake the patriarch of mankind; but Eve
Persisted; yet submiss, though last, replied:
    "With thy permission,[9] then, and thus forewarned,
Chiefly by what thy own last reasoning words
Touched only, that our trial, when least sought,   380
May find us both perhaps far less prepared,
The willinger I go, nor much expect
A foe so proud will first the weaker seek;
So bent, the more shall shame him his repulse."
Thus saying, from her husband's hand her hand   385
Soft she withdrew, and like a wood nymph light,
Oread or dryad, or of Delia's train,[1]
Betook her to the groves, but Delia's self
In gait surpassed and goddesslike deport,
Though not as she with bow and quiver armed,   390
But with such gardening tools as art yet rude,
Guiltless of fire[2] had formed, or angels brought.
To Pales, or Pomona, thus adorned,
Likest she seemed, Pomona when she fled
Vertumnus, or to Ceres in her prime,   395
Yet virgin of Proserpina from Jove.[3]
Her long with ardent look his eye pursued
Delighted, but desiring more her stay.
Oft he to her his charge of quick return
Repeated; she to him as oft engaged   400
To be returned by noon amid the bower,
And all things in best order to invite
Noontide repast, or afternoon's repose.
O much deceived, much failing, hapless Eve,

---

8. Prove, give evidence of.
9. Eve takes a reluctant and extorted permission as free leave to do what she wants. Though apparently submissive, she gets the last word.
1. An "oread" is a nymph of the mountain, a "dryad" one of the wood. "Delia" is Diana or Artemis, goddess of the chase, who when she hunted was accompanied by a train of nymphs.
2. There was no need of fire in Paradise; but that fire is a possession which renders one guilty suggests an overtone of the Prometheus myth.
3. Pales is a Roman goddess of flocks, Pomona a Roman divinity of fruits and orchards. Pomona was wooed by Vertumnus, god of spring, who assumed all sorts of shapes to win her. Ceres, the Mother Nature of the ancients (hence, the word "cereal"), bore Proserpina to Jupiter. All three goddesses are patrons of agriculture, like Eve.

Of thy presumed return![4] Event perverse!   405
Thou never from that hour in Paradise
Found'st either sweet repast, or sound repose;
Such ambush hid among sweet flowers and shades
Waited with hellish rancor imminent[5]
To intercept thy way, or send thee back   410
Despoiled of innocence, of faith, of bliss.
For now, and since first break of dawn, the fiend,
Mere serpent in appearance, forth was come,
And on his quest, where likeliest he might find
The only two of mankind, but in them   415
The whole included race, his purposed prey.
In bower and field he sought, where any tuft
Of grove or garden-plot more pleasant lay,
Their tendance[6] or plantation for delight;
By fountain or by shady rivulet   420
He sought them both, but wished his hap might find
Eve separate; he wished, but not with hope
Of what so seldom chanced; when to his wish,
Beyond his hope, Eve separate he spies,
Veiled in a cloud of fragrance, where she stood,   425
Half spied, so thick the roses bushing round
About her glowed, oft stooping to support
Each flower of slender stalk, whose head though gay
Carnation, purple, azure, or specked with gold,
Hung drooping unsustained, them she upstays   430
Gently with myrtle band, mindless the while
Herself, though fairest unsupported flower,
From her best prop so far, and storm so nigh.[7]
Nearer he drew, and many a walk traversed
Of stateliest covert, cedar, pine, or palm;   435
Then voluble[8] and bold, now hid, now seen
Among thick-woven arborets[9] and flowers
Embordered on each bank, the hand of Eve:
Spot more delicious than those gardens feigned
Or of revived Adonis,[1] or renowned   440
Alcinous, host of old Laertes' son,
Or that, not mystic, where the sapient king[2]
Held dalliance with his fair Egyptian spouse.
Much he the place admired, the person more.
As one who long in populous city pent,   445

4. "Much deceived" carries over; Eve was "much deceived of" (about) her "presumed return."
5. Threatening.
6. Object of their tending.
7. The conceit of the flower-gatherer who is herself gathered is repeated here from IV.270, where it was applied to Proserpina.
8. Rolling (a Latinism).
9. Bushes. "Hand": handiwork.
1. The garden of Adonis was a heavenly bower where Venus' lover was supposed

still to lie in secret, recovering from his wound received on earth (Venus would not allow him to die). Alcinous was king of the Phaeacians. His garden, visited by Odysseus ("old Laertes' son"), is described in the *Odyssey*.
2. Solomon; his "fair Egyptian spouse" is Pharaoh's daughter: Milton is referring to the Song of Solomon vi.2. The fact that it is "not mystic" (i.e., not mythical) distinguishes the Scriptural garden from the "feigned" (line 439) ones of classical legend.

Where houses thick and sewers annoy[3] the air,
Forth issuing on a summer's morn to breathe
Among the pleasant villages and farms
Adjoined, from each thing met conceives delight,
The smell of grain, or tedded[4] grass, or kine,   450
Or dairy, each rural sight, each rural sound:
If chance with nymphlike step fair virgin pass,[5]
What pleasing seemed, for her now pleases more,
She most, and in her look sums all delight.[6]
Such pleasure took the serpent to behold   455
This flowery plat,[7] the sweet recess of Eve
Thus early, thus alone; her heavenly form
Angelic, but more soft, and feminine,
Her graceful innocence, her every air
Of gesture or least action overawed   460
His malice, and with rapine[8] sweet bereaved
His fierceness of the fierce intent it brought:
That space the evil one abstracted stood
From his own evil, and for the time remained
Stupidly good,[9] of enmity disarmed,   465
Of guile, of hate, of envy, of revenge.
But the hot Hell that always in him burns,
Though in mid Heaven, soon ended his delight,
And tortures him now more, the more he sees
Of pleasure not for him ordained: then soon   470
Fierce hate he recollects, and all his thoughts
Of mischief, gratulating,[1] thus excites:
    "Thoughts, whither have ye led me? with what sweet
Compulsion thus transported to forget
What hither brought us? hate, not love, nor hope   475
Of Paradise for Hell, hope here to taste
Of pleasure, but all pleasure to destroy,
Save what is in destroying:[2] other joy
To me is lost. Then let me not let pass
Occasion which now smiles; behold alone   480
The woman, opportune to all attempts,
Her husband, for I view far round, not nigh,
Whose higher intellectual more I shun,
And strength, of courage haughty, and of limb
Heroic built, though of terrestrial mold:[3]   485
Foe not informidable, exempt from wound,[4]
I not; so much hath Hell debased, and pain

3. Make noisome, befoul.
4. Tossed and drying in the sun.
5. I.e., if it chance that with nymph-like step a fair virgin should pass.
6. I.e., in her look sums up, or epitomizes, all delight.
7. Plot.
8. It is a deliberate paradox that her sweetness can ravish his malice; the word is deliberately overviolent.
9. Without his evil, Satan (like many wicked people) is quite dull and ordinary. But at the moment he is stunned.
1. Exulting.
2. What brought Satan to Paradise was not hope of pleasure, but the wish to destroy all pleasure except the pleasure of destruction itself.
3. Made of earth.
4. Adam in the state of innocence is invulnerable.

Enfeebled me, to what I was in Heaven.
She fair, divinely fair, fit love for gods,
Not terrible, though terror be in love   490
And beauty, not approached by stronger hate,
Hate stronger, under show of love well feigned,
The way which to her ruin now I tend."[5]
      So spake the enemy of mankind, enclosed
In serpent, inmate bad, and toward Eve   495
Addressed his way, not with indented wave,
Prone on the ground, as since, but on his rear,
Circular base of rising folds, that towered
Fold above fold a surging maze; his head
Crested aloft, and carbuncle[6] his eyes;   500
With burnished neck of verdant gold, erect
Amidst his circling spires,[7] that on the grass
Floated redundant. Pleasing was his shape,
And lovely; never since of serpent kind
Lovelier, not those that in Illyria changed   505
Hermione and Cadmus,[8] or the god
In Epidaurus;[9] nor to which transformed
Ammonian Jove, or Capitoline was seen,
He with Olympias, this with her who bore
Scipio, the height of Rome.[1] With tract oblique   510
At first, as one who sought access, but feared
To interrupt, sidelong he works his way.
As when a ship by skillful steersman wrought
Nigh river's mouth or foreland, where the wind
Veers oft, as oft so steers, and shifts her sail: 515
So varied he, and of his tortuous train
Curled many a wanton wreath in sight of Eve,
To lure her eye: she busied heard the sound
Of rustling leaves, but minded not, as used
To such disport before her through the field,   520
From every beast, more duteous at her call,
Than at Circean call the herd disguised.[2]
He bolder now, uncalled before her stood:
But as in gaze admiring; oft he bowed
His turret crest, and sleek enameled neck,   525
Fawning, and licked the ground whereon she trod.
His gentle dumb expression turned at length

5. I.e., love and beauty are terrible unless counteracted by hate—as they are being counteracted in Satan, to the ruin of Eve.
6. Deep red, inflamed.
7. Coils. "Redundant": abundantly, to excess.
8. Ovid tells how Cadmus and Harmonia (Milton's "Hermione") were changed to serpents after they retired (in despair at the misfortunes of their children) to Illyria.
9. Aesculapius, god of medicine, had a temple at Epidaurus, from which he sometimes emerged in the form of a serpent.
1. Jupiter Ammon ("Ammonian Jove"), in the form of a snake, was said to have consorted with Olympias to beget Alexander the Great; and in the same way, the Jupiter of the Roman capitol (Jove "Capitoline") was thought to have begotten Scipio Africanus, the savior and leader ("height") of Rome.
2. Circe, who enchanted men into the shape of swine, was attended by an obedient herd in the *Odyssey*.

The eye of Eve to mark his play: he, glad
Of her attention gained, with serpent tongue
Organic, or impulse of vocal air,[3]
His fraudulent temptation thus began.   530
    "Wonder not, sovereign mistress, if perhaps
Thou canst, who art sole wonder; much less arm
Thy looks, the heaven of mildness, with disdain,
Displeased that I approach thee thus, and gaze   535
Insatiate, I thus single, nor have feared
Thy awful brow, more awful thus retired.
Fairest resemblance of thy Maker fair,
Thee all things living gaze on, all things thine
By gift, and thy celestial beauty adore   540
With ravishment beheld, there best beheld
Where universally admired: but here
In this enclosure wild, these beasts among,
Beholders rude, and shallow to discern
Half what in thee is fair, one man except,   545
Who sees thee?[4] (and what is one?) who shouldst be seen
A goddess among gods, adored and served
By angels numberless, thy daily train."
    So glozed[5] the tempter, and his proem tuned;
Into the heart of Eve his words made way,   550
Though at the voice much marveling: at length,
Not unamazed, she thus in answer spake.
"What may this mean? Language of man pronounced
By tongue of brute, and human sense expressed?
The first at least of these I thought denied   555
To beasts, whom God on their creation-day
Created mute to all articulate sound;
The latter I demur,[6] for in their looks
Much reason, and in their actions oft appears.
Thee, serpent, subtlest beast of all the field   560
I knew, but not with human voice endued:[7]
Redouble then this miracle, and say,
How cam'st thou speakable of mute,[8] and how
To me so friendly grown above the rest
Of brutal kind, that daily are in sight?   565
Say, for such wonder claims attention due."
    To whom the guileful tempter thus replied:
"Empress of this fair world, resplendent Eve!
Easy to me it is to tell thee all
What thou command'st and right thou shouldst be obeyed: 570
I was at first as other beasts that graze
The trodden herb, of abject thoughts and low,

3. I.e., Satan either used the actual tongue of the serpent or himself impressed the air with speech.
4. The beasts cannot see the beauty of Eve's soul, only Adam can. Satan's entire speech is couched in the extravagant phrases of the Petrarchan love convention.
5. Flattered. "Proem": introduction.
6. I.e., as to whether rational sense was denied to brutes, I am doubtful.
7. Endowed.
8. To have speech after being dumb.

As was my food, nor aught but food discerned
Or sex, and apprehended nothing high:
Till on a day, roving the field, I chanced   575
A goodly tree far distant to behold
Loaden with fruit of fairest colors mixed,
Ruddy and gold; I nearer drew to gaze;
When from the boughs a savory odor blown,
Grateful to appetite, more pleased my sense   580
Than smell of sweetest fennel,[9] or the teats
Of ewe or goat dropping with milk at even,
Unsucked of lamb or kid, that tend their play.
To satisfy the sharp desire I had
Of tasting those fair apples, I resolved   585
Not to defer: hunger and thirst at once,
Powerful persuaders, quickened at the scent
Of that alluring fruit, urged me so keen.
About the mossy trunk I wound me soon,
For, high from ground, the branches would require   590
Thy utmost reach, or Adam's: round the tree
All other beasts that saw, with like desire
Longing and envying stood, but could not reach.
Amid the tree now got, where plenty hung
Tempting so nigh, to pluck and eat my fill   595
I spared not;[1] for such pleasure till that hour
At feed or fountain never had I found.
Sated at length, ere long I might perceive
Strange alteration in me, to degree
Of reason in my inward powers, and speech   600
Wanted not long, though to this shape retained.[2]
Thenceforth to speculations high or deep
I turned my thoughts, and with capacious mind
Considered all things visible in Heaven,
Or Earth, or middle, all things fair and good: 605
But all that fair and good in thy divine
Semblance, and in thy beauty's heavenly ray
United I beheld: no fair[3] to thine
Equivalent or second, which compelled
Me thus, though importune perhaps, to come   610
And gaze, and worship thee of right declared
Sovereign of creatures, universal dame."
      So talked the spirited[4] sly snake: and Eve
Yet more amazed, unwary thus replied:
      "Serpent, thy overpraising leaves in doubt   615
The virtue of that fruit, in thee first proved.
But say, where grows the tree, from hence how far?

---

9. Milton learned probably from Pliny, the natural historian, that serpents were fond of fennel; popular superstition had it that they drank the milk of sheep and goats.
1. Refrained not.

2. His inward powers, his mental constitution and gift of speech, were changed; but he retained his exterior shape as before.
3. Beauty.
4. Possessed by a spirit, inspired.

For many are the trees of God that grow
In Paradise, and various, yet unknown
To us; in such abundance lies our choice,   620
As leaves a greater store of fruit untouched,
Still hanging incorruptible, till men
Grow up to their provision, and more hands
Help to disburden Nature of her bearth."[5]

 To whom the wily adder, blithe and glad: 625
"Empress, the way is ready, and not long,
Beyond a row of myrtles, on a flat,
Fast by a fountain, one small thicket past
Of blowing[6] myrrh and balm: if thou accept
My conduct, I can bring thee thither soon."   630

 "Lead then," said Eve. He leading swiftly rolled
In tangles, and made intricate seem straight,
To mischief swift.[7] Hope elevates, and joy
Brightens his crest; as when a wandering fire
Compact of unctuous vapor,[8] which the night   635
Condenses, and the cold environs round,
Kindled through agitation to a flame
(Which oft, they say, some evil spirit attends),
Hovering and blazing with delusive light,
Misleads th' amazed night-wanderer from his way   640
To bogs and mires, and oft through pond or pool,
There swallowed up and lost, from succor far:
So glistered the dire snake, and into fraud
Led Eve our credulous mother, to the tree
Of prohibition,[9] root of all our woe: 645
Which when she saw, thus to her guide she spake:

 "Serpent, we might have spared our coming hither,
Fruitless to me, though fruit be here to excess,
The credit of whose virtue rest with thee;[1]
Wondrous indeed, if cause of such effects!   650
But of this tree we may not taste nor touch:
God so commanded, and left that command
Sole daughter of his voice;[2] the rest, we live
Law to ourselves; our reason is our law."

 To whom the Tempter guilefully replied: 655
"Indeed? Hath God then said that of the fruit
Of all these garden trees ye shall not eat,
Yet lords declared of all in Earth or air?"

 To whom thus Eve, yet sinless: "Of the fruit
Of each tree in the garden we may eat,   660
But of the fruit of this fair tree amidst

---

5. So spelled to pun on the idea of trees bearing fruit and thus in a way giving birth to young.
6. Blooming.
7. Milton's physical descriptions of the serpent often have distinct moral overtones, as here.
8. Composed of oily vapor; Milton's theory of the *ignis fatuus*, or will-o'-the-wisp, is strikingly material and "scientific."
9. Prohibited tree (a Hebraism).
1. I.e., you must remain the only evidence of the fruit's power.
2. His one injunction (a literal Hebraism). "The rest": in everything else.

The garden, God hath said, 'Ye shall not eat
Thereof, nor shall ye touch it, lest ye die.' "
    She scarce had said, though brief, when now more bold,
The tempter, but with show of zeal and love   665
To man, and indignation at his wrong,
New part puts on, and as to passion moved,
Fluctuates disturbed, yet comely, and in act
Raised,[3] as of some great matter to begin.
As when of old some orator renowned   670
In Athens or free Rome, where eloquence
Flourished, since mute, to some great cause addressed,
Stood in himself collected, while each part,
Motion, each act, won audience ere the tongue,
Sometimes in height began, as no delay   675
Of preface brooking,[4] through his zeal of right.
So standing, moving, or to height upgrown
The tempter all impassioned thus began:
    "O sacred, wise, and wisdom-giving plant,
Mother of science![5] now I feel thy power   680
Within me clear, not only to discern
Things in their causes, but to trace the ways
Of highest agents, deemed however wise.
Queen of this universe! do not believe
Those rigid threats of death. Ye shall not die;   685
How should ye? By the fruit? it gives you life
To knowledge;[6] by the Threatener? look on me,
Me who have touched and tasted, yet both live,
And life more perfect have attained than Fate
Meant me, by venturing higher than my lot.   690
Shall that be shut to man, which to the beast
Is open? Or will God incense his ire
For such a petty trespass, and not praise
Rather your dauntless virtue, whom the pain
Of death denounced, whatever thing death be,   695
Deterred not from achieving what might lead
To happier life, knowledge of good and evil?
Of good, how just![7] Of evil, if what is evil
Be real, why not known, since easier shunned?
God therefore cannot hurt ye, and be just;   700
Not just, not God; not feared then, nor obeyed:
Your fear itself of death removes the fear.[8]
Why then was this forbid? Why but to awe,
Why but to keep ye low and ignorant,
His worshipers? He knows that in the day   705
Ye eat thereof, your eyes that seem so clear,

---

3. Poised in posture.
4. The orator, as if too much moved to be bothered with a preface, bursts into the middle of his speech.
5. Knowledge.
6. Life in addition to knowledge; or, life with which to enlarge your knowledge.
7. I.e., how just to have knowledge of good!
8. I.e., your fear of death removes your fear of God; since if God inflicts death, he will not be just and hence not God. The serpent's sophism is visible.

Yet are but dim, shall perfectly be then
Opened and cleared, and ye shall be as gods,
Knowing both good and evil, as they know.
That ye should be as gods, since I as man,   710
Internal man,[9] is but proportion meet,
I, of brute, human; ye, of human, gods.
So ye shall die perhaps, by putting off
Human, to put on gods: death to be wished,
Though threatened, which no worse than this can bring.   715
And what are gods that man may not become
As they, participating[1] godlike food?
The gods are first, and that advantage use
On our belief, that all from them proceeds.
I question it; for this fair Earth I see,   720
Warmed by the sun, producing every kind,
Them nothing: If they all things,[2] who enclosed
Knowledge of good and evil in this tree,
That whoso eats thereof forthwith attains
Wisdom without their leave? And wherein lies   725
Th' offense, that man should thus attain to know?
What can your knowledge hurt him, or this tree
Impart against his will if all be his?
Or is it envy, and can envy dwell
In heavenly breasts?[3] These, these, and many more   730
Causes import your need of this fair fruit.
Goddess humane,[4] reach then, and freely taste!"
   He ended, and his words, replete with guile,
Into her heart too easy entrance won:
Fixed on the fruit she gazed, which to behold   735
Might tempt alone, and in her ears the sound
Yet rung of his persuasive words, impregned[5]
With reason, to her seeming, and with truth;
Meanwhile the hour of noon drew on, and waked
An eager appetite, raised by the smell   740
So savory of that fruit, which with desire,
Inclinable now grown to touch or taste,
Solicited her longing eye;[6] yet first
Pausing a while, thus to herself she mused:
   "Great are thy virtues, doubtless, best of fruits,   745
Though kept from man, and worthy to be admired,
Whose taste, too long forborn, at first essay
Gave elocution to the mute, and taught
The tongue not made for speech to speak thy praise:
Thy praise he also who forbids thy use,   750

9. Man in intellectual powers.
1. Sharing.
2. The verb "produced" is understood.
Satan is telling now, not about "God,"
but "the gods."
3. Adapted from Virgil, *Aeneid* I.15.
"Import": imply, suggest.

4. Not so much "human goddess" (a
Satanic paradox) as "kindly," "gracious" goddess.
5. Impregnated.
6. The five senses of Eve—sight, hearing, smell, taste, and touch—are all
solicited by the fruit.

Conceals not from us,[7] naming thee the Tree
Of Knowledge, knowledge both of good and evil;
Forbids us then to taste; but his forbidding
Commends thee more, while it infers the good
By thee communicated, and our want: 755
For good unknown, sure is not had, or had
And yet unknown, is as not had at all.[8]
In plain then, what forbids he but to know?
Forbids us good, forbids us to be wise!
Such prohibitions bind not. But if Death   760
Bind us with after-bands, what profits then
Our inward freedom? In the day we eat
Of this fair fruit, our doom is, we shall die.
How dies the serpent? He hath eaten and lives,
And knows, and speaks, and reasons, and discerns,   765
Irrational till then. For us alone
Was death invented? Or to us denied
This intellectual food, for beasts reserved?
For beasts it seems: yet that one beast which first
Hath tasted, envies not, but brings with joy   770
The good befallen him, author unsuspect,[9]
Friendly to man, far from deceit or guile.
What fear I then, rather what know to fear[1]
Under this ignorance of good and evil,
Of God or death, of law or penalty?   775
Here grows the cure of all, this fruit divine,
Fair to the eye, inviting to the taste,
Of virtue[2] to make wise: what hinders then
To reach, and feed at once both body and mind?"
    So saying, her rash hand in evil hour,   780
Forth reaching to the fruit, she plucked, she eat.[3]
Earth felt the wound, and Nature from her seat[4]
Sighing through all her works gave signs of woe,
That all was lost. Back to the thicket slunk
The guilty serpent, and well might, for Eve   785
Intent now wholly on her taste, naught else
Regarded; such delight till then, as seemed,
In fruit she never tasted, whether true
Or fancied so, through expectation high
Of knowledge; nor was godhead from her thought.[5]   790
Greedily she engorged without restraint,
And knew not eating death:[6] satiate at length,
And heightened as with wine, jocund and boon,[7]

7. God himself, by naming it, has called
attention to the tree's magic powers.
8. An unknown good is like no good at
all. "In plain": i.e., in plain language.
9. A witness beyond suspicion.
1. In her ignorance, Eve does not really
know what to fear and what not to
fear.
2. Power.
3. In the 17th century, an accepted

past tense of "eat."
4. Wherever Nature is hidden, in the
heart of things, she sighs.
5. She expected to achieve godhead immediately.
6. A grim pun. She is eating death and
does not know it; but death is eating
her too. Compare "eating cares" (*L'Allegro*, line 135).
7. Joyous and liberal.

Thus to herself she pleasingly began:
"O sovereign, virtuous, precious of all trees   795
In Paradise! of operation blest
To sapience,[8] hitherto obscured, infamed,
And thy fair fruit let hang, as to no end
Created; but henceforth my early care,
Not without song each morning, and due praise   800
Shall tend thee, and the fertile burden ease
Of thy full branches offered free to all;
Till dieted by thee I grow mature
In knowledge, as the gods who all things know;
Though others[9] envy what they cannot give: 805
For had the gift been theirs, it had not here
Thus grown. Experience, next to thee I owe,
Best guide; not following thee I had remained
In ignorance; thou open'st Wisdom's way,
And giv'st access, though secret she retire.   810
And I perhaps am secret; Heaven is high,
High and remote to see from thence distinct
Each thing on Earth; and other care perhaps
May have diverted from continual watch
Our great Forbidder,[1] safe with all his spies   815
About him. But to Adam in what sort[2]
Shall I appear? Shall I to him make known
As yet my change, and give him to partake
Full happiness with me, or rather not,
But keep the odds[3] of knowledge in my power   820
Without copartner? so to add what wants
In female sex, the more to draw his love,
And render me more equal, and perhaps,
A thing not undesirable, sometime
Superior: for, inferior, who is free?[4]   825
This may be well: but what if God have seen
And death ensue? Then I shall be no more,
And Adam, wedded to another Eve,
Shall live with her enjoying, I extinct;
A death to think. Confirmed then I resolve,   830
Adam shall share with me in bliss or woe:
So dear I love him, that with him all deaths
I could endure, without him live no life."[5]
   So saying, from the tree her step she turned,
But first low reverence done,[6] as to the power   835
That dwelt within, whose presence had infused

8. To the point of wisdom, but also for wise people. "Infamed": without fame, but also, defamed.
9. The gods, i.e., other gods. In saying that God did not give the tree, Eve is merely echoing a lesson learned from the serpent.
1. Now that Eve has fallen, God is a "great Forbidder," and all his gifts in Paradise are forgotten.

2. Guise.
3. Balance.
4. Eve's fatal foolishness implies that the only person in the world who can ever be free is an absolute tyrant.
5. Her affection is not unlike Satan's (IV.374–385) in its destructiveness.
6. Eve's first physical act after falling is idolatry.

Into the plant sciental[7] sap, derived
From nectar, drink of gods. Adam the while
Waiting desirous her return, had wove
Of choicest flowers a garland to adorn   840
Her tresses, and her rural labors crown,
As reapers oft are wont their harvest queen.
Great joy he promised to his thoughts, and new
Solace in her return, so long delayed:
Yet oft his heart, divine[8] of something ill,   845
Misgave him; he the faltering measure[9] felt;
And forth to meet her went, the way she took
That morn when first they parted. By the Tree
Of Knowledge he must pass; there he her met,
Scarce from the tree returning; in her hand   850
A bough of fairest fruit that downy smiled,
New gathered, and ambrosial smell diffused.
To him she hastened, in her face excuse
Came prologue, and apology to prompt,[1]
Which with bland words at will she thus addressed: 855
   "Hast thou not wondered, Adam, at my stay?
Thee I have missed, and thought it long, deprived
Thy presence, agony of love till now
Not felt, nor shall be twice; for never more
Mean I to try, what rash untried I sought,   860
The pain of absence from thy sight. But strange
Hath been the cause, and wonderful to hear:
This tree is not as we are told, a tree
Of danger tasted,[2] nor to evil unknown
Opening the way, but of divine effect   865
To open eyes, and make them gods who taste;
And hath been tasted such. The serpent wise,
Or not restrained as we, or not obeying,
Hath eaten of the fruit, and is become,
Not dead, as we are threatened, but thenceforth   870
Endued with human voice and human sense,
Reasoning to admiration,[3] and with me
Persuasively hath so prevailed, that I
Have also tasted, and have also found
Th' effects to correspond, opener mine eyes   875
Dim erst, dilated spirits, ampler heart,
And growing up to godhead;[4] which for thee
Chiefly I sought, without thee can despise.
For bliss, as thou hast part, to me is bliss,
Tedious, unshared with thee, and odious soon.   880
Thou therefore also taste, that equal lot

7. Knowledge-giving.
8. Foreboding, suspicious.
9. I.e., of his pulse.
1. Her face had an excuse in it, as prologue to an apology which followed after.

2. If tasted.
3. Admirably. "Persuasively": by persuasion.
4. Everything that Eve says she feels is what Satan has told her she will feel.

May join us, equal joy, as equal love;
Lest, thou not tasting, different degree[5]
Disjoin us, and I then too late renounce
Deity for thee, when Fate will not permit."[6]   885
    Thus Eve with countenance blithe her story told;
But in her cheek distemper[7] flushing glowed.
On th' other side, Adam, soon as he heard
The fatal trespass done by Eve, amazed,
Astonied[8] stood and blank, while horror chill   890
Ran through his veins, and all his joints relaxed;
From his slack hand the garland wreathed for Eve
Down dropped, and all the faded roses shed.
Speechless he stood and pale, till thus at length
First to himself he inward silence broke: 895
    "O fairest of creation, last and best
Of all God's works, creature in whom excelled
Whatever can to sight or thought be formed,
Holy, divine, good, amiable, or sweet!
How art thou lost, how on a sudden lost,   900
Defaced, deflowered, and now to death devote?[9]
Rather how hast thou yielded to transgress
The strict forbiddance, how to violate
The sacred fruit forbidden! Some curséd fraud
Of enemy hath beguiled thee, yet unknown,[1]   905
And me with thee hath ruined, for with thee
Certain my resolution is to die.
How can I live without thee, how forgo
Thy sweet converse and love so dearly joined,
To live again in these wild woods forlorn?[2]   910
Should God create another Eve, and I
Another rib afford, yet loss of thee
Would never from my heart; no, no! I feel
The link of nature draw me: flesh of flesh,
Bone of my bone thou art, and from thy state   915
Mine never shall be parted, bliss or woe."
    So having said, as one from sad dismay
Recomforted, and after thoughts disturbed
Submitting to what seemed remediless,
Thus in calm mood his words to Eve he turned: 920
    "Bold deed thou hast presumed, adventurous Eve
And peril great provoked, who thus hath dared
Had it been only coveting to eye
That sacred fruit, sacred[3] to abstinence,
Much more to taste it, under ban to touch.   925

5. Differing rank in the hierarchy of creatures.
6. Contrast Eve's logic when she is alone (lines 817–825).
7. The proportion of Eve's humors—which, in the state of innocence, gave her perfect health—has been disturbed, and she is running a fever.

8. Astonished, perhaps even "petrified." "Blank": empty of mind.
9. Doomed.
1. "Yet unknown" modifies "enemy."
2. Without Eve, Paradise itself is wild and forlorn.
3. Devoted.

But past who can recall, or done undo?
Not God omnipotent, nor Fate! Yet so
Perhaps thou shalt not die, perhaps the fact[4]
Is not so heinous now, foretasted fruit,
Profaned first by the serpent, by him first   930
Made common and unhallowed ere our taste,
Nor yet on him found deadly; he yet lives,
Lives, as thou saidst, and gains to live as man
Higher degree of life: inducement strong
To us, as likely, tasting, to attain   935
Proportional ascent, which cannot be
But to be gods, or angels, demigods.[5]
Nor can I think that God, Creator wise,
Though threatening, will in earnest so destroy
Us his prime creatures, dignified so high,   940
Set over all his works, which in our fall,
For us created, needs with us must fail,
Dependent made; so God shall uncreate,
Be frustrate, do, undo, and labor lose;
Not well conceived of God,[6] who, though his power   945
Creation could repeat, yet would be loath
Us to abolish, lest the adversary
Triúmph and say: 'Fickle their state whom God
Most favors; who can please him long? Me first
He ruined, now mankind; whom will he next?'   950
Matter of scorn, not to be given the foe.
However, I with thee have fixed my lot,
Certain to undergo like doom: if death
Consort with thee, death is to me as life;
So forcible within my heart I feel   955
The bond of nature draw me to my own,
My own in thee, for what thou art is mine;
Our state cannot be severed; we are one,
One flesh; to lose thee were to lose myself."
    So Adam, and thus Eve to him replied: 960
"O glorious trial of exceeding love,
Illustrious evidence, example high!
Engaging me to emulate; but short
Of thy perfection, how shall I attain,
Adam? from whose dear side I boast me sprung,   965
And gladly of our union hear thee speak,
One heart, one soul in both; whereof good proof
This day affords, declaring thee resolved,
Rather than death or aught than death more dread
Shall separate us, linked in love so dear,   970
To undergo with me one guilt, one crime,
If any be, of tasting this fair fruit;

4. Act.
5. Note how Adam agrees first in
Eve's harmless errors about the serpent,
then in her sinful ambition to achieve
a higher form of life.
6. I.e., not a proper conception of God
(as making his actions dependent on
those of an inferior).

Whose virtue (for of good still good proceeds,
Direct, or by occasion[7]) hath presented
This happy trial of thy love, which else   975
So eminently never had been known.
Were it I thought death menaced would ensue[8]
This my attempt, I would sustain alone
The worst, and not persuade thee, rather die
Deserted, than oblige[9] thee with a fact   980
Pernicious to thy peace, chiefly assured
Remarkably so late of thy so true,
So faithful love unequaled;[1] but I feel
Far otherwise th' event; [2] not death, but life
Augmented, opened eyes, new hopes, new joys,   985
Taste so divine, that what of sweet before
Hath touched my sense, flat seems to this, and harsh.
On my experience, Adam, freely taste,
And fear of death deliver to the winds."
    So saying, she embraced him, and for joy   990
Tenderly wept, much won that he his love
Had so ennobled, as of choice to incur
Divine displeasure for her sake, or death.
In recompense (for such compliance bad
Such recompense best merits), from the bough   995
She gave him of that fair enticing fruit
With liberal hand; he scrupled not to eat,
Against his better knowledge, not deceived,
But fondly overcome with female charm.[3]
Earth trembled from her entrails, as again   1000
In pangs, and Nature gave a second groan,
Sky lowered, and muttering thunder, some sad drops
Wept at completing of the mortal sin
Original; while Adam took no thought,
Eating his fill, nor Eve to iterate   1005
Her former trespass feared, the more to soothe
Him with her loved society; that now
As with new wine intoxicated both,
They swim in mirth, and fancy that they feel
Divinity within them breeding wings   1010
Wherewith to scorn the Earth. But that false fruit
Far other operation first displayed,
Carnal desire inflaming; he on Eve
Began to cast lascivious eyes, she him
As wantonly repaid; in lust they burn,   1015
Till Adam thus 'gan Eve to dalliance move:
    "Eve, now I see thou art exact[4] of taste,

7. Indirectly.
8. Result from.
9. Render liable, involve.
1. Now that she knows Adam loves
her, Eve has more misgivings than
ever about involving him in her crime.

2. Result (of eating the apple).
3. See I Timothy ii.14: "And Adam was
not deceived, but the woman being deceived was in the transgression."
4. Exacting, demanding.

And elegant, of sapience[5] no small part,
Since to each meaning savor we apply,
And palate call judicious. I the praise   1020
Yield thee, so well this day thou hast purveyed.[6]
Much pleasure we have lost, while we abstained
From this delightful fruit, nor known till now
True relish, tasting; if such pleasure be
In things to us forbidden, it might be wished,   1025
For this one tree had been forbidden ten.
But come; so well refreshed, now let us play,
As meet is, after such delicious fare;
For never did thy beauty, since the day
I saw thee first and wedded thee, adorned   1030
With all perfections, so enflame my sense
With ardor to enjoy thee, fairer now
Than ever, bounty of this virtuous tree."
    So said he, and forbore not glance or toy[7]
Of amorous intent, well understood   1035
Of[8] Eve, whose eye darted contagious fire.
Her hand he seized, and to a shady bank,
Thick overhead with verdant roof embowered
He led her, nothing loath; flowers were the couch,
Pansies, and violets, and asphodel,   1040
And hyacinth, Earth's freshest, softest lap.
There they their fill of love and love's disport
Took largely, of their mutual guilt the seal,
The solace of their sin, till dewy sleep
Oppressed them, wearied with their amorous play.   1045
    Soon as the force of that fallacious fruit,
That with exhilarating vapor bland
About their spirits had played, and inmost powers
Made err, was now exhaled, and grosser sleep
Bred of unkindly fumes,[9] with conscious dreams   1050
Encumbered, now had left them, up they rose
As from unrest, and each the other viewing,
Soon found their eyes how opened, and their minds
How darkened. Innocence, that as a veil
Had shadowed them from knowing ill, was gone;   1055
Just confidence, and native righteousness,
And honor from about them, naked left
To guilty Shame; he covered, but his robe
Uncovered more.[1] So rose the Danite strong,
Herculean Samson, from the harlot-lap   1060
Of Philistean Dalilah, and waked
Shorn of his strength;[2] they destitute and bare

---

5. Wisdom, but the word comes from Latin *sapere*, "to taste," which gives rise, via another etymology, to the word "savor." Adam's sentence plays rather heavily on these two meanings of *sapere*.
6. Provided for us, provisioned us.
7. Caress.
8. By.

9. Unnatural vapors.
1. They were covered with shame, which made them conscious of their nakedness as they had never been before.
2. See the story of Samson and Delilah, Judges xvi.4–20.

Of all their virtue. Silent, and in face
Confounded, long they sat, as strucken mute;
Till Adam, though not less than Eve abashed,   1065
At length gave utterance to these words constrained:
    "O Eve, in evil hour[3] thou didst give ear
To that false worm,[4] of whomsoever taught
To counterfeit man's voice, true in our fall,
False in our promised rising; since our eyes   1070
Opened we find indeed, and find we know
Both good and evil, good lost, and evil got:
Bad fruit of knowledge, if this be to know,
Which leaves us naked thus, of honor void,
Of innocence, of faith, of purity,   1075
Our wonted ornaments now soiled and stained,
And in our faces evident the signs
Of foul concupiscence; whence evil store,[5]
Even shame, the last of evils; of the first
Be sure then.[6] How shall I behold the face   1080
Henceforth of God or angel, erst with joy
And rapture so oft beheld? Those heavenly shapes
Will dazzle now this earthly[7] with their blaze
Insufferably bright. O might I here
In solitude live savage, in some glade   1085
Obscured, where highest woods, impenetrable
To star or sunlight, spread their umbrage broad,
And brown[8] as evening! Cover me, ye pines,
Ye cedars, with innumerable boughs
Hide me, where I may never see them more![9]   1090
But let us now, as in bad plight, devise
What best may for the present serve to hide
The parts of each from other, that seem most
To shame obnoxious,[1] and unseemliest seen;
Some tree whose broad smooth leaves together sewed,   1095
And girded on our loins, may cover round
Those middle parts, that this newcomer, Shame,
There sit not, and reproach us as unclean."
    So counseled he, and both together went
Into the thickest wood; there soon they chose   1100
The figtree,[2] not that kind for fruit renowned,
But such as at this day, to Indians known,
In Malabar or Deccan[3] spreads her arms

---

3. Even in his misery, Adam cannot resist the word-play on Eve-evil.
4. Serpent, with a connotation of disgust. "Of": by.
5. A store of evil.
6. I.e., since we now feel shame, the
last and worst of evils, we shall soon
experience the first and lesser ones.
7. The noun "nature" or "vision" is
understood.
8. Dark.
9. Cf. Revelation vi.16: "And said to

the mountains and rocks, Fall on us,
and hide us from the face of him that
sitteth on the throne, and from the
wrath of the Lamb."
1. Vulnerable, liable.
2. The banyan, or Indian fig. It has,
in fact, small leaves, but Milton's
knowledge of it came from Gerard's
Herball, where all the details of lines
1104–10 may be found.
3. Sections of southern India.

Branching so broad and long, that in the ground
The bended twigs take root, and daughters grow   1105
About the mother tree, a pillared shade
High overarched, and echoing walks between;
There oft the Indian herdsman, shunning heat,
Shelters in cool, and tends his pasturing herds
At loopholes cut through thickest shade. Those leaves   1110
They gathered, broad as Amazonian targe,[4]
And with what skill they had, together sewed,
To gird their waist; vain covering, if to hide
Their guilt and dreaded shame! O how unlike
To that first naked glory! Such of late   1115
Columbus found th' American, so girt
With feathered cincture,[5] naked else and wild
Among the trees on isles and woody shores.
Thus fenced, and, as they thought, their shame in part
Covered, but not at rest or ease of mind,   1120
They sat them down to weep; nor only tears
Rained at their eyes, but high winds worse within
Began to rise, high passions, anger, hate,
Mistrust, suspicion, discord, and shook sore
Their inward state of mind, calm region once   1125
And full of peace, now tossed and turbulent:
For Understanding ruled not, and the Will
Heard not her lore, both in subjection now
To sensual Appetite, who, from beneath
Usurping over sovereign Reason, claimed   1130
Superior sway.[6] From thus distempered breast,
Adam, estranged in look and altered style,
Speech intermitted thus to Eve renewed:
  "Would thou hadst hearkened to my words, and stayed
With me, as I besought thee, when that strange   1135
Desire of wandering, this unhappy morn,
I know not whence possessed thee! we had then
Remained still happy, not as now, despoiled
Of all our good, shamed, naked, miserable.
Let none henceforth seek needless cause to approve[7]   1140
The faith they owe; when earnestly they seek
Such proof, conclude, they then begin to fail."
  To whom, soon moved with touch of blame, thus Eve:
"What words have passed thy lips, Adam severe?
Imput'st thou that to my default, or will   1145
Of wandering, as thou call'st it, which who knows
But might as ill have happened, thou being by,
Or to thyself perhaps? Hadst thou been there,
Or here th' attempt, thou couldst not have discerned

---

4. Shield. The Amazons, mythical female warriors, carried large crescent-shaped shields.
5. Belt.
6. The psychology of the Fall is made explicit here. The higher faculties of reason, represented by the brain, are in subjection to the lower faculties of appetite, represented by sensuality. Moreover, Adam has lost his superiority over Eve.
7. Test. prove. "Owe": own.

Fraud in the serpent, speaking as he spake;   1150
No ground of enmity between us known,
Why he should mean me ill, or seek to harm?
Was I to have never parted from thy side?
As good have grown there still a lifeless rib.
Being as I am, why didst not thou, the head,[8]   1155
Command me absolutely not to go,
Going into such danger, as thou saidst?
Too facile[9] then, thou didst not much gainsay,
Nay, didst permit, approve, and fair dismiss.
Hadst thou been firm and fixed in thy dissent,   1160
Neither had I transgressed, nor thou with me."
    To whom, then first incensed, Adam replied:
"Is this the love, is this the recompense
Of mine to thee, ingrateful Eve, expressed
Immutable[1] when thou were lost, not I,   1165
Who might have lived and joyed immortal bliss,
Yet willingly chose rather death with thee?
And am I now upbraided as the cause
Of thy transgressing? not enough severe,
It seems, in thy restraint! What could I more?   1170
I warned thee, I admonished thee, foretold
The danger, and the lurking enemy
That lay in wait; beyond this had been force,
And force upon free will hath here no place.
But confidence then bore thee on, secure   1175
Either to meet no danger, or to find
Matter of glorious trial; and perhaps
I also erred in overmuch admiring
What seemed in thee so perfect, that I thought
No evil durst attempt thee! but I rue   1180
That error now, which is become my crime,
And thou th' accuser. Thus it shall befall
Him who, to worth in women overtrusting,
Lets her will rule; restraint she will not brook,[2]
And, left to herself, if evil thence ensue,   1185
She first his weak indulgence will accuse."
    Thus they in mutual accusation spent
The fruitless hours, but neither self-condemning;
And of their vain contést appeared no end.

8. Head of the family, but also the ra-   9. Easy, permissive.
tional director, as the head is to the   1. Shown to be unchangeable.
rest of the body. Cf. I Corinthians xi.3,   2. Accept.
"the head of the woman is the man."

From Book X

Summary   When it is known in Heaven that man has fallen, God sends the Son to pass judgment on the sinners. He receives the confession of Adam and Eve and passes sentence on the sinners—cursing the serpent, condemning Eve to the pains of childbirth, and Adam to those of daily labor; but in mercy he clothes the human couple, both outwardly with the skins of animals and inwardly with his righteousness. Meanwhile Sin and Death, sitting by Hell-gate, feel new strength, and pass across Chaos, leaving a great bridge behind them. On their way, they meet their parent, Satan, returning in triumph. Satan reappears in Pandemonium, and describes to the assembly the success of his venture, but instead of the expected applause is received with a vast hiss—he and all the other devils have been transformed to snakes, in which shape they are tormented with humiliating delusions.

Sin and Death now invest the earth; but God prophesies their ultimate defeat. Now the earth and the elements are rearranged, to replace the previous temperate climate with extremes of heat and cold; and discord enters the animal kingdom too, where hitherto all the creatures have dwelt in peace.

[*Consequences of the Fall*]

                       * * * Thus began
Outrage from lifeless things; but Discord, first
Daughter of Sin, among th' irrational,
Death introduced through fierce antipathy:[1]
Beast now with beast 'gan war, and fowl with fowl,
And fish with fish: to graze the herb[2] all leaving,
Devoured each other; nor stood much in awe
Of man, but fled him, or with countenance grim
Glared on him passing. These were from without
The growing miseries, which Adam saw   715
Already in part, though hid in gloomiest shade,
To sorrow abandoned, but worse felt within,
And in a troubled sea of passion tossed,
Thus to disburden sought with sad complaint:
    "O miserable of happy![3] Is this the end   720
Of this new glorious world, and me so late
The glory of that glory? who now, become
Accursed of blessed, hide me from the face
Of God, whom to behold was then my height
Of happiness! Yet well, if here would end   725
The misery; I deserved it, and would bear
My own deservings; but this will not serve.

---

1. "Discord" is the subject of the sentence, "Death" the object. "Th' irrational" are the beasts.

2. Grass.
3. I.e., change, to misery from happiness.

All that I eat or drink, or shall beget,
Is propagated curse.[4] O voice, once heard
Delightfully, 'Increase and multiply,'
Now death to hear! for what can I increase   730
Or multiply, but curses on my head?
Who, of all ages to succeed, but, feeling
The evil on him brought by me, will curse
My head: "Ill fare our ancestor impure!   735
For this we may thank Adam!' but his thanks
Shall be the execration;[5] so, besides
Mine own that bide upon me, all from me
Shall with a fierce reflux on me redound,
On me, as on their natural center, light   740
Heavy, though in their place.[6] O fleeting joys
Of Paradise, dear bought with lasting woes!
Did I request thee, Maker, from my clay
To mold me man? Did I solicit thee
From darkness to promote me, or here place   745
In this delicious garden? As my will
Concurred not to my being, it were but right
And equal[7] to reduce me to my dust,
Desirous to resign and render back
All I received, unable to perform   750
Thy terms too hard, by which I was to hold
The good I sought not. To the loss of that,
Sufficient penalty, why hast thou added
The sense of endless woes? Inexplicable
Thy justice seems; yet, to say truth, too late   755
I thus contest; then should have been refused
Those terms whatever, when they were proposed.
Thou[8] didst accept them; wilt thou enjoy the good,
Then cavil the conditions? And though God
Made thee without thy leave, what if thy son   760
Prove disobedient, and reproved, retort,
'Wherefore didst thou beget me? I sought it not.'
Wouldst thou admit for his contempt of thee
That proud excuse? Yet him not thy election,[9]
But natural necessity begot.   765
God made thee of choice his own, and of his own
To serve him; thy reward was of his grace;
Thy punishment then justly is at his will.
Be it so, for I submit; his doom is fair,
That dust I am and shall to dust return.   770
O welcome hour whenever! Why delays

4. Whatever prolongs life extends the curse.
5. The only thanks for Adam will be mankind's curses.
6. Adam plays with the notion that natural objects have weight only as long as they are above their "natural" positions; so all curses will flow naturally to him, but they will still be heavy when they have lighted.
7. Just.
8. "Thou," which referred to God in lines 753 and 755, here shifts as Adam suddenly addresses himself.
9. Choice.

His hand to execute what his decree
Fixed on this day? Why do I overlive?
Why am I mocked with death, and lengthened out
To deathless pain? How gladly would I meet   775
Mortality, my sentence, and be earth
Insensible! how glad would lay me down
As in my mother's lap![1] There I should rest
And sleep secure; his dreadful voice no more
Would thunder in my ears; no fear of worse   780
To me and to my offspring would torment me
With cruel expectation. Yet one doubt
Pursues me still, lest all I cannot die;[2]
Lest that pure breath of life, the spirit of man
Which God inspired, cannot together perish   785
With this corporeal clod; then, in the grave,
Or in some other dismal place, who knows
But I shall die a living death? O thought
Horrid, if true! Yet why? It was but breath
Of life that sinned; what dies but what had life   790
And sin? the body properly hath neither.
All of me then shall die: let this appease
The doubt, since human reach no further knows.[3]
For though the Lord of all be infinite,
Is his wrath also? Be it, man is not so,   795
But mortal doomed. How can he exercise
Wrath without end on man whom death must end?
Can he make deathless death? That were to make
Strange contradiction, which to God himself
Impossible is held, as argument   800
Of weakness, not of power.[4] Will he draw out,
For anger's sake, finite to infinite
In punished man, to satisfy his rigor
Satisfied never? That were to extend
His sentence beyond dust and Nature's law;   805
By which all causes else according still
To the reception of their matter act,
Not to th' extent of their own sphere.[5] But say
That death be not one stroke, as I supposed,
Bereaving[6] sense, but endless misery   810
From this day onward, which I feel begun
Both in me and without me, and so last
To perpetuity—Ay me! that fear
Comes thundering back with dreadful revolution

1. Adam's lamentations owe a good deal to the Book of Job iii.
2. Direct from Horace, *Odes* III.xxx.6: *non omnis moriar*.
3. Adam convinces himself, as Milton was apparently convinced, that both soul and body die at death; the corollary is that they are resurrected together.
4. For a man in a state of nature, Adam displays a fine command of medieval theology. He holds that if God contradicts himself, it is a sign of weakness.
5. A maxim of 17th-century physics; all agents (other than God) act according to the capacity of the object, not to the extent of their inherent powers.
6. Taking away.

On my defenseless head! Both death and I   815
Am found eternal, and incorporate[7] both:
Nor I on my part single; in me all
Posterity stands cursed. Fair patrimony
That I must leave ye, sons! O, were I able
To waste it all myself, and leave ye none!   820
So disinherited, how would ye bless
Me, now your curse! Ah, why should all mankind
For one man's fault thus guiltless be condemned,
If guiltless? But from me what can proceed,
But all corrupt, both mind and will depraved,   825
Not to do only, but to will the same
With me?[8] How can they then acquitted stand
In sight of God? Him, after all disputes,
Forced[9] I absolve. All my evasions vain
And reasonings, though through mazes, lead me still   830
But to my own conviction: first and last
On me, me only, as the source and spring
Of all corruption, all the blame lights due;[1]
So might the wrath! Fond[2] wish! Couldst thou support
That burden, heavier than the earth to bear;   835
Than all the world much heavier, though divided
With that bad woman? Thus, what thou desir'st,
And what thou fear'st, alike destroys all hope
Of refuge, and concludes thee miserable[3]
Beyond all past example and future;   840
To Satan only like, both crime and doom.
O Conscience! into what abyss of fears
And horrors hast thou driven me; out of which
I find no way, from deep to deeper plunged!"
    Thus Adam to himself lamented loud   845
Through the still night, not now, as ere man fell,
Wholesome and cool and mild, but with black air
Accompanied, with damps and dreadful gloom;
Which to his evil conscience represented
All things with double terror. On the ground   850
Outstretched he lay, on the cold ground, and oft
Cursed his creation; Death as oft accused
Of tardy execution, since denounced
The day of his offense. "Why comes not Death,"
Said he, "with one thrice-acceptable stroke   855
To end me? Shall Truth fail to keep her word,
Justice divine not hasten to be just?
But Death comes not at call; Justice divine

7. In the same body. Adam is appalled to find that he has become death incarnate; the grammar ("both dead and I / *Am*") displays his shock.
8. Not only will men repeat Adam's sin; their will is corrupted and they will *want* to be fallen like Adam.
9. Perforce.

1. In this discovery that he alone must accept the guilt of mankind, Adam has chosen crucially to be like Christ and unlike Satan—at the very moment when he feels exactly the opposite.
2. Foolish.
3. Shows thee to be miserable.

Mends not her slowest pace for prayers or cries.
O woods, O fountains, hillocks, dales, and bowers! 860
With other echo late I taught your shades
To answer, and resound far other song."
Whom thus afflicted when sad Eve beheld,
Desolate where she sat, approaching nigh,
Soft words to his fierce passion she essayed; 865
But her with stern regard he thus repelled:
    "Out of my sight, thou serpent! that name best
Befits thee, with him leagued, thyself as false
And hateful: nothing wants, but that thy shape,
Like his, and color serpentine, may show 870
Thy inward fraud, to warn all creatures from thee
Henceforth; lest that too heavenly form, pretended[4]
To hellish falsehood, snare them. But for thee
I had persisted happy, had not thy pride
And wandering vanity, when least was safe, 875
Rejected my forewarning, and disdained
Not to be trusted, longing to be seen
Though by the devil himself, him overweening[5]
To overreach, but, with the serpent meeting,
Fooled and beguiled; by him thou, I by thee, 880
To trust thee from my side, imagined wise,
Constant, mature, proof against all assaults;
And understood not all was but a show
Rather than solid virtue, all but a rib
Crooked by nature—bent, as now appears, 885
More to the part sinister[6]—from me drawn;
Well if thrown out, as supernumerary
To my just number found![7] Oh, why did God,
Creator wise, that peopled highest Heaven
With spirits masculine, create at last 890
This novelty on earth, this fair defect
Of nature, and not fill the world at once
With men, as angels, without feminine;
Or find some other way to generate
Mankind?[8] This mischief had not then befallen, 895
And more that shall befall—innumerable
Disturbances on earth through female snares,
And strait conjunction[9] with this sex. For either
He never shall find out fit mate, but such
As some misfortune brings him, or mistake; 900
Or whom he wishes most shall seldom gain,
Through her perverseness, but shall see her gained
By a far worse, or, if she love, withheld

4. Serving as a mask.
5. Overconfident.
6. "On the left hand," as in Latin; also "unlucky."
7. Since men visibly have twelve ribs on both sides, it was supposed that Adam originally had thirteen ribs on his left side, so that he could give up one and still have twelve, an even ("just") number.
8. Ancient traditions of antifeminist thought lie behind these ungenerous speculations.
9. Close connections, i.e., matrimony.

By parents, or his happiest choice too late
Shall meet, already linked and wedlock-bound   905
To a fell[1] adversary, his hate or shame:
Which infinite calamity shall cause
To human life, and household peace confound."
    He added not, and from her turned; but Eve,
Not so repulsed, with tears that ceased not flowing,   910
And tresses all disordered, at his feet
Fell humble, and, embracing them, besought
His peace, and thus proceeded in her plaint:
    "Forsake me not thus, Adam! witness Heaven
What love sincere and reverence in my heart   915
I bear thee, and unweeting[2] have offended,
Unhappily deceived! Thy suppliant[3]
I beg, and clasp thy knees; bereave me not,
Whereon I live, thy gentle looks, thy aid,
Thy counsel in this uttermost distress,   920
My only strength and stay: forlorn of thee,
Whither shall I betake me, where subsist?
While yet we live, scarce one short hour perhaps,
Between us two let there be peace; both joining,
As joined in injuries, one enmity   925
Against a foe by doom express assigned us,
That cruel serpent. On me exercise not
Thy hatred for this misery befallen;
On me already lost, me than thyself
More miserable. Both have sinned, but thou   930
Against God only; I against God and thee,
And to the place of judgement will return,
There with my cries importune Heaven, that all
The sentence, from thy head removed, may light
On me, sole cause to thee of all this woe,   935
Me, me only, just object of his ire."[4]
    She ended weeping; and her lowly plight,
Immovable till peace obtained from fault
Acknowledged and deplored,[5] in Adam wrought
Commiseration. Soon his heart relented   940
Towards her, his life so late and sole delight,
Now at his feet submissive in distress,
Creature so fair his reconcilement seeking,
His counsel, whom she had displeased, his aid;
As one disarmed, his anger all he lost,   945
And thus with peaceful words upraised her soon:
    "Unwary, and too desirous, as before,
So now, of what thou know'st not,[6] who desir'st

1. Bitter.
2. Unintentionally.
3. As a suppliant to thee.
4. Eve too now offers to accept the blame for the Fall; and the moral regeneration of man is henceforth possible.
5. Her suppliant posture ("lowly plight") would not be changed till she obtained forgiveness ("peace") from her admission of her fault, and repentance for it.
6. Adam's remark is rueful but affectionate; Eve is still looking for more trouble than she knows how to handle.

The punishment all on thyself! Alas!
Bear thine own first, ill able to sustain   950
His full wrath, whose thou feel'st as yet least part,[7]
And my displeasure bear'st so ill. If prayers
Could alter high decrees, I to that place
Would speed before thee, and be louder heard,
That on my head all might be visited,   955
Thy frailty and infirmer sex forgiven,
To me committed, and by me exposed.
But rise; let us no more contend, nor blame
Each other, blamed enough elsewhere, but strive
In offices of love, how we may lighten   960
Each other's burden in our share of woe;
Since this day's death denounced, if aught I see,
Will prove no sudden, but a slow-paced evil,
A long day's dying to augment our pain,
And to our seed (O hapless seed!) derived."[8]   965

7. I.e., ill able to sustain the full wrath of God—of whose wrath, so far, you have felt only the least part.
8. Handed down.

Summary   In her despair, Eve proposes to Adam that they refrain from having children, or commit suicide, in order to frustrate Sin and Death, but Adam persuades her to a better resolution. Book X ends with Adam and Eve reconciled to one another, partially reconciled to their fate, and praying forgiveness for their sins.

Book XI. Summary   The prayers of Adam and Eve prove acceptable to God. But while man may now hope for ultimate redemption, he may no longer dwell in Paradise; and Michael, the warrior archangel, is dispatched to explain the sentence, offer some hope for the future, and dismiss mankind from the happy garden. Adam is at first overcome with grief; but the angel encourages him, and while Eve is put in a trance, Adam is raised to the peak of a high hill and shown in a vision the future of the human race as far as the flood of Noah.

From Book XII

Summary   Continuing his instruction of Adam, Michael relates the history of the world from the time of Noah through the coming of Christ, whose ascent into Heaven and triumph over Death after the Crucifixion he describes. The Church which Christ and his apostles leave behind, however, will not be free from troubles caused by greedy and ambitious men; it will require reform. But the reformers will be persecuted and their road will be hard, until at length, in the Last Judgment, Satan and his kingdom will be dissolved, and new heavens and new earths created to exist in eternal bliss.

[The Departure from Eden]

So spake th' archangel Michaël; then paused,
As at the world's great period;[1] and our sire,
Replete with joy and wonder, thus replied:
"O goodness infinite, goodness immense!
That all this good of evil shall produce,   470
And evil turn to good; more wonderful
Than that which by creation first brought forth
Light out of darkness! Full of doubt I stand,
Whether I should repent me now of sin
By me done and occasioned, or rejoice   475
Much more that much more good thereof shall spring;
To God more glory, more good will to men
From God, and over wrath grace shall abound.
But say, if our Deliverer up to Heaven
Must reascend, what will betide the few,   480
His faithful, left among th' unfaithful herd,
The enemies of truth? Who then shall guide
His people, who defend? Will they not deal
Worse with his followers than with him they dealt?"
"Be sure they will," said th' angel; "but from Heaven   485
He to his own a Comforter will send,
The promise of the Father, who shall dwell,
His Spirit, within them, and the law of faith,
Working through love, upon their hearts shall write,
To guide them in all truth, and also arm   490
With spiritual armor, able to resist
Satan's assaults, and quench his fiery darts,
What[2] man can do against them, not afraid,
Though to the death; against such cruelties
With inward consolations recompensed,   495
And oft supported so as shall amaze
Their proudest persecutors.[3] For the Spirit,
Poured first on his Apostles, whom he sends
To evangelize the nations, then on all
Baptized, shall them with wondrous gifts endue[4]   500
To speak all tongues, and do all miracles,
As did their Lord before them. Thus they win
Great numbers of each nation to receive
With joy the tidings brought from Heaven: at length,
Their ministry performed, and race well run,   505
Their doctrine and their story written left,

1. Conclusion.
2. As much as.
3. Milton briefly summarizes here the story of the Christian martyrs.
4. Endow.

They die; but in their room, as they forewarn,
Wolves shall succeed for teachers, grievous wolves,[5]
Who all the sacred mysteries of Heaven
To their own vile advantages shall turn   510
Of lucre and ambition, and the truth
With superstitions and traditions taint,
Left only in those written records pure,
Though not but by the Spirit understood.
Then shall they seek to avail themselves of names,   515
Places, and titles,[6] and with these to join
Secular power, though feigning still to act
By spiritual; to themselves appropriating
The Spirit of God, promised alike and given
To all believers; and, from that pretense,   520
Spiritual laws by carnal[7] power shall force
On every conscience, laws which none shall find
Left them enrolled, or what the Spirit within
Shall on the heart engrave.[8] What will they then,
But force the Spirit of Grace itself, and bind   525
His consort, Liberty? what but unbuild
His living temples,[9] built by faith to stand,
Their own faith, not another's? for, on Earth,
Who against faith and conscience can be heard
Infallible? Yet many will presume: 530
Whence heavy persecution shall arise
On all who in the worship persevere
Of Spirit and Truth; the rest, far greater part,
Will deem in outward rites and specious[1] forms
Religion satisfied; Truth shall retire   535
Bestuck with slanderous darts, and works of faith
Rarely be found. So shall the world go on,
To good malignant, to bad men benign,
Under her own weight groaning,[2] till the day
Appear of respiration[3] to the just   540
And vengeance to the wicked, at return
Of Him so lately promised to thy aid,
The Woman's Seed,[4] obscurely then foretold,
Now amplier known thy Savior and thy Lord;
Last in the clouds from Heaven to be revealed   545

5. To profit by religion was for Milton the lowest of crimes; he felt that priests should serve without pay. In addition, he regularly uses the wolf as an emblem of the Papacy; see *Lycidas*, line 128.
6. The name "Catholic," the place of court preacher, and the title of "bishop," for example.
7. Fleshly, i.e., secular, of this world.
8. I.e., the wolves will enforce laws which have no ancient authority or appeal to the conscience.
9. Individual   believers.   Milton's strict Protestant individualism speaks throughout this passage of protest against persecution.
1. Fair-seeming.
2. This passage, which in isolation appears to offer some justification for viewing the end of the poem as essentially pessimistic, should be set against Adam's earlier statement (lines 470–78) that the Fall was really a fortunate event, and gave rise to more good than evil.
3. Relief, refreshment.
4. Christ, whose Second Coming is here foreseen.

In glory of the Father, to dissolve
Satan with his perverted world; then raise
From the conflagrant mass,[5] purged and refined,
New Heavens, new Earth, ages of endless date
Founded in righteousness and peace and love,   550
To bring forth fruits, joy and eternal bliss."
  He ended, and thus Adam last replied:
"How soon hath thy prediction, seer blest,
Measured this transient world, the race of Time,
Till Time stand fixed! Beyond is all abyss,   555
Eternity, whose end no eye can reach.
Greatly instructed I shall hence depart,
Greatly in peace of thought, and have my fill
Of knowledge, what[6] this vessel can contain;
Beyond which was my folly to aspire.   560
Henceforth I learn that to obey is best,
And love with fear the only God, to walk
As in his presence, ever to observe
His providence, and on him sole depend,
Merciful over all his works, with good   565
Still overcoming evil, and by small
Accomplishing great things, by things deemed weak
Subverting worldly-strong, and worldly-wise
By simply meek; that suffering for truth's sake
Is fortitude to highest victory,   570
And to the faithful, death the gate of life;
Taught this by his example whom I now
Acknowledge my Redeemer ever blest."
  To whom thus also th' angel last replied:
"This having learned, thou hast attained the sum[7]   575
Of wisdom; hope no higher, though all the stars
Thou knew'st by name,[8] and all th' ethereal powers,
All secrets of the deep, all Nature's works,
Or works of God in heaven, air, earth, or sea,
And all the riches of this world enjoy'dst,   580
And all the rule, one empire. Only add
Deeds to thy knowledge answerable;[9] add faith,
Add virtue, patience, temperance; add love,
By name to come called charity, the soul
Of all the rest: then wilt thou not be loath   585
To leave this Paradise, but shalt possess
A Paradise within thee, happier far.
Let us descend now, therefore, from this top
Of speculation;[1] for the hour precise
Exacts[2] our parting hence; and, see! the guards,   590
By me encamped on yonder hill, expect

5. The burning world.
6. As much as.
7. Total.
8. Michael glances back at the rebuke
administered by Raphael in Book VIII

to Adam's astronomical curiosity.
9. Corresponding.
1. Hill of vision.
2. Requires.

Their motion, at whose front[3] a flaming sword,
In signal of remove, waves fiercely round.
We may no longer stay. Go, waken Eve;
Her also I with gentle dreams have calmed,   595
Portending good, and all her spirits composed
To meek submission: thou, at season fit,
Let her with thee partake what thou hast heard;
Chiefly what may concern her faith to know,
The great deliverance by her seed to come   600
(For by the Woman's Seed) on all mankind;
That ye may live, which will be many days,[4]
Both in one faith unanimous; though sad
With cause for evils past, yet much more cheered
With meditation on the happy end."   605
    He ended, and they both descend the hill.
Descended, Adam to the bower where Eve
Lay sleeping ran before, but found her waked;
And thus with words not sad she him received:
    "Whence thou return'st and whither went'st, I know;   610
For God is also in sleep, and dreams advise,
Which he hath sent propitious, some great good
Presaging, since, with sorrow and heart's distress
Wearied, I fell asleep. But now lead on;
In me is no delay; with thee to go   615
Is to stay here; without thee here to stay
Is to go hence unwilling; thou to me
Art all things under Heaven, all places thou,
Who for my willful crime art banished hence.
This further consolation yet secure   620
I carry hence: though all by me is lost,
Such favor I unworthy am vouchsafed,
By me the Promised Seed shall all restore."
    So spake our mother Eve; and Adam heard
Well pleased, but answered not; for now too nigh   625
Th' archangel stood, and from the other hill
To their fixed station, all in bright array,
The cherubim descended; on the ground
Gliding meteorous, as evening mist
Risen from a river o'er the marish[5] glides,   630
And gathers ground fast at the laborer's heel
Homeward returning. High in front advanced,
The brandished sword of God before them blazed,
Fierce as a comet; which with torrid heat,
And vapor as the Libyan air adust,[6]   635
Began to parch that temperate clime; whereat
In either hand the hastening angel caught
Our lingering parents, and to th' eastern gate
Led them direct, and down the cliff as fast

3. Before whom.   5. Marsh (an old form).
4. Adam lived to be 930 (Genesis   6. The scorched climate of Libya, in
v.5).   North Africa, was proverbial.

To the subjected[7] plain; then disappeared.   640
They, looking back, all th' eastern side beheld
Of Paradise, so late their happy seat,[8]
Waved over by that flaming brand;[9] the gate
With dreadful faces thronged and fiery arms.
Some natural tears they dropped, but wiped them soon;   645
The world was all before them, where to choose
Their place of rest, and Providence their guide.
They, hand in hand, with wandering steps and slow,
Through Eden took their solitary way.

1662–67   1667, 1674

7. Low-lying.   9. "Sword," with the extra overtone
8. Home.   of "burning."

Samson Agonistes

Samson Agonistes The figure of Samson, as one finds him in the Book of Judges, does not seem at first glance particularly adaptable to the elevated mode of tragedy. He is a promiscuous, violent fellow, given to riddles and practical jokes—the last of which puts a gruesome end to himself and his enemies. His long shaggy hair, his name (Samson, in Hebrew *Shimshun*), which includes the Hebrew word for "sun," and a persistent association with fire, all suggest a connection with some primitive solar cult, such as can be seen behind the equivalent figure of Hercules. A burly, truculent, and not-very-clever giant, in short; one would not easily see in him the dignified and purifying figure of the tragic sufferer.

But though Samson's rude vigor and vengeful nature appealed to Milton on one level; the story of his fall through the treachery of a woman on another; and the fact of his blindness on still another; there was a last level on which he could in fact be represented as the type and precursor of the Christian hero. He suffered for his people; in the very pit of despair he was rendered suddenly capable of God's revivifying grace; long exercised in physical warfare, he gave evidence in his last heroic action of having learned the principles of spiritual warfare.

Milton approached the idea of tragedy with hesitations and misgivings; for a Puritan of his day, the very idea of a stage play was instinct with moral danger. But the example of the Greeks and of his much-admired Tasso prevailed; he wrote a "closet drama," a drama intended not for the actual stage but for reading. As a play, Dr. Johnson proclaimed it deficient; it had, he said, a beginning and an end but no proper middle. Modern criticism, dissenting as usual from Dr. Johnson and stimulated as usual by his judgment, has exercised itself to find in Samson's spiritual progression during the successive visits of Manoa, Dalila, and Harapha ample psychological movement to sustain both action and interest. This is beyond doubt a useful exercise; but it is useful also to reflect that Samson acts in the end by direction of an inward spirit, a private, intimate inspiration; and that for the coming of this spirit there is no sufficient preparation. "The wind bloweth where it listeth, and thou hearest the sound thereof, but canst not tell whence it cometh, and whither it goeth: so is every one that is born of the Spirit" (John iii.8).

The story of Samson is told in Judges xiii-xvi. "Agonistes" means "in struggle" or "under trial"; it is a term derived from the Greek word for a wrestler and suggests not only that Samson is an athlete of the Lord but that he will wrestle with the pillars.

Samson Agonistes

A DRAMATIC POEM

Of That Sort of Dramatic Poem Which Is Called Tragedy

Tragedy, as it was anciently composed, hath been ever held the gravest, moralest, and most profitable of all other poems: therefore said by Aristotle to be of power, by raising pity and fear, or terror, to purge the mind of those and such-like passions, that is, to temper and reduce them to just measure with a kind of delight, stirred up by reading or seeing those passions well imitated.[1] Nor is Nature wanting in her own effects to make good his assertion; for so, in physic, things of melancholic hue and quality are used against melancholy, sour against sour, salt to remove salt humors.[2] Hence philosophers and other gravest writers, as Cicero, Plutarch, and others, frequently cite out of tragic poets, both to adorn and illustrate their discourse. The Apostle Paul himself thought it not unworthy to insert a verse of Euripides into the text of Holy Scripture, 1 Cor. xv. 33; and Paraeus, commenting on the Revelation, divides the whole book, as a tragedy, into acts, distinguished each by a chorus of heavenly harpings and song between.[3] Heretofore men in highest dignity have labored not a little to be thought able to compose a tragedy. Of that honor Dionysius the elder was no less ambitious than before of his attaining to the tyranny.[4] Augustus Caesar also had begun his *Ajax*, but unable to please his own judgment with what he had begun, left it unfinished. Seneca the philosopher is by some thought the author of those tragedies (at least the best of them) that go under that name. Gregory Nazianzen, a Father of the Church, thought it not unbeseeming the sanctity of his person to write a tragedy, which he entitled *Christ Suffering*.[5] This is mentioned to vindicate tragedy from the small esteem, or rather infamy, which in the account of many it undergoes at this

---

1. Milton is paraphrasing Aristotle's *Poetics* 6.
2. Italian critics like Minturno had applied notions of homeopathic medicine (like cures like) to tragedy; the idea is not Aristotelean. "Physic": medicine.
3. David Paraeus, a 17th-century German Calvinist.
4. Dionysius (4th century B.C.) won a prize at Athens for tragedy, after becoming tyrant of Syracuse.
5. Seneca the philosopher was indeed the author of tragedies; but Gregory Nazianzen, a Greek ecclesiastic of the 4th century, did not write the tragedy *Christ Suffering*, which scholarly opinion of Milton's day attributed to him.

day, with other common interludes—happening through the poet's error of intermixing comic stuff with tragic sadness and gravity, or introducing trivial and vulgar persons—which by all judicious hath been counted absurd, and brought in without discretion, corruptly to gratify the people. And, though ancient tragedy use no prologue,[6] yet using sometimes, in case of self-defense or explanation, that which Martial calls an epistle,[7] in behalf of this tragedy, coming forth after the ancient manner, much different from what among us passes for best, thus much beforehand may be epistled, that chorus is here introduced after the Greek manner, not ancient only, but modern, and still in use among the Italians.[8] In the modeling therefore of this poem, with good reason, the ancients and Italians are rather followed, as of much more authority and fame. The measure of verse used in the chorus is of all sorts, called by the Greeks *Monostrophic*,[9] or rather *Apolelymenon*,[1] without regard had to strophe, antistrophe, or epode, which were a kind of stanzas framed only for the music, then used with the chorus that sung; not essential to the poem, and therefore not material; or, being divided into stanzas or pauses, they may be called *alloeostropha*.[2] Division into act and scene, referring chiefly to the stage (to which this work never was intended), is here omitted.[3]

It suffices if the whole drama be found not produced [4] beyond the fifth act. Of the style and uniformity, and that commonly called the plot, whether intricate or explicit—which is nothing indeed but such economy, or disposition of the fable, as may stand best with verisimilitude and decorum[5]—they only will best judge who are not unacquainted with Aeschylus, Sophocles, and Euripides, the three tragic poets unequaled yet by any, and the best rule to all who endeavor to write tragedy. The circumscription of time wherein the whole drama begins and ends is, according to ancient rule and best example, within the space of twenty-four hours.[6]

6. Prologues and epilogues were frequent on the Restoration stage; Milton sets himself apart from contemporary styles.
7. Martial, the Roman epigrammatist of the 1st century A.D., prefixed an epistle to his book of epigrams.
8. Tasso's tragedy *Re Torrismondo* was modeled closely on classical examples.
9. Not divided into strophe, antistrophe, and epode.
1. Free from stanzaic patterns altogether.
2. With various forms of strophe, irregular.
3. The reader who cares will not find Milton's drama hard to divide into the customary five acts, each ending with a chorus: Act I (Samson and chorus) lines 1–325; II (Samson and Manoa) 326–709; III (Samson and Dalila) 710–1060; IV (Samson and Harapha) 1061–1296; V (Catastrophe) 1297–the end.
4. Led along, drawn out.
5. Decorum, for a Renaissance writer, is not simply solemn or sedate behavior but the use of appropriate and suitable style, depending on speaker, subject, setting, genre, and so on.
6. The so-called "unity of time," limiting dramatic action to 24 hours, was derived from Aristotle's *Poetics* by the Renaissance critic Castelvetro.

The Argument

Samson, made captive, blind, and now in the prison at Gaza,[7] there to labor as in a common workhouse, on a festival day, in the general cessation from labor, comes forth into the open air, to a place nigh, somewhat retired, there to sit a while and bemoan his condition. Where he happens at length to be visited by certain friends and equals of his tribe, which make the chorus, who seek to comfort him what they can; then by his old father, Manoa, who endeavors the like, and withal tells him his purpose to procure his liberty by ransom; lastly, that this feast was proclaimed by the Philistines as a day of thanksgiving for their deliverance from the hands of Samson—which yet more troubles him. Manoa then departs to prosecute his endeavor with the Philistian lords for Samson's redemption; who, in the meanwhile, is visited by other persons, and, lastly, by a public officer to require his coming to the feast before the lords and people, to play or show his strength in their presence. He at first refuses, dismissing the public officer with absolute denial to come; at length persuaded inwardly that this was from God, he yields to go along with him, who came now the second time with great threatenings to fetch him. The chorus yet remaining on the place, Manoa returns full of joyful hope to procure ere long his son's deliverance: in the midst of which discourse an Ebrew[8] comes in haste, confusedly at first, and afterwards more distinctly, relating the catastrophe—what Samson had done to the Philistines, and by accident to himself; wherewith the tragedy ends.

The Persons

SAMSON	HARAPHA of *Gath*
MANOA, *the father of*	*Public Officer*
Samson	*Messenger*
DALILA, *his wife*	*Chorus of Danites*[9]

The Scene, before the Prison in Gaza.

SAMSON. A little onward lend thy guiding hand
　To these dark steps, a little further on;
　For yonder bank hath choice of sun or shade.
　There I am wont to sit, when any chance
　Relieves me from my task of servile toil,　　　　　5
　Daily in the common prison else enjoined me,[1]

---

7. The Philistines, warlike and commercial, lived in Southwest Palestine (the southern coast of modern Israel between, approximately, Tel Aviv and Gaza) in five great cities splendidly named Ashdod, Eshkol, Gaza, Gath, and Ashkalon. They were a wholly urban people as against the largely rural Israelites.
8. Milton follows an old English tradition in transliterating the name "Ebrew."
9. Hebrews of the tribe of Dan, Samson's tribe. When the land of Canaan was divided among the twelve tribes, they received the southern portion, adjacent to the Philistines.
1. The metrical pattern of this line, with its many unaccented syllables and careful placement of the strong word "else," merits careful study.

Where I, a prisoner chained, scarce freely draw
The air, imprisoned also, close and damp,
Unwholesome draught. But here I feel amends—
The breath of heaven fresh blowing, pure and sweet,   10
With day-spring[2] born; here leave me to respire.
This day a solemn feast the people hold
To Dagon,[3] their sea-idol, and forbid
Laborious works. Unwillingly this rest
Their superstition yields me; hence, with leave   15
Retiring from the popular noise, I seek
This unfrequented place, to find some ease—
Ease to the body some, none to the mind
From restless thoughts, that, like a deadly swarm
Of hornets armed, no sooner found alone   20
But rush upon me thronging, and present
Times past, what once I was, and what am now.
Oh, wherefore was my birth from Heaven foretold
Twice by an angel,[4] who at last, in sight
Of both my parents, all in flames ascended   25
From off the altar where an offering burned,
As in a fiery column charioting
His godlike presence, and from some great act
Or benefit revealed to Abraham's race?
Why was my breeding ordered and prescribed   30
As of a person separate to God,
Designed for great exploits,[5] if I must die
Betrayed, captived, and both my eyes put out,
Made of my enemies the scorn and gaze,
To grind in brazen fetters under task   35
With this heaven-gifted strength? O glorious strength,
Put to the labor of a beast, debased
Lower than bondslave! Promise was that I
Should Israel from Philistian yoke deliver;
Ask for this great deliverer now, and find him   40
Eyeless in Gaza, at the mill with slaves,
Himself in bonds under Philistian yoke.
Yet stay; let me not rashly call in doubt
Divine prediction. What if all foretold
Had been fulfilled but through mine own default?   45
Whom have I to complain of but myself,
Who this high gift of strength committed to me,
In what part lodged, how easily bereft me,
Under the seal of silence could not keep,[6]

---

2. Break of day.
3. Dagon's name comes from *dag*, fish, and he seems to have had a fishy shape. His would thus be a marine cult to correspond with that of the many Baals, or land gods of the Philistines. See *Paradise Lost* I.457–66.
4. Before Samson was born an angel foretold that he would begin the delivery of Israel from the Philistines (Judges

xiii.5).
5. Samson was a Nazarite, member of an ascetic group specially dedicated to the service of God. See Numbers vi.
6. I.e., who could not keep silent about the high gift of strength committed to me, or about where it was located, or about how easily it could be taken from me.

But weakly to a woman must reveal it,   50
O'ercome with importunity and tears?
O impotence of mind in body strong!
But what is strength without a double share
Of wisdom? Vast, unwieldy, burdensome,
Proudly secure,[7] yet liable to fall   55
By weakest subtleties; not made to rule,
But to subserve where wisdom bears command.
God, when he gave me strength, to show withal,
How slight the gift was, hung it in my hair.
But peace! I must not quarrel with the will   60
Of highest dispensation,[8] which herein
Haply had ends above my reach to know.
Suffices that to me strength is my bane,
And proves the source of all my miseries—
So many, and so huge, that each apart   65
Would ask a life to wail. But, chief of all,
O loss of sight, of thee I most complain!
Blind among enemies! O worse than chains,
Dungeon, or beggary, or decrepit age!
Light, the prime work of God,[9] to me is extinct,   70
And all her various objects of delight
Annulled, which might in part my grief have eased.
Inferior to the vilest now become
Of man or worm, the vilest here excel me:
They creep, yet see; I, dark in light, exposed   75
To daily fraud, contempt, abuse, and wrong,
Within doors, or without, still as a fool,
In power of others, never in my own—
Scarce half I seem to live, dead more than half.
O dark, dark, dark, amid the blaze of noon,   80
Irrecoverably dark, total eclipse
Without all hope of day!
O first-created beam, and thou great Word,
"Let there be light, and light was over all,"
Why am I thus bereaved thy prime decree? [1]   85
The sun to me is dark
And silent[2] as the moon,
When she deserts the night,
Hid in her vacant interlunar cave.[3]
Since light so necessary is to life,   90
And almost life itself, if it be true
That light is in the soul,
She all in every part,[4] why was the sight

---

7. Confident, free from care (Latin, *cura*).
8. Providence.
9. God's first ("prime") act in creating the world was to say "Let there be light" (Genesis i.3), a phrase Milton paraphrases below.
1. I.e., why am I thus deprived of the first-created (and most important) thing?
2. Unperceived.
3. Ancient astronomers supposed that during the daytime the moon hid in a cave.
4. A famous formula of Plotinus (*Ennead* IV.ii.1) describes the soul as "all in all and all in every part."

To such a tender ball as th' eye confined,
So obvious[5] and so easy to be quenched,   95
And not, as feeling, through all parts diffused,
That she might look at will through every pore?
Then had I not been thus exiled from light,
As in the land of darkness, yet in light,
To live a life half dead, a living death,   100
And buried; but, O yet more miserable!
Myself my sepulcher, a moving grave;
Buried, yet not exempt,
By privilege of death and burial,
From worst of other evils, pains, and wrongs;   105
But made hereby obnoxious[6] more
To all the miseries of life,
Life in captivity
Among inhuman foes.
But who are these? for with joint pace I hear   110
The tread of many feet steering this way;
Perhaps my enemies, who come to stare
At my affliction, and perhaps to insult,
Their daily practice to afflict me more.
CHORUS. This, this is he; softly a while;   115
Let us not break in upon him.
O change beyond report, thought, or belief!
See how he lies at random, carelessly diffused,[7]
With languished head unpropped,
As one past hope, abandoned,   120
And by himself given over,
In slavish habit, ill-fitted weeds [8]
O'er-worn and soiled.
Or do my eyes misrepresent? Can this be he,
That heroic, that renowned,   125
Irresistible Samson? whom, unarmed,
No strength of man, or fiercest wild beast, could withstand: [9]
Who tore the lion as the lion tears the kid;
Ran on embattled armies clad in iron,
And, weaponless himself,   130
Made arms ridiculous, useless the forgery[1]
Of brazen shield and spear, the hammered cuirass,
Chalybean-tempered[2] steel, and frock of mail
Adamantean proof;
But safest he who stood aloof,   135
When insupportably[3] his foot advanced,
In scorn of their proud arms and warlike tools,

---

5. Exposed.
6. Vulnerable, subject.
7. Literally, "poured forth," outstretched.
8. Rags.
9. Judges xiv.5–6 tells the story of Samson ripping apart a lion with his bare hands.

1. Weapons of forged steel, but also fraudulent, exterior protections.
2. The Chalybes lived on the Black Sea and were famous ironworkers. "Adamantean proof": hard as adamant, i.e., diamond.
3. Irresistibly.

Spurned them to death by troops. The bold Ascalonite[4]
Fled from his lion ramp; old warriors turned
Their plated backs under his heel,   140
Or groveling soiled their crested helmets in the dust.
Then with what trivial weapon came to hand,
The jaw of a dead ass, his sword of bone,
A thousand foreskins fell, the flower of Palestine,
In Ramath-lechi, famous to this day; [5]   145
Then by main force pulled up, and on his shoulders bore,
The gates of Azza, post and massy bar,
Up to the hill by Hebron, seat of giants old,
No journey of a Sabbath day, and loaded so,
Like whom the Gentiles feign to bear up Heaven.[6]   150
Which shall I first bewail,
Thy bondage or lost sight,
Prison within prison
Inseparably dark?
Thou art become (O worst imprisonment!)   155
The dungeon of thyself; thy soul
(Which men enjoying sight oft without cause complain),
Imprisoned now indeed,
In real darkness of the body dwells,
Shut up from outward light   160
To incorporate with gloomy night;
For inward light, alas!
Puts forth no visual beam.[7]
O mirror of our fickle state,
Since man on earth unparalleled! [8]   165
The rarer thy example stands,
By how much from the top of wondrous glory,
Strongest of mortal men,
To lowest pitch of abject fortune thou art fallen!
For him I reckon not in high estate   170
Whom long descent of birth,
Or the sphere[9] of fortune, raises;
But thee, whose strength, while virtue was her mate,
Might have subdued the Earth,

---

4. A man from Ascalon, or Ashkalon, one of the five great Philistine cities. "Lion ramp": a lion in the act of attacking its prey, rampant.

5. On one occasion Samson killed a thousand Philistines (i.e., "foreskins", uncircumcised warriors), using the jawbone of an ass (Judges xv.15–17). Judges xvi.3 tells how Samson, to escape his enemies, picked up and carried off the gates of Gaza (Azza).

6. In Greek (or, as Milton calls it, Gentile) mythology, Atlas supports the heavens. From Gaza to Hebron would be about forty miles—no journey for the day of rest.

7. Renaissance physiologists supposed the eye saw by sending forth a "visual beam" which it directed at various objects.

8. I.e., no such example (has been seen) since man (was) on earth. "Fickle": changeable.

9. "Sphere": wheel. Fortune was described as possessing a wheel which merely by rotating automatically interchanged the highest and lowest social positions. Milton's definition of "high estate" is interior and spiritual; he has no interest in the old "Fall of Princes" theme. In fact, the play exactly reverses that theme.

Universally crowned with highest praises. 175

SAMSON. I hear the sound of words; their sense the air
    Dissolves unjointed ere it reach my ear.

CHORUS. He speaks: let us draw nigh. Matchless in might,
    The glory late of Israel, now the grief!
    We come, thy friends and neighbors not unknown, 180
    From Eshtaol and Zora's fruitful vale,
    To visit or bewail thee; or, if better,
    Counsel or consolation we may bring,
    Salve to thy sores: apt words have power to swage[1]
    The tumors of a troubled mind, 185
    And are as balm to festered wounds.

SAMSON. Your coming, friends, revives me; for I learn
    Now of my own experience, not by talk,
    How counterfeit a coin they are who "friends"
    Bear in their superscription (of the most 190
    I would be understood). In prosperous days
    They swarm, but in adverse withdraw their head,
    Not to be found, though sought. Ye see, O friends,
    How many evils have enclosed me round;
    Yet that which was the worst now least afflicts me, 195
    Blindness; for, had I sight, confused with shame,
    How could I once look up, or heave[2] the head,
    Who, like a foolish pilot, have shipwrecked
    My vessel trusted to me from above,
    Gloriously rigged, and for a word, a tear, 200
    Fool! have divulged the secret gift of God
    To a deceitful woman? Tell me, friends,
    Am I not sung and proverbed for a fool
    In every street? Do they not say, "How well
    Are come upon him his deserts"? Yet why? 205
    Immeasurable strength they might behold
    In me; of wisdom nothing more than mean.[3]
    This with the other should at least have paired;[4]
    These two, proportioned ill, drove me transverse.[5]

CHORUS. Tax not divine disposal. Wisest men 210
    Have erred, and by bad women been deceived;
    And shall again, pretend they ne'er so wise.[6]
    Deject not, then, so overmuch thyself,
    Who hast of sorrow thy full load besides.
    Yet, truth to say, I oft have heard men wonder 215
    Why thou should'st wed Philistian women rather
    Than of thine own tribe fairer, or as fair,
    At least of thy own nation, and as noble.

SAMSON. The first I saw at Timna, and she pleased
    Me, not my parents, that I sought to wed 220

1. Assuage.   4. Been equal.
2. Lift.   5. Off the true course.
3. Average.   6. I.e., intend they never so wisely.

The daughter of an infidel.[7] They knew not
That what I motioned[8] was of God; I knew
From intimate impulse, and therefore urged
The marriage on, that, by occasion hence,[9]
I might begin Israel's deliverance—   225
The work to which I was divinely called.
She proving false, the next I took to wife
(O that I never had! fond wish too late!)
Was in the vale of Sorec, Dálila,[1]
That specious monster, my accomplished snare.   230
I thought it lawful from my former act
And the same end, still watching to oppress
Israel's oppressors. Of what now I suffer
She was not the prime cause, but I myself,
Who, vanquished with a peal of words (O weakness!),   235
Gave up my fort of silence to a woman.
CHORUS. In seeking just occasion to provoke
The Philistine, thy country's enemy,
Thou never wast remiss, I bear thee witness;
Yet Israel still serves with all his sons.[2]   240
SAMSON. That fault I take not on me, but transfer
On Israel's governors and heads of tribes,
Who, seeing those great acts which God had done
Singly by me against their conquerors,
Acknowledged not, or not at all considered   245
Deliverance offered. I, on th' other side,
Used no ambition to commend my deeds;[3]
The deeds themselves, though mute, spoke loud the doer.
But they persisted deaf, and would not seem
To count them things worth notice, till at length   250
Their lords, the Philistines, with gathered powers,
Entered Judea seeking me, who then
Safe to the rock of Etham was retired,
Not flying, but forecasting in what place
To set upon them, what advantaged best.   255
Meanwhile the men of Judah, to prevent
The harass of their land, beset me round;
I willingly on some conditions came
Into their hands, and they as gladly yield me
To the uncircumcised[4] a welcome prey,   260
Bound with two cords. But cords to me were threads
Touched with the flame: on their whole host I flew
Unarmed, and with a trivial weapon felled
Their choicest youth; they only lived who fled.[5]

---

7. Judges xiv.1–4 tells the story of
Samson's first decision to marry outside
his own tribe and nation.
8. Intended.
9. I.e., so that it might provide an occasion for me to begin Israel's deliverance.
1. Judges xvi.4.
2. I.e., Israel and the children of Israel

are still in servitude.
3. I.e., sought for no testimonials to my
actions.
4. Foreigners, the people outside the
covenant of Abraham.
5. Judges xv.8–17 tells the tale of Samson's single-handed victory, using a
"trivial weapon," the jawbone of an ass.

Had Judah that day joined, or one whole tribe, 265
They had by this[6] possessed the towers of Gath,
And lorded over them whom now they serve.
But what more oft, in nations grown corrupt,
And by their vices brought to servitude,
Than to love bondage more than liberty, 270
Bondage with ease than strenuous liberty,[7]
And to despise, or envy, or suspect,
Whom God hath of his special favor raised
As their deliverer? If he aught begin,
How frequent to desert him, and at last 275
To heap ingratitude on worthiest deeds!
CHORUS. Thy words to my remembrance bring
How Succoth and the fort of Penuel
Their great deliverer contemned,
The matchless Gideon, in pursuit 280
Of Madian, and her vanquished kings;[8]
And how ingrateful Ephraim
Had dealt with Jephtha, who by argument,
Not worse than by his shield and spear,
Defended Israel from the Ammonite, 285
Had not his prowess quelled their pride
In that sore battle when so many died
Without reprieve, adjudged to death
For want of well pronouncing *Shibboleth*.[9]
SAMSON. Of such examples add me to the roll. 290
Me easily indeed mine[1] may neglect,
But God's proposed deliverance not so.
CHORUS. Just are the ways of God,
And justifiable to men,
Unless there be who think not God at all. 295
If any be, they walk obscure;
For of such doctrine never was there school,
But the heart of the fool,
And no man therein doctor but himself.[2]
    Yet more there be who doubt his ways not just,
As to his own edicts found contradicting; 300
Then give the reins to wandering thought,
Regardless of his glory's diminution,
Till, by their own perplexities involved,
They ravel[3] more, still less resolved,
But never find self-satisfying solution. 305
As if they would confine th' Interminable,[4]
And tie him to his own prescript,

6. By this time.
7. Milton obviously has in mind, not
only early Israel, but also contemporary
England.
8. Judges viii: Succoth and Penuel refused aid to Gideon when he was pursuing the common foe, and he punished
them.

9. Judges xi and xii.
1. My people.
2. Psalm xiv deals with the fool who
says in his heart there is no God. "Doctor": teacher.
3. Become entangled.
4. Infinite.

Who made our laws to bind us, not himself,
And hath full right to exempt   310
Whomso it pleases him by choice
From national obstriction,[5] without taint
Of sin, or legal debt;
For with his own laws he can best dispense.
   He would not else, who never wanted means,   315
Nor in respect of the enemy just cause,
To set his people free,
Have prompted this heroic Nazarite,
Against his vow of strictest purity,
To seek in marriage that fallacious bride,   320
Unclean, unchaste.
   Down, Reason, then; at least, vain reasonings down;
Though Reason here aver
That moral verdict quits her of unclean:
Unchaste was subsequent; her stain, not his.[6]   325
But see! here comes thy reverend sire,
With careful step, locks white as down,[7]
Old Manoa: advise [8]
Forthwith how thou ought'st to receive him.

SAMSON. Ay me! another inward grief, awaked   330
   With mention of that name, renews th' assault.

MANOA. Brethren and men of Dan (for such ye seem,
   Though in this uncouth[9] place), if old respect,
   As I suppose, towards your once gloried friend,
   My son, now captive, hither hath informed[1]   335
   Your younger feet, while mine, cast back with age,
   Came lagging after, say if he be here.

CHORUS. As signal[2] now in low dejected state
   As erst in highest, behold him where he lies.

MANOA. O miserable change! Is this the man,   340
   That invincible Samson, far renowned,
   The dread of Israel's foes, who with a strength
   Equivalent to angels' walked their streets,
   None offering fight; who, single combatant,
   Dueled their armies ranked in proud array,   345
   Himself an army—now unequal match
   To save himself against a coward armed
   At one spear's length? O ever-failing trust
   In mortal strength! and, oh, what not in man
   Deceivable and vain? [3] Nay, what thing good   350

5. Obligation, i.e., the law against marrying Gentiles (Deuteronomy vii.3). The chorus here accepts Samson's argument that God had prompted him inexplicably to marry the woman of Timna.
6. The chorus, having accused the woman of Timna of being unclean (i.e., Gentile and taboo) and unchaste, now admits that since Samson married her at God's instigation she was not unclean to him; and that she was unchaste only after Samson left her. Reason is therefore puzzled.
7. "Careful": full of care; "down": swan's down.
8. Reflect, consider inwardly.
9. Unknown, unfamiliar.
1. Directed.
2. Notable, eminent.
3. I.e., what is there in man that is not deceivable and vain?

Prayed for, but often proves our woe, our bane?
I prayed for children, and thought barrenness
In wedlock a reproach; I gained a son,
And such a son as all men hailed me happy:
Who would be now a father in my stead?   355
Oh, wherefore did God grant me my request,
And as a blessing with such pomp adorned?
Why are his gifts desirable, to tempt
Our earnest prayers, then, given with solemn hand
As graces, draw a scorpion's tail behind?   360
For this did the angel twice descend?[4] for this
Ordained thy nurture holy, as of a plant
Select and sacred? glorious for a while,
The miracle of men; then in an hour
Ensnared, assaulted, overcome, led bound,   365
Thy foes' derision, captive, poor and blind,
Into a dungeon thrust, to work with slaves!
Alas! methinks whom God hath chosen once
To worthiest deeds, if he through frailty err,
He should not so o'erwhelm, and as a thrall   370
Subject him to so foul indignities,
Be it but for honor's sake of former deeds.
SAMSON. Appoint not heavenly disposition,[5] father.
Nothing of all these evils hath befallen me
But justly; I myself have brought them on;   375
Sole author I, sole cause.[6] If aught seem vile,
As vile hath been my folly, who have profaned
The mystery of God, given me under pledge
Of vow, and have betrayed it to a woman,
A Canaanite, my faithless enemy.   380
This well I knew, nor was at all surprised,
But warned by oft experience. Did not she
Of Timna first betray me, and reveal
The secret wrested from me in her height
Of nuptial love professed, carrying it straight   385
To them who had corrupted her, my spies
And rivals?[7] In this other was there found
More faith, who, also in her prime of love,
Spousal embraces, vitiated with gold,
Though offered only, by the scent conceived,   390
Her spurious first-born, treason against me?[8]
Thrice she assayed, with flattering prayers and sighs,
And amorous reproaches, to win from me

4. The angel who announced Samson's birth was sent a second time, in answer to Manoa's request, to give instructions concerning his education and training.
5. I.e., do not presume to control heaven's decisions.
6. Like Adam, *Paradise Lost* X, Samson proves his own resurgent virtue by accepting responsibility for his own faults.
7. Samson's first wife, the woman of Timna, revealed Samson's riddle to his enemies (Judges xiv.8–19).
8. At the mere scent of gold, Dalila conceived a bastard ("spurious") offspring for Samson—treason.

My capital secret,[9] in what part my strength
Lay stored, in what part summed, that she might know;   395
Thrice I deluded her, and turned to sport
Her importunity, each time perceiving
How openly and with what impudence
She purposed to betray me, and (which was worse
Than undissembled hate) with what contempt   400
She sought to make me traitor to myself.[1]
Yet, the fourth time, when, mustering all her wiles,
With blandished parleys, feminine assaults,
Tongue-batteries, she surceased[2] not day nor night
To storm me, over-watched and wearied out,   405
At times when men seek most repose and rest,
I yielded, and unlocked her all my heart,
Who, with a grain of manhood well resolved,
Might easily have shook off all her snares;
But foul effeminacy[3] held me yoked   410
Her bondslave. O indignity, O blot
To honor and religion! servile mind
Rewarded well with servile punishment!
The base degree to which I now am fallen,
These rags, this grinding, is not yet so base   415
As was my former servitude, ignoble,
Unmanly, ignominious, infamous,
True slavery; and that blindness worse than this,
That saw not how degenerately I served.
MANOA. I cannot praise thy marriage-choices, son,   420
Rather approved them not; but thou didst plead
Divine impulsion[4] prompting how thou might'st
Find some occasion to infest our foes.
I state not that; this I am sure, our foes
Found soon occasion thereby to make thee   425
Their captive, and their triumph; thou the sooner
Temptation found'st, or over-potent charms,
To violate the sacred trust of silence
Deposited within thee; which to have kept
Tacit was in thy power. True; and thou bear'st   430
Enough, and more, the burden of that fault;
Bitterly hast thou paid, and still art paying,
That rigid score.[5] A worse thing yet remains:
This day the Philistines a popular feast
Here celebrate in Gaza, and proclaim   435
Great pomp, and sacrifice, and praises loud,
To Dagon, as their god who hath delivered
Thee, Samson, bound and blind, into their hands—

9. The secret Dalila learned was of capital importance; also, it involved the hair on Samson's head (*caput*).
1. Judges xvi.5–20.
2. Forbore.
3. "Effeminacy": uxoriousness, over-

fondness, the fault of Adam.
4. Prudent Manoa mistrusts the inner impulse which is Samson's conscience and the first principle of his life. "Infest": attack.
5. Debt.

Them out of thine, who slew'st them many a slain.[6]
So Dagon shall be magnified,[7] and God,   440
Besides whom is no god, compared with idols,
Disglorified, blasphemed, and had in scorn
By th' idolatrous rout amidst their wine;
Which to have come to pass by means of thee,
Samson, of all thy sufferings think the heaviest,   445
Of all reproach the most with shame that ever
Could have befallen thee and thy father's house.
SAMSON. Father, I do acknowledge and confess
That I this honor, I this pomp, have brought
To Dagon, and advanced his praises high   450
Among the heathen round; to God have brought
Dishonor, obloquy, and oped the mouths
Of idolists and atheists; have brought scandal
To Israel, diffidence[8] of God, and doubt
In feeble hearts, propense[9] enough before   455
To waver, or fall off and join with idols:
Which is my chief affliction, shame and sorrow,
The anguish of my soul, that suffers not
Mine eye to harbor sleep, or thoughts to rest.
This only hope relieves me, that the strife   460
With me hath end. All the contést is now
'Twixt God and Dagon. Dagon hath presumed,
Me overthrown, to enter lists[1] with God,
His deity comparing and preferring
Before the God of Abraham. He, be sure,   465
Will not connive,[2] or linger, thus provoked,
But will arise, and his great name assert.
Dagon must stoop, and shall ere long receive
Such a discomfit as shall quite despoil him
Of all these boasted trophies won on me,   470
And with confusion blank[3] his worshipers.
MANOA. With cause this hope relieves thee; and these words
I as a prophecy receive; for God
(Nothing more certain) will not long defer
To vindicate the glory of his name   475
Against all competition, nor will long
Endure it doubtful whether God be Lord
Or Dagon. But for thee what shall be done?
Thou must not in the meanwhile, here forgot,
Lie in this miserable loathsome plight   480
Neglected. I already have made way
To some Philistian lords, with whom to treat
About thy ransom. Well they may by this [4]
Have satisfied their utmost of revenge,

6. I.e., who slew many a one for them.
7. Glorified.
8. Mistrust.
9. Inclined.
1. Jousting courts as in medieval tour-neys.
2. Hesitate, palter.
3. Confound, turn pale.
4. By this time.

By pains and slaveries, worse than death, inflicted   485
  On thee, who now no more canst do them harm.
SAMSON. Spare that proposal, father; spare the trouble
  Of that solicitation. Let me here,
  As I deserve, pay on my punishment,
  And expiate, if possible, my crime,   490
  Shameful garrulity. To have revealed
  Secrets of men, the secrets of a friend,
  How heinous had the fact been, how deserving
  Contempt and scorn of all; to be excluded
  All friendship, and avoided as a blab,   495
  The mark of fool set on his front! [5] But I
  God's counsel have not kept, his holy secret
  Presumptuously have published, impiously,
  Weakly at least and shamefully: a sin
  That Gentiles in their parables condemn   500
  To their abyss and horrid pains confined.[6]
MANOA. Be penitent, and for thy fault contrite;
  But act not in thy own affliction, son.
  Repent the sin; but, if the punishment
  Thou canst avoid, self-preservation bids;   505
  Or th' execution leave to high disposal,
  And let another hand, not thine, exact
  Thy penal forfeit from thyself. Perhaps
  God will relent, and quit [7] thee all his debt;
  Who ever more approves and more accepts   510
  (Best pleased with humble and filial submission)
  Him who, imploring mercy, sues for life,
  Than who, self-rigorous, chooses death as due; [8]
  Which argues over-just, and self-displeased
  For self-offense more than for God offended.   515
  Reject not, then, what offered means who knows
  But God hath set before us to return thee
  Home to thy country and his sacred house,
  Where thou may'st bring thy offerings, to avert
  His further ire, with prayers and vows renewed.   520
SAMSON. His pardon I implore; but, as for life,
  To what end should I seek it? When in strength
  All mortals I excelled, and great in hopes,
  With youthful courage, and magnanimous thoughts
  Of birth from Heaven foretold and high exploits,   525
  Full of divine instinct, after some proof
  Of acts indeed heroic, far beyond
  The sons of Anak,[9] famous now and blazed,
  Fearless of danger, like a petty god

---

5. Forehead.
6. In classical legend, Tantalus was confined to hell and torment because he betrayed the secrets of the gods, and Prometheus was savagely punished for giving to mankind the secret of fire.

7. Cancel.
8. This is very similar to Adam's argument against suicide in *Paradise Lost* X.1013–30.
9. Giants, described in Numbers xiii.

I walked about, admired of all, and dreaded   530
On hostile ground, none daring my affront.
Then, swoll'n with pride, into the snare I fell
Of fair fallacious looks, venereal trains,[1]
Softened with pleasure and voluptuous life;
At length to lay my head and hallowed pledge   535
Of all my strength in the lascivious lap
Of a deceitful concubine, who shore me,
Like a tame wether,[2] all my precious fleece,
Then turned me out ridiculous, despoiled,
Shaven, and disarmed among my enemies.   540

CHORUS. Desire of wine and all delicious drinks,
   Which many a famous warrior overturns,
   Thou could'st repress; nor did the dancing ruby,
   Sparkling out-poured, the flavor or the smell,
   Or taste, that cheers the heart of gods and men,   545
   Allure thee from the cool crystalline stream.

SAMSON. Wherever fountain or fresh current flowed
   Against the eastern ray, translucent, pure
   With touch ethereal of Heaven's fiery rod,[3]
   I drank, from the clear milky juice allaying   550
   Thirst, and refreshed; nor envied them the grape
   Whose heads that turbulent liquor fills with fumes.

CHORUS. O madness! to think use of strongest wines
   And strongest drinks our chief support of health,
   When God with these forbidden made choice to rear   555
   His mighty champion, strong above compare,
   Whose drink was only from the liquid brook! [4]

SAMSON. But what availed this temperance, not complete
   Against another object more enticing?
   What boots it at one gate to make defence,   560
   And at another to let in the foe,
   Effeminately vanquished? by which means,
   Now blind, disheartened, shamed, dishonored, quelled,
   To what can I be useful? wherein serve
   My nation, and the work from Heaven imposed?   565
   But to sit idle on the household hearth,
   A burdenous drone; to visitance a gaze,[5]
   Or pitied object; these redundant [6] locks,
   Robustious to no purpose, clustering down,
   Vain monument of strength; till length of years   570
   And sedentary numbness craze [7] my limbs
   To a contemptible old age obscure.

---

1. Sensual, sexual lures.
2. A castrated male sheep.
3. The rays of the sun. Samson is saying that wherever water was purest and cleanest, he drank of it—never of wine; "rod" intimates a parallel with Moses, who like Samson brought forth a spring in the middle of the desert.
4. Samson's calling as a Nazarite forbade him the use of wine.
5. A spectacle for visitors.
6. In its Latin sense, "redundant" means "flowing," in the English sense "unnecessary," "unemployed." "Robustious": strong.
7. Weaken, twist.

Here rather let me drudge, and earn my bread,
Till vermin, or the draff of servile food,[8]
Consume me, and oft-invocated death   575
Hasten the welcome end of all my pains.
MANOA. Wilt thou then serve the Philistines with that gift
Which was expressly given thee to annoy them?
Better at home lie bed-rid, not only idle,
Inglorious, unemployed, with age outworn.   580
But God, who caused a fountain at thy prayer
From the dry ground to spring, thy thirst to allay
After the brunt of battle,[9] can as easy
Cause light again within thy eyes to spring,
Wherewith to serve him better than thou hast.   585
And I persuade me so. Why else this strength
Miraculous yet remaining in those locks?
His might continues in thee not for naught,
Nor shall his wondrous gifts be frustrate thus.
SAMSON. All otherwise to me my thoughts portend,   590
That these dark orbs no more shall treat with light,
Nor th' other light of life continue long,
But yield to double darkness nigh at hand:
So much I feel my genial spirits [1] droop,
My hopes all flat: Nature within me seems   595
In all her functions weary of herself;
My race of glory run, and race of shame,
And I shall shortly be with them that rest.
MANOA. Believe not these suggestions, which proceed
From anguish of the mind, and humors black   600
That mingle with thy fancy.[2] I, however,
Must not omit a father's timely care
To prosecute the means of thy deliverance
By ransom or how else: meanwhile be calm,
And healing words from these thy friends admit.   605
SAMSON. Oh, that torment should not be confined
To the body's wounds and sores,
With maladies innumerable
In heart, head, breast, and reins,
But must secret passage find   610
To th' inmost mind,
There exercise all his fierce accidents,[3]
And on her purest spirits prey,
As on entrails, joints, and limbs,
With answerable pains, but more intense,   615
Though void of corporal sense!

8. Garbage given to slaves as food.
9. The story of how Samson, with divine
aid, created a spring in the desert after
the battle with the ass's jawbone, is told
in Judges xv.18–19.
1. Life forces, vital energy.

2. Black bile, the melancholy humor,
was supposed to have specially ill effects
on the imagination.
3. I.e., there put into effect all the fierce
qualities (of torment).

My griefs not only pain me
As a lingering disease,
But, finding no redress, ferment and rage;
Nor less than wounds immedicable   620
Rankle, and fester, and gangrene,
To black mortification.[4]
Thoughts, my tormentors, armed with daily stings,
Mangle my apprehensive tenderest parts,
Exasperate, exulcerate, and raise   625
Dire inflammation, which no cooling herb
Or med'cinal liquor can assuage,
Nor breath of vernal air from snowy Alp.
Sleep hath forsook and given me o'er
To death's benumbing opium as my only cure;   630
Thence faintings, swoonings of despair,
And sense of Heaven's desertion.[5]
    I was his nursling once and choice delight,
His destined from the womb,
Promised by heavenly message [6] twice descending.   635
Under his special eye
Abstemious I grew up and thrived amain;
He led me on to mightiest deeds,
Above the nerve [7] of mortal arm,
Against the uncircumcised, our enemies: 640
But now hath cast me off as never known,
And to those cruel enemies,
Whom I by his appointment had provoked,
Left me, all helpless with th' irreparable loss
Of sight, reserved alive to be repeated [8]   645
The subject of their cruelty or scorn.
Nor am I in the list of them that hope;
Hopeless are all my evils, all remediless.
This one prayer yet remains, might I be heard,
No long petition—speedy death,   650
The close of all my miseries and the balm.
CHORUS. Many are the sayings of the wise,
In ancient and in modern books enrolled,
Extolling patience as the truest fortitude,
And to the bearing well of all calamities,   655
All chances incident to man's frail life,
Consolatories writ
With studied argument, and much persuasion sought,
Lenient [9] of grief and anxious thought.
But with th' afflicted in his pangs their sound   660
Little prevails, or rather seems a tune

4. A medical term for decay.
5. Samson comes close here to suggesting that religious despair is the symptom of a physical condition; cf. Burton's *Anatomy of Melancholy*.
6. Messenger.
7. Sinew, hence, strength.
8. Repeatedly, continually.
9. Soothing (from Latin, *leniens*).

Harsh, and of dissonant mood [1] from his complaint,
Unless he feel within
Some source of consolation from above,
Secret refreshings that repair his strength   665
And fainting spirits uphold. [2]
   God of our fathers! what is man,
That thou towards him with hand so various—
Or might I say contrarious?—
Temper'st thy providence through his short course: 670
Not evenly, as thou rul'st
The angelic orders, and inferior creatures mute,
Irrational and brute? [3]
Nor do I name of men the common rout,
That, wandering loose about,   675
Grow up and perish as the summer fly,
Heads without name, no more remembered;
But such as thou hast solemnly elected,
With gifts and graces eminently adorned,
To some great work, thy glory,   680
And people's safety, which in part they effect.
Yet toward these, thus dignified, thou oft,
Amidst their height of noon,
Changest thy countenance and thy hand, with no regard
Of highest favors past   685
From thee on them, or them to thee of service. [4]
   Nor only dost degrade them, or remit
To life obscured, which were a fair dismission,
But throw'st them lower than thou didst exalt them high,
Unseemly falls in human eye,   690
Too grievous for the trespass or omission;
Oft leav'st them to the hostile sword
Of heathen and profane, their carcasses
To dogs and fowls a prey, or else captíved,
Or to the unjust tribunals, under change of times,   695
And condemnation of the ingrateful multitude. [5]
If these they 'scape, perhaps in poverty
With sickness and disease thou bow'st them down,
Painful diseases and deformed,
In crude [6] old age;   700
Though not disordinate, [7] yet causeless suffering
The punishment of dissolute days. In fine,

---

1. The musical mode, or psychological mood, of the comforter jars on that of the sufferer.
2. Compare Job's answers to his comforters, especially xiv.
3. The chorus feels that the beings above and below man on the Great Chain of Being (the nine orders of angels above, the many mute beasts below) are ruled by a less capricious code than is man.
4. Manoa has already voiced this plaint, lines 368–72.

5. After the Restoration, many Puritan leaders were executed, jailed, or exiled, while even the corpses of some who were dead were exhumed, beheaded, and publicly exhibited.
6. Literally, "raw," but, figuratively, "premature."
7. I.e., though they have not been dissipated (disordinate). Milton resented having the gout, supposed to be a disease of the luxurious.

Just or unjust alike seem miserable,
For oft alike both come to evil end.
    So deal not with this once thy glorious champion,   705
The image of thy strength, and mighty minister.[8]
What do I beg? how hast thou dealt already!
Behold him in this state calamitous, and turn
His labors, for thou canst, to peaceful end.
    But who is this? what thing of sea or land—   710
Female of sex it seems—
That, so bedecked, ornate, and gay,
Comes this way sailing,
Like a stately ship
Of Tarsus, bound for th' isles   715
Of Javan or Gadire,[9]
With all her bravery on, and tackle trim,
Sails filled, and streamers waving,
Courted by all the winds that hold them play;
An amber [1] scent of odorous perfume   720
Her harbinger, a damsel train behind?
Some rich Philistian matron she may seem;
And now, at nearer view, no other certain
Than Dálila thy wife.[2]
SAMSON. My wife! my traitress! let her not come near me.   725
CHORUS. Yet on she moves; now stands and eyes thee fixed,
    About t'have spoke; but now, with head declined,
    Like a fair flower surcharged with dew, she weeps,
    And words addressed seem into tears dissolved,
    Wetting the borders of her silken veil.   730
    But now again she makes address to speak.
DALILA. With doubtful feet and wavering resolution
    I came, still dreading thy displeasure, Samson;
    Which to have merited, without excuse,
    I cannot but acknowledge. Yet, if tears   735
    May expiate (though the fact more evil drew
    In the perverse event than I foresaw),[3]
    My penance hath not slackened, though my pardon
    No way assured. But conjugal affection,
    Prevailing over fear and timorous doubt,   740
    Hath led me on, desirous to behold
    Once more thy face, and know of thy estate,[4]
    If aught in my ability may serve
    To lighten what thou suffer'st, and appease
    Thy mind with what amends is in my power—   745

8. Agent, but with a religious connotation as well.
9. Tarsus (the birthplace of St. Paul) is a trading city in modern Turkey; the isles of Javan are the isles of Greece, supposed to be populated by descendants of Javan, son of Noah's son Japhet. Gadire is modern Cadiz in Spain. Many of these geographical details are to be found an Isaiah II.lxvi, etc.
1. Ambergris.
2. The circling, mocking, derisive description of the chorus carefully holds Samson in suspense till the last minute.
3. I.e., my action turned out worse than I intended.
4. Condition.

Though late, yet in some part to recompense
My rash but more unfortunate misdeed.
SAMSON. Out, out, hyena! [5] These are thy wonted arts,
And arts of every woman false like thee,
To break all faith, all vows, deceive, betray;   750
Then, as repentant, to submit, beseech,
And reconcilement move with feigned remorse,
Confess, and promise wonders in her change—
Not truly penitent, but chief to try
Her husband, how far urged his patience bears,   755
His virtue or weakness which way to assail:
Then, with more cautious and instructed skill,
Again transgresses, and again submits;
That wisest and best men, full oft beguiled,
With goodness principled not to reject   760
The penitent, but ever to forgive,
Are drawn to wear out miserable days,
Entangled with a poisonous bosom-snake,
If not by quick destruction soon cut off,
As I by thee, to ages an example.   765
DALILA. Yet hear me, Samson, not that I endeavor
To lessen or extenuate my offense,
But that, on th' other side, if it be weighed
By itself, with aggravations not surcharged,
Or else with just allowance counterpoised,   770
I may, if possible, thy pardon find
The easier towards me, or thy hatred less.
First granting, as I do, it was a weakness
In me, but incident to all our sex,
Curiosity, inquisitive, importune   775
Of secrets, then with like infirmity
To publish them, both common female faults,
Was it not weakness also to make known,
For importunity, that is for naught,
Wherein consisted all thy strength and safety?   780
To what I did thou show'dst me first the way.
But I to enemies revealed, and should not!
Nor should'st thou have trusted that to woman's frailty: [6]
Ere I to thee, thou to thyself wast cruel.
Let weakness, then, with weakness come to parle, [7]   785
So near related, or the same of kind;
Thine forgive mine, that men may censure thine
The gentler, if severely thou exact not
More strength from me than in thyself was found.

---

5. Apart from being an animal of odious habits and appearance, the hyena was a traditional beast of hypocrisy, supposed to entice men to destruction by its power of imitating the human voice.
6. Like Eve, who wore down Adam with importunity, then blamed him for giving in (*Paradise Lost* IX.1155–61) Dalila blames Samson for doing what she herself has demanded.
7. Parley, agreement.

And what if love, which thou interpret'st hate, 790
The jealousy of love, powerful of sway
In human hearts, nor less in mine towards thee,
Caused what I did? I saw thee mutable
Of fancy; feared lest one day thou would'st leave me,
As her at Timna; sought by all means, therefore, 795
How to endear, and hold thee to me firmest:
No better way I saw than by importuning
To learn thy secrets, get into my power
Thy key of strength and safety. Thou wilt say,
"Why, then, revealed?" I was assured by those 800
Who tempted me that nothing was designed
Against thee but safe custody and hold.
That made for me; I knew that liberty
Would draw thee forth to perilous enterprises,
While I at home sat full of cares and fears, 805
Wailing thy absence in my widowed bed;
Here I should still enjoy thee, day and night,
Mine and love's prisoner, not the Philistines',
Whole to myself, unhazarded abroad,
Fearless at home of partners in my love. 810
These reasons in love's law have passed for good,
Though fond [8] and reasonless to some perhaps;
And love hath oft, well meaning, wrought much woe,
Yet always pity or pardon hath obtained.
Be not unlike all others, not austere 815
As thou art strong, inflexible as steel.
If thou in strength all mortals dost exceed,
In uncompassionate anger do not so.
SAMSON. How cunningly the sorceress displays
Her own transgressions, to upbraid me mine! 820
That malice, not repentance, brought thee hither,
By this appears. I gave, thou say'st, th' example,
I led the way—bitter reproach, but true;
I to myself was false ere thou to me.
Such pardon, therefore, as I give my folly 825
Take to thy wicked deed; which when thou seest
Impartial, self-severe, inexorable,
Thou wilt renounce thy seeking, and much rather
Confess it feigned. Weakness is thy excuse,
And I believe it, weakness to resist 830
Philistian gold. If weakness may excuse,
What murderer, what traitor, parricide,
Incestuous, sacrilegious, but may plead it?
All wickedness is weakness; that plea, therefore,
With God or man will gain thee no remission. 835
But love constrained thee! Call it furious rage
To satisfy thy lust. Love seeks to have love;

8. Foolish.

My love how could'st thou hope, who took'st the way
To raise in me inexpiable [9] hate,
Knowing, as needs I must, by thee betrayed?   840
In vain thou striv'st to cover shame with shame,
Or by evasions thy crime uncover'st more.

DALILA. Since thou determin'st weakness for no plea
In man or woman, though to thy own condemning,
Hear what assaults I had, what snares besides,   845
What sieges girt me round, ere I consented;
Which might have awed the best resolved of men,
The constantest, to have yielded without blame.
It was not gold, as to my charge thou lay'st,
That wrought with me.[1] Thou know'st the magistrates   850
And princes of my country came in person,
Solicited, commanded, threatened, urged,
Adjured by all the bonds of civil duty
And of religion—pressed how just it was,
How honorable, how glorious, to entrap   855
A common enemy, who had destroyed
Such numbers of our nation: and the priest
Was not behind, but ever at my ear,
Preaching how meritorious with the gods
It would be to ensnare an irreligious   860
Dishonorer of Dagon. What had I
To oppose against such powerful arguments?
Only my love of thee held long debate,
And combated in silence all these reasons
With hard contest. At length, that grounded maxim,   865
So rife and celebrated in the mouths
Of wisest men, that to the public good
Private respects must yield,[2] with grave authority
Took full possession of me, and prevailed;
Virtue, as I thought, truth, duty, so enjoining.   870

SAMSON. I thought where all thy circling wiles would end,
In feigned religion, smooth hypocrisy!
But, had thy love, still odiously pretended,
Been, as it ought, sincere, it would have taught thee
Far other reasonings, brought forth other deeds.   875
I, before all the daughters of my tribe
And of my nation, chose thee from among
My enemies, loved thee, as too well thou knew'st;
Too well; unbosomed all my secrets to thee,
Not out of levity, but overpowered   880
By thy request, who could deny thee nothing;
Yet now am judged an enemy. Why, then,

---

9. Inextinguishable.
1. Judges xvi is very explicit that Dalila betrayed Samson for money—eleven hundred pieces of silver offered her by each one of the Philistine lords.

2. Reason of state, political expediency, was in Milton's eyes the worst of all possible motives for an action. Cf. *Paradise Lost* IV. 393–94.

Didst thou at first receive me for thy husband,
Then, as since then, thy country's foe professed?
Being once a wife, for me thou wast to leave   885
Parents and country; nor was I their subject,
Nor under their protection, but my own;
Thou mine, not theirs.[3] If aught against my life
Thy country sought of thee, it sought unjustly,
Against the law of nature, law of nations;   890
No more thy country, but an impious crew
Of men conspiring to uphold their state
By worse than hostile deeds, violating the ends
For which our country is a name so dear;
Not therefore to be obeyed. But zeal moved thee;   895
To please thy gods thou didst it! Gods unable
To acquit themselves and prosecute their foes
But by ungodly deeds, the contradiction
Of their own deity, gods cannot be;
Less therefore to be pleased, obeyed, or feared.   900
These false pretexts and varnished colors failing,
Bare in thy guilt, how foul must thou appear!
DALILA. In argument with men a woman ever
  Goes by the worse,[4] whatever be her cause.
SAMSON. For want of words, no doubt, or lack of breath!   905
  Witness when I was worried with thy peals.
DALILA. I was a fool, too rash, and quite mistaken
  In what I thought would have succeeded best.
  Let me obtain forgiveness of thee, Samson;
  Afford me place to show what recompense   910
  Towards thee I intend for what I have misdone,
  Misguided. Only what remains past cure
  Bear not too sensibly,[5] nor still insist
  To afflict thyself in vain. Though sight be lost,
  Life yet hath many solaces, enjoyed   915
  Where other senses want not their delights—
  At home, in leisure and domestic ease,
  Exempt from many a care and chance to which
  Eyesight exposes, daily, men abroad.
  I to the lords will intercede, not doubting   920
  Their favorable ear, that I may fetch thee
  From forth this loathsome prison house, to abide
  With me, where my redoubled love and care,
  With nursing diligence, to me glad office,
  May ever tend about thee to old age,   925
  With all things grateful cheered, and so supplied
  That what by me thou hast lost thou least shalt miss.
SAMSON. No, no; of my condition take no care;

---

3. I.e., you were under my protection, not theirs.
4. Comes off second best.

5. "Too sensibly": with too great sensitivity.

It fits not; thou and I long since are twain;
Nor think me so unwary or accursed [6]   930
To bring my feet again into the snare
Where once I have been caught. I know thy trains,
Though dearly to my cost, thy gins, and toils.[7]
Thy fair enchanted cup, and warbling charms,
No more on me have power; their force is nulled;   935
So much of adder's wisdom I have learned,
To fence my ear against thy sorceries.[8]
If in my flower of youth and strength, when all men
Loved, honored, feared me, thou alone could hate me,
Thy husband, slight me, sell me, and forgo me,   940
How would'st thou use me now, blind, and thereby
Deceivable, in most things as a child
Helpless, thence easily contemned and scorned,
And last neglected! How would'st thou insult,
When I must live uxorious to thy will   945
In perfect thraldom! how again betray me,
Bearing my words and doings to the lords
To gloss upon, and, censuring, frown or smile! [9]
This jail I count the house of liberty
To thine, whose doors my feet shall never enter.   950
DALILA. Let me approach at least, and touch thy hand.
SAMSON. Not for thy life, lest fierce remembrance wake
My sudden rage to tear thee joint by joint.[1]
At distance I forgive thee, go with that;
Bewail thy falsehood, and the pious works   955
It hath brought forth to make thee memorable
Among illustrious women, faithful wives;
Cherish thy hastened widowhood with the gold
Of matrimonial treason: so farewell.
DALILA. I see thou art implacable, more deaf   960
To prayers than winds and seas. Yet winds to seas
Are reconciled at length, and sea to shore:
Thy anger, unappeasable, still rages,
Eternal tempest never to be calmed.
Why do I humble thus myself, and, suing   965
For peace, reap nothing but repulse and hate,
Bid go with evil omen,[2] and the brand
Of infamy upon my name denounced?
To mix with thy concernments I desist
Henceforth, nor too much disapprove my own.   970

6. I.e., so neglectful or bewitched.
7. "Trains": tricks; "gins": snares;
"toils": nets. The traditional images for
female wiles are heightened by reference
to an enchanting cup and warbled charms
reminiscent of Homer's Circe (*Odyssey*,
X).
8. Psalm lviii verses 4 and 5 describes
the "deaf adder that stoppeth her ear;
which will not hearken to the voice of

charmers, charming never so wisely."
9. Milton's libertarian hatred of censorship and managed liberty is very apparent.
1. What Samson might remember, at the
touch of Dalila, which would lead him
to tear her to pieces, is a problem in
domestic psychology.
2. I.e., dismissed with threats of ill
fame.

Fame, if not double-faced, is double-mouthed.
And with contrary blast proclaims most deeds; [3]
On both his wings, one black, th' other white,
Bears greatest names in his wild airy flight.
My name, perhaps, among the circumcised   975
In Dan, in Judah, and the bordering tribes,
To all posterity may stand defamed,
With malediction mentioned, and the blot
Of falsehood most unconjugal traduced.
But in my country, where I most desire,   980
In Ecron, Gaza, Asdod, and in Gath,
I shall be named among the famousest
Of women, sung at solemn festivals,
Living and dead recorded, who to save
Her country from a fierce destroyer chose   985
Above the faith of wedlock bands; my tomb
With odors [4] visited and annual flowers;
Not less renowned than in Mount Ephraim
Jael, who, with inhospitable guile,
Smote Sisera sleeping, [5] through the temples nailed. 990
Nor shall I count it heinous to enjoy
The public marks of honor and reward
Conferred upon me for the piety
Which to my country I was judged to have shown.
At this whoever envies or repines,   995
I leave him to his lot, and like my own.
CHORUS. She's gone, a manifest serpent by her sting
Discovered in the end, till now concealed.
SAMSON. So let her go. God sent her to debase me,
And aggravate my folly, who committed   1000
To such a viper his most sacred trust
Of secrecy, my safety, and my life.
CHORUS. Yet beauty, though injurious, hath strange power,
After offense returning, to regain
Love once possessed, nor can be easily   1005
Repulsed, without much inward passion [6] felt,
And secret sting of amorous remorse.
SAMSON. Love-quarrels oft in pleasing concord end;
Not wedlock-treachery, endangering life.
CHORUS. It is not virtue, wisdom, valor, wit,   1010
Strength, comeliness of shape, or amplest merit.
That woman's love can win, or long inherit; [7]
But what it is hard is to say,
Harder to hit,

---

3. The figure of Fame, in Milton's youthful poem *On the Fifth of November*,
does indeed have a double tongue, one
for truth and one for lies. Fame or
Rumor was a favorite grotesque allegorical figure in classical poets like Ovid
(*Metamorphoses* XII.43 ff.) and Virgil
(*Aeneid* IV.173 ff.).

4. Perfumes.
5. Jael lured Sisera, who saw in her the
wife of his ally and friend, into a tent,
and there drove a large nail into his
head (Judges iv.17–21).
6. Suffering.
7. Possess.

Which way soever men refer it   1015
(Much like thy riddle, Samson),[8] in one day
Or seven though one should musing sit.
    If any of these, or all, the Timnian bride
Had not so soon preferred
Thy paranymph, worthless to thee compared,   1020
Successor in thy bed,[9]
Nor both so loosely disallied
Their nuptials,[1] nor this last so treacherously
Had shorn the fatal harvest of thy head.
Is it for that [2] such outward ornament   1025
Was lavished on their sex, that inward gifts
Were left for haste unfinished, judgment scant,
Capacity not raised to apprehend
Or value what is best
In choice, but oftest to affect [3] the wrong?   1030
Or was too much of self-love mixed,
Of constancy no root infixed,
That either they love nothing, or not long?
    Whate'er it be, to wisest men and best,
Seeming at first all heavenly under virgin veil,   1035
Soft, modest, meek, demure,
Once joined, the contrary she proves, a thorn
Intestine,[4] far within defensive arms
A cleaving [5] mischief, in his way to virtue
Adverse and turbulent; or by her charms   1040
Draws him awry, enslaved
With dotage, and his sense depraved
To folly and shameful deeds, which ruin ends.
What pilot so expert but needs must wreck,
Embarked with such a steers-mate at the helm?   1045
    Favored of Heaven who finds
One virtuous, rarely found,
That in domestic good combines:
Happy that house! his way to peace is smooth:
But virtue which breaks through all opposition,   1050
And all temptation can remove,
Most shines and most is acceptable above.
    Therefore God's universal law
Gave to the man despotic power
Over his female in due awe,   1055
Nor from that right to part an hour,
Smile she or lour:
So shall he least confusion draw
On his whole life, not swayed

8. Samson's riddle is propounded and answered in Judges xiv, verses 14 and 18.
9. I.e., if any of these ("virtue, . . . ," lines 1010–11) sufficed, Samson's first wife (the Timnian bride) would not have preferred to marry his "paranymph" (best man). See Judges xiv.
1. I.e., nor would both your wives have been so careless about their marriage vows.
2. Because.
3. Desire.
4. An inward thorn, a viper in the bosom.
5. Clinging; a traditional emblem of marriage was the elm and the vine.

By female usurpation, nor dismayed. 1060
    But had we best retire? I see a storm.
SAMSON. Fair days have oft contracted [6] wind and rain.
CHORUS. But this another kind of tempest brings.
SAMSON. Be less abstruse; my riddling days are past.
CHORUS. Look now for no enchanting voice, nor fear 1065
    The bait of honeyed words; a rougher tongue
    Draws hitherward, I know him by his stride,
    The giant Harapha [7] of Gath, his look
    Haughty, as is his pile [8] high-built and proud.
    Comes he in peace? What wind hath blown him hither 1070
    I less conjecture than when first I saw
    The sumptuous Dalila floating this way: [9]
    His habit carries peace, his brow defiance.
SAMSON. Or peace or not, alike to me he comes.
CHORUS. His fraught [1] we soon shall know: he now arrives. 1075
HARAPHA. I come not, Samson, to condole thy chance,
    As these [2] perhaps, yet wish it had not been,
    Though for no friendly intent. I am of Gath;
    Men call me Harapha, of stock renowned
    As Og, or Anak, and the Emims old 1080
    That Kiriathaim held.[3] Thou know'st me now,
    If thou at all art known.[4] Much I have heard
    Of thy prodigious might and feats performed,
    Incredible to me, in this displeased,
    That I was never present on the place 1085
    Of those encounters, where we might have tried
    Each other's force in camp or listed field; [5]
    And now am come to see of whom such noise
    Hath walked about, and each limb to survey,
    If thy appearance answer loud report. 1090
SAMSON. The way to know were not to see, but taste.[6]
HARAPHA. Dost thou already single [7] me? I thought
    Gyves and the mill had tamed thee. O that fortune
    Had brought me to the field where thou art famed
    To have wrought such wonders with an ass's jaw! 1095
    I should have forced thee soon wish [8] other arms,

---

6. Drawn after them.
7. Harapha does not appear at all within the story told in the Book of Judges; Milton invented him with the help of some hints from the image of Goliath in I Samuel xvii and some other giants in II Samuel xxi. *Rapha* means giant in Hebrew.
8. Body; with the suggestion that he is tall as a tower.
9. That the various visitors of Samson are blown hither and yon by the winds of occasion serves to emphasize the deep steadiness of Samson's final resolution.
1. Intent.
2. The chorus of Danites, naturally sympathetic to Samson.
3. Og was a giant King of Bashan in Deuteronomy iii.11; Anak and his sons were giants in Numbers xiii.33; the Emims were giants in Deuteronomy ii. 10–11 and Genesis xiv.5.
4. I.e., you know me now if you know anything; but also "if you are anyone worth knowing." Compare Satan's brag to Zephon and Ithuriel, "Not to know me argues yourselves unknown." *Paradise Lost* IV.830.
5. "Camp": field of battle (from Latin, *campus*); "listed field": lists, tourney-ground.
6. Make a trial of.
7. Challenge; "gyves": chains.
8. Eighteenth-century editors changed "wish" to "with", easing the grammar at the expense of the sense.

Or left thy carcass where the ass lay thrown;
So had the glory of prowess been recovered
To Palestine, won by a Philistine
From the unforeskinned race, of whom thou bear'st   1100
The highest name for valiant acts. That honor,
Certain to have won by mortal duel from thee,
I lose, prevented by thy eyes put out.

SAMSON. Boast not of what thou would'st have done, but do
What then thou would'st; thou seest it in thy hand.   1105

HARAPHA. To combat with a blind man I disdain,
And thou hast need much washing to be touched.

SAMSON. Such usage as your honorable lords
Afford me, assassinated [9] and betrayed;
Who durst not with their whole united powers   1110
In fight withstand me single and unarmed,
Nor in the house with chamber ambushes [1]
Close-banded durst attack me, no, not sleeping,
Till they had hired a woman with their gold,
Breaking her marriage-faith, to circumvent me.   1115
Therefore, without feigned shifts, let be assigned
Some narrow place enclosed, where sight may give thee,
Or rather flight, no great advantage on me;
Then put on all thy gorgeous arms, thy helmet
And brigandine of brass, thy broad habergeon,   1120
Vant-brace and greaves and gauntlet; [2] add thy spear,
A weaver's beam, and seven-times-folded shield:
I only with an oaken staff will meet thee,
And raise such outcries on thy clattered iron,
Which long shall not withhold me from thy head,   1125
That in a little time, while breath remains thee,
Thou oft shalt wish thyself at Gath, to boast
Again in safety what thou would'st have done
To Samson, but shalt never see Gath more.

HARAPHA. Thou durst not thus disparage glorious arms,   1130
Which greatest heroes have in battle worn,
Their ornament and safety, had not spells
And black enchantments, some magician's art,
Armed thee or charmed thee strong, which thou from Heaven
Feign'dst at thy birth was given thee in thy hair,   1135
Where strength can least abide, though all thy hairs
Were bristles ranged like those that ridge the back
Of chafed wild boars or ruffled porcupines.

SAMSON. I know no spells, use no forbidden arts;
My trust is in the Living God, who gave me,   1140

---

9. Treacherously assailed.
1. Samson refers to the four occasions on which Philistines hid in his bedroom while Dalila tried unsuccessfully to betray him to them.
2. "Brigandine": a padded chest-protector, covered with iron scales or rings; "habergeon": a coat of mail, a hauberk;

"vant-brace": a steel cuff for the forearm; greaves protect the shins and thighs, and gauntlets the hands. A weaver's beam, emblem of weightiness, is used to keep threads hanging tautly in a loom. All these military details are from the description of Goliath, I Samuel xvii.4–7.

At my nativity, this strength, diffused
No less through all my sinews, joints, and bones,
Than thine, while I preserved these locks unshorn,
The pledge of my unviolated vow.
For proof hereof, if Dagon be thy god,   1145
Go to his temple, invocate his aid
With solemnest devotion, spread before him
How highly it concerns his glory now
To frustrate and dissolve these magic spells,
Which I to be the power of Israel's God   1150
Avow, and challenge Dagon to the test,
Offering to combat thee, his champion bold,
With th' utmost of his godhead seconded:
Then thou shalt see, or rather to thy sorrow
Soon feel, whose God is strongest, thine or mine.   1155
HARAPHA. Presume not on thy God. Whate'er he be,
Thee he regards not, owns not, hath cut off
Quite from his people, and delivered up
Into thy enemies' hand; permitted them
To put out both thine eyes, and fettered send thee   1160
Into the common prison, there to grind
Among the slaves and asses, thy comrádes,
As good for nothing else, no better service
With those thy boisterous locks; no worthy match
For valor to assail, nor by the sword   1165
Of noble warrior, so to stain his honor,
But by the barber's razor best subdued.
SAMSON. All these indignities, for such they are
From thine,[3] these evils I deserve and more,
Acknowledge them from God inflicted on me   1170
Justly, yet despair not of his final pardon,
Whose ear is ever open, and his eye
Gracious to re-admit the suppliant;
In confidence whereof I once again
Defy thee to the trial of mortal fight,   1175
By combat to decide whose god is God,
Thine, or whom I with Israel's sons adore.
HARAPHA. Fair honor that thou dost thy God, in trusting
He will accept thee to defend his cause,
A murderer, a revolter, and a robber!   1180
SAMSON. Tongue-doughty giant, how dost thou prove me these?
HARAPHA. Is not thy nation subject to our lords?
Their magistrates confessed it when they took thee
As a league-breaker, and delivered bound
Into our hands;[4] for hadst not committed   1185

---

3. Thy people.
4. Judges xiv.8–20 and xv.9–15 describe the episode. Samson when he came to Timna to be married proposed a riddle and a bet to the marriage guests; they got his intended bride to reveal the riddle, and in revenge he killed thirty of their people and left the lady to the "paranymph," or best man. Old Testament Samson is indeed a rude and savage figure; Milton, with characteristic confidence, undertakes his legal defense in everything.

Notorious murder on those thirty men
At Ascalon, who never did thee harm,
Then, like a robber, stripp'dst them of their robes?
The Philistines, when thou hadst broke the league,
Went up with arméd powers thee only seeking,   1190
To others did no violence nor spoil.

SAMSON. Among the daughters of the Philistines
    I chose a wife, which argued me no foe,
    And in your city held my nuptial feast;
    But your ill-meaning politician lords,   1195
    Under pretense of bridal friends and guests,
    Appointed to await me thirty spies,
    Who, threatening cruel death, constrained the bride
    To wring from me, and tell to them, my secret,
    That solved the riddle which I had proposed.   1200
    When I perceived all set on enmity,
    As on my enemies, wherever chanced,
    I used hostility, and took their spoil,
    To pay my underminers in their coin.
    My nation was subjected to your lords! [5]   1205
    It was the force of conquest; force with force
    Is well ejected when the conquered can.
    But I, a private person, whom my country
    As a league-breaker gave up bound, presumed
    Single rebellion, and did hostile acts!   1210
    I was no private,[6] but a person raised,
    With strength sufficient, and command from Heaven,
    To free my country. If their servile minds
    Me, their deliverer sent, would not receive,
    But to their masters gave me up for nought,   1215
    Th' unworthier they; whence to this day they serve.
    I was to do my part from Heaven assigned,
    And had performed it if my known offense
    Had not disabled me, not all your force.
    These shifts refuted, answer thy appellant,[7]   1220
    Though by his blindness maimed for high attempts,
    Who now defies thee thrice to single fight,
    As a petty enterprise of small enforce.[8]

HARAPHA. With thee, a man condemned, a slave enrolled,
    Due by the law to capital punishment?   1225
    To fight with thee no man of arms will deign.

SAMSON. Cam'st thou for this, vain boaster, to survey me,
    To descant on my strength, and give thy verdict?
    Come nearer; part not hence so slight informed;
    But take good heed my hand survey not thee.   1230

HARAPHA. O Baal-zebub! [9] can my ears unused

5. I.e., you argue that my nation was
subjected to your lords.
6. Outlaw.
7. I.e., now that we've disposed of these
dodges, answer your challenger. "Apel-

lant": literally, caller, one who calls
you out.
8. Difficulty.
9. Baal-zebub is Beelzebub, god of the
flies.

Hear these dishonors, and not render death?
SAMSON. No man withholds thee; nothing from thy hand
    Fear I incurable; bring up thy van; [1]
    My heels are fettered, but my fist is free.   1235
HARAPHA. This insolence other kind of answer fits.
SAMSON. Go, baffled coward, lest I run upon thee,
    Though in these chains, bulk without spirit vast,
    And with one buffet lay thy structure low,
    Or swing thee in the air, then dash thee down,   1240
    To the hazard of thy brains and shattered sides.
HARAPHA. By Astaroth,[2] ere long thou shalt lament
    These braveries,[3] in irons loaden on thee.
CHORUS. His giantship is gone somewhat crestfallen,
    Stalking with less unconscionable [4] strides,
    And lower looks, but in a sultry chafe.   1245
SAMSON. I dread him not, nor all his giant brood,
    Though fame divulge him father of five sons,
    All of gigantic size, Goliath chief.[5]
CHORUS. He will directly to the lords, I fear,   1250
    And with malicious counsel stir them up
    Some way or other yet further to afflict thee.
SAMSON. He must allege some cause, and offered fight
    Will not dare mention, lest a question rise
    Whether he durst accept the offer or not;   1255
    And that he durst not plain enough appeared.
    Much more affliction than already felt
    They cannot well impose, nor I sustain,
    If they intend advantage of my labors,
    The work of many hands, which earns my keeping,   1260
    With no small profit daily to my owners.
    But come what will; my deadliest foe will prove
    My speediest friend, by death to rid me hence;
    The worst that he can give to me the best.
    Yet so it may fall out, because their end   1265
    Is hate, not help to me, it may with mine
    Draw their own ruin who attempt the deed.
CHORUS. O, how comely it is, and how reviving
    To the spirits of just men long oppressed,
    When God into the hands of their deliverer   1270
    Puts invincible might,
    To quell the mighty of the earth, th' oppressor,
    The brute and boisterous force of violent men,
    Hardy and industrious to support
    Tyrannic power, but raging to pursue   1275
    The righteous, and all such as honor truth!

1. The vanguard of an army was, naturally, the first group engaged. Samson invites Harapha to start the fight.
2. Moon-goddess of the Philistines, consort of Dagon. See *Paradise Lost* I.437–46.
3. Boasts.
4. Excessive.
5. II Samuel xxi describes four giants "born to the giant in Gath" and slain by David; Milton makes the identification with Harapha on his own.

He all their ammunition
And feats of war defeats,[6]
With plain heroic magnitude of mind
And celestial vigor armed; 1280
Their armories and magazines contemns,
Renders them useless, while
With wingéd expedition [7]
Swift as the lightning glance he executes
His errand on the wicked, who, surprised, 1285
Lose their defense, distracted and amazed.
　　But patience is more oft the exercise
Of saints, the trial of their fortitude,
Making them each his own deliverer,
And victor over all 1290
That tyranny or fortune can inflict.
Either of these is in thy lot,[8]
Samson, with might endued
Above the sons of men; but sight bereaved
May chance to number thee with those 1295
Whom patience finally must crown.[9]
　　This Idol's day hath been to thee no day of rest,
Laboring thy mind
More than the working day thy hands.
And yet, perhaps, more trouble is behind; 1300
For I descry this way
Some other tending; in his hand
A scepter or quaint [1] staff he bears,
Comes on amain, speed in his look.
By his habit I discern him now 1305
A public officer, and now at hand.
His message will be short and voluble.[2]
OFFICER.　Ebrews, the prisoner Samson here I seek.
CHORUS.　His manacles remark [3] him; there he sits.
OFFICER.　Samson, to thee our lords thus bid me say: 1310
This day to Dagon is a solemn feast,
With sacrifices, triumph, pomp, and games;
Thy strength they know surpassing human rate,
And now some public proof thereof require
To honor this great feast, and great assembly. 1315
Rise, therefore, with all speed, and come along,
Where I will see thee heartened and fresh clad,
To appear as fits before th' illustrious lords.
SAMSON.　Thou know'st I am an Ebrew; therefore tell them
Our law forbids at their religious rites 1320
My presence; for that cause I cannot come.

---

6. A touch of the pervasive Miltonic punning.
7. Haste.
8. Fate.
9. The Christian tragedy, like the Christian epic, must center ultimately on an act of passive, not active, fortitude. It is the special achievement of Samson to combine in a single action both qualities.
1. Ornamented.
2. To the point.
3. Distinguish.

OFFICER. This answer, be assured, will not content them.
SAMSON. Have they not sword-players, and every sort
    Of gymnic artists, wrestlers, riders, runners,
    Jugglers and dancers, antics, mummers, mimics,[4]   1325
    But they must pick me out, with shackles tired,
    And over-labored at their public mill,
    To make them sport with blind activity?
    Do they not seek occasion of new quarrels,
    On my refusal, to distress me more,   1330
    Or make a game of my calamities?
    Return the way thou cam'st; I will not come.
OFFICER. Regard thyself; this will offend them highly.
SAMSON. Myself? my conscience, and internal peace.
    Can they think me so broken, so debased   1335
    With corporal servitude, that my mind ever
    Will condescend to such absurd commands?
    Although their drudge, to be their fool or jester,
    And, in my midst of sorrow and heart-grief,
    To show them feats, and play before their god,   1340
    The worst of all indignities, yet on me
    Joined [5] with supreme contempt! I will not come.
OFFICER. My message was imposed on me with speed,
    Brooks no delay: is this thy resolution?
SAMSON. So take it with what speed thy message needs.   1345
OFFICER. I am sorry what this stoutness [6] will produce.
SAMSON. Perhaps thou shalt have cause to sorrow indeed.
CHORUS. Consider, Samson; matters now are strained
    Up to the height, whether to hold or break.
    He's gone, and who knows how he may report   1350
    Thy words by adding fuel to the flame?
    Expect another message, more imperious,
    More lordly thundering than thou well wilt bear.
SAMSON. Shall I abuse this consecrated gift
    Of strength, again returning with my hair   1355
    After my great transgression, so requite
    Favor renewed, and add a greater sin
    By prostituting holy things to idols,
    A Nazarite, in place abominable,
    Vaunting my strength in honor to their Dagon?   1360
    Besides how vile, contemptible, ridiculous,
    What act more execrably unclean,[7] profane?
CHORUS. Where the heart joins not, outward acts defile not.
    Idolatrous, uncircumcised, unclean.
SAMSON. Not in their idol-worship, but by labor   1365
    Honest and lawful to deserve my food
    Of those who have me in their civil power.
CHORUS. Where the heart joins not, outward acts defile not.

---

4. "Gymnic artists": gymnasts; "an-   6. Defiance.
tics": clowns; "mummers": actors.   7. Taboo.
5. Enjoined, ordered.

SAMSON. Where outward force constrains, the sentence holds: [8]
    But who constrains me to the temple of Dagon,   1370
    Not dragging? The Philistian lords command:
    Commands are no constraints. If I obey them,
    I do it freely, venturing to displease
    God for the fear of man, and man prefer,
    Set God behind; which, in his jealousy,   1375
    Shall never, unrepented, find forgiveness.
    Yet that he may dispense with me, or thee,
    Present in temples at idolatrous rites
    For some important cause,[9] thou need'st not doubt.
CHORUS. How thou wilt here come off surmounts my reach.   1380
SAMSON. Be of good courage; I begin to feel
    Some rousing motions in me, which dispose
    To something extraordinary my thoughts.
    I with this messenger will go along—
    Nothing to do, be sure, that may dishonor   1385
    Our Law, or stain my vow of Nazarite.
    If there be aught of presage in the mind,
    This day will be remarkable in my life
    By some great act, or of my days the last.[1]
CHORUS. In time thou hast resolved: the man returns.   1390
OFFICER. Samson, this second message from our lords
    To thee I am bid say: Art thou our slave,
    Our captive, at the public mill our drudge,
    And dar'st thou, at our sending and command,
    Dispute thy coming? Come without delay;   1395
    Or we shall find such engines to assail
    And hamper thee, as thou shalt come of force,
    Though thou wert firmlier fastened than a rock.
SAMSON. I could be well content to try their art,
    Which to no few of them would prove pernicious;   1400
    Yet, knowing their advantages too many,
    Because [2] they shall not trail me through their streets
    Like a wild beast, I am content to go.
    Masters' commands come with a power resistless
    To such as owe them absolute subjection;   1405
    And for a life who will not change his purpose?
    (So mutable are all the ways of men!)
    Yet this be sure, in nothing to comply
    Scandalous or forbidden in our Law.
OFFICER. I praise thy resolution.[3] Doff these links: 1410
    By this compliance thou wilt win the lords
    To favor, and perhaps to set thee free.

---

8. I.e., where outward force constrains, your motto may be right.
9. God will make a special dispensation for Samson to attend idolatrous ceremonies "for some important cause," which Samson cannot yet define but which he intuits.
1. By a classic device of dramatic irony, Samson proposes as alternatives two events which will both simultaneously come true. "Presage": premonition, presight.
2. So that.
3. Decision. "Doff these links": take off these chains.

SAMSON. Brethren, farewell. Your company along
   I will not wish, lest it perhaps offend them
   To see me girt with friends; and how the sight   1415
   Of me, as of a common enemy,
   So dreaded once, may now exasperate them
   I know not. Lords are lordliest in their wine;
   And the well-feasted priest then soonest fired
   With zeal, if aught religion seem concerned; [4]   1420
   No less the people, on their holy-days,
   Impetuous, insolent, unquenchable.
   Happen what may, of me expect to hear
   Nothing dishonorable, impure, unworthy
   Our God, our Law, my nation, or myself;   1425
   The last of me or no I cannot warrant.
CHORUS. Go, and the Holy One
   Of Israel be thy guide
   To what may serve his glory best, and spread his name
   Great among the heathen round;   1430
   Send thee the angel of thy birth, to stand
   Fast by thy side, who from thy father's field
   Rode up in flames after his message told
   Of thy conception, and be now a shield
   Of fire; that Spirit that first rushed on thee   1435
   In the camp of Dan,
   Be efficacious in thee now at need! [5]
   For never was from Heaven imparted
   Measure of strength so great to mortal seed
   As in thy wondrous actions hath been seen.   1440
   But wherefore comes old Manoa in such haste
   With youthful steps? Much livelier than erewhile
   He seems: supposing here to find his son,
   Or of him bringing to us some glad news?
MANOA. Peace with you, brethren! My inducement hither   1445
   Was not at present here to find my son,
   By order of the lords new parted hence
   To come and play before them at their feast.
   I heard all as I came; the city rings,
   And numbers thither flock: I had no will,   1450
   Lest I should see him forced to things unseemly.
   But that which moved my coming now was chiefly
   To give ye part with me [6] what hope I have
   With good success to work his liberty.
CHORUS. That hope would much rejoice us to partake   1455
   With thee. Say, reverend sire; we thirst to hear.
MANOA. I have attempted, one by one, the lords,

---

4. Milton's animus against paid priests, whom he considers particularly likely to contaminate the Word of God with their own private interests and worldly desires, comes out plainly here.

5. Samson's angel, appearing before his birth and at various crises during his life (Judges xiv.6,19; xv.14) is here invoked almost as a tutelary spirit or guardian angel.

6. I.e., to impart to you.

Either at home, or through the high street passing,
With supplication prone and father's tears,
To accept of ransom for my son, their prisoner.   1460
Some much averse I found, and wondrous harsh,
Contemptuous, proud, set on revenge and spite;
That part most reverenced Dagon and his priests:
Others more moderate seeming, but their aim
Private reward, for which both God and State   1465
They easily would set to sale: a third
More generous far and civil, who confessed
They had enough revenged, having reduced
Their foe to misery beneath their fears;
The rest was magnanimity to remit,   1470
If some convenient ransom were proposed.[7]
What noise or shout was that? It tore the sky.
CHORUS. Doubtless the people shouting to behold
    Their once great dread, captive and blind before them,
    Or at some proof of strength before them shown.   1475
MANOA. His ransom, if my whole inheritance
    May compass it, shall willingly be paid
    And numbered down. Much rather I shall choose
    To live the poorest in my tribe, than richest
    And he in that calamitous prison left.   1480
    No, I am fixed not to part hence without him.
    For his redemption all my patrimony,
    If need be, I am ready to forgo
    And quit. Not wanting him, I shall want nothing.
CHORUS. Fathers are wont to lay up for their sons;   1485
    Thou for thy son art bent to lay out all:
    Sons wont to nurse their parents in old age;
    Thou in old age car'st how to nurse thy son,
    Made older than thy age through eyesight lost.
MANOA. It shall be my delight to tend his eyes,   1490
    And view him sitting in his house, ennobled
    With all those high exploits by him achieved,
    And on his shoulders waving down those locks
    That of a nation armed the strength contained.
    And I persuade me God hath not permitted   1495
    His strength again to grow up with his hair
    Garrisoned round about him like a camp
    Of faithful soldiery, were not his purpose
    To use him further yet in some great service—
    Not to sit idle with so great a gift   1500
    Useless, and thence ridiculous, about him.[8]
    And, since his strength with eyesight was not lost,

---

7. The three parties are in effect bigots, swindlers, and gentlemen—three types common enough in Restoration England, with whom Milton and the defeated Puritans must have had frequently to deal.
8. A good deal of the play deals with the concept of relevance and irrelevance; outward weapons and outward strength are often beside the point ("ridiculous") in the face of inward and spiritual powers.

God will restore him eyesight to [9] his strength.
CHORUS. Thy hopes are not ill founded, nor seem vain,
  Of his delivery, and thy joy thereon   1505
  Conceived, agreeable to a father's love;
  In both which we, as next,[1] participate.
MANOA. I know your friendly minds, and—O, what noise!
  Mercy of Heaven! what hideous noise was that?
  Horribly loud, unlike the former shout.   1510
CHORUS. Noise call you it, or universal groan,
  As if the whole inhabitation perished?
  Blood, death, and deathful deeds, are in that noise,
  Ruin,[2] destruction at the utmost point.
MANOA. Of ruin indeed methought I heard the noise.   1515
  Oh! it continues; they have slain my son.
CHORUS. Thy son is rather slaying them; that outcry
  From slaughter of one foe could not ascend.
MANOA. Some dismal accident it needs must be.
  What shall we do, stay here, or run and see?   1520
CHORUS. Best keep together here, lest, running thither,
  We unawares run into danger's mouth.
  This evil on the Philistines is fallen:
  From whom could else a general cry be heard?
  The sufferers then will scarce molest us here;   1525
  From other hands we need not much to fear.
  What if, his eyesight (for to Israel's God
  Nothing is hard) by miracle restored,
  He now be dealing dole [3] among his foes,
  And over heaps of slaughtered walk his way?   1530
MANOA. That were a joy presumptuous to be thought.
CHORUS. Yet God hath wrought things as incredible
  For his people of old; what hinders now?
MANOA. He can, I know, but doubt to think he will;
  Yet hope would fain subscribe, and tempts belief.   1535
  A little stay will bring some notice hither.
CHORUS. Of good or bad so great, of bad the sooner;
  For evil news rides post, while good news baits.[4]
  And to our wish I see one hither speeding—
  An Ebrew, as I guess, and of our tribe.   1540
MESSENGER.[5] O, whither shall I run, or which way fly
  The sight of this so horrid spectacle,
  Which erst [6] my eyes beheld, and yet behold?
  For dire imagination still pursues me.
  But providence or instinct of nature seems,   1545
  Or reason, though disturbed, and scarce consulted,
  To have guided me aright, I know not how,

9. To accompany.
1. "As next": as kinsmen.
2. From Latin *ruina*, downfall.
3. Wreaking havoc.
4. Pauses to renew (bait) the horses.
5. Greek tragedy forbade the representation on stage of actual bloodshed; a messenger is therefore a frequent figure at the end of the Greek tragedy, arriving posthaste from the scene of the final catastrophe, to deliver in a long set speech a descriptive report.
6. A moment ago.

To thee first, reverend Manoa, and to these
My countrymen, whom here I knew remaining,
As [7] at some distance from the place of horror,   1550
So in the sad event too much concerned.

MANOA. The accident was loud, and here before thee
With rueful cry; yet what it was we hear not.
No preface needs; thou seest we long to know.

MESSENGER. It would burst forth; but I recover breath,   1555
And sense distract, to know well what I utter.

MANOA. Tell us the sum; the circumstance defer.

MESSENGER. Gaza yet stands; but all her sons are fallen,
All in a moment overwhelmed and fallen.

MANOA. Sad, but thou know'st to Israelites not saddest   1560
The desolation of a hostile city.

MESSENGER. Feed on that first; there may in grief be surfeit.[8]

MANOA. Relate by whom.

MESSENGER.   By Samson.

MANOA.   That still lessens
The sorrow, and coverts it nigh to joy.

MESSENGER. Ah! Manoa, I refrain too suddenly   1565
To utter what will come at last too soon,
Lest evil tidings, with too rude irruption
Hitting thy agéd ear, should pierce too deep.

MANOA. Suspense in news is torture; speak them out.

MESSENGER. Then take the worst in brief: Samson is dead.   1570

MANOA. The worst indeed! O, all my hopes defeated
To free him hence! but Death, who sets all free,
Hath paid his ransom now and full discharge.
What windy [9] joy this day had I conceived,
Hopeful of his delivery, which now proves   1575
Abortive as the first-born bloom of spring
Nipped with the lagging rear of winter's frost!
Yet, ere I give the reins to grief, say first
How died he; death to life is crown or shame.
All by him fell, thou say'st; by whom fell he?   1580
What glorious hand gave Samson his death's wound?

MESSENGER. Unwounded of his enemies he fell.

MANOA. Wearied with slaughter, then, or how? explain.

MESSENGER. By his own hands.

MANOA.   Self-violence! What cause
Brought him so soon at variance with himself   1585
Among his foes?

MESENGER.   Inevitable cause
At once both to destroy and be destroyed.
The edifice, where all were met to see him,
Upon their heads and on his own he pulled.

MANOA. O lastly over-strong against thyself!   1590
A dreadful way thou took'st to thy revenge.

---

7. The construction "As . . . So . . ." is
equivalent to a "Though . . . Yet . . .".
8. I.e., there may be all too much grief

to follow.
9. Empty and talky.

More than enough we know; but, while things yet
Are in confusion, give us, if thou canst,
Eyewitness of what first or last was done,
Relation more particular and distinct.   1595
MESSENGER. Occasions drew me early to this city;
    And, as the gates I entered with sunrise,
    The morning trumpets festival proclaimed
    Through each high street. Little I had dispatched,
    When all abroad was rumored that this day   1600
    Samson should be brought forth, to show the people
    Proof of his mighty strength in feats and games.
    I sorrowed at his captive state, but minded
    Not to be absent at that spectacle.
    The building was a spacious theater,   1605
    Half round on two main pillars vaulted high,
    With seats where all the lords, and each degree
    Of sort,[1] might sit in order to behold;
    The other side was open, where the throng
    On banks and scaffolds under sky might stand:[2]   1610
    I among these aloof obscurely stood.
    The feast and noon grew high, and sacrifice
    Had filled their hearts with mirth, high cheer, and wine,
    When to their sports they turned. Immediately
    Was Samson as a public servant brought,   1615
    In their state livery clad: before him pipes
    And timbrels;[3] on each side went arméd guards;
    Both horse and foot before him and behind,
    Archers and slingers, cataphracts[4] and spears.
    At sight of him the people with a shout   1620
    Rifted the air, clamoring their god with praise,
    Who had made their dreadful enemy their thrall.
    He patient, but undaunted, where they led him,
    Came to the place; and what was set before him,
    Which without help of eye might be assayed,[5]   1625
    To heave, pull, draw, or break, he still performed
    All with incredible, stupendious force,
    None daring to appear antagonist.
    At length, for intermission sake, they led him
    Between the pillars; he his guide requested   1630
    (For so from such as nearer stood we heard),
    As over-tired, to let him lean a while
    With both his arms on those two massy pillars,
    That to the archéd roof gave main support.
    He unsuspicious led him; which when Samson   1635
    Felt in his arms, with head a while inclined,

1. Of rank.
2. The temple at Gaza comprised a covered pavilion or shell for the gentry, semi-circular in shape and supported at the center of the semi-circle by two pillars; on the open side, under the hot sun, and behind the stage, as it were, sat the common people.
3. Tambourines.
4. Armored horsemen on armored horses.
5. Attempted.

And eyes fast fixed, he stood, as one who prayed,
Or some great matter in his mind revolved:
At last, with head erect, thus cried aloud:
"Hitherto, Lords, what your commands imposed   1640
I have performed, as reason was, obeying,
Not without wonder or delight beheld;
Now, of my own accord,[6] such other trial
I mean to show you of my strength yet greater
As with amaze shall strike all who behold."   1645
This uttered, straining all his nerves,[7] he bowed;
As with the force of winds and waters pent
When mountains tremble,[8] those two massy pillars
With horrible convulsion to and fro
He tugged, he shook, till down they came, and drew   1650
The whole roof after them with burst of thunder
Upon the heads of all who sat beneath,
Lords, ladies, captains, counselors, or priests,
Their choice nobility and flower, not only
Of this, but each Philistian city round,   1655
Met from all parts to solemnize this feast.
Samson, with these immixed, inevitably
Pulled down the same destruction on himself;
The vulgar [9] only 'scaped, who stood without.

CHORUS. O dearly bought revenge, yet glorious!   1660
  Living or dying thou hast fulfilled
  The work for which thou wast foretold
  To Israel, and now li'st victorious
  Among thy slain self-killed;
  Not willingly, but tangled in the fold   1665
  Of dire Necessity,[1] whose law in death conjoined
  Thee with thy slaughtered foes, in number more
  Than all thy life had slain before.

SEMICHORUS. While their hearts were jocund and sublime,[2]
  Drunk with idolatry, drunk with wine   1670
  And fat regorged [3] of bulls and goats,
  Chaunting their idol, and preferring
  Before our living Dread, who dwells
  In Silo, his bright sanctuary,[4]
  Among them he a spirit of frenzy sent,   1675
  Who hurt their minds,
  And urged them on with mad desire
  To call in haste for their destroyer.
  They, only set on sport and play,

6. Latin, *mea sponte,* on spontaneous
impulse of conscience.
7. Muscles.
8. Earthquakes in Milton's day were
supposed to be the effect of escaping
winds and waters imprisoned (pent) beneath the earth.

9. The common people.
1. Samson must not be supposed guilty
of suicide. See above, lines 1586–87.
2. Joyous and exalted.
3. Greedily devoured.
4. Shiloh, where the Israelites established their tabernacle (Joshua xviii.1).

Unweetingly [5] importuned   1680
Their own destruction to come speedy upon them.
So fond are mortal men,
Fallen into wrath divine,
As their own ruin on themselves to invite,
Insensate left, or to sense reprobate,   1685
And with blindness internal [6] struck.

SEMICHORUS. But he, though blind of sight,
Despised, and thought extinguished quite,
With inward eyes illuminated,
His fiery virtue roused   1690
From under ashes into sudden flame,
And as an evening dragon [7] came,
Assailant on the perchéd roosts
And nests in order ranged
Of tame villatic [8] fowl, but as an eagle   1695
His cloudless thunder bolted on their heads.
So Virtue, given for lost,[9]
Depressed and overthrown, as seemed,
Like that self-begotten bird,[1]
In the Arabian woods embossed,[2]   1700
That no second knows nor third,
And lay erewhile a holocaust,[3]
From out her ashy womb now teemed,
Revives, reflourishes, then vigorous most
When most unactive deemed;   1705
And, though her body die, her fame survives,
A secular [4] bird, ages of lives.

MANOA. Come, come; no time for lamentation now,
Nor much more cause. Samson hath quit [5] himself
Like Samson, and heroicly hath finished   1710
A life heroic, on his enemies
Fully revenged; hath left them years of mourning
And lamentation to the sons of Caphtor [6]
Through all Philistian bounds; to Israel
Honor hath left and freedom, let but them   1715
Find courage to lay hold on this occasion;
To himself and father's house eternal fame;
And, which is best and happiest yet, all this
With God not parted from him, as was feared,
But favoring and assisting to the end.   1720
Nothing is here for tears, nothing to wail

5. Unwittingly.
6. The play accomplishes itself by showing the internal blindness of the Philistines at the very moment of Samson's spiritual illumination.
7. Serpent (from Latin, *draco*).
8. Farmyard (from Latin, *villaticus*); "bolted": cast as a thunderbolt.
9. "Given up for lost."
1. The mythical phoenix begets itself out of its own ashes; it is unique, that is, there is only one phoenix alive at any one time, and it lives in the deserts of Arabia.
2. Enclosed, hidden.
3. A sacrifice burned whole on the altar.
4. Living through the centuries (Latin, *saecula*).
5. Acquitted.
6. In Amos ix.7 the Philistines are described as immigrants from Caphtor, i.e. Crete.

Or knock the breast; no weakness, no contempt,
Dispraise, or blame; nothing but well and fair,
And what may quiet us in a death so noble.
Let us go find the body where it lies   1725
Soaked in his enemies' blood, and from the stream
With lavers [7] pure, and cleansing herbs, wash off
The clotted gore. I, with what speed the while [8]
(Gaza is not in plight to say us nay),
Will send for all my kindred, all my friends,   1730
To fetch him hence, and solemnly attend,
With silent obsequy and funeral train,
Home to his father's house. There will I build him
A monument, and plant it round with shade
Of laurel ever green and branching palm,[9]   1735
With all his trophies hung, and acts enrolled
In copious legend, or sweet lyric song.
Thither shall all the valiant youth resort,
And from his memory inflame their breasts
To matchless valor and adventures high;   1740
The virgins also shall, on feastful days,
Visit his tomb with flowers, only bewailing
His lot unfortunate in nuptial choice,
From whence captivity and loss of eyes.

CHORUS.[1] All is best, though we oft doubt   1745
    What th' unsearchable dispose [2]
Of Highest Wisdom brings about,
    And ever best found in the close.
Oft he seems to hide his face,
    But unexpectedly returns,   1750
And to his faithful champion hath in place [3]
    Bore witness gloriously; whence Gaza mourns,
And all that band them to resist
    His uncontrollable intent.
His servants he, with new acquist [4]   1755
Of true experience from this great event,
With peace and consolation hath dismissed,
And calm of mind, all passion spent.   1671

---

7. Basins.
8. I.e., with what speed (I may) in the meanwhile.
9. Leaves of laurel were worn by civic conquerors on triumphal occasions; wreaths of palm were given to victors in the Olympic games. Samson, as both an athletic victor in his *agon* and the favored of Heaven, gets both.
1. The final chorus of the play is cast in the form of a sonnet.
2. Appointment, disposition.
3. On this very spot, at this very instant.
4. Increase, acquisition.

Seventeenth-Century Lyrics

Although the early 17th century witnessed the death of several major art forms—the old English madrigal, the masque, the folk dance—it also experienced a brief revival in the art of lyric poetry. Literary historians conventionally divide the period between the "metaphysical" and "Cavalier" schools, but some poets (like Richard Corbet) do not fit either classification, and some (like Thomas Carew) obligingly fit both. Yet the tone of the English poetry does undergo a pervasive change some time after the turn of the century. The typical Jacobean or Caroline lyric is not exuberant and boisterous, as the lyrics of the Elizabethan age often were: rather, it is touched with a grave, half-melancholy beauty; its feelings are quiet and its techniques restrained. Typically, it is a rather elegant, even an artificial, performance; in this connection, we may note that the word "artificial" sometimes had, in those days, the force of a commendation. For a poem to be the product of artifice was altogether proper.

The lower levels of artifice border on the trifling; and not all the minor lyricists of the 17th century avoided this failing all the time. But even in flowery little tributes to Chloris, Flora, or Amaryllis, the poets often uncovered a true vein of feeling. And sometimes their limitations are themselves a matter of interest. For example, the student of literary modes can trace a notable line of decline in the "gentlemanly" poetry of the century. Measured against the elevated and serious courtier's verse which Sidney and Sir Edward Dyer produced during the 1580's, the "gentleman's verse" of the early 17th century seems increasingly slight. Courtly poets like Sir Kenelm Digby, Aurelian Townshend, Sir William Davenant, and Sir Arthur Gorges were all too often perfunctory and bloodless. In Sir John Suckling one sees a growing quality of willful triviality and conscious carelessness. It is redeemed momentarily in the Cavalier heroics of Richard Lovelace, but fades to a rather formal correctness in Edmund Waller, and in the Restoration lyrics of John Wilmot, Earl of Rochester, it degenerates further into jokes and bawdry. Lyrical impulses of any sort were not, on the whole, sustained long past the Restoration; the rich variety of lyric expression which marked the first forty years of the century has only the slenderest counterpart in the years 1660–1700.

The Restoration lyric declined, in part, as a consequence of new habits of mind, the new prosaic rationalism of Enlightened England. At the same time, the poets were turning to other genres, such as the didactic verse essay and the satiric discourse; and in developing these genres, predominantly discursive in character, the "gentlemanly poets" of midcentury made genuine contributions. The "refinement of our numbers" (it is Dryden's phrase) was the work of men like Waller, Suckling, and John Denham;

what it implied was the development of an art of easy versification—orderly, unstrained, unpadded, fluent, and not necessarily inspired—through which civilized communication could take place between civilized ladies and gentlemen. The best poetry of the age is reaching toward the measured formality of a minuet, yet it has not quite lost the memory of those "native woodnotes wild" which were heard during the preceding age. Whether as somber as Henry King's *Exequy* or as light as Carew's airy trifles, it mingles the natural and the artificial, the casual and the deeply felt emotion, after an altogether distinctive fashion.

RICHARD CORBET
(1582–1635)

Richard Corbet spent his whole adult life in the Church of England, rising to the dignity of two bishoprics (Oxford in 1628, Norwich in 1632). But he never succumbed to the formality of his public positions, and the biographer and anecdote collector John Aubrey has preserved a number of tales, all merry and some indiscreet, of his pranks, retorts, and convivialities. Among others, there is an account of his exchanging the bishop's cassock for the buff jerkin of a ballad singer, and selling out his stock of ballads at a tavern. His verses were published as *Certain Elegant Poems,* twelve years after his death.

A Proper New Ballad
Entitled The Fairies' Farewell, or God-a-Mercy Will

To be sung or whistled, to the tune of *Meadow Brow* by the learned; by the unlearned, to the tune of *Fortune.*

Farewell, rewards and fairies,
Good housewives now may say,
For now foul sluts in dairies
Do fare as well as they;[1]
And though they sweep their hearths no less   5
Than maids were wont to do,
Yet who of late for cleanliness
Finds sixpence in her shoe?

Lament, lament, old abbeys,
The fairies' lost command;   10
They did but change priests' babies,

1. Fairies, it used to be thought, left rewards for good dairymaids and house-wives, while they pinched, punished, and tormented the sluts.

But some have changed your land;[2]
And all your children stolen from thence
Are now grown Puritans;
Who live as changelings ever since,   15
For love of your demesnes.

At morning and at evening both
You merry were and glad,
So little care of sleep or sloth
These pretty ladies had;   20
When Tom came home from labor,
Or Ciss to milking rose,
Then merrily went their tabor,
And nimbly went their toes.

Witness those rings and roundelays   25
Of theirs, which yet remain,
Were footed in Queen Mary's days
On many a grassy plain;[3]
But since of late Elizabeth,
And later James came in,   30
They never danced on any heath
As when the time had been.

By which we note the fairies
Were of the old profession,[4]
Their songs were *Ave Maries*,   35
Their dances were procession;
But now, alas, they all are dead,
Or gone beyond the seas,
Or further from religion fled,
Or else they take their ease.   40

A tell-tale in their company
They never could endure,
And whoso kept not secretly
Their mirth, was punished sure;
It was a just and Christian deed   45
To pinch such black and blue;
Oh, how the commonwealth doth need
Such justices as you!

Now they have left our quarters,
A register[5] they have,   50
Who can preserve their charters,
A man both wise and grave;
A hundred of their merry pranks

2. The fairies only slipped priests' (illegitimate) babies into families; but some worse spirits have now slipped in an illegitimate England in place of the old, merry one.
3. The fairies were thought to dance in rounds or circles, which left marks in the turf; Queen Mary was the last Catholic sovereign of England.
4. Of the Roman Catholic faith. "Merry England" was Catholic; Puritan England, not merry.
5. Keeper of records, registrar.

By one that I could name
Are kept in store; con[6] twenty thanks 55
To William for the same.

To William Chourne of Staffordshire[7]
Give land and praises due,
Who every meal can mend your cheer
With tales both old and true; 60
To William all give audience,
And pray you for his noddle,
For all the fairies' evidence
Were lost if it were addle.

1647

6. Grant.   7. Servant to Dr. Hutten, Corbet's father-in-law.

HENRY KING

(1592–1669)

The son of a bishop, Henry King was an intimate of Donne, Jonson, and Izaak Walton. After attending Westminster School and Oxford University, he entered the church and rose without strain or difficulty from prebend to deacon to dean of Rochester, and in 1642 to the bishopric of Chichester. He survived the deprivations of the Civil Wars, and returned to enjoy his see for nine years after the Restoration. In 1617 he married Anne Berkeley, who died in 1624, and for whom he wrote *The Exequy*. It was printed anonymously, and without King's consent, with other poems of his in 1657. Except for Milton's sonnet on his "late espoused saint," the 17th century produced no poem so direct and poignant in expressing the sentiments of a married lover for his wife.

The Exequy

Accept, thou shrine of my dead saint,
Instead of dirges, this complaint;
And for sweet flowers to crown thy hearse,
Receive a strew[1] of weeping verse
From thy grieved friend, whom thou might'st see 5
Quite melted into tears for thee.

Dear loss! since thy untimely fate
My task hath been to meditate
On thee, on thee; thou art the book,
The library whereon I look, 10
Though almost blind. For thee, loved clay,
I languish out, not live, the day,
Using no other exercise
But what I practice with mine eyes;
By which wet glasses I find out 15

1. Scattering.

How lazily time creeps about
To one that mourns: this, only this,
My exercise and business is.
So I compute the weary hours
With sighs dissolvéd into showers.   20

Nor wonder if my time go thus
Backward and most preposterous;
Thou hast benighted me, thy set[2]
This eve of blackness did beget,
Who wast my day, though overcast   25
Before thou hadst thy noontide passed;
And I remember must in tears,
Thou scarce hadst seen so many years
As day tells hours. By thy clear sun
My love and fortune first did run;   30
But thou wilt never more appear
Folded within my hemisphere,
Since both thy light and motion
Like a fled star is fallen and gone;
And 'twixt me and my soul's dear wish   35
An earth now interposéd is,
Which such a strange eclipse doth make
As ne'er was read in almanac.[3]

I could allow thee for a time
To darken me and my sad clime;   40
Were it a month, a year, or ten,
I would thy exile live till then,
And all that space my mirth adjourn,
So thou wouldst promise to return;
And putting off thy ashy shroud,   45
At length disperse this sorrow's cloud.

But woe is me! the longest date
Too narrow is to calculate
These empty hopes; never shall I
Be so much blest as to descry   50
A glimpse of thee, till that day come
Which shall the earth to cinders doom,
And a fierce fever must calcine[4]
The body of this world—like thine,
My little world! That fit of fire   55
Once off, our bodies shall aspire
To our souls' bliss; then we shall rise
And view ourselves with clearer eyes
In that calm region where no night
Can hide us from each other's sight.   60

2. Setting, death.
3. The earth, which covers her body and so intervenes between her and her husband, is like an eclipse.
4. Burn down to dust.

Meantime, thou hast her, earth: much good
May my harm[5] do thee. Since it stood
With heaven's will I might not call
Her longer mine, I give thee all
My short-lived right and interest   65
In her whom living I loved best;
With a most free and bounteous grief
I give thee what I could not keep.
Be kind to her, and prithee look
Thou write into thy doomsday book   70
Each parcel of this rarity
Which in thy casket shrined doth lie.
See that thou make thy reckoning straight,
And yield her back again by weight;
For thou must audit on thy trust   75
Each grain and atom of this dust,
As thou wilt answer Him that lent,
Not gave thee, my dear monument.

So close the ground, and 'bout her shade
Black curtains draw; my bride is laid.   80

Sleep on, my love, in thy cold bed,
Never to be disquieted!
My last good-night! Thou wilt not wake
Till I thy fate shall overtake;
Till age, or grief, or sickness must   85
Marry my body to that dust
It so much loves; and fill the room
My heart keeps empty in thy tomb.
Stay for me there; I will not fail
To meet thee in that hollow vale.   90
And think not much of my delay;
I am already on the way,
And follow thee with all the speed
Desire can make, or sorrows breed.
Each minute is a short degree,   95
And every hour a step towards thee.
At night when I betake to rest,
Next morn I rise nearer my west
Of life, almost by eight hours' sail,
Than when sleep breathed his drowsy gale.   100

Thus from the sun my bottom[6] steers,
And my day's compass downward bears;
Nor labor I to stem the tide
Through which to thee I swiftly glide.

'Tis true, with shame and grief I yield,   105
Thou like the van first took'st the field,

5. I.e., this event, which harms me so   6. Vessel.
much. "Stood": agreed.

And gotten hast the victory
In thus adventuring to die
Before me, whose more years might crave
A just precedence in the grave.   110
But hark! my pulse like a soft drum
Beats my approach, tells thee I come;
And slow howe'er my marches be,
I shall at last sit down by thee.

The thought of this bids me go on,   115
And wait my dissolution
With hope and comfort. Dear (forgive
The crime), I am content to live
Divided, with but half a heart,
Till we shall meet and never part.   120

ca. 1624   1657

ABRAHAM COWLEY
(1618–1667)

The Muse's Hannibal, as he delighted to call himself, Abraham Cowley
was a poetical prodigy who wrote his first poem at 10 and published his
first volume at 15 years of age. Indeed, he wrote vigorously, in many
genres, throughout his life. Before the Civil Wars, he produced comedies
in Latin and English. A collection of frigidly witty love lyrics in the metaphysical style appeared in 1647 under the title of *The Mistress;* and his
restless pen turned out on various occasions a number of interesting informal essays, including one about himself. His uncompleted epic poem on
King David, the *Davideis*, was large and learned, as epic poems were supposed to be; his irregular odes in imitation of Pindar were felt to be full
of fire and dark rapture. Both these ventures were first published in a volume called *Miscellanies* (1657). When he died, the same year that *Paradise
Lost* was published, Cowley's reputation was lofty indeed. Partly because
of Milton's rise, partly because of the sudden decline of the metaphysical
style, a revulsion of feeling took place immediately after Cowley's death;
and in the next century, Alexander Pope could ask, "Who now reads
Cowley?" Dr. Johnson's low opinion of the metaphysical style may, if it
was not occasioned, at least be partly excused, by the fact that he took
Cowley as the chief poet of the group, and *The Mistress* as Cowley's chef
d'oeuvre. Actually, a modest Horatian poem like *The Wish* represents
Cowley's poetic gifts better than the vast Hannibalistic projects on the
basis of which he was overrated during his life and has been underrated
ever since.

The Wish

Well then; I now do plainly see,
This busy world and I shall ne'er agree;
The very honey of all earthly joy
   Does of all meats the soonest cloy;
   And they, methinks, deserve my pity   5
Who for it can endure the stings,
The crowd, and buzz, and murmurings
   Of this great hive, the city.

Ah, yet, ere I descend to the grave
May I a small house and large garden have!   10
And a few friends, and many books, both true,
   Both wise, and both delightful too!
   And since love ne'er will from me flee,
A mistress moderately fair,
And good as guardian angels are,   15
   Only beloved, and loving me!

O fountains, when in you shall I
Myself, eased of unpeaceful thoughts, espy?
O fields! O woods! when, when shall I be made
   The happy tenant of your shade?   20
   Here's the spring-head of pleasure's flood,
Here's wealthy Nature's treasury,
Where all the riches lie that she
   Has coined and stamped for good.

Pride and ambition here   25
Only in farfetched metaphors appear;
Here naught but winds can hurtful murmurs scatter,
   And naught but Echo flatter.
   The gods, when they descended, hither
From heaven did always choose their way;   30
And therefore we may boldly say
   That 'tis the way, too, thither.

How happy here should I
And one dear she live and, embracing, die!
She who is all the world, and can exclude   35
   In deserts, solitude.
   I should have then this only fear,
Lest men, when they my pleasures see,
Should hither throng to live like me,
   And so make a city here.   40

1647

THOMAS CAREW
(ca. 1594–1640)

Bright, talented, and idle, Thomas Carew was the model of a courtier. He studied law without practicing it; took odd posts and minor diplomatic assignments; and served as an attendant about court. He was witty and debauched and apparently never took much trouble with his verse; yet the poetry he wrote is clean, chiseled, and amazingly perceptive. There is no better introduction to the poetry of Donne than Carew's *Elegy upon the Death of * * * Dr. John Donne*; the *Song* ("Ask me no more") is one of the jewels of court poetry. During his lifetime Carew published only a court masque, *Coelum Brittanicum* (1634); a collection of his poems appeared after his death.

An Elegy upon the Death of the Dean of Paul's, Dr. John Donne[1]

Can we not force from widowed poetry,
Now thou art dead, great Donne, one elegy
To crown thy hearse? Why yet did we not trust,
Though with unkneaded dough-baked prose, thy dust,
Such as the unscissored[2] lect'rer from the flower   5
Of fading rhetoric, short-lived as his hour,
Dry as the sand that measures it,[3] should lay
Upon the ashes on the funeral day?
Have we nor tune, nor voice? Didst thou dispense
Through all our language both words and sense?   10
'Tis sad truth. The pulpit may her plain
And sober Christian precepts still retain;
Doctrines it may, and wholesome uses, frame,
Grave homilies and lectures; but the flame
Of thy brave soul, that shot such heat and light   15
As burnt our earth and made our darkness bright,
Committed holy rapes upon our will,
Did through the eye the melting heart distil,
And the deep knowledge of dark truths so teach
As sense might judge what fancy could not reach,[4]   20
Must be desired forever. So the fire

1. First appearing in the 1633 edition of Donne's poems, this elegy was described as by "Mr. Tho: Carie." It was reprinted in the 1640 edition of Carew's poems, from which our text is taken. 2. I.e., with uncut hair. Whether from grief, poverty, or in imitation of Apollo is not clear. 3. The hourglass was used by preachers to keep track of time. 4. I.e., so that things too abstract and elevated even to be imagined might be made plain to sense. "Desired": missed.

That fills with spirit and heat the Delphic choir,[5]
Which, kindled first by thy Promethean[6] breath,
Glowed here a while, lies quenched now in thy death.
The Muses' garden, with pedantic weeds   25
O'erspread, was purged by thee; the lazy seeds
Of servile imitation thrown away,
And fresh invention planted; thou didst pay
The debts of our penurious bankrupt age—
Licentious thefts, that make poetic rage   30
A mimic fury, when our souls must be
Possessed, or with Anacreon's ecstasy,
Or Pindar's,[7] not their own. The subtle cheat
Of sly exchanges, and the juggling feat
Of two-edged words,[8] or whatsoever wrong   35
By ours was done the Greek or Latin tongue,
Thou hast redeemed, and opened us a mine
Of rich and pregnant fancy, drawn a line
Of masculine expression, which had good
Old Orpheus[9] seen, or all the ancient brood   40
Our superstitious fools admire, and hold
Their lead more precious than thy burnished gold,
Thou hadst been their exchequer, and no more
They in each other's dung had raked for ore.
Thou shalt yield no precedence, but of time   45
And the blind fate of language, whose tuned chime
More charms the outward sense; yet thou mayest claim
From so great disadvantage greater fame,
Since to the awe of thy imperious wit
Our troublesome language bends, made only fit   50
With her tough thick-ribbed hoops, to gird about
Thy giant fancy, which had proved too stout
For their soft melting phrases. As in time
They had the start, so did they cull the prime
Buds of invention many a hundred year,   55
And left the rifled fields, besides the fear
To touch their harvest; yet from those bare lands
Of what is only thine, thy only hands
(And that their smallest work) have gleaned more
Than all those times and tongues could reap before.   60
    But thou art gone, and thy strict laws will be
Too hard for libertines in poetry.

5. The choir of poets, inspired by
Apollo, whose oracle used to be at
Delphi.
6. Donne stole fire from heaven, like
Prometheus, and used it to fill with
spirit and heat the choir of poets.
7. Anacreon (6th and 5th centuries
B.C.) and Pindar (first half of the 5th
century B.C.) were famous Greek lyric
poets.
8. "Sly exchanges": Carew seems to
refer to the habit, frequent in Jonsonian

and Miltonic style, of using English
words in their Latin senses, e.g., "horrid (bristling) spears." "Two-edged
words" might be puns; but as these
were a favorite device of Donne's, this
cannot be the sense. Perhaps "two-
edged words" are not far from "sly exchanges" in meaning.
9. Ancient Greek poet and prophet, so
mythical that he is often used as the
type of all poets.

They will repeal[1] the goodly exiled train
Of gods and goddesses, which in thy just reign
Were banished nobler poems; now with these   65
The silenced tales in the *Metamorphoses*[2]
Shall stuff their lines and swell the windy page,
Till verse, refined by thee in this last age,
Turn ballad-rhyme, or those old idols be
Adored again with new apostasy.   70
   O pardon me, that break with untuned verse
The reverend silence that attends thy hearse,
Whose awful[3] solemn murmurs were to thee,
More than these faint lines, a loud elegy,
That did proclaim in a dumb eloquence   75
The death of all the arts, whose influence,
Grown feeble, in these panting numbers lies
Gasping short-winded accents, and so dies:
So doth the swiftly turning wheel not stand
In th' instant we withdraw the moving hand,   80
But some small time retain a faint weak course
By virtue of the first impulsive force;
And so whilst I cast on thy funeral pile
Thy crown of bays,[4] oh, let it crack awhile
And spit disdain, till the devouring flashes   85
Suck all the moisture up; then turn to ashes.
   I will not draw thee envy to engross
All thy perfections, or weep all the loss;
Those are too numerous for one elegy,
And this too great to be expressed by me.   90
Let others carve the rest; it shall suffice
I on thy grave this epitaph incise:

   Here lies a king, that ruled as he thought fit
   The universal monarchy of wit;
   Here lie two flamens,[5] and both those the best: 95
   Apollo's[6] first, at last the true God's priest.

                                          1633, 1640

Disdain Returned

          He that loves a rosy cheek,
             Or a coral lip admires,
          Or from starlike eyes doth seek
             Fuel to maintain his fires;
          As old Time makes these decay,   5
          So his flames must waste away.

1. Recall, as from banishment.
2. Ovid's tales in the *Metamorphoses* had been a favorite stockpile of poetical properties for Renaissance poets; Donne forwent them, but soon they will return.
3. I.e., awed.
4. The poet's crown.
5. Priests of the Roman religion.
6. I.e., of the god of poetry.

But a smooth and steadfast mind,
 Gentle thoughts and calm desires,
Hearts with equal love combined,
 Kindle never-dying fires.   10
Where these are not, I despise
Lovely cheeks, or lips, or eyes.

No tears, Celia, now shall win
 My resolved heart to return;
I have searched thy soul within,   15
 And find naught but pride and scorn;
I have learned thy arts, and now
 Can disdain as much as thou.
Some power, in my revenge convey
That love to her I cast away.[7]   20

            1640

A Song

Ask me no more where Jove bestows,
When June is past, the fading rose;
For in your beauties orient deep,[8]
These flowers, as in their causes, sleep.[9]

Ask me no more whither do stray   5
The golden atoms of the day;
For in pure love heaven did prepare
Those powders to enrich your hair.

Ask me no more whither doth haste
The nightingale when May is past;   10
For in your sweet dividing[1] throat
She winters, and keeps warm her note.

Ask me no more where those stars light,
That downwards fall in dead of night;
For in your eyes they sit, and there   15
Fixéd become, as in their sphere.

Ask me no more if east or west
The phoenix builds her spicy nest;[2]

---

7. I.e., to a previous mistress.
8. The text permits two readings here: "in your beauties which are orient deep" or "in the orient depths of your beauty." In addition to its reference to the Far East, "orient" implies "pearly" or "lustrous."
9. Aristotelian philosophy suggested that objects often lay latent in their causes—e.g., that in the seed creating man there was a little man (*homunculus*). In Carew's compliment, the lady is a summation of last summer and cause of the next one.
1. Harmonious (from the "division," or musical trill).
2. The phoenix, an Arabian bird, builds her nest from spicy shrubs. She dies every thousand years and a new bird springs from her ashes.

For unto you at last she flies,
And in your fragrant bosom dies.
20

1640

EDMUND WALLER
(1606–1687)

One of the wealthiest of English poets, Waller acquired his estates through
inheritance and a fortunate marriage. He played a wavering role in the
Civil Wars, earning the distrust of both factions; but won universal applause for the mellifluous, effortless clarity of his love poetry. A poised
and fluent production like *Of the Last Verses in the Book* illustrates his
graceful handling of the heroic couplet. His achievements in this line led
the writers of the Restoration and 18th century to hail Waller, with John
Denham, as a "refiner of our numbers"—a polished and dexterous versifier.

Song

> Go, lovely rose!
> Tell her that wastes her time and me
> That now she knows,
> When I resemble[1] her to thee,
> How sweet and fair she seems to be.   5
>
> Tell her that's young,
> And shuns to have her graces spied,
> That hadst thou sprung
> In deserts, where no men abide,
> Thou must have uncommended died.   10
>
> Small is the worth
> Of beauty from the light retired;
> Bid her come forth,
> Suffer herself to be desired,
> And not blush so to be admired.   15
>
> Then die! that she
> The common fate of all things rare
> May read in thee;
> How small a part of time they share
> That are so wondrous sweet and fair!   20

1645

On a Girdle

> That which her slender waist confined,
> Shall now my joyful temples bind;

1. Compare.

No monarch but would give his crown,
His arms might do what this has done.

It was my heaven's extremest sphere,[2]   5
The pale[3] which held that lovely deer;
My joy, my grief, my hope, my love
Did all within this circle move!

A narrow compass! and yet there
Dwelt all that's good, and all that's fair;   10
Give me but what this ribbon bound,
Take all the rest the sun goes round! [4]

1686

Of the Last Verses in the Book

When we for age could neither read nor write,
The subject made us able to indite;
The soul, with nobler resolutions decked,
The body stooping, does herself erect.
No mortal parts are requisite to raise   5
Her that, unbodied, can her Maker praise.
The seas are quiet when the winds give o'er;
So calm are we when passions are no more!
For then we know how vain it was to boast
Of fleeting things, so certain to be lost.   10
Clouds of affection[5] from our younger eyes
Conceal that emptiness which age descries.
The soul's dark cottage, battered and decayed,
Lets in new light through the chinks that time has made;
Stronger by weakness, wiser men become,   15
As they draw near to their eternal home.
Leaving the old, both worlds at once they view,
That stand upon the threshold of the new.

1686

2. The last of the nine concentric crystalline spheres which, according to Ptolemaic astronomy, made up the universe. Hence, the lady's outermost garment.
3. Fence encircling a park. There is, of course. a pun on "deer" in this line.

4. The version of this poem printed in 1645 substituted "Do" for "Did" in line 8, and gave the last couplet as: "Give me but what this ribbon tied, / Take all the sun goes round beside."
5. Passion.

SIR JOHN SUCKLING
(1609–1642)

Blessed with considerable estates, Sir John Suckling won renown of a sort as a gambler, wencher, and general reprobate in the court of Charles I.

On the side, he produced three plays, some fragments of gentlemanly verse, and a prose treatise on natural religion. During the Civil Wars, he played a brief, ineffectual role, raising a troop of a hundred gallant gentlemen in scarlet coats and white doublets, who ran ingloriously before the Scottish armies at Kelso. Later, Suckling took part in a plot to rescue the Earl of Strafford from the Tower of London; but it was discovered, and the ringleaders fled abroad. Shortly thereafter Suckling died at Paris, in poverty and neglect. His poetry, however, had a spry and limber life of its own; during the Restoration, "natural, easy Suckling" was considered the court poet par excellence, the personification of careless, casual grace in verse.

Song

Why so pale and wan, fond lover?
  Prithee, why so pale?
Will, when looking well can't move her,
  Looking ill prevail?
  Prithee, why so pale?   5

Why so dull and mute, young sinner?
  Prithee, why so mute?
Will, when speaking well can't win her,
  Saying nothing do't?
  Prithee, why so mute?   10

Quit, quit, for shame; this will not move,
  This cannot take her.
If of herself she will not love,
  Nothing can make her:
  The devil take her!   15

1638

A Ballad upon a Wedding[1]

I tell thee, Dick,[2] where I have been,
Where I the rarest things have seen,
  Oh, things without compare!
Such sights again cannot be found
In any place on English ground,   5
  Be it at wake[3] or fair.

At Charing Cross,[4] hard by the way
Where we (thou know'st) do sell our hay,
  There is a house with stairs;
And there did I see coming down   10

1. This ballad is traditionally said to describe the wedding of Roger Boyle, Baron Broghill, to Lady Margaret Howard on January 27, 1641; it is part of the humor that the speaker is portrayed as a country bumpkin.
2. "Dick" may well refer to Richard Lovelace; though for the speaker, he is simply a country friend, like "George upon the Green" and "Vincent of the Crown" below.
3. Festival.
4. A suburban center in the 17th century, not far from Haymarket and the present site of Trafalgar Square.

Such folk as are not in our town,
    Forty, at least, in pairs.

Amongst the rest, one pest'lent fine
(His beard no bigger, though, than thine)
    Walked on before the rest.   15
Our landlord looks like nothing to him;
The king (God bless him!), 'twould undo[5] him
    Should he go still so dressed.

At course-a-park,[6] without all doubt,
He should have first been taken out   20
    By all the maids i' th' town,
Though lusty Roger there had been,
Or little George upon the Green,
    Or Vincent of the Crown.

But wot you what? the youth was going   25
To make an end of all his wooing;
    The parson for him stayed.
Yet by his leave, for all his haste,
He did not so much wish all past,
    Perchance, as did the maid.   30

The maid (and thereby hangs a tale),
For such a maid no Whitsun-ale[7]
    Could ever yet produce;
No grape, that's kindly[8] ripe, could be
So round, so plump, so soft as she,   35
    Nor half so full of juice.

Her finger was so small the ring
Would not stay on, which they did bring;
    It was too wide a peck:
And to say truth (for out it must),   40
It looked like the great collar (just)
    About our young colt's neck.

Her feet beneath her petticoat,
Like little mice, stole in and out,
    As if they feared the light;   45
But oh, she dances such a way,
No sun upon an Easter day[9]
    Is half so fine a sight!

He would have kissed her once or twice,
But she would not, she was so nice,[1]   50
    She would not do 't in sight;
And then she looked as who should say,
I will do what I list today;
    And you shall do 't at night.

5. I.e., bankrupt.
6. A country game, in which a girl asks
a boy to chase her.
7. A rural feast held at Whitsuntide
(fifty days after Easter).
8. Naturally, by nature; ripened on the
vine.
9. The sun was often said to dance at
Easter in honor of the Resurrection.
1. Particular, delicate.

Her cheeks so rare a white was on,   55
No daisy makes comparison
 (Who sees them is undone),
For streaks of red were mingled there,
Such as are on a Catherine pear
 (The side that's next the sun).   60

Her lips were red, and one was thin
Compared to that was next her chin
 (Some bee had stung it newly);
But, Dick, her eyes so guard her face
I durst no more upon them gaze   65
 Than on the sun in July.

Her mouth so small, when she does speak,
Thou 'dst swear her teeth her words did break,
 That they might passage get;
But she so handled still the matter,   70
They came as good as ours, or better,
 And are not spent a whit.

If wishing should be any sin,
The parson himself had guilty been
 (She looked that day so purely);   75
And did the youth so oft the feat
At night, as some did in conceit,
 It would have spoiled him, surely.

Just in the nick the cook knocked thrice,
And all the waiters in a trice   80
 His summons did obey;
Each servingman, with dish in hand,
Marched boldly up, like our trained band,[2]
 Presented, and away.

When all the meat was on the table,   85
What man of knife or teeth was able
 To stay to be entreated?
And this the very reason was,
Before the parson could say grace,
 The company was seated.   90

The business of the kitchen's great,
For it is fit that men should eat;
 Nor was it there denied.
Passion o' me, how I run on!
There's that that would be thought upon,   95
 I trow, besides the bride.

Now hats fly off, and youths carouse;
Healths first go round, and then the house;
 The bride's came thick and thick:
And when 'twas named another's health,   100
Perhaps he made it hers by stealth;
 And who could help it, Dick?

2. "Trained bands" were the militia.

O' th' sudden up they rise and dance;
Then sit again and sigh and glance;
    Then dance again and kiss.   105
Thus several ways the time did pass,
Till every woman wished her place,
    And every man wished his!

By this time all were stolen aside
To counsel and undress the bride,   110
    But that he must not know;
But yet 'twas thought he guessed her mind,
And did not mean to stay behind
    Above an hour or so.

When in he came, Dick, there she lay   115
Like new-fallen snow melting away
    ('Twas time, I trow, to part);
Kisses were now the only stay,[3]
Which soon she gave, as who would say,
    "God be with ye,[4] with all my heart."   120

But just as heaven would have to cross it,
In came the bridesmaids with the posset.[5]
    The bridegroom ate in spite,
For had he left the women to 't,
It would have cost two hours to do 't,   125
    Which were too much that night.

At length the candle's out, and now
All that they had not done, they do.
    What that is, who can tell?
But I believe it was no more   130
Than thou and I have done before
    With Bridget and with Nell.

ca. 1641   1646

⭘ Out upon It!

Out upon it! I have loved
    Three whole days together;
And am like to love three more,
    If it prove fair weather.

Time shall molt away his wings,   5
    Ere he shall discover
In the whole wide world again
    Such a constant lover.

---

3. Delay.
4. Some texts read "God b'w'y," i.e., "God be with ye"; others simply "Good Boy!" which improves the meter at the cost of the sense.
5. A drink compounded of hot milk, liquor, and spices.

But the spite on 't is, no praise
    Is due at all to me: 10
Love with me had made no stays
    Had it any been but she.

Had it any been but she,
    And that very face,
There had been at least ere this   15
    A dozen dozen in her place.

                          1659

RICHARD LOVELACE
(1618–1657)

Of an old and wealthy Kentish family, Richard Lovelace was educated at Oxford; he was an attractive, handsome, and witty young man, the very model of a courtier. King Charles and Queen Henrietta Maria admired his demeanor so much, when they visited Oxford in 1636, that they had him created M.A. on the spot. During the wars, Lovelace stood firm for the king. In 1641, he presented a petition to the Long Parliament which earned him a prison term, after which he went abroad; in 1646 he was wounded at Dunkirk while serving with the French army against the Spaniards, and some time later he returned to England, where the Puritan government once more cast him into prison. In the course of this turbulent activity, his estates melted away, and he died in poverty at the early age of 39. Lovelace published *Lucasta* in 1649; and a posthumous volume appeared in 1659, with his remaining writings.

To Althea, from Prison

When Love with unconfinéd wings
Hovers within my gates,
And my divine Althea brings
To whisper at the grates;
When I lie tangled in her hair   5
And fettered to her eye,
The gods[1] that wanton in the air
Know no such liberty.

When flowing cups run swiftly round,
With no allaying Thames,[2]   10
Our careless heads with roses bound,
Our hearts with loyal flames;
When thirsty grief in wine we steep,
When healths and draughts go free,

1. Some versions read "birds" instead of "gods."   2. No mixture of water in the wine.

Fishes, that tipple in the deep, 15
Know no such liberty.

When, like committed linnets,[3] I
With shriller throat shall sing
The sweetness, mercy, majesty,
And glories of my King; 20
When I shall voice aloud how good
He is, how great should be,
Enlargéd winds, that curl the flood,
Know no such liberty.

Stone walls do not a prison make, 25
Nor iron bars a cage;
Minds innocent and quiet take
That for an hermitage.
If I have freedom in my love,
And in my soul am free, 30
Angels alone, that soar above,
Enjoy such liberty.

1649

To Lucasta, Going to the Wars

Tell me not, Sweet, I am unkind
That from the nunnery
Of thy chaste breast and quiet mind,
To war and arms I fly.

True, a new mistress now I chase, 5
The first foe in the field;
And with a stronger faith embrace
A sword, a horse, a shield.

Yet this inconstancy is such
As you too shall adore; 10
I could not love thee, Dear, so much,
Loved I not honor more.

1649

The Grasshopper

TO MY NOBLE FRIEND, MR. CHARLES COTTON[4]

Oh, thou that swing'st upon the waving hair
Of some well-filled oaten beard,

---

3. Caged finches.
4. Lovelace's friend Mr. Charles Cotton, scholar, man of letters, and father of Montaigne's translator, may have appeared to the poet an industrious and prudent ant, compared with himself, the melodious and improvident grasshopper. (Lovelace lost his entire fortune in the Civil Wars.) The circumstances of the poem are evidently those of the interregnum, when a winter of Puritanism seemed to be settling over all civilized feeling in England. For a copious explication of the poem's backgrounds and overtones, see D. C. Allen's article in *Modern Language Quarterly,* XVIII (1957), 35–43.

Drunk every night with a delicious tear
   Dropped thee from heav'n, where now th' art reared,

The joys of earth and air are thine entire,   5
   That with thy feet and wings dost hop and fly;
And when thy poppy [5] works thou dost retire
   To thy carved acorn bed to lie.

Up with the day, the sun thou welcom'st then,
   Sport'st in the gilt-plats [6] of his beams,   10
And all these merry days mak'st merry men,
   Thyself, and melancholy streams.[7]

But ah, the sickle! golden ears are cropped,
   Ceres and Bacchus [8] bid goodnight;
Sharp frosty fingers all your flow'rs have topped,   15
   And what scythes spared, winds shave off quite.

Poor verdant fool! and now green ice! thy joys
   Large and as lasting as thy perch of grass,
Bid us lay in 'gainst winter rain, and poise
   Their floods with an o'erflowing glass.   20

Thou best of men and friends! we will create
   A genuine summer in each other's breast;
And spite of this cold time and frozen fate
   Thaw us a warm seat to our rest.

Our sacred hearths shall burn eternally   25
   As vestal flames; [9] the North wind, he
Shall strike his frost-stretched wings, dissolve, and fly
   This Etna in epitome.[1]

Dropping December shall come weeping in,
   Bewail th'usurping of his reign;   30
But when in showers of old Greek [2] we begin,
   Shall cry, he hath his crown again!

Night as clear Hesper [3] shall our tapers whip
   From the light casements where we play,
And the dark hag from her black mantle strip,   35
   And stick there everlasting day.

---

5. Opiate, sleeping potion.
6. Golden meadows.
7. The three objects of "mak'st merry" are "men," "thyself," and "melancholy streams."
8. The grain and the grape.
9. The vestal virgins, in Rome, were responsible for tending an eternal flame.
1. Boreas, the North wind, "striking" (i.e., folding up) his wings, flees from the underground warmth of Etna, an emblem of the flame of friendship.
2. Greek wine was especially favored in the classical world; drinkers, in classical times, often wore festive crowns at their carousals; and December "crowns," i.e., terminates the year.
3. The tapers are compared to Hesperus, the morning star, which whips night from the sky. Hecate, the dark hag, was sometimes described as the daughter of Night.

Thus richer than untempted kings are we,
That asking nothing, nothing need:
Though lord of all that seas embrace, yet he
That wants himself is poor indeed.

40

1649

TOM A BEDLAM

Many lunatics of the 17th century were classified, by the primitive social codes of the day, as "sturdy beggars" and on this score were whipped from one town to another till they either died or found miserable refuge in the workhouse of their parish. This song, vividly reminiscent of Edgar's mad patter as "Poor Tom" in *King Lear*, survives in a single manuscript in the British Museum. A great deal of it makes use of "canting" terms, or thieves' jargon; it also includes, as in stanza six, some buried learning of the "polite" variety. But its special quality is visionary. This anonymous, dateless, accidentally preserved poem is apocalyptic, free, fiercely ironic, and deeply human.

Tom a Bedlam

From the hag and hungry goblin
That into rags would rend ye,
The spirit that stands by the naked man
In the book of moons [1] defend ye,
That of your five sound senses   5
You never be forsaken,
Nor wander from yourselves with Tom
Abroad to beg your bacon,
    While I do sing, Any food, any feeding,
    Feeding, drink, or clothing;   10
    Come dame or maid, be not afraid,
    Poor Tom will injure nothing.

Of thirty bare years have I
Twice twenty been enraged,
And of forty been three times fifteen   15
In durance soundly caged
On the lordly lofts of Bedlam
With stubble soft and dainty,
Brave bracelets [2] strong, sweet whips ding dong
With wholesome hunger plenty,   20
    And now I sing, etc.

1. A book used by gypsy and astrological fortunetellers.
2. Handcuffs, ironically prettified as the straw pallet of the madman is "stubble soft and dainty."

With a thought I took for Maudlin
And a cruse of cockle pottage,[3]
With a thing thus tall, sky bless you all,
I befell into this dotage.   25
I slept not since the Conquest,
Till then I never waked,
Till the roguish boy of love where I lay
Me found and strip't me naked.
        And now I sing, etc.   30

When I short have shorn my sow's face
And swigged my horny barrel,[4]
In an oaken inn I pound my skin [5]
As a suit of gilt apparrel;
The moon's my constant mistress   35
And the lovely owl my marrow; [6]
The flaming drake and the night crow [7] make
Me music to my sorrow.
        While I do sing, etc.

The palsy plagues my pulses   40
When I prig your pigs or pullen,[8]
Your culvers [9] take, or matchless make
Your chanticleer or sullen.[1]
When I want provant with Humphrey I sup,[2]
And when I am benighted,   45
I walk in Paul's with wandering souls,[3]
Yet never am affrighted.
        But I do sing, etc.

I know more than Apollo,[4]
For oft when he lies sleeping   50
I see the stars at bloody wars
In the wounded welkin weeping;
The moon embrace her shepherd,[5]
And the queen of love her warrior,[6]
While the first doth horn the star of morn,   55

3. A mess of weeds. Sex and a meager diet have reduced Tom to his present state. The "Conquest" may be either the Norman conquest or an erotic defeat, perhaps both.
4. As a "gentleman of the road," the tramp parodies the amenities of polite travelers by scraping off a few bristles and gulping from a leather pottle.
5. The polite traveler pawns (impounds) his suit of clothing to settle his score at an inn, the tramp pawns his skin (all he owns) in a thicket.
6. Wife.
7. The "flaming drake" is a meteor or falling star, the "night crow" an owl, both evil portents.
8. Steal your pigs or poultry.
9. Pigeons.
1. I.e., by stealing hens, I render your rooster a widower, and so sullen.
2. To "dine with Duke Humphrey" is to go hungry.
3. St. Paul's churchyard, supposed to be haunted by ghosts, and perhaps for that reason a good place for a wandering man to get a night's open-air lodging.
4. God of the sun and of daylight; common sense.
5. Diana, goddess of the moon, and her shepherd lover Endymion.
6. Venus and Mars.

And the next the heavenly farrier.[7]
　　While I do sing, etc.

The gypsies, Snap and Pedro,
Are none of Tom's comradoes,
The punk I scorn and the cutpurse sworn,   60
And the roaring boy's bravadoes.[8]
The meek, the white, the gentle
Me handle, touch, and spare not;
But those that cross Tom Rynosseross [9]
Do what the panther dare not.   65
　　Although I sing, etc.

With an host of furious fancies
Whereof I am commander,
With a burning spear and a horse of air,
To the wilderness I wander.   70
By a knight of ghosts and shadows
I summoned am to a tourney
Ten leagues beyond the wide world's end:
Methinks it is no journey.
　　Yet will I sing, etc.   75

7. As the horns of the half-moon some-times seem to embrace the morning star, so Mars, in the mythology, cuckolds ("horns") Vulcan, the husband of Venus and a heavenly farrier, i.e., blacksmith.
8. A punk is a prostitute, a cutpurse a pickpocket, and a roaring boy a drunken, loud-spoken roisterer.
9. Perhaps "rhinoceros," i.e., thick-skinned Tom, in ironic contrast to the two previous lines. The "panther," be-cause his name in Greek means "all-animal," was often supposed to be the most fearsome of beasts.

FRANCIS BACON
(1561–1626)

1597: First edition of the *Essays* (augmented and revised editions in 1612 and 1625).
1605: *The Advancement of Learning.*
1620: *Novum Organum.*
1621: Bacon's disgrace and retirement.

"The wisest, brightest, meanest of mankind"—in these words Pope described the character of Francis Bacon; and the adjectives have clung to his reputation like an evil odor. Nor are they entirely unjust. Bacon was one of those cool, controlled spirits who seem to have such empire over themselves, and over the world, that we are secretly a bit glad when they fail in some shameful and humiliating way. The younger son of a high Elizabethan official, Bacon studied law at Cambridge and Gray's Inn. He then rose steadily and securely through the legal bureaucracy of Elizabeth and James until he stood at the head of his profession, as Lord Chancellor of England. In passing, he sprinkled his career with magisterial essays on human conduct and lordly surveys of human learning. In 1618 he was created Baron Verulam; in 1621, he became Viscount St. Albans. Two months later, he fell from grace with a crash, accused of taking bribes in office, and confessing himself guilty of corruption and neglect. The last five years of his life were spent in retirement. His name has stood since as that of a man a little inhuman in his brilliance but all too human in his frailties.

Informal prose discourse was familiar to the classic writers, but it usually took the form of the epistle, the dialogue, or the impersonal treatise; the essay is essentially a modern form, of Renaissance invention. A series of tentative and often individual formulations, it offers a fluid and casual way of exploring one's relations to the world; it implies an interest in the self which Renaissance men were probably the first to feel. Bacon, who published in 1597, was the first English essayist; indeed, the very first essayist of all, Michel de Montaigne, antedated him by only seventeen years. But Bacon's essays are so different from Montaigne's as to constitute almost a fresh and separate act of creation.

Bacon's essays make little effort to follow the Montaigne pattern of leisurely self-exploration and discursive self-revelation; their sententious clarity compresses complex angles of speculation into a phrase. Bacon gives us a Lord Chancellor's view of the world; he sees it shrewdly, from the outside and from above, and delivers his judgment in sentences. Talking on a topic like *Marriage and Single Life*, he is cold common sense personified; one could not possibly tell from the essay itself whether he was married or not when he wrote it (He waited, actually, to the prudent age of 45 before yielding a hostage to fortune, and he never had any children.)

Montaigne, writing on this topic, would have told us on the first page about his marriage, its pleasures, its problems, his hopes, his fears, his children. The Baconian essay is more formal, more philosophical; it owes more to Seneca. And Bacon's general position in the history of the English essay is fittingly one of solitary eminence. Cowley, his only rival in the 17th century, did not publish till 1661, and then in the vein of Montaigne. It was not till the age of Joseph Addison and Sir Richard Steele, the early 18th century, that Bacon, the founder of the formal essay, acquired his first followers.

But Bacon's greatest achievement is not his *Essays*; rather, it is his scientific writing, all of which he contemplated arranging in one gigantic structure to be known as "The Great Instauration." The "new instrument of learning" announced in *Novum Organum* was to be the second part of this great project; the book represents a preliminary arrangement of the actual field of human learning in relation to man's potential knowledge. The simple audacity of this subject is enough to make one gasp; and the fact is that Bacon shared too many of the mistaken views of the age ever to be able to discriminate truth from falsehood in a wholesale way. Yet this is not the impression with which a reading of *Novum Organum* ultimately leaves us. Though he may have been mistaken in a hundred particulars, the general rightness of Bacon's intellectual method is not open to dispute; and the confidence with which he pointed a new direction for the human mind encouraged and enlightened experimenters in a hundred different disciplines.

The third section of the Great Instauration was to be a natural history of formidable proportions. One fragment which Bacon wrote in connection with this project (probably as early as 1617) is the little fantasy known as *The New Atlantis*. Bacon never finished this sketch, and never published it; it is less pretentious than his other works, and perhaps less polished. Yet it has proved one of the most popular and stimulating things he ever wrote. His idea of a "Solomon's House" devoted to study and research in the natural sciences was certainly responsible for the chartering of the Royal Society, more than thirty years after Bacon's death.

Bacon himself died a martyr to the scientific spirit, though perhaps not as dramatically as one would like: while collecting snow to refrigerate a chicken, he caught a cold and died of bronchitis. Yet of him, more than of any other 17th-century figure, it can be said that if you seek his monument, you have only to look at the world about you. Modern science would have existed without Bacon, but it certainly would not have been modern science as we know it.

From ESSAYS
Of Truth

"What is truth?" said jesting Pilate; and would not stay for an answer.[1] Certainly there be that delight in giddiness,[2] and count it

1. See John xviii.38 for Pilate's idle query to Jesus.

2. Changeability, insecurity of ideas. "That": those who.

a bondage to fix a belief; affecting free-will in thinking, as well as in acting. And though the sects of philosophers of that kind[3] be gone, yet there remain certain discoursing wits, which are of the same veins, though there be not so much blood in them as was in those of the ancients. But it is not only the difficulty and labor which men take in finding out of truth; nor again, that when it is found, it imposeth upon[4] men's thoughts, that doth bring lies in favor; but a natural though corrupt love of the lie itself. One of the later school of the Grecians examineth the matter, and is at a stand to think what should be in it, that men should love lies; where neither they make for pleasure, as with poets; nor for advantage, as with the merchant, but for the lie's sake. But I cannot tell:[5] this same truth is a naked and open daylight, that doth not show the masks and mummeries and triumphs of the world half so stately and daintily as candle lights. Truth may perhaps come to the price of a pearl, that showeth best by day, but it will not rise to the price of a diamond or carbuncle,[6] that showeth best in varied lights. A mixture of a lie doth ever add pleasure. Doth any man doubt that if there were taken out of men's minds vain opinions, flattering hopes, false valuations, imaginations as one would, and the like, but it would leave the minds of a number of men poor shrunken things, full of melancholy and indisposition, and unpleasing to themselves? One of the fathers, in great severity, called poesy *vinum daemonum*,[7] because it filleth the imagination, and yet it is but with the shadow of a lie. But it is not the lie that passeth through the mind, but the lie that sinketh in, and settleth in it, that doth the hurt, such as we spake of before. But howsoever these things are thus in men's depraved judgments and affections, yet truth, which only doth judge itself, teacheth that the inquiry of truth, which is the love-making, or wooing of it, the knowledge of truth, which is the presence of it, and the belief of truth, which is the enjoying of it, is the sovereign good of human nature. The first creature[8] of God, in the works of the days, was the light of the sense; the last was the light of reason; and His sabbath work ever since is the illumination of His Spirit. First, He breathed light upon the face of the matter, or chaos; then He breathed light into the face of man; and still He breatheth and inspireth light into the face of His chosen. The poet that beautified the sect that was otherwise inferior to the rest[9] saith yet excellently well: "It is a pleasure to stand upon the shore, and to see ships tossed upon the sea: a pleasure to stand in the window of a castle,

3. The Greek Skeptics, who taught the uncertainty of all knowledge. "Discoursing wits": discursive minds.
4. Restricts, limits.
5. "I cannot tell," says Bacon, and tells.
6. Ruby.
7. The wine of devils; St. Augustine

is probably being cited.
8. Creation.
9. Lucretius' *On the Nature of Things* expressed the Epicurean creed, which Bacon thought inferior because it emphasized pleasure. The passage cited comprises the first words of Book I.

and to see a battle, and the adventures thereof below: but no pleasure is comparable to the standing upon the vantage ground of truth" (a hill not to be commanded,[1] and where the air is always clear and serene), "and to see the errors, and wanderings, and mists, and tempests, in the vale below": so always that this prospect[2] be with pity, and not with swelling or pride. Certainly, it is heaven upon earth to have a man's mind move in charity, rest in providence, and turn upon the poles of truth.

To pass from theological and philosophical truth to the truth of civil business; it will be acknowledged even by those that practice it not, that clear and round dealing[3] is the honor of man's nature, and that mixture of falsehood is like alloy in coin of gold and silver, which may make the metal work the better, but it embaseth[4] it. For these winding and crooked courses are the goings of the serpent; which goeth basely upon the belly, and not upon the feet. There is no vice that doth so cover a man with shame as to be found false and perfidious; and therefore Montaigne saith prettily, when he inquired the reason why the word of the lie should be such a disgrace, and such an odious charge, saith he, "If it be well weighed, to say that a man lieth is as much as to say that he is brave towards God and a coward towards men."[5] For a lie faces God, and shrinks from man. Surely the wickedness of falsehood and breach of faith cannot possibly be so highly expressed, as in that it shall be the last peal to call the judgments of God upon the generations of men, it being foretold that when Christ cometh, he shall not "find faith upon the earth."[6]

1625

Of Marriage and Single Life[1]

He that hath wife and children hath given hostages to fortune; for they are impediments to great enterprises, either of virtue or mischief. [Certainly the best works, and of greatest merit for the public, have proceeded from the unmarried or childless men,] which both in affection and means have married and endowed the public. Yet it were great reason that those that have children should have greatest care of future times, unto which they know they must transmit their dearest pledges. Some there are who, though they lead a single life, yet their thoughts do end with themselves, and account future times impertinences.[2] Nay, there are some other that account wife and children but as bills of charges. Nay more, there

---

1. Dominated.
2. I.e., provided always that this contemplation.
3. The dealing that Bacon calls "round" we should describe as "square."

4. Debases.
5. *Essays* II.18.
6. Luke xviii.8.
1. The text is that of the 1625 edition.
2. Irrelevant concerns.

are some foolish rich covetous men that take a pride in having no children, because they may be thought so much the richer. For perhaps they have heard some talk, "Such an one is a great rich man," and another except to it, "Yea, but he hath a great charge of children"; as if it were an abatement to his riches. But the most ordinary cause of a single life is liberty, especially in certain self-pleasing and humorous[3] minds, which are so sensible of every restraint, as they will go near to think their girdles and garters to be bonds and shackles. Unmarried men are best friends, best masters, best servants, but not always best subjects, for they are light to run away, and almost all fugitives are of that condition. A single life doth well with churchmen, for charity will hardly water the ground where it must first fill a pool. It is indifferent for judges and magistrates, for if they be facile[4] and corrupt, you shall have a servant five times worse than a wife. For soldiers, I find the generals commonly in their hortatives[5] put men in mind of their wives and children; and I think the despising of marriage amongst the Turks maketh the vulgar soldier more base. Certainly wife and children are a kind of discipline of humanity; and single men, though they be many times more charitable, because their means are less exhaust,[6] yet, on the other side, they are more cruel and hard-hearted (good to make severe inquisitors), because their tenderness is not so oft called upon. Grave natures, led by custom, and therefore constant, are commonly loving husbands, as was said of Ulysses, *Vetulam suam praetulit immortalitati*.[7] Chaste women are often proud and froward, as presuming upon the merit of their chastity. It is one of the best bonds, both of chastity and obedience, in the wife if she think her husband wise, which she will never do if she find him jealous. Wives are young men's mistresses, companions for middle age, and old men's nurses, so as a man may have a quarrel[8] to marry when he will. But yet he was reputed one of the wise men that made answer to the question when a man should marry: "A young man not yet, an elder man not at all."[9] It is often seen that bad husbands have very good wives; whether it be that it raiseth the price of their husbands' kindness when it comes, or that the wives take a pride in their patience. But this never fails, if the bad husbands were of their own choosing, against their friends' consent; for then they will be sure to make good their own folly.

1612, 1625

3. Unbalanced, whimsical.
4. Pliable.
5. Exhortations.
6. Exhausted, drained.
7. "He preferred his old wife to immortality." Ulysses might have had immortality in the company of the nymph Calypso, but preferred to go back to Penelope.
8. Pretext.
9. Thales (6th century B.C.) was the confirmed bachelor who made this remark. He was one of the Seven Sages of Greece.

Of Great Place[1]

Men in great place are thrice servants: servants of the sovereign or state, servants of fame, and servants of business. So as they have no freedom, neither in their persons, nor in their actions, nor in their times. It is a strange desire, to seek power and lose liberty, or to seek power over others and to lose power over a man's self. The rising unto place is laborious, and by pains men come to greater pains; and it is sometimes base, and by indignities men come to dignities. The standing is slippery, and the regress is either a downfall or at least an eclipse, which is a melancholy thing: *Cum non sis qui fueris, non esse cur velis vivere.*[2] Nay, retire men cannot when they would, neither will they when it were reason; but are impatient of privateness,[3] even in age and sickness, which require the shadow; like old townsmen, that will be still sitting at their street door, though thereby they offer age to scorn. Certainly, great persons had need to borrow other men's opinions to think themselves happy; for if they judge by their own feeling, they cannot find it; but if they think with themselves what other men think of them, and that other men would fain be as they are, then they are happy, as it were by report; when perhaps they find the contrary within. For they are the first that find their own griefs, though they be the last that find their own faults. Certainly, men in great fortunes are strangers to themselves, and while they are in the puzzle of business they have no time to tend their health, either of body or mind. *Illi mors gravis incubat, qui notus nimis omnibus, ignotus moritur sibi.*[4] In place there is license to do good and evil, whereof the latter is a curse; for in evil the best condition is not to will, the second not to can.[5] But power to do good is the true and lawful end of aspiring; for good thoughts (though God accept them) yet towards men are little better than good dreams, except they be put in act; and that cannot be without power and place, as the vantage and commanding ground. Merit and good works is the end of man's motion, and conscience[6] of the same is the accomplishment of man's rest; for if a man can be partaker of God's theater,[7] he shall likewise be partaker of God's rest. *Et conversus Deus, ut aspiceret opera quae fecerunt manus suae, vidit quod omnia essent bona nimis;*[8] and then the sabbath.

1. The text is that of the 1625 edition.
2. "When you aren't what you were, there's no reason to live" (Cicero, *Familiar Letters* vii.3).
3. I.e., they object to retirement. "The shadow" is that of retirement, out of the glare of public life.
4. "Death lies heavily on him who, while too well known to everyone else, dies unknown to himself" (Seneca, *Thyestes*).
5. Be able.
6. Consciousness.
7. The world.
8. "And God saw every thing that he had made, and, behold, it was very good" (Genesis i.31).

In the discharge of thy place set before thee the best examples, for imitation is a globe[9] of precepts. And after a time set before thee thine own example; and examine thyself strictly, whether thou didst not best at first. Neglect not also the examples of those that have carried themselves ill in the same place; not to set off thyself by taxing[1] their memory, but to direct thyself what to avoid. Reform, therefore, without bravery, or scandal[2] of former times and persons; but yet set it down to thyself, as well to create good precedents as to follow them. Reduce things to the first institution,[3] and observe wherein and how they have degenerate; but yet ask counsel of both times; of the ancient time what is best, and of the latter time what is fittest. Seek to make thy course regular, that men may know beforehand what they may expect; but be not too positive and peremptory, and express thyself well when thou digressest from thy rule. Preserve the right of thy place, but stir not questions of jurisdiction; and rather assume thy right in silence and *de facto*,[4] than voice it with claims and challenges. Preserve likewise the rights of inferior places, and think it more honor to direct in chief than to be busy in all. Embrace and invite helps and advices touching the execution of thy place, and do not drive away such as bring thee information as meddlers, but accept of them in good part. The vices of authority are chiefly four: delays, corruption, roughness, and facility.[5] For delays, give easy access, keep times appointed, go through with that which is in hand, and interlace not business[6] but of necessity. For corruption, do not only bind thine own hands or thy servants' hands from taking, but bind the hands of suitors also from offering. For integrity used doth the one; but integrity professed and with a manifest detestation of bribery, doth the other. And avoid not only the fault, but the suspicion. Whosoever is found variable and changeth manifestly, without manifest cause, giveth suspicion of corruption. Therefore, always when thou changest thine opinion or course, profess it plainly and declare it, together with the reasons that move thee to change; and do not think to steal it.[7] A servant or a favorite, if he be inward,[8] and no other apparent cause of esteem, is commonly thought but a by-way to close[9] corruption. For roughness, it is a needless cause of discontent; severity breedeth fear, but roughness breedeth hate. Even reproofs from authority ought to be grave, and not taunting. As for facility, it is worse than bribery; for bribes come but now and then; but if importunity or idle respects[1] lead a man, he shall never be without. As Solomon saith, "To respect persons is not good, for such a man will transgress for a piece of bread."[2]

9. World.
1. Blaming.
2. Defaming, imputing evil to. "Bravery": ostentation.
3. I.e., go back to first principles.
4. Without debate as to right and wrong, as a matter of course.
5. Docility, too great obligingness.

6. I.e., do not carry on different businesses at the same time.
7. Change your mind without its being noticed.
8. In his master's confidence.
9. Secret.
1. Irrelevant considerations.
2. Cf. Proverbs xxviii.21.

It is most true that was anciently spoken, "A place showeth the man"; and it showeth some to the better and some to the worse. *Omnium consensu capax imperii, nisi imperasset,*[3] saith Tacitus of Galba; but of Vespasian he saith, *Solus imperantium Vespasianus mutatus in melius:*[4] though the one was meant of sufficiency, the other of manners and affection. It is an assured sign of a worthy and generous spirit, whom honor amends.[5] For honor is, or should be, the place of virtue; and as in nature things move violently to their place and calmly in their place, so virtue in ambition is violent, in authority settled and calm. All rising to great place is by a winding stair; and if there be factions, it is good to side a man's self[6] whilst he is in the rising, and to balance himself when he is placed. Use the memory of thy predecessor fairly and tenderly; for if thou dost not, it is a debt will sure be paid when thou art gone. If thou have colleagues, respect them, and rather call them when they look not for it, than exclude them when they have reason to look to be called. Be not too sensible[7] or too remembering of thy place in conversation and private answers to suitors; but let it rather be said, "When he sits in place he is another man."

1612, 1625

Of Studies[1]

Studies serve for delight, for ornament, and for ability. Their chief use for delight is in privateness[2] and retiring; for ornament, is in discourse; and for ability, is in the judgment and disposition of business. For expert men[3] can execute, and perhaps judge of particulars, one by one; but the general counsels, and the plots and marshaling of affairs, come best from those that are learned. To spend too much time in studies is sloth; to use them too much for ornament is affectation; to make judgment wholly by their rules is the humor[4] of a scholar. They perfect nature, and are perfected by experience; for natural abilities are like natural plants, that need pruning by study; and studies themselves do give forth directions too much at large, except they be bounded in by experience. Crafty men contemn studies, simple men admire them, and wise men use them, for they teach not their own use; but that is a wisdom without them, and above them, won by observation. Read not to contradict and confute, nor to believe and take for granted, nor to find talk and discourse, but to weigh and consider. Some books are to be tasted,

3. "Everyone would have thought him a good ruler, if he had not ruled."
4. "Of all the emperors, only Vespasian changed for the better." "Sufficiency": abilities. "Affection": disposition.
5. I.e., whom promotion improves.
6. For a man to take sides.

7. Sensitive.
1. The text is that of the 1625 edition.
2. Private life.
3. Men of experience, the English adjective being used in its Latin sense, *experti.*
4. Mannerism, implying absurd error.

others to be swallowed, and some few to be chewed and digested; that is, some books are to be read only in parts; others to be read, but not curiously;[5] and some few to be read wholly, and with diligence and attention. Some books also may be read by deputy and extracts made of them by others, but that would be only in the less important arguments and the meaner sort of books; else distilled books are like common distilled waters,[6] flashy things. Reading maketh a full man, conference[7] a ready man, and writing an exact man. And therefore, if a man write little, he had need have a great memory; if he confer little, he had need have a present wit;[8] and if he read little, he had need have more cunning, to seem to know that[9] he doth not. Histories make men wise; poets, witty;[1] the mathematics, subtle; natural philosophy, deep; moral, grave; logic and rhetoric, able to contend. *Abeunt studia in mores.*[2] Nay, there is no stond or impediment in the wit but may be wrought out by fit studies, like as diseases of the body may have appropriate exercises. Bowling is good for the stone and reins,[3] shooting for the lungs and breast, gentle walking for the stomach, riding for the head, and the like. So if a man's wit be wandering, let him study the mathematics; for in demonstrations, if his wit be called away never so little, he must begin again. If his wit be not apt to distinguish or find differences, let him study the schoolmen,[4] for they are *Cymini sectores.* If he be not apt to beat over matters[5] and to call up one thing to prove and illustrate another, let him study the lawyer's cases. So every defect of the mind may have a special receipt.[6]

1597, 1625

From Novum Organum[1]

[*The Idols*]

50

But by far the greatest hindrance and aberration of the human understanding proceeds from the dullness, incompetency, and de-

---

5. Not with care.
6. Infusions of herbs, etc., used as home remedies.
7. Conversation, meetings.
8. Lively intelligence.
9. That which.
1. Imaginative, inventive.
2. "Studies culminate in manners" (Ovid, *Heroides*). "Stond": difficulty.
3. Gall bladder and kidneys.
4. Medieval theologians. The Latin means "dividers of cuminseed," i.e., hairsplitters.
5. Discuss a subject thoroughly.
6. Cure, prescription.
1. *Novum Organum,* or "The New In-

strument of Learning," does not properly represent a work of English literature, since it was written in Latin, for an international scholarly audience. (Bacon rather mistrusted the modern languages, thinking they would "wear away" in time; but Latin was safe.) Still, no history of English ideas can afford to ignore this book; for it was the keystone of Bacon's vast project to renovate the structure of human learning from the ground up. The translation is that of Spedding, Ellis, and Heath, from their edition of the *Works* (1860–64).

Observation was the essential process

ceptions of the senses; in that things which strike the sense outweigh things which do not immediately strike it, though they[2] be more important. Hence it is that speculation commonly ceases where sight ceases; insomuch that of things invisible there is little or no observation. Hence all the working of the spirits enclosed in tangible bodies lies hid and unobserved of men.[3] So also all the more subtle changes of form in the parts of coarser substances (which they commonly call alteration, though it is in truth local motion through exceedingly small spaces) is in like manner unobserved. And yet unless these two things just mentioned be searched out and brought to light, nothing great can be achieved in nature, as far as the production of works is concerned. So again the essential nature of our common air, and of all bodies less dense than air (which are very many), is almost unknown. For the sense by itself is a thing infirm and erring; neither can instruments for enlarging or sharpening the senses do much; but all the truer kind of interpretation of nature is effected by instances and experiments fit and apposite; wherein the sense decides touching the experiment only, and the experiment touching the point in nature and the thing itself.

51

The human understanding is of its own nature prone to abstractions and gives a substance and reality to things which are fleeting. But to resolve nature into abstractions is less to our purpose than to dissect her into parts; as did the school of Democritus,[4] which went further into nature than the rest. Matter rather than forms should be the object of our attention, its configurations and changes of configuration, and simple action, and law of action or motion; for forms are figments of the human mind, unless you will call those laws of action forms.

52

Such then are the idols which I call *Idols of the Tribe;*[5] and which take their rise either from the homogeneity of the substance of the human spirit, or from its preoccupation, or from its narrowness, or

of Bacon's new method; he felt that only observation, long continued and carefully directed, was capable of producing certainty about the operations of nature. As against the true intellectual mean produced by careful observation and controlled experiment, he set the frivolity of the skeptics and the unwarranted confidence of the dogmatists. This argument rises to its height about halfway through the first (destructive) part of the book, in an extended account of the various Idols, or delusive ideas, which mislead and bewilder the human understanding.
2. The latter.
3. Though his views on scientific method were amazingly modern, Bacon's ideas about physical phenomena were those of his age; he believed in subtle spiritual principles which might lie concealed in physical objects, unobserved by men.
4. The school of Democritus, the "laughing philosopher" of ancient Greece (5th century B.C.), held that the world was composed of atoms. Democritus developed the atomic theory, of which Leucippus was the originator; Lucretius (four centuries later) became the great literary exponent of this school.
5. By "Idols" Bacon means delusive images of truth, leading men away from the exact knowledge of science. By "Idols of the Tribe" he denotes particularly generalizations based on inadequate facts—a fault to which all men are prone.

from its restless motion, or from an infusion of the affections, or from the incompetency of the senses, or from the mode of impression.

53

The *Idols of the Cave* take their rise in the peculiar constitution, mental or bodily, of each individual; and also in education, habit, and accident. Of this kind there is a great number and variety; but I will instance those the pointing out of which contains the most important caution, and which have most effect in disturbing the clearness of the understanding.

54

Men become attached to certain particular sciences[6] and speculations, either because they fancy themselves the authors and inventors thereof, or because they have bestowed the greatest pains upon them and become most habituated to them. But men of this kind, if they betake themselves to philosophy and contemplations of a general character, distort and color them in obedience to their former fancies; a thing especially to be noticed in Aristotle, who made his natural philosophy a mere bondservant to his logic, thereby rendering it contentious and well nigh useless. The race of chemists[7] again out of a few experiments of the furnace have built up a fantastic philosophy, framed with reference to a few things; and Gilbert also, after he had employed himself most laboriously in the study and observation of the loadstone, proceeded at once to construct an entire system in accordance with his favorite subject.[8]

55

There is one principal and, as it were, radical distinction between different minds, in respect of philosophy and the sciences, which is this: that some minds are stronger and apter to mark the differences of things, others to mark their resemblances. The steady and acute mind can fix its contemplations and dwell and fasten on the subtlest distinctions: the lofty and discursive mind recognizes and puts together the finest and most general resemblances. Both kinds however easily err in excess, by catching the one at gradations, the other at shadows.

56

There are found some minds given to an extreme admiration of antiquity, others to an extreme love and appetite for novelty; but few so duly tempered that they can hold the mean, neither carping at what has been well laid down by the ancients, nor despising what is well introduced by the moderns. This however turns to the great injury of the sciences and philosophy; since these affectations of antiquity and novelty are the humors of partisans rather than judg-

6. Ideas, bits of information.
7. Alchemists.
8. William Gilbert, author of a famous treatise on the magnet (1600), serves Bacon (rather unfairly) as an example of dogmatism founded on a few limited experiments.

ments; and truth is to be sought for not in the felicity of any age, which is an unstable thing, but in the light of nature and experience, which is eternal. These factions therefore must be abjured, and care must be taken that the intellect be not hurried by them into assent.

57

Contemplations of nature and of bodies in their simple form break up and distract the understanding, while contemplations of nature and bodies in their composition and configuration overpower and dissolve the understanding:[9] a distinction well seen in the school of Leucippus and Democritus as compared with the other philosophies. For that school is so busied with the particles that it hardly attends to the structure; while the others are so lost in admiration of the structure that they do not penetrate to the simplicity of nature. These kinds of contemplation should therefore be alternated and taken by turns; that so the understanding may be rendered at once penetrating and comprehensive, and the inconveniences above mentioned, with the idols which proceed from them, may be avoided.

58

Let such then be our provision and contemplative prudence for keeping off and dislodging the *Idols of the Cave*, which grow for the most part either out of the predominance of a favorite subject, or out of an excessive tendency to compare or to distinguish, or out of partiality for particular ages, or out of the largeness or minuteness of the objects contemplated. And generally let every student of nature take this as a rule—that whatever his mind seizes and dwells upon with peculiar satisfaction is to be held in suspicion, and that so much the more care is to be taken in dealing with such questions to keep the understanding even and clear.

59

But the *Idols of the Market-place* are the most troublesome of all: idols which have crept into the understanding through the alliances of words and names. For men believe that their reason governs words; but it is also true that words react on the understanding; and this it is that has rendered philosophy and the sciences sophistical and inactive. Now words, being commonly framed and applied according to the capacity of the vulgar, follow those lines of division which are most obvious to the vulgar understanding. And whenever an understanding of greater acuteness or a more diligent observation would alter those lines to suit the true divisions of nature, words stand in the way and resist the change. Whence it comes to pass that the high and formal discussions of learned men end oftentimes in disputes about words and names; with which (according to the use[1] and wisdom of the mathematicians) it would be more prudent to begin, and so by means of definitions reduce them to order. Yet

---

9. I.e., reducing nature to first principles is, intellectually, as dangerous as trying to observe all its particulars.
1. Custom.

even definitions cannot cure this evil in dealing with natural and material things; since the definitions themselves consist of words, and those words beget others: so that it is necessary to recur to individual instances, and those in due series and order; as I shall say presently when I come to the method and scheme for the formation of notions and axioms.[2]

60

The idols imposed by words on the understanding are of two kinds. They are either names of things which do not exist (for as there are things left unnamed through lack of observation, so likewise are there names which result from fantastic suppositions and to which nothing in reality responds), or they are names of things which exist, but yet confused and ill-defined, and hastily and irregularly derived from realities. Of the former kind are Fortune, the Prime Mover, Planetary Orbits, Element of Fire, and like fictions which owe their origin to false and idle theories.[3] And this class of idols is more easily expelled, because to get rid of them it is only necessary that all theories should be steadily rejected and dismissed as obsolete.[4]

But the other class, which springs out of a faulty and unskillful abstraction, is intricate and deeply rooted. Let us take for example such a word as *humid*; and see how far the several things which the word is used to signify agree with each other; and we shall find the word *humid* to be nothing else than a mark loosely and confusedly applied to denote a variety of actions which will not bear to be reduced to any constant meaning. For it both signifies that which easily spreads itself round any other body; and that which in itself is indeterminate and cannot solidize; and that which readily yields in every direction; and that which easily divides and scatters itself; and that which easily unites and collects itself; and that which readily flows and is put in motion; and that which readily clings to another body and wets it; and that which is easily reduced to a liquid, or being solid easily melts. Accordingly when you come to apply the word—if you take it in one sense, flame is humid; if in another, air is not humid; if in another, fine dust is humid; if in another, glass is humid. So that it is easy to see that the notion is taken by abstraction only from water and common and ordinary liquids,

---

2. Bacon's mistrust of words, evident here, led the Royal Society to cultivate a plain, stripped prose style for purposes of scientific communication.

3. The "Prime Mover" was a transparent sphere on the outside of the universe, supposed to move all the other spheres; the "Element of Fire" was an area of pure, invisible fire, supposed to exist above the atmosphere. In the nature of things, these concepts could be based on no observation. "Planetary Orbits," on the other hand,

are very real; Bacon may be referring to the old notion of crystalline spheres in which the planets were supposed to be set.

4. Bacon does not really mean "theories" in the inclusive modern sense, but "abstractions loosely invoked to explain particular facts." He is actually restating William of Occam's famous 14th-century principle, known as "Occam's razor," to the effect that "essences must not be multiplied beyond necessity."

without any due verification.

There are however in words certain degrees of distortion and error. One of the least faulty kinds is that of names of substances, especially of lowest species and well-deduced (for the notion of *chalk* and of *mud* is good, of *earth* bad); a more faulty kind is that of actions, as *to generate, to corrupt, to alter*; the most faulty is of qualities (except such as are the immediate objects of the sense), as *heavy, light, rare, dense*, and the like. Yet in all these cases some notions are of necessity a little better than others, in proportion to the greater variety of subjects that fall within the range of the human sense.

61

But the *Idols of the Theater*[5] are not innate, nor do they steal into the understanding secretly, but are plainly impressed and received into the mind from the play-books of philosophical systems and the perverted rules of demonstration. To attempt refutations in this case would be merely inconsistent with what I have already said: for since we agree neither upon principles nor upon demonstrations, there is no place for argument. And this is so far well, inasmuch as it leaves the honor of the ancients untouched. For they are no wise disparaged—the question between them and me being only as to the way. For as the saying is, the lame man who keeps the right road outstrips the runner who takes a wrong one. Nay, it is obvious that when a man runs the wrong way, the more active and swift he is the further he will go astray.

But the course I propose for the discovery of sciences is such as leaves but little to the acuteness and strength of wits, but places all wits and understandings nearly on a level. For as in the drawing of a straight line or a perfect circle, much depends on the steadiness and practice of the hand, if it be done by aim of hand only, but if with the aid of rule or compass, little or nothing; so is it exactly with my plan. But though particular confutations would be of no avail, yet touching the sects and general divisions of such systems I must say something; something also touching the external signs which show that they are unsound; and finally something touching the causes of such great infelicity and of such lasting and general agreement in error; that so the access to truth may be made less difficult, and the human understanding may the more willingly submit to its purgation and dismiss its idols.

62

Idols of the Theater, or of systems, are many, and there can be and perhaps will be yet many more. For were it not that now for many ages men's minds have been busied with religion and theology; and were it not that civil governments, especially monarchies, have

5. I.e., those derived from previous philosophical systems, which misrepresent life by overdramatizing it and mislead men by pretending to show them reality itself.

been averse to such novelties, even in matters speculative; so that men labor therein to the peril and harming of their fortunes—not only unrewarded, but exposed also to contempt and envy; doubtless there would have arisen many other philosophical sects like to those which in great variety flourished once among the Greeks. For as on the phenomena of the heavens many hypotheses may be constructed, so likewise (and more also) many various dogmas may be set up and established on the phenomena of philosophy. And in the plays of this philosophical theater you may observe the same thing which is found in the theater of the poets, that stories invented for the stage are more compact and elegant, and more as one would wish them to be, than true stories out of history.

In general, however, there is taken for the material of philosophy either a great deal out of a few things, or a very little out of many things; so that on both sides philosophy is based on too narrow a foundation of experiment and natural history, and decides on the authority of too few cases. For the rational school of philosophers snatches from experience a variety of common instances, neither duly ascertained nor diligently examined and weighed, and leaves all the rest to meditation and agitation of wit.[6]

There is also another class of philosophers, who having bestowed much diligent and careful labor on a few experiments, have thence made bold to educe and construct systems; wresting all other facts in a strange fashion to conformity therewith.

And there is yet a third class, consisting of those who out of faith and veneration mix their philosophy with theology and traditions; among whom the vanity of some has gone so far aside as to seek the origin of sciences among spirits and genii. So that this parent stock of errors—this false philosophy—is of three kinds; the sophistical, the empirical, and the superstitious. * * *

68

So much concerning the several classes of idols, and their equipage: all of which must be renounced and put away with a fixed and solemn determination, and the understanding thoroughly freed and cleansed; the entrance into the kingdom of man, founded on the sciences, being not much other than the entrance into the kingdom of heaven, whereinto none may enter except as a little child.

1620

6. Bacon's thought contained a concealed element of anti-intellectualism: his enthusiasm for experiment led him to denigrate the value of reason, as very few modern scientists would feel it necessary to do. What he is opposing here is an excessive concern with the forms of logic, as exemplified, he would say, in "the schoolmen."

From The New Atlantis[1]

[Solomon's House]

We came at our day and hour, and I was chosen by my fellows for the private access.[2] We found him in a fair chamber, richly hanged, and carpeted under foot, without any degrees to the state.[3] He was set upon a low throne richly adorned, and a rich cloth of state over his head, of blue satin embroidered. He was alone, save that he had two pages of honor, on either hand one, finely attired in white. His undergarments were the like that we saw him wear in the chariot; but instead of his gown, he had on him a mantle with a cape of the same fine black, fastened about him. When we came in, as we were taught, we bowed low at our first entrance, and when we were come near his chair, he stood up, holding forth his hand ungloved and in posture of blessing; and we every one of us stooped down, and kissed the hem of his tippet.[4] That done, the rest departed, and I remained. Then he warned the pages forth of the room, and caused me to sit down beside him, and spake to me thus in the Spanish tongue:

"God bless thee, my son; I will give thee the greatest jewel I have. For I will impart unto thee, for the love of God and men, a relation of the true state of Solomon's House. Son, to make you know the true state of Solomon's House, I will keep this order. First, I will set forth unto you the end of our foundation. Secondly, the preparations and instruments we have for our works. Thirdly, the several employments and functions whereto our fellows are assigned. And fourthly, the ordinances and rites which we observe.

"The end of our foundation is the knowledge of causes, and secret motions of things; and the enlarging of the bounds of human empire, to the effecting of all things possible.

"The preparations and instruments are these. We have large and deep caves of several depths: the deepest are sunk six hundred

---

1. Sir Thomas More's *Utopia* (1516) set a fashion for imaginary communities with ideal forms of government which was suddenly taken up in the early 17th century. The German Johann Andreae published in 1619 his *Christianopolis;* Thomas Campanella, languishing in a Neapolitan jail, wrote his *City of the Sun* in 1623. Bacon's contribution to the discussion, perhaps because he never completed it, is really tangential to the concept of an ideal commonwealth. His *New Atlantis* is in effect a research establishment which could exist in any society that would tolerate it. Perhaps for that reason, it had an immediate influence beyond that of most full-fledged Utopias; and was largely realized, within thirty years of its publication, in the shape of the Philosophical Society which in 1662 became the Royal Society. Bacon begins by describing an imaginary voyage to the island of Bensalem, supposed to lie in the vicinity of the Bering Straits. Here, after learning about the miraculous diffusion of Christianity to the island, he is invited to visit their most interesting institution, Solomon's House.
2. Audience.
3. I.e., without stairs leading up to the dais.
4. Scarf.

fathoms; and some of them are digged and made under great hills and mountains; so that if you reckon together the depth of the hill, and the depth of the cave, they are, some of them, above three miles deep. For we find that the depth of a hill, and the depth of a cave from the flat, is the same thing; both remote alike from the sun and heaven's beams, and from the open air. These caves we call the lower region, and we use them for all coagulations, indurations,[5] refrigerations, and conservations of bodies. We use them likewise for the imitation of natural mines, and the producing also of new artificial metals, by compositions and materials which we use, and lay there for many years. We use them also sometimes (which may seem strange) for curing of some diseases, and for prolongation of life in some hermits that choose to live there, well accommodated of[6] all things necessary, and indeed live very long; by whom also we learn many things.

"We have burials in several earths, where we put divers cements,[7] as the Chinese do their porcelain. But we have them in greater variety, and some of them more fine. We also have great variety of composts[8] and soils, for the making of the earth fruitful.

"We have high towers, the highest about half a mile in height, and some of them likewise set upon high mountains, so that the vantage of the hill, with the tower, is in the highest of them three miles at least. And these places we call the upper region, accounting the air between the high places and the low as a middle region. We use these towers, according to their several heights and situations, for insolation,[9] refrigeration, conservation, and for the view of divers meteors—as winds, rain, snow, hail;[1] and some of the fiery meteors also. And upon them, in some places, are dwellings of hermits, whom we visit sometimes, and instruct what to observe.

"We have great lakes, both salt and fresh, whereof we have use for the fish and fowl. We use them also for burials of some natural bodies, for we find a difference in things buried in earth, or in air below the earth, and things buried in water. We have also pools, of which some do strain fresh water out of salt, and others by art do turn fresh water into salt. We have also some rocks in the midst of the sea, and some bays upon the shore, for some works wherein is required the air and vapor of the sea. We have likewise violent streams and cataracts, which serve us for many motions; and likewise engines for multiplying and enforcing[2] of winds to set also on going divers motions.

"We have also a number of artificial wells and fountains, made in imitation of the natural sources and baths, as tincted upon[3]

5. Hardenings.
6. Provided with.
7. Clays and pottery mixtures.
8. Manures.
9. Exposure to the sun.

1. Anything that fell from the sky was, in Renaissance terminology, a meteor.
2. Re-enforcing, strengthening.
3. Tinctured with.

vitriol, sulphur, steel, brass, lead, nitre, and other minerals; and again, we have little wells for infusions of many things, where the waters take the virtue[4] quicker and better than in vessels or basins. And amongst them we have a water, which we call Water of Paradise, being by that we do to it, made very sovereign[5] for health and prolongation of life.

"We have also great and spacious houses, where we imitate and demonstrate meteors—as snow, hail, rain, some artificial rains of bodies, and not of water, thunders, lightnings; also generations of bodies in air—as frogs, flies, and divers others.

"We have also certain chambers, which we call chambers of health, where we qualify[6] the air as we think good and proper for the cure of divers diseases, and preservation of health.

"We have also fair and large baths, of several mixtures, for the cure of diseases, and the restoring of a man's body from arefaction;[7] and others for the confirming of it in strength of sinews, vital parts, and the very juice and substance of the body.

"We have also large and various orchards and gardens, wherein we do not so much respect beauty as variety of ground and soil, proper for divers trees and herbs, and some very spacious, where trees and berries are set, whereof we make divers kinds of drinks, besides the vineyards. In these we practice likewise all conclusions[8] of grafting and inoculating, as well of wild-trees as fruit-trees, which produceth many effects. And we make (by art) in the same orchards and gardens trees and flowers to come earlier or later than their seasons, and to come up and bear more speedily than by their natural course they do. We make them also by art greater much than their nature; and their fruit greater and sweeter, and of differing taste, smell, color, and figure, from their nature. And many of them we so order as they become of medicinal use.

"We have also means to make divers plants rise by mixtures of earths without seeds, and likewise to make divers new plants, differing from the vulgar,[9] and to make one tree or plant turn into another.

"We have also parks, and enclosures of all sorts, of beasts and birds; which we use not only for view or rareness, but likewise for dissections and trials,[1] that thereby we may take light what may be wrought upon the body of man. Wherein we find many strange effects: as continuing life in them, though divers parts, which you account vital, be perished and taken forth; resuscitating of some that seem dead in appearance, and the like. We try also all poisons, and other medicines upon them, as well of chirurgery[2] as physic. By art

---

4. Property (of the substances put into water).
5. Efficacious.
6. Modify.
7. Drying up.

8. Theories.
9. Ordinary.
1. Experiments.
2. Surgery.

likewise, we make them greater or taller than their kind is, and contrariwise dwarf them and stay their growth; we make them more fruitful and bearing than their kind is, and contrariwise barren and not generative. Also we make them differ in color, shape, activity, many ways. We find means to make commixtures and copulations of divers kind, which have produced many new kinds,[3] and them not barren, as the general opinion is. We make a number of kinds of serpents, worms, fishes, flies, of putrefaction, whereof some are advanced (in effect) to be perfect creatures, like beasts or birds, and have sexes, and do propagate. Neither do we this by chance, but we know beforehand of what matter and commixture what kind of those creatures will arise.

"We have also particular pools where we make trials upon fishes, as we have said before of beasts and birds.

"We have also places for breed and generation of those kinds of worms and flies which are of special use; such as are with you your silkworms and bees.

"I will not hold you long with recounting of our brew-houses, bake-houses, and kitchens, where are made divers drinks, breads, and meats, rare and of special effects. Wines we have of grapes, and drinks of other juice of fruits, of grains, and of roots, and of mixtures with honey, sugar, manna, and fruits dried and decocted;[4] also of the tears or woundings of trees, and of the pulp of canes. And these drinks are of several ages, some to the age or last[5] of forty years. We have drinks also brewed with several herbs, and roots and spices; yea, with several fleshes and whitemeats;[6] whereof some of the drinks are such as they are in effect meat and drink both, so that divers, especially in age, do desire to live with them, with little or no meat or bread. And above all, we strive to have drinks of extreme thin parts, to insinuate into the body, and yet without all biting, sharpness, or fretting; insomuch as some of them, put upon the back of your hand, will with a little stay[7] pass through to the palm, and yet taste mild to the mouth. We have also waters, which we ripen in that fashion, as they become nourishing, so that they are indeed excellent drink, and many will use no other. Bread we have of several grains, roots, and kernels; yea, and some of flesh, and fish, dried; with divers kinds of leavenings and seasonings; so that some do extremely move appetites; some do nourish so, as divers do live of them, without any other meat, who live very long. So for meats, we have some of them so beaten, and made tender, and mortified,[8] yet without all corrupting, as a weak heat of the stomach will turn them into good chylus,[9] as well as a strong heat would meat other-

---

3. Species.
4. Dissolved in water, by boiling.
5. Duration.
6. Breast of chicken, fish, sometimes cheese.
7. Delay.

8. Softened.
9. Chyle, food in its emulsified and digestible form. Bacon thinks of the stomach as a furnace, which softens food by heat.

wise prepared. We have some meats also, and breads, and drinks, which taken by men, enable them to fast long after; and some other, that used[1] make the very flesh of men's bodies sensibly more hard and tough, and their strength far greater than otherwise it would be.

"We have dispensatories, or shops of medicines; wherein you may easily think, if we have such variety of plants and living creatures more than you have in Europe (for we know what you have), the simples,[2] drugs, and ingredients of medicines, must likewise be in so much the greater variety. We have them likewise of divers ages, and long fermentations. And for their preparations, we have not only all manner of exquisite distillations and separations, and especially by gentle heats, and percolations through divers strainers, yea, and substances; but also exact forms of composition,[3] whereby they incorporate almost as they were natural simples.

"We have also divers mechanical arts, which you have not; and stuffs made by them, as papers, linen, silks, tissues, dainty works of feathers of wonderful luster, excellent dyes, and many others: and shops likewise, as well for such as are not brought into vulgar use amongst us, as for those that are. For you must know, that of the things before recited, many of them are grown into use throughout the kingdom, but yet, if they did flow from our invention, we have of them also for patterns and principals.[4]

"We have also furnaces of great diversities, and that keep great diversity of heats: fierce and quick, strong and constant, soft and mild; blown, quiet; dry, moist; and the like. But above all we have heats, in imitations of the sun's and heavenly bodies' heats, that pass divers inequalities, and (as it were) orbs, progresses, and returns,[5] whereby we produce admirable effects. Besides, we have heats of dungs, and of bellies and maws of living creatures and of their bloods and bodies, and of hays and herbs laid up moist, of lime unquenched, and such like. Instruments also which generate heat only by motion. And farther, places for strong insolations; and again, places under the earth, which by nature or art yield heat. These divers heats we use as the nature of the operation which we intend requireth.

"We have also perspective houses,[6] where we make demonstrations of all lights and radiations, and of all colors; and out of things uncolored and transparent we can represent unto you all several colors, not in rainbows (as it is in gems and prisms), but of themselves single. We represent also all multiplications of light, which we carry to great distance, and make so sharp, as to discern small

---

1. The word "when" is understood here.
2. Herbs.
3. Ways of putting the ingredients of medicines together, making compounds.

4. Models.
5. I.e. the furnaces produce various heats at will.
6. For optical experiments.

points and lines. Also all colorations of light; all delusions and deceits of the sight, in figures, magnitudes, motions, colors; all demonstrations of shadows. We find also divers means, yet unknown to you, of producing of light originally from divers bodies. We procure means of seeing objects afar off, as in the heaven and remote places; and represent things near as afar off, and things afar off as near, making feigned distances. We have also helps for the sight, far above spectacles and glasses in use. We have also glasses and means to see small and minute bodies, perfectly and distinctly; as the shapes and colors of small flies and worms, grains and flaws in gems which cannot otherwise be seen, observations in urine and blood not otherwise to be seen. We make artificial rainbows, halos, and circles about light. We represent also all manner of reflections, refractions, and multiplications of visual beams of objects.

"We have also precious stones of all kinds, many of them of great beauty and to you unknown; crystals likewise; and glasses of divers kinds; and amongst them some of metals vitrificated,[7] and other materials besides those of which you make glass. Also a number of fossils and imperfect minerals, which you have not. Likewise loadstones of prodigious virtue:[8] and other rare stones, both natural and artificial.

"We have also sound-houses, where we practice and demonstrate all sounds and their generation. We have harmonies which you have not, of quarter sounds and lesser slides of sounds. Divers instruments of music likewise to you unknown, some sweeter than any you have; together with bells and rings that are dainty and sweet. We represent small sounds as great and deep; likewise great sounds, extenuate[9] and sharp; we make divers tremblings and warblings of sounds, which in their original are entire.[1] We represent and imitate all articulate sounds and letters, and the voices and notes of beasts and birds. We have certain helps, which set to the ear do further the hearing greatly. We have also divers strange and artificial echoes, reflecting the voice many times, and as it were tossing it; and some that give back the voice louder than it came, some shriller and some deeper; yea, some rendering[2] the voice, differing in the letters or articulate sound from that they receive. We have also means to convey sounds in trunks[3] and pipes, in strange lines and distances.

"We have also perfume-houses, wherewith we join also practices of taste. We multiply smells, which may seem strange: we imitate smells, making all smells to breathe out of other mixtures than those that give them. We make divers imitations of taste likewise, so that they will deceive any man's taste. And in this house we contain also

7. Turned to glass.
8. Strength.
9. Drawn out thin.
1. I.e., we can vary notes which in nature are single.
2. Transforming.
3. Tubes.

a confiture-house, where we make all sweetmeats, dry and moist, and divers pleasant wines, milks, broths, and salads, far in greater variety than you have.

"We have also engine-houses, where are prepared engines and instruments for all sorts of motions. There we imitate and practice to make swifter motions than any you have, either out of your muskets or any engine that you have; and to make them and multiply them more easily and with small force, by wheels and other means, and to make them stronger and more violent than yours are, exceeding your greatest cannons and basilisks.[4] We represent also ordnance and instruments of war and engines of all kinds; and likewise new mixtures and compositions of gunpowder, wildfires burning in water and unquenchable; also fireworks of all variety, both for pleasure and use. We imitate also flights of birds; we have some degrees of flying[5] in the air. We have ships and boats for going under water and brooking[6] of seas, also swimming girdles and supporters. We have divers curious clocks, and other like motions of return, and some perpetual motions. We imitate also motions of living creatures by images of men, beasts, birds, fishes, and serpents; we have also a great number of other various motions, strange for equality,[7] fineness, and subtlety.

"We have also a mathematical-house, where are represented all instruments, as well of geometry as astronomy, exquisitely made.

"We have also houses of deceits of the senses, where we represent all manners of feats of juggling, false apparitions, impostures and illusions, and their fallacies. And surely you will easily believe that we, that have so many things truly natural which induce admiration, could in a world of particulars deceive the senses if we would disguise those things, and labor to make them seem more miraculous. But we do hate all impostures and lies, insomuch as we have severely forbidden it to all our fellows, under pain of ignominy and fines, that they do not show any natural work or thing adorned or swelling, but only pure as it is, and without all affectation of strangeness.

"These are, my son, the riches of Solomon's House.

"For the several employments and offices of our fellows, we have twelve that sail into foreign countries under the names of other nations (for our own we conceal), who bring us the books and abstracts and patterns of experiments of all other parts. These we call Merchants of Light.

"We have three that collect the experiments which are in all books. These we call Depredators.

"We have three that collect the experiments of all mechanical arts, and also of liberal sciences, and also of practices which are not brought into arts. These we call Mystery-men.

4. Cannon, named after the fabulous beast that killed by a beam from its eye.
5. I.e., rudimentary forms of flying.
6. Withstanding.
7. Unusual for their evenness.

"We have three that try new experiments, such as themselves think good. These we call Pioneers or Miners.

"We have three that draw the experiments of the former four into titles and tables, to give the better light for the drawing of observations and axioms out of them. These we call Compilers.

"We have three that bend themselves, looking into the experiments of their fellows, and cast about how to draw out of them things of use and practice for man's life and knowledge, as well for works as for plain demonstration of causes, means of natural divinations, and the easy and clear discovery of the virtues and parts of bodies. These we call Dowry-men or Benefactors.

"Then after divers meetings and consults of our whole number, to consider of the former labors and collections, we have three that take care out of them to direct new experiments, of a higher light, more penetrating into Nature than the former. These we call Lamps.

"We have three others that do execute the experiments so directed, and report them. These we call Inoculators.

"Lastly, we have three that raise the former discoveries by experiments into greater observations, axioms, and aphorisms. These we call Interpreters of Nature.[8]

"We have also, as you must think, novices and apprentices, that the succession of the former employed men do not fail; besides a great number of servants and attendants, men and women. And this we do also: we have consultations, which of the inventions and experiences which we have discovered shall be published, and which not; and take all an oath of secrecy for the concealing of those which we think fit to keep secret; though some of those we do reveal sometimes to the State, and some not.[9]

"For our ordinances and rites, we have two very long and fair galleries: in one of these we place patterns and samples of all manner of the more rare and excellent inventions; in the other we place the statues of all principal inventors. There we have the statue of your Columbus, that discovered the West Indies; also the inventor of ships; your monk that was the inventor of ordnance and of gunpowder;[1] the inventor of music; the inventor of letters; the inventor of printing; the inventor of observations of astronomy; the inventor of works in metal; the inventor of glass; the inventor of silk of the worm; the inventor of wine; the inventor of corn and bread; the inventor of sugars; and all these by more certain tradition than you have. Then we have divers inventors of our own, of excellent works, which since you have not seen, it were too long to

---

8. The total staff of Solomon's House is 36; a generous allowance, by Bacon's estimate, for the project of understanding the natural cosmos. Modern researchers would want a little more staff.
9. Observe Bacon's suspicion of the body politic, and the freedom which he allows to Solomon's House from political pressure.
1. Tradition credits Roger Bacon, a 13th-century monk, with the discovery of gunpowder. Bacon tactfully avoids his name

make descriptions of them; and besides, in the right understanding of those descriptions you might easily err. For upon every invention of value we erect a statue to the inventor, and give him a liberal and honorable reward. These statues are some of brass, some of marble and touchstone,[2] some of cedar and other special woods gilt and adorned; some of iron, some of silver, some of gold.

"We have certain hymns and services, which we say daily of laud and thanks to God for His marvelous works. And forms of prayer, imploring His aid and blessing for the illumination of our labors, and the turning of them into good and holy uses.

"Lastly, we have circuits or visits, of divers principal cities of the kingdom; where, as it cometh to pass, we do publish such new profitable inventions as we think good. And we do also declare natural divinations of diseases, plagues, swarms of hurtful creatures, scarcity, tempests, earthquakes, great inundations, comets, temperature of the year, and divers other things; and we give counsel thereupon, what the people shall do for the prevention and remedy of them."

And when he had said this he stood up; and I, as I had been taught, kneeled down; and he laid his right hand upon my head, and said, "God bless thee, my son, and God bless this relation which I have made. I give thee leave to publish it, for the good of other nations; for we here are in God's bosom, a land unknown." And so he left me; having assigned a value of about two thousand ducats for a bounty to me and my fellows. For they give great largesses, where they come, upon all occasions.

The rest was not perfected.

1627

2. A hard basaltic-type rock.

Prose Ornate and Unadorned

SIR THOMAS BROWNE
(1605–1682)

Sir Thomas Browne of Norwich was one of those meditative, learned, crotchety, humane persons of whom the 17th century seems full to over-flowing. He was born in London, took two degrees at Oxford, and traveled extensively abroad, finally receiving his M.D. degree at Leyden. Aged 32, he settled in Norwich, a little market town amid the broad, flat fens of East Anglia; and there he remained for 45 years, raising a family and practicing his profession. Amid the quiet day-to-day rounds of a country doctor's life, he found time to compose an occasional richly meditated and deeply felt volume of prose reflections. He was knighted by Charles II in 1671, and died ten years later at the age of 76.

Religio Medici ("A Doctor's Faith") is the first of his books. Published in 1643, though written earlier, it is a confession of religious faith, written for his own use; it balances as delicately between skepticism and belief as any essay of Montaigne's, and is written in a gorgeous, bejeweled prose which is at once sweeping and subtle. *Pseudodoxia Epidemica*, known as *Vulgar Errors* (1646), is an encyclopedia of all the delusions, mistakes, and confusions about the world of creatures which had cropped up in Browne's omnivorous reading, along with his confutations of them. From the vantage point of three centuries, it is sometimes hard to tell which is the stranger, the original error or Browne's refutation. But both are likely to be entertaining, for Browne's book is loaded with learning, shot through with whimsical and eccentric opinions, and enlivened by many bizarre digressions.

Finally, in 1658, Browne published in two little treatises the last prose which appeared during his lifetime. *The Garden of Cyrus* is a discussion of the quincunx, or five-spot pattern which results from placing four objects in the corners of a square and one at the intersection of the diagonals. Browne discovers more quincunxes in more varied places than anyone would think possible. His second discourse was occasioned by the discovery near Norwich of some prehistoric urns containing human bones. *Hydriotaphia, Urn-Burial* starts as a simple description of these particular urns, but quickly turns into a discussion of the custom of urn-burial in general, an account of various funeral practices, and finally into a series of intensely poetic meditations on life, death, and the human condition.

Sir Thomas Browne is in effect a metaphysical poet in prose. His learned mind ranges delightedly over a fantastic area of dark and half-forgotten reading, culling a witty comparison here and a curious bit of information there. He relishes the oddity of this information, much of which was exotic and old-fashioned even in his own day; but he is not simply an anti-quarian. He likes to play with ideas, and collapse vast stretches of intellectual distance into boldly compressed metaphors—as when he remarks that "Charles the Fifth can never hope to live within two Methuselahs of Hector." Like the metaphysical poets, Browne was erudite, but his erudition was never an end in itself. Instead, Browne put his curious learning to work, continually drawing acute analogies and surprising parallels to illumine a central vision of the world.

He is most at home in the ages of fabulous darkness and in those areas where doubt melts imperceptibly into faith. His perspectives are so long that in the shadow of his pen even his own age comes to seem mythical and faintly humorous. Under these vast perspectives, the country doctor of Norwich stands among a little group of enlightened skeptics, too humane to accept absolutely any dogma, including the dogma of skepticism, too reverent to think his own mind the measure of mankind, too lively in his curiosity to dismiss even the wildest doctrine without investigation.

From Religio Medici[1]

* * *

40. I am naturally bashful, nor hath conversation, age, or travel been able to effront or enharden me; yet I have one part of modesty which I have seldom discovered in another; that is (to speak truly) I am not so much afraid of death as ashamed thereof. 'Tis the very disgrace and ignominy of our natures, that in a moment can so disfigure us that our nearest friends, wife, and children stand afraid and start at us. The birds and beasts of the field that before in a natural fear obeyed us, forgetting all allegiance begin to prey upon us. This very conceit hath in a tempest disposed and left me willing to be swallowed up in the abyss of waters, wherein I had perished unseen, unpitied, without wondering eyes, tears of pity, lectures of

1. Browne wrote *Religio Medici* about 1635, when he was a little short of 30 years old (see Section 41); he had just returned from his medical studies on the continent, where he had been forced to worship—if he was to worship at all—with communities of different faiths. The essay was written as a form of personal stock-taking, in the shape of a letter to a friend; in 1642 it was printed without Browne's permission, and in 1643 reprinted in an authorized and corrected version. Our text follows the 1643 printing with a few additions, in brackets, from M. Jean-Jacques Denonain's edition based on manuscript copies (Cambridge, 1953).

The title means "A Doctor's Faith," and one might well ask why a doctor should have a special religion of his own, different from a lawyer's or a merchant's. By "faith," however, Browne does not simply mean "creed." He disposes, almost casually, of all the things his age usually meant by "faith"—doctrinal and dogmatic tenets, ceremonies and public observances, an ecclesiastical organization. Not that he is a doubter or a heretic; he accepts the establishment in every detail. But he is interested in something more mysterious and personal, which most of his essay is devoted to exploring; this is a relation to the Christian mystery of faith and resurrection, in which he believes, not because he can explain or defend it but because he cannot. Browne's position, known as "fideism," vigorously separates philosophy from faith and exempts faith from criticism by reason, while at the same time depriving it of reason's support. Previous speculators along these lines, like Montaigne, had explicitly recognized that "fideism" was a dangerous weapon of intellectual foilplay. But for Browne it answered a deep temperamental need.

mortality, and none had said, *"Quantum mutatus ab illo!"*[2] Not that I am ashamed of the anatomy of my parts or can accuse nature for playing the bungler in any part of me or my own vicious life for contracting any shameful disease up on me, whereby I might not call myself as wholesome a morsel for the worms as any.

41. Some, upon the courage of a fruitful issue[3] wherein, as in the truest chronicle, they seem to outlive themselves, can with greater patience away with death. This conceit and counterfeit subsisting in our progenies seems to me a mere fallacy, unworthy the desires of a man that can but conceive a thought of the next world; who, in a nobler ambition, should desire to live in his substance in heaven rather than his name and shadow in the earth. And therefore at my death I mean to take a total adieu of the world, not caring for a monument, history, or epitaph, not so much as the bare memory of my name to be found anywhere but in the universal register of God. I am not yet so cynical as to approve the testament of Diogenes,[4] nor do I altogether allow that *rodomontado* of Lucan—

> *Caelo tegitur, qui non habet urnam.*[5]
> He that unburied lies wants not his hearse,
> For unto him a tomb's the universe.

but commend in my calmer judgment those ingenuous intentions that desire to sleep by the urns of their fathers and strive to go the nearest way unto corruption. I do not envy the temper of crows and daws,[6] nor the numerous and weary days of our fathers before the flood. If there be any truth in astrology, I may outlive a jubilee;[7] as yet I have not seen one revolution of Saturn,[8] nor hath my pulse beat thirty years; and yet, excepting one, have seen the ashes and left underground all the kings of Europe, have been contemporary to three emperors, four Grand Seignieurs,[9] and as many popes. Methinks I have outlived myself and begin to be weary of the sun. I have shaken hands with delight in my warm blood and canicular days.[1] I perceive I do anticipate the vices of age. The world to me is but a dream or mock-show, and we all therein but pantaloons and antics[2] to my severer contemplations.

42. It is not, I confess, an unlawful prayer to desire to surpass the days of our Savior, or wish to outlive that age wherein He thought fittest to die; yet if (as divinity affirms) there shall be no gray hairs in heaven, but all shall rise in the perfect state of men, we do but

2. "How greatly changed from what he was!" The phrase was used by Aeneas of Hector, *Aeneid* II.274; Browne may be referring to an occasion when he was shipwrecked between Ireland and England in 1630.
3. Emboldened by having had children.
4. Diogenes asked his friends not to bury him but to hang him out for a scarecrow.
5. *Pharsalia* VII.819.
6. Traditionally long-lived creatures,

linked here with patriarchs like Noah and Methuselah.
7. Fifty years. Browne lived to 77.
8. Browne was born under Saturn (October 19); he was saturnine (melancholy and philosophical) by temperament; and Saturn completes a heavenly cycle in a little less than thirty years.
9. Sultans of Turkey.
1. Dog days, of July and early August, when summer heat is often at its height.
2. Jokers and clowns.

outlive those perfections in this world to be recalled unto them by a greater miracle in the next, and run on here but to be retrograde hereafter. Were there any hopes to outlive vice or a point to be superannuated from sin, it were worthy our knees to implore the days of Methuselah. But age doth not rectify but incurvate our natures, turning bad dispositions into worser habits, and, like diseases, brings on incurable vices. For every day as we grow weaker in age, we grow stronger in sin, and the number of our days doth but make our sins innumerable. The same vice committed at sixteen is not the same, though it agree in all other circumstances, at forty, but swells and doubles from the circumstance of our ages, wherein, besides the constant and inexcusable habit of transgressing, the maturity of our judgment cuts off pretence unto excuse or pardon.

Every sin, the oftener it is committed the more it acquireth in the quality of evil; as it succeeds in time, so it proceeds in degrees of badness, for as they proceed they ever multiply and, like figures in arithmetic, the last stands for more than all that went before it. [The course and order of my life would be a very death unto another. I use[3] myself to all diets, humors, airs, hunger, thirst, cold, heat, want, plenty, necessity, dangers, hazards. When I am cold I cure not myself by heat; when sick, not by physic. Those that know how I live may justly say I regard not life, nor stand in fear of death.][4] And though I think no man can live well once but he that could live twice, yet for my own part I would not live over my hours past, or begin again the thread of my days—not upon Cicero's ground[5] because I have lived them well, but for fear I should live them worse. I find my growing judgment daily instructs me how to be better, but my untamed affections and confirmed vitiosity makes me daily do worse. I find in my confirmed age the same sins I discovered in my youth. I committed many then because I was a child, and because I commit them still I am yet an infant. Therefore, I perceive a man may be twice a child before the days of dotage, and stand in need of Aeson's bath[6] before threescore.

43. And truly there goes a great deal of providence to produce a man's life unto threescore. There is more required than an able temper for those years. Though the radical humor contain in it sufficient oil for seventy, yet I perceive in some it gives no light past thirty.[7] Men assign not all the causes of long life that write whole books thereof. They that found themselves[8] on the radical

---

3. Accustom.

4. This passage was substituted for most of section 42 and all of section 43 in the manuscript copies and unauthorized editions.

5. In *De Senectute* 23, Cicero supposes the philosopher will be ready to die because he has lived well.

6. A classical fountain of youth.

7. A man's "radical humor" is the basic constitution governing his disposition—phlegm, choler, and so on; Browne compares it to the oil feeding the lamp of life.

8. Base their judgments (as to a man's longevity). Abel, of course, failed to live as long as Adam because Cain killed him.

balsam or vital sulphur of the parts determine not why Abel lived not so long as Adam. There is, therefore, a secret gloom or bottom of our days. 'Twas His wisdom to determine them, but His perpetual and waking providence that fulfills and accomplishes them, wherein the spirits, ourselves, and all the creatures of God in a secret and disputed way do execute His will. Let them not therefore complain of immaturity that die about thirty; they fall but like the whole world, whose solid and well composed substance must not expect the duration and period of its constitution; when all things are completed in it, its age is accomplished, and the last and general fever may as naturally destroy it before six thousand as me before forty. There is therefore some other hand that twines the thread of life than that of nature. We are not only ignorant in antipathies and occult qualities, our ends are as obscure as our beginnings. The line of our days is drawn by night, and the various effects therein by a pencil that is invisible, wherein, though we confess our ignorance, I am sure we do not err if we say it is the hand of God.

44. I am much taken with two verses of Lucan since I have been able not only, as we do at school to construe, but understand them:

> *Victurosque Dei celant ut vivere durent,*
> *Felix esse mori.*[9]
> We're all deluded, vainly searching ways
> To make us happy by the length of days;
> For, cunningly to make's protract this breath
> The Gods conceal the happiness of death.

There be many excellent strains in that poet, wherewith his Stoical genius hath liberally supplied him; and truly there are singular pieces in the philosophy of Zeno and doctrine of the Stoics,[1] which, I perceive, delivered in a pulpit pass for current divinity. Yet herein are they in extremes that can allow a man to be his own assassin and so highly extol the end and suicide of Cato.[2] This is indeed not to fear death but yet to be afraid of life. It is a brave act of valor to contemn death; but where life is more terrible than death, it is then the truest valor to dare to live, and herein religion hath taught us a noble example. For, all the valiant acts of Curtius, Scevola, or Codrus[3] do not parallel or match that one of Job; and sure there is no torture to the rack of a disease, nor any poniards in death itself like those in the way or prologue unto it. *Emori nolo, sed me esse mortuum nihil curo*—"I would not die but care not if I am dead." [4]

Were I of Caesar's religion I should be of his desires, and wish rather to go off at one blow than to be sawed in pieces by the grat-

9. *Pharsalia* IV.519.
1. Zeno was the first of the Stoic philosophers, who taught avoidance of passion and submission to necessity.
2. The younger Cato ("of Utica" from the place of his death) committed suicide (46 B.C.) rather than compromise with Caesar.
3. Curtius, Scevola, and Codrus all suffered (Curtius and Codrus death, Scevola mutilation) in behalf of their country.
4. Cicero, *Tusculan Disputations* I.8.

ing torture of a disease. Men that look no further than their outsides think health an appurtenance unto life, and quarrel with their constitutions for being sick. But I that have examined the parts of man and know upon what tender filaments that fabric hangs, do wonder that we are not always so; and, considering the thousand doors that lead to death, do thank my God that we can die but once. 'Tis not only the mischief of diseases and the villainy of poisons that make an end of us; we vainly accuse the fury of guns and the new inventions of death. 'Tis in the power of every hand to destroy us, and we are beholding unto every one we meet he doth not kill us. There is therefore but one comfort left, that, though it be in the power of the weakest arm to take away life, it is not in the strongest to deprive us of death. God would not exempt Himself from that; the misery of immortality in the flesh He undertook not That was in it immortal.[5] Certainly there is no happiness within this circle of flesh, nor is it in the optics of these eyes to behold felicity. The first day of our jubilee is death. The devil hath therefore failed of his desires: we are happier with death than we should have been without it. There is no misery but in himself, where there is no end of misery; and so indeed in his own sense the Stoic is in the right. He forgets that he can die who complains of misery: we are in the power of no calamity while death is in our own.

45. Now, besides this literal and positive kind of death, there are others whereof divines make mention, and those, I think, not merely metaphorical—as mortification, dying unto sin and the world. Therefore I say every man hath a double horoscope: one of his humanity, his birth; another of his Christianity, his baptism. And from this do I compute or calculate my nativity, not reckoning those *horae combustae*[6] and odd days, or esteeming myself anything before I was my Savior's and enrolled in the register of Christ. Whosoever enjoys not this life, I count him but an apparition, though he wear about him the sensible affections of flesh. In these moral acceptions, the way to be immortal is to die daily; nor can I think I have the true theory of death when I contemplate a skull or behold a skeleton with those vulgar imaginations it casts upon us. I have therefore enlarged that common *memento mori* into a more Christian memorandum: *memento quatuor novissima*,[7] those four inevitable points of us all—death, judgment, heaven, and hell. Neither did the contemplations of the heathens rest in their graves without a further thought of Rhadamanth [8] or some judicial proceeding after death, though in another way and upon suggestion of

5. Christ, who was an immortal in mortal garb, never undertook the burden of physical immortality.
6. Literally, burnt hours, hours when the moon is obscured by the sun; used here as a metaphor for the period between birth and baptism.
7. Remember the four last things. A *memento mori* is a reminder of death, generally a skull.
8. Greek judge of the underworld.

their natural reasons. I cannot but marvel from what sybil or oracle they stole the prophesy of the world's destruction by fire, or whence Lucan learned to say,

> *Communis mundo superest rogus, ossibus astra misturus*—[9]
> There yet remains to th' world one common fire
> Wherein our bones with stars shall make one pyre.

I believe the world grows near its end, yet is neither old nor decayed, nor will ever perish upon the ruins of its own principles. As the work of creation was above nature, so is its adversary, annihilation, without which the world hath not its end but its mutation. Now what fire should be able to consume it thus far without the breath of God, which is the truest consuming flame, my philosophy cannot inform me. Some believe there went not a minute to the world's creation, nor shall there go to its destruction; those six days, so punctually described, make not to them one moment but rather seem to manifest the method and idea of that great work in the intellect of God than the manner how He proceeded in its operation. I cannot dream that there should be at the last day any such judicial proceeding or calling to the bar as indeed the Scripture seems to imply and the literal commentators do conceive. For unspeakable mysteries in the Scripture are often delivered in a vulgar and illustrative way, and, being written unto man, are delivered not as they truly are but as they may be understood. Wherein, notwithstanding, the different interpretations according to different capacities may stand firm with our devotion, nor be any way prejudicial to each single edification.

46. Now, to determine the day and year of this inevitable time is not only convincible and statute-madness but also manifest impiety. How shall we interpret Elias' six thousand years [1] or imagine the secret communicated to a rabbi which God hath denied unto His angels? [2] It had been an excellent query to have posed the devil of Delphos, and must needs have forced him to some strange amphibology.[3] It hath not only mocked the predictions of sundry astrologers in ages past but the prophecies of many melancholy heads in these present, who, neither understanding reasonably things past or present, pretend a knowledge of things to come, heads ordained only to manifest the incredible effects of melancholy and to fulfill old prophecies rather than be the authors of new. "In those days there shall come wars and rumors of wars" [4] to me seems no prophecy but a constant truth, in all times verified since it was

---

9. *Pharsalia* VII.814.
1. According to Jewish tradition, Elijah (Elias) prophesied that 6,000 years would be the ultimate age of the world.
2. In Matthew xxiv.36, Christ says no man knows the hour of the Last Judgment; the "rabbi" is any rabbinical commentator, type of the esoteric exegete.
3. Pagan oracles like that at Delphos (Delphi) were often attributed by Christian writers to the work of daemons or devils; an amphibology is an ambiguous pronouncement, in which the oracles specialized.
4. Matthew xxiv.6.

pronounced. "There shall be signs in the moon and stars." [5] How comes He, then, like a thief in the night when He gives an item of his coming? That common sign drawn from the revelation of Antichrist is as obscure as any; in our common compute he hath been come these many years. But, for my own part, to speak freely, omitting those ridiculous anagrams, I am half of Paracelsus' opinion, and think that Antichrist is the philosopher's stone in divinity,[6] for the discovery and invention whereof, though there be prescribed rules and probable inductions, yet hath hardly any man attained the perfect discovery thereof. That general opinion that the world grows near its end hath possessed all ages past as nearly as ours. I am afraid that the souls that now depart cannot escape that lingering expostulation of the saints under the altar, "*Quousque Domine? How long, O Lord?*"[7] and groan in the expectation of the great jubilee.

47. This is the day that must make good that great attribute of God, His justice; that must reconcile those unanswerable doubts that torment the wisest understandings; and reduce those seeming inequalities and respective distributions in this world to an equality and recompensive justice in the next. This is that one day that shall include and comprehend all that went before it; wherein, as in the last scene, all the actors must enter to complete and make up the catastrophe of this great piece. This is the day whose memory hath only power [8] to make us honest in the dark and to be virtuous without a witness.

Ipsa sui pretium virtus sibi—that "virtue is her own reward" [9] —is but a cold principle and not able to maintain our variable resolutions in a constant and settled way of goodness. I have practiced that honest artifice of Seneca, and, in my retired and solitary imaginations, to detain me from the foulness of vice, have fancied to myself the presence of my dear and worthiest friends, before whom I should lose my head rather than be vicious. Yet herein I found that there was nought but moral honesty, and this was not to be virtuous for His sake Who must reward us at the last. I have tried if I could reach that great resolution of his, [1] to be honest without a thought of heaven or hell, and indeed I found upon a natural inclination and inbred loyalty unto virtue that I could serve her without a livery,[2] yet not in that resolved and venerable way

5. Luke xxi.25.
6. The coming of Antichrist was supposed to foreshadow the Last Judgment; Paracelsus was a doubter. Browne uses the "philosopher's stone" as an emblem of fantastic illusion. The "ridiculous anagrams" were arguments made from the names of the Popes, which, being translated into Greek or Hebrew (where every letter has a numerical value), were sometimes triumphantly added up

to the number of the Beast in the Book of Revelation, i.e., 666.
7. Revelation vi.9–10.
8. The mere thought of which hath power.
9. This was a principle of the Stoic Seneca, who describes his imaginary audience of worthy friends in *Epistle* 25.
1. I.e., Seneca's.
2. Not as a servant, without expectation of wages.

but that the frailty of my nature upon an easy temptation might be induced to forget her. The life, therefore, and spirit of all our actions is the resurrection and stable apprehension that our ashes shall enjoy the fruit of our pious endeavors. Without this, all religion is a fallacy, and those impieties of Lucian, Euripides, and Julian [3] are no blasphemies but subtle verities, and atheists have been the only philosophers.

48. How shall the dead arise is no question of my faith; to believe only possibilities is not faith but mere philosophy. [4] Many things are true in divinity which are neither inducible by reason nor confirmable by sense; and many things in philosophy confirmable by sense, yet not inducible by reason. Thus it is impossible by any solid or demonstrative reasons to persuade a man to believe the conversion of the needle to the north, though this be possible and true and easily credible upon a single experiment unto the sense. I believe that our estranged and divided ashes shall unite again; that our separated dust, after so many pilgrimages and transformations into the parts of minerals, plants, animals, elements, shall at the voice of God return into their primitive shapes and join again to make up their primary and predestinate forms. As at the creation there was a separation of that confused mass into its species, so at the destruction thereof there shall be a separation into its distinct individuals. As at the creation of the world, all the distinct species that we behold lay involved in one mass till the fruitful voice of God separated this united multitude into its several species; so at the last day, when those corrupted relics shall be scattered in the wilderness of forms and seem to have forgot their proper habits, God by a powerful voice shall command them back into their proper shapes and call them out by their single individuals.

Then shall appear the fertility of Adam and the magic of that sperm that hath dilated into so many millions. [What is made to be immortal, nature cannot—nor will the voice of God—destroy. These bodies that we behold to perish were in their created natures immortal, and liable unto death but accidentally and upon forfeit; and therefore they owe not that natural homage unto death as other bodies, but may be restored to immortality with a lesser miracle, and by a bare and easy revocation of the curse return immortal.] [5] I have often beheld as a miracle that artificial resurrec-

3. Lucian, a skeptical mocker, and Julian, an apostate emperor, are rather strangely joined with Euripides, who criticized on the stage certain moral laxities of the Olympian deities.
4. Browne, as fideist, strongly divides faith from philosophy, and boasts (in an earlier section of his essay) of being able to answer all rational criticisms of his faith with a phrase of Tertullian: *Certum est, quia impossibile est.* (It is certain [in faith] because it is impossible [in reason].)
5. Browne's speculation in the manuscript copies that man, despite an "accidental" fall, retains instincts of immortality, verges on heresy and was therefore canceled from the "authorized" editions.

tion and revivification of mercury, how being mortified into thousand shapes it assumes again its own and returns into its numerical self. Let us speak naturally and like philosophers: the forms of alterable bodies in these sensible corruptions perish not, nor, as we imagine, wholly quit their mansions, but retire and contract themselves into their secret and inaccessible parts where they may best protect themselves from the action of their antagonist. A plant or vegetable consumed to ashes, to a contemplative and school-philosopher, seems utterly destroyed and the form to have taken his leave forever. But to a sensible artist [6] the forms are not perished but withdrawn into their incombustible part, where they lie secure from the action of that devouring element. This is made good by experience which can from the ashes of a plant revive the plant and from its cinders recall it into its stalk and leaves again.[7] What the art of man can do in these inferior pieces, what blasphemy is it to affirm the finger of God cannot do in these more perfect and sensible structures? This is that mystical philosophy from whence no true scholar becomes an atheist, but from the visible effects of nature grows up a real divine, and beholds not in a dream, as Ezekiel,[8] but in an ocular and visible object the types of his resurrection.

49. Now, the necessary mansions of our restored selves are those two contrary and incompatible places we call heaven and hell. To define them or strictly to determine what and where these are surpasseth my divinity. That elegant apostle which seemed to have a glimpse of heaven hath left but a negative description thereof: which neither eye hath seen nor ear hath heard, nor can enter into the heart of man. He was translated out of himself to behold it, but, being returned into himself, could not express it.[9] St. John's description by emeralds, chrysolites, and precious stones is too weak to express the material heaven we behold.[1] Briefly, therefore, where the soul hath the full measure and complement of happiness, where the boundless appetite of that spirit remains completely satisfied, that it can neither desire addition nor alteration—that, I think, is truly heaven. And this can only be in the enjoyment of that essence whose infinite goodness is able to terminate the desires of itself and the insatiable wishes of ours: wherever God will thus manifest Himself, there is heaven, though within the circle of this sensible world.

---

6. Browne contrasts a "contemplative" philosopher with a "sensible" artist, i.e., a man who speculates with a man who experiments and founds his conclusions on sense-observations. ·
7. The experiment of reviving a plant from its ashes was many times tried; Browne seems to think it proved successful.
8. Ezekiel xxxvii.5–10 describes a vision of the Resurrection.
9. St. Paul, I Corinthians ii.9, denies that heaven can be visualized.
1. Revelation xxi.19–21 describes a heaven of glittering precious stones.

Thus the soul of man may be in heaven anywhere, even within the limits of his own proper body; and when it ceaseth to live in the body, it may remain in its own soul, that is, its Creator; and thus we may say that St. Paul, whether in the body or out of the body,[2] was yet in heaven. To place it in the empyreal or beyond the tenth sphere is to forget the world's destruction,[3] for when this sensible world shall be destroyed, all shall then be here as it is now there, an empyreal heaven, a *quasi* vacuity; when to ask where heaven is is to demand where the presence of God is, or where we have the glory of that happy vision. Moses, that was bred up in all the learning of the Egyptians, committed a gross absurdity in philosophy when with these eyes of flesh he desired to see God and petitioned his Maker, that is Truth itself, to a contradiction.[4]

Those that imagine heaven and hell neighbors, and conceive a vicinity between these two extremes upon consequence of the parable where Dives discoursed with Lazarus in Abraham's bosom,[5] do too grossly conceive of those glorified creatures whose eyes shall easily out-see the sun and behold without a perspective [6] the extremest distances. For, if there shall be in our glorified eyes the faculty of sight and reception of objects, I could think the visible species there to be in as unlimitable a way as now the intellectual. I grant that two bodies placed beyond the tenth sphere, or in a vacuity according to Aristotle's philosophy, could not behold each other because there wants a body or medium to hand and transport the visible rays of the object unto the sense.[7] But when there shall be a general defect of either medium to convey or light to prepare and dispose that medium, and yet a perfect vision, we must suspend the rules of our philosophy and make all good by a more absolute piece of optics.

50. I cannot tell how to say that fire is the essence of hell; I know not what to make of purgatory, or conceive a flame that can either prey upon or purify the substance of a soul. Those flames of sulphur mentioned in the Scriptures [8] I take not to be understood of this present hell but of that to come, where fire shall make up the

2. St. Paul says he knew a man who had been in heaven, whether in the body or out of the body the saint cannot tell (II Corinthians xii.2–5); Browne's notion that heaven is a state of mind accessible to the fleshly condition represents a private philosophical whimsy.

3. In the old Ptolemaic universe, the tenth sphere was the very outside boundary of the universe. Browne implies that when the sensible world is annihilated, God will be everywhere and everywhere alike.

4. In Exodus xxxiii.18, Moses asked God to contradict himself by becoming physically visible; in verse 20, God rebuked him.

5. The parable is in Luke xvi. Dives (which means "rich" in Latin) is the rich man of the parable.

6. Telescope.

7. Aristotle supposed (*De Anima* II.7) that in a perfect vacuum nothing could be seen, since there would be no medium to transport the "visible emanations" of objects. He would of course have been right about the sense of hearing but not about that of sight.

8. Revelation xxi.8.

complement of our tortures and have a body or subject wherein to manifest its tyranny. Some who have had the honor to be textuary in divinity are of opinion it shall be the same specifical fire with ours. This is hard to conceive, yet I can make good how even that may prey upon our bodies and yet not consume us; for in this material world there are bodies that persist invincible in the powerfullest flames, and though by the action of fire they fall into ignition and liquation, yet will they never suffer a destruction. I would gladly know how Moses with an actual fire calcined or burned the golden calf into powder,[9] for that mystical metal of gold, whose solary and celestial nature I admire, exposed unto the violence of fire, grows only hot and liquifies but consumeth not. So, when the consumable and volatile pieces of our bodies shall be defined into a more impregnable and fixed temper like gold, though they suffer from the action of flames, they shall never perish but lie immortal in the arms of fire.

And surely if this frame must suffer only by the action of this element, there will many bodies escape, and not only heaven but earth will not be at an end but rather a beginning. For, at present it is not earth but a composition of fire, water, earth, and air;[1] but at that time, spoiled of these ingredients, it shall appear in a substance more like itself, its ashes. Philosophers that opinioned the world's destruction by fire did never dream of annihilation, which is beyond the power of sublunary causes, for the last and proper action of that element is but vitrification or a reduction of a body into glass. And therefore some of our chemists facetiously affirm, yea, and urge Scripture for it, that at the last fire all shall be crystallized and reverberated into glass, which is the utmost action of that element. Nor need we fear this term of annihilation or wonder that God will destroy the works of His creation. For, man subsisting, who is and will then truly appear a microcosm, the world cannot be said to be destroyed. For the eyes of God and perhaps also of our glorified selves shall as really behold and contemplate the world in its epitome or contracted essence, as now they do at large and in its dilated substance. In the seed of a plant, to the eyes of God and to the understanding of man, there exist, though in an invisible way, the perfect leaves, flowers, and fruit thereof; for things that are *in posse*[2] to the sense are actually existent to the understanding. Thus God beholds all things, Who contemplates as fully His works in their epitome as in their full volume, and beheld as amply the

---

9. Exodus xxxii.20 says that Moses not only burnt the golden calf and ground it to powder, but strewed it on the water and made the children of Israel drink of it.

1. The four Aristotelian elements.

2. A state of potential being.

whole world in that little compendium of the sixth day [3] as in the scattered and dilated pieces of those five before.

51. Men commonly set forth the torments of hell by fire and the extremity of corporal afflictions, and describe hell in the same method that Mahomet doth heaven. This indeed makes a noise and drums in popular ears; but if this be the terrible piece thereof, it is not worthy to stand in diameter with heaven, whose happiness consists in that part that is best able to comprehend it, that immortal essence, that translated divinity and colony of God, the soul. Surely, though we place hell under earth, the devil's walk and purlieu is about it. Men speak too popularly who place it in those flaming mountains [4] which to grosser apprehensions represent hell. The heart of man is the place the devil dwells in. I feel sometimes a hell within myself; Lucifer keeps his court in my breast, Legion is revived in me.[5] There are as many hells as Anaxagoras' conceited worlds.[6] There was more than one hell in Magdalen when there were seven devils,[7] for every devil is an hell unto himself. He holds enough of torture in his own *ubi* [8] and needs not the misery of circumference to afflict him; and thus a distracted conscience here is a shadow or introduction unto hell hereafter. Who can but pity the merciful intention of those hands that do destroy themselves? The devil, were it in his power, would do the like; which being impossible, his miseries are endless, and he suffers most in that attribute wherein he is impassable,[9] his immortality.

52. I thank God, and with joy I mention it, I was never afraid of hell nor never grew pale at the description of that place. I have so fixed my contemplations on heaven that I have almost forgot the idea of hell, and am afraid rather to lose the joys of the one than endure the misery of the other. To be deprived of them is a perfect hell and needs, methinks, no addition to complete our afflictions. That terrible term hath never detained me from sin, nor do I owe any good action to the name thereof. I fear God, yet am not afraid of Him; His mercies make me ashamed of my sins before His judgments afraid thereof. These are the forced and secondary method of His wisdom, which He useth but as the last remedy and upon provocation; a course rather to deter the wicked than incite the virtuous to His worship. I can hardly think there was ever any scared into

3. Man was made on the sixth day as a summary (microcosm) of the work of the first five.
4. Volcanoes.
5. Lucifer is the devil, Legion (from Mark v.9) the assembly of unclean spirits.
6. Browne has apparently confused Anaxagoras with Anaximander who "con-ceited" (i.e., imagined) an indefinite number of worlds.
7. Luke viii.2 tells the story of Christ's driving seven devils out of Mary Magdalene.
8. Literally, in Latin, *where;* in context, his own self.
9. Inassailable.

heaven. They go the fairest way to heaven that would serve God without a hell; other mercenaries that crouch unto Him in fear of hell, though they term themselves the servants, are indeed but the slaves of the Almighty.

53. And to be true and speak my soul, when I survey the occurrences of my life and call into account the finger of God, I can perceive nothing but an abyss and mass of mercies, either in general to mankind or in particular to myself. And, whether out of the prejudice of my affection or an inverting and partial conceit of His mercies, I know not, but those which others term crosses, afflictions, judgments, misfortunes, to me, who enquire farther into them than their visible effects, they both appear and in event have ever proved the secret and dissembled favors of His affection. It is a singular piece of wisdom to apprehend truly and without passion the works of God, and so well to distinguish His justice from His mercy as not to miscall those noble attributes. Yet it is likewise an honest piece of logic so to dispute and argue the proceedings of God as to distinguish even His judgments into mercies. For God is merciful unto all because better to the worst than the best deserve, and to say He punisheth none in this world, though it be a paradox, is no absurdity. To one that hath committed murder, if the judge should only ordain a fine, it were a madness to call this a punishment and to repine at the sentence rather than admire the clemency of the judge. Thus, our offences being mortal, and deserving not only death but damnation, if the goodness of God be content to traverse and pass them over with a loss, misfortune, or disease, what frenzy were it to term this a punishment rather than an extremity of mercy, and to groan under the rod of His judgments rather than admire the scepter of His mercies!

Therefore to adore, honor, and admire Him is a debt of gratitude due from the obligation of our nature, states, and conditions; and with these thoughts, he that knows them best will not deny that I adore Him. That I obtain heaven and the bliss thereof is accidental and not the intended work of my devotion, it being a felicity I can neither think to deserve nor scarce in modesty to expect. For these two ends of us all, either as rewards or punishments, are mercifully ordained and disproportionally disposed unto our actions; the one being so far beyond our deserts, the other so infinitely below our demerits.

* * *

1635

1642 (*surreptitious*)
1643 (*authentic*)

From Hydriotaphia, Urn-Burial
Chapter V

Now since these dead bones have already outlasted the living ones of Methuselah,[1] and in a yard under ground, and thin walls of clay, outworn all the strong and specious buildings above it, and quietly rested under the drums and tramplings of three conquests;[2] what prince can promise such diuturnity unto his relics, or might not gladly say,

Sic ego componi versus in ossa velim?[3]

Time, which antiquates antiquities, and hath an art to make dust of all things, hath yet spared these minor monuments.

In vain we hope to be known by open and visible conservatories, when to be unknown was the means of their continuation, and obscurity their protection. If they died by violent hands, and were thrust into their urns, these bones become considerable, and some old philosophers would honor them, whose souls they conceived most pure, which were thus snatched from their bodies, and to retain a stronger propension[4] unto them; whereas they weariedly left a languishing corpse, and with faint desires of reunion. If they fell by long and aged decay, yet wrapped up in the bundle of time, they fall into indistinction, and make but one blot with infants. If we begin to die when we live, and long life be but a prolongation of death, our life is a sad composition; we live with death, and die not in a moment. How many pulses made up the life of Methuselah, were work for Archimedes: common counters sum up the life of Moses his man.[5] Our days become considerable, like petty sums, by minute accumulations; where numerous fractions make up but small round numbers; and our days of a span long make not one little finger.[6]

If the nearness of our last necessity[7] brought a nearer conformity unto it, there were a happiness in hoary hairs, and no calamity in half-senses. But the long habit of living indisposeth us for dying; when avarice makes us the sport of death, when even David grew politicly cruel, and Solomon could hardly be said to be the wisest of men.[8] But many are too early old, and before the date of age.

1. Methuselah lived 969 years (Genesis v.27).
2. Roman, Saxon, and Norman. "Diuturnity": long life.
3. "Thus I, when dead, should wish to go to rest" (Tibullus).
4. Attraction. "They" are the philosophers, who traditionally die in bed.
5. I.e., the ordinary man, alluded to in Psalm xc, supposed to be by Moses; it says (verse 10), "The days of our years are three-score years and ten."
6. In certain ancient arithmetics, Browne's note tells us, "the little finger of the right hand, contracted, signified an hundred."
7. I.e., death.
8. David suffered in his last years from the rebellion and death of his son Absalom; Solomon was seduced by fair idolatresses to the service of alien gods.

Adversity stretcheth our days, misery makes Alcmena's nights,[9] and time hath no wings unto it. But the most tedious being is that which can unwish itself, content to be nothing, or never to have been, which was beyond the malcontent of Job, who cursed not the day of his life, but his nativity:[1] content to have so far been as to have a title to future being; although he had lived here but in an hidden state of life, and as it were an abortion.

What song the Sirens sang, or what name Achilles assumed when he hid himself among women, though puzzling questions, are not beyond all conjecture.[2] What time the persons of these ossuaries entered the famous nations of the dead, and slept with princes and counselors, might admit a wide[3] solution. But who were the proprietaries of these bones, or what bodies these ashes made up, were a question above antiquarism; not to be resolved by man, nor easily perhaps by spirits, except we consult the provincial guardians, or tutelary observators.[4] Had they made as good provision for their names as they have done for their relics, they had not so grossly erred in the art of perpetuation. But to subsist in bones, and be but pyramidally extant,[5] is a fallacy in duration. Vain ashes, which in the oblivion of names, persons, times, and sexes, have found unto themselves a fruitless continuation, and only arise unto late posterity, as emblems of mortal vanities, antidotes against pride, vainglory, and madding vices. Pagan vainglories, which thought the world might last forever, had encouragement for ambition; and, finding no Atropos[6] unto the immortality of their names, were never damped with the necessity of oblivion. Even old ambitions had the advantage of ours, in the attempts of their vainglories, who, acting early and before the probable meridian[7] of time, have by this time found great accomplishment of their designs, whereby the ancient heroes have already outlasted their monuments and mechanical preservations. But in this latter scene of time, we cannot expect such mummies unto our memories, when ambition may fear the prophecy of Elias,[8] and Charles the Fifth can never hope to live within two Methuselahs of Hector.[9]

9. Sleeping with Alcmena to beget Hercules, Jove enjoyed himself so much that he forbade the sun to rise for one day; thus there were three nights in a row.

1. Job iii.

2. Suetonius (*Lives of the Twelve Caesars*) says that Tiberius went to the "silly and laughable extreme" of testing grammarians (whom he admired) with these questions.

3. Approximate.

4. Browne, who believed in witches, also believed in angelic protectors, both personal ("tutelary observators") and of more extended jurisdiction ("provincial guardians").

5. Like a pyramid, famous though the person buried within it is long forgotten.

6. Of the three Fates, Clotho, Lachesis, and Atropos, the last-named held the scissors. They cut the threads of mortal life.

7. Noon, midday.

8. "That the earth will last but 6,000 years" [Browne's note]. There is no warrant for this in the Bible.

9. Since Methuselah lived to be 969, Browne's estimate is conservative: Hector, the hero of Troy, had more than three "Methuselahs" head start on Charles V (1500–58).

And therefore, restless inquietude for the diuturnity of our memories unto present considerations seems a vanity almost out of date, and superannuated piece of folly. We cannot hope to live so long in our names as some have done in their persons; one face of Janus[1] holds no proportion unto the other. 'Tis too late to be ambitious. The great mutations of the world are acted, or time may be too short for our designs. To extend our memories by monuments, whose death we daily pray for,[2] and whose duration we cannot hope, without injury to our expectations in the advent of the last day, were a contradiction to our beliefs. We whose generations are ordained in this setting part of time[3] are providentially taken off from such imaginations; and, being necessitated to eye the remaining particle of futurity, are naturally constituted unto thoughts of the next world, and cannot excusably decline the consideration of that duration, which maketh pyramids pillars of snow, and all that's past a moment.

Circles and right lines limit and close all bodies, and the mortal right-lined circle must conclude and shut up all.[4] There is no antidote against the opium of time, which temporally considereth all things: our fathers find their graves in our short memories, and sadly tell us how we may be buried in our survivors. Gravestones tell truth scarce forty years.[5] Generations pass while some trees stand, and old families last not three oaks. To be read by bare inscriptions like many in Gruter,[6] to hope for eternity by enigmatical epithets or first letters of our names, to be studied by antiquaries, who we were, and have new names given us like many of the mummies, are cold consolations unto the students of perpetuity, even by everlasting languages.

To be content that times to come should only know there was such a man, not caring whether they knew more of him, was a frigid ambition in Cardan;[7] disparaging his horoscopal inclination and judgment of himself. Who cares to subsist like Hippocrates' patients, or Achilles' horses in Homer, under naked nominations, without deserts and noble acts, which are the balsam of our memories, the *entelechia*[8] and soul of our subsistences? To be nameless in worthy deeds exceeds[9] an infamous history. The Canaanitish woman lives more happily without a name than Herodias with one.

---

1. Janus, Roman god of doorways and beginnings (hence "January"), had two heads facing in opposite directions, the past and the future.
2. We pray for the "death" and destruction of our graves at the Last Judgment.
3. The image is from the sunset.
4. Θ (*theta*), the first letter of Θάνατος ("death"), symbolizes it.
5. Because old corpses are dug up and replaced with new; see *Hamlet* V.i; and Donne, *The Relic,* lines 3–4.
6. Jan Gruter (1560–1627) was a Dutch scholar who published a collection of Latin inscriptions.
7. Girolamo Cardano, a famous Italian mathematician and occultist of the 16th century. Taking his own horoscope, he found himself destined to great things.
8. Essence, perfection.
9. Is better than.

And who had not rather have been the good thief than Pilate?[1]

But the iniquity of oblivion blindly scattereth her poppy, and deals with the memory of men without distinction to merit of perpetuity. Who can but pity the founder of the pyramids? Herostratus lives that burnt the temple of Diana;[2] he is almost lost that built it. Time hath spared the epitaph of Adrian's horse,[3] confounded that of himself. In vain we compute our felicities by the advantage of our good names, since bad have equal durations, and Thersites is like to live as long as Agamemnon.[4] Who knows whether the best of men be known, or whether there be not more remarkable persons forgot than any that stand remembered in the known account of time? Without the favor of the everlasting register, the first man had been as unknown as the last, and Methuselah's long life had been his only chronicle.

Oblivion is not to be hired: the greater part must be content to be as though they had not been, to be found in the register of God, not in the record of man. Twenty-seven names make up the first story, and the recorded names ever since contain not one living century.[5] The number of the dead long exceedeth all that shall live. The night of time far surpasseth the day, and who knows when was the equinox? Every hour adds unto that current arithmetic,[6] which scarce stands one moment. And since death must be the Lucina[7] of life, and even pagans could doubt whether thus to live were to die; since our longest sun sets at right descensions, and makes but winter arches, and therefore it cannot be long before we lie down in darkness, and have our light in ashes;[8] since the brother of death daily haunts us with dying mementos, and time that grows old in itself bids us hope no long duration; diuturnity is a dream and folly of expectation.

Darkness and light divide the course of time, and oblivion shares with memory a great part even of our living beings; we slightly remember our felicities, and the smartest strokes of affliction leave but short smart upon us. Sense endureth no extremities, and sorrows destroy us or themselves. To weep into stones are fables.[9] Afflictions induce callosities;[1] miseries are slippery, or fall like snow

---

1. The woman of Canaan had faith in Jesus; Herodias asked for the head of John the Baptist (Matthew xv.27–28; Mark vi.22–25). The good thief, crucified beside Christ, had his blessing; Pontius Pilate, the procurator of Judea, typifies the sanctimonious villain.
2. Herostratus of Ephesus set fire to the great temple in that city simply in order to gain a stupid immortality.
3. Adrian (Hadrian) was emperor of Rome in the 2nd century A.D.
4. Thersites, the scurrilous scoffer of the *Iliad,* is contrasted with Agamemnon, the royal leader.

5. Genesis i–v tells the story of the human race from the creation to the flood in 27 names; of all the names since the flood, not 100 ("century") are really living ones.
6. That continual addition.
7. Roman goddess of childbirth, hence, "the deliverance."
8. At funerals, Browne's note says, the Jews place a wax candle in a pot of ashes beside the corpse. The "brother of death" is sleep.
9. Like Niobe, whose grief turned her to stone.
1. Callouses, hardness, indifference.

upon us, which notwithstanding is no unhappy stupidity. To be ignorant of evils to come, and forgetful of evils past, is a merciful provision in nature, whereby we digest the mixture of our few and evil days, and, our delivered senses not relapsing into cutting remembrances, our sorrows are not kept raw by the edge of repetitions. A great part of antiquity contented their hopes of subsistency with a transmigration of their souls: a good way to continue memories, while having the advantage of plural successions, they could not but act something remarkable in such variety of beings, and enjoying the fame of their passed selves, make accumulation of glory unto their last durations. Others, rather than be lost in the uncomfortable night of nothing, were content to recede into the common being, and make one particle of the public soul of all things, which was no more than to return into their unknown and divine original again. Egyptian ingenuity[2] was more unsatisfied, contriving their bodies in sweet consistencies, to attend the return of their souls. But all was vanity, feeding the wind, and folly. The Egyptian mummies, which Cambyses or time hath spared, avarice now consumeth.[3] Mummy is become merchandise, Mizraim cures wounds, and Pharaoh is sold for balsams.

In vain do individuals hope for immortality, or any patent[4] from oblivion, in preservations below the moon; men have been deceived even in their flatteries above the sun, and studied conceits to perpetuate their names in heaven. The various cosmography of that part hath already varied the names of contrived constellations: Nimrod is lost in Orion, and Osiris in the Dog Star.[5] While we look for incorruption in the heavens, we find they are but like the earth, durable in their main bodies, alterable in their parts: whereof beside comets and new stars, perspectives[6] begin to tell tales, and the spots that wander about the sun, with Phaethon's favor,[7] would make clear conviction.

There is nothing strictly immortal but immortality. Whatever hath no beginning may be confident of no end; all others have a dependent being and within the reach of destruction; which is the peculiar[8] of that necessary essence that cannot destroy itself; and the highest strain of omnipotency, to be so powerfully constituted as not to suffer even from the power of itself. But the sufficiency

2. The reference is to embalming practices.
3. The story of Cambyses ravaging Egypt is told in Herodotus, Book III. Powdered mummy was sold in the 17th century as medicine (see Donne, *Love's Alchemy*, line 24). "Mizraim": i.e., Egypt; Mizraim was a son of Ham (Genesis x.6–14).
4. Protection.
5. I.e., the names of the stars change —Osiris to Sirius, Nimrod the mighty hunter (Genesis x.9) to Orion.
6. Telescopes.
7. Phaethon was an unfortunate son of the Sun, who tried to drive his father's chariot and nearly set the universe on fire. His erratic course reminds Browne of spots which wander across the sun's face, and which had only recently been charted by astronomers, starting with Galileo.
8. Characteristic.

of Christian immortality frustrates all earthly glory, and the quality of either state after death makes a folly of posthumous memory. God, who can only[9] destroy our souls, and hath assured our resurrection, either of our bodies or names hath directly promised no duration. Wherein there is so much of chance that the boldest expectants have found unhappy frustration; and to hold long subsistence seems but a scape in oblivion.[1] But man is a noble animal, splendid in ashes, and pompous in the grave, solemnizing nativities and deaths with equal luster, nor omitting ceremonies of bravery[2] in the infamy of his nature.

Life is a pure flame, and we live by an invisible sun within us. A small fire sufficeth for life, great flames seemed too little after death, while men vainly affected precious pyres, and to burn like Sardanapalus;[3] but the wisdom of funeral laws found the folly of prodigal blazes, and reduced undoing fires unto the rule of sober obsequies, wherein few could be so mean as not to provide wood, pitch, a mourner, and an urn.

Five languages secured not the epitaph of Gordianus.[4] The man of God[5] lives longer without a tomb than any by one, invisibly interred by angels, and adjudged to obscurity, though not without some marks directing human discovery. Enoch and Elias,[6] without either tomb or burial, in an anomalous state of being, are the great examples of perpetuity, in their long and living memory, in strict account being still on this side death, and having a late part yet to act upon this stage of earth. If in the decretory term of the world[7] we shall not all die but be changed, according to received translation, the last day will make but few graves; at least quick resurrections will anticipate lasting sepultures; some graves will be opened before they be quite closed, and Lazarus be no wonder.[8] When many that feared to die shall groan that they can die but once, the dismal state is the second and living death, when life puts despair on the damned; when men shall wish the coverings of mountains, not of monuments, and annihilations shall be courted.[9]

While some have studied monuments, others have studiously declined them; and some have been so vainly boisterous that they durst not acknowledge their graves, wherein Alaricus[1] seems most

9. Who alone can.
1. Weak trick against forgetfulness.
2. Proud ceremonies.
3. Sardanapalus burned up a palace full of eunuchs, concubines, and treasures as his funeral pyre; later civilizations often forbade such lavish displays.
4. The epitaph of Gordianus, emperor of Rome (238–244), was written in five languages; but it was obliterated in all of them by his successor, Licinius.
5. Moses (see Deuteronomy xxxiv).
6. Enoch and "Elias" (Elijah) were translated straight to heaven (Genesis v.24; II Kings ii.11).
7. The Last Judgment.
8. Lazarus, the dead man raised by Christ (John xi).
9. The damned soul shrieking for mountains to shield him from the wrath of God was a figure beloved of preachers. See Luke xxiii.30 and Revelation vi.16.
1. Alaric, the Gothic invader, was buried in the bed of the river Busento (A.D. 410).

subtle, who had a river turned to hide his bones at the bottom. Even Sulla,[2] that thought himself safe in his urn, could not prevent revenging tongues, and stones thrown at his monument. Happy are they whom privacy makes innocent, who deal so with men in this world that they are not afraid to meet them in the next; who, when they die, make no commotion among the dead, and are not touched with that poetical taunt of Isaiah.[3]

Pyramids, arches, obelisks were but the irregularities of vainglory, and wild enormities of ancient magnanimity. But the most magnanimous resolution rests in the Christian religion, which trampleth upon pride, and sits on the neck of ambition, humbly pursuing that infallible perpetuity unto which all others must diminish their diameters, and be poorly seen in angles of contingency.[4]

Pious spirits who passed their days in raptures of futurity made little more of this world than the world that was before it, while they lay obscure in the chaos of pre-ordination, and night of their fore-beings. And if any have been so happy as truly to understand Christian annihilation, ecstasies, exolution,[5] liquefaction, transformation, the kiss of the spouse, gustation of God, and ingression into the divine shadow, they have already had an handsome anticipation of heaven; the glory of the world is surely over, and the earth in ashes unto them.

To subsist in lasting monuments, to live in their productions, to exist in their names and predicament of chimeras,[6] was large satisfaction unto old expectations, and made one part of their Elysiums.[7] But all this is nothing in the metaphysics of true belief. To live indeed is to be again ourselves, which being not only an hope but an evidence in noble believers, 'tis all one to lie in St. Innocent's churchyard,[8] as in the sands of Egypt: ready to be anything, in the ecstasy of being ever, and as content with six foot as the *moles* of Adrianus.[9]

> —*Tabesne cadavera solvat,*
> *An rogus, haud refert.*
> —LUCAN

1658

---

2. Roman politician and general, who died 78 B.C.
3. In Isaiah xiv the mighty ones of the earth are taunted with their approaching downfall into hell.
4. The angle of contingency is the smallest possible angle; Browne puns on the idea that all these lesser perpetuities are subject to accident ("contingency").
5. The loosening or freeing of the spirit from the bonds of the body.

6. In the condition of phantasms.
7. The pagan afterworld.
8. In Paris, where bodies soon consume; contrasted with the desert, where they last a long time.
9. Adrian's (Hadrian's) tomb, now Castel San Angelo in Rome, the type of a magnificent mausoleum. The Latin tag is translated, "By the swift funeral pyre or slow decay / (No matter which) the bodies pass away" (Lucan, *Pharsalia* VII.809).

ROBERT BURTON
(1577–1640)

Robert Burton was a quiet Oxford scholar who wrote a book on melancholy. But melancholy was such a strange subject, and Burton was such a strange man, that his book swelled into a vast, overstuffed, rhapsodical account of everything under the sun. From edition to edition it grew, as Burton crammed into it quotations and stories, ideas, digressions, counter-digressions, and scraps of dusty information from his fantastic reading—until finally, it became a world in itself, a kind of magic Robert-Burton-land, in which many people still delight to wander endlessly and without direction.

"Melancholy," for the 17th century, was simply a kind of disease. In a healthy person, the four humors (phlegm, choler, blood, and melancholy) were supposed to be properly tempered, that is, in a state of balance. The predominance of any one would produce an imbalance, an eccentricity, and ultimately a sort of madness. Of all the professions, scholars were popularly supposed to be most prone to melancholy. Their life was sedentary and solitary; the black choler, or bile, pooled up in their livers, stagnated, settled, and finally degenerated, by a drying-out process, to the desperate condition of "adust." We today would call them, at our kindest, neurotics.

Robert Burton early recognized this as his own temper; his cure for the disease (as men still fight fire with fire) was to immerse himself in it. *The Anatomy of Melancholy*, though it was once thought of as a farrago of quaint quotations, is first and foremost a medical treatise; Sir William Osler once called it the greatest medical treatise ever written by a layman. The book is systematically divided into three sections, the first dealing with the definition, causes, symptoms, and properties of melancholy, the second dealing with its cure, and the third describing two particularly stubborn and troublesome varieties of the disease, love melancholy and religious melancholy. Burton takes his function as medical teacher with real seriousness, and his lore represents the very best medical opinion of his day. In spite of his obsolete vocabulary and sometimes primitive theories of causation, many of his insights are still startling in their acuteness.

But aside from his straightforward effort to understand melancholy as a disease, aside from his often-interesting observations as a moralist and social philosopher, Burton is also, in the strict sense, a humorist. He loves to play with words and with concepts; he has a warty sense of the human comedy and of himself as an actor in it. The game he plays with the natural history of melancholy is not unlike that described many years later by Swift, in *A Tale of a Tub*. To divert the monster hysteria from attacking the ship of his sanity, he tosses out diverting, empty barrels of words, quirks, and conceits. There is a mighty rumble of hollow coopers' ware throughout *The Anatomy of Melancholy*; and the spate of words which rushes forth is, as it were, a measure of the anxious pressures behind it.

About Burton's life proper there is not much to say. He came to Oxford in 1593, was elected a scholar of Christ Church in 1599, and stayed there the rest of his life. He never traveled, never married, and lived, as far as

can be told, entirely among his books. In 1621 the first edition of the
Anatomy appeared; later editions, all much augmented, came out in 1624,
1628, 1632, and 1638—not to mention three more in the century, after
Burton's death. It is good to know that Burton, after writing these vast
folios to cure himself of melancholy, did in the end find some relief. Now
and then in later life, it is recorded that he came down with the "vapors";
but he would go down to the bridge at Oxford, to listen to the barge-men
swearing at each other, and laugh himself back into good humor at the
spectacle.

Burton's passion for Democritus, "the laughing philosopher," is easily
understood in the light of this lifelong preoccupation with melancholy. The
Anatomy first came forth under the pseudonym of "Democritus Junior,"
and when Burton addresses the reader in his introduction, he speaks as
"Democritus Junior to the Reader."

From The Anatomy of Melancholy
From *Democritus Junior to the Reader*

* * * How would our Democritus have been affected to see a
wicked caitiff,[1] or "fool, a very idiot, a fungus, a golden ass, a monster of men, to have many good men, wise men, learned men to attend upon him with all submission as an appendix to his riches, for
that respect alone, because he hath more wealth and money, and to
honor him with divine titles, and bombast epithets,"[2] to smother
him with fumes and eulogies, whom they know to be a dizzard,[3] a
fool, a covetous wretch, a beast, etc., "because he is rich"? To see
sub exuviis leonis onagrum, a filthy loathsome carcass, a Gorgon's
head puffed up by parasites,[4] assume this unto himself, glorious
titles, in worth an infant, a Cuman ass, a painted sepulcher, an
Egyptian temple![5] To see a withered face, a diseased, deformed,
cankered complexion, a rotten carcass, a viperous mind, and Epicurean[6] soul set out with orient pearls, jewels, diadems, perfumes,
curious elaborate works, as proud of his clothes as a child of his
new coats; and a goodly person, of an angel-like divine countenance,
a saint, an humble mind, a meek spirit clothed in rags, beg, and now

1. Wretch, criminal.
2. The quoted matter is adapted and
translated from More's *Utopia*, Book
II, "Of Their Journeying or Traveling
Abroad." Burton's prose is so stuffed
with quotations that sources can be
indicated here only for the most extended passages.
3. Idiot. blockhead (analogous to
"dizzy").
4. "*Sub* * * * *onagrum*": an ass in
a lion's skin. Gorgons, in Greek mythology, were three winged women, so
hideous that the sight of them turned

the beholder to stone; their heads were
covered with snakes instead of hair.
5. Glorious without, filthy within. Why
asses from Cumae were considered duller
than other asses cannot be said; but the
expression had long been proverbial.
For "painted sepulcher," see Matthew
xxiii.27.
6. Epicurus' doctrine that absence of
pain is the greatest good was perverted
by popular opinion into an endorsement
of the pursuit of sensual pleasure for its
own sake. "Curious": exquisite.

ready to be starved. To see a silly[7] contemptible sloven in apparel, ragged in his coat, polite in speech, of a divine spirit, wise; another neat in clothes, spruce, full of courtesy,[8] empty of grace, wit, talk nonsense!

To see so many lawyers, advocates, so many tribunals, so little justice; so many magistrates, so little care of the common good; so many laws, yet never more disorders; *tribunal litium segetem*,[9] the tribunal a labyrinth, so many thousand suits in one court sometimes, so violently followed. To see *iniustissimum saepe iuri praesidentem, impium religioni, imperitissimum eruditioni, otiosissimum labori, monstrosum humanitati*.[1] To see a lamb executed, a wolf pronounce sentence, *latro* arraigned, and *fur* sit on the bench,[2] the judge severely punish others, and do worse himself, *eundem furtum facere et punire, rapinam plectere, quum sit ipse raptor*.[3] Laws altered, misconstrued, interpreted *pro* and *con*, as the judge is made by friends, bribed, or otherwise affected as a nose of wax, good today, none tomorrow; or firm in his opinion, cast[4] in his! Sentence prolonged, changed, *ad arbitrium iudicis*,[5] still the same case, "one thrust out of his inheritance, another falsely put in by favor, false forged deeds or wills." *Incisae leges negliguntur*,[6] laws are made and not kept; or if put in execution, they be some silly ones that are punished. As put case it be fornication, the father will disinherit or abdicate[7] his child, quite cashier him (out, villain, begone, come no more in my sight); a poor man is miserably tormented with loss of his estate perhaps, goods, fortunes, good name, forever disgraced, forsaken, and must do penance to the utmost; a mortal sin, and yet make the most of it, *nunquid aliud fecit*, saith Tranio in the poet,[8] *nisi quod faciunt summis nati generibus?* he hath done no more than what gentlemen usually do. * * *

Our *summum bonum*[9] is commodity, and the goddess we adore *Dea Moneta*, Queen Money, to whom we daily offer sacrifice, which steers our hearts, hands, affections, all: that most powerful goddess, by whom we are reared, depressed, elevated, esteemed the sole commandress of our actions, for which we pray, run, ride, go, come, labor, and contend as fishes do for a crumb that falleth into

---

7. Lowly.
8. Courtliness.
9. "The tribunal a thicket of cases."
1. "Often a most unjust man presides over justice, an impious man over religion, a most ignorant man decides questions of learning, a most lazy man questions of labor, a monster questions of humanity."
2. *"Latro"*: a holdup man; *"fur"*: a sneak thief.
3. "The same man commits theft and

punishes it; he deplores the rape when he is himself the rapist."
4. Convicted.
5. At the whim of the judge.
6. "Once engraved, the laws are not enforced."
7. Disown; "cashier": discard.
8. Plautus. Burton cites from *The Haunted House* a phrase to the effect that Tranio did nothing but what the "best people" do.
9. Highest good.

the water. It's not worth, virtue (that's *bonum theatrale*[1]), wisdom, valor, learning, honesty, religion, or any sufficiency for which we are respected, but money, greatness, office, honor, authority; honesty is accounted folly; knavery, policy; men admired out of opinion, not as they are, but as they seem to be: such shifting, lying, cogging,[2] plotting, counterplotting, temporizing, flattering, cozening, dissembling, "that of necessity one must highly offend God if he be conformable to the world, *Cretizare cum Crete*,[3] or else live in contempt, disgrace and misery." One takes upon him temperance, holiness; another austerity; a third an affected kind of simplicity; whenas indeed he, and he, and he, and the rest are "hypocrites, ambidexters,"[4] outsides, so many turning pictures, a lion on the one side, a lamb on the other. How would Democritus have been affected to see these things!

To see a man turn himself into all shapes like a chameleon, or as Proteus, *omnia transformans sese in miracula rerum*,[5] to act twenty parts and persons at once, for his advantage, to temporize and vary like Mercury the Planet,[6] good with good, bad with bad; having a several face, garb, and character for everyone he meets; of all religions, humors, inclinations; to fawn like a spaniel, *mentitis et mimicis obsequiis*,[7] rage like a lion, bark like a cur, fight like a dragon, sting like a serpent, as meek as a lamb, and yet again grin like a tiger, weep like a crocodile, insult over some, and yet others domineer over him, here command, there crouch, tyrannize in one place, be baffled in another, a wise man at home, a fool abroad to make others merry.

To see so much difference betwixt words and deeds, so many parasangs[8] betwixt tongue and heart, men like stage players act variety of parts, give good precepts to others, soar aloft, whilst they themselves grovel on the ground.

To see a man protest friendship, kiss his hand, *quem mallet truncatum videre*,[9] smile with an intent to do mischief, or cozen him whom he salutes, magnify his friend unworthy with hyperbolical eulogiums; his enemy albeit a good man, to vilify and disgrace him, yea all his actions, with the utmost that liver and malice can invent.[1]

To see a servant able to buy out his master, him that carries the

---

1. A "theatrical good," only for show.
2. Tricking at dice.
3. "Be a Cretan at Crete"; i.e., when at Rome do as the Romans do.
4. Double-dealers.
5. "Transforming himself into everything that is monstrous." Proteus, old man of the sea, had the gift of changing shape at will.
6. Because its orbit lies between the sun and that of the earth, the planet Mercury has phases.
7. "With lying and feigned obsequiousness."
8. Persian measure of distance, four miles or less.
9. "Which he would rather see cut off."
1. The liver secretes bile, hence is the seat of malice.

mace more worth than the magistrate, which Plato, lib. 11, *De Leg.*, absolutely forbids,[2] Epictetus abhors. A horse that tills the land fed with chaff, an idle jade[3] have provender in abundance; him that makes shoes go barefoot himself, him that sells meat almost pined; a toiling drudge starve, a drone flourish.

To see men buy smoke for wares, castles built with fools' heads, men like apes follow the fashions in tires,[4] gestures, actions: if the king laugh, all laugh;

> *Rides? majore cachinno*
> *Concutitur, flet si lachrymas conspexit amici.*[5]

Alexander stooped, so did his courtiers; Alphonsus turned his head, and so did his parasites.[6] Sabina Poppea, Nero's wife, wore amber-colored hair, so did all the Roman ladies in an instant; her fashion was theirs.

To see men wholly led by affection,[7] admired and censured out of opinion without judgment: an inconsiderate multitude, like so many dogs in a village, if one bark all bark without a cause: as fortune's fan turns, if a man be in favor, or commanded by some great one, all the world applauds him; if in disgrace, in an instant all hate him, and as at the sun when he is eclipsed, that erst took no notice, now gaze and stare upon him.

To see a man wear his brains in his belly, his guts in his head, an hundred oaks on his back,[8] to devour a hundred oxen at a meal, nay more, to devour houses and towns, or as those anthropophagi,[9] to eat one another.

To see a man roll himself up like a snowball, from base beggary to right worshipful and right honorable titles, unjustly to screw himself into honors and offices; another to starve his genius, damn his soul to gather wealth, which he shall not enjoy, which his prodigal son melts and consumes in an instant.

To see the κακοζηλίαν[1] of our times, a man bend all his forces, means, time, fortunes, to be a favorite's favorite's favorite, etc., a parasite's parasite's parasite, that may scorn the servile world as having enough already.

To see an hirsute beggar's brat that lately fed on scraps, crept and whined, crying to all and for an old jerkin[2] ran on errands, now ruffle in silk and satin, bravely mounted, jovial and polite, now

---

2. In Book XI of *The Laws*. Epictetus was a Stoic philosopher of the 1st century A.D.
3. Horse of inferior breed, worthless beast.
4. Attire.
5. "You laugh? A loud guffaw shakes him. You weep / And with your flowing tears he'll measure keep" (Juvenal iii.100–101).
6. Alexander is Alexander the Great;

Alphonsus any one of numerous kings by that name, who ruled over Spain, Portugal, and Castille.
7. Affectation.
8. I.e., the income from 100 oak trees (chopped down on his estate and sold for lumber) is on his back (in the form of gaudy clothes).
9. Man-eaters, cannibals.
1. Evil ambition.
2. Leather jacket.

scorn his old friends and familiars, neglect his kindred, insult over his betters, domineer over all.

To see a scholar crouch and creep to an illiterate peasant for a meal's meat; a scrivener better paid for an obligation;[3] a falconer receive greater wages than a student; a lawyer get more in a day than a philosopher in a year, better reward for an hour, than a scholar for a twelvemonth's study; him that can paint Thaïs,[4] play on a fiddle, curl hair, etc., sooner get preferment than a philologer or a poet.

To see a fond mother, like Aesop's ape, hug her child to death, a wittol[5] wink at his wife's honesty, and too perspicuous in all other affairs; one stumble at a straw, and leap over a block; rob Peter, and pay Paul; scrape unjust sums with one hand, purchase great manors by corruption, fraud, and cozenage, and liberally to distribute to the poor with the other, give a remnant to pious uses, etc. Penny wise, pound foolish; blind men judge of colors; wise men silent, fools talk; find fault with others, and do worse themselves; denounce that in public which he doth in secret; and which Aurelius Victor[6] gives out of Augustus, severely censure that in a third, of which he is most guilty himself.

To see a poor fellow, or an hired servant venture his life for his new master that will scarce give him his wages at year's end; a country colone[7] toil and moil, till and drudge for a prodigal idle drone, that devours all the gain, or lasciviously consumes with phantastical expenses; a noble man in a bravado to encounter death, and for a small flash of honor to cast away himself; a worldling tremble at an executor, and yet not fear hell-fire;[8] to wish and hope for immortality, desire to be happy, and yet by all means avoid death, a necessary passage to bring him to it.

To see a foolhardy fellow like those old Danes, *qui decollari malunt quam verberari*,[9] die rather than be punished, in a sottish humor embrace death with alacrity, yet scorn to lament his own sins and miseries, or his dearest friends' departures.

To see wise men degraded, fools preferred, one govern towns and cities, and yet a silly woman overrules him at home; command a province, and yet his own servants or children prescribe laws to him, as Themistocles' son did in Greece;[1] "What I will, said he, my mother will, and what my mother will, my father doth." To see

3. Although not a lawyer, a scrivener could draw up simple legal documents like an "obligation" (bond).
4. A famous Egyptian courtesan of antiquity, hence any whore. To "paint" her is to prepare her to ply her trade.
5. Cuckold.
6. Aurelius Victor wrote, ca. 360, a history of the Roman emperors down to Constantine. Augustus was emperor

27 B.C.–A.D. 14.
7. Farm laborer. "Moil": drudge.
8. I.e., a worldly-minded heir fears the legal executor of the will, but not damnation itself.
9. "Who would rather be beheaded than whipped."
1. Themistocles, Athenian general (ca. 525–ca. 460 B.C.); Burton takes the story from Plutarch, *On Education*.

horses ride in a coach, men draw it; dogs devour their masters; towers build masons; children rule; old men go to school; women wear the breeches; sheep demolish towns, devour men, etc.[2] And in a word, the world turned upside downward. *O viveret Democritus!*[3]

To insist in every particular were one of Hercules' labors, there's so many ridiculous instances, as motes[4] in the sun. *Quantum est in rebus inane!* (How much vanity there is in things!) And who can speak of all? *Crimine ab uno disce omnes,*[5] take this for a taste. * * *

1623

2. The enclosure movement, which drove tillers from the soil and replaced them with sheep, is glanced at here.
3. "O, would that Democritus were alive!"
4. Spots.
5. "Learn of all crimes from a single example."

THOMAS HOBBES
(1588–1679)

1628: Discovers Euclid.
1651: Publishes *Leviathan*, returns to England, and makes submission to Cromwell.

Thomas Hobbes was one of the first, and remains one of the most interesting, of English philosophers. Aside from being a man of many ideas, as a philosopher ought to be, he is interesting as a stylist and also as a personality. Alternately bold and timid, radical and reactionary, he raised questions of fundamental importance, even when he did not solve them; his writing is rich both in brilliant insights and amazing oversights, and has generally proved as stimulating to his critics as to his admirers.

Hobbes was born in Armada-year; "twins came forth," he said in his metrical autobiography, "myself and fear." And the yearning for security in an insecure world is perhaps the key to his career. Yet in this, as in every other aspect of his thought, there was a paradox. Yearning for peace, he was willing to sacrifice so many positive convictions that men of all factions grew suspicious of him; and before he died (comfortably in his bed at 90), talk had even been heard of charging the good old gentleman with heresy and burning him at the stake.

Outwardly, at least, his ninety years were uneventful. After taking an A.B. at Oxford in the first years of the century, he was tutor to some of the great houses, and secretary to some of the great men, of England. Among the great men was Francis Bacon, to whom he always professed his indebtedness; it is less easy to estimate what he learned in the course of a number of trips to the Continent. At the age of 40, he discovered Euclid. Thumbing through the volume (which he had picked up by accident in a drawing room), he turned to the 47th Element of Book I, read it, and said emphatically, "By God, this is impossible!" But then he read the demonstration, which referred him to earlier propositions; he read those in turn, and was carried back to axioms with which he could not disagree. The rigor and coherence of geometric method made a lasting impression on him.

Hobbes was in England when the Long Parliament convened in 1640; supposing himself in danger, he promptly left for the Continent; and in Paris he continued to press his speculations. By the age of 55, he had written a preliminary account of his philosophical position, in three treatises, on physical law, human nature, and the state. Owing to the troubled times, their publication was irregular and their immediate influence slight; but the tripartite division of interest which they revealed runs through all of Hobbes's work. Although his political conclusions aroused most interest and opposition, they were always intimately associated with and dependent on his notions of physics and psychology.

While still at Paris, in 1651, he published his best-known book, *Leviathan*; and, late in the same year, seeing Cromwell firmly established in power, he came back to England and made his peace with the Puritan government. The gist of Hobbes's argument in *Leviathan* is that men must have a supreme authority for the sake of quietness, hence any authority which is actually supreme and actually maintaining quiet is to be recognized. These coldly realistic views of Hobbes's were a scandal to the devoted Royalists, whose belief in the divinely bestowed right of kingship kept them in hungry exile from the wicked usurper, Cromwell. But Hobbes, unperturbed by criticism, proceeded to publish the books on physics (*De Corpore*, 1654) and psychology (*De Homine*, 1658) which underlay and provided broad philosophic support for the scandalous views of *Leviathan*.

After the Restoration, Royalist indignation with Hobbes reached a peak when he not only went unpunished for his "defection," but was pensioned by his old friend and former pupil, Charles II. Throughout the Restoration, his outspoken materialism made him a cause of scandal around the court, but his caustic tongue made him feared; and the indolent, cynical king was fond of him. "Here comes the bear to be baited," he used to say whenever Hobbes appeared in court; implying thereby that if the philosopher was bearish and uncouth, those who snapped at him were dogs. In any event, Hobbes survived in intellectual vigor and physical comfort. His philosophic position had been outlined many years before, and the Anglican authorities actively discouraged both the reprinting of his old books and the issuing of new ones; yet his dominion over the minds of men grew steadily during the last half of the century. For his own pleasure, he wrote, but did not publish, a history of his own time (*Behemoth*, published 1680); he translated both the epics of Homer into English verse (1674–75); he squared the circle to his own satisfaction, and quarreled vigorously with John Wallis, the Savilian Professor of Geometry at Oxford, who told him vigorously that he was mistaken; he wrote his autobiography in Latin verses, and sustained himself, generally, to admiration.

The best introduction to *Leviathan* is really the engraving prefixed to the first edition. At the top of the picture is Leviathan himself, the state, represented as a handsome man of superhuman stature. In his right hand he holds the sword of civil power, and in his left hand the staff of a bishop, signifying spiritual power. Before him, dwarfed by his enormous form, is a city. But the curious thing about the giant himself is that his entire body consists of little interlaced people, so tiny that from a distance one cannot distinguish them. Leviathan is in fact the body politic made visible—a social body composed of atoms of individual men, just as the human body is composed of individual cells, the cells composed of tinier atoms, and the atoms of tinier particles still.

Hobbes's view of society, man, and matter is uniformly atomic and reductive. Dissection is his constant study. Every process and every object is to be reduced to its component parts; every word must be divided into its simplest elements, and each of those elements must be defined with absolute clarity before we can talk with certainty about anything at all. Thus our two selections from *Leviathan*, which seem to be about widely different topics, are really to a single point. Reason is a process of adding and subtracting things which are represented by word-counters; it is a way in which man gains control of his naturally chaotic environment. And the public reason embodied in the ruler is strictly analogous. It is a way in which man gains control of a social environment which in nature is absolutely lawless. Hobbes's argument is a classic of mechanical consistency; it combines the magnificent inclusiveness of the old organic view of the world with the vigorous particularity of a new materialism. The materialism horrified most of Hobbes's contemporaries, and to combat it they developed a whole series of brilliant philosophical engines. But it was also a seminal position in its own right. Hobbes presented materialism dogmatically and applied it mechanically; but the 18th-century philosophers—those of France perhaps even more than those of England—developed from it a flexible and skeptical rationalism of great vitality.

From Leviathan
From *Part I, Chapter 5. Of Reason and Science*

When a man reasoneth, he does nothing else but conceive a sum total, from addition of parcels,[1] or conceive a remainder, from subtraction of one sum from another; which, if it be done by words, is conceiving of the consequence of the names of all the parts, to the name of the whole; or from the names of the whole and one part, to the name of the other part. And though in some things, as in numbers, besides adding and subtracting, men name other operations, as multiplying and dividing, yet they are the same; for multiplication is but adding together of things equal; and division, but subtracting of one thing as often as we can. These operations are not incident to numbers only, but to all manner of things that can be added together and taken one out of another. For as arithmeticians teach to add and subtract in numbers; so the geometricians teach the same in lines, figures solid and superficial, angles, proportions, times, degrees of swiftness, force, power, and the like; the

1. Particles, particulars.

logicians teach the same in consequences of words; adding together two names to make an affirmation, and two affirmations to make a syllogism, and many syllogisms to make a demonstration; and from the sum or conclusion of a syllogism, they subtract one proposition to find the other. Writers of politics add together pactions[2] to find men's duties; and lawyers, laws and facts, to find what is right and wrong in the actions of private men. In sum, in what matter soever there is place for addition and subtraction, there also is place for reason; and where these have no place, there reason has nothing at all to do.

Out of all which we may define, that is to say determine, what that is which is meant by this word *reason*, when we reckon it amongst the faculties of the mind. For reason, in this sense, is nothing but reckoning, that is adding and subtracting, of the consequences of general names agreed upon, for the marking and signifying of our thoughts. I say marking them when we reckon by ourselves, and signifying when we demonstrate, or approve our reckonings to other men.

And, as in arithmetic, unpracticed men must, and professors themselves may often, err, and cast up false; so also in any other subject of reasoning, the ablest, most attentive, and most practiced men may deceive themselves, and infer false conclusions; not but that reason itself is always right reason, as well as arithmetic is a certain and infallible art; but no one man's reason, nor the reason of any one number of men, makes the certainty; no more than an account is therefore well cast up because a great many men have unanimously approved it. And therefore, as when there is a controversy in an account, the parties must by their own accord set up, for right reason, the reason of some arbitrator or judge, to whose sentence they will both stand, or their controversy must either come to blows or be undecided, for want of a right reason constituted by nature; so it is also in all debates of what kind soever. And when men that think themselves wiser than all others clamor and demand right reason for judge, yet seek no more but that things should be determined by no other men's reason but their own, it is as intolerable in the society of men, as it is in play after trump is turned, to use for trump on every occasion that suit whereof they have most in their hand. For they do nothing else that will have every of their passions, as it comes to bear sway in them, to be taken for right reason, and that in their own controversies; bewraying[3] their want of right reason by the claim they lay to it.

The use and end of reason is not the finding of the sum and truth of one, or a few consequences, remote from the first definitions, and settled significations of names; but to begin at these, and proceed from one consequence to another. For there can be no certainty of

2. Agreements, contracts.   3. Disclosing.

the last conclusion, without a certainty of all those affirmations and negations on which it was grounded and inferred. As when a master of a family, in taking an account, casteth up the sums of all the bills of expense into one sum; and not regarding how each bill is summed up by those that give them in account, nor what it is he pays for, he advantages himself no more than if he allowed the account in gross, trusting to every of the accountant's skill and honesty. So also in reasoning of all other things, he that takes up conclusions on the trust of authors, and doth not fetch them from the first items in every reckoning, which are the significations of names settled by definitions, loses his labor, and does not know anything, but only believeth.

When a man reckons without the use of words, which may be done in particular things (as when upon the sight of any one thing, we conjecture what was likely to have preceded, or is likely to follow upon it), if that which he thought likely to follow, follows not, or that which he thought likely to have preceded it, hath not preceded it, this is called error; to which even the most prudent men are subject. But when we reason in words of general signification, and fall upon a general inference which is false, though it be commonly called error, it is indeed an absurdity, or senseless speech. For error is but a deception, in presuming that somewhat is past or to come; of which, though it was not past, or not to come, yet there was no impossibility discoverable. But when we make a general assertion, unless it be a true one, the possibility of it is inconceivable. And words whereby we conceive nothing but the sound, are those we call absurd, insignificant, and nonsense. And therefore if a man should talk to me of a round quadrangle, or accidents of bread in cheese,[4] or immaterial substances, or of a free subject, a free will, or any free, but free from being hindered by opposition; I should not say he were in an error, but that his words were without meaning, that is to say, absurd.

I have said before, in the second chapter, that a man did excel all other animals in this faculty, that when he conceived anything whatsoever, he was apt to inquire the consequences of it, and what effects he could do with it. And now I add this other degree of the same excellence, that he can by words reduce the consequences he finds to general rules, called theorems, or aphorisms; that is, he can reason, or reckon, not only in number, but in all other things whereof one may be added unto, or subtracted from another.

But this privilege is allayed[5] by another; and that is, by the privilege of absurdity, to which no living creature is subject but men only. And of men, those are of all most subject to it that profess

---

4. Hobbes uses "accident" in the technical philosophical sense of "secondary quality" (i.e., nonessential accompaniment), but he also glances at the doctrine of transubstantiation, that Christ is present in the sacrament.
5. Modified.

philosophy. For it is most true that Cicero saith of them some-where, that there can be nothing so absurd but may be found in the books of philosophers. And the reason is manifest. For there is not one of them that begins his ratiocination from the definitions, or explications of the names they are to use; which is a method that hath been used only in geometry, whose conclusions have thereby been made indisputable.

(1) The first cause of absurd conclusions I ascribe to the want of method, in that they begin not their ratiocination from definitions; that is, from settled significations of their words; as if they could cast account without knowing the value of the numeral words, one, two, and three.

And whereas all bodies enter into account upon divers considerations, which I have mentioned in the precedent chapter;[6] these considerations being diversely named, divers absurdities proceed from the confusion, and unfit connection of their names into assertions. And therefore:

(2) The second cause of absurd assertions, I ascribe to the giving of names of bodies to accidents, or of accidents to bodies; as they do that say faith is "infused," or "inspired"; when nothing can be poured, or breathed into anything, but body; and that extension is body; that phantasms are spirits, etc.

(3) The third I ascribe to the giving of the names of the accidents of bodies without us, to the accidents of our own bodies; as they do that say the color is in the body, the sound is in the air, etc.

(4) The fourth, to the giving of the names of bodies to names or speeches; as they do that say that there be things universal; that a living creature is genus, or a general thing, etc.

(5) The fifth, to the giving of the names of accidents to names and speeches; as they do that say the nature of a thing is its definition, a man's command is his will, and the like.

(6) The sixth, to the use of metaphors, tropes, and other rhetorical figures, instead of words proper. For though it be lawful to say, for example, in common speech, "the way goeth, or leadeth hither, or thither"; "the proverb says this or that," whereas ways cannot go, nor proverbs speak; yet in reckoning, and seeking of truth, such speeches are not to be admitted.

(7) The seventh, to names that signify nothing, but are taken up and learned by rote from the schools, as *hypostatical, transubstantiate, consubstantiate, eternal-now,* and the like canting of schoolmen.[7]

6. Chapter 4 has argued that bodies may be calculated in several ways: as quantities of matter; as they possess accidents or secondary qualities (e.g., being hot or blue or in motion); as they produce certain effects on us; and as certain names have been assigned to them. On Hobbes's scale of reality, matter ranks highest; hence, the further one abstracts from matter, the greater the risk of error.

7. Hobbes is most suspicious of terms developed by medieval theologians ("schoolmen") to describe and explain religious abstractions.

To him that can avoid these things it is not easy to fall into any absurdity, unless it be by the length of an account; wherein he may perhaps forget what went before. For all men by nature reason alike, and well, when they have good principles. For who is so stupid as both to mistake in geometry, and also to persist in it when another detects[8] his error to him? * * *

Part I, Chapter 13. *Of the Natural Condition of Mankind as Concerning Their Felicity and Misery*

Nature hath made men so equal in the faculties of body and mind as that, though there be found one man sometimes manifestly stronger in body or of quicker mind than another, yet when all is reckoned together, the difference between man and man is not so considerable as that one man can thereupon claim to himself any benefit, to which another may not pretend as well as he. For as to the strength of body, the weakest has strength enough to kill the strongest, either by secret machination, or by confederacy with others that are in the same danger with himself.

And as to the faculties of the mind—setting aside the arts grounded upon words, and especially that skill of proceeding upon general and infallible rules, called science; which very few have, and but in few things; as being not a native faculty, born with us; nor attained, as prudence, while we look after somewhat else—I find yet a greater equality amongst men than that of strength. For prudence is but experience, which equal time equally bestows on all men, in those things they equally apply themselves unto. That which may perhaps make such equality incredible is but a vain conceit of one's own wisdom, which almost all men think they have in a greater degree than the vulgar—that is, than all men but themselves and a few others, whom by fame, or for concurring with themselves, they approve. For such is the nature of men, that howsoever they may acknowledge many others to be more witty, or more eloquent, or more learned, yet they will hardly believe there be many so wise as themselves; for they see their own wit at hand, and other men's at a distance. But this proveth rather that men are in that point equal, than unequal. For there is not ordinarily a greater sign of the equal distribution of anything than that every man is contented with his share.

From this equality of ability ariseth equality of hope in the attaining of our ends. And therefore if any two men desire the same thing, which nevertheless they cannot both enjoy, they become enemies; and in the way to their end (which is principally their own conservation, and sometimes their delectation only) endeavor to destroy or subdue one another. And from hence it comes to pass that where an invader hath no more to fear than another man's single

8. Exposes.

power; if one plant, sow, build, or possess a convenient seat, others may probably be expected to come prepared with forces united, to dispossess and deprive him, not only of the fruit of his labor, but also of his life or liberty. And the invader again is in the like danger of another.

And from this diffidence[9] of one another, there is no way for any man to secure himself so reasonable as anticipation; that is, by force or wiles to master the persons of all men he can, so long, till he see no other power great enough to endanger him, and this is no more than his own conservation requireth, and is generally allowed. Also because there be some, that taking pleasure in contemplating their own power in the acts of conquest, which they pursue farther than their security requires; if others that otherwise would be glad to be at ease within modest bounds, should not by invasion increase their power, they would not be able long time, by standing only on their defense, to subsist. And by consequence, such augmentation of dominion over men being necessary to a man's conservation, it ought to be allowed him.

Again, men have no pleasure, but on the contrary a great deal of grief, in keeping company, where there is no power able to overawe them all. For every man looketh that his companion should value him at the same rate he sets upon himself; and upon all signs of contempt, or undervaluing, naturally endeavors, as far as he dares (which amongst them that have no common power to keep them in quiet, is far enough to make them destroy each other), to extort a greater value from his contemners by damage, and from others by the example.

So that in the nature of man, we find three principal causes of quarrel. First, competition; second, diffidence; thirdly, glory.

The first maketh men invade for gain; the second, for safety; and the third, for reputation. The first use violence to make themselves masters of other men's persons, wives, children, and cattle; the second, to defend them; the third, for trifles, as a word, a smile, a different opinion, and any other sign of undervalue, either direct in their persons, or by reflection in their kindred, their friends, their nation, their profession, or their name.

Hereby it is manifest that during the time men live without a common power to keep them all in awe, they are in that condition which is called war; and such a war as is of every man against every man. For war consisteth not in battle only, or the act of fighting, but in a tract of time wherein the will to contend by battle is sufficiently known, and therefore the notion of time is to be considered in the nature of war, as it is in the nature of weather. For as the nature of foul weather lieth not in a shower or two of rain, but in an inclination thereto of many days together; so the nature of war

9. Lack of faith, mistrust.

consisteth not in actual fighting, but in the known disposition thereto, during all the time there is no assurance to the contrary. All other time is peace.

Whatsoever therefore is consequent to a time of war, where every man is enemy to every man; the same is consequent to the time wherein men live without other security than what their own strength and their own invention shall furnish them withal. In such condition there is no place for industry, because the fruit thereof is uncertain, and consequently no culture of the earth; no navigation, nor use of the commodities that may be imported by sea; no commodious building; no instruments of moving, and removing, such things as require much force; no knowledge of the face of the earth; no account of time; no arts; no letters; no society; and which is worst of all, continual fear, and danger of violent death; and the life of man, solitary, poor, nasty, brutish, and short.

It may seem strange to some man that has not well weighed these things, that nature should thus dissociate, and render men apt to invade and destroy one another; and he may therefore, not trusting to this inference, made from the passions, desire perhaps to have the same confirmed by experience. Let him therefore consider with himself, when taking a journey, he arms himself and seeks to go well accompanied; when going to sleep, he locks his doors; when even in his house he locks his chests; and this when he knows there be laws, and public officers, armed, to revenge all injuries shall be done him; what opinion he has of his fellow subjects, when he rides armed; of his fellow citizens, when he locks his doors; and of his children, and servants, when he locks his chests. Does he not there as much accuse mankind by his actions, as I do by my words? But neither of us accuse man's nature in it. The desires and other passions of man are in themselves no sin. No more are the actions that proceed from those passions, till they know a law that forbids them, which, till laws be made, they cannot know; nor can any law be made, till they have agreed upon the person that shall make it.

It may peradventure be thought there was never such a time nor condition of war as this; and I believe it was never generally so, over all the world; but there are many places where they live so now. For the savage people in many places of America, except the government of small families, the concord whereof dependeth on natural lust, have no government at all and live at this day in that brutish manner, as I said before. Howsoever, it may be perceived what manner of life there would be, where there were no common power to fear; by the manner of life which men that have formerly lived under a peaceful government use to degenerate into in a civil war.[1]

1. Hobbes may well be thinking of such famous accounts of savage civil wars as that of Thucydides (whom he translated).

But though there had never been any time wherein particular men were in a condition of war one against another; yet in all times, kings and persons of sovereign authority, because of their independency, are in continual jealousies, and in the state and posture of gladiators; having their weapons pointing, and their eyes fixed on one another; that is, their forts, garrisons, and guns upon the frontiers of their kingdoms; and continual spies upon their neighbors; which is a posture of war. But because they uphold thereby the industry of their subjects, there does not follow from it that misery which accompanies the liberty of particular men.

To this war of every man against every man, this also is consequent: that nothing can be unjust. The notions of right and wrong, justice and injustice, have there no place. Where there is no common power, there is no law; where no law, no injustice. Force and fraud are in war the two cardinal virtues. Justice and injustice are none of the faculties neither of the body nor mind. If they were, they might be in a man that were alone in the world, as well as his senses and passions. They are qualities that relate to men in society, not in solitude. It is consequent also to the same conditions that there be no propriety,[2] no dominion, no *mine* and *thine* distinct; but only that to be every man's, that he can get; and for so long as he can keep it. And thus much for the ill condition which man by mere nature is actually placed in; though with a possibility to come out of it, consisting partly in the passions, partly in his reason.

The passions that incline men to peace are fear of death, desire of such things as are necessary to commodious living, and a hope by their industry to obtain them. And reason suggesteth convenient articles of peace, upon which men may be drawn to agreement. These articles are they which otherwise are called the Laws of Nature whereof I shall speak more particularly in the two following chapters.

1651

2. Property.

Character-Writers, Historians, Biographers

During the first part of the 17th century, the writing of set "characters" flourished; the second half of the century was a great age of historians and biographers, of diarists and the first writers of prose narratives approximating novels. It is hard not to see here a primitive sort of relationship—as if the same sort of curiosity about human nature were being satisfied in all these various genres.

The "character," as the mode most remote from modern usage, calls for the first word of explanation. Its origin lies in the work of Theophrastus, the pupil, associate, and successor of Aristotle. The *Characters* of Theophrastus perfectly expressed the classifying, "scientific" temper of the 3rd century B.C. They were short lists of things that certain types of people did, loosely analogous to the type characters of New Comedy. Only the "bad" people that Theophrastus described have come down to us; if he wrote about "good" people, those essays have not survived. Thus the character originally had a didactic, even a satiric purpose; and it was inherent in the situation that types, not individuals, should be the chief center of interest.

On the whole, these little prose sketches by Theophrastus were not imitated widely, and do not represent a major literary mode of antiquity. Thumbnail sketches of human types have always been useful in sermons, histories, and various forms of story-telling—witness, for example, the Prologue to the *Canterbury Tales*. But the character as an art form in its own right, a full-length, small-scale literary portrait, was not revived until the early 17th century. The revival was hastened when Isaac Casaubon, in 1592, translated Theophrastus' little book from Greek into Latin, but the brief, feverish vogue of the character between 1600 and 1660 had many other causes. For instance, in early characters like Joseph Hall's *Malcontent* one can see pretty clearly that the form accorded conveniently with the 17th-century theory of "humors" as exemplified in the plays of Jonson. A man's ruling passion, or prevailing humor, could be traced in all the actions of his life, and to expose it to healthful ridicule was socially therapeutic as well as morally sound. In addition, the character-writers were very often men of the world, and while they devoutly continued to profess a didactic purpose, they were clearly delighted to show off their knowledge of people high and low.

From the age of Charles I through the Protectorate and Restoration, England enjoyed a great age of portrait-painting, as the pictures of Anthony

Van Dyck and Peter Lely survive to show us; and the art of portraiture in prose also flourished as never before. In the work of Edward Hyde, Earl of Clarendon, one can distinguish the full-dress formal portrait; this presentation is incidental to a history in the grand style, and while it has the artificial dignity of a formal occasion, it also has a florid and elegant energy, not easily matched outside the sculpture of Bernini. Besides, Clarendon was a good hater; and his best portraits are of political opponents, like Hampden and Cromwell, where his shrewd appraisal of an antagonist's strength is often seen struggling with an active dislike of the man's principles and person.

Clarendon was the greatest painter of portraits in prose, and his history is the most finished example of the historian's art, which the century produced. Clarendon's book is a true history because it offers to derive meaning from a broad panorama of events; unlike chronicles, or books of merely antiquarian interest, it has a design and arrives at a conclusion. Clarendon and his masterpiece do not stand quite alone in the century; at its beginning, Sir Walter Ralegh wrote an eloquent and encyclopedic *History of the World* (1614); and important historical studies of specialized topics were not lacking—witness Selden's *History of Tithes* (1618), and Sprat's *History of the Royal Society* (1667). English antiquarians (Camden, Spelman, Cotton, Selden) were deservedly famous throughout the century. But in the field of historical writing proper, 17th-century England produced few works which can stand on the same shelf with the great Continental historians, Davila, Guicciardini, and Machiavelli. Much more characteristic is the mass of vivid and picturesque narrative, rising out of the Civil Wars, which we are tempted to call "personal history." Such diverse persons as Sir Philip Warwick, Mrs. Lucy Hutchinson, Bishop Gilbert Burnet, the Count de Gramont, the Duchess of Newcastle, and Sir Kenelm Digby produced books which might all be described as "memoirs of their lives, times, and opinions." Intimate, entertaining, and very often unreliable, these books are less histories themselves than the raw materials of histories to be written by other men. Modern students have found in the 17th century a particularly happy testing ground for their historical theories and their literary abilities; the Whig and Tory schools of history founded themselves primarily on differing analyses of 17th-century events.

To call Izaak Walton the father of English biography is certainly an overstatement; yet it is true in the same sense that Clarendon is the father of English historians. Both men brought to the forms in which others had worked before them a new interest in the telling particular fact, a new concern for the perception of human character. Both men were partisans; neither man had any conception of that motivation in depth which is the keynote of modern biography and history. Yet both treat their subjects, not like chroniclers or photographers, but like literary artists who are concerned above all to render the highlights and dramatic shadings.

Walton's biographies rather overshadow accomplishments in this line for the rest of the century. His five lives, describing the careers of four great churchmen and a great lay friend of the church, are not followed in the latter part of the century by any great spate of biographical work. Perhaps the times were too turbulent to produce balanced judgments of such otherwise ideal biographical subjects as Cromwell, Queen Elizabeth, or Sir Walter Ralegh. Yet, just as in history, a vast amount of work was done in accumulating the materials of future biographies. Men like John Aubrey and Anthony à Wood worked on the thin dividing line between biography, antiquarianism, and scandal-mongering. They compiled vast, disorderly dossiers on their contemporaries and predecessors—accounts of their doings and sayings, invaluable for the modern biographer, but which the compilers themselves were scarcely able to cast into proper literary form. Aubrey never even began to try to sort out his muddled notes; and Wood produced only a big biographical dictionary of his university, *Athenae Oxonienses* (1691–92). The century produced some fine autobiographies —an egotistical one by Edward Herbert of Cherbury, a political one by Clarendon, a metrical one by Hobbes, a spiritual one by Bunyan. It was the century of the great diarists, Samuel Pepys and John Evelyn. But one does not exaggerate in saying that Walton is its only great biographer.

JOSEPH HALL
(1574–1656)

Joseph Hall claimed, with some justice, to be the first English satirist; he also managed to be one of the first English character-writers. In fact, he was an indefatigable man, who produced poems, moral essays, works of religious controversy, meditative and contemplative writings, and literary works of every description, besides serving as Bishop of Exeter and later of Norwich. His *Characters of Virtues and Vices*, published in 1608, have an obvious moral intent, explicitly avowed in the Theophrastian title; in addition to its earnest concern with virtue, his mind is dry and witty, his style homely and energetic.

The Malcontent

He is neither well full nor fasting; and though he abound with complaints, yet nothing dislikes[1] him but the present; for what he condemned while it was, once past, he magnifies and strives to recall it out of the jaws of Time. What he hath he sees not, his eyes are so taken up with what he wants; and what he sees he cares not for, because he cares so much for that which is not. When his friend carves him the best morsel, he murmurs that it is a happy feast wherein each one may cut for himself. When a present is sent him, he asks, "Is this all?" and "What, no better?" and so accepts it as if he would have his friend know how much he is bound to him for vouchsafing to receive it. It is hard to entertain him with a pro-portionable[2] gift. If nothing, he cries out of unthankfulness; if little, that he is basely regarded; if much, he exclaims of flattery and ex-pectation of a large requital. Every blessing hath somewhat to dis-parage and distaste it. Children bring cares, single life is wild and

1. Displeases. 2. Appropriate.

solitary; eminency is envious,[3] retiredness obscure; fasting painful, satiety unwieldy; religion nicely[4] severe, liberty is lawless; wealth burdensome, mediocrity contemptible. Everything faulteth either in too much or too little. This man is ever headstrong and self-willed, neither is he always tied to esteem or pronounce according to reason; some things he must dislike he knows not wherefore, but he likes them not; and otherwhere, rather than not censure, he will accuse a man of virtue. Everything he meddleth with he either findeth imperfect or maketh so; neither is there anything that soundeth so harsh in his ear as the commendation of another, whereto yet perhaps he fashionably[5] and coldly assenteth, but with such an after-clause of exception as doth more than mar his former allowance. And if he list not to give a verbal disgrace,[6] yet he shakes his head and smiles, as if his silence should say, "I could, and will not." And when himself is praised without excess, he complains that such imperfect kindness hath not done him right. If but an unseasonable shower cross his recreation, he is ready to fall out with heaven, and thinks he is wronged if God will not take his times when to rain, when to shine. He is a slave to envy and loseth flesh with fretting, not so much at his own infelicity, as at others' good; neither hath he leisure to joy in his own blessings whilst another prospereth.[7] Fain would he see some mutinies, but dare not raise them; and suffers his lawless tongue to walk through the dangerous paths of conceited alterations,[8] but so as in good manners he had rather thrust every man before him when it comes to acting. Nothing but fear keeps him from conspiracies, and no man is more cruel when he is not manacled with danger. He speaks nothing but satires and libels, and lodgeth no guests in his heart but rebels. The inconstant and he agree well in their felicity, which both place in change, but herein they differ: the inconstant man affects that which will be, the malcontent commonly that which was. Finally, he is a querulous cur, whom no horse can pass by without barking at;[9] yea, in the deep silence of night the very moonshine openeth his clamorous mouth; he is the wheel of a well-couched firework that flies out on all sides, not without scorching itself. Every ear was long ago weary of him, and he is now almost weary of himself. Give him but a little respite, and he will die alone, of no other death than others' welfare.

1608

---

3. Exposed to envy.
4. Fastidiously.
5. Conventionally.
6. Slight.
7. In this section of the character, Hall

is glancing at the Puritans.
8. "Imaginary changes" in church government, proposed by the Puritans, were hateful to Hall.
9. Without his barking at it.

SIR THOMAS OVERBURY
(1581–1613)

Sir Thomas Overbury was a courtier, lawyer, and man of affairs, who took service under Robert Carr, later Earl of Somerset. Having opposed his patron's marriage to the divorced Countess of Essex, he was sent to the Tower on a pretext, and there, apparently, slowly poisoned. The whole affair was a mysterious scandal, which aroused much indignant comment by the popular party against the court. A set of *Characters*, some of which were doubtless by Overbury, but many of which were by other hands, remained among his papers, and were published the year after his death, in 1614. Overbury's popular reputation as an innocent victim of courtly intriguers lent wings to their popularity.

A Puritan

Is a diseased piece of Apocrypha:[1] bind him to the Bible, and he corrupts the whole text; ignorance, and fat feed are his founders; his nurses, railing, rabies, and round breeches;[2] his life is but a borrowed blast of wind, for between two religions, as between two doors, he is ever whistling. Truly whose child he is, is yet unknown, for willingly his faith allows no father:[3] only thus far his pedigree is found, Bragger, and he flourished about a time first; his fiery zeal keeps him continually costive,[4] which withers him into his own translation, and till he eat a Schoolman,[5] he is hidebound; he ever prays against nonresidents,[6] but is himself the greatest discontinuer, for he never keeps near his text: anything that the law allows, but marriage, and March beer, he murmurs at; what it disallows and holds dangerous, makes him a discipline. Where the gate stands open, he is ever seeking a stile; and where his learning ought to climb, he creeps through; give him advice, you run into *traditions*, and urge a modest course, he cries out *councils*.[7] His greatest care is to contemn obedience, his last care to serve God handsomely and cleanly; he is now become so cross a kind of teaching, that should the church enjoin

1. The suspect or doubtful books of the Bible.
2. Abuse, madness, and gross fat—with, perhaps, a hit at the Dutch, who wore baggy trousers, and among whom the Protestant sects flourished. "Rabies" may also include a pun on "rabbis"—the text of the original reads "rabbies."
3. The Puritans were much opposed to historical traditions in the church, hence to those early writers known as "fathers of the church." "Bragger" is an imaginary figure of the first ages of history, on the model of Nimrod.
4. Constipated.
5. Puritan hatred of the medieval Schoolmen (all Catholics, naturally) was proverbial. There seems to be a whole series of buried jokes in these opening lines on the Puritan as a book: "bind him to the Bible," "his own translation," and "hidebound" (i.e., bound in leather, but also scrawny, meager, and stubborn).
6. Preachers who do not live among their flock; the Puritan also departs from his duty, i.e., "his text."
7. "Councils" of the church were as odious to Puritans as historical "traditions"—both being ways of adulterating God's pure word with mere human prudence.

clean shirts, he were lousy; more sense than single prayers is not his, nor more in those than still the same petitions:[8] from which he either fears a learned faith, or doubts God understands not at first hearing. Show him a ring, he runs back like a bear; and hates square dealing as allied to caps;[9] a pair of organs blow him out of the parish and are the only clyster pipes[1] to cool him. Where the meat is best, there he confutes most, for his arguing is but the efficacy of his eating: good bits he holds breed good positions, and the Pope he best concludes against in plum broth. He is often drunk, but not as we are, temporally; nor can his sleep then cure him, for the fumes of his ambition make his very soul reel, and that small beer that should allay him (silence) keeps him more surfeited, and makes his heat break out in private houses;[2] women and lawyers are his best disciples; the one, next fruit,[3] longs for forbidden doctrine, the other to maintain forbidden titles, both which he sows amongst them. Honest he dare not be, for that loves order; yet if he can be brought to ceremony, and made but master of it, he is converted.

1614

What a Character Is[4]

If I must speak the schoolmaster's language, I will confess that character comes of this infinite mood χαράξω, that signifieth to engrave, or make a deep impression. And for that cause, a letter (as A, B) is called a character.

Those elements which we learn first, leaving a strong seal in our memories.

Character is also taken from an Egyptian hieroglyphic, for an impress, or short emblem; in little comprehending much.

To square out a character by our English level, it is a picture (real or personal) quaintly drawn, in various colors, all of them heightened by one shadowing.

It is a quick and soft touch of many strings, all shutting up in one musical close; it is wit's descant[5] on any plain song.

1614

8. Puritans were notorious for long, repetitive sermons, but not for logical discourse.
9. The Puritan antipathy to the ceremony of the ring in marriage, compared with a bear's antipathy to the bear ring. "Square dealing" (i.e., honesty) is allied in Puritan eyes to square "caps" (i.e., learning; from the scholar's cap).
1. Enema tubes. The organ is added to the list of Puritan hates.
2. Drunk with ambition, as other men get drunk with ale, the Puritan breaks out in private houses as they do in public houses (taverns).
3. After forbidden fruit, women long for forbidden doctrine.
4. The last of Overbury's characters, this is really the character of a character.
5. Variations.

EDWARD HYDE, EARL OF CLARENDON
(1609–1674)

Edward Hyde was educated at Oxford and during the 1630's practiced law. From about 1641 onward, he was among the chief supporters and advisers of Charles I; he went into exile with the boy who was to become Charles II, and remained the center of the Stuart cause during the Interregnum. After the Restoration, he became Lord Chancellor and Prime Minister to Charles II, but was impeached in 1667 (owing partly to England's ill success in the Dutch War), and spent the last seven years of his life in France.

Clarendon's great *History of the Rebellion* was written in part amid the very events which it describes. For the Muse of history, a short view like this is not an unmixed blessing. But Clarendon's learning—legal, classical, and historical—and the formality of his method save him from many of the failings of partisanship. He wrote as a Lord Chancellor should, with imperial dignity, and he wrote for posterity, which he envisaged as a senatorial assemblage of Lord Chancellors. His *History*, which first appeared in print thirty years after his death, was not only one of the earliest English histories to rise above the level of a chronicle; it served to formulate and crystallize the social philosophy soon to be known as Toryism. As an historical rhetorician and portrait painter, there can be no doubt that Clarendon ranks among the greatest; the strength and resilience of the Tory view of history may be estimated from its present prevalence and influence.

From The History of the Rebellion
[*The Character of John Hampden*]

He was a gentleman of a good family in Buckinghamshire, and born to a fair fortune, and of a most civil and affable deportment. In his entrance into the world, he indulged to himself all the license in sports and exercises and company, which was used by men of the most jolly conversation; afterwards he retired to a more reserved and melancholic society, yet preserving his own natural cheerfulness and vivacity, and above all a flowing courtesy to all men; though they who conversed nearly[1] with him found him growing into a dislike of the ecclesiastical government of the church, yet most believed it rather a dislike of some churchmen, and of some introducements[2] of theirs which he apprehended might disquiet the public peace. He was rather of reputation in his own country, than of public discourse or fame in the kingdom, before the business of

---

1. Intimately.   2. Novelties.

ship-money,[3] but then he grew the argument of all tongues, every man inquiring who and what he was, that durst at his own charge support the liberty and property of the kingdom, and rescue his country from being made a prey to the court; his carriage[4] throughout that agitation was with that rare temper and modesty, that they who watched him narrowly to find some advantage against his person to make him less resolute in his cause, were compelled to give him a just testimony: and the judgment that was given against him infinitely more advanced him, than the service for which it was given. When this Parliament began (being returned knight of the shire[5] for the county where he lived) the eyes of all men were fixed on him as their *Patriae Pater*,[6] and the pilot that must steer their vessel through the tempests and rocks which threatened it. And I am persuaded his power and interest at that time was greater, to do good or hurt, than any man's in the kingdom, or than any man of his rank hath had in any time; for his reputation of honesty was universal, and his affections seemed so publicly guided, that no corrupt or private ends could bias them.

He was of that rare affability and temper in debate, and of that seeming humility and submission of judgment, as if he brought no opinions with him, but a desire of information and instruction, yet he had so subtle a way of interrogating, and under the notion of doubts insinuating his objections, that he left his opinions with those, from whom he pretended to learn and receive them; and even with them, who were able to preserve themselves from his infusions,[7] and discerned those opinions to be fixed in him, with which they could not comply, he always left the character of an ingenious[8] and conscientious person. He was indeed a very wise man, and of great parts,[9] and possessed with the most absolute spirit of popularity, that is, the most absolute faculties to govern the people, of any man I ever knew. For the first year of the Parliament he seemed rather to moderate and soften the violent and distempered humors than to inflame them, but wise and dispassioned men plainly discerned that that moderation proceeded from prudence, and observation that the season was not ripe, rather than that he approved of the moderation, and that he begat many opinions and motions the education[1] whereof he committed to other men, so far disguising his own designs that he seemed seldom to wish more than was concluded, and in many gross conclusions which would hereafter contribute to designs not yet set on foot, when he

3. Charles I tried to collect a tax from the entire kingdom under an ancient law empowering him to tax the harbors of England to support a navy. Hampden legally resisted the third levy of ship-money, and so became the "argument" (subject) of discussion throughout the land.
4. Behavior.

5. The "knight of the shire" represented the whole county, not just a constituency.
6. Father of his country.
7. Insinuations.
8. Ingenuous (in the 17th century, the words were frequently interchanged).
9. Capacities.
1. Leading forward.

found them sufficiently backed by majority of voices, he would withdraw himself before the question, that he might seem not to consent to so much visible unreasonableness, which produced as great a doubt in some, as it did approbation in others of his integrity. What combination soever had been originally with the Scots for the invasion of England, and what farther was entered into afterwards, in favor of them, and to advance any alteration in Parliament, no man doubts was at least with the privity of this gentleman.[2]

After he was amongst those members accused by the King of high treason, he was much altered, his nature and carriage seeming much fiercer than it did before; and without question when he first drew his sword, he threw away the scabbard, for he passionately opposed the overture made by the King for a treaty from Nottingham, and as eminently any expedients that might have produced an accommodation in this[3] that was at Oxford, and was principally relied on to prevent any infusions which might be made into the Earl of Essex towards peace, or to render them ineffectual if they were made; and was indeed much more relied on by that party, than the General himself.[4] In the first entrance into the troubles he undertook the command of a regiment of foot, and performed the duty of a colonel on all occasions most punctually. He was very temperate in diet, and a supreme governor over all his passions and affections, and had thereby a great power over other men's. He was of an industry and vigilance not to be tired out, or wearied by the most laborious, and of parts not to be imposed upon by the most subtle or sharp, and of a personal courage equal to his best parts, so that he was an enemy not to be wished wherever he might have been made a friend, and as much to be apprehended where he was so, as any man could deserve to be, and therefore his death was no less congratulated on the one party than it was condoled on the other. In a word, what was said of Cinna might well be applied to him, *Erat illi consilium ad facinus aptum, consilio autem neque lingua neque manus deerat*, he had a head to contrive, and a tongue to persuade, and a hand to execute any mischief;[5] his death therefore seemed to be a great deliverance to the nation.

[*The Character of Oliver Cromwell*]

He was one of those men, *quos vituperare ne inimici quidem possent, nisi ut simul laudent,*[6] for he could never have done half that

---

2. The English Civil Wars were set off by a Scottish invasion which had actually been invited by the English Parliament. This was done with the "privity" of Hampden, i.e., with his knowledge.
3. I.e., this treaty.
4. The point is that Hampden was an uncompromising member of the Puritan war-party, whereas the Earl of Essex, who was commander in chief of the Parliamentary armies, was too moderate a man for the war-party.
5. Clarendon quotes from memory; the words concern not Cinna but Catiline. They are from Cicero's third oration against Catiline.
6. "Whom not even his enemies could

mischief without great parts of courage and industry and judgment, and he must have had a wonderful understanding in the natures and humors of men, and as great a dexterity in applying them, who from a private and obscure birth (though of a good family), without interest of estate, alliance, or friendships, could raise himself to such a height, and compound and knead such opposite and contradictory tempers, humors, and interests into a consistence that contributed to his designs and to their own destruction, whilst himself grew insensibly powerful enough to cut off those by whom he had climbed in the instant that they projected to demolish their own building. What Velleius Paterculus said of Cinna may very justly be said of him, *Ausum eum quae nemo auderet bonus, perfecisse quae a nullo nisi fortissimo perfici possunt*.[7] Without doubt, no man with more wickedness ever attempted anything, or brought to pass what he desired more wickedly, more in the face and contempt of religion and moral honesty, yet wickedness as great as his could never have accomplished those trophies[8] without the assistance of a great spirit, an admirable circumspection and sagacity, and a most magnanimous resolution. When he appeared first in Parliament he seemed to have a person in no degree gracious, no ornament of discourse, none of those talents which use to reconcile the affections of the standers-by, yet as he grew into place and authority, his parts seemed to be renewed, as if he had concealed faculties till he had occasion to use them; and when he was to act the part of a great man, he did it without any indecency[9] through the want of custom. * * *

He was not a man of blood, and totally declined Machiavel's method,[1] which prescribes upon any alteration of a government, as a thing absolutely necessary, to cut off all the heads of those, and extirpate their families, who are friends to the old; and it was confidently reported that in the Council of Officers, it was more than once proposed that there might be a general massacre of all the royal party, but Cromwell would never consent to it, it may be out of too much contempt of his enemies. In a word, as he had all the wickednesses against which damnation is denounced and for which Hell-fire is prepared, so he had some virtues, which have caused the memory of some men in all ages to be celebrated, and he will be looked upon by posterity as a brave, bad man.

1702–4

---

blame unless at the same time they praised.' The tag has not proved traceable; Clarendon may have invented it.
7. "He dared to undertake things which no good man would have undertaken, and completed projects which only the strongest of men could have completed." Velleius Paterculus, who died ca. 30

A.D., wrote an indignant *History of Rome;* the quotation is from II.xxiv.
8. Great results.
9. Lack of decorum.
1. Machiavelli is cited in his usual role as an exponent of political ruthlessness.

IZAAK WALTON
(1593–1683)

Izaak Walton, who was by profession a London ironmonger, is remembered these days as the author of *The Complete Angler*. This is an early treatise on the art of angling, with interpolated passages of quaintly humorous dialogue; it is consulted nowadays not so much by people who want to catch fish as by people who want to think about fishing from the placid perspective of a library. But to his own generation, Izaak was essentially a pious biographer. A devout Anglican himself, he first turned to biography in the late 30's, just as the Civil Wars were looming; and all his biographical work was done at a time when the English church was under attack from the Puritans, or struggling to re-establish itself after the Restoration. The men whose lives he wrote were ideally suited to be saints and martyrs in a roster of Anglican worthies; or, if they were not ideally suited for the role, Izaak's happy imagination and faculty of forgetting inconvenient details did much to make them so. But if they are not models of scholarly objectivity—how could they be, in that age?—the biographies of Walton are warm and moving compositions of literary art. Certainly he has not been the last man to feel that a good cause justified a little liberty with exact truth.

Walton's life of Dr. John Donne was composed in 1639 and revised repeatedly over a period of nearly 35 years following the death of its subject. Walton might very well have known Donne personally—he was in his late 30's when Donne died—but there is no positive evidence that he actually did so. His biography was composed mostly on the basis of documents and interviews with Donne's surviving friends. While no section of it can be described as teeming with detail, the latter part of Donne's life (from which our selection is taken) is that on which Walton dwells most lovingly and where he gives freest rein to his flights of pious fancy

From The Life of Dr. John Donne[1]
[*Donne Takes Holy Orders*]

I return from my account of the vision to tell the reader that both before Mr. Donne's going into France, at his being there, and after his return, many of the nobility and others that were powerful at court were watchful and solicitous to the king for some secular employment for him. The king had formerly both known and put a

---

1. The present selection begins with Donne in middle life. Walton has broken his account of these middle years with a digression on second sight, occasioned by a vision which Donne is said to have had in France when his wife was ill at home. Izaak then picks up the thread of his narrative with Donne on the threshold of his career in the church. The text is from the fourth edition (1675); "Feb. 15, 1639," the date at the end of the *Life*, is misleading.

value upon his company, and had also given him some hopes of a state-employment; being always much pleased when Mr. Donne attended him, especially at his meals, where there were usually many deep discourses of general learning and very often friendly disputes or debates of religion betwixt His Majesty and those divines whose places required their attendance on him at those times: particularly the Dean of the Chapel, who then was Bishop Montague (the publisher of the learned and eloquent works of His Majesty) and the most Reverend Doctor Andrewes the late learned Bishop of Winchester, who then was the king's almoner.[2]

About this time there grew many disputes that concerned the Oath of Supremacy and Allegiance,[3] in which the king had appeared, and engaged himself by his public writings now extant: and His Majesty discoursing with Mr. Donne concerning many of the reasons which are usually urged against the taking of those oaths, apprehended such a validity and clearness in his stating the questions, and his answers to them, that His Majesty commanded him to bestow some time in drawing the arguments into a method, and then to write his answers to them; and, having done that, not to send, but be his own messenger and bring them to him. To this he presently and diligently applied himself, and within six weeks brought them to him under his own handwriting, as they be now printed; the book bearing the name of *Pseudo-Martyr*, printed *anno* 1610.

When the king had read and considered that book, he persuaded Mr. Donne to enter into the ministry; to which, at that time, he was, and appeared, very unwilling, apprehending it (such was his mistaking modesty) to be too weighty for his abilities: and though His Majesty had promised him a favor, and many persons of worth mediated with His Majesty for some secular employment for him (to which his education had apted[4] him), and particularly the Earl of Somerset[5] when in his greatest height of favor; who being then at Theobald's with the king, where one of the clerks of the council died that night, the Earl posted a messenger for Mr. Donne

---

2. Donne's friends were Richard Montague, later Bishop of Chichester, and famous as an Anglican controversialist and historian; and Lancelot Andrewes, eminent divine, preacher, and translator of the Bible. Both were members of the High-Church, anti-Calvinist wing of the church; both were men of vast learning. As "king's almoner," Andrewes was his Majesty's official almsgiver; Montague, as the king's "publisher," prepared for the press the literary works of which James was so proud.
3. A requirement that they swear unequivocal allegiance to the Crown, under pain of fines and imprisonment, was troubling to the Roman Catholics of England, who claimed that they were

being persecuted for following their consciences in upholding Papal supremacy. The title of Donne's book, *Pseudo-Martyr*, shows the line he took with this argument.
4. Fitted.
5. Robert Carr, a handsome young page about court, had been raised by King James's favor to the rank of Earl of Somerset; and thus had reason to think the king would deny him nothing. He was later disgraced by the scandal surrounding the mysterious death of Sir Thomas Overbury. "Theobald's" was Lord Burghley's country house in Herts, acquired by James as a royal recreation-spot.

to come to him immediately, and at Mr. Donne's coming, said, "Mr. Donne, to testify the reality of my affection, and my purpose to prefer you, stay in this garden till I go up to the king, and bring you word that you are clerk of the council: doubt not my doing this, for I know the king loves you, and know the king will not deny me." But the king gave a positive denial to all requests, and, having a discerning spirit, replied, "I know Mr. Donne is a learned man, has the abilities of a learned divine, and will prove a powerful preacher; and my desire is to prefer him that way, and in that way I will deny you nothing for him." After that time, as he professeth, "the king descended to a persuasion, almost to a solicitation, of him to enter into sacred orders":[6] which, although he then denied not, yet he deferred it for almost three years. All which time he applied himself to an incessant study of textual divinity, and to the attainment of a great perfection in the learned languages, Greek and Hebrew.

In the first and most blessed times of Christianity, when the clergy were looked upon with reverence, and deserved it, when they overcame their opposers by high examples of virtue, by a blessed patience and long suffering, those only were then judged worthy the ministry whose quiet and meek spirits did make them look upon that sacred calling with an humble adoration and fear to undertake it; which indeed requires such great degrees of humility, and labor, and care, that none but such were then thought worthy of that celestial dignity. And such only were then sought out and solicited to undertake it. This I have mentioned because forwardness and inconsideration could not in Mr. Donne, as in many others, be an argument of insufficiency or unfitness;[7] for he had considered long, and had many strifes within himself concerning the strictness of life and competency of learning required in such as enter into sacred orders; and doubtless, considering his own demerits, did humbly ask God with St. Paul, "Lord, who is sufficient for these things?" and with meek Moses, "Lord, who am I?"[8] And sure, if he had consulted with flesh and blood, he had not for these reasons put his hand to that holy plow. But God, who is able to prevail, wrestled with him, as the angel did with Jacob, and marked him; marked him for his own; marked him with a blessing, a blessing of obedience to the motions of his blessed spirit. And then, as he had formerly asked God with Moses, "Who am I?" so now, being inspired with an apprehension of God's particular mercy to him, in the king's and other solicitations of him, he came to ask King David's thankful question, "Lord, who am I, that thou art so mindful of me?"[9] So mindful of me as to

6. A quotation from Donne himself, in the *Devotions upon Emergent Occasions*.

7. I.e., in many men, the fact that they sought a job eagerly might be evidence of their unfitness for it; but not in Donne, for he did not seek it.

8. II Corinthians ii.16 and Exodus iii.11.

9. A paraphrase of Psalm viii.4. Donne's "soliloquy" is, naturally, the work of Walton's imagination—an ef-

lead me for more than forty years through this wilderness of the many temptations and various turnings of a dangerous life; so merciful to me as to move the learnedest of kings to descend to move me to serve at the altar; so merciful to me as at last to move my heart to embrace this holy motion! Thy motions I will and do embrace: and I now say with the blessed Virgin, "Be it with thy servant as seemeth best in thy sight";[1] and so, blessed Jesus, I do take the cup of salvation and will call upon thy name and will preach thy gospel.

Such strifes as these St. Austin[2] had, when St. Ambrose endeavored his conversion to Christianity; with which he confesseth he acquainted his friend Alipius. Our learned author (a man fit to write after no mean copy) did the like. And declaring his intentions to his dear friend Dr. King,[3] then Bishop of London, a man famous in his generation and no stranger to Mr. Donne's abilities (for he had been chaplain to the Lord Chancellor at the time of Mr. Donne's being his lordship's secretary), that reverend man did receive the news with much gladness; and, after some expressions of joy, and a persuasion to be constant in his pious purpose, he proceeded with all convenient speed to ordain him first deacon, and then priest not long after.

Now the English Church had gained a second St. Austin; for I think none was so like him before his conversion, none so like St. Ambrose after it:[4] and if his youth had the infirmities of the one, his age had the excellencies of the other; the learning and holiness of both.

And now all his studies, which had been occasionally diffused, were all concentered in divinity. Now he had a new calling, new thoughts, and a new employment for his wit and eloquence. Now, all his earthly affections were changed into divine love; and all the faculties of his own soul were engaged in the conversion of others: in preaching the glad tidings of remission to repenting sinners and peace to each troubled soul. To these he applied himself with all care and diligence: and now such a change was wrought in him that he could say with David, "O how amiable are thy tabernacles, O Lord God of Hosts!"[5] Now he declared openly, "That when he required a temporal, God gave him a spiritual blessing." And that "he was now gladder to be a doorkeeper in the House of God, than he could be to enjoy the noblest of all temporal employments."

Presently after he entered into his holy profession, the king sent

fort to render vividly the character in conflict.
1. Cf. Luke i.38.
2. Augustine. The reference is to Augustine's conversion, described in the *Confessions*.
3. This is John King (father of Henry King, the poet); he was created bishop of London in 1611.
4. St. Ambrose, the famous bishop of Milan (4th century A.D.), was a pillar of the church against Arianism and exerted a powerful influence in the conversion of Augustine.
5. Cf. Psalm lxxxiv.1.

for him, and made him his Chaplain in Ordinary,[6] and promised to take a particular care for his preferment.

And though his long familiarity with scholars and persons of greatest quality was such as might have given some men boldness enough to have preached to any eminent auditory; yet his modesty in this employment was such that he could not be persuaded to it, but went, usually accompanied with some one friend, to preach privately in some village not far from London; his first sermon being preached at Paddington. This he did till His Majesty sent and appointed him a day to preach to him at Whitehall;[7] and, though much were expected from him, both by His Majesty and others, yet he was so happy (which few are) as to satisfy and exceed their expectations: preaching the Word so, as showed his own heart was possessed with those very thoughts and joys that he labored to distill into others: a preacher in earnest; weeping sometimes for his auditory, sometimes with them; always preaching to himself, like an angel from a cloud, but in none; carrying some, as St. Paul was, to heaven in holy raptures, and enticing others by a sacred art and courtship to amend their lives: here picturing a vice so as to make it ugly to those that practiced it; and a virtue so as to make it be beloved, even by those that loved it not; and all this with a most particular grace and an unexpressible addition of comeliness.[8]

[Donne on His Deathbed]

It is observed that a desire of glory or commendation is rooted in the very nature of man; and that those of the severest and most mortified lives, though they may become so humble as to banish self-flattery, and such weeds as naturally grow there; yet they have not been able to kill this desire of glory, but that like our radical heat,[9] it will both live and die with us; and many think it should do so; and we want not sacred examples to justify the desire of having our memory to outlive our lives; which I mention, because Dr. Donne, by the persuasion of Dr. Fox, easily yielded at this very time[1] to have a monument made for him; but Dr. Fox undertook not to persuade him how, or what monument it should be; that was left to Dr. Donne himself.

A monument being resolved upon, Dr. Donne sent for a carver to make for him in wood the figure of an urn, giving him directions for the compass and height of it; and to bring with it a board, of the just[2] height of his body. These being got, then without delay a choice painter was got to be in readiness to draw his picture, which

6. One of the king's regular staff of chaplains.
7. At court.
8. Having described Donne's decision to take holy orders, Walton proceeds to represent him as a perfect priest—eloquent, laborious, patient, and cheerful. At last, however, he sickened and grew ill; the stage is set for a protracted deathbed scene, such as Donne, Walton, and the 17th century relished enthusiastically.
9. Bodily warmth.
1. Toward the end of his life, in 1631. Dr. Simeon Fox was Donne's physician.
2. Exact.

was taken as followeth. Several charcoal fires being first made in his large study, he brought with him into that place his winding-sheet in his hand, and having put off all his clothes, had this sheet put on him, and so tied with knots at his head and feet, and his hands so placed as dead bodies are usually fitted to be shrouded and put into their coffin or grave. Upon this urn he thus stood with his eyes shut and with so much of the sheet turned aside as might show his lean, pale, and deathlike face, which was purposely turned towards the east, from whence he expected the second coming of his and our Saviour Jesus. In this posture he was drawn at his just height; and when the picture was fully finished, he caused it to be set by his bedside, where it continued and became his hourly object till his death, and was then given to his dearest friend and executor Dr. Henry King,[3] then chief residentiary of St. Paul's, who caused him to be thus carved in one entire piece of white marble, as it now stands in that church;[4] and by Dr. Donne's own appointment, these words were to be affixed to it as his epitaph:

JOHANNES DONNE
Sac. Theol. Profess.

Post varia studia quibus ab annis tenerrimis
fideliter, nec infeliciter incubuit,
instinctu et impulsu Sp. Sancti, monitu
et hortatu

REGIS JACOBI, *ordines sacros*
amplexus, anno sui Jesu, 1614, et suae aetatis 42,
decanatu hujus ecclesiae indutus 27
Novembris, 1621,

exutus morte ultimo die Martii, 1631,
hic licet in occiduo cinere aspicit eum
cujus nomen est Oriens.[5]

And now, having brought him through the many labyrinths and perplexities of a various life, even to the gates of death and the grave, my desire is, he may rest till I have told my reader that I have seen many pictures of him in several habits and at several ages and in several postures; and I now mention this, because I have seen one picture of him, drawn by a curious[6] hand, at his age of eighteen, with his sword, and what other adornments might then

---

3. This is the poet, son of the Bishop of London who had advised Donne to enter holy orders, and himself later Bishop of Chichester. A reproduction of the portrait may be found in Grierson's edition of the poems, Vol. I, opp. p. 369.

4. Donne's tomb was destroyed in the great fire of 1666; only the statue survived, and is still seen in St. Paul's.

5. "John Donne, Professor of Sacred Theology. After various studies, which he plied from his tenderest youth faith-fully and not unsuccessfully, moved by the instinct and impulse of the Holy Spirit and the admonition and encouragement of King James, he took holy orders in the year of our Lord 1614 at the age of 42. On the 27th of November, 1621, he was made deacon of this church; and he died on the last day of March, 1631. Here in the decline and decay of ashes, may he look upon Him whose name is a Rising Sun."

6. Skillful.

suit with the present fashions of youth and the giddy gaieties of that age;[7] and his motto then was—

> How much shall I be changed,
> Before I am changed![8]

And if that young and his now dying picture were at this time set together, every beholder might say, "Lord! how much is Dr. Donne already changed, before he is changed!" And the view of them might give my reader occasion to ask himself with some amazement, "Lord! how much may I also, that am now in health, be changed before I am changed; before this vile, this changeable body shall put off mortality!" and therefore to prepare for it. But this is not writ so much for my reader's memento as to tell him that Dr. Donne would often in his private discourses, and often publicly in his sermons, mention the many changes both of his body and mind; especially of his mind from a vertiginous giddiness; and would as often say, "his great and most blessed change was from a temporal to a spiritual employment"; in which he was so happy, that he accounted the former part of his life to be lost; and the beginning of it to be from his first entering into sacred orders and serving his most merciful God at his altar.

Upon Monday, after the drawing this picture, he took his last leave of his beloved study; and, being sensible of his hourly decay, retired himself to his bedchamber; and that week sent at several[9] times for many of his most considerable friends, with whom he took a solemn and deliberate farewell, commending to their considerations some sentences useful for the regulation of their lives; and then dismissed them, as good Jacob did his sons, with a spiritual benediction. The Sunday following, he appointed his servants, that if there were any business yet undone that concerned him or themselves, it should be prepared against Saturday next; for after that day he would not mix his thoughts with anything that concerned this world; nor ever did; but, as Job, so he "waited for the appointed day of his dissolution."

And now he was so happy as to have nothing to do but to die, to do which he stood in need of no longer time; for he had studied it long and to so happy a perfection that in a former sickness he called God to witness, "he was that minute ready to deliver his soul into his hands, if that minute God would determine his dissolution."[1] In that sickness he begged of God the constancy to be preserved in that estate forever; and his patient expectation to have his immortal soul disrobed from her garment of mortality makes me confident that he now had a modest assurance that his prayers were then heard and his petition granted. He lay fifteen days ear-

7. See the portrait reproduced in Grierson, Vol. I, opp. p. 7.
8. Transformed (i.e., by death).

9. Separate.
1. Walton again quotes from the *Devotions*.

nestly expecting his hourly change; and in the last hour of his last day, as his body melted away and vapored into spirit, his soul having, I verily believe, some revelation of the beatifical vision, he said, "I were miserable if I might not die"; and after those words, closed many periods of his faint breath by saying often, "Thy kingdom come, thy will be done." His speech, which had long been his ready and faithful servant, left him not till the last minute of his life, and then forsook him, not to serve another master (for who speaks like him) but died before him; for that it was then become useless to him that now conversed with God on earth as angels are said to do in heaven, only by thoughts and looks. Being speechless, and seeing heaven by that illumination by which he saw it, he did, as St. Stephen, "look steadfastly into it, till he saw the Son of Man standing at the right hand of God his Father";[2] and being satisfied with this blessed sight, as his soul ascended and his last breath departed from him, he closed his own eyes; and then disposed his hands and body into such a posture as required not the least alteration by those that came to shroud him.

Thus variable, thus virtuous was the life: thus excellent, thus exemplary was the death of this memorable man.

He was buried in that place of St. Paul's Church which he had appointed for that use some years before his death; and by which he passed daily to pay his public devotions to Almighty God (who was then served twice a day by a public form of prayer and praises in that place):[3] but he was not buried privately, though he desired it; for, besides an unnumbered number of others, many persons of nobility, and of eminency for learning, who did love and honor him in his life, did show it at his death by a voluntary and sad attendance of his body to the grave, where nothing was so remarkable as a public sorrow.

To which place of his burial some mournful friends repaired, and, as Alexander the Great did to the grave of the famous Achilles, so they strewed his with an abundance of curious and costly flowers; which course, they (who were never yet known) continued morning and evening for many days, not ceasing, till the stones that were taken up in that church to give his body admission into the cold earth (now his bed of rest) were again by the mason's art so leveled and firmed as they had been formerly, and his place of burial undistinguishable to common view.

The next day after his burial, some unknown friend, some one of the many lovers and admirers of his virtue and learning, wrote this epitaph with a coal on the wall over his grave:

> Reader! I am to let thee know,
> Donne's body only lies below;

2. Cf. Acts vii.55.
3. This phrase clearly shows up as one of Walton's later additions to the *Life;* Walton originally wrote when the forms of liturgy had not been changed.

> For, could the grave his soul comprise,
> Earth would be richer than the skies!

Nor was this all the honor done to his reverend ashes; for, as there be some persons that will not receive a reward for that for which God accounts himself a debtor, persons that dare trust God with their charity and without a witness; so there was by some grateful unknown friend that thought Dr. Donne's memory ought to be perpetuated, an hundred marks sent to his two faithful friends and executors,[4] towards the making of his monument. It was not for many years known by whom; but after the death of Dr. Fox, it was known that it was he that sent it; and he lived to see as lively a representation of his dead friend as marble can express: a statue indeed so like Dr. Donne, that (as his friend Sir Henry Wotton hath expressed himself) "it seems to breathe faintly, and posterity shall look upon it as a kind of artificial miracle."

He was of stature moderately tall; of a straight and equally proportioned body, to which all his words and actions gave an unexpressible addition of comeliness.

The melancholy and pleasant humor were in him so contempered that each gave advantage to the other, and made his company one of the delights of mankind.

His fancy was unimitably high, equaled only by his great wit; both being made useful by a commanding judgment.

His aspect was cheerful, and such as gave a silent testimony of a clear knowing soul, and of a conscience at peace with itself.

His melting eye showed that he had a soft heart, full of noble compassion; of too brave a soul to offer injuries and too much a Christian not to pardon them in others.

He did much contemplate (especially after he entered into his sacred calling) the mercies of Almighty God, the immortality of the soul, and the joys of heaven: and would often say in a kind of sacred ecstasy—"Blessed be God that he is God, only and divinely like himself."

He was by nature highly passionate, but more apt to reluct at[5] the excesses of it. A great lover of the offices of humanity, and of so merciful a spirit that he never beheld the miseries of mankind without pity and relief.

He was earnest and unwearied in the search of knowledge, with which his vigorous soul is now satisfied, and employed in a continual praise of that God that first breathed it into his active body: that body, which once was a temple of the Holy Ghost and is now become a small quantity of Christian dust:

But I shall see it reanimated.

Feb. 15, 1639.   I. W.

                                                            1639, 1675

4. "Dr. King and Dr. Monfort" [marginal note].   5. Oppose.

Topics in Seventeenth-Century Literature

THE VARIETIES OF WIT

The word "wit," which recurs so inevitably in any description of the meta-physical and neoclassic styles, is one of the most bewildering, and yet one of the most important, in the 17th-century critical vocabulary. Sometimes it means "general intelligence"; sometimes it means "repartee"; sometimes it means "recondite learning"; sometimes, any work of literature or amusement. Sometimes it includes a concept called "judgment," and sometimes it is contrasted with and opposed to "judgment." The passages reprinted here illustrate some of the various uses of the word, and some of the problems to which it gave rise. Francis Beaumont, for example, uses the term without any consistency at all, shifting from meaning to meaning, and trusting to the context to inform the reader of what is intended. Sir William Davenant is an almost classic case of confusion; his expressions are as cloudy as his thought is muddled, and it seems clear that Thomas Hobbes in his answer deliberately avoided the word "wit" just because it gave rise to such confusion. But the Hobbesian distinction between judgment and fancy was the cornerstone of a new aesthetic; one which indeed established what T. S. Eliot has called a separation between thought and feeling, a divided sensibility. John Dryden accepts this new position, but with typical caution; allowing that the judicious imitation of folly may be in one general sense, wit; but describing wit more particularly as the spaniel which finds ideas, which are then varied or molded by the judgment to accord with the subject. Finally, in Sir Richard Blackmore, we have an early analogue with Pope's famous one-couplet definition:

> True wit is nature to advantage dressed,
> What oft was thought, but ne'er so well expressed.

Wit is now frankly admitted to be a decorative quality, exterior to "judgment" or "good sense," and subordinate to it. And the 18th century will be concerned with playing variations on this theme, until Wordsworth and Coleridge undertake to set up a whole new critical vocabulary, in which the old distinction between "wit" and "judgment" is replaced by a contrast between "imagination" and the inferior faculties.

From M. Francis Beaumonts Letter to Ben Jonson[1]

* * *

Methinks the little wit° I had is lost   *liveliness*
Since I saw you; for wit is like a rest
Held up[2] at tennis, which men do the best
With the best gamesters. What things have we seen
5 Done at the Mermaid! heard words that have been
So nimble, and so full of subtle flame
As if that every one from whence they came
Had meant to put his whole wit° in a jest,   *intelligence*
And had resolved to live a fool the rest
10 Of his dull life; there where there hath been thrown
Wit° able enough to justify the town   *ingenuity*
For three days past: wit that might warrant be
For the whole town to talk foolishly,
Till that were cancelled; and when that was gone,
15 We left an air behind us, which alone
Was able to make the next two companies
Right witty:° though but downright fools, more wise.   *wisdom*
When I remember this, and see that now
The country gentlemen begin to allow
20 My wit° for dry bobs,[3] then I needs must cry,   *poetry*
I see my days of ballating[4] grow nigh.

* * *

ca. 1608–10   1647

SIR WILLIAM DAVENANT: *From* The Author's Preface to His Much Honored Friend Mr. Hobbes[5]

* * * Wit is the laborious, and the lucky resultances of thought, having towards its excellence (as we say of the strokes of Painting) as well a happinesse, as care. It is a Web consisting of the subtilest threads, and like that of the *Spider*, is considerately[6] woven out of ourselves; for a *Spider* may be said to consider, not onely respecting his solemnesse and tacite posture (like a grave scout in ambush for his Enemy) but because all things done are either from consideration or chance; and the works of chance are accomplishments of

---

1. In *Comedies and Tragedies Written by Francis Beaumont and John Fletcher*, the title goes on to say that the letter was "Written Before He and Master Fletcher Came to London, with Two of the Precedent Comedies Then Not Finisht, Which Deferred Their Merry Meetings at the Mermaid."

2. A rally.
3. Rural jests, coarse and satirical.
4. Balladeering.
5. Prefixed to Davenant's *Gondibert*. Hobbes's reply was published in the same volume.
6. By consideration, artfully.

an instant, having commonly a dissimilitude; but hers are the works of time, and have their contextures alike.

Wit is not onely the luck and labour, but also the dexterity of the thought; rounding the world like the Sun with unimaginable motion; and bringing swiftly home to the memory universall surveyes. It is the Souls *Powder*, which when supprest (as forbidden from flying upward) blows up the restraint; and loseth all force in a farther ascension towards Heaven (the region of' God) and yet by nature is much lesse able to make any inquisition downward towards Hell, the Cell of the Devil; but breaks through all about it (as farre as the utmost it can reach) removes, uncovers, makes way for Light, where darknesse was inclosed, till great bodies are more examinable by being scattered into parcels; and till all that find its strength (but most of mankind are strangers to *Wit*, as *Indians* are to *Powder*) worship it for the effects, as derived from the Deity. It is in Divines Humility, Exemplarinesse, and Moderation:[7] In States-men, Gravity, Vigilance, Benigne Complacency, Secrecy, Patience, and Dispatch. In Leaders of Armies, Valour, Painfulnesse, Temperance, Bounty, Dexterity in Punishing and Rewarding, and a sacred Certitude of Promise: It is in Poets a full comprehension of all recited in all these; and an ability to bring those comprehensions into action, when they shall so farre forget the true measure of what is of greatest consequence to humanity, (which are things righteous, pleasant, and usefull) as to think the delights of greatnesse equal to that of Poesie; or the Chiefs of any Profession more necessary to the World then excellent Poets. * * *

1650

THOMAS HOBBES: *From* The Answer to Sir Will. D'Avenant's Preface Before Gondibert

* * * Time and Education begets experience; Experience begets Memory; Memory begets Judgement and Fancy: Judgement begets the strength and structure, and Fancy begets the ornaments of a Poem. The Ancients therefore fabled not absurdly, in making memory the mother of the Muses.[8] For memory is the World (though not really, yet so as in a looking glass) in which the Judgment (the severer sister) busieth herself in a grave and rigid examination of all the parts of Nature, and in registring by Letters, their order, causes, uses, differences, and resemblances; Whereby the Fancy, when any work of Art is to be performed, findeth her

7. Note that for Davenant, wit is the principle of excellence in any activity; it is simply general intelligence. He is also thinking in terms of the Renaissance theory of epic vision.
8. She was Mnemosyne, goddess of memory.

materials at hand and prepared for use, and needs no more than a swift motion over them, that what she wants, and is there to be had, may not lye too long unespied. So that when she seemeth to fly from one Indies to the other, and from Heaven to Earth, and to penetrate into the hardest matter, and obscurest places, into the future and into her self, and all this in a point of time; the voyage is not very great, her self being all she seeks;[9] and her wonderful celerity, consisteth not so much in motion, as in copious Imagery discreetly ordered, and perfectly registred in the memory. * * *

1650

ABRAHAM COWLEY: Ode of Wit[1]

Tell me, O tell, what kind of thing is *Wit*,
    Thou who *Master* art of it.
For the *First matter* loves *Variety* less;
Less *Women* love 't, either in *Love* or *Dress*.
    A thousand different shapes it bears,   5
    Comely in thousand shapes appears.
Yonder we saw it plain; and here 'tis now,
Like *Spirits* in a *Place*, we know not *How*.

London that vents of *false Ware* so much store,
    In no *Ware* deceives us more.   10
For men led by the *Colour*, and the *Shape*,
Like *Zeuxes Birds* fly to the painted *Grape*;[2]
    Some things do through our Judgment pass
    As through a *Multiplying Glass*.
And sometimes, if the *Object* be too far,   15
We take a *Falling Meteor* for a *Star*.

Hence 'tis a *Wit* that greatest *word* of *Fame*
    Grows such a common Name.
And Wits by our Creation they become,
Just so, as *Tit'lar Bishops* made at *Rome*.[3]   20
    'Tis not a *Tale*, 'tis not a *Jest*
    Admir'd with *Laughter* at a feast,
Nor florid *Talk* which can that *Title* gain;
The *Proofs* of *Wit* for ever must remain.

'Tis not to force some lifeless *Verses* meet   25
    With their five gowty feet.
All ev'ry where, like *Mans*, must be the *Soul*,

9. Here Hobbes is answering directly Davenant's idea that Fancy is a swift traveler.
1. From *Miscellanies*, in Cowley's *Poems* (1656); our text is from the posthumous *Works* (1668).
2. Zeuxis, a celebrated Greek painter of the 5th century B.C., reportedly painted grapes so realistically that the birds pecked at them.
3. Certain churches in Rome have as their titular incumbents cardinals whose real duties are elsewhere; so men are often called "wits" by courtesy.

And *Reason* the *Inferior Powers* controul.
   Such were the *Numbers* which could call
   The *Stones* into the *Theban* wall.[4] 30
Such *Miracles* are ceast; and now we see
No *Towns* or *Houses* rais'd by *Poetrie*.

Yet 'tis not to adorn, and gild each part;
   That shows more *Cost*, then *Art*.
Jewels at *Nose* and *Lips* but ill appear; 35
Rather then *all things Wit*, let *none* be there.
   Several *Lights* will not be seen,
   If there be nothing else between.
Men doubt, because they stand so thick i' th' skie,
If those be *Stars* which paint the *Galaxie*. 40

'Tis not when two like words make up one noise;
   Jests for *Dutch Men*, and *English Boys*.
In which who finds out *Wit*, the same may see
In *An'grams* and *Acrostiques Poetrie*.[5]
   Much less can that have any place 45
   At which a *Virgin* hides her face,
Such *Dross* the *Fire* must purge away; 'tis just
The *Author blush*, there where the *Reader* must.

'Tis not such lines as almost crack the *Stage*
   When *Bajazet*[6] begins to rage. 50
Nor a tall *Meta'phor* in the *Bombast way*,
Nor the dry chips of short lung'd *Seneca*.[7]
   Nor upon all things to obtrude,
   And force some odd *Similitude*.
What is it then, which like the *Power Divine* 55
We only can by *Negatives* define?

In a true piece of *Wit* all things must be,
   Yet all things there *agree*.
As in the *Ark*, joyn'd without force or strife,
All *Creatures* dwelt: all *Creatures* that had *Life*.[8] 60
   Or as the *Primitive Forms* of all
   (If we compare great things with small)
Which without *Discord* or *Confusion* lie,
In that strange *Mirror* of the *Deitie*.[9]

But *Love* that moulds *One Man* up out of *Two*, 65
   Makes me forget and injure you.

4. When Amphion and Zethus were fortifying Thebes, Amphion's performance on the lyre was so moving that the stones rose into place of their own accord.
5. Anagrams and acrostics never stood very high in critical theory; but Cowley here anticipates their rejection as "false wit," a rejection formalized fifty years later by Joseph Addison.
6. A grandiloquent character in Marlowe's *Tamburlaine*.
7. Seneca's influence tended to be toward short, epigrammatic statements.
8. It is hard to tell in what degree Cowley is describing here "the reconciliation of opposites" or a "thick, *Dinglich* texture" or any of the other attributes which modern criticism has found in metaphysical poetry.
9. Cowley posits here a kind of universal first matter, in which the Deity was once directly mirrored, and which contained, in embryo as it were, the whole cosmos.

I took *you* for *my self* sure when I thought
That you in any thing were to be *Taught*.
    Correct my error with thy Pen;
    And if any ask me then,   70
What thing right *Wit*, and height of *Genius* is,
I'll onely shew your *Lines,* and say, '*Tis This*.

1656, 1668

JOHN DRYDEN: [Wit a Nimble Spaniel][1]

    The composition of all poems is, or ought to be, of wit; and wit in the poet, or wit writing (if you will give me leave to use a school-distinction)[2] is no other than the faculty of imagination in the writer, which, like a nimble spaniel, beats over and ranges thro' the field of memory, till it springs the quarry it hunted after; or, without metaphor, which searches over all the memory for the species or ideas of those things which it designs to represent. Wit written is that which is well defin'd, the happy result of thought, or product of imagination. But to proceed from wit, in the general notion of it, to the proper wit of an heroic or historical poem, I judge it chiefly to consist in the delightful imaging of persons, actions, passions, or things. 'Tis not the jerk or sting of an epigram, nor the seeming contradiction of a poor antithesis, (the delight of an ill-judging audience in a play of rhyme,) nor the jingle of a more poor *paronomasia*;[3] neither is it so much the morality of a grave sentence, affected by Lucan, but more sparingly us'd by Virgil; but it is some lively and apt description, dress'd in such colors of speech that it sets before your eyes the absent object as perfectly and more delightfully than nature. So then, the first happiness of the poet's imagination is properly invention, or finding of the thought; the second is fancy, or the variation, deriving, or molding of that thought, as the judgment represents it proper to the subject; the third is elocution, or the art of clothing and adorning that thought, so found and varied, in apt, significant, and sounding words: the quickness of the imagination is seen in the invention, the fertility in the fancy, and the accuracy in the expression.

1667

1. This extract is taken from "An Account of the Ensuing Poem in a Letter to the Honorable Sir Robert Howard," prefixed to *Annus Mirabilis*.
2. Such a distinction as the Schoolmen (medieval theologians) used to make. Dryden is a gentleman, writing for gentlemen.
3. Pun.

JOHN DRYDEN: *From* An Essay on the Dramatic Poetry of the Last Age[4]

* * * I should now speak of the refinement of Wit; but I have been so large on the former subject, that I am forced to contract myself in this. I will therefore only observe to you, that the wit of the last age was yet more incorrect than their language. Shakespeare, who many times has written better than any poet, in any language, is yet so far from writing wit always, or expressing that wit according to the dignity of the subject, that he writes, in many places, below the dullest writer of ours, or any precedent age. Never did any author precipitate himself from such heights of thought to so low expressions, as he often does. He is the very Janus of poets;[5] he wears almost everywhere two faces; and you have scarce begun to admire the one, ere you despise the other. Neither is the luxuriance of Fletcher (which his friends have taxed in him) a less fault than the carelessness of Shakespeare. He does not well always; and, when he does, he is a true Englishman; he knows not when to give over. If he wakes in one scene, he commonly slumbers in another; and, if he pleases you in the first three acts, he is frequently so tired with his labour, that he goes heavily in the fourth, and sinks under his burden in the fifth.

For Ben Jonson, the most judicious of poets, he always writ properly, and as the character required; and I will not contest farther with my friends who call that wit: it being very certain, that even folly itself, well represented, is wit in a larger signification; and that there is fancy, as well as judgment, in it, though not so much or noble: because all poetry being imitation, that of folly is a lower exercise of fancy, though perhaps as difficult as the other; for 'tis a kind of looking downward in the poet, and representing that part of mankind which is below him.

In these low characters of vice and folly lay the excellency of that inimitable writer; who, when at any time he aimed at wit in the stricter sense, that is, sharpness of conceit, was forced either to borrow from the Ancients, as to my knowledge he did very much from Plautus; or, when he trusted himself alone, often fell into meanness of expression. Nay, he was not free from the lowest and most grovelling kind of wit, which we call clenches,[6] of which *Every Man in his Humour* is infinitely full; and, which is worse, the wittiest persons in the drama speak them. * * * I have always acknowledged the wit of our predecessors, with all the veneration which be-

4. This *Essay* was prefixed to the play *The Conquest of Granada*.
5. Janus, Roman god of doors and be-
ginnings, had two faces.
6. Plays on words, puns.

comes me; but, I am sure, their wit was not that of gentlemen; there was ever somewhat that was ill-bred and clownish in it, and which confessed the conversation[7] of the authors. * * *

1672

SIR RICHARD BLACKMORE: *From* An Essay upon Wit

* * * Tho perhaps the Talent which we call Wit, like that of Humour, is as clearly understood by its simple Term,[8] as by the most labour'd Description; an Argument of which is this, That many ingenious Persons, by their unsuccessful Essays to explain it, have rather obscur'd than illustrated its Idea; I will notwithstanding adventure to give the Definition of it, which tho it may fall short of Perfection, yet I imagine will come nearer to it, than any that has yet appear'd. *Wit is a Qualification of the Mind, that raises and enlivens cold Sentiments and plain Propositions, by giving them an elegant and surprizing Turn.*

It is evident, that Wit cannot essentially consist in the Justness and Propriety of the Thoughts, that is, the conformity of our Conceptions to the Objects we conceive; for this is the Definition of Truth, when taken in a Physical Sense; nor in the Purity of Words and Expression, for this may be eminent in the Cold, Didactick Stile, and in the correct Writers of History and Philosophy: But Wit is that which imparts Spirit to our Conceptions and Diction, by giving them a lively and novel, and therefore an agreeable Form: And thus its Nature is limited and diversify'd from all other intellectual Endowments. Wit therefore is the Accomplishment of a warm, sprightly, and fertile Imagination, enrich'd with great Variety of proper Ideas; which active Principle is however under the Direction of a regular Judgment, that takes care of the Choice of just and suitable Materials, prescribes to the lighter Faculties the due Bounds of their Sport and Activity, and assists and guides them, while they imprint on the Conceptions of the Mind their peculiar and delightful Figures. The Addition of Wit to proper Subjects, is like the artful Improvement of the Cook, who by his exquisite Sauce gives to a plain dish, a pleasant and unusual Relish. A Man of this Character works on simple Propositions a rich Embroidery of Flowers and Figures, and imitates the curious Artist, who studs and inlays his prepar'd Steel with Devices of Gold and Silver. But Wit is not only the Improvement of a plain Piece by intellectual Enameling; besides this, it animates and warms a cold Sentiment, and makes it glow with Life and Vigor; and this it effects, as is ex-

7. Revealed both the people with whom and the subjects about which they conversed.
8. Proper name.

press'd in the last Part of the Definition, by giving it an elegant and surprizing Turn. It always conveys the Thought of the Speaker or Writer cloath'd in a pleasing, but foreign Dress, in which it never appear'd to the Hearer before, who however had been long acquainted with it; and this Appearance in the Habit of a Stranger must be admirable, since Surprize naturally arises from Novelty, as Delight and Wonder result from Surprize; which I have more fully explain'd in the former Essay. * * *

1716

THE UNICORN: END OF A LEGEND

Medieval natural histories, being primarily moral in their interests, loved to interpret allegorically the habits of the beasts. Because he never existed, the unicorn lent himself ideally to this purpose. The story of the virgin, who alone can capture (incarnate) him, and the story of his miraculous power against evil are clearly stages leading toward the identification of the unicorn with Christ himself. Unfortunately, scientific skepticism intervened; not only the existence of the unicorn, but the magical efficacy of his horn, was called into question. Finally, the gentlemen of the Royal Society performed a decisive and historic experiment. Under laboratory conditions, they placed a poisonous spider in a circle of powdered unicorn's horn, and proved, beyond a shadow of a doubt, that no mysterious antipathy between the virtuous horn and the evil poison would cause the spider to shrivel up and die. Indeed, only one major problem remained, after their experiment: where did they get the unicorn's horn with which they performed it?

Our materials include some miscellaneous unicorn lore. Early items in the unicorn's story are amusing as they show the slender foundations on which the later myth was built. On the other hand, the foolish and naïve treatise of Alexander Ross illustrates how late the superstitions of the Middle Ages survived, and what dominion they retained over credulous minds. Finally, in the dry, businesslike pages of Sprat's *History of the Royal Society*, the legend, unlike the spider, quietly expires. For all its comic overtones, the experiment with unicorn's horn is one of many which had to be performed in all sober seriousness, in order to clear the way for modern scientific empiricism.

1

He says too that wild asses are taken in its marshes,[1] which have a horn in their foreheads with which they fight like bulls, and not badly; and that the Indians make drinking-cups from this horn, which have such virtue that the man who drinks from one will for one whole day neither fall ill, nor feel pain if wounded, nor be burned by passing through fire, nor even be affected by poisons

1. The Hyphasis River.

which he could not swallow at any other time without harm. These cups are reserved for the king, and only the king may hunt these animals. Apollonius writes that he saw this beast and admired its appearance, and that when Damis asked him if he believed that story about the horn cups, he said: "I will believe it when I find that the king who rules this country never dies." * * *

[Philostratus (3rd century A.D.): from *Life of Apollonius of Tyana* III.ii]

2

Unicornis the Unicorn, which is also called Rhinoceros by the Greeks, is of the following nature.

He is a very small animal like a kid, excessively swift, with one horn in the middle of his forehead, and no hunter can catch him. But he can be trapped by the following stratagem.

A virgin girl is led to where he lurks, and there she is sent off by herself into the wood. He soon leaps into her lap when he sees her, and embraces her, and hence he gets caught.

Our Lord Jesus Christ is also a Unicorn spiritually, about whom it is said: "And he was beloved like the Son of the Unicorns." And in another psalm: "He hath raised up a horn of salvation for us in the house of his son David."

The fact that it has just one horn on its head means what he himself said: "I and the Father are One." Also, according to the Apostle: "The head of Christ is the Lord."

It says that he is very swift because neither Principalities, nor Powers, nor Thrones, nor Dominations could keep up with him, nor could Hell contain him, nor could the most subtle Devil prevail to catch or comprehend him; but, by the sole will of the Father, he came down into the virgin womb for our salvation.

It is described as a tiny animal on account of the lowliness of his incarnation, as he said himself: "Learn from me, because I am mild and lowly of heart."

It is like a kid or scapegoat because the Saviour himself was made in the likeness of sinful flesh, and from sin he condemned sin.

The Unicorn often fights with elephants, and conquers them by wounding them in the belly.

[From a 12th-century Latin bestiary, tr. T. H. White]

3

First, we understand by the word Licorn, a beast born in far distant lands, having a single horn in his forehead, which is taken as a miraculous influence against all poisons, and highly esteemed by

Kings, Princes, and great Lords, and even by the vulgar * * *
Some say that if one dips it in water, and with this water draws a
circle on a table, one may then put within it a scorpion or spider
or toad, and that these beasts will die rather than pass outside the
circle, indeed, that the toad will kill itself.

[Ambroise Paré: from *Discourse on the Licorn* (1582) I, XV]

4

Now let any Reader consider, and observe it as a Thing worthy
of Note, that the true *Unicorns-horn*, sophisticated by no fallacy,[2]
repels all Venom from it self, nor can it assume or draw to it self
any thing of Venom, as is manifest by Experience. Let a living
Spider be put in a Circle made of *Unicorns-horn*, and out of this
Circle it cannot go, or passe over the *Unicorns-horn*, for it shuns
whatsoever is adverse to Venom.

[Basil Valentine: from *Triumphant Chariot of Antimony*,
1400, 1678]

5

The unicorn is a beast that has one horn in its brow, and this
horn is good against poison and pestilential fevers. But one is to
observe that there is very little of the true horn to be found. * * *
I will take this occasion to describe a true test by which one may
know the genuine horn from the false. The test is this: place the
horn in a vessel of any sort of material you like, and with it three
or four live and large scorpions, keeping the vessel covered. If you
find four hours later that the scorpions are dead, or almost lifeless,
the alicorn is a good one, and there is not money enough in the
world to pay for it. Otherwise, it is false.

[David de Pomis: from *Dittionario Novo Hebraico* (1587), tr.
Odell Shepard]

6

As men, to try the precious unicorn's horn,
Make of the powder a preservative circle,
And in it put a spider. * * *

[John Webster: from *The White Devil* II.i]

7

These Beasts are very swift, and their legs have no Articles. They
keep for the most part in the deserts, and live solitary in the tops of
the mountains. There was nothing more horrible than the voice or

2. Adulterated by no inferior products.

braying of it, for the voice is strained above measure. It fighteth both with the mouth and with the heels, with the mouth biting like a Lion, and with the heels kicking like a Horse. It is a beast of an untamable nature, and therefore the Lord himself in *Job* saith, that he cannot be tied with any halter, nor yet accustomed to any cratch or stable. He feareth not Iron nor any iron instrument (as *Isidorus* writeth) and that which is most strange of all other, it fighteth with his own kind, yea with even the females unto death, except when it burneth in lust for procreation; but unto stranger-Beasts, with whom he hath no affinity in nature, he is more sociable and familiar, delighting in their company when they come willing unto him, never rising against them, but proud of their dependence and retinue, keepeth with them all quarters of league & truce, but with his female, when once his flesh is tickled with lust, he groweth tame, gregall and loving, and so continueth till she is filled and great with young, and then returneth to his former hostility. He is an enemy to the Lions, wherefore as soon as ever a Lion seeth a Unicorn, he runneth to a tree for succor, that so when the Unicorn maketh force at him, he may not only avoid his horn, but also destroy him; for the Unicorn in the swiftness of his course runneth against the tree wherein his sharp horn sticketh fast, then when the Lion seeth the Unicorn fastened by the horn without all danger, he falleth upon him and killeth him. These things are reported by the king of *Aethiopia* in an Haebrew Epistle unto the Bishop of Rome.

[Edward Topsell: from *The History of Four-Footed Beasts*, 1607]

8

* * * Lastly, Although we allow it an Antidotal efficacy, and such as the Ancients commended, yet are there some vertues ascribed thereto by Moderns not easily to be received; and it hath surely faln out in this, as other magnified[3] medicines, whose operations effectual in some diseases, are presently extended unto all. That some Antidotal quality it may have, we have no reason to deny; for since Elk's Hoofs and Horns are magnified for Epilepsies, since not only the bone in the heart,[4] but the Horn of a Deer is Alexipharmacal,[5] and ingredient into the confection of Hyacinth, and the Electuary of Maximilian;[6] we cannot without prejudice except against the efficacy of this. But when we affirm it is not only Antidotal to proper venoms, and substances destructive by qualities

---

3. Praised.
4. The roots of the arterial vein and chief artery of the deer, which harden with age and were sometimes likened to a bone.
5. "Expulsive of poisons" [Browne's note].
6. Ancient medical compounds.

we cannot express; but that it resisteth also Sublimate, Arsenick, and poysons which kill by second qualities, that is, by corrosion of parts; I doubt we exceed the properties of its nature, and the promises of experiment will not secure the adventure. * * *

Since therefore there be many Unicorns;[7] since that whereto we appropriate a Horn is so variously described, that it seemeth either never to have been seen by two persons, or not to have been one animal; Since though they agreed in the description of the animal, yet is not the Horn we extol the same with that of the Ancients; Since what Horns soever they be that pass among us, they are not the Horns of one, but several animals: Since many in common use and high esteem are no Horns at all: Since if there were true Horns, yet might their vertues be questioned: Since though we allowed some vertues, yet were not others to be received; with what security a man may rely on this remedy, the mistress of fools[8] hath already instructed some, and to wisdom (which is never too wise to learn) it is not too late to consider. * * *

[Sir Thomas Browne: from *Pseudodoxia Epidemica* (1646) III. 23]

9

* * * If the Ancients adscribed no vertue to this horn, why was it of such account among them? Why did the *Indian* Princes drink out of them, and make Cups and Rings of them, which either they wore on their fingers, or applied to their breasts, but that they knew there was in them an antidotal vertue against poison, as Andreth Baccius (*l. de Unicor.*) sheweth, and the Doctor[9] denyeth not (an Antidotall efficacy, and such as the Ancients commended in this Horn) and yet two lines before, he denies that the Ancients adscribed any vertue to it. But sure it is apparent, that not only there is an occult quality in it against poison, as in the *Elks* Hoof against the falling sicknesse,[1] but also by manifest qualities it works; for *Baccius* proves it to be of an excessive drying quality, and therefore good against worms and putrefaction. And that *Riccius* the Physitian did use sometimes the weight of a scruple, sometimes of ten grains thereof in burning fevers with good successe. That it can resist Arsnick, the same *Baccius* proves, by the experiment which the Cardinal of *Trent* made upon two Pigeons, (*l. de Unic.*) to which he caused some Arsenick to be given: shortly after he gave som scrapings of his Unicorns horn to one of them, which after some symptoms recovered and lived, the other died two hours after it had eaten the Arsenick: The same Horn cured divers pestilential Fevers, and

7. Browne's many unicorns include rhinoceri, oryces, narwhals, and even "four kinds of nasicornous Beetles."
8. Experience is the mistress of fools.

9. I.e., Thomas Browne.
1. The value of elk's hoof against epilepsy was an article of Ross's faith, and even Browne conceded it.

such as were poisoned. Hence then it appears, that this Horn was both commended by the Ancients, namely by *Aelian, Philostrates,* and divers others, as also by modern Physitians, as *Ficinus, Brasavolus, Matthiolus, Mandella,* and many more. It is true that some might not find the vertue of it, either because it was not the true Horn, or the true dosis was not exhibited,[2] or due time was not observed, or else the malignancy of the disease would not yield. For *Interdum docta plus valet arte malum.*[3] But from hence to deny the Horn or its vertue, were all one as to deny Rhubarb, Agarick, Sena, or other Simples,[4] because they do not always produce the wished effect, or work upon all bodies at all times alike. The means to discriminate the true Unicorns horn from the false, are two, to wit; if it cause the liquor in which it is put, to bubble; and secondly, if it sweat when the poison is near it, as *Baccius* tells us. * * *

[Alexander Ross: from *Arcana Microcosmi* (1652)]

10

* * * Experiments[5] of destroying *Mites* by several Fumes: of the equivocal *Generation* of *Insects:* of feeding a *Carp* in the Air: of making Insects with Cheese, and Sack: of killing Water-Newts, Toads, and Sloworms with several Salts: of killing Frogs by touching their skin, with Vinegar, Pitch, or Mercury: of a Spiders not being Inchanted by a Circle of *Unicorns-horn,* or *Irish Earth,*[6] laid round about it. * * *

[Thomas Sprat: from *The History of the Royal Society,* 1667]

2. It was given in wrong amounts.
3. "Sometimes a sickness is stronger than learned art."
4. Herbs.
5. In this extract, Sprat is describing experiments conducted by the Royal Society.

6. The absence of reptiles from Ireland gave rise to superstitions about the magic properties of Irish earth, as early as Giraldus Cambrensis (ca. 1146–ca. 1220); but this is another story and another set of experiments.

The Restoration and the Eighteenth Century

(1660-1798)

1660: Charles II restored to the English throne.
1688–89: The Glorious Revolution: deposition of James II and accession of William of Orange.
1700: Death of John Dryden.
1707: Act of Union unites Scotland and England, which thus become "Great Britain."
1714: Rule by house of Hanover begins with accession of George I.
1744–45: Deaths of Pope and Swift.
1784: Death of Samuel Johnson.
1789: The French Revolution begins.

The years between the restoration of Charles Stuart to the English throne in 1660 and the outbreak of the Revolution in France in 1789 can conveniently be thought of as a single period in the political (and, as we shall see, in the literary) history of England. The kingdom to which Charles returned had just passed through twenty years of civil war and a radical political and religious revolution that would have left a less virile people exhausted. Early in Charles's reign, the people were visited by two frightful calamities that seemed to the superstitious to be the work of a Divine Providence outraged by rebellion and regicide: the plague visited England in 1665, carrying off over 70,000 people in London alone; and in September, 1666, a fire which raged for five days destroyed a large part of the City, burning more than 13,000 houses and leaving about two-thirds of the population homeless. Yet, within two decades of the king's return, the Royal Navy had defeated the navy of Holland, England's greatest maritime and commercial rival; and, in a series of wars fought between 1689 and 1763 against France, the British acquired an empire which included Canada in the west and India in the east Despite the loss of her thirteen North American colonies, Great Britain was able to enter the final struggle with Revolutionary and Napoleonic France as a world power.

Religion and politics were generally inseparable during the 17th century, for until the religious issues of the age were resolved no stable political settlement was possible. Extremes of belief in religion and of opinions in politics had driven to violent and open conflict Crown and Parliament, Anglican and Puritan, during the twenty years preceding the Restoration. Charles came home to the almost universal satisfaction of his subjects, for after the abdication of Richard Cromwell in 1659 had seemed to bring the country to the brink of chaos, Britons were eager to believe that the king would bring order, peace, freedom under law, and a spirit of mildness back into the national life. But the Restoration itself actually postponed rather than solved the nation's problems. Another thirty years had to pass before any sort of adjustment was possible among antagonistic parties which had made the 17th century so turbulent an age in England.

The restoration of the monarchy meant, inevitably, the restoration of the Established Church; and though Charles had promised mildness toward all but a few of his late father's enemies, the bishops and Anglican clergy felt anything but Christian charity toward their Dissenting brothers. In 1662 Parliament reimposed the Book of Common Prayer on all ministers and congregations, and in 1664 religious meetings in which the forms of the Established Church were not followed were declared illegal. Thousands of clergymen resigned their livings, and the jails were filled with Nonconformist preachers who, like John Bunyan, refused to be silenced. In 1673 the triumph of the Establishment was completed by the Test Act, which required all holders of civil and military offices to receive the sacrament according to the Anglican rite and to declare their disbelief in transubstantiation. Thus the two adversaries of the Anglican Church, Protestant Dissenters and Roman Catholics, were alike excluded from public life, though the practice of occasional conformity (i.e., receiving the sacrament in an Anglican church at rare intervals) enabled many Dissenters to comply with the law. Throughout the closing decades of the 17th century, Anglicans associated Nonconformity with revolution, regicide, republicanism, and the rule of the Puritan Saints—hence, with subversion; and with excessive zeal, "enthusiasm" (i.e., belief in private revelation), and irrationality—hence, with absurdity. The scorn and detestation in which Dissenters were held may be measured by the delight that readers took in Samuel Butler's caricature of Presbyterians and Independents in *Hudibras* (1663), an attitude that persisted unchanged for the rest of the century, as Jonathan Swift's *Tale of a Tub*, written about 1697, makes clear. As for the English Catholics, they appeared always as potential traitors of whom anything evil could be believed. Few doubted, for example, that the Great Fire of 1666 had been set by Catholics.

Although ecclesiastical problems seemed to have been quickly and effectively solved, the constitutional issues which had divided Charles I and Parliament were not so readily settled. Charles II had promised to govern through Parliament, but like other members of his family he held strong views on the power and prerogatives of the Crown. Nevertheless, he was content to avoid crises whenever he could, and since he was an astute politician he frequently could. He concealed from his subjects his Catholic sympathies (on his deathbed he received the last rites of the Roman

Church), for he had no wish "to go on his travels" again. The one great religious and constitutional crisis of his reign was the Popish Plot and its political consequences (1678–81)—the unsuccessful attempt of a faction in Parliament to force Charles to accept a bill excluding his Catholic brother, James, Duke of York, from the succession. Except in this instance, where he was successful because of his courage, duplicity, and political skill, Charles allowed no opportunity for a test of strength between Crown and Parliament.

One important result of the political and religious turmoils of the decade following the Popish Plot was the emergence of two clearly defined political parties, Whig and Tory. The party of the court, which supported the king in 1681, came to be called Tories; the king's opponents, Whigs. By the end of the century the two parties had developed opposed attitudes on other important issues. The Tories drew their strength largely from the landed gentry and the country clergy. They were the conservatives of the period: strong supporters of the Crown and of the Established Church as the two great sources of political and social stability, they bitterly (though futilely) opposed toleration of Dissenters and successfully supported the Test Act. They were hostile to the new moneyed interests, whether among the newer nobility or the increasingly well-to-do middle class, for they held that landed wealth is the only responsible wealth. The Whigs were a less homogeneous group: many powerful nobles, jealous of the powers of the Crown, the merchants and financiers of London, a number of bishops and Low Church clergymen, and the Dissenters; these varied groups were united by their policies of toleration and support of commerce.

After James II came to the throne in 1685, an atmosphere of crisis rapidly developed. He was a most maladroit politician and was afflicted with the stubbornness that characterized all Stuart rulers. Determined to relieve Catholics of civil disabilities and to advance the cause of the Roman Church in England, he began a course of action that soon earned him the distrust and opposition of the great majority of his subjects. Claiming the right to set aside laws and to overrule Parliament, he issued in 1687 a Declaration of Indulgence, suspending the Tests and penal laws against both Catholics and Dissenters, and he began to fill the army and the government—not to mention the universities—with his coreligionists. Matters came to a crisis in the summer of 1688, when a son was born to the queen and the prospect of a succession of Catholic monarchs confronted the nation. Secret negotiations paved the way for the arrival in England of the Dutchman William of Orange at the head of a small armed force. He was the leading champion of Protestantism on the Continent and the husband of James's Protestant daughter Mary. Finding resistance to his hostile subjects impossible, James, after sending his wife and the infant prince out of the country, fled to France on December 11. There he was cordially received by Louis XIV, granted a subsidy, and established with his court at St. Germain. For over half a century the possibility of invasion and the forcible restoration first of James, later of his son "the Old Pretender," and finally of his grandson Prince Charles Edward, was a source of anxiety to the English government. Adherents of the exiled family are called Jacobites (from the Latin *Jacobus*, James).

Many Englishmen and a great many more Scots remained loyal to the house of Stuart until there was nothing left of the Jacobite cause but a pleasant sentiment. Two serious Jacobite rebellions actually occurred: in 1715, when the Old Pretender arrived in Scotland to support an uprising against the newly crowned Hanoverian, George I, and more threateningly in 1745, when Prince Charles Edward (the "Bonnie Prince Charlie" of romantic story) came dangerously close to success in his invasion of England, an event which affects the fortunes of the hero in Henry Fielding's novel *Tom Jones.*

It was only with the flight of James that England could begin to bury the past and to turn toward her destiny in the next age. The coming in of William and Mary and the settlement achieved in 1689 were known as the Glorious or Bloodless Revolution, all the more glorious for being bloodless. A more tolerant era was opening, as was made apparent in important acts passed by Parliament in the first year of the new reign. Since the Revolution had been largely achieved by Whigs, Whig principles prevailed during William's reign. In 1689 the Bill of Rights limited the powers of the Crown, reaffirmed the supremacy of Parliament, and guaranteed important legal rights to individuals. Moreover, the Toleration Act, although it did not repeal the Test, did grant freedom of worship to Dissenters. A number of the conflicting elements in the national life were thus reconciled through what proved to be a workable compromise; and with the passage of the Act of Settlement in 1701, settling the succession to the throne upon Sophia, Electress of Hanover, and her descendants (as the granddaughter of James I, she was the closest Protestant relative of the Princess Anne, James II's younger daughter, whose sole surviving child died in that year), the difficult problems that had so long divided England seemed resolved. The principles established in 1689 brought stability and order into English life and endured unaltered in essentials until the Reform Bill of 1832.

During the reign of Anne, the last Stuart monarch (1702–14), a renewal of tension embittered the political atmosphere. On the Continent England led her allies, Holland, Austria, and Bavaria, to victory in the War of the Spanish Succession against France and Spain (1702–13). The hero of the war was the brilliant Captain-General John Churchill, Duke of Marlborough, who, with his duchess, dominated the queen until 1710. The war was a Whig war, supported by powerful Whig lords and the Whig merchants of London, who grew increasingly rich on war profits and who stood to gain by any weakening of the power of France and Spain. The Whigs were anxious to reward the Dissenters for their loyalty by removing the Test. Unfortunately for them, Anne was especially devoted to the church, and when, in 1710, they were made to appear to threaten the health of the Establishment, she dismissed her Whig ministers and called in Robert Harley as Lord Treasurer and the brilliant young Henry St. John as Secretary of State (in charge of foreign relations) to form the Tory ministry which governed England during the last four years of her reign. The Marlboroughs were dismissed, the duke even losing his command in 1711, but not before the royal favor and a grateful nation had made him immensely rich and had given him the land on which he built his famous palace, Blenheim (pronounced *Blen'm*) in memory of the most brilliant victory (pronounced *Blén-hime*) of the war.

It was these Tory ministers whom Defoe and Swift served in their different ways; it was for them that Matthew Prior negotiated the Peace of Utrecht, ratified in 1713. To Swift's despair, a bitter rivalry developed between Harley (then Earl of Oxford) and St. John (then Viscount Bolingbroke) during 1713–14, and as the queen's life faded in the summer of 1714, Bolingbroke succeeded in ousting Oxford, only to have his own ambitions thwarted by the death of Anne and the return to power of the vindictive Whigs with the accession of George I, son of the late Sophia, Electress of Hanover. For a moment it seemed as if this event might not occur without bloodshed, but the crisis quickly passed, the Protestant succession was not immediately opposed by Jacobites, and the Whigs turned happily to investigating the conduct of the former ministers. Harley was imprisoned in the Tower of London (where he remained until 1717), and Bolingbroke, charged with treasonable correspondence with the Pretender, fled to France, where he actually became, for a while, Secretary of State to the Jacobite court. Pardoned in 1723 but denied his seat in the House of Lords, he returned to England and directed the opposition to Robert Walpole, while seeing much of Pope and playing the gentleman-farmer-philosopher at Dawley Farm.

The three Georges who occupied the throne during the rest of the century presided over a nation that grew increasingly prosperous through war, trade, and the beginnings of industrialism. George I (reigned 1714–27) and George II (reigned 1727–60) spoke broken English, had little interest in the affairs of the country. In their hearts they remained petty German princelings even when they were kings of Great Britain, spending as much time as possible in Hanover. Under such circumstances it was inevitable that ministers should become more important and more independent of the Crown than they had been under stronger and more intelligent monarchs. Through the indifference of two kings and the ambition and great abilities of the Whig Prime Minister Sir Robert Walpole, the modern system of ministerial government began to develop. This was the last important contribution of the age to British political institutions. Walpole's long ascendency (1721–42) brought a period of peace and prosperity and of capable government based, paradoxically, on flagrant political corruption. Although Walpole strengthened the importance of the House of Commons in British politics, he nonetheless continued, if he did not increase, the corruption of its members through bribery. He was a practical man and cared little for literature, preferring to spend money on useful journalists and voting Members of Parliament rather than on poets. Thus with two kings who knew nothing of literature and a prime minister who was indifferent to it, English writers could not expect the shower of offices and government sinecures that had made the age of Anne the great age of patronage: Congreve, Steele, Addison, Prior, Swift had expected and obtained such rewards both for their literary eminence and for their service to party. But after 1715, as patronage declined, authors found that they must turn to the publishers, who could pay them well because of the growing reading public. Indeed, Johnson was accustomed to declare that the booksellers of the midcentury had become the patrons of literature.

The long reign of George III (1760–1820), the first Hanoverian monarch born in England, somewhat retarded the development of government through parties and responsible ministers, for the king was determined to rule personally, and he succeeded in doing so to a remarkable degree. This was a dangerous policy for a man who, as a politician, was neither wise nor liberal. He brought the Tories back into power after they had been excluded from office for 46 years, and he did all that he could to crush the long-powerful Whig oligarchy.

INTELLECTUAL BACKGROUND

The political turbulence of the 17th century subsided only gradually during the last decades of the century, and the "peace of the Augustans" did not settle over England until the Protestant succession had been safely accomplished. Analogously, the literature of the Restoration period (1660–1700) did not at once attain the measured pace and disciplined order that we associate with "classic" art. John Dryden himself, the principal writer of the period, retained much of the characteristic boldness and extravagant wit of the literature of the earlier part of the century, delighting, as Johnson remarked, "in wild and daring sallies of sentiment, in the irregular and excentric violence of wit." The period is remarkable for variety: Milton's major poems, relics of an earlier age, appeared in 1667 (*Paradise Lost*) and 1671 (*Paradise Regained* and *Samson Agonistes*). The age that produced Bunyan's *Pilgrim's Progress*, perhaps the greatest literary expression of the Nonconformist conscience, produced also the libertine poems of such court wits as Rochester, Sedley, and Etherege, savage satire like Butler's, the brilliant depiction of the dissolute but elegant manners of the upper classes in the comedies of Etherege, Wycherley, and Congreve, and the rant and bombast of Dryden's rhymed heroic plays. But the general drift was toward classic restraint and good sense; and both Dryden's example, in the works of his maturity, and his numerous critical essays helped to formulate standards and to make the period the foundation on which the neoclassical art of the next century was erected. His literary theories, the poetic language that he shaped, and his metrics determined the dominant literary tendencies of the 18th century.

Perhaps most people think of the Restoration as a period wholly given over to frivolity and debauchery. It is true that Puritan rigidities (never enforced quite as rigorously as sometimes has been made out) were quickly repudiated by the upper classes and that the Saints were rendered impotent by harsh prohibitive laws. It is true that the king was easy-going, pleasure-loving, and amorous, more fond of the society of boon companions than he was of business of state, and lavishly extravagant in squandering public funds on his mistresses. It is true that the court itself was luxurious, immoral, full of intrigue. It is true that all this is vividly reflected in lampoons, satires, and comedies. But the ordinary life of the nation did not radically change. Rural manners, then as now, were conservative and old-fashioned. The London citizens, middle-class and respectable, cherishing much of the independence and piety of Dissent, were scandalized by the behavior of such lewd young men as Rochester and Etherege, who regarded them with contempt and considered their wives and daughters fair game. Even good royalists like John Evelyn and Samuel Pepys often speak anxiously in their diaries of the moral laxness of the court and the danger to the country of the king's example.

Charles himself had serious intellectual interests and was a patron of the arts. He dabbled in chemistry and was interested in the progress of science. A characteristic act was his chartering in 1662 the Royal Society of London for the Improving of Natural Knowledge, thus giving official approval to the scientific movement that Francis Bacon had initiated early in the century and that was just then coming to maturity. The king's love of music and painting led him to import from the Continent composers, musicians, new musical instruments, the French and Italian opera, and painting and painters largely from the Low Countries. His interest in the theater was demonstrated by the chartering of two companies of actors in 1660, both under royal patronage, the King's Players, and the Duke's— the Duke being James, Duke of York.

It is natural, therefore, that the most characteristic art of the period reflected the interests and tastes of those who supported it, as is the case today. Artists addressed themselves to court and "town," the western sub-urbs which were the center of fashion. The middle-class tradesmen who lodged over their shops in the City (i.e., that part of greater London which was once within the city walls and which was then thickly popu-lated—not, as it is today, almost wholly given over to business and fi-nance) were scorned as tasteless barbarians. Except in the theater, litera-ture was not in itself a gainful profession (as it was to become in the 18th century), and writers looked for patronage from the court and the great nobles. Milton, for example, received only £5 for the first edition of *Para-dise Lost*. By the end of the century, however, thanks to the enterprise of the bookseller Jacob Tonson and the new device of publishing books through subscription (i.e., soliciting payment in advance for de luxe copies of a work, in addition to publishing a regular trade edition), Dryden was able to earn between £1000 and £1200 by his translation of the works of Virgil (1697). And Pope's Homer, similarly published between 1715 and 1726, was to prove even more profitable.

Perhaps the most important aspect of the Restoration period is the in-creasing challenge of various forms of secular thought to the old religious orthodoxies which had been matters of life and death since the Reforma-tion. We can observe most clearly in this period the beginnings of the secularization of values and thought that characterizes Western society to-day. As the contentious voices of Roman, Anglican, and Dissenter grew more and more subdued, other interests attracted adventurous minds. Thomas Hobbes in a bold and, to many, shocking book, *Leviathan* (1651), had taught a philosophic materialism and advocated an absolute government as the most efficacious check to human nature, which he described as wholly driven by egoistic and predatory passions. Detested by the church and attacked on all sides, these ideas nonetheless played their role in the lives and writings of some of the more advanced young men, and they provoked by way of reaction in the next century an opti-mistic insistence on the natural goodness of man. A soberer and more ancient tradition was philosophic skepticism. Originating in ancient Greece, skepticism had found its most persuasive recent statement in the essays of the Frenchman Michel de Montaigne (1533–92), whose influence was widespread throughout 17th-century Europe. The skeptic argued that all our knowledge is derived from our senses, but that our senses do not report the world around us accurately, and that therefore reliable knowledge is an impossibility. The safest course is to affirm nothing as absolutely true, to remember that most beliefs are mere opinions, and, where possible, to be guided by the traditional in matters intellectual, political, and ethical. Butler, Dryden, and Rochester, among others, more or less adhered to this doctrine. But though the skeptic remained in doubt about the results of human reasoning, he was not precluded from religious beliefs, for he could assert (as did Dryden after his conversion to Catholicism) that faith alone is necessary for accepting the mysteries of the Christian religion.

The new science, already self-confident if not quite triumphant, was rapidly altering men's view of nature. The members of the Royal Society were all good theists and would have been perplexed had they been told that, in the 19th century, science and religion would come to seem incompatible. Science in the 17th century was principally concerned with the physical sciences—with astronomy, physics, and to a lesser degree, chemistry; and the discoveries in these sciences were reassuring in their revelation of universal and immutable law and order, clear revelations of the wisdom and goodness of God in His creation. Such laws of nature as Boyle's law of the behavior of gases under pressure or Newton's law of gravitation seemed obviously to support the idea that a beneficent, divine intelligence created and directs the universe: they could be reduced to simple mathematical terms and were demonstrably universal and unchanging. The whole creation appeared a revelation of the mind, intent, and nature of the Creator. The truest truths proved to be the clearest, the simplest, the most general. Such truths, while they confirmed the existence of a Deity, seemed at the same time to render unnecessary, even preposterous, the intricate a priori reasoning of Scholastic philosophy, and to promise a time, not remote, when mystery would be banished entirely from nature. Indeed the new religion, Deism or Natural Religion, which had an increasingly wide appeal to "enlightened" minds, deduced its simple rationalistic creed from the Book of Nature, God's first and to many 18th-century men, only valid revelation. The Deists deduced the existence of a Supreme Being or First Cause from the existence of the universe: a creature presupposes a Creator. The laws of nature, the structure of the universe—its regularity, order, and purposefulness—sufficiently proved the reasonableness, goodness, and wisdom of this Creator. Him we can and must revere; but, good though He is, it is demonstrable that He does not punish vice and reward virtue in this life; and therefore, being good and just, He must do so in some future life: hence, we must believe in immortality. Meanwhile, here on earth, it is our duty to co-operate with Nature and the Deity, cultivating as best we can wisdom, virtue, and benevolence. This creed is as simple and as rational as one of Newton's laws; but its complete omission of the "second revelation" of the Scriptures, the scheme of salvation through the vicarious atonement, made it unacceptable to many Christians, although many were attracted by its reasonableness and found it possible to accept both Natural Religion and revealed Christianity.

As the 17th century drew to a close, its temper became more secular, tolerant, and moderate. If it is not quite possible to talk sensibly of an "Age of Reason" in England, it is possible to think of the early decades of the 18th century as a period of good sense, restraint, and reasonableness. "Enthusiasm," that state of mind which asserted the validity of private inspiration and which had fostered a dangerous zeal among the Saints of Dissent, was decried. The new age was willing to settle for the possible within the limits of human intelligence and of the material world. Its temper was expressed by its most influential philosopher, John Locke (1632–1704), in his *Essay Concerning Human Understanding* (1690):

> If by this inquiry into the nature of the understanding, I can discover the powers thereof; how far they reach; to what things they are in any degree proportionate; and where they fail us, I suppose it may be of use to prevail with the busy mind of man to be more cautious in meddling with things exceeding its comprehension; to stop when it is at the utmost extent of its tether; and to sit down in a quiet ignorance of those things which, upon examination, are found to be beyond the reach of our capacities. We should not then perhaps be so forward, out of an affectation of an universal knowledge, to raise questions, and perplex ourselves and others with disputes about things to which our understandings are not suited; and of which we cannot frame in our minds any clear and distinct perceptions, or whereof * * * we have not any notions at all. If we can find out how far the understanding can extend its view; how far it has faculties to attain certainty; and in what cases it can only judge and guess, we may learn to content ourselves with what is attainable by us in this state. * * * Our business here is not to know all things, but those which concern our conduct.

These words might be taken as the creed of 18th-century England. Such a position is Swift's, when he inveighs against metaphysics, abstract logical deductions, and theoretical science; it is similar to Pope's in the *Essay on Man*; it prompts Dr. Johnson to talk of "the business of living"; it helps to account for the emphasis that the Anglican clergy put on good works, rather than faith, as the way to salvation, and for their dislike of emotion and "enthusiasm" in religion.

But if the 18th century brought a recognition of the limitations of man, it also took an optimistic view of his moral nature. Rejecting Hobbes's view of man as in essence a selfish and predatory creature and ignoring politely the Christian doctrine of original sin, 18th-century philosophers asserted that man is naturally good and that he finds his highest happiness in the exercise of virtue and benevolence. Such a view of human nature we describe as "sentimental." It found the source of virtue in men's instinctive and social impulses rather than in a code of conduct sanctioned by divine law. And men began to feel—or to fancy that they felt—exquisite pleasure in the exercise of benevolent impulses. Sentimentalism fostered a benevolism that led to social reforms seldom envisioned in earlier times—to the improvement of jails, to the relief of imprisoned debtors, to the establishment of foundling hospitals and of homes for penitent prostitutes, and ultimately to the abolition of the slave trade; but it also encouraged a ready flow of feeling and tears and a capacity to respond to the joys and sorrows of others which suggests that the period was much more an Age of Feeling than an Age of Reason. The doctrine of the natural goodness of man seemed to many to suggest that it is civilization which corrupts us and that primitive men, "noble savages" who live according to nature, are models of innocence and virtue. Such notions encouraged an interest in primitive societies and even helped to prepare for the enthusiastic reception given the peasant poet Robert Burns, an "original genius," as well as for William Wordsworth's interest in children and in simple, rural people.

As the wave of sentimentalism mounted, a parallel rise of religious feeling occurred after about 1740. The great religious revival known as Methodism was led by John Wesley (1703–91), his brother Charles (1707–88), and George Whitefield (1714–70), all Oxford graduates. The Methodists took their gospel to the common people, preaching the necessity of a conviction of sin, and of conversion, and the joy of the "blessed assurance" of being saved. Often denied the privilege of preaching in village churches, they preached to thousands in the open fields and in barns. The somnolent Anglican Church and the self-assured upper classes were repelled by the emotionalism aroused by Methodist preachers among the lower orders. It seemed as if the irrationality, zeal, and enthusiasm of the Puritan sects were being revived. But the religious awakening persisted, and affected many clergymen and laymen within the Establishment, who, as "Evangelicals," reanimated the church and promoted unworldliness and piety. And yet the insistence of Methodists on faith over works as the way to salvation did not prevent them or their Anglican counterparts from playing important roles in many of the social reforms of the time, especially in helping to abolish slavery and the slave trade.

NEOCLASSICAL LITERARY THEORY

The literature of the period between 1660 and 1785 can conveniently, though perhaps too schematically, be considered as falling into three lesser periods of about forty years each: the first, extending to the death of Dryden in 1700, may be thought of as the period in which English "neoclassical" literature came into being and its critical principles were formulated; the second, ending with the death of Pope in 1744 and of Swift in 1745, brought to its culmination the literary movement initiated by Dryden and his generation; the third, concluding with the death of Johnson in 1784 and the publication of William Cowper's *The Task* in 1785, was a period in which neoclassical principles were confronted by new ideas which contained within themselves the origins of the Romantic movement of the early 19th century.

Seldom in the course of English literature can we find so radical and apparently sudden a change of taste as took place about 1660. But actually the change was not so sudden as it appears. Like the English Renaissance, it was part of a general movement in European culture, seen perhaps at its most impressive in 17th-century France. Described most simply, it was a reaction against the intricacy and occasional obscurity, boldness, and extravagance of European literature of the late Renaissance, in favor of greater simplicity, clarity, restraint, regularity, and good sense in all sorts of writing. This tendency is most readily to be observed in the preference of Dryden and his contemporaries for "easy, natural" wit, which aims to surprise rather than to shock, as did much metaphysical wit. It accompanied, though it was not necessarily caused by, the development of certain rationalistic philosophies and the rise of experimental science, as well as a desire for peace and order after an era of violent extremism.

This movement produced in France the impressive body of classical literature that distinguished the age of Louis XIV. In England it produced a literature that we term "neoclassical," or "Augustan," because it was strongly influenced by the writers of the reign of the first Roman Emperor, Augustus Caesar, just before the beginning of the Christian era. Rome's Augustan Age was a period of stability and peace after the civil war that followed the death of Julius Caesar. Its chief poets, Virgil, Horace, and Ovid, addressed their carefully ordered, disciplined, and polished works to a sophisticated aristocracy, among whom they found generous patrons. Dryden's generation was aware of an analogy between the situations of post-Civil War England and Augustan Rome. Charles seemed in 1660 a kind of Augustus, bringing to England civilized order and enlightened patronage of the arts, which, as in ancient Rome, reflected the interests and taste of the aristocracy. The English Augustans, in fact, were self-consciously Augustan in a way that Wordsworth and Coleridge could not have been self-consciously "Romantic." The image of Augustan Rome and the example of her writers play an active role in the literature of the age.

Charles and his followers, who had spent many years of their exile in France, inevitably brought back to England an admiration of contemporary French literature as well as of French fashions and elegance. But it is a mistake to regard the Restoration, as many historians have done, as a period in which the court and its poets betrayed English genius to French rules and taste. The French critics were of course known and studied in England, and the theories of such writers as Pierre Corneille, René Rapin, and Nicolas Boileau were influential in helping Dryden and his fellows to formulate their own standards. But as, during the period of Italian influence in the 16th century, English literature remained stubbornly English, so now: English writers took what they required from France, but used it for their own ends. It was not Dryden's aim merely to imitate the French poets or for that matter the Latin, but to produce in England works that would be worthy to stand beside theirs. He knew that this could be done only if English literature remained true to its living tradition: Chaucer, Spenser, Shakespeare, Jonson, Donne entered into his literary consciousness as well as Virgil, Horace, Longinus, or Corneille.

It is likely that, had Charles never lived abroad, the English neoclassical period would have come into existence pretty much in the form that it actually assumed. Ben Jonson's classicism (manifested in his poems and comedies and in the critical observations gathered from ancient and Renaissance writers which make up his *Discoveries*) brought to a focus by both example and precept the classicizing tendencies of the English Renaissance. His closed heroic couplets are the model for those of Edmund Waller and Sir John Denham, whom Dryden considered the principal "refiners" of English metrics. One of the lesser "Sons of Ben," Sir John Beaumont, at least as early as 1625—and incidentally in couplets that might have been the very pattern of those of Dryden and Pope—proposed critical standards that became dominant after 1660:

Pure phrase, fit epithets, a sober care
Of metaphors, descriptions clear, yet rare,
Similitudes contracted, smooth and round,
Not vexed by learning, but with Nature crowned:
Strong figures drawn from deep invention's springs,
Consisting less in words, and more in things:
A language not affecting ancient times,
Nor Latin shreds, by which the pedant climbs.

[*To His Late Majesty, Concerning the True Form
of English Poetry*]

Such standards are alien to the poetry of Donne, Crashaw, or Milton; on the other hand they prefigure the poetry of the Augustans, and make evident the fact that a native "classicism" existed side by side with metaphysical poetry. The emphasis on the correct ("pure"), the appropriate ("fit"), restraint and discipline ("sober care"), clarity, the fresh and surprising ("rare"), Nature, strength, freedom from pedantry—these indicate exactly the direction English literature was to take after the Restoration.

What was the prevalent idea of the nature of the poet? He must, of course, be a genius, for all agreed with Horace that the poet is born, not made. But even genius must be trained and disciplined if it is to produce art. The word *poet* is derived from a Greek word meaning "maker," and it is this notion that dominated the Augustans' idea of the poet: he is not a prophet, a visionary, a seer, but the maker of an object, a poem. He must have "invention," the gift of finding materials for his poems—fictional, but representative, images of human actions and of the world in which those actions take place; and he must so vivify, heighten, and order those materials that they seem true pictures of what is, or might or ought to be, or of the evil and folly that we should avoid. For the poet makes this image of life in order to teach, not so much by precept and moral sentences as by examples that move our love and admiration or evoke our fear and detestation. And to teach effectively he must please us by his fictions and by all the ornaments of language, metrics, and rhetoric that belong to his craft.

The materials of poetry must derive from, conform to, and recognizably represent "Nature," a word of many meanings in the neoclassic or any age. The Augustans were especially conscious of one meaning: Nature as the universal, permanent, and representative elements in the moral and intellectual experience of men. External nature—the landscape—both as a source of aesthetic pleasure and as an object of scientific inquiry or religious contemplation attracted the attention of Englishmen throughout the 18th century. But Pope's injunction to the critic, "First follow Nature," has primarily *human* nature and *human* experience in view. Nature is truth in the sense that it includes the permanent, enduring, general truths which have been, are, and will be true for all men, in all times, everywhere. The poet exists not to take us on long voyages to discover the new and unique ("We were the first that ever burst / Into that silent sea") but to reveal the permanent and the representative in human experience through what becomes for us an act of recognition. As Pope says of "true wit" or poetry, it "gives us back an image of our minds."

So Johnson, in Chapter X of *Rasselas*, says that the poet is to examine "not the individual, but the species; to remark general properties and large appearances * * * to exhibit in his portraits of nature such prominent and striking features as recall the original to every mind." Historians during this period studied the particulars of history in order to observe the universal human nature which those particulars reveal; and scientists formulated, after experiment and observation of particulars, universal and permanent laws of nature. Indeed, Sir Isaac Newton's *Principia* (1687) did much to reinforce scientifically the idea of Nature as order, which underlies such a typical 18th-century work as Pope's *Essay on Man*.

But it would be erroneous to assume that this emphasis on the general and the representative excluded the particular from the arts and reduced their material to the merely obvious, typical, and familiar. No art—and no theory of art—can be so simple. Originality, novelty, accuracy of observation were desired in neoclassical as well as in Romantic art. If human nature was held to be uniform, men were known to be infinitely varied; and the task of the artist was so to treat the particular as to render it representative. Thus Pope, after praising the characters of Shakespeare because they are "Nature herself," continued: "But every single character in Shakespeare is as much an individual as those in life itself; it is * * * impossible to find any two alike * * * " And Johnson praised the poet James Thomson because he looked on external nature "with a mind that at once comprehends the vast, and attends to the minute."

But although Nature was "at once the source, and end, and test of art," the poet could learn much from the ancients—the great writers, philosophers, critics, sculptors, and architects of Greece and especially of Rome. They were useful guides not because they were ancient or because they were thought to have some prescriptive authority to command attention and respect, but because they had so truly expressed Nature that, despite changes as radical as those wrought by the establishment of Christianity in Europe, they had lost none of their relevance to the experience of modern men. As Pope said, Homer and Nature were the same; and both Pope and his readers found Horace's satires on Roman society thoroughly applicable to their own world, for Horace had followed Nature, "one clear, unchanged, and universal light."

And how did a poet come to know Nature? Not, certainly, by a life of solitude or rural retirement, or by the intermittent light of visionary gleams. The poet was to be a man living among men and speaking to men, a member of society, an important and functional part of a civilized community that would not be civilized without his presence. Only by living among men and by ceaseless and sympathetic observation of them could he gain the knowledge of Nature required of him as a poet. He was also to supplement his own inevitably limited experience by the wisdom of the past, by studying Nature wherever truthfully represented: in Homer, Virgil, Horace, or Shakespeare.

He could learn also from the ancients how to practice his craft. If a poem is an object to be made, the maker, like an architect or a cabinetmaker, must follow sound principles or botch the job. The ancients—Aristotle in his *Poetics*, Horace in his *Ars Poetica*, Quintilian in his *Institutio Oratoria*, for instance—had left more or less systematized principles (or to use the word current among the Augustans, "rules") by which to order "Nature"—the material of art—into an epic, a tragedy, a dramatic character, an oration. They had deduced these rules from the practice of earlier masters—Homer, Sophocles, the Greek and Roman orators. Italian and French critics during the 16th and 17th centuries invented new rules of their own and refined on and further codified those of the ancients. The rules directed the planning and executing of one or another of the literary "kinds," or genres: epic, tragedy, comedy, pastoral, satire, ode; the choice of language, which must differ from genre to genre; the use of figures and tropes; tone, style, characters. They could serve as a short cut to Nature, for as Pope said, they "are Nature methodized."

In England, actually, the rules were followed in rather a casual way. Most readers were prepared to admit that mere correctness could not recommend a poem which was commonplace in thought and sentiment and unanimated by the vital force of genius. Almost everyone acknowledged that Shakespeare had written the greatest body of drama in modern literature without following the rules of the ancients or the moderns. Indeed, the presence of Shakespeare and the native English suspicion of mere theory prevented English neoclassical literature from being shackled by pedantic critics. In 1765 Samuel Johnson was to brush aside in the name of Shakespeare and good sense two hundred years of critical reverence for the three unities of action, place, and time, a reverence which had not, however, much affected the plotting of English plays during that period.

The idea that each of the literary kinds is distinct and has its own proper material, characters, language, and style, was influential throughout our period. Epic and tragedy, the loftiest and most serious of the kinds, demand noble English, stately verse, heightened diction, splendor of figures and ornaments. (This can be readily understood by examining a few pages of *Paradise Lost*.) Comedy, on the other hand, since it deals not with ideal heroes or great kings and generals as do epic and tragedy, but with ordinary people in daily life, calls for a lower style and natural, unadorned language. This principle was known as the principle of "decorum" or the appropriate; it determined Dryden's definition of wit as "a propriety of thoughts and words; or, in other terms, thoughts and words elegantly adapted to the subject."

Examining the psychological faculties that distinguish the artist from other men, critics fixed upon "wit" as his most important and characteristic endowment. "Wit," like "Nature," is a complicated word of many meanings. Here it implies quickness and liveliness of mind, inventiveness, a readiness to perceive resemblances between things apparently unlike and so to enliven literary discourse with appropriate images, similes, and metaphors. This faculty was often identified with "fancy" or "imagination," and was thought to be irregular, wayward, extravagant, unless curbed and disciplined by another and soberer faculty, "judgment." An excess of imagination was considered dangerous to sanity, and in literature to lead away from Nature and truth to falsehood and such violent and farfetched conceits as we find in the poetry of Donne or Crashaw at their boldest. One task of the age was to tame what seemed the wildness of metaphysical wit into the more reasonable and decorous wit that Dryden described in the passage quoted above. So Pope insists in the *Essay on Criticism*, lines 80–83, on the necessity of a harmonious union of judgment and fancy (which he calls "wit") in a work of literature. Though judgment was to tame, it was not to suppress passion, energy, or originality, but to make them more effective through discipline. Pope expresses the aesthetic ideal of the age succinctly in a traditional image: "The wingéd courser, like a generous horse, / Shows most true mettle when you check his course." Only that literature is true which remains true to universal human experience; and for it to do so, wayward wit or fancy must be firmly guided.

Two more general observations must be made. When Wordsworth, in the Preface to *Lyrical Ballads* (1800), declared that the poems were written "in a selection of the language really used by men," he went on to attack 18th-century poets for their use of an artificial and stock "diction" and to illustrate it by Thomas Gray's sonnet, *On the Death of Richard West*. Coleridge, in *Biographia Literaria* (1817), also had a good deal to say on the subject. Although the bulk of good poetry in the 18th century, as in other times, is written in "a selection of the language really used by men," the special and stylized diction to which the two early Romantics objected did exist, especially in heroic, descriptive, pastoral, and lyric poetry. It is characterized by periphrasis (a roundabout and elegant way of avoiding homely words: "finny tribe" for "fish," or "household feathery people" for "chickens"); frequently used stock phrases, such as "shining sword," "verdant mead," "bounding main," "checkered shade"; words used in their original Latin sense, such as "genial," "gelid," "horrid"; and a fondness for adjectives ending in *y*. This language is much older than the 18th century. It originated in the attempt of Renaissance poets all over Europe to rival the elegant and golden diction of Virgil and other Roman writers. Milton depended on it to help him obtain "answerable style" for the lofty theme of *Paradise Lost*. Dryden used it in his translation of Virgil. Thomson found it suitable in passages of generalized description in *The Seasons*, and Pope employed it, not always happily, in his versions of Homer. Used with discretion it could be both subtle and expressive; but when it became a mannerism as it did with Gray (see stanzas 3 and 4 of his *Eton* ode), or a dead and conventional language used mechanically, as it did with scores of mere versifiers, it properly became an object of contempt. An extreme example of a desire to attain dignity by periphrasis is this absurd translation into poetic diction of the simple sentence, "Hay and straw were burned in the fields of Thessaly":

> There at his words devouring Vulcan feasts
> On all the tribute which Thessalian meads
> Yield to the scythe, and riots on the heaps
> Of Ceres, emptied of the ripened grain.
>
> [Glover's *Leonidas*, 1737]

But such extremes of mannerism are seldom to be found in the works of the good poets of the century.

Finally, there is the matter of versification. Everyone associates the neoclassical period with the "closed" heroic couplet—i.e., a pentameter couplet which more often than not contains within itself a complete statement and so is closed by a semicolon, period, question mark, or exclamation point. Within these two lines it was possible, but neither imperative nor habitual, to attain certain rhetorical or witty effects by the use of parallelism, balance, or antithesis within the couplet as a whole or the individual line. The second line of the couplet might be made closely parallel in structure and meaning to the first, or the two could be played off against each other in antithesis; taking advantage of the fact that normally a pentameter line of English verse contains at some point a slight pause called a "caesura," one part of a line so divided can be made parallel with or antithetical to the other or even to one of the two parts of the following line. This can be illustrated by a passage from Sir John Denham's *Cooper's Hill* (1642), which was quoted and parodied *ad nauseam* for many years. The poem addresses the Thames and builds up a witty comparison between the flow of a river and the flow of verse (italics are the present editor's, to illustrate the rhetorical effects):

> O could I flow like thee, || and make thy stream
> Parallelism: *My* great *example,* || as it is *my theme!*
> Double balance: *Though deep,* yet *clear,* || *though gentle,* yet not *dull,*
> Double balance: *Strong* without *rage,* || without o'erflowing, *full.*

It only remained for Dryden and Pope to bind such passages more tightly together with alliteration and assonance, and the typical metrical-rhetorical wit of the new age had been perfected.

Shortly after the beginning of the 18th century began the vogue of blank verse—the other metrical form most favored by the age. Philosophical poems, descriptive poems, meditative poems, and original or translated epics employed blank verse of one sort or another from Thomson's *Seasons* (1726–30) to Cowper's *The Task* (1785); and the tradition determined Wordsworth's use of the form in *Tintern Abbey* and *The Prelude*. The two chief patterns of blank verse available to the age were the blank verse of Milton in *Paradise Lost* and the dramatic blank verse of Dryden and other Restoration tragic poets. The influence of Milton is easily detected, not by the success with which his manner was imitated, but by the amateur performance of most of those who try to play on his instrument. The dramatic blank verse of the Restoration too often led in 18th-century poetry to a rather disagreeably declamatory and rhetorical manner. But gradually a more lyrical blank verse developed, of which William Cowper is the master; and this more plastic metrical line had a formative influence on the blank verse of William Wordsworth.

RESTORATION LITERATURE, 1660–1700

The critical ideas discussed above determined the characteristics of the typical literature of our period; but it should not be assumed that there was universal agreement on all points or that the literature of the 18th century was monotonously uniform. Writers could assent to the general system of critical theory and at the same time work as individuals; change and experiment went on as always, and from the beginning there was room for different, even opposite, tastes and interests from those that neoclassical literary standards asserted.

The period between 1660 and 1700 was remarkably varied and vigorous. Dryden was the dominant figure, of course, writing in all the important contemporary forms—occasional verse, comedy, tragedy, heroic play, ode, satire, translation, and critical essay—and the variety of Dryden suggests the variety of his age. Both his example and his precepts had great influence, but that influence did not enforce a sterile and pedantic conformity to the rules of critics, but instead gave to the England of his day a *modern* literature, cosmopolitan, to be sure, but possessing the richness and variety that he admired in the Elizabethans, the "God's plenty" that he praised in Chaucer's *Canterbury Tales*.

The prose of the Restoration is a clear indication of the direction in which literature was moving. The styles of Donne's sermons, of Milton's pamphlets, of Sir Thomas Browne's writings, and of the character books (to select four different kinds of earlier 17th-century prose) were quite unsuitable to serve the ends of the new age. They were too elaborate, too involved, too ornate, too insistently musical, or too wittily rhetorical and pointed for mere exposition or social intercourse. The Royal Society decreed that its members must employ only a plain, concise, and utilitarian prose style suitable to the clear communication of scientific truths. Metaphors, similes, and rhetorical flourishes were disapproved because they engaged the emotions, not the reason, and though they were tolerable in poetry, they had no place in rational discourse. Similarly the learned, often pedantic language, the rhetoric and imagery and emotional intensity of earlier 17th-century pulpit oratory gradually gave way to a simplicity and plainness of diction and style entirely appropriate to sermons which sought mainly to inculcate in both the ignorant and the learned a rational morality in the conduct of life, and to avoid anything smacking of religious "enthusiasm." In polite literature, thanks to the example of such writers as Abraham Cowley, Dryden, and Sir William Temple, the ideal of good prose came to be a clear, simple, and natural style which has the ease and poise of well-bred urbane conversation. This is a social prose, designed for a social age. Later, it was available to the writers of periodical essays, such as Addison or Steele, to the novelists of the 18th century, and to the many practitioners of the delightful art of letter-writing, one of the minor literary achievements of the 18th-century. This movement toward clarity and simplicity in prose accompanied a similar movement away from the intricacies of metaphysical wit in verse, which found an early statement in Dryden's *Essay of Dramatic Poesy*.

But if prose was simplified and wit was tamed, the Restoration did not break wholly with the immediate past. It retained the Renaissance admiration for the typically aristocratic heroic ideal as expressed in the "heroic poem" or epic. *Paradise Lost*, carefully modeled though it is on the structure and conventions of ancient epic poetry, did not meet the expectations of most Restoration readers, who associated the heroic poem with "fierce wars and faithful loves" and expected it to offer patterns of ideal virtue and heroism for the emulation of princes and generals. General enthusiasm for Milton's epic did not develop until the early 18th century. The romantic idealism of the heroic mode was most characteristically expressed during the Restoration not in the heroic poem (except for Dryden's translations of the *Aeneid* and of Chaucer's Knight's Tale), but in the heroic play, which Dryden, its foremost practitioner, defined as "a heroic poem in little." The theme of these plays (their vogue lasted from about 1664 to about 1675) was the conflict between love and honor in the hearts of impossibly valorous heroes and impossibly high-minded and attractive ladies. These lovers, amidst the turmoil of battles and busy, bustling intrigue, are driven by erotic passion and heroic pride; they engage in debates on love and points of honor, they utter many fine sentiments, as well as a good deal of rather engaging nonsense, in heroic couplets and bold, figurative, and extravagant language. Typical examples are Dryden's *Conquest of Granada* in two parts (produced in 1670, 1671) and *Aureng-Zebe* (produced in 1675), his last work in this genre. A burlesque of the heroic play, *The Rehearsal* (produced in 1671), by the Duke of Buckingham (see the character of Zimri in Dryden's *Absalom and Achitophel*, lines 554–569, below) and others, raised a laugh at the absurdities of the genre and at Dryden himself, who was caricatured in the person of the playwright, Mr. Bayes.

A great many tragedies were written and produced, but as a rule they are inferior to those of the Elizabethan and Jacobean eras. Dryden achieved one undoubted masterpiece in his blank verse tragedy *All for Love* (produced 1677), based on the story of Antony and Cleopatra. In this play we can observe the effect of neoclassic taste on the drama: Dryden kept the three unities of action, place, and time more exactly, as he remarked, than "the English theater requires"; he consequently greatly simplified the action and therefore drastically reduced the number of characters. Instead of Shakespeare's world-wide panorama, his rapid shifts of scene, his complex characters, we have the last hours of the tragic lovers presented in a static though grand manner and in a plot that is almost too neatly symmetrical. The characters are much simpler and more generalized than are Shakespeare's, and the language and imagery (when Dryden adapts passages from Shakespeare's play) are less involved and more restrained. But though not Shakespeare, *All for Love* is a noble tragedy. The two other eminent tragic poets of the period were Nathaniel Lee (ca. 1649–92), known for violent plots, the wild emotions of his characters, and the extravagance of his rhetoric; and Thomas Otway (1652–85), who excelled in pathos. His two best tragedies, *The Orphan* (produced in 1680) and *Venice Preserved* (produced in 1682), have a rather hothouse emotional quality, but they kept the stage far into the 19th century. Not one enduring tragedy was written during the 18th century. Addison's *Cato* (produced in 1713) is a museum piece, illustrating the frigidity of "correct" and rule-bound tragedy. The long succession of verse tragedy thereafter was cursed by hollow rhetoric, stilted declamation, forced emotion, and conventional diction. George Lillo's *London Merchant* (produced in 1731) in prose, dealing with commonplace characters in mercantile life, took a feeble step in the direction of the sort of realistic, middle-class tragedy with which we are familiar today.

The real distinction of Restoration drama was comedy, which, like its cousin satire, is concerned with criticism of man as a moral and social being. Although Dryden had no great talent for the comic, he produced a number of successful comedies, the best of which have well-constructed plots and amusing dialogue, spiced with quick repartee between gay and emancipated rakes, male and female (as in *Marriage à la Mode*, produced ca. 1672); the worst of them (for instance, *The Kind Keeper*, produced ca. 1678) are often excessively salacious. Thomas Shadwell (ca. 1642–92), later the unhappy object of Dryden's satire, specialized in comedies of humor, following his master Ben Jonson in his own rather clumsy but not incompetent way. But the finest comedies of the period are those of Sir George Etherege (ca. 1635–91), William Wycherley (ca. 1640–1716), William Congreve, and the less accomplished but witty Sir John Vanbrugh (pronounced *Vánbroo* or *Vanbróok*; 1664–1726) and George Farquhar (ca. 1677–1707). These writers excelled in representing—and critically evaluating—the social behavior of the fashionable upper classes of the town, though of course their version of that life is heightened and stylized, not a literal transcript. This sort of comedy—brilliantly witty, cynical in its view of the nature of man, whom it shows to be sensual, egoistic, and predatory—is known as "the comedy of manners," since its concern is to bring the moral and social behavior of its characters to the test of comic laughter. The principal male character is a hero who lives not for military glory but for pleasure and the conquests that he can achieve in his amorous campaigns. The object of his very practical game of sexual intrigue is a beautiful, witty, pleasure-loving, and emancipated lady, every bit his equal in the strategies of love. The two are distinguished not for virtue, but for the good taste, aristocratic good breeding, true wit, sophisticated charm, and well-bred grace with which they conduct the often complicated intrigue that makes up the plot of such comedies. The characters are mainly familiar social types, examples of "manners," good and bad: besides the witty couple who play the leading roles, there are the affected fop; the would-be wit; the outraged cast-off mistress; the jealous (and thereafter ridiculous and unsympathetic) husband; the amorous but hypocritically virtuous wife; the ill-bred booby squire, newly come to town; the witty servant. The best examples of the comedy of manners before William Congreve's *The Way of the World* (produced in 1700) are Etherege's *The Man of Mode* (produced in 1676), William Wycherley's *The Country Wife* (produced ca. 1672–74), and Congreve's earlier *Love for Love* (produced in 1695).

During the 1690's a considerable demand arose for moral reform in both literature and daily life, partly because of the nature of Restoration comedy. "Societies for the Reformation of Manners" were founded with the support of the soberer Anglicans and the resurgent Nonconformists. Their members served not only as propagandists of moral respectability, but also less pleasingly as spies and informers who brought offenders to trial for blasphemy, obscenity, and sexual immorality. The most effective attack on the indecencies of language and situation in comedy was made by the Anglican clergyman Jeremy Collier, whose *Short View of the Immorality and Profaneness of the English Stage* (1698) bore hard on Dryden and Congreve, among others. Collier spoke for the outraged moral sense of the godly middle classes as well as for the church, and his attack helped to discredit "wit" and the wits as subversive of religion and morals. One of the tasks that Steele and Addison undertook in the *Tatler* and *Spectator* and Pope in his *Essay on Criticism*, early in the next century, was to rehabilitate "wit" by making it the servant of social and moral decorum. When Dryden died, a better ordered and more respectable (if not actually more virtuous) society was coming into being.

The literary life of Restoration and 18th-century London differs from that of our own time in no more striking way than in its semipublic and social character. From 1652 and increasingly during the first half of the 18th century, the coffeehouses of London served as informal meeting places for men of all classes, and their popularity did much to promote conversation and the exchange of opinion. At the coffeehouses men could smoke, drink chocolate or coffee, read the newspapers, write and receive letters, exchange news, gossip, and opinions, and observe the oddities of character that the English have always been happy to cultivate. Like-minded men tended to congregate at certain coffeehouses: literary men at Will's in Covent Garden, where Dryden ruled during most of his life in London; scholars and the learned professions at the Grecian; Whigs at St. James's, and so on. Thus the clubs which played an important role in English masculine society came into being, from Addison's imaginary Spectator Club to the brilliant men who formed Johnson's famous Club. The men who frequented the coffeehouses formed an influential element among the reading public and helped to determine the tone of literature, the critical reputation of writers, the success or failure of plays, and the character of such periodicals as the *Tatler* and the *Spectator*. After the middle of the century, certain literary ladies known as bluestockings, led by the wealthy Mrs. Elizabeth Montagu, established the salon and the evening *conversazione* as a means of encouraging literary conversation between the sexes.

EIGHTEENTH-CENTURY LITERATURE, 1700–1745

During the 45 years between the deaths of Dryden and Swift, the literature that Dryden and his contemporaries had created attained full maturity. A new and brilliant group of writers took the stage: Swift, with *A Tale of a Tub* (1704–10); Addison, with his overpraised and vastly popular poetic celebration of Marlborough's victory at Blenheim, *The Campaign* (1705); Prior, with *Poems on Several Occasions* (1707); Steele, with the *Tatler* (1709); and the youthful Pope, in the same year, with his *Pastorals*. On the whole, the literature of this period is chiefly a literature of wit, concerned with civilization, with man in his social relationships; and consequently it is critical and in some degree moral or satiric. It preserves the earlier period's interest in the heroic, but apart from Pope's translations of Homer, no writer succeeded in heroic poetry. It is revealing and characteristic that on the other hand some of the finest works of the period are mock-heroic (individual passages in Swift's *Battle of the Books* and *A Description of a City Shower* and Pope's *Rape of the Lock* and *The Dunciad*) or humorous burlesques of serious classic or modern modes (John Gay's delightful town mock-Georgic, *Trivia, or the Art of Walking the Streets of London*, 1716, or his burlesque of the heroics of Italian opera, *The Beggar's Opera*, produced in 1728). Such literature is addressed to highly sophisticated and cultivated readers, and it reminds us that earlier 18th-century literature retained the aristocratic bias that had marked the literature of the 17th century.

Nevertheless a body of writing that reached a wider audience was coming into being. The reading public expanded steadily throughout the 18th century, and its new recruits were upper-class women and the increasingly numerous rich and leisured people of both sexes in the trading middle class. The popular press flourished, producing a succession of newspapers, literary periodicals in the manner of the *Tatler*, miscellanies of various sorts, and finally, in 1731, the first magazine in the modern sense, the *Gentleman's Magazine*, which was to be followed not only by imitations but also by the appearance of such successful literary reviews as the *Monthly Review* (1749) and the *Critical Review* (1756). The new journalism satisfied the hunger of the less well-educated among the literate for all sorts of information about politics, science, philosophy, literature, as well as for such less edifying materials as scandal and gossip. It also created a demand for writers—not necessarily for geniuses—and, though often on harsh terms, men began to subsist as hack writers and compilers in a milieu that came to be called Grub Street, from the name of an actual street, just as we can speak of the whole sphere of speculative finance and banking as Wall Street. To such writers as Pope and Swift, Grub Street with all its denizens (it was to gain the services of both Johnson and Oliver Goldsmith!) represented a serious threat to humanistic learning, urbane enlightenment, and good taste. But literature became in this period of expanding publication and increasingly numerous readers a gainful profession. Something will shortly be said of the novel, but it may be remarked here that the novel as we know it—a long prose narrative concerned with the actual world and the men and women who inhabit it—very probably could not have come into existence had not these new readers existed. The 18th-century novel supplied the place in the life of the common reader that the heroic poem had occupied in the life of the courtly reader of the past.

During this period certain literary kinds changed very much for the worse. The lyric, one of the glories of the Elizabethan age and the first half of the 17th century, had become in the Restoration a minor and graceful mode, appropriate to a song or a "paper of verses" addressed to a mistress. The wits of Charles II's court could turn out accomplished, conventional poems of this sort which do not lack distinction; and Matthew Prior was their counterpart in the time of William of Orange and Queen Anne. But between 1700 and 1740 lyric poetry became increasingly trivial and empty. Comedy, too, underwent a deplorable change. The moral reform of the 1690's, together with the increasingly optimistic and flattering view of human nature, made the rakes of Restoration comedy seem distasteful libels on humanity. A new sort of comedy, "sentimental comedy," began to replace the old comedy of manners; not only because it is based on the sentimental notion that man is naturally good and that, given a chance, his virtuous feelings and his good heart will triumph over his accidentally acquired vices and follies, but also because its dialogue deals in high moral sentiments rather than wit, and because its virtuous heroines and virtuous (or penitent) heroes suffer misfortunes which move the audience not to laughter, but to tears. One of the pleasures invented in 18th-century Europe was the delicious pleasure of weeping, and sentimental comedy (or, as the French phrased it, *la comédie larmoyante*, "weeping comedy") brought that pleasure to playgoers through many decades. As tragedy froze into rhetoric, comedy dissolved in tears. And the successes enjoyed by John Gay's comic ballad opera *The Beggar's Opera* (1728), or of the laughing comedies of Goldsmith and Sheridan later in the century, could not eradicate the taste for sentimentality. It is a curious fact that although during the 18th century the *theater* prospered and the stage was adorned by a succession of great actors and actresses (the finest being Johnson's pupil and friend, David Garrick), the *drama* declined into a depressing nullity.

On the other hand, of course, satire flourished, its most distinguished practitioners being Pope and Swift, though they are only two among many effective writers. The satirist is usually a conservative, who uses his weapon against those deviations from norms of conduct which threaten to undermine traditional and socially approved behavior. Both Pope and Swift wrote their major satires as Tories, at a time when Britain was dominated by the Whig party. The Tories resisted, but resisted futilely, the social and economic changes which were taking place as England grew from an island kingdom into a world power, and transformed its agrarian into a mercantile economy. They looked with gloomy forebodings on the rising tide of popular taste, on what they considered the invasion and debasement of the polite world by the barbarians from the middle classes and by vulgar and luxurious rich and noble families, and on the increase of corruption in public life. The satire of both Swift and Pope is great because it was animated by moral urgency and heightened by a tragic sense of doom. Pope saw the issue as a struggle between Darkness and Light, Chaos and Order, Barbarism and Civilization: a vision which he expressed in his greatest work, *The Dunciad*. For Swift the issue was one between "right reason" and "madness"—not clinical insanity, of course, but a blindness to anything but one's own private illusions, which is an abandonment of practical reality.

But the great age of satire also produced a wholly different sort of poetry from that which Pope was writing in the 1730's. After 1726, when James Thomson published the first of his nature poems, *Winter*, the poetry of natural description flourished and the characteristic 18th-century English taste for natural and picturesque beauty found expression—not only in poetry, but also in that typical Georgian art, landscape gardening, and finally in the beginning of the art of landscape in water color or oils, which has been England's principal achievement in painting. Nothing could be further from the truth than the assumption of most 19th-century critics and literary historians that a love of external nature was unknown to English literature until the coming of the Romantic poets, a view encouraged by some not disinterested remarks of Coleridge and Wordsworth. But Wordsworth was the heir of 18th-century nature poets: *Tintern Abbey* (1798) not only was written *within* the century, but in most respects is very much a poem *of* the century.

In the course of the century, Englishmen not only admired tamed and ordered nature, in large landscape gardens or cultivated fields, but also early learned to enjoy the more thrilling, emotional pleasure which they began to feel in the presence of what they called "the sublime" in nature: vast spaces, mountainous country, wild and untamed landscape. Whether the enthusiast of nature went to landscape for evidence of the presence of the Deity or merely to enjoy natural beauty, he inevitably learned to feel emotions in the presence of external nature and to examine the quality of his feelings. Before the death of Pope and Swift, in the poetry of Thomson and others, a literature of feeling had come into existence alongside the dominant literature of wit. The development of such a literature of sentiment is perhaps the crucial fact in the literary history of the century after the deaths of Pope and Swift.

THE EMERGENCE OF NEW LITERARY THEMES AND MODES, 1740–1785

The younger generation, the successors of Prior, Thomson, Swift, and Pope, began to make themselves heard in the 1740's, and it was soon evident that a more varied literature was in the making. First we must remark on the appearance in literature of what became a fashionable emotion—melancholy, then often associated with religious musings, but often cultivated also for its own sake, and therefore sentimental. In contrast to the philosophic optimism of Thomson's *Seasons* or Pope's *Essay on Man*, a number of works exploited the themes of night, death, the grave, the charnel house, in a more or less sensational manner. The clergymen Edward Young (1683–1765) gained a European reputation by his blank-verse poem *The Complaint: or Night Thoughts on Life, Death, and Immortality* (1742–46), in nine "Nights," a typical poem of the so-called "graveyard school." The *Night Thoughts* was written to supplement the *Essay on Man*, and in its preoccupation with the life to come and the darker side of Christian thought it is a counterstatement to the secular optimism of the period which found expression in Pope's poem.

During the 1740's, however, melancholy was detached from religion and became rather a literary pose or, with sentimentalists, an emotion to be cultivated for its own peculiar delights. The prototype of the mid-18th-century melancholy poet was Milton's *Il Penseroso*, a night-loving solitary, who sucks pensive sadness from the "far-off curfew" or the swelling organ in the twilight of a Gothic church. Such a figure is most unlike the Augustan poet, a social being, living in a crowded world and little given to the impropriety of the public confession of private feelings. He is rather a not very remote ancestor of such typically Romantic figures as Wordsworth, wandering "lonely as a cloud," of Byron's Childe Harold, brooding over the ruins of Rome, or of the speaker of Keats's sonnet, who, contemplating his own mortal day and the transitoriness of love and beauty, exclaims:

> on the shore
> Of the wide world I stand alone and think,
> Till love and fame to nothingness do sink.

The "pilgrim" in William Collins' *Ode to Evening* and the speaker in Thomas Gray's *Elegy Written in a Country Churchyard* are typical 18th-century Penserosos. The idea of the poet was changing from that of a maker to that of an introspective, brooding confessor; the materials of poetry were becoming rather the inner life and private vision of the poet than the public, social affairs of men.

The growing interest in the medieval found expression in a revival of Gothic architectural styles. The most interesting example of this fashion was Strawberry Hill, the pseudo-Gothic castle which Gray's friend Horace Walpole built for himself near Twickenham. It attracted admiring visitors from all over Europe. The new taste also made possible the interest in the ballad as a literary form. Thomas Percy's publication of *Reliques of*

Ancient English Poetry (1765) is important in this respect, for it influenced the poetic theory and practice of Wordsworth and Coleridge, as may be seen in *Lyrical Ballads* (1798) and also, for example, in Wordsworth's generous praise of the *Reliques* in the *Essay Supplementary to Lyrical Ballads* (1815). Yet other reflections of a taste for the medieval are to be seen in the invention of the Gothic novel—a tale of terror set in the Middle Ages amidst the glooms and intricacies of medieval castles —and in the antiquarian and literary-picturesque interest in medieval life and art that is prominent in such Romantics as Sir Walter Scott, Coleridge, and Keats.

The vogue for Gothic architecture was accompanied in the 1750's and 1760's by a fad for Chinese motifs in architecture and the decorative arts. Both Chinese and Gothic, it should be observed, challenged strict neoclassical theory, which demanded proportion, balance, simplicity, and a serene, harmonious order. The Chinese and the Gothic are characterized by imbalance, asymmetry, intricacy, and dynamic line—curved in the Chinese, vertical in the Gothic; and to classic taste, both seemed fussy, unnecessarily intricate, and ununified. Similarly, medieval literature had been written without benefit of classic rules and was a great deal more fanciful and extravagant than neoclassic canons of taste approved. And yet it increasingly pleased and interested readers of the late 18th century. Homer and Nature were the same, no doubt; but might not the chivalric romance and the manners of feudal Europe be Nature, too? More and more readers were inclined to answer in the affirmative.

The 1740's also saw an attempt to revive lyric poetry, an attempt in which Collins and his friend Joseph Warton (1722–1800) took part. Warton called for an end to didactic and moralizing poetry and for the creation of a poetry of imagination or fancy. What he and Collins wanted was a lyric poetry of feeling and pictorial beauty, not a poetry of wit and intellection. In his *Ode to Fancy*, Warton revealed what the two friends meant by that term. He associated "fancy" with the natural, the wild and spontaneous, with solitude, and with enthusiasm and the passions, and, strikingly, with the visionary. Such a conception of the fancy or imagination emphasizes not rules and the craft of the maker, but original genius, the poet as the seer, as nature's priest; and it suggested to Warton and Collins that true poets should be singers, not conversationalists or orators. It is noteworthy that in this period the English poets Spenser, Shakespeare, and Milton assumed equal importance with Homer, Virgil, and Horace as objects of emulation. Both Warton and Collins wrote "odes," with the mythopoeic poets of ancient Greece very much in their minds, but they were seldom able to attain the freedom of movement essential to genuine lyric expression. Gray never knew Joseph Warton and Collins, but his odes prove that he shared their tastes and aspirations. The actual lyric revival of the 18th century, however, came later, with Thomas Chatterton in Bristol, Robert Burns in Scotland, and William Blake in his own private world.

THE BEGINNING OF THE NOVEL

To say that the modern novel came into existence in the 18th century is not to say that there was no prose fiction before 1700. There were the ancient Greek romances and their modern European imitators; the courtly

Arcadia of Sidney and the humbler fiction of Deloney and Nashe and other Elizabethans; the interminable French romances of the 17th century and their English translations and imitations, loosely constructed, blending aristocratic refinement, chivalric adventure, and courtly love; the tales of the adventures of rogues and the careers of famous criminals; and, in a world apart, Bunyan's vivid allegories of the spiritual adventures of wayfaring and militant Christians and their adversaries. But it remains true that, if we except Daniel Defoe, the creator of the modern novel was Samuel Richardson (1689–1761). It is interesting to observe that both Defoe and Richardson belonged to the middle class and expressed in their works middle-class interests and attitudes. Defoe simply ignored the sentimental and aristocratic refinements of the earlier romances and was content to show his readers not a world as it might be, a heroic world, but their world as it was, populated with believable people who were motivated by the practical concerns that dominate our daily lives. He did not seek—and except through *Robinson Crusoe* (1719) did not often find—readers among the upper classes. He was content to interest shopkeepers, apprentices, and servants, who were already avid readers of tales of crime and adventure, usually heavily laced with pious moral observations.

Richardson, however, caught the attention of all literate Europe. In *Pamela, or Virtue Rewarded* (1740), he once for all established the novel as we know it, as a solid and enduring object in the literary landscape. He brought to the writing of his novels a conventional moral code, a touch of middle-class snobbery, and a surprising insight into the sensibilities of women. His three novels were strikingly new in their minute and subtle analysis of emotions and states of mind. It was while he was compiling a little book of model letters to serve as a guide to the less well-educated that he conceived the idea of telling in a series of letters written by his heroine, Pamela, to her parents, the story of a virtuous servant girl— Pamela herself—in the household of a bachelor, Mr. B——, who resists her master's base designs on her virtue and eventually wins her would-be seducer as her husband. The epistolary method (which he used in all his novels) creates palpable improbabilities; nonetheless, Richardson found that by using it he was able to reveal the thoughts and emotions of his characters more vividly than any of his predecessors had done. Pamela's virtue seems as bogus to the modern reader as it did to Richardson's contemporary Henry Fielding; but there is no denying that Richardson's narrative method allows the reader to share his heroine's experiences to a degree which was quite new in fiction. Richardson's masterpiece is the more involved and gloomy *Clarissa* (1747–48). His third and final novel, *Sir Charles Grandison* (1753–54), is less impressive.

Henry Fielding (1707–54), who loved virtue as much as Richardson did, but to whom goodness was a matter of spontaneity and lack of calculation, not of mere propriety or conformity to a code, considered Pamela a misleading image of virtue; therefore, in 1742, he published *Joseph Andrews*, which begins as an hilarious burlesque of *Pamela* by describing the staunch resistance offered to the lewd advances of Lady Booby by her servant, the virtuous Joseph, brother of Pamela. Expelled for his chastity from Lady Booby's household, he takes to the road, joining the guileless

Parson Adams, who is walking to London to try to sell a bundle of his sermons to a publisher. Their adventures make up what Fielding called "a comic epic in prose." His great novel is *The History of Tom Jones, A Foundling* (1749). The protagonist became the pattern of the sentimental hero of the age: a young man of manly virtues, generous, high-spirited, loyal, and courageous, but impulsive, unreflecting, full of animal spirits and sensuality. The novel is crowded with incident and with varied types of men and women; and critics have agreed with Coleridge's praise of its brilliantly constructed plot. Fielding's sentimentality is not the sentimentality of Richardson, whose dying heroine Clarissa gives full expression to every shade of feeling as she writes her letters, using her coffin as an escritoire; rather it is the sentimentality of a man—of most English men and women of his time—who accepted the curious doctrine that men are naturally good and that our innate love of truth and virtue can in the end save us from our baser selves. Fielding's other important novel, *Amelia* (1751), having as its heroine a long-suffering woman, almost wholly passive, is an example of pathos rather than of Fielding's comic vigor and healthy gusto.

Two other novelists must be mentioned: Tobias Smollett (1721–71) and Laurence Sterne (1713–68). Smollett was a gifted caricaturist, a dealer in grotesque humor and rather strongly flavored comedy. He delighted to depict the seamier side of 18th-century life, its brutality, coarse practical jokes, and strong odors. *Roderick Random* (1748), *Peregrine Pickle* (1751), and *Ferdinand, Count Fathom* (1753) owe something to the picaresque tradition, as, of course, did Fielding's first two novels. Smollett's one masterpiece is an epistolary novel, *Humphry Clinker* (1771), which recounts, through letters written by several members of a traveling party, the comic incidents of a journey through England and Scotland, from the differing points of view of the travelers, some of them "originals" in a high degree.

Sterne, an unclerical clergyman, a humorist, a wit, a consumptive whose disease gave a hectic, heightened quality to his senses and emotions, a masterly recorder of the refinements of sensation, feeling, and thought, produced between 1760 and 1767 his long, brilliant, sentimental-comic, and eccentric novel, *The Life and Opinions of Tristram Shandy*. He deliberately frustrated all the stock expectations of his readers. The plot has not the logical order of a beginning, a middle, and an end; instead it abandons clock time for psychological time, interrupts scenes in order to digress or to recount past or future events, follows whimsically any apparently chance association, digresses for several chapters—in fact, it is designed as an elaborate joke at the reader's expense. And yet the method gets us inside the consciousness of the narrator and the other characters, and into a world peopled by the most engaging of comic characters.

Fielding, Smollett, and Sterne gave to English literature not only vivid scenes from the life of their times, but a gallery of eccentric and original characters that illustrate the interest of the age not only in the ideal and the general, but also in the individual and the unique. The novels of Dickens and of Thackeray in the 19th century owe much to their forerunners in the 18th.

THE CONTINUITY OF THE AUGUSTAN TRADITION

Despite the emergence of new literary forms, materials, and methods after the death of Pope and Swift, the Augustan line continued vigorously throughout the last half of the 18th and even into the 19th century. If the years between 1745 and 1784 were years of change and experiment, they were also the period of Samuel Johnson's greatest achievement and influence. A conservative in literature as in politics and religion, Johnson defended in conversation and in his critical writings the humanistic neo-classicism which he had inherited from the older generation. His two major poems, *London* (1738) and *The Vanity of Human Wishes* (1749), are satirical and ethical and show no influence of the new sensibility of the midcentury. He was loyal to the heroic couplet and to the use of generalized diction. His *Dictionary* (1755) was designed not to fix our language permanently but certainly to retard the process of change and to expel words which he considered superfluous. His critical writings sufficiently reveal his devotion to the standards of Dryden and Pope, though his judgments of particular writers and works were often personal, even idiosyncratic. But his conservatism was saved from pedantry by the empirical bent of his mind and his broad and humanistic learning.

Others of his circle shared his tastes. Sir Joshua Reynolds, the painter and the theorist of art, gave in his presidential *Discourses* before the Royal Academy (1769–90) the most complete and admirably reasoned formulation of classical tenets that the century produced. Edmund Burke (1729–97), the great Whig statesman and orator, and Edward Gibbon (1737–94), the author of *The Decline and Fall of the Roman Empire* (1776–87), shared with Johnson the ability to write prose which unites "the grandeur of generality" in its diction with the stately rhythms of elaborately ordered sentences. Goldsmith, despite the sentiment that characterizes his two major poems, *The Traveler* (1764) and *The Deserted Village* (1770), and his novel, *The Vicar of Wakefield* (1766), was, like Johnson, a literary conservative, and used the couplet of Dryden, though he avoided the older poet's rhetoric and pointed wit. Satire declined as sentimentalism gained the day, but one vigorous satirist—who was not a member of Johnson's circle—must be mentioned: Charles Churchill (1731–64), who coarsened while he continued the satiric tradition of Dryden and Pope. At the very end of Johnson's life appeared the poet George Crabbe, who was to continue the old tradition of the couplet into the next century. Even Cowper's *The Task* (1785), which brings us to the threshold of the Romantic movement, belongs most definitely in the 18th century. Indeed, the Augustan age did not die on that day in 1798 when a small and unsuccessful volume of poems, *Lyrical Ballads*, was published by Wordsworth and Coleridge. We hear the accents of that age from time to time in the poems of both Wordsworth and Coleridge, in many of the poems of Byron, and in Byron's ardent defense of Pope and Dryden, when the new age finally brought those masters to judgment. And we hear its old verities expressed in its own vocabulary in the criticism of that arch-enemy of the Romantic movement, Francis Jeffrey, editor of the *Edinburgh Review*, as when, for example, in a review (1808) of a volume of poems by George Crabbe, he paused to rebuke the (as he believed) affectedly eccentric poet Wordsworth for having written *The Thorn* and one of the Lucy poems:

Now we leave it to any reader of common candor and discernment to say whether these representations of character and sentiment are drawn from that eternal and universal standard of truth and nature, which every one is knowing enough to recognize, and no one great enough to depart from with impunity; or whether they are not formed * * * upon certain fantastic and affected peculiarities in the mind or fancy of the author, into which it is most improbable that many of his readers will enter, and which cannot, in some cases, be comprehended without much effort and explanation.

SAMUEL BUTLER
(1612–1680)

Butler passed his middle years during the "fury" of the Civil War and under the Commonwealth, sardonically observing the behavior and lovingly memorizing the faults of the Puritan rulers. He despised them and found relief for his feelings by satirizing them, though, naturally enough, he could not publish while they were in power. He served as clerk to several Puritan justices of the peace in the west of England, one of whom, according to tradition, was the original of Sir Hudibras (the *s* is pronounced). To Butler these men were fanatics, rapacious rascals, and hypocrites, inhabiting a world populated by only two classes: knaves and their preordained victims, fools.

Hudibras, Part I, was published late in 1662 (the edition bears the date 1663) and pleased the triumphant Royalists. King Charles II admired and often quoted the poem and rewarded its author with a gift of £300; it was, after all, a relief to laugh at what he had earlier hated and feared. The first part, attacking Presbyterians and Independents, proved more vigorous and effective than Parts II and III, which followed in 1664 and 1678 respectively, and which are less unified, since they aim at several different objects: romantic love, sex, astrology, and the new science, among others. After his initial success, Butler was neglected by the men he had pleased. He died in poverty, and not until 1721 was a monument erected in Westminster Abbey to his memory.

Hudibras is a travesty, or burlesque, i.e., it takes a serious subject and debases it by using a low style or distorts it by grotesque exaggeration. Butler carried this mode even into his verse, for he reduced the iambic tetrameter line (used subtly and seriously by such 17th-century poets as John Donne, John Milton, and Andrew Marvell) to something approaching doggerel, and his boldly comic rhymes add to the effect of broad comedy which he sought to create. Burlesque was a popular form of satire during the 17th century, especially after the French poet Paul Scarron published his *Virgile Travesti* (1648), which provoked mirth by retelling the heroic fable of the *Aeneid* in the most vulgar terms. Butler's use of burlesque expresses his contempt for the Puritans and their Commonwealth. Their theology he reduced to absurdity, their religious practices to pretense and self-deception, their morality to imposture and hypocrisy. In short, the history of England from 1642 to 1660 is made to appear mere sound and fury.

Butler took his hero's name from Spenser's *Faerie Queene*, II.ii, where Sir Huddibras appears briefly as the lover of Elissa, who represents sullenness as opposed to high spirits. To a mind like Butler's, chivalric romance seemed contemptibly absurd, and therefore a suitable vehicle for his satiric narrative: Hudibras, the pedantic Presbyterian and his squire Ralph, the Independent, who relies on inner light and inspiration and who talks a deal of mystical nonsense, move in a romantic and hence an irrational world. The questing knight of chivalric romance is degraded into the meddling, hypocritical busybody Hudibras, who goes out, like an officer in Cromwell's army, "a-coloneling" against the popular sport of bearbaiting. The knight and the squire suggest Don Quixote and Sancho Panza, but the temper of Butler's mind is as remote from Cervantes' warm humanity as it is from Spenser's ardent idealism. Butler has one purpose: to degrade those he despises, and no one was ever more successful in finding the means which serve such an end.

Some of Butler's minor satires such as *Upon the Weakness and Misery of Man* and *Upon the Licentious Age of Charles II*, are also impressive; his prose "characters"—not published until they appeared in his *Genuine Remains* (1759)—are as witty as any produced in the century; and the miscellanous reflections in his notebooks give fascinating insights into his mind. Butler had no illusions; he was skeptical in philosophy and conservative in politics, distrusting theoretical reasoning and the new science, disdainful of claims of inspiration and illumination, contemptuous of Catholicism and dubious of bishops, Anglican no less than Roman. It is difficult to think of anything which he approved unless it was peace, common sense, and the wisdom that emerges from the experience of mankind through the ages.

From Hudibras
From *Part I, Canto I*

THE ARGUMENT

Sir Hudibras, his passing worth,
The manner how he sallied forth,
His arms and equipage are shown,
His horse's virtues and his own:
The adventure of the Bear and Fiddle
Is sung, but breaks off in the middle.

When civil fury[1] first grew high,
And men fell out, they knew not why;
When hard words, jealousies, and fears
Set folks together by the ears
And made them fight, like mad or drunk,   5
For Dame Religion as for punk,[2]
Whose honesty they all durst swear for,
Though not a man of them knew wherefore;
When gospel-trumpeter,[3] surrounded
With long-eared rout, to battle sounded,   10
And pulpit, drum ecclesiastic,[4]

---

1. The Civil War between Royalists and Parliamentarians (1642–1649).
2. I.e., a prostitute.
3. A Presbyterian minister, vehemently preaching rebellion. The "long-eared rout" is a mob of Puritans or Roundheads, so called because they wore their hair short instead of in flowing curls

and thus exposed their ears, which to many satirists suggested the long ears of the ass.
4. The Presbyterian clergy were said to have preached the country into civil war. Hence, in pounding their pulpits with their fists, they are said to beat their ecclesiastical drums.

Was beat with fist instead of a stick;
Then did Sir Knight abandon dwelling,
And out he rode a-coloneling.[5]
    A wight he was whose very sight would   15
Entitle him Mirror of Knighthood;
That never bent his stubborn knee
To anything but chivalry,
Nor put up blow but that which laid
Right worshipful on shoulder blade;[6]   20
Chief of domestic knights and errant,
Either for chartel or for warrant;[7]
Great on the bench, great in the saddle,
That could as well bind o'er as swaddle.[8]
Mighty he was at both of these,   25
And styled of war as well as peace.
(So some rats of amphibious nature
Are either for the land or water.)
But here our authors make a doubt
Whether he were more wise or stout.   30
Some hold the one and some the other;
But howsoe'er they make a pother,
The difference was so small his brain
Outweighed his rage but half a grain;
Which made some take him for a tool   35
That knaves do work with, called a fool,
And offer to lay wagers that,
As Montaigne, playing with his cat,
Complains she thought him but an ass,[9]
Much more she would Sir Hudibras   40
(For that's the name our valiant knight
To all his challenges did write).
But they're mistaken very much,
'Tis plain enough he was no such.
We grant, although he had much wit,   45
He was very shy of using it;
As being loath to wear it out,
And therefore bore it not about,
Unless on holidays, or so,
As men their best apparel do.   50
Beside, 'tis known he could speak Greek

5. Here pronounced *có-lo-nel-ing*. "Wight:" a creature.
6. When a man is knighted he kneels and is tapped on the shoulder by his overlord's sword.
7. "Chartel," a written challenge to combat, such as a knight errant sends. But Hudibras, as Justice of the Peace ("domestic knight"), could also issue a "warrant" (a writ authorizing an arrest, a seizure, or a search). Hence he is satirically called "great on the [Justice's] bench" as well as in the saddle. "Errant" was spelled and pronounced *arrant*.
8. Both Justice of the Peace and soldier, he is equally able to "bind over" a malefactor to be tried at the next sessions or in his role of colonel, to beat ("swaddle") him.
9. In his *Apology for Raymond Sebond*, Michel de Montaigne (1533–92), French skeptic and essayist, wondered whether he played with his cat or his cat played with him.

As naturally as pigs squeak;
That Latin was no more difficile
Than to a blackbird 'tis to whistle.
Being rich in both, he never scanted   55
His bounty unto such as wanted,
But much of either would afford
To many that had not one word.
For Hebrew roots, although they're found
To flourish most in barren ground,[1]   60
He had such plenty as sufficed
To make some think him circumcised;
And truly so perhaps he was,
'Tis many a pious Christian's case.

   He was in logic a great critic,   65
Profoundly skilled in analytic.
He could distinguish and divide
A hair 'twixt south and southwest side;
On either which he would dispute,
Confute, change hands, and still confute.   70
He'd undertake to prove, by force
Of argument, a man's no horse;
He'd prove a buzzard is no fowl,
And that a lord may be an owl,
A calf an alderman, a goose a justice,   75
And rooks committee-men and trustees.[2]
He'd run in debt by disputation,
And pay with ratiocination.
All this by syllogism true,
In mood and figure,[3] he would do.   80
   For rhetoric, he could not ope
His mouth but out there flew a trope;[4]
And when he happened to break off
In the middle of his speech, or cough,[5]
He had hard words ready to show why,   85
And tell what rules he did it by.
Else, when with greatest art he spoke,
You'd think he talked like other folk;
For all a rhetorician's rules
Teach nothing but to name his tools.   90
His ordinary rate of speech
In loftiness of sound was rich,
A Babylonish dialect,[6]

1. Hebrew, the language of Adam, was thought of as the primitive language, the one which men in a state of nature would naturally speak.
2. Committees were set up in the counties by Parliament and given authority to imprison Royalists and to sequestrate their estates. "Rooks": a kind of blackbird; slang for "cheats."
3. "Mood" is the form of an argument. The "figure" of a syllogism is "the proper disposition of the middle term with the parts of the question."
4. Figure of speech.
5. Some pulpit orators regarded hemming and coughing as ornaments of speech.
6. Pedants affected the use of foreign words. The allusion is to the Tower of Babel (Genesis xi.4-9).

Which learned pedants much affect.
It was a parti-colored dress 95
Of patched and piebald languages;
'Twas English cut on Greek and Latin,
Like fustian heretofore on satin.[7]
It had an odd promiscuous tone,
As if he had talked three parts in one; 100
Which made some think, when he did gabble,
They had heard three laborers of Babel,
Or Cerberus himself pronounce
A leash of languages at once.[8]
This he as volubly would vent 105
As if his stock would ne'er be spent;
And truly, to support that charge,
He had supplies as vast and large.
For he could coin or counterfeit
New words with little or no wit;[9] 110
Words so debased and hard no stone
Was hard enough to touch them on.
And when with hasty noise he spoke 'em,
The ignorant for current took 'em;
That had the orator, who once 115
Did fill his mouth with pebble-stones
When he harangued,[1] but known his phrase,
He would have used no other ways.
    In mathematics he was greater
Than Tycho Brahe,[2] or Erra Pater: 120
For he, by geometric scale,
Could take the size of pots of ale;
Resolve by sines and tangents straight,
If bread or butter wanted weight;
And wisely tell what hour o' the day 125
The clock does strike, by algebra.
    Beside, he was a shrewd philosopher,
And had read every text and gloss over;
Whate'er the crabbed'st author hath,
He understood by implicit faith; 130
Whatever skeptic could inquire for,
For every *why* he had a *wherefore*;
Knew more than forty of them do,
As far as words and terms could go.
All which he understood by rote 135

7. Clothes made of coarse cloth ("fustian") were slashed so as to display the richer satin lining.
8. The sporting term "leash" denotes a group of three dogs, hawks, deer, etc.; hence, *three* in general. Cerberus was the three-headed dog that guarded the entrance to Hades.
9. The Presbyterians and other sects invented a special religious vocabulary, much ridiculed by Anglicans: "outgoings," "workings-out," "gospel-walking-times," etc.
1. Demosthenes cured a stutter by speaking with pebbles in his mouth.
2. A Danish astronomer (1546–1601). "Erra Pater": Butler's contemptuous name for the popular astrologer William Lilly (1602–81).

And, as occasion served, would quote,
No matter whether right or wrong;
They might be either said or sung.
His notions fitted things so well
That which was which he could not tell,⠀⠀⠀⠀⠀140
But oftentimes mistook the one
For the other, as great clerks have done.[3]
He could reduce all things to acts,
And knew their natures by abstracts;
Where entity and quiddity,[4]⠀⠀⠀⠀⠀145
The ghosts of defunct bodies, fly;
Where truth in person does appear,
Like words congealed in northern air.[5]
He knew what's what, and that's as high
As metaphysic wit can fly.⠀⠀⠀⠀⠀150
⠀⠀In school-divinity[6] as able
As he that hight Irrefragable;[7]
Profound in all the nominal
And real ways beyond them all;
And with as delicate a hand⠀⠀⠀⠀⠀155
Could twist as tough a rope of sand.
And weave fine cobwebs, fit for skull
That's empty when the moon is full;[8]
Such as take lodgings in a head
That's to be let unfurnishéd⠀⠀⠀⠀⠀160
He could raise scruples dark and nice,[9]
And after solve 'em in a trice;
As if divinity had catched
The itch on purpose to be scratched,
Or, like a mountebank,[1] did wound⠀⠀⠀⠀⠀165
And stab herself with doubts profound,
Only to show with how small pain
The sores of faith are cured again;
Although by woeful proof we find
They always leave a scar behind.⠀⠀⠀⠀⠀170
He knew the seat of paradise,[2]

3. Elsewhere Butler wrote: "Notions are but pictures of things in the imagination of man, and if they agree with their originals in nature, they are true, and if not, false." "Clerks": scholars.
4. In the hair-splitting logic of medieval Scholastic philosophy, a distinction was drawn between the "entity" or *being* and the "quiddity" or *essence* of bodies. Butler calls entity and quiddity "ghosts" because they were held to be independent realities and so to survive the bodies in which they lodge.
5. The notion, as old as the Greek wit Lucian, that in arctic regions words freeze as they are uttered and become audible only when they thaw.
6. Scholastic theology.
7. Alexander of Hales (d. 1245) was called "Irrefragable," i.e., unanswer-

able, because his system seemed incontrovertible. The next couplet refers to the debate, continuous throughout the Middle Ages, as to whether the objects of our concepts exist in nature or are mere intellectual abstractions. The "nominalists" denied their objective reality, the "realists" affirmed it.
8. The frenzies of madmen were supposed to wax and wane with the moon (hence "lunatic").
9. Obscure ("dark") and subtle ("nice") intellectual perplexities ("scruples").
1. A seller of quack medicines.
2. The problem of the precise location of the Garden of Eden and the similar problems listed in the ensuing dozen lines had all been the subject of controversy among theologians.

Could tell in what degree it lies;
And, as he was disposed, could prove it
Below the moon, or else above it;
What Adam dreamt of when his bride   175
Came from her closet in his side;
Whether the devil tempted her
By a High Dutch interpreter;
If either of them had a navel;
Who first made music malleable; [2a]   180
Whether the serpent at the fall
Had cloven feet or none at all:
All this without a gloss or comment
He could unriddle in a moment,
In proper terms, such as men smatter   185
When they throw out and miss the matter.

    For his religion, it was fit
To match his learning and his wit:
'Twas Presbyterian true blue,[3]
For he was of that stubborn crew   190
Of errant[4] saints whom all men grant
To be the true church militant,
Such as do build their faith upon
The holy text of pike and gun;
Decide all controversies by   195
Infallible artillery,
And prove their doctrine orthodox
By apostolic blows and knocks;
Call fire, and sword, and desolation
A godly, thorough reformation,   200
Which always must be carried on
And still be doing, never done;
As if religion were intended
For nothing else but to be mended.
A sect whose chief devotion lies   205
In odd, perverse antipathies;[5]
In falling out with that or this,
And finding somewhat still amiss;
More peevish, cross, and splénetic
Than dog distract or monkey sick;   210

2a. Capable of being fashioned into form. Pythagoras is said to have organized sounds into the musical scale.
3. The Scotch Covenanters adopted blue as their color, in contrast to the Royalist red. Blue is the color of constancy; hence, "true blue," staunch, unwavering. This and the next five couplets bitterly recall the violence and fanaticism of the Parliamentary armies in attempting to reform the Anglican Church.
4. A pun: "arrant," meaning "un-mitigated," and "errant," meaning "wandering," were both spelled and pronounced *arrant*. The Puritans frequently called themselves "saints."
5. The hostility of the sects to everything Anglican or Roman Catholic laid them open to the charge of opposing innocent practices out of mere perverse antipathy. Some extreme Presbyterians fasted at Christmas, instead of following the old custom of feasting and rejoicing. Cf. lines 211–12.

That with more care keep holiday
The wrong, than others the right way;
Compound for sins they are inclined to
By damning those they have no mind to;
Still so perverse and opposite   215
As if they worshiped God for spite.
The selfsame thing they will abhor
One way and long another for.
Free-will they one way disavow,[6]
Another, nothing else allow: 220
All piety consists therein
In them, in other men all sin.
Rather than fail, they will defy
That which they love most tenderly;
Quarrel with minced pies and disparage   225
Their best and dearest friend, plum-porridge;
Fat pig and goose itself oppose,
And blaspheme custard through the nose.[7]

* * *

1663

6. By the doctrine of predestination.   7. A reference to the nasal whine of
                                           the pious sectarians.

JOHN BUNYAN
(1628–1688)

1653:   Conversion.
1660–72:   Imprisoned in Bedford jail.
1675:   Second imprisonment in Bedford jail; *The Pilgrim's
           Progress* composed.

Bunyan is one of the most remarkable figures in 17th-century literature.
The son of a poor Bedfordshire tinker (a maker and mender of metal
pots), he received only meager schooling and then learned his father's
craft. Nothing in the circumstances of his early life could have suggested
that he would become a writer known the world over in translations too
numerous to reckon, many of them in languages and dialects of which he
had never heard.

His inner life is fully chronicled in his spiritual autobiography, *Grace
Abounding to the Chief of Sinners* (1666). Here we learn of his humble
parentage, his marriage to a woman (he does not tell us her name) whose
dowry consisted only of two pious tracts, and of his military service—in
the Parliamentary army (though he neglects to say so). But such details
scarcely interest him except as he can use them to reveal the purposes of

Divine Providence. *Grace Abounding* was written to show the way by which a man, convinced of his sins, is led by God's grace through the agonies of spiritual crises to a new birth and the assurance of salvation; and to record how the obscure and sinful tinker was transformed into the eloquent and fearless preacher. Such books abounded in Puritan England and followed a conventional formula; but Bunyan's psychological insight and vivid narrative gifts make *Grace Abounding* one of the most enthralling autobiographies in the language.

As a result of his spiritual struggle and triumph, he joined one of the several groups of Baptists and began his career as a preacher and religious writer. Preachers, both male and female, often even less educated than Bunyan, were common phenomena among the sects during the Commonwealth. They wished no ordination but the "call," and they could dispense with learning since they abounded in inspiration, inner light, and the gifts conferred by the Holy Spirit. In November, 1660, despite Charles II's promised policy of mildness, the Anglican Church began to persecute and silence the Dissenting sects. Jails filled with unlicensed Nonconformist preachers, and John Bunyan was one of the prisoners. Refusing to keep silent, he chose imprisonment and so for twelve years remained in Bedford jail, preaching to his fellow prisoners and writing religious books. Upon his release, he was called to the pastorate of a Nonconformist group in Bedford. It was during a second imprisonment, in 1675, when the Test Act was once again rigorously enforced against Nonconformists, that he wrote his greatest work, *The Pilgrim's Progress from This World to That Which Is to Come* (1678), revised and augmented in the third edition (1679). Bunyan was a prolific writer: Part II of *The Pilgrim's Progress,* dealing with the journey of Christian's wife and children, appeared in 1684; *The Life and Death of Mr. Badman,* in 1680; *The Holy War,* in 1682. But these major works form only a small part of all his writings.

The Pilgrim's Progress is the most successful allegory in our literature. Its basic metaphor—life is a journey—is simple and familiar; the objects that the pilgrim Christian meets are homely and commonplace: a quagmire, the highway, the bypaths and short cuts through pleasant meadows; the inn, the steep hill, the town fair on market day; the river that must be forded—such objects were familiar then, and *mutatis mutandis,* are familiar even in our automotive age. They have the immediacy of daily experience, a quality that recalls the equally homely parables of Jesus, but Bunyan's allegorizing of these details charges them with spiritual significance. Moreover, Bunyan is a superb storyteller: this is, after all, a tale of adventure; he knows how to keep his reader in suspense, and because he was of the folk, how to mingle the romantic and the strange with the familiar. If the road that Christian travels is the King's Highway, it is also a perilous path along which we encounter giants, wild beasts, hobgoblins, and the terrible Apollyon, "the angel of the bottomless pit," with whom Christian must fight. Bunyan's knowledge of human nature keeps the tale firmly based on universal experience—whether in the brilliant and sometimes humorous characterization of other travelers along the way (who represent states of the soul and intellectual or moral attitudes) or in the inevitably right arrangement of Christian's own experiences, from the unforgettable first sight that we catch of him as his reading in the book convinces him of his sins and evokes his cry of terror, to the moving account of his death with Hopeful in the river. Finally, Bunyan's style, modeled on the prose of the English Bible, together with his concrete and living language and carefully observed and vividly rendered details, enable even the simplest reader to share the experiences of the characters. What could be better than the following sentence? "Some cry out against sin even as the mother cries out against her child in her lap, when she calleth it slut and naughty girl, and then falls to hugging and kissing it." Even the conversations on doctrinal matters, tedious though they are, cannot seriously damage so human and dramatic a tale. In a secular age like the present, *The Pilgrim's Progress* is no longer a household book; but it survives in the speech of men who have never read it, for it gave to our language phrases that will doubtless always live: "the slough of despond," "the house beautiful," "Mr. Worldly-Wiseman," "Vanity Fair." And it lives again for anyone who reads beyond the first page.

From The Pilgrim's Progress
FROM THIS WORLD TO THAT WHICH IS TO COME: DELIVERED UNDER THE SIMILITUDE OF A DREAM

[*Christian Sets out for the Celestial City*]

As I walked through the wilderness of this world, I lighted on a certain place where was a Den, and I laid me down in that place to sleep; and, as I slept, I dreamed a dream. I dreamed, and behold I saw a man clothed with rags, standing in a certain place, with his face from his own house, a book in his hand, and a great burden upon his back (*Isaiah lxiv.6; Luke xiv.33; Psalms xxxviii.4; Habakkuk ii.2; Acts xvi.31*). I looked and saw him open the book and read therein; and, as he read, he wept, and trembled; and not being able longer to contain, he brake out with a lamentable cry, saying, "What shall I do?" (*Acts ii.37*).

In this plight, therefore, he went home and refrained himself as long as he could, that his wife and children should not perceive his distress; but he could not be silent long, because that his trouble increased. Wherefore at length he brake his mind to his wife and children; and thus he began to talk to them. O my dear wife, said he, and you the children of my bowels, I your dear friend am in myself undone by reason of a burden that lieth hard upon me; moreover, I am for certain informed that this our city will be burned with fire from heaven, in which fearful overthrow both myself, with thee, my wife, and you, my sweet babes, shall miserably come to ruin, except (the which yet I see not) some way of escape can be found, whereby we may be delivered. At this his relations were sore amazed; not for that they believed that what he had said to them was true, but because they thought that some frenzy distemper[1] had got into his head; therefore, it drawing towards night, and they hoping that sleep might settle his brains, with all haste they got him to bed; but the night was as troublesome to him as the day; wherefore, instead of sleeping, he spent it in sighs and tears. So when the morning was come, they would know how he did. He told them, Worse and worse; he also set to talking to them again, but they began to be hardened. They also thought to drive away his distemper by harsh and surly carriages[2] to him: sometimes they would deride, sometimes they would chide, and sometimes they would quite neglect him. Wherefore he began to retire himself to his chamber, to pray for and pity them, and also to condole his own misery; he would also walk solitarily in the fields, sometimes reading, and sometimes praying; and thus for some days he spent his time.

Now I saw, upon a time, when he was walking in the fields, that he was (as he was wont) reading in this book, and greatly distressed in his mind; and as he read, he burst out, as he had done before, crying, "What shall I do to be saved?"

I saw also that he looked this way and that way, as if he would run; yet he stood still, because (as I perceived) he could not tell which way to go. I looked then, and saw a man named Evangelist[3] coming to him, who asked, Wherefore dost thou cry? (*Job xxxiii.23*). He answered, Sir, I perceive by the book in my hand that I am condemned to die, and after that to come to judgment (*Hebrews ix.27*), and I find that I am not willing to do the first (*Job xvi.21*), nor able to do the second (*Ezekiel xxii.14*). * * *

Then said Evangelist, Why not willing to die, since this life is attended with so many evils? The man answered, Because I fear that this burden that is upon my back will sink me lower than the grave, and I shall fall into Tophet[4] (*Isaiah xxx.33*). And, sir, if I be not fit to go to prison, I am not fit to go to judgment, and from thence to execution; and the thoughts of these things make me cry.[5]

Then said Evangelist, If this be thy condition, why standest thou still? He answered, Because I know not whither to go. Then he gave him a parchment roll, and there was written within, "Fly from the wrath to come" (*Matthew iii.7*).

The man therefore read it, and looking upon Evangelist very carefully,[6] said, Whither must I fly? Then said Evangelist, point-

1. A malady causing madness; the use of "frenzy" as an adjective was not uncommon in the 17th century.
2. Behavior.
3. A preacher of the Gospel; literally, a bearer of good news.
4. The place near Jerusalem where bodies and filth were burned; hence, by association, a name for hell.
5. Cry out.
6. Sorrowfully.

ing with his finger over a very wide field, Do you see yonder wicket-gate?[7] (*Matthew vii.13, 14.*) The man said, No. Then said the other, Do you see yonder shining light? (*Psalms cxix.105; II Peter i.19.*) He said, I think I do. Then said Evangelist, Keep that light in your eye, and go up directly thereto; so shalt thou see the gate; at which when thou knockest it shall be told thee what thou shalt do.

So I saw in my dream that the man began to run. Now, he had not run far from his own door, but his wife and children perceiving it, began to cry after him to return; but the man put his fingers in his ears, and ran on, crying, Life! life! eternal life! (*Luke xiv.26.*) So he looked not behind him, but fled towards the middle of the plain (*Genesis xix.17*).

The neighbors also came out to see him run (*Jeremiah xx.10*); and as he ran some mocked, others threatened, and some cried after him to return; and, among those that did so, there were two that resolved to fetch him back by force. The name of the one was Obstinate, and the name of the other Pliable. Now by this time the man was got a good distance from them; but, however, they were resolved to pursue him, which they did, and in a little time they overtook him. Then said the man, Neighbors, wherefore are ye come? They said, To persuade you to go back with us. But he said, That can by no means be; you dwell, said he, in the City of Destruction (the place also where I was born) I see it to be so; and, dying there, sooner or later, you will sink lower than the grave, into a place that burns with fire and brimstone; be content, good neighbors, and go along with me.

OBST. What! said Obstinate, and leave our friends and our comforts behind us?

CHR. Yes, said Christian (for that was his name), because that ALL which you shall forsake is not worthy to be compared with a little of that which I am seeking to enjoy (*II Corinthians v.17*); and, if you will go along with me, and hold it, you shall fare as I myself; for there, where I go, is enough and to spare (*Luke xv.17*). Come away, and prove my words.

OBST. What are the things you seek, since you leave all the world to find them?

CHR. I seek an inheritance incorruptible, undefiled, and that fadeth not away (*I Peter i.4*), and it is laid up in heaven, and safe there (*Hebrews xi.16*), to be bestowed, at the time appointed, on them that diligently seek it. Read it so, if you will, in my book.

OBST. Tush! said Obstinate, away with your book; will you go back with us or no?

7. A small gate in or beside a larger gate.

CHR. No, not I, said the other, because I have laid my hand to the plow (*Luke ix.62*).

OBST. Come, then, neighbor Pliable, let us turn again, and go home without him; there is a company of these crazed-headed coxcombs,[8] that, when they take a fancy by the end, are wiser in their own eyes than seven men that can render a reason (*Proverbs xxvi.16*).

PLI. Then said Pliable, Don't revile; if what the good Christian says is true, the things he looks after are better than ours; my heart inclines to go with my neighbor.

OBST. What! more fools still? Be ruled by me, go back; who knows whither such a brain-sick fellow will lead you? Go back, go back, and be wise.

CHR. Nay, but do thou come with thy neighbor, Pliable; there are such things to be had which I spoke of, and many more glories besides. If you believe not me, read here in this book; and for the truth of what is expressed therein, behold, all is confirmed by the blood of Him that made it (*Hebrews ix.17–22; xiii.20*).

PLI. Well, neighbour Obstinate, said Pliable, I begin to come to a point,[9] I intend to go along with this good man, and to cast in my lot with him: but, my good companion, do you know the way to this desired place?

CHR. I am directed by a man, whose name is Evangelist, to speed me to a little gate that is before us, where we shall receive instructions about the way.

PLI. Come, then, good neighbor, let us be going. Then they went both together. * * *

[The Slough of Despond]

Now I saw in my dream, that just as they had ended this talk they drew near to a very miry slough,[1] that was in the midst of the plain; and they, being heedless, did both fall suddenly into the bog. The name of the slough was Despond. Here, therefore, they wallowed for a time, being grievously bedaubed with dirt; and Christian, because of the burden that was on his back, began to sink in the mire.

PLI. Then said Pliable, Ah, neighbor Christian, where are you now?

CHR. Truly, said Christian, I do not know.

PLI. At that Pliable began to be offended, and angrily said to his fellow, Is this the happiness you have told me all this while of? If we have such ill speed at our first setting out, what may we expect 'twixt this and our journey's end? May I get out again with my life, you shall possess the brave country alone for me. And, with

---

8. Fools: "fancy": delusion.   1. Pronounce to rhyme with *now*.
9. Decision.

that, he gave a desperate struggle or two, and got out of the mire on that side of the slough which was next[2] to his own house: so away he went, and Christian saw him no more.

Wherefore Christian was left to tumble in the Slough of Despond alone: but still he endeavored to struggle to that side of the slough that was further from his own house, and next to the wicket-gate; the which he did, but could not get out, because of the burden that was upon his back: but I beheld in my dream, that a man came to him, whose name was Help, and asked him what he did there?

CHR. Sir, said Christian, I was bid go this way by a man called Evangelist, who directed me also to yonder gate, that I might escape the wrath to come; and as I was going thither I fell in here.

HELP. But why did not you look for the steps?

CHR. Fear followed me so hard that I fled the next way, and fell in.

HELP. Then said he, Give me thy hand; so he gave him his hand, and he drew him out, and set him upon sound ground, and bid him go on his way.

Then I stepped to him that plucked him out, and said, Sir, wherefore, since over this place is the way from the City of Destruction to yonder gate, is it that this plat[3] is not mended, that poor travelers might go thither with more security? And he said unto me, This miry slough is such a place as cannot be mended; it is the descent whither the scum and filth that attends conviction for sin doth continually run, and therefore it was called the Slough of Despond; for still, as the sinner is awakened about his lost condition, there ariseth in his soul many fears, and doubts, and discouraging apprehensions, which all of them get together, and settle in this place. And this is the reason of the badness of this ground. * * *

Chr. joined by Faithy [Vanity Fair][4]

Then I saw in my dream, that when they were got out of the wilderness, they presently saw a town before them, and the name of that town is Vanity; and at the town there is a fair kept, called Vanity Fair; it is kept all the year long; it beareth the name of Vanity Fair because the town where it is kept is lighter than

2. Nearest.
3. A plot of ground.
4. In this, perhaps the best-known episode in the book, Bunyan characteristically turns one of the most familiar institutions in contemporary England —annual fairs—into an allegory of universal spiritual significance. Christian and his companion Faithful pass through the town of Vanity at the season of the local fair. "Vanity" means "emptiness" or "worthlessness," and hence the fair is an allegory of worldliness and the corruption of the religious life through the attractions of the world. From earliest times numerous fairs were held for stated periods throughout Britain; to them the most important merchants from all over Europe brought their wares. The serious business of buying and selling was accompanied by all sorts of diversions —eating, drinking, and other fleshly pleasures, as well as spectacles of strange animals, acrobats, and other wonders.

vanity; and also because all that is there sold, or that cometh thither, is vanity. As is the saying of the wise, "All that cometh is vanity" (*Ecclesiastes i.2, 14; ii.11, 17; xi.8; Isaiah xl.17*).

This fair is no new-erected business, but a thing of ancient standing; I will show you the original of it.

Almost five thousand years agone, there were pilgrims walking to the Celestial City, as these two honest persons are; and Beelzebub, Apollyon, and Legion,[5] with their companions, perceiving by the path that the pilgrims made, that their way to the city lay through this town of Vanity, they contrived here to set up a fair; a fair wherein should be sold all sorts of vanity, and that it should last all the year long. Therefore at this fair are all such merchandise sold, as houses, lands, trades, places, honors, preferments,[6] titles, countries, kingdoms, lusts, pleasures, and delights of all sorts, as whores, bawds, wives, husbands, children, masters, servants, lives, blood, bodies, souls, silver, gold, pearls, precious stones, and what not.

And, moreover, at this fair there is at all times to be seen jugglings, cheats, games, plays, fools, apes, knaves, and rogues, and that of every kind.

Here are to be seen, too, and that for nothing, thefts, murders, adulteries, false swearers, and that of a blood-red color.

And as in other fairs of less moment, there are the several rows and streets, under their proper names, where such and such wares are vended; so here likewise you have the proper places, rows, streets (viz., countries and kingdoms), where the wares of this fair are soonest to be found. Here is the Britain Row, the French Row, the Italian Row, the Spanish Row, the German Row, where several sorts of vanities are to be sold. But, as in other fairs, some one commodity is as the chief of all the fair, so the ware of Rome and her merchandise[7] is greatly promoted in this fair; only our English nation, with some others, have taken a dislike thereat.

Now, as I said, the way to the Celestial City lies just through this town where this lusty[8] fair is kept; and he that will go to the City, and yet not go through this town, must needs "go out of the world" (*I Corinthians v.10*). The Prince of princes himself, when here, went through this town to his own country, and that upon a fair-day too;[9] yea, and as I think, it was Beelzebub, the chief lord of this fair, that invited him to buy of his vanities; yea, would have made him lord of the fair, would he but have done him reverence

5. Beelzebub, prince of the devils (Matthew xii.24); Apollyon, the Destroyer, "the Angel of the bottomless pit" (Revelation ix.11); Legion, the "unclean spirit" sent by Jesus into the Gadarene swine (Mark v.9).
6. Appointments and promotions to political or ecclesiastical positions.
7. The usages and the temporal power of the Roman Catholic Church.
8. Merry.
9. The temptation of Jesus in the wilderness (Matthew iv.1–11).

as he went through the town. (*Matthew iv.*8; *Luke iv.*5–7.) Yea, because he was such a person of honor, Beelzebub had him from street to street, and showed him all the kingdoms of the world in a little time, that he might, if possible, allure the Blessed One to cheapen[1] and buy some of his vanities; but he had no mind to the merchandise, and therefore left the town, without laying out so much as one farthing upon these vanities. This fair, therefore, is an ancient thing, of long standing, and a very great fair.

Now these pilgrims, as I said, must needs go through this fair. Well, so they did; but, behold, even as they entered into the fair, all the people in the fair were moved, and the town itself as it were in a hubbub about them; and that for several reasons: for

First, The pilgrims were clothed with such kind of raiment as was diverse from the raiment of any that traded in that fair. The people, therefore, of the fair, made a great gazing upon them: some said they were fools, some they were bedlams,[2] and some they are outlandish men. (*I Corinthians ii.*7, 8.)

Secondly, And as they wondered at their apparel, so they did likewise at their speech; for few could understand what they said; they naturally spoke the language of Canaan,[3] but they that kept the fair were the men of this world; so that, from one end of the fair to the other, they seemed barbarians[4] each to the other.

Thirdly, But that which did not a little amuse the merchandisers was that these pilgrims set very light by all their wares; they cared not so much as to look upon them; and if they called upon them to buy, they would put their fingers in their ears, and cry, "Turn away mine eyes from beholding vanity," and look upwards, signifying that their trade and traffic was in heaven. (*Psalms cxix.*37; *Philippians iii.*19, 20.)

One chanced mockingly, beholding the carriages of the men, to say unto them, What will ye buy? But they, looking gravely upon him, said, "We buy the truth" (*Proverbs xxiii.*23). At that there was an occasion taken to despise the men the more; some mocking, some taunting, some speaking reproachfully, and some calling upon others to smite them. At last things came to an hubbub and great stir in the fair, insomuch that all order was confounded. Now was word presently brought to the great one of the fair, who quickly came down, and deputed some of his most trusty friends to take these men into examination, about whom the fair was almost overturned. So the men were brought to examination; and they that sat

---

1. Ask the price of.
2. Lunatics from Bethlehem Hospital, the insane asylum in London. "Outlandish": foreign.
3. The Promised Land, ultimately conquered by the Children of Israel (Joshua iv) and settled by them: hence

the pilgrims speak the language of the Bible and of the true religion. Dissenters were notorious for their habitual use of Biblical language.
4. The Greeks and Romans so designated all those who spoke a foreign tongue.

upon them[5] asked them whence they came, whither they went, and what they did there, in such an unusual garb? The men told them that they were pilgrims and strangers in the world, and that they were going to their own country, which was the Heavenly Jerusalem (*Hebrews xi.13–16*); and that they had given no occasion to the men of the town, nor yet to the merchandisers, thus to abuse them, and to let[6] them in their journey, except it was for that, when one asked them what they would buy, they said they would buy the truth. But they that were appointed to examine them did not believe them to be any other than bedlams and mad, or else such as came to put all things into a confusion in the fair. Therefore they took them and beat them, and besmeared them with dirt, and then put them into the cage, that they might be made a spectacle to all the men of the fair.[7] *Faithful + martyred. Christian continues his journey*

[The River of Death and the Celestial City]

So I saw that when they[7] awoke, they addressed themselves to go up to the City; but, as I said, the reflection of the sun upon the City (for the City was pure gold, *Revelation xxi.18*) was so extremely glorious, that they could not, as yet, with open face behold it, but through an instrument made for that purpose. (*II Corinthians iii.18.*) So I saw that as I went on, there met them two men, in raiment that shone like gold; also their faces shone as the light.

These men asked the pilgrims whence they came; and they told them. They also asked them where they had lodged, what difficulties and dangers, what comforts and pleasures they had met in the way; and they told them. Then said the men that met them, You have but two difficulties more to meet with, and then you are in the City.

Christian then and his companion asked the men to go along with them; so they told them they would. But, said they, you must obtain it by your own faith. So I saw in my dream that they went on together till they came in sight of the gate.

Now I further saw that betwixt them and the gate was a river, but there was no bridge to go over; the river was very deep. At the sight, therefore, of this river, the pilgrims were much stunned;[8] but the men that went with them said, You must go through, or you cannot come at the gate.

The pilgrims then began to inquire if there was no other way to the gate; to which they answered, Yes; but there hath not any, save two, to wit, Enoch and Elijah,[9] been permitted to tread that path, since the foundation of the world, nor shall, until the last

---

5. Interrogated and tried them.
6. Hinder.
7. Christian and his companion, Hopeful. Ignorance, who appears tragically in the final paragraph, had tried to accompany the two pilgrims, but had

dropped behind because of his hobbling gait.
8. Amazed.
9. Both were "translated" alive to heaven (*Genesis v.24, Hebrews xi.5, II Kings ii.11–12*).

trumpet shall sound. (*I Corinthians xv.51, 52.*) The pilgrims then, especially Christian, began to despond in his mind, and looked this way and that, but no way could be found by them by which they might escape the river. Then they asked the men if the waters were all of a depth. They said no; yet they could not help them in that case; for, said they, you shall find it deeper or shallower, as you believe in the King of the place.

They then addressed themselves to the water; and entering, Christian began to sink, and crying out to his good friend Hopeful, he said, I sink in deep waters; the billows go over my head, all his waves go over me! Selah.[1]

Then said the other, Be of good cheer, my brother, I feel the bottom, and it is good. Then said Christian, Ah, my friend, the sorrows of death have compassed me about; I shall not see the land that flows with milk and honey. And with that a great darkness and horror fell upon Christian, so that he could not see before him. Also here he in great measure lost his senses, so that he could neither remember nor orderly talk of any of those sweet refreshments that he had met with in the way of his pilgrimage. But all the words that he spake still tended to discover that he had horror of mind, and heart-fears that he should die in that river, and never obtain entrance in at the gate. Here also, as they that stood by perceived, he was much in the troublesome thoughts of the sins that he had committed, both since and before he began to be a pilgrim. 'Twas also observed that he was troubled with apparitions of hobgoblins and evil spirits; for ever and anon he would intimate so much by words. Hopeful, therefore, here had much ado to keep his brother's head above water; yea, sometimes he would be quite gone down, and then, ere a while, he would rise up again half dead. Hopeful also would endeavor to comfort him, saying, Brother, I see the gate and men standing by to receive us; but Christian would answer, 'Tis you, 'tis you they wait for; you have been Hopeful ever since I knew you. And so have you, said he to Christian. Ah, brother, said he, surely if I was right he would now arise to help me; but for my sins he hath brought me into the snare, and hath left me. Then said Hopeful, My brother, you have quite forgot the text, where it is said of the wicked, "There are no bands in their death, but their strength is firm. They are not in trouble as other men, neither are they plagued like other men" (*Psalms lxxiii.4, 5*). These troubles and distresses that you go through in these waters are no sign that God hath forsaken you, but are sent to try you, whether you will call to mind that which heretofore you have received of his goodness, and live upon him in your distresses.

Then I saw in my dream that Christian was as in a muse[2] a

---

1. A word of uncertain meaning that occurs frequently at the end of a verse in the Psalms. Bunyan may have supposed it to signify the end.
2. A deep meditation.

while, to whom also Hopeful added this word, Be of good cheer. Jesus Christ maketh thee whole. And with that Christian brake out with a loud voice, Oh, I see him again! and he tells me, "When thou passest through the waters, I will be with thee; and through the rivers, they shall not overflow thee" (*Isaiah xliii.2*). Then they both took courage, and the Enemy was after that as still as a stone, until they were gone over. Christian therefore presently found ground to stand upon, and so it followed that the rest of the river was but shallow. Thus they got over. Now, upon the bank of the river on the other side, they saw the two Shining Men again, who there waited for them. Wherefore, being come out of the river, they saluted them saying, We are ministering spirits, sent forth to minister for those that shall be heirs of salvation. Thus they went along towards the gate. * * *

Now when they were come up to the gate, there was written over it in letters of gold, "Blessed are they that do his commandments, that they may have right to the tree of life, and may enter in through the gates into the city" (*Revelation xxii.14*).

Then I saw in my dream, that the Shining Men bid them call at the gate; the which, when they did, some from above looked over the gate, to wit, Enoch, Moses, and Elijah, etc., to whom it was said, These pilgrims are come from the City of Destruction, for the love that they bear to the King of this place; and then the pilgrims gave in unto them each man his certificate, which they had received in the beginning; those, therefore, were carried in to the King, who, when he had read them, said, Where are the men? To whom it was answered, They are standing without the gate. The King then commanded to open the gate, "That the righteous nation," said he, "which keepeth the truth, may enter in" (*Isaiah xxvi.2*).

Now I saw in my dream that these two men went in at the gate; and lo, as they entered, they were transfigured, and they had raiment put on that shone like gold. There was also that met them with harps and crowns, and gave them to them: the harps to praise withal, and the crowns in token of honor. Then I heard in my dream that all the bells in the city rang again for joy, and that it was said unto them, "ENTER YE INTO THE JOY OF OUR LORD" (*Matthew xxv.21*). I also heard the men themselves, that they sang with a loud voice, saying, "BLESSING AND HONOR, GLORY AND POWER, BE TO HIM THAT SITTETH UPON THE THRONE, AND TO THE LAMB FOREVER AND EVER" (*Revelation v.13*).

Now just as the gates were opened to let in the men, I looked in after them, and, behold, the City shone like the sun; the streets also were paved with gold, and in them walked many men, with crowns on their heads, palms in their hands, and golden harps to sing praises withal.

There were also of them that had wings, and they answered one another without intermission, saying, "Holy, holy, holy is the Lord" (*Revelation iv.*8). And after that they shut up the gates, which when I had seen I wished myself among them.

Now while I was gazing upon all these things, I turned my head to look back, and saw Ignorance come up to the riverside; but he soon got over, and that without half that difficulty which the other two men met with. For it happened that there was then in that place one Vain-hope, a ferryman, that with his boat helped him over; so he, as the other, I saw, did ascend the hill to come up to the gate, only he came alone; neither did any man meet him with the least encouragement. When he was come up to the gate, he looked up to the writing that was above, and then began to knock, supposing that entrance should have been quickly administered to him; but he was asked by the men that looked over the top of the gate, Whence came you? and what would you have? He answered, I have eat and drank in the presence of the King, and he has taught in our streets. Then they asked him for his certificate, that they might go in and show it to the King; so he fumbled in his bosom for one, and found none. Then said they, Have you none? But the man answered never a word. So they told the King, but he would not come down to see him, but commanded the two Shining Ones that conducted Christian and Hopeful to the City, to go out and take Ignorance, and bind him hand and foot, and have him away. Then they took him up, and carried him through the air, to the door that I saw in the side of the hill, and put him in there. Then I saw that there was a way to hell, even from the gates of heaven, as well as from the City of Destruction. So I awoke, and behold it was a dream.

1678

JOHN DRYDEN
(1631–1700)

1668: Made poet laureate.
1681: *Absalom and Achitophel.*
ca. 1686: Conversion to Catholicism.
1689: Loss of court offices upon accession of William and Mary.
1697: Translation of Virgil.

Although John Dryden's parents seem to have sided with Parliament against the king, there is no evidence that the poet grew up in a strict

Puritan family. His father, a country gentleman of moderate fortune, gave his son a gentleman's education at Westminster School, under the renowned Dr. Richard Busby, who used the rod as a pedagogical aid in imparting a sound knowledge of the learned languages and literatures to his charges (among others John Locke and Matthew Prior). From Westminster, Dryden went to Trinity College, Cambridge, where he took his A.B. in 1654. He probably held a minor post in Cromwell's government, and if he did so, it was obtained through the influence of his cousin Sir Gilbert Pickering, a member of the Protector's Council. His first important and impressive poem, *Heroic Stanzas* (1659), was written to commemorate the death of Cromwell. It was followed in the next year by *Astraea Redux*, celebrating the return of Charles II to his throne. Years later Dryden's political and religious enemies taunted him with this sudden change of position, as if he had been a political turncoat, ready to change sides whenever he could serve his own interests. The charge has often been repeated, but it is both malicious and stupid: as Dr. Johnson long ago said, "if he changed, he changed with the nation," for in 1660 most Englishmen enthusiastically welcomed the Restoration. During the rest of his life Dryden was to remain entirely loyal to Charles and to his successor James II.

Dryden is the commanding literary figure of the last four decades of the 17th century. He is that rare phenomenon, the man of letters in whose work the image of an age can be discerned. Every important aspect of the life of his times—political, religious, philosophical, artistic—finds expression somewhere in his writings. Dryden is the least personal of our poets. He is not at all the solitary, subjective poet listening to the murmur of his own voice and preoccupied with his own personal view of experience, but rather a citizen of the world commenting publicly on matters of public concern.

From the beginning to the end of his literary career, Dryden's original nondramatic poems are most typically occasional poems, i.e., poems which celebrate particular events of a public character—a coronation, a military victory, a death, a political crisis. Such poems are social and ceremonial, and they demand of the writer tact as well as talent. They are public and formal, blending poetry with rhetoric and oratory, and their tone is that of the forum, not of intimate conversation or private meditation. In varying degrees Dryden's occasional poems have these qualities. His earliest published poem, to be sure, *Upon the Death of Lord Hastings* (1649), belongs stylistically to the tradition of metaphysical poetry, but ten years later, when his next ambitious poem appeared, the *Heroic Stanzas* on the death of Cromwell, he had mastered the tone, language, and manner of grave public speech. His principal achievements in this form are the two poems on the king's return and his coronation; *Annus Mirabilis* (1667), which celebrates the English naval victory over the Dutch and the fortitude of the people of London and the king during the Great Fire, both events of that "wonderful year," 1666; the political poems, the lines on the death of Oldham (1684), the odes, and the masque printed below.

Between 1664 and 1681, however, Dryden was mainly and most seri-

ously a playwright. The newly chartered theaters needed a modern repertory, and Dryden was foremost among those who set vigorously about
supplying the need. As his *Essay of Dramatic Poesy* (1668) shows, he
studied the works of the great playwrights of Greece and Rome, of the
English Renaissance, and of contemporary France, seeking sound theoretical principles on which to construct the new drama that the age demanded. Indeed his fine critical intelligence always supported his creative
powers, and because he took literature seriously and enjoyed discussing it,
he became, it appears almost casually, what Dr. Johnson called him: "the
father of English criticism." His abilities as both poet and dramatist
brought him to the attention of the king, who in 1668 made him poet
laureate. Two years later the post of Historiographer Royal was added
to the laureateship at a combined stipend of £200, well over £2000 in
modern money.

Dryden is not a great playwright, but he was influential in his own time.
He wrote his plays, as he frankly confessed, to please his audiences, which
were not heterogeneous, like Shakespeare's, but were largely drawn from
the court and from the fashionable world that took its standard from the
court. He followed rather than formed the taste of his audiences, producing rhymed heroic plays, in which incredibly noble heroes and heroines
face incredibly difficult choices between their mutual love and the claims
of honor, and the dialogue is conducted in a boldly rhetorical style; comedies of busy intrigue and bright, witty repartee, especially between a male
and female rake; and, later, libretti for the newly introduced dramatic
form, the opera. His one great tragedy—on Antony and Cleopatra—is
All for Love (1677), in blank verse, written more in emulation than in
imitation of Shakespeare.

Between 1678 and 1681, when he was nearing 50, Dryden discovered his
great gift for writing formal verse satire. A quarrel with Thomas Shadwell,
a playwright of some talent, prompted the mock-heroic episode *Mac
Flecknoe*, which was probably written about 1678 but which was not published until 1682. Out of the stresses occasioned by the Popish Plot
(1678) and its political aftermath came his major political satires, *Absalom and Achitophel* (1681), and *The Medal* (1682), his final attack
on the villain of *Absalom and Achitophel*, the Earl of Shaftesbury. Twenty
years' experience as poet and playwright had prepared him technically
for the triumphant achievement that *Absalom and Achitophel* undoubtedly
is. He had completely mastered the heroic couplet, having fashioned it
into an instrument suitable in his hands for every sort of discourse from
the thrust and parry of quick logical argument, to lyric feeling, rapid narrative, or forensic declamation. And he had fashioned a noble, resonant,
and malleable language as well. Thanks to this long discipline, he was
able in one stride to assume his proper place beside the masters of verse
satire: Horace, Juvenal, Persius, in ancient Rome, and Boileau, his French
contemporary.

The consideration of religious and political questions that the events of
1678–81 forced on Dryden brought a new seriousness to his mind and
works. In 1682 he published *Religio Laici*, a poem in which he examined
the grounds of his religious faith and defended the *via media* of the Angli-

can Church against the rationalism of Deism on the one hand and the authoritarianism of Rome on the other. But he had moved closer to Rome than he perhaps realized when he wrote the poem. Charles II died in 1685 and was succeeded by his Catholic brother, James II. Within less than a year Dryden and his two sons were converted to Catholicism. Just when, by whom, and under what circumstances the poet was converted we do not know, but once again his enemies were loud in denouncing his apparent venality. Again the accusation does not survive serious scrutiny. Dryden's court appointments had been renewed promptly on the accession of James, certainly before his conversion. Moreover, as Louis Bredvold has shown, Dryden's early philosophic skepticism (the conviction that the human reason cannot arrive at truth) gave way to fideism (the acceptance by faith alone of Christian mysteries as interpreted by some valid tradition). The development was slow and consistent, and his sincerity is borne out by his steadfast loyalty to the Roman Church after James abdicated and the Protestant William and Mary came in; as a result he was to lose his offices and their much-needed stipends. From his new position as a Roman Catholic, Dryden wrote in 1687 *The Hind and the Panther,* in which he defended the doctrines of his church and the policies (which he knew to be ruinous for the king and his coreligionists) that James was pursuing. Though full of splendid passages, this poem is a rather odd performance. The various religious sects of England are represented by appropriate animals, and, surprisingly enough, we listen to a prolonged theological debate between two of them, the milk-white Hind (the Roman Church) and the spotted Panther (the Anglican Church).

Dryden was now nearing 60, with a family to support on a much-diminished income. With quiet dignity he once more undertook to earn his living. He easily resumed his career as a playwright, producing five more plays before his death. He had occasionally practiced translation in the past and to this minor but, in his time, highly esteemed art he now returned. In 1693 appeared his translations from Juvenal and Persius, with the long dedicatory epistle on satire; and in 1697, his greatest achievement in this mode, the magnificent folio, illustrated, of the works of Virgil. At the very end, two months before his death, came the *Fables Ancient and Modern,* prefaced by one of the finest of his critical essays and made up of superb translations from Ovid, Boccaccio, and Chaucer.

What was the nature of Dryden's achievement? His drama, by and large, belongs entirely to his age, though its influence persisted into the next century. His critical writings established canons of taste and theoretical principles that determined the character of neoclassic literature in the next century. He helped establish a new sort of prose—easy, lucid, plain, and shaped to the cadences of natural speech. This is the prose that we like to think of as "modern," although it is not everywhere evident in our modern age. Johnson praised it for its informality and apparent artlessness:

* * * every word seems to drop by chance, though it falls into its proper place. Nothing is cold or languid; the whole is airy, animated, and vigorous * * * though all is easy, nothing is feeble; though all seems careless, there is nothing harsh * * *

His satire, as vital today as it was nearly 300 years ago, exerted a fruitful influence on the most brilliant verse satirist of the next century, Alexander Pope. The vigor and variety of his metrics made inevitable the long-enduring vogue of the heroic couplet among his successors. At the same time, he created a poetic language that remained the basic language of poetry until the early 19th century and that even the Romantic movement did not wholly destroy. This is not to say that he created the stock "poetic diction" to which Wordsworth and Coleridge justly objected later on, though he added to it and used it judiciously. His language is the superbly civilized language of the Augustan style at its best: dignified, unaffected, precise and always musical—a noble instrument of public speech. Johnson's final estimate remains valid:

By him we were taught *sapere et fari*, to think naturally and express forcibly * * * What was said of Rome, adorned by Augustus, may be applied by an easy metaphor to English poetry embellished by Dryden, *lateritiam invenit, marmoream reliquit*, he found it brick, and he left it marble.

Prologue to *The Tempest*[1]

OR THE ENCHANTED ISLAND

As, when a tree's cut down, the secret root
Lives underground, and thence new branches shoot;
So from old Shakespeare's honored dust, this day
Springs up and buds a new reviving play:
Shakespeare, who (taught by none)[2] did first impart   5
To Fletcher[3] wit, to laboring Jonson art.
He, monarch-like, gave those, his subjects, law;
And is that nature which they paint and draw.
Fletcher reached that which on his heights did grow,
Whilst Jonson crept, and gathered all below.   10
This did his love, and this his mirth digest:
One imitates him most, the other best.
If they have since outwrit all other men,
'Tis with the drops which fell from Shakespeare's pen.
The storm which vanished on the neighboring shore,   15
Was taught by Shakespeare's *Tempest* first to roar.[4]
That innocence and beauty which did smile
In Fletcher, grew on this *Enchanted Isle*.
But Shakespeare's magic could not copied be;
Within that circle none durst walk but he.   20
I must confess 'twas bold, nor would you now

1. In 1667 Dryden collaborated with the poet laureate, Sir William Davenant, in adapting Shakespeare's *Tempest* to the Restoration stage and the tastes of Restoration audiences.
2. The view of Shakespeare as a natural genius, writing without the advantages of classical learning, was a critical commonplace. Compare Jonson's *To the Memory of * * * Shakespeare*, line 31, Milton's *L'Allegro*, lines 131–34, and Dryden's *Essay of Dramatic Poesy*.
3. John Fletcher (1579–1625), who collaborated with Francis Beaumont (ca. 1584–1616) in writing plays. During the early years of the Restoration period, their dramas were the most frequently revived plays "of the last age."
4. Details of the plot of *The Sea-Voyage* (1622), by Fletcher and Philip Massinger, suggest *The Tempest*.

That liberty to vulgar wits[5] allow,
Which works by magic supernatural things;
But Shakespeare's power is sacred as a king's.
Those legends from old priesthood were received,   25
And he then writ, as people then believed.
But if for Shakespeare we your grace implore,
We for our theater shall want it more:
Who by our dearth of youths are forced to employ
One of our women to present a boy;   30
And that's a transformation, you will say,
Exceeding all the magic in the play.
Let none expect in the last act to find
Her sex transformed from man to womankind.
Whate'er she was before the play began,   35
All you shall see of her is perfect man.
Or if your fancy will be farther led
To find her woman, it must be abed.

1667   1670

Epilogue to *Tyrannic Love*

SPOKEN BY MRS. ELLEN,[1] WHEN SHE WAS TO BE CARRIED OFF DEAD BY THE BEARERS

[*To the Bearer.*] Hold, are you mad? you damned confounded
    dog,
I am to rise, and speak the epilogue.
    [*To the Audience.*] I come, kind gentlemen, strange news to tell
    ye,
I am the ghost of poor departed Nelly.
Sweet ladies, be not frighted, I'll be civil;   5
I'm what I was, a little harmless devil:
For after death, we sprites have just such natures
We had for all the world, when human creatures;[2]
And therefore, I that was an actress here,
Play all my tricks in hell, a goblin there.   10
Gallants, look to it, you say there are no sprites;
But I'll come dance about your beds at nights.
And faith you'll be in a sweet kind of taking,
When I surprise you between sleep and waking.
To tell you true, I walk because I die   15
Out of my calling in a tragedy.
O poet, damned dull poet, who could prove
So senseless! to make Nelly die for love!
Nay, what's yet worse, to kill me in the prime

5. The common run of poets.

1. The famous actress Nell Gwynn ("Mrs."—i.e., "Mistress"—was the title given all young unmarried women); her beauty and wit made her not only a favorite of London audiences, but eventually a mistress of Charles II. As he lay dying he was heard to say, "Don't let poor Nelly starve." Her great roles were comic parts, but in *Tyrannic Love* she acted Valeria, the daughter of the wicked Roman Emperor Maximin, who puts to death St. Catharine of Alexandria. Valeria is killed in the general slaughter which ends the play.

2. Pope develops this idea brilliantly in the sylphs and gnomes of *The Rape of the Lock.*

Of Easter term,[3] in tart and cheese-cake time!   20
I'll fit[4] the fop, for I'll not one word say
To excuse his godly out-of-fashion play:
A play, which if you dare but twice sit out,
You'll all be slandered, and be thought devout.
But farewell, gentlemen, make haste to me;   25
I'm sure ere long to have your company.
As for my epitaph, when I am gone,
I'll trust no poet, but will write my own:

Here Nelly lies, who, though she lived a slattern,
Yet died a princess, acting in St. Cathar'n.[5]   30
1669   1670

Epilogue to *The Conquest of Granada*, II[1]

They who have best succeeded on the stage
Have still conformed their genius to their age.
Thus Jonson did mechanic humor[2] show,
When men were dull, and conversation low.
Then comedy was faultless, but 'twas coarse: 5
Cob's[3] tankard was a jest, and Otter's horse.
And, as their comedy, their love was mean;
Except, by chance, in some one labored scene
Which must atone for an ill-written play.
They rose, but at their height could seldom stay.   10
Fame then was cheap, and the first comer sped;
And they have kept it since, by being dead.
But, were they now to write, when critics weigh
Each line, and every word, throughout a play,
None of 'em, no, not Jonson in his height,   15
Could pass, without allowing grains for weight.[4]
Think it not envy, that these truths are told;
Our poet's not malicious, though he's bold.
'Tis not to brand 'em, that their faults are shown,
But, by their errors, to excuse his own.   20
If love and honor[5] now are higher raised,
'Tis not the poet, but the age is praised.
Wit's now arrived to a more high degree;
Our native language more refined and free.
Our ladies and our men now speak more wit   25
In conversation, than those poets writ.

3. One of the four periods of the year when the law courts sit.
4. Punish.
5. The normal pronunciation of *Catharine* at the time.
1. This epilogue, in which Dryden compared unfavorably the manners, the conversation, and the drama of the earlier 17th century with those of his own time, had provoked such hostile criticism that, when he published the play in 1672, he included a long prose defense of his position.

2. The eccentricities of artisans, as opposed to people of the middle and upper classes.
3. A character in Jonson's play *Every Man in His Humor;* "Otter" appears in Jonson's *Epicoene, or the Silent Woman.*
4. Without weighting the scale in his favor. A "grain" is the smallest unit of weight.
5. The two themes of the rhymed heroic play, of which *The Conquest of Granada* is the most distinguished example.

Then, one of these is, consequently, true;
That what this poet writes comes short of you,
And imitates you ill (which most he fears),
Or else his writing is not worse than theirs.   30
Yet, though you judge (as sure the critics will)
That some before him writ with greater skill,
In this one praise he has their fame surpassed,
To please an age more gallant than the last.

1671   1672

Song from The Indian Emperor

Ah, fading joy, how quickly art thou past!
    Yet we thy ruin haste.
As if the cares of human life were few,
    We seek out new:
And follow fate, which would too fast pursue.[1]   5

See how on every bough the birds express
    In their sweet notes their happiness.
    They all enjoy and nothing spare;
But on their mother nature lay their care:
Why then should man, the lord of all below,   10
    Such troubles choose to know
As none of all his subjects undergo?

Hark, hark, the waters fall, fall, fall,
    And with a murmuring sound
    Dash, dash upon the ground.   15
    To gentle slumber's call.

1665   1667

Song from An Evening's Love

1

Calm was the even, and clear was the sky,
    And the new-budding flowers did spring,
When all alone went Amyntas and I
    To hear the sweet nightingale sing.
I sate, and he laid him down by me,   5
    But scarcely his breath he could draw;
For when with a fear, he began to draw near,
    He was dashed with: "A ha ha ha ha!"

2

He blushed to himself, and lay still for a while,
    And his modesty curbed his desire;
But straight I convinced [2] all his fear with a smile,   10

1. Dryden's enemies ridiculed this line   2. Overcame.
as nonsense.

Which added new flames to his fire.
　"O Sylvia," said he, "you are cruel,
　　To keep your poor lover in awe";
Then once more he pressed with his hand to my breast,   15
　But was dashed with: "A ha ha ha ha!"

3

I knew 'twas his passion that caused all his fear,
　And therefore I pitied his case;
I whispered him softly: "There's nobody near,"
　And laid my cheek close to his face: 20
But as he grew bolder and bolder,
　A shepherd came by us and saw,
And just as our bliss we began with a kiss,
　He laughed out with: "A ha ha ha ha!"

1668   1671

Song from Marriage à la Mode

1

Why should a foolish marriage vow,
　Which long ago was made,
Oblige us to each other now,
　When passion is decayed?
We loved, and we loved, as long as we could,   5
　Till our love was loved out in us both;
But our marriage is dead when the pleasure is fled:
　'Twas pleasure first made it an oath.

2

If I have pleasures for a friend,
　And farther love in store,   10
What wrong has he whose joys did end,
　And who could give no more?
'Tis a madness that he should be jealous of me,
　Or that I should bar him of another:
For all we can gain is to give ourselves pain,   15
　When neither can hinder the other.

ca. 1672   1673

Absalom and Achitophel

In 1678 a dangerous crisis, both religious and political, threatened to undo the Restoration settlement and to precipitate England once again into civil war. The Popish Plot and its aftermath not only whipped up extreme anti-Catholic passions, but led between 1679 and 1681 to a bitter political struggle between Charles II (whose adherents came to be called Tories) and the Earl of Shaftesbury (whose followers were termed Whigs). The issues were nothing less than the prerogatives of the Crown and the possible exclusion of the king's Catholic brother, James, Duke of York, from his rightful position as heir

presumptive to the throne. Charles's cool courage and brilliant, if unscrupulous, political genius saved the throne for his brother and gave at
least temporary peace to his people.

Charles was a Catholic at heart—he received the last rites of that
Church on his deathbed—and was eager to do what he could do discreetly
for the relief of his Catholic subjects, who suffered severe civil and religious disabilities imposed by their numerically superior Protestant countrymen. James openly professed the Catholic religion, an awkward fact politically, for he was next in line of succession since Charles had no legitimate children. The household of the duke, as well as that of Charles's
neglected queen, Catherine of Braganza, inevitably became the center of
Catholic life and intrigue at court and consequently of Protestant prejudice and suspicion.

No one understood, however, that the situation was explosive until 1678,
when Titus Oates (a renegade Catholic convert and a man of the most
infamous character) offered sworn testimony of the existence of a Jesuit
plot to assassinate the king, burn London, massacre Protestants, and re-
establish the Roman Church.

The country might have kept its head and come to realize (what no
historian has doubted) that Oates and his confederates were perjured
rascals, as Charles himself quickly perceived. But panic was created by the
discovery of the murdered body of a prominent London Justice of the
Peace, Sir Edmund Berry Godfrey, who a few days before had received
for safekeeping a copy of Oates's testimony. The crime, immediately
ascribed to the Catholics, has never been solved. Fear and indignation
reached a hysterical pitch when the seizure of the papers of the Duke
of York's secretary revealed that he had been in correspondence with the
confessor of Louis XIV regarding the re-establishment of the Roman
Church in England. Before the terror subsided many innocent men were
executed on the increasingly bold and always false evidence of Oates and
his fellows.

The Earl of Shaftesbury, the Duke of Buckingham, and others quickly
took advantage of the situation. With the support of the Commons and
the City of London, they moved to exclude the Duke of York from the
succession. Between 1679 and 1681 Charles and Shaftesbury were engaged in a mighty struggle. The Whigs found a candidate of their own in
the king's favorite illegitimate son, the handsome and engaging Duke of
Monmouth, whom they advanced as a proper successor to his father.
They urged Charles to legitimize him, and when he refused they whispered that there was proof that the king had secretly married Monmouth's
mother. The young man allowed himself to be used against his father.
He was sent on a triumphant progress through western England, where he
was enthusiastically received. Twice an Exclusion Bill nearly passed both
Houses. But by early 1681 Charles had secured his own position by secretly
accepting from Louis XIV a three-year subsidy that made him independent
of Parliament, which had tried to force his hand by refusing to vote him
funds. He summoned Parliament to meet at Oxford in the spring of 1681,
and, a few moments after the Commons had passed the Exclusion Bill, in
a bold stroke he abruptly dissolved Parliament, which never met again
during his reign. Already, as Charles was aware, a reaction had set in

against the violence of the Whigs. In midsummer, when he felt it safe to move against his enemies, Shaftesbury was sent to the Tower, charged with high treason. In November the Grand Jury, packed with Whigs, threw out the indictment, and the earl was free; but his power was broken, and he lived only two more years.

Shortly before the Grand Jury acted, Dryden published anonymously the first part of *Absalom and Achitophel*, apparently hoping to influence their verdict. It is worthy of the occasion which produced it. The issues in question were grave; the chief actors, the most important men in the realm. Dryden, therefore, could not use burlesque and caricature as had Butler, or the mock-heroic as he himself had done in *Mac Flecknoe*. Only a heroic style and manner were appropriate to his weighty material, and the poem is most original in its blending of the heroic and the satiric. Dryden's task called for all his tact and literary skill; he had to mention, but to gloss over, the king's faults: his indolence and love of pleasure; his neglect of his wife and his devotion to his mistresses—conduct which had left him with many children, but no heir except his Catholic brother. He had to deal gently with Monmouth, whom Charles still loved. And he had to present, or appear to present, the king's case objectively.

The remarkable parallels between the rebellion of Absalom against his father King David (II Samuel xiii–xviii) had already been remarked in sermons, satires, and pamphlets. Dryden took the hint and gave contemporary events a due distance and additional dignity by approaching them indirectly through their Biblical analogues. The poem is famous for its brilliant portraits of the king's enemies and friends; but equally admirable are the temptation scene (which, like other passages, is indebted to *Paradise Lost*) and the remarkably astute analysis of the Popish Plot itself.

A second part of *Absalom and Achitophel* appeared in 1682. Most of it is the work of Nahum Tate, but lines 310–509, which include the devastating portraits of Doeg and Og (two Whig poets, Elkanah Settle and Thomas Shadwell) are certainly by Dryden.

Absalom and Achitophel: A Poem

In pious times, ere priestcraft did begin,
Before polygamy was made a sin;
When man on many multiplied his kind,
Ere one to one was cursedly confined;
When nature prompted and no law denied   5
Promiscuous use of concubine and bride;
Then Israel's monarch after Heaven's own heart,[1]
His vigorous warmth did variously impart
To wives and slaves; and, wide as his command,
Scattered his Maker's image through the land.   10
Michal,[2] of royal blood, the crown did wear,
A soil ungrateful to the tiller's care:
Not so the rest; for several mothers bore
To godlike David several sons before.
But since like slaves his bed they did ascend,   15
No true succession could their seed attend.

1. David ("a man after [God's] own heart," according to Acts xiii.22) represents Charles II.

2. "Michal," one of David's wives, represents the childless queen, Catherine of Braganza.

Of all this numerous progeny was none
So beautiful, so brave, as Absalom:[3]
Whether, inspired by some diviner lust,
His father got him with a greater gust,[4]   20
Or that his conscious destiny made way,
By manly beauty, to imperial sway.
Early in foreign fields he won renown,
With kings and states allied to Israel's crown:[5]
In peace the thoughts of war he could remove, 25
And seemed as he were only born for love.
Whate'er he did, was done with so much ease,
In him alone 'twas natural to please;
His motions all accompanied with grace;
And paradise was opened in his face.   30
With secret joy indulgent David viewed
His youthful image in his son renewed:
To all his wishes nothing he denied;
And made the charming Annabel[6] his bride.
What faults he had (for who from faults is free?) 35
His father could not, or he would not see.
Some warm excesses which the law forbore,
Were construed youth that purged by boiling o'er:
And Amnon's murther,[7] by a specious name,
Was called a just revenge for injured fame. 40
Thus praised and loved the noble youth remained,
While David, undisturbed, in Sion[8] reigned.
But life can never be sincerely[9] blest;
Heaven punishes the bad, and proves[1] the best.
The Jews,[2] a headstrong, moody, murmuring race, 45
As ever tried the extent and stretch of grace;
God's pampered people, whom, debauched with ease,
No king could govern, nor no God could please
(Gods they had tried of every shape and size
That god-smiths could produce, or priests devise);[3] 50
These Adam-wits,[4] too fortunately free,
Began to dream they wanted liberty;
And when no rule, no precedent was found,
Of men by laws less circumscribed and bound,
They led their wild desires to woods and caves, 55
And thought that all but savages were slaves.
They who, when Saul[5] was dead, without a blow,

3. James Scott, Duke of Monmouth (1649–85).
4. Relish, pleasure.
5. Monmouth had won repute as a soldier fighting for France against Holland and for Holland against France.
6. Anne Scott, Duchess of Buccleuch (pronounced *Bue-cloo*), a beauty and a great heiress.
7. Absalom killed his half-brother Amnon, who had raped Absalom's sister Tamar (II Samuel xiii.28–29). The parallel with Monmouth is vague. He is known to have committed acts of violence in his youth, but certainly not fratricide.

8. London.
9. Wholly.
1. Tests.
2. The English.
3. Dryden recalls the political and religious controversies which, since the Reformation, had divided England and finally caused civil war.
4. Adam rebelled because he felt that he lacked ("wanted") liberty, since he was forbidden to eat the fruit of one tree.
5. Oliver Cromwell. "Ishbosheth": Saul's son; he stands for Richard Cromwell, who succeeded his father as Lord Protector.

Made foolish Ishbosheth the crown forgo;
Who banished David did from Hebron[6] bring,
And with a general shout proclaimed him king: 60
Those very Jews, who, at their very best,
Their humor[7] more than loyalty expressed,
Now wondered why so long they had obeyed
An idol monarch, which their hands had made;
Thought they might ruin him they could create,   65
Or melt him to that golden calf,[8] a state.
But these were random bolts;[9] no formed design
Nor interest made the factious crowd to join:
The sober part of Israel, free from stain,
Well knew the value of a peaceful reign;   70
And, looking backward with a wise affright,
Saw seams of wounds, dishonest[1] to the sight:
In contemplation of whose ugly scars
They cursed the memory of civil wars.
The moderate sort of men, thus qualified,[2]   75
Inclined the balance to the better side;
And David's mildness managed it so well,
The bad found no occasion to rebel.
But when to sin our biased[3] nature leans,
The careful Devil is still at hand with means;   80
And providently pimps for ill desires:
The Good Old Cause[4] revived, a plot requires.
Plots, true or false, are necessary things,
To raise up commonwealths and ruin kings.
    The inhabitants of old Jerusalem   85
Were Jebusites;[5] the town so called from them;
And theirs the native right.
But when the chosen people[6] grew more strong,
The rightful cause at length became the wrong;
And every loss the men of Jebus bore,   90
They still were thought God's enemies the more.
Thus worn and weakened, well or ill content,
Submit they must to David's government:
Impoverished and deprived of all command,
Their taxes doubled as they lost their land;   95
And, what was harder yet to flesh and blood,
Their gods disgraced, and burnt like common wood.[7]
This set the heathen priesthood[8] in a flame;
For priests of all religions are the same:
Of whatsoe'er descent their godhead be,   100

6. Where David reigned over Judah after the death of Saul and before he became king of Israel (II Samuel i–v). Charles had been crowned in Scotland in 1651.
7. Caprice.
8. The image worshiped by the Children of Israel during the period that Moses spent on Mt. Sinai, receiving the law from God. "A state": a republic.
9. Shots.
1. Disgraceful.
2. Assuaged.

3. Inclined. Cf. *Mac Flecknoe,* line 189 and note.
4. The Commonwealth. Dryden stigmatizes the Whigs by associating them with subversion.
5. Roman Catholics. The original name of Jerusalem (here, London) was Jebus.
6. Protestants.
7. Such oppressive laws against Roman Catholics date from the time of Elizabeth I.
8. Roman Catholic clergy.

Stock, stone, or other homely pedigree,
In his defense his servants are as bold,
As if he had been born of beaten gold.
The Jewish rabbins,[9] though their enemies,
In this conclude them honest men and wise: 105
For 'twas their duty, all the learned think,
To espouse his cause, by whom they eat and drink.
From hence began that Plot, the nation's curse,
Bad in itself, but represented worse;
Raised in extremes, and in extremes decried;   110
With oaths affirmed, with dying vows denied;
Not weighed or winnowed by the multitude;
But swallowed in the mass, unchewed and crude.
Some truth there was, but dashed[1] and brewed with lies,
To please the fools, and puzzle all the wise.   115
Succeeding times did equal folly call,
Believing nothing, or believing all.
The Egyptian[2] rites the Jebusites embraced,
Where gods were recommended by their taste.
Such savory deities must needs be good,   120
As served at once for worship and for food.
By force they could not introduce these gods,
For ten to one in former days was odds;
So fraud was used (the sacrificer's trade):
Fools are more hard to conquer than persuade.   125
Their busy teachers mingled with the Jews,
And raked for converts even the court and stews:[3]
Which Hebrew priests the more unkindly took,
Because the fleece accompanies the flock.[4]
Some thought they God's anointed [4a] meant to slay   130
By guns, invented since full many a day:
Our author swears it not; but who can know
How far the Devil and Jebusites may go?
This Plot, which failed for want of common sense,
Had yet a deep and dangerous consequence: 135
For, as when raging fevers boil the blood,
The standing lake soon floats into a flood,
And every hostile humor, which before
Slept quiet in its channels, bubbles o'er;
So several factions from this first ferment   140
Work up to foam, and threat the government.
Some by their friends, more by themselves thought wise,
Opposed the power to which they could not rise.
Some had in courts been great, and thrown from thence,
Like fiends were hardened in impenitence;   145
Some, by their monarch's fatal mercy, grown
From pardoned rebels kinsmen to the throne,
Were raised in power and public office high;

9. Anglican clergy.
1. Adulterated.
2. French, therefore Catholic. In the next line Dryden sneers at the doctrine of transubstantiation.
3. Brothels.

4. Dryden charges that the Anglican clergy ("Hebrew priests") resented proselytizing by Catholics chiefly because they stood to lose their tithes ("fleece").
4a. The King.

Strong bands, if bands ungrateful men could tie.
    Of these the false Achitophel[5] was first;   150
A name to all succeeding ages cursed:
For close designs, and crooked counsels fit;
Sagacious, bold, and turbulent of wit;[6]
Restless, unfixed in principles and place;
In power unpleased, impatient of disgrace: 155
A fiery soul, which, working out its way,
Fretted the pygmy body to decay,
And o'er-informed the tenement of clay.[7]
A daring pilot in extremity;
Pleased with the danger, when the waves went high,   160
He sought the storms; but, for a calm unfit,
Would steer too nigh the sands, to boast his wit.
Great wits[8] are sure to madness near allied,
And thin partitions do their bounds divide;
Else why should he, with wealth and honor blest,   165
Refuse his age the needful hours of rest?
Punish a body which he could not please;
Bankrupt of life, yet prodigal of ease?
And all to leave what with his toil he won,
To that unfeathered two-legged thing,[9] a son;   170
Got, while his soul did huddled[1] notions try;
And born a shapeless lump, like anarchy.
In friendship false, implacable in hate,
Resolved to ruin or to rule the state.
To compass this the triple bond[2] he broke,   175
The pillars of the public safety shook,
And fitted Israel for a foreign yoke;
Then seized with fear, yet still affecting fame,
Usurped a patriot's all-atoning name.
So easy still it proves in factious times,   180
With public zeal to cancel private crimes.
How safe is treason, and how sacred ill,
Where none can sin against the people's will!
Where crowds can wink, and no offense be known,
Since in another's guilt they find their own!   185
Yet fame deserved, no enemy can grudge;
The statesman we abhor, but praise the judge.
In Israel's courts ne'er sat an Abbethdin[3]

5. Anthony Ashley Cooper, 1st Earl of Shaftesbury (1621–83). He had served in the Parliamentary army and been a member of Cromwell's Council of State. He later helped bring back Charles, and in 1670 was made a member of the notorious Cabal Ministry, which formed an alliance with Louis XIV in which England betrayed her ally, Holland, and joined France in war against that country. In 1672 he became Lord Chancellor, but with the dissolution of the Cabal in 1673 he was removed from office. Lines 146–49 apply perfectly to him.
6. Unruly imagination.
7. The soul is thought of as the animat-

ing principle, the force that puts the body in motion. Shaftesbury's body seemed too small to house his fiery, energetic soul.
8. Men of genius. That genius and madness are akin is a very old idea.
9. Cf. Plato's definition of man: "a featherless biped."
1. Confused, hurried.
2. The Triple Alliance of England, Sweden, and Holland against France, 1668. Shaftesbury helped to bring about the war against Holland in 1672.
3. The chief of the seventy elders who composed the Jewish supreme court. The allusion is to Shaftesbury's serving as Lord Chancellor in 1672–73. Dry-

With more discerning eyes, or hands more clean;
Unbribed, unsought, the wretched to redress;   190
Swift of dispatch, and easy of access.
Oh, had he been content to serve the crown,
With virtues only proper to the gown;
Or had the rankness of the soil been freed
From cockle, that oppressed the noble seed;   195
David for him his tuneful harp had strung,
And Heaven had wanted one immortal song.[4]
But wild Ambition loves to slide, not stand,
And Fortune's ice prefers to Virtue's land.
Achitophel, grown weary to possess   200
A lawful fame, and lazy happiness,
Disdained the golden fruit to gather free,
And lent the crowd his arm to shake the tree.
Now, manifest of[5] crimes contrived long since,
He stood at bold defiance with his prince;   205
Held up the buckler of the people's cause
Against the crown, and skulked behind the laws.
The wished occasion of the Plot he takes;
Some circumstances finds, but more he makes.
By buzzing emissaries fills the ears   210
Of listening crowds with jealousies[6] and fears
Of arbitrary counsels brought to light,
And proves the king himself a Jebusite.
Weak arguments! which yet he knew full well
Were strong with people easy to rebel.   215
For, governed by the moon, the giddy Jews
Tread the same track when she the prime renews;[7]
And once in twenty years, their scribes record,
By natural instinct they change their lord.
Achitophel still wants a chief, and none   220
Was found so fit as warlike Absalom:
Not that he wished his greatness to create
(For politicians neither love nor hate),
But, for he knew his title not allowed,
Would keep him still depending on the crowd,   225
That kingly power, thus ebbing out, might be
Drawn to the dregs of a democracy.[8]
Him he attempts with studied arts to please,
And sheds his venom in such words as these:
    "Auspicious prince, at whose nativity   230
Some royal planet[9] ruled the southern sky;
Thy longing country's darling and desire;

den's praise of Shaftesbury's integrity in this office, by suggesting a balanced judgment, makes his condemnation of the statesman more effective than it might otherwise have been.
4. I.e., David would have had occasion to write one less song of praise to Heaven. The reference may be to II Samuel xxii or to Psalm iv.
5. Detected in.
6. Suspicions.
7. The moon "renews her prime" when her several phases recur on the same day of the solar calendar—i.e., complete a cycle—as happens approximately every twenty years. The crisis between Charles I and Parliament began to grow acute about 1640; Charles II returned in 1660; it is now 1680 and a full cycle has been completed.
8. To Dryden, "democracy" meant popular government. The "dregs of a democracy" would be mob rule.
9. A planet whose influence destines him to kingship.

Their cloudy pillar and their guardian fire:[1]
Their second Moses, whose extended wand
Divides the seas, and shows the promised land;   235
Whose dawning day in every distant age
Has exercised the sacred prophet's rage:
The people's prayer, the glad diviners' theme,
The young men's vision, and the old men's dream![2]
Thee, savior, thee, the nation's vows[3] confess,   240
And, never satisfied with seeing, bless:
Swift unbespoken pomps thy steps proclaim,
And stammering babes are taught to lisp thy name.
How long wilt thou the general joy detain,
Starve and defraud the people of thy reign?   245
Content ingloriously to pass thy days
Like one of Virtue's fools that feeds on praise;
Till thy fresh glories, which now shine so bright,
Grow stale and tarnish with our daily sight.
Believe me, royal youth, thy fruit must be   250
Or gathered ripe, or rot upon the tree.
Heaven has to all allotted, soon or late,
Some lucky revolution of their fate;
Whose motions if we watch and guide with skill
(For human good depends on human will),   255
Our Fortune rolls as from a smooth descent,
And from the first impression takes the bent;
But, if unseized, she glides away like wind,
And leaves repenting Folly far behind.
Now, now she meets you with a glorious prize,   260
And spreads her locks before her as she flies.[4]
Had thus old David, from whose loins you spring,
Not dared, when Fortune called him, to be king,
At Gath[5] an exile he might still remain,
And heaven's anointing[6] oil had been in vain.   265
Let his successful youth your hopes engage;
But shun the example of declining age;
Behold him setting in his western skies,
The shadows lengthening as the vapors rise.
He is not now, as when on Jordan's sand[7]   270
The joyful people thronged to see him land, }
Covering the beach, and blackening all the strand; }
But, like the Prince of Angels, from his height
Comes tumbling downward with diminished light;[8]

1. After their exodus from Egypt under
the leadership of Moses, whose "extended wand" separated the waters of
the Red Sea so that they crossed over
on dry land, the Israelites were led in
their forty-year wandering in the wilderness by a pillar of cloud by day and
a pillar of fire by night. See Exodus
xiii–xiv.
2. Cf. Joel ii.28.
3. Solemn promises of fidelity.
4. Achitophel gives to Fortune the traditional attributes of the allegorical
personification of Opportunity: bald except for a forelock, she can be seized

only as she approaches.
5. Brussels, where Charles spent his
last years in exile. David took refuge
from Saul in Gath (I Samuel xxvii.4).
6. After God rejected Saul, He sent
Samuel to anoint the boy David, as a
token that he should finally come to
the throne (I Samuel xvi.1–13).
7. The seashore at Dover, where Charles
landed (May 25, 1660).
8. Cf. the fall of Satan in *Paradise
Lost*, which dims the brightness of the
archangel. The choice of the undigni-
fied word "tumbling" is deliberate.

Betrayed by one poor plot to public scorn   275
(Our only blessing since his cursed return),
Those heaps of people which one sheaf did bind,
Blown off and scattered by a puff of wind.
What strength can he to your designs oppose,
Naked of friends, and round beset with foes?   280
If Pharaoh's[9] doubtful succor he should use,
A foreign aid would more incense the Jews:
Proud Egypt would dissembled friendship bring;
Foment the war, but not support the king:
Nor would the royal party e'er unite   285
With Pharaoh's arms to assist the Jebusite;
Or if they should, their interest soon would break,
And with such odious aid make David weak.
All sorts of men by my successful arts,
Abhorring kings, estrange their altered hearts   290
From David's rule: and 'tis the general cry,
'Religion, commonwealth, and liberty.'[1]
If you, as champion of the public good,
Add to their arms a chief of royal blood,
What may not Israel hope, and what applause   295
Might such a general gain by such a cause?
Not barren praise alone, that gaudy flower
Fair only to the sight, but solid power;
And nobler is a limited command,
Given by the love of all your native land,   300
Than a successive title,[2] long and dark,
Drawn from the moldy rolls of Noah's ark."
    What cannot praise effect in mighty minds,
When flattery soothes, and when ambition blinds!
Desire of power, on earth a vicious weed,   305
Yet, sprung from high, is of celestial seed:
In God 'tis glory; and when men aspire,
'Tis but a spark too much of heavenly fire.
The ambitious youth, too covetous of fame,
Too full of angels' metal[3] in his frame,   310
Unwarily was led from virtue's ways,
Made drunk with honor, and debauched with praise.
Half loath, and half consenting to the ill
(For loyal blood within him struggled still),
He thus replied: "And what pretense have I   315
To take up arms for public liberty?
My father governs with unquestioned right;
The faith's defender, and mankind's delight,
Good, gracious, just, observant of the laws:
And heaven by wonders has espoused his cause.   320
Whom has he wronged in all his peaceful reign?
Who sues for justice to his throne in vain?
What millions has he pardoned of his foes,

9. Louis XIV of France.
1. Cf. line 82 and note.
2. A title to the crown based on succession.
3. An alternative spelling of *mettle*,
(i.e., spirit). But a pun on "metal" is intended, as is obvious from the pun "angel" (a purely intellectual being and a coin). Ambition caused the revolt of the angels in heaven.

Whom just revenge did to his wrath expose?
Mild, easy, humble, studious of our good,   325
Inclined to mercy, and averse from blood;
If mildness ill with stubborn Israel suit,
His crime is God's beloved attribute.
What could he gain, his people to betray,
Or change his right for arbitrary sway?   330
Let haughty Pharaoh curse with such a reign
His fruitful Nile, and yoke a servile train.
If David's rule Jerusalem displease,
The Dog Star[4] heats their brains to this disease.
Why then should I, encouraging the bad,   335
Turn rebel and run popularly mad?
Were he a tyrant, who, by lawless might
Oppressed the Jews, and raised the Jebusite,
Well might I mourn; but nature's holy bands
Would curb my spirits and restrain my hands: 340
The people might assert[5] their liberty,
But what was right in them were crime in me.
His favor leaves me nothing to require,
Prevents my wishes, and outruns desire.
What more can I expect while David lives?   345
All but his kingly diadem he gives:
And that"— But there he paused; then sighing, said—
"Is justly destined for a worthier head.
For when my father from his toils shall rest
And late augment the number of the blest,   350
His lawful issue shall the throne ascend,
Or the collateral line,[6] where that shall end.
His brother, though oppressed with vulgar spite,
Yet dauntless, and secure of native right,
Of every royal virtue stands possessed;   355
Still dear to all the bravest and the best.
His courage foes, his friends his truth proclaim;
His loyalty the king, the world his fame.
His mercy even the offending crowd will find,
For sure he comes of a forgiving kind.[7]   360
Why should I then repine at heaven's decree,
Which gives me no pretense to royalty?
Yet O that fate, propitiously inclined,
Had raised my birth, or had debased my mind;
To my large soul not all her treasure lent,   365
And then betrayed it to a mean descent!
I find, I find my mounting spirits bold,
And David's part disdains my mother's mold.
Why am I scanted by a niggard birth?[8]

4. Sirius, which in midsummer rises and sets with the sun and is thus associated with the maddening heat of the "dog days."
5. Claim.
6. In the event of Charles's dying without legitimate issue, the throne would constitutionally pass to his brother James, or his descendants, the "collateral line."
7. Race, in the sense of family.
8. I.e., why am I limited by a sordid birth?

My soul disclaims the kindred of her earth;   370
And, made for empire, whispers me within,
'Desire of greatness is a godlike sin.' "
    Him staggering so when hell's dire agent found,[9]
While fainting Virtue scarce maintained her ground,
He pours fresh forces in, and thus replies: 375
    "The eternal God, supremely good and wise,
Imparts not these prodigious gifts in vain:
What wonders are reserved to bless your reign!
Against your will, your arguments have shown,
Such virtue's only given to guide a throne.   380
Not that your father's mildness I contemn,
But manly force becomes the diadem.
'Tis true he grants the people all they crave;
And more, perhaps, than subjects ought to have:
For lavish grants suppose a monarch tame,   385
And more his goodness than his wit[1] proclaim.
But when should people strive their bonds to break,
If not when kings are negligent or weak?
Let him give on till he can give no more,
The thrifty Sanhedrin[2] shall keep him poor;   390
And every shekel which he can receive,
Shall cost a limb of his prerogative.[3]
To ply him with new plots shall be my care;
Or plunge him deep in some expensive war;
Which when his treasure can no more supply,   395
He must, with the remains of kingship, buy.
His faithful friends our jealousies and fears
Call Jebusites, and Pharaoh's pensioners;
Whom when our fury from his aid has torn,
He shall be naked left to public scorn.   400
The next successor, whom I fear and hate,
My arts have made obnoxious to the state;
Turned all his virtues to his overthrow,
And gained our elders[4] to pronounce a foe.
His right, for sums of necessary gold,   405
Shall first be pawned, and afterward be sold;
Till time shall ever-wanting David draw,
To pass your doubtful title into law:
If not, the people have a right supreme
To make their kings; for kings are made for them.   410
All empire is no more than power in trust,
Which, when resumed, can be no longer just.
Succession, for the general good designed,
In its own wrong a nation cannot bind;
If altering that the people can relieve,   415
Better one suffer than a nation grieve.

9. Observe the Miltonic inversion, which helps to maintain the epic tone.
1. Intelligence.
2. The highest judicial counsel of the Jews; here, Parliament.
3. The Whigs hoped to limit the special privileges of the Crown (the royal "prerogative") by refusing to vote money to Charles. He circumvented them by living on French subsidies and refusing to summon Parliament.
4. The chief magistrates and rulers of the Jews. Shaftesbury had won over ("gained") country gentlemen and nobles to his hostile view of James.

The Jews well know their power: ere Saul they chose,[5]
God was their king, and God they durst depose.
Urge now your piety,[6] your filial name,
A father's right, and fear of future fame;   420
The public good, that universal call,
To which even heaven submitted, answers all.
Nor let his love enchant your generous mind;
'Tis Nature's trick to propagate her kind.
Our fond begetters, who would never die,   425
Love but themselves in their posterity.
Or let his kindness by the effects be tried,
Or let him lay his vain pretense aside.
God said he loved your father; could he bring
A better proof than to anoint him king?   430
It surely showed he loved the shepherd well,
Who gave so fair a flock as Israel.
Would David have you thought his darling son?
What means he then, to alienate[7] the crown?
The name of godly he may blush to bear: 435
'Tis after God's own heart[8] to cheat his heir.
He to his brother gives supreme command;
To you a legacy of barren land,[8a]
Perhaps the old harp, on which he thrums his lays,
Or some dull Hebrew ballad in your praise.   440
Then the next heir, a prince severe and wise,
Already looks on you with jealous eyes;
Sees through the thin disguises of your arts,
And marks your progress in the people's hearts.
Though now his mighty soul its grief contains,   445
He meditates revenge who least complains;
And, like a lion, slumbering in the way,
Or sleep dissembling, while he waits his prey,
His fearless foes within his distance draws,
Constrains his roaring, and contracts his paws;   450
Till at the last, his time for fury found,
He shoots with sudden vengeance from the ground;
The prostrate vulgar[9] passes o'er and spares,
But with a lordly rage his hunters tears.
Your case no tame expedients will afford: 455
Resolve on death, or conquest by the sword,
Which for no less a stake than life you draw;
And self-defense is nature's eldest law.
Leave the warm people no considering time;
For then rebellion may be thought a crime.   460
Prevail yourself of what occasion gives,
But try your title while your father lives;
And that your arms may have a fair pretense,[1]

5. Before Saul, the first king of Israel, came to the throne, the Jews were governed by judges. Similarly Oliver Cromwell ("Saul") as Lord Protector took over the reins of government, after he had dissolved the Rump Parliament in 1653.
6. Dutifulness to a parent.

7. In law, to convey the title to property to another person.
8. An irony: cf. line 7, note.
8a. James was given the title of generalissimo in 1678. In 1679 Monmouth was banished and withdrew to Holland.
9. Common people.
1. Pretext.

Proclaim you take them in the king's defense;
Whose sacred life each minute would expose 465
To plots, from seeming friends, and secret foes.
And who can sound the depth of David's soul?
Perhaps his fear his kindness may control.
He fears his brother, though he loves his son,
For plighted vows too late to be undone. 470
If so, by force he wishes to be gained,
Like women's lechery, to seem constrained.[2]
Doubt not; but when he most affects the frown,
Commit a pleasing rape upon the crown.
Secure his person to secure your cause: 475
They who possess the prince, possess the laws."
  He said, and this advice above the rest
With Absalom's mild nature suited best:
Unblamed of life (ambition set aside),
Not stained with cruelty, nor puffed with pride, 480
How happy had he been, if destiny
Had higher placed his birth, or not so high!
His kingly virtues might have claimed a throne,
And blest all other countries but his own.
But charming greatness since so few refuse, 485
'Tis juster to lament him than accuse.
Strong were his hopes a rival to remove,
With blandishments to gain the public love;
To head the faction while their zeal was hot,
And popularly prosecute the Plot. 490
To further this, Achitophel unites
The malcontents of all the Israelites;
Whose differing parties he could wisely join,
For several ends, to serve the same design:
The best (and of the princes some were such), 495
Who thought the power of monarchy too much;
Mistaken men, and patriots in their hearts;
Not wicked, but seduced by impious arts.
By these the springs of property were bent,
And wound so high, they cracked the government. 500
The next for interest sought to embroil the state,
To sell their duty at a dearer rate;
And make their Jewish markets of the throne,
Pretending public good, to serve their own.
Others thought kings an useless heavy load, 505
Who cost too much, and did too little good.
These were for laying honest David by,
On principles of pure good husbandry.[3]
With them joined all the haranguers of the throng,
That thought to get preferment by the tongue. 510
Who follow next, a double danger bring,
Not only hating David, but the king:
The Solymaean rout,[4] well-versed of old
In godly faction, and in treason bold;

2. Forced.
3. Economy.
4. I.e., London rabble. Solyma was a name for Jerusalem.

Cowering and quaking at a conqueror's sword,   515
But lofty to a lawful prince restored;
Saw with disdain an ethnic[5] plot begun,
And scorned by Jebusites to be outdone.
Hot Levites[6] headed these; who, pulled before
From the ark, which in the Judges' days they bore,   520
Resumed their cant, and with a zealous cry
Pursued their old beloved theocracy:
Where Sanhedrin and priest enslaved the nation,
And justified their spoils by inspiration:[7]
For who so fit for reign as Aaron's race,[8]   525
If once dominion they could found in grace?
These led the pack; though not of surest scent,
Yet deepest-mouthed[9] against the government.
A numerous host of dreaming saints[1] succeed,
Of the true old enthusiastic breed: 530
'Gainst form and order they their power employ,
Nothing to build, and all things to destroy.
But far more numerous was the herd of such,
Who think too little, and who talk too much.
These out of mere instinct, they knew not why,   535
Adored their fathers' God and property;
And, by the same blind benefit of fate,
The Devil and the Jebusite did hate:
Born to be saved, even in their own despite,
Because they could not help believing right.   540
Such were the tools; but a whole Hydra more
Remains, of sprouting heads too long to score.
Some of their chiefs were princes of the land:
In the first rank of these did Zimri[2] stand;
A man so various, that he seemed to be   545
Not one, but all mankind's epitome:
Stiff in opinions, always in the wrong;

5. Gentile; here, Roman Catholic.
6. I.e., Presbyterian clergymen. The tribe of Levi, assigned to duties in the tabernacle, carried the ark of the covenant during the forty-year sojourn in the wilderness (Numbers iv). Under the Commonwealth ("in the Judges' days") Presbyterianism became the state religion, and its clergy therefore "bore the ark." The Act of Uniformity (1662) forced the Presbyterian clergy out of their livings: in short, before the Popish Plot, they had been "pulled from the ark." They are represented here as joining the Whigs in the hope of restoring the Commonwealth, "their old beloved theocracy."
7. Observe in these lines the cluster of disparaging words: "cant," "zealous," "inspiration." Dryden shared Samuel Butler's contempt for the irrationality of Dissenters.
8. Priests had to be descendants of Aaron (Exodus xxviii.1; Numbers xviii.7).
9. Loudest. The phrase is applied to hunting dogs. "Pack" and "scent" sustain the image.

1. A term used by certain Dissenters for those elected to salvation. The extreme fanaticism of the "saints" and their claims to inspiration are characterized as a form of religious madness ("enthusiastic").
2. George Villiers, 2nd Duke of Buckingham (1628–87), wealthy, brilliant, dissolute, unstable. He had been an influential member of the Cabal, but after 1673 had joined Shaftesbury in opposition to the Court party. This is the least political of the satirical portraits in the poem. Buckingham had been the chief author of *The Rehearsal* (1671), the play which satirized the heroic play and ridiculed Dryden in the character of Mr. Bayes. Politics gave Dryden an opportunity to retaliate. He comments on this portrait in his *Discourse Concerning the Original and Progress of Satire*. Dryden had two Biblical Zimris in mind: the Zimri destroyed for his lustfulness and blasphemy (Numbers xxv) and the conspirator and regicide of I Kings xvi.8–20 and II Kings ix.31.

Was everything by starts, and nothing long;
But, in the course of one revolving moon,
Was chymist,[3] fiddler, statesman, and buffoon: 550
Then all for women, painting, rhyming, drinking,
Besides ten thousand freaks that died in thinking.
Blest madman, who could every hour employ,
With something new to wish, or to enjoy!
Railing[4] and praising were his usual themes;   555
And both (to show his judgment) in extremes:
So over-violent, or over-civil,
That every man, with him, was God or Devil.
In squandering wealth was his peculiar art:
Nothing went unrewarded but desert.   560
Beggared by fools, whom still he found[5] too late,
He had his jest, and they had his estate.
He laughed himself from court; then sought relief
By forming parties, but could ne'er be chief;
For, spite of him, the weight of business fell   565
On Absalom and wise Achitophel:
Thus, wicked but in will, of means bereft,
He left not faction, but of that was left.

    Titles and names 'twere tedious to rehearse
Of lords, below the dignity of verse.   570
Wits, warriors, Commonwealth's men, were the best;
Kind husbands, and mere nobles, all the rest.
And therefore, in the name of dullness, be
The well-hung Balaam and cold Caleb, free;
And canting Nadab[6] let oblivion damn,   575
Who made new porridge for the paschal lamb.
Let friendship's holy band some names assure;
Some their own worth, and some let scorn secure.
Nor shall the rascal rabble here have place,
Whom kings no titles gave, and God no grace: 580
Not bull-faced Jonas,[7] who could statutes draw
To mean rebellion, and make treason law.
But he, though bad, is followed by a worse,
The wretch who heaven's anointed dared to curse:
Shimei,[8] whose youth did early promise bring   585
Of zeal to God and hatred to his king,
Did wisely from expensive sins refrain,

3. Chemist.
4. Reviling, abusing.
5. **Found out**; "still": **constantly**.
6. The identities of Balaam, Caleb, and Nadab have not been certainly established, although various Whig nobles have been suggested. For Balaam see Numbers xxii–xxiv; for Caleb, Numbers xiii–xiv; for Nadab, Leviticus x.1–2. "Well-hung" may mean "fluent of speech" or "sexually potent" or both; "cold" would contrast with the second meaning of "well-hung." "Canting" points to a Nonconformist, as does the obscure line 576, for Dissenters referred to the Book of Common Prayer contemptuously as "porridge," a hodge-podge, unsubstantial stuff. The "paschal lamb," the lamb slain at the Passover, is Christ.
7. Sir William Jones, Attorney General, had been largely responsible for the passage of the first Exclusion Bill by the House of Commons. He prosecuted the accused in the Popish Plot.
8. Shimei cursed and stoned David when he fled into the wilderness during Absalom's revolt (II Samuel xvi.5–14); his name is used here for one of the two sheriffs of London, Slingsby Bethel, a Whig, former republican, and virulent enemy of Charles. He packed juries with Whigs and so secured the acquittal of enemies of the court, among them Shaftesbury himself.

And never broke the Sabbath, but for gain;
Nor ever was he known an oath to vent,
Or curse, unless against the government.   590
Thus heaping wealth, by the most ready way
Among the Jews, which was to cheat and pray,
The city, to reward his pious hate
Against his master, chose him magistrate.
His hand a vare[9] of justice did uphold;   595
His neck was loaded with a chain of gold.
During his office, treason was no crime;
The sons of Belial[1] had a glorious time;
For Shimei, though not prodigal of pelf,
Yet loved his wicked neighbor as himself.   600
When two or three were gathered to declaim   ⎫
Against the monarch of Jerusalem,   ⎬
Shimei was always in the midst of them;   ⎭
And if they cursed the king when he was by,
Would rather curse than break good company.   605
If any durst his factious friends accuse,
He packed a jury of dissenting Jews;
Whose fellow-feeling in the godly cause
Would free the suffering saint from human laws.
For laws are only made to punish those   610
Who serve the king, and to protect his foes.
If any leisure time he had from power
(Because 'tis sin to misemploy an hour),
His business was, by writing, to persuade
That kings were useless, and a clog to trade;   615
And, that his noble style he might refine,
No Rechabite[2] more shunned the fumes of wine.
Chaste were his cellars, and his shrieval board[3]
The grossness of a city feast abhorred:
His cooks, with long disuse, their trade forgot;   620
Cool was his kitchen, though his brains were hot.
Such frugal virtue malice may accuse,
But sure 'twas necessary to the Jews:
For towns once burnt[4] such magistrates require
As dare not tempt God's providence by fire.   625
With spiritual food he fed his servants well,
But free from flesh that made the Jews rebel;
And Moses' laws he held in more account,
For forty days of fasting in the mount.[5]
To speak the rest, who better are forgot,   630
Would tire a well-breathed witness of the Plot.
Yet, Corah,[6] thou shalt from oblivion pass:

9. Staff.
1. Sons of wickedness. Cf. Milton, *Paradise Lost* I.490–505. Dryden probably intended a pun on Balliol, the Oxford college in which leading Whigs stayed during the brief and fateful meeting of Parliament at Oxford in 1681.
2. An austere Jewish sect that drank

no wine (Jeremiah xxxv.2–19).
3. Sheriff's dinner table.
4. London burned in 1666.
5. Mt. Sinai, where, during a fast of forty days, Moses received the law (Exodus xxxiv.28).
6. Or Korah, a rebellious Levite, swallowed up by the earth because of his

Erect thyself, thou monumental brass,
High as the serpent of thy metal made,[7]
While nations stand secure beneath thy shade.   635
What though his birth were base, yet comets rise
From earthy vapors, ere they shine in skies.
Prodigious actions may as well be done
By weaver's issue,[8] as by prince's son.
This arch-attestor for the public good   640
By that one deed ennobles all his blood.
Who ever asked the witnesses' high race
Whose oath with martyrdom did Stephen grace?[9]
Ours was a Levite, and as times went then,
His tribe were God Almighty's gentlemen.   645
Sunk were his eyes, his voice was harsh and loud,
Sure signs he neither choleric[1] was nor proud:
His long chin proved his wit; his saintlike grace
A church vermilion, and a Moses' face.[2]
His memory, miraculously great,   650
Could plots, exceeding man's belief, repeat;
Which therefore cannot be accounted lies,
For human wit could never such devise.
Some future truths are mingled in his book;
But where the witness failed, the prophet spoke: 655
Some things like visionary flights appear;
The spirit caught him up, the Lord knows where,
And gave him his rabbinical degree,
Unknown to foreign university.[3]
His judgment yet his memory did excel;   660
Which pieced his wondrous evidence so well,
And suited to the temper of the times,
Then groaning under Jebusitic crimes.
Let Israel's foes suspect his heavenly call,
And rashly judge his writ apocryphal;[4]   665
Our laws for such affronts have forfeits made:
He takes his life, who takes away his trade.
Were I myself in witness Corah's place,
The wretch who did me such a dire disgrace
Should whet my memory, though once forgot,   670
To make him an appendix of my plot.
His zeal to heaven made him his prince despise,
And load his person with indignities;

---

crimes (Numbers xvi). Corah is Titus
Oates, the self-appointed, perjured, and
"well-breathed" (long-winded) witness
of the Plot.
7. Moses erected a brazen serpent to
heal the Jews bitten by fiery serpents
(Numbers xxi.4–9). "Brass" also means
"impudence" or "shamelessness."
8. Oates's father, a clergyman, belonged
to an obscure family of ribbon weavers.
9. The first Christian martyr, accused
by false witnesses (Acts vi–vii).

1. Prone to anger.
2. Moses' face shone when he came
down from Mt. Sinai with the tables of
the law (Exodus xxxiv.29–30). Oates's
face suggests high living, not spiritual
illumination.
3. Oates falsely claimed to be a Doctor
of Divinity in the University of Sala-
manca.
4. Not inspired, and hence excluded
from Holy Writ.

But zeal peculiar privilege affords,
Indulging latitude to deeds and words;   675
And Corah might for Agag's murder [5] call,
In terms as coarse as Samuel used to Saul.
What others in his evidence did join
(The best that could be had for love or coin),
In Corah's own predicament will fall;   680
For *witness* is a common name to all.
    Surrounded thus with friends of every sort,
Deluded Absalom forsakes the court:
Impatient of high hopes, urged with renown,
And fired with near possession of a crown.   685
The admiring crowd are dazzled with surprise,
And on his goodly person feed their eyes:
His joy concealed, he sets himself to show,
On each side bowing popularly [6] low;
His looks, his gestures, and his words he frames,   690
And with familiar ease repeats their names.
Thus formed by nature, furnished out with arts,
He glides unfelt into their secret hearts.
Then, with a kind compassionating look,
And sighs, bespeaking pity ere he spoke,   695
Few words he said; but easy those and fit,
More slow than Hybla-drops,[7] and far more sweet.
    "I mourn, my countrymen, your lost estate;
Though far unable to prevent your fate:
Behold a banished man, for your dear cause   700
Exposed a prey to arbitrary laws!
Yet oh! that I alone could be undone,
Cut off from empire, and no more a son!
Now all your liberties a spoil are made; ⎤
Egypt and Tyrus [8] intercept your trade, ⎬   705
And Jebusites your sacred rites invade.   ⎦
My father, whom with reverence yet I name,
Charmed into ease, is careless of his fame;
And, bribed with petty sums of foreign gold,
Is grown in Bathsheba's [9] embraces old;   710
Exalts his enemies, his friends destroys;
And all his power against himself employs.
He gives, and let him give, my right away;
But why should he his own, and yours betray?
He only, he can make the nation bleed,   715
And he alone from my revenge is freed.
Take then my tears (with that he wiped his eyes),

---

5. Agag is probably one of the five Catholic peers executed for the Popish Plot in 1680, most likely Lord Stafford, against whom Oates fabricated testimony; almost certainly not, as is usually suggested, Sir Edmund Berry Godfrey (cf. title note). For "Agag's murder" and Samuel's coarse terms to Saul, see I Samuel xv.

6. "So as to please the crowd" (Johnson's *Dictionary*).
7. The famous honey of Hybla in Sicily.
8. France and Holland.
9. With whom David committed adultery (II Samuel xi); here, Charles II's French mistress, Louise de Keroualle, Duchess of Portsmouth.

'Tis all the aid my present power supplies:
No court-informer can these arms accuse;
These arms may sons against their fathers use: 720
And 'tis my wish, the next successor's reign
May make no other Israelite complain."
   Youth, beauty, graceful action seldom fail;
But common interest always will prevail;
And pity never ceases to be shown   725
To him who makes the people's wrongs his own.
The crowd (that still believe their kings oppress),
With lifted hands their young Messiah bless:
Who now begins his progress to ordain
With chariots, horsemen, and a numerous train;   730
From east to west his glories he displays,[1]
And, like the sun, the promised land surveys.
Fame runs before him as the morning star,
And shouts of joy salute him from afar:
Each house receives him as a guardian god,   735
And consecrates the place of his abode:
But hospitable treats did most commend
Wise Issachar,[2] his wealthy western friend.
This moving court, that caught the people's eyes,
And seemed but pomp, did other ends disguise: 740
Achitophel had formed it, with intent
To sound the depths, and fathom where it went,
The people's hearts; distinguish friends from foes,
And try their strength, before they came to blows.
Yet all was colored with a smooth pretense   745
Of specious love, and duty to their prince.
Religion, and redress of grievances,
Two names that always cheat and always please,
Are often urged; and good King David's life
Endangered by a brother and a wife.[3]   750
Thus, in a pageant show, a plot is made,
And peace itself is war in masquerade.
O foolish Israel! never warned by ill,
Still the same bait, and circumvented still!
Did ever men forsake their present ease,   755
In midst of health imagine a disease;
Take pains contingent mischiefs to foresee,
Make heirs for monarchs, and for God decree?
What shall we think![4] Can people give away
Both for themselves and sons, their native sway?   760
Then they are left defenseless to the sword
Of each unbounded, arbitrary lord:

1. In 1680 Monmouth made a progress through the west of England, seeking popular support for his cause.
2. Thomas Thynne of Longleat. He entertained Monmouth on his journey in the west. "Wise" is, of course, ironic.
3. Titus Oates had sworn that both James, Duke of York, and the Queen were involved in a plot to poison Charles II.
4. In the passage that follows, Dryden states his political philosophy. He bases the royal authority on a covenant entered into by the governor and the governed.

And laws are vain, by which we right enjoy,
If kings unquestioned can those laws destroy.
Yet if the crowd be judge of fit and just,   765
And kings are only officers in trust,
Then this resuming covenant was declared
When kings were made, or is forever barred.
If those who gave the scepter could not tie
By their own deed their own posterity,   770
How then could Adam bind his future race?
How could his forfeit on mankind take place?
Or how could heavenly justice damn us all,
Who ne'er consented to our father's fall?
Then kings are slaves to those whom they command,   775
And tenants to their people's pleasure stand.
Add, that the power for property allowed
Is mischievously seated in the crowd;
For who can be secure of private right,
If sovereign sway may be dissolved by might?   780
Nor is the people's judgment always true:
The most may err as grossly as the few;
And faultless kings run down, by common cry,
For vice, oppression, and for tyranny.
What standard is there in a fickle rout,   785
Which, flowing to the mark,[5] runs faster out?
Nor only crowds, but Sanhedrins may be
Infected with this public lunacy,
And share the madness of rebellious times,
To murder monarchs for imagined crimes.[6]   790
If they may give and take whene'er they please,
Not kings alone (the Godhead's images),
But government itself at length must fall
To nature's state, where all have right to all.
Yet, grant our lords the people kings can make,   795
What prudent men a settled throne would shake?
For whatsoe'er their sufferings were before,
That change they covet makes them suffer more.
All other errors but disturb a state,
But innovation is the blow of fate.   800
If ancient fabrics nod, and threat to fall,
To patch the flaws, and buttress up the wall,
Thus far 'tis duty; but here fix the mark;
For all beyond it is to touch our ark.[7]
To change foundations, cast the frame anew,   805
Is work for rebels, who base ends pursue,
At once divine and human laws control,
And mend the parts by ruin of the whole.

5. An obscure couplet, rare in Dryden. George R. Noyes paraphrases it thus: "The fickle crowd is apparently compared to water, which, after rising to the *mark*, or boundary, it was intended to reach, overflows all the faster."

6. An allusion to the execution of Charles I.
7. Uzzah was struck dead because he sacrilegiously touched the Ark of the Covenant. II Samuel vi. 6–7.

The tampering world is subject to this curse,
To physic their disease into a worse.   810
　　Now what relief can righteous David bring?
How fatal 'tis to be too good a king!
Friends he has few, so high the madness grows:
Who dare be such, must be the people's foes:
Yet some there were, even in the worst of days;   815
Some let me name, and naming is to praise.
　　In this short file Barzillai [8] first appears;
Barzillai, crowned with honor and with years:
Long since, the rising rebels he withstood
In regions waste, beyond the Jordan's flood: 820
Unfortunately brave to buoy the State;
But sinking underneath his master's fate:
In exile with his godlike prince he mourned;
For him he suffered, and with him returned.
The court he practiced, not the courtier's art: 825
Large was his wealth, but larger was his heart:
Which well the noblest objects knew to choose,
The fighting warrior, and recording Muse.
His bed could once a fruitful issue boast;
Now more than half a father's name is lost.   830
His eldest hope,[9] with every grace adorned,
By me (so Heaven will have it) always mourned,
And always honored, snatched in manhood's prime
By unequal fates, and Providence's crime:
Yet not before the goal of honor won, ⎫   835
All parts fulfilled of subject and of son; ⎬
Swift was the race, but short the time to run. ⎭
O narrow circle, but of power divine,
Scanted in space, but perfect in thy line!
By sea, by land, thy matchless worth was known,   840
Arms thy delight, and war was all thy own:
Thy force, infused, the fainting Tyrians [1] propped;
And haughty Pharaoh found his fortune stopped.
Oh ancient honor! Oh unconquered hand,
Whom foes unpunished never could withstand!   845
But Israel was unworthy of thy name:
Short is the date of all immoderate fame.
It looks as Heaven our ruin had designed,
And durst not trust thy fortune and thy mind.
Now, free from earth, thy disencumbered soul   850
Mounts up, and leaves behind the clouds and starry pole:
From thence thy kindred legions mayst thou bring,
To aid the guardian angel of thy king.
Here stop my Muse, here cease thy painful flight;

8. James Butler, Duke of Ormond (1610–88). He was famous for his loyalty to the Stuart cause. He fought for Charles I in Ireland, and when that cause was hopeless, he joined Charles II in his exile abroad. He spent a large fortune in behalf of the King and continued to serve him loyally after the Restoration.
9. Ormond's son, Thomas, Earl of Ossory (1634–80), a famous soldier, and like his father devoted to Charles II.
1. The Dutch.

No pinions can pursue immortal height: 855
Tell good Barzillai thou canst sing no more,
And tell thy soul she should have fled before.
Or fled she with his life, and left this verse
To hang on her departed patron's hearse?
Now take thy steepy flight from heaven, and see 860
If thou canst find on earth another *he*:
Another *he* would be too hard to find;
See then whom thou canst see not far behind.
Zadoc the priest,[2] whom, shunning power and place,
His lowly mind advanced to David's grace: 865
With him the Sagan of Jerusalem,
Of hospitable soul, and noble stem;
Him of the western dome, whose weighty sense
Flows in fit words and heavenly eloquence.
The prophets' sons, by such example led, 870
To learning and to loyalty were bred:
For colleges on bounteous kinds depend,
And never rebel was to arts a friend.
To these succeed the pillars of the laws,
Who best could plead, and best can judge a cause. 875
Next them a train of loyal peers ascend;
Sharp-judging Adriel, the Muses' friend,
Himself a Muse—in Sanhedrin's debate
True to his prince, but not a slave of state:
Whom David's love with honors did adorn, 880
That from his disobedient son were torn.
Jotham of piercing wit, and pregnant thought,
Indued by nature, and by learning taught
To move assemblies, who but only tried
The worse a while, then chose the better side; 885
Nor chose alone, but turned the balance too;
So much the weight of one brave man can do.
Hushai, the friend of David in distress,
In public storms, of manly steadfastness:
By foreign treaties he informed his youth, 890
And joined experience to his native truth.
His frugal care supplied the wanting throne,
Frugal for that, but bounteous of his own:
'Tis easy conduct when exchequers flow,
But hard the task to manage well the low; 895
For sovereign power is too depressed or high,
When kings are forced to sell, or crowds to buy.
Indulge one labor more, my weary Muse,
For Amiel: who can Amiel's praise refuse?
Of ancient race by birth, but nobler yet 900

2. William Sancroft, Archbishop of Canterbury; the Sagan is Henry Compton, Bishop of London; "Him of the western dome" is John Dolben, Dean of Westminster; "The prophets' sons" are the boys of Westminster School, which Dryden had attended; Adriel is John Sheffield, Earl of Mulgrave; Jotham, George Savile, Marquis of Halifax; Hushai, Laurence Hyde, Earl of Rochester; and Amiel is Edward Seymour, Speaker of the House of Commons.

In his own worth, and without title great:
The Sanhedrin long time as chief he ruled,
Their reason guided, and their passion cooled:
So dexterous was he in the crown's defence,
So formed to speak a loyal nation's sense,   905
That, as their band was Israel's tribes in small,
So fit was he to represent them all.
Now rasher charioteers the seat ascend,
Whose loose careers his steady skill commend:
They like the unequal ruler of the day,   910
Misguide the seasons, and mistake the way;
While he withdrawn at their mad labor smiles,
And safe enjoys the sabbath of his toils.
    These were the chief, a small but faithful band ⎫
Of worthies, in the breach who dared to stand, ⎬   915
And tempt the united fury of the land. ⎭
With grief they viewed such powerful engines bent,
To batter down the lawful government:
A numerous faction, with pretended frights,
In Sanhedrins to plume the regal rights;   920
The true successor from the court removed:[3]
The Plot, by hireling witnesses, improved.
These ills they saw, and, as their duty bound,
They showed the king the danger of the wound:
That no concessions from the throne would please,   925
But lenitives[4] fomented the disease;
That Absalom, ambitious of the crown,
Was made the lure to draw the people down;
That false Achitophel's pernicious hate
Had turned the Plot to ruin Church and State: 930
The council violent, the rabble worse;
That Shimei taught Jerusalem to curse.
    With all these loads of injuries oppressed,
And long revolving in his careful breast,
The event of things, at last, his patience tired,   935
Thus from his royal throne, by Heaven inspired,
The godlike David spoke: with awful fear
His train their Maker in their master hear.
    "Thus long have I, by native mercy swayed,
My wrongs dissembled, my revenge delayed: 940
So willing to forgive the offending age,
So much the father did the king assuage.
But now so far my clemency they slight,
The offenders question my forgiving right.
That one was made for many, they contend;   945
But 'tis to rule; for that's a monarch's end.
They call my tenderness of blood, my fear;
Though manly tempers can the longest bear.
Yet, since they will divert my native course,

---

3. The Duke of York had been banished   4. Any medicine that relieves pain.
from England.

'Tis time to show I am not good by force.   950
Those heaped affronts that haughty subjects bring,
Are burdens for a camel, not a king:
Kings are the public pillars of the State,
Born to sustain and prop the nation's weight:
If my young Samson will pretend a call   955
To shake the column, let him share the fall: [5]
But, oh, that yet he would repent and live!
How easy 'tis for parents to forgive!
With how few tears a pardon might be won
From nature, pleading for a darling son!   960
Poor pitied youth, by my paternal care
Raised up to all the height his frame could bear:
Had God ordained his fate for empire born,
He would have given his soul another turn:
Gulled [6] with a patriot's name, whose modern sense
Is one that would by law supplant his prince: 965
The people's brave, the politician's tool;
Never was patriot yet, but was a fool.
Whence comes it that religion and the laws
Should more be Absalom's than David's cause?   970
His old instructor, ere he lost his place,
Was never thought indued with so much grace.[7]
Good heavens, how faction can a patriot paint!
My rebel ever proves my people's saint:
Would *they* impose an heir upon the throne?   975
Let Sanhedrins be taught to give their own.
A king's at least a part of government,
And mine as requisite as their consent;
Without my leave a future king to choose,
Infers a right the present to depose: 980
True, they petition me to approve their choice;
But Esau's hands suit ill with Jacob's voice.[8]
My pious subjects for my safety pray,
Which to secure, they take my power away.
From plots and treasons Heaven preserve my years,   985
But save me most from my petitioners.
Unsatiate as the barren womb or grave;
God cannot grant so much as they can crave.
What then is left but with a jealous eye
To guard the small remains of royalty?   990
The law shall still direct my peaceful sway,
And the same law teach rebels to obey:
Votes shall no more established power control—
Such votes as make a part exceed the whole:
No groundless clamors shall my friends remove,   995
Nor crowds have power to punish ere they prove:
For gods and godlike kings, their care express,
Still to defend their servants in distress.

5. Judges xvi.   7. The Earl of Shaftesbury.
6. Deceived.   8. Genesis xxvii. 22.

O that my power to saving were confined:
Why am I forced, like Heaven, against my mind, ⎫
To make examples of another kind?   ⎬ 1000
Must I at length the sword of justice draw?   ⎭
O curst effects of necessary law!
How ill my fear they by my mercy scan!
Beware the fury of a patient man.   1005
Law they require, let Law then show her face;
They could not be content to look on Grace,
Her hinder parts, but with a daring eye
To tempt the terror of her front and die.⁹
By their own arts, 'tis righteously decreed,   1010
Those dire artificers of death shall bleed.
Against themselves their witnesses will swear,
Till viper-like their mother Plot they tear:
And suck for nutriment that bloody gore,
Which was their principle of life before.   1015
Their Belial with their Belzebub ¹⁰ will fight;
Thus on my foes, my foes shall do me right:
Nor doubt the event; for factious crowds engage,
In their first onset, all their brutal rage.
Then let 'em take an unresisted course,   1020
Retire and traverse, and delude their force:
But when they stand all breathless, urge the fight,
And rise upon 'em with redoubled might:
For lawful power is still superior found,
When long driven back, at length it stands the ground." 1025
    He said. The Almighty, nodding, gave consent;
And peals of thunder shook the firmament.
Henceforth a series of new time began,
The mighty years in long procession ran:
Once more the godlike David was restored,   1030
And willing nations knew their lawful lord.

1681

Mac Flecknoe¹

OR A SATIRE UPON THE TRUE-BLUE-PROTESTANT POET, T. S.

All human things are subject to decay,
And when fate summons, monarchs must obey.

9. Moses was not allowed to see the countenance of Jehovah. Exodus xxxiii. 20–23.
10. Belial, the incarnation of all evil; Beelzebub, a god of the Philistines.
1. The victim of this superb satire, which is cast in the form of a mock-heroic episode, is Thomas Shadwell (1640–92), the playwright, with whom Dryden had been on good terms for a number of years, certainly as late as March, 1678. Shadwell considered himself the successor of Ben Jonson and the champion of the type of comedy that Jonson had written, the "comedy of humors," in which each character is presented under the domination of a single psychological trait or eccentricity, his humor. His plays are not without merit, but they are often clumsy and prolix, and certainly much inferior to Jonson's. For many years he had conducted a public argument with Dryden on the merits of Jonson's comedies, which he thought Dryden undervalued. Exactly what moved Dry-

This Flecknoe found, who, like Augustus,[2] young
Was called to empire, and had governed long;
In prose and verse, was owned, without dispute,
Through all the realms of Nonsense, absolute.   5
This aged prince, now flourishing in peace,
And blest with issue of a large increase,
Worn out with business, did at length debate
To settle the succession of the state;   10
And, pondering which of all his sons was fit
To reign, and wage immortal war with wit,
Cried: " 'Tis resolved; for nature pleads that he
Should only rule, who most resembles me.
Sh——[3] alone my perfect image bears,   15
Mature in dullness from his tender years:
Sh—— alone, of all my sons, is he
Who stands confirmed in full stupidity.
The rest to some faint meaning make pretense,
But Sh—— never deviates into sense.   20
Some beams of wit on other souls may fall,
Strike through, and make a lucid interval;
But Sh——'s genuine night admits no ray,
His rising fogs prevail upon the day.
Besides, his goodly fabric[4] fills the eye,   25
And seems designed for thoughtless majesty:
Thoughtless as monarch oaks that shade the plain,
And, spread in solemn state, supinely reign.

den to attack him is a matter of conjecture: he may simply have grown progressively bored and irritated by Shadwell and his tedious argument. The poem seems to have been written in late 1678 or 1679 and to have circulated only in manuscript, until it was printed in 1682 in a pirated edition by an obscure publisher. By that time, the two playwrights were alienated by politics as well as by literary quarrels. Shadwell was a violent Whig and the reputed author of a sharp attack on Dryden as the Tory author of *Absalom and Achitophel* and *The Medal*. It was probably for this reason that the printer added the subtitle referring to Shadwell's Whiggism in the phrase "true-blue-Protestant poet." Political passions were running high and sales would be helped if the poem seemed to refer to the events of the day.

Whereas Butler had debased and degraded his victims by using burlesque, caricature, and the grotesque, Dryden exposed Shadwell to ridicule by using the devices of mock-epic, which treats the low, mean, or absurd in the grand language, lofty style, and solemn tone of epic poetry. The obvious disparity between subject and style makes the satiric point. In 1678 an execrable Irish poet and playwright, Richard Flecknoe, died. Dryden conceived the idea of presenting Shadwell (the self-proclaimed heir of Ben Jonson, the laureate) as the

son and successor of Flecknoe—hence *Mac* (i.e., son of) *Flecknoe*—from whom he inherits the throne of dullness. Flecknoe in the triple role of king, priest, and poet hails his successor, pronounces a panegyric on his perfect fitness for the throne, anoints and crowns him, foretells his glorious reign, and, as he sinks (leaden dullness cannot soar), leaves his mantle to fall symbolically upon Shadwell's shoulders. The poem abounds in literary allusions—to Roman legend and history and to the *Aeneid;* to Cowley's fragmentary epic, *The Davideis,* and to *Paradise Lost;* and to Shadwell's own plays. Biblical allusions add an unexpected dimension of incongruous dignity to the low scene. The coronation takes place in the City, to the plaudits of the citizens, who are fit to admire only what is dull. In 217 lines Dryden created an image of Shadwell which has fixed his reputation to this day.
2. In 31 B.C. Octavian became the first Roman emperor at the age of 32. He assumed the title Augustus in 27 B.C.
3. Thomas Shadwell. The initial and second letter of the name followed by a dash give the appearance, but only the appearance, of protecting Dryden's victim by concealing his name. A common device in the satire of the period.
4. His body. Shadwell was a corpulent man.

Heywood and Shirley[5] were but types of thee,
Thou last great prophet of tautology.[6]
Even I, a dunce of more renown than they,   30
Was sent before but to prepare thy way;
And, coarsely clad in Norwich drugget,[7] came
To teach the nations in thy greater name.[8]
My warbling lute, the lute I whilom[9] strung,
When to King John of Portugal I sung,   35
Was but the prelude to that glorious day,
When thou on silver Thames didst cut thy way,
With well-timed oars before the royal barge,
Swelled with the pride of thy celestial charge;   40
And big with hymn, commander of a host,
The like was ne'er in Epsom blankets tossed.[1]
Methinks I see the new Arion[2] sail,
The lute still trembling underneath thy nail.
At thy well-sharpened thumb from shore to shore   45
The treble squeaks for fear, the basses roar;
Echoes from Pissing Alley Sh—— call,
And Sh—— they resound from Aston Hall.
About thy boat the little fishes throng,
As at the morning toast[3] that floats along.   50
Sometimes, as prince of thy harmonious band,
Thou wield'st thy papers in thy threshing hand.
St. André's[4] feet ne'er kept more equal time,
Not ev'n the feet of thy own *Psyche's* rhyme;
Though they in number as in sense excel: 55
So just, so like tautology, they fell,
That, pale with envy, Singleton[5] forswore
The lute and sword, which he in triumph bore,
And vowed he ne'er would act Villerius[6] more."
Here stopped the good old sire, and wept for joy   60
In silent raptures of the hopeful boy.
All arguments, but most his plays, persuade,
That for anointed[7] dullness he was made.

5. Thomas Heywood (ca. 1570–1641) and James Shirley (1596–1666), playwrights popular before the closing of the theaters in 1642 but now out of fashion. They are introduced here as "types" (i.e., prefigurings) of Shadwell, in the sense that Solomon was regarded as an Old Testament prefiguring of Christ, the "last [final] great prophet." 6. Unnecessary repetition of meaning in different words. 7. A coarse woolen cloth. 8. The parallel between Flecknoe, as forerunner of Shadwell, and John the Baptist, as forerunner of Jesus, is made plain in lines 32–34 by the use of details and even words taken from Matthew iii.3–4 and John i.23. 9. Formerly. Flecknoe boasted of the patronage of the Portuguese king. 1. A reference to Shadwell's comedy *Epsom Wells* and to the farcical scene in his *Virtuoso*, in which Sir Samuel Hearty is tossed in a blanket. 2. A legendary Greek poet. Returning home by sea, he was robbed and thrown overboard by the sailors, but was saved by a dolphin which had been charmed by his music. 3. Sewage. 4. A French dancer who designed the choreography of Shadwell's opera *Psyche* (1675). Dryden's sneer in the next line at the mechanical metrics of the songs in *Psyche* is justified. 5. John Singleton (d. 1686), a musician at the Theatre Royal. 6. A character in Sir William Davenant's *Siege of Rhodes* (1656), the first English opera. 7. The anticipated phrase is "anointed *majesty*." English kings are anointed with oil at their coronations.

Close to the walls which fair Augusta[8] bind
(The fair Augusta much to fears inclined),   65
An ancient fabric[9] raised to inform the sight,
There stood of yore, and Barbican it hight:
A watchtower once; but now, so fate ordains,
Of all the pile an empty name remains.
From its old ruins brothel houses rise,   70
Scenes of lewd loves, and of polluted joys,
Where their vast courts the mother-strumpets keep,
And, undisturbed by watch, in silence sleep.
Near these a Nursery[1] erects its head,
Where queens are formed, and future heroes bred;   75
Where unfledged actors learn to laugh and cry,
Where infant punks[2] their tender voices try,
And little Maximins[3] the gods defy.
Great Fletcher[4] never treads in buskins here,
Nor greater Jonson dares in socks appear;   80
But gentle Simkin[5] just reception finds
Amidst this monument of vanished minds:
Pure clinches[6] the suburbian Muse affords,
And Panton[7] waging harmless war with words.
Here Flecknoe, as a place to fame well known,   85
Ambitiously design'd his Sh——'s throne;
For ancient Dekker[8] prophesied long since,
That in this pile would reign a mighty prince,
Born for a scourge of wit, and flail of sense;
To whom true dullness should some *Psyches* owe,   90
But worlds of *Misers* from his pen should flow;
Humorists and *Hypocrites*[9] it should produce,
Whole Raymond families, and tribes of Bruce.
    Now Empress Fame had published the renown
Of Sh——'s coronation through the town.   95
Roused by report of Fame, the nations meet,
From near Bunhill, and distant Watling Street.[1]
No Persian carpets spread the imperial way,
But scattered limbs of mangled poets lay;
From dusty shops neglected authors come,   100
Martyrs of pies, and relics of the bum.[2]

---

8. London. The next line alludes to
the fears excited by the Popish Plot
(cf. *Absalom and Achitophel*).
9. Building.
1. The name of a training school for
young actors.
2. Prostitutes.
3. Maximin is the cruel emperor in
Dryden's *Tyrannic Love* (1669), notorious for his bombast.
4. John Fletcher (1579–1625), the
playwright and collaborator with Francis Beaumont (ca. 1584–1616). "Buskins" and "socks" were the symbols of
tragedy and comedy.
5. A popular character in low farces.
6. Puns.
7. Said to have been a celebrated punster.

8. Thomas Dekker (ca. 1572–1632),
the playwright, whom Jonson had satirized in *The Poetaster*.
9. Three of Shadwell's plays; *The Hypocrite*, a failure, was not published.
"Raymond" and "Bruce" (line 94) are
characters in *The Humorists* and *The
Virtuoso* respectively.
1. Since Bunhill is about a quarter of
a mile and Watling Street little more
than half a mile from the site of the
Nursery, where the coronation is held,
Shadwell's fame is narrowly circumscribed. Moreover, his subjects live in
the heart of the City, regarded by men
of wit and fashion as the abode of bad
taste and middle-class vulgarity.
2. Unsold books eventually went to
bakers' shops and privies.

Much Heywood, Shirley, Ogilby[3] there lay,
But loads of Sh—— almost choked the way.
Bilked stationers[4] for yeomen stood prepared,
And Herringman was captain of the guard. 105
The hoary prince in majesty appeared,
High on a throne of his own labors reared.
At his right hand our young Ascanius[5] sate,
Rome's other hope, and pillar of the state.
His brows thick fogs, instead of glories, grace, 110
And lambent dullness played around his face.
As Hannibal did to the altars come,
Sworn by his sire a mortal foe to Rome,[6]
So Sh—— swore, nor should his vow be vain,
That he till death true dullness would maintain; 115
And, in his father's right, and realm's defense,
Ne'er to have peace with wit, nor truce with sense.
The king himself the sacred unction[7] made,
As king by office, and as priest by trade.
In his sinister[8] hand, instead of ball, 120
He placed a mighty mug of potent ale;
Love's Kingdom to his right he did convey,
At once his scepter, and his rule of sway;
Whose righteous lore the prince had practiced young,
And from whose loins recorded *Psyche* sprung. 125
His temples, last, with poppies were o'erspread,
That nodding seemed to consecrate his head.
Just at that point of time, if fame not lie,
On his left hand twelve reverend owls did fly.[9]
So Romulus, 'tis sung, by Tiber's brook, 130
Presage of sway from twice six vultures took.
The admiring throng loud acclamations make,
And omens of his future empire take.
The sire then shook the honors[1] of his head,
And from his brows damps of oblivion shed 135
Full on the filial dullness: long he stood,
Repelling from his breast the raging god;
At length burst out in this prophetic mood:

3. John Ogilby, a translator of Homer and Virgil, ridiculed by both Dryden and Pope as a bad poet.
4. Cheated publishers, who acted as "yeomen" of the guard, led by Henry Herringman, who until 1679 was the publisher of both Shadwell and Dryden.
5. Or Ïulus, son of Aeneas; Virgil referred to him as *"spes altera Romae"* ("Rome's other hope"; *Aeneid* XII. 168). As Troy fell, he was marked as favored by the gods when a flickering ("lambent") flame played round his head (*Aeneid* II.680–84).
6. Hannibal, who almost conquered Rome in 216 B.C., during the 2nd Punic War, took this oath at the age of 9 (Livy xxi.1).
7. The sacramental oil, used in the coronation.
8. Left. During his coronation a British monarch holds two symbols of kingship: a globe ("ball") representing the world in his left hand, a scepter in his right. In lines 121–27, Shadwell's symbols of monarchy—a mug of ale; Flecknoe's dreary play, *Love's Kingdom;* a crown of poppies—suggest heaviness, dullness, drowsiness. The poppies also refer obliquely to Shadwell's addiction to opium.
9. Birds of night, appropriate substitutes for the twelve vultures whose flight confirmed to Romulus the destined site of Rome, of which he was founder and king.
1. Ornaments, hence locks.

"Heavens bless my son, from Ireland let him reign
To far Barbadoes on the western main;[2]   140
Of his dominion may no end be known,
And greater than his father's be his throne;
Beyond *Love's Kingdom* let him stretch his pen!"
He paused, and all the people cried, "Amen."
Then thus continued he: "My son, advance   145
Still in new impudence, new ignorance.
Success let others teach, learn thou from me
Pangs without birth, and fruitless industry.
Let *Virtuosos* in five years be writ;
Yet not one thought accuse thy toil of wit.   150
Let gentle George[3] in triumph tread the stage,
Make Dorimant betray, and Loveit rage;
Let Cully, Cockwood, Fopling, charm the pit,
And in their folly show the writer's wit.
Yet still thy fools shall stand in thy defense,   155
And justify their author's want of sense.
Let 'em be all by thy own model made
Of dullness, and desire no foreign aid;
That they to future ages may be known,
Not copies drawn, but issue of thy own.   160
Nay, let thy men of wit too be the same,
All full of thee, and differing but in name.
But let no alien S—dl—y[4] interpose,
To lard with wit[5] thy hungry *Epsom* prose.
And when false flowers of rhetoric thou wouldst cull, 165
Trust nature, do not labor to be dull;
But write thy best, and top; and, in each line,
Sir Formal's[6] oratory will be thine:
Sir Formal, though unsought, attends thy quill,
And does thy northern dedications[7] fill.   170
Nor let false friends seduce thy mind to fame,
By arrogating Jonson's hostile name.
Let father Flecknoe fire thy mind with praise,
And uncle Ogilby thy envy raise.
Thou art my blood, where Jonson has no part: 175
What share have we in nature, or in art?
Where did his wit on learning fix a brand,
And rail at arts he did not understand?
Where made he love in Prince Nicander's vein,[8]
Or swept the dust in *Psyche's* humble strain?   180

2. Shadwell's empire is vast but empty.
3. Sir George Etherege (ca. 1635–91), a writer of brilliant comedies. In the next couplet Dryden names characters from his plays.
4. Sir Charles Sedley (1638–1701), wit, rake, poet, playwright. Dryden hints that he contributed more than the prologue to Shadwell's *Epsom Wells*.
5. The phrase "lard with wit" recalls a sentence in Burton's *Anatomy of Melancholy*: "They lard their lean books with the fat of others' works * * * "
6. Sir Formal Trifle, the ridiculous and vapid orator in *The Virtuoso*.
7. Shadwell frequently dedicated his works to the Duke of Newcastle and members of his family.
8. In *Psyche*.

Where sold he bargains,[9] 'whip-stitch, kiss my arse,'
Promised a play and dwindled to a farce?[1]
When did his Muse from Fletcher scenes purloin,
As thou whole Eth'rege dost transfuse to thine?
But so transfused, as oil on water's flow,   185
His always floats above, thine sinks below.
This is thy province, this thy wondrous way,
New humors to invent for each new play:
This is that boasted bias[2] of thy mind,
By which one way, to dullness, 'tis inclined;   190
Which makes thy writings lean on one side still,
And, in all changes, that way bends thy will.
Nor let thy mountain-belly make pretense
Of likeness; thine's a tympany[3] of sense.
A tun[4] of man in thy large bulk is writ,   195
But sure thou'rt but a kilderkin of wit.
Like mine, thy gentle numbers feebly creep;
Thy tragic Muse gives smiles, thy comic sleep.
With whate'er gall thou sett'st thyself to write,
Thy inoffensive satires never bite.   200
In thy felonious heart though venom lies,
It does but touch thy Irish pen,[5] and dies.
Thy genius calls thee not to purchase fame
In keen iambics,[6] but mild anagram.
Leave writing plays, and choose for thy command   205
Some peaceful province in acrostic land.
There thou may'st wings display and altars raise,
And torture one poor word ten thousand ways.[7]
Or, if thou wouldst thy different talent suit,
Set thy own songs, and sing them to thy lute."   210
    He said: but his last words were scarcely heard ⎫
For Bruce and Longville had a trap prepared,   ⎬
And down they sent the yet declaiming bard.[8]   ⎭
Sinking he left his drugget robe behind,
Borne upwards by a subterranean wind.   215

9. To "sell bargains" is to answer an innocent question with a coarse or indecent phrase as in this line. "Whip-stitch" is a nonsense word frequently used by Sir Samuel Hearty in *The Virtuoso*.
1. Low comedy which depends largely on situation rather than wit, consistently condemned by Dryden and other serious playwrights.
2. In bowling, the spin given to the bowl that causes it to swerve. Dryden closely parodies a passage in Shadwell's epilogue to *The Humorists*.
3. A swelling in some part of the body caused by wind.
4. A large wine cask. "Kilderkin": a very small cask.
5. Flecknoe was Irish, and so his son must be Irish. Ireland suggested only poverty, superstition, and barbarity to 17th-century Londoners.
6. Sharp satire.
7. "Anagram": the transposition of letters in a word so as to make a new one; "acrostic": a poem in which the first letter of each line, read downward, makes up the name of the person or thing that is the subject of the poem; "wings" and "altars" refer to poems in the shape of these objects as in George Herbert's *Easter Wings* and *The Altar*. Dryden is citing instances of triviality and overingenuity in literature.
8. In *The Virtuoso*, Bruce and Longville play this trick on Sir Formal Trifle while he makes a speech.

⎧ The mantle fell to the young prophet's part,[9]
⎩ With double portion of his father's art.

ca. 1679   1682

To the Memory of Mr. Oldham[1]

Farewell, too little, and too lately known,
Whom I began to think and call my own:
For sure our souls were near allied, and thine
Cast in the same poetic mold with mine.
One common note on either lyre did strike,
And knaves and fools[2] we both abhorred alike.   5
To the same goal did both our studies drive;
The last set out the soonest did arrive.
Thus Nisus[3] fell upon the slippery place,
While his young friend performed and won the race.   10
O early ripe! to thy abundant store
What could advancing age have added more?
It might (what nature never gives the young)
Have taught the numbers[4] of thy native tongue.
But satire needs not those, and wit will shine   15
Through the harsh cadence of a rugged line:[5]
A noble error, and but seldom made,
When poets are by too much force betrayed.
Thy generous fruits, though gathered ere their prime, ⎫
Still showed a quickness;[6] and maturing time   ⎬ 20
But mellows what we write to the dull sweets of rhyme. ⎭
Once more, hail and farewell;[7] farewell, thou young,
But ah too short, Marcellus[8] of our tongue;
Thy brows with ivy, and with laurels bound;[9]
But fate and gloomy night encompass thee around.   25

                                                                            1684

9. When the prophet Elijah was carried to heaven in a chariot of fire borne on a whirlwind, his mantle fell on his successor, the younger prophet Elisha (II Kings.ii.8–14). Flecknoe, prophet of dullness, naturally cannot ascend, but must sink.

1. John Oldham (1653–83), the young poet whose *Satires upon the Jesuits* (1681) won Dryden's admiration. This elegy was published in Oldham's *Remains in Verse and Prose* (1684).

2. The objects of satire.

3. Nisus, on the point of winning a foot race, slipped in a pool of blood; his "young friend" was Euryalus (Virgil, *Aeneid* V.315–39).

4. Metrics, verse.

5. Dryden repeats the Renaissance idea that the satirist should avoid smoothness and affect rough meters ("harsh cadence").

6. Sharpness of flavor.

7. Dryden echoes the famous words that conclude Catullus' elegy to his brother: "*Atque in perpetuum, frater, ave atque vale*" ("And forever, brother, hail and farewell!").

8. The nephew of Augustus, adopted by him as his successor. After winning military fame as a youth, he died at the age of 20. Virgil celebrated him in the *Aeneid* VI.854–86; the last line of Dryden's poem is a reminiscence of *Aeneid* VI.866.

9. The poet's wreath. Cf. Milton's *Lycidas*, lines 1–2.

To the Pious Memory of the Accomplished Young Lady Mrs.[1] Anne Killigrew

EXCELLENT IN THE TWO SISTER ARTS OF POESY AND PAINTING.

AN ODE [1a]

1

Thou youngest virgin-daughter of the skies,
Made in the last promotion of the blest,
Whose palms,[2] new plucked from paradise,

1. "Mrs." means "Mistress," used at this time for our "Miss."

1a. Like Milton's *Lycidas*, Dryden's ode to Anne Killigrew is not so much the expression of private grief as it is a decorous ceremonial gesture dignifying a public occasion. In both poems the death of an individual becomes the point of departure for the treatment of larger topics. The fact that Mrs. Killigrew was not a distinguished poet or painter is irrelevant: her death prompted the poet to consider the arts themselves, their present state in a corrupt age, their central role in civilization, their service to virtue and religion. In the course of the poem, the dead woman is transformed into a symbol of the sister arts themselves, what they are, and what, on earth, they might become. *Lycidas* is an elegy; Dryden's ode combines the elegiac with the lyric and the heroic. Although *Lycidas* is cast in the traditional mode of the pastoral lament, and *Anne Killigrew* in the form of a eulogistic memorial, both poems develop classical and Christian themes which had become conventions of the funeral poem: the death of the young and promising, the praise of his genius and virtues, a lament for the times which suffer such loss, and a consolation, offered by describing the reception of the soul of the dead into heaven.

Dryden's poem, in form, is an irregular ode, a lyric poem which develops a serious theme in a dignified or exalted manner. Two kinds of ode were recognized during the 18th century. To quote Johnson: " * * * the ode is either of the greater or less kind. The less is characterized by sweetness and ease; the greater by sublimity, rapture, and quickness of transition." The greater ode, of which this is the finest example in 17th-century poetry, was associated with the odes of Pindar, the lyric poet of 5th-century Greece, whose intricate metrics, bold imagery, and intense and energetic power were aspired to (seldom with success) by English poets throughout our period. Pindar's odes were rigorously constructed: each was divided into long stanzas, which in turn were subdivided into three parts —called in Greek strophe, antistrophe, and epode—whose metrical structure was repeated throughout the whole poem. Strophes and antistrophes were identical but the epodes followed a different metrical pattern. Such symmetry is not easily attained in English verse because of the paucity of rhymes in our language, but Ben Jonson's *To the Immortal Memory * * * of * * * Sir Lucius Cary and Sir Henry Morison* is strictly Pindaric, as are Thomas Gray's *The Progress of Poesy* and *The Bard* (1757).

In 1656 Abraham Cowley published loose paraphrases of two of Pindar's odes in which he abandoned the formal structure of the originals in favor of irregular meters and irregularly constructed stanzas, while trying to preserve Pindar's rapture, boldness, and sublimity. Thanks to Cowley's popularity, his irregular Pindarics became the standard of what the age considered the loftiest sort of lyric poetry. It was a tempting form for poets who wished to achieve (or to simulate) the loftiest lyric rapture, for the apparent structural disorder could suggest inspired improvisation. The result was a plague of turgid rhetoric in uninteresting irregular meter.

Dryden declared that Cowley's Pindarics lacked "somewhat of a finer turn and more lyrical verse" and that such odes should consist in "the warmth and vigor of fancy, the masterly figures, and the copiousness of imagination" (Ker, *Essays* I.267–268). His superb ear and gift for melodious eloquence enabled him in this poem to raise the greater ode to heights not to be equaled again until Wordsworth wrote his *Ode: Intimations of Immortality*.

The lesser ode, often in this period associated with the odes of Horace, is more quiet and contemplative, more lyrical in mood, and it usually employs an uncomplicated, rather short stanza.

2. The symbol of victory (cf. Revelation vii.9).

In spreading branches more sublimely rise,
Rich with immortal green above the rest;   5
Whether, adopted to some neighboring star,
Thou roll'st above us in thy wandering race,
    Or in procession fixed and regular,
    Moved with the heavens' majestic pace,
    Or called to more superior bliss,   10
Thou tread'st with seraphims the vast abyss:[3]
Whatever happy region is thy place,
Cease thy celestial song a little space;
Thou wilt have time enough for hymns divine,
    Since heaven's eternal year is thine.   15
Hear then a mortal Muse thy praise rehearse,
    In no ignoble verse;
But such as thy own voice did practice here,
When thy first fruits of poesy were given,
To make thyself a welcome inmate there,   20
    While yet a young probationer,
    And candidate of heaven.

2

If by traduction came thy mind,
Our wonder is the less to find
A soul so charming from a stock so good;   25
Thy father was transfused into thy blood:[4]
So wert thou born into the tuneful strain
(An early, rich, and inexhausted vein).
    But if thy pre-existing soul
    Was formed at first with myriads more,   30
It did through all the mighty poets roll
    Who Greek or Latin laurels wore,
And was that Sappho last, which once it was before.[5]
    If so, then cease thy flight, O heaven-born mind!
Thou hast no dross to purge from thy rich ore;   35
Nor can thy soul a fairer mansion find
Than was the beauteous frame she left behind:
Return, to fill or mend the choir of thy celestial kind.

3

May we presume to say that at thy birth
New joy was sprung in heaven, as well as here on earth?   40
For sure the milder planets did combine

3. Dryden is speculating on where the soul of the dead poetess has come to rest: is she the tutelary deity of a planet ("neighboring star")? or of one of the remote "fixed" stars? or does she enjoy the higher ("superior") bliss of having joined the "seraphim," the guardians of the throne of God? (cf. Isaiah vi). Like Milton, Dryden makes use of the Ptolemaic universe of concentric spheres moving around the earth "in procession fixed and regular."

4. The idea that the soul is transmitted by the father at the moment of conception. Since Henry Killigrew had written a tragedy, his daughter is said to have inherited a poet's soul from him. In lines 29–32, Dryden proposes the theory that the soul exists before birth, and less seriously that through the ages it transmigrates from body to body.

5. Mrs. Killigrew is said to have been Sappho (the Greek lyric poetess of the 7th century B.C.) twice: "once before," when her soul transmigrated into Sappho's body, and most recently ("last"), when it inhabited the body of the modern Sappho, Anne Killigrew.

On thy auspicious horoscope to shine,[6]
And even the most malicious were in trine.
Thy brother-angels at thy birth
    Strung each his lyre, and tuned it high,
    That all the people of the sky   45
Might know a poetess was born on earth.
    And then, if ever, mortal ears
Had heard the music of the spheres!
And if no clustering swarm of bees   50
On thy sweet mouth distilled their golden dew,[7]
    'Twas that such vulgar miracles
Heaven had not leisure to renew:
For all the blest fraternity of love
Solemnized there thy birth, and kept thy holiday above.   55

4

O gracious God! how far have we
Profaned thy heavenly gift of poesy!
Made prostitute and profligate the Muse,
Debased to each obscene and impious use,
Whose harmony was first ordained above   60
For tongues of angels, and for hymns of love!
O wretched we! why were we hurried down
    This lubric and adulterate[8] age
(Nay, added fat pollutions of our own)
    To increase the steaming ordures of the stage?   65
What can we say to excuse our second fall?
Let this thy vestal,[9] Heaven, atone for all:
Her Arethusan stream remains unsoiled,
Unmixed with foreign filth, and undefiled;
Her wit was more than man, her innocence a child!   70

5

Art she had none, yet wanted none,
    For nature did that want supply;
So rich in treasures of her own,
    She might our boasted stores defy:
Such noble vigor did her verse adorn   75
That it seemed borrowed where 'twas only born.
Her morals too were in her bosom bred,
    By great examples daily fed,
What in the best of books, her father's life, she read.
And to be read herself she need not fear;   80
Each test and every light her Muse will bear,

6. The familiar idea that character and destiny are determined by the position of the planets at the moment of birth ("horoscope"). Mrs. Killigrew's horoscope was fortunate ("auspicious"): even those planets that are usually baleful ("malicious") were "in trine" —120 degrees apart and hence favorable in their influence.

7. It was said that bees clustered on the lips of the infant Pindar, thus foretelling his greatness as a lyric poet.
8. Lewd and corrupted.
9. I.e., thy virgin. The Roman "vestal" virgins guarded the fire in the Temple of Vesta, goddess of the hearth. For "Arethusan stream," cf. Milton's *Lycidas*, line 85.

Though Epictetus with his lamp were there.[1]
Even love (for love sometimes her Muse expressed)
Was but a lambent flame[2] which played about her breast,
Light as the vapors of a morning dream;   85
So cold herself, whilst she such warmth expressed,
'Twas Cupid bathing in Diana's stream.

6

Born to the spacious empire of the Nine,[3]
One would have thought she should have been content
To manage well that mighty government;   90
But what can young ambitious souls confine?
> To the next realm she stretched her sway,
> For Painture[4] near adjoining lay,
A plenteous province, and alluring prey.
A chamber of dependences[5] was framed   95
(As conquerors will never want pretense,
> When armed, to justify the offense)
And the whole fief in right of Poetry she claimed.
The country open lay without defense;
For poets frequent inroads there had made,   100
> And perfectly could represent
> The shape, the face, with every lineament;
And all the large demains[6] which the dumb Sister swayed,
> All bowed beneath her government,
> Received in triumph wheresoe'er she went.   105
Her pencil[7] drew whate'er her soul designed,
And oft the happy draft surpassed the image in her mind.
> The sylvan scenes[8] of herds and flocks
> And fruitful plains and barren rocks;
> Of shallow brooks that flowed so clear   110
> The bottom did the top appear;
> Of deeper too and ampler floods,
> Which, as in mirrors, showed the woods;
> Of lofty trees, with sacred shades
> And perspectives[9] of pleasant glades,   115
> Where nymphs of brightest form appear,
> And shaggy satyrs standing near,
> Which them at once admire and fear;

1. A collector is said to have paid a large sum for the lamp of the philosopher Epictetus in the faith that owning it would make him wise. Dryden merely means that Anne Killigrew's poems would appear pure even if judged in the light of the most severe Stoic ethical standards.
2. I.e., "a flickering flame." Cf. Dryden's *Mac Flecknoe,* line 111 and note on line 108.
3. The nine Muses, who preside over the arts of literature, the dance, music, and astronomy.
4. The art of painting (a Gallicism).
5. In the elaborate figure that dominates lines 95–98, Dryden alludes to recent peaceful annexations by Louis XIV of France, who in 1679 added most of Alsace, Lorraine, and Luxembourg to his realm through his policy of *"réunions,"* by setting up *"Chambres de Réunions."* These chambers by quasi-legal means awarded to Louis, as overlord, towns, cities, and estates with all their "dependences" or fiefs, i.e., estates held under the feudal system from overlords, to whom the holders owed services and rents.
6. I.e., an estate held in one's own right, as opposed to "fief" (line 98). The "dumb Sister" is the Muse of painting.
7. Painter's brush.
8. Cf. Milton, *Paradise Lost* IV.140.
9. Vistas.

The ruins, too, of some majestic piece,
Boasting the power of ancient Rome or Greece,   120
Whose statues, friezes, columns broken lie,
And, though defaced, the wonder of the eye:[1]
What nature, art, bold fiction e'er durst frame,
Her forming hand gave feature to the name.
So strange a concourse ne'er was seen before   125
But when the peopled ark the whole creation bore.[2]

7

The scene then changed: with bold erected look
Our martial king[3] the sight with reverence strook;
For, not content to express his outward part,
Her hand called out the image of his heart: 130
His warlike mind, his soul devoid of fear,
His high-designing thoughts were figured there,
As when by magic, ghosts are made appear.
Our phoenix queen[4] was portrayed, too, so bright,
Beauty alone could beauty take[5] so right: 135
Her dress, her shape, her matchless grace
Were all observed, as well as heavenly face.
With such a peerless majesty she stands
As in that day she took the crown from sacred hands;[6]
Before a train of heroines was seen,   140
In beauty foremost, as in rank the queen.
Thus nothing to her genius was denied,
  But like a ball of fire, the further thrown,
  Still with a greater blaze she shone,
And her bright soul broke out on every side.   145
What next she had designed, heaven only knows;[7]
To such immoderate growth her conquest rose
That fate alone its progress could oppose.

8

Now all those charms, that blooming grace,
The well-proportioned shape, and beauteous face,   150
Shall never more be seen by mortal eyes:
In earth the much-lamented virgin lies!
  Not wit nor piety could fate prevent;
  Nor was the cruel destiny content
  To finish all the murder at a blow,   155
  To sweep at once her life and beauty too;
But, like a hardened felon, took a pride

---

1. Mrs. Killigrew's landscapes are typical of the ideal classical landscape of
17th-century Italian painters: contrasts
of fruitful plains and barren rocks, water that reflects trees, vistas, classical
ruins, and mythological figures.
2. Noah's ark, which contained all that
survived of created beings.
3. James II, who, as Duke of York,
had won a reputation for courage and
skill while fighting as a soldier with
the French armies in the 1650's and

serving as an admiral during the Eng-
lish-Dutch wars of the 1660's.
4. Mary of Modena, wife of James II,
whose unique beauty is expressed by
the reference to the "phoenix," the fabulous bird, only one of which exists
during each thousand years.
5. I.e., take the likeness of.
6. The queen was crowned by the
"sacred hands" of the Archbishop of
Canterbury.
7. God alone knows.

> To work more mischievously slow,
> And plundered first, and then destroyed.
> O double sacrilege on things divine,
> To rob the relic, and deface the shrine!
>   But thus Orinda died:[8]
> Heaven, by the same disease, did both translate;
> As equal were their souls, so equal was their fate.

160

9

> Meantime her warlike brother[9] on the seas
> His waving streamers to the winds displays,
> And vows for his return with vain devotion pays.
>   Ah, generous youth, that wish forbear;
>   The winds too soon will waft thee here!
> Slack all thy sails, and fear to come,
> Alas, thou know'st not thou art wrecked at home!
> No more shalt thou behold thy sister's face;
> Thou hast already had her last embrace.
> But look aloft, and if thou kenn'st[1] from far,
> Among the Pleiads,[2] a new-kindled star,
> If any sparkles than the rest more bright,
> 'Tis she that shines in that propitious light.

165

170

175

10

> When in mid-air the golden trump shall sound,
>   To raise the nations under ground;
>   When in the Valley of Jehosaphat[3]
> The judging God shall close the book of fate,
>   And there the last assizes[4] keep
>   For those who wake and those who sleep;
>   When rattling bones together fly
>   From the four corners of the sky;
> When sinews o'er the skeletons are spread,
> Those clothed with flesh, and life inspires the dead;
> The sacred poets first shall hear the sound,
> And foremost from the tomb shall bound,
> For they are covered with the lightest ground,
> And straight, with inborn vigor, on the wing,
> Like mounting larks, to the new morning sing.
> There thou, sweet saint, before the choir shalt go,
> As harbinger[5] of heaven, the way to show,
> The way which thou so well hast learned below.

180

185

190

195

1686

---

8. The poetess Katharine Philips (1631–64), fancifully referred to by her admirers as "the matchless Orinda," who, like Anne Killigrew, died of the disfiguring disease, smallpox.

9. Henry Killigrew, an officer in the Royal Navy. Pennons ("streamers") fly from the mast of his ship.

1. Perceivest.

2. The Pleiades, a cluster of stars (six are visible to the unaided eye) in the constellation Taurus.

3. Joel iii.12; **Ezekial xxxvii**.

4. Periodical sessions of superior courts held in each county in England; here, of course, the Last Judgment—at which some will be alive on earth ("wake") and many will have already died ("sleep").

5. One who goes ahead to provide a lodging.

A Song for St. Cecilia's Day[1]

1

From harmony, from heavenly harmony
   This universal frame began:
   When Nature[2] underneath a heap
     Of jarring atoms lay,
   And could not heave her head,   5
The tuneful voice was heard from high:
     "Arise, ye more than dead."
Then cold, and hot, and moist, and dry,
In order to their stations leap,
     And Music's power obey.   10
From harmony, from heavenly harmony
   This universal frame began:
   From harmony to harmony
Through all the compass of the notes it ran,
The diapason[3] closing full in man.   15

2

What passion cannot Music raise and quell![4]
   When Jubal[5] struck the corded shell,
   His listening brethren stood around,
   And, wondering, on their faces fell
   To worship that celestial sound.   20
Less than a god they thought there could not dwell
   Within the hollow of that shell
   That spoke so sweetly and so well.
What passion cannot Music raise and quell!

1. St. Cecilia, a Roman lady, was an early Christian martyr. She has long been regarded as the patroness of music and the supposed inventor of the organ. Celebrations of her festival day (November 22) in England were usually devoted to music and the praise of music, and from about 1683 to 1703 a "Musical Society" in London annually commemorated it with a religious service and a public concert. This concert always included an ode written and set to music for the occasion, of which the two by Dryden (*A Song for St. Cecilia's Day*, 1687, and *Alexander's Feast*, 1697) are the most distinguished. G. B. Draghi, an Italian brought to England by Charles II, set this ode to music, but Handel's fine score, composed in 1739, has completely obscured the original setting. Like the ode to Mrs. Killigrew, this is an irregular ode in the manner of Cowley. In stanzas 3–6 Dryden boldly attempted to suggest in the sounds of his words the characteristic tones of the instruments mentioned.
2. Created nature, ordered by the Divine Wisdom out of chaos, which Dry-

den, adopting the physics of the Greek philosopher Epicurus, describes as composed of the warring and discordant ("jarring") atoms of the four elements: earth, fire, water, air ("cold," "hot," "moist," "dry").
3. The entire compass of tones in the scale. Dryden is thinking of the Chain of Being, the ordered creation from inanimate nature up to man, God's latest and final work. The just gradations of notes in a scale is analogous to the equally just gradations in the ascending scale of created beings. Both are the result of harmony.
4. The power of music to describe, evoke, or subdue emotion ("passion") is a frequent theme in 17th-century literature. In stanzas 2–6 the poet considers music as awakening religious awe, warlike courage, sorrow for unrequited love, jealousy and fury, and the impulse to worship God.
5. According to Genesis iv.21, the inventor of the harp and the organ. Dryden imagines Jubal's harp to have been made of a tortoise shell ("corded shell").

3

The trumpet's loud clangor   25
    Excites us to arms,
With shrill notes of anger,
    And mortal alarms.
The double double double beat
    Of the thundering drum   30
Cries: "Hark! the foes come;
Charge, charge, 'tis too late to retreat."

4

The soft complaining flute
    In dying notes discovers
    The woes of hopeless lovers,   35
Whose dirge is whispered by the warbling lute.

5

Sharp violins[6] proclaim
Their jealous pangs, and desperation,
Fury, frantic indignation,
Depth of pains, and height of passion,   40
    For the fair, disdainful dame.

6

    But O! what art can teach,
    What human voice can reach,
The sacred organ's praise?
    Notes inspiring holy love,   45
Notes that wing their heavenly ways
    To mend the choirs above.

7

Orpheus[7] could lead the savage race;
And trees unrooted left their place,
    Sequacious of the lyre;   50
But bright Cecilia raised the wonder higher:
When to her organ vocal breath was given,
An angel heard, and straight appeared,[8]
    Mistaking earth for heaven.

GRAND CHORUS

As from the power of sacred lays   55
    The spheres began to move,[9]
And sung the great Creator's praise
    To all the blest above;
So, when the last and dreadful hour

6. A reference to the bright tone of the modern violin, introduced into England at the Restoration. The tone of the old-fashioned viol is much duller (Bronson).

7. A legendary poet, son of one of the Muses, who played so wonderfully on the lyre that wild beasts ("the savage race") grew tame and followed him, as did even rocks and trees. "Sequacious of": following.

8. According to the legend, it was Cecilia's piety, not her music, that brought an angel to visit her.

9. As it was harmony which ordered the universe, so it was angelic song ("sacred lays") which put the celestial bodies ("spheres") in motion. The harmonious chord which results from the traditional "music of the spheres" is a hymn of "praise" sung by created nature to its "Creator."

This crumbling pageant[1] shall devour,   60
The trumpet shall be heard on high,[2]
The dead shall live, the living die,
And Music shall untune the sky.

1687

Epigram on Milton[3]

Three poets, in three distant ages born,
Greece, Italy, and England did adorn.
The first in loftiness of thought surpassed,
The next in majesty; in both the last:
The force of Nature could no farther go;   5
To make a third, she joined the former two.

1688

Alexander's Feast[1]

OR THE POWER OF MUSIC; AN ODE IN HONOR OF
ST. CECILIA'S DAY

1

'Twas at the royal feast, for Persia won
      By Philip's[2] warlike son:
  Aloft in awful state
  The godlike hero sate
    On his imperial throne;   5
  His valiant peers were placed around;
Their brows with roses and with myrtles[3] bound:
  (So should desert in arms be crowned).
The lovely Thaïs, by his side,
Sate like a blooming Eastern bride   10
In flower of youth and beauty's pride.
  Happy, happy, happy pair!
    None but the brave,
    None but the brave,
  None but the brave deserves the fair.   15

1. The universe: the stage on which the drama of man's salvation has been acted out.
2. The "last trump" of I Corinthians xv.52, which will announce the Resurrection and the Last Judgment. Dryden develops his theme of harmony as order in such a way as to give full emphasis of the splendid paradox ("Music shall *untune*") in the final line of the ode.
3. Engraved beneath the portrait of Milton in Jacob Tonson's edition of *Paradise Lost* (1688). The "three poets" are Homer, Virgil, Milton.
1. In Dryden's earlier poem for St. Cecilia's Day, music was celebrated primarily as harmony and order, though its power over the passions was also praised. *Alexander's Feast* is devoted entirely to the second theme. It is based upon a well-known episode in the life of Alexander the Great. After the de-

feat of the Persian Emperor Darius III and the fall of the Persian capital, Persepolis (331 B.C.), Alexander held a great feast for his officers. Thaïs, his Athenian mistress, persuaded him to set fire to the palace in revenge for the burning of Athens by the Persians under Xerxes in 480 B.C. According to Plutarch, Alexander was moved by love and wine, not by music; but Dryden, perhaps altering an old tradition that Alexander's musician Timotheus once caused the hero by his flute-playing to start up and arm himself, attributes the burning of Persepolis to the power of music. The original music was by Jeremiah Clarke, but Handel's score of 1736 is better known.
2. King Philip II of Macedonia, father of Alexander the Great.
3. The Greeks and Romans wore wreaths of flowers at banquets. Roses and myrtles are emblems of love.

CHORUS

Happy, happy, happy pair!
None but the brave,
None but the brave,
None but the brave deserves the fair.

2

Timotheus, placed on high   20
    Amid the tuneful choir,
        With flying fingers touched the lyre:
The trembling notes ascend the sky,
        And heavenly joys inspire.
The song began from Jove,   25
Who left his blissful seats above
(Such is the power of mighty love).[4]
A dragon's fiery form belied the god:
Sublime on radiant spires[5] he rode,
        When he to fair Olympia pressed;   30
        And while he sought her snowy breast:
Then, round her slender waist he curled,
And stamped an image of himself, a sovereign of the world.
The listening crowd admire[6] the lofty sound:
"A present deity," they shout around;   35
"A present deity," the vaulted roofs rebound.
        With ravished ears
        The monarch hears,
        Assumes the god,
        Affects to nod,   40
And seems to shake the spheres.[7]

CHORUS

With ravished ears
The monarch hears,
Assumes the god,
Affects to nod,   45
And seems to shake the spheres.

3

The praise of Bacchus[8] then the sweet musician sung,
    Of Bacchus ever fair and ever young:
        The jolly god in triumph comes;
        Sound the trumpets; beat the drums;   50
        Flushed with a purple grace
        He shows his honest face:
Now give the hautboys[9] breath; he comes, he comes!
    Bacchus, ever fair and young
        Drinking joys did first ordain;   55

4. An oracle had declared that Alexander was the son of Zeus ("Jove") by Philip's wife Olympias (not, as Dryden calls her in line 30, "Olympia"), thus conferring on him that semi-divinity often claimed by heroes. Zeus habitually conducted his amours with mortals in the guise of an animal: in this case a dragon.
5. High on shining coils ("radiant spires"). "Spires" for the coils of a serpent is derived from the Latin word *spira*, which Virgil uses in this sense; *Aeneid* II.217. Cf. *Paradise Lost* IX.502.
6. Wonder at.
7. According to Virgil (*Aeneid* X.115) the nod of Jove causes earthquakes.
8. The god of wine.
9. Oboes.

Bacchus' blessings are a treasure,
Drinking is a soldier's pleasure;
   Rich the treasure,
   Sweet the pleasure,
Sweet is pleasure after pain.   60

CHORUS

Bacchus' blessings are a treasure,
Drinking is the soldier's pleasure;
   Rich the treasure,
   Sweet the pleasure,
Sweet is pleasure after pain.   65

4

Soothed with the sound, the king grew vain;
   Fought all his battles o'er again,
And thrice he routed all his foes, and thrice he slew the slain.
The master saw the madness rise,
His glowing cheeks, his ardent eyes;   70
And, while he[1] heaven and earth defied,
Changed his hand, and checked his pride.
   He chose a mournful Muse,
     Soft pity to infuse:
He sung Darius great and good,   75
   By too severe a fate
Fallen, fallen, fallen, fallen,
   Fallen from his high estate,
     And weltering in his blood;
Deserted at his utmost need   80
By those his former bounty fed;
On the bare earth exposed he lies,
With not a friend to close his eyes.[2]
With downcast looks the joyless victor sate,
   Revolving[3] in his altered soul   85
     The various turns of chance below;
And, now and then, a sigh he stole,
   And tears began to flow.

CHORUS

Revolving in his altered soul
   The various turns of chance below;   90
And, now and then, a sigh he stole,
   And tears began to flow.

5

The mighty master smiled to see
That love was in the next degree;
'Twas but[4] a kindred sound to move,   95
For pity melts the mind to love.
   Softly sweet, in Lydian[5] measures,

---

1. Alexander; in line 72, "his hand"
is the hand of Timotheus, "his pride,"
the pride of Alexander.
2. After his final defeat by Alexander,
Darius was assassinated by his own
followers.
3. Pondering.
4. I.e., it was necessary only.
5. In Greek music the Lydian mode
expressed the plaintive and the sad.

Soon he soothed his soul to pleasures.
"War," he sung, "is toil and trouble;
Honor, but an empty bubble.
    Never ending, still beginning, 100
Fighting still, and still destroying:
    If the world be worth thy winning,
Think, O think it worth enjoying.
    Lovely Thaïs sits beside thee, 105
    Take the good the gods provide thee."
The many[6] rend the skies with loud applause;
So Love was crowned, but Music won the cause.
    The prince, unable to conceal his pain,
        Gazed on the fair 110
        Who caused his care,
    And sighed and looked, sighed and looked,
Sighed and looked, and sighed again:
At length, with love and wine at once oppressed,
The vanquished victor sunk upon her breast. 115

CHORUS

*   The prince, unable to conceal his pain,*
*   Gazed on the fair*
*   Who caused his care,*
*   And sighed and looked, sighed and looked,*
Sighed and looked, and sighed again: 120
At length, with love and wine at once oppressed,
The vanquished victor sunk upon her breast.

6

Now strike the golden lyre again:
A louder yet, and yet a louder strain.
Break his bands of sleep asunder, 125
And rouse him, like a rattling peal of thunder.
    Hark, hark, the horrid[7] sound
        Has raised up his head:
        As waked from the dead,
    And amazed, he stares around. 130
"Revenge, revenge!" Timotheus cries,
    "See the Furies[8] arise!
    See the snakes that they rear,
    How they hiss in their hair,
And the sparkles that flash from their eyes! 135
    Behold a ghastly band,
    Each a torch in his hand!
Those are Grecian ghosts, that in battle were slain,
    And unburied remain[9]
    Inglorious on the plain: 140

6. As G. R. Noyes points out, "many" means *meiny*, "a retinue," a spelling that Dryden used elsewhere in his work.
7. Rough, from Latin *horridus*.
8. The Erinyes of the Greeks, avengers of crimes against the natural and the social orders. They are described as women with snakes in their hair and around their waists and arms.
9. According to Greek beliefs, the shades of the dead could not rest until their bodies were buried.

Give the vengeance due
To the valiant crew.
Behold how they toss their torches on high,
How they point to the Persian abodes,
And glittering temples of their hostile gods!"   145
The princes applaud, with a furious joy;
And the king seized a flambeau[1] with zeal to destroy;
Thaïs led the way,
To light him to his prey,
And, like another Helen, fired another Troy.[2]   150

CHORUS

And the king seized a flambeau with zeal to destroy;
Thaïs led the way,
To light him to his prey,
And, like another Helen, fired another Troy.

7

Thus long ago,   155
Ere heaving bellows learned to blow,
While organs yet were mute;
Timotheus, to his breathing flute,
And sounding lyre,
Could swell the soul to rage, or kindle soft desire.   160
At last, divine Cecilia came,
Inventress of the vocal frame;[3]
The sweet enthusiast,[4] from her sacred store,
Enlarged the former narrow bounds,
And added length to solemn sounds,   165
With nature's mother wit, and arts unknown before.
Let old Timotheus yield the prize,
Or both divide the crown:
He raised a mortal to the skies;
She drew an angel down.   170

GRAND CHORUS

At last, divine Cecilia came,
Inventress of the vocal frame;
The sweet enthusiast, from her sacred store,
Enlarged the former narrow bounds,
And added length to solemn sounds,   175
With nature's mother wit, and arts unknown before.
Let old Timotheus yield the prize,
Or both divide the crown:
He raised a mortal to the skies;
She drew an angel down.   180
1697

1. Torch.
2. Helen's elopement to Troy with Paris brought on the Trojan War and the ultimate destruction of the city by the Greeks.
3. Organ.
4. Usually at this time a disparaging word, frequently, though not always, applied to a religious zealot or fanatic. Here it is used approvingly and in its literal sense, "possessed by a god," an allusion to Cecilia's angelic companion referred to in line 170. But see note on *Song for St. Cecilia's Day*, line 53.

The Secular Masque[1]

[*Enter* JANUS.[2]]

JANUS.   Chronos,[3] Chronos, mend thy pace;
          An hundred times the rolling sun
          Around the radiant belt[4] has run
      In his revolving race.
      Behold, behold, the goal in sight;   5
      Spread thy fans,[5] and wing thy flight.

[*Enter* CHRONOS, *with a scythe in his hand, and a great globe on his back, which he sets down at his entrance.*]

CHRONOS.   Weary, weary of my weight,
      Let me, let me drop my freight,
          And leave the world behind.
      I could not bear   10
      Another year
          The load of humankind.

[*Enter* MOMUS,[6] *laughing.*]

MOMUS.   Ha! ha! ha! ha! ha! ha! well hast thou done
          To lay down thy pack,
          And lighten thy back;   15
      The world was a fool, e'er since it begun,
      And since neither Janus, nor Chronos, nor I
          Can hinder the crimes,
          Or mend the bad times,
      'Tis better to laugh than to cry.   20

CHORUS OF ALL THREE.
      'Tis better to laugh than to cry.

JANUS.   Since Momus comes to laugh below,
          Old Time, begin the show,
      That he may see, in every scene,
      What changes in this age have been.   25

CHRONOS.   Then, goddess of the silver bow,[7] begin.

[*Horns, or hunting music within.*]

[*Enter* DIANA.]

DIANA.   With horns and with hounds I waken the day,

---

1. A masque is a dramatic performance, usually mythological in character, that combines poetry, music, dance, and spectacle. Distinctly a courtly form of art, it flourished at the courts of James I and Charles I. This masque, however, was written for public performance as an afterpiece to the revival of Fletcher's *The Pilgrim*, revised by Sir John Vanbrugh, and produced for the financial benefit of Dryden himself. It is a "secular masque" because it celebrates the end of the century, "secular" being derived from the Latin *saeculares*, applied to the games, plays, and shows celebrated in Rome once an "age," a period of 120 years. It is not certain that Dryden lived to see his masque performed.

2. The god of beginnings, who here presides over the opening of the new century.

3. God of time.

4. The sun, in the course of a year, passes through all twelve signs of the zodiac ("the radiant belt").

5. Wings.

6. God of mockery and faultfinding.

7. Diana, the virgin goddess of the moon, a huntress. She symbolizes England before the Civil War, an allusion to James I's passion for the chase.

And hie to my woodland walks away;
I tuck up my robe, and am buskined[8] soon,
And tie to my forehead a wexing[9] moon.   30
I course the fleet stag, unkennel the fox,
And chase the wild goats o'er summits of rocks;
With shouting and hooting we pierce through the sky,
And Echo turns hunter, and doubles the cry.

CHORUS OF ALL.

With shouting and hooting we pierce through the sky,   35
And Echo turns hunter, and doubles the cry.

JANUS.   Then our age was in its prime:
CHRONOS.   Free from rage:
DIANA.   And free from crime:
MOMUS.   A very merry, dancing, drinking,
           Laughing, quaffing, and unthinking time.   40

CHORUS OF ALL.

Then our age was in its prime,
Free from rage, and free from crime;
A very merry, dancing, drinking,
Laughing, quaffing, and unthinking time.
           [*Dance of* DIANA'S *attendants.*]
           [*Enter* MARS.[1]]

MARS.   Inspire[2] the vocal brass, inspire;   45
           The world is past its infant age:
                Arms and honor,
                Arms and honor,
           Set the martial mind on fire,
           And kindle manly rage.   50
           Mars has looked the sky to red;
           And Peace, the lazy good, is fled.
           Plenty, Peace, and Pleasure fly;
                The sprightly green
                In woodland walks no more is seen;   55
           The sprightly green has drunk the Tyrian dye.[3]

CHORUS OF ALL.

Plenty, Peace, etc.

MARS.   Sound the trumpet, beat the drum;
                Through all the world around,
                Sound a reveille, sound, sound,   60
           The warrior god is come.

CHORUS OF ALL.

Sound the trumpet, etc.

MOMUS.   Thy sword within the scabbard keep,
                And let mankind agree;
           Better the world were fast asleep,   65

---

8. Wearing hunting boots.
9. Waxing (i.e., increasing, because in the first quarter).
1. God of war, who represents the period of the Civil War and the Commonwealth.

2. Breathe into.
3. I.e., the costume has changed from the green of the hunter to the crimson of the soldier (at once the color of blood and of "Tyrian dye," known to the ancients as "purple").

     Than kept awake by thee.
     The fools are only thinner,
      With all our cost and care;
     But neither side a winner,
      For things are as they were.   70

CHORUS OF ALL.
     The fools are only, etc.
      [*Enter* VENUS.[4]]

VENUS. Calms appear when storms are past,
     Love will have his hour at last:
     Nature is my kindly care;
     Mars destroys, and I repair;   75
     Take me, take me, while you may;
     Venus comes not every day.

CHORUS OF ALL.
     Take her, take her, etc.

CHRONOS. The world was then so light,
     I scarcely felt the weight;   80
     Joy ruled the day, and Love the night.
     But since the Queen of Pleasure left the ground,[5]
      I faint, I lag,
      And feebly drag
     The ponderous orb around.   85

MOMUS. All, all of a piece throughout:
      [*Pointing to* DIANA.]
     Thy chase had a beast in view;
      [*To* MARS.]
     Thy wars brought nothing about;
      [*To* VENUS.]
     Thy lovers were all untrue.

JANUS. 'Tis well an old age is out: 90
CHRONOS. And time to begin a new.

CHORUS OF ALL.
     All, all of a piece throughout:
     Thy chase had a beast in view;
     Thy wars brought nothing about;
     Thy lovers were all untrue.   95
     'Tis well an old age is out,
     And time to begin a new.

[*Dance of huntsmen, nymphs, warriors, and lovers.*]

              1700

---

4. Goddess of love and beauty, representing the licentious reigns of Charles
II and James II.

5. Sir Walter Scott suggested that this
line refers to the exiled Queen Mary
of Modena, wife of James II.

Criticism   Because Dryden liked to talk about literature, he became
a critic, indeed the first comprehensive critic in England. The Elizabethans, largely impelled by the example of Italian humanists, had produced an interesting and unsystematic body of critical writings. Dryden
could look back to such pioneer works as George Puttenham's *Art of
English Poesy* (1589), Sir Philip Sidney's *Apology for Poetry* (1595),
Samuel Daniel's *Defense of Rhyme* (ca. 1603), and Ben Jonson's *Timber,
or Discoveries* (1641), which is more Jonson's commonplace book than a
collection of critical essays. These and later writings Dryden knew, as he
knew the ancient critics, especially Aristotle, Horace, Quintilian, and
Longinus, and the important contemporary French critics, notably Corneille, Rapin, and Boileau. Taken as a whole, his critical prefaces and
dedications, which appeared between 1664 and 1700, are the work of a
man of independent mind who has made his own synthesis of critical
canons from wide reading, a great deal of thinking, and the constant practice of the art of writing. As a critic he is no man's disciple, and he has
the saving grace of being always willing to change his mind. This unwillingness to construct a rigid and dogmatic critical system has been regarded
by many as mere inconsistency, but recent students of Dryden have held
that it is actually the sign of a lively mind, always capable of growth.

All but a very few of Dryden's critical works (most notably the *Essay of
Dramatic Poesy*) grew out of the works to which they served as prefaces:
comedies, heroic plays, tragedies, translations, poems of various sorts. Each
work posed problems which Dryden was eager to discuss with his readers,
and the topics that he treated proved to be important in the development
of the new literature of which he was the principal apologist. Little that
was pertinent escaped his attention: the processes of literary creation fascinated him and led him to talk of wit, fancy, imagination, and judgment;
the question of the relation of the poet to tradition prompted him to explore earlier literatures in search of safe guides and models; the problems
posed by the new theater and the new drama made it desirable that he,
as a playwright, should reassess the achievement of Shakespeare's generation and should theorize about the nature of the forms of modern drama
from tragedy down to farce; his interest in poetry as a craft started discussions of metrics, language, imagery, metaphors, poetic license, methods
of translation, the literary kinds, the decorum of styles; and always his
ready enthusiasm for great writers evoked warm and generous characteriza-
tions of the genius of other poets: Shakespeare, Jonson, Chaucer, Juvenal,
Horace, Homer, Virgil. For nearly forty years this voice was heard in
the land, and when it was finally silenced, a set of critical standards had
come into existence and the Augustan age was approaching maturity. The
representative selections below may give some insight into how Dryden
helped to order taste and critical standards, while he sacrificed nothing
of that freedom without which the English literary genius could not
function.

From An Essay of Dramatic Poesy[1]
[*Two Sorts of Bad Poetry*]

" * * * I have a mortal apprehension of two poets,[2] whom this victory, with the help of both her wings, will never be able to escape." " 'Tis easy to guess whom you intend," said Lisideius; "and without naming them, I ask you if one of them does not perpetually pay us with clenches[3] upon words, and a certain clownish kind of raillery?[4] if now and then he does not offer at a catachresis[5] or Clevelandism, wresting and torturing a word into another meaning: in fine, if he be not one of those whom the French would call *un mauvais buffon*;[6] one who is so much a well-willer to the satire, that he spares no man; and though he cannot strike a blow to hurt any, yet ought to be punished for the malice of the action, as our witches are justly hanged, because they think themselves so, and suffer deservedly for believing they did mischief, because they meant it." "You have described him," said Crites, "so exactly that I am afraid to come after you with my other extremity of poetry. He is one of those who, having had some advantage of education and converse, knows better than the other what a poet should be,

1. With the reopening of the theaters in 1660, older plays were revived, but, despite their power and charm, they seemed old-fashioned. Although new playwrights, ambitious to create a modern English drama, soon appeared, they were uncertain of their direction. What, if anything, useful could they learn from the dramatic practice of the ancients? Should they ignore the English dramatists of the late 16th and early 17th centuries? Should they make their example the vigorous contemporary drama of France? Dryden addresses himself to these and other problems in this essay, his first extended piece of criticism. Its purpose, he tells us, was "chiefly to vindicate the honor of our English writers from the censure of those who unjustly prefer the French before them." Its method is skeptical: Dryden presents several points of view, but imposes none. The form is a dialogue among friends, like the *Tusculan Disputations* or the *Brutus* of Cicero. Crites praises the drama of the ancients; Eugenius protests against their authority and argues for the idea of progress in the arts; Lisideius urges the excellence of French plays; Neander, speaking in the climactic position, defends the native tradition and the greatness of Shakespeare, Fletcher, and Jonson. The dialogue takes place on June 3, 1665, in a boat on the Thames. The four friends are rowed downstream to listen to the cannonading of the English and Dutch fleets, engaged in battle off the Suffolk coast. As the gunfire recedes they are assured of victory and order their boatman to return to London, and naturally enough they fall to discussing the number of bad poems that the victory will evoke.

2. Probably Robert Wilde and possibly Richard Flecknoe, whom Dryden later ridiculed in *Mac Flecknoe*. Their actual identity is unimportant, for they merely represent two extremes in poetry, both deplorable: the fantastic and extravagant manner of decadent metaphysical wit and its opposite, the flat and the dull. The new poetry was to seek a mean between these extremes. Cf. Pope, *Essay on Criticism* II.239–42 and 289–300.

3. Puns.

4. Boorish banter.

5. The use of a word in a sense remote from its normal meaning: a legitimate figure of speech used by all poets, it had been abused by John Cleveland (1613–58), who was at first admired for his ingenuity, but whose reputation declined rapidly after the Restoration. A Clevelandism: "The marigold, whose courtier's face / *Echoes* the sun * * * "

6. A malicious jester.

but puts it into practice more unluckily than any man; his style and matter are everywhere alike: he is the most calm, peaceable writer you ever read: he never disquiets your passions[7] with the least concernment, but still[8] leaves you in as even a temper as he found you; he is a very Leveler[9] in poetry: he creeps along with ten little words in every line, and helps out his numbers with *for to*, and *unto*, and all the pretty expletives[1] he can find, till he drags them to the end of another line; while the sense is left tired half-way behind it: he doubly starves all his verses, first for want of thought, and then of expression; his poetry neither has wit in it, nor seems to have it; like him in Martial:

> *Pauper videri Cinna vult, et est pauper.*[2]

"He affects plainness, to cover his want of imagination: when he writes the serious way, the highest flight of his fancy is some miserable antithesis, or seeming contradiction; and in the comic he is still reaching at some thin conceit, the ghost of a jest, and that too flies before him, never to be caught; these swallows which we see before us on the Thames are the just resemblance of his wit: you may observe how near the water they stoop, how many proffers they make to dip, and yet how seldom they touch it; and when they do, it is but the surface: they skim over it but to catch a gnat, and then mount into the air and leave it."

[The Wit of the Ancients: The Universal]

" * * * A thing well said will be wit in all languages; and though it may lose something in the translation, yet to him who reads it in the original, 'tis still the same: he has an idea of its excellency, though it cannot pass from his mind into any other expression or words than those in which he finds it. When Phaedria, in the *Eunuch*,[3] had a command from his mistress to be absent two days, and, encouraging himself to go through with it, said, *'Tandem ego non illa caream, si sit opus, vel totum triduum?'*[4]—Parmeno, to mock the softness of his master, lifting up his hands and eyes, cries out, as it were in admiration,[5] *'Hui! universum triduum!'* the elegancy of which *universum*, though it cannot be rendered in our language, yet leaves an impression on our souls: but this happens seldom in him; in Plautus[6] oftener, who is infinitely too bold

---

7. Emotions.
8. Always.
9. The Levelers were radical egalitarians and republicans, a powerful political force in the Puritan Army about 1648. They were suppressed by Cromwell.
1. Words used merely to fill out a line of verse. Cf. Pope, *Essay on Criticism* II.346–47.
2. "Cinna wishes to seem poor, and he is poor" (*Epigrams* VIII.xix).

3. A comedy by the Roman poet Terence (ca. 185–159 B.C.).
4. "Shall I not then do without her, if need be, for three whole days?"
5. Wonder. The wit of Parmeno's exclamation, "Oh, three entire days," depends on *universum*, which suggests that a lover may regard three days as an eternity.
6. Titus Maccus Plautus, Roman comic poet (ca. 254–184 B.C.).

in his metaphors and coining words, out of which many times his
wit is nothing; which questionless was one reason why Horace falls
upon him so severely in those verses:

> *Sed proavi nostri Plautinos et numeros et*
> *Laudavere sales, nimium patienter utrumque,*
> *Ne dicam stolide.*[7]

For Horace himself was cautious to obtrude a new word on his
readers, and makes custom and common use the best measure of
receiving it into our writings:

> *Multa renascentur quae nunc cecidere, cadentque*
> *Quae nunc sunt in honore vocabula, si volet usus,*
> *Quem penes arbitrium est, et jus, et norma loquendi.*[8]

"The not observing this rule is that which the world has blamed
in our satirist, Cleveland: to express a thing hard and unnaturally
is his new way of elocution. 'Tis true no poet but may sometimes
use a catachresis: Virgil does it—

> *Mistaque ridenti colocasia fundet acantho*[9]—

in his eclogue of Pollio; and in his seventh *Aeneid:*

> *mirantur et undae,*
> *Miratur nemus insuetum fulgentia longe*
> *Scuta virum fluvio pictasque innare carinas.*[1]

And Ovid once so modestly that he asks leave to do it:

> *quem, si verbo audacia detur,*
> *Haud metuam summi dixisse Palatia caeli.*[2]

calling the court of Jupiter by the name of Augustus his palace;
though in another place he is more bold, where he says, '*et longas
visent Capitolia pompas.*'[3] But to do this always, and never be able
to write a line without it, though it may be admired by some few
pedants, will not pass upon those who know that wit is best conveyed to us in the most easy language; and is most to be admired
when a great thought comes dressed in words so commonly received that it is understood by the meanest apprehensions, as the

---

7. "But our ancestors too tolerantly
(I do not say foolishly) praised both
the verse and the wit of Plautus" (*Ars
Poetica*, lines 270–72). Dryden mis-
quotes slightly.
8. "Many words that have perished
will be born again, and those shall
perish that are now esteemed, if usage
wills it, in whose power are the judgment, the law, and the pattern of
speech" (*Ars Poetica*, lines 70–72).
9. "[The earth] shall give forth the
Egyptian bean, mingled with the smiling acanthus" (*Eclogues* IV.20). "*Smil-*

ing acanthus" is a catachresis.
1. Actually *Aeneid* VIII.91–93. Dryden's paraphrase makes the point
clearly: "The woods and waters wonder at the gleam / Of shields and
painted ships that stem the stream"
(*Aeneis* VIII.125–26). "Wonder" is a
catachresis.
2. "[This is the place] which, if boldness of expression be permitted, I shall
not hesitate to call the Palace of high
heaven" (*Metamorphoses* I.175–76).
3. "And the Capitol shall see the long
processions" (*Metamorphoses* I.561).

best meat is the most easily digested: but we cannot read a verse of Cleveland's without making a face at it, as if every word were a pill to swallow: he gives us many times a hard nut to break our teeth, without a kernel for our pains. So that there is this difference ·betwixt his satires and Doctor Donne's; that the one gives us deep thoughts in common language, though rough cadence; the other gives us common thoughts in abstruse words: 'tis true in some places his wit is independent of his words, as in that of the *Rebel Scot:*

> Had Cain been Scot, God would have changed his doom;
> Not forced him wander, but confined him home.[4]

"*Si sic omnia dixisset!*[5] This is wit in all languages: it is like mercury, never to be lost or killed:[6] and so that other—

> For beauty, like white powder, makes no noise,
> And yet the silent hypocrite destroys.

You see the last line is highly metaphorical, but it is so soft and gentle that it does not shock us as we read it."

[Shakespeare and Ben Jonson Compared]

"To begin, then, with Shakespeare. He was the man who of all modern, and perhaps ancient poets, had the largest and most comprehensive soul. All the images of Nature were still present to him, and he drew them, not laboriously, but luckily; when he describes anything, you more than see it, you feel it too. Those who accuse him to have wanted learning, give him the greater commendation: he was naturally learned; he needed not the spectacles of books to read Nature; he looked inwards, and found her there. I cannot say he is everywhere alike; were he so, I should do him injury to compare him with the greatest of mankind. He is many times flat, insipid; his comic wit degenerating into clenches, his serious swelling into bombast. But he is always great when some great occasion is presented to him; no man can say he ever had a fit subject for his wit and did not then raise himself as high above the rest of poets,

Quantum lenta solent inter viburna cupressi[7]

The consideration of this made Mr. Hales of Eton[8] say that there was no subject of which any poet ever writ, but he would produce it much better treated of in Shakespeare; and however others are now generally preferred before him, yet the age wherein he lived,

---

4. Lines 63–64.
5. "Had he said everything thus!" (Juvenal, *Satires* X.123–24).
6. Mercury is said to be "killed" if its fluidity is destroyed. The couplet quoted below is from *Rupertismus,*

lines 39–40.
7. "As do cypresses among the bending shrubs" (Virgil, *Eclogues* I.25).
8. The learned John Hales (1584–1656), provost of Eton. He is reputed to have said this to Jonson himself.

which had contemporaries with him Fletcher and Jonson, never equaled them to him in their esteem: and in the last king's[9] court, when Ben's reputation was at highest, Sir John Suckling,[1] and with him the greater part of the courtiers, set our Shakespeare far above him. * * *

"As for Jonson, to whose character I am now arrived, if we look upon him while he was himself (for his last plays were but his dotages), I think him the most learned and judicious writer which any theater ever had. He was a most severe judge of himself, as well as others. One cannot say he wanted wit, but rather that he was frugal of it. In his works you find little to retrench[2] or alter. Wit, and language, and humor also in some measure, we had before him; but something of art[3] was wanting to the drama till he came. He managed his strength to more advantage than any who preceded him. You seldom find him making love in any of his scenes or endeavoring to move the passions; his genius was too sullen and saturnine[4] to do it gracefully, especially when he knew he came after those who had performed both to such an height. Humor was his proper sphere:[5] and in that he delighted most to represent mechanic people.[6] He was deeply conversant in the ancients, both Greek and Latin, and he borrowed boldly from them: there is scarce a poet or historian among the Roman authors of those times whom he has not translated in *Sejanus* and *Catiline*.[7] But he has done his robberies so openly, that one may see he fears not to be taxed by any law. He invades authors like a monarch; and what would be theft in other poets is only victory in him. With the spoils of these writers he so represents old Rome to us, in its rites, ceremonies, and customs, that if one of their poets had written either of his tragedies, we had seen less of it than in him. If there was any fault in his language, 'twas that he weaved it too closely and laboriously, in his serious plays:[8] perhaps, too, he did a little too much Romanize our tongue, leaving the words which he translated almost as much Latin as he found them: wherein, though he learnedly followed the idiom of their language, he did not enough comply with the idiom of ours. If I would compare him with Shakespeare, I must acknowledge him the more correct poet, but Shakespeare the greater wit.[9] Shakespeare was the Homer, or father of our dramatic poets; Jonson was the Virgil, the pattern of elaborate writing; I admire him, but I love Shakespeare. To

9. Charles I.
1. Courtier, poet, playwright, much admired in Dryden's time for his wit and the easy naturalness of his style.
2. Delete.
3. Craftsmanship.
4. Heavy.
5. In Jonson's comedies the characters are seen under the domination of some psychological trait, ruling passion, or affectation—i.e., some "humor"—which makes them unique and ridiculous.
6. I.e., artisans.
7. Jonson's two Roman plays, dated 1605 and 1611 respectively.
8. This is the reading of the first edition. Curiously enough, in the second edition Dryden altered the phrase to "in his comedies especially."
9. Genius.

conclude of him; as he has given us the most correct plays, so in the precepts which he has laid down in his *Discoveries,* we have as many and profitable rules for perfecting the stage, as any wherewith the French can furnish us."

1668

From The Author's Apology for Heroic Poetry and Heroic License[1]

["Boldness" of Figures and Tropes Defended: The Appeal to "Nature"]

* * * They, who would combat general authority with particular opinion, must first establish themselves a reputation of understanding better than other men. Are all the flights of heroic poetry to be concluded bombast, unnatural, and mere madness, because they are not affected with their excellencies? It is just as reasonable as to conclude there is no day, because a blind man cannot distinguish of light and colors. Ought they not rather, in modesty, to doubt of their own judgments, when they think this or that expression in Homer, Virgil, Tasso, or Milton's *Paradise* to be too far strained, than positively to conclude that 'tis all fustian and mere nonsense? 'Tis true there are limits to be set betwixt the boldness and rashness of a poet; but he must understand those limits who pretends to judge as well as he who undertakes to write: and he who has no liking to the whole ought, in reason, to be excluded from censuring of the parts. He must be a lawyer before he mounts the tribunal; and the judicature of one court, too, does not qualify a man to preside in another. He may be an excellent pleader in the Chancery, who is not fit to rule the Common Pleas. But I will presume for once to tell them that the boldest strokes of poetry, when they are managed artfully, are those which most delight the reader.

Virgil and Horace, the severest writers of the severest age, have made frequent use of the hardest metaphors and of the strongest hyperboles; and in this case the best authority is the best argument, for generally to have pleased, and through all ages, must bear the force of universal tradition. And if you would appeal from thence to right reason, you will gain no more by it in effect than,

1. This essay was prefixed to Dryden's *State of Innocence,* the libretto for an opera (never produced), based on *Paradise Lost.* Dryden had been ridiculed for the extravagant and bold imagery and rhetorical figures that are typical of the style of his rhymed heroic plays. This preface is a defense not only of his own predilection for what Samuel Johnson described as "wild and daring sallies of sentiment, in the irregular and eccentric violence of wit," but also of the theory that heroic and idealized materials should be treated in lofty and boldly metaphorical style; hence his definition of "wit" as propriety.

first, to set up your reason against those authors, and, secondly, against all those who have admired them. You must prove why that ought not to have pleased which has pleased the most learned and the most judicious; and, to be thought knowing, you must first put the fool upon all mankind. If you can enter more deeply than they have done into the causes and resorts[2] of that which moves pleasure in a reader, the field is open, you may be heard: but those springs of human nature are not so easily discovered by every superficial judge: it requires philosophy, as well as poetry, to sound the depth of all the passions, what they are in themselves, and how they are to be provoked; and in this science the best poets have excelled. * * * From hence have sprung the tropes[3] and figures, for which they wanted a name who first practiced them and succeeded in them. Thus I grant you that the knowledge of Nature was the original rule, and that all poets ought to study her, as well as Aristotle and Horace, her interpreters.[4] But then this also undeniably follows, that those things which delight all ages must have been an imitation of Nature—which is all I contend. Therefore is rhetoric made an art; therefore the names of so many tropes and figures were invented, because it was observed they had such and such effect upon the audience. Therefore catachreses and hyperboles[5] have found their place amongst them; not that they were to be avoided, but to be used judiciously and placed in poetry as heightenings and shadows are in painting, to make the figure bolder, and cause it to stand off to sight. * * *

[*Wit as "Propriety"*]

* * * [Wit] is a propriety of thoughts and words; or, in other terms, thought and words elegantly adapted to the subject. If our critics will join issue on this definition, that we may *convenire in aliquo tertio*;[6] if they will take it as a granted principle, it will be easy to put an end to this dispute. No man will disagree from another's judgment concerning the dignity of style in heroic poetry; but all reasonable men will conclude it necessary that sublime subjects ought to be adorned with the sublimest, and, consequently, often with the most figurative expressions. * * *

1677

2. Mechanical springs which set something in motion.
3. The use of a word in a figurative sense; "figures," in this phrase, means such figures of speech as metaphors and similes.
4. In the words of the French critic René Rapin, the rules (largely derived from Aristotle's *Poetics* and Horace's *Ars Poetica*) were made in order to "reduce Nature to method." Cf. Pope, *Essay on Criticism* I.88–89.
5. "Catachresis" is the use of a word in a sense remote from its normal meaning; "hyperbole," deliberate overstatement or exaggeration.
6. "To find some means of agreement, in a third term, between the two opposites" [W. P. Ker's note].

From A Discourse Concerning the Original and Progress of Satire[1]
[*The Art of Satire*]

* * * How easy is it to call rogue and villain, and that wittily! But how hard to make a man appear a fool, a blockhead, or a knave without using any of those opprobrious terms! To spare the grossness of the names, and to do the thing yet more severely, is to draw a full face, and to make the nose and cheeks stand out, and yet not to employ any depth of shadowing.[2] This is the mystery of that noble trade, which yet no master can teach to his apprentice; he may give the rules, but the scholar is never the nearer in his practice. Neither is it true that this fineness of raillery[3] is offensive. A witty man is tickled while he is hurt in this manner, and a fool feels it not. The occasion of an offense may possibly be given, but he cannot take it. If it be granted that in effect this way does more mischief; that a man is secretly wounded, and though he be not sensible himself, yet the malicious world will find it out for him; yet there is still a vast difference betwixt the slovenly butchering of a man, and the fineness of a stroke that separates the head from the body, and leaves it standing in its place. A man may be capable, as Jack Ketch's[4] wife said of his servant, of a plain piece of work, a bare hanging; but to make a malefactor die sweetly was only belonging to her husband. I wish I could apply it to myself, if the reader would be kind enough to think it belongs to me. The character of Zimri in my *Absalom*[5] is, in my opinion, worth the whole poem: it is not bloody, but it is ridiculous enough; and he, for whom it was intended, was too witty to resent it as an injury. If I had railed,[6] I might have suffered for it justly; but I managed my own work more happily, perhaps more dexterously. I avoided the mention of great crimes, and applied myself to the representing of blindsides, and little extravagancies; to which, the wittier a man is, he is generally the more obnoxious.[7] It succeeded as I

1. This passage is an excerpt from the long and rambling preface which served as the dedication of a translation of the satires of the Roman satirists Juvenal and Persius to Charles Sackville, 6th Earl of Dorset. The translations were made by Dryden and other writers, among them William Congreve. Dryden traces the origin and development of verse satire in Rome, and in a very fine passage contrasts Horace and Juvenal as satiric poets. It is plain that he prefers the "tragic" satire of Juvenal to the urbane and laughing satire of Horace. But in the passage printed here he praises his own satiric character of Zimri (the Duke of Buckingham) in *Absalom and Achitophel* for the very

reason that it is modeled on Horatian "raillery," not Juvenalian invective.
2. Early English miniaturists prided themselves on the art of giving roundness to the full face without painting in shadows.
3. Satirical mirth, good-natured satire.
4. A notorious public executioner of Dryden's time (d. 1686). His name later became a generic term for all members of his profession.
5. See *Absalom and Achitophel* I.544–68.
6. Reviled, abused. Observe that the verb differed in meaning from its noun, defined above.
7. Liable.

wished; the jest went round, and he was laughed at in his turn who began the frolic. * * *

1693

From The Preface to *Fables Ancient and Modern*[1]
[In Praise of Chaucer]

In the first place, as he is the father of English poetry, I hold him in the same degree of veneration as the Grecians held Homer, or the Romans Virgil. He is a perpetual fountain of good sense; learned in all sciences;[2] and, therefore, speaks properly on all subjects. As he knew what to say, so he knows also when to leave off; a continence which is practiced by few writers, and scarcely by any of the ancients, excepting Virgil and Horace. * * *

Chaucer followed Nature everywhere, but was never so bold to go beyond her; and there is a great difference of being *poeta* and *nimis poeta*,[3] if we may believe Catullus, as much as betwixt a modest behavior and affectation. The verse of Chaucer, I confess, is not harmonious to us; but 'tis like the eloquence of one whom Tacitus commends, it was *auribus istius temporis accommodata*:[4] they who lived with him, and some time after him, thought it musical; and it continues so, even in our judgment, if compared with the numbers[5] of Lydgate and Gower, his contemporaries; there is the rude sweetness of a Scotch tune in it, which is natural and pleasing, though not perfect. 'Tis true I cannot go so far as he who published the last edition of him;[6] for he would make us believe the fault is in our ears, and that there were really ten syllables in a verse where we find but nine; but this opinion is not worth confuting; 'tis so gross and obvious an error that common sense (which is a rule in everything but matters of faith and revelation) must convince the reader that equality of numbers in every verse which we call heroic[7] was either not known, or not always practiced in

1. Dryden's final work, published in the year of his death, was a collection of translations from Homer, Ovid, Boccaccio, and Chaucer, and one or two other pieces. The Preface, in many ways, is Dryden's ripest and finest critical essay. In it, he is not concerned with critical theory or with a formalistic approach to literature; he is simply a man, grown old in the reading and writing of poetry, who is eager to talk informally with his readers about some of his favorite authors. His praise of Chaucer (unusually sympathetic and perceptive for 1700) is animated by that love of great literature which is manifest in everything that Dryden wrote.
2. Branches of learning.
3. A poet (*"poeta"*) and too much of a poet (*"nimis poeta"*). The phrase is not from Catullus but from Martial (*Epigrams* III.44).
4. "Suitable to the ears of that time." Tacitus was a Roman historian and writer on oratory (A.D. ca. 55–ca. 117).
5. Versification. John Lydgate (ca. 1370–ca. 1449) wrote poetry which shows the influence of Chaucer. John Gower (d. 1408), poet and friend of Chaucer.
6. Thomas Speght's Chaucer, which Dryden used, was first published in 1598; the second edition, published in 1602, was reprinted in 1687.
7. The pentameter line. In Dryden's time few readers knew how to pronounce Middle English, especially the syllabic *e*. Moreover, Chaucer's works were

Chaucer's age. It were an easy matter to produce some thousands of his verses which are lame for want of half a foot, and sometimes a whole one, and which no pronunciation can make otherwise. We can only say that he lived in the infancy of our poetry, and that nothing is brought to perfection at the first. * * *

He must have been a man of a most wonderful comprehensive nature, because, as it has been truly observed of him, he has taken into the compass of his *Canterbury Tales* the various manners and humors (as we now call them) of the whole English nation in his age. Not a single character has escaped him. All his pilgrims are severally distinguished from each other; and not only in their inclinations but in their very physiognomies and persons. Baptista Porta[8] could not have described their natures better than by the marks which the poet gives them. The matter and manner of their tales, and of their telling, are so suited to their different educations, humors, and callings that each of them would be improper in any other mouth. Even the grave and serious characters are distinguished by their several sorts of gravity: their discourses are such as belong to their age, their calling, and their breeding; such as are becoming of them, and of them only. Some of his persons are vicious, and some virtuous; some are unlearned, or (as Chaucer calls them) lewd, and some are learned. Even the ribaldry of the low characters is different: the Reeve, the Miller, and the Cook are several[9] men, and distinguished from each other as much as the mincing Lady Prioress and the broad-speaking, gap-toothed Wife of Bath. But enough of this; there is such a variety of game springing up before me that I am distracted in my choice, and know not which to follow. 'Tis sufficient to say, according to the proverb, that here is God's plenty. * * *

1700

known only in corrupt printed texts. As a consequence Chaucer's verse seemed rough and irregular.
8. Giambattista della Porta (ca. 1535–

1615), author of a Latin treatise on physiognomy.
9. Different.

WILLIAM CONGREVE
(1670–1729)

1693: First play, *The Old Bachelor*, produced.
1695: *Love for Love*, a successful comedy.
1700: Failure of *The Way of the World*; Congreve retires from the stage.

On both sides of his family Congreve was descended from well-to-do and prominent county families. His father, a younger son, obtained a commission as lieutenant in the army and removed with his family to Ireland in 1674. There the future playwright was educated at Kilkenny School and Trinity College, Dublin; at both places he was a younger contemporary of Swift, with whom he was always on friendly terms. In 1691 he took rooms in the Middle Temple and began to study law, but like other Templars of fact and fiction he preferred the wit of the coffeehouses and the theater to the aridity of the law. Within a year he had so distinguished himself at Will's Coffeehouse that he had become intimate with the great Dryden himself; and his brief career as a dramatist began shortly thereafter.

The success of *The Old Bachelor* (produced in 1693) immediately established him as the most promising young dramatist in London. It had the then phenomenally long run of fourteen days, and Dryden declared it the best first play he had ever read. *The Double Dealer* (produced in 1693) was a near failure, though it evoked one of Dryden's most graceful and gracious poems, in which he praised Congreve as the superior of Jonson and Fletcher and the equal of Shakespeare. *Love for Love* (produced in 1695) was an unqualified success and remains Congreve's most frequently revived play. In 1697 he brought out a tragedy, *The Mourning Bride*, which enjoyed great popular esteem. But in 1700 Congreve's greatest work, *The Way of the World*, despite a brilliant cast, was a failure. Subsequently, Congreve gave up the stage. He held a minor government post, which, though a Whig, he was allowed to keep during the Tory ministry of Oxford and Bolingbroke; after the accession of George I he was given a more lucrative government sinecure. Despite the political animosities of the first two decades of the century, he managed to remain on friendly terms with Swift and Pope, and Pope dedicated to him his translation of the *Iliad*. His final years were perplexed by poor health, but were made bearable by the love of Henrietta, Duchess of Marlborough, whose last child, a daughter, was in all probability the playwright's.

Although *The Way of the World* has never been remarkably successful on the stage, it remains in the judgment of most critics the finest example of the comedy of manners; it has, then, been esteemed as literature rather than as a stage play. The reasons for its unsuccess in the theater are obvious: the plot is extremely involved and not easy to follow on the stage, while the dialogue, phrased in fastidiously exact and melodious language and subtle cadences, is swift, compact, allusive, poetically rich, and dazzlingly witty, and thus beyond the immediate comprehension of an audience, though utterly delightful to readers who can take their time. In short, Congreve's virtues as a writer, when brought to full maturity, served to frustrate his designs as a dramatist. One unusual quality in this comedy is its serious moral point of view. The characters of the hero and heroine, Mirabell and Millamant, and of the two villains, Fainall and Mrs. Marwood, have a moral complexity which the gay couples and dissolute male and female wits of more typical comedies of the period usually lacked. The play is not simply a frivolous examination of manners in the beau monde. It is informed with a moral insight into the nature of illicit and married love, and though it is no sermon, it seriously examines sexual morality.

The central four, whose complex interrelationships provide the groundwork of the plot, are surrounded by characters who serve in one way or another as foils: Witwoud, the would-be wit, with whom we contrast the true wit of Mirabell and Millamant; Petulant, a "humor" character, who affects bluff candor and cynical realism, but succeeds only in being offensive; and Sir Wilfull Witwoud, the booby squire from the country, who serves with Petulant to throw into relief the high good breeding and fineness of nature of the hero and heroine. Finally there is one of Congreve's finest creations, Lady Wishfort ("wish for it"), who though aging and ugly still longs for love, gallantry, and courtship and who is led by her appetites into the trap that Mirabell lays for her.

Because of the complexity of the plot, a summary of the situation at the rise of the curtain will prove helpful. Mirabell (a reformed rake) is sincerely in love with and wishes to marry Millamant, who, though a coquette and a highly sophisticated wit, is a virtuous woman. Mirabell some time before has married off his former mistress, the daughter of Lady Wishfort, to his friend Fainall. Fainall has grown tired of his wife and has been squandering her money on his mistress, Mrs. Marwood. In order to gain access to Millamant, Mirabell has pretended to pay court to the elderly and amorous Lady Wishfort, who is the guardian of Millamant and as such controls half her fortune. But his game has been spoiled by Mrs. Marwood, who nourishes a secret love for Mirabell, and in order to separate him from Millamant has made Lady Wishfort aware of Mirabell's duplicity. Lady Wishfort now loathes Mirabell for making a fool of her —an awkward situation, since if Millamant should marry without her guardian's consent she would lose half her fortune, and Mirabell cannot afford to marry any but a rich wife. It is at this point that the action begins. Mirabell perfects a plot to get such power over Lady Wishfort as to force her to agree to the marriage, while Millamant continues to doubt whether she wishes to marry at all.

The Way of the World

Dramatis Personae[1]

Men

FAINALL, *in love with* MRS. MARWOOD

MIRABELL, *in love with* MRS. MILLAMANT

WITWOUD } *followers of* MRS. MILLAMANT
PETULANT }

SIR WILFULL WITWOUD, *half brother to* WITWOUD, *and nephew to* LADY WISHFORT

WAITWELL, *servant to* MIRABELL

1. The names of the principal characters reveal their dominant traits: for example, Fainall would *fain* have *all*, with perhaps also the suggestion that he is the complete hypocrite, who *feigns;* Witwoud is the *would-be wit;* Wishfort suggests *wish for it;* Millamant is the lady with a thousand lovers (*mille amants*); Marwood *would* willingly *mar* (injure) the lovers; Mincing has an air of affected gentility (i.e., she *minces*), which sorts ill with her vulgar English. "Mrs." is "Mistresss," a title then used by young unmarried ladies as well as by the married Mrs. Fainall.

Women

LADY WISHFORT, *enemy to* MIRABELL, *for having falsely pretended love to her*

MRS. MILLAMANT, *a fine lady, niece to* LADY WISHFORT, *and loves* MIRABELL

MRS. MARWOOD, *friend to* MR. FAINALL, *and likes* MIRABELL

MRS. FAINALL, *daughter to* LADY WISHFORT, *and wife to* FAINALL, *formerly friend to* MIRABELL

FOIBLE, *woman to* LADY WISHFORT

MINCING, *woman to* MRS. MILLAMANT

BETTY, *waitress at the chocolate house*

PEG, *under-servant to* LADY WISHFORT

DANCERS, FOOTMEN, *and* ATTENDANTS

SCENE—*London.*

Prologue

SPOKEN BY MR. BETTERTON[2]

Of those few fools, who with ill stars are cursed,
Sure scribbling fools, called poets, fare the worst:
For they're a sort of fools which Fortune makes,
And after she has made 'em fools, forsakes.
With nature's oafs 'tis quite a different case,   5
For Fortune favors all her idiot race.
In her own nest the cuckoo eggs we find,
O'er which she broods to hatch the changeling kind.[3]
No portion for her own she has to spare,
So much she dotes on her adopted care.   10
   Poets are bubbles,[4] by the town drawn in,
Suffered at first some trifling stakes to win:
But what unequal hazards do they run!
Each time they write they venture all they've won:
The squire that's buttered still,[5] is sure to be undone.   15
This author, heretofore, has found your favor,
But pleads no merit from his past behavior;
To build on that might prove a vain presumption,
Should grants to poets made, admit resumption:[6]
And in Parnassus he must lose his seat,   20
If that be found a forfeited estate.[7]
   He owns, with toil, he wrought the following scenes,
But if they're naught ne'er spare him for his pains:
Damn him the more; have no commiseration

---

2. Thomas Betterton (ca. 1635–1710), the greatest actor of the period, played Fainall in the original production of this play.

3. Simpletons; children supposed to have been secretly exchanged in infancy for others. The analogy to the "cuckoo," which lays its eggs in the nests of other birds, is obvious.

4. Dupes.

5. Constantly flattered.

6. The crown could both grant and take back ("resume") estates.

7. *Seat* rhymed with *estate;* in the next couplet, *scenes* and *pains* rhymed. A few lines later *scene* is similarly pronounced to rhyme with *maintain,* and *fault* (the *l* being silent) is rhymed with *thought.*

For dullness on mature deliberation.   25
He swears he'll not resent one hissed-off scene ⎤
Nor, like those peevish wits, his play maintain, ⎬
Who, to assert their sense, your taste arraign. ⎦
Some plot we think he has, and some new thought;
Some humor too, no farce; but that's a fault.   30
Satire, he thinks, you ought not to expect,
For so reformed a town,[8] who dares correct?
To please, this time, has been his sole pretense,
He'll not instruct, lest it should give offense.
Should he by chance a knave or fool expose,   35
That hurts none here; sure here are none of those.
In short, our play shall (with your leave to show it)
Give you one instance of a passive poet
Who to your judgments yields all resignation;
So save or damn after your own discretion.   40

Act I—A chocolate house.

SCENE 1

Mirabell and Fainall rising from cards, Betty waiting.

MIRA. You are a fortunate man, Mr. Fainall.

FAIN. Have we done?

MIRA. What you please. I'll play on to entertain you.

FAIN. No, I'll give you your revenge another time, when you are not so indifferent; you are thinking of something else now, and play too negligently. The coldness of a losing gamester lessens the pleasure of the winner. I'd no more play with a man that slighted his ill fortune than I'd make love to a woman who undervalued the loss of her reputation.

MIRA. You have a taste extremely delicate, and are for refining on your pleasures.

FAIN. Prithee, why so reserved? Something has put you out of humor.

MIRA. Not at all. I happen to be grave today, and you are gay; that's all.

FAIN. Confess, Millamant and you quarreled last night after I left you; my fair cousin has some humors that would tempt the patience of a stoic. What, some coxcomb came in, and was well received by her, while you were by?

MIRA. Witwoud and Petulant; and what was worse, her aunt, your wife's mother, my evil genius; or to sum up all in her own name, my old Lady Wishfort came in.

FAIN. O, there it is then—she has a lasting passion for you, and with reason. What, then my wife was there?

MIRA. Yes, and Mrs. Marwood and three or four more, whom I

8. A sarcasm, directed against the general movement to reform manners and morals and, more particularly, against Jeremy Collier's attack on actors and playwrights in his *Short View of the Profaneness and Immorality of the English Stage* (1698).

never saw before. Seeing me, they all put on their grave faces, whispered one another; then complained aloud of the vapors,[9] and after fell into a profound silence.

FAIN. They had a mind to be rid of you.

MIRA. For which good reason I resolved not to stir. At last the good old lady broke through her painful taciturnity, with an invective against long visits. I would not have understood her, but Millamant joining in the argument, I rose and with a constrained smile told her I thought nothing was so easy as to know when a visit began to be troublesome. She reddened and I withdrew, without expecting[1] her reply.

FAIN. You were to blame to resent what she spoke only in compliance with her aunt.

MIRA. She is more mistress of herself than to be under the necessity of such a resignation.

FAIN. What? though half her fortune depends upon her marrying with my lady's approbation?

MIRA. I was then in such a humor that I should have been better pleased if she had been less discreet.

FAIN. Now I remember, I wonder not they were weary of you: last night was one of their cabal[2] nights; they have 'em three times a week, and meet by turns, at one another's apartments, where they come together like the coroner's inquest, to sit upon the murdered reputations of the week. You and I are excluded; and it was once proposed that all the male sex should be excepted; but somebody moved that to avoid scandal there might be one man of the community; upon which Witwoud and Petulant were enrolled members.

MIRA. And who may have been the foundress of this sect? My Lady Wishfort, I warrant, who publishes her detestation of mankind, and full of the vigor of fifty-five, declares for a friend and ratafia;[3] and let posterity shift for itself, she'll breed no more.

FAIN. The discovery of your sham addresses to her, to conceal your love to her niece, has provoked this separation. Had you dissembled better, things might have continued in the state of nature.

MIRA. I did as much as man could, with any reasonable conscience: I proceeded to the very last act of flattery with her, and was guilty of a song in her commendation. Nay, I got a friend to put her into a lampoon and compliment her with the imputation of an affair with a young fellow, which I carried so far that I told her the malicious town took notice that she was grown fat of a sudden; and when she lay in of a dropsy, persuaded her she was reported to be in labor. The devil's in't, if an old woman is to be flattered further, unless a man should endeavor downright personally to debauch her; and that my virtue forbade me. But for the discovery of this amour, I am indebted to your friend, or your wife's friend, Mrs. Marwood.

FAIN. What should provoke her to be your enemy, unless she has

9. Melancholy, the blues.
1. Awaiting.
2. Secret organization designed for in-

trigue.
3. A liqueur flavored with fruit kernels (pronounced *rat-a-fé-a*).

made you advances, which you have slighted? Women do not easily forgive omissions of that nature.

MIRA. She was always civil to me, till of late. I confess I am not one of those coxcombs who are apt to interpret a woman's good manners to her prejudice, and think that she who does not refuse 'em everything, can refuse 'em nothing.

FAIN. You are a gallant man, Mirabell; and though you may have cruelty enough not to satisfy a lady's longing, you have too much generosity not to be tender of her honor. Yet you speak with an indifference which seems to be affected, and confesses you are conscious of a negligence.

MIRA. You pursue the argument with a distrust that seems to be unaffected, and confesses you are conscious of a concern for which the lady is more indebted to you than is your wife.

FAIN. Fie, fie, friend, if you grow censorious I must leave you.—I'll look upon the gamesters in the next room.

MIRA. Who are they?

FAIN. Petulant and Witwoud.—Bring me some chocolate.

MIRA. Betty, what says your clock?

BET. Turned of the last canonical hour,[4] sir.

MIRA. How pertinently the jade answers me! Ha? almost one a clock! [*looking on his watch*]—O, y'are come—

SCENE 2

Mirabell and Footman.

MIRA. Well, is the grand affair over? You have been something tedious.

FOOT. Sir, there's such coupling at Pancras[5] that they stand behind one another, as 'twere in a country dance. Ours was the last couple to lead up; and no hopes appearing of dispatch, besides, the parson growing hoarse, we were afraid his lungs would have failed before it came to our turn; so we drove around to Duke's Place, and there they were riveted in a trice.

MIRA. So, so, you are sure they are married?

FOOT. Married and bedded, sir. I am witness.

MIRA. Have you the certificate?

FOOT. Here it is, sir.

MIRA. Has the tailor brought Waitwell's clothes home, and the new liveries?

FOOT. Yes, sir.

MIRA. That's well. Do you go home again, d'ye hear, and adjourn the consummation till farther order. Bid Waitwell shake his ears, and Dame Partlet[6] rustle up her feathers, and meet me at one a clock by Rosamond's Pond, that I may see her before she returns to her lady: and as you tender your ears, be secret.

4. The hours in which marriage can legally be performed in the Anglican Church, then 8–12 noon.
5. The Church of St. Pancras, like that of St. James in Duke's Place (referred to later in the same speech), was notorious for a thriving trade in unlicensed marriages.
6. Pertelote, the hen-wife of the cock Chauntecleer in Chaucer's Nun's Priest's Tale. Rosamond's Pond was in St. James's Park.

SCENE 3

Mirabell, Fainall, Betty.

FAIN. Joy of your success, Mirabell; you look pleased.

MIRA. Aye, I have been engaged in a matter of some sort of mirth, which is not yet ripe for discovery. I am glad this is not a cabal night. I wonder, Fainall, that you who are married, and of consequence should be discreet, will suffer your wife to be of such a party.

FAIN. Faith, I am not jealous. Besides, most who are engaged are women and relations; and for the men, they are of a kind too contemptible to give scandal.

MIRA. I am of another opinion. The greater the coxcomb, always the more the scandal: for a woman who is not a fool can have but one reason for associating with a man who is one.

FAIN. Are you jealous as often as you see Witwoud entertained by Millamant?

MIRA. Of her understanding I am, if not of her person.

FAIN. You do her wrong; for to give her her due, she has wit.

MIRA. She has beauty enough to make any man think so; and complaisance enough not to contradict him who shall tell her so.

FAIN. For a passionate lover, methinks you are a man somewhat too discerning in the failings of your mistress.

MIRA. And for a discerning man, somewhat too passionate a lover; for I like her with all her faults, nay, like her for her faults. Her follies are so natural, are so artful, that they become her, and those affectations which in another woman would be odious, serve but to make her more agreeable. I'll tell thee, Fainall, she once used me with that insolence that in revenge I took her to pieces; sifted her, and separated her failings; I studied 'em, and got 'em by rote. The catalogue was so large that I was not without hopes, one day or other, to hate her heartily: to which end I so used myself to think of 'em that at length, contrary to my design and expectation, they gave me every hour less and less disturbance, till in a few days it became habitual to me to remember 'em without being displeased. They are now grown as familiar to me as my own frailties, and in all probability in a little time longer I shall like 'em as well.

FAIN. Marry her, marry her; be half as well acquainted with her charms as you are with her defects, and my life on't, you are your own man again.

MIRA. Say you so?

FAIN. Aye, aye, I have experience; I have a wife, and so forth.

SCENE 4

[*To them*] *Messenger.*

MESS. Is one Squire Witwoud here?

BET. Yes. What's your business?

MESS. I have a letter for him, from his brother Sir Wilfull, which I am charged to deliver into his own hands.

BET. He's in the next room, friend—that way.

SCENE 5

Mirabell, Fainall, Betty.

MIRA. What, is the chief of that noble family in town, Sir Wilfull Witwoud?

FAIN. He is expected today. Do you know him?

MIRA. I have seen him. He promises to be an extraordinary person; I think you have the honor to be related to him.

FAIN. Yes; he is half brother to this Witwoud by a former wife, who was sister to my Lady Wishfort, my wife's mother. If you marry Millamant, you must call cousins too.

MIRA. I had rather be his relation than his acquaintance.

FAIN. He comes to town in order to equip himself for travel.

MIRA. For travel! Why the man that I mean is above forty.[7]

FAIN. No matter for that; 'tis for the honor of England that all Europe should know that we have blockheads of all ages.

MIRA. I wonder there is not an Act of Parliament to save the credit of the nation, and prohibit the exportation of fools.

FAIN. By no means, 'tis better as 'tis; 'tis better to trade with a little loss than to be quite eaten up with being overstocked.

MIRA. Pray, are the follies of this knight-errant, and those of the squire his brother, anything related?

FAIN. Not at all. Witwoud grows by the knight, like a medlar[8] grafted on a crab. One will melt in your mouth, and t'other set your teeth on edge; one is all pulp, and the other all core.

MIRA. So one will be rotten before he be ripe, and the other will be rotten without ever being ripe at all.

FAIN. Sir Wilfull is an odd mixture of bashfulness and obstinacy. But when he's drunk, he's as loving as the monster in the *Tempest*;[9] and much after the same manner. To give t'other his due, he has something of good nature, and does not always want wit.

MIRA. Not always; but as often as his memory fails him, and his commonplace of comparisons.[1] He is a fool with a good memory, and some few scraps of other folks' wit. He is one whose conversation can never be approved, yet it is now and then to be endured. He has indeed one good quality, he is not exceptious,[2]

7. The grand tour of the Continent was rapidly becoming a part of the education of gentlemen, but it was usually made in company with a tutor after a young man had graduated from a university, not after a man had passed the age of forty.

8. A fruit eaten when it is overripe. "Crab": crab apple.

9. Trinculo, in the adaptation of Shakespeare's *Tempest* by Sir William Davenant and Dryden (1667), having made Caliban drunk, says: "The poor monster is loving in his drink" (II.2).

1. One recognized sign of wit was the ability to discover quickly resemblances between objects apparently unlike. Witwoud specializes in this kind of wit, but Mirabell suggests that they are all obvious and collected from others, like observations copied in a notebook, or "commonplace" book.

2. Quarrelsome.

for he so passionately affects the reputation of understanding raillery that he will construe an affront into a jest; and call downright rudeness and ill language, satire and fire.

FAIN. If you have a mind to finish his picture, you have an opportunity to do it at full length. Behold the original.

SCENE 6

[*To them*] Witwoud.

WIT. Afford me your compassion, my dears; pity me, Fainall, Mirabell, pity me.

MIRA. I do from my soul.

FAIN. Why, what's the matter?

WIT. No letters for me, Betty?

BET. Did not a messenger bring you one but now, sir?

WIT. Aye, but no other?

BET. No, sir.

WIT. That's hard, that's very hard. A messenger, a mule, a beast of burden, he has brought me a letter from the fool my brother, as heavy as a panegyric in a funeral sermon, or a copy of commendatory verses from one poet to another. And what's worse, 'tis as sure a forerunner of the author as an epistle dedicatory.

MIRA. A fool, and your brother, Witwoud!

WIT. Aye, aye, my half brother. My half brother he is, no nearer upon honor.

MIRA. Then 'tis possible he may be but half a fool.

WIT. Good, good, Mirabell, *le drôle!*[3] Good, good. Hang him, don't let's talk of him. Fainall, how does your lady? Gad, I say anything in the world to get this fellow out of my head. I beg pardon that I should ask a man of pleasure and the town a question at once so foreign and domestic. But I talk like an old maid at a marriage, I don't know what I say: but she's the best woman in the world.

FAIN. 'Tis well you don't know what you say, or else your commendation would go near to make me either vain or jealous.

WIT. No man in town lives well with a wife but Fainall. Your judgment, Mirabell?

MIRA. You had better step and ask his wife, if you would be credibly informed.

WIT. Mirabell.

MIRA. Aye.

WIT. My dear, I ask ten thousand pardons—gad, I have forgot what I was going to say to you.

MIRA. I thank you heartily, heartily.

WIT. No, but prithee excuse me—my memory is such a memory.

MIRA. Have a care of such apologies, Witwoud—for I never knew a fool but he affected to complain, either of the spleen or his memory.

FAIN. What have you done with Petulant?

---

3. The witty fellow.

WIT. He's reckoning his money—my money it was.—I have no luck today.

FAIN. You may allow him to win of you at play—for you are sure to be too hard for him at repartee. Since you monopolize the wit that is between you, the fortune must be his of course.

MIRA. I don't find that Petulant confesses the superiority of wit to be your talent, Witwoud.

WIT. Come, come, you are malicious now, and would breed debates. —Petulant's my friend, and a very honest fellow, and a very pretty fellow, and has a smattering—faith and troth a pretty deal of an odd sort of a small wit: nay, I'll do him justice. I'm his friend, I won't wrong him.—And if he had any judgment in the world—he would not be altogether contemptible. Come, come, don't detract from the merits of my friend.

FAIN. You don't take your friend to be over-nicely bred.

WIT. No, no, hang him, the rogue has no manners at all, that I must own—no more breeding than a bum-bailey,[4] that I grant you.—'Tis pity; the fellow has fire and life.

MIRA. What, courage?

WIT. Hum, faith I don't know as to that—I can't say as to that.— Yes, faith, in a controversy he'll contradict anybody.

MIRA. Though 'twere a man whom he feared, or a woman whom he loved.

WIT. Well, well, he does not always think before he speaks—we have all our failings; you are too hard upon him, you are, faith. Let me excuse him—I can defend most of his faults, except one or two. One he has, that's the truth on't, if he were my brother, I could not acquit him.—That indeed I could wish were otherwise.

MIRA. Aye marry, what's that, Witwoud?

WIT. O, pardon me—expose the infirmities of my friend?—No, my dear, excuse me there.

FAIN. What, I warrant he's unsincere, or 'tis some such trifle.

WIT. No, no, what if he be? 'Tis no matter for that, his wit will excuse that. A wit should no more be sincere than a woman constant; one argues a decay of parts, as t'other of beauty.

MIRA. Maybe you think him too positive?

WIT. No, no, his being positive is an incentive to argument, and keeps up conversation.

FAIN. Too illiterate.

WIT. That! that's his happiness.—His want of learning gives him the more opportunities to show his natural parts.

MIRA. He wants words.

WIT. Aye; but I like him for that now; for his want of words gives me the pleasure very often to explain his meaning.

FAIN. He's impudent.

WIT. No, that's not it.

MIRA. Vain.

WIT. No.

4. Bumbailiff, the lowest kind of arresting officer.

MIRA. What, he speaks unseasonable truths sometimes, because he has not wit enough to invent an evasion.

WIT. Truths! Ha, ha, ha! No, no, since you will have it—I mean, he never speaks truth at all—that's all. He will lie like a chambermaid, or a woman of quality's porter. Now that is a fault.

SCENE 7

[To them] Coachman.

COACH. Is Master Petulant here, mistress?

BET. Yes.

COACH. Three gentlewomen in a coach would speak with him.

FAIN. O brave Petulant, three!

BET. I'll tell him.

COACH. You must bring two dishes of chocolate and a glass of cinnamon water.

SCENE 8

Mirabell, Fainall, Witwoud.

WIT. That should be for two fasting strumpets, and a bawd troubled with wind. Now you may know what the three are.

MIRA. You are free with your friend's acquaintance.

WIT. Aye, aye, friendship without freedom is as dull as love without enjoyment, or wine without toasting; but to tell you a secret, these are trulls whom he allows coach-hire, and something more by the week, to call on him once a day at public places.

MIRA. How!

WIT. You shall see he won't go to 'em because there's no more company here to take notice of him.—Why this is nothing to what he used to do, before he found out this way, I have known him call for himself.—

FAIN. Call for himself? What dost thou mean?

WIT. Mean? Why he would slip you out of this chocolate house, just when you had been talking to him.—As soon as your back was turned—whip he was gone—then trip to his lodging, clap on a hood and scarf, and a mask, slap into a hackney coach, and drive hither to the door again in a trice; where he would send in for himself, that I mean, call for himself, wait for himself, nay and what's more, not finding himself, sometimes leave a letter for himself.

MIRA. I confess this is something extraordinary.—I believe he waits for himself now, he is so long a-coming. O, I ask his pardon.

SCENE 9

Petulant, Mirabell, Fainall, Witwoud, Betty.

BET. Sir, the coach stays.

PET. Well, well; I come.—'Sbud,[5] a man had as good be a pro-

5. God's body.

fessed midwife, as a professed whoremaster, at this rate; to be knocked up and raised at all hours, and in all places. Pox on 'em, I won't come.—D'ye hear, tell 'em I won't come.—Let 'em snivel and cry their hearts out.

FAIN. You are very cruel, Petulant.

PET. All's one, let it pass—I have a humor to be cruel.

MIRA. I hope they are not persons of condition that you use at this rate.

PET. Condition, condition's a dried fig, if I am not in humor.—By this hand, if they were your—a—a—your what-dee-call-'ems themselves, they must wait or rub off,[6] if I want appetite.

MIRA. What-de-call-'ems! What are they, Witwoud?

WIT. Empresses,[7] my dear.—By your what-dee-call-'ems he means sultana queens.

PET. Aye, Roxolanas.

MIRA. Cry you mercy.

FAIN. Witwoud says they are—

PET. What does he say th' are?

WIT. I? Fine ladies I say.

PET. Pass on, Witwoud.—Harkee, by this light his relations—two co-heiresses his cousins, and an old aunt, who loves caterwauling better than a conventicle.[8]

WIT. Ha, ha, ha; I had a mind to see how the rogue would come off.—Ha, ha, ha; gad, I can't be angry with him, if he had said they were my mother and my sisters.

MIRA. No!

WIT. No; the rogue's wit and readiness of invention charm me, dear Petulant.

BET. They are gone, sir, in great anger.

PET. Enough, let 'em trundle. Anger helps complexion, saves paint.

FAIN. This continence is all dissembled; this is in order to have something to brag of the next time he makes court to Millamant, and swear he has abandoned the whole sex for her sake.

MIRA. Have you not left off your impudent pretensions there yet? I shall cut your throat, sometime or other, Petulant, about that business.

PET. Aye, aye, let that pass.—There are other throats to be cut.—

MIRA. Meaning mine, sir?

PET. Not I—I mean nobody.—I know nothing. But there are uncles and nephews in the world—and they may be rivals—What then? All's one for that—

MIRA. How! Harkee, Petulant, come hither—explain, or I shall call your interpreter.

PET. Explain? I know nothing.—Why, you have an uncle, have you not, lately come to town, and lodges by my Lady Wishfort's?

MIRA. True.

PET. Why, that's enough.—You and he are not friends; and if he

6. Make off.
7. "Empresses," like "sultana queens" and "Roxolanas," were terms for prostitutes. Roxolana is the wife of the Sultan in Davenant's *Siege of Rhodes* (1656).
8. Nonconformist religious meeting.

should marry and have a child, you may be disinherited, ha?

MIRA. Where hast thou stumbled upon all this truth?

PET. All's one for that; why, then, say I know something.

MIRA. Come, thou art an honest fellow, Petulant, and shalt make love to my mistress, thou sha't, faith. What hast thou heard of my uncle?

PET. I, nothing, I. If throats are to be cut, let swords clash; snug's the word, I shrug and am silent.

MIRA. O raillery, raillery. Come, I know thou art in the women's secrets.—What, you're a cabalist. I know you stayed at Milla-mant's last night, after I went. Was there any mention made of my uncle or me? Tell me; if thou hadst but good nature equal to thy wit, Petulant, Tony Witwoud, who is now thy competitor in fame, would show as dim by thee as a dead whiting's eye by a pearl of Orient. He would no more be seen by thee than Mer-cury is by the sun: come, I'm sure thou wo't tell me.

PET. If I do, will you grant me common sense then, for the future?

MIRA. Faith, I'll do what I can for thee, and I'll pray that Heaven may grant it thee in the meantime.

PET. Well, harkee.

FAIN. Petulant and you both will find Mirabell as warm a rival as a lover.

WIT. Pshaw, pshaw, that she laughs at Petulant is plain. And for my part—but that it is almost a fashion to admire her, I should —harkee—to tell you a secret, but let it go no further—between friends, I shall never break my heart for her.

FAIN. How!

WIT. She's handsome; but she's a sort of an uncertain woman.

FAIN. I thought you had died for her.

WIT. Umh—no—

FAIN. She has wit.

WIT. 'Tis what she will hardly allow anybody else.—Now, demme, I should hate that, if she were as handsome as Cleopatra. Mira-bell is not so sure of her as he thinks for.

FAIN. Why do you think so?

WIT. We stayed pretty late there last night, and heard something of an uncle to Mirabell, who is lately come to town—and is be-tween him and the best part of his estate. Mirabell and he are at some distance, as my Lady Wishfort has been told; and you know she hates Mirabell, worse than a Quaker hates a parrot, or than a fishmonger hates a hard frost. Whether this uncle has seen Mrs. Millamant or not, I cannot say; but there were items of such a treaty being in embryo; and if it should come to life, poor Mirabell would be in some sort unfortunately fobbed[9] i' faith.

FAIN. 'Tis impossible Millamant should harken to it.

WIT. Faith, my dear, I can't tell; she's a woman and a kind of a humorist.[1]

MIRA. And this is the sum of what you could collect last night.

PET. The quintessence. Maybe Witwoud knows more, he stayed

9. Tricked.   1. A capricious person.

longer.—Besides they never mind him; they say anything before him.

MIRA. I thought you had been the greatest favorite.

PET. Aye, *tête à tête;*[2] but not in public, because I make remarks.

MIRA. You do?

PET. Aye, aye, pox, I'm malicious, man. Now he's soft, you know, they are not in awe of him.—The fellow's well bred, he's what you call a—what-d'ye-call-'em. A fine gentleman, but he's silly withal.

MIRA. I thank you, I know as much as my curiosity requires. Fainall, are you for the Mall?[3]

FAIN. Aye, I'll take a turn before dinner.

WIT. Aye, we'll all walk in the park, the ladies talked of being there.

MIRA. I thought you were obliged to watch for your brother Sir Wilfull's arrival.

WIT. No, no, he's come to his aunt's, my Lady Wishfort. Pox on him, I shall be troubled with him too. What shall I do with the fool?

PET. Beg him for his estate, that I may beg you afterwards, and so have but one trouble with you both.

WIT. O rare Petulant; thou art as quick as fire in a frosty morning; thou shalt to the Mall with us; and we'll be very severe.

PET. Enough, I'm in a humor to be severe.

MIRA. Are you? Pray then walk by yourselves.—Let not us be accessory to your putting the ladies out of countenance with your senseless ribaldry, which you roar out aloud as often as they pass by you; and when you have made a handsome woman blush, then you think you have been severe.

PET. What, what? Then let 'em either show their innocence by not understanding what they hear, or else show their discretion by not hearing what they would not be thought to understand.

MIRA. But hast not thou then sense enough to know that thou ought'st to be most ashamed thyself, when thou hast put another out by countenance?

PET. Not I, by this hand.—I always take blushing either for a sign of guilt, or ill breeding.

MIRA. I confess you ought to think so. You are in the right, that you may plead the error of your judgment in defense of your practice.

> Where modesty's ill manners, 'tis but fit
> That impudence and malice pass for wit.

Act II—St. James's Park.

SCENE 1

Mrs. Fainall and Mrs. Marwood.

MRS. FAIN. Aye, aye, dear Marwood, if we will be happy, we must find the means in ourselves, and among ourselves. Men are ever

---

2. Face to face, i.e., in private.   3. A walk in St. James's Park, one of the fashionable resorts of the day.

in extremes; either doting or averse. While they are lovers, if they have fire and sense, their jealousies are insupportable: and when they cease to love (we ought to think at least) they loathe. They look upon us with horror and distaste; they meet us like the ghosts of what we were, and as from such, fly from us.

MRS. MAR. True, 'tis an unhappy circumstance of life that love should ever die before us; and that the man so often should out-live the lover. But say what you will, 'tis better to be left than never to have been loved. To pass over youth in dull indifference, to refuse the sweets of life because they once must leave us, is as preposterous as to wish to have been born old, because we one day must be old. For my part, my youth may wear and waste, but it shall never rust in my possession.

MRS. FAIN. Then it seems you dissemble an aversion to mankind only in compliance to my mother's humor.

MRS. MAR. Certainly. To be free, I have no taste of those insipid dry discourses with which our sex of force must entertain them-selves apart from men. We may affect endearments to each other, profess eternal friendships, and seem to dote like lovers; but 'tis not in our natures long to persevere. Love will resume his empire in our breasts, and every heart, or soon or late, receive and readmit him as its lawful tyrant.

MRS. FAIN. Bless me, how have I been deceived! Why, you profess a libertine.

MRS. MAR. You see my friendship by my freedom. Come, be as sincere, acknowledge that your sentiments agree with mine.

MRS. FAIN. Never.

MRS. MAR. You hate mankind?

MRS. FAIN. Heartily, inveterately.

MRS. MAR. Your husband?

MRS. FAIN. Most transcendently; aye, though I say it, meritoriously.

MRS. MAR. Give me your hand upon it.

MRS. FAIN. There.

MRS. MAR. I join with you. What I have said has been to try you.

MRS. FAIN. Is it possible? Dost thou hate those vipers men?

MRS. MAR. I have done hating 'em, and am now come to despise 'em; the next thing I have to do is eternally to forget 'em.

MRS. FAIN. There spoke the spirit of an Amazon, a Penthesilea.[4]

MRS. MAR. And yet I am thinking sometimes to carry my aversion further.

MRS. FAIN. How?

MRS. MAR. Faith, by marrying. If I could but find one that loved me very well, and would be thoroughly sensible of ill usage, I think I should do myself the violence of undergoing the cere-mony.

MRS. FAIN. You would not make him a cuckold?

MRS. MAR. No; but I'd make him believe I did, and that's as bad.

MRS. FAIN. Why had not you as good do it?

MRS. MAR. O, if he should ever discover it, he would then know

4. Queen of the Amazons (a legendary nation of women warriors).

the worst, and be out of his pain; but I would have him ever to continue upon the rack of fear and jealousy.

MRS. FAIN. Ingenious mischief! Would thou wert married to Mirabell.

MRS. MAR. Would I were.

MRS. FAIN. You change color.

MRS. MAR. Because I hate him.

MRS. FAIN. So do I; but I can hear him named. But what reason have you to hate him in particular?

MRS. MAR. I never loved him; he is and always was insufferably proud.

MRS. FAIN. By the reason you give for your aversion, one would think it dissembled; for you have laid a fault to his charge of which his enemies must acquit him.

MRS. MAR. O then it seems you are one of his favorable enemies. Methinks you look a little pale, and now you flush again.

MRS. FAIN. Do I? I think I am a little sick o' the sudden.

MRS. MAR. What ails you?

MRS. FAIN. My husband. Don't you see him? He turned short upon me unawares, and has almost overcome me.

SCENE 2

[To them] Fainall and Mirabell.

MRS. MAR. Ha, ha, ha; he comes opportunely for you.

MRS. FAIN. For you, for he has brought Mirabell with him.

FAIN. My dear.

MRS. FAIN. My soul.

FAIN. You don't look well today, child.

MRS. FAIN. D'ye think so?

MIRA. He is the only man that does, madam.

MRS. FAIN. The only man that would tell me so at least; and the only man from whom I could hear it without mortification.

FAIN. O my dear, I am satisfied of your tenderness; I know you cannot resent anything from me, especially what is an effect of my concern.

MRS. FAIN. Mr. Mirabell, my mother interrupted you in a pleasant relation last night. I would fain hear it out.

MIRA. The persons concerned in that affair have yet a tolerable reputation.—I am afraid Mr. Fainall will be censorious.

MRS. FAIN. He has a humor more prevailing than his curiosity, and will willingly dispense with the hearing of one scandalous story to avoid giving an occasion to make another by being seen to walk with his wife. This way, Mr. Mirabell, and I dare promise you will oblige us both.

SCENE 3

Fainall, Mrs. Marwood.

FAIN. Excellent creature! Well, sure if I should live to be rid of my wife, I should be a miserable man.

MRS. MAR. Aye!

FAIN. For having only that one hope, the accomplishment of it of
consequence must put an end to all my hopes; and what a wretch
is he who must survive his hopes! Nothing remains when that
day comes but to sit down and weep like Alexander, when he
wanted other worlds to conquer.

MRS. MAR. Will you not follow 'em?

FAIN. Faith, I think not.

MRS. MAR. Pray let us; I have a reason.

FAIN. You are not jealous?

MRS. MAR. Of whom?

FAIN. Of Mirabell.

MRS. MAR. If I am, is it inconsistent with my love to you that I am
tender of your honor?

FAIN. You would intimate then, as if there were a fellow-feeling between my wife and him.

MRS. MAR. I think she does not hate him to that degree she would
be thought.

FAIN. But he, I fear, is too insensible.

MRS. MAR. It may be you are deceived.

FAIN. It may be so. I do now begin to apprehend it.

MRS. MAR. What?

FAIN. That I have been deceived, Madam, and you are false.

MRS. MAR. That I am false! What mean you?

FAIN. To let you know I see through all your little arts.—Come, you
both love him; and both have equally dissembled your aversion.
Your mutual jealousies of one another have made you clash till
you have both struck fire. I have seen the warm confession red-
dening on your cheeks, and sparkling from your eyes.

MRS. MAR. You do me wrong.

FAIN. I do not.—'Twas for my ease to oversee[5] and willfully neglect
the gross advances made him by my wife; that by permitting her
to be engaged I might continue unsuspected in my pleasures;
and take you oftener to my arms in full security. But could you
think, because the nodding husband would not wake, that e'er
the watchful lover slept?

MRS. MAR. And wherewithal can you reproach me?

FAIN. With infidelity, with loving another, with love of Mirabell.

MRS. MAR. 'Tis false. I challenge you to show an instance that can
confirm your groundless accusation. I hate him.

FAIN. And wherefore do you hate him? He is insensible, and your
resentment follows his neglect. An instance! The injuries you
have done him are a proof: your interposing in his love. What
cause had you to make discoveries of his pretended passion? To
undeceive the credulous aunt, and be the officious obstacle of his
match with Millamant?

MRS. MAR. My obligations to my lady urged me. I had professed a
friendship to her, and could not see her easy nature so abused
by that dissembler.

5. Overlook.

FAIN. What, was it conscience then? Professed a friendship! O the pious friendships of the female sex!

MRS. MAR. More tender, more sincere, and more enduring than all the vain and empty vows of men, whether professing love to us, or mutual faith to one another.

FAIN. Ha, ha, ha; you are my wife's friend too.

MRS. MAR. Shame and ingratitude! Do you reproach me? You, you upbraid me! Have I been false to her, through strict fidelity to you, and sacrificed my friendship to keep my love inviolate? And have you the baseness to charge me with the guilt, unmindful of the merit! To you it should be meritorious that I have been vicious: and do you reflect that guilt upon me, which should lie buried in your bosom?

FAIN. You misinterpret my reproof. I meant but to remind you of the slight account you once could make of strictest ties, when set in competition with your love to me.

MRS. MAR. 'Tis false, you urged it with deliberate malice.—'Twas spoke in scorn, and I never will forgive it.

FAIN. Your guilt, not your resentment, begets your rage. If yet you loved, you could forgive a jealousy, but you are stung to find you are discovered.

MRS. MAR. It shall be all discovered. You too shall be discovered; be sure you shall. I can but be exposed.—If I do it myself, I shall prevent[6] your baseness.

FAIN. Why, what will you do?

MRS. MAR. Disclose it to your wife; own what has passed between us.

FAIN. Frenzy!

MRS. MAR. By all my wrongs I'll do't—I'll publish to the world the injuries you have done me, both in my fame and fortune: with both I trusted you, you bankrupt in honor, as indigent of wealth.

FAIN. Your fame[7] I have preserved. Your fortune has been bestowed as the prodigality of your love would have it, in pleasures which we both have shared. Yet, had not you been false, I had e'er this repaid it.—'Tis true—had you permitted Mirabell with Millamant to have stolen their marriage, my lady had been incensed beyond all means of reconcilement: Millamant had forfeited the moiety[8] of her fortune, which then would have descended to my wife—and wherefore did I marry, but to make lawful prize of a rich widow's wealth, and squander it on love and you?

MRS. MAR. Deceit and frivolous pretense.

FAIN. Death, am I not married? What's pretense? Am I not imprisoned, fettered? Have I not a wife? Nay, a wife that was a widow, a young widow, a handsome widow; and would be again a widow, but that I have a heart of proof, and something of a constitution to bustle through the ways of wedlock and this

6. Anticipate.
7. Good name.
8. Half.

world. Will you yet be reconciled to truth and me?

MRS. MAR. Impossible. Truth and you are inconsistent—I hate you, and shall forever.

FAIN. For loving you?

MRS. MAR. I loathe the name of love after such usage; and next to the guilt with which you would asperse me, I scorn you most. Farewell.

FAIN. Nay, we must not part thus.

MRS. MAR. Let me go.

FAIN. Come, I'm sorry.

MRS. MAR. I care not.—Let me go.—Break my hands, do—I'd leave 'em to get loose.

FAIN. I would not hurt you for the world. Have I no other hold to keep you here?

MRS. MAR. Well, I have deserved it all.

FAIN. You know I love you.

MRS. MAR. Poor dissembling!—O that—Well, it is not yet—

FAIN. What? What is it not? What is it not yet? It is not yet too late—

MRS. MAR. No, it is not yet too late—I have that comfort.

FAIN. It is, to love another.

MRS. MAR. But not to loathe, detest, abhor mankind, myself, and the whole treacherous world.

FAIN. Nay, this is extravagance.—Come, I ask your pardon.—No tears.—I was to blame. I could not love you and be easy in my doubts.—Pray forbear.—I believe you; I'm convinced I've done you wrong; and any way, every way will make amends.—I'll hate my wife yet more, damn her, I'll part with her, rob her of all she's worth, and we'll retire somewhere, anywhere, to another world. I'll marry thee.—Be pacified.—'Sdeath, they come, hide your face, your tears.—You have a mask,[9] wear it a moment. This way, this way, be persuaded.

SCENE 4

Mirabell and Mrs. Fainall.

MRS. FAIN. They are here yet.

MIRA. They are turning into the other walk.

MRS. FAIN. While I only hated my husband, I could bear to see him, but since I have despised him, he's too offensive.

MIRA. O, you should hate with prudence.

MRS. FAIN. Yes, for I have loved with indiscretion.

MIRA. You should have just so much disgust for your husband as may be sufficient to make you relish your lover.

MRS. FAIN. You have been the cause that I have loved without bounds, and would you set limits to that aversion, of which you have been the occasion? Why did you make me marry this man?

MIRA. Why do we daily commit disagreeable and dangerous ac-

9. Often worn in public places by fashionable women of the time in order to preserve their complexions; they were also useful to disguise a woman and so to protect her reputation when she was carrying on an illicit affair.

tions? To save that idol, reputation. If the familiarities of our loves had produced that consequence, of which you were apprehensive, where could you have fixed a father's name with credit, but on a husband? I knew Fainall to be a man lavish of his morals, an interested and professing friend, a false and a designing lover; yet one whose wit and outward fair behavior have gained a reputation with the town, enough to make that woman stand excused who has suffered herself to be won by his addresses. A better man ought not to have been sacrificed to the occasion; a worse had not answered to the purpose. When you are weary of him, you know your remedy.

MRS. FAIN. I ought to stand in some degree of credit with you, Mirabell.

MIRA. In justice to you, I have made you privy to my whole design, and put it in your power to ruin or advance my fortune.

MRS. FAIN. Whom have you instructed to represent your pretended uncle?

MIRA. Waitwell, my servant.

MRS. FAIN. He is an humble servant to Foible,[1] my mother's woman, and may win her to your interest.

MIRA. Care is taken for that.—She is won and worn by this time. They were married this morning.

MRS. FAIN. Who?

MIRA. Waitwell and Foible. I would not tempt my servant to betray me by trusting him too far. If your mother, in hopes to ruin me, should consent to marry my pretended uncle, he might, like Mosca in *The Fox*,[2] stand upon terms; so I made him sure beforehand.

MRS. FAIN. So, if my poor mother is caught in a contract, you will discover the imposture betimes; and release her by producing a certificate of her gallant's former marriage.

MIRA. Yes, upon condition that she consent to my marriage with her niece, and surrender the moiety of her fortune in her possession.

MRS. FAIN. She talked last night of endeavoring at a match between Millamant and your uncle.

MIRA. That was by Foible's direction, and my instruction, that she might seem to carry it more privately.

MRS. FAIN. Well, I have an opinion of your success, for I believe my lady will do anything to get an husband; and when she has this, which you have provided for her, I suppose she will submit to anything to get rid of him.

MIRA. Yes, I think the good lady would marry anything that resembled a man, though 'twere no more than what a butler could pinch out of a napkin.

MRS. FAIN. Female frailty! We must all come to it, if we live to be old, and feel the craving of a false appetite when the true is decayed.

1. I.e., he is Foible's lover.
2. The scheming parasite in Ben Jonson's *Volpone,* who in the end tries to blackmail Volpone. "To stand upon terms" means to insist upon conditions —hence, here, to blackmail.

MIRA. An old woman's appetite is depraved like that of a girl—'tis the greensickness[3] of a second childhood; and like the faint offer of a latter spring, serves but to usher in the fall and withers in an affected bloom.

MRS. FAIN. Here's your mistress.

SCENE 5

[To them] Mrs. Millamant, Witwoud, Mincing.

MIRA. Here she comes, i'faith, full sail, with her fan spread and streamers out, and a shoal of fools for tenders.—Ha, no, I cry her mercy.

MRS. FAIN. I see but one poor empty sculler, and he tows her woman after him.

MIRA. You seem to be unattended, madam.—You used to have the *beau monde*[4] throng after you; and a flock of gay fine perukes hovering round you.

WIT. Like moths about a candle—I had like to have lost my comparison for want of breath.

MILLA. O, I have denied myself airs today. I have walked as fast through the crowd—

WIT. As a favorite just disgraced; and with as few followers.

MILLA. Dear Mr. Witwoud, truce with your similitudes: For I am as sick of 'em—

WIT. As a physician of a good air—I cannot help it, madam, though 'tis against myself.

MILLA. Yet again! Mincing, stand between me and his wit.

WIT. Do, Mrs. Mincing, like a screen before a great fire. I confess I do blaze today, I am too bright.

MRS. FAIN. But dear Millamant, why were you so long?

MILLA. Long! Lord, have I not made violent haste? I have asked every living thing I met for you; I have inquired after you, as after a new fashion.

WIT. Madam, truce with your similitudes.—No, you met her husband, and did not ask him for her.

MIRA. By your leave, Witwoud, that were like inquiring after an old fashion, to ask a husband for his wife.

WIT. Hum, a hit, a hit, a palpable hit,[5] I confess it.

MRS. FAIN. You were dressed before I came abroad.

MILLA. Aye, that's true.—O, but then I had—Mincing, what had I? Why was I so long?

MINC. O mem, your la'ship stayed to peruse a packet of letters.

MILLA. O, aye, letters—I had letters—I am persecuted with letters —I hate letters.—Nobody knows how to write letters; and yet one has 'em, one does not know why.—They serve one to pin up one's hair.

WIT. Is that the way? Pray, madam, do you pin up your hair with

---

3. The anemia that sometimes affects girls at puberty.
4. Fashionable world. "Perukes": periwigs, worn by fashionable men. Cf.

Pope's *Rape of the Lock* I.101.
5. An allusion to the dueling scene in *Hamlet* V.ii.

all your letters? I find I must keep copies.

MILLA. Only with those in verse, Mr. Witwoud. I never pin up my hair with prose. I think I tried once, Mincing.

MINC. O mem, I shall never forget it.

MILLA. Aye, poor Mincing tiffed[6] and tiffed all the morning.

MINC. Till I had the cramp in my fingers, I'll vow, mem. And all to no purpose. But when your la'ship pins it up with poetry, it sits so pleasant the next day as anything, and is so pure and so crips.[7]

WIT. Indeed, so crips?

MINC. You're such a critic, Mr. Witwoud.

MILLA. Mirabell, did you take exceptions last night? O, aye, and went away.—Now I think on't I'm angry.—No, now I think on't I'm pleased—for I believe I gave you some pain.

MIRA. Does that please you?

MILLA. Infinitely; I love to give pain.

MIRA. You would affect a cruelty which is not in your nature; your true vanity is in the power of pleasing.

MILLA. O, I ask your pardon for that—one's cruelty is one's power, and when one parts with one's cruelty, one parts with one's power; and when one has parted with that, I fancy one's old and ugly.

MIRA. Aye, aye, suffer your cruelty to ruin the object of your power, to destroy your lover.—And then how vain, how lost a thing you'll be? Nay, 'tis true: you are no longer handsome when you've lost your lover; your beauty dies upon the instant: for beauty is the lover's gift; 'tis he bestows your charms—your glass is all a cheat. The ugly and the old, whom the looking glass mortifies, yet after commendation can be flattered by it, and discover beauties in it: for that reflects our praises, rather than your face.

MILLA. O, the vanity of these men! Fainall, d'ye hear him? If they did not commend us, we were not handsome! Now you must know they could not commend one, if one was not handsome. Beauty the lover's gift?—Lord, what is a lover, that it can give? Why, one makes lovers as fast as one pleases, and they live as long as one pleases, and they die as soon as one pleases: and then if one pleases one makes more.

WIT. Very pretty. Why, you make no more of making of lovers, madam, than of making so many card-matches.[8]

MILLA. One no more owes one's beauty to a lover than one's wit to an echo.—They can but reflect what we look and say; vain empty things if we are silent or unseen, and want a being.

MIRA. Yet, to those two vain empty things, you owe two of the greatest pleasures of your life.

MILLA. How so?

MIRA. To your lover you owe the pleasure of hearing yourselves praised; and to an echo the pleasure of hearing yourselves talk.

WIT. But I know a lady that loves talking so incessantly she won't

6. Dressed the hair.
7. A dialectal form of "crisp," curly.

8. Matches made by dipping pieces of card in melted sulphur.

give an echo fair play; she has that everlasting rotation of tongue, that an echo must wait till she dies before it can catch her last words.

MILLA. O, fiction; Fainall, let us leave these men.

MIRA. [*aside to* MRS. FAINALL] Draw off Witwoud.

MRS. FAIN. Immediately; I have a word or two for Mr. Witwoud.

SCENE 5

Millamant, Mirabell, Mincing.

MIRA. I would beg a little private audience too.—You had the tyranny to deny me last night, though you knew I came to impart a secret to you that concerned my love.

MILLA. You saw I was engaged.

MIRA. Unkind. You had the leisure to entertain a herd of fools, things who visit you from their excessive idleness, bestowing on your easiness that time, which is the encumbrance of their lives. How can you find delight in such society? It is impossible they should admire you, they are not capable: or if they were, it should be to you as a mortification; for sure to please a fool is some degree of folly.

MILLA. I please myself—besides, sometimes to converse with fools is for my health.

MIRA. Your health! Is there a worse disease than the conversation of fools?

MILLA. Yes, the vapors; fools are physic for it, next to asafetida.[9]

MIRA. You are not in a course of fools?

MILLA. Mirabell, if you persist in this offensive freedom, you'll displease me. I think I must resolve after all not to have you.— We shan't agree.

MIRA. Not in our physic, it may be.

MILLA. And yet our distemper in all likelihood will be the same, for we shall be sick of one another. I shan't endure to be reprimanded nor instructed; 'tis so dull to act always by advice, and so tedious to be told of one's faults.—I can't bear it. Well, I won't have you, Mirabell—I'm resolved—I think—you may go— ha, ha, ha. What would you give that you could help loving me?

MIRA. I would give something that you did not know I could not help it.

MILLA. Come, don't look grave then. Well, what do you say to me?

MIRA. I say that a man may as soon make a friend by his wit, or a fortune by his honesty, as win a woman with plain-dealing and sincerity.

MILLA. Sententious Mirabell! prithee don't look with that violent and inflexible wise face, like Solomon at the dividing of the child in an old tapestry hanging.[1]

MIRA. You are merry, madam, but I would persuade you for a moment to be serious.

9. An evil-smelling drug.
1. The Judgment of Solomon (I Kings iii.16–27) was a favorite subject in painting and tapestry.

MILLA. What, with that face? No, if you keep your countenance, 'tis impossible I should hold mine. Well, after all, there is something very moving in a lovesick face. Ha, ha, ha.—Well I won't laugh, don't be peevish—heigho! Now I'll be melancholy, as melancholy as a watchlight. Well, Mirabell, if ever you will win me, woo me now. Nay, if you are so tedious, fare you well; I see they are walking away.

MIRA. Can you not find in the variety of your disposition one moment—

MILLA. To hear you tell me Foible's married and your plot like to speed.—No.

MIRA. But how you came to know it—

MILLA. Without the help of the devil, you can't imagine; unless she should tell me herself. Which of the two it may have been, I will leave you to consider; and when you have done thinking of that, think of me.

SCENE 7

Mirabell alone.

MIRA. I have something more.—Gone!—Think of you! To think of a whirlwind, though 'twere in a whirlwind, were a case of more steady contemplation, a very tranquility of mind and mansion. A fellow that lives in a windmill has not a more whimsical dwelling than the heart of a man that is lodged in a woman. There is no point of the compass to which they cannot turn, and by which they are not turned; and by one as well as another, for motion, not method, is their occupation. To know this, and yet continue to be in love, is to be made wise from the dictates of reason, and yet persevere to play the fool by the force of instinct. O, here come my pair of turtles[2]—what, billing so sweetly! Is not Valentine's Day over with you yet?

SCENE 8

[To him] Waitwell, Foible.

MIRA. Sirrah Waitwell, why sure you think you were married for your own recreation and not for my conveniency.

WAIT. Your pardon, sir. With submission, we have indeed been solacing in lawful delights, but still with an eye to business, sir. I have instructed her as well as I could. If she can take your directions as readily as my instructions, sir, your affairs are in a prosperous way.

MIRA. Give you joy, Mrs. Foible.

FOIB. O-las, sir, I'm so ashamed—I'm afraid my lady has been in a thousand inquietudes for me. But I protest, sir, I made as much haste as I could.

WAIT. That she did indeed, sir. It was my fault that she did not

2. Turtledoves, remarkable for their affectionate billing and cooing. Birds were popularly supposed to choose their mates on St. Valentine's Day.

make more.

MIRA. That I believe.

FOIB. But I told my lady as you instructed me, sir. That I had a prospect of seeing Sir Rowland your uncle, and that I would put her ladyship's picture in my pocket to show him; which I'll be sure to say has made him so enamored of her beauty that he burns with impatience to lie at her ladyship's feet and worship the original.

MIRA. Excellent, Foible! Matrimony has made you eloquent in love.

WAIT. I think she has profited, sir. I think so.

FOIB. You have seen Madam Millamant, sir?

MIRA. Yes.

FOIB. I told her, sir, because I did not know that you might find an opportunity; she had so much company last night.

MIRA. Your diligence will merit more—in the meantime—

[*Gives money.*]

FOIB. O dear sir, your humble servant.

WAIT. Spouse.

MIRA. Stand off, sir, not a penny. Go on and prosper, Foible. The lease shall be made good and the farm stocked if we succeed.

FOIB. I don't question your generosity, sir. And you need not doubt of success. If you have no more commands, sir, I'll be gone; I'm sure my lady is at her toilet, and can't dress till I come. O dear, I'm sure that [*looking out*] was Mrs. Marwood that went by in a mask; if she has seen me with you I'm sure she'll tell my lady. I'll make haste home and prevent her.[3] Your servant, sir. B'w'y, Waitwell.

SCENE 9

Mirabell, Waitwell.

WAIT. Sir Rowland, if you please. The jade's so pert upon her preferment she forgets herself.

MIRA. Come, sir, will you endeavor to forget yourself—and transform into Sir Rowland.

WAIT. Why, sir, it will be impossible I should remember myself—married, knighted, and attended all in one day! 'Tis enough to make any man forget himself. The difficulty will be how to recover my acquaintance and familiarity with my former self; and fall from my transformation to a reformation into Waitwell. Nay, I shan't be quite the same Waitwell neither—for now I remember me, I'm married and can't be my own man again.

> Aye, there's my grief; that's the sad change of life;
> To lose my title, and yet keep my wife.

3. Arrive before she does. "B'w'y" is a shortened form of "God be with you" (our word "goodbye").

Act III—A room in Lady Wishfort's house.

SCENE 1

Lady Wishfort at her toilet, Peg waiting.

LADY. Merciful, no news of Foible yet?

PEG. No, madam.

LADY. I have no more patience. If I have not fretted myself till I am pale again, there's no veracity in me. Fetch me the red—the red, do you hear, sweetheart? An errant ash color, as I'm a person. Look you how this wench stirs! Why dost thou not fetch me a little red? Didst thou not hear me, mopus?[4]

PEG. The red ratafia does your ladyship mean, or the cherry brandy?

LADY. Ratafia, fool. No, fool. Not the ratafia, fool. Grant me patience! I mean the Spanish paper,[5] idiot—complexion, darling. Paint, paint, paint, dost thou understand that, changeling, dangling thy hands like bobbins before thee? Why dost thou not stir, puppet? Thou wooden thing upon wires.

PEG. Lord, madam, your ladyship is so impatient.—I cannot come at the paint, madam. Mrs. Foible has locked it up and carried the key with her.

LADY. A pox take you both!—Fetch me the cherry brandy then.

SCENE 2

Lady Wishfort.

I'm as pale and as faint, I look like Mrs. Qualmsick, the curate's wife, that's always breeding. Wench, come, come, wench, what art thou doing? Sipping? Tasting? Save thee, dost thou not know the bottle?

SCENE 3

Lady Wishfort, Peg with a bottle and china cup.

PEG. Madam, I was looking for a cup.

LADY. A cup, save thee, and what a cup hast thou brought! Dost thou take me for a fairy, to drink out of an acorn? Why didst thou not bring thy thimble? Hast thou ne'er a brass thimble clinking in thy pocket with a bit of nutmeg? I warrant thee. Come, fill, fill.—So—again. See who that is.—[*One knocks.*]—Set down the bottle first. Here, here, under the table.—What, wouldst thou go with the bottle in thy hand like a tapster? As I'm a person, this wench has lived in an inn upon the road before she came to me, like Maritornes the Asturian[6] in *Don Quixote*. No Foible yet?

PEG. No, madam, Mrs. Marwood.

LADY. O Marwood, let her come in. Come in, good Marwood.

4. Dull, stupid person.
5. Rouge.

6. The servant at the inn where the Don and Sancho Panza are succored.

SCENE 4

[*To them*] *Mrs. Marwood.*

MRS. MAR. I'm surprised to find your ladyship in *deshabillé*[7] at this time of day.

LADY. Foible's a lost thing; has been abroad since morning, and never heard of since.

MRS. MAR. I saw her but now, as I came masked through the park, in conference with Mirabell.

LADY. With Mirabell! You call my blood into my face, with mentioning that traitor. She durst not have the confidence. I sent her to negotiate an affair, in which if I'm detected I'm undone. If that wheedling villain has wrought upon Foible to detect me, I'm ruined. O my dear friend, I'm a wretch of wretches if I'm detected.

MRS. MAR. O madam, you cannot suspect Mrs. Foible's integrity.

LADY. O, he carries poison in his tongue that would corrupt integrity itself. If she has given him an opportunity, she has as good as put her integrity into his hands. Ah dear Marwood, what's integrity to an opportunity? Hark! I hear her—dear friend, retire into my closet,[8] that I may examine her with more freedom. You'll pardon me, dear friend, I can make bold with you. There are books over the chimney—Quarles and Prynne, and the *Short View of the Stage*, with Bunyan's works to entertain you.[9] [*to* PEG] Go, you thing, and send her in.

SCENE 5

Lady Wishfort, Foible.

LADY. O Foible, where hast thou been? What hast thou been doing?

FOIB. Madam, I have seen the party.

LADY. But what hast thou done?

FOIB. Nay, 'tis your ladyship has done, and are to do; I have only promised. But a man so enamored—so transported! Well, if worshiping of pictures be a sin—poor Sir Rowland, I say.

LADY. The miniature has been counted like[1]—but hast thou not betrayed me, Foible? Hast thou not detected me to that faithless Mirabell?—What hadst thou to do with him in the park? Answer me, has he got nothing out of thee?

FOIB. [*aside*] So, the devil has been beforehand with me. What shall I say?—Alas, madam, could I help it if I met that confident thing? Was I in fault? If you had heard how he used me, and

7. In negligee.
8. Private retiring room.
9. Francis Quarles (1592–1644), a religious poet, by 1700 regarded with contempt, but formerly greatly admired, especially among the Puritans; William Prynne (1600–69), Puritan pamphleteer, author of *Histriomastix* (1632), a

violent attack on the stage. For Jeremy Collier's *Short View*, see the Prologue of this play: Congreve, who had been the object of much of Collier's vituperation, slyly identifies his enemy with Puritans and Nonconformists, whom Collier, an ardent high churchman, despised.
1. Considered a likeness.

all upon your ladyship's account, I'm sure you would not suspect my fidelity. Nay, if that had been the worst I could have borne; but he had a fling at your ladyship too; and then I could not hold; but i'faith I gave him his own.

LADY. Me? What did the filthy fellow say?

FOIB. O madam; 'tis a shame to say what he said—with his taunts and his fleers, tossing up his nose. Humh (says he) what, you are a-hatching some plot (says he) you are so early abroad, or catering[2] (says he), ferreting for some disbanded officer, I warrant—half pay is but thin subsistence (says he).—Well, what pension does your lady propose? Let me see (says he) what, she must come down pretty deep now, she's superannuated (says he) and—

LADY. Ods my life, I'll have him—I'll have him murdered. I'll have him poisoned. Where does he eat? I'll marry a drawer[3] to have him poisoned in his wine. I'll send for Robin from Locket's —immediately.

FOIB. Poison him? Poisoning's too good for him. Starve him, madam, starve him; marry Sir Rowland, and get him disinherited. O, you would bless yourself, to hear what he said.

LADY. A villain!—superannuated!

FOIB. Humh (says he) I hear you are laying designs against me too (says he) and Mrs. Millamant is to marry my uncle; (he does not suspect a word of your ladyship) but (says he) I'll fit you for that, I warrant you (says he) I'll hamper you for that (says he) you and your old frippery[4] too (says he). I'll handle you—

LADY. Audacious villain! handle me, would he durst—frippery? old frippery! Was there ever such a foul-mouthed fellow? I'll be married tomorrow, I'll be contracted tonight.

FOIB. The sooner the better, madam.

LADY. Will Sir Rowland be here, say'st thou? When, Foible?

FOIB. Incontinently, madam. No new sheriff's wife expects the return of her husband after knighthood, with that impatience in which Sir Rowland burns for the dear hour of kissing your ladyship's hand after dinner.

LADY. Frippery! Superannuated frippery! I'll frippery the villain, I'll reduce him to frippery and rags. A tatterdemalion—I hope to see him hung with tatters, like a Long Lane penthouse,[5] or a gibbet-thief. A slander-mouthed railer—I warrant the spendthrift prodigal's in debt as much as the million lottery, or the whole court upon a birthday. I'll spoil his credit with his tailor. Yes, he shall have my niece with her fortune, he shall.

FOIB. He! I hope to see him lodge in Ludgate first, and angle into Blackfriars for brass farthings with an old mitten.[6]

2. Procuring (i.e., pimping for Lady Wishfort). When a regiment was "disbanded," its officers went on half pay, often for life.
3. One who draws wine from casks and serves it. Locket's was a fashionable tavern near Charing Cross.
4. Old, cast-off clothes; an insulting metaphor to apply to Lady Wishfort.
5. "Tatterdemalion": ragamuffin. Long Lane was a street where old clothes were sold; "penthouse": a shed, supported by the wall toward which it is inclined.
6. Ludgate was a debtor's prison, adjoined the district of Blackfriars in London. Prisoners begged by letting down

LADY. Aye, dear Foible; thank thee for that, dear Foible. He has
put me out of all patience. I shall never recompose my features
to receive Sir Rowland with any economy of face. This wretch
has fretted me that I am absolutely decayed. Look, Foible.

FOIB. Your ladyship has frowned a little too rashly, indeed, madam.
There are some cracks discernible in the white varnish.

LADY. Let me see the glass.—Cracks, say'st thou? Why I am
arrantly flayed—I look like an old peeled wall. Thou must repair me, Foible, before Sir Rowland comes, or I shall never keep
up to my picture.

FOIB. I warrant you, madam; a little art once made your picture
like you and now a little of the same art must make you like
your picture. Your picture must sit for you, madam.

LADY. But art thou sure Sir Rowland will not fail to come? Or will
a' not fail[7] when he does come? Will he be importunate, Foible,
and push? For if he should not be importunate—I shall never
break decorums.—I shall die with confusion, if I am forced to
advance.—Oh, no, I can never advance.—I shall swoon if he
should expect advances. No, I hope Sir Rowland is better bred
than to put a lady to the necessity of breaking her forms. I won't
be too coy neither—I won't give him despair—but a little disdain
is not amiss; a little scorn is alluring.

FOIB. A little scorn becomes your ladyship.

LADY. Yes, but tenderness becomes me best.—A sort of dyingness
—You see that picture has a sort of a—Ha, Foible? A swimming-
ness in the eyes—Yes, I'll look so—my niece affects it; but she
wants features. Is Sir Rowland handsome? Let my toilet be removed—I'll dress above. I'll receive Sir Rowland here. Is he
handsome? Don't answer me. I won't know: I'll be surprised.
I'll be taken by surprise.

FOIB. By storm, madam. Sir Rowland's a brisk man.

LADY. Is he! O, then he'll importune, if he's a brisk man. I shall
save decorums if Sir Rowland importunes. I have a mortal terror
at the apprehension of offending against decorums. O, I'm glad
he's a brisk man. Let my things be removed, good Foible.

SCENE 6

Mrs. Fainall, Foible.

MRS. FAIN. O Foible, I have been in a fright, lest I should come
too late. That devil Marwood saw you in the park with Mirabell,
and I'm afraid will discover it to my lady.

FOIB. Discover what, madam?

MRS. FAIN. Nay, nay, put not on that strange face. I am privy to
the whole design and know Waitwell, to whom thou wert this
morning married, is to personate Mirabell's uncle, and as such,
winning my lady, to involve her in those difficulties from which
Mirabell only must release her, by his making his conditions to

a mitten on a string; passers-by dropped   7. I.e., will *he* not fail?
coins into it.

have my cousin and her fortune left to her own disposal.

FOIB. O dear madam, I beg your pardon. It was not my confidence in your ladyship that was deficient, but I thought the former good correspondence between your ladyship and Mr. Mirabell might have hindered his communicating this secret.

MRS. FAIN. Dear Foible, forget that.

FOIB. O dear madam, Mr. Mirabell is such a sweet winning gentleman—but your ladyship is the pattern of generosity. Sweet lady, to be so good! Mr. Mirabell cannot choose but to be grateful. I find your ladyship has his heart still. Now, madam, I can safely tell your ladyship our success. Mrs. Marwood had told my lady; but I warrant I managed myself. I turned it all for the better. I told my lady that Mr. Mirabell railed at her. I laid horrid things to his charge, I'll vow; and my lady is so incensed that she'll be contracted to Sir Rowland tonight, she says—I warrant I worked her up, that he may have her for asking for, as they say of a Welsh maidenhead.

MRS. FAIN. O rare Foible!

FOIB. Madam, I beg your ladyship to acquaint Mr. Mirabell of his success. I would be seen as little as possible to speak to him—besides, I believe Madam Marwood watches me. She has a month's mind;[8] but I know Mr. Mirabell can't abide her.—[*Calls.*]—John—remove my lady's toilet. Madam, your servant. My lady is so impatient, I fear she'll come for me if I stay.

MRS. FAIN. I'll go with you up the back stairs, lest I should meet her.

SCENE 7

Mrs. Marwood alone.

MRS. MAR. Indeed, Mrs. Engine,[9] is it thus with you? Are you become a go-between of this importance? Yes, I shall watch you. Why, this wench is the *passe-partout*, a very master key to everybody's strongbox. My friend Fainall,[1] have you carried it so swimmingly? I thought there was something in it; but it seems it's over with you. Your loathing is not from a want of appetite, then, but from a surfeit. Else you could never be so cool to fall from a principal to be an assistant; to procure for him! A pattern of generosity, that I confess. Well, Mr. Fainall, you have met with your match. O, man, man! Woman, woman! The devil's an ass: If I were a painter, I would draw him like an idiot, a driveler with a bib and bells. Man should have his head and horns, and woman the rest of him. Poor simple fiend! Madam Marwood has a month's mind, but he can't abide her.—'Twere better for him you had not been his confessor in that affair without you could have kept his counsel closer. I shall not prove another pattern of generosity.—He has not obliged me to that with those excesses of himself; and now I'll have none of him. Here

8. An inclination (toward Mirabell).
9. A person who serves as an instrument or tool of others in an intrigue.
1. I.e., Mrs. Fainall.

comes the good lady, panting ripe, with a heart full of hope and a head full of care, like any chemist upon the day of projection.[2]

SCENE 8

[To her] Lady Wishfort.

LADY. O dear Marwood, what shall I say for this rude forgetfulness —but my dear friend is all goodness.

MRS. MAR. No apologies, dear madam. I have been very well entertained.

LADY. As I'm a person I am in a very chaos to think I should so forget myself—but I have such an olio[3] of affairs really I know not what to do—[*Calls.*]—Foible—I expect my nephew Sir Wilfull every moment too.—Why, Foible!—He means to travel for improvement.

MRS. MAR. Methinks Sir Wilfull should rather think of marrying than traveling at his years. I hear he is turned of forty.

LADY. O, he's in less danger of being spoiled by his travels.—I am against my nephew's marrying too young. It will be time enough when he comes back and has acquired discretion to choose for himself.

MRS. MAR. Methinks Mrs. Millamant and he would make a very fit match. He may travel afterwards. 'Tis a thing very usual with young gentlemen.

LADY. I promise you I have thought on't—and since 'tis your judgment, I'll think on't again. I assure you I will; I value your judgment extremely. On my word I'll propose it.

SCENE 9

[To them] Foible.

LADY. Come, come Foible—I had forgot my nephew will be here before dinner.—I must make haste.

FOIB. Mr. Witwoud and Mr. Petulant are come to dine with your ladyship.

LADY. O dear, I can't appear till I am dressed. Dear Marwood, shall I be free with you again and beg you to entertain 'em? I'll make all imaginable haste. Dear friend, excuse me.

SCENE 10

Mrs. Marwood, Mrs. Millamant, Mincing.

MILLA. Sure never anything was so unbred as that odious man.— Marwood, your servant.

MRS. MAR. You have a color. What's the matter?

MILLA. That horrid fellow Petulant has provoked me into a flame —I have broke my fan.—Mincing, lend me yours; is not all the powder out of my hair?

---

2. An alchemical term denoting the final step in the transmutation of baser metals into gold.
3. Hodgepodge.

MRS. MAR. No. What has he done?

MILLA. Nay, he has done nothing; he has only talked.—Nay, he has said nothing neither; but he has contradicted everything that has been said. For my part, I thought Witwoud and he would have quarreled.

MINC. I vow, mem, I thought once they would have fitt.

MILLA. Well, 'tis a lamentable thing, I swear, that one has not the liberty of choosing one's acquaintance as one does one's clothes.

MRS. MAR. If we had that liberty, we should be as weary of one set of acquaintance, though never so good, as we are of one suit, though never so fine. A fool and a doily stuff[4] would now and then find days of grace, and be worn for variety.

MILLA. I could consent to wear 'em, if they would wear alike; but fools never wear out—they are such drap-de-Berry[5] things! Without one could give 'em to one's chambermaid after a day or two.

MRS. MAR. 'Twere better so indeed. Or what think you of the play house? A fine gay glossy fool should be given there, like a new masking habit after the masquerade is over,[6] and we have done with the disguise. For a fool's visit is always a disguise, and never admitted by a woman of wit, but to blind her affair with a lover of sense. If you would but appear barefaced now and own Mirabell, you might as easily put off Petulant and Witwoud as your hood and scarf. And indeed 'tis time, for the town has found it: the secret is grown too big for the pretense: 'tis like Mrs. Primly's great belly; she may lace it down before, but it burnishes[7] on her hips. Indeed, Millamant, you can no more conceal it than my Lady Strammel can her face, that goodly face, which in defiance of her Rhenish-wine tea will not be comprehended in a mask.[8]

MILLA. I'll take my death, Marwood, you are more censorious than a decayed beauty, or a discarded toast.[9] Mincing, tell the men they may come up. My aunt is not dressing here; their folly is less provoking than your malice.

SCENE 11

Millamant, Marwood.

MILLA. "The town has found it." What has it found? That Mirabell loves me is no more a secret than it is a secret that you discovered it to my aunt, or than the reason why you discovered it is a secret.

MRS. MAR. You are nettled.

MILLA. You're mistaken. Ridiculous!

MRS. MAR. Indeed, my dear, you'll tear another fan if you don't mitigate those violent airs.

4. A woolen cloth.
5. Coarse woolen cloth, made in the Berry district of France.
6. Fine gentlemen and ladies sometimes donated their old clothes to the playhouses.
7. Spreads out.

8. Lady Strammel (the name means "a lean, ill-favored person") reduces by drinking Rhenish wine, but still her face is too large to be contained ("comprehended") in a mask.
9. A lady to whom toasts are no longer drunk.

MILLA. O silly! Ha, ha, ha. I could laugh immoderately. Poor Mirabell! His constancy to me has quite destroyed his complaisance for all the world beside. I swear, I never enjoined it him, to be so coy.—If I had the vanity to think he would obey me, I would command him to show more gallantry.—'Tis hardly well bred to be so particular on one hand and so insensible on the other. But I despair to prevail, and so let him follow his own way. Ha, ha, ha. Pardon me, dear creature, I must laugh, ha, ha, ha; though I grant you 'tis a little barbarous, ha, ha, ha.

MRS. MAR. What pity 'tis, so much fine raillery, and delivered with so significant gesture, should be so unhappily directed to miscarry.

MILLA. Hae? Dear creature, I ask your pardon—I swear I did not mind you.

MRS. MAR. Mr. Mirabell and you both may think it a thing impossible, when I shall tell him by telling you—

MILLA. O dear, what? For it is the same thing, if I hear it—Ha, ha, ha.

MRS. MAR. That I detest him, hate him, madam.

MILLA. O madam, why so do I—and yet the creature loves me, ha, ha, ha. How can one forbear laughing to think of it?—I am a sibyl[1] if I am not amazed to think what he can see in me. I'll take my death, I think you are handsomer—and within a year or two as young. If you could but stay for me, I should overtake you.—But that cannot be.—Well, that thought makes me melancholy.—Now I'll be sad.

MRS. MAR. Your merry note may be changed sooner than you think.

MILLA. D'ye say so? Then I'm resolved I'll have a song to keep up my spirits.

SCENE 12.

[To them] Mincing.

MINC. The gentlemen stay but to comb,[2] madam, and will wait on you.

MILLA. Desire Mrs. ———[3] that is in the next room to sing the song I would have learnt yesterday. You shall hear it, madam—not that there's any great matter in it—But 'tis agreeable to my humor.

Song. Set by Mr. John Eccles

1

Love's but the frailty of the mind,
    When 'tis not with ambition joined;
A sickly flame, which if not fed expires;
And feeding, wastes in self-consuming fires.

2

'Tis not to wound a wanton boy
    Or amorous youth, that gives the joy;

---

1. A prophetess.
2. I.e., to comb their periwigs.
3. The name of the singer was to be inserted. The music was by John Eccles (d. 1735), a popular composer for the theater.

> But 'tis the glory to have pierced a swain,
> For whom inferior beauties sighed in vain.
>
> 3
>
> Then I alone the conquest prize,
> When I insult a rival's eyes:
> If there's delight in love, 'tis when I see
> That heart which others bleed for, bleed for me.

SCENE 13

[To them] Petulant, Witwoud.

MILLA. Is your animosity composed, gentlemen?

WIT. Raillery, raillery, madam, we have no animosity. We hit off a little wit now and then, but no animosity. The falling out of wits is like the falling out of lovers—we agree in the main, like treble and bass. Ha, Petulant!

PET. Aye, in the main. But when I have a humor to contradict—

WIT. Aye, when he has a humor to contradict, then I contradict too. What, I know my cue. Then we contradict one another like two battledores;[4] for contradictions beget one another like Jews.

PET. If he says black's black—if I have a humor to say 'tis blue— let that pass.—All's one for that. If I have a humor to prove it, it must be granted.

WIT. Not positively must—but it may—it may.

PET. Yes, it positively must, upon proof positive.

WIT. Aye, upon proof positive it must; but upon proof presumptive it only may. That's a logical distinction now, madam.

MRS. MAR. I perceive your debates are of importance and very learn-edly handled.

PET. Importance is one thing, and learning's another; but a debate's a debate, that I assert.

WIT. Petulant's an enemy to learning; he relies altogether on his parts.[5]

PET. No, I'm no enemy to learning; it hurts not me.

MRS. MAR. That's a sign indeed it's no enemy to you.

PET. No, no, it's no enemy to anybody but them that have it.

MILLA. Well, an illiterate man's my aversion. I wonder at the impudence of any illiterate man, to offer to make love.

WIT. That I confess I wonder at too.

MILLA. Ah! to marry an ignorant! that can hardly read or write.

PET. Why should a man be any further from being married though he can't read than he is from being hanged. The ordinary's[6] paid for setting the Psalm, and the parish priest for reading the ceremony. And for the rest which is to follow in both cases, a man may do it without book.—So all's one for that.

MILLA. D'ye hear the creature? Lord, here's company, I'll be gone.

---

4. Rackets used to strike the shuttle-cock, or bird, in the old game from which badminton is descended.

5. Native abilities.

6. The clergyman appointed to prepare condemned prisoners for death.

SCENE 14

Sir Wilfull Witwoud in a riding dress, Mrs. Marwood,
Petulant, Witwoud, Footman.

WIT. In the name of Bartlemew and his Fair,[7] what have we here?

MRS. MAR. 'Tis your brother, I fancy. Don't you know him?

WIT. Not I.—Yes, I think it is he—I've almost forgot him; I have not seen him since the Revolution.[8]

FOOT. Sir, my lady's dressing. Here's company; if you please to walk in, in the meantime.

SIR WIL. Dressing! What, it's but morning here, I warrant, with you in London; we should count it towards afternoon in our parts, down in Shropshire. Why, then belike my aunt han't dined yet—ha, friend?

FOOT. Your aunt, Sir?

SIR WIL. My aunt, sir, yes, my aunt, sir, and your lady, sir; your lady is my aunt, sir.—Why, what do'st thou not know me, friend? Why, then send somebody hither that does. How long hast thou lived with thy lady, fellow, ha?

FOOT. A week, sir; longer than anybody in the house, except my lady's woman.

SIR WIL. Why, then belike thou dost not know thy lady, if thou see'st her, ha, friend?

FOOT. Why truly, sir, I cannot safely swear to her face in a morning, before she is dressed. 'Tis like I may give a shrewd guess at her by this time.

SIR WIL. Well, prithee try what thou canst do; if thou canst not guess, inquire her out, do'st hear, fellow? And tell her her nephew, Sir Wilfull Witwoud, is in the house.

FOOT. I shall, sir.

SIR WIL. Hold ye, hear me, friend; a word with you in your ear. Prithee who are these gallants?

FOOT. Really, sir, I can't tell; there come so many here, 'tis hard to know 'em all.

SCENE 15

Sir Wilfull Witwoud, Petulant, Witwoud, Mrs. Marwood.

SIR WIL. Oons,[9] this fellow knows less than a starling; I don't think a'knows his own name.

MRS. MAR. Mr. Witwoud, your brother is not behind hand in forgetfulness—I fancy he has forgot you too.

WIT. I hope so.—The devil take him that remembers first, I say.

SIR WIL. Save you, gentlemen and lady.

MRS. MAR. For shame, Mr. Witwoud; why don't you speak to him? —And you, sir.

7. A feature of St. Bartholomew's Fair, held during August in Smithfield, London, was the exhibition of monsters and freaks of nature.

8. The "Glorious" Revolution of 1688 that forced the abdication of James II.
9. An uncouth oath: "God's wounds."

WIT. Petulant, speak.

PET. And you, sir.

SIR WIL. [*Salutes* MARWOOD.] No offense, I hope.

MRS. MAR. No sure, sir.

WIT. This is a vile dog, I see that already. No offense! Ha, ha, ha, to him; to him, Petulant, smoke him.[1]

PET. [*surveying him round*] It seems as if you had come a journey, sir. Hem, hem.

SIR WIL. Very likely, sir, that it may seem so.

PET. No offense, I hope, sir.

WIT. Smoke the boots, the boots, Petulant, the boots. Ha, ha, ha.

SIR WIL. Maybe not, sir; thereafter as 'tis meant, sir.

PET. Sir, I presume upon the information of your boots.

SIR WIL. Why, 'tis like you may, sir: If you are not satisfied with the information of my boots, sir, if you will step to the stable, you may inquire further of my horse, sir.

PET. Your horse, sir! Your horse is an ass, sir!

SIR WIL. Do you speak by way of offense, sir?

MRS. MAR. The gentleman's merry, that's all, sir.—[*aside*] 'Slife,[2] we shall have a quarrel betwixt an horse and an ass, before they find one another out. [*aloud*] You must not take anything amiss from your friends, sir. You are among your friends, here, though it may be you don't know it.—If I am not mistaken, you are Sir Wilfull Witwoud.

SIR WIL. Right, lady; I am Sir Wilfull Witwoud, so I write myself; no offense to anybody, I hope; and nephew to the Lady Wishfort of this mansion.

MRS. MAR. Don't you know this gentleman, sir?

SIR WIL. Hum! What, sure, 'tis not—yea by'r Lady, but 'tis— 'sheart,[3] I know not whether 'tis or no.—Yea but 'tis, by the Wrekin.[4] Brother Antony! What, Tony, i'faith! What, do'st thou not know me? By'r Lady, nor I thee, thou art so becravated and so beperriwigged—'sheart, why do'st not speak? Art thou o'erjoyed?

WIT. Odso, brother, is it you? Your servant, brother.

SIR WIL. Your servant! Why, yours, sir. Your servant again—'sheart, and your friend and servant to that—and a—[*Puff.*]—and a flap-dragon[5] for your service, sir: and a hare's foot, and a hare's scut[6] for your service, sir; an you be so cold and so courtly!

WIT. No offense, I hope, brother.

SIR WIL. 'Sheart, sir, but there is, and much offense. A pox, is this your Inns o' Court[7] breeding, not to know your friends and your relations, your elders and your betters?

WIT. Why, Brother Wilfull of Salop,[8] you may be as short as a

1. Make fun of him.
2. "God's life."
3. "God's heart."
4. A solitary mountain peak in Shropshire, near the Welsh border.
5. Something worthless.
6. Rabbit's tail.
7. The buildings—Gray's Inn, Lincoln's Inn, the Inner Temple, the Middle Temple—housing the four legal societies that have the sole right to admit persons to the practice of law.
8. An ancient name of Shropshire. A "Shrewsbury cake" was a "short" cake, in the modern meaning of the term. Witwould puns, using "short" also in the sense of "abrupt."

Shrewsbury cake, if you please. But I tell you 'tis not modish to know relations in town. You think you're in the country, where great lubberly brothers slabber and kiss one another when they meet, like a call of sergeants.[9]—'Tis not the fashion here; 'tis not inded, dear brother.

SIR WIL. The fashion's a fool; and you're a fop, dear brother. 'Sheart, I've suspected this—by'r Lady, I conjectured you were a fop, since you began to change the style of your letters and write in a scrap of paper gilt round the edges, no bigger than a subpoena. I might expect this when you left off "Honored Brother" and "hoping you are in good health," and so forth—to begin with a "Rat me, knight, I'm so sick of a last night's debauch"— 'od's heart, and then tell a familiar tale of a cock and bull, and a whore and a bottle, and so conclude—You could write news before you were out of your time,[1] when you lived with honest Pumple-Nose, the attorney of Furnival's Inn—You could entreat to be remembered then to your friends round the Wrekin. We could have gazettes[2] then, and Dawks's *Letter*, and the Weekly Bill, till of late days.

PET. 'Slife, Witwoud, were you ever an attorney's clerk? Of the family of the Furnivals. Ha, ha, ha!

WIT. Aye, aye, but that was but for a while. Not long, not long; pshaw, I was not in my own power then. An orphan, and this fellow was my guardian; aye, aye, I was glad to consent to that man to come to London. He had the disposal of me then. If I had not agreed to that, I might have been bound 'prentice to a felt-maker in Shrewsbury; this fellow would have bound me to a maker of felts.

SIR WIL. 'Sheart, and better than to be bound to a maker of fops; where, I suppose, you have served your time; and now you may set up for yourself.

MRS. MAR. You intend to travel, sir, as I'm informed.

SIR WIL. Belike I may, madam. I may chance to sail upon the salt seas, if my mind hold.

PET. And the wind serve.

SIR WIL. Serve or not serve, I shan't ask license of you, sir; nor the weather-cock your companion. I direct my discourse to the lady, sir. 'Tis like my aunt may have told you, madam—Yes, I have settled my concerns, I may say now, and am minded to see foreign parts. If an' how that the peace[3] holds, whereby, that is, taxes abate.

9. Witwoud refers to the mutual greetings and felicitations of a group of barristers ("sergeants") newly admitted to the bar.
1. Before he had served out his apprenticeship. Furnival's Inn was one of the Inns of Chancery, attached to Lincoln's Inn. Attorneys were looked down on socially; hence Petulant's ill-natured mirth in his next speech.
2. Newspapers. Dawks's *News-Letter* was a popular source of news in the country. The Weekly Bill was the official list of the deaths occurring in London.
3. The peace established by the Treaty of Ryswick in 1697, which concluded the war against France waged under the leadership of William III by England, the Empire, Spain, and Holland. It endured until the spring of 1702, when the War of the Spanish Succession began.

MRS. MAR. I thought you had designed for France at all adventures.

SIR WIL. I can't tell that; 'tis like I may and 'tis like I may not. I am somewhat dainty[4] in making a resolution, because when I make it I keep it, I don't stand shill I, shall I,[5] then; if I say't, I'll do't. But I have thoughts to tarry a small matter in town, to learn somewhat of your lingo first, before I cross the seas. I'd gladly have a spice of your French as they say, whereby to hold discourse in foreign countries.

MRS. MAR. Here's an academy in town for that use.

SIR WIL. There is? 'Tis like there may.

MRS. MAR. No doubt you will return very much improved.

WIT. Yes, refined like a Dutch skipper from a whale-fishing.

SCENE 16

[To them] Lady Wishfort and Fainall.

LADY. Nephew, you are welcome.

SIR WIL. Aunt, your servant.

FAIN. Sir Wilfull, your most faithful servant.

SIR WIL. Cousin Fainall, give me your hand.

LADY. Cousin Witwoud, your servant; Mr. Petulant, your servant. —Nephew, you are welcome again. Will you drink anything after your journey, nephew, before you eat? Dinner's almost ready.

SIR WIL. I'm very well, I thank you, aunt. However, I thank you for your courteous offer. 'Sheart, I was afraid you would have been in the fashion too, and have remembered to have forgot your relations. Here's your cousin Tony, belike, I mayn't call him brother for fear of offense.

LADY. O, he's a rallier, nephew—my cousin's a wit; and your great wits always rally their best friends to choose.[6] When you have been abroad, nephew, you'll understand raillery better.

[FAIN. *and* MRS. MARWOOD *talk apart.*]

SIR WIL. Why then let him hold his tongue in the meantime, and rail when that day comes.

SCENE 17

[To them] Mincing.

MINC. Mem, I come to acquaint your la'ship that dinner is impatient.

SIR WIL. Impatient? Why then belike it won't stay till I pull off my boots. Sweetheart, can you help me to a pair of slippers?— My man's with his horses, I warrant.

LADY. Fie, fie, nephew, you would not pull off your boots here. Go down into the hall.—Dinner shall stay for you. My nephew's a little unbred; you'll pardon him, madam.—Gentlemen, will you walk? Marwood?

MRS. MAR. I'll follow you, madam—before Sir Wilfull is ready.

4. Scrupulous, cautious.   6. By choice.
5. Shilly-shally.

SCENE 18

Marwood, Fainall.

FAIN. Why then Foible's a bawd, an errant, rank, match-making bawd. And I it seems am a husband, a rank husband; and my wife a very errant, rank wife—all in the way of the world. 'Sdeath, to be a cuckold by anticipation, a cuckold in embryo? Sure I was born with budding antlers like a young satyr, or a citizen's child.[7] 'Sdeath, to be outwitted, to be outjilted—outmatrimonied. If I had kept my speed like a stag, 'twere somewhat, but to crawl after, with my horns like a snail, and be outstripped by my wife 'tis scurvy wedlock.

MRS. MAR. Then shake it off. You have often wished for an opportunity to part, and now you have it. But first prevent their plot.— The half of Millamant's fortune is too considerable to be parted with to a foe, to Mirabell.

FAIN. Damn him, that had been mine—had you not made that fond[8] discovery.—That had been forfeited, had they been married. My wife had added luster to my horns. By that increase of fortune, I could have worn 'em tipped with gold, though my forehead had been furnished like a Deputy-Lieutenant's hall.[9]

MRS. MAR. They may prove a cap of maintenance[1] to you still, if you can away with your wife. And she's no worse than when you had her—I dare swear she had given up her game, before she was married.

FAIN. Hum! That may be—

MRS. MAR. You married her to keep you, and if you can contrive to have her keep you better than you expected, why should you not keep her longer than you intended?

FAIN. The means, the means.

MRS. MAR. Discover to my lady your wife's conduct; threaten to part with her.—My lady loves her and will come to any composition to save her reputation. Take the opportunity of breaking it, just upon the discovery of this imposture. My lady will be enraged beyond bounds and sacrifice niece and fortune and all at that conjuncture. And let me alone to keep her warm; if she should flag in her part, I will not fail to prompt her.

FAIN. Faith, this has an appearance.

MRS. MAR. I'm sorry I hinted to my lady to endeavor a match between Millamant and Sir Wilfull. That may be an obstacle.

FAIN. O, for that matter leave me to manage him; I'll disable him for that; he will drink like a Dane; after dinner, I'll set his hand in.

---

7. "Satyr": a sylvan deity, usually represented with a goat's legs and horns. A cuckold is said to wear horns. Since the wives of "citizens" (merchants living in the old city of London, not the fashionable suburbs) were regarded by the rakes as their natural and easy prey, a "citizen's child" was born to be cuckolded.

8. Foolish.

9. I.e., the great hall in the house of the Deputy Lieutenant of a shire. Fainall imagines it ornamented with numerous antlers taken from deer slain in the hunt. The allusion, of course, is to the horns of a cuckold.

1. In heraldry, a cap with two points like horns.

MRS. MAR. Well, how do you stand affected towards your lady?

FAIN. Why, faith, I'm thinking of it. Let me see—I am married already; so that's over. My wife has played the jade with me—well, that's over too. I never loved her, or if I had, why that would have been over too by this time. Jealous of her I cannot be, for I am certain; so there's an end of jealousy. Weary of her I am and shall be—no, there's no end of that; no, no, that were too much to hope. Thus far concerning my repose. Now for my reputation. As to my own, I married not for it; so that's out of the question. And as to my part in my wife's—why, she had parted with hers before; so bringing none to me, she can take none from me; 'tis against all rule of play that I should lose to one who has not wherewithal to stake.

MRS. MAR. Besides you forget, marriage is honorable.

FAIN. Hum! Faith, and that's well thought on; marriage is honorable, as you say; and if so, wherefore should cuckoldom be a discredit, being derived from so honorable a root?

MRS. MAR. Nay, I know not; if the root be honorable, why not the branches?[2]

FAIN. So, so, why this point's clear. Well, how do we proceed?

MRS. MAR. I will contrive a letter which shall be delivered to my lady at the time when that rascal who is to act Sir Rowland is with her. It shall come as from an unknown hand—for the less I appear to know of the truth, the better I can play the incendiary. Besides, I would not have Foible provoked if I could help it, because you know she knows some passages—nay, I expect all will come out. But let the mine be sprung first, and then I care not if I am discovered.

FAIN. If the worst come to the worst, I'll turn my wife to grass—I have already a deed of settlement of the best part of her estate; which I wheedled out of her; and that you shall partake at least.

MRS. MAR. I hope you are convinced that I hate Mirabell now: you'll be no more jealous?

FAIN. Jealous, no—by this kiss.—Let husbands be jealous; but let the lover still believe: or if he doubt; let it be only to endear his pleasure, and prepare the joy that follows, when he proves his mistress true. But let husbands' doubts convert to endless jealousy; or if they have belief, let it corrupt to superstition and blind credulity. I am single, and will herd no more with 'em. True, I wear the badge, but I'll disown the order. And since I take my leave of 'em, I care not if I leave 'em a common motto to their common crest.

> All husbands must, or pain, or shame, endure;
> The wise too jealous are, fools too secure.

2. I.e., of the cuckold's horns.

Act IV—*Scene continues.*

SCENE 1

Lady Wishfort and Foible.

LADY. Is Sir Rowland coming, say'st thou, Foible? and are things in order?

FOIB. Yes, madam. I have put wax lights in the sconces, and placed the footmen in a row in the hall, in their best liveries, with the coachman and postilion to fill up the equipage.

LADY. Have you pulvilled[3] the coachman and postilion, that they may not stink of the stable, when Sir Rowland comes by?

FOIB. Yes, madam.

LADY. And are the dancers and the music ready, that he may be entertained in all points with correspondence to his passion?

FOIB. All is ready, madam.

LADY. And—well—and how do I look, Foible?

FOIB. Most killing well, madam.

LADY. Well, and how shall I receive him? In what figure shall I give his heart the first impression? There is a great deal in the first impression. Shall I sit?—No, I won't sit—I'll walk.—Aye, I'll walk from the door upon his entrance; and then turn full upon him.—No, that will be too sudden. I'll lie—aye, I'll lie down—I'll receive him in my little dressing-room, there's a couch.—Yes, yes, I'll give the first impression on a couch.—I won't lie neither, but loll and lean upon one elbow; with one foot a little dangling off, jogging in a thoughtful way—yes—and then as soon as he appears, start, aye, start and be surprised, and rise to meet him in a pretty disorder—yes. O, nothing is more alluring than a levee[4] from a couch in some confusion. It shows the foot to advantage and furnishes with blushes and recomposing airs beyond comparison. Hark! There's a coach.

FOIB. 'Tis he, madam.

LADY. O dear, has my nephew made his addresses to Millamant? I ordered him.

FOIB. Sir Wilfull is set in to drinking, madam, in the parlor.

LADY. 'Ods my life, I'll send him to her. Call her down, Foible; bring her hither. I'll send him as I go.—When they are together, then come to me, Foible, that I may not be too long alone with Sir Rowland.

SCENE 2

Mrs. Millamant, Mrs. Fainall, Foible.

FOIB. Madam, I stayed here to tell your ladyship that Mr. Mirabell has waited this half hour for an opportunity to talk with you. Though my lady's orders were to leave you and Sir Wilfull together. Shall I tell Mr. Mirabell that you are at leisure?

---

3. Sprinkled with perfumed powder.   4. A rising.

MILLA. No—What would the dear man have? I am thoughtful and would amuse myself.—Bid him come another time.

> There never yet was woman made,
> Nor shall, but to be cursed.[5]
>> [*Repeating and walking about.*]

That's hard!

MRS. FAIN. You are very fond of Sir John Suckling today, Millamant, and the poets.

MILLA. He? Aye and filthy verses—so I am.

FOIB. Sir Wilfull is coming, madam. Shall I send Mr. Mirabell away?

MILLA. Aye, if you please, Foible, send him away—or send him hither, just as you will, dear Foible. I think I'll see him—Shall I? Aye, let the wretch come.

> Thyrsis, a youth of the inspiréd train.[6]
>> [*Repeating.*]

Dear Fainall, entertain Sir Wilfull.—Thou hast philosophy to undergo a fool, thou art married and hast patience.—I would confer with my own thoughts.

MRS. FAIN. I am obliged to you that you would make me your proxy in this affair, but I have business of my own.

SCENE 3

[*To them*] Sir Wilfull.

MRS. FAIN. O Sir Wilfull; you are come at the critical instant. There's your mistress up to the ears in love and contemplation. Pursue your point, now or never.

SIR WIL. Yes; my aunt will have it so.—I would gladly have been encouraged with a bottle or two, because I'm somewhat wary at first, before I am acquainted; [*This while* MILLA. *walks about repeating to herself.*]—but I hope, after a time, I shall break my mind—that is upon further acquaintance.—So for the present, cousin, I'll take my leave.—If so be you'll be so kind to make my excuse, I'll return to my company.—

MRS. FAIN. O fie, Sir Wilfull! What, you must not be daunted.

SIR WIL. Daunted, no, that's not it; it is not so much for that—for if so be that I set on't, I'll do't. But only for the present, 'tis sufficient till further acquaintance, that's all.—Your servant.

MRS. FAIN. Nay, I'll swear you shall never lose so favorable an opportunity if I can help it. I'll leave you together and lock the door.

---

5. The opening lines of a poem by Sir John Suckling. Impelled by her love to accept Mirabell, but reluctant to give herself, Millamant broods over poems that speak of the brief happiness of lovers and the falseness of men.

6. The first line of Edmund Waller's *Story of Phoebus and Daphne Applied.* In the flight of the virgin nymph from the embraces of the amorous god, Millamant finds an emblem of her relations with Mirabell.

SCENE 4

Sir Wilfull, Millamant.

SIR WIL. Nay, nay, cousin—I have forgot my gloves.—What d'ye do? 'Sheart, a'has locked the door indeed, I think.—Nay, cousin Fainall, open the door.—Pshaw, what a vixen trick is this? Nay, now a'has seen me too.—Cousin, I made bold to pass through, as it were.—I think this door's enchanted.—

MILLA. [*repeating*]

> I prithee spare me, gentle boy,
> Press me no more for that slight toy.[7]

SIR WIL. Anan?[8] Cousin, your servant.

MILLA.—"That foolish trifle of a heart"—Sir Wilfull!

SIR WIL. Yes—your servant. No offense I hope, cousin.

MILLA. [*repeating*]

> I swear it will not do its part,
> Though thou dost thine, employ'st thy power and art.

Natural, easy Suckling!

SIR WIL. Anan? Suckling? No such suckling neither, cousin, nor stripling: I thank heaven I'm no minor.

MILLA. Ah rustic, ruder than Gothic.[9]

SIR WIL. Well, well, I shall understand your lingo one of these days, cousin. In the meanwhile I must answer in plain English.

MILLA. Have you any business with me, Sir Wilfull?

SIR WIL. Not at present, cousin.—Yes, I made bold to see, to come and know if that how you were disposed to fetch a walk this evening, if so be that I might not be troublesome, I would have sought a walk with you.

MILLA. A walk? What then?

SIR WIL. Nay nothing—only for the walk's sake, that's all—

MILLA. I nauseate walking; 'tis a country diversion. I loathe the country and everything that relates to it.

SIR WIL. Indeed! Hah! Look ye, look ye, you do? Nay, 'tis like you may.—Here are choice of pastimes here in town, as plays and the like; that must be confessed indeed.—

MILLA. Ah, *l'étourdi.*[1] I hate the town too.

SIR WIL. Dear heart, that's much—Hah! that you should hate 'em both! Hah! 'tis like you may; there are some can't relish the town, and others can't away with the country—'tis like you may be one of those, cousin.

MILLA. Ha, ha, ha. Yes, 'tis like I may. You have nothing further to say to me?

SIR WIL. Not at present, cousin. 'Tis like when I have an oppor-

7. The first lines of a song by Suckling.
8. "How's that?"
9. To the new age with its classical taste, medieval art, especially architecture, seemed crude ("rude").
1. I.e., "Oh, the silly fellow!" The French phrase forms the title of a comedy by Molière.

tunity to be more private, I may break my mind in some measure.—I conjecture you partly guess—however, that's as time shall try; but spare to speak and spare to speed, as they say.

MILLA. If it is of no great importance, Sir Wilfull, you will oblige me to leave me. I have just now a little business.

SIR WIL. Enough, enough, cousin. Yes, yes, all a case—when you're disposed, when you're disposed. Now's as well as another time; and another time as well as now. All's one for that.—Yes, yes, if your concerns call you, there's no haste; it will keep cold as they say.—Cousin, your servant. I think this door's locked.

MILLA. You may go this way, sir.

SIR WIL. Your servant—then with your leave I'll return to my company.

MILLA. Aye, aye. Ha, ha, ha.

Like Phœbus sung the no less amorous Boy.[2]

SCENE 5
Millamant, Mirabell.

MIRA.

Like Daphne she, as lovely and as coy.

Do you lock yourself up from me, to make my search more curious?[3] Or is this pretty artifice contrived to signify that here the chase must end, and my pursuit be crowned, for you can fly no further?

MILLA. Vanity! No—I'll fly and be followed to the last moment. Though I am upon the very verge of matrimony, I expect you should solicit me as much as if I were wavering at the grate of a monastery,[4] with one foot over the threshold. I'll be solicited to the very last, nay and afterwards.

MIRA. What, after the last?

MILLA. O, I should think I was poor and had nothing to bestow, if I were reduced to an inglorious ease; and freed from the agreeable fatigues of solicitation.

MIRA. But do not you know that when favors are conferred upon instant and tedious solicitation, that they diminish in their value and that both the giver loses the grace, and the receiver lessens his pleasure?

MILLA. It may be in things of common application, but never sure in love. O, I hate a lover that can dare to think he draws a moment's air, independent on the bounty of his mistress. There is not so impudent a thing in nature as the saucy look of an assured man, confident of success. The pedantic arrogance of a very husband has not so pragmatical[5] an air. Ah! I'll never marry, unless I am first made sure of my will and pleasure.

MIRA. Would you have 'em both before marriage? Or will you be

---

2. This, and the line that Mirabell caps it with, are from Waller's poem mentioned in note 6 (above).
3. Intricate, laborious.
4. The grated door of a convent.
5. Self-assured, conceited.

contented with the first now, and stay for the other till after grace?

MILLA. Ah, don't be impertinent.—My dear liberty, shall I leave thee? My faithful solitude, my darling contemplation, must I bid you then adieu? Ay-h adieu—My morning thoughts, agreeable wakings, indolent slumbers, all ye *douceurs,* ye *sommeils du matin,*[6] adieu.—I can't do't, 'tis more than impossible.—Positively, Mirabell, I'll lie abed in a morning as long as I please.

MIRA. Then I'll get up in a morning as early as I please.

MILLA. Ah, idle creature, get up when you will.—and d'ye hear? I won't be called names after I'm married; positively I won't be called names.

MIRA. Names!

MILLA. Aye, as wife, spouse, my dear, joy, jewel, love, sweetheart, and the rest of that nauseous cant, in which men and their wives are so fulsomely familiar—I shall never bear that.—Good Mirabell, don't let us be familiar or fond, nor kiss before folks, like my Lady Fadler[7] and Sir Francis; nor go to Hyde Park together the first Sunday in a new chariot, to provoke eyes and whispers; and then never be seen there together again, as if we were proud of one another the first week, and ashamed of one another ever after. Let us never visit together, nor go to a play together, but let us be very strange[8] and well bred; let us be as strange as if we had been married a great while; and as well bred as if we were not married at all.

MIRA. Have you any more conditions to offer? Hitherto your demands are pretty reasonable.

MILLA. Trifles—as liberty to pay and receive visits to and from whom I please; to write and receive letters, without interrogatories or wry faces on your part; to wear what I please; and choose conversation with regard only to my own taste; to have no obligation upon me to converse with wits that I don't like, because they are your acquaintance; or to be intimate with fools, because they may be your relations. Come to dinner when I please, dine in my dressing room when I'm out of humor, without giving a reason. To have my closet inviolate; to be sole empress of my tea table, which you must never presume to approach without first asking leave. And lastly, wherever I am, you shall always knock at the door before you come in. These articles subscribed, if I continue to endure you a little longer, I may by degrees dwindle into a wife.

MIRA. Your bill of fare is something advanced in this latter account. Well, have I liberty to offer conditions—that when you are dwindled into a wife, I may not be beyond measure enlarged into a husband?

MILLA. You have free leave, propose your utmost, speak and spare not.

MIRA. I thank you. *Imprimis*[9] then, I covenant that your acquaint-

6. I.e., soft (pleasures) and morning naps.
7. "Fondler."
8. Reserved.
9. In the first place, as in legal documents.

ance be general; that you admit no sworn confidante or intimate of your own sex; no she-friend to screen her affairs under your countenance and tempt you to make trial of a mutual secrecy. No decoy duck to wheedle you a fop—scrambling to the play in a mask—then bring you home in a pretended fright, when you think you shall be found out—and rail at me for missing the play, and disappointing the frolic which you had to pick me up and prove my constancy.

MILLA. Detestable *imprimis!* I go to the play in a mask!

MIRA. *Item,*[1] I article, that you continue to like your own face as long as I shall; and while it passes current with me, that you endeavor not to new coin it. To which end, together with all vizards[2] for the day, I prohibit all masks for the night, made of oiled-skins and I know not what—hog's bones, hare's gall, pig water, and the marrow of a roasted cat. In short, I forbid all commerce with the gentlewoman in what-d'ye-call-it court. *Item,* I shut my doors against all bawds with baskets, and pennyworths of muslin, china, fans, atlases,[3] etc. *Item,* when you shall be breeding—

MILLA. Ah! Name it not.

MIRA. Which may be presumed, with a blessing on our endeavors—

MILLA. Odious endeavors!

MIRA. I denounce against all strait lacing, squeezing for a shape, till you mold my boy's head like a sugar loaf; and instead of a man-child, make me father to a crooked billet.[4] Lastly, to the dominion of the tea table I submit.—But with proviso that you exceed not in your province; but restrain yourself to native and simple tea-table drinks, as tea, chocolate, and coffee. As likewise to genuine and authorized tea-table talk—such as mending of fashions, spoiling reputations, railing at absent friends, and so forth—but that on no account you encroach upon the men's prerogative, and presume to drink healths, or toast fellows; for prevention of which, I banish all foreign forces, all auxiliaries to the tea table, as orange brandy, all aniseed, cinnamon, citron and Barbados waters,[5] together with ratafia and the most noble spirit of clary.—But for cowslip-wine, poppy water, and all dormitives,[6] those I allow. These provisos admitted, in other things I may prove a tractable and complying husband.

MILLA. O, horrid provisos! filthy strong waters! I toast fellows, odious men! I hate your odious provisos.

MIRA. Then we're agreed. Shall I kiss your hand upon the contract? And here comes one to be a witness to the sealing of the deed.

---

1. Used to introduce each item in a list. "I article": I stipulate.
2. Masks. Cosmetics were made of materials as repulsive as those that Mirabell names.
3. Rich silk fabrics.

4. I.e., a crooked piece of firewood.
5. All of these "waters" are alcoholic drinks. "Clary": a sweet liqueur made of wine, honey, and spices.
6. Sleeping draughts.

SCENE 6

[To them] Mrs. Fainall.

MILLA. Fainall, what shall I do? Shall I have him? I think I must have him.

MRS. FAIN. Aye, aye, take him, take him. What should you do?

MILLA. Well then—I'll take my death I'm in a horrid fright—Fainall, I shall never say it—well—I think—I'll endure you.

MRS. FAIN. Fy, fy, have him, have him, and tell him so in plain terms: for I am sure you have a mind to him.

MILLA. Are you? I think I have—and the horrid man looks as if he thought so too.—Well, you ridiculous thing you, I'll have you.—I won't be kissed, nor I won't be thanked.—Here kiss my hand though.—So, hold your tongue now, don't say a word.

MRS. FAIN. Mirabell, there's a necessity for your obedience—you have neither time to talk nor stay. My mother is coming; and in my conscience if she should see you, would fall into fits, and maybe not recover, time enough to return to Sir Rowland; who, as Foible tells me, is in a fair way to succeed. Therefore spare your ectasies for another occasion, and slip down the back stairs, where Foible waits to consult you.

MILLA. Aye, go, go. In the meantime I suppose you have said something to please me.

MIRA. I am all obedience.

SCENE 7

Millamant, Mrs. Fainall.

MRS. FAIN. Yonder Sir Wilfull's drunk, and so noisy that my mother has been forced to leave Sir Rowland to appease him; but he answers her only with singing and drinking.—What they may have done by this time I know not, but Petulant and he were upon quarreling as I came by.

MILLA. Well, if Mirabell should not make a good husband, I am a lost thing; for I find I love him violently.

MRS. FAIN. So it seems, for you mind not what's said to you.—If you doubt him, you had best take up with Sir Wilfull.

MILLA. How can you name that superannuated lubber? foh!

SCENE 8

[To them] Witwoud from drinking.

MRS. FAIN. So, is the fray made up, that you have left 'em?

WIT. Left 'em? I could stay no longer—I have laughed like ten christenings—I am tipsy with laughing.—If I had stayed any longer, I should have burst—I must have been let out and pieced in the sides like an unsized camlet.[7]—Yes, yes, the fray is composed; my lady came in like a *nolle prosequi*[8] and stopped the

7. A fabric made by mixing wool and silk; "unsized" because not stiffened with some glutinous substance.

8. A phrase indicating the withdrawal of a lawsuit.

proceedings.

MILLA. What was the dispute?

WIT. That's the jest; there was no dispute. They could neither of 'em speak for rage; and so fell a-sputtering at one another like two roasting apples.

SCENE 9

[To them] Petulant drunk.

WIT. Now, Petulant? All's over, all's well? Gad, my head begins to whim it about.—Why dost thou not speak? Thou art both as drunk and as mute as a fish.

PET. Look you, Mrs. Millamant—if you can love me, dear nymph —say it—and that's the conclusion—pass on, or pass off—that's all.

WIT. Thou hast uttered volumes, folios, in less than decimo sexto,[9] my dear Lacedemonian. Sirrah Petulant, thou art an epitomizer of words.

PET. Witwoud—You are an annihilator of sense.

WIT. Thou art a retailer of phrases, and dost deal in remnants of remnants, like a maker of pincushions. Thou art in truth (metaphorically speaking) a speaker of shorthand.

PET. Thou art (without a figure) just one-half of an ass, and Baldwin[1] yonder, thy half brother, is the rest.—A Gemini of asses split, would make just four of you.

WIT. Thou dost bite, my dear mustard-seed; kiss me for that.

PET. Stand off—I'll kiss no more males.—I have kissed your twin yonder in a humor of reconciliation, till he—[*hiccup*]—rises upon my stomach like a radish.

MILLA. Eh! filthy creature.—What was the quarrel?

PET. There was no quarrel—there might have been a quarrel.

WIT. If there had been words enow between 'em to have expressed provocation, they had gone together by the ears like a pair of castanets.

PET. You were the quarrel.

MILLA. Me!

PET. If I have a humor to quarrel, I can make less matters conclude premises.—If you are not handsome, what then, if I have a humor to prove it?—If I shall have my reward, say so; if not, fight for your face the next time yourself.—I'll go sleep.

WIT. Do, wrap thyself up like a woodlouse, and dream revenge—and hear me, if thou canst learn to write by tomorrow morning, pen me a challenge.—I'll carry it for thee.

PET. Carry your mistress's monkey a spider[2]—go flea dogs, and read

9. "Folios" are books of the largest size, as "decimo sexto" means a book of the smallest size. The Spartans ("Lacedemonians") were men of few words.
1. The name of the ass in the beast epic, *Reynard the Fox*. "Gemini," the twin Roman deities, Castor and Pollux, for whom one of the signs of the zodiac is named.
2. Monkeys were supposed to eat spiders. Petulant scornfully contrasts what he imagines to be Witwoud's technique with his lady and his own more vigorous and direct program for the rest of the evening.

romances—I'll go to bed to my maid.

MRS. FAIN. He's horridly drunk—how came you all in this pickle?

WIT. A plot, a plot, to get rid of the knight—your husband's advice; but he sneaked off.

SCENE 10

Sir Wilfull drunk, Lady Wishfort, Witwoud,
Millamant, Mrs. Fainall.

LADY. Out upon't, out upon't! At years of discretion, and comport yourself at this rantipole[3] rate!

SIR WIL. No offense, aunt.

LADY. Offense? As I'm a person, I'm ashamed of you.—Fogh! how you stink of wine! D'ye think my niece will ever endure such a borachio![4] you're an absolute borachio.

SIR WIL. Borachio!

LADY. At a time when you should commence an amour, and put your best foot foremost—

SIR WIL. 'Sheart, an you grutch[5] me your liquor, make a bill.—Give me more drink, and take my purse.

> [*Sings.*]   Prithee fill me the glass
>   'Till it laugh in my face,
> With ale that is potent and mellow;
>   He that whines for a lass
>   Is an ignorant ass,
> For a bumper[6] has not its fellow.

But if you would have me marry my cousin—say the word and I'll do't—Wilfull will do't, that's the word—Wilfull will do't, that's my crest—my motto I have forgot.[6a]

LADY. My nephew's a little overtaken, cousin—but 'tis with drinking your health—O' my word you are obliged to him—

SIR WIL. *In vino veritas*,[7] aunt.—If I drunk your health today, cousin—I am a borachio. But if you have a mind to be married, say the word, and send for the piper; Wilfull will do't. If not, dust it away, and let's have t'other round.—Tony, 'ods heart, where's Tony?—Tony's an honest fellow, but he spits after a bumper, and that's a fault—

> [*Sings.*]   We'll drink and we'll never ha' done, boys,
>   Put the glass then around with the sun, boys,
> Let Apollo's example invite us;
>   For he's drunk every night,
>   And that makes him so bright,
> That he's able next morning to light us.

The sun's a good pimple,[8] an honest soaker, he has a cellar at your Antipodes. If I travel, aunt, I touch at your Antipodes.—

3. Rakish.
4. Drunkard. The word is Spanish.
5. Grudge.
6. A wineglass filled to the brim; the word comes from the custom of touching (bumping) glasses when drinking toasts.

6a. A coat of arms had a crest—a helmet surmounting the shield—and a motto. In his drunkenness, Sir Wilfull confuses the two.
7. "In wine [there is] truth."
8. Boon companion.

Your Antipodes are a good rascally sort of topsy-turvy fellows.—
If I had a bumper, I'd stand upon my head and drink a health to
'em.—A match or no match, cousin, with the hard name?—aunt,
Wilfull will do't. If she has her maidenhead, let her look to't;
if she has not, let her keep her own counsel in the meantime, and
cry out at the nine months' end.

MILLA. Your pardon, madam, I can stay no longer—Sir Wilfull
grows very powerful. Egh! how he smells! I shall be overcome if
I stay. Come, cousin.

SCENE 11

Lady Wishfort, Sir Wilfull Witwoud, Mr. Witwoud, Foible.

LADY. Smells! he would poison a tallow-chandler and his family.
Beastly creature, I know not what to do with him. Travel, quoth
a'; aye, travel, travel, get thee gone, get thee but far enough, to
the Saracens, or the Tartars, or the Turks—for thou art not fit
to live in a Christian commonwealth, thou beastly pagan.

SIR WIL. Turks, no; no Turks, aunt. Your Turks are infidels, and
believe not in the grape. Your Mahometan, your Mussulman is
a dry stinkard.—No offense, aunt. My map says that your Turk is
not so honest a man as your Christian.—I cannot find by the
map that your Mufti[9] is orthodox—whereby it is a plain case,
that orthodox is a hard word, aunt, and—[*hiccup*]—Greek for
claret.

[*Sings.*]   To drink is a Christian diversion.
        Unknown to the Turk or the Persian:
           Let Mahometan fools
           Live by heathenish rules,
        And be damned over tea cups and coffee.
           But let British lads sing,
           Crown a health to the king,
        And a fig for your sultan and sophy.[1]

    Ah, Tony!

                    [FOIBLE *whispers* LADY W.]

LADY. Sir Rowland impatient? Good lack! what shall I do with this
beastly tumbrel?[2]—Go lie down and sleep, you sot—or as I'm
a person, I'll have you bastinadoed with broomsticks. Call up
the wenches with broomsticks.

SIR WIL. Ahay? Wenches, where are the wenches?

LADY. Dear cousin Witwoud, get him away, and you will bind me
to you inviolably. I have an affair of moment that invades me
with some precipitation—you will oblige me to all futurity.

WIT. Come, knight.—Pox on him, I don't know what to say to
him.—Will you go to a cockmatch?

SIR WIL. With a wench, Tony? Is she a shakebag,[3] sirrah? Let me

9. The Grand Mufti, head of the state
religion of Turkey. Moslems do not use
alcohol.
1. The Shah of Persia.

2. Dung cart. "To bastinado" is to punish by beating the soles of the feet.
3. Gamecock.

bite your cheek for that.

WIT. Horrible! He has a breath like a bagpipe.—Aye, aye, come, will you march, my Salopian?[4]

SIR WIL. Lead on, little Tony—I'll follow thee, my Anthony, my Tantony. Sirrah, thou shalt be my Tantony, and I'll be thy pig.[5]

—And a fig for your sultan and sophy.

LADY. This will never do. It will never make a match—at least before he has been abroad.

SCENE 12

Lady Wishfort, Waitwell disguised as for Sir Rowland.

LADY. Dear Sir Rowland, I am confounded with confusion at the retrospection of my own rudeness—I have more pardons to ask than the Pope distributes in the Year of Jubilee. But I hope where there is likely to be so near an alliance—we may unbend the severity of decorum—and dispense with a little ceremony.

WAIT. My impatience, madam, is the effect of my transport—and till I have the possession of your adorable person, I am tantalized on the rack;[5a] and do but hang, madam, on the tenter[6] of expectation.

LADY. You have excess of gallantry, Sir Rowland; and press things to a conclusion, with a most prevailing vehemence.—But a day or two for decency of marriage.—

WAIT. For decency of funeral, madam. The delay will break my heart—or if that should fail, I shall be poisoned. My nephew will get an inkling of my designs, and poison me—and I would willingly starve him before I die—I would gladly go out of the world with that satisfaction.—That would be some comfort to me, if I could but live so long as to be revenged on that unnatural viper.

LADY. Is he so unnatural, say you? Truly I would contribute much both to the saving of your life, and the accomplishment of your revenge—Not that I respect[7] myself; though he has been a perfidious wretch to me.

WAIT. Perfidious to you!

LADY. O Sir Rowland, the hours that he has died away at my feet, the tears that he has shed, the oaths that he has sworn, the palpitations that he has felt, the trances and the tremblings, the ardors and the ecstasies, the kneelings, and the risings, the heart-heavings and the hand-gripings, the pangs and the pathetic regards of his protesting eyes! Oh, no memory can register.

WAIT. What, my rival! Is the rebel my rival? a'dies.

LADY. No, don't kill him at once, Sir Rowland, starve him gradually inch by inch.

---

4. Inhabitant of Shropshire.
5. St. Anthony (hence "Tantony"), the patron of swineherds, was represented accompanied by a pig.
5a. Waitwell mixes his metaphors. Tantalus, from whose name we derive the word *tantalize*, was not tortured on the rack. In Hades he was placed in a pool of water that receded from his lips when he tried to drink and under fruit trees whose boughs blew out of his reach when he tried to pluck the fruit.
6. A frame for stretching cloth on hooks so that it may dry without losing its original shape (cf. the phrase "to be on tenterhooks").
7. Consider.

WAIT. I'll do't. In three weeks he shall be barefoot; in a month out
at knees with begging an alms—he shall starve upward and upward, till he has nothing living but his head, and then go out
in a stink like a candle's end upon a saveall.[8]

LADY. Well, Sir Rowland, you have the way.—You are no novice
in the labyrinth of love—you have the clue—but as I am a person, Sir Rowland, you must not attribute my yielding to any
sinister appetite, or indigestion of widowhood; nor impute my
complacency to any lethargy of continence.—I hope you do
not think me prone to any iteration of nuptials.—

WAIT. Far be it from me—

LADY. If you do, I protest I must recede—or think that I have made
a prostitution of decorums, but in the vehemence of compassion,
and to save the life of a person of so much importance—

WAIT. I esteem it so—

LADY. Or else you wrong my condescension—

WAIT. I do not, I do not—

LADY. Indeed you do.

WAIT. I do not, fair shrine of virtue.

LADY. If you think the least scruple of carnality was an ingredient—

WAIT. Dear madam, no. You are all camphire[9] and frankincense, all
chastity and odor.

LADY. Or that—

SCENE 13

[To them] Foible.

FOIB. Madam, the dancers are ready, and there's one with a letter,
who must deliver it into your own hands.

LADY. Sir Rowland, will you give me leave? Think favorably, judge
candidly, and conclude you have found a person who would
suffer racks in honor's cause, dear Sir Rowland, and will wait on
you incessantly.[1]

SCENE 14

Waitwell, Foible.

WAIT. Fie, fie!—What a slavery have I undergone; spouse, hast
thou any cordial? I want spirits.

FOIB. What a washy rogue art thou, to pant thus for a quarter of an
hour's lying and swearing to a fine lady?

WAIT. O, she is the antidote to desire. Spouse, thou wilt fare the
worse for't—I shall have no appetite for iteration of nuptials—
this eight and forty hours—by this hand I'd rather be a chairman in the dog days[2]—than act Sir Rowland till this time tomorrow.

8. A small pan inserted into a candlestick to catch the drippings of the
candle.
9. Camphor was considered an effective
antidote to sexual desire.
1. Immediately.

2. I.e., one who carries a sedan chair
during the hottest part of the summer.
July and August were called the "dog
days" because during these months the
Dog Star, Sirius, rises and sets with the
sun.

[*To them*] *Lady with a letter.*

LADY. Call in the dancers.—Sir Rowland, we'll sit, if you please, and see the entertainment.

[*Dance.*]

Now with your permission, Sir Rowland, I will peruse my letter. —I would open it in your presence, because I would not make you uneasy. If it should make you uneasy, I would burn it— speak if it does—but you may see, the superscription is like a woman's hand.

FOIB. [*to him*] By heaven! Mrs. Marwood's, I know it—my heart aches—get it from her.—

WAIT. A woman's hand? No, madam, that's no woman's hand, I see that already. That's somebody whose throat must be cut.

LADY. Nay, Sir Rowland, since you give me a proof of your passion by your jealousy, I promise you I'll make a return, by a frank communication—you shall see it—we'll open it together—look you here.—[*Reads.*]—*Madam, though unknown to you* (Look you there, 'tis from nobody that I know.)—*I have that honor for your character, that I think myself obliged to let you know you are abused. He who pretends to be Sir Rowland is a cheat and a rascal*—O Heavens! what's this?

FOIB. Unfortunate, all's ruined.

WAIT. How, how, let me see, let me see—[*Reads.*]—*A rascal and disguised, and suborned for that imposture*—O villainy! O villainy!—*by the contrivance of*—

LADY. I shall faint, I shall die, oh!

FOIB. [*to him*] Say, 'tis your nephew's hand.—Quickly, his plot, swear, swear it.—

WAIT. Here's a villain! Madam, don't you perceive it, don't you see it?

LADY. Too well, too well. I have seen too much.

WAIT. I told you at first I knew the hand—A woman's hand? The rascal writes a sort of a large hand, your Roman hand—I saw there was a throat to be cut presently. If he were my son, as he is my nephew, I'd pistol him—

FOIB. O treachery! But are you sure, Sir Rowland, it is his writing?

WAIT. Sure? Am I here? Do I live? Do I love this pearl of India? I have twenty letters in my pocket from him in the same character.

LADY. How!

FOIB. O, what luck it is, Sir Rowland, that you were present at this juncture! This was the business that brought Mr. Mirabell disguised to Madam Millamant this afternoon. I thought something was contriving, when he stole by me and would have hid his face.

LADY. How, how!—I heard the villain was in the house indeed; and now I remember, my niece went away abruptly, when Sir Wilfull was to have made his addresses.

FOIB. Then, then, madam, Mr. Mirabell waited for her in her chamber; but I would not tell your ladyship to discompose you when you were to receive Sir Rowland.

WAIT. Enough, his date is short.

FOIB. No, good Sir Rowland, don't incur the law.

WAIT. Law! I care not for law. I can but die, and 'tis in a good cause—my lady shall be satisfied of my truth and innocence, though it cost me my life.

LADY. No, dear Sir Rowland, don't fight. If you should be killed I must never show my face—or be hanged—O, consider my reputation, Sir Rowland—no, you shan't fight—I'll go and examine my niece; I'll make her confess. I conjure you, Sir Rowland, by all your love not to fight.

WAIT. I am charmed, madam, I obey. But some proof you must let me give you—I'll go for a black box, which contains the writings of my whole estate, and deliver that into your hands.

LADY. Aye, dear Sir Rowland, that will be some comfort. Bring the black box.

WAIT. And may I presume to bring a contract to be signed this night? May I hope so far?

LADY. Bring what you will; but come alive, pray come alive. O, this is a happy discovery.

WAIT. Dead or alive I'll come—and married we will be in spite of treachery; aye, and get an heir that shall defeat the last remaining glimpse of hope in my abandoned nephew. Come, my buxom widow:

> E'er long you shall substantial proof receive
> That I'm an arrant[3] knight——

FOIB.   Or arrant knave.

Act V—Scene continues.

SCENE 1

Lady Wishfort and Foible.

LADY. Out of my house, out of my house, thou viper, thou serpent, that I have fostered; thou bosom traitress, that I raised from nothing.—Begone, begone, begone, go, go—that I took from washing of old gauze and weaving of dead hair,[4] with a bleak blue nose over a chafing dish of starved embers, and dining behind a traverse rag,[5] in a shop no bigger than a bird cage—go, go, starve again, do, do.

FOIB. Dear madam, I'll beg pardon on my knees.

3. The two words *errant* ("wandering," as in "knight-errant") and *arrant* ("thorough-going," "notorious") were originally the same and were still pronounced alike. This makes possible Foible's pun.
4. Foible had been a wigmaker.
5. A worn cloth, used to curtain off part of a room.

LADY. Away, out, out, go set up for yourself again.—Do, drive a trade, do, with your three-pennyworth of small ware, flaunting upon a packthread, under a brandy-seller's bulk or against a dead wall by a ballad-monger. Go, hang out an old frisoneer-gorget,[6] with a yard of yellow colberteen again; do; an old gnawed mask, two rows of pins and a child's fiddle; a glass necklace with the beads broken, and a quilted nightcap with one ear. Go, go, drive a trade—these were your commodities, you treacherous trull, this was the merchandise you dealt in when I took you into my house, placed you next myself, and made you governante[7] of my whole family. You have forgot this, have you, now you have feathered your nest?

FOIB. No, no, dear madam. Do but hear me, have but a moment's patience—I'll confess all. Mr. Mirabell seduced me; I am not the first that he has wheedled with his dissembling tongue. Your ladyship's own wisdom has been deluded by him; then how should I, a poor ignorant, defend myself? O madam, if you knew but what he promised me, and how he assured me your ladyship should come to no damage—or else the wealth of the Indies should not have bribed me to conspire against so good, so sweet, so kind a lady as you have been to me.

LADY. No damage? What, to betray me, to marry me to a cast[8] servingman; to make me a receptacle, an hospital for a decayed pimp? No damage? O, thou frontless[9] impudence, more than a big-bellied actress.

FOIB. Pray do but hear me, madam. He could not marry your ladyship, madam.—No, indeed, his marriage was to have been void in law; for he was married to me first, to secure your ladyship. He could not have bedded your ladyship; for if he had consummated with your ladyship, he must have run the risk of the law, and been put upon his clergy.[1]—Yes, indeed, I inquired of the law in that case before I would meddle or make.[2]

LADY. What, then I have been your property, have I? I have been convenient to you, it seems.—While you were catering for Mirabell, I have been broker for you? What, have you made a passive bawd of me?—This exceeds all precedent; I am brought to fine uses, to become a botcher[3] of second-hand marriages between Abigails and Andrews! I'll couple you. Yes, I'll baste you together, you and your philander.[4] I'll Duke's-Place you, as I'm a person. Your turtle is in custody already: you shall coo in the same cage, if there be constable or warrant in the parish.

---

6. A woolen garment that covers the neck and breast. "Colberteen": a French imitation of Italian lace.
7. Housekeeper.
8. Cast off, discharged.
9. Shameless.
1. I.e., pleaded "benefit of clergy," originally the privilege of the clergy to be tried for felony before ecclesiastical, not secular, courts; by Congreve's time it had become the privilege to plead exemption from a penal sentence granted a person who could read and was a first offender.
2. A dialectal phrase; the two words mean approximately the same thing.
3. A mender of old clothes; Lady Wishfort means something like "a patcher-up of marriages." "Abigail" and "Andrew" were generic names for maidservants and servingmen.
4. Lover. For "Duke's Place," see Act I, Scene 2, note 5.

FOIB. O, that ever I was born, O, that I was ever married.—A bride, aye, I shall be a Bridewell-bride.[5] Oh!

SCENE 2

Mrs. Fainall, Foible.

MRS. FAIN. Poor Foible, what's the matter?

FOIB. O madam, my lady's gone for a constable. I shall be had to a justice, and put to Bridewell to beat hemp; poor Waitwell's gone to prison already.

MRS. FAIN. Have a good heart, Foible. Mirabell's gone to give security for him. This is all Marwood's and my husband's doing.

FOIB. Yes, yes, I know it, madam; she was in my lady's closet, and overheard all that you said to me before dinner. She sent the letter to my lady; and that missing effect, Mr. Fainall laid this plot to arrest Waitwell, when he pretended to go for the papers; and in the meantime Mrs. Marwood declared all to my lady.

MRS. FAIN. Was there no mention made of me in the letter?—My mother does not suspect my being in the confederacy? I fancy Marwood has not told her, though she has told my husband.

FOIB. Yes, madam; but my lady did not see that part. We stifled the letter before she read so far. Has that mischievous devil told Mr. Fainall of your ladyship then?

MRS. FAIN. Aye, all's out, my affair with Mirabell, everything discovered. This is the last day of our living together, that's my comfort.

FOIB. Indeed, madam, and so 'tis a comfort if you knew all.—He has been even with your ladyship; which I could have told you long enough since, but I love to keep peace and quietness by my good will. I had rather bring friends together than set 'em at distance. But Mrs. Marwood and he are nearer related than ever their parents thought for!

MRS. FAIN. Say'st thou so, Foible? Canst thou prove this?

FOIB. I can take my oath of it, madam. So can Mrs. Mincing; we have had many a fair word from Madam Marwood, to conceal something that passed in our chamber one evening when you were at Hyde Park—and we were thought to have gone a-walking; but we went up unawares—though we were sworn to secrecy too; Madam Marwood took a book and swore us upon it, but it was but a book of poems.—So long as it was not a Bible-oath, we may break it with a safe conscience.

MRS. FAIN. This discovery is the most opportune thing I could wish. Now, Mincing?

SCENE 3

[To them] Mincing.

MINC. My lady would speak with Mrs. Foible, mem. Mr. Mirabell is with her; he has set your spouse at liberty, Mrs. Foible, and

5. Bridewell was the house of correction for women in London.

would have you hide yourself in my lady's closet, till my old
lady's anger is abated. O, my old lady is in a perilous passion,
at something Mr. Fainall has said; he swears, and my old lady
cries. There's a fearful hurricane, I vow. He says, mem, how
that he'll have my lady's fortune made over to him, or he'll be
divorced.

MRS. FAIN. Does your lady or Mirabell know that?

MINC. Yes, mem, they have sent me to see if Sir Wilfull be sober,
and to bring him to them. My lady is resolved to have him, I
think, rather than lose such a vast sum as six thousand pound.
O, come, Mrs. Foible, I hear my old lady.

MRS. FAIN. Foible, you must tell Mincing that she must prepare to
vouch when I call her.

FOIB. Yes, yes, madam.

MINC. O yes, mem, I'll vouch anything for your ladyship's service,
be what it will.

SCENE 4

Mrs. Fainall, Lady Wishfort, Marwood.

LADY. O my dear friend, how can I enumerate the benefits that I
have received from your goodness? To you I owe the timely discovery of the false vows of Mirabell; to you I owe the detection
of the impostor Sir Rowland. And now you are become an intercessor with my son-in-law, to save the honor of my house,
and compound for the frailties of my daughter. Well, friend,
you are enough to reconcile me to the bad world, or else I would
retire to deserts and solitudes; and feed harmless sheep by groves
and purling streams. Dear Marwood, let us leave the world and
retire by ourselves and be shepherdesses.

MRS. MAR. Let us first dispatch the affair in hand, madam. We shall
have leisure to think of retirement afterwards. Here is one who
is concerned in the treaty.

LADY. O daughter, daughter, is it possible thou should'st be my
child, bone of my bone, and flesh of my flesh, and as I may say,
another me, and yet transgress the most minute particle of severe
virtue? Is it possible you should lean aside to iniquity, who have
been cast in the direct mold of virtue? I have not only been a
mold but a pattern for you, and a model for you, after you were
brought into the world.

MRS. FAIN. I don't understand your ladyship.

LADY. Not understand? Why, have you not been naught?[6] Have
you not been sophisticated? Not understand? Here I am ruined
to compound[7] for your caprices and your cuckoldoms. I must
pawn my plate and my jewels, and ruin my niece, and all little
enough—

MRS. FAIN. I am wronged and abused, and so are you. 'Tis a false
accusation, as false as hell, as false as your friend there, aye, or

6. Wicked. "Sophisticated": corrupted.   7. I.e., come to terms by making a
monetary settlement.

your friend's friend, my false husband.

MRS. MAR. My friend, Mrs. Fainall? Your husband my friend, what do you mean?

MRS. FAIN. I know what I mean, madam, and so do you; and so shall the world at a time convenient.

MRS. MAR. I am sorry to see you so passionate, madam. More temper[8] would look more like innocence. But I have done. I am sorry my zeal to serve your ladyship and family should admit of misconstruction, or make me liable to affront. You will pardon me, madam, if I meddle no more with an affair in which I am not personally concerned.

LADY. O dear friend, I am so ashamed that you should meet with such returns.—You ought to ask pardon on your knees, ungrateful creature; she deserves more from you than all your life can accomplish—O, don't leave me destitute in this perplexity—no, stick to me, my good genius.

MRS. FAIN. I tell you, madam, you're abused—Stick to you? aye, like a leech, to suck your best blood—She'll drop off when she's full. Madam, you shan't pawn a bodkin,[9] nor part with a brass counter, in composition for me. I defy 'em all. Let 'em prove their aspersions; I know my own innocence, and dare stand a trial.

SCENE 5

Lady Wishfort, Marwood.

LADY. Why, if she should be innocent, if she should be wronged after all, ha? I don't know what to think—and I promise you, her education has been unexceptionable—I may say it; for I chiefly made it my own care to initiate her very infancy in the rudiments of virtue, and to impress upon her tender years a young odium and aversion to the very sight of men.—Aye, friend, she would have shrieked if she had but seen a man, till she was in her teens. As I'm a person, 'tis true—she was never suffered to play with a male child, though but in coats. Nay, her very babies[1] were of the feminine gender—O, she never looked a man in the face but her own father, or the chaplain, and him we made a shift to put upon her for a woman, by the help of his long garments, and his sleek face; till she was going in her fifteen.

MRS. MAR. 'Twas much she should be deceived so long.

LADY. I warrant you, or she would never have borne to have been catechized by him; and have heard his long lectures against singing and dancing, and such debaucheries; and going to filthy plays; and profane music-meetings, where the lewd trebles squeek nothing but bawdry, and the basses roar blasphemy. O, she would have swooned at the sight or name of an obscene play-book— and can I think after all this, that my daughter can be naught?

8. Moderation.
9. An ornamental hairpin. "Counter," an imitation coin, used in games of chance.
1. Dolls.

What, a whore? And thought it excommunication to set her foot within the door of a playhouse? O dear friend, I can't believe it, no, no; as she says, let him prove it, let him prove it.

MRS. MAR. Prove it, madam? What, and have your name prostituted in a public court; yours and your daughter's reputation worried at the bar by a pack of bawling lawyers? To be ushered in with an O Yes[2] of scandal; and have your case opened by an old fumbler lecher in a quoif[3] like a man midwife, to bring your daughter's infamy to light; to be a theme for legal punsters, and quibblers by the statute; and become a jest, against a rule of court, where there is no precedent for a jest in any record; not even in Doomsday Book;[4] to discompose the gravity of the bench, and provoke naughty interrogatories in more naughty law-Latin; while the good judge, tickled with the proceeding, simpers under a gray beard, and figes off and on his cushion as if he had swallowed cantharides, or sate upon cowhage.[5]

LADY. O, 'tis very hard!

MRS. MAR. And then to have my young revelers of the Temple[6] take notes, like 'prentices at a conventicle; and after talk it over again in commons, or before drawers in an eating house.

LADY. Worse and worse.

MRS. MAR. Nay, this is nothing; if it would end here 'twere well. But it must after this be consigned by the shorthand writers to the public press; and from thence be transferred to the hands, nay into the throats and lungs of hawkers, with voices more licentious than the loud flounderman's;[7] and this you must hear till you are stunned; nay, you must hear nothing else for some days.

LADY. O, 'tis insupportable. No, no, dear friend, make it up, make it up; aye, aye, I'll compound. I'll give up all, myself and my all, my niece and her all—anything, everything for composition.

MRS. MAR. Nay, madam, I advise nothing; I only lay before you, as a friend, the inconveniencies which perhaps you have overseen.[8] Here comes Mr. Fainall. If he will be satisfied to huddle up all in silence, I shall be glad. You must think I would rather congratulate than condole with you.

SCENE 6

Fainall, Lady Wishfort, Mrs. Marwood.

LADY. Aye, aye, I do not doubt it, dear Marwood. No, no, I do not doubt it.

FAIN. Well, madam; I have suffered myself to be overcome by the importunity of this lady, your friend, and am content you shall enjoy your own proper estate during life; on condition you oblige

2. The formula for opening court, a variant of Old French *Oyez*, "Hear ye."
3. The cap of a sergeant-at-law.
4. Or Domesday Book, the survey of England made in 1085–86 by William the Conqueror.
5. "Figes": fidgets; "cantharides" (or Spanish fly) is an irritant; "cowhage": a plant that causes intolerable itching.
6. The law students at the Temple, one of the Inns of Court.
7. A seller of flounders, well known throughout London for his loud voice.
8. Overlooked.

yourself never to marry, under such penalty as I think convenient.

LADY. Never to marry?

FAIN. No more Sir Rowlands—the next imposture may not be so timely detected.

MRS. MAR. That condition, I dare answer, my lady will consent to, without difficulty; she has already but too much experienced the perfidiousness of men. Besides, madam, when we retire to our pastoral solitude we shall bid adieu to all other thoughts.

LADY. Aye, that's true; but in case of necessity; as of health, or some such emergency—

FAIN. O, if you are prescribed marriage, you shall be considered; I will only reserve to myself the power to choose for you. If your physic be wholesome, it matters not who is your apothecary. Next, my wife shall settle on me the remainder of her fortune, not made over already; and for her maintenance depend entirely on my discretion.

LADY. This is most inhumanly savage; exceeding the barbarity of a Muscovite husband.

FAIN. I learned it from His Czarish Majesty's retinue,[9] in a winter evening's conference over brandy and pepper, amongst other secrets of matrimony and policy, as they are at present practiced in the northern hemisphere. But this must be agreed unto, and that positively. Lastly, I will be endowed, in right of my wife, with that six thousand pound, which is the moiety of Mrs. Millamant's fortune in your possession; and which she has forfeited (as will appear by the last will and testament of your deceased husband, Sir Jonathan Wishfort) by her disobedience in contracting herself against your consent or knowledge; and by refusing the offered match with Sir Wilfull Witwoud, which you, like a careful aunt, had provided for her.

LADY. My nephew was *non compos*,[1] and could not make his addresses.

FAIN. I come to make demands—I'll hear no objections.

LADY. You will grant me time to consider?

FAIN. Yes, while the instrument is drawing, to which you must set your hand till more sufficient deeds can be perfected: which I will take care shall be done with all possible speed. In the meanwhile I will go for the said instrument, and till my return you may balance this matter in your own discretion.

SCENE 7

Lady Wishfort, Mrs. Marwood.

LADY. This insolence is beyond all precedent, all parallel; must I be subject to this merciless villain?

MRS. MAR. 'Tis severe indeed, madam, that you should smart for your daughter's wantonness.

LADY. 'Twas against my consent that she married this barbarian,

9. Peter the Great of Russia visited London in 1698.

1. I.e., *non compos mentis,* "of unsound mind."

but she would have him, though her year was not out.[2]—Ah! her first husband, my son Languish, would not have carried it thus. Well, that was my choice, this is hers; she is matched now with a witness[3]—I shall be mad, dear friend. Is there no comfort for me? Must I live to be confiscated at this rebel-rate?— Here comes two more of my Egyptian plagues,[4] too.

SCENE 8

[To them] Millamant, Sir Wilfull.

SIR WIL. Aunt, your servant.

LADY. Out, caterpillar, call not me aunt; I know thee not.

SIR WIL. I confess I have been a little in disguise,[5] as they say— 'Sheart! and I'm sorry for't. What would you have? I hope I committed no offense, aunt—and if I did, I am willing to make satisfaction; and what can a man say fairer? If I have broke anything, I'll pay for't, and it cost a pound. And so let that content for what's past, and make no more words. For what's to come, to pleasure you I'm willing to marry my cousin. So, pray, let's all be friends. She and I are agreed upon the matter before a witness.

LADY. How's this, dear niece? Have I any comfort? Can this be true?

MILLA. I am content to be a sacrifice to your repose, madam; and to convince you that I had no hand in the plot, as you were misinformed, I have laid my commands on Mirabell to come in person, and be a witness that I give my hand to this flower of knighthood; and for the contract that passed between Mirabell and me, I have obliged him to make a resignation of it in your ladyship's presence.—He is without, and waits your leave for admittance.

LADY. Well, I'll swear I am something revived at this testimony of your obedience; but I cannot admit that traitor—I fear I cannot fortify myself to support his appearance. He is as terrible to me as a Gorgon;[6] if I see him, I fear I shall turn to stone, petrify incessantly.

MILLA. If you disoblige him, he may resent your refusal, and insist upon the contract still. Then 'tis the last time he will be offensive to you.

LADY. Are you sure it will be the last time?—If I were sure of that —Shall I never see him again?

MILLA. Sir Wilfull, you and he are to travel together, are you not?

SIR WIL. 'Sheart, the gentleman's a civil gentleman, aunt, let him come in; why, we are sworn brothers and fellow travelers. We are to be Pylades[7] and Orestes, he and I. He is to be my inter-

2. The conventional period of mourning for a widow was one year.
3. With a vengeance.
4. The plagues visited by Moses on Pharaoh until he agreed to release the Israelites from bondage (Exodus vii– xii).
5. Drunk.
6. In Greek mythology, a hideous monster with snakes in her hair. Her glance turned men to stone.
7. The constant friend who journeyed with Orestes, the son and avenger of the murdered King Agamemnon.

preter in foreign parts. He has been overseas once already; and
with proviso that I marry my cousin, will cross 'em once again,
only to bear me company.—'Sheart, I'll call him in—an I set
on't once, he shall come in; and see who'll hinder him.

[*Goes to the door and hems.*]

MRS. MAR. This is precious fooling, if it would pass; but I'll know
the bottom of it.

LADY. O dear Marwood, you are not going?

MAR. Not far, madam; I'll return immediately.

SCENE 9

Lady Wishfort, Millamant, Sir Wilfull, Mirabell.

SIR WIL. [*aside*] Look up, man, I'll stand by you. 'Sbud an she do
frown, she can't kill you—besides—harkee, she dare not frown
desperately, because her face is none of her own. 'Sheart, an
she should her forehead would wrinkle like the coat of a cream
cheese; but mum for that, fellow traveler.

MIRA. If a deep sense of the many injuries I have offered to so good
a lady, with a sincere remorse, and a hearty contrition, can but
obtain the least glance of compassion, I am too happy—Ah
madam, there was a time—but let it be forgotten—I confess I
have deservedly forfeited the high place I once held of sighing
at your feet. Nay kill me not by turning from me in disdain—I
come not to plead for favor—nay not for pardon. I am a suppliant only for pity—I am going where I never shall behold you
more—

SIR WIL. [*aside*] How, fellow traveler!—You shall go by yourself
then.

MIRA. Let me be pitied first, and afterwards forgotten—I ask no
more.

SIR WIL. By'r Lady a very reasonable request, and will cost you nothing, aunt.—Come, come, forgive and forget, aunt. Why you
must, an you are a Christian.

MIRA. Consider, madam, in reality you could not receive much
prejudice; it was an innocent device; though I confess it had a
face of guiltiness.—It was at most an artifice which love contrived—and errors which love produces have ever been accounted
venial. At least think it is punishment enough that I have lost
what in my heart I hold most dear, that to your cruel indignation, I have offered up this beauty, and with her my peace and
quiet; nay, all my hopes of future comfort.

SIR WIL. An he does not move me, would I may never be o' the
quorum[8]—An it were not as good a deed as to drink, to give
her to him again—I would I might never take shipping.—Aunt,
if you don't forgive quickly I shall melt, I can tell you that. My
contract went no farther than a little mouth glue,[9] and that's

8. Justices of the peace, who were required to be present at the sessions of a
court.
9. Literally, glue to be used by moisten-

ing with the tongue, but here the meaning is "glue made of mere words" and
therefore not binding.

hardly dry.—One doleful sigh more from my fellow traveler and 'tis dissolved.

LADY. Well, nephew, upon your account—Ah, he has a false insinuating tongue.—Well, sir, I will stifle my just resentment at my nephew's request.. I will endeavor what I can to forget—but on proviso that you resign the contract with my niece immediately.

MIRA. It is in writing and with papers of concern, but I have sent my servant for it and will deliver it to you, with all acknowledgments for your transcendent goodness.

LADY. [*aside*] O, he has witchcraft in his eyes and tongue; when I did not see him I could have bribed a villain to his assassination; but his appearance rakes the embers which have so long lain smothered in my breast.—

SCENE 10

[*To them*] *Fainall, Mrs. Marwood.*

FAIN. Your date of deliberation, madam, is expired. Here is the instrument; are you prepared to sign?

LADY. If I were prepared, I am not empowered. My niece exerts a lawful claim, having matched herself by my direction to Sir Wilfull.

FAIN. That sham is too gross to pass on me—though 'tis imposed on you, madam.

MILLA. Sir, I have given my consent.

MIRA. And, sir, I have resigned my pretensions.

SIR WIL. And, sir, I assert my right; and will maintain it in defiance of you, sir, and of your instrument. 'Sheart, an you talk of an instrument, sir, I have an old fox[1] by my thigh shall hack your instrument of ram vellum to shreds, sir. It shall not be sufficient for a *mittimus*[2] or a tailor's measure; therefore withdraw your instrument, sir, or by'r Lady I shall draw mine.

LADY. Hold, nephew, hold.

MILLA. Good Sir Wilfull, respite your valor.

FAIN. Indeed? Are you provided of your guard, with your single beefeater[3] there? But I'm prepared for you; and insist upon my first proposal. You shall submit your own estate to my management and absolutely make over my wife's to my sole use, as pursuant to the purport and tenor of this other covenant. I suppose, madam, your consent is not requisite in this case; nor, Mr. Mirabell, your resignation; nor, Sir Wilfull, your right—You may draw your fox if you please, sir, and make a bear garden[4] flourish somewhere else: for here it will not avail. This, my Lady Wishfort, must be subscribed, or your darling daughter's turned adrift, like a leaky hulk to sink or swim, as she and the current of this lewd town can agree.

---

1. A kind of sword. "Ram vellum": the legal instrument to be signed is written on vellum.
2. A warrant, committing a felon to jail.
3. Yeoman of the guard.
4. The place for bearbaiting, frequented by a vulgar and unruly crowd.

LADY. Is there no means, no remedy, to stop my ruin? Ungrateful wretch! Dost thou not owe thy being, thy subsistance to my daughter's fortune?

FAIN. I'll answer you when I have the rest of it in my possession.

MIRA. But that you would not accept of a remedy from my hands —I own I have not deserved you should owe any obligation to me; or else perhaps I could advise—

LADY. O, what? what? to save me and my child from ruin, from want, I'll forgive all that's past; nay, I'll consent to anything to come, to be delivered from this tyranny.

MIRA. Aye, madam, but that is too late; my reward is intercepted. You have disposed of her who only could have made me a compensation for all my services; but be it as it may, I am resolved I'll serve you. You shall not be wronged in this savage manner.

LADY. How! Dear Mr. Mirabell, can you be so generous at last! But it is not possible. Harkee, I'll break my nephew's match, you shall have my niece yet, and all her fortune, if you can but save me from this imminent danger.

MIRA. Will you? I take you at your word. I ask no more. I must have leave for two criminals to appear.

LADY. Aye, aye, anybody, anybody.

MIRA. Foible is one, and a penitent.

SCENE 11

[To them] Mrs. Fainall, Foible, Mincing.

MRS. MAR. O, my shame! These corrupt things are brought hither to expose me.

[MIRA. *and* LADY *go to* MRS. FAIN. *and* FOIB.]

FAIN. If it must all come out, why let 'em know it, 'tis but *the way of the world*. That shall not urge me to relinquish or abate one tittle of my terms, no, I will insist the more.

FOIB. Yes indeed, madam, I'll take my Bible-oath of it.

MINC. And so will I, mem.

LADY. O Marwood, Marwood, art thou false? My friend deceive me? Hast thou been a wicked accomplice with that profligate man?

MRS. MAR. Have you so much ingratitude and injustice, to give credit against your friend to the aspersions of two such mercenary trulls?

MINC. Mercenary, mem? I scorn your words. 'Tis true we found you and Mr. Fainall in the blue garret; by the same token, you swore us to secrecy upon Messalina's[5] poems. Mercenary? No, if we would have been mercenary, we should have held our tongues; you would have bribed us sufficiently.

FAIN. Go, you are an insignificant thing. Well, what are you the better for this! Is this Mr. Mirabell's expedient? I'll be put off

---

5. Mincing means "Miscellany," a collection of poems by various writers, such as Dryden's popular *Miscellanies*. Mes-salina was the viciously debauched wife of the Roman Emperor Claudius.

no longer. You, thing that was a wife, shall smart for this. I will not leave thee wherewithal to hide thy shame: your body shall be naked as your reputation.

MRS. FAIN. I despise you and defy your malice.—You have aspersed me wrongfully.—I have proved your falsehood.—Go, you and your treacherous—I will not name it, but starve together—perish.

FAIN. Not while you are worth a groat, indeed, my dear. Madam, I'll be fooled no longer.

LADY. Ah, Mr. Mirabell, this is small comfort, the detection of this affair.

MIRA. O, in good time—Your leave for the other offender and penitent to appear, madam.

SCENE 12

[*To them*] *Waitwell with a box of writings*.

LADY. O Sir Rowland—Well, rascal.

WAIT. What your ladyship pleases—I have brought the black box at last, madam.

MIRA. Give it me. Madam, you remember your promise.

LADY. Aye, dear sir.

MIRA. Where are the gentlemen?

WAIT. At hand, sir, rubbing their eyes, just risen from sleep.

FAIN. 'Sdeath, what's this to me? I'll not wait your private concerns.

SCENE 13

[*To them*] *Petulant, Witwoud*.

PET. How now? What's the matter? Who's hand's out?

WIT. Heyday! What, are you all got together, like players at the end of the last act?

MIRA. You may remember, gentlemen, I once requested your hands as witnesses to a certain parchment.

WIT. Aye, I do, my hand I remember—Petulant set his mark.

MIRA. You wrong him, his name is fairly written, as shall appear. You do not remember, gentlemen, anything of what that parchment contained—   [*Undoing the box.*]

WIT. No.

PET. Not I. I writ, I read nothing.

MIRA. Very well, now you shall know. Madam, your promise.

LADY. Aye, aye, sir, upon my honor.

MIRA. Mr. Fainall, it is now time that you should know that your lady, while she was at her own disposal, and before you had by your insinuations wheedled her out of a pretended settlement of the greatest part of her fortune—

FAIN. Sir! Pretended!

MIRA. Yes, sir. I say that this lady while a widow, having, it seems, received some cautions respecting your inconstancy and tyranny of temper, which from her own partial opinion and fondness of you she could never have suspected—she did, I say, by the wholesome advice of friends and of sages learned in the laws of this land, deliver this same as her act and deed to me in trust, and to the uses within mentioned. You may read if you please—[*Holding out the parchment*]—though perhaps what is written on the back may serve your occasions.

FAIN. Very likely, sir. What's here? Damnation?—[*Reads.*] *A deed of conveyance of the whole estate real of Arabella Languish, widow, in trust to Edward Mirabell.* Confusion!

MIRA. Even so, sir, 'tis the way of the world, sir; of the widows of the world. I suppose this deed may bear an elder date than what you have obtained from your lady.

FAIN. Perfidious fiend! Then thus I'll be revenged.

[*Offers to run at* MRS. FAIN.]

SIR WIL. Hold, sir, now you may make your bear garden flourish somewhere else, sir.

FAIN. Mirabell, you shall hear of this, sir, be sure you shall. Let me pass, oaf.

MRS. FAIN. Madam, you seem to stifle your resentment: you had better give it vent.

MRS. MAR. Yes, it shall have vent—and to your confusion, or I'll perish in the attempt.

SCENE THE LAST

Lady Wishfort, Millamant, Mirabell, Mrs. Fainall, Sir Wilfull, Petulant, Witwoud, Foible, Mincing, Waitwell.

LADY. O daughter, daughter, 'tis plain thou hast inherited thy mother's prudence.

MRS. FAIN. Thank Mr. Mirabell, a cautious friend, to whose advice all is owing.

LADY. Well, Mr. Mirabell, you have kept your promise and I must perform mine. First I pardon for your sake Sir Rowland there and Foible.—The next thing is to break the matter to my nephew —and how to do that—

MIRA. For that, madam, give yourself no trouble—let me have your consent.—Sir Wilfull is my friend; he has had compassion upon lovers, and generously engaged a volunteer in this action, for our service; and now designs to prosecute his travels.

SIR WIL. 'Sheart, aunt, I have no mind to marry. My cousin's a fine lady, and the gentleman loves her, and she loves him, and they deserve one another. My resolution is to see foreign parts—I have set on't—and when I'm set on't, I must do't. And if these two gentlemen would travel too, I think they may be spared.

PET. For my part, I say little—I think things are best off or on.

WIT. Igad, I understand nothing of the matter—I'm in a maze yet, like a dog in a dancing school.

LADY. Well, sir, take her, and with her all the joy I can give you.

MILLA. Why does not the man take me? Would you have me give myself to you over again?

MIRA. Aye, and over and over again—[*Kisses her hand.*]—I would
have you as often as possibly I can. Well, Heaven grant I love
you not too well, that's all my fear.[5a]

SIR WIL. 'Sheart, you'll have time enough to toy after you're married; or if you will toy now, let us have a dance in the meantime;
that we who are not lovers may have some other employment,
besides looking on.

MIRA. With all my heart, dear Sir Wilfull. What shall we do for
music?

FOIB. O, sir, some that were provided for Sir Rowland's entertainment are yet within call.

[*A dance.*]

LADY. As I am a person I can hold out no longer.—I have wasted
my spirits so today already, that I am ready to sink under the
fatigue; and I cannot but have some fears upon me yet, that my
son Fainall will pursue some desperate course.

MIRA. Madam, disquiet not yourself on that account; to my knowledge his circumstances are such, he must of force comply. For
my part, I will contribute all that in me lies to a reunion: in the
meantime, madam—[*to* MRS. FAIN.]—let me before these witnesses restore to you this deed of trust; it may be a means, well
managed, to make you live easily together.

> From hence let those be warned, who mean to wed;
> Lest mutual falsehood stain the bridal bed:
> For each deceiver to his cost may find,
> That marriage frauds too oft are paid in kind.

[*Exeunt omnes.*]

Epilogue

SPOKEN BY MRS. BRACEGIRDLE[6]

> After our Epilogue this crowd dismisses,
> I'm thinking how this play'll be pulled to pieces.
> But pray consider, e'er you doom its fall,
> How hard a thing 'twould be to please you all.
> There are some critics so with spleen diseased,   5
> They scarcely come inclining to be pleased;
> And sure he must have more than mortal skill,
> Who pleases anyone against his will.
> Then, all bad poets we are sure are foes,
> And how their number's swelled the town well knows: 10
> In shoals, I've marked 'em judging in the pit; ⎫
> Though they're on no pretence for judgment fit, ⎬
> But that they have been damned for want of wit. ⎭
> Since when, they by their own offenses taught.

5a. Mirabell alludes to Othello's last
speech, in which he speaks of having
loved Desdemona "not wisely but too
well."
6. Anne Bracegirdle (ca. 1663–1748),
the most brilliant actress of her generation. She created the role of Millamant.
Congreve loved her, and it was rumored
that they were secretly married.

Set up for spies on plays, and finding fault.   15
Others there are whose malice we'd prevent; ⎫
Such, who watch plays, with scurrilous intent ⎬
To mark out who by characters are meant.   ⎭
And though no perfect likeness they can trace,
Yet each pretends to know the copied face.   20
These, with false glosses feed their own ill-nature,
And turn to libel, what was meant a *satire*.[7]
May such malicious fops this fortune find,
To think themselves alone the fools designed:
If any are so arrogantly vain,   ⎫   25
To think they singly can support a scene,   ⎬
And furnish fool enough to entertain.   ⎭
For well the learn'd and the judicious know, ⎫
That satire scorns to stoop so meanly low,   ⎬
As any one abstracted fop to show.   ⎭   30
For, as when painters form a matchless face,
They from each fair one catch some different grace,
And shining features in one portrait blend,
To which no single beauty must pretend:
So poets oft do in one piece expose   35
Whole *belles assemblées* of coquettes and beaux.

                                                1700

7. Pronounce *nā-ter* and *sā-ter*.

DANIEL DEFOE
(ca. 1660–1731)

1703:   Pilloried and jailed for political pamphleteering.
1704–13: Editor of the *Review*.
1719:   *Robinson Crusoe*, first of his adventure tales.

By birth, education, and occupations Daniel Defoe was a stranger to the
sphere of refined tastes and classical learning that determined the course
of English literature during his lifetime. Middle-class in his birth, Presbyterian in his religion, he belonged to the vigorous and durable group of
Nonconformist tradesmen who, after the Restoration, slowly increased
their wealth and toward the end of the 17th century began to achieve
political importance.

He began life as a small merchant and for a while prospered; but he was
not overscrupulous in his dealings, and in 1692 he found himself bankrupt, with debts amounting to £17,000. This was the first of his many
financial crises, crises which drove him to make his way, like his own heroes
and heroines, by whatever means presented themselves to his clever
mind and abundant energy. And however double his dealings, he seems
always to have found the way to reconcile them with his genuine Non-

conformist piety. His restless mind was fertile in "projects," both for himself and for the country; and his itch for politics made the role of passive observer impossible for him.

An ardent Whig, he first gained notoriety by political verses and pamphlets, and for one of them, in which he ironically defended the Anglican's hostility to the Dissenter, *The Shortest Way with the Dissenters*, he stood in the pillory three times and was sentenced to jail. He was released through the influence of that astute politician, Robert Harley (later Earl of Oxford), who recognized in Defoe, as he was to do in Swift, a useful ally. For the next eleven years Defoe served his benefactor secretly as a political spy and confidential agent, traveling throughout England and Scotland, reporting and perhaps influencing opinion. As founder and editor of the *Review*, his job was to gain support for Harley's policies, and his Whiggism did not seem to make it difficult for him to follow Harley's lead, even when, in 1710, his master became head of a Tory ministry. It is characteristic of Defoe that, after the fall of the Tories in 1714, he went over to the triumphant Whigs and served them as loyally as he had their enemy.

When he was nearly 60, Defoe's energy and inventiveness enabled him to break new ground, indeed to begin a new career. One of the few books of the century that belong to world literature is *Robinson Crusoe*, which appeared in 1719. It is the first of a series of tales of adventure for which Defoe is now admired, but which brought him little esteem from the polite world, however much they gratified the less cultivated readers in the City or the servants' hall. In this and the other tales which followed, Defoe was able to use all his greatest gifts: the ability to re-create a milieu vividly, through the cumulative effect of carefully observed, often petty details; a special skill in writing relaxed and careless prose which seems to reveal the consciousness of the first-person narrator and which comes alive because the language is the language of actual speech; his wide knowledge of the society in which he lived, both the trading bourgeoisie and the rogues who preyed on them; and his absorption in the spectacle of the lonely human being, whether Crusoe on his island or Moll Flanders in England and Virginia, somehow bending a stubborn and indifferent environment to his own ends of survival or profits. He was interested in the mere processes of living, and there is something of himself in all his protagonists: enormous vitality, ultimate humanity, a scheming and not always edifying ingenuity. In these fictitious autobiographies of adventurers or rogues, Defoe spoke for and to the members of his own class whose interest in property and success he shared.

Robinson Crusoe was followed by *Captain Singleton* (1720); *Moll Flanders* (1722), perhaps his most impressive book; *A Journal of the Plague Year* (1722)—like the earlier ghost story *The Apparition of Mrs. Veal* (1706), a remarkable example of fiction that appears to be reporting from immediate observation; *Colonel Jack* (1722); and *Roxana* (1724), which takes us into vice in high life.

Of these *Colonel Jack* is perhaps the least successful as a whole, but nothing in all Defoe's works excels the brilliant opening episode (slightly condensed below), which describes the early life and the initiation into crime of a nameless, homeless, penniless boy, one of hundreds who populated the streets of London in all seasons, not knowing in the morning where they would sleep at night or whether, in the course of any day, they would eat so much as a crust of bread. The London of Jack, like the London of Moll Flanders, is more a desert than is Crusoe's island, for Crusoe, after all, could start his solitary life handsomely endowed with tools and materials salvaged from the wrecked ship. But Jack faces a city whose indifference to him and his kind leaves him no alternative except to live—if he is to live—on his takings as a pickpocket. Defoe is as much interested in the technique of this craft as he had been in the making of bricks or the selling of hose. Among the many unforgettable scenes in the novel, none is more remarkable than the episode in which Defoe studies the anxiety and responsibility that burden the boy when he suddenly acquires a fairly large sum of money. In such episodes we recognize that Defoe not only has created out of his own experience an apparently real physical world, but has peopled it through unobtrusive art with living men and women.

From The History and Remarkable Life of the Truly Honorable Col. Jacque

COMMONLY CALLED COL. JACK, ETC.

Seeing my life has been such a checkerwork of nature, and that I am able now to look back upon it from a safer distance than is ordinarily the fate of the clan to which I once belonged, I think my history may find a place in the world as well as some who I see are every day read with pleasure, though they have in them nothing so diverting or instructing as I believe mine will appear to be.

My original may be as high as anybody's for aught I know, for my mother kept very good company; but that part belongs to her story more than to mine. All I know of it is by oral tradition, thus: my nurse told me my mother was a gentlewoman, that my father was a man of quality, and she (my nurse) had a good piece of money given her to take me off his hands, and deliver him and my mother from the importunities that usually attend the misfortune of having a child to keep that should not be seen or heard of.

My father, it seems, gave my nurse something more than was agreed for, at my mother's request, upon her solemn promise that she would use me well and let me be put to school; and charged her, that if I lived to come to any bigness, capable to understand the meaning of it, she should always take care to bid me remember that I was a gentleman; and this, he said, was all the education he would desire of her for me; for he did not doubt, he said, but that, some time or other, the very hint would inspire me with thoughts suitable to my birth, and that I would certainly act like a gentleman, if I believed myself to be so. * * *

My nurse was as honest to the engagement she had entered into as could be expected from one of her employment, and particularly as honest as her circumstances would give her leave to be; for she bred me up very carefully with her own son, and with another son of shame like me, whom she had taken upon the same terms.

My name was John, as she told me, but neither she nor I knew anything of a surname that belonged to me; so I was left to call myself Mr. Anything, what I pleased, as fortune and better circumstances should give occasion.

It happened that her own son (for she had a little boy of her own, about one year older than I) was called John too, and about two years after she took another son of shame, as I called it above, to keep as she did me, and his name was John too.

As we were all Johns, we were all Jacks, and soon came to be called so; for at that part of the town where we had our breeding, viz., near Goodman's Fields,[1] the Johns are generally called Jack; but my nurse, who may be allowed to distinguish her own son a little from the rest, would have him called Captain, because, forsooth, he was the eldest.

I was provoked at having this boy called Captain, and I cried, and told my nurse I would be called Captain; for she told me I was a gentleman, and I would be a captain, that I would. The good woman, to keep the peace, told me, aye, aye, I was a gentleman, and therefore I should be above a captain, for I should be a colonel, and that was a great deal better than a captain. "For, my dear," says she, "every tarpaulin,[2] if he gets but to be lieutenant of a press-smack,[3] is called captain, but colonels are soldiers, and none but gentlemen are ever made colonels. Besides," says she, "I have known colonels come to be lords and generals, though they were b——ds at first, and therefore you shall be called Colonel."

Well, I was hushed indeed with this for the present, but not thoroughly pleased, till, a little while after, I heard her tell her own boy that I was a gentleman, and therefore he must call me Colonel; at which her boy fell a-crying, and he would be called Colonel. That part pleased me to the life, that he should cry to be called Colonel, for then I was satisfied that it was above a captain: so universally is ambition seated in the minds of men that not a beggar-boy but has his share of it.

So here was Colonel Jack and Captain Jack. As for the third boy, he was only plain Jack for some years after, till he came to preferment by the merit of his birth, as you shall hear in its place.

---

1. Then an open area near the Tower of London. Jack's boyhood was spent in what is now the crowded East End of London, but what was then a series of villages surrounded by open country.

2. Slang for "sailor." Cf. the modern "tar."

3. A small boat dispatched from a man-of-war under orders to "press" (forcibly conscript) men into naval service.

We were hopeful boys, all three of us, and promised very early, by many repeated circumstances of our lives, that we would be all rogues; and yet I cannot say, if what I have heard of my nurse's character be true, but the honest woman did what she could to prevent it.

Before I tell you much more of our story, it would be very proper to give you something of our several characters, as I have gathered them up in my memory, as far back as I can recover things, either of myself or my brother Jacks, and they shall be brief and impartial.

Captain Jack was the eldest of us all, by a whole year. He was a squat, big, strong-made boy, and promised to be stout when grown up to be a man, but not to be tall. His temper was sly, sullen, reserved, malicious, revengeful; and, withal, he was brutish, bloody, and cruel in his disposition. He was, as to manners, a mere boor, or clown, of a carman-like[4] breed; sharp as a street-bred boy must be, but ignorant and unteachable from a child. He had much the nature of a bulldog, bold and desperate, but not generous at all. All the schoolmistresses we went to could never make him learn, no, not so much as to make him know his letters; and as if he was born a thief, he would steal everything that came near him, even as soon almost as he could speak, and that not from his mother only, but from anybody else, and from us too that were his brethren and companions. He was an original rogue, for he would do the foulest and most villainous things, even by his own inclination; he had no taste or sense of being honest, no, not, I say, to his brother rogues, which is what other thieves make a point of honor of; I mean that of being honest to one another.

The other, that is to say, the youngest of us Johns, was called Major Jack, by the accident following: the lady that had deposited him with our nurse had owned to her that it was a Major of the Guards that was the father of the child, but that she was obliged to conceal his name, and that was enough. So he was at first called John the Major, and afterwards the Major; and at last, when we came to rove together, Major Jack, according to the rest, for his name was John, as I have observed already.

Major Jack was a merry, facetious, pleasant boy, had a good share of wit, especially offhand wit, as they call it; was full of jests and good humor and, as I often said, had something of a gentleman in him. He had a true manly courage, feared nothing, and could look death in the face without any hesitation; and yet, if he had the advantage, was the most generous and most compassionate creature alive. He had native principles of gallantry in him, without anything of the brutal or terrible part that the Captain had; and, in a word, he wanted nothing but honesty to have made him an excellent man. He had learned to read, as I had done; and as he

4. I.e., like a wagoner or teamster.

talked very well, so he wrote good sense and very handsome language, as you will see in the process of his story.

As for your humble servant, Colonel Jack, he was a poor, unhappy, tractable dog, willing enough, and capable too, to learn anything, if he had had any but the devil for his schoolmaster. He set out into the world so early that when he began to do evil, he understood nothing of the wickedness of it, nor what he had to expect for it. I remember very well that when I was once carried before a justice, for a theft which indeed I was not guilty of, and defended myself by argument, proving the mistakes of my accusers, and how they contradicted themselves, the Justice told me it was a pity I had not been better employed, for I was certainly better taught; in which, however, his worship was mistaken, for I had never been taught anything but to be a thief, except, as I said, to read and write, and that was all, before I was ten years old; but I had a natural talent of talking, and could say as much to the purpose as most people that had been taught no more than I. * * *

As for my person, while I was a dirty glass-bottle-house boy,[4a] sleeping in the ashes, and dealing always in the street dirt, it cannot be expected but that I looked like what I was, and so we did all; that is to say, like a "black-your-shoes-your-honor," a beggar boy, a blackguard boy,[5] or what you please, despicable and miserable to the last degree; and yet I remember the people would say of me, "That boy has a good face; if he was washed and well dressed, he would be a good, pretty boy. Do but look what eyes he has; what a pleasant, smiling countenance! 'Tis a pity. I wonder what the rogue's father and mother was," and the like. Then they would call me, and ask me my name, and I would tell them my name was Jack. "But what's your surname, sirrah?" says they. "I don't know," says I. "Who is your father and mother?" "I have none," said I. "What! and never had you any?" said they. "No," says I, "not that I know of." Then they would shake their heads and cry, "Poor boy!" and " 'Tis a pity!" and the like, and so let me go. But I laid up all these things in my heart.

I was almost ten years old, the Captain eleven, and the Major about eight, when the good woman my nurse died. Her husband was a seaman, and had been drowned a little before in the *Gloucester* frigate, one of the king's ships which was cast away going to Scotland with the Duke of York in the time of King Charles II,[6] and the honest woman dying very poor, the parish was obliged to bury her; when the three young Jacks attended her corpse, and I, the Colonel (for we all passed for her own children), was chief

4a. A boy who slept in the warm ashes of a bottle factory.
5. A low, dirty boy of the streets.
6. The frigate, with the Duke of York aboard, was wrecked with great loss of life off the mouth of the river Humber in May, 1682. Cf. Samuel Pepys's account of the disaster in his letter to William Hewer, Edinburgh, May 8. The reference to this event gives us the date of Jack's birth: ca. 1672.

mourner; the Captain, who was the eldest son, going back very sick.

The good woman being dead, we, the three Jacks, were turned loose to the world. As to the parish providing for us, we did not trouble ourselves much about that; we rambled about all three together, and the people in Rosemary Lane and Ratcliff,[7] and that way, knowing us pretty well, we got victuals easily enough and without much begging.

For my particular part, I got some reputation for a mighty civil, honest boy; for if I was sent of an errand, I always did it punctually and carefully, and made haste again; and if I was trusted with anything, I never touched it to diminish it, but made it a point of honor to be punctual to whatever was committed to me, though I was as arrant a thief as any of them in all other cases.

In like case, some of the poorer shopkeepers would often leave me at their door, to look after their shops till they went up to dinner, or till they went over the way to an alehouse, and the like, and I always did it freely and cheerfully, and with the utmost honesty.

Captain Jack, on the contrary, a surly, ill-looked, rough boy, had not a word in his mouth that savored either of good manners or good humor. He would say "Yes" and "No," just as he was asked a question, and that was all, but nobody got anything from him that was obliging in the least. If he was sent of an errand he would forget half of it, and it may be go to play, if he met any boys, and never go at all, or if he went, never come back with an answer, which was such a regardless, disobliging way that nobody had a good word for him, and everybody said he had the very look of a rogue, and would come to be hanged. In a word, he got nothing of anybody for goodwill, but was, as it were, obliged to turn thief for the mere necessity of bread to eat; for if he begged, he did it with so ill a tone, rather like bidding folks give him victuals than entreating them, that one man, of whom he had something given, and knew him, told him one day, "Captain Jack," says he, "thou art but an awkward, ugly sort of a beggar, now thou art a boy; I doubt thou wilt be fitter to ask a man for his purse than for a penny when thou comest to be a man."

The Major was a merry, thoughtless fellow, always cheerful; whether he had any victuals or no, he never complained; and he recommended himself so well by his good carriage that the neighbors loved him, and he got victuals enough, one where or other. Thus we all made a shift, though we were so little, to keep from starving; and as for lodging, we lay in the summertime about the watch house[8] and on bulkheads and shop doors, where we were

7. Rosemary Lane extended eastward from a little south of Goodman's Fields to within a short distance of Glass-house Hill, the site of the factory where the boys slept. Ratcliff, at that time a village near Limehouse, is now swallowed up in the parish of Stepney.
8. The headquarters of the night watch (the feeble equivalent of a police force); "bulkheads" were the roofs of

known. As for a bed, we knew nothing what belonged to it for many years after my nurse died; and in winter we got into the ash holes and nealing-arches[9] in the glass-house, called Dallow's Glass-house, in Rosemary Lane, or at another glass-house in Ratcliff Highway.

In this manner we lived for some years; and here we failed not to fall among a gang of naked, ragged rogues like ourselves, wicked as the devil could desire to have them be at so early an age, and ripe for all the other parts of mischief that suited them as they advanced in years. * * *

Captain Jack in this time fell into bad company, and went away from us, and it was a good while before we ever heard tale or tidings of him, till about half a year, I think, or thereabouts. I understood he was got among a gang of kidnappers, as they were then called, being a sort of wicked fellows that used to spirit people's children away; that is, snatch them up in the dark, and, stopping their mouths, carry them to such houses where they had rogues ready to receive them, and so carry them on board ships bound to Virginia, and sell them.

This was a trade that Horrid Jack, for so I called him when we were grown up, was very fit for, especially the violent part; for if a little child got into his clutches, he would stop the breath of it, instead of stopping its mouth, and never troubled his head with the child's being almost strangled, so he did but keep it from making a noise. There was, it seems, some villainous thing done by this gang about that time, whether a child was murdered among them, or a child otherwise abused; but it seems it was a child of an eminent citizen, and the parent somehow or other got a scent of the thing so that they recovered their child, though in a sad condition, and almost killed. I was too young, and it was too long ago, for me to remember that whole story, but they were all taken up and sent to Newgate[1] and Captain Jack among the rest, though he was but young, for he was not then much above thirteen years old.

What punishment was inflicted upon the rogues of that gang I cannot tell now, but the Captain, being but a lad, was ordered to be three times soundly whipped at Bridewell,[2] my Lord Mayor, or the Recorder, telling him it was done in pity to him, to keep him from the gallows, not forgetting to tell him that he had a hanging look, and bid him have a care on that very account; so remarkable was the Captain's countenance, even so young, and which he heard of afterwards on many occasions. When he was in Bridewell I heard of his misfortune, and the Major and I went to see him; for this was the first news we heard of what became of him.

stalls or booths (or the stalls themselves), projecting from the wall of a shop or house.
9. Where hot glass was allowed to cool slowly.
1. 18th-century London's most notorious prison.
2. A house of correction where prostitutes, vagrants, and apprentices were detained, whipped, and—it was hoped—reformed.

The very day that we went he was called out to be corrected, as they called it, according to his sentence; and as it was ordered to be done soundly, so indeed they were true to the sentence; for the alderman who was the President of Bridewell, and whom I think they called Sir William Turner,[3] held preaching to him about how young he was, and what a pity it was such a youth should come to be hanged, and a great deal more; how he should take warning by it, and how wicked a thing it was that they should steal away poor innocent children, and the like; and all this while the man with a blue badge on lashed him most unmercifully, for he was not to leave off till Sir William knocked with a little hammer on the table.

The poor Captain stamped and danced and roared out like a mad boy; and I must confess I was frighted almost to death, for though I could not come near enough, being but a poor boy, to see how he was handled, yet I saw him afterwards with his back all wealed with the lashes, and in several places bloody, and thought I should have died with the sight of it; but I grew better acquainted with those things afterwards. * * *

The Major and I, though very young, had sensible impressions made upon us for some time by the severe usage of the Captain, and it might be very well said we were corrected as well as he, though not concerned in the crime; but it was within the year that the Major, a good-conditioned, easy boy, was wheedled away by a couple of young rogues that frequented the glass-house apartments, to take a walk with them, as they were pleased to call it. The gentlemen were very well matched; the Major was about twelve years old, and the oldest of the two that led him out was not above fourteen. The business was to go to Bartholomew Fair,[4] and the end of going to Bartholomew Fair was, in short, to pick pockets.

The Major knew nothing of the trade, and therefore was to do nothing; but they promised him a share with them for all that, as if he had been as expert as themselves. So away they went. The two dexterous young rogues managed it so well that by eight o'clock at night they came back to our dusty quarters at the glass-house, and, sitting them down in a corner, they began to share their spoil, by the light of the glass-house fire. The Major lugged out the goods, for as fast as they made any purchase[5] they unloaded themselves, and gave all to him, that, if they had been taken, nothing might be found about them. * * *

He came very early to me, who lay not far from him, and said to

---

3. Turner's first term of office ran from 1669 to 1687, when he was deprived of his alderman's gown because of his loyalty to the Anglican Church. He would have been well known to Defoe's readers as a victim of James II and of certain London Dissenters.

4. Held annually in Smithfield (now a district of central London); famous for its side shows, acrobats, and merry-making; pronounced *Bártlemy*.

5. Anything acquired through theft.

me, "Colonel Jack, I want to speak with you." "Well," said I, "what do you say?" "Nay," said he, "it is business of consequence; I cannot talk here"; so we walked out. As soon as we were come out into a narrow lane by the glass-house, "Look here," says he, and pulls out his little hand almost full of money.

I was surprised at the sight, when he puts it up again, and, bringing his hand out, "Here," says he, "you shall have some of it," and gives me a sixpence and a shilling's worth of the small silver pieces. This was very welcome to me, who, as much as I was of a gentleman, and as much as I thought of myself upon that account, never had a shilling of money together before in all my life, not that I could call my own.

I was very earnest then to know how he came by this wealth, for he had for his share 7s. 6d. in money, the silver thimble, and a silk handkerchief, which was, in short, an estate to him, that never had, as I said of myself, a shilling together in his life.

"And what will you do with it now, Jack?" said I. "I do?" says he. "The first thing I do I'll go into Rag Fair[6] and buy me a pair of shoes and stockings." "That's right," says I, "and so will I too"; so away we went together, and we bought each of us a pair of Rag Fair stockings in the first place for fivepence; not fivepence a pair, but fivepence together; and good stockings they were too, much above our wear, I assure you.

We found it more difficult to fit ourselves with shoes; but at last, having looked a great while before we could find any good enough for us, we found a shop very well stored, and of these we bought two pair for sixteenpence.

We put them on immediately, to our great comfort, for we had neither of us had any stockings to our legs that had any feet to them for a long time. I found myself so refreshed with having a pair of warm stockings on, and a pair of dry shoes—things, I say, which I had not been acquainted with a great while—that I began to call to my mind my being a gentleman, and now I thought it began to come to pass. When we had thus fitted ourselves I said, "Hark ye, Major Jack, you and I never had any money in our lives before, and we never had a good dinner in all our lives. What if we should go somewhere and get some victuals? I am very hungry."

"So we will, then," says the Major; "I am hungry too." So we went to a boiling cook's in Rosemary Lane, where we treated ourselves nobly, and, as I thought with myself, we began to live like gentlemen, for we had three pennyworth of boiled beef, two pennyworth of pudding, a penny brick (as they call it, or loaf), and a whole pint of strong beer, which was sevenpence in all.

N.B.—We had each of us a good mess of charming beef broth into the bargain; and, which cheered my heart wonderfully, all the

6. Held in Rosemary Lane.

while we were at dinner, the maid and the boy in the house, every time they passed by the open box where we sat at our dinner, would look in and cry, "Gentlemen, do you call?" and "Do ye call, gentlemen?" I say, this was as good to me as all my dinner.

Not the best housekeeper in Stepney parish, not my Lord Mayor of London, no, not the greatest man on earth, could be more happy in their own imagination, and with less mixture of grief or reflection, than I was at this new piece of felicity; though mine was but a small part of it, for Major Jack had an estate compared to me, as I had an estate compared to what I had before; in a word, nothing but an utter ignorance of greater felicity, which was my case, could make anybody think himself so exalted as I did, though I had no share of this booty but eighteenpence.

That night the major and I triumphed in our new enjoyment, and slept with an undisturbed repose in the usual place, surrounded with the warmth of the glass-house fires above, which was a full amends for all the ashes and cinders which we rolled in below.

Those who know the position of the glass-houses, and the arches where they neal the bottles after they are made, know that those places where the ashes are cast, and where the poor boys lie, are cavities in the brickwork, perfectly close, except at the entrance, and consequently warm as the dressing room of a bagnio,[7] that it is impossible they can feel any cold there, were it in Greenland or Nova Zembla,[8] and that therefore the boys lie there not only safe, but very comfortably, the ashes excepted, which are no grievance at all to them.

The next day the Major and his comrades went abroad again, and were still successful; nor did any disaster attend them, for I know not how many months; and, by frequent imitation and direction, Major Jack became as dexterous a pickpocket as any of them, and went on through a long variety of fortunes, too long to enter upon now, because I am hastening to my own story, which at present is the main thing I have to set down.

The Major failed not to let me see every day the effects of his new prosperity, and was so bountiful as frequently to throw me a tester,[9] sometimes a shilling; and I might perceive that he began to have clothes on his back, to leave the ash hole, having gotten a society lodging (of which I may give an explanation by itself on another occasion); and which was more, he took upon him to wear a shirt, which was what neither he nor I had ventured to do for three years before, and upward.

But I observed all this while, that though Major Jack was so prosperous and had thriven so well, and not withstanding he was very kind, and even generous, to me, in giving me money upon

---

7. A public bath house.
8. An island group in the Arctic Ocean, north of Russia.
9. Sixpence.

many occasions, yet he never invited me to enter myself into the society or to embark with him, whereby I might have been made as happy as he; no, nor did he recommend the employment to me at all.

I was not very well pleased with his being thus reserved to me. I had learned from him in general that the business was picking of pockets, and I fancied that though the ingenuity of the trade consisted very much in sleight of hand, a good address,[1] and being very nimble, yet that it was not at all difficult to learn; and, especially, I thought the opportunities were so many, the country people that came to London so foolish, so gaping, and so engaged in looking about them, that it was a trade with no great hazard annexed to it, and might be easily learned, if I did but know in general the manner of it, and how they went about it.

The subtle devil, never absent from his business, but ready at all occasions to encourage his servants, removed all these difficulties, and brought me into an intimacy with one of the most exquisite divers, or pickpockets, in the town; and thus our intimacy was of no less a kind than that, as I had an inclination to be as wicked as any of them, he was for taking care that I should not be disappointed.

He was above the little fellows who went about stealing trifles and baubles in Bartholomew Fair and ran the risk of being mobbed for three or four shillings. His aim was at higher things, even at no less than considerable sums of money, and bills[2] for more.

He solicited me earnestly to go and take a walk with him as above, adding that after he had shown me my trade a little, he would let me be as wicked as I would; that is, as he expressed it, that after he had made me capable, I should set up for myself, if I pleased, and he would only wish me good luck. * * *

I hesitated at the matter a great while, objecting the hazard, and telling the story of Captain Jack, my elder brother, as I might call him. "Well, Colonel," says he, "I find you are fainthearted, and to be fainthearted is indeed to be unfit for our trade, for nothing but a bold heart can go through-stitch[3] with this work; but, however, as there is nothing for you to do, so there is no risk for you to run in these things the first time. If I am taken," says he, "you have nothing to do in it; they will let you go free; for it shall easily be made appear, that whatever I have done, you had no hand in it."

Upon these persuasions I ventured out with him; but I soon found that my new friend was a thief of quality, and a pickpocket above the ordinary rank, and that he aimed higher abundantly than my brother Jack. He was a bigger boy than I, a great deal; for though I was now near fifteen years old, I was not big of my age,

1. Dexterity, skill.
2. Bills of exchange or, in modern parlance, bank drafts. In Jack's time they
were drawn by arrangement on merchants.
3. Go through to the end.

and as to the nature of the thing, I was perfectly a stranger to it. I knew indeed what at first I did not, for it was a good while before I understood the thing as an offense. I looked on picking pockets as a kind of trade, and thought I was to go apprentice to it. It is true this was when I was young in the society, as well as younger in years, but even now I understood it to be only a thing for which, if we were caught, we ran the risk of being ducked or pumped, which we called soaking, and then all was over; and we made nothing of having our rags wetted a little; but I never understood, till a great while after, that the crime was capital, and that we might be sent to Newgate for it, till a great fellow, almost a man, one of our society, was hanged for it; and then I was terribly frighted, as you shall hear by and by. * * *

The first day I went abroad with my new instructor, he carried me directly into the City, and as we went first to the waterside, he led me into the long room at the customhouse. We were but a couple of ragged boys at best, but I was much the worse. My leader had a hat on, a shirt, and a neckcloth; as for me, I had neither of the three, nor had I spoiled my manners so much as to have a hat on my head since my nurse died, which was now some years. His orders to me were to keep always in sight, and near him, but not close to him, nor to take any notice of him at any time till he came to me; and if any hurly-burly happened, I should by no means know him, or pretend to have anything to do with him.

I observed my orders to a tittle. While he peered into every corner and had his eye upon everybody, I kept my eye directly upon him, but went always at a distance, and on the other side of the long room, looking as it were for pins, and picking them up out of the dust as I could find them, and then sticking them on my sleeve, where I had at last gotten forty or fifty good pins; but still my eye was upon my comrade, who, I observed, was very busy among the crowds of people that stood at the board doing business with the officers who pass the entries and make the cockets,[4] etc.

At length he comes over to me, and stooping as if he would take up a pin close to me, he put something into my hand, and said, "Put that up, and follow me downstairs quickly." He did not run, but shuffled along apace through the crowd, and went down, not the great stairs which we came in at, but a little narrow staircase at the other end of the long room. I followed, and he found I did, and so went on, not stopping below, as I expected, nor speaking one word to me, till, through innumerable narrow passages, alleys, and dark ways, we were got up into Fenchurch Street, and through Billiter Lane into Leadenhall Street, and from thence into Leadenhall Market.

4. Warrants permitting merchandise to pass through customs. The "long room" was the public lobby where customs fees were paid.

It was not a meat market day, so we had room to sit down upon one of the butchers' stalls, and he bid me lug out. What he had given me was a little leather letter case, with a French almanac stuck in the inside of it, and a great many papers in it of several kinds.

We looked them over, and found there was several valuable bills in it, such as bills of exchange and other notes, things I did not understand; but among the rest was a goldsmith's note,[5] as he called it, of one Sir Stephen Evans, for £300, payable to the bearer, and at demand. Besides this, there was another note for £12, 10s., being a goldsmith's bill too, but I forget the name. There was a bill or two also written in French, which neither of us understood, but which, it seems, were things of value, being called foreign bills accepted.

The rogue, my master, knew what belonged to the goldsmiths' bills well enough, and I observed, when he read the bill of Sir Stephen, he said, "This is too big for me to meddle with"; but when he came to the bill for £12, 10s., he said to me, "This will do. Come hither, Jack"; so away he runs to Lombard Street, and I after him, huddling the other papers into the letter case. As he went along he inquired the name out immediately, and went directly to the shop, put on a good, grave countenance, and had the money paid him without any stop or question asked. I stood on the other side the way looking about the street, as not at all concerned with anybody that way, but observed that when he presented the bill he pulled out the letter case, as if he had been a merchant's boy, acquainted with business, and had other bills about him.

They paid him the money in gold, and he made haste enough in telling[6] it over, and came away, passing by me, and going into Three King Court, on the other side of the way; then we crossed back into Clement's Lane, made the best of our way to Cole Harbor, at the waterside, and got a sculler for a penny to carry us over the water to St. Mary over Stairs,[7] where we landed, and were safe enough.

Here he turns to me; "Colonel Jack," says he, "I believe you are a lucky boy; this is a good job. We'll go away to St. George's Fields[8] and share our booty." Away we went to the Fields, and sitting down in the grass, far enough out of the path, he pulled out the money. "Look here, Jack," says he, "did you ever see the like before in your life?" "No, never," says I; and added very in-

---

5. Goldsmiths received money on deposit and served in the role of the modern banker. Thus a "goldsmith's note" is the equivalent of a modern bank check.
6. Counting; cf. "bank teller."
7. The boys crossed the Thames not far from London Bridge and landed on the south bank at the water-stairs that led up to the church of St. Mary Overie, today the cathedral church of the Borough of Southwark.
8. A large park, with a rather unsavory reputation at that time, not far from Lambeth Palace.

nocently, "Must we have it all?" "We have it!" says he. "who should have it?" "Why," says I, "must the man have none of it again that lost it?" "He have it again!" says he. "What d'ye mean by that?" "Nay, I don't know," says I. "Why, you said just now you would let him have the t'other bill again, that you said was too big for you."

He laughed at me. "You are but a little boy," says he, "that's true, but I thought you had not been such a child neither"; so he mighty gravely explained the thing to me thus: that the bill of Sir Stephen Evans was a great bill for £300, "and if I," says he, "that am but a poor lad, should venture to go for the money, they will presently say, how should I come by such a bill, and that I certainly found it or stole it; so they will stop me," says he, "and take it away from me, and it may bring me into trouble for it too; so," says he, "I did say it was too big for me to meddle with, and that I would let the man have it again, if I could tell how. But for the money, Jack, the money that we have got, I warrant you he should have none of that. Besides," says he, "whoever he be that has lost this letter case, to be sure, as soon as he missed it, he would run to the goldsmith and give notice that if anybody came for the money they would be stopped; but I am too old for him there," says he.

"Why," says I, "and what will you do with the bill? Will you throw it away? If you do, somebody else will find it," says I, "and they will go and take the money." "No, no," says he; "then they will be stopped and examined, as I tell you I should be." I did not know well what all this meant, so I talked no more about that; but we fell to handling the money. As for me, I had never seen so much together in all my life, nor did I know what in the world to do with it, and once or twice I was a-going to bid him keep it for me, which would have been done like a child indeed, for, to be sure, I had never heard a word more of it, though nothing had befallen him.

However, as I happened to hold my tongue as to that part, he shared the money very honestly with me; only at the end he told me, that though it was true he promised me half, yet as it was the first time, and I had done nothing but look on, so he thought it was very well if I took a little less than he did; so he divided the money, which was £12, 10s., into two exact parts, viz, £6, 5s. in each part; then he took £1, 5s. from my part, and told me I should give him that for handsel.[9] "Well," says I, "take it, then, for I think you deserve it all"; so, however, I took up the rest, and "What shall I do with this now," says I, "for I have nowhere to put it?" "Why, have you no pockets?" says he. "Yes," says I; "but they are full of holes." I have often thought since that, and with some

9. A gift expressing good wishes at the beginning of a new undertaking.

mirth too, how I had really more wealth than I knew what to do with; for lodging I had none, nor any box or drawer to hide my money in; nor had I any pocket, but such as I say was full of holes. I knew nobody in the world that I could go and desire them to lay it up for me; for, being a poor naked, ragged boy, they would presently say I had robbed somebody, and perhaps lay hold of me, and my money would be my crime, as they say it often is in foreign countries. And now, as I was full of wealth, behold I was full of care, for what to do to secure my money I could not tell; and this held me so long, and was so vexatious to me the next day, that I truly sat down and cried.

Nothing could be more perplexing than this money was to me all that night. I carried it in my hand a good while, for it was in gold, all but 14*s*.; and that is to say, it was in four guineas, and that 14*s*. was more difficult to carry than the four guineas. At last I sat down and pulled off one of my shoes, and put the four guineas into that; but after I had gone a while, my shoe hurt me so I could not go, so I was fain to sit down again and take it out of my shoe, and carry it in my hand. Then I found a dirty linen rag in the street, and I took that up and wrapped it all together, and carried it in that a good way. I have often since heard people say, when they have been talking of money that they could not get in, "I wish I had it in a foul clout";[1] in truth, I had mine in a foul clout; for it was foul, according to the letter of that saying, but it served me till I came to a convenient place, and then I sat down and washed the cloth in the kennel,[2] and so then put my money in again.

Well, I carried it home with me to my lodging in the glass-house, and when I went to go to sleep I knew not what to do with it. If I had let any of the black crew I was with know of it, I should have been smothered in the ashes for it, or robbed of it, or some trick or other put upon me for it; so I knew not what to do, but lay with it in my hand, and my hand in my bosom. But then sleep went from my eyes. Oh, the weight of human care! I, a poor beggar boy, could not sleep so soon as I had but a little money to keep, who before that could have slept upon a heap of brickbats, or stones, or cinders, or anywhere, as sound as a rich man does on his down bed, and sounder too.

Every now and then dropping asleep, I should dream that my money was lost, and start like one frighted; then, finding it fast in my hand, try to go to sleep again, but could not for a long while; then drop and start again. At last a fancy came into my head that if I fell asleep I should dream of the money, and talk of it in my sleep, and tell that I had money, which if I should do, and one of the rogues should hear me, they would pick it out of my bosom,

---

1. Dirty rag.

2. An open drainage ditch down the middle of a street.

and of my hand too, without waking me; and after that thought I could not sleep a wink more; so that I passed that night over in care and anxiety enough; and this, I may safely say, was the first night's rest that I lost by the cares of this life and the deceitfulness of riches.

As soon as it was day I got out of the hole we lay in, and rambled abroad in the fields toward Stepney, and there I mused and considered what I should do with this money, and many a time I wished that I had not had it; for, after all my ruminating upon it, and what course I should take with it, or where I should put it, I could not hit upon any one thing, or any possible method to secure it, and it perplexed me so that at last, as I said just now, I sat down and cried heartily.

When my crying was over, the case was the same; I had the money still, and what to do with it I could not tell. At last it came into my head that I would look out for some hole in a tree, and seek to hide it there till I should have occasion for it. Big was this discovery, as I then thought it. I began to look about me for a tree; but there were no trees in the fields about Stepney or Mile End that looked fit for my purpose; and if there were any that I began to look narrowly at, the fields were so full of people that they would see if I went to hide anything there; and I thought the people eyed me as it was, and that two men in particular followed me to see what I intended to do.

This drove me farther off, and I crossed the road at Mile End, and in the middle of the town went down a lane that goes away to the Blind Beggar's at Bethnal Green. When I came a little way in the lane I found a footpath over the fields, and in those fields several trees for my turn, as I thought. At last one tree had a little hole in it, pretty high out of my reach, and I climbed up the tree to get it, and when I came there I put my hand in, and found (as I thought) a place very fit, so I placed my treasure there, and was mighty well satisfied with it; but, behold, putting my hand in again to lay it more commodiously, as I thought, of a sudden it slipped away from me, and I found the tree was hollow, and my little parcel was fallen in quite out of my reach, and how far it might go in I knew not; so that, in a word, my money was quite gone, irrecoverably lost. There could be no room so much as to hope ever to see it again, for 'twas a vast great tree.

As young as I was, I was now sensible what a fool I was before, that I could not think of ways to keep my money, but I must come thus far to throw it into a hole where I could not reach it. Well, I thrust my hand quite up to my elbow, but no bottom was to be found, or any end of the hole or cavity. I got a stick of the tree, and thrust it in a great way, but all was one. Then I cried, nay, roared out, I was in such a passion. Then I got down the tree again, then up again, and thrust in my hand again till I scratched my arm and made it bleed, and cried all the while most violently. Then I began to think I had not so much as a halfpenny of it left for a halfpenny roll, and I was hungry, and then I cried again. Then I came away in despair, crying and roaring like a little boy that had been whipped; then I went back again to the tree, and up the tree again, and thus I did several times.

The last time I had gotten up the tree I happened to come down not on the same side that I went up and came down before, but on the other side of the tree, and on the side of the bank also; and, behold, the tree had a great open place in the side of it close to the ground, as old hollow trees often have; and looking into the open place, to my inexpressible joy, there lay my money and my linen rag, all wrapped up just as I had put it into the hole; for the tree being hollow all the way up, there had been some moss or light stuff, which I had not judgment enough to know was not firm, and had given way when it came to drop out of my hand, and so it had slipped quite down at once.

I was but a child, and I rejoiced like a child, for I hallooed quite out loud when I saw it; then I ran to it, and snatched it up, hugged and kissed the dirty rag a hundred times; then danced and jumped about, ran from one end of the field to the other, and, in short, I knew not what; much less do I know now what I did, though I shall never forget the thing, either what a sinking grief it was to my heart when I thought I had lost it, or what a flood of joy over-whelmed me when I had got it again.

While I was in the first transport of my joy, as I have said, I ran about, and knew not what I did; but when that was over I sat down, opened the foul clout the money was in, looked at it, told it, found it was all there, and then I fell a-crying as savorly[3] as I did before, when I thought I had lost it. * * *

Well, I came away with my money, and having taken sixpence out of it, before I made it up again I went to a chandler's shop[4] in Mile End and bought a halfpenny roll and a halfpenny worth of cheese, and sat down at the door after I bought it, and ate it very heartily, and begged some beer to drink with it, which the good woman gave me very freely.

Away I went then for the town, to see if I could find any of my companions, and resolved I would try no more hollow trees for my treasure. As I came along Whitechapel I came by a broker's shop over against the church, where they sold old clothes, for I had nothing on but the worst of rags; so I stopped at the shop, and stood looking at the clothes which hung at the door.

"Well, young gentleman," says a man that stood at the door,

3. With as much gusto.
4. Chandlers made and sold candles, but many also traded in groceries and other provisions.

"you look wishfully. Do you see anything you like, and will your pocket compass a good coat now, for you look as if you belonged to the ragged regiment?" I was affronted at the fellow. "What's that to you," says I, "how ragged I am? If I had seen anything I liked, I have money to pay for it; but I can go where I shan't be huffed at for looking."

While I said this pretty boldly to the fellow, comes a woman out. "What ails you," says she to the man, "to bully away our customers so? A poor boy's money is as good as my Lord Mayor's. If poor people did not buy old clothes, what would become of our business?" And then turning to me, "Come hither, child," says she; "if thou hast a mind to anything I have, you shan't be hectored[5] by him. The boy is a pretty boy, I assure you," says she to another woman that was by this time come to her. "Ay," says t'other, "so he is, a very well-looking child, if he was clean and well dressed, and may be as good a gentleman's son, for anything we know, as any of those that are well dressed. Come, my dear," says she, "tell me what is it you would have." She pleased me mightily to hear her talk of my being a gentleman's son, and it brought former things to my mind; but when she talked of my being not clean and in rags, then I cried.

She pressed me to tell her if I saw anything that I wanted. I told her no, all the clothes I saw there were too big for me. "Come, child," says she, "I have two things here that will fit you, and I am sure you want them both; that is, first, a little hat, and there," says she (tossing it to me), "I'll give you that for nothing. And here is a good warm pair of breeches; I dare say," says she, "they will fit you, and they are very tight and good; and," says she, "if you should ever come to have so much money that you don't know what to do with it, here are excellent good pockets," says she, "and a little fob to put your gold in, or your watch in, when you get it."

It struck me with a strange kind of joy that I should have a place to put my money in, and need not go to hide it again in a hollow tree, that I was ready to snatch the breeches out of her hands, and wondered that I should be such a fool never to think of buying me a pair of breeches before, that I might have a pocket to put my money in, and not carry it about two days together in my hand, and in my shoes and I knew not how; so, in a word, I gave her two shillings for the breeches, and went over into the churchyard and put them on, put my money into my new pockets, and was as pleased as a prince is with his coach and six horses. I thanked the good woman too for the hat, and told her I would come again when I got more money, and buy some other things I wanted; and so I came away. * * *

1722

5. Bullied.

JONATHAN SWIFT
(1667–1745)

1704: A *Tale of a Tub* and *The Battle of the Books.*
1710–14: Alignment with Tories; political writings in defense of the Tory ministry.
1713: Made Dean of St. Patrick's Cathedral, Dublin.
1726: Publication of *Gulliver's Travels.*

Swift—a posthumous child—was born of English parents in Dublin. Through the generosity of an uncle he was educated at Kilkenny School and Trinity College, Dublin; but before he could fix on a career, the troubles that followed upon James II's abdication and his subsequent invasion of Ireland drove him along with other Anglo-Irish to England. Between 1689 and 1699 he was more or less continuously a member of the household of his kinsman Sir William Temple, an urbane, civilized man, a retired diplomat, and a friend of King William. During these years Swift read widely; rather reluctantly decided on the church as a career and so took orders; and discovered his astonishing gifts as a satirist. About 1696–97 he wrote his powerful satires on corruptions in religion and learning, *A Tale of a Tub* and *The Battle of the Books*, which were published in 1704 and reached their final form only in the fifth edition of 1710. These were the years in which he slowly came to maturity. When at the age of 32, he returned to Ireland as chaplain to the Lord Justice, the Earl of Berkeley, he had a clear sense of his genius.

It was at Temple's that Swift met and learned to love the woman whose role in his life has been the cause of much conjecture. Esther Johnson (Swift's "Stella") was the daughter of Temple's steward, and when Swift first knew her she was little more than a child. He educated her, formed her character, and came to love her as he was to love no other person. After Temple's death she removed (at Swift's suggestion) with her lifelong companion, Rebecca Dingley, to Dublin, where she and Swift met constantly, but never alone. To her he wrote the famous journal-letters, later published (1766) as *The Journal to Stella*, during his four-year residence in London when he was working with the Tories; and to her he wrote charming poems. Whether they were secretly married or whether they never married—and in either case why—has been often debated. A marriage of any sort seems most unlikely; and however perplexing their relationship was to others, it was obviously satisfying to each of them. Not even the violent passion that Swift awakened, no doubt unwittingly, in a much younger woman, Hester Vanhomrigh (pronounced *Van-úm-mer-y*), her pleadings and reproaches and early death, could unsettle his devotion to Stella. An enigmatic account of his relations with "Vanessa," as he called Miss Vanhomrigh, is given in his poem *Cadenus and Vanessa.*

The man who gained the lifelong devotion of Stella and evoked the romantic passion of Vanessa was also admired and loved by many of the distinguished men of his time. His friendships with Addison, Pope, Dr. Arbuthnot, John Gay, Prior, Oxford, Bolingbroke, not to mention those with his less brilliant, but pleasant, Irish circle, bear witness to his moral integrity and social charm. The dark side of Swift's nature has been exaggerated at the cost of neglecting the wit and gaiety, the playful humor, and the consciously assumed eccentricities which marked his social behavior. Nor is it tenable that his satires are the product of a diseased mind which was gradually disintegrating throughout his life. Swift suffered most of his adult life from what we now recognize as Ménière's syndrome, which affects the inner ear, causing dizziness, nausea, and deafness. By all these ills he was greatly afflicted, but he was never in any sense insane. After 1739, when he was 72 years old, his infirmities and deafness cut him off from social life and his duties as Dean, and from then on senility advanced inexorably. In 1742 guardians were appointed to administer his affairs, and his last three years were spent in gloom and lethargy. But the writer of the satires was a man in full control of very great intellectual powers.

Because Swift was a clergyman, a spirited controversialist, and a devoted supporter of the Anglican Church as an institution no less important than the Crown itself, he was drawn into politics in both England and Ireland. He was hostile to all who seemed to threaten the Established Church— Deists, freethinkers, Roman Catholics, Nonconformists, or merely Whig politicians. In 1710 he abandoned his old party, the Whig, because he disapproved of its indifference to the welfare of the Anglican Church in Ireland and of its desire to repeal the Test Act, which required all holders of offices of state to take the Sacrament according to the Anglican rites, thus excluding Roman Catholics and Dissenters. Welcomed by the Tories, he became the most brilliant political journalist of the day, serving the government of Oxford and Bolingbroke as editor of the party organ, the *Examiner*, and as author of its most powerful articles, as well as writing longer pamphlets in support of important policies, such as that favoring the Peace of Utrecht (1713). He was greatly valued by the two ministers, who admitted him to social intimacy, though never to their counsels. The reward of his services was not the English bishopric which he had a right to expect, but the Deanship of St. Patrick's Cathedral in Dublin, which came to him in 1713, a year before the death of Queen Anne and the fall of the Tories put an end to all his hopes of preferment in England.

In Ireland, where he lived unwillingly, he became not only an efficient ecclesiastical administrator, but also, in 1724, the leader of Irish resistance to English oppression. Under the pseudonym of "M. B., Drapier," he published the famous series of public letters that aroused the country to refuse to accept £100,000 in new copper coins (minted in England by William Wood, who had obtained his patent through court corruption) which, it was feared, would further debase the coinage of the already poverty-stricken kingdom. Although his authorship of the letters was known to all Dublin, no one could be found to earn the £300 offered by the government for information as to the identity of the Drapier. Swift is still venerated in Ireland as a national hero. He earned the right to refer to himself in the epitaph that he wrote for his tomb as a vigorous defender of liberty.

For all his involvement in public affairs, Swift seems to stand apart from his contemporaries—a striking figure even among the statesmen of the time, a man who towered above other writers by reason of his more profound imagination, mordant wit, and emotional intensity. He has been called a misanthrope, a hater of mankind; and *Gulliver's Travels* has been considered an expression of savage misanthropy. It is true that Swift proclaimed himself a misanthrope in a letter to Pope, declaring that though he loved individuals, he hated mankind in general, and offering a new definition of man as not *animal rationale* ("a rational animal"), but as merely *animal rationis capax* ("an animal *capable* of reason"). This, he declared, is the "great foundation" upon which his "misanthropy" was erected. Swift was stating not his hatred of his fellowmen, but his antagonism to the current optimistic view that human nature is essentially good. To the "philanthropic" flattery that sentimentalism and Deistic rationalism were paying to human nature, Swift opposed a more ancient and plausible view: that human nature is deeply and permanently flawed, and that we can do nothing with or for the human race until we recognize its moral and intellectual limitations. This attitude he was pleased to call "misanthropy." In his epitaph he spoke of the "fierce indignation" which had torn his heart, an indignation that found superb expression in his greatest satires. It was provoked by the constant spectacle of creatures capable of reason, and therefore of reasonable conduct, steadfastly refusing to live up to their capabilities.

Gulliver's Travels is Swift's most universal satire. Although it is full of allusions to recent and contemporary historical events, it is as valid today as it was in 1726, for its objects are man's moral nature and the defective political, economic, and social institutions which, because of his imperfections, he creates. Swift adopts an ancient satirical device: the imaginary voyage. Lemuel Gulliver, the narrator, is a ship's surgeon, a reasonably well-educated man, kindly, resourceful, cheerful, inquiring, patriotic, truthful, and rather unimaginative. He is, in short, a reasonably decent example of humanity, with whom we identify ourselves readily enough. He undertakes four voyages, all of which end disastrously among "several remote nations of the world." In the first, Gulliver is shipwrecked in the empire of Lilliput, where he finds himself a giant among a diminutive people, charmed by their miniature city and amused by their toylike prettiness. But in the end they prove to be treacherous, malicious, ambitious, vengeful, and cruel. As we read we grow disenchanted with the inhabitants of this fanciful kingdom, and then gradually we begin to recognize our likeness to them, especially in the disproportion between our natural pettiness and our boundless and destructive passions. In the second voyage (printed below), Gulliver is abandoned by his shipmates in Brobdingnag, a land of giants, creatures ten times as large as Europeans, as Gulliver had been twelve times as large as the Lilliputians. Naturally enough, he assumes that such monsters must be brutes, but the reverse proves to be the case. Brobdingnag is something of a utopia, governed by a humane and enlightened prince who is the embodiment of moral and political wisdom. In the long interview in which Gulliver pridefully enlarges on the glories of England and her political institutions, the King reduces him to resentful silence by asking questions which reveal the difference between what is and what ought to be in human, especially British, institutions. In Brobdingnag, Gulliver finds himself a Lilliputian, his pride humbled by his helpless state and his human vanity diminished by the realization that his body must have seemed as disgusting to the Lilliputians as do the bodies of the Brobdingnagians to him.

In the third voyage, to Laputa, Swift is chiefly concerned with attacking extremes of theoretical and speculative reasoning, whether in science, politics, or economics. Much of this voyage is an allegory of political life under the administration of the Whig minister, Sir Robert Walpole. The final voyage sets Gulliver between a race of horses, Houyhnhnms (pronounced *Hwin-ims*), who live entirely by reason except for a few well-controlled and muted social affections, and their slaves, the Yahoos, whose bodies are obscene caricatures of the human body, and who have no glimmer of reason, but are mere creatures of appetite and passion.

Swift is one of our greatest writers of prose. He defined a good style as "proper words in proper places," a more complex and difficult saying than at first appears. Clear, simple, concrete diction, uncomplicated syntax, economy and conciseness of language mark all of his writings. His is a style that shuns ornaments and singularity of all kinds, a style that grows more tense and controlled the more fierce the indignation that it is called upon to express. The virtues of his prose are those of his poetry, which only lately has come to be much valued. It is unpoetic poetry, devoid of, indeed as often as not mocking at, inspiration, romantic love, easily assumed literary attitudes, and conventional poetic language. Like the prose it is predominantly satiric in purpose, but not without its moments of comedy and light-heartedness, though written most often not so much to divert as to reform mankind.

A Description of a City Shower

Careful observers may foretell the hour
(By sure prognostics) when to dread a shower:
While rain depends,[1] the pensive cat gives o'er
Her frolics, and pursues her tail no more.
Returning home at night, you'll find the sink[2]   5
Strike your offended sense with double stink.
If you be wise, then go not far to dine;
You'll spend in coach hire more than save in wine.
A coming shower your shooting corns presage,
Old aches throb, your hollow tooth will rage.   10
Sauntering in coffeehouse is Dulman[3] seen;

1. Impends, is imminent. An example of elevated diction used frequently throughout the poem in order to gain a mock dignity, comically inappropriate to the homely and realistic subject.
2. Sewer.

3. A type name (from "dull man"), like Congreve's "Petulant" or "Witwoud." It was commonly believed at this time that the Englishman's tendency to melancholy ("the spleen") was attributable to the rainy climate.

He damns the climate and complains of spleen.
  Meanwhile the South, rising with dabbled wings,
A sable cloud athwart the welkin flings,
That swilled more liquor than it could contain,   15
And, like a drunkard, gives it up again.
Brisk Susan whips her linen from the rope,
While the first drizzling shower is borne aslope:
Such is that sprinkling which some careless quean[4]
Flirts on you from her mop, but not so clean: 20
You fly, invoke the gods; then turning, stop
To rail; she singing, still whirls on her mop.
Not yet the dust had shunned the unequal strife,
But, aided by the wind, fought still for life,
And wafted with its foe by violent gust,   25
'Twas doubtful which was rain and which was dust.
Ah! where must needy poet seek for aid,
When dust and rain at once his coat invade?
Sole coat, where dust cemented by the rain
Erects the nap, and leaves a mingled stain.   30
  Now in contiguous drops the flood comes down,
Threatening with deluge this devoted town.
To shops in crowds the daggled[5] females fly,
Pretend to cheapen goods, but nothing buy.
The Templar[6] spruce, while every spout's abroach,   35
Stays till 'tis fair, yet seems to call a coach.
The tucked-up sempstress walks with hasty strides,
While streams run down her oiled umbrella's sides.
Here various kinds, by various fortunes led,
Commence acquaintance underneath a shed.   40
Triumphant Tories and desponding Whigs
Forget their feuds,[7] and join to save their wigs.
Boxed in a chair[8] the beau impatient sits,
While spouts run clattering o'er the roof by fits,
And ever and anon with frightful din   45
The leather sounds;[9] he trembles from within.
So when Troy chairmen bore the wooden steed,
Pregnant with Greeks impatient to be freed
(Those bully Greeks, who, as the moderns do,
Instead of paying chairmen, run them through[1]),   50
Laocoön struck the outside with his spear,
And each imprisoned hero quaked for fear.[2]

4. Wench, slut.
5. Spattered with mud. "To cheapen": to bargain for.
6. A young man engaged in studying law. In the literature of the period the Templar is usually depicted as neglecting his professional studies for the sake of dissipation and the pursuit of literature. Cf. the Member of the Inner Temple in *Spectator* 2. "Abroach": pouring out water.
7. The Whig ministry had just fallen and the Tories, led by Harley and St. John, were forming the government with which Swift was to be closely associated until the death of the Queen in 1714.
8. Sedan chair.
9. The roof of the sedan chair was made of leather.
1. Run them through with their swords. The bully, always prone to violence, was a familiar figure in London streets and places of amusement.
2. *Aeneid* II.40–53.

Now from all parts the swelling kennels[3] flow,
And bear their trophies with them as they go:
Filth of all hues and odors seem to tell   55
What street they sailed from, by their sight and smell.
They, as each torrent drives with rapid force,
From Smithfield or St. Pulchre's shape their course,
And in huge confluence joined at Snow Hill ridge,
Fall from the conduit prone to Holborn Bridge.[4]   60
Sweepings from butchers' stalls, dung, guts, and blood,
Drowned puppies, stinking sprats,[5] all drenched in mud,
Dead cats, and turnip tops, come tumbling down the flood.[6]

1710

Verses on the Death of Dr. Swift

OCCASIONED BY READING A MAXIM IN ROCHEFOUCAULD [1]

*Dans l'adversité de nos meilleurs amis nous trouvons toujours quelque chose,
qui ne nous déplaît pas.*[2]

As Rochefoucauld his maxims drew
From nature, I believe 'em true:
They argue no corrupted mind
In him; the fault is in mankind.
This maxim more than all the rest   5
Is thought too base for human breast:
"In all distresses of our friends
We first consult our private ends,
While Nature, kindly bent to ease us,
Points out some circumstance to please us."   10
If this perhaps your patience move,
Let reason and experience prove.
We all behold with envious eyes
Our equal raised above our size.
Who would not at a crowded show   15
Stand high himself, keep others low?
I love my friend as well as you,

3. The open gutters in the middle of the street.
4. An accurate description of the drainage system of this part of London—the eastern edge of Holborn and West Smithfield, which lie outside the old walls west and east of Newgate. The great cattle and sheep markets were in Smithfield. The church of St. Sepulchre ("St. Pulchre's") stood opposite Newgate Prison. Holborn Conduit was at the foot of Snow Hill. It drained into Fleet Ditch, an evil-smelling open sewer, at Holborn Bridge.
5. Small herrings.
6. In Falkner's edition of Swift's *Works* (Dublin, 1735) a note almost certainly suggested by Swift points to the concluding triplet, with its resonant final Alexandrine, as a burlesque of a mannerism of Dryden and other Restoration poets, and claims that Swift's ridicule banished the triplet from contemporary poetry.
1. François de La Rochefoucauld (1613–80), writer of witty, cynical maxims. Writing to Pope (November 26, 1725), Swift, opposing the optimistic philosophy that Pope and Bolingbroke were at that time developing, professed to have founded his whole character on these maxims.
2. "In the misfortune of our best friends we always find something that does not displease us."

But why should he obstruct my view?
Then let me have the higher post;
Suppose it but an inch at most.   20
    If in a battle you should find
One, whom you love of all mankind,
Had some heroic action done,
A champion killed, or trophy won;
Rather than thus be overtopped,   25
Would you not wish his laurels cropped?
    Dear honest Ned is in the gout,
Lies racked with pain, and you without:
How patiently you hear him groan!
How glad the case is not your own!   30
    What poet would not grieve to see
His brethren write as well as he?
But rather than they should excel,
He'd wish his rivals all in hell.
    Her end when Emulation misses,   35
She turns to envy, stings, and hisses:
The strongest friendship yields to pride,
Unless the odds be on our side.
    Vain humankind! fantastic race!
Thy various follies who can trace?   40
Self-love, ambition, envy, pride,
Their empire in our hearts divide.
Give others riches, power, and station;
'Tis all on me an usurpation;
I have no title to aspire,   45
Yet, when you sink, I seem the higher.
In Pope I cannot read a line,
But with a sigh I wish it mine:
When he can in one couplet fix
More sense than I can do in six,   50
It gives me such a jealous fit,
I cry, "Pox take him and his wit!"
    I grieve to be outdone by Gay [3]
In my own humorous biting way.
Arbuthnot [4] is no more my friend,   55
Who dares to irony pretend,
Which I was born to introduce,
Refined it first, and showed its use.
St. John,[5] as well as Pulteney, knows

---

3. John Gay (1685–1732), author of
the famous *Beggar's Opera* (1728), intimate friend of Swift and Pope. His
*Trivia, or the Art of Walking the
Streets of London* (1716) owes something to Swift's *City Shower.*
4. Dr. John Arbuthnot, physician and
wit, friend of Swift and Pope. See
Pope's *Epistle to Dr. Arbuthnot.*
5. Henry St. John, Lord Bolingbroke
(see note, Pope's *Essay on Man.* I.1),

though debarred from the House of
Lords and from public office, had become the center of a group of Tories
and discontented young Whigs (of
whom William Pulteney was one) who
united in opposing Sir Robert Walpole,
the chief minister. They published a
political periodical, the *Craftsman*, thus
rivaling Swift in his role of political
pamphleteer and enemy of Sir Robert.

That I had some repute for prose;   60
And, till they drove me out of date,
Could maul a minister of state.
If they have mortified my pride,
And made me throw my pen aside;
If with such talents Heaven hath blessed 'em,   65
Have I not reason to detest 'em?
　　To all my foes, dear Fortune, send
Thy gifts, but never to my friend:
I tamely can endure the first,
But this with envy makes me burst.   70
　　Thus much may serve by way of proem;
Proceed we therefore to our poem.
　　The time is not remote, when I
Must by the course of nature die;
When, I foresee, my special friends   75
Will try to find their private ends:
Though it is hardly understood
Which way my death can do them good;
Yet thus, methinks, I hear 'em speak:
"See how the Dean begins to break!   80
Poor gentleman! he droops apace!
You plainly find it in his face.
That old vertigo⁶ in his head
Will never leave him till he's dead.
Besides, his memory decays;   85
He recollects not what he says;
He cannot call his friends to mind;
Forgets the place where last he dined;
Plies you with stories o'er and o'er,
He told them fifty times before.   90
How does he fancy we can sit
To hear his out-of-fashion wit?
But he takes up with younger folks,
Who for his wine will bear his jokes.
Faith, he must make his stories shorter,   95
Or change his comrades once a quarter;
In half the time he talks them round,
There must another set be found.
　　"For poetry, he's past his prime;
He takes an hour to find a rhyme;   100
His fire is out, his wit decayed,
His fancy sunk, his Muse a jade.⁷
I'd have him throw away his pen—
But there's no talking to some men."
　　And then their tenderness appears   105
By adding largely to my years:
"He's older than he would be reckoned,

6. Johnson in his *Dictionary* authorizes Swift's pronounciation: *ver-ti-go*.
7. A worn-out horse, in contrast to Pegasus, the winged horse of Greek mythology, emblem of poetic inspiration.

And well remembers Charles the Second.
He hardly drinks a pint of wine;
And that, I doubt, is no good sign.   110
His stomach, too, begins to fail;
Last year we thought him strong and hale;
But now he's quite another thing;
I wish he may hold out till spring."
They hug themselves, and reason thus: 115
"It is not yet so bad with us."
    In such a case they talk in tropes,[8]
And by their fears express their hopes.
Some great misfortune to portend
No enemy can match a friend.   120
With all the kindness they profess,
The merit of a lucky guess
(When daily how-d'ye's come of course,
And servants answer, "Worse and worse!")
Would please 'em better, than to tell   125
That God be praised! the Dean is well.
Then he who prophesied the best,
Approves his foresight to the rest:
"You know I always feared the worst,
And often told you so at first."   130
He'd rather choose that I should die,
Than his prediction prove a lie.
Not one foretells I shall recover,
But all agree to give me over.
    Yet, should some neighbor feel a pain   135
Just in the parts where I complain,
How many a message would he send!
What hearty prayers that I should mend!
Inquire what regimen I kept;
What gave me ease, and how I slept,   140
And more lament, when I was dead,
Then all the snivelers round my bed.
    My good companions, never fear;
For though you may mistake a year,
Though your prognostics run too fast,   145
They must be verified at last.
    Behold the fatal day arrive!
    "How is the Dean?"—"He's just alive."
Now the departing prayer is read.
"He hardly breathes"—"The Dean is dead."   150
Before the passing bell begun,
The news through half the town has run.
"Oh! may we all for death prepare!
What has he left? and who's his heir?"
"I know no more than what the news is;   155
'Tis all bequeathed to public uses."
"To public use! a perfect whim!

8. Figures of speech.

What had the public done for him?
Mere envy, avarice, and pride:
He gave it all—but first he died.   160
And had the Dean in all the nation
No worthy friend, no poor relation?
So ready to do strangers good,
Forgetting his own flesh and blood?"
Now Grub Street [9] wits are all employed;   165
With elegies the town is cloyed;
Some paragraph in every paper
To curse the Dean, or bless the Drapier.[1]
  The doctors, tender of their fame,
Wisely on me lay all the blame.   170
"We must confess his case was nice; [2]
But he would never take advice.
Had he been ruled, for aught appears,
He might have lived these twenty years:
For, when we opened him, we found,   175
That all his vital parts were sound."
  From Dublin soon to London spread,
'Tis told at court, "The Dean is dead."
Kind Lady Suffolk,[3] in the spleen,
Runs laughing up to tell the Queen.   180
The Queen, so gracious, mild and good,
Cries, "Is he gone? 'tis time he should.
He's dead, you say; why, let him rot:
I'm glad the medals were forgot.[4]
I promised him, I own; but when?   185
I only was the Princess then;
But now, as consort of the King,
You know, 'tis quite a different thing."
  Now Chartres,[5] at Sir Robert's levee,
Tells with a sneer the tidings heavy: 190
"Why, is he dead without his shoes?"
Cries Bob, "I'm sorry for the news:
Oh, were the wretch but living still,
And in his place my good friend Will! [6]
Or had a miter on his head,   195
Provided Bolingbroke were dead!"
  Now Curll his shop from rubbish drains: [7]

9. Originally a street in London largely inhabited by hack writers; later, a generic term applied to all such writers.
1. It was in the character of "M. B.," a Dublin drapier, that Swift aroused the Irish people to resistance against the importation of Wood's halfpence. See biographical introduction.
2. Delicate; hence demanding careful diagnosis and treatment.
3. George II's mistress, with whom Swift became friendly during his visit to Pope in 1726. "In the spleen": in low spirits. The phrase is ironic, as "laughing" in the next line makes clear.
4. Queen Caroline had promised Swift some medals when she was Princess of Wales during the same year.
5. Col. Francis Chartres, a debauchee often satirized by Pope; Sir Robert Walpole.
6. William Pulteney (see line 59 and its note.)
7. Edmund Curll, shrewd and disreputable bookseller, published pirated works, scandalous biographies, and works falsely ascribed to notable writers of the time.

Three genuine tomes of Swift's remains!
And then, to make them pass the glibber,
Revised by Tibbalds, Moore, and Cibber.[8]   200
He'll treat me as he does my betters,
Publish my will, my life, my letters;
Revive the libels born to die,
Which Pope must bear, as well as I.
        Here shift the scene, to represent   205
How those I love my death lament.
Poor Pope will grieve a month, and Gay
A week, and Arbuthnot a day.
        St. John himself will scarce forbear
To bite his pen, and drop a tear.   210
The rest will give a shrug, and cry,
"I'm sorry—but we all must die!"
        Indifference clad in wisdom's guise
All fortitude of mind supplies:
For how can stony bowels melt   215
In those who never pity felt?
When *we* are lashed, *they* kiss the rod,
Resigning to the will of God.
        The fools, my juniors by a year,
Are tortured with suspense and fear;   220
Who wisely thought my age a screen,
When death approached, to stand between:
The screen removed, their hearts are trembling;
They mourn for me without dissembling.
        My female friends, whose tender hearts   225
Have better learned to act their parts,
Receive the news in doleful dumps:
"The Dean is dead (and what is trumps?)
Then, Lord have mercy on his soul!
(Ladies, I'll venture for the vole.[9])   230
Six deans, they say, must bear the pall.
(I wish I knew what king to call.)
Madam, your husband will attend
The funeral of so good a friend?"
"No, madam, 'tis a shocking sight;   235
And he's engaged tomorrow night:
My Lady Club would take it ill,
If he should fail her at quadrille.
He loved the Dean—(I lead a heart)
But dearest friends, they say, must part.   240
His time was come; he ran his race;
We hope he's in a better place."
        Why do we grieve that friends should die?

8. Lewis Theobald (1688–1744), Shake-speare scholar and editor, already enthroned as King of the Dunces in Pope's *Dunciad* (1728). Like Pope, Swift spells the name phonetically. James Moore-Smyth, poetaster and playwright, an enemy of Pope. Colley Cibber (1671–1757), comic actor, playwright, and supremely untalented poet laureate. He succeeded Theobald as King of the Dunces in the *Dunciad* of 1743.

9. The equivalent in the card game quadrille of bidding a grand slam in bridge.

No loss more easy to supply.
One year is past; a different scene!   245
No further mention of the Dean,
Who now, alas! no more is missed,
Than if he never did exist.
Where's now this favorite of Apollo?
Departed—and his works must follow,   250
Must undergo the common fate;
His kind of wit is out of date.
    Some country squire to Lintot [1] goes,
Inquires for Swift in verse and prose.
Says Lintot, "I have heard the name;   255
He died a year ago."—"The same."
He searches all the shop in vain.
"Sir, you my find them in Duck Lane: [2]
I sent them, with a load of books,
Last Monday to the pastry-cook's.[3]   260
To fancy they could live a year!
I find you're but a stranger here.
The Dean was famous in his time,
And had a kind of knack at rhyme.
His way of writing now is past: 265
The town has got a better taste.
I keep no antiquated stuff;
But spick and span I have enough.
Pray do but give me leave to show 'em:
Here's Colley Cibber's birthday poem.   270
This ode you never yet have seen
By Stephen Duck [4] upon the Queen.
Then here's a letter finely penned
Against the *Craftsman* [5] and his friend;
It clearly shows that all reflection   275
On ministers is disaffection.
Next, here's Sir Robert's vindication,[6]
    And Mr. Henley's last oration.[7]
The hawkers have not got them yet:
Your honor please to buy a set?   280
    "Here's Woolston's tracts,[8] the twelfth edition;
'Tis read by every politician:
The country members, when in town,
To all their boroughs send them down;
You never met a thing so smart;   285

1. Bernard Lintot, the publisher of Pope's Homer and some of his early poems.
2. London street where second-hand books and publishers' "remainders" were sold.
3. To be used as waste paper for lining baking dishes and wrapping parcels.
4. Stephen Duck, "the thresher poet," an agricultural laborer, whose mild poetic gifts brought him to the notice and patronage of Queen Caroline.
5. See line 59 and its note.
6. "Walpole hires a string of party scribblers who do nothing else but write in his defense" [Swift's note].
7. "Orator" John Henley, an Independent preacher, who dazzled unlearned audiences with his oratory and who wrote treatises on elocution.
8. Thomas Woolston (1670–1733), a freethinker, whose *Discourses on the Miracles of Our Saviour* had recently earned him notoriety.

The courtiers have them all by heart;
Those maids of honor (who can read)
Are taught to use them for their creed.
The reverend author's good intention
Has been rewarded with a pension.   290
He does an honor to his gown,
By bravely running priestcraft down;
He shows, as sure as God's in Gloucester,
That Jesus was a grand impostor;
That all his miracles were cheats,   295
Performed as jugglers do their feats:
The Church had never such a writer;
A shame he has not got a miter!"
　　Suppose me dead; and then suppose
A club assembled at the Rose;   300
Where, from discourse of this and that,
I grow the subject of their chat.
And while they toss my name about,
With favor some, and some without,
One, quite indifferent in the cause,   305
My character impartial draws:
　　"The Dean, if we believe report,
Was never ill received at court.
As for his works in verse and prose,
I own myself no judge of those;   310
Nor can I tell what critics thought 'em:
But this I know, all people bought 'em,
As with a moral view designed
To cure the vices of mankind.
　　"His vein, ironically grave,   315
Exposed the fool and lashed the knave,
To steal a hint was never known,
But what he writ was all his own.
　　"He never thought an honor done him,
Because a duke was proud to own him,   320
Would rather slip aside and choose
To talk with wits in dirty shoes;
Despised the fools with stars and garters,
So often seen caressing Chartres.
He never courted men in station,   325
Nor persons held in admiration;
Of no man's greatness was afraid,
Because he sought for no man's aid.
Though trusted long in great affairs,
He gave himself no haughty airs;   330
Without regarding private ends,
Spent all his credit for his friends;
And only chose the wise and good;
No flatterers, no allies in blood;
But succored virtue in distress,   335
And seldom failed of good success;

As numbers in their hearts must own,
Who, but for him, had been unknown.
   "With princes kept a due decorum,
But never stood in awe before 'em.   340
He followed David's lesson just;
In princes never put thy trust:[9]
And would you make him truly sour,
Provoke him with a slave in power.
The Irish senate if you named,   345
With what impatience he declaimed!
Fair Liberty was all his cry,
For her he stood prepared to die;
For her he boldly stood alone;
For her he oft exposed his own.   350
Two kingdoms, just as faction led,
Had set a price upon his head,
But not a traitor could be found,
To sell him for six hundred pound.[1]
   "Had he but spared his tongue and pen,   355
He might have rose like other men;
But power was never in his thought,
And wealth he valued not a groat:
Ingratitude he often found,
And pitied those who meant the wound;   360
But kept the tenor of his mind,
To merit well of human kind:
Nor made a sacrifice of those
Who still were true, to please his foes.
He labored many a fruitless hour,   365
To reconcile his friends in power;
Saw mischief by a faction brewing,
While they pursued each other's ruin.
But finding vain was all his care,
He left the court in mere despair.[2]   370
   "And, oh! how short are human schemes!
Here ended all our golden dreams.
What St. John's skill in state affairs,
What Ormonde's [3] valor, Oxford's cares,
To save their sinking country lent,   375
Was all destroyed by one event.[4]

---

9. Psalm cxlvi.3.
1. In 1714 the government offered £300 for the discovery of the author of Swift's *Public Spirit of the Whigs,* and in 1724 the Irish government offered a similar amount for the discovery of the author of the fourth of Swift's *Drapier's Letters.*
2. The antagonism between the two chief ministers (his dear friends), Robert Harley, Earl of Oxford, and Bolingbroke paralyzed the Tory ministry in the crucial last months of Queen Anne's life and drove Swift to retirement in Ireland, whence he returned in 1714 to make a final effort to heal the breach and save the government. He failed and retired to the country in despair. There he received the news of Anne's death on August 1. The Hanoverian succession brought the Whigs back in triumph, ruined Swift's friends, and brought Swift's public life to a close.
3. James Butler, Duke of Ormonde, who succeeded to the command of the English armies on the Continent, when, in 1711, the Duke of Marlborough was stripped of his offices by Anne. He went into exile in 1714 and was active in Jacobite intrigue.
4. The death of Queen Anne.

Too soon that precious life was ended,
On which alone our weal depended.
When up a dangerous faction starts,[5]
With wrath and vengeance in their hearts;   380
By solemn League and Covenant bound,
To ruin, slaughter, and confound;
To turn religion to a fable,
And make the government a Babel;
Pervert the laws, disgrace the gown,   385
Corrupt the senate, rob the crown;
To sacrifice old England's glory,
And make her infamous in story:
When such a tempest shook the land,
How could unguarded Virtue stand?   390
With horror, grief, despair, the Dean
Beheld the dire destructive scene:
His friends in exile, or the Tower,[6]
Himself within the frown of power,
Pursued by base envenomed pens,   395
Far to the land of slaves and fens;[7]
A servile race in folly nursed,
Who truckle most, when treated worst.
    "By innocence and resolution,
He bore continual persecution;   400
While numbers to preferment rose,
Whose merits were to be his foes;
When even his own familiar friends,
Intent upon their private ends,
Like renegadoes now he feels,   405
Against him lifting up their heels.
    "The Dean did, by his pen, defeat
An infamous destructive cheat;[8]
Taught fools their interest how to know,
And gave them arms to ward the blow.   410
Envy has owned it was his doing,
To save that hapless land from ruin;
While they who at the steerage [9] stood,
And reaped the profit, sought his blood.
    "To save them from their evil fate,   415
In him was held a crime of state.
A wicked monster on the bench,[1]

---

5. Swift's view of the policies of the "dangerous faction" (the Whig party) is hardly impartial. He feared it especially because of its toleration of Dissenters, and so as an enemy of the Church of England.
6. Bolingbroke was in exile; Oxford was sent to the Tower by the Whigs.
7. Ireland.
8. The scheme to introduce Wood's copper halfpence into Ireland in 1723–24.
9. Literally the steering of a ship. Here the direction and management of public affairs in Ireland.
1. William Whitshed, Lord Chief Justice of the King's Bench of Ireland. In 1720, when the jury refused to find Swift's anonymous pamphlet *Proposal for the Universal Use of Irish Manufacture* wicked and seditious, Whitshed sent them back nine times, hoping to force them to another verdict. In 1724 he presided over the trial of Harding, the printer of Swift's fourth *Drapier's Letter*, but again was unable, despite bullying, to force a verdict of guilty.

Whose fury blood could never quench;
As vile and profligate a villain,
As modern Scroggs, or old Tresilian;[2]   420
Who long all justice had discarded,
Nor feared he God, nor man regarded;
Vowed on the Dean his rage to vent,
And make him of his zeal repent:
But Heaven his innocence defends,   425
The grateful people stand his friends;
Not strains of law, nor judge's frown,
Nor topics brought to please the crown,
Nor witness hired, nor jury picked,
Prevail to bring him in convict.   430
    "In exile, with a steady heart,
He spent his life's declining part;
Where folly, pride, and faction sway
Remote from St. John, Pope, and Gay.
    "His friendships there, to few confined,   435
Were always of the middling kind;
No fools of rank, a mongrel breed,
Who fain would pass for lords indeed:
Where titles give no right or power,
And peerage is a withered flower;   440
He would have held it a disgrace,
If such a wretch had known his face.
On rural squires, that kingdom's bane,
He vented oft his wrath in vain;
Biennial squires [3] to market brought: 445
Who sell their souls, and votes for naught;
The nation stripped, go joyful back,
To rob the church, their tenants rack,
Go snacks with rogues and rapparees;[4]
And keep the peace to pick up fees;   450
In every job to have a share,
A jail or barrack to repair;
And turn the tax for public roads,
Commodious to their own abodes.
    "Perhaps I may allow the Dean   455
Had too much satire in his vein;
And seemed determined not to starve it,
Because no age could more deserve it.
Yet malice never was his aim;
He lashed the vice, but spared the name;   460
No individual could resent,
Where thousands equally were meant;
His satire points at no defect,

2. Sir William Scroggs, Lord Chief Justice of England at the time of the Popish Plot, 1678 (see Dryden's *Absalom and Achitophel*), was impeached for his misdemeanors in office in 1680. Sir Robert Tresilian punished with great severity in 1381 men who had participated in the Peasants' Revolt; he was impeached and in 1387 was hanged.
3. Members of the Irish Parliament.
4. Highwaymen.

But what all mortals may correct;
For he abhorred that senseless tribe   465
Who call it humor when they gibe:
He spared a hump, or crooked nose,
Whose owners set not up for beaux.
True genuine dullness moved his pity,
Unless it offered to be witty.   470
Those who their ignorance confessed,
He ne'er offended with a jest;
But laughed to hear an idiot quote
A verse from Horace learned by rote.
    "He knew an hundred pleasant stories,   475
With all the turns of Whigs and Tories:
Was cheerful to his dying day;
And friends would let him have his way.
    "He gave the little wealth he had
To build a house for fools and mad;[5]   480
And showed by one satiric touch,
No nation wanted it so much.
That kingdom he hath left his debtor,
I wish it soon may have a better."

1731   1739

AN ARGUMENT TO PROVE THAT THE

Abolishing of Christianity in England

MAY, AS THINGS NOW STAND, BE ATTENDED WITH
SOME INCONVENIENCES, AND PERHAPS NOT
PRODUCE THOSE MANY GOOD EFFECTS PRO-
POSED THEREBY.[1]

I am very sensible what a weakness and presumption it is, to reason against the general humor and disposition of the world. I remember it was with great justice, and a due regard to the freedom both of the public and the press, forbidden upon several penalties to write, or discourse, or lay wagers against the Union,[2] even before it was confirmed by Parliament, because that was looked upon as a design to oppose the current of the people, which, besides the folly of it, is a manifest breach of the fundamental law that makes this

5. Swift left funds to endow a hospital for the insane.
1. The Test Act of 1673 required all holders of public office to take the sacrament of the Lord's Supper according to the usage of the Church of England; it was directed against Dissenters and Roman Catholics. In 1708 the Whigs (with whom Swift was then allied) were seeking to repeal the Test in Ireland and eventually in England, in an effort to consolidate the support of the Dissenters. Swift believed that repeal would do great harm to the Established Church, and as a good Anglican priest he opposed it with this essay.

Swift's technique is to assume blandly that to argue against the Test Act is to argue against Christianity and the Church, and he constructs his essay accordingly. The basic satiric principle is therefore that of the *reductio ad absurdum*, but this device is surrounded by a host of other ironies.
2. The union of Scotland and England under one crown in 1707.

majority of opinion the voice of God. In like manner, and for the very same reasons, it may perhaps be neither safe nor prudent to argue against the abolishing of Christianity at a juncture when all parties appear so unanimously determined upon the point, as we cannot but allow from their actions, their discourses, and their writings. However, I know not how, whether from the affectation of singularity, or the perverseness of human nature, but so it unhappily falls out that I cannot be entirely of this opinion. Nay, though I were sure an order were issued for my immediate prosecution by the attorney-general, I should still confess that in the present posture of our affairs at home or abroad, I do not yet see the absolute necessity of extirpating the Christian religion from among us.

This perhaps may appear too great a paradox even for our wise and paradoxical age to endure: therefore I shall handle it with all tenderness, and with the utmost deference to that great and profound majority which is of another sentiment.

And yet the curious may please to observe how much the genius of a nation is liable to alter in half an age: I have heard it affirmed for certain by some very old people that the contrary opinion was even in their memories as much in vogue as the other is now; and that a project for the abolishing of Christianity would then have appeared as singular, and been thought as absurd, as it would be at this time to write or discourse in its defense.

Therefore I freely own that all appearances are against me. The system of the Gospel, after the fate of other systems, is generally antiquated and exploded; and the mass or body of the common people, among whom it seems to have had its latest credit, are now grown as much ashamed of it as their betters; opinions, like fashions, always descending from those of quality to the middle sort, and thence to the vulgar, where at length they are dropped and vanish.

But here I would not be mistaken, and must therefore be so bold as to borrow a distinction from the writers on the other side, when they make a difference between nominal and real Trinitarians. I hope no reader imagines me so weak to stand up in the defense of real Christianity, such as used in primitive times (if we may believe the authors of those ages) to have an influence upon men's belief and actions: to offer at the restoring of that would indeed be a wild project; it would be to dig up foundations; to destroy at one blow all the wit, and half the learning of the kingdom; to break the entire frame and constitution of things; to ruin trade, extinguish arts and sciences with the professors of them; in short, to turn our courts, exchanges, and shops into deserts; and would be full as absurd as the proposal of Horace,[3] where he advises the Romans all in a body to

3. *Epode* xvi.

leave their city and seek a new seat in some remote part of the world, by way of cure for the corruption of their manners.

Therefore I think this caution was in itself altogether unnecessary (which I have inserted only to prevent all possibility of caviling), since every candid reader will easily understand my discourse to be intended only in defense of nominal Christianity, the other having been for some time wholly laid aside by general consent as utterly inconsistent with all other present schemes of wealth and power.

But why we should therefore cast off the name and title of Christians, although the general opinion and resolution be so violent for it, I confess I cannot (with submission) apprehend the consequence necessary. However, since the undertakers propose such wonderful advantages to the nation by this project, and advance many plausible objections against the system of Christianity, I shall briefly consider the strength of both, fairly allow them their greatest weight, and offer such answers as I think most reasonable. After which I will beg leave to show what inconveniences may possibly happen by such an innovation, in the present posture of our affairs.

First, one great advantage proposed by the abolishing of Christianity is that it would very much enlarge and establish liberty of conscience, that great bulwark of our nation, and of the protestant religion, which is still too much limited by priestcraft, notwithstanding all the good intentions of the legislature, as we have lately found by a severe instance. For it is confidently reported that two young gentlemen of real hopes, bright wit, and profound judgment, who upon a thorough examination of causes and effects, and by the mere force of natural abilities, without the least tincture of learning, having made a discovery that there was no God, and generously communicating their thoughts for the good of the public, were some time ago, by an unparalleled severity, and upon I know not what obsolete law, broke only for blasphemy. And as it hath been wisely observed, if persecution once begins, no man alive knows how far it may reach, or where it will end.

In answer to all which, with deference to wiser judgments, I think this rather shows the necessity of a nominal religion among us. Great wits love to be free with the highest objects; and if they cannot be allowed a God to revile or renounce, they will speak evil of dignities, abuse the government, and reflect upon the ministry; which I am sure few will deny to be of much more pernicious consequence, according to the saying of Tiberius, *Deorum offensa diis curae*.[4] As to the particular fact related, I think it is not fair to argue from one instance; perhaps another cannot be produced; yet (to the comfort of all those who may be apprehensive of persecution) blasphemy we know is freely spoken a million of times in every

---

4. "Offenses against the gods are the concern of the gods" (Tacitus, *Annals* I.lxxiii).

coffeehouse and tavern, or wherever else good company meet. It must be allowed indeed, that to break an English freeborn officer only for blasphemy, was, to speak the gentlest of such an action, a very high strain of absolute power. Little can be said in excuse for the general; perhaps he was afraid it might give offense to the allies [5] among whom, for aught we know, it may be the custom of the country to believe a God. But if he argued, as some have done, upon a mistaken principle, that an officer who is guilty of speaking blasphemy may some time or other proceed so far as to raise a mutiny, the consequence is by no means to be admitted: for, surely the commander of an English army is likely to be but ill obeyed whose soldiers fear and reverence him as little as they do a deity.

It is further objected against the gospel system that it obliges men to the belief of things too difficult for freethinkers, and such who have shaken off the prejudices that usually cling to a confined education. To which I answer that men should be cautious how they raise objections which reflect upon the wisdom of the nation. Is not everybody freely allowed to believe whatever he pleases, and to publish his belief to the world whenever he thinks fit, especially if it serves to strengthen the party which is in the right? Would any indifferent foreigner who should read the trumpery lately written by Asgil, Tindal, Toland, Coward,[6] and forty more, imagine the Gospel to be our rule of faith, and confirmed by parliaments? Does any man either believe, or say he believes, or desire to have it thought that he says he believes one syllable of the matter? And is any man worse received upon that score, or does he find his want of nominal faith a disadvantage to him in the pursuit of any civil or military employment? What if there be an old dormant statute or two against him? Are they not now obsolete to a degree that Empson and Dudley [7] themselves, if they were now alive, would find it impossible to put them in execution?

It is likewise urged that there are by computation in this kingdom above ten thousand parsons whose revenues, added to those of my lords the bishops, would suffice to maintain at least two hundred young gentlemen of wit and pleasure, and freethinking enemies to priestcraft, narrow principles, pedantry, and prejudices; who might be an ornament to the court and town. And then again, so great a number of able (-bodied) divines might be a recruit to our fleet and armies. This indeed appears to be a consideration of some weight; but then, on the other side, several things deserve to be considered likewise: as, first, whether it may not be thought necessary that in certain tracts of country, like what we call parishes, there shall be one man at least of abilities to read and write. Then it

5. England's principal allies against France in the War of the Spanish Succession were Holland, Austria, Prussia, Portugal, and Savoy.

6. Deistic writers.
7. Two corrupt ministers of Henry VII, notorious for reviving obsolete statutes in subservience to that king's greed.

seems a wrong computation that the revenues of the Church throughout this island would be large enough to maintain two hundred young gentlemen, or even half that number, after the present refined way of living; that is, to allow each of them such a rent [8] as, in the modern form of speech, would make them easy. But still there is in this project a greater mischief behind; and we ought to beware of the woman's folly who killed the hen that every morning laid her a golden egg. For, pray, what would become of the race of men in the next age if we had nothing to trust to beside the scrofulous, consumptive productions, furnished by our men of wit and pleasure, when, having squandered away their vigor, health, and estates, they are forced by some disagreeable marriage to piece up their broken fortunes, and entail rottenness and politeness on their posterity? Now here are ten thousand persons reduced by the wise regulations of Henry the Eighth to the necessity of a low diet and moderate exercise,[9] who are the only great restorers of our breed, without which the nation would in an age or two become one great hospital.

Another advantage proposed by the abolishing of Christianity is the clear gain of one day in seven, which is now entirely lost, and consequently the kingdom one-seventh less considerable in trade, business, and pleasure; besides the loss to the public of so many stately structures now in the hands of the clergy, which might be converted into playhouses, exchanges, markethouses, common dormitories, and other public edifices.

I hope I shall be forgiven a hard word, if I call this a perfect cavil. I readily own there hath been an old custom, time out of mind, for people to assemble in the churches every Sunday, and that shops are still frequently shut, in order, as it is conceived, to preserve the memory of that ancient practice; but how this can prove a hindrance to business or pleasure is hard to imagine. What if the men of pleasure are forced, one day in the week, to game at home instead of the chocolatehouse? Are not the taverns and coffeehouses open? Can there be a more convenient season for taking a dose of physic? Are fewer claps got upon Sundays than other days? Is not that the chief day for traders to sum up the accounts of the week and for lawyers to prepare their briefs? But I would fain know how it can be pretended that the churches are misapplied? Where are more appointments and rendezvouses of gallantry? Where more care to appear in the foremost box with greater advantage of dress? Where more meetings for business? Where more bargains driven of all sorts? And where so many conveniences or incitements to sleep?

8. Income.
9. Swift refers ironically to Henry VIII's expropriation of church lands at the time of the Reformation. Instead of giving them to the church for the support of the clergy, as Swift thought he should have done, he bestowed them on laymen, thus impoverishing the lower clergy, who were deprived of the tithes that would otherwise have been their due.

There is one advantage greater than any of the foregoing proposed by the abolishing of Christianity: that it will utterly extinguish parties among us by removing those factious distinctions of High and Low Church, of Whig and Tory, Presbyterian and Church of England, which are now so many mutual clogs upon public proceedings, and dispose men to prefer the gratifying themselves, or depressing their adversaries, before the most important interest of the state.

I confess, if it were certain that so great an advantage would redound to the nation by this expedient, I would submit and be silent: but will any man say that if the words *whoring, drinking, cheating, lying, stealing,* were by act of Parliament ejected out of the English tongue and dictionaries, we should all awake next morning chaste and temperate, honest and just, and lovers of truth? Is this a fair consequence? Or, if the physicians would forbid us to pronounce the words *pox, gout, rheumatism,* and *stone,* would that expedient serve like so many talismans to destroy the diseases themselves? Are party and faction rooted in men's hearts no deeper than phrases borrowed from religion, or founded upon no firmer principles? And is our language so poor that we cannot find other terms to express them? Are *envy, pride, avarice,* and *ambition* such ill nomenclators that they cannot furnish appellations for their owners? Will not *heydukes* and *mamalukes, mandarins* and *patshaws,* or any other words formed at pleasure, serve to distinguish those who are in the ministry from others who would be in it if they could? What, for instance, is easier than to vary the form of speech, and instead of the *church,* make it a question in politics whether the Monument [1] be in danger? Because religion was nearest at hand to furnish a few convenient phrases, is our invention so barren we can find no others? Suppose, for argument sake, that the Tories favored Margarita, the Whigs Mrs. Tofts, and the Trimmers Valentini,[2] would not *Margaritians, Toftians,* and *Valentinians* be very tolerable marks of distinction? The *Prasini* and *Veniti,*[3] two most virulent factions in Italy, began (if I remember right) by a distinction of colors in ribbons, which we might do with as good a grace about the dignity of the blue and the green, and would serve as properly to divide the court, the Parliament, and the kingdom between them, as any terms of art whatsoever borrowed from religion. Therefore I think there is little force in this objection against Christianity, or prospect of so great an advantage as is proposed in the abolishing of it.

'Tis again objected as a very absurd, ridiculous custom that a set of men should be suffered, much less employed and hired, to bawl one day in seven against the lawfulness of those methods most in use toward the pursuit of greatness, riches, and pleasure, which are

---

1. The column that commemorates the great fire of London, 1666.
2. Singers in the popular Italian opera.
3. Rival factions in the Roman chariot races, violently supported by the populace.

the constant practice of all men alive on the other six. But this objection is, I think, a little unworthy so refined an age as ours. Let us argue this matter calmly; I appeal to the breast of any polite freethinker whether in the pursuit of gratifying a predominant passion he hath not always felt a wonderful incitement, by reflecting it was a thing forbidden; and therefore we see, in order to cultivate this taste, the wisdom of the nation hath taken special care that the ladies should be furnished with prohibited silks and the men with prohibited wine. And indeed, it were to be wished that some other prohibitions were promoted in order to improve the pleasures of the town; which, for want of such expedients begin already, as I am told, to flag and grow languid, giving way daily to cruel inroads from the spleen.[4]

'Tis likewise proposed as a great advantage to the public that if we once discard the system of the Gospel, all religion will of course be banished for ever; and consequently, along with it, those grievous prejudices of education, which under the names of *virtue, conscience, honor, justice*, and the like, are so apt to disturb the peace of human minds, and the notions whereof are so hard to be eradicated by right reason or freethinking, sometimes during the whole course of our lives.

Here first I observe how difficult it is to get rid of a phrase which the world is once grown fond of, though the occasion that first produced it be entirely taken away. For several years past, if a man had but an ill-favored nose, the deep thinkers of the age would some way or other contrive to impute the cause to the prejudice of his education. From this fountain were said to be derived all our foolish notions of justice, piety, love of our country, all our opinions of God, or a future state, heaven, hell, and the like: and there might formerly perhaps have been some pretense for this charge. But so effectual care hath been since taken to remove those prejudices by an entire change in the methods of education that (with honor I mention it to our polite innovators) the young gentlemen who are now on the scene, seem to have not the least tincture of those infusions, or string of those weeds; and, by consequence, the reason for abolishing nominal Christianity upon that pretext is wholly ceased.

For the rest, it may perhaps admit a controversy whether the banishing of all notions of religion whatsoever would be convenient for the vulgar. Not that I am in the least of opinion with those who hold religion to have been the invention of politicians to keep the lower part of the world in awe by the fear of invisible powers; unless mankind were then very different from what it is now: for I look upon the mass or body of our people here in England to be as freethinkers, that is to say, as staunch unbelievers, as any of the highest

4. Melancholy; often a real affliction, but as often affected as a fashionable ailment.

rank. But I conceive some scattered notions about a superior power to be of singular use for the common people, as furnishing excellent materials to keep children quiet when they grow peevish, and providing topics of amusement in a tedious winter night.

Lastly, it is proposed as a singular advantage that the abolishing of Christianity will very much contribute to the uniting of Protestants, by enlarging the terms of communion so as to take in all sorts of Dissenters, who are now shut out of the pale upon account of a few ceremonies which all sides confess to be things indifferent; that this alone will effectually answer the great ends of a scheme for comprehension, by opening a large noble gate, at which all bodies may enter: whereas the chaffering with Dissenters, and dodging about this or t'other ceremony, is but like opening a few wickets [5] and leaving them at jar, by which no more than one can get in at a time, and that, not without stooping, and sideling, and squeezing his body.

To all this I answer that there is one darling inclination of mankind, which usually affects to be a retainer to religion, though she be neither its parent, its godmother, or its friend; I mean the spirit of opposition, that lived long before Christianity, and can easily subsist without it. Let us, for instance, examine wherein the opposition of sectaries [6] among us consists; we shall find Christianity to have no share in it at all. Does the Gospel any where prescribe a starched, squeezed countenance, a stiff, formal gait, a singularity of manners and habit, or any affected modes of speech different from the reasonable part of mankind? Yet, if Christianity did not lend its name to stand in the gap, and to employ or divert these humors, they must of necessity be spent in contraventions to the laws of the land, and disturbance of the public peace. There is a portion of enthusiasm assigned to every nation, which, if it hath not proper objects to work on, will burst out, and set all in a flame. If the quiet of state can be bought by only flinging men a few ceremonies to devour, it is a purchase no wise man would refuse. Let the mastiffs amuse themselves about a sheepskin stuffed with hay, provided it will keep them from worrying the flock. The institution of convents abroad seems in one point a strain of great wisdom, there being few irregularities in human passions that may not have recourse to vent themselves in some of those orders, which are so many retreats for the speculative, the melancholy, the proud, the silent, the politic and the morose, to spend themselves, and evaporate the noxious particles; for each of whom we in this island are forced to provide a several sect of religion, to keep them quiet. And whenever Christianity shall be abolished, the legislature must find some other expedient to employ and entertain them. For what imports it how large a gate you open if there will be always left a number who place a pride and merit in refusing to enter?

5. Small gates. 6. Adherents of one of the dissenting sects.

Having thus considered the most important objections against Christianity and the chief advantages proposed by the abolishing thereof, I shall now with equal deference and submission to wiser judgments as before, proceed to mention a few inconveniences that may happen if the Gospel should be repealed; which perhaps the projectors may not have sufficiently considered.

And first, I am very sensible how much the gentlemen of wit and pleasure are apt to murmur, and be choked at the sight of so many daggled-tail parsons who happen to fall in their way, and offend their eyes. But at the same time, these wise reformers do not consider what an advantage and felicity it is for great wits to be always provided with objects of scorn and contempt, in order to exercise and improve their talents, and divert their spleen from falling on each other or on themselves; especially when all this may be done without the least imaginable danger to their persons.

And to urge another argument of a parallel nature: if Christianity were once abolished, how could the freethinkers, the strong reasoners, and the men of profound learning, be able to find another subject so calculated in all points whereon to display their abilities? What wonderful productions of wit should we be deprived of from those whose genius by continual practice hath been wholly turned upon raillery and invectives against religion, and would therefore never be able to shine or distinguish themselves upon any other subject! We are daily complaining of the great decline of wit among us, and would we take away the greatest, perhaps the only, topic we have left? Who would ever have suspected Asgil for a wit, or Toland for a philosopher, if the inexhaustible stock of Christianity had not been at hand to provide them with materials? What other subject, through all art or nature, could have produced Tindal for a profound author, or furnished him with readers? It is the wise choice of the subject that alone adorns and distinguishes the writer. For had a hundred such pens as these been employed on the side of religion, they would have immediately sunk into silence and oblivion.

Nor do I think it wholly groundless, or my fears altogether imaginary, that the abolishing of Christianity may perhaps bring the Church in danger, or at least put the senate to the trouble of another securing vote. I desire I may not be mistaken; I am far from presuming to affirm or think that the Church is in danger at present, or as things now stand; but we know not how soon it may be so when the Christian religion is repealed. As plausible as this project seems, there may a dangerous design lurk under it. Nothing can be more notorious than that the atheists, deists, Socinians,[7] Antitrinitarians, and other subdivisions of freethinkers are persons of little zeal for the present ecclesiastical establishment: their declared opinion is for repealing the Sacramental Test; they are very

7 The Socinians denied the divinity of Jesus.

indifferent with regard to ceremonies; nor do they hold the *jus divinum* of Episcopacy.[8] Therefore this may be intended as one politic step toward altering the constitution of the Church established, and setting up Presbytery [9] in the stead, which I leave to be further considered by those at the helm.

In the last place, I think nothing can be more plain than that by this expedient, we shall run into the evil we chiefly pretend to avoid; and that the abolishment of the Christian religion will be the readiest course we can take to introduce popery. And I am the more inclined to this opinion because we know it has been the constant practice of the Jesuits to send over emissaries with instructions to personate themselves members of the several prevailing sects among us. So it is recorded that they have at sundry times appeared in the guise of Presbyterians, Anabaptists, Independents, and Quakers, according as any of these were most in credit; so, since the fashion hath been taken up of exploding religion, the popish missionaries have not been wanting to mix with the freethinkers; among whom, Toland, the great oracle of the Antichristians, is an Irish priest, the son of an Irish priest; and the most learned and ingenious author of a book called *The Rights of the Christian Church*, was in a proper juncture reconciled to the Romish faith, whose true son, as appears by an hundred passages in his treatise, he still continues. Perhaps I could add some others to the number; but the fact is beyond dispute, and the reasoning they proceed by is right: for, supposing Christianity to be extinguished, the people will never be at ease till they find out some other method of worship; which will as infallibly produce superstition as this will end in popery.

And therefore, if notwithstanding all I have said, it still be thought necessary to have a bill brought in for repealing Christianity, I would humbly offer an amendment; that instead of the word *Christianity* may be put *religion* in general; which I conceive will much better answer all the good ends proposed by the projectors of it. For, as long as we leave in being a God and his providence, with all the necessary consequences which curious and inquisitive men will be apt to draw from such premises, we do not strike at the root of the evil, though we should ever so effectually annihilate the present scheme of the Gospel. For of what use is freedom of thought, if it will not produce freedom of action, which is the sole end, how remote soever in appearance, of all objections against Christianity? And, therefore, the freethinkers consider it as a sort of edifice wherein all the parts have such a mutual dependence on each other that if you happen to pull out one single nail, the whole fabric must fall to the ground. This was happily expressed by him who had heard of a text brought for proof of the Trinity, which in an ancient manuscript was differently read; he thereupon immedi-

---

8. The divine authority of Anglican bishops, derived from apostolic succession.

9. The Presbyterians opposed episcopacy and set up a democratic form of church government.

ately took the hint, and by a sudden deduction of a long *sorites*,[10] most logically concluded, "Why, if it be as you say, I may safely whore and drink on, and defy the parson." From which, and many the like instances easy to be produced, I think nothing can be more manifest than that the quarrel is not against any particular points of hard digestion in the Christian system, but against religion in general; which, by laying restraints on human nature, is supposed the great enemy to the freedom of thought and action.

Upon the whole, if it shall still be thought for the benefit of Church and State that Christianity be abolished, I conceive, however, it may be more convenient to defer the execution to a time of peace, and not venture in this conjuncture to disoblige our allies, who, as it falls out, are all Christians; and many of them, by the prejudices of their education, so bigoted as to place a sort of pride in the appellation. If upon being rejected by them, we are to trust to an alliance with the Turk, we shall find ourselves much deceived: for, as he is too remote, and generally engaged in war with the Persian emperor, so his people would be more scandalized at our infidelity than our Christian neighbors. Because the Turks are not only strict observers of religious worship, but what is worse, believe a God; which is more than is required of us even while we preserve the name of Christians.

To conclude: whatever some may think of the great advantages to trade by this favorite scheme, I do very much apprehend that in six months time after the act is passed for the extirpation of the Gospel, the Bank and East-India Stock may fall at least one per cent. And since that is fifty times more than ever the wisdom of our age thought fit to venture for the preservation of Christianity, there is no reason we should be at so great a loss merely for the sake of destroying it.

1708

1711

From Gulliver's Travels[1]

A Letter from Captain Gulliver to His Cousin Sympson

I hope you will be ready to own publicly, whenever you shall be called to it, that by your great and frequent urgency you prevailed on me to publish a very loose and uncorrect account of my travels;

10. "An argument when one proposition is accumulated on another" (Johnson's *Dictionary*).

1. Swift's full title for this work was *Travels into Several Remote Nations of the World. In Four Parts. By Lemuel Gulliver, First a Surgeon, and then a Captain of several Ships.* In the first edition (1726), either the bookseller or Swift's friends Charles Ford, Pope, and others, who were concerned in getting the book anonymously into print, altered and omitted so much of the original manuscript (because of its dangerous political implications) that Swift was seriously annoyed. When, in 1735, the Dublin bookseller George Faulkner brought out an edition of Swift's works, the Dean seems to have taken pains, surreptitiously, to see that a more authen-

with direction to hire some young gentlemen of either University to put them in order, and correct the style, as my Cousin Dampier [2] did by my advice, in his book called *A Voyage round the World*. But I do not remember I gave you power to consent that anything should be omitted, and much less that anything should be inserted: therefore, as to the latter, I do here renounce everything of that kind; particularly a paragraph about her Majesty the late Queen Anne, of most pious and glorious memory; although I did reverence and esteem her more than any of human species. But you, or your interpolator, ought to have considered that as it was not my inclination, so was it not decent to praise any animal of our composition before my master Houyhnhnm; and besides, the fact was altogether false; for to my knowledge, being in England during some part of her Majesty's reign, she did govern by a chief Minister; nay, even by two successively; the first whereof was the Lord of Godolphin, and the second the Lord of Oxford; so that you have made me *say the thing that was not*. Likewise, in the account of the Academy of Projectors, and several passages of my discourse to my master Houyhnhnm, you have either omitted some material circumstances, or minced or changed them in such a manner, that I do hardly know mine own work. When I formerly hinted to you something of this in a letter, you were pleased to answer that you were afraid of giving offense; that people in power were very watchful over the press; and apt not only to interpret, but to punish everything which looked like an *inuendo* (as I think you called it). But pray, how could that which I spoke so many years ago, and at above five thousand leagues distance, in another reign, be applied to any of the Yahoos, who now are said to govern the herd; especially, at a time when I little thought on or feared the unhappiness of living under them. Have not I the most reason to complain, when I see these very Yahoos carried by Houyhnhnms in a vehicle, as if these were brutes, and those the rational creatures? And, indeed, to avoid so monstrous and detestable a sight was one principal motive of my retirement hither.[3]

Thus much I thought proper to tell you in relation to yourself, and to the trust I reposed in you.

I do in the next place complain of my own great want of judgment, in being prevailed upon by the intreaties and false reasonings of you and some others, very much against mine own opinion, to suffer my travels to be published. Pray bring to your mind how often I desired you to consider, when you insisted on the motive of

---

tic version of the work was published. This text is the basis of modern editions.

In this letter, first published in 1735, Swift complains, among other matters, of the alterations in his original text made by the publisher, Benjamin Motte,

in the interest of what he considered political discretion.
2. William Dampier (1652–1715), the explorer, whose account of his circumnavigation of the globe Swift had read.
3. To Nottinghamshire.

public good, that the Yahoos were a species of animals utterly incapable of amendment by precepts or examples; and so it hath proved; for instead of seeing a full stop put to all abuses and corruptions, at least in this little island, as I had reason to expect, behold, after above six months warning. I cannot learn that my book hath produced one single effect according to mine intentions; I desired you would let me know by a letter, when party and faction were extinguished; judges learned and upright; pleaders honest and modest, with some tincture of common sense; and Smithfield [4] blazing with pyramids of law books; the young nobility's education entirely changed; the physicians banished; the female Yahoos abounding in virtue, honor, truth, and good sense; courts and levees of great ministers thoroughly weeded and swept; wit, merit, and learning rewarded; all disgracers of the press in prose and verse, condemned to eat nothing but their own cotton,[5] and quench their thirst with their own ink. These, and a thousand other reformations, I firmly counted upon by your encouragement; as indeed they were plainly deducible from the precepts delivered in my book. And, it must be owned that seven months were a sufficient time to correct every vice and folly to which Yahoos are subject; if their natures had been capable of the least disposition to virtue or wisdom; yet so far have you been from answering mine expectation in any of your letters, that on the contrary, you are loading our carrier every week with libels, and keys, and reflections, and memoirs, and second parts; wherein I see myself accused of reflecting upon great statesfolk; of degrading human nature (for so they have still the confidence to style it) and of abusing the female sex. I find likewise, that the writers of those bundles are not agreed among themselves; for some of them will not allow me to be author of mine own travels; and others make me author of books to which I am wholly a stranger.

I find likewise that your printer hath been so careless as to confound the times, and mistake the dates of my several voyages and returns; neither assigning the true year, or the true month, or day of the month; and I hear the original manuscript is all destroyed, since the publication of my book. Neither have I any copy left; however, I have sent you some corrections, which you may insert, if ever there should be a second edition; and yet I cannot stand to them, but shall leave that matter to my judicious and candid readers, to adjust it as they please.

I hear some of our sea Yahoos find fault with my sea language, as not proper in many parts, nor now in use. I cannot help it. In my first voyages, while I was young, I was instructed by the oldest mariners, and learned to speak as they did. But I have since found

4. A part of London containing many bookshops.

5. Presumably their paper.

that the sea Yahoos are apt, like the land ones, to become new fangled in their words; which the latter change every year; insomuch, as I remember upon each return to mine own country, their old dialect was so altered, that i could hardly understand the new. And I observe, when any Yahoo comes from London out of curiosity to visit me at mine own house, we neither of us are able to deliver our conceptions in a manner intelligible to the other.[6]

If the censure of Yahoos could any way affect me, I should have great reason to complain that some of them are so bold as to think my book of travels a mere fiction out of mine own brain; and have gone so far as to drop hints that the Houyhnhnms, and Yahoos have no more existence than the inhabitants of Utopia.

Indeed I must confess that as to the people of Lilliput, Brobdingrag (for so the word should have been spelled, and not erroneously Brobdingnag) and Laputa, I have never yet heard of any Yahoo so presumptuous as to dispute their being, or the facts I have related concerning them; because the truth immediately strikes every reader with conviction. And, is there less probability in my account of the Houyhnhnms or Yahoos, when it is manifest as to the latter, there are so many thousands even in this city, who only differ from their brother brutes in Houyhnhnmland, because they use a sort of a jabber, and do not go naked. I wrote for their amendment, and not their approbation. The united praise of the whole race would be of less consequence to me, than the neighing of those two degenerate Houyhnhnms I keep in my stable; because, from these, degenerate as they are, I still improve in some virtues, without any mixture of vice.

Do these miserable animals presume to think that I am so far degenerated as to defend my veracity; Yahoo as I am, it is well known through all Houyhnhnmland, that by the instructions and example of my illustrious master, I was able in the compass of two years (although I confess with the utmost difficulty) to remove that infernal habit of lying, shuffling, deceiving, and equivocating, so deeply rooted in the very souls of all my species; especially the Europeans.

I have other complaints to make upon this vexatious occasion; but I forbear troubling myself or you any further. I must freely confess that since my last return, some corruptions of my Yahoo nature have revived in me by conversing with a few of your species, and particularly those of mine own family, by an unavoidable necessity; else I should never have attempted so absurd a project as that of reforming the Yahoo race in this kingdom; but I have now done with all such visionary schemes for ever.

1727?   1735

6. Swift was the inveterate enemy of slang.

The Publisher to the Reader

The author of these travels, Mr. Lemuel Gulliver, is my ancient and intimate friend; there is likewise some relation between us by the mother's side. About three years ago Mr. Gulliver, growing weary of the concourse of curious people coming to him at his house in Redriff,[1] made a small purchase of land, with a convenient house, near Newark, in Nottinghamshire, his native country; where he now lives retired, yet in good esteem among his neighbors.

Although Mr. Gulliver were born in Nottinghamshire, where his father dwelt, yet I have heard him say his family came from Oxfordshire; to confirm which, I have observed in the churchyard at Banbury, in that county, several tombs and monuments of the Gullivers.

Before he quitted Redriff, he left the custody of the following papers in my hands, with the liberty to dispose of them as I should think fit. I have carefully perused them three times; the style is very plain and simple; and the only fault I find is that the author, after the manner of travelers, is a little too circumstantial. There is an air of truth apparent through the whole; and indeed the author was so distinguished for his veracity, that it became a sort of proverb among his neighbors at Redriff, when anyone affirmed a thing, to say, it was as true as if Mr. Gulliver had spoke it.

By the advice of several worthy persons, to whom, with the author's permission, I communicated these papers, I now venture to send them into the world; hoping they may be, at least for some time, a better entertainment to our young noblemen, than the common scribbles of politics and party.

This volume would have been at least twice as large, if I had not made bold to strike out innumerable passages relating to the winds and tides, as well as to the variations and bearings in the several voyages; together with the minute descriptions of the management of the ship in storms, in the style of sailors; likewise the account of the longitudes and latitudes, wherein I have reason to apprehend that Mr. Gulliver may be a little dissatisfied; but I was resolved to fit the work as much as possible to the general capacity of readers. However, if my own ignorance in sea affairs shall have led me to commit some mistakes, I alone am answerable for them; and if any traveler hath a curiosity to see the whole work at large, as it came from the hand of the author, I will be ready to gratify him.

As for any further particulars relating to the author, the reader will receive satisfaction from the first pages of the book.

RICHARD SYMPSON

1. Rotherhithe, a district in southern London, below Tower Bridge, then frequented by sailors.

Part II. A Voyage to Brobdingnag

CHAPTER I. *A great storm described. The longboat sent to fetch water; the Author goes with it to discover the country. He is left on shore, is seized by one of the natives, and carried to a farmer's house. His reception there, with several accidents that happened there. A description of the inhabitants.*

Having been condemned by nature and fortune to an active and restless life, in ten months after my return I again left my native country, and took shipping in the Downs on the 20th day of June, 1702, in the *Adventure,* Captain John Nicholas, a Cornish man, Commander, bound for Surat.[2] We had a very prosperous gale till we arrived at the Cape of Good Hope, where we landed for fresh water, but discovering a leak we unshipped our goods and wintered there; for the Captain falling sick of an ague, we could not leave the Cape till the end of March. We then set sail, and had a good voyage till we passed the Straits of Madagascar; but having got northward of that island, and to about five degrees south latitude, the winds, which in those seas are observed to blow a constant equal gale between the north and west from the beginning of December to the beginning of May, on the 19th of April began to blow with much greater violence and more westerly than usual, continuing so for twenty days together, during which time we were driven a little to the east of the Molucca Islands and about three degrees northward of the Line, as our Captain found by an observation he took the 2nd of May, at which time the wind ceased, and it was a perfect calm, whereat I was not a little rejoiced. But he, being a man well experienced in the navigation of those seas, bid us all prepare against a storm, which accordingly happened the day following: for a southern wind, called the southern monsoon, began to set in.

Finding it was likely to overblow,[3] we took in our spritsail, and stood by to hand the foresail; but making foul weather, we looked the guns were all fast, and handed the mizzen. The ship lay very broad off, so we thought it better spooning before the sea, than trying or hulling. We reefed the foresail and set him, we hauled aft the foresheet; the helm was hard aweather. The ship wore bravely. We belayed the fore-downhaul; but the sail was split, and we hauled down the yard and got the sail into the ship, and unbound all the things clear of it. It was a very fierce storm; the sea broke

<hr />

2. In India. The geography of the voyage is simple: The *Adventure,* after sailing up the east coast of Africa to about 5° south of the equator (the "Line"), is blown past India into the Malay Archipelago, north of the islands of Buru and Ceram. The storm then drives the ship northward and eastward, away from the coast of Siberia ("Great Tartary") into the northeast Pacific, at that time unexplored. Brobdingnag lies somewhere in the vicinity of Alaska.

3. This paragraph is taken almost literally from Samuel Sturmy's *Mariner's Magazine* (1669). Swift is ridiculing the use of technical terms by writers of popular voyages.

strange and dangerous. We hauled off upon the lanyard of the whip-staff, and helped the man at helm. We would not get down our topmast, but let all stand, because she scudded before the sea very well, and we knew that the topmast being aloft, the ship was the wholesomer, and made better way through the sea, seeing we had searoom. When the storm was over, we set foresail and mainsail, and brought the ship to. Then we set the mizzen, main topsail and the fore topsail. Our course was east-northeast, the wind was at southwest. We got the starboard tacks aboard, we cast off our weather braces and lifts; we set in the lee braces, and hauled forward by the weather bowlings, and hauled them tight, and belayed them, and hauled over the mizzen tack to windward, and kept her full and by as near as she would lie.

During this storm, which was followed by a strong wind west-southwest, we were carried by my computation about five hundred leagues to the east, so that the oldest sailor on board could not tell in what part of the world we were. Our provisions held out well, our ship was stanch, and our crew all in good health; but we lay in the utmost distress for water. We thought it best to hold on the same course rather than turn more northerly, which might have brought us to the northwest parts of Great Tartary, and into the frozen sea.

On the 16th day of June, 1703, a boy on the topmast discovered land. On the 17th we came in full view of a great island or continent (for we knew not whether) on the south side whereof was a small neck of land jutting out into the sea, and a creek[4] too shallow to hold a ship of above one hundred tons. We cast anchor within a league of this creek, and our Captain sent a dozen of his men well armed in the longboat, with vessels for water if any could be found. I desired his leave to go with them that I might see the country and make what discoveries I could. When we came to land we saw no river or spring, nor any sign of inhabitants. Our men therefore wandered on the shore to find out some fresh water near the sea, and I walked alone about a mile on the other side, where I observed the country all barren and rocky. I now began to be weary, and seeing nothing to entertain my curiosity, I returned gently down towards the creek; and the sea being full in my view, I saw our men already got into the boat, and rowing for life to the ship. I was going to hollow after them, although it had been to little purpose, when I observed a huge creature walking after them in the sea as fast as he could; he waded not much deeper than his knees and took prodigious strides, but our men had the start of him half a league, and the sea thereabouts being full of sharp-pointed rocks, the monster was not able to overtake the boat. This I was afterwards told, for I durst not stay to see the issue of that adventure, but ran as fast as I could the way I first went, and

4. A small bay or cove, affording anchorage.

then climbed up a steep hill, which gave me some prospect of the country. I found it fully cultivated; but that which first surprised me was the length of the grass, which, in those grounds that seemed to be kept for hay, was about twenty foot high.[5]

I fell into a highroad, for so I took it to be, although it served to the inhabitants only as a footpath through a field of barley. Here I walked on for some time, but could see little on either side, it being now near harvest, and the corn[6] rising at least forty foot. I was an hour walking to the end of this field, which was fenced in with a hedge of at least one hundred and twenty foot high, and the trees so lofty that I could make no computation of their altitude. There was a stile to pass from this field into the next: it had four steps, and a stone to cross over when you came to the utmost. It was impossible for me to climb this stile, because every step was six foot high, and the upper stone above twenty. I was endeavoring to find some gap in the hedge when I discovered one of the inhabitants in the next field advancing towards the stile, of the same size with him whom I saw in the sea pursuing our boat. He appeared as tall as an ordinary spire-steeple, and took about ten yards at every stride, as near as I could guess. I was struck with the utmost fear and astonishment, and ran to hide myself in the corn, from whence I saw him at the top of the stile, looking back into the next field on the right hand; and heard him call in a voice many degrees louder than a speaking trumpet; but the noise was so high in the air that at first I certainly thought it was thunder. Whereupon seven monsters like himself came towards him with reaping hooks in their hands, each hook about the largeness of six scythes. These people were not so well clad as the first, whose servants or laborers they seemed to be. For, upon some words he spoke, they went to reap the corn in the field where I lay. I kept from them at as great a distance as I could, but was forced to move with extreme difficulty, for the stalks of the corn were sometimes not above a foot distant, so that I could hardly squeeze my body betwixt them. However, I made a shift to go forward till I came to a part of the field where the corn had been laid by the rain and wind; here it was impossible for me to advance a step, for the stalks were so interwoven that I could not creep through, and the beards of the fallen ears so strong and pointed that they pierced through my clothes into my flesh. At the same time I heard the reapers not above an hundred yards behind me. Being quite dispirited with toil, and wholly overcome by grief and despair, I lay down between two ridges and heartily wished I might there end my days. I bemoaned my desolate widow and fatherless children; I lamented my own folly and willfulness in attempting a second voyage against the advice of all my friends and relations. In this terrible agitation of mind, I could not forbear thinking of Lilliput, whose inhabitants looked upon me as the

5. Swift's intention, not always carried out accurately, is that everything in Brobdingnag should be, in relation to our familiar world, on a scale of ten to one.

6. Wheat, not maize.

greatest prodigy that ever appeared in the world; where I was able to draw an imperial fleet in my hand, and perform those other actions which will be recorded forever in the chronicles of that empire, while posterity shall hardly believe them, although attested by millions. I reflected what a mortification it must prove to me to appear as inconsiderable in this nation as one single Lilliputian would be among us. But this I conceived was to be the least of my misfortunes; for as human creatures are observed to be more savage and cruel in proportion to their bulk, what could I expect but to be a morsel in the mouth of the first among these enormous barbarians who should happen to seize me? Undoubtedly philosophers are in the right when they tell us that nothing is great or little otherwise than by comparison. It might have pleased fortune to let the Lilliputians find some nation where the people were as diminutive with respect to them as they were to me. And who knows but that even this prodigious race of mortals might be equally overmatched in some distant part of the world, whereof we have yet no discovery?

Scared and confounded as I was, I could not forbear going on with these reflections; when one of the reapers approaching within ten yards of the ridge where I lay, made me apprehend that with the next step I should be squashed to death under his foot, or cut in two with his reaping hook. And therefore when he was again about to move, I screamed as loud as fear could make me. Whereupon the huge creature trod short, and looking round about under him for some time, at last espied me as I lay on the ground. He considered a while with the caution of one who endeavors to lay hold on a small dangerous animal in such a manner that it shall not be able either to scratch or to bite him, as I myself have sometimes done with a weasel in England. At length he ventured to take me up behind by the middle between his forefinger and thumb, and brought me within three yards of his eyes, that he might behold my shape more perfectly. I guessed his meaning, and my good fortune gave me so much presence of mind that I resolved not to struggle in the least as he held me in the air about sixty foot from the ground, although he grievously pinched my sides, for fear I should slip through his fingers. All I ventured was to raise mine eyes towards the sun, and place my hands together in a supplicating posture, and to speak some words in an humble melancholy tone, suitable to the condition I then was in. For I apprehended every moment that he would dash me against the ground, as we usually do any little hateful animal which we have a mind to destroy. But my good star would have it that he appeared pleased with my voice and gestures, and began to look upon me as a curiosity, much wondering to hear me pronounce articulate words, although he could not understand them. In the meantime I was not able to forbear groaning and shedding tears and turning my head towards my sides, letting him know, as well as I could, how cruelly I was hurt by the pressure of his thumb and finger. He seemed to apprehend my meaning; for, lifting up the lappet[7] of his coat, he put me gently into it, and immediately ran along with me to his master, who was a substantial farmer, and the same person I had first seen in the field.

The farmer having (as I supposed by their talk) received such an account of me as his servant could give him, took a piece of a small straw about the size of a walking staff, and therewith lifted up the lappets of my coat, which it seems he thought to be some kind of covering that nature had given me. He blew my hairs aside to take a better view of my face. He called his hinds[8] about him, and asked them (as I afterwards learned) whether they had ever seen in the fields any little creature that resembled me. He then placed me softly on the ground upon all four; but I got immediately up, and walked slowly backwards and forwards, to let those people see I had no intent to run away. They all sat down in a circle about me, the better to observe my motions. I pulled off my hat, and made a low bow towards the farmer; I fell on my knees, and lifted up my hands and eyes, and spoke several words as loud as I could; I took a purse of gold out of my pocket, and humbly presented it to him. He received it on the palm of his hand, then applied it close to his eye to see what it was, and afterwards turned it several times with the point of a pin (which he took out of his sleeve), but could make nothing of it. Whereupon I made a sign that he should place his hand on the ground; I then took the purse, and opening it, poured all the gold into his palm. There were six Spanish pieces of four pistoles each, beside twenty or thirty smaller coins. I saw him wet the tip of his little finger upon his tongue, and take up one of my largest pieces, and then another; but he seemed to be wholly ignorant what they were. He made me a sign to put them again into my purse, and the purse again into my pocket, which after offering to him several times, I thought it best to do.

The farmer by this time was convinced I must be a rational creature. He spoke often to me, but the sound of his voice pierced my ears like that of a water mill, yet his words were articulate enough. I answered as loud as I could in several languages, and he often laid his ear within two yards of me, but all in vain, for we were wholly unintelligible to each other. He then sent his servants to their work, and taking his handkerchief out of his pocket, he doubled and spread it on his hand, which he placed flat on the ground with the palm upwards, making me a sign to step into it, as I could easily do, for it was not above a foot in thickness. I thought it my part to obey, and for fear of falling, laid myself at full length upon the handkerchief, with the remainder of which

7. Flap or fold.   8. Farm servants.

he lapped me up to the head for further security, and in this manner carried me home to his house. There he called his wife, and showed me to her; but she screamed and ran back as women in England do at the sight of a toad or a spider. However, when she had a while seen my behavior, and how well I observed the signs her husband made, she was soon reconciled, and by degrees grew extremely tender of me.

It was about twelve at noon, and a servant brought in dinner. It was only one substantial dish of meat (fit for the plain condition of an husbandman) in a dish of about four-and-twenty foot diameter. The company were the farmer and his wife, three children, and an old grandmother. When they were sat down, the farmer placed me at some distance from him on the table, which was thirty foot high from the floor. I was in a terrible fright, and kept as far as I could from the edge, for fear of falling. The wife minced a bit of meat, then crumbled some bread on a trencher,[9] and placed it before me. I made her a low bow, took out my knife and fork, and fell to eat; which gave them exceeding delight. The mistress sent her maid for a small dram cup, which held about two gallons, and filled it with drink; I took up the vessel with much difficulty in both hands, and in a most respectful manner drank to her ladyship's health, expressing the words as loud as I could in English; which made the company laugh so heartily that I was almost deafened with the noise. This liquor tasted like a small cider,[1] and was not unpleasant. Then the master made me a sign to come to his trencher side; but as I walked on the table, being in great surprise all the time, as the indulgent reader will easily conceive and excuse, I happened to stumble against a crust, and fell flat on my face, but received no hurt. I got up immediately, and observing the good people to be in much concern, I took my hat (which I held under my arm out of good manners) and waving it over my head, made three huzzas to show I had got no mischief by my fall. But advancing forwards toward my master (as I shall henceforth call him), his youngest son who sat next him, an arch[2] boy of about ten years old, took me up by the legs, and held me so high in the air that I trembled every limb; but his father snatched me from him, and at the same time gave him such a box on the left ear as would have felled an European troop of horse to the earth, ordering him to be taken from the table. But being afraid the boy might owe me a spite, and well remembering how mischievous all children among us naturally are to sparrows, rabbits, young kittens, and puppy dogs, I fell on my knees, and pointing to the boy, made my master to understand, as well as I could, that I desired his son might be pardoned. The father complied, and the lad took his seat again; whereupon I went to him and kissed his hand, which my master took, and made him stroke me gently with it.

9. A platter.
1. I.e., weak cider.

2. Mischievous.

In the midst of dinner, my mistress's favorite cat leaped into her lap. I heard a noise behind me like that of a dozen stocking weavers at work; and turning my head, I found it proceeded from the purring of this animal, who seemed to be three times larger than an ox, as I computed by the view of her head and one of her paws, while her mistress was feeding and stroking her. The fierceness of this creature's countenance altogether discomposed me, although I stood at the farther end of the table, above fifty foot off, and although my mistress held her fast for fear she might give a spring and seize me in her talons. But it happened there was no danger, for the cat took not the least notice of me when my master placed me within three yards of her. And as I have been always told, and found true by experience in my travels, that flying or discovering[3] fear before a fierce animal is a certain way to make it pursue or attack you, so I resolved in this dangerous juncture to show no manner of concern. I walked with intrepidity five or six times before the very head of the cat, and came within half a yard of her; whereupon she drew herself back, as if she were more afraid of me; I had less apprehension concerning the dogs, whereof three or four came into the room, as it is usual in farmers' houses; one of which was a mastiff, equal in bulk to four elephants, and a greyhound, somewhat taller than the mastiff, but not so large.

When dinner was almost done, the nurse came in with a child of a year old in her arms, who immediately spied me, and began a squall that you might have heard from London Bridge to Chelsea, after the usual oratory of infants, to get me for a plaything. The mother out of pure indulgence took me up, and put me towards the child, who presently seized me by the middle, and got my head in his mouth, where I roared so loud that the urchin was frighted and let me drop; and I should infallibly have broke my neck if the mother had not held her apron under me. The nurse to quiet her babe made use of a rattle, which was a kind of hollow vessel filled with great stones, and fastened by a cable to the child's waist: but all in vain, so that she was forced to apply the last remedy by giving it suck. I must confess no object ever disgusted me so much as the sight of her monstrous breast, which I cannot tell what to compare with so as to give the curious reader an idea of its bulk, shape, and color. It stood prominent six foot, and could not be less than sixteen in circumference. The nipple was about half the bigness of my head, and the hue both of that and the dug so varified with spots, pimples, and freckles that nothing could appear more nauseous: for I had a near sight of her, she sitting down the more conveniently to give suck, and I standing on the table. This made me reflect upon the fair skins of our English ladies, who appear so beautiful to us, only because they are of our own size, and their defects not to be seen but through a magnifying glass, where

---

3. Revealing.

we find by experiment that the smoothest and whitest skins look rough and coarse and ill colored.

I remember when I was at Lilliput, the complexion of those diminutive people appeared to me the fairest in the world; and talking upon this subject with a person of learning there, who was an intimate friend of mine, he said that my face appeared much fairer and smoother when he looked on me from the ground than it did upon a nearer view when I took him up in my hand and brought him close, which he confessed was at first a very shocking sight. He said he could discover great holes in my skin; that the stumps of my beard were ten times stronger than the bristles of a boar, and my complexion made up of several colors altogether disagreeable: although I must beg leave to say for myself that I am as fair as most of my sex and country and very little sunburnt by all my travels. On the other side, discoursing of the ladies in that Emperor's court, he used to tell me one had freckles, another too wide a mouth, a third too large a nose; nothing of which I was able to distinguish. I confess this reflection was obvious enough; which however I could not forbear, lest the reader might think those vast creatures were actually deformed: for I must do them justice to say they are a comely race of people; and particularly the features of my master's countenance, although he were but a farmer, when I beheld him from the height of sixty foot, appeared very well proportioned.

When dinner was done, my master went out to his laborers; and as I could discover by his voice and gesture, gave his wife a strict charge to take care of me. I was very much tired and disposed to sleep, which my mistress perceiving, she put me on her own bed, and covered me with a clean white handkerchief, but larger and coarser than the mainsail of a man-of-war.

I slept about two hours, and dreamed I was at home with my wife and children, which aggravated my sorrows when I awaked and found myself alone in a vast room, between two and three hundred foot wide, and above two hundred high, lying in a bed twenty yards wide. My mistress was gone about her household affairs, and had locked me in. The bed was eight yards from the floor. Some natural necessities required me to get down; I durst not presume to call, and if I had, it would have been in vain with such a voice as mine at so great a distance from the room where I lay to the kitchen where the family kept. While I was under these circumstances, two rats crept up the curtains, and ran smelling backwards and forwards on the bed. One of them came up almost to my face; whereupon I rose in a fright, and drew out my hanger[4] to defend myself. These horrible animals had the boldness to attack me on both sides, and one of them held his forefeet at my collar; but I had the good fortune to rip up his belly before he

4. A short, broad sword.

could do me any mischief. He fell down at my feet; and the other seeing the fate of his comrade, made his escape, but not without one good wound on the back, which I gave him as he fled, and made the blood run trickling from him. After this exploit I walked gently to and fro on the bed, to recover my breath and loss of spirits. These creatures were of the size of a large mastiff, but infinitely more nimble and fierce; so that if I had taken off my belt before I went to sleep, I must have infallibly been torn to pieces and devoured. I measured the tail of the dead rat, and found it to be two yards long, wanting an inch; but it went against my stomach to drag the carcass off the bed, where it lay still bleeding; I observed it had yet some life, but with a strong slash cross the neck, I thoroughly dispatched it.

Soon after, my mistress came into the room, who seeing me all bloody, ran and took me up in her hand. I pointed to the dead rat, smiling and making other signs to show I was not hurt, whereat she was extremely rejoiced, calling the maid to take up the dead rat with a pair of tongs, and throw it out of the window. Then she set me on a table, where I showed her my hanger all bloody, and wiping it on the lappet of my coat, returned it to the scabbard. I was pressed to do more than one thing, which another could not do for me, and therefore endeavored to make my mistress understand that I desired to be set down on the floor; which after she had done, my bashfulness would not suffer me to express myself farther than by pointing to the door, and bowing several times. The good woman with much difficulty at last perceived what I would be at, and taking me up again in her hand, walked into the garden, where she set me down. I went on one side about two hundred yards; and beckoning to her not to look or to follow me, I hid myself between two leaves of sorrel, and there discharged the necessities of nature.

I hope the gentle reader will excuse me for dwelling on these and the like particulars, which however insignificant they may appear to groveling vulgar[5] minds, yet will certainly help a philosopher to enlarge his thoughts and imagination, and apply them to the benefit of public as well as private life, which was my sole design in presenting this and other accounts of my travels to the world; wherein I have been chiefly studious of truth, without affecting any ornaments of learning or of style. But the whole scene of this voyage made so strong an impression on my mind, and is so deeply fixed in my memory, that in committing it to paper I did not omit one material circumstance; however, upon a strict review, I blotted out several passages of less moment which were in my first copy, for fear of being censured as tedious and trifling, whereof travelers are often, perhaps not without justice, accused.

---

5. Commonplace, uncultivated, in contrast to the scientist ("philosopher"); an irony.

CHAPTER II. *A description of the farmer's daughter. The Author carried to a market town, and then to the metropolis. The particulars of his journey.*

My mistress had a daughter of nine years old, a child of towardly parts for her age, very dexterous at her needle, and skillful in dressing her baby.[6] Her mother and she contrived to fit up the baby's cradle for me against night: the cradle was put into a small drawer of a cabinet, and the drawer placed upon a hanging shelf for fear of the rats. This was my bed all the time I stayed with those people, although made more convenient by degrees as I began to learn their language, and make my wants known. This young girl was so handy, that after I had once or twice pulled off my clothes before her, she was able to dress and undress me, although I never gave her that trouble when she would let me do either myself. She made me seven shirts, and some other linen of as fine cloth as could be got, which indeed was coarser than sackcloth, and these she constantly washed for me with her own hands. She was likewise my schoolmistress to teach me the language: when I pointed to anything, she told me the name of it in her own tongue, so that in a few days I was able to call for whatever I had a mind to. She was very good-natured, and not above forty foot high, being little for her age. She gave me the name of *Grildrig*, which the family took up, and afterwards the whole kingdom. The word imports what the Latins call *nanunculus*, the Italian *homunceletino*,[7] and the English *mannikin*. To her I chiefly owe my preservation in that country: we never parted while I was there; I called her my *Glumdalclitch*, or little nurse: and I should be guilty of great ingratitude if I omitted this honorable mention of her care and affection towards me, which I heartily wish it lay in my power to requite as she deserves, instead of being the innocent but unhappy instrument of her disgrace, as I have too much reason to fear.

It now began to be known and talked of in the neighborhood that my master had found a strange animal in the field, about the bigness of a *splacknuck*, but exactly shaped in every part like a human creature, which it likewise imitated in all its actions: seemed to speak in a little language of its own, had already learned several words of theirs, went erect upon two legs, was tame and gentle, would come when it was called, do whatever it was bid, had the finest limbs in the world, and a complexion fairer than a nobleman's daughter of three years old. Another farmer who lived hard by, and was a particular friend of my master, came on a visit on purpose to inquire into the truth of this story. I was immediately produced, and placed upon a table, where I walked as I was commanded, drew my hanger, put it up again, made my reverence to my master's

6. Doll.
7. The Latin and Italian words are Swift's own coinages, as, of course, are the various words from the Brobdingnagian language.

guest, asked him in his own language how he did, and told him he was welcome, just as my little nurse had instructed me. This man, who was old and dimsighted, put on his spectacles to behold me better, at which I could not forbear laughing very heartily, for his eyes appeared like the full moon shining into a chamber at two windows. Our people, who discovered the cause of my mirth, bore me company in laughing, at which the old fellow was fool enough to be angry and out of countenance. He had the character of a great miser, and to my misfortune he well deserved it by the cursed advice he gave my master to show me as a sight upon a market day in the next town, which was half an hour's riding, about two and twenty miles from our house. I guessed there was some mischief contriving when I observed my master and his friend whispering long together, sometimes pointing at me; and my fears made me fancy that I overheard and understood some of their words. But the next morning Glumdalclitch, my little nurse, told me the whole matter, which she had cunningly picked out from her mother. The poor girl laid me on her bosom, and fell a weeping with shame and grief. She apprehended some mischief would happen to me from rude vulgar folks, who might squeeze me to death, or break one of my limbs by taking me in their hands. She had also observed how modest I was in my nature, how nicely I regarded my honor, and what an indignity I should conceive it to be exposed for money as a public spectacle to the meanest of the people. She said her papa and mamma had promised that Grildrig should be hers; but now she found they meant to serve her as they did last year, when they pretended to give her a lamb, and yet, as soon as it was fat, sold it to a butcher. For my own part, I may truly affirm that I was less concerned than my nurse. I had a strong hope, which never left me, that I should one day recover my liberty; and as to the ignominy of being carried about for a monster, I considered myself to be a perfect stranger in the country, and that such a misfortune could never be charged upon me as a reproach, if ever I should return to England; since the King of Great Britain himself, in my condition, must have undergone the same distress.

My master, pursuant to the advice of his friend, carried me in a box the next market day to the neighboring town, and took along with him his little daughter, my nurse, upon a pillion[8] behind him. The box was close on every side, with a little door for me to go in and out, and a few gimlet holes to let in air. The girl had been so careful to put the quilt of her baby's bed into it, for me to lie down on. However, I was terribly shaken and discomposed in this journey, although it were but of half an hour. For the horse went about forty foot at every step, and trotted so high that the agitation was equal to the rising and falling of a ship in a great storm, but much more frequent. Our journey was somewhat further than

8. A pad attached to the hinder part of a saddle, on which a second person, usually a woman, could ride.

from London to St. Albans. My master alighted at an inn which he used to frequent; and after consulting a while with the innkeeper, and making some necessary preparations, he hired the *Grultrud*, or crier, to give notice through the town of a strange creature to be seen at the Sign of the Green Eagle, not so big as a *splacknuck* (an animal in that country very finely shaped, about six foot long), and in every part of the body resembling an human creature, could speak several words and perform an hundred diverting tricks.

I was placed upon a table in the largest room of the inn, which might be near three hundred foot square. My little nurse stood on a low stool close to the table, to take care of me, and direct what I should do. My master, to avoid a crowd, would suffer only thirty people at a time to see me. I walked about on the table as the girl commanded; she asked me questions as far as she knew my understanding of the language reached, and I answered them as loud as I could. I turned about several times to the company, paid my humble respects, said they were welcome, and used some other speeches I had been taught. I took up a thimble filled with liquor, which Glumdalclitch had given me for a cup, and drank their health. I drew out my hanger, and flourished with it after the manner of fencers in England. My nurse gave me part of a straw, which I exercised as a pike, having learned the art in my youth. I was that day shown to twelve sets of company, and as often forced to go over again with the same fopperies, till I was half dead with weariness and vexation. For those who had seen me made such wonderful reports that the people were ready to break down the doors to come in. My master for his own interest would not suffer anyone to touch me except my nurse; and, to prevent danger, benches were set round the table at such a distance as put me out of everybody's reach. However, an unlucky schoolboy aimed a hazelnut directly at my head, which very narrowly missed me; otherwise, it came with so much violence that it would have infallibly knocked out my brains, for it was almost as large as a small pumpion:[9] but I had the satisfaction to see the young rogue well beaten, and turned out of the room.

My master gave public notice that he would show me again the next market day, and in the meantime he prepared a more convenient vehicle for me, which he had reason enough to do; for I was so tired with my first journey, and with entertaining company for eight hours together, that I could hardly stand upon my legs or speak a word. It was at least three days before I recovered my strength; and that I might have no rest at home, all the neighboring gentlemen from an hundred miles round, hearing of my fame, came to see me at my master's own house. There could not be fewer than thirty persons with their wives and children (for the country is very populous); and my master demanded the rate of a

9. Pumpkin.

full room whenever he showed me at home, although it were only to a single family. So that for some time I had but little ease every day of the week (except Wednesday, which is their Sabbath) although I were not carried to the town.

My master finding how profitable I was like to be, resolved to carry me to the most considerable cities of the kingdom. Having therefore provided himself with all things necessary for a long journey, and settled his affairs at home, he took leave of his wife; and upon the 17th of August, 1703, about two months after my arrival, we set out for the metropolis, situated near the middle of that empire, and about three thousand miles distance from our house. My master made his daughter Glumdalclitch ride behind him. She carried me on her lap in a box tied about her waist. The girl had lined it on all sides with the softest cloth she could get, well quilted underneath, furnished it with her baby's bed, provided me with linen and other necessaries, and made everything as convenient as she could. We had no other company but a boy of the house, who rode after us with the luggage.

My master's design was to show me in all the towns by the way, and to step out of the road for fifty or an hundred miles to any village or person of quality's house where he might expect custom. We made easy journeys of not above seven or eight score miles a day: for Glumdalclitch, on purpose to spare me, complained she was tired with the trotting of the horse. She often took me out of my box at my own desire, to give me air and show me the country, but always held me fast by leading strings. We passed over five or six rivers many degrees broader and deeper than the Nile or the Ganges; and there was hardly a rivulet so small as the Thames at London Bridge. We were ten weeks in our journey, and I was shown in eighteen large towns, besides many large villages and private families.

On the 26th day of October, we arrived at the metropolis, called in their language *Lorbrulgrud*, or Pride of the Universe. My master took a lodging in the principal street of the city, not far from the royal palace, and put out bills in the usual form, containing an exact description of my person and parts. He hired a large room between three and four hundred foot wide. He provided a table sixty foot in diameter, upon which I was to act my part, and palisadoed it round three foot from the edge, and as many high, to prevent my falling over. I was shown ten times a day to the wonder and satisfaction of all people. I could now speak the language tolerably well, and perfectly understood every word that was spoken to me. Besides, I had learned their alphabet, and could make a shift to explain a sentence here and there; for Glumdalclitch had been my instructor while we were at home, and at leisure hours during our journey. She carried a little book in her pocket, not much larger than a Sanson's *Atlas;*[1] it was a common treatise for the use of young girls, giving a short account of their religion: out of this she taught me my letters, and interpreted the words.

CHAPTER III. *The Author sent for to Court. The Queen buys him of his master, the farmer, and presents him to the King. He disputes with his Majesty's great scholars. An apartment at Court provided for the Author. He is in high favor with the Queen. He stands up for the honor of his own country. His quarrels with the Queen's dwarf.*

The frequent labors I underwent every day made in a few weeks a very considerable change in my health: the more my master got by me, the more unsatiable he grew. I had quite lost my stomach, and was almost reduced to a skeleton. The farmer observed it, and concluding I soon must die, resolved to make as good a hand of me as he could. While he was thus reasoning and resolving with himself, a *Slardral,* or Gentleman Usher, came from Court, commanding my master to carry me immediately thither for the diversion of the Queen and her ladies. Some of the latter had already been to see me and reported strange things of my beauty, behavior, and good sense. Her Majesty and those who attended her were beyond measure delighted with my demeanor. I fell on my knees and begged the honor of kissing her Imperial foot; but this gracious princess held out her little finger towards me (after I was set on a table), which I embraced in both my arms, and put the tip of it, with the utmost respect, to my lip. She made me some general questions about my country and my travels, which I answered as distinctly and in as few words as I could. She asked whether I would be content to live at Court. I bowed down to the board of the table, and humbly answered that I was my master's slave, but if I were at my own disposal, I should be proud to devote my life to her Majesty's service. She then asked my master whether he were willing to sell me at a good price. He, who apprehended I could not live a month, was ready enough to part with me, and demanded a thousand pieces of gold, which were ordered him on the spot, each piece being about the bigness of eight hundred moidores;[2] but, allowing for the proportion of all things between that country and Europe, and the high price of gold among them, was hardly so great a sum as a thousand guineas would be in England. I then said to the Queen, since I was now her Majesty's most humble creature and vassal, I must beg the favor that Glumdalclitch, who had always tended me with so much care and kindness, and understood to do it so well, might be admitted into her service, and continue to be my nurse and instructor. Her Majesty agreed to my petition, and easily got the farmer's consent, who was glad enough to have his daughter preferred at Court; and the poor girl herself was not able to hide her

1. I.e., over two feet long and about two feet wide.   2. Portuguese coins.

joy. My late master withdrew, bidding me farewell, and saying he had left me in a good service; to which I replied not a word, only making him a slight bow.

The Queen observed my coldness, and when the farmer was gone out of the apartment, asked me the reason. I made bold to tell her Majesty that I owed no other obligation to my late master than his not dashing out the brains of a poor harmless creature found by chance in his field; which obligation was amply recompensed by the gain he had made in showing me through half the kingdom, and the price he had now sold me for. That the life I had since led was laborious enough to kill an animal of ten times my strength. That my health was much impaired by the continual drudgery of entertaining the rabble every hour of the day; and that if my master had not thought my life in danger, her Majestry would not have got so cheap a bargain. But as I was out of all fear of being ill treated under the protection of so great and good an Empress, the Ornament of Nature, the Darling of the World, the Delight of her Subjects, the Phoenix of the Creation; so I hoped my late master's apprehensions would appear to be groundless, for I already found my spirits to revive by the influence of her most august presence.

This was the sum of my speech, delivered with great improprieties and hesitation; the latter part was altogether framed in the style peculiar to that people, whereof I learned some phrases from Glumdalclitch, while she was carrying me to Court.

The Queen, giving great allowance for my defectiveness in speaking, was however surprised at so much wit and good sense in so diminutive an animal. She took me in her own hand, and carried me to the King, who was then retired to his cabinet.[3] His Majesty, a prince of much gravity, and austere countenance, not well observing my shape at first view, asked the Queen after a cold manner how long it was since she grew fond of a *splacknuck*; for such it seems he took me to be, as I lay upon my breast in her Majesty's right hand. But this princess, who hath an infinite deal of wit and humor, set me gently on my feet upon the scrutore,[4] and commanded me to give his Majesty an account of myself, which I did in a very few words; and Glumdalclitch, who attended at the cabinet door, and could not endure I should be out of her sight, being admitted, confirmed all that had passed from my arrival at her father's house.

The King, although he be as learned a person as any in his dominions, had been educated in the study of philosophy and particularly mathematics; yet when he observed my shape exactly, and saw me walk erect, before I began to speak, conceived I might be a piece of clockwork (which is in that country arrived to a very great perfection) contrived by some ingenious artist. But when he heard my voice, and found what I delivered to be regular and ra-

3. A private apartment.　　　　4. Writing desk.

tional, he could not conceal his astonishment. He was by no means satisfied with the relation I gave him of the manner I came into his kingdom, but thought it a story concerted between Glumdalclitch and her father, who had taught me a set of words to make me sell at a higher price. Upon this imagination he put several other questions to me, and still received rational answers, no otherwise defective than by a foreign accent, and an imperfect knowledge in the language, with some rustic phrases which I had learned at the farmer's house, and did not suit the polite style of a court.

His Majesty sent for three great scholars who were then in their weekly waiting (according to the custom in that country). These gentlemen, after they had a while examined my shape with much nicety, were of different opinions concerning me. They all agreed that I could not be produced according to the regular laws of nature, because I was not framed with a capacity of preserving my life, either by swiftness, or climbing of trees, or digging holes in the earth. They observed by my teeth, which they viewed with great exactness, that I was a carnivorous animal; yet most quadrupeds being an overmatch for me, and field mice, with some others, too nimble, they could not imagine how I should be able to support myself, unless I fed upon snails and other insects; which they offered, by many learned arguments, to evince that I could not possibly do. One of them seemed to think that I might be an embryo, or abortive birth. But this opinion was rejected by the other two, who observed my limbs to be perfect and finished, and that I had lived several years, as it was manifest from my beard, the stumps whereof they plainly discovered through a magnifying glass. They would not allow me to be a dwarf, because my littleness was beyond all degrees of comparison; for the Queen's favorite dwarf, the smallest ever known in that kingdom, was nearly thirty foot high. After much debate, they concluded unanimously that I was only *relplum scalcath*, which is interpreted literally, *lusus naturae*;[5] a determination exactly agreeable to the modern philosophy of Europe, whose professors, disdaining the old evasion of *occult causes*, whereby the followers of Aristotle endeavor in vain to disguise their ignorance, have invented this wonderful solution of all difficulties, to the unspeakable advancement of human knowledge.

After this decisive conclusion, I entreated to be heard a word or two. I applied myself to the King, and assured his Majesty that I came from a country which abounded with several millions of both sexes, and of my own stature, where the animals, trees, and houses were all in proportion, and where by consequence I might be as able to defend myself, and to find sustenance, as any of his Majesty's subjects could do here; which I took for a full answer to

5. One of nature's sports, or, roughly, freaks. Swift had contempt for both the medieval schoolmen, who discussed "occult causes," the unknown causes of observable effects, and modern scientists, who, he believed, often concealed their ignorance by using equally meaningless terms.

those gentlemen's arguments. To this they only replied with a smile of contempt, saying that the farmer had instructed me very well in my lesson. The King, who had a much better understanding, dismissing his learned men, sent for the farmer, who by good fortune was not yet gone out of town; having therefore first examined him privately, and then confronted him with me and the young girl, his Majesty began to think that what we told him might possibly be true. He desired the Queen to order that a particular care should be taken of me, and was of opinion that Glumdalclitch should still continue in her office of tending me, because he observed we had a great affection for each other. A convenient apartment was provided for her at Court; she had a sort of governess appointed to take care of her education, a maid to dress her, and two other servants for menial offices; but the care of me was wholly appropriated to herself. The Queen commanded her own cabinet-maker to contrive a box that might serve me for a bedchamber, after the model that Glumdalclitch and I should agree upon. This man was a most ingenious artist, and according to my directions, in three weeks finished for me a wooden chamber of sixteen foot square and twelve high, with sash windows, a door, and two closets, like a London bedchamber. The board that made the ceiling was to be lifted up and down by two hinges, to put in a bed ready furnished by her Majesty's upholsterer, which Glumdalclitch took out every day to air, made it with her own hands, and letting it down at night, locked up the roof over me. A nice[6] workman, who was famous for little curiosities, undertook to make me two chairs, with backs and frames, of a substance not unlike ivory, and two tables, with a cabinet to put my things in. The room was quilted on all sides, as well as the floor and the ceiling, to prevent any accident from the carelessness of those who carried me, and to break the force of a jolt when I went in a coach. I desired a lock for my door to prevent rats and mice from coming in: the smith, after several attempts, made the smallest that ever was seen among them, for I have known a larger at the gate of a gentleman's house in England. I made a shift[7] to keep the key in a pocket of my own, fearing Glumdalclitch might lose it. The Queen likewise ordered the thinnest silks that could be gotten, to make me clothes, not much thicker than an English blanket, very cumbersome till I was accustomed to them. They were after the fashion of the kingdom, partly resembling the Persian, and partly the Chinese, and are a very grave, decent habit.

The Queen became so fond of my company that she could not dine without me. I had a table placed upon the same at which her Majesty ate, just at her left elbow, and a chair to sit on. Glumdalclitch stood upon a stool on the floor, near my table, to assist and take care of me. I had an entire set of silver dishes and plates, and

6. Exact.   7. Contrived.

other neccssaries, which, in proportion to those of the Queen, were not much bigger than what I have seen of the same kind in a London toyshop,[8] for the furniture of a baby-house: these my little nurse kept in her pocket in a silver box and gave me at meals as I wanted them, always cleaning them herself. No person dined with the Queen but the two Princesses Royal, the elder sixteen years old, and the younger at that time thirteen and a month. Her Majesty used to put a bit of meat upon one of my dishes, out of which I carved for myself; and her diversion was to see me eat in miniature. For the Queen (who had indeed but a weak stomach) took up at one mouthful as much as a dozen English farmers could eat at a meal, which to me was for some time a very nauseous sight. She would craunch the wing of a lark, bones and all, between her teeth, although it were nine times as large as that of a full-grown turkey; and put a bit of bread into her mouth as big as two twelve-penny loaves. She drank out of a golden cup, above a hogshead at a draught. Her knives were twice as long as a scythe set straight upon the handle. The spoons, forks, and other instruments were all in the same proportion. I remember when Glumdalclitch carried me out of curiosity to see some of the tables at Court, where ten or a dozen of these enormous knives and forks were lifted up together, I thought I had never till then beheld so terrible a sight.

It is the custom that every Wednesday (which, as I have before observed, was their Sabbath) the King and Queen, with the royal issue of both sexes, dine together in the apartment of his Majesty, to whom I was now become a favorite; and at these times my little chair and table were placed at his left hand, before one of the salt-cellars. This prince took a pleasure in conversing with me, inquiring into the manners, religion, laws, government, and learning of Europe; wherein I gave him the best account I was able. His apprehension was so clear, and his judgment so exact, that he made very wise reflections and observations upon all I said. But I confess that after I had been a little too copious in talking of my own beloved country, of our trade and wars by sea and land, of our schisms in religion and parties in the state, the prejudices of his education prevailed so far that he could not forbear taking me up in his right hand, and stroking me gently with the other, after an hearty fit of laughing, asked me whether I were a Whig or a Tory. Then turning to his first minister, who waited behind him with a white staff, near as tall as the mainmast of the *Royal Sovereign*,[9] he observed how contemptible a thing was human grandeur, which could be mimicked by such diminutive insects as I: "and yet," said he, "I dare engage, these creatures have their titles and distinctions of honor; they contrive little nests and burrows, that they call houses and cities; they make a figure in dress and equipage;[1] they love, they

8. A shop for selling knickknacks.
9. At the English court the Lord Treasurer bore a white staff as the symbol of his office. The *Royal Sover-*

eign was one of the largest ships in the Royal Navy.
1. A carriage and horses, with attendant footmen.

fight, they dispute, they cheat, they betray." And thus he continued on, while my color came and went several times with indignation to hear our noble country, the mistress of arts and arms, the scourge of France, the arbitress of Europe, the seat of virtue, piety, honor, and truth, the pride and envy of the world, so contemptuously treated.

But as I was not in a condition to resent injuries, so, upon mature thoughts, I began to doubt whether I were injured or no. For, after having been accustomed several months to the sight and converse of this people, and observed every object upon which I cast my eyes to be of proportionable magnitude, the horror I had first conceived from their bulk and aspect was so far worn off that if I had then beheld a company of English lords and ladies in their finery and birthday clothes,[2] acting their several parts in the most courtly manner of strutting and bowing and prating, to say the truth, I should have been strongly tempted to laugh as much at them as this King and his grandees did at me. Neither indeed could I forbear smiling at myself when the Queen used to place me upon her hand towards a looking glass, by which both our persons appeared before me in full view together; and there could be nothing more ridiculous than the comparison; so that I really began to imagine myself dwindled many degrees below my usual size.

Nothing angered and mortified me so much as the Queen's dwarf, who being of the lowest stature that was ever in that country (for I verily think he was not full thirty foot high) became so insolent at seeing a creature so much beneath him that he would always affect to swagger and look big as he passed by me in the Queen's antechamber, while I was standing on some table talking with the lords or ladies of the court; and he seldom failed of a smart word or two upon my littleness, against which I could only revenge myself by calling him brother, challenging him to wrestle, and such repartees as are usual in the mouths of Court pages. One day at dinner this malicious little cub was so nettled with something I had said to him that, raising himself upon the frame of Her Majesty's chair, he took me up by the middle, as I was sitting down, not thinking any harm, and let me drop into a large silver bowl of cream, and then ran away as fast as he could. I fell over head and ears, and if I had not been a good swimmer, it might have gone very hard with me; for Glumdalclitch in that instant happened to be at the other end of the room, and the Queen was in such a fright that she wanted presence of mind to assist me. But my little nurse ran to my relief, and took me out, after I had swallowed above a quart of cream. I was put to bed; however, I received no other damage than the loss of a suit of clothes, which was utterly spoiled. The dwarf was soundly whipped, and as a further punishment, forced to drink up the bowl of cream into which he had

2. Courtiers dressed with especial splendor on the monarch's birthday.

thrown me; neither was he ever restored to favor: for soon after the Queen bestowed him to a lady of high quality, so that I saw him no more, to my very great satisfaction; for I could not tell to what extremity such a malicious urchin might have carried his resentment.

He had before served me a scurvy trick, which set the Queen a laughing, although at the same time she were heartily vexed, and would have immediately cashiered him,[3] if I had not been so generous as to intercede. Her Majesty had taken a marrow bone upon her plate, and after knocking out the marrow, placed the bone again in the dish, erect as it stood before; the dwarf watching his opportunity, while Glumdalclitch was gone to the sideboard, mounted upon the stool she stood on to take care of me at meals, took me up in both hands, and squeezing my legs together, wedged them into the marrow bone above my waist, where I stuck for some time, and made a very ridiculous figure. I believe it was near a minute before anyone knew what was become of me, for I thought it below me to cry out. But, as princes seldom get their meat hot, my legs were not scalded, only my stockings and breeches in a sad condition. The dwarf at my entreaty had no other punishment than a sound whipping.

I was frequently rallied by the Queen upon account of my fearfulness, and she used to ask me whether the people of my country were as great cowards as myself. The occasion was this. The kingdom is much pestered with flies in summer, and these odious insects, each of them as big as a Dunstable lark, hardly gave me any rest while I sat at dinner, with their continual humming and buzzing about my ears. They would sometimes alight upon my victuals, and leave their loathsome excrement or spawn behind, which to me was very visible, although not to the natives of that country, whose large optics were not so acute as mine in viewing smaller objects. Sometimes they would fix upon my nose or forehead, where they stung me to the quick, smelling very offensively; and I could easily trace that viscous matter, which our naturalists tell us enables those creatures to walk with their feet upwards upon a ceiling. I had much ado to defend myself against these destable animals, and could not forbear starting when they came on my face. It was the common practice of the dwarf to catch a number of these insects in his hand, as schoolboys do among us, and let them out suddenly under my nose, on purpose to frighten me, and divert the Queen. My remedy was to cut them in pieces with my knife as they flew in the air, wherein my dexterity was much admired.

I remember one morning when Glumdalclitch had set me in my box upon a window, as she usually did in fair days to give me air (for I durst not venture to let the box be hung on a nail out of the window, as we do with cages in England), after I had lifted up one

3. Dismissed him.

of my sashes, and sat down at my table to eat a piece of sweet cake for my breakfast, above twenty wasps, allured by the smell, came flying into the room, humming louder than the drones of as many bagpipes. Some of them seized my cake, and carried it piecemeal away; others flew about my head and face, confounding me with the noise, and putting me in the utmost terror of their stings. However, I had the courage to rise and draw my hanger, and attack them in the air. I dispatched four of them, but the rest got away, and I presently shut my window. These insects were as large as partridges; I took out their stings, found them an inch and a half long, and as sharp as needles. I carefully preserved them all, and having since shown them with some other curiosities in several parts of Europe, upon my return to England I gave three of them to Gresham College,[4] and kept the fourth for myself.

CHAPTER IV. *The country described. A proposal for correcting modern maps. The King's palace, and some account of the metropolis. The Author's way of traveling. The chief temple described.*

I now intend to give the reader a short description of this country, as far as I have traveled in it, which was not above two thousand miles round Lorbrulgrud the metropolis. For the Queen, whom I always attended, never went further when she accompanied the King in his progresses, and there stayed till his Majesty returned from viewing his frontiers. The whole extent of this prince's dominions reacheth about six thousand miles in length, and from three to five in breadth. From whence I cannot but conclude that our geographers of Europe are in a great error by supposing nothing but sea between Japan and California: for it was ever my opinion that there must be a balance of earth to counterpoise the great continent of Tartary; and therefore they ought to correct their maps and charts by joining this vast tract of land to the northwest parts of America, wherein I shall be ready to lend them my assistance.

The kingdom is a peninsula, terminated to the northeast by a ridge of mountains thirty miles high, which are altogether impassable by reason of the volcanoes upon the tops. Neither do the most learned know what sort of mortals inhabit beyond those mountains, or whether they be inhabited at all. On the three other sides it is bounded by the ocean. There is not one seaport in the whole kingdom; and those parts of the coasts into which the rivers issue are so full of pointed rocks, and the sea generally so rough, that there is no venturing with the smallest of their boats; so that these people are wholly excluded from any commerce with the rest of the world. But the large rivers are full of vessels, and abound with excellent fish, for they seldom get any from the sea, because the sea fish are of the same size with those in Europe, and consequently

4. The Royal Society, in its earliest years, met in Gresham College.

not worth catching; whereby it is manifest that nature, in the production of plants and animals of so extraordinary a bulk, is wholly confined to this continent, of which I leave the reasons to be determined by philosophers. However, now and then they take a whale that happens to be dashed against the rocks, which the common people feed on heartily. These whales I have known so large that a man could hardly carry one upon his shoulders; and sometimes for curiosity they are brought in hampers to Lorbrulgrud: I saw one of them in a dish at the King's table, which passed for a rarity, but I did not observe he was fond of it; for I think indeed the bigness disgusted him, although I have seen one somewhat larger in Greenland.

The country is well inhabited, for it contains fifty-one cities, near an hundred walled towns, and a great number of villages. To satisfy my curious reader, it may be sufficient to describe Lorbrulgrud. This city stand upon almost two equal parts on each side the river that passes through. It contains above eighty thousand houses, and about six hundred thousand inhabitants. It is in length three *glongluns* (which make about fifty-four English miles) and two and a half in breadth, as I measured it myself in the royal map made by the King's order, which was laid on the ground on purpose for me, and extended an hundred feet; I paced the diameter and circumference several times barefoot, and computing by the scale, measured it pretty exactly.

The King's palace is no regular edifice, but an heap of buildings about seven miles round: the chief rooms are generally two hundred and forty foot high, and broad and long in proportion. A coach was allowed to Glumdalclitch and me, wherein her governess frequently took her out to see the town, or go among the shops; and I was always of the party, carried in my box, although the girl at my own desire would often take me out, and hold me in her hand, that I might more conveniently view the houses and the people as we passed along the streets. I reckoned our coach to be about a square of Westminster Hall,[5] but not altogether so high; however, I cannot be very exact. One day the governess ordered our coachman to stop at several shops, where the beggars, watching their opportunity, crowded to the sides of the coach, and gave me the most horrible spectacles that ever an English eye beheld. There was a woman with a cancer in her breast, swelled to a monstrous size, full of holes, in two or three of which I could have easily crept, and covered my whole body. There was a fellow with a wen in his neck, larger than five woolpacks, and another with a couple of wooden legs, each about twenty foot high. But the most hateful sight of all was the lice crawling on their clothes. I could see distinctly the limbs of these vermin with my naked eye, much better than those

5. The ancient hall, now incorporated into the Houses of Parliament, where the Law Courts then sat. Swift presum- ably means the square of its breadth (just under 68 feet).

of an European louse through a microscope, and their snouts with which they rooted like swine. They were the first I had ever beheld; and I should have been curious enough to dissect one of them if I had proper instruments (which I unluckily left behind me in the ship), although indeed the sight was so nauseous that it perfectly turned my stomach.

Besides the large box in which I was usually carried, the Queen ordered a smaller one to be made for me, of about twelve foot square and ten high, for the convenience of traveling, because the other was somewhat too large for Glumdalclitch's lap, and cumbersome in the coach; it was made by the same artist, whom I directed in the whole contrivance. This traveling closet was an exact square with a window in the middle of three of the squares, and each window was latticed with iron wire on the outside, to prevent accidents in long journeys. On the fourth side, which had no window, two strong staples were fixed, through which the person that carried me, when I had a mind to be on horseback, put in a leathern belt, and buckled it about his waist. This was always the office of some grave trusty servant in whom I could confide, whether I attended the King and Queen in their progresses, or were disposed to see the gardens, or pay a visit to some great lady or minister of state in the court, when Glumdalclitch happened to be out of order: for I soon began to be known and esteemed among the greatest officers, I suppose more upon account of their Majesties' favor than any merit of my own. In journeys, when I was weary of the coach, a servant on horseback would buckle my box, and place it on a cushion before him; and there I had a full prospect of the country on three sides from my three windows. I had in this closet a field bed and a hammock hung from the ceiling, two chairs and a table, neatly screwed to the floor to prevent being tossed about by the agitation of the horse or the coach. And having been long used to sea voyages, those motions, although sometimes very violent, did not much discompose me.

When I had a mind to see the town, it was always in my traveling closet, which Glumdalclitch held in her lap in a kind of open sedan, after the fashion of the country, borne by four men, and attended by two others in the Queen's livery. The people, who had often heard of me, were very curious to crowd about the sedan; and the girl was complaisant enough to make the bearers stop, and to take me in her hand that I might be more conveniently seen.

I was very desirous to see the chief temple, and particularly the tower belonging to it, which is reckoned the highest in the kingdom. Accordingly one day my nurse carried me thither, but I may truly say I came back disappointed; for the height is not above three thousand foot, reckoning from the ground to the highest pinnacle top; which, allowing for the difference between the size of those people and us in Europe, is no great matter for admiration, nor at all equal in proportion (if I rightly remember) to Salisbury steeple.[6] But, not to detract from a nation to which during my life I shall acknowledge myself extremely obliged, it must be allowed that whatever this famous tower wants in height is amply made up in beauty and strength. For the walls are near an hundred foot thick, built of hewn stone, whereof each is about forty foot square, and adorned on all sides with statues of gods and emperors cut in marble larger than the life, placed in their several niches. I measured a little finger which had fallen down from one of these statues, and lay unperceived among some rubbish, and found it exactly four foot and an inch in length. Glumdalclitch wrapped it up in a handkerchief, and carried it home in her pocket to keep among other trinkets, of which the girl was very fond, as children at her age usually are.

The King's kitchen is indeed a noble building, vaulted at top, and about six hundred foot high. The great oven is not so wide by ten paces as the cupola at St. Paul's:[7] for I measured the latter on purpose after my return. But if I should describe the kitchen grate, the prodigious pots and kettles, the joints of meat turning on the spits, with many other particulars, perhaps I should be hardly believed; at least a severe critic would be apt to think I enlarged a little, as travelers are often suspected to do. To avoid which censure, I fear I have run too much into the other extreme, and that if this treatise should happen to be translated into the language of Brobdingnag (which is the general name of that kingdom) and transmitted thither, the King and his people would have reason to complain that I had done them an injury by a false and diminutive representation.

His Majesty seldom keeps above six hundred horses in his stables: they are generally from fifty-four to sixty foot high. But when he goes abroad on solemn days, he is attended for state by a militia guard of five hundred horse, which indeed I thought was the most splendid sight that could be ever beheld, till I saw part of his army in battalia;[8] whereof I shall find another occasion to speak.

CHAPTER V. *Several adventures that happened to the Author. The execution of a criminal. The Author shows his skill in navigation.*

I should have lived happy enough in that country if my littleness had not exposed me to several ridiculous and troublesome accidents, some of which I shall venture to relate. Glumdalclitch often carried me into the gardens of the court in my smaller box, and would sometimes take me out of it and hold me in her hand, or set me down to walk. I remember, before the dwarf left the Queen, he followed us one day into those gardens; and my nurse having set me down, he and I being close together near some dwarf apple

6. One of the most beautiful Gothic steeples in England is that of Salisbury Cathedral, 404 feet high.
7. The cupola of St. Paul's Cathedral in London is 108 feet in diameter.
8. Battle array.

trees, I must needs show my wit by a silly allusion between him and the trees, which happens to hold in their language as it doth in ours. Whereupon, the malicious rogue watching his opportunity, when I was walking under one of them, shook it directly over my head, by which a dozen apples, each of them near as large as a Bristol barrel, came tumbling about my ears; one of them hit me on the back as I chanced to stoop, and knocked me down flat on my face, but I received no other hurt; and the dwarf was pardoned at my desire, because I had given the provocation.

Another day Glumdalclitch left me on a smooth grassplot to divert myself while she walked at some distance with her governess. In the meantime there suddenly fell such a violent shower of hail that I was immediately by the force of it struck to the ground: and when I was down, the hailstones gave me such cruel bangs all over the body as if I had been pelted with tennis balls;[9] however I made a shift to creep on all four, and shelter myself by lying on my face on the lee side of a border of lemon thyme, but so bruised from head to foot that I could not go abroad in ten days. Neither is this at all to be wondered at, because nature in that country observing the same proportion through all her operations, a hailstone is near eighteen hundred times as large as one in Europe; which I can assert upon experience, having been so curious to weigh and measure them.

But a more dangerous accident happened to me in the same garden when my little nurse, believing she had put me in a secure place, which I often entreated her to do that I might enjoy my own thoughts, and having left my box at home to avoid the trouble of carrying it, went to another part of the garden with her governess and some ladies of her acquaintance. While she was absent and out of hearing, a small white spaniel belonging to one of the chief gardeners, having got by accident into the garden, happened to range near the place where I lay. The dog following the scent, came directly up, and taking me in his mouth, ran straight to his master, wagging his tail, and set me gently on the ground. By good fortune he had been so well taught that I was carried between his teeth without the least hurt, or even tearing my clothes. But the poor gardener, who knew me well, and had a great kindness for me, was in a terrible fright. He gently took me up in both his hands, and asked me how I did; but I was so amazed and out of breath that I could not speak a word. In a few minutes I came to myself, and he carried me safe to my little nurse, who by this time had returned to the place where she left me, and was in cruel agonies when I did not appear nor answer when she called; she severely reprimanded the gardener on account of his dog. But the thing was hushed up and never known at court; for the girl was afraid of the Queen's anger; and truly, as to myself, I thought it

9. 18th-century tennis balls, unlike the modern, were very hard.

would not be for my reputation that such a story should go about.

This accident absolutely determined Glumdalclitch never to trust me abroad for the future out of her sight. I had been long afraid of this resolution, and therefore concealed from her some little unlucky adventures that happened in those times when I was left by myself. Once a kite[1] hovering over the garden made a swoop at me, and if I had not resolutely drawn my hanger, and run under a thick espalier,[2] he would have certainly carried me away in his talons. Another time walking to the top of a fresh molehill, I fell to my neck in the hole through which that animal had cast up the earth, and coined some lie, not worth remembering, to excuse myself for spoiling my clothes. I likewise broke my right shin against the shell of a snail, which I happened to stumble over, as I was walking alone, and thinking on poor England.

I cannot tell whether I were more pleased or mortified to observe in those solitary walks that the smaller birds did not appear to be at all afraid of me; but would hop about within a yard distance, looking for worms and other food with as much indifference and security as if no creature at all were near them. I remember a thrush had the confidence to snatch out of my hand with his bill a piece of cake that Glumdalclitch had just given me for my breakfast. When I attempted to catch any of these birds, they would boldly turn against me, endeavoring to pick my fingers, which I durst not venture within their reach; and then they would hop back unconcerned to hunt for worms or snails, as they did before. But one day I took a thick cudgel, and threw it with all my strength so luckily at a linnet that I knocked him down, and seizing him by the neck with both my hands, ran with him in triumph to my nurse. However, the bird, who had only been stunned, recovering himself, gave me so many boxes with his wings on both sides of my head and body, though I held him at arm's length, and was out of the reach of his claws, that I was twenty times thinking to let him go. But I was soon relieved by one of our servants, who wrung off the bird's neck, and I had him next day for dinner, by the Queen's command. This linnet, as near as I can remember, seemed to be somewhat larger than an English swan.

The Maids of Honor often invited Glumdalclitch to their apartments, and desired she would bring me along with her, on purpose to have the pleasure of seeing and touching me. They would often strip me naked from top to toe and lay me at full length in their bosoms; wherewith I was much disgusted, because, to say the truth, a very offensive smell came from their skins, which I do not mention or intend to the disadvantage of those excellent ladies, for whom I have all manner of respect; but I conceive that my sense was more acute in proportion to my littleness, and that those illus-

1. A bird of prey.   2. A trellis on which fruit trees are trained.

trious persons were no more disagreeable to their lovers, or to each other, than people of the same quality are with us in England. And, after all, I found their natural smell was much more supportable than when they used perfumes, under which I immediately swooned away. I cannot forget that an intimate friend of mine in Lilliput took the freedom in a warm day, when I had used a good deal of exercise, to complain of a strong smell about me, although I am as little faulty that way as most of my sex: but I suppose his faculty of smelling was as nice with regard to me as mine was to that of this people. Upon this point, I cannot forbear doing justice to the Queen, my mistress, and Glumdalclitch, my nurse, whose persons were as sweet as those of any lady in England.

That which gave me most uneasiness among these Maids of Honor, when my nurse carried me to visit them, was to see them use me without any manner of ceremony, like a creature who had no sort of consequence. For they would strip themselves to the skin and put on their smocks in my presence, while I was placed on their toilet[3] directly before their naked bodies; which, I am sure, to me was very far from being a tempting sight, or from giving me any other emotions than those of horror and disgust. Their skins appeared so coarse and uneven, so variously colored, when I saw them near, with a mole here and there as broad as a trencher, and hairs hanging from it thicker than pack-threads, to say nothing further concerning the rest of their persons. Neither did they at all scruple, while I was by, to discharge what they had drunk, to the quantity of at least two hogsheads, in a vessel that held above three tuns. The handsomest among these Maids of Honor, a pleasant frolicsome girl of sixteen, would sometimes set me astride upon one of her nipples, with many other tricks, wherein the reader will excuse me for not being over particular. But I was so much displeased that I entreated Glumdalclitch to contrive some excuse for not seeing that young lady any more.

One day a young gentleman, who was nephew to my nurse's governess, came and pressed them both to see an execution. It was of a man who had murdered one of that gentleman's intimate acquaintance. Glumdalclitch was prevailed on to be of the company, very much against her inclination, for she was naturally tender-hearted: and as for myself, although I abhorred such kind of spectacles, yet my curiosity tempted me to see something that I thought must be extraordinary. The malefactor was fixed in a chair upon a scaffold erected for the purpose, and his head cut off at a blow with a sword of about forty foot long. The veins and arteries spouted up such a prodigious quantity of blood, and so high in the air, that the great *jet d'eau*[4] at Versailles was not equal for the time it lasted; and the head, when it fell on the scaffold floor, gave such a bounce,[5]

3. Toilet table.
4. This fountain rose over forty feet in the air.
5. A sudden noise.

as made me start, although I were at least half an English mile distant.

The Queen, who often used to hear me talk of my sea voyages, and took all occasions to divert me when I was melancholy, asked me whether I understood how to handle a sail or an oar, and whether a little exercise of rowing might not be convenient for my health. I answered that I understood both very well. For although my proper employment had been to be surgeon or doctor to the ship, yet often, upon a pinch, I was forced to work like a common mariner. But I could not see how this could be done in their country, where the smallest wherry was equal to a first-rate man-of-war among us, and such a boat as I could manage would never live in any of their rivers. Her Majesty said, if I would contrive a boat, her own joiner[6] should make it, and she would provide a place for me to sail in. The fellow was an ingenious workman and, by my instructions, in ten days finished a pleasure boat with all its tackling, able conveniently to hold eight Europeans. When it was finished, the Queen was so delighted that she ran with it in her lap to the King, who ordered it to be put in a cistern full of water, with me in it, by way of trial; where I could not manage my two sculls, or little oars, for want of room. But the Queen had before contrived another project. She ordered the joiner to make a wooden trough of three hundred foot long, fifty broad, and eight deep; which being well pitched to prevent leaking, was placed on the floor along the wall in an outer room of the palace. It had a cock near the bottom to let out the water when it began to grow stale, and two servants could easily fill it in half an hour. Here I often used to row for my own diversion, as well as that of the Queen and her ladies, who thought themselves well entertained with my skill and agility. Sometimes I would put up my sail, and then my business was only to steer, while the ladies gave me a gale with their fans; and when they were weary, some of the pages would blow my sail forward with their breath, while I showed my art by steering starboard or larboard as I pleased. When I had done, Glumdalclitch always carried my boat into her closet, and hung it on a nail to dry.

In this exercise I once met an accident which had like to have cost me my life. For one of the pages having put my boat into the trough, the governess who attended Glumdalclitch very officiously[7] lifted me up to place me in the boat; but I happened to slip through her fingers, and should have infallibly fallen down forty feet upon the floor, if by the luckiest chance in the world I had not been stopped by a corking-pin[8] that stuck in the good gentlewoman's stomacher; the head of the pin passed between my shirt and the waistband of my breeches, and thus I was held by the middle in the air until Glumdalclitch ran to my relief.

6. A skilled woodworker.
7. Kindly, dutifully.
8. A pin of the largest size. "Stom-acher": an ornamental covering for the front and upper part of the body.

Another time, one of the servants, whose office it was to fill my trough every third day with fresh water, was so careless to let a huge frog (not perceiving it) slip out of his pail. The frog lay concealed till I was put into my boat, but then seeing a resting place, climbed up, and made it lean so much on one side that I was forced to balance it with all my weight on the other, to prevent overturning. When the frog was got in, it hopped at once half the length of the boat, and then over my head, backwards and forwards, daubing my face and clothes with its odious slime. The largeness of its features made it appear the most deformed animal that can be conceived. However, I desired Glumdalclitch to let me deal with it alone. I banged it a good while with one of my sculls, and at last forced it to leap out of the boat.

But the greatest danger I ever underwent in that kingdom was from a monkey, who belonged to one of the clerks of the kitchen. Glumdalclitch had locked me up in her closet, while she went somewhere upon business or a visit. The weather being very warm, the closet window was left open, as well as the windows in the door of my bigger box, in which I usually lived, because of its largeness and conveniency. As I sat quietly meditating at my table, I heard something bounce in at the closet window, and skip about from one side to the other, whereat, although I was much alarmed, yet I ventured to look out, but stirred not from my seat; and then I saw this frolicsome animal, frisking and leaping up and down, till at last he came to my box, which he seemed to view with great pleasure and curiosity, peeping in at the door and every window. I retreated to the farther corner of my room, or box, but the monkey looking in at every side, put me into such a fright that I wanted presence of mind to conceal myself under the bed, as I might easily have done. After some time spent in peeping, grinning, and chattering, he at last espied me, and reaching one of his paws in at the door, as a cat does when she plays with a mouse, although I often shifted place to avoid him, he at length seized the lappet of my coat (which, being made of that country cloth, was very thick and strong) and dragged me out. He took me up in his right forefoot, and held me as a nurse does a child she is going to suckle, just as I have seen the same sort of creature do with a kitten in Europe: and when I offered to struggle, he squeezed me so hard that I thought it more prudent to submit. I have good reason to believe that he took me for a young one of his own species, by his often stroking my face very gently with his other paw. In these diversions he was interrupted by a noise at the closet door, as if somebody were opening it, whereupon he suddenly leaped up to the window at which he had come in, and thence upon the leads and gutters, walking upon three legs, and holding me in the fourth, till he clambered up to a roof that was next to ours. I heard Glumdalclitch give a shriek at the moment he was carrying me out. The poor girl was almost distracted: that quarter of the palace was all in an uproar; the servants ran for ladders; the monkey was seen by hundreds in the court, sitting upon the ridge of a building, holding me like a baby in one of his forepaws and feeding me with the other, by cramming into my mouth some victuals he had squeezed out of the bag on one side of his chaps, and patting me when I would not eat; whereat many of the rabble below could not forbear laughing; neither do I think they justly ought to be blamed, for without question the sight was ridiculous enough to everybody but myself. Some of the people threw up stones, hoping to drive the monkey down; but this was strictly forbidden, or else very probably my brains had been dashed out.

The ladders were now applied, and mounted by several men; which the monkey observing, and finding himself almost encompassed, not being able to make speed enough with his three legs, let me drop on a ridge tile, and made his escape. Here I sat for some time three hundred yards from the ground, expecting every moment to be blown down by the wind, or to fall by my own giddiness, and come tumbling over and over from the ridge to the eaves. But an honest lad, one of my nurse's footmen, climbed up, and putting me into his breeches pocket, brought me down safe.

I was almost choked with the filthy stuff the monkey had crammed down my throat; but my dear little nurse picked it out of my mouth with a small needle, and then I fell a vomiting, which gave me great relief. Yet I was so weak and bruised in the sides with the squeezes given me by this odious animal that I was forced to keep my bed a fortnight. The King, Queen, and all the Court sent every day to inquire after my health, and her Majesty made me several visits during my sickness. The monkey was killed, and an order made that no such animal should be kept about the palace.

When I attended the King after my recovery, to return him thanks for his favors, he was pleased to rally me a good deal upon this adventure. He asked me what my thoughts and speculations were while I lay in the monkey's paw, how I liked the victuals he gave me, his manner of feeding, and whether the fresh air on the roof had sharpened my stomach. He desired to know what I would have done upon such an occasion in my own country. I told his Majesty that in Europe we had no monkeys, except such as were brought for curiosities from other places, and so small that I could deal with a dozen of them together, if they presumed to attack me. And as for that monstrous animal with whom I was so lately engaged (it was indeed as large as an elephant), if my fears had suffered me to think so far as to make use of my hanger (looking fiercely and clapping my hand upon the hilt as I spoke) when he poked his paw into my chamber, perhaps I should have given him such a wound as would have made him glad to withdraw it with more haste than he put it in. This I delivered in a firm tone, like a person who was jealous lest his courage should be called in question. However, my speech produced nothing else besides a loud laughter, which all the respect due to his Majesty from those about him could not make them contain. This made me reflect how vain an attempt it is for a man to endeavor doing himself honor among those who are out of all degree of equality or comparison with him. And yet I have seen the moral of my own behavior very frequent in England since my return, where a little contemptible varlet, without the least title to birth, person, wit, or common sense, shall presume to look with importance, and put himself upon a foot with the greatest persons of the kingdom.

I was every day furnishing the court with some ridiculous story; and Glumdalclitch, although she loved me to excess, yet was arch enough to inform the Queen whenever I committed any folly that she thought would be diverting to her Majesty. The girl, who had been out of order, was carried by her governess to take the air about an hour's distance, or thirty miles from town. They alighted out of the coach near a small footpath in a field, and Glumdalclitch setting down my traveling box, I went out of it to walk. There was a cow dung in the patch, and I must needs try my activity by attempting to leap over it. I took a run, but unfortunately jumped short, and found myself just in the middle up to my knees. I waded through with some difficulty, and one of the footmen wiped me as clean as he could with his handkerchief; for I was filthily bemired, and my nurse confined me to my box till we returned home, where the Queen was soon informed of what had passed and the footmen spread it about the Court, so that all the mirth, for some days, was at my expense.

CHAPTER VI. *Several contrivances of the Author to please the King and Queen. He shows his skill in music. The King inquires into the state of Europe, which the Author relates to him. The King's observations thereon.*

I used to attend the King's levee[9] once or twice a week, and had often seen him under the barber's hand, which indeed was at first very terrible to behold. For the razor was almost twice as long as an ordinary scythe. His Majesty, according to the custom of the country, was only shaved twice a week. I once prevailed on the barber to give me some of the suds or lather, out of which I picked forty or fifty of the strongest stumps of hair. I then took a piece of fine wood, and cut it like the back of a comb, making several holes in it at equal distance with as small a needle as I could get from Glumdalclitch. I fixed in the stumps so artificially,[1] scraping

9. A morning reception held by a prince or nobleman, sometimes while dressing for the day.
1. Skillfully.

and sloping them with my knife towards the points, that I made a very tolerable comb; which was a seasonable supply, my own being so much broken in the teeth that it was almost useless; neither did I know any artist in that country so nice and exact as would undertake to make me another.

And this puts me in mind of an amusement wherein I spent many of my leisure hours. I desired the Queen's woman to save for me the combings of her Majesty's hair, whereof in time I got a good quantity; and consulting with my friend the cabinetmaker, who had received general orders to do little jobs for me, I directed him to make two chair frames, no larger than those I had in my box, and then to bore little holes with a fine awl round those parts where I designed the backs and seats; through these holes I wove the strongest hairs I could pick out, just after the manner of cane chairs in England. When they were finished, I made a present of them to her Majesty, who kept them in her cabinet, and used to show them for curiosities, as indeed they were the wonder of every one that beheld them. The Queen would have made me sit upon one of these chairs, but I absolutely refused to obey her, protesting I would rather die a thousand deaths than place a dishonorable part of my body on those precious hairs that once adorned her Majesty's head. Of these hairs (as I had always a mechanical genius) I likewise made a neat little purse above five foot long, with her Majesty's name deciphered in gold letters, which I gave to Glumdalclitch by the Queen's consent. To say the truth, it was more for show than use, being not of strength to bear the weight of the larger coins; and therefore she kept nothing in it but some little toys[2] that girls are fond of.

The King, who delighted in music, had frequent consorts[3] at court, to which I was sometimes carried, and set in my box on a table to hear them; but the noise was so great that I could hardly distinguish the tunes. I am confident that all the drums and trumpets of a royal army, beating and sounding together just at your ears, could not equal it. My practice was to have my box removed from the places where the performers sat, as far as I could, then to shut the doors and windows of it, and draw the window curtains, after which I found their music not disagreeable.

I had learned in my youth to play a little upon the spinet. Glumdalclitch kept one in her chamber, and a master attended twice a week to teach her: I call it a spinet, because it somewhat resembled that instrument, and was played upon in the same manner. A fancy came into my head that I would entertain the King and Queen with an English tune upon this instrument. But this appeared extremely difficult: for the spinet was near sixty foot long, each key being almost a foot wide; so that, with my arms extended, I could

2. Trifles.   3. Concerts.

not reach to above five keys, and to press them down required a good smart stroke with my fist, which would be too great a labor and to no purpose. The method I contrived was this: I prepared two round sticks about the bigness of common cudgels; they were thicker at one end than the other, and I covered the thicker ends with a piece of a mouse's skin, that by rapping on them I might neither damage the tops of the keys, nor interrupt the sound. Before the spinet a bench was placed, about four foot below the keys, and I was put upon the bench. I ran sideling upon it that way and this, as fast as I could, banging the proper keys with my two sticks; and made a shift to play a jig, to the great satisfaction of both their Majesties: but it was the most violent exercise I ever underwent, and yet I could not strike above sixteen keys, nor, consequently, play the bass and treble together, as other artists do; which was a great disadvantage to my performance.

The King, who, as I before observed, was a prince of excellent understanding, would frequently order that I should be brought in my box and set upon the table in his closet. He would then command me to bring one of my chairs out of the box, and sit down within three yards distance upon the top of the cabinet, which brought me almost to a level with his face. In this manner I had several conversations with him. I one day took the freedom to tell his Majesty that the contempt he discovered towards Europe, and the rest of the world, did not seem answerable to those excellent qualities of mind that he was master of. That reason did not extend itself with the bulk of the body: on the contrary, we observed in our country that the tallest persons were usually least provided with it. That among other animals, bees and ants had the reputation of more industry, art, and sagacity than many of the larger kinds; and that, as inconsiderable as he took me to be, I hoped I might live to do his Majesty some signal service. The King heard me with attention, and began to conceive a much better opinion of me than he had before. He desired I would give him as exact an account of the government of England as I possibly could; because, as fond as princes commonly are of their own customs (for so he conjectured of other monarchs, by my former discourses), he should be glad to hear of anything that might deserve imitation.

Imagine with thyself, courteous reader, how often I then wished for the tongue of Demosthenes or Cicero, that might have enabled me to celebrate the praise of my own dear native country in a style equal to its merits and felicity.

I began my discourse by informing his Majesty that our dominions consisted of two islands, which composed three mighty kingdoms under one sovereign, beside our plantations in America. I dwelt long upon the fertility of our soil, and the temperature[4] of

4. Temperateness.

our climate. I then spoke at large upon the constitution of an English Parliament, partly made up of an illustrious body called the House of Peers, persons of the noblest blood, and of the most ancient and ample patrimonies. I described that extraordinary care always taken of their education in arts and arms, to qualify them for being counselors born to the king and kingdom; to have a share in the legislature, to be members of the highest Court of Judicature, from whence there could be no appeal; and to be champions always ready for the defense of their prince and country, by their valor, conduct, and fidelity. That these were the ornament and bulwark of the kingdom, worthy followers of their most renowned ancestors, whose honor had been the reward of their virtue, from which their posterity were never once known to degenerate. To these were joined several holy persons, as part of that assembly, under the title of Bishops, whose peculiar business it is to take care of religion, and of those who instruct the people therein. These were searched and sought out through the whole nation, by the prince and his wisest counselors, among such of the priesthood as were most deservedly distinguished by the sanctity of their lives and the depth of their erudition, who were indeed the spiritual fathers of the clergy and the people.

That the other part of the Parliament consisted of an assembly called the House of Commons, who were all principal gentlemen, freely picked and culled out by the people themselves, for their great abilities and love of their country, to represent the wisdom of the whole nation. And these two bodies make up the most august assembly in Europe, to whom, in conjunction with the prince, the whole legislature is committed.

I then descended to the Courts of Justice, over which the Judges, those venerable sages and interpreters of the law, presided, for determining the disputed rights and properties of men, as well as for the punishment of vice, and protection of innocence. I mentioned the prudent management of our treasury, the valor and achievements of our forces by sea and land. I computed the number of our people, by reckoning how many millions there might be of each religious sect, or political party among us. I did not omit even our sports and pastimes, or any other particular which I thought might redound to the honor of my country. And I finished all with a brief historical account of affairs and events in England for about an hundred years past.

This conversation was not ended under five audiences, each of several hours, and the King heard the whole with great attention, frequently taking notes of what I spoke, as well as memorandums of several questions he intended to ask me.

When I had put an end to these long discourses, his Majesty in a sixth audience consulting his notes, proposed many doubts, queries, and objections, upon every article. He asked what methods were used to cultivate the minds and bodies of our young nobility, and in what kind of business they commonly spent the first and teachable part of their lives. What course was taken to supply that assembly when any noble family became extinct. What qualifications were necessary in those who were to be created new lords. Whether the humor[5] of the prince, a sum of money to a Court lady or a prime minister, or a design of strengthening a party opposite to the public interest, ever happened to be motives in those advancements. What share of knowledge these lords had in the laws of their country, and how they came by it, so as to enable them to decide the properties of their fellow subjects in the last resort. Whether they were always so free from avarice, partialities, or want that a bribe or some other sinister view could have no place among them. Whether those holy lords I spoke of were constantly promoted to that rank upon account of their knowledge in religious matters, and the sanctity of their lives, had never been compliers with the times while they were common priests, or slavish prostitute chaplains to some nobleman, whose opinions they continued servilely to follow after they were admitted into that assembly.

He then desired to know what arts were practiced in electing those whom I called Commoners. Whether a stranger with a strong purse might not influence the vulgar voters to choose him before their own landlord or the most considerable gentleman in the neighborhood. How it came to pass that people were so violently bent upon getting into this assembly, which I allowed to be a great trouble and expense, often to the ruin of their families, without any salary or pension: because this appeared such an exalted strain of virtue and public spirit that his Majesty seemed to doubt it might possibly not be always sincere; and he desired to know whether such zealous gentlemen could have any views of refunding themselves for the charges and trouble they were at, by sacrificing the public good to the designs of a weak and vicious prince in conjunction with a corrupted ministry. He multiplied his questions, and sifted me thoroughly upon every part of this head, proposing numberless inquiries and objections, which I think it not prudent or convenient to repeat.

Upon what I said in relation to our Courts of Justice, his Majesty desired to be satisfied in several points: and this I was the better able to do, having been formerly almost ruined by a long suit in chancery, which was decreed for me with costs. He asked what time was usually spent in determining between right and wrong, and what degree of expense. Whether advocates and orators had liberty to plead in causes manifestly known to be unjust, vexatious, or oppressive. Whether party in religion or politics were observed

5. Whim.

to be of any weight in the scale of justice. Whether those pleading orators were persons educated in the general knowledge of equity, or only in provincial, national, and other local customs. Whether they or their judges had any part in penning those laws which they assumed the liberty of interpreting and glossing upon at their pleasure. Whether they had ever at different times pleaded for and against the same cause, and cited precedents to prove contrary opinions. Whether they were a rich or a poor corporation. Whether they received any pecuniary reward for pleading or delivering their opinions. And particularly whether they were ever admitted as members in the lower senate.

He fell next upon the management of our treasury, and said he thought my memory had failed me, because I computed our taxes at about five or six millions a year, and when I came to mention the issues,[6] he found they sometimes amounted to more than double, for the notes he had taken were very particular in this point; because he hoped, as he told me, that the knowledge of our conduct might be useful to him, and he could not be deceived in his calculations. But if what I told him were true, he was still at a loss how a kingdom could run out of its estate like a private person. He asked me, who were our creditors? and where we should find money to pay them? He wondered to hear me talk of such chargeable and extensive wars; that certainly we must be a quarrelsome people, or live among very bad neighbors, and that our generals must needs be richer than our kings.[7] He asked what business we had out of our own islands, unless upon the score of[8] trade or treaty or to defend the coasts with our fleet. Above all, he was amazed to hear me talk of a mercenary standing army[9] in the midst of peace, and among a free people. He said if we were governed by our own consent in the persons of our representatives, he could not imagine of whom we were afraid, or against whom we were to fight; and would hear my opinion whether a private man's house might not better be defended by himself, his children, and family, than by half a dozen rascals picked up at a venture[1] in the streets for small wages, who might get an hundred times more by cutting their throats.

He laughed at my odd kind of arithmetic (as he was pleased to call it) in reckoning the numbers of our people by a computation drawn from the several sects among us in religion and politics. He said he knew no reason why those who entertain opinions prejudicial to the public should be obliged to change, or should not be obliged

6. Expenditures.
7. An allusion to the enormous fortune gained by the Duke of Marlborough, formerly Captain-General of the army, whom Swift detested.
8. For the sake of.
9. Since the declaration of the Bill of Rights (1689), a standing army without authorization by Parliament had been illegal. Swift and the Tories in general were vigilant in their opposition to such an army.
1. By chance.

to conceal them. And as it was tyranny in any government to require the first, so it was weakness not to enforce the second: for a man may be allowed to keep poisons in his closet, but not to vend them about for cordials.[2]

He observed that among the diversions of our nobility and gentry I had mentioned gaming.[3] He desired to know at what age this entertainment was usually taken up, and when it was laid down; how much of their time it employed; whether it ever went so high as to affect their fortunes; whether mean, vicious people, by their dexterity in that art, might not arrive at great riches, and sometimes keep our very nobles in dependence, as well as habituate them to vile companions, wholly take them from the improvement of their minds, and force them, by the losses they have received, to learn and practice that infamous dexterity upon others.

He was perfectly astonished with the historical account I gave him of our affairs during the last century, protesting it was only an heap of conspiracies, rebellions, murders, massacres, revolutions, banishments, the very worst effects that avarice, faction, hypocrisy, perfidiousness, cruelty, rage, madness, hatred, envy, lust, malice, or ambition could produce.

His Majesty in another audience was at the pains to recapitulate the sum of all I had spoken; compared the questions he made with the answers I had given; then taking me into his hands, and stroking me gently, delivered himself in these words, which I shall never forget nor the manner he spoke them in. "My little friend Grildrig, you have made a most admirable panegyric[4] upon your country. You have clearly proved that ignorance, idleness, and vice are the proper ingredients for qualifying a legislator. That laws are best explained, interpreted, and applied by those whose interests and abilities lie in perverting, confounding, and eluding them. I observe among you some lines of an institution which in its original might have been tolerable; but these half erased, and the rest wholly blurred and blotted by corruptions. It doth not appear from all you have said how any one virtue is required towards the procurement of any one station among you; much less that men are ennobled on account of their virtue, that priests are advanced for their piety or learning, soldiers for their conduct or valor, judges for their integrity, senators for the love of their country, or counselors for their wisdom. As for yourself," continued the King, "who have spent the greatest part of your life in traveling, I am well disposed to hope you may hitherto have escaped many vices of your country. But by what I have gathered from your own relation, and the answers I have with much pains wringed and extorted from you, I cannot but conclude the bulk of your natives to be the most pernicious race

2. Medicines to stimulate the heart, or, equally commonly, liqueurs.
3. Gambling.

4. A formal oration in praise of someone or something.

of little odious vermin that nature ever suffered to crawl upon the surface of the earth."

CHAPTER VII. *The Author's love of his country. He makes a proposal of much advantage to the King; which is rejected. The King's great ignorance in politics. The learning of that country very imperfect and confined. Their laws, and military affairs, and parties in the State.*

Nothing but an extreme love of truth could have hindered me from concealing this part of my story. It was in vain to discover my resentments, which were always turned into ridicule: and I was forced to rest with patience while my noble and most beloved country was so injuriously treated. I am heartily sorry as any of my readers can possibly be that such an occasion was given, but this prince happened to be so curious and inquisitive upon every particular that it could not consist either with gratitude or good manners to refuse giving him what satisfaction I was able. Yet thus much I may be allowed to say in my own vindication: that I artfully eluded many of his questions, and gave to every point a more favorable turn by many degrees than the strictness of truth would allow. For I have always borne that laudable partiality to my own country, which Dionysius Halicarnassensis[5] with so much justice recommends to an historian. I would hide the frailties and deformities of my political mother, and place her virtues and beauties in the most advantageous light. This was my sincere endeavor in those many discourses I had with that mighty monarch, although it unfortunately failed of success.

But great allowances should be given to a King who lives wholly secluded from the rest of the world, and must therefore be altogether unacquainted with the manners and customs that most prevail in other nations: the want of which knowledge will ever produce many *prejudices*, and a certain *narrowness of thinking*, from which we and the politer countries of Europe are wholly exempted. And it would be hard indeed if so remote a prince's notions of virtue and vice were to be offered as a standard for all mankind.

To confirm what I have now said, and further, to show the miserable effects of a *confined education*, I shall here insert a passage which will hardly obtain belief. In hopes to ingratiate myself farther into his Majesty's favor, I told him of an invention discovered between three and four hundred years ago, to make a certain powder, into an heap of which the smallest spark of fire falling would kindle the whole in a moment, although it were as big as a mountain, and make it all fly up in the air together, with a noise and agitation

---

5. A Greek rhetorician and historian, who flourished ca. 25 B.C. His history of Rome was written to reconcile the Greeks to their Roman masters.

greater than thunder. That a proper quantity of this powder rammed into an hollow tube of brass or iron, according to its bigness, would drive a ball of iron or lead with such violence and speed as nothing was able to sustain its force. That the largest balls thus discharged would not only destroy whole ranks of an army at once, but batter the strongest walls to the ground; sink down ships with a thousand men in each, to the bottom of the sea; and, when linked together by a chain, would cut through masts and rigging; divide hundreds of bodies in the middle, and lay all waste before them. That we often put this powder into large hollow balls of iron, and discharged them by an engine into some city we were besieging; which would rip up the pavements, tear the houses to pieces, burst and throw splinters on every side, dashing out the brains of all who came near. That I knew the ingredients very well, which were cheap and common; I understood the manner of compounding them, and could direct his workmen how to make those tubes of a size proportionable to all other things in his Majesty's kingdom, and the largest need not be above two hundred foot long; twenty or thirty of which tubes, charged with the proper quantity of powder and balls, would batter down the walls of the strongest town in his dominions in a few hours; or destroy the whole metropolis, if ever it should pretend to dispute his absolute commands. This I humbly offered to his Majesty as a small tribute of acknowledgment in return of so many marks that I had received of his royal favor and protection.

The King was struck with horror at the description I had given of those terrible engines and the proposal I had made. He was amazed how so impotent and groveling an insect as I (these were his expressions) could entertain such inhuman ideas, and in so familiar a manner as to appear wholly unmoved at all the scenes of blood and desolation which I had painted as the common effects of those destructive machines; whereof he said some evil genius, enemy to mankind, must have been the first contriver. As for himself, he protested that although few things delighted him so much as new discoveries in art or in nature, yet he would rather lose half his kingdom than be privy[6] to such a secret, which he commanded me, as I valued my life, never to mention any more.

A strange effect of *narrow principles* and *short views!* that a prince possessed of every quality which procures veneration, love, and esteem; of strong parts, great wisdom, and profound learning; endued with admirable talents for government, and almost adored by his subjects; should from a *nice, unnecessary scruple*, whereof in Europe we can have no conception, let slip an opportunity put into his hands that would have made him absolute master of the lives, the liberties, and the fortunes of his people. Neither do I say this with the least intention to detract from the many virtues of that

6. To share secret knowledge.

excellent King, whose character I am sensible will on this account be very much lessened in the opinion of an English reader: but I take this defect among them to have risen from their ignorance; they not having hitherto reduced politics into a science, as the more acute wits of Europe have done. For I remember very well, in a discourse one day with the King, when I happened to say there were several thousand books among us written upon the art of government, it gave him (directly contrary to my intention) a very mean opinion of our understandings. He professed both to abominate and despise all *mystery, refinement,* and *intrigue,* either in a prince or a minister. He could not tell what I meant by *secrets of state,* where an enemy or some rival nation were not in the case. He confined the knowledge of governing within very *narrow bounds:* to common sense and reason, to justice and lenity,[7] to the speedy determination of civil and criminal causes, with some other obvious topics which are not worth considering. And he gave it for his opinion that whoever could make two ears of corn or two blades of grass to grow upon a spot of ground where only one grew before would deserve better of mankind and do more essential service to his country than the whole race of politicians [7a] put together.

The learning of this people is very defective, consisting only in morality, history, poetry, and mathematics; wherein they must be allowed to excel. But the last of these is wholly applied to what may be useful in life, to the improvement of agriculture and all mechanical arts; so that among us it would be little esteemed. And as to ideas, entities, abstractions, and transcendentals,[8] I could never drive the least conception into their heads.

No law of that country must exceed in words the number of letters in their alphabet, which consists only in two and twenty. But indeed few of them extend even to that length. They are expressed in the most plain and simple terms, wherein those people are not mercurial[9] enough to discover above one interpretation. And to write a comment upon any law is a capital crime. As to the decision of civil causes, or proceedings against criminals, their precedents[1] are so few that they have little reason to boast of any extraordinary skill in either.

They have had the art of printing as well as the Chinese, time out of mind. But their libraries are not very large; for that of the King's, which is reckoned the biggest, doth not amount to above a thousand volumes, placed in a gallery of twelve hundred foot long, from whence I had liberty to borrow what books I pleased. The

7. Mildness.
7a. By "politicians" Swift means something like our modern "political scientists"—theorists.
8. In Swift's time, "transcendental" was practically synonymous with "metaphysical."
9. Changeable.

1. A legal decision or a course of action which comes to serve as a rule in determining similar cases in the future. In the Fourth Voyage of *Gulliver's Travels,* Gulliver is made to say: "It is a maxim among these lawyers that whatever hath been done before may legally be done again. * * * "

Queen's joiner had contrived in one of the Glumdalclitch's rooms a kind of wooden machine five and twenty foot high, formed like a standing ladder; the steps were each fifty foot long. It was indeed a movable pair of stairs, the lowest end placed at ten foot distance from the wall of the chamber. The book I had a mind to read was put up leaning against the wall. I first mounted to the upper step of the ladder, and turning my face towards the book, began at the top of the page, and so walking to the right and left about eight or ten paces according to the length of the lines, till I had gotten a little below the level of mine eyes, and then descending gradually till I came to the bottom: after which I mounted again, and began the other page in the same manner, and so turned over the leaf, which I could easily do with both my hands, for it was as thick and stiff as a pasteboard, and in the largest folios[2] not above eighteen or twenty foot long.

Their style is clear, masculine, and smooth, but not florid; for they avoid nothing more than multiplying unnecessary words or using various expressions. I have perused many of their books, especially those in history and morality. Among the rest, I was much diverted with a little old treatise, which always lay in Glumdalclitch's bedchamber, and belonged to her governess, a grave elderly gentlewoman, who dealt in writings of morality and devotion. The book treats of the weakness of human kind, and is in little esteem, except among the women and the vulgar. However, I was curious to see what an author of that country could say upon such a subject. This writer went through all the usual topics of European moralists: showing how diminutive, contemptible, and helpless an animal was man in his own nature; how unable to defend himself from the inclemencies of the air, or the fury of wild beasts; how much he was excelled by one creature in strength, by another in speed, by a third in foresight, by a fourth in industry. He added that nature was degenerated in these latter declining ages of the world, and could now produce only small abortive births in comparison of those in ancient times. He said it was very reasonable to think, not only that the species of men were originally much larger, but also that there must have been giants in former ages; which, as it is asserted by history and tradition, so it hath been confirmed by huge bones and skulls casually dug up in several parts of the kingdom, far exceeding the common dwindled race of man in our days. He argued that the very laws of nature absolutely required we should have been made in the beginning of a size more large and robust, not so liable to destruction from every little accident of a tile falling from a house, or a stone cast from the hand of a boy, or of being drowned in a little brook. From this way of reasoning, the author drew several moral applications useful in the

2. A book of the largest size.

conduct of life, but needless here to repeat. For my own part, I could not avoid reflecting how universally this talent was spread, of drawing lectures in morality, or indeed rather matter of discontent and repining, from the quarrels we raise with nature. And I believe, upon a strict inquiry, those quarrels might be shown as ill grounded among us as they are among that people.

As to their military affairs, they boast that the King's army consists of an hundred and seventy-six thousand foot and thirty-two thousand horse: if that may be called an army which is made up of tradesmen in the several cities, and farmers in the country, whose commanders are only the nobility and gentry, without pay or reward. They are indeed perfect enough in their exercises, and under very good discipline, wherein I saw no great merit; for how should it be otherwise, where every farmer is under the command of his own landlord, and every citizen under that of the principal men in his own city, chosen after the manner of Venice by ballot?

I have often seen the militia of Lorbrulgrud drawn out to exercise in a great field near the city, of twenty miles square. They were in all not above twenty-five thousand foot, and six thousand horse; but it was impossible for me to compute their number, considering the space of ground they took up. A cavalier mounted on a large steed might be about an hundred foot high. I have seen this whole body of horse, upon a word of command, draw their swords at once, and brandish them in the air. Imagination can figure nothing so grand, so surprising, and so astonishing. It looked as if ten thousand flashes of lightning were darting at the same time from every quarter of the sky.

I was curious to know how this prince, to whose dominions there is no access from any other country, came to think of armies, or to teach his people the practice of military discipline. But I was soon informed, both by conversation and reading their histories. For in the course of many ages they have been troubled with the same disease to which the whole race of mankind is subject: the nobility often contending for power, the people for liberty, and the King for absolute dominion. All which, however happily tempered by the laws of the kingdom, have been sometimes violated by each of the three parties, and have more than once occasioned civil wars, the last whereof was happily put an end to by this prince's grandfather in a general composition;[3] and the militia, then settled with common consent, hath been ever since kept in the strictest duty.

CHAPTER VIII. *The King and Queen make a progress to the frontiers. The Author attends them. The manner in which he leaves the country very particularly related. He returns to England.*

---

3. A political settlement based upon general agreement of all parties.

I had always a strong impulse that I should some time recover my liberty, though it were impossible to conjecture by what means, or to form any project with the least hope of succeeding. The ship in which I sailed was the first ever known to be driven within sight of that coast; and the King had given strict orders that if at any time another appeared, it should be taken ashore, and with all its crew and passengers brought in a tumbrel[4] to Lorbrulgrud. He was strongly bent to get me a woman of my own size, by whom I might propagate the breed: but I think I should rather have died than undergone the disgrace of leaving a posterity to be kept in cages like tame canary birds, and perhaps in time sold about the kingdom to persons of quality for curiosities. I was indeed treated with much kindness: I was the favorite of a great King and Queen, and the delight of the whole Court, but it was upon such a foot as ill became the dignity of human kind. I could never forget those domestic pledges[5] I had left behind me. I wanted to be among people with whom I could converse upon even terms, and walk about the streets and fields without fear of being trod to death like a frog or a young puppy. But my deliverance came sooner than I expected, and in a manner not very common; the whole story and circumstances of which I shall faithfully relate.

I had now been two years in this country; and about the beginning of the third, Glumdalclitch and I attended the King and Queen in progress to the south coast of the kingdom. I was carried as usual in my traveling box, which, as I have already described, was a very convenient closet of twelve foot wide. I had ordered a hammock to be fixed by silken ropes from the four corners at the top, to break the jolts when a servant carried me before him on horseback, as I sometimes desired; and would often sleep in my hammock while we were upon the road. On the roof of my closet, set not directly over the middle of the hammock, I ordered the joiner to cut out a hole of a foot square to give me air in hot weather as I slept, which hole I shut at pleasure with a board that drew backwards and forwards through a groove.

When we came to our journey's end, the King thought proper to pass a few days at a palace he hath near Flanflasnic, a city within eighteen English miles of the seaside. Glumdalclitch and I were much fatigued; I had gotten a small cold, but the poor girl was so ill as to be confined to her chamber. I longed to see the ocean, which must be the only scene of my escape, if ever it should happen. I pretended to be worse than I really was, and desired leave to take the fresh air of the sea with a page whom I was very fond of, and who had sometimes been trusted with me. I shall never forget with what unwillingness Glumdalclitch consented, nor the strict charge she gave the page to be careful of me, bursting at the

4. A farm wagon.   5. His wife and children.

same time into a flood of tears, as if she had some foreboding of what was to happen. The boy took me out in my box about half an hour's walk from the palace, towards the rocks on the seashore. I ordered him to set me down, and lifting up one of my sashes, cast many a wistful melancholy look towards the sea. I found myself not very well, and told the page that I had a mind to take a nap in my hammock, which I hoped would do me good. I got in, and the boy shut the window close down, to keep out the cold. I soon fell asleep: and all I can conjecture is that while I slept, the page, thinking no danger could happen, went among the rocks to look for birds' eggs; having before observed him from my window searching about, and picking up one or two in the clefts. Be that as it will, I found myself suddenly awaked with a violent pull upon the ring which was fastened at the top of my box for the conveniency of carriage. I felt my box raised very high in the air, and then borne forward with prodigious speed. The first jolt had like to have shaken me out of my hammock, but afterwards the motion was easy enough. I called out several times as loud as I could raise my voice, but all to no purpose. I looked towards my windows, and could see nothing but the clouds and sky. I heard a noise just over my head like the clapping of wings, and then began to perceive the woeful condition I was in; that some eagle had got the ring of my box in his beak, with an intent to let it fall on a rock, like a tortoise in a shell, and then pick out my body and devour it. For the sagacity and smell of this bird enable him to discover his quarry at a great distance, although better concealed than I could be within a two-inch board.

In a little time I observed the noise and flutter of wings to increase very fast, and my box was tossed up and down like a sign-post in a windy day. I heard several bangs or buffets, as I thought, given to the eagle (for such I am certain it must have been that held the ring of my box in his beak), and then all on a sudden felt myself falling perpendicularly down for above a minute, but with such incredible swiftness that I almost lost my breath. My fall was topped by a terrible squash, that sounded louder to mine ears than the cataract of Niagara; after which I was quite in the dark for an-other minute, and then my box began to rise so high that I could see light from the tops of my windows. I now perceived that I was fallen into the sea. My box, by the weight of my body, the goods that were in, and the broad plates of iron fixed for strength at the four corners of the top and bottom, floated about five foot deep in water. I did then and do now suppose that the eagle which flew away with my box was pursued by two or three others, and forced to let me drop while he was defending himself against the rest, who hoped to share in the prey. The plates of iron fastened at the bot-tom of the box (for those were the strongest) preserved the balance while it fell, and hindered it from being broken on the surface of the water. Every joint of it was well grooved, and the door did not move on hinges, but up and down like a sash; which kept my closet so tight that very little water came in. I got with much difficulty out of my hammock, having first ventured to draw back the slip-board on the roof already mentioned, contrived on purpose to let in air, for want of which I found myself almost stifled.

How often did I then wish myself with my dear Glumdalclitch, from whom one single hour had so far divided me! And I may say with truth that in the midst of my own misfortune, I could not forbear lamenting my poor nurse, the grief she would suffer for my loss, the displeasure of the Queen, and the ruin of her fortune. Perhaps many travelers have not been under greater difficulties and distress than I was at this juncture, expecting every moment to see my box dashed in pieces, or at least overset by the first violent blast or a rising wave. A breach in one single pane of glass would have been immediate death, nor could anything have preserved the windows but the strong lattice wires placed on the outside against accidents in traveling. I saw the water ooze in at several crannies, although the leaks were not considerable, and I endeavored to stop them as well as I could. I was not able to lift up the roof of my closet, which otherwise I certainly should have done, and sat on the top of it, where I might at least preserve myself from being shut up, as I may call it, in the hold. Or, if I escaped these dangers for a day or two, what could I expect but a miserable death of cold and hunger! I was four hours under these circumstances, expecting and indeed wishing every moment to be my last.

I have already told the reader that there were two strong staples fixed upon that side of my box which had no window and into which the servant, who used to carry me on horseback, would put a leathern belt, and buckle it about his waist. Being in this disconsolate state, I heard, or at least thought I heard, some kind of grating noise on that side of my box where the staples were fixed; and soon after I began to fancy that the box was pulled or towed along in the sea; for I now and then felt a sort of tugging, which made the waves rise near the tops of my windows, leaving me almost in the dark. This gave me some faint hopes of relief, although I was not able to imagine how it could be brought about. I ventured to unscrew one of my chairs, which were always fastened to the floor; and having made a hard shift to screw it down again directly under the slipping-board that I had lately opened, I mounted on the chair, and putting my mouth as near as I could to the hole, I called for help in a loud voice, and in all the languages I understood. I then fastened my handkerchief to a stick I usually carried, and thrusting it up the hole, waved it several times in the air, that if any boat or ship were near, the seamen might conjecture some unhappy mortal to be shut up in the box.

I found no effect from all I could do, but plainly perceived my closet to be moved along; and in the space of an hour or better, that side of the box where the staples were, and had no window, struck against something that was hard. I apprehended it to be a rock, and found myself tossed more than ever. I plainly heard a noise upon the cover of my closet, like that of a cable, and the grating of it as it passed through the ring. I then found myself hoisted up by degrees at least three foot higher than I was before. Whereupon I again thrust up my stick and handkerchief, calling for help till I was almost hoarse. In return to which, I heard a great shout repeated three time, giving me such transports of joy as are not to be conceived but by those who feel them. I now heard a trampling over my head, and somebody calling through the hole with a loud voice in the English tongue: "If there be anybody below, let them speak." I answered, I was an Englishman, drawn by ill fortune into the greatest calamity that ever any creature underwent, and begged, by all that was moving, to be delivered out of the dungeon I was in. The voice replied, I was safe, for my box was fastened to their ship; and the carpenter should immediately come and saw an hole in the cover, large enough to pull me out. I answered, that was needless and would take up too much time, for there was no more to be done but let one of the crew put his finger into the ring, and take the box out of the sea into the ship, and so into the captain's cabin. Some of them, upon hearing me talk so wildly, thought I was mad; others laughed; for indeed it never came into my head that I was now got among people of my own stature and strength. The carpenter came, and in a few minutes sawed a passage about four foot square; then let down a small ladder, upon which I mounted, and from thence was taken into the ship in a very weak condition.

The sailors were all in amazement, and asked me a thousand questions, which I had no inclination to answer. I was equally confounded at the sight of so many pygmies, for such I took them to be, after having so long accustomed my eyes to the monstrous objects I had left. But the Captain, Mr. Thomas Wilcocks, an honest, worthy Shropshire man, observing I was ready to faint, took me into his cabin, gave me a cordial to comfort me, and made me turn in upon his own bed, advising me to take a little rest, of which I had great need. Before I went to sleep I gave him to understand that I had some valuable furniture in my box, too good to be lost, a fine hammock, an handsome field bed, two chairs, a table, and a cabinet; that my closet was hung on all sides, or rather quilted with silk and cotton; that if he would let one of the crew bring my closet into his cabin, I would open it before him and show him my goods. The Captain, hearing me utter these absurdities, concluded I was raving; however (I suppose to pacify me), he promised to give order as I desired, and going upon deck, sent some of his men down into my closet, from whence (as I afterwards found) they drew up all my goods and stripped off the quilting; but the chairs, cabinet, and bedstead, being screwed to the floor, were much damaged by the ignorance of the seamen, who tore them up by force. Then they knocked off some of the boards for the use of the ship; and when they had got all they had a mind for, let the hulk drop into the sea, which, by reason of many breaches made in the bottom and sides, sunk to rights.[6] And indeed I was glad not to have been a spectator of the havoc they made, because I am confident it would have sensibly touched me, by bringing former passages into my mind, which I had rather forget.

I slept some hours, but perpetually disturbed with dreams of the place I had left, and the dangers I had escaped. However, upon waking, I found myself much recovered. It was now about eight o'clock at night, and the Captain ordered supper immediately, thinking I had already fasted too long. He entertained me with great kindness, observing me not to look wildly, or talk inconsistently; and when we were left alone, desired I would give him a relation of my travels, and by what accident I came to be set adrift in that monstrous wooden chest. He said that about twelve o'clock at noon, as he was looking through his glass, he spied it at a distance, and thought it was a sail, which he had a mind to make,[7] being not much out of his course, in hopes of buying some biscuit, his own beginning to fall short. That, upon coming nearer, and finding his error, he sent out his longboat to discover what I was; that his men came back in a fright, swearing they had seen a swimming house. That he laughed at their folly, and went himself in the boat, ordering his men to take a strong cable along with them. That the weather being calm, he rowed round me several times, observed my windows, and the wire lattices that defended them. That he discovered two staples upon one side, which was all of boards, without any passage for light. He then commanded his men to row up to that side, and fastening a cable to one of the staples, ordered his men to tow my chest (as he called it) towards the ship. When it was there, he gave directions to fasten another cable to the ring fixed in the cover, and to raise up my chest with pulleys, which all the sailors were not able to do above two or three foot. He said they saw my stick and handkerchief thrust out of the hole, and concluded that some unhappy man must be shut up in the cavity. I asked whether he or the crew had seen any prodigious birds in the air about the time he first discovered me. To which he answered that, discoursing this matter with the sailors while I was asleep, one of them said he had observed three eagles flying towards the

6. At once; altogether.   7. Overtake.

north, but remarked nothing of their being larger than the usual size (which I suppose must be imputed to the great height they were at), and he could not guess the reason of my question. I then asked the Captain how far he reckoned we might be from land; he said, by the best computation he could make, we were at least an hundred leagues. I assured him that he must be mistaken by almost half; for I had not left the country from whence I came above two hours before I dropped into the sea. Whereupon he began again to think that my brain was disturbed, of which he gave me a hint, and advised me to go to bed in a cabin he had provided. I assured him I was well refreshed with his good entertainment and company, and as much in my senses as ever I was in my life. He then grew serious and desired to ask me freely whether I were not troubled in mind by the consciousness of some enormous crime, for which I was punished at the command of some prince, by exposing me in that chest, as great criminals in other countries have been forced to sea in a leaky vessel without provisions; for although he should be sorry to have taken so ill[8] a man into his ship, yet he would engage his word to set me safe on shore in the first port where we arrived. He added that his suspicions were much increased by some very absurd speeches I had delivered at first to the sailors, and afterwards to himself, in relation to my closet or chest, as well as by my odd looks and behavior while I was at supper.

I begged his patience to hear me tell my story, which I faithfully did from the last time I left England to the moment he first discovered me. And as truth always forceth its way into rational minds, so this honest, worthy gentleman, who had some tincture of learning, and very good sense, was immediately convinced of my candor and veracity. But further to confirm all I had said, I entreated him to give order that my cabinet should be brought, of which I kept the key in my pocket (for he had already informed me how the seamen disposed of my closet). I opened it in his presence and showed him the small collection of rarities I made in the country from whence I had been so strangely delivered. There was the comb I had contrived out of the stumps of the King's beard, and another of the same materials, but fixed into a paring of her Majesty's thumbnail, which served for the back. There was a collection of needles and pins from a foot to half a yard long; four wasp-stings, like joiners' tacks; some combings of the Queen's hair; a gold ring which one day she made me a present of in a most obliging manner, taking it from her little finger, and throwing it over my head like a collar. I desired the Captain would please to accept this ring in return for his civilities, which he absolutely refused. I showed him a corn that I had cut off with my own hand from a Maid of Honor's toe; it was about the bigness of a Kentish pippin,[9] and grown so

8. Evil.   9. Apple.

hard that, when I returned to England, I got it hollowed into a cup and set in silver. Lastly, I desired him to see the breeches I had then on, which were made of a mouse's skin.

I could force nothing on him but a footman's tooth, which I observed him to examine with great curiosity, and found he had a fancy for it. He received it with abundance of thanks, more than such a trifle could deserve. It was drawn by an unskillful surgeon in a mistake from one of Glumdalclitch's men, who was afflicted with the toothache; but it was as sound as any in his head. I got it cleaned, and put it into my cabinet. It was about a foot long, and four inches in diameter.

The Captain was very well satisfied with this plain relation I had given him, and said he hoped when we returned to England I would oblige the world by putting it in paper and making it public. My answer was that I thought we were already overstocked with books of travels; that nothing could now pass which was not extraordinary; wherein I doubted some authors less consulted truth than their own vanity or interest, or the diversion of ignorant readers. That my story could contain little besides common events, without those ornamental descriptions of strange plants, trees, birds, and other animals, or the barbarous customs and idolatry of savage people, with which most writers abound. However, I thanked him for his good opinion, and promised to take the matter into my thoughts.

He said he wondered at one thing very much, which was to hear me speak so loud, asking me whether the King or Queen of that country were thick of hearing. I told him it was what I had been used to for above two years past, and that I admired[1] as much at the voices of him and his men, who seemed to me only to whisper, and yet I could hear them well enough. But, when I spoke in that country, it was like a man talking in the street to another looking out from the top of a steeple, unless when I was placed on a table, or held in any person's hand. I told him I had likewise observed another thing: that when I first got into the ship, and the sailors stood all about me, I thought they were the most little contemptible creatures I had ever beheld. For indeed while I was in that prince's country, I could never endure to look in a glass after mine eyes had been accustomed to such prodigious objects, because the comparison gave me so despicable a conceit[2] of myself. The Captain said that while we were at supper he observed me to look at everything with a sort of wonder, and that I often seemed hardly able to contain my laughter; which he knew not well how to take, but imputed it to some disorder in my brain. I answered, it was very true; and I wondered how I could forbear, when I saw his dishes of the size of a silver threepence, a leg of pork hardly a

1. Wondered at.   2. Notion.

mouthful, a cup not so big as a nutshell; and so I went on, describing the rest of his household stuff and provisions after the same manner. For, although the Queen had ordered a little equipage[3] of all things necessary for me while I was in her service, yet my ideas were wholly taken up with what I saw on every side of me, and I winked at my own littleness, as people do at their own faults. The Captain understood my raillery very well, and merrily replied with the old English proverb, that he doubted[4] mine eyes were bigger than my belly, for he did not observe my stomach so good, although I had fasted all day; and continuing in his mirth, protested he would have gladly given an hundred pounds to have seen my closet in the eagle's bill, and afterwards in its fall from so great an height into the sea; which would certainly have been a most astonishing object, worthy to have the description of it transmitted to future ages: and the comparison of Phaeton[5] was so obvious, that he could not forbear applying it, although I did not much admire the conceit.

The Captain having been at Tonquin,[6] was in his return to England driven northeastward to the latitude of 44 degrees, and of longitude 143. But meeting a trade wind two days after I came on board him, we sailed southward a long time, and coasting New Holland[7] kept our course west-southwest, and then south-southwest till we doubled the Cape of Good Hope. Our voyage was very prosperous, but I shall not trouble the reader with a journal of it. The Captain called in at one or two ports, and sent in his longboat for provisions and fresh water; but I never went out of the ship till we came into the Downs,[8] which was on the third day of June, 1706, about nine months after my escape. I offered to leave my goods in security for payment of my freight; but the Captain protested he would not receive one farthing. We took kind leave of each other, and I made him promise he would come to see me at my house in Redriff.[9] I hired a horse and guide for five shillings, which I borrowed of the Captain.

As I was on the road, observing the littleness of the houses, the trees, the cattle, and the people, I began to think myself in Lilliput. I was afraid of trampling on every traveler I met, and often called aloud to have them stand out of the way, so that I had like to have gotten one or two broken heads for my impertinence.

When I came to my own house, for which I was forced to inquire, one of the servants opening the door, I bent down to go in

---

3. Furnishings.
4. Feared.
5. The son of Apollo, whose unsuccessful attempt to drive the chariot of the sun god resulted in his death, when he was hurled by Zeus from the sky and fell into the river Eridanus, where he drowned.

6. Tonkin, in Indo-China.
7. Australia.
8. The sheltered anchorage between Goodwin Sands and the coast of Kent, near Deal.
9. Rotherhithe, on the south bank of the Thames, slightly below the City.

(like a goose under a gate) for fear of striking my head. My wife ran out to embrace me, but I stooped lower than her knees, thinking she could otherwise never be able to reach my mouth. My daughter kneeled to ask my blessing, but I could not see her till she arose, having been so long used to stand with my head and eyes erect to above sixty foot; and then I went to take her up with one hand by the waist. I looked down upon the servants and one or two friends who were in the house, as if they had been pygmies and I a giant. I told my wife she had been too thrifty; for I found she had starved herself and her daughter to nothing. In short, I behaved myself so unaccountably that they were all of the Captain's opinion when he first saw me, and concluded I had lost my wits. This I mention as an instance of the great power of habit and prejudice.

In a little time I and my family and friends came to a right understanding; but my wife protested I should never go to sea any more, although my evil destiny so ordered that she had not power to hinder me; as the reader may know hereafter. In the meantime I here conclude the second part of my unfortunate voyages.

1726, 1735

Part IV. A Voyage to the Country of the Houyhnhnms [1]

CHAPTER I. *The Author sets out as Captain of a ship. His men conspire against him, confine him a long time to his cabin, set him on shore in an unknown land. He travels up into the country. The Yahoos, a strange sort of animal, described. The Author meets two Houyhnhnms.*

I continued at home with my wife and children about five months in a very happy condition, if I could have learned the lesson of knowing when I was well. I left my poor wife big with child, and accepted an advantageous offer made me to be Captain of the *Adventure,* a stout merchantman of 350 tons; for I understood navigation well, and being grown weary of a surgeon's employment at sea, which however I could exercise upon occasion, I took a skillful young man of that calling, one Robert Purefoy, into my ship. We set sail from Portsmouth upon the 7th day of September, 1710; on the 14th we met with Captain Pocock of Bristol, at Tenariff,[2] who was going to the Bay of Campeachy [3] to cut logwood. On the 16th he was parted from us by a storm; I heard since my return that his ship foundered and none escaped, but one cabin boy. He was an honest man and a good sailor, but a little too positive in his own opinions, which was the cause of his destruction,

---

1. Pronounced Hwín-ims. The word suggests the neigh characteristic of a horse.
2. Teneriffe, one of the Canary Islands.
3. In the Gulf of Mexico.

as it hath been of several others. For if he had followed my advice, he might at this time have been safe at home with his family as well as myself.

I had several men died in my ship of calentures,[4] so that I was forced to get recruits out of Barbadoes and the Leeward Islands, where I touched by the direction of the merchants who employed me; which I had soon too much cause to repent, for I found afterwards that most of them had been buccaneers. I had fifty hands on board; and my orders were that I should trade with the Indians in the South Sea, and make what discoveries I could. These rogues whom I had picked up debauched my other men, and they all formed a conspiracy to seize the ship and secure me; which they did one morning, rushing into my cabin, and binding me hand and foot, threatening to throw me overboard, if I offered to stir. I told them I was their prisoner, and would submit. This they made me swear to do, and then unbound me, only fastening one of my legs with a chain near my bed, and placed a sentry at my door with his piece charged, who was commanded to shoot me dead if I attempted my liberty. They sent me down victuals and drink, and took the government of the ship to themselves. Their design was to turn pirates and plunder the Spaniards, which they could not do, till they got more men. But first they resolved to sell the goods in the ship, and then go to Madagascar for recruits, several among them having died since my confinement. They sailed many weeks, and traded with the Indians; but I knew not what course they took, being kept close prisoner in my cabin, and expecting nothing less than to be murdered, as they often threatened me.

Upon the 9th day of May, 1711, one James Welch came down to my cabin; and said he had orders from the Captain to set me ashore. I expostulated with him, but in vain; neither would he so much as tell me who their new Captain was. They forced me into the long-boat, letting me put on my best suit of clothes, which were as good as new, and a small bundle of linen, but no arms except my hanger; and they were so civil as not to search my pockets, into which I conveyed what money I had, with some other little necessaries. They rowed about a league, and then set me down on a strand. I desired them to tell me what country it was; they all swore, they knew no more than myself, but said that the Captain (as they called him) was resolved, after they had sold the lading, to get rid of me in the first place where they discovered land. They pushed off immediately, advising me to make haste, for fear of being overtaken by the tide, and bade me farewell.

In this desolate condition I advanced forward, and soon got upon firm ground, where I sat down on a bank to rest myself, and con-

4. "A distemper peculiar to sailors, in hot climates; wherein they imagine the sea to be green fields, and will throw themselves into it, if not restrained" (Johnson's *Dictionary*).

sider what I had best to do. When I was a little refreshed, I went up into the country, resolving to deliver myself to the first savages I should meet, and purchase my life from them by some bracelets, glass rings, and other toys, which sailors usually provide themselves with in those voyages, and whereof I had some about me. The land was divided by long rows of trees, not regularly planted, but naturally growing; there was great plenty of grass, and several fields of oats. I walked very circumspectly for fear of being surprised, or suddenly shot with an arrow from behind, or on either side. I fell into a beaten road, where I saw many tracks of human feet, and some of cows, but most of horses. At last I beheld several animals in a field, and one or two of the same kind sitting in trees. Their shape was very singular, and deformed, which a little discomposed me, so that I lay down behind a thicket to observe them better. Some of them coming forward near the place where I lay, gave me an opportunity of distinctly marking their form. Their heads and breasts were covered with a thick hair, some frizzled and others lank; they had beards like goats, and a long ridge of hair down their backs, and the fore parts of their legs and feet; but the rest of their bodies were bare, so that I might see their skins, which were of a brown buff color. They had no tails, nor any hair at all on their buttocks, except about the anus; which, I presume Nature had placed there to defend them as they sat on the ground; for this posture they used, as well as lying down, and often stood on their hind feet. They climbed high trees, as nimbly as a squirrel, for they had strong extended claws before and behind, terminating in sharp points, and hooked. They would often spring, and bound, and leap with prodigious agility. The females were not so large as the males; they had long lank hair on their heads, and only a sort of down on the rest of their bodies, except about the anus, and pudenda. Their dugs hung between their forefeet, and often reached almost to the ground as they walked. The hair of both sexes was of several colors, brown, red, black, and yellow. Upon the whole, I never beheld in all my travels so disagreeable an animal, or one against which I naturally conceived so strong an antipathy. So that thinking I had seen enough, full of contempt and aversion, I got up and pursued the beaten road, hoping it might direct me to the cabin of some Indian: I had not gone far when I met one of these creatures full in my way, and coming up directly to me. The ugly monster, when he saw me, distorted several ways every feature of his visage, and stared as at an object he had never seen before; then approaching nearer, lifted up his forepaw, whether out of curiosity or mischief, I could not tell; but I drew my hanger, and gave him a good blow with the flat side of it; for I durst not strike him with the edge, fearing the inhabitants might be provoked against me, if they should come to know that I had killed or maimed any of their cattle. When the beast felt the smart, he drew back, and roared so loud, that a herd of at least forty came flocking about me from the next field, howling and making odious faces; but I ran to the body of a tree, and leaning my back against it, kept them off, by waving my hanger. Several of this cursed brood getting hold of the branches behind, leaped up into the tree, from whence they began to discharge their excrements on my head; however, I escaped pretty well, by sticking close to the stem of the tree, but was almost stifled with the filth, which fell about me on every side.

In the midst of this distress, I observed them all to run away on a sudden as fast as they could; at which I ventured to leave the tree, and pursue the road, wondering what it was that could put them into this fright. But looking on my left hand, I saw a horse walking softly in the field; which my persecutors having sooner discovered, was the cause of their flight. The horse started a little when he came near me, but soon recovering himself, looked full in my face with manifest tokens of wonder; he viewed my hands and feet, walking round me several times. I would have pursued my journey, but he placed himself directly in the way, yet looking with a very mild aspect, never offering the least violence. We stood gazing at each other for some time; at last I took the boldness, to reach my hand towards his neck, with a design to stroke it; using the common style and whistle of jockies when they are going to handle a strange horse. But, this animal seeming to receive my civilities with disdain, shook his head, and bent his brows, softly raising up his left forefoot to remove my hand. Then he neighed three or four times, but in so different a cadence, that I almost began to think he was speaking to himself in some language of his own.

While he and I were thus employed, another horse came up; who applying himself to the first in a very formal manner, they gently struck each others right hoof before, neighing several times by turns, and varying the sound, which seemed to be almost articulate. They went some paces off, as if it were to confer together, walking side by side, backward and forward, like persons deliberating upon some affair of weight; but often turning their eyes towards me, as it were to watch that I might not escape. I was amazed to see such actions and behavior in brute beasts; and concluded with myself that if the inhabitants of this country were endued with a proportionable degree of reason, they must needs be the wisest people upon earth. This thought gave me so much comfort, that I resolved to go forward until I could discover some house or village, or meet with any of the natives, leaving the two horses to discourse together as they pleased. But the first, who was a dapple grey, observing me to steal off, neighed after me in so expressive a tone that I fancied myself to understand what he meant; whereupon I turned back, and came near him, to expect his farther commands; but concealing my fear as much as I could; for I began to be in some pain, how this adventure might terminate; and the reader will easily believe I did not much like my present situation.

The two horses came up close to me, looking with great earnestness upon my face and hands. The grey steed rubbed my hat all round with his right fore hoof, and discomposed it so much that I was forced to adjust it better, by taking it off, and settling it again; whereat both he and his companion (who was a brown bay) appeared to be much surprised; the latter felt the lappet of my coat, and finding it to hang loose about me, they both looked with new signs of wonder. He stroked my right hand, seeming to admire the softness, and color; but he squeezed it so hard between his hoof and his pastern, that I was forced to roar; after which they both touched me with all possible tenderness. They were under great perplexity about my shoes and stockings, which they felt very often, neighing to each other, and using various gestures, not unlike those of a philosopher, when he would attempt to solve some new and difficult phenomenon.

Upon the whole, the behavior of these animals was so orderly and rational, so acute and judicious, that I at last concluded, they must needs be magicians, who had thus metamorphosed themselves upon some design; and seeing a stranger in the way, were resolved to divert themselves with him; or perhaps were really amazed at the sight of a man so very different in habit, feature, and complexion from those who might probably live in so remote a climate. Upon the strength of this reasoning, I ventured to address them in the following manner: "Gentlemen, if you be conjurers, as I have good cause to believe, you can understand any language; therefore I make bold to let your worships know that I am a poor distressed Englishman, driven by his misfortunes upon your coast; and I entreat one of you, to let me ride upon his back, as if he were a real horse, to some house or village, where I can be relieved. In return of which favor, I will make you a present of this knife and bracelet" (taking them out of my pocket). The two creatures stood silent while I spoke, seeming to listen with great attention; and when I had ended, they neighed frequently towards each other, as if they were engaged in serious conversation. I plainly observed, that their language expressed the passions very well, and the words might with little pains be resolved into an alphabet more easily than the Chinese.

I could frequently distinguish the word *Yahoo*,[5] which was repeated by each of them several times; and although it were impossible for me to conjecture what it meant, yet while the two horses were busy in conversation, I endeavored to practice this word upon my tongue; and as soon as they were silent, I boldly pronounced "Yahoo" in a loud voice, imitating, at the same time, as near as I could, the neighing of a horse; at which they were both visibly sur-

5. Morley suggested that *Yahoo* was compounded from two expressions of disgust, *yah* and *ugh* (or *hoo*) common in the 18th century [Case's note].

prised, and the grey repeated the same word twice, as if he meant to teach me the right accent, wherein I spoke after him as well as I could, and found myself perceivably to improve every time, although very far from any degree of perfection. Then the bay tried me with a second word, much harder to be pronounced; but reducing it to the English orthography, may be spelt thus, *Houyhnhnm*. I did not succeed in this so well as the former, but after two or three farther trials, I had better fortune; and they both appeared amazed at my capacity.

After some farther discourse, which I then conjectured might relate to me, the two friends took their leaves, with the same compliment of striking each other's hoof; and the grey made me signs that I should walk before him; wherein I thought it prudent to comply, till I could find a better director. When I offered to slacken my pace, he would cry, "Hhuun, Hhuun"; I guessed his meaning, and gave him to understand, as well as I could that I was weary, and not able to walk faster; upon which, he would stand a while to let me rest.

CHAPTER II. *The Author conducted by a Houyhnhnm to his house. The house described. The Author's reception. The food of the Houyhnhnms. The Author in distress for want of meat is at last relieved. His manner of feeding in that country.*

Having traveled about three miles, we came to a long kind of building, made of timber, stuck in the ground, and wattled across; the roof was low, and covered with straw. I now began to be a little comforted, and took out some toys, which travelers usually carry for presents to the savage Indians of America and other parts, in hopes the people of the house would be thereby encouraged to receive me kindly. The horse made me a sign to go in first; it was a large room with a smooth clay floor, and a rack and manger extending the whole length on one side. There were three nags, and two mares, not eating, but some of them sitting down upon their hams, which I very much wondered at; but wondered more to see the rest employed in domestic business; the last seemed but ordinary cattle; however this confirmed my first opinion, that a people who could so far civilize brute animals must needs excel in wisdom all the nations of the world. The grey came in just after, and thereby prevented any ill treatment, which the others might have given me. He neighed to them several times in a style of authority, and received answers.

Beyond this room there were three others, reaching the length of the house, to which you passed through three doors, opposite to each other, in the manner of a vista; we went through the second room towards the third; here the grey walked in first, beckoning me to attend; [6] I waited in the second room, and got ready my presents,

6. To wait.

for the master and mistress of the house; they were two knives, three bracelets of false pearl, a small looking glass and a bead necklace. The horse neighed three or four times, and I waited to hear some answers in a human voice, but I heard no other returns than in the same dialect, only one or two a little shriller than his. I began to think that this house must belong to some person of great note among them, because there appeared so much ceremony before I could gain admittance. But, that a man of quality should be served all by horses, was beyond my comprehension. I feared my brain was disturbed by my sufferings and misfortunes; I roused myself, and looked about me in the room where I was left alone; this was furnished as the first, only after a more elegant manner. I rubbed my eyes often, but the same objects still occurred. I pinched my arms and sides, to awake myself, hoping I might be in a dream. I then absolutely concluded that all these appearances could be nothing else but necromancy and magic. But I had no time to pursue these reflections; for the grey horse came to the door, and made me a sign to follow him into the third room; where I saw a very comely mare, together with a colt and foal, sitting on their haunches, upon mats of straw, not unartfully made, and perfectly neat and clean.

The mare soon after my entrance, rose from her mat, and coming up close, after having nicely observed my hands and face, gave me a most contemptuous look; then turning to the horse, I heard the word Yahoo often repeated betwixt them; the meaning of which word I could not then comprehend, although it were the first I had learned to pronounce; but I was soon better informed, to my everlasting mortification: for the horse beckoning to me with his head, and repeating the word, "Hhuun, Hhuun," as he did upon the road, which I understood was to attend him, led me out into a kind of court, where was another building at some distance from the house. Here we entered, and I saw three of those detestable creatures, which I first met after my landing, feeding upon roots, and the flesh of some animals, which I afterwards found to be that of asses and dogs, and now and then a cow dead by accident or disease. They were all tied by the neck with strong withes, fastened to a beam; they held their food between the claws of their forefeet, and tore it with their teeth.

The master horse ordered a sorrel nag, one of his servants, to untie the largest of these animals, and take him into a yard. The beast and I were brought close together; and our countenances diligently compared, both by master and servant, who thereupon repeated several times the word "Yahoo." My horror and astonishment are not to be described, when I observed, in this abominable animal, a perfect human figure; the face of it indeed was flat and broad, the nose depressed, the lips large, and the mouth wide; but these differences are common to all savage nations, where the lineaments of the countenance are distorted by the natives suffering their infants to lie groveling on the earth, or by carrying them on their backs, nuzzling with their face against the mother's shoulders. The fore-feet of the Yahoo differed from my hands in nothing else but the length of the nails, the coarseness and brownness of the palms, and the hairiness on the backs. There was the same resemblance be-tween our feet, with the same differences, which I knew very well, although the horses did not, because of my shoes and stockings; the same in every part of our bodies, except as to hairiness and color, which I have already described.

The great difficulty that seemed to stick with the two horses was to see the rest of my body so very different from that of a Yahoo, for which I was obliged to my clothes, whereof they had no conception; the sorrel nag offered me a root, which he held (after their manner, as we shall describe in its proper place) between his hoof and pastern; I took it in my hand, and having smelled it, returned it to him again as civilly as I could. He brought out of the Yahoo's kennel a piece of ass's flesh, but it smelled so offensively that I turned from it with loathing; he then threw it to the Yahoo, by whom it was greedily devoured. He afterwards showed me a wisp of hay, and a fetlock full of oats; but I shook my head, to signify that neither of these were food for me. And indeed, I now apprehended that I must absolutely starve, if I did not get to some of my own species; for as to those filthy Yahoos, although there were few greater lovers of mankind, at that time, than myself, yet I confess I never saw any sensitive being so detestable on all accounts; and the more I came near them, the more hateful they grew, while I stayed in that coun-try. This the master horse observed by my behavior, and therefore sent the Yahoo back to his kennel. He then put his forehoof to his mouth, at which I was much surprised, although he did it with ease, and with a motion that appeared perfectly natural; and made other signs to know what I would eat; but I could not return him such an answer as he was able to apprehend; and if he had under-stood me, I did not see how it was possible to contrive any way for finding myself nourishment. While we were thus engaged, I ob-served a cow passing by; whereupon I pointed to her, and expressed a desire to let me go and milk her. This had its effect; for he led me back into the house, and ordered a mare-servant to open a room, where a good store of milk lay in earthen and wooden vessels, after a very orderly and cleanly manner. She gave me a large bowl full, of which I drank very heartily, and found myself well refreshed.

About noon I saw coming towards the house a kind of vehicle, drawn like a sledge by four Yahoos. There was in it an old steed, who seemed to be of quality; he alighted with his hind feet for-ward, having by accident got a hurt in his left forefoot. He came to dine with our horse, who received him with great civility. They dined in the best room, and had oats boiled in milk for the second course, which the old horse eat warm, but the rest cold. Their mangers were placed circular in the middle of the room, and divided into several partitions, round which they sat on their haunches upon bosses of straw. In the middle was a large rack with angles answering to every partition of the manger. So that each horse and mare eat their own hay, and their own mash of oats and milk, with much decency and regularity. The behavior of the young colt and foal appeared very modest; and that of the master and mistress extremely cheerful and complaisant to their guest. The grey ordered me to stand by him; and much discourse passed between him and his friend concerning me, as I found by the stranger's often looking on me, and the frequent repetition of the word Yahoo.

I happened to wear my gloves; which the master grey observing, seemed perplexed; discovering signs of wonder what I had done to my forefeet; he put his hoof three or four times to them, as if he would signify, that I should reduce them to their former shape, which I presently did, pulling off both my gloves, and putting them into my pocket. This occasioned farther talk, and I saw the company was pleased with my behavior, whereof I soon found the good effects. I was ordered to speak the few words I understood; and while they were at dinner, the master taught me the names for oats, milk, fire, water, and some others which I could readily pronounce after him, having from my youth a great facility in learning languages.

When dinner was done, the master horse took me aside, and by signs and words made me understand the concern he was in that I had nothing to eat. Oats in their tongue are called *hlunnh*. This word I pronounced two or three times; for although I had refused them at first, yet upon second thoughts, I considered that I could contrive to make a kind of bread, which might be sufficient with milk to keep me alive, till I could make my escape to some other country, and to creatures of my own species. The horse immediately ordered a white mare-servant of his family to bring me a good quantity of oats in a sort of wooden tray. These I heated before the fire as well as I could, and rubbed them till the husks came off, which I made a shift to winnow from the grain; I ground and beat them between two stones, then took water, and made them into a paste or cake, which I toasted at the fire, and eat warm with milk. It was at first a very insipid diet, although common enough in many parts of Europe, but grew tolerable by time; and having been often reduced to hard fare in my life, this was not the first experiment I had made how easily nature is satisfied. And I cannot but observe that I never had one hour's sickness, while I staid in this island. It is true, I sometimes made a shift to catch a rabbit, or bird, by springes [7] made of Yahoos' hairs; and I often gathered wholesome herbs, which I boiled, or eat as salads with my bread; and now and then, for a rarity, I made a little butter, and drank the whey. I was

7. Snares.

at first at a great loss for salt; but custom soon reconciled the want of it; and I am confident that the frequent use of salt among us is an effect of luxury, and was first introduced only as a provocative to drink; except where it is necessary for preserving of flesh in long voyages, or in places remote from great markets. For we observe no animal to be fond of it but man; [8] and as to myself, when I left this country, it was a great while before I could endure the taste of it in anything that I eat.

This is enough to say upon the subject of my diet, wherewith other travelers fill their books, as if the readers were personally concerned whether we fare well or ill. However, it was necessary to mention this matter, lest the world should think it impossible that I could find sustenance for three years in such a country, and among such inhabitants.

When it grew towards evening, the master horse ordered a place for me to lodge in; it was but six yards from the house, and separated from the stable of the Yahoos. Here I got some straw, and covering myself with my own clothes, slept very sound. But I was in a short time better accommodated, as the reader shall know hereafter, when I come to treat more particularly about my way of living.

CHAPTER III. *The Author studious to learn the language, the Houyhnhnm his master assists in teaching him. The language described. Several Houyhnhnms of quality come out of curiosity to see the Author. He gives his master a short account of his voyage.*

My principal endeavor was to learn the language, which my master (for so I shall henceforth call him) and his children, and every servant of his house were desirous to teach me. For they looked upon it as a prodigy, that a brute animal should discover such marks of a rational creature. I pointed to everything, and enquired the name of it, which I wrote down in my journal book when I was alone, and corrected my bad accent, by desiring those of the family to pronounce it often. In this employment, a sorrel nag, one of the under servants, was very ready to assist me.

In speaking, they pronounce through the nose and throat, and their language approaches nearest to the High Dutch or German, of any I know in Europe; but is much more graceful and significant. The Emperor Charles V made almost the same observation, when he said, that if he were to speak to his horse, it should be in High Dutch.[9]

The curiosity and impatience of my master were so great, that he spent many hours of his leisure to instruct me. He was convinced (as he afterwards told me) that I must be a Yahoo, but my

8. Gulliver is, of course, in error. Many animals require salt.
9. The Emperor is supposed to have said that he would speak to his God in Spanish, to his mistress in Italian, and to his horse in German.

teachableness, civility, and cleanliness astonished him; which were qualities altogether so opposite to those animals. He was most perplexed about my clothes, reasoning sometimes with himself whether they were a part of my body; for I never pulled them off till the family were asleep, and got them on before they waked in the morning. My master was eager to learn from whence I came; how I acquired those appearances of reason, which I discovered in all my actions; and to know my story from my own mouth, which he hoped he should soon do by the great proficiency I made in learning and pronouncing their words and sentences. To help my memory, I formed all I learned into the English alphabet, and writ the words down with the translations. This last, after some time, I ventured to do in my master's presence. It cost me much trouble to explain to him what I was doing; for the inhabitants have not the least idea of books or literature.

In about ten weeks time I was able to understand most of his questions; and in three months could give him some tolerable answers. He was extremely curious to know from what part of the country I came, and how I was taught to imitate a rational creature; because the Yahoos (whom he saw I exactly resembled in my head, hands, and face, that were only visible) with some appearance of cunning, and the strongest disposition to mischief, were observed to be the most unteachable of all brutes. I answered that I came over the sea, from a far place, with many others of my own kind, in a great hollow vessel made of the bodies of trees; that my companions forced me to land on this coast, and then left me to shift for myself. It was with some difficulty, and by the help of many signs, that I brought him to understand me. He replied that I must needs be mistaken, or that I *said the thing which was not*. (For they have no word in their language to express lying or falsehood.) He knew it was impossible that there could be a country beyond the sea, or that a parcel of brutes could move a wooden vessel whither they pleased upon water. He was sure no Houyhnhnm alive could make such a vessel, or would trust Yahoos to manage it.

The word Houyhnhnm, in their tongue, signifies a Horse; and in its etymology, the Perfection of Nature. I told my master that I was at a loss for expression, but would improve as fast as I could; and hoped in a short time I should be able to tell him wonders; he was pleased to direct his own mare, his colt, and foal, and the servants of the family to take all opportunities of instructing me; and every day for two or three hours, he was at the same pains himself; several horses and mares of quality in the neighborhood came often to our house, upon the report spread of a wonderful Yahoo, that could speak like a Houyhnhnm, and seemed in his words and actions to discover some glimmerings of reason. These delighted to converse with me; they put many questions, and received such answers as I was able to return. By all which advantages,

I made so great a progress, that in five months from my arrival, I understood whatever was spoke, and could express myself tolerably well.

The Houyhnhnms who came to visit my master, out of a design of seeing and talking with me, could hardly believe me to be a right Yahoo, because my body had a different covering from others of my kind. They were astonished to observe me without the usual hair or skin, except on my head, face, and hands; but I discovered that secret to my master, upon an accident, which happened about a fortnight before.

I have already told the reader, that every night when the family were gone to bed, it was my custom to strip and cover myself with my clothes; it happened one morning early, that my master sent for me, by the sorrel nag, who was his valet; when he came, I was fast asleep, my clothes fallen off on one side, and my shirt above my waist. I awaked at the noise he made, and observed him to deliver his message in some disorder; after which he went to my master, and in a great fright gave him a very confused account of what he had seen; this I presently discovered; for going as soon as I was dressed, to pay my attendance upon his honor, he asked me the meaning of what his servant had reported; that I was not the same thing when I slept as I appeared to be at other times; that his valet assured him, some part of me was white, some yellow, at least not so white, and some brown.

I had hitherto concealed the secret of my dress, in order to distinguish myself as much as possible, from that cursed race of Yahoos; but now I found it in vain to do so any longer. Besides, I considered that my clothes and shoes would soon wear out, which already were in a declining condition, and must be supplied by some contrivance from the hides of Yahoos, or other brutes; whereby the whole secret would be known. I therefore told my master, that in the country from whence I came, those of my kind always covered their bodies with the hairs of certain animals prepared by art, as well for decency, as to avoid inclemencies of air both hot and cold; of which, as to my own person I would give him immediate conviction, if he pleased to command me; only desiring his excuse, if I did not expose those parts that nature taught us to conceal. He said, my discourse was all very strange, but especially the last part; for he could not understand why Nature should teach us to conceal what Nature had given. That neither himself nor family were ashamed of any parts of their bodies; but however I might do as I pleased. Whereupon, I first unbuttoned my coat, and pulled it off. I did the same with my waistcoat; I drew off my shoes, stockings, and breeches. I let my shirt down to my waist, and drew up the bottom, fastening it like a girdle about my middle to hide my nakedness.

My master observed the whole performance with great signs of curiosity and admiration. He took up all my clothes in his pastern, one piece after another, and examined them diligently; he then stroked my body very gently, and looked round me several times; after which he said, it was plain I must be a perfect Yahoo; but that I differed very much from the rest of my species, in the whiteness and smoothness of my skin, my want of hair in several parts of my body, the shape and shortness of my claws behind and before, and my affectation of walking continually on my two hinder feet. He desired to see no more; and gave me leave to put on my clothes again, for I was shuddering with cold.

I expressed my uneasiness at his giving me so often the appellation of Yahoo, an odious animal, for which I had so utter an hatred and contempt. I begged he would forbear applying that word to me, and take the same order in his family, and among his friends whom he suffered to see me. I requested likewise, that the secret of my having a false covering to my body might be known to none but himself, at least as long as my present clothing should last; for as to what the sorrel nag his valet had observed, his honor might command him to conceal it.

All this my master very graciously consented to; and thus the secret was kept till my clothes began to wear out, which I was forced to supply by several contrivances, that shall hereafter be mentioned. In the meantime, he desired I would go on with my utmost diligence to learn their language, because he was more astonished at my capacity for speech and reason, than at the figure of my body, whether it were covered or no; adding that he waited with some impatience to hear the wonders which I promised to tell him.

From thenceforward he doubled the pains he had been at to instruct me; he brought me into all company, and made them treat me with civility, because, as he told them privately, this would put me into good humor, and make me more diverting.

Every day when I waited on him, beside the trouble he was at in teaching, he would ask me several questions concerning myself, which I answered as well as I could; and by those means he had already received some general ideas, although very imperfect. It would be tedious to relate the several steps, by which I advanced to a more regular conversation, but the first account I gave of myself in any order and length was to this purpose:

That, I came from a very far country, as I already had attempted to tell him, with about fifty more of my own species; that we traveled upon the seas, in a great hollow vessel made of wood, and larger than his honor's house. I described the ship to him in the best terms I could; and explained by the help of my handkerchief displayed, how it was driven forward by the wind. That, upon a quarrel among us, I was set on shore on this coast, where I walked forward without knowing whither, till he delivered me from the persecution of those execrable Yahoos. He asked me who made the ship, and how it was possible that the Houyhnhnms of my country would leave it to the management of brutes? My answer was that I durst proceed no farther in my relation, unless he would give me his word and honor that he would not be offended; and then I would tell him the wonders I had so often promised. He agreed; and I went on by assuring him, that the ship was made by creatures like myself, who in all the countries I had traveled, as well as in my own, were the only governing, rational animals; and that upon my arrival hither, I was as much astonished to see the Houyhnhnms act like rational beings, as he or his friends could be in finding some marks of reason in a creature he was pleased to call a Yahoo; to which I owned my resemblance in every part, but could not account for their degenerate and brutal nature. I said farther, that if good fortune ever restored me to my native country, to relate my travels hither, as I resolved to do; everybody would believe that I *said the thing which was not*; that I invented the story out of my own head; and with all possible respect to himself, his family, and friends, and under his promise of not being offended, our countrymen would hardly think it probable, that a Houyhnhnm should be the presiding creature of a nation, and a Yahoo the brute.

CHAPTER IV. *The Houyhnhnms' notion of truth and falsehood. The author's discourse disapproved by his master. The author gives a more particular account of himself, and the accidents of his voyage.*

My master heard me with great appearances of uneasiness in his countenance; because *doubting* or *not believing* are so little known in this country, that the inhabitants cannot tell how to behave themselves under such circumstances. And I remember in frequent discourses with my master concerning the nature of manhood, in other parts of the world, having occasion to talk of *lying* and *false representation*, it was with much difficulty that he comprehended what I meant; although he had otherwise a most acute judgment. For he argued thus: that the use of speech was to make us understand one another, and to receive information of facts; now if anyone *said the thing which was not*, these ends were defeated; because I cannot properly be said to understand him; and I am so far from receiving information, that he leaves me worse than in ignorance; for I am led to believe a thing *black* when it is *white*, and *short* when it is *long*. And these were all the notions he had concerning that faculty of *lying*, so perfectly well understood, and so universally practiced among human creatures.

To return from this digression; when I asserted that the Yahoos were the only governing animals in my country, which my master said was altogether past his conception, he desired to know, whether we had Houyhnhnms among us, and what was their employment; I told him we had great numbers; that in summer they grazed in the fields, and in winter were kept in houses, with hay and oats, where Yahoo servants were employed to rub their skins smooth, comb their manes, pick their feet, serve them with food, and make their beds. "I understand you well," said my master; "it is now very plain from all you have spoken, that whatever share of reason the Yahoos pretend to, the Houyhnhnms are your masters; I heartily wish our Yahoos would be so tractable." I begged his honor would please to excuse me from proceeding any farther, because I was very certain that the account he expected from me would be highly displeasing. But he insisted in commanding me to let him know the best and the worst; I told him he should be obeyed. I owned that the Houyhnhnms among us, whom we called Horses, were the most generous [1] and comely animal we had; that they excelled in strength and swiftness; and when they belonged to persons of quality, employed in traveling, racing, and drawing chariots, they were treated with much kindness and care, till they fell into diseases, or became foundered in the feet; but then they were sold, and used to all kind of drudgery till they died; after which their skins were stripped and sold for what they were worth, and their bodies left to be devoured by dogs and birds of prey. But the common race of horses had not so good fortune, being kept by farmers and carriers, and other mean people, who put them to greater labor, and feed them worse. I described as well as I could, our way of riding; the shape and use of a bridle, a saddle, a spur, and a whip; of harness and wheels. I added, that we fastened plates of a certain hard substance called iron at the bottom of their feet, to preserve their hoofs from being broken by the stony ways on which we often traveled.

My master, after some expressions of great indignation, wondered how we dared to venture upon a Houyhnhnm's back; for he was sure, that the weakest servant in his house would be able to shake off the strongest Yahoo; or by lying down, and rolling upon his back, squeeze the brute to death. I answered that our horses were trained up from three or four years old to the several uses we intended them for; that if any of them proved intolerably vicious, they were employed for carriages; that they were severely beaten while they were young for any mischievous tricks; that the males, designed for the common use of riding or draught, were generally castrated about two years after their birth, to take down their spirits, and make them more tame and gentle; that they were indeed sensible of rewards and punishments; but his honor would please to consider that they had not the least tincture of reason any more than the Yahoos in this country.

It put me to the pains of many circumlocutions to give my master a right idea of what I spoke; for their language doth not abound in variety of words, because their wants and passions are fewer than

1. Noble.

among us. But it is impossible to express his noble resentment at our savage treatment of the Houyhnhnm race; particularly after I had explained the manner and use of castrating horses among us, to hinder them from propagating their kind, and to render them more servile. He said, if it were possible there could be any country where Yahoos alone were endued with reason, they certainly must be the governing animal, because reason will in time always prevail against brutal strength. But, considering the frame of our bodies, and especially of mine, he thought no creature of equal bulk was so ill-contrived for employing that reason in the common offices of life; whereupon he desired to know whether those among whom I lived resembled me or the Yahoos of his country. I assured him that I was as well shaped as most of my age; but the younger and the females were much more soft and tender, and the skins of the latter generally as white as milk. He said I differed indeed from other Yahoos, being much more cleanly, and not altogether so deformed; but in point of real advantage, he thought I differed for the worse. That my nails were of no use either to my fore or hinder feet; as to my forefeet, he could not properly call them by that name, for he never observed me to walk upon them; that they were too soft to bear the ground; that I generally went with them uncovered, neither was the covering I sometimes wore on them of the same shape, or so strong as that on my feet behind. That I could not walk with any security; for if either of my hinder feet slipped, I must inevitably fall. He then began to find fault with other parts of my body; the flatness of my face, the prominence of my nose, my eyes placed directly in front, so that I could not look on either side without turning my head; that I was not able to feed myself without lifting one of my forefeet to my mouth; and therefore nature had placed those joints to answer that necessity. He knew not what could be the use of those several clefts and divisions in my feet behind; that these were too soft to bear the hardness and sharpness of stones without a covering made from the skin of some other brute; that my whole body wanted a fence against heat and cold, which I was forced to put on and off every day with tediousness and trouble. And lastly, that he observed every animal in his country naturally to abhor the Yahoos, whom the weaker avoided, and the stronger drove from them. So that supposing us to have the gift of reason, he could not see how it were possible to cure that natural antipathy which every creature discovered against us; nor consequently, how we could tame and render them serviceable. However, he would (as he said) debate the matter no farther, because he was more desirous to know my own story, the country where I was born, and the several actions and events of my life before I came hither.

I assured him how extremely desirous I was that he should be satisfied in every point; but I doubted much whether it would be possible for me to explain myself on several subjects whereof his honor could have no conception, because I saw nothing in his country to which I could resemble them. That however, I would do my best, and strive to express myself by similitudes, humbly desiring his assistance when I wanted proper words; which he was pleased to promise me.

I said, my birth was of honest parents, in an island called England, which was remote from this country, as many days journey as the strongest of his honor's servants could travel in the annual course of the sun. That I was bred a surgeon, whose trade it is to cure wounds and hurts in the body, got by accident or violence. That my country was governed by a female man, whom we called a queen. That I left it to get riches, whereby I might maintain myself and family when I should return. That in my last voyage, I was Commander of the ship and had about fifty Yahoos under me, many of which died at sea, and I was forced to supply them by others picked out from several nations. That our ship was twice in danger of being sunk; the first time by a great storm, and the second, by striking against a rock. Here my master interposed, by asking me, how I could persuade strangers out of different countries to venture with me, after the losses I had sustained, and the hazards I had run. I said, they were fellows of desperate fortunes, forced to fly from the places of their birth, on account of their poverty or their crimes. Some were undone by lawsuits; others spent all they had in drinking, whoring, and gaming; others fled for treason; many for murder, theft, poisoning, robbery, perjury, forgery, coining false money; for committing rapes or sodomy; for flying from their colors, or deserting to the enemy; and most of them had broken prison. None of these durst return to their native countries for fear of being hanged, or of starving in a jail; and therefore were under a necessity of seeking a livelihood in other places.

During this discourse, my master was pleased often to interrupt me. I had made use of many circumlocutions in describing to him the nature of the several crimes, for which most of our crew had been forced to fly their country. This labor took up several days conversation before he was able to comprehend me. He was wholly at a loss to know what could be the use or necessity of practicing those vices. To clear up which I endeavored to give him some ideas of the desire of power and riches; of the terrible effects of lust, intemperance, malice, and envy. All this I was forced to define and describe by putting of cases, and making suppositions. After which, like one whose imagination was struck with something never seen or heard of before, he would lift up his eyes with amazement and indignation. Power, government, war, law, punishment, and a thousand other things had no terms, wherein that language could express them; which made the difficulty almost insuperable to give my master any conception of what I meant; but being of an excellent understanding, much improved by contemplation and converse, he at last arrived at a competent knowledge of what human nature in our parts of the world is capable to perform; and desired I would give him some particular account of that land, which we call Europe, especially, of my own country.

CHAPTER V. *The Author, at his master's commands, informs him of the state of England. The causes of war among the princes of Europe. The Author begins to explain the English Constitution.*

The reader may please to observe that the following extract of many conversations I had with my master contains a summary of the most material points, which were discoursed at several times for above two years; his honor often desiring fuller satisfaction as I farther improved in the Houyhnhnm tongue. I laid before him, as well as I could, the whole state of Europe; I discoursed of trade and manufactures, of arts and sciences; and the answers I gave to all the questions he made, as they arose upon several subjects, were a fund of conversation not to be exhausted. But I shall here only set down the substance of what passed between us concerning my own country, reducing it into order as well as I can, without any regard to time or other circumstances, while I strictly adhere to truth. My only concern is that I shall hardly be able to do justice to my master's arguments and expressions; which must needs suffer by my want of capacity, as well as by a translation into our barbarous English.

In obedience therefore to his honor's commands, I related to him the Revolution under the Prince of Orange; the long war with France entered into by the said Prince, and renewed by his successor the present queen; wherein the greatest powers of Christendom were engaged, and which still continued. I computed at his request, that about a million of Yahoos might have been killed in the whole progress of it; and perhaps a hundred or more cities taken, and five times as many ships burned or sunk.[2]

He asked me what were the usual causes or motives that made one country to go to war with another. I answered, they were innumerable; but I should only mention a few of the chief. Sometimes the ambition of princes, who never think they have land or people enough to govern; sometimes the corruption of ministers, who engage their master in a war in order to stifle or divert the clamor of the subjects against their evil administration. Difference in opinions hath cost many millions of lives; for instance, whether flesh be bread, or bread be flesh; whether the juice of a certain berry be blood or wine; whether whistling be a vice or a virtue; whether it be better to kiss a post, or throw it into the fire; what is the best color for a coat, whether black, white, red, or grey; and

2. Gulliver relates recent English history: the Glorious Revolution of 1688 and the War of Spanish Succession (1703–13). He greatly exaggerates the casualties in the war.

whether it should be long or short, narrow or wide, dirty or clean;[3] with many more. Neither are any wars so furious and bloody, or of so long continuance, as those occasioned by difference in opinion, especially if it be in things indifferent.[4]

Sometimes the quarrel between two princes is to decide which of them shall dispossess a third of his dominions, where neither of them pretend to any right. Sometimes one prince quarreleth with another, for fear the other should quarrel with him. Sometimes a war is entered upon, because the enemy is too strong, and sometimes because he is too weak. Sometimes our neighbors want the things which we have, or have the things which we want; and we both fight, till they take ours or give us theirs. It is a very justifiable cause of war to invade a country after the people have been wasted by famine, destroyed by pestilence, or embroiled by factions amongst themselves. It is justifiable to enter into a war against our nearest ally, when one of his towns lies convenient for us, or a territory of land, that would render our dominions round and compact. If a prince send forces into a nation, where the people are poor and ignorant, he may lawfully put half of them to death, and make slaves of the rest, in order to civilize and reduce them from their barbarous way of living. It is a very kingly, honorable, and frequent practice, when one prince desires the assistance of another to secure him against an invasion, that the assistant, when he hath driven out the invader, should seize on the dominions himself, and kill, imprison, or banish the prince he came to relieve. Alliance by blood or marriage is a sufficient cause of war between princes; and the nearer the kindred is, the greater is their disposition to quarrel; poor nations are hungry, and rich nations are proud; and pride and hunger will ever be at variance. For these reasons, the trade of a soldier is held the most honorable of all others: because a soldier is a Yahoo hired to kill in cold blood as many of his own species, who have never offended him, as possibly he can.

There is likewise a kind of beggarly princes in Europe, not able to make war by themselves, who hire out their troops to richer nations for so much a day to each man; of which they keep three fourths to themselves, and it is the best part of their maintenance; such are those in many northern parts of Europe.[5]

"What you have told me," said my master, "upon the subject of war, doth indeed discover most admirably the effects of that reason you pretend to; however, it is happy that the shame is greater than the danger; and that Nature hath left you utterly uncapable of doing much mischief; for your mouths lying flat with your faces, you can hardly bite each other to any purpose, unless by

---

3. Gulliver refers to the religious controversies of the Reformation and Counter Reformation: the doctrine of transubstantiation, the use of music in church services, the veneration of the crucifix, and the wearing of priestly vestments.
4. Of little consequence.
5. A satiric glance at George I, who, as Elector of Hanover, had dealt in this trade.

consent. Then, as to the claws upon your feet before and behind, they are so short and tender, that one of our Yahoos would drive a dozen of yours before him. And therefore in recounting the numbers of those who have been killed in battle, I cannot but think that you have *said the thing which is not.*"

I could not forbear shaking my head and smiling a little at his ignorance. And, being no stranger to the art of war, I gave him a description of cannons, culverins, muskets, carabines, pistols, bullets, powder, swords, bayonets, battles, sieges, retreats, attacks, undermines, countermines, bombardments, sea fights; ships sunk with a thousand men; twenty thousand killed on each side; dying groans, limbs flying in the air; smoke, noise, confusion, trampling to death under horses' feet; flight, pursuit, victory; fields strewed with carcasses left for food to dogs, and wolves, and birds of prey; plundering, stripping, ravishing, burning, and destroying. And, to set forth the valor of my own dear countrymen, I assured him that I had seen them blow up a hundred enemies at once in a siege, and as many in a ship; and beheld the dead bodies drop down in pieces from the clouds, to the great diversion of all the spectators.

I was going on to more particulars, when my master commanded me silence. He said, whoever understood the nature of Yahoos might easily believe it possible for so vile an animal, to be capable of every action I had named, if their strength and cunning equaled their malice. But, as my discourse had increased his abhorrence of the whole species, so he found it gave him a disturbance in his mind, to which he was wholly a stranger before. He thought his ears being used to such abominable words, might by degrees admit them with less detestation. That, although he hated the Yahoos of this country, yet he no more blamed them for their odious qualities, than he did a *gnnayh* (a bird of prey) for its cruelty, or a sharp stone for cutting his hoof. But, when a creature pretending to reason could be capable of such enormities, he dreaded lest the corruption of that faculty might be worse than brutality itself. He seemed therefore confident, that instead of reason, we were only possessed of some quality fitted to increase our natural vices; as the reflection from a troubled stream returns the image of an ill-shapen body, not only larger, but more distorted.

He added that he had heard too much upon the subject of war, both in this and some former discourses. There was another point which a little perplexed him at present. I had said that some of our crew left their country on account of being ruined by law: that I had already explained the meaning of the word; but he was at a loss how it should come to pass, that the law which was intended for every man's preservation, should be any man's ruin. Therefore he desired to be farther satisfied what I meant by law, and the dispensers thereof, according to the present practice in my own country; because he thought nature and reason were sufficient guides for a reasonable animal, as we pretended to be, in showing us what we ought to do, and what to avoid.

I assured his honor that law was a science wherein I had not much conversed, further than by employing advocates, in vain, upon some injustices that had been done me. However, I would give him all the satisfaction I was able.

I said there was a society of men among us, bred up from their youth in the art of proving by words multiplied for the purpose, that white is black, and black is white, according as they are paid. To this society all the rest of the people are slaves.

"For example. If my neighbor hath a mind to my cow, he hires a lawyer to prove that he ought to have my cow from me. I must then hire another to defend my right; it being against all rules of law that any man should be allowed to speak for himself. Now in this case, I who am the true owner lie under two great disadvantages. First, my lawyer being practiced almost from his cradle in defending falsehood is quite out of his element when he would be an advocate for justice, which as an office unnatural, he always attempts with great awkwardness, if not with ill-will. The second disadvantage is that my lawyer must proceed with great caution, or else he will be reprimanded by the judges, and abhorred by his brethren, as one who would lessen the practice of the law. And therefore I have but two methods to preserve my cow. The first is to gain over my adversary's lawyer with a double fee; who will then betray his client, by insinuating that he hath justice on his side. The second way is for my lawyer to make my cause appear as unjust as he can; by allowing the cow to belong to my adversary; and this if it be skillfully done, will certainly bespeak the favor of the bench.

"Now, your honor is to know that these judges are persons appointed to decide all controversies of property, as well as for the trial of criminals; and picked out from the most dextrous lawyers who are grown old or lazy; and having been biased all their lives against truth and equity, lie under such a fatal necessity of favoring fraud, perjury, and oppression, that I have known some of them to have refused a large bribe from the side where justice lay, rather than injure the faculty,[6] by doing anything unbecoming their nature or their office.

"It is a maxim among these lawyers, that whatever hath been done before may legally be done again; and therefore they take special care to record all the decisions formerly made against common justice and the general reason of mankind. These, under the name of *precedents*, they produce as authorities to justify the most iniquitous opinions; and the judges never fail of directing accordingly.

6. Profession.

"In pleading, they studiously avoid entering into the merits of the cause; but are loud, violent, and tedious in dwelling upon all circumstances which are not to the purpose. For instance, in the case already mentioned, they never desire to know what claim or title my adversary hath to my cow; but whether the said cow were red or black; her horns long or short; whether the field I graze her in be round or square; whether she were milked at home or abroad; what diseases she is subject to, and the like. After which they consult precedents, adjourn the cause, from time to time, and in ten, twenty, or thirty years come to an issue.

"It is likewise to be observed, that this society hath a peculiar cant and jargon of their own, that no other mortal can understand, and wherein all their laws are written, which they take special care to multiply; whereby they have wholly confounded the very essence of truth and falsehood, of right and wrong; so that it will take thirty years to decide whether the field, left me by my ancestors for six generations, belong to me, or to a stranger three hundred miles off.

"In the trial of persons accused for crimes against the state, the method is much more short and commendable: the judge first sends to sound the disposition of those in power; after which he can easily hang or save the criminal, strictly preserving all the forms of law."

Here my master interposing said it was a pity that creatures endowed with such prodigious abilities of mind as these lawyers, by the description I gave of them must certainly be, were not rather encouraged to be instructors of others in wisdom and knowledge. In answer to which, I assured his honor that in all points out of their own trade, they were usually the most ignorant and stupid generation among us, the most despicable in common conversation, avowed enemies to all knowledge and learning; and equally disposed to pervert the general reason of mankind, in every other subject of discourse as in that of their own profession.

CHAPTER VI. *A continuation of the state of England, under Queen Anne. The character of a first minister in the courts of Europe.*

My master was yet wholly at a loss to understand what motives could incite this race of lawyers to perplex, disquiet, and weary themselves by engaging in a confederacy of injustice, merely for the sake of injuring their fellow animals; neither could he comprehend what I meant in saying they did it for hire. Whereupon I was at much pains to describe to him the use of money, the materials it was made of, and the value of the metals; that when a Yahoo had got a great store of his precious substance, he was able to purchase whatever he had a mind to; the finest clothing, the noblest houses, great tracts of land, the most costly meats and drinks; and have his choice of the most beautiful females. Therefore since money alone was able to perform all these feats, our Yahoos thought they could never have enough of it to spend or to save, as they found themselves inclined from their natural bent either to profusion or avarice. That the rich man enjoyed the fruit of the poor man's labor, and the latter were a thousand to one in proportion to the former. That the bulk of our people was forced to live miserably, by laboring every day for small wages to make a few live plentifully. I enlarged myself much on these and many other particulars to the same purpose, but his honor was still to seek,[7] for he went upon a supposition that all animals had a title to their share in the productions of the earth; and especially those who presided over the rest. Therefore he desired I would let him know what these costly meats were, and how any of us happened to want [8] them. Whereupon I enumerated as many sorts as came into my head, with the various methods of dressing them, which could not be done without sending vessels by sea to every part of the world, as well for liquors to drink, as for sauces, and innumerable other conveniencies. I assured him, that this whole globe of earth must be at least three times gone round, before one of our better female Yahoos could get her breakfast, or a cup to put it in. He said, "That must needs be a miserable country which cannot furnish food for its own inhabitants." But what he chiefly wondered at, was how such vast tracts of ground as I described, should be wholly without fresh water, and the people put to the necessity of sending over the sea for drink. I replied that England (the dear place of my nativity) was computed to produce three times the quantity of food, more than its inhabitants are able to consume, as well as liquors extracted from grain, or pressed out of the fruit of certain trees, which made excellent drink; and the same proportion in every other convenience of life. But, in order to feed the luxury and intemperance of the males, and the vanity of the females, we sent away the greatest part of our necessary things to other countries, from whence in return we brought the materials of diseases, folly, and vice, to spend among ourselves. Hence it follows of necessity, that vast numbers of our people are compelled to seek their livelihood by begging, robbing, stealing, cheating, pimping, forswearing, flattering, suborning, forging, gaming, lying, fawning, hectoring, voting, scribbling, star gazing, poisoning, whoring, canting, libeling, freethinking, and the like occupations; every one of which terms, I was at much pains to make him understand.

That, wine was not imported among us from foreign countries, to supply the want of water or other drinks, but because it was a sort of liquid which made us merry, by putting us out of our senses; diverted all melancholy thoughts, begat wild extravagant imaginations in the brain, raised our hopes, and banished our

7. Still did not understand.   8. Lack.

fears; suspended every office of reason for a time, and deprived us of the use of our limbs, until we fell into a profound sleep; although it must be confessed, that we always awaked sick and dispirited; and that the use of this liquor filled us with diseases, which made our lives uncomfortable and short.

But beside all this, the bulk of our people supported themselves by furnishing the necessities or conveniencies of life to the rich, and to each other. For instance, when I am at home and dressed as I ought to be, I carry on my body the workmanship of an hundred tradesmen; the building and furniture of my house employ as many more; and five times the number to adorn my wife.

I was going on to tell him of another sort of people, who get their livelihood by attending the sick; having upon some occasions informed his honor that many of my crew had died of diseases. But here it was with the utmost difficulty that I brought him to apprehend what I meant. He could easily conceive that a Houyhnhnm grew weak and heavy a few days before his death; or by some accident might hurt a limb. But that nature, who worketh all things to perfection, should suffer any pains to breed in our bodies, he thought impossible; and desired to know the reason of so unaccountable an evil. I told him, we fed on a thousand things which operated contrary to each other; that we eat when we were not hungry, and drank without the provocation of thirst; that we sat whole nights drinking strong liquors without eating a bit, which disposed us to sloth, inflamed our bodies, and precipitated or prevented digestion. That, prostitute female Yahoos acquired a certain malady, which bred rottenness in the bones of those who fell into their embraces; that this and many other diseases were propagated from father to son; so that great numbers come into the world with complicated maladies upon them; that it would be endless to give him a catalogue of all diseases incident to human bodies; for they could not be fewer than five or six hundred, spread over every limb, and joint; in short, every part, external and intestine, having diseases appropriated to each. To remedy which, there was a sort of people bred up among us, in the profession or pretense of curing the sick. And because I had some skill in the faculty, I would in gratitude to his honor let him know the whole mystery and method by which they proceed.

Their fundamental is that all diseases arise from repletion; from whence they conclude, that a great evacuation of the body is necessary, either through the natural passage, or upwards at the mouth. Their next business is, from herbs, minerals, gums, oils, shells, salts, juices, seaweed, excrements, barks of trees, serpents, toads, frogs, spiders, dead men's flesh and bones, birds, beasts and fishes, to form a composition for smell and taste the most abominable, nauseous, and detestable, that they can possibly contrive, which the stomach immediately rejects with loathing, and this they call a vomit. Or else from the same storehouse, with some other poisonous additions, they command us to take in at the orifice above or below (just as the physician then happens to be disposed) a medicine equally annoying and disgustful to the bowels; which relaxing the belly, drives down all before it; and this they call a purge, or a clyster. For nature (as the physicians allege) having intended the superior anterior orifice only for the intromission of solids and liquids, and the inferior posterior for ejection, these artists ingeniously considering that in all diseases nature is forced out of her seat; therefore to replace her in it, the body must be treated in a manner directly contrary, but interchanging the use of each orifice; forcing solids and liquids in at the anus, and making evacuations at the mouth.

But, besides real diseases, we are subject to many that are only imaginary, for which the physicians have invented imaginary cures; these have their several names, and so have the drugs that are proper for them; and with these our female Yahoos are always infested.

One great excellency in this tribe is their skill at prognostics, wherein they seldom fail; their predictions in real diseases, when they rise to any degree of malignity, generally portending death, which is always in their power, when recovery is not, and therefore, upon any unexpected signs of amendment, after they have pronounced their sentence rather than be accused as false prophets, they know how to approve [9] their sagacity to the world by a seasonable dose.

They are likewise of special use to husbands and wives, who are grown weary of their mates; to eldest sons, to great ministers of state, and often to princes.

I had formerly upon occasion discoursed with my master upon the nature of government in general, and particularly of our own excellent constitution, deservedly the wonder and envy of the whole world. But having here accidently mentioned a minister of state, he commanded me some time after to inform him what species of Yahoo I particularly meant by that appellation.

I told him that a first or chief minister of state, whom I intended to describe, was a creature wholly exempt from joy and grief, love and hatred, pity and anger; at least makes use of no other passions but a violent desire of wealth, power, and titles; that he applies his words to all uses, except to the indication of his mind; that he never tells a truth, but with an intent that you should take it for a lie; nor a lie, but with a design that you should take it for a truth; that those he speaks worst of behind their backs are in the surest way to preferment; and whenever he begins to praise you to others or to yourself, you are from that day forlorn. The worst mark you can receive is a promise, especially when it is confirmed

9. Prove.

with an oath; after which every wise man retires, and gives over all hopes.

There are three methods by which a man may rise to be chief minister: the first is by knowing how with prudence to dispose of a wife, a daughter, or a sister; the second, by betraying or undermining his predecessor; and the third is by a furious zeal in public assemblies against the corruptions of the court. But a wise prince would rather choose to employ those who practice the last of these methods; because such zealots prove always the most obsequious and subservient to the will and passions of their master. That, these ministers having all employments at their disposal, preserve themselves in power by bribing the majority of a senate or great council; and at last by an expedient called an Act of Indemnity[1] (whereof I described the nature to him) they secure themselves from after reckonings, and retire from the public, laden with the spoils of the nation.

The palace of a chief minister is a seminary to breed up others in his own trade; the pages, lackies, and porter, by imitating their master, become ministers of state in their several districts, and learn to excel in the three principal ingredients, of insolence, lying, and bribery. Accordingly, they have a subaltern court paid to them by persons of the best rank; and sometimes by the force of dexterity and impudence, arrive through several gradations to be successors to their lord.

He is usually governed by a decayed wench, or favorite footman, who are the tunnels through which all graces are conveyed, and may properly be called, in the last resort, the governors of the kingdom.

One day, my master, having heard me mention the nobility of my country, was pleased to make me a compliment which I could not pretend to deserve: that, he was sure, I must have been born of some noble family, because I far exceeded in shape, color, and cleanliness, all the Yahoos of his nation, although I seemed to fail in strength, and agility, which must be imputed to my different way of living from those other brutes; and besides, I was not only endowed with the faculty of speech, but likewise with some rudiments of reason, to a degree, that with all his acquaintance I passed for a prodigy.

He made me observe, that among the Houyhnhnms, the white, the sorrel, and the iron grey were not so exactly shaped as the bay, the dapple grey, and the black; nor born with equal talents of mind, or a capacity to improve them; and therefore continued always in the condition of servants, without ever aspiring to match out of their own race, which in that country would be reckoned monstrous and unnatural.

---

1. An act passed at each session of Parliament to protect ministers of state who in good faith might have acted illegally.

I made his honor my most humble acknowledgments for the good opinion he was pleased to conceive of me; but assured him at the same time, that my birth was of the lower sort, having been born of plain, honest parents, who were just able to give me a tolerable education; that, nobility among us was altogether a different thing from the idea he had of it; that, our young noblemen are bred from their childhood in idleness and luxury; that, as soon as years will permit, they consume their vigor, and contract odious diseases among lewd females; and when their fortunes are almost ruined, they marry some woman of mean birth, disagreeable person, and unsound constitution, merely for the sake of money, whom they hate and despise. That, the productions of such marriages are generally scrofulous, rickety or deformed children; by which means the family seldom continues above three generations, unless the wife take care to provide a healthy father among her neighbors, or domestics, in order to improve and continue the breed. That a weak diseased body, a meager countenance, and sallow complexion are the true marks of noble blood; and a healthy robust appearance is so disgraceful in a man of quality, that the world concludes his real father to have been a groom or a coachman. The imperfections of his mind run parallel with those of his body; being a composition of spleen, dullness, ignorance, caprice, sensuality, and pride.

Without the consent of this illustrious body, no law can be enacted, repealed, or altered, and these nobles have likewise the decision of all our possessions without appeal.

CHAPTER VII. *The Author's great love of his native country. His master's observations upon the constitution and administration of England, as described by the Author, with parallel cases and comparisons. His master's observations upon human nature.*

The reader may be disposed to wonder how I could prevail on myself to give so free a representation of my own species, among a race of mortals who were already too apt to conceive the vilest opinion of humankind, from that entire congruity betwixt me and their Yahoos. But I must freely confess that the many virtues of those excellent quadrupeds placed in opposite view to human corruptions had so far opened my eyes, and enlarged my understanding, that I began to view the actions and passions of man in a very different light; and to think the honor of my own kind not worth managing; [2] which, besides, it was impossible for me to do before a person of so acute a judgment as my master, who daily convinced me of a thousand faults in myself, whereof I had not the least perception before, and which with us would never be numbered even among human infirmities. I had likewise learned from his example an utter detestation of all falsehood or disguise; and

2. Taking care of.

truth appeared so amiable to me, that I determined upon sacrificing everything to it.

Let me deal so candidly with the reader as to confess that there was yet a much stronger motive for the freedom I took in my representation of things. I had not been a year in this country, before I contracted such a love and veneration for the inhabitants, that I entered on a firm resolution never to return to humankind, but to pass the rest of my life among these admirable Houyhnhnms in the contemplation and practice of every virtue; where I could have no example or incitement to vice. But it was decreed by fortune, my perpetual enemy, that so great a felicity should not fall to my share. However, it is now some comfort to reflect that in what I said of my countrymen, I extenuated their faults as much as I durst before so strict an examiner; and upon every article, gave as favorable a turn as the matter would bear. For, indeed, who is there alive that will not be swayed by his bias and partiality to the place of his birth?

I have related the substance of several conversations I had with my master, during the greatest part of the time I had the honor to be in his service; but have indeed for brevity sake omitted much more than is here set down.

When I had answered all his questions, and his curiosity seemed to be fully satisfied; he sent for me one morning early, and commanding me to sit down at some distance (an honor which he had never before conferred upon me), he said he had been very seriously considering my whole story, as far as it related both to myself and my country; that, he looked upon us as a sort of animals to whose share, by what accident he could not conjecture, some small pittance of reason had fallen, whereof we made no other use than by its assistance to aggravate our natural corruptions, and to acquire new ones which nature had not given us. That we disarmed ourselves of the few abilities she had bestowed; had been very successful in multiplying our original wants, and seemed to spend our whole lives in vain endeavors to supply them by our own inventions. That, as to myself, it was manifest I had neither the strength or agility of a common Yahoo; that I walked infirmly on my hinder feet; had found out a contrivance to make my claws of no use or defense, and to remove the hair from my chin, which was intended as a shelter from the sun and the weather. Lastly, that I could neither run with speed, nor climb trees like my brethren (as he called them) the Yahoos in this country.

That our institutions of government and law were plainly owing to our gross defects in reason, and by consequence, in virtue; because reason alone is sufficient to govern a rational creature; which was therefore a character we had no pretense to challenge, even from the account I had given of my own people; although he manifestly perceived, that in order to favor them, I had concealed many particulars, and often *said the thing which was not.*

He was the more confirmed in this opinion, because he observed that I agreed in every feature of my body with other Yahoos, except where it was to my real disadvantage in point of strength, speed, and activity, the shortness of my claws, and some other particulars where nature had no part; so, from the representation I had given him of our lives, our manners, and our actions, he found as near a resemblance in the disposition of our minds. He said the Yahoos were known to hate one another more than they did any different species of animals; and the reason usually assigned was the odiousness of their own shapes, which all could see in the rest, but not in themselves. He had therefore begun to think it not unwise in us to cover our bodies, and by that invention, conceal many of our deformities from each other, which would else be hardly supportable. But he now found he had been mistaken; and that the dissentions of those brutes in his country were owing to the same cause with ours, as I had described them. For, if (said he) you throw among five Yahoos as much food as would be sufficient for fifty, they will, instead of eating peaceably, fall together by the ears, each single one impatient to have all to itself; and therefore a servant was usually employed to stand by while they were feeding abroad, and those kept at home were tied at a distance from each other. That, if a cow died of age or accident, before a Houyhnhnm could secure it for his own Yahoos, those in the neighborhood would come in herds to seize it, and then would ensue such a battle as I had described, with terrible wounds made by their claws on both sides, although they seldom were able to kill one another, for want of such convenient instruments of death as we had invented. At other times the like battles have been fought between the Yahoos of several neighborhoods without any visible cause; those of one district watching all opportunities to surprise the next before they are prepared. But if they find their project hath miscarried, they return home, and for want of enemies, engage in what I call a civil war among themselves.

That, in some fields of his country, there are certain shining stones of several colors, whereof the Yahoos are violently fond; and when part of these stones are fixed in the earth, as it sometimes happeneth, they will dig with their claws for whole days to get them out, and carry them away, and hide them by heaps in their kennels; but still looking round with great caution, for fear their comrades should find out their treasure. My master said he could never discover the reason of this unnatural appetite, or how these stones could be of any use to a Yahoo; but now he believed it might proceed from the same principle of avarice, which I had ascribed to mankind. That he had once, by way of experiment, privately removed a heap of these stones from the place where one of his Yahoos had buried it, whereupon, the sordid animal missing his treasure, by his loud lamenting brought the whole herd to the place, there miserably howled, then fell to biting and tearing the rest; began to pine away, would neither eat nor sleep, nor work, till he ordered a servant privately to convey the stones into the same hole, and hide them as before; which when his Yahoo had found, he presently recovered his spirits and good humor; but took care to remove them to a better hiding place; and hath ever since been a very serviceable brute.

My master farther assured me, which I also observed myself; that in the fields where these shining stones abound, the fiercest and most frequent battles are fought, occasioned by perpetual inroads of the neighboring Yahoos.

He said it was common when two Yahoos discovered such a stone in a field, and were contending which of them should be the proprietor, a third would take the advantage, and carry it away from them both; which my master would needs contend to have some resemblance with our suits at law; wherein I thought it for our credit not to undeceive him; since the decision he mentioned was much more equitable than many decrees among us; because the plaintiff and defendant there lost nothing beside the stone they contended for; whereas our courts of equity would never have dismissed the cause while either of them had anything left.

My master continuing his discourse said there was nothing that rendered the Yahoos more odious, than their undistinguished appetite to devour everything that came in their way, whether herbs, roots, berries, corrupted flesh of animals, or all mingled together; and it was peculiar in their temper, that they were fonder of what they could get by rapine or stealth at a greater distance, than much better food provided for them at home. If their prey held out, they would eat till they were ready to burst, after which nature had pointed out to them a certain root that gave them a general evacuation.

There was also another kind of root very juicy, but something rare and difficult to be found, which the Yahoos fought for with much eagerness, and would suck it with great delight; it produced the same effects that wine hath upon us. It would make them sometimes hug, and sometimes tear one another; they would howl and grin, and chatter, and reel, and tumble, and then fall asleep in the mud.

I did indeed observe that the Yahoos were the only animals in this country subject to any diseases; which however, were much fewer than horses have among us, and contracted not by any ill treatment they meet with, but by the nastiness and greediness of that sordid brute. Neither has their language any more than a general appellation for those maladies; which is borrowed from the name of the beast, and called *Hnea Yahoo*, or the Yahoo's Evil; and the cure prescribed is a mixture of their own dung and urine, forcibly put down the Yahoo's throat. This I have since often known to have been taken with success, and do here freely recommend it to my countrymen, for the public good, as an admirable specific against all diseases produced by repletion.

As to learning, government, arts, manufactures, and the like, my master confessed he could find little or no resemblance between the Yahoos of that country and those in ours. For he only meant to observe what parity there was in our natures. He had heard indeed some curious Houyhnhnms observe that in most herds there was a sort of ruling Yahoo (as among us there is generally some leading or principal stag in a park) who was always more deformed in body, and mischievous in disposition, than any of the rest. That this leader had usually a favorite as like himself as he could get, whose employment was to lick his master's feet and posteriors, and drive the female Yahoos to his kennel; for which he was now and then rewarded with a piece of ass's flesh. This favorite is hated by the whole herd; and therefore to protect himself, keeps always near the person of his leader. He usually continues in office till a worse can be found; but the very moment he is discarded, his successor, at the head of all the Yahoos in that district, young and old, male and female, come in a body, and discharge their excrements upon him from head to foot. But how far this might be applicable to our courts and favorites, and ministers of state, my master said I could best determine.

I durst make no return to this malicious insinuation, which debased human understanding below the sagacity of a common hound, who hath judgment enough to distinguish and follow the cry of the ablest dog in the pack, without being ever mistaken.

My master told me there were some qualities remarkable in the Yahoos, which he had not observed me to mention, or at least very slightly, in the accounts I had given him of humankind. He said, those animals, like other brutes, had their females in common; but in this they differed, that the she-Yahoo would admit the male while she was pregnant; and that the hes would quarrel and fight with the females as fiercely as with each other. Both which practices were such degrees of infamous brutality, that no other sensitive creature ever arrived at.

Another thing he wondered at in the Yahoos was their strange disposition to nastiness and dirt; whereas there appears to be a natural love of cleanliness in all other animals. As to the two former accusations, I was glad to let them pass without any reply, because I had not a word to offer upon them in defense of my species, which otherwise I certainly had done from my own inclinations. But I could have easily vindicated humankind from the imputation of singularity upon the last article, if there had been any swine in that country (as unluckily for me there were not) which although it may be a sweeter quadruped than a Yahoo, cannot I humbly conceive in justice pretend to more cleanliness; and so his honor himself must have owned, if he had seen their filthy way of feeding, and their custom of wallowing and sleeping in the mud.

My master likewise mentioned another quality, which his servants had discovered in several Yahoos, and to him was wholly unaccountable. He said, a fancy would sometimes take a Yahoo, to retire into a corner, to lie down and howl, and groan, and spurn away all that came near him, although he were young and fat, and wanted neither food nor water; nor did the servants imagine what could possibly ail him. And the only remedy they found was to set him to hard work, after which he would infallibly come to himself. To this I was silent out of partiality to my own kind; yet here I could plainly discover the true seeds of spleen,[3] which only seizeth on the lazy, the luxurious, and the rich; who, if they were forced to undergo the same regimen, I would undertake for the cure.

His Honor had farther observed, that a female Yahoo would often stand behind a bank or a bush, to gaze on the young males passing by, and then appear, and hide, using many antic gestures and grimaces; at which time it was observed, that she had a most offensive smell; and when any of the males advanced, would slowly retire, looking back, and with a counterfeit show of fear, run off into some convenient place where she knew the male would follow her.

At other times, if a female stranger came among them, three or four of her own sex would get about her, and stare and chatter, and grin, and smell her all over; and then turn off with gestures that seemed to express contempt and disdain.

Perhaps my master might refine a little in these speculations, which he had drawn from what he observed himself, or had been told by others; however, I could not reflect without some amazement, and much sorrow, that the rudiments of lewdness, coquetry, censure, and scandal, should have place by instinct in womankind.

I expected every moment that my master would accuse the Yahoos of those unnatural appetites in both sexes, so common among us. But nature it seems hath not been so expert a schoolmistress; and these politer pleasures are entirely the productions of art and reason, on our side of the globe.

CHAPTER VIII. *The Author relateth several particulars of the Yahoos. The great virtues of the Houyhnhnms. The education and exercises of their youth. Their general assembly.*

As I ought to have understood human nature much better than I supposed it possible for my master to do, so it was easy to apply

3. Hypochondria.

the character he gave of the Yahoos to myself and my countrymen; and I believed I could yet make farther discoveries from my own observation. I therefore often begged his honor to let me go among the herds of Yahoos in the neighborhood; to which he always very graciously consented, being perfectly convinced that the hatred I bore those brutes would never suffer me to be corrupted by them; and his honor ordered one of his servants, a strong sorrel nag, very honest and good-natured, to be my guard; without whose protection I durst not undertake such adventures. For I have already told the reader how much I was pestered by those odious animals upon my first arrival. I afterwards failed very narrowly three or four times of falling into their clutches, when I happened to stray at any distance without my hanger. And I have reason to believe, they had some imagination that I was of their own species, which I often assisted myself, by stripping up my sleeves, and shewing my naked arms and breast in their sight, when my protector was with me; at which times they would approach as near as they durst, and imitate my actions after the manner of monkeys, but ever with great signs of hatred; as a tame jackdaw with cap and stockings is always persecuted by the wild ones, when he happens to be got among them.

They are prodigiously nimble from their infancy; however, I once caught a young male of three years old, and endeavored by all marks of tenderness to make it quiet; but the little imp fell a squalling, scratching, and biting with such violence, that I was forced to let it go; and it was high time, for a whole troop of old ones came about us at the noise; but finding the cub was safe (for away it ran) and my sorrel nag being by, they durst not venture near us. I observed the young animal's flesh to smell very rank, and the stink was somewhat between a weasel and a fox, but much more disagreeable. I forgot another circumstance (and perhaps I might have the reader's pardon, if it were wholly omitted) that while I held the odious vermin in my hands, it voided its filthy excrements of a yellow liquid substance, all over my clothes; but by good fortune there was a small brook hard by, where I washed myself as clean as I could; although I durst not come into my master's presence until I were sufficiently aired.

By what I could discover, the Yahoos appear to be the most unteachable of all animals, their capacities never reaching higher than to draw or carry burdens. Yet I am of opinion, this defect ariseth chiefly from a perverse, restive disposition. For they are cunning, malicious, treacherous and revengeful. They are strong and hardy, but of a cowardly spirit, and by consequence insolent, abject, and cruel. It is observed that the red-haired of both sexes are more libidinous and mischievous than the rest, whom yet they much exceed in strength and activity.

The Houyhnhnms keep the Yahoos for present use in huts not far from the house; but the rest are sent abroad to certain fields, where they dig up roots, eat several kinds of herbs, and search about for carrion, or sometimes catch weasels and *luhimuhs* (a sort of wild rat) which they greedily devour. Nature hath taught them to dig deep holes with their nails on the side of a rising ground, wherein they lie by themselves; only the kennels of the females are larger, sufficient to hold two or three cubs.

They swim from their infancy like frogs, and are able to continue long under water, where they often take fish, which the females carry home to their young. And upon this occasion, I hope the reader will pardon my relating an odd adventure.

Being one day abroad with my protector the sorrel nag, and the weather exceeding hot, I entreated him to let me bathe in a river that was near. He consented, and I immediately stripped myself stark naked, and went down softly into the stream. It happened that a young female Yahoo standing behind a bank, saw the whole proceeding; and inflamed by desire, as the nag and I conjectured, came running with all speed, and leaped into the water within five yards of the place where I bathed. I was never in my life so terribly frighted; the nag was grazing at some distance, not suspecting any harm; she embraced me after a most fulsome manner; I roared as loud as I could, and the nag came galloping towards me, whereupon she quitted her grasp, with the utmost reluctancy, and leaped upon the opposite bank, where she stood gazing and howling all the time I was putting on my clothes.

This was matter of diversion to my master and his family, as well as of mortification to myself. For now I could no longer deny that I was a real Yahoo, in every limb and feature, since the females had a natural propensity to me as one of their own species; neither was the hair of this brute of a red color (which might have been some excuse for an appetite a little irregular) but black as a sloe, and her countenance did not make an appearance altogether so hideous as the rest of the kind; for I think, she could not be above eleven years old.

Having already lived three years in this country, the reader I suppose will expect that I should, like other travelers, give him some account of the manners and customs of its inhabitants, which it was indeed my principal study to learn.

As these noble Houyhnhnms are endowed by Nature with a general disposition to all virtues, and have no conceptions or ideas of what is evil in a rational creature; so their grand maxim is to cultivate reason, and to be wholly governed by it. Neither is reason among them a point problematical as with us, where men can argue with plausibility on both sides of a question; but strikes you with immediate conviction; as it must needs do where it is not mingled, obscured, or discolored by passion and interest. I remember it was with extreme difficulty that I could bring my master to understand the meaning of the word "opinion," or how a point could be disputable; because reason taught us to affirm or deny only where we are certain; and beyond our knowledge we cannot do either. So that controversies, wranglings, disputes, and positiveness in false or dubious propositions are evils unknown among the Houyhnhnms. In the like manner when I used to explain to him our several systems of natural philosophy, he would laugh that a creature pretending to reason should value itself upon the knowledge of other people's conjectures, and in things, where that knowledge, if it were certain, could be of no use. Wherein he agreed entirely with the sentiments of Socrates, as Plato delivers them, which I mention as the highest honor I can do that prince of philosophers. I have often since reflected what destruction such a doctrine would make in the libraries of Europe; and how many paths to fame would be then shut up in the learned world.

Friendship and benevolence are the two principal virtues among the Houyhnhnms; and these not confined to particular objects, but universal to the whole race. For a stranger from the remotest part is equally treated with the nearest neighbor, and wherever he goes, looks upon himself as at home. They preserve decency and civility in the highest degrees, but are altogether ignorant of ceremony. They have no fondness for their colts or foals; but the care they take in educating them proceedeth entirely from the dictates of reason. And I observed my master to show the same affection to his neighbor's issue that he had for his own. They will have it that nature teaches them to love the whole species, and it is reason only that maketh a distinction of persons, where there is a superior degree of virtue.

When the matron Houyhnhnms have produced one of each sex, they no longer accompany with their consorts, except they lose one of their issue by some casualty, which very seldom happens; but in such a case they meet again; or when the like accident befalls a person whose wife is past bearing, some other couple bestows on him one of their own colts, and then go together a second time, until the mother be pregnant. This caution is necessary to prevent the country from being overburdened with numbers. But the race of inferior Houyhnhnms bred up to be servants is not so strictly limited upon this article; these are allowed to produce three of each sex, to be domestics in the noble families.

In their marriages they are exactly careful to choose such colors as will not make any disagreeable mixture in the breed. Strength is chiefly valued in the male, and comeliness in the female; not upon the account of love, but to preserve the race from degenerating; for, where a female happens to excel in strength, a consort is

chosen with regard to comeliness. Courtship, love, presents, join-
tures, settlements, have no place in their thoughts, or terms
whereby to express them in their language. The young couple meet
and are joined, merely because it is the determination of their
parents and friends; it is what they see done every day; and they
look upon it as one of the necessary actions in a reasonable being.
But the violation of marriage, or any other unchastity, was never
heard of; and the married pair pass their lives with the same
friendship and mutual benevolence that they bear to all others of
the same species who come in their way, without jealousy, fondness, quarreling, or discontent.

In educating the youth of both sexes, their method is admirable,
and highly deserveth our imitation. These are not suffered to taste
a grain of oats, except upon certain days, till eighteen years old;
nor milk, but very rarely; and in summer they graze two hours in
the morning, and as many in the evening, which their parents
likewise observe; but the servants are not allowed above half that
time; and a great part of the grass is brought home, which they eat
at the most convenient hours, when they can be best spared from
work.

Temperance, industry, exercise, and cleanliness are the lessons
equally enjoined to the young ones of both sexes; and my master
thought it monstrous in us to give the females a different kind of
education from the males, except in some articles of domestic
management; whereby, as he truly observed, one half of our natives
were good for nothing but bringing children into the world; and
to trust the care of their children to such useless animals, he said
was yet a greater instance of brutality.

But the Houyhnhnms train up their youth to strength, speed,
and hardiness, by exercising them in running races up and down
steep hills, or over hard stony grounds; and when they are all in a
sweat, they are ordered to leap over head and ears into a pond or a
river. Four times a year the youth of certain districts meet to show
their proficiency in running, and leaping, and other feats of
strength or agility; where the victor is rewarded with a song made in
his or her praise. On this festival the servants drive a herd of Yahoos
into the field, laden with hay, and oats, and milk for a repast to the
Houyhnhnms; after which these brutes are immediately driven
back again, for fear of being noisome to the assembly.

Every fourth year, at the vernal equinox, there is a representative
council of the whole nation, which meets in a plain about twenty
miles from our house, and continueth about five or six days. Here
they inquire into the state and condition of the several districts;
whether they abound or be deficient in hay or oats, or cows or
Yahoos? And wherever there is any want (which is but seldom) it
is immediately supplied by unanimous consent and contribution.
Here likewise the regulation of children is settled: as for instance,

if a Houyhnhnm hath two males, he changeth one of them with another who hath two females, and when a child hath been lost by any casualty, where the mother is past breeding, it is determined what family in the district shall breed another to supply the loss.

CHAPTER IX. *A grand debate at the general assembly of the Houyhnhnms, and how it was determined. The learning of the Houyhnhnms. Their buildings. Their manner of burials. The defectiveness of their language.*

One of these grand assemblies was held in my time, about three months before my departure, whither my master went as the representative of our district. In this council was resumed their old debate, and indeed, the only debate that ever happened in their country; whereof my master after his return gave me a very particular account.

The question to be debated was whether the Yahoos should be exterminated from the face of the earth. One of the members for the affirmative offered several arguments of great strength and weight, alleging that, as the Yahoos were the most filthy, noisome, and deformed animal which nature ever produced, so they were the most restive and indocible, mischievous, and malicious; they would privately suck the teats of the Houyhnhnms' cows; kill and devour their cats, trample down their oats and grass, if they were not continually watched; and commit a thousand other extravagancies. He took notice of a general tradition, that Yahoos had not been always in their country, but that many ages ago, two of these brutes appeared together upon a mountain; whether produced by the heat of the sun upon corrupted mud and slime, or from the ooze and froth of the sea, was never known. That these Yahoos engendered, and their brood in a short time grew so numerous as to overrun and infest the whole nation. That the Houyhnhnms to get rid of this evil, made a general hunting, and at last enclosed the whole herd; and destroying the older, every Houyhnhnm kept two young ones in a kennel, and brought them to such a degree of tameness as an animal so savage by nature can be capable of acquiring, using them for draft and carriage. That there seemed to be much truth in this tradition, and that those creatures could not be *ylnhniamshy* (or aborigines of the land) because of the violent hatred the Houyhnhnms as well as all other animals bore them; which although their evil disposition sufficiently deserved, could never have arrived at so high a degree, if they had been aborigines, or else they would have long since been rooted out. That the inhabitants taking a fancy to use the service of the Yahoos, had very imprudently neglected to cultivate the breed of asses, which were a comely animal, easily kept, more tame and orderly, without any offensive smell, strong enough for labor, although they yield to the other in agility of body; and if their braying be no agreeable sound, it is far preferable to the horrible howlings of the Yahoos.

Several others declared their sentiments to the same purpose, when my master proposed an expedient to the assembly, whereof he had indeed borrowed the hint from me. He approved of the tradition, mentioned by the honorable member, who spoke before; and affirmed, that the two Yahoos said to be first seen among them, had been driven thither over the sea; that coming to land, and being forsaken by their companions, they retired to the mountains, and degenerating by degrees, became in process of time much more savage than those of their own species in the country from whence these two originals came. The reason of his assertion was that he had now in his possession a certain wonderful Yahoo (meaning myself) which most of them had heard of, and many of them had seen. He then related to them how he first found me; that my body was all covered with an artificial composure of the skins and hairs of other animals; that I spoke in a language of my own, and had thoroughly learned theirs; that I had related to him the accidents which brought me thither; that when he saw me without my covering, I was an exact Yahoo in every part, only of a whiter color, less hairy and with shorter claws. He added how I had endeavored to persuade him that in my own and other countries the Yahoos acted as the governing, rational animal, and held the Houyhnhnms in servitude; that he observed in me all the qualities of a Yahoo, only a little more civilized by some tincture of reason, which however was in a degree as far inferior to the Houyhnhnm race as the Yahoos of their country were to me; that among other things, I mentioned a custom we had of castrating Houyhnhnms when they were young, in order to render them tame; that the operation was easy and safe; that it was no shame to learn wisdom from brutes, as industry is taught by the ant, and building by the swallow (for so I translate the world *lyhannh*, although it be a much larger fowl). That this invention might be practiced upon the younger Yahoos here, which, besides rendering them tractable and fitter for use, would in an age put an end to the whole species without destroying life. That in the meantime the Houyhnhnms should be exhorted to cultivate the breed of asses, which, as they are in all respects more valuable brutes, so they have this advantage, to be fit for service at five years old, which the others are not till twelve.

This was all my master thought fit to tell me at that time, of what passed in the grand council. But he was pleased to conceal one particular, which related personally to myself, whereof I soon felt the unhappy effect, as the reader will know in its proper place, and from whence I date all the succeeding misfortunes of my life.

The Houyhnhnms have no letters, and consequently, their knowledge is all traditional. But there happening few events of any moment among a people so well united, naturally disposed to every virtue, wholly governed by reason, and cut off from all commerce with other nations, the historical part is easily preserved without burdening their memories. I have already observed that they are subject to no diseases, and therefore can have no need of physicians. However, they have excellent medicines composed of herbs, to cure accidental bruises and cuts in the pastern or frog of the foot by sharp stones, as well as other maims and hurts in the several parts of the body.

They calculate the year by the revolution of the sun and the moon, but use no subdivisions into weeks. They are well enough acquainted with the motions of those two luminaries, and understand the nature of eclipses; and this is the utmost progress of their astronomy.

In poetry they must be allowed to excell all other mortals; wherein the justness of their similes, and the minuteness, as well as exactness of their descriptions, are indeed inimitable. Their verses abound very much in both of these, and usually contain either some exalted notions of friendship and benevolence, or the praises of those who were victors in races and other bodily exercises. Their buildings, although very rude and simple, are not inconvenient, but well contrived to defend them from all injuries of cold and heat. They have a kind of tree, which at forty years old loosens in the root, and falls with the first storm; it grows very straight, and being pointed like stakes with a sharp stone (for the Houyhnhnms know not the use of iron), they stick them erect in the ground about ten inches asunder, and then weave in oat straw, or sometimes wattles, betwixt them. The roof is made after the same manner, and so are the doors.

The Houyhnhnms use the hollow part between the pastern and the hoof of their forefeet as we do our hands, and this with greater dexterity than I could at first imagine. I have seen a white mare of our family thread a needle (which I lent her on purpose) with that joint. They milk their cows, reap their oats, and do all the work which requires hands in the same manner. They have a kind of hard flints, which by grinding against other stones they form into instruments that serve instead of wedges, axes, and hammers. With tools made of these flints, they likewise cut their hay, and reap their oats, which there groweth naturally in several fields; the Yahoos draw home the sheaves in carriages, and the servants tread them in certain covered huts, to get out the grain, which is kept in stores. They make a rude kind of earthen and wooden vessels, and bake the former in the sun.

If they can avoid casualties, they die only of old age, and are buried in the obscurest places that can be found, their friends and relations expressing neither joy nor grief at their departure; nor does the dying person discover the least regret that he is leaving the world, any more than if he were upon returning home from a visit to one of his neighbors; I remember my master having once made an appointment with a friend and his family to come to his house upon some affair of importance; on the day fixed, the mistress and her two children came very late; she made two excuses, first for her husband, who, as she said, happened that very morning to *lhnuwnh*. The word is strongly expressive in their language, but not easily rendered into English; it signifies, *to retire to his first Mother*. Her excuse for not coming sooner was that her husband dying late in the morning, she was a good while consulting her servants about a convenient place where his body should be laid; and I observed she behaved herself at our house, as cheerfully as the rest; she died about three months after.

They live generally to seventy or seventy-five years, very seldom to fourscore; some weeks before their death they feel a gradual decay, but without pain. During this time they are much visited by their friends, because they cannot go abroad with their usual ease and satisfaction. However, about ten days before their death, which they seldom fail in computing, they return the visits that have been made by those who are nearest in the neighborhood, being carried in a convenient sledge drawn by Yahoos; which vehicle they use, not only upon this occasion, but when they grow old, upon long journeys, or when they are lamed by any accident. And therefore when the dying Houyhnhnms return those visits, they take a solemn leave of their friends, as if they were going to some remote part of the country, where they designed to pass the rest of their lives.

I know not whether it may be worth observing, that the Houyhnhnms have no word in their language to express anything that is evil, except what they borrow from the deformities or ill qualities of the Yahoos. Thus they denote the folly of a servant, an omission of a child, a stone that cuts their feet, a continuance of foul or unseasonable weather, and the like, by adding to each the epithet of Yahoo. For instance, *hhnm Yahoo, whnaholm Yahoo, ynlhmnd-wihlma Yahoo*, and an ill-contrived house, *ynholmhnmrohlnw Yahoo*.

I could with great pleasure enlarge farther upon the manners and virtues of this excellent people; but intending in a short time to publish a volume by itself expressly upon that subject, I refer the reader thither. And in the meantime, proceed to relate my own sad catastrophe.

CHAPTER X. *The Author's economy, and happy life among the Houyhnhnms. His great improvement in virtue, by conversing with them. Their conversations. The Author hath notice given him by his master that he must depart from the country. He falls into a swoon for grief, but submits. He contrives and finishes a canoe, by the help of a fellow servant, and puts to sea at a venture.*

I had settled my little economy to my own heart's content. My master had ordered a room to be made for me after their manner, about six yards from the house; the sides and floors of which I plastered with clay, and covered with rush mats of my own contriving; I had beaten hemp, which there grows wild, and made of it a sort of ticking; this I filled with the feathers of several birds I had taken with springes made of Yahoos' hairs, and were excellent food. I had worked two chairs with my knife, the sorrel nag helping me in the grosser and more laborious part. When my clothes were worn to rags, I made myself others with the skins of rabbits, and of a certain beautiful animal about the same size, called *nnuhnoh*, the skin of which is covered with a fine down. Of these I likewise made very tolerable stockings. I soled my shoes with wood which I cut from a tree, and fitted to the upper leather, and when this was worn out, I supplied it with the skins of Yahoos, dried in the sun. I often got honey out of hollow trees, which I mingled with water, or eat it with my bread. No man could more verify the truth of these two maxims, that *Nature is very easily satisfied*; and, that *Necessity is the mother of invention*. I enjoyed perfect health of body, and tranquility of mind; I did not feel the treachery or inconstancy of a friend, nor the inquiries of a secret or open enemy. I had no occasion of bribing, flattering, or pimping to procure the favor of any great man, or of his minion. I wanted no fence against fraud or oppression; here was neither physician to destroy my body, nor lawyer to ruin my fortune; no informer to watch my words and actions, or forge accusations against me for hire; here were no gibers, censurers, backbiters, pickpockets, highwaymen, housebreakers, attorneys, bawds, buffoons, gamesters, politicians, wits, splenetics, tedious talkers, controvertists, ravishers, murderers, robbers, virtuosos; no leaders or followers of party and faction; no encouragers to vice, by seducement or examples; no dungeons, axes, gibbets, whipping posts, or pillories; no cheating shopkeepers or mechanics; no pride, vanity or affectation; no fops, bullies, drunkards, strolling whores, or poxes; no ranting, lewd, expensive wives; no stupid, proud pedants; no importunate, overbearing, quarrelsome, noisy, roaring, empty, conceited, swearing companions; no scoundrels raised from the dust upon the merit of their vices; or nobility thrown into it on account of their virtues; no lords, fiddlers, judges, or dancing masters.

I had the favor of being admitted to several Houyhnhnms, who came to visit or dine with my master; where his honor graciously suffered me to wait in the room, and listen to their discourse. Both he and his company would often descend to ask me questions, and receive my answers. I had also sometimes the honor of attending my master in his visits to others. I never presumed to speak, except in answer to a question; and then I did it with inward regret, because it was a loss of so much time for improving myself; but I was infinitely delighted with the station of an humble auditor in such conversations, where nothing passed but what was useful, expressed in the fewest and most significant words; where (as I have already said) the greatest decency was observed, without the least degree of ceremony; where no person spoke without being pleased himself, and pleasing his companions; where there was no interruption, tediousness, heat, or difference of sentiments. They have a notion, that when people are met together, a short silence doth much improve conversation; this I found to be true; for during those little intermissions of talk, new ideas would arise in their minds, which very much enlivened the discourse. Their subjects are generally on friendship and benevolence; on order and economy; sometimes upon the visible operations of nature, or ancient traditions; upon the bounds and limits of virtue; upon the unerring rules of reason; or upon some determinations, to be taken at the next great assembly; and often upon the various excellencies of poetry. I may add, without vanity, that my presence often gave them sufficient matter for discourse, because it afforded my master an occasion of letting his friends into the history of me and my country, upon which they were all pleased to discant in a manner not very advantageous to human kind; and for that reason I shall not repeat what they said; only I may be allowed to observe that his honor, to my great admiration, appeared to understand the nature of Yahoos much better than myself. He went through all our vices and follies, and discovered many which I had never mentioned to him; by only supposing what qualities a Yahoo of their country, with a small proportion of reason, might be capable of exerting; and concluded, with too much probability, how vile as well as miserable such a creature must be.

I freely confess, that all the little knowledge I have of any value was acquired by the lectures I received from my master, and from hearing the discourses of him and his friends; to which I should be prouder to listen, than to dictate to the greatest and wisest assembly in Europe. I admired the strength, comeliness, and speed of the inhabitants; and such a constellation of virtues in such amiable persons produced in me the highest veneration. At first, indeed, I did not feel that natural awe which the Yahoos and all other animals bear towards them; but it grew upon me by degrees, much sooner than I imagined, and was mingled with a respectful love and gratitude, that they would condescend to distinguish me from the rest of my species.

When I thought of my family, my friends, my countrymen, or human race in general, I considered them as they really were, Yahoos in shape and disposition, perhaps a little more civilized, and qualified with the gift of speech; but making no other use of reason than to improve and multiply those vices, whereof their brethren in this country had only the share that nature allotted them. When I happened to behold the reflection of my own form in a lake or fountain, I turned away my face in horror and detestation of myself, and could better endure the sight of a common Yahoo than of my own person. By conversing with the Houyhnhnms, and looking upon them with delight, I fell to imitate their gait and gesture, which is now grown into a habit; and my friends often tell me in a blunt way, that I trot like a horse; which, however, I take for a great compliment; neither shall I disown, that in speaking I am apt to fall into the voice and manner of the Houyhnhnms, and hear myself ridiculed on that account without the least mortification.

In the midst of this happiness, when I looked upon myself to be fully settled for life, my master sent for me one morning a little earlier than his usual hour. I observed by his countenance that he was in some perplexity, and at a loss how to begin what he had to speak. After a short silence, he told me, he did not know how I would take what he was going to say; that, in the last general assembly, when the affair of the Yahoos was entered upon, the representatives had taken offense at his keeping a Yahoo (meaning myself) in his family more like a Houyhnhnm than a brute animal. That he was known frequently to converse with me, as if he could receive some advantage of pleasure in my company; that such a practice was not agreeable to reason or nature, or a thing ever heard of before among them. The assembly did therefore exhort him, either to employ me like the rest of my species, or command me to swim back to the place from whence I came. That the first of these expedients was utterly rejected by all the Houyhnhnms who had ever seen me at his house or their own; for, they alleged, that because I had some rudiments of reason, added to the natural pravity of those animals, it was to be feared, I might be able to seduce them into the woody and mountainous parts of the country, and bring them in troops by night to destroy the Houyhnhnms' cattle, as being naturally of the ravenous kind, and averse from labor.

My master added that he was daily pressed by the Houyhnhnms of the neighborhood to have the assembly's exhortation executed, which he could not put off much longer. He doubted it would be impossible for me to swim to another country; and therefore wished I would contrive some sort of vehicle resembling those I had described to him, that might carry me on the sea; in which work I should have the assistance of his own servants, as well as those of his neighbors. He concluded that for his own part he could have been content to keep me in his service as long as I lived; because he found I had cured myself of some bad habits and dispositions, by endeavoring, as far as my inferior nature was capable, to imitate the Houyhnhnms.

I should here observe to the reader, that a decree of the general assembly in this country is expressed by the word *hnhloayn*, which signifies an exhortation, as near as I can render it; for they have no conception how a rational creature can be compelled, but only advised, or exhorted; because no person can disobey reason without giving up his claim to be a rational creature.

I was struck with the utmost grief and despair at my master's discourse; and being unable to support the agonies I was under, I fell into a swoon at his feet; when I came to myself, he told me that he concluded I had been dead (for these people are subject to no such imbecilities of nature). I answered, in a faint voice, that death would have been too great an happiness; that although I could not blame the assembly's exhortation, or the urgency of his friends; yet in my weak and corrupt judgment, I thought it might consist with reason to have been less rigorous. That I could not swim a league, and probably the nearest land to theirs might be distant above an hundred; that many materials, necessary for making a small vessel to carry me off, were wholly wanting in this country, which, however, I would attempt in obedience and gratitude to his honor, although I concluded the thing to be impossible, and therefore looked on myself as already devoted [4] to destruction. That the certain prospect of an unnatural death was the least of my evils; for, supposing I should escape with life by some strange adventure, how could I think with temper [5] of passing my days among Yahoos, and relapsing into my old corruptions, for want of examples to lead and keep me within the paths of virtue. That I knew too well upon what solid reasons all the determinations of the wise Houyhnhnms were founded, not to be shaken by arguments of mine, a miserable Yahoo; and therefore after presenting him with my humble thanks for the offer of his servants' assistance in making a vessel, and desiring a reasonable time for so difficult a work, I told him I would endeavor to preserve a wretched being; and, if ever I returned to England, was not without hopes of being useful to my own species by celebrating the praises of the renowned Houyhnhnms, and proposing their virtues to the imitation of mankind.

My master in a few words made me a very gracious reply, allowed me the space of two months to finish my boat, and ordered the sorrel nag, my fellow servant (for so at this distance I may presume to call him), to follow my instructions, because I told my master that his help would be sufficient, and I knew he had a tenderness for me.

In his company my first business was to go to that part of the coast where my rebellious crew had ordered me to be set on shore. I got upon a height, and looking on every side into the sea, fancied I saw a small island towards the northeast; I took out my pocket glass, and could then clearly distinguish it about five leagues off, as I computed; but it appeared to the sorrel nag to be only a blue cloud; for, as he had no conception of any country besides his own, so he

4. Doomed.   5. Equanimity.

could not be as expert in distinguishing remote objects at sea, as we who so much converse in that element.

After I had discovered this island, I considered no farther; but resolved, it should, if possible, be the first place of my banishment, leaving the consequence to fortune.

I returned home, and consulting with the sorrel nag, we went into a copse at some distance, where I with my knife, and he with a sharp flint fastened very artificially,[6] after their manner, to a wooden handle, cut down several oak wattles about the thickness of a walking staff, and some larger pieces. But I shall not trouble the reader with a particular description of my own mechanics; let it suffice to say, that in six weeks time, with the help of the sorrel nag, who performed the parts that required most labor, I finished a sort of Indian canoe; but much larger, covering it with the skins of Yahoos, well stitched together, with hempen threads of my own making. My sail was likewise composed of the skins of the same animal; but I made use of the youngest I could get, the older being too tough and thick; and I likewise provided myself with four paddles. I laid in a stock of boiled flesh, of rabbits and fowls; and took with me two vessels, one filled with milk, and the other with water.

I tried my canoe in a large pond near my master's house, and then corrected in it what was amiss, stopping all the chinks with Yahoo's tallow, till I found it staunch, and able to bear me and my freight. And when it was as complete as I could possibly make it, I had it drawn on a carriage very gently by Yahoos, to the seaside, under the conduct of the sorrel nag and another servant.

When all was ready, and the day came for my departure, I took leave of my master and lady, and the whole family, my eyes flowing with tears and my heart quite sunk with grief. But his honor, out of curiosity, and perhaps (if I may speak it without vanity) partly out of kindness, was determined to see me in my canoe; and got several of his neighboring friends to accompany him. I was forced to wait above an hour for the tide, and then observing the wind very fortunately bearing towards the island to which I intended to steer my course, I took a second leave of my master; but as I was going to prostrate myself to kiss his hoof, he did me the honor to raise it gently to my mouth. I am not ignorant how much I have been censured for mentioning this last particular. Detractors are pleased to think it improbable that so illustrious a person should descend to give so great a mark of distinction to a creature so inferior as I. Neither have I forgot how apt some travelers are to boast of extraordinary favors they have received. But, if these censurers were better acquainted with the noble and courteous disposition of the Houyhnhnms, they would soon change their opinion. I paid my respects to the rest of the Houyhnhnms in his honor's company; then getting into my canoe, I pushed off from shore.

6. Artfully.

CHAPTER XI. *The Author's dangerous voyage. He arrives at New Holland, hoping to settle there. Is wounded with an arrow by one of the natives. Is seized and carried by force into a Portuguese ship. The great civilities of the Captain. The Author arrives at England.*

I began this desperate voyage on February 15, 1714/5,[7] at 9 o'clock in the morning. The wind was very favorable; however, I made use at first only of my paddles; but considering I should soon be weary, and that the wind might probably chop about, I ventured to set up my little sail; and thus, with the help of the tide, I went at the rate of a league and a half an hour, as near as I could guess. My master and his friends continued on the shore, till I was almost out of sight; and I often heard the sorrel nag (who always loved me) crying out, "*Hnuy illa nyha maiah Yahoo*," ("Take care of thyself, gentle Yahoo").

My design was, if possible, to discover some small island uninhabited, yet sufficient by my labor to furnish me with necessaries of life, which I would have thought a greater happiness than to be first minister in the politest court of Europe, so horrible was the idea I conceived of returning to live in the society and under the government of Yahoos. For in such a solitude as I desired, I could at least enjoy my own thoughts, and reflect with delight on the virtues of those inimitable Houyhnhnms, without any opportunity of degenerating into the vices and corruptions of my own species.

The reader may remember what I related when my crew conspired against me, and confined me to my cabin, how I continued there several weeks, without knowing what course we took; and when I was put ashore in the longboat, how the sailors told me with oaths, whether true or false, that they knew not in what part of the world we were. However, I did then believe us to be about 10 degrees southward of the Cape of Good Hope, or about 45 degrees southern latitude, as I gathered from some general words I overheard among them, being I supposed to the southeast in their intended voyage to Madagascar. And although this were but little better than conjecture, yet I resolved to steer my course eastward, hoping to reach the southwest coast of New Holland, and perhaps some such island as I desired, lying westward of it. The wind was full west, and by six in the evening I computed I had gone eastward at least eighteen leagues; when I spied a very small island about half a league off, which I soon reached. It was nothing but a rock with one creek,[8] naturally arched by the force of tempests. Here I put in my canoe, and climbing a part of the rock, I could plainly discover land to the east, extending from south to north. I lay all night in my canoe; and repeating my voyage early in the morning, I arrived in seven hours to the southeast point of New Holland. This confirmed me in the opinion I have long entertained, that the maps and

7. I.e., 1714. The year began on March 25th.

8. A bay.

charts place this country at least three degrees more to the east than it really is; which thought I communicated many years ago to my worthy friend Mr. Herman Moll,[9] and gave him my reasons for it, although he hath rather chosen to follow other authors.

I saw no inhabitants in the place where I landed; and being unarmed, I was afraid of venturing far into the country. I found some shellfish on the shore, and eat them raw, not daring to kindle a fire, for fear of being discovered by the natives. I continued three days feeding on oysters and limpets, to save my own provisions; and I fortunately found a brook of excellent water, which gave me great relief.

On the fourth day, venturing out early a little too far, I saw twenty or thirty natives upon a height, not above five hundred yards from me. They were stark naked, men, women, and children round a fire, as I could discover by the smoke. One of them spied me, and gave notice to the rest; five of them advanced towards me, leaving the women and children at the fire. I made what haste I could to the shore, and getting into my canoe, shoved off; the savages observing me retreat, ran after me; and before I could get far enough into the sea, discharged an arrow, which wounded me deeply on the inside of my left knee. (I shall carry the mark to my grave.) I apprehended the arrow might be poisoned; and paddling out of the reach of their darts (being a calm day) I made a shift to suck the wound, and dress it as well as I could.

I was at a loss what to do, for I durst not return to the same landing place, but stood to the north, and was forced to paddle; for the wind, although very gentle, was against me, blowing northwest. As I was looking about for a secure landing place, I saw a sail to the north northeast, which appearing every minute more visible, I was in some doubt whether I should wait for them or no; but at last my detestation of the Yahoo race prevailed; and turning my canoe, I sailed and paddled together to the south, and got into the same creek from whence I set out in the morning, choosing rather to trust myself among these barbarians than live with European Yahoos. I drew up my canoe as close as I could to the shore, and hid myself behind a stone by the little brook, which, as I have already said, was excellent water.

The ship came within half a league of this creek, and sent out her longboat with vessels to take in fresh water (for the place it seems was very well known), but I did not observe it until the boat was almost on shore; and it was too late to seek another hiding place. The seamen at their landing observed my canoe, and rummaging it all over, easily conjectured that the owner could not be far off. Four of them well armed searched every cranny and lurking hole, till at last they found me flat on my face behind the stone. They gazed a while in admiration [1] at my strange uncouth dress;

9. A famous contemporary map maker.   1. Wonder.

my coat made of skins, my wooden-soled shoes, and my furred stockings; from whence, however, they concluded I was not a native of the place, who all go naked. One of the seamen in Portuguese bid me rise, and asked who I was. I understood that language very well, and getting upon my feet, said I was a poor Yahoo, banished from the Houyhnhnms, and desired they would please to let me depart. They admired to hear me answer them in their own tongue, and saw by my complexion I must be an European; but were at a loss to know what I meant by Yahoos and Houyhnhnms, and at the same time fell a laughing at my strange tone in speaking, which resembled the neighing of a horse. I trembled all the while betwixt fear and hatred; I again desired leave to depart, and was gently moving to my canoe; but they laid hold on me, desiring to know what country I was of? whence I came? with many other questions. I told them I was born in England, from whence I came about five years ago, and then their country and ours was at peace. I therefore hoped they would not treat me as an enemy, since I meant them no harm, but was a poor Yahoo, seeking some desolate place where to pass the remainder of his unfortunate life.

When they began to talk, I thought I never heard or saw any thing so unnatural; for it appeared to me as monstrous as if a dog or a cow should speak in England, or a Yahoo in Houyhnhnmland. The honest Portuguese were equally amazed at my strange dress, and the odd manner of delivering my words, which however they understood very well. They spoke to me with great humanity, and said they were sure their Captain would carry me *gratis* to Lisbon, from whence I might return to my own country; that two of the seamen would go back to the ship, to inform the Captain of what they had seen, and receive his orders; in the meantime, unless I would give my solemn oath not to fly, they would secure me by force. I thought it best to comply with their proposal. They were very curious to know my story, but I gave them very little satisfaction; and they all conjectured, that my misfortunes had impaired my reason. In two hours the boat, which went laden with vessels of water, returned with the Captain's commands to fetch me on board. I fell on my knees to preserve my liberty; but all was in vain, and the men having tied me with cords, heaved me into the boat, from whence I was taken into the ship, and from thence into the Captain's cabin.

His name was Pedro de Mendez; he was a very courteous and generous person; he entreated me to give some account of myself, and desired to know what I would eat or drink; said I should be used as well as himself, and spoke so many obliging things, that I wondered to find such civilities from a Yahoo. However, I remained silent and sullen; I was ready to faint at the very smell of him and his men. At last I desired something to eat out of my own canoe; but he ordered me a chicken and some excellent wine, and then directed that I should be put to bed in a very clean cabin. I would not undress myself, but lay on the bedclothes; and in half an hour stole out, when I thought the crew was at dinner; and getting to the side of the ship, was going to leap into the sea, and swim for my life, rather than continue among Yahoos. But one of the seamen prevented me, and having informed the Captain, I was chained to my cabin.

After dinner Don Pedro came to me, and desired to know my reason for so desperate an attempt; assured me he only meant to do me all the service he was able; and spoke so very movingly, that at last I descended to treat him like an animal which had some little portion of reason. I gave him a very short relation of my voyage; of the conspiracy against me by my own men; of the country where they set me on shore, and of my five years residence there. All which he looked upon as if it were a dream or a vision; whereat I took great offense; for I had quite forgot the faculty of lying, so peculiar to Yahoos in all countries where they preside, and consequently the disposition of suspecting truth in others of their own species. I asked him whether it were the custom of his country to *say the thing that was not?* I assured him I had almost forgot what he meant by falsehood; and if I had lived a thousand years in Houyhnhnmland, I should never have heard a lie from the meanest servant. That I was altogether indifferent whether he believed me or no; but however, in return for his favors, I would give so much allowance to the corruption of his nature, as to answer any objection he would please to make; and he might easily discover the truth.

The Captain, a wise man, after many endeavors to catch me tripping in some part of my story, at last began to have a better opinion of my veracity. But he added that since I professed so inviolable an attachment to truth, I must give him my word of honor to bear him company in this voyage without attempting anything against my life; or else he would continue me a prisoner till we arrived at Lisbon. I gave him the promise he required; but at the same time protested that I would suffer the greatest hardships rather than return to live among Yahoos.

Our voyage passed without any considerable accident. In gratitude to the Captain I sometimes sat with him at his earnest request, and strove to conceal my antipathy against humankind, although it often broke out; which he suffered to pass without observation. But the greatest part of the day, I confined myself to my cabin, to avoid seeing any of the crew. The Captain had often entreated me to strip myself of my savage dress, and offered to lend me the best suit of clothes he had. This I would not be prevailed on to accept, abhorring to cover myself with anything that had been on the back of a Yahoo. I only desired he would lend me two clean shirts, which having been washed since he wore them, I believed would not so much defile me. These I changed every second day, and washed them myself.

We arrived at Lisbon, Nov. 5, 1715. At our landing, the Captain forced me to cover myself with his cloak, to prevent the rabble from crowding about me. I was conveyed to his own house; and at my earnest request, he led me up to the highest room backwards.[2] I conjured him to conceal from all persons what I had told him of the Houyhnhnms; because the least hint of such a story would not only draw numbers of people to see me, but probably put me in danger of being imprisoned, or burned by the Inquisition. The Captain persuaded me to accept a suit of clothes newly made; but I would not suffer the tailor to take my measure; however, Don Pedro being almost of my size, they fitted me well enough. He accoutred me with other necessaries, all new, which I aired for twenty-four hours before I would use them.

The Captain had no wife, nor above three servants, none of which were suffered to attend at meals; and his whole deportment was so obliging, added to very good human understanding, that I really began to tolerate his company. He gained so far upon me, that I ventured to look out of the back window. By degrees I was brought into another room, from whence I peeped into the street, but drew my head back in a fright. In a week's time he seduced me down to the door. I found my terror gradually lessened, but my hatred and contempt seemed to increase. I was at last bold enough to walk the street in his company, but kept my nose well stopped with rue, or sometimes with tobacco.

In ten days, Don Pedro, to whom I had given some account of my domestic affairs, put it upon me as a point of honor and conscience that I ought to return to my native country, and live at home with my wife and children. He told me there was an English ship in the port just ready to sail, and he would furnish me with all things necessary. It would be tedious to repeat his arguments, and my contradictions. He said it was altogether impossible to find such a solitary island as I had desired to live in; but I might command in my own house, and pass my time in a manner as recluse as I pleased.

I complied at last, finding I could not do better. I left Lisbon the 24th day of November, in an English merchantman, but who was the Master I never inquired. Don Pedro accompanied me to the ship, and lent me twenty pounds. He took kind leave of me, and embraced me at parting; which I bore as well as I could. During this last voyage I had no commerce with the Master, or any of his men; but pretending I was sick kept close in my cabin. On the fifth of December, 1715, we cast anchor in the Downs about nine in the morning, and at three in the afternoon I got safe to my house at Redriff.

My wife and family received me with great surprise and joy, because they concluded me certainly dead; but I must freely confess, the sight of them filled me only with hatred, disgust, and con-

2. At the rear.

tempt; and the more, by reflecting on the near alliance I had to them. For, although since my unfortunate exile from the Houyhn-hnm country, I had compelled myself to tolerate the sight of Yahoos, and to converse with Don Pedro de Mendez; yet my memory and imaginations were perpetually filled with the virtues and ideas of those exalted Houyhnhnms. And when I began to consider that by copulating with one of the Yahoo species, I had become a parent of more, it struck me with the utmost shame, confusion, and horror.

As soon as I entered the house, my wife took me in her arms, and kissed me; at which, having not been used to the touch of that odious animal for so many years, I fell in a swoon for almost an hour. At the time I am writing, it is five years since my last return to England; during the first year I could not endure my wife or children in my presence, the very smell of them was intolerable; much less could I suffer them to eat in the same room. To this hour they dare not presume to touch my bread, or drink out of the same cup; neither was I ever able to let one of them take me by the hand. The first money I laid out was to buy two young stone-horses,[3] which I keep in a good stable, and next to them the groom is my greatest favorite; for I feel my spirits revived by the smell he contracts in the stable. My horses understand me tolerably well; I converse with them at least four hours every day. They are strangers to bridle or saddle; they live in great amity with me, and friendship to each other.

CHAPTER XII. *The Author's veracity. His design in publishing this work. His censure of those travelers who swerve from the truth. The Author clears himself from any sinister ends in writing. An objection answered. The method of planting colonies. His native country commended. The right of the crown to those countries described by the Author is justified. The difficulty of conquering them. The Author takes his last leave of the reader; proposeth his manner of living for the future; gives good advice, and concludeth.*

Thus, gentle reader, I have given thee a faithful history of my travels for sixteen years, and above seven months; wherein I have not been so studious of ornament as of truth. I could perhaps like others have astonished thee with strange improbable tales; but I rather chose to relate plain matter of fact in the simplest manner and style; because my principal design was to inform, and not to amuse thee.

It is easy for us who travel into remote countries, which are seldom visited by Englishmen or other Europeans, to form descriptions of wonderful animals both at sea and land. Whereas a traveler's chief aim should be to make men wiser and better, and to improve their minds by the bad as well as good example of

3. Stallions.

what they deliver concerning foreign places.

I could heartily wish a law were enacted, that every traveler, before he were permitted to publish his voyages, should be obliged to make oath before the Lord High Chancellor that all he intended to print was absolutely true to the best of his knowledge; for then the world would no longer be deceived as it usually is, while some writers, to make their works pass the better upon the public, impose the grossest falsities on the unwary reader. I have perused several books of travels with great delight in my younger days; but, having since gone over most parts of the globe, and been able to contradict many fabulous accounts from my own observation, it hath given me a great disgust against this part of reading, and some indignation to see the credulity of mankind so impudently abused. Therefore, since my acquaintance were pleased to think my poor endeavors might not be unacceptable to my country; I imposed on myself as a maxim, never to be swerved from, that I would *strictly adhere to truth*; neither indeed can I be ever under the least temptation to vary from it, while I retain in my mind the lectures and example of my noble master, and the other illustrious Houyhnhnms, of whom I had so long the honor to be an humble hearer.

> ———*Nec si miserum Fortuna Sinonem*
> *Finxit, vanum etiam, mendacemque improba finget.*[4]

I know very well how little reputation is to be got by writings which require neither genius nor learning, nor indeed any other talent, except a good memory, or an exact *Journal*. I know likewise, that writers of travels, like dictionary-makers, are sunk into oblivion by the weight and bulk of those who come last, and therefore lie uppermost. And it is highly probable that such travelers who shall hereafter visit the countries described in this work of mine, may be detecting my errors (if there be any) and adding many new discoveries of their own, jostle me out of vogue, and stand in my place, making the world forget that ever I was an author. This indeed would be too great a mortification if I wrote for fame; but, as my sole intention was the PUBLIC GOOD, I cannot be altogether disappointed. For, who can read the virtues I have mentioned in the glorious Houyhnhnms, without being ashamed of his own vices, when he considers himself as the reasoning, governing animal of his country? I shall say nothing of those remote nations where Yahoos preside; amongst which the least corrupted are the Brobdingnagians, whose wise maxims in morality and government it would be our happiness to observe. But I forbear descanting further, and rather leave the judicious reader to his own remarks and applications.

---

4. Virgil, *Aeneid*, II, 79–80. "* * * nor if Fortune had moulded Sinon for mis- ery, will she also in spite mould him as false and lying."

I am not a little pleased that this work of mine can possibly meet with no censurers; for what objections can be made against a writer who relates only plain facts that happened in such distant countries, where we have not the least interest with respect either to trade or negotiations? I have carefully avoided every fault with which common writers of travels are often too justly charged. Besides, I meddle not the least with any party, but write without passion, prejudice, or ill-will against any man or number of men whatsoever. I write for the noblest end, to inform and instruct mankind, over whom I may, without breach of modesty, pretend to some superiority, from the advantages I received by conversing so long among the most accomplished Houyhnhnms. I write without any view towards profit or praise. I never suffer a word to pass that may look like reflection, or possibly give the least offense even to those who are most ready to take it. So that, I hope, I may with justice pronounce myself an Author perfectly blameless; against whom the tribes of answerers, considerers, observers, reflectors, detecters, remarkers will never be able to find matter for exercising their talents.

I confess it was whispered to me that I was bound in duty as a subject of England, to have given in a memorial to a secretary of state, at my first coming over; because, whatever lands are discovered by a subject, belong to the Crown. But I doubt whether our conquests in the countries I treat of would be as easy as those of Ferdinando Cortez over the naked Americans. The Lilliputians, I think, are hardly worth the charge of a fleet and army to reduce them; and I question whether it might be prudent or safe to attempt the Brobdingnagians; or, whether an English army would be much at their ease with the Flying Island over their heads. The Houyhnhnms, indeed, appear not to be so well prepared for war, a science to which they are perfect strangers, and especially against missive weapons. However, supposing myself to be a minister of state, I could never give my advice for invading them. Their prudence, unanimity, unacquaintedness with fear, and their love of their country would amply supply all defects in the military art. Imagine twenty thousand of them breaking into the midst of an European army, confounding the ranks, overturning the carriages, battering the warriors' faces into mummy,[5] by terrible yerks [6] from their hinder hoofs: for they would well deserve the character given to Augustus, *Recalcitrat undique tutus.*[7] But instead of proposals for conquering that magnanimous nation, I rather wish they were in a capacity or disposition to send a sufficient number of their inhabitants for civilizing Europe; by teaching us the first principles of Honor, Justice, Truth, Temperance,

---

5. Pulp.
6. Kicks.
7. Horace, *Satires* II.i.20. "* * * he kicks backward, at every point on his guard."

public Spirit, Fortitude, Chastity, Friendship, Benevolence, and Fidelity. The names of all which Virtues are still retained among us in most languages, and are to be met with in modern as well as ancient authors, which I am able to assert from my own small reading.

But I had another reason which made me less forward to enlarge his majesty's dominions by my discoveries: to say the truth, I had conceived a few scruples with relation to the distributive justice of princes upon those occasions. For instance, a crew of pirates are driven by a storm they know not whither; at length a boy discovers land from the topmast; they go on shore to rob and plunder; they see an harmless people, are entertained with kindness, they give the country a new name, they take formal possession of it for the king, they set up a rotton plank or a stone for a memorial, they murder two or three dozen of the natives, bring away a couple more by force for a sample, return home, and get their pardon. Here commences a new dominion acquired with a title by Divine Right. Ships are sent with the first opportunity; the natives driven out or destroyed, their princes tortured to discover their gold; a free license given to all acts of inhumanity and lust; the earth reeking with the blood of its inhabitants: and this execrable crew of butchers employed in so pious an expedition is a *modern colony* sent to convert and civilize an idolatrous and barbarous people.

But this description, I confess, doth by no means affect the British nation, who may be an example to the whole world for their wisdom, care, and justice in planting colonies; their liberal endowments for the advancement of religion and learning; their choice of devout and able pastors to propagate Christianity; their caution in stocking their provinces with people of sober lives and conversations from this the Mother Kingdom; their strict regard to the distribution of justice, in supplying the civil administration through all their colonies with officers of the greatest abilities, utter strangers to corruption: and to crown all, by sending the most vigilant and virtuous governors, who have no other views than the happiness of the people over whom they preside, and the honor of the king their master.

But, as those countries which I have described do not appear to have any desire of being conquered, and enslaved, murdered, or driven out by colonies, nor abound either in gold, silver, sugar, or tobacco, I did humbly conceive they were by no means proper objects of our zeal, our valor, or our interest. However, if those whom it may concern, think fit to be of another opinion, I am ready to depose, when I shall be lawfully called, that no European did ever visit these countries before me. I mean, if the inhabitants ought to be believed.

But, as to the formality of taking possession in my sovereign's name, it never came once into my thoughts; and if it had, yet as my affairs then stood, I should perhaps in point of prudence and self-preservation have put it off to a better opportunity.

Having thus answered the only objection that can be raised against me as a traveler, I here take a final leave of my courteous readers, and return to enjoy my own speculations in my little garden at Redriff; to apply those excellent lessons of virtue which I learned among the Houyhnhnms; to instruct the Yahoos of my own family as far as I shall find them docible animals; to behold my figure often in a glass, and thus if possible habituate myself by time to tolerate the sight of a human creature; to lament the brutality of Houyhnhnms in my own country, but always treat their persons with respect, for the sake of my noble master, his family, his friends, and the whole Houyhnhnm race, whom these of ours have the honor to resemble in all their lineaments, however their intellectuals came to degenerate.

I began last week to permit my wife to sit at dinner with me, at the farthest end of a long table; and to answer (but with the utmost brevity) the few questions I ask her. Yet the smell of a Yahoo continuing very offensive, I always keep my nose well stopped with rue, lavender, or tobacco leaves. And although it be hard for a man late in life to remove old habits, I am not altogether out of hopes in some time to suffer a neighbor Yahoo in my company, without the apprehensions I am yet under of his teeth or his claws.

My reconcilement to the Yahoo kind in general might not be so difficult, if they would be content with those vices and follies only which nature hath entitled them to. I am not in the least provoked at the sight of a lawyer, a pickpocket, a colonel, a fool, a lord, a gamester, a politician, a whoremonger, a physician, an evidence, a suborner, an attorney, a traitor, or the like: this is all according to the due course of things. But when I behold a lump of deformity, and diseases both in body and mind, smitten with pride, it immediately breaks all the measures of my patience; neither shall I be ever able to comprehend how such an animal and such a vice could tally together. The wise and virtuous Houyhnhnms, who abound in all excellencies that can adorn a rational creature, have no name for this vice in their language, which hath no terms to express anything that is evil, except those whereby they describe the detestable qualities of their Yahoos, among which they were not able to distinguish this of pride, for want of thoroughly understanding human nature, as it showeth itself in other countries, where that animal presides. But I, who had more experience, could plainly observe some rudiments of it among the wild Yahoos.

But the Houyhnhnms, who live under the government of reason, are no more proud of the good qualities they possess, than I should be for not wanting a leg or an arm, which no man in his wits would boast of, although he must be miserable without them. I dwell the longer upon this subject from the desire I have to make the society of an English Yahoo by any means not insupportable; and therefore I here entreat those who have any tincture of this absurd vice, that they will not presume to appear in my sight.

1726, 1735

A Modest Proposal[1]

FOR PREVENTING THE CHILDREN OF POOR PEOPLE IN IRELAND FROM BEING A BURDEN TO THEIR PARENTS OR COUNTRY, AND FOR MAKING THEM BENEFICIAL TO THE PUBLIC

It is a melancholy object to those who walk through this great town[2] or travel in the country, when they see the streets, the roads, and cabin doors, crowded with beggars of the female sex, followed by three, four, or six children, all in rags and importuning every passenger for an alms. These mothers, instead of being able to work for their honest livelihood, are forced to employ all their time in strolling to beg sustenance for their helpless infants, who, as they grow up, either turn thieves for want of work, or leave their dear native country to fight for the Pretender in Spain, or sell themselves to the Barbadoes.[3]

I think it is agreed by all parties that this prodigious number of children in the arms, or on the backs, or at the heels of their mothers, and frequently of their fathers, is in the present deplor-

1. *A Modest Proposal* is an example of Swift's favorite satiric devices used with superb effect. Irony (from the deceptive adjective "modest" in the title to the very last sentence) pervades the piece. A rigorous logic deduces ghastly arguments from a shocking premise so quietly assumed that the reader assents before he is aware of what his assent implies. Parody, at which Swift is adept, allows him to glance sardonically at the by then familiar figure of the benevolent humanitarian (forerunner of the modern sociologist, social worker, economic planner) concerned to correct a social evil by means of a theoretically conceived plan. The proposer, as naïve as he is apparently logical and kindly, ignores and therefore emphasizes for the reader the enormity of his plan. The whole is an elaboration of a rather trite metaphor: "The English are devouring the Irish." But there is nothing trite about the pamphlet, which expresses in Swift's most controlled style his pity for the oppressed, ignorant, populous, and hungry Catholic peasants of Ireland, and his anger at the rapacious English absentee landlords, who were bleeding the country white with the silent approbation of Parliament, ministers, and the Crown.
2. Dublin.
3. James Francis Edward Stuart (1688–1766), the son of James II, was claimant ("Pretender") to the throne of England from which the Glorious Revolution had barred his succession. Catholic Ireland was loyal to him, and Irishmen joined him in his exile on the Continent. Because of the poverty in Ireland, many Irishmen emigrated to the West Indies and other British colonies in America; they paid their passage by binding themselves to work for a stated period for one of the planters.

able state of the kingdom a very great additional grievance; and therefore whoever could find out a fair, cheap, and easy method of making these children sound, useful members of the commonwealth would deserve so well of the public as to have his statue set up for a preserver of the nation.

But my intention is very far from being confined to provide only for the children of professed beggars; it is of a much greater extent, and shall take in the whole number of infants at a certain age who are born of parents in effect as little able to support them as those who demand our charity in the streets.

As to my own part, having turned my thoughts for many years upon this important subject, and maturely weighed the several schemes of other projectors,[4] I have always found them grossly mistaken in their computation. It is true, a child just dropped from its dam may be supported by her milk for a solar year, with little other nourishment; at most not above the value of two shillings, which the mother may certainly get, or the value in scraps, by her lawful occupation of begging; and it is exactly at one year old that I propose to provide for them in such a manner as instead of being a charge upon their parents or the parish, or wanting food and raiment for the rest of their lives, they shall on the contrary contribute to the feeding, and partly to the clothing, of many thousands.

There is likewise another great advantage in my scheme, that it will prevent those voluntary abortions, and that horrid practice of women murdering their bastard children, alas, too frequent among us, sacrificing the poor innocent babes, I doubt, more to avoid the expense than the shame, which would move tears and pity in the most savage and inhuman breast.

The number of souls in this kingdom[5] being usually reckoned one million and a half, of these I calculate there may be about two hundred thousand couple whose wives are breeders; from which number I subtract thirty thousand couples who are able to maintain their own children, although I apprehend there cannot be so many under the present distresses of the kingdom; but this being granted, there will remain an hundred and seventy thousand breeders. I again subtract fifty thousand for those women who miscarry, or whose children die by accident or disease within the year. There only remain an hundred and twenty thousand children of poor parents annually born. The question therefore is, how this number shall be reared and provided for, which, as I have already said, under the present situation of affairs, is utterly impossible by all the methods hitherto proposed. For we can neither employ them in handicraft or agriculture; we neither build houses (I mean in the country) nor cultivate land. They can very seldom pick up a livelihood

4. Devisers of schemes.   5. Ireland.

by stealing till they arrive at six years old, except where they are of towardly[6] parts; although I confess they learn the rudiments much earlier, during which time they can however be looked upon only as probationers, as I have been informed by a principal gentleman in the county of Cavan, who protested to me that he never knew above one or two instances under the age of six, even in a part of the kingdom so renowned for the quickest proficiency in that art.

I am assured by our merchants that a boy or a girl before twelve years old is no salable commodity; and even when they come to this age they will not yield above three pounds, or three pounds and half a crown at most on the Exchange; which cannot turn to account either to the parents or the kingdom, the charge of nutriment and rags having been at least four times that value.

I shall now therefore humbly propose my own thoughts, which I hope will not be liable to the least objection.

I have been assured by a very knowing American of my acquaintance in London, that a young healthy child well nursed is at a year old a most delicious, nourishing, and wholesome food, whether stewed, roasted, baked, or boiled; and I make no doubt that it will equally serve in a fricassee or a ragout.[7]

I do therefore humbly offer it to public consideration that of the hundred and twenty thousand children, already computed, twenty thousand may be reserved for breed, whereof only one fourth part to be males, which is more than we allow to sheep, black cattle, or swine; and my reason is that these children are seldom the fruits of marriage, a circumstance not much regarded by our savages, therefore one male will be sufficient to serve four females. That the remaining hundred thousand may at a year old be offered in sale to the persons of quality and fortune through the kingdom, always advising the mother to let them suck plentifully in the last month, so as to render them plump and fat for a good table. A child will make two dishes at an entertainment for friends; and when the family dines alone, the fore or hind quarter will make a reasonable dish, and seasoned with a little pepper or salt will be very good boiled on the fourth day, especially in winter.

I have reckoned upon a medium that a child just born will weigh twelve pounds, and in a solar year if tolerably nursed increaseth to twenty-eight pounds.

I grant this food will be somewhat dear, and therefore very proper for landlords, who, as they have already devoured most of the parents, seem to have the best title to the children.

Infant's flesh will be in season throughout the year, but more plentiful in March, and a little before and after. For we are told by a grave author, an eminent French physician,[8] that fish being

6. Dutiful, tractable.
7. A highly seasoned meat stew.
8. François Rabelais (ca. 1494–1553), a humorist and a satirist, by no means grave.

a prolific diet, there are more children born in Roman Catholic countries about nine months after Lent than at any other season; therefore, reckoning a year after Lent, the markets will be more glutted than usual, because the number of popish infants is at least three to one in this kingdom; and therefore it will have one other collateral advantage, by lessening the number of Papists among us.

I have already computed the charge of nursing a beggar's child (in which list I reckon all cottagers, laborers, and four fifths of the farmers) to be about two shillings per annum, rags included; and I believe no gentleman would repine to give ten shillings for the carcass of a good fat child, which, as I have said, will make four dishes of excellent nutritive meat, when he hath only some particular friend or his own family to dine with him. Thus the squire will learn to be a good landlord, and grow popular among the tenants; the mother will have eight shillings net profit, and be fit for work till she produces another child.

Those who are more thrifty (as I must confess the times require) may flay the carcass, the skin of which artificially[9] dressed will make admirable gloves for ladies, and summer boots for fine gentlemen.

As to our city of Dublin, shambles[1] may be appointed for this purpose in the most convenient parts of it, and butchers we may be assured will not be wanting; although I rather recommend buying the children alive, and dressing them hot from the knife as we do roasting pigs.

A very worthy person, a true lover of his country, and whose virtues I highly esteem, was lately pleased in discoursing on this matter to offer a refinement upon my scheme. He said that many gentlemen of this kingdom, having of late destroyed their deer, he conceived that the want of venison might be well supplied by the bodies of young lads and maidens, not exceeding fourteen years of age nor under twelve, so great a number of both sexes in every county being now ready to starve for want of work and service; and these to be disposed of by their parents, if alive, or otherwise by their nearest relations. But with due deference to so excellent a friend and so deserving a patriot, I cannot be altogether in his sentiments; for as to the males, my American acquaintance assured me from frequent experience that their flesh was generally tough and lean, like that of our schoolboys, by continual exercise, and their taste disagreeable; and to fatten them would not answer the charge. Then as to the females, it would, I think with humble submission, be a loss to the public, because they soon would become breeders themselves: and besides, it is not improbable that some scrupulous people might be apt to censure such a practice (although indeed very unjustly) as a little bordering upon cruelty;

---

9. Skillfully.   1. Slaughterhouses.

which, I confess, hath always been with me the strongest objection against any project, how well soever intended.

But in order to justify my friend, he confessed that this expedient was put into his head by the famous Psalmanazar,[2] a native of the island Formosa, who came from thence to London above twenty years ago, and in conversation told my friend that in his country when any young person happened to be put to death, the executioner sold the carcass to persons of quality as a prime dainty; and that in his time the body of a plump girl of fifteen, who was crucified for an attempt to poison the emperor, was sold to his Imperial Majesty's prime minister of state, and other great mandarins of the court, in joints from the gibbet, at four hundred crowns. Neither indeed can I deny that if the same use were made of several plump young girls in this town, who without one single groat to their fortunes cannot stir abroad without a chair, and appear at the playhouse and assemblies in foreign fineries which they never will pay for, the kingdom would not be the worse.

Some persons of a desponding spirit are in great concern about that vast number of poor people who are aged, diseased, or maimed, and I have been desired to employ my thoughts what course may be taken to ease the nation of so grievous an encumbrance. But I am not in the least pain upon that matter, because it is very well known that they are every day dying and rotting by cold and famine, and filth and vermin, as fast as can be reasonably expected. And as to the younger laborers, they are now in almost as hopeful a condition. They cannot get work, and consequently pine away for want of nourishment to a degree that if at any time they are accidentally hired to common labor, they have not strength to perform it; and thus the country and themselves are happily delivered from the evils to come.

I have too long digressed, and therefore shall return to my subject. I think the advantages by the proposal which I have made are obvious and many, as well as of the highest importance.

For first, as I have already observed, it would greatly lessen the number of Papists, with whom we are yearly overrun, being the principal breeders of the nation as well as our most dangerous enemies; and who stay at home on purpose to deliver the kingdom to the Pretender, hoping to take their advantage by the absence of so many good Protestants, who have chosen rather to leave their country than stay at home and pay tithes against their conscience to an Episcopal curate.

Secondly, the poorer tenants will have something valuable of their own, which by law may be made liable to distress,[3] and help

2. George Psalmanazar (ca. 1679–1763), a famous imposter. A Frenchman, he imposed himself on English bishops, noblemen, and scientists as a Formosan. He wrote an entirely fictitious account of Formosa, in which he described human sacrifices and cannibalism.

3. Distraint, i.e., the seizing, through legal action, of property for the payment of debts and other obligations.

to pay their landlord's rent, their corn and cattle being already seized and money a thing unknown.

Thirdly, whereas the maintenance of an hundred thousand children, from two years old and upwards, cannot be computed at less than ten shillings a piece per annum, the nation's stock will be thereby increased fifty thousand pounds per annum, besides the profit of a new dish introduced to the tables of all gentlemen of fortune in the kingdom who have any refinement in taste. And the money will circulate among ourselves, the goods being entirely of our own growth and manufacture.

Fourthly, the constant breeders, besides the gain of eight shillings sterling per annum by the sale of their children, will be rid of the charge of maintaining them after the first year.

Fifthly, this food would likewise bring great custom to taverns, where the vintners will certainly be so prudent as to procure the best receipts for dressing it to perfection, and consequently have their houses frequented by all the fine gentlemen, who justly value themselves upon their knowledge in good eating; and a skillful cook, who understands how to oblige his guests, will contrive to make it as expensive as they please.

Sixthly, this would be a great inducement to marriage, which all wise nations have either encouraged by rewards or enforced by laws and penalties. It would increase the care and tenderness of mothers toward their children, when they were sure of a settlement for life to the poor babes, provided in some sort by the public, to their annual profit instead of expense. We should see an honest emulation among the married women, which of them could bring the fattest child to the market. Men would become as fond of their wives during the time of their pregnancy as they are now of their mares in foal, their cows in calf, or sows when they are ready to farrow; nor offer to beat or kick them (as is too frequent a practice) for fear of a miscarriage.

Many other advantages might be enumerated. For instance, the addition of some thousand carcasses in our exportation of barreled beef, the propagation of swine's flesh, and improvement in the art of making good bacon, so much wanted among us by the great destruction of pigs, too frequent at our tables, which are no way comparable in taste or magnificence to a well-grown, fat, yearling child, which roasted whole will make a considerable figure at a lord mayor's feast or any other public entertainment. But this and many others I omit, being studious of brevity.

Supposing that one thousand families in this city would be constant customers for infants' flesh, besides others who might have it at merry meetings, particularly weddings and christenings, I compute that Dublin would take off annually about twenty thousand carcasses, and the rest of the kingdom (where probably they will be sold somewhat cheaper) the remaining eighty thousand.

I can think of no one objection that will possibly be raised against this proposal, unless it should be urged that the number of people will be thereby much lessened in the kingdom. This I freely own, and it was indeed one principal design in offering it to the world. I desire the reader will observe, that I calculate my remedy for this one individual kingdom of Ireland and for no other that ever was, is, or I think ever can be upon earth. Therefore let no man talk to me of other expedients: of taxing our absentees at five shillings a pound: of using neither clothes nor household furniture except what is of our own growth and manufacture: of utterly rejecting the materials and instruments that promote foreign luxury: of curing the expensiveness of pride, vanity, idleness, and gaming in our women: of introducing a vein of parsimony, prudence, and temperance: of learning to love our country, in the want of which we differ even from Laplanders and the inhabitants of Topinamboo:[4] of quitting our animosities and factions, nor acting any longer like the Jews, who were murdering one another at the very moment their city was taken:[5] of being a little cautious not to sell our country and conscience for nothing: of teaching landlords to have at least one degree of mercy toward their tenants: lastly, of putting a spirit of honesty, industry, and skill into our shopkeepers; who, if a resolution could now be taken to buy only our native goods, would immediately unite to cheat and exact upon us in the price, the measure, and the goodness, nor could ever yet be brought to make one fair proposal of just dealing, though often and earnestly invited to it.[6]

Therefore I repeat, let no man talk to me of these and the like expedients, till he hath at least some glimpse of hope that there will ever be some hearty and sincere attempt to put them in practice.

But as to myself, having been wearied out for many years with offering vain, idle, visionary thoughts, and at length utterly despairing of success, I fortunately fell upon this proposal, which, as it is wholly new, so it hath something solid and real, of no expense and little trouble, full in our own power, and whereby we can incur no danger in disobliging England. For this kind of commodity will not bear exportation, the flesh being of too tender a consistence to admit a long continuance in salt, although perhaps I could name a country which would be glad to eat up our whole nation without it.[7]

After all, I am not so violently bent upon my own opinion as

4. I.e., even Laplanders love their frozen, infertile country and the savage tribes of Brazil their jungle more than the Anglo-Irish love Ireland.
5. During the siege of Jerusalem by the Roman Emperor Titus, who captured and destroyed the city in A.D. 70, the city was torn by bloody fights between factions of fanatics.
6. Swift himself had made all these proposals in various pamphlets. In editions printed during his lifetime the various proposals were italicized to indicate that Swift is no longer being ironic.
7. I.e., England.

to reject any offer proposed by wise men, which shall be found equally innocent, cheap, easy, and effectual. But before something of that kind shall be advanced in contradiction to my scheme, and offering a better, I desire the author or authors will be pleased maturely to consider two points. First, as things now stand, how they will be able to find food and raiment for an hundred thousand useless mouths and backs. And secondly, there being a round million of creatures in human figure throughout this kingdom, whose sole subsistence put into a common stock would leave them in debt two millions of pounds sterling, adding those who are beggars by profession to the bulk of farmers, cottagers, and laborers, with their wives and children who are beggars in effect; I desire those politicians who dislike my overture, and may perhaps be so bold to attempt an answer, that they will first ask the parents of these mortals whether they would not at this day think it a great happiness to have been sold for food at a year old in the manner I prescribe, and thereby have avoided such a perpetual scene of misfortunes as they have since gone through by the oppression of landlords, the impossibility of paying rent without money or trade, the want of common sustenance, with neither house nor clothes to cover them from the inclemencies of the weather, and the most inevitable prospect of entailing the like or greater miseries upon their breed forever.

I profess, in the sincerity of my heart, that I have not the least personal interest in endeavoring to promote this necessary work, having no other motive than the public good of my country, by advancing our trade, providing for infants, relieving the poor, and giving some pleasure to the rich. I have no children by which I can propose to get a single penny; the youngest being nine years old, and my wife past childbearing.

1729

JOSEPH ADDISON *and* SIR RICHARD STEELE
(1672–1719)　　　　　　(1672–1729)

1709–11: *Tatler* published.
1711–12: *Spectator* published.
1714:　　*Spectator* resumed (for 80 numbers).

The friendship of Joseph Addison and Richard Steele began when they were schoolboys together at the Charterhouse in London. Their careers ran parallel courses and brought them for a while into fruitful collaboration. Addison, though a man of infinite charm among intimates, was by nature reserved, rather chilly, calculating, ungenerous, and prudent. Steele was impulsive and rakish when young (but ardently devoted to his beautiful wife), imprudent to a degree, and consequently in frequent financial distress. Addison never stumbled in his progress to financial competence, a late marriage to a dowager countess, and a successful political career; walking less surely, Steele experienced many vicissitudes and faced serious financial problems during his last years.

Both men attended Oxford, where Addison took his degree, won a fellowship, and earned a reputation for Latin verse; the less scholarly Steele, however, had only moderate academic success and did not stay for a degree, but left the University to take a commission in the army. For a while he cut a dashing figure in London, even, to his horror, seriously wounding a man in a duel. Both men enjoyed the patronage of the great Whig magnates, and except during the last four years of Queen Anne's reign, when the Tories were in the ascendency, they were generously treated. Steele became editor of the *London Gazette*, an official newspaper that appeared twice a week during the greater part of his editorship, listing government appointments and reporting domestic and foreign news—in short, the first newspaper in the modern sense, for it was very much unlike the news pamphlets or the news letters, written by hand and sent out to subscribers, that one finds in the previous century. Much later, Steele became manager of the Theatre Royal, Drury Lane. Meanwhile he had served in Parliament and been knighted by George I. Addison held more important positions: he was secretary to the Lord Lieutenant of Ireland, and later an Under-Secretary of State; finally, toward the end of his life, he became Secretary of State. Both men wrote plays: Addison's *Cato*, a frigid and very "correct" tragedy, had great success in 1713 because it was received by the town as a political play; and Steele's later plays at Drury Lane (*The Conscious Lovers*, 1722, for instance) were instrumental in establishing the popularity of sentimental comedy throughout the 18th century.

Steele's debts and Addison's loss of office in 1710 were the efficient causes of their journalistic enterprises, through which they developed one of the most characteristic types of 18th-century literature, the periodical essay. Steele's experience as gazetteer had involved him in journalism, and in 1709, when in need of money, he launched the *Tatler* under the pseudonym Isaac Bickerstaff. He sought to attract the largest possible audience: the title was a bid for female readers, and the early fivefold division of each number into departments (dated from four appropriate coffeehouses and the editor's own apartment) dealing respectively with "gallantry, pleasure and entertainment," poetry, learning, news, and personal reflections gave the paper a wide appeal among men. The fifth department soon swallowed up the other four, as the lucubrations of Squire Bickerstaff won readers in coffeehouses and at breakfast tables. The paper appeared thrice weekly from April, 1709, to January, 1711. Steele wrote by far the greater number of *Tatlers*, but Addison contributed helpfully, as did other friends. The *Spectator*, which appeared daily except Sunday from March, 1711, to December, 1712 (and was briefly resumed by Addison in 1714), was the joint undertaking of the two friends, though it was dominated by Addison. The papers had many imitators in their own day and throughout the rest of the century; Johnson's *Rambler* and *Idler* and Goldsmith's brief *Bee* are distinguished instances.

The periodical essay as developed in these two papers admits of no strict definition. It is less formal and purely didactic than the essays of Bacon, less personal than those of Charles Lamb and William Hazlitt in the next century. It deals with the widest possible variety of topics: manners and morals, literature and philosophical ideas, types and characters, fads, fashions, foibles; and these it was necessary to treat lightly and in an agreeable manner. But one topic of the times was wisely avoided in both papers—politics.

Both Steele and Addison were conscious moralists and did not disguise their intention of improving the minds, morals, and manners of their readers. Moral reform had been in the air since the 1690's, and the new society that was coming into existence (and was certainly in some degree the creation of Addison and Steele) was attaining a balance between the morality and respectability of the old, rather Puritan middle class (which was too often narrowly Philistine in taste and outlook) and the wit, grace, and enlightenment of the older aristocratic and fashionable class (which, in the previous century, had too often been libertine in morals and thought). The new social ideal, which the two essayists themselves fostered, stressed moderation, reasonableness, self-control, urbanity, and good taste. Steele's *Tatler* essays on marriage and domestic life held up an ideal which would have provoked the wits of Charles's day to contemptuous laughter. He wrote on any topic that suggested itself as pleasing or useful: the theater, true breeding as against vulgar manners, education, simplicity in dress, the proper use of Sunday, and so on; and he lightly ridiculed common social types such as the prude, the coquette, the "pretty fellow," and the rake. Addison's best *Tatler* essays initiated his study of eccentric or affected characters (to be continued in the *Spectator*), cleverly observed and described with agreeable humor. These essays on social types were a development of the "characters" of the 17th century. The *Tatler* papers quickly won an appreciative audience, and when published in book form, they continued (like those of the *Spectator*) to sell throughout the century. Steele's style is informal, even careless, but for that very reason intimate and engaging. His generous, even sentimental, warmth imparts itself to his style and animates his subject when, as is most often the case, he writes from his heart. It was, he says, "a most exquisite pleasure * * * to trace human life through all its mazes and recesses, and to show much shorter methods than men ordinarily practice to be happy, agreeable, and great." Shortly after Steele discontinued the *Tatler*, John Gay in a pamphlet, *The Present State of Wit*, praised him for banishing or checking follies and persuading the town to virtue, religion, and learning. "In the dress he gives it [learning] 'tis a most welcome guest at tea tables and assemblies, and is relished and caressed by the merchants on the 'Change * * * "

The readers whom Steele had reached and influenced were at hand when the *Spectator* began to appear two months after the last *Tatler*. Steele played a more important role in the paper than Addison had in the *Tatler*, but the *Spectator* is throughout Addisonian. In the second number Steele introduces us to the members of Mr. Spectator's Club (male social life was dominated by clubs during the reign of Queen Anne), who prove to be a man about town, a student of law and literature, a churchman, a soldier, a Tory country squire, and, interestingly enough, a London merchant. These men suggest the readers (other than women) to whom the paper was primarily addressed. As a Whig, Steele was ardently sympathetic with the new moneyed class in the City, and it was evidently his intention to pit the merchant, Sir Andrew Freeport, the representative of the new order, against the Tory Sir Roger de Coverley, who is presented as belonging to a vanishing order. Addison, however, preferred to present Sir Roger in episodes set in town and in the country as an endearing, eccentric character, often absurd but always amiable and innocent. He is a prominent ancestor of a long line of similar characters in fiction during the next two centuries. The social criticism continued, with more wit and raillery than the *Tatler* had usually commanded. Addison's scholarly interests broadened the material to include the popularization of current philosophical notions about man and nature; and he wrote several important series of critical papers: among others, two recommending the ballad of *Chevy Chase* (old ballads had not yet come into fashion), a group distinguishing true and false wit, an extended series of Saturday essays evaluating *Paradise Lost*, and finally, an influential series on "the pleasures of the imagination" which treated the aesthetics of visual beauty in nature and art. Altogether, the *Spectator* fulfilled his ambition (see *Spectator* 10, below) to be considered a modern Socrates. Addison's contributions to the paper are the finest among the vast numbers of 18th-century periodical essays. If his tone is a little superior and his style a bit more fussy than we like today, his keen observation of the life around him, the graceful ease of his learning, his never cruel wit, and, despite the commonplaceness of most of his moral and philosophical reflections, his genuine if occasional originality made him the most agreeable, and consequently the most persuasive, instructor the age could have found.

The best description of Addison's prose is Dr. Johnson's in his *Life of Addison*: "His prose is the model of the middle style; on grave subjects not formal, on light occasions not groveling; pure without scrupulosity, and exact without apparent elaboration; always equable, and always easy, without glowing words or pointed sentences." And he concludes: "Whoever wishes to attain an English style, familiar but not coarse, and elegant but not ostentatious, must give his days and nights to the volumes of Addison," a course of study which a good many aspiring writers during the century seem to have undertaken with some success.

THE PERIODICAL ESSAY: MANNERS
STEELE: [The Gentleman; The Pretty Fellow]
From *The Tatler*, No. 21, Saturday, May 28, 1709

Quidquid agunt homines——
——nostri est farrago libelli.[1]
—JUVENAL, *Satire* I.85–86

White's Chocolate House,[2] May 26

A gentleman has writ to me out of the country a very civil letter, and said things which I suppress with great violence to my vanity.

1. "Whatever men do * * * shall form the motley subject of my book." Steele used this epigraph for all but a very few of the first 62 *Tatlers*.
2. One of the fashionable chocolate houses, from which Steele, in the earlier numbers of the *Tatler*, dated "accounts of gallantry, pleasure, and entertainment."

There are many terms in my narratives which he complains want explaining, and has therefore desired that, for the benefit of my country readers, I would let him know what I mean by a Gentleman, a Pretty Fellow, a Toast, a Coquette, a Critic, a Wit, and all other appellations of those now in the gayer world, who are in possession of these several characters; together with an account of those who unfortunately pretend to them. I shall begin with him we usually call a Gentleman, or man of conversation.

It is generally thought that warmth of imagination, quick relish of pleasure, and a manner of becoming it, are the most essential qualities for forming this sort of man. But anyone that is much in company will observe that the height of good breeding is shown rather in never giving offense, than in doing obliging things. Thus, he that never shocks you, though he is seldom entertaining, is more likely to keep your favor than he who often entertains, and sometimes displeases you. The most necessary talent therefore in a man of conversation, which is what we ordinarily intend by a fine gentleman, is a good judgment. He that has this in perfection is master of his companion, without letting him see it; and has the same advantage over men of any other qualifications whatsoever, as one that can see would have over a blind man of ten times his strength.

This is what makes Sophronius the darling of all who converse with him, and the most powerful with his acquaintance of any man in town. By the light of this faculty, he acts with great ease and freedom among the men of pleasure, and acquits himself with skill and dispatch among the men of business. All which he performs with so much success that, with as much discretion in life as any man ever had, he neither is, nor appears, cunning. But as he does a good office, if he ever does it, with readiness and alacrity, so he denies what he does not care to engage in, in a manner that convinces you that you ought not to have asked it. His judgment is so good and unerring, and accompanied with so cheerful a spirit, that his conversation is a continual feast, at which he helps some, and is helped by others, in such a manner that the equality of society is perfectly kept up, and every man obliges as much as he is obliged: for it is the greatest and justest skill in a man of superior understanding, to know how to be on a level with his companions. This sweet disposition runs through all the actions of Sophronius, and makes his company desired by women, without being envied by men. Sophronius would be as just as he is, if there were no law; and would be as discreet as he is, if there were no such thing as calumny.

In imitation of this agreeable being, is made that animal we call a Pretty Fellow; who being just able to find out that what makes Sophronius acceptable is a natural behavior, in order to the same reputation, makes his own an artificial one. Jack Dimple is his perfect mimic, whereby he is of course the most unlike him of all men living. Sophronius just now passed into the inner room directly forward: Jack comes as fast after as he can for the right and left looking glass, in which he had but just approved himself by a nod at each, and marched on. He will meditate within for half an hour, till he thinks he is not careless enough in his air, and come back to the mirror to recollect his forgetfulness. * * *

STEELE: [Dueling]

From *The Tatler*, No. 25, Tuesday, June 7, 1709

Quidquid agunt homines——
——nostri est farrago libelli.
—JUVENAL, *Satire* I.85–86

White's Chocolate House, June 6

A letter from a young lady, written in the most passionate terms, wherein she laments the misfortune of a gentleman, her lover, who was lately wounded in a duel, has turned my thoughts to that subject, and inclined me to examine into the causes which precipitate men into so fatal a folly. And as it has been proposed to treat of subjects of gallantry in the article from hence, and no one point in nature is more proper to be considered by the company who frequent this place than that of duels, it is worth our consideration to examine into this chimerical groundless humor, and to lay every other thought aside, until we have stripped it of all its false pretenses to credit and reputation amongst men.

But I must confess, when I consider what I am going about, and run over in my imagination all the endless crowd of men of honor who will be offended at such a discourse, I am undertaking, methinks, a work worthy an invulnerable hero in romance, rather than a private gentleman with a single rapier; but as I am pretty well acquainted by great opportunities with the nature of man, and know of a truth that all men fight against their will, the danger vanishes, and resolution rises upon this subject. For this reason, I shall talk very freely on a custom which all men wish exploded, though no man has courage enough to resist it.

But there is one unintelligible word, which I fear will extremely perplex my dissertation, and I confess to you I find very hard to explain, which is the term "satisfaction." An honest country gentleman had the misfortune to fall into company with two or three modern men of honor, where he happened to be very ill treated; and one of the company, being conscious of his offense, sends a note to him in the morning, and tells him he was ready to give him satisfaction. "This is fine doing," says the plain fellow; "last night he sent me away cursedly out of humor, and this morning he fancies it would be a satisfaction to be run through the body."

As the matter at present stands, it is not to do handsome actions denominates a man of honor; it is enough if he dares to defend ill ones. Thus you often see a common sharper in competition with a gentleman of the first rank; though all mankind is convinced that a fighting gamester is only a pickpocket with the courage of an highwayman. One cannot with any patience reflect on the unaccountable jumble of persons and things in this town and nation, which occasions very frequently that a brave man falls by a hand below that of a common hangman, and yet his executioner escapes the clutches of the hangman for doing it. I shall therefore hereafter consider how the bravest men in other ages and nations have behaved themselves upon such incidents as we decide by combat; and show, from their practice, that this resentment neither has its foundation from true reason or solid fame; but is an imposture, made of cowardice, falsehood, and want of understanding. For this work, a good history of quarrels would be very edifying to the public, and I apply myself to the town for particulars and circumstances within their knowledge, which may serve to embellish the dissertation with proper cuts.[1] Most of the quarrels I have ever known have proceeded from some valiant coxcomb's persisting in the wrong, to defend some prevailing folly, and preserve himself from the ingenuity[2] of owning a mistake.

By this means it is called "giving a man satisfaction" to urge your offense against him with your sword; which puts me in mind of Peter's order to the keeper, in *The Tale of a Tub*:[3] "If you neglect to do all this, damn you and your generation forever: and so we bid you heartily farewell." If the contradiction in the very terms of one of our challenges were as well explained and turned into downright English, would it not run after this manner?

"SIR,

"Your extraordinary behavior last night, and the liberty you were pleased to take with me, makes me this morning give you this, to tell you, because you are an ill-bred puppy, I will meet you in Hyde Park an hour hence; and because you want both breeding and humanity, I desire you would come with a pistol in your hand, on horseback, and endeavor to shoot me through the head to teach you more manners. If you fail of doing me this pleasure, I shall say you are a rascal, on every post in town: and so, sir, if you will not injure me more, I shall never forgive what you have done already. Pray, sir, do not fail of getting everything ready; and you will infinitely oblige, sir, your most obedient humble servant, etc." * * *

1. Either woodcuts or engravings on copper plates.
2. Honorable candor.
3. In Swift's satire, the Roman Church is attacked in the character of Peter. The passage (slightly misquoted) satirizes the Pope's practice of issuing indulgences.

STEELE: [The Spectator's Club]

The Spectator, No. 2, Friday, March 2, 1711

———*Haec alii sex*
Vel plures uno conclamant ore.[1]
—JUVENAL, *Satire* VII.166–67

The first of our society is a gentleman of Worcestershire, of ancient descent, a baronet, his name Sir Roger de Coverley. His great-grandfather was inventor of that famous country-dance which is called after him. All who know that shire are very well acquainted with the parts and merits of Sir Roger. He is a gentleman that is very singular in his behavior, but his singularities proceed from his good sense, and are contradictions to the manners of the world only as he thinks the world is in the wrong. However, this humor creates him no enemies, for he does nothing with sourness or obstinacy; and his being unconfined to modes and forms makes him but the readier and more capable to please and oblige all who know him. When he is in town, he lives in Soho Square. It is said he keeps himself a bachelor by reason he was crossed in love by a perverse, beautiful widow of the next county to him. Before this disappointment, Sir Roger was what you call a fine gentleman, had often supped with my Lord Rochester and Sir George Etherege, fought a duel upon his first coming to town, and kicked Bully Dawson in a public coffeehouse for calling him "youngster."[2] But being ill used by the above-mentioned widow, he was very serious for a year and a half; and though, his temper being naturally jovial, he at last got over it, he grew careless of himself, and never dressed afterward. He continues to wear a coat and doublet of the same cut that were in fashion at the time of his repulse, which, in his merry humors, he tells us, has been in and out twelve times since he first wore it. 'Tis said Sir Roger grew humble in his desires after he had forgot this cruel beauty, insomuch that it is reported he has frequently offended in point of chastity with beggars and gypsies; but this is looked upon by his friends rather as matter of raillery than truth. He is now in his fifty-sixth year, cheerful, gay, and hearty; keeps a good house both in town and country; a great lover of mankind; but there is such a mirthful cast in his behavior that he is rather beloved than esteemed. His tenants grow rich, his servants look satisfied, all the young women profess love to him, and the young men are glad of his company; when he comes into a house he calls the servants by their names, and talks all the way upstairs to a visit. I must not omit that Sir Roger is a justice of the quorum;[3] that he fills the chair at a quarter-session with great abil-

1. "Six more at least join their consenting voice."
2. John Wilmot, Earl of Rochester (1647–80), the poet and rake, an intimate of Charles II; Sir George Etherege (ca. 1634–91), playwright, rake, and boon companion of the king and Rochester. Bully Dawson was a notorious sharper of the period.
3. A county justice of the peace, presiding over quarterly sessions of the court.

ities; and, three months ago, gained universal applause by explaining a passage in the Game Act.

The gentleman next in esteem and authority among us is another bachelor, who is a member of the Inner Temple;[4] a man of great probity, wit, and understanding; but he has chosen his place of residence rather to obey the direction of an old humorsome[5] father, than in pursuit of his own inclinations. He was placed there to study the laws of the land, and is the most learned of any of the house in those of the stage. Aristotle and Longinus are much better understood by him than Littleton or Coke.[6] The father sends up, every post, questions relating to marriage articles, leases, and tenures, in the neighborhood; all which questions he agrees with an attorney to answer and take care of in the lump. He is studying the passions themselves, when he should be inquiring into the debates among men which arise from them. He knows the argument of each of the orations of Demosthenes and Tully,[7] but not one case in the reports of our own courts. No one ever took him for a fool, but none, except his intimate friends, know he has a great deal of wit. This turn makes him at once both disinterested and agreeable; as few of his thoughts are drawn from business, they are most of them fit for conversation. His taste of books is a little too just[8] for the age he lives in; he has read all, but approves of very few. His familiarity with the customs, manners, actions, and writings of the ancients makes him a very delicate observer of what occurs to him in the present world. He is an excellent critic, and the time of the play is his hour of business; exactly at five he passes through New Inn, crosses through Russell Court, and takes a turn at Will's[9] till the play begins; he has his shoes rubbed and his periwig powdered at the barber's as you go into the Rose.[1] It is for the good of the audience when he is at a play, for the actors have an ambition to please him.

The person of next consideration is Sir Andrew Freeport, a merchant of great eminence in the city of London, a person of indefatigable industry, strong reason, and great experience. His notions of trade are noble and generous, and (as every rich man has usually some sly way of jesting which would make no great figure were he not a rich man) he calls the sea the British Common. He is acquainted with commerce in all its parts, and will tell you that it

4. One of the Inns of Court, where lawyers resided or had their offices and where students studied law.
5. Full of crotchets.
6. In other words, he is more familiar with the laws of literature than those of England. The *Poetics* of Aristotle and the Greek treatise *On the Sublime* (reputedly by Longinus) were in high favor among the critics of the time. Sir Thomas Littleton, 15th-century jurist, was author of a renowned treatise on *Tenures;* Sir Edward Coke (1552–

1634) was the judge and writer whose *Reports* and *Institutes of the Laws of England* (known as *Coke upon Littleton*) have exerted a great influence on the interpretation of English law.
7. Marcus Tullius Cicero.
8. Exact.
9. The coffeehouse in Covent Garden associated with literature and criticism since Dryden had begun to frequent it in the 1660's.
1. A tavern near Drury Lane.

is a stupid and barbarous way to extend dominion by arms; for true power is to be got by arts and industry. He will often argue that if this part of our trade were well cultivated, we should gain from one nation; and if another, from another. I have heard him prove that diligence makes more lasting acquisitions than valor, and that sloth has ruined more nations than the sword. He abounds in several frugal maxims, among which the greatest favorite is, "A penny saved is a penny got." A general trader of good sense is pleasanter company than a general scholar; and Sir Andrew having a natural unaffected eloquence, the perspicuity of his discourse gives the same pleasure that wit would in another man. He has made his fortunes himself, and says that England may be richer than other kingdoms by as plain methods as he himself is richer than other men; though at the same time I can say this of him, that there is not a point in the compass but blows home a ship in which he is an owner.

Next to Sir Andrew in the clubroom sits Captain Sentry, a gentleman of great courage, good understanding, but invincible modesty. He is one of those that deserve very well, but are very awkward at putting their talents within the observation of such as should take notice of them. He was some years a captain, and behaved himself with great gallantry in several engagements and at several sieges; but having a small estate of his own, and being next heir to Sir Roger, he has quitted a way of life in which no man can rise suitably to his merit who is not something of a courtier as well as a soldier. I have heard him often lament that in a profession where merit is placed in so conspicuous a view, impudence should get the better of modesty. When he has talked to this purpose I never heard him make a sour expression, but frankly confess that he left the world because he was not fit for it. A strict honesty and an even, regular behavior are in themselves obstacles to him that must press through crowds who endeavor at the same end with himself —the favor of a commander. He will, however, in his way of talk, excuse generals for not disposing according to men's desert, or inquiring into it, "for," says he, "that great man who has a mind to help me, has as many to break through to come at me as I have to come at him"; therefore he will conclude that the man who would make a figure, especially in a military way, must get over all false modesty, and assist his patron against the importunity of other pretenders by a proper assurance in his own vindication. He says it is a civil cowardice to be backward in asserting[2] what you ought to expect, as it is a military fear to be slow in attacking when it is your duty. With this candor does the gentleman speak of himself and others. The same frankness runs through all his conversation. The military part of his life has furnished him with many adventures, in the relation of which he is very agreeable to the company; for he is never overbearing, though accustomed to command men

2. Claiming.

in the utmost degree below him; nor ever too obsequious from an habit of obeying men highly above him.

But that our society may not appear a set of humorists[3] unacquainted with the gallantries and pleasures of the age, we have among us the gallant Will Honeycomb, a gentleman who, according to his years, should be in the decline of his life, but having ever been very careful of his person, and always had a very easy fortune, time has made but very little impression either by wrinkles on his forehead or traces in his brain. His person is well turned and of a good height. He is very ready at that sort of discourse with which men usually entertain women. He has all his life dressed very well, and remembers habits[4] as others do men. He can smile when one speaks to him, and laughs easily. He knows the history of every mode, and can inform you from which of the French king's wenches our wives and daughters had this manner of curling their hair, that way of placing their hoods; whose frailty was covered by such a sort of petticoat, and whose vanity to show her foot made that part of the dress so short in such a year. In a word, all his conversation and knowledge has been in the female world. As other men of his age will take notice to you what such a minister said upon such and such an occasion, he will tell you when the Duke of Monmouth[5] danced at court such a woman was then smitten, another was taken with him at the head of his troop in the Park. In all these important relations, he has ever about the same time received a kind glance or a blow of a fan from some celebrated beauty, mother of the present Lord Such-a-one. If you speak of a young commoner that said a lively thing in the House, he starts up: "He has good blood in his veins; Tom Mirabell begot him. The rogue cheated me in that affair; that young fellow's mother used me more like a dog than any woman I ever made advances to." This way of talking of his very much enlivens the conversation among us of a more sedate turn; and I find there is not one of the company but myself, who rarely speak at all, but speaks of him as of that sort of man who is usually called a well-bred, fine gentleman. To conclude his character, where women are not concerned he is an honest, worthy man.

I cannot tell whether I am to account him whom I am next to speak of as one of our company, for he visits us but seldom; but when he does, it adds to every man else a new enjoyment of himself. He is a clergyman, a very philosophic man, of general learning, great sanctity of life, and the most exact good breeding. He has the misfortune to be of a very weak constitution, and consequently cannot accept of such cares and business as preferments in his function would oblige him to; he is therefore among divines what a chamber-counselor is among lawyers. The probity of his mind and the integrity of his life create him followers, as being eloquent or

3. Eccentrics.
4. Clothes.
5. The illegitimate son of Charles II, the ill-fated Absalom of Dryden's *Absalom and Achitophel.*

loud advances others. He seldom introduces the subject he speaks upon; but we are so far gone in years that he observes, when he is among us, an earnestness to have him fall on some divine topic, which he always treats with much authority, as one who has no interest in this world, as one who is hastening to the object of all his wishes and conceives hope from his decays and infirmities. These are my ordinary companions.

ADDISON: [Party Patches]

The Spectator, No. 81, Saturday, June 2, 1711

Qualis ubi audio venantum murmure tigris
Horruit in maculas [1]——
—STATIUS, *Thebaid* II.128

About the middle of last winter I went to see an opera at the theater in the Haymarket, where I could not but take notice of two parties of very fine women that had placed themselves in the opposite side boxes, and seemed drawn up in a kind of battle array one against another. After a short survey of them, I found they were *patched* differently; the faces, on one hand, being spotted on the right side of the forehead, and those upon the other on the left. I quickly perceived that they cast hostile glances upon one another; and that their patches were placed in those different situations as party signals to distinguish friends from foes. In the middle boxes, between these two opposite bodies, were several ladies who patched indifferently on both sides of their faces, and seemed to sit there with no other intention but to see the opera. Upon inquiry I found, that the body of Amazons on my right hand were Whigs; and those on my left, Tories; and that those who had placed themselves in the middle boxes were a neutral party, whose faces had not yet declared themselves. These last, however, as I afterwards found, diminished daily, and took their party with one side or the other; insomuch that I observed in several of them the patches, which were before dispersed equally, are now all gone over to the Whig or Tory side of the face. The censorious say that the men whose hearts are aimed at are very often the occasions that one part of the face is thus dishonored and lies under a kind of disgrace, while the other is so much set off and adorned by the owner; and that the patches turn to the right or to the left, according to the principles of the man who is most in favor. But whatever may be the motives of a few fantastical coquettes, who do not patch for the public good, so much as for their own private advantage, it is certain that there are several women of honor who patch out of principle, and with an eye to the interest of their country. Nay, I am informed that some of them adhere so steadfastly to their party, and are so far from sacrificing their zeal for the public to their

1. Cowley's translation of these lines is quoted in the body of the essay.

passion for any particular person, that in a late draft of marriage articles a lady has stipulated with her husband that, whatever his opinions are, she shall be at liberty to patch on which side she pleases.

I must here take notice, that Rosalinda, a famous Whig partisan, has most unfortunately a very beautiful mole on the Tory part of her forehead; which, being very conspicuous, has occasioned many mistakes, and given an handle to her enemies to misrepresent her face, as though it had revolted from the Whig interest. But whatever this natural patch may seem to intimate, it is well known that her notions of government are still the same. This unlucky mole, however, has misled several coxcombs; and, like the hanging out of false colors, made some of them converse with Rosalinda in what they though the spirit of her party, when on a sudden she has given them an unexpected fire, that has sunk them all at once. If Rosalinda is unfortunate in her mole, Nigranilla is as unhappy in a pimple, which forces her, against her inclinations, to patch on the Whig side.

I am told that many virtuous matrons, who formerly have been taught to believe that this artificial spotting of the face was unlawful, are now reconciled by a zeal for their cause, to what they could not be prompted by a concern for their beauty. This way of declaring war upon one another puts me in mind of what is reported of the tigress, that several spots rise in her skin when she is angry; or as Mr. Cowley has imitated the verses that stand as the motto of this paper,

> ——She swells with angry pride,
> And calls forth all her spots on every side.

When I was in the theater the time above-mentioned, I had the curiosity to count the patches on both sides, and found the Tory patches to be about twenty stronger than the Whig; but to make amends for this small inequality, I the next morning found the whole puppet show filled with faces spotted after the Whiggish manner. Whether or no the ladies had retreated hither in order to rally their forces I cannot tell; but the next night they came in so great a body to the opera that they outnumbered the enemy.

This account of party patches will, I am afraid, appear improbable to those who live at a distance from the fashionable world; but as it is a distinction of a very singular nature, and what perhaps may never meet with a parallel, I think I should not have discharged the office of a faithful Spectator had I not recorded it.

I have, in former papers, endeavored to expose this party rage in women, as it only serves to aggravate the hatreds and animosities that reign among men, and in a great measure deprives the fair sex of those peculiar charms with which nature has endowed them.

When the Romans and Sabines were at war, and just upon the point of giving battle, the women, who were allied to both of them,[2] interposed with so many tears and entreaties that they prevented the mutual slaughter which threatened both parties, and united them together in a firm and lasting peace.

I would recommend this noble example to our British ladies, at a time when their country is torn with so many unnatural divisions that if they continue it will be a misfortune to be born in it. The Greeks thought it so improper for women to interest themselves in competitions and contentions that for this reason, among others, they forbade them, under pain of death, to be present at the Olympic games, notwithstanding these were the public diversions of all Greece.

As our English women excel those of all nations in beauty, they should endeavor to outshine them in all other accomplishments proper to the sex, and to distinguish themselves as tender mothers and faithful wives, rather than as furious partisans. Female virtues are of a domestic turn. The family is the proper province for private women to shine in. If they must be showing their zeal for the public, let it not be against those who are perhaps of the same family, or at least of the same religion or nation, but against those who are the open, professed, undoubted enemies of their faith, liberty, and country. When the Romans were pressed with a foreign enemy, the ladies voluntarily contributed all their rings and jewels to assist the government under a public exigence; which appeared so laudable an action in the eyes of their countrymen, that from thenceforth it was permitted by a law to pronounce public orations at the funeral of a woman in praise of the deceased person, which till that time was peculiar to men. Would our English ladies, instead of sticking on a patch against those of their own country, show themselves so truly public-spirited as to sacrifice every one her necklace against the common enemy, what decrees ought not to be made in favor of them?

Since I am recollecting upon this subject such passages as occur to my memory out of ancient authors, I cannot omit a sentence in the celebrated funeral oration of Pericles, which he made in honor of those brave Athenians that were slain in a fight with the Lacedemonians.[3] After having addressed himself to the several ranks and orders of his countrymen, and shown them how they should behave themselves in the public cause, he turns to the female part of his audience: "And as for you," says he, "I shall advise you in very few words. Aspire only to those virtues that are peculiar to your sex; follow your natural modesty, and think it your greatest commendation not to be talked of one way or other."

2. The Romans had provided themselves with wives by treacherously seizing a number of Sabine women, who were consequently allied by blood to the one side and by marriage to the other.
3. Spartans.

ADDISON: [Sir Roger at Church]

The Spectator, No. 112, Monday, July 9, 1711

'Αθανάτους μὲν πρῶτα θεοὺς, νόμῳ ὡς διάκειται,
Τίμα.[1]

—PYTHAGORAS

I am always very well pleased with a country Sunday, and think, if keeping holy the seventh day were only a human institution, it would be the best method that could have been thought of for the polishing and civilizing of mankind. It is certain the country people would soon degenerate into a kind of savages and barbarians were there not such frequent returns of a stated time, in which the whole village meet together with their best faces, and in their cleanliest habits, to converse with one another upon indifferent subjects, hear their duties explained to them, and join together in adoration of the Supreme Being. Sunday clears away the rust of the whole week, not only as it refreshes in their minds the notions of religion, but as it puts both the sexes upon appearing in their most agreeable forms, and exerting all such qualities are apt to give them a figure in the eye of the village. A country fellow distinguishes himself as much in the churchyard as a citizen[2] does upon the 'Change, the whole parish politics being generally discussed in that place either after sermon or before the bell rings.

My friend Sir Roger, being a good churchman, has beautified the inside of his church with several texts of his own choosing; he has likewise given a handsome pulpit cloth, and railed in the communion table at his own expense. He has often told me that, at his coming to his estate, he found his parishioners very irregular; and that, in order to make them kneel and join in the responses, he gave every one of them a hassock and a Common Prayer book, and at the same time employed an itinerant singing master, who goes about the country for that purpose, to instruct them rightly in the tunes of the Psalms; upon which they now very much value themselves, and indeed outdo most of the country churches that I have ever heard.

As Sir Roger is landlord to the whole congregation, he keeps them in very good order, and will suffer nobody to sleep in it besides himself; for if by chance he has been surprised into a short nap at sermon, upon recovering out of it he stands up and looks about him, and if he sees anybody else nodding, either wakes them himself, or sends his servant to them. Several other of the old

1. "First worship the immortal gods as custom decrees." The first of the so-called Golden Verses of Pythagoras.
2. A citizen of the City of London, hence commonly a merchant. The " 'Change" is the Exchange in London, where merchants met to transact business.

knight's particularities break out upon these occasions; sometimes he will be lengthening out a verse in the Singing-Psalms half a minute after the rest of the congregation have done with it; sometimes, when he is pleased with the matter of his devotion, he pronounces "Amen" three or four times to the same prayer; and sometimes stands up when everybody else is upon their knees, to count the congregation, or see if any of his tenants are missing.

I was yesterday very much surprised to hear my old friend, in the midst of the service, calling out to one John Matthews to mind what he was about, and not disturb the congregation. This John Matthews, it seems, is remarkable for being an idle fellow, and at that time was kicking his heels for his diversion. This authority of the knight, though exerted in that odd manner which accompanies him in all circumstances of life, has a very good effect upon the parish, who are not polite[3] enough to see anything ridiculous in his behavior; besides that the general good sense and worthiness of his character makes his friends observe these little singularities as foils that rather set off than blemish his good qualities.

As soon as the sermon is finished, nobody presumes to stir till Sir Roger is gone out of the church. The knight walks down from his seat in the chancel between a double row of his tenants, that stand bowing to him on each side, and every now and then inquires how such an one's wife, or mother, or son, or father do, whom he does not see at church—which is understood as a secret reprimand to the person that is absent.

The chaplain has often told me that upon a catechizing day, when Sir Roger has been pleased with a boy that answers well, he has ordered a Bible to be given him next day for his encouragement, and sometimes accompanies it with a flitch of bacon to his mother. Sir Roger has likewise added five pounds a year to the clerk's place; and, that he may encourage the young fellows to make themselves perfect in the church service, has promised, upon the death of the present incumbent, who is very old, to bestow it according to merit.

The fair understanding between Sir Roger and his chaplain, and their mutual concurrence in doing good, is the more remarkable because the very next village is famous for the differences and contentions that rise between the parson and the squire, who live in a perpetual state of war. The parson is always preaching at the squire, and the squire, to be revenged on the parson, never comes to church. The squire has made all his tenants atheists and tithe-stealers;[4] while the parson instructs them every Sunday in the dignity of his order, and insinuates to them almost in every sermon that he is a better man than his patron. In short, matters are come to such an extremity that the squire has not said his prayers either in pub-

3. Refined.
4. Farmers who cheat the parson to whom they are bound to pay annual tithes (i.e., a tenth of the produce of their farms).

lic or private this half year; and that the parson threatens him, if
he does not mend his manners, to pray for him in the face of the
whole congregation.

Feuds of this nature, though too frequent in the country, are
very fatal to the ordinary people, who are so used to be dazzled
with riches that they pay as much deference to the understanding
of a man of an estate as of a man of learning; and are very hardly
brought to regard any truth, how important soever it may be, that
is preached to them, when they know there are several men of five
hundred a year who do not believe it.

ADDISON: [Sir Roger at the Assizes[1]]

The Spectator, No. 122, Friday, July 20, 1711

Comes jucundus in via pro vehiculo est.[2]
—PUBLILIUS SYRUS, *Fragments*

A man's first care should be to avoid the reproaches of his own
heart; his next, to escape the censures of the world. If the last interferes with the former, it ought to be entirely neglected; but otherwise there cannot be a greater satisfaction to an honest mind than
to see those approbations which it gives itself seconded by the ap-
plauses of the public. A man is more sure of his conduct when the
verdict which he passes upon his own behavior is thus warranted
and confirmed by the opinion of all that know him.

My worthy friend Sir Roger is one of those who is not only at
peace within himself but beloved and esteemed by all about him.
He receives a suitable tribute for his universal benevolence to mankind in the returns of affection and good will which are paid him
by everyone that lives within his neighborhood. I lately met with
two or three odd instances of that general respect which is shown
to the good old knight. He would needs carry Will Wimble[3] and
myself with him to the county assizes. As we were upon the road,
Will Wimble joined a couple of plain men who rid before us, and
conversed with them for some time, during which my friend Sir
Roger acquainted me with their characters.

"The first of them," says he, "that has a spaniel by his side, is
a yeoman[4] of about an hundred pounds a year, an honest man.
He is just within the Game Act,[5] and qualified to kill an hare or

1. Periodic sessions of superior courts
held by visiting judges throughout England.
2. "An agreeable companion upon the
road is as good as a coach." Addison
substituted *jucundus* for the original's
jacundus ("eloquent").
3. A character used by Addison to
illustrate the injury done to younger
sons of gentlemen by not educating them
for a profession or to trade.
4. A man who owns and cultivates a
small estate. His rank is just below that
of gentleman.
5. This law restricted the right to kill
game to owners of land whose annual
income was £100 or more.

a pheasant. He knocks down a dinner with his gun twice or thrice a week; and by that means lives much cheaper than those who have not so good an estate as himself. He would be a good neighbor if he did not destroy so many partridges; in short he is a very sensible man, shoots flying,[6] and has been several times foreman of the petty jury.[7]

"The other that rides along with him is Tom Touchy, a fellow famous for taking the law of everybody. There is not one in the town where he lives that he has not sued at a quarter sessions. The rogue had once the impudence to go to law with the widow.[8] His head is full of costs, damages, and ejectments; he plagued a couple of honest gentlemen so long for a trespass in breaking one of his hedges, till he was forced to sell the ground it enclosed to defray the charges of the prosecution. His father left him fourscore pounds a year, but he has cast[9] and been cast so often that he is not now worth thirty. I suppose he is going upon the old business of the willow tree."

As Sir Roger was giving me this account of Tom Touchy, Will Wimble and his two companions stopped short till we came up to them. After having paid their respects to Sir Roger, Will told him that Mr. Touchy and he must appeal to him upon a dispute that arose between them. Will, it seems, had been giving his fellow travelers an account of his angling one day in such a hole; when Tom Touchy, instead of hearing out his story, told him that Mr. Such-an-one, if he pleased, might take the law of him for fishing in that part of the river. My friend Sir Roger heard them both, upon a round trot;[1] and after having paused some time, told them, with an air of a man who would not give his judgment rashly, "that much might be said on both sides." They were neither of them dissatisfied with the knight's determination, because neither of them found himself in the wrong by it. Upon which we made the best of our way to the assizes.

The court was sat before Sir Roger came; but notwithstanding all the justices had taken their places upon the bench, they made room for the old knight at the head of them; who, for his reputation in the country, took occasion to whisper in the judge's ear that he was glad his lordship had met with so much good weather in his circuit. I was listening to the proceedings of the court with much attention, and infinitely pleased with that great appearance and solemnity which so properly accompanies such a public administration of our laws, when, after about an hour's sitting, I observed to my great surprise, in the midst of a trial, that my friend Sir Roger

---

6. A true sportsman, he shoots birds only when they are on the wing.
7. The trial jury of twelve in an ordinary civil or criminal case.
8. The woman whom Sir Roger had loved in his youth. She is frequently mentioned in essays that deal with the old knight.
9. Defeated in a lawsuit.
1. While trotting briskly.

was getting up to speak. I was in some pain for him, till I found
he had acquitted himself of two or three sentences, with a look of
much business and great intrepidity.

Upon his first rising the court was hushed, and a general whisper
ran among the country people that Sir Roger was up. The speech
he made was so little to the purpose that I shall not trouble my
readers with an account of it; and I believe was not so much designed by the knight himself to inform the court, as to give him
a figure in my eye, and keep up his credit in the country.

I was highly delighted, when the court rose, to see the gentlemen
of the country gathering about my old friend, and striving who
should compliment him most; at the same time that the ordinary
people gazed upon him at a distance, not a little admiring his courage that was not afraid to speak to the judge.

In our return home we met with a very odd accident which I
cannot forbear relating, because it shows how desirous all who know
Sir Roger are of giving him marks of their esteem. When we were
arrived upon the verge of his estate, we stopped at a little inn to
rest ourselves and our horses. The man of the house had, it seems,
been formerly a servant in the knight's family; and to do honor to
his old master, had some time since, unknown to Sir Roger, put
him up in a signpost before the door; so that the knight's head had
hung out upon the road about a week before he himself knew anything of the matter. As soon as Sir Roger was acquainted with it,
finding that his servant's indiscretion proceeded wholly from affection and good will, he only told him that he had made him too
high a compliment; and when the fellow seemed to think that
could hardly be, added, with a more decisive look, that it was too
great an honor for any man under a duke; but told him at the same
time that it might be altered with a very few touches, and that he
himself would be at the charge of it. Accordingly they got a painter,
by the knight's directions, to add a pair of whiskers to the face,
and by a little aggravation of the features to change it into the
Saracen's Head. I should not have known this story had not the
innkeeper, upon Sir Roger's alighting, told him in my hearing that
his honor's head was brought back last night with the alterations
that he had ordered to be made in it. Upon this my friend, with
his usual cheerfulness, related the particulars above-mentioned, and
ordered the head to be brought into the room. I could not forbear
discovering greater expressions of mirth than ordinary upon the
appearance of this monstrous face, under which, notwithstanding
it was made to frown and stare in a most extraordinary manner, I
could still discover a distant resemblance of my old friend. Sir
Roger, upon seeing me laugh, desired me to tell him truly if I
thought it possible for people to know him in that disguise. I at
first kept my usual silence; but upon the knight's conjuring me to

tell him whether it was not still more like himself than a Saracen, I composed my countenance in the best manner I could, and replied that much might be said on both sides.

These several adventures, with the knight's behavior in them, gave me as pleasant a day as ever I met with in any of my travels.

The Periodical Essay: Ideas
Addison: [The Aims of the Spectator]
The Spectator, No. 10, Monday, March 12, 1711

Non aliter quam qui adverso vix flumine lembum
Remigiis subigit, si bracchia forte remisit,
Atque illum in præceps prono rapit alveus amni.[1]
—virgil, *Georgics* I.201–3

It is with much satisfaction that I hear this great city inquiring day by day after these my papers, and receiving my morning lectures with a becoming seriousness and attention. My publisher tells me that there are already three thousand of them distributed every day. So that if I allow twenty readers to every paper, which I look upon as a modest computation, I may reckon about three-score thousand disciples in London and Westminster, who I hope will take care to distinguish themselves from the thoughtless herd of their ignorant and unattentive brethren. Since I have raised to myself so great an audience, I shall spare no pains to make their instruction agreeable, and their diversion useful. For which reasons I shall endeavor to enliven morality with wit, and to temper wit with morality, that my readers may, if possible, both ways find their account in the speculation of the day. And to the end that their virtue and discretion may not be short, transient, intermitting starts of thought, I have resolved to refresh their memories from day to day, till I have recovered them out of that desperate state of vice and folly into which the age is fallen. The mind that lies fallow but a single day sprouts up in follies that are only to be killed by a constant and assiduous culture. It was said of Socrates that he brought philosophy down from heaven, to inhabit among men; and I shall be ambitious to have it said of me that I have brought philosophy out of closets and libraries, schools and colleges, to dwell in clubs and assemblies, at tea tables and in coffeehouses.

I would therefore in a very particular manner recommend these my speculations to all well-regulated families that set apart an hour in every morning for tea and bread and butter; and would earnestly advise them for their good to order this paper to be punctually

1. "Like him whose oars can hardly force his boat against the current, if by chance he relaxes his arms, the boat sweeps him headlong down the steam."

served up, and to be looked upon as a part of the tea equipage.

Sir Francis Bacon observes that a well-written book, compared with its rivals and antagonists, is like Moses' serpent, that immediately swallowed up and devoured those of the Egyptians.[2] I shall not be so vain as to think that where *The Spectator* appears the other public prints will vanish; but shall leave it to my reader's consideration whether is it not much better to be let into the knowledge of one's self, than to hear what passes in Muscovy or Poland; and to amuse ourselves with such writings as tend to the wearing out of ignorance, passion, and prejudice, than such as naturally conduce to inflame hatreds, and make enmities irreconcilable?

In the next place, I would recommend this paper to the daily perusal of those gentlemen whom I cannot but consider as my good brothers and allies, I mean the fraternity of spectators, who live in the world without having anything to do in it; and either by the affluence of their fortunes or laziness of their dispositions have no other business with the rest of mankind but to look upon them. Under this class of men are comprehended all contemplative tradesmen, titular physicians, fellows of the Royal Society, Templars[3] that are not given to be contentious, and statesmen that are out of business; in short, everyone that considers the world as a theater, and desires to form a right judgment of those who are the actors on it.

There is another set of men that I must likewise lay a claim to, whom I have lately called the blanks of society, as being altogether unfurnished with ideas, till the business and conversation of the day has supplied them. I have often considered these poor souls with an eye of great commiseration, when I have heard them asking the first man they have met with, whether there was any news stirring? and by that means gathering together materials for thinking. These needy persons do not know what to talk of till about twelve o'clock in the morning; for by that time they are pretty good judges of the weather, know which way the wind sits, and whether the Dutch mail be come in.[4] As they lie at the mercy of the first man they meet, and are grave or impertinent all the day long, according to the notions which they have imbibed in the morning, I would earnestly entreat them not to stir out of their chambers till they have read this paper, and do promise them that I will daily instil into them such sound and wholesome sentiments as shall have a good effect on their conversation for the ensuing twelve hours.

But there are none to whom this paper will be more useful than

2. In *The Advancement of Learning*, II, "To the King." But it was the rod of Aaron, not of Moses, that turned into a devouring serpent (Exodus vii. 10-12).

3. Lawyers or students of the law who live or have their offices ("chambers") in the Middle or Inner Temple, one of the Inns of Court.

4. Bringing the latest war news.

to the female world. I have often thought there has not been sufficient pains taken in finding out proper employments and diversions for the fair ones. Their amusements seem contrived for them,
rather as they are women, than as they are reasonable creatures;
and are more adapted to the sex than to the species. The toilet is
their great scene of business, and the right adjusting of their hair
the principal employment of their lives. The sorting of a suit of
ribbons[5] is reckoned a very good morning's work; and if they make
an excursion to a mercer's[6] or a toyshop, so great a fatigue makes
them unfit for anything else all the day after. Their more serious
occupations are sewing and embroidery, and their greatest drudgery
the preparation of jellies and sweetmeats. This, I say, is the state
of ordinary women; though I know there are multitudes of those
of a more elevated life and conversation, that move in an exalted
sphere of knowledge and virtue, that join all the beauties of the
mind to the ornaments of dress, and inspire a kind of awe and respect, as well as love, into their male beholders. I hope to increase
the number of these by publishing this daily paper, which I shall
always endeavor to make an innocent if not an improving entertainment, and by that means at least divert the minds of my female
readers from greater trifles. At the same time, as I would fain give
some finishing touches to those which are already the most beautiful pieces in human nature, I shall endeavor to point all those imperfections that are the blemishes, as well as those virtues which
are the embellishments, of the sex. In the meanwhile I hope these
my gentle readers, who have so much time on their hands, will
not grudge throwing away a quarter of an hour in a day on this
paper, since they may do it without any hindrance to business.

I know several of my friends and well-wishers are in great pain
for me, lest I should not be able to keep up the spirit of a paper
which I oblige myself to furnish every day: but to make them easy
in this particular, I will promise them faithfully to give it over as
soon as I grow dull. This I know will be matter of great raillery
to the small wits; who will frequently put me in mind of my promise, desire me to keep my word, assure me that it is high time to
give over, with many other little pleasantries of the like nature,
which men of a little smart genius cannot forbear throwing out
against their best friends, when they have such a handle given them
of being witty. But let them remember that I do hereby enter my
caveat against this piece of raillery.

5. A set of ribbons to be worn together.
6. A seller of such small-wares as tape, ribbon, fringe. A "toyshop" is a shop where baubles and trifles are sold.

ADDISON: [*Paradise Lost:* General Critical Remarks]

The Spectator, No. 267, Saturday, January 5, 1712

Cedite Romani scriptores, cedite Graii.[1]
—PROPERTIUS, *Elegies* II.xxxiv.65

There is nothing in nature so irksome as general discourses, especially when they turn chiefly upon words. For this reason I shall waive the discussion of that point which was started some years since, Whether Milton's *Paradise Lost* may be called an heroic poem? Those who will not give it that title may call it (if they please) a *divine poem.* It will be sufficient to its perfection, if it has in it all the beauties of the highest kind of poetry; and as for those who allege it is not an heroic poem, they advance no more to the diminution of it, than if they should say Adam is not Aeneas, nor Eve Helen.

I shall therefore examine it by the rules of epic poetry,[2] and see whether it falls short of the *Iliad* or *Aeneid,* in the beauties which are essential to that kind of writing. The first thing to be considered in an epic poem is the fable,[3] which is perfect or imperfect, according as the action which it relates is more or less so. This action should have three qualifications in it. First, it should be but one action. Secondly, it should be an entire action; and thirdly, it should be a great action. To consider the action of the *Iliad, Aeneid,* and *Paradise Lost,* in these three several lights. Homer to preserve the unity of his action hastens into the midst of things, as Horace has observed:[4] had he gone up to Leda's egg, or begun much later, even at the rape of Helen, or the investing of Troy, it is manifest that the story of the poem would have been a series of several actions. He therefore opens his poem with the discord of his princes, and with great art interweaves in the several succeeding parts of it, an account of everything material which relates to them and had passed before that fatal dissension. After the same manner Aeneas makes his first appearance in the Tyrrhene seas,[5] and within sight of Italy, because the action proposed to be celebrated was that of

1. "Yield place, ye Roman and ye Grecian writers, yield."
2. The rules for the conduct of an epic poem, derived out of the poems of Homer and Virgil, the *Poetics* of Aristotle, and the *Ars Poetica* of Horace, had been given their most systematic and complete statement in Père René Le Bossu's *Traité du poème épique* (1675), which was immediately absorbed into English critical thought. Addison writes of *Paradise Lost* with Le Bossu well in sight, but he is no slavish disciple.
3. The plot of a drama or poem.
4. *Ars Poetica,* 147–49. Helen, whose abduction from her husband Menelaus by the Trojan prince Paris brought on the Trojan War, was the daughter of Leda, who was visited by Zeus in the guise of a swan.
5. That part of the Mediterranean Sea west of Italy, bounded by the islands of Sicily, Sardinia, and Corsica.

his settling himself in Latium.[6] But because it was necessary for the reader to know what had happened to him in the taking of Troy, and in the preceding parts of his voyage, Virgil makes his hero relate it by way of episode[7] in the second and third books of the *Aeneid*. The contents of both which books come before those of the first book in the thread of the story, though for preserving of this unity of action, they follow them in the disposition of the poem. Milton, in imitation of these two great poets, opens his *Paradise Lost* with an infernal council plotting the fall of man, which is the action he proposed to celebrate; and as for those great action which preceded, in point of time, the battle of the angels, and the creation of the world (which would have entirely destroyed the unity of his principal action, had he related them in the same order that they happened), he cast them into the fifth, sixth, and seventh books, by way of episode to this noble poem.

Aristotle himself allows that Homer has nothing to boast of as to the unity of his fable, though at the same time that great critic and philosopher endeavors to palliate this imperfection in the Greek poet, by imputing it in some measure to the very nature of an epic poem. Some have been of opinion that the *Aeneid* labors also in this particular, and has episodes which may be looked upon as excrescences rather than as parts of the action. On the contrary, the poem which we have now under our consideration hath no other episodes than such as naturally arise from the subject, and yet is filled with such a multitude of astonishing incidents that it gives us at the same time a pleasure of the greatest variety, and of the greatest simplicity.

I must observe also that as Virgil, in the poem which was designed to celebrate the original of the Roman Empire, has described the birth of its great rival, the Carthaginian commonwealth, Milton with the like art in his poem on the Fall of Man, has related the fall of those angels who are his professed enemies. Besides the many other beauties in such an episode, its running parallel with the great action of the poem hinders it from breaking the unity so much as another episode would have done that had not so great an affinity with the principal subject. In short, this is the same kind of beauty which the critics admire in the *Spanish Friar, or The Double Discovery*,[8] where the two different plots look like counterparts and copies of one another.

The second qualification required in the action of an epic poem is, that it should be an *entire* action. An action is entire when it is complete in all its parts; or as Aristotle describes it, when it con-

---

6. The kingdom of the Latini, where Aeneas was hospitably received when he landed at the mouth of the Tiber. He married Lavinia, the daughter of King Latinus, and later ruled the kingdom.

7. An incidental narration or digression in an epic which arises naturally from the subject but is separable from the main action.
8. A comedy by Dryden.

sists of a beginning, a middle, and an end. Nothing should go before it, be intermixed with it, or follow after it, that is not related to it. As on the contrary, no single step should be omitted in that just and regular process which it must be supposed to take from its original to its consummation. Thus we see the anger of Achilles in its birth, its continuance, and effects; and Aeneas's settlement in Italy, carried on through all the oppositions in his way to it both by sea and land. The action in Milton excels (I think) both the former in this particular: we see it contrived in hell, executed upon earth, and punished by heaven. The parts of it are told in the most distinct manner, and grow out of one another in the most natural method.

The third qualification of an epic poem is its *greatness*. The anger of Achilles was of such consequence that it embroiled the kings of Greece, destroyed the heroes of Troy, and engaged all the gods in factions. Aeneas's settlement in Italy produced the Caesars, and gave birth to the Roman Empire. Milton's subject was still greater than either of the former; it does not determine the fate of single persons or nations, but of a whole species. The united powers of hell are joined together for the destruction of mankind, which they effected in part, and would have completed, had not Omnipotence itself interposed. The principal actors are man in his greatest perfection, and woman in her highest beauty. Their enemies are the fallen angels: the Messiah their friend, and the Almighty their protector. In short, everything that is great in the whole circle of being, whether within the verge of nature, or out of it, has a proper part assigned it in this noble poem.

In poetry, as in architecture, not only the whole, but the principal members, and every part of them, should be great. I will not presume to say, that the book of games in the *Aeneid*, or that in the *Iliad*, are not of this nature, nor to reprehend Virgil's simile of the top, and many other of the same nature in the *Iliad*, as liable to any censure in this particular; but I think we may say, without derogating from those wonderful performances, that there is an unquestionable magnificence in every part of *Paradise Lost*, and indeed a much greater than could have been formed upon any pagan system.

But Aristotle, by the greatness of the action, does not only mean that it should be great in its nature, but also in its duration, or in other words, that it should have a due length in it, as well as what we properly call greatness. The just measure of the kind of magnitude, he explains by the following similitude. An animal, no bigger than a mite, cannot appear perfect to the eye, because the sight takes it in at once, and has only a confused idea of the whole, and not a distinct idea of all its parts: if on the contrary you should suppose an animal of ten thousand furlongs in length, the eye would be so filled with a single part of it, that it could not give the mind an idea of the whole. What these animals are to the eye, a very short or a very long action would be to the memory. The first would be, as it were, lost and swallowed up by it, and the other difficult to be contained in it. Homer and Virgil have shown their principal art in this particular; the action of the *Iliad*, and that of the *Aeneid*, were in themselves exceeding short, but are so beautifully extended and diversified by the invention of episodes, and the machinery[9] of gods, with the like poetical ornaments, that they make up an agreeable story sufficient to employ the memory without overcharging it. Milton's action is enriched with such a variety of circumstances that I have taken as much pleasure in reading the contents of his books as in the best invented story I ever met with. It is possible that the traditions on which the *Iliad* and *Aeneid* were built had more circumstances in them than the history of the Fall of Man, as it is related in Scripture. Besides it was easier for Homer and Virgil to dash the truth with fiction, as they were in no danger of offending the religion of their country by it. But as for Milton, he had not only a very few circumstances upon which to raise his poem, but was also obliged to proceed with the greatest caution in everything that he added out of his own invention. And, indeed, notwithstanding all the restraints he was under, he has filled his story with so many surprising incidents, which bear so close an analogy with what is delivered in Holy Writ, that it is capable of pleasing the most delicate reader, without giving offense to the most scrupulous.

The modern critics have collected from several hints in the *Iliad* and *Aeneid* the space of time which is taken up by the action of each of those poems; but as a great part of Milton's story was transacted in regions that lie out of the reach of the sun and the sphere of day, it is impossible to gratify the reader with such a calculation, which indeed would be more curious than instructive; none of the critics, either ancient or modern, having laid down rules to circumscribe the action of an epic poem with any determined number of years, days, or hours.

This Piece of Criticism on Milton's Paradise Lost *shall be carried on in the following Saturdays' papers.*[1]

9. The technical term (from *deus ex machina*) in critical theory for the supernatural beings who oversee and intervene in the affairs of the characters in epic poems.

1. The series on *Paradise Lost* contains eighteen essays.

ADDISON: [On the Scale of Being]

The Spectator, No. 519, October 25, 1712

*inde hominum pecudumque genus, vitaeque volantum,
et quae marmoreo fert monstra sub aequore pontus.*[1]
—VIRGIL, *Aeneid* VI.728–29

Though there is a great deal of pleasure in contemplating the material world, by which I mean that system of bodies into which nature has so curiously wrought the mass of dead matter, with the several relations which those bodies bear to one another, there is still, methinks, something more wonderful and surprising in contemplations on the world of life, by which I mean all those animals with which every part of the universe is furnished. The material world is only the shell of the universe: the world of life are its inhabitants.

If we consider those parts of the material world which lie the nearest to us and are, therefore, subject to our observations and inquiries, it is amazing to consider the infinity of animals with which it is stocked. Every part of matter is peopled. Every green leaf swarms with inhabitants. There is scarce a single humor in the body of a man, or of any other animal, in which our glasses do not discover myriads of living creatures. The surface of animals is also covered with other animals which are, in the same manner, the basis of other animals that live upon it; nay, we find in the most solid bodies, as in marble itself, innumerable cells and cavities that are crowded with such imperceptible inhabitants as are too little for the naked eye to discover. On the other hand if we look into the more bulky parts of nature, we see the seas, lakes, and rivers teeming with numberless kinds of living creatures. We find every mountain and marsh, wilderness and wood, plentifully stocked with birds and beasts, and every part of matter affording proper necessaries and conveniences for the livelihood of multitudes which inhabit it.

The author of *The Plurality of Worlds*[2] draws a very good argument upon this consideration for the peopling of every planet, as indeed it seems very probable from the analogy of reason that, if no part of matter which we are acquainted with lies waste and useless, those great bodies, which are at such a distance from us, should not be desert and unpeopled, but rather that they should be furnished with beings adapted to their respective situations.

Existence is a blessing to those beings only which are endowed

1. "Thence the race of men and beasts, the life of flying creatures, and the monsters that ocean bears beneath her smooth surface."
2. Bernard de Fontenelle (1657–1757). This delightful book, a series of dialogues between a scientist and a countess concerning the possibility of other inhabited planets and the new astrophysics in general, was published in 1686 in France and beautifully translated by Joseph Glanvill in 1688.

with perception and is, in a manner, thrown away upon dead matter any further than as it is subservient to beings which are conscious of their existence. Accordingly we find from the bodies which lie under observation that matter is only made as the basis and support of animals and that there is no more of the one than what is necessary for the existence of the other.

Infinite Goodness is of so communicative a nature that it seems to delight in the conferring of existence upon every degree of perceptive being. As this is a speculation which I have often pursued with great pleasure to myself, I shall enlarge farther upon it, by considering that part of the scale of beings which comes within our knowledge.

There are some living creatures which are raised but just above dead matter. To mention only that species of shellfish, which are formed in the fashion of a cone, that grow to the surface of several rocks and immediately die upon their being severed from the place where they grow. There are many other creatures but one remove from these, which have no other sense besides that of feeling and taste. Others have still an additional one of hearing; others of smell, and others of sight. It is wonderful to observe by what a gradual progress the world of life advances through a prodigious variety of species before a creature is formed that is complete in all its senses; and, even among these, there is such a different degree of perfection in the sense which one animal enjoys, beyond what appears in another, that, though the sense in different animals be distinguished by the same common denomination, it seems almost of a different nature. If after this we look into the several inward perfections of cunning and sagacity, or what we generally call instinct, we find them rising after the same manner, imperceptibly, one above another, and receiving additional improvements, according to the species in which they are implanted. This progress in nature is so very gradual that the most perfect of an inferior species comes very near to the most imperfect of that which is immediately above it.

The exuberant and overflowing goodness of the Supreme Being, whose mercy extends to all his works, is plainly seen, as I have before hinted, from his having made so very little matter, at least what falls within our knowledge, that does not swarm with life. Nor is his goodness less seen in the diversity than in the multitude of living creatures. Had he only made one species of animals, none of the rest would have enjoyed the happiness of existence; he has, therefore, *specified* in his creation every degree of life, every capacity of being. The whole chasm in nature, from a plant to a man, is filled up with diverse kinds of creatures, rising one over another by such a gentle and easy ascent that the little transitions and deviations from one species to another are almost insensible.

This intermediate space is so well husbanded and managed that there is scarce a degree of perception which does not appear in some one part of the world of life. Is the goodness or wisdom of the Divine Being more manifested in this his proceeding?

There is a consequence, besides those I have already mentioned, which seems very naturally deducible from the foregoing considerations. If the scale of being rises by such a regular progress so high as man, we may by a parity of reason suppose that it still proceeds gradually through those beings which are of a superior nature to him, since there is an infinitely greater space and room for different degrees of perfection between the Supreme Being and man than between man and the most despicable insect. This consequence of so great a variety of beings which are superior to us, from that variety which is inferior to us, is made by Mr. Locke[3] in a passage which I shall here set down after having premised that, notwithstanding there is such infinite room between man and his Maker for the creative power to exert itself in, it is impossible that it should ever be filled up, since there will be still an infinite gap or distance between the highest created being and the Power which produced him:

"That there should be more species of intelligent creatures above us than there are of sensible and material below, is probable to me from hence: That in all the visible corporeal world we see no chasms or no gaps. All quite down from us, the descent is by easy steps and a continued series of things that, in each remove, differ very little from the other. There are fishes that have wings and are not strangers to the airy region; and there are some birds that are inhabitants of the water, whose blood is cold as fishes and their flesh so like in taste that the scrupulous are allowed them on fish days. There are animals so near of kin both to birds and beasts that they are in the middle between both: amphibious animals link the terrestrial and aquatic together; seals live at land and at sea, and porpoises have the warm blood and entrails of a hog, not to mention what is confidently reported of mermaids or seamen. There are some brutes that seem to have as much knowledge and reason as some that are called men; and the animal and vegetable kingdoms are so nearly joined that, if you will take the lowest of one and the highest of the other, there will scarce be perceived any great difference between them; and so on, till we come to the lowest and the most inorganical parts of matter, we shall find everywhere that the several species are linked together and differ but in almost insensible degrees. And when we consider the infinite power and wisdom of the Maker, we have reason to think that it is suitable to the magnificent harmony of the universe and the great design and infinite goodness of the Architect, that the species of creatures should also, by gentle degrees, ascend upward from us

3. John Locke, in his *Essay Concerning Human Understanding* (1690) III.vi. 12.

toward his infinite perfection, as we see they gradually descend from us downward; which, if it be probable, we have reason to be persuaded that there are far more species of creatures above us than there are beneath, we being in degrees of perfection much more remote from the infinite being of God than we are from the lowest state of being and that which approaches nearest to nothing. And yet of all those distinct species we have no clear distinct ideas."

In this system of being, there is no creature so wonderful in its nature, and which so much deserves our particular attention, as man, who fills up the middle space between the animal and intellectual nature, the visible and invisible world, and is that link in the chain of beings which has been often termed the *nexus utriusque mundi*.[4] So that he who, in one respect, is associated with angels and archangels, may look upon a Being of infinite perfection as his father, and the highest order of spirits as his brethren, and may, in another respect, say to corruption, "Thou art my father," and to the worm, "Thou art my mother and my sister."[5]

4. "The binding together of both worlds." 5. Job xvii.14.

ALEXANDER POPE
(1688–1744)

1711: *Essay on Criticism*.
1712: First version of *The Rape of the Lock*.
1713–26: Translating Homer, editing Shakespeare.
1728: The *Dunciad* begins Pope's career as major verse satirist.
1733–34: The *Essay on Man* begins Pope's career as ethical and philosophical poet.

Pope is the only important writer of his generation who was solely a man of letters. Since he could not, as a Roman Catholic, attend a university, vote, or hold public office, he was excluded from the sort of patronage which was freely bestowed by statesmen on most writers during the reign of Anne. This disadvantage he turned into a positive good, for the translation of Homer's *Iliad* and *Odyssey*, which he undertook for profit as well as for fame, gave him ample means to live the life of an independent suburban gentleman. After 1718 he lived hospitably in his villa by the Thames at Twickenham (then pronounced *Twit'nam*), entertaining his friends and converting his five acres of land into a diminutive landscape garden. Almost exactly a century earlier, Shakespeare had earned enough to retire to a country estate at Stratford—but he had been an actor-manager as well as a playwright; Pope, therefore, was the first writer to demonstrate that literature alone could be a gainful profession.

Ill health plagued Pope almost from birth. Delicate as a child, he was early stunted and deformed by tuberculosis of the spine. His father, a well-to-do London merchant, retired from business in the year of the poet's birth, and about 1700 acquired a small property at Binfield in Windsor Forest. In rural surroundings, as the boy's health improved, he early acquired his lifelong taste for natural beauty and for gardening. There he completed by wide reading the desultory schooling that both his ill health and his religion had made inevitable, and, encouraged by his father, he began also to develop his precocious talent for poetry. The removal to Binfield, then, was in every way advantageous. But Pope was never to enjoy good health: in later life he was troubled by violent head-aches, and he suffered from easily exacerbated nerves. This neurotic ir-ritability was a price he had to pay for the sensitive and ardent tempera-ment that helped make him one of our greatest poets. Because of it, he both hated and loved intensely; because of it his responsiveness to beauty in all its forms was unusually acute.

Pope's first striking success as a poet was the *Essay on Criticism* (1711), which earned him the fame of Addison's approval and the notoriety of an intemperate personal attack from the critic John Dennis, who was angered by a casual reference to himself in the poem. *The Rape of the Lock*, both in its original shorter version of 1712 and in its more elaborate version of 1714, established the author of the *Essay on Criticism* as a master not only of metrics and of language, but also of witty, urbane satire. In the earlier work, Pope had excelled all his predecessors in writing a didactic poem after the example of Horace; in the later, he had written the most brilliant mock epic in the language. But there was another vein in Pope's youthful poetry, much of which, concerned as it is with natural beauty and love, reveals a temperament that in a later poet might have been called "Romantic." The *Pastorals* (1709), Pope's first publication, and *Windsor Forest* (1713; much of it was written earlier) are essentially nature poems, abounding in visual imagery and descriptive passages of ideally ordered nature. They remind us that Pope was an amateur painter who delighted in the beauty of external nature, as well as in the artificial beauty of the world of *The Rape of the Lock*. The *Elegy to the Memory of an Unfortunate Lady*, published in the collected poems of 1717, presents the high heroics of romantic love. Looking back to his early poems, Pope said that he had wandered "in Fancy's maze." And even the long task of translating Homer, the "dull duty" of editing Shakespeare, and, in middle age, his preoccupation with ethical and satirical poetry did not extinguish this side of Pope's nature and art. He learned to subordinate, but he did not cease to use, this sensitive awareness of visual beauty in his later poetry.

Pope's early poetry brought him to the attention of literary men, with whom he began to associate in the masculine world of coffeehouse and tavern. His fragile health never permitted him to live the rakish life that he would have liked, but it did not prevent his enjoying the company of some of the most distinguished men of letters of the time. Between 1706 and 1711 he came to know, among many others, William Congreve, William Walsh, the critic and poet, and Richard Steele and Joseph Ad-dison, who, after 1709, were two of the most admired writers of the day. As it happened, all these men were Whigs. Pope was probably indifferent to politics at this time, or at least he could readily ignore politics in the excitement of taking his place among the leading wits of the town. But after the fall of the Whigs in 1710, and the formation of the Tory government under Robert Harley (later Earl of Oxford) and Henry St. John (later Viscount Bolingbroke) party loyalties bred bitterness among the wits as among the politicians.

By 1712 Pope had made the acquaintance of another group of writers, all Tories, who soon became his intimate friends: Jonathan Swift, by then the close associate of Harley and St. John and the principal propagandist for their policies; Dr. John Arbuthnot, physician to the queen, a learned scientist, a wit of the first quality, and a man of deep humanity and utter integrity; John Gay, the poet, who in 1728 was to produce the *Beggar's Opera*, the greatest theatrical success of the century; and Thomas Parnell, a poet of some distinction, who died prematurely in 1718. It was among these men that Pope was to find his lifelong friends; and it was through them that he became the friend and admirer of Oxford, and later the intimate of Bolingbroke. As he grew more intimate with his new circle, he began to drift away from Addison and his earlier friends.

In 1714 this group, at the instigation of Pope, formed a club which was to cooperate in a scheme for satirizing all sorts of false learning and pedantry in philosophy, science, and other branches of knowledge. They were joined by the Earl of Oxford, who attended as often as business permitted. The friends proposed to write jointly the biography of a learned fool whom they named Martinus Scriblerus (Martin the Scribbler), whose life and opinions would be a running commentary on whatever they considered the abuses of learning and the follies of the learned. The death of the queen in August, 1714, brought the venture to a premature end, but not before some amusing episodes had been invented, as the published (probably very much rewritten) version of the *Memoirs of Martinus Scriblerus* (1741), makes plain. The real importance of the club, however, is that it fostered a satiric temper which was to find unexpected expression in such mature works of the friends as *Gulliver's Travels*, the *Dunciad*, and even, perhaps, the *Beggar's Opera*.

"The life of a wit is a warfare on earth," said Pope, generalizing from his own experience. His very success as a poet (and his astonishing precocity brought him success very early) made enemies among the less talented and consequently envious writers, who were to plague him in pamphlets, verse satires, and squibs in the journals throughout his entire literary career. He was to be attacked for his writings, his religion, and his physical deformity. Though he smarted under the jibes of his detractors, he was a fighter who struck back, always giving better than he got. The common notion that he was a malicious, treacherous, venomous man, motivated merely by personal vanity and malice, is the creation of his enemies, and can be accepted by no one who reads the vicious attacks on him published from 1711 to the end of his life. Usually he was not the aggressor, but he never forgot an insult or forgave an injury, and sooner or later he took his revenge—sometimes, it must be admitted, in rather unsavory ways. But he was loved and trusted by many of the most honorable, eminent, and gifted men of his time, and with only a few exceptions (aside from politicians), the objects of his satire are people who would be forgotten today had they not been so humiliatingly preserved to posterity.

Pope's literary warfare began in 1713, when he announced his intention of translating the *Iliad* and sought, with the support of his friends, subscribers to a de luxe edition of the work. Subscribers came in droves, but Pope had enemies as well. The Whig writers who surrounded Addison at Button's Coffee House did all they could through anonymous attacks to hinder the success of the venture, and even (with Addison's knowledge and perhaps encouragement) announced a rival translation by Thomas Tickell, one of Addison's Oxford friends. The eventual success of the first published installment of his *Iliad* in 1715 did not obliterate Pope's just resentment against Addison and his "little senate"; and this resentment found expression in the damaging portrait of Addison (under the name of Atticus), which, years after it was written, was included in Pope's *Epistle to Dr. Arbuthnot* (1735), lines 193–214. The not unjustified attacks on Pope's edition of Shakespeare (1725), especially those by the learned Shakespeare scholar Lewis Theobald (Pope always spelled and pronounced the name "Tibbald" in his satires), led to Theobald's appearance as king of the dunces in the *Dunciad* (1728). In this impressive poem Pope stigmatized his literary enemies as agents of all that he disliked and feared in the literary tendencies of his time—the vulgarization of taste and the arts consequent on the rapid growth of the reading public, the development of journalism, magazines, and other popular and cheap publications, which spread scandal, sensationalism, and political partisanship—in short the new commercial spirit of the nation, which was corrupting not only the arts, but, as Pope saw it, the national life itself.

In the 1730's Pope moved on to philosophical, ethical, and political subjects in the *Essay on Man*, the *Epistles to Several Persons*, and the *Imitations of Horace*. The reigns of George I and George II appeared to him, as to Swift and other Tories, a period of rapid moral, political, and cultural deterioration. The agents of decay seemed in one way or another related to the spread of moneyed (as opposed to landed) wealth, which accounted for the political corruption encouraged by Sir Robert Walpole and the court party, and the increasing influence in all aspects of the national life of a vulgar class of *nouveaux riches*. Pope assumed the role of the champion of traditional civilization: of right reason, humanistic learning, sound art, good taste, and public virtue. For him the supreme value was order —cosmic, political, social, aesthetic—which he saw (or believed he saw) threatened on all sides. It was fortunate that most of his enemies seem to have been designed by nature to illustrate various degrees of unreason, pedantry, bad art, vulgar taste, and, at best, indifferent morals. Personal malice edged his satire, but his art elevated his unhappy victims into symbols of Georgian barbarism.

The principal obstacle between the modern reader and Pope's satires is that they seem to require a vast amount of particular knowledge about a long-vanished age. This is not entirely the case. Although a certain amount of social and political history is helpful, the whole body of Pope's satire can be read and enjoyed without much biographical information. The satirist traditionally deals in generally prevalent evils and generally observable human types, and this is true of Pope, even when he named actual individuals. Usually in the late satires, as in the earlier *Rape*, he used fictional or type names, although he most often had an individual in mind —Sappho, Atossa, Atticus, Sporus; and when he named individuals (as he consistently did in the *Dunciad* and occasionally elsewhere), his purpose was to raise his victims to the bad eminence of typifying some sort of obliquity. Nor need we be concerned with whether or not the moral character of the speaker of the satires is identical with that of Alexander Pope of Twickenham. Pope created a clearly defined person (the "I" of the satires) with the character and personality of one who could freely censure the age. This fictional or semi-fictional figure is the detached observer, somewhat removed from City, town, and court, the centers of corruption; he is the friend of virtuous men, whose friendship for him testifies to his integrity; he is fond of peace, country life, the arts, morality, and truth, and he detests their opposites which flourish in the great world. In such an age, Pope implies, it is impossible for such a man—honest, truthful, blunt—not to write satire. Where even political power and law are subject to the corruptor wealth, no weapon remains to the guardian of the public weal but the "sacred weapon" of satire. This is the satirist whom Pope creates, and to move from him to the private character of Pope is to move away from the poems.

Something must be said about Pope's versification, and the varied styles of his poems. It takes only a little familiarity with his writings to discover how wrong has been the conventional judgment that they are artificial, mechanical, and monotonous. From first to last, the permanent elements of Pope's poetic style are his remarkable rhythmic variety, despite the apparently rigid metrical unit—the heroic couplet—in which he wrote; the precision of meaning and the harmony (or the expressive disharmony, when necessary) of his language; and his superb discipline, which enables him at his characteristic best to achieve maximum conciseness together with maximum complexity. Something of Pope's metrical variety and verbal harmony can be observed in even so short a passage as lines 71–76 of the pastoral *Summer* (1709), lines so lyrical that Handel set them to music. In the passage quoted below (as also in the following quotation), only those rhetorical stresses which distort the normal iambic flow of the verse have been marked; internal pauses within the line are indicated by single and double bars, alliteration and assonance by italics.

> Oh déign to visit our *f*ors*a*ken s*ea*ts,
> The mossy *f*ountains || and the green retr*ea*ts!
> Where'er you wálk || cool gáles shall *f*an the gl*a*de,
> Trées where you sít || shall crowd into a sh*a*de:
> Where'er you tréad || the bl*u*shing *f*lowers shall rise,
> And all things *f*lóurish where you túrn your eyes.

Pope has attained metrical variety here by the free substitution of trochees and spondees for the normal iambs; he has achieved rhythmic variety by arranging phrases and clauses (units of syntax and logic) of different lengths within single lines and couplets, so that the passage moves with the sinuous fluency of thought and feeling, not the mechanical regularity of a metronome; and he has not only chosen musical combinations of words, but has also subtly modulated the harmony of the passage by unobtrusive patterns of alliteration and assonance.

Contrast with this pastoral passage lines 16–25 of the *Epilogue to the*

Satires, Dialogue II (1738), in which Pope is not making music, but is imitating actual conversation so realistically that the metrical pattern and the integrity of the couplet and individual line seem to be destroyed (though in fact they are very much present). The poet-satirist is engaged in a dialogue with a friend who warns him that his satire is too personal, indeed mere libel. The poet is speaking:

> Ye statesmen, | priests of one religion all!
> Ye tradesmen vile || in army, court, or hall!
> Ye reverend atheists. || F. Scandal! | name them, | Who?
>   P. Why that's the thing you bid me not to do.
> Who starved a sister, || who foreswore a debt,
> I never named; || the town's inquiring yet.
> The poisoning dame— | F. You mean— | P. I don't— | F. You do.
>   P. See, now I keep the secret, || and not you!
> The bribing statesman— | F. Hold, || too high you go.
>   P. The bribed elector— || F. There you stoop too low.

In such a passage the language and rhythms of poetry merge with the language and rhythms of impassioned living speech.

A fine example of Pope's ability to derive the maximum of meaning from the most economic use of language and image is the description of the manor house in which lives old Cotta, the miser (*Epistle to Lord Bathurst,* lines 187–196):

> Like some lone Chartreuse stands the good old Hall,
> Silence without, and fasts within the wall;
> No raftered roofs with dance and tabor sound,
> No noontide bell invites the country round;
> Tenants with sighs the smokeless towers survey,
> And turn the unwilling steeds another way;
> Benighted wanderers, the forest o'er,
> Curse the saved candle and unopening door;
> While the gaunt mastiff growling at the gate,
> Affrights the beggar whom he longs to eat.

The first couplet of this passage, which associates the "Hall," symbol of English rural hospitality, with the Grande Chartreuse, the monastery in the French Alps, which, though a place of "silence" and "fasts" for the monks, afforded food and shelter to all travelers, clashes forcefully with the dismal details of Cotta's miserly dwelling; and the meaning of the scene is concentrated in the grotesque image of the last couplet: the half-starved watchdog and the frightened beggar confronting each other in mutual hunger.

But there is another sort of variety within Pope's work as a whole which derives from the poet's respect for the idea that the different kinds of literature have their different and appropriate styles. Thus the *Essay on Criticism,* an informal discussion of literary theory, is written, like Horace's *Ars Poetica,* a similarly didactic poem, in a plain style, relatively devoid of imagery and eloquence, and in the easy language of well-bred talk. *The Rape of the Lock,* being "a heroi-comical poem" (that is, a comic poem that treats trivial material in an epic style), employs the lofty heroic language that Dryden had perfected in his translation of Virgil, and introduces amusing parodies of passages in *Paradise Lost*. The grave epistles that make up the *Essay on Man*, a philosophical discussion of such majestic themes as the Creator and his creation, the universe, and the nature of man, of human society, and of happiness, are written in a stately forensic language and tone and constantly employ the traditional rhetorical figures. The *Imitations of Horace*, and, above all, the *Epistle to Dr. Arbuthnot*, his finest poem "in the Horatian way," reveal Pope's final mastery of the plain style of Horace's epistles and satires and justify his image of himself as the heir of the Roman poet. In short no other poet of the century can equal Pope in the range of his materials, the diversity of his poetic styles, and the sheer mastery of the poet's craft.

From An Essay on Criticism[1]
Part I

'Tis hard to say, if greater want of skill
Appear in writing or in judging ill;
But of the two less dangerous is the offense
To tire our patience than mislead our sense.
Some few in that, but numbers err in this,   5
Ten censure[1a] wrong for one who writes amiss;

1. There is no pleasanter introduction to the canons of taste in the English Augustan age than Pope's *Essay on Criticism*. As Addison said in his review in *Spectator* 253, it assembles the "most known and most received observations on the subject of literature and criticism." Pope was attempting to do for his time what Horace, in his *Ars Poetica*, and what Nicolas Boileau (French poet of the age of Louis XIV), in his *L'Art Poëtique*, had done for theirs. Horace is not only one of Pope's instructors in the principles of criticism; he is also Pope's model in this poem, especially in the simple, conversational language, the tone of well-bred ease, and the deliberately plain style of the *Ars Poetica*—all of which qualities Pope reproduces.

In framing his critical creed, Pope did not try for novelty: he drew from the standard writings of classical antiquity, especially from the *Ars Poetica*, and the *Institutio Oratoria* of the Roman rhetorician Quintilian; from French critical theory of the preceding century; and from Ben Jonson's *Timber, or Discoveries* and the prefaces of John Dryden. He wished merely to give to generally accepted doctrines pleasing and memorable expression. Here one meets the key words of neoclassical criticism: *wit*, *Nature*, *ancients*, *rules*, *genius*. *Wit* in the poem is a word of many meanings—a clever remark, or the man who makes it; a conceit; liveliness of mind; inventiveness; fancy; genius; a genius; poetry itself, among others. *Nature* is an equally ambiguous word, meaning not "things out there," or "the outdoors," but most importantly that which is representative, universal, permanent in human experience as opposed to the idiosyncratic, the individual, the temporary. In line 21, the word comes close to meaning "intuitive knowledge." In line 52, it means that half-personified power manifested in the cosmic order, which in its modes of working is a model for art. The reverence felt by most Augustans for the works of the great writers of ancient Greece and Rome raised the question how far the authority of these *ancients* extended. Were their works to be received as models to be conscientiously imitated? Were the *rules* received from them or deducible from their works to be accepted as prescriptive laws or merely convenient guides? Was individual *genius* to be bound by what has been conventionally held to be *Nature*, by the authority of the *ancients*, and by the legalistic pedantry of *rules*? Or could it go its own way?

In Part I of the *Essay* Pope constructs a harmonious system in which he effects a compromise among all these conflicting forces—a compromise which is typically 18th century in spirit. Part II analyzes the causes of faulty criticism. Part III (not printed here) characterizes the good critic and praises the great critics of the past.
1a. Judge.

A fool might once himself alone expose,
Now one in verse makes many more in prose.
    'Tis with our judgments as our watches, none
Go just alike, yet each believes his own.   10
In poets as true genius is but rare,
True taste as seldom is the critic's share;
Both must alike from Heaven derive their light,
These born to judge, as well as those to write.
Let such teach others who themselves excel,   15
And censure freely who have written well.
Authors are partial to their wit, 'tis true,
But are not critics to their judgment too?
    Yet if we look more closely, we shall find
Most have the seeds of judgment in their mind: 20
Nature affords at least a glimmering light;
The lines, though touched but faintly, are drawn right.
But as the slightest sketch, if justly traced,   ⎫
Is by ill coloring but the more disgraced,   ⎬
So by false learning is good sense defaced: ⎭ 25
Some are bewildered in the maze of schools,
And some made coxcombs² Nature meant but fools.
In search of wit these lose their common sense,
And then turn critics in their own defense:
Each burns alike, who can, or cannot write,   30
Or with a rival's or an eunuch's spite.
All fools have still an itching to deride,
And fain would be upon the laughing side.
If Maevius³ scribble in Apollo's spite,
There are who judge still worse than he can write.   35
    Some have at first for wits, then poets passed,
Turned critics next, and proved plain fools at last.
Some neither can for wits nor critics pass,
As heavy mules are neither horse nor ass.
Those half-learn'd witlings, numerous in our isle,   40
As half-formed insects on the banks of Nile;⁴
Unfinished things, one knows not what to call,
Their generation's so equivocal:
To tell⁵ them would a hundred tongues require,
Or one vain wit's, that might a hundred tire.   45
    But you who seek to give and merit fame,
And justly bear a critic's noble name,
Be sure yourself and your own reach to know,
How far your genius, taste, and learning go;
Launch not beyond your depth, but be discreet,   50
And mark that point where sense and dullness meet.
    Nature to all things fixed the limits fit,
And wisely curbed proud man's pretending wit.
As on the land while here the ocean gains,

---

2. Superficial pretenders to learning.
3. A silly poet alluded to contemptuously by Virgil in *Eclogue III* and by
Horace in *Epode X*.
4. The ancients believed that many
forms of life were spontaneously gen-
erated in the fertile mud of the Nile.
5. Reckon, count.

In other parts it leaves wide sandy plains;   55
Thus in the soul while memory prevails,
The solid power of understanding fails;
Where beams of warm imagination play,
The memory's soft figures melt away.
One science[6] only will one genius fit,   60
So vast is art, so narrow human wit.
Not only bounded to peculiar arts,
But oft in those confined to single parts.
Like kings we lose the conquests gained before,
By vain ambition still to make them more;   65
Each might his several province well command,
Would all but stoop to what they understand.
    First follow Nature, and your judgment frame
By her just standard, which is still the same;
Unerring Nature, still divinely bright,   70
One clear, unchanged, and universal light,
Life, force, and beauty must to all impart,
At once the source, and end, and test of art.
Art from that fund each just supply provides,
Works without show, and without pomp presides.   75
In some fair body thus the informing soul
With spirits feeds, with vigor fills the whole,
Each motion guides, and every nerve sustains;
Itself unseen, but in the effects remains.
Some, to whom Heaven in wit has been profuse,   80
Want as much more to turn it to its use;
For wit and judgment often are at strife,
Though meant each other's aid, like man and wife.
'Tis more to guide than spur the Muse's steed,
Restrain his fury than provoke his speed;   85
The wingèd courser,[7] like a generous horse,
Shows most true mettle when you check his course.
    Those rules of old discovered, not devised,
Are Nature still, but Nature methodized;
Nature, like liberty, is but restrained   90
By the same laws which first herself ordained.
    Hear how learn'd Greece her useful rules indites,
When to repress and when indulge our flights:
High on Parnassus' top her sons she showed,
And pointed out those arduous paths they trod;   95
Held from afar, aloft, the immortal prize,
And urged the rest by equal steps to rise.
Just precepts thus from great examples given,
She drew from them what they derived from Heaven.
The generous critic fanned the poet's fire,   100
And taught the world with reason to admire.
Then criticism the Muse's handmaid proved,

---

6. Branch of learning.
7. Pegasus, associated with the Muses

and poetic inspiration; "generous":
spirited, highly bred.

To dress her charms, and make her more beloved:
But following wits from that intention strayed,
Who could not win the mistress, wooed the maid;   105
Against the poets their own arms they turned,
Sure to hate most the men from whom they learned.
So modern 'pothecaries, taught the art
By doctors' bills[8] to play the doctor's part,
Bold in the practice of mistaken rules,   110
Prescribe, apply, and call their masters fools.
Some on the leaves of ancient authors prey,
Nor time nor moths e'er spoiled so much as they.
Some dryly plain, without invention's aid,
Write dull receipts[9] how poems may be made.   115
These leave the sense their learning to display,
And those explain the meaning quite away.
　　You then whose judgment the right course would steer,
Know well each ancient's proper character;
His fable,[1] subject, scope in every page;   120
Religion, country, genius of his age:
Without all these at once before your eyes,
Cavil you may, but never criticize.
Be Homer's works your study and delight,
Read them by day, and meditate by night;   125
Thence form your judgment, thence your maxims bring,
And trace the Muses upward to their spring.
Still with itself compared, his text peruse;
And let your comment be the Mantuan Muse.[2]
　　When first young Maro in his boundless mind   130
A work to outlast immortal Rome designed,
Perhaps he seemed above the critic's law,
And but from Nature's fountains scorned to draw;
But when to examine every part he came,
Nature and Homer were, he found, the same.   135
Convinced, amazed, he checks the bold design, ⎫
And rules as strict his labored work confine ⎬
As if the Stagirite[3] o'erlooked each line.   ⎭
Learn hence for ancient rules a just esteem;
To copy Nature is to copy them.   140
　　Some beauties yet no precepts can declare,
For there's a happiness as well as care.[4]

---

8. Prescriptions.
9. Formulas for preparing a dish; recipes. Pope himself wrote an amusing burlesque *Receipt to Make an Epic Poem*, first published in the *Guardian* 78 (1713).
1. Plot or story of a play or poem.
2. Virgil, the "young Maro" of the following line, was born in a village adjacent to Mantua in Italy; hence "Mantuan Muse." His epic, the *Aeneid*, was modeled on Homer's *Iliad* and *Odyssey* and was considered to be a refinement

on the Greek poems. Thus it could be thought of as a commentary ("comment") on Homer's poems.
3. Aristotle, native of Stagira, from whose *Poetics* later critics formulated strict rules for writing tragedy and the epic.
4. I.e., no rules ("precepts") can explain ("declare") some beautiful effects in a work of art which can be the result only of inspiration or good luck ("happiness"), not of painstaking labor ("care").

Music resembles poetry, in each }
Are nameless graces which no methods teach, }
And which a master hand alone can reach. } 145
If, where the rules not far enough extend
(Since rules were made but to promote their end)
Some lucky license answer to the full
The intent proposed, that license is a rule.
Thus Pegasus, a nearer way to take, 150
May boldly deviate from the common track.
From vulgar bounds with brave disorder part,
And snatch a grace beyond the reach of art,
Which without passing through the judgment, gains
The heart, and all its end at once attains. 155
In prospects thus, some objects please our eyes, }
Which out of Nature's common order rise, }
The shapeless rock, or hanging precipice. }
Great wits sometimes may gloriously offend,
And rise to faults true critics dare not mend; 160
But though the ancients thus their rules invade
(As kings dispense with laws themselves have made)
Moderns, beware! or if you must offend
Against the precept, ne'er transgress its end;
Let it be seldom, and compelled by need; 165
And have at least their precedent to plead.
The critic else proceeds without remorse,
Seizes your fame, and puts his laws in force.
    I know there are, to whose presumptuous thoughts
Those freer beauties, even in them, seem faults.[5] 170
Some figures monstrous and misshaped appear,
Considered singly, or beheld too near,
Which, but proportioned to their light or place,
Due distance reconciles to form and grace.
A prudent chief not always must display 175
His powers in equal ranks and fair array,
But with the occasion and the place comply,
Conceal his force, nay seem sometimes to fly.
Those oft are stratagems which errors seem,
Nor is it Homer nods, but we that dream. 180
    Still green with bays each ancient altar stands
Above the reach of sacrilegious hands,
Secure from flames, from envy's fiercer rage,
Destructive war, and all-involving age.
See, from each clime the learn'd their incense bring! 185
Here in all tongues consenting[6] paeans ring!
In praise so just let every voice be joined,[7]
And fill the general chorus of mankind.
Hail, bards triumphant! born in happier days,
Immortal heirs of universal praise! 190

5. Pronounced *fawts.*   7. Pronounced *jined.*
6. Agreeing, concurring.

Whose honors with increase of ages grow,
As streams roll down, enlarging as they flow;
Nations unborn your mighty names shall sound,
And worlds applaud that must not yet be found!
Oh, may some spark of your celestial fire,   195
The last, the meanest of your sons inspire
(That on weak wings, from far, pursues your flights,
Glows while he reads, but trembles as he writes)
To teach vain wits a science little known,
To admire superior sense, and doubt their own!   200

Part II

Of all the causes which conspire to blind
Man's erring judgment, and misguide the mind,
What the weak head with strongest bias rules,
Is pride, the never-failing vice of fools.
Whatever Nature has in worth denied,   205
She gives in large recruits[8] of needful pride;
For as in bodies, thus in souls, we find
What wants in blood and spirits swelled with wind:
Pride, where wit fails, steps in to our defense,
And fills up all the mighty void of sense.   210
If once right reason drives that cloud away,
Truth breaks upon us with resistless day.
Trust not yourself: but your defects to know,
Make use of every friend—and every foe.
A little learning is a dangerous thing;   215
Drink deep, or taste not the Pierian spring.[9]
There shallow draughts intoxicate the brain,
And drinking largely sobers us again.
Fired at first sight with what the Muse imparts,
In fearless youth we tempt[1] the heights of arts,   220
While from the bounded level of our mind
Short views we take, nor see the lengths behind;
But more advanced, behold with strange surprise
New distant scenes of endless science rise!
So pleased at first the towering Alps we try,   225
Mount o'er the vales, and seem to tread the sky,
The eternal snows appear already past,
And the first clouds and mountains seem the last;
But, those attained, we tremble to survey
The growing labors of the lengthened way,   230
The increasing prospect tires our wandering eyes,
Hills peep o'er hills, and Alps on Alps arise!
A perfect judge will read each work of wit
With the same spirit that its author writ:
Survey the whole, nor seek slight faults to find   235
Where Nature moves, and rapture warms the mind;

8. Supplies.   sacred to the Muses.
9. The spring in Pieria on Mt. Olympus,   1. Attempt.

Nor lose, for that malignant dull delight,
The generous pleasure to be charmed with wit.
But in such lays as neither ebb nor flow,
Correctly cold, and regularly low,   240
That, shunning faults, one quiet tenor keep,
We cannot blame indeed—but we may sleep.
In wit, as nature, what affects our hearts
Is not the exactness of peculiar parts;
'Tis not a lip, or eye, we beauty call,   245
But the joint force and full result of all.
Thus when we view some well-proportioned dome
(The world's just wonder, and even thine, O Rome![2]),
No single parts unequally surprise,
All comes united to the admiring eyes: 250
No monstrous height, or breadth, or length appear;
The whole at once is bold and regular.
    Whoever thinks a faultless piece to see,
Thinks what ne'er was, nor is, nor e'er shall be.
In every work regard the writer's end,   255
Since none can compass more than they intend;
And if the means be just, the conduct true,
Applause, in spite of trivial faults, is due.
As men of breeding, sometimes men of wit,
To avoid great errors must the less commit,   260
Neglect the rules each verbal critic lays,
For not to know some trifles is a praise.
Most critics, fond of some subservient art,
Still make the whole depend upon a part:
They talk of principles, but notions prize,   265
And all to one loved folly sacrifice.
    Once on a time La Mancha's knight,[3] they say,
A certain bard encountering on the way,
Discoursed in terms as just, with looks as sage,
As e'er could Dennis,[4] of the Grecian stage;   270
Concluding all were desperate sots and fools
Who durst depart from Aristotle's rules.
Our author, happy in a judge so nice,
Produced his play, and begged the knight's advice;
Made him observe the subject and the plot,   275
The manners, passions, unities; what not?
All which exact to rule were brought about,
Were but a combat in the lists left out.
"What! leave the combat out?" exclaims the knight.
"Yes, or we must renounce the Stagirite."   280
"Not so, by Heaven!" he answers in a rage,

2. The dome of St. Peter's, designed by Michelangelo.
3. Don Quixote. The story comes not from Cervantes' novel, but from a spurious sequel to it by Don Alonzo Fernandez de Avellaneda.
4. John Dennis (1657–1734), though one of the leading critics of the time, was frequently ridiculed by the wits for his irascibility and his rather solemn pomposity. Pope apparently did not know Dennis personally, but his jibe at him in Part III of this poem incurred the critic's lasting animosity.

"Knights, squires, and steeds must enter on the stage."
"So vast a throng the stage can ne'er contain."
"Then build a new, or act it in a plain."
    Thus critics of less judgment than caprice,   285
Curious,[5] not knowing, not exact, but nice,
Form short ideas, and offend in arts
(As most in manners), by a love to parts.
    Some to conceit[6] alone their taste confine,
And glittering thoughts struck out at every line;   290
Pleased with a work where nothing's just or fit,
One glaring chaos and wild heap of wit.
Poets, like painters, thus unskilled to trace
The naked nature and the living grace,
With gold and jewels cover every part,   295
And hide with ornaments their want of art.
    True wit is Nature to advantage dressed,
What oft was thought, but ne'er so well expressed;
Something whose truth convinced at sight we find,
That gives us back the image of our mind.   300
As shades more sweetly recommend the light,
So modest plainness sets off sprightly wit;
For works may have more wit than does them good,
As bodies perish through excess of blood.
    Others for language all their care express,   305
And value books, as women men, for dress.
Their praise is still—the style is excellent;
The sense they humbly take upon contént.[7]
Words are like leaves; and where they most abound,
Much fruit of sense beneath is rarely found.   310
False eloquence, like the prismatic glass,
Its gaudy colors spreads on every place;[8]
The face of Nature we no more survey,
All glares alike, without distinction gay.
But true expression, like the unchanging sun,   315
Clears and improves whate'er it shines upon;
It gilds all objects, but it alters none.
Expression is the dress of thought, and still
Appears more decent as more suitable.
A vile conceit in pompous words expressed   320
Is like a clown[9] in regal purple dressed:
For different styles with different subjects sort,
As several garbs with country, town, and court.
Some by old words to fame have made pretense,
Ancients in phrase, mere moderns in their sense.   325
Such labored nothings, in so strange a style,
Amaze the unlearn'd, and make the learned smile;

5. Laboriously careful. "Nice": minutely accurate, over refined.
6. Pointed wit, ingenuity and extravagance, or affectation in the use of figures, especially similes and metaphors.
7. Mere acquiescence.
8. A very up-to-date scientific reference. Newton's *Optics*, which treated of the prism and the spectrum, had been published in 1704, though his theories had been known earlier.
9. Rustic, boor.

Unlucky as Fungoso[1] in the play,
These sparks with awkward vanity display
What the fine gentleman wore yesterday;
And but so mimic ancient wits at best,
As apes our grandsires in their doublets dressed.
In words as fashions the same rule will hold,
Alike fantastic if too new or old:
Be not the first by whom the new are tried,   335
Nor yet the last to lay the old aside.
   But most by numbers[2] judge a poet's song,
And smooth or rough with them is right or wrong.
In the bright Muse though thousand charms conspire,
Her voice is all these tuneful fools admire,   340
Who haunt Parnassus but to please their ear,
Not mend their minds; as some to church repair,
Not for the doctrine, but the music there.
These equal syllables alone require,
Though oft the ear the open vowels tire,[3]   345
While expletives[4] their feeble aid do join,
And ten low words oft creep in one dull line:
While they ring round the same unvaried chimes,
With sure returns of still expected rhymes;
Where'er you find "the cooling western breeze,"   350
In the next line, it "whispers through the trees";
If crystal streams "with pleasing murmurs creep,"
The reader's threatened (not in vain) with "sleep";
Then, at the last and only couplet fraught
With some unmeaning thing they call a thought,   355
A needless Alexandrine[5] ends the song
That, like a wounded snake, drags its slow length along.
Leave such to tune their own dull rhymes, and know
What's roundly smooth or languishingly slow;
And praise the easy vigor of a line   360
Where Denham's strength and Waller's sweetness join.[6]
True ease in writing comes from art, not chance,
As those move easiest who have learned to dance.
'Tis not enough no harshness gives offense,
The sound must seem an echo to the sense.   365
Soft is the strain when Zephyr gently blows,
And the smooth stream in smoother numbers flows;
But when loud surges lash the sounding shore,
The hoarse, rough verse should like the torrent roar.
When Ajax strives some rock's vast weight to throw,   370

---

1. A character in Ben Jonson's comedy *Every Man out of His Humor* (1599).
2. Versification.
3. In lines 345–57 Pope cleverly contrives to make his own metrics or diction illustrate the faults that he is exposing.
4. Words used merely to achieve the necessary number of feet in a line of verse.

5. A line of verse containing six iambic feet; it is illustrated in the next line.
6. Dryden, whom Pope echoes here, considered Sir John Denham (1615–69) and Edmund Waller (1606–87) to have been the principal shapers of the closed pentameter couplet. He had distinguished the "strength" of the one and the "sweetness" of the other.

The line too labors, and the words move slow;
Not so when swift Camilla scours the plain,
Flies o'er the unbending corn, and skims along the main.
Hear how Timotheus'[7] varied lays surprise,
And bid alternate passions fall and rise!   375
While at each change the son of Libyan Jove[8]
Now burns with glory, and then melts with love;
Now his fierce eyes with sparkling fury glow,
Now sighs steal out, and tears begin to flow:
Persians and Greeks like turns of nature[9] found   380
And the world's victor stood subdued by sound!
The power of music all our hearts allow,
And what Timotheus was is Dryden now.
    Avoid extremes; and shun the fault of such
Who still are pleased too little or too much.   385
At every trifle scorn to take offense:
That always shows great pride, or little sense.
Those heads, as stomachs, are not sure the best,
Which nauseate all, and nothing can digest.
Yet let not each gay turn thy rapture move;   390
For fools admire,[1] but men of sense approve:
As things seem large which we through mists descry,
Dullness is ever apt to magnify.
    Some foreign writers, some our own despise;
The ancients only, or the moderns prize.   395
Thus wit, like faith, by each man is applied
To one small sect, and all are damned beside.
Meanly they seek the blessing to confine,
And force that sun but on a part to shine,
Which not alone the southern wit sublimes,   400
But ripens spirits in cold northern climes;
Which from the first has shone on ages past,
Enlights the present, and shall warm the last;
Though each may feel increases and decays,
And see now clearer and now darker days.   405
Regard not then if wit be old or new,
But blame the false and value still the true.
    Some ne'er advance a judgment of their own,
But catch the spreading notion of the town;
They reason and conclude by precedent,   410
And own stale nonsense which they ne'er invent.
Some judge of authors' names, not works, and then
Nor praise nor blame the writings, but the men.
Of all this servile herd the worst is he
That in proud dullness joins with quality,   415
A constant critic at the great man's board,
To fetch and carry nonsense for my lord.

7. The musician in Dryden's *Alexander's Feast*. Pope retells the story of that poem in the following lines.
8. Alexander the Great.
9. Alternations of feelings.
1. Wonder. "Approve": judge favorably only after due deliberation.

What woeful stuff this madrigal would be
In some starved hackney sonneteer or me!
But let a lord once own the happy lines,   420
How the wit brightens! how the style refines!
Before his sacred name flies every fault,
And each exalted stanza teems with thought!
    The vulgar thus through imitation err;
As oft the learn'd by being singular;   425
So much they scorn the crowd, that if the throng
By chance go right, they purposely go wrong.
So schismatics² the plain believers quit,
And are but damned for having too much wit.
Some praise at morning what they blame at night,   430
But always think the last opinion right.
A Muse by these is like a mistress used,
This hour she's idolized, the next abused;
While their weak heads like towns unfortified,
'Twixt sense and nonsense daily change their side.   435
Ask them the cause; they're wiser still, they say;
And still tomorrow's wiser than today.
We think our fathers fools, so wise we grow;
Our wiser sons, no doubt, will think us so.
Once school divines³ this zealous isle o'erspread;   440
Who knew most sentences was deepest read.
Faith, Gospel, all seemed made to be disputed,
And none had sense enough to be confuted.
Scotists and Thomists now in peace remain
Amidst their kindred cobwebs in Duck Lane.⁴   445
If faith itself has different dresses worn,
What wonder modes in wit should take their turn?
Oft, leaving what is natural and fit,
The current folly proves the ready wit;
And authors think their reputation safe,   450
Which lives as long as fools are pleased to laugh.
    Some valuing those of their own side or mind,
Still make themselves the measure of mankind:
Fondly⁵ we think we honor merit then,
When we but praise ourselves in other men.   455
Parties in wit attend on those of state,
And public faction doubles private hate.
Pride, Malice, Folly against Dryden rose,
In various shapes of parsons, critics, beaux;
But sense survived, when merry jests were past;   460
For rising merit will buoy up at last.

2. Those who have divided the church on points of theology. Pope stressed the first syllable, the pronunciation approved by Johnson in his *Dictionary*.
3. The medieval theologians, such as the followers of Duns Scotus and St. Thomas Aquinas mentioned in line 444; "sentences" alludes to Peter Lombard's *Book of Sentences*, a book esteemed by Scholastic philosophers.
4. Street where publishers' remainders and second-hand books were sold.
5. Foolishly.

Might he return and bless once more our eyes,
New Blackmores and new Milbourns must arise.[6]
Nay, should great Homer lift his awful head,
Zoilus[7] again would start up from the dead.   465
Envy will merit, as its shade, pursue,
But like a shadow, proves the substance true;
For envied wit, like Sol eclipsed, makes known
The opposing body's grossness, not its own.
When first that sun too powerful beams displays,   470
It draws up vapors which obscure its rays;
But even those clouds at last adorn its way,
Reflect new glories, and augment the day.
　　Be thou the first true merit to befriend;
His praise is lost who stays till all commend.   475
Short is the date, alas! of modern rhymes,
And 'tis but just to let them live betimes.
No longer now that golden age appears,
When patriarch wits survived a thousand years:
Now length of fame (our second life) is lost,   480
And bare threescore is all even that can boast;
Our sons their fathers' failing language see,
And such as Chaucer is shall Dryden be.[8]
So when the faithful pencil has designed
Some bright idea of the master's mind,   485
Where a new world leaps out at his command,
And ready Nature waits upon his hand;
When the ripe colors soften and unite,
And sweetly melt into just shade and light;
When mellowing years their full perfection give,   490
And each bold figure just begins to live,
The treacherous colors the fair art betray,
And all the bright creation fades away!
　　Unhappy wit, like most mistaken things,
Atones not for that envy which it brings.   495
In youth alone its empty praise we boast,
But soon the short-lived vanity is lost;
Like some fair flower the early spring supplies,
That gaily blooms, but even in blooming dies,
What is this wit, which must our cares employ?   500
The owner's wife, that other men enjoy;
Then most our trouble still when most admired,
And still the more we give, the more required;
Whose fame with pains we guard, but lose with ease,
Sure some to vex, but never all to please;   505

6. Sir Richard Blackmore, physician
and poet, had attacked Dryden for the
immorality of his plays; the Rev. Luke
Milbourn had attacked his translation
of Virgil.
7. A Greek critic of the 4th century
B.C., who wrote a book of carping criticism of Homer.

8. The radical changes that took place
in the English language between the
death of Chaucer in 1400 and the death
of Dryden in 1700 suggested that in
another 300 years Dryden would be
unintelligible. Latin seemed the only
means of attaining enduring fame.

'Tis what the vicious fear, the virtuous shun,
By fools 'tis hated, and by knaves undone!
  If wit so much from ignorance undergo,
Ah, let not learning too commence its foe!
Of old those met rewards who could excel,   510
And such were praised who but endeavored well;
Though triumphs were to generals only due,
Crowns were reserved to grace the soldiers too.
Now they who reach Parnassus' lofty crown
Employ their pains to spurn some others down;   515
And while self-love each jealous writer rules,
Contending wits become the sport of fools;
But still the worst with most regret commend,
For each ill author is as bad a friend.
To what base ends, and by what abject ways,   520
Are morals urged through sacred[9] lust of praise!
Ah, ne'er so dire a thirst of glory boast,
Nor in the critic let the man be lost!
Good nature and good sense must ever join;
To err is human, to forgive divine.   525
  But if in noble minds some dregs remain
Nor yet purged off, of spleen and sour disdain,
Discharge that rage on more provoking crimes,
Nor fear a dearth in these flagitious[1] times.
No pardon vile obscenity should find,   530
Though wit and art conspire to move your mind;
But dullness with obscenity must prove
As shameful sure as impotence in love.
In the fat age of pleasure, wealth, and ease
Sprung the rank weed, and thrived with large increase: 535
When love was all an easy monarch's[2] care,
Seldom at council, never in a war;
Jilts ruled the state, and statesmen farces writ;
Nay, wits had pensions, and young lords had wit;
The fair sat panting at a courtier's play,   540
And not a mask[3] went unimproved away;
The modest fan was lifted up no more,
And virgins smiled at what they blushed before.
The following license of a foreign reign
Did all the dregs of bold Socinus drain;[4]   545
Then unbelieving priests reformed the nation,
And taught more pleasant methods of salvation;
Where Heaven's free subjects might their rights dispute,
Lest God himself should seem too absolute;
Pulpits their sacred satire learned to spare,   550

---

9. Accursed. The phrase imitates Virgil's *"auri sacra fames,"* "accursed hunger for gold" (*Aeneid* III.57).
1. Scandalously wicked.
2. Charles II. The concluding lines of Part II discuss the corruption of wit and poetry under this monarch.
3. A woman wearing a mask.
4. The "foreign reign" refers to William III, a Dutchman. Socinus was the name of two Italian theologians of the 16th century who denied the divinity of Jesus.

And Vice admired to find a flatterer there!
Encouraged thus, wit's Titans braved the skies,
And the press groaned with licensed blasphemies.
These monsters, critics! with your darts engage,
Here point your thunder, and exhaust your rage!
Yet shun their fault, who, scandalously nice,
Will needs mistake an author into vice;
All seems infected that the infected spy,
As all looks yellow to the jaundiced eye.

1709   1711

The Rape of the Lock[1]

AN HEROI-COMICAL POEM

*Nolueram, Belinda, tuos violare capillos;
sed juvat hoc precibus me tribuisse tuis.*
—MARTIAL

TO MRS. ARABELLA FERMOR

Madam,

It will be in vain to deny that I have some regard for this piece,
since I dedicate it to you. Yet you may bear me witness, it was intended only to divert a few young ladies, who have good sense and

1. *The Rape of the Lock* is based upon an actual episode that provoked a quarrel between two prominent Catholic families. Pope's friend John Caryll, to whom the poem is addressed (line 3), suggested that Pope write it, in the hope that a little laughter might serve to soothe ruffled tempers. Lord Petre had cut off a lock of hair from the head of the lovely Arabella Fermor (often spelled "Farmer" and doubtless so pronounced), much to the indignation of the lady and her relatives. In its original version of two cantos and 334 lines, published in 1712, *The Rape of the Lock* was a great success. In 1713 a new version was undertaken against the advice of Addison, who considered the poem perfect as it was first written. Pope greatly expanded the earlier version, adding the delightful "machinery" (i.e., the supernatural agents in epic action) of the Sylphs, Belinda's toilet, the card game, and the visit to the Cave of Spleen in Canto IV, In 1717, with the addition of Clarissa's speech on good humor, the poem assumed its final form.

With supreme tact, delicate fancy, playful wit, and the gentlest satire, Pope elaborated the trivial episode which occasioned the poem into the semblance of an epic in miniature, the most nearly perfect "heroi-comical poem" in English. The poem abounds in parodies and echoes of the *Iliad*, the *Aeneid*, and *Paradise Lost*, thus constantly forcing the reader to compare small things with great. The familiar devices of epic are observed, but the incidents or characters are beautifully proportioned to the scale of mock epic. The *Rape* tells

of war, but it is the drawing-room war between the sexes; it has its heroes and heroines, but they are beaux and belles; it has its supernatural characters ("machinery") but they are Sylphs (borrowed, as Pope tells us in his engaging dedicatory letter, from Rosicrucian lore)—creatures of the air, the souls of dead coquettes, with tasks appropriate to their nature—or the Gnome Umbriel, once a prude on earth; it has its epic game, played on the "velvet plain" of the card table, its feasting heroes, who sip coffee and gossip, its battle, fought with the clichés of compliment and conceits, with frowns and angry glances, with snuff and a bodkin; it has the traditional epic journey to the underworld—here the Cave of Spleen, emblematic of the peevish ill nature of spoiled and hypochondriacal women. And Pope creates a world in which these actions take place, a world that is dense with beautiful objects: brocades, ivory and tortoise shell, cosmetics and diamonds, lacquered furniture, silver teapot, delicate chinaware. It is a world that is constantly in motion and that sparkles and glitters with light, whether the light of the sun, or of Belinda's eyes, or that light into which the "fluid" bodies of the Sylphs seem to dissolve as they flutter in the shrouds and around the mast of Belinda's ship. Though Pope laughs at this world and its creatures— and remembers that a grimmer, darker world surrounds it (III.19–24 and V. 145–48)—he makes us very much aware of its beauty and its charm.

The epigraph may be translated, "I was unwilling, Belinda, to ravish your locks; but I rejoice to have conceded good humor enough to laugh not only at their sex's little un-guarded follies, but at their own. But it was communicated with the air of a secret, it soon found its way into the world. An imperfect copy having been offered to a bookseller, you had the good nature for my sake to consent to the publication of one more correct; this I was forced to, before I had executed half my design, for the machinery was entirely wanting to complete it.

The machinery, Madam, is a term invented by the critics, to signify that part which the deities, angels, or demons are made to act in a poem; for the ancient poets are in one respect like many modern ladies: let an action be never so trivial in itself, they always make it appear of the utmost importance. These machines I determined to raise on a very new and odd foundation, the Rosi-crucian [1a] doctrine of spirits.

I know how disagreeable it is to make use of hard words before a lady; but 'tis so much the concern of a poet to have his works under-stood, and particularly by your sex, that you must give me leave to explain two or three difficult terms.

The Rosicrucians are a people I must bring you acquainted with. The best account I know of them is in a French book called *Le Comte de Gabalis*,[1b] which both in its title and size is so like a novel, that many of the fair sex have read it for one by mistake. According to these gentlemen, the four elements are inhabited by spirits, which they call Sylphs, Gnomes, Nymphs, and Salamanders. The Gnomes or Demons of earth delight in mischief; but the Sylphs, whose habitation is in the air, are the best-conditioned creatures imaginable. For they say, any mortals may enjoy the most intimate familiarities with these gentle spirits, upon a condition very easy to all true adepts, an inviolate preservation of chastity.

As to the following cantos, all the passages of them are as fabulous as the vision at the beginning, or the transformation at the end; (except the loss of your hair, which I always mention with reverence). The human persons are as fictitious as the airy ones; and the character of Belinda, as it is now managed, resembles you in nothing but in beauty.

If this poem had as many graces as there are in your person, or in your mind, yet I could never hope it should pass through the world half so uncensured as you have done. But let its fortune be what it will, mine is happy enough, to have given me this occasion of assuring you that I am, with the truest esteem,

MADAM,
Your most obedient, humble servant,
A. POPE

this to your prayers" (Martial, *Epi-grams* XII.lxxxiv.1–2). Pope substi-tuted his heroine for Martial's Poly-timus. The epigraph is intended to sug-gest that the poem was published at Miss Fermor's request.

1a. A system of arcane philosophy in-troduced into England from Germany in the 17th century.
1b. By the Abbé de Montfaucon de Vil-lars, published in 1670.

Canto I

What dire offense from amorous causes springs,
What mighty contests rise from trivial things,
I sing—This verse to Caryll, Muse! is due:
This, even Belinda may vouchsafe to view:
Slight is the subject, but not so the praise,   5
If she inspire, and he approve my lays.
    Say what strange motive, Goddess! could compel
A well-bred lord to assault a gentle belle?
Oh, say what stranger cause, yet unexplored,
Could make a gentle belle reject a lord?   10
In tasks so bold can little men engage,
And in soft bosoms dwells such mighty rage?
    Sol through white curtains shot a timorous ray,
And oped those eyes that must eclipse the day.
Now lapdogs give themselves the rousing shake,   15
And sleepless lovers just at twelve awake:
Thrice rung the bell, the slipper knocked the ground,[2]
And the pressed watch returned a silver sound.
Belinda still her downy pillow pressed,
Her guardian Sylph prolonged the balmy rest: 20
'Twas he had summoned to her silent bed
The morning dream that hovered o'er her head.
A youth more glittering than a birthnight beau[3]
(That even in slumber caused her cheek to glow)
Seemed to her ear his winning lips to lay,   25
And thus in whispers said, or seemed to say:
    "Fairest of mortals, thou distinguished care
Of thousand bright inhabitants of air!
If e'er one vision touched thy infant thought,
Of all the nurse and all the priest have taught,   30
Of airy elves by moonlight shadows seen,
The silver token, and the circled green,[4]
Or virgins visited by angel powers,
With golden crowns and wreaths of heavenly flowers,
Hear and believe! thy own importance know,   35
Nor bound thy narrow views to things below.
Some secret truths, from learned pride concealed,
To maids alone and children are revealed:
What though no credit doubting wits may give?
The fair and innocent shall still believe.   40
Know, then, unnumbered spirits round thee fly,
The light militia of the lower sky:

2. Belinda thus summons her maid. A "pressed watch" chimes the hour and the quarter-hour when the stem is pressed down.
3. Courtiers wore especially fine clothes on the sovereign's birthday.
4. According to popular belief fairies skim off the cream from jugs of milk left standing overnight and leave a coin ("silver token") in payment. Rings of bright green grass, which are common in England even in winter, were held to be due to the round dances of fairies.

These, though unseen, are ever on the wing,
Hang o'er the box, and hover round the Ring.[5]
Think what an equipage thou hast in air,45
And view with scorn two pages and a chair.[6]
As now your own, our beings were of old,
And once enclosed in woman's beauteous mold;
Thence, by a soft transition, we repair
From earthly vehicles to these of air.50
Think not, when woman's transient breath is fled,
That all her vanities at once are dead:
Succeeding vanities she still regards,
And though she plays no more, o'erlooks the cards.
Her joy in gilded chariots, when alive,55
And love of ombre,[7] after death survive.
For when the Fair in all their pride expire,
To their first elements[8] their souls retire:
The sprites of fiery termagants in flame
Mount up, and take a Salamander's name.[9]60
Soft yielding minds to water glide away,
And sip, with Nymphs, their elemental tea.[1]
The graver prude sinks downward to a Gnome,
In search of mischief still on earth to roam.
The light coquettes in Sylphs aloft repair,65
And sport and flutter in the fields of air.
  "Know further yet; whoever fair and chaste
Rejects mankind, is by some Sylph embraced:
For spirits, freed from mortal laws, with ease
Assume what sexes and what shapes they please.[2]70
What guards the purity of melting maids,
In courtly balls, and midnight masquerades,
Safe from the treacherous friend, the daring spark,
The glance by day, the whisper in the dark,
When kind occasion prompts their warm desires,75
When music softens, and when dancing fires?
'Tis but their Sylph, the wise Celestials know,
Though Honor is the word with men below.
  "Some nymphs there are, too conscious of their face,
For life predestined to the Gnomes' embrace.80
These swell their prospects and exalt their pride,
When offers are disdained, and love denied:
Then gay ideas[3] crowd the vacant brain,

5. The "box" in the theater and the fashionable circular drive ("Ring") in Hyde Park.
6. Sedan chair.
7. The popular card game. See III.27 ff. and note.
8. The four elements out of which all things were believed to have been made were fire, water, earth, and air. One or another of these elements was supposed to be predominant in both the physical and psychological make-up of each human being. In this context they are spoken of as "humors."
9. Pope borrowed his supernatural beings from Rosicrucian mythology. Each element was inhabited by a spirit, as the following lines explain. The salamander is a lizardlike animal, in antiquity believed to live in fire.
1. Pronounce *tay*.
2. Cf. *Paradise Lost* I.427–31; this is one of many allusions to that poem in the *Rape*.
3. Images.

While peers, and dukes, and all their sweeping train,
And garters, stars, and coronets appear,   85
And in soft sounds, 'your Grace' salutes their ear.
'Tis these that early taint the female soul,
Instruct the eyes of young coquettes to roll,
Teach infant cheeks a bidden blush to know,
And little hearts to flutter at a beau.   90
    "Oft, when the world imagine women stray,
The Sylphs through mystic mazes guide their way,
Through all the giddy circle they pursue,
And old impertinence expel by new.
What tender maid but must a victim fall   95
To one man's treat, but for another's ball?
When Florio speaks what virgin could withstand,
If gentle Damon did not squeeze her hand?
With varying vanities, from every part,
They shift the moving toyshop⁴ of their heart;   100
Where wigs with wigs, with sword-knots sword-knots strive,
Beaux banish beaux, and coaches coaches drive.
This erring mortals levity may call;
Oh, blind to truth! the Sylphs contrive it all.
    "Of these am I, who thy protection claim,   105
A watchful sprite, and Ariel is my name.
Late, as I ranged the crystal wilds of air,
In the clear mirror of thy ruling star
I saw, alas! some dread event impend,
Ere to the main this morning sun descend,   110
But Heaven reveals not what, or how, or where:
Warned by the Sylph, O pious maid, beware!
This to disclose is all thy guardian can:
Beware of all, but most beware of Man!"
    He said; when Shock,⁵ who thought she slept too long,   115
Leaped up, and waked his mistress with his tongue.
'Twas then, Belinda, if report say true,
Thy eyes first opened on a billet-doux;
Wounds, charms, and ardors were no sooner read,
But all the vision vanished from thy head.   120
    And now, unveiled, the toilet stands displayed,
Each silver vase in mystic order laid.
First, robed in white, the nymph intent adores,
With head uncovered, the cosmetic powers.
A heavenly image in the glass appears;   125
To that she bends, to that her eyes she rears.
The inferior priestess, at her altar's side,
Trembling begins the sacred rites of Pride.
Unnumbered treasures ope at once, and here
The various offerings of the world appear;   130
From each she nicely culls with curious toil,

4. A shop stocked with baubles and   5. Belinda's lapdog.
trifles.

And decks the goddess with the glittering spoil.
This casket India's glowing gems unlocks,
And all Arabia breathes from yonder box.
The tortoise here and elephant unite,   135
Transformed to combs, the speckled and the white.
Here files of pins extend their shining rows,
Puffs, powders, patches, Bibles,[6] billet-doux.
Now awful Beauty puts on all its arms;
The fair each moment rises in her charms,   140
Repairs her smiles, awakens every grace,
And calls forth all the wonders of her face;
Sees by degrees a purer blush arise,
And keener lightnings quicken in her eyes.
The busy Sylphs surround their darling care,   145
These set the head, and those divide the hair,
Some fold the sleeve, whilst others plait the gown;
And Betty's[7] praised for labors not her own.

Canto II

Not with more glories, in the ethereal plain,
The sun first rises o'er the purpled main,
Than, issuing forth, the rival of his beams
Launched on the bosom of the silver Thames.
Fair nymphs and well-dressed youths around her shone,   5
But every eye was fixed on her alone.
On her white breast a sparkling cross she wore,
Which Jews might kiss, and infidels adore.
Her lively looks a sprightly mind disclose,
Quick as her eyes, and as unfixed as those: 10
Favors to none, to all she smiles extends;
Oft she rejects, but never once offends.
Bright as the sun, her eyes the gazers strike,
And, like the sun, they shine on all alike.
Yet graceful ease, and sweetness void of pride,   15
Might hide her faults, if belles had faults to hide:
If to her share some female errors fall,
Look on her face, and you'll forget 'em all.
This nymph, to the destruction of mankind,
Nourished two locks which graceful hung behind   20
In equal curls, and well conspired to deck
With shining ringlets the smooth ivory neck.
Love in these labyrinths his slaves detains,
And mighty hearts are held in slender chains.
With hairy springes[8] we the birds betray,   25
Slight lines of hair surprise the finny prey,
Fair tresses man's imperial race ensnare,
And beauty draws us with a single hair.
The adventurous Baron the bright locks admired,

6. It has been suggested that Pope intended here not "Bibles," but "bibelots," (trinkets), but this intepretation has not gained wide acceptance.

7. Belinda's maid, the "inferior priestess" mentioned in line 127.

8. Snares; pronounced *sprin-jez.*

He saw, he wished, and to the prize aspired. 30
Resolved to win, he meditates the way,
By force to ravish, or by fraud betray;
For when success a lover's toil attends,
Few ask if fraud or force attained his ends.

    For this, ere Phoebus rose, he had implored 35
Propitious Heaven, and every power adored,
But chiefly Love—to Love an altar built,
Of twelve vast French romances, neatly gilt.
There lay three garters, half a pair of gloves,
And all the trophies of his former loves. 40
With tender billet-doux he lights the pyre,
And breathes three amorous sighs to raise the fire.
Then prostrate falls, and begs with ardent eyes
Soon to obtain, and long possess the prize:
The powers gave ear, and granted half his prayer, 45
The rest the winds dispersed in empty air.

    But now secure the painted vessel glides,
The sunbeams trembling on the floating tides,
While melting music steals upon the sky,
And softened sounds along the waters die. 50
Smooth flow the waves, the zephyrs gently play,
Belinda smiled, and all the world was gay.
All but the Sylph—with careful thoughts oppressed,
The impending woe sat heavy on his breast.
He summons straight his denizens of air; 55
The lucid squadrons round the sails repair:
Soft o'er the shrouds aërial whispers breathe
That seemed but zephyrs to the train beneath.
Some to the sun their insect-wings unfold,
Waft on the breeze, or sink in clouds of gold. 60
Transparent forms too fine for mortal sight,
Their fluid bodies half dissolved in light,
Loose to the wind their airy garments flew,
Thin glittering textures of the filmy dew,
Dipped in the richest tincture of the skies, 65
Where light disports in ever-mingling dyes,
While every beam new transient colors flings,
Colors that change whene'er they wave their wings.
Amid the circle, on the gilded mast,
Superior by the head was Ariel placed; 70
His purple[9] pinions opening to the sun,
He raised his azure wand, and thus begun:

    "Ye Sylphs and Sylphids, to your chief give ear!
Fays, Fairies, Genii, Elves, and Daemons, hear!
Ye know the spheres and various tasks assigned 75
By laws eternal to the aërial kind.
Some in the fields of purest ether play,

9. In 18th-century poetic diction the word might mean "blood-red," "purple," or simply (as is likely here) "brightly colored." The word derives from Virgil, *Eclogue* IX, 40, *purpureous*. An example of the Latinate nature of some poetic diction of the period.

And bask and whiten in the blaze of day.
Some guide the course of wandering orbs on high,
Or roll the planets through the boundless sky.   80
Some less refined, beneath the moon's pale light
Pursue the stars that shoot athwart the night,
Or suck the mists in grosser air below,
Or dip their pinions in the painted bow,
Or brew fierce tempests on the wintry main,   85
Or o'er the glebe[1] distill the kindly rain.
Others on earth o'er human race preside,
Watch all their ways, and all their actions guide:
Of these the chief the care of nations own,
And guard with arms divine the British Throne.   90
  "Our humbler province is to tend the Fair,
Not a less pleasing, though less glorious care:
To save the powder from too rude a gale,
Nor let the imprisoned essences exhale;
To draw fresh colors from the vernal flowers;   95
To steal from rainbows e'er they drop in showers
A brighter wash;[2] to curl their waving hairs,
Assist their blushes, and inspire their airs;
Nay oft, in dreams invention we bestow,
To change a flounce, or add a furbelow.   100
  "This day black omens threat the brightest fair,
That e'er deserved a watchful spirit's care;
Some dire disaster, or by force or slight,
But what, or where, the Fates have wrapped in night:
Whether the nymph shall break Diana's law,[3]   105
Or some frail china jar receive a flaw,
Or stain her honor or her new brocade,
Forget her prayers, or miss a masquerade,
Or lose her heart, or necklace, at a ball;
Or whether Heaven has doomed that Shock must fall.   110
Haste, then, ye spirits! to your charge repair:
The fluttering fan be Zephyretta's care;
The drops[4] to thee, Brillante, we consign;
And, Momentilla, let the watch be thine;
Do thou, Crispissa,[5] tend her favorite Lock;   115
Ariel himself shall be the guard of Shock.
  "To fifty chosen Sylphs, of special note,
We trust the important charge, the petticoat;
Oft have we known that sevenfold fence to fail,
Though stiff with hoops, and armed with ribs of whale.   120
Form a strong line about the silver bound,
And guard the wide circumference around.
  "Whatever spirit, careless of his charge,
His post neglects, or leaves the fair at large,
Shall feel sharp vengeance soon o'ertake his sins,   125

1. Cultiviated field.
2. Cosmetic lotion.
3. Diana was the goddess of chastity.
4. Diamond earrings. Observe the ap-
propriateness of the names of the Sylphs
to their assigned functions.
5. From Latin *crispere*, to curl.

Be stopped in vials, or transfixed with pins,
Or plunged in lakes of bitter washes lie,
Or wedged whole ages in a bodkin's eye;[6]
Gums and pomatums shall his flight restrain,
While clogged he beats his silken wings in vain,   130
Or alum styptics with contracting power
Shrink his thin essence like a riveled[7] flower:
Or, as Ixion[8] fixed, the wretch shall feel
The giddy motion of the whirling mill,
In fumes of burning chocolate shall glow,   135
And tremble at the sea that froths below!"
    He spoke; the spirits from the sails descend;
Some, orb in orb, around the nymph extend;
Some thread the mazy ringlets of her hair;
Some hang upon the pendants of her ear: 140
With beating hearts the dire event they wait,
Anxious, and trembling for the birth of Fate.

Canto III

    Close by those meads, forever crowned with flowers,
Where Thames with pride surveys his rising towers,
There stands a structure of majestic frame,
Which from the neighboring Hampton takes its name.[9]
Here Britain's statesmen oft the fall foredoom   5
Of foreign tyrants and of nymphs at home;
Here thou, great Anna! whom three realms obey,
Dost sometimes counsel take—and sometimes tea.
    Hither the heroes and the nymphs resort,
To taste awhile the pleasures of a court;   10
In various talk the instructive hours they passed,
Who gave the ball, or paid the visit last;
One speaks the glory of the British Queen,
And one describes a charming Indian screen;
A third interprets motions, looks, and eyes;   15
At every word a reputation dies.
Snuff, or the fan, supply each pause of chat,
With singing, laughing, ogling, and all that.
    Meanwhile, declining from the noon of day,
The sun obliquely shoots his burning ray;   20
The hungry judges soon the sentence sign,
And wretches hang that jurymen may dine;
The merchant from the Exchange returns in peace,
And the long labors of the toilet cease.
Belinda now, whom thirst of fame invites,   25
Burns to encounter two adventurous knights,

---

6. A "bodkin" is a blunt needle with a large eye, used for drawing ribbon through eyelets in the edging of women's garments.
7. To "rivel" is to "contract into wrinkles and corrugations" (Johnson's *Dictionary*).
8. In the Greek myth Ixion was punished in the underworld by being bound on an everturning wheel.
9. Hampton Court, the royal palace, about fifteen miles up the Thames from London.

At ombre[1] singly to decide their doom,
And swells her breast with conquests yet to come.
Straight the three bands prepare in arms to join,
Each band the number of the sacred nine.   30
Soon as she spreads her hand, the aërial guard
Descend, and sit on each important card:
First Ariel perched upon a Matadore,
Then each according to the rank they bore;
For Sylphs, yet mindful of their ancient race,   35
Are, as when women, wondrous fond of place.
  Behold, four Kings in majesty revered,
With hoary whiskers and a forky beard;
And four fair Queens whose hands sustain a flower,
The expressive emblem of their softer power;   40
Four Knaves in garbs succinct,[2] a trusty band,
Caps on their heads, and halberts in their hand;
And parti-colored troops, a shining train,
Draw forth to combat on the velvet plain.
  The skillful nymph reviews her force with care;   45
"Let Spades be trumps!" she said, and trumps they were.
  Now move to war her sable Matadores,
In show like leaders of the swarthy Moors.
Spadillio first, unconquerable lord!
Led off two captive trumps, and swept the board.   50
As many more Manillio forced to yield,
And marched a victor from the verdant field.
Him Basto followed, but his fate more hard
Gained but one trump and one plebeian card.
With his broad saber next, a chief in years,   55
The hoary Majesty of Spades appears,
Puts forth one manly leg, to sight revealed,
The rest his many-colored robe concealed.
The rebel Knave, who dares his prince engage,
Proves the just victim of his royal rage.   60
Even mighty Pam,[3] that kings and queens o'erthrew
And mowed down armies in the fights of loo,
Sad chance of war! now destitute of aid,
Falls undistinguished by the victor Spade.
  Thus far both armies to Belinda yield;   65
Now to the Baron fate inclines the field.
His warlike amazon her host invades,

1. The game of ombre which Belinda
plays against the Baron and another
young man is too complicated for complete explication here. Pope has carefully arranged the cards so that Belinda
wins. The Baron's hand is strong enough
to be a threat, but the third player's is
of little account. The hand is played exactly according to the rules of ombre,
and Pope's description of the cards is
equally accurate. Each player holds
nine cards (line 30). The "Matadores"
(line 33), when spades are trumps, are
"Spadillio" (line 49), the ace of spades;
"Manillio" (line 51), the two of spades;
"Basto" (line 53), the ace of clubs;
Belinda holds all three of these. (For a
more complete description of ombre, see
Appendix C, *The Rape of the Lock and
Other Poems*, ed. Geoffrey Tillotson,
in the Twickenham Edition of Pope's
poems, Vol. II.)
2. Girded up.
3. The knave of clubs, the highest trump
in the game of loo.

The imperial consort of the crown of Spades.
The Club's black tyrant first her victim died,
Spite of his haughty mien and barbarous pride. 70
What boots the regal circle on his head,
His giant limbs, in state unwieldy spread?
That long behind he trails his pompous robe,
And of all monarchs only grasps the globe?
    The Baron now his Diamonds pours apace; 75
The embroidered King who shows but half his face,
And his refulgent Queen, with powers combined
Of broken troops an easy conquest find.
Clubs, Diamonds, Hearts, in wild disorder seen,
With throngs promiscuous strew the level green. 80
Thus when dispersed a routed army runs,
Of Asia's troops, and Afric's sable sons,
With like confusion diffcrent nations fly,
Of various habit, and of various dye,
The pierced battalions disunited fall 85
In heaps on heaps; one fate o'erwhelms them all.
    The Knave of Diamonds tries his wily arts,
And wins (oh, shameful chance!) the Queen of Hearts.
At this, the blood the virgin's cheek forsook,
A livid paleness spreads o'er all her look; 90
She sees, and trembles at the approaching ill,
Just in the jaws of ruin, and Codille,[4]
And now (as oft in some distempered state)
On one nice trick depends the general fate.
An Ace of Hearts steps forth: the King unseen 95
Lurked in her hand, and mourned his captive Queen.
He springs to vengeance with an eager pace,
And falls like thunder on the prostrate Ace.
The nymph exulting fills with shouts the sky,
The walls, the woods, and long canals reply. 100
    O thoughtless mortals! ever blind to fate,
Too soon dejected, and too soon elate:
Sudden these honors shall be snatched away,
And cursed forever this victorious day.
    For lo! the board with cups and spoons is crowned, 105
The berries crackle, and the mill turns round;[5]
On shining altars of Japan[6] they raise
The silver lamp; the fiery spirits blaze:
From silver spouts the grateful liquors glide,
While China's earth receives the smoking tide. 110
At once they gratify their scent and taste,
And frequent cups prolong the rich repast.
Straight hover round the fair her airy band;
Some, as she sipped, the fuming liquor fanned,

4. The term applied to losing a hand
at cards.
5. I.e., coffee is roasted and ground.
6. I.e., small, lacquered tables. The word
"altars" suggests the ritualistic character of coffee-drinking in Belinda's
world.

Some o'er her lap their careful plumes displayed,   115
Trembling, and conscious of the rich brocade.
Coffee (which makes the politician wise,
And see through all things with his half-shut eyes)
Sent up in vapors to the Baron's brain
New stratagems, the radiant Lock to gain.   120
Ah, cease, rash youth! desist ere 'tis too late,
Fear the just Gods, and think of Scylla's fate![7]
Changed to a bird, and sent to flit in air,
She dearly pays for Nisus' injured hair!
    But when to mischief mortals bend their will,   125
How soon they find fit instruments of ill!
Just then, Clarissa drew with tempting grace
A two-edged weapon from her shining case:
So ladies in romance assist their knight,
Present the spear, and arm him for the fight.   130
He takes the gift with reverence, and extends
The little engine on his fingers' ends;
This just behind Belinda's neck he spread,
As o'er the fragrant steams she bends her head.
Swift to the Lock a thousand sprites repair,   135
A thousand wings, by turns, blow back the hair,
And thrice they twitched the diamond in her ear,
Thrice she looked back, and thrice the foe drew near.
Just in that instant, anxious Ariel sought
The close recesses of the virgin's thought;   140
As on the nosegay in her breast reclined,
He watched the ideas rising in her mind,
Sudden he viewed, in spite of all her art,
An earthly lover lurking at her heart.
Amazed, confused, he found his power expired,   145
Resigned to fate, and with a sigh retired.
    The Peer now spreads the glittering forfex[8] wide,
To enclose the Lock; now joins it, to divide.
Even then, before the fatal engine closed,
A wretched Sylph too fondly interposed;   150
Fate urged the shears, and cut the Sylph in twain
(But airy substance soon unites again):
The meeting points the sacred hair dissever
From the fair head, forever, and forever!
    Then flashed the living lightning from her eyes,   155
And screams of horror rend the affrighted skies.
Not louder shrieks to pitying heaven are cast,
When husbands, or when lapdogs breathe their last;
Or when rich china vessels fallen from high,
In glittering dust and painted fragments lie!   160

7. Scylla, daughter of Nisus, was turned into a sea bird because, for the sake of her love for Minos of Crete, who was besieging her father's city of Megara, she cut from her father's head the purple lock on which his safety depended. She is not the Scylla of "Scylla and Charybdis."
8. Scissors.

"Let wreaths of triumph now my temples twine,"
The victor cried, "the glorious prize is mine!
While fish in streams, or birds delight in air,
Or in a coach and six the British Fair,
As long as *Atlantis*[9] shall be read,   165
Or the small pillow grace a lady's bed,
While visits shall be paid on solemn days,
When numerous wax-lights in bright order blaze,
While nymphs take treats, or assignations give,
So long my honor, name, and praise shall live!   170
What Time would spare, from Steel receives its date,
And monuments, like men, submit to fate!
Steel could the labor of the Gods destroy,
And strike to dust the imperial towers of Troy;
Steel could the works of mortal pride confound,   175
And hew triumphal arches to the ground.
What wonder then, fair nymph! thy hairs should feel,
The conquering force of unresisted Steel?"

Canto IV

But anxious cares the pensive nymph oppressed,
And secret passions labored in her breast.
Not youthful kings in battle seized alive,
Not scornful virgins who their charms survive,
Not ardent lovers robbed of all their bliss,   5
Not ancient ladies when refused a kiss,
Not tyrants fierce that unrepenting die,
Not Cynthia when her manteau's[1] pinned awry,
E'er felt such rage, resentment, and despair,
As thou, sad virgin! for thy ravished hair.   10
    For, that sad moment, when the Sylphs withdrew
And Ariel weeping from Belinda flew,
Umbriel,[2] a dusky, melancholy sprite
As ever sullied the fair face of light,
Down to the central earth, his proper scene,   15
Repaired to search the gloomy Cave of Spleen.[3]
    Swift on his sooty pinions flits the Gnome,
And in a vapor reached the dismal dome.
No cheerful breeze this sullen region knows,
The dreaded east is all the wind that blows.   20
Here in a grotto, sheltered close from air,
And screened in shades from day's detested glare,
She sighs forever on her pensive bed,
Pain at her side, and Megrim[4] at her head.
    Two handmaids wait the throne: alike in place,   25
But differing far in figure and in face.
Here stood Ill-Nature like an ancient maid,

9. Mrs. Manley's *New Atlantis* (1709) was notorious for its thinly concealed allusions to contemporary scandals.
1. Negligee or loose robe.
2. The name suggests shade and darkness.
3. Ill humor.
4. Headache.

Her wrinkled form in black and white arrayed;
With store of prayers for mornings, nights, and noons,
Her hand is filled; her bosom with lampoons.   30
    There Affectation, with a sickly mien,
Shows in her cheek the roses of eighteen,
Practiced to lisp, and hang the head aside,
Faints into airs, and languishes with pride,
On the rich quilt sinks with becoming woe,   35
Wrapped in a gown, for sickness and for show.
The fair ones feel such maladies as these,
When each new nightdress gives a new disease.
    A constant vapor[5] o'er the palace flies,
Strange phantoms rising as the mists arise;   40
Dreadful as hermit's dreams in haunted shades,
Or bright as visions of expiring maids.
Now glaring fiends, and snakes on rolling spires,[6]
Pale specters, gaping tombs, and purple fires;
Now lakes of liquid gold, Elysian scenes,   45
And crystal domes, and angels in machines.[7]
    Unnumbered throngs on every side are seen
Of bodies changed to various forms by Spleen.
Here living teapots stand, one arm held out,
One bent; the handle this, and that the spout: 50
A pipkin[8] there, like Homer's tripod, walks;
Here sighs a jar, and there a goose pie talks;
Men prove with child, as powerful fancy works,
And maids, turned bottles, call aloud for corks.
    Safe passed the Gnome through this fantastic band,   55
A branch of healing spleenwort[9] in his hand.
Then thus addressed the Power: "Hail, wayward Queen!
Who rule the sex to fifty from fifteen:
Parent of vapors and of female wit,
Who give the hysteric or poetic fit,   60
On various tempers act by various ways,
Make some take physic, others scribble plays;
Who cause the proud their visits to delay,
And send the godly in a pet to pray.
A nymph there is that all your power disdains,   65
And thousands more in equal mirth maintains.
But oh! if e'er thy Gnome could spoil a grace,
Or raise a pimple on a beauteous face,
Like citron-waters[1] matrons' cheeks inflame,
Or change complexions at a losing game;   70

---

5. Emblematic of "the vapors," i.e., hypochondria, melancholy, peevishness, often affected by fashionable women.
6. Coils.
7. Mechanical devices used in the theaters for spectacular effects. The fantasies of neurotic women here merge with the sensational stage effects popular with contemporary audiences.
8. An earthen pot. In *Iliad* XVIII.373–

77, Vulcan furnishes the gods with self-propelling "tripods" (three-legged stools).
9. An herb, efficacious against the spleen. Pope alludes to the golden bough that Aeneas and the Cumaean sybil carry with them for protection into the underworld in *Aeneid* VI.
1. Brandy flavored with orange or lemon peel.

If e'er with airy horns[2] I planted heads,
Or rumpled petticoats, or tumbled beds,
Or caused suspicion when no soul was rude,
Or discomposed the headdress of a prude,
Or e'er to costive lapdog gave disease,   75
Which not the tears of brightest eyes could ease,
Hear me, and touch Belinda with chagrin:[3]
That single act gives half the world the spleen."
   The Goddess with a discontented air
Seems to reject him though she grants his prayer.   80
A wondrous bag with both her hands she binds,
Like that where once Ulysses held the winds;[4]
There she collects the force of female lungs,
Sighs, sobs, and passions, and the war of tongues.
A vial next she fills with fainting fears,   85
Soft sorrows, melting griefs, and flowing tears.
The Gnome rejoicing bears her gifts away,
Spreads his black wings, and slowly mounts to day.
   Sunk in Thalestris'[5] arms the nymph he found,
Her eyes dejected and her hair unbound.   90
Full o'er their heads the swelling bag he rent,
And all the Furies issued at the vent.
Belinda burns with more than mortal ire,
And fierce Thalestris fans the rising fire.
"O wretched maid!" she spread her hands, and cried   95
(While Hampton's echoes, "Wretched maid!" replied),
"Was it for this you took such constant care
The bodkin, comb, and essence to prepare?
For this your locks in paper durance bound,
For this with torturing irons wreathed around?   100
For this with fillets strained your tender head,
And bravely bore the double loads of lead?[6]
Gods! shall the ravisher display your hair,
While the fops envy, and the ladies stare!
Honor forbid! at whose unrivaled shrine   105
Ease, pleasure, virtue, all, our sex resign.
Methinks already I your tears survey,
Already hear the horrid things they say,
Already see you a degraded toast,
And all your honor in a whisper lost!   110
How shall I, then, your helpless fame defend?
'Twill then be infamy to seem your friend!

2. Horns, the symbol of the cuckold, the man whose wife has been unfaithful to him; here "airy," because they exist only in the jealous suspicions of the husband, the victim of the mischievous Umbriel.
3. Ill humor.
4. Aeolus (later conceived of as god of the winds) gave Ulysses a bag containing all the winds adverse to his voyage home. When his ship was in sight of Ithaca, his companions opened the bag and the storms that ensued drove Ulysses far away (*Odyssey* X.19 ff.).
5. The name is borrowed from a queen of the Amazons, hence a fierce and warlike woman. Thalestris, according to legend, traveled 30 days in order to have a child by Alexander the Great. Plutarch denies the story.
6. The frame on which the elaborate coiffures of the day were arranged.

And shall this prize, the inestimable prize,
Exposed through crystal to the gazing eyes,
And heightened by the diamond's circling rays,   115
On that rapacious hand forever blaze?
Sooner shall grass in Hyde Park Circus grow,
And wits take lodgings in the sound of Bow;[7]
Sooner let earth, air, sea, to chaos fall,
Men, monkeys, lapdogs, parrots, perish all!"   120
    She said; then raging to Sir Plume repairs,
And bids her beau demand the precious hairs
(Sir Plume of amber snuffbox justly vain,
And the nice conduct of a clouded cane).
With earnest eyes, and round unthinking face,   125
He first the snuffbox opened, then the case,
And thus broke out—"My Lord, why, what the devil!
Z——ds! damn the lock! 'fore Gad, you must be civil!
Plague on't! 'tis past a jest—nay prithee, pox!
Give her the hair"—he spoke, and rapped his box.   130
    "It grieves me much," replied the Peer again,
"Who speaks so well should ever speak in vain.
But by this Lock, this sacred Lock I swear
(Which never more shall join its parted hair;
Which never more its honors shall renew,   135
Clipped from the lovely head where late it grew),
That while my nostrils draw the vital air,
This hand, which won it, shall forever wear."
He spoke, and speaking, in proud triumph spread
The long-contended honors[8] of her head.   140
    But Umbriel, hateful Gnome, forbears not so;
He breaks the vial whence the sorrows flow.
Then see! the nymph in beauteous grief appears,
Her eyes half languishing, half drowned in tears;
On her heaved bosom hung her drooping head,   145
Which with a sigh she raised, and thus she said:
    "Forever cursed be this detested day,
Which snatched my best, my favorite curl away!
Happy! ah, ten times happy had I been,
If Hampton Court these eyes had never seen!   150
Yet am not I the first mistaken maid,
By love of courts to numerous ills betrayed.
Oh, had I rather unadmired remained
In some lone isle, or distant northern land;
Where the gilt chariot never marks the way,   155
Where none learn ombre, none e'er taste bohea![9]
There kept my charms concealed from mortal eye,
Like roses that in deserts bloom and die.
What moved my mind with youthful lords to roam?
Oh, had I stayed, and said my prayers at home!   160

7. A person born within sound of the bells of St. Mary-le-Bow in Cheapside is said to be a cockney. No fashionable wit would have so vulgar an address.
8. Ornaments, hence locks; a Latinism.
9. A costly sort of tea.

'Twas this the morning omens seemed to tell,
Thrice from my trembling hand the patch box[1] fell;
The tottering china shook without a wind,
Nay, Poll sat mute, and Shock was most unkind!
A Sylph too warned me of the threats of fate,   165
In mystic visions, now believed too late!
See the poor remnants of these slighted hairs!
My hands shall rend what e'en thy rapine spares.
These in two sable ringlets taught to break,
Once gave new beauties to the snowy neck;   170
The sister lock now sits uncouth, alone,
And in its fellow's fate foresees its own;
Uncurled it hangs, the fatal shears demands,
And tempts once more thy sacrilegious hands.
Oh, hadst thou, cruel! been content to seize   175
Hairs less in sight, or any hairs but these!"

Canto V

She said: the pitying audience melt in tears.
But Fate and Jove had stopped the Baron's ears.
In vain Thalestris with reproach assails,
For who can move when fair Belinda fails?
Not half so fixed the Trojan[2] could remain,   5
While Anna begged and Dido raged in vain.
Then grave Clarissa graceful waved her fan;
Silence ensued, and thus the nymph began:
"Say why are beauties praised and honored most,
The wise man's passion, and the vain man's toast?   10
Why decked with all that land and sea afford,
Why angels called, and angel-like adored?
Why round our coaches crowd the white-gloved beaux,
Why bows the side box from its inmost rows?
How vain are all these glories, all our pains,   15
Unless good sense preserve what beauty gains;
That men may say when we the front box grace,
'Behold the first in virtue as in face!'
Oh! if to dance all night, and dress all day,
Charmed the smallpox, or chased old age away,   20
Who would not scorn what housewife's cares produce,
Or who would learn one earthly thing of use?
To patch, nay ogle, might become a saint,
Nor could it sure be such a sin to paint.
But since, alas! frail beauty must decay,   25
Curled or uncurled, since locks will turn to gray;
Since painted, or not painted, all shall fade,
And she who scorns a man must die a maid;

1. A box to hold the ornamental patches of court plaster worn on the face by both sexes. Cf. *Spectator* 81.
2. Aeneas, who forsook Dido at the bidding of the gods, despite her re-proaches and the supplications of her sister Anna. Virgil compares him to a steadfast oak that withstands a storm (*Aeneid* IV.437–43).

What then remains but well our power to use,
And keep good humor still whate'er we lose? 30
And trust me, dear, good humor can prevail
When airs, and flights, and screams, and scolding fail.
Beauties in vain their pretty eyes may roll;
Charms strike the sight, but merit wins the soul."[3]
 So spoke the dame, but no applause ensued; 35
Belinda frowned, Thalestris called her prude.
"To arms, to arms!" the fierce virago cries,
And swift as lightning to the combat flies.
All side in parties, and begin the attack;
Fans clap, silks rustle, and tough whalebones crack; 40
Heroes' and heroines' shouts confusedly rise,
And bass and treble voices strike the skies.
No common weapons in their hands are found,
Like Gods they fight, nor dread a mortal wound.
 So when bold Homer makes the Gods engage, 45
And heavenly breasts with human passions rage;
'Gainst Pallas, Mars; Latona, Hermes arms;
And all Olympus rings with loud alarms:
Jove's thunder roars, heaven trembles all around,
Blue Neptune storms, the bellowing deeps resound: 50
Earth shakes her nodding towers, the ground gives way,
And the pale ghosts start at the flash of day!
 Triumphant Umbriel on a sconce's height
Clapped his glad wings, and sat to view the fight:
Propped on the bodkin spears, the sprites survey 55
The growing combat, or assist the fray.
 While through the press enraged Thalestris flies,
And scatters death around from both her eyes,
A beau and witling perished in the throng,
One died in metaphor, and one in song. 60
"O cruel nymph! a living death I bear,"
Cried Dapperwit, and sunk beside his chair.
A mournful glance Sir Fopling upwards cast,
"Those eyes are made so killing"—was his last.
Thus on Maeander's flowery margin lies 65
The expiring swan, and as he sings he dies.
 When bold Sir Plume had drawn Clarissa down,
Chloe stepped in, and killed him with a frown;
She smiled to see the doughty hero slain,
But, at her smile, the beau revived again. 70
 Now Jove suspends his golden scales in air,
Weighs the men's wits against the lady's hair;
The doubtful beam long nods from side to side;
At length the wits mount up, the hairs subside.
 See, fierce Belinda on the Baron flies, 75

---

3. The speech is a close parody of Pope's own translation of the speech of Sarpedon to Glaucus, first published in 1709 and slightly revised in his version of the *Iliad* (XII.371–96).

With more than usual lightning in her eyes;
Nor feared the chief the unequal fight to try,
Who sought no more than on his foe to die.
   But this bold lord with manly strength endued,
She with one finger and a thumb subdued: 80
Just where the breath of life his nostrils drew,
A charge of snuff the wily virgin threw;
The Gnomes direct, to every atom just,
The pungent grains of titillating dust.
Sudden, with starting tears each eye o'erflows,   85
And the high dome re-echoes to his nose.
   "Now meet thy fate," incensed Belinda cried,
And drew a deadly bodkin[4] from her side.
(The same, his ancient personage to deck,
Her great-great-grandsire wore about his neck,   90
In three seal rings; which after, melted down,
Formed a vast buckle for his widow's gown:
Her infant grandame's whistle next it grew,
The bells she jingled, and the whistle blew;
Then in a bodkin graced her mother's hairs,   95
Which long she wore, and now Belinda wears.)
   "Boast not my fall," he cried, "insulting foe!
Thou by some other shalt be laid as low.
Nor think to die dejects my lofty mind:
All that I dread is leaving you behind!   100
Rather than so, ah, let me still survive,
And burn in Cupid's flames—but burn alive."
   "Restore the Lock!" she cries; and all around
"Restore the Lock!" the vaulted roofs rebound.
Not fierce Othello in so loud a strain   105
Roared for the handkerchief that caused his pain.[5]
But see how oft ambitious aims are crossed,
And chiefs contend till all the prize is lost!
The lock, obtained with guilt, and kept with pain,
In every place is sought, but sought in vain: 110
With such a prize no mortal must be blessed,
So Heaven decrees! with Heaven who can contest?
   Some thought it mounted to the lunar sphere,
Since all things lost on earth are treasured there.
There heroes' wits are kept in ponderous vases,   115
And beaux' in snuffboxes and tweezer cases.
There broken vows and deathbed alms are found,
And lovers' hearts with ends of riband bound,
The courtier's promises, and sick man's prayers,
The smiles of harlots, and the tears of heirs,   120
Cages for gnats, and chains to yoke a flea,
Dried butterflies, and tomes of casuistry.
   But trust the Muse—she saw it upward rise,

---

4. An ornamental pin shaped like a dagger, to be worn in the hair.   5. *Othello* III.iv.

Though marked by none but quick, poetic eyes
(So Rome's great founder to the heavens withdrew,[6]   125
To Proculus alone confessed in view);
A sudden star, it shot through liquid air,
And drew behind a radiant trail of hair.
Not Berenice's locks first rose so bright,[7]
The heavens bespangling with disheveled light.   130
The Sylphs behold it kindling as it flies,
And pleased pursue its progress through the skies.
    This the beau monde shall from the Mall[8] survey,
And hail with music its propitious ray.
This the blest lover shall for Venus take,   135
And send up vows from Rosamonda's Lake.[9]
This Partridge[1] soon shall view in cloudless skies,
When next he looks through Galileo's eyes;
And hence the egregious wizard shall foredoom
The fate of Louis, and the fall of Rome.   140
    Then cease, bright nymph! to mourn thy ravished hair,
Which adds new glory to the shining sphere!
Not all the tresses that fair head can boast,
Shall draw such envy as the Lock you lost.
For, after all the murders of your eye,   145
When, after millions slain, yourself shall die:
When those fair suns shall set, as set they must,
And all those tresses shall be laid in dust,
This Lock the Muse shall consecrate to fame,
And 'midst the stars inscribe Belinda's name.   150

1712   1714

Ode on Solitude[2]

Happy the man whose wish and care
    A few paternal acres bound,
Content to breathe his native air,
        In his own ground.

Whose herds with milk, whose fields with bread,
    Whose flocks supply him with attire,   5
Whose trees in summer yield him shade,
        In winter fire.

6. Romulus, the "founder" and first king of Rome, was snatched to heaven in a storm cloud while reviewing his army in the Campus Martius (Livy I. xvi).

7. Berenice, the wife of Ptolemy III, dedicated a lock of her hair to the gods to ensure her husband's safe return from war. It was turned into a constellation.

8. A walk laid out by Charles II in St. James's Park, a resort for strollers of all sorts.

9. In St. James's Park; associated with unhappy lovers.

1. John Partridge, the astrologer whose annually published predictions had been amusingly satirized by Swift and other wits in 1708. "Galileo's eyes": i.e., a telescope.

2. The hint for this poem was taken from Horace's well-known *Epode II*, which praises the simplicity and innocence of country life, a favorite literary theme in Pope's time.

Blest, who can unconcernedly find
    Hours, days, and years slide soft away,   10
In health of body, peace of mind,
        Quiet by day,

Sound sleep by night; study and ease,
    Together mixed; sweet recreation;
And innocence, which most does please   15
        With meditation.

Thus let me live, unseen, unknown;
    Thus unlamented let me die;
Steal from the world, and not a stone
        Tell where I lie.   20

ca. 1700–1709   1717, 1736

Epistle to Miss Blount[1]

ON HER LEAVING THE TOWN, AFTER THE CORONATION

As some fond virgin, whom her mother's care
Drags from the town to wholesome country air,
Just when she learns to roll a melting eye,
And hear a spark,[2] yet think no danger nigh;
From the dear man unwilling she must sever,   5
Yet takes one kiss before she parts forever:
Thus from the world fair Zephalinda[3] flew,
Saw others happy, and with sighs withdrew;
Not that their pleasures caused her discontent;
She sighed not that they stayed, but that she went.   10
    She went to plain-work,[4] and to purling brooks,
Old-fashioned halls, dull aunts, and croaking rooks:
She went from opera, park, assembly, play,
To morning walks, and prayers three hours a day;
To part her time 'twixt reading and bohea,[5]   15
To muse, and spill her solitary tea,
Or o'er cold coffee trifle with the spoon,
Count the slow clock, and dine exact at noon;[6]
Divert her eyes with pictures in the fire,
Hum half a tune, tell stories to the squire;   20
Up to her godly garret after seven,
There starve and pray, for that's the way to heaven.
    Some squire, perhaps, you take delight to rack,
Whose game is whist, whose treat a toast in sack;
Who visits with a gun, presents you birds,   25

1. Teresa Blount, sister of Pope's life-long friend Martha Blount. The "coronation" was that of George I (1714).
2. A fop, a beau.
3. A fanciful name adopted by Miss Blount.
4. "Needlework, as distinguished from embroidery" (Johnson's *Dictionary*).
5. A costly sort of tea.
6. The fashionable hour for dining in London was three or four o'clock. A noon dinner is a sign of old-fashioned rusticity.

Then gives a smacking buss, and cries—"No words!"
Or with his hounds comes hollowing from the stable,
Makes love with nods and knees beneath a table;
Whose laughs are hearty, though his jests are coarse,
And loves you best of all things—but his horse.   30
    In some fair evening, on your elbow laid,
You dream of triumphs in the rural shade;
In pensive thought recall the fancied scene,
See coronations rise on every green:
Before you pass the imaginary sights   35
Of lords and earls and dukes and gartered knights,
While the spread fan o'ershades your closing eyes;
Then gives one flirt,[7] and all the vision flies.
Thus vanish scepters, coronets, and balls,
And leave you in lone woods, or empty walls!   40
    So when your slave,[8] at some dear idle time
(Not plagued with headaches or the want of rhyme)
Stands in the streets, abstracted from the crew,
And while he seems to study, thinks of you;
Just when his fancy points [9] your sprightly eyes,   45
Or sees the blush of soft Parthenia [1] rise,
Gay [2] pats my shoulder, and you vanish quite;
Streets, chairs, and coxcombs rush upon my sight;
Vexed to be still in town, I knit my brow,
Look sour, and hum a tune—as you may now.   50

1717

Elegy to the Memory of an Unfortunate Lady[3]

    What beckoning ghost, along the moonlight shade
Invites my steps, and points to yonder glade?
'Tis she!—but why that bleeding bosom gored,
Why dimly gleams the visionary sword?
O ever beauteous, every friendly! tell,   5
Is it, in Heaven, a crime to love too well?
To bear too tender, or too firm a heart,
To act a lover's or a Roman's part? [4]
Is there no bright reversion [5] in the sky,
For those who greatly think, or bravely die?   10

---

7. I.e., opens and closes her fan with a jerk.
8. I.e., Pope.
9. Notices
1. Martha Blount.
2. John Gay, the poet.
3. The subject of the poem is fanciful, although Pope had been interested in the misfortunes of two ladies, neither of whom much resembled the subject of this poem. Geoffrey Tillotson has plausibly suggested that lines 79–80 are addressed to the beautiful, witty

Lady Mary Wortley Montagu, to whom Pope was romantically attached at this period. Later the two quarreled bitterly, for reasons no longer ascertainable, and Pope often attacked her in his satires under the pseudonym Sappho.
4. I.e., commit suicide, as the Roman Stoics taught that a man might do if he faced irremediable misery and misfortune.
5. "Succession (to an estate)" (Johnson's *Dictionary*).

Why bade ye else, ye Powers! her soul aspire
Above the vulgar flight of low desire?
Ambition first sprung from your blest abodes;
The glorious fault of angels and of gods: [5a]
Thence to their images on earth it flows,   15
And in the breasts of kings and heroes glows.
Most souls, 'tis true, but peep out once an age,
Dull sullen prisoners in the body's cage:
Dim lights of life, that burn a length of years
Useless, unseen, as lamps in sepulchers;   20
Like Eastern kings a lazy state they keep,
And close confined to their own palace, sleep.
    From these perhaps (ere Nature bade her die)
Fate snatched her early to the pitying sky.
As into air the purer spirits flow,   25
And separate from their kindred dregs below;
So flew the soul to its congenial place.
Nor left one virtue to redeem her race. [6]
    But thou, false guardian of a charge too good,
Thou, mean deserter of thy brother's blood!   30
See on these ruby lips the trembling breath,
These cheeks, now fading at the blast of death;
Cold is that breast which warmed the world before,
And those love-darting eyes must roll no more.
Thus, if Eternal Justice rules the ball,   35
Thus shall your wives, and thus your children fall:
On all the line a sudden vengeance waits,
And frequent hearses shall besiege your gates.
There passengers shall stand, and pointing say
(While the long funerals blacken all the way),   40
Lo these were they, whose souls the Furies steeled,
And cursed with hearts unknowing how to yield.
Thus unlamented pass the proud away,
The gaze of fools, and pageant of a day!
So perish all, whose breast ne'er learned to glow   45
For others' good, or melt at others' woe.
    What can atone (oh, ever-injured shade!)
Thy fate unpitied, and thy rites unpaid?
No friend's complaint, no kind domestic tear
Pleased thy pale ghost, or graced thy mournful bier.   50
By foreign hands thy dying eyes were closed,
By foreign hands thy decent limbs composed,
By foreign hands thy humble grave adorned;
By strangers honored, and by strangers mourned!
What though no friends in sable weeds appear,   55
Grieve for an hour, perhaps, then mourn a year,
And bear about the mockery of woe
To midnight dances, and the public show?

5a. Shakespeare's *Henry VIII* III.ii.   p. 70) has remarked on the "meta-
441-42.   physical" manner of lines 17–28.
6. Family. F. R. Leavis (*Revaluation*,

What though no weeping Loves thy ashes grace,
Nor polished marble emulate thy face?   60
What though no sacred earth allow thee room,
Nor hallowed dirge be muttered o'er thy tomb?[7]
Yet shall thy grave with rising flowers be dressed,
And the green turf lie lightly on thy breast:
There shall the morn her earliest tears bestow,   65
There the first roses of the year shall blow;
While angels with their silver wings o'ershade
The ground, now sacred by thy reliques made.
 So peaceful rests, without a stone, a name,
What once had beauty, titles, wealth, and fame.   70
How loved, how honored once, avails thee not,
To whom related, or by whom begot;
A heap of dust alone remains of thee,
'Tis all thou art, and all the proud shall be!
 Poets themselves must fall, like those they sung,   75
Deaf the praised ear, and mute the tuneful tongue.
Even he, whose soul now melts in mournful lays,
Shall shortly want the generous tear he pays;
Then from his closing eyes thy form shall part,
And the last pang shall tear thee from his heart,   80
Life's idle business at one gasp be o'er,
The Muse forgot, and thou beloved no more!

1717

Epistle to Robert, Earl of Oxford and Mortimer[1]

 Such were the notes thy once-loved Poet[2] sung,
Till Death untimely stopped his tuneful tongue.
Oh, just beheld and lost! admired and mourned!
With softest manners, gentlest arts, adorned!
Blessed in each science! blessed in every strain!   5
Dear to the Muse! to Harley dear—in vain!
 For him thou oft hast bid the world attend,
Fond to forget the statesman in the friend;
For Swift and him despised the farce of state,
The sober follies of the wise and great,   10
Dexterous the craving, fawning crowd to quit,
And pleased to 'scape from flattery to wit.[3]
 Absent or dead, still let a friend be dear
(A sigh the absent claims, the dead a tear);

---

7. In Roman Catholic countries sui-
cides are not given Christian burial.
1. Robert Harley, Lord Treasurer in
the Tory ministry that governed England from 1710 to Queen Anne's death
in 1714, became the Earl of Oxford
and Mortimer, after which he signed
himself "Oxford." Oxford joined Swift,
Pope, the queen's physician Dr. John
Arbuthnot, John Gay, and Thomas Parnell in forming the Martinus Scriblerus
Club in 1713.
2. Thomas Parnell (1679–1718), whose
poems Pope edited in 1722, dedicating
them to Oxford in this Epistle.
3. In the meetings of the Scriblerus
Club.

Recall those nights that closed thy toilsome days,   15
Still hear thy Parnell in his living lays;
Who, careless now of interest, fame, or fate,
Perhaps forgets that Oxford e'er was great;
Or deeming meanest what we greatest call,
Beholds thee glorious only in thy fall.   20
  And sure if aught below the seats divine
Can touch immortals, 'tis a soul like thine;
A soul supreme, in each hard instance tried,
Above all pain, all passion, and all pride,
The rage of power, the blast of public breath,   25
The lust of lucre, and the dread of death.[4]
  In vain to deserts[5] thy retreat is made;
The Muse attends thee to thy silent shade;
'Tis hers the brave man's latest steps to trace,
Rejudge his acts, and dignify disgrace.   30
When Interest calls off all her sneaking train,
And all the obliged desert, and all the vain,
She waits, or to the scaffold or the cell,
When the last lingering friend has bid farewell.
Even now she shades thy evening walk with bays   35
(No hireling she, no prostitute to praise);
Even now, observant of the parting ray,
Eyes the calm sunset of thy various day,
Through fortune's cloud one truly great can see,
Nor fears to tell that Mortimer is he.   40

1722

4. In 1715 Oxford had been impeached on a charge of high treason and imprisoned in the Tower, where he remained until his acquittal in 1717.

5. The word implied not aridity but wildness. Actually Oxford retired to his family estate in Herefordshire.

An Essay on Man

Pope's philosophical poem, *An Essay on Man*, is a fragment of an ambitious but never completed scheme for what the poet referred to as his "ethic work," which was to have been a large survey of man and of the society which he has created. The work is dedicated to Henry St. John (pronounced *Sín-jun*), Viscount Bolingbroke (1678–1751), the brilliant, though erratic, Secretary of State in the Tory ministry of 1710–14, whom Pope had come to know through Swift. After the accession of George I he fled to France, attainted of treason, but was pardoned and allowed to return in 1723. He settled near Pope at Dawley Farm and a close friendship developed between the two men. In their conversations Bolingbroke, who fancied himself a philosopher, helped Pope to formulate the optimistic system that is expounded in this poem, though the notion that Pope merely versified ideas that Bolingbroke furnished him in prose is no longer considered valid.

It is clear that the poem would have been pretty much what it is had the two men never met, for it expresses doctrines widely circulated and generally accepted at the time by enlightened minds throughout Europe.

The *Essay* gives memorable expression to ideas about the nature of the universe and man's place in it, ideas upon which 18th-century optimism rested. The evolutionary theories of the 19th century and the history of the first half of the 20th century have made such optimism untenable today; but this does not mean that the *Essay* is either trivial or cheap.

Pope's purpose is to "vindicate the ways of God to man," a phrase that consciously echoes *Paradise Lost* I.26. Like Milton, Pope faces the problem of the existence of evil in a world presumed to be the creation of a good God (a philosophical work that deals with this problem is called a "theodicy"). *Paradise Lost* is Biblical in content, Christian in doctrine; the *Essay on Man* avoids all specifically Christian doctrines, not because Pope disbelieved them, but because "man," the subject of the poem, includes millions who never heard of Christianity, and Pope is concerned with the universal. Milton tells a mythological story. Pope writes in abstract terms.

The *Essay* is divided into four Epistles. In the first Pope asserts the essential order and goodness of the universe and the rightness of man's place in it. The other Epistles deal with how man may emulate in his nature and in society the cosmic harmony revealed in the first Epistle. The second seeks to show how he may attain a psychological harmony which can become the basis of a virtuous life through the co-operation of self-love and the passions (both necessary to our complete humanity) with reason, the controller and director. The third is concerned with man in society, which, it teaches, was created through the co-operation of self-love (the egoistic drives that motivate us) and social love (our dependence on others, our inborn benevolence). The fourth is concerned with happiness, which lies within the reach of all, for it is dependent upon virtue, which becomes possible when—though only when—self-love is transmuted into love of man and love of God. Such, in brief summary, are Pope's main ideas in the poem. He has given them expression in splendid language, unforgettable phrases (many have detached themselves from the poem and have become a part of our daily speech), and astonishing metrical virtuosity; and though the poem is didactic, it is richly musical and is distinguished by subtly beautiful visual imagery.

From An Essay on Man

TO HENRY ST. JOHN, LORD BOLINGBROKE

Epistle I. Of the Nature and State of Man,
With Respect to the Universe

> Awake, my St. John! leave all meaner things
> To low ambition, and the pride of kings.
> Let us (since life can little more supply
> Than just to look about us and to die)
> Expatiate free[1] o'er all this scene of man;   5

1. Range freely.

A mighty maze! but not without a plan;
A wild, where weeds and flowers promiscuous shoot,
Or garden, tempting with forbidden fruit.
Together let us beat this ample field,
Try what the open, what the covert yield;   10
The latent tracts, the giddy heights, explore
Of all who blindly creep, or sightless soar;
Eye Nature's walks, shoot folly as it flies,
And catch the manners living as they rise;
Laugh where we must, be candid[2] where we can;   15
But vindicate the ways of God to man.[3]

   1. Say first, of God above, or man below,
What can we reason, but from what we know?
Of man, what see we but his station here,
From which to reason, or to which refer?   20
Through worlds unnumbered though the God be known,
'Tis ours to trace him only in our own.
He, who through vast immensity can pierce,
See worlds on worlds compose one universe,
Observe how system into system runs,   25
What other planets circle other suns,
What varied Being peoples every star,
May tell why Heaven has made us as we are.
But of this frame the bearings, and the ties,
The strong connections, nice dependencies,   30
Gradations just, has thy pervading soul
Looked through? or can a part contain the whole?
   Is the great chain, that draws all to agree,
And drawn supports, upheld by God, or thee?

   2. Presumptuous man! the reason wouldst thou find,   35
Why formed so weak, so little, and so blind?
First, if thou canst, the harder reason guess,
Why formed no weaker, blinder, and no less!
Ask of thy mother earth, why oaks are made
Taller or stronger than the weeds they shade?   40
Or ask of yonder argent fields above,
Why Jove's satellites[4] are less than Jove?
   Of systems possible, if 'tis confessed
That Wisdom Infinite must form the best,
Where all must full or not coherent be,   45
And all that rises, rise in due degree;
Then, in the scale of reasoning life, 'tis plain,
There must be, somewhere, such a rank as man:
And all the question (wrangle e'er so long)
Is only this, if God has placed him wrong?   50
   Respecting man, whatever wrong we call,
May, must be right, as relative to all.

2. Kindly.
3. Pope deliberately echoes *Paradise Lost* I.26.
4. In his *Dictionary* Johnson notes and condemns Pope's giving his word four syllables, as in Latin.

In human works, though labored on with pain,
A thousand movements scarce one purpose gain;
In God's, one single can its end produce; 55
Yet serves to second too some other use.
So man, who here seems principal alone,
Perhaps acts second to some sphere unknown,
Touches some wheel, or verges to some goal;
'Tis but a part we see, and not a whole. 60
    When the proud steed shall know why man restrains
His fiery course, or drives him o'er the plains;
When the dull ox, why now he breaks the clod,
Is now a victim, and now Egypt's god:
Then shall man's pride and dullness comprehend 65
His actions', passions', being's use and end;
Why doing, suffering, checked, impelled; and why
This hour a slave, the next a deity.
    Then say not man's imperfect, Heaven in fault;
Say rather, man's as perfect as he ought: 70
His knowledge measured to his state and place,
His time a moment, and a point his space.
If to be perfect in a certain sphere,[5]
What matter, soon or late, or here or there?
The blest today is as completely so, 75
As who began a thousand years ago.

    3. Heaven from all creatures hides the book of Fate,
All but the page prescribed, their present state:
From brutes what men, from men what spirits know:
Or who could suffer Being here below? 80
The lamb thy riot dooms to bleed today,
Had he thy reason, would he skip and play?
Pleased to the last, he crops the flowery food,
And licks the hand just raised to shed his blood.
O blindness to the future! kindly given, 85
That each may fill the circle marked by Heaven:
Who sees with equal eye, as God of all,
A hero perish, or a sparrow fall,
Atoms or systems[6] into ruin hurled,
And now a bubble burst, and now a world. 90
    Hope humbly then; with trembling pinions soar;
Wait the great teacher Death, and God adore!
What future bliss, he gives not thee to know,
But gives that hope to be thy blessing now.
Hope springs eternal in the human breast: 95
Man never is, but always to be blest:
The soul, uneasy and confined from home,
Rests and expatiates in a life to come.
    Lo! the poor Indian, whose untutored mind
Sees God in clouds, or hears him in the wind; 100
His soul proud Science never taught to stray

5. I.e., in one's "state and place."   6. Solar systems.

Far as the solar walk, or milky way;
Yet simple Nature to his hope has given,
Behind the cloud-topped hill, an humbler heaven;
Some safer world in depth of woods embraced,   105
Some happier island in the watery waste,
Where slaves once more their native land behold,
No fiends torment, no Christians thirst for gold!
To be, contents his natural desire,
He asks no angel's wing, no seraph's fire;   110
But thinks, admitted to that equal sky,
His faithful dog shall bear him company.

   4. Go, wiser thou! and, in thy scale of sense,
Weigh thy opinion against Providence;
Call imperfection what thou fancy'st such,   115
Say, here he gives too little, there too much;
Destroy all creatures for thy sport or gust,[7]
Yet cry, if man's unhappy, God's unjust;
If man alone engross not Heaven's high care,
Alone made perfect here, immortal there: 120
Snatch from his hand the balance and the rod,
Rejudge his justice, be the God of God!
In pride, in reasoning pride, our error lies;
All quit their sphere, and rush into the skies.
Pride still is aiming at the blest abodes,   125
Men would be angels, angels would be gods.
Aspiring to be gods, if angels fell,
Aspiring to be angels, men rebel:
And who but wishes to invert the laws
Of order, sins against the Eternal Cause.   130

   5. Ask for what end the heavenly bodies shine,
Earth for whose use? Pride answers, " 'Tis for mine:
For me kind Nature wakes her genial power,
Suckles each herb, and spreads out every flower;
Annual for me, the grape, the rose renew   135
The juice nectareous, and the balmy dew;
For me, the mine a thousand treasures brings;
For me, health gushes from a thousand springs;
Seas roll to waft me, suns to light me rise;
My footstool earth, my canopy the skies."   140
   But errs not Nature from this gracious end,
From burning suns when livid deaths descend,
When earthquakes swallow, or when tempests sweep
Towns to one grave, whole nations to the deep?
"No," 'tis replied, "the first Almighty Cause   145
Acts not by partial, but by general laws;
The exceptions few; some change since all began,
And what created perfect?"—Why then man?
If the great end be human happiness,

---

7. "Sense of tasting" (Johnson's *Dictionary*).

Then Nature deviates; and can man do less?   150
As much that end a constant course requires
Of showers and sunshine, as of man's desires;
As much eternal springs and cloudless skies,
As men forever temperate, calm, and wise.
If plagues or earthquakes break not Heaven's design,   155
Why then a Borgia, or a Catiline?[8]
Who knows but he whose hand the lightning forms,
Who heaves old ocean, and who wings the storms,
Pours fierce ambition in a Caesar's mind,
Or turns young Ammon[9] loose to scourge mankind?   160
From pride, from pride, our very reasoning springs;
Account for moral, as for natural things:
Why charge we Heaven in those, in these acquit?
In both, to reason right is to submit.
    Better for us, perhaps, it might appear,   165
Were there all harmony, all virtue here;
That never air or ocean felt the wind;
That never passion discomposed the mind:
But ALL subsists by elemental strife;
And passions are the elements of life.   170
The general ORDER, since the whole began,
Is kept in Nature, and is kept in man.

    6. What would this man? Now upward will he soar,
And little less than angel, would be more;
Now looking downwards, just as grieved appears   175
To want the strength of bulls, the fur of bears.
Made for his use all creatures if he call,
Say what their use, had he the powers of all?
Nature to these, without profusion, kind,
The proper organs, proper powers assigned;   180
Each seeming want compénsated of course,
Here with degrees of swiftness, there of force;
All in exact proportion to the state;
Nothing to add, and nothing to abate.
Each beast, each insect, happy in its own;   185
Is Heaven unkind to man, and man alone?
Shall he alone, whom rational we call,
Be pleased with nothing, if not blessed with all?
    The bliss of man (could pride that blessing find)
Is not to act or think beyond mankind;   190
No powers of body or of soul to share,
But what his nature and his state can bear.
Why has not man a microscopic eye?

---

8. The Renaissance Italian family of the Borgias were notorious for their crimes: ruthless lust for power, cruelty, rapaciousness, treachery, and murder (especially by poisoning); Cesare Borgia (1476–1507), son of Pope Alexander VI, is here referred to. Lucius Sergius Catiline (ca. 108–62 B.C.), an ambitious, greedy, and cruel conspirator against the Roman state, was denounced in Cicero's famous orations before the senate and in the Forum.
9. Alexander the Great.

For this plain reason, man is not a fly.
Say what the use, were finer optics given,   195
To inspect a mite, not comprehend the heaven?
Or touch, if tremblingly alive all o'er,
To smart and agonize at every pore?
Or quick effluvia[1] darting through the brain,
Die of a rose in aromatic pain?   200
If nature thundered in his opening ears,
And stunned him with the music of the spheres,
How would he wish that Heaven had left him still
The whispering zephyr, and the purling rill?
Who finds not Providence all good and wise,   205
Alike in what it gives, and what it denies?

   7. Far as creation's ample range extends,
The scale of sensual,[2] mental powers ascends:
Mark how it mounts, to man's imperial race,
From the green myriads in the peopled grass: 210
What modes of sight betwixt each wide extreme,
The mole's dim curtain, and the lynx's beam:[3]
Of smell, the headlong lioness between,
And hound sagacious[4] on the tainted green:
Of hearing, from the life that fills the flood,   215
To that which warbles through the vernal wood:
The spider's touch, how exquisitely fine!
Feels at each thread, and lives along the line:
In the nice[5] bee, what sense so subtly true
From poisonous herbs extracts the healing dew: 220
How instinct varies in the groveling swine,
Compared, half-reasoning elephant, with thine!
'Twixt that, and reason, what a nice barrier;[6]
Forever separate, yet forever near!
Remembrance and reflection how allied;   225
What thin partitions sense from thought divide:
And middle natures, how they long to join,
Yet never pass the insuperable line!
Without this just gradation, could they be
Subjected, these to those, or all to thee?   230
The powers of all subdued by thee alone,
Is not thy reason all these powers in one?

   8. See, through this air, this ocean, and this earth,
All matter quick, and bursting into birth.
Above, how high progressive life may go!   235
Around, how wide! how deep extend below!

1. According to the philosophy of Epicurus (adopted by Robert Boyle, the chemist, and other 17th-century scientists), the senses are stirred to perception by being bombarded through the pores by steady streams of "effluvia," incredibly thin and tiny—but material—images of the objects which surround us.
2. Sensory.
3. One of several early theories of vision held that the eye casts a beam of light which makes objects visible.
4. Quick of scent.
5. Exact, accurate.
6. Pronounced *ba-réer*.

Vast Chain of Being! which from God began,
Natures ethereal, human, angel, man,
Beast, bird, fish, insect, what no eye can see,
No glass can reach! from Infinite to thee,   240
From thee to nothing.—On superior powers
Were we to press, inferior might on ours:
Or in the full creation leave a void,
Where, one step broken, the great scale's destroyed:
From Nature's chain whatever link you strike,   245
Tenth or ten thousandth, breaks the chain alike.
  And, if each system in gradation roll
Alike essential to the amazing Whole,
The least confusion but in one, not all
That system only, but the Whole must fall.   250
Let earth unbalanced from her orbit fly,
Planets and suns run lawless through the sky,
Let ruling angels from their spheres be hurled,
Being on being wrecked, and world on world,
Heaven's whole foundations to their center nod,   255
And Nature tremble to the throne of God:
All this dread ORDER break—for whom? for thee?
Vile worm!—oh, madness, pride, impiety!

    9. What if the foot, ordained the dust to tread,
Or hand, to toil, aspired to be the head?   260
What if the head, the eye, or ear repined
To serve mere engines to the ruling Mind?[7]
Just as absurd for any part to claim
To be another, in this general frame:
Just as absurd, to mourn the tasks or pains,   265
The great directing MIND of ALL ordains.
  All are but parts of one stupendous whole,
Whose body Nature is, and God the soul;
That, changed through all, and yet in all the same,
Great in the earth, as in the ethereal frame,   270
Warms in the sun, refreshes in the breeze,
Glows in the stars, and blossoms in the trees,
Lives through all life, extends through all extent,
Spreads undivided, operates unspent,
Breathes in our soul, informs our mortal part,   275
As full, as perfect, in a hair as heart;
As full, as perfect, in vile man that mourns,
As the rapt seraph that adores and burns;
To him no high, no low, no great, no small;
He fills, he bounds, connects, and equals all.   280

    10. Cease then, nor ORDER imperfection name:
Our proper bliss depends on what we blame.
Know thy own point: this kind, this due degree
Of blindness, weakness, Heaven bestows on thee.

7. Cf. I Corinthians xii.14–26.

Submit—In this, or any other sphere,   285
Secure to be as blest as thou canst bear:
Safe in the hand of one disposing Power,
Or in the natal, or the mortal hour.
All Nature is but art, unknown to thee;
All chance, direction, which thou canst not see;   290
All discord, harmony not understood;
All partial evil, universal good:
And, spite of pride, in erring reason's spite,
One truth is clear: Whatever IS, is RIGHT.

From *Epistle II. Of the Nature and State of Man With Respect to Himself, as an Individual*

1. Know then thyself, presume not God to scan;
The proper study of mankind is Man.
Placed on this isthmus of a middle state,
A being darkly wise, and rudely great:
With too much knowledge for the skeptic side,   5
With too much weakness for the Stoic's pride,
He hangs between; in doubt to act, or rest,
In doubt to deem himself a god, or beast;
In doubt his mind or body to prefer,
Born but to die, and reasoning but to err;   10
Alike in ignorance, his reason such,
Whether he thinks too little, or too much:
Chaos of thought and passion, all confused;
Still by himself abused, or disabused;
Created half to rise, and half to fall;   15
Great lord of all things, yet a prey to all;
Sole judge of truth, in endless error hurled:
The glory, jest, and riddle of the world!

* * *

1733

The Universal Prayer

Father of all! in every age,
    In every clime adored,
By saint, by savage, and by sage,
    Jehovah, Jove, or Lord!

Thou Great First Cause, least understood: 5
    Who all my sense confined
To know but this—that thou art good,
    And that myself am blind:

Yet gave me, in this dark estate,
    To see the good from ill;   10

And binding Nature fast in fate,
    Left free the human will.

What conscience dictates to be done,
    Or warns me not to do,
This, teach me more than Hell to shun,   15
    That, more than Heaven pursue.

What blessings thy free bounty gives,
    Let me not cast away;
For God is paid when man receives,
    To enjoy is to obey.   20

Yet not to earth's contracted span,
    Thy goodness let me bound,
Or think thee Lord alone of man,
    When thousand worlds are round:

Let not this weak, unknowing hand   25
    Presume thy bolts to throw,
And deal damnation round the land,
    On each I judge thy foe.

If I am right, thy grace impart,
    Still in the right to stay;   30
If I am wrong, oh teach my heart
    To find that better way.

Save me alike from foolish pride,
    Or impious discontent,
At aught thy wisdom has denied,   35
    Or aught thy goodness lent.

Teach me to feel another's woe,
    To hide the fault I see;
That mercy I to others show,
    That mercy show to me.   40

Mean though I am, not wholly so
    Since quickened by thy breath;
Oh lead me wheresoe'er I go,
    Through this day's life or death.

This day, be bread and peace my lot: 45
    All else beneath the sun,
Thou know'st if best bestowed or not,
    And let thy will be done.

To thee, whose temple is all space,
    Whose altar, earth, sea, skies!   50
One chorus let all being raise!
    All Nature's incense rise!

The First Satire of the Second Book of Horace Imitated[1]

TO MR. FORTESCUE[2]

P. There are (I scarce can think it, but am told),
There are, to whom my satire seems too bold:
Scarce to wise Peter[3] cómplaisant enough,
And something said of Chartres much too rough.
The lines are weak, another's pleased to say,   5
Lord Fanny[4] spins a thousand such a day.
Timorous by nature, of the rich in awe,
I come to counsel learned in the law:
You'll give me, like a friend, both sage and free,[4a]
Advice; and (as you use) without a fee.   10
  F. I'd write no more.
  P.   Not write? but then I think,
And for my soul I cannot sleep a wink.
I nod in company, I wake at night,
Fools rush into my head, and so I write.
  F. You could not do a worse thing for your life.   15
Why, if the nights seem tedious, take a wife:
Or rather truly, if your point be rest,
Lettuce and cowslip wine;[5] *Probatum est.*
But talk with Celsus,[6] Celsus will advise
Hartshorn, or something that shall close your eyes.   20
Or, if you needs must write, write Caesar's[7] praise,

1. In his Preface to the translation of Ovid's *Epistles* (1680), Dryden distinguished three methods of translation: "metaphrase," translating as nearly as possible word for word and line for line; "paraphrase," retaining the sense but not the literal wording of the original (the method that he used in translating Virgil, and Pope in translating Homer); and "imitation," following the general structure of the original, modernizing its allusions to circumstances, manners, and men, and assuming, as he says, "the liberty not only to vary from the words and sense, but to forsake them both" as occasion demands. It is this mode that Pope used in some of his major satires of the 1730's, *Imitations of Horace.*
    Experience had taught him that if in his satires he named actual people, he was charged with cruelty or slander, and if he used fictitious names, they were often identified by gossip with people he had not intended at all. General satire seemed to miss the mark. Satire aimed at individuals aroused sympathy for the victim and antagonism toward the satirist. When Bolingbroke pointed out that his situation was much like that which Horace had treated with wry humor in *Satires* II.i, Pope immediately set about "imitating" it, converting it into a completely contemporary, even a personal poem. It is a vigorous defense of Pope the satirist, who is presented in the heroic role of the disinterested friend and defender of virtue and truth in an evil time.
2. William Fortescue, the eminent lawyer, who, though a Whig and a supporter of Walpole, was a friend of Pope.
3. Peter Walter, a notorious moneylender; Francis Chartres, a debauchee and gambler. Pope mentions them in other satires.
4. John, Lord Hervey. See *Epistle to Dr. Arbuthnot,* line 305 and note. Fannius was a poetaster mentioned contemptuously by Horace (*Satires* I.iv.21–22 and I.x.80).
4a. Frank.
5. Used as soporifics; *"Probatum est"* may be freely rendered "a proved remedy."
6. A Roman writer on medicine, here used as a fictitious name for a physician. "Hartshorn," or buckshorn, was an herb used in treating the eyes and in sleeping potions.
7. George II's.

You'll gain at least a knighthood, or the bays.[8]

P. What? like Sir Richard,[9] rumbling, rough, and fierce,
With arms, and George, and Brunswick crowd the verse?
Rend with tremendous sound your ears asunder,   25
With gun, drum, trumpet, blunderbuss, and thunder?
Or nobly wild, with Budgell's fire and force,
Paint angels trembling round his falling horse?[1]

F. Then all your Muse's softer art display,
Let Carolina[2] smooth the tuneful lay,   30
Lull with Amelia's liquid name the Nine,
And sweetly flow through all the royal line.

P. Alas! few verses touch their nicer ear;
They scarce can bear their laureate twice a year;[3]
And justly Caesar scorns the poet's lays,   35
It is to history he trusts for praise.

F. Better be Cibber, I'll maintain it still,
Than ridicule all taste, blaspheme Quadrille,[4]
Abuse the City's best good men in meter,
And laugh at peers that put their trust in Peter.   40
Even those you touch not, hate you.

P.   What should ail 'em?

F. A hundred smart in Timon[5] and in Balaam:
The fewer still you name, you wound the more;
Bond is but one, but Harpax is a score.[6]

P. Each mortal has his pleasure: none deny   45
Scarsdale his bottle, Darty his ham pie;
Ridotta[7] sips and dances, till she see
The doubling lusters[8] dance as fast as she;
F———[9] loves the senate, Hockley Hole his brother,
Like in all else, as one egg to another.   50
I love to pour out all myself, as plain
As downright Shippen, or as old Montaigne:[1]

---

8. The poet-laureateship.
9. Sir Richard Blackmore (1654–1729),
London physician, knighted by William
III for his Whig principles and his epics.
Pope and all the "wits" laughed at
his poems, with good reason. Observe
the noisy emptiness of lines 23–26, which
are intended to suggest Blackmore's in-
flated style.
1. Eustace Budgell, Addison's cousin,
had sung the praises of the king's horse,
which had been shot out from under
him at the battle of Oudenarde (1708).
George yearned for military glory.
2. Queen Caroline and the Princess
Amelia. Contrast with the bombast of
lines 25–26 the mellifluous emptiness of
lines 30–32.
3. Colley Cibber (1671–1757), the
laureate, wrote execrable official odes
for each New Year and for the king's
birthday.
4. A popular card game.
5. When in his *Epistle to the Earl of
Burlington* (1731) Pope had described

a fictitious "Timon," owner of a vulgar,
ostentatious estate, the town had identified him with the Duke of Chandos and
charged Pope with ingratitude to a
friend. "Balaam": a fictitious London
merchant whose rise and fall Pope recounts in his *Epistle to Lord Bathurst*
(1732).
6. Dennis Bond, a notorious embezzler,
mentioned by name in Pope's *Epistle to
Bathurst*, line 100; "Harpax" (Greek
for "robber") is a type of the miser in
the same poem (lines 91–92).
7. A type name for a pleasure-loving
woman. *Ridotto* is Italian for a social
assembly with music and dancing.
8. Cut-glass chandeliers.
9. Stephen Fox, a Whig politician; "his
brother": Henry, later Lord Holland.
"Hockley Hole" was a bear garden.
1. William Shippen, the plain-spoken
leader of the Jacobites in Parliament.
The essays of Michel de Montaigne
(1533–92) abound in self-revelation.

In them, as certain to be loved as seen,
The soul stood forth, nor kept a thought within;
In me what spots (for spots I have) appear,   55
Will prove at least the medium must be clear.
In this impartial glass, my Muse intends
Fair to expose myself, my foes, my friends;
Publish the present age, but where my text
Is vice too high, reserve it for the next: 60
My foes shall wish my life a longer date,
And every friend the less lament my fate.
My head and heart thus flowing through my quill,
Verse-man or prose-man, term me which you will,
Papist or Protestant, or both between,   65
Like good Erasmus² in an honest mean,
In moderation placing all my glory,
While Tories call me Whig, and Whigs a Tory.
Satire's my weapon, but I'm too discreet
To run amuck, and tilt at all I meet;   70
I only wear it in a land of hectors;
Thieves, supercargoes, sharpers, and directors.³
Save but our army! and let Jove encrust
Swords, pikes, and guns, with everlasting rust!
Peace is my dear delight—not Fleury's⁴ more: 75
But touch me, and no minister so sore.
Whoe'er offends, at some unlucky time
Slides into verse, and hitches in a rhyme,
Sacred to ridicule his whole life long,
And the sad burden of some merry song.   80
    Slander or poison dread from Delia's rage,⁵
Hard words or hanging, if your judge be Page.⁶
From furious Sappho⁷ scarce a milder fate,
P—xed⁸ by her love, or libeled by her hate.
Its proper power to hurt, each creature feels;   85
Bulls aim their horns, and asses lift their heels;
'Tis a bear's talent not to kick, but hug;
And no man wonders he's not stung by Pug.⁹
So drink with Walters, or with Chartres eat,
They'll never poison you, they'll only cheat.   90
    Then, learned sir! (to cut the matter short)
Whate'er my fate, or well or ill at court,

2. Pope admired greatly the Dutch humanist Erasmus (1466–1536).
3. "Hectors": bullies; "supercargoes": officers in charge of the cargoes of merchant ships; "directors": i.e., of the collapsed South Sea Company, whose corruption was revealed by a Parliamentary inquiry when the company failed in 1720. But Pope, whose sympathies lay with the Tories and the landed gentry, is probably thinking generally of trade and finance.
4. Cardinal Fleury, minister of Louis XV of France, whose foreign policy was based on preserving peace.
5. Usually assumed to be Mary Howard. Countess of Delorain, a mistress of George II, who according to gossip had tried, in a fit of jealousy, to poison a Maid of Honor.
6. Sir Francis Page, a judge known for his bullying manner on the bench. Fielding describes him in action in *Tom Jones* VIII.xi.
7. Pope's most violent attack on Lady Mary Wortley Montagu.
8. Poxed, i.e., infected with syphilis.
9. The name of a pet dog or monkey.

Whether old age, with faint but cheerful ray,
Attends to gild the evening of my day,
Or Death's black wing already be displayed,   95
To wrap me in the universal shade;
Whether the darkened room to muse invite,
Or whitened wall provoke the skewer to write,[1]
In durance, exile, Bedlam, or the Mint,[2]
Like Lee or Budgell, I will rhyme and print.   100
    F. Alas, young man! your days can ne'er be long,
In flower of age you perish for a song!
Plums and directors, Shylock and his wife,[3]
Will club their testers, now, to take your life!
    P. What? armed for Virtue when I point the pen,   105
Brand the bold front of shameless guilty men,
Dash the proud gamester in his gilded car;
Bare the mean heart that lurks beneath a star;[4]
Can there be wanting, to defend her cause,
Lights of the Church, or guardians of the laws?   110
Could pensioned Boileau[5] lash in honest strain
Flatterers and bigots even in Louis' reign?
Could laureate Dryden pimp and friar engage,[6]
Yet neither Charles nor James be in a rage?
And I not strip the gilding off a knave,   115
Unplaced,[7] unpensioned, no man's heir, or slave?
I will, or perish in the generous cause.
Hear this, and tremble! you who 'scape the laws.
Yes, while I live, no rich or noble knave
Shall walk the world, in credit, to his grave.   120
To VIRTUE ONLY AND HER FRIENDS A FRIEND,[8]
The world beside may murmur, or commend.
Know, all the distant din that world can keep,
Rolls o'er my grotto,[9] and but soothes my sleep.
There, my retreat the best companions grace,   125
Chiefs out of war, and statesmen out of place.
There St. John mingles with my friendly bowl
The feast of reason and the flow of soul:
And he, whose lightning pierced the Iberian lines,[1]

1. I.e., whether I go mad and am, like other madmen, locked up in a darkened room, or whether I am in prison with a whitewashed wall for paper and a skewer for pen.
2. "Bedlam": Bethlehem Hospital for the insane; "the Mint": an area in Southwark, where debtors were free from arrest. Nathaniel Lee (ca. 1653–92), the tragic poet, was confined for a while in Bedlam. Eustace Budgell, minor poet and relative of Addison, was in financial straits before his suicide in 1737.
3. Pope had thus referred to Lady Mary Wortley Montagu and her husband in his *Epistle to Bathurst*, line 96. A "plum" is slang for a man who (usually

dishonestly) has made £100,000; "testers" are sixpences.
4. The star worn on the chest by Knights of the Garter.
5. Nicolas Boileau-Despréaux (1636–1711), critic and distinguished satirist.
6. In his "Protestant play," *The Spanish Friar* (1681).
7. Holding no public office.
8. A translation of line 70 of Horace's poem, which Pope took as the motto of the satires that he wrote in the 1730's.
9. The subterranean passage under the road that separated his house at Twickenham from his garden became, in Pope's hands, a romantic grotto ornamented with minerals and shells.
1. Charles Mordaunt, Earl of Peter-

Now forms my quincunx,[2] and now ranks my vines,   130
Or tames the genius of the stubborn plain,
Almost as quickly as he conquered Spain.
  Envy must own, I live among the great,
No pimp of pleasure, and no spy of state,
With eyes that pry not, tongue that ne'er repeats,   135
Fond to spread friendships, but to cover heats;
To help who want, to forward who excel;
This, all who know me, know; who love me, tell;
And who unknown defame me, let them be
Scribblers or peers, alike are mob to me.   140
This is my plea, on this I rest my cause—
What saith my counsel, learned in the laws?
    F. Your plea is good. But still I say, beware!
Laws are explained by men—so have a care.
It stands on record, that in Richard's times   145
A man was hanged for very honest rhymes.[3]
Consult the statute: *quart.* I think, it is,
Edwardi sext. or *prim. et quint. Eliz.*
See *Libels, Satires*—here you have it—read.
    P. *Libels* and *satires!* lawless things indeed!   150
But grave *epistles*, bringing vice to light,
Such as a king might read, a bishop write,
Such as Sir Robert[4] would approve—
    F.   Indeed?
The case is altered—you may then proceed;
In such a cause the plaintiff will be hissed,   155
My lords the judges laugh, and you're dismissed.

                                1733

Epistle II. To a Lady[1]

OF THE CHARACTERS OF WOMEN

Nothing so true as what you once let fall,
  "Most women have no characters at all."

borough (1658–1736), won renown in Spain (hence the allusion to "Iberian lines") during the campaign of 1705.
2. Trees or shrubs planted in fives: one at each corner of a square, one in the center.
3. Two rhymers have been suggested by scholars: John Ball, executed under Richard II in 1381 for his role in the Peasants' Revolt, and one Collingbourne, executed under Richard III for treasonable rhymes.
4. Sir Robert Walpole, the Prime Minister.
1. This is one of four poems that Pope grouped together under the title *Epistles to Several Persons*, but that have usually been known by the less appropriate title *Moral Essays.* They were conceived as

parts of Pope's ambitious "ethic work," of which only the first part, the *Essay on Man*, was completed. *Epistle I* treats the characters of men, *Epistle II* the characters of women. The other two epistles are concerned with the use of riches, a subject that engaged Pope's attention during the 1730's, since he distrusted the influence on private morals and public life of the rapidly growing wealth of England under the first Hanoverians.
  Epistle II contains a series of brilliantly executed portraits (the metaphor of portrait painting dominates the poem) which among them illustrate the thesis that women are consistent only in being inconsistent. As we move from portrait to portrait, we not only observe

Matter too soft a lasting mark to bear,
And best distinguished by black, brown, or fair.
    How many pictures[2] of one nymph we view,   5
All how unlike each other, all how true!
Arcadia's countess, here, in ermined pride,
Is, there, Pastora by a fountain side.
Here Fannia, leering on her own good man,
And there, a naked Leda with a swan.[3]   10
Let then the fair one beautifully cry,
In Magdalen's loose hair and lifted eye,
Or dressed in smiles of sweet Cecilia shine,[4]
With simpering angels, palms, and harps divine;
Whether the charmer sinner it, or saint it,   15
If folly grow romantic,[5] I must paint it.
    Come then, the colors and the ground[6] prepare!
Dip in the rainbow, trick her off in air;
Choose a firm cloud, before it fall, and in it
Catch, ere she change, the Cynthia[7] of this minute.   20
    Rufa, whose eye quick-glancing o'er the park,
Attracts each light gay meteor of a spark,
Agrees as ill with Rufa studying Locke,[8]
As Sappho's diamonds with her dirty smock,
Or Sappho at her toilet's greasy task,[9]   25
With Sappho fragrant at an evening masque:
So morning insects that in muck begun,
Shine, buzz, and flyblow in the setting sun.

---

ladies who are changeable and fickle in their own nature, but we also meet a variety of female characters—the affected, the slatternly, the soft-natured, the silly, the lewd, for instance—who remind us that ladies are as variegated as tulips (line 41).

Are the portraits imaginary or do they represent women whom Pope knew and whom his readers could recognize? This question exercised the gossips of Pope's own time and after; and it has occupied the attention of Pope's editors and commentators ever since his death. Many of the portraits indubitably allude to actual women (Sappho); some doubtless are composite (Atossa); others are mere types. Questions of identity, however, pertain rather to Pope's biography and character than to his art. It should matter little if at all to the reader first approaching Pope's satire whether in fact Atossa is Sarah, Duchess of Marlborough, or, as is much more likely, Katherine, Duchess of Buckinghamshire, or, most likely of all, Katherine combined with a few traits of Sarah. Occasionally, perhaps, a lady's name might have hinted to some of Pope's contemporaries that a real person was intended. Today the reader who is not a specialist will do well to neglect particular applications of Pope's satire and to concern himself with the generally, the permanently human, which is always the center of Pope's works.

The "lady" of the title is Martha Blount (1690–1763), Pope's best-loved female friend, to whom he left the bulk of his property.

2. Ladies of the 17th and 18th centuries liked to have themselves painted in the costumes and attitudes of fanciful, mythological, or historical characters.

3. Leda was seduced by Zeus, who approached her in the form of a swan.

4. St. Mary Magdalen was often painted during the 17th century in the attitude described in line 12. St. Cecilia, the reputed inventor of the organ, was traditionally painted in the manner which Pope satirically glances at here.

5. Extravagant.

6. The first coatings of paint on the canvas before the figures in the picture are sketched in.

7. One of the names of Diana, goddess of the moon, a notoriously changeable heavenly body.

8. John Locke, author of *An Essay Concerning Human Understanding* (1690).

9. Lady Mary Wortley Montagu, though beautiful as a young woman, became notorious for her slatternly appearance and personal uncleanliness. Both Sappho and Lady Mary were female poets.

How soft is Silia! fearful to offend,
The frail one's advocate, the weak one's friend: 30
To her, Calista proved her conduct nice,
And good Simplicius asks of her advice.
Sudden, she storms! she raves! You tip the wink,
But spare your censure; Silia does not drink.
All eyes may see from what the change arose,   35
All eyes may see—a pimple on her nose.

    Papillia,[1] wedded to her amorous spark,
Sighs for the shades—"How charming is a park!"
A park is purchased, but the fair he sees
All bathed in tears—"Oh, odious, odious trees!"   40

    Ladies, like variegated tulips, show;
'Tis to their changes half their charms we owe;
Fine by defect, and delicately weak,
Their happy spots the nice admirer take,
'Twas thus Calypso[2] once each heart alarmed,   45
Awed without virtue, without beauty charmed;
Her tongue bewitched as oddly as her eyes,
Less wit than mimic, more a wit than wise;
Strange graces still, and stranger flights she had,
Was just not ugly, and was just not mad;   50
Yet ne'er so sure our passion to create,
As when she touched the brink of all we hate.

    Narcissa's[3] nature, tolerably mild,
To make a wash,[4] would hardly stew a child;
Has even been proved to grant a lover's prayer,   55
And paid a tradesman once to make him stare,
Gave alms at Easter, in a Christian trim,
And made a widow happy, for a whim.
Why then declare good nature is her scorn,
When 'tis by that alone she can be borne?   60
Why pique all mortals, yet affect a name?
A fool to pleasure, yet a slave to fame:
Now deep in Taylor and the *Book of Martyrs*,[5]
Now drinking citron[6] with his Grace and Chartres.
Now conscience chills her, and now passion burns;   65
And atheism and religion take their turns;
A very heathen in the carnal part,

1. The name comes from Latin for "butterfly."
2. The name is borrowed from the fascinating goddess who detained Odysseus on her island for seven years after the fall of Troy, thus preventing his return to his kingdom, Ithaca.
3. Type of extreme self-love. Narcissus, a beautiful youth, fell in love with his own image when he saw it reflected in a fountain.
4. Cosmetic lotion.
5. Jeremy Taylor, 17th-century Anglican divine, whose *Holy Living and Holy Dying* was often reprinted in the 18th century. John Foxe's *Acts and Monu-ments* (usually referred to as Foxe's *Book of Martyrs*), 1563, was a household book in most Protestant families in the 17th and 18th centuries; a record of the Protestants who perished for their faith under the persecution of Mary Tudor (1553–58), it was instrumental in keeping anti-Catholic sentiments alive.
6. I.e., citron-water, brandy flavored with lemon or orange peel. "His Grace" is usually said to be the Duke of Wharton, an old enemy of Swift's and a notorious libertine; Francis Chartres: a debauchee often mentioned by Pope.

Yet still a sad, good Christian at her heart.
    See Sin in state, majestically drunk;
Proud as a peeress, prouder as a punk;   70
Chaste to her husband, frank[6a] to all beside,
A teeming mistress, but a barren bride.
What then? let blood and body bear the fault,
Her head's untouched, that noble seat of thought:
Such this day's doctrine—in another fit   75
She sins with poets through pure love of wit.
What has not fired her bosom or her brain?
Caesar and Tallboy,[7] Charles and Charlemagne.
As Helluo,[8] late dictator of the feast,
The nose of hautgout,[9] and the tip of taste,   80
Criticked your wine, and analyzed your meat,
Yet on plain pudding deigned at home to eat;
So Philomedé,[1] lecturing all mankind
On the soft passion, and the taste refined,
The address, the delicacy—stoops at once,   85
And makes her hearty meal upon a dunce.
    Flavia's a wit, has too much sense to pray;
To toast our wants and wishes, is her way;
Nor asks of God, but of her stars, to give
The mighty blessing, "while we live, to live."   90
Then all for death, that opiate of the soul!
Lucretia's dagger,[2] Rosamonda's bowl.
Say, what can cause such impotence of mind?
A spark too fickle, or a spouse too kind.
Wise wretch! with pleasures too refined to please,   95
With too much spirit to be e'er at ease,
With too much quickness ever to be taught,
With too much thinking to have common thought:
You purchase pain with all that joy can give,
And die of nothing but a rage to live.   100
    Turn then from wits; and look on Simo's mate,
No ass so meek, no ass so obstinate.
Or her, that owns her faults, but never mends,
Because she's honest, and the best of friends:
Or her, whose life the Church and scandal share,   105
Forever in a passion, or a prayer:
Or her, who laughs at hell, but (like her Grace)
Cries, "Ah! how charming, if there's no such place!"
Or who in sweet vicissitude appears
Of mirth and opium, ratafie[3] and tears,   110

6a. "Liberal; generous" (Johnson's *Dictionary*).
7. A crude young man in Richard Brome's comedy *The Jovial Crew* (1641) or the opera adapted from the play (1731); "Charles," as F. W. Bateson points out, was a generic name for a footman in the period.
8. Latin for "glutton."
9. "Anything with a strong relish or strong scent, as overkept venison"

(Johnson's *Dictionary*).
1. The name is Pope's adaptation of a Greek epithet meaning "laughter-loving," frequently applied to Aphrodite, the goddess of love.
2. Lucretia, violated by Tarquin, committed suicide; according to tradition, the "fair Rosamonda," mistress of Henry II, was forced by Queen Eleanor to drink poison.
3. "A fine liquor, prepared from the

The daily anodyne, and nightly draught,
To kill those foes to fair ones, time and thought.
Woman and fool are two hard things to hit,
For true no-meaning puzzles more than wit.
    But what are these to great Atossa's mind?[4]   115
Scarce once herself, by turns all womankind!
Who, with herself, or others, from her birth
Finds all her life one warfare upon earth:
Shines in exposing knaves, and painting fools,
Yet is whate'er she hates and ridicules.   120
No thought advances, but her eddy brain
Whisks it about, and down it goes again.
Full sixty years the world has been her trade,
The wisest fool much time has ever made.
From loveless youth to unrespected age,   125
No passion gratified except her rage.
So much the fury still outran the wit,
The pleasure missed her, and the scandal hit.
Who breaks with her, provokes revenge from hell,
But he's a bolder man who dares be well:[5]   130
Her every turn with violence pursued,
Nor more a storm her hate than gratitude:
To that each passion turns, or soon or late;
Love, if it makes her yield, must make her hate:
Superiors? death! and equals? what a curse!   135
But an inferior not dependent? worse.
Offend her, and she knows not to forgive;
Oblige her, and she'll hate you while you live:
But die, and she'll adore you—Then the bust
And temple rise—then fall again to dust.   140
Last night, her lord was all that's good and great;
A knave this morning, and his will a cheat.
Strange! by the means defeated of the ends,
By spirit robbed of power, by warmth of friends,
By wealth of followers! without one distress   145
Sick of herself through very selfishness!
Atossa, cursed with every granted prayer,
Childless with all her children, wants an heir.
To heirs unknown descends the unguarded store,
Or wanders, Heaven-directed, to the poor.   150
    Pictures like these, dear Madam, to design,
Asks no firm hand, and no unerring line;
Some wandering touches, some reflected light,
Some flying stroke alone can hit 'em right:
For how should equal colors do the knack?[6]   155
Chameleons who can paint in white and black?

kernels of apricots and spirits" (Johnson's *Dictionary*).
4. Atossa, daughter of Cyrus, Emperor of Persia (d. 529 B.C.). If the Duchess of Buckinghamshire is alluded to, the name is appropriate, for she was the natural daughter of James II.
5. Be in her favor.
6. Do the trick.

"Yet Chloe sure was formed without a spot—"
Nature in her then erred not, but forgot.
"With every pleasing, every prudent part,
Say, what can Chloe want?"—She wants a heart.   160
She speaks, behaves, and acts just as she ought;
But never, never, reached one generous thought.
Virtue she finds too painful an endeavor,
Content to dwell in decencies forever.
So very reasonable, so unmoved,   165
As never yet to love, or to be loved.
She, while her lover pants upon her breast,
Can mark[6a] the figures on an Indian chest;
And when she sees her friend in deep despair,
Observes how much a chintz exceeds mohair.   170
Forbid it Heaven, a favor or a debt
She e'er should cancel—but she may forget.
Safe is your secret still in Chloe's ear;
But none of Chloe's shall you ever hear.
Of all her dears she never slandered one,   175
But cares not if a thousand are undone.
Would Chloe know if you're alive or dead?
She bids her footman put it in her head.
Chloe is prudent—Would you too be wise?
Then never break your heart when Chloe dies.   180
    One certain portrait may (I grant) be seen,
Which Heaven has varnished out, and made a *Queen*:[7]
The same forever! and described by all
With Truth and Goodness, as with crown and ball.
Poets heap virtues, painters gems at will,   185
And show their zeal, and hide their want of skill.
'Tis well—but, artists! who can paint or write,
To draw the naked is your true delight.
That robe of quality so struts and swells,
None see what parts of Nature it conceals: 190
The exactest traits of body or of mind,
We owe to models of an humble kind.
If Queensberry[8] to strip there's no compelling,
'Tis from a handmaid we must take a Helen.
From peer or bishop 'tis no easy thing   195
To draw the man who loves his God, or king:
Alas! I copy (or my draft would fail)
From honest Mah'met[9] or plain Parson Hale.
    But grant, in public men sometimes are shown,
A woman's seen in private life alone: 200
Our bolder talents in full light displayed;
Your virtues open fairest in the shade.

6a. Pay attention to.
7. Pope refers as usual to Queen Caroline with disapprobation.
8. The Duchess of Queensberry, whom Pope valued because of her kindness to his friend John Gay, had been a famous beauty.
9. Mahomet, a Turkish servant of George I; Dr. Stephen Hales was an Anglican clergyman and friend of Pope.

Bred to disguise, in public 'tis you hide;
There, none distinguish 'twixt your shame or pride,
Weakness or delicacy; all so nice,   205
That each may seem a virtue, or a vice.
    In men, we various ruling passions find;
In women, two almost divide the kind;
Those, only fixed, they first or last obey,
The love of pleasure, and the love of sway.   210
    That, Nature gives; and where the lesson taught
Is but to please, can pleasure seem a fault?
Experience, this; by man's oppression cursed,
They seek the second not to lose the first.
    Men, some to business, some to pleasure take;   215
But every woman is at heart a rake;
Men, some to quiet, some to public strife;
But every lady would be queen for life.
    Yet mark the fate of a whole sex of queens!
Power all their end, but beauty all the means: 220
In youth they conquer, with so wild a rage,
As leaves them scarce a subject in their age:
For foreign glory, foreign joy, they roam;
No thought of peace or happiness at home.
But wisdom's triumph is well-timed retreat,   225
As hard a science to the fair as great!
Beauties, like tyrants, old and friendless grown,
Yet hate repose, and dread to be alone,
Worn out in public, weary every eye,
Nor leave one sigh behind them when they die.   230
    Pleasures the sex, as children birds, pursue,
Still out of reach, yet never out of view,
Sure, if they catch, to spoil the toy at most,
To covet flying, and regret when lost:
At last, to follies youth could scarce defend,   235
It grows their age's prudence to pretend;
Ashamed to own they gave delight before,
Reduced to feign it, when they give no more:
As hags hold sabbaths,[1] less for joy than spite,
So these their merry, miserable night;   240
Still round and round the ghosts of beauty glide,
And haunt the places where their honor died.
    See how the world its veterans rewards!
A youth of frolics, an old age of cards;
Fair to no purpose, artful to no end,   245
Young without lovers, old without a friend;
A fop their passion, but their prize a sot;
Alive, ridiculous, and dead, forgot!
    Ah friend! to dazzle let the vain design;
To raise the thought, and touch the heart be thine!   250

1. Obscene rites popularly supposed to be held by witches ("hags"); "night," in the next line, refers to evenings on which ladies entertained guests.

That charm shall grow, while what fatigues the Ring[2]
Flaunts and goes down, an unregarded thing:
So when the sun's broad beam has tired the sight,
All mild ascends the moon's more sober light,
Serene in virgin modesty she shines,   255
And unobserved the glaring orb declines.

    Oh! blest with temper, whose unclouded ray
Can make tomorrow cheerful as today;
She, who can love a sister's charms, or hear
Sighs for a daughter with unwounded ear;   260
She, who ne'er answers till a husband cools,
Or, if she rules him, never shows she rules;
Charms by accepting, by submitting sways,
Yet has her humor most, when she obeys;
Let fops or fortune fly which way they will;   265
Disdains all loss of tickets[3] or Codille;
Spleen, vapors, or smallpox, above them all,
And mistress of herself, though China[4] fall.

    And yet, believe me, good as well as ill,
Woman's at best a contradiction still.   270
Heaven, when it strives to polish all it can
Its last best work, but forms a softer man;
Picks from each sex, to make the favorite blest,
Your love of pleasure, our desire of rest:
Blends, in exception to all general rules,   275
Your taste of follies, with our scorn of fools:
Reserve with frankness, art with truth allied,
Courage with softness, modesty with pride;
Fixed principles, with fancy ever new;
Shakes all together, and produces—you.   280
    Be this a woman's fame: with this unblest,
Toasts live a scorn, and queens may die a jest.
This Poebus promised (I forget the year)
When those blue eyes first opened on the sphere;
Ascendant Phoebus watched that hour with care,   285
Averted half your parents' simple prayer;
And gave you beauty, but denied the pelf
That buys your sex a tyrant o'er itself.
The generous god, who wit and gold refines,
And ripens spirits as he ripens mines,[5]   290
Kept dross for duchesses, the world shall know it,
To you gave sense, good humor, and a poet.

1735, 1744

---

2. The fashionable drive in Hyde Park.
3. I.e., lottery tickets; "Codille": the loss of a hand at the card games of ombre or quadrille.
4. Pope refers punningly to the china-ware which fashionable women collected enthusiastically.
5. Phoebus Apollo, as god of poetry "ripens wit"; as god of the sun, he "ripens mines," for respectable scientific theory held that the sun's rays mature precious metals in the earth.

Epistle to Dr. Arbuthnot[1]

Advertisement
TO THE FIRST PUBLICATION OF THIS *Epistle*

This paper is a sort of bill of complaint, begun many years since, and drawn up by snatches, as the several occasions offered. I had no thoughts of publishing it, till it pleased some persons of rank and fortune (the authors of *Verses to the Imitator of Horace*, and of an *Epistle to a Doctor of Divinity from a Nobleman at Hampton Court*) to attack, in a very extraordinary manner, not only my writings (of which, being public, the public is judge) but my person, morals, and family, whereof, to those who know me not, a truer information may be requisite. Being divided between the necessity to say something of myself, and my own laziness to undertake so awkward a task, I thought it the shortest way to put the last hand to this epistle. If it have anything pleasing, it will be that by which I am most desirous to please, the truth and

1. Dr. John Arbuthnot (1667–1735), to whom Pope addressed his best-known verse epistle, was distinguished both as a physician and as a man of wit. He had been one of the liveliest members of the Martinus Scriblerus Club, helping his friends to create the character and shape the career of the learned pedant whose *Memoirs* the Club had undertaken to write.

Pope had long been meditating such a poem, which was to be both an attack on his detractors and a defense of his own character and career. In his usual way he had jotted down hints, lines, couplets, fragments over a period of two decades, but the poem might never have been completed had it not been for two events: Arbuthnot, from his deathbed, wrote to urge Pope to continue his abhorrence of vice and to express it in his writings; and, during 1733, Pope was the victim of two bitter attacks by "persons of rank and fortune," as the "Advertisement" has it. The *Verses Addressed to the Imitator of Horace* was the work of Lady Mary Wortley Montagu, helped by her friend Lord Hervey (pronounced "Harvey"), a close friend and confidant of Queen Caroline; *An Epistle to a Doctor of Divinity from a Nobleman at Hampton Court* was the work of Lord Hervey alone. Lady Mary, it must be admitted, had provocation enough, especially in Pope's recent reference to her in *The First Satire of the Second Book of Horace*, lines 83–84; but Hervey had little to complain of beyond occasional covert references to him as "Lord Fanny." At any rate, the two scurrilous attacks goaded Pope into action, and the poem was completed by

the end of the summer of 1734.

The *Epistle* is a masterpiece of poetic rhetoric. The very fact that it is addressed to Dr. Arbuthnot, a man who had the general approbation of the world because of his kindliness and probity, in some degree seems to guarantee the integrity of the "I" of the poem and to diminish the moral stature of his enemies. This acquisition of virtue through association, an effective stroke, is supported by every device of persuasive rhetoric: reasonable argument and emotional appeals, subtly suggestive imagery, and superbly controlled shifts in tone and style which help to sway the reader's judgment to the side of the speaker. The poem opens in the flat language of commonplace prose discourse, tinged with a wry humor and a tone of exasperation: "Shut, shut the door, good John! (fatigued, I said)" and as it progresses it rises or falls in language and style according to the emotions which the speaker expresses— anger, contempt, amusement, sarcasm, mock self-pity, indignation, hatred, affection, gratitude, tenderness—to return at the end to the homely tone of the opening.

It is not clear that Pope intended the poem to be thought of as a dialogue, as it has usually been printed since Warburton's edition of 1751. The original edition, while suggesting interruptions in the flow of the monologue, kept entirely to the form of a letter. The introduction of the friend, who speaks from time to time, of course converts the original letter into a dramatic dialogue.

the sentiment; and if anything offensive, it will be only to those I am least sorry to offend, the vicious or the ungenerous.

Many will know their own pictures in it, there being not a circumstance but what is true; but I have, for the most part, spared their names, and they may escape being laughed at, if they please.

I would have some of them know, it was owing to the request of the learned and candid friend to whom it is inscribed, that I make not as free use of theirs as they have done of mine. However, I shall have this advantage, and honor, on my side, that whereas, by their proceeding, any abuse may be directed at any man, no injury can possibly be done by mine, since a nameless character can never be found out, but by its truth and likeness. P.

P. Shut, shut the door, good John![2] (fatigued, I said),
Tie up the knocker, say I'm sick, I'm dead.
The Dog Star[3] rages! nay 'tis past a doubt
All Bedlam,[4] or Parnassus, is let out:
Fire in each eye, and papers in each hand,   5
They rave, recite, and madden round the land.
   What walls can guard me, or what shades can hide?
They pierce my thickets, through my grot[5] they glide,
By land, by water, they renew the charge,
They stop the chariot, and they board the barge.   10
No place is sacred, not the church is free;
Even Sunday shines no Sabbath day to me:
Then from the Mint[6] walks forth the man of rhyme,
Happy to catch me just at dinner time.
   Is there a parson, much bemused in beer,   15
A maudlin poetess, a rhyming peer,
A clerk foredoomed his father's soul to cross,
Who pens a stanza when he should engross?[7]
Is there who,[7a] locked from ink and paper, scrawls
With desperate charcoal round his darkened walls?   20
All fly to Twit'nam,[8] and in humble strain
Apply to me to keep them mad or vain.
Arthur,[9] whose giddy son neglects the laws,
Imputes to me and my damned works the cause:
Poor Cornus[1] sees his frantic wife elope,   25
And curses wit, and poetry, and Pope.

2. John Serle, Pope's gardener.
3. Sirius, associated with the period of greatest heat (and hence of madness) because it sets with the sun in late summer. August, in ancient Rome, was the season for reciting poetry.
4. Bethlehem Hospital for the insane in London.
5. See *First Satire of the Second Book of Horace*, line 124 and note.
6. A place in Southwark where debtors were free from arrest (they could not be arrested anywhere on Sundays).
7. Write out legal documents.

7a. Is there some madman who, locked up without ink or paper* * * ?
8. I.e., Twickenham, Pope's villa on the bank of the Thames, a few miles above Hampton Court.
9. Arthur Moore, whose son, James Moore Smythe, dabbled in literature. Moore Smythe had earned Pope's enmity by using in one of his plays some unpublished lines from Pope's *Epistle to a Lady* in spite of Pope's objections.
1. Latin for "horn," the traditional emblem of the cuckold.

Friend to my life (which did not you prolong,
The world had wanted many an idle song)
What drop or nostrum[2] can this plague remove?
Or which must end me, a fool's wrath or love?   30
A dire dilemma! either way I'm sped,[2a]
If foes, they write, if friends, they read me dead.
Seized and tied down to judge, how wretched I!
Who can't be silent, and who will not lie.
To laugh were want of goodness and of grace,   35
And to be grave exceeds all power of face.
I sit with sad civility, I read
With honest anguish and an aching head,
And drop at last, but in unwilling ears,
This saving counsel, "Keep your piece nine years."[3]   40
     "Nine years!" cries he, who high in Drury Lane,[4]
Lulled by soft zephyrs through the broken pane,
Rhymes ere he wakes, and prints before term[5] ends,
Obliged by hunger and request of friends:
"The piece, you think, is incorrect? why, take it,   45
I'm all submission, what you'd have it, make it."
     Three things another's modest wishes bound,
My friendship, and a prologue, and ten pound.
     Pitholeon[6] sends to me: "You know his Grace,
I want a patron; ask him for a place."   50
Pitholeon libeled me—"but here's a letter
Informs you, sir, 'twas when he knew no better.
Dare you refuse him? Curll[7] invites to dine,
He'll write a *Journal*, or he'll turn divine."[8]
Bless me! a packet.—"'Tis a stranger sues,   55
A virgin tragedy, an orphan Muse."
If I dislike it, "Furies, death, and rage!"
If I approve, "Commend it to the stage."
There (thank my stars) my whole commission ends,
The players and I are, luckily, no friends.   60
Fired that the house reject him, "'Sdeath, I'll print it,
And shame the fools—Your interest, sir, with Lintot!"[9]
Lintot, dull rogue, will think your price too much.
"Not, sir, if you revise it, and retouch."
All my demurs but double his attacks;   65
At last he whispers, "Do; and we go snacks."[1]

2. Medicine.
2a. Destroyed; killed (Johnson's *Dictionary*).
3. The advice of Horace in *Ars Poetica* (line 388).
4. I.e., living in a garret in Drury Lane, site of one of the theaters and the haunt of the profligate.
5. One of the four annual periods in which the law courts are in session and with which the publishing season coincided.
6. "A foolish poet of Rhodes, who pretended much to Greek" [Pope's note]; he is Leonard Welsted, who translated Longinus and had attacked and slandered Pope. See line 375.
7. Edmund Curll, shrewd and disreputable bookseller, published pirated works, works falsely ascribed to reputable writers, scandalous biographies, and other ephemera. Pope had often attacked him and had assigned to him a low role in the *Dunciad*.
8. I.e., he will attack Pope in the *London Journal* or write a treatise on theology, as Welsted in fact did.
9. Bernard Lintot, publisher of Pope's Homer and other early works.
1. Go shares.

Glad of a quarrel, straight I clap the door,
"Sir, let me see your works and you no more."
    'Tis sung, when Midas' ears began to spring
(Midas, a sacred person and a king),   70
His very minister who spied them first,
(Some say his queen) was forced to speak, or burst.[2]
And is not mine, my friend, a sorer case,
When every coxcomb perks them in my face?
    A. Good friend, forbear! you deal in dangerous things.   75
I'd never name queens, ministers, or kings;
Keep close to ears, and those let asses prick;
'Tis nothing—— P. Nothing? if they bite and kick?
Out with it, *Dunciad!* let the secret pass,
That secret to each fool, that he's an ass: 80
The truth once told (and wherefore should we lie?)
The queen of Midas slept, and so may I.
    You think this cruel? take it for a rule,
No creature smarts so little as a fool.
Let peals of laughter, Codrus! round thee break,   85
Thou unconcerned canst hear the mighty crack.
Pit, box, and gallery in convulsions hurled,
Thou stand'st unshook amidst a bursting world.
Who shames a scribbler? break one cobweb through,
He spins the slight, self-pleasing thread anew: 90
Destroy his fib or sophistry, in vain;
The creature's at his dirty work again,
Throned in the center of his thin designs,
Proud of a vast extent of flimsy lines.
Whom have I hurt? has poet yet or peer   95
Lost the arched eyebrow or Parnassian sneer?
And has not Colley[3] still his lord and whore?
His butchers Henley? his freemasons Moore?
Does not one table Bavius[4] still admit?
Still to one bishop Philips seem a wit?   100
Still Sappho[5]—— A. Hold! for God's sake—you'll offend.
No names—be calm—learn prudence of a friend.
I too could write, and I am twice as tall;
But foes like these!—— P. One flatterer's worse than all.
Of all mad creatures, if the learn'd are right,   105

2. Midas, king of ancient Lydia, had the bad taste to prefer the flute-playing of Pan to that of Apollo, whereupon the god endowed him with ass's ears. It was his barber (not his wife or his minister) who discovered the secret and whispered it into a hole in the earth. The reference to "queen" and "minister" makes it plain that Pope is alluding to George II, Queen Caroline, and Walpole.
3. Colley Cibber, the laureate (see *First Satire of the Second Book of Horace,* lines 34 ff. and note). John Henley, known as "Orator" Henley, an independent preacher of marked eccentricity, was popular among the lower orders, especially for his elocution.
4. The bad poet alluded to in Virgil's *Eclogues* III. The "Bishop" is Hugh Boulter, Bishop of Armagh; he had employed as his secretary Ambrose Philips (1674–1749), whose insipid and babbling simplicity of manner in poetry earned him the nickname of "Namby-Pamby."
5. Lady Mary Wortley Montagu.

It is the slaver kills, and not the bite.
A fool quite angry is quite innocent:
Alas! 'tis ten times worse when they repent.
　　One dedicates in high heroic prose,
And ridicules beyond a hundred foes;　　　　　　　　110
One from all Grub Street[6] will my fame defend,
And, more abusive, calls himself my friend.
This prints my letters,[7] that expects a bribe,
And others roar aloud, "Subscribe, subscribe!"[8]
　　There are, who to my person pay their court:　　115
I cough like Horace, and, though lean, am short;
Ammon's great son[9] one shoulder had too high,
Such Ovid's nose, and "Sir! you have an eye—"
Go on, obliging creatures, make me see
All that disgraced my betters met in me.　　　　　120
Say for my comfort, languishing in bed,
"Just so immortal Maro[1] held his head":
And when I die, be sure you let me know
Great Homer died three thousand years ago.
　　Why did I write? what sin to me unknown　　　125
Dipped me in ink, my parents', or my own?
As yet a child, nor yet a fool to fame,
I lisped in numbers, for the numbers came.
I left no calling for this idle trade,
No duty broke, no father disobeyed.　　　　　　130
The Muse but served to ease some friend, not wife,
To help me through this long disease, my life,
To second, Arbuthnot! thy art and care,
And teach the being you preserved, to bear.[2]
　　A. But why then publish? P. Granville the polite,　135
And knowing Walsh, would tell me I could write;
Well-natured Garth inflamed with early praise,
And Congreve loved, and Swift endured my lays;
The courtly Talbot, Somers, Sheffield, read;
Even mitered Rochester would nod the head,　　　140
And St. John's self (great Dryden's friends before)
With open arms received one poet more.[3]

6. A term denoting the whole society of literary, political, and journalistic hack writers.

7. In 1726 Curll had surreptitiously acquired and published without permission some of Pope's letters to Henry Cromwell.

8. To ensure the financial success of a work, the public was often asked to "subscribe" to it by taking a certain number of copies before printing was undertaken. Pope's Homer was published thus.

9. Alexander the Great. "Ovid's nose": Ovid's family name Naso suggests the Latin word *nasus* ("nose"), hence the pun.

1. Virgil.

2. Endure.

3. The purpose of this list is to establish Pope as the successor of Dryden and thus to place him far above his Grub-Street persecutors. George Granville, Lord Lansdowne, poet and statesman; Sir Samuel Garth, physician and mock-epic poet; William Congreve, the playwright; the statesmen Charles Talbot, Duke of Shrewsbury; Lord Sommers; John Sheffield, Duke of Buckinghamshire; and Francis Atterbury, Bishop of Rochester, had all been associated with Dryden in his later years and had all encouraged the young Pope.

Happy my studies, when by these approved!
Happier their author, when by these beloved!
From these the world will judge of men and books,   145
Not from the Burnets, Oldmixons, and Cookes.[4]
    Soft were my numbers; who could take offense
While pure description held the place of sense?
Like gentle Fanny's[5] was my flowery theme,
A painted mistress, or a purling stream.   150
Yet then did Gildon[6] draw his venal quill;
I wished the man a dinner, and sat still.
Yet then did Dennis[7] rave in furious fret;
I never answered, I was not in debt.
If want provoked, or madness made them print,   155
I waged no war with Bedlam or the Mint.
    Did some more sober critic come abroad?
If wrong, I smiled; if right, I kissed the rod.
Pains, reading, study are their just pretense,
And all they want is spirit, taste, and sense.   160
Commas and points they set exactly right,
And 'twere a sin to rob them of their mite.
Yet ne'er one sprig of laurel graced these ribalds,
From slashing Bentley down to piddling Tibbalds.[8]
Each wight who reads not, and but scans and spells,   165
Each word-catcher that lives on syllables,
Even such small critics some regard may claim,
Preserved in Milton's or in Shakespeare's name.
Pretty! in amber to observe the forms
Of hairs, or straws, or dirt, or grubs, or worms!   170
The things, we know, are neither rich nor rare,
But wonder how the devil they got there.
    Were others angry? I excused them too;
Well might they rage; I gave them but their due.
A man's true merit 'tis not hard to find;   175
But each man's secret standard in his mind,
That casting weight[9] pride adds to emptiness,
This, who can gratify? for who can guess?
The bard[1] whom pilfered pastorals renown,

4. Thomas Burnet, John Oldmixon, and Thomas Cooke; Pope identifies them in a note as "authors of secret and scandalous history."
5. John, Lord Hervey, whom Pope satirizes in the character of Sporus, lines 305–33 below.
6. Charles Gildon, minor critic and scribbler, who, Pope believed, early attacked him at the instigation of Addison; hence "venal quill."
7. John Dennis (see *Essay on Criticism*, line 270 and its note).
8. Richard Bentley (1662–1742), the eminent classical scholar, seemed to both Pope and Swift the perfect type of the pedant: he is called "slashing" because, in his edition of *Paradise Lost*

(1732), he had set in square brackets all passages which he disliked on the grounds they had been slipped into the poem without the blind poet's knowledge. Lewis Theobald (1688–1744), whose minute learning in Elizabethan literature had enabled him to expose Pope's defects as an editor of Shakespeare in 1726. Pope made him King of the Dunces in the *Dunciad* (1728).
9. The weight that turns the scale; here, the "deciding factor."
1. Ambrose Philips, Pope's rival in pastoral poetry in 1709, when their pastorals were published in Tonson's sixth *Miscellany*. Philips had also translated some Persian tales. Cf. line 100.

Who turns a Persian tale for half a crown, 180
Just writes to make his barrenness appear,
And strains from hard-bound brains eight lines a year:
He, who still wanting, though he lives on theft,
Steals much, spends little, yet has nothing left;
And he who now to sense, now nonsense leaning, 185
Means not, but blunders round about a meaning:
And he whose fustian's so sublimely bad,
It is not poetry, but prose run mad:
All these, my modest satire bade translate,
And owned that nine such poets made a Tate.[2] 190
How did they fume, and stamp, and roar, and chafe!
And swear, not Addison himself was safe.

Peace to all such! but were there one whose fires
True Genius kindles, and fair Fame inspires;
Blessed with each talent and each art to please, 195
And born to write, converse, and live with ease:
Should such a man, too fond to rule alone,
Bear, like the Turk, no brother near the throne;
View him with scornful, yet with jealous eyes,
And hate for arts that caused himself to rise; 200
Damn with faint praise, assent with civil leer,
And without sneering, teach the rest to sneer;
Willing to wound, and yet afraid to strike,
Just hint a fault, and hesitate dislike;
Alike reserved to blame or to commend, 205
A timorous foe, and a suspicious friend;
Dreading even fools; by flatterers besieged,
And so obliging that he ne'er obliged;
Like Cato, give his little senate[3] laws,
And sit attentive to his own applause; 210
While wits and Templars[4] every sentence raise,
And wonder with a foolish face of praise—
Who but must laugh, if such a man there be?
Who would not weep, if Atticus[5] were he?

What though my name stood rubric[6] on the walls 215
Or plastered posts, with claps, in capitals?
Or smoking forth, a hundred hawkers' load,
On wings of winds came flying all abroad?
I sought no homage from the race that write;
I kept, like Asian monarchs, from their sight: 220

2. Nahum Tate (1652–1715), poet laureate (1692–1715). His popular rewriting of Shakespeare's *King Lear* provided a happy ending; he wrote most of Part II of *Absalom and Achitophel.* The line refers to the old adage that it takes nine tailors to make one man.
3. Addison's tragedy *Cato* had been a sensational success in 1713. Pope had written the prologue, in which occurs the line, "While Cato gives his little senate laws." The satirical reference here is to Addison in the role of ar-biter of taste among his friends and admirers, mostly Whigs, at Button's Coffee House. It was these people who had worked against the success of Pope's Homer.
4. Law students.
5. Pope's satiric pseudonym for Addison; Atticus (109–32 B.C.) was a wealthy man of letters and a friend of Cicero, known as a wise and disinterested man.
6. In red letters. "Claps": posters.

Poems I heeded (now berhymed so long)
No more than thou, great George! a birthday song.
I ne'er with wits or witlings passed my days
To spread about the itch of verse and praise;
Nor like a puppy daggled through the town   225
To fetch and carry sing-song up and down;
Nor at rehearsals sweat, and mouthed, and cried,
With handkerchief and orange at my side;
But sick of fops, and poetry, and prate,
To Bufo[7] left the whole Castalian state.   230
　　Proud as Apollo on his forkéd hill,[8]
Sat full-blown Bufo, puffed by every quill;
Fed with soft dedication all day long,
Horace and he went hand in hand in song.
His library (where busts of poets dead   235
And a true Pindar stood without a head)
Received of wits an undistinguished race,
Who first his judgment asked, and then a place:
Much they extolled his pictures, much his seat,[9]
And flattered every day, and some days eat: 240
Till grown more frugal in his riper days,
He paid some bards with port, and some with praise;
To some a dry rehearsal was assigned,
And others (harder still) he paid in kind.
Dryden alone (what wonder?) came not nigh;   245
Dryden alone escaped this judging eye:
But still the great have kindness in reserve;
He helped to bury whom he helped to starve.
　　May some choice patron bless each gray goose quill!
May every Bavius have his Bufo still!   250
So when a statesman wants a day's defense,
Or Envy holds a whole week's war with Sense,
Or simple Pride for flattery makes demands,
May dunce by dunce be whistled off my hands!
Blessed be the great! for those they take away,   255
And those they left me—for they left me Gay;[1]
Left me to see neglected genius bloom,
Neglected die, and tell it on his tomb;
Of all thy blameless life the sole return
My verse, and Queensberry weeping o'er thy urn!   260
Oh, let me live my own, and die so too!
("To live and die is all I have to do")
Maintain a poet's dignity and ease,

---

7. A type of tasteless patron of the arts. The Castalian spring on Mt. Parnassus was sacred to Apollo and the Muses.
8. Mt. Parnassus had two peaks, one sacred to Apollo, one to Bacchus.
9. Pronounced *sate*, and rhymed in next line with "eat" (*ate*). *Seat* means "estate."
1. John Gay (1685–1732), author of the *Beggar's Opera* (1728) and other delightful works, dear friend of Swift and Pope. His failure to obtain patronage from the court intensified Pope's hostility to the Whig administration and the queen. Gay spent the last years of his life under the protection of the Duke and Duchess of Queensberry.

And see what friends, and read what books I please;
Above a patron, though I condescend   265
Sometimes to call a minister my friend.
I was not born for courts or great affairs;
I pay my debts, believe, and say my prayers,
Can sleep without a poem in my head,
Nor know if Dennis be alive or dead.   270
     Why am I asked what next shall see the light?
Heavens! was I born for nothing but to write?
Has life no joys for me? or (to be grave)
Have I no friend to serve, no soul to save?
"I found him close with Swift"—"Indeed? no doubt"   275
Cries prating Balbus, "something will come out."
'Tis all in vain, deny it as I will.
"No, such a genius never can lie still,"
And then for mine obligingly mistakes
The first lampoon Sir Will or Bubo makes.[2]   280
Poor guiltless I! and can I choose but smile,
When every coxcomb knows me by my style?
     Cursed be the verse, how well soe'er it flow,
That tends to make one worthy man my foe,
Give Virtue scandal, Innocence a fear,   285
Or from the soft-eyed virgin steal a tear!
But he who hurts a harmless neighbor's peace,
Insults fallen worth, or Beauty in distress,
Who loves a lie, lame Slander helps about,
Who writes a libel, or who copies out: 290
That fop whose pride affects a patron's name,
Yet absent, wounds an author's honest fame;
Who can your merit selfishly approve,
And show the sense of it without the love;
Who has the vanity to call you friend,   295
Yet wants the honor, injured, to defend;
Who tells whate'er you think, whate'er you say,
And, if he lie not, must at least betray:
Who to the dean and silver bell can swear,
And sees at Cannons what was never there:[3]   300
Who reads but with a lust to misapply,
Make satire a lampoon, and fiction, lie:
A lash like mine no honest man shall dread,
But all such babbling blockheads in his stead.
     Let Sporus[4] tremble—— A. What? that thing of silk,   305
Sporus, that mere white curd of ass's milk?[5]
Satire or sense, alas! can Sporus feel?

2. Sir William Yonge, Whig politician and poetaster; George Bubb ("Bubo") Dodington was a Whig patron of letters.
3. Pope's enemies had accused him of satirizing Cannons, the ostentatious estate of the Duke of Chandos, in his description of Timon's villa in the *Epistle to Burlington*. This Pope quite justly denied. The bell of Timon's chapel was of silver, and there preached a dean who "never mentions Hell to ears polite."
4. John, Lord Hervey, effeminate courtier and confidant of Queen Caroline; see title footnote. The original Sporus was a boy, whom the Emperor Nero publicly married (see Suetonius' life of Nero in *The Twelve Caesars*).
5. Ass's milk was drunk by invalids.

Who breaks a butterfly upon a wheel?
　p. Yet let me flap this bug with gilded wings,
This painted child of dirt, that stinks and stings;　　　　　310
Whose buzz the witty and the fair annoys,
Yet wit ne'er tastes, and beauty ne'er enjoys;
So well-bred spaniels civilly delight
In mumbling of the game they dare not bite.
Eternal smiles his emptiness betray,　　　　　315
As shallow streams run dimpling all the way.
Whether in florid impotence he speaks,
And, as the prompter breathes, the puppet squeaks;
Or at the ear of Eve,[6] familiar toad,
Half froth, half venom, spits himself abroad,　　　　　320
In puns, or politics, or tales, or lies,
Or spite, or smut, or rhymes, or blasphemies.
His wit all seesaw between *that* and *this*,
Now high, now low, now master up, now miss,
And he himself one vile antithesis.　　　　　325
Amphibious thing! that acting either part,
The trifling head or the corrupted heart,
Fop at the toilet, flatterer at the board,
Now trips a lady, and now struts a lord.
Eve's tempter thus the rabbins[7] have expressed,　　　　　330
A cherub's face, a reptile all the rest;
Beauty that shocks you, parts that none will trust,
Wit that can creep, and pride that licks the dust.
　　Not Fortune's worshiper, nor Fashion's fool,
Not Lucre's madman, nor Ambition's tool,　　　　　335
Not proud, nor servile, be one poet's praise,
That if he pleased, he pleased by manly ways:
That flattery, even to kings, he held a shame,
And thought a lie in verse or prose the same:
That not in fancy's maze he wandered long,　　　　　340
But stooped[8] to truth, and moralized his song:
That not for fame, but Virtue's better end,
He stood the furious foe, the timid friend,
The damning critic, half approving wit,
The coxcomb hit, or fearing to be hit;　　　　　345
Laughed at the loss of friends he never had,
The dull, the proud, the wicked, and the mad;
The distant threats of vengeance on his head,
The blow unfelt, the tear he never shed;
The tale revived, the lie so oft o'erthrown,　　　　　350
The imputed trash, and dullness not his own;
The morals blackened when the writings 'scape,
The libeled person, and the pictured shape;[9]

6. "Eve" is the queen. The allusion is to *Paradise Lost* IV.799–809.
7. Scholars of and authorities on Jewish law and doctrine.
8. The falcon is said to "stoop" to its prey when it swoops down and seizes it in flight.
9. Pope's deformity was frequently ridiculed and occasionally caricatured.

Abuse on all he loved, or loved him, spread,
A friend in exile, or a father dead;   355
The whisper, that to greatness still too near,
Perhaps yet vibrates on his Sovereign's ear—
Welcome for thee, fair Virtue! all the past!
For thee, fair Virtue! welcome even the last!
  A. But why insult the poor, affront the great?   360
P. A knave's a knave to me in every state:
Alike my scorn, if he succeed or fail,
Sporus at court, or Japhet[1] in a jail,
A hireling scribbler, or a hireling peer,
Knight of the post[2] corrupt, or of the shire,   365
If on a pillory, or near a throne,
He gain his prince's ear, or lose his own.
  Yet soft by nature, more a dupe than wit,
Sappho[3] can tell you how this man was bit:
This dreaded satirist Dennis will confess   370
Foe to his pride, but friend to his distress:[4]
So humble, he has knocked at Tibbald's door,
Has drunk with Cibber, nay, has rhymed for Moore.
Full ten years slandered, did he once reply?
Three thousand suns went down on Welsted's lie.   375
To please a mistress one aspersed his life;
He lashed him not, but let her be his wife.
Let Budgell charge low Grub Street on his quill,
And write whate'er he pleased, except his will;[5]
Let the two Curlls of town and court,[6] abuse   380
His father, mother, body, soul, and muse.
Yet why? that father held it for a rule,
It was a sin to call our neighbor fool;
That harmless mother thought no wife a whore:
Hear this, and spare his family, James Moore!   385
Unspotted names, and memorable long,
If there be force in virtue, or in song.
  Of gentle blood (part shed in honor's cause,
While yet in Britain honor had applause)
Each parent sprung—— A. What fortune, pray?—— P. Their own,
And better got than Bestia's[7] from the throne.   391
Born to no pride, inheriting no strife,
Nor marrying discord in a noble wife,
Stranger to civil and religious rage,
The good man walked innoxious through his age.   395
No courts he saw, no suits would ever try,

1. Japhet Crook, a notorious forger.
2. One who lives by selling false evidence.
3. Lady Mary Wortley Montagu. "Bit": taken in; deceived.
4. Pope wrote the prologue to Cibber's *Provoked Husband* when that play was performed for Dennis's benefit, shortly before the old critic died.
5. Eustace Budgell attacked the *Grub Street Journal* for publishing what he took to be a squib by Pope charging him with having forged the will of Dr. Matthew Tindal.
6. I.e., the publisher and Lord Hervey.
7. Probably the Duke of Marlborough, whose vast fortune was made through the favor of Queen Anne. The actual Bestia was a corrupt Roman consul.

Nor dared an oath,[8] nor hazarded a lie.
Unlearn'd, he knew no schoolman's subtle art,
No language but the language of the heart.
By nature honest, by experience wise,   400
Healthy by temperance, and by exercise;
His life, though long, to sickness passed unknown,
His death was instant, and without a groan.
Oh, grant me thus to live, and thus to die!
Who sprung from kings shall know less joy than I.   405
    O friend! may each domestic bliss be thine!
Be no unpleasing melancholy mine:
Me, let the tender office long engage,
To rock the cradle of reposing Age,
With lenient arts extend a mother's breath,   410
Make Languor smile, and smooth the bed of Death,
Explore the thought, explain the asking eye,
And keep a while one parent from the sky![9]
On cares like these if length of days attend,
May Heaven, to bless those days, preserve my friend,   415
Preserve him social, cheerful, and serene,
And just as rich as when he served a Queen![1]
A. Whether that blessing be denied or given,
Thus far was right—the rest belong to Heaven.

                                                                  1735

8. As a Catholic, Pope's father refused to take the Oaths of Allegiance and Supremacy, and the oath against the Pope. He thus rendered himself vulnerable to the many repressive anti-Catholic laws then in force.
9. Pope was a tender and devoted son. His mother had died in 1733, and the earliest version of these lines dates from 1731, when the poet was nursing her through a serious illness.
1. Pope alludes to the fact that Arbuthnot, a man of strict probity, left the queen's service no wealthier than when he entered it.

Types of 18th-Century Poetry

MATTHEW PRIOR
(1664–1721)

Prior's distinguished diplomatic achievements cannot concern us here. He became a diplomat through the patronage of Dryden's friend the Earl of Dorset, wit, courtier, and poet, when he was appointed secretary to the embassy at The Hague. His public career culminated in his negotiating for Oxford's Tory ministry the Treaty of Utrecht (1713), which ended the War of the Spanish Succession; but after the fall of the Tories in 1714, Prior was recalled from Paris, placed under house arrest for over a year, and frequently interrogated in the hope that his evidence could be used to bring Oxford to trial as a traitor. Upon his release he found himself out of place and broken in fortune. But the extraordinary success of such friends as Swift and Pope in supporting the publication by subscription of his *Poems on Several Occasions* (1718) secured him a profit of 4,000 guineas, a very large sum at that time, which enabled him to end his life in comfort.

Prior was a representative man of his time: philosophically a skeptic; in public life ambitious and self-seeking, but not corruptible; a wit who entertained no illusions about life and who accepted its darker side and the fallibility of man with grace and irony. In his own words:

> Now in equipage stately, now humbly on foot,
>   Both fortunes he tried, but to neither would trust,
> And whirled in the round, as the wheel turned about,
>   He found riches had wings, and knew man was but dust.

His poetry was the by-product of a busy life—"the fruits of [his] vacant hours," as he once wrote. This pose of being the gentleman amateur he inherited from the Restoration court poets—naturally enough, considering his early association with Dorset and others. And indeed as a lyric poet he stands at the end of the long tradition of *vers de société*, such as was written by the "mob of gentlemen who wrote with ease" at the courts of Charles and James. But Prior was no careless writer: his grace and colloquial simplicity of language are the effects of studied art. His finest pieces are his lyrics, not his official odes and panegyrics. Of his two philosophical poems it is not the serious *Solomon* in weighty language and heroic couplets that attracts readers today, but rather the skeptical and delightfully witty *Alma* (written during his arrest in 1715) in deft octosyllabic couplets and homely conversational language that suggest Swift at his best. William Cowper admired Prior's ability to "make verse speak the language of prose, without being prosaic—to marshal the words of it in such an order as they might naturally take in falling from the lips of an extemporary speaker, yet without meanness, harmoniously, elegantly, and without seeming to displace a syllable for the sake of the rhyme * * * "

The "minor" poems—epigrams, verses to friends and to his mistresses, poems on the joys and transience of love and beauty—are really Prior's major achievement. If they seem light and trivial, they nonetheless are his most serious work, for it was on them that he employed all his artistry in perfecting the familiar style. Irony, wit, and humor keep his tenderness and apparent simplicity from sentimentality, as they save his occasional melancholy from gloom. Cloe and the other ladies whose loves he celebrates were real enough (probably lower-class women of easy virtue, whom he transformed by art into divinities akin to Pope's Belinda). A careful comparison of Prior's love poems with those of Herrick would reveal much about the course of English poetry between 1648 and 1718.

To a Child of Quality Five Years Old

THE AUTHOR FORTY

Lords, knights, and squires, the numerous band
    That wear the fair Miss Mary's fetters,
Were summoned by her high command,
    To show their passions by their letters.

My pen amongst the rest I took,   5
    Lest those bright eyes that cannot read
Should dart their kindling fires, and look
    The power they have to be obeyed.

Nor quality nor reputation
    Forbid me yet my flame to tell;   10
Dear five years old befriends my passion,
    And I may write till she can spell.

For while she makes her silkworms beds
    With all the tender things I swear,
Whilst all the house my passion reads   15
    In papers round her baby's hair,

She may receive and own my flame,
    For though the strictest prudes should know it,
She'll pass for a most virtuous dame,
    And I for an unhappy poet.   20

Then too, alas, when she shall tear
    The lines some younger rival sends,
She'll give me leave to write, I fear,
    And we shall still continue friends;

For, as our different ages move,   25
    'Tis so ordained (would fate but mend it!)

That I shall be past making love
When she begins to comprehend it.

1704

Written in the Beginning of Mézeray's *History of France*[1]

1

Whate'er thy countrymen have done
By law and wit, by sword and gun,
  In thee is faithfully recited:
And all the living world, that view
Thy work, give thee the praises due,
  At once instructed and delighted.   5

2

Yet for the fame of all these deeds,
What beggar in the Invalides,[2]
  With lameness broke, with blindness smitten,
Wished ever decently to die,   10
To have been either Mézeray,
  Or any monarch he has written?

3

It strange, dear author, yet it true is,
That down from Pharamond[3] to Loüis,
  All covet life, yet call it pain: 15
All feel the ill, yet shun the cure:
Can sense this paradox endure?
  Resolve me, Cambrai,[4] or Fontaine.

4

The man in graver tragic known
(Though his best part long since was done)   20
  Still on the stage desires to tarry:
And he who played the Harlequin,
After the jest still loads the scene,
  Unwilling to retire, though weary.

1709

A Better Answer

TO CLOE JEALOUS

Dear Cloe, how blubbered is that pretty face!
Thy cheek all on fire, and thy hair all uncurled!

---

1. François Eudes de Mézeray's *Histoire de France* (1643–51).
2. Louis XIV founded the Hôtel des Invalides in 1670 as a home for ill and disabled soldiers.
3. Traditionally the first king of the Franks; Louis is Louis XIV.

4. The illustrious prelate, moralist, theologian, and literary man François de la Mothe-Fénelon (1651–1715) was Archbishop of Cambrai; Jean de la Fontaine (1621–95), wrote the well-known *Fables*.

Prithee quit this caprice; and (as old Falstaff says)
    Let us e'en talk a little like folks of this world.[1]

How canst thou presume thou hast leave to destroy   5
    The beauties which Venus but lent to thy keeping?
Those looks were designed to inspire love and joy;
    More ordinary eyes may serve people for weeping.

To be vexed at a trifle or two that I writ,
    Your judgment at once and my passion you wrong: 10
You take that for fact which will scarce be found wit:
    Od's life! must one swear to the truth of a song?

What I speak, my fair Cloe, and what I write, shows
    The difference there is betwixt nature and art;
I court others in verse, but I love thee in prose;   15
    And they have my whimsies, but thou hast my heart.

The god of us verse-men (you know, child) the Sun,
    How after his journeys he sets up his rest;
If at morning o'er earth 'tis his fancy to run,
    At night he reclines on his Thetis's breast.[2]   20

So when I am wearied with wandering all day,
    To thee, my delight, in the evening I come;
No matter what beauties I saw in my way—
    They were but my visits, but thou art my home.

Then finish, dear Cloe, this pastoral war;   25
    And let us like Horace and Lydia agree:[3]
For thou art a girl as much brighter than her,
    As he was a poet sublimer than me.

1718

1. Cf. *2 Henry IV* V.iii.101–2.
2. Apollo, god of poetry and of the sun, is said to recline at night on the breast of Thetis, one of the Nereids or sea spirits, because the sun seems to sink into the western ocean.
3. See Horace, *Odes* III.ix.

JAMES THOMSON
(1700–1748)

Perhaps it is significant that Thomson, the first and most popular nature poet of the century, did not see London until he was 25 years old. He grew up in the picturesque border country of Roxboroughshire in Scotland and came to London in 1725, bringing with him, in addition to a memory well stored with images of the external world, the earliest version of his descriptive poem *Winter* in 405 lines of blank verse. Published in 1726, it soon became popular. Thomson went on to publish *Summer* (1727), *Spring* (1728), and *Autumn* in the first collected edition of *The Seasons* (1730), to which he added the *Hymn to the Seasons*. During the next sixteen years, because of constant revisions and additions, the poem grew in length to 5,541 lines. The continued popularity of *The Seasons* is easily demonstrated: between 1730 and 1800 it was printed fifty times; and it continued in favor with readers well into the Romantic period.

Thomson is sometimes said to have been a premature "Romantic," but this is hardly the case, for if he was, then so were all his numerous readers in the second quarter of the century. The success that *Winter* enjoyed shows plainly that the poem was not ahead of its time. It should not be hard to believe that 18th-century readers had as catholic tastes as modern readers have: readers who liked *Winter*, also, in that very year (1726), liked Pope's *Odyssey* and Swift's *Gulliver's Travels*. Thomson's blank verse pleased those who were pleased by Pope's couplets; Swift's simple colloquial language charmed those who were also charmed by Thomson's Latinized diction and not infrequent Miltonic tricks of style. The readers who thrilled to the heroic world of Homer and admired the wit of Swift could also enjoy Thomson's poetry of sentiment and visual imagery. In short, it is plain that when in the Preface to the second edition of *Winter* (1726), Thomson called for a poetry dealing with subjects "such as are fair, useful, and magnificent, [executed] so as at once to please, instruct, surprise, and astonish," he spoke not so much *to* as *for* the common reader.

The Seasons set the fashion for the poetry of natural description. Generations of readers learned to look at the external world through Thomson's eyes and with the emotions which he had taught them to feel. The *eye* dominates the literature of external nature during the 18th century as the *imagination* was to do in the poetry of Wordsworth. And Thomson amazed his readers by his capacity to see: the general effects of light and cloud and foliage or the particular image of a leaf tossed in the gale or the slender feet of a robin or the delicate film of ice at the edge of a brook. As the poem grew, it became an *omnium gatherum* of contemporary ideas and interests: natural history; ideas about the nature of man and society, primitive and civilized; the conception of created nature as a source of religious experience, as an object of religious veneration, as a continuing revelation of the Deity himself.

From The Seasons
From *Summer*

[DAWN]

Young day pours in apace,
And opens all the lawny prospect wide.
The dripping rock, the mountain's misty top
Swell on the sight and brighten with the dawn.   55
Blue through the dusk the smoking currents shine;
And from the bladed field the fearful hare
Limps awkward; while along the forest glade
The wild deer trip, and often turning gaze
At early passenger. Music awakens,   60
The native voice of undissembled joy;

And thick around the woodland hymns arise.
Roused by the cock, the soon-clad shepherd leaves
His mossy cottage, where with peace he dwells,
And from the crowded fold in order drives   65
His flock to taste the verdure of the morn.

[SWIMMING]

Cheered by the milder beam, the sprightly youth
Speeds to the well-known pool, whose crystal depth   1245
A sandy bottom shows. Awhile he stands
Gazing the inverted landscape, half afraid
To meditate the blue profound below;
Then plunges headlong down the circling flood.
His ebon tresses and his rosy cheek   1250
Instant emerge; and through the obedient wave,
At each short breathing by his lip repelled,
With arms and legs according well, he makes,
As humor leads, an easy-winding path;
While from his polished sides a dewy light   1255
Effuses on the pleased spectators round.

[EVENING]

Confessed from yonder slow-extinguished clouds,
All ether softening, sober Evening takes
Her wonted station in the middle air,
A thousand shadows at her beck. First this   1650
She sends on earth; then that of deeper dye
Steals soft behind; and then a deeper still,
In circle following circle, gathers round
To close the face of things. A fresher gale
Begins to wave the wood and stir the stream,   1655
Sweeping with shadowy gust the fields of corn,
While the quail clamors for his running mate.
Wide o'er the thistly lawn, as swells the breeze,
A whitening shower of vegetable down
Amusive[1] floats. The kind impartial care   1660
Of Nature naught disdains: thoughtful to feed
Her lowest sons, and clothe the coming year,
From field to field the feathered seeds she wings.
His folded flock[2] secure, the shepherd home
Hies, merry-hearted; and by turns relieves   1665
The ruddy milkmaid of her brimming pail—
The beauty whom perhaps his witless heart,
Unknowing what the joy-mixed anguish means,
Sincerely loves, by that best language shown
Of cordial glances and obliging deeds.   1670
Onward they pass, o'er many a panting height
And valley sunk and unfrequented; where

---

1. Amusing—i.e. (according to John-   2. Flocks secured for the night within
son's *Dictionary*), "entertaining with   the sheepfold.
tranquility."

At fall of eve the fairy people throng,
In various game and revelry to pass
The summer night, as village stories tell.   1675
But far about they wander from the grave
Of him whom his ungentle fortune urged
Against his own sad breast to lift the hand
Of impious violence. The lonely tower
Is also shunned; whose mournful chambers hold,   1680
So night-struck fancy dreams, the yelling ghost.
    Among the crooked lanes, on every hedge,
The glowworm lights his gem; and, through the dark,
A moving radiance twinkles. Evening yields
The world to Night; not in her winter robe   1685
Of massy Stygian woof, but loose arrayed
In mantle dun. A faint erroneous[3] ray,
Glanced from the imperfect surfaces of things,
Flings half an image on the straining eye;
While wavering woods, and villages, and streams,   1690
And rocks, and mountain-tops that long retained
The ascending gleam are all one swimming scene,
Uncertain if beheld. Sudden to heaven
Thence weary vision turns; where, leading soft
The silent hours of love, with purest ray   1695
Sweet Venus shines; and, from her genial rise,
When daylight sickens, till it springs afresh,
Unrivaled reigns the fairest lamp of night.

                                                                              1727

From *Winter*

[A SNOWSTORM]

    The keener tempests come: and, fuming dun
From all the livid east or piercing north,
Thick clouds ascend, in whose capacious womb   225
A vapory deluge lies, to snow congealed.
Heavy they roll their fleecy world along,
And the sky saddens with the gathered storm.
Through the hushed air the whitening shower descends,
At first thin-wavering; till at last the flakes   230
Fall broad and wide and fast, dimming the day
With a continual flow. The cherished fields
Put on their winter robe of purest white.
'Tis brightness all; save where the new snow melts
Along the mazy current. Low the woods   235
Bow their hoar head; and, ere the languid sun
Faint from the west emits his evening ray,
Earth's universal face, deep-hid and chill,
Is one wild dazzling waste that buries wide
The works of man. Drooping, the laborer-ox   240

---

3. Wandering, irregular.

Stands covered o'er with snow, and then demands
The fruit of all his toil. The fowls of heaven,
Tamed by the cruel season, crowd around
The winnowing store, and claim the little boon
Which Providence assigns them. One alone,   245
The redbreast, sacred to the household gods,
Wisely regardful of the embroiling sky,
In joyless fields and thorny thickets leaves
His shivering mates, and pays to trusted man
His annual visit. Half afraid, he first   250
Against the window beats; then brisk alights
On the warm hearth; then, hopping o'er the floor,
Eyes all the smiling family askance,
And pecks, and starts, and wonders where he is—
Till, more familiar grown, the table crumbs   255
Attract his slender feet. The foodless wilds
Pour forth their brown inhabitants. The hare,
Though timorous of heart, and hard beset
By death in various forms, dark snares, and dogs,
And more unpitying men, the garden seeks,   260
Urged on by fearless want. The bleating kind[4]
Eye the bleak heaven, and next the glistening earth,
With looks of dumb despair; then, sad-dispersed,
Dig for the withered herb through heaps of snow.

1726

4. Genus, class.

THOMAS GRAY
(1716–1771)

The man who wrote the English poem best known and most loved by unsophisticated readers was oddly enough a scholarly recluse who lived the quiet life of a university professor in the stagnant atmosphere of mid-18th-century Cambridge, where toward the end of his life he held the Professorship of Modern History without feeling called upon to give a single lecture. He was educated at Eton College, where he made his first intimate friends—Richard West, Thomas Ashton, and Horace Walpole, the son of the Prime Minister. After a little over four years at Cambridge he left without a degree in order to make the grand tour of France and Italy as the guest of his friend Walpole. Their different interests caused a quarrel, and after two years of traveling Gray returned to England alone. Fortunately, a few years later the quarrel was made up, and Walpole, who was Gray's ardent admirer, was able to play an important role in making his friend's poems public. The death of West in 1742 was a depressing event for Gray, who, still alienated from Walpole, felt keenly the loss of this gifted and congenial friend. The Eton *Ode* and possibly some of the stanzas of the *Elegy Written in a Country Churchyard* are associated with this melancholy event.

After 1742 Gray returned to Cambridge, pursuing his studies and indulging his tastes. He was learned in the classics and modern literatures as well as history, and his curiosity led him to explore the then little-known fields of pre-Elizabethan poetry and old Welsh and Norse literature. He was a connoisseur of painting and music, a careful and scientific observer of nature, and an enthusiastic admirer of wild and picturesque landscape. He seldom left Cambridge except to read in the newly opened British Museum or to go in the summer to the Lake District or to Scotland in search of the sublime and beautiful in nature. He wrote little, for he worked slowly and carefully, fastidiously seeking perfection of form and phrase. His early poetry is a carefully impersonal expression of his own somewhat melancholy temperament: the solitary, brooding speaker of the Eton *Ode* and the *Elegy* is a dramatic projection of Gray and of his personal dilemma: though colored by his own feeling, the poems are not confessions, but public reflections on death, the sorrows of life, and the mysteries of human destiny. The later poems—the two grandiloquent Pindaric odes, *The Progress of Poesy* and *The Bard* (1757), and the translations from Welsh and Norse poetry—are accomplished literary exercises. The living Gray is to be sought in his correspondence, where his genial humor, shy affection, and wide intellectual interests are revealed in some of the most delightful letters of the age that made letter writing an art.

Though Gray never knew Collins and had no association with the Wartons in the 1740's, he shared their interests and many of their tastes. The melancholy of Collins' *Ode to Evening* is that of the opening stanzas of the *Elegy*, and in both poems mood and landscape mutually sustain each other. Like Collins Gray wrote both greater and lesser odes (see title note to Dryden's *Ode to * * * Mistress Anne Killigrew*, above), creating a body of lyric poetry entirely characteristic of the midcentury. Without laying aside his veneration for Dryden, whom he considered his master in versification, he could share his contemporaries' enthusiasm for Spenser and Milton—especially the Milton of the minor poems, whom he often echoes. His evocation of the image of the bard, in the second of the Pindaric odes, is very much in the manner of the period. Gray wrote often in a highly artificial diction and a distorted word order (see the first four stanzas of the Eton *Ode*, for example), for he held that "the language of the age is never the language of poetry," a heresy that earned him the harsh criticism of Wordsworth in his Preface to *Lyrical Ballads*.

The *Elegy* stands alone in Gray's work: it is his one poem that belongs to mankind and that is known in many translations. It speaks to our common humanity through an art so subtle that one can know the poem for many years before becoming aware of its scores of echoes from other poems, its author's sure control of language, imagery, cadence, and his subtle modulation of style and tone. If to express the universal is to be classic, then the *Elegy* is one of our true classics. Dr. Johnson, no friend of Gray's poetry in general, long ago said the final word on this aspect of the poem:

The Churchyard abounds with images which find a mirror in every mind, and with sentiments to which every bosom returns an echo. The four stanzas beginning "Yet even these bones" are to me original: I have never seen the notions in any other place; yet he that reads them here, persuades himself that he has always felt them. Had Gray written often thus, it had been in vain to blame, and useless to praise him.

Ode on a Distant Prospect of Eton College

Ἄνθρωπος· ἱκανὴ πρόφασις εἰς τὸ δυστυχεῖν.[1]
MENANDER

Ye distant spires, ye antique towers,
  That crown the watery glade,
Where grateful Science[2] still adores
  Her Henry's holy shade;[3]
And ye, that from the stately brow   5
Of Windsor's heights the expanse below
  Of grove, of lawn, of mead survey,
Whose turf, whose shade, whose flowers among
Wanders the hoary Thames along
  His silver-winding way.   10

Ah happy hills, ah pleasing shade,
  Ah fields beloved in vain,
Where once my careless childhood strayed,
  A stranger yet to pain!
I feel the gales, that from ye blow,   15
A momentary bliss bestow,
  As waving fresh their gladsome wing,
My weary soul they seem to soothe,
And, redolent of joy and youth,
  To breathe a second spring.   20

Say, Father Thames, for thou hast seen
  Full many a sprightly race
Disporting on thy margent green
  The paths of pleasure trace,
Who foremost now delight to cleave   25
With pliant arm thy glassy wave?
  The captive linnet which enthrall?[4]
What idle progeny succeed[5]
To chase the rolling circle's speed,
  Or urge the flying ball?   30

While some on earnest business bent
  Their murmuring labors ply
'Gainst graver hours, that bring constraint
  To sweeten liberty:
Some bold adventurers disdain   35

1. "I am a man: sufficient reason for being miserable."
2. Learning.
3. Henry VI founded Eton in 1440.
4. Make prisoner.
5. I.e., follow in succession Gray's generation; "rolling circle": a hoop.

The limits of their little reign,
   And unknown regions dare descry:
Still as they run they look behind,
They hear a voice in every wind,
   And snatch a fearful joy.   40

Gay hope is theirs by fancy fed,
   Less pleasing when possessed;
The tear forgot as soon as shed,
   The sunshine of the breast:
Theirs buxom health of rosy hue,   45
Wild wit, invention ever new,
   And lively cheer of vigor born;
The thoughtless day, the easy night,
The spirits pure, the slumbers light,
   That fly the approach of morn.   50

Alas, regardless of their doom,
   The little victims play!
No sense have they of ills to come,
   Nor care beyond today.
Yet see how all around 'em wait   55
The ministers of human fate,
   And black Misfortune's baleful train!
Ah, show them where in ambush stand
To seize their prey the murderous band!
   Ah, tell them they are men!   60

These shall the fury Passions tear,
   The vultures of the mind,
Disdainful Anger, pallid Fear,
   And Shame that skulks behind;
Or pining Love shall waste their youth,   65
Or Jealousy with rankling tooth,
   That inly gnaws the secret heart,
And Envy wan, and faded Care,
Grim-visaged comfortless Despair,
   And Sorrow's piercing dart.   70

Ambition this shall tempt to rise,
   Then whirl the wretch from high,
To bitter Scorn a sacrifice,
   And grinning Infamy.
The stings of Falsehood those shall try,   75
And hard Unkindness' altered eye,
   That mocks the tear it forced to flow;
And keen Remorse with blood defiled,
And moody Madness laughing wild
   Amid severest woe.   80

Lo, in the vale of years beneath
   A grisly troop are seen,

The painful family of Death,
　　More hideous than their queen:
This racks the joints, this fires the veins,　　　85
That every laboring sinew strains,
　　Those in the deeper vitals rage:
Lo, Poverty, to fill the band,
That numbs the soul with icy hand,
　　And slow-consuming Age.　　　90

To each his sufferings: all are men,
　　Condemned alike to groan;
The tender for another's pain,
　　The unfeeling for his own.
Yet ah! why should they know their fate?　　　95
Since sorrow never comes too late,
　　And happiness too swiftly flies.
Thought would destroy their paradise.
No more; where ignorance is bliss,
　　'Tis folly to be wise.　　　100

1742　　　　　　　　　　　　　　　　　　1747

Hymn to Adversity

Ζῆνα . . .
τὸν φρονεῖν βροτοὺς ὁδώ—
σαντα, τῷ πάθει μάθος
θεντα κυρίως ἔχειν.
AESCHYLUS, *Agamemnon* 174–78[1]

Daughter of Jove, relentless power,
Thou tamer of the human breast,
Whose iron scourge and torturing hour
The bad affright, afflict the best!
Bound in thy adamantine chain,　　　5
The proud are taught to taste of pain,
And purple tyrants vainly groan
With pangs unfelt before, unpitied and alone.

When first thy sire to send on earth
Virtue, his darling child, designed,　　　10
To thee he gave the heavenly birth,
And bade to form her infant mind.
Stern rugged nurse! thy rigid lore
With patience many a year she bore:
What sorrow was, thou bad'st her know,　　　15
And from her own she learned to melt at others' woe.

Scared at thy frown terrific, fly
Self-pleasing Folly's idle brood,

---

1. "Zeus, who leads mortals to under-standing, who has established as a fixed ordinance that wisdom comes by suffering."

Wild Laughter, Noise, and thoughtless Joy,
And leave us leisure to be good.   20
Light they disperse, and with them go
The summer friend, the flattering foe;
By vain Prosperity received,
To her they vow their truth, and are again believed.

Wisdom, in sable garb arrayed,   25
Immersed in rapturous thought profound,
And Melancholy, silent maid
With leaden eye, that loves the ground,
Still on thy solemn steps attend:
Warm Charity, the general friend,   30
With Justice, to herself severe,
And Pity, dropping soft the sadly-pleasing tear.

Oh, gently on thy suppliant's head,
Dread Goddess, lay thy chastening hand!
Not in thy Gorgon[2] terrors clad,   35
Nor circled with the vengeful band
(As by the impious thou art seen)
With thundering voice, and threatening mien,
With screaming Horror's funeral cry,
Despair, and fell Disease, and ghastly Poverty.   40

Thy form benign, O Goddess, wear,
Thy milder influence impart,
Thy philosophic train be there
To soften, not to wound, my heart,
The generous spark extinct revive,   45
Teach me to love and to forgive,
Exact my own defects to scan,
What others are, to feel, and know myself a man.

1742   1753

On Lord Holland's Seat Near M——e, Kent[1]

Old, and abandoned by each venal friend,
  Here Holland took the pious resolution
To smuggle some few years, and strive to mend
  A broken character and constitution.

2. The Gorgons were monsters with snaky locks, one glance of whose eyes turned men to stones; the "vengeful band": the Furies.
1. Henry Fox, 1st Baron Holland (1705–74), was, despite his great gifts, one of the most hated statesmen of the century. He changed sides at pleasure, betraying friends and colleagues for his own advantage. As Paymaster-General of the army (1757–65), he amassed a huge fortune. In 1768 Gray saw Holland's estate on a bleak promontory of the coast of Kent near Kingsgate, not far from Margate, which Holland had adorned with a classic villa and simulated Gothic ruins. The idea of the predatory politician's surrounding himself with "mimic desolation" suggested to the poet these lines.

On this congenial spot he fixed his choice,   5
    Earl Goodwin trembled for his neighboring sand;[2]
Here seagulls scream and cormorants rejoice,
    And mariners, though shipwrecked, dread to land.

Here reign the blustering North and blighting East,
    No tree is heard to whisper, bird to sing,   10
Yet Nature cannot furnish out the feast,
    Art he invokes new horrors still to bring.

Now moldering fanes and battlements arise,
    Arches and turrets nodding to their fall,
Unpeopled palaces delude his eyes,   15
    And mimic desolation covers all.

"Ah!" said the sighing peer, "had Bute been true,
    Nor Shelburne's, Rigby's, Calcraft's[3] friendship vain,
Far other scenes than these had blessed our view,
    And realized the ruins that we feign.   20

"Purged by the sword and beautified by fire,
    Then had we seen proud London's hated walls;
Owls might have hooted in St. Peter's choir,[4]
    And foxes stunk and littered in St. Paul's."

1768   1769

Elegy Written in a Country Churchyard

The curfew tolls the knell of parting day,
    The lowing herd wind slowly o'er the lea,
The plowman homeward plods his weary way,
    And leaves the world to darkness and to me.

Now fades the glimmering landscape on the sight,   5
    And all the air a solemn stillness holds,
Save where the beetle wheels his droning flight,
    And drowsy tinklings lull the distant folds;

Save that from yonder ivy-mantled tower
    The moping owl does to the moon complain   10
Of such, as wandering near her secret bower,
    Molest her ancient solitary reign.

Beneath those rugged elms, that yew tree's shade,
    Where heaves the turf in many a moldering heap,

2. Goodwin Sands is a dangerous shoal off Ramsgate. Legend has it that it was once a fertile estate owned by Earl Goodwin.
3. Unscrupulous politicians who had been allied with and had deserted Fox, as Fox himself had been allied with and deserted Pitt and Bute.
4. Westminster Abbey, dedicated to St. Peter; St. Paul's is the cathedral church of the City of London.

Each in his narrow cell forever laid,   15
    The rude[1] forefathers of the hamlet sleep.

The breezy call of incense-breathing Morn,
    The swallow twittering from the straw-built shed,
The cock's shrill clarion, or the echoing horn,[2]
    No more shall rouse them from their lowly bed.   20

For them no more the blazing hearth shall burn,
    Or busy housewife ply her evening care;
No children run to lisp their sire's return,
    Or climb his knees the envied kiss to share.

Oft did the harvest to their sickle yield,   25
    Their furrow oft the stubborn glebe[3] has broke;
How jocund did they drive their team afield!
    How bowed the woods beneath their sturdy stroke!

Let not Ambition mock their useful toil,
    Their homely joys, and destiny obscure;
Nor Grandeur hear with a disdainful smile   30
    The short and simple annals of the poor.

The boast of heraldry,[4] the pomp of power,
    And all that beauty, all that wealth e'er gave,
Awaits alike the inevitable hour.   35
    The paths of glory lead but to the grave.

Nor you, ye proud, impute to these the fault,
    If Memory o'er their tomb no trophies[5] raise,
Where through the long-drawn aisle and fretted[6] vault
    The pealing anthem swells the note of praise.   40

Can storied urn[7] or animated bust
    Back to its mansion call the fleeting breath?
Can Honor's voice provoke[8] the silent dust,
    Or Flattery soothe the dull cold ear of Death?

Perhaps in this neglected spot is laid   45
    Some heart once pregnant with celestial fire;
Hands that the rod of empire might have swayed,
    Or waked to ecstasy the living lyre.

But Knowledge to their eyes her ample page
    Rich with the spoils of time did ne'er unroll;   50
Chill Penury repressed their noble rage,
    And froze the genial current of the soul.

Full many a gem of purest ray serene,
    The dark unfathomed caves of ocean bear:

1. Untaught.
2. The hunter's horn.
3. Soil, turf.
4. Noble birth.
5. An ornamental or symbolic group of figures depicting the achievements of the dead man.
6. Decorated with intersecting lines in relief.
7. A funeral urn with an epitaph inscribed on it; "animated": lifelike.
8. Call forth.

Full many a flower is born to blush unseen,   55
   And waste its sweetness on the desert air.

Some village Hampden,[9] that with dauntless breast
   The little tyrant of his fields withstood;
Some mute inglorious Milton here may rest,
   Some Cromwell guiltless of his country's blood.   60

The applause of listening senates to command,
   The threats of pain and ruin to despise,
To scatter plenty o'er a smiling land,
   And read their history in a nation's eyes,

Their lot forbade: nor circumscribed alone   65
   Their growing virtues, but their crimes confined;
Forbade to wade through slaughter to a throne,
   And shut the gates of mercy on mankind,

The struggling pangs of conscious truth to hide,
   To quench the blushes of ingenuous shame,   70
Or heap the shrine of Luxury and Pride
   With incense kindled at the Muse's flame.

Far from the madding crowd's ignoble strife,
   Their sober wishes never learned to stray;
Along the cool sequestered vale of life   75
   They kept the noiseless tenor of their way.

Yet even these bones from insult to protect
   Some frail memorial still erected nigh,
With uncouth rhymes and shapeless sculpture decked,[1]
   Implores the passing tribute of a sigh.   80

Their name, their years, spelt by the unlettered Muse,
   The place of fame and elegy supply:
And many a holy text around she strews,
   That teach the rustic moralist to die.

For who to dumb Forgetfulness a prey,   85
   This pleasing anxious being e'er resigned,
Left the warm precincts of the cheerful day,
   Nor cast one longing lingering look behind?

On some fond breast the parting soul relies,
   Some pious drops the closing eye requires;   90
Even from the tomb the voice of Nature cries,
   Even in our ashes live their wonted fires.

For thee, who mindful of the unhonored dead
   Dost in these lines their artless tale relate;
If chance, by lonely contemplation led,   95
   Some kindred spirit shall inquire thy fate,

9. John Hampden (1594–1643), who, both as a private citizen and as a Member of Parliament, zealously defended the rights of the people against the autocratic policies of Charles I. A gallant soldier, he was mortally wounded in a skirmish near Oxford.
1. Cf. "the storied urn or animated bust" dedicated inside the church to "the proud" (line 41).

Haply some hoary-headed swain may say,
    "Oft have we seen him at the peep of dawn
Brushing with hasty steps the dews away
    To meet the sun upon the upland lawn.   100

"There at the foot of yonder nodding beech
    That wreathes its old fantastic roots so high,
His listless length at noontide would he stretch,
    And pore upon the brook that babbles by.

"Hard by yon wood, now smiling as in scorn,   105
    Muttering his wayward fancies he would rove,
Now drooping, woeful wan, like one forlorn,
    Or crazed with care, or crossed in hopeless love.

"One morn I missed him on the customed hill,
    Along the heath and near his favorite tree;   110
Another came; nor yet beside the rill,
    Nor up the lawn, nor at the wood was he;

"The next with dirges due in sad array
    Slow through the churchway path we saw him borne.
Approach and read (for thou canst read) the lay,   115
    Graved on the stone beneath yon aged thorn."

THE EPITAPH

Here rests his head upon the lap of Earth
    A youth to Fortune and to Fame unknown.
Fair Science[2] frowned not on his humble birth,
    And Melancholy marked him for her own.   120

Large was his bounty, and his soul sincere,
    Heaven did a recompense as largely send:
He gave to Misery all he had, a tear,
    He gained from Heaven ('twas all he wished) a friend.

No farther seek his merits to disclose,   125
    Or draw his frailties from their dread abode
(There they alike in trembling hope repose),
    The bosom of his Father and his God.

ca. 1742–50   1751
2. Learning.

WILLIAM COLLINS

(1721–1759)

William Collins was born at Chichester and was educated at Winchester
and Oxford. Coming up to London from the university, he tried to establish himself as an author, but he was given rather to planning than to

writing books. He came to know Dr. Johnson, who recorded in the *Lives of the Poets* that he had once "delighted to converse with him." In 1746 Collins published his *Odes on Several Descriptive and Allegorical Subjects*, his part in an undertaking, with his friend Joseph Warton, to create a "new," more lyrical and imaginative poetry than the generation of Dryden and Pope had done. Collins' *Odes*, as their title suggests, are addressed to personified abstractions (Fear, Pity, the Passions) which are rendered vividly and pictorially, in expressive attitudes and allegorical groups. The volume was not much liked; Gray, however, commented favorably on it in private; and the enterprising publisher Robert Dodsley included three of the simpler odes in the first volume of his *Miscellany* (1748). The more ambitious odes were thought to be obscure and too "visionary." In form they represent a new version of the "great" or Cowleian ode (see title note to Dryden's *Anne Killigrew*, above), for Collins gave them at least an approximate regularity of structure, since in several of them strophe and antistrophe are more or less symmetrical. Curiously, however, he departed from the normal Pindaric order of parts by placing epodes between strophes and antistrophes.

Inheriting some money, the poet traveled for a while, but fits of depression gradually deepened into insanity. He spent his last years in Chichester, forgotten by all but a small circle of loyal friends. As the century progressed he gained in reputation, although the tendency to find signs of incipient madness in his vividly realized imaginary figures is regrettable. The Romantics admired his poems and felt akin to him as they did to Thomas Chatterton and Robert Burns. The *Ode to Evening*, which combines a chaste and cool classicism with a delicate feeling for landscape and mood, is one of the delightful poems of the century.

Ode Written in the Beginning of the Year 1746

How sleep the brave[1] who sink to rest
By all their country's wishes blest!
When Spring, with dewy fingers cold,
Returns to deck their hallowed mold,
She there shall dress a sweeter sod   5
Than Fancy's feet have ever trod.

By fairy hands their knell is rung,
By forms unseen their dirge is sung;
There Honor comes, a pilgrim gray,
To bless the turf that wraps their clay,   10
And Freedom shall awhile repair,
To dwell a weeping hermit there!

1746

1. Collins is presumably thinking of those who lost their lives defending England in 1745, when the Scotch Jacobites, led by Bonnie Prince Charlie, penetrated to within 127 miles of London.

Ode to Fear[1]

STROPHE

Thou, to whom the world unknown
With all its shadowy shapes is shown;
Who see'st appalled the unreal scene,
While Fancy lifts the veil between:
    Ah Fear! Ah frantic Fear!   5
    I see, I see thee near.
I know thy hurried step, thy haggard eye!
Like thee I start, like thee disordered fly,
For lo, what monsters in thy train appear!
Danger, whose limbs of giant mold   10
What mortal eye can fixed behold?
Who stalks his round, an hideous form,
Howling amidst the midnight storm,
Or throws him on the ridgy steep
Of some loose hanging rock to sleep: 15
And with him thousand phantoms joined,
Who prompt to deeds accursed the mind:
And those, the fiends, who near allied,
O'er Nature's wounds and wrecks preside;
Whilst Vengeance, in the lurid air,   20
Lifts her red arm, exposed and bare:
On whom that ravening brood of Fate,[2]
Who lap the blood of Sorrow, wait;
Who, Fear, this ghastly train can see,
And look not madly wild, like thee?   25

EPODE

In earliest Greece to thee with partial choice,
    The grief-full Muse[3] addressed her infant tongue;
The maids and matrons, on her awful voice,
    Silent and pale in wild amazement hung.

Yet he, the bard who first invoked thy name,[4]   30
    Disdained in Marathon its power to feel:
For not alone he nursed the poet's flame,
    But reached from virtue's hand the patriot's steel.

But who is he whom later garlands grace,[5]
    Who left a while o'er Hybla's dews to rove,   35

1. About 1744 Collins agreed with a London publisher to furnish a commentary on Aristotle's *Poetics*. The work was abandoned, but the companion odes to Pity and Fear resulted from the undertaking. Aristotle had taught (*Poetics* VI) that the two emotions proper to tragedy are pity and fear and that the function of tragedy is to "purge" the spectators' souls of these emotions.
2. The Erinyes or Furies.
3. The Muse of tragedy, Melpomene.
4. The Greek tragic poet Aeschylus (525–456 B.C.), who fought against the Persians in the Battle of Marathon.
5. Sophocles (ca. 495–ca. 406 B.C.) continued the development of Greek tragedy

With trembling eyes thy dreary steps to trace,
  Where thou and Furies shared the baleful grove?

Wrapped in thy cloudy veil, the incestuous queen[6]
  Sighed the sad call her son and husband heard,
When once alone it broke the silent scene,   40
  And he, the wretch of Thebes, no more appeared.

O Fear, I know thee by my throbbing heart,
  Thy withering power inspired each mournful line;
Though gentle Pity claim her mingled part,
  Yet all the thunders of the scene are thine!   45

ANTISTROPHE

Thou who such weary lengths hast passed,
Where wilt thou rest, mad nymph, at last?
Say, wilt thou shroud in haunted cell,
Where gloomy Rape and Murder dwell?
Or, in some hollowed seat,   50
'Gainst which the big waves beat,
Hear drowning seamen's cries in tempests brought!
Dark power, with shuddering meek submitted thought,
Be mine to read the visions old,
Which thy awakening bards have told: 55
And lest thou meet my blasted view,
Hold each strange tale devoutly true,
Ne'er be I found, by thee o'erawed,
In that thrice-hallowed eve abroad,[7]
When ghosts, as cottage-maids believe,   60
Their pebbled beds permitted leave,
And goblins haunt from fire, or fen,
Or mine, or flood, the walks of men!
  O thou whose spirit most possessed
The sacred seat of Shakespeare's breast!   65
By all that from thy prophet broke,
In thy divine emotions spoke:
Hither again thy fury deal,
Teach me but once like him to feel:
His cypress wreath[8] my meed decree,   70
And I, O Fear, will dwell with thee!

                                                            1746

after Aeschylus. His tragedies *Oedipus
the King* and *Oedipus at Colonus* are
referred to in the following stanzas.
Hybla: a city in Sicily, famed for its
honey.
6. Jocasta; in ignorance she married
her son Oedipus ("the wretch of

Thebes"), who had unwittingly slain his
father on his way to Thebes.
7. Halloween.
8. The ancients associated the dark
green cypress tree with funerals and
mourning; hence the cypress wreath is
the reward ("meed") of the tragic poet.

Ode on the Poetical Character[1]

STROPHE

As once, if not with light regard,
I read aright that gifted bard
(Him whose school above the rest
His loveliest Elfin Queen has blest),[2]
One, only one, unrivaled fair,   5
Might hope the magic girdle wear,
At solemn tourney hung on high,
The wish of each love-darting eye;[3]
Lo! to each other nymph in turn applied,
   As if, in air unseen, some hovering hand,   10
Some chaste and angel-friend to virgin-fame,
   With whispered spell had burst the starting band,
It left unblest her loathed dishonored side;
   Happier, hopeless fair, if never
   Her baffled hand with vain endeavor   15
Had touched that fatal zone to her denied!
Young Fancy thus, to me divinest name,
   To whom, prepared and bathed in Heaven
   The cest of amplest power is given:
To few the godlike gift assigns,   20
To gird their blest, prophetic loins,
And gaze her visions wild, and feel unmixed her flame!

EPODE

The band, as fairy legends say,
Was wove on that creating day,
When He,[4] who called with thought to birth   25
Yon tented sky, this laughing earth,
And dressed with springs, and forests tall,
And poured the main engirting all,
Long by the loved Enthusiast[5] wooed,
Himself in some diviner mood,   30

1. This ode, long held in comparative disregard, has more recently been elevated in critical estimation, for it is now seen as an early, dramatic engagement with one of the central concerns of the Romantic Age—the origin and role of the creative imagination and, indeed, of the poet himself. "It is an allegory," A. S. P. Woodhouse tells us, "whose subject is the *creative imagination* and the poet's passionate desire for its power."

In the strophe an analogy is drawn between the *cestus* or girdle of Venus, which only the chaste can wear, and the cest of Fancy, or the creative imagination. In the epode the act of the creation of the world is presented as an act of the divine imagination.

What is especially new, such critics as Harold Bloom and Northrop Frye suggest, is Collins' implication, in the epode, that "a poet is born from the quasi-sexual union of God and imagina-

tion," or Fancy (lines 30–40). Such a reading animates the personifications in a way that we do not encounter again until the work of William Blake. The poet's creative act is divine, analogous to the creation of the world, and he is born of the divine act.

In the antistrophe, Milton is regarded as the type of poet true enough to wear the girdle of Fancy. Collins pictures himself pursuing the "guiding steps" (line 71) of Milton, as of Spenser (in the epode)—both poet-prophets. He retreats from the elegant school of Waller (and, by implication, that of Pope, as well)—"In vain" (line 72), however, for he lives in an age of sensibility.
2. Edmund Spenser.
3. *Faerie Queene* IV.v tells of the contest of many beautiful ladies for the girdle of Venus.
4. God, on the day of creation.
5. I.e., Fancy.

Retiring, sate with her alone,
And placed her on his sapphire throne;
The whiles, the vaulted shrine around,
Seraphic wires were heard to sound,
Now sublimest triumph swelling,   35
Now on love and mercy dwelling;
And she, from out the veiling cloud,
Breathed her magic notes aloud:
And thou, thou rich-haired Youth of Morn,[6]
And all thy subject life was born!   40
The dangerous Passions kept aloof,
Far from the sainted growing woof:
But near it sate ecstatic Wonder,
Listening the deep applauding thunder:
And Truth, in sunny vest arrayed,   45
By whose the tarsel's [7] eyes were made;
All the shadowy tribes of Mind,
In braided dance their murmurs joined,
And all the bright uncounted Powers
Who feed on Heaven's ambrosial flowers.   50
Where is the bard, whose soul can now
Its high presuming hopes avow?
Where he who thinks, with rapture blind,
This hallow'd work [8] for him designed?

ANTISTROPHE

High on some cliff, to Heaven up-piled,   55
Of rude access, of prospect wild,
Where, tangled round the jealous steep,
Strange shades o'erbrow the valleys deep,
And holy Genii guard the rock,
Its glooms embrown, its springs unlock,   60
While on its rich ambitious head,
An Eden, like his [9] own, lies spread:
I view that oak, the fancied glades among,
By which as Milton lay, his evening ear,
From many a cloud that dropped ethereal dew,   65
Nigh sphered in Heaven its native strains could hear:
On which that ancient trump he reached was hung;
    Thither oft, his glory greeting,
    From Waller's [1] myrtle shades retreating,
With many a vow from Hope's aspiring tongue,   70
My trembling feet his guiding steps pursue;
    In vain—such bliss to one alone,[2]
    Of all the sons of soul was known,
    And Heaven, and Fancy, kindred powers,
    Have now o'erturned the inspiring bowers,   75
Or curtained close such scene from every future view.

1746

6. Apollo, god of the sun and of poetry, associated with the poet himself.
7. The falcon's.
8. The girdle of Fancy.
9. Milton's.

1. Edmund Waller (1606–87). The myrtle is the symbol of love poetry, Waller's poetry is thought of as trivial compared to Milton's grandeur.
2. Milton.

Ode to Evening[1]

If aught of oaten stop, or pastoral song,
May hope, chaste Eve, to soothe thy modest ear,
    Like thy own solemn springs,
    Thy springs and dying gales,
O nymph reserved, while now the bright-haired sun   5
Sits in yon western tent, whose cloudy skirts,
    With brede[2] ethereal wove,
    O'erhang his wavy bed:
Now air is hushed, save where the weak-eyed bat,
With short shrill shrieks flits by on leathern wing,   10
    Or where the beetle winds
    His small but sullen horn,
As oft he rises 'midst the twilight path,
Against the pilgrim borne in heedless hum:
    Now teach me, maid composed,   15
    To breathe some softened strain,
Whose numbers, stealing through thy darkening vale,
May not unseemly with its stillness suit,
    As, musing slow, I hail
    Thy genial loved return!   20
For when thy folding-star[3] arising shows
His paly circlet, at his warning lamp
    The fragrant Hours, and elves
    Who slept in flowers the day,
And many a nymph who wreaths her brows with sedge,   25
And sheds the freshening dew, and, lovelier still,
    The pensive Pleasures sweet,
    Prepare thy shadowy car.
Then lead, calm vot'ress, where some sheety lake
Cheers the lone heath, or some time-hallowed pile   30
    Or upland fallows gray
    Reflect its last cool gleam.
But when chill blustering winds, or driving rain,
Forbid my willing feet, be mine the hut
    That from the mountain's side   35
    Views wilds, and swelling floods,
And hamlets brown, and dim-discovered spires,
And hears their simple bell, and marks o'er all
    Thy dewy fingers draw
    The gradual dusky veil.   40
While Spring shall pour his showers, as oft he wont,
And bathe thy breathing tresses, meekest Eve;

1. Collins borrowed the metrical structure and the rhymeless lines of this ode from Milton's translation of Horace, *Odes* I.5 (1673). The text printed here is based on the revised version, published in Dodsley's *Miscellany* (1748).
2. Embroidery.
3. The evening star, which signals the hour for herding the sheep into the sheepfold.

> While Summer loves to sport
>   Beneath thy lingering light;
> While sallow Autumn fills thy lap with leaves;   45
> Or Winter, yelling through the troublous air,
>   Affrights thy shrinking train,
>   And rudely rends thy robes;
> So long, sure-found beneath the sylvan shed,
> Shall Fancy, Friendship, Science, rose-lipped Health,   50
>   Thy gentlest influence own,
>   And hymn thy favorite name!

1746, 1748

WILLIAM COWPER
(1731–1800)

There are no saner poems in the language than Cowper's, yet they were written by a man who was periodically insane and who, for forty years, lived with the possibility of madness in full view. One form that his madness took was a conviction that he was damned for having committed the unforgivable sin, the "sin against the Holy Ghost." When he recovered from his first attack, in which he had attempted suicide, he was persuaded by his physician that this conviction was a delusion, and he embraced the doctor's own hopeful Evangelical creed. Relieved of his guilts, he felt inwardly assured of salvation and of the healing and sustaining power of divine grace freely extended to him.

From then on, a refugee from life, he found shelter first, in 1765, in the pious family of the Evangelical clergyman, Morley Unwin, and after Unwin's death, with Mrs. Unwin, who gave him exactly the sort of loving shelter that he needed. They were never separated until her death in 1796, by which time Cowper had experienced his final attack of madness. The removal of Mary Unwin and Cowper from Huntington to Olney (pronounced *Own-y*) in 1765 brought the couple under the influence of the strenuous and fervent Evangelical clergyman John Newton. With him Cowper wrote the famous *Olney Hymns*, still familiar to Methodists and other Nonconformists. But here a second attack of madness, in 1773, not only frustrated his planned marriage to Mary, but left him for the rest of his life with the assurance that he had been cast out by God and was inevitably damned. He never again attended divine service, and the main purpose of his life thereafter was to divert his mind by every possible innocent device from the numb despair that was his lot in life. He gardened, he kept pets, he walked, he wrote letters (some of the best of the century), he conversed, he read—and he wrote poetry. When it was published, it brought him a measure of fame that his modest nature could never have hoped for.

Despair could suppress neither his humor and gentle wit nor the religious side of his nature, which finds expression in the poems of the next decade—not only in their ethical point of view, but in the tone of gentle, if wistful, piety that pervades them. The first volume, *Poems* (didactic

and gently satiric verse in heroic couplets), won the praise of Johnson
and the approval of the public. But his major work is *The Task*, undertaken at the bidding—hence the title—of the lively and charming Lady
Austen, who, when he complained that he had no subject, directed him
to write about the sofa in his parlor. It began with a mock-heroic account
of the development of the sofa from a simple stool, but it grew into a
long meditative poem of over five thousand lines in delicately modulated
blank verse. The poet describes in his murmuring voice his small world
of country, village, garden, and parlor, and from time to time he glances
toward the great world to condemn cities and worldliness, war and slavery,
luxury and corruption. The tone is muted, the sensibility delicate, the
language on the whole pure and simple. The truthfulness of Cowper's
description of landscape and of the human figures that animate it, his
moralizing, his generous spirit of humanitarianism, all appealed to the
Englishmen of the late 18th century. His religious piety, domestic sentiment, and humanitarianism made his poems especially acceptable to Methodists and their Anglican counterparts, the Evangelicals, who between
them were transforming the religious life of England and establishing the
values and manners which came to characterize the Victorian age. No
poet of the century expressed more completely the interests and taste of
the new enlightened and religious middle class.

Many of Cowper's themes are identical with Wordsworth's. No doubt a
taste for Cowper's poetry made it easier for some people to accept Wordsworth when he appeared. But the similarity is superficial and deceptive.
Cowper may seem a Wordsworth who never beheld the visionary gleam—
but such a Wordsworth is inconceivable. We may agree today that Cowper was too highly valued by his contemporaries, but it is agreeable to take
up his poems from time to time, and to allow his gentle talk to re-create
for us the serenity and simplicity of life in an English village just before
the French Revolution announced a new era.

From The Task
From *Book I*

[A LANDSCAPE DESCRIBED. RURAL SOUNDS]

Thou[1] knowest my praise of nature most sincere,   150
And that my raptures are not conjured up
To serve occasions of poetic pomp,
But genuine, and art partner of them all.
How oft upon yon eminence our pace
Has slackened to a pause, and we have borne   155
The ruffling wind, scarce conscious that it blew,
While admiration, feeding at the eye,
And still unsated, dwelt upon the scene.
Thence with what pleasure have we just discerned
The distant plow slow moving, and beside   160
His laboring team, that swerved not from the track,

1. Mary Unwin.

The sturdy swain diminished to a boy!
Here Ouse,[2] slow winding through a level plain
Of spacious meads with cattle sprinkled o'er,
Conducts the eye along its sinuous course   165
Delighted. There, fast rooted in their bank,
Stand, never overlooked, our favorite elms,
That screen the herdsman's solitary hut;
While far beyond, and overthwart the stream
That, as with molten glass, inlays the vale,   170
The sloping land recedes into the clouds;
Displaying on its varied side the grace
Of hedgerow beauties numberless, square tower,
Tall spire, from which the sound of cheerful bells
Just undulates upon the listening ear,   175
Groves, heaths, and smoking villages, remote.
Scenes must be beautiful, which, daily viewed,
Please daily, and whose novelty survives
Long knowledge and the scrutiny of years—
Praise justly due to those that I describe.   180
   Nor rural sights alone, but rural sounds,
Exhilarate the spirit, and restore
The tone of languid Nature. Mighty winds,
That sweep the skirt of some far-spreading wood
Of ancient growth, make music not unlike   185
The dash of ocean on his winding shore,
And lull the spirit while they fill the mind;
Unnumbered branches waving in the blast,
And all their leaves fast fluttering, all at once.
Nor less composure waits upon the roar   190
Of distant floods, or on the softer voice
Of neighboring fountain, or of rills that slip
Through the cleft rock, and, chiming as they fall
Upon loose pebbles, lose themselves at length
In matted grass, that with a livelier green   195
Betrays the secret of their silent course.
Nature inanimate employs sweet sounds,
But animated nature sweeter still,
To soothe and satisfy the human ear.
Ten thousand warblers cheer the day, and one   200
The livelong night: nor these alone, whose notes
Nice-fingered art must emulate in vain,
But cawing rooks, and kites that swim sublime
In still repeated circles, screaming loud,
The jay, the pie, and even the boding owl   205
That hails the rising moon, have charms for me.
Sounds inharmonious in themselves and harsh,
Yet heard in scenes where peace forever reigns,
And only there, please highly for their sake.

2. The village of Olney, where Cowper and Mary Unwin were living, is situated
on the river Ouse.

[CRAZY KATE. GYPSIES]

There often wanders one, whom better days
Saw better clad, in cloak of satin trimmed   535
With lace, and hat with splendid ribband bound.
A servingmaid was she, and fell in love
With one who left her, went to sea, and died.
Her fancy followed him through foaming waves
To distant shores; and she would sit and weep   540
At what a sailor suffers; fancy, too,
Delusive most where warmest wishes are,
Would oft anticipate his glad return,
And dream of transports she was not to know.
She heard the doleful tidings of his death—   545
And never smiled again! And now she roams
The dreary waste; there spends the livelong day,
And there, unless when charity forbids,
The livelong night. A tattered apron hides,
Worn as a cloak, and hardly hides, a gown   550
More tattered still; and both but ill conceal
A bosom heaved with never-ceasing sighs.
She begs an idle pin of all she meets,
And hoards them in her sleeve; but needful food,
Though pressed with hunger oft, or comelier clothes,   555
Though pinched with cold, asks never.—Kate is crazed!
   I see a column of slow rising smoke
O'ertop the lofty wood that skirts the wild.
A vagabond and useless tribe there eat
Their miserable meal. A kettle, slung   560
Between two poles upon a stick transverse,
Receives the morsel—flesh obscene of dog,
Or vermin,[3] or, at best, of cock purloined
From his accustomed perch. Hard faring race!
They pick their fuel out of every hedge,   565
Which, kindled with dry leaves, just saves unquenched
The spark of life. The sportive wind blows wide
Their fluttering rags, and shows a tawny skin,
The vellum of the pedigree they claim.
Great skill have they in palmistry, and more   570
To conjure clean away the gold they touch,
Conveying worthless dross into its place;
Loud when they beg, dumb only when they steal.
Strange! that a creature rational, and cast
In human mold, should brutalize by choice   575
His nature; and, though capable of arts
By which the world might profit, and himself,
Self-banished from society, prefer
Such squalid sloth to honorable toil!
Yet even these, though, feigning sickness oft,   580

3. Any small, noxious animal, such as a rat or weasel.

They swathe the forehead, drag the limping limb,
And vex their flesh with artificial sores,
Can change their whine into a mirthful note
When safe occasion offers; and, with dance,
And music of the bladder and the bag,   585
Beguile their woes, and make the woods resound.
Such health and gaiety of heart enjoy
The houseless rovers of the sylvan world;
And, breathing wholesome air, and wandering much,
Need other physic none to heal the effects   590
Of loathsome diet, penury, and cold.

From *Book III*

[THE STRICKEN DEER]

I was a stricken deer, that left the herd
Long since; with many an arrow deep infixed
My panting side was charged, when I withdrew   110
To seek a tranquil death in distant shades.
There was I found by one who had himself
Been hurt by the archers. In his side he bore,
And in his hands and feet, the cruel scars.
With gentle force soliciting[4] the darts,   115
He drew them forth, and healed, and bade me live.
Since then, with few associates, in remote
And silent woods I wander, far from those
My former partners of the peopled scene;
With few associates, and not wishing more.   120
Here much I ruminate, as much I may,
With other views of men and manners now
Than once, and others of a life to come.
I see that all are wanderers, gone astray
Each in his own delusions; they are lost   125
In chase of fancied happiness, still wooed
And never won. Dream after dream ensues;
And still they dream that they shall still succeed.
And still are disappointed. Rings the world
With the vain stir. I sum up half mankind   130
And add two-thirds of the remaining half,
And find the total of their hopes and fears
Dreams, empty dreams.

From *Book IV*

[THE WINTER EVENING]

Hark! 'tis the twanging horn[5] o'er yonder bridge,
That with its wearisome but needful length
Bestrides the wintry flood, in which the moon
Sees her unwrinkled face reflected bright—
He comes, the herald of a noisy world,   5

4. "To endeavor to draw out by the use of gentle force" (*NED*).

5. The post-horn, announcing the arrival of the mail coach.

With spattered boots, strapped waist, and frozen locks;
News from all nations lumbering at his back.
True to his charge, the close-packed load behind,
Yet careless what he brings, his one concern
Is to conduct it to the destined inn: 10
And, having dropped the expected bag, pass on.
He whistles as he goes, light-hearted wretch,
Cold and yet cheerful: messenger of grief
Perhaps to thousands, and of joy to some;
To him indifferent whether grief or joy.   15
Houses in ashes, and the fall of stocks,
Births, deaths, and marriages, epistles wet
With tears that trickled down the writer's cheeks
Fast as the periods from his fluent quill,
Or charged with amorous sighs of absent swains   20
Or nymphs responsive, equally affect
His horse and him, unconscious of them all.
But oh, the important budget![6] ushered in
With such heart-shaking music, who can say
What are its tidings? Have our troops awaked?   25
Or do they still, as if with opium drugged,
Snore to the murmurs of the Atlantic wave?[7]
Is India free, and does she wear her plumed
And jeweled turban with a smile of peace,
Or do we grind her still? The grand debate,[8]   30
The popular harangue, the tart reply,
The logic, and the wisdom, and the wit,
And the loud laugh—I long to know them all;
I burn to set the imprisoned wranglers free,
And give them voice and utterance once again.   35

* * *

O Winter, ruler of the inverted year,   120
Thy scattered hair with sleet like ashes filled,
Thy breath congealed upon thy lips, thy cheeks
Fringed with a beard made white with other snows
Than those of age, thy forehead wrapped in clouds,
A leafless branch thy scepter, and thy throne   125
A sliding car, indebted to no wheels,
But urged by storms along its slippery way,
I love thee, all unlovely as thou seem'st,
And dreaded as thou art! Thou hold'st the sun
A prisoner in the yet undawning east,   130
Shortening his journey between morn and noon,
And hurrying him, impatient of his stay,

---

6. Newspaper.
7. Though a recluse, Cowper followed public affairs with interest. Here he expresses concern for what he considers the inactivity of British arms since the surrender at Yorktown, despite the hostility of France. He was much disturbed by the revelations of the cruelty and rapacity of the British in India (where his old schoolfellow Warren Hastings, Governor of Bengal, had been under attack for his brutal, if efficient, rule), and he longed to see India freed from the tyranny of the East India Company, as Pitt's India Bill of 1784 proposed that it should be.
8. In Parliament, as reported in the newspaper.

Down to the rosy west; but kindly still
Compensating his loss with added hours
Of social converse and instructive ease,   135
And gathering, at short notice, in one group
The family dispersed, and fixing thought,
Not less dispersed by daylight and its cares.
I crown thee king of intimate delights,
Fireside enjoyments, home-born happiness,   140
And all the comforts that the lowly roof
Of undisturbed retirement and the hours
Of long uninterrupted evening know.
No rattling wheels stop short before these gates;
No powdered pert,[9] proficient in the art   145
Of sounding an alarm, assaults these doors
Till the street rings; no stationary steeds
Cough their own knell, while, heedless of the sound,
The silent circle[1] fan themselves, and quake:
But here the needle plies its busy task,   150
The pattern grows, the well-depicted flower,
Wrought patiently into the snowy lawn,[2]
Unfolds its bosom; buds, and leaves, and sprigs,
And curling tendrils, gracefully disposed,
Follow the nimble finger of the fair—   155
A wreath that cannot fade, of flowers that blow
With most success when all besides decay.
The poet's or historian's page, by one
Made vocal for the amusement of the rest;
The sprightly lyre, whose treasure of sweet sounds   160
The touch from many a trembling chord shakes out;
And the clear voice symphonious, yet distinct,
And in the charming strife triumphant still,
Beguile the night, and set a keener edge
On female industry: the threaded steel   165
Flies swiftly, and unfelt the task proceeds.
The volume closed, the customary rites
Of the last meal commence. A Roman meal,
Such as the mistress of the world once found
Delicious, when her patriots of high note,   170
Perhaps by moonlight, at their humble doors,
And under an old oak's domestic shade,
Enjoyed—spare feast!—a radish and an egg!

1785

Lines Written on a Window Shutter at Weston[3]

Farewell, dear scenes, forever closed to me,
Oh, for what sorrows must I now exchange ye!

9. Footmen wore powdered hair.   2. A fine sheer fabric.
1. The audience in the theater.   3. Cowper and Mrs. Unwin lived at

Me miserable![4] how could I escape
Infinite wrath and infinite despair!
Whom Death, Earth, Heaven, and Hell consigned to ruin,   5
Whose friend was God, but God swore not to aid me!

1795

The Castaway

Obscurest night involved the sky,
   The Atlantic billows roared,
When such a destined wretch as I,
   Washed headlong from on board,
Of friends, of hope, of all bereft,   5
His floating home forever left.

No braver chief[1] could Albion boast
   Than he with whom he went,
Nor ever ship left Albion's coast,
   With warmer wishes sent.   10
He loved them both, but both in vain,
Nor him beheld, nor her again.

Not long beneath the whelming brine,
   Expert to swim, he lay;
Nor soon he felt his strength decline,   15
   Or courage die away;
But waged with death a lasting strife,
Supported by despair of life.

He shouted; nor his friends had failed
   To check the vessel's course,   20
But so the furious blast prevailed,
   That, pitiless perforce,
They left their outcast mate behind,
And scudded still before the wind.

Some succor yet they could afford;   25
   And, such as storms allow,
The cask, the coop, the floated cord,
   Delayed not to bestow.
But he (they knew) nor ship, nor shore,
Whate'er they gave, should visit more.   30

Nor, cruel as it seemed, could he
   Their haste himself condemn,

Weston Lodge from 1786 until 1795, when Cowper's relative John Johnson took charge of the dying Mary and the insane poet, removing them to Norfolk. These lines were written just before the move.

4. A poignant echo of Satan in *Paradise Lost* (IV.73–74), when he recognizes that he is forever alienated from God and so is damned.

1. George, Lord Anson (1697–1762), in whose *Voyage* (1748), Cowper, years before writing this poem, had read the story of the sailor washed overboard in a storm.

Aware that flight, in such a sea,
    Alone could rescue them;
Yet bitter felt it still to die   35
Deserted, and his friends so nigh.

He long survives, who lives an hour
    In ocean, self-upheld;
And so long he, with unspent power,
    His destiny repelled;   40
And ever, as the minutes flew,
Entreated help, or cried, "Adieu!"

At length, his transient respite past,
    His comrades, who before
Had heard his voice in every blast,   45
    Could catch the sound no more.
For then, by toil subdued, he drank
The stifling wave, and then he sank.

No poet wept him; but the page
    Of narrative sincere,   50
That tells his name, his worth, his age,
    Is wet with Anson's tear.
And tears by bards or heroes shed
Alike immortalize the dead.

I therefore purpose not, or dream,   55
    Descanting on his fate,
To give the melancholy theme
    A more enduring date:
But misery still delights to trace
Its semblance in another's case.   60

No voice divine the storm allayed,
    No light propitious shone,
When, snatched from all effectual aid,
    We perished, each alone;
But I beneath a rougher sea,   65
And whelmed in deeper gulfs than he.

1799   1803

GEORGE CRABBE
(1754–1832)

Crabbe belongs to the early 19th rather than to the 18th century, but his first successful poem is very much a part of the literature of our period. Born to poverty in a small, decayed Suffolk seaport, Aldeburgh, he was apprenticed to a surgeon, but found it impossible to earn a living by practicing in his native village. In 1780 he went to London, and succeeded neither in finding a patron nor in securing literary employment, until, reduced to desperate straits, he sent an appeal to Edmund Burke, who recognized his merit and gave him timely help. Through Burke's influence *The Library* was published; Dr. Johnson agreed to correct *The Village*; and Crabbe was ordained a minister in the Anglican Church. His appointment as chaplain to the Duke of Rutland enabled him to marry the woman to whom he had long been engaged.

After 1785 he published nothing until 1807, when *The Parish Register* appeared. It was followed by *The Borough* (1810), *Tales* (1812), and *Tales of the Hall* (1819). In these poems, which won the admiration of Wordsworth, Scott, and Byron, Crabbe continued the vein of realism which had distinguished *The Village*, and developed his great gift for narrative and characterization. He was well aware of the difference between his poetry, written in rather prosaic language and heroic couplets, abounding in realistic details and concerned with ordinary people, and that of his two great Romantic contemporaries, Sir Walter Scott and Lord Byron. Scott's medieval and Byron's Oriental tales possessed the charm of the remote and exotic. Crabbe described his own poetry as "poetry without an atmosphere." It is, however, almost always interesting and often dramatic and moving.

The Village was widely read and admired despite the fact that it is not free from faults that Crabbe never overcame: slipshod rhymes, and sometimes flat and often stilted language. But its unrelieved realism and its gloomy darkness of tone set it sharply apart from conventional poems on rural life during the century. Indeed it is an angry, a scornful reply to the sentimental cult of rural simplicity, innocence, and happiness. It glances at the unrealities of the pastoral convention and, somewhat more systematically, it answers Goldsmith's charming idealization of villagers and their life in *The Deserted Village*. Crabbe knew the degrading effect of hopeless poverty, he had observed rural vice, he knew the gulf that sometimes separated the landed gentry from their laboring tenants. Out of recollections of Aldeburgh and the neighboring seacoast he fashioned a setting for his poem in which the penury of a niggardly nature seems the only proper background for the penury of the men who inhabit it. The accuracy and vividness of the details created a poetry of the ugly which is at variance with the long tradition of natural description from Thomson to Cowper.

From The Village

Book I

The village life, and every care that reigns
O'er youthful peasants and declining swains;
What labor yields, and what, that labor past,
Age, in its hour of languor, finds at last;
What form the real picture of the poor, 5
Demand a song—the Muse can give no more.
Fled are those times when, in harmonious strains,

The rustic poet praised his native plains.
No shepherds now, in smooth altérnate verse,
Their country's beauty or their nymphs' rehearse;   10
Yet still for these we frame the tender strain,
Still in our lays fond Corydons[1] complain,
And shepherds' boys their amorous pains reveal,
The only pains, alas! they never feel.
　　On Mincio's[2] banks, in Caesar's bounteous reign,   15
If Tityrus found the Golden Age again,
Must sleepy bards the flattering dream prolong,
Mechanic echoes of the Mantuan song?
From Truth and Nature shall we widely stray,
Where Virgil, not where Fancy, leads the way?   20
　　Yes, thus the Muses sing of happy swains,
Because the Muses never knew their pains.
They boast their peasants' pipes; but peasants now
Resign their pipes and plod behind the plow;
And few, amid the rural tribe, have time   25
To number syllables, and play with rhyme;
Save honest Duck,[3] what son of verse could share
The poet's rapture, and the peasant's care?
Or the great labors of the field degrade,
With the new peril of a poorer trade?   30
　　From this chief cause these idle praises spring,
That themes so easy few forbear to sing;
For no deep thought the trifling subjects ask:
To sing of shepherds is an easy task.
The happy youth assumes the common strain,   35
A nymph his mistress, and himself a swain;
With no sad scenes he clouds his tuneful prayer,
But all, to look like her, is painted fair.
　　I grant indeed that fields and flocks have charms
For him that grazes or for him that farms;   40
But when amid such pleasing scenes I trace
The poor laborious natives of the place,
And see the midday sun, with fervid ray,
On their bare heads and dewy temples play;
While some, with feebler heads and fainter hearts,   45
Deplore their fortune, yet sustain their parts:
Then shall I dare these real ills to hide
In tinsel trappings of poetic pride?
　　No; cast by Fortune on a frowning coast,
Which neither groves nor happy valleys boast;   50
Where other cares than those the Muse relates,
And other shepherds dwell with other mates;
By such examples taught, I paint the cot,

---

1. "Corydon" is a stock name for a shepherd in pastorals, used by both Theocritus and Virgil.
2. Virgil was born near Mantua, in Italy, not far from the river Mincius. Tityrus is one of the speakers in Virgil's *Eclogues* I.
3. Stephen Duck (1705–56), the "Thresher Poet," was a self-educated agricultural laborer whose verses attracted attention and finally won him the patronage of Queen Caroline.

As Truth will paint it, and as bards will not:
Nor you, ye poor, of lettered scorn complain,   55
To you the smoothest song is smooth in vain;
O'ercome by labor, and bowed down by time,
Feel you the barren flattery of a rhyme?
Can poets soothe you, when you pine for bread,
By winding myrtles round your ruined shed?   60
Can their light tales your weighty griefs o'erpower,
Or glad with airy mirth the toilsome hour?
  Lo! where the heath, with withering brake grown o'er,
Lends the light turf that warms the neighboring poor;
From thence a length of burning sand appears,   65
Where the thin harvest waves its withered ears;
Rank weeds, that every art and care defy,
Reign o'er the land, and rob the blighted rye:
There thistles stretch their prickly arms afar,
And to the ragged infant threaten war;   70
There poppies, nodding, mock the hope of toil;
There the blue bugloss paints the sterile soil;
Hardy and high, above the slender sheaf,
The slimy mallow waves her silky leaf;
O'er the young shoot the charlock throws a shade,   75
And clasping tares cling round the sickly blade;
With mingled tints the rocky coasts abound,
And a sad splendor vainly shines around.
So looks the nymph whom wretched arts adorn,
Betrayed by man, then left for man to scorn;   80
Whose cheek in vain assumes the mimic rose,
While her sad eyes the troubled breast disclose;
Whose outward splendor is but folly's dress,
Exposing most, when most it gilds distress.
  Here joyless roam a wild amphibious race,   85
With sullen woe displayed in every face;
Who far from civil arts and social fly,
And scowl at strangers with suspicious eye.
  Here too the lawless merchant of the main
Draws from his plow the intoxicated swain;   90
Want only claimed the labor of the day,
But vice now steals his nightly rest away.
  Where are the swains, who, daily labor done,
With rural games played down the setting sun;
Who struck with matchless force the bounding ball,   95
Or made the ponderous quoit obliquely fall;
While some huge Ajax, terrible and strong,
Engaged some artful stripling of the throng,
And fell beneath him, foiled, while far around
Hoarse triumph rose, and rocks returned the sound?   100
Where now are these?—Beneath yon cliff they stand,
To show the freighted pinnace where to land;[4]

4. Crabbe refers to smuggling.

To load the ready steed with guilty haste;
To fly in terror o'er the pathless waste;
Or, when detected in their straggling course, 105
To foil their foes by cunning or by force;
Or, yielding part (which equal knaves demand),
To gain a lawless passport through the land.
    Here, wandering long amid these frowning fields,
I sought the simple life that Nature yields; 110
Rapine and Wrong and Fear usurped her place,
And a bold, artful, surly, savage race;
Who, only skilled to take the finny tribe,
The yearly dinner, or septennial bribe,[5]
Wait on the shore, and, as the waves run high, 115
On the tossed vessel bend their eager eye,
Which to their coast directs its venturous way;
Theirs, or the ocean's, miserable prey.
    As on their neighboring beach yon swallows stand,
And wait for favoring winds to leave the land, 120
While still for flight the ready wing is spread:
So waited I the favoring hour, and fled;
Fled from these shores where guilt and famine reign,
And cried, "Ah! hapless they who still remain;
Who still remain to hear the ocean roar, 125
Whose greedy waves devour the lessening shore;
Till some fierce tide, with more imperious sway,
Sweeps the low hut and all it holds away;
When the sad tenant weeps from door to door,
And begs a poor protection from the poor!" 130
    But these are scenes where Nature's niggard hand
Gave a spare portion to the famished land;
Hers is the fault, if here mankind complain
Of fruitless toil and labor spent in vain.
But yet in other scenes, more fair in view, 135
Where Plenty smiles—alas! she smiles for few—
And those who taste not, yet behold her store,
Are as the slaves that dig the golden ore,
The wealth around them makes them doubly poor.
    Or will you deem them amply paid in health, 140
Labor's fair child, that languishes with wealth?
Go, then! and see them rising with the sun,
Through a long course of daily toil to run;
See them beneath the dog star's raging heat,
When the knees tremble and the temples beat; 145
Behold them, leaning on their scythes, look o'er
The labor past, and toils to come explore;
See them alternate suns and showers engage,
And hoard up aches and anguish for their age;
Through fens and marshy moors their steps pursue, 150
When their warm pores imbibe the evening dew;

5. Paid to electors by candidates for election to Parliament. Since Parliaments must be elected at least every seven years, the bribes are "septennial."

Then own that labor may as fatal be
To these thy slaves, as thine excess to thee.
    Amid this tribe too oft a manly pride
Strives in strong toil the fainting heart to hide;   155
There may you see the youth of slender frame
Contend, with weakness, weariness, and shame;
Yet, urged along, and proudly loath to yield,
He strives to join his fellows of the field;
Till long-contending nature droops at last,   160
Declining health rejects his poor repast,
His cheerless spouse the coming danger sees,
And mutual murmurs urge the slow disease.
    Yet grant them health, 'tis not for us to tell,
Though the head droops not, that the heart is well;   165
Or will you praise that homely, healthy fare,
Plenteous and plain, that happy peasants share?
Oh! trifle not with wants you cannot feel,
Nor mock the misery of a stinted meal,
Homely, not wholesome; plain, not plenteous; such   170
As you who praise would never deign to touch.
    Ye gentle souls, whom dream of rural ease,
Whom the smooth stream and smoother sonnet please;
Go! if the peaceful cot your praises share,
Go, look within, and ask if peace be there: 175
If peace be his—that drooping weary sire,
Or theirs, that offspring round their feeble fire;
Or hers, that matron pale, whose trembling hand
Turns on the wretched hearth the expiring brand!
    Nor yet can Time itself obtain for these   180
Life's latest comforts, due respect and ease:
For yonder see that hoary swain, whose age
Can with no cares except his own engage;
Who, propped on that rude staff, looks up to see
The bare arms broken from the withering tree,   185
On which, a boy, he climbed the loftiest bough,
Then his first joy, but his sad emblem now.
    He once was chief in all the rustic trade;
His steady hand the straightest furrow made;
Full many a prize he won, and still is proud   190
To find the triumphs of his youth allowed.
A transient pleasure sparkles in his eyes;
He hears and smiles, then thinks again and sighs;
For now he journeys to his grave in pain;
The rich disdain him, nay, the poor disdain;   195
Alternate masters now their slave command,
Urge the weak efforts of his feeble hand;
And, when his age attempts its task in vain,
With ruthless taunts, of lazy poor complain.
    Oft may you see him, when he tends the sheep,   200
His winter charge, beneath the hillock weep;

Oft hear him murmur to the winds that blow
O'er his white locks and bury them in snow,
When, roused by rage and muttering in the morn
He mends the broken hedge with icy thorn: 205
  "Why do I live, when I desire to be
At once from life and life's long labor free?
Like leaves in spring, the young are blown away,
Without the sorrows of a slow decay;
I, like yon withered leaf, remain behind,   210
Nipped by the frost, and shivering in the wind;
There it abides till younger buds come on,
As I, now all my fellow swains are gone;
Then, from the rising generation thrust,
It falls, like me, unnoticed to the dust.   215
  "These fruitful fields, these numerous flocks I see,
Are others' gain, but killing cares to me:
To me the children of my youth are lords,
Cool in their looks, but hasty in their words:
Wants of their own demand their care; and who   220
Feels his own want and succors others too?
A lonely, wretched man, in pain I go,
None need my help, and none relieve my woe;
Then let my bones beneath the turf be laid,
And men forget the wretch they would not aid!"   225
  Thus groan the old, till, by disease oppressed,
They taste a final woe, and then they rest.
  Theirs is yon house that holds the parish poor,
Whose walls of mud scarce bear the broken door;
There, where the putrid vapors, flagging, play,   230
And the dull wheel hums doleful through the day—
There children dwell, who know no parents' care;
Parents, who know no children's love, dwell there!
Heartbroken matrons on their joyless bed,
Forsaken wives, and mothers never wed;   235
Dejected widows with unheeded tears,
And crippled age with more than childhood fears;
The lame, the blind, and, far the happiest they!
The moping idiot and the madman gay.
Here too the sick their final doom receive,   240
Here brought, amid the scenes of grief, to grieve,
Where the loud groans from some sad chamber flow,
Mixed with the clamors of the crowd below;
Here, sorrowing, they each kindred sorrow scan,
And the cold charities of man to man: 245
Whose laws indeed for ruined age provide,
And strong compulsion plucks the scrap from pride;
But still that scrap is bought with many a sigh,
And pride embitters what it can't deny.
  Say ye, oppressed by some fantastic woes,   250
Some jarring nerve that baffles your repose;

Who press the downy couch, while slaves advance
With timid eye to read the distant glance;
Who with sad prayers the weary doctor tease,
To name the nameless ever-new disease;   255
Who with mock patience dire complaints endure,
Which real pain, and that alone, can cure—
How would ye bear in real pain to lie,
Despised, neglected, left alone to die?
How would ye bear to draw your latest breath,   260
Where all that's wretched paves the way for death?

    Such is that room which one rude beam divides,
And naked rafters form the sloping sides;
Where the vile bands that bind the thatch are seen,
And lath and mud are all that lie between,   265
Save one dull pane, that, coarsely patched, gives way
To the rude tempest, yet excludes the day.
Here, on a matted flock, with dust o'erspread,
The drooping wretch reclines his languid head;
For him no hand the cordial cup applies,   270
Or wipes the tear that stagnates in his eyes;
No friends with soft discourse his pain beguile,
Or promise hope till sickness wears a smile.

    But soon a loud and hasty summons calls,
Shakes the thin roof, and echoes round the walls.   275
Anon, a figure enters, quaintly neat,
All pride and business, bustle and conceit;
With looks unaltered by these scenes of woe,
With speed that, entering, speaks his haste to go,
He bids the gazing throng around him fly,   280
And carries fate and physic in his eye:
A potent quack, long versed in human ills,
Who first insults the victim whom he kills;
Whose murderous hand a drowsy Bench protect,[6]
And whose most tender mercy is neglect.   285

    Paid by the parish for attendance here,
He wears contempt upon his sapient sneer;
In haste he seeks the bed where Misery lies,
Impatience marked in his averted eyes;
And, some habitual queries hurried o'er,   290
Without reply, he rushes on the door.
His drooping patient, long inured to pain,
And long unheeded, knows remonstrance vain;
He ceases now the feeble help to crave
Of man; and silent sinks into the grave.   295

    But ere his death some pious doubts arise,
Some simple fears, which "bold bad" men despise:
Fain would he ask the parish priest to prove

6. Crabbe, who had practiced medicine among the poor of Aldeborough, well knew the indifference of the local magistrates ("the drowsy Bench") to the incompetence and callousness of the physician hired by the parish to attend its paupers.

His title certain to the joys above;
For this he sends the murmuring nurse, who calls   300
The holy stranger to these dismal walls;
And doth not he, the pious man, appear,
He, "passing rich with forty pounds a year"?[7]
Ah! no; a shepherd of a different stock:
And far unlike him, feeds this little flock: 305
A jovial youth, who thinks his Sunday's task
As much as God or man can fairly ask;
The rest he gives to loves and labors light,
To fields the morning, and to feasts the night;
None better skilled the noisy pack to guide,   310
To urge their chase, to cheer them or to chide;
A sportsman keen, he shoots through half the day,
And, skilled at whist, devotes the night to play.
Then, while such honors bloom around his head,
Shall he sit sadly by the sick man's bed,   315
To raise the hope he feels not, or with zeal
To combat fears that e'en the pious feel?
    Now once again the gloomy scene explore,
Less gloomy now; the bitter hour is o'er,
The man of many sorrows sighs no more.—   320
Up yonder hill, behold how sadly slow
The bier moves winding from the vale below;
There lie the happy dead, from trouble free,
And the glad parish pays the frugal fee.
No more, O Death! thy victim starts to hear   325
Churchwarden stern, or kingly overseer;
No more the farmer claims his humble bow,
Thou art his lord, the best of tyrants thou!
    Now to the church behold the mourners come,
Sedately torpid and devoutly dumb;   330
The village children now their games suspend,
To see the bier that bears their ancient friend:
For he was one in all their idle sport,
And like a monarch ruled their little court;
The pliant bow he formed, the flying ball,   335
The bat, the wicket, were his labors all;
Him now they follow to his grave, and stand
Silent and sad, and gazing, hand in hand;
While bending low, their eager eyes explore
The mingled relics of the parish poor.   340
The bell tolls late, the moping owl flies round,
Fear marks the flight and magnifies the sound;
The busy priest, detained by weightier care,
Defers his duty till the day of prayer;
And, waiting long, the crowd retire distressed,   345
To think a poor man's bones should lie unblessed.

1780–83   1783

7. Cf. Goldsmith's *Deserted Village*, line 142.

SAMUEL JOHNSON
(1709–1784)

1737:   Settles in London.
1747–55:   At work on the *Dictionary*.
1762:   Pensioned by the Crown.
1765:   Edition of Shakespeare.
1779, 1781: *Lives of the Poets.*

Throughout the 19th century it was generally agreed that although Johnson himself was interesting, especially as a conversationalist, most of his works were unreadable. His poems were condemned as prosaic, his essays as tritely moralistic, his criticism as wrongheaded and tasteless. The case is altered today: a few of the poems, it is agreed, belong with the best of the century; the grave *Rambler* essays, which in his own time established his reputation as a stylist and a moralist, prove not so forbidding as we have been told they are; and the criticism is ranked with that of Dryden and Samuel Taylor Coleridge as the best in English. Boswell's Johnson is chiefly a conversationalist whose talk came hot from a mind that was wise, humane, honest, truthful, and well stored with knowledge drawn from books and experience. The talk is that of a wit and a poet who was quick to seize and to use the unexpected but appropriate image to illuminate truth as it was apprehended by a deeply moral imagination. Any fair examination of Johnson's best writings will demonstrate that for all its studied formality, Johnson's prose possesses most of the virtues of his conversation. The object of the talker and of the moral essayist or critic proves in general to be the same—the search for truth in the wide field of human experience; and the wit and wisdom and energy of Johnson's spontaneous talk are also present in his prose.

Two examples must suffice here. When Mrs. Anna Williams wondered why a man should make a beast of himself through drunkenness, Johnson answered that "he who makes a beast of himself gets rid of the pain of being a man." In this reply Mrs. Williams' tired metaphor is so charged with an awareness of the dark aspects of human life that it comes almost unbearably alive. Such moments characterize Johnson's writings as well. For instance, in reviewing the book of a fatuous would-be philosopher who blandly explained away the pains of poverty by declaring that a kindly providence compensates the poor by making them more hopeful, more healthy, more capable of relishing small pleasures and less sensitive to small annoyances than the rich, Johnson, who had known extreme poverty, retorted: "The poor indeed are insensible of many little vexations which sometimes embitter the possessions and pollute the enjoyment of the rich. They are not pained by casual incivility, or mortified by the mutilation of a compliment; but this happiness is like that of the malefactor who ceases to feel the cords that bind him when the pincers are tearing his flesh."

Johnson had himself known the pains of poverty. During his boyhood and youth, his father's financial circumstances steadily worsened, so that he was forced to leave Oxford before he had taken a degree. An imprudent marriage drove him to open a school which was unsuccessful; and the failure of the school prompted him to attempt to make his way as a writer in London. The years between 1737, when he first arrived there with his pupil David Garrick (later to become the leading actor of his generation), and 1755, when the publication of the *Dictionary* established his reputation, were very difficult. He supported himself at first as best he could by doing hack work for the *Gentleman's Magazine*, but gradually his own original writings began to attract attention, though hardly to support his wife and himself.

In 1746 Johnson published the *Plan* of his *Dictionary*, and the next seven years were occupied in compiling it—although he had been sanguine enough to count on finishing it in three years. Boswell remarks that "the world contemplated with wonder" a work "achieved by one man, while other countries had thought such undertakings fit only for whole academies." When in 1748 Dr. Adams, a friend from Oxford days, questioned his ability to carry out such a work alone in so short a time, and reminded him that the *Dictionary* of the French Academy had been compiled by forty academicians working for forty years, Johnson replied with humorous jingoism: "Sir, thus it is. This is the proportion. Let me see; forty times forty is sixteen hundred. As three to sixteen hundred, so is the proportion of an Englishman to a Frenchman."

Johnson's achievement in compiling the *Dictionary* becomes even greater when it is realized that he was writing some of his best essays and poems during the same period, for although the booksellers who published the *Dictionary* paid him what was then the large sum of £1575, it was not enough to enable him to support his household, buy materials, and pay the wages of the six amanuenses whom he employed year by year until the task was accomplished. He therefore had to exert himself to earn more money by writing. Thus, in 1749, his early tragedy *Irene* (pronounced I-re-ně) was produced at long last by his old friend Garrick, by then not only a successful actor but also the manager of Drury Lane. The play, deservedly, was not a success, though Johnson made some profit from it. In the same year appeared his finest poem, *The Vanity of Human Wishes*. The *Rambler* (1750–52) and the later *Idler* (1758–60), Johnson's very un-Addisonian imitations of the *Spectator*, found admiring readers and spread his reputation as a moralist throughout the island.

Boswell said of the *Rambler* essays that "in no writings whatever can be found more bark and steel [i.e., quinine and iron] for the mind." Moral strength and health; the importance of applying reason to experience; the testing of a man by what he does, not by what he says or merely "feels"; faith in God: these are the centers to which Johnson's moral writings always return. As such critics as Walter Jackson Bate remind us, what Johnson uniquely offers us is the quality of his understanding of the human condition, based on wide reading but always ultimately referred to his own passionate and often anguished experience. Such understanding had to be fought for again and again, as our two selections from the *Prayers and Meditations* show.

Johnson is thought of as the great generalizer, but what gives his generalizations strength is that they are rooted in the particulars of his self-knowledge. He had constantly to fight against what he called "filling the mind" with illusions, in order to avoid the call of duty, his own black melancholy, and the realties of life. The portrait (largely a self-portrait) of

Sober in *Idler* 31 is revealing: he occupies his idle hours with crafts and hobbies, and has now taken up chemistry—he "sits and counts the drops as they come from his retort, and forgets that, whilst a drop is falling, a moment flies away." So clear a vision is some distance away from the secure ease of the Addisonian essay.

His theme of themes is expressed in the title of his poem, *The Vanity of Human Wishes*, by which Johnson means the dangerous but all-pervasive illusion of what we now call wishful thinking, the feverish intrusion of our desires and hopes which distorts reality and interferes with the possibility of sensibly relying on what we have reason to expect. Almost all of Johnson's major writings—verse satire, moral essay, or the prose fable *Rasselas* (1759)—bear this theme. In *Rasselas* it is called "the hunger of imagination, which preys upon life," the seeing of things as one would like them to be, rather than as they are. The travelers who are the fable's protagonists pursue supposed guarantees of happiness; they reflect our naïve hopefulness, against the accumulation of contrary experience, that such a guarantee exists.

During this time of great activity, in which he produced the bulk of his moral writings, Johnson developed his characteristic style: the rotund periods, proceeding through balanced or parallel words; phrases or clauses moving to carefully controlled rhythms, in language that is characteristically general, often Latinate, and frequently polysyllabic. It is a style which is at the opposite extreme from Swift's simplicity or Addison's neatness. In Johnson's writings this style never becomes obscure or turgid, for even a very complex sentence reveals—as it should—the structure of the thought, and the learned words are always precisely used. "Sesquipedalian" words are not so frequent in Johnson's writings as his reputation for using them would imply. He learned many of them when he was reading early scientists to collect words for the *Dictionary*—such words as *obtund, exuberate, fugacity, frigorific,* which most people have been willing to forget. But he used many of these strange words in conversation as well as in his writings, often with a peculiarly Johnsonian felicity, although everyone is familiar with the notoriously infelicitous definition of *network* in the *Dictionary:* "Anything reticulated or decussated, at equal distances, with interstices between the intersections."

After Johnson received his pension in 1762, he no longer had to write for a living, and since he held that "no man but a blockhead" ever wrote for any other reason, he produced as little as he decently could during the last twenty years of his life. His edition of Shakespeare, long delayed, was published in 1765, with its fine preface and its fascinating notes, both textual and explicatory. Johnson's praise of Shakespeare and his discussion and destruction of the doctrine of the three unities are printed below. His last important work is the *Lives of the Poets,* which came out in two parts in 1779 and 1781. These biographical and critical prefaces were written at the instigation of a group of booksellers who had joined together to publish a large collection of the English poets and who wished to give their venture the prestige that it would acquire if Johnson took part in it. The poets to be included (except for four insisted on by Johnson) were selected by the booksellers, and their choice was determined by the current fashions. We have, therefore, a collection that begins with Cowley and Milton and ends with Gray and the poetaster Lord Lyttleton, and that omits poets whom we regard as "standard," such as Chaucer, Spenser, Sidney, or the metaphysicals.

In the *Lives of the Poets* and in the earlier *Life of Richard Savage* (1744), Johnson did much to advance the art of biography in England. The public had long been familiar with biography as panegyric or as scandalous memoir, and therefore Johnson's insistence on truth, even about the subject's defects, and on concrete, often minute, details was a new departure, disliked by many readers, as Boswell was to find when he followed his master's principles both in the *Journal of a Tour to the Hebrides* and in the *Life* itself. "The biographical part of literature is what I love most," Johnson said, for he found every biography useful in revealing human nature and the way men live. His insistence on truth in biography (and knowing that Boswell intended to write his life, he insisted that he should write it truthfully) was due to his conviction that the more truthful such a work is the more useful it will be to all of us who are concerned with the business of living. The value of the lives of the poets varies, for Johnson wrote some more casually than he did others. He is at his best as a critic when he draws up a general character of a writer's genius and when he discusses individual works.

Johnson's taste was conservative, and he therefore liked little in contemporary literature. He valued Richardson for his knowledge of the human heart, but he considered Fielding "low" and immoral, and Sterne merely perversely odd and trivial. Though he loved Collins, he regretted his fanciful subjects and "harsh" diction, and he offended many by his strictures on what he considered Gray's affectations. He poked gentle fun at his friend Thomas Warton's revival of antique words and "Ode, and elegy, and sonnet." But if he was conservative, he was no worshiper of authority, and least of all was he prone to follow mere theory. As a critic Johnson is always the empiricist, testing theory, as he tested all notions, by experience. His attitude toward the rules is perfectly expressed in these words from *Rambler* 156: "It ought to be the first endeavor of a writer to distinguish nature from custom; or that which is established because it is right, from that which is right only because it is established; that he may neither violate essential principles by a desire of novelty, nor debar himself from the attainment of beauties within his view, by a needless fear of breaking rules which no literary dictator has authority to enact." And the perfect illustration of this attitude is his treatment of the long-revered principle of the three dramatic unities in the Preface to Shakespeare.

That there were "essential principles" which any writer must follow seemed to him self-evident. He must adhere to universal truth and experience, i.e., to "Nature"; he must please, but he must also instruct; he must not offend against religion or promote immorality; he must avoid cold and slavish imitation of others, and he must not cultivate "singularity," the eccentrically original. In the passages from the *Lives of the Poets* below, some of his principles are illustrated. The well-known and influential discussion of metaphysical poetry, with its brilliant definition of "wit" as "a kind of *discordia concors*," at once illustrates Johnson's genius for formulating broad philosophical principles and reveals clearly why he equated the general with the natural. The notorious attack on Milton's *Lycidas*, which damaged Johnson's reputation as a critic for over a century, puzzles us until we recall that Johnson himself had his critical singularities, which in this case stood between him and a liking for a very great poem: he was justly contemptuous of 18th-century pastoral poetry, which was always conventional, artificial, and bookish, and which could be produced by mere imitation; and he had a great dislike on religious grounds for the Renaissance habit of mingling pagan and Christian materials in a poem. The praise of Dryden, Pope, and Shakespeare, on the other hand, is admirable because those poets, as was not the case with Donne or Milton, nobly illustrated the literary standards that Johnson respected throughout his career.

The Vanity of Human Wishes[1]

IN IMITATION OF THE TENTH SATIRE OF JUVENAL

Let Observation, with extensive view,
Survey mankind, from China to Peru;
Remark each anxious toil, each eager strife,
And watch the busy scenes of crowded life;
Then say how hope and fear, desire and hate   5
O'erspread with snares the clouded maze of fate,
Where wavering man, betrayed by venturous pride
To tread the dreary paths without a guide,
As treacherous phantoms in the mist delude,
Shuns fancied ills, or chases airy good;   10
How rarely Reason guides the stubborn choice,
Rules the bold hand, or prompts the suppliant voice;
How nations sink, by darling schemes oppressed,
When Vengeance listens to the fool's request.
Fate wings with every wish the afflictive dart,   15
Each gift of nature, and each grace of art;
With fatal heat impetuous courage glows,
With fatal sweetness elocution flows,
Impeachment stops the speaker's powerful breath,
And restless fire precipitates on death.   20

1. *The Vanity of Human Wishes* is an imitation of Juvenal's *Satire X*. Although it closely follows the order and the ideas of the Latin poem, it remains a very personal work, for Johnson has used the Roman Stoic's satire as a means of expressing his own Christian stoicism and his sense of the tragic in human life. He has tried to reproduce in English verse the qualities he thought especially Juvenalian: stateliness, pointed sentences, declamatory grandeur. The poem is difficult because of the extreme compactness of the style: every verse is forced to convey the greatest possible amount of meaning, and as a result the syntax is occasionally obscure. At first the language may seem too general, the frequent personifications mere abstractions. But although Johnson's poetic theory demanded that the poet should deal in the general rather than the particular (cf. his phrase "the grandeur of generality") he certainly did not intend that the general should become the merely abstract: observe, for example, how he makes abstract nouns concrete, active, and dramatic by using them as subjects of active and dramatic verbs: "Hate *dogs* their flight, and Insult *mocks* their end" (line 78). And when the more usual 18th-century combination of general adjective modifying general noun is used, the adjectives are carefully chosen for foreseen effects, as in lines 113–16 (in the first three lines they are used to create a cumulative effect of regal splendor, and in the last line a witty and intellectual impression of Cardinal Wolsey's pride and power): "At once is lost the pride of *awful* state, / The *golden* canopy, the *glittering* plate, / The *regal* palace, the *luxurious* board, / The *liveried* army, and the *menial* lord." The personified abstractions of Collins and Gray, however, are essentially pictorial, grouped in expressive attitudes as they would be in an allegorical painting. A comparison of their method of personification with Johnson's can be readily made by studying Gray's *Eton* ode, stanzas 5–8, along with lines 135–164 of the *Vanity*.

But scarce observed, the knowing and the bold
Fall in the general massacre of gold;
Wide-wasting pest! that rages unconfined,
And crowds with crimes the records of mankind;
For gold his sword the hireling ruffian draws,   25
For gold the hireling judge distorts the laws;
Wealth heaped on wealth, nor truth nor safety buys,
The dangers gather as the treasures rise.
    Let History tell where rival kings command,
And dubious title shakes the madded land,   30
When statutes glean the refuse of the sword,
How much more safe the vassal than the lord,
Low skulks the hind beneath the rage of power,
And leaves the wealthy traitor[2] in the Tower,
Untouched his cottage, and his slumbers sound,   35
Though Confiscation's vultures hover round.
    The needy traveler, serene and gay,
Walks the wild heath, and sings his toil away.
Does envy seize thee? crush the upbraiding joy,
Increase his riches and his peace destroy;   40
New fears in dire vicissitude invade,
The rustling brake[3] alarms, and quivering shade,
Nor light nor darkness bring his pain relief,
One shows the plunder, and one hides the thief.
    Yet still one general cry the skies assails,   45
And gain and grandeur load the tainted gales;
Few know the toiling statesman's fear or care,
The insidious rival and the gaping heir.
    Once more, Democritus,[4] arise on earth,
With cheerful wisdom and instructive mirth,   50
See motley life in modern trappings dressed,
And feed with varied fools the eternal jest:
Thou who couldst laugh where Want enchained Caprice,
Toil crushed Conceit, and man was of a piece;
Where Wealth unloved without a mourner died;   55
And scarce a sycophant was fed by Pride;
Where ne'er was known the form of mock debate,
Or seen a new-made mayor's unwieldy state;
Where change of favorites made no change of laws,
And senates heard before they judged a cause;   60
How wouldst thou shake at Britain's modish tribe,
Dart the quick taunt, and edge the piercing gibe?
Attentive truth and nature to descry,
And pierce each scene with philosophic eye,
To thee were solemn toys or empty show   65
The robes of pleasures and the veils of woe:
All aid the farce, and all thy mirth maintain,
Whose joys are causeless, or whose griefs are vain.

---

2. Johnson first wrote "bonny traitor," recalling the Jacobite uprising of 1745 and the execution of four of its Scot leaders.
3. Thicket.

4. A Greek philosopher of the late 5th century B.C., remembered as the "laughing philosopher" because men's follies only moved him to mirth.

Such was the scorn that filled the sage's mind,
Renewed at every glance on human kind;   70
How just that scorn ere yet thy voice declare,
Search every state, and canvass every prayer.

Unnumbered suppliants crowd Preferment's gate,
Athirst for wealth, and burning to be great;
Delusive Fortune hears the incessant call,   75
They mount, they shine, evaporate, and fall.
On every stage the foes of peace attend,
Hate dogs their flight, and Insult mocks their end.
Love ends with hope, the sinking statesman's door
Pours in the morning worshiper no more;[5]   80
For growing names the weekly scribbler lies,
To growing wealth the dedicator flies;
From every room descends the painted face,
That hung the bright palladium[6] of the place;
And smoked in kitchens, or in auctions sold,   85
To better features yields the frame of gold;
For now no more we trace in every line
Heroic worth, benevolence divine:
The form distorted justifies the fall,
And Detestation rids the indignant wall.   90

But will not Britain hear the last appeal,
Sign her foes' doom, or guard her favorites' zeal?
Through Freedom's sons no more remonstrance rings,
Degrading nobles and controlling kings;
Our supple tribes repress their patriot throats,   95
And ask no questions but the price of votes,
With weekly libels and septennial ale.[7]
Their wish is full to riot and to rail.

In full-blown dignity, see Wolsey[8] stand,
Law in his voice, and fortune in his hand: 100
To him the church, the realm, their powers consign,
Through him the rays of regal bounty shine,
Turned by his nod the stream of honor flows,
His smile alone security bestows:
Still to new heights his restless wishes tower,   105
Claim leads to claim, and power advances power;
Till conquest unresisted ceased to please,
And rights submitted, left him none to seize.
At length his sovereign frowns—the train of state
Mark the keen glance, and watch the sign to hate.   110
Where'er he turns, he meets a stranger's eye,
His suppliants scorn him, and his followers fly;

5. Statesmen gave interviews and received friends and petitioners at levees, or morning receptions.
6. An image of Pallas Athena, which fell from heaven and was preserved at Troy. Not until it was stolen by Diomedes could the city fall to the Greeks.
7. Ministers and even the king freely bought support by bribing members of Parliament, who in turn won elections by buying votes. "Weekly libels": politically motivated lampoons published in the weekly newspapers; "septennial ale": the ale given away by candidates at parliamentary elections, held at least every seven years.
8. Thomas Cardinal Wolsey (ca. 1475–1530), Lord Chancellor and favorite of Henry VIII. Shakespeare dramatized his fall in *Henry VIII*.

At once is lost the pride of awful state,
The golden canopy, the glittering plate,
The regal palace, the luxurious board,   115
The liveried army, and the menial lord.
With age, with cares, with maladies oppressed,
He seeks the refuge of monastic rest.
Grief aids disease, remembered folly stings,
And his last sighs reproach the faith of kings.   120
   Speak thou, whose thoughts at humble peace repine,
Shall Wolsey's wealth, with Wolsey's end be thine?
Or liv'st thou now, with safer pride content,
The wisest justice on the banks of Trent?
For why did Wolsey, near the steeps of fate,   125
On weak foundations raise the enormous weight?
Why but to sink beneath misfortune's blow,
With louder ruin to the gulfs below?
   What gave great Villiers[9] to the assassin's knife,
And fixed disease on Harley's closing life?   130
What murdered Wentworth, and what exiled Hyde,
By kings protected and to kings allied?
What but their wish indulged in courts to shine,
And power too great to keep or to resign?
   When first the college rolls receive his name,   135
The young enthusiast quits his ease for fame;
Resistless burns the fever of renown
Caught from the strong contagion of the gown:
O'er Bodley's dome his future labors spread,
And Bacon's mansion trembles o'er his head.[1]   140
Are these thy views? proceed, illustrious youth,
And Virtue guard thee to the throne of Truth!
Yet should thy soul indulge the generous heat,
Till captive Science yields her last retreat;
Should Reason guide thee with her brightest ray,   145
And pour on misty Doubt resistless day;
Should no false kindness lure to loose delight,
Nor praise relax, nor difficulty fright;
Should tempting Novelty thy cell refrain,
And Sloth effuse her opiate fumes in vain;   150
Should Beauty blunt on fops her fatal dart,
Nor claim the triumph of a lettered heart;
Should no disease thy torpid veins invade,
Nor Melancholy's phantoms haunt thy shade;

9. George Villiers, 1st Duke of Buckingham, favorite of James I and Charles I, was assassinated in 1628. Mentioned in the following lines are: Robert Harley, Earl of Oxford, Chancellor of the Exchequer and later Lord Treasurer under Queen Anne (1710–14), impeached and imprisoned by the Whigs in 1715; Thomas Wentworth, Earl of Strafford, intimate and adviser of Charles I, impeached by the Long Parliament and executed 1641; Edward Hyde, Earl of Clarendon ("to kings allied" because his daughter married James, Duke of York), Lord Chancellor under Charles II; impeached in 1667, he fled to the Continent.
1. "Bodley's dome" is the Bodleian Library, Oxford. Roger Bacon (ca. 1214–94), scientist and philosopher, taught at Oxford, where his study, according to tradition, would collapse when a man greater than he should appear at Oxford.

Yet hope not life from grief or danger free,   155
Nor think the doom of man reversed for thee:
Deign on the passing world to turn thine eyes,
And pause a while from letters, to be wise;
There mark what ills the scholar's life assail,
Toil, envy, want, the patron,[2] and the jail.   160
See nations slowly wise, and meanly just,
To buried merit raise the tardy bust.
If dreams yet flatter, once again attend,
Hear Lydiat's life, and Galileo's end.[3]

Nor deem, when Learning her last prize bestows,   165
The glittering eminence exempt from foes;
See when the vulgar 'scapes, despised or awed,
Rebellion's vengeful talons seize on Laud.[4]
From meaner minds though smaller fines content,
The plundered palace, or sequestered rent;[5]   170
Marked out by dangerous parts he meets the shock,
And fatal Learning leads him to the block:
Around his tomb let Art and Genius weep,
But hear his death, ye blockheads, hear and sleep.

The festal blazes, the triumphal show,   175
The ravished standard, and the captive foe,
The senate's thanks, the gazette's pompous tale,
With force resistless o'er the brave prevail.
Such bribes the rapid Greek[6] o'er Asia whirled,
For such the steady Romans shook the world;   180
For such in distant lands the Britons shine,
And stain with blood the Danube or the Rhine;
This power has praise that virtue scarce can warm,
Till fame supplies the universal charm.

Yet Reason frowns on War's unequal game,   185
Where wasted nations raise a single name,
And mortgaged states their grandsires' wreaths regret
From age to age in everlasting debt;
Wreaths which at last the dear-bought right convey
To rust on medals, or on stones decay.   190

On what foundation stands the warrior's pride,
How just his hopes, let Swedish Charles[7] decide;
A frame of adamant, a soul of fire,
No dangers fright him, and no labors tire;
O'er love, o'er fear, extends his wide domain,   195
Unconquered lord of pleasure and of pain;

2. In the first edition, "garret." For
the reason of the change see Boswell's
Life of Johnson.
3. Thomas Lydiat (1572–1646), Oxford scholar, died impoverished because
of his Royalist sympathies. Galileo
(1564–1642), the famous astronomer,
was imprisoned as a heretic by the
Inquisition in 1633; he died blind.
4. Appointed Archbishop of Canterbury
by Charles I, William Laud followed
rigorously high-church policies and was
executed by order of the Long Parlia-

ment in 1645.
5. During the Commonwealth, the
estates of many Royalists were pillaged
and their incomes confiscated ("sequestered") by the state.
6. Alexander the Great.
7. Charles XII of Sweden (1682–1718).
Defeated by the Russians at Pultowa
(1709), he escaped to Turkey and tried
to form an alliance against Russia
with the sultan. Returning to Sweden,
he attacked Norway and was killed in
the attack on Fredrikshald.

No joys to him pacific scepters yield,
War sounds the trump, he rushes to the field;
Behold surrounding kings their powers combine,
And one capitulate, and one resign;[8]   200
Peace courts his hand, but spreads her charms in vain;
"Think nothing gained," he cries, "till naught remain,
On Moscow's walls till Gothic standards fly,
And all be mine beneath the polar sky."
The march begins in military state,   205
And nations on his eye suspended wait;
Stern Famine guards the solitary coast,
And Winter barricades the realms of Frost;
He comes, nor want nor cold his course delay—
Hide, blushing Glory, hide Pultowa's day: 210
The vanquished hero leaves his broken bands,
And shows his miseries in distant lands;
Condemned a needy supplicant to wait,
While ladies interpose, and slaves debate.
But did not Chance at length her error mend?   215
Did no subverted empire mark his end?
Did rival monarchs give the fatal wound?
Or hostile millions press him to the ground?
His fall was destined to a barren strand,
A petty fortress, and a dubious hand;   220
He left the name at which the world grew pale,
To point a moral, or adorn a tale.
    All times their scenes of pompous woes afford,
From Persia's tyrant to Bavaria's lord.[9]
In gay hostility, and barbarous pride,   225
With half mankind embattled at his side,
Great Xerxes comes to seize the certain prey,
And starves exhausted regions in his way;
Attendant Flattery counts his myriads o'er,
Till counted myriads soothe his pride no more;   230
Fresh praise is tried till madness fires his mind,
The waves he lashes, and enchains the wind;
New powers are claimed, new powers are still bestowed,
Till rude resistance lops the spreading god;
The daring Greeks deride the martial show,   235
And heap their valleys with the gaudy foe;
The insulted sea with humbler thought he gains,
A single skiff to speed his flight remains;
The encumbered oar scarce leaves the dreaded coast
Through purple billows and a floating host.   240
    The bold Bavarian, in a luckless hour,
Tries the dread summits of Caesarean power,

8. Frederick IV of Denmark capitulated to Charles in 1700; Augustus II of Poland resigned his throne to Charles in 1704.
9. Xerxes ("Persia's tyrant") invaded Greece and was totally defeated in the sea battle off Salamis, 480 B.C.; the Elector Charles Albert ("Bavaria's Lord") caused the War of the Austrian Succession (1740–48) when he contested the crown of the Empire with Maria Theresa ("Fair Austria" in line 245).

With unexpected legions bursts away,
And sees defenseless realms receive his sway;
Short sway! fair Austria spreads her mournful charms,   245
The queen, the beauty, sets the world in arms;
From hill to hill the beacon's rousing blaze
Spreads wide the hope of plunder and of praise;
The fierce Croatian, and the wild Hussar,[1]
With all the sons of ravage crowd the war;   250
The baffled prince, in honor's flattering bloom
Of hasty greatness finds the fatal doom;
His foes' derision, and his subjects' blame,
And steals to death from anguish and from shame.

    Enlarge my life with multitude of days!   255
In health, in sickness, thus the suppliant prays;
Hides from himself his state, and shuns to know,
That life protracted is protracted woe.
Time hovers o'er, impatient to destroy,
And shuts up all the passages of joy;   260
In vain their gifts the bounteous seasons pour,
The fruit autumnal, and the vernal flower;
With listless eyes the dotard views the store,
He views, and wonders that they please no more;
Now pall the tasteless meats, and joyless wines,   265
And Luxury with sighs her slave resigns.
Approach, ye minstrels, try the soothing strain,
Diffuse the tuneful lenitives[2] of pain:
No sounds, alas! would touch the impervious ear,
Though dancing mountains witnessed Orpheus[2a] near;   270
Nor lute nor lyre his feeble powers attend,
Nor sweeter music of a virtuous friend,
But everlasting dictates crowd his tongue,
Perversely grave, or positively wrong.
The still returning tale, and lingering jest,   275
Perplex the fawning niece and pampered guest,
While growing hopes scarce awe the gathering sneer,
And scarce a legacy can bribe to hear;
The watchful guests still hint the last offense;
The daughter's petulance, the son's expense,   280
Improve his heady rage with treacherous skill,
And mold his passions till they make his will.

    Unnumbered maladies his joints invade,
Lay siege to life and press the dire blockade;
But unextinguished avarice still remains,   285
And dreaded losses aggravate his pains;
He turns, with anxious heart and crippled hands,
His bonds of debt, and mortgages of lands;
Or views his coffers with suspicious eyes,
Unlocks his gold, and counts it till he dies.   290

1. Hungarian light cavalry.
2. Medicines that relieve pain.
2a. A legendary poet who played on the lyre so beautifully that wild beasts were spellbound.

But grant, the virtues of a temperate prime
Bless with an age exempt from scorn or crime;
An age that melts with unperceived decay,
And glides in modest innocence away;
Whose peaceful day Benevolence endears,   295
Whose night congratulating Conscience cheers;
The general favorite as the general friend:
Such age there is, and who shall wish its end?
    Yet even on this her load Misfortune flings,
To press the weary minutes' flagging wings;   300
New sorrow rises as the day returns,
A sister sickens, or a daughter mourns.
Now kindred Merit fills the sable bier,
Now lacerated Friendship claims a tear;
Year chases year, decay pursues decay,   305
Still drops some joy from withering life away;
New forms arise, and different views engage,
Superfluous lags the veteran[3] on the stage,
Till pitying Nature signs the last release,
And bids afflicted Worth retire to peace.   310
    But few there are whom hours like these await,
Who set unclouded in the gulfs of Fate.
From Lydia's monarch[4] should the search descend,
By Solon cautioned to regard his end,
In life's last scene what prodigies surprise,   315
Fears of the brave, and follies of the wise!
From Marlborough's eyes the streams of dotage flow,
And Swift expires a driveler and a show.[5]
    The teeming mother, anxious for her race,
Begs for each birth the fortune of a face: 320
Yet Vane could tell what ills from beauty spring;[6]
And Sedley cursed the form that pleased a king.
Ye nymphs of rosy lips and radiant eyes,
Whom Pleasure keeps too busy to be wise,
Whom Joys with soft varieties invite,   325
By day the frolic, and the dance by night;
Who frown with vanity, who smile with art,
And ask the latest fashion of the heart;
What care, what rules your heedless charms shall save,
Each nymph your rival, and each youth your slave?   330
Against your fame with Fondness Hate combines,
The rival batters, and the lover mines.
With distant voice neglected Virtue calls,
Less heard and less, the faint remonstrance falls;
Tired with contempt, she quits the slippery reign,   335

3. A veteran of life, not of war.
4. Croesus, the wealthy and fortunate king, was warned by Solon not to count himself happy till he ceased to live. He lost his crown to Cyrus the Great of Persia.
5. John Churchill, Duke of Marlborough, England's brilliant general during most of the War of the Spanish Succession (1702–13); Jonathan Swift, who passed the last four years of his life in utter senility.
6. Anne Vane, mistress of Frederick, Prince of Wales (son of George II). Catherine Sedley, mistress of James II.

And Pride and Prudence take her seat in vain.
In crowd at once, where none the pass defend,
The harmless freedom, and the private friend.
The guardians yield, by force superior plied:
To Interest, Prudence; and to Flattery, Pride.   340
Now Beauty falls betrayed, despised, distressed,
And hissing Infamy proclaims the rest.
    Where then shall Hope and Fear their objects find?
Must dull Suspense corrupt the stagnant mind?
Must helpless man, in ignorance sedate,   345
Roll darkling down the torrent of his fate?
Must no dislike alarm, no wishes rise,
No cries invoke the mercies of the skies?
Inquirer, cease; petitions yet remain,
Which Heaven may hear, nor deem religion vain.   350
Still raise for good the supplicating voice,
But leave to Heaven the measure and the choice.
Safe in His power, whose eyes discern afar
The secret ambush of a specious prayer.
Implore His aid, in His decisions rest,   355
Secure, whate'er He gives, He gives the best.
Yet when the sense of sacred presence fires,
And strong devotion to the skies aspires,
Pour forth thy fervors for a healthful mind,
Obedient passions, and a will resigned;   360
For love, which scarce collective man can fill;
For patience sovereign o'er transmuted ill;
For faith, that panting for a happier seat,
Counts death kind Nature's signal of retreat:
These goods for man the laws of Heaven ordain,   365
These goods He grants, who grants the power to gain;
With these celestial Wisdom calms the mind,
And makes the happiness she does not find.

                                                    1749

To Miss ———[1]

ON HER PLAYING UPON THE HARPSICHORD IN A ROOM HUNG WITH SOME FLOWER-PIECES OF HER OWN PAINTING

        When Stella strikes the tuneful string
        In scenes of imitated spring,
        Where Beauty lavishes her powers
        On beds of never-fading flowers,
        And pleasure propagates around   5
        Each charm of modulated sound,

1. Presumably Alicia Maria Carpenter, daughter of Lord Carpenter and later Countess of Egremont. Smith and Mc-Adam, the editors of Johnson's poems, suggest that Johnson wrote this poem for his friend Henry Harvey to send as his own to Miss Carpenter.

Ah! think not, in the dangerous hour,
The nymph fictitious, as the flower;
But shun, rash youth, the gay alcove,
Nor tempt the snares of wily love.   10
    When charms thus press on every sense,
What thought of flight, or of defense?
Deceitful Hope, and vain Desire,
Forever flutter o'er her lyre,
Delighting, as the youth draws nigh,   15
To point the glances of her eye,
And forming, with unerring art,
New chains to hold the captive heart.
    But on these regions of delight,
Might Truth intrude with daring flight,   20
Could Stella, sprightly, fair and young,
One moment hear the moral song,
Instruction with her flowers might spring,
And Wisdom warble from her string.
    Mark, when from thousand mingled dyes   25
Thou see'st one pleasing form arise,
How active light, and thoughtful shade,
In greater scenes each other aid;
Mark, when the different notes agree
In friendly contrariety,   30
How passion's well-accorded strife
Gives all the harmony of life;
Thy pictures shall thy conduct frame,
Consistent still, though not the same,
Thy music teach the nobler art   35
To tune the regulated heart.

1746

Prologue Spoken by Mr. Garrick[1]

AT THE OPENING OF THE THEATRE ROYAL, DRURY LANE, 1747

When Learning's triumph o'er her barbarous foes
First reared the stage, immortal Shakespeare rose;
Each change of many-colored life he drew,
Exhausted worlds, and then imagined new:
Existence saw him spurn her bounded reign,   5
And panting Time toiled after him in vain.
His powerful strokes presiding Truth impressed,
And unresisted Passion stormed the breast.
    Then Jonson came, instructed from the school
To please in method and invent by rule;   10
His studious patience and laborious art

---

1. David Garrick, the famous actor, had become joint patentee and manager of Drury Lane Theatre. Boswell says that this Prologue is unrivaled "for just and manly dramatic criticism."

By regular approach essayed the heart;
Cold Approbation gave the lingering bays,
For those who durst not censure, scarce could praise.[2]
A mortal born, he met the general doom,   15
But left, like Egypt's kings, a lasting tomb.
    The wits of Charles[3] found easier ways to fame,
Nor wished for Jonson's art, or Shakespeare's flame;
Themselves they studied; as they felt, they writ;
Intrigue was plot, obscenity was wit.   20
Vice always found a sympathetic friend;
They pleased their age, and did not aim to mend.
Yet bards like these aspired to lasting praise,
And proudly hoped to pimp in future days.
Their cause was general, their supports were strong,   25
Their slaves were willing, and their reign was long:
Till Shame regained the post that Sense betrayed,
And Virtue called Oblivion to her aid.
    Then, crushed by rules,[4] and weakened as refined,
For years the power of Tragedy declined;   30
From bard to bard the frigid caution crept,
Till Declamation roared while Passion slept;
Yet still did Virtue deign the stage to tread;
Philosophy remained though Nature fled;
But forced at length her ancient reign to quit,   35
She saw great Faustus[5] lay the ghost of Wit;
Exulting Folly hailed the joyous day,
And Pantomime and Song confirmed her sway.
    But who the coming changes can presage,
And mark the future periods of the stage?   40
Perhaps if skill could distant times explore,
New Behns,[6] new Durfeys, yet remain in store;
Perhaps where Lear has raved, and Hamlet died,
On flying cars new sorcerers may ride;[7]
Perhaps (for who can guess the effects of chance?)   45
Here Hunt may box, or Mahomet may dance.[8]
    Hard is his lot that, here by fortune placed,
Must watch the wild vicissitudes of taste;
With every meteor of caprice must play,
And chase the new-blown bubbles of the day.   50
Ah! let not censure term our fate our choice,
The stage but echoes back the public voice;
The drama's laws, the drama's patrons give,

2. Cf. Dryden's contrast of Shakespeare and Ben Jonson in his *Essay of Dramatic Poesy.*
3. The comic poets of the Restoration period.
4. Cf. Johnson's remarks on the dramatic unities in his preface to Shakespeare.
5. Dr. Faustus at that time was a popular subject for both farce and pantomime.
6. Aphra Behn (1640–89), adventuress, novelist, playwright; Thomas Durfey (1653–1723), satirist and writer of songs and plays.
7. It was a common complaint that the use of increasingly elaborate stage machinery was subordinating drama to mere spectacle.
8. Edward Hunt, a popular pugilist; Mahomet, a tightrope dancer.

For we that live to please, must please to live.
  Then prompt no more the follies you decry,   55
As tyrants doom their tools of guilt to die;
'Tis yours this night to bid the reign commence
Of rescued Nature and reviving Sense;
To chase the charms of Sound, the pomp of Show,
For useful Mirth and salutary Woe;   60
Bid scenic Virtue form the rising age,
And Truth diffuse her radiance from the stage.

1747

On the Death of Dr. Robert Levet[1]

Condemned to Hope's delusive mine,
  As on we toil from day to day,
By sudden blasts, or slow decline,
  Our social comforts drop away.

Well tried through many a varying year,   5
  See Levet to the grave descend;
Officious,[2] innocent, sincere,
  Of every friendless name the friend.

Yet still he fills Affection's eye,
  Obscurely wise, and coarsely kind;   10
Nor, lettered Arrogance, deny
  Thy praise to merit unrefined.

When fainting Nature called for aid,
  And hovering Death prepared the blow,
His vigorous remedy displayed   15
  The power of art without the show.

In Misery's darkest cavern known,
  His useful care was ever nigh,
Where hopeless Anguish poured his groan,
  And lonely Want retired to die.   20

No summons mocked by chill delay,
  No petty gain disdained by pride,
The modest wants of every day
  The toil of every day supplied.

His virtues walked their narrow round,   25
  Nor made a pause, nor left a void;

1. An unlicensed physician, who lived in Johnson's house for many years and who died in 1782. His practice was among the very poor. Boswell wrote: "He was of a strange grotesque appearance, stiff and formal in his manner, and seldom said a word while any company was present."
2. "Kind, doing good offices" (Johnson's *Dictionary*).

And sure the Eternal Master found
    The single talent well employed.

The busy day, the peaceful night,
    Unfelt, uncounted, glided by;   30
His frame was firm, his powers were bright,
    Though now his eightieth year was nigh.

Then with no throbbing fiery pain,
    No cold gradations of decay,
Death broke at once the vital chain,   35
    And freed his soul the nearest way.

1783

A Short Song of Congratulation

Long-expected one and twenty
    Lingering year at last is flown,
Pomp and Pleasure, Pride and Plenty,
    Great Sir John,[1] are all your own.

Loosened from the minor's tether,   5
    Free to mortgage or to sell,
Wild as wind, and light as feather
    Bid the slaves of thrift farewell.

Call the Bettys, Kates, and Jennys
    Every name that laughs at Care,   10
Lavish of your grandsire's guineas,
    Show the spirit of an heir.

All that prey on vice and folly
    Joy to see their quarry fly,
Here the gamester light and jolly   15
    There the lender grave and sly.

Wealth, Sir John, was made to wander,
    Let it wander as it will;
See the jockey, see the pander,
    Bid them come, and take their fill.   20

When the bonny blade carouses,
    Pockets full, and spirits high,
What are acres? What are houses?
    Only dirt, or wet or dry.

If the guardian or the mother   25
    Tell the woes of willful waste,
Scorn their counsel and their pother,
    You can hang or drown at last.

1780   1794

1. Sir John Lade, nephew of Johnson's friend Henry Thrale. He came into his property in 1780, and, as Johnson foretold, he had squandered it all by his death.

Rambler No. 5[1]

[*On Spring*]

TUESDAY, *April 3, 1750*

Et nunc omnis ager, nunc omnis parturit arbos,
Nunc frondent silvae, nunc formosissimus annus.
VIRGIL, *Eclogues* III. v. 56

Now ev'ry field, now ev'ry tree is green;
Now genial nature's fairest face is seen.
ELPHINSTON

Every man is sufficiently discontented with some circumstances of his present state, to suffer his imagination to range more or less in quest of future happiness, and to fix upon some point of time, in which, by the removal of the inconvenience which now perplexes him, or acquisition of the advantage which he at present wants, he shall find the condition of his life very much improved.

When this time, which is too often expected with great impatience, at last arrives, it generally comes without the blessing for which it was desired; but we solace ourselves with some new prospect, and press forward again with equal eagerness.

It is lucky for a man, in whom this temper prevails, when he turns his hopes upon things wholly out of his own power; since he forbears then to precipitate [2] his affairs, for the sake of the great event that is to complete his felicity, and waits for the blissful hour, with less neglect of the measures necessary to be taken in the mean time.

I have long known a person of this temper, who indulged his dream of happiness with less hurt to himself than such chimerical wishes commonly produce, and adjusted his scheme with such address, that his hopes were in full bloom three parts of the year, and in the other part never wholly blasted. Many, perhaps, would be desirous of learning by what means he procured to himself such a cheap and lasting satisfaction. It was gained by a constant practice of referring the removal of all his uneasiness to the coming of the next spring; if his health was impaired, the spring would restore it; if what he wanted was at a high price, it would fall in value in the spring.

The spring, indeed, did often come without any of these effects, but he was always certain that the next would be more propitious; nor was ever convinced that the present spring would fail him

---

icals. Johnson's reputation as a moralist and a stylist was established by these essays; because of them Boswell first conceived the ambition to seek Johnson's acquaintance.

2. "To hurry blindly or rashly" (Johnson's *Dictionary*).

before the middle of summer; for he always talked of the spring as coming till it was past, and when it was once past, everyone agreed with him that it was coming.

By long converse with this man, I am, perhaps, brought to feel immoderate pleasure in the contemplation of this delightful season; but I have the satisfaction of finding many, whom it can be no shame to resemble, infected with the same enthusiasm; for there is, I believe, scarce any poet of eminence, who has not left some testimony of his fondness for the flowers, the zephyrs, and the warblers of the spring. Nor has the most luxuriant imagination been able to describe the serenity and happiness of the golden age, otherwise than by giving a perpetual spring, as the highest reward of uncorrupted innocence.

There is, indeed, something inexpressibly pleasing, in the annual renovation of the world, and the new display of the treasures of nature. The cold and darkness of winter, with the naked deformity of every object on which we turn our eyes, make us rejoice at the succeeding season, as well for what we have escaped, as for what we may enjoy; and every budding flower, which a warm situation brings early to our view, is considered by us as a messenger to notify the approach of more joyous days.

The spring affords to a mind, so free from the disturbance of cares or passions as to be vacant[3] to calm amusements, almost every thing that our present state makes us capable of enjoying. The variegated verdure of the fields and woods, the succession of grateful odors, the voice of pleasure pouring out its notes on every side, with the gladness apparently conceived by every animal, from the growth of his food, and the clemency of the weather, throw over the whole earth an air of gaiety, significantly expressed by the smile of nature.

Yet there are men to whom these scenes are able to give no delight, and who hurry away from all the varieties of rural beauty, to lose their hours, and divert their thoughts by cards, or assemblies, a tavern dinner, or the prattle of the day.

It may be laid down as a position which will seldom deceive, that when a man cannot bear his own company there is something wrong. He must fly from himself, either because he feels a tediousness in life from the equipoise of an empty mind, which, having no tendency to one motion more than another but as it is impelled by some external power, must always have recourse to foreign objects; or he must be afraid of the intrusion of some unpleasing ideas, and, perhaps, is struggling to escape from the remembrance of a loss, the fear of a calamity, or some other thought of greater horror.

Those whom sorrow incapacitates to enjoy the pleasures of contemplation, may properly apply to such diversions, provided

3. "At leisure" (Johnson's *Dictionary*).

they are innocent, as lay strong hold on the attention; and those, whom fear of any future affliction chains down to misery, must endeavor to obviate the danger.

My considerations shall, on this occasion, be turned on such as are burthensome to themselves merely because they want subjects for reflection, and to whom the volume of nature is thrown open, without affording them pleasure or instruction; because they never learned to read the characters.

A French author has advanced this seeming paradox, that *very few men know how to take a walk*; and, indeed, it is true, that few know how to take a walk with a prospect of any other pleasure, than the same company would have afforded them at home.

There are animals that borrow their color from the neighboring body, and, consequently, vary their hue as they happen to change their place. In like manner it ought to be the endeavor of every man to derive his reflections from the objects about him; for it is to no purpose that he alters his position, if his attention continues fixed to the same point. The mind should be kept open to the access of every new idea, and so far disengaged from the predominance of particular thoughts, as easily to accommodate itself to occasional entertainment.

A man that has formed this habit of turning every new object to his entertainment, finds in the productions of nature an inexhaustible stock of materials upon which he can employ himself, without any temptations to envy or malevolence; faults, perhaps, seldom totally avoided by those, whose judgment is much exercised upon the works of art. He has always a certain prospect of discovering new reasons for adoring the sovereign author of the universe, and probable hopes of making some discovery of benefit to others, or of profit to himself. There is no doubt but many vegetables and animals have qualities that might be of great use, to the knowledge of which there is not required much force of penetration, or fatigue of study, but only frequent experiments, and close attention. What is said by the chemists of their darling mercury, is, perhaps, true of everybody through the whole creation, that if a thousand lives should be spent upon it, all its properties would not be found out.

Mankind must necessarily be diversified by various tastes, since life affords and requires such multiplicity of employments, and a nation of naturalists is neither to be hoped, or desired; but it is surely not improper to point out a fresh amusement to those who languish in health, and repine in plenty, for want of some source of diversion that may be less easily exhausted, and to inform the multitudes of both sexes, who are burthened with every new day, that there are many shows which they have not seen.

He that enlarges his curiosity after the works of nature, demonstrably multiplies the inlets to happiness; and, therefore, the younger part of my readers, to whom I dedicate this vernal speculation, must excuse me for calling upon them, to make use at once of the spring of the year, and the spring of life; to acquire, while their minds may be yet impressed with new images, a love of innocent pleasures, and an ardor for useful knowledge; and to remember, that a blighted spring makes a barren year, and that the vernal flowers, however beautiful and gay, are only intended by nature as preparatives to autumnal fruits.

1750

Idler No. 31[1]

[*On Idleness*]

SATURDAY, *November* 18, 1758

Many moralists have remarked, that Pride has of all human vices the widest dominion, appears in the greatest multiplicity of forms, and lies hid under the greatest variety of disguises; of disguises, which, like the moon's *veil of brightness*, are both *its luster and its shade*, and betray it to others, though they hide it from ourselves.

It is not my intention to degrade Pride from this pre-eminence of mischief, yet I know not whether Idleness may not maintain a very doubtful and obstinate competition.

There are some that profess Idleness in its full dignity, who call themselves the Idle, as Busiris in the play "calls himself the Proud";[2] who boast that they do nothing, and thank their stars that they have nothing to do; who sleep every night till they can sleep no longer, and rise only that exercise may enable them to sleep again; who prolong the reign of darkness by double curtains, and never see the sun but to "tell him how they hate his beams";[3] whose whole labor is to vary the postures of indulgence, and whose day differs from their night but as a couch or chair differs from a bed.

These are the true and open votaries of Idleness, for whom she weaves the garlands of poppies, and into whose cup she pours the waters of oblivion; who exist in a state of unruffled stupidity, forgetting and forgotten; who have long ceased to live, and at whose death the survivors can only say, that they have ceased to breathe.

But Idleness predominates in many lives where it is not suspected; for being a vice which terminates in itself, it may be enjoyed without injury to others; and is therefore not watched like Fraud, which endangers property, or like Pride, which naturally seeks its gratifications in another's inferiority. Idleness is a silent and peaceful quality, that neither raises envy by ostentation, nor hatred by opposition; and therefore nobody is busy to censure or detect it.

As Pride sometimes is hid under humility, Idleness is often covered by turbulence and hurry. He that neglects his known duty

---

1. Johnson wrote and published the *Idler*, a periodical similar to the *Rambler*, from 1758 until 1760.
2. Edward Young, *Busiris* (1719), I.13.
3. *Paradise Lost* IV.37.

and real employment, naturally endeavors to crowd his mind with something that may bar out the remembrance of his own folly, and does any thing but what he ought to do with eager diligence, that he may keep himself in his own favor.

Some are always in a state of preparation, occupied in previous measures, forming plans, accumulating materials, and providing for the main affair. These are certainly under the secret power of Idleness. Nothing is to be expected from the workman whose tools are forever to be sought. I was once told by a great master, that no man ever excelled in painting, who was eminently curious about pencils and colors.

There are others to whom Idleness dictates another expedient, by which life may be passed unprofitably away without the tediousness of many vacant hours. The art is, to fill the day with petty business, to have always something in hand which may raise curiosity, but not solicitude, and keep the mind in a state of action, but not of labor.

This art has for many years been practiced by my old friend Sober, with wonderful success. Sober is a man of strong desires and quick imagination, so exactly balanced by the love of ease, that they can seldom stimulate him to any difficult undertaking; they have, however, so much power, that they will not suffer him to lie quite at rest, and though they do not make him sufficiently useful to others, they make him at least weary of himself.

Mr. Sober's chief pleasure is conversation; there is no end of his talk or his attention; to speak or to hear is equally pleasing; for he still fancies that he is teaching or learning something, and is free for the time from his own reproaches.

But there is one time at night when he must go home, that his friends may sleep; and another time in the morning, when all the world agrees to shut out interruption. These are the moments of which poor Sober trembles at the thought. But the misery of these tiresome intervals, he has many means of alleviating. He has persuaded himself that the manual arts are undeservedly overlooked; he has observed in many trades the effects of close thought, and just ratiocination. From speculation he proceeded to practice, and supplied himself with the tools of a carpenter, with which he mended his coalbox very successfully, and which he still continues to employ, as he finds occasion.

He has attempted at other times the crafts of the shoemaker, tinman, plumber, and potter; in all these arts he has failed, and resolves to qualify himself for them by better information. But his daily amusement is chemistry. He has a small furnace, which he employs in distillation, and which has long been the solace of his life. He draws oils and waters, and essences and spirits, which he knows to be of no use; sits and counts the drops as they come from his retort, and forgets that, whilst a drop is falling, a moment flies away.

Poor Sober![4] I have often teased him with reproof, and he has often promised reformation; for no man is so much open to conviction as the Idler, but there is none on whom it operates so little. What will be the effect of this paper I know not; perhaps he will read it and laugh, and light the fire in his furnace; but my hope is that he will quit his trifles, and betake himself to rational and useful diligence.

From The History of Rasselas, Prince of Abyssinia[1]

Chapter I. Description of a Palace in a Valley

Ye who listen with credulity to the whispers of fancy, and pursue with eagerness the phantoms of hope; who expect that age will perform the promises of youth, and that the deficiencies of the present day will be supplied by the morrow—attend to the history of Rasselas, prince of Abyssinia.

Rasselas was the fourth son of the mighty emperor in whose dominions the Father of Waters[2] begins his course; whose bounty

4. Sober represents aspects of Johnson's own character. He was much given to indolence, and he performed chemical experiments in a small laboratory in his garret.

1. Johnson wrote *Rasselas* in January, 1759, during the evenings of one week, a remarkable instance of his ability to write rapidly and brilliantly under the pressure of necessity. His mother lay dying in Lichfield. Her son, famous for his *Dictionary*, was nonetheless oppressed by poverty and in great need of ready money with which to make her last days comfortable, pay her funeral expenses, and settle her small debts. He was paid £100 for the first edition of *Rasselas*, but not in time to attend her deathbed or her funeral. Because of these circumstances, the tale has often been read as an expression of the gloom of the moment; but acquaintance with Johnson's other writings and his conversation makes it plain that the book expresses his settled view of life and what human beings may reasonably expect from it.

Rasselas is a philosophical fable cast in the popular form of an Oriental tale, a type of fiction that owed its popularity to the vogue of the *Arabian Nights*, first translated into English in the early 18th century. Since the work is a fable, we should not approach it as a novel: psychologically credible characters and a series of intricately involved actions that lead to a necessary resolution and conclusion are not to be found in *Rasselas*. The action, the characters, the majestic prose rhythms, and the melancholy resonance of much of the language serve to articulate the theme, which is very similar to that of *The Vanity of Human Wishes*. Johnson formulated it in a magnificent phrase: the "hunger of imagination which preys incessantly upon life" (Chapter XXXII) and which lures us to "listen with credulity to the whispers of fancy and pursue with eagerness the phantoms of hope" (Chapter I). The tale is a gentle satire on one of the perennial topics of satirists, the folly of all of us who stubbornly cling to our illusions despite the evidence of experience. *Rasselas* is not all darkness and gloom, for Johnson's theme invites comic as well as tragic treatment, and some of the episodes evoke that laughter of the mind which is the effect of high comedy. In its main theme, however—the folly of cherishing the dream of ever attaining unalloyed happiness in a world which can never wholly satisfy our desires, however disinterested—and in many of the sayings of its characters, especially of the sage Imlac, *Rasselas* expresses some of Johnson's own deepest convictions.

2. The Nile.

pours down the streams of plenty, and scatters over half the world the harvests of Egypt.

According to the custom which has descended from age to age among the monarchs of the torrid zone, Rasselas was confined in a private palace, with the other sons and daughters of Abyssinian royalty, till the order of succession should call him to the throne.

The place which the wisdom or policy of antiquity had destined for the residence of the Abyssinian princes was a spacious valley[3] in the kingdom of Amhara, surrounded on every side by mountains, of which the summits overhang the middle part. The only passage by which it could be entered was a cavern that passed under a rock, of which it has long been disputed whether it was the work of nature or of human industry. The outlet of the cavern was concealed by a thick wood, and the mouth which opened into the valley was closed with gates of iron, forged by the artificers of ancient days, so massy that no man could, without the help of engines, open or shut them.

From the mountains on every side rivulets descended that filled all the valley with verdure and fertility, and formed a lake in the middle, inhabited by fish of every species, and frequented by every fowl whom nature has taught to dip the wing in water. This lake discharged its superfluities by a stream, which entered a dark cleft of the mountain on the northern side, and fell with dreadful noise from precipice to precipice till it was heard no more.

The sides of the mountains were covered with trees, the banks of the brooks were diversified with flowers; every blast shook spices from the rocks, and every month dropped fruits upon the ground. All animals that bite the grass, or browse the shrub, whether wild or tame, wandered in this extensive circuit, secured from beasts of prey by the mountains which confined them. On one part were flocks and herds feeding in the pastures, on another all the beasts of chase frisking in the lawns; the sprightly kid was bounding on the rocks, the subtle monkey frolicking in the trees, and the solemn elephant reposing in the shade. All the diversities of the world were brought together, the blessings of nature were collected, and its evils extracted and excluded.

The valley, wide and fruitful, supplied its inhabitants with the necessaries of life, and all delights and superfluities were added at the annual visit which the emperor paid his children, when the iron gate was opened to the sound of music, and during eight days everyone that resided in the valley was required to propose whatever might contribute to make seclusion pleasant, to fill up the

3. Johnson had read of the Happy Valley in the Portuguese Jesuit Father Lobo's book on Abyssinia, which he translated in 1735. The description in this and the immediately following paragraphs illustrates well enough Johnson's preference for the "general" over the "particular" (see Chapter X, below). It owes something to the description of the Garden in *Paradise Lost* IV, and Coleridge's *Kubla Khan* owes something to it.

vacancies of attention, and lessen the tediousness of time. Every desire was immediately granted. All the artificers of pleasure were called to gladden the festivity; the musicians exerted the power of harmony, and the dancers showed their activity before the princes, in hope that they should pass their lives in this blissful captivity, to which those only were admitted whose performance was thought able to add novelty to luxury. Such was the appearance of security and delight which this retirement afforded, that they to whom it was new always desired that it might be perpetual; and as those on whom the iron gate had once closed were never suffered to return, the effect of longer experience could not be known. Thus every year produced new schemes of delight and new competitors for imprisonment.

The palace stood on an eminence, raised about thirty paces above the surface of the lake. It was divided into many squares or courts, built with greater or less magnificence according to the rank of those for whom they were designed. The roofs were turned into arches of massy stone, joined with a cement that grew harder by time, and the building stood from century to century, deriding the solstitial rains and equinoctial hurricanes, without need of reparation.

This house, which was so large as to be fully known to none but some ancient officers, who successively inherited the secrets of the place, was built as if suspicion herself had dictated the plan. To every room there was an open and secret passage; every square had a communication with the rest, either from the upper stories by private galleries, or by subterranean passages from the lower apartments. Many of the columns had unsuspected cavities, in which a long race of monarchs had reposited their treasures. They then closed up the opening with marble, which was never to be removed but in the utmost exigencies of the kingdom, and recorded their accumulations in a book, which was itself concealed in a tower, not entered but by the emperor, attended by the prince who stood next in succession.

Chapter II. *The Discontent of Rasselas in the Happy Valley*

Here the sons and daughters of Abyssinia lived only to know the soft vicissitudes of pleasure and repose, attended by all that were skillful to delight, and gratified with whatever the senses can enjoy. They wandered in gardens of fragrance, and slept in the fortresses of security. Every art was practiced to make them pleased with their own condition. The sages who instructed them told them of nothing but the miseries of public life, and described all beyond the mountains as regions of calamity, where discord was always raging, and where man preyed upon man.

To heighten their opinion of their own felicity, they were daily entertained with songs, the subject of which was the *happy valley*.

Their appetites were excited by frequent enumerations of different enjoyments, and revelry and merriment was the business of every hour, from the dawn of morning to the close of even.

These methods were generally successful; few of the princes had ever wished to enlarge their bounds, but passed their lives in full conviction that they had all within their reach that art or nature could bestow, and pitied those whom fate had excluded from this seat of tranquility, as the sport of chance and the slaves of misery.

Thus they rose in the morning and lay down at night, pleased with each other and with themselves; all but Rasselas, who, in the twenty-sixth year of his age, began to withdraw himself from their pastimes and assemblies, and to delight in solitary walks and silent meditation. He often sat before tables covered with luxury, and forgot to taste the dainties that were placed before him; he rose abruptly in the midst of the song, and hastily retired beyond the sound of music. His attendants observed the change, and endeavored to renew his love of pleasure. He neglected their officiousness, repulsed their invitations, and spent day after day on the banks of rivulets sheltered with trees, where he sometimes listened to the birds in the branches, sometimes observed the fish playing in the stream, and anon cast his eyes upon the pastures and mountains filled with animals, of which some were biting the herbage, and some sleeping among the bushes.

This singularity of his humor made him much observed. One of the sages, in whose conversation he had formerly delighted, followed him secretly, in hope of discovering the cause of his disquiet. Rasselas, who knew not that anyone was near him, having for some time fixed his eyes upon the goats that were browsing among the rocks, began to compare their condition with his own.

"What," said he, "makes the difference between man and all the rest of the animal creation? Every beast that strays beside me has the same corporal necessities with myself; he is hungry, and crops the grass, he is thirsty, and drinks the stream, his thirst and hunger are appeased, he is satisfied, and sleeps; he rises again, and he is hungry, he is again fed, and is at rest. I am hungry and thirsty like him, but when thirst and hunger cease, I am not at rest; I am, like him, pained with want, but am not, like him, satisfied with fullness. The intermediate hours are tedious and gloomy; I long again to be hungry that I may again quicken my attention. The birds peck the berries or the corn, and fly away to the groves, where they sit in seeming happiness on the branches, and waste their lives in tuning one unvaried series of sounds. I likewise can call the lutanist and the singer, but the sounds that pleased me yesterday weary me today, and will grow yet more wearisome tomorrow. I can discover within me no power of perception which is not glutted with its proper pleasure, yet I do not feel myself delighted. Man has surely some latent sense for which this place affords no gratification, or he has some desires distinct from sense, which must be satisfied before he can be happy."

After this he lifted up his head, and seeing the moon rising, walked towards the palace. As he passed through the fields, and saw the animals around him, "Ye," said he, "are happy, and need not envy me that walk thus among you, burthened with myself; nor do I, ye gentle beings, envy your felicity, for it is not the felicity of man. I have many distresses from which ye are free; I fear pain when I do not feel it; I sometimes shrink at evils recollected, and sometimes start at evils anticipated. Surely the equity of Providence has balanced peculiar sufferings with peculiar enjoyments."

With observations like these the prince amused himself as he returned, uttering them with a plaintive voice, yet with a look that discovered him to feel some complacence in his own perspicacity, and to receive some solace of the miseries of life from consciousness of the delicacy with which he felt, and the eloquence with which he bewailed them. He mingled cheerfully in the diversions of the evening, and all rejoiced to find that his heart was lightened.

Chapter III. The Wants of Him That Wants Nothing

On the next day his old instructor, imagining that he had now made himself acquainted with his disease of mind, was in the hope of curing it by counsel, and officiously sought an opportunity of conference, which the prince, having long considered him as one whose intellects were exhausted, was not very willing to afford. "Why," said he, "does this man thus intrude upon me; shall I be never suffered to forget those lectures which pleased only while they were new, and to become new again must be forgotten?" He then walked into the wood, and composed himself to his usual meditations; when, before his thoughts had taken any settled form, he perceived his pursuer at his side, and was at first prompted by his impatience to go hastily away; but, being unwilling to offend a man whom he had once reverenced and still loved, he invited him to sit down with him on the bank.

The old man, thus encouraged, began to lament the change which had been lately observed in the prince, and to inquire why he so often retired from the pleasures of the palace, to loneliness and silence. "I fly from pleasure," said the prince, "because pleasure has ceased to please; I am lonely because I am miserable, and am unwilling to cloud with my presence the happiness of others." "You, sir," said the sage, "are the first who has complained of misery in the *happy valley*. I hope to convince you that your complaints have no real cause. You are here in full possession of all that the emperor of Abyssinia can bestow; here is neither labor to be endured nor danger to be dreaded, yet here is all that labor or danger can procure or purchase. Look round and tell me which of your wants is without supply; if you want nothing, how are you unhappy?"

"That I want nothing," said the prince, "or that I know not what I want, is the cause of my complaint; if I had any known want, I should have a certain wish; that wish would excite endeavor, and I should not then repine to see the sun move so slowly towards the western mountain, or lament when the day breaks, and sleep will no longer hide me from myself. When I see the kids and the lambs chasing one another, I fancy that I should be happy if I had something to pursue. But, possessing all that I can want, I find one day and one hour exactly like another, except that the latter is still more tedious than the former. Let your experience inform me how the day may now seem as short as in my childhood, while nature was yet fresh and every moment showed me what I never had observed before. I have already enjoyed too much; give me something to desire."

The old man was surprised at this new species of affliction and knew not what to reply, yet was unwilling to be silent. "Sir," said he, "if you had seen the miseries of the world you would know how to value your present state." "Now," said the prince, "you have given me something to desire. I shall long to see the miseries of the world, since the sight of them is necessary to happiness."[4]

Chapter X. Imlac's History Continued. A Dissertation upon Poetry

"Wherever I went, I found that poetry was considered as the highest learning, and regarded with a veneration somewhat approaching to that which man would pay to the angelic nature. And yet it fills me with wonder that, in almost all countries, the most ancient poets are considered as the best: whether it be that every other kind of knowledge is an acquisition gradually attained, and poetry is a gift conferred at once; or that the first poetry of every nation surprised them as a novelty, and retained the credit by consent which it received by accident at first; or whether, as the province of poetry is to describe nature and passion, which are always the same, the first writers took possession of the most striking objects for description and the most probable occurrences for fiction, and left nothing to those that followed them, but transcription of the same events, and new combinations of the same images—whatever be the reason, it is commonly observed that the early writers are in possession of nature, and their followers of art; that the first excel in strength and invention, and the latter in elegance and refinement.

4. In the chapters here omitted Rasselas, meditating escape, comes to know Imlac, a poet and "man of learning" who has experienced life in all its phases, and who, finally despairing of happiness, has willingly retired to the Happy Valley. Imlac's account of his experiences whets the prince's desire to see the world and make a "choice of life."

"I was desirous to add my name to this illustrious fraternity. I read all the poets of Persia and Arabia, and was able to repeat by memory the volumes that are suspended in the mosque of Mecca. But I soon found that no man was ever great by imitation. My desire of excellence impelled me to transfer my attention to nature and to life. Nature was to be my subject, and men to be my auditors: I could never describe what I had not seen; I could not hope to move those with delight or terror, whose interests and opinions I did not understand.

"Being now resolved to be a poet, I saw everything with a new purpose; my sphere of attention was suddenly magnified; no kind of knowledge was to be overlooked. I ranged mountains and deserts for images and resemblances, and pictured upon my mind every tree of the forest and flower of the valley. I observed with equal care the crags of the rock and the pinnacles of the palace. Sometimes I wandered along the mazes of the rivulet, and sometimes watched the changes of the summer clouds. To a poet nothing can be useless. Whatever is beautiful, and whatever is dreadful, must be familiar to his imagination; he must be conversant with all that is awfully vast or elegantly little. The plants of the garden, the animals of the wood, the minerals of the earth, and meteors of the sky, must all concur to store his mind with inexhaustible variety: for every idea⁵ is useful for the enforcement or decoration of moral or religious truth; and he who knows most will have most power of diversifying his scenes, and of gratifying his reader with remote allusions and unexpected instruction.

"All the appearances of nature I was therefore careful to study, and every country which I have surveyed has contributed something to my poetical powers."

"In so wide a survey," said the prince, "you must surely have left much unobserved. I have lived till now within the circuit of these mountains, and yet cannot walk abroad without the sight of something which I have never beheld before, or never heeded."

"The business of a poet," said Imlac, "is to examine, not the individual, but the species; to remark general properties and large appearances; he does not number the streaks of the tulip, or describe the different shades in the verdure of the forest. He is to exhibit in his portraits of nature such prominent and striking features as recall the original to every mind, and must neglect the minuter discriminations, which one may have remarked and another have neglected, for those characteristics which are alike obvious to vigilance and carelessness.

"But the knowledge of nature is only half the task of a poet; he must be acquainted likewise with all the modes of life. His character requires that he estimate the happiness and misery of every condition; observe the power of all the passions in all their com-

5. Mental image.

binations, and trace the changes of the human mind, as they are modified by various institutions and accidental influences of climate or custom, from the sprightliness of infancy to the despondence of decrepitude. He must divest himself of the prejudices of his age or country; he must consider right and wrong in their abstracted and invariable state; he must disregard present laws and opinions, and rise to general and transcendental[6] truths, which will always be the same. He must, therefore, content himself with the slow progress of his name, contemn the applause of his own time, and commit his claims to the justice of posterity. He must write as the interpreter of nature and the legislator of mankind, and consider himself as presiding over the thoughts and manner of future generations, as a being superior to time and place.

"His labor is not yet at an end; he must know many languages and many sciences; and, that his style may be worthy of his thoughts, must by incessant practice familiarize to himself every delicacy of speech and grace of harmony."

Chapter XI. Imlac's Narrative Continued. A Hint on Pilgrimage

Imlac now felt the enthusiastic fit, and was proceeding to aggrandize his own profession, when the prince cried out: "Enough! thou hast convinced me that no human being can ever be a poet. Proceed with thy narration."

"To be a poet," said Imlac, "is indeed very difficult." "So difficult," returned the prince, "that I will at present hear no more of his labors. Tell me whither you went when you had seen Persia."

"From Persia," said the poet, "I traveled through Syria, and for three years resided in Palestine, where I conversed with great numbers of the northern and western nations of Europe, the nations which are now in possession of all power and all knowledge, whose armies are irresistible, and whose fleets command the remotest parts of the globe. When I compared these men with the natives of our own kingdom, and those that surround us, they appeared almost another order of beings. In their countries it is difficult to wish for anything that may not be obtained; a thousand arts, of which we never heard, are continually laboring for their convenience and pleasure; and whatever their own climate has denied them is supplied by their commerce."

"By what means," said the prince, "are the Europeans thus powerful, or why, since they can so easily visit Asia and Africa for trade or conquest, cannot the Asiatics and Africans invade their coasts, plant colonies in their ports, and give laws to their natural princes? The same wind that carries them back would bring us thither."

"They are more powerful, sir, than we," answered Imlac, "be-

6. "General; pervading many particulars" (Johnson's *Dictionary*).

cause they are wiser; knowledge will always predominate over ignorance, as man governs the other animals. But why their knowledge is more than ours, I know not what reason can be given, but the unsearchable will of the Supreme Being."

"When," said the prince with a sigh, "shall I be able to visit Palestine, and mingle with this mighty confluence of nations? Till that happy moment shall arrive, let me fill up the time with such representations as thou canst give me. I am not ignorant of the motive that assembles such numbers in that place, and cannot but consider it as the center of wisdom and piety, to which the best and wisest men of every land must be continually resorting."

"There are some nations," said Imlac, "that send few visitants to Palestine; for many numerous and learned sects in Europe concur to censure pilgrimage as superstitious, or deride it as ridiculous."

"You know," said the prince, "how little my life has made me acquainted with diversity of opinions. It will be too long to hear the arguments on both sides; you, that have considered them, tell me the result."

"Pilgrimage," said Imlac, "like many other acts of piety, may be reasonable or superstitious, according to the principles upon which it is performed. Long journeys in search of truth are not commanded. Truth, such as is necessary to the regulation of life, is always found where it is honestly sought. Change of place is no natural cause of the increase of piety, for it inevitably produces dissipation of mind. Yet, since men go every day to view the fields where great actions have been performed, and return with stronger impressions of the event, curiosity of the same kind may naturally dispose us to view that country whence our religion had its beginning; and I believe no man surveys those awful scenes without some confirmation of holy resolutions. That the Supreme Being may be more easily propitiated in one place than in another is the dream of idle superstition, but that some places may operate upon our own minds in an uncommon manner is an opinion which hourly experience will justify. He who supposes that his vices may be more successfully combated in Palestine, will, perhaps, find himself mistaken, yet he may go thither without folly; he who thinks they will be more freely pardoned, dishonors at once his reason and religion."

"These," said the prince, "are European distinctions. I will consider them another time. What have you found to be the effect of knowledge? Are those nations happier than we?"

"There is so much infelicity," said the poet, "in the world that scarce any man has leisure from his own distresses to estimate the comparative happiness of others. Knowledge is certainly one of the means of pleasure, as is confessed by the natural desire which every mind feels of increasing its ideas. Ignorance is mere privation, by which nothing can be produced; it is a vacuity in which the soul sits motionless and torpid for want of attraction; and, without knowing why, we always rejoice when we learn, and grieve when we forget. I am therefore inclined to conclude that if nothing counteracts the natural consequence of learning, we grow more happy as our minds take a wider range.

"In enumerating the particular comforts of life, we shall find many advantages on the side of the Europeans. They cure wounds and diseases with which we languish and perish. We suffer inclemencies of weather which they can obviate. They have engines for the despatch of many laborious works, which we must perform by manual industry. There is such communication between distant places that one friend can hardly be said to be absent from another. Their policy removes all public inconveniences; they have roads cut through their mountains, and bridges laid upon their rivers. And, if we descend to the privacies of life, their habitations are more commodious, and their possessions are more secure."

"They are surely happy," said the prince, "who have all these conveniencies, of which I envy none so much as the facility with which separated friends interchange their thoughts."

"The Europeans," answered Imlac, "are less unhappy than we, but they are not happy. Human life is everywhere a state in which much is to be endured, and little to be enjoyed."[7]

Chapter XVI. They Enter Cairo, and Find Every Man Happy

As they approached the city, which filled the strangers with astonishment, "This," said Imlac to the prince, "is the place where travelers and merchants assemble from all the corners of the earth. You will here find men of every character and every occupation. Commerce is here honorable. I will act as a merchant, and you shall live as strangers, who have no other end of travel than curiosity. It will soon be observed that we are rich; our reputation will procure us access to all whom we shall desire to know; you will see all the conditions of humanity, and enable yourself at leisure to make your *choice of life*."

They now entered the town, stunned by the noise, and offended by the crowds. Instruction had not yet so prevailed over habit, but that they wondered to see themselves pass undistinguished along the street, and met by the lowest of the people without reverence or notice. The princess could not at first bear the thought of being leveled with the vulgar, and for some days continued in her chamber, where she was served by her favorite, Pekuah, as in the palace of the valley.

---

7. In the omitted chapters Rasselas and Imlac tunnel through the mountain, starting from a cavern earlier discovered by Rasselas. Laden with wealth and guided by Imlac, Rasselas, his sister Nekayah, and her maid Pekuah escape from the Happy Valley and make their way to Cairo.

Imlac, who understood traffic,[8] sold part of the jewels the next day, and hired a house, which he adorned with such magnificence that he was immediately considered as a merchant of great wealth. His politeness attracted many acquaintance, and his generosity made him courted by many dependents. His table was crowded by men of every nation, who all admired his knowledge, and solicited his favor. His companions, not being able to mix in the conversation, could make no discovery of their ignorance or surprise, and were gradually initiated in the world as they gained knowledge of the language.

The prince had, by frequent lectures, been taught the use and nature of money; but the ladies could not for a long time comprehend what the merchants did with small pieces of gold and silver, or why things of so little use should be received as equivalent to the necessaries of life.

They studied the language two years, while Imlac was preparing to set before them the various ranks and conditions of mankind. He grew acquainted with all who had anything uncommon in their fortune or conduct. He frequented the voluptuous and the frugal, the idle and the busy, the merchants and the men of learning.

The prince being now able to converse with fluency, and having learned the caution necessary to be observed in his intercourse with strangers, began to accompany Imlac to places of resort, and to enter into all assemblies, that he might make his *choice of life*. For some time he thought choice needless, because all appeared to him equally happy. Wherever he went he met gaiety and kindness, and heard the song of joy or the laugh of carelessness. He began to believe that the world overflowed with universal plenty, and that nothing was withheld either from want or merit; that every hand showered liberality, and every heart melted with benevolence: "And who then," says he, "will be suffered to be wretched?"

Imlac permitted the pleasing delusion, and was unwilling to crush the hope of inexperience, till one day, having sat awhile silent, "I know not," said the prince, "what can be the reason that I am more unhappy than any of our friends. I see them perpetually and unalterably cheerful, but feel my own mind restless and uneasy. I am unsatisfied with those pleasures which I seem most to court; I live in the crowds of jollity, not so much to enjoy company as to shun myself, and am only loud and merry to conceal my sadness."

"Every man," said Imlac, "may, by examining his own mind, guess what passes in the minds of others; when you feel that your own gaiety is counterfeit, it may justly lead you to suspect that of your companions not to be sincere. Envy is commonly reciprocal. We are long before we are convinced that happiness is never to be found, and each believes it possessed by others, to keep alive the

8. Commerce.

hope of obtaining it for himself. In the assembly where you passed the last night, there appeared such sprightliness of air, and volatility of fancy, as might have suited beings of an higher order, formed to inhabit serener regions, inaccessible to care or sorrow; yet, believe me, prince, there was not one who did not dread the moment when solitude should deliver him to the tyranny of reflection."

"This," said the prince, "may be true of others, since it is true of me; yet, whatever be the general infelicity of man, one condition is more happy than another, and wisdom surely directs us to take the least evil in the *choice of life.*"

"The causes of good and evil," answered Imlac, "are so various and uncertain, so often entangled with each other, so diversified by various relations, and so much subject to accidents which cannot be foreseen, that he who would fix his condition upon incontestable reasons of preference must live and die inquiring and deliberating."

"But, surely," said Rasselas, "the wise men, to whom we listen with reverence and wonder, chose that mode of life for themselves which they thought most likely to make them happy."

"Very few," said the poet, "live by choice. Every man is placed in his present condition by causes which acted without his foresight, and with which he did not always willingly co-operate; and therefore you will rarely meet one who does not think the lot of his neighbor better than his own."

"I am pleased to think," said the prince, "that my birth has given me at least one advantage over others, by enabling me to determine for myself. I have here the world before me. I will review it at leisure; surely happiness is somewhere to be found."[9]

Chapter XVIII. The Prince Finds a Wise and Happy Man

As he was one day walking in the street, he saw a spacious building which all were, by the open doors, invited to enter: he followed the stream of people, and found it a hall or school of declamation, in which professors read lectures to their auditory. He fixed his eye upon a sage raised above the rest, who discoursed with great energy on the government of the passions. His look was venerable, his action graceful, his pronunciation clear, and his diction elegant. He showed with great strength of sentiment and variety of illustration that human nature is degraded and debased, when the lower faculties predominate over the higher; that when fancy, the parent of passion, usurps the dominion of the mind, nothing ensues but the natural effect of unlawful government, perturbation, and confusion; that she betrays the fortresses of the intellect to rebels, and excites her children to sedition against reason, their lawful sovereign. He compared reason to the sun, of which the light is constant, uniform and lasting; and fancy to a meteor, of bright but transitory luster,

9. In Chapter XVII, here omitted, Rasselas fails to find happiness among the gay and dissipated young men of Cairo.

irregular in its motion, and delusive in its direction.

He then communicated the various precepts given from time to time for the conquest of passion, and displayed the happiness of those who had obtained the important victory, after which man is no longer the slave of fear, nor the fool of hope; is no more emaciated by envy, inflamed by anger, emasculated by tenderness, or depressed by grief; but walks on calmly through the tumults or the privacies of life, as the sun pursues alike his course through the calm or the stormy sky.

He enumerated many examples of heroes immovable by pain or pleasure, who looked with indifference on those modes or accidents to which the vulgar give the names of good and evil. He exhorted his hearers to lay aside their prejudices, and arm themselves against the shafts of malice or misfortune, by invulnerable patience; concluding that this state only was happiness, and that his happiness was in everyone's power.

Rasselas listened to him with the veneration due to the instructions of a superior being, and, waiting for him at the door, humbly implored the liberty of visiting so great a master of true wisdom. The lecturer hesitated a moment, when Rasselas put a purse of gold into his hand, which he received with a mixture of joy and wonder.

"I have found," said the prince at his return to Imlac, "a man who can teach all that is necessary to be known; who, from the unshaken throne of rational fortitude, looks down on the scenes of life changing beneath him. He speaks, and attention watches his lips. He reasons, and conviction closes his periods. This man shall be my future guide; I will learn his doctrines, and imitate his life."

"Be not too hasty," said Imlac, "to trust or to admire the teachers of morality: they discourse like angels, but they live like men."

Rasselas, who could not conceive how any man could reason so forcibly without feeling the cogency of his own arguments, paid his visit in a few days, and was denied admission. He had now learned the power of money, and made his way by a piece of gold to the inner apartment, where he found the philosopher in a room half darkened, with his eyes misty and his face pale. "Sir," said he, "you are come at a time when all human friendship is useless; what I suffer cannot be remedied, what I have lost cannot be supplied. My daughter, my only daughter, from whose tenderness I expected all the comforts of my age, died last night of a fever. My views, my purposes, my hopes are at an end; I am now a lonely being, disunited from society."

"Sir," said the prince, "mortality is an event by which a wise man can never be surprised; we know that death is always near, and it should therefore always be expected." "Young man," answered the philosopher, "you speak like one that has never felt the pangs of separation." "Have you then forgot the precepts," said Rasselas, "which you so powerfully enforced? Has wisdom no strength to arm the heart against calamity? Consider that external things are naturally variable, but truth and reason are always the same." "What comfort," said the mourner, "can truth and reason afford me? Of what effect are they now, but to tell me that my daughter will not be restored?"

The prince, whose humanity would not suffer him to insult misery with reproof, went away, convinced of the emptiness of rhetorical sound, and the inefficacy of polished periods and studied sentences.

Chapter XIX. A Glimpse of Pastoral Life

He was still eager upon the same inquiry; and having heard of a hermit that lived near the lowest cataract of the Nile, and filled the whole country with the fame of his sanctity, resolved to visit his retreat, and inquire whether that felicity which public life could not afford was to be found in solitude; and whether a man whose age and virtue made him venerable could teach any peculiar art of shunning evils, or enduring them.

Imlac and the princess agreed to accompany him, and, after the necessary preparations, they began their journey. Their way lay through fields, where shepherds tended their flocks and the lambs were playing upon the pasture. "This," said the poet, "is the life which has been often celebrated for its innocence and quiet; let us pass the heat of the day among the shepherds' tents, and know whether all our searches are not to terminate in pastoral simplicity."

The proposal pleased them, and they induced the shepherds, by small presents and familiar questions, to tell their opinion of their own state. They were so rude and ignorant, so little able to compare the good with the evil of the occupation, and so indistinct in their narratives and descriptions, that very little could be learned from them. But it was evident that their hearts were cankered with discontent; that they considered themselves as condemned to labor for the luxury of the rich, and looked up with stupid malevolence toward those that were placed above them.

The princess pronounced with vehemence that she would never suffer these envious savages to be her companions, and that she should not soon be desirous of seeing any more specimens of rustic happiness; but could not believe that all the accounts of primeval pleasures were fabulous, and was yet in doubt whether life had anything that could be justly preferred to the placid gratifications of fields and woods. She hoped that the time would come, when, with a few virtuous and elegant companions, she could gather flowers planted by her own hand, fondle the lambs of her own ewe, and listen without care, among brooks and breezes, to one of her maidens reading in the shade.[1]

Chapter XXII. The Happiness of a Life Led According to Nature

Rasselas went often to an assembly of learned men, who met at stated times to unbend their minds and compare their opinions. Their manners were somewhat coarse, but their conversation was instructive, and their disputations acute, though sometimes too violent, and often continued till neither controvertist remembered upon what question they began. Some faults were almost general among them; everyone was desirous to dictate to the rest, and everyone was pleased to hear the genius or knowledge of another depreciated.

In this assembly Rasselas was relating his interview with the hermit, and the wonder with which he heard him censure a course of life which he had so deliberately chosen, and so laudably followed. The sentiments of the hearers were various. Some were of opinion that the folly of his choice had been justly punished by condemnation to perpetual perseverance. One of the youngest among them, with great vehemence, pronounced him an hypocrite. Some talked of the right of society to the labor of individuals, and considered retirement as a desertion of duty. Others readily allowed that there was a time when the claims of the public were satisfied, and when a man might properly sequester himself, to review his life and purify his heart.

One, who appeared more affected with the narrative than the rest, thought it likely that the hermit would in a few years go back to his retreat, and perhaps, if shame did not restrain, or death intercept him, return once more from his retreat into the world. "For the hope of happiness," said he, "is so strongly impressed that the longest experience is not able to efface it. Of the present state, whatever it be, we feel and are forced to confess the misery; yet when the same state is again at a distance, imagination paints it as desirable. But the time will surely come when desire will be no longer our torment, and no man shall be wretched but by his own fault."

"This," said a philosopher who had heard him with tokens of great impatience, "is the present condition of a wise man. The time is already come when none are wretched but by their own fault. Nothing is more idle than to inquire after happiness, which nature has kindly placed within our reach. The way to be happy is to live according to nature, in obedience to that universal and

1. In the omitted chapters the travelers discover the unease and danger of being wealthy, and then find the hermit, who, far from being piously content, is on the point of abandoning his hermitage and returning to society.

unalterable law with which every heart is originally impressed; which is not written on it by precept, but engraven by destiny, not instilled by education, but infused at our nativity. He that lives according to nature will suffer nothing from the delusions of hope, or importunities of desire; he will receive and reject with equability of temper, and act or suffer as the reason of things shall alternately prescribe. Other men may amuse themselves with subtle definitions, or intricate ratiocination. Let them learn to be wise by easier means; let them observe the hind of the forest, and the linnet of the grove; let them consider the life of animals, whose motions are regulated by instinct; they obey their guide, and are happy. Let us therefore, at length, cease to dispute, and learn to live; throw away the encumbrance of precepts, which they who utter them with so much pride and pomp do not understand, and carry with us this simple and intelligible maxim, that deviation from nature is deviation from happiness."

When he had spoken, he looked round him with a placid air, and enjoyed the consciousness of his own beneficence. "Sir," said the prince with great modesty, "as I, like all the rest of mankind, am desirous of felicity, my closest attention has been fixed upon your discourse. I doubt not the truth of a position which a man so learned has so confidently advanced. Let me only know what it is to live according to nature."

"When I find young men so humble and so docile," said the philosopher, "I can deny them no information which my studies have enabled me to afford. To live according to nature, is to act always with due regard to the fitness arising from the relations and qualities of causes and effects; to concur with the great and unchangeable scheme of universal felicity; to co-operate with the general disposition and tendency of the present system of things."

The prince soon found that this was one of the sages whom he should understand less as he heard him longer. He therefore bowed and was silent; and the philosopher, supposing him satisfied, and the rest vanquished, rose up and departed with the air of a man that had co-operated with the present system.[2]

From *Chapter XXVI. The Princess Continues Her Remarks upon Private Life*

Nekayah, perceiving her brother's attention fixed, proceeded in her narrative.

"In families where there is or is not poverty, there is commonly discord. If a kingdom be, as Imlac tells us, a great family, a family likewise is a little kingdom, torn with factions and exposed to revolutions. An unpracticed observer expects the love of parents and

2. In the omitted chapters Rasselas resolves to observe the happiness of men of high position, leaving the study of domestic life to his sister; they report their findings to each other.

children to be constant and equal; but this kindness seldom continues beyond the years of infancy: in a short time the children become rivals to their parents. Benefits are allayed[3] by reproaches, and gratitude debased by envy.

"Parents and children seldom act in concert; each child endeavors to appropriate the esteem or fondness of the parents, and the parents, with yet less temptation, betray each other to their children. Thus, some place their confidence in the father, and some in the mother, and by degrees the house is filled with artifices and feuds.

"The opinions of children and parents, of the young and the old, are naturally opposite, by the contrary effects of hope and despondence, of expectation and experience, without crime or folly on either side. The colors of life in youth and age appear different, as the face of nature in spring and winter. And how can children credit the assertions of parents, which their own eyes show them to be false?

"Few parents act in such a manner as much to enforce their maxims by the credit of their lives. The old man trusts wholly to slow contrivance and gradual progression; the youth expects to force his way by genius, vigor, and precipitance. The old man pays regard to riches, and the youth reverences virtue. The old man deifies prudence; the youth commits himself to magnanimity and chance. The young man, who intends no ill, believes that none is intended, and therefore acts with openness and candor; but his father, having suffered the injuries of fraud, is impelled to suspect, and too often allured to practice it. Age looks with anger on the temerity of youth, and youth with contempt on the scrupulosity[4] of age. Thus parents and children, for the greatest part, live on to love less and less; and, if those whom nature has thus closely united are the torments of each other, where shall we look for tenderness and consolation?"

"Surely," said the prince, "you must have been unfortunate in your choice of acquaintance: I am unwilling to believe that the most tender of all relations is thus impeded in its effects by natural necessity."

"Domestic discord," answered she, "is not inevitably and fatally necessary, but yet is not easily avoided. We seldom see that a whole family is virtuous; the good and evil cannot well agree, and the evil can yet less agree with one another. Even the virtuous fall sometimes to variance, when their virtues are of different kinds, and tending to extremes. In general, those parents have most reverence who most deserve it; for he that lives well cannot be despised.

"Many other evils infest private life. Some are the slaves of servants whom they have trusted with their affairs. Some are kept in continual anxiety to the caprice of rich relations, whom they cannot

3. To allay is "to join anything to another, so as to abate its predominant qualities" (Johnson's *Dictionary*).

4. "Fear of acting in any manner" (Johnson's *Dictionary*).

please, and dare not offend. Some husbands are imperious, and some wives perverse; and, as it is always more easy to do evil than good, though the wisdom or virtue of one can very rarely make many happy, the folly or vice of one may often make many miserable."

"If such be the general effect of marriage," said the prince, "I shall for the future think it dangerous to connect my interest with that of another, lest I should be unhappy by my partner's fault."

"I have met," said the princess, "with many who live single for that reason; but I never found that their prudence ought to raise envy. They dream away their time without friendship, without fondness, and are driven to rid themselves of the day, for which they have no use, by childish amusements, or vicious delights. They act as beings under the constant sense of some known inferiority that fills their minds with rancor, and their tongues with censure. They are peevish at home, and malevolent abroad; and, as the outlaws of human nature, make it their business and their pleasure to disturb that society which debars them from its privileges. To live without feeling or exciting sympathy, to be fortunate without adding to the felicity of others, or afflicted without tasting the balm of pity, is a state more gloomy than solitude; it is not retreat but exclusion from mankind. Marriage has many pains, but celibacy has no pleasures."[5] * * *

Chapter XXIX. *The Debate on Marriage Continued*

"The good of the whole," says Rasselas, "is the same with the good of all its parts. If marriage be best for mankind it must be evidently best for individuals, or a permanent and necessary duty must be the cause of evil, and some must be inevitably sacrificed to the convenience of others. In the estimate which you have made of the two states, it appears that the incommodities of a single life are, in a great measure, necessary and certain, but those of the conjugal state accidental and avoidable.

"I cannot forbear to flatter myself that prudence and benevolence will make marriage happy. The general folly of mankind is the cause of general complaint. What can be expected but disappointment and repentance from a choice made in the immaturity of youth, in the ardor of desire, without judgment, without foresight, without inquiry after conformity of opinions, similarity of manners, rectitude of judgment, or purity of sentiment.

"Such is the common process of marriage. A youth and maiden meeting by chance, or brought together by artifice, exchange glances, reciprocate civilities, go home, and dream of one another. Having little to divert attention, or diversify thought, they find

---

5. In the omitted chapters Rasselas reports that even the highest stations afford no happiness, and the conversation continues.

themselves uneasy when they are apart, and therefore conclude that they shall be happy together. They marry, and discover what nothing but voluntary blindness had before concealed; they wear out life in altercations, and charge nature with cruelty.

"From those early marriages proceeds likewise the rivalry of parents and children: the son is eager to enjoy the world before the father is willing to forsake it, and there is hardly room at once for two generations. The daughter begins to bloom before the mother can be content to fade, and neither can forbear to wish for the absence of the other.

"Surely all these evils may be avoided by that deliberation and delay which prudence prescribes to irrevocable choice. In the variety and jollity of youthful pleasures life may be well enough supported without the help of a partner. Longer time will increase experience, and wider views will allow better opportunities of inquiry and selection: one advantage, as least, will be certain; the parents will be visibly older than their children."

"What reason cannot collect," said Nekayah, "and what experiment has not yet taught, can be known only from the report of others. I have been told that late marriages are not eminently happy. This is a question too important to be neglected, and I have often proposed it to those, whose accuracy of remark, and comprehensiveness of knowledge, made their suffrages worthy of regard. They have generally determined that it is dangerous for a man and woman to suspend their fate upon each other, at a time when opinions are fixed, and habits are established; when friendships have been contracted on both sides, when life has been planned into method, and the mind has long enjoyed the contemplation of its own prospects.

"It is scarcely possible that two traveling through the world under the conduct of chance should have been both directed to the same path, and it will not often happen that either will quit the track which custom has made pleasing. When the desultory levity of youth has settled into regularity, it is soon succeeded by pride ashamed to yield, or obstinacy delighting to contend. And even though mutual esteem produces mutual desire to please, time itself, as it modifies unchangeably the external mien, determines likewise the direction of the passions, and gives an inflexible rigidity to the manners. Long customs are not easily broken: he that attempts to change the course of his own life very often labors in vain; and how shall we do that for others which we are seldom able to do for ourselves?"

"But surely," interposed the prince, "you suppose the chief motive of choice forgotten or neglected. Whenever I shall seek a wife, it shall be my first question, whether she be willing to be led by reason?"

"Thus it is," said Nekayah, "that philosophers are deceived. There are a thousand familiar disputes which reason never can decide; questions that elude investigation, and make logic ridiculous; cases where something must be done, and where little can be said. Consider the state of mankind, and inquire how few can be supposed to act upon any occasions, whether small or great, with all the reasons of action present to their minds. Wretched would be the pair above all names of wretchedness, who should be doomed to adjust by reason every morning all the minute detail of a domestic day.

"Those who marry at an advanced age will probably escape the encroachments of their children; but, in diminution of this advantage, they will be likely to leave them, ignorant and helpless, to a guardian's mercy: or, if that should not happen, they must at least go out of the world before they see those whom they love best either wise or great.

"From their children, if they have less to fear, they have less also to hope, and they lose, without equivalent, the joys of early love, and the convenience of uniting with manners pliant and minds susceptible of new impressions, which might wear away their dissimilitudes by long cohabitation, as soft bodies, by continual attrition, conform their surfaces to each other.

"I believe it will be found that those who marry late are best pleased with their children, and those who marry early with their partners."

"The union of these two affections," said Rasselas, "would produce all that could be wished. Perhaps there is a time when marriage might unite them, a time neither too early for the father, nor too late for the husband."

"Every hour," answered the princess, "confirms my prejudice in favor of the position so often uttered by the mouth of Imlac, 'That nature sets her gifts on the right hand and on the left.' Those conditions, which flatter hope and attract desire, are so constituted that, as we approach one, we recede from another. There are goods so opposed that we cannot seize both, but, by too much prudence, may pass between them at too great a distance to reach either. This is often the fate of long consideration; he does nothing who endeavors to do more than is allowed to humanity. Flatter not yourself with contrarieties of pleasure. Of the blessings set before you make your choice, and be content. No man can taste the fruits of autumn, while he is delighting his scent with the flowers of the spring: no man can, at the same time, fill his cup from the source and from the mouth of the Nile."[6]

6. In Chapter XXX, here omitted, Imlac proposes a visit to the Pyramids.

Chapter XXXI. They Visit the Pyramids

The resolution being thus taken, they set out the next day. They laid tents upon their camels, being resolved to stay among the pyramids till their curiosity was fully satisfied. They traveled gently, turned aside to everything remarkable, stopped from time to time and conversed with the inhabitants, and observed the various appearances of towns ruined and inhabited, of wild and cultivated nature.

When they came to the great pyramid, they were astonished at the extent of the base, and the height of the top. Imlac explained to them the principles upon which the pyramidal form was chosen for a fabric intended to coextend its duration with that of the world; he showed that its gradual diminution gave it such stability as defeated all the common attacks of the elements, and could scarcely be overthrown by earthquakes themselves, the least resistible of natural violence. A concussion that should shatter the pyramid would threaten the dissolution of the continent.

They measured all its dimensions, and pitched their tents at its foot. Next day they prepared to enter its interior apartments, and having hired the common guides, climbed up to the first passage, when the favorite of the princess, looking into the cavity, stepped back and trembled. "Pekuah," said the princess, "of what art thou afraid?" "Of the narrow entrance," answered the lady, "and of the dreadful gloom. I dare not enter a place which must surely be inhabited by unquiet souls. The original possessors of these dreadful vaults will start up before us, and perhaps shut us in forever." She spoke, and threw her arms round the neck of her mistress.

"If all your fear be of apparitions," said the prince, "I will promise you safety. There is no danger from the dead; he that is once buried will be seen no more."

"That the dead are seen no more," said Imlac, "I will not undertake to maintain, against the concurrent and unvaried testimony of all ages, and of all nations. There is no people, rude or learned, among whom apparitions of the dead are not related and believed. This opinion, which perhaps prevails as far as human nature is diffused, could become universal only by its truth; those that never heard of one another would not have agreed in a tale which nothing but experience can make credible. That it is doubted by single cavilers can very little weaken the general evidence; and some who deny it with their tongues confess it by their fears.

"Yet I do not mean to add new terrors to those which have already seized upon Pekuah. There can be no reason why specters should haunt the pyramid more than other places, or why they should have power or will to hurt innocence and purity. Our entrance is no violation of their privileges; we can take nothing from them, how then can we offend them?"

"My dear Pekuah," said the princess, "I will always go before you, and Imlac shall follow you. Remember that you are the companion of the princess of Abyssinia."

"If the princess is pleased that her servant should die," returned the lady, "let her command some death less dreadful than enclosure in this horrid cavern. You know I dare not disobey you; I must go if you command me, but if I once enter, I never shall come back."

The princess saw that her fear was too strong for expostulation or reproof, and, embracing her, told her that she should stay in the tent till their return. Pekuah was yet not satisfied, but entreated the princess not to pursue so dreadful a purpose as that of entering the recesses of the pyramid. "Though I cannot teach courage," said Nekayah, "I must not learn cowardice, nor leave at last undone what I came hither only to do."

Chapter XXXII. *They Enter the Pyramid*

Pekuah descended to the tents, and the rest entered the pyramid. They passed through the galleries, surveyed the vaults of marble, and examined the chest in which the body of the founder is supposed to have been reposited. They then sat down in one of the most spacious chambers to rest a while before they attempted to return.

"We have now," said Imlac, "gratified our minds with an exact view of the greatest work of man, except the wall of China.

"Of the wall it is very easy to assign the motive. It secured a wealthy and timorous nation from the incursions of barbarians, whose unskillfulness in arts made it easier for them to supply their wants by rapine than by industry, and who from time to time poured in upon the habitations of peaceful commerce, as vultures descend upon domestic fowl. Their celerity and fierceness made the wall necessary, and their ignorance made it efficacious.

"But for the pyramids, no reason has ever been given adequate to the cost and labor of the work. The narrowness of the chambers proves that it could afford no retreat from enemies, and treasures might have been reposited at far less expense with equal security. It seems to have been erected only in compliance with that hunger of imagination which preys incessantly upon life, and must be always appeased by some employment. Those who have already all that they can enjoy must enlarge their desires. He that has built for use till use is supplied, must begin to build for vanity, and extend his plan to the utmost power of human performance, that he may not be soon reduced to form another wish.

"I consider this mighty structure as a monument of the insufficiency of human enjoyments. A king, whose power is unlimited, and whose treasures surmount all real and imaginary wants, is compelled to solace, by the erection of a pyramid, the satiety of dominion and tastelessness of pleasures, and to amuse the tediousness of declining life by seeing thousands laboring without end, and one stone, for no purpose, laid upon another. Whoever thou art, that, not content with a moderate condition, imaginest happiness in royal magnificence, and dreamest that command or riches can feed the appetite of novelty with perpetual gratifications, survey the pyramids, and confess thy folly!"[7]

Chapter XLIV. The Dangerous Prevalence[8] of Imagination

"Disorders of intellect," answered Imlac, "happen much more often than superficial observers will easily believe. Perhaps, if we speak with rigorous exactness, no human mind is in its right state. There is no man whose imagination does not sometimes predominate over his reason, who can regulate his attention wholly by his will, and whose ideas will come and go at his command. No man will be found in whose mind airy notions do not sometimes tyrannize, and force him to hope or fear beyond the limits of sober probability. All power of fancy over reason is a degree of insanity; but while this power is such as we can control and repress, it is not visible to others, nor considered as any depravation of the mental faculties; it is not pronounced madness but when it comes ungovernable, and apparently influences speech or action.

"To indulge the power of fiction, and send imagination out upon the wing, is often the sport of those who delight too much in silent speculation. When we are alone we are not always busy; the labor of excogitation is too violent to last long; the ardor of inquiry will sometimes give way to idleness or satiety. He who has nothing external that can divert him must find pleasure in his own thoughts, and must conceive himself what he is not; for who is pleased with what he is? He then expatiates in boundless futurity, and culls from all imaginable conditions that which for the present moment he should most desire, amuses his desires with impossible enjoyments, and confers upon his pride unattainable dominion. The mind dances from scene to scene, unites all pleasures in all combinations, and riots in delights which nature and fortune, with all their bounty, cannot bestow.

"In time, some particular train of ideas fixes the attention; all other intellectual gratifications are rejected; the mind, in weariness

7. Chapters XXXIII-XLIII are here omitted. While the travelers are in the Pyramid, Pekuah is abducted by an Arab chieftain, from whom she is eventually ransomed. The travelers return to Cairo, and Imlac makes the acquaintance of an astronomer, who proves to be mad, having yielded to the delusion that he has learned to control the weather. Chapter XLIII concludes: "Rasselas * * * inquired of Imlac whether he thought such maladies of the mind frequent, and how they were contracted."

8. Predominance.

or leisure, recurs constantly to the favorite conception, and feasts on the luscious falsehood, whenever she is offended with the bitterness of truth. By degrees the reign of fancy is confirmed; she grows first imperious, and in time despotic. Then fictions begin to operate as realities, false opinions fasten upon the mind, and life passes in dreams of rapture or of anguish.

"This, sir, is one of the dangers of solitude, which the hermit has confessed not always to promote goodness, and the astronomer's misery has proved to be not always propitious to wisdom."

"I will no more," said the favorite, "imagine myself the queen of Abyssinia. I have often spent the hours which the princess gave to my own disposal, in adjusting ceremonies and regulating the court; I have repressed the pride of the powerful, and granted the petitions of the poor; I have built new palaces in more happy situations, planted groves upon the tops of mountains, and have exulted in the beneficence of royalty, till, when the princess entered, I had almost forgotten to bow down before her."

"And I," said the princess, "will not allow myself any more to play the shepherdess in my waking dreams. I have often soothed my thoughts with the quiet and innocence of pastoral employments, till I have in my chamber heard the winds whistle, and the sheep bleat; sometimes freed the lamb entangled in the thicket, and sometimes with my crook encountered the wolf. I have a dress like that of the village maids, which I put on to help my imagination, and a pipe on which I play softly, and suppose myself followed by my flocks."

"I will confess," said the prince, "an indulgence of fantastic delight more dangerous than yours. I have frequently endeavored to image the possibility of a perfect government, by which all wrong should be restrained, all vice reformed, and all the subjects preserved in tranquility and innocence. This thought produced innumerable schemes of reformation, and dictated many useful regulations and salutary edicts. This has been the sport, and sometimes the labor, of my solitude; and I start, when I think with how little anguish I once supposed the death of my father and my brothers."

"Such," says Imlac, "are the effects of visionary schemes; when we first form them, we know them to be absurd, but familiarize them by degrees, and in time lose sight of their folly."

Chapter XLV. They Discourse with an Old Man

The evening was now far past, and they rose to return home. As they walked along the bank of the Nile, delighted with the beams of the moon quivering on the water, they saw at a small distance an old man, whom the prince had often heard in the assembly of the sages. "Yonder," said he, "is one whose years have calmed his passions, but not clouded his reason. Let us close the disquisitions of the night by inquiring what are his sentiments of his own state, that we may know whether youth alone is to struggle with vexation, and whether any better hope remains for the latter part of life."

Here the sage approached and saluted them. They invited him to join their walk, and prattled a while, as acquaintance that had unexpectedly met one another. The old man was cheerful and talkative, and the way seemed short in his company. He was pleased to find himself not disregarded, accompanied them to their house, and, at the prince's request, entered with them. They placed him in the seat of honor, and set wine and conserves before him.

"Sir," said the princess, "an evening walk must give to a man of learning like you pleasures which ignorance and youth can hardly conceive. You know the qualities and the causes of all that you behold, the laws by which the river flows, the periods in which the planets perform their revolutions. Everything must supply you with contemplation, and renew the consciousness of your own dignity."

"Lady," answered he, "let the gay and the vigorous expect pleasure in their excursions; it is enough that age can obtain ease. To me the world has lost its novelty; I look round, and see what I remember to have seen in happier days. I rest against a tree, and consider that in the same shade I once disputed upon the annual overflow of the Nile with a friend who is now silent in the grave. I cast my eyes upward, fix them on the changing moon, and think with pain on the vicissitudes of life. I have ceased to take much delight in physical truth; for what have I to do with those things which I am soon to leave?"

"You may at least recreate yourself," said Imlac, "with the recollection of an honorable and useful life, and enjoy the praise which all agree to give you."

"Praise," said the sage with a sigh, "is to an old man an empty sound. I have neither mother to be delighted with the reputation of her son, nor wife to partake the honors of her husband. I have outlived my friends and my rivals. Nothing is now of much importance; for I cannot extend my interest beyond myself. Youth is delighted with applause, because it is considered as the earnest of some future good, and because the prospect of life is far extended; but to me, who am now declining to decrepitude, there is little to be feared from the malevolence of men, and yet less to be hoped from their affection or esteem. Something they may yet take away, but they can give me nothing. Riches would now be useless, and high employment would be pain. My retrospect of life recalls to my view many opportunities of good neglected, much time squandered upon trifles, and more lost in idleness and vacancy. I leave many great designs unattempted, and many great attempts unfinished. My mind is burthened with no heavy crime, and therefore I compose myself to tranquility; endeavor to abstract my thoughts from hopes and cares which, though reason knows them to be vain, still try to keep their old possession of the heart; expect,[9] with serene humility, that hour which nature cannot long delay; and hope to possess, in a better state, that happiness which here I could not find, and that virtue which here I have not attained."

He arose and went away, leaving his audience not much elated with the hope of long life. The prince consoled himself with remarking that it was not reasonable to be disappointed by this account; for age had never been considered as the season of felicity, and if it was possible to be easy in decline and weakness, it was likely that the days of vigor and alacrity might be happy; that the noon of life might be bright, if the evening could be calm.

The princess suspected that age was querulous and malignant, and delighted to repress the expectations of those who had newly entered the world. She had seen the possessors of estates look with envy on their heirs, and known many who enjoy pleasure no longer than they can confine it to themselves.

Pekuah conjectured that the man was older than he appeared, and was willing to impute his complaints to delirious dejection; or else supposed that he had been unfortunate, and was therefore discontented. "For nothing," said she, "is more common than to call our own condition the condition of life."

Imlac, who had no desire to see them depressed, smiled at the comforts which they could so readily procure to themselves, and remembered that, at the same age, he was equally confident of unmingled prosperity, and equally fertile of consolatory expedients. He forebore to force upon them unwelcome knowledge, which time itself would too soon impress. The princess and her lady retired; the madness of the astronomer hung upon their minds, and they desired Imlac to enter upon his office, and delay next morning the rising of the sun.[1]

Chapter XLIX. The Conclusion, in Which Nothing Is Concluded

It was now the time of the inundation of the Nile: a few days after their visit to the catacombs, the river began to rise.

They were confined to their house. The whole region being under water gave them no invitation to any excursions, and being well supplied with materials for talk, they diverted themselves with comparisons of the different forms of life which they had observed, and with various schemes of happiness which each of them had formed.

9. Await.

1. Chapters XLVI-XLVIII are here omitted. The travelers converse with the astronomer and learn that he too regrets his choice of life. A discourse on the nature of the soul (in the penultimate chapter) raises the hope of happiness in a future state.

Pekuah was never so much charmed with any place as the convent of St. Anthony, where the Arab restored her to the princess, and wished only to fill it with pious maidens, and to be made prioress of the order; she was weary of expectation and disgust,[2] and would gladly be fixed in some unvariable state.

The princess thought that, of all sublunary things, knowledge was the best: she desired first to learn all sciences, and then purposed to found a college of learned women, in which she would preside, that, by conversing with the old and educating the young, she might divide her time between the acquisition and communication of wisdom, and raise up for the next age models of prudence, and patterns of piety.

The prince desired a little kingdom, in which he might administer justice in his own person, and see all the parts of government with his own eyes; but he could never fix the limits of his dominion, and was always adding to the number of his subjects.

Imlac and the astronomer were contented to be driven along the stream of life, without directing their course to any particular port.

Of these wishes that they had formed, they well knew that none could be obtained. They deliberated a while what was to be done, and resolved, when the inundation should cease, to return to Abyssinia.[3]

[1]759

From Prayers and Meditations[1]

Easter Eve, 1761

Since the communion of last Easter, I have led a life so dissipated and useless, and my terrors and perplexities have so much increased, that I am under great depression and discouragement; yet I purpose to present myself before God tomorrow, with humble hope that he will not break the bruised reed.

Come unto me all ye that travail.[2]

I have resolved, I hope not presumptuously, till I am afraid to resolve again. Yet hoping in God, I steadfastly purpose to lead a new life. O God, enable me, for Jesus Christ's sake.

2. Aversion.
3. Probably not, as is often suggested, to the Happy Valley (in Chapter I we were told that none who leave the valley can ever return). Presumably the travelers return, with whatever wisdom they have gained, but also with their cherished illusions, to share the common destiny of mankind. But Johnson, hurrying to his conclusion, may have left the place to which they returned vague.

1. During much of his life Johnson observed with prayer and meditation certain seasons: his own birthday, the anniversary of the death of his wife, Good Friday, and Easter. He was accustomed to writing down his prayers and thoughts. This document gives a moving insight into his spiritual struggles and his sense of sin.
2. Matthew xi.28.

Good Friday, 1779, 11 P.M.

I am now to review the last year, and find little but dismal vacuity, neither business nor pleasure; much intended, and little done. My health is much broken; my nights afford me little rest. I have tried opium, but its help is counterbalanced with great disturbance; it prevents the spasms, but it hinders sleep. O God, have mercy on me.

Last week I published the *Lives of the Poets*, written, I hope, in such a manner as may tend to the promotion of piety.

In this last year I have made little acquisition; I have scarcely read anything. I maintain Mrs. [Desmoulins] and her daughter. Other good of myself I know not where to find, except a little charity.

But I am now in my seventieth year; what can be done, ought not to be delayed.

Rambler No. 4

[*On Fiction*]

Saturday, March 31, 1750

Simul et jucunda et idonea dicere vitae.
—HORACE, *Art of Poetry*, 334
And join both profit and delight in one.
—CREECH

The works of fiction with which the present generation seems more particularly delighted are such as exhibit life in its true state, diversified only by accidents that daily happen in the world, and influenced by passions and qualities which are really to be found in conversing with mankind.

This kind of writing may be termed, not improperly, the comedy of romance, and is to be conducted nearly by the rules of comic poetry. Its province is to bring about natural events by easy means, and to keep up curiosity without the help of wonder: it is therefore precluded from the machines[1] and expedients of the heroic romance, and can neither employ giants to snatch away a lady from the nuptial rites, nor knights to bring her back from captivity; it can neither bewilder its personages in deserts, nor lodge them in imaginary castles.

I remember a remark made by Scaliger upon Pontanus,[2] that all his writings are filled with the same images; and that if you take from him his lilies and his roses, his satyrs and his dryads, he will have nothing left that can be called poetry. In like manner, almost

1. The technical term in neoclassical critical theory for the supernatural agents who intervene in human affairs in epic and tragedy.

2. Julius Caesar Scaliger (1484–1558) criticized the Latin poems of the Italian poet Jovianus Pontanus (1426–1503).

all the fictions of the last age will vanish if you deprive them of a hermit and a wood, a battle and a shipwreck.

Why this wild strain of imagination found reception so long in polite and learned ages, it is not easy to conceive; but we cannot wonder that while readers could be procured, the authors were willing to continue it; for when a man had by practice gained some fluency of language, he had no further care than to retire to his closet, let loose his invention, and heat his mind with incredibilities; a book was thus produced without fear of criticism, without the toil of study, without knowledge of nature, or acquaintance with life.

The task of our present writers is very different; it requires, together with that learning which is to be gained from books, that experience which can never be attained by solitary diligence, but must arise from general converse and accurate observation of the living world. Their performances have, as Horace expresses it, *plus oneris quanto veniae minus*,[3] little indulgence, and therefore more difficulty. They are engaged in portraits of which everyone knows the original, and can detect any deviation from exactness of resemblance. Other writings are safe, except from the malice of learning, but these are in danger from every common reader; as the slipper ill executed was censured by a shoemaker who happened to stop in his way at the Venus of Appeles.[4]

But the fear of not being approved as just copiers of human manners is not the most important concern that an author of this sort ought to have before him. These books are written chiefly to the young, the ignorant, and the idle, to whom they serve as lectures of conduct, and introductions into life. They are the entertainment of minds unfurnished with ideas, and therefore easily susceptible of impressions; not fixed by principles, and therefore easily following the current of fancy; not informed by experience, and consequently open to every false suggestion and partial account.

That the highest degree of reverence should be paid to youth, and that nothing indecent should be suffered to approach their eyes or ears, are precepts extorted by sense and virtue from an ancient writer by no means eminent for chastity of thought. The same kind, though not the same degree, of caution, is required in everything which is laid before them, to secure them from unjust prejudices, perverse opinions, and incongruous combinations of images.

In the romances formerly written, every transaction and sentiment was so remote from all that passes among men that the reader was in very little danger of making any applications to himself; the virtues and crimes were equally beyond his sphere of activity; and

3. *Epistles* II.i.170.
4. According to Pliny the Younger (*Naturalis Historia* XXXV.85), the Greek painter Apelles of Kos (4th century B.C.) corrected the drawing of a sandal after hearing a shoemaker criticize it as faulty, but when the flattered artisan dared to find fault with the drawing of a leg, the artist bade him "stick to his last."

he amused himself with heroes and with traitors, deliverers and persecutors, as with beings of another species, whose actions were regulated upon motives of their own, and who had neither faults nor excellencies in common with himself.

But when an adventurer is leveled with the rest of the world, and acts in such scenes of the universal drama as may be the lot of any other man, young spectators fix their eyes upon him with closer attention, and hope, by observing his behavior and success, to regulate their own practices when they shall be engaged in the like part.

For this reason these familiar histories may perhaps be made of greater use than the solemnities of professed morality, and convey the knowledge of vice and virtue with more efficacy than axioms and definitions. But if the power of example is so great as to take possession of the memory by a kind of violence, and produce effects almost without the intervention of the will, care ought to be taken that when the choice is unrestrained, the best examples only should be exhibited; and that which is likely to operate so strongly should not be mischievous or uncertain in its effects.

The chief advantage which these fictions have over real life is that their authors are at liberty, though not to invent, yet to select objects, and to cull from the mass of mankind those individuals upon which the attention ought most to be employed; as a diamond, though it cannot be made, may be polished by art, and placed in such situation as to display that luster which before was buried among common stones.

It is justly considered as the greatest excellency of art to imitate nature; but it is necessary to distinguish those parts of nature which are most proper for imitation: greater care is still required in representing life, which is so often discolored by passion or deformed by wickedness. If the world be promiscuously described, I cannot see of what use it can be to read the account; or why it may not be as safe to turn the eye immediately upon mankind as upon a mirror which shows all that presents itself without discrimination.

It is therefore not a sufficient vindication of a character that it is drawn as it appears; for many characters ought never to be drawn: nor of a narrative that the train of events is agreeable to observation and experience; for that observation which is called knowledge of the world will be found much more frequently to make men cunning than good. The purpose of these writings is surely not only to show mankind, but to provide that they may be seen hereafter with less hazard; to teach the means of avoiding the snares which are laid by Treachery for Innocence, without infusing any wish for that superiority with which the betrayer flatters his vanity; to give the power of counteracting fraud without the temptation to practice it; to initiate youth by mock encounters in the art of necessary defense, and to increase prudence without impairing virtue.

Many writers, for the sake of following nature, so mingle good and bad qualities in their principal personages that they are both equally conspicuous; and as we accompany them through their adventures with delight, and are led by degrees to interest ourselves in their favor, we lose the abhorrence of their faults because they do not hinder our pleasure, or perhaps regard them with some kindness for being united with so much merit.

There have been men indeed splendidly wicked, whose endowments threw a brightness on their crimes, and whom scarce any villainy made perfectly detestable because they never could be wholly divested of their excellencies; but such have been in all ages the great corrupters of the world, and their resemblance ought no more to be preserved than the art of murdering without pain.

Some have advanced, without due attention to the consequence of this notion, that certain virtues have their correspondent faults, and therefore that to exhibit either apart is to deviate from probability. Thus men are observed by Swift to be "grateful in the same degree as they are resentful." This principle, with others of the same kind, supposes man to act from a brute impulse, and pursue a certain degree of inclination without any choice of the object; for, otherwise, though it should be allowed that gratitude and resentment arise from the same constitution of the passions, it follows not that they will be equally indulged when reason is consulted; yet, unless that consequence be admitted, this sagacious maxim becomes an empty sound, without any relation to practice or to life.

Nor is it evident that even the first motions to these effects are always in the same proportion. For pride, which produces quickness of resentment, will obstruct gratitude by unwillingness to admit that inferiority which obligation implies; and it is very unlikely that he who cannot think he receives a favor will acknowledge or repay it.

It is of the utmost importance to mankind that positions of this tendency should be laid open and confuted; for while men consider good and evil as springing from the same root, they will spare the one for the sake of the other, and in judging, if not of others at least of themselves, will be apt to estimate their virtues by their vices. To this fatal error all those will contribute who confound the colors of right and wrong, and, instead of helping to settle their boundaries, mix them with so much art that no common mind is able to disunite them.

In narratives where historical veracity has no place, I cannot discover why there should not be exhibited the most perfect idea of virtue; of virtue not angelical, nor above probability (for what we cannot credit, we shall never imitate), but the highest and purest that humanity can reach, which, exercised in such trials as the various revolutions of things shall bring upon it, may, by conquering some calamities and enduring others, teach us what we may hope, and what we can perform. Vice (for vice is necessary to be shown) should always disgust; nor should the graces of gaiety, nor the dignity of courage, be so united with it as to reconcile it to the mind. Wherever it appears, it should raise hatred by the malignity of its practices, and contempt by the meanness of its stratagems: for while it is supported by either parts or spirit, it will be seldom heartily abhorred. The Roman tyrant was content to be hated if he was but feared;[5] and there are thousands of the readers of romances willing to be thought wicked if they may be allowed to be wits. It is therefore to be steadily inculcated that virtue is the highest proof of understanding, and the only solid basis of greatness; and that vice is the natural consequence of narrow thoughts; that it begins in mistake, and ends in ignominy.

From The Preface to Shakespeare[1]
[*Shakespeare and General Nature*]

The poet of whose works I have undertaken the revision may now begin to assume the dignity of an ancient and claim the privilege of established fame and prescriptive veneration. He has long outlived his century, the term commonly fixed as the test of literary merit.[1a] Whatever advantages he might once derive from personal allusions, local customs, or temporary opinions, have for many years been lost; and every topic of merriment or motive of sorrow which the modes of artificial life afforded him now only obscure the scenes which they once illuminated. The effects of favor and competition are at an end; the tradition of his friendships and his enmities has perished; his works support no opinion with arguments nor

5. The Emperor Tiberius. See Suetonius' *Lives of the Caesars*.
1. This, the finest piece of Shakespeare criticism in the 18th century, is the culmination of a critical tradition that began with Nicholas Rowe's edition of the plays in 1709 (indeed with Dryden's critical remarks on Shakespeare) and that was continued by subsequent editors, notably Pope, Lewis Theobald, and William Warburton. Johnson's topics are in the main the conventional ones of 18th-century Shakespeare criticism: Shakespeare as the poet of nature, not of learning; as the creator of memorable characters; as a poet who supremely expresses and evokes the passions. Johnson follows his tradition in weighing Shakespeare's poetic virtues against his faults and finding that the virtues out-

weigh the faults. No one has praised Shakespeare more nobly and generously. The *Preface* is most original when Johnson attacks and dismisses the long-standing reverence in critical theory for the unities of time and place. By appealing to the experience of the play-goer, he demonstrates that, thanks to the imagination of the spectator, the playwright need not contain his action within a period of twenty-four hours or restrict it to one place throughout the drama.
  Johnson's edition of Shakespeare also contained footnotes and brief introductions to each of the plays. We reprint here the introductory headnote to the two Henry IV plays.
1a. Horace, *Epistles* II.1.39.

supply any faction with invectives; they can neither indulge vanity nor gratify malignity; but are read without any other reason than the desire of pleasure, and are therefore praised only as pleasure is obtained; yet, thus unassisted by interest or passion, they have passed through variations of taste and changes of manners, and, as they devolved from one generation to another, have received new honors at every transmission.

But because human judgment, though it be gradually gaining upon certainty, never becomes infallible, and approbation, though long continued, may yet be only the approbation of prejudice or fashion, it is proper to inquire by what peculiarities of excellence Shakespeare has gained and kept the favor of his countrymen.

Nothing can please many, and please long, but just representations of general nature. Particular manners can be known to few, and therefore few only can judge how nearly they are copied. The irregular combinations of fanciful invention may delight awhile by that novelty of which the common satiety of life sends us all in quest; but the pleasures of sudden wonder are soon exhausted, and the mind can only repose on the stability of truth.

Shakespeare is, above all writers, at least above all modern writers, the poet of nature, the poet that holds up to his readers a faithful mirror of manners and of life. His characters are not modified by the customs of particular places, unpracticed by the rest of the world; by the peculiarities of studies or professions, which can operate but upon small numbers; or by the accidents of transient fashions or temporary opinions: they are the genuine progeny of common humanity, such as the world will always supply and observation will always find. His persons act and speak by the influence of those general passions and principles by which all minds are agitated and the whole system of life is continued in motion. In the writings of other poets a character is too often an individual: in those of Shakespeare it is commonly a species.

It is from this wide extension of design that so much instruction is derived. It is this which fills the plays of Shakespeare with practical axioms and domestic wisdom. It was said of Euripides[2] that every verse was a precept; and it may be said of Shakespeare that from his works may be collected a system of civil and economical prudence. Yet his real power is not shown in the splendor of particular passages, but by the progress of his fable and the tenor of his dialogue; and he that tries to recommend him by select quotations will succeed like the pedant in Hierocles[3] who, when he offered his house to sale, carried a brick in his pocket as a specimen.

It will not easily be imagined how much Shakespeare excels in accommodating his sentiments to real life but by comparing him

2. The Greek tragic poet (ca. 480–406 B.C.). The observation is Cicero's. 3. Hierocles of Alexandria, a Greek philosopher of the 5th century A.D.

with other authors. It was observed of the ancient schools of declamation that the more diligently they were frequented, the more was
the student disqualified for the world, because he found nothing
there which he should ever meet in any other place. The same remark may be applied to every stage but that of Shakespeare. The
theater, when it is under any other direction, is peopled by such
characters as were never seen, conversing in a language which was
never heard, upon topics which will never arise in the commerce
of mankind. But the dialogue of this author is often so evidently
determined by the incident which produces it, and is pursued with
so much ease and simplicity, that it seems scarcely to claim the
merit of fiction, but to have been gleaned by diligent selection out
of common conversation and common occurrences.

Upon every other stage the universal agent is love, by whose
power all good and evil is distributed and every action quickened
or retarded. To bring a lover, a lady, and a rival into the fable; to
entangle them in contradictory obligations, perplex them with
oppositions of interest, and harass them with violence of desires inconsistent with each other; to make them meet in rapture, and
part in agony; to fill their mouths with hyperbolical joy and outrageous sorrow; to distress them as nothing human ever was distressed; to deliver them as nothing human ever was delivered, is the
business of a modern dramatist. For this, probability is violated,
life is misrepresented, and language is depraved. But love is only
one of many passions; and as it has no great influence upon the
sum of life, it has little operation in the dramas of a poet who
caught his ideas from the living world and exhibited only what
he saw before him. He knew that any other passion, as it was regular or exorbitant, was a cause of happiness or calamity.

Characters thus ample and general were not easily discriminated
and preserved; yet perhaps no poet ever kept his personages more
distinct from each other. I will not say with Pope that every speech
may be assigned to the proper speaker,[4] because many speeches
there are which have nothing characteristical; but perhaps though
some may be equally adapted to every person, it will be difficult to
find that any can be properly transferred from the present possessor
to another claimant. The choice is right when there is reason for
choice.

Other dramatists can only gain attention by hyperbolical or aggravated characters, by fabulous and unexampled excellence or de-
pravity, as the writers of barbarous romances invigorated the reader
by a giant and a dwarf; and he that should form his expectations of
human affairs from the play or from the tale would be equally deceived. Shakespeare has no heroes; his scenes are occupied only by
men, who act and speak as the reader thinks that he should himself

4. In the preface to his edition of Shakespeare's plays (1725).

have spoken or acted on the same occasion; even where the agency is supernatural, the dialogue is level with life. Other writers disguise the most natural passions and most frequent incidents so that he who contemplates them in the book will not know them in the world: Shakespeare approximates[5] the remote, and familiarizes the wonderful; the event which he represents will not happen, but, if it were possible, its effects would probably be such as he has assigned; and it may be said that he has not only shown human nature as it acts in real exigencies, but as it would be found in trials to which it cannot be exposed.

This therefore is the praise of Shakespeare, that his drama is the mirror of life; that he who has mazed his imagination in following the phantoms which other writers raise up before him, may here be cured of his delirious ecstasies by reading human sentiments in human language, by scenes from which a hermit may estimate the transactions of the world, and a confessor predict the progress of the passions.

[Shakespeare's Faults. The Three Dramatic Unities]

Shakespeare with his excellencies has likewise faults, and faults sufficient to obscure and overwhelm any other merit. I shall show them in the proportion in which they appear to me, without envious malignity or superstitious veneration. No question can be more innocently discussed than a dead poet's pretensions to renown; and little regard is due to that bigotry which sets candor[6] higher than truth.

His first defect is that to which may be imputed most of the evil in books or in men. He sacrifices virtue to convenience, and is so much more careful to please than to instruct that he seems to write without any moral purpose. From his writings indeed a system of social duty may be selected, for he that thinks reasonably must think morally, but his precepts and axioms drop casually from him; he makes no just distribution of good or evil, nor is always careful to show in the virtuous a disapprobation of the wicked; he carries his persons indifferently through right and wrong, and at the close dismisses them without further care, and leaves their examples to operate by chance. This fault the barbarity of his age cannot extenuate; for it is always a writer's duty to make the world better, and justice is a virtue independent on time or place.

The plots are often so loosely formed that a very slight consideration may improve them, and so carelessly pursued that he seems not always fully to comprehend his own design. He omits opportunities of instructing or delighting which the train of his story seems to force upon him, and apparently rejects those exhibitions

5. Brings near.   6. Kindness.

which would be more affecting for the sake of those which are more easy.

It may be observed that in many of his plays the latter part is evidently neglected. When he found himself near the end of his work, and in view of his reward, he shortened the labor to snatch the profit. He therefore remits his efforts where he should most vigorously exert them, and his catastrophe is improbably produced or imperfectly represented.

He had no regard to distinction of time or place, but gives to one age or nation, without scruple, the customs, institutions, and opinions of another, at the expense not only of likelihood but of possibility. These faults Pope has endeavored, with more zeal than judgment, to transfer to his imagined interpolators. We need not wonder to find Hector quoting Aristotle, when we see the loves of Theseus and Hippolyta combined with the Gothic mythology of fairies.[7] Shakespeare, indeed, was not the only violator of chronology, for in the same age Sidney, who wanted not the advantages of learning, has, in his *Arcadia,* confounded the pastoral with the feudal times, the days of innocence, quiet, and security with those of turbulence, violence, and adventure.

In his comic scenes he is seldom very successful when he engages his characters in reciprocations of smartness and contests of sarcasm; their jests are commonly gross, and their pleasantry licentious; neither his gentlemen nor his ladies have much delicacy, nor are sufficiently distinguished from his clowns by any appearance of refined manners. Whether he represented the real conversation of his time is not easy to determine: the reign of Elizabeth is commonly supposed to have been a time of stateliness, formality, and reserve; yet perhaps the relaxations of that severity were not very elegant. There must, however, have been always some modes of gaiety preferable to others, and a writer ought to choose the best.

In tragedy his performance seems constantly to be worse as his labor is more. The effusions of passion, which exigence forces out, are for the most part striking and energetic; but whenever he solicits his invention, or strains his faculties, the offspring of his throes is tumor,[8] meanness, tediousness, and obscurity.

In narration he affects a disproportionate pomp of diction and a wearisome train of circumlocution, and tells the incident imperfectly in many words which might have been more plainly delivered in few. Narration in dramatic poetry is naturally tedious, as it is unanimated and inactive, and obstructs the progress of the action; it should therefore always be rapid and enlivened by frequent interruption. Shakespeare found it an encumbrance, and instead of

7. In *Troilus and Cressida,* II.2.166, and in *Midsummer Night's Dream,* re- spectively.

8. Inflated grandeur, false magnificence.

lightening it by brevity, endeavored to recommend it by dignity and splendor.

His declamations or set speeches are commonly cold and weak, for his power was the power of nature; when he endeavored, like other tragic writers, to catch opportunities of amplification and, instead of inquiring what the occasion demanded, to show how much his stores of knowledge could supply, he seldom escapes without the pity or resentment of his reader.

It is incident to him to be now and then entangled with an unwieldy sentiment which he cannot well express, and will not reject; he struggles with it awhile, and, if it continues stubborn, comprises it in words such as occur, and leaves it to be disentangled and evolved by those who have more leisure to bestow upon it.

Not that always where the language is intricate the thought is subtle, or the image always great where the line is bulky; the equality of words to things is very often neglected, and trivial sentiments and vulgar[9] ideas disappoint the attention, to which they are recommended by sonorous epithets and swelling figures.

But the admirers of this great poet have most reason to complain when he approaches nearest to his highest excellence, and seems fully resolved to sink them in dejection and mollify them with tender emotions by the fall of greatness, the danger of innocence, or the crosses of love. What he does best, he soon ceases to do. He is not long soft and pathetic without some idle conceit or contemptible equivocation. He no sooner begins to move than he counteracts himself; and terror and pity, as they are rising in the mind, are checked and blasted by sudden frigidity.

A quibble[1] is to Shakespeare what luminous vapors are to the traveler: he follows it at all adventures; it is sure to lead him out of his way, and sure to engulf him in the mire. It has some malignant power over his mind, and its fascinations are irresistible. Whatever be the dignity or profundity of his disquisitions, whether he be enlarging knowledge or exalting affection, whether he be amusing[2] attention with incidents, or enchaining it in suspense, let but a quibble spring up before him, and he leaves his work unfinished. A quibble is the golden apple for which he will always turn aside from his career[3] or stoop from his elevation. A quibble, poor and barren as it is, gave him such delight that he was content to purchase it by the sacrifice of reason, propriety, and truth. A

9. "Mean; low; being of the common rate" (Johnson's *Dictionary*).
1. Pun.
2. "To entertain with tranquility; to fill with thoughts that engage the mind, without distracting it" (Johnson's *Dictionary*).

3. In Greek legend Atalanta refused to marry any man who could not defeat her in a foot race. Hippomenes won her by dropping, as he ran, three of the golden apples of the Hesperides, which she paused to pick up.

quibble was to him the fatal Cleopatra for which he lost the world, and was content to lose it.

It will be thought strange that in enumerating the defects of this writer, I have not yet mentioned his neglect of the unities; his violation of those laws which have been instituted and established by the joint authority of poets and critics.

For his other deviations from the art of writing, I resign him to critical justice without making any other demand in his favor than that which must be indulged to all human excellence: that his virtues be rated with his failings. But from the censure which this irregularity may bring upon him I shall, with due reverence to that learning which I must oppose, adventure to try how I can defend him.

His histories, being neither tragedies nor comedies, are not subject to any of their laws; nothing more is necessary to all the praise which they expect than that the changes of action be so prepared as to be understood; that the incidents be various and affecting, and the characters consistent, natural, and distinct. No other unity is intended, and therefore none is to be sought.

In his other works he has well enough preserved the unity of action. He has not, indeed, an intrigue regularly perplexed and regularly unraveled: he does not endeavor to hide his design only to discover it, for this is seldom the order of real events, and Shakespeare is the poet of nature: but his plan has commonly what Aristotle requires,[4] a beginning, a middle, and an end; one event is concatenated with another, and the conclusion follows by easy consequence. There are, perhaps, some incidents that might be spared, as in other poets there is much talk that only fills up time upon the stage; but the general system makes gradual advances, and the end of the play is the end of expectation.

To the unities of time and place he has shown no regard; and perhaps a nearer view of the principles on which they stand will diminish their value and withdraw from them the veneration which, from the time of Corneille,[5] they have very generally received, by discovering that they have given more trouble to the poet than pleasure to the auditor.

The necessity of observing the unities of time and place arises from the supposed necessity of making the drama credible. The critics hold it impossible that an action of months or years can be possibly believed to pass in three hours; or that the spectator can suppose himself to sit in the theater while ambassadors go and return between distant kings, while armies are levied and towns besieged, while an exile wanders and returns, or till he whom they saw court-

4. *Poetics* VII.
5. Pierre Corneille (1606–84), the French playwright, discussed the unities in his *Discours des trois unités* (1660).

ing his mistress shall lament the untimely fall of his son. The mind revolts from evident falsehood, and fiction loses its force when it departs from the resemblance of reality.

From the narrow limitation of time necessarily arises the contraction of place. The spectator who knows that he saw the first act at Alexandria cannot suppose that he sees the next at Rome, at a distance to which not the dragons of Medea could, in so short a time, have transported him; he knows with certainty that he has not changed his place; and he knows that place cannot change itself, that what was a house cannot become a plain, that what was Thebes can never be Persepolis.

Such is the triumphant language with which a critic exults over the misery of an irregular poet, and exults commonly without resistance or reply. It is time, therefore, to tell him by the authority of Shakespeare that he assumes, as an unquestionable principle, a position which, while his breath is forming it into words, his understanding pronounces to be false. It is false that any representation is mistaken for reality; that any dramatic fable in its materiality was ever credible or, for a single moment, was ever credited.

The objection arising from the impossibility of passing the first hour at Alexandria and the next at Rome supposes that when the play opens the spectator really imagines himself at Alexandria, and believes that his walk to the theater has been a voyage to Egypt, and that he lives in the days of Antony and Cleopatra. Surely he that imagines this may imagine more. He that can take the stage at one time for the palace of the Ptolemies may take it in half an hour for the promontory of Actium. Delusion, if delusion be admitted, has no certain limitation; if the spectator can be once persuaded that his old acquaintances are Alexander and Caesar, that a room illuminated with candles is the plain of Pharsalia or the bank of Granicus, he is in a state of elevation above the reach of reason or of truth, and from the heights of empyrean poetry may despise the circumscriptions of terrestrial nature. There is no reason why a mind thus wandering in ecstasy should count the clock, or why an hour should not be a century in that calenture[6] of the brain that can make the stage a field.

The truth is that the spectators are always in their senses, and know, from the first act to the last, that the stage is only a stage, and that the players are only players. They came to hear a certain number of lines recited with just gesture and elegant modulation. The lines relate to some action, and an action must be in some place; but the different actions that complete a story may be in places very remote from each other; and where is the absurdity of

6. A delirium produced by tropical heat, which causes sailors to leap into the sea under the delusion that it is a green field.

allowing that space to represent first Athens, and then Sicily, which was always known to be neither Sicily nor Athens but a modern theater?

By supposition, as place is introduced, time may be extended; the time required by the fable elapses, for the most part, between the acts; for, of so much of the action as is represented, the real and poetical duration is the same. If, in the first act, preparations for war against Mithridates are represented to be made in Rome, the event of the war may, without absurdity, be represented, in the catastrophe, as happening in Pontus; we know that there is neither war nor preparation for war; we know that we are neither in Rome nor Pontus, that neither Mithridates nor Lucullus are before us. The drama exhibits successive imitations of successive actions; and why may not the second imitation represent an action that happened years after the first, if it be so connected with it that nothing but time can be supposed to intervene? Time is, of all modes of existence, most obsequious[7] to the imagination; a lapse of years is as easily conceived as a passage of hours. In contemplation we easily contract the time of real actions, and therefore willingly permit it to be contracted when we only see their imitation.

It will be asked how the drama moves if it is not credited. It is credited with all the credit due to a drama. It is credited, whenever it moves, as a just picture of a real original; as representing to the auditor what he would himself feel if he were to do or suffer what is there feigned to be suffered or to be done. The reflection that strikes the heart is not that the evils before us are real evils, but that they are evils to which we ourselves may be exposed. If there be any fallacy, it is not that we fancy the players, but that we fancy ourselves, unhappy for a moment; but we rather lament the possibility than suppose the presence of misery, as a mother weeps over her babe when she remembers that death may take it from her. The delight of tragedy proceeds from our consciousness of fiction; if we thought murders and treasons real, they would please no more.

Imitations produce pain or pleasure, not because they are mistaken for realities, but because they bring realities to mind. When the imagination is recreated by a painted landscape, the trees are not supposed capable to give us shade or the fountains coolness; but we consider how we should be pleased with such fountains playing beside us and such woods waving over us. We are agitated in reading the history of *Henry the Fifth;* yet no man takes his book for the field of Agincourt. A dramatic exhibition is a book recited with concomitants that increase or diminish its effect. Familiar comedy is often more powerful on the theater than in the page; imperial tragedy is always less. The humor of Petruchio may be heightened by grimace; but what voice or what gesture can hope to

7. "Obedient; compliant" (Johnson's *Dictionary*).

add dignity or force to the soliloquy of Cato?[8]

A play read affects the mind like a play acted. It is therefore evident that the action is not supposed to be real; and it follows that between the acts a longer or shorter time may be allowed to pass, and that no more account of space or duration is to be taken by the auditor of a drama than by the reader of a narrative, before whom may pass in an hour the life of a hero or the revolutions of an empire.

Whether Shakespeare knew the unities and rejected them by design or deviated from them by happy ignorance, it is, I think, impossible to decide and useless to inquire. We may reasonably suppose that, when he rose to notice, he did not want[9] the counsels and admonitions of scholars and critics, and that he at last deliberately persisted in a practice which he might have begun by chance. As nothing is essential to the fable but unity of action, and as the unities of time and place arise evidently from false assumptions, and, by circumscribing the extent of the drama, lessen its variety, I cannot think it much to be lamented that they were not known by him, or not observed: nor, if such another poet could arise, should I very vehemently reproach him that his first act passed at Venice and his next in Cyprus.[1] Such violations of rules merely positive become the comprehensive genius of Shakespeare, and such censures are suitable to the minute and slender criticism of Voltaire.

> *Non usque adeo permiscuit imis*
> *Longus summa dies, ut non, si voce Metelli*
> *Serventur leges, malint a Caesare tolli.*[2]

Yet when I speak thus slightly of dramatic rules, I cannot but recollect how much wit and learning may be produced against me; before such authorities I am afraid to stand: not that I think the present question one of those that are to be decided by mere authority, but because it is to be suspected that these precepts have not been so easily received but for better reasons than I have yet been able to find. The result of my inquiries, in which it would be ludicrous to boast of impartiality, is that the unities of time and place are not essential to a just drama, that though they may sometimes conduce to pleasure, they are always to be sacrificed to the nobler beauties of variety and instruction; and that a play written with nice observation of critical rules is to be contemplated as an elaborate curiosity, as the product of superfluous and ostentatious art, by which is shown rather what is possible than what is necessary.

8. Petruchio is the hero of Shakespeare's comedy *The Taming of the Shrew*. In Addison's tragedy *Cato* (V.i), the hero soliloquizes on immortality shortly before committing suicide.
9. Lack.

1. As is the case in *Othello*.
2. Lucan, *Pharsalia* III.138–40: "The course of time has not wrought such confusion that the laws would not rather be trampled on by Caesar than saved by Metellus."

He that without diminution of any other excellence shall preserve all the unities unbroken deserves the like applause with the architect who shall display all the orders of architecture in a citadel without any deduction for its strength; but the principal beauty of a citadel is to exclude the enemy, and the greatest graces of a play are to copy nature and instruct life. * * *

[*Henry IV*]

None of Shakespeare's plays are more read than the first and second parts of *Henry the fourth*. Perhaps no author has ever in two plays afforded so much delight. The great events are interesting, for the fate of kingdoms depends upon them; the slighter occurrences are diverting, and, except one or two, sufficiently probable; the incidents are multiplied with wonderful fertility of invention, and the characters diversified with the utmost nicety of discernment, and the profoundest skill in the nature of man.

The prince, who is the hero both of the comic and tragic part, is a young man of great abilities and violent passions, whose sentiments are right, though his actions are wrong; whose virtues are obscured by negligence, and whose understanding is dissipated by levity. In his idle hours he is rather loose than wicked, and when the occasion forces out his latent qualities, he is great without effort, and brave without tumult. The trifler is roused into a hero, and the hero again reposes in the trifler. This character is great, original, and just.[3]

Percy is a rugged soldier, choleric, and quarrelsome, and has only the soldier's virtues, generosity and courage.

But Falstaff, unimitated, unimitable Falstaff, how shall I describe thee? Thou compound of sense and vice; of sense which may be admired but not esteemed, of vice which may be despised, but hardly detested. Falstaff is a character loaded with faults, and with those faults which naturally produce contempt. He is a thief, and a glutton, a coward, and a boaster, always ready to cheat the weak, and prey upon the poor; to terrify the timorous and insult the defenseless. At once obsequious and malignant, he satirizes in their absence those whom he lives by flattering. He is familiar with the prince only as an agent of vice, but of this familiarity he is so proud as not only to be supercilious and haughty with common men, but to think his interest of importance to the duke of Lancaster. Yet the man thus corrupt, thus despicable, makes himself necessary to the prince that despises him, by the most pleasing of all qualities, perpetual gaiety, by an unfailing power of exciting laughter, which is the more freely indulged, as his wit is not of the splendid or ambitious kind, but consists in easy escapes and sallies of levity, which make sport but raise no envy. It must be

3. Exact.

observed that he is stained with no enormous or sanguinary crimes, so that his licentiousness is not so offensive but that it may be borne for his mirth.

The moral to be drawn from this representation is that no man is more dangerous than he that with a will to corrupt, hath the power to please; and that neither wit nor honesty ought to think themselves safe with such a companion when they see Henry seduced by Falstaff.

1765

From LIVES OF THE POETS

From Cowley[1]

[*Metaphysical Wit*]

Wit, like all other things subject by their nature to the choice of man, has its changes and fashions, and at different times takes different forms. About the beginning of the seventeenth century appeared a race of writers that may be termed the metaphysical poets,[2] of whom in a criticism on the works of Cowley it is not improper to give some account.

The metaphysical poets were men of learning, and to show their learning was their whole endeavor; but, unluckily resolving to show it in rhyme, instead of writing poetry they only wrote verses, and very often such verses as stood the trial of the finger better than of the ear; for the modulation was so imperfect that they were only found to be verses by counting the syllables.

If the father of criticism[3] has rightly denominated poetry τέχνη μιμητική, *an imitative art,* these writers will without great wrong lose their right to the name of poets, for they cannot be said to have imitated anything: they neither copied nature nor life; neither painted the forms of matter nor represented the operations of intellect.

Those however who deny them to be poets allow them to be wits. Dryden confesses of himself and his contemporaries that they fall below Donne in it, but maintains that they surpass him in poetry.[4]

If wit be well described by Pope as being "that which has been often thought, but was never before so well expressed,"[5] they cer-

1. Abraham Cowley (1618–67) was much admired during the middle of the 17th century. His reputation began to decline before 1700, but he was remembered as a writer of false wit, especially in his love poems *The Mistress.*
2. Presumably Johnson took this now common designation from a hint in Dryden's *Discourse Concerning the Original and Progress of Satire,* 1693. Dryden condemned Donne because "he

affects the metaphysics * * * and perplexes the minds of the fair sex with nice speculations of philosophy, when he should engage their hearts, and entertain them with the softnesses of love" (*Essays,* ed. W. P. Ker, II.19).
3. Aristotle in his *Poetics.*
4. *Discourse * * * of Satire* (Ker II.102).
5. *Essay on Criticism,* lines 297–98.

tainly never attained nor ever sought it, for they endeavored to be singular in their thoughts, and were careless of their diction. But Pope's account of wit is undoubtedly erroneous; he depresses it below its natural dignity, and reduces it from strength of thought to happiness of language.

If by a more noble and more adequate conception that be considered as wit which is at once natural and new, that which though not obvious is, upon its first production, acknowledged to be just; if it be that which he that never found it, wonders how he missed; to wit of this kind the metaphysical poets have seldom risen. Their thoughts are often new, but seldom natural; they are not obvious, but neither are they just;[6] and the reader, far from wondering that he missed them, wonders more frequently by what perverseness of industry they were ever found.

But wit, abstracted from its effects upon the hearer, may be more rigorously and philosophically considered as a kind of *discordia concors*;[7] a combination of dissimilar images, or discovery of occult resemblances in things apparently unlike. Of wit, thus defined, they have more than enough. The most heterogeneous ideas are yoked by violence together; nature and art are ransacked for illustrations, comparisons, and allusions; their learning instructs, and their subtlety surprises; but the reader commonly thinks his improvement dearly bought, and, though he sometimes admires, is seldom pleased.

From this account of their compositions it will be readily inferred that they were not successful in representing or moving the affections. As they were wholly employed on something unexpected and surprising, they had no regard to that uniformity of sentiment which enables us to conceive and to excite the pains and the pleasure of other minds: they never inquired what on any occasion they should have said or done, but wrote rather as beholders than partakers of human nature; as beings looking upon good and evil, impassive and at leisure; as Epicurean deities making remarks on the actions of men and the vicissitudes of life, without interest and without emotion. Their courtship was void of fondness and their lamentation of sorrow. Their wish was only to say what they hoped had been never said before.

Nor was the sublime more within their reach than the pathetic; for they never attempted that comprehension and expanse of thought which at once fills the whole mind, and of which the first effect is sudden astonishment, and the second rational admiration. Sublimity is produced by aggregation, and littleness by dispersion. Great thoughts are always general, and consist in positions not

---

6. Exact, proper.
7. Literally, "a harmonious discord." Johnson is himself being witty in using this phrase, a familiar philosophical concept denoting the general harmony of God's creation despite its manifold and often contradictory particulars.

limited by exceptions, and in descriptions not descending to minuteness. It is with great propriety that subtlety, which in its original import means exility[8] of particles, is taken in its metaphorical meaning for nicety of distinction. Those writers who lay on the watch for novelty could have little hope of greatness; for great things cannot have escaped former observation. Their attempts were always analytic: they broke every image into fragments, and could no more represent by their slender conceits and labored particularities the prospects of nature or the scenes of life, than he who dissects a sunbeam with a prism can exhibit the wide effulgence of a summer noon.

What they wanted however of the sublime they endeavored to supply by hyperbole;[9] their amplification had no limits: they left not only reason but fancy behind them, and produced combinations of confused magnificence that not only could not be credited, but could not be imagined.

Yet great labor directed by great abilities is never wholly lost: if they frequently threw away their wit upon false conceits, they likewise sometimes struck out unexpected truth: if their conceits were farfetched, they were often worth the carriage.[10] To write on their plan it was at least necessary to read and think. No man could be born a metaphysical poet, nor assume the dignity of a writer by descriptions copied from descriptions, by imitations borrowed from imitations, by traditional imagery and hereditary similes, by readiness of rhyme and volubility of syllables.

1779

From Milton[1]

[*Lycidas*]

One of the poems on which much praise has been bestowed is *Lycidas*; of which the diction is harsh,[2] the rhymes uncertain, and the numbers unpleasing. What beauty there is, we must therefore seek in the sentiments and images. It is not to be considered as

8. Thinness.
9. An image heightened beyond reality (see Johnson's *Dictionary*).
10. In the *Life of Addison*, Johnson wrote: "A simile may be compared to lines converging at a point, and is more excellent as the lines approach from greater distance * * * "
1. Johnson's treatment of Milton as man and poet gave great offense to many ardent Miltonians in his own day and damaged his reputation as a critic in the following century. He did not ad-

mire Milton's character, and he detested his politics and religion. But no one has praised *Paradise Lost* more handsomely. Especially offensive in the 19th century was his attack on *Lycidas*. Johnson disliked modern pastorals, recognizing that the tradition had been worn threadbare. His views on the genre may be read in *Ramblers* 36 and 37.
2. This notorious word does not mean "unmelodious," but "strained, forced, affected, or labored."

the effusion of real passion; for passion runs not after remote allusions and obscure opinions. Passion plucks no berries from the myrtle and ivy, nor calls upon Arethuse and Mincius, nor tells of "rough satyrs and fauns with cloven heel." Where there is leisure for fiction there is little grief.

In this poem there is no nature, for there is no truth; there is no art, for there is nothing new. Its form is that of a pastoral, easy, vulgar, and therefore disgusting:[3] whatever images it can supply are long ago exhausted; and its inherent improbability always forces dissatisfaction on the mind. When Cowley tells of Hervey that they studied together, it is easy to suppose how much he must miss the companion of his labors and the partner of his discoveries;[4] but what image of tenderness can be excited by these lines!

> We drove afield, and both together heard
> What time the grayfly winds her sultry horn,
> Battening our flocks with the fresh dews of night.

We know that they never drove afield, and that they had no flocks to batten; and though it be allowed that the representation may be allegorical, the true meaning is so uncertain and remote that it is never sought because it cannot be known when it is found.

Among the flocks and copses and flowers appear the heathen deities, Jove and Phoebus, Neptune and Aeolus, with a long train of mythological imagery, such as a college easily supplies. Nothing can less display knowledge or less exercise invention than to tell how a shepherd has lost his companion and must now feed his flocks alone, without any judge of his skill in piping; and how one god asks another god what is become of Lycidas, and how neither god can tell. He who thus grieves will excite no sympathy; he who thus praises will confer no honor.

This poem has yet a grosser fault. With these trifling fictions are mingled the most awful and sacred truths, such as ought never to be polluted with such irreverent combinations. The shepherd likewise is now a feeder of sheep, and afterwards an ecclesiastical pastor, a superintendent of a Christian flock. Such equivocations are always unskillful; but here they are indecent,[5] and at least approach to impiety, of which, however, I believe the writer not to have been conscious.

Such is the power of reputation justly acquired that its blaze drives away the eye from nice examination. Surely no man could have fancied that he read *Lycidas* with pleasure had he not known its author.

---

3. I.e., displeasing ("disgusting") because its stale, conventionality made it "vulgar" by putting it within the reach of the many.

4. Cowley's *On the Death of Mr. William Hervey* (1656).

5. Unbecoming, lacking in decorum.

[*L'Allegro. Il Penseroso*]

Of the two pieces, *L'Allegro* and *Il Penseroso*, I believe opinion is uniform; every man that reads them, reads them with pleasure. The author's design is not, what Theobald [1] has remarked, merely to show how objects derived their colors from the mind, by representing the operation of the same things upon the gay and the melancholy temper, or upon the same man as he is differently disposed; but rather how, among the successive variety of appearances, every disposition of mind takes hold on those by which it may be gratified.

The *cheerful* man hears the lark in the morning; the *pensive* man hears the nightingale in the evening. The *cheerful* man sees the cock strut, and hears the horn and hounds echo in the wood; then walks "not unseen" to observe the glory of the rising sun or listen to the singing milkmaid, and view the labors of the plowman and the mower; then casts his eyes about him over scenes of smiling plenty, and looks up to the distant tower, the residence of some fair inhabitant: thus he pursues rural gaiety through a day of labor or of play, and delights himself at night with the fanciful narratives of superstitious ignorance.

The *pensive* man at one time walks "unseen" to muse at midnight, and at another hears the sullen curfew. If the weather drives him home he sits in a room lighted only by "glowing embers"; or by a lonely lamp outwatches the North Star to discover the habitation of separate souls, and varies the shades of meditation by contemplating the magnificent or pathetic scenes of tragic and epic poetry. When the morning comes, a morning gloomy with rain and wind, he walks into the dark trackless woods, falls asleep by some murmuring water, and with melancholy enthusiasm expects some dream of prognostication or some music played by aerial performers.

Both Mirth and Melancholy are solitary, silent inhabitants of the breast that neither receive nor transmit communication: no mention is therefore made of a philosophical friend or a pleasant companion. The seriousness does not arise from any participation of calamity, nor the gaiety from the pleasures of the bottle.

The man of *cheerfulness* having exhausted the country tries what "towered cities" will afford, and mingles with scenes of splendor, gay assemblies, and nuptial festivities; but he mingles a mere spectator as, when the learned comedies of Jonson or the wild dramas of Shakespeare are exhibited, he attends the theater.

The *pensive* man never loses himself in crowds, but walks the cloister or frequents the cathedral. Milton probably had not yet forsaken the Church.

Both his characters delight in music; but he seems to think that

1. Lewis Theobald (1688–1744), the editor of Shakespeare and the enemy of Pope.

cheerful notes would have obtained from Pluto a complete dismission of Eurydice, of whom solemn sounds only procured a conditional release.

For the old age of Cheerfulness he makes no provision; but Melancholy he conducts with great dignity to the close of life. His Cheerfulness is without levity, and his Pensiveness without asperity.

Through these two poems the images are properly selected and nicely distinguished, but the colors of the diction seem not sufficiently discriminated. I know not whether the characters are kept sufficiently apart. No mirth can, indeed, be found in his melancholy; but I am afraid that I always meet some melancholy in his mirth. They are two noble efforts of imagination.

[*Paradise Lost*]

Those little pieces may be dispatched without much anxiety; a greater work calls for greater care. I am now to examine *Paradise Lost*, a poem which, considered with respect to design, may claim the first place, and with respect to performance the second, among the productions of the human mind.

By the general consent of critics the first praise of genius is due to the writer of an epic poem, as it requires an assemblage of all the powers which are singly sufficient for other compositions. Poetry is the art of uniting pleasure with truth, by calling imagination to the help of reason. Epic poetry undertakes to teach the most important truths by the most pleasing precepts, and therefore relates some great event in the most affecting manner. History must supply the writer with the rudiments of narration, which he must improve and exalt by a nobler art, must animate by dramatic energy, and diversify by retrospection and anticipation; morality must teach him the exact bounds and different shades of vice and virtue; from policy and the practice of life he has to learn the discriminations of character and the tendency of the passions, either single or combined; and physiology must supply him with illustrations and images. To put these materials to poetical use is required an imagination capable of painting nature and realizing fiction. Nor is he yet a poet till he has attained the whole extension of his language, distinguished all the delicacies of phrase, and all the colors of words, and learned to adjust their different sounds to all the varieties of metrical modulation.

Bossu is of opinion that the poet's first work is to find a *moral*, which his fable is afterwards to illustrate and establish.[1] This seems to have been the process only of Milton: the moral of other poems is incidental and consequent; in Milton's only it is essential and intrinsic. His purpose was the most useful and the most arduous: "to vindicate the ways of God to man"; to show the reasonableness

---

1. Père le Bossu wrote a treatise on the epic poem, *Traité du Poëme Épique*, 1675, much admired during the late 17th and early 18th centuries.

of religion, and the necessity of obedience to the Divine Law.

To convey this moral there must be a *fable*, a narration artfully constructed, so as to excite curiosity and surprise expectation. In this part of his work Milton must be confessed to have equaled every other poet. He has involved in his account of the Fall of Man the events which preceded, and those that were to follow it: he has interwoven the whole system of theology with such propriety that every part appears to be necessary, and scarcely any recital is wished shorter for the sake of quickening the progress of the main action.

The subject of an epic poem is naturally an event of great importance. That of Milton is not the destruction of a city, the conduct of a colony, or the foundation of an empire. His subject is the fate of worlds, the revolutions of heaven and of earth; rebellion against the Supreme King raised by the highest order of created beings; the overthrow of their host and the punishment of their crime; the creation of a new race of reasonable creatures; their original happiness and innocence, their forfeiture of immortality, and their restoration to hope and peace.

Great events can be hastened or retarded only by persons of elevated dignity. Before the greatness displayed in Milton's poem all other greatness shrinks away. The weakest of his agents are the highest and noblest of human beings, the original parents of mankind; with whose actions the elements consented; on whose rectitude or deviation of will depended the state of terrestrial nature and the condition of all the future inhabitants of the globe.

Of the other agents in the poem, the chief are such as it is irreverence to name on slight occasions. The rest were lower powers;

> of which the least could wield
> Those elements, and arm him with the force
> Of all their regions; [2]

powers which only the control of Omnipotence restrains from laying creation waste, and filling the vast expanse of space with ruin and confusion. To display the motives and actions of beings thus superior, so far as human reason can examine them or human imagination represent them, is the task which this mighty poet has undertaken and performed.

In the examination of epic poems much speculation is commonly employed upon the *characters*. The characters in the *Paradise Lost* which admit of examination are those of angels and of man; of angels good and evil, of man in his innocent and sinful state.

Among the angels the virtue of Raphael is mild and placid, of easy condescension and free communication; that of Michael is regal and lofty, and, as may seem, attentive to the dignity of his own nature. Abdiel and Gabriel appear occasionally, and act as every

2. *Paradise Lost* VI.221.

incident requires; the solitary fidelity of Abdiel is very amiably painted.[3]

Of the evil angels the characters are more diversified. To Satan, as Addison observes, such sentiments are given as suit "the most exalted and most depraved being." [4] Milton has been censured by Clarke for the impiety which sometimes breaks from Satan's mouth. For there are thoughts, as he justly remarks, which no observation of character can justify, because no good man would willingly permit them to pass, however transiently, through his own mind.[5] To make Satan speak as a rebel, without any such expressions as might taint the reader's imagination, was indeed one of the great difficulties in Milton's undertaking, and I cannot but think that he has extricated himself with great happiness. There is in Satan's speeches little that can give pain to a pious ear. The language of rebellion cannot be the same with that of obedience. The malignity of Satan foams in haughtiness and obstinacy; but his expressions are commonly general, and no otherwise offensive than as they are wicked.

The other chiefs of the celestial rebellion are very judiciously discriminated in the first and second books; and the ferocious character of Moloch appears, both in the battle and the council, with exact consistency.

To Adam and to Eve are given during their innocence such sentiments as innocence can generate and utter. Their love is pure benevolence and mutual veneration; their repasts are without luxury and their diligence without toil. Their addresses to their Maker have little more than the voice of admiration and gratitude. Fruition left them nothing to ask, and Innocence left them nothing to fear.

But with guilt enter distrust and discord, mutual accusation, and stubborn self-defense; they regard each other with alienated minds, and dread their Creator as the avenger of their transgression. At last they seek shelter in his mercy, soften to repentance, and melt in supplication. Both before and after the Fall the superiority of Adam is diligently sustained.

Of the *probable* and the *marvelous*,[6] two parts of a vulgar epic poem which immerge the critic in deep consideration, the *Paradise Lost* requires little to be said. It contains the history of a miracle, of Creation and Redemption; it displays the power and the mercy of the Supreme Being: the probable therefore is marvelous, and the marvelous is probable. The substance of the narrative is truth; and as truth allows no choice, it is, like necessity, superior to rule. To the accidental or adventitious parts, as to every thing human, some slight exceptions may be made. But the main fabric is immovably supported.

---

3. *Paradise Lost* V.803 ff.
4. *Spectator* 303.
5. John Clarke, *Essay upon Study*, 1731.

6. Actions in an epic poem which are wonderful because they exceed the probable.

It is justly remarked by Addison [7] that this poem has, by the nature of its subject, the advantage above all others, that it is universally and perpetually interesting. All mankind will, through all ages, bear the same relation to Adam and to Eve, and must partake of that good and evil which extend to themselves.

Of the *machinery*, so called from θεὸς ἀπὸ μηχανῆς [8] by which is meant the occasional interposition of supernatural power, another fertile topic of critical remarks, here is no room to speak, because every thing is done under the immediate and visible direction of Heaven; but the rule is so far observed that no part of the action could have been accomplished by any other means.

Of *episodes* [9] I think there are only two, contained in Raphael's relation of the war in heaven and Michael's prophetic account of the changes to happen in this world. Both are closely connected with the great action; one was necessary to Adam as a warning, the other as a consolation.

To the completeness or *integrity* of the design nothing can be objected; it has distinctly and clearly what Aristotle requires, a beginning, a middle, and an end. There is perhaps no poem of the same length from which so little can be taken without apparent mutilation. Here are no funeral games, nor is there any long description of a shield. The short digressions at the beginning of the third, seventh, and ninth books might doubtless be spared; but superfluities so beautiful who would take away? or who does not wish that the author of the *Iliad* had gratified succeeding ages with a little knowledge of himself? Perhaps no passages are more frequently or more attentively read than those extrinsic paragraphs; and since the end of poetry is pleasure, that cannot be unpoetical with which all are pleased.

The questions, whether the action of the poem be strictly *one*,[1] whether the poem can be properly termed *heroic*, and who is the hero, are raised by such readers as draw their principles of judgment rather from books than from reason. Milton, though he entitled *Paradise Lost* only a "poem," yet calls it himself "heroic song." [2] Dryden, petulantly and indecently, denies the heroism of Adam because he was overcome; but there is no reason why the hero should not be unfortunate except established practice, since success and virtue do not necessarily together. Cato is the hero of Lucan, but Lucan's authority will not be suffered by Quintilian to decide. However, if success be necessary, Adam's deceiver was at last crushed; Adam was restored to his Maker's favor, and therefore may securely resume his human rank.

After the scheme and fabric of the poem must be considered its

7. *Spectator* 273.
8. Aristotle, *Poetics* XV.10. "Deus ex machina," the intervention of supernatural powers into the affairs of men.
9. Incidental but related narratives

within an epic poem. Johnson is citing *Paradise Lost* V.577 ff. and XI.334 ff.
1. I.e., a single action dealing with a single character.
2. *Paradise Lost* IX.25.

component parts, the sentiments, and the diction.

The *sentiments*, as expressive of manners or appropriated to characters, are for the greater part unexceptionably just. Splendid passages containing lessons of morality or precepts of prudence occur seldom. Such is the original formation of this poem that as it admits no human manners till the Fall, it can give little assistance to human conduct. Its end is to raise the thoughts above sublunary cares or pleasures. Yet the praise of that fortitude, with which Abdiel maintained his singularity of virtue against the scorn of multitudes, may be accommodated to all times; and Raphael's reproof of Adam's curiosity after the planetary motions, with the answer returned by Adam, may be confidently opposed to any rule of life which any poet has delivered.[3]

The thoughts which are occasionally called forth in the progress are such as could only be produced by an imagination in the highest degree fervid and active, to which materials were supplied by incessant study and unlimited curiosity. The heat of Milton's mind might be said to sublimate his learning, to throw off into his work the spirit of science, unmingled with its grosser parts.

He had considered creation in its whole extent, and his descriptions are therefore learned. He had accustomed his imagination to unrestrained indulgence, and his conceptions therefore were extensive. The characteristic quality of his poem is sublimity. He sometimes descends to the elegant, but his element is the great. He can occasionally invest himself with grace; but his natural port is gigantic loftiness. He can please when pleasure is required; but it is his peculiar power to astonish.

He seems to have been well acquainted with his own genius, and to know what it was that Nature had bestowed upon him more bountifully than upon others; the power of displaying the vast, illuminating the splendid, enforcing the awful, darkening the gloomy, and aggravating the dreadful: he therefore chose a subject on which too much could not be said, on which he might tire his fancy without the censure of extravagance.

* * *

The defects and faults of *Paradise Lost*, for faults and defects every work of man must have, it is the business of impartial criticism to discover. As in displaying the excellence of Milton I have not made long quotations, because of selecting beauties there had been no end, I shall in the same general manner mention that which seems to deserve censure; for what Englishman can take delight in transcribing passages, which, if they lessen the reputation of Milton, diminish in some degree the honor of our country?

* * *

The plan of *Paradise Lost* has this inconvenience, that it comprises neither human actions nor human manners. The man and

3. *Paradise Lost* VIII.65 ff.

woman who act and suffer are in a state which no other man or woman can ever know. The reader finds no transaction in which he can
be engaged, beholds no condition in which he can by any effort of
imagination place himself; he has, therefore, little natural curiosity
or sympathy.

We all, indeed, feel the effects of Adam's disobedience; we all
sin like Adam, and like him must all bewail our offenses; we have
restless and insidious enemies in the fallen angels, and in the
blessed spirits we have guardians and friends; in the Redemption of
mankind we hope to be included: in the description of heaven and
hell we are surely interested, as we are all to reside hereafter either
in the regions of horror or of bliss.

But these truths are too important to be new: they have been
taught to our infancy; they have mingled with our solitary thoughts
and familiar conversation, and are habitually interwoven with the
whole texture of life. Being therefore not new they raise no unac-
customed emotion in the mind: what we knew before, we cannot
learn; what is not unexpected, cannot surprise.

Of the ideas suggested by these awful scenes, from some we recede with reverence, except when stated hours require their association; and from others we shrink with horror, or admit them only
as salutary inflictions, as counterpoises to our interests and passions.
Such images rather obstruct the career of fancy than incite it.

Pleasure and terror are indeed the genuine sources of poetry; but
poetical pleasure must be such as human imagination can at least
conceive, and poetical terror such as human strength and fortitude
may combat. The good and evil of Eternity are too ponderous for
the wings of wit; the mind sinks under them in passive helplessness,
content with calm belief and humble adoration.

Known truths however may take a different appearance, and be
conveyed to the mind by a new train of intermediate images. This
Milton has undertaken, and performed with pregnancy and vigor
of mind peculiar to himself. Whoever considers the few radical positions which the Scriptures afforded him will wonder by what energetic operation he expanded them to such extent and ramified
them to so much variety, restrained as he was by religious reverence from licentiousness of fiction.

Here is a full display of the united force of study and genius; of a
great accumulation of materials, with judgment to digest and fancy
to combine them: Milton was able to select from nature or from
story, from ancient fable or from modern science, whatever could illustrate or adorn his thoughts. An accumulation of knowledge impregnated his mind, fermented by study and exalted by imagination.

* * *

But original deficience cannot be supplied. The want of human
interest is always felt. *Paradise Lost* is one of the books which the
reader admires and lays down, and forgets to take up again. None

ever wished it longer than it is. Its perusal is a duty rather than a pleasure. We read Milton for instruction, retire harassed and overburdened, and look elsewhere for recreation; we desert our master, and seek for companions.

* * *

Dryden remarks that Milton has some flats among his elevations.[4] This is only to say that all the parts are not equal. In every work one part must be for the sake of others; a palace must have passages, a poem must have transitions. It is no more to be required that wit should always be blazing than that the sun should always stand at noon. In a great work there is a vicissitude [5] of luminous and opaque parts, as there is in the world a succession of day and night. Milton, when he has expatiated in the sky, may be allowed sometimes to revisit earth; for what other author ever soared so high or sustained his flight so long?

* * *

The highest praise of genius is original invention. Milton cannot be said to have contrived the structure of an epic poem, and therefore owes reverence to that vigor and amplitude of mind to which all generations must be indebted for the art of poetical narration, for the texture of the fable, the variation of incidents, the interposition of dialogue, and all the stratagems that surprise and enchain attention. But of all the borrowers from Homer Milton is perhaps the least indebted. He was naturally a thinker for himself, confident of his own abilities and disdainful of help or hindrance; he did not refuse admission to the thoughts or images of his predecessors, but he did not seek them. From his contemporaries he neither courted nor received support; there is in his writings nothing by which the pride of other authors might be gratified or favor gained, no exchange of praise or solicitation of support. His great works were performed under discountenance and in blindness, but difficulties vanished at his touch; he was born for whatever is arduous; and his work is not the greatest of heroic poems, only because it is not the first.

[1]779

From Pope

[Pope's Intellectual Character. Pope and Dryden Compared]

Of his intellectual character, the constituent and fundamental principle was good sense, a prompt and intuitive perception of consonance and propriety. He saw immediately, of his own conceptions, what was to be chosen, and what was to be rejected; and, in

4. Preface to *Sylvae;* see Essays (ed. W. P. Ker), I.268.
5. Change.

the works of others, what was to be shunned, and what was to be copied.

But good sense alone is a sedate and quiescent quality, which manages its possessions well, but does not increase them; it collects few materials for its own operations, and preserves safety, but never gains supremacy. Pope had likewise genius; a mind active, ambitious, and adventurous, always investigating, always aspiring; in its widest searches still longing to go forward, in its highest flights still wishing to be higher; always imagining something greater than it knows, always endeavoring more than it can do.

To assist these powers, he is said to have had great strength and exactness of memory. That which he had heard or read was not easily lost; and he had before him not only what his own meditation suggested, but what he had found in other writers that might be accommodated to his present purpose.

These benefits of nature he improved by incessant and unwearied diligence; he had recourse to every source of intelligence, and lost no opportunity of information; he consulted the living as well as the dead; he read his compositions to his friends, and was never content with mediocrity when excellence could be attained. He considered poetry as the business of his life, and however he might seem to lament his occupation, he followed it with constancy: to make verses was his first labor, and to mend them was his last.

From his attention to poetry he was never diverted. If conversation offered anything that could be improved, he committed it to paper; if a thought, or perhaps an expression more happy than was common, rose to his mind, he was careful to write it; an independent distich was preserved for an opportunity of insertion, and some little fragments have been found containing lines, or parts of lines, to be wrought upon at some other time.

He was one of those few whose labor is their pleasure; he was never elevated to negligence, nor wearied to impatience; he never passed a fault unamended by indifference, nor quitted it by despair. He labored his works first to gain reputation, and afterwards to keep it.

Of composition there are different methods. Some employ at once memory and invention, and, with little intermediate use of the pen, form and polish large masses by continued meditation, and write their productions only when, in their own opinion, they have completed them. It is related of Virgil[1] that his custom was to pour out a great number of verses in the morning, and pass the day in retrenching exuberances and correcting inaccuracies. The method of Pope, as may be collected from his translation, was to write his first thoughts in his first words, and gradually to amplify, decorate, rectify, and refine them.

1. By Suetonius in his brief life of the poet.

With such faculties and such dispositions, he excelled every other writer in *poetical prudence*; he wrote in such a manner as might expose him to few hazards. He used almost always the same fabric of verse; and, indeed, by those few essays which he made of any other, he did not enlarge his reputation. Of this uniformity the certain consequence was readiness and dexterity. By perpetual practice, language had in his mind a systematical arrangement; having always the same use for words, he had words so selected and combined as to be ready at his call. This increase of facility he confessed himself to have perceived in the progress of his translation.

But what was yet of more importance, his effusions were always voluntary, and his subjects chosen by himself. His independence secured him from drudging at a task, and laboring upon a barren topic: he never exchanged praise for money, nor opened a shop of condolence or congratulation. His poems, therefore, were scarce ever temporary. He suffered coronations and royal marriages to pass without a song, and derived no opportunities from recent events, nor any popularity from the accidental disposition of his readers. He was never reduced to the necessity of soliciting the sun to shine upon a birthday, of calling the Graces and Virtues to a wedding, or of saying what multitudes have said before him. When he could produce nothing new, he was at liberty to be silent.

His publications were for the same reason never hasty. He is said to have sent nothing to the press till it had lain two years under his inspection: it is at least certain that he ventured nothing without nice examination. He suffered the tumult of imagination to subside, and the novelties of invention to grow familiar. He knew that the mind is always enamored of its own productions, and did not trust his first fondness. He consulted his friends, and listened with great willingness to criticism; and, what was of more importance, he consulted himself, and let nothing pass against his own judgment.

He professed to have learned his poetry from Dryden, whom, whenever an opportunity was presented, he praised through his whole life with unvaried liberality; and perhaps his character may receive some illustration, if he be compared with his master.

Integrity of understanding and nicety of discernment were not allotted in a less proportion to Dryden than to Pope. The rectitude of Dryden's mind was sufficiently shown by the dismission of his poetical prejudices, and the rejection of unnatural thoughts and rugged numbers. But Dryden never desired to apply all the judgment that he had. He wrote, and professed to write, merely for the people; and when he pleased others, he contented himself. He spent no time in struggles to rouse latent powers; he never attempted to make that better which was already good, nor often to mend what he must have known to be faulty. He wrote, as he tells us, with very little consideration; when occasion or necessity called upon him, he poured out what the present moment happened to supply, and, when once it had passed the press, ejected it from his mind; for when he had no pecuniary interest, he had no further solicitude.

Pope was not content to satisfy; he desired to excel, and therefore always endeavored to do his best: he did not court the candor, but dared the judgment of his reader, and, expecting no indulgence from others, he showed none to himself. He examined lines and words with minute and punctilious observation, and retouched every part with indefatigable diligence, till he had left nothing to be forgiven.

For this reason he kept his pieces very long in his hands, while he considered and reconsidered them. The only poems which can be supposed to have been written with such regard to the times as might hasten their publication were the two satires of *Thirty-Eight*; of which Dodsley[2] told me that they were brought to him by the author, that they might be fairly copied. "Almost every line," he said, "was then written twice over; I gave him a clean transcript, which he sent some time afterwards to me for the press, with almost every line written twice over a second time."

His declaration, that his care for his works ceased at their publication, was not strictly true. His parental attention never abandoned them; what he found amiss in the first edition, he silently corrected in those that followed. He appears to have revised the *Iliad*, and freed it from some of its imperfections; and the *Essay on Criticism* received many improvements after its first appearance. It will seldom be found that he altered without adding clearness, elegance, or vigor. Pope had perhaps the judgment of Dryden; but Dryden certainly wanted the diligence of Pope.

In acquired knowledge, the superiority must be allowed to Dryden, whose education was more scholastic, and who before he became an author had been allowed more time for study, with better means of information. His mind has a larger range, and he collects his images and illustrations from a more extensive circumference of science. Dryden knew more of man in his general nature, and Pope in his local manners. The notions of Dryden were formed by comprehensive speculation, and those of Pope by minute attention. There is more dignity in the knowledge of Dryden, and more certainty in that of Pope.

Poetry was not the sole praise of either; for both excelled likewise in prose; but Pope did not borrow his prose from his predecessor. The style of Dryden is capricious and varied, that of Pope is cautious and uniform; Dryden obeys the motions of his own mind,

2. Robert Dodsley, the publisher.

Pope constrains his mind to his own rules of composition. Dryden is sometimes vehement and rapid; Pope is always smooth, uniform, and gentle. Dryden's page is a natural field, rising into inequalities, and diversified by the varied exuberance of abundant vegetation; Pope's is a velvet lawn, shaven by the scythe, and leveled by the roller.

Of genius, that power which constitutes a poet; that quality without which judgment is cold and knowledge is inert; that energy which collects, combines, amplifies, and animates; the superiority must, with some hesitation, be allowed to Dryden. It is not to be inferred that of this poetical vigor Pope had only a little, because Dryden had more; for every other writer since Milton must give place to Pope; and even of Dryden it must be said that if he has brighter paragraphs, he has not better poems. Dryden's performances were always hasty, either excited by some external occasion, or extorted by domestic necessity; he composed without consideration, and published without correction. What his mind could supply at call, or gather in one excursion, was all that he sought, and all that he gave. The dilatory caution of Pope enabled him to condense his sentiments, to multiply his images, and to accumulate all that study might produce, or chance might supply. If the flights of Dryden therefore are higher, Pope continues longer on the wing. If of Dryden's fire the blaze is brighter, of Pope's the heat is more regular and constant. Dryden often surpasses expectation, and Pope never falls below it. Dryden is read with frequent astonishment, and Pope with perpetual delight.

This parallel will, I hope, when it is well considered, be found just; and if the reader should suspect me, as I suspect myself, of some partial fondness for the memory of Dryden, let him not too hastily condemn me; for meditation and inquiry may, perhaps, show him the reasonableness of my determination.

1781

JAMES BOSWELL
(1740–1795)

1763: Meets Samuel Johnson.
1768: Account of Corsica.
1773: Tour of the Highlands and the Hebrides with Johnson.
1791: *Life of Samuel Johnson.*

The discovery within the last three or four decades of a vast number of James Boswell's personal papers (formerly believed to have been destroyed by his literary executors) has made it possible to know the author of the *Life of Samuel Johnson* better, perhaps, than we can know any other person, dead or living. His published letters and journals (only a portion of those that exist) have made modern readers aware of the serious and absurd, the charming and repellent sides of his character. The journals are the work of a complicated man of genius, who perfected his art as a biographer through his almost lifelong habit of observing himself and recording with unique honesty and completeness his responses to widely varied experience. By the time he met Johnson, when he was only 23, he had already trained himself to listen, to observe, and to remember until he found time to set it all down in writing. Only very rarely, it seems, did he ever take notes of conversations while they were in progress, an action which would quickly have put an end to social discourse. His unusual memory, his instinctive sense of the characteristic, and his disciplined art enabled him in privacy to re-create and vividly preserve the many "scenes" which distinguish his journals as they do the *Life.*

Boswell was the elder son of Alexander Boswell of Auchinleck (pronounced *Aff-léck*) in Ayreshire, a judge who, by virtue of his high office, bore the courtesy title of Lord Auchinleck. As a member of an ancient family and heir to its large estate, Boswell was in the technical sense of the term a gentleman, with entrée into the best circles of Edinburgh and London—not, as he is sometimes represented, a climber who had to toady to his betters. By temperament he was unstable, prone to melancholy, given to romantic excesses of feeling, and thoroughly sensual. The combination of instability and sensuality led him early into the habitual dissipation that ultimately affected his health and shortened his life. After attending the Universities of Edinburgh and Glasgow, and studying law in Utrecht in Holland, he made the grand tour of Germany, Italy, and France, passing through Switzerland where he met and succeeded in captivating the two foremost French men of letters, Rousseau and Voltaire. He visited the beleaguered hero of Corsica, General Pasquale de Paoli, who was leading his people in their revolt against Genoa, and who seemed to European liberals to embody all the civic and military virtues of Republican Rome. Upon returning to England he wrote his first important work, *An Account of Corsica* (1768), which included the journal of his visit to Paoli. It was promptly translated into Dutch, German, French, and Italian, and its young author found himself with a modest European reputation.

By 1769, Boswell was established in what was to prove a successful law practice in Edinburgh and had married his cousin, Margaret Montgomerie. Whenever possible he made a jaunt to London in the spring, where he mingled dissipation with the soberer pleasures of intellectual life, especially in Johnson's circle. In 1773 Johnson, then 64, joined Boswell in a tour of the Highlands and the Hebrides. Boswell delighted in placing his elderly friend in situations which would bring out his essential character, and he was therefore very much pleased to bring Dr. Johnson to Scotland and into the primitive Highlands and the Hebrides, and to watch and record his responses to incidents and people along the way. Almost every aspect of the adventure should have made it impossible, or a least unpleasant. Johnson, far from young and after years of sedentary city living, found himself astride a horse in wild country or in open boats in autumn weather. As a devout Anglican, he was an outspoken enemy of the Presbyterian Church, the national church of Scotland. As a lover of London, he cared little or nothing for scenery and rural life, and even less for such primitive people as the Highlanders were at that time. Moreover, for many years he had half-jestingly, half-seriously, made the Scots as a nation the butt of his satiric wit. But such were Boswell's social tact and Johnson's vigor and curiosity that the tour was a great success. "There have been many people," wrote Boswell of himself, "who built castles in the air, but I believe I am the first that ever attempted to move into them." The trip to the Hebrides is a fine example of this eminently Boswellian trait. Johnson's sober and unflattering account of the trip in his *Journey to the Western Isles of Scotland* (1775) gave some offense to Scottish national pride. Boswell's *Journal of a Tour to the Hebrides* (1785), a preliminary study for the *Life*, is a lively and entertaining diary, kept throughout the journey and approved, at least in part, by Johnson himself.

In 1788, four years after Johnson's death, Boswell abandoned his Scotch practice, removed with his family to London, was admitted to the English bar (but never actually practiced), and, amidst domestic difficulties not made less perplexing by his own frailties, began the *Life*. Fortunately he had the help and encouragement of the distinguished literary scholar Edmond Malone, without whose guidance he might never have finished his task.

The *Life* is the work of an impressive literary artist who was dominated by a Johnsonian regard for accuracy and truth. A lesser craftsman might have been overwhelmed by the very abundance of material that Boswell had to deal with: his own journals, all of Johnson's letters that he could find, his voluminous writings, and every scrap of information that his friends would furnish—all of which had to be collected, verified, and somehow reduced to unity. The *Life* is a record not of Johnson alone but of literary England during the last half of the century. Its pages are populated by men as eminent in their way as was Johnson, most of whom Boswell knew, all of whom are interesting to the reader. But Boswell wrote with his eye on the object, and that object was Samuel Johnson, to whom every detail in the book is relevant, toward whom such eminent persons as Sir Joshua Reynolds, Edmund Burke, Oliver Goldsmith, Lord Chesterfield—even the king himself—always face. Boswell's sense of unity and of proportion is perfect. Although his book is dense with details, they never impede the flow of the narrative. The movement is always forward, individual episodes are designed to reveal the great protagonist in a variety of aspects, and the world that Boswell created and populated is sustained both by the animation of his own imagination and by the vitality of his hero.

Boswell's gift is not only narrative: it is also dramatic. He himself was a good deal of an actor and a superb mimic, with a flair for detecting the characteristic gesture, word, tone, or trait. In reading the journals and the *Life* one often feels that their author is a gifted theatrical improviser, creating dramatic "scenes" (the word is a favorite of his) with living people, and playing simultaneously and with incredible sureness the several roles of contriver of the dialogue, director of the plot, actor in the scene, and applauding audience—for Boswell never failed to watch and applaud or condemn his own curious conduct. The quintessence of Boswell as both a social genius and a literary artist (the two complemented each other) is to be found in his description of his visit to Voltaire: "I placed myself by him. I touched the keys in unison with his imagination. I wish you had heard the music." Boswell's art, as an interviewer, a conversationalist, and a biographer is, like all great art, the product of a deep and humane interpretative imagination. The scene with Voltaire, like all the famous scenes in the *Life*, is contrived with such apparent ease and by seemingly such simple means, that the genius responsible for them may go undetected by the casual reader.

Although the Johnson who has become a part of our heritage is largely Boswell's Johnson, there was much in his life about which Boswell had no first-hand knowledge, and there were aspects of his nature which he did not have much opportunity to observe. When Boswell met him, Johnson was 54, a widower, already established as "Dictionary" Johnson and the author of the *Rambler*, pensioned by the Crown and consequently no longer compelled to earn his living. Boswell knew nothing at first hand of Johnson's boyhood and youth in Lichfield, of his brief stay at Oxford, of his marriage, and of the long, difficult, and heroic years (more than a quarter of a century), during which Johnson made his way up from obscurity to eminence through difficulties that it is painful to imagine. Boswell knew him as the sage, the moralist, the scholar, the critic, and as a man moving in a largely male society in tavern, coffeehouse, and club. The chief glory of the *Life* is the conversation, always dominated by Johnson but not at all a monologue. It is the talk of a man, or rather of men, who have experienced broadly, read widely, observed and reflected on their observations, whose ideas are constantly brought to the test of experience, and whose experience is habitually transmuted into ideas. The book is as large as life and as human as its central character.

From Boswell on the Grand Tour
[*Boswell Interviews Voltaire*[1]]

And whence do I now write to you, my friend?[2] From the château of Monsieur de Voltaire. I had a letter for him from a Swiss colonel at The Hague. I came hither Monday and was presented to him. He received me with dignity and that air of a man who has been much in the world which a Frenchman acquires in perfection. I saw him for about half an hour before dinner. He was not in spirits. Yet he gave me some brilliant sallies. He did not dine with us, and I was obliged to post away immediately after dinner, because the gates of Geneva shut before five and Ferney is a good hour from town. I was by no means satisfied to have been so little time with the monarch of French literature. A happy scheme sprung up in my adventurous mind. Madame Denis, the niece of Monsieur de

1. Voltaire was the name assumed by François Marie Arouet (1694–1778), the most famous French writer of his generation. Playwright, poet, satirist, philosopher, enemy of the church, and irrepressible ironist, after a stormy career he was living in splendor at his chateau at Ferney near the border of Switzerland and France, just outside Geneva. His housekeeper and mistress was his niece Marie-Louise Denis. He and Jean-Jacques Rousseau, whom Boswell had just visited and whose avowed disciple he had become, were deadly enemies.

2. This passage is taken from a letter, dated 28 December, 1764, written to Boswell's closest friend, a young clergyman named William Temple.

Voltaire, had been extremely good to me. She is fond of our language. I wrote her a letter in English begging her interest to obtain for me the privilege of lodging a night under the roof of Monsieur de Voltaire, who, in opposition to our sun, rises in the evening. I was in the finest humor and my letter was full of wit. I told her, "I am a hardy and a vigorous Scot. You may mount me to the highest and coldest garret. I shall not even refuse to sleep upon two chairs in the bedchamber of your maid. I saw her pass through the room where we sat before dinner." I sent my letter on Tuesday by an express. It was shown to Monsieur de Voltaire, who with his own hand wrote this answer in the character of Madame Denis: "You will do us much honor and pleasure. We have few beds. But you will (*shall*) not sleep on two chairs. My uncle, though very sick, hath guessed at your merit. I know it better; for I have seen you longer." * * *

I returned yesterday to this enchanted castle. The magician appeared a very little before dinner. But in the evening he came into the drawing room in great spirits. I placed myself by him. I touched the keys in unison with his imagination. I wish you had heard the music. He was all brilliance. He gave me continued flashes of wit. I got him to speak English, which he does in a degree that made me now and then start up and cry. "Upon my soul this is astonishing!" When he talked our language he was animated with the soul of a Briton. He had bold flights. He had humor. He had an extravagance; he had a forcible oddity of style that the most comical of our *dramatis personae* could not have exceeded. He swore bloodily, as was the fashion when he was in England.[3] He hummed a ballad; he repeated nonsense. Then he talked of our Constitution with a noble enthusiasm. I was proud to hear this from the mouth of an illustrious Frenchman. At last we came upon religion. Then did he rage. The company went to supper. Monsieur de Voltaire and I remained in the drawing room with a great Bible before us; and if ever two mortal men disputed with vehemence, we did. Yes, upon that occasion he was one individual and I another. For a certain portion of time there was a fair opposition between Voltaire and Boswell. The daring bursts of his ridicule confounded my understanding. He stood like an orator of ancient Rome. Tully[4] was never more agitated than he was. He went too far. His aged frame trembled beneath him. He cried, "Oh, I am very sick; my head turns round," and he let himself gently fall upon an easy chair. He recovered. I resumed our conversation, but changed the tone. I talked to him serious and earnest. I demanded of him an honest confession of

---

3. In 1726, in order to avoid imprisonment because of a quarrel with a nobleman, Voltaire had gone into exile in England, where he remained for three years, meeting many distinguished English writers and statesmen and learning to admire the British Constitution and the English principle of religious toleration. His *Lettres philosophiques sur les Anglais* (1734) expressed his admiration of English institutions and is an indirect criticism of France.

4. Marcus Tullius Cicero.

his real sentiments. He gave it me with candor and with a mild eloquence which touched my heart. I did not believe him capable of thinking in the manner that he declared to me was "from the bottom of his heart." He expressed his veneration—his love—of the Supreme Being, and his entire resignation to the will of Him who is All-wise. He expressed his desire to resemble the Author of Goodness by being good himself. His sentiments go no farther. He does not inflame his mind with grand hopes of the immortality of the soul. He says it may be, but he knows nothing of it. And his mind is in perfect tranquility. I was moved; I was sorry. I doubted his sincerity. I called to him with emotion, "Are you sincere? are you really sincere?" He answered "Before God, I am." Then with the fire of him whose tragedies have so often shone on the theater of Paris, he said, "I suffer much. But I suffer with patience and resignation; not as a Christian—but as a man."

Temple, was not this an interesting scene? Would a journey from Scotland to Ferney have been too much to obtain such a remarkable interview? * * *

1764   1928

From The Life of Samuel Johnson, LL.D.
[Plan of the Life]

* * * Had Dr. Johnson written his own life, in conformity with the opinion which he has given, that every man's life may be best written by himself;[1] had he employed in the preservation of his own history, that clearness of narration and elegance of language in which he has embalmed so many eminent persons, the world would probably have had the most perfect example of biography that was ever exhibited. But although he at different times, in a desultory manner, committed to writing many particulars of the progress of his mind and fortunes, he never had persevering diligence enough to form them into a regular composition. Of these memorials a few have been preserved; but the greater part was consigned by him to the flames, a few days before his death.

As I had the honor and happiness of enjoying his friendship for upwards of twenty years; as I had the scheme of writing his life constantly in view; as he was well apprised of this circumstance, and from time to time obligingly satisfied my inquiries, by communicating to me the incidents of his early years; as I acquired a facility in recollecting, and was very assiduous in recording, his conversation, of which the extraordinary vigor and vivacity constituted one of the first features of his character; and as I have spared no pains in obtaining materials concerning him, from every quarter where I could discover that they were to be found, and have been favored

1. *Idler* 84.

with the most liberal communications by his friends; I flatter myself that few biographers have entered upon such a work as this with more advantages; independent of literary abilities, in which I am not vain enough to compare myself with some great names who have gone before me in this kind of writing. * * *

Instead of melting down my materials into one mass, and constantly speaking in my own person, by which I might have appeared to have more merit in the execution of the work, I have resolved to adopt and enlarge upon the excellent plan of Mr. Mason, in his *Memoirs of Gray*.[2] Wherever narrative is necessary to explain, connect, and supply, I furnish it to the best of my abilities; but in the chronological series of Johnson's life, which I trace as distinctly as I can, year by year, I produce, wherever it is in my power, his own minutes, letters, or conversation, being convinced that this mode is more lively, and will make my readers better acquainted with him than even most of those were who actually knew him, but could know him only partially; whereas there is here an accumulation of intelligence from various points, by which his character is more fully understood and illustrated.

Indeed I cannot conceive a more perfect mode of writing any man's life than not only relating all the most important events of it in their order, but interweaving what he privately wrote, and said, and thought; by which mankind are enabled as it were to see him live, and to "live o'er each scene"[3] with him, as he actually advanced through the several stages of his life. Had his other friends been as diligent and ardent as I was, he might have been almost entirely preserved. As it is, I will venture to say that he will be seen in this work more completely than any man who has ever yet lived.

And he will be seen as he really was; for I profess to write, not his panegyric, which must be all praise, but his Life; which, great and good as he was, must not be supposed to be entirely perfect. To be as he was, is indeed subject of panegyric enough to any man in this state of being; but in every picture there should be shade as well as light, and when I delineate him without reserve, I do what he himself recommended, both by his precept and his example. * * *

I am fully aware of the objections which may be made to the minuteness on some occasions of my detail of Johnson's conversation, and how happily it is adapted for the petty exercise of ridicule, by men of superficial understanding and ludicrous fancy; but I remain firm and confident in my opinion, that minute particulars are frequently characteristic, and always amusing, when they relate to a distinguished man. I am therefore exceedingly unwilling that

2. William Mason, poet and dramatist, published his life of Thomas Gray in 1774.   3. Pope's Prologue to Addison's *Cato*, line 4.

anything, however slight, which my illustrious friend thought it worth his while to express, with any degree of point, should perish. * * *

Of one thing I am certain, that considering how highly the small portion which we have of the table-talk and other anecdotes of our celebrated writers is valued, and how earnestly it is regretted that we have not more, I am justified in preserving rather too many of Johnson's sayings, than too few; especially as from the diversity of dispositions it cannot be known with certainty beforehand, whether what may seem trifling to some, and perhaps to the collector himself, may not be most agreeable to many; and the greater number that an author can please in any degree, the more pleasure does there arise to a benevolent mind. * * *

[Johnson's Early Years. Marriage and London]

[1709] Samuel Johnson was born at Lichfield, in Staffordshire, on the 18th of September, N.S.,[4] 1709; and his initiation into the Christian Church was not delayed; for his baptism is recorded, in the register of St. Mary's parish in that city, to have been performed on the day of his birth. His father is there styled *Gentleman*, a circumstance of which an ignorant panegyrist has praised him for not being proud; when the truth is, that the appellation of Gentleman, though now lost in the indiscriminate assumption of *Esquire*, was commonly taken by those who could not boast of gentility. His father was Michael Johnson, a native of Derbyshire, of obscure extraction, who settled in Lichfield as a bookseller and stationer. His mother was Sarah Ford, descended of an ancient race of substantial yeomanry in Warwickshire. They were well advanced in years when they married, and never had more than two children, both sons; Samuel, their first-born, who lived to be the illustrious character whose various excellence I am to endeavor to record, and Nathanael, who died in his twenty-fifth year.

Mr. Michael Johnson was a man of a large and robust body, and of a strong and active mind; yet, as in the most solid rocks veins of unsound substance are often discovered, there was in him a mixture of that disease, the nature of which eludes the most minute inquiry, though the effects are well known to be a weariness of life, an unconcern about those things which agitate the greater part of mankind, and a general sensation of gloomy wretchedness. From him then his son inherited, with some other qualities, "a vile melancholy," which in his too strong expression of any disturbance of the mind, "made him mad all his life, at least not sober." Michael

4. New Style. In 1752 Great Britain adopted the Gregorian Calendar, introduced in 1582 by Pope Gregory XIII, to correct the accumulated inaccuracies of Julius Caesar's calendar, which had been in use since 46 B.C. By 1752 the error amounted to eleven days. Dates before September 2, 1752, must therefore be corrected by adding eleven days or by using the Julian date, followed by "O.S." (Old Style).

was, however, forced by the narrowness of his circumstances to be very diligent in business, not only in his shop, but by occasionally resorting to several towns in the neighborhood, some of which were at a considerable distance from Lichfield. At that time booksellers' shops in the provincial towns of England were very rare, so that there was not one even in Birmingham, in which town old Mr. Johnson used to open a shop every market day. He was a pretty good Latin scholar, and a citizen so creditable as to be made one of the magistrates of Lichfield; and, being a man of good sense, and skill in his trade, he acquired a reasonable share of wealth, of which however he afterwards lost the greatest part, by engaging unsuccessfully in a manufacture of parchment. He was a zealous high-church man and royalist, and retained his attachment to the unfortunate house of Stuart, though he reconciled himself, by casuistical arguments of expediency and necessity, to take the oaths imposed by the prevailing power. * * *

Johnson's mother was a woman of distinguished understanding. I asked his old schoolfellow, Mr. Hector,[5] surgeon of Birmingham, if she was not vain of her son. He said, "She had too much good sense to be vain, but she knew her son's value." Her piety was not inferior to her understanding; and to her must be ascribed those early impressions of religion upon the mind of her son, from which the world afterwards derived so much benefit. He told me that he remembered distinctly having had the first notice of Heaven, "a place to which good people went," and hell, "a place to which bad people went," communicated to him by her, when a little child in bed with her; and that it might be the better fixed in his memory, she sent him to repeat it to Thomas Jackson, their manservant; he not being in the way, this was not done; but there was no occasion for any artificial aid for its preservation. * * *

[1728] That a man in Mr. Michael Johnson's circumstances should think of sending his son to the expensive University of Oxford, at his own charge, seems very improbable. The subject was too delicate to question Johnson upon. But I have been assured by Dr. Taylor[6] that the scheme never would have taken place had not a gentleman of Shropshire, one of his schoolfellows, spontaneously undertaken to support him at Oxford, in the character of his companion; though, in fact, he never received any assistance whatever from that gentleman.

He, however, went to Oxford, and was entered a Commoner of Pembroke College on the 31st of October, 1728, being then in his nineteenth year.

The Reverend Dr. Adams,[7] who afterwards presided over Pembroke College with universal esteem, told me he was present, and

5. Edmund Hector, a lifelong friend of Johnson's.
6. A well-to-do clergyman, who had been Johnson's school fellow in Lich-field.
7. The Rev. William Adams, D.D., elected Master of Pembroke in 1775.

gave me some account of what passed on the night of Johnson's arrival at Oxford. On that evening, his father, who had anxiously accompanied him, found means to have him introduced to Mr. Jorden, who was to be his tutor. * * *

His father seemed very full of the merits of his son, and told the company he was a good scholar, and a poet, and wrote Latin verses. His figure and manner appeared strange to them; but he behaved modestly and sat silent, till upon something which occurred in the course of conversation, he suddenly struck in and quoted Macrobius; and thus he gave the first impression of that more extensive reading in which he had indulged himself.

His tutor, Mr. Jorden, fellow of Pembroke, was not, it seems, a man of such abilities as we should conceive requisite for the instructor of Samuel Johnson, who gave me the following account of him. "He was a very worthy man, but a heavy man, and I did not profit much by his instructions. Indeed, I did not attend him much. The first day after I came to college I waited upon him, and then stayed away four. On the sixth, Mr. Jorden asked me why I had not attended. I answered I had been sliding in Christ Church meadow. And this I said with as much *nonchalance* as I am now talking to you. I had no notion that I was wrong or irreverent to my tutor." Boswell: "That, Sir, was great fortitude of mind." Johnson: "No, Sir; stark insensibility." * * *

[1729] The "morbid melancholy," which was lurking in his constitution, and to which we may ascribe those particularities and that aversion to regular life, which, at a very early period, marked his character, gathered such strength in his twentieth year as to afflict him in a dreadful manner. While he was at Lichfield, in the college vacation of the year 1729, he felt himself overwhelmed with an horrible hypochondria, with perpetual irritation, fretfulness, and impatience; and with a dejection, gloom, and despair, which made existence misery. From this dismal malady he never afterwards was perfectly relieved; and all his labors, and all his enjoyments, were but temporary interruptions of its baleful influence. He told Mr. Paradise[8] that he was sometimes so languid and inefficient that he could not distinguish the hour upon the town-clock. * * *

To Johnson, whose supreme enjoyment was the exercise of his reason, the disturbance or obscuration of that faculty was the evil most to be dreaded. Insanity, therefore, was the object of his most dismal apprehension; and he fancied himself seized by it, or approaching to it, at the very time when he was giving proofs of a more than ordinary soundness and vigor of judgment. That his own diseased imagination should have so far deceived him, is strange; but it is stranger still that some of his friends should have given credit to his groundless opinion, when they had such undoubted

8. John Paradise, a member of the Essex Head Club, which Johnson founded in 1783.

proofs that it was totally fallacious; though it is by no means surprising that those who wish to depreciate him should, since his death, have laid hold of this circumstance, and insisted upon it with very unfair aggravation. * * *

Dr. Adams told me that Johnson, while he was at Pembroke College, "was caressed and loved by all about him, was a gay and frolicsome fellow, and passed there the happiest part of his life." But this is a striking proof of the fallacy of appearances, and how little any of us know of the real internal state even of those whom we see most frequently; for the truth is, that he was then depressed by poverty, and irritated by disease. When I mentioned to him this account as given me by Dr. Adams, he said, "Ah, Sir, I was mad and violent. It was bitterness which they mistook for frolic. I was miserably poor, and I thought to fight my way by my literature and my wit; so I disregarded all power and all authority." * * *

[1734] In a man whom religious education has secured from licentious indulgences, the passion of love, when once it has seized him, is exceedingly strong; being unimpaired by dissipation, and totally concentrated in one object. This was experienced by Johnson, when he became the fervent admirer of Mrs. Porter, after her first husband's death. Miss Porter told me that when he was first introduced to her mother, his appearance was very forbidding: he was then lean and lank, so that his immense structure of bones was hideously striking to the eye, and the scars of the scrofula were deeply visible. He also wore his hair,[9] which was straight and stiff, and separated behind: and he often had, seemingly, convulsive starts and odd gesticulations, which tended to excite at once surprise and ridicule. Mrs. Porter was so much engaged by his conversation that she overlooked all these external disadvantages, and said to her daughter, "This is the most sensible man that I ever saw in my life."

[1735] Though Mrs. Porter was double the age of Johnson, and her person and manner, as described to me by the late Mr. Garrick,[1] were by no means pleasing to others, she must have had a superiority of understanding and talents, as she certainly inspired him with a more than ordinary passion; and she having signified her willingness to accept of his hand, he went to Lichfield to ask his mother's consent to the marriage, which he could not but be conscious was a very imprudent scheme, both on account of their disparity of years and her want of fortune. But Mrs. Johnson knew too well the ardor of her son's temper, and was too tender a parent to oppose his inclinations.

I know not for what reason the marriage ceremony was not performed at Birmingham; but a resolution was taken that it should be at Derby, for which place the bride and bridegroom set out on horseback, I suppose in very good humor. But though Mr. Topham

9. I.e., he wore no wig.
1. David Garrick (1717–79), the most famous actor of his day. In 1736 he was one of Johnson's three pupils in an unsuccessful school at Edial.

Beauclerk[2] used archly to mention Johnson's having told him, with much gravity, "Sir, it was a love marriage on both sides," I have had from my illustrious friend the following curious account of their journey to church upon the nuptial morn:

9th July: "Sir, she had read the old romances, and had got into her head the fantastical notion that a woman of spirit should use her lover like a dog. So, Sir, at first she told me that I rode too fast, and she could not keep up with me; and, when I rode a little slower, she passed me, and complained that I lagged behind. I was not to be made the slave of caprice; and I resolved to begin as I meant to end. I therefore pushed on briskly, till I was fairly out of her sight. The road lay between two hedges, so I was sure she could not miss it; and I contrived that she should soon come up with me. When she did, I observed her to be in tears." * * *

[1737] Johnson now thought of trying his fortune in London, the great field of genius and exertion, where talents of every kind have the fullest scope and the highest encouragement. It is a memorable circumstance that his pupil David Garrick went thither at the same time, with intention to complete his education, and follow the profession of the law, from which he was soon diverted by his decided preference for the stage.[3] * * *

[1744] * * * He produced one work this year, fully sufficient to maintain the high reputation which he had acquired. This was *The Life of Richard Savage;*[4] a man of whom it is difficult to speak impartially without wondering that he was for some time the intimate companion of Johnson; for his character was marked by profligacy, insolence, and ingratitude: yet, as he undoubtedly had a warm and vigorous, though unregulated mind, had seen life in all its varieties, and been much in the company of the statesmen and wits of his time, he could communicate to Johnson an abundant supply of such materials as his philosophical curiosity most eagerly desired; and as Savage's misfortunes and misconduct had reduced him to the lowest state of wretchedness as a writer for bread, his visits to St. John's Gate[5] naturally brought Johnson and him together.

It is melancholy to reflect that Johnson and Savage were some-

2. Topham Beauclerk, a descendant of Charles II and the actress Nell Gwynn. He was brilliant and dissolute.
3. Johnson had hoped to complete his tragedy *Irene* and to get it produced, but ths was not accomplished until Garrick staged it in 1749. Meanwhile Johnson struggled against poverty, at first as a writer and translator for Edward Cave's *Gentleman's Magazine*. He gradually won recognition, but was never financially secure until he was pensioned in 1762. Garrick succeeded in the theater much more rapidly than did Johnson in literature.
4. Richard Savage, poet, courted and gained notoriety by claiming to be the illegitimate son of Earl Rivers and the Countess of Macclesfield, whose husband had divorced her because of her unfaithfulness with Rivers. Savage publicized his claim and persecuted his alleged mother. Johnson and many others believed Savage's story and resented what they considered the lady's inhumanity. Savage was a gifted man, but he lived in poverty as a hack writer, though he was long assisted by Pope and others. He died in a debtor's prison in Bristol in 1743.
5. Where Cave published the *Gentleman's Magazine*.

times in such extreme indigence that they could not pay for a lodging; so that they have wandered together whole nights in the streets. Yet in these almost incredible scenes of distress, we may suppose that Savage mentioned many of the anecdotes with which Johnson afterwards enriched the life of his unhappy companion, and those of other poets.

He told Sir Joshua Reynolds that one night in particular, when Savage and he walked round St. James's Square for want of a lodging, they were not at all depressed by their situation; but in high spirits and brimful of patriotism, traversed the square for several hours, inveighed against the minister, and "resolved they would *stand by their country.*" * * *

[1752] That there should be a suspension of his literary labors during a part of the year 1752[6] will not seem strange when it is considered that soon after closing his *Rambler*, he suffered a loss which, there can be no doubt, affected him with the deepest distress. For on the 17th of March, O.S., his wife died. * * *

The following very solemn and affecting prayer was found, after Dr. Johnson's decease, by his servant, Mr. Francis Barber, who delivered it to my worthy friend the Reverend Mr. Strahan, Vicar of Islington, who at my earnest request has obligingly favored me with a copy of it, which he and I compared with the original:

"April 26, 1752, being after 12 at night of the 25th.

"O Lord! Governor of heaven and earth, in whose hands are embodied and departed spirits, if thou hast ordained the souls of the dead to minister to the living, and appointed my departed wife to have care of me, grant that I may enjoy the good effects of her attention and ministration, whether exercised by appearance, impulses, dreams or in any other manner agreeable to thy government. Forgive my presumption, enlighten my ignorance, and however meaner agents are employed, grant me the blessed influences of thy holy Spirit, through Jesus Christ our Lord. Amen." * * *

One night when Beauclerk and Langton[7] had supped at a tavern in London, and sat till about three in the morning, it came into their heads to go and knock up Johnson, and see if they could prevail on him to join them in a ramble. They rapped violently at the door of his chambers in the Temple,[8] till at last he appeared in his shirt, with his little black wig on the top of his head, instead of a nightcap, and a poker in his hand, imagining, probably, that some ruffians were coming to attack him. When he discovered who they were, and was told their errand, he smiled, and with great good

---

6. Johnson's important works written before the publication of the *Dictionary* are the poems *London* (1738) and *The Vanity of Human Wishes* (1749), the *Life of Savage* (1744), and the essays which made up his periodical *The Rambler* (1750–52).
7. Bennet Langton. As a boy he so much admired the *Rambler* that he

sought Johnson's acquaintance. They became lifelong friends.
8. Since Johnson lived in Inner Temple Lane between 1760 and 1765, the "frisk" could not have taken place in the year of his wife's death, where Boswell, for his own convenience, placed it.

humor agreed to their proposal: "What, is it you, you dogs! I'll have a frisk with you." He was soon dressed, and they sallied forth together into Covent Garden, where the greengrocers and fruiterers were beginning to arrange their hampers, just come in from the country. Johnson made some attempts to help them; but the honest gardeners stared so at his figure and manner and odd interference, that he soon saw his services were not relished. They then repaired to one of the neighboring taverns, and made a bowl of that liquor called *Bishop*,[9] which Johnson had always liked; while in joyous contempt of sleep, from which he had been roused, he repeated the festive lines,

> Short, O short then be thy reign,
> And give us to the world again![1]

They did not stay long, but walked down to the Thames, took a boat, and rowed to Billingsgate. Beauclerk and Johnson were so well pleased with their amusement that they resolved to persevere in dissipation for the rest of the day: but Langton deserted them, being engaged to breakfast with some young ladies. Johnson scolded him for "leaving his social friends, to go and sit with a set of wretched *un-idea'd* girls." Garrick being told of this ramble, said to him smartly, "I heard of your frolic t'other night. You'll be in the *Chronicle*." Upon which Johnson afterwards observed, *"He* durst not do such a thing. His *wife* would not *let* him!" * * *

[The Letter to Chesterfield]

[1754] Lord Chesterfield,[2] to whom Johnson had paid the high compliment of addressing to his Lordship the *Plan* of his *Dictionary*, had behaved to him in such a manner as to excite his contempt and indignation. The world has been for many years amused with a story confidently told, and as confidently repeated with additional circumstances, that a sudden disgust was taken by Johnson upon occasion of his having been one day kept long in waiting in his Lordship's antechamber, for which the reason assigned was that he had company with him; and that at last, when the door opened, out walked Colley Cibber;[3] and that Johnson was so violently provoked when he found for whom he had been so long excluded, that he went away in a passion, and never would return. I remember having mentioned this story to George Lord Lyttelton, who told me he was very intimate with Lord Chesterfield; and holding it as a well-known truth, defended Lord Chesterfield, by saying, that Cibber, who had been introduced familiarly by the back stairs, had

9. A drink made of wine, sugar, and either lemon or orange.
1. Misquoted from Lansdowne's *Drinking Song to Sleep*.
2. Philip Dormer Stanhope, Earl of Chesterfield (1694–1773), statesman, wit, man of fashion. His *Letters*, written for the guidance of his natural son, are famous for their worldly good sense and for their expression of the ideal of an 18th-century gentleman.
3. Colley Cibber (1671–1757), playwright, comic actor, and (after 1730) poet laureate. A fine actor but a very bad poet, Cibber was a constant object of ridicule by the wits of the town. Pope made him King of the Dunces in the *Dunciad* of 1743.

probably not been there above ten minutes. It may seem strange even to entertain a doubt concerning a story so long and so widely current, and thus implicitly adopted, if not sanctioned, by the authority which I have mentioned; but Johnson himself assured me that there was not the least foundation for it. He told me that there never was any particular incident which produced a quarrel between Lord Chesterfield and him; but that his Lordship's continued neglect was the reason why he resolved to have no connection with him. When the *Dictionary* was upon the eve of publication, Lord Chesterfield, who, it is said, had flattered himself with expectations that Johnson would dedicate the work to him, attempted, in a courtly manner, to soothe, and insinuate himself with the sage, conscious, as it should seem, of the cold indifference with which he had treated its learned author; and further attempted to conciliate him, by writing two papers in *The World*, in recommendation of the work; and it must be confessed that they contain some studied compliments, so finely turned, that if there had been no previous offense, it is probable that Johnson would have been highly delighted. Praise, in general, was pleasing to him; but by praise from a man of rank and elegant accomplishments, he was peculiarly gratified. * * *

This courtly device failed of its effect. Johnson, who thought that "all was false and hollow,"[4] despised the honeyed words, and was even indignant that Lord Chesterfield should, for a moment, imagine that he could be dupe of such an artifice. His expression to me concerning Lord Chesterfield, upon this occasion, was, "Sir, after making great professions, he had, for many years, taken no notice of me; but when my *Dictionary* was coming out, he fell a-scribbling in *The World* about it. Upon which, I wrote him a letter expressed in civil terms, but such as might show him that I did not mind what he said or wrote, and that I had done with him."

This is that celebrated letter of which so much has been said, and about which curiosity has been so long excited, without being gratified. I for many years solicited Johnson to favor me with a copy of it, that so excellent a composition might not be lost to posterity. He delayed from time to time to give it me; till at last in 1781, when we were on a visit at Mr. Dilly's,[5] at Southill in Bedfordshire, he was pleased to dictate it to me from memory. He afterwards found among his papers a copy of it, which he had dictated to Mr. Baretti,[6] with its title and corrections, in his own handwriting. This he gave to Mr. Langton; adding that if it were to come into print, he wished it to be from that copy. By Mr. Langton's kindness, I am enabled to enrich my work with a perfect transcript of what the world has so eagerly desired to see.

4. *Paradise Lost* II.112.
5. Southill was the country home of Charles and Edward Dilly, publishers. The firm published all of Boswell's serious works and shared in the publication of Johnson's *Lives of the Poets* (1779–81).
6. Giuseppe Baretti, an Italian writer and lexicographer whom Johnson introduced into his circle.

To the Right Honorable the Earl of Chesterfield

February 7, 1755.

My Lord,

I have been lately informed, by the proprietor of *The World*, that two papers, in which my Dictionary is recommended to the public, were written by your Lordship. To be so distinguished, is an honor, which, being very little accustomed to favors from the great, I know not well how to receive, or in what terms to acknowledge.

When, upon some slight encouragement, I first visited your Lordship, I was overpowered, like the rest of mankind, by the enchantment of your address; and could not forbear to wish that I might boast myself *Le vainqueur du vainqueur de la terre*[7]—that I might obtain that regard for which I saw the world contending; but I found my attendance so little encouraged that neither pride nor modesty would suffer me to continue it. When I had once addressed your Lordship in public, I had exhausted all the art of pleasing which a retired and uncourtly scholar can possess. I had done all that I could; and no man is well pleased to have his all neglected, be it ever so little.

Seven years, my Lord, have now passed since I waited in your outward rooms, or was repulsed from your door; during which time I have been pushing on my work through difficulties of which it is useless to complain, and have brought it, at last, to the verge of publication, without one act of assistance, one word of encouragement, or one smile of favor. Such treatment I did not expect, for I never had a patron before.

The shepherd in Virgil grew at last acquainted with Love, and found him a native of the rocks.[8]

Is not a patron, my Lord, one who looks with unconcern on a man struggling for life in the water, and, when he has reached ground, encumbers him with help? The notice which you have been pleased to take of my labors, had it been early, had been kind; but it has been delayed till I am indifferent, and cannot enjoy it; till I am solitary, and cannot impart it; till I am known, and do not want it. I hope it is no very cynical asperity not to confess obligations where no benefit has been received, or to be unwilling that the public should consider me as owing that to a patron which Providence has enabled me to do for myself.

Having carried on my work thus far with so little obligation to any favorer of learning, I shall not be disappointed though I should conclude it, if less be possible, with less; for I have been long wakened from that dream of hope in which I once boasted myself with so much exultation, my Lord, your Lordship's most humble, most obedient servant,

Sam. Johnson.

"While this was the talk of the town," says Dr. Adams, in a letter to me, "I happened to visit Dr. Warburton,[9] who finding that

7. "The conqueror of the conqueror of the earth." From the first line of Scudéry's epic *Alaric* (1654).
8. *Eclogues* VIII.44.

9. William Warburton, Bishop of Gloucester, friend and literary executor of Pope, editor of Pope and Shakespeare, theological controversialist.

I was acquainted with Johnson, desired me earnestly to carry his compliments to him, and to tell him that he honored him for his manly behavior in rejecting these condescensions of Lord Chesterfield, and for resenting the treatment he had received from him, with a proper spirit. Johnson was visibly pleased with this compliment, for he had always a high opinion of Warburton. Indeed, the force of mind which appeared in this letter was congenial with that which Warburton himself amply possessed."

There is a curious minute circumstance which struck me, in comparing the various editions of Johnson's imitations of Juvenal. In the tenth satire, one of the couplets upon the vanity of wishes even for literary distinction stood thus:

> Yet think what ills the scholar's life assail,
> Pride, envy, want, the *garret*, and the jail.

But after experiencing the uneasiness which Lord Chesterfield's fallacious patronage made him feel, he dismissed the word *garret* from the sad group, and in all the subsequent editions the line stands

> Pride, envy, want, the *patron*, and the jail.

[1762] The accession of George the Third to the throne of these kingdoms[1] opened a new and brighter prospect to men of literary merit, who had been honored with no mark of royal favor in the preceding reign. His present Majesty's education in this country, as well as his taste and beneficence, prompted him to be the patron of science and the arts; and early this year Johnson, having been represented to him as a very learned and good man, without any certain provision, his Majesty was pleased to grant him a pension of three hundred pounds a year. The Earl of Bute,[2] who was then Prime Minister, had the honor to announce this instance of his Sovereign's bounty, concerning which many and various stories, all equally erroneous, have been propagated: maliciously representing it as a political bribe to Johnson, to desert his avowed principles, and become the tool of a government which he held to be founded in usurpation. I have taken care to have it in my power to refute them from the most authentic information. Lord Bute told me that Mr. Wedderburne, now Lord Loughborough, was the person who first mentioned this subject to him. Lord Loughborough told me that the pension was granted to Johnson solely as the reward of his literary merit, without any stipulation whatever, or even tacit understanding that he should write for administration. His Lordship added that he was confident the political tracts which Johnson afterwards did write, as they were entirely consonant with his

1. In 1760.
2. An intimate friend of George III's mother, he early gained an ascendancy over the young prince and was largely responsible for the king's autocratic views. He was hated in England both as a favorite and as a Scot.

own opinions, would have been written by him though no pension had been granted to him.[3] * * *

[A Memorable Year: Boswell Meets Johnson]

[1763] This is to me a memorable year; for in it I had the happiness to obtain the acquaintance of tha⁺ extraordinary man whose memoirs I am now writing; an acquaintance which I shall ever esteem as one of the most fortunate circumstances in my life. * * *

Mr. Thomas Davies the actor, who then kept a bookseller's shop in Russel Street, Covent Garden, told me that Johnson was very much his friend, and came frequently to his house, where he more than once invited me to meet him; but by some unlucky accident or other he was prevented from coming to us. * * *

At last, on Monday the 16th of May, when I was sitting in Mr. Davies's back parlor, after having drunk tea with him and Mrs. Davies, Johnson unexpectedly came into the shop; and Mr. Davies having perceived him through the glass door in the room in which we were sitting, advancing towards us—he announced his awful approach to me, somewhat in the manner of an actor in the part of Horatio, when he addresses Hamlet on the appearance of his father's ghost, "Look, my Lord, it comes." I found that I had a very perfect idea of Johnson's figure, from the portrait of him painted by Sir Joshua Reynolds soon after he had published his *Dictionary*, in the attitude of sitting in his easy chair in deep meditation, which was the first picture his friend did for him, which Sir Joshua very kindly presented to me, and from which an engraving has been made for this work. Mr. Davies mentioned my name, and respectfully introduced me to him. I was much agitated; and recollecting his prejudice against the Scotch, of which I had heard much, I said to Davies, "Don't tell where I come from."—"From Scotland," cried Davies roguishly. "Mr. Johnson," said I, "I do indeed come from Scotland, but I cannot help it." I am willing to flatter myself that I meant this as light pleasantry to soothe and conciliate him, and not as an humiliating abasement at the expense of my country. But however that might be, this speech was somewhat unlucky; for with that quickness of wit for which he was so remarkable, he seized the expression "come from Scotland," which I used in the sense of being of that country; and, as if I had said that I had come away from it, or left it, retorted, "That, Sir, I find, is what a very great many of your countrymen cannot help." This stroke stunned me a good deal; and when we had sat down, I felt myself not a little embarrassed, and apprehensive of what might come next. He then addressed himself to Davies: "What do

3. Johnson's few political pamphlets in the 1770's invariably supported the policies of the Crown. The best-known is his answer to the American colonies, *Taxation No Tyranny* (1775). His dislike of the Americans was in large part due to the fact they owned slaves.

you think of Garrick? He has refused me an order for the play for Miss Williams,[4] because he knows the house will be full, and that an order would be worth three shillings." Eager to take any opening to get into conversation with him, I ventured to say, "O Sir, I cannot think Mr. Garrick would grudge such a trifle to you." "Sir," said he, with a stern look, "I have known David Garrick longer than you have done: and I know no right you have to talk to me on the subject." Perhaps I deserved this check; for it was rather presumptuous in me, an entire stranger, to express any doubt of the justice of his animadversion upon his old acquaintance and pupil. I now felt myself much mortified, and began to think that the hope which I had long indulged of obtaining his acquaintance was blasted. And, in truth, had not my ardor been uncommonly strong, and my resolution uncommonly persevering, so rough a reception might have deterred me forever from making any further attempts. Fortunately, however, I remained upon the field not wholly discomfited. * * *

I was highly pleased with the extraordinary vigor of his conversation, and regretted that I was drawn away from it by an engagement at another place. I had, for a part of the evening, been left alone with him, and had ventured to make an observation now and then, which he received very civilly; so that I was satisfied that though there was a roughness in his manner, there was no ill nature in his disposition. Davies followed me to the door, and when I complained to him a little of the hard blows which the great man had given me, he kindly took upon him to console me by saying, "Don't be uneasy. I can see he likes you very well."

A few days afterwards I called on Davies, and asked him if he thought I might take the liberty of waiting on Mr. Johnson at his chambers in the Temple. He said I certainly might, and that Mr. Johnson would take it as a compliment. So upon Tuesday the 24th of May, after having been enlivened by the witty sallies of Messieurs Thornton, Wilkes, Churchill, and Lloyd,[5] with whom I had passed the morning, I boldly repaired to Johnson. His chambers were on the first floor of No. 1, Inner Temple Lane, and I entered them with an impression given me by the Reverend Dr. Blair,[6] of Edinburgh, who had been introduced to him not long before, and described his having "found the giant in his den"; an expression, which, when I came to be pretty well acquainted with Johnson, I repeated to him, and he was diverted at this picturesque account

---

4. Mrs. Anna Williams (1706–83), a blind poet and friend of Mrs. Johnson. She continued to live in Johnson's house after his wife's death, and habitually sat up to make tea for him whenever he came home.
5. Bonnell Thornton, journalist; Charles Churchill, satirist; Robert Lloyd, poet and essayist. For Wilkes see a later episode. The four were bound together by a common love of wit and dissipation. Boswell enjoyed their company in 1763.
6. The Rev. Hugh Blair (1718–1800), Scottish divine and Professor of Rhetoric and Belles Lettres at the University of Edinburgh.

of himself. Dr. Blair had been presented to him by Dr. James Fordyce.[7] At this time the controversy concerning the pieces published by Mr. James Macpherson, as translations of *Ossian*, was at its height.[8] Johnson had all along denied their authenticity; and, what was still more provoking to their admirers, maintained that they had no merit. The subject having been introduced by Dr. Fordyce, Dr. Blair, relying on the internal evidence of their antiquity, asked Dr. Johnson whether he thought any man of a modern age could have written such poems? Johnson replied, "Yes, Sir, many men, many women, and many children." Johnson, at this time, did not know that Dr. Blair had just published a dissertation, not only defending their authenticity, but seriously ranking them with the poems of Homer and Virgil; and when he was afterwards informed of this circumstance, he expressed some displeasure at Dr. Fordyce's having suggested the topic, and said, "I am not sorry that they got thus much for their pains. Sir, it was like leading one to talk of a book when the author is concealed behind the door."

He received me very courteously; but, it must be confessed that his apartment, and furniture, and morning dress, were sufficiently uncouth. His brown suit of clothes looked very rusty; he had on a little old shriveled unpowdered wig, which was too small for his head; his shirt neck and knees of his breeches were loose; his black worsted stockings ill drawn up; and he had a pair of unbuckled shoes by way of slippers. But all these slovenly particularities were forgotten the moment that he began to talk. Some gentlemen, whom I do not recollect, were sitting with him; and when they went away, I also rose; but he said to me, "Nay, don't go." "Sir," said I, "I am afraid that I intrude upon you. It is benevolent to allow me to sit and hear you." He seemed pleased with this compliment, which I sincerely paid him, and answered, "Sir, I am obliged to any man who visits me." I have preserved the following short minute of what passed this day:

"Madness frequently discovers itself merely by unnecessary deviation from the usual modes of the world. My poor friend Smart showed the disturbance of his mind by falling upon his knees, and saying his prayers in the street, or in any other unusual place. Now although, rationally speaking, it is greater madness not to pray at all than to pray as Smart did, I am afraid there are so many who do not pray, that their understanding is not called in question."

Concerning this unfortunate poet, Christopher Smart, who was confined in a madhouse, he had, at another time, the following

7. A Scottish preacher.
8. Macpherson had imposed on most of his contemporaries, Scottish and English, by convincing them of the genuineness of prose poems which he had concocted but which he claimed to have translated from the original Gaelic of Ossian, a blind epic poet of the 3rd century. The vogue of the poems both in Europe and in America was enormous.

conversation with Dr. Burney.[9] BURNEY. "How does poor Smart do, Sir; is he likely to recover?" JOHNSON. "It seems as if his mind had ceased to struggle with the disease; for he grows fat upon it." BURNEY. "Perhaps, Sir, that may be from want of exercise." JOHNSON. "No, Sir; he has partly as much exercise as he used to have, for he digs in the garden. Indeed, before his confinement, he used for exercise to walk to the ale house; but he was *carried* back again. I did not think he ought to be shut up. His infirmities were not noxious to society. He insisted on people praying with him; and I'd as lief pray with Kit Smart as anyone else. Another charge was that he did not love clean linen; and I have no passion for it." —Johnson continued. "Mankind have a great aversion to intellectual labor; but even supposing knowledge to be easily attainable, more people would be content to be ignorant than would take even a little trouble to acquire it."

Talking of Garrick, he said, "He is the first man in the world for sprightly conversation."

When I rose a second time he again pressed me to stay, which I did. * * *

[*Goldsmith. Sundry Opinions. Johnson Meets His King*]

As Dr. Oliver Goldsmith will frequently appear in this narrative, I shall endeavor to make my readers in some degree acquainted with his singular character. He was a native of Ireland, and a contemporary with Mr. Burke[1] at Trinity College, Dublin, but did not then give much promise of future celebrity. He, however, observed to Mr. Malone,[2] that "though he made no great figure in mathematics, which was a study in much repute there, he could turn an ode of Horace into English better than any of them." He afterwards studied physic at Edinburgh, and upon the Continent; and I have been informed, was enabled to pursue his travels on foot, partly by demanding at universities to enter the lists as a disputant, by which, according to the custom of many of them, he was entitled to the premium of a crown, when luckily for him his challenge was not accepted; so that, as I once observed to Dr. Johnson, he *disputed* his passage through Europe. He then came to England, and was employed successively in the capacities of an usher[3] to an academy, a corrector of the press, a reviewer, and a writer for a newspaper. He had sagacity enough to cultivate assiduously the acquaintance of Johnson, and his faculties were gradually enlarged by the contemplation of such a model. To me and many others it

9. Dr. Charles Burney (1726–1814), historian of music and father of the novelist and diarist Fanny Burney, whom Johnson knew and loved in his old age.
1. Edmund Burke (1729–97), statesman, orator, and political philosopher.

2. Edmond Malone (1741–1812), distinguished editor and literary scholar. He helped Boswell in the writing and publication of the *Life.*
3. An assistant teacher; then a disagreeable and ill-paid job.

appeared that he studiously copied the manner of Johnson, though, indeed, upon a smaller scale.

At this time I think he had published nothing with his name, though it was pretty generally known that *one Dr. Goldsmith* was the author of *An Enquiry into the Present State of Polite Learning in Europe,* and of *The Citizen of the World,* a series of letters supposed to be written from London by a Chinese. No man had the art of displaying, with more advantage as a writer, whatever literary acquisitions he made. "*Nihil quod tetigit non ornavit.*"[4] His mind resembled a fertile, but thin soil. There was a quick, but not a strong vegetation, of whatever chanced to be thrown upon it. No deep root could be struck. The oak of the forest did not grow there; but the elegant shrubbery and the fragrant parterre[5] appeared in gay succession. It has been generally circulated and believed that he was a mere fool in conversation; but, in truth, this has been greatly exaggerated. He had, no doubt, a more than common share of that hurry of ideas which we often find in his countrymen, and which sometimes produces a laughable confusion in expressing them. He was very much what the French call *un étourdi,*[6] and from vanity and an eager desire of being conspicuous wherever he was, he frequently talked carelessly without knowledge of the subject, or even without thought. His person was short, his countenance coarse and vulgar, his deportment that of a scholar awkwardly affecting the easy gentleman. Those who were in any way distinguished, excited envy in him to so ridiculous an excess that the instances of it are hardly credible. When accompanying two beautiful young ladies with their mother on a tour in France, he was seriously angry that more attention was paid to them than to him; and once at the exhibition of the *Fantoccini* in London, when those who sat next him observed with what dexterity a puppet was made to toss a pike, he could not bear that it should have such praise, and exclaimed with some warmth, "Pshaw! I can do it better myself."[7] * * *

I had as my guests this evening at the Mitre Tavern, Dr. Johnson, Dr. Goldsmith, Mr. Thomas Davies, Mr. Eccles, an Irish gentleman, for whose agreeable company I was obliged to Mr. Davies, and the Reverend Mr. John Ogilvie,[8] who was desirous of being in company with my illustrious friend, while I, in my turn, was proud to have the honor of showing one of my countrymen upon what easy terms Johnson permitted me to live with him. * * *

Mr. Ogilvie was unlucky enough to choose for the topic of his

4. "He touched nothing that he did not adorn." From Johnson's epitaph for Goldsmith's monument in Westminster Abbey.
5. A flower garden with beds laid out in patterns.
6. One who acts without thought.

7. It is difficult to believe that Boswell did not recognize that Goldsmith was joking. Indeed, his entire characterization of Goldsmith is not without malice and distortion.
8. An eminent Scottish divine.

conversation the praises of his native country. He began with saying
that there was very rich land round Edinburgh. Goldsmith, who
had studied physic there, contradicted this, very untruly, with a
sneering laugh. Disconcerted a little by this, Mr. Ogilvie then took
new ground, where, I suppose, he thought himself perfectly safe;
for he observed that Scotland had a great many noble wild prospects. JOHNSON. "I believe, Sir, you have a great many. Norway,
too, has noble wild prospects; and Lapland is remarkable for prodigious noble wild prospects. But, Sir, let me tell you, the noblest
prospect which a Scotchman ever sees, is the highroad that leads
him to England!" This unexpected and pointed sally produced a
roar of applause. After all, however, those who admire the rude
grandeur of nature cannot deny it to Caledonia. * * *

At night Mr. Johnson and I supped in a private room at the
Turk's Head Coffeehouse, in the Strand. "I encourage this house,"
said he, "for the mistress of it is a good civil woman, and has not
much business.

"Sir, I love the acquaintance of young people; because, in the
first place, I don't like to think myself growing old. In the next
place, young acquaintances must last longest, if they do last; and
then, Sir, young men have more virtue than old men: they have
more generous sentiments in every respect. I love the young dogs
of this age: they have more wit and humor and knowledge of life
than we had; but then the dogs are not so good scholars. Sir, in my
early years I read very hard. It is a sad reflection, but a true one,
that I knew almost as much at eighteen as I do now. My judgment,
to be sure, was not so good; but I had all the facts. I remember very
well, when I was at Oxford, an old gentleman said to me, 'Young
man, ply your book diligently now, and acquire a stock of knowledge; for when years come upon you, you will find that poring upon
books will be but an irksome task.' " * * *

He again insisted on the duty of maintaining subordination of
rank. "Sir, I would no more deprive a nobleman of his respect than
of his money. I consider myself as acting a part in the great system
of society, and I do to others as I would have them to do to me.
I would behave to a nobleman as I should expect he would behave
to me, were I a nobleman and he Sam. Johnson. Sir, there is one
Mrs. Macaulay[9] in this town, a great republican. One day when I
was at her house, I put on a very grave countenance, and said to
her, 'Madam, I am now become a convert to your way of thinking.
I am convinced that all mankind are upon an equal footing; and
to give you an unquestionable proof, Madam, that I am in earnest,
here is a very sensible, civil, well-behaved fellow citizen, your footman; I desire that he may be allowed to sit down and dine with
us.' I thus, Sir, showed her the absurdity of the leveling doctrine.

9. Mrs. Catharine Macaulay, at this
time much in the public eye as a female
historian and a propounder of libertarian and egalitarian ideas.

She has never liked me since. Sir, your levelers wish to level *down* as far as themselves; but they cannot bear leveling *up* to themselves. They would all have some people under them; why not then have some people above them?" * * *

At supper this night he talked of good eating with uncommon satisfaction. "Some people," said he, "have a foolish way of not minding, or pretending not to mind, what they eat. For my part, I mind my belly very studiously, and very carefully; for I look upon it that he who does not mind his belly will hardly mind anything else." He now appeared to me *Jean Bull philosophe*,[1] and he was, for the moment, not only serious but vehement. Yet I have heard him, upon other occasions, talk with great contempt of people who were anxious to gratify their palates; and the 206th number of his *Rambler* is a masterly essay against gulosity.[2] His practice, indeed, I must acknowledge, may be considered as casting the balance of his different opinions upon this subject; for I never knew any man who relished good eating more than he did. When at table, he was totally absorbed in the business of the moment; his looks seemed riveted to his plate; nor would he, unless when in very high company, say one word, or even pay the least attention to what was said by others, till he had satisfied his appetite, which was so fierce, and indulged with such intenseness, that while in the act of eating, the veins of his forehead swelled, and generally a strong perspiration was visible. To those whose sensations were delicate, this could not but be disgusting; and it was doubtless not very suitable to the character of a philosopher, who should be distinguished by self-command. But it must be owned that Johnson, though he could be rigidly *abstemious*, was not a *temperate* man either in eating or drinking. He could refrain, but he could not use moderately. He told me that he had fasted two days without inconvenience, and that he had never been hungry but once. They who beheld with wonder how much he eat upon all occasions when his dinner was to his taste, could not easily conceive what he must have meant by hunger; and not only was he remarkable for the extraordinary quantity which he eat, but he was, or affected to be, a man of very nice discernment in the science of cookery. * * *

[1767] In February, 1767, there happened one of the most remarkable incidents of Johnson's life, which gratified his monarchical enthusiasm, and which he loved to relate with all its circumstances, when requested by his friends. This was his being honored by a private conversation with his Majesty, in the library at the Queen's house. He had frequently visited those splendid rooms and noble collection of books, which he used to say was more numerous and curious than he supposed any person could have made in the time which the King had employed. Mr. Barnard,

1. I.e., John Bull (the typical hard-headed Englishman) in the role of philosopher.
2. Greediness.

the librarian, took care that he should have every accommodation that could contribute to his ease and convenience, while indulging his literary taste in that place; so that he had here a very agreeable resource at leisure hours.

His Majesty having been informed of his occasional visits, was pleased to signify a desire that he should be told when Dr. Johnson came next to the library. Accordingly, the next time that Johnson did come, as soon as he was fairly engaged with a book, on which, while he sat by the fire, he seemed quite intent, Mr. Barnard stole round to the apartment where the King was, and, in obedience to his Majesty's commands, mentioned that Dr. Johnson was then in the library. His Majesty said he was at leisure, and would go to him; upon which Mr. Barnard took one of the candles that stood on the King's table, and lighted his Majesty through a suite of rooms, till they came to a private door into the library, of which his Majesty had the key. Being entered, Mr. Barnard stepped forward hastily to Dr. Johnson, who was still in a profound study, and whispered him, "Sir, here is the King." Johnson started up, and stood still. His Majesty approached him, and at once was courteously easy.

His Majesty began by observing that he understood he came sometimes to the library; and then mentioning his having heard that the Doctor had been lately at Oxford, asked him if he was not fond of going thither. To which Johnson answered that he was indeed fond of going to Oxford sometimes, but was likewise glad to come back again. The King then asked him what they were doing at Oxford. Johnson answered, he could not much commend their diligence, but that in some respects they were mended, for they had put their press under better regulations, and were at that time printing Polybius. He was then asked whether there were better libraries at Oxford or Cambridge. He answered, he believed the Bodleian was larger than any they had at Cambridge; at the same time adding, "I hope, whether we have more books or not than they have at Cambridge, we shall make as good use of them as they do." Being asked whether All Souls or Christ Church library was the largest, he answered, "All Souls library is the largest we have, except the Bodleian." "Aye," said the King, "that is the public library."

His Majesty inquired if he was then writing anything. He answered, he was not, for he had pretty well told the world what he knew, and must now read to acquire more knowledge. The King, as it should seem with a view to urge him to rely on his own stores as an original writer, and to continue his labors, then said "I do not think you borrow much from anybody." Johnson said he thought he had already done his part as a writer. "I should have thought so too," said the King, "if you had not written so well."—

Johnson observed to me, upon this, that "No man could have paid a handsomer compliment; and it was fit for a king to pay. It was decisive." When asked by another friend, at Sir Joshua Reynolds's, whether he made any reply to this high compliment, he answered, "No, Sir. When the King had said it, it was to be so. It was not for me to bandy civilities with my sovereign." Perhaps no man who had spent his whole life in courts could have shown a more nice and dignified sense of true politeness than Johnson did in this instance. * * *

[Fear of Death]

[1769] When we were alone, I introduced the subject of death, and endeavored to maintain that the fear of it might be got over. I told him that David Hume said to me, he was no more uneasy to think he should *not be* after this life, than that he *had not been* before he began to exist. JOHNSON. "Sir, if he really thinks so, his perceptions are disturbed; he is mad: if he does not think so, he lies. He may tell you, he holds his finger in the flame of a candle, without feeling pain; would you believe him? When he dies, he at least gives up all he has." BOSWELL. "Foote,[3] Sir, told me, that when he was very ill he was not afraid to die." JOHNSON. "It is not true, Sir. Hold a pistol to Foote's breast, or to Hume's breast, and threaten to kill them, and you'll see how they behave." BOSWELL. "But may we not fortify our minds for the approach of death?" Here I am sensible I was in the wrong, to bring before his view what he ever looked upon with horror; for although when in a celestial frame, in his *Vanity of Human Wishes*, he has supposed death to be "kind Nature's signal for retreat," from this state of being to "a happier seat," his thoughts upon this awful change were in general full of dismal apprehensions. His mind resembled the vast amphitheater, the Colosseum at Rome. In the center stood his judgment, which, like a mighty gladiator, combated those apprehensions that, like the wild beasts of the arena, were all around in cells, ready to be let out upon him. After a conflict, he drives them back into their dens; but not killing them, they were still assailing him. To my question, whether we might not fortify our minds for the approach of death, he answered, in a passion, "No, Sir, let it alone. It matters not how a man dies, but how he lives. The act of dying is not of importance, it lasts so short a time." He added (with an earnest look), "A man knows it must be so, and submits. It will do him no good to whine."

I attempted to continue the conversation. He was so provoked that he said, "Give us no more of this"; and was thrown into such a state of agitation that he expressed himself in a way that alarmed

3. Samuel Foote, actor and dramatist, famous for his wit and his skill in mimicry.

and distressed me; showed an impatience that I should leave him, and when I was going away, called to me sternly, "Don't let us meet tomorrow." * * *

[*Ossian. "Talking for Victory"*]

MR. BOSWELL TO DR. JOHNSON

Edinburgh, Feb. 2, 1775.

* * * As to Macpherson, I am anxious to have from yourself a full and pointed account of what has passed between you and him. It is confidently told here that before your book[4] came out he sent to you, to let you know that he understood you meant to deny the authenticity of Ossian's poems; that the originals were in his possession; that you might have inspection of them, and might take the evidence of people skilled in the Erse language; and that he hoped, after this fair offer, you would not be so uncandid as to assert that he had refused reasonable proof. That you paid no regard to his message, but published your strong attack upon him; and then he wrote a letter to you, in such terms as he thought suited to one who had not acted as a man of veracity. * * *

What words were used by Mr. Macpherson in his letter to the venerable sage, I have never heard; but they are generally said to have been of a nature very different from the language of literary contest. Dr. Johnson's answer appeared in the newspapers of the day, and has since been frequently republished; but not with perfect accuracy. I give it as dictated to me by himself, written down in his presence, and authenticated by a note in his own handwriting, "*This, I think, is a true copy.*"

MR. JAMES MACPHERSON,

I received your foolish and impudent letter. Any violence offered me I shall do my best to repel; and what I cannot do for myself, the law shall do for me. I hope I shall never be deterred from detecting what I think a cheat, by the menaces of a ruffian.

What would you have me retract? I thought your book an imposture; I think it an imposture still. For this opinion I have given my reasons to the public, which I here dare you to refute. Your rage I defy. Your abilities, since your Homer, are not so formidable; and what I hear of your morals inclines me to pay regard not to what you shall say, but to what you shall prove. You may print this if you will.

SAM. JOHNSON.

Mr. Macpherson little knew the character of Dr. Johnson if he supposed that he could be easily intimidated; for no man was ever more remarkable for personal courage. He had, indeed, an awful dread of death, or rather, "of something after death"; and what rational man, who seriously thinks of quitting all that he has ever

---

4. Johnson's *Journey to the Western Islands* (1775), in which he had pub-licly expressed his views on the Ossianic poems.

known, and going into a new and unknown state of being, can be without that dread? But his fear was from reflection; his courage natural. His fear, in that one instance, was the result of philosophical and religious consideration. He feared death, but he feared nothing else, not even what might occasion death. Many instances of his resolution may be mentioned. One day, at Mr. Beauclerk's house in the country, when two large dogs were fighting, he went up to them, and beat them till they separated; and at another time, when told of the danger there was that a gun might burst if charged with many balls, he put in six or seven, and fired it off against a wall. Mr. Langton told me that when they were swimming together near Oxford, he cautioned Dr. Johnson against a pool which was reckoned particularly dangerous; upon which Johnson directly swam into it. He told me himself that one night he was attacked in the street by four men, to whom he would not yield, but kept them all at bay, till the watch came up, and carried both him and them to the roundhouse. In the playhouse at Lichfield, as Mr. Garrick informed me, Johnson having for a moment quitted a chair which was placed for him between the side-scenes, a gentleman took possession of it, and when Johnson on his return civilly demanded his seat, rudely refused to give it up; upon which Johnson laid hold of it, and tossed him and the chair into the pit. Foote, who so successfully revived the old comedy, by exhibiting living characters, had resolved to imitate Johnson on the stage, expecting great profits from his ridicule of so celebrated a man. Johnson being informed of his intention, and being at dinner at Mr. Thomas Davies's the bookseller, from whom I had the story, he asked Mr. Davies what was the common price of an oak stick; and being answered sixpence, "Why then, Sir," said he, "give me leave to send your servant to purchase me a shilling one. I'll have a double quantity; for I am told Foote means to *take me off*, as he calls it, and I am determined the fellow shall not do it with impunity." Davies took care to acquaint Foote of this, which effectually checked the wantonness of the mimic. Mr. Macpherson's menaces made Johnson provide himself with the same implement of defense; and had he been attacked, I have no doubt that, old as he was, he would have made his corporal prowess be felt as much as his intellectual. * * *

[1776] I mentioned a new gaming club, of which Mr. Beauclerk had given me an account, where the members played to a desperate extent. JOHNSON. "Depend upon it, Sir, this is mere talk. Who is ruined by gaming? You will not find six instances in an age. There is a strange rout made about deep play: whereas you have many more people ruined by adventurous trade, and yet we do not hear such an outcry against it." THRALE.[5] "There may be few people

5. Johnson met Henry Thrale, the wealthy brewer, and his charming wife Hester in 1765. Thereafter he was domesticated as much as he wished to be

absolutely ruined by deep play; but very many are much hurt in their circumstances by it." JOHNSON. "Yes, Sir, and so are very many by other kinds of expense." I had heard him talk once before in the same manner; and at Oxford he said, he wished he had learnt to play at cards. The truth, however, is that he loved to display his ingenuity in argument; and therefore would sometimes in conversation maintain opinions which he was sensible were wrong, but in supporting which, his reasoning and wit would be most conspicuous. He would begin thus: "Why, Sir, as to the good or evil of card playing——" "Now, said Garrick, "he is thinking which side he shall take." He appeared to have a pleasure in contradiction, especially when any opinion whatever was delivered with an air of confidence; so that there was hardly any topic, if not one of the great truths of religion and morality, that he might not have been incited to argue, either for or against. Lord Elibank[6] had the highest admiration of his powers. He once observed to me, "Whatever opinion Johnson maintains, I will not say that he convinces me; but he never fails to show me that he has good reasons for it." I have heard Johnson pay his Lordship this high compliment: "I never was in Lord Elibank's company without learning something." * * *

[Dinner with Wilkes]

My worthy booksellers and friends, Messieurs Dilly in the Poultry, at whose hospitable and well-covered table I have seen a greater number of literary men than at any other, except that of Sir Joshua Reynolds, had invited me to meet Mr. Wilkes[7] and some more gentlemen on Wednesday, May 15. "Pray," said I, "let us have Dr. Johnson."—"What, with Mr. Wilkes? not for the world," said Mr. Edward Dilly, "Dr. Johnson would never forgive me."—"Come," said I, "if you'll let me negotiate for you, I will be answerable that all shall go well." DILLY. "Nay, if you will take it upon you, I am sure I shall be very happy to see them both here."

Notwithstanding the high veneration which I entertained for Dr. Johnson, I was sensible that he was sometimes a little actuated by the spirit of contradiction, and by means of that I hoped I

at their house at Streatham near London. There he enjoyed the good things of life, as well as the companionship of Mrs. Thrale and her children. Thrale died in 1781. His widow's marriage to Gabriel Piozzi, an Italian musician, in 1784, caused Johnson to quarrel with her and darkened the last months of his life.

6. Prominent in Scottish literary circles. Johnson, who admired him, had visited him on his tour of Scotland with Boswell in 1773.

7. John Wilkes (1727–97) was obnoxious to the Christian and Tory Johnson in every way. He was profane and

dissolute, and his personal life was a public scandal; for over a decade he had been notorious as a courageous, resourceful, and finally victorious opponent of the arbitrary and tyrannical policies of the king and his ministers, and had been the envenomed critic of Lord Bute, to whom Johnson owed his pension. When Johnson met him he had totally defeated his enemies, had served as Lord Mayor, and was again a Member of Parliament, a post from which he had been expelled and driven into exile as an outlaw in 1764. Boswell had found Wilkes a gay and congenial companion in Italy in 1764.

should gain my point. I was persuaded that if I had come upon him with a direct proposal, "Sir, will you dine in company with Jack Wilkes?" he would have flown into a passion, and would probably have answered, "Dine with Jack Wilkes, Sir! I'd as soon dine with Jack Ketch."[8] I therefore, while we were sitting quietly by ourselves at his house in an evening, took occasion to open my plan thus: "Mr. Dilly, Sir, sends his respectful compliments to you, and would be happy if you would do him the honor to dine with him on Wednesday next along with me, as I must soon go to Scotland." JOHNSON. "Sir, I am obliged to Mr. Dilly. I will wait upon him—" BOSWELL. "Provided, Sir, I suppose, that the company which he is to have, is agreeable to you." JOHNSON. "What do you mean, Sir? What do you take me for? Do you think I am so ignorant of the world as to imagine that I am to prescribe to a gentleman what company he is to have at his table?" BOSWELL. "I beg your pardon, Sir, for wishing to prevent you from meeting people whom you might not like. Perhaps he may have some of what he calls his patriotic[9] friends with him." JOHNSON. "Well, Sir, and what then? What care *I* for his *patriotic friends?* Poh!" BOSWELL. "I should not be surprised to find Jack Wilkes there." JOHNSON. "And if Jack Wilkes *should* be there, what is that to *me,* Sir? My dear friend, let us have no more of this. I am sorry to be angry with you; but really it is treating me strangely to talk to me as if I could not meet any company whatever, occasionally." BOSWELL. "Pray forgive me, Sir: I meant well. But you shall meet whoever comes, for me." Thus I secured him, and told Dilly that he would find him very well pleased to be one of his guests on the day appointed.

Upon the much-expected Wednesday, I called on him about half an hour before dinner, as I often did when we were to dine out together, to see that he was ready in time, and to accompany him. I found him buffeting his books, as upon a former occasion, covered with dust, and making no preparation for going abroad. "How is this, Sir?" said I. "Don't you recollect that you are to dine at Mr. Dilly's?" JOHNSON. "Sir, I did not think of going to Dilly's: it went out of my head. I have ordered dinner at home with Mrs. Williams." BOSWELL. "But, my dear Sir, you know you were engaged to Mr. Dilly, and I told him so. He will expect you, and will be much disappointed if you don't come." JOHNSON. "You must talk to Mrs. Williams about this."

Here was a sad dilemma. I feared that what I was so confident I had secured would yet be frustrated. He had accustomed himself

8. After the public hangman, Jack Ketch, died in 1686, his name became the common designation of all those who filled that office.
9. In Tory circles the word had come to be used ironically of those who op- posed the government. The "patriots" considered themselves the defenders of the ancient liberties of the English. They included the partisans of both Wilkes and of the American colonists.

to show Mrs. Williams such a degree of humane attention as frequently imposed some restraint upon him; and I knew that if she should be obstinate, he would not stir. I hastened downstairs to the blind lady's room, and told her I was in great uneasiness, for Dr. Johnson had engaged to me to dine this day at Mr. Dilly's, but that he had told me he had forgotten his engagement, and had ordered dinner at home. "Yes, Sir," said she, pretty peevishly, "Dr. Johnson is to dine at home."—"Madam," said I, "his respect for you is such that I know he will not leave you unless you absolutely desire it. But as you have so much of his company, I hope you will be good enough to forego it for a day; as Mr. Dilly is a very worthy man, has frequently had agreeable parties at his house for Dr. Johnson, and will be vexed if the Doctor neglects him today. And then, Madam, be pleased to consider my situation; I carried the message, and I assured Mr. Dilly that Dr. Johnson was to come, and no doubt he has made a dinner, and invited a company, and boasted of the honor he expected to have. I shall be quite disgraced if the Doctor is not there." She gradually softened to my solicitations, which were certainly as earnest as most entreaties to ladies upon any occasion, and was graciously pleased to empower me to tell Dr. Johnson that all things considered, she thought he should certainly go. I flew back to him, still in dust, and careless of what should be the event, "indifferent in his choice to go or stay";[1] but as soon as I had announced to him Mrs. Williams' consent, he roared, "Frank, a clean shirt," and was very soon dressed. When I had him fairly seated in a hackney coach with me, I exulted as much as a fortune hunter who has got an heiress into a post chaise with him to set out for Gretna Green.[2]

When we entered Mr. Dilly's drawing room, he found himself in the midst of a company he did not know. I kept myself snug and silent, watching how he would conduct himself. I observed him whispering to Mr. Dilly, "Who is that gentleman, Sir?"— "Mr. Arthur Lee."—JOHNSON. "Too, too, too" (under his breath), which was one of his habitual mutterings. Mr. Arthur Lee could not but be very obnoxious to Johnson, for he was not only a *patriot* but an *American*.[3] He was afterwards minister from the United States at the court of Madrid. "And who is the gentleman in lace?" —"Mr. Wilkes, Sir." This information confounded him still more; he had some difficulty to restrain himself, and taking up a book, sat down upon a window seat and read, or at least kept his eye upon it intently for some time, till he composed himself. His feel-

1. Addison's *Cato* V.i.40. Boswell cleverly adapts to his own purpose Cato's words, "Indifferent in his choice to sleep or die."

2. A village just across the Scottish border where runaway couples were married by the local innkeeper or the blacksmith.

3. Johnson was extremely hostile to the rebelling American colonists. On one occasion he said: "I am willing to love all mankind, except an American." Lee had been educated in England and Scotland, and had recently been admitted to the English bar. He had been a loyal supporter of Wilkes.

ings, I dare say, were awkward enough. But he no doubt recollected his having rated me for supposing that he could be at all disconcerted by any company, and he, therefore, resolutely set himself to behave quite as an easy man of the world, who could adapt himself at once to the disposition and manners of those whom he might chance to meet.

The cheering sound of "Dinner is upon the table," dissolved his reverie, and we *all* sat down without any symptom of ill humor. There were present, beside Mr. Wilkes, and Mr. Arthur Lee, who was an old companion of mine when he studied physic at Edinburgh, Mr. (now Sir John) Miller, Dr. Lettsom, and Mr. Slater the druggist. Mr. Wilkes placed himself next to Dr. Johnson, and behaved to him with so much attention and politeness that he gained upon him insensibly. No man eat more heartily than Johnson, or loved better what was nice and delicate. Mr. Wilkes was very assiduous in helping him to some fine veal. "Pray give me leave, Sir—It is better here—A little of the brown—Some fat, Sir—A little of the stuffing—Some gravy—Let me have the pleasure of giving you some butter—Allow me to recommend a squeeze of this orange—or the lemon, perhaps, may have more zest."— "Sir, Sir, I am obliged to you, Sir," cried Johnson, bowing, and turning his head to him with a look for some time of "surly virtue," but, in a short while, of complacency.

Foote being mentioned, Johnson said, "He is not a good mimic." One of the company added, "A merry Andrew, a buffoon." JOHNSON. "But he has wit too, and is not deficient in ideas, or in fertility and variety of imagery, and not empty of reading; he has knowledge enough to fill up his part. One species of wit he has in an eminent degree, that of escape. You drive him into a corner with both hands; but he's gone, Sir, when you think you have got him —like an animal that jumps over your head. Then he has a great range for wit; he never lets truth stand between him and a jest, and he is sometimes mighty coarse. Garrick is under many restraints from which Foote is free." WILKES. "Garrick's wit is more like Lord Chesterfield's." JOHNSON. "The first time I was in company with Foote was at Fitzherbert's. Having no good opinion of the fellow, I was resolved not to be pleased; and it is very difficult to please a man against his will. I went on eating my dinner pretty sullenly, affecting not to mind him. But the dog was so very comical, that I was obliged to lay down my knife and fork, throw myself back upon my chair, and fairly laugh it out. No, Sir, he was irresistible. He upon one occasion experienced, in an extraordinary degree, the efficacy of his powers of entertaining. Amongst the many and various modes which he tried of getting money, he became a partner with a small-beer[4] brewer, and he was to have a share of

4. Weak beer, served in the servants' hall.

the profits for procuring customers amongst his numerous acquaintance. Fitzherbert was one who took his small beer; but it was so bad that the servants resolved not to drink it. They were at some loss how to notify their resolution, being afraid of offending their master, who they knew liked Foote much as a companion. At last they fixed upon a little black boy, who was rather a favorite, to be their deputy, and deliver their remonstrance; and having invested him with the whole authority of the kitchen, he was to inform Mr. Fitzherbert, in all their names, upon a certain day, that they would drink Foote's small beer no longer. On that day Foote happened to dine at Fitzherbert's, and this boy served at table; he was so delighted with Foote's stories, and merriment, and grimace, that when he went downstairs, he told them, 'This is the finest man I have ever seen. I will not deliver your message. I will drink his small beer.' "

Somebody observed that Garrick could not have done this. WILKES. "Garrick would have made the small beer still smaller. He is now leaving the stage; but he will play *Scrub*[5] all his life." I knew that Johnson would let nobody attack Garrick but himself, as Garrick once said to me, and I had heard him praise his liberality; so to bring out his commendation of his celebrated pupil, I said, loudly, "I have heard Garrick is liberal." JOHNSON. "Yes, Sir, I know that Garrick has given away more money than any man in England that I am acquainted with, and that not from ostentatious views. Garrick was very poor when he began life; so when he came to have money, he probably was very unskillful in giving away, and saved when he should not. But Garrick began to be liberal as soon as he could; and I am of opinion, the reputation of avarice which he has had, has been very lucky for him, and prevented his having many enemies. You despise a man for avarice, but do not hate him. Garrick might have been much better attacked for living with more splendor than is suitable to a player: if they had had the wit to have assaulted him in that quarter, they might have galled him more. But they have kept clamoring about his avarice, which has rescued him from much obloquy and envy."

Talking of the great difficulty of obtaining authentic information for biography, Johnson told us, "When I was a young fellow I wanted to write the *Life of Dryden,* and in order to get materials, I applied to the only two persons then alive who had seen him; these were old Swinney,[6] and old Cibber. Swinney's information was no more than this, that at Will's Coffeehouse Dryden had a particular chair for himself, which was set by the fire in winter, and was then called his winter chair; and that it was carried out for him to the balcony in summer, and was then called his summer

---

5. The servant of Squire Sullen in George Farquhar's *Beaux' Stratagem:* a favorite role of Garrick's. 6. Owen Mac Swinney, a playwright.

chair. Cibber could tell no more but that he remembered him a decent old man, arbiter of critical disputes at Will's. You are to consider that Cibber was then at a great distance from Dryden, had perhaps one leg only in the room, and durst not draw in the other." BOSWELL. "Yet Cibber was a man of observation?" JOHN-SON. "I think not." BOSWELL. "You will allow his *Apology* to be well done." JOHNSON. "Very well done, to be sure, Sir. That book is a striking proof of the justice of Pope's remark:

> Each might his several province well command,
> Would all but stoop to what they understand."[7]

BOSWELL. "And his plays are good." JOHNSON. "Yes; but that was his trade; *l'esprit du corps:* he had been all his life among players and play writers. I wondered that he had so little to say in conversation, for he had kept the best company, and learnt all that can be got by the ear. He abused Pindar to me, and then showed me an ode of his own, with an absurd couplet, making a linnet soar on an eagle's wing. I told him that when the ancients made a simile, they always made it like something real."

Mr. Wilkes remarked that "among all the bold flights of Shakespeare's imagination, the boldest was making Birnam Wood march to Dunsinane;[8] creating a wood where there never was a shrub; a wood in Scotland! ha! ha! ha!" And he also observed, that "the clannish slavery of the Highlands of Scotland was the single exception to Milton's remark of 'The mountain nymph, sweet Liberty,'[9] being worshiped in all hilly countries."—"When I was at Inverary," said he, "on a visit to my old friend, Archibald, Duke of Argyle, his dependents congratulated me on being such a favorite of his Grace. I said, 'It is then, gentlemen, truly lucky for me; for if I had displeased the Duke, and he had wished it, there is not a Campbell among you but would have been ready to bring John Wilkes's head to him in a charger. It would have been only

> Off with his head! So much for Aylesbury.'[1]

I was then member for Aylesbury." * * *

Mr. Arthur Lee mentioned some Scotch who had taken possession of a barren part of America, and wondered why they should choose it. JOHNSON. "Why, Sir, all barrenness is comparative. The *Scotch* would not know it to be barren." BOSWELL. "Come, come, he is flattering the English. You have now been in Scotland, Sir, and say if you did not see meat and drink enough there." JOHNSON. "Why yes, Sir; meat and drink enough to give the inhabitants sufficient strength to run away from home." All these quick and lively sallies were said sportively, quite in jest, and with a smile, which

7. *Essay on Criticism* I.66–67.
8. *Macbeth* V.v.30–52.
9. *L'Allegro,* line 36.

1. "Off with his head! So much for Buckingham." A line in Cibber's version of Shakespeare's *Richard III.*

showed that he meant only wit. Upon this topic he and Mr. Wilkes could perfectly assimilate; here was a bond of union between them, and I was conscious that as both of them had visited Caledonia, both were fully satisfied of the strange narrow ignorance of those who imagine that it is a land of famine. But they amused themselves with persevering in the old jokes. When I claimed a superiority for Scotland over England in one respect, that no man can be arrested there for a debt merely because another swears it against him; but there must first be the judgment of a court of law ascertaining its justice; and that a seizure of the person, before judgment is obtained, can take place only if his creditor should swear that he is about to fly from the country, or, as it is technically expressed, is *in meditatione fugae:* WILKES. "That, I should think, may be safely sworn of all the Scotch nation." JOHNSON (to Mr. Wilkes). "You must know, Sir, I lately took my friend Boswell and showed him genuine civilized life in an English provincial town. I turned him loose at Lichfield, my native city, that he might see for once real civility: for you know he lives among savages in Scotland, and among rakes in London." WILKES. "Except when he is with grave, sober, decent people like you and me." JOHNSON (smiling). "And we ashamed of him."

They were quite frank and easy. Johnson told the story of his asking Mrs. Macaulay to allow her footman to sit down with them, to prove the ridiculousness of the argument for the equality of mankind; and he said to me afterwards, with a nod of satisfaction, "You saw Mr. Wilkes acquiesced." * * *

This record, though by no means so perfect as I could wish, will serve to give a notion of a very curious interview, which was not only pleasing at the time, but had the agreeable and benignant effect of reconciling any animosity and sweetening any acidity, which in the various bustle of political contest, had been produced in the minds of two men, who, though widely different, had so many things in common—classical learning, modern literature, wit, and humor, and ready repartee—that it would have been much to be regretted if they had been forever at a distance from each other.

Mr. Burke gave me much credit for this successful "negotiation"; and pleasantly said that there was nothing to equal it in the whole history of the *Corps Diplomatique.* * * *

[Dread of Solitude]

[1777] I talked to him of misery being "the doom of man" in this life, as displayed in his *Vanity of Human Wishes.* Yet I observed that things were done upon the supposition of happiness; grand houses were built, fine gardens were made, splendid places of public amusement were contrived, and crowded with company. JOHNSON. "Alas, Sir, these are all only struggles for happiness. When

I first entered Ranelagh,[2] it gave an expansion and gay sensation to my mind, such as I never experienced anywhere else. But, as Xerxes wept when he viewed his immense army, and considered that not one of that great multitude would be alive a hundred years afterwards, so it went to my heart to consider that there was not one in all that brilliant circle that was not afraid to go home and think; but that the thoughts of each individual there, would be distressing when alone." * * *

["*A Bottom of Good Sense.*" *Bet Flint.*
"*Clear Your Mind of Cant*"]

[1781] Talking of a very respectable author, he told us a curious circumstance in his life, which was that he had married a printer's devil.[3] REYNOLDS. "A printer's devil, Sir! Why, I thought a printer's devil was a creature with a black face and in rags." JOHNSON. "Yes, Sir. But I suppose, he had her face washed, and put clean clothes on her." Then looking very serious, and very earnest: "And she did not disgrace him; the woman had a bottom of good sense." The word *bottom* thus introduced was so ludicrous when contrasted with his gravity, that most of us could not forbear tittering and laughing; though I recollect that the Bishop of Killaloe kept his countenance with perfect steadiness, while Miss Hannah More[4] slyly hid her face behind a lady's back who sat on the same settee with her. His pride could not bear that any expression of his should excite ridicule, when he did not intend it; he therefore resolved to assume and exercise despotic power, glanced sternly around, and called out in a strong tone, "Where's the merriment?" Then collecting himself, and looking awful, to make us feel how he could impose restraint, and as it were searching his mind for a still more ludicrous word, he slowly pronounced, "I say the *woman* was *fundamentally* sensible"; as if he had said, "hear this now, and laugh if you dare." We all sat composed as at a funeral. * * *

He gave us an entertaining account of Bet Flint, a woman of the town, who, with some eccentric talents and much effrontery, forced herself upon his acquaintance. "Bet," said he, "wrote her own Life in verse, which she brought to me, wishing that I would furnish her with a Preface to it" (laughing). "I used to say of her that she was generally slut and drunkard; occasionally, whore and thief. She had, however, genteel lodgings, a spinnet on which she played, and a boy that walked before her chair. Poor Bet was taken up on a charge of stealing a counterpane, and tried at the Old Bailey. Chief Justice ———, who loved a wench, summed up favorably, and she was acquitted. After which Bet said, with a gay and

2. Pleasure gardens in Chelsea, where concerts were held, fireworks displayed, food and drink sold.
3. Apprentice in a print shop.

4. Hannah More (1745–1833), bluestocking and religious writer, one of the promoters of the Sunday School movement.

satisfied air, 'Now that the counterpane is *my own,* I shall make a petticoat of it.'" * * *

[1783] I have no minute of any interview with Johnson till Thursday, May 15, when I find what follows: BOSWELL. "I wish much to be in Parliament, Sir." JOHNSON. "Why, Sir, unless you come resolved to support any administration, you would be the worse for being in Parliament, because you would be obliged to live more expensively." BOSWELL. "Perhaps, Sir, I should be the less happy for being in Parliament. I never would sell my vote, and I should be vexed if things went wrong." JOHNSON. "That's cant,[5] Sir. It would not vex you more in the house than in the gallery: public affairs vex no man." BOSWELL. "Have not they vexed yourself a little, Sir? Have not you been vexed by all the turbulence of this reign, and by that absurd vote of the House of Commons, 'That the influence of the Crown has increased, is increasing, and ought to be diminished?'" JOHNSON. "Sir, I have never slept an hour less, nor eat an ounce less meat. I would have knocked the factious dogs on the head, to be sure; but I was not *vexed.*" BOSWELL. "I declare, Sir, upon my honor, I did imagine I was vexed, and took a pride in it; but it *was,* perhaps, cant; for I own I neither ate less, nor slept less." JOHNSON. "My dear friend, clear your *mind* of cant. You may *talk* as other people do: you may say to a man, 'Sir, I am your most humble servant.' You are *not* his most humble servant. You may say, 'These are bad times; it is a melancholy thing to be reserved to such times.' You don't mind the times. You tell a man, 'I am sorry you had such bad weather the last day of your journey, and were so much wet.' You don't care sixpence whether he is wet or dry. You may *talk* in this manner; it is a mode of talking in society: but don't *think* foolishly." * * *

[Johnson Prepares for Death]

My anxious apprehensions at parting with him this year proved to be but too well founded; for not long afterwards he had a dreadful stroke of the palsy, of which there are very full and accurate accounts in letters written by himself, to show with what composure of mind, and resignation to the Divine Will, his steady piety enabled him to behave. * * *

Two days after he wrote thus to Mrs. Thrale:

"On Monday, the 16th, I sat for my picture, and walked a considerable way with little inconvenience. In the afternoon and evening I felt myself light and easy, and began to plan schemes of life. Thus I went to bed, and in a short time waked and sat up, as has been long my custom, when I felt a confusion and indistinctness in my head, which lasted, I suppose, about half a minute. I was alarmed,

5. "A whining pretension to goodness in formal and affected terms" (Johnson's *Dictionary*).

and prayed God that however he might afflict my body, he would spare my understanding. This prayer, that I might try the integrity of my faculties, I made in Latin verse. The lines were not very good, but I knew them not to be very good: I made them easily, and concluded myself to be unimpaired in my faculties.

"Soon after I perceived that I had suffered a paralytic stroke, and that my speech was taken from me. I had no pain, and so little dejection in this dreadful state, that I wondered at my own apathy, and considered that perhaps death itself, when it should come, would excite less horror than seems now to attend it.

"In order to rouse the vocal organs, I took two drams. Wine has been celebrated for the production of eloquence. I put myself into violent motion, and I think repeated it; but all was vain. I then went to bed and strange as it may seem, I think slept. When I saw light, it was time to contrive what I should do. Though God stopped my speech, he left me my hand; I enjoyed a mercy which was not granted to my dear friend Lawrence,[6] who now perhaps overlooks me as I am writing, and rejoices that I have what he wanted. My first note was necessarily to my servant, who came in talking, and could not immediately comprehend why he should read what I put into his hands.

"I then wrote a card to Mr. Allen,[7] that I might have a discreet friend at hand, to act as occasion should require. In penning this note, I had some difficulty; my hand, I knew not how nor why, made wrong letters. I then wrote to Dr. Taylor to come to me, and bring Dr. Heberden; and I sent to Dr. Brocklesby, who is my neighbor.[8] My physicians are very friendly, and give me great hopes; but you may imagine my situation. I have so far recovered my vocal powers as to repeat the Lord's Prayer with no very imperfect articulation. My memory, I hope, yet remains as it was; but such an attack produces solicitude for the safety of every faculty." * * *

[1784] To Mr. Henry White, a young clergyman, with whom he now formed an intimacy, so as to talk to him with great freedom, he mentioned that he could not in general accuse himself of having been an undutiful son. "Once, indeed," said he, "I was disobedient; I refused to attend my father to Uttoxeter market. Pride was the source of that refusal, and the remembrance of it was painful. A few years ago, I desired to atone for this fault; I went to Uttoxeter in very bad weather, and stood for a considerable time bareheaded in the rain, on the spot where my father's stall used to stand. In contrition I stood, and I hope the penance was expiatory."

"I told him," says Miss Seward,[9] "in one of my latest visits to him, of a wonderful learned pig, which I had seen at Nottingham; and which did all that we have observed exhibited by dogs

---

6. Dr. Thomas Lawrence, president of the Royal College of Physicians and Johnson's own doctor, had died paralyzed shortly before this was written.
7. Edmund Allen, a printer, Johnson's landlord and neighbor.
8. These two physicians attended Johnson on his deathbed.
9. Anna Seward, "the Swan of Lichfield," a poet.

and horses. The subject amused him. 'Then,' said he, 'the pigs are a race unjustly calumniated. *Pig* has, it seems, not been wanting to *man*, but *man* to *pig*. We do not allow *time* for his education, we kill him at a year old.' Mr. Henry White, who was present, observed that if this instance had happened in or before Pope's time, he would not have been justified in instancing the swine as the lowest degree of groveling instinct.[1] Dr. Johnson seemed pleased with the observation, while the person who made it proceeded to remark that great torture must have been employed, ere the indocility of the animal could have been subdued. 'Certainly,' said the Doctor; 'but,' turning to me, 'how old is your pig?' I told him, three years old. 'Then,' said he, 'the pig has no cause to complain; he would have been killed the first year if he had not been *educated*, and protracted existence is a good recompense for very considerable degrees of torture.' "

[*Johnson Faces Death*]

As Johnson had now very faint hopes of recovery, and as Mrs. Thrale was no longer devoted to him, it might have been supposed that he would naturally have chosen to remain in the comfortable house of his beloved wife's daughter,[2] and end his life where he began it. But there was in him an animated and lofty spirit, and however complicated diseases might depress ordinary mortals, all who saw him, beheld and acknowledged the *invictum animum Catonis.*[3] Such was his intellectual ardor even at this time that he said to one friend, "Sir, I look upon every day to be lost, in which I do not make a new acquaintance"; and to another, when talking of his illness, "I will be conquered; I will not capitulate." And such was his love of London, so high a relish had he of its magnificent extent, and variety of intellectual entertainment, that he languished when absent from it, his mind having become quite luxurious from the long habit of enjoying the metropolis; and, therefore, although at Lichfield, surrounded with friends, who loved and revered him, and for whom he had a very sincere affection, he still found that such conversation as London affords, could be found nowhere else. These feelings, joined, probably, to some flattering hopes of aid from the eminent physicians and surgeons in London, who kindly and generously attended him without accepting fees, made him resolve to return to the capital. * * * Death had always been to him an object of terror; so that, though by no means happy, he still clung to life with an eagerness at which many have wondered. At any time when he was ill, he was very much pleased to be told that he looked better. An ingenious mem-

---

1. *Essay on Man* I.221.
2. Lucy Porter.
3. "The unconquered soul of Cato."

An adaptation of a phrase in Horace's *Odes* II.i.24.

ber of the Eumelian Club[4] informs me that upon one occasion
when he said to him that he saw health returning to his cheek,
Johnson seized him by the hand and exclaimed, "Sir, you are one
of the kindest friends I ever had." * * *

Dr. Heberden, Dr. Brocklesby, Dr. Warren, and Dr. Butter,
physicians, generously attended him, without accepting any fees,
as did Mr. Cruikshank, surgeon; and all that could be done from
professional skill and ability was tried, to prolong a life so truly
valuable. He himself, indeed, having, on account of his very bad
constitution, been perpetually applying himself to medical inquiries,
united his own efforts with those of the gentlemen who attended
him; and imagining that the dropsical collection of water which
oppressed him might be drawn off by making incisions in his body,
he, with his usual resolute defiance of pain, cut deep, when he
thought that his surgeon had done it too tenderly.

About eight or ten days before his death, when Dr. Brocklesby
paid him his morning visit, he seemed very low and desponding,
and said, "I have been as a dying man all night." He then emphatically broke out in the words of Shakespeare:

> "Canst thou not minister to a mind diseased;
> Pluck from the memory a rooted sorrow,
> Raze out the written troubles of the brain,
> And with some sweet oblivious antidote
> Cleanse the stuffed bosom of that perilous stuff
> Which weighs upon the heart?"

To which Dr. Brocklesby readily answered, from the same great
poet:

> "Therein the patient
> Must minister to himself."[5]

Johnson expressed himself much satisfied with the application. * * *

Amidst the melancholy clouds which hung over the dying Johnson, his characteristical manner showed itself on different occasions.

When Dr. Warren, in the usual style, hoped that he was better;
his answer was, "No, Sir; you cannot conceive with what accelera-
tion I advance towards death."

A man whom he had never seen before was employed one night
to sit up with him. Being asked next morning how he liked his attendant, his answer was, "Not at all, Sir: the fellow's an idiot; he
is as awkward as a turnspit[6] when first put into the wheel, and
as sleepy as a dormouse."

Mr. Windham[7] having placed a pillow conveniently to support

4. A club to which Boswell and Reynolds belonged.
5. *Macbeth* V.iii.40–46.
6. A dog kept to turn the roasting-spit
by running within a tread-wheel connected to it (*NED*).
7. William Windham, one of Johnson's
younger friends, later a Member of
Parliament.

him, he thanked him for his kindness, and said, "That will do—all that a pillow can do." * * *

Johnson, with that native fortitude, which, amidst all his bodily distress and mental sufferings, never forsook him, asked Dr. Brocklesby, as a man in whom he had confidence, to tell him plainly whether he could recover. "Give me," said he, "a direct answer." The Doctor having first asked him if he could bear the whole truth, which way soever it might lead, and being answered that he could, declared that, in his opinion, he could not recover without a miracle. "Then," said Johnson, "I will take no more physic, not even my opiates; for I have prayed that I may render up my soul to God unclouded." In this resolution he persevered, and, at the same time, used only the weakest kinds of sustenance. Being pressed by Mr. Windham to take somewhat more generous nourishment, lest too low a diet should have the very effect which he dreaded, by debilitating his mind, he said, "I will take anything but inebriating sustenance."

The Reverend Mr. Strahan,[8] who was the son of his friend, and had been always one of his great favorites, had, during his last illness, the satisfaction of contributing to soothe and comfort him. That gentleman's house, at Islington, of which he is Vicar, afforded Johnson, occasionally and easily, an agreeable change of place and fresh air; and he attended also upon him in town in the discharge of the sacred offices of his profession.

Mr. Strahan has given me the agreeable assurance that, after being in much agitation, Johnson became quite composed, and continued so till his death.

Dr. Brocklesby, who will not be suspected of fanaticism, obliged me with the following account:

"For some time before his death, all his fears were calmed and absorbed by the prevalence of his faith, and his trust in the merits and *propitiation* of Jesus Christ." * * *

Johnson having thus in his mind the true Christian scheme, at once rational and consolatory, uniting justice and mercy in the Divinity, with the improvement of human nature, previous to his receiving the Holy Sacrament in his apartment, composed and fervently uttered this prayer:

"Almighty and most merciful Father, I am now as to human eyes, it seems, about to commemorate, for the last time, the death of thy Son Jesus Christ, our Saviour and Redeemer. Grant, O Lord, that my whole hope and confidence may be in his merits, and thy mercy; enforce and accept my imperfect repentance; make this commemoration available to the confirmation of my faith, the establishment

8. The Rev. George Strahan (pronounced *Strawn*), who later published Johnson's *Prayers and Meditations.*

of my hope, and the enlargement of my charity; and make the
death of thy Son Jesus Christ effectual to my redemption. Have
mercy upon me, and pardon the multitude of my offenses. Bless my
friends; have mercy upon all men. Support me, by thy Holy Spirit,
in the days of weakness, and at the hour of death; and receive me,
at my death, to everlasting happiness, for the sake of Jesus Christ.
Amen."

Having * * * made his will on the 8th and 9th of December,
and settled all his worldly affairs, he languished till Monday, the
13th of that month, when he expired, about seven o'clock in the
evening, with so little apparent pain that his attendants hardly perceived when his dissolution took place. * * *

1791

OLIVER GOLDSMITH
(ca. 1730–1774)

It is difficult to distinguish fact from fiction in the accounts that we
have of Goldsmith's first thirty years. Unlike the works of most 18th-
century authors, his writings contain much that is personal, but it is of
little use to biographers, for it has been heightened and romanticized until
it belongs at least as much to fiction as to autobiography. The Goldsmith
legend, which has served as the poet's biography, is to some degree the
creation of Goldmith himself.

He was born in Ireland, the son of an Anglican clergyman whose geni-
ality he inherited and whose improvidence he imitated. He was early disfigured by smallpox and grew up ugly of face, ungraceful of figure, and in
his early years apparently stupid and certainly idle. Nonetheless, he was
sent to Trinity College, Dublin, as a sizar—i.e., a student who did menial
jobs for well-to-do undergraduates—and there he took his A.B. in 1749.
After several false starts in choosing a career, he was sent by a generous
uncle to study medicine at the University of Edinburgh. Instead of taking
a degree, he wandered for a while on the Continent, visiting Holland,
France, Italy, and Switzerland. A much romanticized account of this journey can be read in the story of George Primrose in Goldsmith's novel,
The Vicar of Wakefield (1766). He returned to England in 1756 with
a mysteriously acquired M.D. and tried in vain to support himself as a
physician among the poor in the Borough of Southwark. After serving for
a while as an usher in a school, he drifted into the profession of hack
writer for Ralph Griffiths, the proprietor of the *Monthly Review*, and
later worked for and with the benevolent publisher Edward Newbery. He
first attracted attention by a short book, *An Inquiry into the Present State
of Polite Learning in Europe* (1759), in which he traced what he considered to be the decline of the fine arts in mid-18th-century Europe to
the lack of enlightened patronage and to the malign influence of criticism
and scholarship. From then until his death he earned by his writings very
large sums indeed, but his habitual extravagance and generosity kept him
always in debt, no matter how ample his income. When he was in funds

he lived richly; when he was without money, he borrowed. He died owing the then prodigious sum (for a man whose only source of income was writing) of £2,000.

The variety and excellence of Goldsmith's work is astonishing. His easy and pleasant prose style, his abundant humor, his shrewd observations of character and scene have made his essays constantly popular. His great gift for the comedy of character and situation enabled him to achieve in his two plays, *The Good-Natured Man* (1768) and *She Stoops to Conquer* (1773), a sort of pure and mirthful comedy—uncomplicated by ethical or social criticism and unspoiled by the fashionable sentimentality of the moment—that is unique in the century. His two important poems, *The Traveler, or A Prospect of Society* (1764) and *The Deserted Village*, are distinguished for the purity and harmony of their language. The couplets of *The Deserted Village* lack the rhetoric and formality of Pope's or Johnson's couplets and become almost lyrical in sound and movement.

Goldsmith was an intimate of the circle of brilliant men of whom Johnson was the center. Boswell's description of him in famous scenes in the *Life* is certainly ill-natured and unfair. He was not the inspired idiot, the blundering Irishman with a dash of genius, that Boswell and other members of the group insisted he was. His sly humor, often directed against himself, seems not to have been understood by most of his friends, who took pains to repeat solemnly as examples of Irish "bulls" (verbal blunders) what Goldsmith certainly meant in jest. He was not a profound thinker and his learning was not extensive; but even such hack-work compilations as the *History of Rome*, the *History of Greece*, and the *History of Animated Nature*, which he put together carelessly and rapidly, were ensured a certain life by the charm of his manner and style.

From Letters from a Citizen of the World[1]

Letter XXVI. *The Character of the Man in Black;*
With Some Instances of His Inconsistent Conduct

Though fond of many acquaintances, I desire an intimacy only with a few. The man in black, whom I have often mentioned, is one whose friendship I could wish to acquire, because he possesses my esteem. His manners, it is true, are tinctured with some strange inconsistencies, and he may be justly termed a humorist[2] in a nation of humorists. Though he is generous even to profusion, he affects to be thought a prodigy of parsimony and prudence; though

1. A series of essays (1760–61) in the *Public Ledger*, a newspaper. Imitating a well-established device which had been earlier used by Montesquieu in his *Lettres Persanes* (1721) and others, Goldsmith writes in the character of a philosophical foreigner—in this case a Chinese—who reports regularly to a friend his experiences and observations in contemporary London. The Chinese is the embodiment of benevolence and enlightened good sense, with a touch of naïveté that reveals his innocence: this admirable person serves as the norm by which we judge the world that Goldsmith describes in his good-natured satire. In using a Chinese as his observer, Goldsmith was capitalizing on the current fad for Chinese ornamental buildings in parks and for Chinese motifs in furniture and the decorative arts.
2. An eccentric.

his conversation be replete with the most sordid and selfish maxims, his heart is dilated with the most unbounded love. I have known him profess himself a man-hater, while his cheek was glowing with compassion; and, while his looks were softened into pity, I have heard him use the language of the most unbounded ill nature. Some affect humanity and tenderness, others boast of having such dispositions from nature; but he is the only man I ever knew who seemed ashamed of his natural benevolence. He takes as much pains to hide his feelings, as any hypocrite would to conceal his indifference; but on every unguarded moment the mask drops off, and reveals him to the most superficial observer.

In one of our late excursions into the country, happening to discourse upon the provision that was made for the poor in England, he seemed amazed how any of his countrymen could be so foolishly weak as to relieve occasional objects of charity, when the laws had made such ample provision for their support. "In every parish house,"[3] says he, "the poor are supplied with food, clothes, fire, and a bed to lie on; they want no more, I desire no more myself; yet still they seem discontented. I'm surprised at the inactivity of our magistrates, in not taking up such vagrants, who are only a weight upon the industrious; I'm surprised that the people are found to relieve them, when they must be at the same time sensible that it, in some measure, encourages idleness, extravagance, and imposture. Were I to advise any man for whom I had the least regard, I would caution him by all means not to be imposed upon by their false pretenses: let me assure you, sir, they are impostors, every one of them, and rather merit a prison than relief."

He was proceeding in this strain earnestly, to dissuade me from an imprudence of which I am seldom guilty, when an old man, who still had about him the remnants of tattered finery, implored our compassion. He assured us that he was no common beggar, but forced into the shameful profession to support a dying wife and five hungry children. Being prepossessed against such falsehoods, his story had not the least influence upon me; but it was quite otherwise with the man in black; I could see it visibly operate upon his countenance, and effectually interrupt his harangue. I could easily perceive that his heart burned to relieve the five starving children, but he seemed ashamed to discover his weakness to me. While he thus hesitated between compassion and pride, I pretended to look another way, and he seized this opportunity of giving the poor petitioner a piece of silver, bidding him at the same time, in order that I should hear, go work for his bread, and not tease passengers with such impertinent falsehoods for the future.

As he had fancied himself quite unperceived, he continued, as we proceeded, to rail against beggars with as much animosity as before: he threw in some episodes on his own amazing prudence and

3. The parish poorhouse.

economy, with his profound skill in discovering impostors; he explained the manner in which he would deal with beggars were he a magistrate, hinted at enlarging some of the prisons for their reception, and told two stories of ladies that were robbed by beggarmen. He was beginning a third to the same purpose, when a sailor with a wooden leg once more crossed our walks, desiring our pity, and blessing our limbs. I was for going on without taking any notice, but my friend looking wishfully upon the poor petitioner, bid me stop, and he would show me with how much ease he could at any time detect an impostor.

He now therefore assumed a look of importance, and in an angry tone began to examine the sailor, demanding in what engagement he was thus disabled and rendered unfit for service. The sailor replied in a tone as angrily as he that he had been an officer on board a private ship of war, and that he had lost his leg abroad in defense of those who did nothing at home. At this reply, all my friend's importance vanished in a moment; he had not a single question more to ask: he now only studied what method he should take to relieve him unobserved. He had, however, no easy part to act, as he was obliged to preserve the appearance of ill nature before me, and yet relieve himself by relieving the sailor. Casting, therefore, a furious look upon some bundles of chips which the fellow carried in a string at his back, my friend demanded how he sold his matches; but, not waiting for a reply, desired in a surly tone to have a shilling's worth. The sailor seemed at first surprised at his demand, but soon recollected himself, and presenting his whole bundle, "Here, master," says he, "take all my cargo, and a blessing into the bargain."

It is impossible to describe with what an air of triumph my friend marched off with his new purchase; he assured me that he was firmly of opinion that those fellows must have stolen their goods, who could thus afford to sell them for half value. He informed me of several different uses to which those chips might be applied; he expatiated largely upon the savings that would result from lighting candles with a match, instead of thrusting them into the fire. He averred that he would as soon have parted with a tooth as his money to those vagabonds, unless for some valuable consideration. I cannot tell how long this panegyric upon frugality and matches might have continued, had not his attention been called off by another object more distressful than either of the former. A woman in rags, with one child in her arms and another on her back, was attempting to sing ballads, but with such a mournful voice, that it was difficult to determine whether she was singing or crying. A wretch, who in the deepest distress still aimed at good humor, was an object my friend was by no means capable of withstanding: his vivacity and his discourse were instantly interrupted; upon this occasion his very dissimulation had forsaken him. Even in my presence he immediately applied his hands to his pockets, in order to relieve her; but guess his confusion when he found he had already given away all the money he carried about him to former objects. The misery painted in the woman's visage was not half so strongly expressed as the agony in his. He continued to search for some time, but to no purpose, till, at length recollecting himself, with a face of ineffable good nature, as he had no money, he put into her hands his shilling's worth of matches.

Letter LXXI. The Shabby Beau, the Man in Black,
the Chinese Philosopher, etc., at Vauxhall[1]

The people of London are as fond of walking as our friends at Pekin of riding; one of the principal entertainments of the citizens here in summer is to repair about nightfall to a garden not far from town, where they walk about, show their best clothes and best faces, and listen to a concert provided for the occasion.

I accepted an invitation a few evenings ago from my old friend, the man in black, to be one of a party that was to sup there, and at the appointed hour waited upon him at his lodgings. There I found the company assembled and expecting my arrival. Our party consisted of my friend, in superlative finery, his stockings rolled, a black velvet waistcoat which was formerly new, and a gray wig combed down in imitation of hair; a pawnbroker's widow, of whom, by-the-by, my friend was a professed admirer, dressed out in green damask, with three gold rings on every finger; Mr. Tibbs, the second-rate beau I have formerly described, together with his lady in flimsy silk, dirty gauze instead of linen, and a hat as big as an umbrella.

Our first difficulty was in settling how we should set out. Mrs. Tibbs had a natural aversion to the water,[2] and the widow being a little in flesh, as warmly protested against walking; a coach was therefore agreed upon, which being too small to carry five, Mr. Tibbs consented to sit in his wife's lap.

In this manner, therefore, we set forward, being entertained by the way with the bodings of Mr. Tibbs, who assured us he did not expect to see a single creature for the evening above the degree of a cheesemonger; that this was the last night of the gardens, and that consequently we should be pestered with the nobility and gentry from Thames Street and Crooked Lane,[3] with several other prophetic ejaculations, probably inspired by the uneasiness of his situation.

The illuminations began before we arrived, and I must confess that upon entering the gardens, I found every sense overpaid with

1. Vauxhall (*Vóx-ul*), oldest and most popular of London's pleasure gardens, was situated in Lambeth, on the south bank of the Thames. For a lively account of the resort, see Austin Dobson's *Eighteenth-Century Vignettes*, Series I.
2. She was afraid to go by boat, the normal means of transportation to Vauxhall.
3. These streets, deep in the City, could not produce "nobility and gentry," but only those unfashionable middle-class people whom Tibbs affects to despise.

more than expected pleasure: the lights everywhere glimmering through the scarcely-moving trees, the full-bodied consort[4] bursting on the stillness of the night, the natural consort of the birds in the more retired part of the grove, vying with that which was formed by art; the company gaily dressed looking satisfaction, and the tables spread with various delicacies, all conspired to fill my imagination with the visionary happiness of the Arabian lawgiver,[5] and lifted me into an ecstasy of admiration. "Head of Confucius," cried I to my friend, "this is fine! this unites rural beauty with courtly magnificence; if we except the virgins of immortality that hang on every tree, and may be plucked at every desire, I don't see how this falls short of Mahomet's Paradise!"—"As for virgins," cries my friend, "it is true they are a fruit that do not much abound in our gardens here; but if ladies, as plenty as apples in autumn, and as complying as any houri[6] of them all, can content you, I fancy we have no need to go to heaven for Paradise."

I was going to second his remarks, when we were called to a consultation by Mr. Tibbs and the rest of the company to know in what manner we were to lay out the evening to the greatest advantage. Mrs. Tibbs was for keeping the genteel walk of the garden, where she observed there was always the very best company; the widow, on the contrary, who came but once a season, was for securing a good standing-place to see the waterworks,[7] which she assured us would begin in less than an hour at farthest; a dispute therefore began, and as it was managed between two of very opposite characters, it threatened to grow more bitter at every reply. Mrs. Tibbs wondered how people could pretend to know the polite world who had received all their rudiments of breeding behind a compter;[8] to which the other replied that though some people sat behind compters, yet they could sit at the head of their own tables too, and carve three good dishes of hot meat whenever they thought proper, which was more than some people could say for themselves, that hardly knew a rabbit and onions from a green goose and gooseberries.

It is hard to say where this might have ended, had not the husband, who probably knew the impetuosity of his wife's disposition, proposed to end the dispute by adjourning to a box, and try if there was anything to be had for supper that was supportable. To this we all consented, but here a new distress arose: Mr. and Mrs. Tibbs would sit in none but a genteel box, a box where they might see and be seen; one, as they expressed it, in the very focus of

---

4. Harmonious music.
5. Mohammed, who promised the faithful a Paradise of all sensual delights.
6. One of the voluptuous women who people Mohammed's Paradise.
7. An account of Vauxhall in the *Gentleman's Magazine* XXXV (1765), 354, includes a description of the water-

works as "a curious piece of machinery * * * representing a beautiful landscape in perspective, with a miller's house, a water mill, and a cascade," in which water seemed to flow, turn the mill wheel, foam, and glide away.
8. Counter in a shop.

public view; but such a box was not easy to be obtained, for though we were perfectly convinced of our own gentility, and the gentility of our appearance, yet we found it a difficult matter to persuade the keepers of the boxes to be of our opinion; they chose to re-serve genteel boxes for what they judged more genteel company.

At last, however, we were fixed, though somewhat obscurely, and supplied with the usual entertainment of the place. The widow found the supper excellent, but Mrs. Tibbs thought everything de-testable. "Come, come, my dear," cries the husband, by way of consolation, "to be sure we can't find such dressing here as we have at Lord Crump's or Lady Crimp's; but for Vauxhall dressing it is pretty good; it is not their victuals indeed I find fault with, but their wine; their wine," cries he, drinking off a glass, "indeed, is most abominable."

By this last contradiction the widow was fairly conquered in point of politeness. She perceived now that she had no pretensions in the world to taste, her very senses were vulgar, since she had praised detestable custard, and smacked at wretched wine; she was therefore content to yield the victory, and for the rest of the night to listen and improve. It is true she would now and then forget herself, and confess she was pleased, but they soon brought her back again to miserable refinement. She once praised the painting of the box in which we were sitting, but was soon convinced that such paltry pieces ought rather to excite horror than satisfaction; she ventured again to commend one of the singers, but Mrs. Tibbs soon let her know, in the style of a connoisseur, that the singer in question had neither ear, voice, nor judgment.

Mr. Tibbs, now willing to prove that his wife's pretensions to music were just, entreated her to favor the company with a song; but to this she gave a positive denial, "for you know very well, my dear," says she, "that I am not in voice today, and when one's voice is not equal to one's judgment, what signifies singing? besides, as there is no accompaniment, it would be but spoiling music." All these excuses, however, were overruled by the rest of the com-pany, who, though one would think they already had music enough, joined in the entreaty. But particularly the widow, now willing to convince the company of her breeding, pressed so warmly, that she seemed determined to take no refusal. At last then the lady complied, and after humming for some minutes, began with such a voice, and such affectation, as I could perceive gave but little satisfaction to any except her husband. He sat with rapture in his eye, and beat time with his hand on the table.

You must observe, my friend, that it is the custom of this coun-try, when a lady or gentleman happens to sing, for the company to sit as mute and motionless as statues. Every feature, every limb, must seem to correspond in fixed attention, and while the song con-tinues, they are to remain in a state of universal petrifaction. In this mortifying situation we had continued for some time, listening to the song, and looking with tranquility; when the master of the box came to inform us that the waterworks were going to begin. At this information I could instantly perceive the widow bounce from her seat; but correcting herself, she sat down again, repressed by motives of good breeding. Mrs. Tibbs, who had seen the waterworks a hundred times, resolving not to be interrupted, continued her song without any share of mercy, nor had the smallest pity on our impatience. The widow's face, I own, gave me high entertainment; in it I could plainly read the struggle she felt between good breeding and curiosity; she talked of the waterworks the whole evening before, and seemed to have come merely in order to see them; but then she could not bounce out in the very middle of a song, for that would be forfeiting all pretensions to high life, or high-lived company, ever after. Mrs. Tibbs therefore kept on singing, and we continued to listen, till at last, when the song was just concluded, the waiter came to inform us that the waterworks were over.

"The waterworks over!" cried the widow: "The waterworks over already? That's impossible, they can't be over so soon!"—"It is not my business," replied the fellow, "to contradict your ladyship. I'll run again and see." He went, and soon returned with a confirmation of the dismal tidings. No ceremony could now bind my friend's disappointed mistress; she testified her displeasure in the openest manner; in short, she now began to find fault in turn, and at last, insisted upon going home, just at the time that Mr. and Mrs. Tibbs assured the company that the polite hours were going to begin, and that the ladies would instantaneously be entertained with the horns.

Adieu!
1760–61, 1762

The Deserted Village[1]

Sweet Auburn! loveliest village of the plain,
Where health and plenty cheered the laboring swain,
Where smiling spring its earliest visit paid,

1. *The Deserted Village* is an idealization of English rural life, mingled with poignant memories of the poet's own youth in Lissoy, Ireland. Goldsmith was seriously concerned about the effects of the agricultural revolution then in progress which was being hastened by Enclosure Acts. Either for the sake of more profitable farming or to create vast private parks and landscape gardens, arable land was being taken out of the hands of small proprietors (i.e., "enclosed"), thus displacing yeoman farmers who, like their ancestors, had lived for generations in small villages, grazing their cattle on common land and raising food on small holdings. The only alternative available to many such people was to seek employment in the city or to migrate to America. Goldsmith certainly exaggerates the effects of the enclosures, nor are his diatribes against the debilitating influence of luxury borne out by history; Waterloo and the glories of the 19th century lay ahead for England. In the poem Goldsmith opposes "luxury" (the increase of wealth, the growth of cities, the costly country estates of great noblemen and wealthy merchants) to "rural virtue" (the old agrarian economy which supported a sturdy population of independent peas-

And parting summer's lingering blooms delayed:
Dear lovely bowers of innocence and ease, 5
Seats of my youth, when every sport could please,
How often have I loitered o'er thy green,
Where humble happiness endeared each scene;
How often have I paused on every charm,
The sheltered cot, the cultivated farm, 10
The never-failing brook, the busy mill,
The decent church that topped the neighboring hill,
The hawthorn bush, with seats beneath the shade,
For talking age and whispering lovers made;
How often have I blessed the coming day, 15
When toil remitting lent its turn to play,
And all the village train, from labor free,
Led up their sports beneath the spreading tree,
While many a pastime circled in the shade,
The young contending as the old surveyed; 20
And many a gambol frolicked o'er the ground,
And sleights of art and feats of strength went round,
And still as each repeated pleasure tired,
Succeeding sports the mirthful band inspired;
The dancing pair that simply sought renown, 25
By holding out to tire each other down;
The swain mistrustless of his smutted face,
While secret laughter tittered round the place;
The bashful virgin's sidelong looks of love,
The matron's glance that would those looks reprove: 30
These were thy charms, sweet village! sports like these,
With sweet succession, taught even toil to please;
These round thy bowers their cheerful influence shed,
These were thy charms—But all these charms are fled.
    Sweet smiling village, loveliest of the lawn, 35
Thy sports are fled, and all thy charms withdrawn;
Amidst thy bowers the tyrant's hand is seen,
And desolation saddens all thy green:
One only master grasps the whole domain,
And half a tillage stints thy smiling plain; 40
No more thy glassy brook reflects the day,
But choked with sedges, works its weedy way:
Along thy glades, a solitary guest,
The hollow-sounding bittern guards its nest;
Amidst thy desert walks the lapwing flies, 45
And tires their echoes with unvaried cries.
Sunk are thy bowers, in shapeless ruin all,
And the long grass o'ertops the moldering wall,
And, trembling, shrinking from the spoiler's hand,
Far, far away thy children leave the land. 50
    Ill fares the land, to hastening ills a prey,

ants). His poem is thus at once a nos-
talgic lament for a doomed way of life
and a denunciation of what he regarded
as the corrupting, destructive force of
new wealth.

Where wealth accumulates, and men decay;
Princes and lords may flourish, or may fade;
A breath can make them, as a breath has made;
But a bold peasantry, their country's pride,   55
When once destroyed, can never be supplied.
  A time there was, ere England's griefs began,
When every rood of ground maintained its man;
For him light labor spread her wholesome store,
Just gave what life required, but gave no more: 60
His best companions, innocence and health;
And his best riches, ignorance of wealth.
  But times are altered; Trade's unfeeling train
Usurp the land and dispossess the swain;
Along the lawn, where scattered hamlets rose,   65
Unwieldy wealth, and cumbrous pomp repose;
And every want to opulence allied,
And every pang that folly pays to pride.
These gentle hours that plenty bade to bloom,
Those calm desires that asked but little room,   70
Those healthful sports that graced the peaceful scene,
Lived in each look, and brightened all the green;
These far departing seek a kinder shore,
And rural mirth and manners are no more.
  Sweet Auburn! parent of the blissful hour,   75
Thy glades forlorn confess the tyrant's power.
Here, as I take my solitary rounds,
Amidst thy tangling walks, and ruined grounds,
And, many a year elapsed, return to view
Where once the cottage stood, the hawthorn grew,   80
Remembrance wakes with all her busy train,
Swells at my breast, and turns the past to pain.
  In all my wanderings round this world of care,
In all my griefs—and God has given my share—
I still had hopes my latest hours to crown,   85
Amidst these humble bowers to lay me down;
To husband out life's taper at the close,
And keep the flame from wasting by repose.
I still had hopes, for pride attends us still,
Amidst the swains to show my book-learned skill,   90
Around my fire an evening group to draw,
And tell of all I felt, and all I saw;
And, as an hare whom hounds and horns pursue,
Pants to the place from whence at first she flew,
I still had hopes, my long vexations past,   95
Here to return—and die at home at last.
  O blest retirement, friend to life's decline,
Retreats from care that never must be mine,
How happy he who crowns in shades like these,
A youth of labor with an age of ease;   100
Who quits a world where strong temptations try,
And, since 'tis hard to combat, learns to fly!

For him no wretches, born to work and weep,
Explore the mine, or tempt the dangerous deep;
No surly porter stands in guilty state   105
To spurn imploring famine from the gate;
But on he moves to meet his latter end,
Angels around befriending virtue's friend;
Bends to the grave with unperceived decay,
While Resignation gently slopes the way;   110
And, all his prospects brightening to the last,
His Heaven commences ere the world be passed!
    Sweet was the sound when oft at evening's close,
Up yonder hill the village murmur rose;
There, as I passed with careless steps and slow,   115
The mingling notes came softened from below;
The swain responsive as the milkmaid sung,
The sober herd that lowed to meet their young,
The noisy geese that gabbled o'er the pool,
The playful children just let loose from school;   120
The watchdog's voice that bayed the whispering wind,
And the loud laugh that spoke the vacant² mind;
These all in sweet confusion sought the shade,
And filled each pause the nightingale had made.
But now the sounds of population fail,   125
No cheerful murmurs fluctuate in the gale,
No busy steps the grass-grown footway tread,
For all the bloomy flush of life is fled.
All but yon widowed, solitary thing
That feebly bends beside the plashy spring;   130
She, wretched matron, forced, in age, for bread,
To strip the brook with mantling cresses spread,
To pick her wintry faggot from the thorn,
To seek her nightly shed, and weep till morn;
She only left of all the harmless train,   135
The sad historian of the pensive plain.
    Near yonder copse, where once the garden smiled,
And still where many a garden flower grows wild,
There, where a few torn shrubs the place disclose,
The village preacher's modest mansion rose.   140
A man he was, to all the country dear,
And passing rich with forty pounds a year;
Remote from towns he ran his godly race,
Nor e'er had changed, nor wished to change his place;
Unpracticed he to fawn, or seek for power,   145
By doctrines fashioned to the varying hour;
Far other aims his heart had learned to prize,
More skilled to raise the wretched than to rise.
His house was known to all the vagrant train,
He chid their wanderings, but relieved their pain;   150
The long-remembered beggar was his guest,
Whose beard descending swept his aged breast;

2. Idle.

The ruined spendthrift, now no longer proud,
Claimed kindred there, and had his claims allowed;
The broken soldier, kindly bade to stay,   155
Sate by his fire, and talked the night away;
Wept o'er his wounds, or tales of sorrow done,
Shouldered his crutch, and showed how fields were won.
Pleased with his guests, the good man learned to glow,
And quite forgot their vices in their woe;   160
Careless their merits, or their faults to scan,
His pity gave ere charity began.
    Thus to relieve the wretched was his pride,
And even his failings leaned to Virtue's side;
But in his duty prompt at every call,   165
He watched and wept, he prayed and felt, for all.
And, as a bird each fond endearment tries,
To tempt its new-fledged offspring to the skies,
He tried each art, reproved each dull delay,
Allured to brighter worlds, and led the way.   170
    Beside the bed where parting life was laid,
And sorrow, guilt, and pain, by turns dismayed,
The reverend champion stood. At his control,
Despair and anguish fled the struggling soul;
Comfort came down the trembling wretch to raise,   175
And his last faltering accents whispered praise.
    At church, with meek and unaffected grace,
His looks adorned the venerable place;
Truth from his lips prevailed with double sway,
And fools, who came to scoff, remained to pray.   180
The service past, around the pious man,
With steady zeal each honest rustic ran;
Even children followed with endearing wile,
And plucked his gown, to share the good man's smile.
His ready smile a parent's warmth expressed,   185
Their welfare pleased him, and their cares distressed;
To them his heart, his love, his griefs were given,
But all his serious thoughts had rest in Heaven.
As some tall cliff that lifts its awful form,
Swells from the vale, and midway leaves the storm,   190
Though round its breast the rolling clouds are spread,
Eternal sunshine settles on its head.
    Beside yon straggling fence that skirts the way,
With blossomed furze unprofitably gay,
There, in his noisy mansion, skilled to rule,   195
The village master taught his little school;
A man severe he was, and stern to view,
I knew him well, and every truant knew;
Well had the boding tremblers learned to trace
The day's disasters in his morning face;   200
Full well they laughed with counterfeited glee,
At all his jokes, for many a joke had he;

Full well the busy whisper circling round,
Conveyed the dismal tidings when he frowned;
Yet he was kind, or if severe in aught,   205
The love he bore to learning was in fault;[3]
The village all declared how much he knew;
'Twas certain he could write, and cipher too;
Lands he could measure, terms[4] and tides presage,
And even the story ran that he could gauge.[5]   210
In arguing too, the parson owned his skill,
For even though vanquished, he could argue still;
While words of learned length, and thundering sound,
Amazed the gazing rustics ranged around;
And still they gazed, and still the wonder grew,   215
That one small head could carry all he knew.
    But past is all his fame. The very spot
Where many a time he triumphed, is forgot.
Near yonder thorn, that lifts its head on high,
Where once the signpost caught the passing eye,   220
Low lies that house where nut-brown draughts inspired,
Where graybeard Mirth and smiling Toil retired,
Where village statesmen talked with looks profound,
And news much older than their ale went round.
Imagination fondly stoops to trace   225
The parlor splendors of that festive place:
The whitewashed wall, the nicely sanded floor,
The varnished clock that clicked behind the door;
The chest contrived a double debt to pay,
A bed by night, a chest of drawers by day;   230
The pictures placed for ornament and use,
The twelve good rules,[6] the royal game of goose;
The hearth, except when winter chilled the day,
With aspen boughs, and flowers, and fennel gay,
While broken teacups, wisely kept for show,   235
Ranged o'er the chimney, glistened in a row.
    Vain transitory splendors! Could not all
Reprieve the tottering mansion from its fall!
Obscure it sinks, nor shall it more impart
An hour's importance to the poor man's heart;   240
Thither no more the peasant shall repair
To sweet oblivion of his daily care;
No more the farmer's news, the barber's tale,
No more the woodman's ballad shall prevail;
No more the smith his dusky brow shall clear,   245
Relax his ponderous strength, and lean to hear;

---

3. Since the *l* was silent, "fault" and "aught" rhymed perfectly.
4. Dates on which rent, wages, etc., were due and tenancy began or ended; "tides": feasts and seasons in the church year.
5. Measure the content of casks and other vessels.

6. "The twelve good rules" of conduct, attributed to Charles I, were printed in a broadside that was often seen on the walls of taverns; "goose" was a game in which counters were moved on a board according to the throw of the dice.

The host himself no longer shall be found
Careful to see the mantling bliss[7] go round;
Nor the coy maid, half willing to be pressed,
Shall kiss the cup to pass it to the rest.   250
    Yes! let the rich deride, the proud disdain,
These simple blessings of the lowly train,
To me more dear, congenial to my heart,
One native charm, than all the gloss of art;
Spontaneous joys, where nature has its play,   255
The soul adopts, and owns their first-born sway;
Lightly they frolic o'er the vacant mind,
Unenvied, unmolested, unconfined.
But the long pomp, the midnight masquerade,
With all the freaks of wanton wealth arrayed,   260
In these, ere triflers half their wish obtain,
The toiling pleasure sickens into pain;
And, even while fashion's brightest arts decoy,
The heart distrusting asks if this be joy.
    Ye friends to truth, ye statesmen, who survey   265
The rich man's joys increase, the poor's decay,
'Tis yours to judge how wide the limits stand
Between a splendid and an happy land.
Proud swells the tide with loads of freighted ore,
And shouting Folly hails them from her shore;   270
Hoards, even beyond the miser's wish abound,
And rich men flock from all the world around.
Yet count our gains. This wealth is but a name
That leaves our useful products still the same.
Not so the loss. The man of wealth and pride,   275
Takes up a space that many poor supplied;
Space for his lake, his park's extended bounds,
Space for his horses, equipage, and hounds;
The robe that wraps his limbs in silken sloth
Has robbed the neighboring fields of half their growth;   280
His seat, where solitary sports are seen,
Indignant spurns the cottage from the green;
Around the world each needful product flies,
For all the luxuries the world supplies.
While thus the land adorned for pleasure, all   285
In barren splendor feebly waits the fall.
    As some fair female unadorned and plain,
Secure to please while youth confirms her reign,
Slights every borrowed charm that dress supplies,
Nor shares with art the triumph of her eyes: 290
But when those charms are past, for charms are frail,
When time advances, and when lovers fail,
She then shines forth, solicitous to bless,
In all the glaring impotence of dress.
Thus fares the land, by luxury betrayed;   295
In nature's simplest charms at first arrayed;

7. Foaming bliss, i.e., foaming ale.

But verging to decline, its splendors rise,
Its vistas strike, its palaces surprise;
While scourged by famine from the smiling land,
The mournful peasant leads his humble band;   300
And while he sinks without one arm to save,
The country blooms—a garden, and a grave.
　　Where then, ah where, shall Poverty reside,
To 'scape the pressure of contiguous Pride?
If to some common's fenceless limits strayed,   305
He drives his flock to pick the scanty blade,
Those fenceless fields the sons of wealth divide,
And even the bare-worn common is denied.
　　If to the city sped—What waits him there?
To see profusion that he must not share;   310
To see ten thousand baneful arts combined
To pamper luxury, and thin mankind;
To see those joys the sons of pleasure know,
Extorted from his fellow creature's woe.
Here, while the courtier glitters in brocade,   315
There the pale artist[8] plies the sickly trade;
Here, while the proud their long-drawn pomps display,
There the black gibbet glooms beside the way.
The dome where Pleasure holds her midnight reign,
Here, richly decked, admits the gorgeous train;   320
Tumultuous grandeur crowds the blazing square,
The rattling chariots clash, the torches glare.
Sure scenes like these no troubles e'er annoy!
Sure these denote one universal joy!
Are these thy serious thoughts?—Ah, turn thine eyes   325
Where the poor houseless shivering female lies.
She once, perhaps, in village plenty blest,
Has wept at tales of innocence distressed;
Her modest looks the cottage might adorn,
Sweet as the primrose peeps beneath the thorn;   330
Now lost to all; her friends, her virtue fled,
Near her betrayer's door she lays her head,
And pinched with cold, and shrinking from the shower,
With heavy heart deplores that luckless hour,
When idly first, ambitious of the town,   335
She left her wheel and robes of country brown.
　　Do thine, sweet Auburn, thine, the loveliest train,
Do thy fair tribes participate her pain?
Even now, perhaps, by cold and hunger led,
At proud men's doors they ask a little bread!   340
　　Ah, no. To distant climes, a dreary scene,
Where half the convex world intrudes between,
Through torrid tracts with fainting steps they go,
Where wild Altama[9] murmurs to their woe.
Far different there from all that charmed before,   345
The various terrors of that horrid shore;

8. Artisan.　　　　　　　　　9. The Altamaha River in Georgia.

Those blazing suns that dart a downward ray,
And fiercely shed intolerable day;
Those matted woods where birds forget to sing,
But silent bats in drowsy clusters cling,   350
Those poisonous fields with rank luxuriance crowned,
Where the dark scorpion gathers death around;
Where at each step the stranger fears to wake
The rattling terrors of the vengeful snake;
Where crouching tigers wait their hapless prey,[1]   355
And savage men, more murderous still than they;
While oft in whirls the mad tornado flies,
Mingling the ravaged landscape with the skies.
Far different these from every former scene,
The cooling brook, the grassy vested green,   360
The breezy covert of the warbling grove,
That only sheltered thefts of harmless love.
    Good Heaven! what sorrows gloomed that parting day,
That called them from their native walks away;
When the poor exiles, every pleasure past,   365
Hung round their bowers, and fondly looked their last,
And took a long farewell, and wished in vain
For seats like these beyond the western main;
And shuddering still to face the distant deep,
Returned and wept, and still returned to weep.   370
The good old sire, the first prepared to go
To new-found worlds, and wept for other's woe.
But for himself, in conscious virtue brave,
He only wished for worlds beyond the grave.
His lovely daughter, lovelier in her tears,   375
The fond companion of his helpless years,
Silent went next, neglectful of her charms,
And left a lover's for a father's arms.
With louder plaints the mother spoke her woes,
And blessed the cot where every pleasure rose;   380
And kissed her thoughtless babes with many a tear,
And clasped them close in sorrow doubly dear;
Whilst her fond husband strove to lend relief
In all the silent manliness of grief.
    O luxury! Thou cursed by Heaven's decree,   385
How ill exchanged are things like these for thee!
How do thy potions, with insidious joy,
Diffuse their pleasures only to destroy!
Kingdoms, by thee, to sickly greatness grown,
Boast of a florid vigor not their own.   390
At every draught more large and large they grow,
A bloated mass of rank unwieldy woe;
Till sapped their strength, and every part unsound,
Down, down they sink, and spread a ruin round.
    Even now the devastation is begun,   395
And half the business of destruction done;

---

1. Not the Asiatic tiger, but the puma.

Even now, methinks, as pondering here I stand,
I see the rural Virtues leave the land.
Down where yon anchoring vessel spreads the sail,
That idly waiting flaps with every gale,   400
Downward they move, a melancholy band,
Pass from the shore, and darken all the strand.
Contented Toil, and hospitable Care,
And kind connubial Tenderness are there;
And Piety, with wishes placed above,   405
And steady Loyalty, and faithful Love:
And thou, sweet Poetry, thou loveliest maid,
Still first to fly where sensual joys invade;
Unfit in these degenerate times of shame,
To catch the heart, or strike for honest fame;   410
Dear charming Nymph, neglected and decried,
My shame in crowds, my solitary pride;
Thou source of all my bliss, and all my woe,
That found'st me poor at first, and keep'st me so;
Thou guide by which the nobler arts excel,   415
Thou nurse of every virtue, fare thee well.
Farewell, and O! where'er thy voice be tried
On Torno's cliffs, or Pambamarca's side,[2]
Whether where equinoctial fervors glow,
Or winter wraps the polar world in snow,   420
Still let thy voice, prevailing over time,
Redress the rigors of the inclement clime;
Aid slighted truth, with thy persuasive strain
Teach erring man to spurn the rage of gain;
Teach him that states of native strength possessed,   425
Though very poor, may still be very blest;
That Trade's proud empire hastes to swift decay,
As ocean sweeps the labored mole[3] away;
While self-dependent power can time defy,
As rocks resist the billows and the sky.[4]   430

1770

2. The river Torne in Sweden falls into the Gulf of Bothnia; Pambamarca is a mountain in Ecuador.

3. The laboriously built breakwater.

4. Johnson composed the last four lines of the poem.

Topics in Restoration and Eighteenth-Century Literature

"A GRACE BEYOND THE REACH OF ART"

Throughout the neoclassical period artists and critics were constantly aware of two apparently contrary but valid principles which they had to honor: the principle that any work of art must be constructed according to certain established and tested "rules," and the principle that genius must be left free, even within a system of rules, to achieve its own ends in its own way. The dilemma was an old one, as the selections from *On the Sublime* (traditionally attributed to Longinus, but actually by an unknown Greek rhetorician and critic of the 1st century A.D.) and from the *Institutio Oratoria* by Quintilian, the Roman rhetorician of the same century, make clear. The "rules" were not merely those basic principles of sound construction that any writer freely submits to; they were a set of precepts (too easily reduced to mere formulas) derived by Renaissance critics in Italy from the writings of the ancients, both poets and critics—precepts which legislated the structure, subjects, characters, language and conventions of each of the major literary "kinds": epic, tragedy, comedy.

The poet who was content merely to follow the rules and thereby to be "correct" had been scorned by Longinus and by Horace. Modern critics and poets shared this scorn, especially in England, where an impressive body of literature, from Chaucer to Spenser and Shakespeare, written without benefit of the rules, testified to the sufficiency of original and untutored genius to "follow Nature." Few English critics of the 18th century approved a rigid conformity to the rules, and most were in agreement with Pope, who in *An Essay on Criticism* (lines 141–160), had been careful to emphasize the supreme value of those moments of insight which come to all great artists, enabling them to achieve their greatest effects by ignoring or transcending mere formal correctness, effects which appear to be, in vulgar terms, the result of "inspiration" alone.

Pope calls such effects "grace," a word with a long history in both Greek and Roman critical theory, signifying that ultimate, inexpressible charm which converts the merely formal and regular into vital and animated beauty, and which is the mysterious result of "Nature" and not of "art," or rules. Some such notion as this governed neoclassical critical theory in England and kept criticism from degenerating into tasteless pedantry. The passages printed below show this idea at work during the period in which the rules had their greatest authority.

1930

LONGINUS: [Genius and the Rules]

Come, now, let us take some writer who is really immaculate
and beyond reproach. Is it not worthwhile, on this very point, to
raise the general question whether we ought to give the preference
in poems and prose writings to grandeur with some attendant
faults or to success which is moderate but altogether sound and
free from error? Aye, and further, whether a greater number of
excellences, or excellences higher in quality, would in literature
rightly bear away the palm? * * * For my part, I am well aware
that lofty genius is far removed from flawlessness; for invariable
accuracy incurs the risk of pettiness, and in the sublime, as in great
fortunes, there must be something which is overlooked. It may be
necessarily the case that low and average natures remain as a rule
free from failing and in greater safety because they never run a risk
or seek to scale the heights, while great endowments prove insecure
because of their very greatness. In the second place, I am not ignorant that it naturally happens that the worse side of human
character is always the more easily recognized, and that the memory
of errors remains indelible, while that of excellence quickly dies
away. I have myself noted not a few errors on the part of Homer
and other writers of the greatest distinction, and the slips they
have made afford me anything but pleasure. Still I do not term
them willful errors, but rather oversights of a random and casual
kind, due to neglect and introduced with all the heedlessness of
genius. Consequently I do not waver in my view that excellences
higher in quality, even if not sustained throughout, should always
on a comparison be voted the first place, because of their sheer elevation of spirit, if for no other reason. * * *

[From *On the Sublime* XXXIII (1st century A.D.),
tr. W. Rhys Roberts]

QUINTILIAN: [When to Break the Rules]

Let no one, however, demand from me a rigid code of rules such
as most authors of textbooks have laid down, or ask me to impose
on students of rhetoric a system of laws immutable as fate. * * *
most rules are liable to be altered by the nature of the case, circumstances of time and place, and by hard necessity itself. * * * For
these rules have not the formal authority of laws or decrees of the
plebs, but are with all they contain, the children of expediency. I

will not deny that it is generally expedient to conform to such rules, otherwise I should not be writing now; but if our friend expediency suggests some other course to us, why, we shall disregard the authority of the professors and follow her.

For my part above all things

This I enjoin and urge and urge anew[1]

that in all his pleadings the orator should keep two things constantly in view, what is becoming and what is expedient. But it is often expedient and occasionally becoming to make some modification in the time-honored order. We see the same thing in pictures and in statues. Dress, expression, and attitude are frequently varied. The body, when held bolt upright, has but little grace, for the face looks straight forward, the arms hang by the side, the feet are joined, and the whole figure is stiff from top to toe. But that curve (I might almost have called it motion) with which we are so familiar, gives an impression of action and animation. So, too, the hand will not always be represented in the same position, and the variety given to the expression will be infinite. * * * It has always, therefore, been my custom not to tie myself down to universal or general rules. * * * For rules are rarely of such a kind that their validity cannot be shaken and overthrown in some particular or other. * * * But rules are helpful all the same so long as they indicate the direct road and do not restrict us absolutely to the ruts made by others. For he who thinks it an unpardonable sin to leave the old, old track, must be content to move at much the same speed as a tightrope walker. Thus, for example, we often leave a paved military road to take a short cut or, finding that the direct route is impossible owing to floods having broken down the bridges, are forced to make a circuit, while if our house is on fire and flames bar the way to the front door, we make our escape by breaking through a party wall.

[From *Institutio Oratoria* II.xiii (1st century A.D.), tr. H. E. Butler]

RENÉ RAPIN: [Grace Beyond the Rules]

Yet is there in poetry, as in other arts, certain things that cannot be expressed, which are (as it were) mysteries. There are no precepts to teach the hidden graces, the insensible charms, and all that secret power of poetry which passes to the heart, as there is no method to teach to please. 'Tis a pure effect of Nature. However, Nature alone can never please regularly, unless in the small

1. *Aeneid* III.436.

compositions: there must be the assistance of art to succeed well in the great poems. 'Tis by this help that a genius a little cultivated shall range his thoughts in that admirable order which makes the greatest beauty in the productions of wit: by this order everything becomes delightful, because, as Horace saith, " 'Tis in its place";[2] but this is the work of judgment, as invention is the work of imagination; and this order that keeps all right, and without which, the most beautiful becomes deformed, is a mystery but little known to modern poets.

[From *Réflexions sur la Poétique d'Aristote*, 1674]

JOHN DRYDEN: [Genius is Above Correctness]

* * * I must take leave to tell them that they wholly mistake the nature of criticism who think its business is principally to find fault. Criticism, as it was first instituted by Aristotle, was meant a standard of judging well, the chiefest part of which is to observe those excellencies which should delight a reasonable reader. If the design, the conduct, the thought, and the expressions of a poem be generally such as proceed from a true genius of poetry, the critic ought to pass his judgment in favor of the author. 'Tis malicious and unmanly to snarl at the little lapses of a pen from which Virgil himself stands not exempted. Horace acknowledges that honest Homer nods sometimes:[3] he is not equally awake in every line; * * * And Longinus, who was undoubtedly, after Aristotle, the greatest critic amongst the Greeks, in his twenty-seventh chapter of περὶ Ὕψους,[4] has judiciously preferred the sublime genius that sometimes errs, to the middling, or indifferent one, which makes few faults but seldom or never rises to any excellence. He compares the first to a man of large possessions, who has not leisure to consider of every slight expense, will not debase himself to the management of every trifle: particular sums are not laid out, or spared, to the greatest advantage in his economy, but are sometimes suffered to run to waste, while he is only careful of the main. On the other side, he likens a mediocrity of wit to one of a mean fortune, who manages his store with extreme frugality, or rather parsimony; but who, with fear of running into profuseness, never arrives to the magnificence of living. This kind of genius writes indeed correctly. A wary man he is in grammar, very nice as to solecism or barbarism, judges to a hair of little decencies, knows better than any man what is not to be written, and never hazards himself so far as to fall,

2. For the context of this phrase see *Ars Poetica*, lines 42–45.
3. *Ars Poetica*, line 359.
4. The title of this Greek rhetorical treatise of the 1st century A.D. (traditionally but erroneously attributed to Longinus) is usually translated "On the Sublime."

but plods on deliberately, and as a grave man ought, is sure to put his staff before him * * *

[From *The Author's Apology for Heroic Poetry and Heroic License*, 1677]

SIR WILLIAM TEMPLE: [The Inadequacy of the Rules]

The modern French wits (or pretenders) have been very severe in their censures and exact in their rules, I think to very little purpose; for I know not why they might not have contented themselves with those given by Aristotle and Horace, and have translated them rather than commented upon them, for all they have done has been no more, so as they seem by their writings of this kind rather to have valued themselves than improved anybody else. The truth is, there is something in the genius of poetry too libertine to be confined to so many rules; and whoever goes about to subject it to such constraints loses both its spirit and grace, which are ever native, and never learned, even of the best masters. 'Tis as if, to make excellent honey, you should cut off the wings of your bees, confine them to their hives or their stands, and lay flowers before them, such as you think the sweetest and like to yield the finest extraction; you had as good pull out their stings, and make arrant drones of them. They must range through fields as well as gardens, choose such flowers as they please, and by proprieties[5] and scents they only know and distinguish. They must work up their cells with admirable art, extract their honey with infinite labor, and sever it from the wax with such distinction and choice as belongs to none but themselves to perform or judge. * * *

After all, the utmost that can be achieved or, I think, pretended by any rules in this art is but to hinder some men from being very ill poets, but not to make any man a very good one.

[From *Of Poetry*, 1690]

JOHN HUGHES: ["Curiosa Felicitas"]

Elegance of thought is what we commonly call wit, which adds to propriety,[6] beauty, and pleases our fancy, while propriety entertains our judgment. This depends so much on genius that 'tis impossible to teach it by rules. To the elegance of words, or style, belong all the figures of rhetoric, and to use these to advantage requires a judgment well formed by observation. In this, therefore, as in learning the graces upon an instrument of music, good ex-

5. Properties, attributes.   6. The fitting, the appropriate.

amples are the best instruction. Thus a man may write metaphors, tropes, hyperboles, and all other figures, without the trouble of studying a system of rhetoric; and I believe better, too; for to attend to a great many rules whilst you are writing is the way to make your style stiff and constrained, whereas elegance consists very much in a genteel ease and freedom of expression; it is like a coy mistress, of so nice a humor that to court her too much is the surest way to lose her; and as success in love is owing to good fortune and the natural happiness of pleasing, rather than to fidelity and attendance, so the art of choosing out of several expressions equally proper that which is most graceful is best called a *curiosa felicitas*,[7] which two words seem to comprehend all that can be said upon this head.

[From *Of Style*, 1698]

ROGER DE PILES: [Grace Gains the Heart]

* * * A painter posses es [grace] only as a gift of Nature; he himself does not know whether he possesses it, or in what degree, or how he communicates it to his works. It surprises the spectator, who feels its effect without penetrating to its true cause * * * It can be defined as that which pleases and gains the heart without passing through the judgment.

Grace and beauty are two different things; beauty pleases only by rules, and grace pleases without rules. The beautiful is not always graceful, and the graceful is not always beautiful. But grace joined to beauty is the height of perfection.

[From *L'Idée de Peintre Parfait*, 1699]

JOSEPH ADDISON: [The Beauties of Great Geniuses Independent of Rules]

They [ignorant critics] are often led into those numerous absurdities in which they daily instruct the people by not considering that, first, there is sometimes a greater judgment shown in deviating from the rules of art than in adhering to them; and, secondly, that there is more beauty in the works of a great genius who is ignorant of all the rules of art than in the works of a little genius who not only knows, but scrupulously observes them.

First, we may often take notice of men who are perfectly acquainted with all the rules of good writing, and notwithstanding

7. In his *Satyricon*, Chapter XIV, Petronius (d. A.D. 65) used this phrase to describe the ultimate quality of Horace's poetry. It refers to the impression of ease and rightness (*felicitas*, "happiness") that is the final result of technical mastery and painstaking care (implied in the paradoxical adjective *curiosa*, "careful," "diligent").

choose to depart from them on extraordinary occasions. I could give instances out of all the tragic writers of antiquity who have shown their judgment in this particular, and purposely receded from an established rule of the drama when it has made way for a much higher beauty than the observation of such a rule would have been. Those who have surveyed the noblest pieces of architecture and statuary, both ancient and modern, know very well that there are frequent deviations from art in the works of the greatest masters, which have produced a much nobler effect than a more accurate and exact way of proceeding could have done. This often arises from what the Italians call the *gusto grande* in these arts, which is what we call the sublime in writing.

In the next place, our critics do not seem sensible that there is more beauty in the works of a great genius who is ignorant of the rules of art than in those of a little genius who knows and observes them. * * * Our inimitable Shakespeare is a stumbling-block to the whole tribe of these rigid critics. Who would not rather read one of his plays, where there is not a single rule of the stage observed, than any production of a modern critic where there is not one of them violated! * * *

[From *Spectator* 592, September 10, 1714]

LEONARD WELSTED: [No Precepts Can
Teach Grace]

* * * The secret and soul of good writing is not to be come at through * * * mechanic laws; the main graces and the cardinal beauties of this charming art lie too retired within the bosom of nature and are too fine and subtle an essence to fall under the discussion of pedants, commentators, or trading critics, whether they be heavy prose-drudges or more sprightly essayers in rhyme. These beauties, in a word, are rather to be felt than described. By what precepts shall a writer be taught only to think poetically, or to trace out among the various powers of thought, that particular vein or feature of it which poetry loves, and to distinguish between the good sense which may have its weight and justness in the prose and that which is of the nature of verse? What instruction shall convey to him that flame which can alone animate a work and give it the glow of poetry? * * * Could certain methods be laid down for attaining these excellencies, everyone that pleased might be a poet, as everyone that pleases may be a geometrician, if he will but have due patience and attention. * * *

[From *Dissertation Concerning * * * the
State of Poetry*, 1724]

THE GENERAL AND THE PARTICULAR

This section brings together some opinions of critics of both literature and painting. In view of the fact that neoclassical theory stressed the close kinship between these two arts, considering them "sisters," critics of either art often help us to understand the other. This is especially true of our selections from the *Discourses* of the famous portrait painter Sir Joshua Reynolds, which he delivered between 1769 and 1790 in his role as president of the Royal Academy. They are as relevant to poetry or to literature in general as they are to Reynolds' own art, painting.

The emphasis on the general and representative in art derives from classical antiquity. Aristotle, in a passage in his *Poetics* included below, gave authority to the idea that history deals in particulars, but poetry in universals; and this view of art was confirmed by the observation of the idealized and generalized forms of Greek and Roman sculpture, by the study of the characters in Homer, Virgil, and the ancient dramatists, and by such a formulation of character types as is found in the passage from Horace's *Ars Poetica* printed below. The general could be fruitfully used in those forms of art that deal with the moral and emotional life of man—epic, tragedy, comedy, satire, and heroic or historical sculpture and painting. It was to prove less satisfying to 18th-century readers of descriptive poetry, despite the fact that such 17th-century landscape painters as Claude Lorrain, Nicholas Poussin, and Gasper Poussin had created a beautiful and satisfying landscape of general and ordered natural forms.

It was in regard to the poetry of natural description, which flourished after 1726, the year of James Thomson's *Winter*, that critics began to insist that the poet should render concrete particulars actually observed. This sort of poetry is a prelude to the nature poetry of the Romantic movement, but the two are actually very unlike each other. Different philosophies, different ideas about human consciousness and about the imagination, different interests and emphases separate the largely pictorial nature poetry of the Augustan age from the quasi-religious and often very subjective nature poetry of the Romantics.

Many 19th-century poets and painters prided themselves on their minutely factual observation of the external world, which they often approached in the spirit of the botanist or the zoologist, and sometimes with the eye of an impressionist painter, quick to perceive and to make permanent in art some fleeting and uniquely individual aspect of the external world. One thinks of Coleridge's evening sky, with its "peculiar tint of yellow green"; of Keats's musk rose, "the murmurous haunt of flies on summer eves"; of Tennyson's "black as ash-buds in March"; of Arnold's "Frail-leafed, white anemone." This sort of observation played an increasingly important role in 18th-century nature poetry. Thomson in the *Seasons* had been able to achieve broad, general effects as well as accurately observed details, and to combine them with admirable tact. As time passed many critics stressed the importance of the particular in natural description and demanded some evidence that the poet had observed what he described; still, conservative theorists like Johnson and Reynolds continued to support the older idea that great art is based on general nature. At the turn of the century we hear in John Moir's insistence that genius must particularize, and in William Blake's angry contradictions of the opinions of Reynolds, the very accent of the new generation of romantic artists and theorists who were just appearing on the scene.

ARISTOTLE: [Poetry and History Contrasted]

It is, moreover, evident from what has been said, that it is not the function of the poet to relate what has happened, but what may happen—what is possible according to the law of probability or necessity. The poet and the historian differ not by writing in verse or in prose. The work of Herodotus[1] might be put into verse, and it would still be a species of history, with meter no less than without it. The true difference is that one relates what has happened, the other what may happen. Poetry, therefore, is a more philosophical and a higher thing than history: for poetry tends to express the universal, history the particular. By the universal I mean how a person of given character will on occasion speak or act, according to the law of probability or necessity; and it is this universality at which poetry aims in the names she attaches to the personages. The particular is—for example—what Alcibiades did or suffered.

[From *Poetics* IX.1–liv (3rd century B.C.), tr. S. H. Butcher]

HORACE: [Character Types in Comedy]

Mark in each stage of life how nature veers,
The temper varying with the varying years.   240
What time the tongue has mastered every sound,
And steadier footsteps learn to print the ground,
Behold the schoolboy frolicsome and gay
Scampering to join his comrades at their play,
Vexed with a straw, but soothed as soon as vexed,   245
In tears this moment and in smiles the next.
The beardless youth, his freedom proud to gain,
Loves horses, hounds, and Mars's sunny plain;
Ductile as wax to vice his yielding soul,
Deaf to the warning voice of dull control,   250
Profuse of purse, impatient of delay,

---

1. Greek historian (ca. 480–ca. 425 B.C.).

Taking no thought but for the present day,
Of lofty spirit, of affections strong,
Pleased with what's new, but pleased with nothing long.
Shifting his views, see riper manhood crave   255
Place, power, and patronage—ambition's slave;
Wary betimes each oversight to shun,
And slow to do what he may wish undone.
A thousand ills declining age attend,
Still brooding o'er its bags, still loath to spend,   260
In council cold, and tardy to decide,
In thrifty forecast placing all its pride;
Full of prospective bliss and present pain,
Suspicious and splenetic, fretful, vain;
Loud in the praises of the good old times,   265
And croaking stern rebuke on modern crimes.

[From *Ars Poetica* (late 1st century B.C.), tr. Francis Howes]

SIR WILLIAM DAVENANT: [Poetry and
    History Contrasted]

Lucan,[2] who chose to write the greatest actions that ever were allowed to be true, which for fear of contemporary witnesses obliged him to a very close attendance upon fame, did not observe that such an enterprise rather beseemed an historian than a poet: for wise poets think it more worthy to seek out truth in the passions than to record the truth of actions; and practice to describe mankind just as we are persuaded or guided by instinct, not particular persons as they are lifted or leveled by the force of fate, it being nobler to contemplate the general history of nature than a selected diary of Fortune. And painters are no more than historians when they draw eminent persons, though they term that "drawing to the life"; but when, by assembling divers figures in a larger volume they draw passions, though they term it but story, then they increase in dignity and become poets.

[From Preface to *Gondibert*, 1650]

---

2. Marcus Annaeus Lucanus (A.D. 39–65), author of the historical poem *Phar-* *salia* which dealt with the civil war between Julius Caesar and Pompey.

ANTHONY ASHLEY COOPER, THIRD EARL OF
SHAFTESBURY: [The General and the
Particular in Painting]

A painter, if he has any genius, understands the truth and unity
of design; and knows he is even then unnatural, when he follows
Nature too close and strictly copies life. For his art allows him not
to bring all Nature into his piece, but a part only. However, his
piece, if it be beautiful and carries truth, must be a whole, by itself complete, independent, and withal as great and comprehensive
as he can make it. So that particulars, on this occasion, must yield
to the general design; and all things be subservient to that which is
principal, in order to form a certain easiness of sight: a simple, clear,
and united view, which would be broken and disturbed by the
expression of anything particular or distinct.

Now the variety of Nature is such as to distinguish everything
she forms by a peculiar original character; which, if strictly observed, will make the subject appear unlike to anything extant in
the world besides. But this effort the good poet and painter seek
industriously to prevent. They hate minuteness and are afraid of
singularity; which would make their images or characters appear capricious and fantastical. The mere face-painter, indeed, has little
in common with the poet; but, like the mere historian, copies what
he sees, and minutely traces every feature and odd mark. 'Tis otherwise with the men of invention and design. 'Tis from the many
objects of Nature, and not from a particular one, that those geniuses
form the idea of their work. Thus the best artists are said to have
been indefatigable in studying the best statues, as esteeming them
a better rule than the perfectest human bodies could afford. And
thus some considerable wits have recommended the best poems as
preferable to the best of histories, as better teaching the truth of
characters and nature of mankind.

[From *Sensus Communis* iv.iii, 1709]

SAMUEL JOHNSON: [The Particular in Biography]

The general and rapid narrative of history, which involve a
thousand fortunes in the business of a day, and communicate in-

numerable incidents in one great transaction, afford few lessons applicable to private life, which derives its comforts and its wretchedness from the right or wrong management of things which nothing but their frequency makes considerable * * * and which can have no place in those relations which never descend below the consultation of senates, the motions of armies, and the schemes of conspirators.

I have often thought that there has rarely passed a life of which a judicious and faithful narrative would not be useful. For not only every member has, in the mighty mass of the world, great numbers in the same condition with himself, to whom his mistakes and miscarriages, escapes and expedients, would be of immediate and apparent use; but there is such an uniformity in the state of man, considered apart from adventitious and separate decorations and disguises, that there is scarce any possibility of good or ill, but is common to human kind. A great part of the time of those who are placed at the greatest distance by fortune or by temper must unavoidably pass in the same manner; and though, when the claims of nature are satisfied, caprice and vanity and accident begin to produce discriminations and peculiarities, yet the eye is not very heedful or quick which cannot discover the same causes still terminating their influence in the same effects, though sometimes accelerated, sometimes retarded, or perplexed by multiplied combinations. We are all prompted by the same motives, all deceived by the same fallacies, all animated by hope, obstructed by danger, entangled by desire, and seduced by pleasure. * * *

* * * The business of the biographer is often to pass slightly over those performances and incidents which produce vulgar greatness, to lead the thoughts into domestic privacies, and display the minute details of daily life, where exterior appendages are cast aside, and men excel each other only by prudence and virtue.

[From *Rambler* 60, 1750]

SAMUEL JOHNSON: [The Simplicity of Grandeur]

Poetry cannot dwell upon the minuter distinctions, by which one species differs from another, without departing from that simplicity of grandeur which fills the imagination; nor dissect the latent qualities of things, without losing its general power of gratifying every mind by recalling its conceptions.

[From *Rambler* 36, 1750]

SAMUEL JOHNSON: [*Hudibras* and the Particular]

But human works are not easily found without a perishable part. Of the ancient poets every reader feels the mythology tedious and oppressive. Of *Hudibras*, the manners, being founded on opinions, are temporary and local, and therefore become every day less intelligible and less striking. What Cicero says of philosophy is true likewise of wit and humor, that "time effaces the fictions of opinion and confirms the determinations of Nature."[3] Such manners as depend upon standing relations and general passions are coextended with the race of man; but those modifications of life and peculiarities of practice which are the progeny of error and perverseness, or at best of some accidental influence or transient persuasion, must perish with their parents.

[From *Life of Butler*, 1779]

SAMUEL JOHNSON: [The Grandeur of Generality][4]

The fault of Cowley and perhaps of all the writers of the metaphysical race is that of pursuing his thoughts to their last ramifications, by which he loses the grandeur of generality; for of the greatest things the parts are little; what is little can be but pretty, and by claiming dignity becomes ridiculous. Thus all the power of description is destroyed by a scrupulous enumeration; and the force of metaphors is lost, when the mind by the mention of particulars is turned more upon the original than the secondary sense, more upon that from which the illustration is drawn than that to which it is applied. * * *

[From *Life of Cowley*, 1779]

JOSEPH WARTON: [On Thomson's *Seasons*]

Thomson was blessed with a strong and copious fancy; he hath enriched poetry with a variety of new and original images, which he painted from nature itself, and from his own actual observations: his descriptions have therefore a distinctness and truth,

3. *De Natura Deorum* II.ii.5.
4. For other important remarks on this subject by Johnson see in this volume his *Rasselas*, Chapter X, and the discussion of the representative and the individual in Shakespeare's dramatic characters (Preface to Shakespeare).

which are utterly wanting to those of poets who have only copied from each other, and have never looked abroad on the objects themselves. Thomson was accustomed to wander away into the country for days and for weeks, attentive to "each rural sight, each rural sound"; while many a poet who has dwelt for years in the Strand[5] has attempted to describe fields and rivers, and generally succeeded accordingly. Hence that nauseous repetition of the same circumstances; hence that disgusting impropriety of introducing what may be called a set of hereditary images, without proper regard to the age, or climate, or occasion, in which they were formerly used. * * * Innumerable are the little circumstances in his descriptions totally unobserved by all his predecessors. What poet hath ever taken notice of the leaf that, towards the end of autumn,

> Incessant rustles from the mournful grove,
> Oft startling such as studious walk below,
> And slowly circles through the waving air?[6]

Or who, in speaking of a summer evening, hath ever mentioned

> The quail that clamors for his running mate?[7]

Or the following natural image, at the same time of the year?

> Wide o'er the thistly lawn, as swells the breeze,
> A whitening flower of vegetable down
> Amusive[8] floats.

Where do we find the silence and expectation that precedes an April shower insisted on, as in verse 165 of *Spring*, or where

> The stealing shower is scarce to patter heard
> By such as wander through the forest walks,
> Beneath the umbrageous multitude of leaves.[9]

* * *In no one subject are common poets more confused and unmeaning than in their descriptions of rivers, which are generally said only to wind and to murmur, while their qualities and courses are seldom accurately marked; examine the exactness of the ensuing description, and consider what a perfect idea it communicates to the mind.

> Around the adjoining brook, that purls along
> The vocal grove, now fretting o'er a rock,
> Now scarcely moving through a reedy pool,

5. A busy London street, leading from Temple Bar to Charing Cross.
6. *Autumn*, lines 990–92.
7. *Summer*, line 1657, slightly misquoted.
8. From the verb "to amuse," defined by Johnson as "to entertain with tranquility."
9. *Spring*, lines 177–79.

Now starting to a sudden stream, and now
Gently diffused into a limpid plain,
A various group the herds and flocks compose,
Rural confusion![1]

* * * A minute and particular enumeration of circumstances judiciously selected is what chiefly discriminates poetry from history and renders the former, for that reason, a more close and faithful representation of nature than the latter. And if our poets would accustom themselves to contemplate fully every object before they attempted to describe it, they would not fail of giving their readers more new images than they generally do.

[From *An Essay on the Writings and Genius of Pope*,
Section II, 1756]

HUGH BLAIR: [The Particular in Descriptive Poetry]

Description is the great test of a poet's imagination, and always distinguishes an original from a second-rate genius. To a writer of the inferior class, nature, when at any time he attempts to describe it, appears exhausted by those who have gone before him in the same track. He sees nothing new or particular in the object which he would paint; his conceptions of it are loose and vague; and his expressions, of course, feeble and general. * * * whereas a true poet makes us imagine that we see it before our eyes: he catches the distinguishing features; he gives it the colors of life and reality; he places it in such a light that a painter could copy after him. This happy talent is chiefly owing to a strong imagination, which first receives a lively impression of the object, and then, by employing a proper selection of circumstances in describing it, transmits that impression in all its full force to the imagination of others.

* * * of all the English poems in the descriptive style, the richest and most remarkable are Milton's *Allegro* and *Penseroso*.

[Quotes *Il Penseroso*, lines 65–94]

Here there are no unmeaning expressions. All is particular; all is picturesque; nothing forced or exaggerated, but a simple style and a collection of strong expressive images, which are all of one class and recall a number of similar ideas of the melancholy kind * * *

Everything, as I before said, in description, should be as marked and particular as possible, in order to imprint on the mind a distinct and complete image. A hill, a river, or a lake, rises up more

---

1. *Summer*, lines 480–86.

conspicuous to the fancy, when some particular lake, or river, or hill is specified, than when the terms are left general.

[From Lecture XL, "Didactic Poetry–Descriptive Poetry," in
Lectures on Rhetoric and Belles Lettres, 1783]

SIR JOSHUA REYNOLDS: [The General and the Particular in Painting—The "Grand Style"]

1

All objects which are exhibited to our view by nature, upon close examination will be found to have their blemishes and defects. The most beautiful forms have something about them like weaknesses, minuteness, or imperfections. But it is not every eye that preceives these blemishes. It must be an eye long used to the contemplation and comparison of these forms; and which, by a long habit of observing what any set of objects of the same kind have in common, has acquired the power of discerning what each wants in particular. This long, laborious comparison should be the first study of the painter who aims at the great style. By this means, he acquires a just idea of beautiful forms; he corrects nature by herself, her imperfect state by her more perfect. His eyes being enabled to distinguish the accidental deficiencies, excrescences, and deformities of things, from their general figures, he makes out an abstract idea of their forms more perfect than any one original; and, what may seem a paradox, he learns to design naturally by drawing his figures unlike to any one object. This idea of the perfect state of nature, which the artist calls the ideal beauty, is the great leading principle by which works of genius are conducted. * * *

Thus it is from a reiterated experience and a close comparison of the objects in nature that an artist becomes possessed of the idea of that central form, if I may so express it, from which every deviation is deformity. * * *

To the principle I have laid down, that the idea of beauty in each species of beings is an invariable one, it may be objected that in every particular species there are various central forms which are undeniably beautiful; that in the human figure, for instance, the beauty of Hercules is one, of the Gladiator another, of the Apollo another;[2] which makes so many different ideas of beauty.

It is true, indeed, that these figures are each perfect in their kind, though of different characters and proportions; but still none of

2. Reynolds refers to three well-known Roman statues: the Farnese Hercules (now at Naples), the Apollo Belvedere (in the Vatican), and, according to Robert Wark, the Borghese Warrior (now in the Louvre).

them is the representation of an individual, but of a class. And as there is one general form, which, as I have said, belongs to the human kind at large, so in each of these classes there is one common idea and central form, which is the abstract of the various individual forms belonging to that class. Thus, though the forms of childhood and age differ exceedingly, there is a common form in childhood, and a common form in age, which is more perfect as it is more remote from all peculiarities. * * *

However the mechanic and ornamental arts may sacrifice to fashion, she must be entirely excluded from the art of painting; the painter must never mistake this capricious challenging for the genuine offspring of nature; he must divest himself of all prejudices in favor of his age and country; he must disregard all local and temporal ornaments, and look only on those general habits which are everywhere and always the same; he addresses his works to the people of every country and every age, he calls upon posterity to be his spectators, and says, with Zeuxis,[3] *In aeternitatem pingo.* * * *

[From *Discourse* III, 1770]

2

I am very ready to allow that some circumstances of minuteness and particularity frequently tend to give an air of truth to a piece, and to interest the spectator in an extraordinary manner. Such circumstances, therefore, cannot wholly be rejected: but if there be anything in the art which requires peculiar nicety of discernment, it is the disposition of these minute circumstantial parts; which, according to the judgment employed in the choice, become so useful to truth, or so injurious to grandeur.

However, the usual and most dangerous error is on the side of minuteness: and therefore, I think caution most necessary where most have failed. The general idea constitutes real excellence. All smaller things, however perfect in their way, are to be sacrificed without mercy to the greater * * * Even in portraits, the grace, and, we may add, the likeness, consists more in taking the general air than in observing the exact similitude of every feature.

[From *Discourse* IV, 1771]

3

* * * I do not forget that a painter must have the power of contracting as well as dilating his sight; because he that does not at all express particulars, expresses nothing; yet it is certain that a nice discrimination of minute circumstances and a punctilious delineation of them, whatever excellence it may have * * * never did confer on the artist the character of genius.

3. Greek painter of the 5th century B.C. The phrase "I paint for eternity" is apparently based on an anecdote twice told by Plutarch, once in his *Moralia* ("*De Amicorum Multitudine*") and once in the *Life of Pericles*, Chapter XIII.

The detail of particulars, which does not assist the expression of the main characteristic, is worse than useless; it is mischievous, as it dissipates the attention and draws it from the principal point. It may be remarked that the impression which is left on our mind even of things which are familiar to us is seldom more than their general effect, beyond which we do not look in recognizing such objects. To express this in painting is to express what is congenial and natural to the mind of man, and what gives him by reflection his own mode of conceiving. The other presupposes *nicety* and *research*, which are only the business of the curious and attentive, and therefore does not speak to the general sense of the whole species, in which common, and as I may so call it, mother tongue, everything grand and comprehensive must be uttered. * * *

I remember a landscape painter in Rome, who was known by the name of "Studio," from his patience in high finishing, in which he thought the whole excellence of art consisted; so that he once endeavored, as he said, to represent every individual leaf on a tree. This picture I never saw, but I am very sure that an artist who looked only at the general character of the species, the order of the branches, and the masses of the foliage would in a few minutes produce a more true resemblance of trees than this painter in as many months.

A landscape painter certainly ought to study anatomically (if I may use the expression) all the objects which he paints; but when he is to turn his studies to use, his skill as a man of genius will be displayed in showing the general effect, preserving the same degree of hardness and softness which the objects have in nature; for he applies himself to the imagination, not to the curiosity, and works not for the virtuoso[4] and the naturalist, but for the common observer of life and nature.

[From *Discourse* XI, 1782]

JOHN MOIR: [The Unique Vision of Original Genius]

What is it a truly original genius will not improve? Everything is prolific of novelty in the hand of a master. His ideas are not the crude conceptions of dullness; nor his sentiments either the vapid yawning of a listless, or the insignificant prattle of an empty, heart. He generally plans entirely for himself, and always executes in a manner preceded by nothing similar. The light he strikes out is

---

4. "A man skilled in antique or natural curiosities; a man studious of painting, statuary, or architecture" (Johnson's *Dictionary*).

so singular, and withal so true, that we are equally pleased with what we never saw before, and surprised that we now only see it for the first time. Who, for example, before Virgil, expected to find the fable of the *Iliad* capable of being so beautifull[y] diversified with new elegance and truth, as we find it in the *Aeneid?*

In descriptive poetry, as in landscape painting, fancy has the fullest scope. Here, however, fiction does not consist in feigning objects unknown to the senses, but in embellishing them with colors, endowing them with qualities, connecting them by relations, and disposing them in attitudes and groups of which we have little or no acquaintance. In truth, ideal arrangements are endless. While our affections retain their usual aversion to uniformity, the multifarious objects of our respective senses and faculties must unavoidably admit of new combinations.

This, like every other art, is improved by practice: for the more a fertile imagination creates or fabricates the exercise becomes the easier, new veins of verisimilitude are disclosed, and we may give over for want of patience or strength, but not of materials. The human genius is so versatile, and the original sources of beauty so inexhaustible, that every new inspection of the most common and familiar phenomena of nature discovers a thousand new variations, distinctions, and resemblances, at the same time that it opens up a multiplicity of avenues, where novelty wantons in all her charms, where science displays her happiest attractions, where the fancy is feasted, and the heart at once entertained and made better. * * *

Want of real discrimination is one of the greatest defects in thinking, acting, or writing. It infallibly degrades every species of composition; and indeed is a decisive criterion by which the most genuine offspring of dullness is everywhere known and distinguished. Ordinary minds are seldom struck with anything, because they never particularize or examine the objects of their respective senses. All their literary efforts, whatever departments they may fill, or consequence they may effect, are but an echo, which dies with the sound that begets, or the situation that occasions it. Original genius never rests in generals, never runs in a circle, but gives, in vivid, glowing, and permanent characters, the identical impression it receives.

Perhaps no better account can be given of a quality which, from the beginning of the world, has continued in full possession of universal homage, than that individual minds are distinguished by nature in the formation and structure of the organs by which they respectively operate; that we have all our own way of thinking whenever we do think; and that our sentiments and ideas are never destitute of novelty or justness but when we cease to think.

[From "Originality," *Gleanings or Fugitive Pieces*, 1785]

WILLIAM BLAKE: [The Aesthetic Value of the General Denied]

To generalize is to be an idiot. To particularize is the alone distinction of merit. General knowledges are those knowledges that idiots possess.

What is general nature? is there such a thing? what is general knowledge? is there such a thing? Strictly speaking, all knowledge is particular.

Distinct general form cannot exist. Distinctness is particular, not general.

[From his marginalia in Reynolds's *Discourses*, ca. 1808]

Selected Bibliographies

The symbol ‡ following a title indicates that the
volume is available in a paperbound edition.

SUGGESTED GENERAL READINGS

Histories of England and of English Literature

George Macaulay Trevelyan's *History of England*,‡ rev., 1945, is an excellent survey in one volume; for detailed studies of single periods, see *The Oxford History of England*, 1934–, by a variety of historians, to be published in 14 volumes. The projected 12-volume *Oxford History of English Literature*, edited by F. P. Wilson and Bonamy Dobrée, 1945–, is nearing completion; see the listings below. *A Guide to English Literature*, ed. Boris Ford (1954–61), is available in 6 paperback volumes. Up-to-date one-volume histories are Albert C. Baugh and others, *A Literary History of England*,‡ rev., 1967; Hardin Craig and others, *A History of English Literature*, 1950; and (less densely factual, and more a running literary appreciation) David Daiches, *A Critical History of English Literature*, 2 vols., 1961.

Drama

Allardyce Nicoll, *British Drama*, rev., 1957, and *A History of English Drama, 1660–1900*, 6 vols., rev., 1952–59.

The Novel

The most detailed history is Ernest A. Baker's *History of the English Novel*, 10 vols., 1924–39. Among the short histories are Walter A. Raleigh, *The English Novel*, rev., 1911, which stops at Walter Scott; Wilbur L. Cross, *The Development of the English Novel*, 1930, through R. L. Stevenson; and, more up-to-date, Arnold Kettle, *An Introduction to the English Novel*,‡ 2 vols., 1951–53, and Walter Allen, *The English Novel*,‡ 1954.

Poetry

W. J. Courthope, *A History of English Poetry*, 6 vols., 1895–1910, and H. J. C. Grierson and J. C. Smith, *A Critical History of English Poetry*, rev., 1947. In addition, Douglas Bush's two books, *Mythology and the Renaissance Tradition in English Poetry*,‡ 1932, 1957, and *Mythology and the Romantic Tradition in English Poetry*,‡ 1937, 1957, constitute an excellent running account, from their special perspective, of English poetry from the 16th century through T. S. Eliot. Another book which ranges widely in English poetry from the Middle Ages through the 18th century is E. M. W. Tillyard, *The English Epic and Its Background*,‡ 1954.

Literary Criticism

George Saintsbury, *A History of English Criticism*, 1911, is still referred to. More recent histories of English criticism are J. W. H. Atkins' three books on *The Medieval Phase*, 1943, *The Renascence*, 1947, and *17th and 18th Centuries*,‡ 1951; W. K. Wimsatt, Jr., and Cleanth Brooks, *Literary Criticism: A Short History*,‡ 1957; and René Wellek, *A History of Modern Criticism: 1750–1950*, 1955–, of which four of the projected five volumes have been published.

Reference Works

The Cambridge Bibliography of English Literature, edited by F. W. Bateson, 4 vols., 1941, lists all the books of the major and many minor British authors, together with a large selection from biographical, scholarly, and critical works written about these authors; a supplement edited by George Watson carries the listing of secondary materials to 1955. Literary biographies and critical books published since that time can be found in the "Annual Bibliography" *PMLA;* for separate periods, see the listings below. *Poetry Explication*,‡ rev. by Joseph M. Kuntz, 1962, lists close analyses of English poems, old and recent, and I. F. Bell and Donald Baird, *The English Novel, 1578–1956*,‡ 1958, provides a useful list of 20th-century criticisms of fiction. Further bibliographical aids are described in

Richard D. Altick and Andrew Wright, *Selective Bibliography for the Study of English and American Literature,*‡ 1960, and Arthur G. Kennedy, *A Concise Bibliography for Students of English,* rev., 1954.

For compact biographies of English authors see the multi-volumed *Dictionary of National Biography,* edited by Leslie Stephen and Sidney Lee in 1885–1900, with supplements that carry the work to persons who died up to 1950; condensed biographies will be found in the one-volume *Concise Dictionary of National Biography,* 1939. Handy reference books on authors, works, and various literary terms and allusions are *The Oxford Companion to English Literature,* edited by Paul Harvey, rev., 1946; *The Oxford Companion to the Theater,* edited by Phyllis Hartnoll, rev., 1957; *Dictionary of World Literature,*‡ edited by Joseph T. Shipley, rev., 1953; and *Encyclopedia of Poetry and Poetics,* ed. Alex Preminger and others, 1965. Low-priced handbooks which define and illustrate literary concepts and terms are: M. H. Abrams, *A Glossary of Literary Terms,* 1957; Carl Beckson and Arthur Ganz, *A Reader's Guide to Literary Terms,*‡ 1960; and W. F. Thrall and Addison Hibbard, *A Handbook to Literature,*‡ revised by G. Hugh Holman, 1960.

Albert C. Baugh, *A History of the English Language,* rev., 1957, will be found helpful, as will various treatments of English meters and stanza forms, such as: R. M. Alden, *English Verse,* 1903; T. S. Omond, *English Metrists,* 1921; George R. Stewart, *The Technique of English Verse,* 1930; Enid Hamer, *The Metres of English Verse,* 1930; Paul Fussell, Jr., *Poetic Meter and Poetic Form,*‡ 1966; and *The Structure of Verse: Modern Essays in Prosody,*‡ ed. Harvey Gross, 1966.

Intellectual History and Criticism

Students interested in intellectual history as a background for reading English literature will profit from Arthur O. Lovejoy, *The Great Chain of Being,*‡ 1936, and *Essays in the History of Ideas,*‡ 1948; Marjorie Nicolson, *The Breaking of the Circle,*‡ 1950, *Science and Imagination,*‡ 1956, and *Mountain Gloom and Mountain Glory,*‡ 1959; John Herman Randall, Jr., *The Making of the Modern Mind,* rev., 1940; Basil Willey, *The Seventeenth Century Background,* 1934, *The Eighteenth Century Background,* 1940, and *Nineteenth Century Studies,* 1949; and Joseph Warren Beach, *The Concept of Nature in 19th-Century English Poetry,* 1936, 1956. In addition, the following is a selection from those books in literary history and criticism which have been notably influential in shaping modern approaches to English literature and literary forms: Erich Auerbach, *Mimesis: The Representation of Reality in Western Literature,*‡ 1953; Maud Bodkin, *Archetypal Patterns in Poetry,*‡ 1934; Cleanth Brooks, *The Well Wrought Urn,*‡ 1947; Ronald Crane, *The Languages of Criticism and the Structure of Poetry,*‡ 1953, *The Idea of the Humanities,* 2 vols., 1967; and, as editor, *Critics and Criticism, Ancient and Modern,*‡ 1952; T. S. Eliot, *Selected Essays,*‡ 3rd edition, 1951, and *On Poetry and Poets,*‡ 1957; William Empson, *Seven Types of Ambiguity,*‡ 3rd edition, 1953; Francis Fergusson, *The Idea of a Theater,*‡ 1949; Northrop Frye, *Anatomy of Criticism,* 1957; Henry James, *The Art of the Novel: Critical Prefaces,*‡ 1934; F. R. Leavis, *Revaluation,*‡ 1936, and *The Great Tradition* ‡ (i.e., in the novel), 1948; C. S. Lewis, *The Allegory of Love,*‡ rev., 1938; John Livingston Lowes, *The Road to Xanadu,*‡ rev., 1930; Percy Lubbock, *The Craft of Fiction,*‡ 1926; I. A. Richards, *Principles of Literary Criticism,*‡ 5th edition, 1934, and *Practical Criticism,*‡ 1930; Caroline Spurgeon, *Shakespeare's Imagery,*‡ 1935; Lionel Trilling, *The Liberal Imagination,*‡ 1950, and *The Opposing Self,*‡ 1955; Edmund Wilson, *Axel's Castle: A Study in the Imaginative Literature of 1870–1930,*‡ 1936, and *The Wound and the Bow,*‡ 1941; and Wayne C. Booth, *The Rhetoric of Fiction,*‡ 1961.

THE MIDDLE AGES

The Old English Period

The reader who wishes to acquire historical background for the literature of the period will profit greatly from Dorothy Whitelock's concise study, *The Beginnings of English Society,*‡ Penguin (Pelican), 1952. The most detailed history is F. M. Stenton's authoritative *Anglo-Saxon England,* 2nd edition, 1947. Also highly informative are P. Hunter Blair's *An Introduction to Anglo-Saxon England,*‡ 1956, and *Roman Britain and Early England, 55 B.C.-A.D. 871,*‡ 1963. The classic study of the culture of the primitive Germanic peoples is H. M. Chadwick's *The Heroic Age,* 1912. For those who wish to sample basic historical documents of the period, there are available the translations by G. N. Garmonsway of *The Anglo-Saxon Chronicle,* 1959, and by L. Sherley-Price of Bede's *Ecclesiastical History,* published under the title *A History of the English Church and People,*‡ Penguin, 1955.

All the surviving poetry in Old English is contained in the six volumes edited by G. P. Krapp and E. V. K. Dobbie, *The Anglo-Saxon Poetic Records*, 1931–53, but the absence of glossaries makes this edition difficult for nonspecialists. Excellent texts of the shorter poems translated in this anthology are contained in J. C. Pope's *Seven Old English Poems*,‡ 1966. The standard text of *Beowulf and the Fight of Finnsburg* is F. Klaeber's 3rd edition, 1950; C. L. Wrenn's edition, *Beowulf, with the Finnesburg Fragment*, rev. 1958, is very useful. Modern English translations of many of the Old English poems have been published by C. W. Kennedy under various titles.

Good critical discussion of Old English literature will be found in Volume I of the *Cambridge History of English Literature;* in Kemp Malone's section of *A Literary History of England*,‡ edited by A. C. Baugh, rev 1967; in S. B. Greenfield's *A Critical History of Old English Literature*,‡ 1965; and in C. L. Wrenn, *A Study of Old English Literature*,‡ 1966. The best critical essay on *Beowulf* remains J. R. R. Tolkien's Gollancz lecture, *Beowulf, the Monsters, and the Critics*, 1937. The most exhaustive scholarly discussion is R. W. Chambers' *Beowulf: An Introduction to the Study of the Poem*, 3rd edition, with a supplement by C. L. Wrenn, 1959. W. W. Lawrence's *Beowulf and the Epic Tradition*, 1928, is still of value. Recent works by Dorothy Whitelock, *The Audience of Beowulf*, 1958, A. C. Brodeur, *The Art of Beowulf*, 1959, and Kenneth Sisam, *The Structure of Beowulf*, 1965, mingle fine general criticism with some highly specialized discussion.

The Middle English Period

Good and fairly compact accounts of the history of England between the Norman Conquest and the end of the Middle Ages are contained in the two volumes by Christopher Brooke, *From Alfred to Henry III, 871–1272*,‡ 1961, and George Holmes, *The Later Middle Ages, 1272–1485*,‡ 1962: see also in the Pelican series D. M. Stenton, *English Society in the Early Middle Ages (1066–1307)*,‡ Penguin, 1951, and A. R. Myers, *England in the Late Middle Ages*,‡ Penguin, 1952. Interesting illustrations of life in the Middle Ages, especially in the later centuries, will be found in three books by G. G. Coulton: *Chaucer and His England*,‡ 1908, *The Medieval Scene*,‡ 1930, *Medieval Panorama*,‡ 1938; in Eileen Power's *Medieval People*,‡ 1924; in Edith Rickert's *Chaucer's World*,‡ 1948; in Volume I of G. M. Trevelyan's *Illustrated English Social History, Chaucer's England and the Early Tudors*, 1949; and in R. S. Loomis' *A Mirror of Chaucer's World*,

1965. The spirit of the 15th and late 14th century is brilliantly discussed by J. Huizinga, *The Waning of the Middle Ages*,‡ 1924, 1954.

For general discussions of Middle English literature including Chaucer, see Volume II of the *Cambridge History of English Literature* and A. C. Baugh's section of *A Literary History of England*,‡ edited by Baugh, 1948. W. P. Ker's *English Literature: Medieval*, 1912, is still provocative. D. M. Zesmer's *Guide to English Literature from Beowulf through Chaucer and Medieval Drama*,‡ 1961, is a most useful survey; W. L. Renwick and H. Orton, *The Beginnings of English Literature to Skelton*, rev., 1952, is a good survey with bibliographical notes; also useful is H. S. Bennett, *Chaucer and the Fifteenth Century*, 1947. Edward Vasta's collection of essays by various scholars, *Middle English Survey: Critical Essays*,‡ 1965, will offer stimulation to students of *Piers Plowman, Sir Gawain and the Green Knight*, the drama, and the ballads. Chapters 6–10 of Erich Auerbach's *Mimesis: The Representation of Reality in Western Literature*,‡ translated by W. R. Trask, 1953, while dealing with none of the works included in this anthology, shed much light on the spirit of medieval literature. For the Middle English language, see Helge Kökeritz's *A Guide to Chaucer's Pronunciation*,‡ 1954; Samuel Moore's *Historical Outlines of English Sounds and Inflections*, revised by A. H. Marckwardt, 1951; and John W. Clark's *Early English*,‡ 1957.

For general discussion of non-Chaucerian Middle English literature, see R. M. Wilson, *Early Middle English Literature*, 1939, and E. K. Chambers, *English Literature at the Close of the Middle Ages*, 1954, which between them thoroughly cover the beginning and end of the period. The only recent work attempting to survey the whole non-Chaucerian field is John Speirs' erratic but stimulating *Medieval English Poetry: The Non-Chaucerian Tradition*, 1957. George Kane's *Middle English Literature*, 1951, has good chapters on the romances, the religious lyrics, and *Piers Plowman*. A broad sampling of non-Chaucerian literature in translation is offered by *Medieval English Verse and Poetry*, edited by R. S. Loomis and R. Willard, 1948.

The standard bibliography is J. E. Wells, *A Manual of the Writings in Middle English, 1050–1400*, 1916; nine supplements extend coverage through 1945. A revised edition of Wells's chapter on Middle English romances, under the editorship of J. B. Severs, 1967, has recently appeared.

Geoffrey Chaucer

The standard edition of Chaucer's writing is F. N. Robinson's *The Complete Works of Chaucer*, 2nd edition, 1957. The present editor's anthology of Chaucer's poetry, from which are taken the selections printed here, is helpful to the nonspecialist, as is A. C. Baugh's *Chaucer's Major Poetry*, 1963. Vivid presentations of Chaucer in the background of 14th-century England are found in Marchette Chute's *Geoffrey Chaucer of England*,‡ 1946, and D. S. Brewer's *Chaucer and His Time*, 1963. The raw material for Chaucer's biography is contained in *Chaucer Life-Records*, edited by M. M. Crow and C. C. Olson, 1966. For a succinct account of the sources and literary background of Chaucer's works, see R. D. French's *A Chaucer Handbook*, 2nd edition, 1947; a complete reproduction of the known sources of the *Canterbury Tales* is contained in the scholarly compendium *Sources and Analogues of Chaucer's Canterbury Tales*, edited by W. F. Bryan and Germaine Dempster, 1941, 1958. Muriel Bowden, *A Commentary on the General Prologue to the Canterbury Tales*, 1948, provides a wealth of background information on the individual Canterbury pilgrims. For literary criticism, all the following works contain stimulating material: P. F. Baum, *Chaucer: A Critical Appreciation*, 1958; H. S. Bennett, *Chaucer and the Fifteenth Century*, 1947; D. S. Brewer, *Chaucer*, 1953; B. H. Bronson, *In Search of Chaucer*,‡ 1960; G. K. Chesterton, *Chaucer*, 1932; Nevill Coghill, *The Poet Chaucer*, 1949, and *Geoffrey Chaucer*, 1956; H. S. Corsa, *Chaucer, Poet of Mirth and Morality*, 1964; T. W. Craik, *The Comic Tales of Chaucer*, 1964; W. C. Curry, *Chaucer and the Medieval Sciences*,‡ rev., 1960; Germaine Dempster, *Dramatic Irony in Chaucer*, 1932; Maurice Hussey, A. C. Spearing, and James Winny, *An Introduction to Chaucer*,‡ 1965; G. L. Kittredge, *Chaucer and His Poetry*, 1915; W. W. Lawrence, *Chaucer and the Canterbury Tales*, 1950; Emile Legouis, *Geoffrey Chaucer*, 1913; J. L. Lowes, *Geoffrey Chaucer and the Development of His Genius*, 1934; R. M. Lumiansky, *Of Sondry Folk*, 1955; Kemp Malone, *Chapters on Chaucer*, 1951; J. M. Manly, *Some New Light on Chaucer*, 1926; Charles Muscatine, *Chaucer and the French Tradition*,‡ 1957; H. R. Patch, *On Rereading Chaucer*, 1939; R. O. Payne, *The Key of Remembrance*, 1963; Raymond Preston, *Chaucer*, 1952; R. K. Root, *The Poetry of Chaucer*, 2nd edition, 1922; P. V. D. Shelly, *The Living Chaucer*, 1940; John Speirs, *Chaucer the Maker*, 1951; and J. S. P. Tatlock, *The Mind and Art of Chaucer*, 1950. D. W. Robert-

son's *A Preface to Chaucer*, 1962, is a most learned, stimulating, doctrinaire, and controversial introduction to the reading of Chaucer. The following are collections of critical essays by various writers: *Discussions of the Canterbury Tales*,‡ edited by C. J. Owen, 1961; *Chaucer Criticism: The Canterbury Tales*,‡ edited by R. J. Schoeck and J. Taylor, 1960; and *Chaucer: Modern Essays in Criticism*,‡ edited by E. C. Wagenknecht, 1959. See the prefatory remarks to Chaucer's poems in Robinson's edition and the editor's commentary in his anthology.

The standard bibliographies are E. P. Hammond, *Chaucer: A Bibliographical Manual*, 1908; D. D. Griffith, *Bibliography of Chaucer*, 1955; and W. R. Crawford, *Bibliography of Chaucer 1954–63*, 1967. See also Caroline Spurgeon's *Five Hundred Years of Chaucer Criticism and Allusion, 1357–1900*, 1925.

Sir Gawain and the Green Knight

The standard Middle English text of the poem is that of J. R. R. Tolkien and E. V. Gordon, 1925 (revised by Norman Davis, 1967). Good discussion of various aspects of the poem appear in Marie Borroff's *Sir Gawain and the Green Knight: A Stylistic and Metrical Study*, 1962; L. D. Benson, *Art and Tradition in Sir Gawain and the Green Knight*, 1965 (especially good on the sources); and J. A. Burrow, *A Reading of Sir Gawain and the Green Knight*, 1965. Interesting chapters on the poem are contributed by A. C. Spearing in *Criticism and Medieval Poetry*, 1964, and D. R. Howard in *The Three Temptations: Medieval Man in Search of the World*, 1966.

Piers Plowman

The most handy edition of *Piers Plowman* is W. W. Skeat's *The Vision of William Concerning Piers the Plowman * * *, 2 vols., 1886, which gives all three versions. There are modern translations by H. W. Wells, *The Vision of Piers Plowman*, 1935, and by Nevill Coghill (selections only), *Visions from Piers Plowman*, 1949. The best general account of the poem is in Chapters IV–V of R. W. Chambers' *Man's Unconquerable Mind*, 1939; see also Kane's chapter in *Middle English Literature*. Recent studies by Elizabeth Salter, *Piers Plowman: An Introduction*, 1962, and John Lawlor, *Piers Plowman: An Essay in Criticism*, 1962, are most useful to the beginner, as are chapters on the poem in the works by Howard and Spearing mentioned above under *Sir Gawain and the Green Knight*.

Middle English Lyrics

The best selection of Middle English

lyrics are *Early English Lyrics*,‡ edited by E. K. Chambers and F. Sidgwick, 1921, and *Medieval English Lyrics: A Critical Anthology*, edited by R. T. Davies, 1963; modernized and semi-modernized selections appear in M. R. Adamson's *A Treasury of Middle English Verse*, 1930, and in R. D. Stevick's *One Hundred Middle English Poems*,‡ 1964. For criticism see A. K. Moore, *The Secular Lyric in Middle English*, 1951, and Kane's chapter.

The Second Shepherds' Play; Everyman

The classic work on the medieval drama is E. K. Chambers' *The Medieval Stage*, 1905. More recent is Hardin Craig's exhaustive *English Religious Drama of the Middle Ages*, 1955. For a good discussion of the Middle English mystery cycle, see V. A. Kolve's *The Play Called Corpus Christi*, 1966. Good selections of Middle English plays are presented by J. Q. Adams, *Chief Pre-Shakespearean Dramas*, 1924, and by A. C. Cawley, *Everyman and Medieval Miracle Plays*,‡ 1960. Cawley's *The Wakefield Pageants in the Towneley Cycle*, 1958, has a discussion of the work of the "Wakefield Masters" whose hand is seen in the *Second Shepherds' Play*.

Popular Ballads

The great ballad collection is that of F. J. Child, *The English and Scottish Popular Ballads*,‡ 1882, more available in the somewhat abridged edition by H. C. Sargent and G. L. Kittredge, 1904. For general discussion, see F. B. Gummere, *The Popular Ballads*,‡ 1907; G. H. Gerould, *The Ballad of Tradition*, 1932; W. J. Entwistle, *European Balladry*, 1939; and M. J. C. Hodgart, *The Ballads*,‡ 1950.

Sir Thomas Malory

The Winchester manuscript of Malory's *Morte Darthur*, with full commentary and valuable discussion, is given in Eugène Vinaver's *The Works of Sir Thomas Malory*, 3 vols., 1947; the one-volume edition, Oxford, 1954, contains the text only. The Caxton version is most readily available in *Le Morte D'Arthur*, edited by E. Rhys, 1906. Vinaver's *Malory*, 1929, surveys Malory's life and career. A number of critical problems in Malory's work, especially its unity, are discussed in two collections of essays by various scholars: *Essays on Malory*, edited by J. A. W. Bennett, 1963, and *Malory's Originality*, edited by R. M. Lumianski, 1964. In *The Ill-Framed Knight*, 1966, William Matthews challenges the traditional identification of the author of the *Morte Darthur* with that knight-prisoner, the details of whose stormy career have been unearthed by scholars interested in the book.

A most valuable summary of the Arthurian literary background is R. S. Loomis' *The Development of Arthurian Romance*,‡ 1963.

THE SIXTEENTH CENTURY

General books on the political, social, and economic history of the period are: A. L. Rowse, *The England of Elizabeth*, 1950; J. B. Black, *The Reign of Elizabeth*, 1936; A. F. Pollard, *The History of England, 1547–1603;* J. E. Neale, *Queen Elizabeth I*,‡ 1934; Conyers Read, *Mr. Secretary Walsingham*, 1925; J. D. Mackie, *The Earlier Tudors*, 1952; Katharine Garvin, ed., *The Great Tudors*, 1935; J. E. Neale, *Elizabeth I and Her Parliaments 1559–1581, 1584–1601*,‡ 1953, 1957; D. L. Keir, *The Constitutional History of Modern Britain Since 1485*,‡ 5 ed., 1953; R. H. Tawney, *Religion and the Rise of Capitalism*,‡ 1926; R. H. Tawney and E. Power, *Tudor Economic Documents*, 1924; W. H. Dunham and S. Pargellis, eds., *Complaint and Reform in England*, 1938. H. D. Traill, *Social England*, 1897 and 1901–4; *Shakespeare's England*, 1916.

Discussions of church history include W. H. Frere, *The English Church in the Reigns of Elizabeth and James*, 1911; R. W. Dixon, *History of the Church of England*, 1878–1902; J. H.

Pollen, *The English Catholics in the Reign of Elizabeth*, 1920; A. F. Scott Pearson, *Thomas Cartwright and Elizabethan Puritanism*, 1925; W. Haller, *The Rise of Puritanism*,‡ 1938; A. C. Southern, *Elizabethan Recusant Prose*, 1950; H. C. White, *The Tudor Books of Private Devotion*, 1951.

The important topics of geography and exploration are treated in E. G. R. Taylor, *Tudor Geography, 1485–1583*, 1930, and *Late Tudor and Early Stuart Geography, 1583–1650*, 1934; A. L. Rowse, *Sir Richard Grenville of the Revenge*, 1937; J. A. Williamson, *The Age of Drake*,‡ 1938, 2nd edition, 1946, and *Hawkins of Plymouth*, 1949.

Intellectual history is discussed in E. M. W. Tillyard, *The Elizabethan World Picture*,‡ 1943, 1956; Theodore Spencer, *Shakespeare and the Nature of Man*,‡ 1942; L. B. Wright, *Middle-Class Culture in Elizabethan England*, 1935; F. R. Johnson, *Astronomical Thought in Renaissance England*, 1937; P. Kocher, *Science and Religion in Elizabethan England*, 1953.

Books on the fine arts in Elizabethan

England include: John Stevens, *Music and Poetry in the Early Tudor Court*, 1961; Bruce Pattison, *Music and Poetry of the English Renaissance*, 1948; E. H. Fellowes, *The English Madrigal Composers*, 1921; M. C. Boyd, *Elizabethan Music and Music Criticism*, 1940; W. Chappell, *Popular Music of the Olden Time*, 1855; R. Blomfield, *History of Renaissance Architecture in England*, 1897; J. A. Gotch and W. T. Brown, *Architecture of the Renaissance in England*, 1891–94; T. Garner and A. Stratton, *The Domestic Architecture of England during the Tudor Period*, 1911, 1929; R. Blomfield, *The Formal Garden in England*, 1901; C. H. C. Baker and W. G. Constable, *English Painting of the Sixteenth and Seventeenth Centuries*, 1930; S. Colvin, *Early Engraving and Engravers in England, 1545–1695*, 1905; F. B. Williams, Jr., *Elizabethan England*, 1939.

The standard reference work on Elizabethan drama is E. K. Chambers, *The Elizabethan Stage*, 4 vols., 1923. An introduction is Tucker Brooke's *The Tudor Drama*. See also C. Walter Hodges, *The Globe Restored*, 1954.

The new professions of writing, printing, and publishing are discussed in H. S. Bennett, *English Books and Readers, 1475–1557*, 1952, and *English Books and Readers, 1558–1603*, 1965; J. W. Saunders, "The Stigma of Print," *Essays in Criticism I* (1951) 139–164; E. H. Miller, *The Professional Writer in Elizabethan England*, 1959; D. N. Smith, "Authors and Patrons" in *Shakespeare's England*, Vol. II, 1916; R. B. McKerrow, *An Introduction to Bibliography for Literary Students*, 1928; A. W. Pollard, *Shakespeare's Fight with the Pirates*, 1917; W. W. Greg, *English Literary Autographs*, 1925–32, and (ed.) *Records of the Court of the Stationers' Company*, 1930; Percy Simpson, *Proofreading in the Sixteenth, Seventeenth and Eighteenth Centuries*, 1935.

Useful histories and criticism of literature are: V. de Sola Pinto, *The English Renaissance*, 1938; Helen Morris, *Elizabethan Literature*, 1958; Douglas L. Peterson, *The English Lyric from Wyatt to Donne*, 1966; Maurice Evans, *English Poetry in the Sixteenth Century*,‡ 1955; Douglas Bush, *Prefaces to Renaissance Literature*,‡ 1965; J. M. Berdan, *Early Tudor Poetry*, 1920; Louis B. Wright, *Middle-Class Culture in Elizabethan England*, 1935; Douglas Bush, *Mythology and the Renaissance Tradition in English Poetry*,‡ 1932; Sidney Lee, *The French Renaissance in England*, 1910; Geoffrey Tillotson, *Essays in Criticism and Research*, 1942; E. A. Baker, *The History of the English Novel*, Vol. II, 1929; F. P. Wilson, *Elizabethan and Jacobean*, 1945; Hallett

Smith, *Elizabethan Poetry*, 1952; C. S. Lewis, *English Literature in the Sixteenth Century*, 1954.

The general bibliographies are F. W. Bateson, ed., *Cambridge Bibliography of English Literature*, Vol. I, 1940; Conyers Read, ed., *Bibliography of British History, Tudor Period*, 1933; A. W. Pollard and G. R. Redgrave, eds., *A Short-Title Catalogue of books * * * 1475–1640*, 1927; E. Arber, ed., *A Transcript of the Registers of the Company of Stationers*, 1875–94.

Sir Thomas More

More's life is told in several early biographies, one by his son-in-law William Roper, edited by E. V. Hitchcock, 1935, and another by Nicholas Harpsfield, also edited by Hitchcock, 1932. The standard modern life is *Thomas More*,‡ by R. W. Chambers, 1935. *Utopia* was early translated into English by Ralph Robinson (1551); there are many editions of this translation. Others are by Gilbert Burnet in the 17th century, and the modern translation, by H. V. S. Ogden, 1949.

Important modern commentaries are J. H. Hexter, *More's Utopia: The Biography of an Idea*,‡ 1952; Russell Ames, *Citizen Thomas More and His Utopia*, 1949; Edward L. Surtz, *The Praise of Pleasure: Philosophy, Education and Communism in More's Utopia*, 1957; and the same author's *The Praise of Wisdom: Religious and Moral Problems and Backgrounds of St. Thomas More's Utopia*, 1957.

Sir Thomas Hoby

The Book of the Courtier, with an introduction by Walter Raleigh, Tudor Translations, 1900; Castiglione's original, *Il Cortegiano*, was edited by V. Cian in 1929. A good account of Castiglione is given in Ralph Roeder, *The Man of the Renaissance*, 1933. Hoby's curious diary, *A Booke of the Travaile and Lief of Me*, is edited by E. Powell as *Camden Miscellany X*, 1902. The qualities of Hoby's prose are discussed in F. O. Matthiessen, *Translation, An Elizabethan Art*, 1931.

Richard Hooker

The Laws were edited by J. Keble, 3 vols., 1936, revised by R. W. Church and F. Paget, 1888. There are various editions of individual Books; R. Bayne edited Books I–V in 1907. Izaak Walton wrote the first biography of Hooker; C. J. Sisson's *The Judicious Marriage of Mr. Hooker*, 1940, corrects Walton in many respects. See also E. N. S. Thompson, "Richard Hooker among the Controversialists," *Philological Quarterly*, XX (1941), 454–64; Peter Munz, *The*

Place of Hooker in the History of Thought, 1952; and F. J. Shirley, *Richard Hooker and Contemporary Political Ideas*, 1949.

Sir Thomas Wyatt

The best edition of Wyatt's poetry is by Kenneth Muir, 1949, and additional unpublished poems from the Blage manuscript, 1961. *Tottel's Miscellany* is edited by Hyder E. Rollins, rev. 1965. Recent biographical and critical works are Kenneth Muir, *Life and Letters of Sir Thomas Wyatt*, 1963; Patricia Thomson, *Sir Thomas Wyatt and His Background*, 1965; Raymond Southall, *The Courtly Maker*, 1964; and H. A. Mason, *Humanism and Poetry in the Early Tudor Period*, 1959. Earlier studies are Hallett Smith, "The Art of Sir Thomas Wyatt," *Huntington Library Quarterly* IX (1946) 323–55; E. K. Chambers, *Sir Thomas Wyatt and Some Collected Studies* 1933; and E. M. W. Tillyard, *The Poetry of Sir Thomas Wyatt*, 1929.

Henry Howard, Earl of Surrey

A recent edition of Surrey's poems is by Emrys Jones, 1964; an older one is by F. M. Padelford, rev. 1928. *Tottel's Miscellany* is edited by Hyder E. Rollins, rev. 1965. The most recent biography is by E. Casaday, *Henry Howard, Earl of Surrey*, 1938.

Sir Philip Sidney

The definitive edition of Sidney's poetry is edited by William Ringler, 1962. The complete works are available in the edition of A. Feuillarat, 1912–26. The *Apology* has been edited separately by E. S. Shuckburgh, 1891, and by G. Gregory Smith in *Elizabethan Critical Essays*, 1904.

Recent books on Sidney are Walter R. Davis, *Sidney's Arcadia*, 1965; R. B. Young, *English Petrarke*, 1958; David Kalstone, *Sidney's Poetry*, 1965; R. L. Montgomery, *Symmetry and Sense; the Poetry of Sir Philip Sidney*, 1961.

An important critical article on the poetry is Theodore Spencer, "The Poetry of Sir Philip Sidney," *English Literary History*, XII (1945). 251–78. The biography by Mona Wilson, *Sir Philip Sidney*, 1931, is still the best. Also useful are: J. E. Spingarn, *A History of Literary Criticism in the Renaissance*,‡ 1899; K. O. Myrick, *Sir Philip Sidney as a Literary Craftsman*,‡ 1935; J. W. H. Atkins, *English Literary Criticism: the Renascence*, 1947; John Buxton, *Sir Philip Sidney and the English Renaissance*,‡ 1954; and Frederick S. Boas, *Sir Philip Sidney, Representative Elizabethan, His Life and Writings*, 1955.

Edmund Spenser

The Works of Edmund Spenser: A Variorum Edition, edited by Edwin Greenlaw, C. G. Osgood, F. M. Padelford, and Ray Heffner, 10 vols., 1932–49, summarizes modern scholarly knowledge. A one-volume edition is *The Poetical Works*,‡ edited by J. C. Smith and E. de Selincourt for the Oxford Standard Authors, 1912.

A good introduction for the student is H. S. V. Jones, *A Spenser Handbook*, 1930. Critical works of importance are A. Kent Hieatt, *Short Time's Endless Monument: The Symbolism of the Numbers in Edmund Spenser's Epithalamion*, 1960; Alastair Fowler, *Spenser and the Numbers of Time*, 1964; Graham Hough, *A Preface to The Faerie Queene*,‡ 1962; Pauline Parker, *The Allegory of The Faerie Queene*, 1960; Paul E. McLane, *Spenser's Shepheardes Calender*, 1961; Robert Ellrodt, *Neoplatonism in the Poetry of Spenser*, 1960; William Nelson, *The Poetry of Edmund Spenser*,‡ 1963; William Nelson, ed., *Form and Convention in the Poetry of Edmund Spenser*, 1961; Kathleen Williams, *Spenser's Faerie Queene: World of Glass*, 1966; C. S. Lewis, *The Allegory of Love*,‡ 1936, and *English Literature in the Sixteenth Century*, 1954; J. W. Bennett, *The Evolution of "The Faerie Queene,"* Chicago, 1942; L. Bradner, *Edmund Spenser and "The Faerie Queene,"* Chicago, 1948; and A. C. Hamilton, *The Structure of Allegory in The Faerie Queene*, 1961.

Christopher Marlowe

The standard edition of Marlowe's works is in six volumes, under the general editorship of R. H. Case, 1930. *Dr. Faustus* has been edited by Sir W. W. Greg, in a large parallel-text edition with elaborate commentary, 1950, and a smaller reconstruction of the original text, also 1950. General studies of Marlowe are by Paul Kocher, 1946, by F. S. Boas, 1940, and by John Bakeless, 1937. Most interesting and valuable recent treatments are those by Harry Levin, *The Overreacher*,‡ 1952, and F. P. Wilson, *Marlowe and the Early Shakespeare*, 1953. The circumstances of Marlowe's death are told by their discoverer, Leslie Hotson, in *The Death of Christopher Marlowe*, 1925, and Marlowe's involvement in another fatal quarrel is the subject of Mark Eccles, *Christopher Marlowe in London*, 1934.

Recent critical studies are: Douglas Cole, *Suffering and Evil in the Plays of Christopher Marlowe*, 1962; and J. B. Steane, *Marlowe: A Critical Study*, 1964.

William Shakespeare

On *1 Henry IV* see *The Variorum Shakespeare, Henry the Fourth Part One,* ed. S. B. Hemmingway, 1936; G. B. Evans, "Supplement to Henry IV. Part I" *Shakespeare Quarterly,* VII (1956), 3; John Dover Wilson, *The Fortunes of Falstaff,*‡ 1944; F. P. Wilson, *Marlowe and the Early Shakespeare,* 1953; Irving Ribner, *The English History Play in the Age of Shakespeare,* 1957; L. B. Campbell, *Shakespeare's "Histories,"* 1947; H. Levin, "Falstaff Uncolted," *Modern Language Notes,* LXI (1946), 305–10; E. M. W. Tillyard, *Shakespeare's History Plays,*‡ 1946.

There are many editions of the sonnets, ranging from the convenient paperback Signet edition, 1964, with an introduction by W. H. Auden, to the two-volume *New Variorum* edited by Hyder E. Rollins, 1944. Commentary is extensive and much of it worthless, but sensible guidance may be found in Tucker Brooke's edition, 1936, which attempts a rearrangement; Edward Hubler, *The Sense of Shakespeare's Sonnets,*‡ 1952; J. B. Leishman, *Themes and Variations in Shakespeare's Sonnets,*‡ 1961; *The Riddle of Shakespeare's Sonnets: Essays by Edward Hubler, Northrop Frye, Leslie Fiedler, Stephen Spender and R. P. Blackmur,* 1962; and Hilton Landry, *Interpretations in Shakespeare's Sonnets,* 1963.

The poems have been edited by Hyder E. Rollins in the *New Variorum* edition, 1938. More manageable are the recent editions by F. T. Prince, 1960, and J. C. Maxwell, 1966. William H. Matchett has published *The Phoenix and the Turtle,* 1965. G. Wilson Knight's *The Mutual Flame,* 1955, discusses the sonnets and *The Phoenix and the Turtle.*

The standard scholarly authority on the life and works is E. K. Chambers, *William Shakespeare, A Study of Facts and Problems,* 1930. A well-written and dependable biography for the student and general reader is Marchette Chute, *Shakespeare of London,*‡ 1949. A scrupulously objective account is G. E. Bentley's *Shakespeare: A Biographical Handbook,* 1961. Bibliographies of Shakespearean studies appear in the periodical *Shakespeare Quarterly.*

John Skelton

Stanley E. Fish, *Skelton's Poetry,* 1965; Arthur R. Heiserman, *Skelton and Satire,* 1961; H. L. R. Edwards, *Skelton,* 1949; Ian A. Gordon, *John Skelton,* 1943; L. J. Lloyd, *John Skelton,* 1938; William Nelson, *John Skelton, Laureate,* 1939.

Sir Walter Ralegh

The standard edition of the poems is by A. M. C. Latham, rev. 1950. An important study of Ralegh's ideas is Ernest A. Strathmann, *Sir Walter Ralegh, A Study in Elizabethan Skepticism,* 1951. Recent books include Philip Edwards, *Sir Walter Ralegh,* 1953; Margaret Irwin, *That Great Lucifer,* 1960; W. F. Oakeshott, *The Queen and the Poet,* 1960; A. L. Rowse, *Ralegh and the Throckmortons,* 1962; and Willard M. Wallace, *Sir Walter Raleigh,* 1959.

Robert Southwell

Two studies are Pierre Janelle, *Robert Southwell the Writer,* London, 1935, and Christopher Devlin, *The Life of Robert Southwell, Poet and Martyr,* 1956.

Samuel Daniel

A. C. Sprague has edited *Poems and a Defence of Ryme,*‡ 1930. See also G. K. Brady, *Samuel Daniel,* 1923.

Michael Drayton

The Works of Michael Drayton, edited by J. W. Hebel, 5 vols., 1931–41, is the standard edition. B. H. Newdigate, *Michael Drayton and His Circle,* 1941, is a biography.

Thomas Nashe

R. B. McKerrow's edition *of The Works,* 5 vols., 1904–10, is a great work of scholarship. Volume V contains the best account yet written of Nashe's life, the Martin Marprelate controversy, and the Nashe-Harvey quarrel.

Thomas Campion

Campion's Works are edited by Percival Vivian, Oxford, 1909. A biography is M. W. Kastendieck, *England's Musical Poet: Thomas Campion,* 1938; Campion's settings are reprinted in E. H. Fellowes, ed., *The English School of Lutenist Song-Writers* (Second Series), 1926.

THE SEVENTEENTH CENTURY

Two standard general histories of England during the 17th century are Godfrey Davies, *The Early Stuarts,* 2nd edition, 1959, and G. M. Trevelyan, *England Under the Stuarts,*‡ London, 1949. Clarendon's *History* is a fascinating contemporary document, and Samuel Rawson Gardiner's *History of England * * * from 1603 to 1656,* 10 vols., rev., 1894–96, is rich in facts. Over the past decade or so, a prodigious series of books by Christopher Hill of Oxford, books fundamentally Marxist in their approach, have done much to transfigure our understanding of the 17th-century revolution, seen under its political, economic, and social aspects. One of these, *The Century of Revolution, 1603–1714,*‡ 1966, forms part of the Norton Library History of England.

On the intellectual background of the age, one would do well to consult E. M. W. Tillyard's fascinating little study *The Elizabethan World Picture,*‡ 1943, 1956; Sir Herbert J. C. Grierson's *Cross Currents in English Literature of the 17th Century,*‡ 1929; and Basil Wiley's *The 17th Century Background,*‡ 1934.

General literary histories of the age include Douglas Bush, *English Literature in the Earlier Seventeenth Century,* 1945, and a shorter, less bibliographical introduction, Miss C. V. Wedgwood's *Seventeenth Century English Literature,* 1950.

Special studies of social and economic problems in relation to the intellectual life of the day are Max Weber's *The Protestant Ethic and the Spirit of Capitalism,*‡ translated by Talcott Parsons, 1948, 1958, and R. H. Tawney, *Religion and the Rise of Capitalism,*‡ 1937; also, the various criticisms to which this theory has been subjected by H. R. Trevor-Roper and others should not be overlooked. They are mostly to be found in the *Economic History Review.* William Haller's *The Rise of Puritanism,*‡ 1938, is a classic account of the Puritans viewed through their propaganda; M. M. Knappen also offers a fine historical introduction in his *Tudor Puritanism: A Chapter in the History of Idealism,*‡ 1939. L. C. Knight's *Drama and Society in the Age of Jonson,* 1937, is a shrewd analytic study of a special problem with wide implications.

The growth of science in the 17th century may be studied in Abraham Wolf's *History of Science, Technology, and Philosophy in the 16th and 17th Centuries,* 2nd edition, prep. by D. McKie, 1950; its impact on the daily thought of men is traced by E. A. Burtt, *Metaphysical Foundations of Modern Science,*‡ rev., 1950. A. O. Lovejoy's *The Great Chain of Being: A Study of the History of an Idea,*‡ 1936, is a classic reconstruction of an important Renaissance idea, and an account of how it decayed in the 17th century and after.

The literary criticism of the age is best studied in the documents collected by G. Gregory Smith, *Elizabethan Critical Essays,* 1904, and by J. E. Spingarn, *Critical Essays of the 17th Century,* 1908–9; Donald L. Clark, in *Rhetoric and Poetry in the Renaissance,* 1922; Rosemond Tuve, in *Elizabethan and Metaphysical Imagery,*‡ 1947; and Ruth Wallerstein, in *Studies in 17th Century Poetic,*‡ 1950, have probed into the relation between critical theory and poetic practice. Finally, Wylie Sypher, *Four*

Stages of Renaissance Style,‡ 1955, offers some very interesting and provocative analogies between poetic styles and styles in the graphic arts during the 17th century.

In addition to the references given below for individual poets, the following titles may prove useful for the student of 17th-century poetry: George Saintsbury edited, in three volumes, the texts of the *Minor Poets of the Caroline Period,* 1905–21, and Norman Ault collected some interesting lyrics of the age, *Seventeenth-Century Lyrics,* 1928. Edward Dowden's *Puritan and Anglican,* 1900, and Edmund Gosse's *The Jacobean Poets,* 1894, are older studies which retain a good deal of vitality. A spate of books on the metaphysical poets appeared during the 1930's, of which the best are Joan Bennett's *Four Metaphysical Poets,*‡ 1934, 2nd edition, 1953 (Donne, Herbert, Crashaw, and Vaughan); Helen C. White's *The Metaphysical Poets,*‡ 1936; and J. B. Leishman's book, of the same title, 1934. Louis L. Martz, in *The Poetry of Meditations: A Study of English Religious Literature of the 17th Century,*‡ discusses a traditional mode of thought as it influenced the metaphysicals; and Mario Praz has made several important *Studies in 17th Century Imagery,* 1939. Of particular interest to students of classic myth in the 17th-century poetry is Douglas Bush's erudite *Mythology and the Renaissance Tradition in English Poetry,*‡ 1932, 1963.

John Donne

For nearly fifty years the standard edition of Donne's poems was that in two volumes by Sir Herbert J. C. Grierson, 1912. In 1952 Miss Helen Gardner re-edited the *Divine Poems* and in 1965 added a volume of *Elegies and the Songs and Sonnets.* These new editions alter the text of some poems in some particulars on the basis of new manuscript evidence and offer to redate many of them. It is by no means clear that the text is always improved by the new readings or that the new dating will hold up; one can only say many questions remain open. Under the editorship of G. R. Potter and Evelyn Simpson, a new edition of Donne's *Sermons* has been issued, 10 vols., 1953–59. *A Complete Poetry and Selected Prose,* under the editorship of John Hayward, 1929, is handy and handsome.

All biographies are based more or less directly on Walton's *Life;* the best one currently available is still Sir Edmund Grosse's *Life and Letters of John Donne,* 1899. E. S. LeComte's recent biography, *Grace to a Witty Sinner,* 1965, is more popular in character.

T. S. Eliot's essays on Donne, the

metaphysical poets, and the 17th century have been remarkably influential. They include an essay on "The Metaphysical Poets," originally a review of Grierson's anthology of *Metaphysical Lyrics and Poems* ‡ but reprinted as an independent essay in *Homage to John Dryden*, 1924, in Eliot's *Selected Essays*, 1932, and elsewhere. Eliot also took another, not quite congruent, view of the poet in *A Garland for John Donne*, edited by Theodore Spencer, 1931. Other collections of critical essays have been prepared by Helen Gardner,‡ 1962, and Frank Kermode, 1962.

Pierre Legouis' *Donne the Craftsman*, 1928, was an interesting early study; more recently Arnold Stein has offered close scrutinies of *John Donne's Lyrics*, 1962, and Joan Webber, in *Contrary Music*, 1963, has analyzed Donne's prose style. J. B. Leishman, in *The Monarch of Wit: An Analytical and Comparative Study of the Poetry of John Donne*,‡ 1951 and 1959, provides an analytic survey. Rosemond Tuve's *Elizabethan and Metaphysical Imagery*,‡ 1947, offered a revolutionary, conservative view of Donne's imagery; and Leonard Unger, in *Donne's Poetry and Modern Criticism*, 1950, undertook to survey the whole troubled field. The standard bibliography of Donne, first published by Geoffrey Keynes in 1914, was revised in 1932 and again in 1958.

Ben Jonson

The standard edition of Jonson's works is that of C. H. Herford and Percy and Evelyn Simpson, published by the Clarendon Press in eleven volumes, 1925–52. This edition is meticulous in reproducing the old spellings, and typographically it is very elegant; but to find one's way around in it takes some practice. Of earlier editions, the handiest and most correct (though the text has been modernized) is that of W. Gifford, 9 vols., 1875.

Because Jonson's work falls into several different categories, general introductory accounts of the whole man are few. G. Gregory Smith did a biography for the English Men of Letters series, 1919, and a recent popular life is that of Marchette Chute, *Ben Jonson of Westminster*,‡ 1953. A. C. Swinburne wrote a characteristically acute and enthusiastic *Study of Ben Jonson*, 1889, and Maurice Castelain a weighty *Ben Jonson, l'homme et l'oeuvre*, 1907; both these books, though long out of date, retain the power to instruct and interest.

Special studies of the masques generally, and of Jonson's masques in particular, have been written by Enid Welsford, *The Court Masque*, 1927, Allardyce Nicoll, *Stuart Masques and the Renaissance Stage*, 1937, and Stephen Orgel, *The Jonsonian Masque*, 1965. Wesley Trimpi has written a good account of *Ben Jonson's Poems*, 1962, and C. F. Wheeler has studied *Classical Mythology in the Plays, Masques, and Poems of Ben Jonson*, 1938. There are of course many studies of Jonson as a dramatist, the comedies and satires having received particular attention. Jonas Barish has edited *Ben Jonson*,‡ 1963, a collection of critical essays. In 1938 S. A. Tannenbaum published a *Concise Bibliography* of Jonson, and in 1947 added a Supplement to it.

Robert Herrick

The standard edition is the *Poetical Works*, edited by L. C. Martin, Oxford Standard Authors, 1956. F. W. Moorman produced a full-length study, *Robert Herrick*, 1910; and Marchette Chute, joining Herrick with George Herbert, has described their lives, *Two Gentle Men*, 1959. There is an interesting novel about Herrick by Rose Macaulay, *The Shadow Flies*, 1932.

George Herbert

The standard edition of *The Temple* is that edited by F. E. Hutchinson, 1945. There is an interesting account of Herbert's technical ingenuities by A. Hayes, *Studies in Philology*, XXXV (1938). Margaret Bottrall has written an introductory appreciation, *George Herbert*, 1954, and Rosemond Tuve's *A Reading of George Herbert*, 1952, is a fine exposition of her conservative view of Herbert's imagery. As part of the same revival of interest in Herbert appeared J. H. Summers, *George Herbert, His Religion and His Art*, 1954.

Richard Crashaw

The standard edition is that prepared by L. C. Martin, 1927, 2nd edition, 1957. Two interesting books are those of Ruth Wallerstein, *Richard Crashaw: A Study in Style and Poetic Development*,‡ 1935, and of Austin Warren, *Richard Crashaw: A Study in Baroque Sensibility*,‡ 1939, 1957. Influential ideas about Crashaw are found in William Empson, *Seven Types of Ambiguity*,‡ 1935, 1947, 1953; in Wylie Sypher, *Four Stages of Renaissance Style*, 1955; and in Mario Praz, *The Flaming Heart*, 1958.

Henry Vaughan

The works of Henry Vaughan were edited by L. C. Martin, 1914, 1957; F. E. Hutchinson wrote the standard life, *Henry Vaughan, a Life and an Interpretation*, 1947. Elizabeth Holmes opened up the interesting topic of *Henry Vaughan and the Hermetic Phi-*

losophy, 1932, and there have been a number of studies in this area since.

Andrew Marvell

The standard edition is the *Poems and Letters*, edited by H. M. Margoliouth, 1927, 1952. Pierre Legouis' *André Marvell, poète, puritan, patriote*, 1928, is the most ambitious yet account; in English the nearest competitor is Miss M. C. Bradbrook and Miss Lloyd Thomas, *Andrew Marvell*, 1940. Ruth Wallerstein's *Studies in 17th Century Poetic*,‡ 1950, are knotty and hard to read, but they illuminate the medieval backgrounds of Marvell's thought. H. E. Toliver, *Marvell's Ironic Vision*, 1965, and J. B. Leishman, *The Art of Marvell's Poetry*, 1966, are recent additions to an exegetical corpus which long ago exceeded many-fold in bulk the quantity of text being commented on.

John Milton

Despite occasional textual eccentricities, the opulent Columbia Milton, a complete edition of poetry and prose, 18 vols., 1931–38, is widely accepted as standard; controversy continues over details, however, and anyone interested may consult Harris Fletcher's 4-volume facsimile edition of the *Poetical Works*, 1943–48, Miss Helen Darbishire's radical re-editing of the poetry, 1952–55, and the currently appearing Yale edition of the *Prose Works*, for a spectrum of editorial procedures and principles. Of the annotated editions of *Paradise Lost*, A. W. Verity's text, 1910, is probably still the least cumbersome and the most sensible.

The definitive, monumental biography of Milton is that of David Masson, 7 vols., 1859–94, rev. 1881–96; Sir Walter Raleigh's *Milton*, 1900, is handier to use, less pontifical in tone, and still relevant, though much disputed. Harris Fletcher's *Intellectual Development of John Milton*, 1956–61, 2 vols. projected for several volumes, promises to be in its way as encyclopaedic as Masson. While it takes no account at all of Milton the rebel (in fact, denies his existence), C. S. Lewis's *Preface to Paradise Lost*,‡ 1942, rev., 1960, is bright, persuasive, and enormously useful as a first approach. It may be corrected by A. J. A. Waldock's *Paradise Lost and Its Critics* ‡ 1947; B. Rajan's *Paradise Lost and the 17-Century Reader*, 1947; and G. W. Whiting, *Milton's Literary Milieu*, 1939. E. M. W. Tillyard's handbook, *Milton*, 1930, 1949, is in some ways more acute in setting forth the outstanding problems than J. H. Hanford's *Milton Handbook* 4th edition, 1946. David Daiches, under the short, sufficient title of *Milton*,‡

1961, offers a general introductory survey of the poet's accomplishment; and the beginning student is likely to profit as well, by Marjorie H. Nicolson's *John Milton, a Reader's Guide to his Poetry*,‡ 1963. Collections of critical essays have been edited by A. E. Barker, 1965, and Louis L. Martz, 1966; the latter has also done an informative thematic study of *The Paradise Within*,‡ 1964, which includes discussions of Vaughan and Traherne as well as of Milton.

Specialized studies are beyond enumeration; only a scattering of the most useful can be named here. Robert Bridges has written the best account of *Milton's Prosody*, 2nd edition, 1921; Maurice Kelley has shown the intimate relation of Milton's theology, as expressed in the treatise *On Christian Doctrine* with his views in *Paradise Lost*, in *This Great Argument*, 1941; Malcolm M. Ross, *Poetry and Dogma*, 1954, suggests some of the theological complexities behind Milton's problems with incarnation; F. T. Prince has traced *The Italian Element in Milton's Verse*, 1954; and Theodore Banks has studied *Milton's Imagery*, 1950. An important study of *Samson Agonistes* is that of F. Michael Krouse, *Milton's Samson and the Christian Tradition*, 1949. Douglas Bush, in a series of lectures published as *Paradise Lost in Our Time*, 1945, has defended Milton against his New Critical enemies, and sometimes against his friends. D. H. Stevens did the basic bibliography, a *Reference Guide to Milton from 1800 to the Present Day*, 1930; it was supplemented by Harris Fletcher in *Contributions to a Milton Bibliography*, 1931. But the bibliographers seem to have been falling far behind the current terrifying spate of books and articles on Milton.

Francis Bacon

The big edition of Bacon is *The Works*, 15 vols., edited by Spedding, Ellis, and Heath, 1860–64. Among the biographical introductions may be recommended that done for the English Men of Letters series by R. W. Church, 1884, and two more recent ones, *Francis Bacon: A Biography*, by Mary Sturt, 1932, and *Bacon*, by Charles Williams, 1933. Christopher Hill's *Intellectual Origins of the English Revolution*, 1965, demonstrates most tellingly the existence of a popular scientific tradition, in the vernacular, which lent body and popular support to Bacon's magisterial scientific dicta. An old-fashioned but still interesting book is *Francis Bacon of Verulaam* by Kuno Fischer, translated from the German and published in 1857. Two specialized studies of particular interest are F. H.

Anderson's *The Philosophy of Francis Bacon*, 1948, and K. R. Wallace, *Francis Bacon on Communication & Rhetoric*, 1943.

Prose Ornate and Unadorned

No general study of English prose style during the 17th century has yet been attempted, perhaps because of the diversity and complexity of the topic. G. P. Krapp's classic *The Rise of English Literary Prose*, 1915, carries the story only as far as Hooker. George Williamson's *The Senecan Amble*, 1951, is concerned with only a single, though a very popular, variety of prose style. Other special studies are W. G. Crane's *Wit and Rhetoric in the Renaissance*, 1937, and W. F. Mitchell, *English Pulpit Oratory*, 1932. Morris W. Croll in a series of brilliant articles scattered through *Studies in Philology* XVI and XVIII, *PMLA XXXIX*, the *Schelling Anniversary Papers*, 1923, and the *Revue du seizième siècle*, II (1914), discussed and analyzed the anti-Ciceronian movement. In a similar series of articles, R. F. Jones discussed the influence of the Royal Society on prose style in the later 17th century; these are collected in R. F. Jones, *The Seventeenth Century*, 1951. William Haller's fascinating account of Puritan propaganda techniques in *The Rise of Puritanism*,‡ 1938, is balanced by an account of late-century developments in G. R. Cragg, *From Puritanism to the Age of Reason*,‡ 1950. And the greatest book written in the 17th, or any other century, is discussed by David Daiches, *The King James Version of the English Bible*, 1941, by C. C. Butterworth, *The Literary Lineage of the King James Bible*, 1941, and by a host of others.

Sir Thomas Browne

The standard complete edition of Browne is *The Works of Sir Thomas Browne*, edited in 6 volumes by Geoffrey L. Keynes, 1928–31. General introductory accounts are those of Jeremiah S. Finch, *Sir Thomas Browne: A Doctor's Life of Science and Faith*,‡ 1950, and W. P. Dunn, *Sir Thomas Browne, a Study in Religious Philosophy*, 1950. There is a classic account of the backgrounds of skepticism and fideism in Louis Bredvold, *The Intellectual Milieu of John Dryden*,‡ 1934; this makes frequent reference to Browne.

Jeremy Taylor

Biographies of Taylor have been written by Edmund Gosse, English Men of Letters Series, 1904, and Hugh Ross Williamson, 1952. Logan Pearsall Smith, in his introduction to a selection of Taylor's writings titled *The Golden Grove*, 1930, and W. F.

Mitchell, in his general history of *English Pulpit Oratory*, 1932, comment on aspects of Taylor's orotund prose style. There is a bibliography of Taylor by Robert Gathorne-Hardy appended to the former book.

Robert Burton

The handiest edition of *The Anatomy* for a modern reader is that of Floyd Dell and P. Jordan-Smith, 1927, in which the Latin quotations and tags are translated. Bergen Evans has written, with professional assistance, an interesting study in *The Psychiatry of Robert Burton*, 1944, and W. R. Mueller an analysis of Burton's background called *The Anatomy of Robert Burton's England*, 1952.

Thomas Hobbes

The standard edition of Hobbes is that edited by Sir William Molesworth: *The English Works* in 11 volumes, the *Opera Philosophica* in five, 1839–45. G. C. Robertson in *Hobbes*, 1886, provides a good general introduction, and for the student of literature there is a useful study of the philosopher's literary theory, by C. D. Thorpe, *The Aesthetic Theory of Thomas Hobbes*, 1940. The most recent edition of *Leviathan* has a very perceptive introduction by Michael Oakeshott, 1946. S. I. Mintz, *The Hunting of Leviathan*, 1958, describes the interesting 17th-century reactions to Hobbe's thought.

Character-Writers, Historians, Biographers

A general account of the vogue of the character in England may be found in Benjamin Boyce, *The Theophrastan Character in England to 1642*, 1947. Gwendolyn Murphy has collected many of the best essays in the genre into *A Cabinet of Characters*, 1925, and W. J. Payor has edited *The Overburian Characters*, Percy Reprints XIII, 1936. D. Nichol Smith's *Characters from the Histories & Memoirs of the 17th Century*, 1918, contains, not characters in the strict Theophrastan sense, but verbal portraits of actual 17th-century figures—which in many ways are more interesting. Bibliographies of the genre have been done by Miss Murphy, 1925, and by Chester N. Greenough with the aid of J. Milton French, 1947.

Edward Hyde, Earl of Clarendon

As befits the man who founded the Clarendon Press, Clarendon has always been well printed; the 1888 edition of the *History*, edited by W. Dunn Macray, includes fresh readings and previously suppressed passages. The *Autobiography* was first printed in 1759; and a *Life* in two volumes by Sir Henry Craik supplemented it, 1911. Brian Wormald's *Clarendon: Politics, History, and Religion*, 1951, is the most recent study.

Izaak Walton

A major study of Walton the biographer is David Novarr's *The Making of Walton's Lives*, 1958. Editions of *The Complete Angler* are too numerous to describe; for many years, the book has been one of the classics for the fine-binding trade. A life of Walton by Nicols for the 1836 edition of the *Angler* is said to be particularly meritorious; but no full-length independent biography has yet been published.

THE RESTORATION AND THE EIGHTEENTH CENTURY

The student who wishes to inform himself about English history during the 18th century may consult the relevant chapters in George M. Trevelyan's *History of England*,‡ 1926. Studies in the social life of the period abound—among them H. D. Traill and J. S. Mann, *Social England* (Vol. IV, 1603–1714, and Vol. V, 1714–1815), 1893–97; A. S. Turberville's *English Men and Manners in the Eighteenth Century*,‡ 1926, and as editor, *Johnson's England: An Account of the Life and Manners of His Age*, 2 vols., 1933; Maurice J. Quinlan's *Victorian Prelude: A History of English Manners 1700–1830*, 1941; Sir Walter Besant's illustrated survey *London in the Eighteenth Century*, 1902; M. Dorothy George's *London Life in the Eighteenth Century*,‡ 1925, largely a study of urban poverty; William H. Irving's *John Gay's London Illustrated from the Poetry of the Time*, 1928; Robert J. Allen's *The Clubs of Augustan London*, 1933; and A. R. Humphreys' *The Augustan World: Life and Letters in Eighteenth-Century England*,‡ 1954. B. Sprague Allen's *Tides of English Taste 1619–1800: A Background for the Study of Literature*, 2 vols., 1937, is concerned with architecture, gardening, and the decorative arts, a subject not irrelevant to literature, as the title of Edward Malins' *English Landscaping and Literature, 1760–1840*, 1966 makes explicit.

Helpful books dealing with the intellectual background of the period are: J. H. Randall's *The Making of the Modern Mind*, 1926; Basil Wiley's *The Seventeenth-Century Background*,‡ 1934, and *The Eighteenth-Century Background*,‡ 1940; Arthur O. Lovejoy's *Essays in the History of Ideas*,‡ 1948, and *The Great Chain of Being*,‡ 1942. Paul Hazard's *The European Mind, 1680–1715*,‡ 1953, and *European Thought in the Eighteenth Century: From Montesquieu to Lessing*,‡ 1954, are translations from the French by J. L. May, rapid, readable surveys of intellectual movements on the Continent as well as in England. Peter Gay's *The Enlightenment: An Interpretation*, 1966, is the first half of an inquiry into the accomplishment of the philosophers of the "age of reason." Marjorie H. Nicolson's *Newton Demands the Muse: Newton's "Opticks" and the Eighteenth-Century Poets*,‡ 1946, together with many articles, some of which have been republished in *Science and the Imagination*, 1956, are valuable studies of the relation between science and literature in the period. Primitivistic ideas in the age may be studied in Hoxie Fairchild's *The Noble Savage: A Study in Romantic Naturalism*, 1928, and in Chauncey B. Tinker's *Nature's Simple Plan*, 1922.

The only volume of the *Oxford History of English Literature* dealing with the 18th century that has been published is Bonamy Dobrée's *English Literature in the Early Eighteenth Century, 1700–1740*, 1959. It treats its subject in great detail. Brief surveys of the literature of the age are: George Sherburn's "The Restoration and Eighteenth Century," in A. C. Baugh, ed. *A Literary History of England*,‡ rev. 1967; Alan D. McKillop's *English Literature from Dryden to Burns*, 1948; John Butt's *The Augustan Age*,‡ 1950. A much more detailed study of the literature of the period is Oliver Elton's *A Survey of English Literature 1730–1800*, 2 vols., 1928.

Among books of a general nature that deal with special aspects of literature and taste are James R. Sutherland's *A Preface to Eighteenth-Century Poetry*,‡ 1948, an extremely skillful introduction to a body of poetry that sometimes seems alien to modern readers; Walter Graham's *The Beginnings of English Literary Periodicals 1665–1715*, 1926, and *English Literary Periodicals*, 1930; Allardyce Nicoll's *A History of Restoration Drama, 1660–1700*, *A History of Early Eighteenth-Century Drama, 1700–1750*, and *A History of Late Eighteenth-Century Drama, 1750–1800*, rev., 1952, may be supplemented by Bonamy Dobrée's *Restoration Comedy*, 1924, and *Restoration Tragedy*, 1929, as well as by Arthur Sherbo's *English Sentimental Drama*, 1957. Two recent collections, Earl Miner, ed. *Restoration Dramatists*,‡ 1966, and John Loftis, ed. *Restoration Drama, Modern Essays in Criticism*,‡ 1966, provide studies by various writers; the latter includes several essays on the drama of the early eighteenth century. John Loftis's *The Politics of Drama in Augustan England*, 1963, is a useful interpretation. Satire has been well treated in Ian Jack's *Augustan Satire: Intention and Idiom in English Poetry 1660–1750*,‡ 1952, and James R. Sutherland's *English Satire*,‡ 1955. The important topic of biography was treated by Donald A. Stauffer in *English Biography before 1700*, 1930, and *The Art of Biography in Eighteenth-Century England*, 2 vols., 1941. John N. Morris, *Versions of the Self: Studies in English Autobiography from John Bunyan to John Stuart Mill*, 1966, and Howard Anderson, Philip B. Daghlian, and Irvin Ehrenpreis, eds. *The Familiar Letter in the Eighteenth Century*, 1966, provide introductions to two influential but neglected genres. The novel is treated in detail in E. A. Baker's *The History of the English Novel*, Vol. III (1930), Vol. IV (1930), Vol. V (1934). This work should be supplemented by two excellent modern studies, Ian Watt's *The Rise of the Novel: Studies in Defoe, Richardson and Fielding*,‡ 1957, and Alan D. McKillop's *The Early Masters of English Fiction*, 1956, which deals with Defoe, Richardson, Fielding, Smollett, and Sterne. Sheridan Baker, "The Idea of Romance in the Eighteenth-Century Novel," *Papers of the Michigan Academy of Science, Arts, and Letters*, XLIX, discusses an important aspect of the background of the novel.

Studies of critical movements in this period are numerous and tend to be rather specialized. The two standard collections of neoclassical criticisms are Joel E. Spingarn's *Critical Essays of the Seventeenth Century*, Vols. II and III, 1908 (the preface is not yet outdated), and Scott Elledge's *Eighteenth-Century Critical Essays*, 2 vols., 1961. The best statement of the critical canons of the age is Ronald S. Crane's "Neo-Classical Criticism," in J. T. Shipley, ed. *A Dictionary of World Literature*,‡ 1943. The student may also consult Francis Gallaway's *Reason, Rule, and Revolt in English Classicism*,‡ 1940; René Wellek, *A History of Modern Criticism 1750–1950*, 1955, Vol. I, and William K. Wimsatt, Jr., and Cleanth Brooks, *Literary Criticism: A Short History*,‡ 1957. M. H. Abrams, *The Mirror and the Lamp*,‡ 1953, though primarily concerned with romantic theory, has much to say that is valuable about the 18th century.

Studies that discuss the treatment of external nature in the literature of the period (a theme as important for the 18th as it was for the 19th century) are Christopher Hussey's *The Picturesque: Studies in a Point of View*, 1927, Samuel Holt Monk's *The Sublime: A Study of Critical Theories in Eighteenth-Century England*,‡ 1935, and Marjorie H. Nicolson's *Mountain Gloom and Mountain Glory: The Development of the Aesthetics of the Infinite*,‡ 1959. Sir Kenneth Clark's *The Gothic Revival*, 2nd edition,‡ 1950, is concerned with architecture, but is relevant to literature. Harko G. De Maar's *A History of Modern English Romanticism*, 1924, Vol. I, touches all those movements in art and thought that have conventionally, though perhaps not always wisely, been considered aspects of 18th-century "romanticism."

A group of important books that contain miscellaneous essays and studies by many hands should be consulted: R. F. Jones, and Others Writing in His Honor, *The Seventeenth Century: Studies in the History of English Thought and Literature from Bacon to Pope*, 1951; *Essays of the Eighteenth Century Presented to David Nichol Smith*, 1945; *The Age of Johnson: Essays Presented to Chauncey B. Tinker*,‡ 1949; James L. Clifford and Louis A. Landa, eds. *Pope and His Contemporaries: Essays Presented to George Sherburn*, 1949; Richard C. Boys, ed. *Studies in the Literature of the Augustan Age: Essays Collected in Honor of Arthur E. Case*, 1952; Bernard Schilling, ed. *Essential Articles: English Augustan Backgrounds*, 1961; J. A. Mazzeo, ed. *Reason and Imagination: Studies in the History of Ideas, 1600–1800, In Honor of Marjorie Hope Nicolson*, 1962; Carroll Camden, ed. *Restoration and Eighteenth-Century Literature, Essays in Honor of Alan Dugald McKillop*, 1963; Earl R. Wasserman, ed. *Aspects of the Eighteenth Century*, 1965; Frederick W. Hilles and Harold Bloom, eds. *From Sensibility to Romance, Essays Presented to Frederick A. Pottle*, 1965; Paul Baender and Curt A. Zimansky, eds. *Essays in English Neoclassicism in Memory of Charles B. Woods*, in *Philological Quarterly*, XLV, 1966; Howard Anderson and John S. Shea, eds. *Studies in Criticism and Aesthetics, 1660–1800: Essays in Honor of Samuel H. Monk*, 1967. Cecil A. Moore's *Backgrounds of English Literature 1700–1760*, 1953, contains a valuable essay on nature poetry. James L. Clifford has collected a number of essays of various writers on the period in *Eighteenth-Century English Literature: Modern Essays in Criticism*,‡ 1959. *Studies in English Literature* devotes its summer issue to the Restoration and Eighteenth Century and includes an article reviewing important work on the period published in the preceding year.

Finally, for further and elaborate bibliographies of 18th-century studies, the student may be referred to the bibliography of English literature, 1600–1800, that has appeared annually since 1926 in *Philological Quarterly.*

Samuel Butler

Materials for a full-length biography of Butler do not exist. Of editions of *Hudibras,* Zacharay Grey's, 2 vols., 1744, is still useful for its illustrative notes. The best modern edition is A. R. Waller's, 1905. The same editor's *Characters and Passages from Note-Books,* 1908, is invaluable for studying Butler's opinions; René Lamar has edited *Satires and Miscellaneous Poetry and Prose,* 1928. E. A. Richards' *Hudibras in the Burlesque Tradition,* 1937, is useful. An excellent essay on Butler is included in Ian Jack's *Augustan Satire 1660–1750,‡* 1952.

John Bunyan

Bunyan was a prolific writer: Part II of *The Pilgrim's Progress,* dealing with the journey of Christian's wife and children, appeared in 1684; *The Life and Death of Mr. Badman* in 1680; *The Holy War* in 1682. But these major works form only a small part of all his writings.

The standard life is John Brown's *John Bunyan: His Life, Times, and Work,* 1885, revised by Frank M. Harrison, 1928. The critical edition of *The Pilgrim's Progress* is by J. B. Wharey, 1928, revised by Roger Sharrock,‡ 1960. Among interesting modern studies are George B. Harrison, *John Bunyan: A Study in Personality,* 1928; William Y. Tindall, *John Bunyan, Mechanick, Preacher,* 1934; and Henri A. Talon, *John Bunyan, The Man and His Work,* 1951, a translation from the French.

John Dryden

In 1961 appeared the long-awaited *Life of John Dryden* by Charles E. Ward. Also useful are George Saintsbury's brief *Dryden,* 1881, or the excellent biographical sketch in George R. Noyes' edition of the *Poetical Works,* 2nd edition, 1950. The only edition of the *Works* is the unsatisfactory one in 18 volumes by Sir Walter Scott and George Saintsbury, 1882–93. Of a new edition of the *Works,* begun under the general editorship of the late Edward N. Hooker and carried on under H. T. Swedenberg, Jr., three volumes have appeared: Vol. I, E. N. Hooker and H. T. Swedenberg, Jr., eds. *Poems, 1649–1680,* 1956; Vol. VIII, J. H. Smith and D. MacMillan, eds., 1962, and Vol. IX, J. Loftis and V. A. Dearing, eds., 1966, each contain three parts. A bibliography of work on Dryden is Samuel H. Monk, *John Dryden: A List of Critical Studies—1895 to 1948,* 1950. The poems have been edited by James Kinsley, 4 vols., 1958. The best

(but not complete) edition of the *Essays* is W. P. Ker's, 1900.

The best extended critical study of Dryden's poetry is Mark Van Doren's *The Poetry of John Dryden,* 1920, reissued in 1946 as *John Dryden: A Study of His Poetry ‡.* A. W. Verral's *Lectures of Dryden,* 1914, is valuable, as are T. S. Eliot's two studies, *Homage to John Dryden,* 1924, and *John Dryden the Poet, the Dramatist, the Critic,* 1932. Arthur H. Hoffman's *John Dryden's Imagery,* 1962, is relevant not only to Dryden but also to Augustan poetry in general. Louis I. Bredvold's *The Intellectual Milieu of John Dryden,* 1934, remains a valuable study of Dryden's philosophical, political, and religious ideas although some of its conclusions have been questioned in recent years, notably in Thomas H. Fujimura, "Dryden's *Religio Laici:* An Anglican Poem," *Publication of the Modern Language Association,* LXXVI (1961), 205–217, and in Elias J. Chiasson, "Dryden's Apparent Scepticism in *Religio Laici,*" *Harvard Theological Review,* LIV (1961), 207–221. John C. Aden in *The Critical Opinions of John Dryden, A Dictionary,* 1963, brings together Dryden's critical ideas under convenient headings.

William Congreve

Congreve's *Complete Works* have been edited by Montague Summers, 4 vols., 1923; and the *Plays* by Herbert Davis in 1966. Bonamy Dobrée edited the *Comedies,* 1925, and *The Mourning Bride,* etc., 1928. The best biography is John C. Hodges', *William Congreve the Man,* 1941. Kathleen Lynch's *A Congreve Gallery,* 1951, contains studies of some members of Congreve's circle, including one of Henrietta, Duchess of Marlborough. Criticism of Congreve is abundant in books on Restoration comedy. Modern scholarship is modifying earlier judgments as to the nature and purpose of the comic poets of the Restoration period. Earlier views which have for long been standard (John Palmer's *The Comedy of Manners,* 1913; Bonamy Dobrée's *Restoration Comedy, 1660–1720,* 1924; H. T. E. Perry's *The Comic Spirit in Restoration Drama,* 1925) are being supplemented or revised as knowledge of the period increases. See, for example, Thomas H. Fujimura's *The Restoration Comedy of Wit,* 1952, and Dale Underwood's *Etherege and the Seventeenth-Century Comedy,* 1957. An interesting special study is Paul and Miriam Mueschke's *A New View of Congreve's Way of the World,* 1958.

Daniel Defoe

The best biography of Defoe is James Sutherland's *Defoe,* 1937, rev.,

1950. The *Letters* were edited by George H. Healey, 1955. Among older studies, W. P. Trent's *Daniel Defoe: How to Know Him*, 1916, is still useful, as is A. W. Secord's *Studies in the Narrative Method of Defoe*, 1924. Ian Watt's *The Rise of the Novel*,‡ 1957, contains an interesting study of Defoe's novels in relation to social and economic history. Recent full-length studies include John R. Moore's *Daniel Defoe: Citizen of the Modern World*, 1958; Maximilian E. Novak, *Economics and the Fiction of Daniel Defoe*, 1962, and *Defoe and the Nature of Man*, 1963; G. A. Starr, *Defoe and Spiritual Autobiography*, 1965. J. R. Moore has also provided a useful *Checklist of the Writings of Daniel Defoe*, 1960.

Jonathan Swift

Biographers have found it difficult to write of Swift without advancing some special and private thesis about his character and personal life. Sir Henry Craik's *Life of Jonathan Swift*, 2 vols., 1882, has the advantage of being freer from moral prejudice than any other 19th-century biography of Swift, and the even greater advantage of having been written before the Freudians began to psychoanalyze the Dean. Carl Van Doren's *Swift*, 1930, is readable; and a more recent study, Irvin Ehrenpreis's *The Personality of Jonathan Swift*, 1958, is full of good things as well as of a certain amount of ingenious and not wholly convincing theorizing. Ehrenpreis has so far published two excellent volumes of a three-volume biography: *Mr. Swift and His Contemporaries*, 1962, and *Dr. Swift*, 1968.

The standard edition of the poems is by Sir Harold Williams, 3 vols., 1937, rev., 1958. Joseph Horrell's edition of the *Collected Poems*, 2 vols., The Muses' Library, 1958, is less expensive than Williams' and almost, but not entirely, relies on the canon and text established by Williams in his edition. Herbert Davis's edition of the prose works in 14 volumes, published over a period of years, is now all but complete. Swift's *Correspondence* has been edited by F. Elrington Ball, 6 vols., 1910–14; and by Sir Harold Williams, 5 vols., 1963–65. Distinguished editions of other works are Herbert Davis's *The Drapier's Letters*, 1935; Harold Williams' *Journal to Stella*, 1948; A. C. Guthkelch and D. Nichol Smith, *A Tale of a Tub*, 2nd edition, 1958; and Frank H. Ellis, *A Discourse of the Contests and Dissentions Between the Nobles and the Commons in Athens and Rome*, 1967. Useful bibliographies have been provided by Arthur H. Scouten in his edition of H. Teerink's *A Bibliography of the*

Writings of Jonathan Swift, 1963, Louis A. Landa and James E. Tobin, *Jonathan Swift: A List of Critical Studies Published from 1895 to 1945*, 1945, and James J. Stathis, *A Bibliography of Swift Studies, 1945–65*, 1967.

Critical studies long and short abound. The student should find especially helpful Ricardo Quintana's *The Mind and Art of Jonathan Swift*, 1936, and *Swift: an Introduction*,‡ 1955. Arthur E. Case's *Four Essays on Gulliver's Travels*, 1945, and Maurice Johnson's *The Sin of Wit: Jonathan Swift as a Poet*, 1950, are useful special studies. Most of Herbert Davis's excellent critical pieces on Swift have been brought together in *Jonathan Swift, Essays on his Satire and Other Studies*,‡ 1964; in recent years there have appeared a number of paperbound collections of important essays, particularly those on *Gulliver's Travels*. Milton Voight has summarized the movements in Swift studies in *Swift and the Twentieth Century*, 1964.

Joseph Addison and Sir Richard Steele

There is no scholarly edition of the collected works; the Bohn edition of Addison, 6 vols., 1854–56, rev. and enl., 1869–73, is available in libraries. *Letters* were edited by Walter Graham, 1941. *The Spectator* in five volumes was published by Donald F. Bond, 1965. This is the definitive edition. The authoritative biography of Addison is by Peter Smithers, 1954. Of lives of Steele, George A. Aitken's, 2 vols., 1889, Willard Connely's, 1934, and Calhoun Winton's *Captain Steele: The Early Career of Richard Steele*, 1964, the first of 2 vols., are the best. Rae Blanchard has edited Steele's *Correspondence*, 1941; *Tracts and Pamphlets*, 1944; *Occasional Verse*, Oxford, 1952; and other lesser works. Walter Graham's *English Literary Periodicals*, 1930, may be consulted on both the *Tatler* and the *Spectator*. *The Tatler*, ed. G. A. Aitken, 4 vols., 1898–1899, is the best modern edition of that work.

Alexander Pope

There is no reliable complete edition of all of Pope's works. Defective though it is in many respects, the Victorian edition in 10 volumes by Elwin and Courthope, 1871–89, must still be consulted, though with caution. The excellent Twickenham Edition of the poems, a co-operative undertaking by several scholars (the general editor is John Butt), is now complete in 6 volumes (except for the volumes that will contain the translation of Homer, which are in preparation) and in a convenient single volume with selected notes ‡. Revised editions of individual volumes have appeared from time to time. The introductory and critical materials and the notes are most valuable. Only one volume of Norman Ault's edition of *The Prose Works*, 1936, was published before the editor's death.

No sound biography of Pope exists. George Sherburn's *Early Career of Alexander Pope*, 1934, is authoritative, but unfortunately it does not study the poet's life beyond about 1726. It is an essential book, for it corrects many misinterpretations and distortions of Pope's character and motives that mar earlier biographies. Edith Sitwell's biography ‡ is sentimental; earlier lives were marred by prejudice or misunderstanding. Ault's *New Light on Pope*, 1949, makes important miscellaneous contributions to Pope's biography. Sherburn's edition of the *Correspondence*, 1956, 5 vols., is standard, though it should be supplemented by his publication of some further letters in the *Review of English studies*, new. ser., IX (1958), 388–406. R. H. Griffith, *Alexander Pope: A Bibliography*, 1962, is a 2-volume listing of Pope's writings.

The best detailed critical study of the poems is Geoffrey Tillotson's *On the Poetry of Pope*, 2nd edition, 1950; and the same author's *Pope and Human Nature*, 1958, throws light on a difficult subject. Austen Warren's *Alexander Pope as Critic and Humanist*, 1929, though somewhat dated, is still useful. Much information is gathered up in Robert W. Rogers' *The Major Satires of Alexander Pope*, 1955. Reuben A. Brower's *Alexander Pope: The Poetry of Allusion*, 1959, is an enlightening study of Pope's lifelong habit of felicitous quotation from and adaptation of phrases, images, and ideas from earlier European poets, especially, though not exclusively, from the poets of classical antiquity. Maynard Mack, ed. *Essential Articles for the Study of Alexander Pope*, 1964, conveniently brings together a number of short studies.

Matthew Prior

The complete critical edition of Prior is *Literary Works*, edited by H. B. Wright and M K. Spears, 2 vols., 1959. The older and less complete edition in 2 volumes by A. R. Waller, 1905, 1907, is useful. The best biography is Charles K. Eves' *Matthew Prior, Poet and Diplomatist*, 1939.

James Thomson

The most recent biographical and critical study of Thomson is Douglas Grant's *James Thomson, Poet of "The Seasons,"* 1951. A. D. McKillop has edited *James Thomson, Letters and Documents*, 1958, which contains much about Thomson's friends and the in-terests of his literary circle, and *James Thomson: The Castle of Indolence and Other Poems*, 1961. The most valuable study of the content of *The Seasons* is McKillop's *The Background of Thomson's Seasons*, 1942. For the poetry of natural description see C. V. Deane's *Aspects of Eighteenth-Century Nature Poetry*, 1935. Ralph Cohen, *The Art of Discrimination: Thomson's The Seasons and the Language of Criticism*, 1964, is a valuable work which uses responses to the poem to illustrate the development of critical theory. Patricia Meyer Spacks, *The Poetry of Vision: Five Eighteenth-Century Poets*, 1966, contains a chapter on Thomson, as well as others on Collins, Gray, Smart, and Cowper.

Thomas Gray

The standard edition of Gray's *Works* is that of Edmund Gosse, 4 vols., rev., 1902–6, of the *Correspondence*, that of Paget Toynbee and Leonard Whibley, 3 vols., 1935; of the poems that of H. W. Starr and J. R. Hendrickson, 1966. R. W. Ketton-Cremer's *Thomas Gray*, 1955, is the most recent and the best biography. The best extended critical study is unfortunately in French: Roger Martin's *Essai sur Gray*, 1934. A more specialized study is William P. Jones's *Thomas Gray, Scholar*, 1937. Frederick W. Hilles and Harold Bloom, eds. *From Sensibility to Romance*, 1965, contains studies of the *Elegy* by F. Brady, B. H. Bronson, and I. Jack.

William Collins

The poems have been edited by, among several others, W. C. Bronson, 1898, and by Edmund Blunden, 1929. An interesting recent discovery is a group of Collins's hitherto unpublished verse, edited by J. S. Cunningham in *Drafts & Fragments of Verse*, 1956. E. G. Ainsworth's *Poor Collins*, 1937, is the most detailed biographical and critical study of the poet. A valuable general work, important for understanding Collins and other 18th-century poets, is Chester F. Chapin's *Personification in Eighteenth-Century English Poetry*, 1955.

William Cowper

The poems have been reprinted many times. A convenient modern edition in one volume is H. S Milford's, 4th edition, 1934. Thomas Wright has edited the *Correspondence*, 4 vols., 1904, and *Unpublished and Uncollected Letters*, 1925. Maurice J. Quinlan's *William Cowper*, 1953, is the most recent scholarly biography. See also his useful edition of Cowper's *Memoir* (first published 1816), in *Proceedings of the*

American Philosophical Society XCVII (1953), 359–82. Charles Ryskamp's *William Cowper*, 1959, concentrates on the poet's early life. Bibliographies include Norma Russell, *A Bibliography of William Cowper to 1837*, 1963, which provides a useful sense of the poet's development and of the reception of his work; and Lodwick Hartley, *William Cowper: The Continuing Revaluation, An Essay and a Bibliography of Cowperian Studies from 1895 to 1960*, 1960. Interesting special studies are Gilbert Thomas, *William Cowper and the Eighteenth Century*, 1935, and L. C. Hartley, *William Cowper, Humanitarian*, 1938.

George Crabbe

Crabbe's biography was written by his son, George, in 1834. It has been re-edited by E. M. Forster, 1932, and by Edmund Blunden, 1947. The *Poetical Works*, well edited by A. J. and R. M. Carlyle, were published in 1914. *New Poems*, edited by Arthur Pollard, 1960, contains hitherto unpublished poems. Howard Mills has edited *George Crabbe: Tales (1812) and Other Selected Poems*, 1967. Lilian Haddakin's *Poetry of Crabbe*, 1955, is the only book devoted entirely to a study of the poems.

Samuel Johnson

Others among Johnson's friends besides Boswell wrote of him: notably, Mrs. Hester Lynch Thrale Piozzi, whose *Anecdotes* appeared in 1786; Sir John Hawkins, whose *Life* was published in 1787 and reissued in 1961, edited and abridged by Bertram H. Davis; and Fanny Burney (Mme D'Arblay), from whose diary the Johnsonian passages are found most conveniently in C. B. Tinker's *Dr. Johnson and Fanny Burney*, 1911. James L. Clifford's *Young Sam Johnson*,‡ 1955, is a thorough study of Johnson's early life and a necessary supplement to Boswell's rather sketchy account of Johnson's life before their meeting in 1763. The poems were admirably edited by David Nichol Smith and E. L. McAdam, 1941. The first volume of the new Yale Edition of the *Works*, "Diaries, Prayers, and Annals," edited by E. L. McAdam and Donald and Mary Hyde, was published in 1958: it was followed by Vol. II, W. J. Bate, J. M. Bullitt, L. F. Powell, eds. *The Idler* and *The Adventurer*, 1963; and Vol. VI, E. L. McAdam with George Milne, eds. *Poems*, 1964. R. W. Chapman's edition of the letters, 3 vols., 1952, is authoritative. James L. Clifford, *Johnsonian Studies, 1887–1950. A Survey and Bibliography*, 1951, and J. L. Clifford and O. J. Greene, *Johnsonian Bibliography 1950–1960, A Supplement*, in *Johnsonian Studies* (Cairo), 1962, will soon be brought up to date in a more convenient form.

Some interesting modern studies of Johnson are W. C. B. Watkins' three essays in *Perilous Balance: The Tragic Genius of Swift, Johnson, and Sterne*, 1939; B. H. Bronson's "Johnson Agonistes," 1944 (reissued in *Johnson Agonistes and Other Essays*, 1965); W. J. Bate's *The Achievement of Samuel Johnson*, 1955; W. K. Wimsatt, Jr., *The Prose Style of Samuel Johnson*,‡ 1941; Donald J. Greene's *The Politics of Samuel Johnson*, 1960; and Arieh Sachs' *Passionate Intelligence: Imagination and Reason in the Work of Samuel Johnson*, 1967. *Johnson, Boswell, and Their Circle*, 1965, and Donald J. Greene, ed. *Samuel Johnson, A Collection of Critical Essays*,‡ 1965, bring together short studies by various hands. Aspects of Johnson's criticism are treated in Joseph E. Brown's *The Critical Opinions of Samuel Johnson*, 1926; Jean Hagstrum's *Samuel Johnson's Literary Criticism*, 1952; and Arthur Sherbo's *Samuel Johnson, Editor of Shakespeare*, 1956. Johnson's interesting notes to Shakespeare's comedies, histories, and seven of the tragedies have been reprinted by the Augustan Reprint Society in its publications Nos. 59, 60, 65, 66, 71, 72, 73. G. B. Hill's edition of the *Lives of the Poets*, 1905, has been recently reprinted.

James Boswell

A vast amount has been written about Boswell, much now outmoded by the discovery within the last quarter of a century of Boswell's private papers. Most of this outdated material is now simply ill informed, prejudiced, and worthless. Frederick A. Pottle's *James Boswell, The Earlier Years, 1740–1769*, 1966, makes good use of the private papers. C. B. Tinker's lively and percipient *Young Boswell*, 1922, is useful. Frederick A. Pottle's *The Literary Career of James Boswell*, 1929, was the first attempt to establish the canon of Boswell's writings. The *Letters*, edited by C. B. Tinker, 2 vols., 1924, will have to be supplemented by the recently recovered correspondence, of which one volume has been published: Ralph S. Walker, ed. *The Correspondence of James Boswell and John Johnston of Grange*, 1966. *The Private Papers of James Boswell from Malahide Castle*, edited by Geoffrey Scott and F. A. Pottle, 18 vols., 1928–34, made available the first of Boswell's papers to be discovered. Volumes of the trade edition of the *Journals*, under the general editorship of F. A. Pottle, appear regularly. The *Journal of a Tour to the Hebrides* has been edited, as first published, by

R. W. Chapman, 1924; and, as originally written, by Frederick A. Pottle, 1936. The introductory material and illustrative notes in these volumes and the Malahide papers are of great value. Anthony E. Brown has provided a useful bibliography in "Boswellian Studies: A Bibliography," *Cairo Studies in English,* 1963–66.

A wise and sympathetic brief study of Boswell is B. H. Bronson's "Boswell's Boswell," in *Johnson and Boswell,‡* 1944. *Johnson, Boswell, and Their Circle: Essays Presented to L. F. Powell,* 1965, is a valuable collection. The best edition of the *Life* is L. F. Powell's revised and enlarged edition of the earlier edition by G. B. Hill, 6 vols., 1934–50. A helpful guide through the *Life* is J. L. Smith-Dampier's *Who's Who in Boswell?,* 1935. Mention should perhaps be made of Thomas Babington Macaulay's brilliantly paradoxical, highly prejudiced account of Boswell in his review in 1831 of Croker's edition of the *Life of Johnson.* It blackened Boswell's reputation for nearly a century and its influence is still alive. It is easily available in any of the numerous printings of Macaulay's *Critical and Historical Essays.*

Oliver Goldsmith

The Collected Works of Goldsmith was published by Arthur Friedman in 1966. The most recent biography of Goldsmith is Ralph M. Wardle's *Oliver Goldsmith,* 1957. Sir James Prior's *Life of Oliver Goldsmith,* 2 vols., 1837, is the important biography of the last century. Kathleen C. Balderston has edited the *Collected Letters,* 1928; Austin Dobson edited the *Complete Poetical Works,* 1906, and the *Plays,* 1901. An important addition to the canon of Goldsmith's works was made by Ronald S. Crane in his edition of *New Essays,* 1927.

Note on Poetic Forms and Terminology

RHYTHM AND METER

Verse is generally distinguished from prose as a more compressed and more regularly rhythmic form of statement. This approximate truth underlines the importance of **meter** in poetry, as the means by which rhythm is measured and described.

In the classical languages, meter was established on a **quantitative** basis, by the regular alternation of long and short syllables (that is, syllables classified according to the time taken to pronounce them). Outside of a few experiments (and the songs of Thomas Campion), this system has never proved congenial to English, which distinguishes, instead, between **stressed** and **unstressed,** or accented and unaccented syllables. Two varieties of accented stress may be distinguished. On the one hand, there is the natural stress pattern of words themselves; *sýllable* is accented on the first syllable, *deplórable* on the second, and so on. Then there is the sort of stress which indicates rhetorical emphasis. If the sentence "You went to Greece?" is given a pronounced accent on the last word, it implies "Greece (of all places)?" If the accent falls on the first word, it implies "you (of all people)?" The meter of poetry—that is, its rhythm—is ordinarily built up out of a regular recurrence of accents, whether established as **word accents** or **rhetorical accents;** once started in the reader's mind, it has (like all rhythm) a persistent effect of its own.

The unit which is repeated to give steady rhythm to a poem is called a **poetic foot;** in English it usually consists of accented and unaccented syllables in one of five fairly simple patterns:

The **iambic foot** (or **iamb**) consists of an unstressed followed by a stressed syllable, as in *uníte, repeát,* or *insíst.* Most English verse falls naturally into the iambic pattern.

The **trochaic foot** (**trochee**) inverts this order; it is a stressed followed by an unstressed syllable—for example, *únit, réaper,* or *ínstant.*

The **anapestic foot** (**anapest**) consists of two unstressed syllables followed by a stressed syllable, as in *intercéde, disarránge,* or *Cameróon.*

The **dactylic foot** (**dactyl**) consists of a stressed syllable followed by two unstressed syllables, as in *Wáshington, Écuador,* or *ápplejack.*

The **spondaic foot** (**spondee**) consists of two successive stressed syllables, as in *heartbreak, headline,* or *Kashmir.*

In all the examples above, word accent and the quality of the metrical foot coincide exactly. But the metrical foot may well consist of several words, or, on the other hand, one word may well consist of several metrical feet. *Phótolithógraphy* consists of two excellent dactyls in a single word; *dárk and with spóts on ít,* though it consists of six words rather than one, is also two dactyls—not quite such good ones. When we read a piece of poetry with the intention of discovering its underlying metrical pattern, we are said to **scan** it—that is, we go through it line by line, indicating by conventional signs which are the accented and which the unaccented syllables within the feet (the ictus ′ generally designates accented, the mora ˘ unaccented syllables). We also count the number of feet in each line, or, more properly, **verse**—since a single poetic line is generally called a "verse." Verse lengths are conventionally described in terms derived from the Greek:

Monometer: one foot (of rare occurrence)
Dimeter: two feet (also rare)
Trimeter: three feet
Tetrameter: four feet
Pentameter: five feet
Hexameter: six feet (six iambic feet make an **Alexandrine**)
Heptameter: seven feet (also rare)

Doctor Johnson's little parody of simpleminded poets would thus be scanned this way:

> ˘ ′ ˘ ′ ˘ ′ ˘ ′
> I put my hat upon my head
> ˘ ′ ˘ ′ ˘ ′
> And walked into the Strand,
> ˘ ′ ˘ ′ ˘ ′ ˘ ′
> And there I met another man
> ˘ ′ ˘ ′ ˘ ′
> Whose hat was in his hand.

The poem is iambic in rhythm, alternating tetrameter and trimeter in verse length. The fact that it scans so nicely is, however, no proof that it is good poetry. Quite the contrary. Many of poetry's most subtle effects are achieved by establishing an underlying rhythm and then varying it by means of a whole series of devices, some dramatic and expressive, others designed simply to lend variety and interest to the verse. A well-known sonnet of Shakespeare's (CXVI) begins,

> Let me not to the marriage of true minds
> Admit impediments. Love is not love
> Which alters when it alteration finds,
> Or bends with the remover to remove.

It is perfectly possible, if one crushes all one's sensitivities, to read the first line of this poem as mechanical iambic pentameter:

> ˘ ′ ˘ ′ ˘ ′ ˘ ′ ˘ ′
> Let me not to the marriage of true minds.

But of course nobody ever reads it that way, except to make a point; read with normal English accent and some sense of what it is saying, the line would probably form a pattern something like this:

Let me not to the marriage of true minds,

which is neither pentameter nor in any way iambic. The second line is a little more iambic, but, read for expression, falls just as far short of pentameter:

Admit impediments. Love is not love.

Only in the third and fourth lines of the sonnet do we get verses which read as well as scan like five iambic feet.

The fact is that perfectly regular metrical verse is easy to write and dull to read. Among the devices in common use for varying too regular a pattern are, for instance, the insertion of a trochaic foot among iambics, especially at the opening of a line, where the soft first syllable of the iambic foot often needs stiffening (see line 1 above); the more or less free addition of extra unaccented syllables; and the use of **caesura,** or strong grammatical pause within a line (conventionally indicated, in scanning, by the sign ||). The second line of the sonnet above is a good example of caesura:

Admit impediments. || Love is not love.

The strength of the caesura, and its placing in the line, may be varied to produce striking variations of effect. More broadly, the whole relation between the poem's sound- and rhythm-patterns and its pattern as a sequence of assertions (phrases, clauses, sentences) may be manipulated by the poet. Sometimes his statements fit neatly within the lines, so that each line ends with a strong mark of punctuation; they are then known as **end-stopped lines.** Sometimes the sense flows over the ends of the lines, creating **run-on lines;** this process is also known, from the French, as **enjambment** (literally, "straddling").

End-stopped lines (Marlowe, *Hero and Leander,* First Sestiad, lines 45–48):

So lovely fair was Hero, Venus' nun,
As Nature wept, thinking she was undone,
Because she took more from her than she left,
And of such wondrous beauty her bereft.

Run-on lines (Keats, *Endymion* I.89–93):

Full in the middle of this pleasantness
There stood a marble altar, with a tress
Of flowers budded newly; and the dew
Had taken fairy fantasies to strew
Daisies upon the sacred sward, ° ° °

Following the example of such poets as Blake, Rimbaud, and Whitman, many poets of the 20th century have undertaken to write what is called **free verse**—that is, verse which has neither a fixed metrical foot, nor (consequently) a fixed number of feet in its lines, but which depends for its rhythm on a pattern of cadences, or the rise and fall of the voice in utterance. All freedom in art is of course relative; free verse, with its special aptitude for metrical variety and nervous, colloquial phrasing —its total responsiveness, in other words, to its subject matter—has so successfully established itself that it is now widely recognized as a new and rather demanding form of artistic discipline.

SENSE AND SOUND

The very words of which poetic lines—whether free or traditional—are composed cause them to have different sounds and produce different effects. Polysyllables, being pronounced fast, often cause a line to move swiftly; monosyllables, especially when heavy and requiring distinct accents, may cause it to move heavily, as in Milton's famous line (*Paradise Lost* II.621):

> Rocks, caves, lakes, fens, bogs, dens, and shades of death.

Poetic assertions are often dramatized and reinforced by means of **alliteration**—that is, the use of several nearby words or stressed syllables beginning with the same consonant. When Shakespeare writes (*Sonnet LXIV*),

> Ruin hath taught me thus to ruminate
> That Time will come and take my love away,

the rich, round, vague echoes of the first line contrast most effectively with the sharp anxiety and directness of the alliterative *t*'s in the second. When Dryden starts *Absalom and Achitophel* with that wicked couplet,

> In pious times, ere priestcraft did begin,
> Before polygamy was made a sin,

the satiric undercutting is strongly reinforced by the triple alliteration which links "*pious*" with "*priestcraft*" and "*polygamy*."

Assonance, or repetition of the same or similar vowel sounds within a passage (usually in accented syllables), also serves to enrich it, as in two lines from Keats's *Ode on Melancholy:*

> For shade to shade will come too drowsily,
> And drown the wakeful anguish of the soul.

It is clear that the round, hollow tones of "dr*ow*sily," repeated in "dr*ow*n" and darkening to the full *o*-sound of "s*ou*l," have much to do with the effect of the passage. A related device is **consonance**, or the repetition of a pattern of consonants with changes in the intervening vowels—for example: *linger, longer, languor; rider, reader, raider, ruder.*

Direct verbal imitation of natural sounds (known as **onomatopoeia**) has been much attempted, from Virgil's galloping horse—

> *Quadrupedante putrem sonitu quatit ungula campum*—

to Tennyson's account, in *The Princess*, of

> The moan of doves in immemorial elms
> And murmuring of innumerable bees.

Often ingeniously exploited as a side effect, onomatopoeia is essentially a trick, with about the same value in poetry as it has in music.

RHYME AND STANZA

Rhyme consists of a repetition of accented sounds in words, usually those falling at the end of verse lines. If the rhyme sound is the very last syllable of the line (*rebound, sound*), the rhyme is called **masculine**; if the accented syllable is followed by an unaccented syllable (*hounding,* *bounding*), the rhyme is called **feminine.** Rhymes amounting to three or more syllables, like forced rhymes, generally have a comic effect in English, and have been freely used for this purpose, e.g., by Ogden Nash (*opportunity, impunity; failure, azalea*). Rhymes occurring within a single line are called **internal;** for instance, the Mother-Goose rhyme, "Mary, Mary, quite contrary," or Coleridge's *Ancient Mariner* ("We were the first that ever burst / Into that silent sea"). **Eye rhymes** are words used as rhymes which look alike but actually sound different (for example, *alone, done; remove, love*); **off** rhymes (sometimes called **partial, imperfect,** or **slant rhymes**) are occasionally the result of pressing exigencies or lack of skill, but are also, at times, used deliberately by modern poets for special effects. For instance, a sonnet by Dylan Thomas contains such "rhymes" as *knees, toes; Eve, grave; van, bone; and winter, ladder* (*Holy Sonnet 3*). Pairings like the last two are sometimes loosely described as consonance, rather than rhyme.

Blank verse is unrhymed iambic pentameter; until the recent advent of free verse, it was the only unrhymed measure to achieve general popularity in English. First used by the Earl of Surrey, blank verse was during the 16th century largely dramatic in character. *Paradise Lost* was one of the first nondramatic poems in English to use blank verse. But Milton's authority and his success were so great that during the 18th and 19th centuries blank verse came to be used for a great variety of discursive, descriptive, and philosophical poems—besides remaining the standard metrical form for epics. Thomson's *Seasons*, Cowper's *Task*, Wordsworth's *Prelude*, and Tennyson's *Idylls of the King* were all written in blank verse.

A **stanza** is a recurring unit of a poem, consisting of a number of verses. Certain poetic forms (as a notable example, Pindaric odes) have stanzas comprising a variable number of verses, of varying lengths. Others are more regular, hence easier to describe.

The simplest form of stanza is the **couplet;** it is simply two lines rhyming together. When a single couplet is considered in isolation, it is sometimes called a **distich;** when it includes a complete unified thought, ending with a terminal mark of punctuation, it is called a **closed couplet.** Early metrical experimenters sometimes made couplets which alternated hexameter with pentameter lines in imitation of the classical "elegiac" meter, but the effect in English is somewhat jerky and uneven. Actually, the iambic pentameter couplet seems to work best when it is strict and regular. To regularize it was a work of considerable time and practice. Even as skillful a versifier as Ben Jonson, though he writes iambic pentameter couplets in a poem like *To Penshurst*, has not yet mastered what we call the **heroic couplet.** This is a strictly iambic pentameter couplet, strongly end-stopped, and with the couplets prevailingly closed. Heroic couplets generally are varied by means of a decided caesura, and limited to precisely ten syllables per line. The heroic couplet is the principal form of English neoclassical style. A model of its swift, keen, yet weighty wit is the opening of Dryden's *Absalom and Achitophel*. Occasionally, as in this poem, neoclassic heroic couplets are varied by the introduction of a third rhyme, to make a **tercet** (usually enclosed by a marginal brace); and a striking terminal effect is sometimes achieved by the introduction of an Alexandrine (a line of iambic hexameter) as the third line of the tercet.

Another customary and challenging form of couplet is the **tetrameter, or four-beat couplet.** The more closely rhymes recur, the harder couplets are to manage; in addition, a four-beat line is hard to divide by caesura without splitting it into two tick-tock dimeters. For this reason, tetrameter couplets have posed a perpetual challenge to poets, and still provide an admirable finger-exercise for aspiring versifiers. A model of tetrameter couplets managed with marvelous variety, complexity, and expressiveness is Marvell's *To His Coy Mistress:*

> Thou by the Indian Ganges' side
> Shouldst rubies find; I by the tide
> Of Humber would complain. I would
> Love you ten years before the flood,
> And you should, if you please, refuse
> Till the conversion of the Jews.

English has not done much with rhymes grouped in threes, but has borrowed from Italian the form known as **terza rima,** in which Dante composed his *Divine Comedy.* This form consists of linked groups of three rhymes according to the following pattern: *aba bcb cdc ded,* etc. Shelley's *Ode to the West Wind* is composed in stanzas of terza rima, the poem as a whole ending with a couplet.

Quatrains are stanzas of four lines; the lines usually rhyme alternately, *abab,* or in the second and fourth lines, *abcb.* When they alternate tetrameter and trimeter lines, as in Johnson's little poem about men in hats (above), or as in *Sir Patrick Spens,* they are called **ballad stanza.** This is also the prevailing stanza form of Mother Goose—cf. "Little Miss Muffet / Sat on a tuffet," etc. Dryden's *Annus Mirabilis* and Gray's *Elegy Written in a Country Churchyard* are in heroic quatrains; these rhyme alternately, and employ five-stress iambic verse throughout. Tennyson used for *In Memoriam* a tetrameter quatrain rhymed *abba,* and FitzGerald translated *The Rubáiyát of Omar Khayyám* into a pentameter quatrain rhymed *aaba;* but these forms have not been very generally adopted.

Chaucer's *Troilus and Criseyde* is an early example in English of **rime royal,** a seven-line iambic pentameter stanza consisting essentially of a quatrain dovetailed onto two couplets, according to the rhyme scheme *ababbcc* (the fourth line serves both as the final line of the quatrain and the first line of the first couplet). Closely akin to rime royal, but differentiated by an extra *a*-rhyme between the two *b*-rhymes, is **ottava rima,** that is, an eight-line stanza rhyming *abababcc.* As its name suggests, ottava rima is of Italian origin; it was first used in English by Wyatt. Its final couplet, being less prepared for than in rime royal, and usually set off as a separate verbal unit, has a special witty snap to it, for which Byron found good use in *Don Juan.*

The longest and most intricate stanza generally used for narrative purposes in English is that devised by Edmund Spenser for *The Faerie Queene.* The **Spenserian stanza** has nine lines rhyming *ababbcbcc;* the first eight lines are pentameter, the last line an Alexandrine. Slow-moving, intricate of pattern, and demanding in its rhyme scheme (the *b*-sound recurs four times, the *c*-sound three), the Spenserian stanza has nonetheless appealed widely to poets seeking a rich and complicated metrical form. Keats's *Eve of St. Agnes* and Shelley's *Adonais* are brilliantly successful 19th-century examples of its use.

The **sonnet,** originally a stanza of Italian origin which has developed into an independent lyric form, is usually defined as fourteen lines of iambic pentameter. None of the elements in this definition is absolute. The first sonnet of Sidney's *Astrophel and Stella* is in hexameters, and Milton has one sonnet of twenty lines (*On the New Forcers of Conscience*), while Meredith wrote a whole series of sixteen-line sonnets (*Modern Love*). Most sonnets, however, conform to the definition. Sonnets generally follow one of two conventional rhyme schemes. The **Petrarchan** or **Italian sonnet** is divided into sections of eight lines (**octave**) and six lines (**sestet**), rhyming *abba abba* and *cdecde*. (There are many variations of the rhyme scheme in the sestet; that described is the most frequent.) Under this arrangement, the poet tends to use his octave to state the problem and his sestet to resolve it. The **English** or **Shakespearean** sonnet takes the form of three quatrains and a final couplet, rhyming *abab cdcd efef gg*. The couplet is ideally suited for producing a summary statement or witty twist after the problem has been turned about in the three quatrains. Both these forms represent ideal models, not absolute prescriptions. Many sonnets approximate these patterns without following them precisely; indeed, the term "sonnet" was slow in acquiring any meaning more specific than that of "short lyric poem." Among Donne's *Songs and Sonnets* there is just one sonnet in the more modern sense, *The Token*, and it has eighteen lines.

In the Elizabethan period, the sonnet underwent its most intensive cultivation in connection with themes of courtly love. Perhaps in revulsion, Donne used the sonnet mostly to express religious devotion (*Holy Sonnets, La Corona*), while Milton employed it on satiric, social, or political themes. In Wordsworth, it expanded in the direction of moral reflection and commentary, while G. M. Hopkins loaded it with a rich philosophical and rhetorical complexity which sometimes threatened to swamp the form altogether. But the applications of the sonnet are truly limitless, for it is a form just long and complex enough to provide compressed yet dignified statement of almost any major theme.

In blank verse or irregularly rhymed verse, where stanzaic divisions do not exist or are indistinct, the poetry sometimes falls into **verse paragraphs,** which are in effect divisions of sense like prose paragraphs. This division can be clearly seen in Milton's *Lycidas* or Spenser's *Epithalamion*. In the latter poem, it is reinforced by a **refrain,** which is simply a line repeated at the end of each stanza. Ballads also customarily have refrains; for example, the refrain of *Lord Randall* is

> mother, make my bed soon,
> For I'm weary wi' hunting, and fain wad lie down.

FIGURATIVE LANGUAGE

The act of bringing words together into rich and vigorous poetic lines is a complex and demanding art, impossible to reduce to formula, even if one wanted to. The characteristic way in which a poet works his words, rhythms, sounds, and assertions into a controlled yet vigorous pattern constitutes his **style.** Style is, in poetry as in the other arts, a set of conventions. The poet does not try to recreate raw reality; he attempts to make a formalized arrangement which is analogous to the experience which is his "subject." As a painter has a range of pigments with which to represent the much wider range of natural tones, so the poet has an array of verbal strategies. His task is to find, within his chosen scale, a verbal equivalent for the precise experience he wants to present. Among these strategies the most complex and the most easily overlooked are the varying verbal textures of which poetry may be composed.

In addition to the strictly aural devices of verbal texture, the poet has at his disposal the many resources of figurative language. Here, as in matters of meter, one may distinguish a great variety of devices, some of which we use in everyday speech without special awareness of their names and natures. When we say someone eats "like a horse" or "like a bird," we are using a **simile**, that is, a comparison marked out by a specific word of likening—"like" or "as." When we omit the word of comparison but imply a likeness—as in the sentence, "That hog has guzzled all the champagne"—we are making use of **metaphor.** The **epic simile,** frequent in epic poetry, is an extended simile in which the thing compared is described as an object in its own right, beyond its point of likeness with the main subject. Milton starts to compare Satan to Leviathan, but concludes his simile with the story of a sailor who moored his ship by mistake, one night, to a whale (*Paradise Lost* I.200–208). Metaphors and similes have been complexly but usefully distinguished according to their special effects; they may be, for instance, violent, comic, degrading, decorative.

When we speak of "forty head of cattle" or ask someone to "lend a hand" with a job, we are using **synecdoche**, a figure which substitutes the part for the whole. When we speak of a statement "coming from the White House," or a man much interested in "the turf," we are using **metonymy**, or the substitution of one term for another with which it is closely associated. **Antithesis** is a device for placing opposing ideas in grammatical parallel, as, for example, in the following passage from Pope's *Rape of the Lock* (V.25–30), where there are more examples of antithesis than there are lines:

> But since, alas! frail beauty must decay,
> Curled or uncurled, since locks will turn to gray;
> Since painted, or not painted, all shall fade,
> And she who scorns a man, must die a maid;
> What then remains but well our power to use,
> And keep good humor still whate'er we lose?

Irony is a verbal device which implies an attitude quite different from (and often opposite to) that which is literally expressed. When Job answers his comforters, saying "No doubt but ye are the people, and wisdom shall die with you" (Job xii.2), he is using irony thick to the point of sarcasm. When Eliot writes, in *Whispers of Immortality*, that "Grishkin is nice," the adjective is carefully chosen to let an ironic grimace of distaste appear. And when Donne "proves," in *The Canonization*, that he and his mistress are going to found a new religion of love, he seems to be inviting us to take a subtly ironic attitude toward religion as well as love. Irony is thus a very broad term indeed, which can be applied to double attitudes of many different sorts and tonalities. It is, in effect, a device of **wit** (the felicitous, unexpected juxtaposition of ideas to produce a shock of comic surprise), which, Freud tells us, also involves a double attitude, and may also be either serious or comic.

Because it is easy to see through, **hyperbole**, or willful exaggeration, is a favorite device of irony—which is not to say that it may not be "serious" as well. When she hears that a young man is "dying for love" of her, a sensible girl does not accept this statement literally, but it may convey a serious meaning to her nonetheless. The **pun**, or play on words (known to the learned, sometimes, as **paronomasia**), may also be serious or comic in intent; witness, for example, the famous series of puns in Donne's *Hymn to God the Father*. **Oxymoron** is a figure of flat contradiction—for instance, Milton's famous description of hell as containing "darkness visible" (*Paradise Lost* I.63). A **paradox** is a statement which seems absurd but turns out to have rational meaning after all, usually in some unexpected sense; Donne speaks of fear being great courage and high valor (*Satire III*, line 16), and turns out to mean that fear of God is greater courage than any earthly bravery. The **Petrarchan conceit** was an ingenious, complimentary comparison or turn of thought; Wyatt compares the state of a lover to a ship tossed in a storm, and a hundred different sonneteers explored the possibility of describing their ladies' anatomy in conventional Petrarchan conceits—her teeth like pearls, lips like rubies, hair like finespun gold, etc. On the other hand, the **metaphysical conceit** was a more ingenious many-leveled comparison, worked out in some detail and giving a strong sense of the poet's ingenuity in overcoming obstacles—for instance, Donne's comparison of separated lovers to the legs of a compass (*A Valediction: Forbidding Mourning*) or Herbert's comparison of devotion to a pulley (*The Pulley*).

Images, symbols, and **emblems** are all words with general meaning; in addition, they refer to varieties of figurative language. Broadly speaking, an image is a picture; a symbol is something which stands for something else (it could be a flag, a gesture, or a word); and an emblem is a badge or device. In literary discussion, it is useful to distinguish them as indicating three different relations between the terms of a comparison. If we say a certain man is "strong as a bear," the man is the primary subject of the comparison, and the bear is the secondary subject, by which a notion of the man's strength is conveyed to us. The image maintains clearly this primary-secondary relationship. The symbol, on the other hand, obliterates the distinction between primary and secondary subjects. The swan in Yeats's poem *Leda and the Swan* is no less a swan because it is generating upon Leda a whole new era of human history. The nature of a symbol is to be both a solid object in its own right and the transparent vehicle of a meaning, either public or private, which must be inferred from the symbol. Thus Prufrock (the protagonist of Eliot's poem) "should have been a pair of ragged claws" because he is feeling submerged, invertebrate, hardshelled, a crawler and a sidler. All these attributes are unexpressed, and must be inferred from the concrete symbol of the ragged claws. Finally, an emblem is an object which quite arbitrarily stands for something else. In the 16th and 17th centuries, emblems were little pictures, like heraldic devices, but with moral meanings, to which short explanatory verses were attached. In early

Christian art, the picture of a fish was an emblem of Christ because in Greek the word for "fish," *ichthys,* forms an anagram of "Jesus Christ, Son of God, Saviour." The white rose was the emblem of York, the red rose of Lancaster. The image adorns a meaning, the symbol contains it, the emblem assumes it.

Personification is the attribution of human qualities to an inanimate object (for example, the Sea) or an abstract concept (Freedom); a special variety of it is called (in a term of John Ruskin's invention) the **pathetic fallacy.** When we speak of leaves "dancing" or a lake "smiling," we attribute human traits to nonhuman objects. Ruskin thought this was false and therefore "morbid"; modern criticism tends to view the practice as artistically and morally neutral. A more formal and abstract variety of personification is **allegory,** in which a narrative (such as *Pilgrim's Progress*) is constructed by representing general concepts (Faithfulness, Sin, Despair) as persons. A **fable** (like the Nun's Priest's Tale) represents beasts behaving like humans; a **parable** is a brief story, or simply an observation, with strong moral application; and an **exemplum** is a story told to illustrate a point in a sermon. A special series of devices, nearly obsolete today, used to be available to poets who could count on readers trained in the classics. These were the devices of **classical epithet** and **allusion.** In their simplest form, the classic myths used to provide a repertoire of agreeable stage properties, and a convenient shorthand for expressing emotional attitudes. Picturesque creatures like centaurs, satyrs, and sphinxes, heroes and heroines like Hector and Helen, and the whole pantheon of Olympic deities could be used to make ready reference to a great many aspects of human nature. One does not have to explain the problems of a man who is "cleaning the Augean stables"; if he is afflicted with an "Achilles' heel," or is assailing "Hydra-headed difficulties," his state is clear. These epithets, or descriptive phrases, making reference to mythological stories, suggest in a phrase situations which would normally require cumbersome explanations. Conceivably other mythologies might have served the same end in analogous ways. But because they could be taken for granted as the common possession of all educated readers, the classic myths entered into English literature as early as Chaucer, and are only now passing away as a viable system of allusions. In poets like Spenser and Milton, classical allusion becomes a kind of enormously learned game, in which the poet seeks to make his points as indirectly as possible. For instance, Spenser writes in the *Epithalamion,* lines 328–29:

> Lyke as when Jove with fayre Alcmena lay,
> When he begot the great Tirynthian groom.

The mere mention of Alcmena in the first line suggests, to the knowing reader, Hercules; Spenser's problem in the second line is to find a way of referring to him which is neither redundant nor heavy-handed. "Tirynthian" reminds us of his long connection with the city of Tiryns, stretching our minds (as it were) across his whole career; and "groom" compresses references to a man-child, a servant, and a bridegroom, all of which apply to different aspects of Hercules' history. Thus, far from simply avoiding redundancy, Spenser has enriched the whole texture of his verse, thought, and feeling by his gift for precise classical epithet.

ROBERT M. ADAMS

Index

Regents Park

0   ¼   ½   1 mile
R. M. Chapin, Jr.

Bloomsbury
Square

British
Museum

High Holborn

Duke's
Theatre

Drury Lane

Drury Lane Theatre

Covent Garden Theatre

Will's Coffee
House

Covent Garden

Oxford   Street

Somerset House

Grosvenor
Square

Strand

Berkeley
Square

Haymarket

Trafalgar
Square

Victoria Embankment

Waterloo Bridge

Devonshire
House

Piccadilly

Charing Cross

Brooks's

Pall Mall

Whitehall

River

Hyde
Park

St. James's
Palace

The Mall

St. James's   Park

Westminster Hall

Buckingham
Palace

Belgrave
Square

Westminster
Abbey

Westminster
Bridge

Houses of
Parliament

Lambeth
Palace

CHELSEA

Vauxhall
Gardens